THE
ROSTER
OF
CONFEDERATE
SOLDIERS

1861 – 1865

Volume XIII

Randal, Amos P.
– to –
Shackford, W. E.

M253-394 — M253-428

EDITED BY
Janet B. Hewett

BROADFOOT PUBLISHING COMPANY
Wilmington, NC
1996

"Fine Books Since 1970."

BROADFOOT PUBLISHING COMPANY

1907 Buena Vista Circle * Wilmington, North Carolina 28405

THIS BOOK IS PRINTED ON ACID-FREE PAPER.

ISBN No. 1-56837-306-6 (Multi-Volume Set)

Randal, Amos P. TN 6th (Wheeler's) Cav. Co.I
Randal, A.R. MO 6th Cav. Co.G Comsy.Sgt.
Randal, D.B. AL 3rd Res. Co.C
Randal, Ed MO 2nd Cav. Co.D
Randal, Edmond G. MS Inf. 2nd Bn. Co.B
Randal, George D. GA 2nd Res. Co.C
Randal, George W. TN 37th Inf. Co.D
Randal, George W. TX 8th Cav. Co.A
Randal, H.I. GA Arty. 9th Bn. Co.B Capt.
Randal, H.O. TN 6th (Wheeler's) Cav. Co.I
Randal, Horace TX 28th Cav. Col.
Randal, Horace Gen. & Staff, Cav. 1st Lt.
Randal, J. TX 24th & 25th Cav. (Cons.) Co.B
Randal, Jack TX 8th Cav. Co.A Sgt.
Randal, Jackson H. MO Inf. 4th Regt.St.Guard Co.C Sgt.
Randal, James D. AL 61st Inf. Co.F
Randal, James M. NC 60th Inf. Co.A Drum Maj.
Randal, J.H. LA 4th Cav. Co.F
Randal, John NC 5th Inf. Co.D
Randal, John NC McLean's Bn.Lt.Duty Men Co.B
Randal, John A. TX Cav. 3rd Bn.St.Troops Capt.,AQM
Randal, John H. AL 61st Inf. Co.F
Randal, John L. NC 60th Inf. Co.F Cpl.
Randal, John W. NC 60th Inf. Co.A
Randal, Joseph TX 25th Cav. Co.C
Randal, Joseph W. NC 14th Inf. Co.F
Randal, Joseph W. TX 10th Inf. Co.I
Randal, L.C. TX Cav. Terry's Regt. Co.B
Randal, Leonard, Jr. TX 28th Cav. Co.F Sgt.Maj.
Randal, Leonard, Sr. TX 28th Cav. Co.F Surg.
Randal, Lewis H. TX 13th Cav. Co.C
Randal, M.M. NC 2nd Jr.Res. Co.D
Randal, Roan A. GA Arty. 9th Bn. Co.B 1st Sgt.
Randal, Robert D. GA Inf. 2nd Bn. Co.D
Randal, S.A. AL 61st Inf. Co.F
Randal, Sidney MS 2nd St.Cav. Co.F Adj.
Randal, Stephen MS Inf. 2nd Bn. Co.L
Randal, Thomas FL 2nd Cav. Co.I
Randal, Thomas J. TX 10th Inf. Co.H
Randal, W. GA 55th Inf. Co.E
Randal, William AL 3rd Bn.Res. Flemming's Co.
Randal, William R. NC 16th Inf. Co.F Cpl.
Randall, --- LA 1st (Nelligan's) Inf. Co.K
Randall, A. AR 13th Inf.
Randall, A. GA 10th Inf. Co.K
Randall, A. MS Cav. Ham's Regt. Co.D
Randall, A. TX 12th Inf. Co.B
Randall, A.A. Conf.Cav. Wood's Regt. 2nd Co.F
Randall, Aaron W. VA 1st Cav. Co.F
Randall, Abram E. NC 29th Inf. Co.C Drum.
Randall, Addison GA 14th Inf. Co.B
Randall, Addison P. KY Cav. Buckner Guards 1st Sgt.
Randall, A.J. MS 2nd (Davidson's) Inf. Co.H
Randall, A.J. Conf.Inf. Tucker's Regt. Co.E
Randall, Alax KY 6th Cav. Co.C
Randall, Albert G. MO 8th Cav. Co.C
Randall, Alexander TN 32nd Inf. Co.H
Randall, Alexander VA 14th Cav. Co.H,B
Randall, Alfred GA 60th Inf. Co.H
Randall, Allison SC 14th Inf. Co.A

Randall, Alonzo E. MO Inf. 8th Bn. Co.A
Randall, A.M. AL 28th Inf. Co.B Sgt.
Randall, Amos G. AR Cav. 1st Bn. (Stirman's)
Randall, Andrew MS 3rd Inf. Co.G 2nd Lt.
Randall, Andrew J. AL Inf. 1st Regt. Co.H
Randall, Aquilla VA Mil. 45th Regt. Co.G Capt.
Randall, A.R. FL 2nd Cav. Co.H
Randall, A.R. MO Cav. 4th Regt.St.Guard Co.F Capt.
Randall, A.S. MS St.Cav. 3rd Bn. (Cooper's) Little's Co.
Randall, B. SC 2nd Arty. Co.E
Randall, Benny SC Hvy.Arty. Mathewes' Co.
Randall, B.F. AL 62nd Inf. Co.C
Randall, B.P. SC Lt.Arty. 3rd (Palmetto) Bn. Co.I
Randall, C. LA Miles' Legion Co.A
Randall, Caleb NC 55th Inf. Co.F
Randall, Calvin TN 15th Inf. Co.G
Randall, Carson W. MO 8th Cav. Co.F,C
Randall, Carver SC Cav.Bn. Hampton Legion Co.B Cpl.
Randall, Charles LA 2nd Cav. Co.A
Randall, Charles LA 1st (Nelligan's) Inf. Co.G
Randall, Charles LA 21st (Patton's) Inf. Co.D
Randall, Charles LA 22nd (Cons.) Inf. Co.K
Randall, Charles SC Percival's Cav.
Randall, Charles VA Lt.Arty. Cooper's Co.
Randall, Charles F. AL 2nd Cav. Co.B
Randall, Charles H. Conf.Arty. Braxton's Bn. Co.A
Randall, Charles S. KY Cav. Buckner Guards Orderly Sgt.
Randall, C.W. GA 19th Inf. Beall's Co.
Randall, C.W. MS Grace's Co. (St.Troops)
Randall, C.W. SC 7th Inf. Co.H,A
Randall, C.W. SC 19th Inf. Co.K 2nd Lt.
Randall, D. TX 3rd (Kirby's) Bn.Vol. Co.A
Randall, Dallas AL 50th Inf. Co.E
Randall, Daniel SC Mason's Cav.
Randall, David MO Inf. 5th Regt.St.Guard Co.A
Randall, E. LA 9th Inf. Co.K
Randall, E. SC 2nd St.Troops Co.I
Randall, E. SC Inf.Bn. Co.C Capt.
Randall, E. TX 9th (Nichols') Inf. Surg.
Randall, E. TX Inf. Timmons' Regt. Surg.
Randall, E. TX Waul's Legion Surg.
Randall, E. Gen. & Staff Surg.
Randall, E.D. TX 21st Cav. Co.A
Randall, E.F. SC Inf. 1st (Charleston) Bn. Co.E
Randall, E.F. SC 27th Inf. Co.A
Randall, Elbert W. MS 6th Inf. Co.G
Randall, Eldred SC 19th Inf. Co.K
Randall, Eldred S. SC 6th Inf. Co.E
Randall, Elijah VA 97th Mil. Co.A
Randall, E.W. MS 38th Cav. Co.F
Randall, Ezekiel SC 19th Inf. Co.A Sr.2nd Lt.
Randall, Fayette TX 27th Cav. Co.C
Randall, F.E. SC 7th Inf. 1st Co.H
Randall, Francis SC 14th Inf. Co.H
Randall, Frank AL 7th Cav. Co.E
Randall, George D. AL 41st Inf. Co.C
Randall, George D. GA Inf. 3rd Bn. Co.C
Randall, George H. TN 32nd Inf. Co.H
Randall, G.H. GA 39th Inf. Maj.
Randall, G.W. NC 55th Inf. Co.D
Randall, G.W. SC 19th Inf. Co.A

Randall, H. GA Cav. Alexander's Co. Cpl.
Randall, Hardy J. GA Arty. 9th Bn. Co.B Sr.1st Lt.
Randall, Harvey MO 8th Cav. Co.D,K Jr.2nd Lt.
Randall, Henry SC 1st (Butler's) Inf. Co.I Sgt.
Randall, Henry C. AL 25th Inf. Co.C
Randall, Henry J. GA Phillips' Legion Co.O
Randall, H.G. SC 5th Cav. Co.D
Randall, H.G. SC 2nd Arty. Co.E
Randall, H.G. SC 5th Res. Co.K Sgt.
Randall, H.H. TX 30th Cav. Co.C
Randall, H.J. AR 1st (Dobbin's) Cav. Co.F
Randall, H.J. GA 10th Cav. (St.Guards) Co.A
Randall, Hollowman SC 19th Inf. Co.K
Randall, Horace D. GA Arty. 11th Bn. (Sumter Arty.) Co.A 1st Lt.
Randall, Howard S. MO 3rd Cav. Co.F,A Capt.
Randall, H.P. MS Cav. Hughes' Bn. Co.D
Randall, H.S. MO 4th Inf. Co.G 1st Lt.
Randall, Isaac B. SC 19th Inf. Co.A
Randall, Isaac B. SC Inf.Bn. Co.C Cpl.
Randall, Isaac J. NC 28th Inf. Co.K
Randall, I.W. NC 56th Inf. Co.F
Randall, J.A. MS 39th Inf. Co.A
Randall, J.A. NC 14th Inf. Co.D
Randall, James LA 15th Inf. Co.F
Randall, James MS 38th Cav. Co.A
Randall, James SC 7th Inf. Co.A
Randall, James TN 13th (Gore's) Cav. Capt.
Randall, James VA 12th Cav. Co.B
Randall, James 8th (Wade's) Conf.Cav. Co.E
Randall, James Ruggles' Staff Capt.,ADC
Randall, James F. AL 3rd Inf. Co.B
Randall, James H. NC 55th Inf. Co.D 2nd Lt.
Randall, James L. AL 11th Inf. Co.H
Randall, James W. SC 7th Inf. 1st Co.F
Randall, James W. VA Lt.Arty. Cooper's Co.
Randall, James W.R. MS 6th Inf. Co.G
Randall, J.B. MS 1st (Johnston's) Inf. Co.K
Randall, J.B. MS 8th Inf. Co.H
Randall, J.B. MS 39th Inf.
Randall, J.D. AR 2nd Cav. 1st Co.A 1st Sgt.
Randall, J.D. MS 8th Cav. Co.K
Randall, J.D. Gen. & Staff Capt.,AQM
Randall, Jefferson SC 19th Inf. Co.A
Randall, Jesse F. TN 32nd Inf. Co.H
Randall, J.F. MO Lt.Arty. Barret's Co.
Randall, J.H. TN 19th & 20th (Cons.) Cav. Co.E
Randall, J.H. TN 28th Cav. Co.A Sgt.
Randall, J.J. GA 1st Cav. Co.A
Randall, J.L. AL 41st Inf. Co.C
Randall, J.M. MS Inf. 3rd Bn. (St.Troops) Co.E Surg.
Randall, J.M. SC Lt.Arty. 3rd (Palmetto) Bn. Co.H
Randall, J.M. Gen. & Staff Surg.
Randall, Joel VA 31st Mil. Co.E
Randall, Joel L. AL 11th Inf. Co.H
Randall, John AR Inf. Williamson's Bn. Co.D Capt.
Randall, John LA 14th Inf. Co.G Sgt.
Randall, John MS 39th Inf. Co.A
Randall, John MO Cav. Preston's Bn.
Randall, John MO 1st Inf. Co.A
Randall, John MO 1st & 4th Cons.Inf. Co.A

Randall, John NC 1st Inf. (6 mo. '61) Co.E Music.
Randall, John NC 55th Inf. Co.D
Randall, John 1st Conf.Inf. Co.A,B
Randall, John A. NC 55th Inf. Co.D
Randall, John C. NC 14th Inf. Co.D Sgt.
Randall, John H. AL 2nd Bn. Hilliard's Legion Vol. Co.A
Randall, John K. AL Cav. Murphy's Bn. Co.B
Randall, John K. AL 1st Regt. Mobile Vol. Co.E Cpl.
Randall, John W. NC 16th Inf. Co.B 2nd Lt.
Randall, Joseph TX 9th (Nichols') Inf. Co.H
Randall, Joseph VA 9th Bn.Res. Co.C
Randall, Joseph 1st Chickasaw Inf. White's Co.
Randall, Joseph E. MS 21st Inf. Co.I Cpl.
Randall, J.P. NC 14th Inf. Co.D
Randall, J.W. FL 2nd Cav. Co.H
Randall, J.W. GA 21st Inf. Co.G
Randall, J.W. MO Lt.Arty. Barret's Co.
Randall, J.W. SC 2nd Inf. Co.K
Randall, J.W. SC 17th Inf. Co.C
Randall, J.W. TX 2nd Inf. Co.G
Randall, L. MS Inf. 2nd St.Troops Co.B
Randall, Lafayett SC 19th Inf. Co.A
Randall, Leonard Gen. & Staff Surg.
Randall, L.H. MS 3rd Inf. Co.E
Randall, Manly B. SC 14th Inf. Co.H
Randall, Michael VA 13th Inf. Co.I Cpl.
Randall, Miller H. NC 55th Inf. Co.D
Randall, M.J. MS 39th Inf. Co.A
Randall, M.L. MS 10th Cav. Co.A
Randall, M.L. SC 17th Inf. Co.F Sgt.
Randall, M.L. TN Cav. 17th Bn. (Sanders') Co.C
Randall, Newsom 1st Conf.Eng.Troops Co.H
Randall, N.H. AL 47th Inf. Co.C
Randall, N.G. AL 25th Inf. Co.E
Randall, Oliver P. TX 6th Inf. Co.A Cpl.
Randall, Philip SC 6th Cav. Co.B,G
Randall, Pleasant SC Lt.Arty. 3rd (Palmetto) Bn. Co.I
Randall, P.P. MS 9th Cav. Co.B 2nd Lt.
Randall, P.P. MS Cav. 17th Bn. Co.D 2nd Lt.
Randall, R.H. SC 17th Inf. Co.C
Randall, Richard VA 10th Inf. Co.B
Randall, R.M. TN 15th Inf. Co.G
Randall, R.O. AL 31st Inf. Co.A
Randall, Robert AL 34th Inf. Black's Co.
Randall, Robert MS 43rd Inf. Co.I
Randall, Robt. MO 3rd Cav. Co.D
Randall, Robert VA Lt.Arty. Jackson's Bn.St.Line Co.A
Randall, Robert D. AL 41st Inf. Co.C
Randall, Robert G. MO 3rd Cav. Co.E,B
Randall, Romulus M.S. NC 55th Inf. Co.D Sgt.
Randall, Rowan A. GA 8th Inf. Co.F
Randall, R.S. SC 17th Inf. Co.F Sgt.
Randall, S. AR 1st Inf. Co.B
Randall, Samuel TX 20th Inf. Co.H Surg.
Randall, S.B. TX 5th Inf. Co.D
Randall, Seaborn SC 19th Inf. Co.A
Randall, Silas SC 2nd St.Troops Co.K
Randall, Silas D. NC 55th Inf. Co.D Capt.
Randall, Silas J. TX 31st Cav. Co.H
Randall, S.J. MS 5th Inf. (St.Troops) Co.C Maj.

Randall, Smiley AL 2nd Bn. Hilliard's Legion Vol. Co.A Cpl.
Randall, Smith Conf.Cav. Wood's Regt. 1st Co.A
Randall, Steph A. AL 41st Inf. Co.C
Randall, Stephen MS 48th Inf. Co.L
Randall, Thomas NC 55th Inf. Co.D
Randall, Thomas P. TX Cav. Mann's Regt. Co.A
Randall, Thomas P. TX Cav. Mann's Bn. Co.A Cpl.
Randall, W. SC 2nd Arty. Co.E
Randall, Walter J. MD Inf. 2nd Bn. Co.F Sgt.
Randall, Walter J. VA Inf. 25th Bn. Co.B
Randall, W.B. MO 16th Inf. Co.A
Randall, W.H. AL Mil. 2nd Regt.Vol. Co.E
Randall, W.H. MS 10th Cav. Co.A
Randall, W.H. TN Inf. 2nd Cons.Regt. Co.F
Randall, Whitaker P. TX 1st Inf. Co.L 2nd Lt.
Randall, William GA 37th Inf. Co.F
Randall, William SC 19th Inf. Co.I,K
Randall, William SC 23rd Inf. Co.K
Randall, William VA Lt.Arty. Cooper's Co.
Randall, William F. MS 43rd Inf. Co.I
Randall, William H. AL 1st Regt. Mobile Vol. Co.A
Randall, Wm. H. AL 38th Inf. Co.G
Randall, William H. AL 41st Inf. Co.C
Randall, William H. TN Cav. 17th Bn. (Sanders') Co.C
Randall, William L. LA 1st (Nelligan's) Inf. Co.F,K Capt.
Randall, Wm. L. TX Cav. Border's Regt. Williams' Co.
Randall, William R. TX 14th Cav. Co.K Sgt.
Randall, William W. GA 13th Cav. Co.A
Randall, W.M.G. AL 56th Part.Rangers Co.K Capt.
Randall, W.P. MS 38th Cav. Co.F
Randall, W.R. MS 1st Cav. Co.G Cpl.
Randall, W.R. MO 9th Bn.S.S. Co.C
Randall, W.R. SC 2nd Arty. Co.E
Randall, W.R. TN 12th Inf. Co.A
Randall, W.R. TN 12th (Cons.) Inf. Co.A
Randall, W.R. TN 49th Inf. Co.F
Randall, X.C. GA 17th Inf. Co.K 1st Lt.
Randall, Young A. GA Siege Arty. 28th Bn. Co.C
Randalls, Churchwell TN 25th Inf. Co.C
Randals, Benjamin TN 16th Inf. Co.I Maj.
Randals, Dion C. TN 16th Inf. Co.I
Randals, James VA 7th Cav. Baylor's Co.
Randbrar, J.L. AL 17th Inf. Co.A
Randel, A. MS 2nd (Quinn's St.Troops) Inf. Co.C
Randel, Anderson S. GA 34th Inf. Co.G
Randel, Carver SC 1st St.Troops Co.A
Randel, Ira W. GA 24th Inf. Co.H
Randel, James M. MS 39th Inf. Co.I Capt.
Randel, John LA Inf. 1st Sp.Bn. (Wheat's) New Co.D
Randel, John C. TN 42nd Inf. 2nd Co.K
Randel, John M. TN 10th (DeMoss') Cav. Co.B 2nd Lt.
Randel, Nacy M. TN 10th (DeMoss') Cav. Co.B Sgt.
Randell, A. MS 1st (King's) Inf. (St.Troops) Co.B

Randell, B.J. SC 6th Inf. 1st Co.A, 2nd Co.A 2nd Lt.
Randell, B.J. SC Inf. 7th Bn. (Enfield Rifles) Co.H 1st Lt.
Randell, F.E. SC 2nd Cav. Co.G
Randell, F.M. TN 42nd Inf. Co.C
Randell, F.M. 4th Conf.Inf. Co.H
Randell, Harvey R. TN 14th Inf. Co.F
Randell, James D. SC 1st Arty. Co.B
Randell, James M. MS 43rd Inf. Co.D Cpl.
Randell, James M. NC 64th Inf. Co.C
Randell, J.F. TX Waul's Legion Co.A
Randell, J.J. TN 42nd Inf. Co.C
Randell, J.J. 4th Conf.Inf. Co.H
Randell, John MO 1st N.E. Cav.
Randell, Joseph W. NC 64th Inf. Co.C
Randell, R.C. MS 37th Inf. Co.I
Randell, Samuel J. MS 13th Inf. Co.K Capt.
Randell, Vans FL 1st Inf. Old Co.F Capt.
Randell, W.L. FL 2nd Inf. Co.H
Randells, J.W. KY 2nd (Duke's) Cav.
Randelman, William V. NC 33rd Inf. Co.G
Randels, Joseph NC Cav. 5th Bn. Co.C
Randels, Joseph NC 6th Cav. (65th St.Troops) Co.C
Randen, Joseph LA 14th (Austin's) Bn.S.S. Co.B
Rander, Joseph LA 11th Inf. Co.D
Rander, N. NC 3rd Jr.Res. Co.H
Randerath, Edward GA 9th Inf. Co.F 1st Sgt.
Randill, J. MD Arty. 4th Btty.
Randit, Francis GA 12th Inf. Co.A
Randit, Henry J. GA 12th Inf. Co.A
Randit, Jeremiah GA 12th Inf. Co.A
Randit, Jeremiah M. GA 2nd Cav. Co.G Cpl.
Randit, J.R. GA Lt.Arty. Anderson's Btty.
Randle, --- TX Cav. McCord's Frontier Regt. Co.F
Randle, A.H. TX 2nd Cav. Co.K
Randle, Albert G. MS Inf. 3rd Bn. Co.G
Randle, Alexander MS 2nd Cav. Co.B
Randle, Angus P. AR 15th (Josey's) Inf. Co.C
Randle, Asa F. MS Inf. 5th Bn. Co.A
Randle, Asa F. MS 43rd Inf. Co.I
Randle, Benjamin VA Inf. 23rd Bn. Co.A
Randle, B.F.M. AL 9th Inf. Co.E
Randle, B.P. SC 16th Inf. Co.F
Randle, Charles TX 1st Hvy.Arty. Co.B
Randle, C.L. KY 1st Inf. Co.E Capt.
Randle, C.L. KY 7th Mtd.Inf. Co.A Capt.
Randle, Columbus C. AR 15th (Josey's) Inf. Co.G
Randle, D.A. TX 35th (Brown's) Cav. 2nd Co.B
Randle, David NC 6th Cav. (65th St.Troops) Co.A,F
Randle, David A. TN 11th Inf. Co.H,A
Randle, D.H. MO 5th Cav. Co.C
Randle, E. LA 12th Inf. 2nd Co.M
Randle, E.C. TN 19th & 20th (Cons.) Cav. Co.K
Randle, Edmond D. NC 42nd Inf. Co.K
Randle, Edmund D. NC 14th Inf. Co.H
Randle, Edmund G. MS 48th Inf. Co.B Sgt.
Randle, Edward MO 8th Cav. Co.E
Randle, Edward VA 122nd Mil. Co.F
Randle, Edward T. TX 35th (Brown's) Cav. 2nd Co.B 2nd Lt.
Randle, Edwin D. AR Lt.Arty. Wiggins' Btty. Sgt.

Randle, Elijah P. AL 19th Inf. Co.H
Randle, Emiles LA 2nd Cav. Co.G
Randle, E.O. TN 20th (Russell's) Cav. Co.F
Randle, E.P. TN 15th Inf. Co.A 2nd Lt.
Randle, Ervin AR 7th Inf. Co.I
Randle, E. Troup AL 3rd Inf. Co.D Capt.
Randle, E.W. TN 19th & 20th (Cons.) Cav. Co.A QMSgt.
Randle, F.D. MS 43rd Inf. Co.B
Randle, Fount P. KY 6th Mtd.Inf. Co.F,I Sgt.Maj.
Randle, G.D. TN 30th Inf. Co.E
Randle, George A. VA 58th Mil. Co.C
Randle, George W.L. TX 10th Inf. Co.C
Randle, G.H. AR Mtd.Vol. (St.Troops) Abraham's Co.
Randle, G.W.L. TX Granbury's Cons.Brig. Co.D
Randle, Hamilton F. AL 4th Inf. Co.A
Randle, Harvy O. TN Cav. 2nd Bn. (Biffle's) Co.C Sgt.
Randle, H.C. LA 6th Cav. Co.C Sgt.
Randle, Henry MS Inf. 1st St.Troops Co.G
Randle, H.S. TN 20th (Russell's) Cav. Co.F
Randle, H.S. TN 46th Inf. Co.A
Randle, Isaac W. MS 11th Inf. Co.I
Randle, J. SC 16th Inf. Co.F
Randle, J. TX 3rd (Kirby's) Bn.Vol. Co.A
Randle, J.A. TX Cav. Border's Regt. Maj.
Randle, James GA 11th Cav. Co.D
Randle, James MS Cav. 4th Bn. Co.C
Randle, James TN 19th & 20th (Cons.) Cav. Co.B
Randle, James TN 20th (Russell's) Cav. Co.B
Randle, James C. AL 3rd Inf. Co.D Sgt.
Randle, James C. Gen. & Staff 1st Lt.,ADC
Randle, James E. TN 19th (Biffle's) Cav. Co.H
Randle, James L. GA Frazier's/Graham's Arty.
Randle, James R. MS Inf. 3rd Bn. (St.Troops) Co.E
Randle, James R. TN 50th Inf. Co.H,I Jr.2nd Lt.
Randle, J.C. Ruggles' Staff ADC
Randle, J.E. TN Inf. 3rd Bn. Co.A
Randle, J.G. TX 11th Cav. Co.K
Randle, J.G. TX 35th (Brown's) Cav. 1st Lt.
Randle, J.G. TX Cav. Mann's Regt. Co.B 1st Lt.
Randle, J.H. AR Inf. Cocke's Regt. Co.C
Randle, J.H. TN 18th (Newsom's) Cav. Co.E
Randle, J.H. TN 21st (Wilson's) Cav. Co.H Sgt.
Randle, J.K. 15th Conf.Cav. Co.G
Randle, J.L. LA 3rd (Harrison's) Cav. Co.G
Randle, J.M. SC 13th Inf. Co.E
Randle, J.M. TN 18th (Newsom's) Cav. Co.D Cpl.
Randle, J.M. TN 19th & 20th (Cons.) Cav. Co.H
Randle, J.M. TN 5th Inf. 2nd Co.F
Randle, John VA Inf. 23rd Bn. Co.A
Randle, John A. TX 5th Inf. Co.E
Randle, John A. TX 20th Inf. Co.C
Randle, John A. Gen. & Staff Capt.,AQM
Randle, John D. AR 3rd Inf. Co.A Music.
Randle, John D. MS Inf. 3rd Bn. Co.D
Randle, John E.W. AL 19th Inf. Co.H 1st Sgt.
Randle, John G. LA 13th Bn. (Part.Rangers) Co.E Capt.

Randle, John H. AL Cav. Forrest's Regt.
Randle, John J. LA 28th (Gray's) Inf. Co.H
Randle, John S. MS Inf. 5th Bn. Co.A
Randle, John S. MS 43rd Inf. Co.I
Randle, John T. TX 8th Cav. Co.A
Randle, John W. MS 43rd Inf. Co.B
Randle, John W. NC 28th Inf. Co.D 2nd Lt.
Randle, Joseph VA 58th Mil. Co.H
Randle, J.R. TN 50th (Cons.) Inf. Co.I Jr.2nd Lt.
Randle, J.T. TN Inf. 1st Cons.Regt. Co.I
Randle, J.W. MS 6th Cav. Morgan's Co. Jr.2nd Lt.
Randle, J.W. MS 12th Cav. Co.C 2nd Lt.
Randle, L. MS Inf. 1st Bn. Co.A
Randle, L.C. GA Cav. 29th Bn. Co.E
Randle, L.C. TX 20th Inf. Co.C
Randle, Merritt MS Inf. 1st St.Troops Co.G
Randle, Mirabeau L. MS 11th Inf. Co.I Sgt.
Randle, M.L. MS 6th Cav. Morgan's Co.
Randle, M.L. MS 12th Cav. Co.C
Randle, O.P. TX Granbury's Cons.Brig. Co.A Cpl.
Randle, Oscar E. GA 55th Inf. Co.B
Randle, P.H. TN 46th Inf. Co.G Capt.
Randle, P.M. TX 29th Cav. Co.D
Randle, Richard VA 23rd Cav. 2nd Co.K
Randle, Robert LA Cav. Webb's Co.
Randle, Robert LA 12th Inf. Co.L
Randle, S.M. SC 16th Inf. Co.F
Randle, T.G. TN 5th Inf. Co.A
Randle, T.G. TN 51st (Cons.) Inf. Co.K
Randle, Thomas LA Cav. Webb's Co.
Randle, Thomas G. TN 52nd Inf. Maj.
Randle, Thomas K. MS 30th Inf. Co.F Sgt.
Randle, Thomas S. LA 12th Inf. Co.L
Randle, T.J. TN 5th Inf. 2nd Co.C, 1st Co.F
Randle, Walter H. GA 4th Inf. Co.K
Randle, Walter J. MD 1st Inf. Co.I
Randle, W.G. TN 46th Inf. Co.B Capt.
Randle, W.H. TN 11th Inf. Co.A
Randle, W.H. TX Cav. Border's Regt. Co.K,D 1st Lt.
Randle, Wiley W. AL 27th Inf. Co.C Sgt.
Randle, William MS 2nd Part.Rangers Co.A
Randle, William MO Cav. 9th Regt.St.Guard Co.D 2nd Lt.
Randle, William NC 52nd Inf. Co.I
Randle, William E. MS 26th Inf. Co.D
Randle, William H. AL 15th Bn.Part.Rangers Co.B
Randle, William H. LA 12th Inf. Co.G
Randle, William H. MS Cav. Jeff Davis Legion Co.C
Randle, William H. MS 1st (Patton's) Inf. Co.B Ord.Sgt.
Randle, William H. MS 11th Inf. Co.I
Randle, William J. GA 3rd Inf. Co.A
Randle, William M. NC 37th Inf. Co.B
Randle, William M.G. AL 55th Vol. Co.B,K Capt.
Randle, William P. TN 14th Inf. Co.E Sgt.
Randle, Willis NC 52nd Inf. Co.I Jr.2nd Lt.
Randle, W.L. TX Cav. Terry's Regt. Co.A
Randle, W.N. AL 55th Vol. Co.K
Randle, W.P. MS 7th Cav. Co.A
Randle, W.W. TN 46th Inf. Co.H

Randle, Wyatt MS Inf. 2nd Bn. Co.B Sgt.
Randle, Wyatt MS 48th Inf. Co.B Sgt.
Randleman, Augustus T. NC 28th Inf. Co.F Sgt.
Randleman, Jacob M. NC Res. Co.A
Randles, D.C. TN 13th (Gore's) Cav. Co.I
Randles, Franklin MO 4th Inf. Co.G Cpl.
Randles, Franklin M. MO Cav. Wood's Regt. Co.A Jr.2nd Lt.
Randles, F.W. MO 1st & 4th Cons.Inf. Co.B
Randles, J. TN 15th (Stewart's) Cav. Co.B
Randles, J.H. AL 30th Inf. Co.H
Randles, John AL 49th Inf. Co.H
Randles, John TN Cav. 5th Bn. (McClellan's) Co.F
Randles, John B. AL 7th Inf.
Randles, Joseph NC 16th Inf. Co.E
Randles, Joseph NC 58th Inf. Co.I
Randles, J.T. AL Cav. Moreland's Regt. Co.G
Randles, Silas M. AL 49th Inf. Co.H
Randles, S.R. AL Cav. Moreland's Regt. Co.G
Randles, Stephen TN 25th Inf. Co.A
Randlet, Samuel L. LA 2nd Cav. Co.C Sgt.
Randlett, Andrew J. VA 44th Inf. Co.G
Randling, Thomas MO 1st Inf. Co.H
Randlman, J.B. AR 15th Mil. Co.C
Randnitzky, Frederick GA 1st (Olmstead's) Inf. 1st Co.A
Rando, Guiseppe LA Mil. 6th Regt.Eur.Brig. (Italian Guards Bn.) Co.2
Randol, A.G. MO Cav. 2nd Regt.St.Guard Co.A
Randol, Benjamin LA 21st (Kennedy's) Inf. Co.A
Randol, Benjamin E. VA 34th Mil. Co.A
Randol, C.W. MO Cav. 2nd Regt.St.Guard Co.A
Randol, E.H. TN 20th (Russell's) Cav. QMSgt.
Randol, F.A. MO Cav. 2nd Regt.St.Guard Co.A
Randol, George TN Lt.Arty. Baxter's Co.
Randol, J.G. MO Cav. 2nd Regt.St.Guard Co.A Cpl.
Randol, John MO 7th Cav. Ward's Co.
Randol, John P. MO 8th Cav. Co.C,E
Randol, Joseph C. TX 31st Cav. Co.B Sgt.
Randol, R.G. MO Cav. 2nd Regt.St.Guard Co.A
Randol, Robert G. AR 32nd Inf. Co.B
Randol, Rodolph MO 8th Cav. Co.K
Randol, William GA Inf. 4th Bn. (St.Guards) Co.A
Randol, William J. MO 8th Cav. Co.B
Randol, W.L. LA 2nd Inf. Co.C
Randolf, S.E. GA 12th Inf. Co.I
Randoll, John H. AL 59th Inf. Co.F
Randoll, S.S. AL 59th Inf. Co.F
Randolph, --- MS 2nd Part.Rangers Co.C
Randolph, --- TX Cav. Border's Bn. Co.G Capt.
Randolph, A. LA Mil. Beauregard Regt. Cpl.
Randolph, A. SC 14th Inf. Co.C
Randolph, Abraham AL 27th Inf. Co.K
Randolph, A.C. Lee's Div. Ch.Surg.
Randolph, Addison S. GA 48th Inf. Co.C
Randolph, A.J. MS 25th Inf. Co.K
Randolph, A.J. MO 1st Inf. Co.C
Randolph, A.J. MO 1st & 4th Cons.Inf. Co.A,G
Randolph, A.J. MO 3rd & 5th Cons.Inf.
Randolph, A.J. VA 1st Cav. Surg.
Randolph, A.L. FL Cadets Military Inst. 1st Lt.
Randolph, Algernon S. LA 3rd Inf. Co.A 2nd Lt.
Randolph, Allan VA 4th Cav. Co.I,E

Randolph, A.M. Gen. & Staff Chap.
Randolph, Ananias NC 29th Inf. Co.B
Randolph, Andrew J. TN 2nd (Ashby's) Cav. Co.G
Randolph, Andrew J. TN Cav. 4th Bn. (Branner's) Co.B
Randolph, Andrew J. TN 53rd Inf. Co.G
Randolph, Andrew W. KY 6th Mtd.Inf. Co.B
Randolph, Angus B. LA 8th Inf. Co.E
Randolph, Ansel NC 16th Inf. Co.C
Randolph, Ansil NC 39th Inf. Co.K
Randolph, Augustus LA 8th Inf. Co.D 2nd Lt.
Randolph, B. AL 8th (Hatch's) Cav. Co.F 2nd Lt.
Randolph, B. LA Inf. Pelican Regt. Co.G
Randolph, B. TN 45th Inf. Co.C Sgt.Maj.
Randolph, B.D. VA 54th Mil. Co.C,D
Randolph, B.E. AL 8th (Hatch's) Cav. Co.B Cpl.
Randolph, Benjamin LA Inf. 4th Bn. Co.C
Randolph, Benjamin F. MS 12th Inf. Co.F
Randolph, Benjamin F. MS 19th Inf. Co.G
Randolph, Benjamin Fitz NC 18th Inf. Co.K
Randolph, Benjamin Henry VA 5th Inf. Co.I
Randolph, Benton TX 4th Inf. Co.H 1st Lt.
Randolph, Benton Gen. & Staff, Cav. Capt.
Randolph, Beverly GA 4th (Clinch's) Cav. Co.B
Randolph, Beverly Gen. & Staff Maj.
Randolph, B.L. LA 1st Hvy.Arty. (Reg.) Co.E
Randolph, Blakey J. VA 52nd Inf. Co.D
Randolph, B.M. VA Inf. Hutter's Co.
Randolph, B.N. GA 13th Cav. Co.D
Randolph, Buckner M. VA 49th Inf. Co.C Capt.
Randolph, C.A. VA VMI Co.C
Randolph, Calvin TN 28th (Cons.) Inf. Co.H
Randolph, Calvin TN 84th Inf. Co.D
Randolph, Calvin D. VA 5th Cav. (12 mo. '61-2) Co.A
Randolph, Calvin D. VA Cav. 14th Bn. Co.C Sgt.
Randolph, Calvin D. VA 15th Cav. Co.C
Randolph, Carson P. TN 32nd Inf. Co.F
Randolph, Cater NC 44th Inf. Co.C
Randolph, C.D. VA Inf. 2nd Bn.Loc.Def. Co.D
Randolph, C.H. TX Inf. Carter's Co.
Randolph, Charles NC 2nd Cav. (19th St.Troops) Co.D
Randolph, Charles A. NC 55th Inf. Co.E
Randolph, Charles C. VA 6th Cav. Co.F
Randolph, Charles H. VA 1st Arty. 1st Co.C
Randolph, Charles H. VA 1st Inf. Co.F
Randolph, Charles W. TX 31st Cav. Co.C
Randolph, C.L. TN 41st Inf. Co.E
Randolph, C.L. Johnson's Div. Maj.,QM
Randolph, Clinton TX 1st (Yager's) Cav. Co.K
Randolph, Clinton TX Cav. 8th (Taylor's) Bn. Co.B
Randolph, C.M. Eng. Capt.,Ch.Eng.
Randolph, Daniel F. VA Horse Arty. Lurty's Co.
Randolph, David TN Inf. 154th Sr.Regt. Co.H
Randolph, D.J. TX 21st Cav. Co.A 1st Sgt.
Randolph, D.J. TX 4th Inf. Co.H
Randolph, D.W. MS Inf. 2nd Bn. (St.Troops) Co.B
Randolph, D.W.C. TN 14th Inf. 3rd Lt.
Randolph, E. AR 18th (Marmaduke's) Inf. Co.C
Randolph, E. AR Mil. Desha Cty.Bn. 2nd Lt.

Randolph, E.B. AL 7th Cav. Capt.,ACS
Randolph, E.B. AL Lt.Arty. Goldthwaite's Btty.
Randolph, E.B. Al 46th Inf. Capt.,ACS
Randolph, E.C. VA 7th Cav. 1st Lt.
Randolph, E.C. VA 12th Cav. Co.H Capt.
Randolph, Edmon 3rd Conf.Inf. Co.C
Randolph, Edward G. LA 9th Inf. Co.D Col.
Randolph, Edw. R. LA Mil. Beauregard Bn. Sgt.Maj.
Randolph, Elihu GA 1st Inf. (St.Guards) Co.G
Randolph, Elijah TN 25th Inf. Co.A
Randolph, Elisha NC 16th Inf. Co.C
Randolph, E.R. LA Mil. 4th Regt. 3rd Brig. 1st Div. Co.D Capt.
Randolph, E.R. VA 3rd Inf.Loc.Def. Co.F
Randolph, Eston FL 1st Inf. Old Co.D,G Sgt.
Randolph, E.W. TX Inf. Timmons' Regt. Co.I
Randolph, F. MS 28th Cav. Co.F
Randolph, F. TX 9th (Nichols') Inf. Co.K
Randolph, F. TX Inf. Timmons' Regt. Co.E
Randolph, F. TX Waul's Legion Co.D
Randolph, F.C. AL 7th Cav. Co.A Maj.
Randolph, F.C. AL Lt.Arty. Goldthwaite's Btty. 1st Sgt.
Randolph, Flavius J. AR 9th Inf. Co.C Capt.
Randolph, Francis C. AL 3rd Inf. Co.G
Randolph, Franklin KY 6th Cav. Co.G
Randolph, G.B. AL Cav. 24th Bn. Co.A
Randolph, George W. AL 11th Cav. Co.F
Randolph, George W. KY 2nd Cav.
Randolph, George W. KY 2nd Mtd.Inf. Co.B
Randolph, George W. MS 2nd Part.Rangers Co.F,D Bvt.2nd Lt.
Randolph, George W. TX 22nd Cav. Co.B Sgt.
Randolph, George W. VA 10th Cav. Co.D
Randolph, George W. VA 1st Arty. Col.
Randolph, Geo. W. Gen. & Staff Brig.Gen.,War Res. Secretary
Randolph, G.F. TX 20th Inf. Co.F Cpl.
Randolph, Green TX Cav. Morgan's Regt. Co.A
Randolph, G.W. MS 18th Cav. Co.D
Randolph, G.W. MS 1st (Patton's) Inf. Co.G Sgt.
Randolph, G.W. TX 2nd Inf. Co.G Cpl.
Randolph, H. GA 13th Cav. Co.H
Randolph, H. KY 1st Bn.Mtd.Rifles Co.B
Randolph, H. MS Cav. Davenport's Bn. (St.Troops) Co.B
Randolph, H. TN Inf. 4th Cons.Regt. Co.I Sgt.
Randolph, Harris TN 30th Inf. Co.B Sgt.
Randolph, Henry MS 26th Inf. Co.G
Randolph, Henry W. KY 6th Mtd.Inf.
Randolph, Hesekiah GA 34th Inf. Co.B
Randolph, Hilliard J. GA 9th Inf. (St.Guards) DeLaperriere's Co.
Randolph, Hill J. GA 13th Cav. Co.K 2nd Lt.
Randolph, Hill J., Jr. GA 16th Inf. Ord.Sgt.
Randolph, H.J. GA 13th Cav. Co.A Cpl.
Randolph, H.J. GA 16th Inf. Co.G
Randolph, Hugh J. SC Inf. 7th Bn. (Enfield Rifles) Co.D
Randolph, H.W. GA 13th Cav. Co.I
Randolph, I.M. MO 10th Cav. Co.H
Randolph, Isaac TN Lt.Arty. Polk's Btty. Artif.
Randolph, Isaac H. LA Washington Arty.Bn. Co.2
Randolph, Isham G. TN 18th Inf. Co.C Lt.

Randolph, J. TN Cav. 11th or 4th Regt. Co.D Lt.
Randolph, James GA 41st Inf. Co.C
Randolph, James MS 6th Cav. Co.E
Randolph, James MS Lt.Arty. (The Hudson Btty.) Hoole's Co. Sgt.
Randolph, James NC 29th Inf. Co.B
Randolph, James TN 53rd Inf. Co.G Cpl.
Randolph, James TX Legion Co.B
Randolph, James A. AL 5th Inf. Co.A
Randolph, James A. VA 41st Inf. Co.F Cpl.
Randolph, James B. NC 15th Inf. Co.A Capt.
Randolph, James B. NC 58th Inf. Co.G
Randolph, James B. TN 44th (Cons.) Inf. Co.E Sgt.
Randolph, James B. TN 55th (McKoin's) Inf. Co.H Bvt.2nd Lt.
Randolph, James D. AL Montgomery Guards
Randolph, James E. LA Cav. 18th Bn. Co.D Capt.
Randolph, James E. TN 44th (Cons.) Inf. Co.E Lt.
Randolph, James E. TN 55th (McKoin's) Inf. Co.H
Randolph, Jas. J. AL 62nd Inf.
Randolph, James J. TN Inf. 22nd Bn. Co.D
Randolph, James P. VA 44th Inf. Co.D 1st Sgt.
Randolph, James R. TX 17th Cav. Co.G
Randolph, James W. AR 25th Inf. Co.H
Randolph, James W. TN 41st Inf. Co.D
Randolph, J.B. AL 27th Inf. Co.K
Randolph, J.B. AL Cp. of Instr. Talladega
Randolph, J.B. MS 2nd (Davidson's) Inf. Potts' Co.
Randolph, J.C. GA 13th Cav. Co.D
Randolph, J.E. GA 4th Cav. (St.Guards) White's Co. Sgt.
Randolph, J.E. Conf.Cav. Powers' Regt. Co.D Capt.
Randolph, Jeremiah C. AL 43rd Inf. Co.I
Randolph, Jerry N. MS 26th Inf. Co.G
Randolph, Jesse NC 44th Inf. Co.C
Randolph, Jessee LA 11th Inf. Co.G
Randolph, Jessie A. LA 14th (Austin's) Bn.S.S. Co.A
Randolph, J.F.W. GA 16th Inf. Co.D
Randolph, J.G. TX 25th Cav. Co.B
Randolph, J.H. GA 7th Cav. Co.D
Randolph, J.H. GA Cav. 24th Bn. Co.C
Randolph, J.H. Jones' Staff Surg.
Randolph, J. Innis Eng.,CSA 1st Lt.
Randolph, J.J. TX 11th Inf. Co.B 1st Sgt.
Randolph, J.K. TN Cav. 13th Bn. (Day's) Co.D
Randolph, J.K.P. TN 31st Inf. Co.C Capt.
Randolph, J.M. AL 27th Inf. Co.K
Randolph, J.M. GA 13th Cav. Co.I
Randolph, J.M. GA 13th Cav. Co.K
Randolph, J.M. TX 21st Cav. Co.A
Randolph, J.M. TX 2nd Inf. Co.G
Randolph, J.N. GA 13th Cav. Co.D
Randolph, John GA 41st Inf. Co.C
Randolph, John LA 1st (Nelligan's) Inf. Co.I
Randolph, John NC 2nd Cav. (19th St.Troops) Co.H Capt.
Randolph, John NC 45th Inf. Co.H
Randolph, John TN 18th (Newsom's) Cav. Chap.

Randolph, John TN 31st Inf. Co.C Chap.
Randolph, John TN 84th Inf. Co.D
Randolph, John TX 20th Inf. Co.H
Randolph, John VA Cav. Mosby's Regt.
  (Part.Rangers) Co.D
Randolph, John VA 1st Inf. Co.E
Randolph, John VA Inf. 25th Bn. Co.C 1st Lt.
Randolph, John Sig.Corps,CSA
Randolph, John A.E. TX 1st (Yager's) Cav.
  Co.F
Randolph, John C. GA 34th Inf. Co.E
Randolph, John C. NC 1st Inf. (6 mo. '61) Co.I
Randolph, John E. MS 21st Inf. Co.A
Randolph, John E. NC 27th Inf. Co.H
Randolph, John F. LA Washington Arty.Bn.
  Co.3,2 Cpl.
Randolph, John H. LA 2nd Cav. Co.I
Randolph, John H. TN 14th Inf. Co.I
Randolph, John J. MS 26th Inf. Co.G
Randolph, John L. MS 14th Inf. Co.B
Randolph, John L. TX Cav. Martin's Regt. Co.B
  Capt.
Randolph, John M. NC 29th Inf. Co.A
Randolph, John M. TN Cav. 4th Bn. (Branner's)
  Co.B Cpl.
Randolph, John M. VA 4th Cav. Co.H
Randolph, John R. AL 28th Inf. Co.F
Randolph, John R. TN 32nd Inf. Co.B
Randolph, John R. TN 35th Inf. 2nd Co.F
Randolph, John R. TN 53rd Inf. Co.C
Randolph, John S. AR 25th Inf. Co.H
Randolph, John T. AL 10th Cav.
Randolph, John T. GA 13th Cav. Co.D
Randolph, John T. GA 16th Inf. Co.G
Randolph, John T. NC 3rd Inf. Co.A
Randolph, John W. AR 35th Inf. Co.B
Randolph, John W. TN 2nd (Ashby's) Cav. Co.G
Randolph, John W. TX Waul's Legion Co.A
Randolph, Joseph AR 1st Mtd.Rifles Co.K
Randolph, Joseph AR 25th Inf. Co.H
Randolph, Joseph TX 9th Cav. Co.B
Randolph, Joseph B. MS 26th Inf. Co.C
Randolph, Joseph E. VA 44th Inf. Co.D Sgt.
Randolph, Joseph T. MS St.Cav. Perrin's Bn.
  Co.F 3rd Lt.
Randolph, Joshua M. GA 9th Inf. (St.Guards)
  DeLaperriere's Co.
Randolph, J.R. TN Cav. 12th Bn. (Day's) Co.D
Randolph, J.S. AR 2nd Vol. Co.B
Randolph, J.T. AL 27th Inf. Co.K
Randolph, J.T. AL 57th Inf. Co.K
Randolph, J.T. MS Inf. 2nd St.Troops Co.G
  Sgt.
Randolph, J.T. MO 6th Cav. Co.E Bvt.2nd Lt.
Randolph, J.T. TN 14th Inf. Co.C Sgt.
Randolph, J.T.W. GA 16th Inf. Co.G
Randolph, J.V. TN 28th (Cons.) Inf. Co.H Sgt.
Randolph, J.V. TN 84th Inf. Co.D
Randolph, J.W. AR 1st Mtd.Rifles Co.K
Randolph, J.W. GA 13th Cav. Co.K
Randolph, J.W. TN 15th (Cons.) Cav. Co.A
Randolph, J.W. TN 19th (Biffle's) Cav. Co.G
  Capt.
Randolph, J.W. TN Inf. Spencer's Co.
Randolph, J.W. TX 2nd Inf. Co.G Cpl.
Randolph, J.W. VA 4th Cav. Co.F
Randolph, J.W. VA 8th Cav. Co.K

Randolph, J.W. VA 12th Cav. Co.H 1st Lt.
Randolph, J.W. VA Lt.Arty. W.P. Carter's Co.
Randolph, K. AL 59th Inf. Co.H
Randolph, Lafayette TN 32nd Inf. Co.F
Randolph, L.B. AL 13th Bn.Part.Rangers Co.C
Randolph, L.B. AL 56th Part.Rangers Co.G
Randolph, L.C. NC 5th Cav. (63rd St.Troops)
  Surg.
Randolph, L.C. VA 9th Cav. Surg.
Randolph, L.C. VA 46th Inf. 2nd Co.I 1st Lt.
Randolph, Leroy GA 41st Inf. Co.C Cpl.
Randolph, Levi H. TN 53rd Inf. Co.G
Randolph, Lewis VA Inf. 1st Bn. Co.C 1st Lt.
Randolph, Lewis C. Gen. & Staff Surg.
Randolph, Luther R. GA 34th Inf. Co.D
Randolph, M. TX Inf. 2nd Lt.
Randolph, M.A. AR 26th Inf. Co.K
Randolph, Marion A. VA Inf. 4th Bn.Loc.Def.
  Co.A
Randolph, Mathew NC 3rd Inf. Co.A
Randolph, Mathew P. GA 41st Inf. Co.C
Randolph, M.C. Gen. & Staff Surg.
Randolph, M.E. VA 3rd Inf.Loc.Def. 2nd Co.G
Randolph, Merewether L. VA 21st Inf. Co.F
Randolph, M.L. Sig.Corps,CSA Capt.
Randolph, Morgan NC 58th Inf. Co.G
Randolph, Moses L. LA 11th Inf. Co.B Sgt.
Randolph, M.P. GA 7th Inf. (St.Guards) Co.A
Randolph, Murray W. AR 1st Mtd.Rifles Co.K
Randolph, M.W. GA 16th Inf. Co.D
Randolph, M.W. MS 28th Cav. Co.F
Randolph, N. TX 16th Inf. Co.K 2nd Lt.
Randolph, N. 4th Conf.Eng.Troops Co.E Artif.
Randolph, N. Kellersberg's Corps Sap. &
  Min.,CSA Artif.
Randolph, Napoleon Bonapart VA 6th Inf. Fer-
  guson's Co.
Randolph, Napoleon C. TN 32nd Inf. Co.F
Randolph, N.B. VA 12th Inf. Co.H
Randolph, Nicholas TX Inf. Griffin's Bn. Co.E
Randolph, N.L. GA 10th Inf. Co.C
Randolph, Norman VA Cav. 1st Bn.
  (Loc.Def.Troops) Co.C Sgt.
Randolph, Norman V. VA Cav. Mosby's Regt.
  (Part.Rangers) Co.E
Randolph, P.B. TX 9th (Nichols') Inf. Co.E
  Cpl.
Randolph, P.B. TX 20th Inf. Co.H Sgt.
Randolph, P.C. MS Cav. Ham's Regt. Co.B 2nd
  Lt.
Randolph, Peyton AL 5th Inf. 1st Lt.
Randolph, Peyton 1st Conf.Eng.Troops Maj.
Randolph, Peyton L. GA Inf. 2nd Bn. Co.D
Randolph, P.H. AL Gid Nelson Lt.Arty.
Randolph, P.M. TN 28th (Cons.) Inf. Co.H
Randolph, P.M. TN 84th Inf. Co.D
Randolph, R. AL 7th Cav. Co.E,H 1st Lt.
Randolph, R. AL 7th Cav. Co.G 1st Sgt.
Randolph, R. AL Lt.Ary. Goldthwaite's Btty.
Randolph, R. GA 16th Inf. Co.B
Randolph, R. LA 11th Inf. Co.K 2nd Lt.
Randolph, R.C. AL Mil. 4th Vol. Co.I
Randolph, R.C. MS Cav. Jeff Davis Legion Co.E
  1st Lt.
Randolph, Reuben NC 58th Inf. Co.K
Randolph, R.H. FL 1st Inf. Old Co.G
Randolph, R.H. FL 8th Inf. Co.B

Randolph, R.H. TN Inf. 154th Sr.Regt. Co.A
  1st Lt.
Randolph, R.H. Gen. & Staff Asst.Surg.
Randolph, Richard NC 27th Inf. Co.H
Randolph, Richard H. FL 1st Inf. Co.G
Randolph, R.J. VA 3rd Inf.Loc.Def. Co.C
Randolph, Robert MO 1st N.E. Cav.
Randolph, Robert NC 3rd Inf. Co.A
Randolph, Robert NC 29th Inf. Co.B
Randolph, Robert NC 33rd Inf. Co.B
Randolph, Robert VA 4th Cav. Co.H Lt.Col.
Randolph, Robert C. VA 2nd Inf. Co.C 1st Lt.
Randolph, Robert G. VA 6th Inf. Ferguson's Co.
Randolph, Robert G. VA 12th Inf. Co.H
Randolph, Robert J. TX Cav. Hardeman's Regt.
  Co.E 2nd Lt.
Randolph, R.R. Gen. & Staff Capt.
Randolph, Ryland AL 1st Cav. 1st Co.K Cpl.
Randolph, Ryland AL Lt.Arty. Goldthwaite's
  Btty.
Randolph, Samuel NC 16th Inf. Co.C
Randolph, Samuel NC 45th Inf. Co.H
Randolph, Samuel A. TN 53rd Inf. Co.C
Randolph, Samuel G. AL 27th Inf. Co.K
Randolph, Samuel H. TN 13th Cav. Co.D
Randolph, Samuel H. TN Cav. Newsom's Regt.
  Co.D
Randolph, Samuel W. NC 29th Inf. Co.B
Randolph, S.H. SC 2nd Inf. Co.A
Randolph, S.H. SC 22nd Inf. Co.D
Randolph, S.H. TN 51st (Cons.) Inf. Co.E
Randolph, Shadrach NC 45th Inf. Co.H
Randolph, S. Hawe SC 20th Inf. Co.A
Randolph, S.T. AR 8th Inf. Co.F
Randolph, Stephen S. TN 32nd Inf. Co.H
Randolph, T. AR 11th & 17th (Cons.) Inf. Co.I
Randolph, Tandy K. GA 9th Inf. (St.Guards)
  DeLaperriere's Co. Cpl.
Randolph, T.B. AL Cp. of Instr. Talladega
Randolph, T.D. MS 28th Cav. Co.F Sgt.
Randolph, T.E. FL 2nd Cav. Co.D Cpl.
Randolph, T.E. FL 8th Inf. Co.B
Randolph, T.H. FL 2nd Cav. Co.D
Randolph, Thaddeus D. MS Lt.Arty. (The
  Hudson Btty.) Hoole's Co. 1st Lt.
Randolph, Thomas AR 17th (Griffith's) Inf. Co.C
Randolph, Thomas SC Inf. 7th Bn. (Enfield
  Rifles) Co.A
Randolph, Thomas TN Inf. 3rd Bn. Co.E
Randolph, Thomas VA 6th Inf. 1st Co.B
Randolph, Thomas B. AL 28th Inf. Co.F
Randolph, Thomas E. LA 1st (Nelligan's) Inf.
  Co.I
Randolph, Thomas E. NC 44th Inf. Co.C
Randolph, Thomas E. VA Lt.Arty. Woolfolk's
  Co.
Randolph, Thomas G. TN 55th (McKoin's) Inf.
  Co.H
Randolph, Thomas H.B. VA 2nd Inf. Co.C 1st
  Lt.
Randolph, Thomas Hugh P. Pendleton's Staff Lt.
Randolph, Thomas J. GA 13th Cav. Co.H
Randolph, Thomas J. GA 9th Inf. (St.Guards)
  DeLaperriere's Co.
Randolph, Thomas J. TX 1st (McCulloch's) Cav.
  Co.B Sgt.

Randolph, Thomas J. VA 2nd Cav. Co.K 2nd Lt.

Randolph, Thomas J., Jr. VA 19th Inf. Co.A Sgt.

Randolph, Thomas L. NC 16th Inf. Co.C,A

Randolph, Thomas L. NC 39th Inf. Co.K

Randolph, Thomas L. NC Inf. Thomas Legion 1st Co.A

Randolph, Thomas M. NC 58th Inf. Co.G

Randolph, Thomas W. TX 11th Cav. AQM

Randolph, Thomas W. Gen. & Staff Capt.,QM

Randolph, Tip GA 12th Cav. Co.B

Randolph, T.J., Jr. Gen. & Staff, QM Dept. Maj.

Randolph, T.P. FL Lt.Arty. Dyke's Co. Cpl.

Randolph, T.P. FL Kilcrease Lt.Arty. Sgt.

Randolph, Tucker AL 51st (Part.Rangers) Co.K 1st Lt.

Randolph, Tucker VA 21st Inf. Co.F 1st Sgt.

Randolph, T.W. MS 2nd Part.Rangers Co.F,D Bvt.2nd Lt.

Randolph, T.W. TX Cav. Bourland's Regt. Co.D

Randolph, W. NC 3rd Jr.Res. Co.E

Randolph, Wash R. GA 16th Inf. Co.G,B

Randolph, W.C. TN 43rd Inf. Co.H

Randolph, W.C.N. Gen. & Staff Surg.

Randolph, W.D. FL 2nd Cav. Co.D Sgt.

Randolph, W.F. AL 32nd Inf. Co.I

Randolph, W.F. SC Inf. 7th Bn. (Enfield Rifles) Co.A

Randolph, W.F. SC 23rd Inf. Co.K

Randolph, W.H. LA 2nd Cav. Co.G

Randolph, W.H. TX Cav. W.H. Randolph's Co. Capt.

Randolph, W.H. TX 9th (Nichols') Inf. Co.E

Randolph, William AL 44th Inf. Co.D

Randolph, William AL 44th Inf. Co.E 1st Lt.

Randolph, William FL 1st Inf. Old Co.D,G

Randolph, William GA 28th Inf. Co.C

Randolph, William LA 13th Inf. Co.B

Randolph, William MS 26th Inf. Co.G,C Cpl.

Randolph, William MO 2nd Cav. Co.E

Randolph, William TN 22nd Inf. Co.I

Randolph, William A. LA Washington Arty.Bn. Co.2 Sgt.Maj.

Randolph, William C. MO 10th Cav. Co.A 1st Sgt.

Randolph, William C. TX 22nd Cav. Co.B 1st Lt.

Randolph, William F. VA 6th Cav. Co.F

Randolph, William F. VA Cav. 39th Bn. Co.B Capt.

Randolph, William F. Ewell's Staff Capt.

Randolph, William G. LA 7th Inf. Co.B 2nd Lt.

Randolph, William H. NC 2nd Arty. (36th St.Troops) Co.F

Randolph, William H. VA 5th Inf. Co.D Capt.

Randolph, William J. NC 58th Inf. Co.G

Randolph, William J. VA 19th Cav. Co.F

Randolph, William L. VA 57th Inf. Co.H 2nd Lt.

Randolph, William L. VA Inf. Hutter's Co.

Randolph, William L. Lee's Div. Capt.,Ord.Off.

Randolph, William T. TN 30th Inf. Co.B

Randolph, William T. VA 6th Inf. Co.F

Randolph, William W. VA 2nd Inf. Co.C Capt.

Randolph, William W. Gen. & Staff Capt.,AQM

Randolph, Wilson KY 5th Cav. Co.C

Randolph, W.J. SC 2nd Inf. Co.A

Randolph, W.J. TN 36th Inf. Co.E Sgt.

Randolph, W.L. TX Cav. Terry's Regt. Co.A

Randolph, W.L.O. GA 16th Inf. Co.G Cpl.

Randolph, W.M. GA 13th Cav. Co.D

Randolph, W.M. GA 23rd Inf. Co.A

Randolph, W.M. NC 3rd Inf. Co.A

Randolph, W.S., Jr. MS 28th Cav. Co.F

Randolph, W.S. MS Lt.Arty. 14th Bn. Co.B

Randolph, W.S. MS 9th Inf. Old Co.H

Randolph, W.S., Jr. MS 9th Inf. Old Co.H Cpl.

Randolph, W.W. TN 9th Inf. Co.K Capt.,AQM

Randolph, W. Willon VA 3rd Inf.Loc.Def. Co.A,B, 1st Co.G, 2nd Co.G 2nd Lt.

Randolph, Zachariah AR 3rd Inf. Co.L

Randols, William VA 18th Cav. 1st Co.G

Randon, Francois LA Mil. 1st Regt. French Brig. Co.6

Randon, H.S. TN 19th & 20th (Cons.) Cav. Co.K

Randon, Lewis TX 5th Inf. Co.F

Randon, Robert TX Terry's Mtd.Co. (St.Troops)

Randy, Francois LA 10th Inf. Co.I

Rane, E. AL 89th Mil. Co.G

Rane, Edward AL St.Arty. Co.D

Rane, J. AL 1st Regt. Mobile Vol. Co.I

Rane, Lewis VA Cav. Ferguson's Bn. Morris' Co.

Ranegar, George W. AL 12th Inf. Co.I

Raner, Wyman MS 22nd Inf. Co.B

Ranes, James TN 2nd (Ashby's) Cav. Co.D

Ranes, James M. AR 26th Inf. Co.I

Ranes, Jasper J. NC 47th Inf. Co.E Cpl.

Ranes, John M. AR 26th Inf. Co.I Cpl.

Ranes, Marshall S. NC 22nd Inf. Co.M

Ranes, W.H. VA 11th Cav. Co.D,G

Ranetree, Jackson GA 2nd Cav. Co.F

Ranew, George VA 16th Cav. Co.G

Ranew, M.J. FL Lt.Arty. Dyke's Co.

Raney, A. LA 13th Inf. Co.F

Raney, A.B. TX Inf. Rutherford's Co.

Raney, Albert TX 13th Vol. 1st Co.H

Raney, Albert S. VA Inf. 5th Bn. Co.C Lt.

Raney, Alexander KY 2nd (Duke's) Cav. Co.H

Raney, Alexander R. VA Hvy.Arty. Epes' Co.

Raney, Anda A. LA 19th Inf. Co.A

Raney, B.D. AR 45th Cav. Co.G

Raney, Bennett C. TN 1st (Turney's) Inf. Co.B

Raney, Bradford AR 27th Inf. Co.E 2nd Lt.

Raney, B.V. AL 3rd Inf. Co.B Capt.

Raney, Charles AL 59th Inf. Co.C

Raney, Charles F. Sig.Corps,CSA

Raney, Christopher C. TN 7th Inf. Co.K Drum.

Raney, Claiborn B. TN 41st Inf. Co.K 3rd Lt.

Raney, C.W. NC 5th Cav. (63rd St.Troops) Co.G

Raney, C.W. NC 12th Inf. Co.B,D Sgt.

Raney, D. MS 1st (King's) Inf. (St.Troops) Co.C

Raney, D. MS Inf. 1st Bn.St.Troops (12 mo. '62-3) Co.C

Raney, D.A. TX Cav. McCord's Frontier Regt. Co.H Cpl.

Raney, David MS Cav. Powers' Regt. Co.A

Raney, David TN 40th Inf. Co.I

Raney, David TX 25th Cav. Co.E

Raney, David A. NC 42nd Inf. Co.D Cpl.

Raney, Edward J. FL 2nd Cav. Co.A Sgt.

Raney, Edward J. GA Cav. 29th Bn. Co.A 1st Lt.

Raney, Elijah AR 38th Inf. Co.A 2nd Lt.

Raney, Eli N. MS 1st Lt.Arty. Co.I

Raney, Elisha AR 45th Cav. Co.G

Raney, E.N. MS Cav. 1st Bn. (Montgomery's) St.Troops Hammond's Co. Sgt.

Raney, E.N. MS Cav. Yerger's Regt. Co.A

Raney, Enoch GA 4th Bn.S.S. Co.A

Raney, F.M. AR Inf. Cocke's Regt. Co.F

Raney, Francis M. NC 47th Inf. Co.D

Raney, George NC 12th Inf. Co.B,D

Raney, George A. TX 6th Cav. Co.G 1st Sgt.

Raney, George P. GA Cav. 29th Bn. Co.A

Raney, George W. LA 19th Inf. Co.A

Raney, George W. MS 5th Cav. Co.C

Raney, George W. VA 17th Inf. Co.C

Raney, G.W. AR 58th Mil. Co.E

Raney, G.W. GA 7th Inf. (St.Guards) Co.C

Raney, Henry NC Pris.Guards Howard's Co.

Raney, Henry K. TN 41st Inf. Co.K

Raney, I.H. TN Inf. 2nd Cons.Regt. Co.A 1st Sgt.

Raney, Isaac A. NC 42nd Inf. Co.D

Raney, J. AR 8th Cav. Co.B

Raney, J.A. AR 2nd Vol. Co.D Sgt.

Raney, J.A. AR 14th (McCarver's) Inf. Co.K

Raney, J.A. AR 21st Inf. Co.F

Raney, James AR 13th Inf. Co.G

Raney, James GA 7th Mil.

Raney, James LA 9th Inf. Co.G

Raney, James LA 15th Inf. Co.D

Raney, James MO 1st N.E. Cav. White's Co.

Raney, James MO 6th Cav. Co.B Sgt.

Raney, James MO 1st & 4th Cons.Inf. Co.A

Raney, James MO St.Guard

Raney, James VA 64th Mtd.Inf. Co.C

Raney, James A. TN 1st (Turney's) Inf. Co.D

Raney, James A. TN 17th Inf. Co.K,E

Raney, James F. VA 21st Inf. Co.G

Raney, James H. TN 15th Cav. Co.E

Raney, James K. MS 44th Inf. Co.E

Raney, James P. AL 54th Inf.

Raney, James Polk TN 40th Inf. Co.A Cpl.

Raney, James R. NC 15th Inf. Co.G 1st Sgt.

Raney, James S. AR 1st Mtd.Rifles Co.E

Raney, James T. MS 2nd Cav. Co.K

Raney, James W. LA 1st Cav. Co.H

Raney, James W. LA 8th Inf. Co.E

Raney, J.B. 14th Conf.Cav. Co.G

Raney, J.C. AR 30th Inf. Co.C

Raney, J.C. AR 30th Inf. Co.G

Raney, J.D. AR 37th Inf. Co.C

Raney, J.E. TX Cav. Giddings' Bn. Carrington's Co.

Raney, J.F. AR 38th Inf. Co.B

Raney, J.F. GA Inf. 3rd Bn. Co.F

Raney, J.G. TX 16th Cav. Co.G

Raney, J.H. AR Pine Bluff Arty.

Raney, J.H. AR 2nd Vol. Co.D

Raney, J.H. AR 37th Inf. Co.C

Raney, J.H. TN 6th Inf. Co.A

Raney, J.J. AL 59th Inf. Co.F

Raney, J.J. TN 24th Bn.S.S. Co.B

Raney, J.K. MS 29th Inf. Co.D

Raney, J.M. TN 15th (Stewart's) Cav. Co.E 2nd Lt.

Raney, John GA 50th Inf. Co.G
Raney, John MO Cav. 9th Regt.St.Guard Co.A 3rd Lt.
Raney, John TN 51st (Cons.) Inf. Co.A
Raney, John TX 25th Cav. Co.E
Raney, John A. TN 45th Inf. Co.C
Raney, John B. AL 4th Inf. Co.C
Raney, John C. TN 8th Inf. Co.K
Raney, John D. MS 4th Inf. Co.I
Raney, John H. TN 13th Inf. Co.G 1st Sgt.
Raney, John M. GA 19th Inf. Co.K
Raney, John W. TN Inf. Nashville Bn. Fulcher's Co.
Raney, John Y. MS Nash's Co. (Leake Rangers)
Raney, Joseph AL 56th Part.Rangers Co.H
Raney, Joseph MS 2nd Cav. Co.B
Raney, Joseph TN 24th Inf. Co.F
Raney, Joseph TN 41st Inf. Co.A
Raney, Joseph E. MS 14th Inf. Co.E
Raney, Joseph W. MS 7th Inf. Co.E Cpl.
Raney, Joshua J. AL 2nd Bn. Hilliard's Legion Vol. Co.A
Raney, Josiah GA Cav. 22nd Bn. (St.Guards) Co.D
Raney, Josiah T. AL 2nd Bn. Hilliard's Legion Vol. Co.A
Raney, J.S. AR 38th Inf. Co.B
Raney, J.T. AL 59th Inf. Co.I,F
Raney, J.W. TN 6th Inf. Co.A
Raney, L.L. TN 12th (Green's) Cav. Co.I
Raney, M. AR 38th Inf. Co.B
Raney, Marcus G. AR 1st Mtd.Rifles Co.A
Raney, Marcus L. TN Lyons' Cav. J.C. Stone's Co.A
Raney, Marion TN Inf. 23rd Bn. Co.C
Raney, Marion TN 37th Inf. Co.A
Raney, Mark GA 64th Inf. Co.D
Raney, Matthew KY 6th Mtd.Inf. Co.F
Raney, M.H. AR 13th Inf. Co.G
Raney, Morgan AR 1st Mtd.Rifles Co.E
Raney, Morris KY 12th Cav.
Raney, Munroe MS 3rd Cav. Co.G
Raney, P.C. GA 57th Inf. Co.A
Raney, P.L. GA 50th Inf.
Raney, Reuben A. GA 59th Inf. Co.K
Raney, R.M. GA 7th Inf. (St.Guards) Co.C
Raney, Robert AR Cav. McGehee's Regt. Co.H
Raney, Robert MO Phelan's Regt.
Raney, Robert 9th Conf.Inf. Co.B Sgt.
Raney, Rufus MS Lt.Arty. (Warren Lt.Arty.) Swett's Co.
Raney, S. LA 1st Cav. Co.H
Raney, Samuel MS Lt.Arty. (Warren Lt.Arty.) Swett's Co.
Raney, Samuel MO 1st N.E. Cav. White's Co.
Raney, Samuel SC 16th Inf. Co.F
Raney, Samuel B. TN 37th Inf. Co.A,F
Raney, S.B. AL 37th Inf. Co.A
Raney, S.C. AR 38th Inf. Co.B Ord.Sgt.
Raney, S.G. TN 6th Inf. Co.A
Raney, S.H. AR 2nd Vol. Co.D
Raney, S.H. AR 31st Inf. Co.H Sgt.
Raney, S.J. AL 9th Inf. Co.I
Raney, T. Andrew LA 16th Inf. Co.F
Raney, T.C. TN 7th (Duckworth's) Cav. Co.M
Raney, T.H.C. AL 59th Inf. Co.F
Raney, Theophilus A. VA 54th Inf. Co.E

Raney, Thomas MO 1st N.E. Cav. White's Co., Co.C
Raney, Thomas B. TN 34th Inf. 2nd Co.C
Raney, Thomas J. AR 1st Mtd.Rifles Co.E 1st Lt.
Raney, Thomas J. TN 23rd Inf. 1st Co.A
Raney, Thomas T. MO 16th Inf. Co.K
Raney, T.J. AR 8th Cav. Co.I
Raney, T.J. AR 37th Inf. Co.C
Raney, T.J. TN 35th Inf. 2nd Co.I
Raney, V.A. MS 23rd Inf. Co.A Cpl.
Raney, W.A. MS Inf. Co.B
Raney, Wesley AR 1st Mtd.Rifles Co.E
Raney, W.F. AR 38th Inf. Co.B
Raney, W.H. AL Cp. of Instr. Talladega
Raney, William AL 12th Inf. Co.E
Raney, William GA 56th Inf. Co.G
Raney, William MO 11th Inf. Co.A
Raney, William TN 2nd Cav.
Raney, William TN Inf. 1st Bn. (Colms') Co.B
Raney, William TN 39th Mtd.Inf. Co.D
Raney, William TN 50th (Cons.) Inf. Co.H
Raney, William A. AL 9th (Malone's) Cav. Co.D Cpl.
Raney, William A. VA Cav. Mosby's Regt. (Part.Rangers) Co.H
Raney, William F. AR 1st Mtd.Rifles Co.E
Raney, William H. AL 13th Inf. Co.I
Raney, William H. LA 12th Inf. Co.I
Raney, Wm. J. AL Cp. of Instr. Talladega
Raney, Williamson TN Inf. 23rd Bn. Co.C Sgt.
Raney, W.P. TN 17th Inf. Co.A Sgt.
Raney, W.R. GA Lt.Arty. 12th Bn. 3rd Co.C
Raney, W.V. MS 2nd Cav. Co.C Capt.
Raney, W.V. MS 13th Inf. Co.F
Raney, Wyatt TX 15th Cav. Co.C Far.
Ranford, William NC 66th Inf. Co.E Music.
Ranfrand, W.H. NC 1st Jr.Res. Co.A
Ranfro, R. TX Waul's Legion Co.H
Ranfroe, J.A. TN Inf. 4th Cons.Regt. Co.F
Ranft, J.H. TX 8th Cav. Co.E
Rang, William SC Hvy.Arty. 15th (Lucas') Bn. Co.A
Range, John TX Arty. 4th Bn. Co.B
Range, John TX 8th Inf. Co.B
Rangel, Nativida TX 3rd Inf. Co.F
Rangeley, James H. VA 50th Inf. Co.K 2nd Lt.
Rangely, John J. VA 42nd Inf. Co.G 2nd Lt.
Ranger, Abram GA 63rd Inf. Co.B Asst.Cook
Ranger, A.J. FL Cav. 5th Bn. Co.E
Ranger, Francis LA 15th Inf. Co.D
Ranger, Francis MO Inf. 5th Regt.St.Guard Co.C
Ranger, I. NC 8th Inf. Co.K
Ranger, John L. Conf.Inf. Tucker's Regt. Co.I
Ranghaof, J. AL Cav. Moreland's Regt. Co.F
Rangley, Joseph VA Hvy.Arty. 10th Bn. Co.C
Ranguel, Francisco TX 3rd Inf. Co.G
Ranier, John T. VA 6th Inf. Vickery's Co.
Ranier, John T. VA 16th Inf. 1st Co.H
Ranier, Joseph E. NC 5th Inf. Co.D
Ranier, J.T. Conf.Lt.Arty. Richardson's Bn. Co.C
Rank, Amos LA Inf. 7th Bn. Co.C
Rank, Amos LA 15th Inf. Co.D
Rank, Eugene R. NC 33rd Inf. Co.I
Rank, J. LA C.S. Zouave Bn. Co.B
Rank, J.B. LA 17th Inf. Co.K

Rank, P.A. NC 21st Inf. Co.K
Rank, Philip VA 24th Cav. Co.D
Rank, Philip VA 21st Mil. Co.D
Rank, Phillip VA Cav. 40th Bn. Co.D
Rank, Theodore MS 1st Inf. Co.H
Rank, Thomas W. TX 3rd (Kirby's) Bn.Vol. Co.A
Ranken, William MO 4th Cav. Co.A 1st Sgt.
Rankens, Robert J. MS 32nd Inf. Co.K
Rankhorn, C.M. TN 28th (Cons.) Inf. Co.C Cpl.
Rankhorn, Crawford M. TN 28th Inf. Co.K Cpl.
Rankhorn, G.B. TN Inf. 1st Cons.Regt. Co.F Cpl.
Rankhorn, Green B. TN 16th Inf. Co.G Cpl.
Rankhorn, J.G. TN Inf. 1st Bn. (Colms') Co.C
Rankhorn, J.M. TN 28th (Cons.) Inf. Co.C
Rankin, --- TX Cav. Mann's Regt. Co.H
Rankin, A. NC Loc.Def. Lee's Co. (Silver Greys)
Rankin, A.A. KY 7th Cav. Co.A 1st Lt.
Rankin, Abraham VA 9th Bn.Res. Co.D
Rankin, A.G. AL 34th Inf. Co.F
Rankin, A.J. SC 13th Inf. Co.G
Rankin, A.L. AR 35th Inf. Co.I Cpl.
Rankin, Alex KY 2nd Mtd.Inf. Co.H Cpl.
Rankin, Alexander M. TX 19th Cav. Co.C Sgt.
Rankin, Alexander N. NC 37th Inf. Co.H
Rankin, Alexander V. NC 64th Inf. Co.K
Rankin, Alfred F. NC 45th Inf. Co.E
Rankin, Allen A. KY 5th Cav. 1st Lt.
Rankin, A.M. AR 7th Mil. Co.D
Rankin, Anthony AL Arty. 1st Bn. Co.F
Rankin, Anthony TN 50th Inf. Co.C
Rankin, Anthony L. AR 7th Cav. Co.A
Rankin, Austin TX 19th Cav. Co.C Cpl.
Rankin, A.V. TN 61st Mtd.Inf. Co.D
Rankin, B. TX 9th (Nichols') Inf. Co.K
Rankin, Berry TX 15th Cav. Co.B
Rankin, Berry TX Inf. Whaley's Co.
Rankin, B.F. TN 19th (Biffle's) Cav. Co.F Cpl.
Rankin, Blair L. NC 16th Inf. Co.M Cpl.
Rankin, C.A. KY 1st (Butler's) Cav. Co.E
Rankin, C.A. KY 2nd Cav. Co.E
Rankin, Cephas L. NC 37th Inf. Co.H Cpl.
Rankin, Charles TN Cav. 12th Bn. (Day's) Co.B
Rankin, Charles S. NC 35th Inf. Co.H
Rankin, C.R. MS 6th Inf. Co.H
Rankin, D. Gen. & Staff 1st Lt.,Adj.
Rankin, D.A. AL 5th Inf. New Co.C
Rankin, David TN 5th (McKenzie's) Cav. Co.H Cpl.
Rankin, David VA Inf. 2nd Bn.Loc.Def. Co.A Adj.
Rankin, David B. TN 21st (Carter's) Cav. Co.B
Rankin, David C. SC 1st (Orr's) Rifles Co.E
Rankin, David G. TN 2nd (Robison's) Inf. Co.D
Rankin, D.C. AL 5th Inf. New Co.C
Rankin, D.M. MS 6th Inf. Co.G
Rankin, D.S. LA 13th Bn. (Part.Rangers) Co.F
Rankin, D.V. MS 6th Cav. Co.G
Rankin, D.W. AL Inf. 2nd Regt. Co.C
Rankin, D.W. AL 37th Inf. Co.I Capt.
Rankin, D.W. AL 42nd Inf. Co.A 2nd Lt.
Rankin, E.A.W. AR Lt.Arty. Zimmerman's Btty.
Rankin, Edmon K. AR Inf. Cocke's Regt. Co.B Sgt.

Rankin, Edward MS 7th Inf. Co.D
Rankin, Edwin J. TX 1st (Yager's) Cav. Co.K
Rankin, E.E. TN 4th (McLemore's) Cav. Co.B
Rankin, Ephraim L. NC 49th Inf. Co.H 1st Sgt.
Rankin, E.R. MO Inf. Clark's Regt. Co.A
Rankin, F.M. AR 2nd Inf. Co.A
Rankin, F.M. AR 7th Mil. Co.D
Rankin, George AR 17th (Lemoyne's) Inf. Co.B
Rankin, George A. SC Palmetto S.S. Co.L 1st
    Lt.
Rankin, George Alexander SC 4th Inf. Co.D
    Cpl.
Rankin, George F. MS 7th Inf. Co.D
Rankin, George L. NC 7th Inf. Co.I
Rankin, George T. MS Lt.Arty. 14th Bn. Co.A
    AQM
Rankin, Geo. T. Gen. & Staff Capt.,AQM
Rankin, George W. MS 7th Inf. Co.F Sgt.
Rankin, George W. SC Inf. Holcombe Legion
    Co.H
Rankin, George W. SC Palmetto S.S. Co.L
Rankin, George W. VA 14th Cav. Co.D
Rankin, George W. VA 19th Cav. Co.F
Rankin, G.F. MS 12th Inf. Co.C
Rankin, G.F. SC Inf. 1st (Charleston) Bn. Co.E
Rankin, G.F. SC 27th Inf. Co.A
Rankin, G.L. TN 12th (Green's) Cav. Co.D
Rankin, H.D. NC 2nd Jr.Res. Co.C
Rankin, Henry C. SC 13th Inf. Co.G
Rankin, Henry L. TX 12th Cav. AAQM,
    Comsy.Subs.
Rankin, Hiram MS 3rd Cav.Res. Co.A
Rankin, Hugh AL 42nd Inf. Co.H 1st Sgt.
Rankin, J. AR 13th Mil. Co.G
Rankin, J. KY Morgan's Men Co.C
Rankin, J.A. TX 9th Cav. Co.F Sgt.
Rankin, James TN 2nd (Ashby's) Cav. Co.F
Rankin, James TN Cav. 4th Bn. (Branner's) Co.F
Rankin, James TN 15th (Cons.) Cav. Co.C
Rankin, James TN 15th (Stewart's) Cav. Co.A
Rankin, James TN 30th Inf. Co.C 1st Sgt.
Rankin, James VA 1st Inf. Co.C
Rankin, James VA 89th Mil. Co.H
Rankin, James A. AL 4th Inf. Co.G
Rankin, James A. MS 2nd Inf. (A. of 10,000)
    Co.A
Rankin, James A. MS 29th Inf. Co.A 2nd Lt.
Rankin, James A. NC 7th Inf. Co.I
Rankin, James B. TX 24th Cav. Co.K Sgt.
Rankin, James C. NC 1st Detailed Men Co.B
    Jr.2nd Lt.
Rankin, James E. GA Inf. 2nd Bn. (St.Guards)
    Old Co.D
Rankin, James E. MS Lt.Arty. (Issaquena Arty.)
    Graves' Co. 2nd Lt.
Rankin, James W. VA 4th Inf. Co.C
Rankin, James W. VA 52nd Inf. Co.G
Rankin, J.C. Inf. Bailey's Cons.Regt. Co.A
Rankin, J.C. TX 7th Inf. Co.E
Rankin, J.C.M. TN Cav. 2nd Bn. (Biffle's) Co.B
    Sgt.
Rankin, J.C.M. TN 6th (Wheeler's) Cav. Co.G
Rankin, J.D. Gen. & Staff Surg.
Rankin, J.E. GA Conscr.
Rankin, J.E. KY Lt.Arty. Cobb's Co. Lt.
Rankin, J.E. MO 12th Cav. Co.I
Rankin, J.E. NC 58th Inf. Co.F

Rankin, Jesse GA 1st (Ramsey's) Inf. Co.D Cpl.
Rankin, Jesse T. MS 7th Inf. Co.F 2nd Sr.Lt.
Rankin, J.G. AL Cav. Hardie's Bn.Res. Capt.
Rankin, J.G. TN 35th Inf. 2nd Co.I 1st Lt.
Rankin, J.G. TN Detailed Conscr. Co.B
Rankin, J.H. TN 9th Inf. Co.F
Rankin, J.H. TN 45th Inf. Co.C
Rankin, J.J. TN 14th Cav. Co.A
Rankin, J.J. TN 42nd Inf. Co.D
Rankin, J.J. 4th Conf.Inf. Co.K
Rankin, J.L. GA Hvy.Arty. 22nd Bn. Co.B
Rankin, J.N. Hosp.Stew.
Rankin, J.O. GA 46th Inf. Co.E
Rankin, Joel KY Cav. 2nd Bn. (Dortch's) Co.A
Rankin, Joel F. KY 2nd (Duke's) Cav. Co.E
Rankin, John MS 6th Inf. Co.B
Rankin, John MO 8th Inf. Co.F
Rankin, John TN 35th Inf. Co.L
Rankin, John VA 2nd Inf.Loc.Def. Co.G
Rankin, John VA Inf. 2nd Bn.Loc.Def. Co.A
Rankin, John A. AR 9th Inf. Co.C,K
Rankin, John B., Jr. VA 5th Inf. Co.C
Rankin, John B., Sr. VA 5th Inf. Co.C Drum.
Rankin, John B. VA 52nd Inf. Co.H Drum.
Rankin, John C. GA 45th Inf. Co.E
Rankin, John D.M. NC 16th Inf. Co.M 1st Sgt.
Rankin, John G. GA 38th Inf. Co.B Capt.
Rankin, John G. TN 32nd Inf. Co.G 1st Lt.
Rankin, John G. TX 5th Cav. Co.E
Rankin, John H. NC 45th Inf. Co.B
Rankin, John H. NC 45th Inf. Co.B Sgt.
Rankin, John J. TX Cav. Ragsdale's Bn. 2nd
    Co.C
Rankin, John K. VA 5th Inf. Co.I
Rankin, John M. SC 1st (Orr's) Rifles Co.E
Rankin, John N. NC 23rd Inf. Co.K
Rankin, John R. AR Cav. 1st Bn. (Stirman's)
    Co.A
Rankin, John R. AR Cav. Gordon's Regt. Co.E
Rankin, John T. NC Hvy.Arty. 1st Bn. Co.D,A
    1st Lt.
Rankin, John W. MS 7th Inf. Co.F
Rankin, John W. TX 27th Cav. Co.C Sgt.
Rankin, John Y. TX 25th Cav. Co.E
    Capt.,Comsy.
Rankin, John Y. Granbury's Brig. Maj.,CS
Rankin, Joseph A. MS Inf. Lewis' Co.
Rankin, Joseph J. NC 16th Inf. Co.M
Rankin, Joshua SC 1st (Orr's) Rifles Co.E
Rankin, Joshua SC 2nd Rifles Co.B
Rankin, Josiah S. SC 1st (Orr's) Rifles Co.E
Rankin, J. Pinckney AL 38th Inf. Co.E
Rankin, J.S. TX 15th Inf. 2nd Co.E
Rankin, J.W. AR 32nd Inf. Co.K
Rankin, J.W. NC 27th Inf. Co.B
Rankin, J.W. TN 30th Inf. Co.C
Rankin, J.W. TN 33rd Inf. Co.E
Rankin, J.W. TN 42nd Inf. 2nd Co.E
Rankin, J.W. TN Conscr. (Cp. of Instr.)
Rankin, J.W. 3rd Conf.Eng.Troops Co.B Artif.
Rankin, J.W. Gen. & Staff Hosp.Stew.
Rankin, Lawson L. NC 49th Inf. Co.H 2nd Lt.
Rankin, Leonard VA 9th Cav.
Rankin, M. TX 26th Cav. Co.E
Rankin, Madison J. MO 5th Inf. Co.K Sgt.
Rankin, Madison Jesse MO Inf. 1st Bn. Co.B 1st
    Sgt.

Rankin, Nathaniel P. NC 26th Inf. Co.F Maj.
Rankin, Nat P. NC 5th Cav. (63rd St.Troops)
    Co.I Capt.
Rankin, Patrick VA 1st Inf. Co.C Sgt.
Rankin, Patton H. MS 29th Inf. Co.A Sgt.
Rankin, Peter T. TN 2nd (Smith's) Cav. Rankin's
    Co. Capt.
Rankin, Peter T. TN 4th (McLemore's) Cav.
    Maj.
Rankin, P.H. MS 24th Inf. Co.A
Rankin, R. TN 21st Inf. Co.C
Rankin, R.A. TN 61st Mtd.Inf. Co.A 2nd Lt.
Rankin, R.B. AL 37th Inf. Co.I Cpl.
Rankin, R.B. AR 35th Inf. Co.I
Rankin, R.B. TX 11th Inf. Co.A
Rankin, R.B. TX Inf.Riflemen Arnold's Co.
Rankin, R.C. NC McLean's Bn.Lt.Duty Men
    Co.A
Rankin, R.E. LA Red River S.S. Cassidy's Co.
Rankin, Reuben TN 2nd (Ashby's) Cav. Co.F
Rankin, Reuben TN Cav. 4th Bn. (Branner's)
    Co.F
Rankin, Reubin B. AR Cav. 1st Bn. (Stirman's)
    Co.B
Rankin, R.F. TX 8th Inf. Co.K
Rankin, R.G. Gen. & Staff Capt.,QM
Rankin, Richard A. TN 5th (McKenzie's) Cav.
    Co.H
Rankin, R.N. AR 3rd Cav. Co.B,D Sgt.
Rankin, R.N. AR 3rd Inf. Co.B,D
Rankin, Robert LA 21st (Patton's) Inf. Co.F
Rankin, Robert MO 2nd Cav. Co.G
Rankin, Robert NC 4th Sr.Res. Co.E
Rankin, Robert TX Cav. Terry's Regt. Co.G
Rankin, Robert TX 4th Inf. Co.H
Rankin, Robert A. TN 39th Mtd.Inf. Co.H Cpl.
Rankin, Robert B. AL 42nd Inf. Co.H Cpl.
Rankin, Robert D. VA 19th Cav. Co.F
Rankin, Robert E. LA 1st (Nelligan's) Inf. Co.A
    Sgt.
Rankin, Robert E. LA 25th Inf. Co.A
Rankin, Robert F. SC 1st Arty. Co.C
Rankin, Robert G. NC Hvy.Arty. 1st Bn. Co.A
    Capt.
Rankin, Robert H. TX 16th Inf. Co.I
Rankin, Robert M. AR 7th Cav. Co.A Cpl.
Rankin, Robert M. MS 26th Inf. Co.I
Rankin, Robert S. MO 1st & 4th Cons.Inf. Co.E
    Sr.2nd Lt.
Rankin, Robert S. MO 4th Inf. Co.H 2nd Lt.
Rankin, Robert W. MS 9th Inf. Old Co.I,G Cpl.
Rankin, Robert W. MS 16th Inf. Co.F
Rankin, Robinson W. SC Inf. Hampton Legion
    Co.D
Rankin, R.S. TN 4th (McLemore's) Cav. Co.D
Rankin, R.T. TN 45th Inf. Co.C
Rankin, R.W. GA 1st Reg. Co.C
Rankin, R.W. GA 55th Inf. Co.E
Rankin, R.W. MS 5th Cav. Co.K
Rankin, R.W. TX 5th Cav. Co.D
Rankin, Samuel 1st Conf.Eng.Troops Co.F Artif.
Rankin, Samuel C. NC 45th Inf. Co.B Capt.
Rankin, Samuel E. MS 7th Inf. Co.D 1st Lt.
Rankin, Samuel S. TX 24th Cav. Co.A
Rankin, Stephen AR 1st Mtd.Rifles Co.I
Rankin, T.C. TN 16th (Logwood's) Cav. Co.E
    Sgt.

Rankin, Theo LA 1st Inf.
Rankin, Theopholus MS 8th Cav. Co.A
Rankin, Thomas TX 26th Cav. Co.E
Rankin, Thomas VA 52nd Inf. Co.G
Rankin, Tim VA Inf. 4th Bn.Loc.Def. Co.C
Rankin, Timothy VA 1st Inf. Co.C Cpl.
Rankin, T.J. AR 32nd Inf. Co.K
Rankin, T.J. SC 2nd Arty. Co.E
Rankin, T.W. TN 33rd Inf. Co.E Cpl.
Rankin, Vinton 3rd Conf.Inf. Co.E
Rankin, W.A. TX 26th Cav. Co.E
Rankin, Wade D. NC 49th Inf. Co.H Sgt.
Rankin, Wallace A. NC 49th Inf. Co.H 1st Lt.
Rankin, W.C. LA Inf.Crescent Regt. Co.C
Rankin, W.D. NC Loc.Def. Lee's Co. (Silver Greys)
Rankin, W.D. TN 12th (Green's) Cav. Co.D
Rankin, W.D. Gen. & Staff Asst.Comsy.
Rankin, W.G. AR Inf. Cocke's Regt. Co.B
Rankin, W.G. MO 12th Cav. Co.I
Rankin, W.G. NC 3rd Arty. (40th St.Troops) Co.B
Rankin, Will D. TN 60th Mtd.Inf. Co.I Capt.,Comsy.
Rankin, William GA 31st Inf. Co.A
Rankin, William GA Loc.Bn.
Rankin, William MO Cav. Preston's Bn. Co.A 1st Sgt.
Rankin, William SC 1st (Orr's) Rifles Co.E
Rankin, William TN 35th Inf. Co.L 2nd Lt.
Rankin, William TN 36th Inf. Co.L Ord.Sgt.
Rankin, William A. MS 9th Inf. Old Co.G, New Co.A Capt.
Rankin, William F. TX Cav. Martin's Regt. Co.K,I
Rankin, William G. MO 3rd Cav. Co.I
Rankin, William G. NC 16th Inf. Co.M
Rankin, William H. AR Lt.Arty. Owen's Btty.
Rankin, William H. NC 21st Inf. Co.M Sgt.
Rankin, William J. MS 7th Inf. Co.D Sgt.
Rankin, William J., Jr. MS 7th Inf. Co.D
Rankin, William J. MS 7th Inf. Co.F Capt.
Rankin, William J. TN 61st Mtd.Inf. Co.A
Rankin, William O. GA Inf. 2nd Bn. (St.Guards) Old Co.D
Rankin, William O. TX 15th Inf. 2nd Co.E
Rankin, William R. NC 28th Inf. Co.B Sgt.Maj.
Rankin, William R. NC 37th Inf. Co.H Maj.
Rankin, William S. NC 21st Inf. Co.M Lt.Col.
Rankin, William T. TN 2nd (Robison's) Inf. Co.D
Rankin, William W. AR Cav. 1st Bn. (Stirman's) Co.A
Rankin, William W. AL 32nd Inf. Co.C
Rankin, William W. NC 28th Inf. Co.B
Rankin, W.M. TX 20th Inf. Co.G
Rankin, W. Robertson SC Palmetto S.S. Co.L 2nd Lt.
Rankin, W.W. NC 35th Inf. Co.H
Ranking, C.A. KY 3rd Cav. Co.D
Rankins, A.K. AR Cav. 1st Bn. (Stirman's) Co.E,F
Rankins, A.K. AR 3rd Cav. 2nd Co.E
Rankins, Allen A. KY 11th Cav. Co.A 1st Lt.
Rankins, A.M. AR 15th (N.W.) Inf. Co.K
Rankins, Anderson VA 21st Cav. Co.K
Rankins, C.C. AR 19th (Dawson's) Inf. Co.F

Rankins, C.W. MS 6th Inf. Co.H
Rankins, D.V. 14th Conf.Cav. Co.K
Rankins, D.W. TX 11th Inf. Co.E
Rankins, F. TN 1st (Turney's) Inf. Co.A
Rankins, F.M. AR 34th Inf. Co.I
Rankins, G.W. AR Cav. Gordon's Regt. Co.B
Rankins, Henry NC 1st Inf.
Rankins, J. TN 14th (Neely's) Cav. Co.A
Rankins, J.A. AR 19th (Dawson's) Inf. Co.F
Rankins, J.B. MS 2nd St.Cav. Co.K
Rankins, J.B. MS Cav. Ham's Regt. Co.K
Rankins, J.C. NC 7th Sr.Res. Williams' Co.
Rankins, Jesse MS 2nd St.Cav. Co.K,L
Rankins, John AL 12th Cav. Co.G
Rankins, John 14th Conf.Cav. Co.G
Rankins, John W. KY 4th Mtd.Inf. Co.B Cpl.
Rankins, John W. MS Lt.Arty. (Issaquena Arty.) Graves' Co. Cpl.
Rankins, Joseph C. AL 19th Inf. Co.I
Rankins, J.P. TN 19th Inf. Co.B
Rankins, Malen J.S. AR 33rd Inf. Co.I Cpl.
Rankins, P.P. KY Cav. 2nd Bn. (Dortch's) Co.A
Rankins, Sidney AR 19th (Dawson's) Inf. Co.F
Rankins, V. AR 18th (Marmaduke's) Inf. Co.H
Rankins, William MO Lt.Arty. 1st Field Btty.
Rankins, William D. TN 13th Inf. Co.D,A
Rankins, William H. MS 16th Inf. Co.K
Rankins, William S. VA 18th Cav. Co.I
Rankins, W.P. MS 34th Inf. Co.G
Rankins, W.S. VA 62nd Mtd.Inf. 1st Co.D
Ranlett, A. LA 25th Inf. Co.H 2nd Lt.
Ranley, C. NC 23rd Inf. Co.F
Rannals, John N. VA 114th Mil. Co.A, Mtd.Co.
Rannay, W. KY 1st (Butler's) Cav.
Ranncaville, William MS 8th Cav. Co.C,I
Ranne, W.A. TX 33rd Cav. Co.K 1st Lt.
Ranneconnet, Camerose LA 3rd (Harrison's) Cav. Co.I
Rannels, Andrew J. TX 14th Cav. Co.F
Ranner, J.H. TX 14th Cav. Co.G
Ranner, W.E. FL 10th Inf.
Ranney, B.W. GA Arty. Lumpkin's Co.
Ranney, Charles H. MO 1st N.E. Cav.
Ranney, F.D. TX Cav. Benavides' Regt. Co.G
Ranney, Francis A. Imboden's Brig.Band Music.
Ranney, Fred TX Cav. Benavides' Regt. Co.F
Ranney, George KY 9th Mtd.Inf. Co.C
Ranney, J. LA Miles' Legion Co.A
Ranney, Thomas N. MO 2nd Cav. 2nd Co.K
Ranney, W.C. GA 41st Inf. Co.C
Ranney, William C. GA 42nd Inf. Co.A
Rannon, J.E. NC 2nd Inf. Sgt.
Rannscraft, H. KY 5th Cav. Co.C
Ranny, Bryant R. GA 3rd Cav. Co.E
Ranny, D.W. GA 43rd Inf. Co.A
Rano, Angel TX Cav. Ragsdale's Bn. Co.B
Ranolds, --- AR 24th Inf. Co.A
Ranolds, John GA 15th Inf. Co.G
Ranor, James VA 7th Inf. Co.F
Ranqueta, --- LA Mil. 1st Regt. French Brig. Co.3
Rans, W.H. AL 22nd Inf. Co.I
Ransbarger, Silas VA 8th Cav. Co.L
Ransbarger, Silas A. VA 14th Cav. Co.K,A
Ransberger, Silas A. VA 135th Mil. Co.C
Ransdale, George T. KY 5th Mtd.Inf. Co.E
Ransdale, Luther SC 2nd Arty. Co.C

Ransdall, B.L.F. NC 32nd Inf. Co.K
Ransdall, George W. NC 15th Inf. Co.L
Ransdall, James H. LA 1st Cav. Co.D
Ransdell, Daniel W. KY 3rd Cav. Hosp.Stew.
Ransdell, D.W. KY 3rd Mtd.Inf. Co.D
Ransdell, George C. VA 4th Cav. Co.H
Ransdell, G.T. KY 4th Cav. Co.I
Ransdell, G.W. NC 32nd Inf. Co.K Music.
Ransdell, James AR 30th Inf. Co.E
Ransdell, John E. TN 14th Inf. Co.K Sgt.
Ransdell, M.D. KY 4th Cav. Co.G
Ransdell, Sylvester S. NC 15th Inf. Co.L
Ransdell, Sylvester S. NC 32nd Inf. Co.K Music.
Ransel, Louis LA 21st (Kennedy's) Inf. Co.C
Ransem, S.C. GA 13th Inf. Co.C Sgt.
Ransey, A. AL 8th Inf. Co.G
Ransey, David MO 3rd & 5th Cons.Inf.
Ransey, G.T. SC 2nd St.Troops Co.K
Ransey, J.E. MS 12th Cav. Co.G 3rd Lt.
Ransey, W.H. MS 12th Cav. Co.H
Ransford, G. MS St.Cav. 3rd Bn. (Cooper's) Little's Co.
Ransford, H. GA 3rd Bn. (St.Guards) Co.A
Ransle, Andrew MD 1st Inf. Co.I
Ransley, William LA 7th Inf. Co.E
Ransom, --- TX 23rd Cav. Co.H
Ransom, A.C. TX 17th Inf. Co.C 2nd Lt.
Ransom, A.F. MS 2nd St.Cav. Co.F Sgt.
Ransom, A.F. MS 6th Cav. Morgan's Co.
Ransom, A.F. MS 12th Cav. Co.C
Ransom, A.F. MS 1st (Patton's) Inf. Co.H
Ransom, A.J. TX Cav. Baird's Regt. Co.B 2nd Lt.
Ransom, A.J. TX Waul's Legion Co.A
Ransom, Alfred C. TN 1st (Feild's) Inf. Co.I
Ransom, Andrew J. AR 15th (N.W.) Inf. Co.I Capt.
Ransom, A.R.H. Gen. & Staff Lt.,Asst.Ord.Off.
Ransom, Arthur NC 51st Inf. Co.E
Ransom, Benjamin J. GA 38th Inf. Co.M
Ransom, Benjamin M. TN 2nd (Robison's) Inf. Co.D
Ransom, B.F. GA Inf. Hull's Co.
Ransom, Briscoe B. VA 12th Cav. Co.B
Ransom, B.Y. KY 7th Mtd.Inf. Co.F
Ransom, Charles W. GA 51st Inf. Co.K Sgt.
Ransom, C.M. AR 19th (Dockery's) Inf. Co.B
Ransom, Columbus F. GA Lt.Arty. 12th Bn. 2nd Co.A Cpl.
Ransom, Columbus F. GA 1st (Ramsey's) Inf. Co.A
Ransom, C.R. TN 8th (Smith's) Cav. Co.A
Ransom, C.W. AR 15th Inf. Co.B
Ransom, Daniel TN 4th (Murray's) Cav. Co.E
Ransom, Daniel M. AR 8th Inf. New Co.D
Ransom, David GA 3rd Cav. Co.B
Ransom, David R. TN 45th Inf. Co.I
Ransom, D.M. AR 8th Cav. Co.C
Ransom, Edward Gen. & Staff A.Surg.
Ransom, Elliot E. TX 35th (Brown's) Cav. Co.E Cpl.
Ransom, Ernest LA 1st Hvy.Arty. (Reg.) Co.E
Ransom, G. NC 2nd Inf. Co.H
Ransom, G. SC 2nd Res.
Ransom, G. SC 7th Inf. 2nd Co.B
Ransom, G. SC 26th Inf. Co.D

Ransom, Gabriel SC Cav. 12th Bn. Co.C
Ransom, George M. MS 10th Inf. Co.K
Ransom, George M. MS 11th Inf. Co.K
Ransom, George M. MS 30th Inf. Co.K 2nd Lt.
Ransom, George W. AR 5th Inf. Co.K
Ransom, George W. GA 21st Inf. Co.C
Ransom, George W. GA 55th Inf. Co.D
Ransom, George W. NC 21st Inf. Co.D
Ransom, G.M. TN 8th (Smith's) Cav. Co.A
Ransom, G.T. GA 51st Inf. Co.K
Ransom, G.W. KY 11th Cav. Co.E 1st Lt.
Ransom, G.W. TN 11th (Holman's) Cav. Co.D
Ransom, H.A. TN 1st (Feild's) & 27th Inf.
    (Cons.) Co.A 2nd Lt.
Ransom, Hamilton TX Waul's Legion Co.A
Ransom, H.B. TX 10th Cav. 1st Lt.
Ransom, Henry NC 48th Inf. Co.K
Ransom, Henry A. TN 1st (Feild's) Inf. Co.I
    2nd Lt.
Ransom, Henry B. TX 35th (Likens') Cav. Co.B
    Capt.
Ransom, Henry B. Gen. & Staff 1st Lt.,Adj.
Ransom, Henry T. VA 3rd Lt.Arty. Co.I
Ransom, Henry T. VA Lt.Arty. Clutter's Co.
Ransom, Hughey AL 4th Cav. Co.I
Ransom, Hy. A. KY 6th Mtd.Inf. Co.F 1st Sgt.
Ransom, Irwin B. GA 60th Inf. Co.B
Ransom, Isaac VA 4th Res. Co.C
Ransom, Jacob N. 1st Cherokee Mtd.Vol. 1st
    Co.K
Ransom, James TX 7th Cav. Co.B Black.
Ransom, James B. VA 21st Inf. Co.A
Ransom, James G. AR 26th Inf. Co.B
Ransom, James M. GA 14th Inf. Co.I
Ransom, James M. TX 1st Field Btty. 1st Lt.
Ransom, Jas. M. Gen. & Staff Agent
Ransom, James T. VA 54th Inf. Co.F
Ransom, J.B. MS 22nd Inf. Co.F
Ransom, J.D. AL Cav. 24th Bn. Co.C
Ransom, J.E. KY 7th Mtd.Inf. Co.F
Ransom, J.E. LA 4th Inf. Co.A
Ransom, Jefferson GA 20th Inf. Co.E
Ransom, Jeter MS Cav. Jeff Davis Legion Co.H
Ransom, J.H. AR 1st (Monroe's) Cav. Co.H
Ransom, J.H. MS 41st Inf. Lt.
Ransom, J.H.W. VA 21st Inf. Co.D
Ransom, J.J. GA Phillips' Legion Co.D
Ransom, J.M. GA Hvy.Arty. 22nd Bn. Co.A
Ransom, J.M. TX Waul's Legion Co.A 1st Lt.
Ransom, John TX 2nd Inf. Co.A Cpl.
Ransom, John C. GA 5th Inf. Co.B
Ransom, John C. SC 1st (Orr's) Rifles Co.C
Ransom, John C. Gen. & Staff Capt.,AQM
Ransom, John C. Gen. & Staff AQM
Ransom, John F. MD Arty. 1st Btty. Cpl.
Ransom, John G. SC 2nd Bn.S.S. Co.A
Ransom, John H. GA 20th Inf. Co.E
Ransom, John I. GA 60th Inf. Co.B Cpl.
Ransom, Jno. M. Gen. & Staff Capt.,QM
Ransom, John P. VA 9th Cav. Co.G
Ransom, John W. TN 36th Inf. Co.B
Ransom, Jordan D. GA 41st Inf. Co.E
Ransom, Joseph B. MS 33rd Inf. Co.G
Ransom, L.C. Gen. & Staff Chap.
Ransom, Lem C. AL 20th Inf. Chap.
Ransom, M.A. SC 2nd St.Troops Co.I

Ransom, Matthew W. NC 1st Inf. Lt.Col.
Ransom, Matt W. NC 35th Inf. Col.
Ransom, Medicus Gen. & Staff Surg.
Ransom, M.W. Ransom's Brig. Brig.Gen.
Ransom, N.C. TN 10th & 11th (Cons.) Cav.
    Co.D
Ransom, P. AL 61st Inf. Co.G
Ransom, P.C. VA 3rd Res. Co.I
Ransom, Pleiades O. SC 1st (McCreary's) Inf.
    Co.G Sgt.
Ransom, R. AL Cav. 24th Bn. Co.C
Ransom, R. TX 1st Hvy.Arty. 2nd Co.A
Ransom, R. TX 15th Inf. 1st Co.E
Ransom, R.B. NC 57th Inf. Co.G
Ransom, R.D. MS McCord's Co. (Slate Springs
    Co.)
Ransom, Reuben GA 12th Cav. Co.F 1st Sgt.
Ransom, Richard NC 48th Inf. Co.K
Ransom, Richard NC 52nd Inf. Co.K
Ransom, Richard TN 24th Inf. Co.A 2nd Lt.
Ransom, Richard C. GA 55th Inf. Co.C
Ransom, Robert NC 1st Cav. (9th St.Troops)
    Col.
Ransom, Robert, Jr. Gen. & Staff Maj.Gen.
Ransom, Robert S. VA 57th Inf. Co.I Capt.
Ransom, R.T. VA 54th Mil. Co.E,F
Ransom, R.W. TX 4th Inf. Co.H
Ransom, Samuel H. TN 1st (Feild's) Inf. Co.I
    QM
Ransom, S.H. TN 1st (Feild's) & 27th Inf.
    (Cons.) AQM
Ransom, Simeon LA 19th Inf. Co.A
Ransom, S.M. VA Inf. 25th Bn. Co.D
Ransom, T.H. GA 8th Inf. Co.I
Ransom, Thomas F. GA 20th Inf. Co.E
Ransom, Thomas G. VA 9th Cav. Co.G
Ransom, Thomas P. AL 3rd Inf. Co.H
Ransom, Uriah A. GA 4th Inf. Co.K
Ransom, W. GA Inf. 27th Bn. (NonConscr.)
    Co.A
Ransom, W. LA 12th Inf. Co.A
Ransom, W. SC 2nd Inf. Co.C
Ransom, Wade H. KY Horse Arty. Byrne's Co.
Ransom, Waid TN 4th (Murray's) Cav. Co.E
    Sgt.
Ransom, Walter E. AL 3rd Inf. Co.C Sgt.
Ransom, Washington GA 12th Inf. Co.A
Ransom, W.H. AL 16th Inf. Co.A
Ransom, W.H. TN Inf. 22nd Bn. Co.C
Ransom, Whitman TN 11th (Holman's) Cav.
    Co.C
Ransom, William AL 49th Inf. Co.A
Ransom, William TN 4th (Murray's) Cav. Co.E
Ransom, William A. GA Floyd Legion
    (St.Guards) Co.C Sgt.
Ransom, William A. VA Lt.Arty. Parker's Co.
Ransom, William J. GA Phillips' Legion Co.D
    2nd Lt.
Ransom, William N. SC 1st (Orr's) Rifles Co.C
Ransom, William S. AL Lt.Arty. 20th Bn. Co.A
    Artif.
Ransom, William S. TN 1st (Feild's) Inf. Co.I
Ransom, W.M. TN 8th (Smith's) Cav. Co.A
Ransom, W.P. AR 36th Inf. Co.E
Ransom, W.S. TN 8th (Smith's) Cav. Co.A
Ransom, W.T. AL 13th Inf. Co.F
Ransome, Andrew AL 20th Inf. Co.D Capt.

Ransome, Charles C. VA Lt.Arty. Armistead's
    Co.
Ransome, George AR 15th (N.W.) Inf. Co.I
Ransome, James M. VA Lt.Arty. Hardwicke's
    Co. Artif.
Ransome, R.P. TN Inf. 3rd Cons.Regt. Chap.
Ransome, T.G. VA 44th Inf.
Ransome, William TN 25th Inf. Co.G
Ranson, --- GA 22nd Inf. Co.B
Ranson, A.F. MS Inf. 3rd Bn. (St.Troops) Co.A
Ranson, A.J. AR Inf. Williamson's Bn. Co.A 1st
    Lt.
Ranson, Albert Walter VA 21st Inf. Co.A 1st Lt.
Ranson, A.R.H. Gen. & Staff,PACS Capt.
Ranson, Daniel TN 22nd Inf. Co.K
Ranson, Frank Pegram's Staff Capt.,ADC
Ranson, Grghan N. AR 19th Inf. Co.B
Ranson, Henry C. VA 18th Inf. Co.H
Ranson, Isaac VA 5th Bn.Res. Co.C
Ranson, James M. GA 30th Inf. Co.A
Ranson, James M. TX St.Troops Edgar's Co.
    2nd Lt.
Ranson, J.F. Gen. & Staff 1st Lt.,ADC
Ranson, John GA 28th Inf. Co.G
Ranson, John VA 18th Inf. Co.F Sgt.
Ranson, John J. VA 44th Inf. Co.G
Ranson, John N. VA 12th Inf. Co.A
Ranson, John T. VA 3rd Lt.Arty. Co.D
Ranson, John T. VA Inf. 25th Bn. Co.C Sgt.
Ranson, John W. VA Arty. Paris' Co.
Ranson, John W. VA 21st Inf. Co.A
Ranson, Joseph LA Inf.Crescent Regt. Co.E
Ranson, J.R. TX 13th Vol. Co.E
Ranson, J.R. VA 42nd Inf. Co.D
Ranson, J.T. VA 20th Inf. Co.E
Ranson, Louis LA 7th Cav. Co.H Capt.
Ranson, Mathew KY 1st Bn.Mtd.Rifles Co.E
Ranson, Mathew D. KY 3rd Bn.Mtd.Rifles Co.E
Ranson, Richard T. VA Inf. 25th Bn. Co.C
Ranson, Robert Henry SC 4th Inf. Co.C Cpl.
Ranson, Silas D. VA 26th Inf. Co.F
Ranson, Thomas D. VA 12th Cav. Co.B
Ranson, Thomas D. VA 52nd Inf. Co.I 2nd Lt.
Ranson, Thomas R. VA 5th Cav. 3rd Co.F Cpl.
Ranson, Wade TN Inf. 22nd Bn. Co.K Sgt.
Ranson, W.H.F.A. AR 23rd Inf. Co.I
Ranson, William TN 19th (Biffle's) Cav. Co.D
Ranson, William TN Inf. 22nd Bn. Co.K
Ranson, William A. VA 5th Cav. 3rd Co.F 2nd
    Lt.
Ranson, William A. VA 61st Mil. Co.I 3rd Lt.
Ranson, William D. VA 4th Cav. Co.K
Ranson, William J. AR 1st Cav. Co.B
Ranson, W.W. VA Inf. 25th Bn. Co.H
Ranson, W.W.F.A. AR 30th Inf. Co.I
Ransone, A. Conf.Lt.Arty. Richardson's Bn.
    Co.D
Ransone, A.A. AR 30th Inf. Co.I Cpl.
Ransone, Alexander VA 21st Mil. Co.D
Ransone, Alexander L. VA Lt.Arty. Moore's Co.
Ransone, Augustus A. AR 23rd Inf. Co.I
Ransone, Benjamin F. GA Lt.Arty. (Jo
    Thompson Arty.) Hanleiter's Co.
Ransone, Chesly D. VA 18th Inf. Co.E
Ransone, Edward NC 32nd Inf. Asst.Surg.
Ransone, George W. GA 28th Inf. Co.G 1st Lt.
Ransone, H.C. GA 13th Inf. Co.G

Ransone, James H. VA 26th Inf. Co.E
Ransone, James R. VA 24th Cav. Co.D
Ransone, James R. VA Cav. 40th Bn. Co.D
Ransone, James R. VA 21st Mil. Co.D 1st Lt.
Ransone, John F. VA 9th Inf. Co.E
Ransone, John R. GA 13th Inf. Co.G
Ransone, John W. VA 26th Inf. Co.E Sgt.
Ransone, Julien GA Siege Arty. 28th Bn. Co.C
   Capt.
Ransone, R.L. AR 30th Inf. Co.I
Ransone, Robert L. AR 23rd Inf. Co.I
Ransone, Thomas R. VA 61st Mil. Co.I Cpl.
Ransone, William A. VA 3rd Cav. Co.G
Ransonet, Octave LA Inf.Cons. 18th Regt. &
   Yellow Jacket Bn. Co.D Cpl.
Ransonet, Ovid LA Inf.Cons. 18th Regt. & Yel-
   low Jacket Bn. Co.D
Ransour, John AR 1st (Colquitt's) Inf. Co.K
Ransum, A.J. TX 26th Cav. Co.E
Ransum, Wade H. TN 8th Inf. Co.G
Ransvall, W.J. LA 17th Inf. Co.K
Ransville, Wesley MS 3rd Cav. Co.F
Rant, John NC 48th Inf.
Rante, Felix FL 8th Inf. Co.D Cpl.
Rantero, Victor LA 18th Inf. Co.F
Rantero, Victor LA Inf.Cons. 18th Regt. & Yel-
   low Jacket Bn. Co.F
Rantin, C.C. SC 5th Cav. Co.G
Rantin, C.C. SC 27th Inf. Co.I
Rantin, Charles C. SC Arty. Manigault's Bn. 1st
   Co.A
Rantin, F.C. SC Lt.Arty. Parker's Co. (Marion
   Arty.)
Rantin, J.D. GA 48th Inf. Co.I
Rantin, J.D. Sig.Corps,CSA
Rantin, J.F. AL 9th Inf. Co.K
Rantin, John VA 47th Inf. Co.C
Rantin, John D. GA 42nd Inf. Co.I 1st Sgt.
Rantin, W. GA 3rd Bn. (St.Guards) Co.H
Rantin, William M. GA 42nd Inf. Co.I
Rantley, W.A. SC 1st (McCreary's) Inf. Co.C
Ranton, --- AL 22nd Inf. Co.I
Ranton, H. AL Lt.Arty. 20th Bn. Co.B
Ranton, W.J. AL St.Res. Cpl.
Rantoon, --- TX Cav. Mann's Regt. Co.H
Rants, S. SC 18th Inf.
Ranval, Louis LA C.S. Zoauve Bn. Co.A
Rany, B. AL 17th Inf. Co.F
Rany, Benjamin F. TN 11th Cav. Co.E
Rany, D.P. AR 32nd Inf. Co.D
Rany, James AR 32nd Inf. Co.D
Rany, James KY Jessee's Bn.Mtd.Riflemen Co.C
Rany, James KY Part.Rangers Rowan's Co.
Rany, James K. MS 29th Inf. Co.E
Rany, John A. MS 24th Inf. Co.E Sgt.
Rany, Milus W. GA 35th Inf. Co.H
Rany, Thomas AR 32nd Inf. Co.D
Rany, W.C. AR 10th Inf. Co.D 2nd Lt.
Raoul, Alfred AL Lt.Arty. Phelan's Co.
Raoul, Alfred AL 5th Inf. Old Co.H
Raoul, Alfred Gen. & Staff Surg.
Raoul, R.G. Gen. & Staff Capt.,AQM
Raoul, T. AL 1st Cav. 1st Co.K
Raoul, T.C. AL 7th Cav. Co.E 2nd Lt.
Raoul, Thomas C. AL Lt.Arty. Goldthwaite's
   Btty. Sgt.

Raoul, W.G. LA Washington Arty.Bn. Co.2
Raoul, W.G. Gen. & Staff Capt.,AQM
Rapanie, Matias LA Mil. 5th Regt.Eur.Brig.
   (Spanish Regt.) Co.10
Rape, Agustus D. AL 46th Inf. Co.B Music.
Rape, Allen GA 53rd Inf. Co.B,F
Rape, Andrew J. GA Inf. 10th Bn. Co.D
Rape, Augustus J. TX 35th (Brown's) Cav. Co.K
Rape, B.F. AL 1st Inf. Co.H
Rape, Charles AL Cav. Barbiere's Bn. Brown's
   Co.
Rape, C.M. MS 36th Inf. Co.F
Rape, G. AL 34th Inf. Co.E
Rape, George W. GA 27th Inf. Co.H
Rape, Gustavus AL 24th Inf. Co.I
Rape, G.W. GA 53rd Inf. Co.F
Rape, Henry TX Cav. Border's Regt. Co.C
Rape, Henry N. NC 37th Inf. Co.D
Rape, Henry R. SC 22nd Inf. Co.E
Rape, J.A. 3rd Conf.Cav. Co.A
Rape, Jackson GA 61st Inf. Co.I
Rape, James AL 48th Inf. Co.C
Rape, James GA 53rd Inf. Co.F
Rape, James F. AL 1st Inf. Co.H
Rape, James P. NC 26th Inf. Co.B
Rape, J.H. TX 7th Inf. Co.B
Rape, J.M. NC 2nd Jr.Res. Co.F
Rape, J.M.C.D. GA 39th Inf. Co.E
Rape, John AL 59th Inf. Co.C
Rape, John TX Inf. 3rd St.Troops Co.H
Rape, John A. TN 2nd (Smith's) Cav. Lea's Co.
Rape, John W. AL 3rd Inf. Co.H
Rape, J.S. NC 30th Inf. Co.H
Rape, J.W. GA 8th Inf. (St.Guards) Co.K
Rape, M.A. GA 53rd Inf. Co.B
Rape, Milton GA 3rd Res. Co.A
Rape, Milton A. GA 19th Inf. Co.G
Rape, Milton C. GA 61st Inf. Co.I
Rape, Peter GA 19th Inf. Co.G
Rape, Peter M.D. GA 44th Inf. Co.I
Rape, S. AL 34th Inf. Co.B
Rape, Samuel NC 48th Inf. Co.E
Rape, Samuel M. NC 37th Inf. Co.D
Rape, T.A. TN 26th Inf. Co.G
Rape, T.A. 1st Conf.Inf. 2nd Co.K Sgt.
Rape, Taylor GA 3rd Res. Co.A
Rape, Thomas GA 61st Inf. Co.I
Rape, Thomas W. GA Hvy.Arty. 22nd Bn. Co.F
Rape, W. GA 3rd Res. Co.H
Rape, W.F. TX 17th Cons.Dismtd.Cav. Co.A
Rape, William P. NC 48th Inf. Co.A
Rapel, H.H. AL 32nd Inf. Co.B
Rapelle, F. LA Mil.Cont.Cadets
Rapelt, D. LA Mil. 4th Regt. French Brig. Co.4
Rapen, A. MS 38th Cav. Co.D
Rapen, W.S. NC 3rd Jr.Res. Co.G
Raper, --- FL 1st Cav. Co.A
Raper, A.J. AR 1st (Monroe's) Cav. Co.F
Raper, Alexander AL 12th Inf. Co.H
Raper, Alonzo L. NC 39th Inf. Co.C Sgt.
Raper, Andrew J. AR 11th Inf. Co.I
Raper, Andrew J. AR 23rd Inf. Co.F
Raper, Andrew J. TN 62nd Mtd.Inf. Co.K Sgt.
Raper, B. AL Cav. Moreland's Regt. Co.E
   Capt.
Raper, Caleb NC 17th Inf. (2nd Org.) Co.B
Raper, Caleb NC 66th Inf. Co.E,F,H

Raper, Calvin NC 55th Inf. Co.A
Raper, David Johnathan AL 49th Inf. Co.B
Raper, Deson J. TN 3rd (Lillard's) Mtd.Inf.
   Co.H
Raper, Dison J. TN 62nd Mtd.Inf. Co.K Cpl.
Raper, E. AL Cav. Moreland's Regt. Co.D
Raper, Elijah GA 6th Cav. Co.D
Raper, Elisha NC 48th Inf. Co.B Sgt.Maj.
Raper, Franklin SC 1st (Butler's) Inf. Co.E
Raper, George 2nd Cherokee Mtd.Vol. Co.G
Raper, Henderson MS 42nd Inf. Co.K Cpl.
Raper, H.H. TN 43rd Inf. Co.K
Raper, H.R. AL Cav. Moreland's Regt. Co.D
Raper, J.A. AR 11th & 17th (Cons.) Inf. Co.C
Raper, J.A. 1st Cherokee Mtd.Vol. 1st Co.D 2nd
   Lt.
Raper, Jacob MO 8th Inf. Co.B Cpl.
Raper, James GA 12th Cav. Co.B
Raper, James M. MO 4th Cav. Co.E
Raper, Jesse AL 35th Inf. Co.C
Raper, Jesse MS 42nd Inf. Co.K
Raper, J.M. GA 8th Cav. Old Co.D
Raper, J.M. GA 62nd Cav. Co.D
Raper, J.M. NC Cav. 16th Bn. Co.H
Raper, John MO 4th Cav. Co.E
Raper, John A. NC 17th Inf. (1st Org.) Co.L
Raper, John A. NC 39th Inf. Co.C,G
Raper, John A. Sig.Corps,CSA
Raper, John C. VA 4th Inf. Co.A
Raper, John P. TN 43rd Inf. Co.K
Raper, John R. NC 2nd Cav. (19th St.Troops)
   Co.E Sgt.
Raper, John W. NC 17th Inf. (1st Org.) Co.I
Raper, John W. NC 17th Inf. (2nd Org.) Co.L
Raper, Joseph MS 32nd Inf. Co.I
Raper, Joseph J. MS 26th Inf. Co.C
Raper, J.P. TN 1st (Carter's) Cav. Co.B
Raper, J.W. MO 15th Cav. Co.B
Raper, Larkin W. TN 39th Mtd.Inf. Co.K
Raper, L.T. NC Loc.Def. Croom's Co.
Raper, M. NC 2nd Jr.Res. Co.H
Raper, Matthew AR 2nd Inf. Co.D
Raper, Meredith H. TN 39th Mtd.Inf. Co.K Cpl.
Raper, M.H. NC Loc.Def. Croom's Co.
Raper, Milton AL 19th Inf. Co.B
Raper, Monroe TN 62nd Mtd.Inf. Co.K Cpl.
Raper, Newton TN 62nd Mtd.Inf. Co.K
Raper, Newton J. TN 2nd (Ashby's) Cav. Co.G
Raper, Newton J. TN Cav. 4th Bn. (Branner's)
   Co.B
Raper, Noah GA Lt.Arty. 14th Bn. Co.C
Raper, Noah GA Lt.Arty. Ferrell's Btty.
Raper, P. TN 29th Inf. Co.B
Raper, P.G. 1st Conf.Cav. 2nd Co.A
Raper, Robert MS 2nd Inf. Co.E
Raper, Robert NC 4th Cav. (59th St.Troops)
   Co.H Cpl.
Raper, Robinson NC 50th Inf. Co.E
Raper, S.A. NC 45th Inf. Co.K Sgt.
Raper, Stephen MS 10th Cav. Co.E
Raper, Thomas TN 62nd Mtd.Inf. Co.K
Raper, William MS 42nd Inf. Co.K
Raper, William MO 8th Inf. Co.B
Raper, William NC 4th Cav. (59th St.Troops)
   Co.H
Raper, William NC 5th Inf. Co.G
Raper, William TN 8th (Smith's) Cav. Co.H

Raper, William TN 62nd Mtd.Inf. Co.G
Raper, William Horse Arty. White's Btty.
Raper, William C. NC 45th Inf. Co.B
Raper, William J. VA 4th Inf. Co.A
Raper, William R. MO 4th Cav. Co.E
Raper, William T. TN 59th Mtd.Inf. Co.E
Raper, W.J. AL 18th Bn.Vol. Co.C
Raper, W.P. NC 45th Inf. Co.K
Rapert, F.A. AR 38th Inf. Old Co.I, Co.H
Rapert, Francis A. AR Inf. Ballard's Co.
Rapert, J. MO 15th Cav. Co.L
Rapert, James J. AR 38th Inf. Old Co.I, Co.H
Rapert, L.D. AR 38th Inf. Old Co.I, Co.H
Rapestock, Antoine AR 23rd Inf. Co.E
Raphael, A.J. TX 2nd Inf. Co.B Music.
Raphael, Aristilde LA Mil. 1st Native Guards
Raphael, E. TX 5th Cav. Co.H
Raphael, H.J. Gen. & Staff Capt.,AQM
Raphael, H.T. AL 8th Inf. AQM
Raphael, J. TX Inf. Houston Bn. Co.D Cpl.
Raphael, N.W. LA Inf.Crescent Regt. Co.G
Raphail, H.J. LA 1st Cav. Co.G
Raphail, Samuel VA 54th Mil. Co.E,F
Rapheal, Abraham VA 9th Inf. Co.B
Raphel, Eugene F. MD 1st Cav. Co.C
Raphel, L. VA 54th Mil. Co.E,F
Raphene, Francois LA 3rd Inf. Co.G
Rapheune, F. LA Siege Train Bn.
Rapheune, T. LA Arty. Hutton's Co. (Crescent
  Arty.,Co.A)
Rapid, Edward NC 54th Inf. Co.F
Rapier, Charles KY 9th Mtd.Inf. Co.B
Rapier, E.S. LA Inf.Crescent Regt. Co.I 1st Sgt.
Rapier, J.L. LA C.S. Zouave Bn. Sgt.Maj.
Rapier, John LA C.S. Zouave Bn. Sgt.Maj.
Rapier, John L. LA Inf. 7th Bn. Co.A
Rapier, L. LA Inf.Crescent Regt. Co.C
Rapier, Richard KY 8th Cav. Co.K
Rapier, T.G. VA 3rd Inf.Loc.Def. Co.C
Rapier, Thomas LA 21st (Patton's) Inf.
Rapilje, George R. AL 1st Regt. Mobile Vol.
  Butt's Co.
Rapjohn, George W. MS 29th Inf. Co.B
Rapley, W.F. AR 12th Bn.S.S. Maj.
Raply, W.F. MO Inf. 3rd Bn.St.Guard Maj.
Rapmann, Henry LA C.S. Zouave Bn. Co.D
Rapp, A. LA Mil. Orleans Guards Regt. Co.H
Rapp, Benjamin F. VA 4th Inf. Co.H
Rapp, David P. VA 6th Bn.Res. Co.E
Rapp, F. LA 30th Inf. Co.F
Rapp, Francis GA 30th Inf. Co.F
Rapp, George W. LA 22nd Inf. Jones' Co.
Rapp, J.K. MS Lt.Arty. (Warren Lt.Arty.)
  Swett's Co. 2nd Lt.
Rapp, John LA Miles' Legion Co.F
Rapp, John D. VA 135th Mil. Co.B
Rapp, John E. MS Lt.Arty. (Warren Lt.Arty.)
  Swett's Co.
Rapp, John H. VA 26th Inf. Co.I
Rapp, John M. TX 5th Cav. Co.H
Rapp, John T. VA Cav. Moorman's Co. Sgt.
Rapp, Joseph A. VA 135th Mil. Co.B Sgt.
Rapp, J.T. VA 22nd Inf. Co.A
Rapp, L.F. LA 30th Inf. Co.F
Rapp, Peter LA Mil. 4th Regt. 2nd Brig. 1st Div.
  Co.K
Rapp, Samuel A. VA 135th Mil. Co.B

Rappe, Fran LA Mil. Chalmette Regt. Co.K
Rapper, J. NC 67th Inf. Co.C
Rappier, L. LA 18th Inf. Co.H
Rappin, Charles LA Mil. British Guard Bn. Bur-
  rowes' Co. Cpl.
Rappleye, Guyon LA Inf. 1st Sp.Bn. (Rightor's)
  Co.E
Rappleyre, John VA Lt.Arty. Jackson's Bn.
  St.Line Co.A
Rappold, George GA Inf. (RR Guards) Preston's
  Co.
Rappold, J.M. VA 8th Inf. Co.I
Rappold, John GA Inf. 18th Bn. (St.Guards)
  Co.B
Rappoldt, C. LA Miles' Legion Co.E
Rapson, A. Conf.Cav. Wood's Regt. Co.K
Raquemore, J.P. AL 4th Res. Co.I
Raquet, Charles M. TX Inf.Riflemen Arnold's
  Co.
Raquette, P. LA Mil. 3rd Regt.Eur.Brig. (Garde
  Francaise) Co.4
Raquit, Condy TX Cav. 1st Bn.St.Troops Capt.
Raral, T.C. AL 7th Cav. Co.E 2nd Lt.
Rarden, Joseph VA 17th Cav. Co.G
Rardin, Samuel F. KY 4th Cav. McGraw's Co.
Rardon, Joseph P. VA 17th Cav. Co.G
Raredon, Dennis MS 44th Inf. Co.K
Raredon, J. VA 54th Mil. Co.G
Raredoni, T. VA 54th Mil. Co.G
Rarefield, T.J. GA 3rd Res. Co.B
Rarerack, John AR 19th (Dockery's) Inf. Co.F
Rareshide, Edwin P. LA 21st (Patton's) Inf.
  Co.A Capt.
Rareshide, E.P. Gen. & Staff Capt.,Asst.Comsy.
Rareshide, H. LA 1st Hvy.Arty. (Reg.) Co.I
Rareshide, Henry LA 21st (Patton's) Inf. Co.A
  2nd Lt.
Rareshide, John LA 21st (Patton's) Inf. Co.A
  Capt.
Rarey, Henry LA 1st (Strawbridge's) Inf. Co.F
Rarick, John AR Lt.Arty. 5th Btty.
Rariden, John MS 21st Inf. Co.G
Rarishide, John H. MS Conscr.
Rarris, S.R. MS 1st Cav. Co.D
Rary, Henry NC 42nd Inf. Co.D
Rary, W.A. NC 66th Inf. Co.G
Ras, Isadore LA Mil. 2nd Regt. French Brig.
  Co.5
Rasberry, --- TX Cav. Good's Bn. Co.B
Rasberry, Abner NC 3rd Arty. (40th St.Troops)
  Co.F
Rasberry, Abner NC Loc.Def. Croom's Co.
Rasberry, A.C. MO 7th Cav. Co.K
Rasberry, Alexander J. NC 8th Bn.Part.Rangers
  Co.A,C
Rasberry, Alex J. NC 3rd Arty. (40th St.Troops)
  Co.F
Rasberry, Allen NC 8th Bn.Part.Rangers Co.A,C
Rasberry, Allen NC 3rd Arty. (40th St.Troops)
  Co.F
Rasberry, Allen NC 1st Inf. (6 mo. '61) Co.I
Rasberry, Allen R. GA 64th Inf. Co.C 1st Sgt.
Rasberry, A.R. MS 46th Inf. Co.H
Rasberry, Benjamin LA 16th Inf. Co.K
Rasberry, Benjamin F. MS 31st Inf. Co.G,A 1st
  Lt.
Rasberry, B.F. MS 6th Inf. Co.D

Rasberry, Dan C. LA 14th Inf. Co.F Cpl.
Rasberry, F.M. MS 15th Inf. Co.K
Rasberry, Francis M. Conf.Cav. Wood's Regt.
  Co.E
Rasberry, G.B. NC Unassign.Conscr.
Rasberry, Green AL Cav. 24th Bn. Co.A
Rasberry, Green AL 29th Inf. Co.A
Rasberry, Green S. AL 53rd (Part.Rangers) Co.K
Rasberry, Green S. LA 9th Inf. Co.D
Rasberry, G.S. AL Cp. of Instr. Talladega
Rasberry, Henry H. NC 1st Inf. (6 mo. '61) Co.I
Rasberry, Henry H. NC 61st Inf. Co.E Jr.2nd
  Lt.
Rasberry, I.H. TN 19th (Biffle's) Cav. Co.F
Rasberry, James MO Inf. 4th Regt.St.Guard
  Co.C
Rasberry, James H. LA 28th (Gray's) Inf. Co.I
Rasberry, James W. AR 17th (Griffith's) Inf.
  Co.B
Rasberry, Jasper N. TX 11th Inf. Co.K
Rasberry, J.F. AL 42nd Inf. Co.F
Rasberry, J.M. GA 40th Inf. Co.K
Rasberry, J.M. GA 66th Inf. Co.H 1st Lt.
Rasberry, J.N. AL 56th Part.Rangers Co.K
Rasberry, J.N. TX Cav. Wells' Regt. Co.G
Rasberry, John AL 18th Inf. Co.F
Rasberry, John L. AR 3rd Inf. Co.C
Rasberry, John R. NC 61st Inf. Co.E
Rasberry, John T. MS 1st Lt.Arty. Co.I
Rasberry, John W. LA 28th (Gray's) Inf. Co.I
Rasberry, Joseph C. MS 31st Inf. Co.G Sgt.
Rasberry, L.C. LA 9th Inf. Co.D
Rasberry, Madison AL 29th Inf. Co.D
Rasberry, Madison R. MS 15th Inf. Co.K
Rasberry, M.W. GA 2nd Brig.St.Troops Capt.
Rasberry, M.W. GA 3rd Bn. (St.Guards) Co.F
Rasberry, Pinkney MS 31st Inf. Co.I
Rasberry, Reuben L. 1st Conf.Inf. 1st Co.D Sgt.
Rasberry, R.H. AL 42nd Inf. Co.I
Rasberry, Richard J. LA Inf. 4th Bn. Co.C
Rasberry, Robert TN 5th Inf. 2nd Co.C
Rasberry, Robert J. LA 9th Inf. Co.C
Rasberry, S.S. MS Cav. Jeff Davis Legion Co.B
Rasberry, T.B. MS Inf. 3rd Bn. (St.Troops)
  Co.A
Rasberry, T.D. MS 9th Cav. Co.E
Rasberry, T.D. TN Cav. 17th Bn. (Sanders')
  Co.B
Rasberry, Thomas C. MS 27th Inf. Co.E
Rasberry, Titus MS 10th Cav. Co.F
Rasberry, W. AR 35th Inf. Co.A Cpl.
Rasberry, W.C. AL Mil. 2nd Regt.Vol. Co.B
Rasberry, W.C. AL 42nd Inf. Co.I
Rasberry, W.G. MS 6th Inf. Co.D
Rasberry, William G., Jr. MS 1st Lt.Arty. Co.I
Rasberry, Willis J. NC 1st Cav. (9th St.Troops)
  Co.H
Rasberry, Willis J. NC 8th Bn.Part.Rangers Co.A
  Capt.
Rasberry, Willis J. NC 66th Inf. Co.F Capt.
Rasberry, W.M. TN 19th & 20th (Cons.) Cav.
  Co.K
Rasberry, W.M. TN 20th (Russell's) Cav. Co.E
Rasbery, James LA 28th (Thomas') Inf. Co.B
Rasbery, J.B. LA 4th Res. Co.E Sgt.
Rasbery, J.H. Exch.Bn. 1st Co.B,CSA

Rasbery, William G. LA 28th (Thomas') Inf.
  Co.B
Rasborn, Jos. LA 13th Bn. (Part.Rangers) Co.F
Rasborough, J. MS 18th Cav. Co.K
Rasburn, T. AL 11th Inf. Co.F
Rasbury, Allen GA 36th (Villepigue's) Inf. Co.D
Rasbury, Allen P. GA 7th Inf. Co.K
Rasbury, J.F. TX 22nd Inf. Co.I 1st Lt.
Rasbury, J.M. GA Lt.Arty. 14th Bn. Co.D
Rasbury, J.M. GA Lt.Arty. King's Btty.
Rasbury, John A. 7th Conf.Cav. Co.F
Rasbury, John A. 8th (Dearing's) Conf.Cav.
  Co.G
Rasbury, John M. GA 64th Inf. Co.C 2nd Lt.
Rasbury, J.W. AR 19th (Dockery's) Inf. Co.K
  1st Sgt.
Rasbury, Mansel W. GA Cobb's Legion Co.A,G
Rasbury, Reuben L. GA 36th (Villepigue's) Inf.
  Co.D Cpl.
Rasbury, Reuben L. GA Cobb's Legion Co.B,G
Rasbury, Richard J. LA 31st Inf. Co.C
Rasbury, T.J. AR 51st Mil. Co.H
Rasbury, William NC 51st Inf. Co.I
Rasbury, W.M. GA 64th Inf. Co.C
Rasch, Emile LA 10th Inf. Co.F
Rasch, F.A. LA Mil. Orleans Guards Regt. Co.A
Rasche, Frank LA 10th Inf. Co.F Sgt.
Raschel, Sebast LA 2nd Cav. Co.D
Rasco, Avry L. MS 43rd Inf. Co.H
Rasco, C.J. AL 14th Inf. Co.I
Rasco, E.D. TX 12th Inf. Co.D
Rasco, Edward H. AL Cp. of Instr. Talladega
Rasco, George W. AL 46th Inf. Co.G
Rasco, J. AL Talladega Cty.Res. J. Lucius' Co.
  Cpl.
Rasco, J. TN 12th Inf. Co.E
Rasco, J.A. AL 32nd & 58th (Cons.) Inf.
Rasco, James L. GA Inf. 10th Bn. Co.A Sgt.
Rasco, J.H. AL 3rd Res. Co.B
Rasco, John TX 20th Cav. Co.H Sgt.
Rasco, John A. AL Mil. 4th Vol. Co.G
Rasco, Jules LA Miles' Legion Co.G
Rasco, L. AL Cp. of Instr. Talladega
Rasco, Lindsay MS 25th Inf. Co.C
Rasco, L.T. AL 58th Inf. Co.H
Rasco, L.T. AL Cp. of Instr. Talladega
Rasco, R.C.W. AL 17th Inf. Co.H
Rasco, R.C.W. AL 32nd & 58th (Cons.) Inf.
  Cpl.
Rasco, R.C.W. AL 58th Inf. Co.H Cpl.
Rasco, S.H. TN 12th Inf. Co.E
Rasco, Smith S. NC 1st Arty. (10th St.Troops)
  Co.I
Rasco, Thomas AL 23rd Inf. Co.E
Rasco, T.V. LA 58th Inf. Co.H
Rasco, W.E. AL Mil. 4th Vol. Co.G
Rasco, William SC 20th Inf. Co.L
Rascock, James P. TN 25th Inf. Co.A Bvt.2nd
  Lt.
Rascoe, A.H. SC 21st Inf. Co.F
Rascoe, A.L. KY 7th Mtd.Inf. Co.K
Rascoe, B.W. Trans-MS Conf.Cav. 1st Bn. Co.A
Rascoe, Daniel SC 8th Inf. Co.K
Rascoe, Gabriel TX 2nd Cav. Co.A
Rascoe, George W. SC 8th Inf. Co.G
Rascoe, Harris SC 24th Inf. Co.B
Rascoe, H.E. MS 3rd Cav. Co.I

Rascoe, Henry NC 6th Inf. Co.H
Rascoe, Jesse AL Cav. Lewis' Bn. Co.D
Rascoe, J.F. SC 21st Inf. Co.E
Rascoe, John NC 6th Inf. Co.H
Rascoe, John F. NC 6th Inf. Co.K Cpl.
Rascoe, John R. SC 8th Inf. Co.G
Rascoe, John R. TN Inf. 22nd Bn. Co.A
Rascoe, Joseph E. TN 9th (Ward's) Cav. Co.C
Rascoe, Joshua TX 12th Cav. Co.K
Rascoe, Joshua TX 20th Cav. Co.H
Rascoe, Josiah TX 20th Cav. Co.H
Rascoe, Laban Taylor TX 20th Cav. Co.G
  Bugler
Rascoe, Leonidas TX 20th Cav. Co.H
Rascoe, L.J. LA 58th Inf. Co.H
Rascoe, Lycurgus TX 6th Cav. Co.B
Rascoe, M.L. TN 46th Inf. Co.G 1st Sgt.
Rascoe, Peter NC 1st Inf. (6 mo. '61) Co.L
Rascoe, Solen TX 20th Cav. Co.H
Rascoe, T.J. KY 1st Inf. Co.E
Rascoe, W. Trans-MS Conf.Cav. 1st Bn. Co.B
Rascoe, William SC Cav. 19th Bn. Co.E
Rascoe, William A. NC 6th Inf. Co.K
Rascoe, William E. AL Cav. Lewis' Bn. Co.D
Rascoe, William L. SC 21st Inf. Co.F
Rascoe, W.R. SC 4th St.Troops Co.K
Rascoe, W.S. AR 25th Inf. Co.C Sgt.
Rascow, W.L. SC 23rd Inf. Co.G
Rasdall, L.W. KY Cav.
Rasdon, Albert MO 15th Cav. Co.K
Rasdon, W. AR 38th Inf. Co.H
Rasdon, William MO 15th Cav. Co.K
Rasdon, Wilz MO 15th Cav. Co.K
Rase, A.D. AL 23rd Inf. Co.F Music.
Rase, Alfred A. AL 16th Inf. Co.C
Rase, Columbus F.A. TN 19th Inf. Co.D
Rase, Mont MO 9th Inf. Co.D
Rase, N.B. AR 38th Inf. Co.C
Rasenborough, T.J. TX 1st Inf. Co.F
Rasenick, Jacob W. VA 72nd Mil.
Rasenick, James VA 72nd Mil.
Rasenick, James P. VA 72nd Mil.
Rasenick, John VA 72nd Mil.
Rasenick, N.B. VA 72nd Mil.
Rasenick, Steph VA 72nd Mil.
Raser, George W. VA 34th Mil. Co.C
Raser, L.J. SC Post Guard Senn's Co.
Rash, A.B. VA Conscr. Cp.Lee Co.A
Rash, A. Clay KY 11th Cav. Co.A
Rash, Asa GA 39th Inf. Co.H
Rash, Asa NC 55th Inf. Co.B Sgt.
Rash, Benjamin NC 6th Sr.Res. Co.D
Rash, Beverly NC 4th Inf. Co.H
Rash, Burris NC 54th Inf. Co.E
Rash, Cornelius N. VA Loc.Def. Chappell's Co.
Rash, Daniel GA 9th Inf. Co.K
Rash, Frank KY 12th Cav. Co.A
Rash, George L. MS 15th Inf. Co.I 2nd Cpl.
Rash, H. VA 1st (Farinholt's) Res. Co.K
Rash, Henry NC 55th Inf. Co.B
Rash, Henry H. AR 14th (Powers') Inf. Co.E
Rash, Hubbard B. KY 7th Mtd.Inf. Co.B
Rash, Israel NC 55th Inf. Co.B
Rash, J. LA Mil. Fire Bn. Co.B
Rash, J.A. TN Inf. 1st Cons.Regt. Co.C 1st Sgt.
Rash, James NC 64th Inf. Co.C
Rash, James A. TN 28th Inf. Co.E

Rash, James A. TN 28th (Cons.) Inf. Co.D 1st
  Sgt.
Rash, James B. NC Unassign.Conscr.
Rash, James M. GA Cobb's Legion Co.F
Rash, James S. VA 56th Inf. Co.I
Rash, J.C. NC 13th Inf. Co.C
Rash, J.E. TN Inf. 1st Cons.Regt. Co.C
Rash, J.E. TN 28th (Cons.) Inf. Co.D
Rash, John AL 2nd Cav. Co.E
Rash, John NC 60th Inf. Co.A Cpl.
Rash, Joseph AR 7th Cav. Co.K
Rash, Joseph NC Cav. 5th Bn. Co.C
Rash, Joseph NC 6th Cav. (65th St.Troops)
  Co.C,H
Rash, Joseph NC 4th Inf. Co.H
Rash, Joseph NC 58th Inf. Co.I
Rash, Joseph W. TN 34th Inf. Co.G
Rash, Joshua A. TN 28th Inf. Co.E Cpl.
Rash, Leander NC 54th Inf. Co.E
Rash, Leroy S. AR Inf. Clayton's Co.
Rash, Levi NC 5th Sr.Res. Co.A
Rash, Lewis NC 55th Inf. Co.B
Rash, L.P. NC 18th Inf. Co.F
Rash, Martin NC 64th Inf. Co.C
Rash, Melvill NC 23rd Inf. Co.B
Rash, Merida NC 33rd Inf. Co.C
Rash, Munsey NC 60th Inf. Co.A
Rash, Noah NC 23rd Inf. Co.B
Rash, Payton NC 58th Inf. Co.M
Rash, Peter VA Loc.Def. Tayloe's Co.
Rash, Peyton NC 6th Cav. (65th St.Troops)
  Co.H,K
Rash, Reuben A. NC 52nd Inf. Co.F
Rash, Richard M. NC 28th Inf. Co.F
Rash, Robert GA 2nd (Stapleton's) St.Troops
  Co.E Cpl.
Rash, Robert NC 28th Inf. Co.F
Rash, Robert A. VA 9th Inf. 1st Co.H, 2nd
  Co.H, Co.B
Rash, Robert A. VA Inf. 28th Bn. Co.C
Rash, Ryland L. Conf.Cav. Wood's Regt. Co.B
  1st Sgt.
Rash, S. NC 42nd Inf. Co.D
Rash, S.A. TX Cav. Hardeman's Regt. Co.D
Rash, Thomas A. VA 9th Inf. 1st Co.H, 2nd
  Co.H, Co.B
Rash, Thomas A. VA Inf. 28th Bn. Co.C
Rash, Thomas J. TN 28th Inf. Co.E
Rash, Thomas V. AR 14th (Powers') Inf. Co.E
Rash, T.J. TN Inf. 1st Cons.Regt. Co.C
Rash, T.J. TN 28th (Cons.) Inf. Co.D
Rash, Tobe KY 12th Cav. Co.A
Rash, Uriah NC 44th Inf. Co.H
Rash, W.F. AL 18th Bn.Vol. Co.B Cpl.
Rash, W.H. KY 7th Cav. Co.B
Rash, Wiley H. KY 7th Mtd.Inf. Co.B
Rash, William MS 2nd Cav.
Rash, William MO 2nd Cav.
Rash, William TN Cav. Shaw's Bn. Hamilton's
  Co.
Rash, William C. NC 54th Inf. Co.E
Rash, William F. TN 34th Inf. Co.G
Rash, William H. AR 14th (Powers') Inf. Co.E
Rash, William H. VA Inf. 5th Bn. Co.E Sgt.
Rash, William H. VA 53rd Inf. Co.B
Rash, W.K. NC 5th Sr.Res. Co.A

Rash, W.M. TX Cav. Saufley's Scouting Bn. Co.C

Rash, W.R. TN 21st (Wilson's) Cav. Co.H Cpl.

Rash, Zenah M. NC 52nd Inf. Co.F Cpl.

Rasha, H. LA Mil. 4th Regt. 1st Brig. 1st Div. Co.A Sgt.

Rashbrooks, Samuel LA 4th Inf. Co.I

Rasheels, W.A. TN 21st (Carter's) Cav. Co.G

Rasher, Benjamin AL 3rd Cav. Co.E

Rasimi, Joseph KY 2nd (Duke's) Cav. Co.F

Rasimi, Jos. E. AL 21st Inf. Co.E

Rasin, M.M. LA Arty. Moody's Co. (Madison Lt.Arty.) 2nd Lt.

Rasin, M.M. VA Lt.Arty. Woolfolk's Co.

Rasin, William I. MD 1st Cav. Co.E Capt.

Raskey, Joseph SC 2nd Arty. Co.C

Raskilley, J.H. TN 38th Inf. 1st Co.A

Rasler, A. TX 20th Inf. Co.K

Rasler, J. TX 20th Inf. Co.K

Rasley, G.W. TX 12th Inf. Co.E

Rasmerson, C. TX 13th Vol. 2nd Co.H

Rasmes, Franklin TX 20th Bn.St.Troops Co.B

Rasmus, J. GA Cav. 29th Bn. Co.G

Rasmusan, Andrew LA 22nd Inf. Co.E Sgt.

Rasmussen, Charles TX 22nd Inf. Co.K

Rasmuzan, A. LA 22nd (Cons.) Inf. Co.E Sgt.

Rasnake, Charles VA 72nd Mil.

Rasnake, J.N. VA 72nd Mil.

Rasnek, J.J. MO Cav. Coleman's Regt. Co.B

Rasnes, James GA 20th Inf. Co.B

Rasnick, Charles VA Cav. Ferguson's Bn. Stevenson's Co.

Rasnick, Charles C. VA 29th Inf. Co.G

Rasnick, Jasper N. VA 37th Inf. Co.I

Rasnick, John VA 29th Inf. Co.G

Rasnick, Lafayette VA 16th Cav. Co.A

Rasnick, Lafayette VA Cav. Ferguson's Bn. Stevenson's Co.

Rasnick, Oliver VA 16th Cav. Co.A

Rasnick, Oliver VA Cav. Ferguson's Bn. Stevenson's Co.

Rasnick, William P. VA 25th Cav. Co.B

Rasnicke, Johnson VA 29th Inf. Co.A

Rasnike, Elijah VA 21st Cav. 1st Co.E

Rasnike, James VA 21st Cav. 1st Co.E

Rasnike, Johnson VA 21st Cav. 1st Co.E

Rasnike, N.B. VA 21st Cav. 1st Co.E

Rasnike, William VA 21st Cav. 1st Co.E

Rasor, George TN 14th Inf. Co.A

Rasor, J. AL 22nd Inf. Co.F

Rasor, J.C. SC 5th St.Troops Co.D Cpl.

Rasor, John AR 2nd Inf. Co.A

Rasor, John M. SC 1st (Orr's) Rifles Co.G Sgt.

Rasor, T.C. AL 22nd Inf. Co.F

Rasor, W.J. 1st Conf.Cav. 2nd Co.A Sgt.

Raspail, L. LA Mil. 3rd Regt. French Brig. Co.4

Raspberrie, James C. AL 36th Inf. Co.E

Raspberry, Ben MS 1st (Patton's) Inf. Co.H Sgt.

Raspberry, E.J. AL 29th Inf. Co.H

Raspberry, George LA 22nd (Cons.) Inf. Co.G

Raspberry, Green AL 44th Inf. Co.F,E,H

Raspberry, G.S. AL 10th Inf. Co.E

Raspberry, G.S. AL Cp. of Instr. Talladega

Raspberry, Harrison AR 2nd Cav. Co.I

Raspberry, J.P. AL 15th Inf. Co.F

Raspberry, J.P. AL Cp. of Instr. Talladega

Raspberry, Logan L. TX 24th Cav. Co.D Cpl.

Raspberry, P.C. AL 29th Inf. Co.H Cpl.

Raspberry, Sanders GA 6th Inf. Co.I

Raspberry, W.G., Jr. AL 29th Inf. Co.H

Raspberry, W.G., Sr. AL 29th Inf. Co.H

Raspberry, William G. MS Inf. 2nd Bn. Co.C Cpl.

Raspberry, William G. MS 48th Inf. Co.C Cpl.

Raspberry, W.R. AL 29th Inf. Co.D

Raspburry, A.R. TN 20th (Russell's) Cav. Co.E

Raspbury, Newton AL 11th Inf. Co.F

Raspbury, Richard F. AL 11th Inf. Co.F

Raspbury, William R. AL 11th Inf. Co.F

Rasplery, B.F. MS 8th Cav. Co.K

Rass, David TX Cav. Giddings' Bn. Carr's Co.

Rasser, B.H. GA Lt.Arty. Ferrell's Btty. Cpl.

Rasser, J.P. Gen. & Staff Contr.Surg.

Rasser, L.J. NC 67th Inf. Co.C

Rassignol, Henry GA Inf. 1st Conf.Bn. Asst.Surg.

Rassman, R.S. MS Scouts Montgomery's Co.

Rassner, H. TN 9th Inf. Co.I

Rassom, James TN 19th (Biffle's) Cav. Co.D

Rasson, B.F. MO Robertson's Regt.St.Guard Co.12

Rasson, James Conf.Cav. Baxter's Bn. Co.C

Rassunur, Henry TN Conscr. (Cp. of Instr.)

Rast, A.D. AL Inf. 1st Regt. Co.G

Rast, D.M. AL Cav. Moreland's Regt. Co.I

Rast, D.W. SC 26th Inf. Co.G 2nd Lt.

Rast, F.M. SC 2nd Arty. Co.F

Rast, F.M. SC 11th Res. Co.H

Rast, F.M. SC 20th Inf. Co.B

Rast, Fred M. SC 25th Inf. Co.G

Rast, G.D. SC 2nd Inf. Co.I Sgt.

Rast, G.D. SC 2nd St.Troops Co.C Cpl.

Rast, G.D. SC 20th Inf. Co.B Sgt.

Rast, H.D. LA 1st Hvy.Arty. (Reg.) Co.C

Rast, Horace D. AL Lt.Arty. 2nd Bn. Co.E

Rast, Horace D. AL 3rd Inf. Co.H

Rast, J.A. SC 2nd Inf. Co.I

Rast, Jacob E. SC 1st (Hagood's) Inf. 1st Co.A

Rast, Jacob E. SC 25th Inf. Co.G Sgt.

Rast, Jacob S. SC 20th Inf. Co.B

Rast, James D. AL 10th Cav. Co.I,L

Rast, James H. AL 53rd (Part.Rangers) Co.K,H Cpl.

Rast, James L. SC 20th Inf. Co.B

Rast, James T. SC 1st (Hagood's) Inf. 1st Co.D

Rast, J.D. AL Cav. Moreland's Regt. Co.I

Rast, J.N. SC Lt.Arty. J.T. Kanapaux's Co. (Lafayette Arty.)

Rast, John A. SC 20th Inf. Co.B

Rast, John L. AR Cav. Wright's Regt. Co.B

Rast, Joshua C. SC 20th Inf. Co.B

Rast, J.T. SC 25th Inf. Co.F

Rast, J.W. AL 3rd Inf. Co.H

Rast, L.P. SC 2nd Arty. Co.F Cpl.

Rast, L.P. SC 1st (Hagood's) Inf. 1st Co.C

Rast, Melvin J.D. AL Cav. 5th Bn. Hilliard's Legion Co.D

Rast, M.J. SC 2nd Arty. Co.C

Rast, M.J. SC 2nd St.Troops Co.C

Rast, M.J. SC 11th Res. Co.H

Rast, M.J.D. 10th Conf.Cav. Co.D Ord.Sgt.

Rast, Paul J. AL 3rd Inf. Co.H Sgt.

Rast, P.D. SC Lt.Arty. J.T. Kanapaux's Co. (Lafayette Arty.)

Rast, P.D. SC Mil. 16th Regt. Co.D Bvt.2nd Lt.

Rast, Thomas F. SC 20th Inf. Co.B

Rast, T.M. SC 2nd Arty. Co.F

Rast, William AL Cav. Moreland's Regt. Co.B

Rast, William MS 8th Inf. Co.A

Rast, William J.A. FL 9th Inf. Co.K

Rast, W.J. AL Cav. Moreland's Regt. Co.I

Rast, W.J. MS 26th Inf. Co.A Jr.2nd Lt.

Rast, W.M.N. AL Arty. 1st Bn. Co.C

Rast, W.M.N. SC 6th Cav. Co.H 1st Sgt.

Rast, W.R. SC Mil. 14th Regt. Co.C

Rast, W.T. AL 53rd (Part.Rangers) Co.E

Rasted, Charles SC Lt.Arty. Walter's Co. (Washington Arty.)

Raston, Charles A. VA Cav. 1st Bn. (Loc.Def.Troops) Co.C

Raston, H. AL 24th Inf. Co.H

Rat, David 1st Cherokee Mtd.Rifles Co.F

Rat, D.B. 1st Squad. Cherokee Mtd.Vol. Co.A

Rat, John 1st Cherokee Mtd.Rifles Co.G

Rat, W.M. 1st Cherokee Mtd.Vol. 1st Co.E

Ratan, J.F. MS Cav. Davenport's Bn. (St.Troops) Co.B Sgt.

Ratan, W.J. AL Inf. 2nd Regt. Co.G

Rataree, Asa TN 46th Inf. Co.A

Rataree, T. SC 16th & 24th (Cons.) Inf. Co.K

Rataree, T.D. SC 5th Inf. 2nd Co.B

Ratares, T.J. TN 46th Inf. Co.I

Ratch, J.W., Jr. Gen. & Staff Capt.,AAG

Ratcherside, James H. AR Inf. Hardy's Regt. Co.D Cpl.

Ratchford, E.C. NC 11th (Bethel Regt.) Inf. Co.A

Ratchford, G.R. SC 3rd Bn.Res. Co.D

Ratchford, J.A. 8th (Wade's) Conf.Cav. Co.B

Ratchford, James A. SC 1st Cav. Co.H 2nd Lt.

Ratchford, J.G. AR 10th Inf. Co.D

Ratchford, J.H. NC 28th Inf. Co.B

Ratchford, John A. NC 37th Inf. Co.H

Ratchford, John F. NC 37th Inf. Co.H

Ratchford, J.S. TX 14th Inf. Co.D

Ratchford, J.W. Lee's Corps Maj.,AAG

Ratchford, Moses NC 38th Inf. Co.C

Ratchford, R.B. AR 2nd Inf. Co.I

Ratchford, R.C. AR 1st Mtd.Rifles Co.K

Ratchford, Robert NC 23rd Inf. Co.H 1st Lt.

Ratchford, Robert C. AR 25th Inf. Co.I

Ratchford, Robert M. NC 38th Inf. Co.C

Ratchford, R.W. SC 1st Cav. Co.H

Ratchford, T.D. 8th (Wade's) Conf.Cav. Co.B

Ratchford, V.B. AL Cav. Falkner's Co. Black.

Ratchford, V.B. 8th (Wade's) Conf.Cav. Co.B

Ratchford, W.A. NC 49th Inf. Co.H

Ratchford, W.E. 8th (Wade's) Conf.Cav. Co.B

Ratchford, William GA 3rd Cav. Co.C

Ratchwood, Fra TN 21st Inf. Co.E

Ratclif, Joel GA 48th Inf. Co.D

Ratclife, W.P. TN 45th Inf. Co.B

Ratcliff, Albert M. NC 25th Inf. Co.C Sgt.

Ratcliff, Alonzo TX 22nd Inf. Co.K

Ratcliff, A.N. MS 38th Cav. Co.D

Ratcliff, Andrew VA 51st Inf. Co.B

Ratcliff, A.S.M. MS 33rd Inf. Co.K

Ratcliff, A.T. TX 1st Inf. Co.G

Ratcliff, A.V. AL 15th Bn.Part.Rangers Co.C

Ratcliff, A.V. MS 37th Inf. Co.B

Ratcliff, B.B. MS 8th Inf. Co.H

Ratcliff, Benjamin F. AR 9th Inf. Co.C
Ratcliff, Benjamin F. LA 28th (Gray's) Inf. Co.B
Ratcliff, Benjamin O. FL 10th Inf. Co.C
Ratcliff, C. AL 27th Inf. Co.H 1st Lt.
Ratcliff, Calvin N. MS 18th Inf. Co.B
Ratcliff, Charles W. VA 5th Cav. 2nd Co.F
Ratcliff, Cook VA Cav. 37th Bn. Co.G
Ratcliff, Curtis FL 10th Inf. Co.D Sgt.
Ratcliff, Daniel AL 3rd Cav. Co.D
Ratcliff, Daniel AR 16th Inf. Co.E 1st Sgt.
Ratcliff, David AR 16th Inf. Co.E
Ratcliff, David TX 37th Cav. Co.E
Ratcliff, David VA 17th Cav. Co.H
Ratcliff, Dennis NC 23rd Inf. Co.A
Ratcliff, Doremus C. LA 31st Inf. Co.A 1st Lt.
Ratcliff, E. GA 1st (Olmstead's) Inf. Co.G
Ratcliff, E. GA 10th Inf. Co.B
Ratcliff, E.B. TX 1st Inf. Co.F Sgt.
Ratcliff, Edward B. MD 1st Cav. Co.E,D
Ratcliff, Edward T. TX 13th Cav. Co.K
Ratcliff, Edwin GA 1st (Symons') Res. Co.F,K
    Sgt.
Ratcliff, Elijah TX 2nd Cav. Co.G
Ratcliff, Elisha P. MS 27th Inf. Co.B
Ratcliff, F. AR 45th Cav. Co.K
Ratcliff, Fidelio NC 60th Inf. Co.E
Ratcliff, Francis VA 45th Inf. Co.D
Ratcliff, Francis M. NC 62nd Inf. Co.C
Ratcliff, Franklin MS Inf. (Res.) Berry's Co.
Ratcliff, Fredrick J. FL 10th Inf. Co.C
Ratcliff, George AL 3rd Cav. Co.C Sgt.
Ratcliff, George D. AL 3rd Cav. Co.D
Ratcliff, Geo. N. MO 3rd Inf. Co.K
Ratcliff, Gilford TX 30th Cav. Co.D
Ratcliff, Graham NC 17th Inf. (2nd Org.) Co.B
Ratcliff, H. MS 38th Cav. Co.D
Ratcliff, Hamilton A. AL 6th Inf. Co.I
Ratcliff, H.H. MS 7th Inf. Co.C
Ratcliff, Hiram B. MS Cav. 24th Bn. Co.B
Ratcliff, H.J. LA 28th (Gray's) Inf. Co.H
Ratcliff, Holloway H. MS 22nd Inf. Co.E Sgt.
Ratcliff, Homond MO 15th Cav. Co.K
Ratcliff, Howard VA Inf. 23rd Bn. Co.D
Ratcliff, H.W. AR 1st Vol. Kelsey's Co. Sgt.
Ratcliff, I.M. MS Cav. 3rd Bn.Res. Co.C
Ratcliff, Isaac KY 2nd Bn.Mtd.Rifles Co.D
Ratcliff, J. AL 27th Inf. Co.I
Ratcliff, J.A. MS 24th Inf. Co.E
Ratcliff, Jackson LA Inf. 9th Bn. Co.B
Ratcliff, James NC 62nd Inf. Co.C
Ratcliff, James VA 8th Cav. Co.F
Ratcliff, James 4th Conf.Eng.Troops Artif.
Ratcliff, James A. TX 13th Cav. Co.K
Ratcliff, James A. VA 22nd Cav. Co.F
Ratcliff, James C. FL 10th Inf. Co.D Sgt.
Ratcliff, James M.H. GA 4th (Clinch's) Cav.
    Co.B
Ratcliff, James R. LA 28th (Gray's) Inf. Co.H
Ratcliff, James R. TX 36th Cav. Co.D
Ratcliff, James T. GA Lt.Arty. 12th Bn. 1st
    Co.A
Ratcliff, James T. GA 63rd Inf. Co.A
Ratcliff, J.B. MS 2nd (Quinn's St.Troops) Inf.
    Co.B
Ratcliff, J.B. VA 5th Cav. Co.H Sgt.
Ratcliff, Jeff M. VA Inf. 23rd Bn. Co.D
Ratcliff, Jehu M. VA 21st Cav. 2nd Co.G

Ratcliff, Jeremiah NC 62nd Inf. Co.C 2nd Lt.
Ratcliff, Jesse H. AR 1st (Colquitt's) Inf. Co.G
Ratcliff, J.N. MS Inf. 2nd Bn. (St.Troops) Co.B
    QMSgt.
Ratcliff, Job TX 30th Cav. Co.D
Ratcliff, John VA 22nd Cav. Co.F
Ratcliff, John VA 25th Cav. Co.H
Ratcliff, John B. MS Cav. 24th Bn. Co.B
Ratcliff, John B. NC 39th Inf. Co.H
Ratcliff, John C. MS 19th Inf. Co.G
Ratcliff, John D. MS Cav. 24th Bn. Co.E,B
Ratcliff, John J. AL 3rd Cav. Co.D
Ratcliff, John M. AR 33rd Inf. Co.F
Ratcliff, John N. VA 19th Cav. Co.A
Ratcliff, John N. VA 3rd Cav. & Inf.St.Line
    Co.A
Ratcliff, John R. VA 45th Inf. Co.D
Ratcliff, John R. VA 50th Inf. Co.I
Ratcliff, John T. KY 5th Mtd.Inf. Co.A,K Capt.
Ratcliff, John T. LA 28th (Gray's) Inf. Co.H
    Sgt.
Ratcliff, John T. MS 21st Inf. Co.I
Ratcliff, Joseph TX 30th Cav. Co.D
Ratcliff, Joseph VA 45th Inf. Co.D
Ratcliff, Joseph Conf.Cav. Wood's Regt. 2nd
    Co.A
Ratcliff, Joshua H. TX 30th Cav. Co.D Sgt.
Ratcliff, J.R. TX 9th (Nichols') Inf. Co.I
Ratcliff, J.W. LA 13th Bn. (Part.Rangers) Co.B
Ratcliff, J.W. VA 17th Cav. Co.B
Ratcliff, Lewis VA 22nd Cav. Co.F
Ratcliff, Lewis G. VA 51st Inf. Co.D
Ratcliff, L.W. MS 46th Inf. Co.F
Ratcliff, Marion KY 2nd Bn.Mtd.Rifles Co.D
Ratcliff, Marion NC 16th Inf. Co.F
Ratcliff, Marion J. NC 29th Inf. Co.C 2nd Lt.
Ratcliff, Martin V. AR 24th Inf. Co.G
Ratcliff, Nathaniel G. NC 43rd Inf. Co.K Sgt.
Ratcliff, Peter MS 7th Inf. Co.C Sgt.
Ratcliff, Peter MS 22nd Inf. Co.E
Ratcliff, Porter LA 17th Inf. Co.K
Ratcliff, R.A. TN 19th (Biffle's) Cav. Co.E
Ratcliff, Redmond LA 17th Inf. Co.K
Ratcliff, R.H. VA Inf. 23rd Bn. Co.D
Ratcliff, Richard TX 2nd Cav. Co.G
Ratcliff, Richard VA 22nd Cav. Co.F
Ratcliff, Richard 1st Cherokee Mtd.Rifles Co.C
Ratcliff, Richard J. MS 33rd Inf. Co.C
Ratcliff, Richard S. VA 45th Inf. Co.L
Ratcliff, R.K. TX 13th Cav. Co.K
Ratcliff, Robert GA 32nd Inf. Co.C
Ratcliff, Rose 1st Cherokee Mtd.Vol. 2nd Co.G
Ratcliff, Rowland LA 1st Hvy.Arty. (Reg.) Co.D
Ratcliff, R.S. VA Inf. 23rd Bn. Co.C
Ratcliff, Samuel MS 22nd Inf. Co.E
Ratcliff, Samuel TX 3rd Cav. Co.G
Ratcliff, Samuel TX 6th Inf. Co.E
Ratcliff, Samuel H. MS 3rd Inf. Co.I
Ratcliff, Shadrach VA Cav. Ferguson's Bn. Mor-
    ris' Co.
Ratcliff, T. MS Hall's Co.
Ratcliff, Thomas AR 18th Inf. Co.I
Ratcliff, Thomas J. NC 29th Inf. Co.C
Ratcliff, Thomas W. MS 1st Lt.Arty. Co.E
Ratcliff, Thompson TX Inf. Griffin's Bn. Co.A
Ratcliff, T.J. AR 1st Vol. Kelsey's Co.
Ratcliff, V.B. MS 9th Inf. Co.I

Ratcliff, V.B. MS 41st Inf. Co.C
Ratcliff, Walter H. VA 1st Inf. Co.F
Ratcliff, Washington NC 43rd Inf. Co.K Sgt.
Ratcliff, W.C. SC Inf. 7th Bn. (Enfield Rifles)
    Co.A,F
Ratcliff, W.F. NC 60th Inf. Co.E
Ratcliff, W.F. Conf.Cav. 7th Bn. Co.C 1st Lt.
Ratcliff, William AR Cav. Harrell's Bn. Co.A
Ratcliff, William GA 10th Inf. Co.D
Ratcliff, William GA Inf. 19th Bn. (St.Guards)
    Co.B
Ratcliff, William LA 17th Inf. Co.K
Ratcliff, William TN 11th (Holman's) Cav. Co.G
Ratcliff, William TN 14th Inf.
Ratcliff, William TN 37th Inf. Co.C
Ratcliff, William TX Cav. 1st Regt.St.Troops
    Co.B
Ratcliff, William TX 2nd Cav. Co.G
Ratcliff, William TX 16th Cav. Co.B
Ratcliff, William VA 18th Cav. 2nd Co.G
Ratcliff, William VA Cav. 34th Bn. Co.A,D
Ratcliff, Wm. VA Loc.Def. Morehead's Co.
Ratcliff, William VA Wade's Regt.Loc.Def.
    Co.D
Ratcliff, William B. FL 10th Inf. Co.D 2nd Lt.
Ratcliff, William C. MS Cav. 24th Bn. Co.B
Ratcliff, William H. TN Holman's Bn.
    Part.Rangers Co.B
Ratcliff, William J. NC 17th Inf. (1st Org.) Co.B
Ratcliff, William R. MS 7th Inf. Co.C
Ratcliff, William R. MS 21st Inf. Co.I
Ratcliff, William S. LA 28th (Gray's) Inf. Co.H
Ratcliff, William S. MS Cav. 24th Bn. Co.B
Ratcliff, W.P. Gen. & Staff Chap.
Ratcliff, W.R. TX 11th (Spaight's) Bn.Vol. Co.D
Ratcliff, Y.R. MS 4th Inf. Co.H
Ratcliff, Z.R. MS 6th Inf. Co.B
Ratcliffe, --- VA Cav. 34th or 37th Bn. Capt.
Ratcliffe, A.A. AL 8th Cav. Co.E Sgt.
Ratcliffe, Alexander H. VA 49th Inf. Co.B 2nd
    Lt.
Ratcliffe, Benjamin H. VA 32nd Inf. Co.C
Ratcliffe, Benjamin K. MS 44th Inf. Co.K
Ratcliffe, B.J. SC 7th Cav. Co.K
Ratcliffe, C.H. LA 27th Inf. Co.A 2nd Lt.
Ratcliffe, Charles W. VA 4th Cav. Co.H
Ratcliffe, C.P. LA 4th Inf. Co.A Sgt.
Ratcliffe, C.W. VA 11th Cav. Co.I
Ratcliffe, Daniel 1st Squad. Cherokee Mtd.Vol.
    Co.A
Ratcliffe, E.B. TX Cav. Waller's Regt. Co.F
Ratcliffe, Eli NC 43rd Inf. Co.I
Ratcliffe, George B. VA 3rd Cav. 1st Co.I Sgt.
Ratcliffe, George B. VA 5th Cav. Co.H Sgt.
Ratcliffe, George E. AL 51st (Part.Rangers)
    Co.K
Ratcliffe, George E. VA Cav. Mosby's Regt.
    (Part.Rangers) Co.D
Ratcliffe, George E. VA 21st Inf. Co.B
Ratcliffe, George T. VA 9th Cav. Co.H Sgt.
Ratcliffe, Isaac KY 2nd Cav. Co.D
Ratcliffe, Isaiah LA Cav. Webb's Co.
Ratcliffe, James GA 1st (Ramsey's) Inf. Co.D
Ratcliffe, James VA 19th Cav. Co.K
Ratcliffe, James E. VA 49th Inf. Co.B
Ratcliffe, James W. VA 1st St.Res. Co.A
Ratcliffe, Jeremiah VA 1st Cav. Co.G

Ratcliffe, J.H. MS 46th Inf. Co.F
Ratcliffe, John AL 11th Inf. Co.K
Ratcliffe, John KY 13th Cav. Co.D
Ratcliffe, John MO 3rd Inf. Co.E
Ratcliffe, John VA 32nd Inf. Co.C
Ratcliffe, John 1st Cherokee Mtd.Rifles Co.B
Ratcliffe, John R. VA 17th Inf. Co.D
Ratcliffe, John W. VA 1st Inf. Co.B
Ratcliffe, Joseph TX 1st Inf. Co.M
Ratcliffe, J.S. MS Inf. 2nd Bn. (St.Troops) Co.B
Ratcliffe, Nathan KY 10th (Diamond's) Cav. Co.L
Ratcliffe, Peter VA 16th Cav. Co.C
Ratcliffe, Richard LA Cav. Webb's Co.
Ratcliffe, Richard M. VA 49th Inf. Co.B
Ratcliffe, R.M. LA 3rd Inf. Co.F
Ratcliffe, Robert MO Cav. Freeman's Regt.
Ratcliffe, Robert K. VA 1st Arty. Co.I
Ratcliffe, Ro K. VA Lt.Arty. 38th Bn. Co.B
Ratcliffe, R.P. KY 3rd Mtd.Inf. Co.A Capt.
Ratcliffe, Samuel C. TX 22nd Cav. Co.F
Ratcliffe, Samuel W. GA 10th Inf. Co.D
Ratcliffe, Silas VA Inf. French's Bn. Co.B
Ratcliffe, S.S. MS 5th Inf. Co.B
Ratcliffe, T.G. LA 6th Inf. Co.A
Ratcliffe, Walter H. VA 1st Arty. 1st Co.C
Ratcliffe, W.H. AL 51st (Part.Rangers) Co.K Capt.
Ratcliffe, W.H. SC 7th Cav. Co.K
Ratcliffe, William AR 6th Inf. Co.A 3rd Lt.
Ratcliffe, William B. VA Cav. 1st Bn. Co.C
Ratcliffe, William B. VA 1st St.Res. Co.B
Ratcliffe, William D. AR 26th Inf. Co.F
Ratcliffe, William P. AL 15th Part.Rangers Co.B
Ratcliffe, William P. VA 1st Arty. Co.D
Ratcliffe, William T. VA 3rd Cav. Co.F
Ratcliffe, William T. VA Lt.Arty. Ellett's Co. Cpl.
Ratcliffe, W.J. VA Lt.Arty. Ellett's Co. Sgt.
Ratcliffe, W.J. 4th Conf.Eng.Troops 1st Lt.
Ratcliffe, W.P. AL 56th Part.Rangers Co.B
Ratcliffer, Jacob VA 4th Inf. Co.A
Rate, John B. VA 15th Inf. Co.B
Ratecan, A.J. Mead's Conf.Cav. Co.H
Rategan, John LA 1st (Nelligan's) Inf. Co.C
Ratelle, Alphonse LA Mil. 2nd Regt. French Brig. Co.1
Raten, W.H. AR 1st Inf. Co.G
Rateree, J.L. SC 6th Res. Co.C
Rateree, John SC 6th Res. Co.E
Rateree, Thomas SC 24th Inf. Co.H
Rateree, Wiley AR Lt.Arty. Rivers' Btty.
Raterree, Asa C. KY 10th Cav. Co.A
Raterree, Asa C. TN 10th Cav. Co.A
Ratford, James R. VA 4th Res. Co.F Sgt.
Ratford, J.M. AR 12th Inf. Co.D Jr.2nd Lt.
Rath, Lewis C. GA Arty. 9th Bn. Co.A
Rath, M. LA Mil. Lewis Guards
Rath, Martin LA Arty. Castellanos' Btty.
Rath, Peter M. LA 21st (Patton's) Inf. Co.I
Rath, William NC Wallace's Co. (Wilmington RR Guard)
Rathbone, Berry H. NC 62nd Inf. Co.A
Rathbone, D.C. LA 1st Cav. Co.I
Rathbone, G.W. MS 1st (Patton's) Inf. Co.H
Rathbone, G.W. MS 4th Inf.
Rathbone, G.W. MS 14th Inf.

Rathbone, G.W. MS 20th Inf. Co.B
Rathbone, G.W. MS 43rd Inf. Co.C
Rathbone, Hiram NC 25th Inf. Co.C
Rathbone, Hyram NC 62nd Inf. Co.A
Rathbone, Jacob M. NC 29th Inf. Co.E
Rathbone, James D. AL City Troop (Mobile) Arrington's Co.A
Rathbone, James H. NC 6th Inf. Co.E Band
Rathbone, James M. NC 62nd Inf. Co.A
Rathbone, J.D. 15th Conf.Cav. Co.F
Rathbone, Jesse NC 62nd Inf. Co.A
Rathbone, John NC 25th Inf. Co.C
Rathbone, John H. NC 29th Inf. Co.E
Rathbone, Joseph NC 29th Inf. Co.E
Rathbone, Lorenzo D. NC 25th Inf. Co.C
Rathbone, Maxil NC Inf. Thomas Legion Co.E
Rathbone, Purnel NC 62nd Inf. Co.A
Rathbone, Russel NC Inf. Thomas Legion Co.E
Rathbone, Russel M. NC Inf. Thomas Legion Co.E
Rathbone, Silas G. NC 62nd Inf. Co.A
Rathbone, T. GA Lt.Arty. 12th Bn. 2nd Co.D,F
Rathbone, Thomas NC 6th Inf. Co.E
Rathbone, Tillmon GA 54th Inf. Co.K
Rathbone, Tilman GA 37th Inf. Co.H
Rathbone, William NC 29th Inf. Co.E
Rathbone, William C. NC 62nd Inf. Co.A
Rathbone, William C. TN 37th Inf. Co.C
Rathborne, E.C. LA Inf. 9th Bn. Co.I
Rathbun, George S. MO 5th Cav. Co.F Capt.
Rathbun, George S. MO St.Guard Lt.Col.,Judge Advocate
Rathbun, Lysander LA Cav. Webb's Co. Sgt.
Rathbun, Morris LA 19th Inf. Co.A
Rathbun, Philander A. LA 19th Inf. Co.A QMSgt.
Rathbun, Thomas S. TN 1st (Feild's) Inf.
Rathburn, D.C. LA 3rd (Wingfield's) Cav. Co.I
Rathburn, Joel TX 24th & 25th Cav. (Cons.) Co.E Sgt.
Rathburn, R.W. TN 5th Inf. 2nd Co.D
Rathburne, Joseph MO 8th Cav. Co.A
Rather, A.S.P. MO 7th Cav. Old Co.A
Rather, C.C. TX 37th Cav. Co.K
Rather, Christopher C. TX 14th Cav. Co.B Sgt.
Rather, Daniel, Jr. MS 17th Inf. Co.G Cpl.
Rather, E.R. MS 1st (Percy's) Inf. Co.D
Rather, E.R. MS 3rd Inf. Co.C
Rather, Geo. T. AL 5th Cav. Co.D
Rather, George T. AL 7th Cav. Co.D
Rather, Henry C. TX 35th (Brown's) Cav. Co.K
Rather, Hewitt M. TX 14th Cav. Co.B
Rather, I.T. MS 3rd Cav. Co.B Cpl.
Rather, I.T. MS 1st (King's) Inf. (St.Troops) Co.D
Rather, John AR 34th Inf. Co.B
Rather, John R. MO 7th Cav. Old Co.A
Rather, John W. TN 18th Inf. Co.C
Rather, J.W. AL 35th Inf. Co.B 2nd Lt.
Rather, Nathaniel H. TX 14th Cav. Co.B Sgt.
Rather, William D. MS 14th Inf. Co.B
Rather, William S. TX 6th Cav. Co.H AQM
Rather, W.S. TX Cav. Baird's Regt. Co.B Capt.
Rathers, John MO 8th Cav. Co.C
Rathers, Nathaniel MO 8th Cav. Co.E
Rathers, Robert MS 1st Inf. Co.D
Rathers, Robert MS 5th Inf. Co.D

Rathert, Henry LA 7th Inf. Co.K
Rathford, William TN 35th Inf. Co.L
Rathford, W.T. MO Cav. Wood's Regt.
Rathlen, Lewis MS 12th Inf. Co.K
Rathrock, G.M. TN 10th Inf. Co.G
Rathwell, Richard AL Lt.Arty. 20th Bn. Co.A,B
Rathwell, Richard AL 6th Inf. Co.H
Ratican, B.P. KY 1st Inf. Co.H 2nd Lt.
Ratican, Daniel P. LA 9th Inf. Co.F Sgt.
Ratican, D.P. KY 3rd Cav. Co.I 3rd Lt.
Ratican, R.E. AL 5th Inf. New Co.G
Ratican, Robert Emmett AL Lt.Arty. 2nd Bn. Co.D
Raticin, James AL 11th Cav. Co.E
Ratier, E.N. LA Inf. 10th Bn. Co.C 2nd Lt.
Ratigan, B.W. KY 2nd Mtd.Inf. Co.F Sgt.
Ratigan, John TX 5th Inf. Co.B
Ratigan, Peter SC 1st Arty. Co.H
Ratin, J.H. AL 3rd Inf. Co.B
Ra Tirce, Samuel MO 8th Inf. Co.K
Ratissean, A.A. TX 1st Hvy.Arty. Co.C
Ratlaw, E.P. TX Cav. (Dismtd.) Chisum's Regt. Co.E
Ratledge, Daniel TN 3rd (Lillard's) Mtd.Inf. Co.H
Ratledge, Daniel R. TN 26th Inf. Co.D
Ratledge, David TN 3rd (Lillard's) Mtd.Inf. Co.G
Ratledge, David TN 3rd (Lillard's) Mtd.Inf. Co.H
Ratledge, D.J. 7th Conf.Cav. Co.G,M
Ratledge, D.R. TN 63rd Inf. Co.B
Ratledge, Isaac 7th Conf.Cav. Co.G,M
Ratledge, James F. TN 59th Mtd.Inf. Co.G
Ratledge, John TN 39th Mtd.Inf. Co.B Sgt.
Ratledge, Joseph TN 63rd Inf. Co.B
Ratledge, L.P. 7th Conf.Cav. Co.G,M
Ratledge, M.D. TN 63rd Inf. Co.G
Ratledge, Thomas TN 26th Inf. Co.E
Ratledge, Thomas TN 39th Mtd.Inf. Co.B
Ratledge, Thomas TN 63rd Inf. Co.G
Ratledge, W.H. NC Cav. 16th Bn. Co.E
Ratledge, William H. 7th Conf.Cav. Co.G,M
Ratleff, John VA 64th Mtd.Inf. 2nd Co.F
Ratleff, John A. VA 54th Inf. Co.A
Ratlege, B.J. NC 34th Inf. Co.C
Ratler, Stephen NC Inf. Thomas Legion
Ratlett, J.T. MS 21st Inf. Co.I
Ratley, Calvin NC 51st Inf. Co.F
Ratley, Hinant NC 3rd Arty. (40th St.Troops) Co.K
Ratley, John TN 44th (Cons.) Inf. Co.E
Ratley, John TX 21st Cav. Co.H
Ratley, John R. TN 55th (McKoin's) Inf. Co.H
Ratley, Joseph NC 31st Inf. Co.A
Ratley, Joseph NC 51st Inf. Co.F
Ratley, Richard NC 31st Inf. Co.A
Ratley, Richard C. NC 51st Inf. Co.E
Ratley, T.J. LA 27th Inf. Co.I
Ratley, Wallace 1st Cherokee Mtd.Vol. 2nd Co.E
Ratley, William NC Walker's Bn. Thomas' Legion Co.A
Ratlidge, James GA 60th Inf. Co.F
Ratlidge, Joseph TN 3rd (Lillard's) Mtd.Inf. Co.G
Ratlief, John H. VA 51st Inf. Co.B
Ratlief, S. GA 5th Res. Co.D

Ratlif, A. AR 58th Mil. Co.B
Ratlif, J. AR 58th Mil. Co.B
Ratlif, J.A. TX 20th Inf. Co.F
Ratlif, James W. AL 19th Inf. Co.C
Ratlif, William B. AR Cav. Nave's Bn. Co.C
Ratlife, W.W. 3rd Conf.Cav. Co.D
Ratliff, A. LA Hvy.Arty. 8th Bn. Co.2
Ratliff, Aaron AR 35th Inf. Co.E
Ratliff, Abednago KY 10th (Diamond's) Cav.
  Co.G
Ratliff, Alderrine VA Inf. 21st Bn. 2nd Co.F
Ratliff, Alfred MS 18th Inf. Co.A
Ratliff, Alfred VA 54th Inf. Co.E
Ratliff, A.P.S. VA 20th Cav. Co.C Sr.2nd Lt.
Ratliff, Archer S. VA 25th Inf. 1st Co.G
Ratliff, A.W. KY 10th (Diamond's) Cav. Co.D
Ratliff, Benjamin MS 28th Cav. Co.G
Ratliff, Benjamin MS Inf. 1st Bn.St.Troops (12
  mo. '62-3) Co.B
Ratliff, B.F. TX 20th Inf. Co.F
Ratliff, B.P. MS 32nd Inf. Co.C
Ratliff, Burrel W. MS 1st (Johnston's) Inf. Co.K
Ratliff, Burwell MS Cav. Ham's Regt. Co.F
Ratliff, B.W. MS 2nd Cav. Co.H
Ratliff, B.Y. TX 10th Cav. Co.A
Ratliff, Calvin MS 33rd Inf. Co.E
Ratliff, Campbell VA 48th Inf. Co.G
Ratliff, C.C. VA Lt.Arty. Fry's Co.
Ratliff, Charles A. VA 4th Inf. Co.L
Ratliff, Charles H. NC 31st Inf. Co.B
Ratliff, Cullen C. TX 27th Cav. Co.L
Ratliff, D. VA 59th Inf. 2nd Co.D
Ratliff, David MS Cav. Ham's Regt. Co.F
Ratliff, David S. VA 4th Res. Co.C
Ratliff, DeKalb AL 29th Inf. Co.C
Ratliff, Elijah AL 29th Inf. Co.C
Ratliff, Ely MS 2nd (Davidson's) Inf. Co.K
  Teamster
Ratliff, Evan AL 44th Inf. Co.B
Ratliff, Evin W. TN 23rd Inf. 1st Co.A, Co.B
Ratliff, Ezekiel M. KY 5th Mtd.Inf. Co.C
Ratliff, Floyd VA 86th Mil. Co.D
Ratliff, F.M. MS 39th Inf. Co.B
Ratliff, F.M. TN 2nd (Walker's) Inf. Co.B Cpl.
Ratliff, Frank 2nd Conf.Inf. Co.D Cpl.
Ratliff, Frederick KY 10th (Diamond's) Cav.
  Co.G
Ratliff, F.T. MO 16th Inf. Co.A
Ratliff, G.A. NC 1st Jr.Res. Co.I
Ratliff, G.B. MS 1st (Percy's) Inf. Co.F
Ratliff, G.B. MS 22nd Inf. Co.G
Ratliff, George H. VA 54th Inf. Co.I
Ratliff, George N. MO 3rd Inf. Co.K
Ratliff, George S. VA Horse Arty. McClanahan's
  Co.
Ratliff, George S. VA 162nd Mil. Co.C
Ratliff, George W. VA 4th Res. Co.H,I
Ratliff, German J. VA 48th Inf. Co.G
Ratliff, Given VA 62nd Mtd.Inf. Co.D
Ratliff, Granville VA 17th Cav. Co.B
Ratliff, Green B. MS 33rd Inf. Co.E
Ratliff, G.W. TX 21st Cav. Co.F
Ratliff, H. VA 4th Res. Co.D
Ratliff, Harrison KY 10th (Diamond's) Cav.
  Co.D
Ratliff, Ira W. MS 6th Inf. Co.B Sgt.
Ratliff, Ira W. MS 21st Inf. Co.G

Ratliff, Isaac P. VA 4th Inf. Co.L
Ratliff, J. AL 29th Inf. Co.C 1st Sgt.
Ratliff, J. LA 27th Inf. Co.K
Ratliff, Jacob KY 5th Mtd.Inf. Co.G
Ratliff, Jacob M. KY 10th (Diamond's) Cav.
  Co.G
Ratliff, Jacob M. VA Inf. 21st Bn. 2nd Co.F 1st
  Lt.
Ratliff, James, Jr. AL 29th Inf. Co.C
Ratliff, James, Sr. AL 29th Inf. Co.C
Ratliff, James KY 10th (Diamond's) Cav. Co.C
Ratliff, James MS 1st (King's) Inf. (St.Troops)
  Co.B
Ratliff, James MO Inf. Perkins' Bn. Co.B
Ratliff, James TX 20th Inf. Co.K
Ratliff, James VA Cav. 34th Bn. Co.G
Ratliff, James VA Inf. 1st Bn. Co.E
Ratliff, James VA Inf. 21st Bn. 2nd Co.F
Ratliff, James A. VA 63rd Inf. Co.B
Ratliff, James C. NC 13th Inf. Co.H Sgt.
Ratliff, James F. NC 43rd Inf. Co.I Cpl.
Ratliff, James F. VA 17th Cav. Co.A Sgt.
Ratliff, James Floyd VA 8th Cav. 1st Co.D
Ratliff, James L. KY 10th (Diamond's) Cav.
  Co.D 1st Sgt.
Ratliff, James L. KY 5th Mtd.Inf. Co.G Capt.
Ratliff, James M. MS 18th Inf. Co.A
Ratliff, James M. TX 36th Cav. Co.B
Ratliff, James M. VA 24th Inf. Co.A
Ratliff, James N. GA Cav. 16th Bn. (St.Guards)
  Co.F
Ratliff, James O. VA 19th Cav. Co.I
Ratliff, James P. NC 45th Inf. Co.G
Ratliff, James P. VA 4th Inf. Co.L
Ratliff, James P. VA 52nd Inf. Co.K
Ratliff, James R. MS 2nd Inf. Co.E
Ratliff, James S. AR Lt.Arty. 5th Btty.
Ratliff, James T. KY 10th (Diamond's) Cav.
  Co.C
Ratliff, James T. VA Inf. 21st Bn. 2nd Co.F
Ratliff, James W. MS Cav. Jeff Davis Legion
  Co.B
Ratliff, James W. MS 1st Lt.Arty. Co.A
Ratliff, Jasper MS 28th Cav. Co.G
Ratliff, J.B. TX Cav. McDowell's Co.
Ratliff, J.D. AL 29th Inf. Co.C
Ratliff, Jeremiah AL 28th Inf. Co.D
Ratliff, Jeremiah AL 29th Inf. Co.C 1st Sgt.
Ratliff, Jesse MS 28th Cav. Co.G
Ratliff, Jesse B. TX 26th Cav. Co.B, 2nd Co.G
Ratliff, J.F. VA 59th Inf. 2nd Co.D
Ratliff, J.M. AL 48th Inf. Co.A 1st Sgt.
Ratliff, J.M. TX 21st Cav. Co.D
Ratliff, J.N. NC 1st Jr.Res. Co.I
Ratliff, J.N. TN 48th (Nixon's) Inf. Co.K
Ratliff, John AL 12th Cav. Co.C
Ratliff, John AL 3rd Res. Co.H
Ratliff, John AL 29th Inf. Co.C
Ratliff, John AL 48th Inf. Co.F
Ratliff, John KY 2nd (Duke's) Cav. Co.G
Ratliff, John KY 10th (Diamond's) Cav. Co.D
Ratliff, John KY 5th Mtd.Inf. Co.G
Ratliff, John MS 28th Cav. Co.G
Ratliff, John MS 3rd Inf. (St.Troops) Co.B
Ratliff, John MS 9th Inf. New Co.C
Ratliff, John MO 12th Inf. Co.F
Ratliff, John TN 48th (Nixon's) Inf. Co.D

Ratliff, John TN 48th (Voorhies') Inf. Co.D Sgt.
Ratliff, John VA 24th Inf. Co.K
Ratliff, John VA 29th Inf. Co.H
Ratliff, John D. TX 18th Cav. Co.K 2nd Lt.
Ratliff, John M. KY 10th (Diamond's) Cav.
  Co.F,G 1st Lt.
Ratliff, John M. KY 5th Mtd.Inf. Co.G
Ratliff, John M. VA Inf. 21st Bn. 2nd Co.F 1st
  Sgt.
Ratliff, John N. VA 10th Bn.Res. Co.E
Ratliff, John P. VA 54th Inf. Co.A
Ratliff, John S. KY 10th (Diamond's) Cav. Co.I
  Capt.
Ratliff, John W. KY 3rd Bn.Mtd.Rifles Co.D
Ratliff, John W. KY Horse Arty. Byrne's Co.
Ratliff, John W. TX 27th Cav. Co.L
Ratliff, Jonathan VA 62nd Mtd.Inf. 2nd Co.G
Ratliff, Joseph E. VA 45th Inf. Co.H
Ratliff, Joseph N. TN 54th Inf. Co.E
Ratliff, Joshua AL 48th Inf. Co.F Cpl.
Ratliff, Joshua B. TX 26th Cav. Co.B, 2nd Co.G
  2nd Lt.
Ratliff, Josiah R. LA 27th Inf. Co.H
Ratliff, J.T. MS Cav. Ham's Regt. Co.B Sgt.
Ratliff, Julions W. GA 32nd Inf. Co.C
Ratliff, Julius KY 10th (Diamond's) Cav. Co.I
Ratliff, J.W. KY 3rd Cav. Co.G
Ratliff, J.W. MS 28th Cav. Co.G
Ratliff, Leonard VA 19th Cav. Co.E
Ratliff, Levi AL 48th Inf. Co.F
Ratliff, Lewis B. VA 11th Bn.Res. Co.A Cpl.
Ratliff, Little S.B.J. AL 11th Inf. Co.K
Ratliff, Mark AL Pris.Guard Freeman's Co.
Ratliff, Martin AL 28th Inf. Co.C
Ratliff, Mathias VA 54th Inf. Co.E
Ratliff, Meshack KY 10th (Diamond's) Cav.
  Co.G 1st Lt.
Ratliff, Milbern C. TN 1st (Turney's) Inf. Co.H
Ratliff, Milburn AL 18th Bn.Vol. Co.A
Ratliff, Moses KY 10th (Diamond's) Cav. Co.I
Ratliff, Newton VA 11th Regt.Rangers Co.A
Ratliff, Obed TN 48th (Nixon's) Inf. Co.K
Ratliff, Obed TN 54th Inf. Co.E
Ratliff, Owen TN 48th (Nixon's) Inf. Co.K
Ratliff, Owen TN 54th Inf. Co.E
Ratliff, Owen VA 22nd Inf. Co.D
Ratliff, Phil VA 51st Inf. Co.H,A,B
Ratliff, R. GA 5th Res. Co.K
Ratliff, R. MS 5th Cav. Co.B
Ratliff, Richard TX 8th Inf. Co.D
Ratliff, Richard VA Cav. 34th Bn. Co.G
Ratliff, Richard VA Cav. McFarlane's Co.
Ratliff, Richard VA Inf. 45th Bn. Co.E
Ratliff, Richard Conf.Cav. 6th Bn.
Ratliff, Richard H. KY 10th (Diamond's) Cav.
  Co.G Sgt.
Ratliff, Richard M. TX 18th Cav. Co.K
Ratliff, R.L. FL 1st (Res.) Inf. Co.B
Ratliff, R.L. MS Inf. 1st Bn.St.Troops (30 days
  '64) Co.G
Ratliff, Robert TN 60th Mtd.Inf. Co.C
Ratliff, Robert VA Cav. 34th Bn. Co.G 2nd Lt.
Ratliff, Robert VA Cav. McFarlane's Co.
Ratliff, Robert Conf.Cav. 6th Bn.
Ratliff, Rufus M. MS 18th Inf. Co.A
Ratliff, S. KY 10th (Diamond's) Cav. Co.I Sgt.

Ratliff, Samuel Conf.Cav. 7th Bn. Co.C Bvt.2nd Lt.
Ratliff, Samuel H. MS 6th Inf. Co.B
Ratliff, Samuel H. TN 1st (Turney's) Inf. Co.H
Ratliff, S.F. TX 1st Hvy.Arty. 2nd Co.A
Ratliff, S.H. MS 14th (Cons.) Inf. Co.A
Ratliff, Shadrich KY 10th (Diamond's) Cav. Co.G Cpl.
Ratliff, Silas KY 10th (Diamond's) Cav. Co.G
Ratliff, Silas O. VA 45th Inf. Co.H
Ratliff, Silas W. KY 10th (Diamond's) Cav. Co.D
Ratliff, Simeon MS 16th Inf. Co.E
Ratliff, Sparrel VA Inf. 21st Bn. 2nd Co.F Capt.
Ratliff, Sponil KY 10th (Diamond's) Cav. Co.C
Ratliff, Stephen C. MS 43rd Inf. Co.E
Ratliff, Tazwell M. VA 54th Inf. Co.I
Ratliff, Thomas AL 29th Inf. Co.C
Ratliff, Thomas MS 1st (King's) Inf. (St.Troops) Co.G Cpl.
Ratliff, Thomas VA 17th Cav. Co.A
Ratliff, Thomas VA 24th Inf. Co.K
Ratliff, Thomas VA 54th Inf. Co.E
Ratliff, Thomas C. VA 17th Inf. Co.G
Ratliff, Thomas J. MS 18th Inf. Co.A
Ratliff, Thomas M. VA 4th Inf. Co.L
Ratliff, Thompson KY 10th (Diamond's) Cav. Co.C
Ratliff, T.J. MS 2nd (Davidson's) Inf. Co.K
Ratliff, T.J. TX 20th Inf. Co.F
Ratliff, Tyre KY 10th (Diamond's) Cav. Co.C Sgt.
Ratliff, Van B. MS Lt.Arty. (Brookhaven Lt.Arty.) Hoskins' Btty.
Ratliff, V.R. VA 24th Inf. Co.A
Ratliff, Warren R. MS 16th Inf. Co.E Sgt.
Ratliff, Warren R. MS 33rd Inf. Co.E 3rd Lt.
Ratliff, Warwick C. VA 52nd Inf. Co.K
Ratliff, W.B. NC 5th Cav. (63rd St.Troops) Co.D
Ratliff, W.E. MS Cav. 24th Bn. Co.E
Ratliff, Wesley W. MS 21st Inf. Co.G
Ratliff, W.G. TX 21st Inf. Co.A
Ratliff, William AL 12th Cav. Co.C
Ratliff, William AL 12th Inf. Co.E
Ratliff, William AL 24th Inf. Co.I
Ratliff, William AL 28th Inf. Co.C
Ratliff, William, Jr. AL 29th Inf. Co.C
Ratliff, William KY 7th Cav. Co.E
Ratliff, William KY 10th (Diamond's) Cav. Co.C Capt.
Ratliff, William KY 10th (Diamond's) Cav. Co.I Cpl.
Ratliff, William LA 11th Inf. Co.G
Ratliff, William MS 28th Cav. Co.G Capt.
Ratliff, William MS Cav. Ham's Regt. Co.B 1st Sgt.
Ratliff, William MS 6th Inf. Co.B Sgt.
Ratliff, William MS 18th Inf. Co.A Capt.
Ratliff, William MO 12th Cav. Co.K
Ratliff, William NC 1st Cav. (9th St.Troops) Co.H
Ratliff, William NC Walker's Bn. Thomas' Legion Co.A
Ratliff, William TX 22nd Inf. Co.H
Ratliff, William VA 19th Cav. Co.I
Ratliff, William VA 25th Inf. 1st Co.G

Ratliff, Wm. VA Loc.Def. Morehead's Co.
Ratliff, William A. KY 10th (Diamond's) Cav. Co.C
Ratliff, William A. VA Inf. 21st Bn. 2nd Co.F
Ratliff, William B., Sr. AL 29th Inf. Co.C
Ratliff, Wm. B. AL Cp. of Instr. Talladega
Ratliff, William B. LA 7th Inf. Co.F Capt.
Ratliff, William C. TN 23rd Inf. 1st Co.A, Co.B
Ratliff, William E. MS 3rd Inf. Co.C Capt.
Ratliff, William H. AL 24th Inf. Co.F
Ratliff, William H.H. AL 11th Inf. Co.K
Ratliff, William J. TX Inf. Griffin's Bn. Co.E
Ratliff, William J. 4th Conf.Eng.Troops Co.E 1st Lt.
Ratliff, William M. AL 28th Inf. Co.K
Ratliff, William N. TN Cav. 9th Bn. (Gantt's) Co.D Cpl.
Ratliff, William O.B. KY 10th (Diamond's) Cav. Co.D Sgt.
Ratliff, William O.B. KY 5th Mtd.Inf. Co.G Cpl.
Ratliff, William S. GA 2nd Cav. Co.G
Ratliff, William T. MS 7th Cav. Co.D Cpl.
Ratliff, William T. MS 1st Lt.Arty. Co.A Capt.
Ratliff, William W. MS 6th Inf. Co.B
Ratliff, W.J. GA Inf. 9th Bn. Co.B
Ratliff, W.N. TN 11th Inf. Co.H
Ratliff, W.P. KY 9th Mtd.Inf. Co.F
Ratliff, W.P. TN Inf. 23rd Bn. Co.B Cpl.
Ratliff, W.P. 20th Conf.Cav. 2nd Co.I
Ratliff, W.Q. LA Mil.Cav. (Jeff Davis Rangers) Norwood's Co.
Ratliff, W.R. TX 21st Inf. Co.H
Ratliff, W.T. NC 14th Inf. Co.H
Ratliff, Z. AR 45th Cav. Co.F
Ratliff, Z. AR 1st Vol. Co.K
Ratliff, Z.L. MS Cav. 3rd Bn.Res. Co.C
Ratliff, Z.L. MS 5th Cav. Co.E
Ratliff, Z.W. MS Cav. Yerger's Regt. Co.A
Ratliffe, Arch TX Cav. Morgan's Regt. Co.A
Ratliffe, A.S. VA 62nd Mtd.Inf. 2nd Co.A
Ratliffe, David F. NC 5th Cav. (63rd St.Troops) Co.D Sgt.
Ratliffe, Derius VA Inf. 26th Bn. Co.H
Ratliffe, J.E. AR 3rd Cav. Co.H
Ratliffe, John A. GA 35th Inf. Co.I Cpl.
Ratliffe, Joseph KY 5th Mtd.Inf. Co.H,G,F Capt.
Ratliffe, Marcellus VA 5th Inf. Co.L
Ratliffe, R. MS 2nd Cav. 2nd Co.G
Ratliffe, Richard MS 15th Inf. Co.E
Ratliffe, Robert TX 4th Cav. Co.F
Ratliffe, Samuel MS 15th Inf. Co.E
Ratliffe, T.N. GA 5th Res. Co.D
Ratliffe, Valentine VA 30th Bn.S.S. Co.D
Ratliffe, W.A. TX Cav. 1st Regt.St.Troops Co.C
Ratliffe, W.E. Bradford's Corps Scouts & Guards Co.A
Ratliffe, William E. TX 22nd Cav. Co.F
Ratlige, Asberry TN 3rd (Lillard's) Mtd.Inf. Co.F
Ratling Goard Rider 1st Cherokee Mtd.Rifles Co.D
Ratlips, J.R. LA Cav. Gober's Regt.
Ratree, W.L. SC 17th Inf. Co.I
Ratrie, Henry H. VA 6th Cav. Co.K
Ratrie, John M. VA Cav. 39th Bn. Co.B

Ratsburg, Jacob MS 8th Inf. Co.H,I
Ratsford, John AR 36th Inf. Co.K
Rattan, Augustus AL Arty. 1st Bn. Co.A
Rattan, C.C. TX 22nd Cav. Co.I Cpl.
Rattan, David TX 9th Cav. Co.G
Rattan, Hampton TX 22nd Cav. Co.C
Rattan, M.E. TX 9th Cav. Co.G
Rattan, Thomas TX Cav. Martin's Regt. Co.I
Rattan, Thomas H. TX 37th Cav. Co.B
Rattan, V. TX 23rd Cav. Co.F
Rattans, John TX 22nd Cav. Co.I Capt.
Rattelte, Eugene LA Mil. British Guard Bn. Burrowes' Co.
Ratten, J.G. AR 1st Cav. Co.I
Ratten, M.B. AL 22nd Inf. Co.B
Ratteree, James SC 17th Inf. Co.D
Ratteree, James W. GA 36th (Broyles') Inf. Co.B
Ratteree, John AR 35th Inf. Co.D Cpl.
Ratteree, John GA 64th Inf. Co.A Music.
Ratteree, Joseph SC 17th Inf. Co.D
Ratteree, L.D. SC 6th Inf. 1st Co.G
Ratteree, L.L. SC 17th Inf. Co.D
Ratteree, Robert SC 17th Inf. Co.D
Ratteree, Thomas SC 3rd Bn.Res. Co.C
Ratteree, Thomas SC 17th Inf. Co.D
Ratteree, T.J. TN 5th Inf. Co.A
Ratterree, Alexander J.K.P. GA 42nd Inf. Co.K
Ratterree, Henry SC 5th Inf. 2nd Co.D
Ratterree, Henry M. AR 26th Inf. Co.A
Ratterree, J. SC 12th Inf. Co.H
Ratterree, James GA 22nd Inf. Co.C Cpl.
Ratterree, John GA 42nd Inf. Co.K
Ratterree, John SC 5th Inf. 2nd Co.B
Ratterree, John SC 5th St.Troops Co.K
Ratterree, Leonard A. GA 42nd Inf. Co.K Sgt.
Ratterree, Robert AR 3rd Inf. Co.I
Ratterree, William L. NC 49th Inf. Co.F
Ratterru, John TN Lt.Arty. Baxter's Co.
Rattervee, Robert AR Inf. 2nd Bn. Co.B
Ratti, Domenico LA Mil. Cazadores Espanoles Regt. Co.1
Rattigan, Neut LA 17th Inf. Co.I
Rattin, H. TX 32nd Cav. Co.B
Rattison, A. TX Inf. 1st St.Troops Beihler's Co.A
Rattisseau, A.A. TX 1st Hvy.Arty. Co.C
Rattle, Hinnant NC 31st Inf. Co.A
Rattler, H.T. 1st Chickasaw Inf. Kesner's Co.
Rattler, J.T. GA 41st Inf. Co.C
Rattley, Elam GA 64th Inf. Co.G Cpl.
Rattlif, James L. FL 1st (Res.) Inf. Co.B
Rattliff, Alfred E. TN 33rd Inf. Co.D Sgt.
Rattliff, John N. VA Inf. 9th Bn. Duffy's Co.C
Rattliff, Peter VA Cav. Caldwell's Bn. Hankins' Co.
Rattliff, S.B. VA Cav. Caldwell's Bn. Hankins' Co.
Rattliff, William 3rd Conf.Eng.Troops Co.A
Rattliff, Z.W. MS St.Cav. 3rd Bn. (Cooper's) 2nd Co.A
Rattling, George LA 20th Inf. Co.H
Rattling Gourd 1st Cherokee Mtd.Vol. 2nd Co.B
Rattling Gourd 1st Cherokee Mtd.Vol. 1st Co.E, 2nd Co.C
Rattlingourd 1st Cherokee Mtd.Vol. 1st Co.D
Ratton, --- AL 22nd Inf. Co.K
Ratton, F. Brush Bn.

Ratton, Thomas H. TX 1st Bn.S.S. Co.A
Ratton, Volney Brush Bn.
Ratton, W.O. MS Cav. Jeff Davis Legion Co.I
Rattree, Alexander SC 17th Inf. Co.D
Ratts, A.H. TX Cav. 2nd Regt.St.Troops Co.G
Ratts, Burrell R. NC 49th Inf. Co.C
Ratts, Hiram C. NC 42nd Inf. Co.F
Ratts, Thomas O. NC 42nd Inf. Co.A Cpl.
Ratty, Patrick VA 12th Cav. Co.F
Rau, C. TX Inf. 1st St.Troops Martin's Co.A
Rau, C.H. VA 2nd Cav. Music.
Rau, Charles O. TN 60th Mtd.Inf. Co.L
Rau, Edward SC Lt.Arty. 3rd (Palmetto) Bn.
    Co.D
Rau, Edward SC Sea Fencibles Symons' Co. 1st
    QM
Rau, George GA Lt.Arty. (Jackson Arty.) Mas-
    senburg's Btty.
Rau, H. LA 20th Inf. Co.D
Rau, Henry W. KY 4th Mtd.Inf. Co.I
Rau, John NC Mil. Clark's Sp.Bn. Co.B
Rau, Louis TX 2nd Inf. Co.F
Rau, Paul LA Mil. Fire Bn. Co.F
Raube, Fred TX Waul's Legion Co.C Drum.
Raubottom, Charles F. TX 35th (Brown's) Cav.
    Co.H
Rauch, A. LA Miles' Legion Co.A
Rauch, Fritz TX 3rd Inf. Co.K
Rauch, Fritz TX 16th Inf. Co.B
Rauch, H.J. SC 14th Inf. Co.B 3rd Lt.
Rauch, Jacob SC 14th Inf. Co.B
Rauch, John MS 3rd (St.Troops) Cav. Co.K
Rauch, Joseph TX 18th Cav. Co.B Cpl.
Rauch, Lewis Conf.Inf. Tucker's Regt. Co.B
Rauch, Louis SC 1st Pioneers Co.B
Rauch, M. LA Washington Arty.Bn. Co.1
Rauch, P.J. MS 3rd (St.Troops) Cav. Co.K
Rauch, Samuel N. SC 14th Inf. Co.B Cpl.
Rauch, William W. SC 20th Inf. Co.K
Rauchart, E. VA 54th Mil. Co.H
Raudean, A. LA Lt.Arty. LeGardeur, Jr.'s Co.
    (Orleans Guard Btty.)
Raudit, J.R. GA Lt.Arty. 14th Bn. Co.B
Raudnitzky, Frederick GA 1st Bn.S.S. Co.B
Raue, T.A. AL 94th Mil. Co.A
Raugh, Bernard AR 8th Inf. New Co.A
Raughton, Isaiah AL 12th Inf. Co.K
Rauhman, Henry A. LA 4th Inf. Co.B Capt.
Raul, Adolph LA Lewis' Regt. Co.B
Raul, John SC 24th Inf. Co.G
Raul, Lewis SC 15th Inf. Co.C
Raulan, P.B. AL 48th Inf. Co.D Sgt.
Rauland, Charles 1st Conf.Inf. 1st Co.F
Raule, Alex LA Bienville Res.
Raulerson, Aaron FL 2nd Inf. Co.C Cpl.
Raulerson, D. GA 7th Cav. Co.G
Raulerson, David GA Cav. 24th Bn. Co.A
Raulerson, Frank FL Cav. 5th Bn. Co.G
Raulerson, H. FL 2nd Cav. Co.F
Raulerson, Hardy FL 1st Cav. Co.G
Raulerson, Harris FL 3rd Inf. Co.K
Raulerson, J. FL Cav. 5th Bn. Co.H
Raulerson, Jackson FL 3rd Inf. Co.K
Raulerson, Jacob FL 1st Cav. Co.D
Raulerson, James FL 3rd Inf. Co.I
Raulerson, James W. GA 26th Inf. Co.D
Raulerson, J.F. FL Cav. 5th Bn. Co.H Sgt.

Raulerson, J.N. GA 4th (Clinch's) Cav. Co.K,A
Raulerson, J.N. GA Hvy.Arty. 22nd Bn. Co.E
    Cpl.
Raulerson, Moses L. FL 7th Inf. Co.D Sgt.
Raulerson, R. FL Cav. 5th Bn. Co.H
Raulerson, Russell GA Mtd.Inf. (Pierce
    Mtd.Vol.) Hendry's Co.
Raulerson, Samuel FL 4th Inf. Co.D Cpl.
Raulerson, Thomas S. GA 4th (Clinch's) Cav.
    Co.A,K Cpl.
Raulerson, Wade H. FL 7th Inf. Co.F
Raulerson, W.H. FL Cav. 5th Bn. Co.H
Raulerson, William H. FL 7th Inf. Co.B
Raulerson, William J. FL 4th Inf. Co.D
Raulerson, William T. FL 7th Inf. Co.F
Raulerson, W.J. FL 2nd Inf. Co.C
Raulerston, Liberty F. FL Cav. 5th Bn.
Raulin, Oscar D. LA 8th Inf. Co.F
Raulin, Rene LA 3rd (Harrison's) Cav. Co.K,A
Raulins, T. KY 1st (Helm's) Cav. New Co.G
Raulison, John FL 1st (Res.) Inf. Co.G
Raulison, West FL 1st (Res.) Inf. Co.G
Rauls, H.C. LA 31st Inf. Co.K
Rauls, James VA 2nd St.Res. Co.I
Rauls, James L. SC 21st Inf. Co.A
Rauls, James N. AL Cav. Barbiere's Bn.
    Goldsby's Co.
Rauls, J.F. AL Mobile City Troop
Rauls, J.J. GA Inf. 25th Bn. (Prov.Guard) Co.D
Rauls, J.L. AR 24th Inf. Co.A
Rauls, Joseph R. NC 17th Inf. (2nd Org.) Co.H
Rauls, Richard N. VA Hvy.Arty. A.J. Jones' Co.
Raulston, James R. TN 18th Inf. Co.G
Raulston, J.B. MS 8th Cav. Co.I
Raulston, Samuel TN 5th (McKenzie's) Cav.
    Co.D
Raulston, W.E. AR 1st (Monroe's) Cav. Co.E
    Capt.
Raulston, W.E. AR 5th Inf. Co.G
Raulston, W.E. AR 50th Mil. Co.G
Raulston, William D. AL 6th Inf. Co.K
Rault, Joseph LA Mil. 3rd Regt.Eur.Brig. (Garde
    Francaise) Frois' Co.
Raum, --- VA VMI Co.A
Raum, J.M. AL Cav. Murphy's Bn. Co.B
Raum, J.M. 15th Conf.Cav. Co.G
Raum, Robert H. LA 1st (Nelligan's) Inf. Co.I
Raum, T. AL 51st (Part.Rangers) Co.H
Raum, W.C. Conf.Cav. Wood's Regt. 1st Co.G
    Capt.
Raum, William C. Conf.Cav. Raum's Co. Capt.
Rauman, E. LA Bickham's Co. (Caddo Mil.)
Raumback, Christian LA Mil. Mech.Guard
Raun, W.H. TX Cav. 2nd Bn.St.Troops Hub-
    bard's Co.
Rauner, Lambert AR 17th (Griffith's) Inf. Co.A
Raunere, Lambert AR 11th & 17th (Cons.) Inf.
    Co.I
Rauney, H.J. Gen. & Staff, QM Dept. Maj.
Raupp, Albert GA 36th (Villepigue's) Inf. Co.D
Raus, James VA 53rd Inf. Co.F
Raus, William AL 1st Regt.Conscr. Co.F
Rausberger, Adolphus MO Cav. Jackman's Regt.
    Co.D
Rausberger, Andrew MO Cav. Jackman's Regt.
    Co.D

Rausberger, Robert MO Cav. Jackman's Regt.
    Co.D
Rausberry, John N. AL 61st Inf. Co.I
Rausch, A.H. VA 59th Inf. 1st Sgt.
Rausch, Henry 1st Conf.Eng.Troops Co.D Artif.
Rausch, Peter LA Mil. 1st Regt. 3rd Brig. 1st
    Div. Co.E
Rauschenberg, A. GA Phillips' Legion Co.B
    Ch.Music.
Rauschenberg, Leopold TX 2nd Inf. Co.F Cpl.
Rauschert, Edward VA 54th Mil. Co.E,F
Rause, B.S. MS Cav. 17th Bn. Co.E
Rause, Charles S. MS Cav. 17th Bn. Co.E
Rauserman, R.C. VA 12th Cav. Co.K
Rausey, J.T. SC 11th Res. Co.A
Raush, Henry VA Hvy.Arty. 20th Bn. Co.A
Raush, J. LA Mil. 3rd Regt. French Brig. Co.7
Raushenberg, Charles GA 1st Inf. (St.Guards)
    Co.I
Rausher, H. TN 15th Inf. Co.I
Raushide, John LA 22nd Inf. Co.A
Rausin, E. TN 26th Inf. Co.F
Rauson, Peter Conf.Lt.Arty. 1st Reg.Btty.
Rauson, Thomas D. VA 2nd Inf. Co.G
Rausseau, Calvin C. TN 4th (McLemore's) Cav.
    Co.K
Rausseau, Henry W. FL 5th Inf. Co.B
Raussecuy, George AL 18th Inf. Co.B
Rausshort, Edward VA 54th Mil. Co.E,F
Rauten, Edw. LA Mtd.Rifles Miller's Ind.Co.
Rauten, J.W. TN 4th (McLemore's) Cav. Co.C
Rauters, T.M. AL 30th Inf. Co.E
Rauth, Charles VA 1st Cav.
Rauton, T.A. NC 2nd Home Guards Co.G Capt.
Rautz, S.B. LA 5th Cav. Co.E
Ravan, Benjamin LA 14th Inf. Co.I
Ravan, Benjamin LA 31st Inf. Co.A
Ravan, Charles SC 13th Inf. Co.F
Ravan, Erwin GA 65th Inf. Co.F
Ravan, J. LA 13th Bn. (Part.Rangers) Co.B
Ravan, J. LA 3rd Inf. Co.H
Ravan, J. SC 6th Cav. Co.H
Ravan, James GA 65th Inf. Co.F
Ravan, John GA 65th Inf. Co.F
Ravan, John SC 7th Inf. 2nd Co.I
Ravan, Thomas SC 13th Inf. Co.F
Ravan, William GA Inf. 11th Bn. (St.Guards)
    Co.A
Ravanel, St.J. SC 24th Inf. Surg.
Ravanell, Anthony P. MS 18th Inf. Co.F
Ravel, G.W. MO 12th Cav.
Ravel, Julius LA 13th Inf. Co.H
Ravell, Martin TX 26th Cav. Co.F
Ravells, Allen SC 18th Inf.
Ravely, Joseph P. TN Cav. Newsom's Regt.
    Co.C 1st Lt.
Raven, Charles FL 4th Inf. Co.C
Raven, Edward NC 6th Sr.Res. Co.D
Raven, Herman L. TX 16th Inf. Co.G
Raven, H.H. TX 21st Cav. Co.B
Raven, Hugh H. TX 1st (McCulloch's) Cav.
    Co.D Bugler
Raven, J.A. AL 51st (Part.Rangers) Co.H Cpl.
Ravena, Francis E. TX 2nd Inf. Co.D Sgt.
Ravena, Jacob KY 4th Cav. Co.D
Ravenal, W.F. SC Rutledge Mtd.Riflemen &
    Horse Arty. Trenholm's Co.

Ravencraft, G. LA 3rd Cav. Co.E
Ravencraft, Solomon MO 3rd Inf. Co.F
Ravencraft, Uriah KY Cav. 1st Bn. Co.A
Ravencrans, William B. KY 1st (Butler's) Cav. Co.A
Ravencroft, J. LA 3rd (Wingfield's) Cav. Co.E
Ravenel, A.F. SC Mil.Arty. 1st Regt. Parker's Co.
Ravenel, Daniel, Jr. SC Mil.Arty. 1st Regt. Parker's Co.
Ravenel, Daniel, Jr. SC Lt.Arty. Parker's Co. (Marion Arty.)
Ravenel, Edmund, Jr. GA Inf. 26th Bn. Asst.Surg.
Ravenel, Edmund SC Lt.Arty. Parker's Co. (Marion Arty.)
Ravenel, Edmund, Jr. Gen. & Staff A.Surg.
Ravenel, Edward SC Cav. Walpole's Co.
Ravenel, Elias Prioleau SC 1st Arty. Co.G,I 1st Lt.
Ravenel, F.G. SC Mil.Arty. 1st Regt. Parker's Co. Bvt.2nd Lt.
Ravenel, Francis G. Gen. & Staff 1st Lt.,ADC
Ravenel, James SC 8th Bn.Res. Co.A
Ravenel, J.R.P. SC Lt.Arty. Parker's Co. (Marion Arty.)
Ravenel, Samuel SC 1st Mil.
Ravenel, S.P. Gen. & Staff Capt.,Comsy.
Ravenel, S. Prioleau SC 1st Arty. Regt.Comsy.
Ravenel, Stephen SC 24th Inf. Surg.
Ravenel, St.J. SC Mil. 16th Regt. Surg.
Ravenel, St.Julien Gen. & Staff Surg.
Ravenel, Thomas P. SC 2nd Cav. Co.B
Ravenel, Thomas P. SC 4th Cav. Co.K
Ravenel, Thomas P. SC Mil. Trenholm's Co.
Ravenel, T.P. SC 2nd Cav. Co.B
Ravenel, T.P. SC 4th Cav. Co.K
Ravenel, W.F. SC Mil. Trenholm's Co.
Ravenel, William SC Mil. 1st Regt. (Charleston Res.) 1st Lt.,QM
Ravenel, William, Jr. SC Bn.St.Cadets Co.B
Ravenel, William C. SC 25th Inf. Surg.
Ravenel, Wm. C. Gen. & Staff Surg.
Ravenell, H.L. SC 4th Bn.Res. Co.B
Ravenna, Francesco LA Mil. 6th Regt.Eur.Brig. (Italian Guards Bn.) Co.2
Ravenna, J.M. 4th Conf.Eng.Troops Co.E Artif.
Ravenna, J.M. Kellersberg's Corps Sap. & Min.,CSA Artif.
Ravennac, Fritz LA Mil. 2nd Regt. 2nd Brig. 1st Div. Co.I
Ravens, --- LA 5th Cav. Co.I
Ravens, A.W. MS Inf. 3rd Bn. (St.Troops) Co.F
Ravens, B. James GA 2nd Res. Co.B
Ravens, James B. GA 10th Cav. (St.Guards) Co.B 2nd Lt.
Ravens, R.S. LA 13th Bn. (Part.Rangers) Co.E
Ravenscraft, Charles B. MO Inf. 8th Bn. Co.B
Ravenscraft, Charles B. MO 9th Inf. Co.F
Ravenscraft, George W. LA 4th Inf. Co.A, Old Co.G
Ravenscraft, G.W. LA 3rd (Wingfield's) Cav. Co.E
Ravenscraft, Humphrey KY 2nd Cav. Co.B
Ravenscraft, John H. MO 1st N.E. Cav.
Ravenscraft, L. LA 3rd (Wingfield's) Cav. Co.E
Ravenscraft, Uriah KY 3rd Bn.Mtd.Rifles Co.A

Ravenscraft, William KY 2nd (Duke's) Cav. Co.E
Ravenscroft, A. GA Inf. (Loc.Def.) Whiteside's Nav.Bn. Co.B
Ravenscroft, Charles MO 1st Inf. Co.A
Ravenscroft, Joseph LA 13th Inf. Co.C
Ravenscroft, R.H. MO Inf. 4th Regt.St.Guard Co.F 1st Lt.
Raver, J. AR 5th Inf. Co.C
Ravere, Jacob GA 17th Inf. Co.C
Raverty, Arthur TX 1st Hvy.Arty. Co.G
Ravesies, Edmond AL 15th Bn.Part.Rangers Co.B Sgt.
Ravesies, Edmund AL 3rd Cav. Co.E
Ravesies, Edmund Conf.Cav. Wood's Regt. 1st Co.D
Ravesies, Paul AL 3rd Cav. Co.E Capt.
Ravesies, Paul Conf.Cav. Wood's Regt. 1st Co.D Capt.
Raveur, Joseph LA Mil. 1st Regt. French Brig. Co.7
Ravier, Joseph Shecoe's Chickasaw Bn.Mtd.Vol. Co.A
Raviere, R.T. AL 37th Inf. Co.C Sgt.
Ravinel, W.H. SC 5th Res. Co.D
Ravins, J.W. TN 20th (Russell's) Cav. Co.F
Ravis, Henry AL 51st (Part.Rangers) Co.E
Ravis, Henry AL 57th Cav. Co.G
Ravises, A.H. AL 8th Inf. Co.E Capt.
Ravisies, Ed AL 56th Part.Rangers Co.B Sgt.
Ravisies, E.P. AL 21st Inf. Co.K
Ravoult, A. AL St.Arty. Co.D
Ravssies, Ed AL 8th (Hatch's) Cav. Co.H 2nd Lt.
Ravur, H. LA Mil. 3rd Regt. French Brig. Co.4
Raw, Chs. LA Mil. 4th Regt. 1st Brig. 1st Div. Co.E
Raw, Charles H. VA 17th Inf. Co.C Bugler
Raw, Gustavus L. VA 17th Inf. Co.C
Raw, James W. VA 7th Cav. Co.C
Raw, James W. VA 146th Mil. Co.E Cpl.
Raw, John LA 22nd Inf. Co.D
Raw, John H. VA 7th Cav. Co.C
Raw, John H. VA 136th Mil. Co.D
Raw, Samuel VA 136th Mil. Co.E
Raw, Samuel C. VA 7th Cav. Co.K
Rawby, S.J. AL 1st Cav. 2nd Co.D,A
Rawden, C.G. GA 42nd Inf. Co.A
Rawden, Levi TN 6th (Wheeler's) Cav. Co.I
Rawdon, J.G. TN Cav. 9th Bn. (Gantt's) Co.F
Rawdon, John TN Cav. 9th Bn. (Gantt's) Co.F
Rawes, John MS 1st Lt.Arty. Co.H
Rawes, W.S. AL 38th Inf. Co.I Cpl.
Rawhuff, James MS 17th Inf. Co.E
Rawings, C.E. VA 13th Cav.
Rawl, B. SC 2nd Inf. Co.K
Rawl, Benjamin SC 20th Inf. Co.K
Rawl, C. SC 2nd St.Troops Co.A
Rawl, C. SC 15th Inf. Co.C
Rawl, David SC Cav. 14th Bn. Co.C
Rawl, E. SC 15th Inf. Co.C
Rawl, Elijah A. SC 20th Inf. Co.K Cpl.
Rawl, Franklin SC 15th Inf. Co.C
Rawl, Jacob E. SC 9th Inf. Co.K Jr.2nd Lt.
Rawl, James E. SC 13th Inf. Co.K Cpl.
Rawl, J.E. SC 5th Cav. Co.I Cpl.
Rawl, J.E. SC 1st Inf. Co.O

Rawl, J.E. SC Palmetto S.S. Co.F 1st Lt.
Rawl, J.S. SC 3rd Inf. Co.C
Rawl, J.W. SC 2nd Inf. Co.K
Rawl, O.D. SC 7th Inf. Co.H
Rawl, O.D. SC 15th Inf. Co.C
Rawl, Philip J. SC 20th Inf. Co.K
Rawl, S.E. SC 1st Inf. Co.O
Rawl, T. SC 2nd St.Troops Co.A
Rawlan, W. GA 10th Inf. Co.G
Rawland, C. GA 36th (Villepigue's) Inf. Co.F
Rawland, E. AL 55th Vol. Co.E
Rawland, E.S. NC 1st Jr.Res. Co.B
Rawle, Edward W. LA 1st Hvy.Arty. (Reg.) Co.A,D,H Capt.
Rawle, Elijah H. Gen. & Staff Surg.
Rawle, E.W. Wheeler's Staff Capt.,AIG
Rawle, Francis LA 1st (Nelligan's) Inf. Co.C Capt.
Rawle, Francis LA Inf. 1st Sp.Bn. (Rightor's) New Co.C Capt.
Rawle, Francis Gordon's Div. Maj.,QM
Rawle, Frank LA 10th Inf. AQM
Rawle, James M. FL Cav. 5th Bn. Co.B,D
Rawle, John LA Inf. 1st Sp.Bn. (Rightor's) Co.A
Rawle, John Gen. & Staff, Arty. Maj.
Rawleigh, William S. VA 9th Cav. Co.D
Rawlenn, J. FL Cav. 5th Bn. Co.H
Rawlenn, W.H. FL Cav. 5th Bn. Co.H
Rawlens, James TN 21st (Wilson's) Cav. Co.G Cpl.
Rawlerson, Elias FL 5th Inf. Co.B Cpl.
Rawlerson, Jackson FL 5th Inf. Co.B Cpl.
Rawlerson, John G. FL 5th Inf. Co.B 2nd Lt.
Rawlerson, William FL 9th Inf. Co.B
Rawlens, Benjamin F. MS Inf. 7th Bn. Co.B 2nd Lt.
Rawles, Charles C. NC 5th Inf. Co.G 2nd Lt.
Rawles, Charles C. VA 13th Cav. Co.I Sgt.
Rawles, Donald LA 9th Inf. Co.F
Rawles, E. Gen. & Staff Hosp.Stew.
Rawles, Elbert VA 6th Inf. 2nd Co.E
Rawles, Elisha 8th (Dearing's) Conf.Cav. Co.E
Rawles, Ethelbert VA 61st Inf. Co.F
Rawles, F. MS 24th Inf. Co.E
Rawles, Felix S. MS 24th Inf. Co.F
Rawles, Felix S. MS 27th Inf. Co.B Sgt.
Rawles, F.M. TN 33rd Inf. Co.H Sgt.
Rawles, George FL 8th Inf. Co.K
Rawles, Greg P. GA 2nd Bn.S.S. Co.B
Rawles, G.W. MS Inf. 7th Bn. Co.B
Rawles, H. Jackson TX 13th Cav. Co.K
Rawles, I. TX 14th Inf. Co.C
Rawles, Irwin H. TX 25th Cav. Co.C
Rawles, J. SC 21st Inf. Co.K
Rawles, J. VA 2nd Inf.Loc.Def. Co.G
Rawles, J. VA Inf. 2nd Bn.Loc.Def. Co.A
Rawles, James GA 1st Res. Co.E Cpl.
Rawles, James GA 48th Inf. Co.E
Rawles, James J. TX 8th Cav. Co.A
Rawles, James M. LA Arty. Green's Co. (LA Guard Btty.)
Rawles, James R. NC 11th (Bethel Regt.) Inf. Co.C
Rawles, J.B. SC 5th Inf. 2nd Co.E
Rawles, J.C. AL 17th Inf. Co.D
Rawles, Jesse MS Cp.Guard (Cp. of Instr. for Conscr.)

Rawles, J. Henry NC 17th Inf. (1st Org.) Co.G
Rawles, J.M. TN 1st (Feild's) Inf. Co.L
Rawles, John B. NC 5th Inf. Co.H
Rawles, John H. AR Inf. Hardy's Regt. Co.K
  Sgt.
Rawles, John McG. NC 17th Inf. (2nd Org.)
  Co.A
Rawles, Joseph L. NC 17th Inf. (2nd Org.) Co.H
Rawles, Jo. W. TN 8th Inf. Co.E Sgt.
Rawles, J.T. MS 27th Inf. Co.B Sgt.
Rawles, Martin SC 5th Inf. 2nd Co.F,E
Rawles, P. FL 1st (Res.) Inf. Co.C
Rawles, Reuben TN 12th (Cons.) Inf. Sgt.
Rawles, Reuben TN 47th Inf. Co.E Sgt.
Rawles, R.I. AL 6th Cav. Co.A
Rawles, Samuel A. LA Inf.Cons.Crescent Regt.
  Co.C
Rawles, S.E. FL 2nd Cav. Co.D
Rawles, Thomas VA Lt.Arty. 38th Bn. Co.A
Rawles, Thomas VA 49th Inf. 1st Co.G
Rawles, Thomas J. VA 41st Inf. Co.K
Rawles, W.A. TN 6th Inf. Co.A
Rawles, W.E. MS 38th Cav. Co.I
Rawles, W.G. TN 1st (Feild's) Inf. Co.L Sgt.
Rawles, W.G. TN Inf. Nashville Bn. Fulcher's
  Co.
Rawles, William NC 17th Inf. (1st Org.) Co.G
Rawles, William H. VA 12th Inf. Co.C
Rawles, William T. GA 2nd Bn.S.S. Co.B
Rawles, W.J. Gen. & Staff Capt.
Rawles, W.R. AR Inf. Hardy's Regt.
Rawlet, James VA 25th Mil. Co.B
Rawlet, John VA 25th Mil. Co.C
Rawlet, Phillip VA 25th Mil. Co.B
Rawlett, James S. VA 9th Cav. Co.I
Rawlett, Thomas AR 8th Cav. Co.D
Rawley, Darius N. TN 11th Inf. Co.G,B,D Sgt.
Rawley, George W. NC 21st Inf. Co.H
Rawley, Hugh S. NC 14th Inf. Co.G Cpl.
Rawley, J.A. GA Cav. 12th Bn. (St.Guards)
  Co.A
Rawley, James Conf.Reg.Inf. Brooks' Bn. Co.C
Rawley, John H. VA 18th Cav. 2nd Co.G
Rawley, J.W. NC 14th Inf. Co.G 1st Sgt.
Rawley, J.W. TN 20th Inf. Co.C 1st Lt.
Rawley, Lafayette TN 8th Inf. Co.E,G
Rawley, P.J. TN 8th Inf. Co.G
Rawley, P.R. VA 26th Cav. Co.I Lt.
Rawley, R.G. TX 2nd Inf. Co.G
Rawley, Rheuben VA 3rd Bn. Valley Res. Co.A
Rawley, Robert P. NC 21st Inf. Co.I 2nd Lt.
Rawley, Robert P. TX 22nd Cav. Co.D Cpl.
Rawley, Robert P. VA Cav. 47th Bn. Co.C
  Jr.2nd Lt.
Rawley, Taylor L. NC 13th Inf. Co.K 1st Lt.
Rawley, Taylor L. NC 14th Inf. Co.G Sgt.
Rawling, August TX Inf. 1st St.Troops Sheldon's
  Co.B
Rawling, Edward G. AR Mil. Desha Cty.Bn.
  Capt.
Rawlings, --- MS Arty. Byrne's Btty.
Rawlings, A.K. TN Cav. 16th Bn. (Neal's) Co.C
Rawlings, Anderson L. TX 19th Cav. Co.I
Rawlings, Andrew J. KY 4th Cav. Co.D Sgt.
Rawlings, B.C. VA Lt.Arty. Ellett's Co.
Rawlings, B.C. VA 30th Inf. Co.D
Rawlings, Benjamin C. VA 30th Inf. Co.D Capt.

Rawlings, Benjamin L. NC 6th Inf. Co.E Cpl.
Rawlings, B.F. GA 5th Res. Co.K
Rawlings, B.F. TX Cav. Crump's Regt.
Rawlings, B.W.S. LA 14th Inf. Co.F
Rawlings, C.A. SC 1st Inf. Co.A
Rawlings, Carrol H. AR 8th Cav. 1st Lt.
Rawlings, C.H. TN Lt.Arty. Tobin's Co.
Rawlings, Charles GA 1st (Ramsey's) Inf. Co.E
Rawlings, Charles GA 32nd Inf. Co.E
Rawlings, Charles VA 3rd Lt.Arty. Co.D
Rawlings, Charles VA Hvy.Arty. Coleman's Co.
  Sgt.
Rawlings, Charles A. SC 1st (McCreary's) Inf.
  Co.C
Rawlings, Charles H. VA 6th Cav. Co.K
Rawlings, Daniel MS 9th Inf. Co.G
Rawlings, Daniel MS 10th Inf. New Co.B
Rawlings, Daniel TN Inf. 22nd Bn. Co.E,B
Rawlings, E. KY 3rd Bn.Mtd.Rifles Co.A
Rawlings, E.B. GA 28th Inf. Co.B 3rd Lt.
Rawlings, Edward G. VA 21st Inf. Co.F 2nd Lt.
Rawlings, E.J. KY 4th Cav. Co.D
Rawlings, E.J. VA 3rd (Archer's) Bn.Res. Co.B
Rawlings, E.W. GA 12th (Robinson's) Cav.
  (St.Guards) Co.G
Rawlings, Ezekiel KY 1st Bn.Mtd.Rifles Co.A
Rawlings, F.M. LA 15th Inf. Co.I
Rawlings, F.M. NC 2nd Jr.Res. Co.K
Rawlings, Franklin P. TX 8th Inf.
Rawlings, George W. MS 3rd Inf. Co.C
Rawlings, Henry FL 4th Inf. Co.B
Rawlings, Henry H. TX 19th Cav. Co.C Lt.
Rawlings, H.H. KY 1st (Butler's) Cav. Co.E
Rawlings, H.H. KY 2nd Cav. Co.I
Rawlings, Hinchly A. TX 8th Inf. Co.D Sgt.
Rawlings, I.M. TN 19th Inf. Co.A
Rawlings, Isham GA 3rd Inf. 1st Co.I
Rawlings, J.A. VA Inf. 28th Bn. Co.D
Rawlings, J.A. VA 59th Inf. 3rd Co.I
Rawlings, James MS 5th Inf. (St.Troops) Co.C
Rawlings, James VA Hvy.Arty. Coleman's Co.
Rawlings, James VA 4th Bn.Res. Co.D 2nd Lt.
Rawlings, James VA 59th Inf. Co.I
Rawlings, James A. VA 3rd Arty. Co.E
Rawlings, James L. VA 9th Cav. Co.E
Rawlings, James M. VA 13th Cav. Co.D
Rawlings, James M. VA Lt.Arty. Arch.
  Graham's Co.
Rawlings, James S. TN 3rd (Forrest's) Cav.
  Co.A
Rawlings, James S. TN Inf. 154th Sr.Regt. 1st
  Co.B
Rawlings, James W. VA 8th Inf. Co.B
Rawlings, James W. VA 12th Inf. Co.H
Rawlings, James W. VA 21st Inf. Co.G Sgt.
Rawlings, Jesse NC 17th Inf. (2nd Org.) Co.I
Rawlings, J.G. GA Inf. 1st Loc.Troops Barnes'
  Lt.Arty.Co.
Rawlings, J.H. LA 27th Inf. Co.H Cpl.
Rawlings, J.H. MO Inf. Clark's Regt. Co.C
Rawlings, J.H. TN Hvy.Arty. Johnston's Co.
Rawlings, J.L. TN 4th Inf. Co.A
Rawlings, J.M. VA 2nd Arty. Co.E
Rawlings, John AR 2nd Mtd.Rifles Co.I Capt.
Rawlings, John AR Gipson's Bn.Mtd.Riflemen
  Capt.

Rawlings, John AR Cav. Gordon's Regt. Co.I
  Capt.
Rawlings, John MO Lt.Arty. 1st Btty.
Rawlings, John VA 61st Inf. Co.G Cpl.
Rawlings, John G. TN 36th Inf. Co.I 2nd Lt.
Rawlings, Jno. G. Gen. & Staff Hosp.Stew.
Rawlings, John H. VA 9th Cav. Co.I
Rawlings, John H. VA Hvy.Arty. 18th Bn. Co.A
  Sgt.
Rawlings, John H. VA 25th Mil. Co.C
Rawlings, John J. VA Inf. 5th Bn. Co.A
Rawlings, John J. VA 59th Inf. 3rd Co.I
Rawlings, John L. VA 30th Inf. Co.D Jr.2nd Lt.
Rawlings, John W. TN 4th (McLemore's) Cav.
  Co.E
Rawlings, Joseph B. VA Hvy.Arty. Coleman's
  Co. Sgt.
Rawlings, J.W. AR Mil. Desha Cty.Bn.
Rawlings, J.W. TN 13th Inf. Co.G
Rawlings, J.W. TN 21st Inf. Co.C
Rawlings, Logan MO 5th Inf. Co.A Sgt.
Rawlings, M.R. MS 9th Inf. Old Co.H, New
  Co.A
Rawlings, Nathan S. LA 14th Inf. Co.F
Rawlings, N.L.W. AR 7th Inf. Co.B
Rawlings, O.F. MO Inf. Clark's Regt. Co.C
Rawlings, Perry KY 4th Cav. Co.D
Rawlings, Perry KY 9th Mtd.Inf. Co.I
Rawlings, Peter B. VA 61st Inf. Co.G
Rawlings, Peyton J. VA 23rd Inf. Co.A 2nd Lt.
Rawlings, P.H. VA 2nd Arty. Co.E
Rawlings, P.H.H. VA 21st Inf. Co.G
Rawlings, R.G. LA 31st Inf. Co.F 1st Sgt.
Rawlings, Richard TN 3rd (Forrest's) Cav. Co.A
Rawlings, Richard H. VA 6th Cav. Co.I
Rawlings, R.J.H. TN 2nd (Walker's) Inf. Co.E
Rawlings, R.M. TN 7th (Duckworth's) Cav.
  Co.A
Rawlings, Robert VA Hvy.Arty. Coleman's Co.
Rawlings, Robert L. VA Hvy.Arty. Coleman's
  Co.
Rawlings, Robt. R. AL 36th Inf. Co.H
Rawlings, Roderick TX 6th Cav. Co.F 1st Sgt.
Rawlings, R.R. AL Mil. 4th Vol. Co.I
Rawlings, S.A. MO 3rd Regt.St.Guards Lt.Col.
Rawlings, Sam T. KY 2nd Cav.
Rawlings, Samuel D. TN 43rd Inf. Co.C
Rawlings, Samuel T. VA 61st Inf. Co.G
Rawlings, S.H. TN 3rd (Forrest's) Cav. Co.A
Rawlings, S.H. TN Inf. 154th Sr.Regt. 1st Co.B
Rawlings, Thomas TN 16th Inf. Co.I
Rawlings, Thomas K. TN 35th Inf. Co.L 1st Lt.
Rawlings, Thomas K. TN 36th Inf. Co.L 1st Lt.
Rawlings, Thomas N. MS 3rd Inf. Co.C
Rawlings, Thomas W. LA Inf. 1st Sp.Bn.
  (Wheat's) Old Co.D
Rawlings, T.W. LA Inf. 7th Bn. Co.B
Rawlings, T.W. LA 15th Inf. Co.I
Rawlings, V.A. TN 3rd (Forrest's) Cav. Co.H
Rawlings, V.A. TN Inf. 8th Bn. Co.A
Rawlings, W. GA 63rd Inf. Co.C
Rawlings, W.A. VA 21st Inf. Co.G
Rawlings, W.A. VA 59th Inf. 3rd Co.I
Rawlings, W.E. TN Cav. 16th Bn. (Neal's) Co.C
  Far.
Rawlings, William GA 1st (Ramsey's) Inf. Co.E
Rawlings, William NC 1st Inf. (6 mo. '61) Co.I

Rawlings, William A. LA Inf. 9th Bn. Co.A
Rawlings, William A. NC 17th Inf. (2nd Org.) Co.I
Rawlings, William M. MO 2nd Inf. Co.H
Rawlings, William M. VA 21st Inf. Co.G
Rawlings, William T. VA 1st Arty. Co.E
Rawlings, William T. VA Hvy.Arty. 18th Bn. Co.C
Rawlings, William W. VA Arty. Kevill's Co.
Rawlings, W.W. TN 16th Inf. Co.I Cpl.
Rawlins, Alexander H. TX 6th Cav. Co.F
Rawlins, C.F. AR 3rd Cav. Co.A
Rawlins, Daniel FL 8th Inf. Co.H
Rawlins, Daniel H. TN 14th Inf. Co.L
Rawlins, David S. GA 35th Inf. Co.F
Rawlins, Dolphin T. VA 2nd Inf. Co.A 1st Sgt.
Rawlins, E.A. VA Mil. 98th Regt.
Rawlins, Edward A. VA 2nd Arty. Co.D Cpl.
Rawlins, Edward A. VA Inf. 22nd Bn. Co.D
Rawlins, Fayette W. VA 2nd Inf. Co.G
Rawlins, Francis TX 6th Cav. Co.F
Rawlins, F.W. VA Cav. 35th Bn.
Rawlins, George TX 6th Cav. Co.F
Rawlins, George W. GA 49th Inf. Co.K
Rawlins, I.F. GA 35th Inf. Co.F
Rawlins, Isaac GA Cav. 22nd Bn. (St.Guards) Co.I Sgt.
Rawlins, Isham G. GA 35th Inf. Co.F Cpl.
Rawlins, J. GA Inf. 25th Bn. (Prov.Guard) Co.D
Rawlins, James A. GA 35th Inf. Co.F
Rawlins, James A. VA 27th Inf. Co.C Hosp.Stew.
Rawlins, James T. FL 5th Inf. Co.I Cpl.
Rawlins, J.L. GA 21st Inf. Co.F
Rawlins, J.M. MS Conscr. Detailed on SC of D.
Rawlins, John AL 9th Inf. Co.F Cpl.
Rawlins, John FL 1st Cav. Co.B
Rawlins, John GA 42nd Inf. Co.B
Rawlins, John LA 31st Inf. Co.C
Rawlins, John A. MO Cav. Wood's Regt. Co.C
Rawlins, John R. AL Inf. 1st Regt. Co.F Sgt.
Rawlins, John S. TX 6th Cav. Co.F
Rawlins, Joseph E. VA 2nd Inf. Co.A
Rawlins, J.S. TN 9th Inf. Co.L
Rawlins, Marcellus F. VA 23rd Inf. Co.K
Rawlins, Matthew H. GA 35th Inf. Co.F
Rawlins, Nicholas GA Cav. 22nd Bn. (St.Guards) Co.F
Rawlins, O.H.P. GA 42nd Inf. Co.B
Rawlins, R. TX 19th Inf. Co.A
Rawlins, R.A. TX 6th Cav. Co.F Capt.
Rawlins, R.F. AL 40th Inf. Co.I
Rawlins, Robert FL 10th Inf. Co.B
Rawlins, Robert M. GA 35th Inf. Co.F Capt.
Rawlins, R.S. TN 11th Cav. Co.F
Rawlins, R.S. TX 11th Cav. Co.F
Rawlins, R.S. TX 9th (Young's) Inf. Co.H
Rawlins, Samuel VA 115th Mil. Co.C
Rawlins, Samuel T. KY 2nd Mtd.Inf. Co.H
Rawlins, T.F. Exch.Bn. 1st Co.C,CSA
Rawlins, Thomas TX 16th Inf. Co.D
Rawlins, Thomas F. TX 6th Cav. Co.F,C
Rawlins, T.W. GA Cav. 20th Bn. Co.D
Rawlins, V.A. TN 12th (Green's) Cav. Co.K
Rawlins, Virgil TN 16th (Logwood's) Cav. Co.C
Rawlins, Walter H. VA Cav. 39th Bn. Co.B Cpl.

Rawlins, William SC 1st (Butler's) Inf. Co.E
Rawlins, William B. TX 6th Cav. Co.F
Rawlins, William J. GA 35th Inf. Co.F
Rawlins, William M. GA 35th Inf. Co.F 1st Lt.
Rawlins, William W. VA 41st Inf. Co.E Sgt.
Rawlinson, A.A. AL 53rd (Part.Rangers) Co.D
Rawlinson, Abram S. SC 1st (Hagood's) Inf. 1st Co.A
Rawlinson, Abram S. SC 25th Inf. Co.G
Rawlinson, Daniel MO 7th Cav. Co.H
Rawlinson, Elbert A. AL 44th Inf. Co.E
Rawlinson, F.C. MS Lt.Arty. (Jefferson Arty.) Darden's Co.
Rawlinson, H. SC 5th Bn.Res. Co.A
Rawlinson, James FL 9th Inf. Co.E,K
Rawlinson, James B. AL 3rd Cav. Co.H
Rawlinson, J.M. SC 17th Inf. Co.E Cpl.
Rawlinson, John D. MS 44th Inf. Co.K
Rawlinson, John L. AL 3rd Cav. Co.H
Rawlinson, J.W. SC Lt.Arty. J.T. Kanapaux's Co. (Lafayette Arty.)
Rawlinson, Lewis F. GA 2nd Bn.S.S. Co.E Cpl.
Rawlinson, Louis F. AL 58th Inf. Co.K Cpl.
Rawlinson, Moses A. SC 1st (Hagood's) Inf. 1st Co.A
Rawlinson, Moses A. SC 25th Inf. Co.G
Rawlinson, Robert T.C. AL 45th Inf. Co.D
Rawlinson, S.E. MS 7th Inf. Co.K
Rawlinson, William SC 25th Inf. Co.G
Rawlinson, W.W. AL 45th Inf. Co.E
Rawlison, Benjamin AL 6th Inf. Co.G
Rawlison, George SC 1st (McCreary's) Inf. Co.B
Rawlison, John Horse Arty. White's Btty.
Rawlison, Robert AR 2nd Inf. Co.B
Rawlman, J.D. NC 57th Inf. Co.G
Rawls, --- TX 35th (Brown's) Cav. Co.K
Rawls, A.B. FL 1st (Res.) Inf. Co.L
Rawls, A.B.F. MS 2nd (Quinn's St.Troops) Inf. Co.G 1st Sgt.
Rawls, Abner P. NC Lt.Arty. 3rd Bn. Co.B,C
Rawls, Albert J. VA 16th Inf. Co.A
Rawls, Alexander NC 44th Inf. Co.B 1st Sgt.
Rawls, Alfred D. NC 2nd Inf. Co.I
Rawls, Allen AR 5th Inf. Co.H
Rawls, Allen MO Lt.Arty. 13th Btty.
Rawls, Allen TN 15th (Stewart's) Cav. Co.C
Rawls, Andrew J. FL 6th Inf. Co.C Sgt.
Rawls, Andrew J. VA 5th Cav. (12 mo. '61-2) Co.G
Rawls, Ansel SC Palmetto S.S. Co.F
Rawls, B.E. AL 33rd Inf. Co.F Cpl.
Rawls, Benjamin NC 17th Inf. (2nd Org.) Co.E
Rawls, Benjamin F. LA 8th Inf. Co.G,D
Rawls, B.F. LA 13th Bn. (Part.Rangers) Co.F
Rawls, Bob SC 1st Inf. Band
Rawls, C. SC 6th Inf. Co.A
Rawls, C.E. SC Palmetto S.S. Co.F
Rawls, Charles AL City Troop (Mobile) Arrington's Co.A
Rawls, Charles AL St.Arty. Co.C Cpl.
Rawls, Charles C. VA 5th Cav. (12 mo. '61-2) Co.G Sgt.
Rawls, Charles D. FL 2nd Inf. Co.B,E Cpl.
Rawls, Charles R. VA 5th Cav. (12 mo. '61-2) Winfield's Co.
Rawls, Charles R. VA 13th Cav. Co.D Sgt.
Rawls, Charles R. VA 46th Inf. 2nd Co.F

Rawls, Cloyd AR 26th Inf. Co.D
Rawls, D. MS Inf. 2nd Bn. Co.F
Rawls, D. MS 48th Inf. Co.F
Rawls, Daniel GA Cav. 22nd Bn. (St.Guards) Co.F
Rawls, David P. GA 50th Inf. Co.F
Rawls, DeKalb TN 8th Inf. Co.E
Rawls, DeKalb 1st Conf.Cav. 2nd Co.G
Rawls, D.L. MS 6th Inf. Co.F
Rawls, D.L. Gen. & Staff Surg.
Rawls, E. GA 62nd Cav. Co.L
Rawls, E. SC Palmetto S.S. Co.F
Rawls, Edwin S. VA 41st Inf. Co.I
Rawls, Eli J. SC 20th Inf. Co.I
Rawls, Elijah GA 12th (Robinson's) Cav. (St.Guards) Co.B
Rawls, Elijah H. GA Inf. 10th Bn. Co.A Surg.
Rawls, Elijah W. VA 16th Inf. Co.A
Rawls, Elisha GA 59th Inf. Co.D
Rawls, Elisha VA 5th Cav. (12 mo. '61-2) Co.G
Rawls, Elisha VA 13th Cav. Co.I
Rawls, Elisha VA 24th Cav. Co.K
Rawls, Elisha VA 41st Inf. Co.K
Rawls, Elisha (of W.) VA 59th Mil. Riddick's Co.
Rawls, Ephraim MS 7th Inf. Co.F Cpl.
Rawls, Ezra SC 9th Inf. Co.K
Rawls, Felix M. TX 36th Cav. Co.K
Rawls, F.M. GA 29th Inf. Co.I,C
Rawls, Francis H. VA 59th Mil. Arnold's Co. 2nd Lt.
Rawls, Francis W. GA 21st Inf. Co.B
Rawls, Frank H. VA 14th Inf. Co.A
Rawls, G.B. GA 7th Inf. (St.Guards) Co.H Sgt.
Rawls, G.C. AL 6th Inf. Co.I
Rawls, George AL 6th Inf. Co.I
Rawls, George C. TX 24th Cav. Co.A
Rawls, George E. AL 36th Inf. Co.F Cpl.
Rawls, George T. VA 3rd Inf. Co.G
Rawls, G.W. LA 13th Bn. (Part.Rangers) Co.F
Rawls, H. GA 2nd Inf. Co.D
Rawls, H. MS Rogers' Co.
Rawls, H.A. SC 9th Inf. Co.K
Rawls, H.A. SC Palmetto S.S. Co.F
Rawls, Hamilton H. AL 6th Inf. Co.I
Rawls, Henry AL 17th Bn.S.S. Co.A
Rawls, Henry AL 19th Inf. Co.K,I
Rawls, Henry A. VA 59th Mil. Arnold's Co.
Rawls, Henry C. GA 53rd Inf. Co.F
Rawls, Hosey NC Lt.Arty. 3rd Bn. Co.C
Rawls, H.S. TN 8th Inf. Co.E
Rawls, H.S. TN 38th Inf. 2nd Co.A
Rawls, Isaiah NC 1st Cav. (9th St.Troops) Co.H
Rawls, J. GA 4th (Clinch's) Cav. Co.D
Rawls, J. GA Lt.Arty. Clinch's Btty. Cpl.
Rawls, J. GA 5th Res. Co.A
Rawls, J. MS 2nd St.Cav. Co.G
Rawls, James MS 2nd (Quinn's St.Troops) Inf. Co.G
Rawls, James NC 55th Inf. Co.H
Rawls, James E. VA 5th Cav. (12 mo. '61-2) Co.G Cpl.
Rawls, James E. VA 13th Cav. Co.I Sgt.
Rawls, James E. VA 41st Inf. Co.I Cpl.
Rawls, James H. AL 47th Inf. Co.D 1st Sgt.
Rawls, James H. NC 31st Inf. Co.F

Rawls, James J. TX 11th (Spaight's) Bn.Vol. Co.D
Rawls, James M. GA 51st Inf. Co.D
Rawls, James M. MS 20th Inf. Co.A
Rawls, James P. SC 2nd Cav. Co.C
Rawls, James R. NC 1st Inf. (6 mo. '61) Co.L
Rawls, James W. FL 1st Cav. Co.H Sgt.
Rawls, James W. MS 14th Inf. Co.H
Rawls, J.B. AL Mil. 4th Vol. Gantt's Co. Cpl.
Rawls, J.B. LA 2nd Res.Corps Co.H Sgt.
Rawls, J.C. AL 1st Regt.Conscr. Co.K
Rawls, J.C. TX 25th Cav. Co.K Cpl.
Rawls, J.C. TX 11th (Spaight's) Bn.Vol. Co.D
Rawls, Jesse GA 41st Inf. Co.A Sgt.
Rawls, Jesse MS 7th Inf. Co.B
Rawls, Jesse NC 17th Inf. (2nd Org.) Co.A
Rawls, J.F. GA 54th Inf. Co.I 1st Lt.
Rawls, J.G. SC Cav. 4th Bn. Co.B
Rawls, J.G. SC 1st Inf. Co.A
Rawls, J.H. TX 9th (Nichols') Inf. Co.H
Rawls, J.M. GA 55th Inf. Co.E
Rawls, J.M. TN Inf. Nashville Bn. Felts' Co.
Rawls, John AR Inf. Hardy's Regt.
Rawls, John GA 44th Inf. Co.A
Rawls, John LA 8th Inf. Co.G Cpl.
Rawls, John SC Cav. 10th Bn. Co.A
Rawls, John A. VA 5th Cav. (12 mo. '61-2) Winfield's Co.
Rawls, John A. VA 13th Cav. Co.D
Rawls, John B. NC 52nd Inf. Co.C
Rawls, John C. GA 50th Inf. Co.F
Rawls, John D. AL 7th Inf. Co.A
Rawls, John F. NC 2nd Inf. Co.I
Rawls, John G. FL 1st Cav. Co.I 2nd Lt.
Rawls, John G. SC 2nd Cav. Co.C
Rawls, John H. NC 44th Inf. Co.B
Rawls, John H. TX 3rd Cav. Co.E
Rawls, John L. MS 11th Inf. Co.D
Rawls, John R. VA 5th Cav. (12 mo. '61-2) Winfield's Co.
Rawls, John R. VA 46th Inf. 2nd Co.F
Rawls, John Robert VA 13th Cav. Co.D
Rawls, John T. VA 41st Inf. Co.I Cpl.
Rawls, John W. TX 11th (Spaight's) Bn.Vol. Co.D
Rawls, John W. TX Inf. Griffin's Bn. Co.C
Rawls, Joseph GA Lt.Arty. 12th Bn. 2nd Co.D
Rawls, Joseph GA 50th Inf. Co.F
Rawls, Joseph A. NC Lt.Arty. 3rd Bn. Co.C
Rawls, Joseph J. NC 1st Arty. (10th St.Troops) Co.K
Rawls, Joshua M. NC 31st Inf. Co.K
Rawls, J.P. SC Cav. 4th Bn. Co.B
Rawls, J.S. GA 29th Inf. Co.I,C
Rawls, J.T. SC 4th Cav. Co.B
Rawls, J.T. SC 25th Mil.
Rawls, J.T. TN Inf. Nashville Bn. Felts' Co.
Rawls, Julius J. VA 16th Inf. Co.A
Rawls, Julius J. VA Inf. Cohoon's Bn. Co.A
Rawls, Junius FL 4th Inf. Co.I Music.
Rawls, J.W. TN 14th (Neely's) Cav. Co.D 1st Sgt.
Rawls, Kenneth J. NC 17th Inf. (2nd Org.) Co.F Cpl.
Rawls, Kenneth J. NC 31st Inf. Co.F
Rawls, L. SC 7th Inf. Co.H
Rawls, Luther VA 41st Inf. Co.K

Rawls, M. SC 12th Inf. Co.B
Rawls, M. SC Palmetto S.S. Co.I
Rawls, Martin J. LA 13th Bn. (Part.Rangers) Co.F 1st Sgt.
Rawls, M.D. AL 8th Inf. Co.B
Rawls, Michael FL 1st Cav. Co.D
Rawls, Michael NC 55th Inf. Co.H
Rawls, M.M. SC 9th Inf. Co.K
Rawls, Morgan GA 54th Inf. Lt.Col.
Rawls, M.R. TX 11th (Spaight's) Bn.Vol. Co.D Sgt.
Rawls, Nathaniel VA Hvy.Arty. A.J. Jones' Co.
Rawls, N.B. TX 11th (Spaight's) Bn.Vol. Co.D
Rawls, Noah S. AL 3rd Inf. Co.I
Rawls, O.H.P. GA Cav. 22nd Bn. (St.Guards) Co.A Cpl.
Rawls, Oliver L. AL 17th Inf. Co.I
Rawls, Prior L. GA 29th Inf. Co.C
Rawls, R.A. MS 9th Bn.S.S. Co.B Cpl.
Rawls, R.E. FL Lt.Arty. Dyke's Co.
Rawls, R.E. FL Kilcrease Lt.Arty.
Rawls, R.E. FL 2nd Inf. Co.D
Rawls, R.G. TN 11th (Spaight's) Bn.Vol. Co.D
Rawls, Robert VA 41st Inf. Co.I
Rawls, Robert A. MS 7th Inf. Co.A
Rawls, Samuel B. FL 1st Inf. Old Co.C,H
Rawls, Samuel H. TN 5th Inf. 2nd Co.G
Rawls, S.B. FL 2nd Cav. Co.F
Rawls, S.B. FL 4th Inf. Co.G
Rawls, Seaborn E. FL 1st Inf. Old Co.A,B
Rawls, Seaborn W. AL Inf. 1st Regt. Co.F
Rawls, Simeon AL 11th Inf. Co.D
Rawls, T.F. GA 53rd Inf. Co.G 1st Lt.
Rawls, T.F. MS 7th Inf. Co.A
Rawls, T.G. AL 21st Inf. Co.C
Rawls, Theodore SC 20th Inf. Co.I
Rawls, Thomas MS 11th Inf. Co.D
Rawls, Thomas F. GA 1st (Ramsey's) Inf. Co.A
Rawls, Thomas J. FL 4th Inf. Co.G Capt.
Rawls, Thomas O. TX 27th Cav. Co.C
Rawls, T.J. AL 21st Inf. Co.C
Rawls, T.J. GA Siege Arty. Campbell's Ind.Co.
Rawls, T.J. GA 50th Inf. Co.E
Rawls, T.J. TX 20th Bn.St.Troops Co.A
Rawls, T.W. SC 4th Cav. Co.B
Rawls, W. GA 62nd Cav. Co.L
Rawls, W. SC 5th Inf. Co.E
Rawls, W.B. AL Inf. 2nd Regt. Co.G
Rawls, W.B. AL 43rd Inf. Co.F
Rawls, William GA 44th Inf. Co.A
Rawls, William NC 31st Inf. Co.F
Rawls, William SC 17th Inf. Co.K
Rawls, William (of W.) VA 59th Mil. Arnold's Co.
Rawls, William (of W.) VA 59th Mil. Hunter's Co.
Rawls, William 2nd Conf.Eng.Troops Co.A
Rawls, William A. TN 14th (Neely's) Cav. Co.D 2nd Lt.
Rawls, William A.L. FL 7th Inf. Co.B
Rawls, William B. AL 17th Inf. Co.D
Rawls, William C. FL 8th Inf. Co.K
Rawls, William C. NC 17th Inf. (1st Org.) Co.F
Rawls, William C. NC 17th Inf. (2nd Org.) Co.A
Rawls, William H. NC 3rd Arty. (40th St.Troops) Co.H

Rawls, William H. VA 41st Inf. Co.C
Rawls, William J. AL 5th Inf. New Co.G
Rawls, William J. TX 13th Cav. Co.G
Rawls, William R. NC Lt.Arty. 3rd Bn. Co.C
Rawls, William S. AL Inf. 2nd Regt. Co.D
Rawls, William S. AL 38th Inf. Co.I
Rawls, William S. FL 9th Inf. Co.G
Rawls, William S. MS 11th Inf. Co.D
Rawls, William T. FL 3rd Inf. Co.I
Rawls, William T.E. LA 8th Inf. Co.G
Rawls, William W. AL 3rd Cav. Co.C
Rawls, William W. TX Inf. Griffin's Bn. Co.C Music.
Rawls, William W. VA 16th Inf. Co.A Sgt.
Rawls, Willis J. NC 8th Inf. Co.G
Rawls, W.P. TX 1st Inf. Co.E
Rawls, W.W. TX 21st Inf. Co.C
Rawls, Z. AL 32nd Inf. Co.D
Rawls, Z.A. GA 54th Inf. Co.I
Rawlston, James TN 2nd (Ashby's) Cav. Co.B
Rawlston, James TN 20th Inf. Co.K
Rawlston, James TN 39th Mtd.Inf. Co.B
Rawlston, Michael TN 62nd Mtd.Inf. Co.C
Rawlston, Robert GA Cav. 16th Bn. (St.Guards) Co.E Cpl.
Rawlston, W. TN 20th Inf. Co.K
Raworth, G.F. SC 2nd Arty. Co.E 2nd Lt.
Raws, Ames TN 19th (Biffle's) Cav. Co.B
Raws, George MS Lt.Arty. English's Co.
Raws, R. AL 37th Inf. Co.H
Rawson, C. GA 43rd Inf. Co.H
Rawson, C.H. MS 41st Inf. Co.C
Rawson, Charles AR 5th Inf. Co.G 1st Sgt.
Rawson, Charles A. VA 61st Inf. Co.D
Rawson, C.L. MS 41st Inf. Co.C
Rawson, C.W. GA 4th Inf. QMSgt.
Rawson, E. AL 8th Inf. Co.C
Rawson, E.E. GA Inf. Ezzard's Co.
Rawson, E.P. GA 51st Inf. Co.K
Rawson, F.M. VA 8th Cav. Co.E
Rawson, F.S. GA Inf. 1st City Bn. (Columbus) Co.D
Rawson, F.S. GA Inf. 19th Bn. (St.Guards) Co.A
Rawson, H.H. MS 6th Cav. Co.G Cpl.
Rawson, H.H. MS 5th Inf. (St.Troops) Co.C
Rawson, J. MS 4th Inf. Co.K
Rawson, James TX 14th Inf. Co.A
Rawson, James Gen. & Staff Hosp.Stew.
Rawson, James W. NC 6th Inf. Co.C
Rawson, John GA Inf. 23rd Bn.Loc.Def. Sims' Co.D
Rawson, John MS 8th Inf. Co.H
Rawson, John C. MS 13th Inf. Co.K
Rawson, John E. LA Mil. Beauregard Bn. Frobus' Co.
Rawson, Joseph G. GA 51st Inf. Co.A
Rawson, Joseph V. VA 8th Cav. Co.E
Rawson, Lewis TN 48th (Voorhies') Inf. Co.G
Rawson, Loyd S. GA 51st Inf. Co.K Ord.Sgt.
Rawson, Middleton M. GA 16th Inf. Co.G
Rawson, Robert TN 2nd (Robison's) Inf. Co.G
Rawson, Robert J. MS 13th Inf. Co.K
Rawson, W. AL 45th Inf. Co.A
Rawson, William MS 4th Inf. Co.K
Rawson, W.S. GA 21st Inf. Co.C
Rawton, J.M. 8th (Wade's) Conf.Cav. Co.K
Rawyer, T.J. AL 9th Inf. Co.C

Raxsdale, Frank M. LA 16th Inf. Co.E Maj.
Raxter, Charles C. NC 25th Inf. Co.E
Raxter, Charles C. SC 1st Arty. Co.G
Raxter, Samuel NC 62nd Inf. Co.E
Ray, --- TX Cav. 4th Regt.St.Troops Co.G
Ray, A. AL Mil. 4th Vol. Co.D
Ray, A. AL 26th (O'Neal's) Inf. Co.A
Ray, A. NC 8th Sr.Res. Williams' Co.
Ray, A. SC 2nd Arty. Co.G
Ray, A.A. NC 3rd Inf. Co.C
Ray, Aaron AL Inf. 1st Regt. Co.A
Ray, Aaron TN 16th Cav.
Ray, Aaron TX 14th Cav. Co.A
Ray, A.B. KY 8th Mtd.Inf. Co.D
Ray, A.B. MS 5th Cav. Co.I
Ray, Abel D. NC 21st Inf. Co.H
Ray, Abner VA 57th Inf. Co.B
Ray, Abraham MO 3rd Cav.
Ray, Abraham MO 3rd Inf. Co.K
Ray, Abraham SC 22nd Inf. Co.C
Ray, Absalom TN 19th Inf.
Ray, A.C. GA 9th Inf. Co.E QMSgt.
Ray, A.C. MS 2nd (Davidson's) Inf. Co.E
Ray, A.C. NC 31st Inf. Co.K
Ray, A.C. 1st Conf.Cav. 1st Co.E Sgt.
Ray, A.D. AL 50th Inf. Co.H Capt.
Ray, A.D. AR 24th Inf. Co.H
Ray, A.D. AR Inf. Hardy's Regt. Co.E
Ray, A.D. MO 6th Cav. Co.E
Ray, A.D. SC 7th Res. Co.C Cpl.
Ray, Adam LA Hvy.Arty. 2nd Bn. Co.F
Ray, Adams LA 18th Inf. Co.B
Ray, Addison NC 1st Cav. (9th St.Troops) Co.D
Ray, A.E. AL 61st Inf. Co.A
Ray, A.E. TN 45th Inf. Co.F
Ray, A.F. TX 20th Inf. Co.I
Ray, A.G. TN Inf. 23rd Bn. Co.C Sgt.
Ray, A.H. NC 6th Cav. (65th St.Troops) Lt.
Ray, A.J. AL 7th Cav. Co.E
Ray, A.J. AL Cav. 24th Bn. Co.B Lt.
Ray, A.J. AL 17th Inf. Co.K,D
Ray, A.J. GA 15th Inf. Co.B
Ray, A.J. GA 37th Inf. Co.E
Ray, A.J. MS 27th Inf. Co.A
Ray, A.J. SC 13th Inf. Co.A
Ray, A.J. TN 44th (Cons.) Inf. Co.G
Ray, Albert NC 2nd Inf. Co.H
Ray, Albert NC 29th Inf. Co.D,B
Ray, Albert N. TN 24th Inf. 2nd Co.H, Co.M
Ray, Alcibiades AL 61st Inf. Co.B
Ray, Alex TN 21st & 22nd (Cons.) Cav. Co.D
Ray, Alex TN 22nd (Barteau's) Cav. Co.D
Ray, Alexander AL Lt.Arty. 20th Bn. Co.A
Ray, Alexander AL 38th Inf. Co.F
Ray, Alexander AL 38th Inf. Co.K
Ray, Alexander AL 48th Inf.
Ray, Alexander AR 15th Mil. Co.A
Ray, Alexander KY Cav. 2nd Bn. (Dortch's) Co.H
Ray, Alexander KY 7th Cav. Co.E
Ray, Alexander MS Inf. 3rd Bn. Co.H
Ray, Alexander NC 1st Inf. (6 mo. '61) Co.H
Ray, Alexander NC 53rd Inf. Co.D Capt.
Ray, Alexander SC 1st (Butler's) Inf. Co.I
Ray, Alexander TN 13th (Gore's) Cav. Co.C
Ray, Alexander TN 28th Inf. Co.G,B
Ray, Alexander TN 28th (Cons.) Inf. Co.K

Ray, Alexander B. MD 1st Inf. Co.D
Ray, Alexander C. AL 10th Cav.
Ray, Alexander S. AL 50th Inf. Co.H 2nd Lt.
Ray, Alf MS 6th Cav. Co.B
Ray, Allen NC 38th Inf. Co.K
Ray, Allen W. GA 12th Inf. Co.A
Ray, Allin GA Cav. 22nd Bn. (St.Guards) Co.I
Ray, Alonzo GA Inf. 2nd Bn. Co.B
Ray, A.M. GA 5th Mil. Co.C
Ray, Amos G. MS 9th Inf. Old Co.C
Ray, Amos G. TN 45th Inf. Co.C
Ray, A.N. GA 24th Inf. Co.H
Ray, A.N. TN Inf. 3rd Cons.Regt. Co.K
Ray, Anderson AL 36th Inf. Co.D
Ray, Andrew AL 47th Inf. Co.E 2nd Lt.
Ray, Andrew AR 20th Inf. Co.H
Ray, Andrew MO 7th Cav. Co.E 1st Sgt.
Ray, Andrew VA Hvy.Arty. 18th Bn. Co.E
Ray, Andrew C. SC Inf. Holcombe Legion Co.K
Ray, Andrew J. AL 18th Inf. Co.H
Ray, Andrew J. AR 8th Inf. New Co.G
Ray, Andrew J. AR 9th Inf. Co.E Sgt.
Ray, Andrew J. MS 2nd Part.Rangers Co.E
Ray, Andrew J. MS 19th Inf. Co.K
Ray, Andrew J. NC 18th Inf. Co.G
Ray, Andrew J. TN 55th (McKoin's) Inf. Duggan's Co.
Ray, Andrew P. MS St.Cav. Perrin's Bn. Co.B
Ray, Andrew R. TN 44th Inf. Co.K
Ray, Andrew R. TN 44th (Cons.) Inf. Co.F
Ray, Andrew T. AL 13th Inf. Co.D
Ray, Andrew W. Wheeler's Scouts,CSA Capt.
Ray, Andy M. GA 3rd Cav. (St.Guards) Co.B Cpl.
Ray, Angus NC 24th Inf. Co.G
Ray, Angus J. NC 3rd Inf. Co.C
Ray, Angus P. NC 4th Cav. (59th St.Troops) Co.E
Ray, Ansalom MS Lt.Arty. (Issaquena Arty.) Graves' Co.
Ray, Ansolom KY 4th Mtd.Inf. Co.B
Ray, A.P. MS 1st Lt.Arty. Co.E
Ray, A.P. SC 23rd Inf. Co.G
Ray, Archibald GA 52nd Inf. Co.D
Ray, Archibald NC 24th Inf. Co.G
Ray, Archibald NC 33rd Mil. Ray's Co.
Ray, Archibald NC 38th Inf. Co.K
Ray, Archibald SC 8th Inf. Co.H
Ray, Archibald TN 1st Inf. Co.D
Ray, Archibald A. NC 35th Inf. Co.C Cpl.
Ray, Archibald B. NC 3rd Inf. Co.B
Ray, Archy TX 16th Inf. Co.C
Ray, Arthur GA 47th Inf. Co.F
Ray, A.S. AL 27th Inf. Co.I Sgt.
Ray, A.S. AL 50th Inf. Co.H
Ray, A.S. GA 1st (Olmstead's) Inf. Co.F
Ray, A.S. NC Cumberland Cty.Bn. Detailed Men Co.B
Ray, Asa AL 54th Inf. Co.E 2nd Lt.
Ray, Asa 4th Conf.Inf. Co.D 2nd Lt.
Ray, Ashford NC 2nd Arty. (36th St.Troops) Co.I
Ray, Aug. J. LA 1st Hvy.Arty. (Reg.) Co.G
Ray, Augustus AL 44th Inf. Co.I 2nd Lt.
Ray, Augustus H. GA 36th (Villepigue's) Inf. Co.B
Ray, Augustus H. 1st Conf.Inf. Co.B Jr.2nd Lt.

Ray, Augustus W. GA 4th Inf. Co.A
Ray, A.W. KY 10th (Johnson's) Cav. Co.A Capt.
Ray, A.W. KY 8th Mtd.Inf. Co.D 1st Sgt.
Ray, A.W. MS 1st Lt.Arty. Co.C
Ray, B. KY Inf. 44th Regt. Co.B
Ray, B. NC 16th Inf. Co.C
Ray, Bart SC 2nd Arty. Co.G
Ray, B.B. MS Inf. 2nd St.Troops Co.E
Ray, B.B. TX 22nd Inf. Co.I Cpl.
Ray, Benjamin GA 1st (Olmstead's) Inf. Co.H
Ray, Benjamin GA 36th (Broyles') Inf. Co.K
Ray, Benjamin LA 3rd Inf. Co.I
Ray, Benjamin MO 8th Bn. Co.F
Ray, Benjamin MO 9th Inf. Co.K
Ray, Benjamin 1st Conf.Inf. 2nd Co.C
Ray, Benjamin B. MO 1st N.E. Cav. Co.H
Ray, Benjamin F. AL Mil. 4th Vol. Co.H
Ray, Benjamin F. FL Cav. 5th Bn. Co.I
Ray, Benjamin F. GA 22nd Inf. Co.D
Ray, Benjamin F. MO Inf. Clark's Regt. Co.A
Ray, Benjamin H. AL 43rd Inf. Co.E
Ray, Benjamin L. SC Horse Arty. (Washington Arty.) Vol. Hart's Co.
Ray, Benjamin L. SC Arty.Bn. Hampton Legion Co.A
Ray, Bennett TX 16th Inf. Co.I
Ray, B.F. AL St.Res.
Ray, B.F. GA 8th Inf. Co.I
Ray, B.F. MO 9th Inf. Co.B
Ray, B.G. SC 3rd Cav. Co.A
Ray, B.G. SC 2nd Arty. Co.G
Ray, B.H. TN 13th (Gore's) Cav. Co.C
Ray, B.H. Inf. Bailey's Cons.Regt. Co.B
Ray, B.H. TX 7th Inf. Co.F
Ray, B.J. AL 31st Inf. Co.E
Ray, B.M. NC 15th Inf. Co.D
Ray, Bose AL Inf. 1st Regt. Co.A
Ray, Brace NC 53rd Inf. Co.F
Ray, Bradford GA 1st (Olmstead's) Inf. Co.H
Ray, Brantley M. NC 49th Inf. Co.B
Ray, B.T. GA Cav. 22nd Bn. (St.Guards) Co.C
Ray, Buckner NC 6th Sr.Res. Co.K 2nd Lt.
Ray, Burruss F. MS 4th Inf. Co.K
Ray, Burwell J. NC 3rd Inf. Co.K
Ray, C. MS 2nd (Quinn's St.Troops) Inf. Co.C Cpl.
Ray, C. MS 6th Inf. Co.G
Ray, C. NC 3rd Jr.Res. Co.B
Ray, Calvin NC 4th Bn.Jr.Res. Co.B
Ray, Calvin TN Inf. 154th Sr.Regt. Co.F Bvt.2nd Lt.
Ray, Calvin S. AL Cav. Lenoir's Ind.Co.
Ray, Calvin S. NC 24th Inf. Co.G
Ray, Caswell NC 30th Inf. Co.D
Ray, C.B.S. SC 2nd Arty. Co.G Sgt.
Ray, C.B.S. SC 1st (Hagood's) Inf. 1st Co.G
Ray, C.C. AR 1st (Dobbin's) Cav. Co.B
Ray, C.C. AR 2nd Inf. Co.D
Ray, C.C. GA Inf. 2nd Bn. (St.Guards) Co.C Cpl.
Ray, C.C. MO Cav. Coffee's Regt. Co.D 2nd Lt.
Ray, Chalmon VA 57th Inf. Co.F
Ray, Charles MS Cav. Powers' Regt. Co.E
Ray, Charles MS 19th Inf. Co.C
Ray, Charles TX 16th Inf. Co.C,I

Ray, Charles VA 18th Cav. Co.G
Ray, Charles A. GA Inf. 9th Bn. Co.D
Ray, Charles A. MS 3rd (St.Troops) Cav. Co.F Sgt.
Ray, Charles A. MS 26th Inf. Co.G 1st Lt.
Ray, Charles B. SC 17th Inf. Co.H
Ray, Charles C. AL 4th Cav. Co.A
Ray, Charles E. TN 37th Inf. Co.A
Ray, Charles K. SC Horse Arty. (Washington Arty.) Vol. Hart's Co.
Ray, Charles K. SC Arty.Bn. Hampton Legion Co.A
Ray, Charles W. AR 4th Inf. Co.G
Ray, Charles W. NC 14th Inf. Co.E
Ray, Charles W. TN 41st Inf. Co.K
Ray, Chesley VA 22nd Inf. Co.K
Ray, Christopher C. AL 62nd Inf. Co.D
Ray, Churchill C. GA 42nd Inf. Co.I
Ray, Cicero B. AL 26th Inf.
Ray, C.J. 1st Conf.Cav. 2nd Co.B
Ray, C.L. GA 13th Cav. Co.F
Ray, C.L. NC 3rd Arty. (40th St.Troops) Co.H
Ray, C.M. NC 7th Sr.Res. Watts' Co.
Ray, C.M. NC 63rd Bn.Home Guards 1st Lt.
Ray, C.M. TN 17th Inf. Co.A
Ray, C.M.G. TN Inf. 1st Cons.Regt. Co.E
Ray, C.M.G. TN 9th Inf. Co.H
Ray, Colen G., Jr. FL 6th Inf. Co.H
Ray, Colen G., Sr. FL 6th Inf. Co.H
Ray, Columbus W. VA 4th Inf. Co.A
Ray, Cornelius NC 50th Inf. Co.H
Ray, C.P. AR 1st Mtd.Rifles Co.D
Ray, C.P. KY 7th Mtd.Inf. Co.K Capt.
Ray, C.P. MS 25th Inf. Co.C Capt.
Ray, C.P. 2nd Conf.Inf. Co.C Capt.
Ray, Creely NC 6th Inf. Co.F
Ray, C.S. AL 62nd Inf. Co.F
Ray, Curtis TX 21st Cav. Co.H
Ray, Cyrus N. TN 38th Inf. Co.I
Ray, D. GA Arty. Pruden's Btty.
Ray, D. SC 2nd Inf. Co.G
Ray, D. TN Cav. Cox's Bn. Co.C
Ray, D. VA 5th Bn.Res. Co.B
Ray, D.A. NC 1st Jr.Res. Co.H
Ray, Dallas AL 22nd Inf. Co.C
Ray, Dallas M. AL 25th Inf. Co.C
Ray, Daniel AL Inf. 1st Regt. Co.A
Ray, Daniel NC 33rd Mil. Ray's Co.
Ray, Daniel NC 38th Inf. Co.K
Ray, Daniel SC Lt.Arty. 3rd (Palmetto) Bn. Co.E
Ray, Daniel TN Cav. 12th Bn. (Day's) Co.C
Ray, Daniel TX 14th Cav. Co.H
Ray, Daniel VA 57th Inf. Co.C
Ray, Daniel McN. NC 24th Inf. Co.G
Ray, Daniel W. AR 33rd Inf. Co.G
Ray, Daniel W. GA 4th Inf. Co.A
Ray, David AR 6th Inf. Co.B
Ray, David AR 30th Inf. Co.H Cpl.
Ray, David GA Arty. Maxwell's Reg.Lt.Btty. Music.
Ray, David GA 1st Reg. Co.D Music.
Ray, David GA 49th Inf. Co.B
Ray, David GA 60th Inf. Co.E
Ray, David KY 4th Mtd.Inf. Co.G
Ray, David NC 33rd Mil. Ray's Co. Cpl.
Ray, David, Jr. NC 38th Inf. Co.K
Ray, David, Sr. NC 38th Inf. Co.K

Ray, David NC 50th Inf. Co.H
Ray, David TN 19th & 20th (Cons.) Cav. Co.C
Ray, David VA 7th Cav. Co.I
Ray, David VA 2nd St.Res. Co.B
Ray, David VA 146th Mil. Co.E
Ray, David 2nd Conf.Eng.Troops Co.A
Ray, David A. NC 30th Inf. Co.D Cpl.
Ray, David B. NC 34th Inf. Co.D
Ray, David F. MO 6th Cav. Co.E
Ray, David H. NC 1st Inf. (6 mo. '61) Co.H
Ray, David Hamilton NC 5th Inf. Co.A 2nd Lt.
Ray, David J. NC 2nd Bn.Loc.Def.Troops Co.B 1st Lt.
Ray, David L. AR 3rd Inf. Co.G
Ray, David L. MO Inf. Clark's Regt. Co.A
Ray, David M. NC 29th Inf. Co.B Capt.
Ray, David M. NC 34th Inf. Co.I
Ray, David M. TX 16th Cav. Co.G Hosp.Stew.
Ray, David N. AL 50th Inf. Co.H Cpl.
Ray, David R. GA 9th Inf. Co.C
Ray, David S. NC 56th Inf. Co.D 1st Lt.
Ray, D.B. AL 46th Inf. Co.B
Ray, D.B. MS 5th Cav. Co.I Sgt.
Ray, D.B. NC 1st Inf. (6 mo. '61) Co.C
Ray, D.C. FL 2nd Inf. Co.B
Ray, D.E. KY 5th Cav. Co.I
Ray, D.E. MS 2nd Cav. Co.A
Ray, Dempsey A. GA Inf. 10th Bn. Co.A
Ray, Dempsey E. MS 15th Inf. Co.I
Ray, D.G. AL 15th Inf. Co.F
Ray, D.H. AL 51st (Part.Rangers) Co.F
Ray, D.H. TX 1st Hvy.Arty. Co.K
Ray, D.M. AL Inf. 1st (Loomis') Bn. Co.C
Ray, D.M. AL 24th Inf. Co.K
Ray, D.M. AL Cp. of Instr. Talladega
Ray, D.M. Gen. & Staff Hosp.Stew.
Ray, D.N. AL 25th Inf. Co.C
Ray, Doctor F. AL 18th Bn.Vol. Co.C Cpl.
Ray, Doctor F. AL 33rd Inf. Co.C Cpl.
Ray, D.R. NC 3rd Bn.Sr.Res. Durham's Co.
Ray, D.S. GA Cav. 24th Bn. Co.B,C 1st Lt.
Ray, Duncan SC Hvy.Arty. 15th (Lucas') Bn. Co.C
Ray, Duncan K. NC 2nd Bn.Loc.Def.Troops Co.D
Ray, Duncan K. NC 33rd Mil. Ray's Co. Sgt.
Ray, Duncan S. GA 57th Inf. Co.A
Ray, Duncan W. SC 9th Inf. Co.B Lt.Col.
Ray, D.W. AL 11th Cav. Co.I
Ray, D.W. GA 1st Lt.Duty Men Co.A
Ray, D.W. GA Inf. 14th Bn. (St.Guards) Co.E
Ray, D.W. Exch.Bn. 3rd Co.B,CSA
Ray, E. MS 6th Cav. Co.F
Ray, E. MS 1st Lt.Arty. Co.B
Ray, E. MS Inf. 3rd Bn. (St.Troops) Co.E
Ray, E. TX Conscr.
Ray, E.D. VA Inf. 26th Bn. Co.I
Ray, Ed K. TX 1st (Yager's) Cav. Co.H
Ray, Edwin S. SC 5th Inf. 1st Co.K Sgt.
Ray, Edwin S. Gen. & Staff Asst.Surg.
Ray, E.E. TX 7th Field Btty. Guidon
Ray, E.G. MS Inf. 2nd Bn. Co.K
Ray, E.G. MS 48th Inf. Co.K
Ray, E.G. 8th (Wade's) Conf.Cav. Co.F
Ray, E.H. AR 38th Inf. Co.K
Ray, Elah KY 10th (Diamond's) Cav. Co.D
Ray, Eli KY 5th Mtd.Inf. Co.G

Ray, Eli NC 61st Inf. Co.G
Ray, Eli TN 10th (DeMoss') Cav. Co.B
Ray, Eli TN 18th (Newsom's) Cav. Co.G
Ray, Elias SC 2nd Arty. Co.G
Ray, Elias SC 1st (Hagood's) Inf. 1st Co.G
Ray, Elijah AL Inf. 1st Regt. Co.A,K
Ray, Elijah AL 22nd Inf. Co.C
Ray, Elijah AL 57th Inf. Co.B
Ray, Elijah NC 44th Inf. Co.G
Ray, Elijah SC 5th Inf. 1st Co.A
Ray, Elijah SC Palmetto S.S. Co.A Sgt.
Ray, Elijah 4th Conf.Inf. Co.D
Ray, Eli S. TN Cav. Newsom's Regt. Co.C
Ray, Elisha AL 42nd Inf. Co.C
Ray, Elisha AL 48th Inf. Co.B
Ray, Elisha MS 15th Inf. Co.I
Ray, Elisha B. NC 3rd Inf. Co.I
Ray, Ellis S. VA 42nd Inf. Co.F
Ray, Elza TN 48th (Nixon's) Inf. Co.F
Ray, Elza TN 54th Inf. Co.A
Ray, E.M. NC 47th Inf. Co.E
Ray, Enoch AL 18th Inf. Co.A
Ray, Enoch KY 1st (Butler's) Cav. Co.A
Ray, Enock GA 65th Inf. Co.A
Ray, Erastus H. NC 47th Inf. Co.E 1st Lt.
Ray, Ervin NC 16th Inf. Co.C
Ray, E.S. TN 31st Inf. Co.B
Ray, E.T. SC 10th Inf. Co.E
Ray, Eugene A. AR 1st (Colquitt's) Inf. Co.I Sgt.
Ray, Eusibeous VA 57th Inf. Co.B
Ray, E.W. AL 14th Inf. Co.C Jr.2nd Lt.
Ray, E.W. NC 64th Inf. Co.G
Ray, E.W. TX 21st Cav. Co.C Cpl.
Ray, F. TX 24th & 25th Cav. Co.I
Ray, Farrah J. NC 6th Cav. (65th St.Troops) Co.D
Ray, Farrow NC 1st Cav. (9th St.Troops) Co.A
Ray, F.B. AR 19th (Dawson's) Inf. Co.K Sgt.
Ray, F.F. SC Inf. 1st (Charleston) Bn. Co.D
Ray, F.G. AR 32nd Inf. Co.D Sgt.
Ray, F.H. FL Cav. 3rd Bn. Co.A
Ray, F.L. LA 26th Inf. Co.A
Ray, F.M. GA 51st Inf. Co.C
Ray, F.M. LA 3rd Inf. Co.I
Ray, F.M. TN Lt.Arty. Morton's Co.
Ray, F.M. TN 35th Inf. Co.L
Ray, F.M. TN 52nd Inf. Co.B Cpl.
Ray, F.M. VA 2nd Inf.Loc.Def. Co.A
Ray, F.M. VA Inf. 2nd Bn.Loc.Def. Co.C
Ray, Fountain P. Gen. & Staff Chap.
Ray, F.R. TN 23rd Inf. 2nd Co.F
Ray, Francis NC 15th Inf. Co.D
Ray, Francis NC 49th Inf. Co.B
Ray, Francis TN 6th (Wheeler's) Cav. Co.K
Ray, Francis C. GA 30th Inf. Co.K
Ray, Francis H. AL Mil. 4th Vol. Co.A
Ray, Frank LA Inf. McLean's Co.
Ray, Frank TX 1st (Yager's) Cav. Co.A
Ray, Frank TX Cav. 3rd (Yager's) Bn. Co.A Cpl.
Ray, Frank VA 2nd Arty. Co.E
Ray, Franklin AL 7th Inf. Co.G
Ray, Franklin GA 50th Inf. Co.I
Ray, Franklin L. MS 16th Inf. Co.C Cpl.
Ray, Fred TN 51st (Cons.) Inf. Co.B
Ray, Frederick SC 1st (Butler's) Inf. Co.I,H

Ray, Frederick J. AL 36th Inf. Co.K
Ray, F.S. TN Cav. 16th Bn. (Neal's) Co.B 1st Cpl.
Ray, F.T. SC 27th Inf. Co.D
Ray, G.A. TX Cav. 1st Regt.St.Troops Co.A
Ray, G.A. TX 13th Vol. Co.G
Ray, Gains R. SC 13th Inf. Co.A
Ray, Garrett D. NC 58th Inf. Co.C
Ray, Garrett D. NC 64th Inf. Co.A Lt.
Ray, General TN 41st Inf. Co.G
Ray, George AL 29th Inf. Co.C
Ray, George AR 7th Cav. Co.K
Ray, George NC 44th Inf. Co.E
Ray, George TN Lt.Arty. Phillips' Co. Artif.
Ray, George TN Inf. 22nd Bn. Co.K
Ray, George Conf.Reg.Inf. Brooks' Bn. Co.A
Ray, George A. AL 46th Inf. Co.B
Ray, George A. NC 56th Inf. Co.D,H
Ray, George C. VA 4th Cav. Chap.
Ray, George D. NC 2nd Arty. (36th St.Troops) Co.B Black.
Ray, George D. NC Lt.Arty. 13th Bn. Co.B
Ray, George Duffie NC 33rd Mil. Ray's Co.
Ray, George F. VA 14th Inf. Co.H
Ray, George F. VA 38th Inf. Co.A
Ray, George F.H. GA 24th Inf. Co.B
Ray, George H. AL 35th Inf. Co.B
Ray, George H. TN 37th Inf. Co.A Cpl.
Ray, George H. VA 3rd Cav. Chap.
Ray, George H. Conf.Cav. 6th Bn. Co.G
Ray, Geo. H. Gen. & Staff Chap.
Ray, George J. TN 28th Inf. Co.E
Ray, George L. AL 46th Inf. Co.E
Ray, George L. TN 28th Inf. Co.E
Ray, George M. AL 63rd Inf. Co.B,K
Ray, George M. AR 1st Vol. Co.C Sgt.
Ray, George M. NC 31st Inf. Co.E
Ray, George M. TN 8th Inf. Co.G Cpl.
Ray, George S. LA 28th (Gray's) Inf. Co.H
Ray, George T. MO Inf. Clark's Regt. Co.A
Ray, George W. AL Arty. 1st Bn. Co.F Cpl.
Ray, George W. AL Lt.Arty. 2nd Bn. Co.F
Ray, George W. AL 1st Regt.Conscr. Co.G
Ray, George W. AL 25th Inf. Co.C Cpl.
Ray, George W. AL 59th Inf. Co.B
Ray, George W. AL 2nd Bn. Hilliard's Legion Vol. Co.E
Ray, George W. AR 23rd Inf. Co.C
Ray, George W. GA 3rd Cav. Co.E Sgt.
Ray, George W. GA 7th Inf. (St.Guards) Co.K Sgt.
Ray, George W. MS 5th Inf. Co.A
Ray, George W. MS 9th Inf. New Co.C
Ray, George W. NC 1st Cav. (9th St.Troops) Co.A Saddler
Ray, George W. NC Cav. 5th Bn. Co.D
Ray, George W. NC 6th Cav. (65th St.Troops) Co.D,B
Ray, George W. TN 25th Inf. Co.D
Ray, George W. TN 25th Inf. Co.K
Ray, George W. TX Cav. Waller's Regt. Co.B
Ray, G.F. SC 2nd Arty. Co.G
Ray, G.F. SC 1st (Hagood's) Inf. 1st Co.G
Ray, G.G. MS Inf. 2nd Bn. Co.K
Ray, G.G. MS 48th Inf. Co.K
Ray, G.G. 8th (Wade's) Conf.Cav. Co.F
Ray, G.H. GA Lt.Arty. 12th Bn.

Ray, G.H. TN 12th Inf. Co.F
Ray, Gilbert NC 38th Inf. Co.K
Ray, Gilbert C. NC 5th Cav. (63rd St.Troops) Co.A
Ray, Gilbert C. NC 2nd Arty. (36th St.Troops) Co.B
Ray, Gilbert C. NC Lt.Arty. 13th Bn. Co.B
Ray, Gilbert G. NC 2nd Bn.Loc.Def.Troops Co.B
Ray, G.J. TN 28th (Cons.) Inf. Co.D
Ray, G.L. TN Inf. 1st Cons.Regt. Co.C
Ray, G.L. TN 28th (Cons.) Inf. Co.D
Ray, Green MS 13th Inf. Co.I Cpl.
Ray, Greenbury B. AR 19th (Dockery's) Inf. Co.B,D Sgt.
Ray, G.S. TN 5th Inf. 2nd Co.K
Ray, G.T. MO 9th Inf. Co.B
Ray, Gustavus Conf.Cav. Clarkson's Bn. Ind.Rangers Co.B
Ray, G.W. MS 6th Cav. Co.F
Ray, G.W. MS Inf. 3rd Bn. (St.Troops) Co.F
Ray, G.W. MO St.Guard
Ray, G.W. TN 8th Cav. Co.C
Ray, G.W. TN 25th Inf. Co.B Sgt.
Ray, G.W. TN 63rd Inf. Co.C
Ray, G.W. TX 6th Cav. Co.C
Ray, H. MS 1st (Patton's) Inf. Co.A
Ray, H. MO Inf. 3rd Regt.St.Guard Co.E 2nd Lt.
Ray, H. TX Waul's Legion Co.D
Ray, H.A. AL 20th Inf. Co.A
Ray, H.A. TN Inf. 154th Sr.Regt. Co.I
Ray, Hamilton J. MO 1st Cav. Co.A Sgt.
Ray, Hamp MS Inf. 3rd Bn. (St.Troops) Co.A
Ray, Harris AR 3rd Inf. Co.E
Ray, Harriss AR Inf. 2nd Bn. Co.C
Ray, H.B. AL 53rd (Part.Rangers) Co.E Cpl.
Ray, H.B. GA 11th Cav. Co.C
Ray, H.D. MO 15th Cav. Co.C
Ray, H.D. VA 5th Inf.
Ray, Henderson NC 26th Inf. Co.D
Ray, Henry MS 12th Cav. Co.B
Ray, Henry NC Cav. 5th Bn. Co.D
Ray, Henry NC 6th Cav. (65th St.Troops) Co.A
Ray, Henry NC 6th Cav. (65th St.Troops) Co.D
Ray, Henry NC Cav. 7th Bn. Co.A
Ray, Henry TN 16th Cav.
Ray, Henry VA 22nd Cav. Co.D
Ray, Henry VA 37th Inf. Co.I,G
Ray, Henry B. NC 29th Inf. Co.B
Ray, Henry B. VA Lt.Arty. Carpenter's Co.
Ray, Henry B. VA 27th Inf. Co.A
Ray, Henry C. NC 30th Inf. Co.D
Ray, Henry H. NC 1st Cav. (9th St.Troops) Co.A
Ray, Henry L. VA 45th Inf. Co.G
Ray, Henry L. 1st Conf.Inf. Co.B 2nd Lt.
Ray, Henry P. VA 50th Inf. Co.F
Ray, Henry P. Nitre & Min. Bureau War Dept.,CSA
Ray, Hezekiah TN 27th Inf. Co.A
Ray, H.G.B. MS 13th Inf. Co.G
Ray, H.H. SC 3rd Inf. Co.D Sgt.
Ray, H.H. TN 19th & 20th (Cons.) Cav. Co.I 1st Sgt.
Ray, Hilton H. NC Cav. 5th Bn. Co.D 2nd Lt.

Ray, Hilton H. NC 6th Cav. (65th St.Troops) Co.D,B 1st Lt.
Ray, Hiram AL 27th Inf. Co.I Cpl.
Ray, Hiram GA 11th Cav. (St.Guards) Godfrey's Co.
Ray, Hiram GA 1st (Olmstead's) Inf. Co.H
Ray, Hiram A. NC Cav. 5th Bn. Co.A
Ray, Hiram A. NC 6th Cav. (65th St.Troops) Co.A
Ray, Hiram A. NC Cav. 14th Bn. Co.D 2nd Lt.
Ray, Hiram A. NC 64th Inf. Co.F
Ray, Hiram R. NC Cav. 5th Bn. Co.A
Ray, Hiram W. KY 10th (Johnson's) Cav. New Co.I
Ray, H.J. MS 30th Inf. Co.D
Ray, H.J. MO 1st & 3rd Cons.Cav. Sgt.
Ray, H.L. AL 27th Inf. Co.I Capt.
Ray, H.L. AL 27th Inf. Co.I
Ray, H.L. AR 3rd Inf. (St.Troops) Co.A
Ray, H.L. Gen. & Staff Surg.
Ray, H.M. MS 10th Cav. Co.H
Ray, H.M. SC 17th Inf. Co.H,F Capt.
Ray, H.M. TN 25th Inf. Co.B Sgt.
Ray, H.M. Conf.Cav. Baxter's Bn. Co.A
Ray, Horace C. AR 2nd Cav. Co.C
Ray, Horace E. NC 17th Inf. (2nd Org.) Co.H
Ray, Hosea TX 9th (Nichols') Inf. Co.F
Ray, Howell GA 45th Inf. Co.B
Ray, Hugh NC 34th Inf. Co.D
Ray, Hugh SC Palmetto S.S. Co.M
Ray, Hugh M. NC 26th Inf. Co.H
Ray, Huston TN 8th Inf. Co.I
Ray, I.L. TN 35th Inf. Co.G Cpl.
Ray, I.P. TN 19th Inf. Co.H 2nd Lt.
Ray, Ira VA 22nd Cav. Co.D
Ray, Ira VA 37th Inf. Co.G
Ray, Ira VA 46th Inf. 2nd Co.E
Ray, Iradall TN 15th (Stewart's) Cav. Co.A Sgt.
Ray, Irvin L. AL Inf. 1st Regt. Co.A
Ray, Isaac AR 3rd Inf. Co.F
Ray, Isaac TX 34th Cav. Co.I
Ray, Isaac H. TN 25th Inf. Co.B Cpl.
Ray, Isaac L. AL 13th Inf. Co.C
Ray, Isaac N. AL Inf. 1st Regt. Co.H 2nd Lt.
Ray, Isaac O. MS 21st Inf. Co.D
Ray, Isaac T. KY 4th Mtd.Inf. Co.I
Ray, Isaac W. AR 3rd Cav. Co.F
Ray, Isicha B. NC 29th Inf. Co.B
Ray, I.T. TN 15th (Stewart's) Cav. Co.C
Ray, I.W. LA Maddox's Regt.Res.Corps Co.B
Ray, J. AL 1st Cav. Co.D
Ray, J. AR 13th Mil. Co.E
Ray, J. AR 37th Inf. Co.C
Ray, J. GA Lt.Arty. (Arsenal Btty.) Hudson's Co.
Ray, J. LA Mil. 4th Regt. French Brig. Co.2
Ray, J. TN 20th Inf. Co.E
Ray, J. 20th Conf.Cav. Co.E
Ray, J. Gillum's Regt. Co.G
Ray, J.A. AR 1st Mtd.Rifles Co.F
Ray, J.A. AR 38th Inf. Co.K
Ray, J.A. AR Inf. Cocke's Regt. Co.K,F
Ray, J.A. GA 49th Inf. Co.D
Ray, J.A. KY 8th Mtd.Inf. Co.D Sgt.
Ray, J.A. SC Lt.Arty. 3rd (Palmetto) Bn. Co.I
Ray, J.A. TN 31st Inf. Co.B Cpl.
Ray, J.A. TX Cav. Wells' Regt. Co.D

Ray, Jabez M. TX 16th Inf. Co.I
Ray, Jack KY 10th (Johnson's) Cav. New Co.I
Ray, Jackson AR 14th (McCarver's) Inf. Co.A
Ray, Jackson KY 5th Mtd.Inf. Co.G
Ray, Jackson MO 9th Inf. Co.B
Ray, Jackson NC 5th Sr.Res. Co.H
Ray, Jackson H. MS 11th Inf. Co.D
Ray, Jacob NC 6th Inf. Co.E
Ray, Jacob L. AL 36th Inf. Co.D
Ray, James AL Inf. 1st Regt. Co.A
Ray, James AL Mil. 2nd Regt.Vol. Co.A
Ray, James AL 11th Inf. Co.G
Ray, James AL 18th Inf. Co.A
Ray, James AL 46th Inf. Co.H
Ray, James AL 59th Inf. Co.C
Ray, James AL Randolph Cty.Res. B.C. Raney's
Co.
Ray, James AR 1st Inf. Co.C
Ray, James AR 5th Inf. Co.C
Ray, James AR 8th Inf. New Co.H
Ray, James AR Inf. Cocke's Regt. Co.F Sgt.
Ray, James GA Cav. 37th Regt. Co.F
Ray, James GA 6th Mil.
Ray, James GA 51st Inf. Co.C
Ray, James MS 1st Cav.Res. Co.K
Ray, James MS Lt.Arty. (The Hudson Btty.)
Hoole's Co.
Ray, James MS 2nd Inf. Co.I
Ray, James MS 5th Inf. Co.B Lt.
Ray, James MS 5th Inf. (St.Troops) Co.C
Ray, James MS 22nd Inf. Co.E
Ray, James MS 33rd Inf. Co.A
Ray, James MS 43rd Inf. Co.A
Ray, James NC 1st Cav. (9th St.Troops) Co.A
Ray, James NC 3rd Inf. Co.I
Ray, James NC 21st Inf. Co.L
Ray, James SC 15th Inf. Co.D
Ray, James TN 1st (Carter's) Cav. Co.B
Ray, James TN 20th (Russell's) Cav. Co.E
Ray, James TN Inf. 1st Bn. (Colms') Co.C
Ray, James TN 14th Inf. Co.E
Ray, James TN 28th Inf. Co.E Cpl.
Ray, James TN 28th (Cons.) Inf. Co.D
Ray, James TN 28th (Cons.) Inf. Co.E
Ray, James TN 46th Inf. Co.K
Ray, James TN 54th Inf. Co.A
Ray, James TN 84th Inf. Co.A
Ray, James TX Cav. Wells' Regt. Co.D
Ray, James TX 11th Inf. Co.K
Ray, James TX 14th Inf. Co.C
Ray, James VA 37th Inf. Co.G Sgt.
Ray, James A. AR 9th Inf. Co.G
Ray, James A. GA 3rd Cav. (St.Guards) Co.A
Cpl.
Ray, James A. GA 15th Inf. Co.C
Ray, James A. GA 15th Inf. Co.K
Ray, James A. GA 34th Inf. Co.K 2nd Lt.
Ray, James A. NC 29th Inf. Co.D
Ray, James A. TN 31st Inf. Co.B 2nd Lt.
Ray, James B. KY 6th Mtd.Inf. Co.D Sgt.
Ray, James B. NC 29th Inf. Co.B
Ray, James B. NC Hill's Bn.Res. Co.A 2nd Lt.
Ray, James B. TN 28th Inf. Co.I Cpl.
Ray, James C. TN 19th & 20th (Cons.) Cav.
Co.C
Ray, James C. TN 17th Inf. Co.A
Ray, James C. TX Waul's Legion Co.A Sgt.

Ray, James C. Gen. & Staff Hosp.Stew.
Ray, James D. AL 2nd Bn. Hilliard's Legion
Vol. Co.A Cpl.
Ray, James E. AR 23rd Inf. Co.C
Ray, James E. GA 39th Inf. Co.B
Ray, James F. GA 13th Cav. Co.E,H Capt.
Ray, James F. GA 2nd Inf. Co.A Cpl.
Ray, James F. MS 2nd (Davidson's) Inf. Co.G
1st Cpl.
Ray, James F. SC Inf. Holcombe Legion Co.A
Ray, James Franklin NC 38th Inf. Co.K
Ray, James G. AL 42nd Inf. Co.C
Ray, James H. NC 47th Inf. Co.E
Ray, James H. TX 3rd Cav. Co.K
Ray, James H. VA 11th Inf. Co.K Cpl.
Ray, James H.C. AL 13th Inf. Co.F
Ray, James J. MO 1st N.E. Cav.
Ray, James J. NC Cav. 5th Bn. Co.D
Ray, James J. NC 6th Cav. (65th St.Troops)
Co.D,B
Ray, James K. TN 7th Inf. Co.G
Ray, James L. AL 6th Inf. Co.I
Ray, James L. KY 10th (Diamond's) Cav. Co.D
Ray, James L. KY 5th Mtd.Inf. Co.G
Ray, James L. NC 6th Inf. Co.F
Ray, James L. TN 1st (Turney's) Inf. Co.H
Ray, James L. TX 10th Cav. Co.A Cpl.
Ray, James M. AL 4th Inf. Co.K Cpl.
Ray, James M. AL 44th Inf. Co.D
Ray, James M. AL 2nd Bn. Hilliard's Legion
Vol. Co.F
Ray, James M. GA 30th Inf. Co.K
Ray, James M. MS 2nd Cav. Co.E
Ray, James M. MS 2nd St.Cav. 1st Co.C,F 1st
Lt.
Ray, James M. MS Inf. 1st Bn. Ray's Co. Capt.
Ray, James M. MS 8th Inf. Co.G
Ray, James M. MS 24th Inf. Co.C
Ray, James M. MS 30th Inf. Co.D
Ray, James M. MS 30th Inf. Co.G
Ray, James M. MS 31st Inf. Co.D
Ray, James M. NC Cav. 5th Bn. Co.D
Ray, James M. NC 6th Cav. (65th St.Troops)
Co.D,B
Ray, James M. NC Cav. 14th Bn. Co.C
Ray, James M. NC 25th Inf. Co.K 1st Lt.
Ray, James M. NC 29th Inf. Co.B
Ray, James M. NC 60th Inf. Co.F Lt.Col.
Ray, James M. SC 9th Res. Co.F
Ray, James M. TX 17th Inf. Co.K
Ray, James Moore NC 64th Inf. Co.A 1st Lt.
Ray, James N. GA 49th Inf. Co.D
Ray, James O. TN 13th Cav. Co.A
Ray, James O. TN 18th (Newsom's) Cav. Co.B
2nd Lt.
Ray, James O. TN Cav. Newsom's Regt. Co.C
Ray, James P. GA 7th Inf. Co.H
Ray, James P. GA 36th (Broyles') Inf. Co.F
Ray, James P. GA 42nd Inf. Co.I
Ray, James P. VA Cav. 46th Bn. Co.F
Ray, James S. AL 46th Inf. Co.E
Ray, James S. MS 12th Inf. Co.H
Ray, James S. MO 5th Cav. Co.F
Ray, James T. GA 4th (Clinch's) Cav. Co.D
Ray, James T. GA 51st Inf. Co.D Sgt.
Ray, James T. NC 49th Inf. Co.C 1st Sgt.
Ray, James T. TN 46th Inf. Co.D

Ray, James U. SC 17th Inf. Co.H Sgt.
Ray, James W. AL 48th Inf. Co.K
Ray, James W. MS 1st Lt.Arty. Co.E,C
Ray, James W. MS 2nd Inf. Co.D Cpl.
Ray, James W. MS 31st Inf. Co.I
Ray, James W. VA Hvy.Arty. 10th Bn. Co.D
Ray, James William TN 34th Inf. Co.D,H
Ray, James Y. TX 7th Inf. Co.F,C
Ray, Jasper J. GA 3rd Cav. (St.Guards) Co.B
Ray, Jasper N. AL 18th Inf. Co.I
Ray, Jasper N. AL 42nd Inf. Co.H
Ray, J.B. AL 2nd Cav. Co.I
Ray, J.B. AL Inf. 2nd Regt. Co.I
Ray, J.B. AL 15th Inf. Co.H
Ray, J.B. AR 50th Mil. Co.A
Ray, J.B. LA Inf. 4th Bn. Co.B Sgt.
Ray, J.B. LA Inf. Pelican Regt. Co.F Sgt.
Ray, J.B. MS 7th Cav. Co.G
Ray, J.B. MS 2nd (Davidson's) Inf. Co.G
Ray, J.B. NC 29th Inf. Co.B
Ray, J.B. TN 4th (McLemore's) Cav. Co.I Sgt.
Ray, J.B. TN 5th Inf. 2nd Co.K
Ray, J.B. TX 18th Inf. Co.H Cpl.
Ray, J.B. 4th Conf.Inf. Co.G
Ray, J. Benjamin GA 1st (Symons') Res. Co.K
Ray, J. Benjamin GA Inf. 18th Bn. (St.Guards)
Co.C
Ray, J.C. AL Cav. Forrest's Regt. Sgt.
Ray, J.C. AL 5th Inf. New Co.D
Ray, J.C. AL 49th Inf. Co.K
Ray, J.C. AR 5th (St.Troops) Inf. Davis' Co.
Ray, J.C. AR 13th Mil. Co.A
Ray, J.C. AR Willett's Co.
Ray, J.C. GA 32nd Inf. Co.I
Ray, J.C. MS 10th Cav. Co.G
Ray, J.C. NC 3rd Inf. Co.C
Ray, J.C. SC 13th Inf. Co.A
Ray, J.C. TN 18th (Newsom's) Cav. Co.A
Ray, J.C. TN Inf. 154th Sr.Regt. Co.I
Ray, J.C. TX 30th Cav. Co.D
Ray, J.C. TX 19th Inf. Co.E Sgt.
Ray, J.C. 1st Conf.Eng.Troops Co.B
Ray, J.C. Hosp.Stew.
Ray, J.D. AL 59th Inf. Co.F Cpl.
Ray, J.D. AR 19th (Dockery's) Inf. Co.C
Ray, J.D. SC Inf. Hampton Legion Co.H
Ray, J.D. TN 47th Inf. Co.H
Ray, J.D. Gen. & Staff A.Post Surg.
Ray, J.E. LA 3rd Inf. Co.H
Ray, J.E. TX 22nd Inf. Co.E Cpl.
Ray, J.E. Brush Bn.
Ray, Jeremiah SC 15th Inf. Co.B
Ray, Jesse MS 7th Cav. Co.G Sgt.
Ray, Jesse MS 30th Inf. Co.K Cpl.
Ray, Jesse MS 31st Inf. Co.I
Ray, Jesse MO 4th Cav. Co.E
Ray, Jesse NC 1st Cav. (9th St.Troops) Co.A
Ray, Jesse NC 16th Inf. Co.H
Ray, Jesse SC Inf. 3rd Bn. Co.D
Ray, Jesse TN 12th (Green's) Cav. Co.D
Ray, Jessee MS 2nd (Davidson's) Inf. Co.G Sgt.
Ray, Jesse M. AR Cav. Crabtree's (46th) Regt.
Co.D
Ray, J.F. AL 23rd Inf. Co.B
Ray, J.F. GA 9th Inf. (St.Guards) Co.C
Ray, J.F., Jr. MS 7th Cav. Co.G
Ray, J.F., Sr. MS 7th Cav. Co.G

Ray, J.F. MS 2nd Inf. Co.C Sgt.
Ray, J.F. SC Arty. Manigault's Bn. 1st Co.B
Ray, J.F. TN 12th Inf. Co.F
Ray, J.F. TX 11th Cav. Co.K Cpl.
Ray, J.G. AL 37th Inf. Co.H
Ray, J.G. TX 15th Inf. 2nd Co.G
Ray, J.G. Bell's Co.A,CSA
Ray, J.H. MO St.Guard
Ray, J.H. NC Mallett's Bn. Co.C
Ray, J.H. SC 15th Inf. Co.B
Ray, J.H. TN 17th Inf. Co.A
Ray, J.H. TX 20th Inf. Co.F
Ray, J.H. Nitre & Min. Bureau War Dept.,CSA
Ray, J.J. AL Cav. Forrest's Regt.
Ray, J.J. AL 22nd Inf. Co.A
Ray, J.J. AR 27th Inf. Co.I
Ray, J.J. LA 17th Inf. Co.G
Ray, J.J. MS 3rd (St.Troops) Cav. Co.H
Ray, J.J. MS 14th (Cons.) Inf. Co.E
Ray, J.J. SC 2nd Arty. Co.B
Ray, J.J. TN 18th (Newsom's) Cav. Co.A
Ray, J.K. TN Cav. Nixon's Regt. Co.K
Ray, J.L. AL 18th Inf. Co.I
Ray, J.L. AL 40th Inf. Co.E,D
Ray, J.L. AL 61st Inf. Co.I
Ray, J.L. GA Lt.Arty. 12th Bn. 3rd Co.B
  Music.
Ray, J.L. TX 3rd Cav. Co.K Cpl.
Ray, J.L. VA 3rd Arty. Co.E
Ray, J.M. AL Inf. 1st Regt. Co.A
Ray, J.M. AL 20th Inf. Co.D
Ray, J.M. AR 32nd Inf. Co.E
Ray, J.M. GA 11th Cav. (St.Guards) Smith's Co.
  3rd Lt.
Ray, J.M. MS 2nd Cav. Co.I,B
Ray, J.M. MS 2nd (Davidson's) Inf. Co.A
Ray, J.M. MS 2nd (Davidson's) Inf. Co.G Sgt.
Ray, J.M. MS 39th Inf. Co.E 1st Sgt.
Ray, J.M. MO 7th Cav. Co.B
Ray, J.M. TN 9th Inf. Co.F
Ray, J.N. AL 16th Inf. Co.D
Ray, J.N. AL 31st Inf. Co.K
Ray, Jo. B. TN 16th Inf. Co.E
Ray, John AL 7th Cav. Co.I
Ray, John AL Gid Nelson Lt.Arty.
Ray, John AL 10th Inf. Co.A,H
Ray, John AL 17th Inf. Co.K
Ray, John AL 50th Inf. Co.F
Ray, John AL 59th Inf. Co.C
Ray, John AR 47th (Crandall's) Cav. Co.B
Ray, John AR 24th Inf. Co.F
Ray, John AR Inf. Hardy's Regt. Co.D
Ray, John FL 11th Inf. Co.C
Ray, John FL Conscr.
Ray, John GA 1st Inf.
Ray, John GA 30th Inf. Co.B
Ray, John GA 49th Inf. Co.K
Ray, John GA 54th Inf. Co.E
Ray, John GA 65th Inf. Co.A
Ray, John GA Phillips' Legion Co.E
Ray, John KY 10th (Johnson's) Cav. Co.A Sgt.
Ray, John LA 2nd Cav. Co.E
Ray, John LA 2nd Inf. Co.H
Ray, John LA 25th Inf. Co.H Sgt.
Ray, John LA Mil. Chalmette Regt. Co.K
Ray, John LA Sabine Res.

Ray, John MS Cav. 1st Bn. (Montgomery's)
  St.Troops Co.C
Ray, John MS 3rd (St.Troops) Cav. Co.F
Ray, John MS 6th Cav. Co.L
Ray, John MS 8th Cav. Co.E
Ray, John MS St.Cav. Perrin's Bn. Co.H
Ray, John MS Cav. Yerger's Regt. Co.F
Ray, John MO 1st N.E. Cav. Co.H
Ray, John MO Cav. Poindexter's Regt.
Ray, John MO 1st Inf. Co.E
Ray, John MO 8th Inf. Co.F
Ray, John NC 3rd Inf. Co.G
Ray, John NC 6th Inf. Co.F
Ray, John NC 6th Sr.Res. Co.H
Ray, John NC 8th Sr.Res. McLean's Co.
Ray, John NC 12th Inf. Co.A Capt.
Ray, John NC 15th Inf. Co.H
Ray, John NC 16th Inf. Co.C
Ray, John NC 26th Inf. Co.C
Ray, John NC 32nd Inf. Co.E,F Capt.
Ray, John NC 50th Inf. Co.H
Ray, John SC 3rd St.Troops Co.C Cpl.
Ray, John SC 5th St.Troops Co.H
Ray, John SC 9th Res. Co.H
Ray, John TN 24th Inf. Co.B
Ray, John TN 46th Inf. Co.A
Ray, John TN Inf. 154th Sr.Regt. Co.I
Ray, John VA 2nd Inf. Co.B Cpl.
Ray, John VA 22nd Inf. Swann's Co.
Ray, John VA 37th Inf. Co.G
Ray, John VA 57th Inf. Co.B
Ray, John VA 59th Inf. 2nd Co.K
Ray, John 1st Cherokee Mtd.Vol. 2nd Co.K
Ray, John A. AL 16th Inf. Co.C
Ray, John A. AL 50th Inf. Co.B Capt.
Ray, John A. AR 8th Cav. Co.H
Ray, John A. AR 7th Inf. Co.H Cpl.
Ray, John A. MS 6th Inf. Co.I Druggist
Ray, John A. MS 11th Inf. Co.K
Ray, John A. MO Cav. Freeman's Regt. Co.F
Ray, John A. NC 1st Cav. (9th St.Troops) Co.A
Ray, John A. NC 6th Cav. (65th St.Troops)
  Co.D,B
Ray, John A. SC 1st (McCreary's) Inf. Co.E
Ray, John A. TX 15th Cav. Co.D Sgt.
Ray, John A. VA Lt.Arty. Penick's Co.
Ray, John B. GA Inf. 2nd Bn. Co.B Sgt.
Ray, John B. NC 29th Inf. Co.B,D
Ray, John B. NC 56th Inf. Co.D
Ray, John B. NC 56th Inf. Co.E
Ray, John B. TX 16th Cav. Co.G Sgt.
Ray, John B. VA 61st Inf. Co.G
Ray, John C. AL 6th Cav. Co.K
Ray, John C. AL 5th Bn.Vol. Co.B
Ray, John C. AR 14th (Powers') Inf. Co.A
Ray, John C. MS 9th Inf. Old Co.C
Ray, John C. TN 8th Cav. Co.F
Ray, John C. TN Inf. 28th Bn. Co.C
Ray, John C. TX 1st (McCulloch's) Cav. Co.C
Ray, John C. TX 1st (Yager's) Cav. Co.H
Ray, John C. TX 10th Cav. Co.A
Ray, John C. TX 17th Cav. Co.H
Ray, John D. AL Inf. 1st Regt. Co.A
Ray, John D. AL 13th Inf. Co.D
Ray, John D. AL 44th Inf. Co.I
Ray, John D. GA 1st (Ramsey's) Inf. Co.A
Ray, John D. NC 2nd Inf. Co.I

Ray, John D. NC 56th Inf. Co.E
Ray, John D. SC 1st (Hagood's) Inf. 1st Co.A
Ray, John E. GA Phillips' Legion Co.M,L
Ray, John E. LA 31st Inf. Co.C Sgt.
Ray, John E. TN 5th Inf. 1st Co.C AQM
Ray, John E. Gen. & Staff Capt.,AQM
Ray, John F. MS 1st Lt.Arty. Co.B
Ray, John F. MS 34th Inf. Co.K
Ray, John F. MO 3rd Inf. Co.D
Ray, John F. TN 13th Inf. Co.D,A
Ray, John F. VA Cav. 46th Bn. Co.F
Ray, John G. AL 6th Cav. Co.K
Ray, John H. FL Cav. 3rd Bn. Co.B
Ray, John H. GA 10th Inf.
Ray, John H. GA Inf. 14th Bn. (St.Guards) Co.E
  2nd Lt.
Ray, John H. KY 5th Mtd.Inf. Co.A
Ray, John H. KY 7th Mtd.Inf. Co.K
Ray, John H. MS 25th Inf. Co.C Cpl.
Ray, John H. NC 1st Cav. (9th St.Troops) Co.A
Ray, John H. NC Cav. 5th Bn. Co.D
Ray, John H. NC 16th Inf. Co.C Sgt.
Ray, John H. NC 26th Inf. Co.E
Ray, John H. NC 47th Inf. Co.E
Ray, John H. 15th Conf.Cav. Co.D
Ray, John H.Z. MS 2nd Inf. Co.B Cpl.
Ray, John J. GA 49th Inf. Co.B Cpl.
Ray, John J. MS 14th Inf. Co.H
Ray, John J. NC 6th Cav. (65th St.Troops) Co.C
Ray, John J. NC Cav. 7th Bn. Co.C
Ray, John J. NC 26th Inf. Co.B
Ray, John J.M. GA Cav. 29th Bn. Co.E
Ray, John K. NC 3rd Cav. (41st St.Troops)
  Co.D 1st Lt.
Ray, John K. NC 33rd Mil. Ray's Co. 1st Lt.
Ray, John L. GA 49th Inf. Co.C Sgt.
Ray, John L. LA 12th Inf. Co.A
Ray, John L. NC 39th Inf. Co.H
Ray, John M. GA 41st Inf. Co.I
Ray, John M. MS 10th Inf. Co.K Sgt.
Ray, John M. NC 1st Cav. (9th St.Troops) Co.A
Ray, John M. NC Cav. 5th Bn. Co.D
Ray, John M. NC 6th Cav. (65th St.Troops)
  Co.D
Ray, John M.J. KY 10th Cav. Co.A
Ray, John P. FL 8th Inf. Co.E
Ray, John P. GA 38th Inf. Co.D
Ray, John P. NC 29th Inf. Co.D
Ray, John Q. NC 6th Cav. (65th St.Troops)
  Co.C
Ray, John R. AL 59th Inf. Co.F
Ray, John R. AL 2nd Bn. Hilliard's Legion Vol.
  Co.A
Ray, John R. AL Cp. of Instr. Talladega
Ray, John R. GA 16th Inf. Co.C Sgt.
Ray, John R. GA 40th Inf. Co.E
Ray, John R. GA Cobb's Legion Co.H
Ray, John R. KY 2nd (Woodward's) Cav. Co.G
  Sgt.
Ray, John R. MS 24th Inf. Co.L
Ray, John R. NC Hvy.Arty. 1st Bn. Co.A
Ray, John S. AR 31st Inf. Co.B
Ray, John S. LA Cav. Cole's Co.
Ray, John S. MS 25th Inf. Co.C Sgt.
Ray, John S. MS 30th Inf. Co.D 1st Sgt.
Ray, John S. NC 1st Cav. (9th St.Troops) Co.I
Ray, John S. NC 6th Inf. Co.F

Ray, John S. NC 38th Inf. Co.K 1st Lt.
Ray, John S. TN 28th Inf. Co.I 2nd Lt.
Ray, John Smith NC 33rd Mil. Ray's Co.
Ray, John T. AL 46th Inf. Co.E
Ray, John T. GA Inf. 10th Bn. Co.A
Ray, John T. GA 15th Inf. Co.D
Ray, John T. GA Inf. 18th Bn. Co.C
Ray, John T. NC 15th Inf. Co.H
Ray, John T. SC 1st (Butler's) Inf. Co.A Cpl.
Ray, John T. SC 13th Inf. Co.A
Ray, John T. TX 3rd Cav. Co.B
Ray, John T. TX 37th Cav. Co.H
Ray, John T.V. TX 37th Cav. Co.G
Ray, John W. AL 14th Inf. Co.K
Ray, John W. AL 24th Inf. Co.E Capt.
Ray, John W. AR 7th Inf. Co.C
Ray, John W. GA 36th (Broyles') Inf. Co.K
Ray, John W. NC Cav. 5th Bn. Co.D
Ray, John W. NC 6th Cav. (65th St.Troops)
    Co.B,D
Ray, John W. NC 2nd Inf. Co.A
Ray, John W. NC 13th Inf. Co.B
Ray, John W. SC 13th Inf. Co.B
Ray, John W. TN 54th Inf. Co.H
Ray, John W. TX 10th Cav. Co.C
Ray, John W. 4th Conf.Inf. Co.F
Ray, Jonathan AR 6th Inf. Co.B 2nd Lt.
Ray, Jonathan 1st Conf.Eng.Troops Co.H Artif.
Ray, Jonathan A. AL 7th Cav. Co.M
Ray, Jones D. TX 37th Cav. Co.K,D
Ray, Joseph GA 19th Inf. Co.A
Ray, Joseph GA Phillips' Legion Co.E
Ray, Joseph GA Smith's Legion Co.C
Ray, Joseph KY 6th Mtd.Inf. Co.D Cpl.
Ray, Joseph KY 8th Mtd.Inf. Co.D Cpl.
Ray, Joseph LA 3rd (Harrison's) Cav. Co.K
Ray, Joseph MS 2nd Inf. Co.D
Ray, Joseph SC 1st (Hagood's) Inf. 2nd Co.F
Ray, Joseph TN 16th Inf. Co.G
Ray, Joseph TN 48th (Nixon's) Inf. Co.C
Ray, Joseph TN 48th (Voorhies') Inf. Co.F
Ray, Joseph TN 50th Inf. Co.F,H
Ray, Joseph TX 1st (McCulloch's) Cav. Co.G
Ray, Joseph VA 20th Cav. Co.I
Ray, Joseph VA 51st Inf. Co.D
Ray, Joseph Conf.Cav. 6th Bn. Co.E
Ray, Joseph A. NC 34th Inf. Co.D,K
Ray, Joseph A. TN 5th Inf. Co.A
Ray, Joseph B. MS 23rd Inf. Co.H
Ray, Joseph G. TX Cav. 8th (Taylor's) Bn. Co.A
Ray, Joseph H. GA 23rd Inf. Co.F
Ray, Joseph J. AL 11th Inf. Co.G
Ray, Joseph J. TN 4th Inf. Co.I
Ray, Joseph L. NC Cav. 5th Bn. Co.A
Ray, Joseph L. NC 16th Inf. Co.C
Ray, Joseph M. NC 29th Inf. Co.D
Ray, Joseph S. MS 34th Inf. Co.H
Ray, Joseph S. TN 37th Inf. Co.A
Ray, Jos. T. AL 22nd Inf. Co.C
Ray, Joseph T. NC Cav. 5th Bn. Co.A
Ray, Joseph T. NC 64th Inf. Co.D
Ray, Joshua MO Cav. Freeman's Regt. Co.L
Ray, J.P. AR Inf. Cocke's Regt. Co.C
Ray, J.P. GA Lt.Arty. 12th Bn. 3rd Co.C
Ray, J.P. VA 26th Cav. Co.F
Ray, J.P. Eng.,CSA
Ray, J.P.M. MS 4th Inf. Co.K

Ray, J.R. AL Cp. of Instr. Talladega
Ray, J.R. AR 1st (Monroe's) Cav. Co.A
Ray, J.R. GA 4th Cav. (St.Guards) Deadwyler's
    Co.
Ray, J.R. KY 3rd Mtd.Inf. Co.G
Ray, J.R. MS 22nd Inf. Co.I
Ray, J.R. MO 11th Inf. Co.E
Ray, J.R. TN 42nd Inf. Co.A
Ray, J.R. TX 17th Inf. Co.C
Ray, J.R. TX 19th Inf. Co.H Sgt.
Ray, J.S. GA 41st Inf. Co.I Cpl.
Ray, J.S. KY 7th Cav. Co.K
Ray, J.S. KY 7th Mtd.Inf. Co.K
Ray, J.S. NC 7th Sr.Res. Bradshaw's Co.
Ray, J.S. TN 28th (Cons.) Inf. Co.I 2nd Lt.
Ray, J.S. TX St.Troops Hampton's Co.
Ray, J.T. AL 31st Inf. Co.F,E
Ray, J.T. AL 41st Inf. Co.F
Ray, J.T. GA 22nd Inf. Co.D
Ray, J.T. KY 7th Cav. Co.B Sgt.
Ray, J.T. LA 27th Inf. Co.G
Ray, J.T. MS 2nd Cav. Co.I
Ray, J.T. MS Inf. 1st Bn. Ray's Co. Sgt.
Ray, J.T. MS Inf. 2nd Bn. Co.K
Ray, J.T. MS 31st Inf. Co.K
Ray, J.T. MS 48th Inf. Co.K
Ray, J.T. SC 3rd Inf. Co.D 2nd Lt.
Ray, J.W. AL 2nd Cav. Co.B
Ray, J.W. AL 25th Inf. Co.C
Ray, J.W. AR 2nd Cav. Co.G
Ray, J.W. AR 5th Inf. Co.H
Ray, J.W. MS 5th Cav. Co.C
Ray, J.W. MS Cav. 6th Bn. Prince's Co.
Ray, J.W. MO 9th Inf. Co.B
Ray, J.W. MO Inf. Clark's Regt. Co.A
Ray, J.W. MO St.Guard
Ray, J.W. TN Cav. 12th Bn. (Day's) Co.C
Ray, J.W. TX 4th Cav. Co.D
Ray, J.W. TX 9th Cav. Co.C Cpl.
Ray, J.W. 2nd Conf.Eng.Troops Co.A
Ray, J.Y. NC 16th Inf. Co.C
Ray, J.Y. Inf. Bailey's Cons.Regt. Co.B
Ray, J.Y. TX Granbury's Cons.Brig. Co.C
Ray, J.Y. TX 7th Inf. Co.F,A
Ray, Kelsie NC 29th Inf. Co.B
Ray, L. MS Cav.
Ray, L.A. TN 44th (Cons.) Inf. Co.G
Ray, Lauchlin NC 33rd Mil. Ray's Co. Capt.
Ray, Lauchlin NC 38th Inf. Co.K
Ray, Lavender GA 1st Cav. Co.H
Ray, Lavender R. Gen. & Staff Lt.,A.Ord.Off.
Ray, L.B. MO Cav. Schnabel's Bn. Co.F
Ray, L.C. LA Inf. 4th Bn. Co.B
Ray, L.C. LA Inf. Pelican Regt. Co.F
Ray, L.D. TN 28th Cav. Co.G Capt.
Ray, Leander T. NC 58th Inf. Co.C
Ray, Lee T. TN 19th Inf. Co.D
Ray, Lenard R. GA 4th Inf. Co.B
Ray, Leonadas NC 1st Cav. (9th St.Troops)
    Co.K
Ray, Leonard L. MS 4th Inf. Co.K
Ray, Leonidas TN 28th Inf. Co.I Music.
Ray, Leroy TN 48th (Nixon's) Inf. Co.F
Ray, Leroy TN 53rd Inf. Co.I
Ray, Leroy C. NC 58th Inf. Co.C
Ray, Levi T. MS 26th Inf. Co.G
Ray, Lewis AL 32nd Inf. Co.A

Ray, Lewis SC 1st St.Troops Co.K
Ray, Lewis TN 29th Inf. Co.C
Ray, Lewis A. TN Inf. 55th (McKoin's) Bn.
    Duggan's Co.
Ray, L.L., Jr. MS 4th Inf. Co.K
Ray, L.M. MS Inf. 2nd St.Troops
Ray, Lochlin Sig.Corps,CSA
Ray, Luke R. AR 37th Inf. Co.I Cpl.
Ray, Luney TN 35th Inf. Co.G
Ray, M. GA Lt.Arty. Ritter's Co.
Ray, M. LA 28th (Thomas') Inf.
Ray, M. NC Allen's Co. (Loc.Def.)
Ray, M.A. AR 19th (Dockery's) Inf. Co.G
Ray, Madison TN Cav. 9th Bn. (Gantt's) Co.F
Ray, Madison TN 48th (Nixon's) Inf. Co.F Cpl.
Ray, Madison TN 54th Inf. Co.A
Ray, Madison VA 37th Inf. Co.I,G
Ray, Major W. AL 31st Inf. Co.E
Ray, Malachi B. AL Inf. 1st Regt. Co.B
Ray, Malcom, Jr. NC 35th Inf. Co.C 2nd Lt.
Ray, Malcom, Sr. NC 35th Inf. Co.C
Ray, Marcus D.L. KY 2nd Mtd.Inf. Co.A
Ray, Marion MD Arty. 3rd Btty.
Ray, Marion MS 7th Cav. Co.G Sgt.
Ray, Marion MS 2nd (Davidson's) Inf. Co.G 1st
    Cpl.
Ray, Marion NC 3rd Inf. Co.G
Ray, Marion TN 37th Inf. Co.K
Ray, Marion A. AL 63rd Inf. Co.A
Ray, Mark TN 84th Inf. Co.B
Ray, Martin GA 52nd Inf. Co.D
Ray, Martin TN 1st Inf. Co.D
Ray, Martin L. AR 3rd Cav. Co.H
Ray, Martin L. NC 5th Cav. (63rd St.Troops)
    Co.A
Ray, Martin V. TN 1st Hvy.Arty.
Ray, M.E. AL 63rd Inf.
Ray, Meek MS 28th Cav. Co.H
Ray, Michael AL Gorff's Co. (Mobile Pulaski
    Rifles)
Ray, Michael VA 27th Inf. Co.B Cpl.
Ray, Middleton SC 6th Cav. Co.H
Ray, Middleton SC 7th Res. Co.G
Ray, Middleton SC Inf. Holcombe Legion Co.I
    1st Lt.
Ray, Milton S. TN 37th Inf. Co.A 1st Lt.
Ray, M.L. TN 28th (Cons.) Inf. Co.H
Ray, M.L. TN 84th Inf. Co.D
Ray, Monroe MS 7th Cav. Co.C
Ray, Monroe M. GA 40th Inf. Co.E
Ray, Montraville NC 16th Inf. Co.C
Ray, Moses AL 12th Cav. Co.D Sgt.
Ray, Moses TX 19th Inf. Co.I Cpl.
Ray, Moses J. MO 3rd Inf. Co.D
Ray, M.P. AR 14th (Powers') Inf. Co.C
Ray, M.R. AR 19th (Dockery's) Inf. Co.K
Ray, M.V. LA 3rd Inf. Co.I
Ray, M.V. MS 4th Inf. Co.K Sgt.
Ray, M.V. TN 27th Inf. Co.B
Ray, M.V. TX 14th Inf. Co.I
Ray, N. TN 22nd Cav. Co.F
Ray, N. NC 50th Inf. Co.A
Ray, N.A. GA Cav. 29th Bn. Co.E
Ray, N.A. NC 3rd Jr.Res. Co.H
Ray, Nathan GA Cav. 16th Bn. (St.Guards) Co.C
Ray, Nathan GA 7th Inf. Co.H
Ray, Nathan GA 65th Inf. Co.B

Ray, Nathan B. NC 16th Inf. Co.C
Ray, Nathaniel MS 10th Cav. Co.B,E
Ray, Nathaniel MS 33rd Inf. Co.A
Ray, Nathaniel B. MO Cav. Snider's Bn. Co.C Sgt.
Ray, Neal SC Inf. 7th Bn. (Enfield Rifles) Co.D
Ray, Neill NC 33rd Mil. Ray's Co.
Ray, Neill NC 38th Inf. Co.K
Ray, Neill A. NC 7th Bn.Jr.Res. Co.A
Ray, Neill A. NC 26th Inf. Co.H
Ray, Neill W. NC 6th Inf. Co.D Capt.
Ray, Nelson TN 25th Inf. Co.D,B
Ray, Nelson TN 28th (Cons.) Inf. Co.K
Ray, Nelson TN 84th Inf. Co.F
Ray, Nelson 1st Conf.Inf. 2nd Co.K
Ray, Newton NC 42nd Inf. Co.K
Ray, Newton F. MS 43rd Inf. Co.D
Ray, Newton M. GA 65th Inf. Co.A
Ray, N.F. MS 5th Cav. Co.I
Ray, Niven NC 31st Inf. Co.I Cpl.
Ray, Nivin NC 50th Inf. Co.H
Ray, N.J. TN 24th Inf. Co.A
Ray, N.M. GA 63rd Inf. Co.A
Ray, N.M. GA Smith's Legion Co.B
Ray, N.M. NC Mil. Clark's Sp.Bn. Co.D Lt.
Ray, Oliver P. AL 61st Inf. Co.H
Ray, Oliver P. TX 16th Cav. Co.G
Ray, Otey VA 2nd Inf.Loc.Def. Co.K
Ray, Otey VA Inf. 2nd Bn.Loc.Def. Co.B
Ray, Ovide LA 18th Inf. Co.C
Ray, Ozias TN 37th Inf. Co.G
Ray, P. LA 2nd Cav. Co.E
Ray, P.A. LA Pointe Coupee Arty. Prov.Capt.
Ray, Patrick TN 52nd Inf.
Ray, Patrick VA 10th Cav. Co.A
Ray, Patrick VA Inf. 1st Bn. Co.D
Ray, Patrick W. NC 39th Inf. Co.H
Ray, Payton VA 57th Inf. Co.B
Ray, P.B. NC 21st Inf. Co.L Sgt.
Ray, Perry AL 26th (O'Neal's) Inf. Co.D
Ray, Perry TX 22nd Cav. Co.D,I
Ray, Perry TX Cav. Baird's Regt. Co.D,C
Ray, Perry TX 22nd Inf. Co.I
Ray, Peter AR 7th Cav. Co.K Sgt.
Ray, Peter TN 13th (Gore's) Cav. Co.F
Ray, Peter TN 8th Inf. Co.F
Ray, Peter A. NC 2nd Cav. (19th St.Troops) Co.K Black.
Ray, Peter L. MS 33rd Inf. Co.K
Ray, Pharoah J. NC Cav. 5th Bn. Co.D
Ray, Philip SC Inf. Holcombe Legion Co.A
Ray, Phillip S. TN 25th Inf. Co.B Cpl.
Ray, P.L. MS 2nd Cav. Co.A
Ray, Pleasant TN Cav. Welcker's Bn.
Ray, Polk TN 13th (Gore's) Cav. Co.C
Ray, Porter T. MS 4th Inf. Co.K
Ray, P.T. AL 18th Inf. Co.I
Ray, P.T. GA 2nd Inf. Co.H
Ray, R. AL 10th Inf. Co.A
Ray, R. AR 13th Inf. Co.B 2nd Sgt.
Ray, R.A. GA Floyd Legion (St.Guards) Co.B
Ray, R.A. LA 2nd Cav. Co.E
Ray, R.A. MS 41st Inf. Co.B
Ray, R.A. TX 5th Inf. Co.G
Ray, Randal M. TN 18th Inf. Co.E 1st Lt.
Ray, Randolph TN 5th Inf. 1st Co.C, Co.A
Ray, Ransom G. AL 6th Inf. Co.L

Ray, R.B. AL Cav. Forrest's Regt.
Ray, R.B. TN 18th (Newsom's) Cav. Co.A
Ray, R.B. TN 19th & 20th (Cons.) Cav. Co.C
Ray, R.C. AR 8th Inf. New Co.K
Ray, R.C. TN 46th Inf. Co.D
Ray, Reilly AL 27th Inf. Co.I
Ray, Reuben KY 5th Mtd.Inf. Co.G
Ray, Reuben M. GA 39th Inf. Co.D,K Cpl.
Ray, R.F. AL 38th Inf. Co.E
Ray, R.F. SC 15th Inf. Co.B
Ray, R.F. SC 18th Inf. Co.C Sgt.
Ray, R.F. TN 23rd Inf. 2nd Co.F
Ray, R.H. TX 8th Cav. Co.I
Ray, R.H. TX Arty. (St.Troops) Good's Co.
Ray, Rice GA 1st (Symons') Res. Co.I
Ray, Richard AR 19th (Dawson's) Inf. Co.K
Ray, Richard KY 1st (Butler's) Cav. Co.A
Ray, Richard MS 13th Inf. Co.E
Ray, Richard NC 5th Sr.Res. Co.H
Ray, Richard NC 54th Inf. Co.G
Ray, Richard H.L. MS 10th Inf. Old Co.G, New Co.H 1st Lt.
Ray, Right TN 2nd (Walker's) Inf. Co.B
Ray, Riley H. NC 60th Inf. Co.D
Ray, Ritton NC 3rd Bn.Sr.Res. Durham's Co.
Ray, Ritton D. NC 15th Inf. Co.H
Ray, R.L. MS 2nd (Davidson's) Inf. Co.G Lt.
Ray, R.L. MS 10th Inf. New Co.K 1st Sgt.
Ray, R.L. SC 3rd Inf. Co.D 1st Sgt.
Ray, Robert AL 4th Res. Co.E
Ray, Robert AL 23rd Inf. Co.D
Ray, Robert AR 1st (Crawford's) Cav. Co.B
Ray, Robert AR 30th Inf. Co.H 1st Sgt.
Ray, Robert GA 12th Cav. Co.K
Ray, Robert KY 2nd Cav.
Ray, Robert LA 3rd (Harrison's) Cav. Co.A
Ray, Robert MS 11th Inf. Co.K
Ray, Robert NC Walker's Bn. Thomas' Legion Co.A
Ray, Robert TN Cav. Clark's Ind.Co.
Ray, Robert TN 60th Mtd.Inf. Co.E
Ray, Robert TX 20th Cav. Co.D Sgt.
Ray, Robert 3rd Conf.Eng.Troops Co.D Artif.
Ray, Robert A. AL 22nd Inf. Co.C
Ray, Robert A. GA 4th Res. Co.K
Ray, Robert A. GA 38th Inf. Co.D Sgt.
Ray, Robert A. MS 19th Inf. Co.G
Ray, Robert C. Gen. & Staff, Medical Dept. Surg.
Ray, Robert F. MS 2nd St.Cav. Co.F
Ray, Robert F. MS St.Cav. 2nd Bn. (Harris') Co.C,L
Ray, Robert H. TX 21st Cav. Co.H
Ray, Robert J. TX 15th Cav. Co.E
Ray, Robert M. VA 14th Cav. Co.M Sr.2nd Lt.
Ray, Robert M. VA Cav. 36th Bn. Co.B 1st Lt.
Ray, Robert P. TN 34th Inf. Co.D Cpl.
Ray, Robert S. FL 6th Inf. Co.F
Ray, Robert T. TX Cav. Morgan's Regt. Co.B
Ray, Ross NC 6th Cav. (65th St.Troops) Co.A
Ray, Ross SC 5th St.Troops Co.G
Ray, R.P. GA 2nd Res. Co.A
Ray, R.R. GA 7th Inf. (St.Guards) Co.L
Ray, R.T. AL 47th Inf. Co.E Cpl.
Ray, R.T. SC 13th Inf. Co.A Cpl.
Ray, Russell B. MS 4th Inf. Co.K
Ray, R.Y. AL 14th Inf. Co.F

Ray, R.Y. AR 19th (Dockery's) Inf. Co.H
Ray, S. AL Cav. Hardie's Bn.Res. S.D. McClellan's Co.
Ray, S. AL 16th Inf. Co.H
Ray, S. AR Mil. Louis' Co.
Ray, S. GA Lt.Arty. (Arsenal Btty.) Hudson's Co.
Ray, S. GA 5th Inf. Co.D
Ray, S. GA Inf. 27th Bn. Co.A
Ray, S. GA Inf. (Loc.Def.) Hamlet's Co.
Ray, S. Conf.Lt.Arty. Richardson's Bn. Co.A
Ray, S.A. AL 2nd Inf. Co.A
Ray, Samuel AL 62nd Inf. Co.A
Ray, Samuel MO 9th Inf. Co.B
Ray, Samuel MO Inf. Clark's Regt. Co.A
Ray, Samuel NC 1st Cav. (9th St.Troops) Co.A Black.
Ray, Samuel TN 32nd Inf. Co.B
Ray, Samuel TN Inf. 154th Sr.Regt. Co.I
Ray, Samuel C. NC 29th Inf. Co.D
Ray, Samuel F. TN 60th Mtd.Inf. Co.K
Ray, Samuel H. VA 2nd Inf. Co.B 2nd Lt.
Ray, Samuel J. SC 18th Inf. Co.C 1st Lt.
Ray, Samuel L. TX 6th Cav. Co.C
Ray, Samuel M. MS 24th Inf. Co.L
Ray, Samuel P. NC 16th Inf. Co.C
Ray, Samuel T. AL 2nd Bn. Hilliard's Legion Vol. Co.C
Ray, Samuel W. NC 2nd Jr.Res. Co.B
Ray, Samuel W. TN 1st Cav. Co.I
Ray, S.B. AL 13th Bn.Part.Rangers Co.D
Ray, S.B. AL 56th Part.Rangers Co.H
Ray, S.B. AR 2nd Inf. Co.K
Ray, S.B. MS 5th Cav. Co.I
Ray, S.B. MS 1st (King's) Inf. (St.Troops) Co.H
Ray, S.C. MS 2nd Cav. Co.A
Ray, S.D. VA Inf. 26th Bn. Co.I
Ray, S.E. GA Inf. 1st Loc.Troops (Augusta) Co.F
Ray, S.F. FL Cav. 3rd Bn. Co.B
Ray, S.F. LA 27th Inf. Co.G
Ray, S.F. LA Res.Corps Doyle's Co.
Ray, S.F. 15th Conf.Cav. Co.D
Ray, S.G. SC 17th Inf. Co.H,F 1st Lt.
Ray, S.G. Gen. & Staff Capt.,ACS
Ray, Sidney TN 22nd (Barteau's) Cav. Co.D
Ray, Sidney George GA 3rd Cav. Co.G
Ray, Silas M. NC 29th Inf. Co.H
Ray, Silas R. AL 1st Regt. Co.A
Ray, Simon SC 10th Inf. Co.C
Ray, Sion VA Lt.Arty. Penick's Co.
Ray, Sion W. AL 2nd Bn. Hilliard's Legion Vol. Co.A
Ray, S.J. TN 20th (Russell's) Cav. AQM
Ray, S.J. TN 46th Inf. ACS
Ray, S.L. TN 23rd Inf. 2nd Co.F
Ray, S.O. MS 41st Inf. Co.B
Ray, Solomon AL 28th Inf. Co.F
Ray, Solomon TX 22d Cav. Co.B
Ray, S.P. TN 34th Inf. 2nd Co.C
Ray, S.P.C. GA Inf. 25th Bn. (Prov.Guard) Co.G
Ray, Spencer GA Inf. 14th Bn. (St.Guards) Co.E
Ray, Spottswood D. VA 4th Inf. Co.C
Ray, S.T. AL Res. Desheay's Co.
Ray, Stephen AL 12th Inf. Co.C
Ray, Stephen B. AL 22nd Inf. Co.G

Ray, Stephen B. AL 39th Inf. Co.G Cpl.
Ray, Stephen J. AL 16th Inf. Co.C
Ray, S.U. GA 23rd Inf. Co.E
Ray, S.Y.L. 8th (Wade's) Conf.Cav. Co.H 1st Lt.
Ray, Sylvester TN 33rd Inf. Co.G
Ray, Sylvester 3rd Conf.Eng.Troops Co.B
Ray, Sylvester Eng.Dept. Polk's Corps A. of TN Sap. & Min. Co.,CSA
Ray, T.A. TX 14th Inf. Co.I
Ray, T.B. NC 3rd Bn.Sr.Res. Durham's Co.
Ray, T.C. TX 22nd Inf. Co.F
Ray, T.F. SC 7th Res. Co.C
Ray, T.G. MS 26th Inf. Co.G
Ray, T.H. AL 31st Inf. Co.C
Ray, T.H. GA Lt.Arty. 12th Bn. 3rd Co.C Cpl.
Ray, Thaddeus A. NC 17th Inf. (1st Org.) Co.F Cpl.
Ray, Thaddeus A. NC 17th Inf. (2nd Org.) Co.E Sgt.
Ray, Theo. AL Gid Nelson Lt.Arty.
Ray, Theophilus H. AL 18th Inf. Co.C
Ray, Thomas AL 1st Cav. 1st Co.C
Ray, Thomas AL 18th Inf. Co.D
Ray, Thomas AL 31st Inf. Co.G
Ray, Thomas AL 41st Inf. Co.B
Ray, Thomas AL City Guards Lockett's Co.
Ray, Thomas GA 65th Inf. Co.A
Ray, Thomas GA Smith's Legion Co.B
Ray, Thomas KY 3rd Mtd.Inf. Co.I Sgt.
Ray, Thomas MS Inf. 2nd Bn. Co.F
Ray, Thomas NC 6th Inf. Co.F
Ray, Thomas NC 15th Inf. Co.B
Ray, Thomas NC 56th Inf. Co.M 2nd Lt.
Ray, Thomas SC 2nd Arty. Co.B 1st Sgt.
Ray, Thomas SC Horse Arty. (Washington Arty.) Vol. Hart's Co.
Ray, Thomas TN 13th (Gore's) Cav. Co.F
Ray, Thomas TN 3rd (Clack's) Inf. Co.K
Ray, Thomas TN 8th Inf. Co.F
Ray, Thomas TN 35th Inf. Co.L
Ray, Thomas TN 36th Inf. Co.L
Ray, Thomas TN 84th Inf. Co.G
Ray, Thomas TX 4th Cav. Co.E
Ray, Thomas TX 1st Hvy.Arty. Co.F Music.
Ray, Thomas TX 4th Inf. (St.Troops) Co.B Music.
Ray, Thomas B. AR 17th (Lemoyne's) Inf. Co.H 3rd Lt.
Ray, Thomas B. AR 21st Inf. Co.G 3rd Lt.
Ray, Thomas B. NC 29th Inf. Co.K Sgt.
Ray, Thomas C. MS 10th Inf. Old Co.H
Ray, Thomas C. NC Cav. 5th Bn. Co.D 2nd Lt.
Ray, Thomas C. NC 24th Inf. Co.K Music.
Ray, Thomas C. TN 37th Inf. Co.A
Ray, Thomas E. AL 4th Inf. Co.E
Ray, Thomas G. MS 19th Inf. Co.K
Ray, Thomas H. GA 7th Inf. Co.K Sgt.
Ray, Thomas H. MS 1st Lt.Arty. Co.B
Ray, Thomas J. AL 41st Inf. Co.I Cpl.
Ray, Thomas J. AR 8th Cav. Co.H
Ray, Thomas J. AR 7th Inf. Co.H
Ray, Thomas J., Jr. GA 3rd Cav. (St.Guards) Co.A
Ray, Thomas J. GA Siege Arty. 28th Bn. Co.C
Ray, Thomas J. MS 3rd Inf. Co.C
Ray, Thomas J. MS 23rd Inf. Co.C

Ray, Thomas J. MS 34th Inf. Co.H
Ray, Thomas J. TN 11th Cav.
Ray, Thomas J. TN 12th (Green's) Cav. Co.B 2nd Lt.
Ray, Thomas J. TN 2nd (Robison's) Inf. Co.E
Ray, Thomas L. NC 6th Inf. Co.K
Ray, Thomas M. GA 1st (Olmstead's) Inf. Stiles' Co.
Ray, Thomas M. GA Inf. 18th Bn. Co.B
Ray, Thomas N. GA 22nd Inf. Co.K
Ray, Thomas N. NC 3rd Inf. Co.I
Ray, Thomas P. MS 48th Inf. Co.F
Ray, Thomas R. LA 12th Inf. Co.K
Ray, Thomas R. TN 37th Inf. Co.K
Ray, Thomas S. AR 23rd Inf. Co.I Cpl.
Ray, Thomas S. AR 30th Inf. Co.O,I
Ray, Thomas S. VA Lt.Arty. Penick's Co.
Ray, Thomas W. NC 29th Inf. Co.D
Ray, Th. R. LA 4th Eng.Troops Co.I
Ray, T.I. LA 22nd Inf. Co.F
Ray, T.J. AL 44th Inf. Co.I Cpl.
Ray, T.J. GA 1st Reg. Co.B
Ray, T.J., Jr. GA Inf. 9th Bn. Co.A
Ray, T.J. GA 16th Inf. Co.C
Ray, T.J. MS 8th Cav. Co.F
Ray, T.J. MS Inf. 3rd Bn. (St.Troops) Co.F
Ray, T.J. MS 41st Inf. Co.L
Ray, T.J. SC 3rd Inf. Co.D
Ray, T.J. TN 6th (Wheeler's) Cav. Co.L
Ray, T.J. TN 23rd Inf. 2nd Co.F
Ray, T.J. TX Cav. Waller's Regt. Co.B
Ray, T.L. AL 15th Inf. Co.H
Ray, T.L. GA Cav. (St.Guards) Bond's Co.
Ray, T.M. MO Cav. Schnabel's Bn. Co.F
Ray, T.M. TN 17th Inf. Co.F
Ray, T.M. 4th Conf.Inf. Co.B
Ray, T. Murphy NC 27th Inf. Co.G
Ray, Troy L. TX 1st Hvy.Arty. Co.K 1st Lt.
Ray, Tryon TX 11th (Spaight's) Bn.Vol. Co.E
Ray, Turner MS 2nd Inf. Co.I
Ray, T.W. GA Lt.Arty. 12th Bn. 3rd Co.B Music.
Ray, T.W. SC Inf. Holcombe Legion Co.E
Ray, T.W. TN 46th Inf. Co.D
Ray, Tyler NC Cav. 5th Bn. Co.A
Ray, V.P. AL 61st Inf. Co.H
Ray, W. LA 13th Bn. (Part.Rangers) Co.B
Ray, W. MS Arty. (Wesson Arty.) Kittrell's Co.
Ray, W.A. AL 31st Inf. Co.D Cpl.
Ray, W.A. MS 5th Cav. Co.I
Ray, W.A. TN 45th Inf. Co.D
Ray, W.A. TX Cav. 1st Regt.St.Troops Co.G
Ray, Warren H. NC 39th Inf. Co.H
Ray, Warren S. MS 9th Inf. Old Co.C
Ray, Warren S. TN Inf. 23rd Bn. Co.C
Ray, Washington LA 18th Inf. Co.B
Ray, Washington MS 7th Cav. Co.C
Ray, Washington TN 25th Inf. Co.B Sgt.
Ray, W.B. AL Cav. Musgrove's Bn. Co.B
Ray, W.B. AL 3rd Inf. Co.L
Ray, W.B. AL 14th Inf. Co.F
Ray, W.B. TN 12th (Cons.) Inf. Co.F
Ray, W.B. TN 22nd Inf. Co.D
Ray, W.B. Trans-MS Conf.Cav. 1st Bn. Co.D
Ray, W.C. KY 7th Mtd.Inf. Co.K
Ray, W.C. MS 28th Cav. Co.A
Ray, W.C. MS Inf. 3rd Bn. Co.I

Ray, W.D. AL 7th Inf. Co.F 1st Sgt.
Ray, W.D. AL 31st Inf. Co.I
Ray, W.D. AR 6th Inf. Co.B
Ray, W.D. AR 33rd Inf. Co.G
Ray, W.D. LA 17th Inf. Co.E Cpl.
Ray, W.E. GA 11th Cav. Co.A
Ray, W.E. GA Inf. 14th Bn. (St.Guards) Co.E
Ray, W.E. GA 16th Inf. Co.C
Ray, W.E. GA 45th Inf. Co.E
Ray, W.E. MS 28th Cav. Co.A
Ray, W.E. MS Inf. 2nd Bn. Co.K
Ray, W.E. MS 48th Inf. Co.K
Ray, W.E. 8th (Wade's) Conf.Cav. Co.F
Ray, W.F. AR 1st Mtd.Rifles Co.I
Ray, W.F. NC 5th Cav. (63rd St.Troops)
Ray, W.F. TN 5th Inf. 2nd Co.K 1st Sgt.
Ray, W.G. LA 19th Inf. Co.C
Ray, W.H. AL 4th Cav. Co.A
Ray, W.H. AL 7th Cav. Co.D
Ray, W.H. GA 46th Inf. Co.B
Ray, W.H. KY 2nd Cav. Co.C
Ray, W.H. MS 28th Cav. Co.A Capt.
Ray, W.H. MS 28th Cav. Co.A
Ray, W.H. MO Lt.Arty. 2nd Field Btty.
Ray, W.H. SC 1st Cav. Co.B
Ray, W.H. SC 13th Inf. Co.E
Ray, W.H. TN 18th (Newsom's) Cav. Co.A
Ray, W.H. TN 19th & 20th (Cons.) Cav. Co.C
Ray, W.H. TN 27th Inf. Co.B
Ray, W.H. VA 2nd Cav. Co.D
Ray, W.H.H. GA 32nd Inf. Co.I
Ray, W.H.H. SC 13th Inf. Co.A
Ray, Wilbern NC 6th Cav. (65th St.Troops) Co.A,E
Ray, Wilberne NC Cav. 7th Bn. Co.A
Ray, Wiley F. MS 1st Lt.Arty. Co.B
Ray, Wiley P. NC 14th Inf. Co.E
Ray, Wiley R. NC 39th Inf. Co.H
Ray, William AL Inf. 1st Regt. Co.A
Ray, William AL 3rd Res. Co.I
Ray, William AL 4th Res. 1st Co.D
Ray, Wm. AL 36th Inf. Co.D
Ray, William AL 41st Inf. Co.D
Ray, William AR 1st Vol. Co.C Cpl.
Ray, William AR 5th Inf. Co.H
Ray, William AR 18th Inf. Co.H
Ray, William GA 11th Cav. Co.H
Ray, William GA Inf. 4th Bn. (St.Guards) Co.B
Ray, William GA 43rd Inf. Co.C
Ray, William GA 47th Inf. Co.F
Ray, William GA 49th Inf. Co.B
Ray, William KY 10th (Johnson's) Cav. New Co.F
Ray, William LA 1st Hvy.Arty. (Reg.) Co.A
Ray, William LA 19th Inf. Co.B
Ray, William LA 28th (Thomas') Inf.
Ray, William LA 31st Inf. Co.C
Ray, William MS 5th Cav. Co.I Sgt.
Ray, William MS 18th Cav. Co.I
Ray, William MS Cav. Davenport's Bn. (St.Troops) Co.A
Ray, William MS 1st Lt.Arty. Co.H
Ray, William MS 6th Inf. Co.C
Ray, William MS 15th (Cons.) Inf. Co.K
Ray, William MS 30th Inf. Co.K Capt.
Ray, William MO 5th Cav. Co.A
Ray, William MO 7th Cav. Ward's Co.

Ray, William MO Arty. Jos. Bledsoe's Co.
Ray, William MO 3rd & 5th Cons.Inf.
Ray, William MO Inf. Perkins' Bn.
Ray, William NC 1st Cav. (9th St.Troops) Co.A
Ray, William NC 1st Cav. (9th St.Troops) Co.K
Ray, William NC 15th Inf. Co.H
Ray, William NC 47th Inf. Co.I
Ray, William NC Walker's Bn. Thomas' Legion Co.H
Ray, William SC 1st (Hagood's) Inf. 1st Co.A Sgt.
Ray, William SC 1st (Hagood's) Inf. 1st Co.G, 2nd Co.E
Ray, William SC 3rd Inf. Co.I
Ray, William SC 6th Inf. 1st Co.H, 2nd Co.B Cpl.
Ray, William SC 9th Res. Co.H
Ray, William TN 1st (Carter's) Cav. Co.B Sgt.
Ray, William TN 2nd (Ashby's) Cav. Co.G
Ray, William TN Cav. 4th Bn. (Branner's) Co.B
Ray, William TN Cav. Nixon's Regt. Co.K
Ray, William TN Inf. 1st Cons.Regt. Co.G Sgt.
Ray, William TN 16th Inf. Co.C
Ray, William TN 19th Inf. Co.D
Ray, William TN 28th Inf. Co.A
Ray, William TN 28th (Cons.) Inf. Co.B Sgt.
Ray, William TN 34th Inf. Co.D
Ray, William TN 60th Mtd.Inf. Co.K 2nd Lt.
Ray, William TN 62nd Mtd.Inf. Co.G
Ray, William TN Inf. 154th Sr.Regt. Co.I
Ray, William TX 1st Field Btty.
Ray, William TX 13th Vol. Co.E
Ray, William TX 16th Inf. Co.I
Ray, William VA 22nd Inf. Swann's Co.
Ray, William A. GA 36th (Broyles') Inf. Co.H Cpl.
Ray, William A. GA 40th Inf. Co.D
Ray, William A. GA 59th Inf. Co.I
Ray, William A. GA Cobb's Legion Co.C
Ray, William A. MS 20th Inf. Co.A
Ray, William A. MS 43rd Inf. Co.D
Ray, William A. NC 29th Inf. Co.B 1st Lt.
Ray, William A. NC 49th Inf. Co.D Cpl.
Ray, William A. NC 64th Inf. Co.F 3rd Lt.
Ray, William B. AL 6th Inf. Co.L
Ray, William B. GA 41st Inf. Co.I
Ray, William B. MS 4th Inf. Co.G
Ray, William B. NC 29th Inf. Co.B
Ray, William B. NC 30th Inf. Co.D Music.
Ray, William B. SC 2nd Rifles Co.B
Ray, William C. AL 41st Inf. Co.I Sgt.
Ray, William C. MS 9th Inf. Old Co.C
Ray, William C. MS 15th Inf. Co.F
Ray, William C. MS 19th Inf. Co.G
Ray, William C. NC 25th Inf. Co.E
Ray, William C. NC 39th Inf. Co.H
Ray, William C. NC 64th Inf. Co.A Cpl.
Ray, William D. KY 4th Cav. Co.A Maj.
Ray, William D. NC 3rd Cav. (41st St.Troops) Co.D
Ray, William E. AL 3rd Bn.Res. Co.C
Ray, William E. NC 15th Inf. Co.L
Ray, William E. NC 32nd Inf. Co.K
Ray, William E. TX 11th Inf. Co.K
Ray, William F. AR 9th Inf. Co.G
Ray, William F. FL 6th Inf. Co.B
Ray, William F. MO 11th Inf. Co.K Cpl.

Ray, William F. TX 10th Cav. Co.C Cpl.
Ray, William G. MS 19th Inf. Co.K
Ray, William G. NC 6th Inf. Co.B Sgt.
Ray, William G. TX 15th Inf. 2nd Co.G
Ray, William G.M. TN 37th Inf. Co.A
Ray, William H. AL 13th Inf. Co.D
Ray, William H. AR 8th Inf. New Co.G
Ray, William H. AR 14th (McCarver's) Inf. Co.H
Ray, William H. AR Inf. Crawford's Bn.
Ray, William H. GA 51st Inf. Co.G
Ray, William H. LA 9th Inf. Co.C
Ray, William H. MS 1st Lt.Arty. Co.C
Ray, William H. MS 17th Inf. Co.D Cpl.
Ray, William H. NC 2nd Inf. Co.H
Ray, William H. NC 16th Inf. Co.F
Ray, William H. NC 29th Inf. Co.D
Ray, William H. NC 58th Inf. Co.C
Ray, William H. SC Lt.Arty. 3rd (Palmetto) Bn. Co.A
Ray, William H. SC 1st (McCreary's) Inf. Campbell's Co.
Ray, William H. TN 28th Inf. Co.E
Ray, William H. VA Cav. 39th Bn. Co.A
Ray, William I. MS 2nd Regt.Res. Co.K
Ray, William J. MS 23rd Inf. Co.C
Ray, William J. MO Inf. 3rd Bn. Co.F
Ray, William J. MO Inf. 3rd Regt.St.Guard Co.H 1st Lt.
Ray, William J. MO 6th Inf. Co.H
Ray, William J.C. MS 6th Inf. Co.G Cpl.
Ray, William K. NC 6th Inf. Co.B
Ray, William L. GA 11th Cav. Co.I Sgt.
Ray, William L. GA 52nd Inf. Co.I 1st Sgt.
Ray, William L. TN 13th (Gore's) Cav. Co.H
Ray, William L. TX 6th Inf. Co.H
Ray, William M. AL Cav. Forrest's Regt.
Ray, William M. AR 23rd Inf. Co.C
Ray, William M. AR 27th Inf. New Co.B Cpl.
Ray, William M. GA 42nd Inf. Co.I
Ray, William M. MS 27th Inf. Co.I
Ray, William M. NC 29th Inf. Co.D Color Sgt.
Ray, William M. TN 18th (Newsom's) Cav. Co.A
Ray, William Miles MO 8th Inf. Co.E Cpl.
Ray, William P. AL 17th Inf. Co.E
Ray, William P. GA 51st Inf. Co.E
Ray, William P. MO 10th Inf. Co.A
Ray, William P. VA Lt.Arty. 12th Bn. Co.C
Ray, William P. VA Lt.Arty. Taylor's Co. Cpl.
Ray, William P. VA 50th Inf. Co.F
Ray, William R. GA 4th Res. Co.E,K
Ray, William R. GA 15th Inf. Co.K
Ray, William R. NC 27th Inf. Co.G
Ray, William R. VA 57th Inf. Co.B
Ray, William S. NC Cav. 5th Bn. Co.A
Ray, William S. NC Inf. 2nd Bn. Co.A Sgt.
Ray, William S. TX 14th Cav. Co.H
Ray, William T. AL 22nd Inf. Co.I
Ray, William T. AL 50th Inf. Co.E
Ray, William T. GA 36th (Broyles') Inf. Co.F
Ray, William T. MS 43rd Inf. Co.A
Ray, William T. MO 2nd Inf. Co.G
Ray, William T. VA 20th Cav. Co.I
Ray, William T. VA 60th Inf. Co.G
Ray, William T. 4th Conf.Eng.Troops Cpl.
Ray, William W. AR 28th Inf. Co.C

Ray, William W. GA 22nd Inf. Co.K
Ray, William W. KY 12th Cav. Co.A,E
Ray, Willis AR Inf. Hardy's Regt. Co.D
Ray, Willis NC 3rd Inf. Co.I
Ray, Willis T. SC 13th Inf. Co.B
Ray, Wilson MS 30th Inf. Co.K
Ray, Wilson NC Cav. 5th Bn. Co.A
Ray, Wilson SC Inf. 1st (Charleston) Bn. Co.B,G
Ray, Wilson SC 7th Res. Co.D
Ray, Wilson SC 27th Inf. Co.K,B
Ray, Winchester AL 38th Inf. Co.F
Ray, W.J. AR 47th (Crandall's) Cav. Co.D
Ray, W.J. GA 49th Inf. Co.D
Ray, W.J. TN 12th (Green's) Cav. Co.B Sgt.
Ray, W.M. GA 63rd Inf. Co.E
Ray, W.M. TN Inf. 154th Sr.Regt. Co.I
Ray, W.N. TX 24th & 25th Cav. (Cons.) Co.E
Ray, W.N. TX Cav. Border's Regt. Co.C
Ray, W.P. GA Conscr.
Ray, W.P. NC 1st Jr.Res. Co.G
Ray, W.P. SC 5th St.Troops Co.E
Ray, W.P. SC 7th Res. Co.D
Ray, W.R. NC Loc.Def. Lee's Co. (Silver Greys)
Ray, W.S. LA 28th (Gray's) Inf. Co.H
Ray, W.S. MS 1st Lt.Arty. Co.C
Ray, W.S. NC 2nd Conscr. Co.B
Ray, W.S. NC 64th Inf. Co.D
Ray, W.S. TN 21st (Wilson's) Cav. Co.A
Ray, W.S. TN Inf. 154th Sr.Regt. Co.I
Ray, W.S. TX St.Troops Hampton's Co.
Ray, W.T. GA Cherokee Legion (St.Guards) Co.B
Ray, W.T. MO 7th Cav. Co.B
Ray, W.W. AL 8th Inf.
Ray, W.W. AL 9th Inf.
Ray, W.W. TX 23rd Cav. Co.D Sgt.
Ray, Y.B. TX 4th Inf. Co.C
Ray, Y.B. TX 5th Inf. Co.G
Ray, Young D. NC 42nd Inf. Co.K
Ray, Young W. AL 14th Inf. Co.K
Ray, Zachariah GA Inf. 40th Bn. Co.B
Ray, Zeddock D. NC 30th Inf. Co.D Sgt.
Rayal, T. GA 5th Res. Co.H
Rayall, J.R. GA 5th Res. Co.B
Rayals, W.A. TN 20th Inf. Co.G Cpl.
Rayan, James LA Mil. Irish Regt. Co.F
Rayane, John H. LA Mil. Borge's Co. (Garnet Rangers)
Raybaut, E. LA Mil. 3rd Regt. French Brig. Co.4
Raybon, A. SC 2nd Res.
Raybon, C. GA 1st (Olmstead's) Inf. Stiles' Co.
Raybon, C. GA Inf. 18th Bn. Co.B
Raybon, Charles FL 4th Inf. Co.C
Raybon, F. MS 38th Cav. Co.G
Raybon, J.F. FL Conscr.
Raybon, John FL 11th Inf. Co.E
Raybon, John TN 15th (Stewart's) Cav. Co.G
Raybon, Richard NC 2nd Arty. (36th St.Troops) Co.E
Raybon, Silas GA 1st Inf. Co.H
Raybon, W.J. AL Cav. Lewis' Bn. Co.B Sgt.
Rayborg, F. MO Lt.Arty. Von Phul's Co.
Rayborn, Asa AL Lt.Arty. Kolb's Btty.
Rayborn, Berry AR 37th Inf. Co.D
Rayborn, C.F. GA Inf. 27th Bn. Co.F

Rayborn, Henry NC 1st Inf. Co.I
Rayborn, H.M. AR 37th Inf. Co.D
Rayborn, James F. FL 5th Inf. Co.E
Rayborn, J.L. Conf.Cav. Powers' Regt. Co.H 1st Lt.
Rayborn, John FL 4th Inf. Co.E
Rayborn, John A. AR 1st (Monroe's) Cav. Co.A
Rayborn, John G. TN 25th Inf. Co.B
Rayborn, John J. MS Cav. Hughes' Bn. Co.H
Rayborn, John M. TN 25th Inf. Co.F Cpl.
Rayborn, Leroy TX 13th Cav. Co.A
Rayborn, Noah MS 9th Inf. Co.C
Rayborn, Robert MO 4th Inf. Co.I
Rayborn, Samuel H. MS 9th Inf. Old Co.C
Rayborn, Thomas MS Cav. 17th Bn. Co.F
Rayborn, Thomas MO 8th Inf. Co.E Cpl.
Rayborn, Thomas M. 1st Conf.Cav. 2nd Co.C
Rayborn, T.M. TN 4th (Murray's) Cav. Co.D
Rayborn, William AR 37th Inf. Co.D
Rayborn, William MS 2nd (Quinn's St.Troops) Inf. Co.G
Rayborn, William NC 1st Inf. Co.I
Rayborn, Willis GA 40th Inf. Co.G Cpl.
Rayborn, Willis MO 4th Cav. Co.D,B
Rayborne, A. TX 13th Cav. Co.C
Rayborne, Noah MS 8th Cav. Co.A 2nd Lt.
Rayborne, W.T. LA 4th Inf. Co.I 1st Sgt.
Raybourn, G.P. GA 36th (Villepigue's) Inf. Co.K
Raybourn, R.L. MS 18th Cav. Co.C,G
Raybourne, George W. AR 2nd Mtd.Rifles Co.C
Raybu, Macke AL 3rd Bn.Res. Jackson's Co.
Raybun, Davis AL 3rd Bn.Res. Jackson's Co.
Raybun, Elijah Z. GA 22nd Inf. Co.B
Raybun, James H. GA 48th Inf. Co.A
Raybun, John M. LA 31st Inf. Co.I Jr.2nd Lt.
Raybun, Thomas AL 3rd Bn.Res. Jackson's Co.
Raybun, William GA 48th Inf. Co.A
Rayburn, A. MS 22nd Inf. Co.D
Rayburn, A.J. TN 16th Inf. Co.C
Rayburn, Andrew D. MS 42nd Inf. Co.I
Rayburn, Andrew J. MO 9th Inf. Co.C
Rayburn, Benjamin AR 3rd Inf. Co.B
Rayburn, C.J. AL 61st Inf. Co.G
Rayburn, Cyrus MS 30th Inf. Co.H
Rayburn, D. AL 23rd Inf. Co.A,C Cpl.
Rayburn, D.M. AR 5th Inf. Co.E
Rayburn, Elisha T. AR 1st (Monroe's) Cav. Steward's Co.
Rayburn, E.M. AR 25th Inf. Co.D
Rayburn, F.G. MS Rogers' Co.
Rayburn, Frazier G. MS Inf. (Res.) Berry's Co.
Rayburn, G.W. AR 1st (Monroe's) Cav. Co.A
Rayburn, H. GA 1st Res.
Rayburn, H.B. VA Inf. 26th Bn. Co.C
Rayburn, Henry LA 20th Inf. Co.G
Rayburn, Henry C. TN 13th (Gore's) Cav. Co.B
Rayburn, H.J. KY 3rd Cav.
Rayburn, H.J. KY 3rd Mtd.Inf. Co.H
Rayburn, H.J. Cent.Div. KY Sap. & Min.,CSA
Rayburn, H.N. MS 18th Cav. Co.G Sgt.
Rayburn, H.N. MS 34th Inf. Co.I 2nd Lt.
Rayburn, Hodge TX Inf. Whaley's Co.
Rayburn, Howel A. TX 12th Cav. Co.C
Rayburn, James AR Cav. Wright's Regt. Co.H
Rayburn, James MS 1st (Johnston's) Inf. Co.E
Rayburn, James SC Manigault's Bn.Vol. Co.B
Rayburn, James A. KY 2nd Mtd.Inf. Co.D Sgt.

Rayburn, James H. MS 11th (Perrin's) Cav. Co.C
Rayburn, James H. MS 21st Inf. Co.F 2nd Lt.
Rayburn, J.D. MS 3rd Cav. Co.F
Rayburn, J.H. MS 3rd Cav. Co.D
Rayburn, J.J. LA 27th Inf. Co.I
Rayburn, J.J. MS 46th Inf. Co.B
Rayburn, J.L. AL 46th Inf. Co.I
Rayburn, J.M. AL Cp. of Instr. Talladega
Rayburn, John AL 9th Inf. Co.K Capt.
Rayburn, John AR 50th Mil. Co.C Sgt.
Rayburn, John LA 17th Inf. Co.C
Rayburn, John MO Cav. Freeman's Regt. Co.F
Rayburn, John 4th Conf.Inf. Co.G
Rayburn, John D. MS 1st Bn.S.S. Co.C
Rayburn, J.P. AR 7th Cav. Co.D
Rayburn, J.Q. MS St.Cav. Perrin's Bn. Co.E Capt.
Rayburn, J.Q. MS 36th Inf. Co.D 1st Lt.
Rayburn, J.T. MS 1st Cav. Co.E
Rayburn, J.V. AR 5th Inf. Co.E Sgt.
Rayburn, L.M. TX 8th Cav. Co.E Maj.
Rayburn, Louis J. GA 22nd Inf. Co.B
Rayburn, Milton V. TX 12th Cav. Co.C
Rayburn, M.M. AR 30th Inf. Co.L,A
Rayburn, M.T. AR Cav. Gordon's Regt. Co.B Cpl.
Rayburn, M.V. AR Cav. Davies' Bn. Co.E
Rayburn, N. MS 22nd Inf. Co.K Cpl.
Rayburn, Noah M. MS 22nd Inf. Co.K Sgt.
Rayburn, R. AL 63rd Inf. Co.F
Rayburn, R.A. MS 29th Inf. Co.D
Rayburn, R.H. TX 35th (Brown's) Cav. Co.I
Rayburn, Richard AL 3rd Cav. Co.C
Rayburn, R.O. MS 11th (Perrin's) Cav. Co.C
Rayburn, R.O. MS 3rd Inf. (St.Troops) Co.D
Rayburn, Robert AL 38th Inf. Co.B
Rayburn, Robert TN 4th (McLemore's) Cav. Co.F
Rayburn, R.W. AL 9th Inf. Co.D
Rayburn, Samuel AL Lt.Arty. 2nd Bn. Co.D Sgt.
Rayburn, Samuel TN Lt.Arty. Browne's Co.
Rayburn, Samuel K. AL 48th Inf. Co.E Capt.
Rayburn, S.E. TN 17th Inf. Co.G
Rayburn, S.P. MS 1st Bn.S.S. Co.D
Rayburn, S.R. GA 48th Inf. Co.A
Rayburn, S.S. MO 2nd Cav. Co.D Sgt.
Rayburn, S.S. MO 10th Inf. Co.B
Rayburn, Stephen LA 26th Inf. Co.G
Rayburn, Thomas MO Cav. Freeman's Regt. Co.F
Rayburn, W. MO 1st Cav. Co.D
Rayburn, W.A. AR 50th Mil. Co.C
Rayburn, W.A. MS 25th Inf. Co.H Capt.
Rayburn, W.A. 2nd Conf.Inf. Co.H Capt.
Rayburn, W.A. Walthall's Div. Maj.
Rayburn, W.C. AR 5th Inf. Co.E Capt.
Rayburn, W.C. MO Cav. Davies' Bn. Maj.
Rayburn, W.C.A. MS 22nd Inf. Co.K Lt.
Rayburn, W.G. TN 4th (McLemore's) Cav. Co.F
Rayburn, W.H. AR 1st (Monroe's) Cav. Co.A
Rayburn, William AR Cav. Wright's Regt. Co.H
Rayburn, William AR 3rd Inf. Co.B
Rayburn, William A. MS 1st Bn.S.S. Maj.
Rayburn, William A. MS Gage's Co. (Wigfall Guards) 2nd Lt.

Rayburn, William B. TN 10th (DeMoss') Cav. Co.F
Rayburn, William B. TX 2nd Cav. Co.H
Rayburn, William C. MS 11th (Perrin's) Cav. Co.C
Rayburn, Wm. P. Gen. & Staff, Medical Dept. Surg.
Rayburn, William R. GA 22nd Inf. Co.B
Rayburn, Willis MS 2nd (Quinn's St.Troops) Inf. Co.B
Rayburn, W.K. TN 4th (McLemore's) Cav. Co.F
Rayburn, W.L. LA Washington Arty.Bn. Co.6 Can.
Rayburn, W.R. AL 38th Inf. Co.H
Rayburne, William KY Inf. Ficklin's Bn. Co.B
Raycroft, N.W. AR 1st (Dobbin's) Cav. Co.A
Raycroft, R.W. TN 47th Inf. Co.D Cpl.
Raydel, H. LA 2nd Inf. Co.D
Rayden, Adam AR 35th Inf. Co.C
Rayder, J.J. TN 12th Inf. Co.I
Rayder, J.J. TN 12th (Cons.) Inf. Co.I
Raydon, Timothy TN 2nd (Robison's) Inf. Co.E
Raydor, Wm. B. AR 1st (Colquitt's) Inf. Co.D
Raye, Henry MS 7th Cav. Co.I
Raye, Henry TN 55th (McKoin's) Inf. James' Co.
Raye, Josiah TN 55th (McKoin's) Inf. James' Co.
Raye, L. MS 7th Cav. Co.I
Raye, Thomas GA 47th Inf. Co.E
Rayel, Edward AL Mil. 4th Vol. Co.C
Rayel, James T. TX 19th Cav. Co.G
Rayel, John E. AL Mil. 4th Vol. Co.C
Rayellior, J. LA 3rd (Harrison's) Cav. Co.C
Rayers, D. AL 37th Inf. Co.C
Rayes, Julius TX Cav. Benavides' Regt. Co.D
Rayes, Pedro TX 8th Inf. Co.G
Rayfield, Adam AL Cp. of Instr. Talladega
Rayfield, A.W. AL Cp. of Instr. Talladega
Rayfield, B. GA Cav. 19th Bn. Co.C
Rayfield, Benjamin F. AL 10th Inf. Co.K
Rayfield, Edward J. NC 1st Arty. (10th St.Troops) Co.K
Rayfield, George W. AL 18th Inf. Co.D
Rayfield, Hy SC 2nd Arty. Co.E
Rayfield, James AL 1st Regt. Legion Co.C
Rayfield, James A. NC 6th Inf. Co.B
Rayfield, James D. VA 39th Inf. Co.K
Rayfield, J.B. 10th Conf.Cav. Co.H
Rayfield, John MO Cav. Clardy's Bn. Farris' Co.
Rayfield, John SC 26th Inf. Co.B
Rayfield, John H. AL St.Arty. Co.A
Rayfield, John W. AL 3rd Bn. Hilliard's Legion Vol. Co.C Cpl.
Rayfield, J.W. AL 60th Inf. Co.B Cpl.
Rayfield, L.H. AL 62nd Inf. Co.D
Rayfield, Littleton S. VA 16th Inf. 2nd Co.H, Co.G 1st Sgt.
Rayfield, Littleton S. VA 39th Inf. Co.A 1st Sgt.
Rayfield, L.S. VA Loc.Def. Ezell's Co. 1st Lt.
Rayfield, Lyttleton S. VA 54th Mil. Co.A
Rayfield, Moulton MS 14th Inf. Co.H
Rayfield, N. GA Lt.Arty. Howell's Co.
Rayfield, Noah H. AL 62nd Inf. Co.D
Rayfield, Thomas AL 11th Inf. Co.F
Rayfield, Thomas C. AL 24th Inf. Co.D
Rayfield, Thomas C. AL 28th Inf. Co.A

Rayfield, Tully R. VA 39th Inf. Co.I
Rayfield, Tully R. VA 46th Inf. 4th Co.F
Rayfield, W.C. MD 1st Inf. Co.F Cpl.
Rayfield, William FL 11th Inf. Co.I
Rayfield, William VA 32nd Inf. Co.A
Rayfield, William H. AL 30th Inf. Co.A Music.
Rayfield, William W. AL St.Arty. Co.A
Rayfield, Windslow NC 25th Inf. Co.I
Rayfield, W.K. AL 60th Inf. Co.B
Rayford, A.C. VA Lt.Arty. 38th Bn. Co.B
Rayford, Albert N. VA 9th Inf. Co.B
Rayford, Alfred R. AL St.Arty. Co.A
Rayford, A.R. AL 9th Cav. Co.A
Rayford, D. AL St.Arty. Co.C
Rayford, Dudley AL Mobile City Troop
Rayford, Edward AL 1st Bn.Cadets Co.A
Rayford, Edwin VA 9th Inf. Co.B
Rayford, Everette VA 9th Inf. Co.B
Rayford, George LA 1st Hvy.Arty. (Reg.) Co.C
Rayford, H.C. LA Inf. 4th Bn. Co.B
Rayford, Henry B. GA 12th Inf. Co.A
Rayford, J. GA 16th Inf.
Rayford, James H. NC 32nd Inf. Co.G
Rayford, Jethro VA 16th Inf. Co.D
Rayford, John LA 20th Inf. Co.G 2nd Cpl.
Rayford, John J. AL Mil. 4th Vol. Co.A
Rayford, John T. LA 13th & 20th Inf. Co.H,A
   Cpl.
Rayford, John T. LA Herrick's Co. (Orleans
   Blues)
Rayford, J.W. AR 6th Inf. 1st Co.B
Rayford, Malashia AR 20th Inf. Co.B
Rayford, M.H. AL Mil. 2nd Regt.Vol. Co.E
Rayford, N.B. TN Lt.Arty. Polk's Btty.
Rayford, Philip T. MS 1st Cav. Co.K
Rayford, R. TX 1st Hvy.Arty. Co.K
Rayford, W. AL Mobile City Troop
Rayford, William M. MS 5th Inf. (St.Troops)
   Co.D
Rayhill, W.H. VA 22nd Inf. Co.K
Rayhill, William VA 60th Inf. Co.C
Raykandall, Abe TX Cav. Wells' Regt.
Raykeendall, --- TX Cav. Wells' Regt.
Rayl, George W. TN 43rd Inf. Co.K
Rayl, John F. NC 30th Inf. Co.K
Rayl, L.P. LA 1st Cav. Co.I Sgt.
Rayl, W.T. GA 1st (Fannin's) Res. Co.K
Rayl, Wyatt T. GA 2nd Res. Co.D
Rayland, Gideon VA 2nd Inf.Loc.Def. Co.E
Rayland, W.A.N. AR 1st Mtd.Rifles Co.F
Rayle, Bartlett Y. NC 33rd Inf. Co.I 2nd Lt.
Rayle, Charles TN 8th (Smith's) Cav. Co.B
Rayle, E.A. NC 1st Inf. Co.A
Rayle, G.W. AL 9th Inf. Co.F
Rayle, Wyatt W. GA 2nd Cav. Co.E
Raylmue, E. AL 6th Inf. Co.A Cpl.
Raylor, J.B. AL 26th Cav. Co.E
Raylor, Piny AR 8th Cav. Co.L
Raymann, Louis VA 1st Inf. Co.K
Raymee, J.R. MO 12th Inf. Co.I
Raymer, B.A. AR 8th Cav. Peoples' Co.
Raymer, Benj. B. AR 26th Inf. Co.I
Raymer, Elias FL 1st Inf. New Co.E
Raymer, George F. TX 4th Cav. Co.A
Raymer, Jacob SC 1st (Butler's) Inf. Co.C,H
Raymer, J.C. TN 55th (McKoin's) Inf. Joyner's
   Co.

Raymer, J.H. MO Inf. 5th Regt.St.Guard Co.B
   Cpl.
Raymer, John N. TN 55th (McKoin's) Inf.
   Joyner's Co.
Raymer, Nat NC 4th Inf. Co.C Music.
Raymer, P.H. AR 1st (Dobbin's) Cav. Co.A
Raymer, W.R. TN Inf. Nashville Bn. Felts' Co.
Raymon, Thomas A. KY 1st Bn.Mtd.Rifles Co.A
Raymon, W.H. VA 12th Inf. Co.E
Raymond, A.H. LA 7th Inf. Co.E
Raymond, Antoine LA Mil. 1st Native Guards
Raymond, Arthur LA 10th Inf. Co.G 1st Lt.
Raymond, Benjamin LA Arty. Moody's Co.
   (Madison Lt.Arty.)
Raymond, C.C. MD Arty. 2nd Btty.
Raymond, Ch. LA Mil. 1st Regt. French Brig.
   Co.1
Raymond, Charles LA Washington Arty.Bn.
   Co.3
Raymond, Charles LA 22nd Inf. Co.B
Raymond, Charles MS 1st Lt.Arty. Co.H
Raymond, Charles TX 1st Hvy.Arty. 2nd Co.F
Raymond, Charles TX 15th Field Btty.
Raymond, Charles TX 3rd Inf. Co.G
Raymond, Charles A. VA Lt.Arty. Thompson's
   Co.
Raymond, Daniel GA 4th (Clinch's) Cav. Co.K,I
Raymond, D.H. LA 4th Inf. Co.F
Raymond, E. LA Mil. Orleans Guards Regt.
   Co.D
Raymond, Ebenezer NC 2nd Arty. (36th
   St.Troops) Co.K
Raymond, Edward F. Gen. & Staff Asst.Surg.
Raymond, Frank LA 5th Inf. Co.E
Raymond, G. GA 1st (Fannin's) Res.
Raymond, G.B. AR 26th Inf. Co.B
Raymond, George LA Washington Arty.Bn.
Raymond, George E. VA 9th Inf. 2nd Co.A
Raymond, G.J. GA Inf. 14th Bn. (St.Guards)
   Co.C
Raymond, H. LA Mil. 3rd Regt. French Brig.
   Co.1
Raymond, Henry H. SC 20th Inf. Co.B
Raymond, H.H. SC 4th Cav. Co.L
Raymond, I. 7th Conf.Cav.
Raymond, J. AR Cav. McGehee's Regt. Co.F
Raymond, Jas. Gen. & Staff, Comsy.Dept.
Raymond, J.M. NC 18th Inf. Co.G
Raymond, John AR 1st Mtd.Rifles Co.D
Raymond, John LA 22nd Inf. D.H. Marks' Co.
Raymond, John TX 5th Cav. Co.C
Raymond, Joseph VA 59th Inf. 3rd Co.D
Raymond, Joseph S. VA 4th Inf. Co.I Sgt.
Raymond, J.T. VA Inf. 25th Bn. Co.G
Raymond, J.W. AL 40th Inf. Co.I
Raymond, J.W. LA 17th Inf. Co.D
Raymond, L. KY 9th Mtd.Inf. Co.H
Raymond, O.G. SC 3rd Cav. Co.F
Raymond, O.G. SC 1st Mtd.Mil. 2nd Lt.
Raymond, Patrick LA 1st (Nelligan's) Inf. Co.G
   1st Sgt.
Raymond, Peter MO Lt.Arty. Farris' Btty. (Clark
   Arty.)
Raymond, R. LA Mil. 3rd Regt. French Brig.
   Co.4
Raymond, Richard S. LA 7th Inf. Co.H
Raymond, S.P. MS 41st Inf. Co.E

Raymond, S.R. 1st Conf.Cav. Co.I
Raymond, Thomas A. KY Jessee's Bn.Mtd.
   Riflemen Co.A
Raymond, W.C. LA Mil.Conf.Guards Regt.
   Co.D 1st Sgt.
Raymond, William TN 18th Inf. Co.B
Raymond, William D. KY 2nd Mtd.Inf. Co.C
Raymond, William M. LA 17th Inf. Co.D
   Sr.2nd Lt.
Raymond, William M. NC 20th Inf. Co.G
Raymond, W.L. AR Lt.Arty. Owen's Btty.
Raymond, W.M. GA 20th Inf. Co.G
Raymond, W.M. TN 10th (DeMoss') Cav. Co.D
Raymond, W.S. TN 12th (Green's) Cav. Co.D
Raymond, W.S. TN 16th (Logwood's) Cav.
   Co.G
Raymond, W.T. VA Cav. Mosby's Regt.
   (Part.Rangers) Co.E
Raymondet, C. LA 18th Inf. Co.E
Raymor, Clay TN 9th (Ward's) Cav. Co.A Cpl.
Raymur, A. GA 54th Inf. Co.F
Raymur, A.J. GA 54th Inf. Co.F
Raymur, William A. GA 5th Inf. Co.F,A
Raynal, A. LA Mil. 1st Native Guards 1st Sgt.
Raynal, A. LA Mil.Cont.Cadets Capt.
Raynal, Peter N. GA Inf. 18th Bn. Co.A Jr.2nd
   Lt.
Raynal, P.N. GA 1st (Olmstead's) Inf. Screven's
   Co. Sgt.
Raynal, P.S. LA Washington Arty.Bn. Co.6
   Can.
Raynaud, Paul Sap. & Min. Gallimard's Co.,CSA
   1st Sap.
Rayne, R.S. LA 11th Inf. Co.L
Rayne, William W. LA 5th Inf. New Co.A 1st
   Sgt.
Rayner, Aaron, Jr. MS Inf. 2nd St.Troops Co.D
Rayner, Aaron, Sr. MS Inf. 2nd St.Troops Co.D
Rayner, Aaron MS 46th Inf. Co.I Sgt.
Rayner, Allen MS 18th Inf. Co.A
Rayner, Allen NC 24th Inf. Co.E
Rayner, Benjamin S. MS 29th Inf. Co.K
Rayner, B.F. MS 46th Inf. Co.I
Rayner, Brookfield NC 5th Inf. Co.D
Rayner, Bryant MS 36th Inf. Co.I
Rayner, Cyrus T. VA Lt.Arty. E.J. Anderson's
   Co. Cpl.
Rayner, Ervin W. NC 18th Inf. Co.E
Rayner, Gaston TX 8th Cav. Co.A
Rayner, George LA 26th Inf. Co.E
Rayner, Gov. R. MS 1st (Patton's) Inf. Co.K
Rayner, G.W. AL 12th Inf. Co.G
Rayner, Henry M. NC 8th Inf. Co.E
Rayner, Hinton NC 2nd Inf. Co.E
Rayner, James NC 8th Sr.Res. Daniel's Co.
Rayner, James T. NC 1st Inf. (6 mo. '61) Co.L
Rayner, James T. NC 11th (Bethel Regt.) Inf.
   Co.C 1st Lt.
Rayner, J.C. NC 66th Inf. Co.H
Rayner, Jesse VA Inf. 1st Bn. Co.B
Rayner, J.G. NC 1st Arty. (10th St.Troops) Co.E
Rayner, John A. NC 4th Cav. (59th St.Troops)
   Co.F
Rayner, John C. NC 30th Inf. Co.E
Rayner, John J. NC 67th Inf. Co.H
Rayner, John L. NC 67th Inf. Co.H
Rayner, Juan TN 3rd (Forrest's) Cav. Co.A

Rayner, Juan T. TN Inf. 154th Sr.Regt. Co.E
Rayner, K. TN Inf. 1st Cons.Regt. Co.A Cpl.
Rayner, Kenneth NC 17th Inf. (2nd Org.) Co.F
Rayner, Kenneth TN 6th Inf. Co.A
Rayner, L. TN 12th (Green's) Cav. Co.E
Rayner, Lovet NC 30th Inf. Co.K
Rayner, Luck TN 4th Inf. Co.D
Rayner, Marshall NC 46th Inf. Co.E
Rayner, Prentiss MS 9th Cav. Co.G
Rayner, Prince MS 6th Inf. Co.D
Rayner, Robert C. MS 18th Inf. Co.A
Rayner, S.S. MS 1st Cav.Res. Co.B
Rayner, S.S. MS Inf. 2nd St.Troops Co.D
Rayner, T. AL 38th Inf. Co.K
Rayner, T.A. TN 6th Inf. Co.A
Rayner, Thomas VA 13th Inf. Co.F
Rayner, Washington MS 9th Cav. Co.G
Rayner, William H. MS 31st Inf. Co.F
Rayner, William H. NC 24th Inf. Co.E
Rayner, W.S. TN 7th (Duckworth's) Cav. Co.M
Rayner, Z.C. MS 5th Inf. (St.Troops) Co.B
Raynes, A.G. VA 1st Inf. Co.I
Raynes, Archibald G. VA Lt.Arty. Arch.
    Graham's Co.
Raynes, A.W. GA 63rd Inf. Co.D
Raynes, G.L. GA 12th Cav. Co.D
Rayncs, Henry VA 6th Cav. Co.C
Raynes, Henry VA Cav. Caldwell's Bn. Taylor's
    Co.
Raynes, Herod GA 22nd Inf. Co.D
Raynes, Jacob VA 6th Cav. Co.C
Raynes, J.C. MS 8th Inf. Co.A
Raynes, John VA Cav. Caldwell's Bn. Taylor's
    Co.
Raynes, J.W. AR 2nd Inf. Co.G
Raynes, J.W. GA Cobb's Legion Co.K
Raynes, Leyton D. VA 58th Mil. Co.B
Raynes, Noah VA 6th Cav. Co.C
Raynes, Reuben VA 6th Cav. Co.C
Raynes, Samuel VA 21st Cav. 2nd Co.I
Raynes, W. GA 24th Inf. Co.G
Raynes, Zack VA 6th Cav. Co.C
Rayney, J. LA 8th Inf.
Rayney, John MS 9th Cav. Co.B
Rayney, Samuel SC 3rd Res. Co.E
Rayney, W. KY 1st (Butler's) Cav. Co.E
Rayney, W.H. AR 2nd Inf. Co.I
Raynham, Thomas LA 4th Inf. Co.D
Raynhart, J.W. TN 19th (Biffle's) Cav. Co.I
    Cpl.
Raynola, --- Echols' Staff Capt.
Raynold, B.D. GA 13th Cadets
Raynold, Charles AL 12th Inf. Co.A
Raynold, H.A. MS 18th Cav. Co.A 1st Lt.
Raynolds, C.J. LA 7th Cav. Co.K
Raynolds, David TX 11th Cav. Co.D
Raynolds, J.C. NC Arty. 1st Lt.
Raynolds, John Mead's Conf.Cav. Co.F
Raynolds, Larkin TX Cav. Hardeman's Regt.
    Co.B
Raynolds, Middelton W. GA Inf. White's Co.
    Cpl.
Raynor, Aaron MS 5th Inf. (St.Troops) Co.B
Raynor, C.T. VA Lt.Arty. 38th Bn. Co.C Cpl.
Raynor, Guilford NC 8th Sr.Res. Broadhurst's
    Co.
Raynor, G.W. MS 5th Inf. (St.Troops) Co.B

Raynor, Henry AR 32nd Inf. Co.A
Raynor, H.H. MS 6th Inf. Co.B
Raynor, Jason NC 8th Sr.Res. Broadhurst's Co.
Raynor, John LA Inf. 1st Sp.Bn. (Wheat's) New
    Co.D
Raynor, John NC 8th Bn.Part.Rangers Co.B,C
Raynor, L. TN 16th (Logwood's) Cav. Co.I
Raynor, Lawrence TN 1st Hvy.Arty. 1st Co.C,
    2nd Co.A
Raynor, Lewis AR 14th (Powers') Inf. Co.G
Raynor, Lewis AR Inf. Cocke's Regt. Co.G
Raynor, Lovell TN 16th (Logwood's) Cav. Co.D
Raynor, Richard NC 2nd Arty. (36th St.Troops)
    Co.C
Raynor, Samuel NC 2nd Inf. Co.E
Raynor, V.A. NC Detail
Raynor, William H. AR 32nd Inf. Co.A
Rayon, Joseph LA Seige Train Bn. Co.D
Rays, J.G. GA 22nd Inf. Co.C
Raysdelly, A.A. AL 21st Inf. Co.D
Rayser, G.W. NC 2nd Inf.
Raysor, Alfred FL Cav. 5th Bn. Co.C
Raysor, B.S. SC 5th Cav. Co.C
Raysor, B.S. SC Cav. 17th Bn. Co.D
Raysor, B.S. SC 11th Inf. Co.H
Raysor, C.A. SC Arty. Fickling's Co. (Brooks
    Lt.Arty.)
Raysor, C.A. SC Arty. Manigault's Bn. Co.E
Raysor, Charles A. SC Hvy.Arty. Gilchrist's Co.
    (Gist Guard)
Raysor, Edgar H. FL 5th Inf. Co.G Sgt.
Raysor, George FL Cav. 5th Bn. Co.C Cpl.
Raysor, George FL 5th Inf. Co.G
Raysor, George D. FL 5th Inf. Co.G 1st Lt.
Raysor, G.W. SC 1st Mtd.Mil. Smith's Co. 1st
    Sgt.
Raysor, G.W. SC 5th Cav. Co.C 2nd Lt.
Raysor, G.W. SC Cav. 17th Bn. Co.D 2nd Lt.
Raysor, H.C. SC 1st Mtd.Mil. Blakewood's Co.
    1st Lt.
Raysor, Henry C. SC 3rd Cav. Co.E Capt.
Raysor, J.C. SC Hvy.Arty. Gilchrist's Co. (Gist
    Guard)
Raysor, J.C. SC Arty. Manigault's Bn. Co.E
Raysor, J.C. SC 2nd Inf. Co.I,G
Raysor, J.M. SC 7th Cav. Co.G
Raysor, J.M. SC Rutledge Mtd.Riflemen &
    Horse Arty. Trenholm's Co.
Raysor, J.M. SC 11th Inf. Sheridan's Co.
Raysor, John M. FL 5th Inf. Co.F,G Sgt.
Raysor, Leonidas M. SC Horse Arty.
    (Washington Arty.) Vol. Hart's Co.
Raysor, L.M. GA 8th Inf. Co.B
Raysor, Michael O. FL 3rd Inf. Co.H
Raysor, P.A. SC 20th Inf. Co.D
Raysor, Peter A. SC Cav. 14th Bn. Co.D Capt.
Raysor, T.E. SC 11th Inf. Co.H Capt.
Rayzor, G. KY 6th Cav. Co.I
Razall, Charles W. TN Inf. 154th Sr.Regt.
Razer, Winston J. TN Inf. 154th Sr.Regt. Co.H
Razor, Adam KY 1st (Butler's) Cav. Co.C
Razor, Adam KY 3rd Cav. Co.C
Razor, David KY 1st (Butler's) Cav. Co.C
Razor, David KY 3rd Cav. Co.C
Razor, Henry KY 3rd Cav. Co.C
Razor, J.R. KY 3rd Cav. Grant's Co.
Razor, Nathaniel KY 4th Cav. Co.G

Razor, Nathaniel KY 5th Mtd.Inf. Co.E
Razor, Thomas J. TN 48th (Voorhies') Inf. Co.K
Razor, W. KY 3rd Cav. Grant's Co.
Razzile, B.H. AL 10th Inf.
Rchards, Michael NC 2nd Jr.Res. Co.C
Rchards, William AL 3rd Inf. Co.C
Rea, Albert S. MS 40th Inf. Co.I
Rea, A.M. AL 27th Inf. Co.G Sgt.
Rea, A.M. MS 10th Inf. Old Co.B
Rea, Andrew A. VA 56th Inf. Co.H
Rea, Andrew J. GA Arty. 9th Bn. Co.
Rea, Andrew M. MS 2nd Inf. Co.C,H
Rea, A.T. VA 19th Inf. Co.K
Rea, C.H. AL 29th Inf. Co.H
Rea, C.H. 2nd Conf.Eng.Troops Co.C Sgt.
Rea, Con MS 46th Inf. Co.F Maj.
Rea, C.S. TN 20th Inf. Co.D
Rea, D.A. GA 10th Inf. Co.E
Rea, David A. VA 42nd Inf. Co.G
Rea, David B. NC 5th Cav. (63rd St.Troops)
    Co.F
Rea, David J. NC 49th Inf. Co.F
Rea, D.B. NC 1st Cav. (9th St.Troops) Co.C
Rea, Edward G. TX 6th Inf. Co.E
Rea, E.K. 8th (Wade's) Conf.Cav. Co.K
Rea, Elijah K. AL Lt.Arty. Hurt's Btty.
Rea, Frank VA 59th Inf. 2nd Co.A
Rea, George A. VA 1st Inf. Co.II
Rea, George H. AL 3rd Inf. Co.B
Rea, George W. MS 1st (Percy's) Inf. Co.A
Rea, George W. MS 36th Inf. Co.G 1st Lt.
Rea, G.W. AR Cav. Harrell's Bn. Co.A
Rea, H.C. TX 30th Cav. Co.K
Rea, J. LA 18th Inf. Co.H
Rea, James AL Inf.Crescent Regt. Co.C
Rea, James NC 35th Inf. Co.H
Rea, James TX 30th Cav. Co.K
Rea, James H. MO 5th Cav. Co.A
Rea, James H. VA 19th Inf. Co.K
Rea, James M. MO 16th Inf. Co.G
Rea, James M. NC 30th Inf. Co.K
Rea, Jesse VA 2nd Inf.Loc.Def. Co.I Cpl.
Rea, Jesse VA 52nd Inf. Co.D
Rea, J.K. NC 1st Inf. (6 mo. '61) Co.C
Rea, J.K.L. AR 45th Mil. Co.B Cpl.
Rea, J.L. NC 1st Cav. (9th St.Troops) Co.C
Rea, J.M. MS 2nd Cav.Res. Co.F
Rea, J.M. NC 1st Cav. (9th St.Troops) Co.C
Rea, John AL 26th (O'Neal's) Inf. Co.H
Rea, John MS 5th Inf. Co.B 1st Cpl.
Rea, John MS 5th Inf. (St.Troops) Co.I Sgt.
Rea, John TN 17th Inf. Co.H
Rea, John TX 19th Cav. Co.A
Rea, John A. VA 19th Inf. Co.K
Rea, John A. VA 46th Inf. 2nd Co.D
Rea, John B. MO 16th Inf. Co.G
Rea, John C. AR 27th Inf. Co.A Capt.
Rea, John H. MS 35th Inf. Co.A
Rea, John H. TX Cav. 2nd Regt.St.Troops Co.I
Rea, John K. NC 4th Sr.Res. Co.G
Rea, John T. TN 53rd Inf. Co.K
Rea, Joseph C. TN 53rd Inf. Co.K
Rea, J.S. GA 10th Inf. Co.E
Rea, J.W. TX 25th Cav.
Rea, L. TN 12th (Cons.) Inf. Co.B
Rea, Lee NC 4th Sr.Res. Co.G
Rea, Luke AL 18th Inf. Co.C

Rea, Major W. AL 42nd Inf. Co.K
Rea, M.D. AR Cav. Harrell's Bn. Co.A
Rea, Obadiah VA 42nd Inf. Co.G
Rea, Pinkney C. NC Hvy.Arty. 10th Bn. Co.D,C
Rea, Pinkney C. NC 35th Inf. Co.F
Rea, R. AL Chas. A. Herts' Co.
Rea, R.B. VA 7th Inf. Co.I
Rea, Reuben F. MS 40th Inf. Co.I Sgt.
Rea, Richard R. GA 2nd Res. Co.C Cpl.
Rea, R.N. MS 8th Inf. Co.H
Rea, R.N. MS 46th Inf. Co.F 1st Lt.
Rea, Robert AL 27th Inf. Co.G
Rea, Robert NC 1st Cav. (9th St.Troops) Co.C
Rea, Robert M. AL 11th Inf. Co.K
Rea, Robert W. MS 36th Inf. Co.G,D
Rea, R.R. NC 1st Cav. (9th St.Troops) Co.C
Rea, Ryland B. VA 56th Inf. Co.H
Rea, Samuel SC 1st (Butler's) Inf. Co.C
Rea, Samuel SC 16th Inf. Co.I
Rea, Samuel H. MS 43rd Inf. Co.H
Rea, Samuel R. MS 3rd Cav.Res. Co.F
Rea, Sanford V. GA Cherokee Legion
    (St.Guards) Co.G Sgt.
Rea, Stephen AL Cp. of Instr. Talladega Co.D
Rea, Tho. B. AR 33rd Inf. Co.A
Rea, Thomas J. AR 2nd Inf.
Rea, Thomas M. MS Jefferson Arty.
Rea, Thomas M. MS 1st (Patton's) Inf. Co.K
Rea, Thomas M. MS 12th Inf. Co.D
Rea, Thomas R. LA Mil. 2nd Regt. 3rd Brig. 1st
    Div. Co.E 3rd Lt.
Rea, Thomas S. MS 2nd Inf. Co.C
Rea, W. VA 46th Inf. Co.D
Rea, W.A. MS 2nd Cav.Res. Co.F
Rea, Washington S. MO 16th Inf. Co.G
Rea, William MS Cav. 17th Bn. Co.D 3rd Lt.
Rea, William MS Lt.Arty. (Jefferson Arty.) Dar-
    den's Co.
Rea, William MS 44th Inf. Co.G Cpl.
Rea, William MO 5th Cav. Co.H
Rea, William NC 1st Inf. (6 mo. '61) Co.M
Rea, William A. NC 1st Cav. (9th St.Troops)
    Co.C Far.
Rea, William D. NC 11th (Bethel Regt.) Inf.
    Co.F 2nd Lt.
Rea, William F. NC 43rd Inf. Co.B
Rea, William J. AL 29th Inf. Co.H
Rea, William J. MS 12th Inf. Co.D Capt.
Rea, William M. TN 53rd Inf. Co.K
Rea, William P. NC 1st Inf. (6 mo. '61) Co.B
Rea, William R. AR 25th Inf. Co.B 1st Sgt.
Rea, William T. VA 19th Inf. Co.K Sgt.
Rea, Willis C. AL 27th Inf. Co.G
Rea, W.J. AR 45th Mil. Co.B
Rea, Zepheniah R. VA 56th Inf. Co.H
Reab, A.R. GA Lt.Arty. 12th Bn. 2nd Co.D,F
    Sgt.
Reabold, Robert MS Lt.Arty. (Jefferson Arty.)
    Darden's Co.
Reaburn, John H. VA Cav. Hounshell's Bn.
    Co.C
Reaburn, R.A. VA Arty. Bryan's Co.
Reaburn, Robert A. VA 108th Mil. Co.A,
    Lemons' Co. Sgt.
Reaburn, William H. VA 14th Cav. Co.I,G
Reaburn, William H. VA Arty. Bryan's Co.
Reace, A.B. TN 20th (Russell's) Cav. Co.B

Reace, Alexander VA 14th Cav. 1st Co.F
Reace, Alexander VA Cav. 36th Bn. Co.E
Reace, Alexander C. TN 29th Inf. Co.C 2nd Lt.
Reace, Alvin AR 7th Cav. Co.G
Reace, Ignatious SC Lt.Arty. 3rd (Palmetto) Bn.
    Co.I
Reace, J.C. NC 6th Inf. Co.C
Reace, William NC 58th Inf. Co.M
Reace, William H. KY 1st (Butler's) Cav. Co.C
Reach, A.J. AL 50th Inf. Co.F
Reach, Andrew J. VA 8th Inf. Co.I Cpl.
Reach, George W. GA 21st Inf. Co.B
Reach, G.S. TN Lt.Arty. Tobin's Co.
Reach, James C., Jr. AL 44th Inf. Co.B
Reach, Jeremiah M., Jr. AL 62nd Inf. Co.A
Reach, Jeremiah M., Sr. AL 62nd Inf. Co.A
Reach, J.W. TN 19th & 20th (Cons.) Cav. Co.F
Reach, J.W. TN 20th (Russell's) Cav. Co.A
Reach, J.W. TN 12th Inf. Co.D
Reach, T.G. TN 19th & 20th (Cons.) Cav. Co.D
Reach, T.G. TN 20th (Russell's) Cav. Co.D
Reach, Theophilous AL 44th Inf. Co.B
Read, A.B. Gen. & Staff Asst.Comsy.
Read, Abner A. AL 3rd Inf. Co.C
Read, Abraham VA 11th Cav. Co.C
Read, A.D. GA Inf. 9th Bn. Co.C
Read, A.D. VA 3rd Res. Co.G Capt.
Read, Adolphus D. VA 11th Inf. Co.E 2nd Lt.
Read, Adolphus E. Gen. & Staff Surg.
Read, A.E. LA Miles' Legion Co.A
Read, A.E. TN 7th (Duckworth's) Cav. Co.I
Read, A.H. GA 64th Inf. Asst.Surg.
Read, A.J. TX 5th Inf. Co.F
Read, A.L. GA Cav. 22nd Bn. (St.Guards) Co.C
    Capt.
Read, Alexander TN 22nd Inf. Looney's Co.
Read, Alexander C. LA 5th Inf. Co.D Comsy.
    Sgt.
Read, Alexander H. VA 27th Inf. Co.A
Read, Allen TN 27th Inf. Co.K
Read, Alvan E. LA Inf. 1st Sp.Bn. (Wheat's)
    New Co.D 2nd Lt.
Read, Alvan R. VA Hvy.Arty. Read's Co. Capt.
Read, Alvan S. LA 4th Inf. Co.F
Read, Amos TN 15th (Stewart's) Cav. Co.C
Read, Amos W. VA 8th Cav. Co.G
Read, Amos W. VA Inf. 45th Bn. Co.C
Read, Andrew A. GA 11th Inf. Co.A
Read, Andrew H. Gen. & Staff Asst.Surg.
Read, Arthor AR 15th Mil. Co.D
Read, A.S. VA 19th Cav. Co.I
Read, A.S. VA Cav. 37th Bn. Co.H
Read, Asa AL 10th Inf. Co.G Cpl.
Read, A.T. TN 7th (Duckworth's) Cav. Co.M
Read, A.W. VA 34th Mil. (1st) A.Surg.
Read, A.W. Gen. & Staff Surg.
Read, B. AL 31st Inf. Co.D
Read, B.C. GA 11th Cav. Co.H
Read, Benjamin KY Inf. Ficklin's Bn. Co.C
Read, Benjamin F. TX 35th (Brown's) Cav. Co.I
    Cpl.
Read, Benjamin F. TX 13th Vol. 3rd Co.I
Read, Benj. H. Gen. & Staff, Adj.Gen.Dept.
    Capt.
Read, B.F. TN 49th Inf. Co.K
Read, B.F. Inf. Bailey's Cons.Regt. Co.E

Read, B.H. SC Cav. DeSaussure's Squad. Co.B
    1st Lt.
Read, Burgest NC 6th Cav. (65th St.Troops)
    Co.K,B Sgt.
Read, Calvin VA 190th Mil. Co.G Cpl.
Read, C.C. AL Cav. Moreland's Regt. Co.C
Read, C.E. LA Inf. 9th Bn. Co.A
Read, C.H. VA 3rd Inf.Loc.Def. Co.A
Read, Charles VA 59th Inf. 2nd Co.A
Read, Charles F. VA 14th Inf. Co.F
Read, Charles H. AL 1st Bn.Cadets Co.A,B 2nd
    Lt.
Read, Charles H. AL 21st Inf. Co.A
Read, Charles W. TN 16th Inf. Co.C
Read, Christopher C. TX 22nd Inf. Co.C Sgt.
Read, Clement C. AL 58th Inf. Co.F,E 2nd Lt.
Read, Clement C. VA Arty. Paris' Co. 1st Sgt.
Read, Columbus W. LA 1st (Nelligan's) Inf.
    Co.G
Read, C.P. AL 32nd & 58th (Cons.) Inf. 2nd Lt.
Read, C.P. VA 3rd Res. Co.G
Read, D. TX Cav. Giddings' Bn. Carr's Co.
Read, David AL 1st Regt. Mobile Vol. Baas' Co.
Read, David AR 33rd Inf. Co.G
Read, David TN 49th Inf. Co.K
Read, David K. NC 30th Inf. Co.G
Read, David S. VA 28th Inf. Co.I Sgt.
Read, D.B. TN 84th Inf. Co.C
Read, D.B. VA 9th Bn.Res. Co.D
Read, D.J. AL Cav. Murphy's Bn. Co.C
Read, D.J. MS Inf. 7th Bn. Co.B
Read, D.W. LA Inf. 9th Bn. Co.A
Read, E. KY Cav. Thompson's Co.
Read, E.C. TN 16th Inf. Co.C 1st Lt.
Read, Edmond TN 23rd Inf. Co.B
Read, Edmund S. VA Inf. 26th Bn. Co.B Capt.
Read, Edmund T. VA 34th Inf. Co.H
Read, Eldridge H. TN 24th Inf. 2nd Co.G
Read, Elias VA Inf. 45th Bn. Co.C
Read, Elisha TN 37th Inf. Co.C
Read, F.B. AR 2nd Vol. Co.D Comsy.Sgt.
Read, Fleming VA 57th Inf. Co.C
Read, F.N. AR Lt.Arty. Owen's Btty. Teamster
Read, F.N. VA Inf. 26th Bn. AQM
Read, F.N. Gen. & Staff Capt.,AQM
Read, Francis W. Gen. & Staff Capt.,Comsy.
Read, Frank J. LA Mil. Beauregard Regt. Co.B
    Capt.
Read, Frederick N. VA 22nd Inf. Co.H 1st Sgt.
Read, F.S. MO 10th Inf. Co.B Sgt.
Read, G. VA Wade's Regt.Loc.Def. Co.D
Read, Garrett L. TN 60th Mtd.Inf. Co.H
    Ord.Sgt.
Read, G.D. GA Inf. 1st Bn. (St.Guards) Co.D
    Cpl.
Read, G.D. GA Inf. City Bn. (Columbus) Co.C
Read, G.D. KY 6th Mtd.Inf. Co.E
Read, George VA Cav. 39th Bn. Co.D
Read, George VA 20th Inf. Co.G
Read, George VA Mil. Scott Cty.
Read, George VA Conscr. Cp.Lee Co.A
Read, George Conf.Cav. Wood's Regt. Co.L
Read, George B. VA 42nd Inf. Co.C Cpl.
Read, George F. GA 40th Inf. Co.G Sgt.
Read, George H. VA Hvy.Arty. 19th Bn. 3rd
    Co.E
Read, George H. VA 39th Inf. Co.A Sgt.

Read, George S. VA Hvy.Arty. 19th Bn. 3rd Co.E
Read, Geo. T. AR 1st (Colquitt's) Inf. Co.D
Read, George T. KY 1st (Butler's) Cav.
Read, George W. VA Hvy.Arty. 18th Bn. Co.C Sgt.
Read, G.L. GA 1st Inf. (St.Guards) Co.B
Read, G.L. TN 37th Inf. Co.C
Read, G.W. TN 30th Inf. Co.D Cpl.
Read, G.W. VA 14th Cav. Co.C,B
Read, H. KY Cav. 2nd Bn. (Dortch's) Co.D Sgt.
Read, Harold P. VA 49th Inf. Co.H Cpl.
Read, Henry GA 40th Inf. Co.G
Read, Henry C. AL 34th Inf. Co.K
Read, Henry N. VA 18th Inf. Co.K
Read, Henry W. VA 18th Inf. Co.D
Read, Hiram AL Auburn Home Guards Vol. Darby's Co.
Read, Hiram J. GA 4th (Clinch's) Cav. Co.C
Read, Hiram J. GA 26th Inf. Atkinson's Co.B
Read, H.J. MS Inf. 1st Bn.St.Troops (30 days '64) Co.C
Read, H.P. VA Inf. 44th Bn. Co.E
Read, Hugh K. AL 11th Inf. Co.H
Read, I.F. GA 1st Inf. (St.Guards) Co.B
Read, Isaac VA 14th Cav. Co.B
Read, Isaac Nitre & Min. Bureau War Dept.,CSA Maj.
Read, Isaac A. VA Arty. Paris' Co.
Read, Isaac A. VA 20th Inf. Co.G
Read, Isaac H. VA Arty. Paris' Co.
Read, J. GA 10th Inf.
Read, J. GA Conscr.
Read, J. MS 16th Inf. Co.D
Read, J.A. AR 2nd Inf. Co.G
Read, J.A. GA 63rd Inf. Co.C
Read, Jackson TN Cav. 12th Bn. (Day's) Co.B
Read, Jacob GA 1st Reg. Co.D Capt.
Read, Jacob GA Arty. Maxwell's Reg.Lt.Btty. Capt.
Read, James AR 10th (Witt's) Cav. Co.G
Read, James KY 7th Cav. Co.A
Read, James MS 6th Inf. Co.H
Read, James MS 24th Inf. Co.G
Read, James TN 28th (Cons.) Inf. Co.K
Read, James TN 49th Inf. Co.K
Read, James TN 84th Inf. Co.F
Read, James Inf. Bailey's Cons.Regt. Co.E
Read, James A. AR 17th (Lemoyne's) Inf. Co.B
Read, James B. GA 1st (Olmstead's) Inf. Read's Co. Capt.
Read, James B. VA 5th Cav. Co.K
Read, James B. VA 58th Inf. Co.E
Read, Jas. B. Gen. & Staff Surg.
Read, James E. NC 1st Arty. (10th St.Troops) Co.H
Read, James H. GA 48th Inf. Co.C Sgt.
Read, James H. TX 2nd Cav. Co.C Capt.
Read, James H. VA 87th Mil. Co.D
Read, James K. VA Horse Arty. Shoemaker's Co. Sgt.
Read, James L. TN 41st Inf. Co.H
Read, James L. TX 22nd Cav. Co.E Capt.
Read, James M. AR 1st (Colquitt's) Inf. Co.D
Read, James M. MS 31st Inf. Co.C
Read, James T. AL 21st Inf. Co.A

Read, James W. MS Cav. Shelby's Co. (Bolivar Greys)
Read, James W. VA 27th Inf. Co.A
Read, James W. VA 38th Inf. Co.D
Read, Jasper MS 6th Inf. Co.H
Read, J.B. Gen. & Staff Capt.,Comsy.
Read, J.C. TN 7th (Duckworth's) Cav. Co.F
Read, J.C. VA Cav. 37th Bn. Co.H
Read, J.D. MS 3rd Inf. Co.K Lt.
Read, J.E. VA 1st Res. Co.I
Read, Jesse GA 17th Inf. Co.B
Read, Jesse MS Conscr.
Read, Jesse TN 12th (Cons.) Inf. Co.E
Read, Jesse Hare VA 2nd Cav. Co.G
Read, J. Greene AR 31st Inf. Co.B Sgt.
Read, J.H. MS 3rd Inf. Co.B
Read, J.H. NC 2nd Cav. (19th St.Troops) Co.I
Read, J.H. VA 1st Inf. Co.H
Read, J.H. VA Inf. 26th Bn. Co.C
Read, J. Harleston, Jr. SC 21st Inf. Co.A 2nd Lt.
Read, J. Harleston, Sr. SC 21st Inf. Co.A Maj.
Read, J.J. TN Inf. 4th Cons.Regt. Co.G
Read, J.J. TX Cav. Waller's Regt. Co.B Sgt.
Read, J.L. LA 25th Inf. Co.D
Read, J.M. VA Conscr. Cp.Lee
Read, J.O. KY 6th Mtd.Inf. Co.B
Read, John LA Washington Arty.Bn. Co.5
Read, John LA 6th Inf.
Read, John LA 31st Inf. Co.D
Read, John MS Cav. Yerger's Regt. Co.B
Read, John MS 6th Inf. Co.H
Read, John MS 9th Inf. Old Co.E
Read, John SC 6th Cav. Co.H
Read, John TN 7th Inf. Co.A
Read, John TX 11th Cav. Co.K
Read, John 2nd Corps Comsy.Sgt.
Read, John A. TN 39th Mtd.Inf. Co.H 2nd Lt.
Read, John A. VA Horse Arty. Shoemaker's Co.
Read, John C. MS 20th Inf. Co.F
Read, John F. GA 20th Inf. Co.A Cpl.
Read, John H. MS 23rd Inf. Co.B
Read, John H. VA Lt.Arty. W.H. Rice's Co. Sgt.
Read, John J. LA 25th Inf. Co.D
Read, John J. MS Inf. 3rd Bn. Co.K
Read, John L. VA 34th Mil. (2) A.Surg.
Read, John L. Gen. & Staff, A. of N.VA Asst.Surg.
Read, John P. VA Inf. 26th Bn. Co.E
Read, John P.W. GA Lt.Arty. Fraser's Btty. Capt.
Read, John P.W. GA 10th Inf. 1st Co.K Capt.
Read, John P.W. VA Lt.Arty. 38th Bn. Maj.
Read, John R. MO 10th Inf. Co.H
Read, John W. MO 1st N.E. Cav. Co.E,L
Read, Joseph A. GA 48th Inf. Co.G Sgt.
Read, Joseph D. MS Inf. 3rd Bn. Co.K 1st Lt.
Read, Joshua B. KY 8th Cav. Co.K,B Lt.
Read, J.P.W. VA 1st Arty. Co.K,L Capt.
Read, J.R. AR 27th Inf. Co.I
Read, J.R. TX 29th Cav. Co.I
Read, J.R. TX 11th (Spaight's) Bn.Vol. Co.D
Read, J.T. Gen. & Staff, Medical Dept. Surg.
Read, J.W. AL Cav. 4th Bn. (Love's) Co.C
Read, J.W. MS 6th Inf. Co.E
Read, Lancelot W. VA 39th Inf. Co.D

Read, Lawrence TN 39th Mtd.Inf. Co.H
Read, Lemuel M. TX 22nd Inf. Co.C
Read, Lewis H. VA 14th Inf. Co.F
Read, Littleton D. VA 16th Inf. 2nd Co.H
Read, Littleton D. VA 39th Inf. Co.I
Read, Littleton D. VA 61st Inf. Co.I,K Sgt.
Read, Littleton D. VA Inf. Cohoon's Bn. Co.C Sgt.
Read, Littleton S. VA 39th Inf. Co.A 1st Lt.
Read, Little W. VA 14th Inf. Co.E
Read, L.L. TN 49th Inf. Co.K
Read, L.L. Inf. Bailey's Cons.Regt. Co.E
Read, Lloyd H. KY 6th Mtd.Inf. Co.B
Read, M.A. VA 60th Inf. Co.G
Read, Marion AR 23rd Inf. Co.G Music.
Read, Martin W. TX 3rd Cav. Co.G
Read, Milton AL 2nd Cav. Co.A
Read, Morel MO 7th Cav. Co.H
Read, N. GA Conscr.
Read, Nathan L. GA Inf. 4th Bn. (St.Guards) Co.A
Read, Nat. V. NC 22nd Inf. Co.G
Read, N.C. VA Lt.Arty. R.M. Anderson's Co.
Read, N.C. VA 1st St.Res. Co.F
Read, N.C. VA 20th Inf. Co.G
Read, Newton GA Inf. 14th Bn. (St.Guards) Co.E
Read, N.G. Conf.Lt.Arty. Richardson's Bn. Co.D
Read, N.M. VA Lt.Arty. Griffin's Co.
Read, N.M. Gen. & Staff Asst.Surg.
Read, Noah F. TN 60th Mtd.Inf. Co.H 1st Lt.
Read, Nugent M. VA 28th Inf. Co.I,E 2nd Lt.
Read, Oscar E. KY 6th Mtd.Inf. Co.F,I
Read, Owen GA 19th Inf. Co.K
Read, Peter TN 12th (Cons.) Inf. Co.E
Read, Raymond GA 5th Inf. Co.C
Read, R.D. AL 48th Inf.
Read, Reuben TX 7th Cav. Co.K
Read, Rhesa TX 29th Cav. Co.I Surg.
Read, Rhesa W. Gen. & Staff Surg.
Read, Richard VA Horse Arty. Shoemaker's Co.
Read, Richard M. MS 16th Inf. Co.F
Read, Richard W. VA 21st Inf. Co.A
Read, Robert TN 39th Mtd.Inf. Co.H
Read, Robert VA 1st St.Res. Co.A
Read, Robert VA Inf. 26th Bn. Co.C
Read, Robert F. MS 43rd Inf. Co.D
Read, Robert G. MS 42nd Inf. Co.F
Read, Robert J. VA 24th Inf. Co.K 2nd Lt.
Read, Robert S. KY 4th Cav. Cpl.
Read, Russel F. GA 48th Inf. Co.G Sgt.
Read, R.W. MS Cp.Guard (Cp. of Instr. for Conscr.)
Read, S. GA 59th Inf. Co.G
Read, Samuel KY 4th Mtd.Inf. Co.E
Read, Samuel NC 58th Inf. Co.F
Read, Samuel TN 27th Inf. Co.I
Read, Samuel C. TN Cav. 12th Bn. (Day's) Co.D
Read, Samuel R. TN 2nd (Robison's) Inf. Co.H
Read, S.H. GA 46th Inf. Co.B
Read, Spence A. TN 2nd (Ashby's) Cav. Co.F
Read, Stephen P. VA 14th Inf. Co.F Capt.
Read, T.A. AL 12th Cav. Co.D
Read, T.B. TX 21st Inf. Co.G
Read, Thomas AR 17th (Lemoyne's) Inf. Co.B
Read, Thomas KY 7th Cav. Co.B,C

Read, Thomas TN 2nd (Ashby's) Cav. Co.K
Read, Thomas TN 59th Mtd.Inf. Co.D
Read, Thomas A. AL 34th Inf. Co.K
Read, Thomas A. VA 6th Inf. Co.K
Read, Thomas A. VA 14th Inf. Co.F
Read, Thomas B. LA 12th Inf. Co.M
Read, Thomas B. TN 20th Inf. Co.K Ch.Music.
Read, Thomas G. VA 33rd Inf. Co.I Sgt.
Read, Thomas N. VA 56th Inf. Co.I 1st Sgt.
Read, Thomas W. MS 18th Inf. Co.H
Read, Thomas W. NC 56th Inf. Co.H
Read, T.J. TX Cav. Giddings' Bn. Carr's Co.
Read, T.N. VA 14th Cav. Co.B
Read, T.W. MO Inf. Clark's Regt. Co.C
Read, W. Conf.Inf. Tucker's Regt. Co.F
Read, W.A. TX 11th (Spaight's) Bn.Vol. Co.D
Read, W.B. TN 84th Inf. Co.F
Read, W.D. TN 19th & 20th (Cons.) Cav. Co.K
Read, W.E. AL 12th Cav. Co.D
Read, Wesley TX 22nd Inf. Co.C
Read, W.H. TN 19th (Biffle's) Cav. Co.B
Read, William AL Inf. 2nd Regt. Co.H
Read, William GA Inf. 18th Bn. Co.C Cook
Read, William KY 2nd (Duke's) Cav. Co.E
Read, William KY 2nd (Woodward's) Cav. Co.E
Read, William MS 27th Inf. Co.E
Read, William MO 1st N.E. Cav. Co.E
Read, William MO Cav. Freeman's Regt. Co.C
Read, William MO Cav. Schnabel's Bn.
Read, Wm. MO St.Guard
Read, William SC Palmetto S.S. Co.F
Read, William TN 39th Mtd.Inf. Co.H
Read, William TX 21st Inf. Co.G
Read, William VA Lt.Arty. 38th Bn. Co.D
Read, William VA 39th Inf. Co.I
Read, William VA 58th Inf. Co.E
Read, William A. MS 40th Inf. Co.B
Read, William B. TN 15th Cav. Co.H Black.
Read, William F. AL Inf. 2nd Regt. Co.E
Read, William F. VA Hvy.Arty. 18th Bn.
Read, William F. Conf.Inf. 1st Bn. 2nd Co.C
Read, William H. GA 48th Inf. Co.G
Read, William H. KY 6th Mtd.Inf. Co.F,I Sgt.
Read, William H. TX 5th Cav. Co.I
Read, William H. TX 37th Cav. Co.F
Read, William H. VA 32nd Inf. Co.F
Read, William H.C. AR 1st (Crawford's) Cav. Co.C
Read, William J. LA 16th Inf. Co.I
Read, William J. MS 48th Inf. Co.A
Read, William M. TN 2nd (Smith's) Cav.
Read, William M. VA 1st Arty. Co.D 2nd Lt.
Read, William M. VA Arty. B.H. Smith's Co. 2nd Lt.
Read, William M. VA 34th Inf. Co.C
Read, William M. VA 61st Inf. Co.A
Read, William P. AL 2nd Cav. Co.A
Read, William S. TX 36th Cav. Co.B
Read, William T. AL 21st Inf. Co.A
Read, William T. TX 22nd Inf. Co.C Sgt.
Read, W.J. AL 1st Inf. Co.E
Read, W.J. AL 8th Inf. Co.D
Read, W.J. GA 40th Inf. Co.H
Read, W.J. LA Washington Arty.Bn. Co.5
Read, W.O. NC 21st Inf. Co.C
Read, W.O. TN 6th (Wheeler's) Cav.
Read, W.P. LA 31st Inf. Co.D

Read, Young TN 34th Inf. Co.I
Readdick, A.J. GA 4th (Clinch's) Cav. Co.D
Readdick, F. GA 4th (Clinch's) Cav. Co.D Sgt.
Readdick, Francis FL 2nd Inf. Co.K
Readdick, George FL 2nd Inf. Co.K
Readdick, John GA 4th (Clinch's) Cav. Co.D,F Capt.
Readdick, Peter FL 2nd Inf. Co.K Cpl.
Readdy, Andrew GA 12th Inf. Co.H
Readdy, George GA Cav. 2nd Bn. Co.E
Readdy, G.F. GA 45th Inf. Co.A
Readdy, John 14th Conf.Cav. Co.A
Readdy, Thomas J. GA 14th Inf. Co.B
Reade, C. VA VMI Co.G
Reade, Edward B. NC 24th Inf. Co.A
Reade, J.H. TN 7th (Duckworth's) Cav. Co.D 2nd Lt.
Reade, Julian Logan's Staff Capt.
Reade, M. VA 36th Inf. Co.G
Reade, R.J. AL Cp. of Instr. Talladega
Reader, Abijah AL 40th Inf. Co.I,D
Reader, A.G. 2nd Cherokee Mtd.Vol. Co.C
Reader, A.J. AL 18th Inf. Co.B
Reader, B. AR Inf. Sparks' Co.
Reader, Elias 1st Cherokee Mtd.Vol. 1st Co.E, 2nd Co.C
Reader, E.P. TN 23rd Inf. Co.C
Reader, George W. SC 20th Inf. Co.K
Reader, Henry MS Inf. 2nd Bn. (St.Troops) Co.D
Reader, Henry VA 54th Inf. Co.C
Reader, James TN 10th Inf. Co.B
Reader, J.B. SC 26th Inf. Co.F
Reader, J.N. GA Cobb's Legion Co.A
Reader, John AR 15th (Josey's) Inf. Co.F
Reader, John TX 5th Inf. Co.H
Reader, John VA 54th Inf. Co.C
Reader, John P. TX 13th Vol. 2nd Co.I,B
Reader, Joseph MS Cav. Ham's Regt. Co.I
Reader, Joseph TX 13th Vol. 2nd Co.I,B
Reader, Joseph W. SC 20th Inf. Co.K Sgt.
Reader, L.T. AL 27th Inf. Co.E
Reader, M. AL 34th Inf. Co.D
Reader, N. AL 18th Inf. Co.G
Reader, Nathan AL 40th Inf. Co.I
Reader, Newton S. AL 21st Inf. Co.B Sgt.
Reader, N.L. AL 18th Inf. Co.B Cpl.
Reader, Thomas J. MS Cav. Ham's Regt. Co.I
Reader, W. AL 34th Inf. Co.D
Reader, W.A. AL Cav. Forrest's Regt.
Reader, W.A. TN 19th & 20th (Cons.) Cav. Co.C
Reader, William TN 41st Inf. Co.E
Reader, William A. TN 18th (Newsom's) Cav. Co.A
Reader, William F. TX 24th Cav. Co.E
Reader, William J. MS 31st Inf. Co.D
Reader, William N. AL 63rd Inf. Co.D
Reader, W.J. TX 10th Inf. Co.C
Reader, W.L. AL 18th Inf. Co.B
Reader, Z. AL 40th Inf. Co.I
Readey, G.F. GA 5th Cav. Co.C
Readfearn, W.J. NC 1st Jr.Res. Co.I
Readford, Benjamin F. TX 20th Inf. Co.A
Readford, Samuel S. TX 20th Inf. Co.A
Readhimer, L.J. LA 2nd Cav. Co.G

Readhimer, William W. LA 12th Inf. 1st Co.M, Co.C
Readick, William E. GA 1st (Olmstead's) Inf. Gordon's Co. Sgt.
Readick, William E. GA 63rd Inf. Co.B 2nd Lt.
Reading, Abram B. MS 21st Inf. Co.A
Reading, Charles H. AL 29th Inf. Co.G
Reading, Hugh MO St.Guard
Reading, J.A. KY 7th Cav. Co.A
Reading, James AL 8th (Hatch's) Cav. Co.D
Reading, James MO 9th Bn.S.S. Co.A
Reading, Jay MO 9th Bn.S.S. Co.A
Reading, Jay MO St.Guard
Reading, J.M. TN 30th Inf. Co.H
Reading, John AR 51st Mil. Co.D
Reading, John GA Lt.Arty. King's Btty.
Reading, Joseph W. MO Robertson's Regt. St.Guard Co.7
Reading, M. AR 51st Mil. Co.D
Reading, M.C. TX 14th Inf. Co.H
Reading, Moses C. KY 1st (Butler's) Cav. Co.G
Reading, R.G. LA 9th Inf. Co.E 1st Lt.
Reading, Samuel AR 3rd Cav. Co.D
Reading, T.R. MS 19th Inf. Co.C Capt.
Reading, William LA 1st Hvy.Arty. (Reg.) Co.A
Readiss, J.F. AL City Guards Lockett's Co.
Readling, C.T. NC Lt.Arty. 3rd Bn. Co.C
Readling, James M. NC 20th Inf. Co.B
Readling, Solomon NC 57th Inf. Co.F
Readman, A.L. SC 10th Inf. Co.B
Readman, A.P. LA Red River S.S.
Readman, George W. LA 16th Inf. Co.H
Readman, H.T. LA 16th Inf. Co.H
Readman, John LA Red River S.S.
Readman, J.W. MS 4th Cav. Co.B
Readman, Samuel MO 7th Cav. Old Co.A
Readmon, H.H. MS 1st Cav. Co.A
Readmon, James A. NC 4th Inf. Co.H
Readmond, Mortimer GA Cav. 2nd Bn. Co.E
Readmond, W. SC 9th Res. Co.K
Readon, J.G. AR 58th Mil. Co.C
Readon, J.J. SC Inf. Hampton Legion Co.C
Readon, S.W. TN 4th (McLemore's) Cav. Co.I
Readon, W.M. Nitre & Min. Bureau War Dept.,CSA Clerk
Readus, William G. AR 36th Inf. Co.B Cpl.
Ready, Abner GA Lt.Arty. Milledge's Co.
Ready, Abner GA 3rd Inf. 1st Co.I
Ready, Abraham VA 11th Cav. Co.E
Ready, A.J. AL 3rd Bn.Res. Co.C
Ready, Andrew J. AL 3rd Bn.Res. Jackson's Co.
Ready, B. SC 1st (Butler's) Inf. Co.D
Ready, B. SC 2nd St.Troops Co.I
Ready, Baziel SC 5th Res. Co.D
Ready, C.F. Sap. & Min.,CSA
Ready, Charles AR 2nd Cav. Co.I
Ready, Charles A. AL 3rd Inf. Co.I
Ready, Charles F. AR 26th Inf. Co.I
Ready, D. VA 9th Bn.Res. Co.D
Ready, Daniel LA 13th Inf. Co.K
Ready, David VA 136th Mil. Co.E
Ready, Edward S. AL 3rd Inf. Co.I Capt.
Ready, Elias A. TN 2nd (Smith's) Cav. Cpl.
Ready, E.M. SC 20th Inf. Co.B
Ready, Emanuel GA 1st (Olmstead's) Inf. Co.I
Ready, Emanuel SC 6th Inf. 2nd Co.D
Ready, E.R. SC 1st Arty. Co.I

41

Ready, E.S. Gen. & Staff Maj.
Ready, F.M. GA 2nd Res. Co.I
Ready, Francis M. TX Cav. Martin's Regt. Co.I
Ready, George A. TN 1st (Turney's) Inf. Co.D
Ready, George W. TN 7th Inf. Co.H Sgt.
Ready, H. MO 6th Cav. Co.C
Ready, H.C. AR 20th Inf. Co.H
Ready, H.C. AR 37th Inf. Co.A
Ready, Henry LA 14th Inf. Co.H
Ready, Hiram MO 4th Cav. Co.A,H
Ready, Horace TN 23rd Inf. Co.E Col.
Ready, James SC 1st Mtd.Mil. Johnson's Co.
Ready, James SC 3rd Cav. Co.K
Ready, J.D. SC 1st Res. Co.L
Ready, Jerry TN Cav. 9th Bn. (Gantt's) Co.A
Ready, J.F. SC 3rd Cav. Co.K
Ready, J.L. GA 12th (Robinson's) Cav. (St.Guards) Co.D
Ready, John AL 18th Inf. Co.B
Ready, John GA 2nd Bn.S.S. Co.D
Ready, John SC 22nd Inf. Co.A
Ready, John TN 10th Inf. Co.E
Ready, John VA 17th Inf. Co.G
Ready, John VA 26th Inf. 1st Co.B
Ready, John A. TN 7th Inf. Co.F
Ready, John J. GA 5th Inf. Co.B Sgt.
Ready, John L. AL 8th Inf. Co.K
Ready, John O. NC Inf. 144th Regt. Co.E
Ready, Joshua VA 7th Cav. Co.I
Ready, J.P. SC 3rd Cav. Co.K
Ready, J.P. SC 1st Bn.S.S. Co.A
Ready, J.P. SC 27th Inf. Co.E
Ready, J.W. AL 5th Inf. New Co.A
Ready, J.W. SC 22nd Inf. Co.I
Ready, Lawrence AL 18th Inf. Co.B
Ready, Lawrence GA 2nd Bn.S.S. Co.D
Ready, Leroy R. AL 19th Inf. Co.I
Ready, M. SC 1st Mtd.Mil. Evans' Co.
Ready, M. SC 11th Res. Co.A
Ready, Manuel SC 9th Inf. Co.H
Ready, Martin LA 10th Inf. Co.D Sgt.
Ready, Mat SC 20th Inf. Co.B
Ready, Matthew AR 8th Inf. New Co.E
Ready, Michael MS 7th Inf. Co.H
Ready, Michael VA 27th Inf. Co.B
Ready, Mike SC 2nd St.Troops Co.K
Ready, M.M. AL 33rd Inf. Co.E 1st Lt.
Ready, Owen TX 1st Hvy.Arty. Co.D
Ready, Philip VA Lt.Arty. B.Z. Price's Co.
Ready, Robert A. AR 9th Inf. Co.E
Ready, Robert H. TX Cav. Martin's Regt. Co.C,I 1st Sgt.
Ready, Samuel SC 22nd Inf. Co.A 2nd Lt.
Ready, S.W. AL 17th Inf. Co.I
Ready, Thomas L. TN 1st (Turney's) Inf. Co.D
Ready, Tim TX 1st Hvy.Arty. Co.C
Ready, Timothy TX Lt.Arty. Jones' Co.
Ready, W.F. TX 1st Hvy.Arty. Co.D Sgt.
Ready, W.F. TX 15th Field Btty. Cpl.
Ready, William GA 10th Inf. Co.D
Ready, William LA 5th Inf. Co.B
Ready, William SC 1st Inf. Co.C 1st Lt.
Ready, William SC Inf. Holcombe Legion Co.D
Ready, William TN 84th Inf. Co.C
Ready, William H. MO Inf. 3rd Bn. Co.E
Ready, William H. MO 6th Inf. Co.C Ord.Sgt.
Ready, Wm. J. Gen. & Staff 1st Lt.,Adj.

Ready, William M. NC 7th Inf. Co.I
Ready, Willis A. TX 14th Cav. Co.H
Ready, W.J. SC 14th Inf. Co.B
Ready, W.J. SC 14th Inf. Adj.
Reafort, J.P. VA 1st Cav. Co.B
Reagan, --- TX Cav. 4th Regt.St.Troops Co.D
Reagan, --- TX Cav. 4th Regt.St.Troops Co.F
Reagan, --- TX 33rd Cav. Co.D Cpl.
Reagan, --- TX 8th Inf. Co.G
Reagan, A.A. TN 13th (Gore's) Cav. Co.C Bvt.2nd Lt.
Reagan, A.A. TN 25th Inf. Co.F
Reagan, Absalom TN 5th (McKenzie's) Cav. Co.A Far.
Reagan, A.C.B. TX Res.Corps.
Reagan, A.J. MS 31st Inf. Co.A
Reagan, A.J. TN 5th (McKenzie's) Cav. Co.A Capt.
Reagan, Alfred H. MS 33rd Inf. Co.A
Reagan, Alfred L. FL 5th Inf. Co.K
Reagan, Andrew SC Hvy.Arty. Gilchrist's Co. (Gist Guard)
Reagan, Andy NC 6th Inf. Co.A Cpl.
Reagan, A.T. AR 30th Inf. Co.F
Reagan, A.T. TX 13th Vol. Co.B
Reagan, B. Conf.Inf. 8th Bn. Co.E Sgt.
Reagan, Benjamin P. TN 3rd (Lillard's) Mtd.Inf. Co.H, 2nd Co.K
Reagan, B.T. Mead's Conf.Cav. Co.F
Reagan, C.A. TN 13th (Gore's) Cav. Co.C
Reagan, C.G. AR 2nd Mtd.Rifles Co.K Capt.
Reagan, Charles TX 14th Cav. Co.D
Reagan, Charles C. MS 31st Inf. Co.A
Reagan, Charles H. AL 49th Inf. Co.E
Reagan, Claibourn G. AR 34th Inf. Co.K 3rd Lt.
Reagan, Con TN 15th Inf. 2nd Co.F
Reagan, Daniel H. NC 14th Inf. Co.F
Reagan, Daniel M. Gen. & Staff Contr.Surg.
Reagan, D.M. TX Inf. Whaley's Co.
Reagan, E. LA Mil. Bragg's Bn. Fowler's Co.
Reagan, E.A. TN 10th (DeMoss') Cav. Co.E
Reagan, E.H. MS Cav. 2nd Bn.Res. Co.E Cpl.
Reagan, E. Mc. TX 19th Inf. Co.B
Reagan, E.O. MS 29th Inf. Co.K
Reagan, F. LA Mil. Chalmette Regt. Co.E
Reagan, F.M. AL 55th Vol. Co.G
Reagan, F.M. TN 10th (DeMoss') Cav. Asst.Surg.
Reagan, Frank NC 1st Inf. Co.D
Reagan, F.W. GA Inf. 1st Loc.Troops (Augusta) Barnes' Lt.Arty.Co. Cpl.
Reagan, Gorum NC 45th Inf. Co.I
Reagan, G.P. TX 33rd Cav. Co.D
Reagan, G.W. MS 26th Inf. Co.A
Reagan, H. TN 15th (Stewart's) Cav. Co.D
Reagan, H.C. AR Lt.Arty. Rivers' Btty. 2nd Lt.
Reagan, Henry MO 1st Inf. Co.A
Reagan, H.J. SC 19th Inf. Co.H
Reagan, J. GA 5th Res. Co.B
Reagan, J. TX Cav. 4th Regt.St.Troops Co.H 1st Lt.
Reagan, J.A. TN Cav. 16th Bn. (Neal's) Co.B
Reagan, James LA 20th Inf. Co.G
Reagan, James LA 22nd Inf. Co.A
Reagan, James LA Herrick's Co. (Orleans Blues)
Reagan, James MS 6th Cav. Co.E
Reagan, James NC Inf. Thomas Legion Co.I

Reagan, James TX 9th Cav. Co.D
Reagan, James H. NC 25th Inf. Co.D
Reagan, James H. NC Inf. Thomas Legion Co.F
Reagan, James H. TN 13th (Gore's) Cav. Co.C
Reagan, James H. TX 6th Cav. Co.C Ch.Bugler
Reagan, James M. LA 19th Inf. Co.B
Reagan, James M. MO Cav. Coleman's Regt. Co.C
Reagan, James M. SC 19th Inf. Co.H
Reagan, James M. TN 9th (Ward's) Cav.
Reagan, James M. TX 11th Inf. Co.C 2nd Lt.
Reagan, J.B. TN 24th Inf. Co.F
Reagan, J.B. TX Cav. Wells' Regt. Co.A 2nd Lt.
Reagan, J.C. TN 10th (DeMoss') Cav. Co.E
Reagan, J.D. TN 13th (Gore's) Cav. Co.C
Reagan, J.E. TN 13th (Gore's) Cav. Co.C
Reagan, Jefferson GA Cav. (St.Guards) Bond's Co.
Reagan, Jesse MS 11th (Perrin's) Cav. Co.E Sgt.
Reagan, Jesse H. MS Lt.Arty. (The Hudson Btty.) Hoole's Co.
Reagan, J.H. GA 8th Inf. Co.A
Reagan, J.H. TN 25th Inf. Co.F
Reagan, J.J. TN 10th (DeMoss') Cav. Co.E
Reagan, J.L. LA 6th Cav. Co.C
Reagan, J.M. MS 28th Cav. Co.E
Reagan, J.M. MS Morgan's Co. (Morgan Riflemen)
Reagan, J.M. TX 7th Cav. Co.F Sgt.
Reagan, J.M. TX 33rd Cav. Co.D
Reagan, John AL Mil. 3rd Vol. Co.G
Reagan, John GA Inf. 2nd Bn. Co.B Cpl.
Reagan, John LA 1st Hvy.Arty. (Reg.) Co.B
Reagan, John LA 13th Inf. Co.I
Reagan, John NC 7th Sr.Res. Davie's Co.
Reagan, John TN 2nd (Walker's) Inf. Co.F
Reagan, John A. NC 23rd Inf. Co.K
Reagan, John B. TX 3rd Cav. Co.C
Reagan, John B. TX Cav. Wells' Bn. Co.A 2nd Lt.
Reagan, John C. NC 13th Inf. Co.A
Reagan, John C. TN 43rd Inf. Co.E
Reagan, John D. MS 25th Inf. Co.A
Reagan, John H. TX 22nd Inf. Co.G
Reagan, John R. TN 1st (Feild's) Inf. Co.K Sgt.
Reagan, John T. LA Arty. Moody's Co. (Madison Lt.Arty.)
Reagan, John T. MS 31st Inf. Co.A
Reagan, Joseph NC Inf. Thomas Legion Co.H
Reagan, Joseph T. MS Arty. (Seven Stars Arty.) Roberts' Co.
Reagan, J.R. GA 8th Inf. Co.G
Reagan, J.R. GA 60th Inf. Co.E
Reagan, J.R. TN Inf. 1st Cons.Regt. Co.B
Reagan, J.W. AL 31st Inf. Co.D
Reagan, J.W. GA Mil. 12th Regt. Co.C
Reagan, J.W. TX 12th Cav. Co.K
Reagan, Ker B. GA 5th Inf. Co.B
Reagan, Lenoir TN Cav. 16th Bn. (Neal's) Co.B 1st Lt.,Adj.
Reagan, Leroy NC 45th Inf. Co.I
Reagan, Lewis L. AL 4th Inf. Co.I
Reagan, M.A. AL 51st (Part.Rangers) Co.D
Reagan, Marcus A. SC 6th Cav. Co.E
Reagan, Mardis TN 53rd Inf. Co.A 2nd Lt.

Reagan, Merryweather G. TX 1st (Yager's) Cav. Co.A

Reagan, Merryweather G. TX Cav. 3rd (Yager's) Bn. Co.A

Reagan, Michael AL City Guards Lockett's Co.

Reagan, Michael LA 1st Hvy.Arty. (Reg.) Co.D

Reagan, Michael W. TX 11th (Spaight's) Bn.Vol. Co.E

Reagan, M.V. MS 8th Cav. Co.B Sgt.

Reagan, M.V. MS 28th Cav. Co.E Sgt.

Reagan, M.V. MS 4th Inf. Co.F Cpl.

Reagan, M.V. MS 44th Inf. Co.E

Reagan, M.V. MS Morgan's Co. (Morgan Riflemen) 1st Lt.

Reagan, M.W. TX 21st Inf. Co.B

Reagan, Nathan H. TN 59th Mtd.Inf. Co.G

Reagan, N.C. LA 2nd Inf. Co.B

Reagan, N.C. LA Res.Corps.

Reagan, Neal C. LA 16th Inf. Co.G 2nd Lt.

Reagan, N.M. TX 7th Cav. Co.F

Reagan, P. AL 8th Inf. Co.H

Reagan, P. AR 1st (Colquitt's) Inf. Co.F

Reagan, Pat Conf.Inf. 8th Bn. Co.A

Reagan, Patrick GA Arty. Maxwell's Reg. Lt.Btty.

Reagan, Patrick GA 1st Reg. Co.D

Reagan, Peter NC 3rd Inf. Co.G

Reagan, Peter L. MS 31st Inf. Co.A

Reagan, P.G. TX 16th Cav. Co.E

Reagan, Pleasant Y. TX 16th Cav. Co.K Cpl.

Reagan, P.M. MS 31st Inf. Co.A

Reagan, R. AL 17th Inf. Co.H

Reagan, R.A. TX 12th Cav. Co.K

Reagan, R.B. GA Inf. 25th Bn. (Prov.Guard) Co.B

Reagan, Robert AL 24th Inf. Co.E

Reagan, Robert F. NC 37th Inf. Co.H

Reagan, Sam AL 4th (Russell's) Cav. Co.I

Reagan, S.B. MS 9th Inf. Co.K 1st Sgt.

Reagan, Simpson GA 12th Mil.

Reagan, Stephen R. GA 42nd Inf. Co.E

Reagan, T. LA Mil. Chalmette Regt. Co.E

Reagan, Thomas AR 15th Mil. Co.B

Reagan, Thomas LA 1st (Strawbridge's) Inf. Co.A

Reagan, Thomas B. MS 31st Inf. Co.D Sgt.

Reagan, Thomas L.B.E. MS 44th Inf. Co.C

Reagan, Thomas R. TX 16th Cav. Co.B Cpl.

Reagan, Timothy MS 2nd (Quinn's St.Troops) Inf. Co.B

Reagan, Timothy TN 5th Inf. 1st Co.C

Reagan, W.A. TX 15th Inf. 2nd Co.G

Reagan, W.B.L. Gen. & Staff 1st Lt.,Adj.

Reagan, W.C. TX 9th Cav. Co.F

Reagan, W.C. TX Cav. Giddings' Bn. Carrington's Co. Sgt.

Reagan, W.D. Gen. & Staff, Cav. Col.

Reagan, W.E. GA 42nd Inf. Co.F

Reagan, West TX 8th Inf. Co.K

Reagan, W.G. GA 1st Reg. Co.C Cpl.

Reagan, W.G. GA Inf. (Loc.Def.) Hamlet's Co.

Reagan, William AL 55th Vol. Co.G

Reagan, William LA 11th Inf. Co.A

Reagan, William LA 13th Inf. Co.I,F Sgt.

Reagan, William NC 25th Inf. Co.D

Reagan, William TN 13th (Gore's) Cav. Co.A

Reagan, William TN 13th (Gore's) Cav. Co.F

Reagan, William TN 28th Inf. Co.B

Reagan, William TX 20th Inf. Co.F

Reagan, William A. TX 13th Vol. Co.E

Reagan, William J. TN 25th Inf. Co.F Adj.

Reagan, William M. GA Arty. 9th Bn. Co.C

Reagan, William S. TN 3rd (Lillard's) Mtd.Inf. Co.C

Reagan, William T. TN 43rd Inf. Co.E

Reagan, W.J. TN 84th Inf. Co.B

Reagan, W.R. TX 30th Cav. Co.F

Reagan, W.T. AR 35th Inf. Co.H 1st Sgt.

Reagan, Y.P. SC 7th Inf. 2nd Co.C, Co.G

Reagan, Z.H. TN 5th (McKenzie's) Cav. Co.C

Reagan, Z.P. TX 9th Cav. Co.B

Reagen, James J. GA 42nd Inf. Co.F

Reagen, Robert J. FL Milton Lt.Arty. Dunham's Co.

Reager, --- TN 37th Inf. Asst.Surg.

Reager, Benjamin F. AR Boon's Bn.

Reager, Francis M. TX 4th Inf. Co.D

Reager, George TX 37th Cav. 2nd Co.I Cpl.

Reager, George F. VA 13th Inf. 2nd Co.B

Reager, George W. VA 6th Cav. Co.B

Reager, Joseph VA 49th Inf. Co.E

Reager, Lewis VA 6th Cav. Co.B

Reager, Lewis VA 34th Mil. Co.A

Reager, Lewis A. VA 17th Inf. Co.B

Reager, Milton AR 1st (Monroe's) Cav. Palmer's Co.

Reagget, James AL 15th Inf. Co.H

Reagh, Anderson M. MS 2nd Inf. Co.C,F

Reagh, James MS Inf. 3rd Bn. (St.Troops) Co.A 1st Cpl.

Reagh, J.C. MS 2nd Inf. Co.F

Reagh, J.C. MS 41st Inf. Co.E

Reagh, John W. MS 11th Inf. Co.I

Reagh, Robert H. MS 14th Inf. Co.K

Reagh, Robert H. MS 14th (Cons.) Inf. Co.F

Reagin, C.G. TN 17th Inf. Co.D Sgt.

Reagin, Cumegys AL 50th Inf. Co.B

Reagin, Harrison T. GA Cobb's Legion Co.C

Reagin, Haydon C. GA Cobb's Legion Co.C

Reagin, Henry B. GA 7th Inf. Co.D

Reagin, H.W. SC 3rd Inf. Co.C

Reagin, James M. GA 7th Inf. Co.D Sgt.

Reagin, J.B. SC 2nd Cav. Co.G

Reagin, J.B. SC 3rd Inf. Co.C

Reagin, J.J. GA Lt.Arty. Ritter's Co.

Reagin, John A. TN 62nd Mtd.Inf. Co.C Cpl.

Reagin, J.W. SC 3rd Inf. Co.C,A

Reagin, Oliver GA 35th Inf. Co.B

Reagin, T.E. SC 4th Cav. Co.I

Reagin, Thomas SC Cav. 12th Bn. Co.B

Reagin, Thomas C. TN 32nd Inf. Co.H

Reagin, Thomas C. TN 35th Inf. 2nd Co.F

Reagin, Thomas J. TN 1st (Turney's) Inf. Co.B 1st Sgt.

Reagin, W.B. GA 18th Inf. Co.B Sgt.

Reagin, William GA 35th Inf. Co.B Sgt.

Reagin, William 3rd Conf.Inf. Co.D

Reagin, William D. GA Cobb's Legion Co.C Cpl.

Reagin, Wilson GA 35th Inf. Co.B

Reagin, Young MS 35th Inf. Co.K

Reagins, W.H. TN Inf. Nashville Bn. Cattles' Co.

Reagle, James L. VA Mil. Carroll Cty.

Reagon, J. AR Inf. Sparks' Co.

Reagon, J.A. 2nd Conf.Inf. Co.A

Reagon, Thomas B. AR 15th (Josey's) Inf. Co.A

Reagor, --- TX Cav. 4th Regt.St.Troops Co.H

Reagor, Anthony W. AR 1st (Colquitt's) Inf. Co.G

Reagor, Benjamin F. AR Cav. Logan's Regt. Co.I

Reagor, Benjamin F. TX 19th Cav. Co.A

Reagor, George A. TN 41st Inf. Co.K

Reagor, J.A. TN Inf. 23rd Bn. Co.C 1st Sgt.

Reagor, James D. TX 19th Cav. Co.A

Reagor, John F. TX 19th Cav. Co.A

Reagor, John R. TN 19th Cav. Co.E

Reagor, John W. TN Inf. 23rd Bn. Co.C Sgt.

Reagor, Joseph A. TN 45th Inf.

Reagor, L.S. TX 7th Inf. Co.C

Reagor, Rober J. TN 37th Inf. Co.A

Reagor, Robert J. TN Inf. 23rd Bn. Co.C

Reagor, Samuel L. TN 37th Inf. Co.A Capt.

Reagor, William J. TN 41st Inf. Co.K

Reags, P.A. MD Cav. 2nd Bn. Co.A

Reah, Robert C. NC 6th Cav. (65th St.Troops) Surg.

Reahard, David G. MO Lt.Arty. Landis' Co.

Reahard, D.G. MO Lt.Arty. 1st Btty.

Real, A. LA Mil. 3rd Regt. French Brig. Co.2 Cpl.

Real, Albert SC 24th Inf. Co.K

Real, Charles TN Inf. 22nd Bn. Co.C

Real, G.W. MS 31st Inf. Co.A

Real, J.H. AL 5th Cav. Co.B

Real, J.H. AL 26th (O'Neal's) Inf. Co.B

Real, J.L. NC 1st Inf. Co.G

Real, John MO Inf. 4th Regt.St.Guard Co.B

Real, John VA 18th Cav. Co.H

Real, Valentine MO Inf. 4th Regt.St.Guard Co.B

Reale, Joseph LA 28th (Thomas') Inf. Co.K

Reall, R.B. AR 38th Inf. Co.A

Reals, John H. AL 46th Inf. Co.C

Realy, Carles W. MS Cav. Semple's Co.

Realy, John TX 9th (Nichols') Inf. Co.G

Ream, Abraham K. AR 23rd Inf. Co.G

Ream, Charles H. VA 13th Inf. Co.K

Ream, David M. MS 11th Inf. Co.C

Ream, David M. VA 18th Cav. Co.D 1st Lt.

Ream, David M. VA 10th Inf. Co.F 2nd Lt.

Ream, James W. VA 11th Cav. Co.D Cpl.

Ream, James W. VA 13th Inf. Co.K

Ream, John MO Cav. Coffee's Regt.

Ream, N.B. Gen. & Staff Maj.,CS

Ream, R. AR Mil. Borland's Regt. Woodruff's Co.

Ream, Robert L. AR Cav. 1st Bn. (Stirman's) Co.H Capt.

Ream, Robert L. TX 27th Cav. Co.B 2nd Lt.

Ream, Robert L. Stirman's Regt.S.S. Co.H 1st Lt.

Ream, Smp. GA 12th Mil.

Ream, Sylvester TX 30th Cav. Co.I

Ream, T.M. Gen. & Staff Maj.,Surg.

Ream, V. Gen. & Staff 1st Lt.,AAQM

Reamar, Daniel A. VA 136th Mil. Co.B

Reamer, B.F. MS 1st Lt.Arty. Music.

Reamer, Feness M. VA 97th Mil. Co.K

Reamer, Frank T. KY 2nd (Woodward's) Cav. Co.D 1st Sgt.

Reamer, Frank T. TN 1st (Feild's) Inf. Co.C
Reamer, John MD 1st Cav. Co.A
Reamer, John C. NC 4th Inf. Co.C
Reamer, John D.S. VA 10th Inf. Co.B
Reamer, Marion F. VA Lt.Arty. Utterback's Co.
Reamer, Solomon P. VA 33rd Inf. Co.I
Reamer, Solomon P. VA 97th Mil. Co.D
Reamer, Solomon P. VA Guards & Scouts Rockingham Cty. Sgt.
Reamer, W.D. NC 4th Inf. Co.C
Reames, Albert SC 2nd Arty. Co.K
Reames, Asa C. MS 29th Inf. Co.C
Reames, B.T. LA Inf. 9th Bn. Co.A
Reames, Charles LA Mil. Chalmette Regt. Hosp.Stew.
Reames, Churchwell TN 33rd Inf. Co.G
Reames, C.W. LA Mil. Chalmette Regt. Co.C
Reames, D.B. LA 3rd Inf. Co.K
Reames, Edward H. VA 18th Inf. Co.K Cpl.
Reames, George VA 62nd Mtd.Inf. Co.F
Reames, George W. NC 30th Inf. Co.G
Reames, H.B. LA 3rd Inf. Co.E
Reames, H.M. SC 2nd Inf. Co.D Cpl.
Reames, Irwin NC 25th Inf. Co.G
Reames, Isham D. VA 9th Inf. Co.C
Reames, James TN 33rd Inf. Co.G
Reames, James VA 18th Inf. Co.G
Reames, Jefferson SC 2nd Arty. Co.K
Reames, John LA 4th Inf. Co.D
Reames, Jordan SC 2nd Arty. Co.B,K
Reames, Joshua NC 25th Inf. Co.G
Reames, Joshua A. GA 29th Inf. Co.G
Reames, Laban R. VA Inf. 5th Bn. Co.E
Reames, Laborn R. VA 53rd Inf. Co.B
Reames, Leonard SC 2nd Arty. Co.K
Reames, L.I. SC 8th Res.
Reames, L. Ira SC 5th Cav. Co.H
Reames, L.W. VA 1st (Farinholt's) Res. Co.I Cpl.
Reames, P.A. Conf.Cav. Powers' Regt. Co.F Lt.
Reames, Peter S. VA Inf. 5th Bn. Co.E
Reames, Peter S. VA 53rd Inf. Co.B Sgt.
Reames, Reuben NC 25th Inf. Co.G
Reames, Rhodes E. AR Lt.Arty. Wiggins' Btty.
Reames, Richard B. VA Inf. 5th Bn. Co.E
Reames, Ridley SC 2nd Arty. Co.K
Reames, Robert H. VA 3rd (Archer's) Bn.Res. Co.B
Reames, Stephen E. VA Inf. 5th Bn. Co.E
Reames, Stephen E. VA 53rd Inf. Co.B Cpl.
Reames, Thomas MS 29th Inf. Co.C
Reames, Thomas B. LA 11th Inf. Co.H
Reames, Thomas D. VA Inf. 5th Bn. Co.B
Reames, W.H. VA 1st (Farinholt's) Res. Co.F 2nd Lt.
Reames, W.H. VA Averett's Bn.Res. 2nd Lt.
Reames, William H. VA 18th Inf. Co.G
Reames, William L. VA Inf. 5th Bn. Co.E 2nd Lt.
Reames, W.J. LA 2nd Inf. Co.I 1st Lt.
Reames, W.R. TN 20th Inf. Co.H
Reamey, Henry C. VA 24th Inf. Co.H Cpl.
Reamey, James A. VA 34th Inf. Co.B
Reamey, John S. VA 24th Inf. Co.H
Reamey, Pressley G. VA Cav. 15th Bn. Co.A
Reamey, Richard R. VA 55th Inf. Co.E
Reamey, Robert G. VA 111th Mil. Co.5

Reamey, Robert L. VA 55th Inf. Co.E
Reams, --- TX Cav. McCord's Frontier Regt. Co.K
Reams, B.B. AL Cav. (St.Res.) Young's Co.
Reams, Benjamine MO St.Guard
Reams, Benjamin F. VA 14th Inf. Co.I
Reams, B.M. GA 24th Inf. Co.E
Reams, C.E. LA 25th Inf. Co.I
Reams, C.W. LA 16th Inf. Co.A Cpl.
Reams, Erasmus VA 2nd Arty. Co.A Cpl.
Reams, Erasmus N. VA Arty. Dance's Co.
Reams, Frederick Spann SC 5th Cav. Co.H
Reams, F.S. SC Cav. 14th Bn. Co.A
Reams, G.A. AL Talladega Cty.Res. R.N. Ware's Cav.Co.
Reams, George W. TN 11th (Holman's) Cav. Co.G
Reams, George W. TN Holman's Bn. Part.Rangers Co.B
Reams, George W. 3rd Conf.Eng.Troops Co.A
Reams, G.H. TN 3rd (Forrest's) Cav. Co.B
Reams, J.A. TN 50th (Cons.) Inf. Co.C
Reams, J.C. VA Loc.Def. Wood's Co.
Reams, Jefferson SC 22nd Inf. Co.A
Reams, J.H. TN 3rd (Clack's) Inf. Co.F 3rd Lt.
Reams, J.M. GA 34th Inf. Co.I
Reams, J.M. TN 31st Inf. Co.B Cpl.
Reams, John NC 1st Inf. Co.F
Reams, John TN 10th (DeMoss') Cav. Co.A
Reams, John TN 11th (Holman's) Cav. Co.G
Reams, John TN Holman's Bn.Part.Rangers Co.B
Reams, John A. TN 50th Inf. Co.C
Reams, John C. VA 41st Inf. Co.B
Reams, John H. VA Lt.Arty. Montgomery's Co. Artif.
Reams, John H. VA 18th Inf. Co.K
Reams, John W. NC 43rd Inf. Co.B
Reams, Joshua FL 5th Inf. Co.D
Reams, L.D. TX Conscr.
Reams, Levi E. AR 19th (Dockery's) Inf. Cons.Co.E,K,D
Reams, N.H. TN 31st Inf. Co.C Ord.Sgt.
Reams, P.A. LA 2nd Inf. Co.I Sgt.
Reams, Richard NC 1st Jr.Res. Co.K
Reams, Richard S. VA 2nd Arty. Co.A
Reams, Richard S. VA Arty. Dance's Co.
Reams, Robert GA 27th Inf. Co.E
Reams, Robert TN 22nd Cav.
Reams, R.Y. TN 39th Mtd.Inf. Co.A
Reams, S.B. TN 3rd (Forrest's) Cav. Co.B
Reams, T.B. VA Loc.Def. Tayloe's Co.
Reams, Thomas B. GA Siege Arty. 28th Bn. Co.E Cpl.
Reams, T.T. GA Inf. 1st Bn. (St.Guards) Co.E
Reams, W.A. TN 12th (Green's) Cav. Co.B
Reams, William AR 27th Inf. Co.E
Reams, William LA Miles' Legion Co.A
Reams, William SC 4th Inf. Co.K
Reams, William SC Palmetto S.S. Co.L Cpl.
Reams, William VA Inf. Mileham's Co.
Reams, William L. VA Hvy.Arty. Epes' Co.
Reams, William M. NC 43rd Inf. Co.B
Reams, W.L. VA Mtd.Guard 4th Congr.Dist.
Reamy, Baldwin M. VA 9th Cav. Sandford's Co.
Reamy, Baldwin M. VA 15th Cav. Co.A Cpl.

Reamy, Baldwin M. VA Cav. 15th Bn. Co.A Cpl.
Reamy, B.M. VA 5th Cav.
Reamy, H.D. VA 47th Inf. Co.C Sgt.
Reamy, James C. VA 9th Cav. Co.C
Reamy, James O. VA 41st Mil. Co.E 2nd Lt.
Reamy, James S. VA 9th Cav. Co.I
Reamy, Joseph J. VA 9th Cav. Co.I
Reamy, Joseph J. VA 25th Mil. Co.A
Reamy, P.E. VA 5th Cav.
Reamy, Presley G. VA 15th Cav. Co.A
Reamy, Prestley G. VA 9th Cav. Sandford's Co.
Reamy, Robert G. VA 9th Cav. Sandford's Co.
Reamy, Robert G. VA 15th Cav. Co.A
Reamy, Robert G. VA Cav. 15th Bn. Co.A
Reamy, Robert L. VA 41st Mil. Co.E
Reamy, R.T. VA 47th Inf. Co.C Sgt.
Reamy, Thomas B. VA 9th Cav. Co.A
Reamy, Thomas J. VA 9th Cav. Co.B
Reamy, Thomas J. VA Lt.Arty. Thornton's Co.
Reamy, William A. VA 6th Inf. Co.K
Reamy, William A. VA 9th Cav. Co.C
Reamy, William A. VA 41st Mil. Co.E
Reamy, William J. VA 9th Cav. Co.K Cpl.
Reamy, William J. VA 41st Mil. Co.D Sgt.
Rean, --- TX 24th & 25th Cav. (Cons.)
Rean, John SC 22nd Inf. Co.A
Reand, Joseph LA Inf.Cons. 18th Regt. & Yellow Jacket Bn. Co.K
Reand, O. LA 22nd (Cons.) Inf. Co.E
Reand, Omer LA Mil. 4th Regt. 2nd Brig. 1st Div. Co.A 2nd Lt.
Reando, J. TX Conscr.
Reane, T.H. MS 31st Inf. Co.D
Reanes, Walter VA 2nd Inf.Loc.Def. Co.C
Reaney, Henry J. NC 1st Arty. (10th St.Troops) Co.K
Reaney, H.L. GA Inf. 1st Loc.Troops (Augusta) Barnes' Lt.Arty.Co.
Reaney, John LA 8th Inf. Co.B
Reaney, John E. NC 1st Arty. (10th St.Troops) Co.K Sgt.
Reaney, John P. VA 3rd Inf. Co.E Sgt.
Reaney, John T. VA 47th Inf. Co.C
Reaney, Matthew LA 8th Inf. Co.B
Reaney, William T. GA 48th Inf. Co.C
Reans, H.H. TN 20th Cav. Co.B
Reans, Josiah H. LA 3rd Inf. Co.I
Reany, J.C. AL 24th Inf. Co.G
Reany, J.T. MS 22nd Inf.
Reany, T.M. Eng.,CSA 2nd Asst.Eng.
Reap, Daniel NC 42nd Inf. Co.C
Reap, Edward C. AR 9th Inf. Old Co.B, Co.K
Reap, Ephraim NC 42nd Inf. Co.C
Reap, J. AR 30th Inf. Co.C
Reap, Lawson NC 8th Bn.Jr.Res. Co.B
Reap, Michael LA 22nd Inf. D.H. Marks' Co.
Reap, Richard G. AR Lt.Arty. Owen's Btty.
Reap, Richard G. AR 9th Inf. Old Co.B, Co.K
Reap, Samuel H. AR 1st (Colquitt's) Inf. Co.I
Reapass, --- VA Cav. 47th Bn. Co.B
Reapi, L. AL 4th Inf.
Rear, James AR 37th Inf. Co.K
Rearburn, Robert A. VA Lt.Arty. 13th Bn. Co.B
Rearden, C. SC 13th Inf. Co.C
Rearden, Daniel TN 6th Inf. Co.F
Rearden, Jimmy Conf.Cav. 6th Bn. Co.C

Rearden, Lorenzo D. SC 15th Inf. Co.K
Rearden, Martin TN 11th Inf. Co.K,G
Rearden, Michael VA 34th Inf. Co.C
Rearden, Robert N. SC 7th Inf. 1st Co.F, 2nd Co.F Sgt.
Rearden, William E. SC 7th Inf. 1st Co.F, 2nd Co.F Cpl.
Rearden, William W. AL 6th Inf. Co.L
Rearden, William W. AL 47th Inf. Co.D 2nd Lt.
Reardin, Michael 9th Conf.Inf. Co.B
Reardon, Bat AL 4th Res. Co.B
Reardon, Bryant NC Hvy.Arty. 10th Bn. Co.B
Reardon, C. AL Inf. 2nd Regt. Co.I
Reardon, C. MO Cav. Woodson's Co.
Reardon, Charles MO 1st Cav.
Reardon, Charles Conf.Inf. 1st Bn. Co.I
Reardon, Daniel AR Lt.Arty. Key's Btty.
Reardon, Daniel LA 3rd Inf. Co.E
Reardon, David A. NC Hvy.Arty. 10th Bn. Co.B
Reardon, D.C. NC 32nd Inf. Co.G,C
Reardon, D.E. SC 25th Inf. Co.I
Reardon, Drury W. NC 2nd Cav. (19th St.Troops) Co.D
Reardon, E. LA 1st (Strawbridge's) Inf. Co.D
Reardon, Edward GA 45th Inf. Co.C
Reardon, George William SC Lt.Arty. 3rd (Palmetto) Bn. Co.E,G Sgt.
Reardon, Henry F. VA 6th Inf. Co.G
Reardon, H.F. Gen. & Staff Capt.,Dist.Off.
Reardon, H.F. Nitre & Min. Bureau War Dept.,CSA Capt.
Reardon, J. KY Jessee's Bn.Mtd.Riflemen Co.C
Reardon, J. LA Mil. 1st Regt. 2nd Brig. 1st Div. Co.E
Reardon, James LA Inf.Crescent Regt. Co.D
Reardon, James NC Hvy.Arty. 10th Bn. Co.B
Reardon, James E. SC 7th Inf. 1st Co.F, 2nd Co.F Capt.
Reardon, J.B. AL Vol. Meador's Co.
Reardon, Jerry KY 1st Inf. Co.G
Reardon, J.J. SC 23rd Inf. Co.I
Reardon, John AL 3rd Cav. Co.E
Reardon, John AR 11th Inf. Co.D
Reardon, John AR 11th & 17th (Cons.) Inf. Co.D
Reardon, John GA 25th Inf. Co.A
Reardon, John LA 21st (Patton's) Inf. Co.A
Reardon, John SC 16th Inf. Co.A
Reardon, John TN 2nd (Walker's) Inf. Co.F
Reardon, John TN 15th Inf. Co.H
Reardon, John VA 1st Lt.Arty. Co.B
Reardon, John VA 2nd Inf. Co.C
Reardon, John Conf.Cav. Wood's Regt. 1st Co.D
Reardon, John A. GA Inf. 1st Loc.Troops (Augusta) Co.A
Reardon, John E. AR 6th Inf. Co.A Capt.
Reardon, John F. NC 15th Inf. Co.F
Reardon, John W. AR 1st (Colquitt's) Inf. Co.G
Reardon, John W. VA 52nd Inf. Co.H
Reardon, J.P. AL 19th Inf. Co.F Cpl.
Reardon, J.W. GA 19th Inf. Co.D
Reardon, Lewis NC Hvy.Arty. 10th Bn. Co.B
Reardon, L.M. VA Cav. Mosby's Regt. (Part. Rangers) Co.E
Reardon, Louis VA Vol. Taylor's Co.
Reardon, M. LA Inf. 4th Bn. Co.D
Reardon, M. LA Inf. Pelican Regt. Co.F

Reardon, Martin LA 21st (Patton's) Inf.
Reardon, Mathew LA Arty. Moody's Co. (Madison Lt.Arty.)
Reardon, Michael MD Cav. 2nd Bn. Co.B Sgt.
Reardon, Michael MO 1st Inf. Co.F
Reardon, Michael VA Lt.Arty. Moore's Co.
Reardon, Michael VA Lt.Arty. Thompson's Co.
Reardon, Mike TN 21st Inf. Co.B
Reardon, P. AL 48th Mil. Co.A
Reardon, Patrick AL St.Arty. Co.D
Reardon, Patrick LA 21st (Patton's) Inf. Co.A
Reardon, Patrick MO Cav. 3rd Bn. Co.D
Reardon, Patrick TN 1st Hvy.Arty. Co.F, 2nd Co.D
Reardon, Patrick VA Inf. 1st Bn. Co.C
Reardon, P.V. VA Cav. Mosby's Regt. (Part. Rangers) Co.E
Reardon, Robert SC Inf. 1st (Charleston) Bn. Co.A
Reardon, Robert SC 2nd Inf. Co.D
Reardon, S.B. AR 6th Inf. Co.A N.C.S. Sgt.
Reardon, S.M. SC 9th Inf. Co.C
Reardon, Thomas R. VA 54th Mil. Co.B
Reardon, Timothy AL 19th Inf. Co.F
Reardon, Timothy AL 20th Inf. Co.F
Reardon, T.J. LA Inf. 1st Sp.Bn. (Rightor's) Co.D
Reardon, William MO 1st Inf. Co.F
Reardon, William TN 13th Inf. Co.A
Reardon, William M. MS 1st Lt.Arty. Co.K
Reardon, W.W. AL Vol. Meador's Co.
Reardy, Philip T. AL Lt.Arty. 2nd Bn. Co.E Sgt.
Reardy, P.T. AL St.Arty. Co.D Sgt.
Reariden, James J. TN Lt.Arty. Barry's Co.
Rearley, Wain NC 37th Inf.
Reary, Hugh LA 22nd Inf. Co.B
Reasce, G.C. AL 7th Cav. Co.D
Rease, George H. VA 5th Inf. Co.G
Rease, John S. AR 27th Inf. Co.F
Rease, J.R. TN 12th (Cons.) Inf. Co.F
Rease, L.J. GA 8th Cav. Co.B
Rease, W.B. MO 4th Cav. Co.I
Rease, William J. VA 2nd Arty. Co.K
Rease, W.R. TX 4th Inf. Co.C
Reasenover, Jacob Shecoe's Chickasaw Bn. Mtd.Vol. Co.A Cpl.
Reasenover, John TX 16th Cav. Co.C
Reasenover, J.R. TN 12th (Green's) Cav. Co.A
Reaser, A.F. MO 9th (Elliott's) Cav. Co.K
Reaser, Jacob B. MO 9th (Elliott's) Cav. Co.K Capt.
Reaser, James VA Inf. 26th Bn. Co.D,B
Reaser, John VA 146th Mil. Co.E
Reaser, Louis LA 5th Inf. Co.G 1st Sgt.
Reaser, Philip VA Inf. 26th Bn. Co.D
Reaser, Samuel VA Inf. 26th Bn. Co.D
Reaser, Samuel H. VA 136th Mil. Co.E Cpl.
Reaser, T.H. NC 2nd Arty. (36th St.Troops) Co.H
Reaser, W.W. VA 2nd Inf. Co.G
Reaser, William H. VA 136th Mil. Co.E
Reashe, Nicholas MS 18th Cav. Co.K
Reaside, John AL Loc.Def. & Sp.Serv. Toomer's Co.
Reasler, William L. SC 11th Inf. Co.C
Reasoile, H.L. LA 22nd Inf. Co.D

Reason, James TN 12th (Green's) Cav. Co.C
Reason, James TN 16th (Logwood's) Cav. Co.I
Reason, Joseph MS 29th Inf. Co.B
Reason, Joseph VA Lt.Arty. Douthat's Co.
Reason, Levi W. 7th Conf.Cav. 2nd Co.I Sgt.
Reason, M. GA 12th Mil.
Reason, P. LA Inf.Cons.Crescent Regt. Co.L
Reason, Raleigh NC 2nd Inf. Co.D,B
Reason, Redin NC Cav. 16th Bn. Co.B
Reason, Reuben KY 10th Cav. Co.D Cpl.
Reason, Riley NC 61st Inf. Co.H
Reason, S. NC 15th Inf. Co.M
Reason, T.R. SC 10th Inf. Co.K
Reason, William W. VA Lt.Arty. Douthat's Co.
Reasoner, Gilbert M. TN 2nd (Robison's) Inf. Co.G
Reasoner, John C. AL 4th Inf. Co.I,F Cpl.
Reasoner, J.W. TX 29th Cav. Co.K
Reasoner, J.W. TX 34th Cav. Co.K
Reasoner, William AR 11th & 17th (Cons.) Inf. Co.I
Reasoner, William V. LA 3rd Inf. Co.F
Reasoner, W.V. AR Inf. Cocke's Regt. Co.F
Reasonover, George W. TN 7th Inf. Co.A 1st Sgt.
Reasonover, James L. TN 4th Cav. Co.A
Reasonover, James L. TN Cav. Allison's Squad. Co.A Sgt.
Reasonover, J.B. TN 55th (McKoin's) Inf. James' Co.
Reasonover, John Shecoe's Chickasaw Bn. Mtd.Vol. Co.A
Reasonover, John B. TN 44th (Cons.) Inf. Co.C
Reasonover, John M. TN 53rd Inf. Co.C
Reasonover, Jordan TX 11th Inf. Co.E
Reasonover, Joseph B. AL 33rd Inf. Co.B
Reasonover, P.B. TX 11th Inf. Co.E
Reasonover, Robert N. MS 9th Inf. Old Co.E
Reasonover, Thomas TN 53rd Inf. Co.H 2nd Lt.
Reasonover, Thomas B. TN 53rd Inf. Co.C
Reasonover, Thomas J. MS 29th Inf. Co.I
Reasonover, William J. TN 32nd Inf. Co.B Cpl.
Reasons, Allen M. MS 2nd Part.Rangers Co.F Capt.
Reasons, A.M. MS 4th Inf. Co.F 3rd Lt.
Reasons, Cotton NC 1st Inf. Co.H
Reasons, G.F. TN 47th Inf. Co.B
Reasons, Grandison B. TN 32nd Inf. Co.E 1st Lt.
Reasons, Grandison B. TN 35th Inf. 2nd Co.K 1st Lt.
Reasons, Joseph T. NC Hvy.Arty. 1st Bn. Co.B
Reasons, Lafayette W. MS 44th Inf. Co.C 1st Lt.
Reasons, Levi W. NC 1st Inf. (6 mo. '61) Co.A
Reasons, N.P. TX 37th Cav. Mullins' Co.
Reasons, R. Conf.Cav. Wood's Regt. 2nd Co.M
Reasons, R.D. MS 9th Inf. Old Co.H, New Co.A
Reasons, Redden W. NC 13th Inf. Co.G
Reasons, Redding 7th Conf.Cav. 2nd Co.I
Reasons, Riley NC 42nd Inf. Co.B
Reasons, Samuel NC 17th Inf. (2nd Org.) Co.C
Reasons, William KY 3rd Mtd.Inf. Co.B
Reasons, William M. MS 15th Inf. Co.H Capt.
Reasons, W.R. AR 37th Inf. Co.I
Reasor, Daniel S. VA Inf. 21st Bn. Co.A 3rd Lt.

45

Reaves, Jerry P. NC 2nd Arty. (36th St.Troops) Co.I

Reasor, Daniel S. VA 64th Mtd.Inf. Co.A 2nd Lt.

Reasor, James H. VA Inf. 21st Bn. Co.A Cpl.

Reasor, James H. VA 64th Mtd.Inf. Co.A Cpl.

Reasor, James M. KY 14th Cav. Co.B

Reasor, William KY 6th Mtd.Inf. Co.A

Reasor, William A.J. VA Inf. 21st Bn. Co.A

Reasor, William A.J. VA 64th Mtd.Inf. Co.A

Reasor, William A.J. VA 94th Mil. Co.A Sgt.

Reasser, John VA Arty. C.F. Johnston's Co.

Reatherford, A. AR 35th Inf. Co.A

Reatherford, B. AR 35th Inf. Co.A

Reatherford, J.H. MS 7th Cav. Co.K

Reathmire, John 9th Conf.Inf. Co.B

Reaton, John AL 27th Inf.

Reaton, Simeon MS 35th Inf. Co.C

Reau, Jean LA Mil.Bn. French Vol. 1st Lt.

Reaud, Victor LA Mil. Lartigue's Co. (Bienville Guards) 1st Lt.

Reausaux, S.R. MS Lt.Arty. (Jefferson Arty.) Darden's Co.

Reave, Laurence A.R. GA 63rd Inf. Co.A Cpl.

Reavell, J.H. MS 9th Inf. Co.I

Reaver, Alfred TX 33rd Cav. Co.A

Reaves, A. GA 12th Cav. Co.C

Reaves, A. GA Cav. 22nd Bn. (St.Guards) Co.I

Reaves, A. GA 8th Inf. Co.A

Reaves, A. MS 2nd St.Cav. Co.K

Reaves, A. SC 22nd Inf. Co.F

Reaves, A.B. AR 24th Inf. Co.D Cpl.

Reaves, A.B. AR Inf. Hardy's Regt. Co.C 2nd Lt.

Reaves, A.B. MS 1st (King's) Inf. (St.Troops) D. Love's Co. 2nd Lt.

Reaves, A.C. MS 29th Inf. Co.C

Reaves, A.H. TN 3rd (Forrest's) Cav. Co.E

Reaves, Alexander NC 20th Inf. Co.I

Reaves, Algernon S. AL 13th Inf. Co.D Capt.

Reaves, Andrew J. AL 12th Inf. Co.H

Reaves, A.R. 10th Conf.Cav. Co.B

Reaves, Asael TX Waul's Legion Co.F

Reaves, Asa J. GA 41st Inf. Co.H

Reaves, Asher NC 5th Inf. Co.C

Reaves, A.T. SC 22nd Inf. Co.F

Reaves, A.W. AL Cav. 24th Bn. Co.A

Reaves, B. MS 2nd St.Cav. Co.G

Reaves, B. 4th Conf.Inf. Co.E

Reaves, Barham SC Inf. Holcombe Legion Co.B

Reaves, Barram SC 13th Inf. Co.I

Reaves, Barry G. AR 8th Inf. Old Co.I

Reaves, Benjamin SC 1st (McCreary's) Inf. Co.H

Reaves, Benjamin SC 9th Res. Co.I

Reaves, Benjamin TN 14th Inf. Co.D

Reaves, Benjamin L. MS 31st Inf. Co.B

Reaves, Benjamin T. TN 4th Inf. Co.D Sgt.

Reaves, B.F. AL 46th Inf. Co.C

Reaves, B.N. AL 9th Cav. Co.C

Reaves, B.T. TN Inf. 3rd Cons.Regt. Co.D

Reaves, Burrell F. SC Palmetto S.S. Co.H

Reaves, Burton W. MS Inf. 3rd Bn. Co.G Sgt.

Reaves, B.W. AL 30th Inf. Co.E

Reaves, C. MS 27th Inf. Co.G

Reaves, C. TX 17th Inf. Co.I

Reaves, C.A. NC 14th Inf. Co.D

Reaves, C.C. AL Cav. 4th Bn. (Love's) Co.C

Reaves, C.G. AR 45th Cav. Co.A

Reaves, C.G. AR 38th Inf. Co.K

Reaves, C.H. AL 58th Inf. Co.B

Reaves, C.H. GA 2nd Cav. Co.D

Reaves, Charles NC Cav. 5th Bn. Co.D

Reaves, Charles I.W. SC 4th Cav. Co.F

Reaves, Charles K. GA 2nd Bn.S.S. Co.D 1st Sgt.

Reaves, Charles L. NC 8th Inf. Co.K Ch.Cook

Reaves, Charles W. TN Cav. Newsom's Regt. Co.C

Reaves, Columbus C. AL 1st Regt.Conscr. Co.A

Reaves, C.S. TN 51st (Cons.) Inf. Co.I

Reaves, C.W. SC 1st (McCreary's) Inf. Co.E Cpl.

Reaves, D. AR 32nd Inf. Co.B

Reaves, D. GA 5th Res. Co.I Sgt.

Reaves, D.A. FL 5th Inf.

Reaves, Daniel FL 3rd Inf. Co.H

Reaves, David MS 34th Inf. Co.G

Reaves, David SC Inf. 7th Bn. (Enfield Rifles) Co.D

Reaves, David TN 24th Inf. Co.I

Reaves, David E. GA 10th Inf. Co.F

Reaves, David R. SC Inf. 7th Bn. (Enfield Rifles) Co.D

Reaves, D.M. AL 1st Inf. Co.G

Reaves, D.M. SC Inf. 9th Bn. Co.A

Reaves, D.M. SC 26th Inf. Co.A

Reaves, D.R. SC 2nd Inf. Co.G

Reaves, Drury V. LA 19th Inf. Co.H

Reaves, D.S. AL Cav. 4th Bn. (Love's) Co.C

Reaves, Duff TN 4th Inf. Co.D

Reaves, Dugald F. NC 18th Inf. Co.H

Reaves, D.W. TN 38th Inf. Co.E

Reaves, E. AL 22nd Inf. Co.E

Reaves, E. TN 10th (DeMoss') Cav. Co.A

Reaves, Edward A. GA 3rd Cav. (St.Guards) Co.F Sgt.

Reaves, Edward C. NC 3rd Inf. Co.F

Reaves, Edwin NC 35th Inf. Co.I

Reaves, E.G. AL Cav. Hardie's Bn.Res. Co.I

Reaves, E.G. AL 3rd Inf. Co.G

Reaves, E.G. AL 30th Inf. Co.E

Reaves, E.H. AR 7th Cav. Co.B

Reaves, Eldridge W. AL 13th Inf. Co.D 2nd Lt.

Reaves, Elijah N.B. TN 1st (Feild's) Inf. Co.H

Reaves, Elijah N.B. TN 48th (Voorhies') Inf. Co.K

Reaves, E.N.B. TN Inf. Sowell's Detach.

Reaves, Eralbun C. AL 13th Inf. Co.D

Reaves, Ervan TN 24th Bn.S.S. Co.B

Reaves, Ervin T. AL 1st Bn. Hilliard's Legion Vol. Co.B

Reaves, E.T. KY 9th Cav. Co.G

Reaves, E.W. GA 4th Res. Co.B Sgt.

Reaves, Fountain M. AR 1st (Colquitt's) Inf. Co.G

Reaves, F.R. TN 49th Inf. Co.I

Reaves, F.R. Inf. Bailey's Cons.Regt. Co.D

Reaves, Francis M. GA Inf. 1st Conf.Bn. Co.D

Reaves, Franklin NC 4th Cav. (59th St.Troops) Co.E

Reaves, G. AL 49th Inf. Co.K

Reaves, G.E. SC 7th Inf. 2nd Co.G

Reaves, George AL 39th Inf. Co.D

Reaves, George TN 33rd Inf. Co.K

Reaves, George D. VA 59th Inf. 3rd Co.C

Reaves, George L. GA 41st Inf. Co.H Cpl.

Reaves, George S. NC 20th Inf. Co.G Cpl.

Reaves, George W. AR 9th Inf. Co.D

Reaves, George W. AR 33rd Inf. Co.G Sgt.

Reaves, George W., Jr. GA 13th Inf. Co.A

Reaves, George W. NC 18th Inf. Co.C

Reaves, George W. NC 20th Inf. Co.D

Reaves, George W. NC 24th Inf. Co.I

Reaves, George W. TN 1st (Feild's) Inf. Co.H

Reaves, G.S. AL 48th Inf. Co.K

Reaves, G.W. AR 11th & 17th (Cons.) Inf. Co.H,K

Reaves, G.W. SC 26th Inf. Co.K

Reaves, G.W. TN 10th (DeMoss') Cav. Co.A

Reaves, H. KY 8th Mtd.Inf. Co.C

Reaves, Hanes NC 7th Bn.Jr.Res. Co.B

Reaves, Hardy V. LA 2nd Inf. Co.D

Reaves, Haywood NC 24th Inf. Co.I

Reaves, H.B. AL Cp. of Instr. Talladega

Reaves, Henry NC 2nd Inf. Co.C

Reaves, Henry 1st Choctaw Mtd.Rifles Co.G

Reaves, Henry Green MS 7th Cav. Co.E

Reaves, Henry R. SC 1st (McCreary's) Inf. Co.H

Reaves, H.J. GA 13th Inf. Co.A

Reaves, H.J. TX Waul's Legion Co.G

Reaves, Holden AR 8th Cav. Co.B

Reaves, H.P. TN 84th Inf. Co.F 1st Lt.

Reaves, Hudson TN 24th Bn.S.S. Co.A

Reaves, Hunter B. AL Cav. Holloway's Co.

Reaves, Huston TN Inf. Sowell's Detach. 2nd Lt.

Reaves, I.B. MS 9th Cav. Co.K

Reaves, I.J. AL Cav. 5th Bn. Hilliard's Legion Co.E

Reaves, I.J. 10th Conf.Cav. Co.E

Reaves, Irvin B. AL Cav. Moses' Squad. Co.B Cpl.

Reaves, Isham W. SC 13th Inf. Co.I

Reaves, J. GA 5th Res. Co.I

Reaves, J.A. MS Cav. 3rd Bn.Res. Co.A

Reaves, James AL Cav. Lenoir's Ind.Co.

Reaves, James AR 34th Inf. Co.D

Reaves, James FL 3rd Inf. Co.H

Reaves, James GA 43rd Inf. Co.A

Reaves, James NC Mil. Clark's Sp.Bn. D.N. Bridgers' Co.

Reaves, James TN 11th Inf. Co.I

Reaves, James A. FL 9th Inf. Co.A Cpl.

Reaves, James B. GA 19th Inf. Co.I

Reaves, James B. GA 39th Inf. Co.D

Reaves, James B. MS Inf. 3rd Bn. Co.G 1st Lt.

Reaves, James H. GA 3rd Inf. Co.K

Reaves, James K.P. TN 1st (Feild's) Inf. Co.H

Reaves, James S. NC 1st Inf. Co.H

Reaves, James T. GA Lt.Arty. Scogin's Btty. (Griffin Lt.Arty.)

Reaves, James W. NC 28th Inf. Co.I

Reaves, Jasper AL 11th Inf. Co.G

Reaves, Jasper AR 5th Inf. Co.F

Reaves, J.B. GA 62nd Cav. Co.I Cpl.

Reaves, J.B. MS Inf. 7th Bn. Co.F

Reaves, J.B. NC Mil. Clark's Sp.Bn. Co.I

Reaves, J.B. TN Lt.Arty. Sparkman's Co.

Reaves, J.C. KY 3rd Mtd.Inf. Co.K

Reaves, Jerry E. TX 37th Cav. Co.K

Reaves, Jerry P. NC 2nd Arty. (36th St.Troops) Co.I

Reaves, Jess MO Cav. Fristoe's Regt. Co.A

46

Reaves, Jess MO Cav. Fristoe's Regt. Co.A
Reaves, Jesse AL 18th Inf. Co.K
Reaves, Jesse NC 52nd Inf. Co.B
Reaves, Jesse W. AR 3rd Inf. Co.B
Reaves, J.F. GA 2nd Cav. Co.D
Reaves, J.F.M. GA 11th Cav. Co.I
Reaves, J.G. AL Cav. Hardie's Bn.Res. S.D. McClellan's Co. Sgt.
Reaves, J.H. AR 7th Cav. Co.B
Reaves, J.H. GA 1st Cav. Co.D
Reaves, J.H. NC 80th Regt.
Reaves, J.H. SC 8th Inf. Co.M,F
Reaves, J.J. MS 5th Inf. (St.Troops) Co.B
Reaves, J.J. TN 24th Inf. Co.I
Reaves, J.L. LA 25th Inf. Co.I
Reaves, J.L. MS 48th Inf. Co.B
Reaves, J.L. SC Cav. 12th Bn. Co.D Sgt.
Reaves, J.L. TN 16th (Logwood's) Cav. Co.C
Reaves, J.M. AL Cp. of Instr. Talladega
Reaves, J.M. GA Inf. 27th Bn. (NonConscr.) Co.A
Reaves, John AL 3rd Cav. Co.B
Reaves, John AL 3rd Res. Co.E
Reaves, John AL 4th Inf. Co.K
Reaves, John AL 30th Inf. Co.F
Reaves, John AR 45th Mil. Co.D
Reaves, John NC 2nd Arty. (36th St.Troops) Co.D
Reaves, John NC 15th Inf. Co.D
Reaves, John NC 49th Inf. Co.B
Reaves, John SC 22nd Inf. Co.F
Reaves, John TN 9th (Ward's) Cav. Co.C
Reaves, John TN Cav. Allison's Squad.
Reaves, John TN Inf. 23rd Bn. Co.C Cpl.
Reaves, John TN 49th Inf. Co.B
Reaves, John TX 19th Inf. Co.D
Reaves, John A. GA 41st Inf. Co.H
Reaves, John A. MS 3rd Inf. (St.Troops) Co.C Sgt.
Reaves, John A. SC 13th Inf. Co.I
Reaves, John Anderson MS 7th Cav. Co.E
Reaves, John B. NC 38th Inf. Co.D
Reaves, John E. NC 2nd Arty. (36th St.Troops) Co.E
Reaves, John G. NC Hvy.Arty. 1st Bn. Co.C
Reaves, John H. SC 5th Inf. 1st Co.E, 2nd Co.H
Reaves, John J. MS 31st Inf. Co.B Cpl.
Reaves, John L. MS Inf. 2nd Bn. Co.B
Reaves, John P. NC 25th Inf. Co.E
Reaves, John Q. NC 5th Inf. Co.C
Reaves, John R. NC 2nd Jr.Res. Co.A Cpl.
Reaves, John T. AR 23rd Inf. Co.E
Reaves, John T. NC 51st Inf. Co.G
Reaves, John W. AL 13th Inf. Co.A
Reaves, John W. GA 44th Inf. Co.C 2nd Lt.
Reaves, Jonas L. AR 5th Inf. Co.C
Reaves, Joseph GA 49th Inf. Co.B
Reaves, Joseph SC Lt.Arty. Beauregard's Co.
Reaves, Joseph J. AL 1st Bn. Hilliard's Legion Vol. Co.B
Reaves, Joseph L. SC 4th Cav. Co.F Bvt.2nd Lt.
Reaves, Joseph L. SC 1st Inf. Co.K
Reaves, Joseph S. FL 5th Inf. Co.H
Reaves, Joseph T. NC 18th Inf. Co.C
Reaves, Josiah GA Inf. 17th Bn. (St.Guards) McCarty's Co.

Reaves, Josiah GA 23rd Inf. Co.F Sgt.
Reaves, Josiah P. TN Cav. 9th Bn. (Gantt's) Co.D Sgt.
Reaves, J.P. AR 18th Inf. Co.I
Reaves, J.P. TN 42nd Inf. Co.A
Reaves, J.R. LA 31st Inf. Co.D
Reaves, J.R. SC 14th Inf. Co.B
Reaves, J.S. AL 30th Inf. Co.E
Reaves, J.T. AR 1st Cav. Co.B
Reaves, J.T. MS 2nd St.Cav. Co.A
Reaves, Julius F.A. NC 3rd Inf. Co.F
Reaves, J.W. AL 9th (Malone's) Cav. Co.M
Reaves, J.W. AL 48th Inf. Co.K
Reaves, J.W. GA 13th Inf. Co.A
Reaves, J.W. MS 18th Cav. Co.G
Reaves, J.W. MS Inf. 8th Bn. Co.B
Reaves, J.W. SC 7th Inf. 1st Co.L, 2nd Co.L, Co.D 2nd Lt.
Reaves, L.E. TN 24th Inf. 1st Co.H, Co.I Cpl.
Reaves, Levi NC Hvy.Arty. 10th Bn. Co.A
Reaves, Levi SC 20th Inf. Co.A
Reaves, L.P. TN 51st (Cons.) Inf. Co.I
Reaves, L.R. TN 51st Inf. Co.C Sgt.
Reaves, Marcus A. FL 3rd Inf. Co.D
Reaves, Mathew TN 24th Bn.S.S. Co.A Comsy.Sgt.
Reaves, Mathew L. AR 5th Inf. Co.C
Reaves, M.B. FL Inf. 1st (Res.) Co.F
Reaves, M.C. TX 24th Cav. Co.I
Reaves, McD. AL 21st Inf. Co.F
Reaves, M.L. MS Cav. 3rd Bn.Res. Co.A Sgt.
Reaves, M.L. MS 3rd Inf. (St.Troops) Co.B Sgt.
Reaves, M.W. AL 37th Inf. Co.C,D
Reaves, Nathan R. MS Lt.Arty. Stanford's Co.
Reaves, Newton TN Inf. Sowell's Detach.
Reaves, N.L. MO Cav. Fristoe's Regt. Co.A
Reaves, Noah MS Inf. 1st Bn.St.Troops (12 mo. '62-3) Co.A
Reaves, N.W. MS 1st (Johnston's) Inf. Co.K Cpl.
Reaves, N.W. TN 44th (Cons.) Inf. Co.G 1st Sgt.
Reaves, Oliver A. GA 44th Inf. Co.G
Reaves, P.G. AR 27th Inf. Co.A
Reaves, P.L. NC 47th Inf. Co.I
Reaves, R. VA 24th Cav. Co.G
Reaves, R.A. NC 53rd Inf. Co.C
Reaves, Ransom Columbus MS 7th Cav. Co.E
Reaves, R.C. SC 14th Inf. Co.C
Reaves, R.E. AL 1st Bn. Hilliard's Legion Vol. Co.B
Reaves, Redden TN Inf. Sowell's Detach.
Reaves, Reubin GA 27th Inf. Co.I
Reaves, R.H. MS Cav. 3rd (St.Troops) Co.A
Reaves, Rheubin GA Mayer's Co. (Appling Cav.)
Reaves, Richard NC 62nd Inf. Co.E
Reaves, Richard R. NC 18th Inf. Co.E
Reaves, Riley A.C. GA 39th Inf. Co.D
Reaves, R.K. GA Arty. Lumpkin's Co.
Reaves, Robert TN Inf. Sowell's Detach.
Reaves, Robert D. AR 1st (Dobbins') Cav. Co.B
Reaves, Robert D. NC 50th Inf. Co.H Sgt.
Reaves, Robert M. GA 5th Cav. Co.I
Reaves, Robert S. AR 36th Inf. Co.H
Reaves, Robertus W. AL 25th Inf. Co.B 1st Sgt.
Reaves, R.R. AR 45th Cav. Co.A

Reaves, R.R. AR 38th Inf. New Co.I Cpl.
Reaves, Rufus K. GA 3rd Inf. Co.K Comsy.Sgt.
Reaves, R.W. GA 43rd Inf. Co.K
Reaves, S. GA 16th Inf. Co.B
Reaves, Samuel NC 52nd Inf. Co.F
Reaves, Samuel A. NC 18th Inf. Co.C
Reaves, Samuel F. NC 2nd Arty. (36th St.Troops) Co.G
Reaves, Samuel F. NC 20th Inf. Co.D
Reaves, Samuel J. FL 3rd Inf. Co.H
Reaves, Samuel W. NC 2nd Arty. (36th St.Troops) Co.E
Reaves, S.E.A. AL 59th Inf. Co.F Capt.
Reaves, S.H. AR Inf. Hardy's Regt. Co.F
Reaves, S.J. TN 24th Inf. 1st Co.H, Co.I
Reaves, S.L. TN 3rd (Forrest's) Cav. Co.H
Reaves, S.L. TN 38th Inf. Co.L
Reaves, Solomon NC 8th Sr.Res. Jacobs' Co., McNeill's Co.
Reaves, Solomon TX 13th Vol. 1st Co.F
Reaves, S.T. TX 1st Bn.S.S. Co.B Cook
Reaves, Stephen TN 19th (Biffle's) Cav. Co.B
Reaves, Stephen E.A. AL 2nd Bn. Hilliard's Legion Vol. Co.A Capt.
Reaves, Stephen G. GA 10th Inf. Co.F
Reaves, T.E. AL 51st (Part.Rangers) Co.C
Reaves, T.F. TN 24th Bn.S.S. Co.A
Reaves, Thomas MO 1st N.E. Cav. White's Co.
Reaves, Thomas NC 3rd Inf. Co.F
Reaves, Thomas NC Mil. Clark's Sp.Bn. D.N. Bridgers' Co.
Reaves, Thomas TN 38th Inf. 2nd Co.H
Reaves, Thomas J. MS 11th Inf. Co.D
Reaves, Thomas L. VA 14th Inf. Co.K
Reaves, Thomas W. AL 43rd Inf. Co.G Sgt.
Reaves, Thompson GA 2nd Cav. Co.D
Reaves, Thompson GA Cav. Arnold's Co.
Reaves, Timothy NC 51st Inf. Co.C
Reaves, T.J. AL 15th Inf. Co.D Cpl.
Reaves, T.K. GA 8th Inf. Co.E
Reaves, T.L. 15th Conf.Cav.
Reaves, T.P. AR 27th Inf. Co.G
Reaves, T.W. TN 16th (Logwood's) Cav. Co.C
Reaves, W. TN 31st Inf. Co.I
Reaves, W.A. AL 10th Inf. Co.K
Reaves, W.A. 4th Conf.Inf. Co.E
Reaves, Washington AL 10th Inf. Co.D
Reaves, W.B. KY 8th Mtd.Inf. Co.C
Reaves, W.B. MS 1st (Johnston's) Inf. Co.K
Reaves, W.B. TX Cav. Mann's Regt. Co.H
Reaves, W.E. AR 30th Inf. Co.B
Reaves, Wesley D. MS Inf. 3rd Bn. Co.G
Reaves, W.F. TX 1st Hvy.Arty. Co.H
Reaves, W.F.M. TN Inf. 154th Sr.Regt. Co.K
Reaves, W.H. AL 8th (Livingston's) Cav. Co.C
Reaves, W.H. AR 13th Inf. Co.K
Reaves, W.H. TN 12th (Green's) Cav. Co.H
Reaves, Wiley J. TN 48th (Voorhies') Inf. Co.K Sgt.
Reaves, William AR 8th Inf. New Co.C
Reaves, William AR Inf. Cocke's Regt. Co.K
Reaves, William GA 22nd Inf. Co.F
Reaves, William GA Inf. 25th Bn. (Prov.Guard) Co.F
Reaves, William LA 10th Inf. Co.K,E
Reaves, William MS 35th Inf. Co.E

47

Reaves, William MS Walsh's Co. (Muckalusha Guards)
Reaves, William NC 26th Inf. Co.A
Reaves, William NC 35th Inf. Co.I
Reaves, William NC 66th Inf. Co.I
Reaves, William SC 22nd Inf. Co.F
Reaves, William TN 10th (DeMoss') Cav. Co.A
Reaves, William TN 21st & 22nd (Cons.) Cav. Co.F
Reaves, William A. AR 1st (Crawford's) Cav. Co.C
Reaves, William A. GA 31st Inf. Co.G
Reaves, William A. NC 31st Inf. Co.C
Reaves, William A. SC 14th Inf. Co.C
Reaves, William A. TN 33rd Inf. Co.G
Reaves, William B. NC 26th Inf. Co.A Cpl.
Reaves, William C. GA 22nd Inf. Co.D
Reaves, William D. GA Lt.Arty. Scogin's Btty. (Griffin Lt.Arty.)
Reaves, William F. MS 2nd St.Cav. Co.A
Reaves, William F. NC 20th Inf. Co.D
Reaves, William H. NC 22nd Inf. Co.I
Reaves, William H. NC 24th Inf. Co.I Cpl.
Reaves, William J. GA 40th Inf. Co.G
Reaves, William M. VA 2nd Inf.Loc.Def. Co.K
Reaves, W.J. TN 11th Inf. Co.H
Reaves, W.M. MS 7th Cav. Co.H
Reaves, W.M. TN 15th (Cons.) Cav. Co.E
Reaves, Woodson MO 1st N.E. Cav. White's Co.
Reaves, W.R. AL 51st (Part.Rangers) Co.C
Reaves, W.R. SC 13th Inf. Co.I
Reaves, W.W. MS 6th Inf. Co.B
Reaves, Zachariah SC 15th Inf. Co.F Cpl.
Reaves, Zeb AR 27th Inf. Co.B
Reavie, Joseph TX Cav. Madison's Regt. Co.A
Reavie, M.E. TX Cav. Madison's Regt. Co.A
Reavie, M.R. TX Cav. Madison's Regt. Co.A
Reavill, Charles F. TX 8th Cav. Co.A Sgt.
Reavis, A.H. NC 9th Bn.S.S. Co.A
Reavis, A.J. MO St.Guard W.H. Taylor's Co.
Reavis, Asa NC 3rd Inf. Co.H
Reavis, Benjamin H. KY 3rd Cav. Co.B
Reavis, Benjamin W. GA Phillips' Legion Co.C
Reavis, B.H. KY 7th Cav. Co.B
Reavis, B.H. TX Cav. Gano's Squad. Co.B
Reavis, David NC 3rd Inf. Co.H
Reavis, D.J. TN 41st Inf. Co.C
Reavis, Giles NC 9th Bn.S.S. Co.A
Reavis, Gov. MS 2nd Part.Rangers Co.C
Reavis, H. AL 5th Bn. (Blount's) Vol. Co.D 1st Lt.
Reavis, J. AL 18th Inf. Co.G
Reavis, James NC 5th Sr.Res. Co.H
Reavis, James TN 18th (Newsom's) Cav. Co.K
Reavis, James TN 122nd Regt. Capt.
Reavis, James A. MO Arty. Lowe's Co.
Reavis, James A. NC 2nd Cav. (19th St.Troops) Co.B
Reavis, James L. TN 28th Inf. Co.A Sgt.
Reavis, James M. AL 25th Inf. Co.C
Reavis, James M. NC 9th Bn.S.S. Co.A
Reavis, James R. NC 12th Inf. Co.F
Reavis, Jesse NC 55th Inf. Co.H Sgt.
Reavis, J.F. NC 9th Bn.S.S. Co.A
Reavis, J.F. NC 21st Inf. Co.B
Reavis, J.G. NC 9th Bn.S.S. Co.A Ord.Sgt.
Reavis, J.G. NC 21st Inf. Co.B Cpl.

Reavis, J.G. TN 7th (Duckworth's) Cav. Co.A
Reavis, J.H. NC 5th Sr.Res. Co.H
Reavis, J.H. VA 2nd Inf.Loc.Def. Co.K
Reavis, J.H. VA Inf. 2nd Bn.Loc.Def. Co.B
Reavis, J.M. NC 21st Inf. Co.B
Reavis, John AR 6th Inf. New Co.F Sgt.
Reavis, John E. MO 10th Cav. Co.H
Reavis, John H. TN Cav. 16th Bn. (Neal's) Co.D
Reavis, Joseph NC 5th Sr.Res. Co.H
Reavis, Joseph H. NC 30th Inf. Co.D
Reavis, J.P.H. NC 9th Bn.S.S. Co.A
Reavis, J.W. TN 8th (Smith's) Cav. Co.A
Reavis, Nathan NC 28th Inf. Co.C
Reavis, Robert TN 18th (Newsom's) Cav. Co.K
Reavis, Samuel NC 23rd Inf. Co.G
Reavis, Samuel NC 42nd Inf. Co.B
Reavis, Samuel NC 42nd Inf. Co.D
Reavis, T.C. NC 23rd Inf. Co.G
Reavis, T.H. TX 18th Inf. Co.G 1st Lt.
Reavis, Thomas J.P. GA 3rd Cav. Co.F
Reavis, W.A. AL Cav. 4th Bn. (Love's) Co.B
Reavis, William A. NC 1st Cav. (9th St.Troops) Co.E Cpl.
Reavis, William J. GA 14th Inf. Co.A
Reavis, Willis W. MS 26th Inf. Co.D
Reavs, A.M. TN 19th (Biffle's) Cav. Co.E Sgt.
Reavs, Thomas LA 28th (Gray's) Inf. Co.H
Reavs, William GA Cav. 9th Bn. (St.Guards) Co.E
Reavy, Hugh AL 1st Regt. Mobile Vol. British Guard Co.A
Reavy, Hugh LA 22nd (Cons.) Inf. Co.B
Reay, A.M. MS 7th Inf. Co.C
Reay, Charles S. AR 1st (Monroe's) Cav. Co.G
Reay, Jerman F. VA 24th Inf. Co.H
Reay, Joseph O. VA 24th Inf. Co.H
Reay, William H. VA 24th Inf. Co.H
Reazor, J.C. TX 12th Cav. Co.F
Rebat, Jean LA Mil. French Co. of St.James
Rebb, George A. GA 7th Inf. (St.Guards) Co.E
Rebbell, Charles NC 5th Inf. Co.D Cpl.
Rebbman, F.J. SC Lt.Arty. Wagener's Co. (Co.A,German Arty.)
Rebbman, J. SC Mil. 1st Regt. (Charleston Res.) Co.B
Rebbman, J.J. SC Charleston Arty. Co.A
Rebe, A. TX 14th Field Btty.
Rebe, J.R. AL 69th Regt. Co.D
Rebeen, H. TN 15th Inf. Co.I
Rebel, Moses VA 25th Cav. Co.K
Reben, Henry VA Inf. 1st Bn.Loc.Def. Co.A,E
Reben, Henry P. VA 34th Inf. Co.A
Rebenholtz, Charles LA 6th Inf.
Rebens, George W. GA 41st Inf. Co.K
Reber, E.H. MS 6th Inf. Co.I Sgt.
Reber, P. LA Mil. 3rd Regt.Eur.Brig. (Garde Francaise) Co.1
Reberger, B.C. KY 2nd Mtd.Inf. Co.K
Rebesmann, Edward VA Inf. Lyneman's Co.
Rebhuhn, Henry LA Mil. 4th Regt.Eur.Brig. Co.C
Rebight, John TX Cav. Bourland's Regt. Co.K Black.
Reble, William F. SC Arty.Bn. Hampton Legion Co.B
Rebley, William J. TN 4th (Murray's) Cav. Co.C Sgt.

Rebmann, Jean LA C.S. Zouave Bn. Co.B
Rebnack, Fritz LA 20th Inf. Co.C
Rebon, C. LA 8th Cav. Co.K
Rebon, William AL 31st Inf. Co.A
Rebouche, A. LA Cav. Benjamin's Co.
Rebouche, A. LA Arty. Hutton's Co. (Crescent Arty.,Co.A)
Rebouil, Henry LA Mil. 1st Native Guards Cpl.
Rebren, J.W. FL 1st Inf. New Co.D
Rebsamen, Edward VA Inf. Lyneman's Co.
Rebsamen, Edward LA C.S. Zouave Bn. Co.F
Rebuffe, Henry LA 13th Inf. Co.D
Rebuffe, Henry Sap. & Min. Gallimard's Co.,CSA 1st Sap.
Reburn, C. KY 10th (Johnson's) Cav. New Co.F
Reca, William 18th Inf.
Recaho, Francis LA 22nd (Cons.) Inf. Co.G
Recaho, Francis LA 28th (Thomas') Inf. Co.G
Recant, Jules LA Inf.Cons.Crescent Regt.
Recards, G.A. LA Mil. 4th Regt. 1st Brig. 1st Div. Co.E
Rece, Asa TX Cav. McCord's Frontier Regt. Co.F
Rece, Walter J. AR Lt.Arty. 5th Btty.
Rece, Warren P. VA 8th Cav. Co.E
Recel, Jacob SC 19th Inf. Co.G
Recendes, Cevero TX Cav. 3rd (Yager's) Bn. Co.A
Recendes, Pedro TX Cav. 3rd (Yager's) Bn. Co.A
Rechard, F.D. AL Lt.Arty. 2nd Bn. Co.D
Rechey, Moses S. NC 11th (Bethel Regt.) Inf.
Rechie, David MS Cav. 1st Res. Co.D
Rechords, R.S. TN 50th (Cons.) Inf. Co.C
Reck, A.J. MS 27th Inf. Co.H
Reckard, Andrew J. MS Unassign.Conscr.
Reckard, Andrew J. NC Unassign.Conscr.
Reckard, John E. TN Cav. Newsom's Regt.
Reckely, Simon TN 61st Mtd.Inf. Co.B
Reckenbacker, Emanuel J. SC 5th Cav. Co.A
Recker, Daniel AR 10th (Witt's) Cav. Co.G
Recker, Ernst H. TX 4th Field Btty. Sgt.
Recker, Frederick TX 4th Field Btty.
Recker, Jacob H. VA 62nd Mtd.Inf. 2nd Co.F
Reckes, W. 1st Cherokee Mtd.Vol. 1st Co.B
Reckins, --- TX Cav. Good's Bn. Co.C
Recklefsen, August TX 3rd Inf. Co.D
Reckley, Mason NC Inf. Thomas Legion 2nd Co.A
Reckold, Benard VA 18th Inf.
Recks, W.L. NC 66th Inf. Co.G
Recob, I. MO Cav. Williams' Regt. Co.H
Reconlley, Peter LA 3rd (Harrison's) Cav. Co.C
Recor, Charles L. LA 1st Cav. Co.K
Record, Adam M. NC 3rd Cav. (41st St.Troops) Co.D
Record, Adam M. NC Hvy.Arty. 10th Bn. Co.B
Record, A.J. NC 5th Inf. Co.K
Record, A.M. NC Mallett's Bn. (Cp.Guard) Co.C Sgt.
Record, B. MO 6th Cav. Co.C
Record, David P. NC 26th Inf. Co.G
Record, F.M. TX Cav. Wells' Regt. Co.B
Record, Francis M. TX Cav. Wells' Bn. Co.B
Record, Frank M. TX 18th Cav. Witt's Co.
Record, George H. MS 21st Inf. Co.A
Record, G.W. TN 51st (Cons.) Inf. Co.C

Record, I.S. MO Cav. Fristoe's Regt. Co.H

48

Record, I.S. MO Cav. Fristoe's Regt. Co.H
Record, James K.P. Gen. & Staff Capt.,AQM
Record, James M. NC 1st Arty. (10th St.Troops) Co.I
Record, James M. NC 2nd Arty. (36th St.Troops) Co.A
Record, James S. TN 27th Inf. Co.I Cpl.
Record, J.F. TN 21st (Wilson's) Cav. Co.H
Record, J.F. TN 21st & 22nd (Cons.) Cav. Co.E Sgt.
Record, J.J. TX 9th (Young's) Inf. Co.A
Record, J.K.P. TX 14th Cav. Dr.M.
Record, J.L. MS Inf. 2nd Bn. (St.Troops) Co.E
Record, John TN 1st Btty.
Record, John TX Cav. Wells' Regt. Co.B
Record, John TX Arty. (St.Troops) Good's Co.
Record, John E. TN 21st (Wilson's) Cav. Co.D
Record, John E. TN 27th Inf. Co.A
Record, John J. NC 26th Inf. Co.G Cpl.
Record, John S. MO 4th Cav. Co.E
Record, Joseph W. TX 19th Cav. Co.K Cpl.
Record, J.S.M. TX Arty. Douglas' Co.
Record, M.D. TN 16th Inf. Co.E
Record, Newton K. TX 27th Cav. Co.G Sr.2nd Lt.
Record, S.D. TN 51st (Cons.) Inf. Co.C
Record, S.S. KY 3rd Mtd.Inf. Co.B
Record, S.S. TX 9th (Young's) Inf. Co.A Cpl.
Record, S.S. TX Lt.Inf. & Riflemen Maxey's Co. (Lamar Rifles) Cpl.
Record, Sylvester TX 9th Cav. Co.A Cpl.
Record, Thomas D. NC 26th Inf. Co.G Sgt.
Record, W.D. TN 35th Inf. 3rd Co.F
Record, W.M. TN 21st Cav. Co.H
Recter, Samuel TX 18th Inf. Co.K
Recter, Thomas TN 28th (Cons.) Inf. Co.K
Recton, N.W. TX Cav. Giddings' Bn. Pickerell's Co.
Recton, W.G. TX Cav. Giddings' Bn. Pickerell's Co.
Rector, A.B. NC 18th Inf. Co.B
Rector, A.J. VA 63rd Inf. Co.C
Rector, Albert W. VA 7th Inf. Co.E
Rector, Albin VA Lt.Arty. 38th Bn. Co.A Cpl.
Rector, Albin VA 49th Inf. 1st Co.G
Rector, Alex P. MS 4th Inf. Co.A
Rector, Alfred W. VA 11th Inf. Co.I
Rector, Amos J. AL 43rd Inf. Co.I
Rector, A.P. MS 41st Inf. Co.F
Rector, Asa H. VA 6th Cav. Co.A
Rector, Banks Shecoe's Chickasaw Bn.Mtd.Vol. Co.A
Rector, Battle VA 6th Cav. Co.H
Rector, Benjamin TN Cav. 12th Bn. (Days') Co.F
Rector, Benjamin TN 60th Mtd.Inf. Co.C
Rector, Bennet VA 63rd Inf. Co.C 1st Lt.
Rector, B.F. TX 11th Inf. Co.A
Rector, Burnett VA Mil. Grayson Cty.
Rector, Caleb C. VA 6th Cav. Co.A Cpl.
Rector, C.D. NC 55th Inf. Co.H
Rector, Chandler P. VA 6th Cav. Co.F
Rector, Charles H. VA Lt.Arty. 38th Bn. Co.A
Rector, Charles H. VA 49th Inf. 1st Co.G
Rector, Charles H. VA 60th Inf. Co.G 1st Lt.
Rector, Charles W. NC 16th Inf. Co.C
Rector, Creed F. VA 63rd Inf. Co.K Sgt.

Rector, D. GA 4th Inf.
Rector, D.F. MO Inf. Clark's Regt. Co.A
Rector, D.L. SC 6th Cav. Co.H
Rector, D.L. SC 16th Inf. Co.D
Rector, D.M. MO 6th Cav. Co.A
Rector, E. NC 64th Inf. Co.F
Rector, Edward W. VA Cav. Mosby's Regt. (Part.Rangers) Co.A
Rector, Edward W. VA 2nd Inf. Co.G
Rector, Elihu NC 64th Inf. Co.C
Rector, Elihu W. NC 18th Inf. Co.D
Rector, Elihu W. NC 37th Inf. Co.D
Rector, Enos VA 63rd Inf. Co.C 1st Sgt.
Rector, Enos VA Mil. Grayson Cty.
Rector, E.S. TX 9th (Young's) Inf. Co.I
Rector, F.A. AR 17th (Griffith's) Inf. Col.
Rector, F.A. AR 35th Inf. Col.
Rector, F.N. AR 20th Inf. Co.I
Rector, Frank Armstrong Gen. & Staff Maj.,QM
Rector, Franklin NC 64th Inf. Co.F
Rector, Franklin VA 34th Mil. Co.A
Rector, G.B. MO 1st N.E. Cav.
Rector, G.B. MO 2nd Inf.
Rector, George TN 2nd (Ashby's) Cav. Co.H
Rector, George TN Cav. 4th Bn. (Branner's) Co.A
Rector, George A. TX 22nd Cav. Co.K Sgt.
Rector, George S. VA 36th Inf. 2nd Co.E 2nd Lt.
Rector, Gilbright NC 38th Inf. Co.F
Rector, Green MO 1st N.E. Cav.
Rector, H. TX 8th Inf. Co.G
Rector, H. VA 42nd Inf. Co.H
Rector, Hamilton KY 2nd Mtd.Inf. Co.E
Rector, Harvey MO 1st Cav. Co.I
Rector, H.B. GA Inf. 17th Bn. (St.Guards) Fay's Co.
Rector, Henry B. GA 66th Inf. Co.E
Rector, Henry J. VA Lt.Arty. 12th Bn. 1st Co.A
Rector, Henry J. VA Lt.Arty. Utterback's Co.
Rector, H.M. TN 19th Inf. Co.D Sgt.
Rector, H.M. VA Lt.Arty. King's Co. Cpl.
Rector, H.N. VA 7th Cav. Co.A
Rector, Hugh NC 38th Inf. Co.G
Rector, Isaac E. TN 13th (Gore's) Cav. Co.C
Rector, Isaiah VA 8th Cav. Co.C
Rector, Jackson TX Inf. 2nd St.Troops Co.C
Rector, Jackson B. TN 13th (Gore's) Cav. Co.C
Rector, Jacob MO Cav. Hunter's Regt. Co.A
Rector, Jacob N. NC 16th Inf. Co.E 2nd Lt.
Rector, James MO 7th Cav.
Rector, James NC 14th Inf. Co.F
Rector, James NC Walker's Bn. Thomas' Legion Co.A
Rector, James C. VA 63rd Inf. Co.C
Rector, James C. VA Mil. Grayson Cty.
Rector, James E. AL 26th Inf. Co.D
Rector, James E. TN 1st (Carter's) Cav. Co.D
Rector, James E. Whitfield's Brig. Capt.
Rector, James H. NC 64th Inf. Co.N
Rector, James P. TX 22nd Cav. Co.K 1st Sgt.
Rector, James P. TX 4th Inf. Co.F
Rector, James P. TX Inf. Cunningham's Co.
Rector, James Pendleton TX 8th Cav. Co.H
Rector, James W. VA 4th Cav. Co.H
Rector, J.B. MO Beck's Co.
Rector, J.E. TN 13th (Gore's) Cav. Co.C

Rector, Jesse TX 15th Inf. 2nd Co.E
Rector, Jesse S. TN 1st (Carter's) Cav. Co.A
Rector, Jesse S. TN Cav. 16th Bn. (Neal's) Co.C
Rector, J.F. AL 26th (O'Neal's) Inf. Co.D
Rector, J.H. MO 6th Cav. Co.B
Rector, J.M. MO 6th Cav. Co.G
Rector, J.M. VA Lt.Arty. King's Co.
Rector, Joel SC 1st St.Troops Co.K
Rector, John NC Cav. 5th Bn. Co.A Sgt.
Rector, John NC 6th Cav. (65th St.Troops) Co.A
Rector, John NC 54th Inf. Co.B
Rector, John VA 63rd Inf. Co.C
Rector, John VA Mil. Grayson Cty.
Rector, John A. NC 6th Inf. Co.A
Rector, John B. TX 8th Cav. Co.D
Rector, John D. Gen. & Staff 1st Lt.,ADC
Rector, John E. NC 38th Inf. Co.F
Rector, John H. MO 3rd Cav. Co.B
Rector, John H. Conf.Cav. Clarkson's Bn. Ind.Rangers Co.E
Rector, John W., Jr. VA 31st Inf. Co.C
Rector, Joseph TX 11th Inf. Co.A Cpl.
Rector, Joseph W. AR 7th Inf. Co.H 2nd Lt.
Rector, Joseph W. AR 27th Inf. Co.G Bvt.2nd Lt.
Rector, Joseph W. MO Cav. Freeman's Regt. Co.F Sr.2nd Lt.
Rector, J.P. SC Lt.Arty. 3rd (Palmetto) Bn. Co.A
Rector, J.R. TN 13th (Gore's) Cav. Co.C
Rector, J.W. NC 1st Bn.Jr.Res. Co.A
Rector, K.K. TX 8th Cav. Co.D Sgt.
Rector, L. TX Inf. Timmons' Regt. Co.F
Rector, L. TX Waul's Legion Co.C
Rector, Leland W. VA 6th Bn.Res. Co.D Sgt.
Rector, Lewis NC Inf. Thomas Legion Co.K 1st Lt.
Rector, L.T. VA 4th Cav. Co.H
Rector, Mack AL 48th Inf. Co.G,E
Rector, Marion MO 6th Cav. Co.F
Rector, Marion VA Lt.Arty. 38th Bn. Co.A
Rector, Marion VA 49th Inf. 1st Co.G
Rector, Mark TN 8th Cav. Co.I
Rector, Merit KY 4th Cav. Co.G
Rector, Micager NC Cav. 5th Bn. Co.A
Rector, Micager NC 6th Cav. (65th St.Troops) Co.A
Rector, Monroe NC 64th Inf. Co.A
Rector, Nathaniel G. SC 6th Inf. 1st Co.K Sgt.
Rector, Newton C. NC 7th Inf. Co.K
Rector, N.G. SC 3rd Res. Co.E Cpl.
Rector, N.G. SC 11th Inf. Co.B
Rector, P. MS 9th Bn.S.S. Co.A
Rector, P.H. MS 2nd Inf. (A. of 10,000) Co.G
Rector, P.H. MO 6th Cav. Co.G
Rector, R.C. AL 26th (O'Neal's) Inf. Co.D 2nd Lt.
Rector, Richard 3rd Conf.Eng.Troops Co.D
Rector, Richard H. VA 6th Cav. Co.A
Rector, Robert LA 2nd Cav. Co.G
Rector, Samuel L. NC 14th Inf. Co.F
Rector, S.H. TX 11th Inf. Co.A
Rector, Stephen MO Cav. Snider's Bn. Co.D
Rector, T.H. TN 13th (Gore's) Cav. Co.C
Rector, Theophilus TX 11th Inf. Co.A
Rector, Thomas Gen. & Staff, Comsy.Dept. Capt.

Rector, Thomas B. TX 22nd Cav. Co.K Cpl.
Rector, Thomas B. VA Lt.Arty. 12th Bn. 1st Co.A Cpl.
Rector, Thomas B. VA Lt.Arty. Utterback's Co. Cpl.
Rector, Thomas C. TX Cav. Martin's Regt. Co.K
Rector, Thomas M. VA 7th Inf. Co.E
Rector, Thomas M. VA 11th Inf. Co.I
Rector, Thomas S. VA 11th Inf. Co.A Sgt.
Rector, Thomas W. TN 26th Inf. Co.C
Rector, T.M. TX 8th Cav. Co.D
Rector, V.B. TN 61st Mtd.Inf. Co.A
Rector, W.A. TN 13th (Gore's) Cav. Co.I
Rector, W.B. TN 13th (Gore's) Cav. Co.C
Rector, Warren VA 4th Res. Co.B
Rector, W.F. Gen. & Staff Adj.
Rector, W.G. TX 17th Cons.Dismtd.Cav. Co.D Capt.
Rector, W.H. KY 2nd (Woodward's) Cav. Co.A,B Ord.Sgt.
Rector, Wiley G. VA 63rd Inf. Co.C
Rector, Wiley S. VA Mil. Grayson Cty.
Rector, Willa E. NC 37th Inf. Co.G
Rector, William MO 3rd Cav. Co.G
Rector, William MO 6th Cav. Co.G
Rector, William TN 28th Inf. Co.K
Rector, William VA 1st Inf.
Rector, William VA 4th Res. Co.B
Rector, William VA 63rd Inf. Co.C
Rector, William VA Mil. Grayson Cty.
Rector, William A. VA 7th Cav. Co.A
Rector, William B. VA 42nd Inf. Co.I Capt.
Rector, William C. TN 13th (Gore's) Cav. Co.C
Rector, William C. VA 7th Cav. Co.A
Rector, William E. VA 8th Inf. Co.K
Rector, William F. AR 30th Inf. Adj.
Rector, William F. VA 7th Cav. Co.A
Rector, William G. TX 10th Inf. Co.F Capt.
Rector, William J. TN 28th Inf. Co.K
Rector, William L. VA 11th Inf. Co.C
Rector, W.J. TN 13th (Gore's) Cav. Co.C
Rector, W.J. TX 1st Bn.S.S. Co.D
Rector, W.S. TN 26th Inf. Co.E
Rector, Wyatt NC 16th Inf. Co.B Cpl.
Red, A.A. TX Cav. Border's Regt. Co.E
Red, A. Gad GA 65th Inf. Co.I
Red, Alson MS 8th Inf. Co.B Jr.2nd Lt.
Red, A.M. TX Cav. 1st Bn.St.Troops Co.A
Red, A.R. SC 2nd Arty. Co.E Sgt.
Red, Bartley SC 11th Res. Co.C
Red, C.A. GA Cav. 21st Bn. Co.A
Red, Cornelius A. GA 3rd Inf. Co.G
Red, C.W.J. SC Arty. Ind.Co.A
Red, David J. MS 25th Inf. Co.A Capt.
Red, D.J. MS 1st Bn.S.S. Co.B Capt.
Red, D.J. MS Inf. (Red Rebels) D.J. Red's Co. Capt.
Red, D.J. 2nd Conf.Inf. Co.A Capt.
Red, Elijah MS 8th Inf. Co.B
Red, Elisha MS 3rd (St.Troops) Cav. Co.B
Red, F.H. SC 21st Inf. Co.H
Red, F.M. TN 38th Inf. Co.G
Red, Franklin F. SC 14th Inf. Co.F
Red, George W. GA 3rd Cav. Co.F Sgt.
Red, George W. SC Hvy.Arty. Mathewes' Co.
Red, G.M. MS 4th Inf. Co.C Cpl.
Red, G.W. MS 11th (Perrin's) Cav. Co.K

Red, G.W. SC Arty. Manigault's Bn.
Red, J. SC Percival's Cav.
Red, James GA 36th (Broyles') Inf. Co.E
Red, James (MD) MS S.W. Red's Co. (St.Troops) Stew.
Red, James I. GA 43rd Inf. Co.I
Red, James J. AL 12th Inf. Co.H
Red, James L. SC Hvy.Arty. Mathewes' Co.
Red, James M. GA 36th (Broyles') Inf. Co.E
Red, J.B.F. GA Phillips' Legion Co.C Cpl.
Red, Jeff SC Inf. Holcombe Legion Co.D
Red, J.J. AL 5th Cav. Co.C
Red, J.L. SC Arty. Manigault's Bn.
Red, John AL 13th Bn.Part.Rangers Co.D
Red, John AL 56th Part.Rangers Co.K
Red, John GA 1st (Olmstead's) Inf. Gordon's Co.
Red, John GA Inf. 4th Bn. (St.Guards) Co.B
Red, John GA 63rd Inf. Co.F
Red, John C. SC Hvy.Arty. Mathewes' Co.
Red, Josiah J. AL 41st Inf. Co.A
Red, J.R. AL 5th Cav. Co.C
Red, J.W. MS Adams' Co. (Holmes Cty.Ind.)
Red, Levy L. MS Cav. Garland's Bn. Co.C
Red, Martin SC Hvy.Arty. Mathewes' Co.A
Red, Meshack GA 36th (Broyles) Inf. Co.E
Red, M.H. TX 35th (Likens') Cav. Co.I
Red, N.H. TX 37th Cav. Mullins' Co.
Red, R.A. AL 11th Inf. Co.G
Red, R.A. AL 41st Inf. Co.A
Red, R.B. MS 8th Inf. Co.B
Red, Reuben A. SC Hvy.Arty. Mathewes' Co.
Red, S. SC 2nd Arty. Co.E
Red, S. SC Hvy.Arty. Mathewes' Co.
Red, Samuel SC 19th Inf. Co.B
Red, Samuel SC Inf.Bn. Co.C
Red, Samuel W. MS 12th Cav. Co.E Capt.
Red, Samuel W. MS 12th Inf. Co.I 1st Lt.
Red, Samuel W. MS S.W. Red's Co. (St.Troops) Capt.
Red, S.C. TX 4th Cav. Co.K
Red, S.W. MS Adams' Co. (Holmes Cty.Ind.) 1st Lt.
Red, T.F. AL 5th Cav. Co.G
Red, Thos. AL 18th Inf. Co.C
Red, Thomas GA Cherokee Legion (St.Guards) Co.B
Red, Thomas J. MS 33rd Inf. Co.C
Red, T.J. MS 8th Inf. Co.B Sgt.
Red, Washington J. SC Hvy.Arty. Mathewes' Co.
Red, W.C. MS 4th Inf. Co.C Capt.
Red, William GA 32nd Inf. Co.C
Red, William GA Inf. (Jones Hussars) Jones' Co.
Red, William B. GA 36th (Broyles') Inf. Co.E Cpl.
Red, William W. SC Hvy.Arty. Mathewes' Co.
Red, W.M. SC Hvy.Arty. Mathewes' Co.
Red, W.M. SC 11th Res. Co.F
Red, W.T. AL 5th Cav. Co.G
Red, W.W. AL 11th Inf. Co.G
Redan, Hardy MS 26th Inf. Co.G
Redaught, John W. FL 7th Inf. Co.H 1st Sgt.
Red Bird 1st Cherokee Mtd.Rifles Co.C
Red Bird 1st Cherokee Mtd.Rifles Co.F
Red Bird 1st Cherokee Mtd.Rifles Co.G
Red Bird 1st Cherokee Mtd.Vol. 2nd Co.H
Red Bird, Daniel 1st Cherokee Mtd.Rifles Co.A

Redbird, Jack 1st Cherokee Mtd.Rifles Co.G
Redbird, Jesse 1st Cherokee Mtd.Rifles Co.G
Redcliff, William Kellersberg's Corps Sap. & Min.,CSA Sgt.
Redd, --- VA VMI Co.C 2nd Lt.
Redd, A.F. VA VMI Co.C 2nd Lt.
Redd, A.L. AL 15th Bn.Part.Rangers Co.D
Redd, A.L. VA Lt.Arty. R.M. Anderson's Co.
Redd, Alfred VA 61st Inf. Co.F
Redd, Allison L. AL 56th Part.Rangers Co.D Sgt.
Redd, Alonzo NC 3rd Cav. (41st St.Troops) Co.B Cpl.
Redd, A.M. SC Inf. Holcombe Legion Co.D Music.
Redd, Andrew J. VA 51st Mil. Co.B
Redd, Archibald VA 41st Inf. Co.I
Redd, Asa A. TX Cav. Hardeman's Regt. Co.A
Redd, Barney FL 5th Inf. Co.C
Redd, Barney VA 1st St.Res. Co.F
Redd, B.J. FL Lt.Arty. Dyke's Co.
Redd, C.A. AL 46th Inf. Capt.,AQM
Redd, C.F. GA Cav. Nelson's Ind.Co.
Redd, C.F. GA Cav. Ragland's Co.
Redd, C.F. Shelby's Brig. ADC
Redd, Charles GA Cav. Nelson's Ind.Co.
Redd, Charles A. Gen. & Staff Capt.,AQM
Redd, Charles E. VA 3rd Cav. Co.K
Redd, Christopher C. NC 1st Arty. (10th St.Troops) Co.I Jr.2nd Lt.
Redd, Christopher C. NC 2nd Arty. (36th St.Troops) Co.A Cpl.
Redd, Clarence M. VA Cav. 40th Bn. Co.F
Redd, Clarence M. VA 21st Inf. Co.F
Redd, David KY 2nd (Woodward's) Cav. Co.A,B
Redd, D.J. TN Inf. 23rd Bn. Co.D
Redd, Duncan FL 8th Inf. Co.K
Redd, E. FL Lt.Arty. Dyke's Co.
Redd, Edmond M. VA 6th Cav. Co.G
Redd, Edward MS Cav. Jeff Davis Legion Co.A
Redd, Edward T. VA Mil. 33rd Regt. Capt.
Redd, E.M. VA 4th Cav. Co.G
Redd, E.T. VA 10th Cav. Co.I
Redd, F. GA Cav. Nelson's Ind.Co.
Redd, F. GA Cav. Ragland's Co.
Redd, Francis D. VA 3rd Cav. Co.K 2nd Lt.
Redd, Francis M. NC 3rd Inf. Co.E
Redd, George S. VA 26th Inf. Co.C
Redd, G.T. FL 11th Inf. Co.G 2nd Lt.
Redd, Isaac A. FL 5th Inf. Co.C
Redd, J. GA Cav. Nelson's Ind.Co.
Redd, J. GA Cav. Ragland's Co.
Redd, Jacob NC 3rd Inf. Co.E
Redd, Jacob H. NC 4th Cav. (59th St.Troops) Co.C
Redd, James E. VA 26th Inf. Co.C
Redd, James J. GA 50th Inf. Co.H
Redd, James S. VA 18th Inf. Co.A
Redd, Jesse TN 4th Inf. Co.C Sgt.
Redd, J.F. TN Inf. 23rd Bn. Co.B
Redd, J.K. GA 2nd Inf. Co.G Sgt.
Redd, John AL 5th Inf. Co.C
Redd, John SC 2nd St.Troops Co.K
Redd, John A. AL 11th Inf. Co.G
Redd, John A. VA 3rd Cav. Co.K
Redd, John H. VA 3rd Cav. Co.K

Redd, John H. VA 18th Inf. Co.B Sgt.
Redd, John H. VA 24th Inf. Co.H
Redd, John H. VA 53rd Inf. Co.E
Redd, John K. GA 64th Inf. Co.F Capt.
Redd, John O. VA 64th Mil. Campbell's Co.
Redd, John R. VA 24th Cav. Co.F
Redd, John W. AL Inf. 1st Regt. Co.E
Redd, John W. VA 3rd Cav. Co.K
Redd, John W. VA 26th Inf. Co.C
Redd, Joseph T. VA 3rd Cav. Co.K
Redd, Joshua AL 2nd Cav. Co.I
Redd, Joshua AL 16th Inf. Co.D
Redd, Joshua AL 17th Inf. Co.B
Redd, J.T. MS 1st (Patton's) Inf. Co.A
Redd, J.T. Gen. & Staff A.Surg.
Redd, L.B. MO Inf. Perkins' Bn.
Redd, Lewellyn W. VA 1st Arty. Co.D
Redd, Lindsey VA 13th Inf. 2nd Co.B
Redd, L.L. 14th Conf.Cav. Co.C
Redd, Marcus L.F. NC 3rd Inf. Co.E Capt.
Redd, Mark TN 41st Inf. Co.A
Redd, M.B. LA 8th Cav. Co.E Capt.
Redd, Mordica KY 5th Cav. Co.A
Redd, M.W. TN 8th Inf. Co.D
Redd, N.L. GA 2nd Inf. Co.G
Redd, N.L. GA Inf. 19th Bn. (St.Guards) Co.D
  2nd Lt.
Redd, O.F. MO 5th Cav. Co.A 1st Sgt.
Redd, Phillip D. VA 13th Inf. 2nd Co.E Sgt.
Redd, Polk D. VA Cav. Mosby's Regt. (Part.
  Rangers) Co.E
Redd, Reuben B. AL 37th Inf. Co.D
Redd, R.H. GA 38th Inf. Co.E
Redd, Richard MO 5th Cav. Co.A
Redd, Richard L. VA 56th Inf. Co.G
  Comsy.Sgt.
Redd, Robert NC 52nd Inf. Co.C
Redd, Robert VA 41st Inf. Co.I
Redd, Robert Leigh VA 3rd Cav. Co.K
Redd, Robert S. KY 5th Cav. Co.A Cpl.
Redd, S. MO 10th Inf. New Co.B
Redd, Samuel TN 16th (Logwood's) Cav. Co.D
Redd, Samuel C. VA Cav. 40th Bn. Co.F
Redd, Samuel R. MO 5th Cav. Co.A QMSgt.
Redd, S.B. MO 1st Cav. Co.A
Redd, Seth VA 13th Inf. 2nd Co.B
Redd, S.G. TN 15th (Cons.) Cav. Co.I
Redd, S.G. TN Cav. Nixon's Regt. Co.A
Redd, Siglee NC 3rd Cav. (41st St.Troops)Co.H
Redd, Siglee NC 3rd Inf. Co.E Cpl.
Redd, S.J. TX 33rd Cav. Co.C
Redd, Thomas AL 16th Inf. Co.F
Redd, Thomas VA 53rd Inf. Co.D Sgt.
Redd, Thomas D. KY 4th Cav. Co.G
Redd, Thomas H. KY 5th Cav. Co.A Cpl.
Redd, Toliver C. FL 5th Inf. Co.C
Redd, T.S. MS 12th Inf. Co.G
Redd, W.A. LA 2nd Inf. Co.D Capt.
Redd, W.A. MO 5th Cav. 1st Lt.,Adj.
Redd, Wade W. FL 5th Inf. Co.C
Redd, Wiley VA 59th Mil. Hunter's Co.
Redd, William GA 3rd Cav. Co.B
Redd, William GA 2nd Inf. Co.G
Redd, William, Jr. GA 2nd Inf. Adj.
Redd, William GA Inf. (GA Defend.) Chapman's
  Co.

Redd, William A. MO 2nd Regt.St.Guards 1st
  Lt.
Redd, William J. FL 1st Inf. Old Co.E
Redd, William J. FL 8th Inf. Co.E Cpl.
Redd, William P. TN 1st (Feild's) Inf. Co.C,A
Redd, William S. VA 13th Inf. 1st Co.B, 2nd
  Co.B
Redd, William S. VA 24th Inf. Co.H 2nd Lt.
Redd, William W. AL 37th Inf. Co.D
Redd, W.J. TN 3rd (Forrest's) Cav. Co.E 2nd
  Lt.
Redd, W.K. MS Cav. Vivion's Co.
Redd, Zephaniah W. NC 51st Inf. Co.G
Redd, Z.J. FL 2nd Inf.
Redd, Z.J. GA 8th Inf. Co.G
Reddan, James LA 25th Inf. Co.H
Reddan, J.K. AR 1st (Monroe's) Cav. Co.B
Reddell, Aquila AR 14th (Powers') Inf. Co.K
Reddell, George R. AR 14th (Powers') Inf. Co.K
Reddell, James A. TN 3rd (Clack's) Inf. Co.K
  Sgt.
Reddell, J.T. MS Cav. Powers' Regt. Co.C
Reddell, Vincent R. AR 14th (Powers') Inf. Co.K
Reddels, R.N. AR 11th Inf. 3rd Lt.
Redden, Adolph VA Mtd.Riflemen St.Martin's
  Co. 2nd Lt.
Redden, Adolphe LA 7th Inf. Co.B
Redden, Allen AL 35th Inf. Co.B
Redden, Allen NC 25th Inf. Co.D
Redden, Asburry F. SC 14th Inf. Co.C
Redden, David W. MS 37th Inf. Co.B
Redden, G.C. TX 18th Inf. Co.G
Redden, George W. VA 28th Inf. Co.E,I
Redden, George W. 4th Conf.Inf. Co.F
Redden, G.L. TN 11th Inf. Co.K
Redden, G.W. AL 15th Bn.Part.Rangers Co.D
Redden, G.W. VA 42nd Inf. Co.E
Redden, H. SC Inf. 1st (Charleston) Bn. Co.D
Redden, H. TX 1st Inf. Co.M
Redden, Harrison VA 30th Bn.S.S. Co.A
Redden, Henry SC Inf. 3rd Bn. Co.A
Redden, Henry SC 9th Res. Co.B
Redden, Hollis TN 17th Inf. Co.B
Redden, Horace NC 56th Inf. Co.G
Redden, H.R. SC 9th Res. Co.B
Redden, James AR 62nd Mil. Co.D QMSgt.
Redden, James LA 12th Inf. Co.E
Redden, James A. NC 44th Inf. Co.F
Redden, James O. MS Inf. 2nd Bn. Co.H
Redden, James O. MS 48th Inf. Co.H
Redden, James P. NC 35th Inf. Co.G
Redden, J.L. TN 11th Inf. Co.E,K
Redden, John MS Inf. 2nd Bn. (St.Troops) Co.C
Redden, John G. MS 37th Inf. Co.B
Redden, John H. VA 30th Bn.S.S. Co.A
Redden, John M. NC 35th Inf. Co.G
Redden, John T. KY Cav. Buckner Guards
Redden, J.S. LA 3rd (Wingfield's) Cav. Co.F
  1st Lt.
Redden, J.W. AL 34th Inf. Co.F
Redden, J.W. TN 11th Inf. Co.K
Redden, J.W. TN 17th Inf. Co.B
Redden, Larkin AL 22nd Inf. Co.C
Redden, M.C. NC 16th Inf. Co.I
Redden, M.P. VA 28th Inf. 2nd Co.C
Redden, R.D. AL 26th (O'Neal's) Inf. Maj.

Redden, R.H. LA 3rd (Wingfield's) Cav. Co.F
  Sgt.
Redden, Reuben L. AL 26th (O'Neal's) Inf. Co.F
  Cpl.
Redden, R.M. AR 32nd Inf. Co.B
Redden, Robert H. TN 42nd Inf. Co.B
Redden, Robert S. NC 56th Inf. Co.G
Redden, S.W. TN 16th Inf. Co.E
Redden, Thomas B. KY Horse Arty. Byrne's Co.
  Sgt.
Redden, Thomas C. NC 49th Inf. Co.D
Redden, Wade H. GA 36th (Villepigue's) Inf.
  Co.E,F
Redden, W.H. TN 15th (Cons.) Cav. Co.F
Redden, William VA 60th Inf. Co.C
Redden, William C. MO 9th (Elliott's) Cav. Co.B
Redden, William C. MO 12th Inf. Co.H
Redden, William E. AR 24th Inf. Co.G
Redden, William J. AR 8th Cav. Co.F
Redden, W.T. TX 1st Inf. Co.M
Reddett, R.W. MS 5th Cav. Co.C
Reddett, T.W. TN 21st Inf. Co.A
Reddic, J.F. SC 1st (McCreary's) Inf. Co.D
Reddic, J.M. TN 21st (Wilson's) Cav. Co.K
Reddick, Abraham TN 37th Inf. Co.K
Reddick, Albert TN 26th Inf. Co.D
Reddick, Annual NC 46th Inf. Co.G
Reddick, B.J. LA 15th Inf. Co.B Sgt.
Reddick, C. GA 12th (Robinson's) Cav.
  (St.Guards) Co.B
Reddick, Chas. VA 9th Cav. Co.C
Reddick, Columbus 15th Conf.Cav. Co.I
Reddick, D. GA 4th (Clinch's) Cav. Co.E
Reddick, D. GA 9th Inf. (St.Guards) Co.A Sgt.
Reddick, David L. NC 56th Inf. Co.K
Reddick, Desaix MO Lt.Arty. 1st Field Btty.
Reddick, E.L. TX 3rd Cav. Co.B Sgt.
Reddick, Elias H. SC 19th Inf. Co.E
Reddick, Frank TN 15th (Cons.) Cav. Co.C
Reddick, G.A. TN 1st (Feild's) Inf. Co.L Sgt.
Reddick, G.A. TN Inf. Nashville Bn. Fulcher's
  Co.
Reddick, George K. NC 33rd Inf. Co.K
Reddick, G.W. TN Inf. 154th Sr.Regt. Co.A
Reddick, Henry L. NC 7th Inf. Co.D
Reddick, Henry W. FL 1st Inf. New Co.E, Co.A
  1st Lt.
Reddick, H.L. NC 1st Inf. Co.D
Reddick, Humphrey TN 15th (Cons.) Cav. Co.C
Reddick, Hymbrick SC 8th Inf. Co.A
Reddick, I.F. SC 1st Inf. Co.B
Reddick, J.A. NC 7th Inf. Co.D
Reddick, Jacob GA 8th Cav. New Co.I Jr.2nd
  Lt.
Reddick, Jacob GA Cav. 20th Bn. Co.D Jr.2nd
  Lt.
Reddick, Jacob G. GA Cav. 2nd Bn. Co.F Sgt.
Reddick, Jacob G. GA 5th Cav. Co.B Sgt.
Reddick, James TN 1st (Feild's) Inf. Co.L
Reddick, James TN 5th Inf. 2nd Co.C
Reddick, James D. MO 3rd Cav. Co.F Cpl.
Reddick, James H. GA Inf. 5th Bn. (St.Guards)
  Co.C
Reddick, James T. NC 3rd Inf. Co.A
Reddick, James W. MO 8th Inf. Co.E
Reddick, J.B. TN 15th Inf. 2nd Co.F

51

Redding, John MO Inf. Clark's Regt. Co.E

Reddick, J.E. SC Lt.Arty. 3rd (Palmetto) Bn. Co.C
Reddick, J.E. TN 1st (Feild's) Inf. Co.F
Reddick, Jeff TN 55th (Brown's) Inf. Co.B
Reddick, J.F. SC Arty. Manigault's Bn. 2nd Co.C Cpl.
Reddick, J.F. SC Arty. Zimmerman's Co. (Pee Dee Arty.)
Reddick, J.J. GA Hvy.Arty. 22nd Bn. Co.E
Reddick, John GA 1st Bn.S.S. Co.C
Reddick, John GA 32nd Inf. Co.K
Reddick, John NC Cav. 12th Bn. Co.B
Reddick, John NC 1st Jr.Res. Co.K
Reddick, John NC Unassign.Conscr.
Reddick, John TN 15th (Cons.) Cav. Co.C
Reddick, John TX 34th Cav. Co.H
Reddick, John B. AR 1st (Colquitt's) Inf. Co.F
Reddick, John B. TN 11th Inf. Co.D Bvt.2nd Lt.
Reddick, John L. VA 24th Inf. Co.C Cpl.
Reddick, John M. FL 2nd Inf. Co.E Ch.Bugler
Reddick, John M. NC 22nd Inf. Co.L
Reddick, John M. Band Finegan's Brig. Ch.Music.
Reddick, John P. FL 1st (Res.) Inf. Co.A
Reddick, John R. TN 22nd Inf. Co.I
Reddick, John W. GA 55th Inf. Co.A
Reddick, John W. NC Inf. 71st Regt.
Reddick, Joseph AR 15th (N.W.) Inf. Emergency Co.I
Reddick, Joseph NC 46th Inf. Co.G
Reddick, J.P. TN 24th Inf. Co.E
Reddick, J.R. TN 15th (Stewart's) Cav. Co.E Sgt.
Reddick, J.W.B. TN 15th Inf. Co.B Drum.
Reddick, Loftin TX 3rd (Kirby's) Bn.Vol. Co.A
Reddick, Loftin TX 20th Inf. Co.A Sgt.
Reddick, M. MS Cav. Yerger's Regt. Co.B
Reddick, M. Conf.Inf. 1st Bn. 2nd Co.B Sgt.
Reddick, M.A. NC 5th Cav. (63rd St.Troops) Co.D
Reddick, M.M. FL 1st Inf. New Co.E Sgt.
Reddick, M.V. TN 55th (Brown's) Inf. Co.B
Reddick, N.L. Gen. & Staff Capt.
Reddick, N.M. GA 61st Inf. Co.C 1st Sgt.
Reddick, N.T. NC 1st Jr.Res. Co.K
Reddick, P.W. GA 2nd (Stapleton's) St.Troops Sgt.
Reddick, P.W. GA 61st Inf. Co.C
Reddick, R. Exch.Bn. 2nd Co.C,CSA
Reddick, R.B. Forrest's Scouts T. Henderson's Co.
Reddick, R.H. MS 10th Inf. Old Co.D Sgt.
Reddick, R.J. LA 14th Inf. Co.D
Reddick, Samuel C. FL 2nd Cav. Co.C 1st Lt.
Reddick, T.F. GA Cav. 20th Bn. Co.D
Reddick, T.H. GA Lt.Arty. (Jackson Arty.) Massenburg's Btty.
Reddick, T.H. GA 55th Inf. Co.A
Reddick, Thomas GA 32nd Inf.
Reddick, T.L.D. NC Townsend's Co. (St.Troops)
Reddick, W.A. GA 12th Mil.
Reddick, Washington SC 8th Inf. Co.A
Reddick, William GA Cav. 16th Bn. (St.Guards) Co.B

Reddick, William NC Hvy.Arty. 10th Bn. Co.A
Reddick, William NC 33rd Inf. Co.B
Reddick, William 1st Choctaw & Chickasaw Mtd.Rifles 1st Co.K Sgt.
Reddick, William A. MS 15th Inf. Co.H 2nd Lt.
Reddick, William H. NC 31st Inf. Co.F
Reddick, William H. SC 8th Inf. Co.A Cpl.
Reddick, William T. NC 3rd Inf. Co.A
Reddick, Willis TN 15th (Stewart's) Cav. Co.C
Reddick, W.R. TN 31st Inf. Co.I
Reddick, W.T. SC 8th Inf. Co.F
Reddick, W.T. 1st Conf.Eng.Troops Co.K
Reddick, W.W. TN 15th Inf. Co.A
Reddick, W.W. TN 31st Inf. Co.I
Reddick, Zachariah TN 37th Inf. Co.K
Reddicks, Asa S. TN 41st Inf. Co.A Sgt.
Reddicks, J.A. TX 21st Cav. Co.F
Reddie, James MD Inf. 2nd Bn. Co.E Cpl.
Reddig, William S. LA 1st (Nelligan's) Inf. Co.I
Reddill, S. TN 51st (Cons.) Inf. Co.I
Reddin, A. AL 19th Inf. Co.A 2nd Lt.
Reddin, Andrew NC 53rd Inf. Co.C
Reddin, Daniel K. VA Hvy.Arty. 19th Bn. Co.D
Reddin, George MS Cav. Powers' Regt. Co.C
Reddin, George B. MS 2nd Cav. Co.F
Reddin, George W. GA 35th Inf. Co.D
Reddin, G.W. GA Lt.Arty. 14th Bn. Co.D
Reddin, G.W. GA Lt.Arty. King's Btty.
Reddin, H. SC 27th Inf. Co.D
Reddin, Henry KY 4th Cav. Co.G
Reddin, Isaac K. AR Inf. Hardy's Regt. Co.F
Reddin, Jacob KY 4th Cav. Co.G
Reddin, James KY 4th Cav. Co.G
Reddin, James S. GA 65th Inf. Co.G
Reddin, J.E. MS Lt.Arty. 14th Bn. Co.C
Reddin, John KY 4th Cav. Co.G
Reddin, R.M. AR Cav. McGehee's Regt. Co.F
Reddin, Thomas KY 7th Cav. Co.K
Reddin, Thomas LA C.S. Zouave Bn.
Reddin, Thomas J. GA 41st Inf. Co.E
Reddin, W. GA 11th Inf. Co.F
Reddin, William GA Lt.Arty. 14th Bn. Co.D
Reddin, William GA Lt.Arty. King's Btty.
Reddin, William H. TN 53rd Inf. Co.C
Reddin, W.M. GA 20th St.Mil. Capt.
Reddin, W.S. AR 19th (Dockery's) Inf. Cons. Co.E,D
Reddin, Y. KY 4th Cav. Co.G
Redding, A.F. GA Inf. 14th Bn. (St.Guards) Co.A Sgt.
Redding, Alfred NC Inf. 2nd Bn. Co.F
Redding, Alonzo AL Inf. 2nd Regt. Co.F,E Bvt.2nd Lt.
Redding, Alonzo Conf.Inf. 1st Bn. 2nd Co.C 2nd Lt.
Redding, A.M. MO Cav. 7th Regt.St.Guard Co.F 2nd Lt.
Redding, Anderson S. GA Inf. 2nd Bn. Co.C
Redding, Arthur M. AL 57th Inf. Co.B
Redding, August B. Gen. & Staff AQM
Redding, Augustus B. GA 31st Inf. Co.G AQM
Redding, B.B. GA Arty. 11th Bn. (Sumter Arty.) New Co.D,C
Redding, Benjamin F. NC 22nd Inf. Co.I
Redding, Benjamin J. GA 26th Inf. Co.C
Redding, B.J. FL 8th Inf. Co.A

Redding, Charles F. GA Cav. 8th Bn. (St.Guards) Co.D Capt.
Redding, Charles F. GA 27th Inf. Adj.
Redding, Charles H. AL 7th Inf. Co.E
Redding, Chas. H. AL 29th Inf. Co.G
Redding, Charles H. AL Vol. Lee, Jr.'s Co.
Redding, Charles R. GA Inf. 2nd Bn. Co.C Capt.
Redding, Columbus C. GA 41st Inf. Co.E
Redding, Crawford GA 12th Inf. Co.A
Redding, D.A. LA 22nd (Cons.) Inf. Co.G
Redding, Daniel S. GA 45th Inf. Co.D Capt.
Redding, D.F. TX 32nd Cav. Co.B
Redding, Edward Q. NC 4th Inf. Co.E 2nd Lt.
Redding, Elhannan GA 26th Inf. Co.C
Redding, Eli D. MS 34th Inf. Co.I
Redding, F. GA 29th Inf. Co.F
Redding, F.W. MS 3rd Cav. Co.E
Redding, George KY Cav. 1st Bn. Revill's Co.
Redding, George L. AR 16th Inf. Co.C
Redding, George W. AL 56th Part.Rangers Co.D
Redding, George W. GA 24th Inf. Co.D
Redding, George W. MS 42nd Inf. Co.C
Redding, G.W. GA 5th Inf. Co.K
Redding, G.W. FL 1st (Res.) Inf.
Redding, Henry C. AR Cav. 1st Bn. (Stirman's) Co.H
Redding, Henry C. TX 27th Cav. Co.B
Redding, Henry G. TX Cav. Waller's Regt. Co.B
Redding, Henry P. TN 13th Inf. Co.K
Redding, Henry T. FL Lt.Arty. Perry's Co.
Redding, H.R. TX 10th Cav. Co.B
Redding, Isaac AR Lt.Arty. Thrall's Btty.
Redding, J. AR 11th & 17th (Cons.) Inf. Co.I
Redding, J. FL 1st (Res.) Inf. Co.D
Redding, J.A. AR 19th (Dawson's) Inf. Co.E
Redding, James GA 29th Inf. Co.F
Redding, James GA Cherokee Legion (St.Guards) Co.E
Redding, James NC 1st Arty. (10th St.Troops) Co.C
Redding, James SC 10th Inf. Co.K
Redding, James Conf.Cav. Clarkson's Bn. Ind.Rangers Co.G
Redding, James A. GA Siege Arty. 28th Bn. Co.K Cpl.
Redding, James H. KY 3rd Cav. Co.A
Redding, James M. AL 3rd Res. Co.H
Redding, James M. AL 4th Inf. Co.D
Redding, James M. GA 4th Bn.S.S. Co.A
Redding, James M. GA 8th Inf. (St.Guards) Co.D
Redding, James Oliver LA 28th (Gray's) Inf. Co.F
Redding, James P. GA 64th Inf. Co.I Sgt.
Redding, James V. NC 54th Inf. Co.G
Redding, J.B. MS 8th Cav. Co.D
Redding, J.B. TX 4th Inf. (St.Troops) Co.D
Redding, J.C. MS 2nd Part.Rangers Co.K
Redding, J.E. AL 8th Cav. Co.D
Redding, J.E. AL 8th (Hatch's) Cav. Co.D
Redding, J.E. MS Lt.Arty. Merrin's Btty.
Redding, J.L. GA 2nd Inf. Co.K Sgt.
Redding, John AR 35th Inf. Co.D
Redding, John GA Lt.Arty. 14th Bn. Co.B,F
Redding, John GA Lt.Arty. Anderson's Btty.
Redding, John MO Inf. Clark's Regt. Co.E

Redding, John NC 54th Inf. Co.G
Redding, John A. MS 30th Inf. Co.E
Redding, John B. TX 10th Cav. Co.B
Redding, John C. GA 13th Inf. Co.A
Redding, John C. GA 44th Inf. Co.H Capt.
Redding, John H. AL 20th Inf. Co.I,H Sgt.
Redding, John M. GA 5th Inf. Co.F,A Cpl.
Redding, John M. GA 14th Inf. Co.A
Redding, John M. GA 45th Inf. Co.D
Redding, John P. NC 3rd Arty. (40th St.Troops) Co.D Surg.
Redding, John T. AL 20th Inf. Co.C
Redding, John W. GA Cav. 1st Bn.Res. Co.C
Redding, Jordan T. GA 5th Inf. Co.F,A
Redding, Jordon NC 3rd Bn.Sr.Res. Durham's Co.
Redding, Joseph AL 41st Inf. Co.A
Redding, Joseph MO Cav. Poindexter's Regt.
Redding, Joseph MO Arty. Lowe's Co.
Redding, Joseph A. LA 12th Inf. Co.H
Redding, Joseph A. MO Lt.Arty. 3rd Btty.
Redding, Joseph W. MO 5th Inf. Co.H
Redding, J.P. GA 10th Cav.
Redding, J.P. GA 2nd Inf. Cpl.
Redding, J.P. GA 2nd Inf. Co.C Cpl.
Redding, J.Q. TX 32nd Cav. Co.B
Redding, J.R., 2nd AR 17th (Griffith's) Inf. Co.C
Redding, J.R. AR 35th Inf. Co.D
Redding, J.R. GA 12th Inf. Co.F Sgt.
Redding, J.T. AR 27th Inf. Co.E
Redding, J.T. GA 12th Inf. Co.F
Redding, L. MS 27th Inf. Co.C
Redding, Lee R. FL 4th Inf. Co.G
Redding, Leonidas R. GA 31st Inf. Co.E Capt.
Redding, L.J.B. MS 24th Inf. Co.K
Redding, Luke TN 46th Inf. Co.G
Redding, L.W. TX Cav. Waller's Regt. Co.D
Redding, Marion AR 35th Inf. Co.D
Redding, M.C. TX 19th Inf. Co.F
Redding, McCoy C. TX 12th Cav. Co.I
Redding, M.N. NC 3rd Arty. (40th St.Troops) Co.G Cpl.
Redding, M.N. NC Lt.Arty. 13th Bn. Co.E Cpl.
Redding, M.R. GA 28th Inf. Co.E
Redding, Nathan E. NC Unassign.Conscr.
Redding, N.M. FL 8th Inf. Co.A 3rd Lt.
Redding, P., 1st AR 17th (Griffith's) Inf. Co.C
Redding, Pinckney GA 4th Bn.S.S. Co.A
Redding, Pinkney GA Inf. 3rd Bn. Co.G
Redding, Ples. J. AR 16th Inf. Co.A Cpl.
Redding, R.B. GA 8th Inf. Co.E
Redding, R.D. AL Mil. 4th Vol. Co.I Cpl.
Redding, Richard MO Searcy's Bn.S.S. Co.C
Redding, Richard R. MS 15th Inf. Co.D
Redding, Robert J. GA 46th Inf. Co.B Capt.
Redding, Robert M. MS 1st (Johnston's) Inf. Co.F Sgt.
Redding, Solomon W. MS 18th Cav. Co.B,K Sgt.
Redding, S.W. MS 2nd Part.Rangers Co.K
Redding, S.W. MS 7th Cav. Co.K
Redding, T.A. GA 43rd Inf. Co.A
Redding, T.C. FL Cav. 5th Bn. Co.G
Redding, T.C. MS 2nd Part.Rangers Co.K
Redding, Thomas AR 7th Cav. Co.L
Redding, Thomas NC 6th Sr.Res. Co.D

Redding, Thomas B. FL 1st Cav. Co.D
Redding, Thomas C. FL 5th Inf. Co.D
Redding, Thomas C. GA 11th Cav. (St.Guards) Groover's Co.
Redding, Thomas P. GA 64th Inf. Co.H
Redding, Thomas J. GA 6th Inf. (St.Guards) Co.D 1st Sgt.
Redding, Thomas W. TN 6th Inf. Co.I
Redding, T.J. TN 19th (Biffle's) Cav. Co.D
Redding, T.W. MS Blythe's Bn. (St.Troops) Co.A Sgt.
Redding, W. GA Cav. 16th Bn. (St.Guards) Co.F Cpl.
Redding, W.A. AL Lt.Arty. Kolb's Btty.
Redding, W.A. LA 17th Inf. Co.F
Redding, Wade H. FL 9th Inf. Co.D,F
Redding, Walter C. MS 3rd Inf. Co.F
Redding, Watson W. NC 22nd Inf. Co.I Sgt.
Redding, W.H. AL 51st (Part.Rangers) Co.I
Redding, W.H. GA Lt.Arty. Pritchard's Co. (Washington Arty.)
Redding, W.H. Lt.Arty. Dent's Btty.,CSA
Redding, W.H. 1st Conf.Inf. 1st Co.F
Redding, William GA 4th Res. Co.A,F
Redding, William KY 7th Cav. Co.A
Redding, William KY 8th Cav. Co.H
Redding, William MO Lt.Arty. Barret's Co.
Redding, William NC 58th Inf. Co.E
Redding, William A. AL Arty. 4th Bn. Hilliard's Legion Co.B
Redding, William A. FL 7th Inf. Co.A
Redding, William A. GA Inf. 2nd Bn. Co.D 2nd Lt.
Redding, William A. GA 42nd Inf. Co.A
Redding, William A. GA 43rd Inf. Co.A
Redding, William A. NC 37th Inf. Co.F 2nd Lt.
Redding, William C. GA Inf. 2nd Bn. Co.C
Redding, William C. GA 24th Inf. Co.D
Redding, William D. GA 27th Inf. Co.G Capt.
Redding, William G. GA 12th Inf. Co.F
Redding, William H. NC 56th Inf. Co.D,H
Redding, William J. AR 19th Inf. Co.F
Redding, William L. MS 16th Inf. Co.C
Redding, William M. TX 1st (McCulloch's) Cav. Co.B Cpl.
Redding, William R. GA 13th Inf. Co.E Capt.
Redding, William W. MS 34th Inf. Co.I 1st Lt.
Redding, William W. NC 56th Inf. Co.D Cpl.
Redding, W.J. GA Cav. 2nd Bn. Co.C
Redding, W.J. GA 5th Cav. Co.E
Redding, W.J. TX Cav. 3rd (Yager's) Bn. Co.B 1st Sgt.
Redding, W.J. TX Cav. Border's Regt. Co.H 2nd Lt.
Redding, W.N. FL 1st (Res.) Inf. Co.D
Redding, W.R. TN 27th Inf. Co.B
Redding, W.T. AR 19th (Dawson's) Inf. Co.E
Redding, W.Y. GA 1st (Fannin's) Res. Co.C
Reddinger, Samuel VA 157th Mil. Co.B
Reddings, Alexander TN 48th (Voorhies') Inf. Co.I
Reddington, H. AL 5th Inf. Co.A
Reddington, H.T. TX 17th Cons.Dismtd.Cav. 1st Co.G, Co.E
Reddington, James KY 9th Mtd.Inf. Co.I
Reddington, James LA Washington Arty.Bn. Co.1

Reddington, James NC 54th Inf. Co.I
Reddington, James P. LA 1st (Nelligan's) Inf. Co.C
Reddington, James P. LA Inf. 1st Sp.Bn. (Rightor's) 2nd Co.C
Reddington, Jeremiah LA 5th Inf. Co.K
Reddington, William GA 1st (Olmstead's) Inf. Read's Co., Gordon's Co.
Reddins, Mitchell NC 52nd Inf. Co.G
Reddish, Augustus W. MO Cav. 3rd Bn. Co.B Cpl.
Reddish, D. GA 1st (Symons') Res. Co.F
Reddish, Garrett NC 3rd Inf. Co.I
Reddish, Isham SC 24th Inf. Co.E
Reddish, Isham SC 24th Inf. Co.E Cpl.
Reddish, J. AL 12th Cav. Co.F Capt.
Reddish, Jackson FL 2nd Cav. Co.K
Reddish, Jackson FL 10th Inf. Co.A
Reddish, James H. AL 40th Inf. Co.B
Reddish, John Logan AL 3rd Cav. Co.D Sgt.Maj.
Reddish, Paul J. GA 61st Inf. Co.B
Reddish, Peter SC 24th Inf. Co.E
Reddish, Phillip MO 2nd Cav. Co.C,A
Reddish, Phillip W. MO Cav. 3rd Bn. Co.B
Reddish, Riley SC Hvy.Arty. 15th (Lucas') Bn. Co.C
Reddish, Thompson K. MO Cav. 3rd Bn. Co.B
Reddish, William NC 3rd Inf. Co.I
Reddish, William T. GA 54th Inf. Co.B
Reddish, William W. GA 25th Inf. Co.I
Reddit, John J. FL 7th Inf. Co.F
Redditt, Augustus L MS 20th Inf. Co.C Cpl.
Redditt, David F. NC 1st Arty. (10th St.Troops) Co.K Sgt.
Redditt, David F. NC 61st Inf. Co.B 1st Lt.
Redditt, David L. MS 20th Inf. Co.C Cpl.
Redditt, G.W. TN 38th Inf. Co.I
Redditt, James NC 4th Inf. Co.E
Redditt, Robert W. GA Brig.
Redditt, R.W. MS Cav. 6th Bn. Prince's Co.
Redditt, Samuel TN 51st Inf. Co.B
Redditt, T.W. 9th Conf.Inf. Co.H
Redditt, William TX 3rd Cav. Co.E
Redditt, William A. NC 3rd Arty. (40th St.Troops) Co.C
Redditt, William Antoinie LA 17th Inf. Co.A Lt.Col.
Redditt, William H. NC 5th Inf. Co.D
Reddle, John AR 8th Cav. Co.H
Reddle, Sanford S. 14th Conf.Cav. Co.H Sgt.
Reddle, Thomas J. AR 8th Cav. Co.H
Reddlees, William H. AL 14th Inf. Co.D
Reddling, M. GA Lt.Arty. Barnwell's Btty.
Reddoch, Daniel MS Inf. 7th Bn. Co.G
Reddoch, James O. MS Inf. 7th Bn. Co.G 1st Sgt.
Reddock, A. NC Townsend's Co. (St.Troops)
Reddock, I. AL 6th Cav. Co.A
Reddock, J.A. MS Cav. 1st Bn. (McNair's) St.Troops Co.B
Reddock, J.D. AL 6th Cav. Co.A Sgt.
Reddock, J.D. AL 15th Inf. Co.I
Reddock, J.D. AL 37th Inf. Co.K 2nd Lt.
Reddock, John L. MS 7th Inf. Co.I
Reddock, J.V. MS 46th Inf. Co.B
Reddock, Martin C. MS 7th Inf. Co.I

Reddock, William C. AL 61st Inf. Co.D
Reddock, William M. AL 63rd Inf. Co.B,G
Reddock, William R. MS 7th Inf. Co.I
Reddoe, James S. AL 37th Inf. Co.K
Reddon, I.J. LA 3rd (Wingfield's) Cav. Co.F
   2nd Lt.
Reddus, W.G. AR Mil. Louis' Co.
Reddy, Andrew GA 26th Inf. Co.B
Reddy, George SC Inf. Holcombe Legion Co.D
Reddy, J.A. SC Inf. Holcombe Legion Co.D
Reddy, James SC 1st Bn.S.S. Co.B
Reddy, James SC 8th Bn.Res. Co.C
Reddy, James SC 27th Inf. Co.F
Reddy, James F. SC 1st (Hagood's) Inf. 1st Co.G
Reddy, Joel NC 1st Inf.
Reddy, John MS Cav. Garland's Bn. Co.A
Reddy, John MS Inf. 2nd Bn. Co.A 1st Sgt.
Reddy, John MS 7th Inf. Co.H
Reddy, John MS 48th Inf. Co.A 1st Sgt.
Reddy, John SC 27th Inf. Co.F
Reddy, Richard GA 1st Bn.S.S. Co.C
Reddy, R.W. SC 1st Inf. Co.B
Reddy, R.W. SC 21st Inf. Co.G Capt.
Reddy, T.J. SC 2nd Arty. Co.A
Reddy, William SC 1st Bn.S.S. Co.B
Reddy, William SC 27th Inf. Co.F
Reddy, William Conf.Cav. Wood's Regt. Co.K
Redeau, Henry LA Washington Arty.Bn. Co.3
Redeker, F. TX 16th Inf. Co.E
Redel, Fred TN 15th Inf. Co.K
Redell, John H. AR Cav. 1st Bn. (Stirman's)
   Co.B
Redelstorff, John MS Cav. Jeff Davis Legion
   Co.B
Reden, H. TX 7th Cav. Co.E
Reden, James A. NC 28th Inf. Co.E
Redenbaugh, F.B. MO Robertson's Regt.
   St.Guard Co.3
Redenbaugh, Frederick B. MO 5th Cav. Co.E
Redenhower, D.R. AR Inf. Cocke's Regt. Co.C
   1st Sgt.
Reder, C. Eng.Dept. Polk's Corps A. of TN Sap.
   & Min. Co.,CSA
Reder, Calvin 3rd Conf.Eng.Troops Co.B Cpl.
Reder, Christoph TX 16th Inf. Co.F
Reder, Jackson TX Inf. 1st St.Troops Co.F
Reder, James MO 15th Cav. Co.B
Reder, John AR 2nd Vol. Co.B
Reder, Louis LA Mil. 4th Regt.Eur.Brig. Co.D
   1st Lt.
Redesick, R.W. LA 28th (Gray's) Inf. Co.K
Red Eye FL McBride's Co. (Indians)
Redfearn, Alfred NC 4th Cav. (59th St.Troops)
   Co.A
Redfearn, Alfred NC 23rd Inf. Co.A
Redfearn, Alfred SC 1st (Butler's) Inf. Co.E
Redfearn, A.T. NC 4th Cav. (59th St.Troops)
   Co.A
Redfearn, Berry J. NC 23rd Inf. Co.A Cpl.
Redfearn, D.A. NC Cav. 4th Regt. (59th
   St.Troops) Co.A
Redfearn, David A. SC Lt.Arty. Kelly's Co.
   (Chesterfield Arty.)
Redfearn, David T. NC 3rd Arty. (40th
   St.Troops) Co.G
Redfearn, E. GA 5th Res. Co.C

Redfearn, George W. NC 4th Cav. (59th
   St.Troops) Co.A
Redfearn, G.W. NC 1st Jr.Res. Co.I
Redfearn, H. TN 12th (Cons.) Inf. Co.H
Redfearn, H. TN 22nd Inf. Co.C
Redfearn, Harrison MS 1st Cav. Co.B
Redfearn, James T. MS 29th Inf. Co.B
Redfearn, James T. NC 23rd Inf. Co.A
Redfearn, John NC 23rd Inf. Co.A Cpl.
Redfearn, John W. NC 3rd Arty. (40th
   St.Troops) Co.G
Redfearn, John W. NC 14th Inf. Co.C
Redfearn, Joseph N. NC 43rd Inf. Co.I
Redfearn, J.W. NC 1st Jr.Res. Co.I
Redfearn, Malachi G. NC 3rd Arty. (40th
   St.Troops) Co.G
Redfearn, William NC 4th Cav. (59th St.Troops)
   Co.A
Redfearn, William D. NC 23rd Inf. Co.A 1st Lt.
Redfearn, William M. MS 39th Inf. Co.I
Redfearn, Wilson C. NC 23rd Inf. Co.A
Redfearn, Z.T. SC 26th Inf. Co.B
Redfern, Asbury VA 10th Inf. Co.A Music.
Redfern, Charles E. VA 27th Inf. Co.G
Redfern, E.T. NC Allen's Co. (Loc.Def.)
Redfern, J.N. NC Allen's Co. (Loc.Def.) Cpl.
Redfern, John GA 59th Inf. Co.B
Redfern, Robert S. NC 43rd Inf. Co.I
Redfern, W. GA 59th Inf. Co.B
Redfield, C.G. MS Conscr.
Redfield, E.F. 3rd Conf.Cav. Co.G
Redfield, Festus S. TX 17th Cav. Co.G
Redfield, Frank LA 1st (Nelligan's) Inf. Co.K
   Sgt.
Redfield, F.S. 3rd Conf.Eng.Troops Co.H
Redfield, F.S. Sap. & Min.,CSA
Redfield, Henry LA 17th Inf. Co.A
Redfield, James MS 22nd Inf. Co.D
Redfield, Sidney LA 17th Inf. Co.A
Redfield, Syd. AL 17th Inf. Co.K
Redfield, Thomas LA 1st (Strawbridge's) Inf.
   Co.D
Redfiern, Andrew GA 15th Inf. Co.K
Redfiern, E.W. GA 15th Inf. Co.K
Redfiern, James GA 15th Inf. Co.K
Redfor, C.E. VA 3rd Inf.Loc.Def. Co.F
Redford, A. AL 7th Inf. Co.D
Redford, Anderson Mead's Conf.Cav. Co.E
Redford, Andrew J. VA 15th Inf. Co.G
Redford, B.C. TN 3rd (Forrest's) Cav.
   Asst.Surg.
Redford, Ben C. KY 10th (Johnson's) Cav.
   Asst.Surg.
Redford, Benjamin VA 15th Inf. Co.G
Redford, Benj. C. Gen. & Staff Asst.Surg.
Redford, Channing E. VA 1st Inf. Co.A
Redford, Channing E. VA 12th Inf. Co.G Cpl.
Redford, Cornelius A. VA 1st Inf. Co.G
Redford, Edward G. VA 53rd Inf. Co.C
Redford, Edward G. VA Inf. Montague's Bn.
   Co.D
Redford, Edward W. VA Inf. 23rd Bn. Co.H
Redford, E.G. VA Hvy.Arty. 18th Bn. Co.C
Redford, E.G. VA Inf. 25th Bn. Co.D
Redford, E.W. KY 3rd Mtd.Inf. Co.K
Redford, Fred P. VA Cav. 1st Bn. Co.B 2nd Lt.
Redford, George E. VA 1st Inf. Co.H

Redford, Isaac MO 6th Cav. Co.F
Redford, James KY 1st Inf. Co.I
Redford, James VA Inf. 25th Bn. Co.G
Redford, James H. LA 1st (Nelligan's) Inf. Co.H
   Cpl.
Redford, James H. TN 6th Inf. Co.I
Redford, James M. MO 10th Cav. Co.H
Redford, James M. VA 53rd Inf. Co.I Cpl.
Redford, J.B. SC 2nd Inf. Co.D
Redford, J.D. TN 18th Inf. Co.I
Redford, Jesse E. MO 10th Cav. Co.A
Redford, J.M. VA Inf. Montague's Bn. Co.B
Redford, John VA Hvy.Arty. 18th Bn. Co.C
Redford, John A. TN 44th (Cons.) Inf. Co.I
Redford, John R. VA Lt.Arty. Ellett's Co.
   Comsy.Sgt.
Redford, Joseph F. VA Inf. 4th Bn.Loc.Def.
   Co.C
Redford, J.T. AR 19th (Dockery's) Inf. Co.B
Redford, J.T. KY 8th Mtd. Inf. Co.I 1st Lt.
Redford, J.W. NC 32nd Inf. Co.G
Redford, L. VA 1st St.Res. Co.F
Redford, Marcus L. VA Hvy.Arty. 10th Bn.
   Co.A
Redford, M.L. 1st Conf.Eng.Troops Co.D Artif.
Redford, M.W. TN 4th Inf. Co.H
Redford, Nathan MO 10th Cav. Co.A
Redford, N.H. MO Lt.Arty. 4th (Harris') Field
   Btty. Sgt.
Redford, Noah H. MO 10th Cav. Co.H
Redford, N.T. VA Inf. 1st Bn.Loc.Def. Co.E,F
   1st Sgt.
Redford, N.T. VA Inf. 25th Bn. Co.A
Redford, N.W. VA 2nd St.Res. Co.C Cpl.
Redford, R.F. MO 10th Cav. Co.H
Redford, R.F. VA Lt.Arty. 12th Bn. Co.B
Redford, Richard T. VA Lt.Arty. W.P. Carter's
   Co.
Redford, R.F. VA 1st St.Res. Co.F Cpl.
Redford, Robert VA 1st St.Res. Co.B
Redford, Robert Spann MS Inf. 1st St.Troops
   Co.D Sgt.
Redford, Rogers AL 38th Inf. Co.B
Redford, Smith VA Lt.Arty. Cayce's Co.
Redford, Thomas VA Inf. 4th Bn. Co.F
Redford, W. AR 2nd Inf. Co.I
Redford, W. VA 3rd Inf.Loc.Def. Co.F
Redford, W.A. 3rd Conf.Inf. QMSgt.
Redford, W.H. VA 3rd Inf.Loc.Def. Co.I
Redford, William NC 1st Inf. Co.I
Redford, William TX Cav. Border's Regt. Co.D
Redford, William F. VA Lt.Arty. W.P. Carter's
   Co.
Redford, William J. VA Lt.Arty. Kirkpatrick's
   Co.
Redford, William P. VA 1st Cav. Co.G Sgt.
Redford, W.J. VA Hanover Rifles Co.D
Redgeway, L.S. TX Cav. Giddings' Bn. Onins'
   Co.
Redgister, J.S. AL 6th Inf. Co.A
Redgiway, Elijah MO 10th Cav. Co.D
Redgood, R.A. GA Cav. 29th Bn.
Redgood, S.J. AL 37th Inf. Co.C
Redgway, George W. VA 53rd Inf. Co.I
Redicheck, Frederick A. MO Inf. 3rd Bn. Co.A
Redick, Epinetus NC 30th Inf. Co.F

Redick, Hymbrick SC 1st (Hagood's) Inf. 2nd Co.B
Redick, James M. TN Inf. Nashville Bn. Felts' Co.
Redick, John H. MO 10th Inf. Co.A
Redick, J.P. AL 63rd Inf. Co.F
Redick, L.B. TN Inf. Nashville Bn. Felts' Co.
Redick, M.L. NC Townsend's Co. (St.Troops)
Redick, W.T. SC 26th Inf. Co.G
Redifer, Henry Morgan's,CSA
Redilsheimer, H. GA Inf. 14th Bn. (St.Guards) Co.B
Redimemd, Robert VA 8th Cav. 1st Co.D
Redin, Alvin NC Hvy.Arty. 10th Bn. Co.C
Redin, George W. LA 31st Inf. Co.I
Redin, S.C. AL 34th Inf. Co.F
Redin, William GA Inf. (Richmond Factory Guards) Barney's Co.
Redin, William MO Cav. Schnabel's Bn. Co.F
Reding, A.M. TN 30th Inf. Co.H
Reding, G.W. TX 4th Inf. (St.Troops) Co.D
Reding, James AR 7th Cav. Co.B
Reding, James M. TX 37th Cav. 2nd Co.I Sgt.
Reding, J.B. TX 24th Cav. Co.B
Reding, John A. LA 28th (Gray's) Inf. Co.I
Reding, John S. MO Cav. 11th Regt.St.Guard Comsy.
Reding, M.C. LA 1st Inf. Co.G
Reding, William 1st Cherokee Mtd.Vol. 1st Co.C
Reding, William M. TX Waul's Legion Co.B 1st Lt.
Redinger, J.P. AL 5th Inf. Co.B
Redington, Hiram TX 18th Cav. Co.E
Redington, Obediah TX 18th Cav. Co.E
Redington, William GA 63rd Inf. Co.B
Redins, Jonathan L. MS 2nd St.Cav. Co.F
Redis, James AR Lt.Arty. Thrall's Btty.
Redis, James H. MS Inf. 2nd Bn. Co.C Cpl.
Redis, James H. MS 48th Inf. Co.C Sgt.
Redish, D. FL 1st (Res.) Inf. Co.I
Redish, David GA Mayer's Co. (Appling Cav.)
Redish, D.L. SC 4th Cav. Co.G
Redish, Drew GA Mayer's Co. (Appling Cav.)
Redish, George GA Mayer's Co. (Appling Cav.)
Redish, Joshua GA 29th Inf. Co.H
Reditt, J.P. TN 30th Inf. Co.C
Redka, Fred TX Cav. Waller's Regt. Co.A
Redle, V.R. AR 7th Cav. Co.C
Redler, --- LA Mil. 3rd Regt.Eur.Brig. (Garde Francaise) Co.5
Redley, A. SC 12th Inf. Co.K
Redley, J.S. Gen. & Staff Capt.,Comsy.
Redlick, J. AL 8th Inf. Co.G
Redling, George W. NC 33rd Inf. Co.A
Redling, R.T. AR 11th Inf. Co.G Sgt.
Redling, William A. NC 33rd Inf. Co.C
Redling, W.J. KY 6th Mtd.Inf. Co.B
Redlit, Oliver NC 67th Inf. Co.G Cpl.
Redman, A. MO Lt.Arty. Welsh's Co.
Redman, Alexander K. SC 24th Inf. Co.H
Redman, Allen SC 20th Inf. Co.D
Redman, A.P. LA 2nd Cav. Co.G
Redman, Archibald TN 44th (Cons.) Inf. Co.I
Redman, A.W. AR 32nd Inf. Co.K
Redman, Benjamin MS Inf. 2nd Bn. (St.Troops) Co.C

Redman, Benjamin TN Inf. 1st Bn. (Colms') Co.C Cpl.
Redman, Benjamin TN 50th (Cons.) Inf. Co.K 1st Sgt.
Redman, Benjamin F. MO Searcy's Bn.S.S.
Redman, Benson VA Inf. 21st Bn. 1st Co.D
Redman, Brian VA 6th Inf. Co.C
Redman, C. TX 1st (Yager's) Cav. Co.D Bugler
Redman, C.E. KY 6th Mtd.Inf. Co.I
Redman, Christopher TX Cav. 3rd (Yager's) Bn. Co.D
Redman, C.J. AL 57th Inf. Co.K
Redman, C.M. MS 11th (Perrin's) Cav. Co.K
Redman, C.P. LA 16th Inf. Co.H
Redman, David LA 1st Cav. Co.D
Redman, David TN 1st (Carter's) Cav. Co.L
Redman, Edward MO 1st & 3rd Cons.Cav. Co.E
Redman, Elisha VA Inf. 1st Bn. Co.C Sgt.
Redman, Elisha VA 8th Inf. Co.K
Redman, F. LA 21st (Kennedy's) Inf. Co.A
Redman, F. SC 23rd Inf. Co.C
Redman, F.M. GA 3rd Cav. Co.E
Redman, Franklin NC 13th Inf. Co.C
Redman, Franklin NC 52nd Inf. Co.D
Redman, Franklin A. NC 54th Inf. Co.E Cpl.
Redman, F.S. NC 6th Inf. Co.A
Redman, G.B. MO 16th Inf. Co.A
Redman, George AL 39th Inf. Co.K
Redman, George Conf.Cav. Clarkson's Bn. Ind.Rangers Co.A
Redman, George W. AL 50th Inf. Co.C
Redman, George W. NC 54th Inf. Co.E
Redman, George W. TN 3rd (Clack's) Inf.
Redman, Green D. MO 10th Cav. Co.C
Redman, G.S. Conf.Cav. Clarkson's Bn. Ind. Rangers Co.G
Redman, G.W., Sr. NC 54th Inf. Co.E
Redman, G.W. TN 5th (McKenzie's) Cav.Co.C
Redman, G.W. TN 11th (Holman's) Cav. Co.B
Redman, H. MO 10th Inf. Co.B
Redman, H.A. AL 6th Inf. Co.E
Redman, H.A. NC 54th Inf. Co.E
Redman, H.B. VA Inf. 21st Bn. 2nd Co.C
Redman, Henry VA Lt.Arty. W.P. Carter's Co.
Redman, Henry B. VA 64th Mtd.Inf. Co.C Sgt.
Redman, Hugh AR 31st Inf. Co.F
Redman, J. AR 58th Mil. Co.A
Redman, J.A. KY 8th Mtd.Inf. Co.C
Redman, Jacob NC 29th Inf. Co.E
Redman, Jacob SC 2nd St.Troops Co.G
Redman, James FL 3rd Inf. Co.A
Redman, James LA 14th Inf. Co.A
Redman, James LA 20th Inf. Co.C
Redman, James MO 11th Inf. Co.G
Redman, James NC 6th Cav. (65th St.Troops) Co.A
Redman, James B. MO 1st Cav. Co.I Sgt.
Redman, James L. AL 10th Inf. Co.I
Redman, James M. VA Inf. 21st Bn. 1st Co.D, 2nd Co.C
Redman, James M. VA 64th Mtd.Inf. Co.C
Redman, Jasper NC Inf. Thomas Legion Co.F
Redman, J.B. GA 43rd Inf. Co.F Cpl.
Redman, J.B. MS 3rd Cav. Co.F
Redman, J.C. AL 11th Inf. Co.I
Redman, J.E. VA 2nd Bn.Res. Co.A

Redman, Jesse Conf.Cav. Clarkson's Bn. Ind. Rangers Co.A
Redman, J.G. TN Conscr. (Cp. of Instr.)
Redman, J.H. KY 1st (Butler's) Cav. Co.E
Redman, J.H. TN 4th (McLemore's) Cav. Co.D
Redman, J.L. SC 20th Inf. Co.A
Redman, J.M. GA 56th Inf. Co.D
Redman, Jobe R. NC 6th Cav. (65th St.Troops) Co.A,I Sgt.
Redman, John AL 3rd Bn.Res. Co.H Cpl.
Redman, John AL 15th Inf. Co.I
Redman, John KY 3rd Bn.Mtd.Rifles Co.B
Redman, John LA 13th & 20th Inf. Co.D
Redman, John MS 6th Cav. Co.E
Redman, John MS 5th Inf. (St.Troops) Co.B
Redman, John Conf.Cav. Clarkson's Bn. Ind. Rangers Co.A Sgt.
Redman, John Lt.Arty. Dent's Btty.,CSA
Redman, John C. TN 6th (Wheeler's) Cav. Co.F 1st Lt.,Adj.
Redman, John F. VA 54th Inf. Co.H
Redman, John G. TN 26th Inf. Co.A Cpl.
Redman, John G. VA 38th Inf. 1st Co.I
Redman, John H. VA Inf. 21st Bn. 1st Co.D, 2nd Co.C
Redman, John H. VA 64th Mtd.Inf. Co.C
Redman, John H. VA 111th Mil. Co.8
Redman, John P. MO 5th Inf. Co.C Sgt.
Redman, John T. NC 54th Inf. Co.E
Redman, John T. VA 10th Cav. Co.B
Redman, John T. VA 14th Inf. 2nd Co.G Sgt.
Redman, John W. MS Cav. Stockdale's Bn. Co.B
Redman, John W. NC 54th Inf. Co.E Sgt.
Redman, Joseph GA 3rd Cav. Co.E
Redman, Joseph TN 37th Inf. Co.B
Redman, J.P. NC 60th Inf. Co.K
Redman, J.R. GA 39th Inf. Co.G 1st Lt.
Redman, J.T. GA 24th Inf. Co.A
Redman, J.W. SC Hvy.Arty. 15th (Lucas') Bn. Co.B Sgt.
Redman, J.W. SC 25th Inf. Co.D
Redman, J.W. 3rd Conf.Cav. Co.G
Redman, Lafayette AR 8th Cav. Co.H
Redman, Lafayette AR 14th (McCarver's) Inf. Co.D
Redman, Lewis J. MS 8th Inf. Co.K,A
Redman, L.H. NC 60th Inf. Co.K
Redman, Lloyd KY 6th Mtd.Inf. Co.G Sgt.
Redman, M. AL 15th Inf. Co.K
Redman, M.B. SC 1st Cav. Co.I Cpl.
Redman, M.B. SC 11th Inf. Sheridan's Co.
Redman, Michael GA 25th Inf. Co.C
Redman, M.T. AL 57th Inf. Co.C Jr.2nd Lt.
Redman, N.A. AL 6th Inf. Co.E
Redman, N.C. TN Cav. Welcker's Bn. Kincaid's Co.
Redman, Nelson C. TN 43rd Inf. Co.F
Redman, O.M. MS 2nd St.Cav. Co.H
Redman, Patrick TN 10th Inf.
Redman, Peter AL 6th Cav. Co.A
Redman, Peter F. MO Douglas' Regt.
Redman, P.F. MO Searcy's Bn.S.S.
Redman, Reuben J. GA 34th Inf. Co.H
Redman, Robert NC Inf. Thomas Legion Co.F
Redman, Robert VA 44th Inf. Co.I
Redman, Robert A. AL 13th Inf. Co.G
Redman, Robert H. VA 1st Inf. Co.D

55

Redman, Rufus H. NC 2nd Detailed Men Co.C
Jr.2nd Lt.
Redman, S. LA 3rd (Wingfield's) Cav. Co.F
Redman, Samuel L. TN 9th Inf. Co.H
Redman, Samuel M. AR 23rd Inf. Co.C
Redman, Sanford GA 52nd Inf. Co.G
Redman, Solomon TN Inf. 1st Bn. (Colms')
Co.A
Redman, Solomon TN 50th (Cons.) Inf. Co.B
Redman, Stephen LA 1st Cav. Co.C
Redman, Stephen VA 57th Inf. Co.K
Redman, Stephen 14th Conf.Cav. Co.G
Redman, T.B. TN 7th (Duckworth's) Cav. Co.F
Redman, Thomas LA 4th Inf. Co.B
Redman, Thomas SC Arty. Ferguson's Bn. Co.C
Redman, Thomas TN 30th Inf. Co.D
Redman, Thomas VA Inf. 1st Bn. Co.C
Redman, Thomas 14th Conf.Cav. Co.G
Redman, Thomas C. VA 40th Inf. Co.C 1st Lt.
Redman, Thomas J. TN 20th Inf. Co.D Sgt.Maj.
Redman, Thomas S. VA 12th Cav. Co.B
Redman, Thomas W. NC 1st Cav. (9th
St.Troops) Co.B
Redman, Thomas W. NC 54th Inf. Co.E 1st Sgt.
Redman, Tilghman VA 49th Inf. 1st Co.G
Redman, Tilman VA Lt.Arty. 38th Bn. Co.A
Redman, T.S. SC 11th Inf. Sheridan's Co.
Redman, T.W. 3rd Conf.Cav. Co.B
Redman, W. AL 30th Inf. Co.B
Redman, W. KY 3rd Bn.Mtd.Rifles Co.B Sgt.
Redman, W. SC Mil. 1st Regt. (Charleston Res.)
Co.B
Redman, W.A. AR Mil. Desha Cty.Bn.
Redman, Washington KY 4th Cav. Co.I
Redman, Washington S. NC 2nd Inf. Co.A
Redman, W.H. TN Cav. Jackson's Co. Sgt.
Redman, Wilford VA 6th Cav. Co.A
Redman, William KY 3rd Mtd.Inf. Co.D,I Cpl.
Redman, William MO 11th Inf. Co.G
Redman, William MO 16th Inf. Co.A
Redman, William TN Inf. 1st Bn. (Colms') Co.A
Redman, William TN 50th (Cons.) Inf. Co.B
Redman, William H. AR 15th Mil. Co.C
Redman, William H. TN 39th Mtd.Inf. Co.K
Cpl.
Redman, William M. MO Cav. 3rd Bn. Co.A
Redman, William R. VA 2nd Inf. Co.A Lt.
Redman, William T.C. GA 6th Inf. (St.Guards)
Pittman's Co. Cpl.
Redman, William W. NC 54th Inf. Co.E Sgt.
Redman, Willis TX 27th Cav. Co.H
Redman, Wood MO 12th Cav. Co.F
Redmand, H. LA Washington Arty.Bn. Co.4
Redmand, J.W.C. SC 20th Inf. Co.B
Redmeyer, M. LA Mil. 3rd Regt. 1st Brig. 1st
Div. Co.G
Redmon, Archibald TN 23rd Inf. Co.E
Redmon, A.T. NC 1st Bn.Jr.Res. Co.A
Redmon, Calvin AL 12th Cav. Co.B
Redmon, Cary AL 57th Inf. Co.K
Redmon, C.B. AL Cav. 4th Bn. (Love's) Co.C
Redmon, C.G. SC 11th Inf. Co.C Sgt.
Redmon, Charles B. AL Hardy's Co. (Eufaula
Minute Men)
Redmon, Clement AL 22nd Inf. Co.K
Redmon, Daniel M. NC 29th Inf. Co.C

Redmon, D.M. MS Cav. Part.Rangers Rhodes'
Co.
Redmon, E. SC 20th Inf. Co.D
Redmon, F.C. MO 10th Inf. Co.B
Redmon, George KY 9th Cav. Co.C 1st Sgt.
Redmon, George W. GA 3rd Inf. Co.L Sgt.
Redmon, G.W. TN Holman's Bn.Part.Rangers
Co.A
Redmon, Isaac SC 20th Inf. Co.D Sgt.
Redmon, J.A. SC 20th Inf. Co.D
Redmon, James NC Cav. 5th Bn. Co.A
Redmon, James NC 64th Inf. Co.G
Redmon, James Kinchen NC 6th Inf. Co.C
Redmon, J.B. MO 1st & 3rd Cons.Cav.
Redmon, Jesse TN 16th Inf. Co.A
Redmon, J.L. SC 1st Bn.S.S. Co.A
Redmon, J.L. SC 27th Inf. Co.E
Redmon, J.M. TN 23rd Inf. Co.C
Redmon, J.M. TX Cav. McCord's Frontier Regt.
Co.D Sgt.
Redmon, Job SC 1st (Hagood's) Inf. 1st Co.B,
2nd Co.K
Redmon, Jobe R. NC Cav. 5th Bn. Co.A Sgt.
Redmon, Joseph NC 21st Inf. Co.G
Redmon, J.W. TX Cav. McCord's Frontier Regt.
Co.D
Redmon, M. GA 5th Cav. Co.C
Redmon, N.A. AL 22nd Inf. Co.K
Redmon, N.C. TN 28th Cav. Co.I
Redmon, P.A. NC 60th Inf. Co.C Cpl.
Redmon, Richard TX 4th Inf. Co.K
Redmon, Robert W. AL 61st Inf. Co.F
Redmon, R.W. TN Cav. Williams' Co.
Redmon, Wm. P. AL 22nd Inf. Co.K
Redmon, William P. AL 57th Inf. Co.K
Redmond, A. MO Lt.Arty. Walsh's Co.
Redmond, Albert J. NC 12th Inf. Co.E
Redmond, Archy TN 55th (McKoin's) Inf.
McEwen, Jr.'s Co.
Redmond, B.F. MS Cav. Part.Rangers Rhodes'
Co.
Redmond, B.F. 14th Conf.Cav. Co.F
Redmond, Charles AL Lt.Arty. Kolb's Btty.
Redmond, D. GA Inf. 1st Loc.Troops (Augusta)
Dearing's Cav. Co.
Redmond, David LA Res.Corps
Redmond, Dennis LA 7th Inf. Co.F
Redmond, D.M. 14th Conf.Cav. Co.F Sgt.
Redmond, Duncan NC 1st Inf. Co.D
Redmond, Edward MO 1st Cav. Co.I
Redmond, F.M. LA 11th Inf. Co.I
Redmond, F.M. LA 20th Inf. Co.D,A
Redmond, F.M. MS 9th Bn.S.S. Co.C
Redmond, Frank P. NC Moseley's Co. (Sampson
Arty.)
Redmond, George S. MD 1st Inf. Co.H
Redmond, George T. VA Cav. 39th Bn. Co.B
2nd Lt.
Redmond, G.F. GA 3rd Cav. Co.E
Redmond, H.O. MS 1st Lt.Arty. Co.B
Redmond, I.H. AL 59th Inf. Co.G
Redmond, Isaac B. VA 11th Inf. Co.D
Redmond, J. LA Lt.Arty. Fenner's Btty.
Redmond, James AL Gorff's Co. (Mobile Pulaski
Rifles)
Redmond, James GA 1st (Olmstead's) Inf. Co.B

Redmond, James GA Inf. (High Shoals Defend.)
Medlin's Ind.Co.
Redmond, James TX 4th Field Btty. Sgt.
Redmond, James B. GA 27th Inf. Co.D Cpl.
Redmond, J.M. AL 24th Bn. Co.B
Redmond, Job TN 37th Inf. Co.I
Redmond, John LA Arty. Kean's Btty. (Orleans
Ind.Arty.)
Redmond, John LA Inf. 1st Sp.Bn. (Rightor's)
Co.F
Redmond, John LA Mil.Conf.Guards Regt. Co.I
Redmond, John MS 3rd Inf. Co.H
Redmond, John MS 9th Inf. New Co.B
Redmond, John MS 10th Inf. Co.G
Redmond, John MO 1st Inf. Co.E 1st Lt.
Redmond, John MO 1st & 4th Cons.Inf.
Co.B,D,E 1st Lt.
Redmond, John W.C. SC 2nd Arty. Co.B
Redmond, John W.D. SC 14th Inf. Co.A
Redmond, Joseph LA Mil.Conf.Guards Regt.
Co.I
Redmond, J.T. VA Cav. Mosby's Regt.
(Part.Rangers) Co.F
Redmond, M. LA Mil.Conf.Guards Regt. Co.I
Jr.2nd Lt.
Redmond, M. VA Hvy.Arty. 19th Bn. 1st Co.E
Redmond, Michael GA Hvy.Arty. 22nd Bn.
Co.F
Redmond, Michael GA 1st (Olmstead's) Inf.
Bonaud's Co.
Redmond, Michael VA 1st Inf. Co.C
Redmond, Morgan AL Gorff's Co. (Mobile
Pulaski Rifles)
Redmond, Morgan SC 1st Arty. Co.G
Redmond, Morgan VA 44th Inf. Co.E
Redmond, Newton SC 8th Bn.Res. Co.C
Redmond, P. GA Inf. 1st Loc.Troops (Augusta)
Co.D
Redmond, P. LA Hvy.Arty. 2nd Bn. Co.D
Redmond, P. SC Hvy.Arty. 15th (Lucas') Bn.
Co.B
Redmond, Robert VA 11th Bn.Res. Co.C
Redmond, Samuel VA 6th Cav. Co.H
Redmond, Samuel R. GA Inf. 8th Bn. Co.E
Redmond, S.M. AR 3rd Inf. Co.C
Redmond, S.M. NC 1st Cav. (9th St.Troops)
Co.G Cpl.
Redmond, Stanley P. AL 47th Inf. Co.A Sgt.
Redmond, T. LA Mil. Lewis Guards
Redmond, Thaddeus NC 6th Inf. Co.C
Redmond, Thomas LA 6th Inf. Co.B Capt.
Redmond, Tim LA Mil.Conf.Guards Regt. Co.I
Redmond, Uriah GA 12th Cav. Co.D
Redmond, W.H. AR Inf. Cocke's Regt. Co.B
Redmond, W.H. VA 56th Inf. Co.G
Redmond, William AL 16th Inf. Co.G
Redmond, William GA 46th Inf. Co.G
Redmond, William LA Washington Arty.Bn.
Co.4
Redmond, William LA Inf. Jeff Davis Regt. Co.F
Redmond, William MS 20th Inf. Co.E
Redmond, William NC 17th Inf. (2nd Org.) Co.I
Redmond, William VA 17th Cav. Co.A
Redmond, William R. TN 2nd (Robison's) Inf.
Co.G
Redmond, Wyatt T. VA 56th Inf. Co.G
Redmouth, John 1st Creek Mtd.Vol. Co.G

Redner, William NC 33rd Inf.
Rednouer, Henry LA 30th Inf. Co.C
Rednower, James KY 5th Mtd.Inf. Co.F
Redon, O. LA Mil. 3rd Reg.Eur.Brig. (Garde
   Francaise) Frois' Co.
Redrich, G.G. GA 54th Inf. Co.F
Redrick, Robert MS Lt.Arty. (Warren Lt.Arty.)
   Swett's Co.
Redrick, W.S. TN 15th Inf. 2nd Co.F Sgt.
Redrick, W.S. 3rd Conf.Eng.Troops Co.C Artif.
Redruff, --- 1st Conf.Cav. 2nd Co.F
Redsall, James E. TX 5th Inf. Co.A
Redshaw, T.S. MO St.Guard
Redsleeves, K.W. NC 1st Bn.Jr.Res. Co.C
Redsleve, John G. NC Inf. Thomas Legion Co.C
Redsleve, Morgamin H. NC Inf. Thomas Legion
   Co.C
Redslie, J.R. MS 12th Inf. Cpl.
Redus, --- TX Cav. Mann's Regt. Co.K
Redus, Blewitt S. MS 14th Inf. Co.C
Redus, E. MS 1st (Foote's) Inf. (St.Troops)
   Hobart's Co. Orderly Sgt.
Redus, Enoch B. MS 30th Inf. Co.I Sgt.
Redus, George TX 33rd Cav. Co.A Cpl.
Redus, James B. MS 1st (Patton's) Inf. Co.C
Redus, James B. MS 43rd Inf. Co.F Sgt.
Redus, James F. AL 18th Inf. Co.I
Redus, James F. AR 7th Inf. Co.K
Redus, James W. TX 36th Cav. Co.D Cpl.
Redus, J.F. AL Cp. of Instr. Talladega
Redus, J.M. LA 4th Inf. Co.C
Redus, J.M. MS Inf. 3rd Bn. (St.Troops) Co.A
Redus, Jo. MS T.P. Montgomery's Co. Off.
Redus, John TX 33rd Cav. Co.A
Redus, John C. MS Inf. 1st Bn.St.Troops (12
   mo. '62-3) Co.B
Redus, John W. MS St.Cav. 2nd Bn. (Harris')
   Co.A
Redus, J.W. MS 28th Cav. Co.B
Redus, J.W. MS Wilson's Co. (Ponticola Guards)
Redus, Len R. MS 22nd Inf. Co.F
Redus, Leonard H. MS Cav. 24th Bn. Co.E 1st
   Lt.
Redus, Leonard H. MS 12th Inf. Co.D Sgt.
Redus, L.S. AR 8th Cav.
Redus, L.W. MS 9th Inf. Old Co.I,K
Redus, L.W. TN 22nd (Barteau's) Cav. Co.G
Redus, Samuel MS T.P. Montgomery's Co.
Redus, Samuel B. MS Cav. 24th Bn. Co.E
Redus, Samuel E. MS 11th (Perrin's) Cav. Co.H
Redus, Thomas MS 22nd Inf. Co.F
Redus, W.A. AL 10th Cav. Co.I
Redus, W. Frank MS 9th Inf. Old Co.D
Redus, William TX 4th Inf. Co.D
Redus, William TX Res.Corps 1st Lt.
Redus, William D. MS 24th Inf. Co.D
Redus, William J. Conf.Cav. Wood's Regt. 2nd
   Co.G
Redus, William M. AL 35th Inf. Co.G 1st Lt.
Redus, W.J. MS 1st (Johnston's) Inf. Co.I Sgt.
Redus, W.J. MS 9th Inf. Old Co.K
Redus, W.R. MS T.P. Montgomery's Co.
Redutts, L. LA 3rd (Harrison's) Cav. Co.C
Redvert, James TN 1st (Turney's) Inf. Co.G
Redway, M.A. Gen. & Staff Surg.
Redweyne, F.M. GA 3rd Cav. Co.A
Redwine, A.T. TN 37th Inf. Co.I

Redwine, Benjamin F. AR Inf. Ballard's Co.
Redwine, Benjamin F. MO 6th Inf. Co.K
Redwine, B.F. MO Inf. 1st Bn. Co.C
Redwine, Bramwell VA Cav. McFarlane's Co.
Redwine, Charles C. VA 25th Cav. Co.G
Redwine, Charles C. VA 64th Mtd.Inf. Co.K
Redwine, C.L. GA 10th Cav. (St.Guards) Co.E
Redwine, C.L. Gen. & Staff AASurg.
Redwine, C.M. LA 9th Inf. Co.K Cpl.
Redwine, Columbus M. LA 12th Inf. 2nd Co.M
   Sgt.
Redwine, C.W. MS 18th Cav. Co.E
Redwine, D. TX Cav. Hardeman's Regt. Co.C
Redwine, David VA Inf. 21st Bn. 1st Co.E Sgt.
Redwine, David B. VA Inf. 21st Bn. Co.A
Redwine, David B. VA 64th Mtd.Inf. Co.A
Redwine, D.C. MO 12th Inf. Co.A
Redwine, E.L. TN 28th Cav. Co.C Sgt.
Redwine, Elbert Mead's Conf.Cav. Co.I Sgt.
Redwine, Elbert S. VA Lt.Arty. Jeffress' Co.
Redwine, G.A. NC 2nd Inf. Co.B
Redwine, G.O. NC 2nd Jr.Res. Co.B
Redwine, Green D. NC 7th Inf. Co.F
Redwine, Green D. NC 42nd Inf. Co.I 3rd Lt.
Redwine, H.T. GA 39th Inf. Co.K
Redwine, J. NC 1st Jr.Res. Co.C
Redwine, J.A. AL 5th Cav. Co.E
Redwine, J.A. TX 13th Vol. Co.G
Redwine, Jacob J. TX 37th Cav. Co.E
Redwine, James A. MS Cav. 18th Bn. Co.E
Redwine, James M. NC 7th Inf. Co.F
Redwine, James N. GA 39th Inf. Co.C,D
Redwine, James O. GA Inf. 1st Conf.Bn. Co.D
   Capt.
Redwine, James O. GA 30th Inf. Co.H Capt.
Redwine, James W. TX 10th Inf. Co.E
Redwine, J.C. MO 12th Inf. Co.A
Redwine, Jerome B. VA Inf. 21st Bn. Co.A
Redwine, Jerome B. VA 64th Mtd.Inf. Co.A
Redwine, Jessie F. AR 15th (Josey's) Inf. Co.G
Redwine, J.H. MS 1st (Johnston's) Inf. Co.G
Redwine, J.M. TX 32nd Cav. Co.F Sgt.
Redwine, Joel Jacob TX 20th Cav. Co.A
Redwine, John C. VA Inf. 21st Bn. Co.A
Redwine, John C. VA 64th Mtd.Inf. Co.K
Redwine, John F. NC 42nd Inf. Co.E
Redwine, John R. AR 45th Mil. Co.E Capt.
Redwine, Joseph TN 26th Inf. Co.C
Redwine, Joseph TX Cav. Martin's Regt. Co.F
   1st Lt.
Redwine, Joseph VA Inf. 23rd Bn. Co.D Sgt.
Redwine, Joshua N. VA Inf. 21st Bn. Co.A
Redwine, Joshua N. VA 64th Mtd.Inf. Co.A
Redwine, Joshua R. VA 64th Mtd.Inf. Co.A
Redwine, J.R. AR 7th Cav. Co.C
Redwine, J.S. GA 39th Inf. Co.B,K
Redwine, L.A. GA 11th Cav. Co.K
Redwine, L.J. GA 1st (Fannin's) Res. Co.I
Redwine, L.S. GA 39th Inf. Co.C
Redwine, Martin C. LA 2nd Inf. Co.F Maj.
Redwine, M.T. GA 11th Cav. Co.B
Redwine, Peter W. NC 6th Inf. Co.G
Redwine, P.L. MS 7th Inf. Co.H 2nd Lt.
Redwine, P.L.N. MS 1st (Johnston's) Inf. Co.G
   1st Sgt.
Redwine, Ras. TX 10th Cav. Co.E Maj.
Redwine, Rheuben J. GA 24th Inf. Co.H

Redwine, R.M. MS 18th Cav. Co.E
Redwine, Rufus TX 10th Cav. Co.E
Redwine, Sam L. AR 45th Mil. Co.C Capt.
Redwine, Thomas W. NC 35th Inf. Co.F Capt.
Redwine, Thomas W. NC 42nd Inf. Co.I Capt.
Redwine, T.M. MO 12th Inf. Co.A
Redwine, William NC 7th Inf. Co.F
Redwine, William E. LA 28th (Gray's) Inf. Co.I
   Jr.2nd Lt.
Redwine, William J. GA Arty. 9th Bn. Co.B
Redwine, William J. GA 36th (Villepigue's) Inf.
   Co.F
Redwine, William M. GA 41st Inf. Co.D 1st Lt.
Redwine, William R. NC 7th Inf. Co.F
Redwine, William S. NC 8th Inf. Co.D
Redwine, William T. GA 39th Inf. Co.B,D
Redwine, W.P. AR 32nd Inf. Co.F
Redwine, W.P. AR 45th Mil. Co.F
Redwine, W.P. GA 10th Inf. Co.I 1st Lt.
Redwood, --- VA VMI Co.B,A Cpl.
Redwood, A.C. MD 1st Cav. Co.C
Redwood, Allen C. VA 55th Inf. Co.C
Redwood, George MS 44th Inf. Co.A Sgt.Maj.
Redwood, George E. AL 19th Inf. Surg.
Redwood, George E. Gen. & Staff, Inf. 1st
   Lt.,Dr.M.
Redwood, George Edward Gen. & Staff, Medical
   Dept. Surg.
Redwood, George R. AL 43rd Inf. Co.C,K 1st
   Lt.
Redwood, H. VA 3rd Inf.Loc.Def. Co.B
Redwood, James D. VA Cav. 1st Bn. Co.A
Redwood, James J. VA 3rd Cav. Co.D
Redwood, John H. VA 1st St.Res. Co.A
Redwood, John M. AL 3rd Inf. Co.A
Redwood, John T. LA 7th Inf. Co.H
Redwood, John T. VA 4th Inf. Co.I
Redwood, Joseph C. VA 1st St.Res. Co.A 1st
   Sgt.
Redwood, J.W. MD 1st Cav. Co.C
Redwood, J.W. VA 3rd Inf.Loc.Def. Co.B
Redwood, Leroy H. AL Cav. Murphy's Bn.
   Co.B 1st Sgt.
Redwood, Leroy Henry MS Inf. 1st St.Troops
   Co.G
Redwood, R.H. AL 8th (Hatch's) Cav. Maj.
Redwood, R.H. AL 21st Inf. Maj.,Surg.
Redwood, R.H. AL 62nd Inf. Co.F Capt.
Redwood, R.H., Jr. LA 7th Inf. Co.H
Redwood, R.H., Jr. Gen. & Staff, Inf. 1st
   Lt.,Dr.M.
Redwood, Robt. H. Gen. & Staff Surg.
Redwood, W.F. AL Mil. 2nd Regt.Vol. Co.E
Redwood, W.F. VA VMI Co.A Cpl.
Redwood, W.H., Jr. AL 21st Inf. Co.K
Redwood, William TX 1st Hvy.Arty. Co.I
Redwood, William H. TX 16th Inf. Lt.Col.
Redwood, William H. VA 1st St.Res. Co.E Cpl.
Ree, J. TX Cav. Baird's Regt. Co.A
Ree, J.B. MO 7th Cav. Co.F
Ree, John GA 3rd Cav. Co.I
Ree, R.E. MS 36th Inf. Co.C
Ree, S. TX Cav. Border's Regt. Co.C
Ree, T. TX Cav. Border's Regt. Co.C
Ree, W.H. AL 28th Inf. Co.A
Ree, William MO Cav. Ford's Bn. Co.F

Reeber, Fred TN Inf. 154th Sr.Regt. Co.K 1st Lt.

Reece, ---, 1st TX Cav. McCord's Frontier Regt. Co.F

Reece, ---, 2nd TX Cav. McCord's Frontier Regt. Co.F

Reece, Aaron B. NC 58th Inf. Co.E

Reece, A.B. TN 19th & 20th (Cons.) Cav. Co.B

Reece, A.C. GA 34th Inf. Co.B

Reece, Adam M. VA 24th Inf. Co.G Cpl.

Reece, Adison H. AR 31st Inf. Co.D

Reece, A.H. NC 21st Inf. Co.H

Reece, A.J. GA Inf. 11th Bn. Co.C

Reece, Alfred C. GA 38th Inf. Co.B,D

Reece, Allen NC 5th Sr.Res. Co.H

Reece, A.M. AR 16th Inf. Co.F Sgt.

Reece, A.M. VA 29th Inf. Co.D

Reece, Amos M. NC 25th Inf. Co.F

Reece, Andrew TN 55th (McKoin's) Inf. Dillehays' Co.

Reece, Antney NC 21st Inf. Co.C

Reece, Asberry H. NC 28th Inf. Co.I

Reece, Ben MO 10th Inf. Co.B

Reece, Benjamin A. GA 3rd Cav. Co.F,K Cpl.

Reece, Benjamin F. NC 3rd Inf. Co.G

Reece, Bennett MO 6th Cav. Co.K

Reece, C. VA 34th Inf. Co.B

Reece, Caleb TN 44th (Cons.) Inf. Co.C

Reece, Caleb TN 55th (McKoin's) Inf. Dillehay's Co. Sgt.

Reece, Calvin NC 42nd Inf. Co.B

Reece, C.C. MS 7th Cav. Co.A

Reece, Charles A. MS 2nd Inf. Co.A

Reece, Charles A. MS 26th Inf. Co.C

Reece, Charles A. VA 8th Cav. 2nd Co.D 2nd Lt.

Reece, C.J. MS 46th Inf. Co.E

Reece, Clemens TX Cav. Baylor's Regt. Co.F

Reece, C.M. MS 1st Cav.Res. Co.C

Reece, C.M. TN Inf. 1st Cons.Regt. Co.D

Reece, C.T. 3rd Conf.Inf. Co.C

Reece, David AR 30th Inf. Co.E

Reece, D.S. TN 55th (McKoin's) Inf. Day's Co.

Reece, D.W. TX Cav. McCord's Frontier Regt. Co.H

Reece, E. AL 36th Inf. Co.I

Reece, E. NC 6th Inf. Co.B

Reece, E.C. GA 23rd Inf. Co.B

Reece, Edmond NC 64th Inf. Co.D

Reece, Elijah NC 64th Inf. Co.F

Reece, Elza B. NC 24th Inf. Co.B Sgt.

Reece, Enoch NC 48th Inf. Co.K

Reece, E.P. TN Cav. Allison's Squad. Co.B Sgt.

Reece, E.P. TN 24th Inf. Co.F

Reece, Erasmus D. MS Inf. 3rd Bn. (St.Troops) Co.E

Reece, Evan H. NC 28th Inf. Co.I

Reece, F.H. TN Inf. Sowell's Detach.

Reece, F.J. TN 10th (DeMoss') Cav. Co.F

Reece, F.J. TN Cav. Napier's Bn. Co.C

Reece, Francis M. TX 19th Cav. Co.B

Reece, G. TN Inf. 2nd Cons.Regt. Co.K

Reece, G.C. SC 13th Inf. Co.F

Reece, George J. AL 19th Inf. Co.F

Reece, George M. NC 42nd Inf. Co.B

Reece, George W. TN 42nd Inf. 2nd Co.K

Reece, Green W. SC 13th Inf. Co.F Cpl.

Reece, Griffith TN 11th Inf. Co.K

Reece, Harvey MO 6th Cav. Co.K

Reece, Henry LA 14th Inf. Co.B

Reece, Henry MS 6th Cav. Co.C

Reece, Henry Exch.Bn. Co.D,CSA

Reece, Henry C. VA 8th Cav. 2nd Co.D

Reece, Henry L. TX 11th (Spaight's) Bn.Vol. Co.B,C

Reece, Henry P. MS St.Cav. Perrin's Bn. Co.F

Reece, Hiram AL Lt.Arty. Phelan's Co.

Reece, H.P. AL 3rd Res. Co.G

Reece, H.P. TX 12th Cav. Co.A

Reece, H.R. AR Inf. Cocke's Regt. Co.H

Reece, Hugh NC 37th Inf. Co.E

Reece, Hyrum GA 34th Inf. Co.B

Reece, Ira NC 3rd Cav. (41st St.Troops) Co.B

Reece, Ira NC 18th Inf. Co.I

Reece, Isaac A. NC 64th Inf. Co.I

Reece, Isaac N. NC 25th Inf. Co.F

Reece, J. GA Cav. 1st Bn.Res. Co.E

Reece, J. MS 1st Bn.St.Guards Co.A

Reece, Jacob NC 6th Cav. (65th St.Troops) Co.A,F

Reece, James AR 45th Cav. Co.L

Reece, James AR 27th Inf. Co.F

Reece, James GA 1st (Symons') Res. Co.E

Reece, James GA Inf. 11th Bn. (St.Guards) Co.C

Reece, James MO 2nd Cav. Co.D

Reece, James SC Arty. Stuart's Co. (Beaufort Vol.Arty.)

Reece, James SC 1st St.Troops Co.G

Reece, James SC 3rd Res. Co.C

Reece, James VA 4th Res. Co.F

Reece, James VA 27th Inf. Co.G

Reece, James VA 29th Inf. Co.D

Reece, James VA 58th Mil. Co.C

Reece, James A. MS St.Cav. Perrin's Bn. Co.F

Reece, James C. NC 2nd Cav. (19th St.Troops) Co.F

Reece, James M. GA 6th Cav. Co.D Cpl.

Reece, James M. GA Smith's Legion Ralston's Co. Cpl.

Reece, James M. TN 24th Inf. Co.I

Reece, James M. TN 44th (Cons.) Inf. Co.E

Reece, James O. MS 2nd Inf. Co.A

Reece, James W. TN 24th Inf. 2nd Co.H, Co.M

Reece, Jasper AL 10th Cav.

Reece, Jasper NC 62nd Inf. Co.K

Reece, Jasper N. AR 36th Inf. Co.F Cpl.

Reece, J.C. AL 29th Inf. Co.C Sgt.

Reece, J.C. LA 3rd Inf. Co.H

Reece, J.D. NC 5th Cav. (63rd St.Troops) Co.D

Reece, J.E. MO Inf. 1st Bn. Co.C

Reece, Jeremiah GA 38th Inf. Co.B

Reece, Jeremiah NC 62nd Inf. Co.I Drum.

Reece, Jesse VA 29th Inf. Co.D Cpl.

Reece, Jesse VA 54th Inf. Co.G

Reece, Jessee W. AL 24th Inf. Co.H

Reece, J.G. VA 1st (Farinholt's) Res. Co.E

Reece, J.H. AR 11th Inf. Co.G

Reece, J.H. AR 11th & 17th (Cons.) Inf. Co.G

Reece, J.H. TN 20th Inf. Co.K

Reece, J.I. MS 12th Cav. Co.G

Reece, J.J. GA Smith's Legion Co.F

Reece, J.L. AR Inf. Hardy's Regt. Co.E

Reece, J.L. GA Smith's Legion Co.F

Reece, J.L. MS Inf. 2nd St.Troops Co.I

Reece, J.M. NC 5th Cav. (63rd St.Troops) Co.D

Reece, J.M. TN 45th Inf. Co.B

Reece, J.M. VA 34th Inf. Co.B

Reece, Joel TN Cav. Jackson's Co.

Reece, John GA Cav. Young's Co. (Alleghany Troopers)

Reece, John NC 2nd Inf. Co.A Fifer

Reece, John NC 13th Inf. Co.B

Reece, John NC 24th Inf. Co.B

Reece, John NC 48th Inf. Co.K

Reece, John TN 37th Inf. Co.C

Reece, John TN Inf. 154th Sr.Regt. Co.A Cpl.

Reece, John TX 32nd Cav. Co.K

Reece, John TX Cav. Wells' Regt. Co.A

Reece, John A. GA 23rd Inf. Co.B

Reece, John A. VA 22nd Inf. Co.C Music.

Reece, John B. SC 3rd Res. Co.G

Reece, John C. MS 23rd Inf. Co.A

Reece, John C. MS 26th Inf. Co.C 2nd Lt.

Reece, John E. VA 12th Cav. Co.H

Reece, John H. GA 8th Inf. Co.H Capt.

Reece, John H. VA 60th Inf. 2nd Co.H

Reece, John H. 1st Conf.Inf. 2nd Co.G Capt.

Reece, John M. NC Mallett's Bn. Co.E

Reece, John Q. GA Cobb's Legion Co.E Sgt.

Reece, John R.A. VA 9th Inf. Co.B Sgt.

Reece, John S. MO Cav. Fristoe's Regt. Co.F Cpl.

Reece, John T. AL 24th Inf. Co.H

Reece, John T. MS 26th Inf. Co.I 2nd Lt.

Reece, John V. NC 25th Inf. Co.F Music.

Reece, John V. NC 62nd Inf. Co.I Cpl.

Reece, John W. TX 37th Cav. Co.C

Reece, John W. VA Cav. 47th Bn. Co.C Sgt.

Reece, Jonathan TN 60th Mtd.Inf. Co.C

Reece, Jonathan K. NC 25th Inf. Co.F

Reece, J.O.P. TN 8th Inf. Co.D

Reece, Joseph MS 7th Cav. Co.A

Reece, Joseph GA 2nd Inf. Co.F

Reece, Joseph L. VA 8th Cav. Co.E

Reece, Joseph M. NC 5th Cav. (63rd St.Troops) Co.E

Reece, Joseph W. TX Cav. McCord's Frontier Regt. Co.H

Reece, Jourdan TX Cav. Morgan's Regt. Co.B

Reece, J.S. TN Cav. Allison's Squad. Co.B Capt.

Reece, J.S. TN 24th Inf. Co.F Sgt.

Reece, J.T. TX 18th Cav. Co.K

Reece, Julius TN Lt.Arty. Burroughs' Co.

Reece, J.W. AL 34th Inf. Co.C

Reece, J.W. MS 3rd Inf. Co.D

Reece, Lafayette H. TN 48th (Nixon's) Inf. Co.E Sgt.

Reece, Larkin W. NC 6th Cav. (65th St.Troops) Co.A,F Black.

Reece, Leonard E. NC Inf. Thomas Legion Co.C

Reece, Leroy TN 9th (Ward's) Cav. Co.F

Reece, Leroy TN 44th (Cons.) Inf. Co.C

Reece, Leroy TN 55th (McKoin's) Inf. Dillehay's Co.

Reece, Levi NC 64th Inf. Co.D

Reece, L.L. MS 26th Inf. Co.C

Reece, L.S. NC 7th Sr.Res. Boon's Co.

Reece, Madison GA 43rd Inf. Co.L,C

Reece, Marion TN 22nd Inf. Co.I

Reece, Martin NC 64th Inf. Co.D Fifer
Reece, Matt GA 6th Cav. Co.I
Reece, Maxwell AR 4th Inf. Co.H
Reece, M.C. AR 24th Inf. Co.H
Reece, M.C. AR Inf. Hardy's Regt. Co.E
Reece, M.H. VA 28th Inf. Co.K
Reece, Nathan S. NC 21st Inf. Co.A
Reece, Oliver P. GA Cobb's Legion Co.E
Reece, O.M. LA 26th Inf. Co.G
Reece, Oscar C. MO 5th Inf. Co.A
Reece, Perrender MS 26th Inf. Co.I
Reece, Quiller F. GA 6th Cav. Co.F
Reece, Reuben P. GA 38th Inf. Co.B
Reece, Richard L. TN 55th (McKoin's) Inf. Dillehay's Co.
Reece, Risdon VA 36th Inf. Co.F
Reece, Robert VA 63rd Inf. Co.F
Reece, Robert M. TN Holman's Bn.Part.Rangers Co.B
Reece, Robert W. GA 23rd Inf. Co.F
Reece, S. TN 28th (Cons.) Inf. Co.C
Reece, Samuel VA 3rd Res. Co.F
Reece, Samuel B. TN 40th Inf. Co.K
Reece, S.C. NC 18th Inf. Co.K
Reece, Solon VA 8th Cav. 2nd Co.D Cpl.
Reece, T.A. AL 13th Inf. Co.C
Reece, T.A. NC 21st Inf. Co.B
Reece, T. Heber VA 8th Cav. 2nd Co.D
Reece, Thomas GA 65th Inf. Co.D
Reece, Thomas GA Smith's Legion Co.F
Reece, Thomas TX 12th Cav. Co.A
Reece, Thomas B. GA 3rd Cav. Co.F,K Sgt.
Reece, Thomas E. TN 37th Inf. Co.C
Reece, Tiera T. AR 4th Inf. Co.H
Reece, W. GA Cav. 1st Bn.Res. Co.E
Reece, W. MO St.Guard
Reece, W. VA Cav. 37th Bn. Co.F
Reece, Wade H. TN 24th Inf. 2nd Co.H, Co.M
Reece, Warren GA 43rd Inf. Co.L
Reece, W.D. GA 57th Inf. Co.A
Reece, W.D. GA Conscr.
Reece, W.D. NC 9th Bn.S.S. Co.A
Reece, W.D. NC 22nd Inf. Co.M
Reece, W.E. SC Inf.Bn. Co.D Cpl.
Reece, W.G. AR 10th Inf. Co.E
Reece, W.H. AL 51st (Part.Rangers) Co.C
Reece, W.H. TN Inf. Spencer's Co.
Reece, W.H. TX 19th Cav. Co.I
Reece, Wiley TN 40th Inf. Co.K
Reece, Wm. AL 26th Inf. Sgt.
Reece, William GA 23rd Inf. Co.F
Reece, William GA Cherokee Legion (St.Guards) Co.D
Reece, William NC 3rd Inf. Co.G
Reece, William TN Cav. 16th Bn. (Neal's) Co.E
Reece, William VA 29th Inf. 2nd Co.F
Reece, William B. MO 3rd Cav. Co.F
Reece, William E. NC 25th Inf. Co.C
Reece, William Elbert SC 19th Inf. Co.D
Reece, William H. AL 41st Inf. Co.G
Reece, William H. GA 6th Cav. Co.F
Reece, William H. MS 32nd Inf. Co.A
Reece, William H. TN 24th Inf. 2nd Co.H, Co.M
Reece, William J. NC 64th Inf. Co.D
Reece, William L. NC 25th Inf. Co.F
Reece, William M. GA 52nd Inf. Co.I

Reece, William P. GA Smith's Legion Standridge's Co.
Reece, William P. MS 30th Inf. Co.D
Reece, William T. AL Nitre & Min. Corps Young's Co.
Reece, William T. GA 28th Inf. Co.D Cpl.
Reece, Willis VA 54th Inf. Co.G
Reece, Wilson GA Cobb's Legion Co.E
Reece, Winston NC 21st Inf. Co.H
Reece, W.J. MS Inf. 1st Bn.St.Troops (30 days '64) Co.D
Reece, W.J. TN 18th Inf. Co.K
Reece, W.J. TN 45th Inf. Co.F
Reece, W.J. TN 55th (McKoin's) Inf. Day's Co.
Reece, W.M. KY 2nd (Duke's) Cav. Co.F
Reece, W.P. TX 9th Cav. Co.D
Reece, Z.C. AR 10th Inf. Co.E Sgt.
Reecer, Abraham Brush Bn.
Reecer, C.V.A. MD Weston's Bn. Co.B
Reecer, John TX Cav. Martin's Regt. Co.F
Reecer, Luke TX Cav. Martin's Regt. Co.F
Reechy, James H. Gen. & Staff Chap.
Reecse, Levi SC 22nd Inf. Co.D
Reed, --- TX Cav. 4th Regt.St.Troops Co.A
Reed, --- TX Cav. 4th Regt.St.Troops Co.H
Reed, --- TX Cav. Border's Regt. Co.H
Reed, --- TX Cav. Mann's Regt. Co.H Sgt.
Reed, --- TX Cav. McCord's Frontier Regt. Co.E
Reed, --- VA 10th Inf. Co.H
Reed, A. AR 30th Inf. Co.A
Reed, A. GA 63rd Inf. Co.G
Reed, A. LA Inf.Crescent Regt. Co.A
Reed, A. MS 2nd St.Cav. Co.K
Reed, A. MS 11th (Perrin's) Cav. Co.K
Reed, A. MS 5th Inf. Co.E Capt.
Reed, A. TN 18th (Newsom's) Cav. Co.K
Reed, A. TX Cav. Baird's Regt. Co.G
Reed, A. VA 62nd Mtd.Inf. 1st Co.D
Reed, A. Conf.Cav. Clarkson's Bn. Ind.Rangers Co.G
Reed, A.A. GA 4th Cav. (St.Guards) Gower's Co.
Reed, A.A. MO 16th Inf. Co.D
Reed, Aaron LA 5th Inf. Co.F
Reed, Aaron MS 36th Inf. Co.A
Reed, A.B. AL Randolph Cty.Res. D.A. Self's Co.
Reed, A.B. AR 34th Inf. Co.B
Reed, Abe TX 11th Cav. Co.K
Reed, Abnet MS 11th (Perrin's) Cav. Co.D Maj.
Reed, Abraham MO 3rd Cav. Co.K
Reed, Abraham VA 10th Cav. Co.A
Reed, Abraham MS St.Cav. Perrin's Bn. Co.C Maj.
Reed, A.C. SC 1st (McCreary's) Inf. Campbell's Co.
Reed, A.C. SC 13th Inf. Co.E
Reed, Acy MS 15th Inf. Co.K
Reed, A.D. AR 62nd Mil. Co.F Cpl.
Reed, A.D. VA 51st Inf. Band Prin.Music.
Reed, A.E. SC 1st St.Troops Co.C
Reed, A.G. GA 1st (Symons') Res. Co.I
Reed, A.G. GA 11th Inf.
Reed, A.G. LA 18th Inf. Co.H
Reed, A.G. MS Arty. (Wesson Arty.) Kittrell's Co.
Reed, A.G. MS 5th Inf. (St.Troops) Co.I

Reed, A.J. AL 26th (O'Neal's) Inf. Co.E
Reed, A.J. AR Cav. 1st Bn. (Stirman's) Co.E Music.
Reed, A.J. GA 6th Cav. Co.C Cpl.
Reed, A.J. GA 7th Inf. Co.H Cpl.
Reed, A.J. GA 11th Inf. Co.C
Reed, A.J. GA 18th Inf. Co.F
Reed, A.J. GA Smith's Legion Stiff's Co.
Reed, A.J. KY 3rd Mtd.Inf. Co.G Cpl.
Reed, A.J. MS Inf. 2nd St.Troops Co.D
Reed, A.J. MS 43rd Inf. Co.F
Reed, A.J. TN 43rd Inf. Co.B
Reed, A.J. TX Inf. 1st St.Troops White's Co.D
Reed, A.J. TX 9th (Young's) Inf. Co.K
Reed, A.J. VA 8th Cav.
Reed, A.L. AL 5th Inf. Co.A
Reed, Albert SC 1st Arty. Co.A Laundress
Reed, Albert M. AR 6th Inf. Co.K Sgt.
Reed, Albert R. AL 6th Inf. Co.L,K
Reed, Alex VA 20th Cav. Co.H
Reed, Alexander AR 8th Inf. New Co.A
Reed, Alexander AR 38th Inf. Old Co.I, Co.H
Reed, Alexander LA 6th Inf. Co.D
Reed, Alex. MS 8th Cav. Co.K
Reed, Alexander MO 3rd Cav. Co.K
Reed, Alexander TX 18th Cav. Co.D
Reed, Alexander TX 22nd Cav. Co.G
Reed, Alexander VA 52nd Inf. Co.I
Reed, Alexander T. MS 31st Inf. Co.G
Reed, Alfred AL 59th Inf. Co.K
Reed, Alfred LA Inf. Weatherly's Bn. Co.D
Reed, Alfred TN 18th Inf. Co.D
Reed, Allen MS 2nd St.Cav. Co.A
Reed, Allen MS 23rd Inf. Co.A
Reed, Allen TN 10th (DeMoss') Cav. Co.K Sgt.
Reed, Allen TN 21st & 22nd (Cons.) Cav. Co.I Sgt.
Reed, Allison TN 39th Mtd.Inf. Co.A
Reed, Alphonce LA 28th (Thomas') Inf. Co.K
Reed, A.M. TN 20th Inf. Co.E
Reed, A.M. TX Cav. Border's Regt. Co.E
Reed, Amos MS 7th Cav. Co.H
Reed, Amos VA 54th Inf. Co.D
Reed, Amos VA 64th Mtd.Inf. Co.E
Reed, Amos VA Mil. Scott Cty.
Reed, Amos S. TX Cav. Madison's Regt. Co.D
Reed, Amos W. VA 190th Mil. Co.E
Reed, Amus VA Inf. 21st Bn. 2nd Co.E
Reed, A.N. NC 42nd Inf. Co.D
Reed, And. J. MO Lt.Arty. Farris' Btty. (Clark Arty.)
Reed, Andrew GA 19th Inf. Co.K
Reed, Andrew LA 13th Inf. Co.B
Reed, Andrew MS Cav. 3rd Bn. (Ashcraft's) Co.E,F
Reed, Andrew MO Cav. Clardy's Bn. Co.C
Reed, Andrew TX 22nd Inf. Co.E
Reed, Andrew VA 5th Inf. Co.I
Reed, Andrew A. GA 21st Inf. Co.A
Reed, Andrew B. AL 16th Inf. Co.H
Reed, Andrew H. NC 58th Inf. Co.F
Reed, Andrew J. GA 11th Inf. Co.G
Reed, Andrew J. MS 33rd Inf. Co.A
Reed, Andrew J. NC 37th Inf. Co.G
Reed, Andrew J. TN 3rd (Clack's) Inf. Co.A
Reed, Andrew J. TX 17th Cons.Dismtd.Cav. Co.H

Reed, Andrew J. TX Cav. Hardeman's Regt.
Co.B
Reed, Andrew J. VA 4th Res. Co.H,I
Reed, Andrew J.D. TN 23rd Inf. 1st Co.A, Co.B
Reed, Anthony VA 18th Cav. Co.I
Reed, Archibald AL Mil. 2nd Regt.Vol. Co.B
Reed, Arthur NC 3rd Arty. (40th St.Troops)
Co.D
Reed, Arthur TN 37th Inf. Co.C
Reed, Asa MS 35th Inf. Co.C
Reed, A.W. LA 2nd Res.Corps Co.I
Reed, A.W. MO Cav. 1st Regt.St.Guard Co.A
Reed, B. AL 19th Inf. Co.C Sgt.
Reed, B. AL 23rd Inf. Co.G
Reed, B. AL 30th Inf. Co.E
Reed, B. MO 6th Cav. Co.D Cpl.
Reed, B. TN 1st (Carter's) Cav. Co.E
Reed, B.A. AL 12th Cav. Co.A
Reed, Baily Conf.Cav. Clarkson's Bn. Ind.
Rangers Co.A
Reed, Baxter NC Walker's Bn. Thomas' Legion
Co.E
Reed, Bemis GA 40th Inf. Co.B
Reed, Ben Trans-MS Conf.Cav. 1st Bn. E
Reed, Ben. F. KY 1st (Butler's) Cav. Co.G
Reed, Beniah VA Lt.Arty. G.B. Chapman's Co.
Reed, Beniah VA 108th Mil. Co.F
Reed, Benjamin VA 37th Inf. Co.F 1st Lt.
Reed, Benjamin F. AL 8th Cav. Co.B Cpl.
Reed, Benjamin F. GA 4th Inf. Co.D
Reed, Benjamin F. SC Inf. 3rd Bn. Co.B
Reed, Benjamin F. TN 41st Inf. Co.K
Reed, Benjamin R. GA 3rd Cav. (St.Guards)
Co.D
Reed, Benjamin T. VA 39th Inf. Co.F
Reed, Berry VA Hvy.Arty. Coleman's Co.
Reed, B.B. AL Cav. Moses' Squad. Co.A
Reed, B.F. AL 17th Inf. Co.E 1st Lt.
Reed, B.F. AR Inf. Cocke's Regt. Co.B
Reed, B.F. GA Phillips' Legion Co.E
Reed, B.F. TX 11th Inf. Co.E Cpl.
Reed, B.F. TX 16th Inf. Co.D
Reed, B.F. TX 17th Inf. Co.E
Reed, B.F. Shelley's Staff Capt.,AQM
Reed, Birdwell NC Lt.Arty. Thomas' Legion
Levi's Btty.
Reed, Black TN Cav. Welcker's Bn. Kincaid's
Co.
Reed, Bluford VA Cav. Swann's Bn. Sweeny's
Co.
Reed, Bluford VA 151st Mil. Co.F
Reed, B.M. AL 5th Inf. New Co.I
Reed, B.M. TX 10th Cav. Co.A
Reed, Booker KY 9th Cav. Co.I Sgt.
Reed, Booker KY 9th Mtd.Inf. Co.B
Reed, B.P. SC 6th Inf. Co.D
Reed, B.R. TN 9th (Ward's) Cav. Co.E
Reed, Brownlow TN 19th Inf. Co.E
Reed, Buck TN 50th Inf. Co.E
Reed, Burges NC Cav. 5th Bn. Co.B Sgt.
Reed, C. KY 9th Cav. Co.A
Reed, C.A. AL 5th Inf. New Co.E
Reed, C.A. KY 2nd (Duke's) Cav. Co.C Lt.
Reed, C.A. KY Morgan's Men Co.C Sgt.
Reed, C.A. SC 7th Cav. Co.A
Reed, C.A. SC Rutledge Mtd.Riflemen & Horse
Arty. Trenholm's Co.

Reed, Calvin VA Inf. 23rd Bn. Co.B
Reed, Calvin J. MS 4th Inf. Co.A
Reed, Carson AR Inf. Hardy's Regt. Co.D
Reed, C.C. AL Brew Cav.
Reed, C.C. MS Inf. 2nd St.Troops Co.E 2nd Lt.
Reed, C.C. TN Cav. 16th Bn. (Neal's) Co.E
2nd Lt.
Reed, C.C. TN 29th Inf. Co.H Sgt.
Reed, C.C.E. 8th (Wade's) Conf.Cav. Co.B
Reed, C.H. MS 2nd (Davidson's) Inf. Potts' Co.
Reed, C.H. MS 32nd Inf. Co.G Sgt.
Reed, Chas. AR 4th St.Inf. Co.C 1st Lt.
Reed, Charles KY 3rd Mtd.Inf. Co.D
Reed, Charles LA 5th Inf. Co.I
Reed, Charles LA 14th Inf. Co.G Jr.2nd Lt.
Reed, Charles LA Inf. McLean's Co.
Reed, Charles MS 23rd Inf.
Reed, Charles NC 29th Inf. Co.H
Reed, Charles TN 6th (Wheeler's) Cav. Co.G
Reed, Charles VA 10th Cav. Co.D
Reed, Charles VA Arty. Kevill's Co.
Reed, Charles VA 3rd Inf. Co.B
Reed, Charles VA 54th Inf. Co.I
Reed, Charles Horse Arty. White's Btty.
Reed, Charles Bradford's Corps Scouts & Guards
Co.B
Reed, Charles A. TX 13th Cav. Co.A
Reed, Charles A. TX 21st Cav. Co.E 1st Lt.
Reed, Charles A. VA 60th Inf. 2nd Co.H
Reed, Charles E. TX 6th Cav. Co.G
Reed, Charles H. GA Arty. (Chatham Arty.)
Wheaton's Co.
Reed, Charles L. AR 1st Field Btty.
Reed, Charles L. AR Inf. Crawford's Bn. Co.B
Sgt.
Reed, Charles L. 1st Conf.Inf. 2nd Co.D
Reed, Charles L. 1st Conf.Inf. 2nd Co.D, 2nd
Co.K Capt.
Reed, Charles T. FL Inf. 2nd Bn. Co.F
Reed, Charles W. TN 11th Cav. Co.H
Reed, Charles W. VA 8th Inf. Co.G 1st Sgt.
Reed, Charlton GA Brooks' Co. (Terrell
Lt.Arty.)
Reed, Chesley MO 11th Inf. Co.A
Reed, Chilton KY 2nd (Duke's) Cav. Co.H Sgt.
Reed, Christopher W. VA Cav. 35th Bn. Co.E,F
2nd Lt.
Reed, C.L. AR 19th (Dawson's) Inf. Co.H Sgt.
Reed, C.L. TN 26th Inf. Co.G 2nd Lt.
Reed, Clark GA 8th Cav. Co.A
Reed, Clark GA 62nd Cav. Co.A
Reed, Clement MS 9th Inf. Old Co.B, New Co.I
Cpl.
Reed, Clement P. AL 18th Inf. Co.H
Reed, Clemons O. AL 4th Cav.
Reed, Clemons O. AL 16th Inf. Co.H
Reed, Colston H. VA 5th Inf. Co.H
Reed, Columbus MO 12th Cav. Co.A
Reed, C.P. AL 58th Inf. Co.F
Reed, C.W. VA 31st Mil. Co.B Capt.
Reed, Cyrus MO 1st Cav. Co.E
Reed, Cyrus MO 2nd Cav. Co.C
Reed, D. MO Cav. 2nd Bn.St.Guard Co.A Capt.
Reed, Dallas TN 44th (Cons.) Inf. Co.I
Reed, Daniel MO 8th Inf. Co.C
Reed, Daniel TX 5th Cav. Co.D 1st Lt.
Reed, Daniel VA 12th Cav. Co.D

Reed, Daniel VA 62nd Mtd.Inf. 2nd Co.H Cpl.
Reed, Daniel Conf.Reg.Inf. Brooks' Bn. Co.A
Reed, Daniel Cherokee Regt. Miller's Co.
Reed, Daniel G. SC Inf. 7th Bn. (Enfield Rifles)
Co.B
Reed, Daniel O. 1st Conf.Inf. 2nd Co.D
Reed, Daniel W. MO 6th Inf. Co.B
Reed, David AL 2nd Cav. Co.D
Reed, David AL 26th Inf. Co.I 2nd Lt.
Reed, David AL 50th Inf. Co.F
Reed, David AR Lt.Arty. Key's Btty.
Reed, David GA Arty. St.Troops Pruden's Btty.
Reed, David LA Hvy.Arty. 8th Bn. Co.3
Reed, David LA Siege Train Bn. Co.D
Reed, David MS 11th (Perrin's) Cav. Co.B
Reed, David MO 2nd Cav. Co.C,K Capt.
Reed, David MO 15th Cav. Co.C Capt.
Reed, David MO 10th Inf. Co.K
Reed, David TN 14th (Neely's) Cav. Co.F
Reed, David VA 23rd Cav. Co.E
Reed, David VA Cav. 41st Bn. Co.E
Reed, David VA 38th Inf. 2nd Co.I
Reed, David 1st Conf.Cav. 2nd Co.G
Reed, David 1st Seminole Mtd.Vol. Sgt.Maj.
Reed, David A. LA 28th (Gray's) Inf. Co.D
Reed, David B. VA 30th Bn.S.S. Co.E Cpl.
Reed, David C. KY 3rd Bn.Mtd.Rifles Co.E
Reed, David C.G. MS Inf. 3rd Bn. Co.C
Reed, David H. GA 12th Inf. Co.G
Reed, D.B. TN 8th (Smith's) Cav. Co.E
Reed, D.B.R. FL 2nd Inf. Co.A
Reed, D.C. AR 1st (Monroe's) Cav. Co.E
Reed, D.C. AR 21st Mil. Co.E
Reed, D.C. TX 3rd Cav. Co.E
Reed, D.C. Trans-MS Conf.Cav. 1st Bn. Co.C
Sgt.
Reed, D.F. AR 15th (Johnson's) Inf. Co.D
Reed, D.G. MS Cav. Jeff Davis Legion Co.B
Cpl.
Reed, D.H. Gen. & Staff 1st Lt.,ADC
Reed, D.J. 15th Conf.Cav. Co.H
Reed, D.J. Gen. & Staff,PACS Maj.
Reed, D.M. VA 7th Cav. Glenn's Co.
Reed, D.N. TX 33rd Cav. Co.D
Reed, Dorsey VA Cav. 41st Bn. Co.E Sgt.
Reed, D.S. TX Cav. Baird's Regt. Co.G
Reed, D.S. TX 17th Inf. Co.I
Reed, Duff G. Wheeler's Staff Maj.
Reed, D.W. MO Inf. 3rd Bn. Co.C
Reed, D.W. TN 1st (Feild's) & 27th Inf. (Cons.)
Co.I
Reed, D.W. TN 27th Inf. Co.F
Reed, D.W. TX 11th (Spaight's) Bn.Vol. Co.A
Reed, E. KY 1st (Butler's) Cav. Co.F
Reed, E. KY Morgan's Men Beck's Co.
Reed, E. LA Siege Train Bn. Co.D
Reed, E. MS 18th Cav. Co.G
Reed, E. TX 9th Cav. Co.C
Reed, E. VA Horse Arty. J.W. Carter's Co.
Reed, E.A. GA Boddie's Co. (Troup
Cty.Ind.Cav.)
Reed, E.A. TN 21st (Wilson's) Cav. Co.C
Reed, E.A. TN 21st & 22nd (Cons.) Cav. Co.G
Reed, Edmund S. VA 26th Inf. Co.I
Reed, Edward AR 30th Inf. Co.K
Reed, Edward LA C.S. Zouave Bn. Co.D
Reed, Edward MO 2nd Cav. Co.C,K

Reed, Edward MO Cav. 2nd Bn.St.Guard Co.B
Reed, Edward W. KY 6th Mtd.Inf. Co.B
Reed, E.H. AR 2nd Inf. Co.G
Reed, E.J. VA 23rd Cav. Co.A
Reed, Elbert NC Walker's Bn. Thomas' Legion Co.A
Reed, Eli AR 34th Inf. Co.E
Reed, Elias AL Cav. Lewis' Bn. Co.E
Reed, Elias VA 60th Inf. Co.I
Reed, Elias VA 151st Mil. Co.F
Reed, Elijah MS Cav. Hughes' Bn. Co.C
Reed, Elijah NC 37th Inf. Co.G
Reed, Elisha W. TN 15th Cav. Co.E
Reed, Ellich R. GA Cav. Nelson's Ind.Co.
Reed, Elliott SC 2nd Arty. Co.B
Reed, E.M. TX 21st Cav. Co.C
Reed, Emile LA 1st Hvy.Arty. (Reg.) Co.D
Reed, Emile LA Hvy.Arty. 8th Bn. Co.3
Reed, Emmett W. VA 9th Cav. Co.C
Reed, E.S. SC 2nd Arty. Co.B
Reed, E.T. GA Phillips' Legion Co.B
Reed, E.T. TX 17th Inf. Co.I
Reed, Euphrades T. AR 1st (Colquitt's) Inf. Co.I 2nd Lt.
Reed, Ewel MO 3rd Cav. Co.C
Reed, Ezekiel MS 2nd (Quinn's St.Troops) Inf. Co.A
Reed, Ezekiel TN 18th Inf. Co.D
Reed, Ezra R. TN 10th Inf. Co.C
Reed, F.B. AR 21st Inf. Co.F Comsy.Sgt.
Reed, F.F. VA 47th Inf. Co.G
Reed, Finis E. AL 28th Inf. Co.I
Reed, F.J. GA 13th Inf. Co.D
Reed, Fleming VA 51st Inf. Co.H
Reed, F.M. AR 17th (Lemoyne's) Inf. Co.A
Reed, F.M. MO 11th Inf. Co.F
Reed, F.M. TN 27th Inf. Co.D
Reed, F.R. KY 3rd Bn.Mtd.Rifles Co.C 1st Lt.
Reed, Francis MO 1st Cav. Co.B
Reed, Francis M. TX 15th Inf. 2nd Co.E
Reed, Frank AL 5th Cav. Co.E
Reed, Frederick MO Inf. 3rd Bn. Co.F
Reed, Frederick MO 6th Inf. Co.H
Reed, Frederick S. GA Lt.Arty. Guerard's Btty.
Reed, Fritz LA 7th Inf. Co.K Drum.
Reed, F.S. GA Brooks' Co. (Terrell Lt.Arty.)
Reed, F.T. AL 21st Inf. Co.C Cpl.
Reed, F.T. AL 26th (O'Neal's) Inf. Co.K Sgt.
Reed, F.T. VA 8th Inf. Co.G
Reed, F.T. Gen. & Staff AASurg.
Reed, F.T. Gen. & Staff Pvt.Physician
Reed, F.Y. AR 19th (Dawson's) Inf. Co.D
Reed, G. AL 5th Inf. Co.I
Reed, G. KY 12th Cav. Co.E
Reed, G. MO 1st N.E. Cav. Co.G
Reed, G.A. LA 17th Inf. Co.D Sgt.
Reed, Galveston M. AR Cav. Wright's Regt. Co.D Capt.
Reed, Galveston M. AR 26th Inf. Co.A,E 1st Lt.
Reed, Garland TN 20th (Russell's) Cav. Co.B
Reed, Garnett TN 13th (Gore's) Cav. Co.F
Reed, Garrott TN 13th (Gore's) Cav. Co.E
Reed, G.C. Gen. & Staff Capt.,AQM
Reed, George AL 28th Inf. Co.E
Reed, George AL 48th Inf. Co.E
Reed, George AL 48th Inf. Co.G
Reed, George AR 32nd Inf. Co.F

Reed, George AR 45th Mil. Co.D Cpl.
Reed, George MS 35th Inf. Co.G
Reed, George MO 1st Cav. Co.I
Reed, George MO 10th Cav. Co.G
Reed, George TN Cav. Welcker's Bn. Kincaid's Co.
Reed, George TN 19th Inf. Co.E
Reed, George VA 54th Mil. Co.G
Reed, George VA 89th Mil. Co.A
Reed, George Mead's Conf.Cav. Co.D
Reed, George Conf.Inf. 8th Bn. Co.B
Reed, George Conf.Inf. Tucker's Regt. Co.H
Reed, George Sig.Corps,CSA
Reed, George A. AR Cav. Gordon's Regt. Co.E 2nd Lt.
Reed, George A. AR 2nd Inf. Co.G
Reed, George A. AR 15th Mil. Co.C Sgt.
Reed, George A. VA 111th Mil. Co.8
Reed, George B. AL 6th Inf. Co.G Sgt.
Reed, George E. AL 40th Inf. Co.H
Reed, Geo. E. AL Cp. of Instr. Talladega
Reed, George F. VA 52nd Inf. Co.G
Reed, George F. Gen. & Staff, Arty. 1st Lt.
Reed, George H. AL 48th Inf. New Co.G
Reed, George I. GA Phillips' Legion Co.A
Reed, George L. AL 28th Inf. Co.B
Reed, George M.D. TN 55th (McKoin's) Inf. McEwen, Jr.'s Co.
Reed, George P.L. TX 4th Inf. Co.H Hosp.Stew.
Reed, Geo. P.L. Gen. & Staff Hosp.Stew.
Reed, George R. LA 5th Cav. Co.I Sgt.
Reed, George R. NC 37th Inf. Co.G
Reed, George R. Inf. School of Pract. Co.C
Reed, George T. AL 58th Inf. Co.A,H
Reed, George T. TX 13th Cav. Co.A Sgt.
Reed, George W. AL 5th Inf. New Co.E Capt.
Reed, George W. AL 22nd Inf. Co.E
Reed, George W. AR 1st (Monroe's) Cav. Palmer's Co.
Reed, George W. AR 2nd Inf. Co.G
Reed, George W. AR 26th Inf. Co.A,E Cpl.
Reed, George W. AR 32nd Inf. Co.A
Reed, George W. GA 35th Inf. Co.E
Reed, George W. MS 15th Inf. Co.H
Reed, George W. MS 21st Inf. Co.F
Reed, George W. TN 42nd Inf. Co.A Cpl.
Reed, George W. TN 63rd Inf. Co.D
Reed, George W. VA 17th Cav. Co.A
Reed, George W. VA 2nd Inf. Co.D
Reed, George W. VA 5th Inf. Co.C
Reed, George W. VA 13th Inf. Co.I, 2nd Co.B
Reed, George W. VA 22nd Inf. Co.B
Reed, George W. VA 22nd Inf. Co.F
Reed, George W. VA 22nd Inf. Co.I
Reed, George W. VA 27th Inf. 2nd Co.H
Reed, George W. VA 55th Inf. Co.E
Reed, George W. VA 146th Mil. Co.H
Reed, George W. 4th Conf.Inf. Co.G
Reed, George Washington VA 8th Cav. 1st Co.D Black.
Reed, G.F. TN 4th Inf. Co.C
Reed, G.F. Forrest's Scouts T. Henderson's Co.
Reed, G.G. TN 13th (Gore's) Cav. Co.F
Reed, G.H. VA 8th Cav. Co.H Sgt.
Reed, G.H.C. Gen. & Staff AASurg.

Reed, Gideon B. VA Patrol Guard 11th Congr. Dist. (Mtd.)
Reed, G.J. AL 1st Regt. Mobile Vol. Bass' Co.
Reed, G.J. AL 4th Res. Co.B
Reed, Godfrey VA 18th Cav. Co.B
Reed, G.R. TN 1st (Feild's) & 27th Inf. (Cons.) Co.I
Reed, G.R. TN 27th Inf. Co.F
Reed, Granville TX 9th Cav. Co.F
Reed, Green B. AL 16th Inf. Co.A
Reed, G.T. AL 18th Inf. Co.I
Reed, G.T. AL 32nd & 58th (Cons.) Inf.
Reed, G.V. AR 20th Inf. Co.K
Reed, G.W. AL 9th Inf. Co.B
Reed, G.W. AL 18th Inf. Co.I
Reed, G.W. AL 19th Inf. Co.K
Reed, G.W. AR 15th (Josey's) Inf. 1st Co.G
Reed, G.W. LA 19th Inf. Co.K Cpl.
Reed, G.W. MS Arty. (Wesson Arty.) Kittrell's Co.
Reed, G.W. MS 13th Inf. Co.K
Reed, G.W. MO 4th Inf. Co.D
Reed, G.W. NC 48th Inf. Co.H
Reed, G.W. TN 16th (Logwood's) Cav. Co.H
Reed, G.W. TN 22nd (Barteau's) Cav. Co.H
Reed, G.W. TN 23rd Inf. Co.H
Reed, G.W. TN 45th Inf. Co.C
Reed, G.W. TX 28th Cav. Co.C,K
Reed, G.W. TX 2nd Inf. Co.G
Reed, G.W. TX 11th Inf. Co.E
Reed, G.W. 1st Conf.Cav. Co.I
Reed, H. AL 59th Inf. Co.E
Reed, H. AR 8th Inf. New Co.K 2nd Lt.
Reed, H. GA 52nd Inf. Co.G
Reed, H. MS 3rd Inf. (St.Troops) Co.H
Reed, H. MS 5th Inf. Co.A
Reed, H. NC 2nd Cav. (19th St.Troops) Co.A
Reed, H. NC McLean's Bn.Lt.Duty Men Co.A
Reed, H. TX Inf. 1st St.Troops Beihler's Co.A
Reed, H.A. VA 8th Cav. Co.H
Reed, Hamilton VA Inf. 26th Bn. Co.C
Reed, Harden MO 12th Inf. Co.D
Reed, Hardy SC 24th Inf. Co.D
Reed, Harrison AL Arty. 4th Bn. Hilliard's Legion Co.E
Reed, Harrison VA 4th Inf. Co.B
Reed, H.B. TN 28th Cav. Co.C
Reed, H.B. TN 18th Inf. Co.H
Reed, H.B. TN 47th Inf. Co.H
Reed, H.C. AL 48th Inf. Co.K
Reed, H.C. FL 2nd Inf. Co.K
Reed, H.C. GA 41st Inf. Co.C
Reed, H.D. KY 10th (Johnson's) Cav. New Co.B
Reed, Henderson VA Lt.Arty. G.B. Chapman's Co. 1st Lt.
Reed, Henderson VA 108th Mil. Co.F, Lemons' Co. 1st Lt.
Reed, Henry AL 8th (Hatch's) Cav. Co.H
Reed, Henry AR 15th Mil. Co.E
Reed, Henry AR 19th (Dawson's) Inf. Co.C
Reed, Henry AR 31st Inf. Co.B
Reed, Henry GA 2nd Bn.S.S. Co.B
Reed, Henry LA C.S. Zouave Bn. Co.A Cpl.
Reed, Henry MS 10th Inf. New Co.E, Co.N
Reed, Henry NC 6th Sr.Res. Co.G
Reed, Henry NC 7th Sr.Res. Clinard's Co.
Reed, Henry NC 60th Inf. Co.C Cpl.

Reed, Henry TX 5th Cav. Co.D
Reed, Henry VA Hvy.Arty. 19th Bn. 2nd Co.C
Reed, Henry A. AR 2nd Mtd.Rifles Co.B
Reed, Henry C. AL Seawell's Btty. (Mohawk Arty.) 1st Sgt.
Reed, Henry C. LA 1st Hvy.Arty. (Reg.) Co.A Sgt.
Reed, Henry C. MS 13th Inf. Co.E
Reed, Henry C. NC 32nd Inf. Co.B
Reed, Henry C. TX 14th Cav. Co.G
Reed, Henry C. VA Hvy.Arty. 19th Bn. 2nd Co.C
Reed, Henry H. AL Pris.Guard Freeman's Co.
Reed, Henry H. MS 43rd Inf. Co.B
Reed, Henry J. VA 11th Cav. Co.B
Reed, Henry J. VA 14th Mil. Co.C
Reed, Henry M. NC 37th Inf. Co.G Cpl.
Reed, Henry S. AL 8th Cav. Co.H
Reed, Henry S. NC 2nd Bn.Loc.Def.Troops Co.G
Reed, Henry S. NC 50th Inf. Co.F
Reed, H.F. AL 49th Inf. Co.I
Reed, H.G. AR 27th Inf. Old Co.B
Reed, H.H. AL 26th (O'Neal's) Inf. Co.E Capt.
Reed, H.H. AL Pris.Guard Freeman's Co.
Reed, H.H. AL Supp.Force 2nd Congr.Dist. Reed's Co. Capt.
Reed, Hill J. NC 2nd Cav. (19th St.Troops) Co.C
Reed, Hill J. NC Lt.Arty. 13th Bn. Co.A Guidon
Reed, Hill J. NC 17th Inf. (1st Org.) Co.I Sgt.
Reed, Hillary F. VA 8th Cav. 2nd Co.D
Reed, Hinas VA 46th Mil. Co.B
Reed, H.J. AL 8th Inf. Co.E
Reed, H.P. LA 17th Inf. Co.D
Reed, H.R. KY 10th Cav. Co.E
Reed, H.S. GA 3rd Inf.
Reed, H.S. MO Inf. 4th Regt.St.Guard Co.A
Reed, H.S. VA 17th Cav. Co.B
Reed, H.T. MS Arty. (Wesson Arty.) Kittrell's Co.
Reed, H.T. SC 22nd Inf. Co.D
Reed, H.T. TN 38th Inf. 2nd Co.H 1st Sgt.
Reed, Hugh AR 7th Bn. Co.A 2nd Lt.
Reed, Hugh AR 32nd Inf. Co.D
Reed, Hugh LA 22nd Inf. Co.A
Reed, Humphrey VA Inf. 21st Bn. 2nd Co.E
Reed, Humphrey VA 54th Inf. Co.I
Reed, Humphrey VA 64th Mtd.Inf. Co.E
Reed, Humphrey VA Mil. Scott Cty.
Reed, Humphrey L. VA Mil. Carroll Cty.
Reed, H.W. GA 1st Cav. Co.E
Reed, I.C. KY 7th Cav. Co.A
Reed, I.C. MO 8th Cav. Co.H
Reed, I.N. TX 11th Inf. Co.E
Reed, Ira LA Inf. 4th Bn. Co.C
Reed, Isaac MO 8th Inf. Co.C
Reed, Isaac MO Robertson's Regt.St.Guard Co.8
Reed, Isaac TN 45th Inf. Co.I
Reed, Isaac A. GA 7th Inf. Co.H Sgt.
Reed, Isaac A. LA 6th Inf. Co.D Capt.,AQM
Reed, Isaac A. Gen. & Staff Capt.,AQM
Reed, Isaac B. AR 15th Inf. Co.G
Reed, Isaac H. Conf.Cav. Wood's Regt. 1st Co.A
Reed, Isaac R. AR 2nd Inf. Co.G
Reed, Isaac S. AR 6th Inf. New Co.D

Reed, Isaac S. TN 43rd Inf. Co.C
Reed, Isaac W. MO Cav. Freeman's Regt. Co.B
Reed, I.T. MS Cav. 2nd Bn.Res. Co.I
Reed, I.W. TN 50th Inf. Co.G
Reed, Izeria GA 40th Inf. Co.H
Reed, J. AL 26th (O'Neal's) Inf. Co.G
Reed, J. AL 59th Inf. Co.E
Reed, J. AR 1st (Dobbin's) Cav. Co.E
Reed, J. AR 35th Inf. Co.A
Reed, J. GA 1st Reg. Co.E
Reed, J. KY 10th Cav. Co.G
Reed, J. LA Arty. King's Btty.
Reed, J. MS 8th Cav. Co.D
Reed, J. MS 11th (Perrin's) Cav. Co.K
Reed, J. MS 15th (Cons.) Inf. Co.A
Reed, J. TN 4th Inf. Sgt.
Reed, J. TN 51st (Cons.) Inf. Co.B
Reed, J.A. GA 1st Bn.S.S. Co.D Cpl.
Reed, J.A. KY 10th (Johnson's) Cav. New Co.B
Reed, J.A. LA 2nd Inf. Co.I
Reed, J.A. MO 2nd Inf. Co.H
Reed, J.A. TN 3rd (Clack's) Inf. Co.E
Reed, J.A. TX 11th Inf. Co.H
Reed, J.A. VA 3rd Cav. Co.K
Reed, Jackson LA Arty. Hutton's Co. (Crescent Arty.Co.A)
Reed, Jackson TN 18th Inf. Co.A
Reed, Jackson VA 22nd Cav. Co.B
Reed, Jackson J. AL 41st Inf. Co.A
Reed, Jacob MS 7th Cav. Co.B
Reed, Jacob TX 36th Cav. Co.K Black.
Reed, Jacob G. TX 34th Cav. Co.C
Reed, Jacob H. VA 108th Mil. Co.F, McNeer's Co.
Reed, James AL 19th Inf. Co.K
Reed, James AL 60th Inf. Co.K
Reed, James AL 1st Bn. Hilliard's Legion Vol. Co.C
Reed, James AR 2nd Mtd.Rifles Co.E
Reed, James AR 34th Inf. Co.E
Reed, James GA 19th Inf. Sgt.
Reed, James GA 23rd Inf. Co.A
Reed, James KY 4th Mtd.Inf. Co.F
Reed, James LA 2nd Cav. Co.A
Reed, James MD 1st Cav. Co.B
Reed, James MD Inf. 2nd Bn. Co.D
Reed, James MS 2nd Cav. Co.A
Reed, James MS 2nd St.Cav. Co.A
Reed, James MS Cav. Davenport's Bn. (St.Troops) Co.A
Reed, James MS Cav. Drane's Co. (Choctaw Cty.Res.)
Reed, James MS 5th Inf. Co.E
Reed, James MO 1st & 3rd Cons.Cav. Co.E
Reed, James MO 2nd Cav. Co.B
Reed, James MO Cav. 3rd Bn. Co.E Sgt.
Reed, James MO 10th Inf. Co.D
Reed, James MO 10th Inf. Co.K
Reed, James MO 12th Inf. Co.I
Reed, James NC 21st Inf. Co.H
Reed, James NC 37th Inf. Co.G Capt.
Reed, James NC Walker's Bn. Thomas' Legion 2nd Co.D
Reed, James SC 2nd Cav. Co.D
Reed, James SC 2nd Arty. Co.B
Reed, James SC 11th Res. Co.C
Reed, James SC 25th Inf. Co.H

Reed, James TN 18th Inf. Co.H Sgt.
Reed, James TN 42nd Inf. Co.A
Reed, James TX 12th Cav. Co.I
Reed, James TX 24th Cav. Co.C
Reed, James TX Cav. Wells' Regt. Co.E
Reed, James TX Waul's Legion Co.B
Reed, James VA 3rd Cav.
Reed, James VA Cav. Mosby's Regt. (Part. Rangers)
Reed, James VA 8th Inf. Co.E
Reed, James VA 54th Mil. Co.A
Reed, James VA 108th Mil. Co.F, McNeer's Co.
Reed, James VA Res.Forces Thurston's Co.
Reed, James 4th Conf.Inf. Co.G
Reed, James Conf.Reg.Inf. Brooks' Bn. Co.A
Reed, James Conf.Inf. Tucker's Regt. Co.I
Reed, James A. AR 21st Inf. Co.I
Reed, James A. MS 2nd Inf. Co.G
Reed, James A. VA 52nd Inf. Co.E
Reed, James A. Conf.Cav. Wood's Regt. 2nd Co.G
Reed, James B. AL 16th Inf.
Reed, James B. AL 21st Inf. Co.C
Reed, James B. GA 47th Inf. Co.A Cpl.
Reed, James B. TN 43rd Inf. Co.H
Reed, James B. VA 9th Cav. Sandford's Co. Sgt.
Reed, James B. VA 15th Cav. Co.A Sgt.
Reed, James B. VA Cav. 15th Bn. Co.A Sgt.
Reed, James C. AR 3rd Inf. Co.G
Reed, James C. MS Cav. 1st Bn. (Miller's) Cole's Co.
Reed, James C. MO 7th Cav. Co.D
Reed, James C. TN Cav. Welcker's Bn. Kincaid's Co.
Reed, James C. TN 44th Inf. Co.K
Reed, James C. TN 44th (Cons.) Inf. Co.F
Reed, James C. TX 9th Field Btty.
Reed, James C. VA Lt.Arty. J.D. Smith's Co. Sgt.
Reed, James D. AL 3rd Inf. Co.C
Reed, James D. AL 26th (O'Neal's) Inf. Co.K
Reed, James D. TX 25th Cav. Co.D 1st Lt.
Reed, James D. TX 1st Inf. Co.H
Reed, James E. NC 17th Inf. (2nd Org.) Co.C
Reed, James E., 2nd NC 66th Inf. Co.G
Reed, James F. NC 42nd Inf. Co.D
Reed, James F. VA 5th Inf. Co.H
Reed, James G. AL 30th Inf. Co.D Sgt.
Reed, James G. TN 14th (Neely's) Cav. Reed's Co. Capt.
Reed, James H. AL 16th Inf. Co.K
Reed, James H. AR 35th Inf. Co.C QMSgt.
Reed, James H. KY Kirkpatrick's Bn. Co.B QMSgt.
Reed, James H. NC 52nd Inf. Co.G
Reed, James H. TX Cav. McCord's Frontier Regt. Co.F
Reed, James H. TX 9th (Nichols') Inf. Co.B Cpl.
Reed, James H. TX 22nd Inf. Co.G 1st Sgt.
Reed, James H. VA 22nd Inf. Co.F
Reed, James J. AL 27th Inf. Co.A
Reed, James J. 1st Conf.Inf. 2nd Co.D Cpl.
Reed, James K.P. TN 1st (Feild's) Inf. Co.G Cpl.
Reed, James M. AL 36th Inf. Co.C

Reed, James M. AL 55th Vol. Co.B
Reed, James M. AL 62nd Inf. Co.A
Reed, James M. MS 36th Inf. Co.A
Reed, James M. NC Cav. 7th Bn. Co.C
Reed, James M. TX Cav. Baylor's Regt. Co.E
Reed, James M. TX 2nd Inf. Co.E
Reed, James M. VA 8th Cav. 2nd Co.D
Reed, James M. VA 2nd Inf. Co.D
Reed, James P. AR 17th (Griffith's) Inf. Co.G
Reed, James P. TX 22nd Cav. Co.G Cpl.
Reed, James P. TX 36th Cav. Co.C
Reed, James P. TX Cav. Giddings' Bn. Co.A
Reed, James R. MS 2nd Inf. Co.A
Reed, James R. TN 27th Inf. Co.F
Reed, James R. TX 1st Inf. Co.H
Reed, James Robert VA 34th Inf. Co.K
Reed, James S. NC 37th Inf. Co.G Cpl.
Reed, James T. AR 35th Inf. Co.K
Reed, James T. KY 4th Mtd.Inf. Co.I Sgt.
Reed, James T. NC Unassign.Conscr.
Reed, James T. VA 47th Inf. Co.C
Reed, James W. GA 4th Res. Co.D Cpl.
Reed, James W. GA 7th Inf. Co.H
Reed, James W. MO Searcy's Bn.S.S. Co.C
Reed, James W. SC Cav. 14th Bn. Co.D Capt.
Reed, James W. SC Hvy.Arty. Mathewes' Co.
Reed, James W. VA 6th Cav. Co.K
Reed, James W.D. VA 20th Cav. Co.D
Reed, James Y. SC Inf. 3rd Bn. Co.B
Reed, Jasper AR 3rd Inf. Co.B
Reed, Jasper GA 11th Inf. Co.C
Reed, Jasper MO 2nd Inf. Co.E
Reed, J.B. AR 2nd Cav. Co.B
Reed, J.B. AR 8th Cav. Co.E
Reed, J.B. AR Inf. Cocke's Regt. Co.H
Reed, J.B. GA 7th Inf. (St.Guards) Co.A
Reed, J.B. LA Mil.Crescent Cadets
Reed, J.B. MS 5th Cav. Co.H
Reed, J.B. MS 41st Inf. Co.B 3rd Lt.
Reed, J.B. TN 3rd (Forrest's) Cav. Co.D
Reed, J.B. TN 18th Inf. Co.F
Reed, J.B. TX 23rd Cav. Co.A Sgt.
Reed, J.B. TX 32nd Cav. Co.F
Reed, J.B. TX 15th Inf. 2nd Co.G
Reed, J.B. Gen. & Staff, Subs.Dept. Capt.,ACS
Reed, J.C. AL 36th Inf. Co.I
Reed, J.C. AR 3rd Inf. (St.Troops) Co.A Music.
Reed, J.C. AR 7th Inf. Co.A
Reed, J.C. MS 15th (Cons.) Inf. Co.G
Reed, J.C. TN 15th & 37th Regt.Vol. (Cons.)
Co.C Cpl.
Reed, J.C. TN 42nd Inf. Co.D
Reed, J.C. TX 26th Cav. 2nd Co.G
Reed, J.C. TX 2nd Inf. Co.A
Reed, J.C. TX 4th Inf. Co.E
Reed, J.C. VA Cav. Swann's Bn. Watkins' Co.
Reed, J.C. 4th Conf.Inf. Co.K
Reed, J.C. Brig.Brass Band 2nd Brig. Price's Div.
AR Dist.,CSA Music.
Reed, J.D. GA 16th Inf. Co.C
Reed, J.D. GA 1st Bn.S.S. Co.D Cpl.
Reed, J.D. LA 12th Inf. Co.F
Reed, J.D. MS 1st (Percy's) Inf. Co.B
Reed, J.D. MS 12th Inf. Co.F
Reed, J.E. MS 8th Cav. Co.F
Reed, J.E. NC 66th Inf. Co.G
Reed, Jeff MS Shields' Co.

Reed, Jefferson MS 23rd Inf.
Reed, Jehu NC Walker's Bn. Thomas' Legion
Co.B
Reed, Jeptha GA 12th (Robinson's) Cav.
(St.Guards) Co.G
Reed, Jeremiah TX 21st Cav. Co.L
Reed, Jerry GA Inf. 1st Loc.Troops (Augusta)
Barnes' Lt.Arty.Co. Cpl.
Reed, Jesse AR 34th Inf. Co.K
Reed, Jesse GA Inf. 5th Bn. (St.Guards) Co.C
Reed, Jesse GA 6th Inf. Co.F 2nd Lt.
Reed, Jesse NC 60th Inf. Co.C
Reed, Jesse SC 2nd Rifles Co.F,G
Reed, Jesse TN 9th (Ward's) Cav. Co.D
Reed, Jesse TN 12th Inf. Co.G
Reed, Jesse C. AR 35th Inf. Co.C Drum Maj.
Reed, Jessee MS 15th Inf. Co.H
Reed, Jesse F. GA 17th Inf. Co.B
Reed, Jesse G. MO Robertson's Regt.St.Guard
Co.9
Reed, Jesse J. TN 3rd (Clack's) Inf. Co.G
Reed, Jesse V. AR 17th (Griffith's) Inf. Co.C
Reed, Jesse W. FL Inf. 2nd Bn. Co.A
Reed, Jesse W. 1st Conf.Eng.Troops Co.K Sgt.
Reed, J.F. AL 8th Inf. Co.B Sgt.
Reed, J.F. AR 19th (Dawson's) Inf. Co.B Surg.
Reed, J.F. MS 10th Cav. Co.B
Reed, J.F. TX 11th Inf. Co.H
Reed, J.F.M. SC 3rd Bn.Res. Co.D
Reed, J.G. AR 32nd Inf. Co.B
Reed, J.G. TN 47th Inf. Co.I Cpl.
Reed, J.H. AR 11th Inf. Co.B
Reed, J.H. GA 4th Cav. (St.Guards) Pirkle's Co.
Reed, J.H. GA 55th Inf. Co.K
Reed, J.H. KY 11th Cav. Co.C
Reed, J.H. MS 46th Inf. Co.D
Reed, J.H. TN 18th Inf. Co.H
Reed, J.H. VA 14th Cav. Co.H
Reed, J.H. VA Cav. Mosby's Regt. (Part.
Rangers) Co.G
Reed, Jimsey 1st Creek Mtd.Vol. 1st Co.C Sgt.
Reed, J.J. TN 47th Inf. Co.H
Reed, J.J. TX 1st Hvy.Arty. Co.K
Reed, J.J. Gen. & Staff 2nd Lt.,Dr.M.
Reed, J.J.M. TX 11th Inf. Co.E
Reed, J.K. MS Inf. Lewis' Co. Sgt.
Reed, J.K.P. TX 17th Inf. Co.K
Reed, J.L. AL Cav. Hardie's Bn.Res. S.D.
McClellan's Co.
Reed, J.L. AR 19th (Dawson's) Inf. Co.I
Reed, J.L. GA Cav. 1st Bn.Res. Co.E
Reed, J.L. GA 16th Inf. Co.K
Reed, J.L. LA 2nd Cav. Co.B
Reed, J.L. LA 3rd Inf. Co.D
Reed, J.L. TN 1st (Feild's) Inf. Co.H
Reed, J.L. TN 35th Inf. 2nd Co.I
Reed, J.M. AL 48th Inf. Co.H
Reed, J.M. AR 31st Inf. Co.F
Reed, J.M. MS Cav. Ham's Regt. Co.A
Reed, J.M. NC Elliott's Co.
Reed, J.M. TN 5th (McKenzie's) Cav. Co.B
Reed, J.M. TN 39th Mtd.Inf. Co.A
Reed, J.M. TX 10th Cav. Co.F
Reed, J.M. TX 9th (Young's) Inf. Co.K Cpl.
Reed, J.M. VA 6th Bn.Res. Co.C
Reed, J.M.C. GA 3rd Bn. (St.Guards) Co.G
Sr.2nd Lt.

Reed, J.O. SC Inf. Hampton Legion Co.A
Reed, Joe MS 1st (Percy's) Inf. Co.H
Reed, Joel LA 8th Cav. Co.E Cpl.
Reed, Joel NC 37th Inf. Co.G
Reed, Joel E. MS 43rd Inf. Co.B
Reed, Joel P. GA 7th Inf. Co.H
Reed, Joel S. GA 4th Res. Co.D
Reed, John AL 20th Inf. Co.H
Reed, John AL 26th (O'Neal's) Inf. Co.E Sgt.
Reed, John AR 1st Mtd.Rifles Co.B
Reed, John AR 45th Cav. Co.B
Reed, John AR 10th Mil. Cpl.
Reed, John AR 26th Inf. Co.H 1st Sgt.
Reed, John AR 34th Inf. Co.A
Reed, John GA 8th Inf. Co.E
Reed, John KY 9th Cav. Co.B
Reed, John KY Fields' Co. (Part.Rangers)
Reed, John KY 3rd Mtd.Inf. Co.G
Reed, John KY 5th Mtd.Inf. Co.B
Reed, John KY 5th Mtd.Inf. Co.C
Reed, John LA Mil. 3rd Regt. 1st Brig. 1st Div.
Co.H
Reed, John LA 5th Inf. Co.K
Reed, John MS Arty. (Wesson Arty.) Kittrell's
Co.
Reed, John MS 2nd (Quinn's St.Troops) Inf. Co.I
Reed, John MS 35th Inf. Co.D
Reed, John MO Cav. Fristoe's Regt. Co.D Cpl.
Reed, John MO Cav. Snider's Bn. Co.B
Reed, John MO Cav. Snider's Bn. Co.D
Reed, John MO Beck's Co.
Reed, Jno. MO St.Guard
Reed, John NC 28th Inf. Co.A
Reed, John NC 32nd Inf. Co.C
Reed, John SC 1st (Orr's) Rifles Co.C
Reed, John TN 3rd (Forrest's) Cav.
Reed, John TN 4th Cav. Co.A
Reed, John TN 21st (Wilson's) Cav. Co.A
Reed, John TN Cav. Jackson's Co.
Reed, John TN 13th Inf. Co.I
Reed, John TN 32nd Inf. Co.K
Reed, John TN 41st Inf. Co.F
Reed, John TN 44th Inf. Co.C
Reed, John TN 44th (Cons.) Inf. Co.K
Reed, John TN 46th Inf. Co.A
Reed, John TN 50th Inf. Co.F
Reed, John TX 11th Cav. Co.H
Reed, John TX Cav. (Dismtd.) Chisum's Regt.
Co.E
Reed, John TX Cav. Waller's Regt. Co.B
Reed, John TX 1st Hvy.Arty. Co.K
Reed, John TX 2nd Inf. Co.I
Reed, John VA 7th Cav. Co.C
Reed, John VA 9th Cav. Sandford's Co.
Reed, John VA 15th Cav. Co.A
Reed, John VA Cav. 15th Bn. Co.A
Reed, John VA 20th Cav. Co.F
Reed, John VA Cav. McNeill's Co.
Reed, John VA Cav. O'Ferrall's Bn. Co.B
Reed, John VA Lt.Arty. 13th Bn. Co.C
Reed, John VA Hvy.Arty. 20th Bn. Co.B
Reed, John VA 4th Res. Co.H
Reed, John VA 25th Inf. 1st Co.K
Reed, John VA 38th Inf. 2nd Co.I
Reed, John VA 49th Inf. Co.B Cpl.
Reed, John VA 108th Mil. McNeer's Co.
Reed, John VA 3rd Cav. & Inf.St.Line Co.D

Reed, John VA Res.Forces Clark's Co.
Reed, John 14th Conf.Cav. Co.A
Reed, John Conf.Cav. Clarkson's Bn. Ind.
    Rangers Co.B
Reed, John Conf.Inf. 8th Bn. Co.C
Reed, John 1st Seminole Mtd.Vol. 1st Lt.
Reed, John, Sr. 1st Seminole Mtd.Vol. 2nd Lt.
Reed, John Bradford's Corps Scouts & Guards
    Co.B
Reed, John A. AR 1st Cav. Co.E
Reed, John A. AR 2nd Mtd.Rifles Co.G Sgt.
Reed, John A. NC 37th Inf. Co.G
Reed, John A. TX 14th Cav. Co.A
Reed, John B. AR 33rd Inf. Co.I Cpl.
Reed, John B. KY 6th Mtd.Inf. Co.B Cpl.
Reed, John B. MS 2nd Cav. Co.D Sgt.
Reed, John B. TN 16th (Logwood's) Cav. Co.B
Reed, John B. VA 19th Cav. Co.C
Reed, John C. AL 19th Inf. Co.B
Reed, John C. MS 26th Inf. Co.B Sgt.
Reed, John C. MS 43rd Inf. Co.B
Reed, John C. NC 25th Inf. Co.A
Reed, John C. NC 56th Inf. Co.A
Reed, John C. SC 1st Arty. Co.D
Reed, John C. VA 17th Cav. Co.B,K
Reed, John C. VA 151st Mil. Co.F
Reed, John D. AR 7th Cav. Co.L
Reed, John D. GA 6th Inf. Co.F
Reed, John D. KY 11th Cav. Co.A Sgt.
Reed, John D. TN 7th Inf. Co.K
Reed, John G. AL 49th Inf. Co.G Sgt.
Reed, John G. TN 43rd Inf. Co.K Ord.Sgt.
Reed, John G. TN 47th Inf. Co.H Sgt.
Reed, John H. AR 2nd Cav. Co.D
Reed, John H. AR 33rd Inf. Co.I
Reed, John H. GA Conscr.
Reed, John H. KY 4th Cav. Co.B
Reed, John H. MS Inf. 2nd Bn. Co.A Cpl.
Reed, John H. MS 48th Inf. Co.A Cpl.
Reed, John H. NC 16th Inf. Co.I
Reed, John H. TN 39th Inf. Co.B
Reed, John H. TX 11th Inf. Co.E
Reed, John H. VA 23rd Cav. Co.G
Reed, John H. VA 26th Inf. 1st Co.B Cpl.
Reed, John J. VA 2nd Inf. Co.B
Reed, John James 2nd Inf.
Reed, John L. GA 4th Res. Co.D 1st Sgt.
Reed, John L., Jr. GA 7th Inf. (St.Guards) Co.K
    Sgt.
Reed, John L., Sr. GA 7th Inf. (St.Guards) Co.K
    1st Sgt.
Reed, John L. NC 4th Sr.Res. Co.F
Reed, John L. TN 13th Inf. Co.D
Reed, John L. TN 27th Inf. Co.F
Reed, John L. TX 36th Cav. Co.G
Reed, John L. VA Cav. 34th Bn. Co.C
Reed, John M. LA 13th Bn. (Part.Rangers) Co.F
Reed, John M. MS 1st (Percy's) Inf. Co.A
Reed, John M. MS 36th Inf. Co.A
Reed, John M. MS 41st Inf. Co.G Sgt.
Reed, John M. NC 42nd Inf. Co.D
Reed, John M. TN Inf. 23rd Bn. Co.D
Reed, John M. TN 27th Inf. Co.E Fifer
Reed, John M. VA 42nd Inf. Co.B
Reed, John M. VA 108th Mil. Co.F, McNeer's
    Co.
Reed, John N. GA Brooks' Co. (Terrell Lt.Arty.)

Reed, John P. AR Inf. 2nd Bn. Co.B
Reed, John P. GA 11th Inf. Co.H
Reed, John P. TX 15th Inf. Co.A
Reed, John R. AR 26th Inf. Co.D
Reed, John R. TX 9th Field Btty.
Reed, John R. VA 146th Mil. Co.H
Reed, John S. AR 47th (Crandall's) Cav. Co.H
Reed, John S. MO Cav. Freeman's Regt. Co.B
Reed, John T. AL Mil. 4th Vol. Co.B
Reed, John T. AL 10th Inf. Co.B Music.
Reed, John T. MO 4th Cav. Co.G
Reed, John T. TN 31st Inf.
Reed, John T. VA 6th Cav. Co.A
Reed, John T. 4th Conf.Eng.Troops Co.H
Reed, John V. GA 35th Inf. Co.G
Reed, John W. AL 60th Inf. Co.K
Reed, John W. AL 1st Bn. Hilliard's Legion Vol.
    Co.C
Reed, John W. AR 2nd Inf. Co.A
Reed, John W. AR 17th (Griffith's) Inf. Co.D
Reed, John W. GA 53rd Inf. Co.E Music.
Reed, John W. MO 2nd Inf. Co.F,E
Reed, John W. NC 27th Inf. Co.B
Reed, John W. NC 48th Inf. Co.K 2nd Lt.
Reed, John W. TN 1st Cav.
Reed, John W. TN 37th Inf. Co.F
Reed, John W. VA 20th Cav. Co.D
Reed, John W. VA Cav. Mosby's Regt.
    (Part.Rangers) Co.D
Reed, John W. VA 1st Lt.Arty. Co.C Sgt.
Reed, John W. VA Lt.Arty. Cutshaw's Co. Sgt.
Reed, John W. VA 51st Mil. Co.C
Reed, John W. VA 52nd Inf. Co.C
Reed, Jonas VA Patrol Guard 11th Congr.Dist.
    (Mtd.)
Reed, Jonathan VA Mil. Scott Cty.
Reed, Jordan GA 11th Inf. Co.G
Reed, Joseph AL 16th Inf. Co.H
Reed, Joseph AR 8th Inf. New Co.C
Reed, Joseph AR 33rd Inf. Co.I Sgt.
Reed, Joseph AR 38th Inf. Old Co.I, Co.H
Reed, Joseph AR Inf. Cocke's Regt. Co.B
Reed, Joseph GA 11th Cav. Co.G
Reed, Joseph LA 1st (Nelligan's) Inf. Co.F
Reed, Joseph MS 6th Cav. Co.B,L
Reed, Joseph MS 2nd (Quinn's St.Troops) Inf.
    Co.I
Reed, Joseph MS 27th Inf. Co.L
Reed, Joseph MO 2nd Inf. Co.K
Reed, Joseph MO Cav. Freeman's Regt. Co.C
Reed, Joseph TN Conscr. (Cp. of Instr.)
Reed, Joseph TX 30th Cav. Co.I
Reed, Joseph TX Cav. Baird's Regt. Co.A
Reed, Joseph VA 5th Cav.
Reed, Joseph VA 8th Cav. Co.F
Reed, Joseph VA 45th Inf. Co.F
Reed, Joseph VA 108th Mil. Co.F
Reed, Joseph 1st Conf.Inf. 2nd Co.C
Reed, Joseph B. MS 36th Inf. Co.A
Reed, Joseph C. VA 1st Lt.Arty. Co.C
Reed, Joseph C. VA Lt.Arty. Cutshaw's Co.
Reed, Joseph C. VA 51st Mil. Co.C
Reed, Joseph E. VA 9th Cav. Sandford's Co.
    Sgt.
Reed, Joseph E. VA 15th Cav. Co.A
Reed, Joseph E. VA Cav. 15th Bn. Co.A Sgt.
Reed, Joseph E. VA 111th Mil. Co.5 Cpl.

Reed, Joseph H. VA Lt.Arty. G.B. Chapman's
    Co.
Reed, Joseph M. MO 16th Inf. Co.D Sgt.
Reed, Joseph R. AR 1st Cav. Co.A
Reed, Jos. W. VA 19th Cav. Co.B
Reed, Joseph W. VA 9th Mil. Co.A
Reed, Joseph W. VA 26th Inf. Co.I
Reed, Joshua MO Inf. 8th Bn. Co.A
Reed, Joshua MO 9th Inf. Co.A,H
Reed, Joshua B. KY 2nd Cav. Co.B Lt.
Reed, Joshua D. VA 6th Inf. Ferguson's Co.
Reed, Joshua D. VA 12th Inf. Co.H
Reed, Joshua H. GA 4th Res. Co.D
Reed, Joshua H. GA 7th Inf. (St.Guards) Co.K
    Cpl.
Reed, Josua H. VA 108th Mil. Lemons' Co.
Reed, J.P. AL 9th (Malone's) Cav. Co.I
Reed, J.P. GA 3rd Res. Co.E
Reed, J.P. GA Phillips' Legion Co.C,M
Reed, J.P. LA 16th Inf. Co.K,G
Reed, J.P. SC Simons' Co.
Reed, J.P. TN 6th Inf. Co.D
Reed, J.R. AL Inf. 2nd Regt. Co.B
Reed, J.R. AL 42nd Inf. Co.K
Reed, J.R. MS 10th Cav. Co.A
Reed, J.R. SC 25th Inf. Co.H
Reed, J.R. TN 21st (Wilson's) Cav. Co.C 1st
    Sgt.
Reed, J.R. TN 21st & 22nd (Cons.) Cav. Co.G
    1st Sgt.
Reed, J.S. AL 10th Inf. Co.A Cpl.
Reed, J.S. AR 11th Inf. Co.B
Reed, J.S. AR 11th & 17th (Cons.) Inf. Co.A,C
Reed, J.S. GA 2nd Res. Co.I
Reed, J.S. TN 39th Mtd.Inf. Co.A
Reed, J.S. TX 13th Vol. Co.B
Reed, J.T. AL 38th Inf. Co.H
Reed, J.T. AR 34th Inf. Co.G
Reed, J.T. MS Cav. (St.Troops) Gamblin's Co.
Reed, J.W. AL 13th Bn.Part.Rangers Co.B
Reed, J.W. AL 56th Part.Rangers Co.F
Reed, J.W. AL 1st Inf. Co.I
Reed, J.W. AL 15th Inf. Co.C
Reed, J.W. AL 32nd & 58th (Cons.) Inf.
Reed, J.W. AR 8th Inf. Co.C
Reed, J.W. AR 11th & 17th (Cons.) Inf. Co.K
Reed, J.W. GA 3rd Bn. (St.Guards) Co.C
Reed, J.W. GA 13th Inf. Co.G
Reed, J.W. GA 27th Inf. Co.D
Reed, J.W. GA Inf. (E. to W.Point Guards)
    Matthews' Co.
Reed, J.W. MO 1st N.E. Cav. Co.G
Reed, J.W. SC 1st (McCreary's) Inf. Co.D
Reed, J.W. SC 11th Res. Co.G 1st Lt.
Reed, J.W. SC Inf. 13th Bn. Co.E
Reed, J.W. SC Mil. 16th Regt. Sigwald's Co.
    Ex.Sgt.
Reed, J.W. TN 9th Inf. Co.I Cpl.
Reed, J.W. TX Cav. Bourland's Regt. Co.C
Reed, J.W. TX Cav. Coopwood's Spy Co.
Reed, J.W. TX 9th (Young's) Inf. Co.A
Reed, J.W. VA 18th Cav. Co.H
Reed, L. TX Cav. Morgan's Regt. Co.G
Reed, Larkin M. NC 37th Inf. Co.G
Reed, L.D. AL 26th Inf. Co.K
Reed, L.E. Hosp.Stew.

Reed, Leander NC Walker's Bn. Thomas' Legion 2nd Co.D
Reed, Legrand VA 49th Inf. Co.B
Reed, Lemuel AR 1st (Colquitt's) Inf. Co.E
Reed, Lemuel C. TX 28th Cav. Co.K,A
Reed, Leroy MS Cav. Ham's Regt. Co.A 1st Lt.
Reed, Leroy MS St.Cav. Perrin's Bn. Co.B
Reed, Leroy MS 26th Inf. Co.B Cpl.
Reed, Leroy MS 30th Inf. Co.C
Reed, Leroy MS 32nd Inf. Co.I
Reed, Leroy MO 2nd Inf. Co.A 1st Lt.
Reed, Levi AR 1st Mtd.Rifles Co.F
Reed, Levi AR Lt.Arty. Marshall's Btty.
Reed, Levi AR 4th Inf. Co.C
Reed, Levy TN Inf. 23rd Bn. Co.D
Reed, Lewis A. GA Inf. 1st Loc.Troops (Augusta) Co.H
Reed, Lewis V. Conf.Cav. Wood's Regt. 1st Co.A
Reed, L.H. TX 3rd Cav. Co.C
Reed, Littlebury W. VA Hvy.Arty. Coleman's Co.
Reed, London TN Cav. 12th Bn. (Day's) Co.D
Reed, Louis C. TX 29th Cav. Co.A
Reed, Louis W. TX Cav. 6th Bn. Co.E
Reed, Loyd VA Vol. Taylor's Co.
Reed, L.P. AR 15th Mil. Co.A
Reed, L.T. KY 9th Mtd.Inf. Co.C
Reed, L.V. LA 3rd (Harrison's) Cav. Co.A
Reed, Lyman C. LA 1st Cav. Co.D
Reed, M. AL Inf.
Reed, Madison LA Lt.Arty. 6th Field Btty. (Grosse Tete Flying Arty.)
Reed, Manuel MD 1st Cav. Co.B
Reed, Marion K. FL 5th Inf. Co.B
Reed, Martin AL Arty. 1st Bn. Co.C
Reed, Martin L. MS 31st Inf. Co.I 2nd Lt.
Reed, Martin V. LA 31st Inf. Co.E
Reed, Mathias NC 48th Inf. Co.K
Reed, Maxwell K. TN 23rd Inf. 1st Co.A, Co.B
Reed, M.B. TN 26th Inf. Co.B,H
Reed, M.C. MO Inf. 3rd Bn. Co.B
Reed, M. Columbus MO 6th Inf. Co.A
Reed, M.D. NC 30th Inf. Co.A
Reed, M.H. AR 34th Inf. Co.E
Reed, M.H. VA Cav. 34th Bn. Co.B
Reed, Michael LA 1st (Strawbridge's) Inf. Co.F
Reed, Michael MS 34th Inf. Co.A
Reed, Miles NC 3rd Arty. (40th St.Troops) Co.D
Reed, Miles TX Cav. Ragsdale's Co.
Reed, Milton TX Cav. Baylor's Regt. Co.B
Reed, Mitchel AR Inf. Cocke's Regt. Co.B
Reed, Mitchell AR 8th Inf. New Co.C
Reed, M.J. GA 10th Inf. Co.F
Reed, Monroe 1st Conf.Inf. 2nd Co.D
Reed, Morgan KY 7th Mtd.Inf. Co.F
Reed, Moses MO 12th Inf. Co.A
Reed, Moses W. AR Inf. Ballard's Co.
Reed, M.R. TX 17th Inf. Co.I
Reed, M.W. AR 16th Inf. Co.K
Reed, N. AL 12th Inf. Co.G
Reed, Nathaniel AL 1st Cav. Co.A
Reed, Nathaniel AL 12th Cav. Co.A
Reed, Nathaniel AL 19th Inf. Co.C Sgt.
Reed, Nathaniel TX Cav. Madison's Regt. Co.E
Reed, Nathaniel G. VA Lt.Arty. Moore's Co.
Reed, Nathaniel I. GA 24th Inf. Co.H

Reed, N.B. TN 24th Inf. 1st Co.G
Reed, N.D. GA 19th Inf. Co.F
Reed, N.D. TX 1st Inf. Co.G
Reed, N.G. LA 9th Inf. Co.K,A
Reed, Nicholas TN 60th Mtd.Inf. Co.A
Reed, Nimrod TN 13th (Gore's) Cav. Co.G Cpl.
Reed, N.J. GA 42nd Inf. Co.D
Reed, N.J. 1st Conf.Cav. 1st Co.D
Reed, N.K. GA 19th Inf. Co.F
Reed, N.M. AL Cp. of Instr. Talladega
Reed, Noah MO 16th Inf. Co.K
Reed, Noel TN 44th (Cons.) Inf. Co.C
Reed, Noel TN 55th (McKoin's) Inf. Dillehay's Co.
Reed, Obadiah AR 4th Inf. Co.I
Reed, Oliver TX 6th Cav. Co.A
Reed, Oliver P. MS 31st Inf. Co.I
Reed, Oscar D. TX 12th Cav. Co.I
Reed, Oscar J. SC 5th Cav. Co.D
Reed, Oty. T. VA 42nd Inf. Co.B
Reed, Owen TN 61st Mtd.Inf. Co.A
Reed, P. AL Inf. 2nd Regt. Co.G
Reed, P. AL 26th (O'Neal's) Inf. Co.E 1st Sgt.
Reed, P. GA 31st Inf. Co.E
Reed, P. MS 12th Inf. Co.C
Reed, P. TX 1st Hvy.Arty. Co.K
Reed, P.A. MS 4th Inf. Co.A
Reed, Patrick LA 9th Inf. Co.K,A
Reed, Patrick LA 13th Inf. Co.G,E
Reed, Patrick MS 4th Inf. Co.K
Reed, P.D. GA 10th Inf. Co.I Cpl.
Reed, Perry TN Cav. 16th Bn. (Neal's) Co.E
Reed, Perry TN 29th Inf. Co.H
Reed, Peter TN 12th Inf. Co.G
Reed, Peter T. VA 62nd Mtd.Inf. 2nd Co.H
Reed, P.F. AL 6th Cav. Co.H
Reed, P.H. KY 12th Cav. Co.A,I 1st Sgt.
Reed, P.H. TN 20th Inf. Co.H
Reed, Philip GA 28th Inf. Co.E
Reed, Philip VA 157th Mil. Co.B 1st Sgt.
Reed, Phillip VA 5th Cav. Co.D
Reed, Pinkney TN 55th (McKoin's) Inf. Dillehay's Co.
Reed, Pinkney L. TX 1st (McCulloch's) Cav. Co.D Cpl.
Reed, P.L. TN 33rd Cav. Co.A
Reed, Pleasant MS 42nd Inf. Co.C
Reed, Pleasant TX 21st Cav. Co.L
Reed, Pleasant TX 24th Cav. Co.C
Reed, Prentiss TX 21st Cav. Co.I
Reed, R. VA 2nd Inf.Loc.Def. Co.I
Reed, R.A. AL 26th Inf. Co.C
Reed, R.A. AR Cav. McGehee's Regt. Co.A
Reed, R.A. Gen. & Staff Capt.,AQM
Reed, Rasmus J. MS Cav. 1st Bn. (Miller's) Cole's Co.
Reed, Raymond S. GA 55th Inf. Co.D
Reed, R.B. AL Cav. Hardie's Bn.Res. S.D. McClellan's Co.
Reed, R.B. AL 26th (O'Neal's) Inf. Co.E
Reed, R.C. TN 11th (Holman's) Cav. Co.K
Reed, R.D. TN 9th (Ward's) Cav. Co.E
Reed, R.D. TN Lt.Arty. Morton's Co.
Reed, R.D.P. VA 26th Inf. Co.H
Reed, Reuben C. VA 49th Inf. Co.B
Reed, Reuben R. TN 15th Inf. Co.I Cpl.

Reed, R.F. AR Cav. Crabtree's (46th) Regt. Co.H
Reed, R.F. AR 32nd Inf. Co.H
Reed, R.H. LA 5th Inf. Chap.
Reed, R.H. TN 21st (Wilson's) Cav. Co.H
Reed, R.H. TN 21st & 22nd (Cons.) Cav. Co.H
Reed, R.H. TN 1st (Feild's) & 27th Inf. (Cons.) Co.I
Reed, R.H. TN 27th Inf. Co.F Lt.
Reed, Richard LA C.S. Zouave Bn. Co.F
Reed, Richard C. TX 2nd Inf. Co.E
Reed, Richard F. AR 8th Inf. New Co.C
Reed, Richard H. VA 26th Inf. Co.I
Reed, Richard R. TN 3rd (Clack's) Inf. Co.A
Reed, Richard S. VA 7th Inf. Co.C
Reed, Richard T. TN 15th Cav. Co.A
Reed, Riley VA Inf. 7th Bn.Loc.Def. Co.C
Reed, R.J. AL 28th Inf. Co.I
Reed, R.J. NC 32nd Inf. Co.B
Reed, R.M. GA 52nd Inf. Co.G
Reed, R.M. MS Cav. 1st Bn. (Montgomery's) St.Troops Hammond's Co.
Reed, R.N. GA Tiller's Co. (Echols Lt.Arty.)
Reed, R.O. TX 17th Inf. Co.I Sgt.
Reed, Robt. AL 48th Inf. Co.C
Reed, Robert AR 5th Inf. Co.B
Reed, Robert GA 23rd Inf. Co.A
Reed, Robert LA 13th Inf. Co.B Cpl.
Reed, Robert LA Mil.Cont.Regt. Kirk's Co.
Reed, Robert MO 7th Cav. Co.D
Reed, Robert MO 3rd Inf. Co.A
Reed, Robert TN 21st (Wilson's) Cav. Co.D
Reed, Robert TN 17th Inf. Co.A
Reed, Robert TN 42nd Inf. Co.A
Reed, Robert 4th Conf.Inf. Co.G
Reed, Robert C. TN Holman's Bn.Part.Rangers Co.D
Reed, Robert D. TN 4th (McLemore's) Cav. Co.B
Reed, Robert E. LA 31st Inf. Co.E
Reed, Robert G. AR 33rd Inf. Co.G
Reed, Robert H. NC 3rd Bn.Sr.Res. Co.C
Reed, Robert M. AL 4th (Russell's) Cav. Co.D
Reed, Robert M. TN 34th Inf. Co.B
Reed, Robert N. GA Inf. 1st Loc.Troops (Augusta) Co.G
Reed, Robert P. AR Cav. 1st Bn. (Stirman's) Co.E
Reed, Robert R. GA 23rd Inf. Co.E Cpl.
Reed, Robert S. AL 19th Inf. Co.C 2nd Lt.
Reed, Robert W. VA 31st Mil. QM
Reed, Robert W. Gen. & Staff Capt.,QM
Reed, Romanzo L. NC 18th Inf. Co.G Cpl.
Reed, R.P. MO Cav. 3rd Bn. Co.A
Reed, R.P. TN 21st & 22nd (Cons.) Cav. Co.H Sgt.
Reed, R.P. TX 22nd Inf. Co.E Sgt.
Reed, R.P. Ord.Scouts & Guards Click's Co.,CSA
Reed, R.T. AL 22nd Inf. Co.E
Reed, Ruben C. AL 8th Cav. Co.H 2nd Lt.
Reed, Ruben C. AL 28th Inf. Co.E
Reed, Ruffis R. AL 4th (Russell's) Cav.
Reed, Rufus TN 37th Inf. Co.F Comsy.
Reed, Rufus TN 44th (Cons.) Inf. Co.G
Reed, R.W. GA 64th Inf. Co.B
Reed, R.W. KY 1st (Helm's) Cav. Old Co.G

Reed, S. AL 18th Inf. Co.I
Reed, S. AR 35th Inf. Co.A Cpl.
Reed, S. TX Cav. Bone's Co.
Reed, S. TX Cav. Terry's Regt. Co.I
Reed, S.A. AL 5th Bn.Vol. Sgt.
Reed, S.A. AL 26th (O'Neal's) Inf. Co.K Sgt.
Reed, S.A. TN 15th (Cons.) Cav. Co.F Cpl.
Reed, S.A. TN 15th (Stewart's) Cav. Co.H
Reed, S.A. TN 22nd Inf. Co.I
Reed, Samuel AL Cav. Hardie's Bn.Res. Co.C
Reed, Samuel AL 49th Inf. Co.H
Reed, Samuel AR 34th Inf. Co.E
Reed, Samuel GA 7th Inf. Co.H Cpl.
Reed, Samuel MD 1st Inf. Co.G
Reed, Samuel MS 21st Inf. Co.E
Reed, Samuel MS 26th Inf. Co.H,K
Reed, Samuel TN 14th Cav. Co.E
Reed, Samuel TN 32nd Inf. Co.K
Reed, Samuel TX Cav. 2nd Regt.St.Troops Co.B
Reed, Samuel A. TX Cav. Baylor's Regt. Co.E
Reed, Samuel A. TX 11th Inf. Co.E
Reed, Samuel A. VA 22nd Inf. Co.B Cpl.
Reed, Samuel C. MO 2nd Inf. Co.B Cpl.
Reed, Samuel E. AL 4th Cav. Co.M
Reed, Samuel F. VA 27th Inf. Co.G
Reed, Samuel H. MO 1st Inf. Co.B
Reed, Sam. H. MO 1st & 4th Cons.Inf. Co.D
Reed, Samuel H. Conf.Cav. Wood's Regt. Co.B
Reed, Samuel J. SC 2nd Arty. Co.B Capt.
Reed, Samuel J. TN 3rd (Forrest's) Cav.
Reed, Samuel J. TX 14th Cav. Co.G Cpl.
Reed, Samuel L. AR 8th Inf. New Co.B
Reed, Samuel P. AR 5th Inf. Co.G
Reed, Samuel W. AR 15th (Josey's) Inf. Co.D Sgt.
Reed, S.B. MO 11th Inf. Co.F
Reed, S.C. AL 12th Inf. Co.G
Reed, S.D. AL 12th Cav. Co.C
Reed, S.G. TN 39th Mtd.Inf. Co.A Cpl.
Reed, S.H. MS Inf. 2nd Bn. Co.L
Reed, S.H. MS 15th Inf. Co.K
Reed, S.H. MS 48th Inf. Co.L
Reed, S.H. SC 25th Inf. Co.D
Reed, Shipman AR 11th & 17th (Cons.) Inf. Co.K
Reed, Shipman AR 17th (Griffith's) Inf. Co.D
Reed, Shipman TN Inf. 23rd Bn. Co.D
Reed, Sidney KY 2nd Mtd.Inf. Co.A Sgt.
Reed, Silas AL 31st Inf.
Reed, S.K. AR 34th Inf. Co.B
Reed, S.L. TX Cav. Terry's Regt. Co.D
Reed, S.M. AR 8th Cav. Co.E
Reed, S.M. GA 7th Inf. Co.H
Reed, S.N. AR 1st (Monroe's) Cav. Co.E
Reed, S.N. VA Arty. 3rd Bn. Co.D
Reed, Solomon S. TX 15th Cav. Co.B Cpl.
Reed, Spencer A. TN Cav. 4th Bn. (Branner's) Co.F
Reed, S.S. TX 28th Cav. Co.C,K
Reed, Stephen AR 21st Mil. Co.E
Reed, Stephen KY Inf. Ficklin's Bn.
Reed, Sternbell KY 5th Mtd.Inf. Co.F
Reed, Sumner W. GA 9th Inf. (St.Guards) Co.F
Reed, Sumners AL Res. J.G. Rankin's Co.
Reed, S.W. NC 32nd Inf. Co.B
Reed, Sylvester AL 53rd (Part.Rangers) Co.B
Reed, Sylvester LA 12th Inf. Co.A

Reed, Sylvester D. AL Cav. Lewis' Bn. Co.E
Reed, T. LA Mil. Chalmette Regt. Co.B
Reed, T. TN 27th Inf. Co.D
Reed, T.A.K. GA 60th Inf. Co.I
Reed, T.B. MS 3rd Inf. ACS
Reed, T.B. Gen. & Staff Maj.,Comsy.
Reed, T.C. AL 28th Inf. Co.D
Reed, T.C. MS 28th Cav. Co.A
Reed, T.C. TN 21st (Wilson's) Cav. Co.D Cpl.
Reed, T.C. TN 21st & 22nd (Cons.) Cav. Co.H
Reed, T.C. TX 27th Cav. Co.K
Reed, T.F. AR 34th Inf. Co.B
Reed, T.H. MS 2nd Cav. Co.A
Reed, Thomas AL Randolph Cty.Res. B.C. Raney's Co.
Reed, Thomas AR Cav. Gordon's Regt. Co.B
Reed, Thomas AR 2nd Inf. Co.D Cpl.
Reed, Thomas AR 21st Inf. Co.A
Reed, Thomas AR 21st Inf. Co.D
Reed, Thomas GA Inf. 1st Loc.Troops (Augusta) Co.G
Reed, Thomas GA 3rd Bn. (St.Guards) Co.B
Reed, Thomas KY 2nd (Duke's) Cav. Co.F
Reed, Thomas KY 4th Cav. Co.B
Reed, Thomas KY 12th Cav. Co.F
Reed, Thomas LA Lt.Arty. Fenner's Btty.
Reed, Thomas LA 28th (Thomas') Inf. Co.K Sgt.
Reed, Thomas MS 1st Lt.Arty. Co.E
Reed, Thomas MS Lt.Arty. (Jefferson Arty.) Darden's Co.
Reed, Thomas MS 31st Inf. Co.G
Reed, Thomas MO 16th Inf. Co.F
Reed, Thomas NC 37th Inf. Co.G
Reed, Thomas NC 52nd Inf. Co.G
Reed, Thomas TN 3rd (Clack's) Inf. Co.A Cpl.
Reed, Thomas TN 23rd Inf. 2nd Co.A
Reed, Thomas VA 20th Cav. Co.F,E 3rd Lt.
Reed, Thomas VA 24th Bn.Part.Rangers Co.A
Reed, Thomas VA 30th Bn.S.S. Co.B
Reed, Thomas VA 31st Inf. Co.C
Reed, Thomas VA 114th Mil. Co.K
Reed, Thomas Conf.Lt.Arty. 1st Reg.Btty. Sgt.
Reed, Thomas 1st Choctaw & Chickasaw Mtd.Rifles 1st Co.K Bugler
Reed, Thomas B. AR 1st (Colquitt's) Inf. Co.K
Reed, Thomas B. LA 1st (Strawbridge's) Inf. Co.K,E,F
Reed, Thomas B. LA 9th Inf. Co.A Cpl.
Reed, Thomas B. MS 17th Inf. Co.K
Reed, Thomas B. SC 11th Inf. Co.B
Reed, Thomas B. TX Inf. Griffin's Bn. Co.B
Reed, Thomas B. Gen. & Staff Maj.,CS
Reed, Thomas C. TX 24th Cav. Co.D
Reed, Thomas D. VA Lt.Arty. J.D. Smith's Co.
Reed, Thomas F. MS 46th Inf. Co.E
Reed, Thomas J. TN 15th Inf. Co.E
Reed, Thomas J. TX 16th Inf. Co.D
Reed, Thomas L. AL Cav. 8th Regt. (Livingston's) Co.I
Reed, Thomas L. AL Cav. Moses' Squad. Co.A
Reed, Thomas M. MO 1st N.E. Cav. Price's Co.M
Reed, Thomas M. TX 13th Cav. Co.A
Reed, Thomas N. 1st Conf.Inf. 2nd Co.D
Reed, Thomas P. TN 7th Inf. Co.C Cpl.
Reed, Thomas P. VA 3rd Inf. Co.A

Reed, Thomas S. NC 13th Inf. Co.H
Reed, Thomas S. TN 55th (Brown's) Inf. Co.C
Reed, Thomas W. TN 53rd Inf. Co.G
Reed, Thomas W. TX Cav. 6th Bn. Co.D
Reed, Thomas W. TX 19th Cav. Bugler
Reed, Thomas W. VA 4th Inf. Co.I
Reed, Thompson H. GA Phillips' Legion Co.M
Reed, Tillman AL 12th Inf. Co.G
Reed, Tipton B. AL 19th Inf. Co.D Sgt.
Reed, T.J. AR 12th Inf. Col.
Reed, T.J. GA 54th Inf. Co.B
Reed, T.J. KY 3rd Mtd.Inf. Co.L
Reed, T.J. TN 12th Inf. Co.E
Reed, T.J. TX 1st Inf. Co.G
Reed, T.J. Exch.Bn. 1st Co.A,CSA
Reed, T.L. MO 6th Cav. Co.F
Reed, T.M. SC 12th Inf. Co.H
Reed, T.M. TX 9th Cav. Co.H
Reed, T.M. TX Lt.Inf. & Riflemen Maxey's Co. (Lamar Rifles)
Reed, T.R. TN 9th (Ward's) Cav. Co.E
Reed, T.R. TN Conscr. (Cp. of Instr.)
Reed, Turner KY 2nd Bn.Mtd.Rifles Co.E Sgt.
Reed, T.W. MS 10th Inf. Old Co.K
Reed, T.W. SC 6th Res. Co.E
Reed, T.W. TX 21st Cav. Co.E
Reed, T.W. VA Inf. 25th Bn. Co.D
Reed, T.W. 20th Conf.Cav. Co.A
Reed, Valentine LA 1st Hvy.Arty. (Reg.) Co.A
Reed, Vardiman M. MO Cav. 3rd Bn. Co.A Sgt.
Reed, Venira C. VA 17th Cav. Co.D
Reed, Vincent A. VA 2nd Cav. Co.H
Reed, Virgil M. GA 23rd Inf. Co.H
Reed, W. LA 25th Inf. Co.F
Reed, W.A. AR Cav. Gordon's Regt. Co.E
Reed, W.A. AR 14th (McCarver's) Inf. Co.E
Reed, W.A. GA Inf. 1st City Bn. (Columbus) Co.A
Reed, W.A. GA 20th Inf. Co.D
Reed, W.A. KY 3rd Mtd.Inf. Co.G Cpl.
Reed, W.A. TN 45th Inf. Co.C
Reed, Walden MO 12th Inf. Co.D
Reed, Walter AL 22nd Inf. Co.G
Reed, W.A.P. GA 15th Inf. Co.H
Reed, W.A.P. GA Inf. 23rd Bn.Loc.Def. Pendergrass' Co.C
Reed, Warren TX Granbury's Cons.Brig. Co.A
Reed, Warren TX 6th Inf. Co.F
Reed, Washington MS 34th Inf. Co.B Cpl.
Reed, Washington Sig.Corps,CSA
Reed, Watson LA 31st Inf. Co.E
Reed, W.B. AR Cav. Crabtree's (46th) Regt. Co.H
Reed, W.B. AR 50th Mil. Co.C
Reed, W.B. VA 7th Cav. Glenn's Co.
Reed, W.C. AL 47th Inf. Co.D
Reed, W.C. AR 1st (Dobbin's) Cav. Co.C
Reed, W.C. MS Arty. (Wesson Arty.) Kittrell's Co.
Reed, W.C. NC 1st Inf. Co.D
Reed, W.C. TN 15th (Cons.) Cav. Co.I
Reed, W.C. TN 13th Inf. Co.E
Reed, W.D. AL Cp. of Instr. Talladega
Reed, W.D. LA 22nd (Cons.) Inf. Co.D
Reed, W.D. MS 23rd Inf. Co.A
Reed, W.D. TN 19th & 20th (Cons.) Cav.

Reed, Wesley KY 10th (Diamond's) Cav. Co.H
Reed, Wesley VA 8th Cav. Co.H
Reed, W.F. AL Pris.Guard Freeman's Co.
Reed, W.F. GA Cav. 29th Bn.
Reed, W.F. GA 3rd Bn. (St.Guards) Co.F
Reed, W.F. SC Mil. Charbonnier's Co.
Reed, W.G. TN 41st Inf. 1st Lt.
Reed, W.G. Gen. & Staff 2nd Lt.,Dr.M.
Reed, W.H. AL 7th Cav. Co.H
Reed, W.H. AL 26th (O'Neal's) Inf. Co.K
Reed, W.H. AR 37th Inf. Co.A
Reed, W.H. GA Cav. 1st Bn.Res.
Reed, W.H. KY 5th Cav. Co.E 1st Sgt.
Reed, W.H. KY 9th Cav. Co.A
Reed, W.H. TN 5th (McKenzie's) Cav. Co.A
Reed, W.H. TX 29th Cav. Co.I
Reed, W.H. TX Cav. Terry's Regt. Co.A
Reed, W.H. TX 22nd Inf. Co.E
Reed, W.M. VA 42nd Inf.
Reed, Wiley KY 5th Mtd.Inf. Co.B
Reed, Wiley C. AL Cp. of Instr. Talladega
Reed, Wiley J. GA 35th Inf. Co.E
Reed, Wiley J. TN 25th Inf. Co.I Capt.
Reed, Wilie TX 21st Cav. Co.I
Reed, Willas D. VA 4th Res. Co.I
Reed, William AL Lt.Arty. 2nd Bn. Co.B
Reed, Wm. AL 26th Inf. Co.E
Reed, William AL 55th Vol. Co.G
Reed, William AR 7th Cav. Co.L
Reed, William AR 16th Inf. Co.K
Reed, William AR 18th (Marmaduke's) Inf. Co.F Capt.
Reed, William AR 27th Inf. Co.G Cpl.
Reed, William AR 30th Inf. Co.A
Reed, William AR 34th Inf. Co.B
Reed, William AR Inf. Cocke's Regt. Co.B
Reed, William GA Cav. Logan's Co. (White Cty. Old Men's Home Guards)
Reed, William GA 3rd Inf. Co.G Cpl.
Reed, William GA 16th Inf. Co.C
Reed, William GA 21st Inf.
Reed, William GA 60th Inf. Co.E
Reed, William KY 8th Mtd.Inf. Co.D
Reed, William LA 2nd Res.Corps Co.B
Reed, William LA 2nd Res.Corps Co.I
Reed, William LA 18th Inf. Co.K
Reed, William LA Inf. Weatherly's Bn. Co.D
Reed, William MD Cav. 2nd Bn. Co.D 1st Lt.
Reed, William MS 2nd St.Cav. Co.A 2nd Lt.
Reed, William MS 1st Inf. Co.A
Reed, William MS 7th Inf. Co.A
Reed, Wm. MS Cav. 2nd Regt.Res. Sgt.
Reed, William MS 34th Inf. Co.A
Reed, William MO 3rd Cav. Co.H
Reed, William MO 4th Cav. Co.A
Reed, William MO Lt.Arty. Parsons' Co.
Reed, William MO Inf. 4th Regt.St.Guard Co.C
Reed, William MO 11th Inf. Co.C
Reed, William MO 11th Inf.
Reed, William MO 16th Inf. Co.F
Reed, William MO Thompson's Command
Reed, William NC Walker's Bn. Thomas' Legion 2nd Co.D
Reed, William SC Mil. 1st Regt. (Charleston Res.) Co.A
Reed, William SC 1st (McCreary's) Inf. Campbell's Co.L

Reed, William TN 3rd (Forrest's) Cav. Co.A 3rd Lt.
Reed, William TN Lt.Arty. Baxter's Co.
Reed, William TN 17th Inf. Co.A
Reed, William TN 19th Inf. Co.E
Reed, William TN 42nd Inf. Co.D Sgt.
Reed, William TN 42nd Inf. 1st Co.H
Reed, William TN 53rd Inf. Co.G
Reed, William TX 21st Cav. Co.I
Reed, William TX 1st Hvy.Arty. Co.K
Reed, William TX 11th Inf. Co.H
Reed, William TX Inf. Griffin's Bn. Co.B
Reed, William VA 12th Cav. Co.F
Reed, William VA Horse Arty. G.W. Brown's Co.
Reed, William VA 4th Res. Co.H,I
Reed, William VA 8th Inf. Co.A
Reed, William VA 25th Mil. Co.C
Reed, William VA 52nd Inf. Co.C
Reed, William 3rd Conf.Inf. Co.F Capt.
Reed, William A. AR 15th Mil. Co.C Sgt.
Reed, William A. NC 45th Inf. Co.C
Reed, William A. SC 22nd Inf. Co.D
Reed, William A.P. GA 34th Inf. Co.G
Reed, William B. AL 50th Inf.
Reed, William B. GA 64th Inf. Co.F
Reed, William B. TN 3rd (Forrest's) Cav. Co.H Black.
Reed, William B. TN 33rd Inf. Co.D
Reed, William B. VA 12th Cav. Co.A
Reed, William B. VA 2nd Inf. Co.H
Reed, William B. VA 31st Inf. Co.I
Reed, William B. VA 52nd Inf. Co.I
Reed, William C. TN 3rd (Forrest's) Cav.
Reed, William C. TX 16th Inf. Co.F
Reed, William C. VA Lt.Arty. J.D. Smith's Co.
Reed, William D. AL 1st Cav.
Reed, William D. AR 7th Inf. Co.H
Reed, William D. TX 17th Inf. Co.E 3rd Lt.
Reed, William E. VA 12th Cav. Co.C
Reed, William F. FL 5th Inf. Co.B
Reed, William F. LA 21st (Patton's) Inf. Co.B Cpl.
Reed, William F. NC 9th Bn.S.S. Co.A
Reed, William G. GA 63rd Inf. Co.G 2nd Lt.
Reed, William G. MS 4th Inf. Co.K,C
Reed, William H. AR 12th Inf. Co.D Jr.2nd Lt.
Reed, William H. KY 5th Mtd.Inf. Co.C
Reed, William H. LA 1st Hvy.Arty. (Reg.) Co.H
Reed, William H. MO 8th Cav. Reed's Co. 2nd Lt.
Reed, William H. MO 2nd Inf. Co.B
Reed, William H. NC 5th Inf. Co.B
Reed, William H. VA 5th Inf. Co.K
Reed, William H. VA 32nd Inf. 2nd Co.K
Reed, William H. VA 55th Inf. Co.A
Reed, William J. AL 19th Inf. Co.E Sgt.
Reed, William J. AR 2nd Cav. Co.C Sgt.
Reed, William J. MS 16th Inf. Co.D
Reed, William J. TN 2nd Cav. 1st Lt.
Reed, William J. TN 2nd (Robison's) Inf. Co.B 1st Lt.
Reed, William J. VA 6th Cav. Co.K
Reed, William L. TX 24th Cav. Co.F
Reed, William L. TX Cav. Hardeman's Regt. Co.B
Reed, William M. AL 56th Part.Rangers Co.F

Reed, William M. TN 53rd Inf. Co.A
Reed, William M. VA 15th Inf. Co.B
Reed, William P. AR 8th Cav. Co.H
Reed, William P. GA Inf. 11th Bn. (St.Guards) Co.B
Reed, William P. GA 35th Inf. Chap.
Reed, William P. GA 36th (Broyles') Inf. Co.E
Reed, William P. LA 18th Inf. Co.D
Reed, William P. TX 11th Cav. Co.F Cpl.
Reed, Wm. P. Gen. & Staff Chap.
Reed, William S. LA 7th Inf. Co.A
Reed, William S. TX 15th Cav. Co.B Sgt.
Reed, William T. AL 12th Cav. Co.A
Reed, William T. AL Cp. of Instr. Talladega
Reed, William T. AR 9th Inf. Co.C
Reed, William T. KY 2nd Cav. Co.F
Reed, William T. LA 2nd Inf. Cpl.
Reed, William T. MD Inf. 2nd Bn. Co.G
Reed, William T. VA 26th Cav. Co.F
Reed, William T. VA Cav. 46th Bn. Co.F
Reed, William W. SC 12th Inf. Co.G Sgt.
Reed, Will K. AL 26th (O'Neal's) Inf. Co.H
Reed, Wilson GA 24th Inf. Co.E
Reed, W.J. AL 22nd Inf. Co.E
Reed, W.J. AR Inf. Cocke's Regt. Co.H Cpl.
Reed, W.J. AR 35th Inf. Co.B
Reed, W.J. GA 11th Inf. Co.C
Reed, W.J. GA Phillips' Legion Co.C
Reed, W.J. MS 6th Inf. Co.E Sgt.
Reed, W.J. 20th Conf.Cav. Co.B
Reed, W.L. AL Cav. Hardie's Bn.Res. Co.C
Reed, W.L. GA 2nd Inf. Co.B
Reed, W.L. TN 47th Inf. Co.K
Reed, W.M. AL 13th Bn.Part.Rangers Co.B
Reed, W.M. MS 5th Cav. Lt.Col.
Reed, W.M. TN 8th (Smith's) Cav. Co.G
Reed, W.M. TN 55th (Brown's) Inf. Lt.Col.
Reed, W.M. VA Lt.Arty. Barr's Co.
Reed, W.M. Gen. & Staff, Adj.Gen. Dept. Capt.
Reed, W.N. AL 12th Cav. Co.B
Reed, W.N. KY 4th Cav. Co.G
Reed, W.N. MS 2nd St.Cav. Co.G Sgt.
Reed, W.P. GA 1st Cav. Co.K,B Sgt.
Reed, W.P. LA Mil. 4th Regt. 3rd Brig. 1st Div. Co.A Cpl.
Reed, W.P. LA Inf.Cons. 18th Regt. & Yellow Jacket Bn. Co.E
Reed, W.P. NC 7th Sr.Res. Watts' Co.
Reed, W.R. MO 4th Inf. Co.E
Reed, W.S. VA Inf. 25th Bn. Co.G Capt.
Reed, W.S. Gen. & Staff,PACS Capt.
Reed, W. Shelby Gen. & Staff, Mil.Dept. Capt.,ADC
Reed, W.T. AL Pris.Guard Freeman's Co.
Reed, W.T. MS Cav. (St.Troops) Gamblin's Co.
Reed, W.T. MS 46th Inf. Co.F
Reed, W.T. TX Inf. Timmons' Regt. Co.I
Reed, W.W. GA 5th Res. Co.E
Reed, W.W. GA Inf. 17th Bn. (St.Guards) Fay's Co.
Reed, W.W. MS 2nd (Davidson's) Inf. Co.A
Reed, W.W. MS 9th Inf. Co.D
Reed, W.W. MS 9th Bn.S.S. Co.A
Reed, W.W. SC 2nd Inf. Co.F
Reed, W.W. TX Cav. Bourland's Regt. Co.G
Reed, Wyly M. TN 55th (McKoin's) Inf. Co.I Capt.

Reed, Younger TN 2nd (Robison's) Inf. Co.H
Reed, Zachariah M. GA 34th Inf. Co.E
Reed, Zalmon MS 42nd Inf. Co.C
Reed, Zenon LA 28th (Thomas') Inf. Co.K
Reedar, J.W. KY 7th Cav. Co.D
Reede, --- AL 12th Inf. Co.E
Reede, Alexander VA Cav. 46th Bn. Co.A
Reede, C.C.E. AL Cav. Falkner's Co.
Reede, E.S. MS St.Cav. 3rd Bn. (Cooper's) 1st Co.A
Reede, George LA 1st Hvy.Arty. (Reg.) Co.B
Reede, G.W. AL 43rd Inf. Co.A,E
Reede, J.A. TN 30th Inf. Co.E
Reede, J.S. LA 27th Inf. Co.B
Reede, R. LA 27th Inf. Co.B
Reede, V.K. LA 27th Inf. Co.B
Reede, William TN Cav. 16th Bn. (Neal's) Co.E
Reede, William 4th Conf.Inf. Co.K
Reedeker, Lewis LA 22nd Inf. D.H. Marks' Co.
Reeder, --- AL 26th (O'Neal's) Inf. Lt.Col.
Reeder, A.D. TX 10th Cav. Co.A
Reeder, A.J. VA 18th Cav. Co.A Sgt.
Reeder, Alfred AL Mobile City Troop
Reeder, Alfred A. AL Mil. 2nd Regt.Vol. Co.B
Reeder, A.M. SC 3rd Inf. Co.B
Reeder, A.M. SC 5th St.Troops Co.C
Reeder, A.M. SC 9th Res. Co.F Sgt.
Reeder, A.M. SC Post Guard Senn's Co.
Reeder, A.N. TX 10th Cav. Co.A
Reeder, Andrew J. TN 25th Inf. Co.H
Reeder, Andrew J. VA 25th Inf. 2nd Co.B
Reeder, A.V. NC 55th Inf. Co.I
Reeder, A.W. SC Inf. Holcombe Legion Co.G
Reeder, B.F. SC 22nd Inf. Co.K
Reeder, C. TN Inf. 154th Sr.Regt. Co.A Sgt.
Reeder, Charles AL 4th (Roddey's) Cav. Co.F
Reeder, Claborn MO Inf. 4th Regt.St.Guard Co.D 2nd Lt.
Reeder, Claiborne MO 6th Inf. Co.D
Reeder, Daniel AR 5th Inf. Co.E
Reeder, David MS Cav. Jeff Davis Legion Co.B
Reeder, D.D. AR Inf. Hardy's Regt. Co.G
Reeder, D.H. TN Inf. 3rd Bn. Co.A
Reeder, E.C. AR Inf. Hardy's Regt. Co.G
Reeder, E.E. AR Inf. Hardy's Regt. Co.G
Reeder, Elijah MS Cav. Jeff Davis Legion Co.B
Reeder, Elijah TN 13th (Gore's) Cav. Co.B
Reeder, Ernest LA Mil. 4th Regt. 1st Brig. 1st Div. Co.C
Reeder, G.H. TN Conscr. (Cp. of Instr.)
Reeder, Gideon S. VA 62nd Mtd.Inf. 2nd Co.E
Reeder, H. 2nd Conf.Eng.Troops Co.A
Reeder, Henry MS Inf. Lewis' Co.
Reeder, H.M. TX Cav. McCord's Frontier Regt. Co.E
Reeder, Isaac MS 31st Inf. Co.A Sgt.
Reeder, J. TX 2nd Inf. Co.C
Reeder, J.A. MS 2nd Cav. Co.E
Reeder, Jacob KY 3rd Mtd.Inf. Co.G
Reeder, James A. KY 2nd Mtd.Inf. Co.K
Reeder, James H. SC 22nd Inf. Co.D
Reeder, James J. SC Inf. Holcombe Legion Co.G Bvt.2nd Lt.
Reeder, James W. KY 3rd Mtd.Inf. Co.G
Reeder, Jasper AR Cav. Gordon's Regt. Co.A
Reeder, J.B. SC 2nd Res.
Reeder, J.F. AL Cp. of Instr. Talladega

Reeder, J.H. SC 22nd Inf. Co.K 2nd Lt.
Reeder, J.J. SC 9th Res. Co.F
Reeder, J.K. AR 36th Inf. Co.I
Reeder, J.L. SC Cav. 2nd Bn.Res. Co.H Sgt.
Reeder, J.L. SC 7th Inf. Co.K
Reeder, J.N. GA Inf. 9th Bn. Co.A
Reeder, John AR 15th (Josey's) Inf. 1st Co.G
Reeder, John KY 3rd Mtd.Inf. Co.G
Reeder, John LA 4th Cav. Co.F
Reeder, John MS Wilson's Co. (Ponticola Guards)
Reeder, John TN 10th Inf. Co.D
Reeder, John E. VA 8th Inf. Co.A
Reeder, John H. SC Inf. Holcombe Legion Co.G
Reeder, John H.L. TN 11th Inf. Co.K
Reeder, John W. AR Inf. Hardy's Regt. Co.I Bvt.2nd Lt.
Reeder, John W. KY 3rd Mtd.Inf. Co.G
Reeder, John W. KY 6th Mtd.Inf. Co.I
Reeder, John W. LA 9th Inf. Co.A
Reeder, Joseph MS Standefer's Co. 1st Sgt.
Reeder, Joseph TX 3rd Cav. Co.E
Reeder, Joseph C. AR 19th (Dawson's) Inf. Co.B
Reeder, Joseph W. VA 19th Cav. Co.C Capt.
Reeder, Joseph W. VA 3rd Cav. & Inf.St.Line Co.D 2nd Lt.
Reeder, J.R.C. SC 3rd Inf. Co.B Sgt.
Reeder, J.S. SC 9th Res. Co.K
Reeder, J.W. AL 4th (Roddey's) Cav. Co.F
Reeder, J.W. AR Lt.Arty. Etter's Btty.
Reeder, J.W. AR 19th (Dawson's) Inf. Co.I
Reeder, J.W. GA 20th Inf. Co.K Sgt.
Reeder, J.W. 10th Conf.Cav. Co.A
Reeder, Levi MO 12th Inf. Co.B
Reeder, Lewis TN 14th Inf. Co.C
Reeder, Lewis T. SC 1st (Orr's) Rifles Co.F 1st Lt.
Reeder, L.G. TN 1st Cav. Co.C
Reeder, L.L. AR Inf. Hardy's Regt. Co.I Sgt.
Reeder, M.B. SC 1st Regt. Charleston Guard Co.A
Reeder, M.H. GA Inf. 2nd Bn. (St.Guards) Co.C
Reeder, Nathaniel GA 16th Inf. Co.H Capt.
Reeder, Noah NC 44th Inf. Co.H
Reeder, Oscar MO 5th Cav. Co.D
Reeder, Oscar MO Cav. Stallard's Co.
Reeder, P.H. AL 9th Inf. Co.D
Reeder, Philip T. MD Inf. 2nd Bn. Co.B 1st Sgt.
Reeder, P.M. TN 2nd (Ashby's) Cav. Co.B,E
Reeder, R.C. AL 42nd Inf. Co.I Capt.
Reeder, Reuben A. AL 4th (Roddey's) Cav. Co.F
Reeder, Richmond C. AL Mil. 2nd Regt.Vol. Co.B 2nd Lt.
Reeder, R.S. SC Inf. 1st (Charleston) Bn. Co.D
Reeder, R.S. SC 27th Inf. Co.D
Reeder, Samuel TN 1st Hvy.Arty. Co.L QMSgt.
Reeder, Samuel TN Hvy.Arty. Johnston's Co.
Reeder, Samuel D. AR 20th Inf. Co.A Sgt.
Reeder, Samuel N. AR 18th (Marmaduke's) Inf. Co.G 1st Lt.
Reeder, Samuel P. KY 1st (Butler's) Cav. Co.D
Reeder, Samuel P. KY 1st Inf. Co.D Sgt.
Reeder, S.D. MS 20th Inf. Co.A Cpl.
Reeder, Simon LA Mil. Mech.Guard
Reeder, Simon H. VA 25th Cav. Co.F Sgt.
Reeder, Simon H. VA 54th Inf. Co.I Cpl.

Reeder, S.N. AR Pine Bluff Arty. 1st Lt.
Reeder, S.N. 3rd Conf.Inf. Co.G Lt.
Reeder, T.H. SC 2nd Arty. Co.K
Reeder, T.H. SC Arty. Manigault's Bn. 1st Co.A
Reeder, T.H. SC 2nd Inf. Co.I
Reeder, Thomas AL Cav. Barbiere's Bn. Truss' Co.
Reeder, Thomas AR 17th (Griffith's) Inf. Co.H
Reeder, Thomas TN 13th (Gore's) Cav. Co.E Sgt.
Reeder, Thomas TN 3rd (Lillard's) Mtd.Inf. Co.C
Reeder, Thomas TN 25th Inf. Co.H Cpl.
Reeder, Thomas TX 15th Cav. Co.I
Reeder, Thomas TX 20th Cav. Co.C
Reeder, T.J. AR 11th & 17th (Cons.) Inf. Co.H,K
Reeder, T.M. SC 1st (Orr's) Rifles Co.F
Reeder, W. LA 17th Inf. Co.H
Reeder, W. TX 37th Cav. Co.E
Reeder, William AL Mobile City Troop Sgt.
Reeder, William SC Arty. Manigault's Bn. 1st Co.A
Reeder, William SC 2nd Inf. Co.F
Reeder, William SC 9th Res. Co.F Sgt.
Reeder, William SC Mil. 17th Regt. Buist's Co.
Reeder, William SC 20th Inf. Co.F
Reeder, William C. AL 9th Inf. Co.D 1st Lt.
Reeder, William F. TX 25th Cav. Co.C
Reeder, William H. TN 4th (McLemore's) Cav. Co.D
Reeder, William L. MS 2nd Inf. Co.I
Reeder, William T. AL 28th Inf. Co.G,C
Reeder, W.J. AR 1st (Monroe's) Cav. Co.D
Reeder, W.L. TX 20th Cav.
Reeder, W.M. 1st Conf.Cav. 2nd Co.A
Reeder, W.M. 1st Conf.Cav. 2nd Co.B
Reeder, W.T. Trans-MS Conf.Cav. 1st Bn. Co.E
Reedey, C. GA 2nd Mil. Co.H
Reedish, W.H. SC 2nd Arty. Co.F
Reedon, H.F. NC 50th Inf. Co.C
Reeds, J.M. KY 3rd Mtd.Inf. Co.L
Reeds, J.M. TN 12th Inf. Co.E Sgt.
Reeds, Josiah M. TX 17th Inf. Co.C
Reedus, G.W. MS Inf. 2nd St.Troops Co.G
Reedus, W.F. MS 34th Inf. Co.K
Reedy, Abraham VA 146th Mil. Co.E Cpl.
Reedy, Abram VA 50th Inf. Co.D
Reedy, Abram VA Mil. Grayson Cty.
Reedy, A.J. MS 35th Inf. Co.F
Reedy, Andrew VA 50th Inf. Co.D
Reedy, Ben F. TX 17th Cons.Dismtd.Cav. Co.E, 1st Co.G
Reedy, Benjamin F. TX 18th Cav. Co.C
Reedy, B.G. GA Inf. 19th Bn. (St.Guards) Co.B
Reedy, Calvin N. NC 26th Inf. Co.A
Reedy, C.F. 3rd Conf.Eng.Troops Co.H Cpl.
Reedy, Chrisley VA Inf. 23rd Bn. Co.E
Reedy, Christopher VA 21st Cav. 1st Co.E, 2nd Co.I
Reedy, Christopher C. NC McMillan's Co. Sgt.
Reedy, Christophy C. VA 50th Inf. Co.D
Reedy, David VA 7th Cav. Co.K
Reedy, David VA 10th Cav. Co.H
Reedy, David R. VA 37th Inf. Co.F
Reedy, David W. TX 18th Cav. Co.C
Reedy, Dennis LA 5th Inf. Co.B

Reedy, E.A. TN 8th (Smith's) Cav. Co.E
Reedy, Eli VA 58th Mil. Co.K
Reedy, Elias VA 50th Inf. Co.D
Reedy, Elijah H. VA 37th Inf. Co.F
Reedy, Ezekiel J. VA Inf. 23rd Bn. Co.A Sgt.
Reedy, Frank E. VA 43rd Inf. Co.G
Reedy, Franklin VA 63rd Inf. Co.C
Reedy, Frederick NC 25th Inf. Co.D
Reedy, George AL 58th Inf.
Reedy, George E. AL 55th Vol. Co.J,K Sgt.
Reedy, George N. VA 4th Cav. Co.C
Reedy, George W. NC 58th Inf. Co.L
Reedy, George W. TX 18th Cav. Co.C
Reedy, George W. VA 33rd Inf. Co.B
Reedy, Grane. W. VA Mil. Grayson Cty.
Reedy, Granville W. VA 63rd Inf. Co.C
Reedy, Harman VA 33rd Inf. Co.B
Reedy, H.J. MS 1st (Patton's) Inf. Halfacre's Co.
Reedy, Isaac VA 7th Cav. Co.B
Reedy, Isaac VA 33rd Inf. Co.B
Reedy, Isaac VA 51st Inf. Co.I
Reedy, Israel VA 33rd Inf. Co.B
Reedy, Jackson VA 50th Inf. Co.D
Reedy, Jacob VA Cav. 37th Bn. Co.D
Reedy, Jacob VA 33rd Inf. Co.B,A
Reedy, Jacob VA Mil. Grayson Cty.
Reedy, James C. MS 23rd Inf. Co.G Cpl.
Reedy, James H. Gen. & Staff Cadet
Reedy, James M. MO 10th Inf. Co.E
Reedy, James M. VA 50th Inf. Co.D
Reedy, James W. VA 50th Inf. Co.D
Reedy, J.B. MS 26th Inf. Co.F
Reedy, J.C. MS 10th Inf. New Co.K Cpl.
Reedy, J.C. 7th Conf.Cav. Co.K Lt.
Reedy, Jesse NC 26th Inf. Co.A
Reedy, J.H. AL 4th (Russell's) Cav. Co.F
Reedy, John AR 2nd Inf. Co.B
Reedy, John TN 2nd (Walker's) Inf. Co.K
Reedy, John VA Cav. O'Ferrall's Bn. Co.B
Reedy, John VA 33rd Inf. Co.B
Reedy, John 9th Conf.Inf. Co.A
Reedy, John C. GA 31st Inf. Co.B 2nd Lt.
Reedy, John H. LA 6th Inf. Co.B
Reedy, John J. MS 7th Cav. Co.B 2nd Lt.
Reedy, John J. MS 23rd Inf. Co.G
Reedy, John W. AR 3rd Inf. Co.G Maj.
Reedy, Joseph VA 11th Cav. Co.C
Reedy, Joseph VA 51st Inf. Co.I
Reedy, J.T. AL 20th Inf. Co.A
Reedy, J.W. LA 2nd Inf. Co.D
Reedy, Levi VA 9th Bn.Res. Co.D 1st Lt.
Reedy, Linnville VA Inf. French's Bn. Powers' Co.D, Co.B
Reedy, Loque AL 4th (Russell's) Cav. Co.F,A
Reedy, M. LA Mil. British Guard Bn. Coburn's Co.
Reedy, Mitchel C. VA Inf. 23rd Bn. Co.A
Reedy, Philip VA 58th Mil. Co.I
Reedy, P.W. AL 20th Inf. Co.A
Reedy, Riley VA 63rd Inf. Co.C
Reedy, Riley VA Mil. Grayson Cty.
Reedy, Romanus VA 62nd Mtd.Inf. 2nd Co.K
Reedy, Samuel MS 2nd Cav. Co.A,H
Reedy, Samuel VA 4th Inf. Co.D
Reedy, Samuel VA 33rd Inf. Co.B
Reedy, Samuel VA Mil. Washington Cty.
Reedy, Solomon VA 63rd Inf. Co.C

Reedy, Solomon VA Mil. Grayson Cty.
Reedy, T.B. MS 7th Cav. Co.B
Reedy, Thomas AL 9th Inf. Co.B
Reedy, Thomas GA Hvy.Arty. 22nd Bn. Co.C
Reedy, Thomas SC Hvy.Arty. 15th (Lucas') Bn. Co.A Cpl.
Reedy, Thomas B. MS 23rd Inf. Co.G
Reedy, W.A. AL 20th Inf. Co.A
Reedy, Wilborn VA Inf. French's Bn. Co.B
Reedy, William NC 52nd Inf. Co.K
Reedy, William TN 17th Inf. Co.D
Reedy, William VA Mil. Grayson Cty.
Reedy, William A. AR 33rd Inf. Co.E
Reedy, William B. VA 37th Inf. Co.F,K
Reedy, William H. VA 33rd Inf. Co.B Sgt.
Reedy, W.J. TX Cav. 1st Regt.St.Troops Co.A Capt.
Reedy, W.J. TX Cav. Border's Regt. Co.D Jr.2nd Lt.
Reedy, W.M. SC 1st Cav. Co.D
Reedy, W.P. AL Inf. 2nd Regt. Co.I
Reedy, W.P. AL 63rd Inf. Co.I
Reedy, W.S. TX 5th Inf. Co.E
Reefo, Theodor C. 1st Conf.Inf. 1st Co.F
Reeg, Cristof LA Mil. 4th Regt. 1st Brig. 1st Div. Co.A
Reegan, John AL 1st Regt. Mobile Vol. Co.K 3rd Lt.
Reegs, F. AL 6th Inf. Co.M Lt.
Reeh, Andree LA Mil. Cazadores Espanoles Regt. Co.D Sgt.
Reeh, Christian TX 33rd Cav. Co.B
Reeh, Rudolph TX 36th Cav. Co.F
Reekes, Saul H. KY Cav. Malone's Regt.
Reekes, Thomas E. NC 12th Inf. Co.D,B
Reeks, George C. AL 61st Inf. Co.A
Reeks, J.I. TN 42nd Inf. Co.C
Reeks, John LA Supp.Force Co.A
Reeks, John B. LA Inf. 11th Bn. Co.C Cpl.
Reeks, John G. SC Palmetto S.S. Co.I
Reeks, John T. LA 14th (Austin's) Bn.S.S. Co.A
Reel, Albert NC 3rd Arty. (40th St.Troops) Co.D Cpl.
Reel, Andrew TN 13th (Gore's) Cav. Co.C
Reel, Daniel NC 22nd Inf. Co.K
Reel, Daniel M. TX 32nd Cav. Co.D
Reel, Daniel R. NC 52nd Inf. Co.H
Reel, David VA 14th Mil. Co.B
Reel, Ed TN 35th Inf. Co.H
Reel, Edward MS 15th Inf. Co.K
Reel, Edward D. MS 27th Inf. Co.A
Reel, George MS 8th Cav. Co.K Cpl.
Reel, George W. TN 13th (Gore's) Cav. Co.C
Reel, Henry SC 5th Res. Co.E
Reel, Henry SC 6th Inf. Co.E
Reel, Jackson MS 15th Inf. Co.K
Reel, Jacob AR 4th Vol. Hutchinson's Co.
Reel, Jacob VA 25th Inf. 1st Co.K
Reel, James H. NC Mallett's Bn. (Cp.Guard) Co.B
Reel, James M. NC 2nd Inf. Co.F Sgt.
Reel, J.J. TN Inf. 154th Sr.Regt. Co.C
Reel, John MS 27th Inf. Co.A Music.
Reel, John NC 49th Inf. Co.A
Reel, J.P. MS Inf. 2nd St.Troops Co.M
Reel, J.S. TN 13th (Gore's) Cav. Co.C
Reel, J.W. 2nd Conf.Inf. Co.G

Reel, M.A. AR 1st Mtd.Rifles Co.D
Reel, M.A. AR 2nd Mtd.Rifles Co.G
Reel, M.A. AR 2nd Inf.
Reel, Martin VA 25th Inf. 2nd Co.E
Reel, Ml. LA Mil. 4th Regt. 1st Brig. 1st Div. Co.K
Reel, Oscar AR 23rd Inf. Co.A
Reel, Peter MS 8th Cav. Co.K
Reel, Peter H. TN 43rd Inf. Co.C
Reel, Philip W. AR 9th Inf. New Co.I Sgt.
Reel, Philip W. MS 25th Inf. Co.G Sgt.
Reel, P.W. 3rd Conf.Inf. Co.G Sgt.
Reel, Standafer NC Cav. 7th Bn. Co.E
Reel, Stanopher NC 6th Cav. (65th St.Troops) Co.D,E
Reel, Thomas L. MS 12th Inf. Co.I
Reel, William NC 58th Inf. Co.F
Reel, William C. VA 62nd Mtd.Inf. 2nd Co.H
Reel, William P. AR 24th Inf. Co.F
Reel, William P. AR Inf. Hardy's Regt. Co.D
Reel, W.P. AR 12th Inf. Co.K
Reeley, I.E. LA Red River S.S.
Reels, W.I. GA Siege Arty. Campbell's Ind.Co.
Reely, Benjamin F. VA 57th Inf. Co.F
Reely, George VA 58th Mil. Co.F
Reem, J.W. LA Mil.Conf.Guards Regt. Co.G Sgt.
Reeme, John M. MS 1st Lt.Arty. Co.F
Reemer, Alfred KY 5th Cav. Co.G
Reems, Benjamin L. SC Inf. Hampton Legion Co.B
Reems, Felix SC 1st (Orr's) Rifles Co.A
Reems, H. TN Inf. 4th Cons.Regt. Co.C
Reen, John F. GA Inf. 18th Bn. (St.Guards) Co.E
Reen, S.W. VA Cav. Mosby's Regt. (Part. Rangers) Co.D
Reen, Timothy AL 14th Inf. Co.E
Reene, Richard LA 9th Inf.
Reeny, Andrew J. VA 45th Inf. Co.E
Reep, Adam NC 46th Inf. Co.K
Reep, Albert M. NC 32nd Inf. Co.D,E
Reep, Christopher NC 32nd Inf. Co.D,E
Reep, Daniel NC 4th Sr.Res. Co.K
Reep, Daniel A. NC 32nd Inf. Co.D,E
Reep, George NC 49th Inf. Co.K
Reep, Jesse NC 34th Inf. Co.E
Reep, John NC 23rd Inf. Co.D
Reep, Jonas NC 23rd Inf. Co.K
Reep, Jones GA 38th Inf. Co.I Sgt.
Reep, Joseph L. AR 25th Inf. Co.H
Reep, Laban NC 34th Inf. Co.E
Reep, Lawson NC 4th Bn.Jr.Res. Co.B
Reep, Marcus D. AR 2nd Mtd.Rifles Co.C
Reep, Obed NC 23rd Inf. Co.K
Reep, P.A. NC 2nd Jr.Res. Co.C
Reep, Peter NC 23rd Inf. Co.B
Reep, Peter VA 14th Cav. Co.L
Reep, Peter VA 17th Cav. Co.I
Reep, Thomas NC 11th (Bethel Regt.) Inf. Co.I
Reep, William J. AR 1st (Colquitt's) Inf. Co.I
Rees, A.C. GA Cav. 7th Bn. (St.Guards) Co.G
Rees, A.E. KY 8th Mtd.Inf. Co.G Sgt.
Rees, A.J. MS Inf. 1st Bn. Co.A
Rees, A.J. TN 11th Inf. Co.G
Rees, Alonzo TX Cav. McCord's Frontier Regt. Co.A Capt.

Rees, Alson NC 6th Cav. (65th St.Troops) Co.E
Rees, A.M. GA 23rd Inf. Co.F
Rees, B. MO 2nd Cav. Co.D
Rees, Berryman T. SC 7th Res. Co.H Sgt.
Rees, B.F. SC 27th Inf. Co.C
Rees, B.T. SC Inf. 1st (Charleston) Bn. Co.F
Rees, C. TX 17th Field Btty. Sgt.
Rees, C.M. TN 8th Inf. Co.D
Rees, C.R. VA 2nd St.Res. Co.C
Rees, Daniel A. TX Cav. McCord's Frontier Regt. 2nd Co.A
Rees, David M. NC 25th Inf. Co.A
Rees, David N. KY 1st Inf. Co.C
Rees, David N. KY 6th Cav. Sgt.
Rees, Elijah VA 25th Inf. 2nd Co.A Cpl.
Rees, E.M. SC 1st St.Troops Co.C
Rees, Fred VA 15th Inf. Co.K
Rees, F.W. AL Cav.
Rees, George GA 54th Inf. Music.
Rees, George F. TX 21st Inf. Co.B
Rees, G.M. TX Cav. McCord's Frontier Regt. Co.F
Rees, G.W. TN 41st Inf. Co.A
Rees, H. KY 2nd (Duke's) Cav. Co.A
Rees, Haman VA 62nd Mtd.Inf. 2nd Co.H
Rees, Henry AR 45th Mil. Co.A
Rees, Henry F. GA 1st Reg. Co.I,C Cpl.
Rees, Horace C. VA 8th Inf. Co.B
Rees, Hyson KY 9th Mtd.Inf. Co.D
Rees, J. TN 31st Inf. Co.I
Rees, James NC 25th Inf. Co.A
Rees, James TX 5th Inf. Co.F
Rees, James M. MS 42nd Inf. Co.H
Rees, James M. TX 13th Cav. Co.G
Rees, James N. NC 4th Inf. Co.I
Rees, James Sanford TN 40th Inf. Co.A
Rees, J.G. MS 18th Cav. Co.H,F
Rees, J.M. MS 2nd St.Cav. Co.H Sgt.
Rees, John VA 7th Cav. Co.I 2nd Lt.
Rees, John VA 58th Mil. Co.E
Rees, John B. TX 2nd Cav. 1st Co.F Bugler
Rees, John B. TX Cav. Morgan's Regt. Co.I
Rees, John C. GA Inf. 1st Loc.Troops (Augusta) Dearing's Cav.Co.
Rees, John H. KY 1st Inf. Co.C
Rees, John M. AL 14th Inf. Co.D
Rees, John M. KY 9th Mtd.Inf. Co.D Sgt.
Rees, John S. VA 13th Inf. Co.K
Rees, Jordan L. MS 26th Inf. Co.C Ord.Sgt.
Rees, J.S. AR 45th Mil. Co.A
Rees, J.T. MS Cav. Ham's Regt. Capt.
Rees, L.S. NC Unassign.Conscr.
Rees, Lucius G. GA Arty. 11th Bn. (Sumter Arty.) Co.A 1st Lt.
Rees, M. TX Waul's Legion Co.A
Rees, Marion M. MS 42nd Inf. Co.H Cpl.
Rees, Martin V. MS 42nd Inf. Co.H
Rees, Martin V. NC 64th Inf. Co.G
Rees, Mary TN 41st Inf. Co.A
Rees, Mathew C. MS 42nd Inf. Co.H
Rees, Michael LA Mil. 3rd Regt. 1st Brig. 1st Div. Co.C Cpl.
Rees, N.B. TN Inf. 23rd Bn. Co.A
Rees, N.B. TN 41st Inf. Co.A
Rees, N.S. KY 9th Mtd.Inf. Co.E Sgt.
Rees, N.S. TN Inf. 23rd Bn. Co.A 1st Sgt.
Rees, N.S. TN 41st Inf. Co.A

Rees, Orlando C. TX 13th Cav. Co.G
Rees, Orlando U. TX 13th Cav. Co.G
Rees, Oscar C. MO 3rd Inf. Co.A
Rees, Oscar C. MO Inf. 3rd Regt.St.Guard Co.C 3rd Lt.
Rees, Peter TN 26th Inf. Co.K
Rees, Peter O.A. TX Cav. McCord's Frontier Regt. 2nd Co.A Jr.2nd Lt.
Rees, Raymond R. GA Arty. 11th Bn. (Sumter Arty.) Co.B
Rees, Riley AL Cp. of Instr. Talladega
Rees, Robert TN 8th Inf. Co.H
Rees, Robert TN 41st Inf. Co.A
Rees, Robert M. SC 22nd Inf. Co.B Sgt.
Rees, S. NC 26th Inf. Co.C
Rees, Samuel TN 28th Inf. Co.H
Rees, S.B. Exch.Bn. 1st Co.A,CSA
Rees, Susan TN 41st Inf. Co.A Laundress
Rees, Thad. J. 7th Conf.Cav. Co.A Sgt.
Rees, Thomas B. GA Inf. 11th Bn. (St.Guards) Co.B Sgt.
Rees, Thomas B. VA 1st St.Res. Co.H
Rees, Thomas C. GA 12th (Robison's) Cav. (St.Guards) Co.K
Rees, Thomas F. GA 45th Inf. Co.D
Rees, Thomas S. TN 2nd (Smith's) Cav. Thomason's Co. Sgt.
Rees, Thomas S. 3rd Conf.Cav. Co.I Capt.
Rees, T.M. TN 41st Inf. Co.A
Rees, Walt E. LA Inf. 1st Sp.Bn. (Rightor's) Co.F
Rees, W.G. TN 16th Inf. Co.H
Rees, W.H. KY 9th Mtd.Inf. Co.E
Rees, W.H. MS 2nd St.Cav. Co.H
Rees, W.H. TN Inf. 23rd Bn. Co.A Sgt.
Rees, William GA 2nd Cav. (St.Guards) Co.B
Rees, William MS 6th Cav. Co.H
Rees, William MS 5th Inf. Co.A Sgt.
Rees, William MS 41st Inf. Co.G Sgt.
Rees, William TN Inf. 1st Cons.Regt. Co.F
Rees, William VA 25th Inf. 2nd Co.A
Rees, William Cunningham TN 40th Inf. Co.A
Rees, William M. AR 20th Inf. Co.G 1st Lt.
Rees, William N. 3rd Conf.Cav. Co.C,I
Rees, William P. GA 6th Cav. Co.A Sgt.
Rees, William P. NC 16th Inf. Co.I Music.
Rees, Winchester KY 9th Mtd.Inf. Co.D
Rees, W.J. Gen. & Staff Surg.
Rees, W.S. TN 41st Inf. Co.A
Rees, W.T. 7th Conf.Cav. Co.A
Rees, Zopha S. SC 22nd Inf. Co.B
Reese, --- AR 36th Inf. Co.K 3rd Lt.
Reese, --- SC 4th Cav. Co.C
Reese, A. GA Cav. 29th Bn. Co.G
Reese, A. LA 18th Inf. Co.H
Reese, A. LA Inf.Crescent Regt. Co.H
Reese, A. LA Inf.Cons.Crescent Regt. Co.G,L
Reese, A. VA Inf. 1st Bn.Loc.Def. Co.C
Reese, Aaron GA Cherokee Legion (St.Guards) Co.D
Reese, Aaron NC 6th Cav. (65th St.Troops) Co.C,D Black.
Reese, Aaron NC Cav. 7th Bn. Co.E,D Black.
Reese, Aaron TN 1st (Feild's) Inf. Co.D
Reese, Aaron J. AL 42nd Inf. Co.K
Reese, Abner R. VA 53rd Inf. Co.F
Reese, Abner R. VA Inf. Montague's Bn. Co.C

Reese, Abraham TN 24th Inf. 2nd Co.H
Reese, A.H. MS 35th Inf. Co.C 2nd Lt.
Reese, A.H. SC 7th Cav. Co.D
Reese, A.H. SC Cav.Bn. Holcombe Legion Co.B
Reese, A.H. TX 15th Cav. Co.I
Reese, A.H. TX 32nd Cav. Co.I
Reese, A.H. TX 11th (Spaight's) Bn.Vol. Co.G
Reese, A.H. Gen. & Staff A.Surg.
Reese, A. Henry AL 62nd Inf. Co.A
Reese, A.J. GA Inf. 1st Loc.Troops (Augusta) Co.B
Reese, A.J. GA 10th Inf. Co.F
Reese, A.J. GA Phillips' Legion Co.E 1st Lt.
Reese, A.J. TN 7th (Duckworth's) Cav. Co.E
Reese, A.J. TN 8th Inf. Co.D
Reese, A.J. TN 12th (Cons.) Inf. Co.G
Reese, A.J. TN 22nd Inf. Co.E
Reese, Alb. LA 21st (Kennedy's) Inf. Co.F
Reese, Alexander TN 39th Mtd.Inf. Co.A
Reese, Alexander VA 64th Mtd.Inf. Co.B
Reese, Alfred GA Cherokee Legion (St.Guards) Co.D
Reese, Alfred TN Cav. 16th Bn. (Neal's) Co.E
Reese, Alson NC Cav. 7th Bn. Co.E
Reese, Alson E. NC 62nd Inf. Co.E
Reese, Anderson W. GA Carlton's Co. (Troup Cty.Arty.)
Reese, Anderson W. GA 2nd Inf. Stanley's Co.
Reese, Andrew 1st Cherokee Mtd.Vol. 1st Co.G
Reese, Andrew 1st Squad. Cherokee Mtd.Vol. Co.A
Reese, Andrew J. MS 42nd Inf. Co.H
Reese, Andrew J. TN 20th Cav.
Reese, Augustus C. AL 3rd Inf. Co.H Sgt.
Reese, Augustus F. AR Inf. 1st Bn. Co.F
Reese, Augustus J. GA 3rd Inf. Co.D
Reese, Augustus R. NC 38th Inf. Co.B
Reese, A.W. GA 1st Reg. Co.M,D 2nd Lt.
Reese, B. MO 11th Inf. Co.G Cpl.
Reese, Bailey NC 62nd Inf. Co.K
Reese, Bailey P. TN Cav. 7th Bn. (Bennett's) Co.B
Reese, Bailey P. TN 22nd (Barteau's) Cav. Co.E
Reese, Benjamin GA 48th Inf. Co.K
Reese, Benjamin F. TN 32nd Inf. Co.A
Reese, Benjamin N. MO Cav. 7th Regt.St.Guard Co.D 1st Lt.
Reese, Benjamin T. VA Inf. 5th Bn. Co.E
Reese, Benjamin T. VA 53rd Inf. Co.B
Reese, Benton MO 10th Cav. Co.B
Reese, Beverly M. NC Inf. 2nd Bn. Co.C Cpl.
Reese, Beverly M. VA 59th Inf. 3rd Co.G
Reese, B.N. LA 19th Inf. Co.G
Reese, B.N. 1st Cherokee Mtd.Vol. 2nd Co.I
Reese, B.P. TN 21st & 22nd (Cons.) Cav. Co.B
Reese, B.P. Gen. & Staff Surg.
Reese, B.W. AL 11th Inf. Co.G
Reese, C. TX 9th (Nichols') Inf. Co.G
Reese, C.A.H. VA 8th Cav. Co.D
Reese, Carlos AL 4th Inf. Co.G Cpl.
Reese, Carlos, Jr. AL 28th Inf. Co.C AQM
Reese, Carlos Lee's Corps Capt.,QM
Reese, Carlos, Jr. Gen. & Staff AQM
Reese, C.B. AL 10th Cav. Co.F
Reese, C.E. Gen. & Staff Hosp.Stew.
Reese, C.H. AL Lt.Arty. Phelan's Co.
Reese, Charles KY 3rd Mtd.Inf. Co.I

Reese, Charles LA 13th & 20th Inf. Co.K Sgt.
Reese, Charles MS 6th Inf. Co.C
Reese, Charles TX 6th Inf. Co.C
Reese, Charles A. VA 21st Mil. Co.D
Reese, Charles A. VA 34th Inf. Co.A
Reese, Charles E. AL 44th Inf. Co.A
Reese, C.M. TN 8th Inf. Co.D
Reese, Columbus GA 15th Inf. Co.E
Reese, Columbus C. GA 48th Inf. Co.B
Reese, Columbus C. 7th Conf.Cav. Co.E
Reese, C.P. AR 20th Inf. Co.G
Reese, Crawford J. GA 3rd Inf. Co.D 2nd Lt.
Reese, C.T. AR 15th (Josey's) Inf. Co.E
Reese, Curtis GA 48th Inf. Co.K
Reese, Cuthbert TX 11th (Spaight's) Bn.Vol. Co.C
Reese, Cuthbert TX 21st Inf. Co.E
Reese, D. GA Lt.Arty. Pritchard's Co. (Washington Arty.)
Reese, D.A. TN 47th Inf. Co.G
Reese, Daniel C. NC 53rd Inf. Co.E Sgt.
Reese, David TX 14th Inf. Co.C
Reese, David A. NC 2nd Cav. (19th St.Troops) Co.B Sgt.
Reese, David C. AL 55th Vol. Co.B
Reese, David F. AL 47th Inf. Co.B
Reese, David G. VA 64th Mtd.Inf. Co.I 1st Lt.
Reese, David L. NC 56th Inf. Co.K
Reese, David N. KY 4th Cav. Co.C
Reese, David N. KY Jessee's Bn.Mtd.Riflemen Co.A Sgt.
Reese, D.G. Gen. & Staff Capt.,MSK
Reese, Dosius Lt.Arty. Dent's Btty.,CSA
Reese, Drew W. FL 5th Inf. Co.G
Reese, Drury W. FL 11th Inf. Co.E
Reese, E. LA C.S. Zouave Bn. Co.F
Reese, E. SC 1st St.Troops Co.B
Reese, Ed GA Cav. Nelson's Ind.Co.
Reese, Ed GA Cav. Ragland's Co.
Reese, Edmund VA 2nd Arty. Co.D
Reese, Edmund VA Inf. 22nd Bn. Co.D
Reese, Edward LA 20th Inf. Co.K
Reese, Edward F. SC 1st (Hagood's) Inf. 1st Co.D Sgt.
Reese, Edwin AL Crawford's Co.
Reese, E.F. SC Conscr.
Reese, E.H. GA 1st (Olmstead's) Inf. Co.F
Reese, E.H. GA 10th Inf. Co.C
Reese, E.H. 3rd Conf.Eng.Troops Co.H Artif.
Reese, E.J.H. MS 3rd Inf. (St.Troops) Co.A
Reese, Elias S. TN 28th Inf. Co.G
Reese, Elihu M. SC 1st (Orr's) Rifles Co.L Cpl.
Reese, Elijah VA 62nd Mtd.Inf. 2nd Co.E
Reese, Elisha NC 64th Inf. Co.G
Reese, E.M. SC Prov.Guard Hamilton's Co.
Reese, Emmett VA 61st Inf. Co.G
Reese, Enoch D. GA Inf. 1st Loc.Troops (Augusta) Co.G
Reese, Eugene AL 3rd Cav. Co.H Sgt.
Reese, Eugene MO 5th Inf. Co.K
Reese, E.W. SC 2nd Inf. Co.D
Reese, E.W. SC Inf. Holcombe Legion Co.G Music.
Reese, F. TX 33rd Cav. Co.K
Reese, Felix F. GA 48th Inf. Co.B
Reese, F.M. GA 22nd Inf. Co.I
Reese, Francis M. GA 48th Inf. Co.B

Reese, Francis M. GA 65th Inf. Co.D,I
Reese, Francis M. NC Lt.Arty. 3rd Bn. Co.A
Reese, Francis M. TN 1st (Turney's) Inf. Co.G Cpl.
Reese, Franklin NC 62nd Inf. Co.I
Reese, Frederick C. GA Cav. 10th Bn. (St.Guards) Co.D
Reese, G. SC 27th Inf. Co.G
Reese, G.A. GA Arty. 11th Bn. (Sumter Arty.) New Co.C
Reese, Garrett GA 26th Inf. Co.B
Reese, George AL 44th Inf. Co.A 1st Lt.
Reese, George AL 45th Inf. Co.C
Reese, George AL Auburn Home Guards Vol. Darby's Co.
Reese, George GA Lt.Arty. Croft's Btty. (Columbus Arty.)
Reese, George 1st Cherokee Mtd.Vol. 1st Co.G
Reese, George 1st Squad. Cherokee Mtd.Vol. Co.A Sgt.
Reese, George F. TX 11th (Spaight's) Bn.Vol. Co.E
Reese, George G. VA 54th Inf. Co.E
Reese, George W. AL 19th Inf. Co.C
Reese, George W. AL 25th Inf. Co.D
Reese, George W. AL Cp. of Instr. Talladega
Reese, George W. GA Arty. (Macon Lt.Arty.) Slaten's Co. Sgt.
Reese, George W. GA 20th Inf. Co.A
Reese, George W. TX 3rd Cav. Co.H
Reese, Gibson VA 62nd Mtd.Inf. 2nd Co.E
Reese, Gilbert R. TN Cav. 12th Bn. (Day's) Co.E
Reese, Giles NC 62nd Inf. Co.K
Reese, G.N. TX 3rd Cav. Co.H
Reese, G.T. VA Inf. 44th Bn. Co.C
Reese, G.W. MS 28th Cav. Co.D Cpl.
Reese, G.W. TN 12th Inf. Co.B
Reese, G.W. TN 12th (Cons.) Inf. Co.A
Reese, H. VA Loc.Def. Earhart's Co.
Reese, H. Conf.Arty. McLaughlin's Bn. 1st Lt.
Reese, H.A. AL 26th (O'Neal's) Inf. Co.E Sgt.
Reese, Handsell GA 5th Inf. Co.D
Reese, Harriss NC 3rd Cav. (41st St.Troops) Co.B
Reese, H.B. LA 18th Inf. Co.I
Reese, H.B. LA Inf.Crescent Regt. Co.I
Reese, H.B. MS 12th Cav. Co.G
Reese, H.C. AR 34th Inf. Co.E
Reese, H.C. GA 3rd Bn. (St.Guards) Co.C
Reese, H.E. GA 46th Inf. Co.E
Reese, Henry AL 14th Inf. Co.A
Reese, Henry AL 49th Inf. Co.B
Reese, Henry GA 36th (Villepigue's) Inf. Co.I
Reese, Henry KY 10th Cav. Co.B
Reese, Henry NC Inf. Thomas Legion Co.I
Reese, Henry TN 29th Inf. Co.F
Reese, Henry B. TX 1st Inf. Co.C
Reese, Henry C. GA 10th Inf. Co.F
Reese, Henry C. GA Cobb's Legion Co.I
Reese, Henry C. NC 25th Inf. Co.A
Reese, Henry T. MS 11th (Perrin's) Cav. Co.H
Reese, Hiram KY 2nd Cav. Co.D Capt.
Reese, Hiram S. TN 22nd Inf.
Reese, Hiram S. TN 32nd Inf. Co.A
Reese, Hiram W. VA 64th Mtd.Inf. Co.B
Reese, H.L. LA 1st Cav. Robinson's Co.

Reese, H.L. TN Arty. Ramsey's Btty.
Reese, H.L. TX 21st Inf. Co.E
Reese, H.L. VA Inf. 1st Bn.Loc.Def. Co.C
Reese, H.N. AL Cp. of Instr. Talladega Walthall's Bn. Fowler's Co.
Reese, Horace AL 3rd Inf. Co.H Sgt.
Reese, Houston KY 14th Cav. Co.B
Reese, Hugh G. KY 2nd (Duke's) Cav. Co.K
Reese, H.V. GA 3rd Cav. Co.I
Reese, H.W. AL 31st Inf. Co.A
Reese, I.I. VA Inf. 44th Bn. Co.C
Reese, I.P. MO 8th Cav. Co.H
Reese, Isaac VA 50th Inf. Co.A
Reese, Isaac VA 62nd Mtd.Inf. 2nd Co.E
Reese, Isaac VA 64th Mtd.Inf. Co.A
Reese, Isaac N. VA Inf. 1st Bn.Loc.Def. Co.C
Reese, Isaac N. VA 45th Inf. Co.B
Reese, Isaac T. AR 25th Inf. Co.A
Reese, Isaac W. GA 3rd Inf. Co.D Cpl.
Reese, Isaac W. GA 66th Inf. Co.G 1st Lt.
Reese, J. AL Cav.
Reese, J. AL 47th Inf. Co.B
Reese, J. LA Inf. Pelican Regt. Co.H 1st Sgt.
Reese, J. MS 8th Cav. Co.I
Reese, J. TN 9th (Ward's) Cav. Kirkpatrick's Co.
Reese, J.A. SC 20th Inf. Co.L
Reese, James AL Inf. 1st Regt. Co.G
Reese, James AR 4th Bn. Co.C
Reese, James GA Cav. Lee's Bn. Co.H,M
Reese, James GA Inf. 1st Loc.Troops (Augusta) Co.C
Reese, James GA Inf. (Jones Hussars) Jones' Co.
Reese, James LA 11th Inf. Co.B
Reese, James LA 20th Inf. Co.I,D,E 1st Sgt.
Reese, James MS 6th Cav. Co.H,C
Reese, James MO St.Guard
Reese, James NC Unassign.Conscr.
Reese, James SC 2nd Cav. Co.K
Reese, James TN 21st Inf. Co.I
Reese, James TX 11th (Spaight's) Bn.Vol. Co.F
Reese, James VA 53rd Inf. Co.F
Reese, James VA Mil. Carroll Cty.
Reese, James VA Inf. Montague's Bn. Co.C
Reese, James A. VA 2nd Arty. Co.D
Reese, James A. VA Inf. 22nd Bn. Co.D
Reese, James B. SC 1st (Orr's) Rifles Co.K
Reese, James B. TN 2nd (Robison's) Inf. Co.I
Reese, James C. GA 30th Inf. Co.D
Reese, James E. AL 5th Bn.Vol. Co.C Capt.
Reese, James F. TN 43rd Inf. Co.B
Reese, James H. NC 7th Inf. Co.I
Reese, James J. GA 10th Inf. Co.F
Reese, James J. GA 65th Inf. Co.I
Reese, James L. GA Inf. 5th Bn. (St.Guards) Co.F
Reese, James L. GA 41st Inf. Co.F
Reese, James L. GA 65th Inf. Co.D
Reese, James M. TN 55th (McKoin's) Inf. Co.F
Reese, James M. VA 58th Inf. Co.F
Reese, James R. GA Cav. 7th Bn. (St.Guards) Co.F
Reese, James S. AL Cav. 1st Bn. Co.A
Reese, James T. AL Arty. 1st Bn. Maj.,Surg.
Reese, James T. Gen. & Staff Surg.
Reese, James W. GA 3rd Inf. Co.D Band Music.
Reese, James W. GA 6th Inf. Co.A

Reese, Jarrett GA 36th (Broyles') Inf. Co.B
Reese, Jasper GA 2nd Inf. Co.F
Reese, Jasper GA 6th Inf. Co.A
Reese, Jasper GA 59th Inf. Co.I
Reese, Jasper VA 50th Inf. Co.A
Reese, J.B. AL Inf. 1st Regt. Co.D
Reese, J.B. AL 63rd Inf. Co.G
Reese, J.B. GA 8th Inf. Co.D
Reese, J.B. TX 28th Cav. Co.F
Reese, J.C. GA 2nd Inf. Co.D
Reese, J.C. GA Floyd Legion (St.Guards) Co.I
Reese, J.C.D. AL 26th (O'Neal's) Inf. Co.A
   Sgt.
Reese, J.D. MS 3rd Inf. (A. of 10,000) Co.A 1st
   Cpl.
Reese, J.D. MS 15th Inf. Co.F
Reese, J.D. SC 24th Inf. Co.B 1st Sgt.
Reese, J.E. AR 36th Inf. Co.K
Reese, Jeptha AL 16th Inf. Co.E
Reese, Jeptha SC 2nd Rifles Co.B
Reese, Jesse GA 22nd Inf. Co.H Cpl.
Reese, J.F. AL Inf. 1st Regt. Co.G
Reese, J.F. TX 5th Inf. Co.K
Reese, J.G. AR 19th (Dawson's) Inf. Co.C
Reese, J.H. GA 6th Cav. Co.I
Reese, J.H. GA 8th Inf. Co.D
Reese, J.H. TX 11th Inf. Co.E
Reese, J.H. 7th Conf.Cav. Co.C Cpl.
Reese, J.J. GA Inf. 5th Bn. (St.Guards) Co.D
   2nd Lt.
Reese, J.J. MS 43rd Inf. Co.C
Reese, J.J. TN 3rd (Lillard's) Mtd.Inf. Lt.Col.
Reese, J.J. 3rd Conf.Cav. Co.K Sgt.
Reese, J.L. GA 39th Inf. Co.K
Reese, J.L. MS 46th Inf. Co.H
Reese, J.M. GA 3rd Cav. Co.I
Reese, J.N. NC 62nd Inf. Co.K
Reese, Joe C. VA Mil. Carroll Cty.
Reese, Joel GA 48th Inf. Co.K
Reese, Joel Brown MO 5th Inf. Co.K 1st Lt.
Reese, Joel J. GA 12th Inf. Co.A
Reese, Joel W. GA 3rd Res. Co.I Cpl.
Reese, Joel W. VA Hvy.Arty. Wright's Co.
Reese, John AL 27th Inf. Co.K
Reese, John GA 43rd Inf. Co.L,C Cpl.
Reese, John MS 11th (Perrin's) Cav. Co.H
Reese, John NC Inf. 2nd Bn. Co.G
Reese, John NC 54th Inf. Co.F
Reese, John NC 62nd Inf. Co.K
Reese, John SC 3rd Res. Co.I
Reese, John VA Inf. 44th Bn. Co.C
Reese, John VA 94th Mil. Co.A
Reese, John A. GA 46th Inf. Co.F Sgt.
Reese, John A. SC 1st (Orr's) Rifles Co.L Cpl.
Reese, John A. TN 9th (Ward's) Cav. Co.E
Reese, John A. TN 15th Cav. Co.E
Reese, John A. VA 25th Inf. 2nd Co.E
Reese, John A. VA 52nd Inf. Co.E
Reese, John B. AL 46th Inf. Co.E
Reese, John Chappel GA 1st (Ramsey's) Inf.
   Co.B Sgt.
Reese, John Charles Galloway TX 20th Cav.
   Co.D
Reese, John E. VA 5th Cav. (12 mo. '61-2)
   Co.D
Reese, John E. VA 13th Cav. Co.B
Reese, John E. VA Loc.Def. Scott's Co. Sgt.

Reese, John F. MO 10th Cav. Co.A
Reese, John G. VA 53rd Inf. Co.F
Reese, John G. VA Inf. Montague's Bn. Co.C
Reese, John H. TX 25th Cav. Co.H
Reese, John H. TX Cav. Wells' Regt. Co.C
Reese, John J. NC Unassign.Conscr.
Reese, John J. VA 18th Inf. Co.G
Reese, John J. Gen. & Staff Capt.,AAG
Reese, John Jeff TN 3rd (Lillard's) Mtd.Inf.
   Co.A
Reese, John L. AL Auburn Home Guards Vol.
   Darby's Co.
Reese, John L. Gen. & Staff 1st Lt.,Adj.
Reese, John M. NC 4th Bn.Jr.Res. Maj.
Reese, John M. VA 77th Mil. Co.B
Reese, John McNary VA 11th Cav. Co.D
Reese, John M.N. GA 5th Inf. Co.I 1st Lt.
Reese, John P. GA 37th Inf. Co.I
Reese, John P. MS 44th Inf. Co.E
Reese, John S. AL 3rd Inf. Co.C
Reese, John S. AL 45th Inf. Co.I
Reese, John S. NC 2nd Cav. (19th St.Troops)
   Co.F
Reese, Johnson 1st Cherokee Mtd.Vol. 1st Co.G
   Sgt.
Reese, John T. SC 7th Inf. 1st Co.I
Reese, John T. TX 24th Cav. Co.E Sgt.
Reese, John V. VA 64th Mtd.Inf. Co.I
Reese, John W. NC 60th Inf. Co.F
Reese, John W. TX 12th Cav. Co.D 1st Lt.
Reese, John W. VA 19th Inf. Co.H
Reese, John W. VA 38th Inf. Co.G
Reese, John Y. TN 8th Inf. Co.K Sgt.
Reese, Jonathan R. AL 42nd Inf. Co.K
Reese, Jordan GA 8th Inf. Co.E
Reese, Jordan TX 24th Cav. Co.E
Reese, Joseph GA 9th Inf. (St.Guards) Co.B
Reese, Joseph GA 61st Inf. Co.I
Reese, Joseph NC 3rd Bn.Sr.Res. Durham's Co.
Reese, Joseph NC Jones' Co. (Supp.Force) Cpl.
Reese, Joseph TN 55th (Brown's) Inf. Co.H
Reese, Joseph B. GA 1st (Ramsey's) Inf. Co.K
Reese, Joseph B. GA 20th Inf. Co.D
Reese, Joseph B. GA 44th Inf. Co.F Capt.
Reese, Joseph C. VA 29th Inf. Co.I
Reese, Joseph E. AL 4th Inf. Co.G Cpl.
Reese, Joseph H. MS 15th Inf. Co.F Cpl.
Reese, Joseph H. TX 11th (Spaight's) Bn.Vol.
   Co.C
Reese, Joseph J. GA Inf. 2nd Bn. Co.A
Reese, Joseph J. GA 55th Inf. Co.H
Reese, Joseph M. NC 22nd Inf. Co.M
Reese, Joseph M. VA 38th Inf. Co.G
Reese, Joseph M.D. NC Inf. 2nd Bn. Co.F
Reese, Joseph W. LA 1st (Strawbridge's) Inf.
   Co.I
Reese, Joseph W. TN 3rd (Lillard's) Mtd.Inf.
   Co.A 1st Lt.
Reese, J.P. AL 17th Inf. Co.F
Reese, J.P. AL 46th Inf. Co.E
Reese, J.P. MO 7th Cav. Co.D
Reese, J.S. AL 54th Inf. Co.B
Reese, J.S. SC Lt.Arty. Jeter's Co. (Macbeth
   Lt.Arty.)
Reese, J.S. TN Lt.Arty. Rice's Btty.
Reese, J.S. TN 38th Inf. 1st Co.A
Reese, J.S. TN 55th (Brown's) Inf. Co.H

Reese, J.T. AL 25th Inf. Surg.
Reese, J.T. AL 34th Inf. Co.C
Reese, J.T. GA 2nd Cav. (St.Guards) Co.C
Reese, J.T. GA Inf. Arsenal Bn. (Columbus)
   Co.A Sgt.
Reese, J.T. TN Conscr. (Cp. of Instr.) Co.B
Reese, J.W. AL Arty. 1st Bn. Co.G
Reese, J.W. GA 11th Cav. (St.Guards) McGriff's
   Co.
Reese, J.W. MO Inf. 1st Regt.St.Guard Co.B
   Capt.
Reese, J.W. 3rd Conf.Cav. Co.K Sgt.
Reese, K.W. TX 12th Cav. Co.D
Reese, L. SC 4th Cav. Co.C
Reese, Lafayet H. TN 54th Inf. Dooley's Co.
Reese, Lafayette R. MS 44th Inf. Co.E
Reese, L.D. SC 7th Inf. Co.D
Reese, Leonidas P. AL 33rd Inf. Co.I
Reese, Levi SC Cav. 10th Bn. Co.B
Reese, Lewis B. MO Inf.
Reese, Lewis C. AL 3rd Inf. Co.H
Reese, L.G. GA Brooks' Co. (Terrell Lt.Arty.)
Reese, L.H. GA 59th Inf. Co.I
Reese, Littleton AL 3rd Cav. Co.H
Reese, Lloyd B. KY 2nd Mtd.Inf. Co.B
Reese, Louis GA 6th Inf. Co.A
Reese, Louis GA 59th Inf. Co.I
Reese, Louis C. AL Lt.Arty. 2nd Bn. Co.E
Reese, Louis H. GA 6th Inf. Co.A
Reese, L.S. TN 28th (Cons.) Inf.
Reese, Lucius J. GA 1st Reg. 2nd Lt.
Reese, M. TX Inf. Timmons' Regt. Co.G
Reese, Mat. AR 26th Inf. Co.C
Reese, Matthew VA 2nd Arty. Co.D
Reese, Matthew A. VA Inf. 22nd Bn. Co.D
Reese, Matthew E. GA 48th Inf. Co.B
Reese, M.E. 10th Conf.Cav. Co.B 1st Lt.
Reese, Merril GA 48th Inf. Co.B
Reese, Milton E. AL Cav. 5th Bn. Hilliard's
   Legion Co.B 1st Lt.
Reese, Milton E. GA 4th Inf. Co.D
Reese, Morris H. VA 22nd Inf. Co.A Fifer
Reese, Moses SC Inf. Holcombe Legion Co.F
Reese, Moses 7th Conf.Cav. Co.E
Reese, Murray 1st Squad. Cherokee Mtd.Vol.
   Co.A
Reese, M.V. TN Inf. 3rd Cons.Regt. Co.E
Reese, M.V. TN 41st Inf. Co.E
Reese, N.B. VA Rockbridge Cty.Res. Bacon's
   Co.
Reese, Newton GA 6th Inf. Co.A
Reese, Newton R. AL Arty. 1st Bn. Co.A,D,E
Reese, Nicholas M. TX 18th Inf. Co.B
Reese, N.W. AL 16th Inf. Co.D
Reese, O.B. GA 2nd Inf. Co.H
Reese, O.B. TN 2nd (Ashby's) Cav. Co.I
Reese, O.H.P. MS 35th Inf. Co.C
Reese, O.L. GA 1st (Fannin's) Res. Co.F
Reese, Orlando B. TN Cav. 4th Bn. (Branner's)
   Co.E
Reese, Parker VA 63rd Inf. 1st Co.I
Reese, Perry AL Stacey Cav.
Reese, Peter NC 67th Inf. Co.K
Reese, Peter VA 52nd Inf. Co.C
Reese, P.F. SC 7th Inf. Co.C
Reese, Pleasant H. GA 13th Inf. Co.I
Reese, R. AL 22nd Inf. Co.E

Reese, R. NC 3rd Cav. (41st St.Troops) Co.B
Reese, R.C. MS 44th Inf. Co.E
Reese, Redman T. GA 3rd Cav. Co.G 1st Lt.
Reese, Randall H. NC 2nd Cav. (19th St.Troops) Co.H Capt.
Reese, Richard NC Lt.Arty. 3rd Bn. Co.A
Reese, Richard VA 1st Arty. Co.I
Reese, Richard VA Lt.Arty. 38th Bn. Co.B
Reese, Richard H. VA Hvy.Arty. Wright's Co.
Reese, Richard J. TX 1st (Yager's) Cav. Co.A Cpl.
Reese, Richard J. TX Cav. 3rd (Yager's) Bn. Co.A
Reese, Richard L. AL 37th Inf. Co.D 1st Lt.
Reese, Riley AL Cp. of Instr. Talladega
Reese, R.M. NC Snead's Co. (Loc.Def.)
Reese, Robert AL 28th Inf. Co.C
Reese, Robert TN 4th (McLemore's) Cav. Co.D
Reese, Robert C. VA Inf. 5th Bn. Co.F
Reese, Robert T. VA Hvy.Arty. Epes' Co. Sgt.
Reese, Robert W. TN 11th (Holman's) Cav. Co.G
Reese, Rody 1st Cherokee Mtd.Vol. 2nd Co.I
Reese, R.R. NC 62nd Inf. Co.K
Reese, Rufus M. TN 2nd (Robison's) Inf. Co.I Cpl.
Reese, S. GA 66th Inf. Co.G
Reese, S. MS 2nd St.Cav. Co.H
Reese, Sampson TX 3rd Cav. Co.K
Reese, Samuel VA 1st Cav. Co.E
Reese, Samuel B. AL 54th Inf. Co.K
Reese, Samuel B. NC 54th Inf. Co.F
Reese, Samuel S. TX 3rd Cav. Co.H
Reese, Seaborn GA 9th Inf. (St.Guards) Co.B
Reese, S.H. GA 46th Inf. Co.E
Reese, Sidney SC 5th Inf. 2nd Co.C
Reese, Simon GA 1st (Ramsey's) Inf.
Reese, S.J. MO 6th Cav. Co.D
Reese, S.L. LA 3rd Inf. Co.H
Reese, Sol. D. GA 22nd Inf. Co.I
Reese, Solomon MO Henry Cty.Regt.
Reese, Stephen TN 15th Inf. 2nd Co.F
Reese, Stephen VA 63rd Inf. 1st Co.I, Co.E,F
Reese, Stephen H. VA 50th Inf. 1st Co.G
Reese, S.W. AL 7th Cav. Co.A
Reese, S.W. AL 19th Inf. Co.C
Reese, S.W. AR Cav. Witherspoon's Bn. Co.C 3rd Lt.
Reese, S.W. AR 19th (Dawson's) Inf. Co.C
Reese, Sydney SC 3rd Res. Co.I
Reese, Sylvanus VA 21st Inf. Co.C
Reese, T. GA Lt.Arty. Pritchard's Co. (Washington Arty.)
Reese, T. GA Inf. (NonConscr.) Howard's Co.
Reese, Talbot Lt.Arty. Dent's Btty.,CSA
Reese, T.B. GA Phillips' Legion Co.E
Reese, T.B. 3rd Conf.Cav. Co.G
Reese, Thomas GA Inf. 1st Loc.Troops (Augusta) Co.C
Reese, Thomas TX 37th Cav. Co.A
Reese, Thomas 3rd Conf.Cav. Co.C
Reese, Thomas A. FL 1st Cav. Co.H Music.
Reese, Thomas E. NC 2nd Cav. (19th St.Troops) Co.H
Reese, Thomas E. NC 62nd Inf. Co.K
Reese, Thomas J. AL 6th Cav. N.C.S. Sgt.Maj.
Reese, Thomas S. TN 1st (Turney's) Inf. Co.B

Reese, Thomas T.T. MS 15th Inf. Co.F
Reese, T.J.C. TX Cav. McCord's Frontier Regt. Co.F
Reese, T.M. AL 26th (O'Neal's) Inf. Co.E Comsy.Sgt.
Reese, T.M. GA 5th Res. Co.F
Reese, T.M. GA Inf. 27th Bn. (NonConscr.) Co.B
Reese, Toliver GA 48th Inf. Co.K
Reese, Travis AL 32nd & 58th (Cons.) Inf. Sgt.
Reese, Travis AL 58th Inf. Co.I,B Sgt.
Reese, T.S. AL 6th Cav. Co.C
Reese, T.S. TN 6th (Wheeler's) Cav. Co.A
Reese, Uriah GA 48th Inf. Co.K
Reese, W. GA 43rd Inf. Co.F
Reese, W. KY Morgan's Men Co.E
Reese, W.A. TN Inf. 4th Cons.Regt. Co.K Capt.
Reese, W.A. TN 12th (Cons.) Inf. Co.A Sgt.
Reese, W.A. TN 47th Inf. Co.I
Reese, W.A. TN 48th (Nixon's) Inf. Co.E 2nd Lt.
Reese, Wade TN 24th Inf. 2nd Co.H, Co.M
Reese, Wade H. TN 9th (Ward's) Cav. Co.F
Reese, Wade Hampton GA 20th Inf. Co.K
Reese, W.B. MO Inf. Winston's Regt. Co.A
Reese, W.B. Gen. & Staff Capt.,AAG
Reese, W.D. AL 21st Inf. Co.D
Reese, W.D. AL 26th (O'Neal's) Inf. Co.E Sgt.
Reese, W.D. GA 5th Inf. Co.B
Reese, W.D. GA 5th Res. Co.C
Reese, W.D. TN 4th Inf. Maj.,Surg.
Reese, W.D. TN 40th Inf. Co.D 1st Lt.
Reese, W.E. LA Lt.Arty. Fenner's Btty.
Reese, W.E. MS Inf. 2nd St.Troops Co.G
Reese, W.E. SC 1st Inf. Co.A
Reese, W.E. SC 6th Inf. 2nd Co.H
Reese, W.F. NC 53rd Inf. Co.A
Reese, W.H. GA 1st Cav. Co.K
Reese, W.H. GA Cav. Gartrell's Co.
Reese, William AL 3rd Cav. Co.I
Reese, William AL 1st Inf. Co.D
Reese, Wm. AL 19th Inf. Co.D
Reese, William GA 48th Inf. Co.B
Reese, William KY 2nd (Duke's) Cav. Co.H
Reese, William KY 2nd (Duke's) Cav. Co.K
Reese, William SC 1st Inf. Co.H
Reese, William TN Cav. 16th Bn. (Neal's) Co.E
Reese, William TN 40th Inf. Co.K
Reese, William TX 24th Cav. Co.E
Reese, William VA 53rd Inf. Co.F
Reese, William VA Inf. Montague's Bn. Co.C
Reese, William 1st Cherokee Mtd.Vol. 1st Co.C Cpl.
Reese, William Conf.Inf. Tucker's Regt. Co.B
Reese, William A. TN 12th Inf. Co.B Capt.
Reese, William A. VA Inf. 5th Bn. Co.B
Reese, William A. VA Inf. 5th Bn. Co.F
Reese, William A. VA 53rd Inf. Co.F
Reese, William B. GA 21st Inf. Co.K
Reese, William B. TN 11th Cav. Co.C
Reese, William C. AL 54th Inf. Co.B
Reese, William C. GA 64th Inf. Co.F
Reese, William D. VA 77th Mil. Co.B, Blue's Co.
Reese, Wm. D.B. AL 14th Inf. Co.A
Reese, William E. MS 15th Inf. Co.F

Reese, William E. SC 9th Inf. Co.B
Reese, William F. AL 3rd Inf. Co.D
Reese, William F. GA Arty. Baker's Co.
Reese, Wm. F. TX Cav. Crump's Regt. Co.O Lt.
Reese, William H. GA 44th Inf. Ord.Sgt.
Reese, William H. NC 15th Inf. Co.A
Reese, William J. AL Jeff Davis Arty. Capt.
Reese, William J. MS 5th Inf. (St.Troops) Co.C
Reese, William J. TN 15th Cav. Co.F
Reese, William J. TN 44th (Cons.) Inf. Co.H
Reese, William J. VA Inf. 2nd Bn. Co.A
Reese, William M. AL Jeff Davis Arty.
Reese, William M. GA 3rd Cav. (St.Guards) Co.C
Reese, William N. VA 28th Inf. Co.K
Reese, William O. GA 1st Inf. Co.G 1st Lt.
Reese, William P. MS Inf. Comfort's Co.
Reese, William P. SC 5th Cav. Co.A Cpl.
Reese, William P. TN 2nd (Robison's) Inf. Co.C Cpl.
Reese, William S. VA 24th Inf. Co.E
Reese, William W. GA Inf. 8th Bn. Co.G
Reese, W.J. GA 12th (Robinson's) Cav. (St.Guards) Co.E 2nd Lt.
Reese, W.J. GA Lt.Arty. Van Den Corput's Co.
Reese, W.J. GA 1st St.Line 1st Lt.
Reese, W.J. Conf.Arty. R.C.M. Page's Bn. 1st Lt.
Reese, W.L. AL 20th Inf. Asst.Surg.
Reese, W.L. GA 60th Inf. AASurg.
Reese, W.L. NC 6th Inf. Asst.Surg.
Reese, W.L. VA 20th Inf. Co.C
Reese, W. Lewis Gen. & Staff Asst.Surg.
Reese, W.M. GA Cobb's Legion Co.I
Reese, W.N. AL 17th Inf. Co.F
Reese, W.N. AL 19th Inf. Co.C,A
Reese, W.P. AL Cav. Roddey's Escort
Reese, W.P. SC Cav. 14th Bn. Co.B
Reese, W.P. Gen. & Staff Surg.
Reese, W.R. NC 3rd Cav. (41st St.Troops) Co.B
Reese, W.R. VA 19th Cav. Co.F
Reese, W.S. AL 1st Cav. 1st Co.K,E Capt.
Reese, W.S. AL 1st Bn. Hilliard's Legion Vol. Co.A
Reese, W.S. AL 60th Inf. Co.F
Reese, W.T. FL 1st Inf. Old Co.D
Reese, W.T. GA Siege Arty. 28th Bn. Co.B Cpl.
Reese, W.W. AR 19th (Dawson's) Inf. Co.C
Reese, Z.T. GA 10th Mil.
Reesee, Payton TX 30th Cav. Co.H
Reesee, R.D. MO Cav. Coleman's Regt. Co.B
Reeser, Benjamin TX 16th Cav. Co.E
Reeser, Jacob VA 27th Inf. Co.E
Reeser, James TX 16th Cav. Co.E
Reeser, James M. KY 2nd (Duke's) Cav. Quirk's Co.
Reeser, Milton G. TN Cav. 12th Bn. (Day's) Co.B Cpl.
Reeser, Thomas TX 16th Cav. Co.E
Reeser, T.M. MS 1st Cav.
Reeser, T.M. MS 7th Cav. Co.I
Reeshman, H. MS 1st Bn.S.S. Co.B
Reesner, Henry NC 18th Inf. Co.G
Reesner, H.H. AL 46th Inf. Co.G
Reeson, E.B. MO Cav. Freeman's Regt. Co.B

Reeson, H.M. VA 4th Res. Co.I
Reesor, W.F. LA 31st Inf. Co.D
Reetoe, W.G. TX Cav. Giddings' Bn. Co.E
Reeton, J.F. AL 28th Inf. Co.L
Reeve, A.D. GA 6th Cav. Co.I
Reeve, Baron D. GA 4th Inf. Co.F 2nd Bvt.Lt.
Reeve, David J.B. VA 21st Inf. Co.F
Reeve, Decatur L. GA 4th Inf. Co.F
Reeve, Edward MO 1st Inf. Co.B
Reeve, Edward P. VA 1st Inf. Co.D Capt.
Reeve, Edward W. GA Arty. 9th Bn. Co.B
Reeve, G.T GA 2nd Res. Co.H
Reeve, J.D. AL 5th Cav.
Reeve, John J. VA 21st Inf. Co.F Sgt.
Reeve, John J. VA Inf. Hutter's Co.
Reeve, John J. Stevenson's Staff Maj.,AAG
Reeve, Joseph C. TN 53rd Inf. Co.D
Reeve, Joseph G. LA Inf. 1st Sp.Bn. (Rightor's) Co.F
Reeve, Nathan H. TN Lt.Arty. Burrough's Co.
Reeve, O.C. LA 26th Inf. Co.B
Reeve, Richard LA 9th Inf. Co.C
Reeve, Ruben C.N. AL 28th Inf. Co.E
Reeve, William F.N. GA Arty. 9th Bn. Co.B
Reeve, William H. TN Greer's Regt.Part.Rangers Co.A
Reeve, W.J.C. GA 1st (Olmstead's) Inf. Co.G
Reeve, W.J.C. GA 2nd Res. Co.H
Reevees, L.B. MS Inf. 3rd Bn. (St.Troops) Co.F
Reever, A.C. MO Inf. 4th Regt.St.Guard Co.E
Reever, D.C. MO Inf. 4th Regt.St.Guard Co.E
Reever, William R. MO Inf. 4th Regt.St.Guard Co.E
Reeves, --- AL 25th Inf. Co.B
Reeves, --- GA 19th Inf. Co.I Sgt.
Reeves, --- TX Cav. McCord's Frontier Regt. Co.K
Reeves, --- VA Scott's Bn.Loc.Def. 3rd Sgt.
Reeves, A. TX 5th Inf. Martindale's Co.
Reeves, A. TX Inf. Timmons' Regt. Co.C
Reeves, A.A. GA 1st Cav. Co.K
Reeves, A.A. GA 12th Cav. Co.H
Reeves, A.A. GA 13th Inf. Co.I
Reeves, A.A. GA 44th Inf. Co.G
Reeves, A.A. TX Cav. 1st Bn.St.Troops Co.E
Reeves, A.A.J. MS 32nd Inf. Co.F
Reeves, A.B. GA 7th Inf. (St Guards) Co.F 1st Sgt.
Reeves, A.B. MS Lt.Arty. Lomax's Co.
Reeves, Abner GA 6th Inf. (St.Guards) Co.I
Reeves, Abner GA 44th Inf. Co.I
Reeves, Abner MS 38th Cav. Co.A
Reeves, Abner TN 16th (Logwood's) Cav. Co.F 3rd Lt.
Reeves, Absalom KY 1st Inf.
Reeves, A.I. MS 24th Inf. Co.B Cpl.
Reeves, A.J. AL 31st Inf. Co.H Lt.
Reeves, A.J. MS 2nd (Davidson's) Inf. Co.A 2nd Lt.
Reeves, A.J. TN Inf. 1st Bn. (Colms') Co. 2nd Lt.
Reeves, A.J. TN Inf. 4th Cons.Regt. Co.H
Reeves, Albert NC 16th Inf. Co.L
Reeves, Albert NC Inf. Thomas Legion Co.E
Reeves, Albert M. TN 1st (Feild's) Inf. Co.G
Reeves, Albert R. KY 13th Cav. Co.C
Reeves, Alexander MS 33rd Inf. Co.C

Reeves, Alexander A.J. MS 2nd (Davidson's) Inf. Co.A
Reeves, Alfred GA 20th Inf. Co.H
Reeves, A.L.M. GA 1st (Fannin's) Res. Co.F
Reeves, Alonzo GA 43rd Inf. Co.B
Reeves, A.M. NC Cav. McRae's Bn. Co.C 2nd Lt.
Reeves, Amos M. TX 18th Cav. Co.F
Reeves, Amos W. GA Hvy.Arty. 22nd Bn. Co.A
Reeves, A.N. MO 10th Inf. Co.F
Reeves, Anderson MS 11th Inf. Co.A
Reeves, Anderson P. NC 29th Inf. Co.C Cpl.
Reeves, Andrew AR 1st (Dobbin's) Cav.
Reeves, Andrew GA 41st Inf. Co.B
Reeves, Andrew TN 34th Inf. Co.A
Reeves, Andrew J. GA 51st Inf. Co.E
Reeves, Andrew J. MS 30th Inf. Co.A Cpl.
Reeves, Andrew M. NC 26th Inf. Co.A Sgt.
Reeves, Andrew W. AL 47th Inf. Co.B,A
Reeves, Aquilla GA Inf. 25th Bn. (Prov.Guard) Co.C
Reeves, A.R. AL 1st Inf. Co.G
Reeves, Archibald MS 44th Inf. Co.L
Reeves, Archibald T. AL 13th Inf. Co.K 2nd Lt.
Reeves, Archie T. TX 1st (Yager's) Cav. Co.C
Reeves, Asael TX Cav. 1st Regt.St.Troops Co.C
Reeves, A.T. 20th Conf.Cav. 1st Co.H
Reeves, Athiel NC 44th Inf. Co.F
Reeves, Atlas J. TN 32nd Inf. Co.E,K
Reeves, Augustus GA 12th Cav. Co.H
Reeves, Augustus A. GA 7th Inf. (St.Guards) Co.D
Reeves, Avery TN 1st (Turney's) Inf. Co.F
Reeves, A.W. GA 1st Inf. (St.Guards) Co.A 2nd Lt.
Reeves, A.W. GA Inf. 27th Bn. Martin's Co.
Reeves, A.W. GA 63rd Inf. Co.G
Reeves, B. LA 19th Inf. Co.I
Reeves, B. MS 9th Cav. Co.E
Reeves, B.A. KY 3rd Mtd.Inf. Co.M
Reeves, Benjamin GA Cav. Roswell Bn. Co.A
Reeves, Benjamin TX Cav. Morgan's Regt. Co.E
Reeves, Benjamin F. GA 8th Inf. (St.Guards) Co.D
Reeves, Benjamin F. GA 55th Inf. Co.F
Reeves, Benjamin H. FL 6th Inf. Co.H
Reeves, Benjamin H. GA 13th Inf. Co.I
Reeves, Benjamin L. TX 1st (Yager's) Cav. Co.C
Reeves, Benjamin L. TX Cav. 3rd (Yager's) Bn. Co.C
Reeves, B.N. AL 15th Inf. Co.F
Reeves, Boliver B. MS 30th Inf. Co.H Cpl.
Reeves, Brantley A. NC 34th Inf. Co.K
Reeves, Burgess AL 13th Inf. Co.K
Reeves, B.W. AL 30th Inf. Co.E
Reeves, B.W. AR 37th Inf. Co.K 1st Sgt.
Reeves, C. AL 1st Inf. Co.I
Reeves, C. MS 1st Inf. Co.B
Reeves, C. Exch.Bn. 2nd Co.A, 3rd Co.B,CSA
Reeves, Calvin AR 23rd Inf. Co.K
Reeves, Calvin MS 26th Inf. Co.F
Reeves, Calvin NC 2nd Detailed Men Co.F Jr.2nd Lt.
Reeves, Calvin NC 22nd Inf. Co.F 2nd Lt.
Reeves, Calvin TN 13th Inf. Co.A

Reeves, C.B. MO Inf. 2nd Regt.St.Guard Co.C 3rd Lt.
Reeves, C.B. SC 2nd St.Troops Co.E
Reeves, C.B. SC 17th Inf. Co.G
Reeves, C.C. AL 29th Inf. Co.G Sgt.
Reeves, C.C. MS 43rd Inf. Co.B
Reeves, C.D. SC 11th Inf. Co.H
Reeves, C.G. AR 45th Cav. Co.A
Reeves, Charles AL 1st Inf.
Reeves, Charles GA 48th Inf. Co.K Cpl.
Reeves, Charles MS 4th Cav. Co.C Cpl.
Reeves, Charles MS Cav. Hughes' Bn. Co.A
Reeves, Charles NC 1st Cav. (9th St.Troops) Co.A
Reeves, Charles NC 6th Cav. (65th St.Troops) Co.B,D
Reeves, Charles A. AL Inf. 1st Regt. Co.G
Reeves, Charles A. TX Waul's Legion Co.C
Reeves, Charles B. KY 14th Cav. Co.D,A
Reeves, Charles K. GA 5th Inf. Co.B Sgt.
Reeves, Charles L. NC 42nd Inf. Co.B Sgt.
Reeves, Charles L. NC Pris.Guards Howard's Co. 3rd Lt.
Reeves, Charles L. TX 1st Inf. Co.G
Reeves, Charles R. MS 20th Inf. Co.C
Reeves, Charles S. TN 51st Inf. Co.E
Reeves, Charles W. TN 21st (Wilson's) Cav. Co.E
Reeves, Charley TX 8th Inf. Co.E
Reeves, Chisten M. AL 1st Bn. Hilliard's Legion Vol. Co.B
Reeves, Christopher G. AR 1st Vol. Co.C
Reeves, Cicero GA 36th (Broyles') Inf. Co.K
Reeves, Cicero NC 1st Cav. (9th St.Troops) Co.A
Reeves, C.J. GA 2nd Cav. (St.Guards) Co.A
Reeves, C.L. GA 63rd Inf. Co.E
Reeves, C.L. NC 5th Inf. Co.E Sgt.
Reeves, C.L. NC 22nd Inf. Co.G
Reeves, Clem W.J. TN 32nd Inf. Co.I
Reeves, C.M. AL 12th Inf. Co.D
Reeves, C.M. GA Cav. (St.Guards) Bond's Co.
Reeves, C.M. TX 18th Inf. Co.H
Reeves, Coleman AL 31st (Part.Rangers) Co.F Sgt.
Reeves, Columbus D. AL 13th Inf. Co.I Drum.
Reeves, C.S. Gen. & Staff Asst.Surg.
Reeves, C.W. AL 17th Inf. Co.K
Reeves, C.W. TN 21st & 22nd (Cons.) Cav. Co.F
Reeves, D. SC Lt.Arty. 3rd (Palmetto) Bn. Co.I
Reeves, D. VA 1st (Farinholt's) Res. Co.E
Reeves, Daniel NC 18th Inf. Co.A
Reeves, Daniel TN 62nd Mtd.Inf. Co.F
Reeves, Daniel D. VA Lt.Arty. 38th Bn. Co.B
Reeves, Daniel L. GA Floyd Legion (St.Guards) Co.G,I
Reeves, Daniel M. AL 10th Inf. Co.I
Reeves, David FL Inf. 2nd Bn. Co.C
Reeves, David FL 10th Inf. Co.H
Reeves, David NC 18th Inf. Co.A
Reeves, David TN Cav. 7th Bn. (Bennett's) Co.E
Reeves, David TN 22nd (Barteau's) Cav. Co.G Sgt.
Reeves, David TN 48th (Voorhies') Inf.
Reeves, David VA Cav. Mosby's Regt. (Part. Rangers) Co.F

Reeves, David P. TN 28th Inf. Co.C 1st Lt.
Reeves, David W. AL 1st Inf. Co.H Cpl.
Reeves, David W. NC 16th Inf. Co.F
Reeves, D.C. AL 31st Inf. Co.H
Reeves, D.D. AL 25th Inf. Co.B
Reeves, Dimer W. TX Cav. Morgan's Regt. Co.B
Reeves, D.M. TX 19th Inf. Co.A
Reeves, Douglas TX 23rd Cav. Co.H
Reeves, D.P. TN 28th (Cons.) Inf. Co.C 1st Lt.
Reeves, Drewry GA 3rd Inf. Co.A Sgt.
Reeves, Drewry GA 20th Inf. Co.H
Reeves, Dyer SC 3rd Res. Co.D
Reeves, E.B. TX 20th Inf. Co.E Music.
Reeves, E.D. MS 37th Inf. Co.E
Reeves, Edmond 1st Conf.Eng.Troops Co.D Artif.
Reeves, Edmund VA Hvy.Arty. 18th Bn. Co.C
Reeves, Edward AL 39th Inf. Co.A
Reeves, Edward MO 1st & 4th Cons.Inf. Co.D,B
Reeves, Edward NC 11th (Bethel Regt.) Inf. Co.G
Reeves, Edward B. TX 2nd Cav. Co.E Bugler
Reeves, Edward Y. MS 43rd Inf. Co.E 1st Lt.
Reeves, E.G. AL 30th Inf. Co.I
Reeves, E.G. MS Cav. Powers' Regt. Co.D
Reeves, E.H. AL 31st Inf. Co.H
Reeves, E.H. GA 13th Inf. Co.D
Reeves, E.H. TN 28th (Cons.) Inf. Co.F
Reeves, E.H. TN 84th Inf. Co.B
Reeves, E. Henry AR 34th Inf. Co.E
Reeves, E.J. MS 2nd (Quinn's St.Troops) Inf. Co.I Cpl.
Reeves, E.L. AR 19th (Dockery's) Inf. Co.F
Reeves, Elbert C. TN 29th Inf. Co.G
Reeves, Elijah M. NC 34th Inf. Co.K
Reeves, Elijah T. KY 14th Cav. Co.D
Reeves, Elisha MS Cav. Garland's Bn. Co.A
Reeves, E.M. SC 2nd Arty. Co.A
Reeves, Emory G. AL 3rd Cav. Co.G
Reeves, Enoch O. GA 21st Inf. Co.G Sgt.
Reeves, E.R. TX Cav. Baylor's Regt. Co.K
Reeves, Ervin KY 3rd Mtd.Inf. Co.E
Reeves, E.T. AL 60th Inf. Co.H
Reeves, E.T. KY 4th Cav. Co.G
Reeves, Evander W. MS 37th Inf. Co.E
Reeves, E.Y. MS 10th Cav. Co.A Cpl.
Reeves, Ezekiel B. AL 10th Inf. Co.I Cpl.
Reeves, F. Exch.Bn. 2nd Co.C,CSA
Reeves, F.A.M. GA 12th Cav. Co.H
Reeves, F.A.M. GA 13th Inf. Co.I
Reeves, F.E. SC 1st Cav. Co.E
Reeves, Fidelia F. NC 16th Inf. Co.F
Reeves, F.J. TN 11th Inf. Co.H
Reeves, F.L. TN 47th Inf. Co.A Sgt.
Reeves, F.M. AR 10th Mil.
Reeves, F.M. GA 30th Inf. Co.H
Reeves, F.M. MS 43rd Inf. Co.B
Reeves, F.M. TN Cav. Jackson's Co.
Reeves, F.M. Conf.Cav. Clarkson's Bn. Ind. Rangers Co.A,F
Reeves, Francis MO 1st & 4th Cons.Inf. Co.B,K 2nd Lt.
Reeves, Francis M. AR Cav. Harrell's Bn. Co.B
Reeves, Francis M. AL 18th Inf. Co.A
Reeves, Francis M. AL 3rd Bn. Hilliard's Legion Vol. Co.E

Reeves, Francis S. MD 1st Inf. Co.H
Reeves, Franklin GA 13th Inf. Co.D 1st Sgt.
Reeves, Franklin E. NC 34th Inf. Co.K
Reeves, Frank M. TN 7th Inf. Co.B Music.
Reeves, Freeman KY 2nd (Duke's) Cav. Co.K
Reeves, F.S. VA 2nd St.Res. Co.B
Reeves, G.B. AL 15th Inf. Co.F Cpl.
Reeves, G.B. AL Inf. 60th Regt. Co.H
Reeves, G.B. SC 13th Inf. Co.I
Reeves, G.C. KY 7th Mtd.Inf. Co.C
Reeves, George AL 8th Inf. Co.F
Reeves, George MS 3rd Cav. Co.A
Reeves, George MS 3rd Inf. Co.A
Reeves, George SC 24th Inf. Co.C
Reeves, George SC 25th Inf. Co.E
Reeves, George B. MS 42nd Inf. Co.A Cpl.
Reeves, George C. MS 11th Inf. Co.K
Reeves, George C. VA Cav. 39th Bn. Co.A
Reeves, George D. VA 4th Res. Co.B
Reeves, George L. AR 8th Inf. New Co.F
Reeves, George L. AR 14th (McCarver's) Inf. Co.E
Reeves, George N. AL Lt.Arty. 20th Bn. Co.A Artif.
Reeves, George N. AL 6th Inf. Co.L
Reeves, George R. GA 20th Inf. Co.H
Reeves, George R. TX 11th Cav. Co.C Col.
Reeves, George W. AL 4th (Russell's) Cav. Co.I Cpl.
Reeves, George W. AL 2nd Bn. Hilliard's Legion Vol. Co.C Cpl.
Reeves, George W. AR 17th (Griffith's) Inf. Co.H
Reeves, George W. NC 26th Inf. Co.A 1st Lt.
Reeves, George W. TX Cav. Ragsdale's Bn. Co.A
Reeves, George W. TX 17th Inf. Co.I
Reeves, George W. TX Waul's Legion Co.C
Reeves, George W. VA 5th Inf. Co.C
Reeves, Gideon W. AL 13th Inf. Co.K
Reeves, Gilbert FL 9th Inf. Co.A
Reeves, G.J. MS Cav. Ham's Regt. Co.E 2nd Lt.
Reeves, G.J. MS 2nd (Davidson's) Inf. Co.A Cpl.
Reeves, G.K. VA 1st (Farinholt's) Res. Co.E Cpl.
Reeves, G.N. AR 7th Cav. Co.B
Reeves, G.R. TX 1st Hvy.Arty. Co.I
Reeves, G.W. AL 59th Inf. Co.A Cpl.
Reeves, G.W. AR 35th Inf. Co.E
Reeves, G.W. GA 7th Cav. Co.E
Reeves, G.W. GA Cav. 21st Bn. Co.B
Reeves, G.W. GA 53rd Inf. Co.D
Reeves, G.W. MS 7th Cav. Co.B
Reeves, G.W. MS Inf. 3rd Bn. (St.Troops) Co.D
Reeves, G.W. MO Cav. Coffee's Regt. Co.G
Reeves, G.W. SC 1st Cav. Co.I
Reeves, G.W. TN 8th Inf. Co.B
Reeves, H. AR 10th Mil.
Reeves, H. AR 10th Mil. Co.F
Reeves, H. AR 12th Bn.S.S. Co.C
Reeves, H. GA Inf. 1st Loc.Troops (Augusta) Co.E
Reeves, H. GA 1st (Ramsey's) Inf. Co.I
Reeves, H. SC 1st Cav. Co.E
Reeves, H. SC 4th Cav. Co.C

Reeves, H. TN 10th (DeMoss') Cav. Co.F
Reeves, H. TN Cav. Napier's Bn. Co.C
Reeves, Hardin NC 5th Sr.Res. Co.B
Reeves, Harris P.H. MO 10th Inf. Co.F Cpl.
Reeves, Harvey AL 10th Inf. Co.A
Reeves, Haywood GA 21st Inf. Co.G
Reeves, H.B. GA 13th Inf. Co.D
Reeves, H.C. GA Hvy.Arty. 22nd Bn. Co.A
Reeves, H.C. GA 13th Inf. Co.I
Reeves, H.D. LA 30th Inf. Co.E
Reeves, Henry AR 1st Mtd.Rifles Co.G
Reeves, Henry AR Inf. 4th Bn. Co.A
Reeves, Henry GA 7th Inf. (St.Guards) Co.K
Reeves, Henry GA 43rd Inf. Co.B
Reeves, Henry MO Lt.Arty. McDonald's Co.
Reeves, Henry MO 6th Inf. Co.D
Reeves, Henry B. NC 1st Inf. Co.C
Reeves, Henry C. TX 1st (Yager's) Cav. Co.C Bugler
Reeves, Henry C. TX Cav. 3rd (Yager's) Bn. Co.C
Reeves, Henry H. GA 31st Inf. Co.G Cpl.
Reeves, Henry S. GA 50th Inf. Co.F Capt.
Reeves, H.H. Horse Arty. White's Btty.
Reeves, Hickman B. AL 30th Inf. Co.E
Reeves, Hiram GA 3rd Res. Co.K,G
Reeves, Hiram GA 66th Inf. Co.E
Reeves, Hiram MS Cav. Hughes' Bn. Co.A
Reeves, Hiram SC Lt.Arty. 3rd (Palmetto) Bn. Co.F
Reeves, Hiram SC Arty. Bachman's Co. (German Lt.Arty.)
Reeves, H.J. TN 10th (DeMoss') Cav. Co.F
Reeves, Holden AR 11th Inf. Co.F
Reeves, H.P. AR 32nd Inf. Co.G
Reeves, H.P. TX Waul's Legion Co.H
Reeves, Hugh C. NC 28th Inf. Co.G
Reeves, Hugh C. NC 44th Inf. Co.G
Reeves, Hughey GA 2nd Cav. Co.E
Reeves, Humphrey P. GA Arty. 9th Bn. Co.A,E
Reeves, Humphry P. LA 31st Inf. Co.B Cpl.
Reeves, Huston TN 48th (Voorhies') Inf. Co.G 2nd Lt.
Reeves, H.W. MS 2nd (Quinn's St.Troops) Inf. Co.I 2nd Lt.
Reeves, I.E. TN Inf. 2nd Cons.Regt. Co.H
Reeves, I.J. AL 20th Inf. Co.B
Reeves, I.M. LA 7th Cav. Co.A
Reeves, Ira E. GA 46th Inf. Co.G
Reeves, Irvin P. GA 23rd Inf. Co.C
Reeves, Isaac LA 10th Inf. Co.K Cpl.
Reeves, Isaac MS 4th Cav. Co.C
Reeves, Isaac MS Hughes' Bn. Co.A
Reeves, Isaac E. TN 29th Inf. Co.G Capt.
Reeves, Isaac H. AL 10th Inf. Co.I Cpl.
Reeves, Isaac N. MS 16th Inf. Co.F
Reeves, Ishma W. GA 19th Inf. Co.I 4th Sgt.
Reeves, J. AL 9th Inf.
Reeves, J. AL 31st Inf. Co.C
Reeves, J. AR 1st (Monroe's) Cav. Co.H
Reeves, J. LA 22nd Inf. Co.B
Reeves, J. MS Mtd.Inf. (St.Troops) Maxey's Co.
Reeves, J. TN 21st & 22nd (Cons.) Cav. Co.C
Reeves, J. TN 28th (Cons.) Inf. Co.K 2nd Lt.
Reeves, J. TX 11th (Spaight's) Bn.Vol. Co.A
Reeves, J.A. GA Hvy.Arty. 22nd Bn. Co.A
Reeves, J.A. GA 8th Inf. Co.H

Reeves, J.A. GA 69th Inf. 1st Co.A
Reeves, J.A. SC 1st (Butler's) Inf. Co.C
Reeves, J.A. TX Cav. Benavides' Regt. Co.G
Reeves, J.A. TX 2nd Inf. Co.E
Reeves, J.A. Conf.Cav. Clarkson's Bn. Ind.
  Rangers Co.A
Reeves, Jack. MS Cav. Garland's Bn. Co.A
Reeves, Jackson NC 1st Bn.Jr.Res. Co.C Sgt.
Reeves, Jacob GA 44th Inf. Co.D
Reeves, Jacob L. FL 6th Inf. Co.C
Reeves, J.A.J. GA 38th Inf. Co.A
Reeves, James AL 56th Part.Rangers Co.C
Reeves, James AL 37th Inf. Co.C
Reeves, James AR 7th Cav. Co.K
Reeves, James AR 7th Inf. Co.I
Reeves, James AR 9th Inf. Co.A
Reeves, James AR 11th Inf. Co.F
Reeves, James AR 37th Inf. Co.B Sgt.
Reeves, James GA 27th Inf. Co.G
Reeves, James GA 48th Inf.
Reeves, James GA Cobb's Legion
Reeves, James KY 3rd Mtd.Inf. Co.F
Reeves, James LA 1st Hvy.Arty. (Reg.) Co.D
Reeves, James LA 9th Inf. Co.C
Reeves, James LA 10th Inf. Co.K Sgt.
Reeves, James LA 22nd (Cons.) Inf. Co.B
Reeves, James MO 3rd Inf. Co.D
Reeves, James MO Inf. 4th Regt.St.Guard Co.E
Reeves, James MO 12th Inf. Co.D
Reeves, James NC 2nd Inf. Co.H
Reeves, James NC 55th Inf. Co.G
Reeves, James TN 29th Inf. Co.E
Reeves, James TX 33rd Cav. Co.D Cpl.
Reeves, James TX Cav. Ragsdale's Bn. Co.A
Reeves, James A. AL 13th Inf. Co.G
Reeves, James A. AL 19th Inf. Co.E
Reeves, James A. GA 46th Inf. Co.G
Reeves, James A. MS 20th Inf. Co.G
Reeves, James B. GA 19th Inf. Co.I
Reeves, James B. NC 1st Inf. Co.C
Reeves, James C. NC 34th Inf. Co.K Cpl.
Reeves, James C. SC 20th Inf. Co.H
Reeves, James C. TN 54th Inf. Co.E
Reeves, James E. TN 28th Inf. Co.C Sgt.
Reeves, James E. TX 10th Cav. Co.K
Reeves, James F. GA Inf. 25th Bn. (Prov.Guard)
  Co.C
Reeves, James F. MS 26th Inf. Co.G Sgt.
Reeves, James G. GA 55th Inf. Co.F Sgt.
Reeves, James H. GA 44th Inf. Co.D
Reeves, James J. AL 19th Inf. Co.F
Reeves, James J. TX 18th Inf. Co.D
Reeves, James L. AL 6th Cav. Co.H,F Cpl.
Reeves, James L. AL 3rd Bn. Hilliard's Legion
  Vol. Co.E
Reeves, James L. VA 26th Inf. Co.D
Reeves, James M. AL 32nd Inf. Co.K
Reeves, Jas. M. AL Cp. of Instr. Talladega
Reeves, James M. GA 3rd Cav. Co.A
Reeves, James M. GA 6th Inf. Co.B
Reeves, James M. GA 23rd Inf. Co.D 2nd Lt.
Reeves, James M. NC 29th Inf. Co.C
Reeves, James M. TN 23rd Inf. Co.E
Reeves, James M. VA 5th Inf. Co.C
Reeves, James N. MS 35th Inf. Co.H
Reeves, James R. AL Low's Regt. Co.E
Reeves, James R. GA 41st Inf. Co.B

Reeves, James R. SC 2nd Rifles Co.L
Reeves, James S. NC 61st Inf. Co.C Cpl.
Reeves, James T. GA 60th Inf. 1st Co.A
Reeves, James T. NC 53rd Inf. Co.D
Reeves, James T. TX 1st (McCulloch's) Cav.
  Co.E
Reeves, James W. GA Inf. 3rd Bn. Co.C
Reeves, James Weldon TX 20th Cav. Co.D
Reeves, Jarrett A. AR 14th (Powers') Inf. Co.K
Reeves, Jasper GA 42nd Inf. Co.G
Reeves, J.B. GA 13th Inf. Co.D
Reeves, J.B. TN 47th Inf. Co.A
Reeves, J.C. AL 7th Cav. Co.H
Reeves, J.C. AL 8th (Livingston's) Cav. Co.B
Reeves, J.C. AR 30th Inf. Co.F
Reeves, J.C. GA 9th Inf. Co.K
Reeves, J.C. LA 31st Inf. Co.F
Reeves, J.C. MS 4th Inf. Co.C
Reeves, J.C. SC 2nd Rifles Co.F
Reeves, J.D. GA 46th Inf. Co.F
Reeves, J.D. MS 43rd Inf. Co.B
Reeves, J.D. SC 2nd Inf. Co.I
Reeves, J.D. TN Lt.Arty. Phillips' Co.
Reeves, J.E. GA Floyd Legion (St.Guards) Co.F
Reeves, J.E. MS 1st (Foote's) Inf. (St.Troops)
  Hobart's Co.
Reeves, J.E. TN Inf. 1st Cons.Regt. Co.C 2nd
  Lt.
Reeves, J.E. TN 28th (Cons.) Inf. Co.A 2nd Lt.
Reeves, J.E. TX 11th Cav. AASurg.
Reeves, J.E. TX 20th Bn.St.Troops Co.B
Reeves, Jefferson G. SC Lt.Arty. 3rd (Palmetto)
  Bn. Co.D
Reeves, Jeremiah GA Conscr.
Reeves, Jery TX 10th Cav. Co.K
Reeves, Jesse AL 4th Cav. Co.L,F
Reeves, Jesse AL 10th Inf. Co.A
Reeves, Jesse AL 18th Inf. Co.E,K
Reeves, Jesse AL 46th Inf. Co.A
Reeves, Jesse GA 15th Inf. Co.E
Reeves, Jesse NC 44th Inf. Co.F
Reeves, Jesse TN 9th Inf. Co.F
Reeves, Jesse VA 60th Inf. Co.B
Reeves, Jesse A. NC 26th Inf. Co.A 2nd Lt.
Reeves, Jessee W. AL 17th Inf. Co.K
Reeves, Jessee W. AR 1st (Crawford's) Cav.
  Co.E
Reeves, Jesse W. NC 62nd Inf. Co.E
Reeves, J.F. GA Cav. Alexander's Co. Sgt.
Reeves, J.F. MS 32nd Inf. Co.K,F
Reeves, J.H. AL 62nd Inf. Co.C,K
Reeves, J.H. GA 27th Inf. Co.E
Reeves, J.H. KY 3rd Mtd.Inf. Co.M
Reeves, J.H. LA 3rd (Wingfield's) Cav. Co.C
Reeves, J.H. LA 16th Inf. Co.H
Reeves, J.H. MS 6th Inf. Co.E
Reeves, J.H. SC 4th Cav. Co.D
Reeves, J.H. TN 22nd (Barteau's) Cav. Co.I
Reeves, J.H. TN 47th Inf. Co.H
Reeves, J.H. VA Horse Arty. G.W. Brown's Co.
Reeves, J.H. Conf.Cav. Clarkson's Bn. Ind.
  Rangers Co.F
Reeves, J. Henry AR 7th Cav. Co.B
Reeves, J.H.W. TN 22nd Inf. Co.F
Reeves, J.J. AL 60th Inf. Co.H
Reeves, J.J. AL 61st Inf. Co.H
Reeves, J.J. AR 27th Inf. Old Co.B

Reeves, J.J. TN 21st & 22nd (Cons.) Cav. Co.C
Reeves, J.J. TN 22nd (Barteau's) Cav. Co.K
Reeves, J.J. TX 10th Cav. Co.B
Reeves, J.J. Gen. & Staff AASurg.
Reeves, J.J.R. AR 8th Cav. Co.E
Reeves, J. Judson TX 18th Inf. Co.E
Reeves, J.L. AR 10th Mil. Co.G
Reeves, J.L. TN 11th (Holman's) Cav. Co.D
Reeves, J.L. VA Inf. 4th Bn.Loc.Def. Co.A
Reeves, J.M. AL 4th Res. Co.E
Reeves, J.M. AL 14th Inf. Co.I
Reeves, J.M. AL 15th Inf. Co.C
Reeves, J.M. AL 37th Inf. Co.C
Reeves, J.M. AL 38th Inf. Co.G Cpl.
Reeves, J.M. GA Cav. 8th Bn. (St.Guards) Co.B
Reeves, J.M. GA 1st Inf. (St.Guards) Co.A
Reeves, J.M. GA 31st Inf. Co.D
Reeves, J.M. LA 2nd Cav. Co.G
Reeves, J.M. LA 18th Inf. Co.K
Reeves, J.M. LA 30th Inf. Co.D
Reeves, J.M. TN 13th Inf. Co.G
Reeves, J.N. GA 31st Inf. Co.G
Reeves, J.N. Conf.Cav. Clarkson's Bn. Ind.
  Rangers Co.F
Reeves, J.N. Gen. & Staff Chap.
Reeves, Joel AL 18th Inf. Co.E,K
Reeves, Joel AR 50th Mil. Co.G
Reeves, Joel P. NC 49th Inf. Co.C
Reeves, John AL 7th Cav. Graves' Co.
Reeves, John AL Cav. Lewis' Bn. Co.D
Reeves, John AL Lt.Arty. 2nd Bn. Co.E
Reeves, John AL Cp. of Instr. Talladega Co.A
Reeves, John AL Recruits
Reeves, John AR 1st (Crawford's) Cav. Co.A
Reeves, John AR 2nd Inf. Co.B
Reeves, John AR 4th Inf. Co.E
Reeves, John AR 10th Mil.
Reeves, John GA 1st Cav. Co.G
Reeves, John GA 2nd Cav. Co.E
Reeves, John GA 4th Inf.
Reeves, John GA 23rd Inf. Co.G
Reeves, John GA 40th Inf. Co.G
Reeves, John LA Cav. Benjamin's Co.
Reeves, John LA 10th Inf. Co.K
Reeves, John MS Cav. 17th Bn. Co.A
Reeves, John MS 3rd Inf. Co.A Cpl.
Reeves, John MO 1st N.E. Cav. Price's Co.M
Reeves, John NC 1st Cav. (9th St.Troops) Co.K
Reeves, John SC Inf. 3rd Bn. Co.F
Reeves, John Inf. Bailey's Cons.Regt. Co.D
Reeves, John TX 1st (McCulloch's) Cav. Co.H
Reeves, John TX Cav. Benavides' Regt. Co.G
Reeves, John TX 11th Inf.
Reeves, John VA Horse Arty. G.W. Brown's Co.
Reeves, John Trans-MS Conf.Cav. 1st Bn.
Reeves, John A. GA 13th Inf. Co.D
Reeves, John A. GA 23rd Inf. Co.G
Reeves, John A. GA 36th (Broyles') Inf. Co.K
Reeves, John A. GA 38th Inf. Co.B
Reeves, John A. MS 37th Inf. Co.A
Reeves, John A. NC 29th Inf. Co.H 2nd Lt.
Reeves, John A. SC 1st (Orr's) Rifles Co.D
Reeves, John A. TX Cav. Morgan's Regt. Co.B
Reeves, John A.J. AL Inf. 1st Regt. Co.G
Reeves, Johnathan N. GA 37th Inf. Co.C
Reeves, John B. GA 44th Inf. Co.E

Reeves, John D. GA 1st (Fannin's) Res. Co.G
Reeves, John D. GA 17th Inf. Co.I
Reeves, John D. MS 1st (Patton's) Inf. Co.C
Reeves, John E. AL 39th Inf. Co.A
Reeves, John F. NC 26th Inf. Co.C
Reeves, John F. VA 8th Inf. Co.H
Reeves, John G. TX Cav. Martin's Regt. Co.D
  2nd Lt.
Reeves, John H. GA 3rd Cav. Co.G
Reeves, John H. SC Arty. Bachman's Co.
  (German Lt.Arty.)
Reeves, John H. TX 15th Cav. Co.H
Reeves, John J. SC 2nd Inf. Co.H
Reeves, John M. AL 18th Inf. Co.H
Reeves, John M. FL 8th Inf. Co.B
Reeves, John M. MS 7th Inf. Co.B Sgt.
Reeves, John M. MS 15th (Cons.) Inf. Co.H
Reeves, John M. MS 20th Inf. Co.C
Reeves, John M. VA Courtney Arty.
Reeves, John Q. SC 3rd Cav. Co.C
Reeves, John Q. SC Mil.Cav. 4th Regt.
  Howard's Co.
Reeves, John Quincy Adams TN 6th Inf. Co.H
Reeves, John R. AR 23rd Inf. Co.D
Reeves, John R. TN 6th Inf. Co.C Cpl.
Reeves, John R. 3rd Conf.Cav. Co.E 1st Sgt.
Reeves, Johnson TX 4th Cav. Co.C
Reeves, John T. GA 3rd Inf. Co.A
Reeves, John T. TX Cav. Ragsdale's Bn. Co.A
Reeves, John W. GA 12th Inf. Co.C Sgt.
Reeves, John W. GA 14th Inf. Co.C
Reeves, John W. MS 11th (Perrin's) Cav. Co.F
Reeves, John W. NC 28th Inf. Co.G
Reeves, John W. TN 7th Inf. Co.H
Reeves, John W. VA 31st Mil. Co.I
Reeves, John W.L. GA Inf. Alexander's Co.
Reeves, John W.L. GA Cobb's Legion Co.G
Reeves, Jonathan TX 8th Inf. Co.E,K Cpl.
Reeves, Jonathan F. AL Cav. Lewis' Bn. Co.E
Reeves, Jonathan J. TN 48th (Voorhies') Inf.
Reeves, Jordan TX 19th Inf. Co.A
Reeves, Joseph AL 18th Inf. Co.L
Reeves, Joseph AL 58th Inf. Co.G
Reeves, Joseph GA Inf. Alexander's Co. Sgt.
Reeves, Joseph TX Cav. Martin's Regt. Co.D
  Sgt.
Reeves, Joseph TX 11th Inf. Co.F
Reeves, Joseph A. AL 3rd Bn. Hilliard's Legion
  Vol. Co.E
Reeves, Joseph A. AR 6th Inf. Co.H 1st Lt.
Reeves, Joseph A. GA Inf. (Collier's Guards)
  Collier's Co. Sgt.
Reeves, Joseph C. MS Page's Co. (Lexington
  Guards)
Reeves, Joseph C. TX 24th Cav. Co.G Sgt.
Reeves, Joseph G. LA Lt.Arty. Fenner's Btty.
  Bugler
Reeves, Joseph H. MS 26th Inf. Co.G Sgt.
Reeves, Joseph M. AL 1st Bn. Hillard's Legion
  Vol. Co.B
Reeves, Joseph M. NC Coast Guards Galloway's
  Co.
Reeves, Joseph T. MS 38th Cav. Co.K
Reeves, Joseph W. GA 37th Inf. Co.I
Reeves, Joseph W. GA 38th Inf. Co.B
Reeves, Joshua NC Unassign.Conscr.
Reeves, Joshua H. MS 34th Inf. Co.K

Reeves, Joshua W. AR 18th Inf. Co.H
Reeves, J.P. MS 1st Cav.Res. Co.E
Reeves, J.P. MS 8th Inf. Co.B
Reeves, J.P. SC 2nd Inf. Co.K,H
Reeves, J.R. MS 7th Cav. Co.E
Reeves, J.S. AR Cav. Gordon's Regt. Co.F
Reeves, J.S. MS 33rd Inf. Co.K
Reeves, J.S. NC 29th Inf. Co.F
Reeves, J.S. NC 61st Inf. Co.G
Reeves, J.T. AR 20th Inf. Co.E Sgt.
Reeves, J.T. GA Cav. 22nd Bn. (St.Guards)
  Co.F
Reeves, J.T. GA Hvy.Arty. 22nd Bn. Co.A
Reeves, J.T. GA 23rd Inf. Co.H
Reeves, J.T. MS 7th Cav. Co.H
Reeves, J.T. MS 10th Cav. Co.D
Reeves, J.T. NC 6th Sr.Res. Co.A
Reeves, J.T. TN 9th Inf. Co.F
Reeves, J.T. TX 4th Inf. Co.D
Reeves, Julius C. NC 44th Inf. Co.F
Reeves, J.W. AL 30th Inf. Co.B
Reeves, J.W. AR 7th Cav. Co.B
Reeves, J.W. AR 3rd Inf. Co.K
Reeves, J.W. FL 1st (Res.) Inf. Co.I
Reeves, J.W. GA 19th Inf. Co.F
Reeves, J.W. GA 40th Inf. Co.G Cpl.
Reeves, J.W. LA 9th Inf. Co.B
Reeves, J.W. MO 12th Inf. Co.G
Reeves, J.W. TX Cav. Border's Regt. Co.I
Reeves, K.H. SC 4th Cav. Co.G
Reeves, K.H. SC 11th Inf. Sheridan's Co. Cpl.
Reeves, King H. AL 61st Inf. Co.G
Reeves, L. AL 29th Inf. Co.K
Reeves, L. SC Cav. 17th Bn. Co.D
Reeves, L. SC 11th Inf. Sheridan's Co.
Reeves, L.A. GA 13th Inf. Co.D
Reeves, Landen C. VA 1st Cav. Surg.
Reeves, Laomi NC 3rd Inf. Co.B
Reeves, L.B. MS Cav. 3rd Bn. (Ashcraft's)
  Co.C,F
Reeves, L.C. MS 15th (Cons.) Inf. Co.H
Reeves, L. Claiborne MS 20th Inf. Co.G
Reeves, Lemuel TX 33rd Cav. Co.C
Reeves, Levi SC Arty. Bachman's Co. (German
  Lt.Arty.)
Reeves, Levi SC 3rd Res. Co.I Cpl.
Reeves, Lewis SC 5th Cav. Co.C Sgt.
Reeves, Lewis T. TX 11th Cav. Co.C
Reeves, L.F. MS Inf. 3rd Bn. Co.I
Reeves, L.F. MS 26th Inf. Co.B
Reeves, L.F. MS 32nd Inf. Co.I
Reeves, Loftin AL 13th Inf. Co.F
Reeves, Loftin M. AL 13th Inf. Co.K
Reeves, Logan NC 3rd Inf. Co.A
Reeves, Lucius AL Inf. 1st Regt. Co.G
Reeves, Lucius Q.C. AL Inf. 1st Regt. Co.E
  Sgt.
Reeves, Lycurgus W. VA Cav. 39th Bn. Co.D
Reeves, M. AR 3rd Inf. Co.K
Reeves, M. GA 56th Inf. Co.F
Reeves, Malachi TX Inf. Currie's Co.
Reeves, Malachi W. NC 29th Inf. Co.C 1st Lt.
Reeves, Malakiah AR 1st (Monroe's) Cav. Co.C
Reeves, Malichiah TX 1st Inf. Co.I Sgt.
Reeves, Mark GA Phillips' Legion Co.M
Reeves, Marshall Morgan's Quirk's Co.,CSA
Reeves, Matthew TN 45th Inf. Co.I

Reeves, M.D. AL 57th Inf. Co.H
Reeves, Melvin AL 37th Inf. Co.C,D
Reeves, M.G. AR Inf. Adams' Regt. Moore's
  Co.
Reeves, M.G. GA 13th Inf. Co.I
Reeves, M.H. TX 3rd Cav. Co.D
Reeves, Micager AR Inf. 2nd Bn. Co.B
Reeves, Millege C. AL 18th Inf. Co.A
Reeves, Milton H. AL 18th Inf. Co.A
Reeves, Mincher L. NC 62nd Inf. Co.C
Reeves, Morgan SC 13th Inf. Co.I
Reeves, Moses S. GA Inf. Cobb Guards Co.A
Reeves, M.S. SC Mil. 1st Regt. (Charleston
  Res.) Co.J Cpl.
Reeves, M.W. GA 1st Cav. Co.K
Reeves, M.W. MS 27th Inf. Co.I
Reeves, Nathan TN 44th Inf. Co.B
Reeves, Nathaniel G. TN 1st (Feild's) Inf. Co.H
  Cpl.
Reeves, Newel W. MS 1st (Johnston's) Inf. Co.K
Reeves, Newton TN 48th (Nixon's) Inf. Co.A
Reeves, Newton TN 48th (Voorhies') Inf. Co.G
Reeves, N.G. TN Cav. Nixon's Regt. Co.I
Reeves, Noah GA 8th Inf. Co.H
Reeves, Noah V. AL 28th Inf. Co.E
Reeves, Norburns P. AL 10th Inf. Co.K
Reeves, N.P. AL 31st Inf. Co.K Capt.
Reeves, N.P. Gen. & Staff Surg.
Reeves, N.W. MS 32nd Inf. Co.F 2nd Lt.
Reeves, N.W. TN 55th (McKoin's) Inf. Bound's
  Co.
Reeves, Oliver C. MS 27th Inf. Co.G
Reeves, Peachey H. VA 52nd Inf. Co.D
Reeves, Perry G. AR 2nd Vol. Co.A
Reeves, Peter MS 3rd Inf. Co.A Cpl.
Reeves, Peter MS 20th Inf. Co.C Cpl.
Reeves, P.G. AR 32nd Inf. Co.E
Reeves, P.G. AR Inf. Adams' Regt. Co.G
Reeves, P.H. TX 30th Cav. Co.H
Reeves, P.J. GA 63rd Inf. Co.G
Reeves, Pleasant W. GA 41st Inf. Co.K
Reeves, P.P. TX 9th Cav. Co.C
Reeves, P.W. AR 18th Inf. Co.H Capt.
Reeves, P.W. 3rd Conf.Cav. Co.G
Reeves, R. AL 1st Bn.Cadets Co.A
Reeves, R., Dr. AR 9th Inf. Co.D Sr.2nd Lt.
Reeves, Raburn H. FL 6th Inf. Co.B Capt.
Reeves, Raibon FL 10th Inf. Love's Co. Bvt.2nd
  Lt.
Reeves, Randall GA Lt.Arty. 12th Bn. 1st Co.A
Reeves, Randal R. GA 63rd Inf. Co.A
Reeves, Ransom AL 12th Inf. Co.I,G
Reeves, Ransom B. LA 10th Inf. Co.E Sgt.
Reeves, R.B. AR 18th Inf. Co.D
Reeves, R.B. GA 13th Inf. Co.D
Reeves, R.B. LA 6th Inf.
Reeves, R.B. MS Grace's Co. (St.Troops) Cpl.
Reeves, R.C. MS 8th Inf. Co.K
Reeves, R.C. TN 45th Inf. Co.I
Reeves, Reddines TN 48th (Voorhies') Inf. Co.C
Reeves, Reuben A. TX 37th Cav. Co.E Capt.
Reeves, R.F. TN 43rd Inf. Co.C
Reeves, R.F. TN 48th (Nixon's) Inf. Co.A
Reeves, R.H. GA 8th Cav. Co.C 1st Sgt.
Reeves, R.H. GA 62nd Cav. Co.C 1st Sgt.
Reeves, R.H. GA 1st (Fannin's) Res. Co.I
Reeves, R.H. KY 7th Mtd.Inf. Co.I

Reeves, R.H. LA 8th Cav. Co.A
Reeves, R.H. MS 32nd Inf. Co.F
Reeves, R.H. SC 21st Inf. Co.L Ord.Sgt.
Reeves, R.H. TX Waul's Legion Co.F
Reeves, Richard AL 42nd Inf. Co.I
Reeves, Richard FL 1st Mil. Cpl.
Reeves, Richard TN 40th Inf. Co.F
Reeves, Richard E. NC 28th Inf. Maj.
Reeves, Richard H. MS 8th Inf. Co.D
Reeves, R.J. LA Inf.Cons.Crescent Regt. Co.N
Reeves, R.M. AL 3rd Res. Co.G
Reeves, R.M. GA Cav. 2nd Bn. Co.A
Reeves, R.O. TX Cav. Bourland's Regt. Ord.Sgt.
Reeves, Robert AR 9th Inf. Co.A
Reeves, Robert AR 18th Inf. Co.C
Reeves, Robert GA 13th Inf. Co.D
Reeves, Robert GA 27th Inf. Co.G
Reeves, Robert NC 18th Inf. Co.A Cpl.
Reeves, Robert TN Cav. Jackson's Co.
Reeves, Robert TN 48th (Nixon's) Inf. Co.A
Reeves, Robert TN 48th (Voorhies') Inf. Co.G
Reeves, Robert TX 25th Cav. Co.D
Reeves, Robert F. VA 52nd Inf. Co.D
Reeves, Robert N. GA 40th Inf. Co.I Sgt.
Reeves, Robert P. TX 11th Cav. Co.C 2nd Lt.
Reeves, Robert R. SC 2nd Cav. Co.B
Reeves, Robert W. TN 1st (Turney's) Inf. Co.C
Reeves, Rodolphus MS 8th Inf. Co.B
Reeves, R.R. AL 60th Inf. Co.H
Reeves, R.R. AL 1st Bn. Hilliard's Legion Vol. Co.B
Reeves, R.R. AR 1st Vol. Co.I
Reeves, R.S. AR 15th (Josey's) Inf. 1st Co.G
Reeves, Rufus H. TN 29th Inf. Co.G
Reeves, R.W. AL 14th Inf. Co.A
Reeves, R.W. AL 22nd Inf. Co.C Capt.
Reeves, S. AL 1st Inf. Co.I
Reeves, S. GA 5th Cav. Co.C
Reeves, S. SC Cav. 10th Bn. Co.C
Reeves, Sampson W. AL Lt.Arty. Phelan's Co.
Reeves, Sampson Witt AL 5th Inf. Old Co.H
Reeves, Samuel MS 6th Cav. Co.G
Reeves, Samuel, Jr. NC 5th Inf. Co.E Capt.
Reeves, Samuel Gen. & Staff AASurg.
Reeves, Samuel H. AR 1st (Crawford's) Cav. Co.H Cpl.
Reeves, Samuel J. TX 10th Inf. Co.F
Reeves, Samuel R. AR Cav. Harrell's Bn. Co.B
Reeves, Samuel R. AR 3rd Inf. Co.B
Reeves, Samuel R. AR 14th (Powers') Inf. Co.E
Reeves, Samuel W. LA 4th Cav. Co.E
Reeves, Sanders NC 2nd Inf. Co.K
Reeves, S.C. TN 9th Inf. Co.K Cpl.
Reeves, S.D. TN Inf. 2nd Cons.Regt. Co.D
Reeves, S.D. TN 47th Inf. Co.B Cpl.
Reeves, S.E. AL 5th Cav. Co.G
Reeves, S.F. MS 4th Inf. Co.H Sgt.
Reeves, S.H. AR 24th Inf. Co.C
Reeves, S.H. TN 22nd (Barteau's) Cav. Co.I Capt.
Reeves, S.H. TN 47th Inf. Co.H 1st Lt.
Reeves, Sherwood A. TX 1st (McCulloch's) Cav. Co.K Sgt.
Reeves, Sherwood A. TX 1st (Yager's) Cav. Co.I

Reeves, Sherwood A. TX Cav. 8th (Taylor's) Bn. Co.D Sgt.
Reeves, Sidney F. MS 20th Inf. Co.C
Reeves, Simeon E. AL 4th (Russell's) Cav. Co.D
Reeves, Simon GA 27th Inf. Co.G
Reeves, S.J. AL 7th Cav. Co.H
Reeves, S.M. MS 6th Cav. Co.B Cpl.
Reeves, S.M. MS Cav. Davenport's Bn. (St.Troops) Co.A Cpl.
Reeves, S.O. Al 9th (Malone's) Cav. Co.I Sgt.
Reeves, Solomon S. FL 3rd Inf. Co.H Music.
Reeves, S.S. MS 7th Inf. Co.C
Reeves, S.T. AL 8th (Livingston's) Cav. Co.B Cpl.
Reeves, S.T. GA 8th Inf. Co.H
Reeves, Stephen MS 7th Inf. Co.H
Reeves, Stephen NC 5th Inf. Co.A Cpl.
Reeves, Stephen C. AR 8th Inf. New Co.E
Reeves, Stephen F. GA 21st Inf. Co.G
Reeves, Stephen G. GA 1st Mil. Co.D Sgt.
Reeves, Stephen Z. MS 16th Inf. Co.E
Reeves, Stinson GA 7th Inf. Co.C
Reeves, T.B. MS 2nd Part.Rangers Co.K
Reeves, T.B. MS 20th Inf. Co.G
Reeves, T.B. TN 19th & 20th (Cons.) Cav.
Reeves, T.C. SC 2nd Inf. Co.H
Reeves, T.H. MS 12th Inf. Co.G
Reeves, Thomas AL 11th Inf. Co.G
Reeves, Thomas AL 13th Inf. Co.K
Reeves, Thomas AR 10th Cav.
Reeves, Thomas GA 3rd Inf. Co.A
Reeves, Thomas GA 66th Inf. Co.E
Reeves, Thomas, Jr. MS Inf. 3rd Bn. Co.E
Reeves, Thomas MS 27th Inf. Co.G
Reeves, Thomas MO 10th Inf.
Reeves, Thomas NC 61st Inf. Co.G
Reeves, Thomas B. TN Inf. 3rd Bn. Co.A
Reeves, Thomas B. TX 11th Cav. Co.C
Reeves, Thomas C. NC 16th Inf. Co.F
Reeves, Thomas D. TX 2nd Cav. Co.B ACS
Reeves, Thos. D. Gen. & Staff Capt.,ACS
Reeves, Thomas F. Wheeler's Scouts,CSA
Reeves, Thomas G. MS 28th Cav. Co.D
Reeves, Thomas H. VA 52nd Inf. Co.D
Reeves, Thomas J. SC 2nd Inf. Co.H 2nd Lt.
Reeves, Thomas J. SC 5th Inf. 2nd Co.H
Reeves, Thomas J. VA 5th Inf. Co.C Sgt.
Reeves, Thomas L. GA 4th Inf. Co.G
Reeves, Thomas M. TN 16th Inf. Co.C
Reeves, Thomas R. MS 36th Inf. Co.I,C
Reeves, Thos. T. GA 8th Inf. Co.H
Reeves, Thomas W. AR 18th Inf. Co.H Cpl.
Reeves, Thomas W. TN 16th (Logwood's) Cav. Co.B
Reeves, Thompson GA 11th Inf. Co.H
Reeves, T.J. GA 53rd Inf. Co.B
Reeves, T.J. LA 3rd (Wingfield's) Cav. Co.A
Reeves, T.J. SC 13th Inf. Co.I
Reeves, T.N. MS 12th Inf. Co.G
Reeves, Toliver M. AL 19th Inf. Co.D
Reeves, T.S. MS 2nd Cav. Co.B
Reeves, T.S. TX 2nd Inf. Co.C 1st Sgt.
Reeves, T.T. GA 3rd Inf. Co.D
Reeves, T.W. TN 45th Inf. Co.I
Reeves, W.A. AR 6th Inf. Old Co.F
Reeves, W.A. KY 1st (Helm's) Cav. Co.G 1st Lt.

Reeves, W.A. SC 2nd Arty. Co.A
Reeves, W.A. TX Inf. 2nd St.Troops Co.E
Reeves, Walter GA Arty. Maxwell's Reg. Lt.Btty.
Reeves, Walter GA Inf. Cobb Guards Cullens' Co.
Reeves, Walter KY 2nd Cav.
Reeves, Walter W. GA 1st Reg. Co.F,B,D
Reeves, Warren GA 27th Inf. Co.G
Reeves, W.B. LA 31st Inf. Co.F
Reeves, W.B. MS 43rd Inf. Co.B
Reeves, W.C. SC 5th Inf. 1st Co.I
Reeves, W.C. TN Inf. 1st Cons.Regt. Co.D
Reeves, W.C. TN 8th Inf. Co.B
Reeves, W.D. GA 9th Inf. (St.Guards) Co.C
Reeves, W.D. SC 1st (Orr's) Rifles Co.A
Reeves, W.D. TN 47th Inf. Co.A
Reeves, W.E. AR 8th Inf. New Co.F
Reeves, W.E. AR 14th (McCarver's) Inf. Co.E
Reeves, W.E. GA 1st (Fannin's) Res. Co.F
Reeves, Wesley AL 37th Inf. Co.C
Reeves, Wesley MO 8th Cav. Co.C
Reeves, Westley TN 16th (Logwood's) Cav. Co.F
Reeves, W.F. TN 42nd Inf. 2nd Co.H
Reeves, W.H. GA 5th Res. Co.M
Reeves, W.H. GA 63rd Inf. Co.A
Reeves, W.H. MS 14th Inf. Co.K
Reeves, W.H. MS 43rd Inf. Co.B
Reeves, W.H. TN 13th Inf. Co.G
Reeves, Whitson A. NC 44th Inf. Co.F
Reeves, Wiley NC 8th Sr.Res. McNeill's Co.
Reeves, Wiley N. GA Arty. 9th Bn. Co.C
Reeves, Wiley Stanhope MS Inf. 1st Bn. Co.D Cpl.
Reeves, William AL 2nd Cav. Co.B
Reeves, William AL Inf. 1st Regt. Co.G
Reeves, William AL 13th Inf. Co.K
Reeves, William AL 17th Inf. Co.D
Reeves, William AR 7th Cav. Co.B
Reeves, William AR Inf. 2nd Bn. Co.B
Reeves, William AR 2nd Vol. Co.A
Reeves, William AR 18th Inf. Co.G
Reeves, William AR 23rd Inf. Co.K Cpl.
Reeves, William GA 1st Reg. Co.H
Reeves, William GA 6th Inf. (St.Guards) Co.I Cpl.
Reeves, William KY 3rd Cav.
Reeves, William MS 1st Cav. Co.H
Reeves, William MS 1st (King's) Inf. (St.Troops) Co.G
Reeves, William MS 2nd (Quinn's St.Troops) Inf. Co.I
Reeves, William MS 5th Inf. (St.Troops) Co.C
Reeves, William MS 27th Inf. Co.H
Reeves, William MO 6th Cav. Co.I
Reeves, William NC 8th Bn.Part.Rangers Co.F
Reeves, William TX 11th Cav. Co.G
Reeves, William TX 32nd Cav. Co.K Cpl.
Reeves, William TX Cav. St.Troops Doughty's Co.
Reeves, William TX 18th Inf. Co.H
Reeves, William VA 25th Cav. Co.G
Reeves, William Conf.Inf. Tucker's Regt. Co.F
Reeves, William A. GA Cav. 29th Bn. Co.E Cpl.
Reeves, William A. GA Inf. 3rd Bn. Co.D

Reeves, William A. GA 4th Bn.S.S. Co.B
Reeves, William A. GA 20th Inf. Co.H
Reeves, William A. GA 23rd Inf. Co.D,B Sgt.
Reeves, William A. NC 62nd Inf. Co.E
Reeves, William A. TN 32nd Inf. Co.I
Reeves, William B. AL 13th Inf. Co.K
Reeves, William B. MS 1st (Johnston's) Inf. Co.K
Reeves, William C. GA 27th Inf. Co.E 2nd Lt.
Reeves, William C. NC 61st Inf. Co.G
Reeves, William E. AR 23rd Inf. Co.C 2nd Lt.
Reeves, William E. MS 2nd (Quinn's St.Troops) Inf. Co.I Sgt.
Reeves, William E. MS 33rd Inf. Co.H
Reeves, William H. GA 35th Inf. Co.C
Reeves, William H. NC 29th Inf. Co.C
Reeves, William H. TN 6th Inf. Co.D
Reeves, William Henry NC 22nd Inf. Co.E
Reeves, William Hickason MS Inf. 1st St.Troops Co.D
Reeves, William J. GA Cav. 1st Gordon Squad. (St.Guards) Reeves' Co. Capt.
Reeves, William J. GA 44th Inf. Co.A
Reeves, William J. GA 52nd Inf. Co.C
Reeves, Wm. J. SC 13th Inf. Co.I
Reeves, Wm. J. Gen. & Staff A.Surg.
Reeves, William L. GA 10th Inf. Co.C
Reeves, William L. LA 18th Inf. Co.K Sgt.
Reeves, William M. AL 63rd Inf. Co.G,B
Reeves, Wm. M. AL Cp. of Instr. Talladega
Reeves, William M. GA 44th Inf. Co.D
Reeves, William N. AL 15th Inf. Co.F
Reeves, William N. AL Arty. 4th Bn. Hilliard's Legion Co.C Lt.Col.
Reeves, William P. AR 20th Inf. Co.H,I,C
Reeves, William P. GA 38th Inf. Co.A
Reeves, William P.T. TX 1st Hvy.Arty. Co.E
Reeves, William R. MS 16th Inf. Co.E
Reeves, William T. TN 48th (Voorhies') Inf.
Reeves, William T. TX 31st Cav. Co.C
Reeves, William W. AL Cav. 4th Bn. (Love's) Co.A
Reeves, William W. GA 35th Inf. Co.C
Reeves, William W. Conf.Cav. Wood's Regt. Co.G
Reeves, Wills NC 29th Inf. Co.C
Reeves, Wilson NC 6th Sr.Res. Co.A
Reeves, Wilson G. AR 5th Inf. Co.F
Reeves, W.J. AL 33rd Inf. Co.K Sgt.
Reeves, W.J. MS 4th Cav. Co.I
Reeves, W.J. TX Cav. 1st Bn.St.Troops Co.C
Reeves, W.L. AL 8th Inf. Co.D
Reeves, W.L. LA 7th Cav. Co.A
Reeves, W.L. SC 2nd Arty. Co.I
Reeves, W.L. TN 19th & 20th (Cons.) Cav. Co.F
Reeves, W.L. TN 20th (Russell's) Cav. Co.A
Reeves, W.L. TN 47th Inf. Co.B
Reeves, W.M. KY 1st (Helm's) Cav. New Co.G
Reeves, W.M. MO Cav. 3rd Bn. Co.H
Reeves, W.N. AL Lt.Arty. Kolb's Btty. Capt.
Reeves, W.N. GA 27th Inf. Co.E Sgt.
Reeves, Woodson MO Cav. 3rd Bn. Co.G,H
Reeves, W.P. GA 13th Inf. Co.I
Reeves, W.P. MS 2nd (Davidson's) Inf. Co.A
Reeves, W.P. MS 9th Inf. Co.F
Reeves, W.P. MS 10th Inf. New Co.G Cpl.

Reeves, Wright R. NC Mallett's Bn. (Cp.Guard) Co.B
Reeves, W.S. AL 12th Cav. Col.
Reeves, W.S. AL 18th Inf. Co.G
Reeves, W.S. AR 18th Inf. Co.G
Reeves, W.S. GA 6th Inf. (St.Guards) Co.I
Reeves, W.S. TX 23rd Cav. Co.D
Reeves, W. Stanhope MS 2nd Part.Rangers Co.E Cpl.
Reeves, W.T. AL 7th Cav. Co.G
Reeves, W.T. MS 6th Cav. Co.H
Reeves, W.T. TX 1st Hvy.Arty. Co.D
Reeves, W.W. GA Hvy.Arty. 22nd Bn. Co.A
Reeves, W.W. GA 60th Inf. 1st Co.A
Reeves, W.W. NC 1st Bn.Jr.Res. Co.D Sgt.
Reeves, Y.D. Gen. & Staff Capt.,ACS
Reeves, Z. TX Cav. Benavides' Regt. Co.G
Reeves, Zebediah AR 27th Inf. Co.G
Reeves, Z.T. TX Cav. Benavides' Regt. Co.G
Reevis, David R. AL 30th Inf. Co.B
Reevis, E.R. MO Cav. Coleman's Regt.
Reevis, John GA Cav. 1st Bn.Res. Co.C
Reevly, G.W. VA 56th Inf. Co.G 1st Sgt.
Reevs, A.H. GA 2nd Inf.
Reevs, G.W. AL 3rd Inf. Co.G
Reevs, J.K.P. AL 13th Inf. Co.K
Reevs, J.K.P. TN Cav. Jackson's Co.
Reevy, B. AL 3rd Bn.Res. Jackson's Co.
Reevy, Thomas VA 41st Inf. 1st Co.E
Reevy, William C. MO 9th Inf. Co.K
Reeyes, Pedro TX 3rd Inf. Co.F
Refearin, Samuel B. MS 2nd St.Cav. Co.A
Refeld, William AR 1st (Colquitt's) Inf. Co.K Cpl.
Reffe, C. TX Inf. 3rd St.Troops Co.B
Reffett, James KY 10th (Diamond's) Cav. Co.A
Reffitt, H. KY 3rd Bn.Mtd.Rifles Co.B
Refile, A. AR Mil. Desha Cty.Bn.
Refo, C.L. SC 22nd Inf. Co.A
Refo, T. GA Lt.Arty. Pritchard's Co. (Washington Arty.)
Refo, Theodore E. GA 36th (Villepigue's) Inf. Co.F
Refo, W.A. GA 3rd Bn. (St.Guards) Co.H 2nd Lt.
Refo, W.A. GA Inf. Exempts Roberts' Co. 2nd Lt.
Refoe, C.L. SC 2nd St.Troops Co.I
Refoe, T.E. Lt.Arty. Dent's Btty.,CSA
Refoil, George W. MO 7th Cav. Wheeler's Co.
Refras, Robert LA 28th (Gray's) Inf. Co.B
Regalado, Francisco TX Cav. Ragsdale's Bn. Co.D
Regalia, Antonio VA Cav. 32nd Bn. Co.A
Regan, Addison NC 2nd Arty. Co.I
Regan, A.J. TX 13th Vol. 2nd Co.B
Regan, Alexander GA 1st (Olmstead's) Inf. Co.A
Regan, Alexander C. GA 1st (Olmstead's) Inf. Gordon's Co.
Regan, Alexander C. GA 63rd Inf. Co.B,K Sgt.
Regan, Asa LA Inf.Cons.Crescent Regt. Co.D
Regan, Authorniles NC 18th Inf. Co.B
Regan, Benjamin VA Inf. 6th Bn.Loc.Def. Co.A
Regan, C. KY 10th (Johnson's) Cav. Co.E
Regan, Charles NC Townsend's Co. (St.Troops)
Regan, Charles F. NC 2nd Cav. (19th St.Troops) Co.I

Regan, C.K. MS 4th Cav. Co.B
Regan, Daniel NC 31st Inf. Co.A
Regan, Daniel 2nd Conf.Eng.Troops Co.A
Regan, Edward VA 60th Inf. Co.F
Regan, E.M. VA Inf. 25th Bn. Co.E
Regan, Green B. NC 6th Sr.Res. Co.D
Regan, H.C. NC 2nd Jr.Res. Co.C
Regan, H.C. NC 27th Inf. Co.F
Regan, Hugh B. NC 31st Inf. Co.A Sgt.
Regan, J. AL 3rd Inf. Co.B
Regan, J. KY 1st (Butler's) Cav. Co.E
Regan, James AL Lt.Arty. 2nd Bn. Co.E
Regan, James LA 6th Inf. Co.E
Regan, James MS 8th Cav. Co.B
Regan, James MS 44th Inf. Co.L
Regan, James NC 24th Inf. Co.A
Regan, James Inf. School of Pract. Co.C
Regan, James W. LA 31st Inf. Co.B
Regan, James W. NC 12th Inf. Co.D
Regan, James W. NC 24th Inf. Co.G
Regan, J.B. GA Cav. 29th Bn. Co.G
Regan, Jerry TN 2nd (Walker's) Inf. Co.K
Regan, Jerry 9th Conf.Inf. Co.A
Regan, J.L. 4th Conf.Inf. Co.K
Regan, John AL Seawell's Btty. (Mohawk Arty.)
Regan, John AL 8th Inf. Co.I
Regan, John GA 1st (Olmstead's) Inf. Co.E
Regan, John LA 14th Inf. Co.H
Regan, John LA C.S. Zouave Bn. Co.C
Regan, John LA C.S. Zouave Bn. Co.D
Regan, John NC 24th Inf. Co.G Lt.
Regan, John TN Arty. Bibb's Co. Cpl.
Regan, John VA 1st Inf. Co.I
Regan, John VA 44th Inf. Co.E 1st Sgt.
Regan, John 1st Conf.Eng.Troops Co.K
Regan, John D. MS 1st Bn.S.S. Co.B
Regan, John F. AR 47th (Crandall's) Cav. Co.A
Regan, John J. LA 6th Cav. Co.C
Regan, John M. MS 30th Inf. Co.A
Regan, Joseph MS Inf. 2nd Bn. Co.F Capt.
Regan, Joseph MS 48th Inf. Co.F Capt.
Regan, Joseph NC 24th Inf. Co.G
Regan, Joseph T. MS Cav. 24th Bn. Co.C
Regan, Michael AL 8th Inf. Co.I
Regan, Michael LA 1st (Strawbridge's) Inf. Co.D,K Sgt.
Regan, Michael LA 7th Inf. Co.D
Regan, Mike TN 1st Hvy.Arty. 2nd Co.D
Regan, M.O. TX 2nd Inf. Co.C
Regan, Neill NC 2nd Arty. (36th St.Troops) Co.I
Regan, Onslow NC 24th Inf. Co.G Sgt.
Regan, Patrick TN 10th Inf. Co.A
Regan, Patrick A. LA 3rd (Harrison's) Cav. Co.A
Regan, Phillip M. MS Inf. 5th Bn. Co.C
Regan, Ralph NC 18th Inf. Co.D
Regan, Rufus NC 7th Inf. Co.D
Regan, S. GA 13th Cav. Co.K
Regan, Sidney NC 31st Inf. Co.E
Regan, Span GA 10th Mil.
Regan, Stephen MS 3rd Inf. Co.C
Regan, Steven MS 5th Cav. Co.A
Regan, Thomas AL Inf. 2nd Regt. Co.G
Regan, Thomas G. MS 16th Inf. Co.E
Regan, Thomas T. NC 12th Inf. Co.C
Regan, Timothy TN 10th Inf. Co.A
Regan, T.S. LA 1st Inf. Co.A

Regan, W. LA 11th Inf. Co.K 1st Sgt.
Regan, Washington NC 2nd Arty. (36th St.Troops) Co.B
Regan, W.B. VA 6th Cav. Co.C
Regan, W.D. LA 17th Inf. Co.C
Regan, William AL Inf. 1st Regt. Co.B
Regan, William LA 5th Inf. Co.G 1st Sgt.
Regan, William LA 8th Inf. Co.A
Regan, William LA 13th & 20th Inf. Co.A
Regan, William LA 20th Inf. Co.E Sgt.
Regan, William LA 20th Inf. Co.I Sgt.
Regan, William D. NC 24th Inf. Co.G Cpl.
Regan, William J. NC 24th Inf. Co.G
Regan, Willis A. MS 38th Cav. Co.I
Regan, W.L. Bradford's Corps Scouts & Guards Co.A
Regan, W.P. MS 38th Cav. Co.I
Regan, W.S. MS 38th Cav. Co.I Cpl.
Regans, George H. FL 4th Inf. Co.A
Regans, James GA 8th Inf. Co.G
Regans, James L. NC 52nd Inf. Co.G
Regans, R.A. GA 10th Inf. Co.H
Regans, Robert A. FL 4th Inf. Co.A
Regans, Robert G. GA 20th Inf. Co.E
Regans, Jacob J. NC Inf. 2nd Bn. Co.G
Regdon, Thomas LA 4th Cav. Co.C
Regeans, C.H. AL Cav. Roddey's Escort
Regel, Charles TX 3rd Inf. Co.D
Regell, John MS Inf. 1st St.Troops Co.G
Regen, I.S. Blake's Scouts,CSA
Regen, Joseph S. TN 4th (McLemore's) Cav. Co.F
Regensburger, Abraham MS 21st Inf. Co.E
Regensburger, David LA 6th Inf. Co.B
Reger, A.G. VA 31st Inf. Co.H Capt.
Reger, Albert G. VA 25th Inf. Maj.
Reger, Ezra VA 62nd Mtd.Inf. 2nd Co.H Jr.2nd Lt.
Reger, G.J. VA 14th Cav. Co.C Lt.
Reger, Isaac N. VA 31st Inf. Co.I 2nd Lt.
Reger, Jerome J. VA 25th Inf. 2nd Co.B 1st Lt.
Reger, Joel VA 62nd Mtd.Inf. 2nd Co.H
Reger, John H. VA 25th Inf. 2nd Co.B
Reger, Lorenzo D. VA 31st Inf. Co.C
Reger, Monroe C. VA 25th Inf. 2nd Co.B 2nd Lt.
Reger, Napoleon B. VA 25th Inf. 2nd Co.B 1st Lt.
Reger, Nimrod D. VA 31st Inf. Co.I Sgt.
Regerson, William TX 21st Cav. Co.C
Regerte, J.M. AL Conscr. Cpl.
Regester, B.T. NC 2nd Inf. Co.A
Regestr, Daniel B. NC 2nd Arty. (36th St.Troops) Co.H
Regg, Charles TN 1st (Feild's) Inf. Co.E 2nd Lt.
Reggan, D.A. NC 8th Sr.Res. McLean's Co.
Reggan, Daniel J. AL 53rd (Part.Rangers) Co.D
Reggan, John W. AL 53rd (Part.Rangers) Co.D
Regges, C.J. MS 16th Inf. Co.D
Regges, John F. MS 16th Inf. Co.D Cpl.
Reggin, T. TN 45th Inf. Co.D
Reggins, A. AR 8th Cav. Co.A
Reggins, George GA 4th Res. Co.G
Reggins, T.J. GA 13th Inf. Co.A
Regginsburg, Samuel A. VA 24th Cav. Co.E
Reggio, A. LA Dreux's Cav. Co.A

Reggio, A.N. LA Lt.Arty. LeGardeur, Jr.'s Co. (Orleans Guard Btty.)
Reggio, A.N. MO Lt.Arty. Barret's Co.
Reggio, C.E. LA Lt.Arty. LeGardeur, Jr.'s Co. (Orleans Guard Btty.)
Reggio, C.E. MO Lt.Arty. Barret's Co.
Reggio, Charles E. LA Dreux's Cav. Co.A
Reggio, Gus. A. LA 30th Inf. Co.F
Reggio, J. LA 22nd (Cons.) Inf. Co.E
Reggio, L. LA Mil. Orleans Guards Regt. Co.H
Reggio, L.O. LA 22nd (Cons.) Inf. Co.E
Reggio, O. LA Mil. Orleans Guards Regt. Co.H
Reggio, Octave LA 18th Inf. Co.E
Reggio, Pit LA Mil.Mtd.Rangers Plaquemines
Reggs, Harvey MS 22nd Inf. Co.D
Regholds, J.J. AL Cav. Hardie's Bn.Res. S.D. McClellan's Co.
Regian, Oliver LA 3rd (Harrison's) Cav. Co.F
Regins, A.J. AR 27th Inf. Co.D
Regins, N. TX Cav. Sutton's Co.
Reginsberger, David VA Inf. 25th Bn. Co.G
Region, Bankston MS 46th Inf. Co.A
Region, Joel TN Cav. 9th Bn. (Gantt's) Co.C
Regions, B. 14th Conf.Cav. Co.K
Registe, William GA 3rd Inf.
Register, Aaron FL Inf. 2nd Bn. Co.F
Register, Abraham FL 10th Inf. Co.B
Register, Abraham FL 10th Inf. Co.C
Register, A.J. TN Inf. Nashville Bn. Fulcher's Co.
Register, Alfred G. GA 14th Inf. Co.H
Register, Allen NC 1st Arty. (10th St.Troops) Co.F
Register, Anthony J. FL 4th Inf. Co.B
Register, Benjamin T. NC 7th Inf. Co.C
Register, Brown AL 6th Inf. Co.B
Register, Burrel FL 11th Inf. Co.F Cpl.
Register, Burrell M. NC 51st Inf. Co.B
Register, Burwell FL Campbellton Boys
Register, C. LA 2nd Cav. Co.G
Register, Calvin GA Inf. 10th Bn. Co.B
Register, Calvin SC 21st Inf. Co.G
Register, Charles B. GA 20th Inf. Co.B
Register, Chester A. FL 5th Inf. Co.F
Register, Chester A. FL 10th Inf. Co.C
Register, Cullen NC 5th Inf. Co.A
Register, Daniel NC 7th Inf. Co.C
Register, Daniel NC 27th Inf. Co.A
Register, David FL 10th Inf. Co.B
Register, David GA 14th Inf. Co.H
Register, David NC Hvy.Arty. 1st Bn. Co.B
Register, David R. GA 57th Inf. Co.C
Register, D.D. FL 10th Inf. Co.B
Register, D.D. FL Conscr.
Register, Dickson S. NC Hvy.Arty. 1st Bn. Co.B
Register, E.A. AL 15th Cav. Co.C
Register, E.A. AL 6th Inf. Co.A
Register, Edward M. NC 30th Inf. Co.A
Register, Elias AL 6th Inf. Co.B
Register, Elias FL 11th Inf. Co.F
Register, Elias NC 18th Inf. Co.C
Register, Elias D. AL 6th Inf. Co.B
Register, Elijah F. GA 14th Inf. Co.H
Register, Elmer G. AL 3rd Inf. Co.B
Register, Erwin AL 61st Inf. Co.I
Register, Ezekiel A. FL Campbellton Boys Sr.2nd Lt.

Register, Ezekiel A. FL Cav. (Marianna Drag.) Smith's Co.
Register, Ezekiel A. 15th Conf.Cav. Co.B
Register, F. GA 29th Inf. Co.I
Register, Francis FL 1st Cav. Co.E
Register, Francis FL Inf. 2nd Bn. Co.C
Register, Francis FL 10th Inf. Co.B
Register, Francis M. AL 57th Inf. Co.G
Register, Frederick J. NC 18th Inf. Co.E
Register, George FL 2nd Cav. Co.I
Register, George FL Cav. 5th Bn. Co.F
Register, George R. NC 51st Inf. Co.B
Register, George W. FL 1st Cav. Co.G Sgt.
Register, G.G. TN Cav. Welcker's Bn. Kincaid's Co.
Register, G.G. TN 62nd Mtd.Inf. Co.G
Register, Gibson NC Wallace's Co. (Wilmington RR Guard)
Register, Gibson S. MS 16th Inf. Co.F
Register, Green AL Cav. Chisolm's Co.
Register, Guilford GA 26th Inf. Co.D
Register, Guilford A. GA 50th Inf. Co.G
Register, G.W. FL 10th Inf. Co.E
Register, Harmon H. NC 5th Cav. (63rd St.Troops) Co.C Sgt.
Register, Harmon H. NC 20th Inf. Faison's Co.
Register, Harrison TX 13th Cav. Co.K
Register, Henry NC 8th Bn.Part.Rangers Co.B
Register, Henry NC 66th Inf. Co.C Sgt.
Register, Herman H. NC 1st Inf. (6 mo. '61) Co.F
Register, I. TN 3rd (Forrest's) Cav.
Register, Ira SC 21st Inf. Co.B
Register, Irving GA 25th Inf. Co.E
Register, Irwin GA 38th Inf. 2nd Co.I
Register, Ivy FL 9th Inf. Co.F
Register, J. FL 2nd Cav. Co.K
Register, J. GA Arty. 11th Bn. (Sumter Arty.) Old Co.C
Register, Jackson AL 6th Inf. Co.B
Register, Jackson FL 6th Inf. Co.E
Register, James AL 39th Inf. Co.A
Register, James FL 2nd Inf. Co.G
Register, James FL 4th Inf. Co.K
Register, James SC 21st Inf. Co.B
Register, James C. SC 21st Inf. Co.H
Register, James E. NC 51st Inf. Co.C
Register, James F. FL 1st Cav. Co.G Sgt.
Register, James L. GA 14th Inf. Co.H
Register, James M. MS 40th Inf. Co.A
Register, Jason FL 1st (Res.) Inf. Co.B
Register, J.C. GA Inf. 2nd Bn. (St.Guards) New Co.D
Register, Jeff GA 63rd Inf. Co.H
Register, Jenkins NC 3rd Arty. (40th St.Troops) Co.A
Register, J.L.D. GA 64th Inf. Co.A 1st Sgt.
Register, J.L.D. 1st Conf.Inf. 2nd Co.C
Register, J.M. GA Inf. 18th Bn. Co.B
Register, J.N. AL 57th Inf. Co.F
Register, Joe TX 3rd (Kirby's) Bn.Vol. Co.C
Register, Joel LA 16th Inf. Co.E
Register, Joel TX 24th & 25th Cav. (Cons.) Co.B
Register, Joel TX 25th Cav. Co.F
Register, John AL 61st Inf. Co.I
Register, John FL 1st Inf. Old Co.E Sgt.
Register, John GA 1st (Symons') Res. Co.G

Register, John GA 14th Inf. Co.H
Register, John GA 38th Inf. 2nd Co.I
Register, John NC 8th Bn.Part.Rangers Co.F
Register, John NC 2nd Arty. (36th St.Troops) Co.D
Register, John NC 66th Inf. Co.I
Register, John TN 1st (Feild's) Inf. Co.L
Register, John TN Inf. Nashville Bn. Fulcher's Co.
Register, John Sig.Corps,CSA
Register, John A. AL 57th Inf. Co.F
Register, John D. FL 6th Inf. Co.E
Register, John F. AL 6th Cav. Co.K
Register, John N. NC 51st Inf. Co.G
Register, John P. GA Inf. 10th Bn. Co.B Sgt.
Register, John R. AL 57th Inf. Co.I
Register, John R. NC 5th Cav. (63rd St.Troops) Co.C
Register, John R. NC 1st Arty. (10th St.Troops) Co.I
Register, John R. NC 20th Inf. Faison's Co.
Register, John R. NC 61st Inf. Co.A
Register, John S. AL 6th Inf. Co.A
Register, John S. FL Cav. 5th Bn. Co.I
Register, John T. GA Inf. 10th Bn. Co.B
Register, John T. GA 50th Inf. Co.G Cpl.
Register, John W. AL 53rd (Part.Rangers) Co.B
Register, John W. GA 4th (Clinch's) Cav. Co.C
Register, John W. Conf.Cav. Wood's Regt. 1st Co.A Cpl.
Register, Joseph M. FL 11th Inf. Co.K
Register, Joseph P. GA 63rd Inf. Co.H
Register, J.R. AL 57th Inf. Co.F
Register, J.S. AL Cav. Chisolm's Co.
Register, J.T. GA Inf. 2nd Bn.
Register, L. GA 26th Inf. Co.D
Register, Lewis S. NC 3rd Inf. Co.B
Register, Maxwell LA 16th Inf. Co.E
Register, M.G. FL Cav. 5th Bn. Co.I
Register, Miles GA 50th Inf. Co.G
Register, Miles NC 2nd Inf. Co.F
Register, Miles C. NC 2nd Arty. (36th St.Troops) Co.I
Register, Mitchell FL 5th Inf. Co.B
Register, Nathan NC 2nd Arty. (36th St.Troops) Co.K
Register, Newton F. NC 20th Inf. Co.I
Register, Noel P. AL 3rd Inf. Co.B
Register, Octavius B. LA Inf.Cons.Crescent Regt. Co.N
Register, O.P. FL 9th Inf. Co.D
Register, Osborn J. GA 42nd Inf. Co.I 2nd Lt.
Register, Owen NC 2nd Arty. (36th St.Troops) Co.I
Register, Perry GA 11th Cav. (St.Guards) Johnson's Co.
Register, Peter E. GA 7th Inf. Co.F
Register, Pierce AL 1st Inf. Co.E
Register, R. GA 54th Inf. Co.E
Register, R. NC 2nd Inf. Co.F
Register, Rice P. NC 20th Inf. Co.I
Register, Richard NC 51st Inf. Co.C
Register, Robert M. GA 14th Inf. Co.H
Register, Robert M. NC 51st Inf. Co.C
Register, Rufus K. NC 1st Arty. (10th St.Troops) Co.E
Register, S. GA Mil. Camden Cty. (Mtd.)

Register, Samuel FL 10th Inf. Co.B Cpl.
Register, Samuel GA 11th Cav. (St.Guards) Staten's Co.
Register, Samuel C. NC 30th Inf. Co.E
Register, Samuel E. GA Inf. 18th Bn. Co.C
Register, Samuel R. NC 51st Inf. Co.B
Register, Samuel W. GA 50th Inf. Co.G
Register, Shadrach F. NC 2nd Arty. (36th St.Troops) Co.D
Register, Stephen GA 4th (Clinch's) Cav.
Register, Stephen W. AL 17th Inf. Co.K
Register, Talcut S. GA 14th Inf. Co.H
Register, Thomas AL 57th Inf. Co.I
Register, Thomas FL 6th Inf. Co.E
Register, Thomas FL 11th Inf. Co.F
Register, Thomas NC 30th Inf. Co.C
Register, Thomas A. NC McDugald's Co.
Register, Thomas P. GA 14th Inf. Co.H Cpl.
Register, Travis NC 8th Sr.Res. Bryan's Co.
Register, W. GA Cav. Floyd's Co.
Register, Warren GA 1st (Symons') Res. Co.G
Register, Washington GA 49th Inf. Co.G
Register, W.G. VA Lt.Arty. Griffin's Co.
Register, William FL 1st Cav. Co.C
Register, William FL 10th Inf. Co.B
Register, William FL 11th Inf. Co.F
Register, William GA Arty. 11th Bn. (Sumter Arty.) Old Co.C
Register, William GA 3rd Res. Co.C
Register, William GA 14th Inf. Co.H
Register, William SC 10th Inf. Co.B
Register, William B. FL 2nd Inf. Co.F
Register, William D. 4th Conf.Inf. Co.D Cpl.
Register, William J. NC 2nd Arty. (36th St.Troops) Co.I
Register, William K. AL 1st Inf. Co.K
Register, William O. NC 7th Inf. Co.C
Register, William R. GA 26th Inf. Atkinson's Co.B
Register, W.R. GA 4th (Clinch's) Cav.
Regler, Henry GA Cav. 1st Bn.Res. McKinney's Co.
Regley, A. VA 23rd Inf. Co.F
Regley, Fred Conf.Inf. 8th Bn. Co.B
Regley, William NC 64th Inf. Co.M
Regnand, Arthur VA 14th Cav. Crawford's Co.
Regnand, Arthur VA 17th Cav. Co.F
Regnault, C.H. VA Arty. Young's Co.
Regnault, Charles H. VA 1st Arty. 2nd Co.C Cpl.
Regnault, Charles H. VA Lt.Arty. 1st Bn. Co.C
Regner, F. AL 38th Inf. Co.K
Regner, Fred TX 6th Cav. Co.A
Regner, Frederick LA C.S. Zouave Bn. Co.C
Regon, Norton W. AL 42nd Inf. Co.K
Regsdale, G. MS 1st (King's) Inf. (St.Troops) Co.G
Regstaff, W.M. AL McDonald's Cav. Co.K
Reguber, J. GA 40th Inf. Co.K
Regus, J. LA Mil. 3rd Regt. 1st Brig. 1st Div. Co.G
Reh, W.F. VA Horse Arty. D. Shanks' Co.
Reh, W.T. TX 11th (Spaight's) Bn.Vol. Co.B
Rehage, M. LA Mil. 4th Regt.Eur.Brig. Co.E
Rehagen, Leopold TN 1st (Feild's) Inf. Co.E
Rehard, George VA 58th Mil. Co.F
Rehard, Peter VA 58th Mil. Co.F

Rehbein, J.F. LA Inf.Crescent Regt. Co.G Sgt.
Rehberg, Charles GA 59th Inf. Co.A Cpl.
Rehberg, William GA 59th Inf. Co.A Cpl.
Rehburg, Henry GA 17th Inf. Co.D
Rehburg, John GA 59th Inf. Co.A
Rehe, Jacob LA Miles' Legion
Rehean, T. TX 8th Inf. Co.G
Rehen, J. AR 37th Inf. Co.K
Reherd, James E. VA 23rd Cav. Co.B
Reherd, Lewis VA 10th Inf. Co.B
Rehile, Thomas AL Mil. 3rd Vol. Co.E
Rehill, Edward VA 9th Cav. Co.A
Rehkoff, Henry TX 1st Hvy.Arty. Co.K Ord.Sgt.
Rehkopf, William TN Inf. 3rd Bn. Co.G
Rehm, B. AL St.Arty. Co.D
Rehm, Ben AL Gorff's Co. (Mobile Pulaski Rifles) Surg.
Rehm, Benedict AL 1st Regt. Mobile Vol. Co.E
Rehm, Frederick VA Lt.Arty. Moore's Co.
Rehm, Frederick VA 55th Inf. Co.F
Rehm, George A. VA Lt.Arty. Clutter's Co.
Rehmann, C. TX 3rd Inf. 2nd Co.A
Rehmen, William AR 15th Inf. Co.A
Rehner, Richard TX Arty. 4th Bn. Co.B
Rehner, Richard TX 8th Inf. Co.B Music.
Rehnold, Henry TN 1st Hvy.Arty. Co.K
Reholee, J.W. NC 2nd Inf.
Rehorst, J. MS 2nd (Quinn's St.Troops) Inf. Co.H
Rehse, John SC Horse Arty. (Washington Arty.) Vol. Hart's Co.
Rehwinkle, R. LA Inf. 4th Bn. Co.E
Reiaks, J.J. AL 8th Cav.
Reibe, F. TX 5th Cav. Co.E Music.
Reibe, J.F. TX 5th Cav. Co.E
Reiber, Fred TN Inf. 154th Sr.Regt. Co.E Lt.
Reiber, John LA Inf.Cons.Crescent Regt. Co.E
Reibert, Aug. TN Hvy.Arty. Sterling's Co.
Reibnitz, D. LA Mil. 4th Regt.Eur.Brig. Co.D
Reice, G.D. VA 12th Cav. Co.F
Reice, James M. NC 8th Bn.Jr.Res. Co.A
Reice, John, No.1 AR 9th Inf. Co.A
Reice, John, No.2 AR 9th Inf. Co.A
Reich, August GA 1st (Symons') Res. Co.B,C
Reich, B.F. NC 21st Inf. Co.K
Reich, C. TX 16th Inf. Co.G
Reich, C. TX Vol. Benton's Co. 1st Lt.
Reich, Charles E.C. NC 22nd Inf. Co.F
Reich, Constantine NC 21st Inf. Co.K
Reich, Cornelius TX 4th Inf. Co.D 1st Lt.
Reich, E.B. MS 2nd Cav. Co.E
Reich, E.B. MS Cav. 3rd Bn. (Ashcraft's) Co.A Jr.2nd Lt.
Reich, Ephraim W. NC 22nd Inf. Co.G
Reich, F. GA Inf. (GA Defend.) Chapman's Co.
Reich, G.A. NC 9th Bn.S.S. Co.B
Reich, G.F. NC 21st Inf. Co.K
Reich, Henry NC 57th Inf. Co.D
Reich, Isaac NC 33rd Inf. Co.H
Reich, J. LA Mil. Orleans Fire Regt. Co.C
Reich, James AL 22nd Inf. Co.E
Reich, James TX 13th Vol. 2nd Co.D
Reich, James TX 15th Inf. 2nd Co.H
Reich, James A. NC 9th Bn.S.S. Co.B
Reich, James A. NC 21st Inf. Co.D Music.
Reich, J.E. NC 21st Inf. Co.E

Reich, J.H. NC 9th Bn.S.S. Co.B
Reich, John LA Mil. Fire Bn. Co.C
Reich, John LA Mil. Mech.Guard
Reich, John TX 36th Cav. Co.H
Reich, John H. NC 4th Bn.Jr.Res. Co.B
Reich, John L. NC 33rd Inf. Co.I
Reich, Joseph H. NC 21st Inf. Co.E
Reich, Joseph H. NC 33rd Inf. Co.I Sgt.
Reich, L.A. AR Inf. Cocke's Regt. Co.F
Reich, Lewis NC 21st Inf. Co.K
Reich, L.J. NC 57th Inf. Co.D
Reich, N.B. NC 7th Sr.Res. Clinard's Co., Holland's Co.
Reich, O.A. TX 11th Field Btty.
Reich, Parmliew NC 21st Inf. Co.D
Reich, Reuben NC 57th Inf. Co.A
Reich, Timothy NC 7th Sr.Res. Holland's Co., Clinard's Co.
Reich, W.A. NC 26th Inf. Music.
Reich, William NC 21st Inf. Co.K
Reichard, A. LA Mil. McPherson's Btty. (Orleans Howitzers)
Reichard, A. LA Inf.Cons.Crescent Regt. Co.G
Reichard, A. LA Mil. Orleans Fire Regt. Co.H
Reichard, Augustus LA 20th Inf. Col.
Reichard, Chr. LA 21st (Kennedy's) Inf. Co.C
Reichard, Christian LA 20th Inf. New Co.B
Reichard, E.F. LA Washington Arty.Bn. Co.5
Reichard, J. LA Inf.Crescent Regt. Co.I
Reichard, R. LA Mil. 2nd Regt. 2nd Brig. 1st Div. Co.G
Reichard, Theodull LA Inf.Crescent Regt. Co.F
Reichardt, F.A. TX Cav. Waller's Regt. Menard's Co.
Reichardt, J.F. TX Cav. Waller's Regt. Menard's Co.
Reichardt, William TX 4th Field Btty. Cpl.
Reichart, S. LA Mil. 3rd Regt. 2nd Brig. 1st Div. Co.C
Reicharyer, Frank TX Cav. Ford's Regt. Sgt.
Reichel, H. TX Inf. 4th Bn. (Oswald's) Co.A
Reichel, John George SC 1st (Orr's) Rifles Co.C
Reichelt, William LA Miles' Legion Co.E
Reichenbarch, John Charles LA 10th Inf. Co.K
Reicher, August LA Mil. 4th Regt. 1st Brig. 1st Div. Co.B
Reichert, C.F. FL Cav. 5th Bn. Co.F
Reichert, Chs. LA Mil. Lafayette Arty. Ord.Sgt.
Reichert, F. GA Arty. (Macon Lt.Arty.) Slaten's Co.
Reichert, George LA Millaudon's Co. (Jefferson Mtd.Guards,Co.B)
Reichert, Jacob F. FL 5th Inf. Co.G
Reichert, John FL 5th Inf. Co.G
Reichert, T. AR 51st Mil. Co.F
Reichert, William S. FL 5th Inf. Co.G
Reicherzer, Theodore TX 33rd Cav. Co.F 1st Sgt.
Reichie, A.W. SC Mil. 1st Regt.Rifles Chichester's Co.
Reichie, G. SC Mil. 1st Regt.Rifles Chichester's Co.
Reichie, States F. TX 13th Vol. 2nd Co.G Ord.Sgt.
Reichler, F. LA Arty. Hutton's Co. (Crescent Arty.,Co.A)
Reichler, F. LA Mil. 1st Regt. French Brig. Co.2

Reichling, J.H. LA Mil. 1st Regt. French Brig. Co.5
Reichman, A. VA 3rd Inf.Loc.Def. Co.K
Reichman, August VA 2nd Regt.Res. Co.B
Reichman, H. 2nd Conf.Inf. Co.A
Reichman, H. Gillum's Regt. Co.F
Reichman, Henry MS 25th Inf. Co.A
Reichman, Henry MS 29th Inf. Co.K
Reichman, Joseph TN Inf. 3rd Bn. Co.F
Reichman, Louis LA 21st (Patton's) Inf. Co.I
Reichner, J. LA Arty. Watson Btty.
Reichner, William LA Mil. 4th Regt. 1st Brig. 1st Div. Co.E
Reichsradt, L. SC 1st Regt. Charleston Guard Co.D
Reichter, Leopold TX Lt.Arty. Hughes' Co.
Reichtman, Fred. LA Mil. 4th Regt. 3rd Brig. 1st Div. Co.C,H
Reichwein, Richard P. VA 12th Inf. Co.D Sgt.
Reichwine, J.P. VA 1st St.Res. Co.B
Reick, H.J. MS 6th Inf. Co.I
Reickardt, C. TX Inf. 1st St.Troops Martin's Co.A
Reicke, Anthony W. SC Lt.Arty. Walter's Co. (Washington Arty.)
Reicke, G. SC 25th Inf. Co.B
Reicke, George SC Arty. Manigault's Bn. 1st Co.A
Reicke, John C.A. SC Lt.Arty. Walter's Co. (Washington Arty.)
Reicke, Louis AL 47th Inf. Co.D
Reid, --- MS 3rd Cav. Chap.
Reid, --- VA VMI Co.D,C
Reid, --- Hosp.Stew.
Reid, A. GA 40th Inf. Co.G
Reid, A.A.F. GA Cav. 22nd Bn. (St.Guards) Co.D 1st Sgt.
Reid, A.B. GA Inf. 25th Bn. (Prov.Guard) Co.B Sgt.
Reid, A.B. GA 64th Inf. Co.B
Reid, A.B. TN 55th (McKoin's) Inf. Bounds' Co.
Reid, Abner L. AL 20th Inf. Co.K
Reid, Abraham MS 5th Inf. (St.Troops) Co.B Cpl.
Reid, Abraham MS 37th Inf. Co.K
Reid, A.C. GA Conscr.
Reid, A.C. SC Lt.Arty. 3rd (Palmetto) Bn. Co.A
Reid, A.C. TN 14th (Neely's) Cav. Co.G Capt.
Reid, A.C. TN 6th Inf. Co.K Cpl.
Reid, A.D. AR Lt.Arty. Zimmerman's Btty.
Reid, A.G. NC 5th Cav. (63rd St.Troops) Co.F
Reid, A.H. GA 66th Inf. Co.F Capt.
Reid, A.H. VA Lt.Arty. Penick's Co. Sgt.
Reid, A.H. VA 3rd Inf.Loc.Def. Co.B
Reid, A.H. Conf.Lt.Arty. Richardson's Bn. Co.A Sgt.
Reid, A.J. FL Lt.Arty. Perry's Co.
Reid, A.J. GA Arty. 11th Bn. (Sumter Arty.) Old Co.C Sgt.
Reid, A.J. LA 18th Inf. Co.I
Reid, A.J. LA Inf.Crescent Regt. Co.C Sgt.
Reid, A.J. LA Inf.Cons.Crescent Regt. Co.G
Reid, Albert SC 1st Arty. Co.A
Reid, Albium M. AL 41st Inf. Co.E
Reid, Alexander MS 37th Inf. Co.K Cpl.
Reid, Alexander TN 39th Mtd.Inf. Co.B
Reid, Alexander TX 1st (Yager's) Cav. Co.F

Reid, Alexander TX 4th Cav. Co.H
Reid, Alexander H. GA 12th Inf. Co.G
Reid, Alexander H. VA Lt.Arty. Carpenter's Co.
Reid, Alexander S. GA 12th Inf. Co.G AQM
Reid, Alex L. TN 1st (Feild's) Inf. Co.C
Reid, Alfred L. NC 49th Inf. Co.E Sgt.
Reid, Alfred L.W. LA 12th Inf. Co.B
Reid, Alfred T. GA Lt.Arty. Scogin's Btty. (Griffin Lt.Arty.)
Reid, Allen AR Cav. 1st Bn. (Stirman's) Co.F Sgt.
Reid, A.M. AL Talladega Cty.Res. D.M. Reid's Co. Sgt.
Reid, A.M. AR 15th (Johnson's) Inf. Co.C 3rd Lt.
Reid, Americus R. GA 5th Inf. Co.B 2nd Lt.
Reid, Amos MS 37th Inf. Co.K
Reid, Andrew MS 10th Inf. New Co.G
Reid, Andrew NC 5th Sr.Res. Co.D
Reid, Andrew, Jr. SC 5th Cav. Co.B
Reid, Andrew, Jr. SC Cav. 17th Bn. Co.C
Reid, Andrew J. GA 22nd Inf. Co.F Cpl.
Reid, Andrew J. TN 3rd (Lillard's) Mtd.Inf. Co.C
Reid, Andrew N. NC 2nd Cav. (19th St.Troops) Co.B
Reid, Anthony VA 114th Mil. Co.F
Reid, A.P. AL 12th Inf. Co.F Sgt.
Reid, A.P. AL 14th Inf. Co.K
Reid, A.P. VA 15th Cav. Co.H
Reid, A.R. Gen. & Staff Lt.
Reid, Archibald C. MS 26th Inf. Co.A 1st Sgt.
Reid, Arthur VA 37th Inf. Co.H,F
Reid, A.S. Grimes' Div. Capt.,AQM
Reid, Ashley TX 4th Inf. Co.C
Reid, Ashley TX Inf. Townsend's Co. (Robertson Five S.)
Reid, Augustus MS 18th Cav. Wimberly's Co.A
Reid, Augustus Conf.Reg.Inf. Brooks' Bn. Co.D
Reid, Augustus T. GA 6th Inf. (St.Guards) Co.I 1st Sgt.
Reid, A.W. AL 56th Part.Rangers Co.I
Reid, A.W. AL 55th Vol. Co.I
Reid, A.W. TN 42nd Inf. 1st Co.I
Reid, Bailey AR Cav. Gordon's Regt. Co.C
Reid, Bailey MO Inf. Clark's Regt. Co.E
Reid, Baty GA Inf. 9th Bn. Co.A
Reid, Benjamin GA 27th Inf. Co.D
Reid, Benjamin A. MS 30th Inf. Co.H
Reid, Benjamin P. SC 2nd St.Troops Co.G
Reid, Benson TX 11th Inf. Co.G
Reid, B.F. KY 8th & 12th (Cons.) Cav. Co.F 2nd Lt.
Reid, B.F. LA 13th Bn. (Part.Rangers) Co.E
Reid, Boling AL 63rd Inf. Co.A 1st Lt.
Reid, Braddock TN 24th Inf. 2nd Co.H, Co.M
Reid, B.S. TX 12th Cav. Co.D
Reid, B.S. TX 33rd Cav. Co.E Sgt.
Reid, Burgess G. NC 22nd Inf. Co.A
Reid, Burgis G. NC 58th Inf. Co.H
Reid, C. MS 3rd Inf. (St.Troops) Co.H
Reid, C. VA VMI Co.C
Reid, C.A. GA 27th Inf. Co.G
Reid, C.A. NC 4th Cav. (59th St.Troops) Co.B Sgt.
Reid, Caleb D. 3rd Conf.Cav. Co.D
Reid, Caleb J. MS 15th Inf. Co.D

Reid, Caloway TX 7th Inf. Co.K Cpl.
Reid, Caloway TX 13th Vol. Co.M, 2nd Co.C Cpl.
Reid, Calvin H. NC 7th Inf. Co.F Sgt.
Reid, C.C.E. AL 29th Inf. Co.A
Reid, C.F. TX 7th Inf. Co.F
Reid, C.H. AL 29th Inf. Co.F
Reid, C.H. LA Inf.Crescent Regt. Co.B
Reid, C.H. MS 12th Cav. Co.I
Reid, C.H. SC Inf. 1st (Charleston) Bn. Co.D
Reid, C.H. SC 27th Inf. Co.D
Reid, Charles VA Mtd.Riflemen Balfour's Co.
Reid, Charles VA 9th Inf. Co.K
Reid, Charles VA 61st Inf. Co.H
Reid, Charles Sig.Corps,CSA
Reid, Chas. A. AL 5th Inf. New Co.E
Reid, Charles A. NC 47th Inf. Co.G
Reid, Charles C. 1st Squad. Cherokee Mtd.Vol. Co.A Ord.Sgt.
Reid, Charles S. FL 8th Inf. Co.B
Reid, Charlie W. AR 16th Inf. Co.A 2nd Lt.
Reid, Christopher R. SC Inf. Hampton Legion Co.E
Reid, C.L. SC Palmetto S.S. Co.C
Reid, Claiborne TX 20th Inf. Co.E
Reid, C.M. GA 19th Inf. Co.F
Reid, C.N. SC 2nd Rifles Co.B
Reid, Corrin AR 3rd Cav. Co.C
Reid, C.P. AL 32nd & 58th (Cons.) Inf. Lt.
Reid, C.W. TX 15th Inf. 2nd Co.E Sgt.
Reid, Cyrenas TN 27th Inf. Co.D
Reid, D. Conf.Reg.Inf. Brooks' Bn. Co.A
Reid, Daniel AL Arty. 1st Bn. Co.A
Reid, Daniel VA 58th Mil. Co.H
Reid, Daniel Conf.Reg.Inf. Brooks' Bn. Co.A
Reid, Daniel S. GA 1st Reg. Co.E
Reid, David AL 95th Mil. Co.D 1st Lt.
Reid, David NC 34th Inf. Co.E
Reid, David TN 6th Inf. Co.L
Reid, David TN 55th (Brown's) Inf. Ford's Co.
Reid, David VA Hvy.Arty. 20th Bn. Co.B
Reid, David B. VA Mil. Washington Cty.
Reid, David C. SC 1st (Orr's) Rifles Co.C
Reid, David H. NC 42nd Inf. Co.I 2nd Lt.
Reid, David K. AR Inf. 4th Bn. Co.B
Reid, David L. VA 14th Cav. Co.I
Reid, David M.B. MS 26th Inf. Co.A Capt.
Reid, David S. NC 4th Bn.Jr.Res. Co.A Sgt.
Reid, Davis AL 58th Inf. Co.D
Reid, D.B. KY 12th Cav. Co.F Sgt.
Reid, D.D. TX 4th Cav. Co.A
Reid, Dennis AL 29th Inf. Co.B
Reid, D.F. SC 13th Inf. Co.G
Reid, D.H. MS 20th Inf. Co.G
Reid, D.H. NC 2nd Cav. (19th St.Troops) Co.I
Reid, D.M. TN 36th Inf. Co.F
Reid, Doctor S. AL 5th Bn.Vol. Co.B
Reid, Dorsey VA 18th Cav. Co.F
Reid, Dorsey VA 23rd Cav. Co.E Sgt.
Reid, Dorsey VA 114th Mil. Co.D Cpl.
Reid, D.P. Gen. & Staff QM
Reid, D.R. AR 36th Inf. Co.K
Reid, Drury GA 49th Inf. Co.E 1st Sgt.
Reid, D.S. NC 3rd Jr.Res. Co.A Lt.
Reid, Dudley W. MO Cav. Freeman's Regt. Co.F

Reid, D.W. GA 2nd Cav. Co.K
Reid, D.W. GA 11th Cav. (St.Guards) McGriff's Co.
Reid, E. MS 4th Cav. Co.D
Reid, E. NC 5th Sr.Res. Co.K
Reid, E.A. MS 5th Cav. Co.K Cpl.
Reid, E.C. TN 45th Inf. Co.A
Reid, E.C. VA 11th Cav. Co.I
Reid, Edward AR 8th Inf. New Co.A
Reid, Edward B. GA 12th Inf. Co.G
Reid, Edward C. VA 5th Cav. 2nd Co.F
Reid, Edward Monroe TX 24th Cav. Co.H
Reid, E.H. MO 1st & 4th Cons.Inf. Co.E 2nd Lt.
Reid, Elbert W. MS 33rd Inf. Co.C
Reid, Elijah H. MO 4th Inf. Co.H Sgt.
Reid, Elisha M. GA 11th Inf. Co.A
Reid, Ella MS 37th Inf. Co.F
Reid, Emanuel NC 7th Sr.Res. Clinard's Co., Holland's Co.
Reid, Enoch MS 22nd Inf. Co.A
Reid, E.P. NC 22nd Inf. Co.B Sgt.
Reid, Ephraim AL 4th (Roddey's) Cav. Co.H
Reid, Eugene A. MS 5th Inf. Co.K
Reid, Evan SC 20th Inf. Co.A
Reid, Evan R. MS 11th Inf. Co.H 1st Lt.
Reid, F. GA 6th Inf. (St.Guards) Co.A
Reid, F. LA 22nd Inf. Co.E
Reid, F. LA 22nd (Cons.) Inf. Co.E
Reid, F. LA Inf.Crescent Regt. Co.C
Reid, F.B. AR 14th (McCarver's) Inf. Co.K Sgt.
Reid, Felix C. GA 15th Inf. Co.D 1st Sgt.
Reid, Ferdinand C. VA 2nd Cav. Co.I Cpl.
Reid, F.H. TX 25th Cav. Co.F
Reid, F.H. Evans' Brig. Maj.,CS
Reid, F.M. MO 1st & 4th Cons.Inf. Co.E
Reid, F.P. MS 44th Inf. Co.A
Reid, Francis Gen. & Staff Maj.,Comsy.
Reid, Francis M. AL 10th Inf. Co.A
Reid, Francis M. MO Inf. 3rd Regt.St.Guard Co.B 1st Lt.
Reid, Francis M. MO 4th Inf. Co.H Sgt.
Reid, Francis M. TX 30th Cav. Co.A Cpl.
Reid, Frank LA 18th Inf. Co.I
Reid, Frank P. MS 14th Inf. Co.K
Reid, Frank S. VA 25th Inf. 2nd Co.H
Reid, Frank T. TN Lt.Arty. Morton's Co. Ord.Sgt.
Reid, Frederick MO 2nd Inf. Co.K
Reid, Frederick VA 60th Inf. Co.K
Reid, Frs. W. GA 1st (Olmstead's) Inf. Gallie's Co. Sgt.
Reid, F.T. TN 4th (McLemore's) Cav. Co.F
Reid, G. GA 11th Inf. Co.K
Reid, Gaston C. VA 22nd Inf. Co.F
Reid, G.B. AL 19th Inf. Co.K
Reid, G.D. LA Mil.Conf.Guards Regt. Co.F
Reid, G.E. AL 23rd Inf. Co.F 2nd Lt.
Reid, George AL 5th Inf. New Co.F
Reid, George MS 28th Cav. Co.B Sgt.
Reid, George MS Lt.Arty. (Madison Lt.Arty.) Richards' Co.
Reid, George MS 1st (Patton's) Inf. Co.G Sgt.
Reid, George MS 11th Inf. Co.H
Reid, George SC 25th Inf. Co.A
Reid, George VA Lt.Arty. Douthat's Co.
Reid, George B. MO 1st Cav. QMSgt.

Reid, George C. Gen. & Staff AQM
Reid, George F. MS 17th Inf. Co.D
Reid, George F. NC 37th Inf. Co.I
Reid, George H. SC 9th Inf. Co.F
Reid, George L. MS 43rd Inf. Co.C
Reid, George R. GA Cav. 22nd Bn. (St.Guards) Co.D Capt.
Reid, George R. MS 10th Inf. Old Co.I
Reid, George W. AR Cav. 1st Bn. (Stirman's) Co.F Sgt.
Reid, George W. AR 15th (Josey's) Inf. Co.F
Reid, George W. GA 49th Inf. Co.E
Reid, George W. GA 53rd Inf. Co.K
Reid, George W. NC 7th Inf. Co.B
Reid, George W. NC 14th Inf. Co.I
Reid, George W. SC 20th Inf. Co.A
Reid, George W. VA 12th Cav. Co.I
Reid, George W. VA 12th Cav. Co.B
Reid, George W. VA Rockbridge Cty.Res. Bacon's Co.
Reid, G.F. GA 40th Inf. Co.G
Reid, G.H. GA 56th Inf. Co.H Cpl.
Reid, G.H. SC Lt.Arty. Garden's Co. (Palmetto Lt.Btty.)
Reid, G.H. VA 29th Inf. Co.B Sgt.
Reid, G.J. AL Mil. 2nd Regt.Vol. Co.F
Reid, G.L. GA 16th Inf. Co.G
Reid, Glen H. AL 48th Inf. New Co.G
Reid, G.N. SC 1st (Butler's) Inf. Co.C
Reid, G.P. LA 2nd Inf. Co.C
Reid, Griffin GA 22nd Inf. Co.F
Reid, Gus C. TN Cav. Nixon's Regt. Co.D Capt.
Reid, G.W. AL 29th Inf. Co.F
Reid, G.W. LA Inf. Pelican Regt. Co.D
Reid, G.W. NC 1st Jr.Res. Co.E
Reid, G.W. SC 6th Inf. 2nd Co.A
Reid, G.W. SC 10th Inf. Co.H
Reid, G.W. TX Cav. 1st Regt.St.Troops Co.F
Reid, H. GA Cav. 9th Bn. (St.Guards) Co.B 1st Sgt.
Reid, H. TX Cav. Giddings' Bn. Weisiger's Co.
Reid, H. TX Inf. 1st Bn. (St.Troops) Co.D
Reid, Harrison NC 4th Bn.Jr.Res. Co.B
Reid, Harrison P. MS 11th Inf. Co.B
Reid, Hayne D. SC Lt.Arty. 3rd (Palmetto) Bn. Co.F 1st Sgt.
Reid, Hayne D. SC 1st (McCreary's) Inf. Co.B Sgt.
Reid, H.B. SC 3rd Inf. Co.E
Reid, H.C. GA Cav. 19th Bn. Co.A
Reid, H.C. NC 1st Inf. (6 mo. '61) Co.B
Reid, H.C. SC 16th Inf. Co.G
Reid, H.C. VA 4th Cav. Co.C Sgt.
Reid, H. Conner NC 5th Cav. (63rd St.Troops) Co.F Sgt.
Reid, H.D. SC 1st Inf. Co.L Cpl.
Reid, H.E. TN 24th Inf. Co.C
Reid, Henry MO 4th Cav. Co.H
Reid, Henry NC 13th Inf. Co.G
Reid, Henry SC 2nd Bn.S.S. Co.A
Reid, Henry TX 19th Cav. Co.D
Reid, Henry TX Cav. Ragsdale's Bn. Co.E
Reid, Henry C. GA 52nd Inf. Co.K
Reid, Henry L. AL Lt.Arty. 2nd Bn. Co.E
Reid, Henry L. GA 10th Inf. Co.H Music.
Reid, Henry L. GA 49th Inf. Co.E

Reid, Henry L. LA 1st Hvy.Arty. (Reg.) Co.C
Reid, Henry M. VA 4th Cav. Co.C
Reid, Henry T. GA 1st Cav. Co.E,F Cpl.
Reid, Henry T. MS 11th (Perrin's) Cav. Co.E
Reid, H.G. NC 45th Inf. Co.C Cpl.
Reid, H.H. AL Cp. of Instr. Talladega
Reid, H.I. LA 4th Cav. Co.G
Reid, Hillory H. AL 17th Inf. Co.K Hosp.Stew.
Reid, Hiram GA Cherokee Legion (St.Guards) Co.I Cpl.
Reid, H.J. MS 1st Cav. Co.K Cpl.
Reid, H.K. NC 1st Inf. (6 mo. '61) Co.B
Reid, H.L.W. KY 1st Inf. Co.F
Reid, H.L.W. TN 8th (Smith's) Cav. Co.A
Reid, H.M. GA 19th Inf. Co.F
Reid, H.M. TN 33rd Inf. Co.I
Reid, H.N. SC 1st (McCreary's) Inf. Co.B
Reid, Horace K. VA 61st Inf. Co.G Sgt.
Reid, H.P. AL 23rd Inf. Co.F Capt.
Reid, H.T. GA 19th Inf. Co.F
Reid, H.T. SC 1st (Butler's) Inf. Co.G
Reid, Hugh TX Home Guards Killough's Co.
Reid, Hugh J. MS 22nd Inf. Co.G Lt.Col.
Reid, Hugh K. NC 53rd Inf. Co.B Music.
Reid, Hugh M. AL 28th Inf. Co.E Cpl.
Reid, Humphrey GA Mil. 6th Regt. Co.E Lt.
Reid, H.W. GA Cav. 9th Bn. (St.Guards) Co.E Sgt.
Reid, Hyatt D. MO 11th Inf. Co.I
Reid, I.A. GA 37th Inf. Co.E 3rd Lt.
Reid, I.H. 2nd Conf.Eng.Troops Co.D
Reid, Ingram P. NC 7th Inf. Co.B
Reid, Ira GA 40th Inf. Co.H
Reid, Irvin NC 28th Inf. Co.A Sgt.
Reid, Isaac AR 10th Inf. Co.H
Reid, Isaac NC 28th Inf. Co.A
Reid, Isaac C. VA 7th Cav. Co.D
Reid, J. AL 45th Inf. Co.K
Reid, J. AL 50th Inf.
Reid, J. AR 1st (Dobbin's) Cav. Co.A
Reid, J. GA Siege Arty. 28th Bn. Co.I
Reid, J. MS 13th Inf. Co.G
Reid, J. SC Lt.Arty. 3rd (Palmetto) Bn. Co.A
Reid, J. VA 5th Cav. 2nd Co.F Sgt.
Reid, J.A. MS Hightower's Co.
Reid, J.A. GA Inf. 8th Bn. Co.A Cpl.
Reid, J.A. GA 27th Inf. Co.D
Reid, J.A. MS 16th Inf. Co.C
Reid, J.A. NC Snead's Co. (Loc.Def.)
Reid, J.A. SC 2nd Cav. Co.H
Reid, J.A. TN 3rd (Forrest's) Cav. Co.C Cpl.
Reid, J.A. VA 82nd Mil. Co.A 1st Surg.
Reid, J.A. Hill's Div. 1st Lt.
Reid, J.A.B. NC 12th Inf. Co.K
Reid, Jabez M. GA 15th Inf. Co.G
Reid, Jackson MS 22nd Inf. Co.A
Reid, Jackson NC 26th Inf. Co.A
Reid, Jackson SC Lt.Arty. 3rd (Palmetto) Bn. Co.F Teamster
Reid, Jacob NC 31st Inf. Co.G Cook
Reid, Jacob TX Cav. Hardeman's Regt. Co.E Sgt.
Reid, Jacob VA 62nd Mtd.Inf. 2nd Co.M
Reid, Jacob VA Burks' Regt.Loc.Def.
Reid, Jacob F. NC 28th Inf. Co.A
Reid, Jacob V. SC 1st (Hagood's) Inf. 1st Co.A
Reid, James AL 5th Inf. New Co.F

Reid, James AL 8th Inf. Co.E
Reid, James AL 12th Inf. Co.H
Reid, James AL 38th Inf. Co.D
Reid, James AR 3rd Inf. Co.B
Reid, James GA 40th Inf. Co.G
Reid, James LA 4th Inf. Co.D Capt.
Reid, James MS Cav. 24th Bn. Co.C
Reid, James NC 7th Sr.Res. Clinard's Co., Holland's Co.
Reid, James SC 6th Inf. 1st Co.B, 2nd Co.A
Reid, James TX Cav. 1st Regt.St.Troops Co.D
Reid, James TX 12th Cav. Co.D
Reid, James VA 4th Cav. Co.B
Reid, James VA 42nd Inf. Co.I
Reid, James Conf.Reg.Inf. Brooks' Bn. Co.A
Reid, James A. GA Inf. (Anderson Guards) Anderson's Co. 1st Lt.
Reid, James A. NC 4th Inf. Co.C
Reid, James A. VA 11th Inf. Co.G
Reid, James C. NC 24th Inf. Co.K
Reid, James C. 1st Conf.Eng.Troops Co.A,B
Reid, James D. TX 18th Inf. Co.C
Reid, James E. AL 4th Cav. Co.M
Reid, James E. GA 66th Inf. Co.D
Reid, James E. VA 5th Cav. (12 mo. '61-2) Co.I
Reid, James F. GA Cav. 7th Bn. (St.Guards) Co.F
Reid, James F. GA 49th Inf. Co.D
Reid, James F. TX 9th (Young's) Inf. Co.K
Reid, James Greer TN 6th Inf. Co.H
Reid, James H. AL 22nd Inf. Co.E
Reid, James H. GA 12th Inf. Co.G
Reid, James H. TN 4th Inf. Co.A
Reid, James H. VA 19th Cav. Co.G,C,K
Reid, James H. VA 11th Inf. Co.K
Reid, James L. GA 4th Inf. Co.G
Reid, James L. NC 9th Bn.S.S. Co.B Cpl.
Reid, James L. NC 21st Inf. Co.E
Reid, James L.B. GA 21st Inf. Co.F
Reid, James M. AR 3rd Inf. Co.B
Reid, James M. GA 6th Inf. Co.A 1st Lt.
Reid, James M. MS 5th Inf. Co.I
Reid, James M. NC 6th Cav. (65th St.Troops) Co.C,G
Reid, James M. SC Cav. 10th Bn. Co.B 2nd Lt.
Reid, James M. SC Lt.Arty. Garden's Co. (Palmetto Lt.Btty.)
Reid, James M. SC 2nd Inf. Co.A
Reid, James M. SC 20th Inf. Co.A
Reid, James M. TX Cav. Baylor's Regt. Co.H Cpl.
Reid, James N. TN 29th Inf. Co.B 2nd Lt.
Reid, James P. AL 19th Inf. Co.D
Reid, James P. TN 42nd Inf. 1st Co.I
Reid, James R. MS 27th Inf. Co.H
Reid, James R. NC 3rd Arty. (40th St.Troops) Co.G
Reid, James Rufus NC 4th Inf. Co.C 1st Lt.
Reid, James S. AR Cav. 1st Bn. (Stirman's) Co.F Cpl.
Reid, James S. GA 3rd Inf. Co.D Lt.Col.
Reid, James S. MS Lt.Arty. (Madison Lt.Arty.) Richards' Co. 1st Lt.
Reid, James S. TX 13th Cav. Co.E Teamster
Reid, James T. AL 1st Bn.Cadets Co.A
Reid, James T. MS 33rd Inf. Co.C
Reid, James T. SC 1st (Orr's) Rifles Co.E Capt.

Reid, James T. VA 5th Cav. Co.G Cpl.
Reid, James T. VA 12th Inf. Co.B
Reid, James T.S. VA 6th Inf. Co.G
Reid, James W. NC 4th Sr.Res. Co.E 1st Lt.
Reid, James W., Jr. TN 14th (Neely's) Cav. Co.I
Reid, James W. VA Lt.Arty. 38th Bn. Co.C
Reid, James W. VA Lt.Arty. Carpenter's Co.
Reid, J.B. GA 2nd Cav. Co.E
Reid, J.B. GA 6th Inf. (St.Guards) Co.K
Reid, J.B. GA Inf. 40th Bn. Co.D 1st Lt.
Reid, J.B. MS 1st Lt.Arty. Co.D
Reid, J.B. NC 49th Inf. Co.G
Reid, J.B. SC 3rd Cav. Co.F
Reid, J.B. TX 13th Vol. 2nd Co.B
Reid, J.C. GA 9th Inf. Co.B
Reid, J.C. MS 1st Cav. Co.K 2nd Lt.
Reid, J.C. SC 1st Cav. Co.H
Reid, J.C. SC 2nd Inf. Co.A,G Sgt.
Reid, J.C. SC 6th Res. Co.E
Reid, J.C. TN 8th (Smith's) Cav. Co.A
Reid, J.C. TX 17th Inf. Co.B Sgt.
Reid, J.D. GA Inf. 8th Bn. Co.A
Reid, J.D. MS 28th Cav. Co.A
Reid, J.D. TN 51st Inf. Co.K Cpl.
Reid, J.D. TN 51st (Cons.) Inf. Co.G Cpl.
Reid, J.E. AL 1st Inf. Co.G
Reid, J.E. AL 28th Inf. Co.I
Reid, J.E. MS 6th Cav. Co.F
Reid, Jeremiah NC 17th Inf. (2nd Org.) Co.F
Reid, Jesse MS 35th Inf. Co.A
Reid, Jesse NC 7th Inf. Co.K
Reid, Jesse NC Inf. Thomas Legion 2nd Co.A
Reid, Jesse VA Inf. 1st Bn. Co.E
Reid, Jesse B. MS 27th Inf. Co.F
Reid, Jessee B. MS 24th Inf. Co.G
Reid, Jesse J. NC 1st Inf. (6 mo. '61) Co.I
Reid, Jesse J. NC 24th Inf. Co.D
Reid, Jesse L. TN 4th (McLemore's) Cav. Co.K
Reid, Jesse W. NC 7th Inf. Co.K
Reid, Jesse Walton SC 4th Inf. Co.C
Reid, J.F. MS Cav. Ham's Regt. Co.H Cpl.
Reid, J.F. MS Inf. 2nd St.Troops Co.A
Reid, J.F. Gen. & Staff Surg.
Reid, J.H. AL 9th (Malone's) Cav. Co.B Sgt.
Reid, J.H. LA 18th Inf. Co.C
Reid, J.H. LA 18th Inf. Co.H
Reid, J.H. TN 6th Inf. Co.L
Reid, J.H. TN 55th (Brown's) Inf. Ford's Co.
Reid, J.H. VA Lt.Arty. 13th Bn. Co.A
Reid, J.H. VA 8th Inf. Co.B
Reid, J.H. VA 54th Mil. Co.H
Reid, J.J. NC Mallett's Bn. (Cp.Guard) Co.A Lt.
Reid, J.J. SC 4th Cav. Co.C
Reid, J.J. VA 23rd Cav. Co.A
Reid, J.L. AL 42nd Inf. Co.K
Reid, J.L. GA Cobb's Legion Co.A
Reid, J.L. MS 1st Lt.Arty.
Reid, J.L. NC 1st Inf. (6 mo. '61) Co.B
Reid, J.L. SC 4th Inf. Co.B
Reid, J.M. AL 26th (O'Neal's) Inf. Co.A
Reid, J.M. LA 4th Cav. Co.G
Reid, J.M. MS 1st (Johnston's) Inf. Co.I
Reid, J.M. MS 14th Inf. Co.E
Reid, J.M. SC 4th Cav. Co.C 2nd Lt.
Reid, J.M. SC 3rd Inf. Co.E
Reid, J.M. TN 8th (Smith's) Cav. Co.A

Reid, J.M. TX 19th Inf. Co.H
Reid, J.N. SC 20th Inf. Co.D
Reid, J.N. TN 29th Inf. Co.B
Reid, Joel E. MS 14th Inf. Co.K
Reid, John, Jr. AL 1st Regt. Mobile Vol. Co.E Sgt.
Reid, John, Jr. AL 4th Res. Co.C Jr.2nd Lt.
Reid, John AL 27th Inf. Co.K
Reid, John AR Cav. Gordon's Regt. Co.D
Reid, John AR 3rd Inf. Co.B
Reid, John AR 8th Inf. New Co.A
Reid, John AR 13th Mil. Co.A
Reid, John GA 62nd Cav. Co.L
Reid, John GA 28th Inf. Co.C
Reid, John GA 40th Inf. Co.G
Reid, John MS Cav. 24th Bn. Co.C
Reid, John MS Inf. 3rd Bn. (St.Troops) Co.D
Reid, John MS 35th Inf. Co.A
Reid, John NC 4th Sr.Res. Co.G
Reid, John NC 21st Inf. Co.H
Reid, John NC 25th Inf. Co.H Cpl.
Reid, John NC 39th Inf. Co.I 1st Lt.
Reid, John SC 7th Cav. Co.G
Reid, John SC Rutledge Mtd.Riflemen & Horse Arty. Trenholm's Co.
Reid, John TN Cav. Nixon's Regt. Co.B
Reid, John TN 55th (Brown's) Inf. Co.H
Reid, John TX 1st (Yager's) Cav. Co.F
Reid, John TX 25th Cav. Co.F
Reid, John TX Cav. Waller's Regt. Co.D 1st Lt.
Reid, John TX 11th Inf. Co.G
Reid, John VA 15th Cav. Co.H
Reid, John VA Cav. Young's Co.
Reid, John VA Hvy.Arty. 19th Bn. 2nd Co.C
Reid, John VA 2nd Inf.Loc.Def. Co.D Cpl.
Reid, John VA Inf. 6th Bn.Loc.Def. Co.A
Reid, John VA 11th Bn.Res. Co.E Cpl.
Reid, John VA 42nd Inf. Co.I
Reid, John 8th (Dearing's) Conf.Cav. Co.E
Reid, John 15th Conf.Cav. Co.G
Reid, John Price's Div. Maj.,ACS
Reid, John A. GA 1st (Fannin's) Res. Co.G,F
Reid, John A. VA 27th Inf. Co.E
Reid, John B. GA Inf. 2nd Bn. Co.D
Reid, John B., Jr. GA 21st Inf. Co.F
Reid, John B., Sr. GA 21st Inf. Co.F
Reid, John B. GA 41st Inf. Co.E 1st Lt.
Reid, John B. Gen. & Staff Lt.,ACS
Reid, John C. AL 8th Inf. Co.A 1st Lt.
Reid, John C. AL 28th Inf. Col.
Reid, John C. AL 32nd & 58th (Cons.) Inf.
Reid, John C. AL 58th Inf. Co.I,B
Reid, John C. GA 8th Inf. Co.I Capt.
Reid, John C. NC 37th Inf. Co.I Sgt.
Reid, John C. NC 45th Inf. Co.C Sgt.
Reid, John E. VA 60th Inf. Co.K
Reid, John F. NC 53rd Inf. Co.B
Reid, John F. TX 33rd Cav. Co.E
Reid, John G. AR Reid's St.Btty. Capt.
Reid, John H. GA 23rd Inf. Co.A
Reid, John H. LA Inf.Crescent Regt. Co.C
Reid, John H. NC 7th Inf. Co.F
Reid, John H. SC 20th Inf. Co.A
Reid, John J. NC Mallett's Bn. 2nd Lt.
Reid, John K. FL 7th Inf. Co.H
Reid, John L. NC 37th Inf. Co.C
Reid, John L. VA 5th Cav.

Reid, John M. AL 50th Inf. Co.A
Reid, John M. AL 55th Vol. Co.I N.C.S. Comsy.Sgt.
Reid, John M. GA 25th Inf. Co.H
Reid, John M. KY 4th Mtd.Inf. Co.K
Reid, John M.L. MO Lt.Arty. 3rd Btty. Sr.1st Lt.
Reid, John N. LA 28th (Gray's) Inf. Co.C
Reid, John R. AL 42nd Inf. Co.D
Reid, John R. AR 25th Inf. Co.C
Reid, John R. MD 1st Cav. Co.C
Reid, John R. MS 24th Inf. Co.G Cpl.
Reid, John R. VA 12th Cav. Co.I
Reid, John R. VA Cav. Mosby's Regt. (Part. Rangers) Co.A
Reid, John R. VA 146th Mil. Co.K
Reid, John S. GA Lt.Arty. (Jo Thompson Arty.) Hanleiter's Co.
Reid, John S. GA 3rd Inf. Co.B Capt.
Reid, John S. VA Lt.Arty. Grandy's Co.
Reid, John S. VA 6th Inf. Vickery's Co.
Reid, John S. VA 16th Inf. 1st Co.H
Reid, John T. AL Lt.Arty. 2nd Bn. Co.E
Reid, John T. MS 17th Inf. Co.D
Reid, John T. NC 22nd Inf. Co.K Hosp.Stew.
Reid, John T. TX Cav. Baylor's Regt. Co.D
Reid, John W. AL 20th Inf. Co.A
Reid, John W. AL 25th Inf. Co.D
Reid, John W. GA 19th Inf. Co.K
Reid, John W. NC 13th Inf. Co.B Music.
Reid, John W. SC 1st (Orr's) Rifles Co.B Sgt
Reid, John W. TX 4th Cav. Co.H
Reid, John W. TX 17th Cav. Co.A Sgt.
Reid, John W. TX Inf.Riflemen Arnold's Co.
Reid, John W. VA Lt.Arty. Carpenter's Co.
Reid, John W. VA Lt.Arty. Carpenter's Co. Sgt.
Reid, John W. VA Inf. 1st Bn. Co.D
Reid, John W. VA 11th Inf. Co.B
Reid, John Wilson VA 2nd Cav. Co.G
Reid, Jonas G.B. GA Cobb's Legion Co.F
Reid, Jonathan VA Lt.Arty. Douthat's Co.
Reid, Joseph GA 11th Cav. Co.C Capt.
Reid, Joseph GA Cav. Young's Co. (Alleghany Troopers)
Reid, Joseph GA 1st (Fannin's) Res. Co.G
Reid, Joseph MS 28th Cav. Co.B
Reid, Joseph MS 38th Cav. Co.I
Reid, Joseph MS Inf. 3rd Bn. (St.Troops) Co.F
Reid, Joseph MS 35th Inf. Co.A
Reid, Joseph SC 1st Cav. Co.F
Reid, Joseph SC 16th Inf. Co.H
Reid, Joseph B. SC 1st (Orr's) Rifles Co.A Cpl.
Reid, Joseph B. SC 2nd Rifles Co.H 1st Sgt.
Reid, Joseph B. TN 4th (McLemore's) Cav. Co.K
Reid, Joseph B. VA 15th Cav. Co.H Sgt.
Reid, Joseph C. TX Cav. 1st Regt.St.Troops Co.D
Reid, Joseph C. VA Lt.Arty. Carpenter's Co. Cpl.
Reid, Joseph Davis MS Lt.Arty. (Madison Lt.Arty.) Richards' Co.
Reid, Joseph E. MS Inf. 3rd Bn. (St.Troops) Co.F
Reid, Joseph H. VA 7th Cav. Co.A
Reid, Joseph H.L. MS 26th Inf. Co.A
Reid, Joseph J. NC 15th Inf. Co.K 2nd Lt.

Reid, Joseph M. NC 39th Inf. Co.I Sgt.
Reid, Joseph N. SC 1st (Hagood's) Inf. 1st Co.A
Reid, Joseph R. GA 27th Inf. Co.D Sgt.
Reid, Joseph S. MS 20th Inf. Co.G Capt.
Reid, Joseph S. VA 4th Cav. Co.H Sgt.
Reid, Joshua D. VA 54th Mil. Co.E,F
Reid, Josiah TX 17th Cav. Co.B Cpl.
Reid, J.P. AL 17th Inf. Co.G
Reid, J.P. AL 55th Vol. Co.I
Reid, J.P. AL 58th Inf. Co.C
Reid, J.P. GA Arty. 11th Bn. (Sumter Arty.) Old Co.C, Co.B
Reid, J.P. SC Mil. 1st Regt. (Charleston Res.) Co.B Sgt.
Reid, J.P. SC Palmetto S.S. Co.C
Reid, J.Q. AR Lt.Arty. Zimmerman's Btty.
Reid, J.R. AL 62nd Inf. Co.D
Reid, J.R. NC 1st Arty. (10th St.Troops) Co.A
Reid, J.R. SC 3rd Cav. Co.F
Reid, J.R. SC 11th Inf. Co.E
Reid, J.R. VA Lt.Arty. W.P. Carter's Co.
Reid, J.S. AR 1st (Monroe's) Cav. Co.D
Reid, J.S. GA 6th Cav. Co.I 1st Lt.
Reid, J.S. MS 1st (Johnston's) Inf. Co.I
Reid, J.S. NC Inf.
Reid, J.S. TN 50th (Cons.) Inf. Co.C Capt.
Reid, J.S. Conf.Lt.Arty. Richardson's Bn. Co.C
Reid, J.T. GA 7th Cav. Co.A
Reid, J.T. GA Cav. 21st Bn. Co.A
Reid, J.T. GA Inf. 8th Bn. Lt.Col.
Reid, J.T. LA 18th Inf. Co.C
Reid, J.T. TN 50th Inf. Co.C Capt.
Reid, J.T. VA 54th Mil. Co.C,D
Reid, J.T.S. Johnston's Command 1st Lt.,Adj.Gen.
Reid, J.T.V. 1st Conf.Eng.Troops Co.K Sgt.
Reid, J.V. SC 20th Inf. Co.D
Reid, J.W. AL 9th (Malone's) Cav. Co.B 1st Sgt.
Reid, J.W. AL Cp. of Instr. Talladega
Reid, J.W. GA 2nd Cav. Co.L
Reid, J.W. LA 2nd Inf. Co.K
Reid, J.W. LA Res.Corps
Reid, J.W. MS Cav. 3rd Bn.Res. Co.C
Reid, J.W. MO 12th Inf. Co.C
Reid, J.W. NC 6th Cav. (65th St.Troops) Co.A
Reid, J.W. NC 2nd Jr.Res. Co.B
Reid, J.W. SC 2nd Inf. Co.K
Reid, J.W. TN 14th (Neely's) Cav. Co.F Cpl.
Reid, J.W. TN 6th Inf. Co.K
Reid, J.W. VA 25th Inf. 2nd Co.H
Reid, J.W. VA 114th Mil. Co.G
Reid, J.W. Gen. & Staff Rec. as Maj.,AAG
Reid, J.Y. NC 4th Sr.Res. Co.K,G
Reid, J.Y. NC 7th Inf. Co.B
Reid, L.A. GA Lt.Arty. 12th Bn. Co.F
Reid, Lemuel AL 44th Inf. Co.K
Reid, Lemuel SC 1st St.Troops Co.I 2nd Lt.
Reid, Lemuel SC 5th Res. Co.H 1st Sgt.
Reid, Lemuel N. MS 11th Inf. Co.H
Reid, Leon E. Gen. & Staff Hosp.Stew.
Reid, Leonidas E. VA 24th Inf. Co.C
Reid, Leonidas E. Hosp.Stew.
Reid, Leonodes GA 1st Cav. Co.E,F
Reid, L.F. AL 49th Inf. Co.A
Reid, L.H. NC 1st Arty. (10th St.Troops) Co.K
Reid, L.H. NC Lt.Arty. 13th Bn. Co.D Sgt.Maj.

Reid, Louis H. NC 2nd Arty. (36th St.Troops) Co.G 1st Sgt.
Reid, L.S. NC 45th Inf. Co.C
Reid, L.S. Davis' Brig. Maj.,QM
Reid, Luther R. MS 1st Lt.Arty. Co.G
Reid, Luther R. MS 21st Inf. Co.H 1st Sgt.
Reid, L.W. TN 11th (Holman's) Cav. Co.C
Reid, L.W. VA 36th Inf. Lt.Col.
Reid, M. AL 50th Inf. Co.F
Reid, M. NC 49th Inf. Co.G
Reid, M. SC 1st Arty. Co.K
Reid, M. SC 3rd Inf. Co.F
Reid, Madden P. AL Inf. 1st Regt. Co.C
Reid, Madison VA 19th Cav. Co.G
Reid, Malon NC 2nd Inf. Co.I
Reid, Malon NC 58th Inf. Co.H
Reid, Marcus B. AL 51st (Part.Rangers) Co.E
Reid, Marcus B. VA 146th Mil. Co.K
Reid, Martin VA 18th Cav. Co.F
Reid, Martin V. VA 114th Mil. Co.D
Reid, Martin V.B. AL 32nd Inf. Co.B
Reid, Martin V.B. NC 24th Inf. Co.K
Reid, Matthew H. NC 22nd Inf. Co.H
Reid, M.C. VA Loc.Def. Durrett's Co.
Reid, McCager KY 7th Cav. Co.C
Reid, McClure TX Cav. Baylor's Regt. Co.D Cpl.
Reid, M.D.L. GA 8th Inf. Co.K
Reid, Michael MS 24th Inf. Co.G 3rd Lt.
Reid, Michael NC 45th Inf. Co.A
Reid, Michael A. TN 36th Inf. Co.F
Reid, Milton L. AL 28th Inf. Co.F
Reid, M.J. GA 19th Inf. Co.F
Reid, M.M. GA 27th Inf. Co.D
Reid, M.V. TN 29th Inf. Co.B
Reid, M.V. TN 62nd Mtd.Inf. Co.B Sgt.
Reid, N.B. AL 20th Inf. Co.A
Reid, N. Byan AL 28th Inf. Co.I
Reid, N.C. MS 5th Cav. Co.A
Reid, Newton H. SC 1st (Orr's) Rifles Co.D
Reid, Newton M. GA 5th Inf. Co.B
Reid, N.J. GA 7th Inf. Co.G
Reid, N.J. GA 56th Inf. Co.K
Reid, N.M. GA Inf. 25th Bn. (Prov.Guard) Co.B Cpl.
Reid, N.W. SC 20th Inf. Co.A
Reid, O.H. TX 12th Cav. Co.D
Reid, O.H. TX 3rd (Kirby's) Bn.Vol. Co.B
Reid, O.J. SC Cav. 17th Bn. Co.A
Reid, O.L. GA Conscr.
Reid, Oliver C. TX 18th Inf. Co.I
Reid, Oscar VA 6th Cav. Co.A Cpl.
Reid, Oscar W. GA 1st (Olmstead's) Inf. Co.C
Reid, Owen GA 36th (Broyles') Inf. Co.D
Reid, Owen GA 36th (Villepigue's) Inf. Co.E
Reid, Owen 1st Conf.Inf. 1st Co.E
Reid, P. Conf.Inf. 1st Bn. 2nd Co.E
Reid, Patrick TX 6th Inf. Co.I
Reid, P.C. GA Conscr.
Reid, Peter VA 17th Inf. Co.B
Reid, Peter C. VA 7th Cav. Co.D 1st Lt.
Reid, Peter C. VA 97th Mil. Co.M Maj.
Reid, Peter H. GA 66th Inf. Co.A
Reid, Philip F. AL 3rd Inf. Co.G
Reid, Philip P. Conf.Inf. 1st Bn. 2nd Co.A
Reid, Phillip F. AL Lt.Arty. Lee's Btty.

Reid, Phillip P. GA Inf. 25th Bn. (Prov.Guard) Co.A
Reid, R. FL 2nd Cav. Co.K
Reid, R. SC Lt.Arty. 3rd (Palmetto) Bn. Co.I
Reid, R. Conf.Cav. Wood's Regt. Co.D Sgt.
Reid, R.A. AL Lowndes Rangers Vol. Fagg's Co.
Reid, R.A. AR 30th Inf. Co.D
Reid, R.A. GA Cav. 9th Bn. (St.Guards) Co.E Capt.
Reid, R.A. GA 1st (Fannin's) Res. Co.F Cpl.
Reid, R.A. Gen. & Staff AQM
Reid, Randol SC 3rd Res. Co.G
Reid, Raymond MS Part.Rangers Smyth's Co. Cpl.
Reid, Raymond J. FL 2nd Inf. Co.H Adj.
Reid, R.C. SC 15th Inf. Co.A
Reid, Reading AL 29th Inf. Co.F Cpl.
Reid, Redman VA 49th Inf. Co.A
Reid, Reuben A. GA 40th Inf. Co.G
Reid, Reuben D. GA 56th Inf. Co.H Cpl.
Reid, Reubin MS 35th Inf. Co.G
Reid, R.F. GA 19th Inf. Co.F
Reid, R.G.C. SC 6th Inf. 1st Co.A, 2nd Co.A
Reid, R.H. NC 23rd Inf. Co.H Sgt.
Reid, Rhesa AL 18th Inf. Co.L.
Reid, Rhesa T. GA 19th Inf. Co.F
Reid, Richard VA Lt.Arty. W.P. Carter's Co.
Reid, Richard A. GA 12th Inf. QM
Reid, Richard B. MS 15th Inf. Co.G
Reid, Richard G. VA 15th Cav. Co.F
Reid, Richard J. VA 49th Inf. Co.A 2nd Lt.
Reid, Richard W. FL 5th Inf. Co.A ACS
Reid, Richie AL 58th Inf. Co.G
Reid, R.J. AL 26th Inf. Co.G
Reid, R.J. AL 42nd Inf. Co.I
Reid, R.J. GA 28th Inf. Co.C
Reid, R.J. Gen. & Staff 1st Lt.,Adj.
Reid, R.M. GA 40th Inf. Co.G
Reid, R.M. SC 20th Inf. Co.D
Reid, R.N. KY 12th Cav. Co.C
Reid, Robert AL 8th (Livingston's) Cav. Co.H
Reid, Robert AL 50th Inf. Co.G
Reid, Robert MS 1st Lt.Arty. Co.D
Reid, Robert MS Inf. 2nd Bn. Co.F
Reid, Robert MS 26th Inf. Co.A
Reid, Robert MS 48th Inf. Co.F
Reid, Robert TN 38th Inf. 1st Co.H
Reid, Robert VA Cav. Young's Co.
Reid, Robert VA Lt.Arty. Douthat's Co.
Reid, Robert VA 1st Inf. Co.B
Reid, Robert VA 46th Inf. 2nd Co.A
Reid, Robert A. GA Inf. 5th Bn. (St.Guards) Co.F
Reid, Robert A. GA 26th Inf. 1st Co.G
Reid, Robert A. GA 29th Inf. Co.E
Reid, Robert A. TN 29th Inf. Co.B 2nd Lt.
Reid, Robert C. VA 11th Inf. Co.G
Reid, Robert E. VA 9th Inf. Co.D
Reid, Robert F. MS 10th Inf. New Co.B
Reid, Robert G. AR 24th Inf. Co.B
Reid, Robert G. AR Inf. Hardy's Regt. Co.B
Reid, Robt. M. AL 49th Inf. Co.A 1st Lt.
Reid, Robert M. GA 19th Inf. Co.F
Reid, Robert R. GA 22nd Inf. Co.F
Reid, Robert S. NC 34th Inf. Co.G 2nd Lt.
Reid, Robert S. TX 20th Inf. 1st Lt.

Reid, Robert S. Gen. & Staff AAAG
Reid, Robt. V. Gen. & Staff Asst.Surg.
Reid, Roswell SC 16th Inf. Co.G
Reid, R.R. Gen. & Staff, QMDept. Capt.
Reid, R.R. Gen. & Staff Capt.,AQM
Reid, R.R.S. MS 19th Inf. Co.A
Reid, Rufus TN 55th (McKoin's) Inf. Bounds' Co.
Reid, Rufus J. Gen. & Staff Capt.,QM
Reid, R.V. GA 13th Inf. Co.A Surg.
Reid, R.W. MS Rogers' Co. Music.
Reid, R.W. VA 2nd Cav. Co.I
Reid, R.W. VA Cav. 36th Bn. Co.D
Reid, R.W. Conf.Cav. Wood's Regt. Co.H
Reid, Samuel FL Lt.Arty. Dyke's Co.
Reid, Samuel GA 29th Inf. Co.E
Reid, Samuel GA Inf. (Milledgeville Guards) Caraker's Co. Cpl.
Reid, Samuel MS 11th Inf. Co.H
Reid, Samuel SC 1st (Orr's) Rifles Co.E
Reid, Samuel SC 23rd Inf. Co.F
Reid, Samuel C. NC Hvy.Arty. 10th Bn. Co.D
Reid, Samuel D. MS 1st Cav.Res. Co.I
Reid, Samuel D. VA 6th Cav. Co.H
Reid, Samuel G. AL Montgomery Guards Sgt.
Reid, Samuel H. MS 17th Inf. Co.D
Reid, Samuel O. SC 1st (Orr's) Rifles Co.G
Reid, Samuel P. GA 1st Reg. Co.B Cpl.
Reid, Samuel T. GA 3rd Inf. Co.B
Reid, Samuel T. GA 6th Inf. (St.Guards) Co.C
Reid, Samuel V. AR 3rd Inf. Co.H Capt.
Reid, Samuel W. SC 20th Inf. Co.A
Reid, Samuel W. TX 4th Cav. Co.H
Reid, S.B. GA Cav. 20th Bn. Co.E Jr.2nd Lt.
Reid, S.C. MO 2nd Inf. Co.B Cpl.
Reid, S.C. SC 2nd Rifles Co.B
Reid, S.D. TX 12th Cav. Co.D
Reid, S.D. TX 33rd Cav. Co.E Cpl.
Reid, S.E. AL 28th Inf. Co.D
Reid, S.H. SC 2nd St.Troops Co.G
Reid, S.H. SC 26th Inf. Co.E
Reid, S.H. TN 3rd (Lillard's) Mtd.Inf. Co.C
Reid, Silas T. GA 7th Inf. Co.D
Reid, S.J. TX 23rd Cav. Co.A
Reid, S.M. SC 18th Inf. Co.B Cpl.
Reid, Smith VA 33rd Inf. Co.D
Reid, Smith VA 114th Mil. Co.D
Reid, S.N. SC 3rd Inf. Co.C
Reid, S.N. Gen. & Staff, Subs.Dept. Maj.,Ch.CS
Reid, Solomon AL 48th Inf. Co.I
Reid, S.P. GA 23rd Inf. Co.B Sgt.
Reid, S.P. SC 3rd Inf. Co.C
Reid, S.T. GA 9th Inf. (St.Guards) Co.A
Reid, Stephen C. SC 1st (Orr's) Rifles Co.A
Reid, Stephen D. TX 37th Cav. Co.H
Reid, S.V. Gen. & Staff Maj.
Reid, S.W. GA 6th Cav. Co.D
Reid, S. Warren SC 20th Inf. Co.F 1st Sgt.
Reid, T.A. TN 6th Inf. Co.K
Reid, T.A.R. SC 6th Inf. 2nd Co.A
Reid, T.B. SC Lt.Arty. 3rd (Palmetto) Bn. Co.I
Reid, T.B. SC 16th Inf. Co.D
Reid, T.D. AL City Troop (Mobile) Arrington's Co.A
Reid, T.G. SC 9th Inf. Co.F
Reid, T.G. SC Palmetto S.S. Co.B

Reid, T. Golden SC Lt.Arty. Garden's Co. (Palmetto Lt.Btty.) Sgt.

86

Reid, T. Golden SC Lt.Arty. Garden's Co. (Palmetto Lt.Btty.) Sgt.
Reid, Thadeus W. AL 20th Inf. Co.K
Reid, Thomas AL 42nd Inf. Co.D
Reid, Thomas AL 46th Inf. Co.C
Reid, Thomas AR 14th (McCarver's) Inf. Co.C Cpl.
Reid, Thomas MS 7th Inf. Co.C
Reid, Thomas MS 35th Inf. Co.A
Reid, Thomas SC 3rd Res. Co.G Cpl.
Reid, Thomas VA 22nd Inf. Co.A
Reid, Thomas Inf. School of Pract. Powell's Detach. Co.C Cpl.
Reid, Thomas B. GA 21st Inf. Co.F
Reid, Thomas B. MS 11th Inf. Co.H
Reid, Thomas B. MS 22nd Inf. Co.A
Reid, Thomas C. GA 57th Inf. Co.I
Reid, Thomas D. AL Arty. 1st Bn. Co.B
Reid, Thomas D. MS 13th Inf. Co.F Hosp.Stew.
Reid, Thomas D. 15th Conf.Cav. Co.F
Reid, Thomas J. AR 25th Inf. Co.I
Reid, Thomas J. TN 32nd Inf. Asst.Surg.
Reid, Thomas L. AL Vol. Meador's Co. Sgt.
Reid, Thomas L. MS 24th Inf. Co.C Sgt.
Reid, Thomas M. MS Inf. 3rd Bn. (St.Troops) Co.F
Reid, Thomas N. SC 12th Inf. Co.F,H
Reid, Thomas W. GA 7th Inf. (St.Guards) Co.E
Reid, Thomas W. LA 1st Hvy.Arty. (Reg.) Co.E
Reid, Thomas W. MS 9th Inf. New Co.D
Reid, Thomas W. SC 13th Inf. Co.G
Reid, Thomas Z. GA 5th Inf. Co.B
Reid, Thornton VA 19th Cav. Co.G
Reid, Timothy NC 20th Inf. Co.B
Reid, T.J. AL Cp. of Instr. Talladega Co.F
Reid, T.J. AR 2nd Cav. Co.E Maj.
Reid, T.J. TN Inf. 4th Cons.Regt. Asst.Surg.
Reid, T.J. TN 13th Inf. Co.B
Reid, T.J. Gen. & Staff,PACS Asst.Surg.
Reid, T.N. Evans' Brig. Maj.,CS
Reid, T.R. MS Cav. 1st Bn. (McNair's) St.Troops Co.E
Reid, T.R. TN 24th Inf. Co.C
Reid, T.S. SC 6th Inf. 1st Co.A, 2nd Co.A
Reid, Tunis H. AL 31st Inf.
Reid, W. NC 4th Inf. Co.C
Reid, W.A. AL 18th Inf. Co.F
Reid, W.A. AL 58th Inf. Co.F
Reid, W.A. SC 18th Inf. Co.B
Reid, W.A. SC Inf. Holcombe Legion Co.B
Reid, W.A. Gen. & Staff, A. of TN Cap.,AIG
Reid, Wallace TN Lt.Arty. Morton's Co.
Reid, Walter H. VA 5th Cav. 2nd Co.F 2nd Lt.
Reid, Walter H. VA 6th Cav. Co.K
Reid, Warren D. MS 11th Inf. Co.H 1st Sgt.
Reid, W.B. TN 13th Inf. Co.B
Reid, W.C. AL 3rd Inf. Co.I
Reid, W.C. SC 6th Inf. 1st Co.A, 2nd Co.A
Reid, W.C. TN 16th (Logwood's) Cav. Co.D
Reid, W.C. VA 13th Cav. Co.K
Reid, W.C. Forrest's Scouts T. Henderson's Co.,CSA
Reid, W.D. AL 29th Inf. Co.F
Reid, W.E. NC Lt.Arty. 13th Bn. Co.D
Reid, W.E. NC 23rd Inf. Co.H
Reid, W.E. 1st Conf.Eng.Troops Co.K
Reid, Wesley VA 27th Inf. Co.F

Reid, W.F. GA Inf. 5th Bn. (St.Guards) Co.A Cpl.
Reid, W.F. NC 4th Bn.Jr.Res. Co.C Sgt.
Reid, W.H. MO 2nd Inf. Co.B
Reid, W.H. SC 16th Inf. Co.G Sgt.
Reid, W.H. SC 20th Inf. Co.D
Reid, W.H. TN 14th (Neely's) Cav. Co.G 2nd Lt.
Reid, W.H. TN Cav. Nixon's Regt. Co.D 2nd Lt.
Reid, W.H. TX 20th Cav. Co.K
Reid, W.H. TX Granbury's Cons.Brig. Co.C
Reid, W.H. VA 11th Cav. Co.I 1st Lt.
Reid, W.H. Gen. & Staff Rec. as Maj.,AIG
Reid, Wilborn P. NC 6th Cav. (65th St.Troops) Co.A,E
Reid, Wilbur L. VA 25th Cav. Co.E 1st Lt.
Reid, Wiley MS 35th Inf.
Reid, William AL 30th Inf. Co.I
Reid, William GA Arty. 11th Bn. (Sumter Arty.) Co.D
Reid, William GA Arty. Maxwell's Reg.Lt.Btty.
Reid, William GA 1st Inf. (St.Guards) Co.D
Reid, William GA 5th Res. Co.A
Reid, William GA 15th Inf. Co.D
Reid, William GA 22nd Inf. Co.F
Reid, William MS 22nd Inf. Co.A
Reid, William MS 35th Inf. Co.A
Reid, William NC Lt.Arty. Thomas' Legion Levi's Btty.
Reid, William NC 22nd Inf. Co.A Cpl.
Reid, William NC 43rd Inf. Co.G
Reid, William NC 49th Inf. Co.F
Reid, William SC Lt.Arty. 3rd (Palmetto) Bn. Co.A
Reid, William TN 36th Inf. Co.F
Reid, William TX 15th Inf. Co.I Capt.
Reid, William VA Inf. 1st Bn. Co.D
Reid, Wm. A. AL Cp. of Instr. Talladega
Reid, William A. GA 4th Inf. Co.B
Reid, William A. GA 19th Inf. Co.F
Reid, William A. GA Inf. 27th Bn. Co.F Jr.2nd Lt.
Reid, William A. LA 1st Cav. Co.C 2nd Lt.
Reid, William A. LA 1st (Strawbridge's) Inf. Co.F,A Capt.
Reid, William A. MO Cav. Freeman's Regt. Co.F
Reid, William A. NC 22nd Inf. Co.H
Reid, William A. VA 17th Cav. Co.A 1st Lt.
Reid, William B. VA 14th Cav. Co.A
Reid, William B. VA 3rd Inf.Loc.Def. Co.B 2nd Lt.
Reid, William B. VA 135th Mil. Co.C Capt.
Reid, William C. VA 5th Cav. 2nd Co.F
Reid, William C. VA 5th Cav. (12 mo. '61-2) Co.B
Reid, William C. VA Cav. 14th Bn. Co.A
Reid, William C. VA Hvy.Arty. 10th Bn. Co.B
Reid, William D. LA 31st Inf. Co.A Sgt.
Reid, William E. AR 3rd Inf. Co.B
Reid, William E. NC 2nd Arty. (36th St.Troops) Co.G
Reid, William F. NC 2nd Cav. (19th St.Troops) Co.B
Reid, William F. NC 21st Inf. Co.B

Reid, William F. SC Mil. 1st Regt. (Charleston Res.) Co.A
Reid, William G. SC 12th Inf. Co.H Sgt.
Reid, William G. SC 12th Inf. Co.H
Reid, William G. VA 11th Cav. Co.C
Reid, William G. VA 58th Mil. Co.B Sgt.
Reid, Wm. H. AL 36th Inf. Co.C
Reid, William H. AR 3rd Inf. Co.I
Reid, William H. GA 3rd Inf. Co.I
Reid, William H. GA Cobb's Legion Co.C
Reid, William H. KY 4th Mtd.Inf. Co.H
Reid, William H. NC 5th Cav. (63rd St.Troops) Co.F
Reid, William H. TX 7th Inf. Co.K
Reid, William H. VA 6th Cav. Co.H
Reid, William H. VA 1st Arty. Co.A
Reid, William H. VA Lt.Arty. W.P. Carter's Co.
Reid, William H. VA 32nd Inf. 1st Co.K
Reid, William H. VA 52nd Inf. Co.E
Reid, William H.A. VA 11th Inf. Co.K
Reid, William H.C. AR 1st (Colquitt's) Inf. Co.G
Reid, William Hume TN 6th Inf. Co.H
Reid, William J. LA 17th Inf. Co.G
Reid, William J. NC 2nd Cav. (19th St.Troops) Co.B
Reid, William L. AL Jeff Davis Arty.
Reid, William M. SC 20th Inf. Co.A
Reid, William N. MS 2nd Part.Rangers Co.F,D
Reid, William N. VA 52nd Inf. Co.E
Reid, Wm. O. Gen. & Staff Chap.
Reid, William P. VA 8th Inf. Co.B 1st Sgt.
Reid, William R. GA 21st Inf. Co.F
Reid, William S., Sr. VA Horse Arty. Shoemaker's Co. Cpl.
Reid, William T. AR Inf. 4th Bn. Co.B
Reid, William T. GA 3rd Inf. Co.B 2nd Lt.
Reid, William T. GA Inf. 27th Bn. Co.F Capt.
Reid, William T. MS 9th Inf. Old Co.D
Reid, William T. MO Inf. Perkins' Bn. Co.A
Reid, William T. NC 26th Inf. Co.I
Reid, William W. SC 3rd Inf. Co.B
Reid, William W. SC 3rd Inf. Co.E
Reid, W.J. AL Lt.Arty. Ward's Btty.
Reid, W.J. AL 8th Inf. Co.D
Reid, W.J. GA 18th Inf. Co.D
Reid, W.J. GA Inf. 18th Bn. (St.Guards) Adam's Co. Cpl.
Reid, W.J. SC 3rd Bn.Res. Co.B
Reid, W.J. VA 11th Cav. Co.I Sgt.
Reid, W.J. VA Lt.Arty. Moore's Co.
Reid, W.L. MO Cav. Ford's Bn. Co.D 1st Sgt.
Reid, W.L. SC Cav. Hawthorne's Bn. Co.A Clerk
Reid, W.L.J. SC 28th Inf. AQM
Reid, W.L.J. 2nd Corps Capt.,AQM
Reid, W.M. AR 1st (Monroe's) Cav. Co.K
Reid, W.M. GA Lt.Arty. Barnwell's Btty.
Reid, W.M. GA 5th Inf. Co.B
Reid, W.M. NC 11th (Bethel Regt.) Inf. Co.H
Reid, W.M. SC Lt.Arty. Garden's Co. (Palmetto Lt.Btty.)
Reid, W.M. SC 9th Inf. Co.F
Reid, Woods LA 31st Inf. Co.A
Reid, W.P. LA Mil. Leeds' Guards Regt. Co.F
Reid, W.R. Finegan's Brig. Capt.,ACS
Reid, W.S. GA Lt.Arty. Barnwell's Btty. Cpl.
Reid, W.S. GA Arty. Maxwell's Reg.Lt.Btty.

Reid, W.S. GA 9th Inf. (St.Guards) Co.A
Reid, W.S. TN 12th (Green's) Cav. Co.E
Reid, W.T. AR Lt.Arty. Zimmerman's Btty.
Reid, W.T. MS 14th (Cons.) Inf. Co.A
Reid, W.W. GA 3rd Res. Co.C
Reid, W.W. MS 10th Inf. New Co.G, Co.P
Reid, W.W. MS 35th Inf. Co.G
Reid, W.W. SC 12th Inf. Co.H
Reid, W.W. TN Cav. 1st Bn. (McNairy's) Co.C Cpl.
Reid, W.W. TN 21st & 22nd (Cons.) Cav. Co.K
Reid, W.W. TN 22nd (Barteau's) Cav. Co.B
Reid, Zachariah B. GA 1st (Olmstead's) Inf. Co.C
Reidel, A. SC Mil. 16th Regt. Lawrence's Co.
Reidel, F. TX 8th Inf. Co.G
Reidell, August SC Inf.Loc.Def. Estill's Co.
Reider, George LA Mil. Chalmette Regt. Co.E
Reider, John J. VA 23rd Inf. Co.I
Reider, Michael LA Mil. Mech.Guard
Reider, P.M. TN Cav. 5th Bn. (McClellan's) Co.C
Reidheimer, J.G. LA 2nd Cav. Co.G
Reiding, R.J. GA 11th Inf. Capt.
Reidle, Charles TX 3rd Inf. Co.G Cpl.
Reidlesheimer, A. GA Lt.Arty. (Jackson Arty.) Massenburg's Btty.
Reidling, Joseph W.M. GA Cobb's Legion Co.H
Reidner, J.M. TX 14th Field Btty.
Reidt, H. VA 2nd St.Res. Co.B Cpl.
Reidt, Henry VA 15th Inf. Co.K
Reidt, Peter VA 24th Bn.Part.Rangers Cropper's Co.
Reidt, Peter VA 1st Inf. Co.K
Reidy, C. AL Cav. 24th Bn. Co.A Bugler
Reidy, Charles AL 8th Cav. Co.F
Reidy, Levi KY 4th Mtd.Inf. Co.B Cpl.
Reidy, S.L. AL 31st Inf. Co.C,B Sgt.
Reien, Carl LA 20th Inf. Co.D, Old Co.B
Reierson, Christian A. TX 3rd Cav. Co.G
Reierson, Otto TX 3rd Cav. Co.G
Reifel, Michael LA 5th Inf. Co.C
Reifert, L. TX 4th Cav. Co.C
Reiff, Charles Conf.Inf. 8th Bn. Co.D
Reiff, J. LA Mil. 3rd Regt.Eur.Brig. (Garde Franciase) Co.5
Reiff, John TX 4th Field Btty.
Reiff, Robert S. AR 34th Inf. Co.A
Reiff, S.D. AR Cav. Gordon's Regt. Co.F
Reiffel, Charles LA Pointe Coupee Arty.
Reiffert, Emil TX Arty. 4th Bn. Co.B
Reiffert, Emil TX 8th Inf. Co.B
Reift, Jacob LA Mil. Chalmette Regt. Co.D
Reift, John TX 1st Hvy.Arty. Co.C
Reigar, John A. MO 12th Inf. Co.E 1st Sgt.
Reigart, John T. TX 8th Inf. Co.I
Reigart, Joseph LA Mil. 1st Regt. 2nd Brig. 1st Div. Co.D
Reiger, George H. MS 1st (Johnston's) Inf. Co.D 1st Sgt.
Reiger, G.H. MS 5th Cav. Co.K
Reiger, G.H. MS 22nd Inf. Co.C 1st Lt.
Reiger, J. LA 21st (Kennedy's) Inf. Co.F Sgt.
Reiger, J.A. MS 1st (Johnston's) Inf. Co.D
Reiger, J.H. MS 9th Inf. Old Co.I
Reiger, J.J. LA Mil. 2nd Regt. 2nd Brig. 1st Div. Co.B

Reiger, T.K. MS 1st (Johnston's) Inf. Co.D
Reiger, T.K. MS 7th Inf. Co.H
Reiger, William J. Conf.Cav. Wood's Regt. 2nd Co.G
Reigh, J.C. MS 14th Inf. Co.E
Reigh, M.A. MS 14th Inf. Co.E
Reigh, Nelson TN 26th Inf. Co.G
Reigh, R. TN 25th Inf. Co.K
Reigh, Robert AL 4th Res. Co.F Sgt.
Reighley, D.H. SC 4th Cav. Co.B
Reighley, D.H. SC Cav. 10th Bn. Co.A
Reighley, G.W. SC 4th Cav. Co.B
Reighley, G.W. SC Cav. 10th Bn. Co.A
Reighley, James T. SC 5th Inf. 2nd Co.C
Reighley, M. SC 4th Cav. Co.B
Reighley, M. SC Cav. 10th Bn. Co.A
Reighley, William SC 23rd Inf. Co.F
Reighlie, William SC 6th Res. Co.A
Reighman, Arthur VA 17th Cav. Co.G
Reigman, Michael TX Res.Corps Co.A
Reigner, J.K. VA 7th Inf. Co.F
Reigner, William AL 36th Inf. Co.H
Reigor, Joseph A. VA Lt.Arty. Moore's Co.
Reik, D.H. MS 6th Inf. Co.I
Reikee, Henry AR 4th Inf. Co.I
Reil, Patrick LA 13th Inf. Co.A
Reil, Thomas LA 13th Inf. Co.A Cpl.
Reil, Valentine LA Mil. 4th Regt. 1st Brig. 1st Div. Co.I
Reil, Valentine LA 8th Inf. Co.B
Reile, Christian TX Comal Res.
Reileigh, J.H. AR 11th & 17th (Cons.) Inf. Co.E Cpl.
Reiler, C. LA Bn.
Reiler, Charles LA C.S. Zouave Bn. Co.A,D Sgt.
Reiler, Charles VA Lt.Arty. Page's Co.
Reiler, Charles VA Lt.Arty. J.D. Smith's Co.
Reiley, Archibald McD. LA Mil.Cav. (Jeff Davis Rangers) Norwood's Co. Orderly Sgt.
Reiley, Charles W. MS 16th Inf. Co.K
Reiley, Francis J. VA 13th Inf. Co.G Lt.
Reiley, G. TX 20th Inf. Co.C,A
Reiley, H.F. NC Snead's Co. (Loc.Def.)
Reiley, I.R. NC Snead's Co. (Loc.Def.)
Reiley, James KY 4th Cav.
Reiley, Jerome B. TX 15th Inf. 2nd Co.D
Reiley, John MD Arty. 2nd Btty.
Reiley, John MS 29th Inf. Co.I
Reiley, John VA 57th Inf. Co.H
Reiley, John C. VA Lt.Arty. 38th Bn. Co.D
Reiley, John H. SC Hvy.Arty. 15th (Lucas') Bn. Co.A
Reiley, Pat TN 2nd (Walker's) Inf. Co.I
Reiley, Patrick LA 1st Hvy.Arty. (Reg.) Co.B
Reiley, Patrick MD Cav. 2nd Bn. Co.C Sgt.
Reiley, P.S. LA 1st (Nelligan's) Inf. Co.H
Reiley, P.S. LA Inf. 1st Sp.Bn. (Rightor's) Co.D
Reiley, Richard LA 1st (Nelligan's) Inf. Co.C Cpl.
Reiley, Robert M. MS 16th Inf. Co.K
Reiley, Samuel W. MS 16th Inf. Co.K
Reiley, S.J. LA 3rd (Wingfield's) Cav. Co.B
Reiley, Thomas LA 1st Hvy.Arty. (Reg.) Co.B
Reiley, William TN 2nd (Walker's) Inf. Co.H
Reiley, W.L. VA 5th Cav. Co.G
Reilley, Bernard LA 20th Inf. New Co.E

Reilley, Edward MS 1st Lt.Arty. Co.E
Reilley, Edward MS 33rd Inf. Co.H
Reilley, F. LA 14th Inf. Co.A
Reilley, Jack LA 11th Inf. Co.K
Reilley, James GA 1st Reg. Co.M
Reilley, James LA 20th Inf. New Co.E
Reilley, John GA 1st Reg. Co.M
Reilley, John LA 5th Inf. Co.B 1st Lt.
Reilley, John LA 11th Inf. Co.K
Reilley, John TN 15th Inf. Co.B 1st Sgt.
Reilley, John D. SC Cav.Bn. Hampton Legion Co.A
Reilley, J.P. LA Inf. 1st Sp.Bn. (Rightor's) Co.D
Reilley, P. LA Mil. British Guard Bn. West's Co.
Reilley, Patrick VA Lt.Arty. Brander's Co.
Reilley, Patrick VA Inf. 1st Bn. Co.B
Reilley, Thomas LA 1st (Strawbridge's) Inf. Co.I
Reilley, Thomas D. 1st Conf.Inf. 1st Co.F
Reilley, Thomas T. LA 1st (Nelligan's) Inf. Co.E
Reilly, --- TX 24th & 25th Cav. (Cons.) Co.B
Reilly, Andrew GA Hvy.Arty. 22nd Bn. Co.C
Reilly, Andrew J. LA 14th Inf. Co.E Sgt.
Reilly, B. VA 2nd St.Res. Co.N
Reilly, Bernard LA 11th Inf. Co.L
Reilly, Charles GA 25th Inf. Co.A Cpl.
Reilly, Charles LA 10th Inf. Co.E,A
Reilly, Charles LA 18th Inf. Co.I
Reilly, Cornelius LA Inf. 1st Sp.Bn. (Wheat's) New Co.D
Reilly, Daniel GA 1st (Olmstead's) Inf. Co.A,B
Reilly, Daniel LA 15th Inf. Co.D
Reilly, Daniel M. VA 5th Inf. Co.B
Reilly, Daniel M. VA 27th Inf. 2nd Co.H Cpl.
Reilly, Ed. W. MS 21st Inf. Co.A
Reilly, Edward LA Mil. Beauregard Regt. Co.C
Reilly, Edward TN 15th Inf. Co.H
Reilly, E.J. SC 19th Inf. Co.D
Reilly, Francis GA 1st (Olmstead's) Inf. Co.B
Reilly, Francis TN Lt.Arty. McClung's Co.
Reilly, Francis TX Cav. Morgan's Regt. Co.I
Reilly, Frank LA Conscr.
Reilly, George Conf.Inf. Tucker's Regt. Co.C Cpl.
Reilly, George S. LA 11th Inf. Co.L
Reilly, George V. VA 27th Inf. Co.G
Reilly, G.W. AL 13th Inf. Co.E
Reilly, Hugh GA 25th Inf. Co.A
Reilly, James AL Arty. 1st Bn. Co.D
Reilly, James GA 1st (Olmstead's) Inf. Co.B
Reilly, James LA 11th Inf. Co.L
Reilly, James NC 1st Arty. (10th St.Troops) Co.D Maj.
Reilly, James SC 1st (McCreary's) Inf. Co.K
Reilly, James SC Inf. 3rd Bn. Co.F
Reilly, James Conf.Inf. Tucker's Regt. Co.K
Reilly, Jas. Gen. & Staff Maj.
Reilly, James H. TX 3rd Inf. Co.G Sgt.
Reilly, J.B. TX 14th Inf. Co.G 1st Sgt.
Reilly, Jeremiah SC 1st (McCreary's) Inf. Co.K
Reilly, Jerome B. TX 13th Vol. 1st Co.F
Reilly, John GA 1st (Olmstead's) Inf. Co.B
Reilly, John GA Inf. 18th Bn. Co.A Sgt.
Reilly, John, No.1 GA 47th Inf. Co.A
Reilly, John, No.2 GA 47th Inf. Co.A
Reilly, John, No.3 GA 47th Inf. Co.A
Reilly, John LA Mil. 2nd Regt. 3rd Brig. 1st Div. Co.A

Reilly, John LA 5th Inf. Co.A
Reilly, John LA 20th Inf. Co.K,I Cpl.
Reilly, John LA Mil. Irish Regt. Laughlin's Co.
Reilly, John MD Cav. 2nd Bn. Co.A
Reilly, John NC 8th Inf. Co.F
Reilly, John SC Mil. 1st Regt. (Charleston Res.) Co.A
Reilly, John SC Inf.Loc.Def. Estill's Co.
Reilly, John TX 3rd Inf. Co.G Sgt.
Reilly, John C. SC 11th Inf. 1st Co.I, 2nd Co.I 2nd Lt.
Reilly, John D. SC 2nd Cav. Co.I Sgt.
Reilly, John O. GA 20th Inf. Co.A
Reilly, Josiah LA Miles' Legion Co.A
Reilly, M. LA Miles' Legion Co.A
Reilly, Malachi SC 1st Arty. Co.E
Reilly, Michael GA Arty. Maxwell's Reg.Lt.Btty. Sgt.
Reilly, Michael GA 1st Reg. Co.D
Reilly, Michael GA 1st (Olmstead's) Inf. Co.A
Reilly, Michael GA 47th Inf. Co.A 1st Sgt.
Reilly, Michael LA 13th Inf. Co.G,E
Reilly, Michael SC 1st (McCreary's) Inf. Co.K
Reilly, Michael TN 37th Inf.
Reilly, Michael W. AL St.Arty. Co.A
Reilly, Mike LA 11th Inf. Co.C
Reilly, O. VA 10th Cav. Co.A
Reilly, P. LA Mil. Orleans Fire Regt. Co.H
Reilly, Pat VA 2nd St.Res. Co.L
Reilly, Pat VA Inf. 2nd Bn.Loc.Def. Co.A
Reilly, Patrick GA Hvy.Arty. 22nd Bn. Co.E
Reilly, Patrick GA 1st (Olmstead's) Inf. Guilmartin's Co.
Reilly, Patrick LA 10th Inf. Co.C
Reilly, Patrick LA 20th Inf. Co.G
Reilly, Patrick VA 31st Inf. Co.H
Reilly, Patrick Conf.Inf. Tucker's Regt. Co.K
Reilly, P.E. LA Mil. British Guard Bn. Hamilton's Co.
Reilly, Peter GA 1st (Olmstead's) Inf. Co.B Bvt.2nd Lt.
Reilly, Peter LA 14th Inf. Co.K Cpl.
Reilly, P.H. SC 1st (McCreary's) Inf. Co.L 1st Sgt.
Reilly, P.S. LA 28th (Gray's) Inf. Co.H
Reilly, Richard TX 1st Inf. Co.C
Reilly, Robert LA 5th Inf. Co.E,B
Reilly, T. LA 27th Inf. Co.G 1st Lt.
Reilly, Thomas AL Arty. 1st Bn. Co.D
Reilly, Timothy GA 1st (Olmstead's) Inf. Co.B Sgt.
Reilly, T.J.D. VA 1st St.Res. Co.E
Reilly, William GA Inf. 18th Bn. Co.A
Reilly, William SC Inf.Loc.Def. Estill's Co.
Reilly, William Exch.Bn. 2nd Co.A,CSA
Reilly, William W. GA 10th Inf. Co.F Cpl.
Reilly, W.L. SC 2nd Inf. Co.A
Reilman, Daniel LA Mil. 4th Regt. 2nd Brig. 1st Div. Co.B
Reilman, J. LA Mil. 2nd Regt. 3rd Brig. 1st Div. Co.C
Reils, Jacob SC Lt.Arty. Wagener's Co. (Co.A, German Arty.) Cpl.
Reils, John SC 1st Regt. Charleston Guard Co.G
Reily, Albert G. LA 11th Inf. Co.I
Reily, Albert G. LA 20th Inf. Co.D

Reily, Francis VA Horse Arty. J.W. Carter's Co. Cpl.
Reily, F.S. MO Inf. Perkins' Bn.
Reily, George GA 25th Inf. Co.C
Reily, Hezekiah TX 19th Cav. Co.H
Reily, James AL 18th Inf.
Reily, James TX 4th Cav. Col.
Reily, J.B. SC Lt.Arty. Walter's Co. (Washington Arty.)
Reily, J.C. VA 31st Mil. Maj.
Reily, John LA 5th Inf. Co.G,B
Reily, John Gen. & Staff Capt.,Comsy.
Reily, John W. Gen. & Staff AAG
Reily, John Y. MS 16th Inf. Co.K
Reily, Joseph C. LA 1st Cav. Co.E Capt.
Reily, Joseph C. VA 1st Inf. Co.E
Reily, J.P. LA 1st (Nelligan's) Inf. Co.H
Reily, J.R. 20th Conf.Cav. Co.C
Reily, Michael LA 1st Hvy.Arty. (Reg.) Co.I
Reily, Owen TN 21st Inf. Co.D
Reily, P. LA Arty. Watson Btty.
Reily, Pat LA Hvy.Arty. 8th Bn. Co.A
Reily, Patrick VA Hvy.Arty. 19th Bn. 3rd Co.C
Reily, Philip K. VA 1st Inf. Co.E
Reily, Philip K. VA 7th Inf. Co.H
Reily, Suter VA 122nd Mil.
Reily, S.W. LA 3rd (Wingfield's) Cav. Co.I 2nd Lt.
Reily, T.J. AL 63rd Inf. Co.H
Reily, Wesley MS Conscr.
Reim, John M. MS 7th Inf. Co.E
Reiman, H. MD Arty. 2nd Btty.
Reiman, Henry LA 22nd Inf. Co.D
Reimbolter, Christopher SC Arty.Bn. Hampton Legion Co.A
Reimer, Augustus AR 15th (Josey's) Inf. Co.B Music.
Reimerdes, A. LA 27th Inf. Co.I
Reimers, John AL 24th Inf. Co.D
Reimes, George LA 1st Hvy.Arty. (Reg.) Co.F
Reimond, Emile TX 19th Cav. Co.B Ens.
Reimonencq, F. LA Mil. 1st Regt. French Brig. Co.2
Reimonencq, F. LA Mil. 3rd Regt.Eur.Brig. (Garde Francaise) Co.2
Reims, Thomas AR 27th Inf. Co.G
Reimschussel, G. TX 3rd Inf. Co.B
Reimshard, Fred. AR Lt.Arty. Marshall's Btty.
Rein, George Adam TX Lt.Arty. Jones' Co.
Rein, Jacob LA Mil.Cont.Regt. Mitchell's Co.
Rein, John 14th Conf.Cav. Co.G
Rein, John George TX Lt.Arty. Jones' Co.
Rein, W.D. TX Inf. 1st St.Troops Shields' Co.B
Reina, Frank LA 6th Inf. Co.C
Reina, Ventura LA Mil. 5th Regt.Eur.Brig. (Spanish Regt.) Co.9
Reinach, Aaron S. VA 12th Inf. Co.C
Reinach, D. MS 1st Cav. Co.H
Reinach, Isadore VA 12th Inf. Co.C Music.
Reinach, J. AL 1st Regt. Mobile Vol. Baas' Co.
Reinarch, G. AL 43rd Inf. Co.F
Reinartz, F. TX 7th Cav. Co.B
Reinarz, Frederick TX 36th Cav. Co.F
Reinauer, M.S. Conf.Cav. Wood's Regt. 1st Co.G
Reinbold, John MS 4th Cav. Co.C
Reinbolt, John LA 22nd Inf. Co.A

Reine, F. KY 1st (Butler's) Cav. Co.A
Reine, F. LA Inf. 1st Sp.Bn. (Rightor's) Co.A
Reine, F. LA 18th Inf. Co.E
Reine, F. LA Inf.Cons. 18th Regt. & Yellow Jacket Bn. Co.B
Reine, F. VA Hvy.Arty. 18th Bn. Co.E
Reine, Francois LA 28th (Thomas') Inf. Co.E
Reine, Joseph A. LA Ogden's Cav. Co.D
Reine, M. LA Lt.Arty. Holmes' Btty.
Reine, M. LA Mil. Chalmette Regt. Co.G
Reinebold, John MS Cav. Hughes' Bn. Co.A
Reinecke, Arthur LA 22nd Inf. Co.C
Reinecke, Arthur LA 22nd (Cons.) Inf. Co.G
Reinecke, August. LA 6th Inf. Co.G
Reinecke, C. TX Waul's Legion Co.F Music.
Reinecke, F. LA Mil. 1st Chasseurs a pied Co.1 Cpl.
Reinecke, F. LA Mil. 1st Chasseurs a pied Co.3
Reinecke, F. TX 4th Inf. (St.Troops) Co.F
Reinecke, Frank LA 22nd Inf. Co.C
Reinecke, Frank LA 22nd (Cons.) Inf. Co.C
Reinecke, Fred LA 22nd Inf. Co.C 1st Sgt.
Reinecke, Fred G. SC Arty.Bn. Hampton Legion Co.B
Reinecke, J. LA Mil. 1st Chasseurs a pied Co.3
Reinecke, John LA 22nd Inf. Co.C
Reinecke, John L. LA 22nd (Cons.) Inf. Co.C
Reinecke, Louis TX Arty. 4th Bn. Co.B
Reinecke, Louis TX 8th Inf. Co.B
Reinecke, T.F. LA 22nd (Cons.) Inf. Co.C 2nd Lt.
Reinecker, J. LA Mil.Conf.Guards Regt. Co.G
Reineger, --- TX 33rd Cav. Co.B
Reineke, G.O. LA Mil. Orleans Guards Regt. Co.G,B
Reineman, Frederick TX 2nd Inf. Co.B
Reiner, Anthony LA Mil. 3rd Regt. 1st Brig. 1st Div. Co.I
Reiner, Fred LA Mil. 3rd Regt. 1st Brig. 1st Div. Co.D
Reines, --- TN 3rd (Forrest's) Cav. Co.D
Reines, J.M. GA 5th Inf.
Reines, John M. VA 4th Res. Co.F
Reineth, Albert LA Mil. 1st Chasseurs a pied Co.5
Reineth, William LA Mil. 1st Chasseurs a pied Co.5 Sgt.
Reiney, William A. VA 15th Cav. Co.H
Reinfrank, Adolph LA 6th Inf. Co.D
Reinfred, Joseph LA Mil. 3rd Regt. 1st Brig. 1st Div. Co.H
Reinfro, J.J. LA 28th (Thomas') Inf. Co.B
Reinglee, Conrad LA Mil. 2nd Regt. 2nd Brig. 1st Div. Co.F
Reinhard, Charles Gen. & Staff Hosp.Stew.
Reinhard, F. TX 33rd Cav. Co.E
Reinhard, Frd. LA Mil. 3rd Regt. 3rd Brig. 1st Div. Co.H Music.
Reinhardt, Alex S. AR 3rd Inf. Co.A
Reinhardt, A.M. AR 1st (Monroe's) Cav. Co.A
Reinhardt, A.M. AR 25th Inf. Co.C Capt.
Reinhardt, A.T. AR 1st (Monroe's) Cav. Co.A
Reinhardt, A.T. AR 25th Inf. Co.C
Reinhardt, B.F. LA Mil.Conf.Guards Regt. Co.G
Reinhardt, Charles NC 11th (Bethel Regt.) Inf. Co.I
Reinhardt, C.W. AL 25th Inf. Co.C Music.

Reinhardt, Daniel M. NC 23rd Inf. Co.K 2nd Lt.
Reinhardt, D.M. AR 37th Inf. Co.D
Reinhardt, Fred Bradford's Corps Scouts & Guards Co.A
Reinhardt, George L. AL 4th Inf. Co.C
Reinhardt, J. LA Mil. 3rd Regt. 3rd Brig. 1st Div. Co.D
Reinhardt, J. VA 1st St.Res. Co.C
Reinhardt, James L. NC 16th Inf. Co.M
Reinhardt, James W. NC 1st Inf. (6 mo. '61) Co.K
Reinhardt, J.F. NC 1st Cav. (9th St.Troops) Co.C
Reinhardt, J.H. GA 16th Inf. Co.G Sgt.
Reinhardt, J.J. NC 57th Inf. Co.E
Reinhardt, J.M. SC 1st (Butler's) Inf. Co.G
Reinhardt, John TX 3rd Inf. Co.H
Reinhardt, John D. MS 24th Inf. Co.H
Reinhardt, John D. MS 34th Inf. Co.K
Reinhardt, John H. AL 24th Inf. Co.K
Reinhardt, John T. NC 1st Inf. (6 mo. '61) Co.K
Reinhardt, Lewis VA 15th Inf. Co.K
Reinhardt, L.H. VA 5th Bn.Res.
Reinhardt, Louis TX Arty. 4th Bn. Co.A
Reinhardt, Louis TX Arty. (St.Troops) Good's Co.
Reinhardt, Louis TX 8th Inf. Co.A
Reinhardt, M. TX Waul's Legion Co.C
Reinhardt, M.A. TX 10th Cav. Co.B
Reinhardt, Mattus TX Cav. Ragsdale's Bn. Co.C
Reinhardt, M.C. NC 20th Inf. Co.B
Reinhardt, M.R. AL Inf. 1st (Loomis') Bn. Co.C
Reinhardt, Robert P. NC 11th (Bethel Regt.) Inf. Co.I
Reinhardt, Robert P. NC 12th Inf. Co.A
Reinhardt, R.S. TX 10th Cav. Co.B Cpl.
Reinhardt, Wallace A. NC 46th Inf. Co.K
Reinhardt, Wallace M. NC 1st Inf. (6 mo. '61) Co.K 1st Lt.
Reinhardt, W.D. TN 23rd Inf. Co.C Capt.
Reinhardt, W.P. NC 16th Inf. Co.M
Reinhart, A.M. GA 43rd Inf. Co.A Capt.
Reinhart, B. LA Mil. 3rd Regt.Eur.Brig. (Garde Francaise)
Reinhart, Benjamin AL 5th Inf. Co.K
Reinhart, Benjamin F. AL 6th Inf. Co.K,M
Reinhart, C. AL 1st Regt. Mobile Vol. Baas' Co.
Reinhart, C.A. TN Hvy.Arty. Sterling's Co.
Reinhart, Charles AL 4th Res. Co.B
Reinhart, Charles LA 1st (Strawbridge's) Inf. Co.K,G,E
Reinhart, Charles LA 6th Inf. Co.D
Reinhart, Charles Sap. & Min. Gallimard's Co. 1st Sap.
Reinhart, Christian AL 3rd Res. Co.H
Reinhart, Francis M. MO 9th Inf. Co.G
Reinhart, George L. GA 43rd Inf. Co.A Sgt.
Reinhart, George L. GA Cherokee Legion (St.Guards) Co.C
Reinhart, Hannum H. NC 3rd Cav. (41st St.Troops) Co.C Capt.
Reinhart, Henry LA 22nd Inf. Co.B
Reinhart, Henry LA 22nd (Cons.) Inf. Co.B
Reinhart, Jacob LA 20th Inf. Co.A
Reinhart, J.H. GA 23rd Inf. Co.G
Reinhart, J.J. GA 5th Inf. (St.Guards) Rucker's Co.

Reinhart, Joseph VA 1st Cav. Co.F 2nd Lt.
Reinhart, Julius GA 1st (Symons') Res. Co.K
Reinhart, Michael LA 10th Inf. Co.F
Reinhart, Milton GA Cherokee Legion (St.Guards) Co.C
Reinhart, M.L. TN Cav. Napier's Bn. Co.D
Reinhart, William LA Mil. 1st Regt. 3rd Brig. 1st Div.
Reinhart, William L. VA 12th Cav. Co.D
Reinhart, William W. VA 57th Inf. Co.H
Reinhdt, J.P.H. TX 19th Inf. Co.H
Reinheart, A.M.M. GA 43rd Inf. Co.A Capt.
Reinheart, Andrew NC 57th Inf. Co.B
Reinheart, Augustus M. GA 2nd Inf. Co.F
Reinheart, James F. MO 5th Inf. Co.A
Reinheart, John NC 57th Inf. Co.B
Reinheart, Joseph M. GA Cav. 22nd Bn. (St.Guards) Co.H
Reinhern, Jacques LA 30th Inf. Co.E
Reinicke, F. LA Mil. 4th Regt.Eur.Brig. Co.C
Reinig, Charles TN 15th Inf. Co.I
Reinig, Franz TN 15th Inf. Co.I
Reinig, John A. TN Hvy.Arty. Sterling's Co. Jr.2nd Lt.
Reiniger, George TX Res.Corps Co.D
Reinike, Ernst LA Mil. Chalmette Regt. Co.A
Reinike, John NC 2nd Inf. Co.B
Reininger, Hy LA 1st Cav. Co.I
Reininger, John G. TX 36th Cav. Co.F
Reinken, H. LA 20th Inf. Co.F
Reinmiller, John TX 34th Cav. Co.C
Reinmuth, L. LA Mil. 4th Regt.Eur.Brig. Co.F
Reinoch, William AR 15th (Johnson's) Inf. Co.C
Reins, B.F. VA Lt.Arty. 38th Bn. Co.C
Reins, Euphrates AL 7th Cav. Co.B
Reins, George VA 58th Mil. Co.D
Reins, Henry F. LA Arty. 1st Field Btty.
Reins, J. TN Lt.Arty. Tobin's Co.
Reins, John KY 12th Cav.
Reins, John M. VA 5th Inf. Co.L,H
Reins, John P. VA 24th Inf. Co.C
Reins, J.P. VA 8th Cav. Co.H
Reins, Lawrence S. VA 6th Inf. Co.C
Reins, R. VA 4th Inf. Co.C
Reins, Thomas SC 5th St.Troops Co.G
Reinshagen, John LA Mil. 4th Regt.Eur.Brig. Co.D
Reinsted, J.A. SC Inf. Holcombe Legion Co.G
Reintz, Augustus VA 30th Inf. Music.
Reintz, John VA 30th Inf. Co.I Music.
Reintzell, George W. VA Lt.Arty. Arch. Graham's Co.
Reipschlager, F.C.F. AL 8th Inf. Co.H Sgt.
Reira, Albert 15th Conf.Cav. Co.D
Reira, Anthony 15th Conf.Cav. Co.D
Reires, W.J. Gen. & Staff Surg.
Reis, B.B. NC 2nd Home Guards Co.A
Reis, Charles MO 1st Inf. Co.I
Reis, F. LA Mil. Fire Bn. Co.E
Reis, G. TX 6th Inf. Co.I
Reis, J. LA Inf.Crescent Regt.
Reis, Jacob MO 1st Inf. Co.I
Reis, John LA 1st (Strawbridge's) Inf. Co.D
Reis, Louis LA C.S. Zouave Bn. Co.F
Reis, Maurice MS 10th Inf. New Co.B
Reis, William LA 1st (Strawbridge's) Inf. Co.E

Reisberg, W.C. GA Siege Arty. 28th Bn. Co.F Adj.
Reisch, Charles LA Mil. Orleans Fire Regt. Co.A
Reise, --- LA Mil. 2nd Regt. 2nd Brig. 1st Div. Co.A
Reise, Henry AL 17th Inf. Co.D
Reisel, --- TX 1st Hvy.Arty. Co.A
Reisen, J. AL 31st Inf. Co.G
Reisener, P. AL 25th Inf. Co.H
Reisert, Conrad AL 12th Inf. Co.C
Reisig, J. TX Inf. Timmons' Regt. Co.B
Reising, Jabus TX Inf. Timmon's Regt. Co.B
Reisinger, John A. MO 4th Cav. Co.K
Reisinger, William VA 42nd Inf. Co.E 1st Lt.
Reisler, David GA 37th Inf. Co.H
Reisler, John GA 37th Inf. Co.F
Reisner, Henry H. AL 12th Inf. Co.K
Reisner, J. TX Lt.Arty. Dege's Bn.
Reisner, Julius TX 6th Field Btty.
Reisner, Theo TX 6th Field Btty.
Reisner, T.J. TN 4th (McLemore's) Cav. Co.I Sgt.
Reisner, William P. AL 12th Inf. Co.K
Reisons, R.H. NC 43rd Inf. Co.G
Reisor, J.J. AR 6th Inf. Co.I Cpl.
Reisor, S.M. MO Cav. Freeman's Regt. Co.L
Reiss, C.E. LA 13th Inf. Co.E Ord.Sgt.
Reiss, Emil Conf.Arty. Palmer's Bn. QMSgt.
Reiss, Emille GA Lt.Arty. Pritchard's Co. (Washington Arty.) QMSgt.
Reiss, Emille GA 36th (Villepigue's) Inf. Co.F
Reiss, Emille 1st Conf.Inf. 1st Co.F
Reiss, G. LA 11th Inf. Co.G
Reiss, H. LA Mil. 2nd Regt. 2nd Brig. 1st Div. Co.G
Reiss, Jacob LA Mil. 1st Regt. French Brig. Co.6
Reisser, David E. GA Lt.Arty. Fraser's Btty. Sgt.
Reisser, David E. GA 10th Inf. 1st Co.K Sgt.
Reissert, Charles AL 1st Regt. Mobile Vol. Co.E
Reissig, Julius TX Waul's Legion Co.D
Reissinger, Adam LA 13th Inf. Co.E
Reist, Louis LA O'Hara's Co. (Pelican Guards,Co.B)
Reister, Charles LA Mil. Orleans Fire Regt. Co.A
Reister, John VA 39th Inf. Co.L
Reister, John E. VA 39th Inf. Co.K Lt.
Reister, Joseph LA Mil. 4th Regt. 2nd Brig. 1st Div. Co.C
Reister, Peter VA 39th Inf. Co.L
Reister, P.P. VA Inf. 1st Bn.Loc.Def. Co.F,D
Reiter, Anthony TX 2nd Inf. Co.B
Reiter, Christian LA Mil. 1st Regt. 3rd Brig. 1st Div. Co.C
Reiter, E. LA Mil. 3rd Regt.Eur.Brig. (Garde Francaise)
Reith, --- LA Mil. 2nd Regt. French Brig. Co.3
Reith, George H. VA 1st St.Res. Co.E
Reith, Jonah TN Cav. 7th Bn. (Bennett's)
Reitz, Henry TX 4th Field Btty.
Reitzel, Christian NC 21st Inf. Co.D
Reitzel, Michael M. NC 27th Inf. Co.E
Reitzel, Robert NC 4th Bn.Jr.Res. Co.A
Reitzell, Henry C. NC 27th Inf. Co.B
Reitzell, James H. LA 3rd Inf. Co.C

Reitzell, James H. LA 12th Inf. Co.D
Reitzell, Joseph LA 31st Inf. Co.B
Reitzell, Samuel H. LA 12th Inf. Co.K
Reitzenstein, Julius TX Comal Res. Cpl.
Reitzenstein, L. LA Mil. 1st Regt. 2nd Brig. 1st Div.
Reitzer, Ambrose TX Conscr.
Reitzer, August TX 26th Cav. Co.H
Reitzer, Joseph TX 2nd Cav. Co.B
Reively, John TN 43rd Inf. Co.K
Reives, Absalom 1st Conf.Cav. 2nd Co.B
Reives, Daniel MS Inf. 2nd St.Troops Co.A
Reives, G. LA 3rd (Harrison's) Cav. Co.I
Reives, Jackson L. NC 1st Bn.Jr.Res. Co.A
Reives, James P. TN 11th Cav.
Reives, J.H. AL 17th Inf. Co.H
Reives, John A. NC 2nd Bn.Loc.Def.Troops Co.F
Reives, John T. TX 13th Vol. 1st Co.H Sgt.
Reives, J.T. GA 4th Inf. Co.G
Reives, R. KY Cav. 2nd Bn. (Dortch's) Co.D Ord.Sgt.
Reives, R.M. GA 12th (Wright's) Cav. (St.Guards) Thiot's Co.
Reives, Thomas NC 64th Inf. Co.N
Reives, W.H. TN 19th Inf. Co.A
Reives, William MS 2nd Cav. Co.I
Reives, W.J. GA Cav. 9th Bn. (St.Guards) Co.E
Reives, W.J. TX 15th Cav. Co.F
Reizor, William MO 7th Cav.
Reke, T.S. TX Inf. Chambers' Bn.Res.Corps Co.C
Rekin, Albert LA 5th Inf. Co.D 1st Lt.
Relburne, Smith AL 3rd Res. Co.K
Releght, William AR 15th (Johnson's) Inf. Co.E
Reley, R.M. MS 5th Inf. (St.Troops) Co.F
Relf, J. LA Mil.Conf.Guards Regt. Co.A
Relf, J.S. LA Mil.Conf.Guards Regt. Co.C
Relf, Samuel LA Mil. 1st Native Guards
Relf, T.E. LA Mil. 1st Native Guards
Relf, William LA Lt.Arty. Bridges' Btty.
Relf, William SC Arty. Manigault's Bn. 1st Co.B, Co.D
Relfe, M.S. AL Montgomery Guards
Relfe, William S. MO Cav. 3rd Regt.St.Guard Co.A 3rd Lt.
Relfe, W.R. AL Lt.Arty. Goldthwaite's Btty.
Relfe, W.S. MO Cav. 1st Bn.St.Guard Co.A 3rd Lt.
Relimpio, Frank LA 7th Inf. Co.G
Relin, S. VA 48th Inf. Co.K
Rell, James KY 8th Mtd.Inf. Co.C
Rell, John VA 18th Cav. 2nd Co.E
Rellen, William LA 8th Cav. Co.G
Rellentruce, J.T. VA 3rd Res. Co.H
Reller, Eulogio TX Cav. Ragsdale's Bn. 1st Co.C Bugler
Relles, Andres TX Cav. Benavides' Regt. Co.B
Relles, Juardelos TX Cav. Benavides' Regt. Co.E
Relles, Polinario TX 8th Inf. Co.C
Relles, Richard TX Cav. Madison's Regt. Co.E
Rellett, W.R. NC 2nd Jr.Res. Co.A
Rellin, F. LA 2nd Inf. Co.D
Relling, J. TX 14th Field Btty.
Relph, Alexander F. NC 33rd Inf. Co.E
Relph, Dorsey NC 56th Inf. Co.C
Relph, Josiah NC 56th Inf. Co.C

Relph, Robert NC 35th Inf. Co.I
Relseewe, F. LA C.S. Zouave Bn. Co.A
Remacle, Joseph AL 3rd Inf. Co.K
Remacle, Joseph LA 1st Hvy.Arty. (Reg.) Co.G
Remacle, Joseph LA Arty. Castellanos' Btty.
Remacle, P. LA 21st (Kennedy's) Inf. Co.B
Remacle, Passerany LA 21st (Kennedy's) Inf. Co.B
Reman, E.A. GA 11th Inf.
Remanee, E.W. GA 1st Inf. Co.E
Remans, J.C. KY 2nd (Duke's) Cav. Co.L
Remasser, Louis AL Mil. Bligh's Co.
Rembell, Ephraim TX 2nd Field Btty.
Remberg, P. LA Mil. 1st Chasseurs a pied Co.7
Rembert, A.J. MS 1st (King's) Inf. (St.Troops) Co.C
Rembert, Andrew J. MS Cav. 24th Bn. Co.E Cpl.
Rembert, Andrew J. MS Arty. (Seven Stars Arty.) Roberts' Co.
Rembert, Charles C. MS Cav. 24th Bn. Co.C
Rembert, Charles C. MS Arty. (Seven Stars Arty.) Roberts' Co.
Rembert, E.B. MS 4th Cav. Co.F
Rembert, Edward J. Gen. & Staff Surg.
Rembert, E.T. SC 4th St.Troops Co.I Cpl.
Rembert, E.T. SC 5th Bn.Res. Co.B 2nd Lt.
Rembert, E.W. GA 37th Inf. Ens.
Rembert, F.M. MS 3rd (St.Troops) Cav. Co.E
Rembert, Franklin J. MS 4th Cav. Co.E
Rembert, Franklin J. MS Cav. Hughes' Bn. Co.D
Rembert, H.M. LA 26th Inf. Co.B
Rembert, James E. GA Inf. 3rd Bn. Co.B
Rembert, James E. GA 37th Inf. Co.A
Rembert, James E. SC 2nd Cav. Co.A
Rembert, J.M. AL 21st Inf. Co.C Capt.
Rembert, John GA 20th Inf. Co.G
Rembert, John SC 4th St.Troops Co.A
Rembert, John A. MS Arty. (Seven Stars Arty.) Roberts' Co.
Rembert, Joseph GA Inf. City Bn. (Columbus) Co.A
Rembert, J.P. MS 1st (King's) Inf. (St.Troops) Co.B
Rembert, L.M. SC 2nd Inf. Co.D Cpl.
Rembert, Madison C. MS 36th Inf. Co.G
Rembert, Robert LA 2nd Cav. Co.B
Rembert, S. SC 7th Cav. Co.A
Rembert, S. SC Arty. Melchers' Co. (Co.B, German Arty.)
Rembert, Tho. J. TN 38th Inf. Co.I
Rembert, Thomas J. MS 29th Inf. Co.I Cpl.
Rembert, Thomas L. MS Arty. (Seven Stars Arty.) Roberts' Co.
Rembert, Thomas M. SC 7th Cav. Co.K Cpl.
Rembert, T.L. MS Cav. 24th Bn. Co.C
Rembert, Tom M. SC 2nd Inf. Co.A,E
Rembert, W.D. MO 6th Cav. Co.C
Rembert, W.E. LA 2nd Inf. Co.D
Rembrandt, J. VA 2nd St.Res. Co.D
Rembrandt, John SC 5th Bn.
Remburt, A.J. TN 12th (Green's) Cav. Co.K
Remendo, Jose LA Mil. 5th Regt.Eur.Brig. (Spanish Regt.) Co.5
Remer, B. Francis MO Lt.Arty. 3rd Btty.
Remer, David NC 46th Inf. Co.B

Remer, D.W. TX 1st Mil. Surg.
Remer, D.W. Gen. & Staff Surg.
Remerez, Juan TX 8th Inf. Co.E
Remero, Theogene LA Conscr.
Remerz, Domingo TX 17th Cons.Dismtd.Cav. Co.A
Remesburg, Joseph VA Cav. 41st Bn. 3rd Co.H
Remey, Francis SC 1st Arty. Co.K
Remford, Franklin O. VA 122nd Mil. Co.A
Remfrey, Samuel TX Arty. 4th Bn. Co.A
Remfrey, Samuel TX 8th Inf. Co.A Music.
Remi, Leon MD 1st Cav. Co.F
Remick, J. TX 33rd Cav. Co.E
Remick, W. TX St.Troops Teel's Co.
Remick, William TX 1st (Yager's) Cav. Co.C
Remick, William TX Cav. 3rd (Yager's) Bn. Co.C
Remine, William KY 10th (Diamond's) Cav. Co.C
Remines, Gabriel VA 45th Inf. Co.A
Remines, Harvey VA Inf. 23rd Bn. Co.D
Remines, James H. VA 29th Inf. Co.H
Remines, Samuel VA Inf. 23rd Bn. Co.D
Remines, William VA 45th Inf. Co.A
Remines, William R. VA 16th Cav. Co.I
Remington, A. KY 8th Cav. Co.F
Remington, Abner H. FL 5th Inf. Co.I,G Sgt.
Remington, Benjamin F. KY 2nd (Duke's) Cav. Co.E Capt.
Remington, B.F. KY Morgan's Men Co.E
Remington, Edward LA 7th Inf. Co.B
Remington, E.S. GA 8th Inf. Co.B
Remington, E.S. GA 29th Inf. Co.F
Remington, James KY 5th Mtd.Inf. Co.D
Remington, James A. KY 2nd Mtd.Inf. Co.F Sgt.
Remington, John A. KY 5th Cav. Co.D
Remington, John E. KY Kirkpatrick's Bn. Co.C
Remington, Leroy KY 4th Mtd.Inf. Co.K
Remington, Samuel W. KY 5th Cav. Co.D
Remington, Thos. GA 3rd Inf. Co.F
Remington, W. SC 12th Inf. Co.E
Remington, W.A. GA Inf. 17th Bn. (St.Guards) Fay's Co.
Remington, William 1st Conf.Cav. 2nd Co.F
Remington, William F. VA Hvy.Arty. 18th Bn. Co.E Sgt.
Remington, W.T. LA Mil. Leeds' Guards Regt. Co.F
Remis, G. GA 6th Mil.
Remke, Bey VA 2nd Inf.Loc.Def. Co.E
Remken, Charles B. Gen. & Staff Surg.
Remler, Charles M. LA 21st (Kennedy's) Inf. Co.B
Remley, Charles VA 108th Mil. Co.F
Remley, G.T. SC 11th Inf. 2nd Co.I
Remley, H.T. SC 3rd Cav. Co.A
Remley, J.A. VA Burks' Regt.Loc.Def.
Remley, James AL 37th Inf. Co.I
Remley, James AL 42nd Inf. Co.H
Remley, John SC 2nd St.Troops Co.H
Remley, John D. AL Arty. 1st Bn. Co.B
Remley, John W. FL Lt.Arty. Perry's Co. Cpl.
Remley, Thomas VA Cav. 37th Bn. Co.K Sgt.
Remley, W. SC 3rd Cav. Co.B
Remley, W.H. SC Post Guard Senn's Co.
Remley, W.H. VA Cav. Hounshell's Bn. Co.C

Remlinger, E. MS Inf. 2nd Bn. Co.I
Remlinger, Ed. TN 34th Inf. Co.E
Remlinger, Edmund MS 48th Inf. Co.I
Remly, Allen VA 22nd Inf. Co.D
Remly, Austin VA 22nd Inf. Co.D
Remly, Conard VA 20th Cav. Co.A
Remly, Henry H. VA 22nd Inf. Co.D
Remly, Mason VA 22nd Inf. Co.D
Remmel, James E. VA 24th Cav. Co.F
Remmell, John LA 1st (Strawbridge's) Inf. Co.G
Remmer, Wilson MS 1st (King's) Inf. (St.Troops) Co.F
Remmick, William GA 64th Inf. Co.I
Remmington, D. KY 5th Cav. Co.F
Remmington, M.L. KY 2nd Mtd.Inf. Co.K Sgt.
Remmington, W.T. NC 33rd Inf. Co.C
Remner, J.L. AR 1st (Cons.) Inf. Co.C
Remon, J. LA Mil. 3rd Regt.Eur.Brig. (Garde Francaise) Co.6
Remondet, Claude LA 30th Inf. Locoul's Co.
Remondet, Eugene D. LA 4th Inf. Co.D Cpl.
Remondet, H.H. LA 4th Inf. Co.D 1st Sgt.
Remore, R.L. AL 15th Inf. Co.E
Remous (Colored) MS 41st Inf. Co.K
Remp, Fred TX Waul's Legion Co.B
Remp, R. LA Mil. Fire Bn. Co.A
Remperson, D.S. AR 10th Inf. Co.I
Rempp, C. SC Lt.Arty. Wagener's Co. (Co.A, German Arty.)
Rempp, Jacob LA Mil. 4th Regt. 2nd Brig. 1st Div. Co.B 2nd Lt.
Rempson, C.P. SC 4th St.Troops Co.G
Rempson, Hamilton AL Cav. Hardie's Bn.Res. Co.A
Rempson, John NC 21st Inf. Co.K
Rempson, John NC 48th Inf. Co.K
Remsburg, William VA 151st Mil. Co.C
Remsen, E.O. LA Inf.Crescent Inf. Co.C
Remsen, E.O. LA Inf.Cons.Crescent Regt. Co.G
Remsen, Stephen FL 4th Inf. Co.D
Remsey, R.M. TN Cav. 12th Bn. (Day's) Co.E
Remshard, Christian LA Lewis' Regt. Co.B
Remshart, Robert Bruce GA 7th Cav. Co.F
Remshart, Robert Bruce GA Cav. 21st Bn. Co.B,E Cpl.
Remshart, William C. GA Arty. (Chatham Arty.) Wheaton's Co.
Remshart, William Wallce GA Cav. 21st Bn. Co.B 1st Sgt.
Remsheart, William W. GA Hvy.Arty. 22nd Bn. Co.D
Remshell, Jule TX 33rd Cav. Co.K Music.
Remson, Charles F. AL Cav. Bowie's Co.
Remson, Charles F. 8th (Wade's) Conf.Cav. Co.A
Remson, E.O. LA 18th Inf. Co.C
Remson, James B. GA 15th Inf. Co.G 1st Sgt.
Remson, James B. SC 1st (Butler's) Inf. Co.C Cpl.
Remson, John R. GA Mil. Camden Cty. (Mtd.) 2nd Lt.
Remson, Rem GA 15th Inf. Co.G Cpl.
Remson, Thomas H. GA 15th Inf. Co.C,G 2nd Lt.
Remus, H. AL Mobile Fire Bn. Mullany's Co.
Remus, Henry LA Mil. Leeds' Guards Regt. Co.F

Remus, Peter AL 8th Inf. Co.G
Remy, A. LA Mil. 1st Native Guards
Remy, Alexandre LA 10th Inf. Co.G
Remy, Charles LA 1st Hvy.Arty. (Reg.) Co.B
Remy, F. LA Mil. 1st Native Guards
Remy, F. LA Mil. 1st Regt. French Brig. Co.1
Remy, J.J. LA Mil. 1st Native Guards 1st Sgt.
Remy, John H. AL Lt.Arty. 2nd Bn. Co.E 1st Sgt.
Remy, J.P.H. AR Cav. Gordon's Regt. Co.E
Remy, L. LA 22nd Inf. Gomez's Co.
Remy, N. Anton LA 20th Inf. Co.F
Remy, O. LA Mil. 1st Native Guards
Remy, Philip Alfred LA 1st Hvy.Arty. (Reg.) Co.H,I
Remy, P. Louis LA Washington Arty.Bn. Co.4
Remy, T. LA Mil. 1st Native Guards
Remy, Taylor Gen. & Staff, Subs.Dept. Capt.
Remy, William H. AL Lt.Arty. 2nd Bn. Co.E
Ren, Edward VA 9th Inf. Co.D
Rena, A. TX Inf. 1st St.Troops Whitehead's Co.
Renager, Nathan NC 4th Sr.Res. Co.D
Renalds, James M. VA 4th Cav. Co.C
Renan, F.M. SC Mil. 16th Regt. Sigwald's Co. Ex.Lt.
Renan, F.M. TX 30th Cav. Co.D
Renan, George TN 1st (Carter's) Cav. Co.K
Renan, Lawrence TX 17th Field Btty.
Renan, T.P. NC 13th Inf. Co.K
Renand, A. LA C.S. Zouave Bn. Co.D Capt.
Renanteau, P. LA Mil. 1st Regt. French Brig. Co.1
Renao, S. 1st Chickasaw Inf. Hansell's Co.
Renard, Ch. LA Mil. 3rd Regt. French Brig. Co.1
Renaud, --- LA Mil. 2nd Regt. French Brig. Co.2
Renaud, Alfred LA 6th Inf. Co.C
Renaud, Aristide LA 8th Inf. Co.C
Renaud, C. LA Mil. 2nd Regt. French Brig. Co.2 Cpl.
Renaud, Desiré LA Conscr.
Renaud, Edouard LA Mil. 2nd Regt. French Brig. Co.6
Renaud, Emile LA Mil. 1st Chasseurs a pied Co.A
Renaud, Emile LA 22nd Inf. Co.B
Renaud, Gustave LA 22nd Inf. Co.C
Renaud, Gustave LA 22nd (Cons) Inf. Co.C
Renaud, Henry LA 8th Inf. Co.C
Renaud, J. LA Mil. Beauregard Bn. Co.D
Renaud, J.C. LA 22nd Inf. Co.C Artif.
Renaud, J.C. LA 22nd (Cons.) Inf. Co.C Cpl.
Renaud, J.K. LA Lt.Arty. Fenner's Btty. Cpl.
Renaud, John LA 4th Inf. Co.H Cpl.
Renaud, John K. LA Inf. 1st Sp.Bn. (Rightor's) Co.F
Renaud, N. LA Mil. 3rd Regt.Eur.Brig. (Garde Francaise) Co.2
Renaud, W.H. LA Lt.Arty. Fenner's Btty.
Renaud, William H. LA Mil.Conf.Guards Regt. Co.C
Renaudin, P. LA Mil. Fire Bn. Co.E
Renauld, Nichola AL City Troop (Mobile) Arrington's Co.A
Renauld, Nicholas 15th Conf.Cav. Co.F
Renaut, H.S. LA Inf.Cons.Crescent Regt. Co.H
Rencan, John D. AL 19th Inf. Co.K

Rench, Daniel MO 10th Cav. Co.K
Rench, John VA 1st Cav. 2nd Co.K
Rench, John V. MD 1st Cav. Co.K
Rench, Michael MO 10th Cav. Co.K
Rench, Michael MO 9th Inf. Co.C
Rench, William MD 3rd Regt.
Rench, William MO 10th Cav. Co.K
Rencher, Abraham AL 36th Inf. Co.A
Rencher, C.R. MS Conscr.
Rencher, Daniel W. AL 5th Bn.Vol. Co.A
Rencher, J.H. MS 2nd St.Cav. Co.E
Rencher, John G. NC 33rd Inf. Co.K 1st Lt.
Rencher, John G. NC Mallett's Bn. (Cp.Guard) Co.B 2nd Lt.
Rencher, John G. Gen. & Staff 2nd Lt.,Dr.M.
Rencher, P. MS 2nd (Davidson's) Inf. Co.G
Rencher, W.C. NC Cumberland Cty.Bn. Detailed Men Co.B Capt.
Rencher, William AL 1st Inf. Co.C
Rencher, William C. Gen. & Staff 2nd Lt.,Dr.M.
Rencher, W.P. MS 2nd St.Cav. Co.E
Rendall, John D. MS 22nd Inf. Co.D Capt.
Rendall, J.S. LA Bickham's Co. (Caddo Mil.)
Rendall, W.J. NC 28th Inf. Co.D
Rendelhuber, S. TN Inf. 3rd Bn. Co.C
Rendelin, William MO Robertson's Regt. St.Guard Co.12
Render, James GA 12th (Robinson's) Cav. (St.Guards) Co.F
Render, Robert GA 12th (Robinson's) Cav. (St.Guards) Co.F
Rendet, P.C. Gen. & Staff ADC
Rendleman, A.H. NC 5th Inf. Co.H
Rendleman, Andrew NC 42nd Inf. Co.D
Rendleman, George W. NC 6th Inf. Co.A
Rendleman, J.A. NC 57th Inf. Co.C
Rendleman, Jacob M. NC Res. Co.A
Rendleman, J.L. NC 57th Inf. Co.C
Rendleman, J.M. GA 34th Inf. Co.F
Rendleman, John M. NC 52nd Inf. Co.H
Rendleman, John M. NC 57th Inf. Co.G 2nd Lt.
Rendleman, Lawson M. NC 4th Inf. Co.K
Rendleman, Pinkney L. NC 23rd Inf. Co.K
Rendleman, Samuel H. NC 52nd Inf. Co.H 2nd Lt.
Rendleman, Tobias L. NC 6th Inf. Co.G
Rendon, Andre LA 2nd Inf. Co.B Sgt.
Rendon, Dionicio TX 33rd Cav. 1st Co.H
Rendon, Dionicio TX Cav. Benavides' Regt. Co.A
Rendon, J. GA 19th Inf. Co.G
Rendon, Theofilo TX 8th Inf. Co.I Music.
Rendon, Ynacio TX Cav. 3rd (Yager's) Bn. Co.A
Rendot, Jules Gen. & Staff Capt.,AAG
Rendue, J.F. TX 9th (Nichols') Inf. Co.G
Rendue, J.F. TX Waul's Legion Co.A
Rene, Charles M. LA Inf. 7th Bn. Co.A 1st Lt.
Rene, C.M. LA C.S. Zouave Bn. Co.E Capt.
Rene, H. TX 16th Inf. Co.E
Renean, J.H. AL 8th Inf. Co.B
Renean, J.T. AR Inf. Hardy's Regt. Co.H
Renean, J.W. AR 1st (Dobbin's) Cav. Co.B
Renean, M.L. AR 1st (Dobbin's) Cav. Co.H
Renean, Russell R. GA 50th Inf. Co.E 1st Sgt.
Renean, William L. MS 2nd Inf. Co.K Sgt.
Reneau, B.S. AL 15th Inf. Co.H

Reneau, Charles F. TX 19th Inf. Co.A
Reneau, F.C. MS Bradford's Co. (Conf.Guards Arty.)
Reneau, George W. GA 6th Cav. 1st Co.K Sgt.
Reneau, George W. KY Part.Rangers Rowan's Co. Sgt.
Reneau, George W. Conf.Cav. 6th Bn. Sgt.
Reneau, G.W. KY Jessee's Bn.Mtd.Riflemen Co.C Sgt.
Reneau, Henry L. AR 5th Inf. Co.B
Reneau, Henry L. MS Cav. 1st Bn. (Miller's) Co.A
Reneau, H.L. MS 1st Cav. Co.H
Reneau, James AR 2nd Inf. Co.G Sgt.
Reneau, James M. TX 24th Cav. Co.C
Reneau, J.B. MS 1st Cav. Co.K
Reneau, J.F. LA 2nd Inf. Co.G Sgt.
Reneau, John AL St.Arty. Co.C
Reneau, John AL 21st Inf. Co.A
Reneau, John C. AL 49th Inf. Co.I
Reneau, John C. TX 31st Cav. Co.B
Reneau, John L. TN 9th Inf. Co.B
Reneau, Joshua B. MS Cav. 1st Bn. (Miller's) Cole's Co.
Reneau, J.T. AR 24th Inf. Co.K
Reneau, J.W. AL 8th Inf. Co.B
Reneau, Marcus LaF. AR 4th Inf. Co.B
Reneau, M.L. AR 32nd Inf. Co.B
Reneau, N.S. Gen. & Staff Vol.ADC
Reneau, T. SC 25th Inf. Co.H
Reneau, T.S. TX 8th Cav. Co.B
Reneau, William Ed MS 17th Inf. Co.H
Reneau, William Edward TN 12th (Green's) Cav. Co.I 2nd Lt.
Reneau, William H. MS 2nd Part.Rangers Co.B
Reneck, John MS 21st Inf. Co.G
Reneck, R.L. MO 12th Cav. Co.H
Renegar, Calvin TN 8th Inf. Co.K
Renegar, Davidson TN 44th (Cons.) Inf. Co.A
Renegar, George Wilson TN 41st Inf. Co.G Sgt.
Renegar, G.W. GA Cav. Gartrell's Co.
Renegar, G.W. TN 41st Inf. Co.A
Renegar, Henry G. TN 41st Inf. Co.G Cpl.
Renegar, Jacob TN 41st Inf. Co.A
Renegar, Jasper TN 44th (Cons.) Inf. Co.A
Renegar, J.H. TN 41st Inf. Co.A
Renegar, John T. TN 44th Inf. Co.I
Renegar, John T. TN 44th (Cons.) Inf. Co.A
Renegar, Nicholas TN 41st Inf. Co.A
Renegar, Sanford TN 41st Inf. Co.A
Renegar, Sanford Mead's Conf.Cav. Co.H
Renegar, W.G. NC Allen's Co. (Loc.Def.)
Renegar, William F. TN 8th Inf. Co.K Cpl.
Reneger, Napoleon VA 5th Cav. 1st Co.F
Renehen, Patrick TN 5th Inf. 1st Co.C
Reneicke, A. LA Mil. 1st Chasseurs a pied Co.1
Reneker, W.P. MS 23rd Inf. Co.D
Renels, Isaac AR 8th Cav. Co.A
Rener, Daniel AL 21st Inf. Co.B
Rener, J.M. TX 14th Cav. Co.D
Rener, William E. TX Cav. Wells' Regt. Co.C
Renew, Aaron GA 51st Inf. Co.H
Renew, A.J. FL Inf. 2nd Bn. Co.E
Renew, A.J. GA 51st Inf. Co.H
Renew, Anderson FL 5th Inf. Co.E
Renew, Basel SC Hvy.Arty. Mathewes' Co. Sgt.
Renew, George SC Hvy.Arty. Mathewes' Co.

Renew, H.J. GA 1st Reg.
Renew, H.W. GA Arty. 11th Bn. (Sumter Arty.) Co.A
Renew, J. FL Cav. 5th Bn. Co.B
Renew, J. GA 3rd Res. Co.C
Renew, James SC Hvy.Arty. Mathewes' Co.
Renew, Richard SC Hvy.Arty. Mathewes' Co.
Renew, Timothy FL 6th Inf. Co.A
Renew, William FL 5th Inf. Co.E
Renew, William GA 51st Inf. Co.H
Renfin, N. SC Lt.Arty. 3rd (Palmetto) Bn. Co.K
Renford, E. GA 5th Res. Co.E
Renford, G. VA 54th Mil. Co.E,F
Renfre, William E. MO 4th Cav. Co.B
Renfren, E. GA 38th Inf. Co.C
Renfrew, Alfred MS 7th Inf. Co.A
Renfrew, Cyrus KY 2nd (Duke's) Cav. Co.E
Renfrew, G.B. SC Hvy.Arty. 15th (Lucas') Bn. Co.B
Renfrew, James KY 2nd (Duke's) Cav. Co.E
Renfrew, Jesse MS Yerger's Co. (St.Troops)
Renfrew, Jesse A. TX 16th Cav. Co.F
Renfrew, J. Martin MO Inf. 3rd Bn. Co.E
Renfrew, John H. NC 56th Inf. Co.E Sgt.
Renfrew, John M. GA 19th Inf. Co.C
Renfrew, Joseph W. MO 8th Cav. Co.B
Renfrew, Marcus MO 3rd Inf. Co.F
Renfrew, Nathaniel J. FL 1st Cav. Co.I Cpl.
Renfrew, Neal AL 15th Inf. Co.L
Renfrew, Seaborn AL 61st Inf. Co.A
Renfrew, T. AL 15th Inf. Co.L
Renfrew, William Cary NC 50th Inf. Co.C 1st Sgt.
Renfro, A.B. AL 22nd Inf. Co.K 1st Lt.
Renfro, Absalom J. AL Lt.Arty. 2nd Bn.
Renfro, Alexander H. AL 17th Inf.B.S.S. Cpl.
Renfro, Alfred LA 8th Inf. Co.B
Renfro, Alfred TN Lt.Arty. Weller's Co. Cpl.
Renfro, Andrew J. AR 4th Inf. Co.E
Renfro, B. MS 1st (King's) Inf. (St.Troops) Co.G
Renfro, Benjamin F., Jr. AR 4th Inf. Co.E Cpl.
Renfro, B.A. TN 48th (Nixon's) Inf. Co.H
Renfro, B.H. AL 48th Inf. Co.D
Renfro, B.H. TX 7th Cav. Co.D
Renfro, B.H. TX 12th Field Btty.
Renfro, Bunk A. TN 54th Inf. Co.E
Renfro, B.W. TN 3rd (Clack's) Inf. Co.E
Renfro, Columbus GA 13th Inf. Co.F
Renfro, David NC 58th Inf. Co.C
Renfro, David K. TX Inf. Cotton's Co. 3rd Lt.
Renfro, David T. KY 4th Cav. Co.B,D
Renfro, E.W. TX 12th Cav. Co.A
Renfro, E.W. TX Cav. Terry's Regt. Co.F
Renfro, Forney AL 37th Inf. Co.G,E Sgt.
Renfro, Francis M. TN 7th Inf. Co.E
Renfro, G.D. TX Granbury's Cons.Brig. Co.I
Renfro, George D. TX 24th Cav. Co.C Cpl.
Renfro, George W. AR 4th Inf. Co.E Ord.Sgt.
Renfro, George W. TN 1st (Carter's) Cav. Co.G
Renfro, George W. TN 62nd Mtd.Inf. Co.D Chap.
Renfro, George W. TX 31st Cav. Co.B
Renfro, G.H. TN Inf. 23rd Bn. Co.E
Renfro, Granville C. VA 22nd Cav. Co.A
Renfro, G.W. TN 7th (Duckworth's) Cav. Co.G
Renfro, G.W. TN Lt.Arty. Kain's Co.
Renfro, G.W. Gen. & Staff Chap.

Renfro, Henry MO 3rd Inf. Co.C
Renfro, Henry TN 62nd Mtd.Inf. Co.A
Renfro, Henry C. TX Inf. Griffin's Bn. Co.C
Renfro, Henry M. TN Detailed Conscr. Co.B 1st Sgt.
Renfro, Hugh M. TN 5th Inf. 1st Co.C, Co.A
Renfro, I.P. AL 4th (Russell's) Cav. Co.F
Renfro, Isaac TX Cav. 3rd (Yager's) Bn. Co.A Sgt.
Renfro, Isaac J. TX 30th Cav. Co.I
Renfro, Isaac P. TX 22nd Inf. Co.D 1st Sgt.
Renfro, Isaac P. TX Waul's Legion Co.B Capt.
Renfro, Isaac W. TX Inf. Griffin's Bn. Co.C
Renfro, J. AR 58th Mil. Co.D
Renfro, J. MS 1st (King's) Inf. (St.Troops) Co.G
Renfro, J.A. TN Inf. 23rd Bn. Co.E
Renfro, J.A. TN Inf. Spencer's Co.
Renfro, James KY 12th Cav. Co.F
Renfro, James MS 3rd (St.Troops) Cav. Co.A
Renfro, James MS 28th Cav. Co.G
Renfro, James MO 10th Cav. Co.B
Renfro, James TN 19th Inf. Co.D
Renfro, James VA 22nd Cav. Co.A
Renfro, James A. MS 2nd Inf. Co.F
Renfro, James Asberry MS 34th Inf. Co.A
Renfro, James H. AL 11th Inf. Co.G
Renfro, James M. AL 10th Inf. Co.G 1st Lt.
Renfro, J.D. TX 7th Cav. Co.D Sgt.
Renfro, J.D. TX 12th Field Btty.
Renfro, Jesse MS Cav. 3rd Bn.Res. Co.D
Renfro, Jesse B. TX Cav. 6th Bn. Co.E Sgt.
Renfro, J.F. TX 29th Cav. Co.C
Renfro, J.J.D. AL 10th Inf. Chap.
Renfro, J.L. TN Inf. 3rd Cons.Regt. Co.H
Renfro, J.L. TX 10th Cav. Co.G
Renfro, John AL Lt.Arty. 2nd Bn. Co.F Black.
Renfro, John GA 6th Inf. (St.Guards) Co.A Cpl.
Renfro, John MO 2nd Cav. Co.F
Renfro, John NC 64th Inf. Co.L
Renfro, John TN 1st (Carter's) Cav. Co.G
Renfro, John TN 7th (Duckworth's) Cav. Co.G
Renfro, John TN 19th (Biffle's) Cav. Co.C
Renfro, John A. AL 24th Inf. Co.K,A
Renfro, John A. KY 9th Mtd.Inf. Co.E
Renfro, John B. TX 13th Cav. Co.D Chap.
Renfro, John D. MS 23rd Inf. Co.K
Renfro, John F. MO 6th Cav. Co.A
Renfro, John H. TX 13th Cav. Co.C Sgt.
Renfro, John H.B. MO 5th Inf. Co.G
Renfro, John M. MO 6th Inf. Co.C
Renfro, John P. TX 14th Cav. Co.G 2nd Lt.
Renfro, John T. TN 6th (Wheeler's) Cav. Co.H
Renfro, John W. TN 12th (Cons.) Inf. Co.F Sgt.
Renfro, John W. TX 10th Inf. Co.C
Renfro, John W. VA 64th Mtd.Inf. Co.E
Renfro, Jo. R. KY 6th Mtd.Inf. Co.E
Renfro, Joseph KY 6th Mtd.Inf. Co.F Cpl.
Renfro, J.S. AL 12th Inf. Co.G
Renfro, J.T. GA Cav. 6th Bn. (St.Guards) Co.B Cpl.
Renfro, J.W. AL 18th Inf. Co.E,D
Renfro, J.W. MO 7th Cav. Co.D
Renfro, J.W. TX 11th Field Btty.
Renfro, J.W. TX 21st Inf. Co.C
Renfro, Lewis MS 34th Inf. Co.A
Renfro, Lewis MO 6th Cav. Co.A
Renfro, Lewis TX 29th Cav. Co.C

Renfro, Mark R. MS Cav. 24th Bn. Co.E
Renfro, Marshall TN 2nd (Robison's) Inf. Co.B
Renfro, Marshall TN 48th (Voorhies') Inf. Co.A
Renfro, Moasmus LA 31st Inf. Co.B
Renfro, Moses MS 28th Cav. Co.G
Renfro, Nathaniel TN 23rd Inf. Co.G
Renfro, N.E. AL 4th Res. Co.H
Renfro, Osborn MS 28th Cav. Co.G
Renfro, P. TN 22nd (Barteau's) Cav. Co.D
Renfro, Peter MS 28th Cav. Co.G
Renfro, Peter F. TX 1st Inf. Co.I
Renfro, Peter F. TX Inf. Cotton's Co.
Renfro, Pleas R. TN Cav. 7th Bn. (Bennett's) Co.A
Renfro, R.A. TX 11th Inf. Co.B
Renfro, R.C. GA 64th Inf. Co.I
Renfro, R.C. MS 28th Cav. Co.G
Renfro, R.C. TX Cav. McCord's Frontier Regt. Co.E
Renfro, Redding MS 18th Inf. Co.C
Renfro, Reding MS 1st (Percy's) Inf. Co.K
Renfro, Samuel MO 10th Cav. Co.B Sgt.
Renfro, S.H. MO 6th Cav. Co.A
Renfro, S.J. GA 3rd Res. Co.D
Renfro, Skelton T. MO Cav. 3rd Bn. Co.B
Renfro, S.P. MO 7th Cav. Co.B
Renfro, Sylvester N. TX 31st Cav. Co.B Sgt.
Renfro, T.A. TN 51st Inf. Co.I 2nd Lt.
Renfro, T.A. TN 51st (Cons.) Inf. Co.D
Renfro, Tarlton A. TN 48th (Nixon's) Inf. Co.H Ord.Sgt.
Renfro, Tarlton A. TN 54th Inf. Co.C Cpl.
Renfro, Thomas GA 27th Inf. Co.E Capt.
Renfro, Thomas NC 29th Inf. Co.I
Renfro, Thomas Mead's Conf.Cav. Co.C
Renfro, Thomas B. AL Nitre & Min.Corps Young's Co.
Renfro, Thomas B. TX 27th Cav. Co.C
Renfro, Thomas F. MO 6th Cav. Co.A 2nd Lt.
Renfro, T.J. AL Pris.Guard Freeman's Co. Music.
Renfro, T.J. AR 1st (Dobbin's) Cav. Co.A 2nd Lt.
Renfro, T.M. Exch.Bn. 1st Co.C,CSA
Renfro, Virgil C. TX 17th Cav. Co.D Cpl.
Renfro, W.C. NC Cav. 16th Bn. Co.F
Renfro, W.C. TX 7th Cav. Co.H
Renfro, W.H. TN 51st Inf. Co.I Sgt.
Renfro, W.H. TN 51st (Cons.) Inf. Co.D
Renfro, Wilkerson B. TN 48th (Voorhies') Inf. Co.B
Renfro, William AR Lt.Arty. Key's Btty.
Renfro, William TN Lt.Arty. Weller's Co.
Renfro, William TN 3rd (Clack's) Inf. Co.E
Renfro, William TN 32nd Inf. Co.B
Renfro, William TN 35th Inf. 2nd Co.F
Renfro, William TX 15th Cav. Co.B,K
Renfro, William TX 18th Cav. Co.I
Renfro, William A. TN 62nd Mtd.Inf. Co.A
Renfro, William B. VA 22nd Cav. Co.A
Renfro, William B. VA 37th Inf. Co.D
Renfro, William G. NC 29th Inf. Co.I
Renfro, William H. MS 23rd Inf. Co.G
Renfro, William J. AL 37th Inf. Co.D,E
Renfro, William J. TN 48th (Voorhies') Inf. Co.B
Renfro, William S. TX 10th Inf. Co.C

Renfro, William Thomas AL 5th Inf. New Co.B Jr.2nd Lt.
Renfro, Willis TN Inf. 2nd Cons.Regt. Co.B
Renfro, W.S. KY 7th Cav. Co.C
Renfrod, John M. GA Inf. Alexander's Co.
Renfrod, Obd. C. GA Inf. Alexander's Co.
Renfroe, Alexander H. AL 39th Inf. Co.E
Renfroe, Allen GA 21st Inf. Co.I
Renfroe, Andrew J. GA 1st (Olmstead's) Inf. Co.E
Renfroe, B. GA 32nd Inf. Co.A
Renfroe, B.F. MS 6th Inf. Co.C
Renfroe, Bidcar P. Conf.Cav. Wood's Regt. Co.B
Renfroe, Charles M. AR 30th Inf. Co.H
Renfroe, C.L. AL 15th Inf. Co.G
Renfroe, C.L. GA Inf. Arsenal Bn. (Columbus) Co.A 2nd Lt.
Renfroe, Commodore L. GA 21st Inf. Co.I
Renfroe, David TX 1st Inf. Co.I Sgt.
Renfroe, Doctor B. TN 32nd Inf. Co.H
Renfroe, E. AL 15th Inf. Co.L
Renfroe, Edward E. VA Lt.Arty. Woolfolk's Co.
Renfroe, Elisha AL 1st Inf.
Renfroe, Elisha FL 5th Inf. Co.C
Renfroe, Elisha D. AL 63rd Inf. Co.C
Renfroe, Enoch GA 9th Inf. Co.F Cpl.
Renfroe, Enoch W. GA 30th Inf. Co.D Sgt.
Renfroe, Eugene MS 12th Cav. Co.I
Renfroe, G.A. GA Siege Arty. 28th Bn. Co.D Cpl.
Renfroe, G.C. AL 5th Inf. New Co.A
Renfroe, George GA Inf. City Bn. (Columbus) Williams' Co.
Renfroe, George MS 28th Cav. Co.G
Renfroe, George A. GA Cav. 1st Bn.Res. McKinney's Co. Sgt.
Renfroe, Green C. AL 15th Inf. Co.G Sgt.Maj.
Renfroe, Greene FL 10th Inf. Co.F
Renfroe, G.W. AR 1st Mtd.Rifles Ord.Sgt.
Renfroe, H. AL 34th Inf. Co.F
Renfroe, H. GA 5th Res. Co.C Cpl.
Renfroe, H. TN 2nd (Ashby's) Cav. Co.A
Renfroe, H.A. GA 32nd Inf. Co.E
Renfroe, Harrison AL 3rd Bn.Res. Co.A
Renfroe, I.S. AL 34th Inf. Co.I
Renfroe, J. GA 5th Res. Co.C
Renfroe, J. 4th Conf.Inf. Co.H
Renfroe, James GA Inf. 3rd Bn. Co.H
Renfroe, James GA 37th Inf. Co.K
Renfroe, James TN Cav. 12th Bn. (Day's) Co.E
Renfroe, James TN Conscr. (Cp. of Instr.)
Renfroe, James VA Mil. Scott Cty.
Renfroe, James A. TX 6th Cav. Co.G
Renfroe, James F. GA 12th Inf. Co.B Sgt.
Renfroe, James M. MS 9th Inf. Old Co.I
Renfroe, James M. Conf.Cav. Wood's Regt. Co.B
Renfroe, James P. FL 5th Inf. Co.C
Renfroe, Jarred GA 9th Inf. Co.F Cpl.
Renfroe, J.E. GA Inf. Clemons' Co.
Renfroe, Jesse GA 7th Inf. Co.D
Renfroe, J.G. FL Cav. 3rd Bn. Co.C
Renfroe, J.G. 15th Conf.Cav. Co.E
Renfroe, J.G.C. FL 4th Inf. Co.F
Renfroe, J.H. GA Inf. Arsenal Bn. (Columbus) Co.A 1st Lt.
Renfroe, J.I. GA 28th Inf. Co.B
Renfroe, J.J. GA Lt.Arty. 12th Bn. 3rd Co.E

Renfroe, J.J.D. Gen. & Staff Chap.
Renfroe, Joel FL Cav. 5th Bn. Co.G
Renfroe, John AL Inf. 2nd Regt. Co.K
Renfroe, John GA 49th Inf. Co.C
Renfroe, John MO 12th Inf. Co.C
Renfroe, John TN 1st (Carter's) Cav. Co.G
Renfroe, John A. GA 60th Inf. Co.A
Renfroe, John A. MS 1st Lt.Arty. Co.I
Renfroe, John A. NC Inf. 2nd Bn. Co.E Sgt.
Renfroe, John B. Gen. & Staff Chap.
Renfroe, John C. FL Cav. 3rd Bn. Co.A
Renfroe, John F. AL Pris.Guard Freeman's Co.
Renfroe, John F. GA 6th Inf. Co.C
Renfroe, John G. GA 2nd Inf. Co.C
Renfroe, John J. GA 49th Inf. Co.H,C
Renfroe, John J. MS 33rd Inf. Co.C
Renfroe, John M. GA 7th Inf. Co.D
Renfroe, John S. MS 9th Inf. Old Co.I
Renfroe, John S. Conf.Cav. Wood's Regt. Co.B
Renfroe, John W. MS 21st Inf. Co.K Capt.
Renfroe, John W. VA Mil. Scott Cty.
Renfroe, Joseph GA Lt.Arty. 12th Bn. 3rd Co.B
Renfroe, Josiah GA 1st (Ramsey's) Inf. Co.E
Renfroe, J.P. TX Cav. 1st Bn.St.Troops Co.C Capt.
Renfroe, Mathew AL 39th Inf. Co.C
Renfroe, M.S. TN 38th Inf. Co.C 3rd Lt.
Renfroe, M.S.F. FL Cav. 5th Bn. Co.I
Renfroe, Nathan G. FL 7th Inf. Co.C
Renfroe, Nathaniel D. AL 5th Bn.Vol. Co.B 2nd Lt.
Renfroe, N.E. FL Cav. 5th Bn. Co.I
Renfroe, Peter AL 22nd Inf. Co.H
Renfroe, Peter AL 39th Inf. Co.C
Renfroe, Peter MS 33rd Inf. Co.C
Renfroe, Phillip AL 39th Inf. Co.C
Renfroe, Raby TX 28th Cav. Co.I
Renfroe, R.C. GA Siege Arty. 28th Bn. Co.I
Renfroe, R.C.G. TN Cav. Jackson's Co.
Renfroe, Robert 2nd Cherokee Mtd.Vol. Co.C
Renfroe, R.T.R. GA 61st Inf. Co.C
Renfroe, Rubin TN Lt.Arty. Tobin's Co.
Renfroe, S.A. AL 22nd Inf. Co.H
Renfroe, Samson A. AL 39th Inf. Co.C
Renfroe, Samuel TN 38th Inf. Co.D
Renfroe, Seaborn FL 11th Inf. Co.L 2nd Lt.
Renfroe, Solomon R. GA 61st Inf. Co.I
Renfroe, S.P. AR 13th Inf. Co.F
Renfroe, S.S. AL 9th Inf. Co.G
Renfroe, Stephen GA Conscr.
Renfroe, T.B. Mead's Conf.Cav. Co.A
Renfroe, Thomas MS 33rd Inf. Co.F
Renfroe, Thomas TN 2nd (Ashby's) Cav. Co.A
Renfroe, Thomas TN Cav. 5th Bn. (McClellan's) Co.A
Renfroe, Thomas M. AL 15th Inf. Co.G Lt.
Renfroe, Thomas M. TX Cav. Madison's Regt. Co.F
Renfroe, Virgil A. FL 1st Cav. Co.F
Renfroe, W. AL 15th Inf. Co.A
Renfroe, W.H. AL 22nd Inf. Co.H
Renfroe, W.H. AL 63rd Inf. Co.F
Renfroe, W.H. GA 1st (Ramsey's) Inf. Co.E Cpl.
Renfroe, W.H. GA 32nd Inf. Co.E 1st Lt.
Renfroe, W.H. MS 2nd Part. Co.D Capt.
Renfroe, William GA 3rd Res. Co.B

Renfroe, William GA 13th Inf. Co.F 2nd Lt.
Renfroe, William GA 30th Inf. Co.D
Renfroe, William H. GA 49th Inf. Co.C
Renfroe, William N. LA 31st Inf. Co.I
Renfroe, William P. GA Phillips' Legion Co.A
Renfroe, William S. GA 12th Inf. Co.H 2nd Lt.
Renfroe, W.J. GA 5th Res. Co.K
Renfroid, Rufus NC 67th Inf. Co.G
Renfrow, A.P. FL 9th Inf. Co.E
Renfrow, Barclay TN 3rd (Clack's) Inf. Co.F
Renfrow, G.A. GA 59th Inf. Co.C
Renfrow, George AR 10th Mil.
Renfrow, George TN 39th Mtd.Inf. Co.F
Renfrow, George W. AR 35th Inf. Co.B
Renfrow, George W. LA 31st Inf. Co.E
Renfrow, G.W. AR 34th Inf. Co.E
Renfrow, J. TN 42nd Inf. Co.C
Renfrow, J. TX 1st Hvy.Arty. Co.A
Renfrow, James K.P. MO 10th Cav. Co.H Sgt.
Renfrow, J.H. AR 45th Mil. Co.A
Renfrow, J.M. AR 18th Inf. Co.G
Renfrow, John TN 39th Mtd.Inf. Co.F Lt.
Renfrow, John TX 11th Inf. Co.K
Renfrow, John W. AL 4th (Russell's) Cav. Co.D
  Sgt.
Renfrow, John W. AR 2nd Inf. Co.H Sgt.
Renfrow, John W. VA Inf. 21st Bn. 2nd Co.E
Renfrow, Josiah AR 14th (Powers') Inf. Co.D
Renfrow, Marion MS 3rd Inf. Co.K Cpl.
Renfrow, Marion J. GA 66th Inf. Co.E
Renfrow, Marion W. FL 4th Inf. Co.F
Renfrow, Mark MS 1st Lt.Arty. Co.B
Renfrow, Michael J. MS 23rd Inf. Co.G
Renfrow, Moses MS 7th Inf. Co.E
Renfrow, M.S. MS 9th Inf. New Co.I
Renfrow, P. MS 1st (King's) Inf. (St.Troops)
  Co.F
Renfrow, P.B. NC 2nd Jr.Res. Co.H
Renfrow, Perry V.B. NC 30th Inf. Co.I Sgt.
Renfrow, Philip MO 5th Inf. Co.D
Renfrow, Riley MO Cav. Freeman's Regt. Co.F
Renfrow, Robert AR 2nd Cav. Co.B
Renfrow, Robert AR 2nd Inf. Co.B
Renfrow, R.T. TN 3rd (Clack's) Inf. Co.F
Renfrow, Samuel AR 14th (Powers') Inf. Co.D
Renfrow, Seaborn AL 1st Regt.Conscr. Co.H
Renfrow, Stephen GA Inf. 25th Bn. (Prov.Guard)
  Co.C
Renfrow, T.B. AL 12th Inf. Co.G
Renfrow, Thomas J. AR 2nd Cav. Co.D
Renfrow, T.J. AR 8th Cav. Co.B
Renfrow, Van MS 3rd Inf. Co.K
Renfrow, W.E. AR 30th Inf. Co.F
Renfrow, Wm. GA Conscr.
Renfrow, William MS 7th Inf. Co.E
Renfrow, William MS 21st Inf. Co.C
Renfrow, William MO 15th Cav. Co.C
Renfrow, William NC 1st Jr.Res. Co.A
Renfrow, W.P. GA 2nd Cav. Co.F
Renfrow, W.P. GA 7th Inf. (St.Guards) Co.F
Renfrow, W.W. TX 37th Cav. Co.K
Renfrowe, R.B. NC 2nd Jr.Res. Co.H
Renfru, Washington TN Lt.Arty. Weller's Co.
Rengol, W.D. NC 57th Inf. Co.E 1st Lt.
Rengsdorf, J. LA Mil.Squad. Guides d'Orleans
Renhee, J. MS 12th Inf.
Reni, M. KY 11th Cav. Co.I 2nd Lt.

Renick, --- TX Cav. Good's Bn. Co.A
Renick, --- TX Cav. Mann's Regt. Co.C
Renick, A.J. MS 2nd Cav.Res. Co.I
Renick, A.R. TX 5th Cav. Co.I
Renick, Calvin B. VA Cav. Moorman's Co. Sgt.
Renick, C.B. VA 14th Cav. Co.A,E
Renick, Chatham E. MO Inf. 1st Regt.St.Guard
  Co.K Capt.
Renick, Chatham E. MO Inf. 3rd Bn. Co.C Sgt.
Renick, Chatham E. MO 6th Inf. Co.B Sgt.
Renick, Edwin L. MO Inf. 3rd Bn. Co.C
Renick, Edwin L. MO 6th Inf. Co.B
Renick, F.A. VA 14th Cav. Co.A,E
Renick, F.F. MO 12th Cav. Co.H
Renick, G.A. MS Cav. Russell's Co.
Renick, H.P. MO 2nd Cav. 3rd Co.K
Renick, J.A. AL 35th Inf. Co.H
Renick, James MO 5th Cav. Co.G Cpl.
Renick, James VA 9th Cav. Sandford's Co.
  Black.
Renick, James M. TX 1st (Yager's) Cav. Co.C
  1st Sgt.
Renick, James M. TX Cav. 3rd (Yager's) Bn.
  Co.C
Renick, James W. MO 4th Inf. Co.H
Renick, J.M. MO 3rd & 5th Cons.Inf.
Renick, John S. MO Inf. 1st Regt.St.Guard Co.K
  3rd Lt.
Renick, Joseph MS Cav. Russell's Co.
Renick, J.W. MO 1st & 4th Cons.Inf. Co.E,C
Renick, M. TX 30th Cav. Co.D
Renick, Matthew LA 7th Inf. Co.H Cpl.
Renick, Robert MO Cav. 1st Regt.St.Guard
  Capt.
Renick, Robert MO 12th Cav. Chap.
Renick, Robert TX 30th Cav. Co.D
Renick, Robert VA 14th Cav. Co.A,E
Renick, Robert Gen. & Staff Chap.
Renick, Robert F. MO 1st & 4th Cons.Inf.
  Co.C,E 1st Lt.
Renick, Robert F. MO 4th Inf. Co.H 1st Lt.
Renick, R.R. MO 7th Cav. Co.K
Renick, Thomas MS Cav. Russell's Co.
Renick, Thomas MO 5th Cav. Co.G
Renick, Thomas J. MS 34th Inf. Co.H
Renick, William H. MO Cav. Slayback's Regt.
  Co.H Cpl.
Renick, William J. MS 14th Inf. Co.E
Renicke, Charles LA 21st (Patton's) Inf. Co.A
Renicke, Charles LA 22nd (Cons.) Inf. Co.I
Renier, J.B. LA Mil. 1st Native Guards
Reniew, J.M. GA 9th Inf. Co.K
Renifoy, W.J. AL 53rd (Part.Rangers) Co.F Sgt.
Reniger, David NC 38th Inf. Co.B
Reninger, Thomas NC 4th Inf. Co.H
Renis, I. LA 2nd Res.Corps Co.A
Renis, J. NC 2nd Inf. Co.B
Renison, J.F. MO 11th Inf. Co.G
Renker, John TX 4th Inf. (St.Troops) Co.C
Renkin, H. SC 1st Regt. Charleston Guard Co.G
Renkl, Gregor GA Inf. 1st Loc.Troops (Augusta)
  Co.A
Renkle, A.D. TX 15th Cav. Co.H
Renley, Moses MS 8th Inf. Co.E Sgt.
Renn, Calvin NC 53rd Inf. Co.C
Renn, Cornelius M. VA 45th Inf. Co.D
  Ch.Music.

Renn, G.P. NC 1st Jr.Res. Co.A Cpl.
Renn, G.W. VA Lt.Arty. Griffin's Co.
Renn, James R. NC 14th Inf. Co.K
Renn, J.H. NC 8th Inf. Co.D Cpl.
Renn, John NC 13th Inf. Co.K
Renn, John C. VA Lt.Arty. Griffin's Co.
Renn, John C. VA 9th Inf. 1st Co.A
Renn, Joseph J. NC 12th Inf. Co.C
Renn, Lewis NC 23rd Inf. Co.G
Renn, W.L.W. MS Lt.Arty. 14th Bn. Co.B
Rennard, Edward VA Lt.Arty. Clutter's Co.
Rennard, J.W. GA 3rd Cav. Co.D
Rennart, Henry TX Comal Cty.Bn.Res. Co.A
Rennbald, J. MS Inf. 2nd Bn. (St.Troops) Co.A
Renneau, James TX 17th Cav. Co.C Cpl.
Renneau, John D. MS Inf. 3rd Bn. Co.F Sgt.
Renneau, Louis L. AL 6th Inf. Co.E Sgt.
Renneck, James VA 111th Mil. Co.5
Rennegar, L.R. NC 4th Inf. Co.H
Renneker, F.W. SC 25th Inf. Co.B
Renneker, J.H. SC 25th Inf. Co.B
Rennels, Alfred LA 1st (Strawbridge's) Inf. Co.G
Rennels, Jacob VA 19th Cav. Co.H
Rennels, John LA 1st Cav. Co.F Sgt.
Rennemore, Jacob TN Cav. Nixon's Regt. Co.H
Renner, Addison VA 1st Cav. Co.A
Renner, Amos VA 31st Mil. Co.I
Renner, Amos L. VA 23rd Cav. 2nd Co.K
Renner, Asa VA 31st Mil. Co.I
Renner, David TN 61st Mtd.Inf. Co.D
Renner, Frank LA 13th Inf. Co.B
Renner, G. GA 11th Mil.
Renner, George TX Cav. Bourland's Regt.
  Doomas' Co.
Renner, Henry VA 31st Mil. Co.I
Renner, Isaac TN 51st Inf. Capt.
Renner, Isaac VA 51st Mil. Co.D Lt.
Renner, James A. VA Cav. 39th Bn. Co.A
Renner, James A. VA 51st Mil. Co.D 2nd Lt.
Renner, James H. VA 31st Mil. Co.I
Renner, John TN 61st Mtd.Inf. Co.D
Renner, John I.W. VA 51st Mil. Co.G
Renner, Joseph VA 31st Mil. Co.I
Renner, Moses TN 61st Mtd.Inf. Co.D
Renner, Peter LA Mil. 1st Regt. 3rd Brig. 1st
  Div. Co.G
Renner, Peter W. VA 1st Cav. Co.A
Renner, William A. TN Cav. 16th Bn. (Neal's)
  Co.E
Rennert, J. TN Hvy.Arty. Sterling's Co.
Rennett, W. SC Mil.Arty. 1st Regt. Walter's Co.
Rennett, William SC Lt.Arty. J.T. Kanapaux's
  Co. (Lafayette Arty.) Teamster
Rennew, John P. SC Hvy.Arty. Mathewes' Co.
Rennick, --- TX Cav. 4th Regt.St.Troops Co.G
Rennick, A.T. KY 1st Inf. Co.E Sgt.
Rennick, A.T. KY 7th Mtd.Inf. Co.B 2nd Lt.
Rennick, Att TN 3rd (Forrest's) Cav. Co.A
Rennick, Att TN Inf. 154th Sr.Regt. 1st Co.B
Rennick, Att Conf.Inf. 1st Bn. Co.F 1st Lt.
Rennick, H. TX 8th Cav. Co.C
Rennick, H.T. SC 3rd Inf. Co.E
Rennick, John A. AR 1st Mtd.Rifles Co.F
Rennick, John A. AR Mil. Borland's Regt.
  Pulaski Lancers Co.
Rennick, Robert D. KY 7th Mtd.Inf. Co.B Sgt.

Rennick, Samuel Wat KY 7th Mtd.Inf. Co.B 1st Lt.

Rennicks, John MS Griffin's Co. (Madison Guards)

Rennie, Alexander Shecoe's Chickasaw Bn. Mtd.Vol. Adj.

Rennie, George H. VA 21st Inf. Co.F Sgt.

Rennie, James LA 30th Inf. Co.F

Rennie, James B. VA Cav. 1st Bn. (Loc.Def. Troops) Co.C

Rennie, Joseph R. VA Cav. 1st Bn. (Loc.Def. Troops) Co.C Cpl.

Rennie, Joseph R. VA 1st Arty. Co.K

Rennie, William AL 1st Regt. Mobile Vol. British Guard Co.B

Rennie, William GA 2nd Inf. 1st Co.B

Rennie, William GA 26th Inf. Co.E,F

Rennier, A. TX 24th & 25th Cav. (Cons.) Co.H

Rennington, R.A. SC 2nd Inf. Co.E

Rennington, W.T. LA Mil. Leeds' Guards

Renno, Alonzo AL Cav. Lewis' Bn. Co.E

Renno, Henry KY 7th Cav. Co.C

Renno, Henry KY 3rd Mtd.Inf. Co.M

Renno, Henry NC 62nd Inf. Co.I

Renno, John NC Inf. Thomas Legion Co.C

Renno, John A. SC 1st (McCreary's) Inf. Co.C

Renno, John E. NC 60th Inf. Co.A Cpl.

Renno, Lewis MS 1st (Percy's) Inf. Co.A

Renno, Lewis MS 36th Inf. Co.B

Renno, Nathan AL Lt.Arty. Ward's Btty.

Renno, Samuel MS 1st (Percy's) Inf. Co.A

Renno, Samuel MS 39th Inf. Co.F

Renno, Stephenson AL Lt.Arty. Ward's Btty.

Renno, W.H. VA Inf. 1st Bn. Co.B

Renno, William AL Cav. Lewis' Bn. Co.E

Renno, William NC Inf. Thomas Legion Co.C Sgt.

Rennoe, John H. VA 15th Cav. Co.H

Rennoe, John L. VA 17th Inf. Co.F

Rennolds, Albert VA 55th Inf. Co.F Capt.

Rennolds, C.W. MS Inf. 3rd Bn. (St.Troops) Co.E

Rennolds, Edwin H. TN 5th Inf. 2nd Co.D 2nd Lt.

Rennolds, George M. MS 2nd St.Cav. Co.A

Rennolds, J.S. TN 5th Inf. 2nd Co.D Cpl.

Rennolds, Thomas VA 55th Inf. Co.F

Rennolds, William R. MS Cav. 1st Bn. (Miller's) Bowles' Co. Sgt.

Rennolds, William R. VA 55th Inf. Co.F

Renny, T.B. AR 7th Mil. Co.B

Rennyson, James B. LA 18th Inf. Co.H 2nd Lt.

Reno, Benjaman AL 48th Inf. Co.F

Reno, F.M. TX 32nd Cav. Co.K

Reno, George MO Inf. Perkins' Bn. Co.D

Reno, George W. LA 12th Inf. Co.H

Reno, Henry VA 5th Cav. Co.B

Reno, J.A. AL 28th Inf. Co.L

Reno, Jasper N. TX 19th Cav. Co.I Sgt.

Reno, John A. TN 28th (Cons.) Inf. Co.L

Reno, Joseph L. LA 12th Inf. Co.H 1st Lt.

Reno, Lewis VA 5th Cav. Co.B

Reno, Neil AL 23rd Inf. Co.D

Reno, S. MS 6th Inf. Co.F

Reno, Solomon AR 2nd Mtd.Rifles Co.G

Reno, Thomas F. MS Inf. 3rd Bn. Co.F

Reno, W.D. AR 1st (Monroe's) Cav. Co.D

Reno, W.H.C. VA 24th Bn.Part.Rangers Co.E

Reno, William AR Cav. Harrell's Bn. Co.B Cpl.

Reno, William MS Inf. 3rd Bn. Co.F

Reno, William C. TX 22nd Cav. Co.D Hosp.Stew.

Reno, William C. TX 37th Cav. Co.B

Reno, William H. KY 1st Inf. Co.I

Reno, William Henry LA 1st (Nelligan's) Inf. Co.H

Reno, W.J. AR 1st (Monroe's) Cav. Co.D

Reno, W.W. AL 48th Inf. Co.G,E

Renoe, Alexander VA 49th Inf. Co.A

Renoe, Cornelius AL Cp. of Instr. Talladega

Renoe, George VA Cav. Ferguson's Bn. Parks' Co.

Renoe, Henry VA 6th Cav. Co.H

Renoe, John F. VA 49th Inf. Co.A

Renoe, Joseph VA 49th Inf. Co.A

Renoe, Robert A. VA 49th Inf. Co.A

Renoe, William A. VA 49th Inf. Co.A

Renois, H. LA 2nd Cav. Co.D

Renois, Victor LA Inf.Cons.Crescent Regt. Co.G

Renojsky, W. TN Inf. 3rd Bn. Co.G

Renol, William M. AL 28th Inf. Co.B

Renolds, Archer VA 21st Inf. Co.K

Renolds, Edmond M. MO Cav. Schnabel's Bn. Co.B

Renolds, George 1st Cherokee Mtd.Vol. 1st Co.C

Renolds, I.M. VA 9th Inf. Co.F

Renolds, John M. VA 7th Inf. Co.A

Renolds, Rowdy 9th Conf.Inf. Co.F

Renolds, William L. MS Inf. (Red Rebels) D.J. Red's Co.

Renolds, Wilson L. AR 33rd Inf. Co.A Cpl.

Renols, Samuel VA 52nd Inf. Co.F

Renom, William F. VA 15th Cav.

Renouse, W.H. LA Cav. Lott's Co. (Carroll Drag.)

Renow, Alonzo AL 12th Cav. Co.C

Renow, J.C. Exch.Bn. Co.E,F,CSA

Renox, James LA Ogden's Cav. Co.F Cpl.

Rensan, J.S. TX Cav. 1st Regt.St.Troops Co.E

Rensch, Charles LA 26th Inf. Co.D

Renshaw, A.C. TN 9th Inf. Paine's Co.

Renshaw, A.C. TN 38th Inf. Co.E

Renshaw, A.D. TX 22nd Inf. Co.E Capt.

Renshaw, Arthur TX 19th Cav. Co.G

Renshaw, H., Jr. LA Inf.Crescent Regt. Co.B

Renshaw, Henry LA Mil.Conf.Guards Regt. Co.B 3rd Lt.

Renshaw, Henry F. TX 19th Cav. Co.G

Renshaw, Iredell R. VA Lt.Arty. B.Z. Price's Co.

Renshaw, J.A. 3rd Conf.Eng.Troops Co.C Sgt.

Renshaw, J.A. Central Div. KY Sap. & Min.,CSA

Renshaw, James KY Arty. McEnnis' Detach.

Renshaw, James TX 3rd Cav. Co.F

Renshaw, James L. TX 19th Cav. Co.G

Renshaw, James P. MS 29th Inf. Co.K

Renshaw, J.F. TX 12th Inf. Co.F Cpl.

Renshaw, John TN 18th Inf. Co.C

Renshaw, John B. TX 19th Cav. Co.G

Renshaw, J.R. LA Mil. British Guard Bn. Coburn's Co.

Renshaw, N.F. KY 10th (Diamond's) Cav. Co.D

Renshaw, N.F. KY 2nd Bn.Mtd.Rifles Co.B

Renshaw, Noble F. KY 1st Bn.Mtd.Rifles Co.D

Renshaw, Noble F. KY 5th Mtd.Inf. Co.C

Renshaw, R.H. VA 122nd Mil. Co.D 2nd Lt.

Renshaw, Robert N. Gen. & Staff, A. of N.VA Capt.,AQM

Renshaw, Samuel P. KY 5th Mtd.Inf. Co.E

Renshaw, S.P. KY 4th Cav. Co.K,C

Renshaw, T.N. NC Mil. 120th Regt. Co.A 1st Lt.

Renshaw, W.A. AL 4th Cav. Co.M

Renshaw, William TN 1st (Carter's) Cav. Co.M

Renshaw, William TN 63rd Inf. Co.D,K

Renshaw, William J. AR 23rd Inf. Co.A,H Sgt.

Renshaw, William T. MD Arty. 4th Btty.

Renshaw, William T. VA 40th Inf. Co.I

Rensler, F. LA Mil. Mooney's Co. (Saddlers Guards)

Rent, J. TX 36th Cav. Co.I

Rent, W.R. GA 56th Inf. Co.F

Rentbron, J.H. NC 27th Inf. Co.A

Renteirs, Jacob SC 1st Inf. Co.M

Renter, John F. NC 4th Inf. Co.K Cpl.

Renteria, Juan Bta. LA Mil. 5th Regt.Eur.Brig. (Spanish Regt.) Co.2

Rentfro, E.W. TX 21st Cav. Co.A

Rentfro, George W. AR 9th Inf. Co.C

Rentfro, Jake KY 5th Mtd.Inf. Co.E

Rentfro, James A. TX 18th Inf. Co.B

Rentfro, James I. NC 50th Inf. Co.E

Rentfro, J.H. NC Loc.Def. Croom's Co.

Rentfro, William H. GA 27th Inf. Co.E Maj.

Rentfro, W.L. KY 5th Mtd.Inf. Co.E

Rentfroe, A.W. GA 19th Inf. Co.C

Rentfroe, E.T. 3rd Conf.Cav. Co.G

Rentfroe, S.H. FL 1st (Res.) Inf. Co.I

Rentfrow, Braswell NC 55th Inf. Co.A

Rentfrow, Braswell NC Mil. Clark's Sp.Bn. Co.I

Rentfrow, Burkett NC 55th Inf. Co.A

Rentfrow, Calvin NC 43rd Inf. Co.C

Rentfrow, David NC 4th Inf. Co.F

Rentfrow, David C. GA 4th Inf. Co.A Cpl.

Rentfrow, D.L. AR 10th Inf. Co.I,K

Rentfrow, G.W. AR 2nd Cav. Co.D

Rentfrow, H. NC 6th Cav. (65th St.Troops) Co.H

Rentfrow, James NC 1st Arty. (10th St.Troops) Co.F

Rentfrow, John T. NC 2nd Inf. Co.B

Rentfrow, Perry NC 2nd Cav. (19th St.Troops) Co.E Cpl.

Rentfrow, Perry NC 2nd Inf. Co.B

Rentfrow, Ransom NC 43rd Inf. Co.C

Rentfrow, Ruffin NC 38th Inf. Co.D

Rentfrow, Rufus NC 2nd Cav. (19th St.Troops) Co.E

Rentfrow, Samuel AR 27th Inf. Co.F

Rentfrow, Stephen NC 43rd Inf. Co.C

Rentfrow, Thomas NC Mallett's Bn. Co.F

Rentfrow, William GA 13th Inf. Co.F

Rentfrow, William F. GA 41st Inf. Co.K

Rentfrow, William V. NC 4th Cav. (59th St.Troops) Co.H Sgt.

Renth, Henry W. AL 24th Inf. Co.D

Rentiers, J.G. SC 2nd Inf. Co.A,G Cpl.

Rentler, --- TX 6th Field Btty.

Renton, John AL 4th Res. Co.H

Rentort, Piere VA Cav. 32nd Bn. Co.A

Rentrop, L.F. LA 26th Inf. Co.B
Rentrope, A.A. LA 2nd Cav. Co.B
Rentrope, Alcie AL 2nd Cav. Co.B
Rentry, R.A. GA 4th (Clinch's) Cav. Co.H
Rents, Artemus GA 11th Cav. (St.Guards)
    Johnson's Co.
Rents, G.W. GA 47th Inf. Co.F
Rentye, Ezekiel GA 51st Inf. Co.E
Rentz, --- LA 13th Inf. Co.F
Rentz, A. GA 4th (Clinch's) Cav. Co.H
Rentz, Aaron GA Mayer's Co. (Appling Cav.)
Rentz, Aaron SC 11th Inf. Co.K
Rentz, Aaron M. GA 47th Inf. Co.F
Rentz, Adam GA 8th Cav. Co.B
Rentz, Benjamin AL 43rd Inf. Co.B
Rentz, Calvin GA 5th Inf. Co.G
Rentz, Charles GA 26th Inf. Co.H
Rentz, Charles SC 11th Res. Co.L
Rentz, Ezekeel GA 62nd Cav. Co.B
Rentz, George S. GA Phillips' Legion Co.D Sgt.
Rentz, George W. AL 43rd Inf. Co.B
Rentz, G.W. SC 11th Inf. Co.K Sgt.
Rentz, Isaac, Jr. SC 17th Inf. Co.G
Rentz, J. AL 21st Inf. Co.C
Rentz, Jacah S. GA 27th Inf. Co.I
Rentz, Jacob AL 43rd Inf. Co.B
Rentz, Jacob SC 11th Inf. Co.K
Rentz, Jacob SC 11th Inf. Co.K Sgt.
Rentz, Jacob, Jr. SC 11th Inf. Co.K
Rentz, Jacob G. SC 17th Inf. Co.H
Rentz, James M. LA 2nd Inf. Co.F
Rentz, J.C. SC 2nd St.Troops Co.E
Rentz, J.D. SC 1st (Hagood's) Inf. 1st Co.F, 2nd
    Co.G
Rentz, J.F. AL 105th Co.H
Rentz, J.J. AL 12th Inf. Co.F
Rentz, John SC 27th Inf. Co.G
Rentz, John H. GA 51st Inf. Co.G Cpl.
Rentz, John W. AL 12th Inf. Co.H
Rentz, John W. AL 13th Inf. Co.A Adj.
Rentz, John W. Gen. & Staff 1st Lt.,Adj.
Rentz, Joseph SC 2nd Arty. Co.C
Rentz, J.W. SC 1st Bn.S.S. Co.C
Rentz, J.W. SC 2nd Inf. Co.K
Rentz, J.W. SC 22nd Inf. Co.F
Rentz, Peter GA 51st Inf. Co.G
Rentz, Samuel R. GA 12th Inf. Co.I
Rentz, Simon P. LA 13th Bn. (Part.Rangers)
    Co.F
Rentz, S.P. SC 5th Cav. Co.I
Rentz, T.H. GA Cav. Gartrell's Co.
Rentz, T.L. LA 27th Inf. Co.E
Rentz, Uzziah SC 17th Inf. Co.G
Rentz, W.A. SC Hvy.Arty. 15th (Lucas') Bn.
    Co.C
Rentz, W.A. SC 1st (Hagood's) Inf. 1st Co.F,
    2nd Co.G
Rentz, W.G. LA 1st Res. Co.D
Rentz, William AL 43rd Inf. Co.B Cpl.
Rentz, William GA 51st Inf. Co.G
Rentz, William D. GA 26th Inf. Co.G
Rentz, William J. GA 8th Cav. Co.B
Rentz, William J. GA 62nd Cav. Co.B
Rentze, Adam GA 62nd Cav. Co.B
Rentze, Charles SC 11th Inf. Co.D
Rentze, Ezekiel GA 8th Cav. Co.B
Rentze, J.C. SC 8th Bn.Res. Co.C

Rentze, J.C. SC 11th Res. Co.B
Rentze, J.P. SC 8th Bn.Res. Co.C
Renwick, J.P. LA 3rd Inf. Co.B Sgt.Maj.
Renwick, M.A. SC Cav. 19th Bn. Co.B
Renwick, M.A. SC 20th Inf. Co.M
Renwick, Nathan AL 31st Inf. Co.B
Renwick, William LA 5th Inf. Co.C
Renwick, William W. LA 12th Inf. Co.F 1st Lt.
Renwick, W.P. LA 3rd Inf. Co.B 2nd Lt.
Reny, D.M. AL 25th Inf. Co.C
Reny, Thomas AR 34th Inf. Co.I Sgt.
Renyew, J.W. TN 3rd (Lillard's) Mtd.Inf. Co.I
Renz, George LA Mil.Cont.Regt. Lang's Co.
Renz, Jann AL 20th Inf. Co.C
Renz, L. LA 6th Inf. Co.G Cpl.
Renz, Michael TN 2nd (Walker's) Inf. Co.D
Reobia, Joseph LA Mil. Leeds' Guards Regt.
    Co.E
Reoffet, David MO Cav. Poindexter's Regt.
Reohe, William LA 6th Inf. Co.B
Reoiese, Felix GA 1st Reg. Co.A
Reonis, John TN 3rd (Lillard's) Mtd.Inf. Co.D
Reordan, Michael TN 5th Inf.
Reordon, John MS Inf. (Red Rebels) D.J. Red's
    Co.
Repap, Edward VA 16th Cav. Co.F
Repass, Alford VA 45th Inf. Co.B
Repass, Augustus VA Cav. 34th Bn. Co.B Sgt.
Repass, Augustus VA 4th Res. Co.E
Repass, Augustus VA 36th Inf. 2nd Co.G
Repass, Austin VA 36th Inf. 2nd Co.G
Repass, Daniel VA 51st Inf. Music.
Repass, Edward VA 45th Inf. Co.A
Repass, Edwin VA Cav. 37th Bn. Co.K
Repass, Eli VA 11th Bn.Res. Co.A
Repass, Eli VA Mil. Stowers' Co.
Repass, Elias VA 26th Cav. Ord.Sgt.
Repass, Elias VA Cav. 47th Bn. Co.B
Repass, Elias VA Inf. French's Bn. Co.D
Repass, Elias Gen. & Staff Ord.Sgt.
Repass, Elijah VA 26th Cav. Hosp.Stew.
Repass, Elijah VA Cav. 47th Bn. Co.B
Repass, Elijah VA 45th Inf. Co.K
Repass, Elijah VA Inf. French's Bn. Co.D
Repass, F.F. VA 26th Cav. Co.H
Repass, Frank VA 22nd Cav. Co.G
Repass, Frederick F. VA Cav. 47th Bn. Co.B
Repass, Fredrick F. VA 54th Inf. Co.F
Repass, G.B. VA 4th Res. Co.E
Repass, George F. VA 51st Inf. Co.C
Repass, Gordon VA 1st Inf. Co.E
Repass, Gordon VA 4th Res. Co.E
Repass, Henry L. VA 45th Inf. Co.B
Repass, H.F. VA 45th Inf. Co.B
Repass, H.S. VA 4th Res. Co.E
Repass, Isaac M. VA Lt.Arty. French's Co. Cpl.
Repass, Isaac M. VA 86th Mil. Co.F
Repass, J.A. VA Mil. Stowers' Co.
Repass, James L. VA 51st Inf. Music.
Repass, Joel VA 36th Inf. 2nd Co.G
Repass, John VA Loc.Def. Patterson's Co.
Repass, Joseph VA 4th Res. Co.G Cpl.
Repass, L.T. VA 4th Res. Co.E
Repass, Newton H. VA 51st Inf. Co.C 2nd Lt.
Repass, R.F. VA 8th Cav. Co.A
Repass, Rufus B. VA 51st Inf. Music.
Repass, Samuel R. VA 29th Inf. Co.A

Repass, Stephen VA Mil. Stowers' Co.
Repass, Stephen A. VA 28th Inf. Co.I 2nd Lt.
Repass, Thomas A. VA 45th Inf. Co.A 1st Sgt.
Repass, Thomas J. VA 51st Inf. Co.C
Repass, Walter VA 45th Inf. Co.B
Repass, W.G. Conf.Cav. 7th Bn. Maj.
Repass, William VA 6th Bn.Res. Co.C Cpl.
Repass, William F. VA 51st Inf. Co.C
Repass, William G. VA 51st Inf. Co.F Capt.
Repass, William G. VA Inf. French's Bn. Co.B
Repeeser, A. LA Miles' Legion Co.B
Repel, John LA Mil. 4th Regt. 2nd Brig. 1st Div.
    Co.E
Repete, A. LA Mil. 2nd Regt. French Brig. Co.8
Repete, Anto. LA Mil. 5th Regt.Eur.Brig.
    (Spanish Regt.) Co.8
Repetto, Guiseppe LA Mil. 6th Regt.Eur.Brig.
    (Italian Guards Bn.) Co.3
Rephas, Elias VA 45th Inf. Co.D Sgt.
Repition, A. Paul, Jr. Gen. & Staff 2nd
    Lt.,Dr.M.
Repiton, A. Paul, Jr. NC 1st Arty. (10th
    St.Troops) Co.E Sgt.
Repiton, A. Paul NC Lt.Arty. 3rd Bn. Co.C
Repiton, A. Paul Gen. & Staff Chap.
Repp, Jonathan TX 12th Inf. Co.G
Repp, Michael 14th Conf.Cav. Co.G
Reppard, H.C. GA 1st (Symons') Res. Co.C
Reppetoe, John E. VA Lt.Arty. Sturdivant's Co.
Reppette, C. LA Mil. 4th Regt. French Brig.
    Co.4
Reppette, D. LA Mil. 4th Regt. French Brig.
    Co.4
Reppond, Battiace F. LA 31st Inf. Co.H
Reppond, Ettienne A. LA 31st Inf. Co.H
Reppond, James LA 25th Inf. Co.E
Reppond, Lewis LA 25th Inf. Co.E
Reppond, Paul LA 25th Inf. Co.E
Repsher, Isaac TN Lt.Arty. Tobin's Co.
Repsher, J.J. AL 4th Res. Co.C
Repsher, L. AL 7th Cav. Co.A
Repss, Albert VA 22nd Cav. Co.C
Reptii, Barney KY 4th Cav. Co.B
Repton, Henry M. NC 2nd Jr.Res. Co.A
Requa, A.C. TX 1st Bn.S.S. Co.A 3rd Lt.
Requa, Austin C. TX 37th Cav. Co.B
Requa, Joseph TX 1st Hvy.Arty. Co.E
Requa, Justin C. TX 1st Bn.S.S. Co.A 3rd Lt.
Requier, H.F. LA Mil.Conf.Guards Regt. Co.H
Reras, Martin LA Mil. 3rd Regt. 1st Brig. 1st
    Div. Co.H
Rerdle, M.C. GA Brooks' Co. (Terrell Lt.Arty.)
    Cpl.
Rerg, John TX 1st Hvy.Arty. Co.F
Reridon, Thomas LA 13th Inf. Co.I
Rerrington, Joriah AL 62nd Inf. Co.A
Rerry, H. MS 8th Cav. Co.K
Rerse, I.L. TX 11th Inf. Co.H
Rertson, Thomas NC 1st Jr.Res. Co.E
Rese, Enoch SC 3rd Res. Co.I
Resee, J.W. AR 1st (Dobbin's) Cav. Co.K
Resell, Alex KY 11th Cav. Co.B
Resendes, G. TX 8th Inf. Co.C
Reser, Thomas A. MS Graves' Co. (Copiah
    Horse Guards)
Reseur, James M. TN Cav. 2nd Bn. (Biffle's)
    Co.D Cpl.

Reseur, John A. TN Cav. 2nd Bn. (Biffle's)
  Co.D 3rd Lt.
Resh, Y. George MS 18th Cav. Co.K
Resher, Green B.G. MS 8th Inf. Co.D Cpl.
Resides, James F. AR Mil. Borland's Regt.
  Pulaski Lancers
Resin, John W. NC 2nd Arty. (36th St.Troops)
  Co.A
Resinger, Henry MO 7th Cav. Co.D Sgt.
Resinger, John A. MO 3rd Cav. Co.K
Resinger, Thomas SC 15th Inf. Co.C
Resinger, Thomas M. LA 31st Inf. Co.I
Reskridge, R.W. MS 5th Inf. (St.Troops) Co.H
Resler, W.H.C. VA Cav. 35th Bn. Co.B
Resly, T. NC 4th Cav. (59th St.Troops) Co.H
Resnar, Henry VA Hvy.Arty. Wright's Co.
Resor, James W. VA 7th Inf. Co.A
Resor, Peter D. VA 8th Inf. Co.K
Resor, Reuben KY 10th (Johnson's) Cav. Co.D
  Cpl.
Resor, Ruben KY 8th Cav. Co.D
Respass, Francis H. VA 61st Mil. Co.C
Respass, George NC 1st Inf. Co.G
Respass, Isaiah NC 2nd Cav. (19th St.Troops)
  Co.G
Respass, Lee M. GA 4th Inf. Co.H
Respass, Richard W. NC 42nd Inf. Co.B 2nd Lt.
Respass, William I. GA 1st (Ramsey's) Inf.
Respass, W.W. LA 2nd Inf. Co.H
Respass, W.W. LA 19th Inf. Co.G
Respass, Z. GA 5th Res. Co.D Sgt.
Respberry, L.W. AR 13th Inf. Co.H
Respbery, Allen AR 13th Inf. Co.H
Respbery, William AR 13th Inf. Co.H
Respes, Henry NC 2nd Arty. (36th St.Troops)
  Co.G
Respess, Francis VA 26th Inf. Co.D
Respess, Henry NC 1st Arty. (10th St.Troops)
  Co.K
Respess, James C. GA 5th Inf. Co.K
Respess, James H. NC 17th Inf. (2nd Org.) Co.H
Respess, James T. NC 61st Inf. Co.I Capt.
Respess, James T. NC 61st Inf. Co.B Sgt.
Respess, J.J. NC 1st Arty. (10th St.Troops) Co.K
Respess, John J. NC 61st Inf. Co.B
Respess, John R. GA Res. Capt.
Respess, J.T. GA 6th Inf. Co.G
Respess, Richard NC 2nd Arty. (36th St.Troops)
  Co.B
Respess, Richard F. NC 3rd Inf. Co.I
Respess, Richard W. AL 10th Inf. Co.F
Respess, Richard W. NC 17th Inf. (1st Org.)
  Co.H
Respess, Richard W. NC 61st Inf. Co.H 2nd Lt.
Respess, R.W. NC Lt.Arty. 13th Bn. Co.B
Respess, Washington H. VA 61st Mil. Co.E
Respess, W.C. AL 18th Inf. Co.I
Respess, William C. KY 2nd Cav.
Respess, William H. VA 61st Mil. Co.E 1st Sgt.
Respess, William O. NC 1st Arty. (10th
  St.Troops) Co.K
Respess, William O. NC 3rd Inf. Co.I
Respess, William T. GA Inf. Atwater's Co. 1st
  Lt.
Respess, W.L. AL 16th Inf. Co.B
Respess, W.M. AL 57th Inf. Co.H
Respondie, Peter TX 35th (Brown's) Cav. Co.C

Respress, Francis VA 61st Mil. Co.B
Resse, Lucian L. GA 6th Inf. (St.Guards) Co.B
Resseau, R. LA Mil. Lewis Guards
Ressell, G. VA 10th Cav. Co.A
Ressing, Wm. L. AL 48th Mil. Co.A
Ressles, F.M. GA 48th Inf. Co.A
Resslon, Thomas TN 2nd (Robison's) Inf. Co.E
Ressman, Christian TX Cav. 8th (Taylor's) Bn.
  Co.C Sgt.
Ressmann, Christian TX 1st (Yager's) Cav. Co.E
  Sgt.
Ressorat, Jacob LA Mil. 4th Regt. 1st Brig. 1st
  Div. Co.I
Rest, W.H. GA 9th Inf. Co.K
Resta, Charles TX 1st Hvy.Arty. Co.B
Restelle, John LA O'Hara's Co. (Pelican
  Guards,Co.B)
Rester, D.F. AR 19th (Dockery's) Inf. Co.F
Rester, Francis M. AL 55th Vol. Co.E
Rester, Francis M. LA 12th Inf. Co.E Cpl.
Rester, G. MS 38th Cav. Co.C
Rester, Gideon LA 5th Cav. Co.I
Rester, Hiram AL 36th Inf. Co.E
Rester, J.W. LA 3rd (Wingfield's) Cav. Co.A
Rester, Lemuel MS 22nd Inf. Co.A Cpl.
Rester, Liberty AR 19th (Dockery's) Inf. Co.F
Rester, Thomas J. LA 12th Inf. Co.E
Rester, William MS 38th Cav. Co.C
Rester, Wilson AL Lt.Arty. 2nd Bn. Co.B
Restler, Henry GA 4th Regt.St.Troops Co.E
Restol, John AR Cav. Gordon's Regt. Co.A
Reston, John A. TN 20th Inf. Co.F
Reston, L. MS 38th Cav. Co.I
Reston, W.J. VA 8th Cav. Co.E
Restor, A.G. MS Cav. 1st Bn. (McNair's)
  St.Troops Co.C
Restucci, Andrea LA Mil. 6th Regt.Eur.Brig.
  (Italian Guards Bn.) Co.3
Retart, H. SC Mil. 16th Regt. Eason's Co.
Retby, A.J. TX 9th (Young's) Inf. Co.I
Retch, Lugart TN Cav. 9th Bn. (Gantt's)
Retcher, T.J. GA 1st Res.
Retchey, Henry J. NC 2nd Inf. Co.B
Retchman, A. VA 2nd St.Res. Co.B
Reteer, Jno. H. AL Coosa Guard J.W. Suttle's
  Co.
Retherford, Allen VA 51st Inf. Co.I
Retherford, Anderson VA 51st Inf. Co.I
Retherford, B.J. GA 50th Inf. Co.I
Retherford, Claiborn D. TX 11th (Spaight's)
  Bn.Vol. Co.C
Retherford, D.F. GA Cav. Russell's Co.
Retherford, D.F. MS 11th (Perrin's) Cav. Co.K
Retherford, D.R. AL 27th Inf. Co.H
Retherford, F. TN 19th (Biffle's) Cav. Co.L
Retherford, Fielding GA 13th Cav. Co.I
Retherford, George AL 33rd Inf. Co.A
Retherford, George W. VA 2nd Inf. Co.D
Retherford, Harvey VA 51st Inf. Co.I
Retherford, Henry MO Inf. Clark's Regt. Co.G
Retherford, Henry Conf.Cav. Clarkson's Bn.
  Ind.Rangers Co.E
Retherford, Isaac AL 34th Inf. Co.E
Retherford, James VA 51st Inf. Co.C
Retherford, James J. VA 51st Inf. Co.I
Retherford, Jefferson VA 51st Inf. Co.I

Retherford, John Conf.Cav. Clarkson's Bn.
  Ind.Rangers Co.C
Retherford, John R. MO 7th Inf. Co.A
Retherford, J.L. MS 11th (Perrin's) Cav. Co.K
Retherford, John GA 1st Inf. (St.Guards) Co.C
Retherford, John TN 3rd (Lillard's) Mtd.Inf. 1st
  Co.K
Retherford, R.A. MS 5th Inf. Co.C
Retherford, Stephen VA 51st Inf. Co.I Cpl.
Retherford, Thompson VA 51st Inf. Co.I
Retherford, William H. AL 27th Inf. Co.H
Retherford, William P. TN 19th Inf. Co.H
Retherford, W.W. GA 11th Cav. (St.Guards)
  Godfrey's Co.
Rethmires, John TN 21st Inf. Co.I
Rethosky, W. 14th Conf.Cav. Co.F
Retif, A. LA Mil. Delery's Co. (St.Bernard
  Horse Rifles Co.)
Retif, Armand LA Lt.Arty. LeGardeur, Jr.'s Co.
  (Orleans Guard Btty.)
Retif, L.E. LA Mil. Delery's Co. (St.Bernard
  Horse Rifles Co.)
Retif, P.E. LA Mil. Delery's Co. (St.Bernard
  Horse Rifles Co.)
Retif, P.E. LA Lt.Arty. LeGardeur, Jr.'s Co.
  (Orleans Guard Btty.) Artif.
Retkke, P. TX Waul's Legion Co.A
Retly, B.F. AL Conscr.
Reton, J.A. AR 35th Inf. Co.H
Retorking, Remon 1st Choctaw & Chickasaw
  Mtd.Rifles 3rd Co.H
Retshek, Konstantin TX 5th Field Btty.
Retshek, Konstantin TX 5th Field Btty.
Rettberg, William LA 8th Inf. Co.F
Retter, Fred LA 17th Inf. Co.F
Retter, Henry LA C.S. Zouave Bn. Co.F,C
Retter, John T. VA 61st Inf. Co.D
Retter, Joseph VA 7th Cav. Co.K
Retter, S.J. TN 21st & 22nd (Cons.) Cav. Co.K
Retter, T. LA Mil. Orleans Fire Regt. Co.G
Rettig, Charles TX 10th Cav. Co.G
Rettiger, John VA 22nd Inf. Co.G
Rettigg, Paul 1st Choctaw & Chickasaw
  Mtd.Rifles 1st Co.K
Rettinger, I. VA 1st Bn.Res. Co.B
Retwood, A. SC 1st Cav. Co.I
Retzer, G.W. AR 1st Vol. Co.E
Retzer, G.W. AR 38th Inf. Co.D
Retzloff, B. TX Waul's Legion Co.C
Retzner, A. LA 4th Inf. Co.F
Reuben GA Cav. 1st Bn. Lamar's Co. Wag.
Reuber, --- LA Mil. 2nd Regt. French Brig. Co.2
Reubke, H. TX 1st Hvy.Arty. Co.B
Reubun 1st Choctaw Mtd.Rifles Co.D
Reubush, William H. VA 52nd Inf. Co.F Cpl.
Reucher, Abe AL 63rd Inf. Co.K,H
Reudelhuber, Franz TN Inf. 3rd Bn. Co.F
Reudelhuber, George TN Inf. 3rd Bn. Co.F
Reudelhuber, P. LA Miles' Legion Co.A
Reuden, T.C. GA 1st Inf. Co.A
Reuder, J.F. TX Inf. Timmons' Regt. Co.G
Reuis, J.W. TN 13th (Gore's) Cav. Co.D Lt.
Reul, Jacob TN 15th Inf. Co.K
Reuler, F. LA Mil. 4th Regt. French Brig. Co.4
  Cpl.
Reumph, Jacob MS Cav. Powers' Regt. Co.C
Reupsch, W. AL 1st Regt. Mobile Vol. Co.C

Reurick, John GA Inf. 18th Bn. (St.Guards) Co.E
Reuse, Henry GA 8th Cav. Co.K
Reuser, John J. AR 1st Inf. Sgt.
Reuser, Louis TX 6th Inf. Co.I
Reuss, J.M. TX 8th Inf. Co.B Capt.
Reuss, Joseph M. TX Arty. 4th Bn. Co.B Capt.
Reuss, William TX Lt.Arty. Jones' Co.
Reutch, M. MO 1st Brig.St.Guard
Reuter, Henri LA 11th Inf. Co.D
Reuter, J. LA 22nd Inf. Co.C
Reuter, John SC 3rd Cav. Co.G
Reuter, John SC Inf. 1st (Charleston) Bn. Co.F
Reuter, John TX 4th Cav. Co.G
Reuter, Joseph VA 2nd Inf.Loc.Def. Co.G
Reuter, Joseph VA Inf. 2nd Bn.Loc.Def. Co.A
Reuter, Louis SC 1st Arty. Co.E
Reutez, W.J. GA 55th Inf. Co.H
Reutez, Z. GA 55th Inf. Co.H
Reuth, J.M. NC Hair's Bn. Co.H
Reuth, William LA 1st Hvy.Arty. (Reg.) Music.
Reutter, Antoine LA Mil. 1st Regt. French Brig. Co.6
Reutz, M.M. AL 3rd Cav. Co.C
Revark, J. Joel GA Cav. 21st Bn. Co.B,E Cpl.
Revas, L. LA 18th Inf. Co.F
Revas, L. LA Inf.Cons. 18th Regt. & Yellow Jacket Bn. Co.F
Revault, Alexander AL 1st Regt. Mobile Vol. Co.E
Revdry, Thomas TN 3rd (Forrest's) Cav. Co.A
Reve, B.M. TN 9th Cav. Co.A
Reveace, William NC McMillan's Co.
Reveer, Isaac P. VA Mtd.Res. Rappahannock Dist. Sale's Co.
Reveer, James VA 92nd Mil. Co.A Fifer
Reveere, John AL 1st Bn.Cadets Co.B
Reveil, David GA Lt.Arty. (Jo Thompson Arty.) Hanleiter's Co.
Reveill, David KY 9th Cav. Co.B
Revel, A. AL 60th Inf. Co.C
Revel, Alfred AL 3rd Bn. Hilliard's Legion Vol. Co.D
Revel, B.M. TN 47th Inf. Co.F
Revel, Charles GA 59th Inf. Co.C
Revel, Duke AR 37th Inf. Co.C Sgt.
Revel, E. TN Inf. 3rd Cons.Regt. Co.G
Revel, E.H. NC 34th Inf. Co.H
Revel, George H. VA 41st Inf. Co.H
Revel, George W. SC 21st Inf. Co.K
Revel, George W. VA 5th Inf. Co.F
Revel, G.W. MO 10th Cav.
Revel, G.W. SC Inf. 9th Bn. Co.F
Revel, Haywood AL 57th Inf. Co.D
Revel, H.B. NC 34th Inf. Co.H
Revel, Henry MS 13th Inf. Co.K
Revel, Henry Denton MO 8th Inf. Co.C Sgt.
Revel, H.S. GA 3rd Res. Co.E
Revel, J.A. SC 1st (Hagood's) Inf. 2nd Co.B
Revel, James MS 15th Bn.S.S. Co.A
Revel, James G. NC 1st Arty. (10th St.Troops) Co.A
Revel, James H. NC 1st Cav. (9th St.Troops) Co.K
Revel, James K. MO 8th Cav. Co.A
Revel, J.H. MS 41st Inf. Co.C
Revel, Joe TN 4th Inf. Co.C Cpl.
Revel, John VA Hvy.Arty. 20th Bn. Co.B

Revel, John W. NC 38th Inf. Co.I
Revel, J.W. TN Cav. Jackson's Regt.
Revel, J.W. NC 56th Inf. Co.F
Revel, J.W. SC 20th Inf. Co.C
Revel, M.J. VA Arty. C.F. Johnston's Co.
Revel, Parker VA 41st Inf. Co.H Sgt.
Revel, R.H. NC 34th Inf. Co.H
Revel, Robert R. NC 34th Inf. Co.H Sgt.
Revel, R.W. GA 46th Inf. Co.D
Revel, Samuel AL 1st Cav. C.H. Colvin's Co.I
Revel, Sanders GA 31st Inf. Co.G Cpl.
Revel, Shepard Wm. AL 22nd Inf. Co.I
Revel, Stephen Hamilton AL 22nd Inf. Co.I
Revel, Thomas TN 38th Inf. Co.D
Revel, Thomas J. MO 8th Cav. Co.A
Revel, William VA 41st Inf. Co.H
Revel, William H. VA 41st Inf. Co.H
Reveld, D.W. GA 5th Res. Co.H
Reveley, --- VA Arty.Detach. VMI
Reveley, George O. VA Hvy.Arty. 20th Bn. Co.A
Reveley, J.P. TN 6th Inf. Co.C
Reveley, W.W. Gen. & Staff 1st Lt.,AADC
Revelin, Francis TN 9th Inf. Co.B
Revell, A.M. TN 7th (Duckworth's) Cav. Co.F
Revell, Benjamin MO 8th Cav. Co.A
Revell, B.T. NC 1st Jr.Res. Co.K Sgt.
Revell, Elijah A. FL 3rd Inf. Co.D Music.
Revell, George A. VA 9th Inf. Co.G
Revell, George W. SC 1st Arty. Co.E
Revell, G.W. SC 26th Inf. Co.G Sgt.
Revell, H.N. TN 7th (Duckworth's) Cav. Co.F
Revell, James GA 59th Inf. Co.C
Revell, James A. FL 3rd Inf. Co.D
Revell, J.C. SC Cav.Bn. Holcombe Legion Co.A
Revell, J.N. FL Cav. 5th Bn. Co.D
Revell, John W. MS 18th Inf. Co.A
Revell, Joseph MO 8th Cav. Co.A
Revell, J.R. SC Arty. Zimmerman's Co. (Pee Dee Arty.)
Revell, Leopold LA C.S. Zouave Bn. Co.B
Revell, M.G. VA 18th Inf. Co.H
Revell, M.H. SC 1st Cav. Co.C
Revell, Noah MO 8th Cav. Co.G,B
Revell, Randall VA 9th Inf. Co.G
Revell, Samuel E. MO Cav. 3rd Bn. Co.F
Revell, Samuel K. FL 3rd Inf. Co.D Cpl.
Revell, S. Calvin FL 5th Inf. Co.I
Revell, S.E. MO 3rd Cav. Co.F
Revell, Stephen J. FL 3rd Inf. Co.K
Revell, Sydney E. FL 5th Inf. Co.I
Revell, W.H. GA 2nd Res. Co.H
Revell, William MO 5th Inf. Co.F
Revell, William J. VA 3rd Inf. Co.H
Revell, W.M. SC 26th Inf. Co.G
Revelle, Able W. GA 21st Inf. Co.H
Revelle, James M. GA 21st Inf. Co.H Sgt.
Revelle, T.B. TX 9th Cav. Co.B Cpl.
Revellion, J.J. LA Inf.Cons. 18th Regt. & Yellow Jacket Bn. Co.E
Revells, Alfred FL 5th Inf. Co.E
Revells, Andrew H. NC 52nd Inf. Co.B
Revells, James AL 16th Inf. Co.K
Revells, Riley FL 5th Inf. Co.E
Revels, B.F. TN 19th (Biffle's) Cav. Co.K
Revels, David SC 23rd Inf. Co.A Cook
Revels, E. TN 31st Inf. Co.E

Revels, Eli NC 51st Inf. Co.F
Revels, George M. SC 6th Inf. 1st Co.F, 2nd Co.I
Revels, George W. FL 6th Inf. Co.F,E
Revels, G.W. SC 3rd Bn.Res. Co.E
Revels, G.W. SC 5th St.Troops Co.A
Revels, G.W. SC 6th Res. Co.B
Revels, Henry FL 10th Inf. Co.B
Revels, Henry NC 51st Inf. Co.F
Revels, Henry A. FL 5th Inf. Co.F
Revels, Henson NC Hvy.Arty. 1st Bn. Co.A
Revels, H.M. AL 12th Inf. Co.D
Revels, James SC Hvy.Arty. 15th (Lucas') Bn. Co.A
Revels, Jeremiah H. FL Parson's Co.
Revels, John FL 2nd Inf. Co.G Sgt.
Revels, John GA 5th Res. Co.G
Revels, John B. FL 7th Inf. Co.A
Revels, John J. SC 18th Inf. Co.G
Revels, Jonathan NC 51st Inf. Co.F
Revels, Jonathan NC McDugald's Co.
Revels, J.T. NC 57th Inf. Co.K
Revels, M. TN 40th Inf. Co.C
Revels, M. TN 42nd Inf. 2nd Co.E
Revels, Owen FL 4th Inf. Co.C
Revels, Owen J. FL 10th Inf. Co.A
Revels, Randol FL Sp.Cav. 1st Bn. Co.B
Revels, Stephen AL 3rd Bn. Hilliard's Legion Vol. Co.E
Revels, Stephen SC 18th Inf. Co.G
Revels, Stephen J. FL 6th Inf. Co.A
Revels, Steven FL 10th Inf. Davidson's Co.
Revels, Thomas SC 23rd Inf. Co.F
Revels, William E. FL 2nd Cav. Co.B
Revels, William E. FL 10th Inf. Co.A
Revels, William R. FL Inf. 2nd Bn. Co.B
Revels, William R. FL 10th Inf. Co.G
Revels, Willis SC Cav. 12th Bn. Co.C
Revels, W.J. TN 31st Inf. Co.E
Revely, James M. TN 39th Mtd.Inf. Co.H
Revely, Joseph P. TN 21st (Wilson's) Cav. Co.E 1st Lt.
Revely, T.H. TX 5th Inf. Co.A
Revely, Thomas C. SC Arty. Fickling's Co. (Brooks Lt.Arty.)
Revely, W.J. TN Inf. 22nd Bn. Co.C 1st Sgt.
Revely, W.W. SC Hvy.Arty. 15th (Lucas') Bn. Co.C 1st Lt.
Revely, W.W. SC Arty. Childs' Co. Lt.
Reven, Henry P. Conf.Hvy.Arty. Montague's Bn. Co.A
Revena, John KY 5th Mtd.Inf. Co.A
Rever, A.K. TX Inf. 2nd St.Troops Co.H
Revera, M. LA 3rd Inf. Co.G
Revercomb, Henry VA Lt.Arty. Thompson's Co.
Revercomb, John VA 13th Inf. 1st Co.B Sgt.
Revercomb, John C. VA 52nd Inf. Co.D 1st Sgt.
Revercomb, William C. VA 97th Mil. Co.F
Revere, Charles VA 34th Inf.
Revere, E.H. VA Lt.Arty. Woolfolk's Co. Cpl.
Revere, Elias H. VA Arty. Fleet's Co. Cpl.
Revere, Elias H. VA 55th Inf. Co.B
Revere, Francis AL Vol. Rabby's Coast Guard Co. No.1
Revere, G. VA Inf. 4th Bn.Loc.Def. Co.E
Revere, Joel VA 55th Inf. Co.I

Revere, Joel VA 109th Mil. Co.B
Revere, John AL Lt.Arty. 2nd Bn. Co.A
Revere, John M. VA 55th Inf. Co.H Sgt.
Revere, J.W. AL 1st Regt. Mobile Vol. Baas' Co.
Revere, Nicholas J. VA 55th Inf. Co.C
Revere, Peter VA 9th Mil. Co.B
Revere, Robert V. VA 55th Inf. Co.H
Revere, Samuel F. GA Arty. 11th Bn. (Sumter Arty.) New Co.C
Revere, Samuel F. GA 9th Inf. Co.A
Revere, T.B. LA Miles' Legion Co.E
Revere, Thomas S. VA 9th Mil. Co.B
Revere, W.H. VA Inf. 6th Bn.Loc.Def. Co.A
Revere, William A. GA Siege Arty. 28th Bn. Co.D
Revere, William M. VA 55th Inf. Co.H
Revere, Wyatt H. VA 2nd Inf.Loc.Def. Co.D
Revernbill, John VA 3rd Cav. Co.H
Reves, A.J. AL 8th Inf. Co.H
Reves, Andrew M. NC McMillan's Co. 3rd Lt.
Reves, Cicero NC McMillan's Co.
Reves, Enoch C. VA 45th Inf. Co.C
Reves, F.M. MO Inf. Clark's Regt. Co.D
Reves, Frederick GA 7th Inf. (St.Guards) Co.D
Reves, George M. TX 19th Inf. Co.I Sgt.Maj.
Reves, Giles NC Cav. 5th Bn. Co.D
Reves, G.W. AR 15th (N.W.) Inf. Co.I
Reves, Henry T. MO 15th Cav. Co.A
Reves, Horton S. NC 22nd Inf. Co.K 2nd Lt.
Reves, H.R. TN 3rd (Lillard's) Mtd.Inf. Co.K
Reves, I.N. MO Inf. Clark's Regt. Co.D
Reves, J. GA Hvy.Arty. 22nd Bn. Co.A
Reves, J.A. AL 50th Inf. Co.C
Reves, James T. MS 34th Inf. Co.C
Reves, Jesse F. NC 22nd Inf. Co.F Capt.
Reves, J.H. AL 8th Inf. Co.B
Reves, J.H. MO Inf. Clark's Regt. Co.D
Reves, John SC 20th Inf. Co.A
Reves, John C. AL 11th Inf. Co.A
Reves, John C. NC 22nd Inf. Co.F Sgt.
Reves, John M. MS 2nd (Quinn's St.Troops) Inf. Co.G
Reves, J.S. NC 5th Sr.Res. Co.H
Reves, Preston B. NC 22nd Inf. Co.F Capt.
Reves, Timothy AR Cav. Reves' Co. Capt.
Reves, Timothy MO 15th Cav. Co.A Capt.
Reves, Wesley MO 15th Cav. Co.A
Reves, W.H. TN 2nd Cav. Co.A
Reves, William KY 13th Cav. Co.K
Reves, William B. LA 25th Inf. Co.I
Reves, W.W. AL 7th Cav. Co.A
Revett, C. LA 20th Inf. New Co.E
Revett, F. Conf.Lt.Arty. 1st Reg.Btty.
Revett, John B. LA 18th Inf.
Revett, Joseph 4th Conf.Eng.Troops Co.K Sgt.
Revett, L. Conf.Lt.Arty. 1st Reg.Btty.
Revette, Thomas TN 13th Inf. Co.A
Revette, Transmire LA 13th Inf. Co.A
Revial, David M. KY 4th Mtd.Inf.
Revice, Calvin NC 1st Bn.Jr.Res. Co.E
Reviel, H.J. MO Inf. 4th Regt.St.Guard Co.E
Revier, Andrew G. GA Lt.Arty. Scogin's Btty. (Griffin Lt.Arty.)
Revier, J. AL 1st Regt. Mobile Vol. Co.K
Revier, J.G. GA Inf. 9th Bn. Co.E

Revier, J.M. TN 6th (Wheeler's) Cav. Co.A Sgt.
Revier, J.M. TX 32nd Cav. Co.I
Revier, John F. TN 1st Cav.
Revier, John H. TN Cav. 2nd Bn. (Biffle's) 3rd Lt.
Revier, John K. GA 22nd Inf. Co.F
Reviere, E. GA 2nd Inf.
Reviere, Erasmus GA 2nd Cav. Co.G
Reviere, George GA 61st Inf. Co.G
Reviere, George H. VA 30th Inf. Music.
Reviere, James F. GA Lt.Arty. Scogin's Btty. (Griffin Lt.Arty.)
Reviere, J.K. TX 14th Inf. Co.F
Reviere, J.L. TX 14th Inf. Co.F
Reviere, John W. AL Mil. 2nd Regt.Vol. Co.F
Reviere, Lawson VA Hvy.Arty. 20th Bn. Co.E
Reviere, R.A. LA Miles' Legion Co.E
Reviere, Talionis L. FL Cav. (Marianna Drag.) Smith's Co.
Reviere, Thomas R. GA Lt.Arty. Scogin's Btty. (Griffin Lt.Arty.)
Revierre, A. LA Miles' Legion Co.F,C
Revil, Gabet LA Mil. 4th Regt. French Brig. Co.4 Sr.2nd Lt.
Revil, Joseph 3rd Conf.Eng.Troops Co.C Artif.
Revill, D.L. KY 4th Cav. Co.G Capt.
Revill, D.L. KY 2nd Mtd.Inf. Co.E
Revill, D.S. AL 33rd Inf. Co.A
Revill, Floyd H. GA 26th Inf. 1st Co.G
Revill, Floyd H. GA 29th Inf. Co.E
Revill, G.W. SC Lt.Arty. 3rd (Palmetto) Bn. Co.E
Revill, Henry NC 31st Inf. Co.A
Revill, Henry M. AL 33rd Inf. Co.A,C Cpl.
Revill, H.M. AL 12th Inf. Co.D
Revill, James H. GA 1st (Ramsey's) Inf. Co.D
Revill, J.E. KY 4th Cav. Co.G 2nd Lt.
Revill, J.H. GA 1st (Ramsey's) Inf. Co.D
Revill, Joseph C. KY 4th Cav. Co.G 2nd Lt.
Revill, J.R. FL 2nd Cav. Co.G Cpl.
Revill, M.L. AL 33rd Inf. Co.A
Revill, Moses G. VA 9th Inf. Co.D
Revill, Richard R. TN 5th Inf. Co.I
Revill, S.E. KY 1st (Butler's) Cav.
Revill, W.A. AL 33rd Inf. Co.A
Revill, Warren M. LA 9th Inf. Co.F
Revill, William A. AL 18th Inf. Co.A
Reville, Charles MS Inf. 1st St.Troops Co.G
Reville, D.W. GA 12th Inf.
Reville, Ed. LA Mil. 1st Regt. 2nd Brig. 1st Div.
Reville, J.C. SC 7th Cav. Co.I
Revilleod, Joseph LA Mil. 2nd Regt. French Brig. Co.5
Revillion, J.J. LA 18th Inf. Co.D
Revills, John NC 21st Inf. Co.H Drum.
Revills, William C. NC 21st Inf. Co.H Fifer
Revils, Jeremiah F. FL 9th Inf. Co.C Music.
Revils, Levin NC 42nd Inf. Co.B
Revils, Levin NC 61st Inf. Co.H
Revis, A.B. TX Cav. Martin's Regt. Co.F
Revis, Andrew H. NC 52nd Inf. Co.F
Revis, Andrew W. TX Cav. Martin's Regt. Co.F
Revis, A.W. NC 64th Inf. Co.B
Revis, Benjamin TN Inf. 23rd Bn. Co.C
Revis, Daniel NC 6th Inf. Co.I
Revis, Daniel TN 11th (Holman's) Cav. Co.C

Revis, D.J. TN Inf. Spencer's Co.
Revis, D.W. NC 64th Inf. Co.B
Revis, Edward AR 34th Inf. Co.E
Revis, Edward B. TX 35th (Likens') Cav. Co.A
Revis, Henry W. NC 64th Inf. Co.D
Revis, James NC 64th Inf. Co.B
Revis, James TN 8th Cav. Co.D 1st Lt.
Revis, James A. NC 64th Inf. Co.D
Revis, James J. MO 4th Cav. Co.I
Revis, James W. TN 16th Inf. Co.K 2nd Lt.
Revis, J.E. 1st Conf.Cav. 1st Co.B Cpl.
Revis, Jeremiah SC 20th Inf. Co.A
Revis, J.J. TN Inf. 23rd Bn. Co.C
Revis, J.N. TN 36th Inf. Co.A
Revis, John AR 34th Inf. Co.F
Revis, John NC 4th Inf. Co.C
Revis, John NC 64th Inf. Co.B
Revis, John TN 13th (Gore's) Cav. Co.D
Revis, John A. TN 34th Inf. 2nd Co.C
Revis, John C. TN 16th Inf. Co.K
Revis, John E. NC 4th Inf. Co.G
Revis, John P. GA Cherokee Legion (St.Guards) Co.B Sgt.
Revis, John W. NC 4th Inf. Co.H
Revis, Joseph W. NC 5th Sr.Res. Co.K
Revis, J.P. GA 36th (Broyles') Inf. Co.E
Revis, J.W. TN 13th (Gore's) Cav. Co.D 1st Lt.
Revis, N. MO Cav. Snider's Bn.
Revis, P.W. NC 62nd Inf. Co.K Sgt.
Revis, R.A. TN 19th & 20th (Cons.) Cav. Co.H
Revis, Robert W. NC 64th Inf. Co.D
Revis, Samuel NC 18th Inf. Co.F
Revis, Samuel H. MO 2nd Inf. Co.E
Revis, T.D. NC 64th Inf. Co.B
Revis, T.H. NC 60th Inf. Co.I
Revis, Thomas E. GA 20th Inf. Co.F
Revis, Thomas F. NC 29th Inf. Co.H
Revis, Thomas J.P. GA 42nd Inf. Co.C
Revis, William AR 33rd Inf. Co.D
Revis, William NC 4th Inf. Co.H
Revis, William TN 16th Inf. Co.K
Revis, William S. NC 6th Inf. Co.B
Revis, William T. TX 13th Cav. Co.A
Revis, Wilson O. TX 13th Cav. Co.A
Revis, W.M. TN 13th (Gore's) Cav. Co.D
Revison, S.T. TN 28th (Cons.) Inf.
Revit, John MS 18th Cav. Wimberly's Co.A
Revitte, Transmire LA 3rd Inf. Co.A
Revoe, John AL City Troop (Mobile) Arrington's Co.A
Revoil, Arthur LA Mil. 1st Native Guards Sgt.Maj.
Revoile, Alphonse LA 10th Inf. Co.G Sr.2nd Lt.
Revol, --- LA Mil. 1st Regt. French Brig. Co.3
Revol, C. LA Mil. 4th Regt. French Brig. Co.1
Revuts, Charles L. NC 42nd Inf. Co.A
Rew, Edward Young MS Inf. (Res.) Berry's Co.
Rew, E.J. MS 5th Inf. (St.Troops) Co.C
Rew, George E. VA 46th Inf. 4th Co.F
Rew, James H. TX 9th (Nichols') Inf. Co.B Cpl.
Rew, J.M. NC 35th Inf. Co.H
Rew, R.Y. AL 23rd Inf. Co.I Capt.
Rew, Washington W. VA Lt.Arty. Thompson's Co.
Rew, Washington W. VA 61st Inf. Co.H 2nd Lt.
Rew, William B. AL 3rd Res. Co.I
Rewarde, G. LA Washington Arty.Bn. Co.5

Rewden, George W. TN 19th (Biffle's) Cav. Co.A

Rewden, William TN 19th (Biffle's) Cav. Co.A

Rewels, James VA 79th Mil. Co.2

Rewgvist, Charles Conf.Inf. 8th Bn.

Rewis, A.J. FL 9th Inf. Co.E,H Music.

Rewis, Andrew FL 3rd Inf. Co.I Music.

Rewis, General E. GA 61st Inf. Co.B

Rewis, James GA 61st Inf. Co.B

Rewis, James J. GA 61st Inf. Co.B Music.

Rewis, James M. GA 61st Inf. Co.B

Rewis, James M. GA 61st Inf. Co.H

Rewis, John GA 50th Inf. Co.C

Rewis, John GA 50th Inf. Co.G

Rewis, Noah GA 4th Inf. Co.E

Rewis, Obediah FL 3rd Inf. Co.I

Rewis, Randal FL 9th Inf. Co.E,H Music.

Rewis, Robert R. GA 61st Inf. Co.B

Rewke, W. LA Mil. 4th Regt. 1st Brig. 1st Div. Co.K

Rex, C.M. VA Lt.Arty. 38th Bn. Co.B

Rex, E.A. MO 11th Inf. Co.B

Rex, Ely H. VA 31st Inf. Co.A

Rex, George MS 16th Inf. Co.D

Rex, George W. NC 37th Inf. Co.F

Rex, Henry J. AL 13th Inf. Co.F

Rex, Jacob W. VA 1st Arty. Co.I,H Jr.1st Lt.

Rex, John TN 4th (Murray's) Cav. Co.H

Rex, John TN 28th (Cons.) Inf. Co.E

Rex, John TN 84th Inf. Co.A

Rex, John VA 31st Inf. Co.A

Rex, John S. VA 20th Cav. Co.B

Rex, William AR 27th Inf. Co.G

Rex, William NC 4th Sr.Res. Co.B

Rexell, J. VA 8th Cav. Co.G

Rexford, R.H. TX Cav. Waller's Regt. Co.D

Rexroad, Aaron VA 25th Inf. 1st Co.E, 2nd Co.E

Rexroad, Addison VA 25th Inf. 2nd Co.K

Rexroad, Addison VA 62nd Mtd.Inf. 2nd Co.K

Rexroad, A.J. VA 46th Inf. 2nd Co.D

Rexroad, Ammi VA 62nd Mtd.Inf. 2nd Co.K

Rexroad, Augustus VA 46th Mil. Co.C

Rexroad, Esau VA 8th Cav. Co.G

Rexroad, George J. VA 25th Inf. 2nd Co.K

Rexroad, George J. VA 62nd Mtd.Inf. 2nd Co.K

Rexroad, George M. of Geo. VA 62nd Mtd.Inf. 2nd Co.K

Rexroad, George M. of H. VA 62nd Mtd.Inf. 2nd Co.K

Rexroad, Harvey VA 8th Cav. Co.G

Rexroad, Isaac VA 8th Cav. Co.G

Rexroad, Israel VA 8th Cav. Co.G

Rexroad, Jacob VA 25th Inf. 1st Co.E, 2nd Co.E

Rexroad, Jacob VA 25th Inf. 2nd Co.K

Rexroad, J.M. VA 10th Bn.Res. Co.D

Rexroad, Joseph VA 10th Bn.Res. Co.D

Rexroad, Laban VA 25th Inf. 2nd Co.K

Rexroad, M. VA 10th Bn.Res. Co.D

Rexroad, Nariel VA 25th Inf. 2nd Co.K Cpl.

Rexroad, N.N. VA 19th Inf. Co.I

Rexroad, Samuel VA 46th Mil. Co.C Cpl.

Rexroad, Solomon VA 25th Inf. 2nd Co.K

Rexroad, Solomon VA 46th Mil. Co.C,B

Rexroad, William VA 46th Mil. Co.C

Rexroad, William VA 62nd Mtd.Inf. 2nd Co.K

Rexroade, Andrew VA 31st Inf. Co.B

Rexroads, William H. VA 17th Cav. Co.H Cpl.

Rexrode, Andrew VA 162nd Mil. Co.C

Rexrode, Augustus VA 25th Inf. 2nd Co.E

Rexrode, Daniel H. VA 31st Inf. Co.E

Rexrode, Daniel H. VA 162nd Mil. Co.B

Rexrode, George A. VA 31st Inf. Co.E

Rexrode, Henry VA 25th Inf. 2nd Co.E

Rexrode, Henry A. VA 162nd Mil. Co.B

Rexrode, Hezekiah VA 14th Mil. Co.C

Rexrode, Joseph VA 162nd Mil. Co.A

Rexrode, Michael VA 162nd Mil. Co.A

Rexrode, Solomon J. VA 31st Inf. Co.E

Rexrode, Sylvester W. VA 31st Inf. Co.E

Rexrode, Sylvester W. VA 162nd Mil. Co.B

Rexrode, William J. VA 31st Inf. Co.E

Rexrode, William J. VA 162nd Mil. Co.B

Rexrodes, Peter MO St.Guard

Rey, Alexander VA 42nd Inf. Co.F

Rey, Armand LA Mil. 1st Native Guards Drum.

Rey, C.A. AL Conscr.

Rey, D.H. Gen. & Staff,PACS 2nd Lt.

Rey, E.G. GA 17th Inf.

Rey, Hippolyte LA Mil. 1st Native Guards Cpl.

Rey, H. Louis LA Mil. 1st Native Guards Capt.

Rey, J.A. GA 39th Inf. Co.B 1st Lt.

Rey, Jacob LA 8th Inf. Co.B

Rey, James M. GA 19th Inf. Co.D

Rey, James M. VA Hvy.Arty. 19th Bn. Co.A Drum.

Rey, Jean LA Mil. 3rd Regt. French Brig. (Garde Francaise) Frois Co.

Rey, J.L. VA 2nd St.Res. Co.G

Rey, Joseph LA Mil. 1st Native Guards Cpl.

Rey, J.S. GA 30th Inf. Co.B

Rey, J.T. AR 36th Inf. 2nd Lt.

Rey, Leon LA Mil. 1st Native Guards

Rey, Octave LA Mil. 1st Native Guards 2nd Lt.

Rey, P. LA 14th Inf. Co.F

Rey, P.C. LA Mil. French Co. of St.James

Rey, Thomas W. VA Horse Arty. E. Graham's Co.

Rey, T.J. TN Douglass' Bn.Part.Rangers Lytle's Co.

Rey, William AL 53rd (Part.Rangers) Co.K

Rey, William TN Inf. 1st Cons.Regt. Co.K

Rey, William T. VA Lt.Arty. 38th Bn. Co.C

Rey, William T. VA Lt.Arty. E.J. Anderson's Co.

Rey, W.N. TX Cav. Baird's Regt. Co.B

Rey, W.S. AL St.Guards

Rey, Xavier LA Mil. 2nd Regt. French Brig. Co.7

Reyal, Eugene S. AL 8th Inf. Co.A

Reyals, A. AL 6th Cav. Co.A

Reyanlds, W.F. TX 16th Cav. Capt.

Reyborne, Charles 2nd Conf.Eng.Troops Co.D Artif.

Reybourd, H. TX Inf. 1st St.Troops Biehler's Co.

Reybourn, J. AR 38th Inf. Co.B

Reyburn, A.J. MO 12th Inf. Co.C

Reyburn, B. LA 26th Inf. Co.H

Reyburn, G.W. AL 38th Inf. Co.B

Reyburn, Jesse AR 18th (Marmaduke's) Inf. Co.C

Reyburn, J.W. AR Cav. Anderson's Unatt.Bn. Co.C 1st Lt.

Reyburn, M.R. VA 21st Cav. Co.K Sgt.

Reyburn, Thomas MO 12th Cav. Co.E,H Sgt.

Reyburn, William AR 7th Cav. Co.D

Reyburn, William J. VA 37th Inf. Co.H

Reyburn, W.W. AR Mil. Borland's Regt. Woodruff's Co. Ord.Sgt.

Reye, J.M. MS Wilson's Co. (Ponticola Guards)

Reye, W.H. TN 12th (Cons.) Inf. Co.G

Reyels, Jac SC Mil.Arty. 1st Regt. Werner's Co. Cpl.

Reyer, C.C. AL 11th Cav. Co.D

Reyer, John LA 14th Inf. Co.G

Reyes, F. LA Mil. 1st Native Guards 2nd Lt.

Reyes, Francisco TX 8th Inf. Co.C

Reyes, Francisco TX Cav. Benavides' Regt. Co.C

Reyes, Juan LA Mil. 5th Regt.Eur.Brig. (Spanish Regt.) Co.4

Reyes, Juan TX St.Troops Teel's Co.

Reyes, Lewis TX Trevino's Squad. Part. Mtd.Vol.

Reyes, Manuel (1) TX 8th Field Btty.

Reyes, Mig'l. LA Mil. 5th Regt.Eur.Brig. (Spanish Regt.) Co.8

Reyes, Peter TX 2nd Cav. Co.I

Reyes, Prehendre TX Cav. Hardeman's Regt. Co.F

Reyes, Prejedes TX Cav. Ragsdale's Bn. 1st Co.A

Reyes, Refugio TX Cav. Benavides' Regt. Co.C

Reyes, Refugio TX 8th Inf. Co.C

Reyes, S. LA Inf.Cons.Crescent Regt. Co.K

Reyes, Thomas C. GA 1st (Olmstead's) Inf. Co.K Cpl.

Reyes, Victor (2) TX 8th Field Btty.

Reyff, J. LA Mil. 3rd Regt.Eur.Brig. (Garde Francaise) Co.7

Reygan, George W. MS 30th Inf. Co.F

Reyland, G.L. AL Talladega Cty.Res. Cunningham's Co.

Reyle, M.A. NC 68th Inf. Co.D Sgt.

Reymeyer, Chs. LA Mil. 3rd Regt. 1st Brig. 1st Div. Co.G

Reymon, George E. VA 41st Inf. Co.C

Reymy, Henry AR 9th Inf. Co.H 3rd Lt.

Reynaldos, Enrique LA Mil. 5th Regt.Eur.Brig. (Spanish Regt.) Co.3

Reynaldos, Jose LA Mil. 5th Regt.Eur.Brig. (Spanish Regt.) Co.3

Reynalds, L.S. AR Mil. 1st Bn.

Reynalds, Stephen M. AR 1st (Dobbin's) Cav. Co.B

Reynalds, Thomas VA Cav. 36th Bn. Co.C

Reynand, Thomas LA 4th Cav. Co.A

Reynard, George H. VA 10th Inf. 1st Co.C, Co.F

Reynard, Joseph H. VA 33rd Inf. Co.C

Reynaud, A.G. AR 2nd Cav. Co.D

Reynaud, A.G. Gen. & Staff ACS

Reynaud, Augustus KY 9th Mtd.Inf. Co.H

Reynaud, L.F. LA Cav. 2nd Bn. (St.Guards) Adj.

Reynaud, L.F. LA 4th Inf. Co.F

Reynaud, L.F. LA Asst.Supt.A.Recon. Capt.

Reynaud, Lucien LA Mil. 6th Regt.Eur.Brig. (Italian Guards Bn.) Co.5 Cpl.

Reynaud, Songy LA 7th Inf. Co.F 2nd Lt.

Reynaux, Andre LA 18th Inf. Co.G
Reynds, J.F. MS 1st Cav.Res. Co.H
Reynes, Charles E. LA 22nd Inf. 1st Lt.
Reynes, E.H. GA Inf. 1st Loc.Troops (Augusta) Co.B
Reynes, E.H. LA Lt.Arty. LeGardeur, Jr.'s Co. (Orleans Guard Btty.) 1st Sgt.
Reynes, J.H. GA 5th Res.
Reyney, J.F. TN 48th (Voorhies') Inf. Co.G Cpl.
Reynhardt, Henry MS 48th Inf. Co.E Capt.
Reynold, Ely AL 62nd Inf. Co.H
Reynold, George AR Lt.Arty. Wiggins' Btty.
Reynold, John C. GA 18th Inf. Co.F 1st Lt.
Reynold, J.T. AR 2nd Cav. Co.E
Reynold, Marion AL 42nd Inf. Co.I
Reynold, W. GA 5th Res. Co.H
Reynold, W.W. TN Cav. J.J. Parton's Co.
Reynolds, --- TX Cav. Border's Regt. Co.K
Reynolds, --- TX Cav. Good's Bn. Co.C
Reynolds, --- TX Cav. Good's Bn. Co.E
Reynolds, A. GA 7th Inf. (St.Guards) Co.G
Reynolds, A. GA Inf. 27th Bn.
Reynolds, A.A. GA 11th Cav. Co.K
Reynolds, A.A. TN 45th Inf. Co.G
Reynolds, A.A. VA 22nd Inf. Co.I
Reynolds, A.B. TX 11th Inf. Co.A Sgt.
Reynolds, Abner M. GA 16th Inf. Co.B Capt.
Reynolds, Absolom 1st Chickasaw Inf. White's Co. 1st Sgt.
Reynolds, A.C. TX 9th (Young's) Inf. Co.D Sgt.
Reynolds, A.C. TX 12th Inf. Co.C
Reynolds, A.C. VA 28th Inf. Co.B
Reynolds, A.C. Gen. & Staff, Ord.Dept. Ord.Sgt.
Reynolds, A.C. Sig.Corps,CSA
Reynolds, A.D. VA 5th Bn.Res. Co.I Maj.
Reynolds, A.D. Gen. & Staff ACS
Reynolds, Addison VA 47th Inf. Co.B
Reynolds, A.F. GA 28th Inf. Co.B
Reynolds, A.H. AR 19th (Dockery's) Inf. Co.F
Reynolds, A.H. VA 42nd Inf. Co.H
Reynolds, A.J. AL 8th Cav. Co.G
Reynolds, A.J. AL 14th Inf. Co.G Cpl.
Reynolds, A.J. AR 37th Inf. Co.D
Reynolds, A.J. KY Cav. 2nd Bn. (Dortch's) Co.C Sgt.
Reynolds, A.J. KY 10th (Johnson's) Cav. Co.A 1st Sgt.
Reynolds, A.J. KY Moran's Men Co.G 1st Sgt.
Reynolds, A.J. MS Inf. 3rd Bn. (St.Troops) Co.C
Reynolds, A.J. MS 40th Inf. Co.K
Reynolds, A.J. TN Lt.Arty. Rice's Btty.
Reynolds, A.J. TN 4th Inf. Co.E
Reynolds, A.J. TN 35th Inf. Co.G, 2nd Co.D
Reynolds, A.J. TX 7th Cav. Co.F
Reynolds, A.J. TX 7th Field Btty.
Reynolds, A.J. VA 22nd Inf. Co.C Music.
Reynolds, A.J. Wheeler's Scouts,CSA
Reynolds, A.L. AL 6th Cav. Co.C,B
Reynolds, A.L. TN 6th (Wheeler's) Cav. Co.D 2nd Lt.
Reynolds, Albert D. VA 9th Cav. Co.D
Reynolds, Alec MS 36th Inf. Co.F,E

Reynolds, Alexander AR 1st (Crawford's) Cav. Co.B
Reynolds, Alexander GA 12th Cav. Co.D
Reynolds, Alexander GA Inf. 2nd Bn. Co.C Cpl.
Reynolds, Alexander NC 2nd Arty. (36th St.Troops) Co.E
Reynolds, Alexander NC 20th Inf. Co.C
Reynolds, Alexander VA 42nd Inf. Co.A
Reynolds, Alexander SC 2nd Inf. Co.F
Reynolds, Alexandrew SC 24th Inf. Co.K
Reynolds, Alex W. VA 50th Inf. Col.
Reynolds, Alex W. Gen. & Staff Brig.Gen.
Reynolds, Alfred MS 5th Cav. Co.A
Reynolds, Alfred MS 3rd Inf. (St.Troops) Co.H
Reynolds, Alfred 1st Chickasaw Inf. Gregg's Co. Sgt.
Reynolds, Alfred H. AL 21st Inf. Co.K
Reynolds, Alfred R. NC 2nd Arty. (36th St.Troops) Co.G
Reynolds, Allen MS 34th Inf. Co.H
Reynolds, Alonzo AL 8th Inf. Co.K
Reynolds, Alonzo L. TN Cav. 11th Bn. (Gordon's) Co.F Music.
Reynolds, Alpheus GA Cobb's Legion Co.F
Reynolds, Anderson 2nd Cherokee Mtd.Vol. Co.F
Reynolds, Anderson J. GA 27th Inf. Co.D
Reynolds, Andrew MO St.Guard
Reynolds, Andrew Chapman MS Inf. 1st St.Troops Co.G
Reynolds, Andrew J. AL 36th Inf. Co.I
Reynolds, Andrew J. GA 11th Inf. Co.B
Reynolds, Andrew J. GA 14th Inf. Co.D
Reynolds, Andrew J. LA 31st Inf. Co.E
Reynolds, Andrew J. MS 11th (Perrin's) Cav. Co.E
Reynolds, Andrew J. NC 61st Inf. Co.E
Reynolds, Andrew J. VA 37th Inf. Co.G
Reynolds, Andrew J. VA 189th Mil. Co.C
Reynolds, A.P. GA Inf. (Newton Factory Employees) Russell's Co.
Reynolds, A.P. MO 6th Cav. Co.B
Reynolds, Aplin H. GA 43rd Inf. Co.H
Reynolds, A. Pope SC 19th Inf. Co.F
Reynolds, A.R. GA 13th Cav. Co.I Sgt.
Reynolds, A.R. GA 3rd Res. Co.I
Reynolds, Arch A. VA 157th Mil. Co.A
Reynolds, Archer VA 44th Inf. Co.A
Reynolds, Archer L. VA Hvy.Arty. 20th Bn. Co.A
Reynolds, Archibald A. VA 30th Bn.S.S. Co.A
Reynolds, Archilaus P. VA 36th Inf. 2nd Co.E
Reynolds, Arthur E. MS 26th Inf. Col.
Reynolds, Arthur M. MS 2nd Inf. Co.A
Reynolds, Arthur M. MS 26th Inf. Co.D Cpl.
Reynolds, A.S. MD Arty. 2nd Btty.
Reynolds, A.S. VA Arty. Wise Legion
Reynolds, Asa B. VA 54th Inf. Co.D
Reynolds, A.W. GA 54th Inf. Co.D
Reynolds, B.A. Eng.,CSA 1st Lt.
Reynolds, Barnard H. VA 16th Cav. Co.A 2nd Lt.
Reynolds, Barnard H. VA Cav. Ferguson's Bn. Stevenson's Co. 2nd Lt.
Reynolds, Barton T. VA 57th Inf. Co.E
Reynolds, B.C. AL Cav. Moreland's Regt. Co.A

Reynolds, B.C. AR 11th Inf. Co.A
Reynolds, B.C. GA 3rd Cav. Co.H
Reynolds, B.C. MS 6th Cav. Co.E
Reynolds, Benajah H. GA 1st Cav. Co.C
Reynolds, Benjamin AL Cav. Holloway's Co. 1st Sgt.
Reynolds, Benjamin, Jr. AL 3rd Inf. Co.A
Reynolds, Benjamin GA 3rd Res. Co.G
Reynolds, Benjamin TX 4th Inf. Co.H 2nd Lt.
Reynolds, Benjamin VA 30th Bn.S.S. Co.F
Reynolds, Benjamin F. AR 8th Inf. New Co.G
Reynolds, Benjamin F. GA 8th Cav. Co.A
Reynolds, Benjamin F. GA 13th Cav. Co.A Adj.
Reynolds, Benj. F. GA 62nd Cav. Co.H Sgt.
Reynolds, Benjamin F. GA 18th Inf. Co.F 2nd Lt.
Reynolds, Benjamin F. GA Floyd Legion (St.Guards) Co.C
Reynolds, Benjamin F. SC 22nd Inf. Co.C
Reynolds, Benjamin F. VA 19th Inf. Co.B
Reynolds, Benjamin H. NC 20th Inf. Co.G
Reynolds, Benjamin J. VA Lt.Arty. 38th Bn. Co.D
Reynolds, Benjamin L. FL 2nd Cav. Co.F
Reynolds, Benjamin L. FL 9th Inf. Co.E,H Capt.
Reynolds, Bennett GA 13th Cav. Co.A Sgt.
Reynolds, Bennett SC 2nd Inf. Co.F
Reynolds, Bernard VA 48th Inf. Co.K
Reynolds, Bernard A. AL Cav. Lenoir's Ind.Co.
Reynolds, B.F. AR 1st (Dobbin's) Cav. Co.A
Reynolds, B.F. VA 11th Bn.Res. Co.B 2nd Lt.
Reynolds, B.F. GA 8th Cav. Co.A
Reynolds, B.F. GA 62nd Cav. Co.H Sgt.
Reynolds, B.F. MO Robertson's Regt.St.Guard Co.10
Reynolds, B.F. TN 3rd (Clack's) Inf. Co.I Cpl.
Reynolds, B.F. TX 7th Field Btty.
Reynolds, B.H. AL 34th Inf. Co.F
Reynolds, B.H. VA 72nd Mil.
Reynolds, Bibb VA 53rd Inf. Co.I Music.
Reynolds, Bibb VA Inf. Montague's Bn. Co.B Music.
Reynolds, B.M. KY 1st Inf.
Reynolds, Brice S. KY 4th Mtd.Inf. Co.A Music.
Reynolds, Bunberry NC 51st Inf. Co.H
Reynolds, B.W. VA 28th Inf. Co.A
Reynolds, B.W. 1st Conf.Cav. 1st Co.B
Reynolds, B.W.F. AL 11th Cav. Co.F
Reynolds, C. LA Mil. British Guard Bn. West's Co.
Reynolds, C. MO 6th Cav. Co.I
Reynolds, C. TN 9th Inf. Co.I
Reynolds, C. TN Conscr. (Cp. of Instr.)
Reynolds, C.A. AL 58th Inf. Co.G
Reynolds, C.A. VA 54th Mil. Co.H
Reynolds, Caleb NC 37th Inf. Co.H
Reynolds, Caleb SC 1st St.Troops Co.D
Reynolds, Caleb SC 5th Res. Co.F
Reynolds, Calvin W. AL 20th Inf. Co.E
Reynolds, Cardwell M. VA 4th Cav. & Inf. St.Line 1st Co.I
Reynolds, C.C. GA 13th Cav. Co.C
Reynolds, C.C. LA 2nd Inf. Co.D Cpl.
Reynolds, C.D. TX Cav. Hardeman's Regt. Co.C

Reynolds, C.H. VA 22nd Inf. Co.H
Reynolds, C.H. Exch.Bn. Co.E,CSA
Reynolds, Chappel AL 34th Inf. Breedlove's Co.
Reynolds, Charles KY 3rd Mtd.Inf. Co.F,B
Reynolds, Charles LA 7th Inf. Co.G
Reynolds, Charles MD Cav. 2nd Bn. Co.D,B
Reynolds, Charles TN 15th Inf. Co.C
Reynolds, Charles TX 13th Cav. Co.E
Reynolds, Charles VA 6th Inf. 2nd Co.B
Reynolds, Charles Conf.Inf. Tucker's Regt. Co.D
Reynolds, Charles A. VA 6th Inf. Ferguson's Co.
Reynolds, Charles A. VA 12th Inf. Co.H
Reynolds, Charles C. TX 16th Inf. Co.G
Reynolds, Charles D. MS 42nd Inf. Co.H
Reynolds, Charles G. VA 22nd Inf. Co.H
Reynolds, Charles H. AL 12th Inf. Co.H
Reynolds, Charles H. MS Lt.Arty. Stanford's Co.
Reynolds, Charles H. NC 30th Inf. Co.A
Reynolds, Charles J. AR 2nd Mtd.Rifles Co.C
Reynolds, Charles L. TN 2nd (Robison's) Inf. Co.B 1st Lt.
Reynolds, Charles L. VA 28th Inf. Co.B
Reynolds, Charles P. SC 2nd Rifles Co.E
Reynolds, Charles W. GA 3rd Inf. Co.K Sgt.
Reynolds, Chesley N. VA 2nd Cav. Co.K
Reynolds, Christopher MO 6th Cav. Co.D
Reynolds, Christopher MO Cav. Hunter's Regt. Co.A
Reynolds, Christopher NC 1st Inf. Co.D
Reynolds, Christopher A. AL 18th Inf. Co.L Sgt.
Reynolds, Churchill TN 5th Inf. Co.D
Reynolds, Churchwell TN 9th Inf. Co.D
Reynolds, C.J. TN 28th (Cons.) Inf. Co.E
Reynolds, C.L. AR 24th Inf. Co.D 1st Lt.
Reynolds, C.L. AR Inf. Hardy's Regt. Co.C 1st Lt.
Reynolds, C.L. NC 57th Inf. Co.A 1st Sgt.
Reynolds, C.L. TN 2nd (Ashby's) Cav. Co.A Sgt.
Reynolds, C.L. TN Cav. 5th Bn. (McClellan's) Co.A Sgt.
Reynolds, Clement MO 16th Inf. Co.E
Reynolds, Clifton GA 28th Inf. Co.E Sgt.
Reynolds, C.M. SC Inf. 13th Bn. Co.B
Reynolds, C.M. VA 46th Inf. 1st Co.I 1st Lt.
Reynolds, C.M. VA Burks' Regt.Loc.Def. Shield's Co.
Reynolds, Coleman VA 38th Inf. Co.B
Reynolds, Collin, Jr. VA Inf. 4th Bn.Loc.Def. Co.E
Reynolds, Columbus L. NC 21st Inf. Co.D
Reynolds, Corbin M. VA 60th Inf. Co.F 1st Lt.
Reynolds, C.P. AL 53rd (Part.Rangers) Co.H Sgt.
Reynolds, C. Shepperd LA Arty. Watson Btty.
Reynolds, C.T. GA Cav. 29th Bn. Co.G
Reynolds, C.W. AR 7th Cav. Co.G
Reynolds, C.W. FL 4th Inf. Co.G
Reynolds, D. AL 53rd (Part.Rangers) Co.G
Reynolds, D. GA Lt.Arty. Ritter's Co.
Reynolds, D. MD Arty. 3rd Btty.
Reynolds, D.A. NC 4th Inf. Co.C
Reynolds, Danford SC 22nd Inf. Co.A
Reynolds, Daniel AL 3rd Cav. Co.E

Reynolds, Daniel AL 62nd Inf. Co.H
Reynolds, Daniel VA 67th Mil. Co.E
Reynolds, Daniel Conf.Cav. Wood's Regt. 1st Co.D
Reynolds, Daniel C. NC 29th Inf. Co.C
Reynolds, Daniel H. AR 1st Mtd.Rifles Co.A Col.
Reynolds, Daniel H. Gen. & Staff,PACS Brig.Gen.
Reynolds, Daniel M. AL 51st (Part.Rangers) Co.B Cpl.
Reynolds, Daniel M. GA 18th Inf. Co.I
Reynolds, Daniel W. NC 21st Inf. Co.M
Reynolds, David AL Cav. Forrest's Regt.
Reynolds, David MO 1st & 3rd Cons.Cav. Co.H
Reynolds, David MO Cav. 3rd Bn. Co.B
Reynolds, David NC 44th Inf. Co.F
Reynolds, David NC 46th Inf. Co.F
Reynolds, David TN 18th (Newsom's) Cav. Co.H
Reynolds, David TN 35th Inf. 1st Co.A, 2nd Co.D
Reynolds, David TX 12th Inf. Co.C
Reynolds, David VA 22nd Inf. Co.F
Reynolds, David D. GA Arty. 9th Bn. Co.A
Reynolds, David O. TN 3rd (Clack's) Inf. Co.G
Reynolds, David S. GA 15th Inf. Co.K
Reynolds, David T. FL 2nd Inf. Co.E 1st Lt.
Reynolds, D.C. SC Lt.Arty. 3rd (Palmetto) Bn. Co.E
Reynolds, Dempsey NC 51st Inf. Co.H
Reynolds, Dennis MO 6th Inf. Co.K
Reynolds, D.F. MS 2nd (Davidson's) Inf. Co.G
Reynolds, D.F. MS 32nd Inf. Co.A Capt.
Reynolds, D.H. TN 19th & 20th (Cons.) Cav. Co.D
Reynolds, D.L. TN 47th Inf. Co.C
Reynolds, D.M. Exch.Bn. 1st Co.A,CSA
Reynolds, D.N. TN 12th Inf. Co.C
Reynolds, D.O. MS 2nd Part.Rangers Co.K
Reynolds, D.O. MO 7th Cav. Co.K
Reynolds, Doctor S. TN 34th Inf. 2nd Co.C
Reynolds, Doctor Samuel TN 4th Cav.
Reynolds, D.R. TX 9th (Young's) Inf. Co.D 2nd Lt.
Reynolds, Drury J. SC Inf. Holcombe Legion Co.A
Reynolds, D.T. AL Randolph Cty.Res. Shepherd's Co.
Reynolds, D.W. AR 1st Vol. Kelsey's Co.
Reynolds, D.W. LA Hvy.Arty. 2nd Bn. Co.B
Reynolds, D.W. LA 2nd Inf. Co.B
Reynolds, D.W. MO Inf. 1st Bn. Co.C
Reynolds, D.W. MO 3rd Inf. Co.I
Reynolds, D.W. MO 12th Inf. Co.G Capt.
Reynolds, E. AL 27th Inf.
Reynolds, E. LA 3rd (Wingfield's) Cav. Co.D
Reynolds, E. LA Mil. 3rd Regt. 3rd Brig. 1st Div. Co.B
Reynolds, E. NC 5th Sr.Res. Co.A
Reynolds, E. NC 5th Sr.Res. Co.K
Reynolds, E.B. SC 5th Cav. Co.G
Reynolds, E.B. SC Cav. 17th Bn. Co.B
Reynolds, E.B. SC 5th St.Troops Co.E
Reynolds, E.B. SC 7th Res. Co.D
Reynolds, E.B. TX 32nd Cav. Co.D
Reynolds, Ebenezer MO Inf. 3rd Bn. Co.F

Reynolds, Ebenezer MO 6th Inf. Co.H
Reynolds, E.C. MS 3rd Cav. Co.F Sgt.
Reynolds, E.C. SC 6th Cav. Co.I
Reynolds, E.C. SC 26th Inf. Co.G
Reynolds, Ed. B. SC 1st Mtd.Mil. Fripp's Co.
Reynolds, Edmen AR 14th (Powers') Inf. Co.E
Reynolds, Edmond W. AR 3rd Inf. Co.H
Reynolds, Edmund P. MO 16th Inf. Co.A 1st Lt.,Adj.
Reynolds, Edward AR 7th Cav. Co.M
Reynolds, Edward AR 16th Inf. Co.A
Reynolds, Edward AR 35th Inf. Co.H
Reynolds, Edward GA 10th Mil.
Reynolds, Edward GA 47th Inf. Co.D
Reynolds, Edward TX 9th (Nichols') Inf. Co.B
Reynolds, Edward TX 18th Inf. Co.K Cpl.
Reynolds, Edward VA 9th Cav. Sandford's Co.
Reynolds, Edward VA 15th Cav. Co.A
Reynolds, Edward VA Cav. 15th Bn. Co.A
Reynolds, Edward VA 17th Cav. Co.B Sgt.
Reynolds, Edward VA 111th Mil. Co.2
Reynolds, Edward J. TX 17th Cav. Co.B
Reynolds, Edward P. FL 3rd Inf. Co.K
Reynolds, Edward S. NC 64th Inf. Co.H Jr.2nd Lt.
Reynolds, Edward S. VA Hvy.Arty. 20th Bn. Co.B Sgt.
Reynolds, Edward S. VA Inf. Cohoon's Bn. Co.A 2nd Lt.
Reynolds, Edwin O. MS Inf. 3rd Bn. Co.K Music.
Reynolds, E.E. NC 16th Inf. Co.H
Reynolds, E.F. SC 16th Inf. Co.H Sgt.
Reynolds, E. Fox NC 33rd Inf. Co.I Sgt.
Reynolds, E.G. TN 13th (Gore's) Cav. Co.C
Reynolds, E.G. TN 25th Inf. Co.F
Reynolds, Egbert AL 45th Inf. Co.H
Reynolds, E.H. SC 24th Inf. Co.K
Reynolds, E.J. AL 1st Cav. 1st Co.B
Reynolds, E.L. TN 3rd (Clack's) Inf. Co.G
Reynolds, Eldridge J. GA 38th Inf. Co.B
Reynolds, Elias TX 12th Inf. Co.C
Reynolds, Elijah AL 51st (Part.Rangers) Co.B
Reynolds, Elijah AR 3rd Inf. Co.F
Reynolds, Elijah NC 34th Inf. Co.K
Reynolds, Elijah SC 8th Inf. Co.A
Reynolds, Elijah TN 28th Cav. Capt.
Reynolds, Elijah TN 1st (Turney's) Inf. Co.A Capt.
Reynolds, Elijah VA 5th Cav. Co.B
Reynolds, Elisha KY 5th Mtd.Inf. Co.B
Reynolds, Elisha NC Unassign.Conscr.
Reynolds, Elisha TN 16th Inf. Co.C
Reynolds, Elisha C. MS Inf. 3rd Bn. Co.F Sgt.
Reynolds, Ellis AL 3rd Res. Co.K
Reynolds, Ellis LA 7th Inf. Co.E
Reynolds, E.M. AR 36th Inf. Co.I
Reynolds, Emanuel AR 14th (Powers' Inf. Co.G
Reynolds, Enoch NC 5th Inf. Co.I
Reynolds, Enos VA Inf. 26th Bn. Co.B
Reynolds, Enos VA 166th Mil. Co.A
Reynolds, Enos F. VA Cav. Hounshell's Bn. Thurmond's Co.
Reynolds, Erasmus J. GA Lt.Arty. 12th Bn. 3rd Co.A
Reynolds, E.S. TX 32nd Cav. Co.B

Reynolds, E.T. AR 15th (Johnson's) Inf. Co.E Sgt.

Reynolds, E.T. TN 5th Inf. 2nd Co.F

Reynolds, Ethan N. LA 7th Inf. Co.H

Reynolds, Evans NC 13th Inf. Co.H

Reynolds, E.W. MS Lt.Arty. Stanford's Co.

Reynolds, E.W. MS 4th Inf. Co.A Sgt.

Reynolds, E.W. SC 7th Inf. 1st Co.K, 2nd Co.K

Reynolds, E.W. SC Inf. Hampton Legion Co.G

Reynolds, Ezekiel E. TN 4th (McLemore's) Cav. Co.D

Reynolds, Ezra VA 22nd Cav. Co.B

Reynolds, F.A. AL 10th Cav. Co.D

Reynolds, Fenton M. VA 22nd Inf. Co.H

Reynolds, F.H. AL St.Arty. Co.C

Reynolds, F.H. AL 21st Inf. Co.A

Reynolds, F.H. TN 13th (Gore's) Cav. Co.C

Reynolds, F.J. VA 72nd Mil. Cpl.

Reynolds, F.L. NC 48th Inf. Co.K Sgt.

Reynolds, Flavius M. VA 6th Bn.Res.

Reynolds, Fletcher S.H. NC 60th Inf. Co.C Capt.

Reynolds, Floyd VA 22nd Inf. Co.C Sgt.

Reynolds, Floyd VA 189th Mil. Co.C

Reynolds, F.M. AL St.Arty. Co.C

Reynolds, F.M. AR 19th (Dockery's) Inf. Co.B

Reynolds, F.M. SC 5th Inf. 2nd Co.I

Reynolds, F.M. SC 6th Inf. 1st Co.I

Reynolds, F.M. TX 24th & 25th Cav. (Cons.) Co.B

Reynolds, Fowler SC Inf. Holcombe Legion Co.A

Reynolds, F.R. AR 19th Inf. Co.K

Reynolds, Francis M. AL 24th Inf. Co.I

Reynolds, Francis M. GA 43rd Inf. Co.H

Reynolds, Francis M. SC 1st St.Troops Co.D

Reynolds, Francis M. SC 5th Res. Co.E Sgt.

Reynolds, Francis S.H. SC 1st (Hagood's) Inf. 1st Co.A

Reynolds, Frank A. NC 39th Inf. Lt.Col.

Reynolds, Franklin NC 53rd Inf. Co.E

Reynolds, Franklin M. GA 8th Inf. Co.E

Reynolds, Frederick S. VA 36th Inf. Co.F

Reynolds, Freeman J. MS 3rd Inf. Co.D

Reynolds, G. GA Cav. 20th Bn. Co.A

Reynolds, G.A. AR 1st (Cons.) Inf. Co.2

Reynolds, G.A. TN 12th (Green's) Cav. Co.A

Reynolds, G.A. TN 6th Inf. Co.A Cpl.

Reynolds, G.A. TN 47th Inf. Co.C Cpl.

Reynolds, Galen O. AL Lt.Arty. Phelan's Co.

Reynolds, Garnett B. MS 19th Inf. Co.D

Reynolds, Garret F. GA 5th Inf. Co.K

Reynolds, George AL Res. J.G. Rankin's Co.

Reynolds, George GA Cav. 20th Bn. Co.G

Reynolds, George GA Cav. 21st Bn. Co.D

Reynolds, George GA Inf. (GA RR Guards) Porter's Co.

Reynolds, George LA 13th Bn. (Part.Rangers) Co.A

Reynolds, George TN 10th (DeMoss') Cav. Co.E

Reynolds, George TN 15th (Stewart's) Cav. Co.A

Reynolds, George TX Cav. Wells' Bn. Co.A

Reynolds, George VA Cav. Caldwell's Bn. Graham's Co.

Reynolds, George VA Rockbridge Cty.Res. Miller's Co.

Reynolds, George A. TX 22nd Cav. Co.F

Reynolds, George B. VA 3rd Res. Co.E 2nd Lt.

Reynolds, George C. AR 37th Inf. Co.F

Reynolds, George E. VA 46th Inf. 2nd Co.K

Reynolds, George F. AL 4th Res. Co.A

Reynolds, George F. MS 3rd Inf. Co.D

Reynolds, George K. MS 28th Cav. Co.G

Reynolds, George N. SC 1st Arty. Co.B 1st Lt.

Reynolds, George S. VA 28th Inf. 2nd Co.C

Reynolds, George T. NC 28th Inf. Co.I

Reynolds, George T. TX 19th Cav. Co.E

Reynolds, George W. AL 1st Cav. 1st Co.B

Reynolds, George W. AL 4th Cav. Co.D

Reynolds, George W. AL 8th Cav. Co.G

Reynolds, Geo. W. AL 25th Inf. Co.I

Reynolds, George W. AR 1st Cav. Co.K

Reynolds, George W. AR Cav. Harrell's Bn. Co.A

Reynolds, George W. FL 5th Inf. Co.G Cpl.

Reynolds, George W. GA 64th Inf. Co.H

Reynolds, George W. KY 5th Mtd.Inf. Co.F

Reynolds, George W. LA Washington Arty.Bn. Co.4

Reynolds, George W. LA 28th (Gray's) Inf. Co.G Sgt.

Reynolds, George W. MS 2nd Inf. Co.A Cpl.

Reynolds, George W. MS 9th Inf. Old Co.E

Reynolds, George W. MS 26th Inf. Co.D Sgt.

Reynolds, George W. MS 29th Inf. Co.I Capt.

Reynolds, George W. TN 4th (McLemore's) Cav. Co.A

Reynolds, George W. TX 13th Cav. Co.B

Reynolds, George W. TX 37th Cav. Co.C Lt.

Reynolds, George W. VA 16th Cav. Co.I Cpl.

Reynolds, George W. VA Lt.Arty. Fry's Co.

Reynolds, George W. VA Hvy.Arty. Patteson's Co.

Reynolds, George W. VA Inf. 5th Bn. Co.A

Reynolds, George W. VA 51st Inf. Co.D

Reynolds, George W. VA 52nd Inf. Co.A Cpl.

Reynolds, George W. VA 53rd Inf. Co.H

Reynolds, G.I. TN 3rd (Clack's) Inf. Co.B

Reynolds, G.I. VA 14th Inf. Co.D

Reynolds, Gilbert M. AL 11th Inf. Co.C

Reynolds, Gilford D. TX 27th Cav. Co.C

Reynolds, Gilford G. MS 2nd Inf. Co.A

Reynolds, G.J. GA 5th Res. Co.C,E

Reynolds, G.L. SC Gregg's Cav.

Reynolds, G.M. AR 3rd Inf. Co.A

Reynolds, G.M. AR 27th Inf. Old Co.B Cpl.

Reynolds, G.M. AR 27th Inf. Co.I

Reynolds, G.N. Gen. & Staff Maj.

Reynolds, G.P. Conf.Cav. Wood's Regt. Co.L

Reynolds, Grouchy G. TX 10th Inf. Co.E

Reynolds, G.S. AL 31st Inf. Co.G

Reynolds, Gus LA Inf. Jeff Davis Regt. Co.F

Reynolds, G.W. AL Cav. Hardie's Bn.Res. Co.D

Reynolds, G.W. AL Lt.Arty. Clanton's Btty.

Reynolds, G.W. FL 11th Inf. Co.C 2nd Lt.

Reynolds, G.W. GA 3rd Res. Co.D

Reynolds, G.W. MS 18th Cav. Wimberly's Co.

Reynolds, G.W. MS 15th Inf. Co.K

Reynolds, G.W. MS 46th Inf. Co.F

Reynolds, G.W. MO 1st Inf. Co.K Cpl.

Reynolds, G.W. TN 8th (Smith's) Cav. Co.A

Reynolds, G.W. TN 11th (Holman's) Cav. Co.B Sgt.

Reynolds, G.W. TN 15th (Cons.) Cav. Co.C

Reynolds, G.W. TN Cav. Napier's Bn. Co.B

Reynolds, G.W. TN 3rd (Lillard's) Mtd.Inf. Co.F 2nd Lt.

Reynolds, H. AL 5th Inf. Co.A

Reynolds, H. GA Cav. 21st Bn. Co.A

Reynolds, H. GA Floyd Legion (St.Guards) Co.B

Reynolds, H. MS 24th Inf. Co.E

Reynolds, H. MO 12th Inf. Co.G

Reynolds, Hal G. Moore's Staff Maj.,Vol.ADC

Reynolds, Hardin A. TN 45th Inf. Co.G

Reynolds, Hardon VA Cav. 36th Bn. Co.C

Reynolds, Harmon GA 1st Mil. Co.C

Reynolds, Harvey NC 28th Inf. Co.C

Reynolds, Hasting SC 12th Inf. Co.C

Reynolds, H.C. AL 5th Inf. Co.K Cpl.

Reynolds, H.C. AL 51st (Part.Rangers) Co.I 2nd Lt.

Reynolds, H.C. MO Lt.Arty. Farris' Btty. (Clark Arty.) Sgt.

Reynolds, Henry AL 22nd Inf. Co.B

Reynolds, Henry AR 15th Mil. Co.F

Reynolds, Henry AR 35th Inf. Co.H

Reynolds, Henry GA 8th Cav. Co.A

Reynolds, Henry GA Cav. 21st Bn. Co.A

Reynolds, Henry GA 62nd Cav. Co.H

Reynolds, Henry GA Lt.Arty. Barnwell's Btty.

Reynolds, Henry GA 14th Inf. Co.G

Reynolds, Henry KY 13th Cav. Co.D

Reynolds, Henry MS 2nd Inf. (A. of 10,000) Co.H

Reynolds, Henry NC 17th Inf. (1st Org.) Co.I

Reynolds, Henry TN 39th Mtd.Inf. Co.D

Reynolds, Henry TX 14th Cav. Co.C

Reynolds, Henry VA 22nd Inf. Co.K

Reynolds, Henry VA 47th Inf. 2nd Co.G

Reynolds, Henry VA 60th Inf. Co.A

Reynolds, Henry Conf.Reg.Inf. Brooks' Bn. Co.D

Reynolds, Henry A. MS 38th Cav. Co.A

Reynolds, Henry C. VA 1st Cav. Co.F

Reynolds, Henry C. VA 6th Inf. 1st Co.E

Reynolds, Henry C. VA 61st Inf. Co.D

Reynolds, Henry G. GA Inf. 10th Bn. Co.B

Reynolds, Henry G. VA 46th Inf. 2nd Co.C 2nd Lt.

Reynolds, Henry H. AL Lt.Arty. 20th Bn. Co.A,B

Reynolds, Henry H. AL 6th Inf. Co.B

Reynolds, Henry J. MS 36th Inf. Co.I 3rd Lt.

Reynolds, Henry S. VA 6th Inf. Co.G

Reynolds, Henry S. VA 6th Inf. Co.H 2nd Lt.

Reynolds, Henry S. 1st Conf.Inf. 2nd Co.H

Reynolds, Henry S. Gen. & Staff Capt.,Asst.Comsy.

Reynolds, Henry T. AL 37th Inf. Co.H 1st Lt.

Reynolds, Hey C. FL 11th Inf. Co.C

Reynolds, Hezekiah AL 22nd Inf. Co.B Music.

Reynolds, H.G. MS 7th Inf. Co.K

Reynolds, H.G. MS Cp.Guard (Cp. of Instr. for Conscr.)

Reynolds, Hines AL 34th Inf. Black's Co. Music.

Reynolds, Hiram TX 18th Inf. Co.K

Reynolds, Hiram C. NC 29th Inf. Co.A Cpl.

Reynolds, H.J. Conf.Cav. Powers' Regt. Co.G Sgt.

Reynolds, H.J. Bradford's Corps Scouts & Guards Co.A

Reynolds, H.M. GA 10th Cav. (St.Guards) Co.K Cpl.

Reynolds, H.M. TX 11th Cav. Co.B

Reynolds, H.P. AL Mil. 4th Vol. Co.K Cpl.

Reynolds, H.P. GA 4th Res. Co.I

Reynolds, H.R. AR 10th Inf. Co.F,C

Reynolds, H.R. AR 26th Inf. Co.G

Reynolds, H.R. FL 5th Inf. Co.I

Reynolds, H.S. AR 1st (Monroe's) Cav. Co.G

Reynolds, H.S. VA 3rd Inf.Loc.Def. Co.K

Reynolds, Hugh AL 3rd Inf. Co.E

Reynolds, Hugh AR 14th (Powers') Inf. Co.F 2nd Lt.

Reynolds, Hugh LA 20th Inf. Co.G

Reynolds, Hugh LA Herrick's Co. (Orleans Blues)

Reynolds, Hugh MS 18th Cav. Co.A 1st Lt.

Reynolds, Hugh MO 3rd Cav. Co.K

Reynolds, Hugh MO Cav. Fristoe's Regt. Co.A

Reynolds, Hugh MO Inf. 1st Bn. Co.C

Reynolds, Hugh MO 6th Inf. Co.K

Reynolds, Hugh A. MS 30th Inf. Co.F Maj.

Reynolds, Hughey VA 57th Inf. Co.E

Reynolds, H.W.W. LA 2nd Cav. Co.G

Reynolds, H.W.W. LA Washington Arty.Bn. Co.6 Can.

Reynolds, H.W.W. 4th Conf.Eng.Troops 2nd Lt.

Reynolds, Hyram G. MS 22nd Inf. Co.E

Reynolds, I.C. MO 4th Cav. Co.G

Reynolds, I.H. NC 1st Cav. (9th St.Troops.) Co.G

Reynolds, Ira SC 19th Inf. Co.F Cpl.

Reynolds, Ira, Jr. VA 6th Bn.Res. Co.G

Reynolds, Isaac MO 9th Bn.S.S. Co.F

Reynolds, Isaac TN 8th Inf. Co.B

Reynolds, Isaac TX Cav. Saufley's Scouting Bn. Co.B

Reynolds, Isaac TX 9th (Nichols') Inf. Co.B

Reynolds, Isaac VA 27th Inf. Co.C

Reynolds, Isaac D. NC 2nd Arty. (36th St.Troops) Co.G Fifer

Reynolds, Isaac H. AL Inf. 1st Regt. Co.G 1st Sgt.

Reynolds, Isaac R. TN Arty. Marshall's Co. Artif.

Reynolds, Isaac V. VA 16th Cav. Co.A Sgt.

Reynolds, Isaac V. VA Cav. Ferguson's Bn. Stevenson's Co. Sgt.

Reynolds, Isaac V. VA 72nd Mil.

Reynolds, Isaiah VA Cav. 36th Bn. Co.C

Reynolds, Isaiah C. VA 28th Inf. 2nd Co.C

Reynolds, Isham NC 20th Inf. Co.G Sgt.

Reynolds, Isham TN 39th Mtd.Inf. Co.D 2nd Lt.

Reynolds, J. AL 9th (Malone's) Cav. Co.E

Reynolds, J. AL 3rd Res. Co.C

Reynolds, J. GA Inf. 1st Loc.Troops (Augusta) Co.K

Reynolds, J. GA 5th Res. Co.B

Reynolds, J. GA Inf. 27th Bn. Co.F

Reynolds, J. LA 15th Inf. Co.K

Reynolds, J. LA Mil. Irish Regt. O'Brien's Co.

Reynolds, J. MS 27th Inf. Co.L

Reynolds, J. MO 12th Inf. Co.G

Reynolds, J. MO St.Guard

Reynolds, J. TN 4th Cav. Co.B

Reynolds, J. TX 13th Vol. 2nd Co.B

Reynolds, J. TX 18th Inf. Co.B

Reynolds, J.A. AL 18th Inf. Co.L

Reynolds, J.A. AL 26th (O'Neal's) Inf. Co.H

Reynolds, J.A. AR 10th Inf. Co.K

Reynolds, J.A. GA 9th Inf. Co.B

Reynolds, J.A. GA 16th Inf. Co.B

Reynolds, J.A. GA Inf. 18th Bn. Co.A

Reynolds, J.A. SC 16th & 24th (Cons.) Inf. Co.H 2nd Lt.

Reynolds, J.A. VA 14th Cav. Co.C

Reynolds, J.A. Gen. & Staff Chap.

Reynolds, Jabez S. VA 46th Inf. 2nd Co.C

Reynolds, Jack TN 11th Cav. Co.A

Reynolds, Jackson GA 14th Inf. Co.K

Reynolds, Jackson GA 51st Inf. Co.I

Reynolds, Jackson TX 22nd Cav. Co.K

Reynolds, Jackson J. GA Inf. 10th Bn. Co.B

Reynolds, Jackson V. AR 32nd Inf. Co.A

Reynolds, Jacob AL 10th Inf. Co.G

Reynolds, Jacob NC 23rd Inf. Co.B

Reynolds, Jacob TN 29th Inf. Co.F

Reynolds, Jacob H. TX 30th Cav. Co.E Jr.2nd Lt.

Reynolds, Jacob V. VA 28th Inf. Co.B Cpl.

Reynolds, James AL 8th Inf. Co.K

Reynolds, James AL 9th Inf. Co.K

Reynolds, James AL 34th Inf. Co.H

Reynolds, James AL 34th Inf. Breedlove's Co.

Reynolds, James AR Cav. 1st Bn. (Stirman's) Co.B Sgt.

Reynolds, James AR Cav. 1st Bn. (Stirman's) Co.E

Reynolds, James AR 7th Inf. Co.F

Reynolds, James GA Cav. 20th Bn. Co.A,F

Reynolds, James GA 1st (Symons') Res. Co.K

Reynolds, James GA 47th Inf. Co.A

Reynolds, James GA 63rd Inf. Co.K

Reynolds, James KY 1st (Butler's) Cav. Co.K

Reynolds, James KY 2nd Cav. Co.A

Reynolds, James KY 6th Cav. Co.G

Reynolds, James KY 4th Mtd.Inf. Co.H

Reynolds, James LA Cav. 18th Bn. Co.C

Reynolds, James LA 18th Inf. Co.I

Reynolds, James LA Mil. British Guard Bn. Burrowes' Co.

Reynolds, James MO 2nd Cav. Co.F

Reynolds, James MO 1st Inf. Co.A

Reynolds, James MO Inf. 3rd Bn. Co.F

Reynolds, James NC 2nd Arty. (36th St.Troops) Co.G

Reynolds, James NC 5th Inf. Co.A

Reynolds, James NC 7th Sr.Res. Williams' Co.

Reynolds, James NC 39th Inf. Co.K

Reynolds, James SC 7th Inf. Co.A

Reynolds, James SC 15th Inf. Co.K

Reynolds, James TN 10th & 11th (Cons.) Cav. Co.B

Reynolds, James TN 15th (Stewart's) Cav. Co.A

Reynolds, James TN 4th Inf. Co.B

Reynolds, James TN 10th Inf. Co.E

Reynolds, James TN 19th Inf. Co.A Cpl.

Reynolds, James TX 13th Cav. Co.B

Reynolds, James TX 20th Cav. Co.E

Reynolds, James TX Cav. Wells' Bn. Co.A

Reynolds, James TX 5th Inf. Co.B

Reynolds, James VA 8th Cav. Co.H

Reynolds, James VA 19th Cav. Co.I

Reynolds, James VA 3rd Bn. Valley Res. Co.A

Reynolds, James VA 10th Inf. Co.L

Reynolds, James VA 11th Inf. Co.H

Reynolds, James VA 24th Inf. Co.H

Reynolds, James VA 28th Inf. Co.E

Reynolds, James VA 64th Mtd.Inf. Co.K

Reynolds, James Conf.Cav. Wood's Regt. 1st Co.G Sgt.

Reynolds, James 1st Choctaw & Chickasaw Mtd.Rifles 1st Co.E Cpl.

Reynolds, James A. AL Lt.Arty. 20th Bn. Co.A,B

Reynolds, James A. GA Arty. 11th Bn. (Sumter Arty.) Co.A

Reynolds, James A. GA 11th Inf. Co.E

Reynolds, James A. GA 16th Inf. Co.K

Reynolds, James A. NC 28th Inf. Co.C

Reynolds, James A. VA 22nd Inf. Co.K

Reynolds, James A. VA 28th Inf. Co.B

Reynolds, James B. AL 25th Inf. Co.D,H

Reynolds, Jas. B. GA Conscr.

Reynolds, James C. AL 3rd Inf. Co.A

Reynolds, James C. GA 1st Cav. Co.A

Reynolds, James C. GA 18th Inf. Co.F

Reynolds, James C. GA Floyd Legion (St.Guards) Co.B Sgt.

Reynolds, James C. SC 1st Arty. Co.H,G 2nd Lt.

Reynolds, James C. VA 21st Inf. Co.I

Reynolds, Jas. C. Gen. & Staff 2nd Lt.,Dr.M.

Reynolds, James D. NC Inf. 2nd Bn. Co.B

Reynolds, James E. GA 5th Res. Co.A

Reynolds, James E. MS 11th Inf. Co.K

Reynolds, James E. MS 30th Inf. Co.K 1st Sgt.

Reynolds, James F. GA 18th Inf. Co.F

Reynolds, James F. MO 6th Inf. Co.H

Reynolds, James F. VA 4th Inf. Co.H

Reynolds, James G. LA 5th Inf. Co.E

Reynolds, James G. NC Cav. 5th Bn. Co.A

Reynolds, James G. NC Cav. 14th Bn. Co.E

Reynolds, James G. NC Inf. 2nd Bn. Co.H

Reynolds, James H. GA Cav. 7th Bn. (St.Guards) Co.D

Reynolds, James H. GA 4th Inf. Co.I Cpl.

Reynolds, James H. GA 42nd Inf. Co.A

Reynolds, James H. MS 8th Inf. Co.K

Reynolds, James H. MS 27th Inf. Co.B

Reynolds, James H. NC 29th Inf. Co.I,D,B

Reynolds, James H. SC 12th Inf. Co.C

Reynolds, James H. SC 22nd Inf. Co.C

Reynolds, James H. TN 3rd (Clack's) Inf. Co.B Cpl.

Reynolds, James H. VA Cav. 36th Bn. Co.C

Reynolds, James H. VA 11th Bn.Res. Co.E Cpl.

Reynolds, James H. VA 28th Inf. 2nd Co.C

Reynolds, James H. VA 28th Inf. Co.F

Reynolds, James J. AL 24th Inf. Co.I

Reynolds, James J. GA 1st (Ramsey's) Inf. Co.G

Reynolds, James K. GA 28th Inf. Co.E

Reynolds, James L. MS 26th Inf. Co.B,K

Reynolds, James L. TN 3rd (Clack's) Inf. Co.G

Reynolds, James L. TX 27th Cav. Co.H Sgt.

Reynolds, James L. TX 15th Inf. 2nd Co.F

Reynolds, James M. AL Lt.Arty. Clanton's Btty.

Reynolds, James M. AL Inf. 1st Regt. Co.E, 3rd Co.G Cpl.

Reynolds, James M. AL 8th Inf. Co.D

Reynolds, James M. AL 13th Inf. Co.D

Reynolds, James M. GA 1st Cav. Co.G

Reynolds, James M. GA 48th Inf. Co.G

Reynolds, James M. GA 57th Inf. Co.H

Reynolds, James M. GA 61st Inf. Co.F

Reynolds, James M. MO 9th Bn.S.S. Co.F

Reynolds, James M. TN 4th Cav.

Reynolds, James M. TN 39th Mtd.Inf. Co.F Cpl.

Reynolds, James M. TN 54th Inf. Hollis' Co. 1st Lt.

Reynolds, James M. VA 9th Cav. Co.H

Reynolds, James M. VA 86th Mil. Co.D

Reynolds, James P. NC Cumberland Cty.Bn. Detailed Men Co.B

Reynolds, James P. TX 30th Cav. Co.E

Reynolds, James R. GA Inf. 10th Bn. Co.B

Reynolds, James R. GA 15th Inf. Co.D

Reynolds, James R. GA 15th Inf. Co.E

Reynolds, James R. GA 15th Inf. Co.K

Reynolds, James R. GA Phillips' Legion Co.A

Reynolds, James R. VA 19th Inf. Co.K

Reynolds, James R. VA Inf. 26th Bn. Co.B

Reynolds, James Riley MO 8th Inf. Co.E

Reynolds, James S. AL 40th Inf. Co.B

Reynolds, James S. TX 4th Inf. Co.G

Reynolds, James S. VA 2nd Arty. Co.A

Reynolds, James S. VA Inf. 22nd Bn. Co.A Sgt.

Reynolds, James T. AR 3rd Inf. (St.Troops) Co.B Cpl.

Reynolds, James T. AR 16th Inf. Co.E

Reynolds, James T. AR 19th (Dockery's) Inf. Co.A 3rd Lt.

Reynolds, James T. FL 1st Cav. Co.G

Reynolds, James T. VA 42nd Inf. Co.F

Reynolds, James W. AL 22nd Inf. Co.G

Reynolds, James W. AL 45th Inf. Co.H

Reynolds, James W. AR 31st Inf. Co.C Cpl.

Reynolds, James W. GA 13th Cav. Co.G

Reynolds, James W. GA 36th (Villepigue's) Inf. Co.A

Reynolds, James W. GA 59th Inf. Co.I

Reynolds, James W. KY 12th Cav.

Reynolds, James W. MO 1st Cav. Co.F Sgt.

Reynolds, James W. TX 1st Inf. Co.H

Reynolds, James W. VA 9th Cav. Co.G

Reynolds, James W. VA 5th Inf. Co.L

Reynolds, James W.B. TX Inf. Griffin's Bn. Co.B Cpl.

Reynolds, Jasper TN 6th (Wheeler's) Cav. Co.D Black.

Reynolds, Jasper TN Cav. 11th Bn. (Gordon's) Co.F

Reynolds, Jasper VA Cav. 36th Bn. Co.C

Reynolds, Jasper M. VA 52nd Inf. Co.A

Reynolds, Jasper N. VA Prov.Guard Avis' Co.

Reynolds, J.B. AL St.Res. Palmer's Co.

Reynolds, J.B. GA 55th Inf. Co.F

Reynolds, J.B. MS 2nd Cav. Co.F,G

Reynolds, J.B. MS 4th Cav. Co.D

Reynolds, J.B. MS St.Cav. Perrin's Bn. Co.D

Reynolds, J.B. MS Lt.Arty. (Jefferson Arty.) Darden's Co.

Reynolds, J.B. MS 37th Inf. Co.D

Reynolds, J.B. MO 9th Inf. Co.F

Reynolds, J.B. NC 62nd Inf. Co.B

Reynolds, J.C. AL 15th Bn.Part.Rangers Co.E

Reynolds, J.C. AL Inf. 2nd Regt. Co.G

Reynolds, J.C. AL 37th Inf. Co.D

Reynolds, J.C. AL 42nd Inf. Co.I

Reynolds, J.C. AL Res. McQueen's Co.

Reynolds, J.C. AR 1st Inf. Co.F

Reynolds, J.C. GA 3rd Bn. (St.Guards) Co.H

Reynolds, J.C. GA Inf. Exempts Roberts' Co. Sgt.

Reynolds, J.C. MS 8th Cav. Co.H

Reynolds, J.C. MS 28th Cav. Co.L

Reynolds, J.C. SC 7th Inf. 1st Co.K, 2nd Co.K

Reynolds, J.C. TX 8th Cav. Co.F

Reynolds, J.C. VA 1st Cav. Co.F 2nd Lt.

Reynolds, J.C. Conf.Inf. 1st Bn. 2nd Co.E

Reynolds, J.C.J. MS 1st Lt.Arty. Co.I

Reynolds, J.D. AL 62nd Inf. Co.H

Reynolds, J.D. GA 4th Res. Co.C

Reynolds, J.D. Conf.Cav. Powers' Regt. Co.I Sr.2nd Lt.

Reynolds, J.D. Gen. & Staff Asst.Surg.

Reynolds, J.E. AL 53rd (Part.Rangers) Co.D

Reynolds, J.E. AL 66th Inf. Co.F

Reynolds, J.E. GA 55th Inf. Co.D

Reynolds, J.E. MS Inf. 2nd St.Troops Co.A

Reynolds, J.E. MO Cav. 3rd Bn. Co.H

Reynolds, J.E. VA 3rd Cav. Co.A

Reynolds, J.E. 2nd Conf.Eng.Troops Co.A

Reynolds, J.E. Exch.Bn. 3rd Co.B,CSA Cpl.

Reynolds, Jehu NC 7th Inf. Co.D

Reynolds, Jeptha V. GA Inf. 3rd Bn. Co.E

Reynolds, Jeptha V. GA 37th Inf. Co.C

Reynolds, Jeremiah FL 7th Inf. Co.C

Reynolds, Jesse GA 62nd Cav. Co.H

Reynolds, Jesse MO 5th Inf. Co.B,D

Reynolds, Jesse TN 44th Inf. Co.C 1st Lt.

Reynolds, Jesse TN 44th (Cons.) Inf. Co.K 1st Lt.

Reynolds, Jesse TN Conscr. (Cp. of Instr.) Co.B

Reynolds, Jesse TX 17th Cons.Dismtd.Cav. Co.B

Reynolds, Jesse TX 24th & 25th Cav. (Cons.) Co.B

Reynolds, Jesse E. NC 33rd Inf. Co.G

Reynolds, Jessee AR 10th Inf. Co.F,C

Reynolds, Jessee L. KY 6th Cav. Co.C

Reynolds, Jesse F. MO Cav. Freeman's Regt. Co.F

Reynolds, J.F. AR 27th Inf. New Co.C

Reynolds, J.F. GA 11th Cav. (St.Guards) Bruce's Co.

Reynolds, J.F. GA 31st Inf. Co.H

Reynolds, J.F. LA 13th Inf. Co.G

Reynolds, J.F. TX Cav. Hardeman's Regt. Co.A

Reynolds, J.G. GA Inf. 2nd Bn. (St.Guards) Co.A Capt.

Reynolds, J.G. TN 43rd Inf. Co.D

Reynolds, J.G. TX 20th Bn.St.Troops Co.B

Reynolds, J.H. AL 51st (Part.Rangers) Co.H

Reynolds, J.H. AL 22nd Inf. Co.G

Reynolds, J.H. AL 31st Inf. Co.E

Reynolds, J.H. GA 5th Res. Co.L

Reynolds, J.H. KY 1st (Helm's) Cav. Co.B

Reynolds, J.H. LA Lt.Arty. 3rd Btty. (Benton's)

Reynolds, J.H. LA 3rd Inf. Co.F

Reynolds, J.H. LA 6th Inf. Co.A Cpl.

Reynolds, J.H. LA Bickham's Co. (Caddo Mil.) 2nd Lt.

Reynolds, J.H. MS 32nd Inf. Co.G

Reynolds, J.H. MO Robertson's Regt.St.Guard Co.1

Reynolds, J.H. MO Ord.Dept.St.Guard 1st Lt.

Reynolds, J.H. NC 1st Cav. (9th St.Troops) Co.G

Reynolds, J.H. TN 11th Cav. Co.L

Reynolds, J.H. TN Cav. Woodward's Co.

Reynolds, J.H. TN 3rd (Clack's) Inf. Co.F

Reynolds, J.H. Parson's Brig. Capt.,AQM

Reynolds, J.I. FL 1st (Res.) Inf. Co.E

Reynolds, J.J. AL Cav. Moreland's Regt. Co.A

Reynolds, J.J. AL 41st Inf. Co.G

Reynolds, J.J. AL Cp. of Instr. Talladega Co.D

Reynolds, J.J. GA 63rd Inf. Co.C

Reynolds, J.J. LA Inf.Crescent Regt. Co.I

Reynolds, J.J. TN Lt.Arty. Phillips' Co.

Reynolds, J.J. VA 3rd Res. Co.G

Reynolds, J. Jones GA Cobb's Legion Co.F

Reynolds, J.K. NC 20th Inf. Co.K

Reynolds, J.L. GA 8th Cav. Co.A

Reynolds, J.L. SC Lt.Arty. Parker's Co. (Marion Arty.)

Reynolds, J.L. TX 32nd Cav. Co.K

Reynolds, J.L.B. TX 35th (Brown's) Cav. Co.A

Reynolds, J.L.B. TX 13th Vol. 1st Co.B

Reynolds, J.M. AL 56th Part.Rangers Co.I

Reynolds, J.M. AL 15th Inf. Co.F

Reynolds, J.M. AR 10th Inf. Co.F

Reynolds, J.M. GA 1st (Fannin's) Res. Co.D

Reynolds, J.M. GA 13th Inf. Co.A

Reynolds, J.M. GA 40th Inf. Co.C

Reynolds, J.M. GA Phillips' Legion Co.A

Reynolds, J.M. LA Mil. Chalmette Regt. Co.D Cpl.

Reynolds, J.M. MS 7th Inf. Co.K

Reynolds, J.M. NC 14th Inf. Co.G

Reynolds, J.M. SC Arty. Stuart's Co. (Beaufort Vol.Arty.)

Reynolds, J.M. TN 19th (Biffle's) Cav. Co.B Capt.

Reynolds, J.M. TN 46th Inf. Co.C

Reynolds, J.M. VA Lt.Arty. R.M. Anderson's Co.

Reynolds, J.M. VA 2nd Inf.Loc.Def. Co.I

Reynolds, J.M. VA Inf. 2nd Bn.Loc.Def. Co.G

Reynolds, J.M. VA 60th Inf. Co.B

Reynolds, J.N. MO Cav. Schnabel's Bn. Co.F

Reynolds, J.N. TX 12th Inf. Co.C

Reynolds, J.N. VA Inf. 26th Bn. Co.B

Reynolds, Jo. MS Lt.Arty. Turner's Co.

Reynolds, J.O. VA 21st Inf. Co.E

Reynolds, Job MS 5th Cav. Co.G Cpl.

Reynolds, Job MS St.Cav. Perrin's Btty. Co.B

Reynolds, Job MS 30th Inf. Co.C

Reynolds, Joberry AL 3rd Cav. Co.G

Reynolds, Joel TX 10th Cav. Co.I

Reynolds, John AL 53rd (Part.Rangers) Co.G

Reynolds, John AL 56th Part.Rangers Co.E

Reynolds, John AL Lt.Arty. Clanton's Btty. Cpl.

Reynolds, John AL Inf. 1st Regt. Co.K

Reynolds, John AL 22nd Inf. Co.G

Reynolds, John AL 29th Inf. Co.F

Reynolds, John AL 34th Inf. Black's Co.

Reynolds, John AL 39th Inf. Co.I
Reynolds, John AR Cav. Harrell's Bn. Co.D
Reynolds, John AR 37th Inf. Co.D
Reynolds, John FL 9th Inf. Co.G
Reynolds, John GA Cav. 7th Bn. (St.Guards) Co.D
Reynolds, John GA 8th Cav. Co.A
Reynolds, John GA 62nd Cav. Co.H Cpl.
Reynolds, John GA Lt.Arty. Barnwell's Btty.
Reynolds, John GA 1st Reg. Co.A
Reynolds, John GA 4th Inf. Co.C
Reynolds, John GA Inf. 25th Bn. (Prov.Guard) Co.F
Reynolds, John GA 29th Inf. Co.D
Reynolds, John GA 43rd Inf. Co.I
Reynolds, John KY 6th Cav. Co.G
Reynolds, John KY 13th Cav. Co.A
Reynolds, John KY 5th Mtd.Inf. Co.F
Reynolds, John LA 1st Cav. Co.H
Reynolds, John LA Cav. 18th Bn. Co.F 2nd Lt.
Reynolds, John LA Cav. Cole's Co.
Reynolds, John LA Inf. 1st Sp.Bn. (Wheat's) Co.B
Reynolds, John LA Mil. 4th Regt. 1st Brig. 1st Div. Co.G
Reynolds, John LA 9th Inf. Co.G
Reynolds, John LA 12th Inf. 1st Co.M
Reynolds, John LA 16th Inf. Co.H Cpl.
Reynolds, John LA 1st Res. Co.E
Reynolds, John LA Mil. British Guard Bn. West's Co.
Reynolds, John MS 22nd Inf. Co.D
Reynolds, John MS 31st Inf. Co.E
Reynolds, John MS 44th Inf. Co.H
Reynolds, John MO 9th (Elliott's) Cav. Co.B
Reynolds, John MO 9th (Elliott's) Cav. Co.I
Reynolds, John MO Lt.Arty. 2nd Field Btty.
Reynolds, John MO Inf. 1st Bn. Co.C
Reynolds, John MO 6th Inf. Co.K
Reynolds, John NC 52nd Inf. Co.G
Reynolds, John NC 64th Inf. Co.F
Reynolds, John SC 6th Inf. 1st Co.I
Reynolds, John SC Manigault's Bn.Vol. Co.C
Reynolds, John SC Palmetto S.S. Co.M
Reynolds, John TN Lt.Arty. Scott's Co.
Reynolds, John TN 39th Mtd.Inf. Co.D
Reynolds, John TN 61st Mtd.Inf. Co.B
Reynolds, John TX 5th Cav. Co.H Cpl.
Reynolds, John TX 37th Cav. Co.C
Reynolds, John TX Cav. Martin's Regt. Co.A
Reynolds, John TX Cav. Wells' Bn. Co.A
Reynolds, John TX 2nd Inf. Co.E
Reynolds, John TX 10th Inf. Co.F
Reynolds, John TX 13th Vol. 1st Co.K
Reynolds, John TX Home Guards Killough's Co.
Reynolds, John VA 12th Cav. Co.F
Reynolds, John VA 20th Cav. Co.I
Reynolds, John VA Lt.Arty. Cayce's Co.
Reynolds, John VA Inf. 1st Bn. Co.E
Reynolds, John VA 11th Inf. Co.K
Reynolds, John VA 22nd Inf. Co.F
Reynolds, John VA 25th Mil. Co.C
Reynolds, John VA 38th Inf. Co.C
Reynolds, John VA 135th Mil. Co.I
Reynolds, John A. AL 13th Inf. Co.I Cpl.
Reynolds, John A. GA 18th Inf. Co.F
Reynolds, John A. GA 24th Inf. Chap.

Reynolds, John A. MO 2nd Inf. Co.E
Reynolds, John A. NC 2nd Arty. (36th St.Troops)
Reynolds, John A. VA 5th Inf. Co.L
Reynolds, John A. VA 22nd Inf. Co.C
Reynolds, John A. VA 23rd Inf. Co.G
Reynolds, John A. VA 27th Inf. Co.B
Reynolds, John A. VA 189th Mil. Co.C
Reynolds, John B. GA 17th Inf. Co.D,E
Reynolds, John B. GA 27th Inf. Co.D
Reynolds, John B. TN 16th Inf. Co.D
Reynolds, John B. VA 46th Inf. 2nd Co.C
Reynolds, John C. AR 37th Inf. Co.F
Reynolds, John C. GA 50th Inf. Co.E 1st Sgt.
Reynolds, John C. NC 44th Inf. Co.F
Reynolds, John C. TX 18th Cav. Co.G,K
Reynolds, John C. VA 29th Inf. Co.A
Reynolds, John C. VA 60th Inf. Co.D
Reynolds, John Caswell GA 18th Inf. Co.F
Reynolds, John C.C. AL 6th Inf. Co.F,I
Reynolds, John D. AR 14th (Powers') Inf. Co.E
Reynolds, John D. GA 17th Inf.
Reynolds, John D. NC 60th Inf. Asst.Surg.
Reynolds, John D. TN 3rd (Clack's) Inf. Co.G Sgt.
Reynolds, John D. VA 22nd Inf. Co.D
Reynolds, John E. GA Cobb's Legion Co.F
Reynolds, John E. MS 37th Inf. Co.D
Reynolds, John E. NC 2nd Inf. Co.E
Reynolds, John E. NC 2nd Bn.Loc.Def.Troops Co.A
Reynolds, John E. VA 9th Cav. Co.G
Reynolds, John E. VA 22nd Inf. Co.C
Reynolds, John E. VA 189th Mil. Co.C
Reynolds, John F. AL 28th Inf. Co.A
Reynolds, John F. AL 32nd Inf. Co.G
Reynolds, John F. TX 14th Cav. Co.B
Reynolds, John F. TX Cav. Sutton's Co.
Reynolds, John F. VA 22nd Inf. Co.I
Reynolds, John F. VA 23rd Inf. Co.D
Reynolds, John F. VA 189th Mil. Co.C
Reynolds, John F. Gen. & Staff Asst.Surg.
Reynolds, John G. AL 20th Inf. Co.E Cpl.
Reynolds, John G. Gen. & Staff, Arty.,PACS Capt.
Reynolds, John H. AL Cp. of Instr.Talladega
Reynolds, John H. LA 21st (Kennedy's) Inf. Co.B Cpl.
Reynolds, John H. NC 60th Inf. Co.F Lt.
Reynolds, John H. SC 15th Inf. Co.A
Reynolds, John H. TX 15th Inf. 2nd Co.F
Reynolds, John H. VA Lt.Arty. G.B. Chapman's Co.
Reynolds, John H. VA 11th Inf. Co.H
Reynolds, John H. VA 38th Inf. Co.B
Reynolds, John H. VA 53rd Inf. Co.I
Reynolds, John H. 1st Conf.Inf. 2nd Co.H Sgt.
Reynolds, John J. LA 17th Inf. Co.E
Reynolds, John J., Jr. VA Lt.Arty. 13th Bn. Co.C
Reynolds, John J., Sr. VA Lt.Arty. 13th Bn. Co.C
Reynolds, John J. VA Hvy.Arty. 20th Bn. Co.D
Reynolds, John J. VA Lt.Arty. 38th Bn. Co.D
Reynolds, John J. VA Courtney Arty. Artif.
Reynolds, John J. VA Lt.Arty. Hardwicke's Co.
Reynolds, John J. VA 50th Inf. Co.K

Reynolds, John L. GA 21st Inf. Co.F
Reynolds, John L. VA 28th Inf. Co.B
Reynolds, John M. AL 45th Inf. Co.K
Reynolds, John M. GA Inf. 10th Bn. Co.B
Reynolds, John M. GA 16th Inf. Co.K
Reynolds, John M. GA 29th Inf. Co.D
Reynolds, John M. SC 2nd Inf. Co.F
Reynolds, John M. SC 11th Inf. Co.A
Reynolds, John M. SC 19th Inf. Co.F Sgt.
Reynolds, John M. Gen. & Staff Asst.Surg.
Reynolds, John N. GA 14th Inf. Co.D
Reynolds, John N. LA 3rd (Harrison's) Cav. Co.F
Reynolds, John O. VA 2nd Arty. Co.A 1st Sgt.
Reynolds, John O. VA Inf. 22nd Bn. Co.A 1st Lt.
Reynolds, John P. MS 16th Inf. Co.F
Reynolds, John R. LA 9th Inf. Co.C Cpl.
Reynolds, John R. MS Cav. Buck's Co.
Reynolds, John R. NC 30th Inf. Co.A
Reynolds, John R. SC Hvy.Arty. 15th (Lucas') Bn. Co.C
Reynolds, John R. SC Arty. Childs' Co.
Reynolds, John R. SC Arty. Lee's Co. Cpl.
Reynolds, John S. SC 16th & 24th (Cons.) Inf. Co.G Sgt.
Reynolds, John S. SC 24th Inf. Co.I Cpl.
Reynolds, John S. VA 57th Inf. Co.E 2nd Lt.
Reynolds, Johnson VA 14th Cav. Co.K
Reynolds, Johnson VA 51st Inf. Co.A
Reynolds, John T. AL 41st Inf. Co.H
Reynolds, John T. GA 2nd Cav.
Reynolds, John T. MS 24th Inf. Co.E
Reynolds, John T. NC 21st Inf. Co.H
Reynolds, John T. NC 64th Inf. Co.H Capt.
Reynolds, John T. TN 29th Inf. Co.F Sgt.Maj.
Reynolds, John W. AL Inf. 1st Regt. Co.D, 3rd Co.G
Reynolds, John W. AL 25th Inf.
Reynolds, John W. AL 26th (O'Neal's) Inf. Co.H Cpl.
Reynolds, John W. AL 30th Inf. Co.I
Reynolds, John W. AL Cav. 5th Bn. Hilliard's Legion Co.C
Reynolds, John W. GA 3rd Cav. Co.C
Reynolds, John W. GA 8th Cav. Co.A
Reynolds, John W. GA 62nd Cav. Co.H
Reynolds, John W. GA 1st Inf. Co.I
Reynolds, John W. GA 2nd Inf. Co.D Cpl.
Reynolds, John W. GA 4th Inf. Co.E
Reynolds, John W. GA 22nd Inf. Co.H
Reynolds, John W. MS 29th Inf. Co.I Cpl.
Reynolds, John W. NC 2nd Bn.Loc.Def.Troops Co.D
Reynolds, John W. TX Cav. Martin's Regt. Co.B
Reynolds, John W. VA 6th Cav. Co.I
Reynolds, John W. VA 23rd Inf. Co.D
Reynolds, John W. VA 57th Inf. Co.G
Reynolds, John W. VA 79th Mil. Co.4 2nd Lt.
Reynolds, John W. 10th Conf.Cav. Co.G Cpl.
Reynolds, John W. 1st Conf.Inf. Co.A
Reynolds, John Ward VA 38th Inf. Co.B
Reynolds, Jonathan VA Inf. 26th Bn. Co.E
Reynolds, Jonathan W. VA 36th Inf. 2nd Co.E
Reynolds, Joseph AL 1st Cav. 2nd Co.C
Reynolds, Joseph AR 15th (N.W.) Inf. Co.A

Reynolds, Joseph GA Inf. 1st City Bn.
  (Columbus) Co.D
Reynolds, Joseph LA 1st Hvy.Arty. (Reg.) Co.B
  Cpl.
Reynolds, Joseph LA Arty. Kean's Btty. (Orleans
  Lt.Arty.) Cpl.
Reynolds, Joseph MS Inf. 7th Bn. Co.C
Reynolds, Joseph MO 2nd Cav. Co.F
Reynolds, Joseph MO 6th Cav. Co.B
Reynolds, Joseph NC 16th Inf. Co.E
Reynolds, Joseph NC 60th Inf. Co.D
Reynolds, Joseph SC 6th Inf. 1st Co.I
Reynolds, Joseph SC 12th Inf. Co.C
Reynolds, Joseph SC Palmetto S.S. Co.M
Reynolds, Joseph TN Cav. 9th Bn. (Gantt's)
Reynolds, Joseph TX 9th (Nichols') Inf. Co.B
Reynolds, Joseph TX 18th Inf. Co.K
Reynolds, Joseph VA 16th Cav. Co.C
Reynolds, Joseph VA 20th Cav. Co.G
Reynolds, Joseph VA 20th Cav. Co.H
Reynolds, Joseph VA 3rd (Archer's) Bn.Res.
  Co.A
Reynolds, Joseph VA 11th Bn.Res. Co.B
Reynolds, Joseph VA 27th Inf. Co.C
Reynolds, Joseph VA 46th Inf. 1st Co.G
Reynolds, Joseph A. SC 24th Inf. Co.K 1st Sgt.
Reynolds, Joseph B. GA 5th Inf. Co.C
Reynolds, Joseph B. GA 48th Inf. Co.C
Reynolds, Joseph B. MS 1st (Patton's) Inf. Co.K
Reynolds, Joseph B. VA 6th Cav. Co.I
Reynolds, Joseph D. VA 21st Inf. Co.I
Reynolds, Joseph D., 1st VA 38th Inf. Co.B
Reynolds, Joseph D., 2nd VA 38th Inf. Co.B
Reynolds, Joseph E. VA 22nd Inf. Co.C
Reynolds, Joseph E. VA 189th Mil. Co.C
Reynolds, Joseph F. MO 3rd & 5th Cons.Inf.
Reynolds, Joseph F. VA 5th Bn.Res. Co.A
Reynolds, Joseph H. MS 27th Inf. Co.C
Reynolds, Joseph H. NC 33rd Inf. Co.A
Reynolds, Joseph J.D. VA 38th Inf. Co.B
Reynolds, Joseph M. GA Cav. 7th Bn.
  (St.Guards) Co.D Cpl.
Reynolds, Joseph M. MS Cav. 24th Bn. Co.E
Reynolds, Joseph M. MS Arty. (Seven Stars
  Arty.) Roberts' Co.
Reynolds, Joseph M. TX 18th Cav. Co.G
Reynolds, Joseph P. NC 16th Inf. Co.F Sgt.
Reynolds, Joseph R. MS 8th Cav. Co.C
Reynolds, Joseph S. VA Lt.Arty. Moore's Co.
Reynolds, Joseph S. VA Lt.Arty. Thompson's
  Co.
Reynolds, Joseph T. GA 14th Inf. Co.D
Reynolds, Joseph W. GA Lt.Arty. Milledge's Co.
Reynolds, Joseph W. MO Searcy's Bn.S.S.
Reynolds, Joshua MO Robertson's Regt.St.Guard
  Co.1
Reynolds, Joshua NC 64th Inf. Co.F
Reynolds, Joshua TX 2nd Cav. Co.D
Reynolds, Joshua TX 12th Inf. Co.A
Reynolds, Joshua D. LA Washington Arty.Bn.
  Co.4 Sgt.
Reynolds, Josiah AL 13th Inf. Co.I
Reynolds, Josiah MS Inf. 7th Bn. Co.C
Reynolds, Josiah L. MS 17th Inf. Co.F
Reynolds, J.P. AL 18th Inf. Co.A
Reynolds, J.P. AL 48th Inf. Co.K
Reynolds, J.P. SC Mil. 17th Regt. Buist's Co.

Reynolds, J.Q. VA 4th Cav. Co.C
Reynolds, J.R. AL 8th Inf. Co.G,D
Reynolds, J.R. AL 63rd Inf. Co.E
Reynolds, J.R. MS Inf. 1st Bn. Co.C
Reynolds, J.R. MS 35th Inf. Co.C
Reynolds, J.R. TN 22nd Inf. Co.I
Reynolds, J.S. AL 9th Inf. Co.I
Reynolds, J.S. AR 11th & 17th (Cons.) Inf.
  Co.A
Reynolds, J.S. GA 1st Cav. Co.G,I
Reynolds, J.S. GA Lt.Arty. Daniell's Btty.
Reynolds, J.S. GA Arty. Maxwell's Reg.Lt.Btty.
  Artif.
Reynolds, J.S. VA Inf. Montague's Bn. Co.B
Reynolds, J.T., Jr. AL 12th Inf. Co.B
Reynolds, J.T. AL 22nd Inf. Co.G
Reynolds, J.T. AL 62nd Inf. Co.B
Reynolds, J.T. AR 35th Inf. Co.H
Reynolds, J.T. GA Cav. Roswell Bn. Co.A
Reynolds, J.T. GA 3rd Res. Co.I
Reynolds, J.T. MS 28th Cav. Co.I
Reynolds, J.T. TN 3rd (Forrest's) Cav. 1st Co.E
Reynolds, J.T. TN 8th Inf. Co.B
Reynolds, J.T. TX 21st Cav. Co.C
Reynolds, J.T. TX Cav. Border's Regt. Co.B
Reynolds, J.T. VA Cav. 36th Bn. Co.C
Reynolds, Julius C. AL Cav.Res. Brooks' Co.
Reynolds, J.W. AL 20th Inf. Co.K
Reynolds, J.W. AR 2nd Mtd.Rifles Co.K Sgt.
Reynolds, J.W. AR Lt.Arty. Marshall's Btty.
Reynolds, J.W. AR 27th Inf. Co.E
Reynolds, J.W. FL 1st (Res.) Inf. Co.H Cpl.
Reynolds, J.W. GA 2nd Bn.Troops & Def.
  (Macon) Co.A
Reynolds, J.W. GA 3rd Inf. Sgt.
Reynolds, J.W. GA 5th Inf. Co.K
Reynolds, J.W. GA Inf. 25th Bn. (Prov.Guard)
  Co.A
Reynolds, J.W. GA Inf. (High Shoals Defend.)
  Medlin's Ind.Co.
Reynolds, J.W. LA 1st Inf. Co.C
Reynolds, J.W. LA Inf. 4th Bn. Co.E
Reynolds, J.W. MS Cav. 3rd Bn. (Ashcraft's)
  Co.C Cpl.
Reynolds, J.W. SC 1st (Butler's) Inf. Co.I
Reynolds, J.W. SC 7th Inf. 1st Co.K, 2nd Co.K
  Sgt.
Reynolds, J.W. TN 1st Hvy.Arty. Co.L
Reynolds, J.W. TN 4th Inf. Co.K
Reynolds, J.W. TX 34th Cav. Co.K
Reynolds, J.W. VA 17th Inf. Co.C
Reynolds, J.W. VA 21st Inf.
Reynolds, J.W. 7th Conf.Cav. Co.D
Reynolds, L. AR 3rd Inf. Co.K
Reynolds, L. GA Cav. 1st Bn.Res. Tufts' Co.
Reynolds, L. MO 9th Inf. Co.F Cpl.
Reynolds, L. NC 23rd Inf. Co.H
Reynolds, L. SC 6th Inf. Co.E
Reynolds, Lafayette TN 29th Inf. Co.K
Reynolds, Lafayette VA Lt.Arty. 13th Bn. Co.C
Reynolds, Lafayette VA Lt.Arty. 38th Bn. Co.D
Reynolds, Lafayette P. MS 2nd Inf. Co.A 1st Lt.
Reynolds, Larkin LA 12th Inf. Co.D
Reynolds, Larkin B. GA 18th Inf. Co.F Cpl.
Reynolds, L.B. SC 6th Inf. 1st Co.C, Co.E
Reynolds, L.B. SC 17th Inf. Co.B
Reynolds, Lee LA Inf. McLean's Co.

Reynolds, Lee VA 59th Inf. 2nd Co.A
Reynolds, Lee L. KY 1st Bn.Mtd.Rifles Co.B
Reynolds, Lemuel AL 45th Inf. Co.G
Reynolds, Lemuel M. AR Cav. Harrell's Bn.
  Co.K
Reynolds, Lemuel M. 1st Choctaw & Chickasaw
  Mtd.Rifles 1st Co.E Lt.Col.
Reynolds, Leroy W. TN 3rd (Clack's) Inf. Co.G
Reynolds, Levi GA Cav. 8th Bn. (St.Guards)
  Co.B
Reynolds, Levi KY 10th (Johnson's) Cav. Co.D
Reynolds, Lewis GA 1st Cav. Co.C
Reynolds, Lewis MS Inf. 7th Bn. Co.C
Reynolds, Lewis SC 1st St.Troops Co.D Sgt.
Reynolds, Lewis SC 5th Res. Co.F Sgt.
Reynolds, Lewis VA 20th Cav. Co.I
Reynolds, Lewis H. VA 17th Inf. Co.K
Reynolds, Lewis L. MO 1st N.E. Cav. Co.D 1st
  Sgt.
Reynolds, Lewis R. AL 10th Inf. Co.D
Reynolds, L.F.C. VA 4th Inf. Co.H
Reynolds, L.F.R. LA 2nd Inf. Co.I
Reynolds, Littleton MS 7th Inf. Co.C
Reynolds, L.M. AR 1st Cav. Co.F
Reynolds, Lorenzo D. GA Arty. 11th Bn.
  (Sumter Arty.) Old Co.C, Co.A
Reynolds, Louis MO Cav. 3rd Bn. Co.G Sgt.
Reynolds, Lucian NC 51st Inf. Co.H
Reynolds, Lucian NC 61st Inf. Co.H
Reynolds, Luther J. VA 23rd Inf. Co.G
Reynolds, L.W. AR 2nd Inf. Old Co.C, Co.B
Reynolds, M. AR Cav. Woosley's Bn. Co.B
Reynolds, M. NC 22nd Inf. Co.I
Reynolds, M. SC 7th Cav. Co.F
Reynolds, M. TX Cav. 2nd Regt.St.Troops Co.E
Reynolds, M. TX Cav. Wells' Regt. Co.H
Reynolds, M.A. AL 37th Inf. Co.H
Reynolds, M.A. AL Cp. of Instr. Talladega
Reynolds, M.A. TX 9th (Young's) Inf. Co.C
Reynolds, Malachi AR 14th (McCarver's) Inf.
  Co.E
Reynolds, Malcom R. TX 19th Cav. Co.D
Reynolds, Mansfield GA 4th (Clinch's) Cav.
  Co.F
Reynolds, Marion MS Arty. (Seven Stars Arty.)
  Roberts' Co.
Reynolds, Marion J. GA 1st Cav. Co.C 2nd Lt.
Reynolds, Mark AR 7th Cav. Co.G Sgt.
Reynolds, Mark D. AR 14th (Powers') Inf. Co.G
Reynolds, Mark W. NC 2nd Arty. (36th
  St.Troops) Co.G Sgt.
Reynolds, Marshal AR 34th Inf. Co.F
Reynolds, Martin MS 24th Inf. Co.A
Reynolds, Martin NC 37th Inf. Co.K
Reynolds, Martin SC 1st Arty. Co.H
Reynolds, Mathew GA 20th Inf. Co.K
Reynolds, Matthew NC 34th Inf. Co.E
Reynolds, Maus AL 9th Inf. Co.E
Reynolds, M.C. AR 15th Mil. Co.F
Reynolds, M.C. AR 35th Inf. Co.H
Reynolds, McCord AL Inf. 1st Regt. Co.H Cpl.
Reynolds, Mellvin TN 62nd Mtd.Inf. Co.B Cpl.
Reynolds, Meridith B. MS 42nd Inf. Co.H
Reynolds, Michael C. VA 58th Inf. Co.G Sgt.
Reynolds, Michael J. TX 13th Cav. Co.F 2nd
  Lt.
Reynolds, Milton VA 16th Cav. Co.I

Reynolds, Mitchell A. MS 11th Inf. Co.A
Reynolds, M.J. AL 18th Inf. Co.A
Reynolds, M.M. LA 11th Inf. Co.G
Reynolds, M.M. LA Mil. Orleans Fire Regt. Lt.Col.
Reynolds, Monroe M. MS 2nd Inf. Co.K
Reynolds, Montgomery AR Inf. 1st Bn. Co.A
Reynolds, Montraville MO Cav. Wood's Regt.
Reynolds, M.O.P. AL 29th Inf. Co.E
Reynolds, Mordica J. GA Cav. 7th Bn. (St.Guards) Co.D Cpl.
Reynolds, Moses KY 6th Cav. Co.C
Reynolds, Moses TX 1st Inf. Co.H
Reynolds, M.P. AL 7th Cav. Co.D
Reynolds, M.R. SC 4th St.Troops Co.E
Reynolds, Murdock C. NC 2nd Arty. (36th St.Troops) Co.G
Reynolds, M.W. GA 9th Inf. (St.Guards) Culp's Co.
Reynolds, M.W. TX 34th Cav. Co.K
Reynolds, N. MS 41st Inf. Co.H
Reynolds, N.A. NC 22nd Inf. Co.F 1st Lt.
Reynolds, Napoleon B. TX 14th Cav. Co.E Sgt.
Reynolds, Napoleon J. GA 21st Inf. Co.B 2nd Lt.
Reynolds, Nathan A. NC 37th Inf. Co.H
Reynolds, Nathaniel NC 22nd Inf. Co.F
Reynolds, Nathaniel TN 30th Inf. Co.F Wag.
Reynolds, N.C. AR 1st Field Btty. (McNally's)
Reynolds, N.C. MO Lt.Arty. Farris' Btty. (Clark Arty.) Cpl.
Reynolds, N.C. TX 31st Cav. Co.H
Reynolds, Needham AR 1st (Crawford's) Cav. Co.I
Reynolds, Nelson MS 14th Inf. Co.K Bugler
Reynolds, Newman VA 108th Mil. Co.C
Reynolds, N.J. GA 1st Cav. Co.F Capt.
Reynolds, N.J. Crews' Brig. Maj.
Reynolds, Norval MS Inf. 7th Bn. Co.C
Reynolds, N.S. TX Cav. 2nd Bn.St.Troops Wilson's Co.
Reynolds, N.T. VA 54th Inf. Co.D
Reynolds, O.B. VA 27th Inf. Co.E
Reynolds, O.L. AL 18th Inf. Co.E,K
Reynolds, Oliver P. TX 13th Cav. Co.F 1st Lt.
Reynolds, Osburn V. SC 12th Inf. Co.C
Reynolds, Owen, No.1 TN 2nd (Walker's) Inf. Co.I Cpl.
Reynolds, Owen, No.2 TN 2nd (Walker's) Inf. Co.I
Reynolds, P. MO Cav. Williams' Regt.
Reynolds, P. SC 5th Cav. Co.D
Reynolds, P. SC Cav. 17th Bn. Co.A
Reynolds, P. TN 1st (Carter's) Cav. Co.C
Reynolds, P. TN 5th Inf. 2nd Co.H
Reynolds, P. TX 24th & 25th Cav. (Cons.) Co.B
Reynolds, P. TX 25th Cav. Co.A
Reynolds, P. Grimes' Brig. Capt.,AQM
Reynolds, Paris VA 30th Bn.S.S. Co.A
Reynolds, Patrick MD 1st Inf. Co.B
Reynolds, Patrick MS Lt.Arty. English's Co. Cpl.
Reynolds, Patrick TN 5th Inf. Co.M
Reynolds, Patrick TX 2nd Cav. Co.I Cpl.
Reynolds, P.B. VA 50th Inf. Co.K
Reynolds, Perry G. AR 9th Inf. Co.F
Reynolds, Peter AL 49th Inf. Co.A

Reynolds, Peter LA Inf. 1st Sp.Bn. (Wheat's) Co.A
Reynolds, Peter LA 15th Inf. Co.D
Reynolds, Peter NC 2nd Inf. Co.E
Reynolds, Peter NC 51st Inf. Co.H
Reynolds, Peter SC 16th Inf. Co.A
Reynolds, Peter J. VA 22nd Cav. Co.E
Reynolds, P.G. AR 10th Inf. Co.K
Reynolds, P.G. SC Inf. 6th Bn. Co.B
Reynolds, P.G. SC 26th Inf. Co.H Cpl.
Reynolds, P.H. GA 1st Cav. Co.H
Reynolds, P.H. GA Cav. 10th Bn. (St.Guards) Co.E
Reynolds, Philip J. VA 22nd Cav. Co.E 2nd Lt.
Reynolds, Phillip TN 59th Mtd.Inf. Co.E
Reynolds, Phillip H. AR Inf. 2nd Bn. Co.C
Reynolds, Phillip H. AR 3rd Inf. Co.E
Reynolds, Pinkney MS Inf. 7th Bn. Co.C
Reynolds, P.J. AR 6th Inf. Co.G
Reynolds, Pleasant M.B. TN Cav. 17th Bn. (Sanders') Co.A
Reynolds, P.M. LA 15th Inf.
Reynolds, P.M. TN 18th (Newsom's) Cav. Co.H
Reynolds, P.M.B. AL Cav. Forrest's Regt.
Reynolds, Powhatan W. VA 28th Inf. Co.D
Reynolds, Powell B. KY 5th Mtd.Inf. Co.D
Reynolds, P.R. MS 2nd Inf.
Reynolds, Preston VA 28th Inf. Co.I
Reynolds, Preston VA 157th Mil. Co.A
Reynolds, Pryor KY 12th Cav. Co.H
Reynolds, Pryor NC 45th Inf. Capt.,AQM
Reynolds, P.S. AR 36th Inf. Co.I Music.
Reynolds, P.S. AL Cp. of Instr. Talladega Co.D
Reynolds, R. GA 6th Inf. (St.Guards) Sims' Co.
Reynolds, R. MS Hall's Co.
Reynolds, R. SC 5th Cav. Co.D
Reynolds, R. SC Cav. 17th Bn. Co.A
Reynolds, R.A. AL 18th Inf. Co.E,K
Reynolds, R.A. GA 3rd Res. Co.I
Reynolds, R.A. VA 34th Inf. Co.B
Reynolds, R.A. VA 72nd Mil.
Reynolds, Raf P. TN 5th (McKenzie's) Cav. Co.C
Reynolds, Ralph C. VA 28th Inf. Co.B Sgt.
Reynolds, Randle VA 60th Inf. Co.B
Reynolds, Randul VA 46th Inf. 1st Co.C
Reynolds, Ransom SC 6th Inf. 1st Co.I
Reynolds, R.B. AR 27th Inf. Co.G
Reynolds, R.B. AR Mil. Louis' Co.
Reynolds, R.B. SC 3rd Cav. Co.B
Reynolds, R.B. SC 5th Cav. Co.G Cpl.
Reynolds, R.B. SC Cav. 17th Bn. Co.B
Reynolds, R.B. Gen. & Staff Maj.,QM (Declined)
Reynolds, R.C. LA Inf.Cons.Crescent Regt. Co.E
Reynolds, R.C. TN 38th Inf. 2nd Co.K Sgt.
Reynolds, R.D. TX 9th (Young's) Inf. Co.C
Reynolds, R.D. VA 2nd Bn.Res. Co.B
Reynolds, R.E. VA Lt.Arty. Grandy's Co.
Reynolds, Reuben VA 60th Inf. Co.G
Reynolds, Reuben A. VA 22nd Cav. Co.E
Reynolds, Reuben O. MS 11th Inf. Co.I Col.
Reynolds, Reubin E. GA 31st Inf. Co.F
Reynolds, R.G. GA Cav. 29th Bn. Co.A
Reynolds, R.G. GA 6th Inf. (St.Guards) Sims' Co. Cpl.

Reynolds, R.H. AL 22nd Inf. Co.K
Reynolds, R.H. VA Lt.Arty. Barr's Co.
Reynolds, R.H. VA Lt.Arty. Jackson's Bn.St.Line Co.A
Reynolds, R.H.L. GA Cav. 9th Bn. (St.Guards) Co.A,F Cpl.
Reynolds, Rhodstl AL 51st (Part.Rangers) Co.B
Reynolds, Richard FL 1st Inf. Old Co.B
Reynolds, Richard MO 1st N.E. Cav. Co.E
Reynolds, Richard SC 5th Res. Co.C
Reynolds, Richard VA 40th Inf. Co.C
Reynolds, Richard J. MS 36th Inf. Co.I
Reynolds, Richard R. GA 3rd Inf. Co.G
Reynolds, Richard T. AR 26th Inf. Co.B
Reynolds, Richard W. MS 1st Bn.S.S. Co.B
Reynolds, Riley MS 5th Inf. (St.Troops) Co.B Sgt.
Reynolds, R.J. AL 37th Inf. Co.B
Reynolds, R.J. AR Inf. Cocke's Regt. Co.D
Reynolds, R.J. GA 5th Res. Co.E
Reynolds, R.J. TN 5th Inf. 1st Co.H
Reynolds, R.K. MS 18th Cav. Co.A
Reynolds, R.L. TX 21st Inf. Co.I
Reynolds, R.M. AR 27th Inf. Old Co.B 1st Sgt.
Reynolds, R.M. SC Arty. Stuart's Co. (Beaufort Vol.Arty.)
Reynolds, R.M. SC 21st Inf. Co.K
Reynolds, R.M. TX 5th Inf. Co.D
Reynolds, R. Martin GA 53rd Inf. Co.K
Reynolds, Robert GA Cherokee Legion (St.Guards) Co.B
Reynolds, Robert GA Cobb's Legion Co.A
Reynolds, Robert LA 25th Inf. Co.E
Reynolds, Robert MO Cav. Wood's Regt.
Reynolds, Robert SC Cav.Bn. Hampton Legion Co.C
Reynolds, Robert NC Lt.Arty. Thomas' Legion Levi's Btty. Cpl.
Reynolds, Robert TN 10th Inf. Co.B Cpl.
Reynolds, Robert TN 11th Inf. Co.D
Reynolds, Robert TN 12th Inf. Co.C
Reynolds, Robert TN 60th Mtd.Inf. Co.L
Reynolds, Robert TX Cav. 2nd Regt. Co.B
Reynolds, Robert VA Lt.Arty. E.J. Anderson's Co.
Reynolds, Robert VA Inf. 1st Bn. Co.E
Reynolds, Robert VA 50th Inf. Co.C
Reynolds, Robert A. GA Cobb's Legion Co.F
Reynolds, Robert A. VA 21st Inf. Co.C
Reynolds, Robert B. SC 1st Arty. Co.D Cpl.
Reynolds, Robert D. AL 6th Cav. Co.H,F Sgt.
Reynolds, Robert F. GA 61st Inf. Co.I
Reynolds, Robert H. MS 2nd Inf. Co.D
Reynolds, Robert J. GA 25th Inf. Co.E
Reynolds, Robert L. TX Inf. Griffin's Bn. Co.A
Reynolds, Robert L. VA 40th Inf. Co.B Sgt.Maj.
Reynolds, Robert M. GA 14th Inf. Co.I Cpl.
Reynolds, Robert N. LA 6th Inf. Co.A
Reynolds, Robert O. SC 11th Inf. Co.E
Reynolds, Robert R. GA 29th Inf. Co.H
Reynolds, Robert R. 1st Conf.Inf. 2nd Co.H
Reynolds, Roberts GA Arty. Baker's Co.
Reynolds, Roberts GA 1st Inf. Co.H
Reynolds, Robert T. GA 14th Inf. Co.B
Reynolds, Robert W. KY 6th Cav. Co.C
Reynolds, Rod P. KY 2nd Mtd.Inf. Co.H

Reynolds, Roling SC 12th Inf. Co.C
Reynolds, Roswell L. VA 22nd Inf. Co.H
Reynolds, R.P. TN 63rd Inf. Co.H Sgt.
Reynolds, R.R. FL 10th Inf. Love's Co.
Reynolds, R.R. GA 4th (Clinch's) Cav.
Reynolds, R.R. GA 11th Cav. (St.Guards) Staten's Co. Cpl.
Reynolds, R.R. TN 19th (Biffle's) Cav. Co.B
Reynolds, R.S. FL 2nd Inf. Co.F
Reynolds, R.S. GA Inf. 19th Bn. (St.Guards) Co.F
Reynolds, R.S. MS 7th Inf. Co.C
Reynolds, R.T. VA 2nd St.Res. Co.A Cpl.
Reynolds, Rufus R. FL 6th Inf. Co.B
Reynolds, R.W. AL 6th Cav. Co.G
Reynolds, R.W. SC Gregg's Cav.
Reynolds, R.W. TX 24th & 25th Cav. (Cons.) Co.A
Reynolds, R.W. VA 4th Cav. Co.K
Reynolds, R.W. VA 6th Cav. Co.G
Reynolds, R.W. 1st Conf.Cav. 2nd Co.G 1st Lt.
Reynolds, S. GA 16th Inf. Co.C
Reynolds, S. SC 6th Cav. Co.H Cpl.
Reynolds, S. SC Inf. Hampton Legion Co.H
Reynolds, Samuel AR Cav. Harrell's Bn. Co.D
Reynolds, Samuel AR 18th (Marmaduke's) Inf. Co.K Cpl.
Reynolds, Samuel GA 3rd Inf. Co.K
Reynolds, Samuel GA 24th Inf. Co.B
Reynolds, Samuel GA 66th Inf. Co.K
Reynolds, Samuel LA Inf. 11th Bn. Co.D
Reynolds, Samuel LA Inf.Cons.Crescent Regt. Co.B
Reynolds, Samuel MS 37th Inf. Co.E
Reynolds, Samuel MO 6th Cav. Co.B
Reynolds, Samuel SC 6th Cav. Co.H
Reynolds, Samuel SC Inf. 1st (Charleston) Bn. Co.C
Reynolds, Samuel SC 27th Inf. Co.H
Reynolds, Samuel TN 54th Inf. Co.A
Reynolds, Samuel TX 29th Cav. Co.K
Reynolds, Samuel A. AR Cav. Wright's Regt. Co.E
Reynolds, Samuel B. GA 14th Inf. Co.I
Reynolds, Samuel E. TN 14th Inf. Co.E
Reynolds, Samuel F. NC 20th Inf. Co.G Sgt.
Reynolds, Samuel F. TX 29th Cav. Co.E
Reynolds, Samuel H. TX 2nd Cav. 1st Co.F
Reynolds, Samuel H. TX Cav. Morgan's Regt. Co.I
Reynolds, Samuel H. Morgan's Co.I,CSA
Reynolds, Samuel H. Gen. & Staff, Inf. Lt.Col.
Reynolds, Samuel M. VA 21st Inf. Co.I
Reynolds, Samuel N. AL 25th Inf. Co.D
Reynolds, Samuel N. TX 18th Cav. Co.G
Reynolds, Samuel S. AR 14th (Powers') Inf. Co.E
Reynolds, Samuel T. VA 14th Inf. Co.E Music.
Reynolds, Sanford SC 14th Inf. Co.E
Reynolds, S.D. TN 29th Inf. Co.F Adj.
Reynolds, Seaborn MS 33rd Inf. Co.B
Reynolds, Seabron MS 22nd Inf. Co.F
Reynolds, Seburn GA 59th Inf. Co.K
Reynolds, S.F. TX 1st Inf. Co.D
Reynolds, S.F. VA 16th Cav. Co.G 1st Lt.
Reynolds, S.H. AR 26th Inf. Co.C Cpl.

Reynolds, S.H. VA Cav. Mosby's Regt. (Part.Rangers) Co.D
Reynolds, Shelton VA 22nd Inf. Co.C
Reynolds, Sherod MS 7th Cav. Co.B
Reynolds, Silas VA 22nd Inf. Swann's Co.H
Reynolds, Silas VA 52nd Inf. Co.F
Reynolds, Silas F. VA Cav. Ferguson's Bn. Ferguson's Co., Parks' Co. 1st Lt.
Reynolds, Silas T. VA 17th Cav. Co.E
Reynolds, Silas T. VA 151st Mil. Co.B
Reynolds, Silas W. VA 59th Inf. 2nd Co.K
Reynolds, Simeon D. TN 62nd Mtd.Inf. Co.F Maj.
Reynolds, Simon GA 1st Cav. Co.C Sgt.
Reynolds, Simon H. NC 29th Inf. Co.A
Reynolds, Simon H. NC Walker's Bn. Thomas' Legion Co.B
Reynolds, Simpson S. MO Armstrong's Conscr.
Reynolds, S.J. GA 1st Cav. Co.D Cpl.
Reynolds, S.J. GA Cav. 9th Bn. (St.Guards) Co.A,F 3rd Lt.
Reynolds, S.J. VA 10th Bn.Res. Co.D
Reynolds, S. Kirk Gen. & Staff AASurg.
Reynolds, S.L. GA 55th Inf. Co.K
Reynolds, S.M. MO 1st Inf. Co.K 4th Sgt.
Reynolds, S.M. TN Lt.Arty. Rice's Btty.
Reynolds, S.M. TX Cav. Morgan's Regt. Co.E
Reynolds, S.M. VA Inf. 7th Bn.Loc.Def. Co.A
Reynolds, S.N. KY 13th Cav. Co.D Cpl.
Reynolds, S.R. AL 51st (Part.Rangers) Co.B
Reynolds, Stafford P. VA 42nd Inf. Co.E
Reynolds, Stancil J. MS 1st Lt.Arty. Co.A
Reynolds, Starling MS Inf. 7th Bn. Co.D
Reynolds, Starling B. NC 2nd Arty. (36th St.Troops) Co.G Drum.
Reynolds, Stephen AR 2nd Mtd.Rifles Co.C
Reynolds, Stephen MS Inf. 7th Bn. Co.D
Reynolds, Stephen E. VA 6th Cav. Co.G
Reynolds, Stephen J. VA 162nd Mil. Co.A
Reynolds, Stephen W. VA Hvy.Arty. 10th Bn. Co.C
Reynolds, Stephen W. VA 1st Inf. Co.G
Reynolds, S.W. AL 34th Inf. Co.F
Reynolds, S.W. TN 38th Inf. 2nd Co.K
Reynolds, S.W. TX 31st Cav. Co.H
Reynolds, Swallding GA 13th Inf. Co.K
Reynolds, Sylvester S. TX Inf. Griffin's Bn. Co.A
Reynolds, T. TN 21st & 22nd (Cons.) Cav. Co.C
Reynolds, T. SC Inf. Hampton Legion Co.G
Reynolds, Tandy K. AR 9th Inf. Old Co.B, Co.F
Reynolds, Taylor TN 22nd (Barteau's) Cav. Co.K
Reynolds, T.B. AL 26th (O'Neal's) Inf. Co.I
Reynolds, T.B. GA 3rd Bn. (St.Guards) Co.H
Reynolds, T.B. GA Inf. Exempts Roberts' Co.
Reynolds, T.B. MS 2nd St.Cav. Co.G
Reynolds, T.D. TX 12th Inf. Co.E
Reynolds, Terrel VA 157th Mil. Co.A
Reynolds, Terrill VA 28th Inf. Co.I
Reynolds, T.F. MS 7th Inf. Co.C
Reynolds, Th. LA 21st (Kennedy's) Inf. Co.F
Reynolds, T.H. NC 57th Inf. Co.D Cpl.
Reynolds, T.H. TN 40th Inf. Co.F
Reynolds, Th. H. SC Lt.Arty. Wagener's Co. (Co.A,German Arty.)

Reynolds, Thaddeus W. TX 27th Cav. Co.I 2nd Lt.
Reynolds, Thaddius W. LA 5th Inf. Co.D 1st Lt.
Reynolds, Tho VA 46th Inf. Co.L
Reynolds, Thomas AL 1st Cav. 1st Co.B Cpl.
Reynolds, Thomas AL 1st Bn.Cadets Co.C
Reynolds, Thomas AL 18th Inf. Co.D
Reynolds, Thomas AR Mil. Desha Cty.Bn.
Reynolds, Thomas AR Inf. Cocke's Regt. Co.D
Reynolds, Thomas GA 1st Cav. Co.H
Reynolds, Thomas GA 4th Inf. Co.I
Reynolds, Thomas GA 48th Inf. Co.C
Reynolds, Thomas GA 56th Inf. Co.E
Reynolds, Thomas GA Cobb's Legion Co.I
Reynolds, Thomas KY 13th Cav. Co.K Cpl.
Reynolds, Thomas KY 4th Mtd.Inf. Co.I
Reynolds, Thomas LA 1st (Strawbridge's) Inf. Co.E,G
Reynolds, Thomas LA Mil. 4th Regt. 1st Brig. 1st Div. Co.D
Reynolds, Thomas LA 8th Inf. Co.K
Reynolds, Thomas LA 11th Inf. Co.A
Reynolds, Thomas LA 13th Inf. Co.A
Reynolds, Thomas MS Lt.Arty. Stanford's Co.
Reynolds, Thomas MS 19th Inf. Co.C
Reynolds, Thomas NC 31st Inf. Co.G Cook
Reynolds, Thomas SC Arty. Ferguson's Bn. Co.A
Reynolds, Thomas SC 12th Inf. Co.C
Reynolds, Thomas TN 19th Inf. Co.H
Reynolds, Thomas TX 11th Inf. Co.H
Reynolds, Thomas VA 47th Inf. Co.D
Reynolds, Thomas VA 59th Inf. 3rd Co.F
Reynolds, Thomas VA Loc.Def. Morehead's Co.
Reynolds, Thomas Shecoe's Chickasaw Bn.Mtd.Vol. Co.A Cpl.
Reynolds, Thomas C. Gen. & Staff Col., Vol.Aide
Reynolds, Thomas E. VA 11th Inf. Co.K
Reynolds, Thomas E. VA 48th Inf. Co.H
Reynolds, Thomas E. VA 64th Mtd.Inf. 1st Lt.
Reynolds, Thomas G. MS 2nd Inf. Co.A
Reynolds, Thomas G. MS 17th Inf. Co.E
Reynolds, Thomas Greene AL Lt.Arty. 2nd Bn. Co.D Sgt.
Reynolds, Thomas H. GA Inf. 3rd Bn. Co.A
Reynolds, Thomas H. GA 40th Inf. Co.I
Reynolds, Thomas H. VA 49th Inf. Co.E Cpl.
Reynolds, Thomas J. MS 11th Inf. Co.A
Reynolds, Thomas J. MO 1st Cav. Co.H
Reynolds, Thomas J. SC 2nd Rifles Co.G
Reynolds, Thomas J. TN 14th Inf. Co.G Sgt.
Reynolds, Thomas J. TX 4th Cav. Co.H
Reynolds, Thomas J. VA 8th Inf. Co.H
Reynolds, Thomas K. AL 40th Inf. Co.B
Reynolds, Thomas L. TN Lt.Arty. McClung's Co.
Reynolds, Thomas M. NC 60th Inf. Co.F Sgt.
Reynolds, Thomas N. MO Cav. 3rd Bn. Co.E
Reynolds, Thomas P. GA Lt.Arty. Milledge's Co.
Reynolds, Thomas P. GA 3rd Inf. 1st Co.I
Reynolds, Thomas W. MS 1st Lt.Arty. Co.D
Reynolds, Thomas W. VA 21st Inf. Co.I
Reynolds, Tilghman D. VA 59th Inf. Co.K
Reynolds, T.J. GA 60th Inf. Co.K
Reynolds, T.J. MS Cav. Jeff Davis Legion Co.C

Reynolds, T.J. MS 3rd Inf. Co.D 1st Lt.
Reynolds, T.J. TX 37th Cav. Co.E
Reynolds, T.J. VA 72nd Mil.
Reynolds, T.J. 1st Conf.Cav. 2nd Co.B 1st Lt.
Reynolds, T.K. GA 53rd Inf. Co.I
Reynolds, T.M. VA Lt.Arty. R.M. Anderson's Co.
Reynolds, Tom P. TN 22nd Inf. Co.A Sgt.
Reynolds, T.P. TN 12th (Cons.) Inf. Co.C Sgt.
Reynolds, T.S. GA 3rd Bn. (St.Guards) Co.D Sgt.
Reynolds, T.S. LA Cav. Greenleaf's Co. (Orleans Lt.Horse)
Reynolds, Turner S. VA Hvy.Arty. 19th Bn. Co.A
Reynolds, T.W. LA 9th Inf. Co.B
Reynolds, T.Z. SC 22nd Inf. Co.G
Reynolds, Uriah AL 45th Inf. Co.B
Reynolds, Verlin NC 21st Inf. Co.I
Reynolds, Vivion S. VA 6th Cav. Co.I
Reynolds, W. AR 8th Inf. New Co.E
Reynolds, W. GA Lt.Arty. Barnwell's Btty.
Reynolds, W. GA Lt.Arty. Ritter's Co.
Reynolds, W. MD Arty. 3rd Btty.
Reynolds, W. MO Cav. Woodson's Co.
Reynolds, W. NC 2nd Arty. (36th St.Troops) Co.A
Reynolds, W. VA 22nd Inf. Co.I
Reynolds, W. VA 72nd Mil.
Reynolds, W. 2nd Conf.Inf. Co.A
Reynolds, W.A. AR 36th Inf. Co.I
Reynolds, W.A. AR Inf. Cocke's Regt. Co.I
Reynolds, W.A. GA 55th Inf. Co.D
Reynolds, W.A. TN 50th Inf. Co.B
Reynolds, W.A. VA 22nd Inf. Co.C
Reynolds, Walter W. MS 36th Inf. Co.I
Reynolds, W.B. AL 9th (Malone's) Cav. Co.B
Reynolds, W.B. LA Inf.Cons.Crescent Regt. Co.E
Reynolds, W.B. MO 2nd Cav. Capt.
Reynolds, W.B. SC 3rd Cav. Co.B
Reynolds, W.B. TX 21st Cav. Co.C Cpl.
Reynolds, W.B.E. AR 15th Mil. Co.A
Reynolds, W.C. AL 21st Inf. Co.K
Reynolds, W.C. AR 19th (Dawson's) Inf. Co.G 1st Lt.
Reynolds, W.C. AR 32nd Inf. Co.D
Reynolds, W.C. GA Cobb's Legion Co.D
Reynolds, W.C. LA 13th Bn. (Part.Rangers) Co.D
Reynolds, W.C. LA 2nd Inf. Co.D 1st Lt.
Reynolds, W.C. SC 14th Inf. Co.A
Reynolds, W.C. VA Inf. 25th Bn. Co.G
Reynolds, W.C. Sig.Corps,CSA Sgt.
Reynolds, W.D. AR 2nd Inf. Co.F
Reynolds, W.D. AR 37th Inf. Co.B
Reynolds, W.D. MO 6th Cav. Co.B
Reynolds, W.D. TN 3rd (Clack's) Inf. Co.I
Reynolds, W.D. NC 2nd Dist. Capt.,Ch.CS
Reynolds, W.E. AR 35th Inf. Co.H
Reynolds, W.E. NC 5th Sr.Res. Co.A
Reynolds, W.E. TN 11th Inf. Co.C
Reynolds, Wesley AR 18th Inf. Co.K
Reynolds, Wesley KY 5th Mtd.Inf. Co.F
Reynolds, Wesly B. TN 19th (Biffle's) Cav. Co.B
Reynolds, W.F. AL 45th Inf. Co.H

Reynolds, W.F. SC 18th Inf. Co.F
Reynolds, W.F. TX 24th Cav. Co.H,I
Reynolds, W.F. TX 24th & 25th Cav. (Cons.) Co.I
Reynolds, W.F. TX Waul's Legion Co.D Sgt.
Reynolds, W.G. MS Inf. 2nd St.Troops Co.G
Reynolds, W.G. TN 11th (Holman's) Cav. Co.C
Reynolds, W.G. VA 5th Cav. Co.B
Reynolds, W.H. AL Inf. 1st Regt. Co.E
Reynolds, W.H. AL 34th Inf. Co.F
Reynolds, W.H. AL 49th Inf. Co.E
Reynolds, W.H. AR 15th Mil. Co.F
Reynolds, W.H. AR 35th Inf. Co.I
Reynolds, W.H. GA Inf. 1st Conf.Bn. Co.E 1st Sgt.
Reynolds, W.H. MS 40th Inf. Co.K
Reynolds, W.H. TN 19th & 20th (Cons.) Cav. Co.K
Reynolds, W.H. TN 20th (Russell's) Cav. Co.K
Reynolds, W.H. TN 1st (Feild's) & 27th Inf. (Cons.) Co.I
Reynolds, W.H. TN 5th Inf. 2nd Co.F
Reynolds, W.H. TN 27th Inf. Co.E Sgt.
Reynolds, W.H.H. TN 42nd Inf. Co.A
Reynolds, W.H.H. 4th Conf.Inf. Co.G Cpl.
Reynolds, Wiley AR Inf. Cocke's Regt. Co.I
Reynolds, William AL 5th Inf. New Co.A
Reynolds, William AL 15th Inf. Co.H
Reynolds, William AL 16th Inf. Co.D
Reynolds, William AL 33rd Inf.
Reynolds, William AL 55th Vol. Co.E
Reynolds, William AR 1st (Monroe's) Cav. Palmer's Co.
Reynolds, William AR 15th Mil. Co.A
Reynolds, William AR 17th (Lemoyne's) Inf. Co.C
Reynolds, William AR 18th Inf. Co.K
Reynolds, William AR 21st Inf. Co.C
Reynolds, William GA 12th Cav. Co.B
Reynolds, William GA 1st (Fannin's) Res. Co.C
Reynolds, William GA 6th Inf. (St.Guards) Co.H
Reynolds, William GA 13th Inf. Co.G
Reynolds, William GA Inf. 27th Bn. Co.A
Reynolds, William GA 28th Inf. Co.B
Reynolds, William GA 41st Inf. Co.G
Reynolds, William KY 1st (Butler's) Cav. Co.G
Reynolds, William KY 6th Cav. Co.G
Reynolds, William KY 13th Cav. Co.E
Reynolds, William LA Cav. Cole's Co.
Reynolds, William MD Cav. 2nd Bn. Co.D
Reynolds, William MS 6th Inf. Co.D
Reynolds, William MS 39th Inf. Co.B
Reynolds, William MS 42nd Inf.
Reynolds, William MO 5th Cav. Co.D
Reynolds, William MO 7th Cav. Co.A
Reynolds, William MO 8th Cav. Co.A
Reynolds, William MO Cav. Schnabel's Bn. Co.B Lt.
Reynolds, William MO 3rd Inf. Co.I
Reynolds, William MO Inf. 3rd Bn. Co.F
Reynolds, William MO 5th Inf. Co.B
Reynolds, William MO 6th Inf. Co.H
Reynolds, William MO Robertson's Regt. St.Guard Co.11
Reynolds, William NC 2nd Arty. (36th St.Troops) Co.A
Reynolds, William NC 22nd Inf. Co.F

Reynolds, William NC 49th Inf. Co.I
Reynolds, William NC 60th Inf. Co.D,C
Reynolds, William SC 5th Res. Co.F
Reynolds, William SC 18th Inf. Co.F
Reynolds, William SC 23rd Inf. Co.C 1st Sgt.
Reynolds, William SC Cav.Bn. Holcombe Legion Co.D
Reynolds, William TN 1st (Carter's) Cav. Co.C
Reynolds, William TN 3rd (Forrest's) Cav. Co.D
Reynolds, William TN Cav. Shaw's Bn. Hamilton's Co.
Reynolds, William TN 24th Bn.S.S. Co.B
Reynolds, William TN 42nd Inf. 1st Co.K
Reynolds, William TX 32nd Cav. Co.K
Reynolds, William TX Granbury's Cons.Brig. Co.H
Reynolds, William TX 9th (Nichols') Inf. Co.F
Reynolds, William TX 9th (Young's) Inf. Co.B
Reynolds, William TX 9th (Young's) Inf. Co.C Cpl.
Reynolds, William VA 11th Cav. Co.G
Reynolds, William VA Cav. 15th Bn. Co.D
Reynolds, William VA Lt.Arty. Pegram's Co.
Reynolds, William VA 12th Inf. Branch's Co.
Reynolds, William VA 15th Inf. Co.C
Reynolds, William VA 16th Inf. Co.K
Reynolds, William VA 27th Inf. Co.D
Reynolds, William VA 41st Mil. Co.B
Reynolds, William 3rd Conf.Eng.Troops Co.D
Reynolds, William A. VA 28th Inf. 2nd Co.C
Reynolds, William A. VA 51st Inf. Co.D
Reynolds, William B. AL 46th Inf. Co.H
Reynolds, William B. MO St.Guards Capt.
Reynolds, William B. VA 22nd Inf. Co.F
Reynolds, William C. SC 8th Inf. Co.A 3rd Lt.
Reynolds, William C. VA 6th Inf. 1st Co.B
Reynolds, William C. VA 22nd Inf. Co.H
Reynolds, William C. VA 46th Inf. 1st Co.G, Co.I
Reynolds, William C. VA Inf. Cohoon's Bn. Co.A Sgt.
Reynolds, William C. 3rd Conf.Eng.Troops Co.E 1st Sgt.
Reynolds, William D. NC 8th Jr.Res. Co.B
Reynolds, William D. TN 2nd (Smith's) Cav.
Reynolds, William D. VA 54th Mil. Co.G
Reynolds, William E. VA 22nd Inf. 2nd Co.C 1st Sgt.
Reynolds, William E. VA 47th Inf. 2nd Co.G
Reynolds, William F. AL 18th Inf. Co.A
Reynolds, William F. AL 61st Inf. Co.F
Reynolds, William F. LA 1st (Nelligan's) Inf. Co.F
Reynolds, William F. TN 13th (Gore's) Inf. Co.C Cpl.
Reynolds, William F. TN 34th Inf. 2nd Co.C
Reynolds, William G. GA 5th Res. Co.H
Reynolds, William G. MS 2nd Inf. (A. of 10,000) Co.A 2nd Lt.
Reynolds, William G. MS 8th Inf. Co.K
Reynolds, William G. MS 27th Inf. Co.B Cpl.
Reynolds, William G. MS 29th Inf. Co.A Capt.
Reynolds, William G. TN 28th Inf. Co.C Sgt.
Reynolds, William G. VA 57th Inf. Co.E
Reynolds, William H. AR 6th Inf. Old Co.D, Co.H

Reynolds, William H. GA 26th Inf. 1st Co.G
Cpl.
Reynolds, William H. GA 29th Inf. Co.E Cpl.
Reynolds, William H. GA 44th Inf. Co.K
Reynolds, William H. GA 49th Inf. Co.I
Reynolds, William H. GA 50th Inf. Co.F
Reynolds, William H. MS 19th Inf. Co.K
Reynolds, William H. MS 26th Inf. Co.I
Reynolds, William H. NC 2nd Arty. (36th
St.Troops) Co.K
Reynolds, William H. TN 9th Cav. Co.F
Reynolds, William H. VA 9th Cav. Sandford's
Co.
Reynolds, William H. VA 15th Cav. Co.A
Reynolds, William H. VA Cav. 15th Bn. Co.A
Reynolds, William H. VA Hvy.Arty. 20th Bn.
Co.A
Reynolds, William H. VA Lt.Arty. Fry's Co.
Reynolds, William H. VA 22nd Inf. Co.C
Reynolds, William H. VA 30th Bn.S.S. Co.F
Reynolds, William H. VA 44th Inf. Co.A
Reynolds, William H. VA 46th Inf. 2nd Co.C
Reynolds, William H. VA 50th Inf. Co.C
Reynolds, William H. VA 189th Mil. Co.C
Reynolds, William H. VA Mil. Carroll Cty.
Reynolds, William H. Conf.Inf. Tucker's Regt.
Co.E
Reynolds, William H.H. Conf.Cav. Wood's Regt.
Co.K
Reynolds, William J. GA 1st (Symons') Res.
Co.K
Reynolds, William J. GA 15th Inf. Co.K
Reynolds, William J. GA 59th Inf. Co.I
Reynolds, William J. NC 44th Inf. Co.F
Reynolds, William J. TX 18th Cav. Co.G
Reynolds, William J. VA Lt.Arty. J.R. Johnson's
Co.
Reynolds, William K. NC Walker's Bn. Thomas'
Legion Co.B Cpl.
Reynolds, William L. AR 26th Inf. Co.C Sgt.
Reynolds, William L. VA 4th Cav. Co.H
Reynolds, William L. VA Cav. Mosby's Regt.
(Part.Rangers) Co.B
Reynolds, William M. AL Conscr. Echols' Co.
Reynolds, William M. AR 3rd Inf. Co.C
Reynolds, William M. LA 31st Inf. Co.G
Reynolds, William M. SC 7th Inf. 1st Co.K, 2nd
Co.K Sgt.
Reynolds, William M. TN 34th Inf. 2nd Co.C
Reynolds, William M. TX Cav. 6th Bn. Co.E
Reynolds, William M. TX 18th Cav. Co.A
Reynolds, William M. VA Cav. Hounshell's Bn.
Reynolds, William M. VA Horse Arty. Lurty's
Co. Sgt.
Reynolds, William M. VA 24th Inf. Co.G
Reynolds, William M. VA 56th Inf. Co.C
Reynolds, William M. VA Rockbridge Cty.Res.
Bacon's Co.
Reynolds, William McD. VA 22nd Inf. Co.D
Reynolds, William O. VA Lt.Arty. J.D. Smith's
Co.
Reynolds, William P. AL 13th Inf. Co.D
Reynolds, Wm. P. AL 15th Inf. Co.H
Reynolds, William P. GA 52nd Inf. Co.I
Reynolds, William P. MS 30th Inf. Co.C
Reynolds, William P. NC 13th Inf. Co.H Music.
Reynolds, William R. GA 4th Bn.S.S. Co.C

Reynolds, William R. LA Collins' Scouts
Physician
Reynolds, William R. MS Lt.Arty. Stanford's
Co.
Reynolds, William R. NC 45th Inf. Co.B
Reynolds, William R. VA 21st Cav. Co.F
Reynolds, William S. GA 44th Inf. Co.E Sgt.
Reynolds, William S. MS 1st Cav.Res. Co.A
Capt.
Reynolds, William S. MS 14th Inf. Co.B 2nd Lt.
Reynolds, William Sarby MS 2nd Cav. Co.F 1st
Lt.
Reynolds, William T. MS 1st Bn.S.S. Co.B
Reynolds, William T. MS 22nd Inf. Co.B
Reynolds, William T. SC 7th Res. Co.H
Reynolds, William T. TX 10th Inf. Co.E Cpl.
Reynolds, William T.I. AL 3rd Inf. Co.D
Reynolds, William V. VA 21st Inf. Co.I 1st Sgt.
Reynolds, William W. AR 15th (N.W.) Inf. Co.F
Lt.Col.
Reynolds, William W. GA 20th Inf. Co.E
Reynolds, William W. GA 60th Inf. Co.K
Reynolds, Willis AL 51st (Part.Rangers) Co.B
Reynolds, Willis SC 7th Res. Co.D
Reynolds, Willis J. LA 1st Hvy.Arty. (Reg.)
Co.E
Reynolds, Wilson NC 5th Sr.Res. Co.B
Reynolds, W.J. AL Lt.Arty. Clanton's Btty.
Reynolds, W.J. AL 20th Inf. Co.K
Reynolds, W.J. AL 30th Inf. Co.B
Reynolds, W.J. AL 45th Inf. Co.K
Reynolds, W.J. GA Siege Arty. 28th Bn. Co.K
Reynolds, W.J. GA 23rd Inf. Co.C
Reynolds, W.J. MS 39th Inf. Co.D Cpl.
Reynolds, W.J. SC 5th Bn.Res. Co.D
Reynolds, W.J. TX 35th (Brown's) Cav. Co.C
Reynolds, W.K.P. AR 11th Inf. Co.E
Reynolds, W.L. MO 1st N.E. Cav.
Reynolds, W.L. MO 5th Inf. Co.E
Reynolds, W.L. SC Cav. 14th Bn. Co.A
Reynolds, W.L. TN 4th Inf. Co.C
Reynolds, W.M. GA 54th Inf. Co.D
Reynolds, W.M. MO Cav. Wood's Regt. Co.H
Reynolds, W.M. TN Inf. 23rd Bn. Co.D
Reynolds, W.M. TX 33rd Cav. Co.F Sgt.
Reynolds, W.N. TN 16th (Logwood's) Cav. Co.I
1st Lt.
Reynolds, W.N. TN 9th Inf. Co.E
Reynolds, W.P. GA Inf. 2nd Bn. (St.Guards)
New Co.D
Reynolds, W.P. GA Inf. (Newton Factory
Employees) Russell's Co.
Reynolds, W.P. MS 32nd Inf. Co.A
Reynolds, W.P. NC 45th Inf. Co.D
Reynolds, W.P. SC 3rd Inf. Co.I
Reynolds, W.P. TN 19th (Biffle's) Cav. Co.B
Reynolds, W.P. TX 28th Cav. Co.M
Reynolds, W.P. TX 14th Inf. 2nd Co.K
Reynolds, W.R. GA Cav. 20th Bn. Co.C
Reynolds, W.R. GA 46th Inf. Co.B
Reynolds, W.R. SC 13th Inf. Co.B
Reynolds, W.R. VA 9th Cav. Co.F
Reynolds, W.R. VA 10th Inf. Co.L
Reynolds, W.R.C. TX Cav. Border's Regt. Co.C
Reynolds, W.R.F. SC 5th Cav. Co.K
Reynolds, W.S. GA Lt.Arty. Daniell's Btty.
Reynolds, W.S. MS Inf. 1st Bn. Co.C

Reynolds, W.T. GA 10th Cav. Co.D Sgt.
Reynolds, W.T. GA Lt.Arty. Barnwell's Btty.
Cpl.
Reynolds, W.T. SC Inf. 1st (Charleston) Bn.
Co.B
Reynolds, W.T. TN 55th (Brown's) Inf. Co.H
Reynolds, W.T. TX Granbury's Cons.Brig. Co.E
Cpl.
Reynolds, W.T.J. 7th Conf.Cav. Co.D
Reynolds, W.W. AL 11th Cav. Co.A
Reynolds, W.W. MS 3rd Inf. (St.Troops) Co.K
Reynolds, W.W. TN 8th (Smith's) Cav. Co.L
Reynolds, W.W. TN Lt.Arty. Rice's Btty.
Reynolds, W.W. TN 42nd Inf. Co.G
Reynolds, W.W. TX Cav. McCord's Frontier
Regt. Capt.,AQM
Reynolds, W.W. Gen. & Staff Capt.,AQM
Reynolds, Wyatt VA 38th Inf. Co.B
Reynolds, Z.A. GA 40th Inf. Co.H
Reynoldson, John T. AL 17th Inf. Co.H
Reynols, J. GA 19th Inf. Co.F
Reynols, John 2nd Conf.Eng.Troops Co.H
Reynols, J.W. MS 1st Cav.Res. Co.H
Reynols, J.W. 3rd Conf.Eng.Troops Co.H
Reynols, T.J. GA 5th Inf. (St.Guards) Rucker's
Co.
Reynols, W.H. MO Cav. Stallard's Co.
Reynols, Willey 3rd Conf.Eng.Troops Co.H
Reynor, J.B. GA 3rd Cav. Co.G
Reynor, John G. AL 9th Cav. Co.C
Reyonalds, Robert TX 2nd Cav. Co.B
Reyriver, A. LA Mil. Orleans Guards Regt.
Co.A
Reysin, J.B. LA Mil. 4th Regt. French Brig.
Co.5
Rezean, R. LA Inf. 16th Bn. (Conf.Guards
Resp.Bn.) Co.A
Rezeau, T. FL 1st Inf. New Co.K
Rezell, R.L. AL 5th Inf. Co.I
Rgge, Christian TX Res.Corps Co.C
Rhabjohn, James MS 13th Inf. Co.G
Rhaim, Phillip AL Mil. 4th Vol. Co.G
Rhaimes, James B. FL 2nd Cav. Co.A Black.
Rhaimes, Levi FL 2nd Cav. Co.A
Rhaimes, Nathan FL 2nd Cav. Co.A
Rhaimes, Nathan FL Cav. 5th Bn. Co.E
Rhame, F.M. SC Cav. 14th Bn. Co.A Jr.2nd Lt.
Rhame, Franklin M. SC 5th Cav. Co.H 2nd Lt.
Rhame, George S. SC 20th Inf. Co.G 3rd Lt.
Rhame, George W. SC 5th Cav. Co.E
Rhame, G.W. SC Vol. Simons' Co. Sgt.
Rhame, G.W. SC Manigault's Bn.Vol. Co.A
Rhame, James O. SC Inf. Hampton Legion Co.C
Rhame, J.B. SC 1st Mtd.Mil. Christopher's Co.
1st Lt.
Rhame, J.F. SC Arty. Manigault's Bn. 2nd Co.C
Rhame, John B. SC Inf. Hampton Legion Co.C
Rhame, John E. SC 2nd Cav. Co.A
Rhame, Joseph F. SC Lt.Arty. 3rd (Palmetto) Bn.
Co.E,G,K QMSgt.
Rhame, Joseph F. SC 2nd Inf. Co.D Music.
Rhame, J.V. LA 17th Inf. Co.D
Rhame, J.V. LA Inf.Crescent Regt. Co.F
Rhame, T.A. SC 5th Cav. Co.H
Rhame, T.B. SC Lt.Arty. 3rd (Palmetto) Bn.
Co.G,K
Rhame, T.B. SC Arty. Manigault's Bn. 2nd Co.C

Rhame, Thomas A. SC Cav. 14th Bn. Co.A
Rhame, Thomas B. SC 20th Inf. Co.G
Rhame, William F. SC 2nd Cav. Co.K
Rhame, William F. SC Cav.Bn. Hampton Legion
  Co.B
Rhames, C.H. GA Cav. 29th Bn. Co.G
Rhames, E. SC 7th (Ward's) Bn.St.Res. Co.F
Rhames, E. SC 21st Inf. Co.A
Rhames, Francis A. AL 12th Inf. Co.D
Rhames, John GA Cav. 29th Bn. Co.G
Rhames, John NC 2nd Jr.Res. Co.B
Rhames, Lawton F. FL Lt.Arty. Perry's Co.
Rhames, M.C. AL 12th Inf. Co.D
Rhames, N. SC 21st Inf. Co.A
Rhames, William E. FL 10th Inf. Co.K
Rhamsey, Washington W. FL 6th Inf. Co.K
Rhaney, C.E. GA Siege Arty. 28th Bn. Co.K
Rhea, --- VA Hvy.Arty. 19th Bn. Co.C
Rhea, A. TN 13th Inf. Co.B
Rhea, A. TX 30th Cav. Co.F Sgt.
Rhea, Aaron TN Cav. 16th Bn. (Neal's) Co.A
Rhea, Aaron TN Cav. Welcker's Bn. Co.A
Rhea, A.B. TN 44th (Cons.) Inf. Co.B 1st Lt.
Rhea, A.B. TN Inf. Spencer's Co. 2nd Lt.
Rhea, Abijah TN 29th Inf. Co.D
Rhea, Abraham Gen. & Staff Surg.
Rhea, Adam TN 35th Inf. 2nd Co.D
Rhea, A.J. KY 8th Mtd.Inf. Co.F
Rhea, Alexander W. NC 16th Inf. Co.M
Rhea, Andrew B. TN 44th Inf. Co.E 3rd Lt.
Rhea, Andrew J. MS 27th Inf. Co.C
Rhea, Archy W. TN Cav. 4th Bn. (Branner's)
  Co.E
Rhea, A.W. SC 17th Inf. Co.C
Rhea, A.W. TN 2nd (Ashby's) Cav. Co.I
Rhea, A.W. Gen. & Staff Surg.
Rhea, Beauford NC 2nd Cav. (19th St.Troops)
  Co.A
Rhea, Christian W. TX Waul's Legion Co.E Sgt.
Rhea, C.M. AR 8th Cav. Co.E Cpl.
Rhea, C.W. TX 26th Cav. 1st Co.G
Rhea, C.W. TX 9th (Nichols') Inf. Atchison's
  Co.
Rhea, Daniel W. AR 8th Cav.
Rhea, David TN 3rd (Clack's) Inf. Co.G Capt.
Rhea, David TN Inf. 4th Cons.Regt. Co.C Capt.
Rhea, D.W. AR Gordon's Cav. Co.B
Rhea, D.W. Exch.Bn. 3rd Co.B,CSA
Rhea, Edw. D. MO 4th Cav. Asst.Surg.
Rhea, Edward W. NC 16th Inf. Co.B Sgt.
Rhea, Edwin R. VA 37th Inf. Co.A,K
Rhea, Elbert Lafayette KY 9th Mtd.Inf. Co.H
Rhea, Elbert Lafayette TX Inf. W. Cameron's
  Co.
Rhea, Elias VA 37th Inf. Co.I Cpl.
Rhea, Ellison T. TN 3rd (Lillard's) Mtd.Inf.
  Co.H, 2nd Co.K 1st Sgt.
Rhea, Enoch AR 2nd Inf. Co.G
Rhea, E.T. AL 9th (Malone's) Cav. Co.M
Rhea, F.M. TN 3rd (Clack's) Inf. Co.H
Rhea, Francis A. MS 27th Inf. Co.C
Rhea, George LA 3rd (Wingfield's) Cav. Co.I
Rhea, George VA 54th Mil. Co.E,F
Rhea, George D. TN Sullivan Cty.Res.
  (Loc.Def.Troops) Witcher's Co.
Rhea, George J. AL 4th Inf. Co.I

Rhea, George Jones TN 3rd (Lillard's) Mtd.Inf.
  Co.C
Rhea, George W. VA 41st Inf. 1st Co.E
Rhea, George W.H. MS 17th Inf. Co.D Cpl.
Rhea, G.W. MS 9th Inf. Co.C
Rhea, Hamilton TN 59th Mtd.Inf. Co.I Cpl.
Rhea, H.B. GA 11th Cav. Co.C
Rhea, Henry TN Cav. 16th Bn. (Neal's) Co.A
Rhea, Henry K. NC 60th Inf. Co.C 2nd Lt.
Rhea, Henry Wesley KY 10th (Johnson's) Cav.
  Bennett's Co.
Rhea, H.G. AR 8th Cav. Co.E
Rhea, Hiram T. MS 15th Inf. Co.G
Rhea, H.S. AL 28th Inf. Co.L
Rhea, Hugh AL 3rd Inf. Co.A
Rhea, Hugh AL 3rd Res. Co.A Capt.
Rhea, Hugh B. TN Cav. 16th Bn. (Neal's) Co.A
Rhea, Hugh B. NC Walker's Bn. Thomas'
  Legion Co.A Sgt.
Rhea, J. MO 5th Cav. Co.K
Rhea, J.A. NC 29th Inf. Co.D
Rhea, J.A. TX 2nd Inf. Co.C
Rhea, Jacob H. VA 30th Bn.S.S. Co.E Sgt.
Rhea, Jacob H. VA Mil. Washington Cty.
Rhea, James AL 12th Inf. Co.H
Rhea, James NC 14th Inf. Co.C,D
Rhea, James TN Cav. 12th Bn. (Day's) Co.B
Rhea, James TN 26th Inf. Co.F
Rhea, James VA 37th Inf. Co.H
Rhea, James A. NC 16th Inf. Co.L
Rhea, James A. NC Inf. Thomas Legion Co.E
Rhea, James A. TN 1st (Carter's) Cav. Co.F
Rhea, James A. TN 19th Inf. Co.G 1st Lt.
Rhea, James A. TN 60th Mtd.Inf. Maj.
Rhea, James A. 1st Conf.Cav. 2nd Co.K
Rhea, James C. TX 6th Cav. Co.D
Rhea, James D. TN Sullivan Cty.Res.
  (Loc.Def.Troops) Witcher's Co. Sgt.
Rhea, James H. AL 3rd Res. Co.H
Rhea, James H. TN Conscr. (Cp. of Instr.)
Rhea, James H. VA 11th Inf. Co.K Cpl.
Rhea, James H. VA 37th Inf. Co.H
Rhea, James L. TN Sullivan Cty.Res.
  (Loc.Def.Troops) Witcher's Co.
Rhea, James M. NC 16th Inf. Co.B Cpl.
Rhea, James M. TX 5th Inf. Co.B
Rhea, James M. VA Hvy.Arty. 18th Bn. Co.B
Rhea, James N. NC 52nd Inf. Co.C
Rhea, James W. VA 48th Inf. Co.K
Rhea, J.D. AR 19th (Dockery's) Inf. Co.C
Rhea, Jesse NC 2nd Arty. (36th St.Troops) Co.F
Rhea, J.H. AR 8th Inf. New Co.A
Rhea, J.H. GA 11th Cav. Co.C
Rhea, J.H. KY 8th Mtd.Inf. Co.F
Rhea, J.H. MO 15th Cav. Co.E
Rhea, J.H. TN 59th Mtd.Inf. Co.I
Rhea, J.J. SC 17th Inf. Co.K
Rhea, J.M. NC 1st Cav. (9th St.Troops) Co.G
Rhea, John NC 4th Cav. (59th St.Troops) Co.F
  Cpl.
Rhea, John TN 59th Mtd.Inf. Co.B
Rhea, John VA Hvy.Arty. 18th Bn. Co.B
Rhea, John A. TN 3rd (Forrest's) Cav. QMSgt.
Rhea, John A. TN Sullivan Cty.Res.
  (Loc.Def.Troops) Witcher's Co.
Rhea, John A. VA 37th Inf. Co.A 1st Lt.
Rhea, John C. TN 29th Inf. Co.D

Rhea, John D. AR 3rd (Cons.) Inf. Co.1
Rhea, John G. 1st Cherokee Mtd.Vol. 2nd Co.A
Rhea, John H. NC 2nd Cav. (19th St.Troops)
  Co.A
Rhea, John H. NC 16th Inf. Co.A
Rhea, John H. NC 39th Inf. Co.K
Rhea, John H. NC Inf. Thomas Legion 1st Co.A
Rhea, John H. TN 19th Inf. Co.G 2nd Lt.
Rhea, John L. TN 19th Inf. Co.G
Rhea, John M. NC 62nd Inf. Co.A
Rhea, John O. TX 30th Cav. Co.A Bugler
Rhea, John P. NC 16th Inf. Co.B 2nd Lt.
Rhea, John P. TN 63rd Inf. Co.F
Rhea, John R. VA 2nd Cav. Co.B
Rhea, John S. TN 13th (Gore's) Cav. Co.H
  Bvt.2nd Lt.
Rhea, John S. VA 18th Cav. 2nd Co.G
Rhea, John S. VA 25th Inf. 1st Co.G
Rhea, John S. VA 62nd Mtd.Inf. 2nd Co.A
Rhea, John W. NC 39th Inf. Co.F 1st Lt.
Rhea, John W. TX 6th Cav. Co.D
Rhea, John W. VA 37th Inf. Co.H
Rhea, Joseph TN Lt.Arty. Burroughs' Co. Sgt.
Rhea, Joseph TN 19th Inf. Co.G Sgt.
Rhea, Joseph VA 8th Cav. Co.A
Rhea, Joseph VA 63rd Inf. Co.E
Rhea, Joseph B. TN 62nd Mtd.Inf. Co.G
Rhea, Joseph G. TN 62nd Mtd.Inf. Co.F
Rhea, Joseph M. VA 37th Inf. Co.H Cpl.
Rhea, Joseph S. TN Vol. (Loc.Def.Troops)
  McLin's Co.
Rhea, J.R. AR 1st (Monroe's) Cav. Co.F 1st Lt.
Rhea, J.T. TX Inf. Chambers' Bn.Res.Corps
  Co.C
Rhea, J.W. AL 3rd Res. Co.G
Rhea, J.Z. NC 64th Inf. Co.G,D
Rhea, L.C. TN 11th (Holman's) Cav. Co.K
Rhea, Leonidas NC 25th Inf. Co.D
Rhea, Lewis TN Inf. 2nd Cons.Regt. Co.E
Rhea, Lewis TN 3rd (Lillard's) Mtd.Inf. Co.H,
  2nd Co.K Cpl.
Rhea, Lewis TN 59th Mtd.Inf. Co.E
Rhea, L.S. TN 18th Inf. Co.D
Rhea, M. MS Inf. 3rd Bn. Co.I
Rhea, M. SC 12th Inf. Co.B
Rhea, Mathew TN 13th Inf. Co.A 1st Lt.
Rhea, Matthew TN 63rd Inf. Co.F
Rhea, M.D.L. TX 26th Cav. Co.C
Rhea, Moses B. MO 7th Cav. Co.B
Rhea, M.R. TN 5th (McKenzie's) Cav. Co.H
Rhea, M.R. TN Blair's Co. (Loc.Def.Troops)
Rhea, O.J. KY 9th Mtd.Inf. Co.A Sgt.
Rhea, Ozias TN 59th Mtd.Inf. Co.G
Rhea, Peter MO Cav. 1st Regt.St.Guard Co.C
Rhea, Peter H. MO St.Guard Sgt.
Rhea, P.M.G. NC 2nd Cav. (19th St.Troops)
  Co.A
Rhea, Ralston MO 11th Inf. Co.E
Rhea, R.B. TN 63rd Inf. Co.F A.Ord.Sgt.
Rhea, R.B. TN Sullivan Cty.Res. (Loc.Def.
  Troops) White's Co.
Rhea, R.C. Gen. & Staff Contr.Surg.
Rhea, R.H. KY 2nd Cav.
Rhea, R.H. TX Cav. Morgan's Regt. Co.G
Rhea, Robert AL Cav. Moreland's Regt. Co.H
Rhea, Robert TN 19th Inf. Co.F 2nd Lt.
Rhea, Robert A. SC 12th Inf. Co.A

Rhea, Robert F. TN 29th Inf. Co.D
Rhea, Robert H. KY 9th Mtd.Inf. Co.H
Rhea, Robert H. TN 18th Inf. Co.D
Rhea, Robert H. TX Inf. W. Cameron's Co.
Rhea, Robert J. TN 19th Inf. Co.G
Rhea, Robert L. VA 37th Inf. Co.A
Rhea, Robert M. TN 63rd Inf. Co.F Sgt.
Rhea, R.P. TN Sullivan Cty.Res. (Loc.Def.
    Troops) Witcher's Co.
Rhea, R.P. TX Cav. Morgan's Regt. Co.G
Rhea, Rufus B. AL 19th Inf. Co.F Capt.
Rhea, Rufus W. TN 1st (Turney's) Inf. Co.G
Rhea, R.W. TX 33rd Cav. Co.K
Rhea, R.W. VA 54th Mil. Co.E,F
Rhea, Samuel NC 26th Inf. Co.A Sgt.
Rhea, Samuel NC Walker's Bn. Thomas' Legion
    1st Co.D
Rhea, Samuel TN 1st (Carter's) Cav. Co.I
Rhea, Samuel TN Blair's Co. (Loc.Def.Troops)
Rhea, Samuel VA 14th Cav. Co.H
Rhea, Samuel M. GA 11th Inf. Co.F
Rhea, Samuel M. TN 3rd (Lillard's) Mtd.Inf.
    Co.H,K
Rhea, Samuel M. TN 59th Mtd.Inf. Co.E
Rhea, Samuel W. TN 63rd Inf. Co.F Sgt.
Rhea, Seaberd F. AR 27th Inf. Co.A
Rhea, Shelton MO 11th Inf. Co.E
Rhea, Simon VA 54th Mil. Co.A
Rhea, Starlin TN 7th Inf. Co.D
Rhea, Stephen VA Lt.Arty. Jeffress' Co.
Rhea, Stephen VA 48th Inf. Co.K
Rhea, Stephens NC 39th Inf. Co.E,A
Rhea, Theodore, Jr. AL 18th Inf. Co.C
Rhea, Theodore, Sr. AL 18th Inf. Co.C
Rhea, Thomas AL 18th Inf. Co.I,C
Rhea, Thomas VA 37th Inf. Co.H
Rhea, Thomas D. AR Cav. Davies' Bn. Co.A
Rhea, Thomas T. VA 25th Inf. 1st Co.G
Rhea, Thomas W. TX 1st (McCulloch's) Cav.
    Co.H
Rhea, Thomas W. TX Cav. Morgan's Regt. Co.B
Rhea, W.A. KY 8th Mtd.Inf. Co.F Cpl.
Rhea, W.A. TN 3rd (Forrest's) Cav. Co.H
Rhea, Walter MS 2nd Part.Rangers Co.C
Rhea, Warren TN Cav. 16th Bn. (Neal's) Co.A
Rhea, Weston H. TN 2nd (Robison's) Inf. Co.E
    AQM
Rhea, W.F. GA Cobb's Legion Co.A
Rhea, W.G. AL Cav. Moreland's Regt. Co.E
Rhea, W.H. AL 12th Cav. Co.A
Rhea, W.H. TN 16th Inf. Co.H Sgt.
Rhea, W.H. VA 6th Bn.Res. Co.F
Rhea, W.H. Cheatham's Div. Capt.
Rhea, William NC 25th Inf. Co.D
Rhea, Wm. NC 25th Inf. Co.D
Rhea, William SC 17th Inf. Co.K
Rhea, William TX 1st (Yager's) Cav. Co.F
Rhea, William VA 54th Mil. Co.H
Rhea, William A. TN 5th (McKenzie's) Cav.
    Co.H
Rhea, William A. TN Cav. 17th Bn. (Sanders')
    Co.A 1st Sgt.
Rhea, William A. TX 6th Cav. Co.D Capt.
Rhea, William B. AL 43rd Inf. Co.K
Rhea, William H. AL 19th Inf. Co.F Sgt.
Rhea, William H. AR 37th Inf. Co.I Sgt.
Rhea, William H. VA 1st Cav. Co.D

Rhea, William H. VA Hvy.Arty. 18th Bn. Co.B
Rhea, William H. VA 37th Inf. Co.A
Rhea, William M. AL Cav. Moreland's Regt.
    Co.H
Rhea, William M. 1st Conf.Cav. 2nd Co.K
Rhea, William R. TN 19th Inf. Co.G Sgt.
Rhea, William S. NC 14th Inf. Co.D
Rhea, William T. MO 7th Cav. Co.B
Rhea, William W.A. NC 39th Inf. Co.A,F
Rhea, W.M. AL 4th Cav. QMSgt.
Rhea, W.M. MS Inf. 3rd Bn. Co.I
Rhea, W.P. TN 17th (Marshall's) Cav. Capt.
Rhea, W.P. TN 63rd Inf. Co.F 1st Lt.
Rheam, G.W. LA 5th Inf. Co.B
Rheames, Charles LA Miles' Legion Co.A
Rheames, H. LA 3rd (Harrison's) Cav. Co.C
Rheams, Daniel LA 1st Hvy.Arty. (Reg.) Co.G
Rheams, Daniel M. LA 4th Inf. Co.K
Rheams, D.M. LA Inf. 9th Bn. Co.B Cpl.
Rheams, F.R. KY 10th (Johnson's) Cav. Co.A
Rheams, John LA 2nd Cav.
Rheams, John M. LA 9th Inf. Co.G Cpl.
Rheams, L.T. LA 4th Inf. Co.A Sgt.
Rheams, Samuel M. LA 16th Inf. Co.D Sgt.
Rheams, Vinsen VA 23rd Cav. Co.M Cpl.
Rheams, V.K. LA 9th Inf. Co.G
Rheams, W.E. FL Inf. 2nd Bn. Co.D
Rhear, Robert H. AL 9th Inf. Co.E 1st Sgt.
Rheder, H. LA Mil. 3rd Regt. 3rd Brig. 1st Div.
    Co.H 1st Sgt.
Rhee, Reinhard TX 1st (Yager's) Cav. Co.E
Rhee, W.P. MS 18th Cav. Wimberly's Co.A
Rheedy, L.B. AL 4th Inf. Co.F
Rheems, William E. FL 3rd Inf. Co.E
Rheen, James VA 10th Bn.Res. Co.E
Rheiling, John H. VA 6th Inf. Ferguson's Co.
Rheiling, John H. VA 12th Inf. Co.H
Rheim, Calvin AR 15th (Johnson's) Inf. Co.D
Rheim, George MS Lt.Arty. English's Co.
Rheim, James J. VA 17th Inf. Co.C
Rheim, John E. NC 38th Inf. Co.G Capt.
Rheim, Joseph A. NC 38th Inf. Co.G
Rheim, William G. VA 17th Inf. Co.C
Rhein, Peter TX 2nd Inf. Co.B
Rheinaman, Henry MS 16th Inf. Co.I
Rheiner, Adam AR 15th (Josey's) Inf. Co.D
Rheiner, G.P. TX 33rd Cav. Co.B
Rheinhardt, Jacob H. GA Cherokee Legion
    (St.Guards) Co.B Sgt.
Rheinhardt, Lewis W. GA Cherokee Legion
    (St.Guards) Co.B
Rheinhardt, V. LA Mil.Squad. Guides d'Orleans
Rheinhardt, W.A. TN 10th Cav. Co.B
Rheinhart, A. TX 8th Field Btty.
Rheinhart, A. TX Lt.Arty. Dege's Bn.
Rheinhart, John H. GA Cherokee Legion
    (St.Guards)
Rheinheimer, J.W. MS 1st (King's) Inf.
    (St.Troops) Co.E
Rheinlander, Chr. TX 7th Cav. Co.B
Rheinlander, J. LA Mil. 4th Regt.Eur.Brig. Co.F
Rheinlander, John LA Mil. 3rd Regt. 3rd Brig.
    1st Div. Co.H
Rheinlander, John TX 5th Cav. Co.D
Rheinwald, J.S. MS 40th Inf. Co.H
Rhem, F. Conf.Lt.Arty. Richardson's Bn. Co.D
Rhem, Frederick VA Lt.Arty. Thompson's Co.

Rhem, John W. NC 1st Arty. (10th St.Troops)
    Co.I
Rhem, William NC 1st Arty. (10th St.Troops)
    Co.B Cpl.
Rhenark, J.C. SC 7th Inf. 1st Co.L, 2nd Co.L
Rhenark, William AR 1st (Dobbin's) Cav. Co.K
Rhenark, W.J. TN 38th Inf. 2nd Co.A
Rhendy, R.B.T. MO 3rd Inf. Co.B
Rheney, Elisha A. GA Cobb's Legion Co.L
Rheney, John M. GA 57th Inf. Co.C
Rheney, John W. GA Cobb's Legion Co.E Sgt.
Rheney, J.W. GA 31st Inf. Co.K
Rheney, W.C. GA 52nd Inf. Co.C
Rheney, William C. GA 57th Inf. Co.C
Rheo, David TN Cav. 12th Bn. (Day's) Co.D
Rhese, John C.M. SC Arty.Bn. Hampton Legion
    Co.A
Rhet, H.S. SC 2nd St.Troops Co.H
Rhetonsky, W. MS Cav.Part.Rangers Rhodes'
    Co.
Rhett, A.B. SC Rhett's Co. Capt.
Rhett, A. Burnett SC Arty. Fickling's Co.
    (Brooks Lt.Arty.) Capt.
Rhett, A. Burnett SC 2nd Inf. Co.K Capt.
Rhett, A. Burnett Arty. Rhett's Bn.,CSA Maj.
Rhett, Albert SC Arty. Stuart's Co. (Beaufort
    Vol.Arty.) Cpl.
Rhett, Albert M. Gen. & Staff Capt.,AQM
Rhett, Alfred SC 1st Arty. Co.B Col.
Rhett, Benjamin Gen. & Staff Surg.
Rhett, B.S., Jr. SC 4th Cav. Co.K
Rhett, B.S. SC Mil.Cav. Rutledge's Co.
Rhett, Chas. M. Gen. & Staff AQM
Rhett, Edmund, Jr. SC 2nd Bn.S.S. Co.A Capt.
Rhett, Grimke SC 1st (McCreary's) Inf. Co.H
    2nd Lt.
Rhett, Grimke Gen. & Staff 1st Lt.,Adj.
Rhett, H. SC Mil. Charbonnier's Co. Cpl.
Rhett, H.S. SC 11th Res. Co.K
Rhett, John T. SC 2nd Cav. Co.H Bvt.2nd Lt.
Rhett, John T. SC Cav.Bn. Hampton Legion
    Co.D Sgt.
Rhett, Julius M. SC 1st Arty. Co.C,D,A,B,F
    Capt.
Rhett, Robert W. SC 1st (McCreary's) Inf. Co.I
    2nd Lt.
Rhett, Roland SC Mil.Cav. Rutledge's Co.
Rhett, Roland Gen. & Staff Maj.,QM
Rhett, Thos. G. Gen. & Staff Maj.
Rhett, Thos. S. Gen. & Staff, Arty. Col.
Rhett, T.M.S. SC 1st (Butler's) Inf. Co.E,F
    2nd Lt.
Rhett, T.S. SC Arty. Stuart's Co. (Beaufort
    Vol.Arty.)
Rhett, T.S. SC 11th Inf. Co.A
Rhett, W.H. SC Bn.St.Cadets Co.A
Rheunn, Calvin AR 6th Inf. Co.I
Rhew, A.H. NC 1st Jr.Res. Co.I
Rhew, Allen NC 1st Jr.Res. Co.I
Rhew, Allen NC 43rd Inf. Co.F
Rhew, Isaac N. NC 24th Inf. Co.A
Rhew, James H. NC 56th Inf. Co.D,H Cpl.
Rhew, Jefferson NC 1st Inf. Co.F
Rhew, John MS 3rd Cav. Co.C
Rhew, Jno. MS Inf. 4th St.Troops Co.L
Rhew, John NC Inf. 13th Bn. Co.A Cpl.

Rhew, John W. NC 2nd Cav. (19th St.Troops) Co.K

Rhew, John W. NC 66th Inf. Co.A Cpl.

Rhew, J.T. NC 50th Inf. Co.A

Rhew, J.W. MS 1st Cav. Co.D

Rhew, Ruffin NC 7th Sr.Res. Davie's Co.

Rhew, Silas M. NC Inf. 13th Bn. Co.A

Rhew, Silas M. NC 66th Inf. Co.A

Rhew, W.A. AR Cav. McGehee's Regt. Co.H

Rhew, Walker NC 31st Inf. Co.E

Rhew, William NC Inf. 13th Bn. Co.A

Rhew, William TX 2nd Cav. Co.G

Rhew, William L. NC 2nd Cav. (19th St.Troops) Co.K

Rhew, William L. NC 44th Inf. Co.C Sgt.

Rhew, William M. NC 56th Inf. Co.D

Rhew, William M. NC 66th Inf. Co.A

Rhew, William N. NC 24th Inf. Co.A

Rhew, William P. MS Inf. 3rd Bn. Co.F

Rhey, A.J. KY 12th Cav. Co.B Cpl.

Rhey, James E. TN Lt.Arty. Burroughs' Co.

Rhidenhour, John W. NC 13th Inf. Co.F

Rhieme, Charles LA 21st (Patton's) Inf. Co.I

Rhiems, James J. MD Arty. 2nd Btty.

Rhiems, W.G. MD Arty. 2nd Btty.

Rhienhart, Charles LA 15th Inf. Co.A Hosp.Stew.

Rhiga, A.W. TN 62nd Mtd.Inf. Surg.

Rhiley, Thomas TX Inf. 1st St.Troops Lawrence's Co.

Rhim, John W. NC 67th Inf. Co.B

Rhimer, A. SC 6th Res. Co.I

Rhimer, Thomas H. NC 42nd Inf. Co.G

Rhimes, J.L. GA 1st (Symons') Res. Co.D

Rhimes, John GA 1st (Symons') Res. Co.D Sgt.

Rhind, Cadwallader D.C. GA 5th Cav. Co.B

Rhine, A. TX 29th Cav. Co.I

Rhine, A.M. NC 3rd Jr.Res. Co.E

Rhine, A.M. NC 11th (Bethel Regt.) Inf. Co.H

Rhine, David TX 16th Cav. Co.A QM

Rhine, David Gen. & Staff Capt.,AQM

Rhine, D.W. NC 42nd Inf. Co.B 2nd Lt.

Rhine, D.W. NC 57th Inf. Co.E Capt.

Rhine, G.W.V. 1st Conf.Cav. 2nd Co.F

Rhine, Isaac TX 34th Cav. Co.B

Rhine, James VA 97th Mil. Co.H

Rhine, J.G. TX Inf. 3rd St.Troops Co.A

Rhine, J.H. AR 5th Inf. Co.D

Rhine, J.J. NC 37th Inf. Co.C

Rhine, John TX 17th Cav. Co.D

Rhine, Joseph N. KY 4th Mtd.Inf. Co.D

Rhine, J.W. NC 1st Cav. (9th St.Troops)

Rhine, Luther NC 42nd Inf. Co.B

Rhine, Michael AR 3rd Inf. Co.D

Rhine, N. SC 6th Res. Co.H

Rhine, Noah SC 3rd Bn.Res. Co.B

Rhine, Noah SC Post Guard Senn's Co.

Rhine, P. TX Inf. Houston Bn. Co.C Sgt.

Rhine, Richard GA 1st Inf. Co.A

Rhine, Thomas J. AR 5th Inf. Co.D

Rhine, T.W. AR Inf. Cocke's Regt. Co.G

Rhine, William A. NC 32nd Inf. Co.D,E

Rhineacre, William VA 62nd Mtd.Inf. 2nd Co.M

Rhinebold, John MS 12th Inf. Co.K

Rhinehardt, Gustavus VA 23rd Inf. Co.H

Rhinehardt, John W. NC 37th Inf. Co.K

Rhinehart, --- LA Inf. 7th Bn. Co.B

Rhinehart, A.C. VA 62nd Mtd.Inf. 2nd Co.M

Rhinehart, Andrew J. VA 97th Mil. Co.I

Rhinehart, A.P. VA 12th Cav. Co.D

Rhinehart, A.R. VA 10th Inf. 2nd Co.C

Rhinehart, B.B. GA 9th Inf. Co.B

Rhinehart, C. NC 5th Sr.Res. Co.E

Rhinehart, Charles Hosp.Stew.

Rhinehart, D.C. NC 7th Inf. Co.H

Rhinehart, Edmund AR 23rd Inf. Co.E

Rhinehart, F. MS 38th Cav. Co.D

Rhinehart, F. NC 6th Inf. Co.K

Rhinehart, Fidilla M. NC 25th Inf. Co.C

Rhinehart, George C. VA 7th Cav. Co.C 1st Sgt.

Rhinehart, Harvey VA 97th Mil. Co.E

Rhinehart, Hiram VA 4th Bn.Res.

Rhinehart, Jacob NC 62nd Inf. Co.C

Rhinehart, John LA Inf. 1st Sp.Bn. (Wheat's) Old Co.D

Rhinehart, John LA 15th Inf. Co.I

Rhinehart, John SC 2nd St.Troops Co.I

Rhinehart, John A. TX 16th Cav. Co.A

Rhinehart, John H. MS 44th Inf. Co.I

Rhinehart, John W. LA 31st Inf. Co.G

Rhinehart, Joseph NC Inf. 62nd Regt. Co.C

Rhinehart, Joseph A. AR 1st (Crawford's) Cav. Co.D

Rhinehart, J.R. AR 34th Inf. Co.B

Rhinehart, M. GA 9th Inf. Co.B

Rhinehart, M. LA 31st Inf. Co.F Jr.2nd Lt.

Rhinehart, Martin E. TN 19th Inf. Co.B

Rhinehart, Powell GA 39th Inf. Edwards' Co.

Rhinehart, Samuel VA 18th Cav. Co.I

Rhinehart, Samuel VA 97th Mil. Co.C

Rhinehart, William AR 12th Inf. Co.E

Rhinehart, William NC 7th Inf. Co.B

Rhinehart, William J. AR 6th Inf. New Co.D

Rhinehart, William L. NC 62nd Inf. Co.C

Rhinehart, W.L. AR 1st (Monroe's) Cav. Co.B

Rhineheart, Adam VA Cav. O'Ferrall's Bn. Co.C

Rhineheart, Dewitt J. VA 7th Cav. Co.H

Rhineheart, Franklin M. MO Inf. 8th Bn. Co.C

Rhineheart, James C. NC 16th Inf. Co.L

Rhineheart, John VA 7th Cav. Co.I

Rhineheart, Sumpter D. SC 5th Res. Co.K

Rhineheart, William GA 21st Inf. Co.K

Rhineheart, William NC 62nd Inf. Co.C Drum.

Rhineheart, William TN 5th (McKenzie's) Cav. Co.I

Rhiner, Daniel Conf.Cav. 7th Bn. Co.B Bvt.2nd Lt.

Rhiner, Samuel J. TN 17th Inf. Co.C

Rhines, John AL 4th Inf. Co.K

Rhinewald, Henderson H. MS 40th Inf. Co.H

Rhoad, David F.C. AL 36th Inf. Co.G

Rhoad, J.A. SC 4th Cav. Co.G

Rhoad, J.A. SC Cav. 10th Bn. Co.C

Rhoad, J.L. SC 8th Bn.Res. Fishburne's Co.

Rhoades, Achilles VA 6th Cav. Co.I Cpl.

Rhoades, A.M. AL 7th Cav. Co.K

Rhoades, Andrew Jackson TX 13th Cav. Co.A

Rhoades, B.A. AR 11th & 17th (Cons.) Inf. Co.C Cpl.

Rhoades, Daniel TX Cav. Martin's Regt. Co.G

Rhoades, Daniel B. AL 18th Inf. Co.H

Rhoades, David AR Lt.Arty. Key's Btty.

Rhoades, David NC Cav. McRae's Bn.

Rhoades, David NC 29th Inf. Co.H

Rhoades, F.Y. TX 8th Cav. Co.B

Rhoades, G.A. VA 14th Cav. Co.I

Rhoades, G.B. KY 6th Mtd.Inf. Co.F

Rhoades, G.C. TN 38th Inf. Co.D

Rhoades, G.E. NC 1st Jr.Res. Co.D

Rhoades, George A. VA 5th Inf. Co.L

Rhoades, G.J. TN 7th (Duckworth's) Cav. Co.D

Rhoades, Hardin J. NC 22nd Inf. Co.H

Rhoades, Jabes M. AR 11th & 17th (Cons.) Inf. Co.C Sgt.

Rhoades, Jacob H. GA 6th Inf. Co.F

Rhoades, James M. AR 11th & 17th (Cons.) Inf. Co.C

Rhoades, James S. GA 6th Inf. Co.F

Rhoades, J.K. MS 1st Bn.S.S. Co.A

Rhoades, J.L. MO 12th Cav. Co.G

Rhoades, J.N. AL 25th Inf. Co.A Sgt.

Rhoades, John VA Lt.Arty. J.S. Brown's Co.

Rhoades, John VA Lt.Arty. Taylor's Co.

Rhoades, John VA 46th Inf. 1st Co.K

Rhoades, Jonathan TX 6th Cav. Co.C

Rhoades, Joseph AR 7th Inf. Co.F

Rhoades, J.P. MO 3rd Inf. Co.E

Rhoades, J.T. TN 11th (Holman's) Cav. Co.H

Rhoades, J.W. GA 37th Inf. Co.E

Rhoades, J.W. KY Jessee's Bn.Mtd.Riflemen Co.C Sgt.

Rhoades, Reuben VA 2nd Cav. Co.E

Rhoades, R.H. GA 15th Inf. Co.D

Rhoades, R.H. TN 7th (Duckworth's) Cav. Co.D

Rhoades, R.H. TX 9th Cav. Co.D

Rhoades, Richard B. VA 7th Inf. Co.C Sgt.

Rhoades, Tarphy C. MS 19th Inf. Co.G

Rhoades, Thomas TX 25th Cav. Co.D

Rhoades, W.A. GA 6th Inf. Co.F

Rhoades, Warwick F. MO 1st Inf. Co.K

Rhoades, W.F. MO 3rd & 5th Cons.Inf.

Rhoades, William MO 1st & 4th Cons.Inf. Co.B

Rhoades, William A. VA 58th Inf. Co.C

Rhoades, William F. VA 2nd Cav. Co.E

Rhoades, William H. AL 17th Inf. Co.E

Rhoades, W.L. AR 8th Cav. Co.K

Rhoades, W.N. SC 25th Inf. Co.I

Rhoads, A.F. AR Inf. Hardy's Regt. Co.G

Rhoads, A.J. GA 31st Inf. Co.E

Rhoads, Andrew J. NC 22nd Inf. Co.G

Rhoads, B.L. KY 2nd (Woodward's) Cav. Co.D

Rhoads, C.E. LA 1st Hvy.Arty. (Reg.) Co.I Sgt.

Rhoads, D. TX Cav. McCord's Frontier Regt. Co.H

Rhoads, Daniel TN 27th Inf. Co.G

Rhoads, D.S. MS 6th Cav. Co.F

Rhoads, Edwin R. VA 31st Inf. Co.C

Rhoads, E.H. TN 27th Inf. Co.G Sgt.

Rhoads, Emerson TX 20th Cav. Co.F

Rhoads, E.T. TX Vol. Benton's Co.

Rhoads, G.A. GA 31st Inf. Co.E

Rhoads, George LA Mil. Orleans Fire Regt.

Rhoads, George W. AR 31st Inf. Co.E

Rhoads, G.M. TX 26th Cav. Co.A

Rhoads, G.W. AR 36th Inf. Co.D

Rhoads, J. MO 3rd St.Guards Sgt.

Rhoads, James NC 62nd Inf. Co.F

Rhoads, James H. TN 20th Cav.

Rhoads, J.M. TX Cav. Terry's Regt. Co.A

Rhoads, John B. NC 64th Inf. Co.E Cmsy.

Rhoads, John D. AL Cav. 4th Bn. (Love's) Co.A
Rhoads, John S. MS 14th Inf. Co.D
Rhoads, John W. TN 41st Inf. Co.D
Rhoads, L. MS 13th Inf. Co.D
Rhoads, M.P. TN 22nd Inf. Co.E
Rhoads, P. VA 3rd Res. Co.A
Rhoads, R. AR 36th Inf. Co.D
Rhoads, Robert H. MS 1st Cav.Res. Co.H 1st Sgt.
Rhoads, T. TX Granbury's Cons.Brig. Co.K
Rhoads, T.H. MO 12th Cav. Co.G
Rhoads, Thomas AL 5th Cav. Co.B Cpl.
Rhoads, Thomas J. TX Cav. Martin's Regt. Co.G
Rhoads, W. TN 15th Inf. Co.E
Rhoads, W.A. MS 26th Inf. Co.E
Rhoads, W.C. AL 5th Cav. Co.B Sgt.
Rhoads, William VA Cav. Ferguson's Bn. Ferguson's Co., Parks' Co.
Rhoads, William J. TX 6th Cav. Co.C
Rhoads, W.R. MS 23rd Inf. Co.G
Rhoady, Marcus M. MO 9th Inf. Co.G Adj.
Rhoan, B.T. GA 13th Inf. Co.C
Rhoards, William MS 8th Inf. Co.B
Rhoda, Hugo TX 17th Inf. Co.K
Rhoda, Robert TX 26th Cav. Co.K
Rhode, Ab MS Inf. 1st Bn.St.Troops (30 days '64) Co.B
Rhode, Charles AL Arty. 1st Bn. Co.A
Rhode, Charles TX 27th Cav. Co.D
Rhode, D. SC Inf. 1st (Charleston) Bn. Co.F
Rhode, D. SC 27th Inf. Co.C
Rhode, Daniel W. TX 27th Cav. Co.D
Rhode, David J. TX 27th Cav. Co.D
Rhode, G. TX 5th Field Btty.
Rhode, H.C. SC 1st Cav. Co.I
Rhode, Henry LA 4th Inf.
Rhode, Hugo TX 4th Cav. Co.B
Rhode, James SC 1st Cav. Co.I
Rhode, Joel TX 27th Cav. Co.D
Rhode, John FL 5th Inf. Co.H 1st Sgt.
Rhode, John VA 59th Mil. Arnold's Co.
Rhode, John C. TX 27th Cav. Co.D
Rhode, John P. TX 27th Cav. Co.D Cpl.
Rhode, N.M. 15th Conf.Cav. Co.E
Rhode, R.A. FL 1st (Res.) Inf. Co.L
Rhode, Richard VA 59th Mil. Arnold's Co.
Rhode, Thomas J. TX 27th Cav. Co.D
Rhode, William B. TX 27th Cav. Co.D
Rhode, W.J. AR 17th (Griffith's) Inf. Co.B Sgt.
Rhode, W.J. SC 1st Cav. Co.I Sgt.
Rhodeffer, William H. VA 9th Bn.Res. Co.C
Rhoden, C.J. SC 19th Inf. Co.B
Rhoden, E. SC 2nd St.Troops Co.I
Rhoden, E. SC 7th Inf. Co.F
Rhoden, Elisha GA Inf. 3rd Bn. Co.G
Rhoden, Elisha GA 4th Bn.S.S. Co.A
Rhoden, Enoch SC 5th Res. Co.K
Rhoden, H. SC Lt.Arty. Beauregard's Co.
Rhoden, Hansford SC 5th Res. Co.K
Rhoden, Henry H. FL 8th Inf. Co.I
Rhoden, Isam J. FL 8th Inf. Co.I
Rhoden, James B. TN 44th (Cons.) Inf. Co.F
Rhoden, James R. MS Cav. Jeff Davis Legion Co.D
Rhoden, James T. FL 8th Inf. Co.I

Rhoden, J.H. TN Holman's Bn.Part.Rangers Co.C
Rhoden, John GA 1st Reg. Co.I,E
Rhoden, John SC 6th Inf. Co.1
Rhoden, John SC 19th Inf. Co.K
Rhoden, John A.J. FL 8th Inf. Co.I
Rhoden, Levy J. FL 8th Inf. Co.I
Rhoden, L.M. SC 22nd Inf. Co.A
Rhoden, M. AL 11th Cav. Co.A
Rhoden, Martin GA 3rd Inf. 1st Co.I
Rhoden, Martin V. GA Lt.Arty. Milledge's Co.
Rhoden, Miles SC 19th Inf. Co.K
Rhoden, Thomas A. SC 17th Inf. Co.G Sgt.
Rhoden, W. SC Lt.Arty. Beauregard's Co.
Rhoden, Wiley SC 19th Inf. Co.A
Rhoden, William FL 1st Cav. Co.D
Rhoden, William SC 2nd Arty. Co.E
Rhoden, William SC 17th Inf. Co.H
Rhoden, W.W. GA 16th Inf. Co.G
Rhodenberg, William AL 9th (Malone's) Cav. Co.G
Rhodenhizer, Daniel K. VA Arty. Paris' Co.
Rhodenhizer, William H. VA 28th Inf. Co.B
Rhodenizer, James VA Lt.Arty. Douthat's Co.
Rhodenmier, George A. TN 1st Hvy.Arty. 2nd Co.C,B 2nd Lt.
Rhoder, John B. LA Inf. 1st Sp.Bn. (Wheat's) New Co.E
Rhodes, --- AL 22nd Inf. Co.C
Rhodes, --- AL 22nd Inf. Co.I
Rhodes, --- LA Mil. Beauregard Bn. Co.D
Rhodes, ---, 2nd SC Inf. 1st (Charleston) Bn. Co.A
Rhodes, --- TX Cav. Steele's Command Co.B
Rhodes, A. GA Lt.Arty. 12th Bn. Co.F
Rhodes, A. GA 63rd Inf. Co.A
Rhodes, A. LA 5th Cav. Co.E
Rhodes, A. SC Inf. Hampton Legion Co.A
Rhodes, Aaron E. VA 28th Inf. Co.I
Rhodes, Abraham VA 3rd (Chrisman's) Bn.Res. Co.C
Rhodes, Abraham VA 136th Mil. Co.A
Rhodes, Adam C. AR 3rd Inf. Co.C Cpl.
Rhodes, A.E. NC 27th Inf. Co.I
Rhodes, A.F. LA Inf. 4th Bn. Co.E
Rhodes, A.G. SC 9th Res. Co.I
Rhodes, A.H. NC 4th Cav. (59th St.Troops) Co.C
Rhodes, A.H. NC 1st Inf. (6 mo. '61) Co.E
Rhodes, A.J. SC 21st Inf. Co.B
Rhodes, A.J.K. NC 55th Inf. Co.G
Rhodes, A.L. AR 15th Mil. Co.D
Rhodes, A.L. LA 3rd Inf. Co.E
Rhodes, Alamong VA 23rd Cav. Co.A
Rhodes, Alexander C. AR 3rd Inf. Co.I
Rhodes, Alex. M. AL 1st Cav. Co.L
Rhodes, Alfred GA 22nd Inf. Co.A
Rhodes, Alvah AL 36th Inf. Co.C
Rhodes, A.M. AL 8th (Livingston's) Cav. Co.B Cpl.
Rhodes, A.M. MS 46th Inf. Co.F Cpl.
Rhodes, A.M. SC 5th St.Troops Co.I
Rhodes, A.M. SC 9th Res. Co.E
Rhodes, Ambrose NC 24th Inf. Co.C
Rhodes, Amon SC 1st Arty. Co.C,F
Rhodes, Amos L. FL 11th Inf. Co.F
Rhodes, Anderson AL 59th Inf. Co.H

Rhodes, Anderson AL Arty. 4th Bn. Hilliard's Legion Co.A,D
Rhodes, Andrew NC 25th Inf. Co.H
Rhodes, Andrew J. AL 18th Inf. Co.H
Rhodes, Andrew J. GA 1st (Ramsey's) Inf. Co.D
Rhodes, Andrew J. GA Inf. (Richmond Factory Guards) Barney's Co.
Rhodes, Andrew J. KY 9th Mtd.Inf. Co.H
Rhodes, Andrew J. NC Inf. 13th Bn. Co.A
Rhodes, Andrew J. NC 66th Inf. Co.A,E
Rhodes, Andrew J. TX Cav. McCord's Frontier Regt. 2nd Co.A
Rhodes, Andrew J. VA 19th Inf. Co.F
Rhodes, Anthony VA 146th Mil. Co.A
Rhodes, Anthony H. NC 3rd Inf. Co.G 1st Lt.
Rhodes, Arnold TX 13th Cav. Co.H
Rhodes, Arthur AR 1st (Colquitt's) Inf. Co.G
Rhodes, Asa M. AL 57th Inf. Co.E
Rhodes, A.T. AL 1st Inf. Co.G
Rhodes, A.T. AL Res. Belser's Co.
Rhodes, Augustus TN 5th Inf. 1st Co.C
Rhodes, Austin C. NC 22nd Inf. Co.H
Rhodes, A.V. TN 35th Inf. Co.L
Rhodes, A.W. MS 29th Inf. Co.C
Rhodes, A.W. TN 18th Inf. Co.I
Rhodes, A.W. TX Cav. 2nd Regt.St.Troops Co.K Cpl.
Rhodes, B. MS 12th Cav. Co.L Sgt.
Rhodes, B.A. AR 11th Inf. Co.H
Rhodes, Baron D.K. TX Cav. Baylor's Regt. Co.D
Rhodes, Battle NC 1st Arty. (10th St.Troops) Co.I
Rhodes, Battle NC 2nd Arty. (36th St.Troops) Co.A
Rhodes, Benjamin AL 33rd Inf. Co.H
Rhodes, Benjamin AL 55th Vol. Co.J,K
Rhodes, Benjamin GA 3rd Cav. (St.Guards) Co.C
Rhodes, Benjamin GA 10th Inf. Co.H
Rhodes, Benjamin VA 7th Cav. Co.H
Rhodes, Benjamin F. GA 51st Inf. Co.H
Rhodes, Benjamin F. MO Searcy's Bn.S.S. Co.C
Rhodes, Benjamin F. NC 2nd Inf. Co.G
Rhodes, Benjamin F. SC 5th St.Troops Co.H
Rhodes, Bennet B. TX 17th Cons.Dismtd.Cav. Co.K
Rhodes, Bennett TX 17th Cav. Co.E
Rhodes, Bennett B. NC 4th Inf. Co.F
Rhodes, Berry FL Cav. 3rd Bn. Co.A
Rhodes, Berry 15th Conf.Cav. Co.A
Rhodes, B.F. LA 1st (Nelligan's) Inf. Co.C Sgt.
Rhodes, B.F. SC 9th Res. Co.I
Rhodes, B.F. SC Post Guard Senn's Co.
Rhodes, B.F. VA 4th Cav.
Rhodes, B.J. TN 21st (Wilson's) Cav. Co.H
Rhodes, B.J. TN 21st & 22nd (Cons.) Cav. Co.H,E
Rhodes, Boyd AR 47th (Crandall's) Cav. McCoy's Co.
Rhodes, B.R. TX 7th Cav. Co.D
Rhodes, Brantley NC 3rd Cav. (41st St.Troops) Co.H
Rhodes, Brantley F. NC 2nd Cav. (19th St.Troops) Co.K
Rhodes, Bryant J. NC 27th Inf. Co.A Sgt.
Rhodes, Bunyan AR 3rd Cav. Co.F

Rhodes, C. KY Cav. Thompson's Co.
Rhodes, C. LA Mil. Lewis Guards
Rhodes, Caleb NC 4th Sr.Res. Co.E
Rhodes, Calvin AL 37th Inf. Co.A
Rhodes, Calvin NC 33rd Inf. Co.D
Rhodes, C.A.W. MO 1st N.E. Cav.
Rhodes, C.B. MO Searcy's Bn.S.S. Co.C Lt.
Rhodes, C.B. SC 4th St.Troops Co.E 1st Sgt.
Rhodes, C.C. LA Hvy.Arty. 2nd Bn. Co.B
Rhodes, C.E. AL 8th (Hatch's) Cav. Co.G Capt.
Rhodes, C.E. LA Inf. 7th Bn. Co.C
Rhodes, C.E. LA 18th Inf. Co.E
Rhodes, C.E. LA Inf.Crescent Regt. Co.C
Rhodes, C.E. LA Miles' Legion Ord.Sgt.
Rhodes, Charles AR 18th Inf. Co.K
Rhodes, Charles GA 4th Res. Co.B
Rhodes, Charles KY 10th Cav. Co.E,F
Rhodes, Charles LA Inf.Crescent Regt. Co.D
Rhodes, Charles SC Lt.Arty. 3rd (Palmetto) Bn. Co.K
Rhodes, Charles SC Cav.Bn. Holcombe Legion Co.E Bugler
Rhodes, Charles TX 29th Cav. Co.K,H
Rhodes, Charles A. VA 22nd Inf. Co.B
Rhodes, Charles H. GA 10th Inf. Co.B Sgt.
Rhodes, Charles H. VA 4th Cav. Co.B 2nd Lt.
Rhodes, Chas. H. Gen. & Staff Capt.,QM
Rhodes, Charles J. KY 10th (Johnson's) Cav. Co.E
Rhodes, Charles L. VA Horse Arty. Jackson's Co.
Rhodes, Charley GA Inf. 27th Bn. Co.F
Rhodes, Charley MO Inf. 5th Regt.St.Guard Co.D
Rhodes, Christian MO Inf. 4th Regt.St.Guard Co.B
Rhodes, Christopher NC 23rd Inf. Co.H
Rhodes, Christopher VA 22nd Inf. Co.D
Rhodes, Christopher VA 135th Mil. Co.F
Rhodes, Clark TN 2nd (Ashby's) Cav. Co.H Capt.
Rhodes, Clark TN Cav. 4th Bn. (Branner's) Co.A
Rhodes, Claudius Jasper NC 6th Inf. Co.C
Rhodes, Columbus AL Lt.Arty. Ward's Btty.
Rhodes, C.P. SC Lt.Arty. 3rd (Palmetto) Bn. Co.H,I
Rhodes, C.P. SC 16th Inf. Co.D
Rhodes, Daley AR 2nd Inf. Co.K
Rhodes, Dan VA 88th Mil.
Rhodes, Daniel MS 6th Inf. Co.D
Rhodes, Daniel MO Cav. Freeman's Regt. Co.H,G
Rhodes, Daniel NC 49th Inf. Co.H
Rhodes, Daniel VA 34th Inf. Co.D
Rhodes, Daniel B. GA 10th Inf. Co.G
Rhodes, Daniel R. VA Lt.Arty. 12th Bn. 2nd Co.A
Rhodes, Daniel R. VA Lt.Arty. Sturdivant's Co.
Rhodes, David AR 7th Inf. Co.H
Rhodes, David NC 34th Inf. Co.E 2nd Lt.
Rhodes, David NC Mallett's Co.
Rhodes, David F. NC 23rd Inf. Co.B
Rhodes, David M. TX 27th Cav. Co.I,N
Rhodes, David S. VA 51st Mil. Co.A 2nd Lt.
Rhodes, David V. NC 54th Inf. Co.I 2nd Lt.

Rhodes, D.B. SC Arty. Stuart's Co. (Beaufort Vol.Arty.) 1st Bugler
Rhodes, D.B. SC 11th Inf. Co.A
Rhodes, D.B.F. TX 1st (Yager's) Cav. Co.H
Rhodes, D.B.F. TX Cav. 8th (Taylor's) Bn. Co.E
Rhodes, D.B.F. TX St.Troops Edgar's Co.
Rhodes, D.C. TN Cav. 1st Bn. (McNairy's) Co.B
Rhodes, D.C. TN 22nd (Barteau's) Cav. Co.A
Rhodes, D.E. AL Cav. Lewis' Bn.
Rhodes, D.H. AL 29th Inf. Co.D
Rhodes, D.S. MS Inf. 3rd Bn. (St.Troops) Co.F
Rhodes, Durant NC 68th Inf. Co.F
Rhodes, E. AR 6th Inf. Co.E
Rhodes, E. FL Cav. 5th Bn. Co.C
Rhodes, E. LA 1st Cav. Co.G
Rhodes, E. LA Washington Arty.Bn. Co.5
Rhodes, E. VA 19th Cav. Co.I
Rhodes, E.B. AL 39th Inf. Co.H
Rhodes, Ed. T. TX 8th Cav. Co.I Sgt.
Rhodes, Edward SC 27th Inf. Co.B Music.
Rhodes, Edward A. GA 18th Inf. Co.B
Rhodes, Edward A. NC 11th (Bethel Regt.) Inf. Co.C 2nd Lt.
Rhodes, Edwd. A. NC 35th Inf. Dr.M.
Rhodes, Edward H. NC 3rd Inf. Co.G Capt.
Rhodes, Edwin D. GA 49th Inf. Co.D 1st Lt.
Rhodes, Edwin H. VA 1st St.Res. Co.E
Rhodes, E.E. SC 8th Inf. Co.F
Rhodes, E.E. SC 18th Inf. Co.I
Rhodes, E.H. FL 2nd Cav. Co.D
Rhodes, E.L. AL 12th Inf. Co.D
Rhodes, Eldred J. SC 1st (McCreary's) Inf. Co.G
Rhodes, Eldridge J. GA 6th Inf. Co.H Cpl.
Rhodes, Eli AL Arty. 1st Bn. Co.F
Rhodes, Eli NC 16th Inf. Co.M
Rhodes, Eli NC 25th Inf. Co.A
Rhodes, Eli NC Mallett's Co.
Rhodes, Elias AL Arty. 1st Bn. Co.B
Rhodes, Elijah AR 12th Inf. Co.E
Rhodes, Elijah NC 47th Inf. Co.F
Rhodes, Emanuel VA 9th Bn.Res. Co.A
Rhodes, Emanuel VA 58th Mil. Co.F
Rhodes, Emory VA Lt.Arty. Griffin's Co.
Rhodes, Emory VA 9th Inf. 1st Co.A
Rhodes, Enoch A. GA Phillips' Legion Co.B
Rhodes, Ephraim SC 19th Inf. Co.B
Rhodes, Ephraim SC Inf.Bn. Co.C
Rhodes, E.T. AL 7th Cav. Co.K,A
Rhodes, E.T. AL 18th Inf. Co.C
Rhodes, E.T. AL 22nd Inf. Co.E
Rhodes, Everett TX 32nd Cav. Co.D
Rhodes, Evin NC 2nd Inf. Co.G
Rhodes, E.W. MS 6th Inf. Co.I
Rhodes, E.W. MS 14th (Cons.) Inf. Co.C
Rhodes, E.W. VA 5th Cav. Co.D
Rhodes, Felix MS 7th Cav. 1st Co.H
Rhodes, Felix M. MS 19th Inf. Co.K
Rhodes, Fennius F. MO Lt.Arty. 2nd Field Btty.
Rhodes, F.J. MS 3rd Inf. Co.E
Rhodes, Fletcher MO 7th Cav. Co.I
Rhodes, Fletcher MO Inf. 4th Regt.St.Guard Co.B
Rhodes, F.M. AL 59th Inf. Co.H
Rhodes, F.M. AL Arty. 4th Bn. Hilliard's Legion Co.D

Rhodes, F.M. GA 1st (Symons') Res. Co.J
Rhodes, F.M. MS 18th Cav. Co.E
Rhodes, Francis M. VA 28th Inf. Co.I
Rhodes, Frank VA 25th Cav. Co.E
Rhodes, Franklin VA 56th Inf. Co.H
Rhodes, Franklin A. NC 61st Inf. Co.H 1st Lt.
Rhodes, Franklin A. NC 42nd Inf. Co.B
Rhodes, Frank T. 1st Choctaw & Chickasaw Mtd.Rifles 1st Co.K
Rhodes, Frederick S. VA 58th Mil. Co.D
Rhodes, F.S. GA Lt.Arty. 12th Bn. 2nd Co.D
Rhodes, F.W. AL St.Arty. Co.D
Rhodes, G. LA Mil. 4th Regt. 3rd Brig. 1st Div. Co.H
Rhodes, G.A. GA 2nd Inf. Co.K
Rhodes, G.A. VA 30th Bn.S.S. Co.F
Rhodes, Gabriel AL 20th Inf. Co.I
Rhodes, G.B. GA 10th Inf. Co.K Lt.
Rhodes, George KY 1st (Butler's) Cav. Co.G
Rhodes, George MD 1st Inf. Co.B
Rhodes, George MD 1st Inf. Co.E
Rhodes, George MO 5th Cav. Co.C Jr.2nd Lt.
Rhodes, George SC 27th Inf. Co.I
Rhodes, George VA 4th Inf. Co.H
Rhodes, George A. NC Inf. 13th Bn. Co.A
Rhodes, George A. NC 66th Inf. Co.A
Rhodes, George C. GA Inf. 1st Loc.Troops (Augusta) Co.D
Rhodes, George C. NC 67th Inf. Co.H
Rhodes, George D. MS 23rd Inf. Co.E
Rhodes, George L. GA 65th Inf. Co.B
Rhodes, George L. GA Smith's Legion Anderson's Co.
Rhodes, George T. MS Packer's Co. (Pope Guards)
Rhodes, George T. VA 24th Inf. Co.E
Rhodes, George W. AL 17th Inf. Co.C Music.
Rhodes, George W. GA 18th Inf. Co.D
Rhodes, George W. MO 1st N.E. Cav.
Rhodes, George W. NC 2nd Inf. Co.G
Rhodes, George W. NC 25th Inf. Co.H Drum.
Rhodes, George W. NC 25th Inf. Co.I
Rhodes, G.F. GA Arty. St.Troops Pruden's Btty.
Rhodes, G.F. TN 3rd (Clack's) Inf. Co.H
Rhodes, G.H. AL 29th Inf. Co.D
Rhodes, G.M. TN 11th Inf. Co.H
Rhodes, Granville M. TN Cav. 2nd Bn. (Biffle's) Co.D
Rhodes, Greenberry GA 15th Inf. Co.A
Rhodes, G.T. GA Inf. 27th Bn. Co.E
Rhodes, G.W. AL Lt.Arty. Clanton's Btty.
Rhodes, G.W. KY 1st (Butler's) Cav. Co.F Sgt.
Rhodes, G.W. KY 1st (Helm's) Cav. New Co.A
Rhodes, G.W. SC 1st (Butler's) Inf. Co.B
Rhodes, G.W. TX 12th Inf. Co.A
Rhodes, H. LA 13th Bn. (Part.Rangers) Co.D
Rhodes, H. TN Cav. Nixon's Regt. Co.G
Rhodes, H. TN 48th (Nixon's) Inf. Co.F
Rhodes, H. VA 2nd Bn.Res. Co.B
Rhodes, Hardy B. NC 4th Cav. (59th St.Troops) Co.C 3rd Lt.
Rhodes, Harman M. TX 35th (Brown's) Cav. Co.K
Rhodes, Harmann M. TX 13th Vol. 3rd Co.I
Rhodes, Harry TN 3rd (Forrest's) Cav. Co.A
Rhodes, H.C. SC 11th Inf. Sheridan's Co.
Rhodes, H.D. AR 15th Mil. Co.D

Rhodes, Henderson TN 16th Inf. Co.I
Rhodes, Henry LA 5th Cav. Co.C
Rhodes, Henry GA 8th Inf. Co.I
Rhodes, Henry SC 19th Inf. Co.B
Rhodes, Henry SC Inf.Bn. Co.C
Rhodes, Henry VA 8th Bn.Res. Co.A
Rhodes, Henry A. NC 4th Cav. (59th St.Troops) Co.C Cpl.
Rhodes, Henry A. VA 146th Mil. Co.A
Rhodes, Henry N. GA Cobb's Legion Co.A
Rhodes, Henry W. TX Arty. 4th Bn. Co.A
Rhodes, Herod KY 13th Cav. Co.E
Rhodes, Hezekiah NC 50th Inf. Co.B
Rhodes, Hezekiah TN 54th Inf. Co.H
Rhodes, Hezekiah VA 56th Inf. Co.H
Rhodes, H.H. SC Arty. Melchers' Co. (Co.B,German Arty.)
Rhodes, H.H. TN 21st (Wilson's) Cav. Co.H
Rhodes, Hiram J. AL 13th Inf. Co.D
Rhodes, H.N. LA 8th Inf. Co.C
Rhodes, Holden J. VA Hvy.Arty. 10th Bn. Co.A
Rhodes, Horace VA 88th Mil.
Rhodes, Horace L. LA 9th Inf. Co.C
Rhodes, H.S. AL 3rd Bn.Res. Co.C
Rhodes, H.T. AL 13th Inf. Co.G
Rhodes, H.W. 1st Conf.Cav. Co.I
Rhodes, I.C. GA 29th Inf.
Rhodes, I.N. MS Lt.Arty. Stanford's Co.
Rhodes, Ingerham AL 19th Inf. Co.C
Rhodes, Ingraham AL Cp. of Instr. Talladega
Rhodes, Ingram NC 13th Inf. Co.I
Rhodes, Isaac GA 63rd Inf. Co.E
Rhodes, Isaac TX 7th Cav. Co.A
Rhodes, Isaac TX Cav. Waller's Regt. Co.D
Rhodes, Isaac VA 51st Mil. Co.A
Rhodes, Isaac B. TX 19th Cav. Co.A Sgt.
Rhodes, Isaac F. MS 23rd Inf. Co.A 3rd Lt.
Rhodes, Isham AR 26th Inf. Co.K
Rhodes, J. AL 1st Cav. Co.G
Rhodes, J. AL 2nd Regt.Eng. Co.C
Rhodes, J. GA 8th Inf. Co.I
Rhodes, J. GA 29th Inf. Co.I
Rhodes, J. GA 49th Inf. Co.D
Rhodes, J. KY 11th Cav. Co.E
Rhodes, J. LA 1st Cav. Co.B
Rhodes, J. MS 8th Inf. Co.B
Rhodes, J. SC 10th Inf. Co.A
Rhodes, J. TN 19th & 20th (Cons.) Cav. Co.E
Rhodes, J. TX Cav. Baird's Regt. Co.C
Rhodes, J. Conf.Reg.Inf. Brooks' Bn. Co.A
Rhodes, J.A. TN 3rd (Clack's) Inf. Co.H
Rhodes, J.A. TX 9th (Young's) Inf. Co.B
Rhodes, Jabes M. AR 11th Inf. Co.H
Rhodes, Jabez M. GA 12th Cav. Co.H
Rhodes, Jabez R. GA 36th (Villepigue's) Inf. Co.D Capt.
Rhodes, Jabez R. 1st Conf.Inf. 1st Co.D, 2nd Co.C Capt.
Rhodes, Jackson VA 9th Bn.Res. Co.A Sgt.
Rhodes, Jacob AL Arty. 1st Bn. Co.B Cpl.
Rhodes, Jacob AR 27th Inf. Co.G
Rhodes, Jacob 1st Seminole Mtd.Vol.
Rhodes, Jacob G. NC 8th Bn.Part.Rangers Co.F Cpl.
Rhodes, Jacob G. NC 66th Inf. Co.I Cpl.
Rhodes, Jacob H. NC 11th (Bethel Regt.) Inf. Co.I Sgt.

Rhodes, Jacob K. MS Packer's Co. (Pope Guards)
Rhodes, Jacob M. TN 20th Cav. Co.D
Rhodes, Jacob N. VA 1st Cav. Co.C
Rhodes, Jacob N. VA 10th Cav. Co.H
Rhodes, Jacob N. VA Lt.Arty. Arch. Graham's Co.
Rhodes, Jacob P. VA 58th Mil. Co.D
Rhodes, Jacob S. AL 4th (Roddey's) Cav. Co.M
Rhodes, James AL 17th Inf. Co.B
Rhodes, James AL 20th Inf. Co.E,A
Rhodes, James AR 3rd Inf. Co.I
Rhodes, James AR 26th Inf. Co.K
Rhodes, James AR 32nd Inf. Co.B
Rhodes, James FL Lt.Arty. Dyke's Co.
Rhodes, James FL 6th Inf. Co.K Music.
Rhodes, James GA 64th Inf. Co.B
Rhodes, James MO 15th Cav. Co.A
Rhodes, James SC 1st Arty. Co.K
Rhodes, James SC Inf. 1st (Charleston) Bn. Co.A
Rhodes, James SC Inf. 9th Bn. Co.A
Rhodes, James SC 26th Inf. Co.A
Rhodes, James TN 19th & 20th (Cons.) Cav. Co.K
Rhodes, James TN 20th (Russell's) Cav. Co.E
Rhodes, James TN 21st (Wilson's) Cav. Co.H
Rhodes, James TN 21st & 22nd (Cons.) Cav. Co.H
Rhodes, James TN 11th Inf. Co.K,H
Rhodes, James TX 37th Cav. 2nd Co.I
Rhodes, James VA 58th Mil. Co.D
Rhodes, James Conf.Reg.Inf. Brooks' Bn. Co.A
Rhodes, James A. MS Cav. 24th Bn. Co.A
Rhodes, James B. NC 18th Inf. Co.G
Rhodes, James C. AL 57th Inf. Co.D
Rhodes, James D. TX 20th Inf. Co.F
Rhodes, James E. MO 1st N.E. Cav.
Rhodes, James E. NC 31st Inf. Co.H Sgt.
Rhodes, James E. VA 61st Inf. Co.F
Rhodes, James F. NC 26th Inf. Co.D
Rhodes, James H. NC 31st Inf. Co.K 1st Sgt.
Rhodes, James H. NC 55th Inf. Co.G
Rhodes, James H. VA 10th Bn.Res. Co.E
Rhodes, James J. SC 9th Inf. Co.G
Rhodes, James L. AL 3rd Inf. Co.I
Rhodes, James M. AR 11th Inf. Co.H
Rhodes, James M. VA 1st Arty. Co.H,G
Rhodes, James O. TX 19th Inf. Co.H
Rhodes, James P. GA 65th Inf. Co.B
Rhodes, James R. GA 4th Inf. Co.E
Rhodes, James R. MS Hamer's Co. (Salem Cav.)
Rhodes, James S. SC 18th Inf. Co.E Sgt.
Rhodes, James T. AR 6th Inf. Co.C Sgt.
Rhodes, James W. AL 40th Inf. Co.G
Rhodes, James W. GA Inf. 9th Bn. Co.B
Rhodes, James W. GA 48th Inf. Co.C
Rhodes, James W. GA 56th Inf. Co.G
Rhodes, James W. SC Inf. Hampton Legion Co.B
Rhodes, James W. VA Cav. 35th Bn. Co.F
Rhodes, Janis TN 44th (Cons.) Inf. Co.E
Rhodes, Jasper Hartem TX 20th Cav. Co.E
Rhodes, Jasper N. SC 1st (Orr's) Rifles Co.K
Rhodes, J.B. AL 34th Inf. Co.C
Rhodes, J.B. AR 15th Inf. Co.D
Rhodes, J.B. GA 63rd Inf. Co.E
Rhodes, J.B. NC 8th Bn.Part.Rangers Co.E,B

Rhodes, J.B. NC 66th Inf. Co.H
Rhodes, J.B. SC 1st (Butler's) Inf. Co.D
Rhodes, J.B. SC 3rd St.Troops Co.D
Rhodes, J.B. SC 7th Inf. 1st Co.G
Rhodes, J.B. SC 8th Inf. Co.M
Rhodes, J.B. SC 21st Inf. Co.B
Rhodes, J.B. SC 21st Inf. Co.H
Rhodes, J.B. TN Cav. 1st Bn. (McNairy's) Co.D
Rhodes, J.B. TN 21st (Wilson's) Cav. Co.H
Rhodes, J.B. TN 21st & 22nd (Cons.) Cav. Co.H
Rhodes, J.B. TX 25th Cav. Co.D
Rhodes, J.B. TX 28th Cav. Co.C
Rhodes, J.C. AR 30th Inf. Co.E
Rhodes, J.C. MO Inf. 4th Regt.St.Guard Co.B
Rhodes, J.C. NC Home Guards
Rhodes, J.C. SC 1st (Hagood's) Inf. 2nd Co.H
Rhodes, J.C. TN 12th (Cons.) Inf. Co.G
Rhodes, J.C. TN 22nd Inf. Co.E
Rhodes, J.C. TX 13th Vol. 2nd Co.H
Rhodes, J.C. VA 17th Cav. Co.G
Rhodes, J.C.H. MS Inf. 4th St.Troops Co.A Sgt.
Rhodes, J.D. AL 17th Inf. Co.C
Rhodes, J.D. SC 8th Inf. Co.F
Rhodes, J.D. SC 11th Res. Co.G 3rd Lt.
Rhodes, J.D. SC Inf. Hampton Legion Co.G
Rhodes, J.D. TN 8th (Smith's) Cav. Co.F
Rhodes, J.E. MO Inf. 5th Regt.St.Guard Co.B
Rhodes, J.E. SC 8th Bn.Res. Co.C
Rhodes, Jerry S. FL 7th Inf. Co.H
Rhodes, Jesse AL 40th Inf. Co.G
Rhodes, Jesse Franklin NC 48th Inf. Co.B
Rhodes, Jesse H. MS Lt.Arty. Yates' Btty.
Rhodes, Jesse M. NC 32nd Inf. Co.B
Rhodes, Jesse M. TX 35th (Brown's) Cav. Co.K
Rhodes, Jesse M. TX 13th Vol. 3rd Co.I
Rhodes, Jesse N. MS 33rd Inf. Co.I
Rhodes, Jethro P. VA 61st Inf. Co.F Sgt.
Rhodes, J.F. MS 7th Cav. Co.G
Rhodes, J.F. SC Arty. Zimmerman's Co. (Pee Dee Arty.)
Rhodes, J.F. SC 1st (Hagood's) Inf. 2nd Co.H
Rhodes, J.F. SC 1st (McCreary's) Inf. Co.D
Rhodes, J.F. TN 28th Cav. Co.A 1st Lt.
Rhodes, J.F.H. MS 41st Inf. Co.C
Rhodes, J.H. AL 9th Inf. Co.D
Rhodes, J.H. AR 1st (Cons.) Inf. Co.G
Rhodes, J.H. AR 10th Inf. Co.I,K Sgt.
Rhodes, J.H. MS 3rd Inf. Co.C Sgt.
Rhodes, J.H. NC 3rd Cav. (41st St.Troops) Co.B
Rhodes, J.H. NC 53rd Inf. Co.C
Rhodes, J.H. TN Cav. Nixon's Regt. Co.G
Rhodes, J.H. TN 35th Inf. Co.L
Rhodes, J.J. FL Lt.Arty. Dyke's Co.
Rhodes, J.J. FL Kilcrease Lt.Arty.
Rhodes, J.J. SC 3rd Inf. Co.G Sgt.
Rhodes, J.J. SC 8th Inf. Co.M Sgt.
Rhodes, J.J. SC 21st Inf. Co.B
Rhodes, J.K.P. AL 62nd Inf. Co.E
Rhodes, J.L. AR Inf. Cocke's Regt. Co.G
Rhodes, J.L. KY 10th (Johnson's) Cav. Co.E
Rhodes, J.L. KY Cav. Thompson's Co.
Rhodes, J.M. AL 5th Inf. Co.B
Rhodes, J.M. AL 15th Inf. Co.K
Rhodes, J.M. AR 2nd Inf. New Co.E
Rhodes, J.M. AR 11th & 17th (Cons.) Inf. Co.G
Rhodes, J.M. AR Unassign.Conscr.

Rhodes, J.M. GA Siege Arty. 28th Bn. Co.K
Rhodes, J.M. GA Siege Arty. Campbell's
  Ind.Co.
Rhodes, J.M. GA 54th Inf. Sgt.
Rhodes, J.M. MS 36th Inf. Co.C
Rhodes, J.M. SC 18th Inf. Co.E
Rhodes, J.M. TN 9th Inf. Co.D
Rhodes, J.N. MS Lt.Arty. 14th Bn. Co.A
Rhodes, J.N. MS Lt.Arty. 14th Bn. Co.B
Rhodes, J.N. MS Lt.Arty. Yates' Btty.
Rhodes, J.N. Trans-MS Conf.Cav. 1st Bn. Co.E
Rhodes, Joel T. MS 17th Inf. Co.H
Rhodes, John AL Cav. Co.A
Rhodes, John AL 17th Inf. Co.K
Rhodes, John AL 20th Inf. Co.H
Rhodes, John AL 22nd Inf. Co.D
Rhodes, John AL Inf.
Rhodes, John AL 40th Inf. Co.G
Rhodes, John AL 41st Inf. Co.G
Rhodes, John AR 15th Inf.
Rhodes, John AR 20th Inf. Co.D Sgt.
Rhodes, John GA 7th Cav. Co.F
Rhodes, John GA Cav. 21st Bn. Co.E
Rhodes, John GA 62nd Cav. Co.L
Rhodes, John GA Arty. St.Troops Pruden's Btty.
Rhodes, John GA Inf. 1st Loc.Troops (Augusta)
  Co.F
Rhodes, John GA Inf. 1st Conf.Bn. Co.C
Rhodes, John GA 5th Inf. Co.F
Rhodes, John GA Inf. 5th Bn. (St.Guards) Co.E
Rhodes, John GA 66th Inf. Co.F
Rhodes, John GA Inf. (Ogeechee Minute Men)
  Garrison's Co.
Rhodes, John KY 4th Cav. Co.F
Rhodes, John MS 5th Cav. Co.H
Rhodes, John MO 9th (Elliott's) Cav. Co.A
Rhodes, John MS 26th Inf. Co.B
Rhodes, John MO Cav. Freeman's Regt. Co.A
Rhodes, John NC 1st Inf. Co.E
Rhodes, John NC 25th Inf. Co.A
Rhodes, John NC 32nd Inf. Co.F,A
Rhodes, John NC 66th Inf. Co.H
Rhodes, John SC 5th Cav. Co.C
Rhodes, John SC 1st Arty. Co.H
Rhodes, John SC Lt.Arty. M. Ward's Co. (Wac-
  camaw Lt.Arty.)
Rhodes, John SC 3rd Res. Co.D
Rhodes, John SC 8th Inf. Co.M
Rhodes, John SC 21st Inf. Co.G Cpl.
Rhodes, John TX 16th Cav. Co.B
Rhodes, John TX 1st Bn.S.S. Co.A,E
Rhodes, John VA 24th Cav. Co.K
Rhodes, John 8th (Dearing's) Conf.Cav. Co.E
Rhodes, John A. AL 10th Inf. Co.G
Rhodes, John A. GA 51st Inf. Co.K
Rhodes, John A. NC 48th Inf. Co.B
Rhodes, John A. NC 54th Inf. Co.D
Rhodes, John B. MS 9th Inf. Old Co.E
Rhodes, John B. SC 1st (McCreary's) Inf. Co.G
  Cpl.
Rhodes, John C. GA 60th Inf. Co.K Cpl.
Rhodes, John C. TN 27th Inf. Co.I Sgt.
Rhodes, John D. NC 2nd Arty. (36th St.Troops)
  Co.E
Rhodes, John D. VA Hvy.Arty. 20th Bn. Co.D
Rhodes, John D. VA Lt.Arty. Cutshaw's Co.
Rhodes, John D. VA Horse Arty. Jackson's Co.

Rhodes, John F. AR 2nd Mtd.Rifles Co.H
Rhodes, John F. SC 18th Inf. Co.E
Rhodes, John F. SC 18th Inf. Co.I
Rhodes, John H. GA Lt.Arty. 12th Bn. Co.F
  Sgt.
Rhodes, John H. GA 1st (Ramsey's) Inf. Co.D
Rhodes, John H. GA 3rd Res. Co.I
Rhodes, John H. MO Mtd.Inf. Boone's Regt.
  Rickett's Co.
Rhodes, John H. NC 2nd Inf. Co.G
Rhodes, John H. NC 25th Inf. Co.H
Rhodes, John H. VA 10th Cav. Co.H 2nd Lt.
Rhodes, John H. VA Lt.Arty. Griffin's Co. Cpl.
Rhodes, John H. VA 9th Inf. 1st Co.A
Rhodes, John J. AL 8th Cav. Co.H
Rhodes, John J. NC 39th Inf. Co.A Drum.
Rhodes, John J. SC Arty. Stuart's Co. (Beaufort
  Vol.Arty.) 1st Lt.
Rhodes, John J. SC 11th Inf. Co.A 1st Lt.
Rhodes, John J. TX 4th Inf. (St.Troops) Co.E
Rhodes, John J. VA 5th Inf. Co.K
Rhodes, John J. VA Prov.Guard Avis' Co.
Rhodes, John L. VA Horse Arty. McClanahan's
  Co.
Rhodes, John L. VA 146th Mil. Co.A Cpl.
Rhodes, John M. AL 18th Inf. Co.H Sgt.
Rhodes, John M. AR 11th Inf. Co.G Wagon M.
Rhodes, John M. AR 33rd Inf. Co.D
Rhodes, John M. GA Hvy.Arty. 22nd Bn.
Rhodes, John M. VA 10th Cav. Co.H
Rhodes, John O. SC 5th Cav. Co.K
Rhodes, John P. TX 27th Cav. Co.D Cpl.
Rhodes, John Q. VA Loc.Def. Mallory's Co.
Rhodes, John T. GA 40th Inf. Co.F
Rhodes, John W. AL 10th Inf. Co.E
Rhodes, John W. AR 1st (Crawford's) Cav.
  Co.D
Rhodes, John W. AR 9th Inf. Co.C
Rhodes, John W. AR 15th (Johnson's) Inf. Co.C
Rhodes, John W. MS 31st Inf. Co.C
Rhodes, John W. MO 1st N.E. Cav.
Rhodes, John W. VA Cav. 39th Bn. Co.C Cpl.
Rhodes, John W. VA 60th Inf. Co.K
Rhodes, Jonathan SC 1st Arty. Co.H
Rhodes, Jonathan SC Lt.Arty. M. Ward's Co.
  (Waccamaw Lt.Arty.)
Rhodes, Jonathan B. AL 1st Regt.Conscr. Co.I
Rhodes, Joseph AL Arty. 4th Bn. Hilliard's
  Legion Co.A
Rhodes, Joseph FL 10th Inf. Co.C
Rhodes, Joseph GA Cav. Russell's Co.
Rhodes, Joseph GA 49th Inf. Co.E
Rhodes, Joseph NC 5th Cav. (63rd St.Troops)
  Co.K
Rhodes, Joseph NC 4th Sr.Res. Co.E
Rhodes, Joseph SC 2nd Res. Co.K
Rhodes, Joseph SC 21st Inf. Co.B
Rhodes, Joseph VA 4th Res. Co.C
Rhodes, Joseph VA 8th Bn.Res. Co.D
Rhodes, Joseph VA 58th Mil. Co.F
Rhodes, Joseph C. TX 18th Cav. Co.K
Rhodes, Joseph E. NC 55th Inf. Co.G
Rhodes, Joseph H. NC 17th Inf. (2nd Org.) Co.C
Rhodes, Joseph M. TX 11th Inf. Co.K
Rhodes, Joseph P. NC 20th Inf. Co.G
Rhodes, Joseph R. VA Loc.Def. Mallory's Co.
Rhodes, Joseph W. GA Mil.Inf.Res.

Rhodes, Joseph W. TX 13th Cav. Co.B
Rhodes, Josiah AL 61st Inf. Co.D
Rhodes, Josiah GA Siege Arty. 28th Bn. Co.D
Rhodes, Josiah VA 51st Mil. Co.A
Rhodes, Josiah D. GA 14th Inf. Co.I
Rhodes, Jo. Wesley SC 20th Inf. Co.F
Rhodes, J.P. LA 19th Inf. Co.C Sgt.
Rhodes, J.P. SC 11th Inf. Sheridan's Co.
Rhodes, J.P. VA 23rd Cav. Co.B
Rhodes, J.Q.S. SC 3rd Regt.Res.
Rhodes, J.R. GA 18th Inf. Co.D
Rhodes, J.R. GA 55th Inf. Co.B Cpl.
Rhodes, J.R. SC Arty. Stuart's Co. (Beaufort
  Vol.Arty.)
Rhodes, J.R. VA 88th Mil.
Rhodes, J.R. Forrest's Scouts T.N. Kizer's
  Co.,CSA
Rhodes, J.S. AR 12th Inf. Co.H
Rhodes, J.S. SC Mil.Arty. 1st Regt. Tupper's
  Co.
Rhodes, J.S. SC 27th Inf. Co.I
Rhodes, J.T. SC 8th Inf. Co.F 2nd Lt.
Rhodes, J.T. TN 8th (Smith's) Cav. Co.A
Rhodes, J.T. TN Douglass' Bn.Part.Rangers Cof-
  fee's Co.
Rhodes, J.W. AL Arty. 1st Bn. Co.D
Rhodes, J.W. AL 19th Inf. Co.G
Rhodes, J.W. GA Cav. Allen's Co.
Rhodes, J.W. GA Inf. 1st Loc.Troops (Augusta)
  Co.D
Rhodes, J.W. GA Inf. 23rd Bn.Loc.Def. Pen-
  dergrass' Co.
Rhodes, J.W. LA 1st Cav. Co.G
Rhodes, J.W. LA 2nd Inf. Co.H
Rhodes, J.W. MS 37th Inf. Co.D
Rhodes, J.W. SC 18th Inf. Co.E
Rhodes, J.W. SC Prov.Guard Hamilton's Co.
Rhodes, J.W. TN 13th Inf. Co.I
Rhodes, J.W. TX Cav. 6th Bn. Co.B
Rhodes, J.W. TX 1st Inf. Co.C
Rhodes, J.W. VA Lt.Arty. Otey's Co.
Rhodes, J.W. Sig.Corps,CSA
Rhodes, Kena VA 61st Inf. Co.F
Rhodes, King A.J. AL 54th Inf. Co.E
Rhodes, King James NC 56th Inf. Co.E Capt.
Rhodes, L.A. MS 32nd Inf. Co.A
Rhodes, Lafayette MS 30th Inf. Co.D
Rhodes, Lafayette VA 7th Cav. Co.D 1st Lt.
Rhodes, L.D. MS 6th Inf. Co.I 2nd Lt.
Rhodes, L.D. MS Inf. Cooper's Co. 2nd Lt.
Rhodes, L.E. Forrest's Scouts T.N. Kizer's
  Co.,CSA
Rhodes, Leander E. TN 51st (Cons.) Inf. Co.C
  3rd Lt.
Rhodes, Leander E. TN 52nd Inf. Co.F 1st Lt.
Rhodes, Lemuel B. FL 7th Inf. Co.A 1st Lt.
Rhodes, Levi C. MS 42nd Inf. Co.I
Rhodes, Levi J. NC 5th Cav. (63rd St.Troops)
  Co.K
Rhodes, Levin TX 37th Cav. 2nd Co.I
Rhodes, Lewis NC 33rd Inf. Co.D
Rhodes, L.J. Forrest's Scouts T.N. Kizer's
  Co.,CSA
Rhodes, L.L AR 19th (Dawson's) Inf. Co.B
Rhodes, L.L. MS 8th Inf. Co.C 2nd Lt.
Rhodes, L.N. AR 30th Inf. Co.B
Rhodes, Louis B. GA Inf. 2nd Bn. Co.B

Rhodes, Lyman P. VA 19th Cav. Co.C
Rhodes, M. SC 5th Bn.Res. Co.B
Rhodes, M. TN 16th (Logwood's) Cav. Co.I
Rhodes, M.A. MS Cav. Jeff Davis Legion Co.D
Rhodes, Mansel AL 33rd Inf. Co.H
Rhodes, Mansfield TN Cav. 1st Bn. (McNairy's) Co.B
Rhodes, Marcus A. TX Cav. Mann's Regt. Co.A,K
Rhodes, Marcus M. MO Inf. 8th Bn. Co.C
Rhodes, Marmaduke C. NC 32nd Inf. Co.B
Rhodes, M.C. NC 17th Inf. (1st Org.) Co.A
Rhodes, M.C. NC 17th Inf. (2nd Org.) Co.B
Rhodes, Mc. W. TX Cav. Mann's Regt. Co.A,I Cpl.
Rhodes, M.E. MS 42nd Inf. Co.I
Rhodes, M.G. AL Cav. Hardie's Bn.Res. Co.A
Rhodes, M.G. AR 12th Inf. Co.H
Rhodes, Milloch W. TX 27th Cav. Co.D
Rhodes, Milton NC 39th Inf. Co.B
Rhodes, Milton VA 136th Mil. Co.A Cpl.
Rhodes, Milton VA 146th Mil. Co.D
Rhodes, Milton N. VA Cav. 35th Bn. Co.E
Rhodes, M.J. AL 22nd Inf. Co.H
Rhodes, M.J. KY 7th Mtd.Inf. Co.A
Rhodes, M.M. MO Robertson's Regt.St.Guard Co.2
Rhodes, Morgan MO Inf. 5th Regt.St.Guard Co.B
Rhodes, M.P. TN 12th (Cons.) Inf. Co.G Cpl.
Rhodes, Nathaniel H. NC 22nd Inf. Co.K
Rhodes, N.E. SC 1st Arty. Co.E
Rhodes, N.E. SC 5th St.Troops Co.C
Rhodes, Newton H. TX 28th Cav. Co.K
Rhodes, Newton H. TX 11th Inf. Co.E
Rhodes, Newton M. AL 17th Inf. Co.B
Rhodes, N.G. MS Cav. Part.Rangers Rhodes' Co. 1st Lt.
Rhodes, N.G. 14th Conf.Cav. Co.F Capt.
Rhodes, N. Green LA 1st Cav. Co.C Sgt.
Rhodes, N.H. GA 1st (Olmstead's) Inf. Co.F
Rhodes, N.H. GA 54th Inf. Co.D,H
Rhodes, N.H. 2nd Conf.Eng.Troops Co.D Sgt.
Rhodes, N.J. GA 18th Inf. Co.A
Rhodes, N.O. TN 9th Inf. Co.D Cpl.
Rhodes, Noah E. SC 9th Res. Co.G Cpl.
Rhodes, Noel NC 18th Inf. Co.I
Rhodes, N.S. AL 27th Inf. Co.C
Rhodes, N.S. MS Inf. 3rd Bn. Co.H
Rhodes, O.A. MS 14th (Cons.) Inf. Co.C
Rhodes, O.D. TN 13th (Gore's) Cav. Co.A
Rhodes, O.L. VA 7th Bn.Res. Co.B
Rhodes, Oliver A. MS 6th Inf. Co.I
Rhodes, Owen R. GA 18th Inf. Co.D 2nd Lt.
Rhodes, P. AL 19th Inf. Co.D
Rhodes, P. AL 40th Inf. Co.G
Rhodes, P. MO 6th Cav. Co.I
Rhodes, Perry VA Cav. 41st Bn. Co.B
Rhodes, Peter M. AL 4th (Roddey's) Cav. Co.F
Rhodes, Philip B. VA Hvy.Arty. 10th Bn. Co.A
Rhodes, Pleasant B. AL 24th Inf. Co.I
Rhodes, Pleasant N. AL 10th Inf. Co.B
Rhodes, Preston VA 7th Cav. Co.I 1st Sgt.
Rhodes, R. LA Mil. British Guard Bn. Burrowes' Co.
Rhodes, R.A. TX 4th Inf. Co.D
Rhodes, Radford GA Cobb's Legion Co.A

Rhodes, Ralzymon A. MS 33rd Inf. Co.H
Rhodes, R.C. MS 1st Bn.S.S. Co.D
Rhodes, R.C. MS 9th Bn.S.S. Co.C
Rhodes, R.C. MS 29th Inf. Co.C
Rhodes, Reuben VA 13th Inf. Co.A
Rhodes, R.H. MS 5th Inf. (St.Troops) Co.D 2nd Lt.
Rhodes, R.H. NC 5th Inf. Div.Commander
Rhodes, Richard GA 62nd Cav. Co.L
Rhodes, Richard GA 22nd Inf. Co.B
Rhodes, Ricahrd MO Cav. Freeman's Regt. Co.A
Rhodes, Richard NC 2nd Inf. Co.G
Rhodes, Richard TX 23rd Cav. Co.F Cpl.
Rhodes, Richard VA 24th Cav. Co.K
Rhodes, Richard VA 14th Inf. Co.A
Rhodes, Richard, Jr. VA 19th Inf. Co.F
Rhodes, Richard 8th (Dearing's) Conf.Cav. Co.E
Rhodes, Richard 14th Conf.Cav.
Rhodes, Richard A. MS 33rd Inf. Co.D 1st Sgt.
Rhodes, R.J. SC 8th Inf. Co.C
Rhodes, R.J. TN 3rd (Forrest's) Cav. Co.E
Rhodes, R.L. GA 3rd Cav. Co.H
Rhodes, Robert AL 33rd Inf. Co.H
Rhodes, Robert TN 11th Inf. Co.G
Rhodes, Robert A. TX 35th (Brown's) Cav. Co.K Sgt.
Rhodes, Robert A. TX 13th Vol. 3rd Co.I
Rhodes, Robert H. GA 2nd Cav. (St.Guards) Co.A Sgt.
Rhodes, Robert H. GA 49th Inf. Co.D Cpl.
Rhodes, Robert H. NC 5th Cav. (63rd St.Troops) Co.A
Rhodes, Robert H. NC 11th (Bethel Regt.) Inf. Co.C Sgt.Maj.
Rhodes, Robert M. GA 2nd Cav. Co.C
Rhodes, Robert M.H. GA 15th Inf. Co.D
Rhodes, Robert P. VA 19th Inf. Co.F
Rhodes, R.S. NC 45th Inf. Co.H,D
Rhodes, R.W. MO 7th Cav. Co.D,K
Rhodes, S. GA 10th Inf. Co.K
Rhodes, S.A. AL 3rd Inf. Co.D
Rhodes, S.A. TN 51st (Cons.) Inf. Co.G
Rhodes, Sabastian GA Inf. 27th Bn. Co.F
Rhodes, Samuel AR 24th Inf. Co.K
Rhodes, Samuel AR 27th Inf. Co.G
Rhodes, Samuel GA Cav. 20th Bn. Co.E
Rhodes, Samuel LA Res.Corps Scott's Co.
Rhodes, Samuel MO Cav. Preston's Bn. Co.C
Rhodes, Samuel VA 33rd Inf. Co.B
Rhodes, Samuel A. VA 2nd Arty. Co.I
Rhodes, Samuel A. VA Inf. 22nd Bn. Co.G
Rhodes, Samuel A. 3rd Conf.Cav. Co.D
Rhodes, Samuel B. NC Unassign.Conscr.
Rhodes, Samuel D. MS 39th Inf. Co.B 2nd Lt.
Rhodes, Samuel D. NC 8th Bn.Jr.Res. Co.C
Rhodes, Samuel J. MO 1st N.E. Cav.
Rhodes, Samuel J. TX 28th Cav. Co.K
Rhodes, Samuel J. TX 11th Inf. Co.E
Rhodes, Samuel M. NC 17th Inf. (1st Org.) Co.A
Rhodes, Samuel M. NC 17th Inf. (2nd Org.) Co.B
Rhodes, Samuel M. NC 32nd Inf. Co.B
Rhodes, Sandford 1st Conf.Inf. 2nd Co.H
Rhodes, Sanford NC 45th Inf. Co.A
Rhodes, S.B. NC 25th Inf.

Rhodes, S.B. TN 42nd Inf. Co.I
Rhodes, S.D. AR Inf. Hardy's Regt. Co.H Cpl.
Rhodes, S.D. NC 3rd Jr.Res. Co.G
Rhodes, S.F. AL 31st Inf. Co.D
Rhodes, S.F. MS 1st Cav.Res. Co.D
Rhodes, S.H. TN 16th (Logwood's) Cav. Co.I
Rhodes, Simeon GA 15th Inf. Co.A
Rhodes, Simion AR 7th Inf. Co.B
Rhodes, Simon B. MS 42nd Inf. Co.I
Rhodes, S.L. AR 26th Inf. Co.G
Rhodes, Solomon NC 5th Sr.Res. Co.K
Rhodes, S.P. AL 22nd Inf. Co.I
Rhodes, S.R. SC 7th Cav. Co.F
Rhodes, S.T. AL 23rd Inf. Co.G
Rhodes, S.T. VA Lt.Arty. Carrington's Co.
Rhodes, Stephen L. LA 19th Inf. Co.A
Rhodes, Stephen R. SC Cav. Tucker's Co.
Rhodes, Sydney VA Cav. 35th Bn. Co.H
Rhodes, T. AL 33rd Inf. Co.B
Rhodes, T.A. AL Cp. of Instr. Talladega Co.A
Rhodes, T. Augustus SC 1st (McCreary's) Inf. Co.H Sgt.
Rhodes, T.C. AL Conscr.
Rhodes, T.H. SC 11th Inf. Co.K
Rhodes, Thaddeus M. TX Cav. 3rd (Yager's) Bn. Rhodes' Co. Capt.
Rhodes, Thomas AL 5th Inf. Co.D
Rhodes, Thomas AL 12th Inf. Co.D
Rhodes, Thomas AL 48th Inf. Co.B Cpl.
Rhodes, Thomas GA 3rd Cav. (St.Guards) Co.D
Rhodes, Thomas GA 7th Inf. (St.Guards) Co.C
Rhodes, Thomas MS 6th Inf. Co.A
Rhodes, Thomas TN 51st (Cons.) Inf. Co.C
Rhodes, Thomas TX 25th Cav. Co.D
Rhodes, Thomas A. AL Inf. 1st Regt. Co.G
Rhodes, Thomas B. AR 26th Inf. Co.F 2nd Lt.
Rhodes, Thomas C. MS Cav. Part.Rangers Rhodes' Co. Capt.
Rhodes, Thomas D. VA Lt.Arty. Carrington's Co.
Rhodes, Thomas E. LA 16th Inf. Co.C 1st Sgt.
Rhodes, Thomas E. LA Mil. Chalmette Regt. Co.C 1st Sgt.
Rhodes, Thomas G. TX 22nd Inf. Co.C
Rhodes, Thomas J. AL Inf. 1st Regt. Co.D
Rhodes, Thomas J. GA 23rd Inf. Co.E
Rhodes, Thomas J. NC 27th Inf. Co.B 1st Sgt.
Rhodes, Thomas L. VA 1st Arty. Co.H
Rhodes, Thomas M. MS 19th Inf. Co.G Cpl.
Rhodes, Thomas P. TX 8th Inf. Co.D
Rhodes, Thomas R. GA Inf. 1st Loc.Troops (Augusta) Co.A
Rhodes, Thomas S. MS 30th Inf. Co.D
Rhodes, Thomas W. NC 39th Inf. Co.B Cpl.
Rhodes, T.J. GA 49th Inf. Co.D
Rhodes, T.J. MS 8th Inf. Co.B
Rhodes, T.J. MS 23rd Inf. Co.E
Rhodes, T.J. TX Cav. Co.D
Rhodes, T.M. AL Mil. 4th Vol. Co.I
Rhodes, T.M. LA 7th Inf. Co.B
Rhodes, Travis C. GA 4th Inf. Co.D
Rhodes, Tyre TN 6th (Wheeler's) Cav. Co.K
Rhodes, Virgil VA Cav. 46th Bn. Co.D
Rhodes, W. AL 62nd Inf. Co.F
Rhodes, W. GA 6th Cav. 1st Co.K Sgt.
Rhodes, W. SC 16th Inf. Co.D
Rhodes, W. VA 56th Inf. Co.H

Rhodes, W.A. AL 22nd Inf. Co.B
Rhodes, W.A. AL Cp. of Instr. Talladega
Rhodes, W.A. GA Siege Arty. Campbell's Ind.Co.
Rhodes, W.A. TN 42nd Inf. Co.C
Rhodes, W.A. 4th Conf.Inf. Co.H
Rhodes, W.A.C. VA Cav. 47th Bn. Co.A
Rhodes, Walter VA 19th Inf. Co.C
Rhodes, Walter VA 46th Inf. 2nd Co.I
Rhodes, Walter VA Loc.Def. Mallory's Co.
Rhodes, W.C. MS 9th Cav. Co.E Sgt.
Rhodes, W.C. MS 10th Cav. Co.F Sgt.
Rhodes, W.C. MS 1st (Johnston's) Inf. Co.I
Rhodes, W.C. NC 31st Inf. Co.C
Rhodes, W.C. SC 2nd Arty. Co.F
Rhodes, W.C. TN Cav. 17th Bn. (Sanders') Co.B Sgt.
Rhodes, W.D. AR 19th Inf. Co.H Sgt.
Rhodes, Wesley AR 2nd Cav. Co.E
Rhodes, Wesley NC 3rd Bn.Sr.Res. Durham's Co.
Rhodes, Wesley NC Jones' Co. (Supp.Force)
Rhodes, Wesley VA 51st Mil. Co.A
Rhodes, Weston T. MS 19th Inf. Co.G
Rhodes, W.F. GA 1st (Symons') Res. Co.I
Rhodes, W.H. AL 3rd Inf. Co.H
Rhodes, W.H. AR 2nd Cav. Co.E
Rhodes, W.H. AR 6th Inf. Co.C
Rhodes, W.H. GA Lt.Arty. 12th Bn. Co.F
Rhodes, W.H. GA 3rd Res. Co.I
Rhodes, W.H. MO Cav. 2nd Regt.St.Guard Co.A
Rhodes, W.H. TN 5th Inf. 2nd Co.G
Rhodes, W.H. TN 27th Inf. Co.H Sgt.
Rhodes, W.H. TX Cav. McCord's Frontier Regt. Co.C
Rhodes, Whitmill N. FL 5th Inf. Co.G
Rhodes, W.I. LA Cav. 22nd Regt. Co.G
Rhodes, Wiley TN 10th Inf. Co.B
Rhodes, William AR 2nd Mtd.Rifles Co.A
Rhodes, William AR 4th Inf. Co.C
Rhodes, William AR Inf. Hardy's Regt. Co.H
Rhodes, William GA 29th Inf. Co.I
Rhodes, William KY 6th Mtd.Inf. Co.A
Rhodes, William KY Part.Rangers Rowan's Co. Cpl.
Rhodes, William LA 7th Inf. Co.B
Rhodes, William LA 27th Inf. Co.G
Rhodes, William MO Cav. Preston's Bn. Co.C
Rhodes, William MO Cav. Wood's Regt. Co.H
Rhodes, William NC 7th Inf. Co.D
Rhodes, William NC 25th Inf. Co.I
Rhodes, William NC 31st Inf. Co.H
Rhodes, William NC 58th Inf. Co.F
Rhodes, William SC Lt.Arty. 3rd (Palmetto) Bn. Co.H,I
Rhodes, William SC 8th Inf. Co.M,F Bvt.2nd Lt.
Rhodes, William TN Cav. 1st Bn. (McNairy's) Co.B
Rhodes, William TN 13th Inf. Co.C
Rhodes, William TN 26th Inf. Co.A
Rhodes, William TX 26th Cav. Co.F,A Cpl.
Rhodes, William TX 37th Cav. 2nd Co.I
Rhodes, William TX Cav. Baylor's Regt. Co.C
Rhodes, William A. LA 19th Inf. Co.G
Rhodes, William A. NC 31st Inf. Co.A

Rhodes, William A. NC 56th Inf. Co.D
Rhodes, William A. TN 27th Inf. Co.I
Rhodes, William A. TN 27th Inf. Co.I Sgt.
Rhodes, William A. TN 44th Inf. Co.G Capt.
Rhodes, William A. TX 1st (McCulloch's) Cav. Co.C
Rhodes, William A. TX Cav. 8th (Taylor's) Bn. Co.E
Rhodes, William A. VA Rockbridge Cty.Res. Bacon's Co.
Rhodes, William B. NC 8th Inf. Co.A
Rhodes, William B. NC 25th Inf. Co.F
Rhodes, William Burton NC 6th Inf. Co.C
Rhodes, William C. NC 47th Inf. Co.C
Rhodes, William D. AR 6th Inf. New Co.D
Rhodes, William D. NC 3rd Cav. (41st St.Troops) Co.B
Rhodes, William D. NC 18th Inf. Co.C
Rhodes, William D. SC 5th Cav. Co.H
Rhodes, William E. NC 56th Inf. Co.D
Rhodes, William E. SC 2nd Arty. Co.D
Rhodes, William F. AL 24th Inf. Co.I
Rhodes, William F. GA 48th Inf. Co.D
Rhodes, William H. AL 6th Inf. Co.I
Rhodes, William H. AL 48th Inf. Co.I
Rhodes, Wm. H. AL Cp. of Instr. Talladega
Rhodes, William H. AR 9th Inf. Co.C
Rhodes, William H. GA 4th Inf. Co.C
Rhodes, William H. GA 15th Inf. Co.D
Rhodes, William H. MO 1st N.E. Cav.
Rhodes, William H., Jr. VA 21st Inf. Co.D
Rhodes, William H.H. MS 17th Inf. Co.H
Rhodes, William J. AL 18th Inf. Co.H
Rhodes, William J. AL 31st Inf. Co.G 2nd Lt.
Rhodes, William J. MS 40th Inf. Co.E
Rhodes, William J. NC 20th Inf. Faison's Co.
Rhodes, William J. NC 25th Inf. Co.H
Rhodes, William J. NC 61st Inf. Co.A
Rhodes, William L. FL 2nd Inf. Co.F
Rhodes, William L. TX 8th Cav. Co.H
Rhodes, William Lee MD 1st Inf. Co.G
Rhodes, William M. AL 31st Inf. Co.D
Rhodes, William M. AL 62nd Inf. Co.K
Rhodes, William M. GA 14th Inf. Co.I
Rhodes, William M. GA 23rd Inf. Co.B
Rhodes, William M. GA 30th Inf. Co.B
Rhodes, William M. MS 23rd Inf. Co.G Cpl.
Rhodes, William M. 1st Conf.Inf. 2nd Co.H, Co.A
Rhodes, William N. GA 13th Inf. Co.F
Rhodes, William P. AL 3rd Res. Co.H Sgt.
Rhodes, William P. NC 2nd Cav. (19th St.Troops) Co.K
Rhodes, William R. GA Inf. Taylor's Co.
Rhodes, William R. TX 1st (Yager's) Cav. Co.H
Rhodes, William S. TN 18th Inf. Co.I
Rhodes, William S. TN 20th Inf. Co.H 2nd Lt.
Rhodes, William T. TX 18th Inf. Co.I
Rhodes, William W. GA 3rd Cav. (St.Guards) Co.C
Rhodes, William W. GA 12th (Wright's) Cav. (St.Guards) Wright's Co.
Rhodes, William W. NC 26th Inf. Co.C
Rhodes, William W.G. VA 44th Inf. Co.K
Rhodes, Wilson TN 9th Inf. Co.H
Rhodes, Wilson TN 19th Inf. Co.E
Rhodes, Wilson A. VA 10th Cav. Co.H

Rhodes, W.J. AL 23rd Inf. Co.K 1st Lt.
Rhodes, W.J. GA 18th Inf. Co.A
Rhodes, W.J. KY 7th Mtd.Inf. Co.E
Rhodes, W.J. LA 17th Inf. Co.E
Rhodes, W.J. MS 30th Inf. Co.D Cpl.
Rhodes, W.J. SC 11th Inf. Sheridan's Co. Cpl.
Rhodes, W.J. TN Inf. 154th Sr.Regt. Co.D
Rhodes, W.K. TN 20th Cav. Co.H
Rhodes, W.L. TX 5th Inf. Co.B
Rhodes, W. Lee VA 8th Cav. Capt.
Rhodes, W.M. MS 10th Inf. New Co.K Cpl.
Rhodes, W.M. MO Cav. Fristoe's Regt. Co.G
Rhodes, W.P. GA Arty. St.Troops Pruden's Btty.
Rhodes, W.P. GA Inf. 1st Loc.Troops (Augusta) Co.C
Rhodes, W.P. GA Inf. 18th Bn. (St.Guards) Adams' Co.
Rhodes, W.R. AR 37th Inf. Co.A
Rhodes, W.R. TN 18th (Newsom's) Cav. Co.H
Rhodes, W.R. TN 9th Inf. Co.F 2nd Lt.
Rhodes, W.R. TX 20th Inf. Co.I
Rhodes, W.S. SC 1st (Hagood's) Inf. 2nd Co.H Cpl.
Rhodes, W.T. AL Arty. 1st Bn. Co.D
Rhodes, W.T. KY 8th Cav. Co.K
Rhodes, W.W. GA 3rd Res. Co.I
Rhodes, W.W. MS 1st Cav.Res. Co.D Cpl.
Rhodes, W.W. MS 36th Inf. Co.D
Rhodes, W.W. TX Cav. 6th Bn. Co.B Cpl.
Rhodes, Wyley KY 10th (Johnson's) Cav. New Co.B
Rhodifer, George VA 18th Cav. Co.I
Rhodin, Joe TX 29th Cav. Co.D
Rhodius, Ch. TX 4th Cav. Co.G
Rhodon, William MS 38th Cav. Co.C
Rhods, B. AL 40th Inf. Co.G
Rhods, Benjamin F. NC 60th Inf. Co.D
Rhods, Davids AL 29th Inf. Co.B
Rhods, H.S. AL 3rd Bn.Res. Jackson's Co.
Rhods, Jacob TX 18th Cav. Co.A
Rhods, Jesse NC 60th Inf. Co.D
Rhods, John M. VA 146th Mil. Co.B Sgt.
Rhods, Pleasant TN Cav. Newsom's Regt. Co.H
Rhods, Robert H. GA 3rd Cav. (St.Guards) Co.D
Rhods, Ruffus TN Cav. Newsom's Regt. Co.E
Rhods, T.J. TX Cav. McCord's Frontier Regt. Co.H
Rhods, William AL 3rd Bn.Res. Jackson's Co.C
Rhods, William SC 16th & 24th (Cons.) Inf. Co.B
Rhods, Willis A. VA 146th Mil. Co.B 1st Sgt.
Rhods, W.S. TN 15th (Stewart's) Cav. Co.F
Rhodus, G.D. SC 23rd Inf. Co.I
Rhodus, Isaac MS 33rd Inf. Co.B
Rhodus, James J. MS 33rd Inf. Co.B
Rhodus, J.G. SC 5th Bn.Res. Co.F 2nd Lt.
Rhodus, Joel G. SC 25th Inf. Co.K
Rhodus, Reeves MS 16th Inf. Co.E
Rhody, A. LA Mil. British Guard Bn. Coburn's Co.
Rhody, Josiah TN Lt.Arty. Kain's Co.
Rhody, J.S. LA Mil. British Guard Bn. Coburn's Co.
Rhody, William H. FL 1st Inf. New Co.K
Rhody, William H. LA 18th Inf. Co.I
Rhoe, John J. TX 28th Cav. Co.K
Rhoger, A.C. MS 43rd Inf. Co.H

Rhoi, Henderson MO 15th Cav. Co.A
Rholand, Frederick W. MO Cav. Slayback's
   Regt. Co.E
Rholater, Nicholas AL 19th Inf. Co.G
Rholeder, J.J. GA 17th Inf. Co.G
Rholeder, J.J. VA Inf. 25th Bn. Co.D
Rholeman, Fred LA Mil. Mooney's Co.
   (Saddlers Guards) Cpl.
Rholetter, Frederick W. VA Lt.Arty. Pegram's
   Co.
Rhom, Robert NC 49th Inf. Co.A
Rhoman, Joseph VA 2nd St.Res. Co.L
Rhome, B.C. TX 18th Inf. Co.K 1st Lt.
Rhome, R.J. TX Vol. Rainey's Co. 3rd Lt.
Rhome, Romulus J. TX 1st Inf. Co.H 2nd Lt.
Rhone, George W. TX 13th Cav. Co.B
Rhone, James AL 20th Inf. Co.F
Rhone, J.L. NC 4th Cav. (59th St.Troops) Co.K
Rhone, Robertus AL 20th Inf. Co.F
Rhoney, John G. NC 4th Sr.Res. Co.C
Rhoney, T. GA 25th Inf. Co.E
Rhoney, W.P. NC 3rd Jr.Res. Co.E Cpl.
Rhoor, George 3rd Conf.Inf. Co.B
Rhoor, John 3rd Conf.Inf. Co.B
Rhorer, Frank LA 7th Inf. Co.D
Rhorer, G.H. LA Inf.Crescent Regt. Co.K
Rhorer, J.N. LA Cav. Benjamin's Co.
Rhorer, Jos. LA Mil. 3rd Regt.Eur.Brig. (Garde
   Francaise) Co.4 Cpl.
Rhorer, Milton M. LA Conscr. Clerk
Rhorer, S.A. LA 25th Inf. Co.H 2nd Lt.
Rhorer, William B. MO Cav. 3rd Bn. Co.D
Rhote, J.C. TX 13th Cav. Co.F
Rhoten, C.D. KY 9th Mtd.Inf. Co.E
Rhoten, Henry VA 48th Inf. Co.B
Rhoten, Henry VA 48th Inf. Co.C
Rhoten, William VA 48th Inf. Co.B
Rhoters, George TN 13th (Gore's) Cav. Co.G
Rhoton, A.C. LA 25th Inf. Co.K Jr.2nd Lt.
Rhoton, Benjamin W. TN 44th Inf. Co.H
Rhoton, C.D. TN Inf. 23rd Bn. Co.A
Rhoton, David J. VA 25th Cav. Co.A
Rhoton, D.J. VA Mil. Scott Cty.
Rhoton, Dutton VA 25th Cav. Co.A
Rhoton, Elisha J. TN 44th Inf. Co.H
Rhoton, Elisha J. TN 44th (Cons.) Inf. Co.A
Rhoton, Henry VA 25th Cav. Co.A
Rhoton, Jacob Gen. & Staff 2nd Lt.,Dr.M.
Rhoton, Jacob P. TN 2nd (Ashby's) Cav. Co.I
   Sgt.
Rhoton, Jacob Peck TN Cav. 4th Bn. (Branner's)
   Co.E Sgt.
Rhoton, James F. TN 44th (Cons.) Inf. Co.A
Rhoton, L.J. TN 37th Inf. Co.C Cpl.
Rhoton, Tolbert VA 45th Inf. Co.C
Rhoton, T.T. TN Inf. 23rd Bn. Co.A
Rhoton, T.W. TN 37th Inf. Co.C Sgt.
Rhoton, W.B. KY 9th Mtd.Inf. Co.E
Rhoton, W.B. TN Inf. 23rd Bn. Co.A
Rhoton, William VA 45th Inf. Co.D
Rhoton, William A. VA 45th Inf. Co.D
Rhotramelle, A.J. 2nd Cherokee Mtd.Vol. Co.E
   Cpl.
Rhotramelle, D.W. 2nd Cherokee Mtd.Vol. Co.E
Rhotramelle, Henry 2nd Cherokee Mtd.Vol. Co.E
Rhotramelle, James H. 2nd Cherokee Mtd.Vol.
   Co.E Cpl.

Rhotramelle, J.L. 2nd Cherokee Mtd.Vol. Co.E
Rhotramelle, William 2nd Cherokee Mtd.Vol.
   Co.E
Rhotschley, W. VA 2nd St.Res. Co.H Sgt.
Rhould, --- LA Mil. 1st Regt. 2nd Brig. 1st Div.
   Co.B
Rhu, Charles TN 1st (Feild's) Inf. Co.E
Rhuark, J.C. SC Lt.Arty. M. Ward's Co. (Wac-
   camaw Lt.Arty.)
Rhuark, Stancil B. SC 10th Inf. Co.M 1st Sgt.
Rhuben, H. GA 44th Inf. Co.A
Rhubottom, C.F. TX Cav. Waller's Regt. Good's
   Co.
Rhubottom, Charles F. TX 35th (Brown's) Cav.
   Co.H
Rhubottom, Charles F. TX 13th Vol. 2nd Co.A
Rhudd, Archibald VA Inf. 23rd Bn. Co.D
Rhudicele, C.M. LA 17th Inf. Co.E
Rhudy, George VA 45th Inf. Co.K
Rhudy, James VA 14th Cav. Co.G
Rhudy, James L. VA 4th Inf. Co.F
Rhudy, S.F. VA 7th Cav. Preston's Co.
Rhudy, S.F. VA 14th Cav. Co.G
Rhudy, S.G. GA Floyd Legion (St.Guards) Co.E
   Sgt.
Rhudy, Stephen F. VA 4th Inf. Co.F
Rhudy, Stephen M. VA 29th Inf. Co.H
Rhudy, Stephen T. GA 29th Inf. Co.I,D
Rhudy, W.F. VA 14th Cav. Co.G
Rhudy, William J. VA Mil. Grayson Cty.
Rhue, Edward NC 1st Arty. (10th St.Troops)
   Co.G
Rhue, J.M. NC 3rd Cav. (41st St.Troops) Co.B
Rhue, John LA 1st Hvy.Arty. (Reg.) Co.H,D
Rhyan, John KY 10th (Johnson's) Cav. New
   Co.C
Rhyme, H.W. GA Arty. Lumpkin's Co. Sgt.
Rhymer, David VA 29th Inf. Co.B
Rhymer, David H. VA 46th Inf. Co.A
Rhymer, Joseph NC 15th Inf. Co.D
Rhymes, Augustus W. LA 19th Inf. Co.D
   Drum.
Rhymes, G.W. TX 24th & 25th Cav. (Cons.)
   Co.E
Rhymes, H.C. LA 27th Inf. Co.B
Rhymes, Henry H. TX 27th Cav. Co.D,E
Rhymes, H.W. GA 9th Inf. (St.Guards) Co.C
   Cpl.
Rhymes, James A. MS 16th Inf. Co.C
Rhymes, James A. MS 36th Inf. Co.B
Rhymes, Jesse J. MS 6th Inf. Co.G,F
Rhymes, J.H. LA 27th Inf. Co.B
Rhymes, J.H. TX 25th Cav. Co.C
Rhymes, John H. TX 9th (Nichols') Inf. Co.H
Rhymes, L.J. MS Inf. 1st Bn.St.Troops (12 mo.
   '62-3) Co.F
Rhymes, R.L. MS 3rd Inf. (St.Troops) Co.F
Rhymes, Stephen GA 1st Bn.S.S. Co.A Cpl.
Rhymes, Stephen GA 25th Inf. Co.C
Rhyn, H.J. AR 15th (Johnson's) Inf. Co.C
Rhynard, Henry MS Inf. 2nd Bn. Co.E Cpl.
Rhynars, D.K. TX 35th (Brown's) Cav. Co.A
Rhyne, A.B. NC 49th Inf. Co.H
Rhyne, Adam A. NC 4th Sr.Res. Co.E Capt.
Rhyne, Adam M. NC 42nd Inf. Co.K 2nd Lt.
Rhyne, Alexander A. NC 28th Inf. Co.B
Rhyne, Alfred NC 37th Inf. Co.H

Rhyne, Alfred M. NC 28th Inf. Co.B Cpl.
Rhyne, A.M. NC 1st Inf. (6 mo. '61) Co.B Cpl.
Rhyne, Ambrose NC 28th Inf. Co.B
Rhyne, A.P. NC 49th Inf. Co.H Cpl.
Rhyne, Arthur M. NC 8th Bn.Jr.Res. Co.B
Rhyne, Caleb NC 34th Inf. Co.E
Rhyne, C.M. NC 4th Cav. (59th St.Troops) Co.E
Rhyne, David NC 11th (Bethel Regt.) Inf. Co.E
Rhyne, Dunlap W. MS 1st Bn.S.S. Co.B
Rhyne, Eli S. NC 18th Inf. Co.A Cpl.
Rhyne, Eli S. NC 49th Inf. Co.H
Rhyne, F.M. MS Inf. 2nd Bn. Co.K
Rhyne, F.M. MS 7th Inf. Co.H
Rhyne, F.M. MS 48th Inf. Co.K
Rhyne, Francis M. MS 1st (Johnston's) Inf. Co.K
Rhyne, George NC 57th Inf. Co.G
Rhyne, George C. NC 28th Inf. Co.B
Rhyne, George F. VA Lt.Arty. Lowry's Co.
Rhyne, Henry NC 37th Inf. Co.H
Rhyne, Henry M. NC 37th Inf. Co.H
Rhyne, H.W. MS Cav. Ham's Regt. Co.F
Rhyne, J.A. GA 43rd Inf. Co.A 2nd Lt.
Rhyne, Jacob H. NC 4th Sr.Res. Co.E
Rhyne, Jacob K. NC 4th Sr.Res. Co.E
Rhyne, Jacob S. GA Cherokee Legion
   (St.Guards) Co.B
Rhyne, James A. GA Cherokee Legion
   (St.Guards) Co.A
Rhyne, James T. MS 4th Inf. Co.G
Rhyne, J.B. NC 49th Inf. Co.H
Rhyne, J.E. MS Inf. 2nd Bn. Co.K
Rhyne, J.E. MS 48th Inf. Co.K
Rhyne, J.E. NC 49th Inf. Co.H Sgt.
Rhyne, J.E. 8th (Wade's) Conf.Cav. Co.F
Rhyne, J.J. NC 2nd Jr.Res. Co.C
Rhyne, Joel W. MS 1st (Johnston's) Inf. Co.K
   2nd Lt.
Rhyne, John AR Cav. Gordon's Regt. Co.K
Rhyne, John NC 37th Inf. Co.F
Rhyne, John C. NC 16th Inf. Co.M
Rhyne, John H. AR 24th Inf. Co.F
Rhyne, John L. NC 49th Inf. Co.H Sgt.
Rhyne, John P. GA Cherokee Legion (St.Guards)
   Co.B
Rhyne, John T. MS 1st Bn.S.S. Co.B
Rhyne, John Y. MS 25th Inf. Co.A
Rhyne, Jonas NC 57th Inf. Co.G
Rhyne, Joseph NC 16th Inf. Co.M
Rhyne, Joseph W. NC 16th Inf. Co.M
Rhyne, Josiah AR 15th (Johnson's) Inf. Co.C
Rhyne, Michael P. TX 18th Inf. Co.B
Rhyne, Miles A. NC 16th Inf. Co.M
Rhyne, M.H. AR 62nd Mil. Co.C
Rhyne, M.H. NC 49th Inf. Co.H Sgt.
Rhyne, M.S. NC 49th Inf. Co.H
Rhyne, Peyton S. NC 37th Inf. Co.H
Rhyne, P.J. NC 4th Cav. (59th St.Troops) Co.E
Rhyne, R.C. MS 1st (Johnston's) Inf. Co.K
Rhyne, R.E. MS 14th (Cons.) Inf. Co.K
Rhyne, Robert D. NC 28th Inf. Co.B Capt.
Rhyne, Robert W. NC 4th Inf. Co.H
Rhyne, Thos. MO St.Guard
Rhynehart, William GA 5th Inf. (St.Guards)
   Everitt's Co.
Rhynhardt, Mike VA 10th Cav. Co.I
Riaale, C. AL Inf. 1st Regt. Co.H
Riach, George S. AL 1st Bn.Cadets Co.A

Riach, John MD 1st Cav. Co.C
Riadon, Allen KY 5th Mtd.Inf. Co.C
Riadon, William KY 5th Mtd.Inf. Co.C
Rial, Adam S. AR 26th Inf. Co.A,B Sgt.
Rial, Charles W. NC 6th Inf. Co.H Cpl.
Rial, John LA 17th Inf. Co.E Cpl.
Rial, Tims LA 17th Inf. Co.E 1st Sgt.
Rial, Walter D. TX 10th Inf. Co.G
Riale, John C. NC 7th Bn.Jr.Res. Co.A
Riales, C.H. MS 9th Inf. New Co.C
Riales, E.F. MS 9th Inf. New Co.C
Riales, J.C. MS 24th Inf. Co.I
Riales, John P. MS 9th Inf. New Co.C
Riales, Samuel MS 9th Inf. New Co.C
Riall, E.H. MS Inf. 4th St.Troops Co.E
Rialle, W. FL 1st (Res.) Inf.
Rialls, George W. MS 7th Inf. Co.G
Rials, Christopher C. MS Cav. Hughes' Bn.
   Co.D
Rials, Christopher R. MS 36th Inf. Co.E Sgt.
Rials, Edmond LA 28th (Gray's) Inf. Co.K
Rials, Edward AL 18th Inf. Co.H
Rials, Eli MS 9th Inf. Old Co.C
Rials, G.W. MS 1st Lt.Arty. Co.F
Rials, G.W. MS Horse Arty. Cook's Co.
Rials, G.W. TN 48th (Voorhies') Inf. Co.G
Rials, Harrison MS 1st Cav.Res. Co.I
Rials, Henry AL 18th Inf. Co.H
Rials, Henry LA 28th (Gray's) Inf. Co.K,H
Rials, I.M. MS Cav. Powers' Regt. Co.D Cpl.
Rials, Jacob AL 37th Inf. Co.K
Rials, Jacob AL 57th Inf. Co.C
Rials, James MS 9th Inf. Co.C
Rials, James F.A. AL Auburn Home Guards Vol.
   Darby's Co.
Rials, James R. AL 33rd Inf. Co.A
Rials, Jesse MS 33rd Inf. Co.D
Rials, Jessee AR 2nd Cav. Co.C
Rials, Jesse M. MS Cav. 24th Bn. Co.B
Rials, J.M. MS Horse Arty. Cooks' Co.
Rials, J.M. 20th Conf.Cav. Co.D
Rials, John AL 18th Inf. Co.A
Rials, John AL 32nd Inf. Co.F
Rials, John AL 34th Inf. Co.H
Rials, John MS 7th Inf. Co.E
Rials, John SC Inf. 7th Bn. (Enfield Rifles) Co.C
Rials, John H. AL 23rd Inf. Co.B
Rials, Joseph MS 42nd Inf. Co.I
Rials, J.P. SC Mil. 1st Regt. (Charleston Res.)
   Co.B
Rials, J.T. TN 48th (Voorhies') Inf. Co.G
Rials, Samuel AL 33rd Inf. Co.A Music.
Rials, Samuel LA Inf. 4th Bn. Co.F
Rials, S.M. MS Res.
Rials, Ves MS St.Cav. 3rd Bn. (Cooper's) 1st
   Co.A
Rials, W. MS 9th Inf. New Co.G
Rials, W. MS 9th Bn.S.S. Co.C
Rials, W.E. MS 1st Lt.Arty. Co.F
Rials, W.E. MS Horse Arty. Cook's Co.
Rials, Wiley NC 2nd Arty. (36th St.Troops)
   Co.B
Rials, William SC 10th Inf. 2nd Co.G
Rialy, T. TN 10th Inf. Co.H
Rian, John A. 1st Conf.Inf. Co.A
Rian, John J. VA 42nd Inf. Co.D
Rian, John W. AR 18th Inf. Co.F

Riancho, Franco. LA Mil. 5th Regt.Eur.Brig.
   (Spanish Regt.) Co.4
Rianhard, William MD Weston's Bn. Co.A
Rianhart, J. VA 2nd Inf. Co.F
Rianherd, William H. MD 1st Inf. Co.C
Riani, A. VA 2nd St.Res. Co.K
Riani, J. VA 2nd St.Res. Co.K
Rians, John F. SC 2nd Rifles Co.A
Riardon, Mark MO Inf. Winston's Regt. Co.A
Rias, Francisco TX 4th Field Btty.
Riason, Charles M. TX 31st Cav. Co.A
Ribas Y Castanos, Jose LA Mil. 5th Regt.
   Eur.Brig. (Spanish Regt.) Co.6
Ribau, J. LA Mil. 4th Regt. French Brig. Co.6
Ribaud, Jean LA Mil. 1st Native Guards
Ribble, Edward J. TX 19th Cav. Co.E
Ribble, George W. MO 12th Inf. Co.K
Ribble, Henry VA Wade's Regt.Loc.Def. Co.E
Ribble, H.W. TX 5th Cav. Co.K
Ribble, John W. VA Lt.Arty. Griffin's Co.
Ribble, John W. VA 9th Inf. 1st Co.A
Ribblin, G.W. NC 42nd Inf. Co.B
Ribby, J.H. AR 1st Cav. Co.B
Ribelin, Jesse NC 38th Inf. Co.A
Riber, A. LA Mil. Orleans Guards Regt. Co.H
Riber, C. LA Mil. 4th Regt. French Brig. Co.6
Ribera, J. MD. LA Mil. Cazadores Espanoles
   Regt. Co.1 Sgt.
Ribera, Juan TX Cav. Ragsdale's Bn. 1st Co.A
Ribera, Mauricis TX Cav. Ragsdale's Bn. 1st
   Co.A
Ribero, Anto. LA Mil. 5th Regt.Eur.Brig.
   (Spanish Regt.) Co.2
Ribero, D. TX 8th Inf. Co.C
Ribero, Manuel LA Mil. 5th Regt.Eur.Brig.
   (Spanish Regt.) Co.4
Ribero, Thomas GA Siege Arty. 28th Bn. Co.F
   2nd Lt.
Ribero, Thomas L. GA 5th Inf. Co.I,H,L,M 2nd
   Lt.
Riberon, A. AL 21st Inf. Co.G
Riberon, F. GA Cav. Floyd's Co.
Ribers, Thomas L. GA 2nd Bn.S.S. Co.A 1st
   Sgt.
Ribes, Bernardo LA Mil. 5th Regt.Eur.Brig.
   (Spanish Regt.) Co.7
Ribes, Eduardo TX Cav. Benavides' Regt. Co.E
Ribet, E.J. AL Cav. Murphy's Bn. Co.C
Ribet, E.J. AL St.Arty. Co.C
Ribet, E.J. AL Mil. 2nd Regt.Vol. Co.C
Ribet, H. LA Mil. 1st Chasseurs a pied Co.2
Ribler, W.R. Gen. & Staff Asst.Surg.
Riblet, George J. VA 19th Cav. Co.D
Riblet, John S. VA 29th Cav. Co.D
Riblett, Michael VA 25th Inf. 1st Co.E
Riblett, Michael VA 62nd Mtd.Inf. 2nd Co.I
Riblette, M. VA 18th Cav. Co.A
Ribley, Adolphus TX 19th Cav. Co.D
Riblin, J.L. NC 5th Cav. (63rd St.Troops) Co.H
Ribold, Jacob TX 19th Inf. Co.A,C
Ribot, Francisco LA Mil. Cazadores Espanoles
   Regt. Surg.
Ribrion, Jules LA Mil. 2nd Regt. French Brig.
   Co.5 Cpl.
Ribron, D.M. GA 26th Inf. Co.K
Ribron, F. GA 4th (Clinch's) Cav. Co.C

Ribuffad, Francois LA Mil. 2nd Regt. French
   Brig. Co.7
Rica, Francois LA Mil. 3rd Regt. 2nd Brig. 1st
   Div.
Ricamore, George MD Cav. 2nd Bn. Co.D
Ricamore, George VA 12th Cav. Co.B
Ricard, C. SC 6th Inf. Co.B
Ricard, James Daniel AL Lt.Arty. 2nd Bn. Co.D
Ricard, John MO Lt.Arty. Barret's Co.
Ricard, Levi W. MS 42nd Inf. Co.I
Ricard, L.H. TN 31st Inf. Co.D
Ricard, Stephen AL 5th Inf. New Co.C
Ricardini, L. LA 21st (Kennedy's) Inf. Co.D
Ricardo, Benjamin LA Inf.Cons.Crescent Regt.
   Co.L
Ricardy, John B. TN Arty. Ramsey's Btty.
Ricau, A. LA Mil. 1st Regt. French Brig. Co.4
Ricau, Fulgence LA Mil. 1st Regt. French Brig.
   Co.4 Capt.
Ricau, J.F. LA Mil. 1st Regt. French Brig.
   Capt.
Ricau, P. LA Mil. 1st Regt. French Brig. Co.4
Ricau, V. LA Mil. 1st Regt. French Brig. Co.4
   Sgt.
Ricaud, --- LA Mil. 2nd Regt. French Brig. Co.2
Ricaud, Benjamin R. VA 2nd Inf. Co.I,C
Ricaud, J.M. LA Mil. French Co. of St.James
Ricca, F.G. TX 25th Cav. Co.I
Ricca, L.G. TX 24th & 25th Cav. (Cons.) Co.H
Ricciardi, Francesco LA Mil. 6th Regt.Eur.Brig.
   (Italian Guards Bn.) Co.2
Rice, --- AL Mil. 3rd Vol. Co.A
Rice, --- TX Cav. Border's Regt. Co.K
Rice, --- TX Cav. McCord's Frontier Regt. Co.E
Rice, --- TX Cav. McCord's Frontier Regt. Co.F
Rice, A. AL 13th Bn.Part.Rangers Co.B
Rice, A. AL Cp. of Instr. Talladega
Rice, A. GA 3rd Res. Co.E
Rice, A. LA Mil.Conf.Guards Regt. Co.F
Rice, A.A. AL Inf. 36th Regt. Co.B
Rice, A.A. Gen. & Staff Surg.
Rice, Aaron AL 26th (O'Neal's) Inf. Co.F
Rice, Aaron GA Hvy.Arty. 22nd Bn. Co.E
Rice, A.B. VA Lt.Arty. Otey's Co.
Rice, A.B. VA Inf. 25th Bn. Co.D
Rice, Abraham B. GA 64th Inf. Co.C
Rice, A.D. TX 3rd Cav. Co.E
Rice, Addison Emit SC 4th Inf. Co.C Sgt.
Rice, A.E. SC Inf. 13th Bn. Co.E Sgt.
Rice, A.F. VA 20th Inf. Co.H 1st Lt.
Rice, A.G. GA 18th Inf. Co.B
Rice, A. Glenn Gen. & Staff Col.,Vol.ADC
Rice, A.H. AL 5th Cav. Co.G Capt.
Rice, A.H. AL 7th Inf. Co.D
Rice, A.H. GA 60th Inf. Co.H 2nd Lt.
Rice, A.H. KY 2nd Cav.
Rice, A.H. TN 1st (Carter's) Cav. Co.C
Rice, A.H. TN 3rd (Forrest's) Cav. Amis' Co.
Rice, A.H. 3rd Conf.Cav. Co.G
Rice, A.J. AR 20th Inf. Co.D
Rice, A.J. MO Cav. Freeman's Regt. Co.G
Rice, A.J. TN 17th Inf. Co.I Sgt.
Rice, A.J. TX Res.Corps Co.I
Rice, A.J. 3rd Conf.Cav. Co.G Bvt.2nd Lt.
Rice, A.J. Gen. & Staff Lt.,Ord.Off.
Rice, Albert KY 3rd Cav. Co.B,E
Rice, Albert F. VA 40th Inf. Co.F 1st Lt.

123

Rice, D.P. SC Arty. Stuart's Co. (Beaufort Vol.Arty.)

Rice, Alexander AL Cp. of Instr. Talladega
Rice, Alexander MO 1st N.E. Cav. Co.F
Rice, Alexander TN 25th Inf. Co.B
Rice, Alexander TX Cav. Morgan's Regt. Co.E
Rice, Alexander C. AL 36th Inf. Co.B
Rice, Alfred NC 14th Inf. Co.F
Rice, Alfred G. KY 10th (Diamond's) Cav. 1st Lt.
Rice, Alfred G. KY 5th Mtd.Inf. Co.A,K Bvt.2nd Lt.
Rice, Alfred G. KY Fields' Co. (Part.Rangers)
Rice, Allen G. NC 4th Inf. Co.B
Rice, A.M. TN 12th Inf. Co.B
Rice, Amedia TN 1st (Carter's) Cav. Co.D
Rice, Amos M. NC 20th Inf. Co.D Cpl.
Rice, Anderson P. Conf.Inf. 1st Bn. 2nd Co.A Sgt.
Rice, Andrew J. AL 16th Inf. Co.C 1st Sgt.
Rice, Andrew J. KY 5th Mtd.Inf. Co.F
Rice, Andrew J. VA 28th Inf. Co.G
Rice, Andrew J. VA 58th Inf. Co.C
Rice, A.P. TX 20th Inf. Co.I
Rice, A.P. TX Inf. Timmons' Regt. Co.I
Rice, Apling GA 7th Inf. Co.D
Rice, A.R. TX 4th Inf. Co.B
Rice, Archabal W. GA 41st Inf. Co.B
Rice, A.S. TX 4th Inf. Co.B
Rice, Asa AL 56th Part.Rangers Co.F
Rice, Asa G. NC 45th Inf. Co.H
Rice, Asa M. GA 38th Inf. Co.I,F
Rice, Asa S. TX Cav. Mann's Regt. Co.A
Rice, Augustus AL 1st Cav. 2nd Co.C Bugler
Rice, Augustus H. GA 45th Inf. Co.G
Rice, A.W. TX 15th Inf. 2nd Co.D
Rice, A.W. VA 19th Cav. Co.A
Rice, B. AL 48th Inf. Co.C
Rice, B. VA 54th Mil. Co.E,F
Rice, Barton M. GA 14th Inf. Co.E Sgt.
Rice, B.B. SC 1st St.Troops Co.B
Rice, B.B. SC 22nd Inf. Co.G
Rice, B.E. KY 3rd Bn.Mtd.Rifles Co.D
Rice, Benjamin AL 47th Inf. Co.I
Rice, Benjamin MO Lt.Arty. 13th Btty.
Rice, Benjamin MO 16th Inf. Co.A
Rice, Benjamin VA 11th Inf. Co.K
Rice, Benjamin 1st Conf.Inf. 2nd Co.F
Rice, Benjamin B. TN Lt.Arty. Lynch's Co.
Rice, Benjamin C. AR 1st Mtd.Rifles Co.H
Rice, Benjamin C. AR 9th Inf. Co.F
Rice, Benjamin F. VA 12th Cav. Co.I
Rice, Benjamin F. VA 58th Inf. Co.C
Rice, Benjamin H. NC 7th Inf. Co.B
Rice, Benjamin J. GA Cherokee Legion (St.Guards) Co.K
Rice, Benjamin L. FL 4th Inf. Co.K Music.
Rice, Benjamin M. AL 36th Inf. Co.K
Rice, Bernard NC Currituck Guard J.W.F. Bank's Co.
Rice, Berry NC 47th Inf. Co.A
Rice, Berry VA 12th Cav. Co.I
Rice, B.F. GA Inf. 1st Conf.Bn. Co.B
Rice, B.F. SC 5th Cav. Co.A
Rice, Bird AR 34th Inf. Co.I
Rice, Bird C. AR 15th (N.W.) Inf. Co.C,I
Rice, B.L. MO Cav. Coleman's Regt. Co.A
Rice, Blakely MS 26th Inf. Co.E

Rice, B.M. AL Cp. of Instr. Talladega
Rice, Boyd C. NC 2nd Arty. (36th St.Troops) Co.G
Rice, Bramwell VA 1st Cav. Co.I
Rice, Bryan NC 44th Inf. Co.C
Rice, Bryant C. MS 3rd Inf. Co.A Cpl.
Rice, B.S. KY 1st Bn.Mtd.Rifles Co.E
Rice, B.S. KY Field's Co. (Part.Rangers) AASurg.
Rice, B.S. Gen. & Staff AASurg.
Rice, B.W. GA 2nd Inf. Co.K Sgt.
Rice, C. AL Cp. of Instr. Talladega
Rice, C. LA Mil.Conf.Guards Regt. Co.F
Rice, C.A. GA 11th Cav. Co.D
Rice, C.A. MS 1st Lt.Arty. Asst.Surg.
Rice, C.A. MS 4th Inf. Surg.
Rice, C.A. MS 9th Inf. New Co.A
Rice, C.A. Gen. & Staff Surg.
Rice, Caleb AR 26th Inf. Co.C
Rice, Calvin SC 5th Cav. Co.I
Rice, Calvin SC Cav. 14th Bn. Co.D
Rice, Calvin VA 1st Arty. 3rd Co.C
Rice, Calvin VA Lt.Arty. 1st Bn. Co.C
Rice, Calvin VA Arty. Young's Co.
Rice, Calvin C. GA Cobb's Legion Co.F
Rice, Calvin Clark MS Inf. 1st St.Troops Co.G Sgt.
Rice, Campbell KY 2nd Bn.Mtd.Rifles Co.A
Rice, Carroll M. AR 13th Inf. Co.H
Rice, C.C. AR 2nd Cav. Co.G
Rice, C.C. MO 12th Cav. Co.I Sgt.
Rice, C.C. TN 38th Inf. Co.D
Rice, C.D. Gen. & Staff Surg.
Rice, C.F. KY 2nd (Duke's) Cav. Co.L
Rice, C.H. SC Bn.St.Cadets Co.B 2nd Lt.
Rice, Charles AL 26th (O'Neal's) Inf.
Rice, Charles AR Mil. Desha Cty.Bn.
Rice, Charles MD Cav. 2nd Bn. Co.D
Rice, Charles MS 9th Inf. Co.A
Rice, Charles MO 16th Inf. Co.D
Rice, Charles NC 4th Inf. Co.I
Rice, Charles TN 7th (Duckworth's) Cav. Co.H
Rice, Charles TN 34th Inf. Co.F
Rice, Charles TX 30th Cav. Co.E
Rice, Charles VA Hvy.Arty. 10th Bn. Co.C
Rice, Charles VA 60th Inf. Co.K
Rice, Charles A. LA Inf.Crescent Regt. Co.I,C
Rice, Charles E. AL St.Arty. Co.A
Rice, Charles E. LA Miles' Legion Co.A Cpl.
Rice, Charles E. VA 97th Mil. Co.B
Rice, Charles F. MO Inf. Perkins' Bn. Co.A
Rice, Charles H. AL 13th Inf. Co.E Sgt.
Rice, Charles H. SC Horse Arty. (Washington Arty.) Vol. Hart's Co.
Rice, Charles H. VA 37th Mil. Co.D
Rice, Charles J. GA 57th Inf. Co.A
Rice, Charles J. TX 5th Inf. Co.E
Rice, Charles L. VA Inf. 21st Bn. 2nd Co.D
Rice, Charles L. VA 64th Mtd.Inf. Co.D
Rice, Charles R. AL 8th Inf. Co.H 1st Lt.
Rice, Charles W. KY Cav. Jenkins' Co.
Rice, Charlton H. KY 8th Cav. Co.D Cpl.
Rice, Cicero N. TX 11th (Spaight's) Bn.Vol. Co.C Sgt.
Rice, C.J. GA 29th Inf. Co.B
Rice, C.L. AR 19th (Dawson's) Inf. Co.K
Rice, C.L. GA Inf. 5th Bn. (St.Guards) Co.C

Rice, C.L. GA Inf. 9th Bn. Co.E
Rice, Clarence VA 9th Cav. Co.C
Rice, Clarence VA Murphy's Co.
Rice, Clay MS 9th Cav. AQM
Rice, Clay TN Cav. 17th Bn. (Sanders') Co.A Capt.,AQM
Rice, Clay Gen. & Staff AQM
Rice, Clemons GA 1st (Fannin's) Res. Co.H
Rice, C.M. VA 3rd Res. Co.D
Rice, C.N. TX 21st Inf. Co.E Sgt.
Rice, C.O. AR 13th Inf. Co.H
Rice, Columbus E. MS Cav. 4th Bn. Sykes' Co.
Rice, Columbus E. 8th (Wade's) Conf.Cav. Co.G Sgt.
Rice, Cornelias A. MS 12th Inf. Co.A Asst.Surg.
Rice, Cornelius LA 8th Inf. Co.C
Rice, Cornelius A. Gen. & Staff Surg.
Rice, C.S.O. TN 7th (Duckworth's) Cav. Co.M 2nd Lt.
Rice, C.T. TN 1st (Carter's) Cav. Co.D 2nd Lt.
Rice, C.W. AR 35th Inf. Co.F
Rice, C.Y. TN 1st (Carter's) Cav. Co.L 2nd Lt.
Rice, D. TX 1st Hvy.Arty. Co.K
Rice, D.A. LA Washington Arty.Bn. Co.5 Sgt.
Rice, D.A. MO Lt.Arty. Barret's Co. Capt.
Rice, Daniel LA 1st Hvy.Arty. (Reg.) Co.A
Rice, Daniel LA 18th Inf. Co.C
Rice, Daniel TN 11th Inf. Co.C
Rice, Daniel TN 34th Inf. Co.H
Rice, Daniel 1st Conf.Eng.Troops Co.F Artif.
Rice, Daniel C. KY 7th Cav. Co.G,A
Rice, Daniel S. AL 6th Inf. Co.E Sgt.
Rice, Daniel W. VA 58th Inf. Co.C 2nd Lt.
Rice, Danyel KY 11th Cav. Co.H
Rice, David GA 38th Inf. Co.H
Rice, David KY 13th Cav.
Rice, David TN 41st Inf. Co.I Sgt.
Rice, David TN 61st Mtd.Inf. Co.A
Rice, David TX 8th Cav. Co.G
Rice, David VA 14th Cav. Co.B
Rice, David VA Inf. Cohoon's Bn. Co.A,B
Rice, David A. GA 36th (Villepigue's) Inf. Co.E
Rice, David A. NC 16th Inf. Co.L
Rice, David A. Lt.Arty. Dent's Btty,CSA
Rice, David B. NC 13th Inf. Co.C
Rice, David C. TX 27th Cav. Co.I
Rice, David D. GA 18th Inf. Co.B
Rice, David E. MS 2nd Inf. Co.K
Rice, David H. SC 11th Res. Capt.,AQM
Rice, David H. TN 11th Inf. Co.K 1st Lt.
Rice, David J. AR Cav. Wright's Regt. Co.D Cpl.
Rice, David P. AL Cav. Lewis' Bn. Co.E
Rice, David P. GA 2nd Inf. 1st Co.B
Rice, David P. GA 26th Inf. Co.E 2nd Lt.
Rice, Dekalb LA 19th Inf. Co.A
Rice, Dempsey GA 26th Inf. Co.E
Rice, D.H. SC 8th Inf. Co.E
Rice, D.H. SC 17th Inf. Co.H 1st Lt.
Rice, D.J. TN 7th (Duckworth's) Cav. Co.L,M
Rice, D.K. TX 1st Inf. Co.C Capt.
Rice, Doctor S. AL Cav. Lewis' Bn. Co.E
Rice, Dolison S. NC 7th Inf. Co.E Cpl.
Rice, Dorsey NC 4th Cav. (59th St.Troops) Co.F
Rice, D.P. SC Arty. Stuart's Co. (Beaufort Vol. Arty.)

Rice, Duncan C. VA 34th Inf. Co.C
Rice, D.W. AL 48th Inf. Co.D
Rice, D.W. TN 21st (Wilson's) Cav. Co.C
Rice, D.W. TN 21st & 22nd (Cons.) Cav. Co.F
Rice, E. AL St.Troops
Rice, E. SC Mil. 3rd Regt. Co.H
Rice, E. VA 37th Inf. Co.C
Rice, E.B. AL 5th Cav. Capt.,AAAG
Rice, E.B. AL 7th Inf. Co.D Cpl.
Rice, E.B. SC Palmetto S.S. Co.C Sgt.
Rice, E.C. TX Waul's Legion Co.B
Rice, E.D. GA 18th Inf. Co.B
Rice, Ed. C. AL Gid Nelson Lt.Arty.
Rice, Edward F. GA 7th Inf. Co.K
Rice, Edward T. MS 44th Inf. Co.L
Rice, Edward T. VA 18th Inf. Co.F
Rice, Edwin AR 3rd Cav. Co.F
Rice, Edwin KY 1st Bn.Mtd.Rifles Co.E
Rice, Edwin KY 5th Mtd.Inf. Co.D
Rice, Edwin E. TX Inf. Timmons' Regt. Adj.
Rice, Edwin E. TX Waul's Legion Co.A
  Sgt.Maj.
Rice, E.E. TX Inf. Timmons' Regt. Adj.
Rice, E.F. AL 48th Inf. Co.K 1st Lt.
Rice, E.H. AR Inf. Cocke's Regt. Co.G 1st Sgt.
Rice, E.H. MO Cav. Schnabel's Bn. Co.D
Rice, E.J. AL 13th Bn.Part.Rangers Co.B Capt.
Rice, E.J. AL 56th Part.Rangers Co.F Capt.
Rice, E.J. LA Inf. 9th Bn. Co.B Cpl.
Rice, Elbert A. GA 4th Res. Co.E,K
Rice, Elijah TN 53rd Inf. Co.F
Rice, Elisha AL 22nd Inf. Co.F
Rice, Elisha P. TX 2nd Inf. Co.E
Rice, Eli T. AL Cav. Lewis' Bn. Co.D
Rice, Enoch B. SC 4th Inf. Co.B
Rice, Enoch H. AR 14th (Powers') Inf. Co.B
Rice, E.P. LA Inf. 4th Bn. Co.F
Rice, Evan VA 55th Inf. Co.A Lt.Col.
Rice, F. GA 46th Inf.Co.H
Rice, F.A. AR 34th Inf. Co.I
Rice, F.A. TX Cav. 3rd Regt.St.Troops Co.A
Rice, F.A. TX Inf. Houston Bn. Capt.
Rice, F.A. TX Loc.Def. Perry's Co. (Fort Bend
  Scouts)
Rice, F.B. KY 2nd (Duke's) Cav. Co.A Cpl.
Rice, F.B. KY 5th Cav. Co.G
Rice, F.C. GA Cherokee Legion (St.Guards)
  Co.F
Rice, Felix LA Mil. 4th Regt. 3rd Brig. 1st Div.
  Co.F 3rd Lt.
Rice, Fleming B. KY 14th Cav. Co.A Cpl.
Rice, F.M. AL 15th Inf. Co.H
Rice, F.M. MO 4th Cav. Co.G
Rice, F.M. MO Cav. Coffee's Regt. Co.F
Rice, Frances Cheatham's Div. Ch.Surg.
Rice, Francis TN 15th Inf.
Rice, Francisco TN 4th (McLemore's) Cav.
  Co.K Capt.
Rice, Francis E. VA Lt.Arty. B.Z. Price's Co.
Rice, Francis E. VA Lt.Arty. W.H. Rice's Co.
Rice, Francis E. VA 97th Mil. Co.B 1st Sgt.
Rice, Francis M. AR 14th (Powers') Inf. Co.A
Rice, Francis M. KY 7th Cav. Co.G,C
Rice, Francis M. TX 13th Cav. Co.B
Rice, Francis M. 1st Conf.Inf. 2nd Co.F
Rice, Francis W. VA Inf. 22nd Bn. Co.B
Rice, Frank TN 15th Inf. Surg.

Rice, Frank TN 15th Inf. Co.B
Rice, Fred KY 2nd Mtd.Inf. Co.E
Rice, Frederick L. NC 3rd Arty. (40th St.Troops)
  Co.D
Rice, Freeman MS 1st Lt.Arty. Co.B
Rice, F.S. Gen. & Staff Lt.,AAQM
Rice, F.T. TN 9th Inf. Co.K Sgt.
Rice, F.T. TN 13th Inf. Co.I
Rice, F.W. VA Inf. 25th Bn. Co.D
Rice, F.Z. NC 3rd Cav. (41st St.Troops) Co.C
Rice, G. FL 2nd Inf. Co.M
Rice, G. NC 47th Inf. Co.A
Rice, G.A. TN 19th (Biffle's) Cav. Co.G
Rice, Gabriel P. NC Walker's Bn. Thomas'
  Legion Co.F
Rice, Gabriel P. TN 5th (McKenzie's) Cav. Co.K
Rice, G.B. GA Inf. 18th Bn. Co.A,B,C Cpl.
Rice, G.C. LA 18th Inf. Co.F
Rice, George AL 13th Bn.Part.Rangers Co.B
Rice, George AL 56th Part.Rangers Co.F
Rice, George LA 21st (Kennedy's) Inf. Co.D
Rice, George MS 44th Inf. Co.K
Rice, George MO 7th Cav. Old Co.A Cpl.
Rice, George NC 52nd Inf. Co.A
Rice, George TN 18th Inf. Co.K
Rice, George A. AL 13th Inf. Co.E
Rice, George A. AR Inf. Crawford's Bn. Co.B
  2nd Lt.
Rice, George A. GA 1st (Olmstead's) Inf. 2nd
  Lt.
Rice, George B. GA 1st (Olmstead's) Inf.
  Screven's Co. Cpl.
Rice, George C. LA Inf.Crescent Regt. Co.I
Rice, George C. LA Inf.Cons.Crescent Regt.
  Co.G,N Cpl.
Rice, George C. MD 1st Cav. Co.A,D
Rice, George D. GA Cav. 9th Bn. (St.Guards)
  Co.B Capt.
Rice, George D. GA Lt.Arty. 12th Bn. 1st Co.A
Rice, George D., Jr. GA 36th (Villepigue's) Inf.
  Co.E
Rice, George D. GA 63rd Inf. Co.A
Rice, George D. GA Phillips' Legion Co.L
Rice, George D. 1st Conf.Inf. 1st Co.E
Rice, George D. Gen. & Staff 2nd Lt.,Dr.M.
Rice, George F. LA Washington Arty.Bn.
Rice, George F. TX 27th Cav. Co.F
Rice, George H. MS 16th Inf. Co.D
Rice, George L. GA 16th Inf. Co.D Sgt.
Rice, Geo. N. AL 35th Inf. Co.A
Rice, George R. AL 4th (Roddey's) Cav. Co.H
  1st Sgt.
Rice, George R. FL 4th Inf. Co.K
Rice, George R. MS Cav. 4th Bn. Roddey's Co.
Rice, George T. GA 61st Inf. Co.F
Rice, George T. MD Arty. 4th Btty. 3rd Lt.
Rice, George T. VA Arty. Forrest's Co.
Rice, George W. AL 36th Inf. Co.I
Rice, George W. AL 48th Inf. Co.B
Rice, George W. AR 1st (Colquitt's) Inf. Co.G
Rice, George W. AR 8th Inf. New Co.A
Rice, George W. AR 9th Inf. Co.F
Rice, George W. MS 21st Inf. Co.F
Rice, George W. MS 27th Inf. Co.D
Rice, George W. NC Cav. 5th Bn. Co.A
Rice, George W. NC 64th Inf. Co.F Sgt.
Rice, George W. TN 14th Inf. Co.H

Rice, George W. TX 18th Cav. Co.C
Rice, George W. TX 18th Cav. Co.F
Rice, George W. VA 5th Cav.
Rice, George W. VA 10th Cav. Co.K
Rice, George W. VA 11th Inf. Co.C
Rice, George W. VA 19th Inf. Co.C
Rice, George W. VA 30th Bn.S.S. Co.C
Rice, George W. VA 166th Mil. Co.D
Rice, G.H. TN 19th (Biffle's) Cav. Co.I
Rice, Gideon B. NC 1st Arty. (10th St.Troops)
  Co.I
Rice, Gideon B. NC 67th Inf. Co.B
Rice, Gilbert C. GA 1st (Olmstead's) Inf.
  Screven's Co. 2nd Lt.
Rice, Gilbert C. GA Inf. 18th Bn. Co.A,C Capt.
Rice, Giles MO 2nd Inf. Co.K
Rice, G.L.D. GA 12th (Robinson's) Cav.
  (St.Guards) Co.B
Rice, G.P. AL 1st Cav. 1st Co.C
Rice, G.P. AL 5th Cav. Co.D 1st Lt.
Rice, G.P. MS Lt.Arty. 14th Bn. Co.C
Rice, G.P. MS Lt.Arty. Merrin's Btty.
Rice, Grant TN 9th (Ward's) Cav. Co.F
Rice, Greek P. MS 29th Inf. Co.B Jr.2nd Lt.
Rice, Griffin D. VA 40th Inf. Co.C
Rice, G.S. AL 56th Part.Rangers Co.F
Rice, G.S. TN 12th Inf. Co.B 2nd Lt.
Rice, G.S. TN 12th (Cons.) Inf. Co.A 2nd Lt.
Rice, Gustavious VA 37th Mil. Co.D
Rice, G.W. AL 5th Cav. Co.B
Rice, G.W. GA 3rd Bn.S.S. Co.A Sgt.
Rice, G.W. GA 18th Inf. Co.K
Rice, H. LA Mil.Conf.Guards Regt. Co.F Sgt.
Rice, H. LA Mil.Conf.Guards Regt. Co.F
Rice, H. MS 3rd Inf. (A. of 10,000) Co.A
Rice, H. 1st Chickasaw Inf. Wallace's Co.
Rice, H.A. KY 10th (Diamond's) Cav. Co.H
Rice, H.A. TX 17th Inf. Co.K Sgt.
Rice, Hampton A. TN 39th Mtd.Inf. Co.I 1st Lt.
Rice, Harry MS Lt.Arty. (Brookhaven Lt.Arty.)
  Hoskins' Btty. Cpl.
Rice, Harvey MS 20th Inf. Co.I
Rice, Harvey C. NC Inf. Thomas Legion Co.E
Rice, Harvy KY 5th Cav. Co.I
Rice, H.B. SC 2nd St.Troops Co.E
Rice, H.C. GA 3rd Inf.
Rice, Henry GA 56th Inf. Co.G Cpl.
Rice, Henry KY 4th Mtd.Inf. Cpl.
Rice, Henry MO 5th Cav. Co.A
Rice, Henry NC Inf. Thomas Legion Co.I
Rice, Henry TN Cav. 11th Bn. (Gordon's) Co.E
Rice, Henry TN 15th Inf. Co.C Capt.
Rice, Henry VA 14th Cav. Co.B
Rice, Henry VA Lt.Arty. Clutter's Co.
Rice, Henry C. TN 41st Inf. Co.I Sgt.
Rice, Henry C. VA 20th Inf. Co.G
Rice, Henry C. VA 38th Inf. Co.C
Rice, Henry D.M. AR 2nd Mtd.Rifles Hawkins'
  Co.
Rice, Henry D.M. TX 27th Cav. Co.A
Rice, Henry H. NC Hvy.Arty. 10th Bn. Co.D
Rice, Henry H. NC 25th Inf. Co.B
Rice, Henry M. MS 11th Inf. Co.A 1st Sgt.
Rice, Henry T. GA Cav. 1st Bn.Res. Co.C
Rice, Henry W. SC 27th Inf. Co.G
Rice, Henry W. TX 14th Cav. Co.H
Rice, H.F. SC 1st (McCreary's) Inf.

Rice, H.F. SC 4th Inf. Co.B
Rice, H.F. SC Palmetto S.S. Co.C
Rice, H.F. TX 7th Inf. Co.F
Rice, H.F. Sig.Corps,CSA
Rice, H.G. TX 8th Cav. Co.K
Rice, Hiram A. KY Fields' Co. (Part.Rangers)
Rice, Hiram A. KY 5th Mtd.Inf. Co.D 1st Lt.
Rice, H.J. GA Inf. 9th Bn. Co.C
Rice, H.M. TN Cav. 16th Bn. (Neal's) Co.B
Rice, H.M. 3rd Conf.Cav. Co.G
Rice, Holman VA 3rd Res. Co.D
Rice, Horace TN Inf. 2nd Cons.Regt. Col.
Rice, Horace TN 29th Inf. Co.E Col.
Rice, H.T. VA Lt.Arty. Snead's Co.
Rice, H.W. NC 27th Inf. Co.G
Rice, H.W. SC 1st Mtd.Mil. Anderson's Co.
Rice, H.W. SC 4th Cav. Co.K
Rice, H.W. SC Arty. Stuart's Co. (Beaufort
    Vol.Arty.) Gy.Cpl.
Rice, H.W. SC 1st Bn.S.S. Co.C
Rice, H.W. SC 2nd St.Troops Co.E
Rice, H.W. SC 8th Bn.Res. Co.C Sgt.
Rice, H.W. SC 11th Inf. Co.A Cpl.
Rice, H.W. SC Mil. 17th Regt. Rogers' Co.
Rice, H.W. SC 20th Inf. Co.B
Rice, H.W. Sig.Corps,CSA
Rice, I.B. TN 50th (Cons.) Inf. Co.C
Rice, Ibzan L. SC 4th Inf. Co.B
Rice, Ignatius NC 8th Inf. Co.B Cpl.
Rice, I.R. TN 50th Inf. Co.C
Rice, Ira AL 12th Cav. Co.G
Rice, Irwin AL 11th Cav. Co.G
Rice, Isaac GA 17th Inf. Co.C
Rice, Isaac NC 25th Inf. Co.B 1st Lt.
Rice, Isaac NC 64th Inf. Co.F
Rice, Isaac NC 64th Inf. Co.G
Rice, Isaac R. NC Walker's Bn. Thomas' Legion
    Co.B
Rice, Isadore L. GA 3rd Inf. Co.K
Rice, Isaiah AL 55th Vol. Co.F
Rice, Isaiah TN 42nd Inf. 1st Co.E
Rice, Isiah AL 18th Bn.Vol. Co.C
Rice, Issac R. AL 47th Inf. Co.F
Rice, I.Y. TN Cav. Nixon's Regt. Co.A 1st Sgt.
Rice, J. AL 49th Inf. Co.H
Rice, J. AL 63rd Inf. Co.I
Rice, J. KY Jessee's Bn.Mtd.Riflemen Co.C
Rice, J. SC 2nd St.Troops Co.I
Rice, J. TX 4th Inf. (St.Troops) Co.H
Rice, J. VA 42nd Inf. Co.D
Rice, J. VA 45th Inf. Co.F
Rice, J.A. AL 1st Regt. Mobile Vol. Co.A
Rice, J.A. AL Mil. 2nd Regt.Vol. Co.E
Rice, J.A. GA 57th Inf. Co.A
Rice, Jackson GA 6th Cav. 1st Co.K
Rice, Jackson KY Part.Rangers Rowan's Co.
Rice, Jackson Gen. & Staff Capt.,Ch.Ord.Off.
Rice, Jacob MO 1st N.E. Cav. Co.B
Rice, Jacob SC 3rd Inf. Co.E
Rice, Jacob VA 58th Mil. Co.H
Rice, Jacob A. MO 5th Inf. Co.H
Rice, Jacob A. MO St.Guard
Rice, Jacob F. AL 6th Inf. Co.D
Rice, Jacob F. NC 25th Inf. Co.B
Rice, James AL 12th Cav. Co.A
Rice, James AL 56th Part.Rangers Co.F Cpl.
Rice, James AL 3rd Res. Co.E

Rice, James AL 47th Inf. Co.H
Rice, James AL 55th Vol. Co.F Cpl.
Rice, James AR Cav. Wright's Regt. Co.A
Rice, James AR Lt.Arty. 5th Btty.
Rice, James GA 3rd Cav. Co.K
Rice, James GA Siege Arty. 28th Bn. Co.D
Rice, James GA 3rd Inf. Co.H
Rice, James GA 7th Inf. (St.Guards) Co.G
Rice, James GA 18th Inf. Co.H
Rice, James GA 65th Inf. Co.F Cpl.
Rice, James GA Smith's Legion Co.D
Rice, James KY 8th Cav. Co.H
Rice, James KY 10th (Johnson's) Cav. Co.D
Rice, James LA 1st Hvy.Arty. (Reg.) Co.G
Rice, James LA 9th Inf. Co.G
Rice, James LA 14th Inf. Co.F
Rice, James MS 12th Inf. Co.E
Rice, James MO 10th Cav. Co.F
Rice, James NC 3rd Arty. (40th St.Troops) Co.D
Rice, James NC 64th Inf. Co.F
Rice, James SC 1st (Orr's) Rifles Co.E
Rice, James SC 2nd Rifles Co.B
Rice, James SC 7th Inf. 2nd Co.I
Rice, James TN 15th (Cons.) Cav. Co.A Sgt.
Rice, James TN 19th & 20th (Cons.) Cav. Co.K
Rice, James TN 20th (Russell's) Cav. Co.E
Rice, James TN 29th Inf. Co.K
Rice, James TN 42nd Inf. 1st Co.E
Rice, James TX 9th Cav. Co.K
Rice, James VA Inf. 4th Bn.Loc.Def. Co.D
Rice, James A. MO Arty. Lowe's Co.
Rice, James B. GA 24th Inf. Co.F
Rice, James B. VA 37th Mil. Co.A
Rice, James B. VA 58th Inf. Co.C
Rice, James C. VA Hvy.Arty. 10th Bn. Co.B
Rice, James D. AL Inf. 1st Regt. Co.K Cpl.
Rice, James E. KY 4th Mtd.Inf. Co.C
Rice, James H. FL 6th Inf. Co.H 2nd Lt.
Rice, James H. MS 35th Inf. Co.E Cpl.
Rice, James H. SC Lt.Arty. Garden's Co. (Pal-
    metto Lt.Btty.) Sgt.
Rice, James H. SC 2nd Inf. Co.B
Rice, James H. SC 16th Inf. Co.E
Rice, James H. TX 12th Inf. Co.A
Rice, James H. 8th (Wade's) Conf.Cav. Co.G
Rice, James H. Wheeler's Scouts,CSA
Rice, James J. TN 3rd (Lillard's) Mtd.Inf. 2nd
    Co.K
Rice, James J. VA 38th Inf. Co.H
Rice, James K. AL 38th Inf. Co.F
Rice, James L. KY 7th Mtd.Inf. 1st Co.K Cpl.
Rice, James L. NC 58th Inf. Co.H
Rice, James L. TN 2nd (Ashby's) Cav. Co.I
Rice, James L. TN Cav. 4th Bn. (Branner's)
    Co.E
Rice, James L. TN 20th Inf. Co.C Capt.
Rice, James L. VA 10th Inf. Co.H
Rice, James L. VA 57th Inf. Co.A
Rice, James M. KY 14th Cav. Co.B
Rice, James M. MS 2nd Inf. Co.E
Rice, James M. MS 14th Inf. Co.G
Rice, James M. MS 20th Inf. Co.G
Rice, James M. MS 31st Inf.
Rice, James M. MO 10th Cav. Co.E
Rice, James M. NC 16th Inf. Co.L
Rice, James M. NC 64th Inf. Co.F
Rice, James M. NC Inf. Thomas Legion Co.E

Rice, James M. TN 29th Inf. Co.E 2nd Lt.
Rice, James M. TN 38th Inf. Co.F Color Sgt.
Rice, James M. VA 27th Inf. 1st Co.H 1st Lt.
Rice, James N. TN 7th (Duckworth's) Cav. Co.B
Rice, James O. NC 60th Inf. Co.C Cpl.
Rice, James P. AL 20th Inf. Co.I Cpl.
Rice, James P. MO 10th Cav. Co.E Capt.
Rice, James P. MO St.Guards Co.F
Rice, James P. VA 38th Inf. Co.E Sgt.
Rice, James R. AR 10th Cav.
Rice, James R. GA Hvy.Arty. 22nd Bn. Co.F
Rice, James R. GA Lt.Arty. 14th Bn. Co.A Sgt.
Rice, James R. GA Lt.Arty. Havis' Btty. 2nd Lt.
Rice, James R. GA 1st (Ramsey's) Inf. Co.C
    Sgt.
Rice, James R. GA Inf. 2nd Bn. Co.C N.C.S.
    Comsy.Sgt.
Rice, James R. VA 9th Inf. Co.B
Rice, James R. VA 61st Inf. Co.D
Rice, James S. AR 13th Inf. Co.E Cpl.
Rice, James T. GA 39th Inf. Co.G
Rice, James T. NC 12th Inf. Co.F
Rice, James T. TN 7th Inf. Co.G Music.
Rice, James T. TN 48th Inf. Co.K Music.
Rice, James W. NC 25th Inf. Co.I
Rice, James W. TN 26th Inf. Co.C 3rd Lt.
Rice, Jay GA 41st Inf. Co.K,E
Rice, J.B. AR 15th (N.W.) Inf. Co.I
Rice, J.B. TN 2nd Cav. Co.F
Rice, J.C. GA 52nd Inf. Co.B
Rice, J.C. LA 3rd Inf. Co.I Cpl.
Rice, J.C. 3rd Conf.Cav. Co.G
Rice, J.D. GA 2nd (Stapleton's) St.Troops Co.E
    Sgt.
Rice, J.D. GA 38th Inf. Co.H
Rice, J.D. NC 6th Inf. Co.C
Rice, J.D. VA 8th Cav. 2nd Co.D
Rice, J.E. MS 8th Cav. Co.F
Rice, J.E. MO 16th Inf. Co.F
Rice, J.E. Gen. & Staff Ord.Off.
Rice, Jeremiah J. TX 11th (Spaight's) Bn.Vol.
    Co.C
Rice, Jesse LA 21st (Kennedy's) Inf. Co.C
Rice, Jesse TN Cav. 16th Bn. (Neal's) Co.B
Rice, Jesse NC 64th Inf. Co.F
Rice, Jesse NC 64th Inf. Co.K
Rice, Jesse NC Walker's Bn. Thomas' Legion
    Co.B
Rice, Jesse TN 37th Inf. Co.C
Rice, Jesse TX 8th Cav. Co.B
Rice, Jesse VA Inf. 2nd Bn.Loc.Def. Co.G Cpl.
Rice, Jessee GA 12th (Robinson's) Cav.
    (St.Guards) Co.B
Rice, Jessee W. MS 3rd Inf. Co.A,K
Rice, Jesse E. NC 6th Cav. (65th St.Troops)
    Co.E
Rice, Jesse R. NC 3rd Arty. (40th St.Troops)
    Co.B
Rice, Jesse W. AL 42nd Inf. Co.E
Rice, J.F. KY 3rd Cav. Co.I Sgt.
Rice, J.F. NC 8th Inf. Co.H
Rice, J.F. TN 45th Inf. Co.F
Rice, J.F. TX 28th Cav. Co.B
Rice, J.G. GA 11th Cav. (St.Guards) Johnson's
    Co.
Rice, J.H. AL Gid Nelson Lt.Arty.
Rice, J.H. GA Inf. 1st Conf.Bn. Co.B Sgt.

Rice, J.H. GA 2nd (Stapleton's) St.Troops Co.H
　Sgt.
Rice, J.H., Jr. GA 52nd Inf. Co.D
Rice, J.H., Sr. GA 52nd Inf. Co.D
Rice, J.H. LA Inf. 9th Bn. Co.C
Rice, J.H. MO 2nd Inf. Co.D
Rice, J.H. TN 1st Inf. Co.D
Rice, J.H. TN 45th Inf. Co.H
Rice, J.H. TN Inf. Nashville Bn. Fulcher's Co.
Rice, J.H. VA 22nd Inf. Co.H
Rice, J.H. Morgan's Co.D, CSA
Rice, J.I.J. SC 11th Res. Co.E
Rice, J.J. GA 32nd Inf. Co.F
Rice, J.J. SC 2nd St.Troops Co.E
Rice, J.J. TN 21st (Wilson's) Cav. Co.C Capt.
Rice, J.J. TX 21st Inf. Co.E
Rice, J.L. AL 50th Conf.Inf. Co.H
Rice, J.L. AR 36th Inf. Co.E
Rice, J.L. SC 2nd Inf. Co.I
Rice, J.L. SC Palmetto S.S. Co.C
Rice, J.L. TX 4th Inf. Co.I
Rice, J.L. TX 20th Inf. Capt.
Rice, J.M. AL 6th Cav. Co.A
Rice, J.M. MS 2nd Cav. Co.E
Rice, J.M. MS Hall's Co.
Rice, J.M. SC Lt.Arty. Wagener's Co. (Co.A,
　German Arty.)
Rice, J.N. MO 12th Cav. Co.E
Rice, J.N. SC 1st Bn.S.S. Co.A
Rice, J.N. SC 27th Inf. Co.E
Rice, J.N. TX Cav. (Dismtd.) Chisum's Regt.
　Co.I
Rice, J.O. AR 6th Inf. Co.I
Rice, Joab NC 3rd Arty. (40th St.Troops) Co.D
Rice, Jobe AR 25th Inf. Co.K
Rice, Joel VA Inf. 21st Bn. Co.A
Rice, Joel VA 64th Mtd.Inf. Co.I
Rice, Joel A. GA 3rd Inf. Co.H
Rice, Joel D. MS 21st Inf. Co.F
Rice, Joel D. MS 27th Inf. Co.D
Rice, Joel T. AL 20th Inf. Co.I
Rice, Joel W. AR 1st Mtd.Rifles Co.E
Rice, John AL 18th Bn.Vol. Co.A
Rice, John AL 30th Inf. Co.E
Rice, John AL 44th Inf. Co.D,E Cpl.
Rice, John AL 61st Inf. Co.F
Rice, John GA Hvy.Arty. 22nd Bn. Co.F Sgt.
Rice, John GA 1st Reg. Co.F
Rice, John GA 6th Inf.
Rice, John GA 7th Inf. Co.D
Rice, John GA 25th Inf. Co.E
Rice, John GA 43rd Inf. Co.L
Rice, John GA 65th Inf. Co.F
Rice, John GA Smith's Legion Co.D
Rice, John KY 11th Cav. Co.B
Rice, John LA Inf. 1st Sp.Bn. (Wheat's) New
　Co.E
Rice, John LA 28th (Gray's) Inf. Co.F
Rice, John LA Bickham's Co. (Caddo Mil.)
Rice, John MS 12th Cav. Co.I
Rice, John MO 7th Cav. Co.F
Rice, John NC Inf. 2nd Bn. Co.G
Rice, John NC 29th Inf. Co.D
Rice, John SC 20th Inf. Co.A
Rice, John TN 9th (Ward's) Cav. Co.F Ord.Sgt.
Rice, John TN 19th (Biffle's) Cav. Co.I
Rice, John TN 7th Inf. Co.I

Rice, John TX 1st (Yager's) Cav. Co.D
Rice, John TX Cav. 3rd (Yager's) Bn. Co.D
Rice, John TX 4th Cav. Co.I Sgt.
Rice, John TX 12th Cav. Co.D
Rice, John TX 21st Cav. Co.K
Rice, John TX 23rd Cav. Co.E
Rice, John TX 37th Cav. Co.E
Rice, John TX Cav. McCord's Frontier Regt.
　Co.I
Rice, John TX 4th Inf. Co.K
Rice, John TX Waul's Legion Co.B
Rice, John VA 31st Mil. Co.D
Rice, John VA 37th Mil. Co.A
Rice, John VA 40th Inf. Co.C
Rice, John VA 59th Inf. 3rd Co.G
Rice, John VA 67th Mil. Co.A
Rice, John 3rd Conf.Cav. Co.G
Rice, John A. MO 9th Inf. Co.G
Rice, John A. Gen. & Staff Asst.Surg.
Rice, John B. NC 17th Inf. (1st Org.) Co.L Cpl.
Rice, John B. NC 17th Inf. (2nd Org.) Co.A
Rice, John B. TN 14th (Neely's) Cav. Co.F 1st
　Lt.
Rice, John B. VA 10th Inf. Co.G
Rice, John C. AL 10th Inf. Co.K
Rice, John C. GA 36th (Broyles') Inf. Co.I
Rice, John C. VA 25th Inf. 2nd Co.H Cpl.
Rice, John D. TX 36th Cav. Co.K
Rice, John D. TX 37th Cav. 2nd Co.I
Rice, John D. VA 5th Bn.Res. Co.H Capt.
Rice, John D. VA 58th Inf. Co.C
Rice, John E. AL 28th Inf. Co.F
Rice, John E. VA 58th Inf. Co.C
Rice, John F. GA 64th Inf. Co.E 1st Lt.
Rice, John F. KY 7th Cav. Co.F
Rice, John F. MS 5th Inf. (St.Troops) Co.D
Rice, John F. MS 37th Inf. Co.K
Rice, John F. VA Lt.Arty. Montgomery's Co.
Rice, John F., Jr. VA 23rd Inf. Co.I
Rice, John G. GA Hvy.Arty. 22nd Bn. Co.E
Rice, John H. AL 19th Inf. Co.B
Rice, John H. AL 48th Inf. New Co.G
Rice, John H. KY 2nd (Duke's) Cav. Co.E
Rice, John H. SC 16th Inf. Co.E 1st Sgt.
Rice, John H. TN 5th (McKenzie's) Cav. Co.I
Rice, John H. 1st Conf.Inf. 2nd Co.G Sgt.
Rice, John H. Gen. & Staff Asst.Surg.
Rice, John J. TN 13th Inf. Co.I 3rd Lt.
Rice, John M. NC 1st Inf. (6 mo. '61) Co.E
Rice, John M. NC 60th Inf. Co.A
Rice, John M. VA Arty. Wise Legion
Rice, John M. Conf.Lt.Arty. Stark's Bn. Co.D
Rice, John N. NC 25th Inf. Co.I
Rice, John O. VA 55th Inf. Co.M Sgt.
Rice, John P. KY Cav. Jenkins' Co. Cpl.
Rice, John P. SC Inf. Hampton Legion Co.E
Rice, John P. TX Arty. 4th Bn. Co.A
Rice, John P. VA 5th Cav. Co.A
Rice, John Q. AR Willett's Co. Cpl.
Rice, John R. TX 13th Cav. Co.C
Rice, John T. GA 10th Cav. (St.Guards) Co.C
Rice, John W. KY 3rd Mtd.Inf. Co.E
Rice, John W. MS Inf. 3rd Bn. Co.B
Rice, John W. MS 14th Inf. Co.G
Rice, John W. MS 20th Inf. Co.G
Rice, John W. NC 35th Inf. Co.H
Rice, John W. VA 48th Inf. Co.D

Rice, John W. Conf.Cav. Wood's Regt. Co.B
Rice, John Y. NC Lt.Arty. 3rd Bn. Co.C
Rice, Jonathan TX Cav. 6th Bn. Co.C Sgt.
Rice, Jonathan W. TX 18th Cav. Co.A
Rice, Jordan SC 3rd Res. Co.I
Rice, Joseph AL Cp. of Instr. Talladega
Rice, Joseph GA 11th Cav. Co.E
Rice, Joseph GA 2nd Inf. Co.F
Rice, Joseph LA Mil. 4th Regt. 2nd Brig. 1st
　Div. Co.C
Rice, Joseph MO 1st Inf. Co.E
Rice, Joseph MO 1st & 4th Cons.Inf. Co.F
Rice, Joseph TN Cav. 12th Bn. (Day's) Co.D
　2nd Lt.
Rice, Joseph TN 21st (Wilson's) Cav. Co.F
Rice, Joseph TN Inf. 2nd Cons.Regt. Co.E
Rice, Joseph TN 39th Mtd.Inf. Co.I
Rice, Joseph TX 5th Cav. Co.G
Rice, Joseph TX 35th (Brown's) Cav. Co.A
Rice, Joseph TX 35th (Likens') Cav. Co.A
Rice, Joseph VA 189th Mil. Co.C
Rice, Joseph 3rd Conf.Cav. Co.B Black.
Rice, Joseph A. AL Cav. Holloway's Co.
Rice, Joseph A. AL 3rd Inf. Co.H
Rice, Joseph A. NC 49th Inf. Co.C
Rice, Joseph A. VA 10th Inf. Co.B 1st Sgt.
Rice, Joseph C. TN 29th Inf. Co.H Color Sgt.
Rice, Joseph D. VA 37th Mil. Co.A
Rice, Joseph E. VA 11th Inf. Co.C
Rice, Joseph E. VA 42nd Inf. Co.D
Rice, Joseph J. MS 19th Inf. Co.K Cpl.
Rice, Joseph M. NC Walker's Bn. Thomas'
　Legion Co.B
Rice, Joseph P. VA 37th Mil. Co.A
Rice, Joseph P. VA 40th Inf. Co.C
Rice, Joseph S. VA 7th Cav. Co.H
Rice, Joseph S. VA 40th Inf. Co.C
Rice, Joseph S. VA 146th Mil. Co.A
Rice, J.P. AL 9th Inf. Co.I
Rice, J.P. MO 12th Cav. Co.I
Rice, J.P. SC Inf. Hampton Legion Co.C
Rice, J.P. TX 8th Inf. Co.A Cpl.
Rice, J.R. AL Cav. Moreland's Regt. Co.A
Rice, J.S. NC 11th (Bethel Regt.) Inf. Co.H
Rice, J.S. TN 7th (Duckworth's) Cav. Co.M
Rice, J.T. AL 8th Cav. Co.A
Rice, J.T. AR 35th Inf. Co.F
Rice, J.T. GA 13th Cav. Co.I,K
Rice, J.T. TN 38th Inf. Co.F
Rice, J.T. VA 3rd Res. Co.D
Rice, J.T. VA 4th Res.
Rice, Julius F. TN 26th Inf. Co.C Sgt.
Rice, Julius T. AL Mil. 4th Vol. Co.B Cpl.
Rice, J.W. AL 47th Inf. Co.E
Rice, J.W. AR 38th Inf. Co.A
Rice, J.W. GA 13th Cav. Co.I
Rice, J.W. GA Inf. 25th Bn. (Prov.Guard) Co.D
Rice, J.W. GA Cobb's Legion Co.E
Rice, J.W. LA Allston's Res.Corps
Rice, J.W. MO Cav. Freeman's Regt. Co.F
Rice, J.W. MO Cav. Fristoe's Regt. Co.L
Rice, J.W. NC 1st Cav. (9th St.Troops) Co.B
Rice, J.W. SC 1st (Hagood's) Inf. 1st Co.K, 2nd
　Co.A Cpl.
Rice, J.W. TN 19th (Biffle's) Cav. Co.G Sgt.
Rice, J.W. TN Inf. 4th Cons.Regt. Co.E
Rice, J.W. TN 31st Inf. Co.H

Rice, J.W. TN 45th Inf. Co.H
Rice, J.Y. TN 12th Inf. Co.B
Rice, J.Y. TN 12th (Cons.) Inf. Co.A
Rice, K.G. KY Cav.
Rice, K.W. GA Hvy.Arty. 22nd Bn. Co.F
Rice, L. AR 7th Inf. Co.G
Rice, L. GA Inf. 1st Loc.Troops (Augusta) Co.K
Rice, L. GA 32nd Inf. Co.F
Rice, L. LA 25th Inf. Co.D 1st Lt.
Rice, L. VA 9th Cav. Co.C
Rice, L.A. SC 2nd Arty. Co.B 1st Lt.
Rice, Laben TX 1st (Yager's) Cav. Co.D Bugler
Rice, Labin TX Cav. 3rd (Yager's) Bn. Co.D
Rice, Larkin SC 14th Inf. Co.K
Rice, L.C. LA Mil. Vermillion Regt. Co.B Capt.
Rice, L.C. SC 2nd Arty. Co.I
Rice, L.C. SC Arty. Stuart's Co. (Beaufort Vol. Arty.)
Rice, L.C. SC 1st St.Troops Co.G Sgt.
Rice, L.C. SC 3rd Res. Co.C
Rice, L.C. SC Bn.St.Cadets Co.B
Rice, Leander W. NC Inf. 2nd Bn. Co.C
Rice, Lemuel L. NC 33rd Inf. Co.F
Rice, Lemuel S. NC 4th Cav. (59th St.Troops) Co.F
Rice, Leroy VA 42nd Inf. Co.F
Rice, Lewis LA Arty. Kean's Btty. (Orleans Ind.Arty.)
Rice, Lewis MO 16th Inf. Co.E
Rice, Lewis VA 18th Cav. 2nd Co.E Cpl.
Rice, L.H. NC 60th Inf. Co.I
Rice, L.L. NC 6th Inf. Co.C
Rice, L.L. SC 2nd Inf. Co.I
Rice, Llewellyn MS 12th Inf. Co.B
Rice, L.M. AL 26th (O'Neal's) Inf. Co.I
Rice, L.M. KY Cav.
Rice, Louis VA 54th Inf. Co.G
Rice, L.S. AL 8th (Livingston's) Cav. Co.A
Rice, Luallen A. SC 1st (Orr's) Rifles Co.C Sgt.
Rice, Luke GA 1st (Symons') Res. Co.K
Rice, Luther G. VA 40th Inf. Co.E Sgt.
Rice, Luther W. TN 14th Inf. Co.L Bugler
Rice, Luther W. VA Lt.Arty. B.Z. Price's Co. Music.
Rice, L.W. TX 4th Inf. Co.I
Rice, L.W. VA 59th Inf. 3rd Co.G
Rice, M. AL 27th Inf. Co.F Bvt.2nd Lt.
Rice, M. AR 1st (Monroe's) Cav. Co.L
Rice, M. GA Inf. 1st Loc.Troops (Augusta) Co.I
Rice, M. TX Cav. Bourland's Regt. Co.C
Rice, M. VA 10th Inf. Co.G
Rice, Madison AR Cav. Wright's Regt. Co.A
Rice, Madison L. AR 10th Cav.
Rice, Marcus L. NC 60th Inf. Co.F
Rice, Marion KY 11th Cav. Co.H
Rice, Marion NC Cav. 5th Bn. Co.A
Rice, Marion TN Inf. 1st Bn. (Colms') Co.B
Rice, Marion TN 39th Mtd.Inf. Co.I
Rice, Marion F. MS Cav. 4th Bn. Sykes' Co.
Rice, Marion F. 8th (Wade's) Conf.Cav. Co.G 1st Sgt.
Rice, Marshall VA 36th Inf. 2nd Co.C
Rice, Marshall VA 86th Mil. Co.B
Rice, Martin MS 21st Inf. Co.F
Rice, Martin TN 45th Inf. Co.I
Rice, Mathew S., Jr. GA 3rd Inf. Co.G Lt.
Rice, Mat J. AL 17th Inf. Asst.Surg.

Rice, Matthias TX 11th Inf. Co.F
Rice, M.D.E. VA Cav. 46th Bn. Co.C
Rice, M.F. AR 11th Inf. Co.C
Rice, M.F. AR 11th & 17th (Cons.) Inf. Co.C Color Cpl.
Rice, M.F. TN 1st (Carter's) Cav. 2nd Lt.
Rice, Micajah LA Inf. 9th Bn. Co.C
Rice, Michael MD Walters' Co. (Zarvona Zouaves)
Rice, Michael VA Hvy.Arty. 19th Bn. 3rd Co.C
Rice, Michael Conf.Lt.Arty. 1st Reg.Btty.
Rice, Michael T. Inf. School of Pract. Co.B
Rice, Miles F. AR Cav. Poe's Bn. Co.A
Rice, M.J. SC 5th Cav. Co.I Bvt.2nd Lt.
Rice, M.J. SC Cav. 14th Bn. Co.D Sgt.
Rice, M.J. Gen. & Staff Asst.Surg.
Rice, M.L. AR 20th Inf. Co.D
Rice, Moses AL 3rd Res. Co.E
Rice, Moses NC 4th Cav. (59th St.Troops) Co.E
Rice, M.P. NC 3rd Jr.Res. Co.I
Rice, M.P. NC 7th Bn.Jr.Res. Co.C
Rice, M.R.F. TN Inf. 154th Sr.Regt. Co.A
Rice, M.T. LA 3rd Inf. Co.I
Rice, M.W. GA Hvy.Arty. 22nd Bn. Co.F
Rice, M.W. NC 5th Sr.Res. Co.E
Rice, N. TN 12th (Cons.) Inf. Co.G
Rice, Napoleon B. NC 1st Inf. (6 mo. '61) Co.L
Rice, Napoleon B. NC 11th (Bethel Regt.) Inf. Co.C
Rice, Nathan TN 22nd Inf. Co.E
Rice, Nathan H. TN 3rd (Forrest's) Cav. Co.C
Rice, N.B. VA Inf. 25th Bn. Co.D
Rice, Neathan MO Cav. Fristoe's Regt. Co.L
Rice, Nelson Conf.Reg.Inf. Brooks' Bn. Co.B
Rice, Newton GA 5th Inf. Co.A
Rice, N.G. GA 32nd Inf. Co.F Sgt.
Rice, N.H. AL 9th Inf. Co.I
Rice, N.H. GA 17th Inf. Co.C
Rice, Nimrod AR 15th (N.W.) Inf. Co.C
Rice, N.N. KY 10th (Johnson's) Cav. New Co.C
Rice, Noah NC 3rd Arty. (40th St.Troops) Co.D
Rice, Noah NC 60th Inf. Co.B
Rice, N.R. AR 34th Inf. Co.I
Rice, N.W. GA Inf. 9th Bn. Co.C
Rice, N.W. GA 37th Inf. Co.F
Rice, O. MS 1st Cav. Co.C
Rice, O.A. TN 29th Inf. Co.E
Rice, O.D. KY 7th Cav. Co.F,G
Rice, O.F. AL 63rd Inf. Col.
Rice, O.F. Gen. & Staff,PACS Maj.
Rice, Olin F. MO 1st Inf. Co.E Capt.
Rice, Orville A. TN 60th Mtd.Inf. Co.B Sgt.
Rice, O.S. GA Inf. 2nd Bn.
Rice, O.S. GA Inf. 19th Bn. (St.Guards) Co.F
Rice, O.S. GA Inf. City Bn. (Columbus) Co.B
Rice, Oscar KY Horse Arty. Byrne's Co. Teamster
Rice, O.T. TN 27th Inf. Co.A
Rice, Othaniel MS Cav. 4th Bn. Sykes' Co.
Rice, Othaniel 8th (Wade's) Conf.Cav. Co.G
Rice, Owen AL 9th Inf.
Rice, Owen VA Hvy.Arty. 19th Bn. 3rd Co.C
Rice, P., Jr. LA Mil.Conf.Guards Regt. Co.F
Rice, Parker A. GA 41st Inf. Co.F
Rice, Pascal 2nd Conf.Inf. Co.G
Rice, Paschal MS 25th Inf. Co.G
Rice, Paschall AR 9th Inf. New Co.I

Rice, Patrick AL Arty. 1st Bn. Co.D
Rice, Paul S. TN Cav. 17th Bn. (Sanders') Co.A
Rice, P.C. MO Cav. Coleman's Regt. Co.K
Rice, Peter AL 40th Inf. Co.F
Rice, Peter GA 65th Inf. Co.F
Rice, Peter GA Smith's Legion Co.D
Rice, Peyton W. VA Lt.Arty. 13th Bn. Co.B
Rice, P.H. MS 2nd (Quinn's St.Troops) Inf. Co.C
Rice, P.H. TX Cav. 4th Regt.St.Troops Co.A
Rice, P.H. 3rd Conf.Cav. Co.G Capt.
Rice, P.H.C. VA Inf. 25th Bn. Co.D
Rice, Philip J. NC 3rd Arty. (40th St.Troops) Co.H
Rice, Prie L. MO Inf. 3rd Bn. Co.A
Rice, Pryor L. MO 6th Inf. Co.E
Rice, P.S. TN Arty. Marshall's Co. Cpl.
Rice, P.S. TN 5th Inf. 2nd Co.C, 1st Co.F
Rice, R. AL 11th Cav. Co.G
Rice, R. MO Cav. Snider's Bn. Co.B Sgt.
Rice, R.A. TN 51st Inf. Co.K
Rice, R.A. TN 51st (Cons.) Inf. Co.G
Rice, R.B. SC 3rd Cav. Co.A Cpl.
Rice, Reuben AR 38th Inf. Old Co.I, Co.H
Rice, Reuben MO Cav. Coffee's Regt. Co.C
Rice, R.G. TX 3rd (Kirby's) Bn.Vol. Co.B Music.
Rice, R.H. LA Inf. 4th Bn. Co.D Cpl.
Rice, R.H. LA Inf. Pelican Regt. Co.F Cpl.
Rice, R.H. MS Cav. Brown's Co. (Foster Creek Rangers)
Rice, Richard MO 3rd Inf. Co.B
Rice, Richard P. GA 1st (Olmstead's) Inf. Co.E Cpl.
Rice, Richard P. LA Mil.Cont.Regt. Mitchell's Co.
Rice, Richardson NC 47th Inf. Co.B
Rice, Richard T. VA 23rd Inf. Co.I
Rice, R.J. VA Cav. 47th Bn. Co.A 1st Lt.
Rice, R.J. Gen. & Staff Lt.,Ord.Off.
Rice, R.L. AR 38th Inf. Co.C
Rice, R.M. GA 5th Res. Co.A Sgt.
Rice, R.N. TX 4th Inf. Co.I
Rice, Robert KY 3rd Cav. Co.E
Rice, Robert KY 7th Cav. Co.E
Rice, Robert KY 11th Cav. Co.B Forage M.
Rice, Robert MS 10th Cav. Co.B Forage M.
Rice, Robert NC 2nd Inf. Co.K
Rice, Robert NC 48th Inf. Co.D
Rice, Robert SC 12th Inf. Co.K
Rice, Robert F. VA 10th Cav. Co.D
Rice, Robert F. VA 24th Cav. Co.G
Rice, Robert F. VA 15th Inf. Co.D
Rice, Robert H. MS 4th Cav. Co.E
Rice, Robert H. TN Cav. 12th Bn. (Day's) Co.A
Rice, Robert J. VA Lt.Arty. 38th Bn. Co.D Cpl.
Rice, Robert L. NC 44th Inf. Co.A Capt.
Rice, Robert W. VA 9th Cav. Co.C
Rice, Robert W. VA Murphy's Co.
Rice, Rolley TN Lt.Arty. Huggins' Co.
Rice, R.S. TN Arty. Marshall's Co. Cpl.
Rice, R. Sidney VA Lt.Arty. B.Z. Price's Co. Capt.
Rice, R. Sidney VA Lt.Arty. W.H. Rice's Co. 1st Lt.
Rice, Rufus GA 40th Inf. Co.D
Rice, Rufus N. AR Cav. Wright's Regt. Co.A

Rice, Rufus W. AR Hardy's Inf.
Rice, R.W. TN 14th (Neely's) Cav. Co.F
Rice, R.W. TN 6th Inf. Co.K
Rice, S. LA Mil. Orleans Fire Regt. Co.H
Rice, S.A. TX 21st Inf. Co.E
Rice, S.A. VA 2nd Inf.Loc.Def. Co.A 1st Lt.
Rice, S.A. VA Inf. 2nd Bn.Loc.Def. Co.C 1st Lt.
Rice, Samuel AL 40th Inf. Co.H
Rice, Samuel GA 11th Inf. Co.K
Rice, Samuel KY 5th Cav. Co.I
Rice, Samuel KY 9th Cav. Co.F
Rice, Samuel MO 7th Cav. Co.F Cpl.
Rice, Samuel MO 8th Cav. Co.G Cpl.
Rice, Samuel MO 2nd Inf. Co.H 1st Lt.
Rice, Samuel MO Inf. 3rd Regt.St.Guard Co.G 2nd Lt.
Rice, Samuel TX 17th Cav. 1st Co.I
Rice, Samuel TX 28th Cav. Co.B
Rice, Samuel VA 1st Cav. Co.E
Rice, Samuel VA 27th Inf. 1st Co.H 1st Lt.
Rice, Samuel A. TX 11th (Spaight's) Bn.Vol. Co.C
Rice, Samuel C. GA Lt.Arty. 14th Bn. Co.A
Rice, Samuel C. GA Lt.Arty. Havis' Btty.
Rice, Samuel D. VA 23rd Inf. Co.G Capt.
Rice, Samuel F. AL Arty. 1st Bn. Co.A 2nd Lt.
Rice, Samuel G. VA 58th Inf. Co.C Cpl.
Rice, Samuel L. GA 12th Cav. Co.B
Rice, Samuel M. TX 9th Cav. Co.I
Rice, Samuel S. VA 9th Cav. Co.D
Rice, Samuel S. VA 37th Mil. Co.A Cpl.
Rice, Sandford M. MS 29th Inf. Co.C
Rice, Sanford 1st Conf.Inf. 2nd Co.F
Rice, S.C. NC 13th Inf. Co.D
Rice, S.D. GA 22nd Inf. Co.I
Rice, S.D. TX Inf. Chambers' Bn.Res.Corps Co.C
Rice, S.D. 1st Conf.Eng.Troops Black.
Rice, S.E. TX 6th & 15th (Cons.) Vol. Co.H Capt.
Rice, Septimus C. TN 24th Inf. 2nd Co.G
Rice, S.F. AL Rebels
Rice, Simon AR 18th Inf. Co.E Capt.
Rice, S.L. TX 14th Inf. Co.H
Rice, S.M. AR Rangers
Rice, S.M. SC Lt.Arty. Jeter's Co. (Macbeth Lt.Arty.)
Rice, S.M. TN 9th Inf. Co.K Cpl.
Rice, Smithen W. VA 36th Inf. 2nd Co.D
Rice, Sol. D. MS 9th Inf. Old Co.F
Rice, Solomon C. AL 4th Inf. Co.H
Rice, Solon KY 2nd (Duke's) Cav. Co.I
Rice, S.P. TN 12th (Cons.) Inf. Co.A
Rice, Spencer NC Walker's Bn. Thomas' Legion Co.B
Rice, Stephen TN 42nd Inf. 2nd Co.H
Rice, Stephen A. NC 3rd Cav. (41st St.Troops) Co.C 2nd Lt.
Rice, Stephen A. VA 18th Inf. Co.A Sgt.
Rice, Stephen C. NC 3rd Cav. (41st St.Troops) Co.C
Rice, Stephen E. TX 6th Inf. Co.H Capt.
Rice, Stephen H. GA 61st Inf. Co.F 2nd Lt.
Rice, Stephen J. VA 27th Inf. Co.G
Rice, Stephen M. VA 10th Inf. Co.H

Rice, Stephen W. NC 2nd Cav. (19th St.Troops) Co.B Regt.Mail Carrier
Rice, Stephen W. VA 20th Cav. Co.K 1st Lt.
Rice, Stephen W. VA Cav. 36th Bn. Co.D
Rice, Stewart NC 4th Sr.Res. Co.I
Rice, Sylus GA 17th Inf. Co.B
Rice, T. AL 26th (O'Neal's) Inf. Co.I
Rice, T. AL Talladega Cty.Res. J.T. Smith's Co.
Rice, T. GA Inf. 40th Bn. Co.A
Rice, T. KY Morgan's Men Co.C
Rice, T.A. VA Hvy.Arty. 20th Bn. Co.C
Rice, T.D. VA 10th Cav. Co.B
Rice, T.E. Gen. & Staff Asst.Surg.
Rice, T.F. AL Cp. of Instr. Talladega
Rice, T.F. MS 1st (King's) Inf. (St.Troops) Co.E
Rice, T.F. TN 7th (Duckworth's) Cav. Co.M
Rice, T.H. VA 4th Cav. Co.K
Rice, Theodore TX 1st Hvy.Arty. Co.K
Rice, Thomas AR Lt.Arty. Rivers' Btty.
Rice, Thomas GA 40th Inf. Co.F
Rice, Thomas KY 3rd Cav. Co.H
Rice, Thomas KY 5th Cav. Co.H
Rice, Thomas KY 7th Cav. Co.B
Rice, Thomas KY 11th Cav. Co.B
Rice, Thomas LA Arty. 1st Field Btty.
Rice, Thomas LA 1st (Nelligan's) Inf. Co.E Capt.
Rice, Thomas MS 3rd Inf. (A. of 10,000) Co.A
Rice, Thomas MS 40th Inf. Co.E
Rice, Thomas MO 10th Inf.
Rice, Thomas NC Cav. 5th Bn. Co.A
Rice, Thomas NC 16th Inf. Co.B
Rice, Thomas NC 64th Inf. Co.F Ord.Sgt.
Rice, Thomas SC Inf. Hampton Legion Co.E
Rice, Thomas TN 9th Inf. Co.L,D
Rice, Thomas VA 92nd Mil. Co.C
Rice, Thomas Conf.Inf. 1st Bn. 2nd Co.C Cpl.
Rice, Thomas A. AR 15th (N.W.) Inf. Co.C
Rice, Thomas A. VA Burks' Regt.Loc.Def. Ammen's Co.
Rice, Thomas B. NC 47th Inf. Co.A
Rice, Thomas B. VA Cav. Mosby's Regt. (Part.Rangers) Co.C
Rice, Thomas C. VA 3rd Cav. Co.H 1st Lt.
Rice, Thomas C. VA 58th Inf. Co.C
Rice, Thomas D. VA 53rd Inf. Co.D
Rice, Thomas F. AL 8th (Hatch's) Cav. Co.A 2nd Lt.
Rice, Thomas F. GA Cobb's Legion Co.B
Rice, Thomas F. TX 3rd Cav. Co.I
Rice, Thomas G. NC 3rd Cav. (41st St.Troops) Co.C
Rice, Thomas G. NC 57th Inf. Co.H
Rice, Thomas H. AL Inf. 2nd Regt. Co.F,E Cpl.
Rice, Thomas H. KY 3rd Cav.
Rice, Thomas H. TN 6th Inf. Co.H 2nd Lt.
Rice, Thomas H. TN 31st Inf. Co.I
Rice, Thomas H. VA 20th Inf. Co.E
Rice, Thomas J. AR 9th Inf. Co.F,C 1st Lt.
Rice, Thomas J. MS 14th Inf. Co.H
Rice, Thomas J. TX 13th Vol. 2nd Co.C,I,B
Rice, Thomas J. VA 9th Cav. Co.K
Rice, Thomas L. TN 3rd (Lillard's) Mtd.Inf. 2nd Co.K
Rice, Thomas N. VA 58th Inf. Co.C
Rice, Thomas R. TX 2nd Cav. Co.G Sgt.
Rice, Thomas S. NC Cav. 5th Bn. Co.A

Rice, Thomas S. NC 57th Inf. Co.K Sgt.
Rice, Thomas S. NC 64th Inf. Co.D
Rice, T.J. AL 12th Inf. Co.B
Rice, T.J. AR 1st Mtd.Rifles Co.I Capt.
Rice, T.J. TN 12th Inf. Co.B Cpl.
Rice, T.J. TN 12th (Cons.) Inf. Co.A
Rice, T.M.C. Gen. & Staff Asst.Surg.
Rice, T.P. TN 24th Inf. Co.E
Rice, Trevor GA 3rd Inf. Co.K
Rice, T.S. MO Cav. Coleman's Regt. Co.A
Rice, T.S. NC Mallett's Co.
Rice, T.T. VA 1st Bn.Res. Co.A
Rice, Tullius M.C. GA Inf. 2nd Bn. Co.B Asst.Surg.
Rice, T.W. TN Lt.Arty. Rice's Btty. Capt.
Rice, T.W. TN 38th Inf. 1st Co.A 1st Lt.
Rice, U.A. GA Cav. 22nd Bn. (St.Guards) Co.C
Rice, Ulysses SC 1st (McCreary's) Inf. Co.H
Rice, Ulysses A. GA 48th Inf. Co.G Capt.
Rice, V.A. GA Inf. (Madison Cty.Home Guard) Milner's Co. Sgt.
Rice, Van A. GA 4th Res. Co.C
Rice, Venallen GA Inf. (Madison Cty.Home Guard) Milner's Co.
Rice, Vincent GA 30th Inf. Co.C
Rice, Vincent KY 9th Cav. Co.F
Rice, Vincent VA 40th Inf. Co.G
Rice, W. AR 2nd Cav. Co.G
Rice, W. KY 1st (Butler's) Cav. Co.E
Rice, W. KY 3rd Cav. Co.D
Rice, W. MS 1st (King's) Inf. (St.Troops) Co.D
Rice, W.A. AL 13th Inf. Co.H
Rice, W.A. GA 43rd Inf. Co.E
Rice, W.A. TN 21st (Wilson's) Cav. Co.C
Rice, W.A. TX 7th Field Btty. Cpl.
Rice, Walter C. VA 40th Inf. Co.F Sgt.
Rice, Warren J. AL 28th Inf. Co.L
Rice, Watford MS Lt.Arty. (Brookhaven Lt.Arty.) Hoskins' Btty. Artif.
Rice, W.B. AL 51st (Part.Rangers) Co.G
Rice, W.B. AL Lt.Arty. Phelan's Co.
Rice, W.B. SC 1st (Hagood's) Inf. 1st Co.K Capt.
Rice, W.B. TN 10th (DeMoss') Cav. Co.F
Rice, W.B. TN Cav. Napier's Bn. Co.C Sgt.
Rice, W.B. TN 11th Inf. Co.I
Rice, W.B. Gen. & Staff AASurg.
Rice, W.C. AR Cav. Carlton's Regt. Co.B 2nd Lt.
Rice, W.C. AR 1st (Colquitt's) Inf. Co.I
Rice, W.C. GA 3rd Cav. Co.B
Rice, W.C. GA Cav. 19th Bn. Co.A
Rice, W.C. KY 1st (Helm's) Cav. Old Co.G
Rice, W.C. VA 37th Mil. 2nd Co.B
Rice, W.C. 10th Conf.Cav. Co.F
Rice, W.D. AL 38th Inf. Co.A
Rice, W.D. TN 12th (Green's) Cav. Co.C
Rice, Wesley NC Cav. 5th Bn. Co.A,B
Rice, Wesley NC 6th Cav. (65th St.Troops) Co.K
Rice, Wesley NC 64th Inf. Co.F
Rice, W.F. AL 50th Inf. Co.H 1st Lt.
Rice, W.F. AR 10th Inf. Co.H
Rice, W.F. SC Arty. Manigault's Bn. 1st Co.A, 2nd Co.B
Rice, W.F. TX Cav. 3rd (Yager's) Bn. Co.D
Rice, W.G. KY 2nd (Duke's) Cav. Co.L Cpl.

Rice, W.G. MS Lt.Arty. (Madison Lt.Arty.) Richards' Co.
Rice, W.H. AL 21st Inf. Co.A
Rice, W.H. GA 1st (Olmstead's) Inf. Screven's Co., Stiles' Co.
Rice, W.H. GA 3rd Bn. (St.Guards) Co.C
Rice, W.H. GA Inf. 18th Bn. Co.A,B,C Cpl.
Rice, W.H. KY 2nd (Woodward's) Cav. Co.A
Rice, W.H. LA Inf.Crescent Regt. Co.E
Rice, W.H. MO 2nd & 6th Cons.Inf. Co.F
Rice, W.H. TX 12th Inf. Co.F Sgt.
Rice, Wiley GA 2nd Res. Co.C Cpl.
Rice, Wilkinson SC 14th Inf. Co.K
Rice, William AL 6th Cav. Co.E
Rice, William AL Cav. Hardie's Bn.Res. Co.C
Rice, William AL 19th Inf. Co.C
Rice, William AR 21st Inf. Co.I
Rice, William AR 24th Inf. Co.I
Rice, William AR 35th Inf. Co.F
Rice, William GA 3rd Cav. Co.B
Rice, William GA 2nd Inf. Co.F
Rice, William GA 2nd Res. Co.A
Rice, William GA 25th Inf. Co.E
Rice, William GA Cherokee Legion (St.Guards) Co.B
Rice, William KY 7th Cav. Co.B
Rice, William KY 3rd Mtd.Inf. Co.K
Rice, William LA 25th Inf. Co.C
Rice, William LA Mil. Mooney's Co. (Saddlers Guards)
Rice, William MO 1st N.E. Cav. Co.B
Rice, William MO 10th Cav. Co.A,K
Rice, William MO 16th Inf. Co.E
Rice, William MO Inf. Clark's Regt. Co.B
Rice, William NC Inf. 2nd Bn. Co.C
Rice, William NC 6th Inf. Co.K
Rice, William NC 13th Inf. Co.G
Rice, William NC 33rd Inf. Co.F
Rice, William NC 52nd Inf. Co.A
Rice, William NC 64th Inf. Co.D
Rice, William TN 3rd (Forrest's) Cav. Co.C Sgt.
Rice, William TN 25th Inf. Co.B Cpl.
Rice, William TN 45th Inf. Co.C
Rice, William TN 62nd Mtd.Inf. Co.D
Rice, William TX 14th Inf. Co.B
Rice, William VA Inf. 4th Bn.Loc.Def. Co.B
Rice, William VA 48th Inf. Co.D
Rice, William VA 59th Inf. 3rd Co.G Cpl.
Rice, William Brush Bn.
Rice, William A. GA 20th Inf. Co.D
Rice, William A. NC 25th Inf. Co.I
Rice, William A. SC 1st (McCreary's) Inf. Co.B
Rice, William A. SC 1st Inf. Co.L
Rice, William A. TN 24th Inf. 2nd Co.G, Co.L 1st Lt.,Adj.
Rice, William A. VA 10th Cav. Co.B
Rice, William A. VA 11th Inf. Co.C
Rice, William A. VA 53rd Inf. Co.H
Rice, William B. AL 41st Inf. Co.F
Rice, William B. TN 24th Inf. Co.E Bvt.2nd Lt.
Rice, William C. NC 1st Inf. Co.F
Rice, William C. VA 38th Inf. Co.C
Rice, William C.W. VA 52nd Inf. 2nd Co.B
Rice, William D. AR 20th Inf. Co.A
Rice, William D. NC 4th Cav. (59th St.Troops) Co.F

Rice, William D. VA Cav. 39th Bn. Co.D
Rice, William D. VA Lt.Arty. Montgomery's Co.
Rice, William D. VA 58th Inf. Co.C Cpl.
Rice, William E. GA 2nd Inf. Co.E Cpl.
Rice, William E. NC Inf. Thomas Legion 2nd Co.A
Rice, William G. NC 49th Inf. Co.C
Rice, William G. SC Inf. 3rd Bn. Co.A Lt.Col.
Rice, William G. VA 58th Inf. Co.A Cpl.
Rice, William H. GA 12th (Robinson's) Cav. (St.Guards) Co.B
Rice, William H. GA 22nd Inf. Co.D
Rice, William H. GA 61st Inf. Co.F
Rice, William H. MO 1st N.E. Cav. Co.D
Rice, William H. MO 1st N.E. Cav. Co.H Sgt.
Rice, William H. MO 2nd Inf. Co.C
Rice, William H. MO 9th Inf. Co.C
Rice, William H. MO 9th Bn.S.S. Co.F
Rice, William H. TN 10th Cav. Co.A
Rice, William H. VA 9th Cav. Co.C
Rice, William H. VA Lt.Arty. W.H. Rice's Co. Capt.
Rice, William H. VA 26th Inf. Co.I
Rice, William H. VA 56th Inf. Co.H
Rice, William H. VA 57th Inf. Co.H
Rice, Wm. Henry Gen. & Staff, Nitre & Min. Asst.Supt.
Rice, William J. AL 19th Inf. Co.D
Rice, William J. MO 9th Inf. Co.G
Rice, William J. TX 13th Cav. Co.C
Rice, William J. VA Inf. 22nd Bn. Co.B
Rice, William L. TN 7th Cav. Chap.
Rice, William L. VA 37th Inf. Co.A 2nd Lt.
Rice, William M. KY 1st Bn.Mtd.Rifles Co.E
Rice, William M. KY 5th Mtd.Inf. Co.D Cpl.
Rice, William M. TX 22nd Cav. Co.E
Rice, William N. TX 3rd Cav. Co.I
Rice, William P. NC 60th Inf. Co.A Cpl.
Rice, William P. TN 2nd (Ashby's) Cav. Co.I
Rice, William P. TN Cav. 4th Bn. (Branner's) Co.E
Rice, William P. TN 7th Inf. Co.K
Rice, William P. TX 14th Cav. Co.H
Rice, William R. AL Cav. 4th Bn. (Love's) Co.A Sgt.Maj.
Rice, William R. MO 12th Cav. Co.I 2nd Lt.
Rice, William R. NC 25th Inf. Co.B
Rice, William R. SC 1st Arty. Co.G
Rice, William Richard SC 4th Inf. Co.C
Rice, William S. GA 8th Inf. (St.Guards) Co.G
Rice, Wm. S. GA Conscr.
Rice, William S. TX 3rd Cav. Co.I Ens.
Rice, William T. AL 3rd Cav. Co.H
Rice, William T. AL Inf. 1st Regt. Co.K
Rice, William T. MS 9th Cav.
Rice, William T. TN Cav. 17th Bn. (Sanders') Co.A
Rice, William T. TN 39th Mtd.Inf. Co.F
Rice, William T. TX 24th Cav. Co.E
Rice, William T. VA 3rd Res. Co.D
Rice, William V.V. LA 8th Inf. Co.A
Rice, William W. AL 3rd Bn.Res. Co.B Cpl.
Rice, William W. MO 3rd Inf. Co.K Sgt.
Rice, William Walter MO 8th Inf. Co.I
Rice, Willis KY 1st (Butler's) Cav. Co.E
Rice, Willis KY 4th Cav. Co.D
Rice, Willis KY 3rd Bn.Mtd.Rifles Co.A

Rice, Willis F. GA 8th Inf. Co.E
Rice, Wilson NC Cav. 5th Bn. Co.A
Rice, Wilson NC 37th Inf. Co.F
Rice, Wilson NC 64th Inf. Co.A
Rice, Wilson NC 64th Inf. Co.K
Rice, Wilson TN 60th Mtd.Inf. Co.F
Rice, W.J. AL 8th Inf. Co.E
Rice, W.J. GA 38th Inf. Co.H
Rice, W.J. MS 12th Inf. Co.D Capt.
Rice, W.J. NC 64th Inf. Co.K
Rice, W.J. TN 50th Inf. Co.C Sgt.
Rice, W.L. TN 26th Inf. Co.E
Rice, W.O. TN Inf. 3rd Bn. Co.E
Rice, W.P. AL 15th Cav. Co.D 1st Lt.
Rice, W.P. AL Talladega Cty.Res. D.M. Reid's Co.
Rice, W.P. FL Cav. 3rd Bn. Co.B 2nd Lt.
Rice, W.P. TX 8th Cav. Co.D
Rice, W.P. 15th Conf.Cav. Co.D 1st Lt.
Rice, W.R. MS Cav. Jeff Davis Legion Co.H
Rice, W.R. SC 24th Inf. Co.F
Rice, W.S. AL 50th Inf. Co.H
Rice, W.S. TX 20th Inf. Co.D
Rice, W.T. NC 1st Cav. (9th St.Troops) Co.B
Rice, W.T. NC 22nd Inf. Co.K
Rice, W.T. TX 24th & 25th Cav. (Cons.) Co.E
Rice, M.V. LA Inf. 9th Bn. Co.F
Rice, W.W. AL 9th Inf. Co.C
Rice, W.W. SC Rutledge Mtd.Riflemen & Horse Arty. Trenholm's Co.
Rice, W.W. TX Waul's Legion Co.B
Rice, Z.A. GA 3rd Bn. (St.Guards) Co.G 1st Lt.
Rice, Zachariah A. GA Cobb's Legion Co.B Capt.
Rice, Zephaniah J. VA Lt.Arty. Montgomery's Co.
Rice, Zeras AL 36th Inf. Co.H Cpl.
Rice, Z.S. TX Inf. Chambers' Bn.Res.Corps Co.D
Riceland, N. LA Mil. 3rd Regt. 3rd Brig. 1st Div. Co.E
Riceman, William VA 60th Inf. Co.K
Ricewick, P. AR Cav. Gordon's Regt. Co.D
Ricgans, Dolby AL 30th Inf. Co.A
Rich, --- AL 25th Inf. Co.H
Rich, --- FL Lt.Arty. Dyke's Co.
Rich, --- TX 1st (McCulloch's) Cav. Co.F
Rich, A. GA 18th Inf. Co.H
Rich, A. LA 22nd Inf. Co.E
Rich, A. NC 22nd Inf. Co.E
Rich, A. TX 7th Cav. Co.E
Rich, A.B. AR 7th Inf. Co.F
Rich, A.B. AR 34th Inf. Co.H Sgt.
Rich, A.C. GA Cav. 1st Gordon Squad. (St.Guards) Co.A
Rich, A.E. GA Inf. 1st Bn. (St.Guards) AQM
Rich, A.E. GA Inf. 1st City Bn. (Columbus) Co.D
Rich, A.G. LA 6th Cav. Co.A
Rich, A.J. AL 46th Inf. Co.I,B
Rich, A.J. GA 54th Inf. Co.C
Rich, Albert NC 3rd Inf. Co.G
Rich, Alfred NC 29th Inf.
Rich, A.M. AR 17th (Griffith's) Inf. Co.E 2nd Lt.
Rich, A.M. FL 1st Inf.
Rich, A.M. FL 10th Inf. Co.D

Rich, A.M. GA 59th Inf. Co.A
Rich, Andrew J. GA 52nd Inf. Co.G
Rich, Andrew J. TN 44th (Cons.) Inf. Co.B
Rich, B. NC 3rd Jr.Res. Co.H
Rich, Barron DeCalb AL 1st Inf. Co.B
Rich, B.D. 3rd Conf.Cav. Co.K
Rich, Benjamin NC 7th Bn.Jr.Res. Co.A
Rich, Benjamin T. FL 5th Inf. Co.H Jr.2nd Lt.
Rich, B.I. AL Inf. 1st Regt. Co.E
Rich, Byrd S. TN 2nd (Smith's) Cav. Cpl.
Rich, Calvin KY 7th Cav. Co.A
Rich, C.C. AL 9th Inf. Co.K
Rich, C.C. NC 1st Jr.Res. Co.F
Rich, C.C. TN Cav. 12th Bn. (Day's) Co.F
Rich, Charles LA 22nd Inf. Jones' Co.
Rich, Charles N. TN 37th Inf. Co.E
Rich, Christopher C. NC 30th Inf. Co.E
Rich, Clarkson J. NC 48th Inf. Co.B
Rich, Curtis W. TN 1st (Turney's) Inf. Co.C
Rich, D.A. MO 12th Inf. Co.A
Rich, Daniel NC Inf. 2nd Bn. Co.F
Rich, Daniel NC 54th Inf. Co.K
Rich, Daniel R. NC 13th Inf. Co.E
Rich, Daniel T. FL 8th Inf. Co.B
Rich, David NC 46th Inf. Co.B
Rich, David A. GA 17th Inf. Co.D
Rich, Davis NC 46th Inf. Co.G
Rich, D.E. MS Inf. (Res.) Berry's Co.
Rich, D.N. MS Inf. 1st Bn.St.Troops (30 days
'64) Co.D
Rich, E. NC 48th Inf.
Rich, E. TN Lt.Arty. Winston's Co.
Rich, Edward NC McDugald's Co.
Rich, Edward C. NC Hvy.Arty. 10th Bn. Co.D
Rich, Edward R. MD 1st Cav. Co.E Cpl.
Rich, Elezar NC 55th Inf. Co.G 1st Sgt.
Rich, Elijah A.J. GA 59th Inf. Co.A 2nd Lt.
Rich, Elisha TN Lt.Arty. Winston's Co.
Rich, Eugene LA 3rd (Harrison's) Cav. Co.B
Rich, Eugene LA 4th Inf. Co.A
Rich, Eugene L. TX 17th Inf. Co.I
Rich, F.A. GA 11th Cav. Co.D
Rich, F.S. AR Cav. 1st Bn. (Stirman's) Co.E
Rich, F.S. AR 34th Inf. Co.C Sgt.
Rich, G.B. GA Mayer's Co. (Appling Cav.)
Rich, George C. SC 7th Cav. Co.G
Rich, George C. SC Rutledge Mtd.Riflemen &
Horse Arty. Trenholm's Co.
Rich, George C. SC Mil. 1st Regt.Rifles Palmer's
Co.
Rich, George L. TX 17th Cons.Dismtd.Cav.
Co.B 1st Sgt.
Rich, George L. TX 24th Cav. Co.G Sgt.
Rich, George W. FL 6th Inf. Co.G
Rich, George W. GA 59th Inf. Co.A Cpl.
Rich, George W. GA Inf. Cobb Guards Co.B
Rich, George W. NC 2nd Cav. (19th St.Troops)
Co.F
Rich, George W. TX 12th Inf. Co.H Sgt.
Rich, G.L. TX 25th Cav. Co.A
Rich, G.W. FL Kilcrease Lt.Arty.
Rich, G.W. NC 52nd Inf. Co.I
Rich, Hawood NC 8th Sr.Res. Bryan's Co.
Rich, Henry AL 23rd Inf. Co.F
Rich, Henry MO Inf. 1st Bn. Co.A
Rich, Henry MO 5th Inf. Co.K
Rich, Henry J. TN 44th (Cons.) Inf. Co.A

Rich, Henry M. NC 13th Inf. Co.E Cpl.
Rich, Henry T. NC 53rd Inf. Co.F Sgt.
Rich, Hiram N. VA 48th Inf. Co.D
Rich, H.P. GA 39th Inf. Co.I Music.
Rich, Huddle H. VA 21st Cav. Co.K
Rich, I. LA Mil. 4th Regt. French Brig. Co.3
Rich, I.J. MS 10th Inf. New Co.K
Rich, I.J. MS 23rd Inf. Co.G
Rich, Isaac GA 50th Inf. Co.F
Rich, Isaac TN 19th Inf. Co.A
Rich, Isaac O. NC 42nd Inf. Co.E Sgt.
Rich, Isham NC 38th Inf. Co.D
Rich, J. SC Mil. 1st Regt. (Charleston Res.)
Co.B
Rich, J.A. GA 6th Inf. Co.H
Rich, J.A. GA Inf. Grubbs' Co.
Rich, J.A. TN 15th (Cons.) Cav. Co.B
Rich, J.A. VA 2nd Cav.
Rich, Jack AL Cav. Lewis' Bn. Co.C Sgt.
Rich, Jackson TX 22nd Cav. Co.B
Rich, Jacob FL Cav. 5th Bn. Co.B
Rich, Jacob FL Kilcrease Lt.Arty.
Rich, Jacob FL 6th Inf. Co.B
Rich, Jacob MS 1st (King's) Inf. (St.Troops)
Co.E
Rich, Jacob N. TN 60th Mtd.Inf. Co.H
Rich, James AL 8th Inf. Co.H
Rich, James AL 13th Inf. Co.H
Rich, James AL 20th Inf. Co.E
Rich, James AL 25th Inf. Co.D
Rich, James AL 30th Inf. Co.H
Rich, James AR 37th Inf. Co.K
Rich, James AR 50th Mil. Co.G
Rich, James MS 28th Cav. Co.H
Rich, James MS 2nd Inf. (A. of 10,000) Co.G
Rich, James MS 3rd Inf. (St.Troops) Co.K
Rich, James TN 12th (Green's) Cav. Co.F
Rich, James TN 47th Inf. Co.F
Rich, James A. NC 13th Inf. Co.E
Rich, James D. GA Inf. 8th Bn. Co.B
Rich, James E. GA 50th Inf. Co.F
Rich, James E. GA 51st Inf. Co.C
Rich, James E. TX 37th Inf. Co.E
Rich, James L. GA Cobb's Legion Co.B,G
Rich, James M. NC Walker's Bn. Thomas'
Legion Co.H Sgt.
Rich, James O. NC 3rd Arty. (40th St.Troops)
Co.H Cpl.
Rich, James O. NC 30th Inf. Co.A
Rich, James R. GA 18th Inf. Co.H Music.
Rich, James S. GA 3rd Cav. Co.G
Rich, James S. GA 35th Inf. Co.G,C
Rich, James W. GA Phillips' Legion Co.H,B
Rich, J.C. AL 44th Inf. Co.B
Rich, J.C. AR 25th Inf. Co.H
Rich, J.C. AR 34th Inf. Co.H 1st Sgt.
Rich, J.C. TX 30th Cav. Co.H
Rich, J.E. NC 66th Inf. Co.C
Rich, Jeremiah VA Inf. 23rd Bn. Co.A
Rich, Jeremiah K.P. TN 37th Inf. Co.E
Rich, J.H. AL 18th Inf. Co.K
Rich, J.H. LA 28th (Gray's) Inf. Co.A
Rich, J.M. MS Cp.Guard (Cp. of Instr. for
Conscr.)
Rich, J.M. NC 14th Inf. Co.G
Rich, J.M. TX 18th Inf. Co.G
Rich, J.M. TX 18th Inf. Co.K

Rich, J.N. GA 3rd Bn.S.S. Co.F
Rich, J.N. VA 34th Inf. Co.C
Rich, Joe KY Lt.Arty. Cobb's Co.
Rich, John AL 2nd Cav. Co.A Black.
Rich, John AL 25th Inf. Co.D
Rich, John AL 55th Vol. Co.G
Rich, John NC 38th Inf. Co.D
Rich, John NC 46th Inf. Co.B
Rich, John NC 54th Inf. Co.B
Rich, John TN 2nd (Ashby's) Cav. Co.B
Rich, John TN Cav. Shaw's Bn. Hamilton's Co.
Rich, John TN 8th Inf. Co.H
Rich, John TN 42nd Inf. 1st Co.H
Rich, John A. TN Vol. (Loc.Def.Troops)
McLin's Co.
Rich, John A. VA Hvy.Arty. 18th Bn. Co.B
Rich, John A.M. GA 7th Inf. Co.D
Rich, John B. FL Kilcrease Lt.Arty.
Rich, John B. FL 6th Inf. Co.B
Rich, John B. MS 8th Inf. Co.G
Rich, John F. FL 5th Inf. Co.H Sgt.
Rich, John F. NC 31st Inf. Co.K
Rich, John J. TN Cav. Allison's Squad. Co.B
Rich, John L. NC 6th Inf. Co.A
Rich, John L. TN 37th Inf. Co.K
Rich, John M. GA Inf. (Anderson Guards) An-
derson's Co.
Rich, John M. NC Inf. 2nd Bn. Co.F
Rich, John M. NC 15th Inf. Co.M Cpl.
Rich, John M. NC 32nd Inf. Co.I
Rich, John M. TX 9th (Nichols') Inf. Co.B
Rich, John N. NC 1st Arty. (10th St.Troops)
Co.C
Rich, John R. NC 29th Inf. Co.C Color Sgt.
Rich, John S. SC 15th Inf. Co.K Cpl.
Rich, John W. MO Inf. Perkins' Bn. Co.E
Rich, John W. NC 2nd Cav. (19th St.Troops)
Co.F
Rich, John W. NC 39th Inf. Co.F
Rich, John W. SC 1st (Orr's) Rifles Co.F
Rich, Jordan G. GA 50th Inf. Co.F
Rich, Joseph KY 7th Cav. Co.G
Rich, Joseph NC Inf. 2nd Bn. Co.F
Rich, Joseph TN 60th Mtd.Inf. Co.H
Rich, Joseph A. NC 25th Inf. Co.C,I
Rich, Joseph M. TN 44th Inf. Co.I
Rich, Joseph M. TN 44th (Cons.) Inf. Co.A
Rich, J.S. GA 9th Inf. (St.Guards) Co.F
Rich, J.S. GA 13th Inf. Co.C
Rich, J.S. SC 7th Inf. 2nd Co.K
Rich, J.T. GA 59th Inf. Co.A
Rich, J.W. TN 12th (Cons.) Inf. Co.E
Rich, L. SC Mil. 1st Regt. (Charleston Res.)
Co.B
Rich, Leander KY 10th (Diamond's) Cav. Co.A
Rich, Leander KY 5th Mtd.Inf. Co.E
Rich, Lewis SC 5th Res. Co.I
Rich, Lewis J. NC 12th Inf. Co.C
Rich, Lewis J. NC 43rd Inf. Co.A
Rich, Lewis M. NC 5th Cav. (63rd St.Troops)
Co.C
Rich, L.M. NC 30th Inf. Co.A
Rich, L.M. TX 2nd Cav. 2nd Co.F
Rich, Lot. NC 2nd Arty. (36th St.Troops) Co.A
Rich, Lott NC Moseley's Co. (Sampson Arty.)
Rich, Louis TX 1st Hvy.Arty. Co.C
Rich, Lucius L. MO 1st Inf. Col.

Rich, L.W. NC 3rd Arty. (40th St.Troops) Co.H
Rich, M. SC Mil. 1st Regt. (Charleston Res.)
  Co.B
Rich, M.A. MS 7th Cav. Co.F
Rich, M.A. MS 2nd (Davidson's) Inf. Co.C
Rich, Marshal H. TN 4th (McLemore's) Cav.
  Co.K
Rich, Marshall Mead's Conf.Cav. Co.B
Rich, Martin P. GA Smith's Legion Anderson's
  Co.
Rich, Martin V. GA 6th Cav. Co.F
Rich, M.H. Mead's Conf.Cav. Co.D
Rich, Milton NC Inf. 2nd Bn. Co.F
Rich, N. NC 22nd Inf. Co.I
Rich, N.A. AL 48th Inf. Co.K
Rich, Newton AL 7th Inf. Co.B
Rich, N.G. NC 5th Cav. (63rd St.Troops) Co.H
Rich, N.G. SC 21st Inf. Co.C
Rich, Noah AL Lt.Arty. 2nd Bn. Co.D
Rich, Noah TN Lt.Arty. Browne's Co.
Rich, Noah TN Lt.Arty. Kain's Co.
Rich, Obadiah KY 10th (Johnson's) Cav. New
  Co.C
Rich, Oliver P. AL 47th Inf. Co.E
Rich, Owen A. NC 5th Cav. (63rd St.Troops)
  Co.C
Rich, P. LA Mil. 3rd Regt. 1st Brig. 1st Div.
  Co.H
Rich, Peter TN 11th Inf. Co.G,B
Rich, Peter M. NC 25th Inf. Co.C Drum.
Rich, Philemon M. NC 15th Inf. Co.B
Rich, Philip SC 1st Regt. Charleston Guard Co.I
Rich, Pinkney NC 5th Cav. (63rd St.Troops)
  Co.C
Rich, Pinkney NC 12th Inf. Co.C
Rich, Pinkney NC 55th Inf. Co.G Cpl.
Rich, R.A. MO 12th Inf. Co.C
Rich, Reuben GA 4th Res. Co.K
Rich, Rile TN 4th (Murray's) Cav. Co.D
Rich, Rile 1st Conf.Cav. 2nd Co.C
Rich, Robert NC 46th Inf. Co.B
Rich, Robert TX 19th Inf. Co.B
Rich, Robert TX Conscr.
Rich, Robert A. TX Cav. 8th (Taylor's) Bn.
  Co.B Cpl.
Rich, Robert H. TX 1st (Yager's) Cav. Co.K
  Sgt.
Rich, R.P. TN 4th (Murray's) Cav. Co.F
Rich, R.P. TN 8th (Smith's) Cav. Co.I
Rich, Rudolph AR 6th Inf. Co.E
Rich, S. AL 4th Inf. Co.A
Rich, S. AL 24th Inf. Co.A
Rich, Samuel TX 28th Cav. Co.M Cpl.
Rich, Samuel TX 14th Inf. 2nd Co.K Cpl.
Rich, Samuel C. NC 42nd Inf. Co.F
Rich, S.C. MS 9th Cav. Co.D
Rich, S.E. GA 54th Inf. Co.C
Rich, S. Fielding AR 15th (N.W.) Inf. Emer-
  gency Co.I
Rich, Shadrach AL Cav. 24th Bn. Co.A
Rich, Solomon H. GA 6th Cav. Co.F
Rich, Solomon J. GA 52nd Inf. Co.G
Rich, Stanford TN 28th Inf. Co.C Sgt.
Rich, Stephen MS 9th Cav. Co.D
Rich, T. AL 25th Inf. Co.H
Rich, Thomas AL 12th Cav. Co.G
Rich, Thomas FL 2nd Cav. Co.E

Rich, Thomas MS 3rd Inf. Co.E
Rich, Thomas TN 60th Mtd.Inf. Co.H
Rich, Thomas A. AL 47th Inf. Co.E
Rich, Thomas J. GA Mil. 12th Regt. Co.H
Rich, Thomas J. TN 44th Inf. Co.I
Rich, Thomas J. TN 44th (Cons.) Inf. Co.A Sgt.
Rich, Timothy MO 11th Inf. Co.C,B
Rich, T.W. AR 50th Mil. Co.B
Rich, W. LA 22nd (Cons.) Inf. Co.H
Rich, W. NC 22nd Inf. Co.I
Rich, Wade H. NC 26th Inf. Co.F
Rich, W.A.J. KY 8th Mtd.Inf. Co.E
Rich, Washington GA 50th Inf. Co.F
Rich, W.D. AL 9th Inf. Co.K
Rich, W.D. TN 1st (Carter's) Cav. Co.M
Rich, W.E. TN Cav. 1st Bn. (McNairy's) Co.E
Rich, W.E. TN 22nd (Barteau's) Cav. Co.C
  Cpl.
Rich, Wesley NC 24th Inf. Co.D
Rich, W.F. GA 3rd Res. Co.G
Rich, W.H. SC 23rd Inf. Co.B
Rich, W.H. TN 13th Inf.
Rich, William AL 20th Inf. Co.C
Rich, William KY 10th (Diamond's) Cav. Co.A
  Cpl.
Rich, William KY 5th Mtd.Inf. Co.E
Rich, William MS 9th Inf. New Co.G
Rich, William MO 11th Inf. Co.C Sgt.
Rich, William TN Cav. 12th Bn. (Day's) Co.F
Rich, William TN Lt.Arty. Kain's Co.
Rich, William A. NC 22nd Inf. Co.E
Rich, William C. AL 25th Inf. Co.D
Rich, William H. GA Inf. 1st Loc.Troops
  (Augusta) Co.A
Rich, William H. NC 51st Inf. Co.K
Rich, William H. SC 6th Cav. Co.D 1st Lt.
Rich, William J. GA 38th Inf. Co.I,C
Rich, William L. AR 50th Mil. Co.B Cpl.
Rich, William P. NC 24th Inf. Co.D
Rich, William P. NC 45th Inf. Co.E
Rich, William R. GA Inf. 8th Bn. Co.B
Rich, William R. MS 8th Inf. Co.G
Rich, William R. NC 26th Inf. Co.F
Rich, William V. TN 37th Inf. Co.E
Rich, William W. GA 18th Inf. Co.H
Rich, William W. GA 52nd Inf. Co.G 1st Sgt.
Rich, William W. GA Phillips' Legion Co.B
  Lt.Col.
Rich, W.J. AR 34th Inf. Co.H
Rich, W.J.M. MO 12th Inf. Co.C
Rich, W.L. AR 1st (Monroe's) Cav. Co.A
Rich, W.T. AL 3rd Cav. Co.E
Rich, W.T. Conf.Cav. Wood's Regt. 1st Co.D
Rich, Zachariah MS 8th Inf. Co.G
Rich, Zachariah NC 2nd Arty. (36th St.Troops)
  Co.C
Richadson, R. Trans-MS Conf.Cav. 1st Bn. Co.A
Richard GA 1st Bn.S.S. Co.A Music.
Richard SC Mil. 16th Regt. Triest's Co. Colored
  Cook
Richard, A. LA 7th Cav. Co.K
Richard, A. LA Odgen's Cav. Co.H
Richard, A. LA Mil. 1st Native Guards
Richard, A. LA 18th Inf. Co.H
Richard, A. LA 28th (Gray's) Inf. Co.D
Richard, A. LA Inf.Crescent Regt. Co.D
Richard, Aaron NC Inf. 2nd Bn. Co.G

Richard, Abraham A. LA 16th Inf. Co.K
Richard, A.C. GA Cav. 10th Bn. (St.Guards)
  Co.D
Richard, Ad. LA Mil. St.James Regt. Gaudet's
  Co.
Richard, Adolphe LA Miles' Legion Co.H
Richard, A.E. LA 18th Inf. Co.F
Richard, Aime LA Arty. Landry's Co.
  (Donaldsonville Arty.) QMSgt.
Richard, Alexander V. LA 26th Inf. Co.C
Richard, Alexandre LA 18th Inf. Co.B
Richard, Alfred TX 25th Cav. Co.H
Richard, Amedee LA 1st Hvy.Arty. (Reg.) Co.C
Richard, Anderson VA 4th Cav. & Inf.St.Line
  1st Co.I
Richard, Andre LA Mil. 2nd Regt. French Brig.
  Co.6
Richard, Apolinaire LA 1st Hvy.Arty. (Reg.)
  Co.C
Richard, Aristide LA Inf. 10th Bn. Co.E
Richard, Armand LA 18th Inf. Co.K 2nd Lt.
Richard, Arthur LA 2nd Cav. Co.K
Richard, Augustus MS 3rd Inf. Co.A Sgt.
Richard, Aurelien LA 18th Inf. Co.K 1st Sgt.
Richard, A.W. TX 16th Inf. Co.A Sgt.Maj.
Richard, B.H. TN Sullivan Cty.Res.
  (Loc.Def.Troops) Witcher's Co.
Richard, C. LA 7th Cav. Co.D
Richard, Camille LA 28th (Thomas') Inf. Co.K
  Sgt.
Richard, Charle VA Lt.Arty. Brander's Co.
Richard, Charles LA 13th Inf. Co.F 1st Lt.
Richard, Charles LA 18th Inf. Co.G
Richard, Charles LA Inf.Cons. 18th Regt. & Yel-
  low Jacket Bn. Co.G
Richard, Charles TX 16th Inf. Co.A
Richard, Chs. B. VA Res. Keyser's Co.
Richard, Charles E. VA Mtd.Riflemen Balfour's
  Co.
Richard, Charles J. LA Arty. 1st Field Btty.
  QMSgt.
Richard, Charles Q. LA Siege Train Bn. Co.D
Richard, Cheri LA 30th Inf. Co.H,G,B
Richard, Clairville LA 1st Hvy.Arty. (Reg.)
  Co.C
Richard, C.P. LA 18th Inf. Co.B
Richard, C.P. LA Inf.Cons. 18th Regt. & Yellow
  Jacket Bn. Co.B
Richard, C.S. LA 2nd Cav. Co.A
Richard, D. LA 28th (Gray's) Inf. Co.A
Richard, D.E.S. NC 14th Inf. Co.I
Richard, D.I. AL 21st Inf. Co.G
Richard, D.L. LA 2nd Res.Corps 1st Lt.
Richard, E. LA 7th Cav. Co.K
Richard, E. LA Mil. Orleans Guards Regt. Co.I
Richard, Edgar LA 3rd Inf. Co.A
Richard, Edmond O. LA 18th Inf. Co.B
Richard, Entwine LA 7th Cav. Co.D
Richard, Eugene LA Inf.Cons. 18th Regt. & Yel-
  low Jacket Bn. Co.A
Richard, Eugene V. LA Inf. 10th Bn. Co.A,C
Richard, Euphreme LA Lovell's Scouts
Richard, F. LA Mil. 3rd Regt. French Brig. Co.6
Richard, F. LA Inf. 10th Bn. Co.B
Richard, F.A. TX 25th Cav.
Richard, Felix LA Inf.Cons. 18th Regt. & Yel-
  low Jacket Bn. Co.B

Richard, Fergus LA 4th Inf. Co.F Sgt.
Richard, Ferris LA 7th Cav. Co.G
Richard, Francis FL 3rd Inf. Co.A
Richard, Francisco LA 30th Inf. Co.D
Richard, Franklin TX Arty. Douglas' Co.
Richard, George LA Inf.Crescent Regt. Co.A
Richard, George LA Inf.Cons.Crescent Regt. Co.C
Richard, George NC 7th Sr.Res. Fisher's Co.
Richard, G.R. SC 1st (McCreary's) Inf. Co.G
Richard, G.W. TN Sullivan Cty.Res. (Loc.Def.Troops) Witcher's Co.
Richard, H. LA Mil. LaFourche Regt.
Richard, H. SC Palmetto S.S. Co.F
Richard, Hardy N. FL 10th Inf. Co.A 2nd Lt.
Richard, Henry AR 51st Mil. Co.F
Richard, Henry GA 51st Inf. Co.E
Richard, Howard VA 35th Inf. Co.H
Richard, Howard VA Cav. 35th Bn. Co.H
Richard, Isaac VA Bn.Res. Co.A
Richard, Isaac VA 51st Mil. Co.G
Richard, Isaiah VA 51st Mil. Co.G
Richard, J. AR Mil. Desha Cty.Bn.
Richard, J. GA 1st Troops & Defences (Macon) Co.C
Richard, J. LA Mil. 1st Native Guards
Richard, J. LA 1st Res. Co.H
Richard, J. LA Mil. 3rd Regt. French Brig. Co.3
Richard, J. LA 4th Inf. Co.F
Richard, J. LA Inf. 10th Bn. Co.G
Richard, J. LA 18th Inf. Co.H
Richard, J. LA 18th Inf. Co.I
Richard, J. LA Inf.Cons. 18th Regt. & Yellow Jacket Bn. Co.H
Richard, J.A. LA Arty. 5th Field Btty. (Pelican Lt.Arty.)
Richard, James A. VA Cav. 39th Bn. Co.C
Richard, James M. AL 38th Inf. Co.G
Richard, James M. FL Lt.Arty. Perry's Co.
Richard, James M. GA 1st Inf. (St.Guards)
Richard, James R. FL 4th Inf. Co.B Cpl.
Richard, J.D. LA 18th Inf. Co.A
Richard, J.D. LA Inf.Cons. 18th Regt. & Yellow Jacket Bn. Co.A
Richard, J.D. LA 28th (Thomas') Inf. Co.A
Richard, Jerassin LA 28th (Thomas') Inf. Co.A
Richard, J.F. MS Cav. 17th Bn. Co.C 3rd Lt.
Richard, Job T. FL 1st Cav. Co.G
Richard, Job T. FL 10th Inf. Co.A Sgt.
Richard, John AL 32nd Inf. Co.F
Richard, John GA Cav. Dorough's Bn.
Richard, John GA 43rd Inf. Co.E
Richard, John LA 7th Cav. Co.D
Richard, John LA Arty. Landry's Co. (Donaldsonville Arty.)
Richard, John NC 15th Inf. Co.H
Richard, John Gen. & Staff Contr.Surg.
Richard, John C. FL 10th Inf. Co.A Capt.
Richard, John F. VA 97th Mil. Co.F Cpl.
Richard, John L. VA 56th Inf. Co.H
Richard, John O. LA 8th Inf. Co.F
Richard, John O. LA 26th Inf. Co.E Jr.2nd Lt.
Richard, John W. AL 4th Cav. Co.E
Richard, Joissin TX 11th (Spaight's) Bn.Vol. Co.E
Richard, Jones FL McBride's Co. (Indians)

Richard, Joseph LA Mtd.Part.Rangers Bond's Co.
Richard, Joseph LA Mil.Cav.Squad. (Ind. Rangers Iberville)
Richard, Joseph LA Arty. 5th Field Btty. (Pelican Lt.Arty.)
Richard, Joseph LA 10th Inf. Co.K
Richard, Joseph LA 11th Inf. Co.B
Richard, Joseph A. GA 36th (Broyles') Inf.
Richard, Joseph E. LA 4th Inf. Co.D
Richard, Joseph V. LA 28th (Thomas') Inf. Co.K
Richard, J.P. LA Inf.Cons.Crescent Regt. Co.E
Richard, J.R. GA 4th (Clinch's) Cav. Co.B
Richard, J.T. LA Mil. 3rd Regt. 3rd Brig. 1st Div. Co.C
Richard, Jules LA 3rd Inf. Co.A Sgt.
Richard, L. LA 6th Inf. Co.C
Richard, L. LA Inf.Cons. 18th Regt. & Yellow Jacket Bn. Co.G
Richard, Laurant TX 8th Inf. Co.A
Richard, Lemuel H. AL 23rd Inf. Co.E
Richard, Leonidas GA 13th Inf. Co.D
Richard, Lewis LA 15th Bn.S.S. (Weatherly's) Co.D
Richard, Lewis J. LA 2nd Res.Corps Co.H
Richard, Louis LA 18th Inf.
Richard, Louis LA 26th Inf. Co.F
Richard, Lre. LA 2nd Res.Corps Co.B
Richard, M. LA 7th Cav. Co.K
Richard, M. LA Conscr.
Richard, Mansel J. LA Mtd.Part.Rangers Bond's Co.
Richard, M.J. LA 2nd Cav. Co.A
Richard, M.P. NC 6th Inf. Co.I
Richard, Myer SC 25th Inf. Co.D Sgt.
Richard, N. LA 30th Inf. Co.A
Richard, Narcisse LA 3rd Inf. Co.A
Richard, Nicholas AR 2nd Inf. Co.B Cpl.
Richard, O. LA 2nd Cav. Co.I
Richard, O. LA Arty. 5th Field Btty. (Pelican Lt.Arty.)
Richard, Octave LA 2nd Res.Corps Co.H Cpl.
Richard, Octave LA 4th Inf. Co.H
Richard, Onezime LA 28th (Thomas') Inf. Co.A
Richard, Osceola FL 10th Inf. Co.A
Richard, P.A. LA 3rd Inf. Co.A
Richard, Paul TX 11 (Spaight's) Bn.Vol. Vo.E
Richard, P.D. LA 7th Cav. Co.B
Richard, Philippe LA Conscr.
Richard, Pierre LA 3rd Inf. Co.A
Richard, Pierre LA 27th Inf. Co.D
Richard, Pierre A. LA 11th Inf. Co.B Sgt.
Richard, Pierre O. LA 26th Inf. Co.E Sgt.
Richard, Placide LA 18th Inf. Co.K
Richard, P.J. LA 2nd Res.Corps Co.A
Richard, P.V. LA Inf. 10th Bn. Co.G
Richard, R. Gen. & Staff Maj.,AIG
Richard, Raphael, Jr. LA 18th Inf. Co.B 1st Sgt.
Richard, S. AR Mil. Desha Cty.Bn.
Richard, S. LA Inf. 10th Bn. Co.G
Richard, S. TX Inf. Griffin's Bn. Co.F
Richard, Silvaine LA 15th Inf. Co.C Cpl.
Richard, Simon LA 7th Cav. Co.K
Richard, Simon LA Mil. St.James Regt. Co.E Sgt.
Richard, Sosthene LA 15th Inf. Co.C

Richard, Sothine LA Inf. 16th Bn. (Conf.Guards Resp.Bn.) Co.B
Richard, T. LA Arty. 5th Field Btty. (Pelican Lt.Arty.)
Richard, T. LA 18th Inf. Co.D
Richard, T. LA Inf.Crescent Regt.
Richard, Telesphore 14th Conf.Cav. Co.D Cpl.
Richard, Theodule LA Inf.Crescent Regt. Co.A
Richard, Theodule LA Inf.Cons.Crescent Regt. Co.C
Richard, Theogene LA 7th Cav. Co.D
Richard, Theojean LA Inf.Crescent Regt. Co.A
Richard, Theojean LA Inf.Cons.Crescent Regt. Co.C
Richard, Theop LA Mil. St.Martin's Regt. Co.I 1st Lt.
Richard, Theophile LA Inf.Cons. 18th Regt. & Yellow Jacket Bn. Co.D
Richard, Thomas TN 48th (Voorhies') Inf. Co.I
Richard, Thomas VA 2nd Arty. Co.K
Richard, Uriah VA 51st Mil. Co.G
Richard, V. LA 1st Cav. Co.I
Richard, V. LA Inf. 10th Bn. Co.G
Richard, V. TX Cav. Ragsdale's Bn. Co.B
Richard, V. TX 21st Inf. Co.D
Richard, Valmon LA 28th (Thomas') Inf. Co.K
Richard, Valsin LA 28th (Thomas') Inf. Co.A
Richard, Victor LA 28th (Thomas') Inf. Co.A
Richard, Victoria TX Inf. Griffin's Bn. Co.E
Richard, Victorine TX 11th (Spaight's) Bn.Vol. Co.D
Richard, W. LA 18th Inf. Co.H
Richard, W.E. LA 2nd Cav. Co.A
Richard, W.E. LA Mtd.Part.Rangers Bond's Co. Sgt.
Richard, W.E.M. SC Palmetto S.S. Co.I Sgt.
Richard, W.H. VA 11th Cav. Co.H
Richard, White TX 11th Cav. Co.C Sgt.
Richard, William GA 46th Inf. Co.H
Richard, William LA Conscr.
Richard, Wm. VA 42nd Inf. Co.B
Richard, William A. VA 10th Inf. Co.K
Richard, William E. AL 24th Inf. Co.D 1st Sgt.
Richard, William H. TN 48th (Voorhies') Inf. Co.B
Richard, Willis R. NC 55th Inf. Co.E
Richardet, William B. AR Lt.Arty. Thrall's Btty. Sgt.
Richards, --- LA Mil.Crescent Cadets
Richards, --- TX 25th Cav. Co.E
Richards, --- VA 46th Inf. Co.I
Richards, A. AL Talladega Cty.Res. W.Y. Hendrick's Co.
Richards, A. LA 1st Cav. Co.A
Richards, A. LA 3rd (Harrison's) Cav. Co.I Sgt.
Richards, A. LA Mil.Cont.Regt. Kirk's Co.
Richards, A. TN 7th (Duckworth's) Cav. Co.F
Richards, A. TX 24th & 25th Cav. (Cons.) Co.H
Richards, A. VA 30th Bn.S.S. Co.E
Richards, A.A. AL 30th Inf. Co.F
Richards, Aaron AL 44th Inf. Co.A
Richards, Adam Conf.Inf. Tucker's Regt. Co.H
Richards, Adolphus VA Cav. Mosby's Regt. (Part.Rangers) Co.B,C Maj.
Richards, A.F. SC 16th Inf. Co.A
Richards, A.J. AL Cav. Barlow's Co.
Richards, A.J. AR 2nd Inf. Co.I Cpl.

Richards, A.J. GA 11th Inf. Co.G
Richards, A.J. GA 17th Inf. Co.I
Richards, A.J. TN 1st (Carter's) Inf. Co.M
Richards, A.J. TN 29th Inf. Co.K
Richards, A.J. TN 60th Mtd.Inf. Co.L
Richards, A.J. VA Loc.Def. Ezell's Co.
Richards, A.J. 15th Conf.Cav. Co.C
Richards, A. Keene Gen. & Staff Vol.ADC
Richards, A.L. MS Cav. 24th Bn. Co.F Cpl.
Richards, A.L. MS Wilkinson Cty. Minute Men
  Co.B 2nd Lt.
Richards, Albert NC 1st Inf. Co.H
Richards, Alex TN Detailed Conscr. Co.B
Richards, Alexander LA C.S. Zouave Bn.
Richards, Alexander NC 34th Inf. Co.E
Richards, Alexander TN 39th Mtd.Inf. Co.G
Richards, Alexander TN 59th Mtd.Inf. Co.C
Richards, Alexandria TN 50th Inf. Co.F Capt.
Richards, Alfred TX 21st Cav. Co.G
Richards, Alfred VA 50th Inf. 1st Co.G
Richards, Alfred VA 63rd Inf. 1st Co.I
Richards, Alick SC 12th Inf. Co.K
Richards, Allison Trans-MS Conf.Cav. 1st Bn.
  Co.D
Richards, Alonzo AL 11th Cav. Co.D
Richards, A.M. TX 12th Inf. Co.C
Richards, Amon MS 20th Inf. Co.E
Richards, Amos VA Lt.Arty. 13th Bn. Co.C
Richards, Anderson VA 21st Cav. Co.B Cpl.
Richards, Anderson R. VA 57th Inf. Co.C
Richards, Andrew J. AL 37th Inf. Co.I,D
Richards, Andrew J. GA 19th Inf. Co.I
Richards, Andrew J. GA 30th Inf. Co.K Sgt.
Richards, Andrew J. GA 56th Inf.
Richards, Andrew J. TN 1st (Feild's) Inf. Co.A
Richards, Andrew J. VA Lt.Arty. Brander's Co.
Richards, Andrew J. VA 6th Bn.Res. Co.E
Richards, A.P. LA 4th Inf. Co.I
Richards, Archibald T. VA QM Dept. Agent
Richards, A.T. VA 11th Cav. Co.F Capt.
Richards, A.W. GA 18th Inf. Co.M
Richards, A.W. GA 28th Inf. Co.F
Richards, B. SC 5th Cav. Co.K 2nd Lt.
Richards, Bailey P. TN 7th Inf. Co.B
Richards, Bender TN 13th (Gore's) Cav. Co.G
Richards, Benjamin TN 26th Inf. Co.K
Richards, Benjamin TN 59th Mtd.Inf. Co.C
Richards, Benjamin, Jr. TN Sullivan Cty.Res.
  (Loc.Def.Troops) Witcher's Co.
Richards, Benjamin, Sr. TN Sullivan Cty.Res.
  (Loc.Def.Troops) Witcher's Co.
Richards, Benjamin D. VA Cav. McNeill's Co.
Richards, Benjamin W. NC 12th Inf. Co.G
Richards, Berry SC 9th Res. Co.G 1st Lt.
Richards, B.F. AL 37th Inf. Co.H
Richards, B. Frank VA 10th Inf. Co.G
Richards, B.M. AL 8th (Hatch's) Cav. Co.K
Richards, Bolin VA Cav. 37th Bn. Co.G
Richards, Bruce W. VA 57th Inf. Co.G
Richards, Burwell A. GA 4th Inf. Co.A
Richards, C. VA 42nd Inf. Co.B
Richards, C.C. LA 2nd Inf. Co.K
Richards, C.C. TX 12th Inf. Co.I
Richards, C.F. MO Inf. 4th Regt.St.Guard Co.B
  Sgt.
Richards, Charles AR Cav. Gordon's Regt. Co.I

Richards, Charles LA 28th (Thomas') Inf. Co.D
  1st Sgt.
Richards, Charles Conf.Lt.Arty. 1st Reg.Btty.
Richards, Charles Inf. School of Pract. Powell's
  Detach. Powell's Co.
Richards, Charles A. AL 10th Inf. Co.C
Richards, Charles C. VA 10th Inf. Co.G
Richards, Charles E. KY 5th Cav. Co.E 2nd Lt.
Richards, Charles E. TX 1st Hvy.Arty. Co.D 1st
  Lt.
Richards, Charles E. VA 24th Cav. Co.B
Richards, Charles E. VA Hvy.Arty. 19th Bn. 3rd
  Co.E
Richards, Charles E. VA 1st Inf. Co.B
Richards, Charles E. Gen. & Staff, Eng.
  Capt.,AACS
Richards, Charles G. AL 4th Res. Co.A
Richards, Charles H. TN 26th Inf. Co.I
Richards, Charles H. TX 3rd Cav. Co.E
Richards, Charles H. VA 2nd Inf. Co.C
Richards, Charles H. VA 13th Inf. Co.C Capt.
Richards, Charles H. 3rd Conf.Eng.Troops Co.C
Richards, Charles M. MS 3rd Cav. Co.I 1st Lt.
Richards, Charles M. VA 40th Inf. Co.E
Richards, Charles P. VA 24th Inf. Co.D
Richards, Charles S. TX 24th Cav. Co.C
Richards, Charles T. GA 56th Inf. Co.C
Richards, Charles W. MS 17th Inf. Co.A
Richards, Claiborne C. MS 9th Inf. New Co.D
Richards, Clinton G. AR 2nd Inf. Co.H Music.
Richards, C.M. AL 56th Part.Rangers Co.I
Richards, C.M. AR 1st (Dobbin's) Cav. Co.F
  Lt.
Richards, C.M. TN 9th Inf. Co.F Sgt.
Richards, Columbus TN 60th Mtd.Inf. Co.H
Richards, C.R. AL 21st Inf. Co.K
Richards, C.R. Central Div. KY Sap. &
  Min.,CSA
Richards, Cyrus W. MS 31st Inf. Co.I Capt.
Richards, D. AR Lt.Arty. Marshall's Btty.
Richards, D.A. MS Lt.Arty. Merrin's Btty.
  Jr.2nd Lt.
Richards, Daniel M. AL 25th Inf. Co.E Capt.
Richards, Daniel M. MS 31st Inf. Co.D
Richards, Daniel M. SC 14th Inf. Co.F
Richards, Daniel Mc. SC 13th Inf. Co.I
Richards, Daniel T. VA 1st Cav. 1st Co.D 2nd
  Lt.
Richards, Daniel T. VA 6th Cav. Co.D Lt.Col.
Richards, Daniel U. FL 2nd Cav. Co.A
Richards, David LA Inf. 1st Sp.Bn. (Wheat's)
  Co.A
Richards, David MS Lt.Arty. 14th Bn. Co.C
  Jr.2nd Lt.
Richards, David VA 16th Cav. Co.K Black.
Richards, David VA Cav. Ferguson's Bn. Noun-
  nan's Co.
Richards, David A. VA 1st Inf. Co.A
Richards, David B. VA 38th Inf. Co.H
Richards, David R. TN 41st Inf. Co.B
Richards, David T. FL 6th Inf. Co.G
Richards, David T. FL Campbellton Boys
Richards, D.M. AL Inf. 1st (Loomis') Bn. Co.E
  Capt.
Richards, Doc TN 19th & 20th (Cons.) Cav.
  Co.D
Richards, D.R. TN 13th (Gore's) Cav. Co.I

Richards, Dulany M. VA Cav. Mosby's Regt.
  (Part.Rangers) Co.A
Richards, D.W. TN 10th Cav. Co.L
Richards, D.W. TN 18th (Newsom's) Cav. Co.H
Richards, E. GA Inf. 14th Bn. (St.Guards) Co.B
  Cpl.
Richards, E. GA Inf. 18th Bn. (St.Guards) Co.E
  Cpl.
Richards, E. LA 4th Inf. Co.D
Richards, Edward NC 2nd Jr.Res. Co.I
Richards, Edward TN 44th (Cons.) Inf. Co.I
Richards, Edward D. MS 20th Inf. Co.E
Richards, Edward D. TN 55th (McKoin's) Inf.
  Co.I
Richards, Edward D. Gen. & Staff Hosp.Stew.
Richards, Edwin GA 10th Inf. Co.D Capt.
Richards, E.L. NC 1st Arty. (10th St.Troops)
  Co.B
Richards, Eldridge TN Cav. 12th Bn. (Day's)
  Co.A
Richards, Eldridge TN 39th Mtd.Inf. Co.G
Richards, Eli GA 43rd Inf. Co.C
Richards, Eli A. VA 57th Inf. Co.C Cpl.
Richards, Elijah VA 59th Mil. Riddick's Co.
Richards, Elmer E. MS 20th Inf. Co.E Sgt.
Richards, E.M. GA 7th Cav. Co.F
Richards, E.M. GA Cav. 21st Bn. Co.E
Richards, Emanuel R. TN 39th Mtd.Inf. Co.G
Richards, E.P. MS 44th Inf. Co.A,K Sgt.
Richards, Ephriam A. MS 30th Inf. Co.E
Richards, Ephrim MS 18th Inf. Co.F
Richards, E.R. GA Cav. 1st Bn.Res. Tufts' Co.
  Sgt.
Richards, E.T. AR 15th (Johnson's) Inf. Co.E
  Cpl.
Richards, E.W. AL 4th Inf. Co.E
Richards, E.W. TX 5th Cav. Co.D Capt.
Richards, E.W. Gen. & Staff Hosp.Stew.
Richards, F. LA Mil. British Guard Bn. Coburn's
  Co.
Richards, F., Jr. SC Mil. Trenholm's Co.
Richards, F. SC 8th Bn.Res. Co.A
Richards, F. SC Bn.St.Cadets Co.A
Richards, F. VA 13th Inf. Co.A
Richards, F.A. TX Cav. Baird's Regt.
Richards, Fleming VA 21st Cav. Co.B
Richards, Fleming B. VA 54th Inf. Co.B
Richards, F.M. AL 51st (Part.Rangers) Co.G
  Sgt.
Richards, F.M. AR 6th Inf. New Co.F
Richards, F.M. AR 11th Inf. Co.E
Richards, F.M. AR 11th & 17th (Cons.) Inf.
  Co.E
Richards, F.M. AR 12th Inf. Co.A
Richards, F.M. FL 2nd Cav. Co.A
Richards, Fontaine VA 57th Inf. Co.H
Richards, Francis LA 1st Hvy.Arty. (Reg.) Co.C
Richards, Francis LA Miles' Legion Co.A
Richards, Francis M. FL Cav. 5th Bn. Co.E
Richards, Francis M. GA 26th Inf.
Richards, Francis M. TN 34th Inf. Co.I
Richards, Frank MO Cav. Coffee's Regt. Co.C
Richards, Franklin VA 10th Inf. Co.L
Richards, Franklin VA 82nd Mil. Co.C
Richards, Fred TX 32nd Cav. Co.K
Richards, Frederick SC Cav. Walpole's Co.
Richards, Fred'k Gen. & Staff Capt.,ACS

Richards, F.W. AR 10th Inf. Co.E Sgt.
Richards, Gabriel M. AL 62nd Inf. Co.A
Richards, G.B. AR Cav. Witherspoon's Bn.
Richards, George LA 7th Cav. Co.D
Richards, George MS Cav. Drane's Co. (Choctaw Cty.Res.)
Richards, George MO 2nd Inf. Co.C
Richards, George NC 26th Inf. Co.B Sgt.
Richards, George SC 8th Inf. Co.C
Richards, George TN Hvy.Arty. Caruthers' Btty.
Richards, George TX 2nd Field Btty.
Richards, George TX Cav. Benavides' Regt. Co.F
Richards, George VA 22nd Cav. Co.G Sgt.
Richards, George 1st Conf.Cav. 1st Co.C
Richards, George Conf.Cav. Wood's Regt. Co.L
Richards, George B. MD 1st Inf. Co.I
Richards, George B. VA Lt.Arty. J.D. Smith's Co.
Richards, George C. TN 1st (Feild's) Inf. Co.L 1st Lt.
Richards, George C. TN Inf. Nashville Bn. Fulcher's Co. 2nd Lt.
Richards, George D. TX 16th Inf. Co.A
Richards, George H. VA 1st Inf. Co.A
Richards, George H. VA 1st Inf. Co.H
Richards, George H. VA 1st St.Res. Co.E,I Sgt.
Richards, George H. VA 17th Inf. Co.E
Richards, George I. GA 37th Inf. Co.I
Richards, George J. GA Inf. 3rd Bn. Co.C Cpl.
Richards, George R. LA 11th Inf. Co.L
Richards, George W. AL 43rd Inf. Co.F
Richards, George W. FL 2nd Cav. Co.A
Richards, George W. FL Cav. 5th Bn. Co.E
Richards, George W. GA 41st Inf. Co.G
Richards, George W. NC 7th Inf. Co.F
Richards, George W. NC 15th Inf. Co.E
Richards, George W. TN Detailed Conscr. Co.B 2nd Lt.
Richards, George W. VA 6th Cav. Co.I
Richards, George W. VA 20th Cav. Co.E
Richards, George W. VA 1st Arty. Co.H Sgt.
Richards, George W. VA 31st Inf. Co.C
Richards, George W. VA 42nd Inf. Co.C
Richards, George W. Conf.Arty. McIntosh's Bn. Asst.Surg.
Richards, George W. Conf.Lt.Arty. Richardson's Bn. Asst.Surg.
Richards, George W. Conf.Inf. 1st Bn. 2nd Co.A
Richards, Geo. W. Gen. & Staff Asst.Surg.
Richards, G.H. VA 12th Inf. Co.G
Richards, Giles W. AL 37th Inf. Co.H
Richards, G.N. MO 2nd Arty.
Richards, Graham NC 2nd Jr.Res. Co.I
Richards, Graham NC 33rd Inf. Co.H
Richards, Gregg G. SC Arty. Manigault's Bn. 1st Co.A
Richards, G.W. AL Cav. Forrest's Regt.
Richards, G.W. GA Inf. 25th Bn. (Prov.Guard) Co.A
Richards, G.W. GA 59th Inf.
Richards, G.W. TN 7th (Duckworth's) Cav. Co.F Sgt.
Richards, G.W. TN 3rd (Lillard's) Mtd.Inf. 1st Co.K
Richards, G.W. TN 26th Inf. Co.K Sgt.
Richards, G.W. TN 63rd Inf. Co.E

Richards, G.W. 3rd Conf.Cav. Co.D
Richards, H. TN 19th & 20th (Cons.) Cav. Co.D
Richards, H.A. VA 2nd St.Res. Co.I
Richards, Harvey R. NC 48th Inf. Co.I
Richards, H.C. AL Loc.Def. & Sp.Serv. Toomer's Co.
Richards, Henderson MS Cav. 4th Bn. Roddey's Co.
Richards, Henry AL 39th Inf. Co.D
Richards, Henry GA 1st (Olmstead's) Inf. Co.A
Richards, Henry GA 1st (Olmstead's) Inf. Gordon's Co.
Richards, Henry GA 63rd Inf. Co.B
Richards, Henry MS 20th Inf. Co.E
Richards, Henry VA Cav. Mosby's Regt. (Part. Rangers) Co.C
Richards, Henry B. MO Cav. 3rd Regt.St.Guard Comsy.
Richards, Henry B. VA 9th Cav. Co.G
Richards, Henry Joseph MS 1st Lt.Arty. Co.A
Richards, Henry R. KY 10th Cav. Co.E
Richards, Hezekiah TN 7th Cav. Co.E
Richards, Hiram NC 27th Inf. Co.G
Richards, H. Goddard LA Mil. British Guard Bn. Hamilton's Co.
Richards, H.H. GA Floyd Legion (St.Guards) Co.F 1st Sgt.
Richards, H.H. NC 44th Inf. Co.F
Richards, Hiram H. SC 5th Inf. 1st Co.D, 2nd Co.D 1st Lt.
Richards, H.J. AL 46th Inf. Co.B
Richards, H.L. AL Cp. of Instr. Talladega Co.E
Richards, Howard VA Lt.Arty. W.H. Chapman's Co.
Richards, H.P. GA 1st (Fannin's) Res. Co.D
Richards, H.R. GA 63rd Inf. Co.F,D
Richards, H.R. TX 7th Cav. Co.H
Richards, H.S. AL 58th Inf. Co.A
Richards, H.T. AL 23rd Inf. Co.F Cpl.
Richards, Hugh J. TN 59th Mtd.Inf. Co.I
Richards, H.W. VA 42nd Inf. Co.B
Richards, Hy. M. LA Washington Arty.Bn. Co.5
Richards, I. MO Lt.Arty. 1st Btty.
Richards, I.C. MS 4th Cav. Co.A
Richards, I.M. AL 63rd Inf. Co.C
Richards, Ira J. TN Cav. 9th Bn. (Gantt's) Co.C
Richards, Isaac TN 43rd Inf. Co.C
Richards, Isaac M. NC 58th Inf. Co.H
Richards, Isaac N. TN 25th Inf. Co.B
Richards, J. AL 1st Regt. Mobile Vol. Co.K
Richards, J. AR 51st Mil. Co.F
Richards, J. GA Cav. 6th Bn. (St.Guards) Co.C
Richards, J. KY Morgan's Men Co.C
Richards, J. LA Inf.Crescent Regt. Co.C
Richards, J. MS Cav. 3rd Bn. (Ashcraft's) Co.C
Richards, J. MO 2nd Cav. Co.D
Richards, J. NC 3rd Bn.Sr.Res. Co.A
Richards, J.A. SC 16th Inf. Co.I
Richards, J.A. TN 8th (Smith's) Cav. Co.E
Richards, J.A. 8th (Wade's) Conf.Cav. Co.K
Richards, Jacob TN 19th Inf. Co.K
Richards, Jacob D. FL Cav. 5th Bn. Co.B
Richards, Jacob S. MO 8th Cav. Co.K
Richards, James AL 12th Cav. Co.F
Richards, James AL 15th Bn.Part.Rangers Co.E
Richards, James AL 56th Part.Rangers Co.E Cpl.

Richards, James GA Arty. 11th Bn. (Sumter Arty.) Old Co.C, Co.B
Richards, James GA Smith's Legion Co.C Cpl.
Richards, James MS Inf. 2nd Bn. (St.Troops) Co.B
Richards, James MO 8th Cav. Co.F
Richards, James MO Inf. 4th Regt.St.Guard Co.C
Richards, James MO 16th Inf. Co.G
Richards, James NC 7th Inf. Co.K
Richards, James SC 12th Inf. Co.G
Richards, James TN 7th (Duckworth's) Cav. Co.F
Richards, James TN 19th (Biffle's) Cav. Co.D
Richards, James TN 26th Inf. Co.K
Richards, James TN 60th Mtd.Inf. Co.L
Richards, James VA 34th Inf. Co.D
Richards, James VA 40th Inf. Co.B
Richards, James VA 41st Mil. Co.B
Richards, James 3rd Conf.Cav. Co.F
Richards, James A. TN 2nd (Smith's) Cav.
Richards, James A. TN 59th Mtd.Inf. Co.E 2nd Lt.
Richards, James C. VA 7th Inf. Co.C
Richards, James E. AR 2nd Inf. Co.D Capt.
Richards, James F. AL 46th Inf. Co.K
Richards, James F. TN 2nd (Smith's) Cav. Rankin's Co.
Richards, James F. TN 4th (McLemore's) Cav. Co.H
Richards, James H. GA 1st (Olmstead's) Inf. Co.G
Richards, James H. GA 56th Inf. Co.D 3rd Lt.
Richards, James H. SC Lt.Arty. 3rd (Palmetto) Bn. Co.A
Richards, James H. TN Cav. 2nd Bn. (Biffle's) Co.D
Richards, James H. VA 7th Cav. Co.I
Richards, James J. AR 33rd Inf. Co.E
Richards, James K.P. TN Cav. 12th Bn. (Day's) Co.A
Richards, James M. AL 37th Inf. Co.H
Richards, James M. AR 15th (N.W.) Inf. Co.G Capt.
Richards, James O. AL 32nd Inf. Co.I Sgt.
Richards, James P. VA 7th Inf. Co.C
Richards, James R. FL 8th Inf. Co.G
Richards, James S. TN 39th Mtd.Inf. Co.F 2nd Lt.
Richards, James T. GA 65th Inf. Co.B Cpl.
Richards, James T.B. TX 8th Cav. Co.A Cpl.
Richards, James W. MO 10th Inf. Co.K
Richards, James W. TN 19th Inf. Co.K
Richards, James W. TX 37th Cav. Co.K
Richards, James W. VA 9th Cav. Co.E
Richards, James W. VA Lt.Arty. J.S. Brown's Co.
Richards, James W. VA Lt.Arty. Taylor's Co.
Richards, James W. VA 46th Inf. 1st Co.K
Richards, Jasper M. GA 40th Inf. Co.I
Richards, J.B. GA 1st Inf. (St.Guards) Co.A
Richards, J.B. MO Inf. 4th Regt.St.Guard Co.B 1st Lt.
Richards, J.C. GA 2nd Inf. Co.A
Richards, J.C. GA 18th Inf. Co.M
Richards, J.C. GA 19th Inf. Co.I
Richards, J.C. MS 3rd (St.Troops) Cav. Co.H

Richards, J.C.M. TX 11th (Spaight's) Bn.Vol. Co.D
Richards, J.D. AL 4th Cav. Co.F
Richards, J.D. AL Cav. Forrest's Regt.
Richards, J.D. FL Kilcrease Lt.Arty.
Richards, J.D. GA Inf. 14th Bn. (St.Guards) Co.H
Richards, J.D. GA 19th Inf. Co.I
Richards, J.D. TN 18th (Newsom's) Cav. Co.A
Richards, J.E. VA 3rd Inf.Loc.Def. 1st Co.G
Richards, Jehu T. MS 31st Inf. Co.C
Richards, Jeremiah P. KY 5th Mtd.Inf. Co.C Cpl.
Richards, Jesse MO 9th Bn.S.S. Co.C
Richards, Jesse MO 16th Inf. Co.G
Richards, Jessee AR 36th Inf. Co.B
Richards, Jesse H. VA 38th Inf. Co.A
Richards, Jesse N. VA 38th Inf. Co.H
Richards, J.F. MO 9th Bn.S.S. Co.C
Richards, J.F. MO Inf. Clark's Regt. Co.A
Richards, J.F. TN 23rd Inf. Co.E
Richards, J.G. SC 10th Inf. Chap.
Richards, J.G. Gen. & Staff Chap.
Richards, J.H. AL 14th Inf. Co.E
Richards, J.H. KY 5th Cav. Co.F
Richards, J.H. MS 6th Cav. Co.H Capt.
Richards, J.H. MS 31st Inf. Co.C
Richards, J.J. MS Part.Rangers Smyth's Co.
Richards, J.J. AL 18th Inf. Co.B Sgt.
Richards, J.J. AL 25th Inf. Co.E
Richards, J.J. GA Inf. Exempts Roberts' Co.
Richards, J.J. Conf.Cav. Wood's Regt. 2nd Co.M
Richards, J.L. AL 4th Cav.
Richards, J.L. AL Cav. 4th Bn. (Love's) Co.C
Richards, J.M. AL 5th Inf. New Co.A
Richards, J.M. AL 62nd Inf. Co.A
Richards, J.M. GA 28th Inf. Co.F
Richards, J.M. MS Conscr.
Richards, J.M. MS 1st (King's) Inf. (St.Troops) Co.K Sgt.
Richards, J.M. TX Cav. Bourland's Regt. Co.G
Richards, J.M. VA Cav. Mosby's Regt. (Part. Rangers) Co.H
Richards, J.M.D. AL 4th Res. Co.E Sgt.
Richards, J.M.D. TN 50th Inf. Co.C
Richards, J.N. AR 21st Inf. Co.E
Richards, J.N. AR 31st Inf. Co.F Sgt.
Richards, Joel A. AL 14th Inf. Co.I Cpl.
Richards, John AR 8th Cav. Peoples' Co.
Richards, John AR Cav. Gordon's Regt. Co.I
Richards, Jno. AR Cav. Woosley's Bn. Co.A
Richards, John FL 1st (Res.) Inf. Co.E
Richards, John FL 4th Inf. Co.B 2nd Lt.
Richards, John GA Hvy.Arty. 22nd Bn. Co.D
Richards, John GA 9th Inf. (St.Guards) Culp's Co. Cpl.
Richards, John GA 40th Inf. Co.B
Richards, John GA Inf. White's Co. Cpl.
Richards, John LA Inf. 1st Sp.Bn. (Wheat's) New Co.D
Richards, John LA 16th Inf. Co.A Music.
Richards, John LA 17th Inf. Co.G,A Music.
Richards, John MS 6th Cav. Co.K Sgt.
Richards, John MS 11th (Perrin's) Cav. Co.H Cpl.
Richards, John MS 6th Inf. Co.D

Richards, John NC 1st Arty. (10th St.Troops) Co.D
Richards, John SC Inf. Hampton Legion Co.K
Richards, John TN 3rd (Lillard's) Mtd.Inf. 2nd Co.K, Co.H
Richards, John TN 14th Inf. Co.G
Richards, John TN 19th Inf. Co.B
Richards, John TN 29th Inf. Co.K
Richards, John TN 61st Mtd.Inf. Co.C
Richards, John VA Cav. 39th Bn. Co.B
Richards, John VA 4th Res. Co.I
Richards, John A. AL 13th Inf. Co.C
Richards, John A. TN 19th Inf. Co.H Ord.Sgt.
Richards, John A. VA 136th Mil. Co.C Capt.
Richards, John A. 1st Creek Mtd.Vol. 2nd Co.D
Richards, John B. GA 20th Inf. Co.F 1st Lt.
Richards, John B. TX 5th Inf. Co.F Cpl.
Richards, John B. VA 1st Cav. 2nd Co.D
Richards, John C. GA 28th Inf. Co.F
Richards, John C. LA 7th Inf. Co.A
Richards, John C. SC 5th Cav. Co.K Sgt.
Richards, John C. SC 20th Inf. Co.A
Richards, John E. MO Cav. Slayback's Regt. Co.A Sgt.
Richards, John F. AL 20th Inf. Co.K
Richards, John G. FL 2nd Cav. Co.A
Richards, John H. AL 9th (Malone's) Cav. Co.B
Richards, John H. GA 1st Ord.Bn. Co.G
Richards, John H. MO 8th Cav. Co.A,K,B
Richards, John H. MO Inf. 4th Regt.St.Guard Co.B Cpl.
Richards, John H. VA 7th Cav. Co.K
Richards, John J. AL 42nd Inf. Co.E Cpl.
Richards, John L. GA Cobb's Legion Co.A
Richards, John M. NC 22nd Inf. Co.G
Richards, John M. SC 22nd Inf. Co.B
Richards, John N. AR 4th Inf. Co.E
Richards, John N. LA 19th Inf. Co.B
Richards, John O. VA 24th Inf. Co.D
Richards, John P. GA 2nd St.Line Ens.
Richards, John P. GA 30th Inf. Co.K
Richards, John R. AL 25th Inf. Co.E
Richards, John R. VA 51st Mil. Co.G
Richards, John R. VA 56th Inf. Co.H 2nd Lt.
Richards, John S. LA 3rd Inf. Co.H Maj.
Richards, John S. NC 34th Inf. Asst.Surg.
Richards, John S. NC 38th Inf. Asst.Surg.
Richards, John S. Gen. & Staff Asst.Surg.
Richards, John T. GA 36th (Villepigue's) Inf. Co.A
Richards, John T. GA 43rd Inf. Co.D
Richards, John T. 1st Conf.Inf. Co.A
Richards, John W. AL 41st Inf. Co.G
Richards, John W. GA 59th Inf. Co.E
Richards, John W. TX 18th Cav. Co.A
Richards, John Wesley NC 56th Inf. Co.F
Richards, Joseph AL 1st Cav. Co.H
Richards, Joseph GA Arty. 11th Bn. (Sumter Arty.) Old Co.C, Co.B
Richards, Joseph GA 23rd Inf. Co.H
Richards, Joseph LA 19th Inf. Co.K
Richards, Joseph MS 1st Lt.Arty. Co.G
Richards, Joseph SC 20th Inf. Co.A
Richards, Joseph TN 40th Inf. Co.K
Richards, Joseph VA 4th Cav. Co.C
Richards, Joseph VA Lt.Arty. W.H. Chapman's Co.

Richards, Joseph VA 82nd Mil. Co.C
Richards, Joseph B. KY 2nd Mtd.Inf. Co.I
Richards, Joseph F. MO Cav. Snider's Bn. Co.B 2nd Lt.
Richards, Joseph F. MO 9th Inf. Co.B Jr.2nd Lt.
Richards, Joseph I. TN 26th Inf. Co.A
Richards, Joseph I. 3rd Conf.Eng.Troops Co.C
Richards, Joseph N. AL 11th Inf. Co.G
Richards, Joseph R. VA Cav. 35th Bn. Co.F 2nd Lt.
Richards, Joshua I. MS 10th Inf. Old Co.I 2nd Lt.
Richards, Josh. J. MS Part.Rangers Smyth's Co.
Richards, Josiah VA 57th Inf. Co.A
Richards, J.P. TX 20th Inf. Co.G
Richards, J.R. AL Inf. 1st (Loomis') Bn. Co.E
Richards, J.R. AL Cp. of Instr. Talladega
Richards, J.R. GA 22nd Inf. Co.K
Richards, J.R. MO Cav. Williams' Regt. Co.K
Richards, J.R. TN 13th (Gore's) Cav. Co.I
Richards, J.S. LA Inf.Cons.Crescent Regt. Co.G
Richards, J.S. MS 2nd (Davidson's) Inf. Co.K
Richards, J.S. MS 32nd Inf. Co.C
Richards, J.S. VA 1st St.Res. Co.I
Richards, J.S. VA 88th Mil. A.Surg.
Richards, J.S. Gen. & Staff Maj.
Richards, J.T. MS 6th Cav. Co.F
Richards, J.T. MS Inf. 3rd Bn. (St.Troops) Co.F
Richards, J.T. TN 20th Inf. Co.E
Richards, Julius AL 3rd Inf. Co.H
Richards, J.V. LA Mil.Conf.Guards Regt. Co.H 1st Sgt.
Richards, J.V. Forrest's Scouts T. Henderson's Co.,CSA Cpl.
Richards, J.W. AL 18th Inf. Co.B
Richards, J.W. GA 2nd Inf. Co.C
Richards, J.W. GA 19th Inf. Co.I
Richards, J.W. MS 29th Inf. Co.E
Richards, J.W. SC 4th Bn.Res. Co.E
Richards, J.W. SC 9th Res. Co.E
Richards, J.W. TN 2nd (Walker's) Inf. Co.F
Richards, J.W. TX 10th Cav. Co.B
Richards, K.H. TX 11th Inf. Co.H
Richards, King D. VA 57th Inf. Co.A
Richards, L.A. VA 48th Inf. Co.B
Richards, Lafayette TN 21st Cav.
Richards, Latanious A. LA 1st Cav. Co.D
Richards, L.B. MS 4th Inf. Co.A
Richards, L.D.S. TN 26th Inf. Co.K
Richards, L.E. TX 7th Cav. Co.I
Richards, Levi SC 22nd Inf. Co.B
Richards, Lewis VA Cav. 35th Bn. Co.A
Richards, Lewis E. VA 40th Inf. Co.B
Richards, Littleton B. MS 31st Inf. Co.I
Richards, Louis SC 1st Arty. Co.B
Richards, Louis SC 1st Arty. Co.I
Richards, Louis SC 1st (Butler's) Inf. Co.F
Richards, M. LA Washington Arty.Bn. Co.2,4
Richards, M. LA 17th Inf. Co.G Music.
Richards, Major NC 43rd Inf. Co.D
Richards, Martin AR Brown's Btty.
Richards, Mat MS 29th Inf. Co.D
Richards, Maurins LA 26th Inf. Co.E
Richards, Mike LA 16th Inf. Co.A Music.
Richards, Milas G. MO 8th Cav. Co.K,B
Richards, Milton V. GA 21st Inf. Co.D Cpl.

Richards, Moses VA 23rd Cav. Co.I
Richards, Moses V. MS 20th Inf. Co.E
Richards, Nelson VA 19th Cav. Co.A
Richards, Newton TN 39th Mtd.Inf. Co.G
Richards, Newton TN Conscr. (Cp. of Instr.)
Co.B
Richards, Noal A. MS 20th Inf. Co.E
Richards, O. LA Mil. LaFourche Regt.
Richards, O.D. TX 14th Inf. Co.E
Richards, P.A. MS 4th Cav. Co.I
Richards, P.D. LA Mil.Conf.Guards Regt. Co.I
1st Sgt.
Richards, Peter AL 8th Inf. Co.E
Richards, P.H. TX 10th Field Btty.
Richards, Pleasant MO 4th Cav. Co.I
Richards, P.M. MO Lt.Arty. 3rd Field Btty.
Richards, Powhatan VA 21st Cav. 2nd Co.G
Richards, Powhatan VA 57th Inf. Co.G Cpl.
Richards, Quintus VA 9th Cav. Co.E
Richards, R. GA Inf. 1st City Bn. (Columbus)
Co.C
Richards, R.A. TX 17th Cons.Dismtd.Cav. Co.B
Cpl.
Richards, R.A. TX 25th Cav. Co.G
Richards, Raleigh FL Milton Lt.Arty. Dunham's
Co.
Richards, Ralph AL 1st Bn.Cadets Co.A,B
Richards, Randle NC Inf. 2nd Bn. Co.G
Richards, R.C. AL Cav. Forrest's Regt.
Richards, R.C. MS 2nd (Davidson's) Inf. Potts'
Co.
Richards, R.C. TN 18th (Newsom's) Cav. Co.A
Richards, R.C. VA 10th Inf. Co.L
Richards, Reuben TX 26th Cav. Co.I
Richards, Reuben MS 9th Inf. New Co.H Jr.2nd
Lt.
Richards, Reuben MS 10th Inf. Old Co.I
Richards, R.H. GA Boddie's Co. (Troup
Cty.Ind.Cav.)
Richards, R.H. MO Inf. 5th Regt.St.Guard Co.D
Richards, R.H. TN 18th Inf. Co.A
Richards, Richard VA 13th Inf. Co.A
Richards, R.J. FL Cav. 5th Bn. Co.I
Richards, R.L. VA 13th Inf. Co.F
Richards, R.M. MS 4th Inf. Co.A
Richards, R.M. TX 28th Cav. Co.D
Richards, Robert GA Lt.Arty. (Jackson Arty.)
Massenburg's Btty.
Richards, Robert GA 20th Inf. Co.A
Richards, Robert GA Inf. Pool's Co. Sgt.
Richards, Robert TX 19th Cav. Co.K
Richards, Robert VA Lt.Arty. Fry's Co.
Richards, Robert VA 42nd Inf. Co.B
Richards, Robert VA 46th Inf. 1st Co.K
Richards, Robert B. GA 13th Cav.
Richards, Robert C. VA 41st Mil. Co.B
Richards, Robert D. AL 63rd Inf. Co.D Cpl.
Richards, Robert E. AR 3rd Inf. Co.D
Richards, Robert J. AL 54th & 57th Inf. Co.B
Sgt.
Richards, Robert L. GA 7th Inf. Co.F Sgt.
Richards, Robert M. AL 49th Inf. Co.H
Richards, Robert W.R. TX 13th Cav. Co.B
Richards, Roscoe NC 27th Inf. Co.G Sgt.
Richards, R.R. GA 1st (Olmstead's) Inf. Stiles'
Co.
Richards, R.R. GA Inf. 1st Conf.Bn. Co.C Sgt.

Richards, R.R. GA Inf. 14th Bn. (St.Guards)
Co.B Sgt.
Richards, R.R. GA Inf. 18th Bn. Co.B
Richards, R.S. AL 14th Inf. Co.K Lt.
Richards, R.S. LA 5th Cav. Co.I
Richards, R.S. LA 2nd Inf. Co.K Sgt.
Richards, R.S. TN 50th Inf. Co.C
Richards, R.T. VA 9th Cav. Co.E
Richards, Rudolph GA 63rd Inf. Co.D
Richards, Rudolph R. GA Hvy.Arty. 22nd Bn.
Co.C 1st Sgt.
Richards, Rufus M. MS 31st Inf. Co.I
Richards, Rufus S. LA 28th (Gray's) Inf. Co.I
Capt.
Richards, R.W. GA 13th Cav. Co.C 2nd Lt.
Richards, R.W. GA 66th Inf. Co.H
Richards, S. AL 1st Regt. Mobile Vol. Baas' Co.
Richards, S. AL 9th Inf. Co.D
Richards, S. MS 9th Cav. Co.A 2nd Lt.
Richards, S. TX Cav. 1st Bn.St.Troops Co.A
Richards, S. TX 5th Cav. Co.I
Richards, S. TX 17th Cons.Dismtd.Cav. Co.G
Richards, S. TX Cav. Ragsdale's Bn. Co.B
Richards, S. VA 57th Inf. Co.A
Richards, Samuel AR 8th Inf. New Co.C
Richards, Samuel AR 32nd Inf. Co.H 2nd Lt.
Richards, Samuel B. VA 1st Cav. Co.H
Richards, Samuel J. FL 6th Inf. Co.C
Richards, Samuel L. TX 8th Cav. Co.A
Richards, Samuel R. VA 42nd Inf. Co.B
Richards, S.B. Carson AL 36th Inf. Co.B
Richards, S.C. AL 26th (O'Neal's) Inf. Co.I
Sgt.
Richards, S.F. AL 46th Inf. Co.K
Richards, S.G. MO 16th Inf. Co.I
Richards, Sidney NC 24th Inf. Co.K Cpl.
Richards, Simeon MS Cav. 17th Bn. Co.A Lt.
Richards, Sirenius C. AL 10th Cav.
Richards, S.M. TX 28th Cav. Co.H
Richards, Smith NC 35th Inf. Co.B Sgt.
Richards, S.P. GA 3rd Bn. (St.Guards) Co.H
Richards, S.P. GA Inf. Exempts Roberts' Co.
Richards, S.R. TN Inf. 3rd Cons.Regt. Co.A
Richards, S.R. TN Inf. 154th Sr.Regt. Co.A
Richards, Stephen TN 35th Inf. Co.H 2nd Lt.
Richards, Stratford H. TX 18th Cav. Co.A
Jr.2nd Lt.
Richards, T. KY 3rd Cav. Co.I
Richards, T. LA Mil. LaFourche Regt.
Richards, T.A. AR 15th (Johnson's) Inf. Co.E
Richards, T.D. AL Cav. 4th Bn. (Love's) Co.C
Richards, T.D. TX 24th & 25th Cav. (Cons.)
Co.F
Richards, T.H. GA 19th Inf. Co.F
Richards, Theodule V. LA 7th Cav. Co.H
Richards, Thomas AL 48th Inf. Co.I
Richards, Thomas KY 1st (Butler's) Cav. Co.D
Ch.Bugler
Richards, Thomas MO Inf. 4th Regt.St.Guard
Co.C
Richards, Thomas NC 26th Inf. Co.B
Richards, Thomas SC 1st Inf. Co.E
Richards, Thomas TN 14th (Neely's) Cav. Co.F
Richards, Thomas TN 2nd (Robison's) Inf. Co.D
Richards, Thomas VA 1st Bn.Res. Co.H
Richards, Thomas VA 34th Inf. Fray's Co.,
Co.D

Richards, Thomas A. AL 42nd Inf. Co.E
Richards, Thomas B. AL 37th Inf. Co.H Capt.
Richards, Thomas D. AR Cav. Wright's Regt.
Co.D
Richards, Thomas Didimus TX 24th Cav. Co.H
Richards, Thomas E. AL Inf. 1st Regt. Co.A
Richards, Thomas J. AL 1st Regt.Conscr. Co.E
Richards, Thos. J. AL 15th Inf. Co.E
Richards, Thomas J. AL 21st Inf. Co.G
Richards, Thomas J. AL 39th Inf. Co.D
Richards, Thomas J. AL Conscr. Echols' Co.
Richards, Thomas J. MS Lt.Arty. (Madison
Lt.Arty.) Richards' Co. Capt.
Richards, Thomas J. MS 10th Inf. Old Co.I
Music.
Richards, Thomas P. GA 1st Reg. Co.B
Richards, Thomas P. VA 21st Cav. Co.K
Richards, Thomas S. AL 6th Cav. Co.L Capt.
Richards, Thomas S. GA Carlton's Co. (Troup
Cty.Arty.)
Richards, Thomas W. AL Cav. 4th Bn. (Love's)
Co.B
Richards, Thomas W. MS 9th Bn.S.S. Co.C
Capt.
Richards, Thomas W. MS 10th Inf. Old Co.K
Capt.
Richards, Tilmond B. NC 22nd Inf. Co.A
Richards, Titus GA Phillips' Legion Co.A
Richards, Titus VA 9th Cav. Co.E
Richards, T.J. MS 24th Inf. Co.F
Richards, T.L. MO 9th Inf. Co.B
Richards, T.L. TN 13th Inf. Co.B Cpl.
Richards, T.M. TN 21st (Wilson's) Cav. Co.A
Cpl.
Richards, T.M. TX 28th Cav. Co.H
Richards, T.S. AL 6th Inf. Co.L Capt.
Richards, T.W. LA 28th (Thomas') Inf. Co.D
1st Sgt.
Richards, T.W. MS 9th Inf. Co.D Capt.
Richards, T.W. VA 1st Cav. Co.N
Richards, T.W. VA Cav. Mosby's Regt.
(Part.Rangers) Co.A
Richards, V. GA Inf. 1st Loc.Troops (Augusta)
Co.K
Richards, Valsin LA 22nd (Cons.) Inf. Co.G
Richards, Vernon GA 1st (Symons') Res. Co.K
Richards, Vernon GA Inf. 18th Bn. (St.Guards)
Co.C
Richards, Victor LA 7th Cav. Co.H
Richards, W. TN 42nd Inf. Co.C
Richards, W. TX Cav. 3rd (Yager's) Bn. Co.D
Richards, W. 4th Conf.Inf. Co.H
Richards, Walter TN 3rd (Forrest's) Cav. Co.A
Richards, Walter TN 3rd (Lillard's) Mtd.Inf.
Co.A
Richards, W.B. MS 35th Inf. Co.H Sgt.
Richards, W.B. TX 18th Cav. Co.B
Richards, W.B.B. GA Inf. (Collier Guards) Col-
lier's Co.
Richards, W.B.B. GA Inf. Jackson's Co.
Richards, W.C. AR 1st (Monroe's) Cav. Co.D
Richards, W.C. GA Hvy.Arty. 22nd Bn. Co.F
Richards, W.C. LA Mil.Cont.Regt. Kirk's Co.
Richards, W.C. MS 9th Inf. Col.
Richards, W.C. MS 9th Bn.S.S. Maj.
Richards, W.C. MS 10th Inf. Old Co.D 1st Lt.
Richards, W.C.B. TX 8th Cav. Co.A

Richards, W.E. TX 12th Cav. Co.B
Richards, Wesley W. AL 6th Inf. Co.B,K
Richards, W.F. TX 10th Cav. Co.G
Richards, W.G. AL 26th (O'Neal's) Inf. Co.I
   Sgt.
Richards, W.G. AR 15th (Johnson's) Inf. Co.E
   Cpl.
Richards, W.G. GA 3rd Bn. (St.Guards) Co.E
Richards, W.G. GA 56th Inf. Co.D Cpl.
Richards, W.H. AL 20th Inf. Co.B
Richards, W.H. LA Inf.Crescent Regt. Co.E
Richards, W.H. TN Inf. 154th Sr.Regt. Co.A
Richards, White TX Cav. Martin's Regt. Co.D
Richards, Wiley W. TN 39th Mtd.Inf. Co.G
Richards, Willard MS Inf. 2nd St.Troops Co.F
   1st Cpl.
Richards, William AL 2nd Cav. Co.B Cpl.
Richards, William AL Cav. Forrest's Regt.
Richards, William AL 1st Regt.Conscr. Co.K
Richards, William AL 12th Inf. Co.I
Richards, William AL 46th Inf. Co.H
Richards, William AR 7th Cav. Co.G
Richards, William AR Lt.Arty. Marshall's Btty.
Richards, William AR 15th Mil. Co.B
Richards, William GA 43rd Inf. Co.C
Richards, William MS Lt.Arty. (Madison
   Lt.Arty.) Richards' Co.
Richards, William MS 2nd (Davidson's) Inf.
   Potts' Co.
Richards, William MO 8th Cav. Co.A
Richards, William MO Inf. 4th Regt.St.Guard
   Co.E
Richards, William NC 4th Cav. (59th St.Troops)
   Co.E
Richards, William TN 1st (Carter's) Cav. Co.M
Richards, William TN 7th (Duckworth's) Cav.
   Co.F
Richards, William TN Cav. 9th Bn. (Gantt's)
   Co.C
Richards, William TN 18th (Newsom's) Cav.
   Co.A
Richards, William TN 19th & 20th (Cons.) Cav.
   Co.A
Richards, William TN 51st Inf. Co.F
Richards, William TN 55th (McKoin's) Inf. Co.C
Richards, William TX 22nd Cav. Co.E
Richards, William TX 31st Cav. Co.B
Richards, William VA 19th Cav. Co.B
Richards, William VA 23rd Cav. Co.I
Richards, William VA Inf. 2nd Bn.Loc.Def.
   Co.D
Richards, William VA 24th Inf. Co.A
Richards, William VA 33rd Inf. Co.H
Richards, William VA 36th Inf. 1st Co.C, 2nd
   Co.D
Richards, William VA 54th Inf. Co.A
Richards, William A. AL 37th Inf. Co.H
Richards, William A. GA Phillips' Legion Co.A
Richards, William A. VA 1st Bn.Res. Co.H,A
Richards, William A. VA 34th Inf. Fray's Co.,
   Co.D
Richards, William Anthony VA 10th Cav. Co.C
Richards, William B. FL 5th Inf. Co.G Sgt.
Richards, William B. GA Inf. 3rd Bn. Co.C Sgt.
Richards, William B. GA 8th Inf. (St.Guards)
   Co.I

Richards, William B. GA Inf. 25th Bn. (Prov.
   Guard) Co.C 2nd Lt.
Richards, William B. GA 30th Inf. Co.K Capt.
Richards, William B. GA 36th (Broyles') Inf.
   Co.E 1st Lt.
Richards, William B. VA 17th Inf. Co.B 2nd Lt.
Richards, Wm. B. Gen. & Staff Maj.,QM
Richards, William C. GA 12th Inf. Co.H
Richards, William C. GA 42nd Inf. Co.B
Richards, William C. GA 45th Inf. Co.A
Richards, William Draden MS 8th Cav. Co.A
Richards, William E. VA 6th Inf. 2nd Co.E
Richards, William F. GA Arty. 11th Bn. (Sumter
   Arty.) Co.A
Richards, William F. NC 24th Inf. Co.D Cpl.
Richards, William F. TX 8th Cav. Co.A 1st Sgt.
Richards, William H. AL Cav. 4th Bn. (Love's)
   Co.B
Richards, William H. LA Washington Arty.Bn.
   Co.5
Richards, William H. NC 12th Inf. Co.G
Richards, William J. MS 42nd Inf. Co.D
Richards, William L. TN 13th (Gore's) Cav.
   Co.B
Richards, William Lawrence TX 24th Cav. Co.H
Richards, William M. NC 61st Inf. Co.B Sgt.
Richards, William N. FL 6th Inf. Co.C
Richards, William N. VA 10th Inf. Co.L
Richards, William S. TN 55th (McKoin's) Inf.
   Dillehay's Co.
Richards, William T. GA 24th Inf. Co.E
Richards, William T. VA 21st Cav. Co.F, 2nd
   Co.C
Richards, William W. VA Lt.Arty. Motley's Co.
Richards, William W. VA 38th Inf. Co.A
Richards, Williard MS 5th Inf. (St.Troops) Co.H
Richards, Willis Tiberius TX 20th Cav. Co.A
Richards, W.M. AL 5th Cav. Co.B
Richards, W.M. GA 19th Inf. Co.I
Richards, W.M. TX Cav. Martin's Regt. Co.G
   2nd Lt.
Richards, W.N. AL 18th Inf. Co.B
Richards, W.N. VA 82nd Mil. Co.D
Richards, W.P. GA 2nd Inf. Co.A
Richards, W.S. LA Mil. Orleans Guards Regt.
   Co.F
Richards, W.S. TN 44th (Cons.) Inf. Co.C
Richards, W.T. LA Mil.Conf.Guards Regt. Co.G
   2nd Lt.
Richards, W.T., Jr. LA Inf.Crescent Regt. Co.A
Richards, W.T. Exch.Bn. 3rd Co.B,CSA
Richards, W.W. AL Cav. Forrest's Regt.
Richards, W.W. AL Mil. 2nd Regt.Vol. Co.E
Richards, W.W. AL 15th Inf. Co.F
Richards, W.W. AL 21st Inf. Co.K
Richards, W.W. TN 18th (Newsom's) Cav. Co.H
Richards, W.W. TN 51st (Cons.) Inf. Co.F
Richardsen, G.T. VA 4th Cav. & Inf.St.Line 1st
   Co.I Cpl.
Richardson, --- KY 7th Cav. Co.G
Richardson, --- SC 27th Inf. Co.H
Richardson, --- TX 24th & 25th Cav. (Cons.)
   Co.F
Richardson, --- TX 24th & 25th Cav. (Cons.)
   Co.H
Richardson, --- TX Cav. Border's Regt. Co.B
Richardson, A. AR 1st Cav. Co.C

Richardson, A. GA Inf. 2nd Bn. (St.Guards) Old
   Co.D
Richardson, A. GA 47th Inf. Co.K
Richardson, A. MS Inf. 1st Bn. Ray's Co.
Richardson, A. MS 3rd Inf. Co.K
Richardson, A. NC 1st Bn.Jr.Res. Co.D
Richardson, A. TX 17th Cons.Dismtd.Cav. Co.A
Richardson, A. TX 21st Inf. Co.A Sgt.
Richardson, A. TX 21st Inf. Co.H
Richardson, Aaron K. GA 35th Inf. Co.H Capt.
Richardson, Abel GA 11th Inf. Co.G
Richardson, Abner VA 1st St.Res. Co.C Sgt.
Richardson, Abner VA 42nd Inf. Co.F
Richardson, Abner VA 63rd Inf. Co.C
Richardson, Abner 1st Chickasaw Inf. Gregg's
   Co.
Richardson, Abram TX 31st Cav. Co.B
Richardson, A.C. LA 9th Inf. 1st Lt.
Richardson, A.C. TX 3rd Cav. Co.B
Richardson, A.C. TX 18th Inf. Co.G Sgt.
Richardson, A.C. TX Inf.Riflemen Arnold's Co.
Richardson, A.C. VA Lt.Arty. 1st Bn. Co.B
Richardson, A.C. VA Arty. Richardson's Co.
Richardson, A.D. SC 7th Cav. Co.I
Richardson, A.D. SC 9th Inf. Co.F
Richardson, A.D. SC 21st Inf. Co.D
Richardson, A.D. SC Cav.Bn. Holcombe Legion
   Co.A
Richardson, A.D. Gen. & Staff Surg.
Richardson, Adcock TX 11th (Spaight's) Bn.Vol.
   Co.E
Richardson, A.F. MS 46th Inf. Co.K Sgt.
Richardson, A.F. TX 1st Inf. Co.D
Richardson, A.F. VA 59th Inf. 2nd Co.F Cpl.
Richardson, A.G. TX 29th Cav. Co.C
Richardson, A.H. VA Lt.Arty. 1st Bn. Co.B
Richardson, A.H. VA Arty. Richardson's Co.
Richardson, A.H.A. AL 14th Inf. Co.B
Richardson, A.I. AL Conscr.
Richardson, A.J. NC 3rd Arty. (40th St.Troops)
   Co.H
Richardson, A.J. NC Lt.Arty. 13th Bn. Co.F
Richardson, A.J. SC 6th Cav. Co.I
Richardson, A.J. SC 10th Inf. Co.A
Richardson, A.J. TN Inf. 2nd Cons.Regt. Co.C
Richardson, A.J. TN 3rd (Clack's) Inf. Co.K
Richardson, A.J. TN 11th Inf. Co.E
Richardson, A.J. VA Mtd.Guard 4th Congr.Dist.
Richardson, A.K. GA 8th Inf. (St.Guards) Co.G
   Capt.
Richardson, A.K. GA 18th Inf. Co.B
Richardson, A.L. GA 3rd Cav. Co.E
Richardson, Albert KY 4th Mtd.Inf. Co.K
Richardson, Albert LA 5th Inf. New Co.A 2nd
   Lt.
Richardson, Alexander AL Lt.Arty. 2nd Bn.
   Co.B Cpl.
Richardson, Alexander AL 36th Inf. Co.A
Richardson, Alexander GA 36th (Broyles') Inf.
   Co.K
Richardson, Alexander MD 1st Cav.
Richardson, Alex. MD 1st Inf.
Richardson, Alexander SC Hvy.Arty. 15th
   (Lucas') Bn. Co.B
Richardson, Alexander TX 10th Inf. Co.B
Richardson, Alexander H. NC 44th Inf. Co.H
Richardson, Alexander H. NC 52nd Inf. Co.E

Richardson, Alexander H. VA 1st Arty. Co.B
Richardson, Alexander H. VA 32nd Inf. 1st
 Co.H
Richardson, Alfred KY 10th (Johnson's) Cav.
 New Co.F Capt.
Richardson, Alfred NC 2nd Jr.Res. Co.H
Richardson, Alfred VA 38th Inf. Co.C
Richardson, Alfred J. MS 11th (Perrin's) Cav.
 Co.D
Richardson, Alfred V. NC 45th Inf. Co.E
Richardson, Allen MS 23rd Inf. Co.K
Richardson, Allen NC Inf. 2nd Bn. Co.F Sgt.
Richardson, Allen NC 34th Inf. Co.A
Richardson, Allen E. GA 46th Inf. Co.E
Richardson, Allen H. NC 48th Inf. Co.F
Richardson, Alonzo AL 4th Inf. Co.B
Richardson, Alphonso NC 5th Cav. (63rd
 St.Troops) Co.E Artif.
Richardson, Alvin NC 37th Inf. Co.K
Richardson, A.M. NC Cav. 16th Bn. Co.E
Richardson, A.M. TX Home Guards Killough's
 Co.
Richardson, A.M. VA Lt.Arty. R.M. Anderson's
 Co.
Richardson, A.M. VA 3rd Inf.Loc.Def. Co.K
Richardson, A.M. 7th Conf.Cav. Co.M
Richardson, Amatus M. NC 4th Inf. Co.H
Richardson, Amos MS 14th (Cons.) Inf. Co.G
Richardson, Amos MS 43rd Inf. Co.A
Richardson, Amos NC 4th Cav. (59th St.Troops)
 Co.A
Richardson, Amos TX 6th Cav. Co.B 2nd Lt.
Richardson, Amos TX 11th (Spaight's) Bn.Vol.
 Co.A Sgt.
Richardson, Amos VA Inf. 44th Bn.
Richardson, Amos N. NC 44th Inf. Co.E
Richardson, Ande MS 11th (Perrin's) Cav. Co.B
Richardson, Andrew TX 11th (Spaight's) Bn.Vol.
 Co.D
Richardson, Andrew VA Cav. Mosby's Regt.
 (Part.Rangers) Co.C
Richardson, Andrew VA 22nd Inf. Co.K
Richardson, Andrew VA 26th Inf. Co.C
Richardson, Andrew J. GA 30th Inf. Co.D
Richardson, Andrew J. MO 10th Inf. Co.D
Richardson, Andrew J. SC 10th Inf. Co.F Cpl.
Richardson, Andrew J. VA 23rd Inf. Co.A Maj.
Richardson, Andrew P. VA Inf. Tomlin's Bn.
 Co.A
Richardson, Anson MO Cav. 1st Regt.St.Guard
 Co.A
Richardson, A.O. TX 4th Cav. Co.I
Richardson, A.O. TX 1st Hvy.Arty. Co.D
Richardson, A.P. AL 31st Inf. Co.C,B
Richardson, Applewhite NC 24th Inf. Co.C Cpl.
Richardson, Applewhite, Jr. NC 24th Inf. Co.C
Richardson, A.R. SC 1st Mtd.Mil. Smart's Co.
Richardson, A.R. SC 5th Cav. Co.B Sgt.
Richardson, A.R. SC Cav. 17th Bn. Co.C Sgt.
Richardson, Arch TX 11th (Spaight's) Bn.Vol.
 Co.D
Richardson, Archer C. VA 1st Arty. Co.B
Richardson, Armistead TX 17th Cav. Co.H
Richardson, Armstead FL 5th Inf. Co.A
Richardson, Arney SC Arty. Gregg's Co.
 (McQueen Lt.Arty.)

Richardson, Arney SC Arty. Manigault's Bn. 1st
 Co.C
Richardson, Arthur AL 41st Inf. Co.B
Richardson, A.S. VA 24th Cav. Co.H Cpl.
Richardson, A.S. VA 47th Inf.
Richardson, A.S. Gen. & Staff 1st Lt.,Dr.Off.
Richardson, Asbery H. AR 33rd Inf. Co.G
Richardson, Atwell S. VA 28th Inf. Co.K
Richardson, Augustine VA 53rd Inf. Co.B 1st
 Sgt.
Richardson, Augustus AL Cav. 4th Bn. (Love's)
 Co.A
Richardson, Auley NC 3rd Inf. Co.E
Richardson, A.W. AL 2nd Cav. Co.D
Richardson, A.W. AL 3rd Inf. Co.F
Richardson, A.W. AR 35th Inf. Co.I
Richardson, A.W. GA 8th Cav. Old Co.I
Richardson, A.W. GA 62nd Cav. Co.I
Richardson, A.W. SC 2nd Arty. Co.H
Richardson, A.W. TN 8th Inf. Co.F 2nd Lt.
Richardson, B. FL 2nd Cav. Co.H
Richardson, B. GA 5th Inf. Co.C
Richardson, B. MO 2nd Cav. Co.E
Richardson, B. MO Inf. Perkins' Bn. Co.B
Richardson, B. NC 8th Sr.Res. Kelly's Co.
Richardson, B. TX 11th (Spaight's) Bn.Vol.
 Co.D
Richardson, B. Bradford's Corps Scouts & Guards
 Co.A
Richardson, B.A. TN 19th (Biffle's) Cav. Co.B
Richardson, Bailey VA 61st Mil. Co.G
Richardson, Balaam AR Cav. Harrell's Bn. Co.B
Richardson, Bardin MS Inf. 3rd Bn. (St.Troops)
 Co.D
Richardson, Baylis GA 35th Inf. Co.E
Richardson, Benjamin VA 23rd Cav. Co.M
Richardson, Benjamin VA 61st Inf. Co.D
Richardson, Benjamin A. VA Arty. Kevill's Co.
Richardson, Benjamin C. VA 14th Inf. Co.C
Richardson, Benjamin E. VA 57th Inf. Co.F
Richardson, Benjamin F. MS 2nd Inf. Co.E 3rd
 Lt.
Richardson, Benjamin F. MS 8th Inf. Co.E
Richardson, Benjamin F. VA Lt.Arty. Pegram's
 Co.
Richardson, Benjamin F. VA 41st Inf. Co.A
Richardson, Benjamin M. LA 28th (Gray's) Inf.
 Co.B
Richardson, Benjamin W. VA 1st St.Res. Co.E
 Maj.
Richardson, Benjamin W. VA 12th Inf. Branch's
 Co.
Richardson, Benjamin W. VA 16th Inf. Co.K
Richardson, Berry TN 42nd Inf. Co.A
Richardson, Berry 4th Conf.Inf. Co.G
Richardson, B.F. AR Inf. Cocke's Regt. Co.K,F
Richardson, B.F. SC Palmetto S.S. Co.D
Richardson, B.F. TN 39th Mtd.Inf. Co.K
Richardson, B.F. VA 2nd Arty. Co.H
Richardson, B.F. VA 15th Inf. Co.A
Richardson, B.F. VA Inf. 22nd Bn. Co.H
Richardson, B.G. MS 3rd Inf. Co.B
Richardson, Bird VA 54th Inf. Co.I
Richardson, B.J. TX Inf. 1st St.Troops Sheldon's
 Co.
Richardson, B.L. GA Phillips' Legion Co.B

Richardson, Bonner Conf.Cav. Wood's Regt.
 Co.K
Richardson, Booker VA 54th Inf. Co.F
Richardson, Bowling VA 15th Inf. Co.I
Richardson, B.P. TN 50th Inf. Co.B
Richardson, Briant AL 55th Vol. Co.B,K
Richardson, Brinkley F. NC 48th Inf. Co.F
 Capt.
Richardson, Brinkly J. NC 26th Inf. Co.B Sgt.
Richardson, Brl. LA 4th Inf. Old Co.G
Richardson, Bryant AL 36th Inf. Co.A
Richardson, Bryant AL Arty. 4th Bn. Hilliard's
 Legion Co.B
Richardson, Bryant H. NC 24th Inf. Co.C
Richardson, Bryant W. AL 27th Inf. Co.C
Richardson, B.T. AL 37th Inf. Co.G
Richardson, Burrell LA 3rd (Wingfield's) Cav.
 Co.E
Richardson, B.W. TN 11th Inf. Co.K
Richardson, C. GA 17th Inf. Co.C
Richardson, C. NC 1st Inf. Co.I
Richardson, C. NC 1st Bn.Jr.Res. Co.D
Richardson, C. TN 14th Inf. Co.E
Richardson, C. TX Conscr.
Richardson, Caleb NC 22nd Inf. Co.F
Richardson, Canady NC 26th Inf. Co.A
Richardson, Carroll TN 13th (Gore's) Cav. Co.A
Richardson, Carter KY 7th Mtd.Inf. Co.F
Richardson, C.B. GA 1st (Olmstead's) Inf. Stiles'
 Co.
Richardson, C.B. GA Inf. 18th Bn. Co.B
Richardson, C.B. MS Lt.Arty. (Jefferson Arty.)
 Darden's Co. 2nd Lt.
Richardson, C.C. MS Hall's Co.
Richardson, C.C. VA Lt.Arty. Hankins' Co.
Richardson, C.E. MS 10th Inf. New Co.B, Co.O
Richardson, C.E. SC 23rd Inf. Asst.Surg.
Richardson, C.H. GA 6th Inf. Co.C 1st Lt.
Richardson, C.H. VA 5th Cav. Co.H
Richardson, Charles MO Cav. Poindexter's Regt.
 Co.G
Richardson, Charles SC 1st (Butler's) Inf. Co.I
 Music.
Richardson, Charles TX 8th Inf. Co.C,D 1st
 Sgt.
Richardson, Charles VA Hvy.Arty. 10th Bn.
 Co.A
Richardson, Charles VA 1st St.Res. Co.C
Richardson, Charles VA Inf. 2nd Bn.Loc.Def.
 Co.B
Richardson, Charles VA 53rd Inf. Co.F
Richardson, Charles VA 58th Inf. Co.D
Richardson, Charles Conf.Lt.Arty. Richardson's
 Bn. Lt.Col.
Richardson, Charles Conf.Reg.Inf. Brooks' Bn.
 Co.B
Richardson, Charles A. VA 15th Inf. Co.B
Richardson, Charles B. VA 26th Inf. Co.K
Richardson, Charles E. NC 52nd Inf. Co.C Sgt.
Richardson, Charles E.H. VA 9th Inf. Co.K
Richardson, Charles F. VA Lt.Arty. Armistead's
 Co.
Richardson, Charles F. VA 61st Mil. Co.E
Richardson, Charles H. GA 57th Inf. Co.E Capt.
Richardson, Charles M. SC 5th Cav. Co.H
Richardson, Charles P. SC Inf. Hampton Legion
 Co.D

Richardson, Charles R. VA Lt.Arty. Sturdivant's Co.

Richardson, Charles R. VA 18th Inf. Co.F

Richardson, Charles S. TN 48th (Voorhies') Inf. Co.H Sgt.

Richardson, Charles T. VA Lt.Arty. Douthat's Co.

Richardson, Charles T. VA 28th Inf. Co.H,A Asst.Surg.

Richardson, Chas. T. Gen. & Staff Asst.Surg.

Richardson, Charles W. LA 1st Cav. Co.E

Richardson, Charles W. LA 1st Hvy.Arty. (Reg.) Co.F

Richardson, Charles W. VA 7th Cav. Co.E

Richardson, Charles W. VA 17th Inf. Co.B

Richardson, Chester A. LA 16th Inf. Co.D

Richardson, Christopher KY 10th (Diamond's) Cav. Co.G

Richardson, Clement L. NC 4th Cav. (59th St.Troops) Co.A 1st Sgt.

Richardson, Clem L. NC 23rd Inf. Co.A Sgt.

Richardson, Clinton VA 28th Inf. Co.D

Richardson, Clinton C. VA 2nd Cav. Co.A

Richardson, C.M. GA Cav. (St.Guards) Bond's Co.

Richardson, C.O. SC Arty. Fickling's Co. (Brooks Lt.Arty.)

Richardson, C.O. SC 2nd Inf. Co.K

Richardson, Colas VA 3rd Cav. Co.F

Richardson, Columbus NC 4th Sr.Res. Co.A

Richardson, Cornelius H. VA 32nd Inf. Co.C

Richardson, Cornelius J. NC 1st Jr.Res. Co.D Capt.

Richardson, C.P. SC Palmetto S.S. Co.I

Richardson, C.S. GA 6th Inf. Surg.

Richardson, C.S. Gen. & Staff Asst.Surg.

Richardson, C.T. GA 8th Cav. Old Co.I

Richardson, C.T. GA 62nd Cav. Co.I

Richardson, C.T. MS 35th Inf. Co.I

Richardson, C.T. NC Mil. Clark's Sp.Bn. Co.D 3rd Cpl.

Richardson, C.W. GA 2nd Inf. Co.K

Richardson, C.W. KY Morehead's Regt. (Part. Rangers) Co.A

Richardson, C.Y. SC Mil. 1st Regt. (Charleston Res.) Co.I 2nd Lt.

Richardson, D. FL Lt.Arty. Dyke's Co.

Richardson, D. FL 2nd Inf. Co.D

Richardson, D. GA Arty. Lumpkin's Co.

Richardson, D. GA 32nd Inf. Co.D Cpl.

Richardson, D. KY 7th Cav. Co.C

Richardson, D. SC 2nd Inf. Co.K

Richardson, D. TN 12th (Cons.) Inf. Co.G

Richardson, D.A. NC 3rd Inf. Co.C

Richardson, D.A. VA 12th Inf. Co.G

Richardson, Dan Gen. & Staff Capt.,QM

Richardson, Daniel AL 9th (Malone's) Cav. Co.E

Richardson, Daniel AR 1st (Colquitt's) Inf. Co.H

Richardson, Daniel KY Cav. 2nd Bn. (Dortch's) Co.B

Richardson, Daniel KY 3rd Cav. Co.K

Richardson, Daniel NC 61st Inf. Co.I

Richardson, Daniel SC 7th Cav. Co.A

Richardson, Daniel SC Cav. Tucker's Co.

Richardson, Daniel TN 47th Inf. Co.D Cpl.

Richardson, Daniel D. GA 38th Inf. Co.K

Richardson, Daniel K. VA 3rd Cav. Co.G

Richardson, Daniel P. AR 33rd Inf. Co.F Sgt.

Richardson, David AL 11th Cav. Co.G

Richardson, David AL 3rd Res. Co.H

Richardson, David GA 3rd Bn.S.S. Co.F

Richardson, David GA 9th Inf. (St.Guards) Co.G

Richardson, David GA 64th Inf. Co.H

Richardson, David GA Phillips' Legion Co.B

Richardson, David NC 34th Inf. Co.K

Richardson, David NC 48th Inf. Co.D

Richardson, David NC 61st Inf. Co.I

Richardson, David SC 3rd Inf. Co.C

Richardson, David TN 13th (Gore's) Cav. Co.B

Richardson, David VA 1st St.Res. Co.F

Richardson, David VA 2nd Inf.Loc.Def. Co.C Sgt.

Richardson, David VA Inf. 2nd Bn.Loc.Def. Co.E Sgt.

Richardson, David VA 36th Inf. Co.A

Richardson, David B. TN 48th (Voorhies') Inf. Co.F

Richardson, David C. GA Siege Arty. 28th Bn. Co.C

Richardson, David C. LA 2nd Inf. Co.F

Richardson, David C. VA Lt.Arty. Parker's Co. Cpl.

Richardson, David G.W. SC 1st (Orr's) Rifles Co.D

Richardson, David M. MO 5th Cav. Co.E

Richardson, David N. AL 3rd Bn.Res. Co.B

Richardson, David P. VA 157th Mil. Co.A

Richardson, David S. MO 12th Cav. Co.F Bvt.2nd Lt.

Richardson, Davis T. Gen. & Staff Asst.Surg.

Richardson, D.B. MO 10th Inf. Co.A

Richardson, D.C. GA 4th (Clinch's) Cav. Co.E,K

Richardson, D.C. GA Cav. 12th Bn. (St.Guards) Co.E

Richardson, D.C. GA 10th Inf.

Richardson, D.C. TX 2nd Inf. QM

Richardson, D.C. VA Conscr. Cp.Lee Co.B

Richardson, D.D. AL 14th Inf. Co.B Sgt.

Richardson, D.E. MS 43rd Inf. Co.L

Richardson, Decatur FL St.Mil. 1st Regt. Capt.

Richardson, Dellett B. TX 12th Cav. Co.F

Richardson, Dempsey NC 17th Inf. (2nd Org.) Cpl.

Richardson, Dempsey L. NC 17th Inf. (1st Org.) Co.L Cpl.

Richardson, D.F. KY 1st (Butler's) Cav. Co.F

Richardson, D.F. KY 1st (Helm's) Cav. New Co.A

Richardson, D.F. MO 16th Inf. Co.K

Richardson, D.H. GA 3rd Res. Co.A

Richardson, D.H. TX 12th Cav. Co.E Cpl.

Richardson, D.H.W. NC 15th Inf. Co.B

Richardson, D.K. TX Cav. Terry's Regt. Co.B

Richardson, D.L. TN 38th Inf. 2nd Co.A

Richardson, D.N. TX 12th Cav. Co.C

Richardson, Drury NC 5th Sr.Res. Co.B

Richardson, Drury TN 41st Inf. Co.A

Richardson, D.S. KY 6th Cav. Co.D

Richardson, D.S.C. SC 1st Arty. Co.I

Richardson, D.T. TX 7th Inf. Asst.Surg.

Richardson, Dudley S. MO 4th Cav. Co.B

Richardson, Dudley T. TX Conscr.

Richardson, D.W. AL Inf. 2nd Regt. Co.G Cpl.

Richardson, D.W. SC 21st Inf. Co.I Cpl.

Richardson, D.W. Conf.Inf. 1st Bn. 2nd Co.E

Richardson, E. AL Cav. Barlow's Co.

Richardson, E. AR 7th Inf. Co.K Drum.

Richardson, E. GA 11th Inf. Co.K

Richardson, E. GA 55th Inf. Co.H

Richardson, E. SC Mil.Arty. 1st Regt. Werner's Co.

Richardson, E. SC Lt.Arty. Wagener's Co. (Co.A,German Arty.)

Richardson, E. LA Mil. Chalmette Regt. Co.C

Richardson, E. TX 4th Inf. (St.Troops) Co.E

Richardson, E.A. VA Lt.Arty. 1st Bn. Co.B Cpl.

Richardson, E.A. VA Arty. Richardson's Co. Cpl.

Richardson, E.A. VA 3rd Res. Co.D

Richardson, E.B. GA 1st (Symons') Res. Co.A 1st Sgt.

Richardson, E.B. SC 5th Cav. Co.B

Richardson, E.B. SC Cav. 17th Bn. Co.C

Richardson, E.D. SC 1st Arty. Co.B Cpl.

Richardson, E.D. SC 3rd St.Troops Co.D Sgt.

Richardson, E.D. SC 10th Inf. Co.M 1st Lt.

Richardson, E.D. TN 6th (Wheeler's) Cav. Co.F

Richardson, Ed. TN 50th Inf. Co.B

Richardson, Ed Bradford's Corps Scouts & Guards Co.A

Richardson, Edgar GA Carlton's Co. (Troup Cty.Arty.) Cpl.

Richardson, Edgar GA 2nd Inf. Stanley's Co.

Richardson, Edmond A. GA 4th Inf. Co.C

Richardson, Edmund FL 3rd Inf. Co.F

Richardson, Edom GA Lt.Arty. 12th Bn. 3rd Co.C

Richardson, Edward MS 20th Inf. Co.C

Richardson, Edward NC 53rd Inf. Co.C

Richardson, Edward TN 17th Inf. Co.H Cpl.

Richardson, Edward TN 53rd Inf. Co.B Cpl.

Richardson, Edward A. TX 27th Cav. Co.I

Richardson, Edward B. Conf.Cav. Wood's Regt. Co.K

Richardson, Edward F. VA Hvy.Arty. 18th Bn. Co.B

Richardson, Edward G. VA 28th Inf. Co.A Sgt.

Richardson, Edward L. NC 3rd Cav. (41st St.Troops) Co.I

Richardson, Edwin R. AL Lt.Arty. Ward's Btty. 2nd Lt.

Richardson, E.F. SC 21st Inf. Co.I

Richardson, E.G. MO Arty.Regt.St.Guard Co.B Capt.

Richardson, E.G. NC 12th Inf. Co.M Cpl.

Richardson, E.G. NC 54th Inf. Co.E

Richardson, E.H. MO Inf. 3rd Regt.St.Guard Co.K Capt.

Richardson, E.J. MO 10th Inf. Co.A

Richardson, E.J. TN 50th Inf. Co.A

Richardson, E.J. VA 32nd Inf. 2nd Co.K

Richardson, E.L. MS 15th (Cons.) Inf. Co.H 3rd Sgt.

Richardson, Elbert NC 6th Sr.Res. Co.E

Richardson, Elbert NC 26th Inf. Co.A

Richardson, Elbridge G. Gen. & Staff Rec. for Maj.,QM

Richardson, Eldridge A. VA 1st Arty. Co.B Cpl.

Richardson, Eldridge A. VA 32nd Inf. 1st Co.H

Richardson, Eleas M. AL 19th Inf. Co.E
Richardson, Eli NC 22nd Inf. Co.F
Richardson, Eli NC Alleghany Grays Doughton's Co.
Richardson, Elias GA 55th Inf. Co.H
Richardson, Elias S. VA 26th Inf. Co.C
Richardson, Elijah GA 62nd Cav. Co.B 2nd Lt.
Richardson, Elijah GA Siege Arty. 28th Bn. Co.K Sgt.
Richardson, Elijah VA 24th Inf. Co.H
Richardson, Elijah VA 54th Mil. Co.E,F
Richardson, Elijah J. MS 32nd Inf. Co.E
Richardson, Elisha GA 8th Cav. Co.B
Richardson, Elisha GA 62nd Cav. Co.B
Richardson, Elisha D. GA 51st Inf. Co.I Sgt.
Richardson, Eli T. GA 29th Inf. Co.K
Richardson, Elwood NC Inf. 2nd Bn. Co.F
Richardson, Ely C. TN 41st Inf. Co.H
Richardson, E.M. AL 23rd Inf. Co.E Cpl.
Richardson, E.M. GA 2nd Cav. Co.G
Richardson, E.N. MS 11th Inf. Co.B
Richardson, Enoch NC 48th Inf. Co.D
Richardson, E.P. TX 9th Cav. Co.A
Richardson, Ephriam L. MS 20th Inf. Co.G Sgt.
Richardson, E.R. MS 43rd Inf. Co.K
Richardson, E.R. NC 26th Inf. Co.B
Richardson, Erlander M. AL 11th Inf. Co.C Sgt.
Richardson, E.S. TN 8th Inf. Co.B
Richardson, Esge G. MO 8th Inf. Co.B
Richardson, Eugene A. VA 18th Inf. Co.B
Richardson, Evain TN 4th (Murray's) Cav. Co.F
Richardson, Evan D. VA 6th Bn.Res. Co.D Capt.
Richardson, Even J. TN 8th (Smith's) Cav. Co.I
Richardson, Everett TX 7th Cav. Co.F Sgt.
Richardson, E.W. LA Miles' Legion Co.A
Richardson, Ezekiel MO Inf. Perkins' Bn. Co.A 2nd Lt.
Richardson, F. GA 55th Inf. Co.H
Richardson, F.B. SC 5th Bn.Res. Co.B
Richardson, F.B. Gen. & Staff Surg.
Richardson, F.D. SC Mil. 18th Regt. Ord.Sgt.
Richardson, F.E. AL 2nd Cav. Co.H Capt.
Richardson, Federick GA 62nd Cav. Co.B
Richardson, F.H. VA 42nd Inf. Co.F
Richardson, F.L. LA Washington Arty.Bn. Co.5
Richardson, Fleming W. VA 21st Mil. Co.D
Richardson, Fleming W. VA 34th Inf. Co.A
Richardson, Floyd VA 63rd Inf. Co.G
Richardson, Floyd VA Mil. Carroll Cty.
Richardson, F.M. GA Inf. 2nd Bn. (St.Guards) New Co.D 1st Lt.
Richardson, F.M. GA 50th Inf. Co.I
Richardson, F.M. LA 28th (Gray's) Inf. Co.E
Richardson, F.M. TN 28th (Cons.) Inf. Co.F Cpl.
Richardson, F.M. TN 84th Inf. Co.B Cpl.
Richardson, F.R. MS 11th (Perrin's) Cav. Co.B
Richardson, F.R. TN 37th Inf. Co.D
Richardson, F.R. TX 24th Cav. Co.G
Richardson, Francis H. VA 42nd Inf. Music.
Richardson, Frank AR 1st (Colquitt's) Inf. Co.G
Richardson, Frank AR 11th & 17th (Cons.) Inf. Co.A
Richardson, Frank LA 2nd Cav. Co.I
Richardson, Frank LA 13th Inf. Co.G
Richardson, Frank 14th Conf.Cav. Co.C

Richardson, Frederick GA 8th Cav. Co.B
Richardson, Frederick LA 5th Inf. Co.F Capt.
Richardson, Frederick NC 1st Inf. Co.E
Richardson, Frederick VA 61st Mil. Co.G
Richardson, Frederick H. MS St.Cav. Perrin's Bn. Co.C
Richardson, Frederick H. MS 20th Inf. Co.G
Richardson, Fred H. MS 15th (Cons.) Inf. Co.H
Richardson, F.T. KY 6th Cav. Co.E
Richardson, Furney W. NC 24th Inf. Co.C
Richardson, F.W. AL Talladega Cty.Res. B.H. Ford's Co.
Richardson, G. SC Mil.Arty. 1st Regt. Harms' Co.
Richardson, G. SC 2nd Inf. Co.D
Richardson, G. SC 14th Inf. Co.B
Richardson, G. VA 10th Cav. 2nd Co.E
Richardson, G. Bradford's Corps Scouts & Guards
Richardson, G.A. NC 66th Inf. Co.D
Richardson, Gabriel A. VA 50th Inf. Co.K Cpl.
Richardson, Gaines MO 1st N.E. Cav. Co.L
Richardson, G.B. GA 12th (Wright's) Cav. (St.Guards) Brannen's Co.
Richardson, G.B. MS 41st Inf. Co.C
Richardson, G.C. MS 38th Cav. Co.D
Richardson, G.C. VA Lt.Arty. 1st Bn. Co.B
Richardson, G.D. KY 10th Cav. Co.E
Richardson, G.D. TX 28th Cav. Co.F
Richardson, General GA 6th Res. Co.B
Richardson, General NC 48th Inf. Co.E
Richardson, George FL 2nd Cav. Co.B
Richardson, George GA 10th Inf. Co.A
Richardson, George MO 11th Inf. Co.I
Richardson, George NC 12th Inf. Co.B,D Cook
Richardson, George NC 26th Inf. Co.B
Richardson, George NC 47th Inf. Co.D
Richardson, George NC 48th Inf. Co.F
Richardson, George NC Walker's Bn. Thomas' Legion Co.A
Richardson, George TN 6th Inf. Co.F Sgt.
Richardson, George TN 21st Inf. Co.H
Richardson, George VA 23rd Cav. Co.M
Richardson, George VA 1st St.Res. Co.C
Richardson, George 3rd Conf.Cav. Co.F
Richardson, George A. NC 8th Bn.Part.Rangers Co.A
Richardson, George B. NC Hvy.Arty. 10th Bn. Co.A Sgt.
Richardson, George B. TN 1st (Feild's) Inf. Co.H
Richardson, George C. VA 1st Arty. Co.B
Richardson, George C. VA Arty. Richardson's Co.
Richardson, George C. VA 9th Inf. Co.I
Richardson, George C. VA 21st Inf. Co.G
Richardson, George D. KY 1st (Helm's) Cav. New Co.A 1st Lt.
Richardson, George D. VA Inf. 25th Bn. Co.C
Richardson, George E. AL 20th Inf. Co.A
Richardson, George E. VA 3rd Cav. 1st Co.I Cpl.
Richardson, George E. VA 5th Cav. Co.H Sgt.
Richardson, George E.C. VA 32nd Inf. 1st Co.H Cpl.
Richardson, George H. VA 15th Cav. Co.H
Richardson, George H. VA 17th Inf. Co.D

Richardson, George L. LA Mil. McPherson's Btty. (Orleans Howitzers)
Richardson, George L. VA 42nd Inf. Co.A 2nd Lt.
Richardson, George N. TN 19th Inf. Co.K
Richardson, George P. LA 2nd Inf.
Richardson, George P. LA 16th Inf. Co.A
Richardson, George P. LA 27th Inf. Co.A
Richardson, George R. TN 21st (Wilson's) Cav. Co.E
Richardson, George R. TN Cav. Newsom's Regt. Co.C
Richardson, George S. LA 1st (Nelligan's) Inf. Co.G Sgt.
Richardson, George S. TN Inf. 3rd Bn. Co.C Sgt.
Richardson, George S. VA 41st Mil. Co.A
Richardson, George T. GA 19th Inf. Co.C
Richardson, George T. VA 21st Cav. Co.B Cpl.
Richardson, George T. VA Lt.Arty. R.M. Anderson's Co.
Richardson, George T. VA 4th Inf. Co.E
Richardson, George T. VA 38th Inf. Co.E
Richardson, George W. AL 18th Inf. Co.A
Richardson, George W. AL 18th Inf. Co.D
Richardson, George W. GA 11th Inf. Co.G
Richardson, George W. MD 1st Cav. Co.G
Richardson, George W. MS 11th (Perrin's) Cav. Co.G
Richardson, George W. MS 20th Inf. Co.G
Richardson, George W. MS 43rd Inf. Co.K
Richardson, George W. NC 1st Arty. (10th St.Troops) Co.K
Richardson, George W. NC 22nd Inf. Co.F
Richardson, George W. SC 2nd Cav. Co.K
Richardson, George W. SC 16th Inf. Co.A 3rd Lt.
Richardson, George W. SC 20th Inf. Co.I
Richardson, George W. SC Cav.Bn. Hampton Legion Co.B
Richardson, George W. TX 12th Cav. Co.E
Richardson, George W. VA 3rd Cav. 1st Co.I Cpl.
Richardson, George W. VA 5th Cav. Co.H
Richardson, George W. VA Lt.Arty. B.Z. Price's Co.
Richardson, George W. VA 15th Inf. Co.A
Richardson, G.H. AL 37th Inf. Co.G
Richardson, G.H. AL 42nd Inf. Co.B
Richardson, G.H. MS 7th Cav. Co.B
Richardson, G.H. TN 3rd (Forrest's) Cav. Co.B
Richardson, G.H. VA Cav. Mosby's Regt. (Part.Rangers) Co.H
Richardson, Gilbert NC 32nd Inf. Co.B
Richardson, Gilly Sap. & Min. G.W. Maxson's Co.,CSA
Richardson, G.L. NC 7th Inf. Co.E
Richardson, G.L. TN 9th Inf. Co.B Sgt.
Richardson, G.N. MO 9th Bn.S.S. Co.B
Richardson, Goodman NC 44th Inf. Co.H
Richardson, G.R. MO 2nd Inf. Co.G
Richardson, G.R. TN 21st & 22nd (Cons.) Cav. Co.F
Richardson, Green KY 5th Mtd.Inf. Co.F
Richardson, Green LA Miles' Legion Co.B Cpl.
Richardson, Green TN 4th (Murray's) Cav. Co.B
Richardson, Green TN Inf. 32nd Bn. Co.H

Richardson, Green VA Burks' Regt.Loc.Def.
  Sprinkle's Co.
Richardson, Green L. NC 52nd Inf. Co.D
Richardson, Griffin SC Hvy.Arty. 15th (Lucas')
  Bn. Co.C
Richardson, G.T. TX 9th Cav. Co.K
Richardson, Guignard SC Hvy.Arty. 15th
  (Lucas') Bn. Co.A,B Capt.
Richardson, G.W. AL 9th Inf. Co.I Sgt.
Richardson, G.W. AR 1st (Monroe's) Cav. Co.L
Richardson, G.W. FL Cav. 3rd Bn. Co.C
Richardson, G.W. FL 11th Inf. Co.C
Richardson, G.W. MD Arty. 2nd Btty.
Richardson, G.W. MS 6th Inf. Co.A 1st Lt.
Richardson, G.W. MS 35th Inf. Co.I Sgt.
Richardson, G.W. NC Cav. 16th Bn. Co.E
Richardson, G.W. NC Townsend's Co.
  (St.Troops)
Richardson, G.W. SC 1st (Butler's) Inf. Co.A
Richardson, G.W. SC 9th Inf. Co.B
Richardson, G.W. SC 12th Inf. Co.F
Richardson, G.W. TN 21st Cav. Co.E
Richardson, G.W. TN 26th Cav. Co.C
Richardson, G.W. TX 13th Cav. Co.K
Richardson, G.W. VA 17th Cav. Co.G
Richardson, G.W. VA 47th Inf. Col.
Richardson, G.W. 7th Conf.Cav. Co.G,M
Richardson, G.W. 15th Conf.Cav. Co.E
Richardson, H. AL 11th Cav. Co.G 1st Sgt.
Richardson, H. AL 53rd (Part.Rangers) Co.G
Richardson, H. AL 1st Regt.Conscr. Co.D
Richardson, H. AL 19th Inf. Co.G
Richardson, H. AR 24th Inf. Co.E
Richardson, H. GA Hardwick Mtd.Rifles
Richardson, H. GA 47th Inf. Co.K
Richardson, H. GA 55th Inf. Co.H
Richardson, H. LA 4th Cav. Co.B 2nd Lt.
Richardson, H. MD Arty. 2nd Bn.
Richardson, H. MS 41st Inf. Co.B
Richardson, H. TN 21st Inf. Co.D
Richardson, H. TX Cav. Terry's Regt. Co.K
Richardson, H. VA 4th Cav. Co.A
Richardson, H. VA 3rd Inf.Loc.Def. Co.F
Richardson, H. Gen. & Staff Capt.,AQM
Richardson, Haden VA 54th Inf. Co.K
Richardson, Hamtn. VA 3rd Cav. Co.I
Richardson, Hannan E. VA 1st Arty. Co.B, 3rd
  Co.C
Richardson, Hardy LA 9th Inf. Co.I Capt.
Richardson, Hardy TX 11th (Spaight's) Bn.Vol.
  Co.C
Richardson, Hardy 1st Conf.Eng.Troops Co.H
  Artif.
Richardson, Hardy C. LA 9th Inf. Co.I Cpl.
Richardson, Hardy H. NC 31st Inf. Co.B
Richardson, Harman E. VA 32nd Inf. 1st Co.H
Richardson, Harmon E. VA Lt.Arty. 1st Bn.
  Co.C Bugler
Richardson, Harris H. NC 24th Inf. Co.C 1st
  Sgt.
Richardson, Harry TN 2nd (Walker's) Inf. Co.E
  Cpl.
Richardson, Harvey GA 60th Inf. Co.I
Richardson, Harvey TN 5th (McKenzie's) Cav.
  Co.H
Richardson, Harvey TN 26th Inf. Co.A
Richardson, Harvey TN Conscr. (Cp. of Instr.)

Richardson, H.B. AL 89th Mil. Co.E
Richardson, H.B. AL Loc.Def. & Sp.Serv.
  Toomer's Co.
Richardson, H.C. AR Cav. Gordon's Regt.
  Walker's Co.
Richardson, H.C. AR 7th Inf. Co.E
Richardson, H.C. AR 32nd Inf. Co.G
Richardson, H.C. MO St.Guard
Richardson, H.C. SC 2nd Cav. Co.G
Richardson, H. Clay KY 2nd Mtd.Inf. Co.G
Richardson, H.D. TX 3rd Cav. Co.G
Richardson, H.E. GA 2nd Cav. Co.I
Richardson, Henley VA 51st Inf. Co.G Capt.
Richardson, Henry AR Lt.Arty. Rivers' Btty.
  Cpl.
Richardson, Henry FL 11th Inf. Co.C
Richardson, Henry GA 62nd Cav. Co.B
Richardson, Henry GA Lt.Arty. 12th Bn. 3rd
  Co.C Sgt.
Richardson, Henry KY 10th (Johnson's) Cav.
  New Co.F
Richardson, Henry MS 2nd Part.Rangers Co.H
Richardson, Henry MS 15th Bn.S.S. Co.A Cpl.
Richardson, Henry TN 13th Cav. Co.C
Richardson, Henry TN Douglass'
  Bn.Part.Rangers Perkins' Co.
Richardson, Henry TN Cav. Newsom's Regt.
  Co.C
Richardson, Henry VA 38th Inf. Co.A
Richardson, Henry B. LA 6th Inf. Co.D
Richardson, Henry B. Ewell's Staff Eng.Capt.
Richardson, Henry C. LA 7th Inf. Co.K
Richardson, Henry C. VA 15th Inf. Co.I
Richardson, Henry C. VA 34th Inf. Co.I
Richardson, Henry D. VA 50th Inf. Co.K
Richardson, Henry G. AL 4th Inf. Co.H
Richardson, Henry H. AL 12th Inf. Co.B,D
Richardson, Henry H. AL 24th Inf. Co.H
Richardson, Henry H.H. GA 36th (Villepigue's)
  Inf. Co.G Sgt.
Richardson, Henry J. MS 24th Inf. Co.H,I
Richardson, Henry L. NC 17th Inf. (2nd Org.)
  Co.B
Richardson, Henry L. SC Arty. Gregg's Co.
  (McQueen Lt.Arty.) Cpl.
Richardson, Henry L. SC Arty. Manigault's Bn.
  1st Co.C Cpl.
Richardson, Henry L. SC 10th Inf. Co.C Cpl.
Richardson, Henry S. FL 7th Inf. Co.D
Richardson, Henry V. LA 6th Inf. Co.H Music.
Richardson, Henry W. GA 2nd Cav. Co.D
Richardson, Henry W. GA 10th Cav. (St.Guards)
  Co.G Sgt.
Richardson, Henry W. VA 51st Inf. Co.E,C
Richardson, Hez. LA 19th Inf. Co.G
Richardson, H.F. GA 2nd Cav. Co.D
Richardson, H.F. GA 11th Inf. Co.G
Richardson, H.F. TN 5th (McKenzie's) Cav.
  Co.A 1st Bugler
Richardson, H.G. VA 2nd Arty. Co.E 2nd Lt.
Richardson, H.H. AL 34th Inf. Co.B
Richardson, H.H. FL 1st (Res.) Inf. Co.C
Richardson, H.H. TN 1st (Feild's) Inf. Co.F
Richardson, H.H. TN 9th Inf. Co.K 1st Lt.
Richardson, H.H. Lt.Arty. Dent's Btty.,CSA 1st
  Lt.
Richardson, Hillery E. GA 30th Inf. Co.K

Richardson, Hillery G. VA 44th Inf. Co.G Capt.
Richardson, Hiram TN 7th Cav. Co.B Sgt.
Richardson, Hiram E. GA 61st Inf. Co.I
Richardson, Hiram O. AL 38th Inf. Co.D
Richardson, H.J. 3rd Conf.Eng.Troops Co.G
Richardson, H.L. AL 16th Inf. Co.C Cpl.
Richardson, H.N. MS 1st (King's) Inf.
  (St.Troops) Co.B
Richardson, H.O. AL Cp. of Instr. Talladega
Richardson, Hobert KY 4th Mtd.Inf. Co.K
Richardson, Hopkins R. MS 11th Inf. Co.B
Richardson, Horatio N. NC 3rd Inf. Co.I
Richardson, Howard MD 1st Cav. Co.A
Richardson, Howard MO Cav. Poindexter's Regt.
Richardson, H.S. AL Inf. 2nd Regt. Co.F
Richardson, H.S. GA 17th Inf. Co.G
Richardson, H.S. TX Cav. 6th Bn. Co.A
Richardson, H.T. AL 46th Inf. Co.B
Richardson, H.T. VA 1st Cav. Co.E
Richardson, Hugh MS 43rd Inf. Co.K
Richardson, Hugh W. GA 1st Cav. Co.C
Richardson, H.W. AL 1st Inf. Co.G
Richardson, H.W. AL Inf. 2nd Regt. Co.E
Richardson, H.W. GA Arty. Lumpkin's Co. Sgt.
Richardson, H.W. SC 4th Cav. Co.K
Richardson, I. AR 1st Field Btty.
Richardson, I. TN Cav. Nixon's Regt. Co.C
  Cpl.
Richardson, I.D. VA 32nd Inf. Co.C
Richardson, I.F. SC Inf. Hampton Legion Co.D
Richardson, I.H. MS 15th (Cons.) Inf. Co.K
Richardson, Incil NC 2nd Inf. Co.D
Richardson, Ira J. GA 2nd Cav. Co.I
Richardson, I.S. SC 7th Cav. Co.I
Richardson, Isaac AR 15th Mil. Co.H Cpl.
Richardson, Isaac KY 1st (Helm's) Cav. New
  Co.A
Richardson, Isaac LA 1st Cav. Co.H
Richardson, Isaac MS 14th (Cons.) Inf. Co.G
Richardson, Isaac NC 61st Inf. Co.I
Richardson, Isaac TN 4th (McLemore's) Cav.
  Co.E
Richardson, Isaac TX 21st Cav. Co.L
Richardson, Isaac TX 24th Cav. Co.C
Richardson, Isaac TX 34th Cav. Co.H
Richardson, Isaac H. AL 9th Inf. Co.I
Richardson, Isaac J. VA 54th Inf. Co.E
Richardson, Isaac N. SC 12th Inf. Co.H
Richardson, Isaiah VA 39th Inf. Co.F
Richardson, Isaiah C. GA Inf. 2nd Bn. Co.C
Richardson, Isham NC 61st Inf. Co.I
Richardson, Isham TX 14th Cav. Co.E 3rd Lt.
Richardson, Isom P. AL 16th Inf. Co.C
Richardson, Israel M. GA Cav. 29th Bn. Co.E
Richardson, I.T. AL 21st Inf. Co.H
Richardson, J. AL 1st Cav. Co.G
Richardson, J. AL 7th Cav. Co.C
Richardson, J. FL 5th Inf. Co.I
Richardson, J. GA 1st (Symons') Res. Co.B Lt.
Richardson, J. GA 5th Res. Co.C
Richardson, J. GA 8th Inf. Co.B
Richardson, J. GA Inf. 14th Bn. (St.Guards)
  Co.E
Richardson, J. KY Cav. 2nd Bn. (Dortch's) Co.A
Richardson, J. MS Cav. 4th Bn. Co.B Cpl.
Richardson, J. MS Inf. 1st Bn. Ray's Co.
Richardson, J. MO 11th Inf. Co.G

Richardson, J. NC 2nd Rifles
Richardson, J. SC 7th Cav. Co.A
Richardson, J. TN 3rd (Forrest's) Cav.
Richardson, J. TX 3rd Inf. 2nd Co.C
Richardson, J. TX 3rd (Kirby's) Bn.Vol. Co.C
Richardson, J. 8th (Wade's) Conf.Cav. Co.D Cpl.
Richardson, J.A. AL 4th Cav. Co.A
Richardson, J.A. AR 3rd Inf. Co.K
Richardson, J.A. AR 20th Inf. Co.G
Richardson, J.A. AR 27th Inf. Co.F
Richardson, J.A. AR 35th Inf. Co.I
Richardson, J.A. GA Hvy.Arty. 22nd Bn. Co.A
Richardson, J.A. GA 19th Inf. Co.C 1st Lt.
Richardson, J.A. GA Inf. 40th Bn. Co.F
Richardson, J.A. GA 52nd Inf. Co.B
Richardson, J.A. MS 5th Cav. Co.E,I
Richardson, J.A. MS 11th (Perrin's) Cav. Co.D
Richardson, J.A. MS 12th Cav. Co.A
Richardson, J.A. MS 35th Inf. Co.D
Richardson, J.A. MO Cav. Coffee's Regt. Co.C
Richardson, J.A. TN 3rd (Clack's) Inf. Co.E
Richardson, J.A. TX 7th Inf. Co.B
Richardson, J.A. TX 11th (Spaight's) Bn.Vol. Co.B
Richardson, J.A. TX 13th Vol. 4th Co.I
Richardson, J.A. TX 21st Inf. Co.A
Richardson, J.A. Gen. & Staff 2nd Lt.,Dr.M.
Richardson, Jack AL 5th Cav. Co.I
Richardson, Jack P. AL 1st Regt. Mobile Vol. Co.A 1st Sgt.
Richardson, Jack P. TN Lt.Arty. Winston's Co.
Richardson, Jackson TN 41st Inf. Co.A
Richardson, Jackson W.J. AL 11th Inf. Co.I
Richardson, Jacob SC 11th Inf. Co.K
Richardson, James AL 11th Cav. Co.G
Richardson, James AL 27th Inf. Co.E Bvt.2nd Lt.
Richardson, James AL 57th Inf. Co.I
Richardson, James AR Lt.Arty. Rivers' Btty.
Richardson, James FL 2nd Cav. Co.H,K
Richardson, James FL Cav. Pickett's Co. Far.
Richardson, James GA 3rd Cav. Co.K
Richardson, James GA Hvy.Arty. 22nd Bn. Co.A
Richardson, James GA Siege Arty. 28th Bn. Co.G
Richardson, James GA 8th Inf. (St.Guards) Co.G
Richardson, James GA 18th Inf. Co.B Lt.
Richardson, James GA 31st Inf. Co.G
Richardson, James GA 42nd Inf.
Richardson, James GA Cobb's Legion Co.C
Richardson, James KY 2nd Cav. Co.F
Richardson, James KY 9th Cav. Co.A
Richardson, James KY 7th Mtd.Inf. Co.F
Richardson, James LA 1st Cav. Co.H
Richardson, James LA 28th (Gray's) Inf. Co.E
Richardson, James MS 1st (Percy's) Inf. Co.K
Richardson, James MS 14th (Cons.) Inf. Co.G
Richardson, James MS 30th Inf. Co.K
Richardson, James MS 43rd Inf. Co.A
Richardson, James MO 4th Cav. Co.B
Richardson, James, Sr. NC 34th Inf. Co.A
Richardson, James NC 37th Inf. Co.K
Richardson, James NC 58th Inf. Co.L
Richardson, James SC 11th Inf. Co.K
Richardson, James TN 9th (Ward's) Cav. Co.E
Richardson, James TN 28th Inf. Co.K

Richardson, James TN 41st Inf. Co.A
Richardson, James TN 48th (Nixon's) Inf. Co.I
Richardson, James TN 54th Inf. Ives' Co.
Richardson, James TN 55th (Brown's) Inf. Co.D
Richardson, James TN 55th (McKoin's) Inf. Co.I
Richardson, James TX 2nd Cav. Co.K
Richardson, James TX 13th Cav. Co.A
Richardson, James TX Cav. Frontier Bn. Co.B
Richardson, James TX Cav. McCord's Frontier Regt. Co.I
Richardson, James VA Hvy.Arty. 19th Bn. Co.C
Richardson, James VA 46th Inf. 1st Co.C
Richardson, James VA 53rd Inf. Co.B Capt.
Richardson, James VA 60th Inf. Co.B
Richardson, James VA 115th Mil. Co.B
Richardson, James VA Inf. Tomlin's Bn. Co.A Capt.
Richardson, James A. GA 1st Reg. Co.G 1st Sgt.
Richardson, James A. KY 4th Cav. Co.A
Richardson, James A. NC 53rd Inf. Co.I
Richardson, James A. SC 2nd Rifles Co.A
Richardson, James A. TN Lt.Arty. Baxter's Co.
Richardson, James A. VA 15th Inf. Co.B Sgt.
Richardson, James B. MO 10th Inf. Co.A
Richardson, James B. SC 4th Cav. Co.K
Richardson, James B. VA 16th Inf. Co.E
Richardson, James C. LA Ouachita Res.Corps Williams' Co.
Richardson, James C. VA 1st Arty. Co.B Sgt.
Richardson, James C. VA Lt.Arty. 1st Bn. Co.B Sgt.
Richardson, James C. VA Arty. Richardson's Co. Sgt.
Richardson, James C. VA 32nd Inf. 1st Co.H Cpl.
Richardson, James D. MS 22nd Inf. Co.D,B
Richardson, James D. MO 5th Inf. Co.B Cpl.
Richardson, James D. NC 47th Inf. Co.E
Richardson, James D. TN 8th Cav. Co.F
Richardson, James D. VA 14th Inf. Co.C
Richardson, James D. VA 26th Inf. Co.K
Richardson, James D. VA 28th Inf. Co.K
Richardson, James D.H. TN 42nd Inf. Co.B
Richardson, James E. NC 18th Inf. Co.K Color Sgt.
Richardson, James F. LA 6th Inf. Co.H
Richardson, James F. LA 8th Inf. Co.K
Richardson, James F. LA Inf. 11th Bn. Co.F
Richardson, James F. TN 9th Cav.
Richardson, James F. TX 15th Cav. Co.D
Richardson, James F. TX Cav. Baylor's Regt. Co.C
Richardson, James G. LA 2nd Inf. Co.C Comsy.
Richardson, James G. NC 34th Inf. Co.A Sgt.
Richardson, James G. TN 25th Inf. Co.H
Richardson, James G. VA 28th Inf. Co.E Cpl.
Richardson, James G. 3rd Conf.Eng.Troops Co.C Artif.
Richardson, James G. Gen. & Staff Maj.
Richardson, James H. AL Cav. 5th Bn. Hilliard's Legion Co.A
Richardson, James H. KY 2nd Mtd.Inf. Co.D
Richardson, James H. MO 3rd Inf. Co.A Sgt.
Richardson, James H. NC 45th Inf. Co.E
Richardson, James H. NC 49th Inf. Co.F
Richardson, James H. TN 44th (Cons.) Inf. Co.I

Richardson, James H., 1st VA 5th Cav. Co.E
Richardson, James H., 2nd VA 5th Cav. Co.E
Richardson, James H. VA 20th Inf. Co.D
Richardson, James H. VA 58th Inf. Co.D
Richardson, James H. VA 61st Mil. Co.B
Richardson, James H. VA 109th Mil. Co.B
Richardson, James I. NC 48th Inf. Co.E
Richardson, James J. GA 11th Inf. Co.H
Richardson, James J. TN 16th Inf. Co.F,K
Richardson, James K. TN 2nd Cav. Co.E
Richardson, James K.P. VA 58th Inf. Co.B Cpl.
Richardson, James L. AL 51st (Part.Rangers) Co.A
Richardson, James L. AL 2nd Inf. Co.A
Richardson, James L. GA 7th Inf. Co.E
Richardson, James L. LA Washington Arty.Bn. Co.2
Richardson, James L. TN 4th Inf. Co.K 2nd Lt.
Richardson, James L. Conf.Inf. 1st Bn. Co.I, 2nd Co.A
Richardson, James M. GA Inf. 2nd Bn. (St.Guards) Co.B
Richardson, James M. GA 4th Bn.S.S. Co.C Cpl.
Richardson, James M. GA 18th Inf. Co.B
Richardson, Jas. M. GA Conscr.
Richardson, James M. MO 11th Inf. Co.E
Richardson, James M. NC 21st Inf. Maj.
Richardson, James M. NC 26th Inf. Co.B
Richardson, James M. SC 2nd Rifles Co.G
Richardson, James M. TN 1st (Feild's) Inf. Co.K
Richardson, James M. TN 2nd (Robison's) Inf. Co.A
Richardson, James M. TN 22nd Inf. Co.C Capt.
Richardson, James M. TX 11th (Spaight's) Bn.Vol. Co.C
Richardson, James N. FL 6th Inf. Co.D
Richardson, James P. AL 45th Inf. Co.I
Richardson, James P. NC 4th Cav. (59th St.Troops) Co.A
Richardson, James P. SC 10th Inf. Co.A 2nd Lt.
Richardson, Jas. P. Gen. & Staff Asst.Surg.
Richardson, James R. GA 11th Inf. Co.G
Richardson, James R. LA 28th (Gray's) Inf. Co.E
Richardson, James R. MO Cav. 3rd Bn. Co.A Cpl.
Richardson, James R. MO Lt.Arty. 1st Field Btty.
Richardson, James R. NC 18th Inf. Co.H,C
Richardson, James R. NC 31st Inf. Co.D Cpl.
Richardson, James R. VA 4th Inf. Co.B
Richardson, James S. LA 19th Inf. Co.B,D
Richardson, James T. GA 31st Inf. Co.C Cpl.
Richardson, James T. LA 12th Inf. Co.H
Richardson, James T. SC 2nd Rifles Co.L
Richardson, James T. VA 2nd Arty. Co.H
Richardson, James T. VA Inf. 22nd Bn. Co.H
Richardson, James T. VA 26th Inf. Co.C
Richardson, James W. AL 27th Inf. Co.C
Richardson, James W. GA 4th (Clinch's) Cav. Co.K,A
Richardson, James W. GA 8th Cav. Co.B
Richardson, James W. GA 62nd Cav. Co.B
Richardson, James W. GA 3rd Inf. Co.D
Richardson, James W. GA 26th Inf. Co.K
Richardson, James W. GA 31st Inf. Co.K

Richardson, James W. SC 1st Arty. Co.C
Richardson, James W. SC Arty. Manigault's Bn.
  1st Co.C
Richardson, James W. SC Inf. 1st (Charleston)
  Bn. Co.C Music.
Richardson, James W. TN 28th Inf. Co.I Sgt.
Richardson, James W. VA Arty. Kevill's Co.
Richardson, James W. VA 16th Inf. Co.C Sgt.
Richardson, James W. VA 17th Inf. Co.D
Richardson, James W. VA 41st Inf. 1st Co.E
Richardson, Jasper GA 2nd Inf. Co.F
Richardson, J.B. AL 1st Regt. Mobile Vol. Co.A
Richardson, J.B. GA 7th Inf. Co.I
Richardson, J.B. GA 29th Inf. Co.D
Richardson, J.B. GA 55th Inf. Co.A Sgt.
Richardson, J.B. GA Phillips' Legion Co.L
Richardson, J.B. SC 4th Cav. Co.K
Richardson, J.C. AL 56th Part.Rangers Co.D
Richardson, J.C. AL 23rd Inf. Co.I
Richardson, J.C. GA Cav. Russell's Co.
Richardson, J.C. GA 45th Inf. Co.A
Richardson, J.C. MS 5th Inf. (St.Troops) Co.F
Richardson, J.C. TN 17th Inf. Co.C
Richardson, J.C. TX Cav. 2nd Regt.St.Troops
  Co.E
Richardson, J.C. TX Cav. W.H. Randolph's Co.
Richardson, J.C. TX Inf. Rutherford's Co.
Richardson, J.C. Gen. & Staff Maj.,Comsy.
Richardson, J.D. GA 3rd Res. Co.F
Richardson, J.D. LA 28th (Gray's) Inf. Co.B
  Cpl.
Richardson, J.D. SC 15th Inf. Co.E
Richardson, J.D. TN 3rd (Clack's) Inf. Co.E
Richardson, J.D. TN Inf. 4th Cons.Regt. Co.K
Richardson, J.D. TN 45th Inf. Co.C Adj.
Richardson, J.D. TX 4th Cav. Co.I
Richardson, J.D. VA 7th Cav. ACS
Richardson, J.D. VA Hvy.Arty. 20th Bn. Co.C
  Cpl.
Richardson, J.D. Gen. & Staff Chap.
Richardson, J.D.H. TX Cav. 6th Bn. Co.B Far.
Richardson, J.E. AL 26th (O'Neal's) Inf. Co.I
Richardson, J.E. LA 3rd (Wingfield's) Cav.
  Co.D
Richardson, J.E. MO St.Guard 2nd Lt.
Richardson, J.E. NC 2nd Arty. (36th St.Troops)
  Co.B
Richardson, Jefferson L. AL 27th Inf. Co.C
Richardson, Jehu R. AL 42nd Inf. Co.D
Richardson, Jesse GA 52nd Inf. Co.B Lt.
Richardson, Jesse GA Phillips' Legion Co.C
  Cpl.
Richardson, Jesse TN 24th Inf. Co.E
Richardson, Jesse TN 25th Inf. Co.G
Richardson, Jesse C. AR 3rd Inf. Co.C
Richardson, Jesse C. AR 33rd Inf. Co.G Sgt.
Richardson, Jesse F. NC 44th Inf. Co.E
Richardson, Jesse M. VA 42nd Inf. Co.A Maj.
Richardson, J.F. GA 3rd Inf. Co.E
Richardson, J.F. MS 5th Inf. Co.G
Richardson, J.F. NC 4th Sr.Res. Co.I
Richardson, J.F. SC 7th Inf. 2nd Co.D
Richardson, J.F. TN 12th (Cons.) Inf. Co.H
Richardson, J.F. TN 22nd Inf. Co.C
Richardson, J.G. GA 3rd Cav. (St.Guards) Co.B
Richardson, J.G. GA Cav. 29th Bn. Co.H
Richardson, J.G. GA 1st Res. Co.B

Richardson, J.G. SC 10th Inf. Co.L
Richardson, J.G. SC 21st Inf. Co.I
Richardson, J.G. Gen. & Staff Maj.,Comsy.
Richardson, J.H. AL 7th Cav. Co.I
Richardson, J.H. AL 11th Inf. Co.H
Richardson, J.H. FL 2nd Inf. Co.F
Richardson, J.H. FL Cav. 3rd Bn. Co.A
Richardson, J.H. GA Inf. 1st Loc.Troops
  (Augusta) Co.C
Richardson, J.H. GA 3rd Res. Co.A
Richardson, J.H. MO 8th Inf. Co.G
Richardson, J.H. SC Inf. 3rd Bn. Co.D,E
Richardson, J.H. SC 21st Inf. Co.I Cpl.
Richardson, J.H. SC 25th Inf. Co.F
Richardson, J.H. TN 8th (Smith's) Cav. Co.I
Richardson, J.H. TN 55th (Brown's) Inf. Co.I
Richardson, J.H. TN 61st Mtd.Inf. Co.E
Richardson, J.H. TX 3rd Cav. Co.A
Richardson, J.H. TX 7th Cav. Co.F
Richardson, J.H. TX 28th Cav. Co.F
Richardson, J.H. TX 13th Vol. 1st Co.K
Richardson, J.H. TX 15th Inf. 2nd Co.F
Richardson, J.H. VA Lt.Arty. Snead's Co.
Richardson, J.H. VA 2nd St.Res. Co.I
Richardson, J.H. VA 47th Inf. Co.F
Richardson, J.H.P. AL 35th Inf. Co.B
Richardson, J.J. AL Inf. 1st (Loomis') Bn. Co.E
  2nd Lt.
Richardson, J.J. AL 25th Inf. Co.E 1st Lt.
Richardson, J.J. AL 32nd & 58th (Cons.) Inf.
  Co.K
Richardson, J.J. AR 37th Inf. Co.A
Richardson, J.J. GA Cav. 6th Bn. (St.Guards)
  Co.F
Richardson, J.J. MS St.Troops (Peach Creek
  Rangers) Maxwell's Co. 1st Sgt.
Richardson, J.J. SC Cav. 14th Bn. Co.D
Richardson, J.J. SC Cav. Tucker's Co. Cpl.
Richardson, J.J. SC 6th Inf. 1st Co.D
Richardson, J.J. TN 12th Inf. Co.I 2nd Lt.
Richardson, J.J. TN 12th (Cons.) Inf. Co.I 2nd
  Lt.
Richardson, J.J. TX 3rd Cav. Co.K
Richardson, J.J. TX 3rd Cav. Co.F Sgt.
Richardson, J.K. TX 3rd Cav. Co.K
Richardson, J.L. GA 1st Cav. Co.D,E
Richardson, J.L. GA Cav. Logan's Co. (White
  Cty. Old Men's Home Guards)
Richardson, J.L. GA Lt.Arty. Guerard's Btty.
Richardson, J.L. GA 2nd Res. Co.H
Richardson, J.L. GA 6th Inf. Co.B
Richardson, J.L. GA 19th Inf. Co.E
Richardson, J.L. MS Stewart's Co. (Yalobusha
  Rangers)
Richardson, J.L. TN 55th (Brown's) Inf. Co.F
Richardson, J.L.D. SC 13th Inf. Co.H
Richardson, J.M. AL 8th Inf. Co.K
Richardson, J.M. AL 27th Inf. Co.E
Richardson, J.M. AL 63rd Inf. Co.E
Richardson, J.M. AR 2nd Cav. Co.D
Richardson, J.M. GA Lt.Arty. 12th Bn. 3rd
  Co.C Sgt.
Richardson, J.M. GA 1st Reg. Co.C,B
Richardson, J.M. GA Inf. 9th Bn. Co.A
Richardson, J.M. GA 15th Inf. Co.H
Richardson, J.M. LA 1st Cav. Co.B

Richardson, J.M. MS 2nd (Quinn's St.Troops)
  Inf. Co.C
Richardson, J.M. MS 37th Inf. Co.G Capt.
Richardson, J.M. MO 2nd Cav. Co.D
Richardson, J.M. MO 6th Cav. Co.A
Richardson, J.M. NC 1st Jr.Res. Co.E
Richardson, J.M. SC 4th Cav. Co.K
Richardson, J.M. SC 7th Cav. Co.F
Richardson, J.M. SC Cav. Tucker's Co.
Richardson, J.M. SC 22nd Inf. Co.H Capt.
Richardson, J.M. TN 15th (Cons.) Cav. Co.F
Richardson, J.M. TN 8th Inf. Co.F Cpl.
Richardson, J.M. TN 9th Inf. Co.B
Richardson, J.M. TX 11th Inf. Co.G
Richardson, J.M. VA 15th Cav. Co.H
Richardson, J.N. MS 5th Inf. Co.E 1st Sgt.
Richardson, J.O. GA 47th Inf. Co.H Sgt.
Richardson, Job AL 18th Inf. Co.G
Richardson, John AL 8th Inf. Co.F
Richardson, John AL 19th Inf. Co.G
Richardson, John AL 28th Inf. Co.L
Richardson, John AL 43rd Inf. Co.K Sgt.
Richardson, John AL 50th Inf. Co.K
Richardson, John AR 27th Inf. New Co.B
Richardson, John FL 1st Cav. Co.B Sgt.
Richardson, John FL 1st (Res.) Cav. Co.F
Richardson, John GA 13th Cav. Co.K
Richardson, John, Jr. GA Arty. (Chatham Arty.)
  Wheaton's Co.
Richardson, John, Jr. GA 1st (Olmstead's) Inf.
  Claghorn's Co.
Richardson, John GA 10th Inf. Co.K
Richardson, John KY Morgan's Men Co.D
Richardson, John LA 7th Cav. Co.F
Richardson, John LA Arty. Green's Co. (LA
  Guard Btty.)
Richardson, John LA Washington Arty.Bn. Co.1
Richardson, John LA 1st (Nelligan's) Inf. Co.C,
  1st Co.B
Richardson, John LA Inf. 1st Sp.Bn. (Rightor's)
  New Co.C
Richardson, John MS 7th Cav. Co.C
Richardson, John MS Cav. Garland's Bn. Co.C
Richardson, John MS Inf. 1st Bn. Ray's Co.
Richardson, John MS Inf. 3rd Bn. Co.A
Richardson, John MS 11th Inf. Co.C Lt.
Richardson, John MS 15th (Cons.) Inf. Co.K
Richardson, John MS 26th Inf. Co.B Sgt.
Richardson, John MS 32nd Inf. Co.I Music.
Richardson, John MS 41st Inf. Co.L Capt.
Richardson, John MS 43rd Inf. Co.A
Richardson, John MO 9th (Elliott's) Cav. Co.B
Richardson, John MO Cav. Freeman's Regt.
  Co.G
Richardson, John MO Cav. Williams' Regt. Co.E
Richardson, John MO St.Guard
Richardson, John NC Inf. 2nd Bn. Co.F
Richardson, John NC 5th Sr.Res. Co.B
Richardson, John NC 5th Sr.Res. Co.H
Richardson, John NC 34th Inf. Co.A
Richardson, John NC 37th Inf. Co.K
Richardson, John NC 48th Inf. Co.F
Richardson, John NC 49th Inf. Co.I
Richardson, John NC 53rd Inf. Co.F
Richardson, John NC Walker's Bn. Thomas'
  Legion Co.A
Richardson, John SC 2nd Cav. Co.B

Richardson, John SC Arty. Stuart's Co. (Beaufort Vol.Arty.)

Richardson, John SC 12th Inf. Co.C

Richardson, John TN Cav. 1st Bn. (McNairy's) Co.D

Richardson, John TN 4th (Murray's) Cav. Co.D

Richardson, John TN 14th (Neely's) Cav. Co.F

Richardson, John TN 13th Inf. Co.K 2nd Lt.

Richardson, John TN Inf. 22nd Bn. Co.E

Richardson, John TN 43rd Inf. Co.C

Richardson, John TN 43rd Inf. Co.D

Richardson, John TX 2nd Cav. Co.K

Richardson, John TX 12th Cav. Co.E

Richardson, John TX 15th Cav. Co.C

Richardson, John TX 17th Cav. Co.K

Richardson, John TX 25th Cav. Co.F Cpl.

Richardson, John TX 32nd Cav. Co.F

Richardson, John TX 33rd Cav. Co.B

Richardson, John TX 34th Cav. Co.D 2nd Lt.

Richardson, John TX Cav. McCord's Frontier Regt. Co.I

Richardson, John TX 11th (Spaight's) Bn.Vol. Co.A

Richardson, John VA 2nd Bn.Res. Co.A

Richardson, John VA 39th Inf. Co.A

Richardson, John VA 56th Inf. Co.F Capt.

Richardson, John 1st Conf.Cav. 2nd Co.C

Richardson, John 3rd Conf.Cav. Co.F

Richardson, John 1st Conf.Inf. 2nd Co.I

Richardson, John 4th Conf.Inf. Co.E

Richardson, John A. AL 7th Cav. Co.B

Richardson, John A. AL 36th Inf. Co.G

Richardson, John A. GA 62nd Cav. Co.I Capt.

Richardson, John A. GA 1st (Olmstead's) Inf. Co.C

Richardson, John A. GA 41st Inf. Co.B

Richardson, John A. NC 2nd Cav. (19th St.Troops) Co.G

Richardson, John A. NC 2nd Arty. (36th St.Troops) Co.I Lt.Col.

Richardson, John A. NC 45th Inf. Co.E

Richardson, John A. TX 11th (Spaight's) Bn.Vol. Co.C,A

Richardson, John A. VA 3rd Cav. Co.F

Richardson, John A. VA Cav. Mosby's Regt. (Part.Rangers) Co.C

Richardson, John A. GA 21st Inf. Co.D

Richardson, John B. LA Washington Arty.Bn. Co.1,2 Capt.

Richardson, John C. AR 9th Inf. Old Co.B, Co.F

Richardson, John C. GA 38th Inf. Co.I 1st Sgt.

Richardson, John C. MO 10th Inf. Co.A Sgt.

Richardson, John C. NC 48th Inf. Co.D

Richardson, John C. NC 58th Inf. Co.G 2nd Lt.

Richardson, John C. VA 136th Mil. Co.H

Richardson, John D. AL 63rd Inf. Co.B

Richardson, John D. MD Arty. 4th Btty. Sgt.

Richardson, John D. NC 45th Inf. Co.D

Richardson, John D. SC Arty. Stuart's Co. (Beaufort Vol.Arty.)

Richardson, John D. VA 3rd Cav. Co.K

Richardson, John D. VA 9th Cav. Co.G

Richardson, John D. VA 11th Inf. Co.B

Richardson, John D. VA 58th Inf. Co.D

Richardson, Jno. D. Gen. & Staff Maj.,QM

Richardson, Jno. D. Gen. & Staff 1st Lt.,ADC

Richardson, John F. TX 32nd Cav. Co.E Sgt.

Richardson, John F. VA 51st Inf. Co.B

Richardson, John G. FL 1st Inf. Old Co.H

Richardson, John G. FL 7th Inf. Co.D Sgt.

Richardson, John G. KY 8th Mtd.Inf. Co.F

Richardson, John G. VA Hvy.Arty. Wright's Co.

Richardson, John H. AL 54th Inf. Co.D

Richardson, John H. MS 23rd Inf. Co.C

Richardson, John H. MO 1st N.E. Cav. Co.H

Richardson, John H. SC 1st (McCreary's) Inf. Co.G

Richardson, John H. TN 17th Inf. Co.C

Richardson, John H. TX 12th Inf. Co.G

Richardson, John H. VA 7th Cav. Capt.

Richardson, John H. VA Cav. 39th Bn. Maj.

Richardson, John H. VA 2nd Arty. Co.H

Richardson, John H. VA 4th Inf. Co.E Sgt.

Richardson, John H. VA 6th Inf. Co.K

Richardson, John H. VA 9th Inf. Co.K

Richardson, John H. VA 15th Inf. Co.I

Richardson, John H. VA Inf. 22nd Bn. Co.H

Richardson, John H. VA 42nd Inf. Co.F

Richardson, John H. VA 46th Inf. Lt.Col.

Richardson, John H. Sig.Corps,CSA

Richardson, John I. TX 12th Cav. Co.F 2nd Lt.

Richardson, John J. AL 5th Inf. Co.A

Richardson, John K. TX 3rd Cav. Co.F Cpl.

Richardson, John M. MO 8th Inf. Co.D

Richardson, John M. NC 43rd Inf. Co.B

Richardson, John M. SC 1st (Hagood's) Inf. 1st Co.H

Richardson, John M. TN 15th (Stewart's) Cav. Co.F Sgt.

Richardson, John M. VA 20th Inf. Co.H

Richardson, John M. VA Inf. 25th Bn. Co.E Sgt.

Richardson, Jno. M. Gen. & Staff Capt.,AA,IG

Richardson, John N. MS 21st Inf. Co.E

Richardson, John P. AL 19th Inf. Co.E

Richardson, John P. VA 36th Inf. Co.C

Richardson, John P. VA 59th Inf. 2nd Co.F

Richardson, John Q. NC 52nd Inf. Maj.

Richardson, John R. AL 36th Inf. Co.A

Richardson, John R. AR 8th Inf. New Co.F Capt.

Richardson, John R. AR 14th (McCarver's) Inf. Co.B 2nd Lt.

Richardson, John R. AR 27th Inf. Co.G 1st Lt.

Richardson, John R. MS 33rd Inf. Co.H Sgt.

Richardson, John R. MO 4th Cav. Co.B

Richardson, John R. MO Cav. Preston's Bn. Co.B

Richardson, John R. NC Inf. 2nd Bn. Co.F Sgt.

Richardson, John R. NC 23rd Inf. Co.A Sgt.

Richardson, John R. NC 37th Inf. Co.K

Richardson, John R. VA 26th Inf. Co.C

Richardson, John R. VA 58th Inf. Co.D

Richardson, John R. VA 61st Mil. Co.A Cpl.

Richardson, John S. AR 1st Mtd.Rifles Co.K

Richardson, John S. GA Inf. 14th Bn. (St.Guards) Co.A

Richardson, John S. SC 2nd Inf. Co.D Capt.

Richardson, John S. VA 14th Inf. Co.C

Richardson, John S. VA 38th Inf. Co.C

Richardson, John S. VA 51st Inf. Co.H

Richardson, John S. Gen. & Staff Capt.,AQM

Richardson, Johnson M. GA 29th Inf. Co.K

Richardson, John T. LA Arty. Green's Co. (LA Guard Btty.)

Richardson, John T. LA 1st (Nelligan's) Inf. Co.C, 1st Co.B

Richardson, John T. LA Inf. 1st Sp.Bn. (Rightor's) New Co.C

Richardson, John T. LA 8th Inf. Co.F

Richardson, John T. LA 28th (Gray's) Inf. Co.I

Richardson, John T. NC 28th Inf. Co.E

Richardson, John T. VA Cav. Young's Co. 1st Sgt.

Richardson, John T. VA 14th Inf. Co.E Sgt.

Richardson, John T. 15th Conf.Cav. Co.H Sgt.

Richardson, John T.R. VA 14th Inf. Co.C

Richardson, John W. AL 41st Inf. Co.G

Richardson, John W. GA 3rd Inf. Co.C,D

Richardson, John W. GA 3rd Inf. Co.L

Richardson, John W. GA Inf. Fuller's Co. 1st Sgt.

Richardson, John W. GA Inf. (High Shoals Defend.) Medlin's Ind.Co.

Richardson, John W. KY 1st (Butler's) Cav. Co.A

Richardson, John W. KY 1st (Helm's) Cav. Co.A

Richardson, John W. MS 15th Inf. Co.G

Richardson, John W. NC 26th Inf. Co.B 2nd Lt.

Richardson, John W. TN 14th Cav. Co.F Capt.

Richardson, John W. TN 48th (Voorhies') Inf. Co.F Cpl.

Richardson, John W. VA 21st Cav. Co.B

Richardson, John W. VA 1st Arty. Co.A

Richardson, John W. VA Lt.Arty. W.P. Carter's Co.

Richardson, John W. VA 3rd Inf. Co.F Music.

Richardson, John W. VA 23rd Inf. Co.A

Richardson, John W. VA 32nd Inf. 1st Co.K

Richardson, John W. Gen. & Staff Capt., Comsy.Off.

Richardson, Jonathan TN 26th Inf. 1st Co.H

Richardson, Jonathan H. NC 5th Inf. Co.C

Richardson, Joseph GA 3rd Res. Co.K

Richardson, Joseph GA 11th Inf. Co.B

Richardson, Joseph GA 19th Inf. Co.B

Richardson, Joseph KY 9th Mtd.Inf. Co.A

Richardson, Joseph MS Inf. 3rd Bn. Co.C

Richardson, Joseph MO 2nd Cav. Co.E

Richardson, Joseph MO 3rd Cav. Co.A

Richardson, Joseph NC 21st Inf. Co.M

Richardson, Joseph NC 26th Inf. Co.A

Richardson, Joseph NC 45th Inf. Co.G,B

Richardson, Joseph NC 52nd Inf. Co.H

Richardson, Joseph NC 53rd Inf. Co.E Cpl.

Richardson, Joseph SC Inf. 9th Bn. Co.E Cpl.

Richardson, Joseph SC 26th Inf. Co.I

Richardson, Joseph TN 25th Inf. Co.B

Richardson, Joseph TX 26th Cav. Co.I

Richardson, Joseph VA 9th Mil. Co.B

Richardson, Joseph VA Inf. 23rd Bn. Co.A

Richardson, Joseph VA 55th Inf. Co.F

Richardson, Joseph 1st Conf.Eng.Troops Co.F Artif.

Richardson, Joseph Gen. & Staff AASurg.

Richardson, Joseph A. TN 15th (Stewart's) Cav. Co.B 2nd Lt.

Richardson, Joseph A.T. TN 1st (Feild's) Inf. Co.H

Richardson, Joseph B. NC 34th Inf. Co.A

Richardson, Joseph C. NC 53rd Inf. Co.C Capt.
Richardson, Joseph C. TN 25th Inf. Co.D Cpl.
Richardson, Joseph D. MO Searcy's Bn.S.S.
   Co.F
Richardson, Joseph E. VA 2nd Arty. Co.A
Richardson, Joseph E. VA Inf. 22nd Bn. Co.A
Richardson, Joseph G. MS 11th Inf. Co.B Sgt.
Richardson, Joseph H. KY 1st Inf. Co.I
Richardson, Joseph H. NC 47th Inf. Co.I
Richardson, Joseph H. NC 53rd Inf. Co.F
Richardson, Joseph H. VA 42nd Inf. Co.F
Richardson, Joseph J. SC 10th Inf. Co.A
Richardson, Joseph L. GA 4th Inf. Co.E
Richardson, Joseph L. VA Hvy.Arty. Epes' Co.
Richardson, Joseph L. VA 3rd Inf. Co.C
Richardson, Joseph M. MS 35th Inf. Co.H
Richardson, Joseph M. SC 12th Inf. Co.I
Richardson, Joseph M. VA Lt.Arty. Parker's Co.
   Music.
Richardson, Joseph S. AL 41st Inf. Co.E
Richardson, Joseph S. NC 4th Cav. (59th
   St.Troops) Co.G
Richardson, Josephus S. GA 38th Inf. Co.K
Richardson, Joseph W. LA 1st (Nelligan's) Inf.
   Co.H
Richardson, Joshua LA 1st Hvy.Arty. (Reg.)
   Co.H
Richardson, Joshua NC 34th Inf. Co.A 1st Cpl.
Richardson, Joshua TX 30th Cav. Co.E
Richardson, J.P. AL Mil. 2nd Regt.Vol. Co.D
   3rd Lt.
Richardson, J.P. GA 64th Inf. Co.I
Richardson, J.P. MS 4th Inf. Co.G Chap.
Richardson, J.P. MS 46th Inf. Co.K
Richardson, J.P. TN 4th Inf. Co.G 1st Lt.
Richardson, J.P. TN 48th (Nixon's) Inf. Co.K
Richardson, J.P. TN 54th Inf. Co.E
Richardson, J.R. AL 4th (Russell's) Cav. Co.A
Richardson, J.R. AL Inf. 2nd Regt. Co.B
Richardson, J.R. AL 62nd Inf. Co.C
Richardson, J.R. AR 1st Inf. Co.A
Richardson, J.R. GA 31st Inf. Co.G
Richardson, J.R. SC Arty. Gregg's Co.
   (McQueen Lt.Arty.)
Richardson, J.R. SC Arty. Manigault's Bn. 1st
   Co.C
Richardson, J.R. SC 12th Inf. Co.C
Richardson, J.R. SC 12th Inf. Co.C
Richardson, J.R. SC 21st Inf. Co.I
Richardson, J.R. TN 38th Inf. 2nd Co.A
Richardson, J.R. TX 20th Bn.St.Troops Co.A
Richardson, J.S. AR 2nd Cav. Co.C Sgt.Maj.
Richardson, J.S. GA 1st Inf. Co.C
Richardson, J.S. NC 21st Inf. Co.M
Richardson, J.S. SC 5th Bn.Res. Co.B
Richardson, J.S. SC 21st Inf. Co.I
Richardson, J.S. SC 23rd Inf. AQM
Richardson, J.S. TN 15th (Cons.) Cav. Co.F
Richardson, J.S. TN 4th Inf. Co.K
Richardson, J.S. TX 14th Cav. Co.A
Richardson, J.S. VA Cav. 37th Bn. Co.E Sgt.
Richardson, J.S. VA 44th Inf. Co.B
Richardson, J.S. 1st Conf.Inf. 2nd Co.C
Richardson, J.S. Conf.Inf. Tucker's Regt. Co.I
Richardson, J.S. Gen. & Staff Asst.Surg.
Richardson, J.T. AL Cav. Murphy's Bn. Co.C
   Cpl.

Richardson, J.T. AR 8th Inf. New Co.F
Richardson, J.T. MS Inf. 3rd Bn. Co.I
Richardson, J.T. SC 5th Cav. Co.I
Richardson, J.T. SC Cav. 14th Bn. Co.D
Richardson, J.T. TX Granbury's Cons.Brig.
   Asst.Surg.
Richardson, J.T. TX 12th Inf. Co.I
Richardson, J.V. AR 32nd Inf. Co.C 1st Sgt.
Richardson, J.V. MO Cav. Ford's Bn. Co.C
   Capt.
Richardson, J.W. AL 2nd Cav. Co.H
Richardson, J.W. AL Cav. 4th Bn. (Love's)
   Co.C
Richardson, J.W. AL 1st Regt.Conscr. Co.D
Richardson, J.W. AL Inf. 2nd Regt. Co.E
Richardson, J.W. AL 17th Inf. Co.H
Richardson, J.W. GA Cav. 19th Bn. Co.E
Richardson, J.W. GA Lt.Arty. Fraser's Btty.
Richardson, J.W. GA 5th Res. Co.C
Richardson, J.W. GA 55th Inf. Co.H
Richardson, J.W. KY 3rd Mtd.Inf. Co.B
Richardson, J.W. MS Cav. 4th Bn. Co.A
Richardson, J.W. MS 44th Inf. Co.A
Richardson, J.W. NC 21st Inf. Co.L
Richardson, J.W. SC Arty. Gregg's Co.
   (McQueen Lt.Arty.)
Richardson, J.W. TN Cav. Nixon's Regt. Co.I
Richardson, J.W. TN 8th Inf. Co.G
Richardson, J.W. TN 28th (Cons.) Inf. Co.D
   Sgt.
Richardson, J.W. TN 38th Inf. Co.D
Richardson, J.W. TN 43rd Inf. Co.G Cpl.
Richardson, J.W. TN 50th Inf. Co.C
Richardson, J.W. TX 18th Inf. Co.A Capt.
Richardson, J.W. VA 4th Cav. & Inf.St.Line 1st
   Co.I
Richardson, J.W. 8th (Wade's) Conf.Cav. Co.C
Richardson, J.W. 10th Conf.Cav. Co.K
Richardson, J.Y.D. LA 4th Inf. Co.A
Richardson, J.Z. NC 6th Inf. Co.G
Richardson, K. TX 20th Cav. Co.F
Richardson, K. TX 13th Vol. 1st Co.K Cpl.
Richardson, K. TX 21st Inf. Co.H
Richardson, Kinsey TX 11th (Spaight's) Bn.Vol.
   Co.D
Richardson, L. FL 2nd Cav. Co.H
Richardson, L. GA 55th Inf. Co.H
Richardson, L. KY 3rd Cav. Co.A Sgt.
Richardson, L. LA 3rd Inf. Co.H
Richardson, L. MS 39th Inf. Co.B
Richardson, L. Gen. & Staff AASurg.
Richardson, L.A. TX 21st Inf. Co.E
Richardson, Larkin A. TX 11th (Spaight's)
   Bn.Vol. Co.C
Richardson, Lat VA 53rd Inf. Co.F
Richardson, Lawson E.G. AR Cav. Nave's Bn.
   Co.E
Richardson, L.B. GA 8th Cav. Old Co.I
Richardson, L.B. GA 62nd Cav. Co.I
Richardson, L.B. MS 14th (Cons.) Inf. Co.F
Richardson, L.B. TN 8th (Smith's) Cav. Co.D
   Ord.Sgt.
Richardson, L.B. TX 30th Cav. Co.H
Richardson, L. Bryant MS 14th Inf. Co.K
Richardson, L.C. TX Cav. 6th Bn. Co.C
Richardson, L.C. 1st Cherokee Mtd.Vol. 1st Co.I
Richardson, L.D. VA Mil. Carroll Cty.

Richardson, Leopold LA 1st (Nelligan's) Inf.
   Co.G
Richardson, Leroy C. VA 28th Inf. Co.D
Richardson, Leslie LA 1st Hvy.Arty. (Reg.)
   Co.A
Richardson, Lever GA 3rd Bn. (St.Guards) Co.B
   Capt.
Richardson, Levi TN 39th Mtd.Inf. Co.K
Richardson, Lewis AR 27th Inf. Co.F
Richardson, Lewis GA 8th Cav. Co.B
Richardson, Lewis GA 62nd Cav. Co.B
Richardson, Lewis MS 18th Inf. Co.D Sgt.
Richardson, Lewis VA 63rd Inf. Co.G
Richardson, Lewis L. GA 1st (Olmstead's) Inf.
   Co.C
Richardson, Lewis L. LA 12th Inf. 1st Co.M,
   Co.C
Richardson, Lewis S. TX 19th Cav. Co.K
Richardson, Lewis T. Gen. & Staff Rec. for
   Asst.Surg.
Richardson, L.H. MS 11th (Perrin's) Cav. Co.H
   Cpl.
Richardson, L.H. 4th Conf.Eng.Troops
Richardson, L.J. GA 31st Inf. Co.E Ch.Music.
Richardson, L.J. LA 19th Inf. Co.B
Richardson, L.M. AR 45th Cav. Co.C
Richardson, L.M. AR 7th Inf. Co.D
Richardson, L.M. AR 38th Inf. Co.D
Richardson, L.M. MS Inf. 3rd Bn. (St.Troops)
   Co.A
Richardson, L.M. NC 6th Inf. Co.B
Richardson, L.M. TX Cav. Terry's Regt. Co.C
Richardson, Logan P. VA 42nd Inf. Co.F
Richardson, Lorenzo D. VA 63rd Inf. Co.G, 2nd
   Co.I
Richardson, Lot VA 58th Inf. Co.D
Richardson, Louis MS 28th Cav. Co.A
Richardson, Louis VA Mil. Carroll Cty.
Richardson, Lovin NC 44th Inf. Co.H Sgt.
Richardson, Loyd M. NC 52nd Inf. Co.E
Richardson, L.R. TN Lt.Arty. Scott's Co.
Richardson, L.T. MO Cav. Fristoe's Regt. Co.F
Richardson, Lucian W. VA 1st Arty. Co.B Capt.
Richardson, Lucian W. VA 32nd Inf. 1st Co.H
   2nd Lt.
Richardson, Luther H.J. AL 11th Inf. Co.I
Richardson, L.W. TN 4th Cav. Co.B
Richardson, L.W. VA Lt.Arty. 1st Bn. Co.B
   Capt.
Richardson, L.W. VA Arty. Richardson's Co.
   Capt.
Richardson, M. GA 62nd Cav. Co.H
Richardson, M. MO 3rd Inf. Co.G
Richardson, M. SC 18th Inf. Co.A
Richardson, M. Gen. & Staff,PACS Asst.Surg.
Richardson, M.A. AL 7th Cav. Co.I
Richardson, M.A. AL 25th Inf. Co.E
Richardson, M.A. MS 12th Cav. Co.D
Richardson, Macager TN 25th Inf. Co.G
Richardson, Madison M. MS 23rd Inf. Co.E
Richardson, Malachi GA 2nd Res. Co.F Capt.
Richardson, Malachi GA 3rd Inf. Co.H
Richardson, Manly NC 2nd Arty. (36th
   St.Troops) Co.B
Richardson, Marcus TN 7th (Duckworth's) Cav.
   Co.I

Richardson, Marcus C. VA 23rd Cav. Co.D 1st Lt.

Richardson, Marcus C. VA Lt.Arty. Douthat's Co.

Richardson, Marcus C. VA 28th Inf. Co.H

Richardson, Marcus F. VA 23rd Cav. Co.D Capt.

Richardson, Marion SC 10th Inf. Co.L

Richardson, Marion TN 40th Inf. Co.H

Richardson, Mark AL 9th Inf. Co.I

Richardson, Martin L. GA 3rd Inf. Co.B

Richardson, Mason VA 53rd Inf. Co.C

Richardson, Mason C. NC 48th Inf. Co.E

Richardson, Mat TN 8th Inf. Co.F

Richardson, Mathew W. VA 26th Inf. Co.K

Richardson, Mathias NC McMillan's Co.

Richardson, Mathias SC 1st Arty. Co.A Cpl.

Richardson, Matthew LA Miles' Legion Co.B 1st Sgt.

Richardson, Matthew J. VA 3rd Cav. Co.A

Richardson, Matthias SC 1st St.Troops Co.A

Richardson, M.B. AL 53rd (Part.Rangers) Co.K

Richardson, M.B. GA 12th Cav. Co.A

Richardson, M.C. NC 3rd Cav. (41st St.Troops)

Richardson, Mered TX Cav. McCord's Frontier Regt. Co.I

Richardson, Meredith NC 61st Inf. Co.I

Richardson, M.F. VA 7th Cav. Co.E Sgt.

Richardson, M.G. GA 7th Inf. Co.G

Richardson, M.H. MS 12th Inf. Co.C Music.

Richardson, M.H. MS Rogers' Co. Music.

Richardson, M.H. MS Cp.Guard (Cp. of Instr. for Conscr.)

Richardson, Miles O. AL Inf. 1st Regt. Co.G

Richardson, Millington KY 6th Cav. Co.E

Richardson, Milton GA Inf. 9th Bn. Co.A Cpl.

Richardson, Milton TN 37th Inf. Co.D

Richardson, M.J. NC 4th Sr.Res. Co.I

Richardson, M.L. AL 7th Inf. Co.K

Richardson, M.L. AR 8th Inf. New Co.E

Richardson, M.L. MD 1st Cav. Co.D Capt.

Richardson, M.L. VA Cav. Mosby's Regt. (Part.Rangers) Co.C

Richardson, M.M. AR 15th Inf. Co.C

Richardson, M.M. GA Inf. 9th Bn. Co.A

Richardson, M.M. GA 37th Inf. Co.D 1st Lt.

Richardson, Morgan J. GA 1st Cav. Co.C

Richardson, Morgan J. GA 29th Inf. Co.D

Richardson, Morgan M. MS 11th Inf. Co.B

Richardson, Moses GA 16th Inf. Co.H Capt.

Richardson, Moses GA 42nd Inf. Co.D

Richardson, Moses GA 52nd Inf. Asst.Surg.

Richardson, Moses MS Inf. 7th Bn. Co.G

Richardson, Moses M. GA Inf. 40th Bn. Co.B Cpl.

Richardson, Moses M. GA 41st Inf. Co.E

Richardson, M.R. TN Cav. 1st Bn. (McNairy's) Co.E

Richardson, M.S. TN 38th Inf. 2nd Co.A

Richardson, M.T. TN 7th Cav. Co.C

Richardson, M.V. AR 27th Inf. Old Co.C, Co.D Capt.

Richardson, M.V. MS 6th Inf. Co.C

Richardson, M.V. MS 9th Bn.S.S. Co.C

Richardson, M.V. TN Inf. 1st Cons.Regt. Co.D

Richardson, M.V. TN 8th Inf. Co.F

Richardson, M.V.B. MS 7th Inf. Co.B

Richardson, M.W. AR 26th Inf. Co.E

Richardson, M.W. NC 48th Inf. Co.F

Richardson, M.W. TN 19th (Biffle's) Cav. Co.D

Richardson, M.W. Conf.Cav. Wood's Regt. Co.K

Richardson, N. NC 22nd Inf. Co.I

Richardson, N. TN 8th Cav. Co.G

Richardson, N.A. MO 10th Inf. Co.A

Richardson, Napoleon B. AL 12th Inf. Co.I

Richardson, Nat GA Inf. Taylor's Co.

Richardson, Nathan GA 2nd Inf. Co.F

Richardson, Nathan TN 21st (Carter's) Cav. 1st Lt.

Richardson, Nathan VA 1st Arty. Co.E,F 2nd Lt.

Richardson, Nathan VA 32nd Inf. Co.G 2nd Lt.

Richardson, Nathaniel AL 12th Inf. Co.F

Richardson, Nathan P. AL 41st Inf. Co.B 2nd Lt.

Richardson, N.B. MS 11th (Perrin's) Cav. Co.G

Richardson, N.B. MS Hudson's Co. (Noxubee Guards) Cpl.

Richardson, N.D. AL 19th Inf. Surg.

Richardson, N.D. Gen. & Staff, Medical Dept. Surg.

Richardson, Nestor F. VA 9th Inf. Co.K

Richardson, Nestor F. Sig.Corps,CSA Cpl.

Richardson, Newton GA 43rd Inf. Co.B

Richardson, Newton GA 52nd Inf. Co.C

Richardson, N. Green VA 51st Inf. Co.B

Richardson, Nicholas S. VA Arty. Forrest's Co.

Richardson, Nicholas T. MD Arty. 4th Btty.

Richardson, Nick D. AL 50th Inf. Co.E Surg.

Richardson, Noah NC 26th Inf. Co.G

Richardson, Noah TN 25th Inf. Co.G

Richardson, Noah T. AL 4th Inf. Co.D

Richardson, Nolley MS 3rd Inf. (St.Troops) Co.H

Richardson, N.P. TN 12th (Cons.) Inf. Co.D

Richardson, N.P. TN 22nd Inf. Co.H Bvt.2nd Lt.

Richardson, N.P. TX 20th Inf. Co.D Capt.

Richardson, N.T. VA 2nd Inf.Loc.Def. Co.K

Richardson, N.T. VA Inf. 2nd Bn.Loc.Def. Co.B

Richardson, O.A. VA 54th Mil. Co.H

Richardson, O. Clay MS 38th Cav. Co.I

Richardson, O.H.P. AR Inf. Hardy's Regt. Co.F 1st Lt.

Richardson, O.L. 3rd Conf.Eng.Troops Co.E Cpl.

Richardson, Oliver MS 43rd Inf. Co.K

Richardson, Oliver H.P. AR 1st (Colquitt's) Inf. Co.A 2nd Lt.

Richardson, Oliver H.P. AR 24th Inf. Co.G 3rd Lt.

Richardson, Oliver L. VA Lt.Arty. Lowry's Co.

Richardson, Oliver P. AR Lt.Arty. Rivers' Btty. 1st Lt.

Richardson, Oliver P. GA 6th Inf. Co.H

Richardson, Oliver P. GA 65th Inf. Co.G

Richardson, Oliver P. SC 10th Inf. Co.A 1st Lt.

Richardson, O.P. GA 18th Inf. Co.B

Richardson, O.R. MS 23rd Inf. Co.E

Richardson, Orang. C. MS Page's Co. (Lexington Guards)

Richardson, Orion C. MS 17th Inf. Co.B

Richardson, Othelo D. TX 14th Cav. Co.E

Richardson, P. GA Inf. (Loc.Def.) Whiteside's Nav.Bn. Co.A

Richardson, P. VA 14th Cav. Co.G

Richardson, P.A. Bradford's Corps Scouts & Guards Co.A

Richardson, P.C. GA 47th Inf. Co.K

Richardson, P.C. MS 28th Cav. Co.A 1st Lt.

Richardson, P.C. TN Cav. Jackson's Co.

Richardson, P.D. VA Inf. 25th Bn. Co.D

Richardson, P.D. VA 46th Inf. 2nd Co.B

Richardson, P.E. GA Cav. 1st Bn.Res. McKinney's Co.

Richardson, P.E. GA 5th Inf. (St.Guards) Johnston's Co.

Richardson, Perry NC 12th Inf. Co.H

Richardson, Perry NC 32nd Inf. Co.H

Richardson, Peter LA 28th (Gray's) Inf. Co.B

Richardson, Peter MO 2nd N.E. Cav. (Franklin's Regt.) Co.B

Richardson, Peter NC Inf. 2nd Bn. Co.F

Richardson, Peter TN 4th (Murray's) Cav. Co.B

Richardson, Peter TN Inf. 22nd Bn. Co.H

Richardson, Peter TX 14th Inf. Co.A Cpl.

Richardson, Peter VA 28th Inf. Co.D

Richardson, Peter VA 42nd Inf. Co.B

Richardson, Peter VA 58th Inf. Co.D

Richardson, Peter H. MS 26th Inf. Co.F,G

Richardson, Peyton B. MS 12th Inf. Co.A

Richardson, Peyton G. VA 54th Inf. Co.I

Richardson, P.G. SC 21st Inf. Co.I

Richardson, P.L. AR 27th Inf. Old Co.C, Co.D 1st Lt.,Adj.

Richardson, Pleasant NC 5th Sr.Res. Co.C

Richardson, P.M. MS 41st Inf. Co.B

Richardson, P.M. MO Lt.Arty. Barret's Co. Artif.

Richardson, P.N. TN Lt.Arty. Morton's Co. Harness Maker

Richardson, P.O. MO 9th Inf. Co.C

Richardson, P.O. MO Inf. Clark's Regt. Co.B

Richardson, Preston C. TN 1st (Feild's) Inf. Co.H

Richardson, P.T. AL Inf. 2nd Regt. Co.B

Richardson, P.T. AL 42nd Inf. Co.B Cpl.

Richardson, Quincy J. VA 41st Inf. Co.A

Richardson, R. GA Phillips' Legion Co.B

Richardson, R. MS Cav. Polk's Ind.Co. (Polk Rangers)

Richardson, R. TN 16th Inf. Co.A

Richardson, R. TX 2nd Inf. Co.H

Richardson, R. TX 3rd (Kirby's) Bn.Vol. Co.C

Richardson, R. TX 20th Inf. Co.G

Richardson, R. VA 22nd Inf. Co.H

Richardson, R.A. TX Inf. 1st St.Troops Saxton's Co.

Richardson, R.B. GA 8th Cav. Old Co.I

Richardson, R.B. GA 62nd Cav. Co.I

Richardson, R.B. MS 12th Cav. Co.D

Richardson, R.B. MS 10th Inf. Old Co.C

Richardson, R.C. LA 2nd Cav. Co.B

Richardson, R.C. SC 4th Cav. Co.K

Richardson, R.C. TX 7th Inf. Co.K

Richardson, R.D. AR 19th (Dockery's) Inf. Co.G

Richardson, R.D. MO 4th Cav. Co.B

Richardson, R.E. MS 38th Cav. Surg.

Richardson, R.E. SC 3rd Inf. Co.A Capt.

Richardson, R.E. VA 3rd Inf.Loc.Def. Co.E

Richardson, Reuben SC 6th Cav. Co.B
Richardson, Reuben VA 16th Cav. Co.F
Richardson, R.F. NC 52nd Inf. Co.D
Richardson, R.G. VA Inf. 22nd Bn. Co.H
Richardson, R.H. GA 41st Inf. Co.B
Richardson, Richard GA 9th Inf. Co.I
Richardson, Richard MD Arty. 1st Btty.
Richardson, Richard MS 12th Inf. Co.E Capt.
Richardson, Richard NC 34th Inf. Co.A
Richardson, Richard B. VA Lt.Arty. Douthat's
Co. Cpl.
Richardson, Richard B. VA 28th Inf. Co.H,A
Cpl.
Richardson, Richard B. 1st Conf.Eng.Troops
Co.G Sgt.
Richardson, Richard C., Jr. SC Inf. Hampton
Legion Co.C
Richardson, Richard H. VA 32nd Inf. Co.C
Richardson, Richard J. 14th Inf. Co.C
Richardson, Rich. C. Gen. & Staff Asst.Surg.
Richardson, Richmond AR 24th Inf. Co.D
Richardson, Riley R. MS 15th (Cons.) Inf. Co.H
Richardson, Riley R. MS 20th Inf. Co.G
Richardson, Riley S. TN 24th Inf. 2nd Co.H,
Co.M
Richardson, Rily D. TX 18th Cav. Co.A
Richardson, Rives B. VA 6th Inf. Co.K
Richardson, R.J. AL 60th Inf. Co.B
Richardson, R.J. GA 11th Inf. Co.G
Richardson, R.L. AL 5th Inf. New Co.I
Richardson, R.M. MS 3rd Inf. Co.E
Richardson, R.M. MS 23rd Inf. Co.E
Richardson, R.M. SC 4th St.Troops Co.A
Richardson, R.M. TX 24th Cav. Co.G
Richardson, R.M. TX Cav. Martin's Regt. Co.D
Richardson, R.N. TN Inf. 1st Cons.Regt. Co.B
Richardson, R.N.C. LA Mil. Chalmette Regt.
Co.A
Richardson, R.O. GA 2nd Inf. Co.F
Richardson, R.O. 2nd Conf.Eng.Troops Co.F
Richardson, Robert AR 33rd Inf. Co.G
Richardson, Robert GA 7th Inf. Co.E
Richardson, Robert GA 53rd Inf. Co.K
Richardson, Robert KY 2nd Mtd.Inf.
Richardson, Robert LA 2nd Inf. Co.C
Richardson, Robert LA 13th Inf. Co.B,H
Richardson, Robert LA 17th Inf. Co.D Col.
Richardson, Robert LA 17th Inf. Co.K Cpl.
Richardson, Robert MS 35th Inf. Co.F
Richardson, Robert NC 37th Inf. Co.B
Richardson, Robert NC 56th Inf. Co.C Cook
Richardson, Robert SC 1st (Butler's) Inf. Co.I
Richardson, Robert TN 35th Inf. Co.B
Richardson, Robert TX Waul's Legion Co.A
Richardson, Robert VA 38th Inf. Co.C Cpl.
Richardson, Robert VA 157th Mil. Co.B
Richardson, Robt. Gen. & Staff 1st Lt.,Adj.
Richardson, Robert A. VA 24th Inf. Co.G Capt.
Richardson, Robert B. GA 44th Inf. Co.A
Richardson, Robert B. VA 1st Arty.
Richardson, Robert B. VA Hvy.Arty. 10th Bn.
Asst.Surg.
Richardson, Robert B. VA 32nd Inf. 1st Co.H
Richardson, Robt. B. Gen. & Staff Asst.Surg.
Richardson, Robert C. VA Inf. 25th Bn. Co.C
Cpl.

Richardson, Robert D. Trans-MS Conf.Cav. 1st
Bn. Sgt.Maj.
Richardson, Robert E. TN 12th (Green's) Cav.
Sgt.
Richardson, Robert E. TX Cav. Hardeman's
Regt. Co.B
Richardson, Robert F. MS Inf. 3rd Bn. Co.C
Color Cpl.
Richardson, Robert G. NC 45th Inf. Co.E
Richardson, Robert H. VA 14th Inf. 2nd Co.G
Sgt.
Richardson, Robert H. VA 38th Inf. 1st Co.I
Richardson, Robert J. AL 3rd Bn. Hilliard's
Legion Vol. Co.C
Richardson, Robert J. MO Cav. Freeman's Regt.
Co.A
Richardson, Robert J. Conf.Cav. Wood's Regt.
Co.K Sgt.
Richardson, Robert L. AL 32nd Inf. Co.G
Richardson, Robert L. SC 2nd Rifles Co.G
Richardson, Robert N. TN 1st (Feild's) Inf. Co.D
Richardson, Robert P. SC 1st (Orr's) Rifles Co.D
Richardson, Robert P. VA 56th Inf. Co.K
Richardson, Robert R. MS Gordon's Co.
(Loc.Guard Wilkinson Cty.)
Richardson, Robert R. TX 11th Inf. Co.B Sgt.
Richardson, Robert S. VA 14th Inf. Co.C Cpl.
Richardson, Robert S. VA 44th Inf. Co.D
Richardson, Robert V. TN 12th (Green's) Cav.
Col.
Richardson, Ro. E. VA Lt.Arty. R.M. Ander-
son's Co. Cpl.
Richardson, Ro. E. Gen. & Staff Surg.
Richardson, Rolla S. GA 9th Inf. Co.C
Richardson, R.P. TN Cav. Kizer's Regt. Brooks'
Co.
Richardson, R.P. TX 28th Cav. Co.F
Richardson, R.R. AL 8th Inf. Co.K Sgt.
Richardson, R.R. LA Inf. 1st Sp.Bn. (Rightor's)
Co.D
Richardson, R.S. AL Cav. (St.Res.) Young's Co.
Sgt.
Richardson, R.S. AR Inf. Cocke's Regt.
Cons.Co.C,I
Richardson, R.S. GA Lt.Arty. 12th Bn. 3rd Co.C
Richardson, R.S. NC 4th Cav. (59th St.Troops)
Co.C
Richardson, R.T. AR 13th Inf. Co.E
Richardson, R.T. KY 7th Mtd.Inf. 1st Co.K
Richardson, Rudolph VA 2nd Arty. Co.H
Richardson, Rudolph VA Inf. 22nd Bn. Co.H
Richardson, Ruffin B. NC 5th Inf. Co.C
Richardson, Ruffin H. NC 24th Inf. Co.C 2nd
Lt.
Richardson, Rufus TN 42nd Inf. 2nd Co.F
Richardson, Rufus E. VA 20th Cav. Co.B
Richardson, Rufus R. MS 16th Inf. Co.K
Richardson, Russel G. VA 54th Inf. Co.E
Richardson, R.V. Gen. & Staff,PACS Col.
Richardson, R.W. AL 34th Inf. Co.D
Richardson, R.W. GA 56th Inf. Co.G
Richardson, R.W. GA Floyd Legion (St.Guards)
Co.B Cpl.
Richardson, R.W. KY 10th (Diamond's) Cav.
Co.B
Richardson, R.W. SC 1st Mtd.Mil. Smart's Co.
Richardson, R.W. SC 3rd Cav. Co.F

Richardson, S. AL 43rd Inf. Co.C
Richardson, S. AR 15th (Johnson's) Inf. Co.F
Richardson, S. GA 6th Cav.
Richardson, S. GA 54th Inf. Co.C
Richardson, S. KY 3rd Bn.Mtd.Rifles Co.B
Richardson, S. MO St.Guard
Richardson, S. NC 38th Inf. Co.K
Richardson, S. TX 33rd Cav. Co.H
Richardson, S. TX 21st Inf. Co.A Cpl.
Richardson, Sampson D. NC 26th Inf. Co.B
Richardson, Sampson M. KY 5th Mtd.Inf. Co.A
Cpl.
Richardson, Sampson M. VA Lt.Arty. 13th Bn.
Co.C
Richardson, Samuel AL Inf. 2nd Regt. Co.H,E
Richardson, Samuel AL 45th Inf. Co.G
Richardson, Samuel AL 63rd Inf. Co.A
Richardson, Samuel GA 61st Inf. Co.H
Richardson, Samuel LA 1st Inf.
Richardson, Samuel MO Cav. Williams' Regt.
Co.E
Richardson, Samuel NC 26th Inf. Co.G
Richardson, Samuel NC 32nd Inf. Co.E,F
Richardson, Samuel TN 25th Inf. Co.G
Richardson, Samuel TN 31st Inf. Co.B Cpl.
Richardson, Samuel TX Cav. 2nd Bn.St.Troops
Co.A
Richardson, Samuel TX 11th Inf. Co.D
Richardson, Samuel VA 5th Cav. (12 mo. '61-2)
Co.E
Richardson, Samuel VA Inf. 25th Bn. Co.A 3rd
Cook
Richardson, Samuel VA 38th Inf. Co.A
Richardson, Samuel Conf.Inf. 1st Bn. 2nd Co.C
1st Sgt.
Richardson, Samuel A. VA 28th Inf. Co.A
Richardson, Samuel C. VA 13th Cav. Co.G Cpl.
Richardson, Samuel E. VA 58th Inf. Co.D Sgt.
Richardson, Samuel H. AL 3rd Inf. Co.B
Richardson, Sam'l. H. Gen. & Staff Asst.Comsy.
Richardson, Samuel J. NC 48th Inf. Co.F
Richardson, Samuel J. TX 2nd Cav. 1st Co.F
Capt.
Richardson, Samuel J. TX Cav. Morgan's Regt.
Co.I Capt.
Richardson, Samuel L. MS 1st Lt.Arty. Co.A
Richardson, Samuel L. NC 48th Inf. Co.F
Richardson, Samuel M. SC Lt.Arty. 3rd (Pal-
metto) Bn. Co.G,K Sr.2nd Lt.
Richardson, Samuel M. SC 1st (Orr's) Rifles
Co.G
Richardson, Samuel N. NC 18th Inf. Co.K
Comsy.Sgt.
Richardson, Samuel R. GA 17th Inf. Co.B
Richardson, Samuel R. TX 2nd Cav. Co.K
Richardson, Samuel S. VA 38th Inf. Co.A
Richardson, Samuel T. TN 1st (Feild's) Inf.
Co.K
Richardson, Samuel T. TX 4th Cav. Co.H
Richardson, Saul VA 72nd Mil.
Richardson, S.C. SC 1st Mtd.Mil. Smart's Co.
Richardson, S.C. SC 5th Cav. Co.B
Richardson, S.C. TN 10th (DeMoss') Cav. Co.I
Richardson, S.C. SC Cav. 17th Bn. Co.C
Richardson, S.C.C. Gen. & Staff Asst.Surg.
Richardson, S.D. LA 5th Cav. Capt.
Richardson, S.E. LA Ogden's Cav. Lt.

Richardson, S.E. LA Inf. 9th Bn. Co.B 1st Lt.
Richardson, S. Elliott VA 61st Mil. Co.I
Richardson, Seth VA 3rd Cav.
Richardson, Seth VA 58th Inf. Co.D
Richardson, Seth VA 61st Mil. Co.G
Richardson, S.F. SC 3rd Inf. Co.A
Richardson, S.H. Exch.Bn. 1st Co.A,CSA Cpl.
Richardson, S.H. Gen. & Staff Capt.,AQM
Richardson, Shepard D. VA 26th Inf. Co.D
Richardson, S.I. TX 22nd Inf. Co.I Cpl.
Richardson, Sidney H. LA 6th Cav. Co.C
Richardson, Simeon MO 3rd Cav. Co.F Sgt.
Richardson, Simeon MO Cav. Freeman's Regt. Co.F
Richardson, Sinclair GA Inf. 9th Bn. Co.A
Richardson, Sineclair GA 37th Inf. Co.D
Richardson, Singleton W. GA Inf. 9th Bn. Co.A 1st Sgt.
Richardson, S.J. GA 3rd Bn.S.S. Co.A
Richardson, S.J. GA 18th Inf. Co.B
Richardson, S.J. KY 6th Mtd.Inf. Co.E
Richardson, S.J. MS 6th Cav. Co.H
Richardson, S.J. MO Inf. Perkins' Bn. Co.B
Richardson, S.J. VA 46th Inf. 2nd Co.B
Richardson, S.L. TN 48th (Nixon's) Inf. Co.I
Richardson, S.M. MO Cav. Poindexter's Regt.
Richardson, S.N. NC 2nd Arty. (36th St.Troops) Co.B
Richardson, S.N. SC 12th Inf. Co.H
Richardson, S.N. Morgan's Co.A,CSA
Richardson, S.O. TX Cav. 2nd Regt.St.Troops Co.C
Richardson, Sol. B. FL 5th Inf. Co.I
Richardson, Sol M. MO 9th Inf. Co.D Cpl.
Richardson, Soloman GA 8th Cav. Co.B
Richardson, Solomon GA 62nd Cav. Co.B
Richardson, Solomon S. TN 32nd Inf. Co.C Cpl.
Richardson, S.P. NC 21st Inf. Co.L
Richardson, S.P. TX 9th Cav. Co.K
Richardson, S.T. TX 1st Bn.S.S. Co.A,E
Richardson, S.T. TX 12th Inf. Co.G Cpl.
Richardson, Stephen GA 47th Inf. Co.K
Richardson, Stephen SC 21st Inf. Co.L
Richardson, Stephen D. AL 42nd Inf. Co.C
Richardson, Stephen W. AR 33rd Inf. Co.K
Richardson, Steven TX 11th (Spaight's) Bn.Vol. Co.A Cpl.
Richardson, Summerson KY 5th Mtd.Inf. Co.F
Richardson, S.W. GA 37th Inf. Co.D
Richardson, S.W. GA 54th Inf. Co.H
Richardson, S.W. MO Inf. Clark's Regt. Co.C
Richardson, S.W. TX 5th Inf. Co.G
Richardson, S.W. 1st Conf.Eng.Troops Co.F
Richardson, Sydney J. GA 21st Inf. Co.I Cpl.
Richardson, Sylvanus S. NC 26th Inf. Co.B
Richardson, Sylvester LA 3rd (Wingfield's) Cav. Co.A Cpl.
Richardson, Sylvester H. VA 53rd Inf. Co.B 2nd Lt.
Richardson, Sylvester H. VA Inf. Tomlin's Bn. Co.A Sgt.
Richardson, T. AL Cp. of Instr. Talladega
Richardson, T. GA 20th Inf. Co.A
Richardson, T. VA 1st (Farinholt's) Res. Co.E
Richardson, T.A. AR 24th Inf. Co.D 1st Sgt.
Richardson, T.B. SC Arty. Manigault's Bn. Co.A

Richardson, T.B. SC Arty. Melchers' Co. (Co.B,German Arty.)
Richardson, T.C. MS 1st Lt.Arty. Co.I Sgt.
Richardson, T.C. VA 46th Inf. 2nd Co.B
Richardson, T.C. VA 58th Inf. Co.D
Richardson, T.C. VA Loc.Def. Morehead's Co.
Richardson, T.D. SC 11th Inf. Co.H
Richardson, T.E. VA Loc.Def. Scott's Co.
Richardson, T.E. Gen. & Staff 1st Lt.,Adj.
Richardson, Temple MO 3rd Inf. Co.F Cpl.
Richardson, Temple B. MO 2nd Regt.St.Guards
Richardson, Tertutlus AL 38th Inf. Co.D
Richardson, T.G. Gen. & Staff Surg.
Richardson, Th. AR 13th Inf. Co.H
Richardson, T.H. GA 8th Inf. Co.H Cpl.
Richardson, T.H. GA 22nd Inf. Co.G
Richardson, Th. LA 8th Cav. Co.I
Richardson, T.H. TN 38th Inf. Co.D
Richardson, T.H. TX 3rd Cav. Co.G
Richardson, T.H. Gen. & Staff Capt.,AQM
Richardson, Theodore TN 6th (Wheeler's) Cav. Co.K
Richardson, Theophilus VA 5th Cav. Co.A
Richardson, Theos VA 11th Cav. Co.K Capt.
Richardson, Thomas AL 11th Inf. Co.C
Richardson, Thomas AL 45th Inf. Co.F
Richardson, Thomas AR 27th Inf. Co.G
Richardson, Thomas AR 32nd Inf. Co.C
Richardson, Thomas GA 18th Inf. Co.B
Richardson, Thomas MD Cav. 2nd Bn.
Richardson, Thomas MS 43rd Inf. Co.D Sgt.
Richardson, Thomas MO 1st N.E. Cav. Co.L
Richardson, Thomas MO 3rd Cav. Co.H
Richardson, Thomas MO 11th Inf. Co.D
Richardson, Thomas MO Inf. Perkins' Bn. Co.C
Richardson, Thomas NC 1st Inf. Dr.M. First Class
Richardson, Thomas SC 5th Inf. 1st Co.C
Richardson, Thomas SC Inf. 7th Bn. (Enfield Rifles) Co.E Sgt.
Richardson, Thomas SC 12th Inf. Co.C
Richardson, Thomas SC 21st Inf. Co.I
Richardson, Thomas TN 5th Inf. 2nd Co.H
Richardson, Thomas TN 21st Inf. Sgt.
Richardson, Thomas TN 25th Inf. Co.B Sgt.
Richardson, Thomas TN 25th Inf. Co.B
Richardson, Thomas TN 25th Inf. Co.G
Richardson, Thomas TN 25th Inf. Co.I
Richardson, Thomas TN 28th Inf. Co.I
Richardson, Thomas TN 31st Inf. Co.B Cpl.
Richardson, Thomas VA 36th Inf. Co.A Cpl.
Richardson, Thomas VA 42nd Inf. Co.A Sgt.
Richardson, Thomas VA 42nd Inf. Co.F
Richardson, Thomas VA 42nd Inf. Co.K 1st Sgt.
Richardson, Thomas VA 51st Inf. Co.B
Richardson, Thomas VA 157th Mil. Co.B
Richardson, Thomas VA Res.Forces Thurston's Co.
Richardson, Thomas Eng.,CSA Sgt.
Richardson, Thomas A. GA 6th Inf. (St.Guards) Co.D
Richardson, Thomas A. VA 37th Mil. Co.E
Richardson, Thomas C. GA Phillips' Legion Co.C
Richardson, Thomas C. VA 21st Inf. Co.A
Richardson, Thomas D. SC 2nd Cav. Co.B

Richardson, Thomas D. SC 1st (Orr's) Rifles Co.H
Richardson, Thomas E. AR 1st Vol. Co.G
Richardson, Thomas E. LA 28th (Gray's) Inf. Co.E
Richardson, Thomas E. MO Cav. Ford's Bn. Co.C 1st Lt.
Richardson, Thomas E. TN 47th Inf. 1st Lt.,Adj.
Richardson, Thomas E. VA 12th Inf. Co.K Cpl.
Richardson, Thomas F. KY 2nd Mtd.Inf. Co.A
Richardson, Thomas F. VA Lt.Arty. 38th Bn. Co.D Sgt.
Richardson, Thomas H. MO 10th Cav. Co.I
Richardson, Thomas H.J. LA 27th Inf. Co.C
Richardson, Thomas J. AL 23rd Inf. Co.I,E
Richardson, Thomas J. GA 36th (Villepigue's) Inf. Co.A Sgt.
Richardson, Thomas J. MS 5th Inf. Co.I
Richardson, Thomas J. VA Cav. 39th Bn. Co.D
Richardson, Thomas J. VA Inf. 23rd Bn. Co.F
Richardson, Thomas J. VA 38th Inf. Co.A
Richardson, Thomas J. 1st Conf.Inf. Co.A Sgt.
Richardson, Thomas L. TN 53rd Inf. Co.G
Richardson, Thomas N. MO 1st Inf. Co.F
Richardson, Thomas N. NC 52nd Inf. Co.C
Richardson, Thomas P. TN 48th (Nixon's) Inf. Co.H
Richardson, Thomas P. VA 21st Inf. Co.A
Richardson, Thos. P. Gen. & Staff Surg.
Richardson, Thomas W. NC 35th Inf. Co.D 1st Lt.
Richardson, Thomas W. SC 5th Inf. 1st Co.H
Richardson, Thomas W. VA 41st Inf. 2nd Co.G 1st Sgt.
Richardson, Thomas W. VA 60th Inf. Co.D
Richardson, Thom S. VA 3rd Res. Co.F
Richardson, T.I. TN Cav. Nixon's Regt. Co.C
Richardson, T.J. AL 8th Inf. Co.K
Richardson, T.J. GA 17th Inf. Co.H
Richardson, T.J. GA 31st Inf. Co.C Cpl.
Richardson, T.J. LA 27th Inf. Co.F
Richardson, T.J. MD Arty. 2nd Btty.
Richardson, T.J. MS 11th Inf. Co.D
Richardson, T.J. MS 46th Inf. Co.K
Richardson, T.J. MO 4th Inf.
Richardson, T.J. SC 16th & 24th (Cons.) Inf. Co.E
Richardson, T.J. TN 16th Inf. Co.A
Richardson, T.J. TN Inf. 154th Sr.Regt. Co.K Sgt.
Richardson, T. Jefferson SC 16th Inf. Co.A
Richardson, T.J.M. TX Cav. 3rd Regt.St.Troops Col.
Richardson, T.J.M. TX 25th Cav. Co.E Capt.
Richardson, T.J.M. TX Cav. Waller's Regt. Goode's Co.
Richardson, T.M. TX 20th Cav. Co.H
Richardson, T.M. Forrest's Scouts T.N. Kizer's Co.,CSA
Richardson, T.M.C. MS 1st Lt.Arty. Co.A
Richardson, T.N. MS 6th Cav. Co.H
Richardson, T.P. LA 17th Inf. Surg.
Richardson, T.P. SC 2nd St.Troops Co.F
Richardson, T.R. MS 3rd Bn.
Richardson, T.R. NC 56th Inf. Co.C
Richardson, T.S. VA Hvy.Arty. 20th Bn. Co.C

Richardson, Turner MO Cav. Snider's Bn. Co.C
Richardson, Turner J. TN 20th Inf. Co.A
Richardson, T.W. SC 6th Inf. 2nd Co.B
Richardson, T.W. SC Palmetto S.S. Co.D
Richardson, T.Y. MS 11th Inf. Co.D
Richardson, V. NC Home Guards
Richardson, Van V. NC 18th Inf. Co.H Capt.
Richardson, Vinton NC 2nd Jr.Res. Co.A
Richardson, W. GA 16th Inf. Co.C Sgt.
Richardson, W. MD Arty. 2nd Btty.
Richardson, W. MS 46th Inf. Co.E
Richardson, W. NC 5th Sr.Res. Co.B
Richardson, W. SC Bn.St.Cadets Co.B
Richardson, W. TN 12th (Green's) Cav. Co.A
  Cpl.
Richardson, W. TN 21st Inf. Co.C
Richardson, W. TX 11th (Spaight's) Bn.Vol.
  Co.B
Richardson, W. TX 13th Vol. 4th Co.I
Richardson, W. 2nd Corps Hosp.Stew.
Richardson, W.A. AL 2nd Cav. Co.H
Richardson, W.A. GA Lt.Arty. 12th Bn. 3rd
  Co.C
Richardson, W.A. LA 3rd (Wingfield's) Cav.
  Co.H
Richardson, W.A. LA 30th Inf. Co.D
Richardson, W.A. MO 12th Cav. Co.D
Richardson, W.A. SC 9th Res. Co.B
Richardson, W.A. VA Cav. Mosby's Regt.
  (Part.Rangers) Co.H
Richardson, W.A.B. GA 8th Cav. Old Co.I
Richardson, W.A.B. GA 62nd Cav. Co.I
Richardson, Wade H. LA 1st Cav. Co.E
Richardson, Wade H. LA 4th Inf. Co.K
Richardson, Wade H. SC Inf. 3rd Bn. Co.B
Richardson, Walker AL 36th Inf. Co.C
Richardson, Wallace P. MD Arty. 2nd Btty.
Richardson, Walter SC Inf. Hampton Legion
  Co.B
Richardson, Walter B. MS 20th Inf. Co.G
Richardson, Walter H. VA 18th Inf. Co.F
Richardson, Walter S. SC 19th Inf. Co.D
Richardson, Watkins VA 5th Cav. 1st Co.F 1st
  Sgt.
Richardson, W.B. GA Cav. 15th Bn. (St.Guards)
  Allen's Co.
Richardson, W.B. GA 57th Inf. Asst.Surg.
Richardson, W.B. KY 1st (Helm's) Cav. Co.A
Richardson, W.B. KY 2nd (Woodward's) Cav.
  Co.A Cpl.
Richardson, W.B. LA 7th Cav. Co.D Ord.Sgt.
Richardson, W.B. MS 1st (Patton's) Inf. Half-
  acre's Co. Cpl.
Richardson, W.B. MS 19th Inf. Co.A
Richardson, W.B. MS 46th Inf. Comsy.
Richardson, W.B. NC 32nd Inf. Chap.
Richardson, W.B. NC 51st Mil. Col.
Richardson, W.B. NC 52nd Inf. Co.F
Richardson, W.B. SC 2nd Inf. Co.K
Richardson, W.B. TN Cav. Woodward's Co.
Richardson, W.B. Conf.Cav. Wood's Regt. Co.K
Richardson, W.B. Gen. & Staff Chap.
Richardson, W.B. Gen. & Staff Asst.Surg.
Richardson, W.C. AR 26th Inf. Co.E
Richardson, W.C. Gen. & Staff Hosp.Stew.
Richardson, W.C.W. MS 41st Inf. Co.L 2nd Lt.
Richardson, W.D. AL 60th Inf. Co.B

Richardson, W.D. GA 46th Inf. Co.A
Richardson, W.D. TX 4th Field Btty.
Richardson, W.D. TX 1st Inf. Co.L Sgt.
Richardson, W.E. GA 8th Cav. Old Co.I
Richardson, W.E. GA 62nd Cav. Co.I
Richardson, W.E. NC Cav. 16th Bn. Co.I
Richardson, W.E. TN 48th (Nixon's) Inf. Co.I
  Comsy.
Richardson, W.E. VA 1st (Farinholt's) Res. Co.E
Richardson, W.E.M. SC 4th Inf. Co.I Cpl.
Richardson, Wesley MO 5th Cav. Co.A
Richardson, Wesley Benton LA 27th Inf. Co.C
  Cpl.
Richardson, West AL 11th Cav. Co.G
Richardson, W.F. AL 13th Inf. Co.D
Richardson, W.F. FL 2nd Inf. Asst.Surg.
Richardson, W.F. GA 1st (Olmstead's) Inf. Co.F
  Sgt.
Richardson, W.F. GA 25th Inf. Pritchard's Co.
  Sgt.
Richardson, W.F. MO Inf. 1st Regt.St.Guard
  Co.D
Richardson, W.F. TN 13th (Gore's) Cav. Co.C
Richardson, W.F. VA Cav. 1st Bn. Co.A
Richardson, W.F. 2nd Conf.Eng.Troops Co.E
  1st Sgt.
Richardson, W.F. Gen. & Staff Asst.Surg.
Richardson, W.F.M. TN 1st (Carter's) Cav.
  Co.M
Richardson, W.G. AR 14th (Powers') Inf. Co.C
Richardson, W.G. AR 38th Inf. Co.D
Richardson, W.G. LA 16th Inf. Co.F Sgt.Maj.
Richardson, W.G. SC Lt.Arty. 3rd (Palmetto)
  Bn. Co.K Sgt.
Richardson, W.G. SC Lt.Arty. Garden's Co.
  (Palmetto Lt.Btty.)
Richardson, W.G. TN 7th (Duckworth's) Cav.
  Co.A Sgt.
Richardson, W.G. TN 28th (Cons.) Inf. Co.K,D
Richardson, W.G. Gen. & Staff Surg.
Richardson, W.H. AL 3rd Res. Co.C
Richardson, W.H. AL 17th Inf. Co.H Sgt.
Richardson, W.H. AL 19th Inf. Co.G
Richardson, W.H. AL 34th Inf. Co.B
Richardson, W.H. AR 15th (Johnson's) Inf. Co.B
Richardson, W.H. GA 7th Inf. Co.H,I
Richardson, W.H. LA 17th Inf. Surg.
Richardson, W.H. MS 14th (Cons.) Inf. Co.F
Richardson, W.H. MS Inf. Cooper's Co.
Richardson, W.H. NC 7th Sr.Res. Watts' Co.
Richardson, W.H. SC Arty. Gregg's Co.
  (McQueen Lt.Arty.)
Richardson, W.H. SC Arty. Manigault's Bn. 1st
  Co.C
Richardson, W.H. SC 9th Inf. Co.K
Richardson, W.H. SC 20th Inf. Co.I
Richardson, W.H. TX Waul's Legion Co.H
Richardson, W.H. VA 5th Cav. Co.H
Richardson, W.H. 10th Conf.Cav. Co.D
Richardson, W.H. 1st Conf.Inf. 2nd Co.I
Richardson, W.H., Jr. Gen. & Staff 2nd
  Lt.,Dr.M.
Richardson, W.H.H. SC 5th Inf. 1st Co.C Cpl.
Richardson, W.H.H. SC Palmetto S.S. Co.D
  Sgt.
Richardson, Wigton W. VA 58th Inf. Co.D
Richardson, Will AL 1st Regt. Mobile Vol. Co.C

Richardson, William AL Arty. 1st Bn. Co.C
Richardson, William AL 21st Inf.
Richardson, William, Jr. AL 26th (O'Neal's) Inf.
  Co.G 1st Lt.
Richardson, William AL 50th Inf. Co.E Capt.
Richardson, William, Jr. AL 50th Inf. Co.E 1st
  Lt.
Richardson, William AL 50th Inf. Co.K
Richardson, Wm. AL Cp. of Instr. Talladega
Richardson, William AR 1st (Crawford's) Cav.
  Co.H
Richardson, William AR 15th Mil. Co.C
Richardson, William AR 17th (Lemoyne's) Inf.
  Co.E
Richardson, William AR Inf. Hardy's Regt. Co.B
  Cpl.
Richardson, William FL 2nd Inf. Co.G,M
  Ch.Music.
Richardson, William GA Cav. 8th Bn.
  (St.Guards) Co.B
Richardson, William GA 5th Inf. Co.F
Richardson, William GA 11th Inf. Co.G
Richardson, William GA 16th Inf. Co.K
Richardson, William GA 51st Inf. Co.I
Richardson, William LA 13th Inf. Co.G,K 1st
  Lt.
Richardson, William MS 4th Cav. Co.H
Richardson, William MS 11th (Perrin's) Cav.
  Co.B
Richardson, William MS Cav. Hughes' Bn. Co.B
Richardson, William MS 12th Inf. Co.C Music.
Richardson, William MS 24th Inf. Co.K
Richardson, William, Jr. MS 26th Inf. Co.B
Richardson, William, Sr. MS 26th Inf. Co.B
Richardson, William MS 39th Inf. Co.C
Richardson, William MS 43rd Inf. Co.A
Richardson, William MO Cav. 1st Regt.St.Guard
  Co.F
Richardson, William MO 7th Cav. Co.H
Richardson, William MO Cav. 12th Regt.
  St.Guard Co.C 2nd Lt.
Richardson, William NC 3rd Cav. (41st
  St.Troops) Co.I
Richardson, William NC Inf. 2nd Bn. Co.B
Richardson, William NC 5th Inf. Co.C 2nd Lt.
Richardson, William NC 6th Sr.Res. Co.H
Richardson, William NC 21st Inf. Co.M
Richardson, William NC 37th Inf. Co.K
Richardson, William NC 53rd Inf. Co.F
Richardson, William NC 67th Inf. Co.K
Richardson, William SC 1st Arty. Co.A
Richardson, William SC Arty. Gregg's Co.
  (McQueen Lt.Arty.)
Richardson, William SC Arty. Manigault's Bn.
  1st Co.C
Richardson, William SC 12th Inf. Co.C
Richardson, William, Jr. TN 8th (Smith's) Cav.
  Co.I
Richardson, William TN 14th (Neely's) Cav.
  Co.F
Richardson, William TN Lt.Arty. Morton's Co.
Richardson, William TN 23rd Inf. Co.G
Richardson, William TN 25th Inf. Co.B
Richardson, William TN 26th Inf. Co.K
Richardson, William TN 38th Inf. 1st Co.K
Richardson, William TN 41st Inf. Co.A
Richardson, William TN 45th Inf. Co.E

Richardson, William TN 63rd Inf. Co.K
Richardson, William TX 3rd Cav. Co.E
Richardson, William TX 12th Cav. Co.G
Richardson, William TX 13th Cav. Co.I
Richardson, William TX 37th Cav. Co.A
Richardson, William TX 7th Inf. Co.H Cpl.
Richardson, William TX 19th Inf. Co.A
Richardson, William VA 15th Cav. Co.H
Richardson, William VA Hvy.Arty. 18th Bn.
  Co.B
Richardson, William VA 4th Inf. Co.E
Richardson, William VA 17th Inf. Co.B 3rd Lt.
Richardson, William VA 26th Inf. Co.D
Richardson, William VA 26th Inf. Co.K
Richardson, William VA 39th Inf. Co.A
Richardson, William VA 50th Inf. Co.I
Richardson, William VA 56th Inf. Co.F
Richardson, William 4th Conf.Eng.Troops Cpl.
Richardson, William A. AL 41st Inf. Co.B
Richardson, William A. AL Cav. 5th Bn. Hil-
  liard's Legion Co.D Black.
Richardson, William A. GA 42nd Inf. Co.D
Richardson, William A. MS 1st Lt.Arty. Co.E
  Cpl.
Richardson, William A. NC 37th Inf. Co.K
Richardson, William A. VA 3rd Res. Co.F
Richardson, William A. VA 42nd Inf. Co.A Sgt.
Richardson, William A. 10th Conf.Cav. Co.D
  Black.
Richardson, William B. GA 6th Inf. (St.Guards)
  Co.F
Richardson, William B. SC 20th Inf. Co.I
Richardson, William B. TN 16th Inf. Co.A
Richardson, William B. VA 28th Inf. Co.I,E
Richardson, William C. AL Mil. 4th Vol. Co.C
Richardson, William C. AL Cp. of Instr. Tal-
  ladega
Richardson, William C. GA 1st Inf. (St.Guards)
  Co.H
Richardson, William C. GA 2nd Inf. Co.K Lt.
Richardson, William C. GA 11th Inf. Co.H Fifer
Richardson, William C. TN 4th (McLemore's)
  Cav. Co.K
Richardson, William C. TN 53rd Inf. Co.A Maj.
Richardson, William C. VA 22nd Cav. Co.D
Richardson, William C. VA 2nd Arty. Co.D
Richardson, William C. VA Lt.Arty. B.Z. Price's
  Co.
Richardson, William D. AL 3rd Bn. Hilliard's
  Legion Vol. Co.C
Richardson, William D. NC 21st Inf. Co.H
Richardson, William D. SC 12th Inf. Co.C
Richardson, William D. TX 11th Inf. Co.K
Richardson, William D.H. VA 38th Inf. Co.A
Richardson, William E. NC 48th Inf. Co.F
Richardson, William E. TX 4th Inf. Co.K
Richardson, William E. VA 4th Inf. Co.I
Richardson, William E. VA 50th Inf. Co.K
Richardson, Wm. E. Gen. & Staff Capt.,ACS
Richardson, William F. AL 18th Inf. Co.D
Richardson, William F. GA 45th Inf. Co.H
Richardson, Wm. F. MO St.Guard
Richardson, William F., Sr. TN 8th (Smith's)
  Cav. Co.I
Richardson, William F. TX 13th Cav. Co.C Cpl.
Richardson, William F. TX 1st Inf. Co.L Sgt.
Richardson, William F.S. SC 5th Inf. 1st Co.K

Richardson, William F.S. SC Palmetto S.S. Co.K
Richardson, William G. TN 28th Inf. Co.I
Richardson, William G. TN 28th (Cons.) Inf.
  Co.D Cpl.
Richardson, William H. AL 3rd Cav. Co.A
Richardson, William H. AL Inf. 1st Regt. Co.B
  2nd Lt.
Richardson, William H. AL 3rd Bn.Res. Co.C
Richardson, William H. AL 4th Inf. Co.B Cpl.
Richardson, William H. AL 11th Inf. Co.C,B
  Lt.
Richardson, William H. AL 45th Inf. Co.I
Richardson, William H. AL Cav. 5th Bn. Hil-
  liard's Legion Co.D
Richardson, William H. GA 1st Cav. Co.C
Richardson, William H. GA 41st Inf. Co.B Cpl.
Richardson, William H. GA 50th Inf. Co.I
Richardson, William H. LA 2nd Inf. Co.C Sgt.
Richardson, William H. LA 8th Inf. Co.E
Richardson, William H. LA 22nd (Cons.) Inf.
  Surg.
Richardson, William H. MD Cav. 2nd Bn. Co.F
  1st Lt.
Richardson, William H. MS 5th Inf. Co.E
Richardson, William H. MS 14th Inf. Co.K
Richardson, William H. MO 1st N.E. Cav.
Richardson, William H. MO Cav. Poindexter's
  Regt.
Richardson, William H. MO Lt.Arty. 3rd Btty.
Richardson, William H. MO Lt.Arty. Landis'
  Co.
Richardson, William H. MO 5th Inf. Co.H
Richardson, William H. TN 4th Inf. Co.I
Richardson, William H. TX 10th Cav. Co.G
  Cpl.
Richardson, William H. VA 3rd Cav. 1st Co.I
Richardson, William H. VA 3rd Cav. 2nd Co.I
Richardson, William H. VA 12th Cav.
Richardson, William H. VA 9th Inf. Co.F
Richardson, William H. VA 9th Mil. Co.B
Richardson, William H. VA 198th Mil.
  Adj.Gen.
Richardson, William H. VA Mil. Carroll Cty.
Richardson, William H. Conf.Cav. Wood's Regt.
  Co.C
Richardson, Wm. H. Gen. & Staff Adj.Gen.
Richardson, Wm. H. Gen. & Staff Surg.
Richardson, William J. FL 11th Inf. Co.C
Richardson, William J. GA 3rd Cav. Co.K
Richardson, William J. GA Siege Arty. 28th Bn.
  Co.H
Richardson, William J. GA 11th Inf. Co.H 3rd
  Lt.
Richardson, William J. KY 4th Mtd.Inf. Co.H
Richardson, William J. SC 1st Arty. Co.D
Richardson, William J. TX 12th Cav. Co.E
Richardson, William J. TX Cav. Martin's Regt.
  Co.G Cpl.
Richardson, William J. VA 24th Cav. Co.I
Richardson, William J. VA 23rd Inf. Co.H
Richardson, William J. VA 44th Inf. Co.D
Richardson, William J. 8th (Dearing's) Conf.Cav.
  Co.D
Richardson, William James VA 9th Inf. Co.D
  Maj.
Richardson, William K. VA 28th Inf. Co.D
Richardson, William L. KY 7th Cav. Co.H

Richardson, William L. TN 4th Cav. Co.I
Richardson, William M. AL 43rd Inf. Co.B 1st
  Lt.
Richardson, William M. AR 31st Inf. Co.E Sgt.
Richardson, William M. FL 3rd Inf. Co.H
Richardson, William M. FL 5th Inf. Co.G
Richardson, William M. GA 38th Inf. Co.K
Richardson, William M. GA 44th Inf. Co.A
Richardson, William M. LA Arty. Green's Co.
  (LA Guard Btty.)
Richardson, William M. LA 1st (Nelligan's) Inf.
  1st Co.B
Richardson, William M. LA 19th Inf. Co.H
Richardson, William M. TN 1st (Feild's) Inf.
  Co.K
Richardson, William M. TX 11th (Spaight's)
  Bn.Vol. Co.C Jr.2nd Lt.
Richardson, Wm. M. TX 21st Inf. Co.F Jr.2nd
  Lt.
Richardson, William M. VA 3rd Cav. Co.K
Richardson, William M. VA 28th Inf. Co.A
Richardson, William N. AL 15th Inf. Co.H
  Capt.
Richardson, William N. VA 53rd Inf. Co.B
Richardson, William N. VA Inf. Tomlin's Bn.
  Co.A
Richardson, William P. LA Arty. Green's Co.
  (LA Guard Btty.)
Richardson, William P. LA 13th Inf. Co.H,D
  Capt.
Richardson, William P. MS Inf. 5th Bn. Co.A
Richardson, William P. MS 24th Inf. Co.H Sgt.
Richardson, William P. NC 15th Inf. Co.B Cpl.
Richardson, William P. VA 12th Inf. Co.F
Richardson, Wm. P. VA Inf. 57th Regt. Co.F
Richardson, Wm. P. Gen. & Staff Asst.Surg.
Richardson, William R. NC 18th Inf. Co.H
Richardson, William R. TN 18th (Newsom's)
  Cav. Co.A
Richardson, William R. TN 32nd Inf. Co.K
Richardson, William R. VA Inf. 25th Bn. Co.C
Richardson, William R. VA 63rd Inf. Co.K
Richardson, William S. FL 9th Inf. Co.A
Richardson, William S. SC Lt.Arty. 3rd (Pal-
  metto) Bn. Co.G,K Bvt.2nd Lt.
Richardson, William S. SC 9th Inf. Co.D 1st Lt.
Richardson, William T. AL 30th Inf. Co.I
Richardson, William T. FL 7th Inf. Co.D Sgt.
Richardson, William T. KY 2nd Mtd.Inf. Co.H
  Cpl.
Richardson, William T. VA Cav. 1st Bn. Co.C
  Cpl.
Richardson, William T. VA 5th Cav. Co.E
Richardson, William T. VA 21st Cav. 2nd Co.E
Richardson, William T. VA 1st St.Res. Co.K
Richardson, William T. VA 39th Inf. Co.A
Richardson, William T. VA 55th Inf. Co.G Sgt.
Richardson, William T. VA 56th Inf. Co.K
Richardson, William Tyler 1st Conf.Eng.Troops
  Co.F Artif.
Richardson, William U. NC 2nd Arty. (36th
  St.Troops) Co.I
Richardson, William W. AR 14th (McCarver's)
  Inf. Co.B
Richardson, William W. GA Inf. 2nd Bn. Co.C
  1st Lt.

151

Richburg, John W. SC 23rd Inf. Co.I

Richardson, William W. MS 9th Inf. New Co.D Sgt.
Richardson, William W. NC 3rd Inf. Co.K
Richardson, William W. NC 24th Inf. Co.C
Richardson, William W. NC 26th Inf. Co.B Sr.2nd Lt.
Richardson, William W. NC 30th Inf. Co.K
Richardson, William W. NC 47th Inf. Co.E
Richardson, William W. VA Goochland Lt.Arty.
Richardson, William W. VA 53rd Inf. Co.E,B
Richardson, Willis MS 15th Bn.S.S. Co.A
Richardson, Wilson E. AL 3rd Inf. Co.A
Richardson, Wilson E. AL 27th Inf. Co.K
Richardson, Wilson E. TN 54th Inf. Ives' Co.
Richardson, Wilson G. MS 11th Inf. Co.G
Richardson, Wilson L. LA 27th Inf. Co.C
Richardson, W.J. AL 1st Regt.Conscr. Co.D
Richardson, W.J. GA Cav. 2nd Bn. Co.B
Richardson, W.J. GA 5th Cav. Co.F
Richardson, W.J. GA 62nd Cav. Co.L
Richardson, W.J. GA 29th Inf. Co.D
Richardson, W.J. KY 2nd Mtd.Inf. Co.G
Richardson, W.J. MS 1st Lt.Arty. Co.I
Richardson, W.J. TN 3rd (Clack's) Inf. Co.B
Richardson, W.J. TN Inf. 4th Cons.Regt. Co.C
Richardson, W.J. TN 23rd Inf. Co.B
Richardson, W.L. GA Lt.Arty. Guerard's Btty.
Richardson, W.L. GA 54th Inf. Co.H
Richardson, W.L. MS 19th Inf. Co.A
Richardson, W.L. TN 38th Inf. 2nd Co.A Bvt.2nd Lt.
Richardson, W.L. TX 32nd Cav. Co.F 2nd Lt.
Richardson, W.L. TX Vol. Rainey's Co.
Richardson, W.L. Morgan's Co.A,CSA
Richardson, W.M. AL 23rd Inf. Co.I,E
Richardson, W.M. AR 24th Inf. Co.E
Richardson, W.M. GA 2nd Cav. Co.I Ord.Sgt.
Richardson, W.M. SC Lt.Arty. Garden's Co. (Palmetto Lt.Btty.)
Richardson, W.M. TN 4th (Murray's) Cav. Co.F
Richardson, W.M. TX Granbury's Cons.Brig. Co.C
Richardson, W.M. Fort's Scouts,CSA
Richardson, W.M.C. AR 14th (McCarver's) Inf. Co.I
Richardson, W.M.C. AR 21st Inf. Co.B
Richardson, W.P. AL Inf. 2nd Regt. Co.E
Richardson, W.P. MS 2nd St.Cav. Co.G
Richardson, W.P. MS 9th Cav. Co.E
Richardson, W.P. MS 10th Cav. Co.F
Richardson, W.P. TN Cav. 17th Bn. (Sanders') Co.B
Richardson, W.P. TX 30th Cav. Co.E
Richardson, W.R. AL Cp. of Instr. Talladega
Richardson, W.R. AR 16th Inf. Co.K Music.
Richardson, W.R. AR 27th Inf. Co.F Music.
Richardson, W.R. MS 2nd Cav. Co.D
Richardson, W.R. MS 2nd (Davidson's) Inf. Co.G Music.
Richardson, W.R. MS 14th (Cons.) Inf. Co.I
Richardson, W.R. MS 33rd Inf. Co.H
Richardson, W.R. MS 38th Inf. Co.F
Richardson, W.R. MS 43rd Inf. Co.F
Richardson, W.R. MS Conscr.
Richardson, W.R. SC Arty. Gregg's Co. (McQueen Lt.Arty.)

Richardson, W.R. SC Arty. Manigault's Bn. 1st Co.C
Richardson, W.R. TN 10th (DeMoss') Cav. Co.F
Richardson, W.R. TN 19th (Biffle's) Cav. Co.B
Richardson, W.R. TX 9th (Nichols') Inf. Co.E
Richardson, W.R. TX 20th Inf. Co.H
Richardson, W.S. GA 29th Inf. Co.A
Richardson, W.S. MS Inf. 1st Bn. Co.C
Richardson, W.S. MS 35th Inf. Co.F
Richardson, W.S. TX St.Troops Gould's Co. (Clarksville Lt.Inf.)
Richardson, W.T. AL 1st Inf. Co.F
Richardson, W.T. AL 13th Inf. Co.I
Richardson, W.T. GA 18th Inf. Co.B
Richardson, W.T. SC 3rd Cav. Co.D
Richardson, W.T. TN 11th Inf. Co.C,E Cpl.
Richardson, W.T. TN 11th Inf. Co.K
Richardson, W.T. TN 38th Inf. 2nd Co.A
Richardson, W.T. TN 45th Inf. Co.C 2nd Lt.
Richardson, W.W. AL Inf. 2nd Regt. Co.B
Richardson, W.W. AL 4th Inf. Co.K Lt.
Richardson, W.W. AL 4th Res. Co.E
Richardson, W.W. AL 37th Inf. Co.G
Richardson, W.W. AL 42nd Inf. Co.B
Richardson, W.W. AR 8th Inf. New Co.F
Richardson, W.W. GA 1st Cav. Co.K
Richardson, W.W. LA 3rd Inf. Co.H
Richardson, W.W. MS 10th Inf. Old Co.H
Richardson, W.W. SC 12th Inf. Co.H
Richardson, W.W. TX Cav. 1st Regt.St.Troops Co.C
Richardson, W.W. TX 28th Cav. Co.I
Richardson, Wylie A. SC 1st (Hagood's) Inf. 2nd Co.D
Richardson, Y.B. GA Arty. 9th Bn. Co.B
Richardson, Zachariah T. TN 48th (Voorhies') Inf.
Richardson, Zealaus NC 2nd Arty. (36th St.Troops) Co.A
Richardson, Z.F. TX 24th Cav. Co.D
Richardson, Z.W. AR 1st (Monroe's) Cav. Co.D
Richardsone, C.B. GA Arty. Maxwell's Reg. Lt.Btty. 2nd Lt.
Richarme, Jean LA Mil. Lartigue's Co. (Bienville Guards)
Richarson, F.M. GA 3rd Inf. Co.E
Richart, D.M. Gen. & Staff Surg.
Richart, John O. KY 8th Cav. Co.I
Richarts, John LA 4th Inf. Co.A Band Music.
Richartt, F. TX 12th Inf. Co.A Music
Richasse, J. LA Mil. 2nd Regt. French Brig. Co.8
Richasse, J. LA Mil. 4th Regt. French Brig. Co.2
Richay, --- GA Inf. City Bn. (Columbus) Williams' Co.
Richberg, Ben AL 1st Bn. Hilliard's Legion Vol. Co.B
Richberg, F.J. AL 25th Inf. Co.B
Richberg, J. AL 25th Inf. Co.B
Richberg, R.E. AL 17th Inf. Co.F
Richberg, R.W. MS 1st (King's) Inf. (St.Troops) Co.H
Richbourg, A.J. SC 23rd Inf. Co.I Sgt.Maj.
Richbourg, A.M. SC 4th St.Troops Co.D
Richbourg, A.M. SC 5th Bn.Res. Co.F
Richbourg, Augustus B. SC Inf. Hampton Legion Co.C

Richbourg, B. Rufus SC 19th Inf. Co.E Capt.
Richbourg, C.C. SC 19th Inf. Co.E
Richbourg, Edwin SC Inf. Hampton Legion Co.C
Richbourg, E.J. SC 6th Inf. 2nd Co.C Sgt.
Richbourg, Eli N. SC Inf. Hampton Legion Co.C
Richbourg, G.W. SC 4th Cav. Co.D
Richbourg, G.W. SC 23rd Inf. Co.I
Richbourg, H. SC Mil. Trenholm's Co.
Richbourg, H.F. SC Manigault's Bn.Vol. Co.B
Richbourg, J.A. SC 21st Inf. Co.C
Richbourg, J.A.H. SC 23rd Inf. Co.K
Richbourg, J.D. SC 4th St.Troops Co.D
Richbourg, J.D. SC 5th Bn.Res. Co.F
Richbourg, J.E. SC 21st Inf. Co.C
Richbourg, J.F. SC 5th Bn.Res Co.F
Richbourg, J.F.D. SC 19th Inf. Co.E Cpl.
Richbourg, J.F.W. SC 9th Inf. Co.D
Richbourg, J.F.W. SC 19th Inf. Co.E 3rd Lt.
Richbourg, J.H. SC 21st Inf. Co.C
Richbourg, J.J. SC 1st Inf. Co.N
Richbourg, J.J.T. SC 19th Inf. Co.E
Richbourg, Joseph E. MS 14th Inf. Co.C
Richbourg, J.T. SC 9th Inf. Co.C
Richbourg, L.F. SC 6th Inf. 2nd Co.C
Richbourg, Reuben L.G. SC 19th Inf. Co.E
Richbourg, R.H. SC Cav. 14th Bn. Co.A
Richbourg, R.N. SC 1st Inf. Co.A
Richbourg, R.N. SC 23rd Inf. Co.I
Richbourg, R.N. SC Post Guard Senn's Co. 2nd Lt.
Richbourg, Rufus Gen. & Staff 2nd Lt.,Dr.M.
Richbourg, Rufus N. SC 1st (McCreary's) Inf. Co.C 1st Sgt.
Richbourg, Rufus N. SC Inf. Hampton Legion Co.C
Richbourg, S.C. 4th St.Troops Co.D
Richbourg, S.J. MS Cav. Jeff Davis Legion Co.H Sgt.
Richburg, B.D. SC 25th Inf. Co.I
Richburg, Benjamin AL 61st Inf. Co.E
Richburg, Daniel FL 3rd Inf. Co.C
Richburg, Daniel M. AL 22nd Inf. Co.I
Richburg, David S. AL 57th Inf. Co.F
Richburg, Ephram AL 53rd (Part.Rangers) Co.B
Richburg, F.L. SC 2nd Inf. Co.A,C
Richburg, Flud M. MS 40th Inf. Co.D Cpl.
Richburg, George M. AL 25th Inf. Co.K Cpl.
Richburg, H. MS Lt.Arty. Lomax's Co.
Richburg, H.A. AL 62nd Inf. Co.B
Richburg, H.C. AL Cav. Barlow's Co.
Richburg, H.C. 15th Conf.Cav. Co.C
Richburg, H.E. AL 53rd (Part.Rangers) Co.H
Richburg, Isaac FL 10th Inf. Co.A
Richburg, J. AL 25th Inf. Co.B
Richburg, J. AL 1st Bn. Hilliard's Legion Vol. Co.B
Richburg, J.A.H. SC 2nd Inf. Co.D
Richburg, James TN Lt.Arty. Tobin's Co.
Richburg, J.E. SC 3rd St.Troops Co.A
Richburg, J.F.W. SC Hvy.Arty. 15th (Lucas') Bn. Co.A
Richburg, J.G. MS 14th (Cons.) Inf. Co.F
Richburg, J.J. SC 15th Inf. Co.D
Richburg, J.M. AL 53rd (Part.Rangers) Co.H
Richburg, Joab E. AL 18th Inf. Co.A
Richburg, John M. AL 25th Inf. Co.B
Richburg, John W. SC 23rd Inf. Co.I

Richburg, Joseph N. AL 18th Inf. Co.A
Richburg, J.S. AL Cav. Murphy's Bn. Co.B
Richburg, J.S. 15th Conf.Cav. Co.G
Richburg, J.W. AL 23rd Inf. Co.I
Richburg, J.W. GA 42nd Inf.
Richburg, L.F. VA Lt.Arty. W.P. Carter's Co.
Richburg, M. AL 25th Inf. Co.B
Richburg, Nathaniel FL 3rd Inf. Co.C
Richburg, Pinkey S. SC 23rd Inf. Co.I
Richburg, Sanders J. AL Cav. 4th Bn. (Love's) Co.A Sgt.
Richburg, W.D. AL 23rd Inf. Co.B
Richburg, W.N. AL 23rd Inf. Co.I
Richburg, W.W. MS 1st Cav.Res. Co.K
Richburg, W.W. MS 40th Inf. Co.D
Richburge, John W. AL 1st Bn. Hilliard's Legion Vol. Co.B
Richburgh, J.E. SC 25th Inf. Co.I
Richburgh, J.H. SC 25th Inf. Co.I
Richburgh, J.N. SC 25th Inf. Co.I
Richburgh, J.T. SC 25th Inf. Co.I
Richburn, W.R. AL St.Res.
Richbury, J.W. AL 60th Inf. Co.H
Richbury, William M. AL 37th Inf. Co.C
Richder, Joseph GA Cav. 1st Bn. Brailsford's Co.
Richder, Joseph GA 5th Cav. Co.H
Richdsen, James Conf.Cav. Baxter's Bn. Co.C
Riche, A. LA Mil. 3rd Regt. French Brig. Co.7
Riche, C.L. LA 18th Inf. Co.C,G
Riche, C.S. LA Inf.Cons. 18th Regt. & Yellow Jacket Bn. Co.H
Riche, H.C. GA Cav. 9th Bn. (St.Guards) Co.A
Riche, Henry LA 2nd Cav. Co.C
Riche, James P. AL 9th (Malone's) Cav. Co.H
Riche, John W. AL 58th Inf. Co.I
Riche, L. LA 28th (Gray's) Inf. Cpl.
Riche, Louis LA 2nd Cav. Co.H Cpl.
Riche, Robert J. MS 8th Inf. Co.I Cpl.
Riche, S. LA Inf.Crescent Regt. Co.H
Riche, Salvador LA Inf.Cons.Crescent Regt. Co.G,C
Richeau, Emile MO 6th Inf. Co.I
Richeaux, Emile MO Lt.Arty. Parsons' Co.
Richee, Burton AR 14th (Powers') Inf. Co.F
Richee, H.J. AL 3rd Res. Co.A
Richee, Louis AL 42nd Inf. Co.G Cpl.
Richee, W.M. AL 3rd Res. Co.A
Richel, Fred LA 28th (Gray's) Inf. Co.G
Richelop, J. LA Mil. 4th Regt. French Brig. Co.5
Richelson, Henry LA 1st (Strawbridge's) Inf. Co.H
Richelt, William LA Miles' Legion Co.E
Richen, John VA Inf. Cohoon's Bn. Co.A
Richenbacker, F. SC 1st (Hagood's) Inf. 2nd Co.B
Richener, Antoine LA Mil. 6th Regt.Eur.Brig. (Italian Guards Bn.)
Richer, Charles TX 3rd Cav. Co.G
Richerd, John T. GA Cav. 16th Bn. (St.Guards) Co.K
Richerson, D. TN Cav. Clark's Ind.Co.
Richerson, E. GA Cav. Dorough's Bn.
Richerson, J.W. GA 51st Inf. Co.I
Richerson, R. GA Lt.Arty. 12th Bn.
Richers, Robert TX 4th Cav. Co.G

Richerson, A.M. VA 21st Cav. 2nd Co.I
Richerson, Andrew VA 79th Mil. Co.3 Cpl.
Richerson, Andrew J. TN 3rd (Lillard's) Mtd.Inf. Co.H
Richerson, Austin VA 47th Inf. 2nd Co.K
Richerson, Benjamin GA 66th Inf. Co.F
Richerson, B.N. TX 13th Vol. Co.G
Richerson, Charles M. TX 22nd Cav. Co.G Cpl.
Richerson, Daniel KY 9th Cav. Co.I
Richerson, D.M. TN 22nd (Nixon's) Cav. Co.C
Richerson, D.R. VA 21st Cav. 2nd Co.D
Richerson, Elias 15th Conf.Cav. Co.C
Richerson, E.R. SC Inf. 9th Bn. Co.E
Richerson, F.B. VA 30th Inf. Surg.
Richerson, F.B. Gen. & Staff Surg.
Richerson, George G. VA 9th Cav. Co.B
Richerson, George R. VA 20th Inf. Co.I
Richerson, Isaac AR 8th Cav. Co.A
Richerson, Isaac TN 19th (Biffle's) Cav. Co.I
Richerson, James VA 21st Cav. 2nd Co.I
Richerson, James D. MS 2nd St.Cav. Co.A
Richerson, James H. 10th Conf.Cav. Co.A
Richerson, James R. VA 9th Cav. Co.B Sgt.Maj.
Richerson, J.H. TN 15th Inf. Co.E
Richerson, J.H. VA 21st Cav. 2nd Co.D
Richerson, J.L. MS 29th Inf. Co.D
Richerson, John AR 23rd Inf. Co.E
Richerson, John GA Murray Cav. Asher's Co.
Richerson, John NC Walker's Bn. Thomas' Legion Co.A
Richerson, John TN 19th (Biffle's) Cav. Co.I
Richerson, John VA Inf. 38th Regt. Co.C
Richerson, John J. VA 47th Inf. 2nd Co.K
Richerson, John R. VA 5th Cav. 3rd Co.F
Richerson, John W. VA 30th Inf. Co.E
Richerson, Jonathan AR Inf. 1st Bn. Co.B
Richerson, J.T. AL 27th Inf. Co.A
Richerson, M.R. MS 1st Inf. Co.C
Richerson, Nathaniel VA 10th Cav. Co.C Capt.
Richerson, Peter VA 57th Inf. Co.C
Richerson, S.B. AL Cav. Barlow's Co.
Richerson, S.B. 15th Conf.Cav. Co.C Sgt.
Richerson, S.E. VA 5th Cav. 3rd Co.F
Richerson, S.G. MO 8th Inf. Co.H
Richerson, Thos. VA Mtd.Res. Rappahanock Dist. Sale's Co.
Richerson, Thomas E. VA 30th Inf. Co.F
Richerson, Thomas P. TN 54th Inf. Co.C
Richerson, Thomas W. VA 30th Inf. Co.E
Richerson, T.S. AL 27th Inf. Co.A Sgt.
Richerson, T.S. MS Inf. 3rd Bn. Co.I
Richerson, W.A. AL 32nd Inf. Co.G
Richerson, William MS 5th Inf. (St.Troops) Co.I
Richerson, Wm. VA Mtd.Res. Rappahanock Dist. Sale's Co.
Richerson, William VA 30th Inf. Co.E
Richerson, William VA 57th Inf. Co.C
Richerson, William A. VA 9th Cav. Co.B
Richerson, William H.C. VA 30th Inf. Co.E
Richerson, William M. TN 3rd (Lillard's) Mtd.Inf. Co.H Cpl.
Richerson, William W. GA Siege Arty. 28th Bn. Co.E
Richert, Albert D. LA 4th Inf. Co.K 1st Sgt.
Richert, F. MS 18th Cav. Co.F
Richerts, George LA Ogden's Cav. Co.I

Richerts, James MS 9th Inf. New Co.K
Riches, Richard VA 3rd (Archer's) Bn.Res. Co.D 1st Sgt.
Richeson, --- VA VMI Co.B
Richeson, Jesse V. VA 19th Inf. Co.H 1st Lt.
Richeson, Levi W. TN 59th Mtd.Inf. Co.E
Richeson, Madison VA 5th Cav. Co.A, 3rd Co.F
Richeson, P.S. VA 21st Inf. Co.F
Richeson, R.A. LA 3rd Inf. Co.G
Richeson, William VA 1st Inf. Co.D
Richeson, William P. VA 30th Inf. Co.D
Richeson, W.R. VA 21st Inf. Co.F
Richetion, Bryant GA Cav. Newbern's Co. (Coffee Revengers)
Richetson, John GA 1st (Symons') Res. Co.K
Richett, Michael AL 18th Inf. Co.F
Richette, Michel Sap. & Min. Gallimard's Co.,CSA 1st Sap.
Richey, Able W. MS 17th Inf. Co.K
Richey, A.C. GA 15th Inf. Co.B
Richey, Addison 8th (Wade's) Conf.Cav. Co.E
Richey, A.J. AL 42nd Inf. Co.G 1st Lt.
Richey, A.J. KY 3rd Bn.Mtd.Rifles
Richey, A.J. TX 14th Inf. Co.I Fifer
Richey, Alex TN 3rd (Lillard's) Mtd.Inf. Co.H, 2nd Co.K
Richey, Alexander M. MS 2nd Part.Rangers Co.F
Richey, Alfred AL 40th Inf. Co.K
Richey, Alfred AL Cp. of Instr. Talladega
Richey, Alfred GA 2nd Inf. Co.A Sgt.
Richey, Alva A. AL 41st Inf. Co.K
Richey, Andrew KY 9th Cav. Co.B
Richey, Andrew LA 1st Cav. Co.G
Richey, Andrew SC 5th Res. Co.A
Richey, Andrew TX Lt.Inf. & Riflemen Maxey's Co. (Lamar Rifles)
Richey, Andrew J. MS 1st (Patton's) Inf. Co.C Cpl.
Richey, Andrew J. MS 35th Inf. Co.H Sgt.
Richey, Andrew J. TX 1st (McCulloch's) Cav. Co.K
Richey, Andrew J. TX 1st (Yager's) Cav. Co.I
Richey, A.P. GA Cav. 19th Bn. Co.A
Richey, A.P. 10th Conf.Cav. Co.F
Richey, B. TX 34th Cav. Co.C
Richey, B.A. TX 7th Cav. Co.F
Richey, Barney TX 9th (Young's) Inf. Co.E
Richey, Barney L. TX 19th Cav. Co.E 1st Lt.
Richey, B.F. Gen. & Staff Capt.,AQM
Richey, B.L. AL Lt.Arty. Tarrant's Btty.
Richey, Caleb MS Shields' Co.
Richey, Charles AL 48th Inf. Co.K
Richey, Charles LA 25th Inf. Co.C
Richey, Charles A. TN 37th Inf. Co.D Drum.
Richey, C.L. LA 5th Inf. Band Music.
Richey, Clark AL 41st Inf. Co.C Ens.
Richey, C.M. SC 20th Inf. Co.F,M Sgt.
Richey, C.P. MS 5th Inf. Co.G 2nd Lt.
Richey, D. NC 3rd Inf. Co.F
Richey, David L. SC 20th Inf. Co.A
Richey, David L. TN Lt.Arty. Barry's Co. Cpl.
Richey, David L. TX 34th Cav. Co.C 2nd Lt.
Richey, D.B. AL 7th Inf. Co.B
Richey, E. SC 13th Inf. Co.A
Richey, Eben NC 28th Inf. Co.K
Richey, Edward F. AR 25th Inf. Co.K 1st Lt.

Richey, E.G. MS 3rd Inf.
Richey, Elam SC 3rd Inf. Co.B,A
Richey, Frank AL Cp. of Instr. Talladega
Richey, Franklin GA 65th Inf. Co.E Sgt.
Richey, George B. SC 1st (Orr's) Rifles
Richey, George W. MO 5th Inf. Co.B
Richey, George W. KY 4th Mtd.Inf. Co.K
Richey, George W. SC 1st Arty. Co.F
Richey, George W. SC 1st (McCreary's) Inf. Co.G
Richey, G.H. MS 10th Inf. Old Co.D Sgt.
Richey, G.H. 8th (Wade's) Conf.Cav. Co.E Jr.2nd Lt.
Richey, G.W. SC 4th Inf. Co.I
Richey, Hamilton W. AR Inf. 1st Bn. Co.C
Richey, Henry TN 10th Cav.
Richey, Henry H. KY 1st Bn.Mtd.Rifles Co.D
Richey, H.H. KY 3rd Bn.Mtd.Rifles
Richey, Hugh LA 3rd (Wingfield's) Cav. Co.G
Richey, H.W. MO Cav. Coleman's Regt. Co.F 1st Lt.
Richey, Isaac SC 4th Bn.Res. Co.B
Richey, Isaac C. SC 6th Res. Co.A
Richey, J. AL 31st Inf. Co.D
Richey, J. AR 35th Inf. Co.A
Richey, J.A. GA Inf. 8th Bn. Co.A
Richey, J.A. MS 10th Inf. Old Co.D Cpl.
Richey, Jabes SC 1st St.Troops Co.A
Richey, James GA Cav. 19th Bn. Co.A
Richey, James GA Inf. 4th Bn. (St.Guards) Co.G Sgt.
Richey, James 10th Conf.Cav. Co.F
Richey, James A. GA 13th Cav. Co.G
Richey, James A. GA 18th Inf. Co.E
Richey, James A. SC 1st Cav. Co.A Teamster
Richey, James A. SC 1st (Orr's) Rifles Co.B
Richey, James A. TX 5th Cav. Co.G
Richey, James D. AR 1st Mtd.Rifles Co.E
Richey, James D. GA 3rd Cav.
Richey, James I. VA 1st Inf. Co.F
Richey, James J. VA 1st Arty. 1st Co.C
Richey, James R. SC 1st Arty. Co.F
Richey, James W. SC 2nd Rifles Co.A
Richey, J.E. AL Cp. of Instr. Talladega
Richey, J.E. TX 15th Inf. Co.C Sgt.
Richey, J.E.A. TN 47th Inf. Co.C
Richey, Jeptha W. MS 22nd Inf. Co.K
Richey, J.F. AL 37th Inf. Co.H
Richey, J.H. TN Inf. 3rd Bn. Co.D
Richey, J.J. SC 4th Bn.Res. Co.B
Richey, J.J. SC Inf. Holcombe Legion Co.F
Richey, J.L. TX Lt.Inf. & Riflemen Maxey's Co. (Lamar Rifles)
Richey, J.N. SC 1st St.Troops Co.A
Richey, John AL 41st Inf. Co.C QMSgt.
Richey, John LA Miles' Legion Co.C
Richey, John MS 10th Inf. Co.I
Richey, John NC 48th Inf. Co.C
Richey, John SC 1st Cav. Co.F
Richey, John SC Cav. A.C. Earle's Co.
Richey, John SC 4th Inf. Co.B
Richey, John SC Palmetto S.S. Co.C
Richey, John TN 62nd Mtd.Inf. Co.E Lt.
Richey, John Gillum's Regt. Whitaker's Co.
Richey, John A. TN Inf. 22nd Bn. Co.A
Richey, John D. TX 22nd Cav. Co.H
Richey, John L. TX 32nd Cav. Co.G Cpl.

Richey, John T. KY 1st Bn.Mtd.Rifles Co.D
Richey, John T. KY 3rd Bn.Mtd.Rifles Co.F
Richey, John W. TX 1st (Yager's) Cav. Co.I
Richey, Joseph AL Cav. Hardie's Bn.Res. Co.E
Richey, Joseph SC 12th Inf. Co.K
Richey, Joseph TX 2nd Inf. Co.A
Richey, Joseph C. NC 11th (Bethel Regt.) Inf. Co.I
Richey, Joseph G. GA 36th (Broyles') Inf. Co.B
Richey, Joshua KY 13th Cav. Co.B,I
Richey, J.R. SC Cav. A.C. Earle's Co.
Richey, J.R. SC Inf. 13th Bn. Co.A
Richey, J.R. VA Cav. 37th Bn. Co.B
Richey, J.S. SC 1st (Butler's) Inf. Co.I
Richey, J.S.P. SC 1st Cav. Co.F,H Sgt.
Richey, J.T. AL Inf. 2nd Regt. Co.A
Richey, J.T. AL 42nd Inf. Co.G
Richey, J.W. AL 10th Inf. Co.E
Richey, J.W. AL 39th Inf. Co.C
Richey, J.W. MS 15th Inf. Co.K
Richey, J.W. SC 5th Res. Co.H
Richey, L.D. AL 37th Inf. Co.H Sgt.
Richey, Leander C. MS 31st Inf. Co.A Sgt.
Richey, M.L. AL 42nd Inf. Co.G 1st Lt.
Richey, M.W. NC 5th Sr.Res. Co.D
Richey, Oliver SC 1st Cav. Co.G,A
Richey, P.A. NC 57th Inf. Co.A
Richey, R. TX 20th Bn.St.Troops Co.A
Richey, R.A. GA Cav. 10th Bn. (St.Guards) Co.A
Richey, R.J. AL 7th Cav. Co.I
Richey, Robert AL 3rd Inf. Co.E
Richey, Robert SC 1st St.Troops Co.F
Richey, Robert SC Inf. Hampton Legion Co.K
Richey, Robert TN 59th Mtd.Inf. Co.H
Richey, Robert C. AL 41st Inf. Co.K
Richey, Robert G. AR Inf. Clayton's Co.
Richey, Robert N. AR 15th (Johnson's) Inf. Co.B Sgt.
Richey, Robert W. MS 23rd Inf. Co.D
Richey, R.R. AL 12th Inf. Co.G
Richey, R.W. AL Home Guards Pollard's Co.
Richey, R.W. MS 7th Cav. Co.G
Richey, R.W. TX 5th Inf. Co.G
Richey, S. TX 25th Cav. Co.B
Richey, Samuel N. MS 41st Inf. Co.G
Richey, Samuel Thompson SC 19th Inf. Co.I Cpl.
Richey, S.H. TN 10th (DeMoss') Cav. Co.G
Richey, Steven D. MS Inf. 3rd Bn. Co.C Sgt.
Richey, S.W. Lockman's Staff Capt.,AQM
Richey, Taylor KY 1st Bn.Mtd.Rifles Co.D
Richey, Thadeus AL 49th Inf. Co.D
Richey, T.J. AL 4th Res. Co.F Cpl.
Richey, T.J. AR 19th (Dawson's) Inf. Co.G Sgt.
Richey, T.M. MO 11th Inf. Co.E
Richey, T.S. MS 18th Cav. Co.G
Richey, T.S. MS 1st (Johnston's) Inf. Co.D Cpl.
Richey, W.B. MS 7th Cav. Co.H
Richey, W.B. MS 2nd Inf. (A. of 10,000) Co.G
Richey, W.F. MS 18th Cav. Co.G
Richey, W.F. MS 1st (Johnston's) Inf. Co.D
Richey, W.F. MS 9th Inf. Co.H
Richey, W.F. MS 22nd Inf.
Richey, W.G. MS St.Cav. 2nd Bn. (Harris') Co.C
Richey, William TN 55th (Brown's) Inf. Co.H

Richey, William TN 59th Mtd.Inf. Co.H
Richey, William TX Cav. Madison's Regt. Co.C
Richey, William Brush Bn.
Richey, William A. AL 10th Inf. Co.E
Richey, William A. SC 1st Cav. Co.G Teamster
Richey, William B. MS 1st Cav.
Richey, William B. MS 35th Inf. Co.H Sgt.
Richey, William F. MS 41st Inf. Co.G
Richey, William F. NC 11th (Bethel Regt.) Inf. Co.E
Richey, William F. NC 48th Inf. Co.C
Richey, William H. TN 3rd (Lillard's) Mtd.Inf. Co.A
Richey, William J. MS 48th Inf. Co.L Sgt.
Richey, William L. GA Inf. 3rd Bn. Co.A Black.
Richey, William P. AR Inf. 1st Bn. Co.C Sgt.
Richey, William P. NC 48th Inf. Co.C
Richey, William T. AR Inf. Clayton's Co.
Richey, William W. TX Cav. Madison's Regt. Co.A Cpl.
Richey, Wilson MS 31st Inf. Co.I
Richey, W.J. MS St.Cav. 2nd Bn. (Harris') Co.C
Richey, W.J. TX 18th Inf. Co.G Jr.2nd Lt.
Richey, W.L. AL 48th Inf. Co.K
Richey, W.L. GA Lt.Arty. Van Den Corput's Co.
Richey, W.M. AL Talladega Cty.Res. W.Y. Hendrick's Co.
Richey, W.M. MS 2nd Cav. Co.H
Richey, W.M. MS 7th Cav. Co.B
Richey, W.T. AR 8th Cav. Co.D
Richfelt, Charles LA Inf. 7th Bn. Co.C
Richford, John MS 11th Inf. Co.E
Richford, R.C. GA 1st Troops & Def. (Macon) Co.B
Richford, William TN 5th Inf. Co.L
Richia, --- TX Lt.Arty. Dege's Bn.
Richia, H.C. TX 6th Field Btty.
Richie, Aaron NC 57th Inf. Co.F
Richie, Absalom TX Waul's Legion Co.A
Richie, A.C. GA 15th Inf. Co.B
Richie, A.J. AL 6th Inf. Co.K
Richie, Albert MS 2nd Inf. Co.B
Richie, Andrew J. KY Horse Arty. Byrne's Co.
Richie, Andrew J. TX Cav. 8th (Taylor's) Bn. Co.D
Richie, A.W. MS 31st Inf. Co.I
Richie, Benjamin VA 58th Mil. Co.G
Richie, Benjamin H. MS 16th Inf. Co.C
Richie, B.T. GA 18th Inf. Co.K
Richie, Charles NC 6th Inf. Co.G
Richie, Charles TX 1st (McCulloch's) Cav. Co.I
Richie, C.M. SC Cav. 19th Bn. Co.B Sgt.
Richie, David AR 2nd (Cons.) Inf. Co.4
Richie, David GA Brooks' Co. (Terrell Lt.Arty.)
Richie, David LA 8th Inf. Co.I
Richie, David 2nd Conf.Eng.Troops Co.D Artif.
Richie, David L. SC 2nd Inf. Co.A
Richie, D.C. LA 3rd (Harrison's) Cav. Co.K
Richie, D.L. AR 45th Cav. Co.G
Richie, Eli TN 62nd Mtd.Inf. Co.E
Richie, Ewell LA 8th Inf. Co.I
Richie, George VA 58th Mil. Co.E
Richie, George VA 129th Mil. Buchanon's Co.
Richie, George A. VA 11th Cav. Co.C
Richie, George W. VA 11th Cav. Co.C

Richie, G.W. AL 63rd Inf. Co.E
Richie, G.W. NC 57th Inf. Co.A
Richie, Henry AR 32nd Inf. Co.D
Richie, Henry KY 8th Cav. Co.G
Richie, Henry G. AR 38th Inf. Co.M
Richie, Henry W. NC 6th Inf. Co.G
Richie, Hiram AR 16th Inf. Co.I
Richie, H.M. NC 4th Inf. Co.A
Richie, Ira MO 8th Inf. Co.G
Richie, Isaac VA 58th Mil. Co.G
Richie, J. NC 57th Inf. Co.A
Richie, J.A. TX 6th Cav. Co.A
Richie, Jacob M. NC 6th Inf. Co.G
Richie, James AL 2nd Cav. Co.A Cpl.
Richie, James MO 10th Inf. Co.A
Richie, James TN 16th (Logwood's) Cav. Co.F
Richie, James VA 2nd St.Res. Co.D
Richie, James D. TX 19th Cav. Co.I Cpl.
Richie, James H. TN Inf. 18th Regt. Chap.
Richie, James J. VA Lt.Arty. Cayce's Co.
Richie, James M. MS 13th Inf. Co.E Sgt.
Richie, James S. TX 10th Inf. Co.E
Richie, J.B. MO Cav. Ford's Bn. Co.D
Richie, Jessie LA 26th Inf. Co.E
Richie, J.F. AR 7th Bn. Co.E 2nd Lt.
Richie, J.H. MO Cav. Ford's Bn. Co.D
Richie, J.M. NC 3rd Jr.Res. Co.E
Richie, John NC 28th Inf. Co.D
Richie, John VA Lt.Arty. Carpenter's Co.
Richie, John President's Guard,CSA
Richie, John A. TN 59th Mtd.Inf. Co.E
Richie, John J. GA 45th Inf. Co.F
Richie, John M. AL 40th Inf. Co.K
Richie, John W. TX 1st (McCulloch's) Cav.
 Co.K
Richie, John W. TX Cav. 8th (Taylor's) Bn.
 Co.D
Richie, Joseph AL 2nd Cav. Co.A
Richie, Josiah VA Inf. 26th Bn. Co.E
Richie, J.R. TX 27th Cav. Co.K
Richie, J.T. TN 12th (Green's) Cav. Co.H Cpl.
Richie, Lewis D. AL Inf. 1st Regt. Co.D
Richie, Luther A. MS 2nd Inf. Co.B 2nd Lt.
Richie, M. MS Rogers' Co.
Richie, Martin V. AL 10th Inf. Co.D
Richie, Patrick T. TX 19th Cav. Co.G
Richie, Peter VA 58th Mil. Co.G
Richie, Peter VA 146th Mil. Co.F
Richie, Philip VA 25th Inf. 1st Co.F
Richie, R. MO Cav. Ford's Bn. Co.D
Richie, R.C. MS 12th Cav. Co.D
Richie, Robert MO Cav. Freeman's Regt.
 Wolfe's Co.
Richie, Robert R. TX 7th Cav. Co.F
Richie, Robert S. AL 45th Inf. Co.I
Richie, Samuel KY 8th Cav. Co.C
Richie, Samuel T. MO 10th Inf. Co.H
Richie, S.H. TN Cav. Napier's Bn. Co.D
Richie, Thomas S. TX 8th Cav. Co.E
Richie, Warren SC 7th Inf. 1st Co.D
Richie, Wash TN 16th (Logwood's) Cav. Co.F
Richie, W.B. MS 6th Cav. Co.K Jr.2nd Lt.
Richie, W.B. TN 12th (Green's) Cav. Co.H
Richie, William AR 7th Inf. Co.I Cpl.
Richie, William MS 2nd Cav. Co.F
Richie, William VA Lt.Arty. Penick's Co. Sgt.
Richie, William C. TX 27th Cav. Co.B

Richie, William H. AL 29th Inf. Co.B
Richie, William M. MS 5th Inf. (St.Troops) Co.A
Richie, William M. NC 6th Inf. Co.G
Richie, William Nichol MS 1st Lt.Arty. Co.A
 Cpl.
Richie, William P. AR 45th Cav. Co.G Cpl.
Richie, Wilson M. MS 2nd Inf. Co.B
Richie, Wilson W. TN 59th Mtd.Inf. Co.E
Richie, W.J. MS Cav. Ham's Regt. Co.E
Richiee, R.B. GA 4th Cav. (St.Guards) Cannon's
 Co.
Richins, J. TX Cav. Wells' Regt. Co.F
Richinson, J.R. GA 1st (Symons') Res. Co.E
Richirdson, Jackson AL Pickens' Cty.Supp.Force
Richirdson, W.E. LA Ogden's Cav. Co.I
Richison, Andrew TN 39th Mtd.Inf. Co.F
Richison, George VA Lt.Arty. G.B. Chapman's
 Co.
Richison, James W. TX 16th Cav. Co.K
Richison, R. NC 7th Inf. Co.C
Richison, Samuel KY 4th Cav. Co.D
Richler, J. TX 20th Inf. Co.B
Richler, Tiluid TX 20th Inf. Co.B
Richley, Randolph GA 5th Cav. Bugler
Richlman, George LA Mil. Lafayette Arty.
Richm, L., Jr. LA Mil. 4th Regt.Eur.Brig. Co.D
Richman, Daniel VA 79th Mil. Co.1
Richman, D.G. TX 12th Inf. Co.B
Richman, H. TX 8th Field Btty.
Richman, H. VA 18th Cav. Co.H
Richman, H.C. AR 1st Mtd.Rifles Co.E
Richman, Henry VA 14th Mil. Co.E
Richman, Henry VA 14th Mil. Co.F Cpl.
Richman, Henry VA 62nd Mtd.Inf. 1st Co.D
Richman, Herrod VA Inf. 23rd Bn. Co.G
Richman, J., Jr. VA Mil. Scott Cty.
Richman, Jacob VA 79th Mil. Co.1
Richman, John AR 35th Inf. Co.K
Richman, John VA Cav. Hounshell's Bn. Thur-
 mond's Co.
Richman, Samuel MS 2nd Inf. Co.H
Richman, T.L. VA 79th Mil. Co.1
Richmon, Arthur VA 190th Mil. Co.G
Richmon, J.W. MS 6th Inf. Co.C
Richmond, --- Conf.Hvy.Arty. F.W. Smith's Bn.
 Asst.Surg.
Richmond, --- 1st Creek Mtd.Vol Co.G
Richmond, A. MS Inf. 3rd Bn. Co.E
Richmond, Abraham VA 33rd Inf. Co.G
Richmond, A.C. GA 32nd Inf. Co.E Cpl.
Richmond, A.J. MO 6th Cav. Co.A
Richmond, A.J. NC 12th Inf.
Richmond, Albert AL 1st Cav. 1st Co.B
Richmond, Andrew KY 4th Cav. Co.H
Richmond, Andrew MS 15th Inf. Co.E
Richmond, Andrew MS 33rd Inf. Co.G
Richmond, Augustus MS 13th Inf. Co.B
Richmond, B. TN 7th (Duckworth's) Cav. Co.E
Richmond, Benjamin KY 2nd (Woodward's) Cav.
 Co.A
Richmond, Benjamin F. VA 25th Cav. Co.C
 Sgt.
Richmond, Benjamin F. VA 50th Inf. Co.A
Richmond, Benjamin F. 7th Conf.Cav. Co.H Lt.
Richmond, B.F. KY 10th (Diamond's) Cav.
 Co.B 3rd Lt.
Richmond, Caleb Gen. & Staff 1st Lt.,ADC

Richmond, Carol NC 39th Inf. Co.A
Richmond, C.H. AR 7th Cav. Co.E Sgt.
Richmond, C.H. NC 45th Inf. Co.I Cpl.
Richmond, Charles N. LA 6th Inf. Co.C
Richmond, Cyrus H. KY 10th Cav. Martin's Co.
Richmond, C.W. AR 10th Mil.
Richmond, D. VA 2nd St.Res. Co.I
Richmond, Daniel VA Hvy.Arty. 18th Bn. Co.E
Richmond, Daniel W.K. NC 13th Inf. Co.D 2nd
 Lt.
Richmond, Danie W. NC 4th Cav. (59th
 St.Troops) Co.B QMSgt.
Richmond, David MO 7th Cav. Co.D
Richmond, David MO 8th Cav. Co.H
Richmond, David J. VA 25th Cav. Co.C
Richmond, Drayton G. TX 17th Cav. Co.H
Richmond, D.S. TX 11th Cav. Co.D 2nd Lt.
Richmond, Edward L. MS 17th Inf. Co.B
Richmond, E.L. MS 3rd Cav. Co.E Capt.
Richmond, E.W.D. TN 50th Inf. Co.K
Richmond, Ezekiel J. AR 31st Inf. Co.C
Richmond, F. AL 1st Regt. Mobile Vol. Baas'
 Co.
Richmond, F. AL 4th Res. Co.B
Richmond, F. VA 2nd St.Res. Co.I
Richmond, F.M. LA 17th Inf. Co.E
Richmond, Frank TN 28th (Cons.) Inf. Co.I 1st
 Lt.
Richmond, George MS Cav. 3rd Bn.Res. Co.C
Richmond, George G. MO Cav. Poindexter's
 Regt.
Richmond, G.G. MO 3rd Inf. 2nd Lt.
Richmond, G.O. MS Inf. 2nd Bn. (St.Troops)
 Co.C
Richmond, G.W. KY 3rd Mtd.Inf. Co.K
Richmond, H. MS 11th Inf. Co.K
Richmond, H. TX 20th Inf. Co.A
Richmond, H.A. GA 1st (Symons') Res. Co.B
Richmond, H.A. NC 7th Sr.Res. Mitchell's Co.
Richmond, H.C. AR 38th Inf. Co.B
Richmond, H.C. MO 6th Cav. Co.C
Richmond, H.C. NC 26th Inf. Co.G
Richmond, Henry NC 13th Inf. Co.A
Richmond, Henry VA 25th Inf. 1st Co.F
Richmond, Henry VA 62nd Mtd.Inf. 2nd Co.F
Richmond, Henry C. NC 4th Cav. (59th
 St.Troops) Co.B Sgt.
Richmond, Henry C. TN 12th (Green's) Cav.
 Co.C
Richmond, Henry C.T. VA 64th Mtd.Inf. Co.I
Richmond, Henry P. GA 2nd Inf. Capt.
Richmond, Henry P. GA 2nd Bn.S.S. Co.C
 Capt.,AQM
Richmond, Henry P. Gen. & Staff Capt.,AQM
Richmond, H.I. VA 1st Res. Co.B
Richmond, H.W. TN 13th Inf. Co.C Music.
Richmond, Iverson G. MS 33rd Inf. Co.B 2nd
 Lt.
Richmond, J.A. MS 18th Cav. Co.C
Richmond, J.A. TX Cav. 3rd (Yager's) Bn. Co.B
Richmond, Ja VA 64th Mtd.Inf. Co.C
Richmond, Jacob VA 60th Inf. Co.I
Richmond, James LA 14th Inf. Co.I
Richmond, James VA Cav. O'Ferrall's Bn. Co.B
Richmond, James B. NC 4th Cav. (59th
 St.Troops) Co.B
Richmond, James B. NC 13th Inf. Co.D

Richmond, James B. VA 50th Inf. Co.A Sgt.
Richmond, James B. VA 64th Mtd.Inf. Co.G Lt.Col.
Richmond, James C. TX 12th Inf. Co.I
Richmond, James D. LA 28th (Gray's) Inf. Co.I
Richmond, James D. MO Lt.Arty. 3rd Btty.
Richmond, James D. MO 3rd Inf. Co.F
Richmond, Jas. H. VA Inf. 26th Bn. Co.G
Richmond, James L. NC 24th Inf. Co.D
Richmond, James L. SC 6th Inf. 1st Co.C, 2nd Co.G
Richmond, James M. TX 17th Cav. Co.E
Richmond, James M. TX 17th Cons.Dismtd.Cav. Co.K Drum Maj.
Richmond, James P. TN 7th Inf. Co.G
Richmond, James W. VA 25th Cav. Co.C
Richmond, James W. VA Mil. Scott Cty.
Richmond, James Y. NC 56th Inf. Co.H
Richmond, J.A.S. LA 25th Inf. Co.C
Richmond, Jasper W. MS 48th Inf. Co.F Cpl.
Richmond, J.C. MO 6th Cav. Co.A
Richmond, J.D. TX 28th Cav. Co.B
Richmond, Jesse W. LA Hvy.Arty. 2nd Bn. Co.C
Richmond, J.G. MS 1st (Percy's) Inf. Co.D
Richmond, J.G. TX 19th Inf. Co.C Ch.Music.
Richmond, J.H. TN 4th (Murray's) Cav. Co.H
Richmond, J.L. NC 3rd Arty. (40th St.Troops) Co.G
Richmond, J.L. NC Lt.Arty. 13th Bn. Co.E
Richmond, J. Lafayette MS 12th Inf. Co.F
Richmond, J.M. SC 1st (Orr's) Rifles Asst.Surg.
Richmond, John MO 12th Inf. Co.C
Richmond, John TN 4th (Murray's) Cav. Co.H
Richmond, John TN 13th Inf. Co.C
Richmond, John TX 19th Inf. Co.B
Richmond, John D. AR 25th Inf. Co.K
Richmond, John D. TX 17th Cav. Co.H
Richmond, John J. TN 36th Inf. Co.D
Richmond, John L. TX 2nd Cav. Co.I
Richmond, John M. NC 3rd Cav. (41st St.Troops) Co.C
Richmond, John M. NC 5th Inf. Asst.Surg.
Richmond, John M. NC 23rd Inf. Asst.Surg.
Richmond, Jno. M. Gen. & Staff Asst.Surg.
Richmond, John T. SC 13th Inf. Co.A
Richmond, John W. MS 40th Inf. Co.B Sgt.
Richmond, Jonathan VA 25th Cav. Co.C
Richmond, Jonathan VA Mil. 5th Div. 17th Brig. Brig.Gen.
Richmond, Jonathan, Jr. VA 50th Inf. Co.A Capt.
Richmond, Jonathan VA 64th Mtd.Inf. Co.C 2nd Lt.
Richmond, Joseph KY 12th Cav. Co.B
Richmond, Joseph TN Jackson's Cav.
Richmond, Joseph H. TN 9th (Ward's) Cav. Co.D
Richmond, Joseph T. MS 18th Inf. Co.D
Richmond, J.S. MS 1st Lt.Arty. Co.F
Richmond, J.W. KY 4th Cav. Co.H
Richmond, J.W. KY 5th Mtd.Inf. Co.A
Richmond, J.W. MS Inf. 2nd Bn. Co.F
Richmond, J.W. TN 24th Inf. 1st Co.H
Richmond, Leonidas MS 34th Inf. Co.E
Richmond, Leonidas Gen. & Staff AASurg.

Richmond, Lineas KY 2nd (Woodward's) Cav. Co.A,B Sgt.
Richmond, Logan MS 34th Inf. Co.E
Richmond, Lovett A. TN 7th Inf. Co.G Cpl.
Richmond, M. AR 38th Inf. Co.B
Richmond, M. MS Inf. 3rd Bn. Co.E
Richmond, M.A. MS 10th Inf. Old Co.A, New Co.K
Richmond, Marion Berry MS 1st Lt.Arty. Co.A
Richmond, Matthew MS 42nd Inf. Co.A
Richmond, M.D. MO Cav. Coleman's Regt. Co.F
Richmond, Moses VA 30th Bn.S.S. Co.A
Richmond, N.W. MS 18th Cav. Co.C
Richmond, Parkinson VA 36th Inf. 2nd Co.C
Richmond, P.H. MO 6th Cav. Co.A,I 2nd Lt.
Richmond, R.F. TN 15th (Cons.) Cav. Co.C
Richmond, R.F. TN 47th Inf. Co.D Sgt.
Richmond, Richard Mead's Conf.Cav. Co.E
Richmond, Robert NC 3rd Arty. (40th St.Troops) Co.K
Richmond, Robert NC 61st Inf. Co.C
Richmond, Robert A. AR 17th (Lemoyne's) Inf. Co.H 1st Sgt.
Richmond, Robert F. TN 28th Inf. Co.I 1st Lt.
Richmond, Robert G. LA 12th Inf. Co.H
Richmond, Robert G. LA 28th (Gray's) Inf. Co.I Cpl.
Richmond, Robert H. AR 21st Inf. Co.E,G 1st Lt.
Richmond, Robert J. VA 25th Cav. Co.C 2nd 2nd Lt.
Richmond, Robert J. VA Mil. Scott Cty.
Richmond, Saul M. TN 36th Inf. Co.D
Richmond, S.D. NC 49th Inf. Adj.
Richmond, Sidney MO 12th Inf. Co.C
Richmond, Silas J. Conf.Cav. 6th Bn. Co.G
Richmond, Stephen D. NC 13th Inf. Co.C 1st Sgt.
Richmond, T.B. MS 40th Inf. Co.E Jr.2nd Lt.
Richmond, T.D. MS 22nd Inf. Co.G 2nd Lt.
Richmond, Thomas TN 10th Inf. Co.E
Richmond, Thomas Bradford's Corps Scouts & Guards Co.A
Richmond, Thomas B. VA 37th Inf. Co.D
Richmond, Thomas D. MS 33rd Inf. Co.E 1st Sgt.
Richmond, Thomas D. NC 6th Inf. Co.H
Richmond, T.J. TX 9th Cav. Co.F,I
Richmond, W. TX 13th Vol. Co.E
Richmond, Washington TX 17th Cav. Co.E
Richmond, Washington TX 17th Cons. Dismtd.Cav. Co.K
Richmond, W.B. Gen. & Staff, Inf. 1st Lt.
Richmond, W.D. AR 4th Cav. Co.F
Richmond, W.D. AR Mil. Desha Cty.Bn. 1st Lt.
Richmond, W.D. MS St.Cav. Perrin's Bn. Co.E
Richmond, W.D. TN 9th (Ward's) Cav. Co.B
Richmond, W.H. MO Cav. Coleman's Regt. Co.B 2nd Lt.
Richmond, Wiley TN 55th (McKoin's) Inf. McEwen, Jr.'s Co.
Richmond, William AR 8th Cav. Peoples' Co.
Richmond, William AR Cav. Wright's Regt. Co.F
Richmond, William LA 13th Bn. (Part.Rangers) Co.E Cpl.

Richmond, William MS 1st Cav.Res. Co.D
Richmond, William NC 57th Inf. Co.D
Richmond, William VA 64th Mtd.Inf. Co.A
Richmond, William VA 64th Mtd.Inf. Co.I Capt.
Richmond, William VA 5th Cav.Arty. & Inf. St.Line Co.I
Richmond, William C. TN 36th Inf. Co.D
Richmond, William D. MS 11th (Perrin's) Cav. Co.K
Richmond, William D. NC 6th Inf. Co.H Sgt.
Richmond, William F. VA Mil. Scott Cty.
Richmond, William H. MO 8th Inf. Co.B Bvt.2nd Lt.
Richmond, William H. VA 36th Inf. 2nd Co.C
Richmond, William I TX 4th Inf. Co.K
Richmond, William T. MS 9th Inf. Old Co.B, New Co.C
Richmond, W.L. LA 13th Bn. (Part.Rangers) Co.D
Richom, William LA 5th Inf. Co.D
Richordesen, J.S. TN 30th Inf. Co.F
Richoux, Anto. LA Mil. 5th Regt.Eur.Brig. (Spanish Regt.) Co.6
Richson, John P. VA 36th Inf. Co.C
Richson, Samuel KY 1st (Butler's) Cav. Co.B
Richt, A. 4th Conf.Inf. Co.A
Richtentall, John LA Mil. 3rd Regt. 1st Brig. 1st Div. Co.E
Richter, A. TX 15th Field Btty.
Richter, A.P. GA 5th Res. Co.C,E 2nd Lt.
Richter, August TX 5th Field Btty.
Richter, August TX 3rd Inf.
Richter, Bernhard TX 3rd Inf. Co.H
Richter, B.F. LA Mil. Fire Bn. Co.F 2nd Lt.
Richter, C. LA Mil.Squad. Guides d'Orleans Brig.
Richter, Ch. TX 16th Inf. Co.E
Richter, Charles TX Comal Res. Co.A Lt.
Richter, Charles W., Jr. GA 3rd Inf. Co.D
Richter, Ed F. GA Siege Arty. Campbell's Ind.Co. Cpl.
Richter, Edmund VA 12th Inf. Co.A Sgt.
Richter, Edward TX 1st Hvy.Arty. Co.C
Richter, Edwin SC 5th Inf. 1st Co.A 1st Lt.
Richter, Edwin SC 5th St.Troops Co.M
Richter, E.H. TX 14th Inf. Co.F
Richter, Ernst GA 1st Reg. Sgt.,Ch.Music.
Richter, F. LA Mil.Squad. Guides d'Orleans Cavalier
Richter, F. TX 2nd Inf. Co.F
Richter, F. TX 16th Inf. Co.E
Richter, Frank TX Conscr.
Richter, George 20th Conf.Cav. Co.D
Richter, H. TX Inf. Timmons' Regt. Co.D
Richter, H. TX Waul's Legion Co.F
Richter, Henry LA Mil. 2nd Regt. 2nd Brig. 1st Div. Co.C
Richter, Henry TX 12th Inf. Co.K Ch.Music.
Richter, H.P. GA Inf. 23rd Bn.Loc.Def. Sims' Co.
Richter, J.H. TX Inf. 1st St.Troops Shield's Co.B Cpl.
Richter, J.J. SC 7th Cav. Co.D
Richter, J.J. SC 1st (Hagood's) Inf. 1st Co.B
Richter, J.J. SC Cav.Bn. Holcombe Legion Co.B
Richter, John SC 4th St.Troops Co.G

Richter, John TX 2nd Cav. Co.C
Richter, John VA 12th Inf. Co.K
Richter, John N. SC 9th Inf. Co.B
Richter, Leopold TX 15th Field Btty.
Richter, Maurice TX 1st Field Btty.
Richter, Robert VA 1st Inf. Co.K
Richter, Robert VA Inf. Lyneman's Co. Sgt.
Richter, W.G.J. FL 1st Inf. New Co.I 2nd Lt.
Richtor, John TX Cav. Baylor's Regt. Co.A
Richu, J.N. AL 28th Inf. Co.G
Richwine, John P. VA 18th Cav. Co.D
Richwood, B.F. SC Arty. Manigault's Bn. 1st
   Co.B Bvt.2nd Lt.
Richwood, George C. FL 1st Inf. Old Co.H,
   New Co.A 3rd Lt.
Richy, A. LA 4th Inf. Co.B
Richy, A.H. TX 5th Inf. Co.K
Richy, Benjamin GA 4th Cav. (St.Guards)
   Gower's Co.
Richy, George MD Cav. 2nd Bn. Co.B
Richy, James VA 23rd Cav. Co.M Jr.2nd Lt.
Richy, James M. GA 34th Inf. Co.H
Richy, J.H. TN 18th Inf. Chap.
Richy, John Robert SC 4th Inf. Co.D
Richy, Joseph LA Mil. Knaps' Co. (Fausse River
   Guards) 1st Lt.
Richy, Joseph VA 11th Cav. Co.G
Richy, Joseph VA 25th Inf. 1st Co.G
Richy, William VA 11th Cav. Co.G
Rici, Antonio LA 5th Inf. Co.I
Rick, A. TN 42nd Inf. 2nd Co.I
Rick, John NC 28th Inf. Co.C
Rick, John VA 1st Inf. Co.K
Rick, Joseph MO 6th Cav. Co.E Sgt.
Rick, M.L. NC 2nd Jr.Res. Co.E
Rick, Nathaniel LA C.S. Zouave Bn. Co.F
Rick, Ransom MS 1st Inf. Co.D
Rickand, S.R. AL 36th Inf. Co.F
Rickar, W.C. Morgan's Co.E,CSA
Rickarby, William D. LA 7th Inf. Co.G Capt.
Rickard, Alex. NC 6th Sr.Res. Co.C
Rickard, Asher W. VA 136th Mil. Co.E
Rickard, Benjamin AL 23rd Inf. Co.A
Rickard, Calvin VA Res. Keyser's Co.
Rickard, Emanuel R. NC 48th Inf. Co.B
Rickard, G. Conf.Inf. Tucker's Regt. Co.G
Rickard, Henry AL Mil. 3rd Vol. Co.B
Rickard, J. AL 4th Inf. Co.B
Rickard, J.A. AR 2nd Cav. Co.E
Rickard, James R. VA 2nd Inf. Co.B Music.
Rickard, J.D. AR 2nd Cav. Co.E
Rickard, J.L. VA Inf. 1st Bn.Loc.Def. Co.B
Rickard, J.O. AL 4th Inf. Co.D
Rickard, John LA 10th Inf. Co.F
Rickard, John VA 3rd (Chrisman's) Bn.Res.
   Co.C
Rickard, John H. VA 7th Cav. Co.K
Rickard, John T. AL 23rd Inf. Co.I
Rickard, Lewis N. NC 48th Inf. Co.B
Rickard, Miles M. MS 11th Inf. Co.D
Rickard, Peter S. NC 48th Inf. Co.B
Rickard, Richard AL 51st (Part.Rangers) Co.H
   Cpl.
Rickard, Samuel MO Cav. Clardy's Bn. Co.B
Rickard, William A. VA 7th Cav. Co.D
Rickard, William C. VA 7th Inf. Co.E
Rickard, William E. AL 28th Inf. Co.A

Rickards, George V. FL 7th Inf. Co.K
Rickards, R.A. VA 13th Inf. Co.F
Rickardson, Joseph AL 10th Cav. Co.C
Rickars, Y.W. NC 56th Inf. Co.F
Rickart, Henry LA 22nd Inf. Co.A Cpl.
Rickart, J.D. TX 24th & 25th Cav. (Cons.) Co.G
Rickborn, Hammond A. SC Hvy.Arty.
   Mathewes' Co.
Ricke, Antoine 1st Conf.Eng.Troops Co.E Artif.
Ricke, Anton TX 26th Cav. Co.F
Ricke, Anton Kellersberg's Corps Sap. &
   Min.,CSA
Ricke, F. AL Cp. of Instr. Talladega
Ricke, J. TX Inf. 4th Bn. (Oswald's) Co.B
Ricke, John 4th Conf.Eng.Troops Co.E Artif.
Ricke, John Kellersberg's Corps Sap. &
   Min.,CSA Artif.
Ricke, Joseph 4th Conf.Eng.Troops Co.E Artif.
Ricke, Joseph Kellersberg's Corps Sap. &
   Min.,CSA Artif.
Ricke, Martin TX 1st Hvy.Arty. Co.C
Rickels, B. MS 3rd Inf. (St.Troops) Co.C
Rickels, Edward T. MS 22nd Inf. Co.G
Rickels, E.H. SC Mil.Arty. 1st Regt. Harms' Co.
Rickels, E.H. SC Arty. Melchers' Co.
   (Co.B,German Arty.)
Rickels, E.N. AL 9th Inf. Co.B
Rickels, H. SC 1st Regt. Charleston Guard Co.G
   Cpl.
Rickels, Jerry L. AL Cav. Lewis' Bn. Co.E
Rickels, John GA Carlton's Co. (Troup
   Cty.Arty.)
Rickels, L.H. AL 58th Inf. Co.A
Rickenbacker, E. SC 2nd St.Troops Co.C 1st
   Sgt.
Rickenbacker, E. SC 11th Res. Co.H Sgt.
Rickenbacker, E.J. SC Cav. 14th Bn. Co.B
Rickenbacker, F.N. SC 1st (Hagood's) Inf. 1st
   Co.C 2nd Lt.
Rickenbacker, H.K. SC Inf. Hampton Legion
   Co.H
Rickenbacker, Jacob AL 20th Inf. Co.A
Rickenbacker, Jacob D. SC 5th Cav. Co.A
Rickenbacker, J.D. SC Cav. 14th Bn. Co.B
Rickenbacker, J.D. SC 2nd Arty. Co.F
Rickenbacker, J.D. SC 1st (Hagood's) Inf. 1st
   Co.C
Rickenbacker, N. SC 25th Inf. Co.F
Rickenbacker, P.H. SC Inf. Hampton Legion
   Co.H
Rickenbacker, T.E. SC Cav. 14th Bn. Co.B
Rickenbacker, T.E. SC 1st (Hagood's) Inf. 1st
   Co.C, 2nd Co.B 1st Lt.
Rickenbacker, Telifus E. SC 5th Cav. Co.A
Rickenbacker, W.J. SC Inf. Hampton Legion
   Co.H
Rickenbacker, William J. SC 1st (Hagood's) Inf.
   1st Co.D
Rickenbaker, H.L. SC 2nd Arty. Co.C
Rickenbaker, Medicus SC 2nd Arty. Co.C Capt.
Ricker, --- LA Mil. 3rd Regt. 2nd Brig. 1st Div.
   Co.C
Ricker, A.G. TX Cav. 1st Regt.St.Troops Co.B
Ricker, B. VA Inf. 1st Bn.Loc.Def. Co.C
Ricker, Charles LA 1st (Strawbridge's) Inf.
   Co.E,G
Ricker, Charles LA 21st (Kennedy's) Inf. Co.F

Ricker, Charles TX Inf. 2nd St.Troops Co.H
Ricker, Daniel MO 10th Inf. Co.H
Ricker, George AR 13th Inf. Co.E
Ricker, George AR Mil. Desha Cty.Bn.
Ricker, George KY 7th Mtd.Inf. 1st Co.K
Ricker, Henry LA 7th Inf. Co.E
Ricker, Henry LA 20th Inf. New Co.B
Ricker, Henry LA 21st (Kennedy's) Inf. Co.C
Ricker, Henry A. AL 21st Inf. Co.E
Ricker, John MS 3rd (St.Troops) Cav. Co.E
Ricker, John MS 1st (King's) Inf. (St.Troops)
   Co.B Sgt.
Ricker, John G. LA 6th Inf. Co.B
Ricker, Orrin GA 61st Inf. Co.I
Ricker, Samuel L. NC 64th Inf. Co.I
Ricker, W. LA 3rd (Wingfield's) Cav. Co.H
Ricker, William 1st Cherokee Mtd.Vol.
   Ch.Bugler
Ricker, William D. GA 41st Inf. Co.G
Rickerby, Robert AR 2nd Inf. Co.B
Rickerick, M.H. VA 31st Mil. Co.B
Rickerman, Miles NC 29th Inf. Co.H Cpl.
Rickers, W.A. GA 7th Inf.
Rickerson, A. GA 1st (Olmstead's) Inf. Gordon's
   Co.
Rickerson, B. GA Lt.Arty. Pritchard's Co.
   (Washington Arty.)
Rickerson, B. TN Lt.Arty. Scott's Co.
Rickerson, Benjamin GA Inf. 27th Bn. Co.B
Rickerson, Emereld GA 27th Inf. Co.K
Rickerson, F. AR 19th (Dockery's) Inf. Co.F
   Sgt.
Rickerson, G.W. GA 45th Inf. Co.A
Rickerson, Henry R. GA 12th Inf. Co.G
Rickerson, James M. FL 5th Inf. Co.C
Rickerson, J.H. GA Inf. 27th Bn. Co.C
Rickerson, Leonard GA 26th Inf. Co.K
Rickerson, Manning GA 1st (Olmstead's) Inf.
   Gordon's Co.
Rickerson, T. TN Lt.Arty. Scott's Co.
Rickerson, T.C. GA 1st (Olmstead's) Inf. Gor-
   don's Co.
Rickerson, Thomas W. GA 45th Inf. Co.K Sgt.
Rickerson, T.L. GA Lt.Arty. Pritchard's Co.
   (Washington Arty.)
Rickerson, Vincent GA Cav. 20th Bn. Co.G
Rickerson, Vincent GA Cav. 21st Bn. Co.D
Rickerson, W. GA Cav. 1st Bn.Res. Tufts' Co.
Rickerson, Whitfield GA Siege Arty. 28th Bn.
   Co.E
Rickerson, William J. GA 1st (Olmstead's) Inf.
   Co.C
Rickert, August TN 15th Inf. Co.I
Rickert, David A. NC 33rd Inf. Co.A
Rickert, Eli P. NC 48th Inf. Co.C
Rickert, Henry LA 22nd (Cons.) Inf. Co.A Cpl.
Rickert, Henry NC 33rd Inf. Co.A
Rickert, Henry H. NC 34th Inf. Co.D Ord.Sgt.
Rickert, J.A. NC 57th Inf. Co.B
Rickert, J.E. LA Mil. 4th Regt.Eur.Brig. Co.F
   Capt.
Rickert, John M. NC 4th Inf. Co.C
Rickert, Marks TN 15th Inf. Co.I Capt.
Rickert, Max TN 15th Inf. Co.I Capt.
Rickert, William T. NC 4th Inf. Co.A Music.
Rickerts, William NC 1st Arty. (10th St.Troops)
   Co.D

Rickertson, Hiram GA 1st Bn.S.S. Co.B
Rickes, A. TX 8th Field Btty.
Rickes, A. TX Lt.Arty. Dege's Bn.
Rickes, G. TX 4th Inf. (St.Troops) Co.A
Ricket, Thomas TN 35th Inf. Co.H
Ricket, W.O. AL Talladega Cty.Res. G.M. Gamble's Co.
Rickets, D.P. TN 19th (Biffle's) Cav. Co.F
Rickets, Edward TX 3rd Inf. Co.H
Rickets, Howard S. LA Miles' Legion Co.B
Rickets, J.A. MS Cav. 1st Res. Co.F
Rickets, J.A. 20th Conf.Cav. 1st Co.H Sgt.
Rickets, James Ervin SC 4th Cav. Co.A
Rickets, J.L. MS 1st Cav.Res. Co.F
Rickets, J.L. 20th Conf.Cav. 1st Co.H
Rickets, John AL 4th (Russell's) Cav. Co.I,H
Rickets, John TN 27th Inf. Co.A
Rickets, John 3rd Conf.Cav. Co.G Cpl.
Rickets, John C. MO Arty. Jos. Bledsoe's Co.
Rickets, John E. SC Cav. 12th Bn. Co.A
Rickets, John J. TN 42nd Inf. 2nd Co.K
Rickets, J.W. TN 4th (McLemore's) Cav. Co.C Sgt.
Rickets, Marcus H. AR 15th Inf. Co.F
Rickets, Peter SC 19th Inf. Co.I
Rickets, R. TN 21st Inf. Co.I Sgt.
Rickets, R.S. LA 2nd Cav. Co.I
Rickets, Russel H. TN 27th Inf. Co.I Sgt.
Rickets, S.A. AR 15th (Johnson's) Inf. Co.C
Rickets, Samuel A. TN Cav. Allison's Squad. Co.B
Rickets, S.R. AL 45th Inf. Co.K
Rickets, T.R. TN 19th (Biffle's) Cav. Co.F Music.
Rickets, W. SC 21st Inf. Co.E
Rickets, William SC 20th Inf. Co.E
Rickets, W.L. MS 1st Cav.Res. Co.F Sgt.
Rickets, W.L. TN 4th (McLemore's) Cav. Co.C
Rickets, W.L. 20th Conf.Cav. 1st Co.H
Ricketson, A. GA 63rd Inf. Co.K
Ricketson, B. TN Arty. Marshall's Co.
Ricketson, Benjamin GA 1st (Olmstead's) Inf. Gordon's Co.
Ricketson, Benjamin GA 63rd Inf. Co.K
Ricketson, E. GA 63rd Inf. Co.K
Ricketson, F. GA 63rd Inf. Co.K
Ricketson, Ivey GA 50th Inf. Co.C
Ricketson, James GA 50th Inf. Co.C
Ricketson, J.L. GA 22nd Inf. Co.H
Ricketson, John H. TN Arty. Marshall's Co.
Ricketson, John P. GA 26th Inf. Co.I,A
Ricketson, Joseph GA 1st (Olmstead's) Inf. Gordon's Co.
Ricketson, Joseph GA 63rd Inf. Co.K
Ricketson, Manning GA 63rd Inf. Co.K
Ricketson, O. AL 8th Inf. Co.D
Ricketson, T. TN Arty. Marshall's Co.
Ricketson, T.C. GA 63rd Inf. Co.K
Ricketson, William O. GA 48th Inf. Co.B Sgt.
Ricketson, William S. GA 15th Inf. Co.D Lt.
Rickett, Alexander NC 39th Inf. Co.E
Rickett, Hartly S. VA 63rd Inf. Co.B
Rickett, Jeremiah NC 39th Inf. Co.E
Rickett, J.H. LA Inf.Cons.Crescent Regt. Co.K
Rickett, Joel H. AL 10th Inf. Co.I
Rickett, Joel H. AL 39th Inf. Co.I
Rickett, John TN 62nd Mtd.Inf. Co.B

Rickett, P. AR 46th (Crabtree's) Cav. Co.F
Rickett, Richard M. VA 5th Inf. Co.B
Rickett, Richard M. VA 27th Inf. 2nd Co.H
Rickett, Richard T. TX 14th Cav. Co.A
Rickett, Thomas MO 11th Inf. Co.C
Rickett, W. AL 3rd Cav. Co.C
Rickett, W.A. AR 21st Inf. Co.K
Ricketts, --- VA VMI Co.C
Ricketts, A.I. MO Cav. Fristoe's Regt. Co.A
Ricketts, Alexander NC 26th Inf. Co.K
Ricketts, Andrew J. MO Inf. 8th Bn. Co.B
Ricketts, Andrew M. TN Cav. 9th Bn. (Gantt's) Co.E
Ricketts, Augustus VA Lt.Arty. Cayce's Co.
Ricketts, B. TN 31st Inf. Co.H Cpl.
Ricketts, Baron C. LA Pointe Coupee Arty. Cpl.
Ricketts, Benjamin NC 6th Inf. Co.D
Ricketts, Benjamin F. TX 6th Cav. Co.F Sgt.
Ricketts, Charles W. TN Cav. 9th Bn. (Gantt's) Co.E Sgt.
Ricketts, Daniel MD Cav. 2nd Bn. Co.A
Ricketts, Drury P. MS 1st Lt.Arty. Co.L
Ricketts, E. LA Washington Arty.Bn. Co.5
Ricketts, E. VA Cav. Mosby's Regt. (Part. Rangers) Co.F
Ricketts, E.D. KY 6th Mtd.Inf. Co.B AQM
Ricketts, E.D. Conf.Cav. 6th Bn. AQM
Ricketts, E.D. Gen. & Staff Capt.,AQM
Ricketts, Edward VA 2nd Inf.Loc.Def. Co.D
Ricketts, Edward VA Inf. 6th Bn.Loc.Def. Co.A
Ricketts, Edwill VA Lt.Arty. Kirkpatrick's Co.
Ricketts, Edwin VA Lt.Arty. Kirkpatrick's Co.
Ricketts, Elisha GA Inf. (Anderson Guards) Anderson's Co.
Ricketts, Ephraim A. MS 26th Inf. Co.C
Ricketts, George Conf.Inf. Tucker's Regt. Co.I
Ricketts, George W. NC 23rd Inf. Co.A
Ricketts, H.H. VA 4th Cav. Co.H
Ricketts, Jacob MS 43rd Inf. Co.B
Ricketts, James AR 15th (N.W.) Inf. Emergency Co.I Cpl.
Ricketts, James VA 4th Inf. Co.H
Ricketts, James VA 38th Inf. Co.H Cpl.
Ricketts, James A. AL 6th Inf. Co.I
Ricketts, James A. KY 6th Mtd.Inf. Co.B Sgt.
Ricketts, James L. MS Inf. 2nd Bn. Co.B Cpl.
Ricketts, James L. MS 48th Inf. Co.B Sgt.
Ricketts, James P. TX 27th Cav. Co.B
Ricketts, James W. MS 1st Lt.Arty. Co.I Sgt.
Ricketts, James W. TN 7th Inf. Co.F Sgt.
Ricketts, J.C. MS 26th Inf. Co.C
Ricketts, John AR 34th Inf. Co.F
Ricketts, John Elias VA 34th Mil. Co.A
Ricketts, John R. MO 3rd Cav. Co.D Sr.2nd Lt.
Ricketts, John W. KY 9th Mtd.Inf. Co.H
Ricketts, John W. VA Hvy.Arty. 19th Bn. Co.D
Ricketts, John W. VA 38th Inf. Co.A
Ricketts, Joseph O. TX 31st Cav. Co.A
Ricketts, Joseph W. KY 9th Mtd.Inf. Co.C
Ricketts, J.T. TN 6th Inf. Co.B
Ricketts, Lewis H. VA Cav. 35th Bn. Co.F
Ricketts, Lucian C. VA 8th Cav. Co.E
Ricketts, Luther C. KY 1st Bn.Mtd.Rifles Co.D Sgt.
Ricketts, Luther C. KY 3rd Bn.Mtd.Rifles Co.F 1st Lt.
Ricketts, Matthew M. MS 26th Inf. Co.K,C

Ricketts, Melvel S. MO 9th (Elliott's) Cav. Co.H
Ricketts, Melvin S. AR 15th (N.W.) Inf. Co.F
Ricketts, Moses B. KY 2nd Mtd.Inf. Co.E
Ricketts, Palmer M. GA Arty. 9th Bn. Co.A
Ricketts, Reuben VA 38th Inf. Co.E
Ricketts, Richard S. GA 12th Inf. Co.B
Ricketts, Robert S. Sig.Corps,CSA
Ricketts, R.R. TN 21st (Wilson's) Cav. Co.H
Ricketts, R.R. TN 21st & 22nd (Cons.) Cav. Co.H
Ricketts, Rufus MO Mtd.Inf. Boone's Regt.
Ricketts, S.A. AR 15th (N.W.) Inf. Co.G
Ricketts, S.R. AL 45th Inf. Co.K
Ricketts, Stephen R. AL 1st Regt.Conscr. Co.G
Ricketts, Thomas VA Lt.Arty. Kirkpatrick's Co. Sgt.
Ricketts, Thomas B. TX 27th Cav. Co.B
Ricketts, Thomas M. TN Cav. 9th Bn. (Gantt's) Co.E Sgt.
Ricketts, T.R. TN 19th (Biffle's) Cav. Co.F Music.
Ricketts, W. MS 1st Lt.Arty. Sgt.
Ricketts, W.A. TN 13th Inf. Co.C
Ricketts, W.A. TX 17th Inf. Co.I Sgt.
Ricketts, William D. TN 7th Inf. Co.F
Ricketts, William H. AL 38th Inf. Co.B
Ricketts, William H. VA 13th Inf. Co.A Sgt.
Ricketts, William H. VA 22nd Inf. Co.A Cpl.
Ricketts, William H. VA 151st Mil. Co.B Orderly Sgt.
Ricketts, William M. AL Lt.Arty. Ward's Btty.
Ricketts, W.L. AR 34th Inf. Co.F
Ricketts, W.L. MS 40th Inf. Co.D
Ricketts, W.L. TN 19th (Biffle's) Cav. Co.F
Ricketts, W.M. AR 34th Inf.
Rickey, August AL 20th Inf. Co.B
Rickey, Frederick AL Cp. of Instr. Talladega
Rickey, J.F. GA 42nd Inf. Co.G
Rickey, John MO Inf. Perkins' Bn. Co.F
Rickey, Joseph VA Cav. 31st Regt. Co.G
Rickey, Robert AL 12th Cav. Co.G
Rickford, Alonzo LA Inf. 10th Bn.
Rickford, Thomas TX 1st Hvy.Arty. Co.B
Rickhow, E.J. MS Inf. 2nd Bn. Co.F
Rickhow, E.J. MS 48th Inf. Co.F
Rickhow, G.H. TX 24th Cav. Co.A Sgt.
Rickhow, Leslie TX 26th Cav. Co.A
Rickhow, S.J. TX 13th Vol. 2nd Co.C
Rickhow, William TX 26th Cav. Co.A Sgt.
Rickie, George LA 25th Inf. Co.H
Rickister, E. SC Palmetto S.S. Co.M
Rickits, Charles 1st Seminole Mtd.Vol.
Rickitts, Albert G. VA 8th Cav. Co.E
Rickitts, William M. AL 9th Inf. Co.K
Rickland, W.R. AL 8th Inf. Co.D
Rickle, Christoff TX Comal Res.
Ricklefsen, August TX 1st (Yager's) Cav. Co.F 1st Sgt.
Rickles, Edmond T. MS 30th Inf. Co.I
Rickles, E.F. SC Mil. 1st Regt. (Charleston Res.) Co.F
Rickles, H. SC Mil. 1st Regt. (Charleston Res.) Co.F
Rickles, H. SC Mil. 16th Regt. Triest's Co.
Rickles, James R. GA 60th Inf. Co.A
Rickles, James R. NC Inf. 2nd Bn. Co.E
Rickles, James W. AL 28th Inf. Co.C

Rickles, Jeremiah KY 2nd (Duke's) Cav. Co.G
Rickles, Jeremiah A. MS 33rd Inf. Co.F
Rickles, J.H. SC Mil. 16th Regt. Bancroft, Jr.'s Co.
Rickles, John MS 35th Inf. Co.D
Rickles, J.S. AL 12th Cav. Co.E
Rickles, Wilson H. MS 30th Inf. Co.I
Rickleson, Henry LA Inf. 9th Bn. Co.B
Rickley, John GA Inf. 1st Bn. (St.Guards) Co.D
Rickley, John GA 17th Inf. Co.F
Rickman, Ab TN 25th Inf. Co.A
Rickman, Abram VA Hvy.Arty. Wright's Co.
Rickman, A.P. AL 21st Inf. Co.K
Rickman, A.T. AL 41st Inf. Co.K
Rickman, Berry G. TN 10th (DeMoss') Cav. Co.H Capt.
Rickman, B.F. MS Morgan's Co. (Morgan Riflemen) Sgt.
Rickman, B.G. TN 10th (DeMoss') Cav. Co.H Capt.
Rickman, Bine MO 8th Inf. Co.B Music.
Rickman, Caleb A. NC 16th Inf. Co.I
Rickman, C.P. TN 17th Inf. Co.F
Rickman, Daniel MO Inf. Perkins' Bn. Co.D Sgt.
Rickman, Eli MS 15th Inf. Co.H
Rickman, E.M. TN 17th Inf. Co.F
Rickman, Ethelbert T. VA 3rd Inf. 2nd Co.K
Rickman, E.W. MS 8th Cav. Co.B
Rickman, E.W. MS 28th Cav. Co.E
Rickman, E.W. MS 4th Inf. Co.F Sgt.
Rickman, Francis M. MS 15th Inf. Co.H
Rickman, Henry C. MS 33rd Inf. Co.H
Rickman, Henry C. VA 21st Inf. Co.A
Rickman, H.J. AL 41st Inf. Co.C
Rickman, Horatio VA 24th Inf. Co.C
Rickman, Isaac W. VA Cav. McFarlane's Co.
Rickman, Isaac W. Conf.Cav. 6th Bn.
Rickman, James C. TN 48th (Nixon's) Inf. Co.I
Rickman, James E. MO Cav. 1st Regt.St.Guard Co.C
Rickman, James F. TN 17th Cav. Co.F
Rickman, James M. TN 11th Cav.
Rickman, J.B. KY 7th Mtd.Inf. Co.H
Rickman, J.B. TN 46th Inf. Co.D
Rickman, J.B. TN 55th (Brown's) Inf. Co.D
Rickman, Jennings VA 14th Inf. Co.K
Rickman, J.F. MS 28th Cav. Co.E
Rickman, J.F. TN 17th Inf. Co.F
Rickman, J.H. GA 4th Cav. (St.Guards) Cannon's Co.
Rickman, J.H. GA 11th Cav.
Rickman, J.H. VA 1st (Farinholt's) Res. Co.D
Rickman, J.N. KY 9th Mtd.Inf. Co.A
Rickman, John AR 17th (Griffith's) Inf. Co.G
Rickman, John NC 25th Inf. Co.H
Rickman, John TN 11th Cav.
Rickman, John Conf.Cav. Baxter's Bn. Co.C Sgt.
Rickman, John H. VA 3rd Inf. 2nd Co.K
Rickman, John J. NC 18th Inf. Co.B
Rickman, John L. TN 42nd Inf. 2nd Co.K 1st Sgt.
Rickman, John N. TN 48th (Nixon's) Inf. Co.I
Rickman, John P. AR 8th Inf. New Co.A
Rickman, Joseph TN 25th Inf. Co.C
Rickman, Joseph A. TN 25th Inf. Co.C

Rickman, Joseph W. NC Inf. 69th Regt. Co.A
Rickman, L.A. TN 17th Inf. Co.F
Rickman, Marquis L. NC 16th Inf. Co.I
Rickman, Monroe MS 32nd Inf. Co.C
Rickman, N.D.F. TN 6th Inf. Co.A
Rickman, Peter AL 40th Inf. Co.B
Rickman, Phillip R. NC 1st Cav. (9th St.Troops) Co.K
Rickman, R.F. Horse Arty White's Btty.
Rickman, Robert F. 1st Conf.Cav. 2nd Co.E
Rickman, S.A. MS 32nd Inf. Co.C Cpl.
Rickman, Thomas LA 1st Hvy.Arty. (Reg.) Co.I
Rickman, Thomas Inf. School of Pract. Powell's Command Co.B
Rickman, Thomas V. VA 3rd Inf. 2nd Co.K
Rickman, W.A. MS 7th Cav. Co.F
Rickman, W.C. MS 33rd Inf. Co.H
Rickman, W.C. TN 11th (Holman's) Cav. Co.C
Rickman, W.E. AR 3rd Inf. (St.Troops) Co.A
Rickman, W.H. TN 48th (Nixon's) Inf. Co.I
Rickman, William AL 16th Inf. Co.C
Rickman, William NC 7th Sr.Res. Watts' Co.
Rickman, William NC 60th Inf. Co.K
Rickman, William C. NC 1st Cav. (9th St.Troops) Co.K
Rickman, William G. AL 41st Inf. Co.C
Rickman, William R. NC 25th Inf. Co.E
Rickman, William R NC Inf. 69th Regt. Co.A
Rickman, William R. VA Arty. Paris' Co.
Rickman, William T. TN Cav. 7th Bn. (Bennett's) Co.A
Rickman, W.T. TN 22nd (Barteau's) Cav. Co.D Capt.
Rickmon, David W. NC 60th Inf. Co.D Sgt.
Rickmon, Jesse W. NC 60th Inf. Co.D Cpl.
Rickmon, John VA 16th Cav. Co.A
Rickmon, P.H. VA Inf. 25th Bn. Co.B
Rickmon, W.A. MS Cav. Ham's Regt. Co.A
Rickmond, Peter NC 21st Inf. Co.L
Rickner, Henry LA 4th Inf. Co.H
Rickner, Samuel MO 11th Inf. Co.A
Ricks, --- GA 54th Inf. Co.A Sgt.
Ricks, --- GA 59th Inf. Co.K
Ricks, A. TX 2nd Cav. Co.K
Ricks, Aaron G. GA 50th Inf. Co.C
Ricks, Adolph MS Cav. Part.Rangers Rhodes' Co.
Ricks, A.E. NC 3rd Arty. (40th St.Troops) Co.H
Ricks, A.G. 14th Conf.Cav. Co.F
Ricks, A.J. GA 16th Inf. Co.K Cpl.
Ricks, Albert MS Cav. Part.Rangers Rhodes' Co.
Ricks, Albert 14th Conf.Cav. Co.F
Ricks, Allfree LA Sabine Res.
Ricks, A.M. AL Cp. of Instr. Talladega
Ricks, A.M. Lt.Arty. Dent's Btty.,CSA
Ricks, Amirald TX 28th Cav. Co.G 1st Sgt.
Ricks, Amos NC 3rd Bn.Sr.Res. Williams' Co.
Ricks, Andrew M. GA 35th Inf. Co.C
Ricks, Arthur W. GA 48th Inf. Co.F
Ricks, Augustus H. NC 3rd Cav. (41st St.Troops) Co.G
Ricks, B. SC Lt.Arty. Garden's Co. (Palmetto Lt.Btty.)
Ricks, B.B. NC 1st Arty. (10th St.Troops) Co.A
Ricks, Benjamin B. NC 3rd Arty. (40th St.Troops) Co.G

Ricks, Benjamin S., Jr. MS 28th Cav. Co.I 1st Lt.
Ricks, Burton A. NC 15th Inf. Co.I
Ricks, Button NC 1st Jr.Res. Co.A
Ricks, C. Trans-MS Conf.Cav. 1st Bn. Co.C
Ricks, Charles W. GA 35th Inf. Co.C
Ricks, Collin A. VA 24th Cav. Co.K
Ricks, Collin A. VA 3rd Inf. Co.D Cpl.
Ricks, Collin A. 8th (Dearing's) Conf.Cav. Co.E
Ricks, Cullen T. NC 32nd Inf. Co.C,D
Ricks, David A. 9th Conf.Inf. Co.G Commanding Co.
Ricks, David B. NC Lt.Arty. 13th Bn. Co.F
Ricks, David W. NC 39th Inf. Co.G
Ricks, D.B. NC 3rd Arty. (40th St.Troops) Co.H
Ricks, D.L. FL Sp.Cav. 1st Bn. Co.B 1st Sgt.
Ricks, D.L. GA 32nd Inf. Co.G 1st Lt.
Ricks, D.M. GA Cav. 29th Bn. Co.H
Ricks, E. 14th Conf.Cav. Co.F
Ricks, Edward MS Cav. Part.Rangers Rhodes' Co.
Ricks, Edward MS 19th Inf. Co.K
Ricks, Edward TX 2nd Cav. Co.K
Ricks, Edwards MS Conscr.
Ricks, Edward T. SC 26th Inf. Co.E
Ricks, Edwin NC 1st Inf. Co.F
Ricks, E.T. SC Lt.Arty. M. Ward's Co. (Waccamaw Lt.Arty.)
Ricks, F. AL Randolph Cty.Res. J. Hightower's Co.
Ricks, F. TN 1st Hvy.Arty. 2nd Co.C
Ricks, F. 14th Conf.Cav. Co.F
Ricks, Feranond MS Cav. Part.Rangers Rhodes' Co.
Ricks, G. MS 3rd Inf. Co.B
Ricks, G.D. NC 4th Cav. (59th St.Troops) Co.H
Ricks, George TX 25th Cav. Co.I
Ricks, George E. GA Lt.Arty. (Jackson Arty.) Massenburg's Btty. Cpl.
Ricks, George H. GA 57th Inf. Co.A
Ricks, George M.C. NC 37th Inf. Co.E
Ricks, George T. VA Lt.Arty. 12th Bn. Co.B
Ricks, G.H. GA 61st Inf. Co.C
Ricks, Guilford NC 43rd Inf. Co.C
Ricks, G.W. TX 17th Inf. Co.F,C
Ricks, H. GA Cav. 20th Bn. Co.B
Ricks, Hampton GA 63rd Inf. Co.H
Ricks, Henry TX 2nd Cav. Co.K
Ricks, I.J. GA Hvy.Arty. 22nd Bn. Co.B
Ricks, Isaac TX 28th Cav. Co.H,G
Ricks, Isaac D. GA 26th Inf. Co.C
Ricks, J.A. AL 8th (Livingston's) Cav. Co.A
Ricks, Jacob GA 3rd Res. Co.I
Ricks, James GA 12th (Robinson's) Cav. (St.Guards) Co.H
Ricks, James H. GA 32nd Inf. Co.G Cpl.
Ricks, James R. VA Inf. 44th Bn. Co.D 1st Lt.
Ricks, James R. VA 54th Mil. Co.C,D
Ricks, James R. Sig.Corps,CSA
Ricks, James S. NC 1st Inf. Co.F
Ricks, James W. GA 50th Inf. Co.F
Ricks, James W. NC 15th Inf. Co.I
Ricks, J.D. AR 1st (Monroe's) Cav. Co.B
Ricks, Jerome NC 3rd Arty. (40th St.Troops) Co.H
Ricks, Jesse B. GA 35th Inf. Co.C

Ricks, Jethro NC 3rd Arty. (40th St.Troops)
  Co.H
Ricks, Jethro D. NC 15th Inf. Co.I
Ricks, J.H. AL 40th Inf. Co.K
Ricks, J.J. AL 14th Inf. Co.H
Ricks, J.J. TN Inf. 4th Cons.Regt. Co.K
Ricks, J.J. TN 51st Inf. Co.C Ord.Sgt.
Ricks, J.J. TN 51st (Cons.) Inf. Co.I
Ricks, J.L. TX 7th Cav. Co.E
Ricks, John GA 50th Inf. Co.C
Ricks, John A. NC 30th Inf. Co.I Sgt.
Ricks, John A. TX 31st Cav. Co.C
Ricks, John A. VA 49th Inf. 3rd Co.G
Ricks, John B. LA Inf.Cons.Crescent Regt. Co.F
Ricks, John E. NC 32nd Inf. Co.H
Ricks, John H. GA 35th Inf. Co.C
Ricks, John L. MS 17th Inf. Co.A
Ricks, John M. GA 31st Inf. Co.I Cpl.
Ricks, John Q. LA 3rd (Wingfield's) Cav. Co.C
Ricks, John R. AL Eufaula Lt.Arty.
Ricks, John R. GA 61st Inf. Co.C Cpl.
Ricks, John R. MS Inf. 1st Bn.St.Troops (12 mo.
  '62-3) Co.C Sgt.
Ricks, John R. MS 33rd Inf. Co.F
Ricks, John R.A. GA 11th Inf. Co.I Sgt.
Ricks, John T. GA Hvy.Arty. 22nd Bn. Co.B
Ricks, John T. GA 25th Inf. 1st Co.K
Ricks, John T. TX Res.Corps
Ricks, John W. MS 15th Inf. Co.I
Ricks, Joseph VA 10th Cav. 1st Co.E, Co.A
Ricks, Joseph D. VA 49th Inf. 3rd Co.G
Ricks, Joshua NC 54th Inf. Co.F
Ricks, J.W. LA 3rd (Wingfield's) Cav. Co.E
  Sgt.
Ricks, J.W. TN 14th (Neely's) Cav. Co.D 1st
  Lt.
Ricks, J.W. TN 31st Inf. Co.F
Ricks, J. Wilson NC 45th Inf. Co.K
Ricks, L.R. GA 3rd Res. Co.H
Ricks, Lucien C. GA 61st Inf. Co.I Sgt.
Ricks, M. TX 11th Inf. Co.B
Ricks, M.C. TN 14th (Neely's) Cav. Co.D
Ricks, Nero NC 12th Inf. Co.H Cpl.
Ricks, Nero NC 32nd Inf. Co.H Cpl.
Ricks, Orlando NC 45th Inf. Co.B
Ricks, Petty H. LA 31st Inf. Co.E
Ricks, Pleasant A. NC 27th Inf. Co.B
Ricks, P.W. AL 6th Cav. Co.E
Ricks, R.H. NC 1st Arty. (10th St.Troops) Co.A
Ricks, Richard GA 31st Inf. Co.I
Ricks, Richard TX 2nd Cav. Co.K
Ricks, R.J. LA 25th Inf. Co.B
Ricks, R.J. MS Inf. 3rd Bn. (St.Troops) Co.F
Ricks, R.M. GA Lt.Arty. Barnwell's Btty. Cpl.
Ricks, Robert F. NC 15th Inf. Co.I Cpl.
Ricks, Robert F. 1st Conf.Cav. 2nd Co.E 2nd Lt.
Ricks, Robert H. NC 3rd Arty. (40th St.Troops)
  Co.G
Ricks, Robert H. NC 1st Inf. (6 mo. '61) Co.A
Ricks, Robert M. AL Hardy's Co. (Eufaula
  Minute Men)
Ricks, Robert V. NC 55th Inf. Co.E Cpl.
Ricks, R.R. GA Inf. 14th Bn. (St.Guards) Co.D
Ricks, Ruffin NC 2nd Cav. (19th St.Troops)
  Co.E
Ricks, Ruffin NC 47th Inf. Co.D
Ricks, R.W. TN 16th (Logwood's) Cav. Co.G

Ricks, Samuel GA 50th Inf. Co.F
Ricks, Samuel GA Cobb's Legion Co.A
Ricks, Samuel Conf.Inf. 1st Bn. 2nd Co.A
Ricks, Samuel J. MS 5th Inf. Co.K
Ricks, Samuel W. NC 39th Inf. Co.C,G
Ricks, Seaborn L. GA Inf. 10th Bn. Co.D
Ricks, Simond D. GA 48th Inf. Co.F
Ricks, Spencer D. NC 47th Inf. Co.D
Ricks, S.R. GA 4th Res. Co.F
Ricks, S.T. MS Cav. Williams' Co.
Ricks, T. Trans-MS Conf.Cav. 1st Bn. Co.D
Ricks, Thomas A. NC 2nd Cav. (19th St.Troops)
  Co.E
Ricks, Thomas C. NC 12th Inf. Co.O
Ricks, Thomas H. LA Inf.Crescent Regt. Co.C
  Sgt.
Ricks, Thomas H. LA Inf.Cons.Crescent Regt.
  Co.G Sgt.
Ricks, Thomas H. MO 2nd Inf. Co.F
Ricks, T.L. TX 37th Cav. Co.E
Ricks, W. LA Inf. 1st Bn. (St.Guards) Co.B
Ricks, W. NC 1st Arty. (10th St.Troops) Co.E
Ricks, W.B. MS 28th Cav. Co.I
Ricks, W.H. GA 11th Cav. Co.C
Ricks, Wiley TX 2nd Cav. Co.K
Ricks, William NC 17th Inf. (2nd Org.) Co.I
Ricks, William A. GA Inf. 10th Bn. Co.B
Ricks, William B. MS 1st Cav.Res. Co.I Sgt.
Ricks, William C. TN 3rd (Forrest's) Cav.
Ricks, William E. NC 45th Inf. Co.K
Ricks, William G. GA 48th Inf. Co.F 1st Sgt.
Ricks, William J. GA 35th Inf. Co.C
Ricks, William L. TX 25th Cav. Co.I,G
Ricks, William M. NC 2nd Cav. (19th St.Troops)
  Co.F
Ricks, William W. GA Hvy.Arty. 22nd Bn. Co.B
Ricks, William W. GA 25th Inf. 1st Co.K
Ricks, W.J. LA 16th Inf. Co.K Cpl.
Ricks, W.L. TX Inf. Griffin's Bn. Co.E
Ricks, W.W. GA 7th Cav. Co.B
Ricks, W.W. GA Cav. 21st Bn. Co.C
Ricks, W.W. LA 3rd (Wingfield's) Cav. Co.E
Ricks, W.W. NC 39th Inf. Co.C
Ricksby, A.B. GA 63rd Inf. Co.I
Rickson, John S. GA 25th Inf.
Ricles, John GA 43rd Inf. Co.G
Ricman, James C. TN 54th Inf. Ives' Co.
Ricman, John N. TN 54th Inf. Ives' Co.
Ricon, Charles H. TN 49th Inf. Co.A Cpl.
Ricon, Charles H. Inf. Bailey's Cons.Regt. Co.G
Ricon, Junius A. Eng.,CSA 1st Lt.
Ricord, Isaac VA 8th Bn.Res. Co.D
Ricord, J.K.P. Gen. & Staff Capt.,AQM
Ricou, Julius A. MS 37th Inf. Co.K
Ricou, Justin LA Mil. 3rd Regt.Eur.Brig. (Garde
  Francaise) Co.6
Ricsky, S. TX 24th & 25th Cav. (Cons.) Co.B
Rictenwald, John LA Miles' Legion Co.B Sgt.
Rictor, H. AR Inf. Cocke's Regt. Co.K
Riculfi, J.N. LA Mil. 5th Regt.Eur.Brig.
  (Spanish Regt.) Co.5 Sgt.
Ridan, Aug. LA Mil. 4th Regt. 1st Brig. 1st Div.
  Co.D
Ridanor, Joel W. VA 18th Cav. Co.D Cpl.
Ridd, A.G. GA Cav. Pemberton's Co. 1st Lt.
Ridd, George C. MS 15th (Cons.) Inf. Co.I 2nd
  Cpl.

Ridd, J.T. KY 4th Cav. Co.B
Ridde, J.W. MS 6th Cav. Co.C
Riddee, J. GA 5th Res. Co.A
Riddee, Jones B. AR Cav. 1st Bn. (Stirman's)
  Co.C
Riddel, B.F. VA 19th Cav. Co.A
Riddel, J.E. AL Cp. of Instr. Talladega
Riddeley, R. 3rd Conf.Eng.Troops Co.H 2nd Lt.
Riddell, A.A. VA 18th Cav. Co.D 1st Sgt.
Riddell, Andrew B. VA Goochland Lt.Arty.
Riddell, Charles VA 10th Cav. Co.I
Riddell, Charles Conf.Cav. Raum's Co. Ord.Sgt.
Riddell, E. KY 4th Cav. Co.I
Riddell, George TX Inf. Griffin's Bn.
Riddell, George W. AL 15th Bn.Part.Rangers
  Co.B
Riddell, George W. AL 56th Part.Rangers Co.B
Riddell, Hugh LA Mil.Conf.Guards Regt. Co.K
Riddell, Isaac A. MS 33rd Inf. Co.F
Riddell, J.E. MS 4th Inf. Co.G
Riddell, Jerry C. VA Goochland Lt.Arty.
Riddell, Jesse MS 28th Cav. Co.B
Riddell, J.M. VA 1st St.Res. Co.F
Riddell, John KY Shelby Co.
Riddell, John M. KY 8th Cav. Bvt.2nd Lt.
Riddell, John M. VA Inf. 22nd Bn. Co.H
Riddell, John T. MS 4th Inf.
Riddell, John W. TX 21st Cav. Co.B 1st Sgt.
Riddell, Matthew M. VA 46th Inf. Co.H
Riddell, Richard J. VA 56th Inf. Co.F
Riddell, Robert R. KY 10th Cav. Co.A
Riddell, Samuel A. AL 33rd Inf. Co.C Cpl.
Riddell, Samuel L. NC 3rd Arty. (40th
  St.Troops) Co.K 1st Sgt.
Riddell, Samuel W. VA 2nd Bn.Res. Co.A Cpl.
Riddell, S.T. SC 1st Bn.S.S. Co.C
Riddell, S.W. VA Goochland Lt.Arty.
Riddell, Thomas C. MS 31st Inf. Co.E
Riddell, Thomas J. VA Goochland Lt.Arty.
Riddell, Wesley AL 16th Inf.
Riddell, William SC 1st Bn.S.S. Co.C
Riddell, William H. MS 4th Inf.
Riddell, William Pitt Gen. & Staff Surg.
Riddell, William R. VA Inf. 22nd Bn. Co.H
Riddell, W.L. MS 28th Cav. Co.B
Riddell, W.M. TN 48th (Nixon's) Inf. Co.K
Riddelle, John M. VA 2nd Arty. Co.H
Riddelle, W.B. VA 2nd Arty. Co.H
Riddells, Burnett TX Cav. Baird's Regt. Co.A
Riddels, James W. MO Cav. Fristoe's Regt.
  Co.K
Riddels, John H. MO Cav. Fristoe's Regt. Co.K
Ridder, Harry VA Cav. McNeill's Co.
Riddick, A.J. TN 9th Inf. Co.B
Riddick, Alexander NC 33rd Inf. Co.E
Riddick, Amos VA 9th Inf. Co.I
Riddick, Amos VA 59th Mil. Riddick's Co.
Riddick, Archibald VA 16th Inf. Co.B 1st Lt.
Riddick, Archibald VA 59th Mil. Riddick's Co.
Riddick, Archibald C. NC 17th Inf. (2nd Org.)
  Co.A
Riddick, Benjamin L. VA Inf. 5th Bn. Co.A
Riddick, C.E. SC 5th Inf. Co.B Sgt.
Riddick, Charles VA Cav. Mosby's Regt.
  (Part.Rangers) Co.G
Riddick, Charles E.C. NC 5th Inf. Co.B,F 1st
  Lt.

Riddick, Charles H. VA 5th Cav. (12 mo. '61-2) Co.G

Riddick, Charles H. VA 13th Cav. Co.C Capt.

Riddick, Columbus FL Cav. 3rd Bn. Co.D

Riddick, David NC 5th Inf. Co.H Comsy.Sgt.

Riddick, David E. NC 2nd Cav. (19th St.Troops) Co.C Sgt.

Riddick, David E. VA Inf. Cohoon's Bn. Co.D

Riddick, Elbert T. NC 27th Inf. Co.F 1st Lt.

Riddick, Elisha R. AL 53rd (Part.Rangers) Co.B Bvt.2nd Lt.

Riddick, F.M. TN 9th Inf. Co.B

Riddick, George W. VA 59th Mil. Riddick's Co. Cpl.

Riddick, G.W. TN 9th Inf. Co.B

Riddick, Isaac S. NC 5th Inf. Co.H

Riddick, Isaac S., Jr. NC 5th Inf. Co.H

Riddick, James NC 20th Inf. Co.C

Riddick, James VA 14th Inf. Co.A

Riddick, James VA 59th Mil. Arnold's Co.

Riddick, James (of J.) VA 59th Mil. Hunter's Co.

Riddick, James (of W.) VA 59th Mil. Arnold's Co.

Riddick, James A. VA Inf. 5th Bn. Co.A Sgt.

Riddick, James A. VA 53rd Inf. Co.H 2nd Lt.

Riddick, James E. VA 24th Cav. Co.I Cpl.

Riddick, James E. VA 1st Inf. Co.G 1st Lt.

Riddick, James E. VA 1st St.Res. Co.K Capt.

Riddick, James E., Jr. VA 1st St.Res. Co.K Drum.

Riddick, James E. VA 59th Mil. Riddick's Co. Capt.

Riddick, James E. 8th (Dearing's) Conf.Cav. Co.D

Riddick, James W. NC 34th Inf. Adj.

Riddick, James W. VA 9th Inf. Co.K

Riddick, James W. Gen. & Staff Capt.,AAG

Riddick, Jethro VA 13th Cav. Co.C

Riddick, Jethro VA 59th Mil. Riddick's Co.

Riddick, Jethro B. VA 41st Inf. Co.I Capt.

Riddick, J.H. TN Inf. 3rd Bn. Co.D

Riddick, J.K. GA 62nd Cav. Co.L

Riddick, J.L. NC 68th Inf.

Riddick, Job NC Lt.Arty. 3rd Bn. Co.B

Riddick, John NC 1st Inf. (6 mo. '61) Co.M

Riddick, John TN 15th (Stewart's) Cav. Co.E

Riddick, John E. TN 2nd Cav. Co.I

Riddick, John F. AL 53rd (Part.Rangers) Co.B 1st Lt.

Riddick, John G. NC 5th Inf. Co.B 1st Sgt.

Riddick, John R. VA 59th Mil. Riddick's Co.

Riddick, Jno. T. Gen. & Staff 2nd Lt.,Dr.M.

Riddick, Joseph VA Inf. Cohoon's Bn. Co.D

Riddick, Joseph H. NC 27th Inf. Co.F

Riddick, Julian F. VA 16th Inf. Co.A

Riddick, Julian F. Gen. & Staff,PACS Lt.

Riddick, M. Gen. & Staff,PACS Capt.,AAG

Riddick, Mills VA 9th Inf. Co.I

Riddick, Mills E. VA 5th Cav. (12 mo. '61-2) Co.G

Riddick, Reuben NC 5th Inf. Co.H

Riddick, R.H. MS 6th Cav. Co.K

Riddick, Richard B. MS 2nd Part.Rangers Co.I 1st Lt.

Riddick, Richard B. MS 1st Bn.S.S. Co.C Jr.2nd Lt.

Riddick, Richard E. VA 3rd Inf.Loc.Def. Co.A

Riddick, Richard H. NC 34th Inf. Col.

Riddick, Richard T. VA 5th Cav. (12 mo. '61-2) Co.G

Riddick, Richard T. Sig.Corps,CSA

Riddick, Robert MS 21st Inf. Co.F

Riddick, Robert VA Hvy.Arty. 18th Bn. Co.B

Riddick, Robert VA 41st Inf. 1st Co.E

Riddick, Robert E. VA 3rd Inf. Co.F

Riddick, Robert H. VA 5th Cav. (12 mo. '61-2) Co.G

Riddick, Robert H. VA 13th Cav. Co.K

Riddick, Roscoe T. NC 5th Inf. Co.B Capt.

Riddick, Rufus M. NC 5th Inf. Co.B,A Sgt.

Riddick, Rufus M. VA 16th Inf. Co.B

Riddick, Samuel A. VA 5th Cav. (12 mo. '61-2) Co.H

Riddick, Samuel A. VA 13th Cav. Co.A

Riddick, Simon NC 52nd Inf. Co.C

Riddick, Solomon VA Inf. Cohoon's Bn. Co.D

Riddick, Solon MS 29th Inf. Co.D

Riddick, Stephen D.C. AR 1st Inf. Co.F

Riddick, Thomas NC 27th Inf. Co.F

Riddick, Thomas VA 59th Mil. Arnold's Co.

Riddick, Thomas J. NC 52nd Inf. Co.C

Riddick, Thomas J. VA Inf. Cohoon's Bn. Co.D

Riddick, Thomas S. VA 1st Inf. Co.H Sgt.

Riddick, Thomas T. NC 27th Inf. Co.F Cpl.

Riddick, T.J. AL 4th (Russell's) Cav. Co.B

Riddick, V.L. AR 6th Inf. Co.K

Riddick, Washington L. VA 5th Cav. (12 mo. '61-2) Co.G 2nd Lt.

Riddick, Wash. L. Gen. & Staff, Adj.Gen.Dept. Capt.

Riddick, W.H. AR 6th Inf. Co.K

Riddick, William A. MS 8th Cav. Co.C

Riddick, William Archibald NC 5th Inf. Co.B,F 2nd Lt.

Riddick, William B. MS 2nd Part.Rangers Co.I

Riddick, William B. VA 2nd St.Res. Co.F

Riddick, William Bat. VA Inf. 25th Bn. Co.E

Riddick, William B.S. VA Inf. Cohoon's Bn. Co.D

Riddick, William H. VA Inf. Cohoon's Bn. Co.D 2nd Lt.

Riddick, William H.H. NC 33rd Inf. Co.E Cpl.

Riddick, William J. NC 20th Inf. Co.C

Riddick, William J. VA 3rd Inf.Loc.Def. Co.A

Riddick, William M. NC 5th Inf. Co.B

Riddick, Willie G. NC 3rd Cav. (41st St.Troops) Co.I 2nd Lt.

Riddick, Willis S. VA 59th Mil. Riddick's Co.

Riddick, W.J. VA 1st St.Res. Co.D

Riddick, W.S. TN 5th (McKenzie's) Cav. Co.D

Riddicks, John VA Loc.Def. Mallory's Co.

Riddill, William M. TN 54th Inf. Co.G

Ridding, F. FL Cav. 5th Bn. Cpl.

Ridding, Rufus M. NC 42nd Inf. Co.G

Riddish, John NC 47th Inf. Co.E

Riddle, ---, 1st TX Cav. McCord's Frontier Regt. Co.F

Riddle, ---, 2nd TX Cav. McCord's Frontier Regt. Co.F

Riddle, A. AR Lt.Arty. Zimmerman's Btty.

Riddle, A.B. AL 29th Inf. Co.A

Riddle, A.B. AL 31st Inf. Co.E

Riddle, Abel NC 46th Inf. Co.H

Riddle, A.G. VA 17th Cav. Co.F Lt.

Riddle, A.J. AL 50th Inf. Co.C

Riddle, A.J. MO St.Guard

Riddle, Albert M. LA Arty. Green's Co. (LA Guard Btty.) 2nd Lt.

Riddle, Alen MO Cav. Fristoe's Regt. Co.D

Riddle, Alex. AL Randolph Cty.Res. D.A. Self's Co.

Riddle, Alex NC Cumberland Cty.Bn.Detailed Men Co.A

Riddle, Alexander TN 37th Inf. Co.A

Riddle, Alexander TX 10th Inf. Co.C Cpl.

Riddle, Alfred VA 17th Cav. Co.G

Riddle, Allen VA 14th Cav. Crawford's Co. 2nd Lt.

Riddle, Alvis NC 5th Cav. (63rd St.Troops) Co.G

Riddle, A.M. GA 32nd Inf. Co.E Cpl.

Riddle, A.M.C. TN 19th Inf. Co.A

Riddle, And. B. VA Inf. 25th Bn Co.B

Riddle, Anderson MO 8th Inf. Co.G

Riddle, Anderson D. GA 45th Inf. Co.A 1st Lt.

Riddle, Anderson M. GA Cav. 7th Bn. (St.Guards) Co.B Sgt.

Riddle, Anderson M. GA 1st (Ramsey's) Inf. Co.E

Riddle, Andrew VA 5th Inf. Co.A

Riddle, Andrew A. TN 3rd (Lillard's) Mtd.Inf. Co.E

Riddle, Andrew J. MO Cav. Wood's Regt. Co.E

Riddle, Andrew J. MO Inf. 8th Bn. Co.B

Riddle, Andrew J. MO 9th Inf. Co.F

Riddle, Andrew J. NC 29th Inf. Co.B

Riddle, Archibald A. VA 10th Inf. Co.F

Riddle, Ariel MS 2nd Inf. Co.C

Riddle, A.T. AL Gid Nelson Lt.Arty. Sgt.

Riddle, Austin TN 2nd (Ashby's) Cav. Co.C

Riddle, Auston TN Cav. 5th Bn. (McClellan's) Co.D

Riddle, A.W. AL Talladega Cty.Res. J.T. Smith's Co.

Riddle, B. AL Talladega Cty.Res. J. Hurst's Co.

Riddle, B. AL Cp. of Instr. Talladega

Riddle, B. SC 5th Res. Co.D

Riddle, Bartis TN 40th Inf. Co.K

Riddle, Benjamin AL Cp. of Instr. Talladega

Riddle, Benjamin VA 38th Inf. Co.H

Riddle, Benjamin VA 53rd Inf. Co.I

Riddle, Benjamin 3rd Conf.Cav. Co.K

Riddle, Benjamin F. VA 57th Inf. Co.D

Riddle, Berry SC Inf. 3rd Bn. Co.E

Riddle, Berry SC 9th Res. Co.E Cpl.

Riddle, Berryman SC 22nd Inf. Co.B

Riddle, B.F. VA 94th Mil. Co.A

Riddle, B.L. MO 11th Inf. Co.D Sgt.

Riddle, B.M. 3rd Conf.Cav. Co.I

Riddle, Calvin MO 7th Cav. Co.B

Riddle, Calvil MO Cav. Coffee's Regt.

Riddle, Cato NC 46th Inf. Co.H

Riddle, C.C. TX 21st Inf. Co.C

Riddle, C.C. VA 7th Inf. Co.F

Riddle, Charles KY 2nd (Duke's) Cav. Co.A

Riddle, Charles MD Arty. 1st Btty.

Riddle, Charles C. MD Cav. 2nd Bn. Co.C

Riddle, Charles M. MS 26th Inf. Co.H

Riddle, Columbus AL 45th Inf. Co.F

Riddle, C.V. AL Inf. 2nd Regt. Co.D

Riddle, C.V. AL 31st Inf. Co.E Sgt.

Riddle, C.V. AL 38th Inf. Co.I
Riddle, Cyrus C. TX Inf. Griffin's Bn. Co.C
Riddle, D. AR 38th Inf. Co.K
Riddle, Daniel L. NC 46th Inf. Co.H Cpl.
Riddle, David AL 5th Inf. New Co.B
Riddle, David GA Inf. 11th Bn. (St.Guards)
    Co.C
Riddle, David C. NC 53rd Inf. Co.E
Riddle, D.B. SC Inf. 3rd Bn. Co.E
Riddle, D.E. TX Cav. Sutton's Co.
Riddle, D.E. TX 22nd Inf. Co.A
Riddle, D.G. AL 8th Inf. Co.B
Riddle, D.L. SC Inf. 3rd Bn. Co.E
Riddle, D.W. NC 61st Inf. Co.D Cpl.
Riddle, E. TX 22nd Inf. Co.A
Riddle, Edmond R. AL Cav. Bowie's Co.
Riddle, Edmond R. 8th (Wade's) Conf.Cav. Co.A
Riddle, Edmund 1st Choctaw & Chickasaw
    Mtd.Rifles 2nd Co.H
Riddle, Elias TN 8th Inf. Co.H
Riddle, Elija AR 1st (Crawford's) Cav. Co.B
Riddle, Elijah TN 4th (Murray's) Cav. Co.F
Riddle, E.M. TX Waul's Legion Co.B
Riddle, Ephraim T. GA 65th Inf. Co.A
Riddle, Eugene M. TX 1st (McCulloch's) Cav.
    Co.I
Riddle, F.B. NC Inf. Thomas Legion Co.C
Riddle, F.G. TX Inf. Chambers' Bn.Res.Corps
    Co.D
Riddle, Fielden SC Inf. 3rd Bn. Co.E
Riddle, F.M. 1st Conf.Inf. 2nd Co.E
Riddle, Francis MS 20th Inf. Co.H
Riddle, Franklin VA Cav. 36th Bn. Co.C
Riddle, Franklin T. VA 64th Mtd.Inf. Co.I
Riddle, Fred C. KY 1st Bn.Mtd.Rifles Co.C
Riddle, Frederick F. VA 64th Mtd.Inf. Co.H
Riddle, F.S. VA 64th Mtd.Inf. Co.G
Riddle, Garland TN 61st Mtd.Inf. Co.H
Riddle, Garrett NC 58th Inf. Co.C
Riddle, George AL 37th Inf. Co.I
Riddle, George AR Cav. Wright's Regt. Co.F
Riddle, George GA 28th Inf. Co.E
Riddle, George NC 53rd Inf. Co.E
Riddle, George W. NC 30th Inf. Co.H
Riddle, George W. NC 46th Inf. Co.H Music.
Riddle, George W TN 1st (Turney's) Inf. Co.H,F
Riddle, George W. VA 53rd Inf. Co.I
Riddle, George W. 1st Choctaw & Chickasaw
    Mtd.Rifles Co.A Sgt.
Riddle, G.M.A.C. SC 18th Inf. Co.H 2nd Lt.
Riddle, G.R. AR Lt.Arty. Zimmerman's Btty.
Riddle, Graydon SC 9th Res. Co.E
Riddle, G.W. TX 21st Inf. Co.C
Riddle, G.W. VA Inf. Montague's Bn. Co.B
Riddle, Hamilton H. NC 46th Inf. Co.H
Riddle, Harmon W. TX 17th Cav. Co.A
Riddle, Harmon W. TX Inf.Riflemen Arnold's
    Co.
Riddle, Harrison VA 33rd Inf. Co.I
Riddle, Haywood Y. TN 55th (McKoin's) Inf.
    Dillehay's Co. 1st Lt.
Riddle, Henry MO 11th Inf. Co.C
Riddle, Henry TX Cav. 1st Bn.St.Troops Co.C
Riddle, Henry A. TX 15th Cav. Co.H
Riddle, Henry F. TX 11th Inf. Co.I
Riddle, Henry O. AL 35th Inf. Co.C
Riddle, Henry R. AL 4th Inf. Co.H

Riddle, H.G. Maple's Staff 1st Lt.,AAAG
Riddle, Hiram AL 45th Inf. Co.B
Riddle, H.O. MS 35th Inf. Co.C
Riddle, Horace J. MS 1st Lt.Arty. Co.E
Riddle, H.W. TX Inf. 2nd St.Troops Co.C 1st
    Lt.
Riddle, H.Y. TN 44th (Cons.) Inf. Co.C 1st Lt.
Riddle, Isaac M. NC Walker's Bn. Thomas'
    Legion Co.C
Riddle, Isaac R. TX 11th Inf. Co.D 1st Sgt.
Riddle, Isearrel 1st Choctaw & Chickasaw
    Mtd.Rifles 3rd Co.D
Riddle, J. KY 6th Cav. Co.K
Riddle, J. LA Mil. 3rd Regt. 1st Brig. 1st Div.
    Co.G
Riddle, J. LA Mil.Crescent Cadets
Riddle, J. TX Inf. 1st St.Troops Whitehead's Co.
Riddle, J. TX 21st Inf. Co.C
Riddle, J. VA Lt.Arty. 12th Bn. Co.B
Riddle, J.A. NC 61st Inf. Co.D
Riddle, J.A. SC Inf. 3rd Bn. Co.E 1st Lt.
Riddle, James AR 4th Inf. Co.H
Riddle, James AR 8th Inf. New Co.C Cpl.
Riddle, James KY 5th Cav. Co.I
Riddle, James KY 10th (Johnson's) Cav. New
    Co.F
Riddle, James NC 48th Inf. Co.D Cpl.
Riddle, James TX 33rd Cav. Co.B Cpl.
Riddle, James TX 1st Hvy.Arty. Co.K
Riddle, James VA 18th Cav. Co.C
Riddle, James VA 33rd Inf. Co.I
Riddle, James VA 34th Inf. Co.D
Riddle, James C. VA 12th Inf. Co.E
Riddle, James E. NC 64th Inf. Co.D
Riddle, James H. NC 29th Inf. Co.B Music.
Riddle, James H. VA Cav. Thurmond's Co.
Riddle, James L. MS 26th Inf. Co.F
Riddle, James M. GA 14th Inf. Co.A
Riddle, James M. KY 4th Mtd.Inf. Co.C
Riddle, James M. NC 58th Inf. Co.A
    Hosp.Stew.
Riddle, James M. SC 2nd Inf. Co.E 2nd Lt.
Riddle, James M. SC 3rd Inf. Co.K,D
Riddle, James M. TN 2nd Inf.
Riddle, James R. VA 13th Cav. Co.G
Riddle, James R. VA 28th Inf. Co.D
Riddle, James R. VA 31st Inf. Co.D Cpl.
Riddle, James S. VA 1st Cav. 2nd Co.D
Riddle, James T. AL 29th Inf. Co.A
Riddle, James T. MS 26th Inf. Co.I
Riddle, James W. GA 1st Cav.
Riddle, Jasper M. TX 7th Inf. Co.I
Riddle, J.B. TX Cav. McCord's Frontier Regt.
    Co.C
Riddle, J. Craig VA 13th Cav. Co.B Capt.
Riddle, J.E. AL 31st Inf. Co.G
Riddle, J.E. AL Cp. of Instr. Talladega
Riddle, Jefferson AR 34th Inf. Co.E
Riddle, Jerre Mead's Conf.Cav. Co.D
Riddle, Jerry 1st Choctaw Mtd.Rifles Co.H 2nd
    Lt.
Riddle, Jerry 1st Choctaw & Chickasaw
    Mtd.Rifles 3rd Co.F 2nd Lt.
Riddle, Jesse AL 45th Inf. Co.F
Riddle, Jesse MS 4th Inf. Co.H
Riddle, Jesse NC 55th Inf. Co.B
Riddle, Jesse SC 2nd Arty. Co.B,K

Riddle, J.G. AR Inf. Cocke's Regt. Co.G Sgt.
Riddle, J.G. MS 14th Inf. Co.C
Riddle, J.G. TX 22nd Inf. Co.A
Riddle, J.H. AR 8th Inf. New Co.C
Riddle, J.H. MS 33rd Inf. Co.F
Riddle, J.H. VA 5th Cav.Arty. & Inf.St.Line
    Co.I
Riddle, J.J. TX 30th Cav. Chap.
Riddle, J.J. TX Cav. McCord's Frontier Regt.
    Co.E
Riddle, J.J. TX 7th Inf. Co.A
Riddle, J.J. Gen. & Staff Chap.
Riddle, J.L. MS 32nd Inf. Co.G
Riddle, J.L. NC 49th Inf. Co.G
Riddle, J.M. AL 10th Cav. Sgt.
Riddle, J.M. KY 7th Cav. Co.D 2nd Lt.
Riddle, J.M. KY 11th Cav. Co.D 2nd Lt.
Riddle, J.M. MS 10th Cav. Co.B Sgt.
Riddle, J.M. SC Inf. 3rd Bn. Co.E
Riddle, J.M. SC 6th Inf. 2nd Co.D
Riddle, John AL 49th Inf. Co.C Cpl.
Riddle, John LA Arty. Castellanos' Btty.
Riddle, John MO Lt.Arty. 13th Bn.
Riddle, John NC 6th Sr.Res. Co.H
Riddle, John NC 58th Inf. Co.B
Riddle, John NC 58th Inf. Co.G
Riddle, John TN 37th Inf. Co.I
Riddle, John VA 21st Inf. Co.I
Riddle, John VA 42nd Inf. Co.F
Riddle, John VA 47th Inf. Co.E
Riddle, John Gen. & Staff Asst.Comsy.
Riddle, John A. AL 29th Inf. Co.A
Riddle, John A. VA 38th Inf. Co.B Sgt.
Riddle, John B. MO 4th Cav. Co.A
Riddle, John B. MO Cav. Preston's Bn. Co.A
Riddle, John E. AL 36th Inf. Co.I
Riddle, John H. VA 2nd Arty. Co.K
Riddle, John H. VA 21st Inf. Co.I
Riddle, John H. VA Inf. 22nd Bn. Co.A
Riddle, John H. VA 36th Inf. 2nd Co.E
Riddle, John J. NC 48th Inf. Co.G
Riddle, John K. AR 1st (Dobbin's) Cav. Wilson's
    Co.
Riddle, John L. TX Cav. Sutton's Co. 2nd Lt.
Riddle, John M. TX Cav. Morgan's Regt. Co.E
    2nd Lt.
Riddle, John M. VA 13th Inf. Co.K
Riddle, John N. VA 2nd Inf. Co.E
Riddle, John R. MO Lt.Arty. McDonald's Co.
Riddle, John R. MO 6th Inf. Co.D
Riddle, John T. AL 45th Inf. Co.F
Riddle, John T. AL 50th Inf. Co.E
Riddle, John T. MS 20th Inf. Co.K
Riddle, John T. MO Cav. Freeman's Regt. Co.F
Riddle, John W. GA 14th Inf. Co.A
Riddle, John W. VA Lt.Arty. Carpenter's Co.
Riddle, Jones AR 34th Inf. Co.E
Riddle, Joseph TN 4th (Murray's) Cav. Co.F 1st
    Lt.
Riddle, Joseph TX Inf. Griffin's Bn. Co.C
Riddle, Joseph 1st Choctaw & Chickasaw
    Mtd.Rifles 3rd Co.F Sgt.
Riddle, Joseph B. AR 23rd Inf. Co.G
Riddle, Joseph B.F. NC 23rd Inf. Co.H 1st Lt.
Riddle, Joseph N. VA 7th Cav. Co.B Sgt.
Riddle, Joshua A. NC 6th Sr.Res. Co.E
Riddle, J.R. Jackson's Co,CSA

Riddle, J.S. SC 3rd Inf. Co.F,C
Riddle, J.T. MS Inf. 2nd St.Troops Co.G
Riddle, J.T. MS Inf. 2nd Bn. Co.L
Riddle, J.T. MS 30th Inf. Co.D
Riddle, J.T. MS 48th Inf. Co.L
Riddle, J.W. MS 4th Inf. Co.H
Riddle, J.W. TN Inf. 23rd Bn. Co.D
Riddle, L. SC Inf. 3rd Bn. Co.E
Riddle, L.D. VA 60th Inf. Co.G Cpl.
Riddle, Leonidas A. VA 31st Inf. Co.D
Riddle, Lewis NC 16th Inf. Co.C
Riddle, Lewis SC 2nd St.Troops Co.F
Riddle, Lewis TX Cav. Morgan's Regt. Co.A
Riddle, Lewis TX 16th Inf. Co.D Ens.
Riddle, Lewis A. VA 53rd Inf. Co.I
Riddle, L.F. AR 34th Inf. Co.E
Riddle, Madison Green MO Inf. 1st Bn. Co.A
Riddle, Marion SC Inf. 3rd Bn. Co.E Cpl.
Riddle, Marvil M. NC 25th Inf. Co.K
Riddle, Melmoth SC Inf. 3rd Bn. Co.E
Riddle, Mortimer LA Arty. Green's Co. (LA
    Guard Btty.)
Riddle, Mortimer LA 1st (Nelligan's) Inf. 1st
    Co.B
Riddle, Mortimer A. LA 1st (Nelligan's) Inf. 1st
    Co.B Ens.
Riddle, Moses 1st Choctaw Mtd.Rifles Co.H
Riddle, M.R. TX Cav. Crump's Regt. Co.C
Riddle, M.S. GA Inf. Bard's Co. 1st Sgt.
Riddle, N. VA Conscr. Cp.Lee Co.B
Riddle, Nathan NC 58th Inf. Co.A
Riddle, Nathaniel NC 6th Sr.Res. Co.E
Riddle, Nathaniel VA 53rd Inf. Co.I
Riddle, Nathaniel W. AL 43rd Inf. Co.E 2nd Lt.
Riddle, N.B. AR Inf. Cocke's Regt. Co.G
Riddle, N.B. LA 5th Cav. Co.H
Riddle, Nelson LA Mil. Chalmette Regt. Co.F
Riddle, Newton SC 9th Res. Co.C
Riddle, O.R. TX 9th (Young's) Inf. Co.C
Riddle, O.S. MO 10th Cav. Co.I
Riddle, O.S. MO 1st & 4th Cons.Inf. Co.E
Riddle, O.S. MO 4th Inf. Co.E
Riddle, Oscar MO Lt.Arty. Farris' Btty. (Clark
    Arty.)
Riddle, Patrick P. AL 10th Inf. Co.H 1st Lt.
Riddle, Patrick P. AL 44th Inf. Co.K Capt.
Riddle, Philip AR 1st (Monroe's) Cav. Co.A
Riddle, Philip AR 50th Mil. Co.G
Riddle, Pinkney TN 2nd (Ashby's) Cav. Co.C
Riddle, Pinkney TN Cav. 5th Bn. (McClellan's)
    Co.D
Riddle, Pleasant F. TN 5th (McKenzie's) Cav.
    Co.B
Riddle, Randolph TN 34th Inf. 2nd Co.C
Riddle, R.F. TN 34th Inf. Co.K
Riddle, R.H. AR 38th Inf. Co.K
Riddle, Richard NC 5th Cav. (63rd St.Troops)
    Co.G
Riddle, Richard NC 8th Sr.Res. McLean's Co.
Riddle, Richard VA 47th Inf. Co.E
Riddle, Ritchard MO 3rd Cav. Co.H
Riddle, R.L. TN Lt.Arty. Winston's Co.
Riddle, R.M. TX Cav. Morgan's Regt. Co.E
Riddle, R.N. AR 11th Inf. Co.C Cpl.
Riddle, Robert MO Todd's Co.
Riddle, Robert NC 58th Inf. Co.G 1st Sgt.
Riddle, Robert VA 1st St.Res. Co.D

Riddle, Robert L. TN 35th Inf. 3rd Co.F Cpl.
Riddle, Robert R. KY Cav. Chenoweth's Regt.
    Co.A
Riddle, Robert S. AL 9th Inf. Co.F
Riddle, Robert T. AL 50th Inf.
Riddle, Rowland MS 32nd Inf. Co.A
Riddle, Samuel AL 32nd Inf. Co.C Cpl.
Riddle, Samuel NC 5th Sr.Res. Co.A
Riddle, Samuel NC 29th Inf. Co.B
Riddle, Samuel NC 58th Inf. Co.C
Riddle, Samuel TN 9th (Ward's) Cav. Co.E
Riddle, Samuel TN 17th Inf.
Riddle, Samuel TN 20th Inf. Co.F
Riddle, Samuel TN 33rd Inf. Co.G Cpl.
Riddle, Simeon AL 41st Inf. Co.B
Riddle, Simeon SC 5th Res. Co.K
Riddle, Simpkins SC 7th Inf. 1st Co.H
Riddle, Spencer VA Hvy.Arty. 10th Bn. Co.E
Riddle, S.T. SC 27th Inf. Co.G
Riddle, S.W. Inf. Bailey's Cons.Regt. Co.A 1st
    Sgt.
Riddle, S.W. TX 7th Inf. Co.I 1st Sgt.
Riddle, S.W.H. TN 9th (Ward's) Cav. Kirkpat-
    rick's Co.
Riddle, T. KY 10th (Johnson's) Cav. Co.E
Riddle, T.B. AL Lt.Arty. 20th Bn. Co.A
Riddle, T.B. MO 11th Inf. Co.D Cpl.
Riddle, T.B. TX 21st Inf. Co.C
Riddle, T.C. NC 42nd Inf. Co.D
Riddle, T.E. MS 26th Inf. Co.H
Riddle, T.G. AL 34th Inf. Co.B
Riddle, T.G. SC Inf. 3rd Bn. Co.E
Riddle, T.G. SC Inf. Holcombe Legion Co.E
Riddle, T.G. TN 20th (Russell's) Cav. Co.K
Riddle, T.H. KY 6th Cav. Co.K
Riddle, Thomas AL 9th (Malone's) Cav. Co.L,D
Riddle, Thos. AL 55th Vol. Co.F
Riddle, Thomas AR 5th Inf. Co.H
Riddle, Thomas AR 34th Inf. Co.I
Riddle, Thomas MS Inf. 8th Bn. Co.D
Riddle, Thomas MS 13th Inf. Co.A
Riddle, Thomas MS 25th Inf. Co.B
Riddle, Thomas NC 46th Inf. Co.H
Riddle, Thomas TX 10th Cav. Co.E
Riddle, Thomas TX 1st Hvy.Arty. Co.K
Riddle, Thomas TX 18th Inf. Co.I
Riddle, Thomas VA 33rd Inf. Co.I
Riddle, Thomas 2nd Conf.Inf. Co.B
Riddle, Thomas B. TX Inf. Griffin's Bn. Co.C
Riddle, Thomas C. VA 53rd Inf. Co.I
Riddle, Thomas E. AR 7th Mil. Co.A
Riddle, Thomas F. MO 2nd Inf. Co.C
Riddle, Thomas H. NC 16th Inf. Co.I
Riddle, Thomas H. NC 60th Inf. Co.C 2nd Lt.
Riddle, Thomas J. MS 20th Inf. Co.K
Riddle, Thomas J. TN 59th Mtd.Inf. Co.D Cpl.
Riddle, Thomas M.S. MS 5th Inf. Co.F
Riddle, Thomas R. SC 1st (McCreary's) Inf.
    Co.K
Riddle, Thomas R. SC 9th Inf. Co.A
Riddle, Thomas W. TX 37th Cav. Co.H
Riddle, T.J. AL 9th Inf. Co.C Music.
Riddle, T.J. AL 30th Inf. Co.D
Riddle, T.J. AL 31st Inf. Co.D
Riddle, T.L. SC 2nd Arty. Co.K
Riddle, T.R. SC 3rd Inf. Co.F
Riddle, Tyre TN Inf. 23rd Bn. Co.C Cpl.

Riddle, Tyree A. MS 7th Cav. Co.E
Riddle, Ulysses TN 48th (Voorhies') Inf.
Riddle, Vaden GA 1st Cav. Co.F 1st Sgt.
Riddle, W. SC 1st (Hagood's) Inf. 2nd Co.H
Riddle, W.A. AL 22nd Inf. Co.F
Riddle, W.A. TN 6th (Wheeler's) Cav. Co.K
Riddle, Walter H. VA 64th Mtd.Inf. Co.H
Riddle, Warler R. VA 94th Mil. Co.A
Riddle, Watkins P. VA 44th Inf. Co.C,I
Riddle, W.B. VA Inf. Montague's Bn. Co.B
Riddle, W.D. AL Cav. Barbiere's Bn. Co.G
Riddle, W.D. SC Inf. 3rd Bn. Co.E
Riddle, Wesley TN 35th Inf. 3rd Co.F
Riddle, W.F. MS 12th Cav. Co.B
Riddle, W.F. MS 35th Inf. Co.C
Riddle, W.F. TX 21st Inf. Co.C
Riddle, W.H. MS 20th Inf. Co.K
Riddle, W.H. MS 33rd Inf. Co.F
Riddle, W.H. TX Cav. Border's Regt. Co.B
Riddle, W.H.H. AL 51st (Part.Rangers) Co.D
Riddle, W.H.H. AL 31st Inf. Co.B
Riddle, W.H.H. MO Cav. Schnabel's Bn.
Riddle, Wiley NC Cumberland Cty.Bn.Detailed
    Men Co.A
Riddle, William KY 4th Cav. Co.H
Riddle, William NC 5th Cav. (63rd St.Troops)
    Co.G
Riddle, William NC 1st Jr.Res Co.E
Riddle, William NC 18th Inf. Co.G
Riddle, William SC 5th Res. Co.K
Riddle, William SC 27th Inf. Co.G
Riddle, William TN 6th (Wheeler's) Cav. Co.H
Riddle, William TN 48th (Voorhies') Inf. Co.D
Riddle, William TX 2nd Inf. Co.I
Riddle, William A. TN 32nd Inf. Co.E
Riddle, William B. VA 53rd Inf. Co.I
Riddle, William C. MO Cav. Fristoe's Regt.
    Co.D Sgt.
Riddle, William F. TX Inf. Griffin's Bn. Co.C
Riddle, William G. TN 2nd Cav. Co.C
Riddle, William H. GA 31st Inf. Co.B
Riddle, William H. TN Cav. 11th Bn. (Gordon's)
    Co.B
Riddle, William H. VA 64th Mtd.Inf. Co.H
Riddle, William H.H. AR 14th (Powers') Inf.
    Co.C
Riddle, William J. MS 13th Inf. Co.A
Riddle, William J. MS 14th Inf. Co.G
Riddle, William J. VA 17th Cav. Co.K,C
Riddle, William J. VA 36th Inf. 2nd Co.E
Riddle, William L. MS 11th Inf. Co.K
Riddle, William M. AL 6th Inf. Co.F
Riddle, William M. KY 11th Cav. Chap.
Riddle, William P. LA 1st Cav. Co.C
Riddle, William P. NC Cav. 14th Bn. Co.K
Riddle, William P. NC 58th Inf. Co.G
Riddle, William S. MS 10th Cav. Co.A,D
Riddle, William S. VA 108th Mil. Co.B Capt.
Riddle, W.J. 1st Choctaw & Chickasaw
    Mtd.Rifles Co.A
Riddle, W.M. 20th Conf.Cav. Co.C
Riddle, W.N. TX Cav. McCord's Frontier Regt.
    Co.F
Riddle, Woodard NC 35th Inf. Co.D
Riddle, W.P. AL 2nd Cav. Co.C
Riddle, W. Pope Gen. & Staff Surg.
Riddle, W.R. TN 40th Inf. Co.B

163

Rider, Henry LA 1st Hvy.Arty. (Reg.) Co.B

Riddle, W.S. MS Inf. 3rd Bn. (St.Troops) Co.A

Riddle, W.S. TN Cav. 17th Bn. (Sanders') Co.C

Riddle, W.S. TN 1st Hvy.Arty. 3rd Co.B

Riddle, W.S. TX 11th Cav. Co.I

Riddle, W.W. TN Lt.Arty. Winston's Co.

Riddle, Zebidee VA 52nd Inf. Co.C

Riddleback, August VA Inf. 1st Bn. Co.B

Riddlebarger, Charlston VA 57th Inf. Co.K

Riddlebarger, E. VA 5th Inf. Co.M

Riddlebarger, H.H. VA 10th Inf. 2nd Co.C Lt.

Riddlebarger, Joseph VA Cav. McNeill's Co.

Riddlebarger, Joseph W. VA 5th Inf. Co.C

Riddleberger, H.H. VA 23rd Cav. Co.G Capt.

Riddleberger, H.H. VA Cav. O'Ferrall's Bn. Co.B Capt.

Riddleberger, M.V. VA Hvy.Arty. 20th Bn. Co.C

Riddlehoover, William SC 7th Inf. 1st Co.E, 2nd Co.E

Riddlemoser, Alfred MD Inf. 2nd Bn. Co.D Cpl.

Riddlemoser, David MD Inf. 2nd Bn. Co.D

Riddlemoser, Joseph MD Inf. 2nd Bn. Co.D

Riddlemoser, Joseph A. VA 5th Inf. Co.L

Riddler, Clement LA Mil. 4th Regt. 1st Brig. 1st Div. Co.K

Riddles, E.A. AR Inf. Cocke's Regt. Co.I

Riddles, G.T. AR 7th Mil. Co.C

Riddles, Isham G. AL 4th (Russell's) Cav. Co.I

Riddles, James AL 49th Inf. Co.D

Riddles, R.N. AR 11th & 17th (Cons.) Inf. Co.C 3rd Lt.

Riddles, R.W. AR Inf. Cocke's Regt. Co.I

Riddles, S.H. AR Inf. Cocke's Regt. Co.H

Riddlesbarger, Dinquid VA 60th Inf. Co.K

Riddlesbarger, Frederick VA 59th Inf. 1st Co.G

Riddlesbarger, M. VA Inf. 26th Bn. Co.D

Riddlesbarger, Samuel VA 59th Inf. 1st Co.G

Riddlesberger, Frederick VA 60th Inf. Co.D

Riddlesberger, Samuel VA 60th Inf. Co.D

Riddlesima, Adolphus GA 36th (Villepigue's) Inf. Co.C

Riddlesperger, John H. MS 23rd Inf. Co.G Capt.

Riddlesperger, Samuel V. MS 23rd Inf. Co.G,L 2nd Lt.

Riddlesperger, S.V. MS 10th Inf. New Co.K

Riddlesperger, W.H. GA Phillips' Legion Co.D

Riddlespurger, W.H. TX 3rd Cav. Co.D

Riddlespurger, William AL 9th (Malone's) Cav. Co.L

Riddley, George MS St.Cav. 2nd Bn. (Harris') Co.C

Riddley, Moses H. GA 23rd Inf. Co.B

Riddley, P. TN 61st Mtd.Inf. Co.H

Riddley, S. TX 1st Hvy.Arty. Co.K

Riddling, A.B. AR 6th Inf. New Co.F

Riddling, G.Y. 20th Conf.Cav. Co.M

Riddling, W.A. NC 30th Inf. Co.C

Riddly, S. AL 12th Inf. Co.H

Riddock, James D. AL 37th Inf. Co.K 2nd Lt.

Riddock, Joseph SC 1st (McCreary's) Inf. Co.I Sgt.

Riddock, Joseph SC 1st Inf. Co.M Cpl.

Rideau, L. LA 30th Inf. Co.F

Rideau, P. LA Mil. 3rd Regt.Eur.Brig. (Garde Francaise) Co.7 Sgt.

Rideau, P. LA Mil. Orleans Guards Regt. Co.C

Rideau, Rene LA 13th Inf. Co.D

Ridel, Elijah TN 8th (Smith's) Cav. Co.I

Rideley, James MS St.Cav. 2nd Bn. (Harris') Co.C

Ridell, Frederick C. KY 10th Cav. Co.E Capt.

Ridely, Thomas G. Gen. & Staff A.2nd Lt., Vol.ADC

Riden, B.F. TN 38th Inf. Co.F

Riden, H.P. TN 38th Inf. Co.F

Riden, Josephus GA 34th Inf. Co.E

Riden, J.T. GA Cav. Gartrell's Co.

Riden, J.T.M. GA 8th Inf. (St.Guards) Co.E

Riden, Mastin W. GA Cobb's Legion Co.C

Ridenbury, Daniel TN 55th (McKoin's) Inf. James' Co.

Ridener, John TN 19th Inf. Co.D

Ridener, John P. AL 5th Bn.Vol. Co.B

Ridener, William M. TN 19th Inf. Co.D

Ridenhour, Aaron W. NC 8th Inf. Co.H

Ridenhour, Anderson J. NC 13th Inf. Co.F

Ridenhour, Augustus B. GA 1st (Ramsey's) Inf. Co.B

Ridenhour, Daniel H. NC 8th Inf. Co.H Music.

Ridenhour, D.D. GA 5th Inf. (St.Guards) Brooks' Co.

Ridenhour, D.E. NC 5th Inf. Co.F

Ridenhour, D.H. NC 1st Jr.Res. Co.G

Ridenhour, Edward NC 7th Inf. Co.F

Ridenhour, E.N. NC 4th Sr.Res. Co.F

Ridenhour, F.F. GA 5th Inf. (St.Guards) Everitt's Co. Cpl.

Ridenhour, Franklin A. NC 28th Inf. Co.D

Ridenhour, George VA 67th Mil. Co.C

Ridenhour, J. GA Inf. (NonConscr.) Howard's Co.

Ridenhour, J.D. GA 3rd Cav. Co.D

Ridenhour, John GA Inf. 27th Bn. (NonConscr.) Co.C 1st Sgt.

Ridenhour, John M. NC 42nd Inf. Co.E

Ridenhour, Jonas E. NC 8th Inf. Co.H

Ridenhour, Joseph NC 54th Inf. Co.H

Ridenhour, J.W. NC 1st Jr.Res. Co.G

Ridenhour, J.W. NC 57th Inf. Co.F

Ridenhour, L.A.S. NC 8th Inf. Co.H

Ridenhour, Losson NC 13th Inf. Co.F

Ridenhour, Rufus C. NC 8th Inf. Co.H

Ridenhour, T.F. GA 2nd Inf. Co.G

Ridenhour, William NC 28th Inf. Co.D

Ridenhour, William W. GA Arty. 9th Bn. Co.C Sr.2nd Lt.

Ridenor, Alfred VA Cav. 41st Bn. Co.A

Ridenor, Branson VA 18th Cav. Co.D

Ridenor, David VA 18th Cav. Co.D

Ridenor, George VA 18th Cav. Co.D

Ridenor, Lafayette VA 18th Cav. Co.D

Ridenor, Levi VA 18th Cav. Co.D

Ridenor, Philip VA Cav. 41st Bn. Co.A

Ridenour, Adam VA 136th Mil. Co.C

Ridenour, Addison VA 16th Cav. Co.D

Ridenour, Addison VA 49th Inf. Co.D

Ridenour, Alfred VA 18th Cav. 1st Co.G

Ridenour, Amos VA Lt.Arty. Carpenter's Co.

Ridenour, Amos VA Lt.Arty. Cutshaw's Co.

Ridenour, Amos VA 51st Mil. Co.A

Ridenour, Daniel VA 51st Mil. Co.A

Ridenour, David VA 136th Mil. Co.C

Ridenour, Elias G. VA 146th Mil.

Ridenour, George VA 136th Mil. Co.E

Ridenour, George A. VA 136th Mil. Co.C Cpl.

Ridenour, Hampson VA Lt.Arty. Cutshaw's Co.

Ridenour, Hampton VA Lt.Arty. Carpenter's Co.

Ridenour, Isaac VA 136th Mil. Co.E

Ridenour, Jacob VA 146th Mil.

Ridenour, John W. VA 49th Inf. Co.D

Ridenour, Lafayette VA 136th Mil. Co.H

Ridenour, Milton VA 146th Mil.

Ridenour, Philip W. VA 23rd Cav. Co.A

Ridenour, Robert LA 2nd Inf. Co.B

Ridens, James NC 60th Inf. Co.B

Ridens, James C. MO 3rd Cav. Co.D Cpl.

Ridens, J.M. TN 4th Inf. Co.K

Ridens, John H. TX 10th Inf. Co.F

Ridens, Kinson GA Cav. Roswell Bn. Co.C

Ridens, W.H. MO Cav. Freeman's Regt. Co.G

Ridens, W.J. TN 10th (DeMoss') Cav. Co.A

Rideout, Benjamin J. VA 3rd Inf. Co.D

Rideout, Giles VA 12th Inf. 2nd Co.I

Rideout, Robert A. VA 12th Inf. Co.F

Rideout, Thomas H. TX 1st (McCulloch's) Cav. Co.B

Rideout, W.T. AL 26th (O'Neal's) Inf. Co.B Cpl.

Rider, A. 1st Cherokee Mtd.Vol. 1st Co.B 1st Sgt.

Rider, A.C. AL 27th Inf. Co.K

Rider, A.H. GA Inf. 8th Bn. Co.C

Rider, A.J. GA 11th Cav. Co.E

Rider, Albert G. VA 4th Inf. Co.A

Rider, Alexander NC Walker's Bn. Thomas' Legion Co.E

Rider, Alexander TN 62nd Mtd.Inf. Co.K

Rider, Alexandria VA 19th Cav. Co.I

Rider, Amos H. GA 40th Inf. Co.D

Rider, A.T. VA 10th Inf. Co.L

Rider, C.J. GA 11th Cav. Co.E

Rider, C.L. Conf.Inf. Tucker's Regt. Co.E Sgt.

Rider, C.P. Wilson VA Cav. 46th Bn. Co.C

Rider, David GA 43rd Inf. Co.I

Rider, Douglass VA 24th Cav. Co.C

Rider, Douglass VA Lt.Arty. W.P. Carter's Co.

Rider, D.W. TN 2nd (Ashby's) Cav. Co.K

Rider, D.W. TN Cav. 5th Bn. (McClellan's) Co.E

Rider, E.C. VA 89th Mil. Maj.

Rider, Edward TN 34th Inf. Co.H

Rider, Emile LA 3rd Inf. Co.D

Rider, F.M. TX 5th Cav. Co.D

Rider, F.M. TX 8th Inf. Co.F Cpl.

Rider, Fountain W. VA 4th Inf. Co.D Sgt.

Rider, Francis M. GA 52nd Inf. Co.D,A

Rider, F.W. VA 8th Cav. Co.A

Rider, George MD Cav. 2nd Bn. Co.C

Rider, George MO Inf. 8th Bn. Co.D

Rider, George MO Quantrill's Co.

Rider, George SC 1st Arty. Co.G

Rider, George H. VA 51st Inf. Co.C

Rider, George W. MD Inf. 2nd Bn. Co.G

Rider, George W. VA 60th Inf. Co.A Sgt.

Rider, G.M. MO 12th Cav. Co.K

Rider, Harvy V. TN 61st Mtd.Inf. Co.B

Rider, Henry GA 11th Cav. Co.E

Rider, Henry LA 1st Hvy.Arty. (Reg.) Co.B

Rider, Henry P. MO Cav. Wood's Regt.
Asst.Surg.
Rider, Henry W. TX 17th Cav. Co.H
Rider, Hesekiah VA 2nd Cav.St.Line McNeel's
Co.
Rider, Hezekiah H. VA 19th Cav. Co.F
Rider, H.P. MS 40th Inf. Asst.Surg.
Rider, H.P. Gen. & Staff Asst.Surg.
Rider, I.P. MO 8th Cav. Co.G Sgt.
Rider, Isaiah VA Lt.Arty. Hardwicke's Co.
Rider, Jacob M. VA 52nd Inf. Co.K
Rider, James GA 11th Cav. Co.E
Rider, James GA Inf. 11th Bn. (St.Guards) Co.B
Rider, James A. VA 4th Inf. Co.A
Rider, James F. VA 4th Inf. Co.A
Rider, James G. VA Hvy.Arty. 20th Bn. Co.C
Rider, James H. VA 4th Inf. Co.A
Rider, James Henry MO 5th Inf. Co.I
Rider, James L. GA 1st (Ramsey's) Inf. Co.H
Rider, James M. AR 4th Inf. Co.I Sgt.
Rider, James R.T. VA 19th Cav. Co.F
Rider, James W. VA 1st Cav. 2nd Co.K
Rider, James W. VA 8th Cav. Co.H
Rider, James W. VA 19th Cav. Co.I
Rider, James W. VA Horse Arty. Jackson's Co.
QMSgt.
Rider, James W. VA 31st Inf. Co.I
Rider, J.C. GA 11th Cav. Co.E
Rider, J.H. TN Cav. 16th Bn. (Neal's) Co.B
Rider, J.L. GA 52nd Inf. Co.D Cpl.
Rider, J.M. MO Quantrill's Co.
Rider, J.M. TN 2nd (Ashby's) Cav. Co.K
Rider, J.M. TN Cav. 5th Bn. (McClellan's) Co.E
Rider, John AL 40th Inf. Co.F
Rider, John AR 1st Mtd.Rifles Co.F
Rider, John AR 1st (Monroe's) Cav. Co.E
Rider, John AR 4th Inf. Co.H
Rider, John MO 1st Inf. Co.H
Rider, John MO Inf. 8th Bn. Co.D
Rider, John VA 1st Bn.Res. Co.H
Rider, John William VA 2nd Inf. Co.G,H Sgt.
Rider, Joseph GA 52nd Inf. Co.D
Rider, Joseph S. VA 7th Cav. Co.D
Rider, Joseph S. VA 31st Inf. Co.E Sgt.
Rider, J.P. MO Cav. 2nd Regt.St.Guard Co.A
Rider, J.P. MO 7th Cav. Co.G Sgt.
Rider, J.T. GA 5th Res. Co.A
Rider, J.T. TN 1st (Carter's) Cav. Co.F
Rider, J.W. VA 59th Inf. 1st Co.B
Rider, L. VA 26th Cav. Co.C
Rider, Lafayette TN 1st (Feild's) Inf. Co.E
Rider, Luke VA Cav. 46th Bn. Co.C
Rider, Luke VA 31st Inf. Co.A
Rider, Martin J. MO 12th Cav. Co.C 1st Lt.
Rider, Martin L. MD 1st Inf. Co.A,G
Rider, Martin L. MD Inf. 2nd Bn. Co.C,G
Rider, Michael M. VA 31st Inf. Co.H 2nd Lt.
Rider, Moses GA 43rd Inf. Co.I
Rider, M.T. VA Lt.Arty. Ellett's Co. Artif.
Rider, M.V. GA 36th (Broyles') Inf. Co.C,H
Rider, M.W. MO 2nd Inf. Co.C Capt.
Rider, Nathaniel SC 1st Arty. Co.K
Rider, Richard TN 1st Hvy.Arty. Co.B Sgt.
Rider, Richard VA Inf. 26th Bn.
Rider, Richard H. VA 31st Inf. Co.B
Rider, Richard H. VA 162nd Mil. Co.C
Rider, Robert TN 59th Mtd.Inf. Co.E

Rider, R.R. TN 2nd (Ashby's) Cav. Co.G
Rider, Samuel GA 6th Cav. Co.B
Rider, Samuel GA 11th Cav. Co.E
Rider, Samuel GA 43rd Inf. Co.I
Rider, Samuel GA Smith's Legion
Rider, Samuel R. NC Walker's Bn. Thomas'
Legion Co.E
Rider, S.S. VA 4th Inf. Co.A
Rider, Thomas VA 20th Cav. Co.C
Rider, Thomas A. VA Cav. 47th Bn. Co.B
Rider, T.L. 1st Cherokee Mtd.Vol. 1st Co.B
Rider, T.R. TN 46th Inf. Co.E
Rider, W. AR Mil. Borland's Regt. Peyton Rifles
Rider, W.A. GA Inf. 17th Bn. (St.Guards)
Stocks' Co.
Rider, W.H. AR 1st Mtd.Rifles Co.F
Rider, William AR Lt.Arty. Marshall's Btty. Sgt.
Rider, William TN 5th (McKenzie's) Cav. Co.A
Rider, William TN Arty. Ramsey's Btty.
Rider, William TX 6th Inf. Co.B
Rider, William VA 21st Cav. Co.A
Rider, William VA 11th Inf. Co.H
Rider, William VA 58th Inf. Co.K
Rider, William Conf.Arty. Marshall's Co.
Rider, William C. GA 43rd Inf. Co.I
Rider, William H. AR 4th Inf. Co.H
Rider, William H. VA Horse Arty. Jackson's Co.
Rider, Wright TN 62nd Mtd.Inf. Co.K
Riders, J.E. TN 1st Inf. Co.D
Riders, W.J. MS 31st Inf. Co.G
Rides, H.A. AL Cav. Hardie's Bn.Res. Co.D
Ridesperger, A.S. MS 2nd St.Cav. Co.A
Ridg, Green B. AR 33rd Inf. Co.I
Ridgall, James VA Inf. 25th Bn. Co.A
Ridgall, P.L. GA 23rd Inf. Co.G
Ridgaway, A.J. TN 19th & 20th (Cons.) Cav.
Co.K
Ridgaway, J.A. GA Arty. Martin's Bn.
Ridgaway, Richard VA 28th Inf. Co.D
Ridgaway, Watson VA 28th Inf. Co.D
Ridgdell, J.W. SC 11th Res. Co.K Sgt.
Ridge 1st Cherokee Mtd.Rifles Co.K
Ridge, A.J. TX 17th Inf. Co.D Capt.
Ridge, Amos AR 33rd Inf. Co.I
Ridge, Amos MO 10th Cav. Co.D
Ridge, B.C. MO 5th Cav. Co.I 2nd Lt.
Ridge, Calvin P. AR 2nd Inf. Co.D
Ridge, Coleman TN 34th Inf. Co.F
Ridge, D. SC 14th Inf. Co.G
Ridge, David LA 2nd Inf. Co.G
Ridge, David TN 3rd (Lillard's) Mtd.Inf. Co.E
Ridge, David TN 39th Mtd.Inf. Co.B
Ridge, F.M. AL 4th (Russell's) Cav. Co.E
Ridge, Francis M. TX 12th Cav. Co.I Sgt.
Ridge, Godfrey MS 31st Inf. Co.G
Ridge, Green TX Cav. Wells' Regt. Co.H
Ridge, Green B. TX 27th Cav. Co.G
Ridge, Green J. AR 35th Inf. Co.B
Ridge, H.B. Conf.Cav. Wood's Regt. Co.L
Ridge, Herman 1st Cherokee Mtd.Vol. 1st Co.D,
2nd Co.G
Ridge, Hiram TN 2nd (Robison's) Inf. Co.C
Ridge, Isaac S. TN 23rd Inf. Co.C Sgt.
Ridge, J. AR Inf. Sparks' Co.
Ridge, James TN 23rd Inf. Co.C
Ridge, James TX 10th Inf. Co.B
Ridge, James A. AR 23rd Inf. Co.E

Ridge, J.G. AR 51st Mil. Co.F
Ridge, John LA 15th Inf. Co.G
Ridge, John TN 10th Inf. Co.A
Ridge, John TN 34th Inf. Co.F
Ridge, John TX 20th Cav. Co.H
Ridge, John 1st Cherokee Mtd.Rifles Co.F
Ridge, John 1st Cherokee Mtd.Rifles Co.G
Ridge, John H. AR Cav. 1st Bn. (Stirman's)
Co.B
Ridge, John H. SC 1st (Butler's) Inf. Co.A
Ridge, John H. SC 14th Inf. Co.G
Ridge, John W. AR 35th Inf. Co.B
Ridge, Joseph VA 146th Mil. Co.H
Ridge, J.T. AR 35th Inf. Co.B
Ridge, J.W. AL 4th (Russell's) Cav. Co.E
Ridge, Logan A. NC Hvy.Arty. 10th Bn. Co.A
Ridge, Michael TN Lt.Arty. Morton's Co.
Ridge, Patrick TN 34th Inf. Co.F
Ridge, Robert TN 18th Inf. Co.B
Ridge, Robert R. TX 12th Cav. Co.I
Ridge, T.Q. AR 8th Cav. Co.I
Ridge, William NC 2nd Inf. Co.I
Ridge, William TX 12th Cav. Co.I
Ridge, William Greenbery TX 20th Cav. Co.H
Ridge, William L. SC 1st (Butler's) Inf. Co.A,H
Cpl.
Ridge, Willis NC 52nd Inf. Co.B
Ridge, W.L. SC 14th Inf. Co.G
Ridge, W.S. LA 2nd Inf. Co.B 2nd Lt.
Ridge, W.S. LA Res.Corps
Ridge chu we skah 1st Cherokee Mtd.Rifles Co.G
Ridgedell, Benjamin R. GA 25th Inf. Co.K
Ridgedell, Israel J. MS 1st Lt.Arty. Co.A
Ridgedell, Theodore LA Miles' Legion Co.C
Ridgedell, Thomas LA Miles' Legion Co.C
Ridgedell, Young LA Miles' Legion Co.C
Ridgel, James MD Inf. 2nd Bn. Co.D
Ridgel, James MD Walters' Co. (Zarvona
Zouaves)
Ridgel, N.A. SC 4th St.Troops Co.D
Ridgel, Richard MO 6th Cav. Co.D
Ridgel, R.M. SC 4th St.Troops Co.D
Ridgele, John W. VA 40th Inf. Co.F
Ridgeley, John MD 1st Cav. Co.C
Ridgeley, John J. LA 1st Hvy.Arty. (Reg.) Co.A
Ridgeley, R.W. GA Inf. 1st City Bn. (Columbus)
Co.C
Ridgeley, Samuel VA 1st Cav. 2nd Co.K
Ridgeley, Thomas MD 1st Cav. Co.A
Ridgell, Andrew R. AR 33rd Inf. Co.D
Ridgell, Arkansas AR Lt.Arty. Owen's Btty.
Ridgell, Arkansas AR 3rd Inf. Co.C
Ridgell, B.R. AL 32nd Inf. Co.H Cpl.
Ridgell, D. GA Cav. 29th Bn. Co.G
Ridgell, Daniel P. TX Cav. 8th (Taylor's) Bn.
Co.E
Ridgell, D.P. TX 1st (MuCulloch's) Cav. Co.C
Ridgell, D.W. SC 2nd St.Troops Co.B
Ridgell, D.W. SC 7th Inf. 2nd Co.E, Co.C
Ridgell, F. LA Miles' Legion Co.F
Ridgell, Felix SC 14th Inf. Co.D
Ridgell, J.B. SC 7th Inf. 1st Co.E, 2nd Co.E
Ridgell, Joel S. AL 42nd Inf. Co.C
Ridgell, Joseph W. AR 33rd Inf. Co.D Cpl.
Ridgell, J.S. MS Inf. 2nd Bn. (St.Troops) Co.B
Ridgell, Norris SC 19th Inf. Co.F
Ridgell, Robert FL 10th Inf. Co.F

Ridgell, R.R. AR 2nd Cav. Co.E
Ridgell, Swiney AR 3rd Inf. Co.C
Ridgell, Tudor T. SC 14th Inf. Co.D
Ridgell, W. AL 17th Inf. Co.G
Ridgell, W.C. SC 7th Inf. 1st Co.E, 2nd Co.E
  Cpl.
Ridgell, William J. AR 1st (Colquitt's) Inf. Co.A
Ridgely, Charles L. FL 3rd Inf. Co.B Capt.
Ridgely, John MD 1st Cav. Co.A
Ridgely, Randolph GA Cav. 2nd Bn. Co.F
  Bugler
Ridgely, Randolph Gen. & Staff 2nd Lt.,Dr.M.
Ridgely, Randolph Gen. & Staff 1st Lt.,ADC
Ridgely, Samuel MD 1st Cav. Co.K
Ridgely, Samuel VA Cav. Mosby's Regt.
  (Part.Rangers) Co.F
Ridgely, T.A. VA 15th Cav. Co.B
Ridgeman, G. GA 45th Inf. Co.C
Ridgen, Frank TX St.Troops Teel's Co.
Ridgeon, Frank TX 2nd Field Btty.
Ridges, J. GA 31st Inf. Co.C
Ridgesby, Barney NC 64th Inf. Co.C
Ridgesby, William NC 64th Inf. Co.C
Ridgeway, A. VA 30th Bn.S.S. Co.D
Ridgeway, Abe MS St.Troops (Peach Creek
  Rangers) Maxwell's Co.
Ridgeway, A.H. TN 31st Inf. Co.K
Ridgeway, A.J. TN 20th (Russell's) Cav. Co.K
Ridgeway, A.J. TN 46th Inf. Co.F Sgt.
Ridgeway, Allen GA 55th Inf. Co.I
Ridgeway, Basil VA 54th Inf. Co.K
Ridgeway, B.C. AL Cp. of Instr. Talladega
Ridgeway, Ben F. Gen. & Staff Capt.,AQM
Ridgeway, B.F. TN 46th Inf. Co.F AQM
Ridgeway, Bradley AL 2nd Cav. Co.C
Ridgeway, Bradley MS Cav. Jeff Davis Legion
  Co.C
Ridgeway, B.T. LA 19th Inf. Co.F
Ridgeway, C.T. VA 10th Bn.Res. Co.E
Ridgeway, D.A. GA 1st Troops & Def. (Macon)
  Co.D
Ridgeway, D.A. MS Conscr.
Ridgeway, David SC 16th Inf. Co.E
Ridgeway, D.C. SC 6th Cav. Co.A,D
Ridgeway, Early W. LA 12th Inf. Co.H
Ridgeway, E.L. TN 46th Inf. Co.F
Ridgeway, Elijah SC 16th Inf. Co.E
Ridgeway, E.R. SC 6th Cav. Co.A
Ridgeway, E. Thomas AL 3rd Cav. Co.A
Ridgeway, E. Thomas Conf.Cav. Wood's Regt.
  Co.C
Ridgeway, George AL 61st Inf. Co.E
Ridgeway, George MO 1st N.E. Cav. Co.B
Ridgeway, George H. AL 9th Inf. Co.I
Ridgeway, Henry H. AL 13th Inf. Co.G
Ridgeway, Hewlett S. GA 35th Inf. Co.C
Ridgeway, H.W. SC 23rd Inf. Co.K
Ridgeway, I.A. TN 19th & 20th (Cons.) Cav.
  Co.D Cpl.
Ridgeway, J.A. SC 23rd Inf. Co.I
Ridgeway, J.A. SC 23rd Inf. Co.K
Ridgeway, J.A. TN 20th (Russell's) Cav. Co.K
Ridgeway, James A. KY Morehead's Regt.
  (Part.Rangers)
Ridgeway, James J. MO 6th Inf. Co.C
Ridgeway, Jarret TX 19th Inf. Co.F
Ridgeway, Jasper TN 55th (Brown's) Inf. Co.D

Ridgeway, J.E. AR 10th Inf. Co.G
Ridgeway, J.H. GA 45th Inf. Co.I
Ridgeway, J.H. TN 46th Inf. Co.F
Ridgeway, J.K.P. TX Waul's Legion Co.F
Ridgeway, J.M. SC 23rd Inf. Co.I
Ridgeway, J.M. SC 25th Inf. Co.I
Ridgeway, J.N. SC 21st Inf. Co.C
Ridgeway, J.N. SC 25th Inf. Co.I
Ridgeway, John MO 10th Cav. Co.D 2nd Sgt.
Ridgeway, John MO 9th Inf. Co.E
Ridgeway, John MO Inf. Clark's Regt. Co.A
Ridgeway, John C.J. AL 11th Inf. Co.B
Ridgeway, John J. MO Cav. Poindexter's Regt.
Ridgeway, John T. MO 4th Cav. Co.D
Ridgeway, John W. VA 12th Cav. Co.I
Ridgeway, John W. VA 42nd Inf. Co.B
Ridgeway, Joseph VA 12th Cav. Co.I
Ridgeway, Joseph A. GA Lt.Arty. Pritchard's
  Co. (Washington Arty.)
Ridgeway, Joseph A. GA 36th (Villepigue's) Inf.
  Co.F
Ridgeway, Joseph A. 1st Conf.Inf. 1st Co.F
Ridgeway, Josiah 1st Creek Mtd.Vol. Co.G
Ridgeway, Josiah J. VA 12th Cav. Co.B
Ridgeway, J.S. AL 48th Inf. Co.D 1st Lt.
Ridgeway, J.S. SC 7th Cav. Co.I
Ridgeway, J.S. SC Cav.Bn. Holcombe Legion
  Co.A
Ridgeway, J.T. VA Cav. Mosby's Regt.
  (Part.Rangers) Co.G
Ridgeway, J.W. MO Cav. Snider's Bn. Co.A
Ridgeway, J.W. SC 4th St.Troops Co.I
Ridgeway, J.W. TN 31st Inf. Co.K
Ridgeway, Laurence M. SC Inf. Hampton Legion
  Co.C
Ridgeway, L.D. GA 13th Inf. Co.K
Ridgeway, L.M. SC 5th Bn.Res. Co.F
Ridgeway, L.M. SC Post Guard Senn's Co.
Ridgeway, Marion TX 19th Inf. Co.F
Ridgeway, M.I. MD Arty. 1st Btty.
Ridgeway, Michael A. Gen. & Staff Asst.Surg.
Ridgeway, M.L. LA 1st Inf. Co.F
Ridgeway, Mordici J. MD 1st Cav. Co.E
Ridgeway, Newton VA 12th Cav. Co.I
Ridgeway, O.C. 3rd Conf.Eng.Troops Co.D
Ridgeway, Orace MO 1st N.E. Cav. Co.M 1st
  Lt.
Ridgeway, P.E. SC 7th Cav. Co.I
Ridgeway, P.E. SC Cav.Bn. Holcombe Legion
  Co.A
Ridgeway, Q.J. TN 3rd (Forrest's) Cav. 1st Co.B
Ridgeway, Reuben F. SC 25th Inf. Co.I Sgt.
Ridgeway, R.F. SC 4th St.Troops Co.D
Ridgeway, R.F. SC 5th Bn.Res. Co.F
Ridgeway, R.F. VA 3rd Bn. Valley Res. Co.A
Ridgeway, Richard A. TX 22nd Cav. Co.B
Ridgeway, Richard F. LA Inf.Cons.Crescent
  Regt. Co.B
Ridgeway, Richard S. VA 6th Cav. Co.D
Ridgeway, R.S. TX Cav. Benavides' Regt. Co.H
Ridgeway, Samuel VA 2nd Inf. Co.G
Ridgeway, S.C. SC 7th Inf. 2nd Co.B
Ridgeway, S.J. GA 1st (Fannin's) Res. Co.D
Ridgeway, Spencer W. TX 18th Cav. Co.F
Ridgeway, Thadious N. AL 47th Inf. Co.K
Ridgeway, Thomas AL 50th Inf. Co.B

Ridgeway, W.A. TN 19th & 20th (Cons.) Cav.
  Co.K 3rd Lt.
Ridgeway, W.A. TN 20th (Russell's) Cav. Co.K
  Bvt.2nd Lt.
Ridgeway, William AR 24th Inf. Co.F
Ridgeway, William AR Inf. Hardy's Regt. Co.D
Ridgeway, William GA 42nd Inf. Co.G
Ridgeway, William LA 7th Inf. Co.I
Ridgeway, William, Jr. VA 50th Inf. Co.F Sgt.
Ridgeway, William 3rd Conf.Eng.Troops Co.D
Ridgeway, William G. VA 114th Mil. Co.D
Ridgeway, William H. VA 49th Inf. Co.D
Ridgeway, William L.H. GA 4th Bn.S.S. Co.C
Ridgeway, William M. GA 45th Inf. Co.I Cpl.
Ridgeway, William P. TX 2nd Cav. 2nd Co.F
Ridgeway, W.L.H. GA Inf. 9th Bn. Co.C
Ridgeway, W.M. TN 15th (Cons.) Cav. Co.H
Ridgeway, W.M. TN 12th Inf. Co.G
Ridgeway, W.M. TN 12th (Cons.) Inf. Co.E
Ridgeway, W.P. TX Cav. Benavides' Regt. Co.H
Ridgeway, W.W. AR 19th Inf.
Ridgeway, W.W. TN 20th (Russell's) Cav. Co.K
Ridgill, A.G. LA Washington Arty.Bn. Co.2
Ridgill, John W. LA Washington Arty.Bn. Co.2
Ridgill, P.L. SC 23rd Inf. Co.I
Ridgill, R.A. SC 23rd Inf. Co.I Cpl.
Ridgill, Robert V. FL 7th Inf. Co.C
Ridgill, William J.W. SC Inf. Hampton Legion
  Co.C
Ridgley, Randolph VA Cav. 39th Bn. Co.B
Ridgon, George W. NC Inf. 13th Bn. Co.C
Ridgsby, W.J. GA 10th Cav. Co.I
Ridgway, --- TX Cav. Steele's Command Co.A
Ridgway, A. TN 16th Cav. Co.E
Ridgway, Abner C. MS 42nd Inf. Co.B
Ridgway, Abram VA 157th Mil. Co.B
Ridgway, Absalom 3rd Conf.Eng.Troops Co.D
Ridgway, Amos VA 31st Inf. Co.K
Ridgway, Andrew VA 67th Mil. Co.A
Ridgway, Benjamin H. AL 1st Bn. Hilliard's
  Legion Vol. Co.B
Ridgway, B.H. AL 60th Inf. Co.H
Ridgway, Charles T. VA 25th Inf. 2nd Co.B 2nd
  Lt.
Ridgway, C.T. VA 3rd (Chrisman's) Bn.Res.
  Co.E
Ridgway, D.A. AL 9th (Malone's) Cav. Co.G,C
Ridgway, D. Alex TN 7th (Duckworth's) Cav.
  Co.C
Ridgway, E.B. AR 7th Inf. Co.A
Ridgway, F.M. TX 5th Inf. Co.D
Ridgway, George R. VA 58th Inf. Co.C
Ridgway, G.M. TN 5th Inf. 1st Co.H Cpl.
Ridgway, H.J. VA 67th Mil. Co.A
Ridgway, J. VA 21st Cav. Co.B
Ridgway, J.B. AL 14th Inf. Co.H
Ridgway, J.C. AR 2nd Mtd.Rifles Co.E
Ridgway, Jesse H. AL 1st Bn. Hilliard's Legion
  Vol. Co.B
Ridgway, J.H. AL 60th Inf. Co.H
Ridgway, J.J. AL 4th (Russell's) Cav. Co.A
Ridgway, J.J. MO Inf. 3rd Bn. Co.E
Ridgway, J.K. TX Inf. Timmons' Regt. Co.C
Ridgway, John MO Inf. Clark's Regt. Co.H
Ridgway, John H. VA 108th Mil. Co.F, Lemons'
  Co.
Ridgway, John J. SC 16th Inf. Co.E

Ridgway, John L. TX Waul's Legion Co.A
Ridgway, John N. GA Cobb's Legion Co.C,H
Ridgway, John N. VA 58th Inf. Co.D
Ridgway, John W. VA 58th Inf. Co.B
Ridgway, Joseph P. VA 58th Inf. Co.D Sgt.
Ridgway, Leander F. TX 1st (McCulloch's) Cav. Co.A
Ridgway, Leander F. TX Waul's Legion Co.A
Ridgway, M.A. AL 1st Bn. Hilliard's Legion Vol. Co.B Capt.
Ridgway, Marion TX 14th Inf. Co.H
Ridgway, Michael N. AL 47th Inf. Co.D Asst.Surg.
Ridgway, Richard VA 8th Bn.Res. Co.A
Ridgway, Richard F. LA Inf. 11th Bn. Co.D
Ridgway, R.S. VA 1st Cav. 1st Co.D
Ridgway, Sidney P. VA 58th Inf. Co.C 1st Sgt.
Ridgway, S. Paine KY 3rd Mtd.Inf. Co.E Capt.
Ridgway, S.T. TN 5th Inf. 2nd Co.D
Ridgway, Thomas VA 11th Cav. Co.K
Ridgway, T.J. TX 17th Inf. Co.A
Ridgway, William VA 28th Cav. Co.D Cpl.
Ridgway, William VA Cav. 37th Bn. Co.G
Ridgway, William C. VA 58th Inf. Co.D Capt.
Ridgway, William G. VA 33rd Inf. Co.A
Ridgway, William H. TX Waul's Legion Co.A 2nd Lt.
Ridgway, William J. TN 3rd (Clack's) Inf. Co.A 2nd Lt.
Ridgway, Willis W. AL 1st Bn. Hilliard's Legion Vol. Co.B
Ridgway, W.J. MS Inf. 1st St.Troops Co.I Cpl.
Ridgway, W.J. MS 5th Inf. Co.K
Ridgway, W.R. TN 5th Inf. 1st Co.H
Ridgway, W.W. TN 5th Inf. 1st Co.H
Riding, C.A. VA 25th Cav. Co.D
Riding, George D. TN 11th Inf. Co.A
Riding, H.H. AR 12th Inf. Co.G
Riding, J. LA 3rd Inf. Co.A
Riding, J.F. MS 6th Inf. Co.C
Riding, J.W. AR Inf. Hardy's Regt. Co.E
Riding, William TX Cav. Martin's Regt. Co.B
Ridinger, George H. VA 4th Res. Co.H
Ridinger, J.P. MS Cav. Jeff Davis Legion Co.D
Ridinger, M.M. TN 35th Inf. Co.G
Ridings, C. AL 1st Cav. Co.B
Ridings, Charles A. VA 23rd Cav. Co.D,G
Ridings, E.T. TN 11th Inf. Co.A
Ridings, Frederick W. VA Lt.Arty. Cutshaw's Co.
Ridings, Frederick W. VA 51st Mil. Co.A
Ridings, Fred W. VA Lt.Arty. Carpenter's Co.
Ridings, George GA Cobb's Legion Co.E
Ridings, George C. VA Lt.Arty. Carpenter's Co.
Ridings, George C. VA Lt.Arty. Cutshaw's Co.
Ridings, George E. VA 51st Mil. Co.A
Ridings, H. MO Lt.Arty. Von Phul's Co.
Ridings, H.D. MO 5th Cav. Co.A
Ridings, James C. AR 18th (Marmaduke's) Inf. Co.K
Ridings, James C. MS 14th Inf. Co.E
Ridings, J.C. 3rd Conf.Inf. Co.G
Ridings, J.G. LA 3rd Inf. Co.A
Ridings, J.J. TN 24th Bn.S.S. Co.A Sgt.
Ridings, Joel P. Forrest's Cav. Lyon's Escort, CSA

Ridings, John C. GA Cherokee Legion (St.Guards) Co.D Sgt.
Ridings, John G. LA 31st Inf. Co.A
Ridings, John W. VA 51st Mil. Co.D
Ridings, Joseph C. NC 54th Inf. Co.I Sgt.
Ridings, J.P. VA 136th Mil. Co.A Sgt.
Ridings, P.H. MS 2nd Cav.Res. Co.C
Ridings, P.H. MS Inf. 3rd Bn. (St.Troops) Co.B
Ridings, Pinckney NC Cav. 7th Bn. Co.E
Ridings, Pinkney NC 6th Cav. (65th St.Troops) Co.E
Ridings, Rice R. GA Cherokee Legion (St.Guards) Co.D
Ridings, Samuel F. MO Cav. Freeman's Regt.
Ridings, Thomas LA 31st Inf. Co.A
Ridings, Thomas TN 27th Inf. Co.K
Ridings, Thomas W. VA Lt.Arty. Cutshaw's Co.
Ridings, Thomas W. VA 51st Mil. Co.A
Ridings, T.W. VA Lt.Arty. Carpenter's Co.
Ridings, W.H. MS Inf. 3rd Bn. (St.Troops) Co.B
Ridings, William P. NC 64th Inf. Co.E
Ridins, James O. GA 36th (Broyles') Inf. Co.E
Ridle, C.C. VA 11th Cav. Co.C
Ridle, M. AL 6th Cav. Co.E
Ridleberger, Joseph VA 11th Cav. Co.C
Ridlehoover, A.J. SC 2nd Arty. Co.K
Ridlehoover, George N. MS 44th Inf. Co.I
Ridlehoover, G.N. MS 9th Bn. S.S. Co.B
Ridlehoover, Jacob E. MS 44th Inf. Co.I
Ridlehoover, Joseph SC 2nd Arty. Co.B,K Sgt.
Ridlehoover, Simeon M. LA 9th Inf. Co.H
Ridlehoover, Sumter SC 2nd Arty. Co.K
Ridlehower, S. AL Talladega Cty.Res. I. Stone's Co.
Ridlehuber, G.C. SC 7th Cav. Co.E
Ridlehuber, G.C. SC Cav.Bn. Holcombe Legion Co.C Sgt.
Ridlehuber, Henry Walter SC 1st (McCreary's) Inf. Co.B 1st Sgt.
Ridlehuber, H.W. SC 1st Inf. Co.L
Ridlehuber, W.F. SC 13th Inf. Co.H Cpl.
Ridlehuber, William SC 1st Inf. Co.L
Ridlehuber, W.L. SC 20th Inf. Co.F,M
Ridlesperger, A.S. MS 7th Cav. Co.G
Ridlesperger, J.K. MS 2nd St.Cav. Co.A
Ridlesperger, Samuel Van Buren MS Inf. 1st Bn. Co.D 3rd Lt.
Ridley, --- VA VMI Co.G Cpl.
Ridley, Adam SC 12th Inf. Co.K
Ridley, Adolphus H. MS 14th Inf. Co.G
Ridley, Alonzo TX Cav. Madison's Regt. Maj.
Ridley, Benjamin Conf.Inf. Tucker's Regt. Co.G Cpl.
Ridley, B.L. Stewart's Corps Lt.,ADC
Ridley, C.A. MO Cav. Stallard's Co. Sgt.
Ridley, C.H. TN 1st (Feild's) & 27th Inf. (Cons.) Co.F 2nd Lt.
Ridley, Charles LA Inf. McLean's Co.
Ridley, Charles VA 46th Inf. Co.C
Ridley, Charles VA 59th Inf. 2nd Co.A
Ridley, Charles A. GA 35th Inf. Co.D
Ridley, Charles B. GA 41st Inf. Co.E Sgt.
Ridley, Christopher H. TN 1st (Feild's) Inf. Co.D 2nd Lt.
Ridley, Cicero A.S. GA 19th Inf. Co.E
Ridley, C.M. SC 12th Inf. Co.K Sgt.
Ridley, Cornelius C. GA 41st Inf. Co.I

Ridley, C.S. Gen. & Staff 1st Lt.,ADC
Ridley, D. GA Inf. Collier's Co.
Ridley, David VA 47th Inf. Co.B
Ridley, Dee TX 9th (Young's) Inf. Co.K Capt.
Ridley, D.L. GA 5th Res. Co.G
Ridley, G. GA 32nd Inf. Co.B
Ridley, G.A. GA 32nd Inf. Co.F
Ridley, G.C. TN Cav. 1st Bn. (McNairy's) Co.A
Ridley, G.C. TN 3rd (Forrest's) Cav. Co.F Sgt.
Ridley, G.C. TN 22nd (Barteau's) Cav. Co.A
Ridley, George AL 18th Bn.Vol. Co.C
Ridley, George AL 33rd Inf. Co.C
Ridley, George C. TN 9th (Ward's) Cav. Co.F 2nd Lt.
Ridley, George C. Gen. & Staff Capt.,AAG
Ridley, George R. TN 20th Inf. Co.E
Ridley, George V. TX 21st Cav. Co.E
Ridley, G.W. NC 27th Inf.
Ridley, H.B. AL 7th Inf. Co.E
Ridley, Henry AR 30th Inf. Co.K
Ridley, Henry GA 36th (Broyles') Inf. Co.H
Ridley, H.M. TN 12th (Cons.) Inf. Co.G
Ridley, H.M. TN 22nd Inf. Co.G
Ridley, I.L. TN 4th Cav. Surg.
Ridley, J. GA 32nd Inf. Co.B
Ridley, J.A. MS 14th (Cons.) Inf. Co.F
Ridley, Jack GA Conscr.
Ridley, James A. MS 14th Inf. Co.G
Ridley, James A. TN 23rd Inf. Co.E Capt.
Ridley, James B. NC Cav. 7th Bn. Co.C
Ridley, James B. TN 2nd (Robison's) Inf. Co.A
Ridley, James H. AL 14th Inf. Co.L Music.
Ridley, James M. TX 1st Inf. 2nd Co.K Drum.
Ridley, James P. Wheeler's Scouts,CSA
Ridley, James S. TN 11th Inf. ACS
Ridley, J.B. TN 20th (Russell's) Cav. Co.D
Ridley, J.B. TN 47th Inf. Co.G
Ridley, J.E.B. TN 20th Inf. Co.I Cpl.
Ridley, Jerome S. TN Inf. 11th Regt. ACS
Ridley, J.J. TN 6th (Wheeler's) Cav. Co.C
Ridley, J.K.P. TN 20th Inf. Co.E
Ridley, J.L. LA 17th Inf. Co.D Lt.
Ridley, J.L. TN Cav. 1st Bn. (McNairy's) Co.A
Ridley, J.L. TN 19th & 20th (Cons.) Cav. Co.B
Ridley, J.L. TN 20th (Russell's) Cav. Co.B
Ridley, J.M. GA 13th Inf. Co.K
Ridley, John AR 8th Inf. New Co.E Music.
Ridley, John NC 62nd Inf. Co.D
Ridley, John NC Inf. Thomas Legion Co.G
Ridley, John D. VA 4th Inf. Co.E 2nd Lt.,Adj.
Ridley, John D. Gen. & Staff 1st Lt.,Adj.
Ridley, John S. GA 57th Inf. Co.D
Ridley, Jonathan FL 11th Inf. Co.F
Ridley, Joseph D. FL 6th Inf. Co.D
Ridley, Joseph W. GA 18th Inf. Co.I
Ridley, J.S. Gen. & Staff Maj.,Comsy
Ridley, J.S. Gen. & Staff Capt.,ACS
Ridley, J.S. Gen. & Staff Surg.
Ridley, J.W. TN 20th (Russell's) Cav. Co.B
Ridley, J.W. TN 15th Inf. Co.D
Ridley, K. TN 1st (Feild's) Inf. Co.G
Ridley, Lucas TN 2nd (Robison's) Inf. Co.A
Ridley, M.V. AR 8th Inf. New Co.A Music.
Ridley, N.B. SC 20th Inf. Co.A
Ridley, N.T. GA 8th Cav. Co.K
Ridley, N.T. GA 62nd Cav. Co.K
Ridley, R. VA 13th Cav. Co.H

Ridley, Richard R. TX 17th Cons.Dismtd.Cav.
Co.K
Ridley, Robert AL 3rd Bn. Hilliard's Legion Vol.
Co.B
Ridley, Robert B. GA 4th Inf. Co.B Bvt.2nd Lt.
Ridley, Robert C. MS 4th Inf. Co.A Sgt.
Ridley, Robert H. TX 10th Cav. Co.C
Ridley, Robert W. AL Inf. 1st Regt. Co.E Sgt.
Ridley, R.R. TX 14th Inf. 1st Co.K
Ridley, Samuel J. TN 1st Cav.
Ridley, Samuel Jones MS 1st Lt.Arty. Co.A
Capt.
Ridley, Samuel W. GA 10th Inf. Co.G Cpl.
Ridley, S.J. TN 20th Inf. Co.I
Ridley, T.J. AR 36th Inf. Co.E
Ridley, T.J. Central Div. KY Sap.& Min.,CSA
2nd Lt.
Ridley, T.L. TN 5th Inf. 2nd Co.F
Ridley, V.B. TX 8th Cav. Co.I
Ridley, Washington G. TN 2nd (Robison's) Inf.
Co.F 2nd Lt.
Ridley, W.B. GA Cobb's Legion Co.D
Ridley, William TN 3rd (Lillard's) Mtd.Inf.
Co.D Sgt.
Ridley, William F. NC Cav. 7th Bn. Co.C
Ridley, William G. VA 6th Inf. Co.G
Ridley, William T. TN 20th Inf. Co.E Capt.
Ridley, Winston MS Inf. 3rd Bn. Co.H
Ridley, W.J. GA 14th Inf. Co.G
Ridley, W.L. SC 20th Inf. Co.A
Ridley, W.R. TX 21st Cav. Co.E
Ridley, W.T. TN 55th (Brown's) Inf. Co.F
Ridley, Y.L. Sig.Corps,CSA Sgt.
Ridley, Young L. AR 1st (Colquitt's) Inf. Co.G
Ridlin, H.C. AR 33rd Inf. Co.F
Ridlin, S.D. AR 37th Inf. Co.K
Ridling, Alexander NC 33rd Inf. Co.C
Ridling, George Thomas MS 8th Cav. Co.A
Ridling, G.M. GA 36th (Broyles') Inf. Co.F
Ridling, G.W. AR 24th Inf. Co.H
Ridling, Henry C. AR 24th Inf. Co.F
Ridling, Henry C. AR Inf. Hardy's Regt. Co.D
Ridling, J.K.P. GA Cobb's Legion Co.B
Ridling, John H. AR 33rd Inf. Co.E
Ridling, John P. GA Cobb's Legion Co.D
Ridling, J.R. NC 33rd Inf.
Ridling, J.U. GA 2nd Res. Co.H
Ridling, J.U. GA Conscr.
Ridling, M.F. AR 6th Inf. Co.B
Ridling, M.L. AR 6th Inf. Co.B Cpl.
Ridling, M.V. GA Lt.Arty. Barnwell's Btty.
Ridling, M.V. GA Lt.Arty. Daniell's Btty.
Ridling, M.V. GA 38th Inf. Co.A
Ridling, R.T. AR 37th Inf. Co.I 2nd Lt.
Ridling, Thomas C. GA 38th Inf. Co.A
Ridling, W.C. AR Inf. 1st Bn. Co.A
Ridling, William J. GA 36th (Broyles') Inf. Co.F
Ridling, W.J. AR 6th Inf. Co.B
Ridly, J.B. TN Cav. Nixon's Regt. Co.I
Ridly, Joseph TN 29th Inf. Co.B
Ridly, Richard R. TX 18th Inf. Co.L Cpl.
Ridly, William M. TX Conscr.
Ridman, Charles B. AL 6th Cav. Co.H
Ridny, TX Cav. 8th (Taylor's) Bn. Co.D
Ridor, J.W. VA Hvy.Arty. 19th Bn. 3rd Co.C
Ridout, Charles A. MS 11th Inf. Co.D
Ridout, David C. VA 12th Inf. Co.F

Ridout, David T. VA 56th Inf. Co.B
Ridout, Henry TX 17th Inf. Co.K
Ridout, James VA 14th Inf. Co.F
Ridout, James J. VA 12th Inf. Co.F
Ridout, John TN 16th (Logwood's) Cav. Co.B
Ridout, John H. VA 12th Inf. Co.F
Ridout, Reese TX 4th Cav. Co.B Cpl.
Ridout, Thomas H. TX 17th Inf. Co.K
Ridout, William TX 17th Inf. Co.K Cpl.
Ridout, William D. TN 38th Inf. Co.I 2nd Lt.
Ridout, William D. VA 12th Inf. Co.F
Ridpath, James VA Inf. 23rd Bn. Co.C
Ridpath, John G. VA 50th Inf. Co.I Sgt.
Ridus, L.H. MS 24th Inf. Co.E 1st Lt.
Ridus, S.B. MS 5th Cav. Co.D
Ridway, John L. MS 4th Cav. Co.A
Ridway, Otho W. VA 8th Bn.Res. Co.A
Ridwell, George MO 1st N.E. Cav. Co.G
Rieber, Charles TX 8th Cav. Co.G
Rieber, Edward TX Cav. Ragsdale's Bn. 1st
Co.A
Rieber, George TX 3rd Inf. Co.H
Riech, George AL Mil. 3rd Vol. Co.G Sgt.
Riech, Louis GA 8th Inf. Co.F
Riecherzer, Adolph TX 5th Cav. Co.C
Riechsrath, L. SC Mil. 16th Regt. Steinmeyer,
Jr.'s Co.
Rieck, Frank B. LA 2nd Inf. Co.B
Rieck, Lewis AL 4th Inf. Co.D
Riecke, G. SC Lt.Arty. Wagener's Co. (Co.A,
German Arty.) Cpl.
Riecke, Henry W. GA 1st (Olmstead's) Inf. 1st
Co.A
Riecke, Henry W. GA 1st Bn.S.S. Co.B
Ried, A. TX 17th Cons.Dismtd.Cav. Co.I
Black.
Ried, A.M. MS 11th (Cons.) Cav. Co.F Cpl.
Ried, Andrew S. VA 11th Inf. Co.K
Ried, A.T. GA Hvy.Arty. 22nd Bn. Co.B
Ried, C.C. 1st Cherokee Mtd.Vol. 2nd Co.I
Ried, Cyrus MS Inf. 2nd St.Troops Co.H
Ried, Francis M. AL 11th Inf. Co.B
Ried, F.T. Gen. & Staff Pvt. Physician
Ried, George L. MS 10th Cav. Co.C
Ried, George W. NC 34th Inf. Co.K
Ried, H. NC 3rd Jr.Res. Co.B
Ried, I.D.C. MS 11th (Perrin's) Cav. Co.B
Ried, J. TX 17th Cons.Dismtd.Cav. Co.G
Ried, James MS 2nd St.Cav. Co.I
Ried, Jas. A. NC Lt.,ADC
Ried, James C. NC 11th (Bethel Regt.) Inf. Co.E
Ried, J.L. MS Condrey's Co. (Bull Mtn.Invinc.)
Ried, J.L. TX Cav. McCord's Frontier Regt.
Co.F
Ried, John F. TN 4th Inf. Co.C Cpl.
Ried, John M. TN 42nd Inf. 1st Co.I 2nd Lt.
Ried, John S. GA Smith's Legion
Ried, J.S. GA 6th Cav. Co.I 1st Lt.
Ried, Lovick MS Condrey's Co. (Bull Mtn.
Invinc.)
Ried, Malan NC 22nd Inf. Co.A
Ried, Nicholas MS 10th Inf. Co.N, New Co.E
Ried, R. VA Inf. 2nd Bn.Loc.Def. Co.G
Ried, R.A. VA Lt.Arty. King's Co.
Ried, R.L. AR 1st (Crawford's) Cav. Co.H
Ried, Robert NC 34th Inf. Co.H
Ried, Rodger A. VA 50th Inf. Co.E

Ried, T.A. TN Inf. 1st Cons.Regt. Co.A Cpl.
Ried, Thomas C. AL 28th Inf. Co.D
Ried, W.F. NC 3rd Jr.Res. Co.C Sgt.
Ried, William MS 38th Cav. Co.I
Ried, William A. MS Inf. 3rd Bn. Co.G Sgt.
Ried, William A.J. AL 28th Inf. Co.D Cpl.
Ried, William F. GA 57th Inf. Co.D
Ried, W.R. MO 2nd Inf. Co.K
Ried, W.R. NC 34th Inf. Co.H
Rieddel, A. TX 14th Field Btty.
Rieddel, J. LA Mil.Squad. Guides d'Orleans
Cavalier
Riede, --- TX Cav. Good's Bn. Co.B
Riedel, C. TX 6th Inf. Co.I
Riedel, E. TX 6th Inf. Co.I
Riedel, Edward LA 4th Inf. Co.B 2nd Lt.
Riedel, F. TX 6th Inf. Co.I
Riedel, Frank TX 7th Cav. Co.B
Riedel, Jacob TX 3rd Inf. Co.K
Riedel, M. TX 6th Inf. Co.I Music.
Rieder, Hengues Sap. & Min. Gallimard's Co.,
CSA 1st Sap.
Rieder, Hughes LA 18th Inf. Co.C,E
Riedinger, D. LA Mil. Orleans Fire Regt. Co.A
Rief, F. VA 2nd St.Res. Co.H
Riefe, Louis MS 21st Inf. Co.H
Rieff, A.V. AR 1st (Monroe's) Cav. Co.D Maj.
Rieff, C.C. AR 1st (Monroe's) Cav. Co.D
Rieff, John W. AR 34th Inf. Co.A
Rieff, J. Ten AR Cav. Gordon's Regt. Co.F
Capt.
Rieffel, Charles LA Arty. Watson Btty.
Forage M.
Rieffel, Ed LA Mil. Orleans Guards Regt. Co.H
Rieffel, Edward LA 22nd Inf. Co.C
Rieffel, Edward LA 22nd (Cons.) Inf. Co.C
Rieffel, Octave LA Mil. 1st Native Guards
Riege, John GA 22nd Inf. Co.C
Rieger, Benjamin TX 6th Inf. Co.B
Rieger, J.A. MO 10th Inf. Co.G
Rieger, Joseph A. VA Lt.Arty. Thompson's Co.
Riehl, H. TN 1st Hvy.Arty. 2nd Co.C
Riehl, H. TN Hvy.Arty. Sterling's Co.
Riehl, J.B. LA Mil. 1st Regt. French Brig. Co.5
Riehm, Lorenz TX Conscr.
Riekert, Peter LA Mil. Mech.Guard
Rieley, Charles B. VA 2nd Inf. Co.I
Rieley, J. TX Waul's Legion Co.A
Rieley, James AR 6th Inf.
Rieley, John TX 5th Inf. Co.A
Rieley, John J. VA 2nd Inf. Co.I
Rieley, J.T. GA 39th Inf. Co.E Sgt.
Rieley, Lewis H. VA 2nd Cav. Co.C
Rieley, Michael VA 7th Cav. Co.I
Rieley, Owen LA Mil. Bragg's Bn. Schwartz's
Co.
Rieley, Robert W. VA 2nd Cav. Co.C Sgt.
Rieley, Samuel R. VA 2nd Cav. Co.C
Rieley, Thomas VA 54th Mil. Co.E,F
Rieley, W. GA 5th Res. Co.E
Rieley, William A. VA 6th Cav. Co.D
Rieley, W.P. LA Inf.Cons. 18th Regt. & Yellow
Jacket Bn. Co.E
Rielley, Thomas J.D. VA 54th Mil. Co.E,F
Riells, John LA 1st Hvy.Arty. (Reg.) Co.G,I
Rielly, Edward GA 1st (Olmstead's) Inf. Co.D
Cpl.

Rielly, James LA 6th Inf. Co.I
Rielly, Jas. Gen. & Staff, Arty. Maj.
Rielly, John W. GA Cav. 1st Bn. Lamar's Co., Brailsford's Co. Sgt.
Rielly, Mike LA Mil. 2nd Regt. 3rd Brig. 1st Div.
Rielly, P. LA Mil. 3rd Regt. 1st Brig. 1st Div. Co.K
Rielly, Pat. LA 1st Hvy.Arty. (Reg.) Co.E
Riels, John MS Inf. 7th Bn. Co.B
Riely, --- TX 5th Cav. Co.E
Riely, Brent VA 23rd Cav. Co.M
Riely, F. MD Cav. 2nd Bn. Co.F
Riely, James P. VA 1st Cav. 1st Co.D
Riely, James P. VA 6th Cav. Co.D
Riely, John GA Siege Arty. 28th Bn. Co.E
Riely, John P. VA 17th Inf. Co.H
Riely, John W. VA 4th Inf. Co.I
Riely, John W. Gen. & Staff Lt.Col.
Riely, Michael VA 17th Inf. Co.G
Riely, Patrick VA 17th Inf. Co.G Sgt.
Riely, W. MD Cav. 2nd Bn. Co.A
Riely, W.B. MD 1st Cav. Co.G
Riely, William AR 15th Inf. Co.A Sgt.
Riely, William A. VA 1st Cav. 1st Co.D
Rieman, A. LA Mil. 4th Regt.Eur.Brig. Co.B
Rieman, Emile SC Arty.Bn. Hampton Legion Co.A Cpl.
Riemann, Emile SC Horse Arty. (Washington Arty.) Vol. Hart's Co.
Riemenschneider, H.V. TX 12th Inf. Co.A
Riemenschneider, Lorenz TX 36th Cav. Co.G
Riemer, Adam AR 15th (Josey's) Inf. Co.D
Riemer, G. TX Waul's Legion Co.C
Rien, Henrich TN 15th Inf. Co.H
Riend, N. LA Mil. 4th Regt. 2nd Brig. 1st Div. Co.A
Rienhard, George LA O'Hara's Co. (Pelican Guards,Co.B)
Rienhardt, M.R. AL 25th Inf. Co.C
Rienhart, Nathaniel F. GA 23rd Inf. Co.G 1st Lt.
Rienow, William LA Mil. 4th Regt. 1st Brig. 1st Div. Co.D Orderly
Rienzi, Joseph MO 2nd Cav. Co.H Sgt.
Rier, William MS Inf. 2nd Bn. Co.F
Rier, William MS 48th Inf. Co.F
Riera, A. AL 15th Cav. Co.D
Riera, Albert FL Cav. 3rd Bn. Co.B
Riera, Anthony FL Cav. 3rd Bn. Co.B
Riera, Ramon LA Mil. 5th Regt.Eur.Brig. (Spanish Regt.) Co.4
Rierden, Lawrence TX 6th Inf. Co.D
Rierdon, Mark MO 4th Cav. Co.I
Rierson, Andrew J. VA Cav. 47th Bn. Aldredge's Co.
Rierson, C.A. TX Vol. Rainey's Co.
Rierson, C.N. MO 2nd Inf. Co.F
Rierson, H.W. NC 21st Inf. Co.F Sgt.
Rierson, James NC 53rd Inf. Co.H
Rierson, J.J. MS Inf. 2nd Bn. Co.F
Rierson, J.J. MS 48th Inf. Co.F
Rierson, John Henry TX 20th Cav. Co.C 2nd Lt.
Rierson, John W. NC 21st Inf. Co.G
Rierson, John W. NC 53rd Inf. Co.G Maj.
Rierson, Samuel M. NC 52nd Inf. Co.D 2nd Lt.

Rierson, S.W. NC 21st Inf. Co.G
Rierson, William D. NC 21st Inf. Co.F
Rierson, William P. NC 53rd Inf. Co.H 1st Sgt.
Rierton, Michael TN Inf. 154th Sr.Regt. Co.C
Ries, August LA 2nd Inf. Co.B
Ries, August Conf.Inf. Tucker's Regt. Co.B
Ries, C.F. VA 2nd Inf.Loc.Def. Co.K
Ries, C.F. VA Inf. 2nd Bn.Loc.Def. Co.B
Ries, Charles F. LA 1st (Nelligan's) Inf. Co.C,A
Ries, Chr. LA Mil. 4th Regt.Eur.Brig. Co.B
Ries, Christian Conf.Inf. Tucker's Regt. Co.B
Ries, F.J. LA Mil.Conf.Guards Regt. Co.F Sgt.
Ries, H. LA 18th Inf. Co.G
Ries, Henry LA Mil. 3rd Regt. 1st Brig. 1st Div. Co.D
Ries, Hy LA Inf.Crescent Regt. Co.D
Ries, John H. LA 7th Cav. Co.K Lt.
Ries, M. LA 21st (Kennedy's) Inf. Co.D 1st Sgt.
Ries, Phillip LA 21st (Kennedy's) Inf. Co.C
Riesbeck, J. LA Mil.Squad. Guides d'Orleans
Riesdorf, Adam KY 2nd Cav. Co.C
Riese, Adam LA 20th Inf. Co.C
Riese, S. TN Arty. Stewart's Co.
Riesel, H. TX Inf. 4th Bn. (Oswald's) Co.B
Riesel, Henry TX 1st Hvy.Arty. Co.C
Riesner, Theo. TX Lt.Arty. Dege's Bn.
Riesner, W.P. AL 46th Inf. Co.G
Rieter, Aug. LA Mil. 3rd Regt. 3rd Brig. 1st Div. Co.C
Rietti, David C. MS 10th Inf.
Rietti, D.C. MS 9th Inf. Co.G
Rietti, J.C. MS 9th Inf. Co.G 1st Sgt.
Rietto, John G. MS 10th Inf. New Co.D, Co.A 1st Sgt.
Rieu, --- LA Mil.3rd Regt.Eur.Brig. (Garde Francaise) Co.5
Rieux, Felix LA Mil. 6th Regt.Eur.Brig. (Italian Guards Bn.)
Rieves, A.B.C. VA 3rd (Archer's) Bn.Res. Co.C
Rieves, Andrew NC 6th Cav. (65th St.Troops) Co.B
Rieves, C.A.B. MS 44th Inf. Co.H
Rieves, E.N.B. TN 48th (Nixon's) Inf. Co.C
Rieves, F.A. AR Lt.Arty. Owen's Btty.
Rieves, G.H. AL 59th Inf. Co.K
Rieves, Henry NC 4th Inf. Co.H
Rieves, Henry D. TX Inf. Griffin's Bn. Co.D
Rieves, H.F. AL 33rd Inf. Co.F
Rieves, I.C. Gillum's Regt. Co.F
Rieves, I.E. AL 2nd Cav. Co.G
Rieves, J. TX 14th Field Btty.
Rieves, James A. VA 3rd (Archer's) Bn.Res. Co.C
Rieves, James M. MS 37th Inf. Co.E
Rieves, J.B. GA Floyd Legion (St.Guards) Co.B Cpl.
Rieves, John C. MS Cav. 6th Bn. Prince's Co.
Rieves, John T. TX 35th (Brown's) Cav. Co.F Sgt.
Rieves, J.T. AR 37th Inf. Co.A
Rieves, J.T. MS Scouts Morphis' Ind.Co.
Rieves, M.A. MS Part.Rangers Armistead's Co.
Rieves, N.C. TX 8th Cav. Co.F
Rieves, Perry NC Inf. 2nd Bn. Co.F
Rieves, Peter AL 21st Inf. Co.I
Rieves, R.H. GA 22nd Inf. Co.E
Rieves, Richard AL Mil. 2nd Regt.Vol. Co.B

Rieves, Richard B. TN 2nd (Robison's) Inf. Co.K
Rieves, R.M. MO 11th Inf. Co.H
Rieves, Stanfield AR 1st Mtd.Rifles Co.B
Rieves, Thomas W 8th (Dearing's) Conf.Cav. Co.C Sgt.
Rieves, William MS 1st (Patton's) Inf. Co.B
Rieves, William H.C. NC 26th Inf. Co.G
Rieves, W.J. AR 18th Inf. Co.D Sgt.
Rieves, Woodson MO 9th Bn.S.S. Co.D
Rievis, David R. NC 8th Sr.Res. Daniel's Co.
Rievs, William R. NC 11th (Bethel Regt.) Inf. Co.E
Riezart, Remy LA Mil. 3rd Regt. 1st Brig. 1st Div. Co.H
Rife, A.J. MS T.P. Montgomery's Co.
Rife, Andrew J. MS 35th Inf. Co.G
Rife, Archibald S. VA 52nd Inf. Co.C
Rife, David J. VA 5th Inf. Co.H
Rife, David M. VA Cav. Hounshell's Bn. Thurman's Co.
Rife, David M. VA 52nd Inf. Co.C
Rife, Furnandus VA 1st Cav.St.Line Co.A
Rife, Gerard VA 5th Inf. Co.H
Rife, Gorden W. VA Cav. 34th Bn. Co.A
Rife, Grandvill VA 129th Mil. Buchanon's Co.
Rife, Gustavus H. MO 12th Inf. Co.K Cpl.
Rife, J. TX Cav. Baird's Regt. Co.C
Rife, James MS 12th Cav. Co.I Sgt.
Rife, J.H. MD Cav. 2nd Bn. Co.C
Rife, J.M. MS T.P. Montgomery's Co.
Rife, John VA 1st Cav.St.Line Co.A
Rife, John J. VA 8th Bn.Res. Co.B
Rife, Joseph LA 1st (Strawbridge's) Inf. Co.A
Rife, J.W. LA Inf. 4th Bn. Co.E
Rife, Lewis VA Mtd.Riflemen Balfour's Co.
Rife, N.F. VA Lt.Arty. Fry's Co.
Rife, Patison VA 1st Cav.St.Line Co.A
Rife, Stewart S. VA Inf. 26th Bn. Co.F
Rife, Thomas E. TX 36th Cav. Co.H
Rife, William VA 67th Mil. Co.C
Rife, William E. MS 35th Inf. Co.G Cpl.
Rife, William W. MS Cav. Jeff Davis Legion Co.A
Riff, Joseph LA 13th Inf. Co.D
Riffaler, Henry TN 41st Inf.
Riffe, Abram MO Robertson's Regt.St.Guard Co.11
Riffe, Fernandez VA 36th Inf. 1st Co.B
Riffe, Gordon W. VA 22nd Cav. Co.B Capt.
Riffe, Henry M. VA Inf. 45th Bn. Co.A
Riffe, Jacob VA 146th Mil. Co.E
Riffe, Jeremiah KY 2nd Bn.Mtd.Rifles Co.D 2nd Lt.
Riffe, J.M. AR 1st Mtd.Rifles Co.B
Riffe, J.M. MO 3rd Inf. Co.I
Riffe, John VA 17th Cav. Co.H
Riffe, John VA 36th Inf. 1st Co.B, 2nd Co.D
Riffe, John H. AR 32nd Inf. Co.K
Riffe, John S. VA Lt.Arty. G.B. Chapman's Co. Cpl.
Riffe, John S. VA 166th Mil. Ballard's Co.
Riffe, Joshua AR 1st (Colquitt's) Inf. Co.B
Riffe, J.P. AR 6th Inf. New Co.C
Riffe, J.P. AR 12th Inf. Co.A Sgt.
Riffe, Lewis VA Inf. 45th Bn. Co.D
Riffe, Lewis F. VA Inf. 26th Bn. Co.F
Riffe, Louis VA 22nd Cav. Co.B Cpl.

Riffe, Owen S. VA 30th Bn.S.S. Co.A Sgt.

Riffe, R.K. MO 12th Cav. Co.K Cpl.

Riffe, Samuel C. VA Lt.Arty. G.B. Chapman's
Co.

Riffe, Samuel C. VA 166th Mil. Ballard's Co.

Riffe, William VA Inf. 45th Bn. Co.D

Riffe, William D. VA Inf. 26th Bn. Co.C

Riffe, William L. TX 16th Cav. Co.K Sgt.

Riffee, Amos D. VA 22nd Inf. Co.B

Riffee, George A. VA 9th Inf. 1st Co.A

Riffee, Hezekiah VA 17th Cav. Co.H

Riffee, Jacob VA 5th Inf. Co.K

Riffee, John VA Cav. 46th Bn. Co.D

Riffee, Samuel VA 60th Inf. Co.G

Riffett, Thomas KY 5th Mtd.Inf.

Riffey, David VA 25th Cav. Co.F

Riffey, George VA 48th Inf. Co.B

Riffey, James VA 157th Mil. Co.B

Riffey, John AR 23rd Inf. Co.H

Riffey, N. VA 22nd Inf. Co.F

Riffey, Noah VA 157th Mil. Co.B

Riffey, William H. VA 12th Cav. Co.K

Riffie, George A. VA Lt.Arty. Griffin's Co.

Riffie, Jacob VA Cav. 35th Bn. Co.A

Riffie, William VA 30th Bn.S.S. Co.C

Rifflard, J.L. LA Mil. Orleans Guards Regt.
Co.A

Riffle, A.C. VA 20th Cav. Co.C

Riffle, Anthony VA 3rd Cav. & Inf.St.Line Co.A

Riffle, A.R. VA 31st Inf. Co.F

Riffle, Benjamin VA 19th Cav. Co.B

Riffle, Charles VA 62nd Mtd.Inf. 2nd Co.G

Riffle, Edward R. VA 19th Cav. Co.B Cpl.

Riffle, G.W. VA 20th Cav. Co.C

Riffle, Henry KY 3rd Cav. Co.A

Riffle, Isaac VA 62nd Mtd.Inf. 2nd Co.G

Riffle, Isaac VA 3rd Cav. & Inf.St.Line Co.A

Riffle, Jeremiah KY 2nd Cav. Co.D 2nd Lt.

Riffle, Martin VA 22nd Inf. Co.E

Riffle, Martin V. VA 14th Cav. Co.L

Riffle, Martin V. VA 17th Cav. Co.I

Riffle, William TN Inf. Harman's Regt. Co.K

Riffle, William A. VA 22nd Inf. Co.E Cpl.

Riffo, A.J. AL 12th Inf. Co.G

Riffy, Harvy W. VA 11th Cav. Co.B

Rigand, L. GA Cobb's Legion Co.K

Rigant, Jules TX Lt.Arty. Jones' Co.

Rigany, I.I. NC Inf. 2nd Bn. Co.G

Rigaud, Joseph LA Mil. 2nd Regt. French Brig.
Co.5

Rigbey, A.J. VA 51st Mil.

Rigbey, James J. FL 2nd Cav. Co.A

Rigby, A.D. TX 1st Inf. Co.M

Rigby, A.H. TX Cav. Waller's Regt. Menard's
Co. Jr.2nd Lt.

Rigby, A.H TX 20th Inf. Co.K Cpl.

Rigby, Allen Samuel SC 5th Cav. Co.H Cpl.

Rigby, B.J. TX Cav. Waller's Regt. Menard's
Co.

Rigby, C.P. SC 1st Cav. Co.E

Rigby, C.R. TN 46th Inf. Co.C

Rigby, C.S. SC 1st Cav. Co.E

Rigby, E.G. AL 23rd Inf. Co.A

Rigby, E.L. SC 24th Inf. Co.C

Rigby, Eli TX 9th (Nichols') Inf. Co.I

Rigby, Eli TX 20th Inf. Co.K Music.

Rigby, G.O. MS Cav. 3rd Bn.Res. Co.C

Rigby, Irwin GA 3rd Res. Co.B

Rigby, J. GA 5th Res. Co.B

Rigby, James J. FL 11th Inf. Co.H

Rigby, J.C. SC 2nd Inf. Co.I

Rigby, Jesse AL 3rd Bn.Res. Co.C

Rigby, Jesse AL St.Res. Co.C

Rigby, J.F. AL 28th Inf. Co.C

Rigby, John GA 35th Inf. Co.D

Rigby, John O. TX 25th Cav. Co.D Sgt.

Rigby, John R. MS 20th Inf. Co.H

Rigby, Lawson AL 40th Inf. Co.D

Rigby, Russell E. TX Cav. Baylor's Regt. Co.E

Rigby, S.A. SC Cav. 14th Bn. Co.A

Rigbys, S.M. MS 36th Inf. Co.F

Rigby, S.T. AL 23rd Inf. Co.C,A

Rigby, Stephen J. AL 36th Inf. Co.G

Rigby, Tillman AL Lt.Arty. 20th Bn. Co.A

Rigby, W.B. TN 46th Inf. Co.C Cpl.

Rigby, William NC 1st Inf. Co.G

Rigby, William TX 28th Cav. Co.E

Rigby, William TX 20th Inf. Co.K 1st Lt.

Rigby, William B. TX Cav. Baylor's Regt. Co.E

Rigby, William J. MS 15th Inf. Co.A

Rigbys, John MS 1st (Percy's) Inf. Co.I

Rigdan, John GA 3rd Inf. Co.C

Rigdell, J.W. GA 11th Cav. (St.Guards) Staten's
Co.

Rigden, Jo Berry SC 2nd Rifles Co.H

Rigden, Joe Berry AL 19th Inf. Co.H

Rigden, John H. SC 2nd Rifles Co.H

Rigden, J.W. LA 13th Bn. (Part.Rangers) Co.F

Rigden, Miles SC 2nd Rifles Co.H

Rigden, Thomas B. SC 2nd Rifles Co.H

Rigden, William H. SC 2nd Rifles Co.H

Rigdin, G.W. AL 29th Inf. Co.K

Rigdon, Adam W. GA 47th Inf. Co.F

Rigdon, Benjamin NC 2nd Arty. (36th St.Troops)
Co.I

Rigdon, Benjamin NC 3rd Arty. (40th St.Troops)
Co.G

Rigdon, Benjamin H. AL 29th Inf. Co.K

Rigdon, B.G. GA 49th Inf. Co.F

Rigdon, B.H. SC Lt.Arty. Beauregard's Co.

Rigdon, Daniel R. GA 9th Inf. Co.I

Rigdon, Edward M. GA 2nd Res. Co.C

Rigdon, Edward M. GA 26th Inf. Co.K

Rigdon, E.H. MS 5th Inf. (St.Troops) Co.D

Rigdon, Enoch H. MS Lt.Arty. Turner's Co.

Rigdon, Enoch H. MS 14th Inf. Co.B

Rigdon, Ephraim AR 3rd Cav. Co.K

Rigdon, Ephraim M. LA 16th Inf. Co.I

Rigdon, George B. MO 11th Inf. Co.H

Rigdon, Green B. GA 47th Inf. Co.F

Rigdon, G.W. NC Mil. Clark's Sp.Bn. Co.A

Rigdon, Henry H. GA 47th Inf. Co.F

Rigdon, Jacob, Jr. LA Res.Corps Allston's Co.

Rigdon, James MS 22nd Inf. Co.G

Rigdon, J.J. LA 6th Cav.

Rigdon, J.M. MS 5th Inf. (St.Troops) Co.A

Rigdon, J.M. SC 2nd Rifles Co.B

Rigdon, John T. AL 29th Inf. Co.G

Rigdon, S.L. TX 16th Inf. Co.D

Rigdon, S.T. GA Cav. 8th Bn. (St.Guards) Co.B

Rigdon, T.C. GA 1st (Symons') Res. Co.F,E

Rigdon, Thomas S. GA 49th Inf. Co.F

Rigdon, W. GA Inf. Rigdon Guards Jr.2nd Lt.

Rigdon, William AL 29th Inf. Co.K

Rigdon, William GA 9th Inf. Co.I

Rigdon, W.J. LA 4th Cav. Co.E

Rigdon, Wyly GA 9th Inf. Co.I

Rigel, John B. TX 3rd Inf. 1st Co.A

Rigell, Jason GA 31st Inf. Co.C

Rigell, W.H. GA 10th Mil.

Rigell, W.T. GA 7th Cav. Co.E

Rigell, W.T. GA Cav. 21st Bn. Co.B

Rigello, Antonio LA 10th Inf. Co.I Sgt.

Riger, Emil LA Mil. Chalmette Regt. Co.G

Riger, Joseph LA Inf. 10th Bn. Co.H

Riger, Ph. LA Mil. Chalmette Regt. Co.G

Rigethe, James LA 5th Inf. Co.I

Rigg, G.W. TX 17th Cons.Dismtd.Cav. Co.D

Rigg, G.W. TX 18th Cav. Co.F

Rigg, Henry B. KY 4th Cav. Co.B

Rigg, James NC 8th Bn.Part.Rangers Co.C

Rigg, John F. MS 16th Inf. Co.D Cpl.

Rigg, R.A. TX Cav. McCord's Frontier Regt.
Co.C

Rigg, R.C. MO 1st & 3rd Cons.Cav. Co.D 2nd
S.Sgt.

Rigg, Richard C. MO 1st Cav. Co.E

Rigg, Robert Gen. & Staff, Ord.Dept.

Rigg, W.A. TX 17th Cons.Dismtd.Cav. Co.D

Rigg, William MS 18th Inf. Co.H

Rigg, William VA 8th Cav. Co.I

Rigg, William C. Gen. & Staff Asst.Surg.

Riggan, B.A. VA 2nd Inf.Loc.Def. Co.D

Riggan, Benjamin J. MS 2nd Inf. Co.H

Riggan, B.F. MS 2nd St.Cav. 1st Co.C,F 1st
Sgt.

Riggan, B.F. MS 43rd Inf. Co.C

Riggan, Charles D. NC 30th Inf. Co.B

Riggan, Charles S. NC 30th Inf. Co.B

Riggan, Daniel N. TN 7th Inf. Co.K

Riggan, Daniel R. NC 14th Inf. Co.A

Riggan, George W. NC 46th Inf. Co.C

Riggan, Gideon B. NC 46th Inf. Co.C

Riggan, Isham S. NC 30th Inf. Co.B

Riggan, James NC 31st Inf. Co.E

Riggan, James M. AR 37th Inf. Co.H

Riggan, James V. MS Inf. 3rd Bn. (St.Troops)
Co.B

Riggan, J.B. MS 2nd Cav. Co.I

Riggan, Jeremiah B. NC 46th Inf. Co.C

Riggan, J.F. NC 3rd Bn.Sr.Res. Williams' Co.

Riggan, J.F. NC 12th Inf. Co.K

Riggan, J.L. MS 2nd Cav. Co.I

Riggan, J.L. MS 43rd Inf. Co.E

Riggan, J.N. MS 5th Inf. Co.A

Riggan, John AR 3rd Inf. Co.I

Riggan, John SC 7th Res. Co.G

Riggan, John G. NC 46th Inf. Co.C

Riggan, John H. NC 12th Inf. Co.F

Riggan, John H. NC 43rd Inf. Co.G

Riggan, Joseph M. NC 28th Inf. Co.A

Riggan, J.W. MS Inf. 3rd Bn. (St.Troops) Co.B

Riggan, Mathew H. NC 1st Inf. Co.I

Riggan, Minga E. NC 30th Inf. Co.B

Riggan, Mingo E. NC 46th Inf. Co.C 1st Sgt.

Riggan, Peter R. NC 46th Inf. Co.C

Riggan, Richard NC 1st Inf. Co.I

Riggan, Robert H. NC 54th Inf. Co.H

Riggan, Shugar A. NC 30th Inf. Co.B

Riggan, W. NC Mallett's Bn. (Cp.Guard)

Riggan, W.C. MS 2nd St.Cav. 1st Co.C

Riggan, W.C. MS 5th Inf. Co.A 1st Sgt.
Riggan, Willoughby VA Hvy.Arty. 19th Bn.
Co.A
Riggans, J.C. AR 2nd Cav. Co.E
Riggans, W. AL 35th Inf. Co.E
Riggart, J.P. SC 13th Inf. Co.D
Riggen, Joseph MS 2nd Cav. Co.B
Riggen, Linzey MS 2nd Cav. Co.B
Riggen, R.T. KY 9th Cav. Co.H Capt.
Riggens, R.G. GA 26th Inf. Co.E
Rigger, W. LA 30th Inf. Co.A
Riggers, Samuel MO 11th Inf. Co.H
Riggin, Austin V. MO Inf. 4th Regt.St.Guard
Co.C
Riggin, George W. MO Inf. 4th Regt.St.Guard
Co.C
Riggin, G.F. TX 4th Inf. Co.D
Riggin, H.C. TX 3rd Cav. Co.B
Riggin, Henry C. AR Lt.Arty. Rivers' Btty. 2nd
Lt.
Riggin, Henry C. 1st Choctaw & Chickasaw
Mtd.Rifles 1st Co.K 1st Sgt.
Riggin, Isaac N. MS 12th Inf. Co.A
Riggin, Jesse B. VA Hvy.Arty. 18th Bn. Co.C
Riggin, Jessee MS 1st Lt.Arty. Co.F
Riggin, John GA Inf. 25th Bn. (Prov.Guard)
Co.A
Riggin, John H. MO 5th Inf. Co.I Sgt.Maj.
Riggin, Jno. H. Gen. & Staff Chap.
Riggin, John W. MS 22nd Inf. Co.B
Riggin, J.W. Gen. & Staff Surg.
Riggin, P.B. Forrest's Scouts A. Harvey's
Co.,CSA
Riggin, R.T. SC 3rd Bn.Res. Co.D
Riggin, Thomas D. MO Inf. 4th Regt.St.Guard
Co.C
Riggin, William T. LA 28th (Gray's) Inf. Co.I,F
Riggings, James SC 12th Inf. Co.G
Riggins, Abner AL 12th Inf. Co.G
Riggins, A.D. GA 28th Inf. Co.E Bvt.2nd Lt.
Riggins, A.L. GA 18th Inf. Co.M
Riggins, A.L. GA 28th Inf. Co.F
Riggins, Allen SC 2nd Rifles Co.L,B
Riggins, Allen SC 3rd Inf. Co.I 1st Sgt.
Riggins, Allen SC 3rd Res. Co.I 1st Sgt.
Riggins, A.R. SC 22nd Inf. Co.F
Riggins, Asberry G. AR 14th (Powers') Inf.
Co.B Cpl.
Riggins, B.B. AL 44th Inf. Co.H
Riggins, Britton W. GA 55th Inf. Co.F
Riggins, Carter AL 43rd Inf. Co.A Sgt.
Riggins, Cave J. TN 49th Inf. Co.A
Riggins, Cave J. Inf. Bailey's Cons.Regt. Co.G
Riggins, Charles A. VA 14th Inf. Co.E
Riggins, Charles D. NC 4th Sr.Res. Co.I
Riggins, C.M. TN 43rd Inf. Co.H
Riggins, David VA Arty. J.W. Drewry's Co.
Riggins, Dolby AL 44th Inf. Co.E
Riggins, Edward T. VA 3rd Cav. Co.A Cpl.
Riggins, Ellick GA Cav. 22nd Bn. (St.Guards)
Co.G
Riggins, F.A. GA 20th Inf. Co.K
Riggins, Francis M. MO 1st Cav. Co.B
Riggins, Franklin M. MO 2nd Cav. 3rd Co.K
Riggins, George B. TN 14th Inf. Co.L
Riggins, George D. AR 34th Inf. Co.A
Riggins, George L. KY Cav. Bolen's Ind.Co.

Riggins, George T. MO 2nd Cav. 3rd Co.K
Riggins, George W. MO 2nd Cav. Co.K
Riggins, Geo. W. Gen. & Staff Surg.
Riggins, G.L. TN Cav.
Riggins, Green B. NC 6th Sr.Res. Co.F Sgt.
Riggins, J. AL 30th Inf. Co.A
Riggins, J. GA Lt.Arty. Clinch's Btty.
Riggins, J. SC Cav. 10th Bn. Co.B
Riggins, James GA 2nd Inf. 1st Co.B
Riggins, James GA 26th Inf. Co.E
Riggins, James NC 4th Inf. Co.I
Riggins, James E. AL 11th Inf. Co.A
Riggins, Jas. E. AL 21st Inf. Co.C
Riggins, James M. GA 23rd Inf. Co.G
Riggins, James M. NC 48th Inf. Co.K
Riggins, James R. AR 14th (Powers') Inf. Co.B
Riggins, Jasper GA 56th Inf. Co.D
Riggins, J.D. TN 49th Inf. Co.G
Riggins, J.D. Inf. Bailey's Cons.Regt. Co.C
Riggins, J.E. AL 43rd Inf. Co.D
Riggins, Jesse B. VA Arty. J.W. Drewry's Co.
Riggins, J.H. MS Cav. 3rd Bn. (Ashcraft's) Co.F
Riggins, J.J. MS 8th Cav. Co.G
Riggins, J.M. SC 4th Inf. Co.H
Riggins, J.N. TN 17th Inf. Co.B Sgt.
Riggins, Joel TN 14th Inf. Co.G 1st Sgt.
Riggins, John AR 14th (Powers') Inf. Co.B
Riggins, John AR 34th Inf. Co.A
Riggins, John B. GA Cav. Hendry's Co.
(Atlantic & Gulf Guards) Sgt.
Riggins, John B. GA 26th Inf. Co.E
Riggins, John H. GA 24th Inf.
Riggins, John H. TN Cav. 16th Bn. (Neal's)
Co.B
Riggins, John J. VA 18th Inf. Co.F
Riggins, John M. MO Cav. 7th Regt.St.Guard
Co.D 3rd Lt.
Riggins, J.R. GA 26th Inf. Co.E 2nd Lt.
Riggins, Levi VA 32nd Inf. 2nd Co.K
Riggins, Levi VA 115th Mil. Co.D
Riggins, Moses T. NC 2nd Inf. Co.F
Riggins, M.W. GA 6th Inf. (St.Guards) Co.E
Sgt.
Riggins, Napoleon B. MO 2nd Cav. 3rd Co.K
Riggins, Nathaniel NC 33rd Inf. Co.I
Riggins, Newton GA 56th Inf. Co.D
Riggins, Nicholas A. TN 14th Inf. Co.L
Riggins, Peter NC 35th Inf. Co.F
Riggins, Reuben TN 49th Inf. Co.A
Riggins, R.J. SC 5th Inf. 2nd Co.D
Riggins, Robert NC 7th Inf. Co.D
Riggins, Robert TN 1st Cav.
Riggins, Robert D. VA 38th Inf. Co.G
Riggins, Robert G. GA Cav. Hendry's Co.
(Atlantic & Gulf Guards)
Riggins, Robert G. GA 26th Inf. Co.F
Riggins, Robert R. MO 1st Cav. Co.B Sgt.
Riggins, Robert R. MO 2nd Cav. 3rd Co.K Sgt.
Riggins, R.W. TN 17th Inf. Co.B Cpl.
Riggins, Samuel H. AL 4th Cav. Co.I
Riggins, Silas W. TN 19th Inf. Co.H
Riggins, Stephen E. VA Arty. J.W. Drewry's
Co.
Riggins, T.G. AL 23rd Inf. Co.G
Riggins, Thomas GA 4th (Clinch's) Cav. Co.G
Riggins, Thomas TN 19th Inf. Co.H
Riggins, Thomas TN 43rd Inf. Co.D

Riggins, Thomas G. AL Inf. 32nd Regt. Co.F
Riggins, Thomas H. AR 26th Inf. Co.F Cpl.
Riggins, Thomas P. VA 1st Arty. Co.G
Riggins, Thomas P. VA 32nd Inf. 1st Co.I
Riggins, T.T. TN 49th Inf. Co.G
Riggins, W.B. GA 53rd Inf. Co.H
Riggins, William GA 3rd Cav. Co.F
Riggins, William GA 26th Inf. Co.F
Riggins, William SC 22nd Inf. Co.F
Riggins, William H. VA 56th Inf. Co.A
Riggins, William J. AR 27th Inf. Co.K
Riggins, William P. SC 1st (Orr's) Rifles Co.A
Riggins, William W. AL 4th Cav.
Riggins, William W. GA 50th Inf. Co.A
Riggle, A. VA 51st Mil. Co.F
Riggle, Abraham MO Inf. 3rd Bn. Co.A
Riggle, A.F. MO 9th Bn.S.S. Co.C
Riggle, A.F. MO 16th Inf. Co.D
Riggle, A.J. MO 9th Bn.S.S. Co.C
Riggle, B. LA 1st Cav. Co.I
Riggle, Calvin TN 2nd (Smith's) Cav. Rankin's
Co.
Riggle, Calvin TN 4th (McLemore's) Cav. Co.H
Riggle, Ezekiel VA 48th Inf. Co.F
Riggle, George VA 2nd Inf. Co.I
Riggle, George W. VA 21st Cav. Co.K
Riggle, Jacob MO Inf. 3rd Bn. Co.A
Riggle, Jacob MO 9th Bn.S.S. Co.C Cpl.
Riggle, Jacob MO 16th Inf. Co.D
Riggle, J.M. AL 4th (Russell's) Cav. Co.E
Riggle, John MO 16th Inf. Co.B
Riggle, John D. TX 7th Inf.
Riggle, John W. TX 10th Cav. Co.A 2nd Lt.
Riggle, John W. TX Inf. Yarbrough's Co. (Smith
Cty.Lt.Inf.)
Riggle, John W. VA 2nd Inf. Co.I
Riggle, John W. VA 37th Inf. Co.K
Riggle, Joseph VA 20th Cav. Co.A
Riggle, N.P. MO 16th Inf. Co.D
Riggle, Phillip LA 21st (Kennedy's) Inf. Co.B
Riggle, Reuben S. TX 18th Cav. Co.B 1st Sgt.
Riggle, Wallace S. TX 3rd Cav. Co.K Sgt.
Riggle, William VA 48th Inf. Co.F
Riggle, Zachariah W. VA 48th Inf. Co.F
Riggleman, Harvey VA 25th Inf. 1st Co.K
Riggleman, Jacob VA 31st Inf. Co.F Cpl.
Riggleman, Josh. A. VA 62nd Mtd.Inf. 2nd Co.F
Riggleman, Joshua A. VA 25th Inf. 2nd Co.E
Riggleman, Washington VA 25th Inf. 2nd Co.E
Rigglemen, William VA 11th Cav. Co.C
Riggles, Jacob MO 2nd Inf. Co.H
Riggles, John TX 14th Inf. Co.B
Riggon, W.H. AL 42nd Inf. Co.K,H
Riggs, --- SC Inf. 1st (Charleston) Bn. Co.A
Riggs, --- TX Cav. Good's Bn. Co.C
Riggs, --- TX Cav. Good's Bn. Co.D
Riggs, --- TX Cav. Steele's Command Co.A
Riggs, A.B. GA 1st (Symons') Res. Co.D
Riggs, A.B. NC 12th Inf. Co.M
Riggs, Abraham B. GA 61st Inf. Co.B,K
Riggs, A.J. NC 27th Inf. Co.A Sgt.
Riggs, Albert NC 3rd Cav. Co.H
Riggs, Albert E. AL Lt.Arty. Phelan's Co.
Riggs, Alexander VA 8th Cav. Co.F
Riggs, Alphis B. NC 32nd Inf. Co.B
Riggs, A.S. GA 1st Cav. Co.E
Riggs, Augustus L. MS 2nd Inf. Co.K

Riggs, Azariah J. NC 1st Arty. (10th St.Troops) Co.F 1st Lt.
Riggs, B. TX 4th Cav. Co.D
Riggs, Barrus NC 3rd Inf. Co.G
Riggs, Bazel M. NC 3rd Inf. Co.G Drum.
Riggs, Benjamin F. KY 2nd (Duke's) Cav. Co.B 2nd Lt.
Riggs, Benjamin F. KY 2nd Mtd.Inf. Co.H
Riggs, Benjamin H. AL 3rd Cav. Co.C
Riggs, Benjamin H. MS 7th Inf. Asst.Surg.
Riggs, Benjamin H. SC Hvy.Arty. 15th (Lucas') Bn. Co.C
Riggs, Benjamin H. SC Arty. Childs' Co.
Riggs, Benjamin H. SC Arty. Lee's Co.
Riggs, Benj. H. Gen. & Staff Surg.
Riggs, Benjamin S. SC 1st (McCreary's) Inf. Co.H,C
Riggs, B.F. MO 10th Cav. Co.F
Riggs, B.H. MS 9th Inf. Surg.
Riggs, B.K. AR 27th Inf. Co.I 2nd Lt.
Riggs, Bryan NC 3rd Arty. (40th St.Troops) Co.G
Riggs, Bryant NC 2nd Arty. (36th St.Troops) Co.I
Riggs, C. AR 1st (Monroe's) Cav. Co.E
Riggs, C. NC 1st Jr.Res. Co.I
Riggs, C. NC 3rd Inf. Co.C
Riggs, Calvin AL 8th Cav. Co.A
Riggs, C.H. AL 18th Inf. Co.I
Riggs, Charles TX Cav. Baird's Regt. Co.B
Riggs, Charles VA 8th Cav. Co.I
Riggs, Charles P. AL 3rd Cav. Co.H Bugler
Riggs, Christopher C. NC 28th Inf. Co.A Sgt.
Riggs, Clarence R. NC Loc.Def. Griswold's Co.
Riggs, Clesly AR 50th Mil. Co.G
Riggs, Cole MS 16th Inf. Co.D
Riggs, Cyrus AR 10th Mil.
Riggs, D.A. LA 13th Inf. Co.G
Riggs, Daniel NC 18th Inf. Co.I,D,F
Riggs, David AR 12th Inf. Co.D
Riggs, Dickson NC 5th Inf. Co.I
Riggs, E.C. MO Robertson's Regt.St.Guard Co.9
Riggs, Ed. LA Inf. 1st Sp.Bn. (Wheat's) Co.D
Riggs, Edward W.O. NC 3rd Inf. Co.G
Riggs, E.J. LA Inf. 1st Sp.Bn. (Wheat's) Co.D
Riggs, Ellis GA 11th Cav. (St.Guards) Johnson's Co.
Riggs, E.S. LA 2nd Inf. Co.D
Riggs, Esom VA 8th Cav. 2nd Co.D
Riggs, Everett L. NC 1st Arty. (10th St.Troops) Co.G
Riggs, Everett L. NC 17th Inf. (2nd Org.) Co.G
Riggs, Felix L. KY 13th Cav. Co.D
Riggs, F.M. TN 12th (Cons.) Inf. Co.G
Riggs, F.M. TN 22nd Inf. Co.G
Riggs, Francis M. AR 27th Inf. Co.K
Riggs, Francis M. NC 21st Inf. Co.F
Riggs, Francis M. TN 3rd (Forrest's) Cav. Co.E
Riggs, G. NC 3rd Jr.Res. Co.C
Riggs, G. NC 4th Bn.Jr.Res. Co.C
Riggs, G. TX Cav. Wells' Regt. Co.H
Riggs, G.A. KY 3rd Cav. Grant's Co.
Riggs, G.A.A. LA Inf. 4th Bn. Co.E
Riggs, G.A.D. AR 7th Inf. Co.B
Riggs, G.D. KY 1st (Butler's) Cav. Co.D
Riggs, George AL 32nd Inf. Co.B

Riggs, George NC 3rd Cav. (41st St.Troops) Co.F
Riggs, George TN Douglass' Bn.Part.Rangers Coffee's Co.
Riggs, George TX Inf. 3rd St.Troops Co.B
Riggs, George C. NC 3rd Inf. Co.G
Riggs, George S. FL 7th Inf. Co.C Music.
Riggs, George S. FL Brig.Band,CSA Music.
Riggs, George T. TN 11th (Holman's) Cav. Co.H
Riggs, George W. MS 42nd Inf. Co.C
Riggs, George W. NC 4th Cav. (59th St.Troops) Co.B
Riggs, George W. NC 28th Inf. Co.A
Riggs, Gustaverus KY 4th Mtd.Inf. Co.D
Riggs, G.W. AR 2nd Cav. Co.G
Riggs, H. MS Condrey's Co. (Bull Mtn.Invinc.) Cpl.
Riggs, H.A. GA 47th Inf. Co.C Cpl.
Riggs, Harper SC 11th Res. Co.G
Riggs, Harvey MS 1st (Johnston's) Inf. Co.I
Riggs, Harvey MS 7th Inf. Co.H
Riggs, Harvey MS 41st Inf. Co.E
Riggs, Haywood NC 2nd Inf. Co.F
Riggs, H.C. TN 12th (Cons.) Inf. Co.G
Riggs, H.C. TN 22nd Inf. Co.G
Riggs, H.C. TX Cav. 2nd Bn.St.Troops Co.A
Riggs, H.C. TX 22nd Inf. Co.A Sgt.
Riggs, Henderson E. AL 42nd Inf. Co.K Cpl.
Riggs, Henry TX 11th (Spaight's) Bn.Vol. Co.E
Riggs, Henry TX 21st Inf. Co.E
Riggs, Henry VA Cav. 47th Bn. Co.B
Riggs, Hiram AR Cav. Gordon's Regt. Co.D
Riggs, Hiram F. AR 35th Inf. Co.B
Riggs, I. NC 27th Inf. Co.I Music.
Riggs, Isaac NC 3rd Cav. (41st St.Troops) Co.F
Riggs, Isaac NC 8th Inf. Co.A
Riggs, Isaac SC 1st Arty. Co.A
Riggs, Isaac SC 1st (McCreary's) Inf. Co.H
Riggs, Isaac SC 27th Inf. Co.I
Riggs, Isaac D.H. SC 1st Arty. Co.A
Riggs, Isaac M. MO 2nd Inf. Co.D
Riggs, Isaac N. NC 3rd Inf. Co.G
Riggs, I.T. TN 1st Cav. Co.A
Riggs, J. NC 12th Inf. Co.I
Riggs, Jacob GA 47th Inf. Co.C
Riggs, James AR Cav. Harrell's Bn. Co.D
Riggs, James AR 14th (Powers') Inf. Co.G
Riggs, James GA 47th Inf. Co.C
Riggs, James KY 12th Cav. Co.F
Riggs, James LA 3rd (Harrison's) Cav.
Riggs, James LA 27th Inf. Co.G
Riggs, James TN Holman's Bn.Part.Rangers Co.B
Riggs, James TN 60th Mtd.Inf. Co.H
Riggs, James TX 30th Cav. Co.C
Riggs, James B. NC 61st Inf. Co.K
Riggs, James Lou TX 6th Cav. Co.H
Riggs, James M. AR 7th Inf. Co.H 1st Lt.
Riggs, James M. AR 27th Inf. Co.I Lt.Col.
Riggs, James M. GA 10th Cav. (St.Guards) Co.D Cpl.
Riggs, James M. TN 39th Mtd.Inf. Co.E
Riggs, James R. AR 14th (Powers') Inf. Co.B
Riggs, James R. AR 27th Inf. Co.K
Riggs, James R. MS 27th Inf. Co.G Sgt.
Riggs, James S. AL 10th Inf. Co.A Cpl.

Riggs, James T. AR 3rd Cav. Co.G
Riggs, James T. AR 33rd Inf. Co.K
Riggs, James W. NC 24th Inf. Co.B
Riggs, Jasper GA 47th Inf. Co.C
Riggs, Jasper N. TN 60th Mtd.Inf. Co.H
Riggs, J.C. AR 35th Inf. Old Co.F
Riggs, J.C. MO 11th Inf. Co.H
Riggs, J.C. TN 1st (Feild's) & 27th Inf. (Cons.) Co.G
Riggs, J.D.E. LA 7th Inf. Co.B 1st Lt.
Riggs, J.D.H. SC 7th Inf. Co.A
Riggs, Jesse FL 4th Inf. Co.D
Riggs, Jesse MO 10th Inf. Co.F
Riggs, Jesse MO Cav. Freeman's Regt. Co.A
Riggs, Jesse TN 60th Mtd.Inf. Co.C
Riggs, Jessee AR 38th Inf. Co.M
Riggs, J.F.M. AR 35th Inf. Old Co.F
Riggs, J.F.M. MO 11th Inf. Co.H
Riggs, J.H. AR 62nd Mil. Co.D
Riggs, J.H. MS 3rd Inf. Co.I
Riggs, J.H. NC 3rd Bn.Sr.Res. Durham's Co.
Riggs, J.K. TN Douglass' Bn.Part.Rangers Coffee's Co.
Riggs, J.L. AR 1st (Monroe's) Cav. Co.B
Riggs, J.L. AR Lt.Arty. Hart's Btty.
Riggs, J.M. AL 9th Inf.
Riggs, J.M. FL 10th Inf. Co.A Cpl.
Riggs, J.M. GA 19th Inf.
Riggs, J.M. MS 9th Inf. Music.
Riggs, J.M. MS 10th Inf. Old Co.B Music.
Riggs, Joel AL 3rd Cav. Co.F
Riggs, Joel VA Cav. 37th Bn. Co.D
Riggs, John KY 7th Cav. Co.C
Riggs, John LA 8th Inf. Co.H
Riggs, John MS 41st Inf. Co.L Sgt.
Riggs, John NC 2nd Cav. (19th St.Troops) Co.K
Riggs, John NC 1st Arty. (10th St.Troops) Co.D Sgt.
Riggs, John NC 7th Sr.Res. Mitchell's Co.
Riggs, John SC 11th Inf. Co.G 1st Sgt.
Riggs, John TN 2nd (Ashby's) Cav. Co.I
Riggs, John TN 1st (Feild's) Inf. Co.K
Riggs, John, Sr. TN 1st (Feild's) Inf. Co.C
Riggs, John, Jr. TN 1st (Feild's) Inf. Co.K
Riggs, John TX 1st (Yager's) Cav. Co.F 1st Sgt.
Riggs, John TX 4th Inf. Co.F
Riggs, John TX Mtd.Coast Guards St.Troops Graham's Co. 1st Sgt.
Riggs, John TX Nolan's Regt.
Riggs, John VA 8th Cav. Co.I
Riggs, John VA 22nd Inf. Swann's Co.
Riggs, John VA 36th Inf. Capt.
Riggs, John A. MS 11th Inf. Co.C
Riggs, John A. TN 37th Inf. Co.C Sgt.
Riggs, John B. NC 3rd Inf. Co.G
Riggs, John C. TN 1st (Feild's) Inf. Co.G
Riggs, John D. NC 1st Arty. (10th St.Troops) Co.I
Riggs, John E. LA Conscr.
Riggs, John H. AL 10th Inf. Co.A
Riggs, John L. AR 6th Inf. 1st Co.B
Riggs, John L. AR 24th Inf. Co.G
Riggs, John M. NC 67th Inf. Co.B
Riggs, John P. TN Lt.Arty. Lynch's Co.
Riggs, John R. NC 61st Inf. Co.K
Riggs, John S. AR 12th Inf. Co.E
Riggs, John S. TX 7th Field Btty.

Riggs, John T. KY Cav. 2nd Bn. (Dortch's) Co.D

Riggs, John T. NC 1st Arty. (10th St.Troops) Co.G

Riggs, John T. NC 17th Inf. (2nd Org.) Co.B

Riggs, John W. AR 35th Inf. Co.B

Riggs, John W. FL 4th Inf. Co.G

Riggs, Joseph AR 10th Mil. Co.D

Riggs, Joseph MS 9th Cav. Co.D

Riggs, Joseph MS Cav. 17th Bn. Co.F

Riggs, Joseph NC 8th Inf. Co.A

Riggs, Joseph NC 32nd Inf. Co.B

Riggs, Joseph E. NC 61st Inf. Co.K

Riggs, Joseph S. VA 37th Inf. Co.D

Riggs, Joshua MD 1st Cav. Co.A Sgt.

Riggs, Joshua VA 1st Cav. 2nd Co.K

Riggs, Joshua D.E. FL 7th Inf. Co.B 1st Lt.

Riggs, J.R. TN 11th (Holman's) Cav. Co.H Sgt.

Riggs, J.S. AR 6th Inf. New Co.F

Riggs, J.S. TN Cav. 16th Bn. (Neal's) Co.B 1st Cpl.

Riggs, J.W. GA 47th Inf. Co.C

Riggs, J.W. VA Cav. Mosby's Regt. (Part. Rangers) Co.D

Riggs, Lafayette NC 4th Inf. Co.I

Riggs, Lafayette VA 29th Inf. 1st Co.F Sgt.

Riggs, Lafayette M. VA 64th Mtd.Inf. Co.H Sgt.

Riggs, L.C. SC 16th & 24th (Cons.) Inf. Co.C

Riggs, L.C. SC 24th Inf. Co.A

Riggs, Leonidas TX 1st (Yager's) Cav. Co.F

Riggs, Lot NC 1st Cav. (9th St.Troops) Co.A

Riggs, L.S. AZ Cav. Herbert's Bn. Helm's Co. Cpl.

Riggs, L.S. AR 2nd Cav. Co.G

Riggs, L.Y. TN 30th Inf. Co.A

Riggs, Madison VA Cav. 47th Cav. Co.B

Riggs, Mark L. TN Inf. 154th Sr.Regt. Co.E Capt.

Riggs, Martin TN 59th Mtd.Inf. Co.A

Riggs, M.C. VA 3rd Inf.Loc.Def. Co.F

Riggs, Nathaniel T. NC 4th Cav. (59th St.Troops) Co.B

Riggs, N.B. TN 12th (Cons.) Inf. Co.G

Riggs, N.B. TN 22nd Inf. Co.G Sgt.

Riggs, P.B. AR 10th Mil. Co.D Cpl.

Riggs, Pleasant M. TN 37th Inf. Co.C

Riggs, Presley B. AR 35th Inf. Co.B

Riggs, P.W. TX 30th Cav. Co.C

Riggs, R. NC 21st Inf. Co.F

Riggs, R. SC Cav. 17th Bn. Co.D

Riggs, R. VA 24th Cav. Co.F

Riggs, R.A. TN 10th Cav. Co.B

Riggs, R.A. TN 1st (Feild's) & 27th Inf. (Cons.) Co.G

Riggs, R.D. NC 42nd Inf. Co.D

Riggs, Reuben MD 1st Cav. Co.A

Riggs, R.H. LA 2nd Inf. Co.D Cpl.

Riggs, Rial NC 7th Mil. Co.C Sgt.

Riggs, Richard AL 1st Regt. Mobile Vol. Co.A

Riggs, Richard AL 4th Res. Co.B

Riggs, Richard NC 12th Inf. Co.M

Riggs, Richard NC 32nd Inf. Co.B

Riggs, Richard SC 11th Inf. Co.G

Riggs, Robert AR 33rd Inf. Co.F

Riggs, Robert LA Inf.Cons.Crescent Regt.

Riggs, Robert A. TN 1st (Feild's) Inf. Co.G Sgt.

Riggs, Robert S. NC 61st Inf. Co.K

Riggs, R.R. FL Lt.Arty. Perry's Co.

Riggs, R.T. SC Mil. 18th Regt.

Riggs, Rubin AR 31st Inf. Co.C

Riggs, Samuel LA Conscr.

Riggs, Samuel TX Cav. Madison's Regt. Co.A 1st Sgt.

Riggs, Sidney AZ Cav. Herbert's Bn. Oury's Co.

Riggs, Sion B. AL 25th Inf. Co.D

Riggs, Sion B. AL Cp. of Instr. Talladega

Riggs, S.L. TN Cav. 16th Bn. (Neal's) Co.B

Riggs, S.M. TX 4th Inf. Co.I Sgt.

Riggs, S.P. TN 59th Mtd.Inf. Co.A

Riggs, Stephen LA 27th Inf. Co.D

Riggs, Stephen J. GA 9th Inf. Co.I

Riggs, T.E. AL 9th Inf.

Riggs, Thomas AR Lt.Arty. Hart's Btty.

Riggs, Thomas AR 8th Inf. New Co.G

Riggs, Thomas AR 14th (McCarver's) Inf. Co.A

Riggs, Thomas AR 15th (N.W.) Inf. Co.D

Riggs, Thomas LA 7th Cav. Co.B

Riggs, Thomas LA Inf. 1st Sp.Bn. (Wheat's) New Co.D

Riggs, Thomas NC 1st Arty. (10th St.Troops) Co.C

Riggs, Thomas NC 5th Inf. Co.I

Riggs, Thomas NC 7th Sr.Res. Davie's Co.

Riggs, Thomas TN 16th (Logwood's) Cav. Co.F

Riggs, Thomas TX 21st Cav. Co.D

Riggs, Thomas Gen. & Staff 1st Lt.,Adj.

Riggs, Thomas D. AR Inf. Cocke's Regt. Co.I Sgt.

Riggs, Thomas E. AL 10th Inf. Co.C

Riggs, Thomas J. NC 28th Inf. Co.A

Riggs, Thomas J. TN Holman's Bn.Part.Rangers Co.D

Riggs, Thomas J. TN 1st (Feild's) Inf. Co.K

Riggs, Thomas L. SC 1st (Hagood's) Inf. 1st Co.D

Riggs, T.J. AL 42nd Inf. Co.K

Riggs, T.J. MS Condrey's Co. (Bull Mtn.Invinc.)

Riggs, T.J. TN 11th (Holman's) Cav. Co.K

Riggs, T.L. SC 16th & 24th (Cons.) Inf. Co.C Cpl.

Riggs, T.L. SC 24th Inf. Co.A Cpl.

Riggs, T.W. TN 35th Inf. 1st Co.D Cpl.

Riggs, Virgil AR 7th Cav. Co.B

Riggs, Virgil AR 16th Inf. Co.C

Riggs, W. NC 1st Jr.Res. Co.I

Riggs, W.C. AL Morris' Co. (Mtd.)

Riggs, W.C. AR 37th Inf. Co.B

Riggs, W.C. KY 9th Mtd.Inf. Co.F

Riggs, W.F. TN 8th (Smith's) Cav. Co.A

Riggs, Wiley NC 23rd Inf. Co.F

Riggs, William AR 10th Mil. Co.D

Riggs, William GA 50th Inf. Co.G

Riggs, William KY 13th Cav. Co.F Sgt.

Riggs, William KY 5th Mtd.Inf. Co.C

Riggs, William MO 1st Cav. Co.A

Riggs, William MO 4th Inf. Co.A

Riggs, William MO 8th Inf. Co.H,A

Riggs, William NC 12th Inf. Co.M

Riggs, William NC 32nd Inf. Co.B

Riggs, William TN 31st Inf. Co.H Sgt.

Riggs, William TN 59th Mtd.Inf. Co.A

Riggs, William TN Sullivan Cty.Res. (Loc.Def. Troops) Trevitt's Co.

Riggs, William TX Cav. Giddings' Bn. Carr's Co.

Riggs, William 3rd Conf.Cav. Co.B

Riggs, William A. LA Conscr.

Riggs, William A. TX 18th Cav. Co.F

Riggs, William B. SC 1st (McCreary's) Inf. Co.H

Riggs, William B. TN Cav. 16th Bn. (Neal's) Co.C Comsy.Sgt.

Riggs, William B. TN 1st (Feild's) Inf. Co.K

Riggs, William C. TX 8th Inf. Co.E

Riggs, William F. NC 61st Inf. Co.K

Riggs, William F. TN 4th (McLemore's) Cav. Co.A

Riggs, William F. VA 8th Cav. 2nd Co.D Comsy.Sgt.

Riggs, William H. TN 48th (Voorhies') Inf.

Riggs, William H. VA 54th Inf. Co.H

Riggs, William P. AR 3rd Cav. Co.G

Riggs, William P. KY 13th Cav. Co.A

Riggs, William R. NC 2nd Inf. Co.F

Riggs, William R. NC 6th Inf. Co.B

Riggs, William R. TX 9th Cav. Co.H

Riggs, William S. AR 35th Inf. Co.B

Riggs, William S. GA 61st Inf. Co.B

Riggs, William S. TN 8th Cav. Co.C

Riggs, William S. TX 6th Cav. Co.H 2nd Lt.

Riggs, Wilson GA 3rd Inf. Co.D

Riggs, Woodson T. TN 60th Mtd.Inf. Co.H Sgt.

Riggs, W.T. LA 2nd Inf. Co.D

Riggs, Zadoc NC 1st Arty. (10th St.Troops) Co.D Bugler

Riggs, Z.C. MS 1st Cav. Co.I

Riggsbee, A.G. NC 15th Inf. Co.M

Riggsbee, Alexander J. NC 15th Inf. Co.D

Riggsbee, Alexander J. NC 49th Inf. Co.B

Riggsbee, Carney C. NC 5th Inf. Co.E Sgt.

Riggsbee, Elbert NC 15th Inf. Co.D Sgt.

Riggsbee, Elbert NC 49th Inf. Co.B

Riggsbee, Francis M. NC 15th Inf. Co.D

Riggsbee, Hawkins NC 11th (Bethel Regt.) Inf. Co.G

Riggsbee, Hyder D. FL 5th Inf. Co.B

Riggsbee, Jefferson NC Lt.Arty. 13th Bn. Co.E

Riggsbee, John A. NC 15th Inf. Co.D 1st Sgt.

Riggsbee, John A. NC 49th Inf. Co.B 1st Sgt.

Riggsbee, John M. NC 15th Inf. Co.D

Riggsbee, John M. NC 49th Inf. Co.B 2nd Lt.

Riggsbee, John W. NC 15th Inf. Co.D

Riggsbee, John W. NC 49th Inf. Co.B

Riggsbee, Jones E. NC 15th Inf. Co.D

Riggsbee, Jones E. NC 49th Inf. Co.B Fifer

Riggsbee, Larkins E. NC 15th Inf. Co.D

Riggsbee, Larkins J. NC 49th Inf. Co.B

Riggsbee, L.H. NC Mallett's Bn. Co.F

Riggsbee, Lucian H. NC 15th Inf. Co.D

Riggsbee, Revel NC 15th Inf. Co.D

Riggsbee, Revel NC 49th Inf. Co.B

Riggsbee, Sidney B. TN 22nd (Barteau's) Cav. Co.F

Riggsbee, S.M. NC 15th Inf. Co.M

Riggsbee, S.M. NC 32nd Inf. Co.I Sgt.

Riggsbee, Thomas S. NC 49th Inf. Co.B

Riggsbee, T.S. NC 15th Inf. Co.D

Riggsbee, T.S. NC 32nd Inf. Co.I

Riggsbee, William L. NC 49th Inf. Co.B

Riggsbee, W.L. NC 15th Inf. Co.D

Riggsbey, William H. NC 5th Inf. Co.E
Riggsby, A.G. NC 32nd Inf. Co.I
Riggsby, Archibald B. NC 54th Inf. Co.H
Riggsby, Christopher C. NC 54th Inf. Co.H
Riggsby, Frank NC 32nd Inf. Co.G
Riggsby, J.A. TN 8th (Smith's) Cav. Co.E
Riggsby, Jobe NC 54th Inf. Co.H
Riggsby, John C. Lt.Arty. Dent's Btty.,CSA Sgt.
Riggsby, Mark NC 6th Inf. Co.I
Righetti, Giacomo LA 30th Inf. Co.D
Righine, Edward VA 48th Inf. Co.A
Right, --- TN 20th Inf. Co.H
Right, Albert GA 1st (Olmstead's) Inf. Co.B
Right, Albert GA 1st Bn.S.S. Co.A
Right, Alexander NC Inf. Thomas Legion Co.K
  Drum.
Right, Andrew VA 1st Cav. Co.F
Right, Bayless KY 5th Mtd.Inf. Co.K
Right, Benjamin AR 34th Inf. Co.H
Right, Benjamin KY 5th Mtd.Inf. Co.E
Right, C. VA 46th Inf. Co.F
Right, Cidney D.J. AL 5th Bn.Vol. Co.B
Right, Charles AR 34th Inf. Co.H
Right, Edwin VA 5th Cav. Co.B
Right, George VA 19th Cav. Co.K Cpl.
Right, George H. VA 49th Inf. Co.E
Right, G.W. MO 16th Inf. Co.I
Right, G.W. SC 1st St.Troops Co.B
Right, Henry NC 6th Cav. (65th St.Troops) Co.C
Right, Henry SC 7th Cav. Co.H
Right, Henry SC Cav.Bn. Holcombe Legion
  Co.E
Right, Jack NC Inf. Thomas Legion Co.K
Right, James MS 33rd Inf. Co.D
Right, James F. MS 33rd Inf. Co.D,B
Right, James J. VA 54th Inf. Co.I
Right, James N. VA 59th Inf. 2nd Co.C
Right, J.C. VA Mil. Grayson Cty.
Right, J.H. GA 28th Inf. Co.F Cpl.
Right, J.L. GA 28th Inf. Co.F
Right, J.O. AR Inf.
Right, John E. NC Inf. 2nd Bn. Co.A
Right, Joseph AR 7th Cav. Co.G
Right, Joseph H. NC 39th Inf. Co.B
Right, Lion AR 2nd Inf. Co.G
Right, N. TX 2nd Inf. Co.E
Right, Powell KY 10th (Diamond's) Cav. Co.A
Right, Powell KY 5th Mtd.Inf. Co.E
Right, Rankin MO 2nd Inf. Co.I
Right, R.B. NC Inf. Thomas Legion Co.K
Right, Robert AR 17th (Griffith's) Inf. Co.E
Right, Thomas MS 25th Inf. Co.B
Right, Thomas 2nd Conf.Inf. Co.B
Right, Thomas C. NC Inf. Thomas Legion Co.K
  Cpl.
Right, William NC 3rd Jr.Res. Co.B
Right, William E. GA 12th Inf. Co.G
Right, William J. AR 24th Inf. Co.G Sgt.
Rightenhower, James MO 15th Cav. Co.I
Righter, George W. KY 9th Cav. Co.K
Righter, John VA 19th Cav. Co.D Capt.
Righter, Peter B. VA 19th Cav. Co.D
Rightmer, E. TX 35th (Brown's) Cav. Co.E
Rightmer, Rainey F. TX 7th Field Btty.
Righton, Gotlit TN 10th Inf. Co.A
Righton, H.Y. SC Charleston Arsenal Bn. Co.E
  2nd Lt.

Righton, S.A. Gen. & Staff Capt.,Comsy.
Righton, S.A.W. NC 57th Inf. Capt.,Comsy.
Rightor, N.H. LA Inf. 1st Sp.Bn. (Rightor's)
  Co.E Lt.Col.
Rights, Alexander J. NC 21st Inf. Co.D
Rights, E.A. NC 7th Sr.Res. Holland's Co.
Rights, William NC 4th Bn.Jr.Res. Co.B
Rightsel, M. NC 26th Inf. Co.G
Rightsel, Samuel NC 21st Inf. Co.G
Rightsel, Samuel NC 26th Inf. Co.G
Rightsell, C.J. TX Cav. Baird's Regt. Co.D
Rightsell, James M. TN 3rd (Lillard's) Mtd.Inf.
  Co.A
Rightsman, Alfred NC 26th Inf. Co.G Music.
Rightstine, Adam VA 2nd Inf. Co.B
Rightzel, John NC 26th Inf. Co.G
Rigland, --- NC 15th Inf. Co.M
Rigle, Caswell AL 55th Vol. Co.I
Rigle, Jesse TX 11th Cav. Co.H
Rigle, L. NC 16th Inf. Co.C
Rigler, Dallas M. NC 37th Inf. Co.I 2nd Lt.
Rigler, George H. NC 1st Inf. (6 mo. '61) Co.B
Rigler, J. AR 6th Inf. Co.A
Rigler, John AR Inf. Cocke's Regt. Co.C
Rigler, John R. NC 5th Cav. (63rd St.Troops)
  Co.F
Rigley, A.H. TX 25th Cav. Lt.
Rigley, M. MS 39th Inf. Co.I
Rigmaiden, A. LA Inf.Crescent Regt. Co.A
Rigmaiden, Albert LA Inf.Cons.Crescent Regt.
  Co.C
Rigmaiden, Albert TX Cav. Ragsdale's Bn. Co.A
Rigmaiden, James LA 16th Inf. Co.G
Rigmaider, H. LA 2nd Cav. Co.A
Rigmaider, Jacob LA 7th Cav. Co.A
Rigmarden, Jacob LA 2nd Cav. Co.E
Rigmasden, Ed TX Cav. Ragsdale's Bn. Co.A
Rigna, Henry VA 57th Inf. Co.E
Rigna, Nathan VA 57th Inf. Co.E
Rigna, Townsend VA 57th Inf. Co.E
Rignault, M. TX Cav. Bourland's Regt. Co.E
Rigney, B. MS 18th Cav. Co.H
Rigney, Charles TN 34th Inf. Co.I
Rigney, Charles W. VA 38th Inf. Co.B
Rigney, C.N. MS 12th Inf. Co.F
Rigney, E. LA Mil.Conf.Guards Regt. Co.K
Rigney, Elijah VA 4th Res. Co.F
Rigney, Elijah VA 63rd Inf. Co.K
Rigney, F.J. AL 27th Inf. Co.F
Rigney, H. AR 30th Inf. Co.I
Rigney, H. TX 23rd Cav. Co.B
Rigney, Harrison TN Lt.Arty. McClung's Co.
Rigney, H.B. MO Inf. Clark's Regt. Co.E
Rigney, H.B. Conf.Cav. Clarkson's Bn. Ind.
  Rangers Co.A,G
Rigney, H.C. VA 22nd Cav. Co.G
Rigney, H.C. VA 45th Inf. Co.G
Rigney, Henly C. VA Mil. Carroll Cty.
Rigney, Henry AR 9th Inf. Co.H 2nd Lt.
Rigney, Henry KY 7th Cav. Co.H,A
Rigney, Isaac L. VA 24th Inf. Co.A
Rigney, James M. TX 22nd Cav. Co.C Black.
Rigney, J.C. AR 58th Mil. Co.A Cpl.
Rigney, Jehu H. VA 24th Inf. Co.C
Rigney, J.M. MS 2nd Cav. Co.D
Rigney, J.M. MS Blythe's Bn. (St.Troops) Co.A
Rigney, John LA Inf. 7th Bn. Co.C

Rigney, John LA 15th Inf. Co.K
Rigney, John TN 1st Hvy.Arty. Co.L, 3rd Co.A
Rigney, John H. MS 9th Inf. Old Co.I Sgt.
Rigney, Leander A. VA 24th Inf. Co.C
Rigney, Levi W. VA 21st Inf. Co.I
Rigney, Simon TN 34th Inf. Co.I
Rigney, T. VA Conscr. Cp.Lee Co.B
Rigney, Thomas GA 1st (Fannin's) Res. Co.A
Rigney, Thomas J. LA 14th Inf. Co.I
Rigs, D. LA 3rd (Wingfield's) Cav. Co.I
Rigs, James R. MO Cav. Schnabel's Bn. Co.A
Rigs, W.C. AL 51st (Part.Rangers) Co.E
Rigsbee, Albert J. AR 31st Inf. Co.M
Rigsbee, Gaston E. NC 7th Inf. Co.G
Rigsbee, Henry Jackson NC 6th Inf. Co.C
Rigsbee, Jeff NC 3rd Arty. (40th St.Troops)
  Co.G
Rigsbee, John NC 3rd Arty. (40th St.Troops)
  Co.G
Rigsbee, John NC Lt.Arty. 13th Bn. Co.E
Rigsbee, J.W. NC Lt.Arty. 13th Bn. Co.E
Rigsbee, Redding NC 7th Inf. Co.G
Rigsbee, Sidney B. Cav. 7th Bn. (Bennett's) Co.D
Rigsbee, T. NC 1st Jr.Res. Co.I
Rigsbee, Warren NC 7th Inf. Co.G
Rigsbee, William NC Inf. 2nd Bn. Co.H
Rigsbee, William C. NC 30th Inf. Co.I
Rigsber, A.B. GA 10th Inf. Co.B
Rigsbey, Archibald VA Inf. 23rd Bn. Co.E
Rigsbey, James E. TN 15th (Stewart's) Cav.
  Co.G
Rigsbey, Milus KY 5th Mtd.Inf. Co.F
Rigsbey, S.J. AL 25th Inf. Co.B
Rigsbey, William L. AL 13th Inf. Co.E
Rigsby, A. TX 7th Cav. Co.E
Rigsby, Aaron TN Detailed Conscr. Co.B
Rigsby, Aaron TN Sullivan Cty.Res.
  (Loc.Def.Troops) Trevitt's Co.
Rigsby, A.B. 7th Conf.Cav. Co.B
Rigsby, A.J. GA 10th Mil.
Rigsby, A.J. TX 1st Inf. Co.F Capt.
Rigsby, Alexander L. TN Inf. 22nd Bn. Co.H
Rigsby, Alex L. TN 4th (Murray's) Cav. Co.B
Rigsby, Allen J. GA 7th Inf. (St.Guards) Co.E
Rigsby, Allen T. AL 13th Inf. Co.K
Rigsby, Almond TN 4th (Murray's) Cav. Co.B
Rigsby, Almond TN Inf. 22nd Bn. Co.H
Rigsby, A.M. GA 45th Inf. Co.K
Rigsby, Ben F. AR 3rd Cav. Co.F
Rigsby, Benjamin AL 15th Bn.Part.Rangers Co.E
Rigsby, Benjamin AL 17th Inf. Co.B
Rigsby, Benjamin F. AR 25th Inf. Co.B
Rigsby, Benjamin F. TX 13th Cav. Co.K
Rigsby, Canada TN Inf. 1st Bn. (Colms') Co.C
Rigsby, Caswell NC 47th Inf. Co.I
Rigsby, David S. TN 4th (McLemore's) Cav.
  Co.G
Rigsby, Elijah GA 31st Inf. Co.K
Rigsby, F.V. NC 1st Jr.Res. Co.H
Rigsby, Gaston NC 1st Jr.Res. Co.I
Rigsby, George W. AR 3rd Cav. Co.F
Rigsby, George W. AR 25th Inf. Co.B
Rigsby, G.S. VA Goochland Lt.Arty.
Rigsby, H. AL 7th Cav. Co.A Cpl.
Rigsby, James TN Inf. 1st Bn. (Colms') Co.C
Rigsby, James TN 16th Inf. Co.A
Rigsby, James A. AR 3rd Cav. Co.F

Rigsby, James E. VA Goochland Lt.Arty.
Rigsby, James L. TN 43rd Inf. Co.C
Rigsby, James M. TX 13th Cav. Co.K
Rigsby, James R. GA 17th Inf. Co.D
Rigsby, J.C. GA Siege Arty. 28th Bn. Co.K
  Cpl.
Rigsby, J.D. TN Inf. 1st Bn. (Colms') Co.C
Rigsby, J.M. TN 13th (Gore's) Cav. Co.I
Rigsby, John TN 7th (Duckworth's) Cav. Co.G
Rigsby, John A. GA Inf. Cobb Guards Co.A
Rigsby, John C. AL Inf. 1st Regt. Co.A
Rigsby, John H. KY 5th Mtd.Inf. Co.K
Rigsby, John T. AL 11th Inf. Co.G
Rigsby, John W. AL 13th Inf. Co.K
Rigsby, John W. GA 1st (Ramsey's) Inf. Co.D
Rigsby, J.R. AL 30th Inf. Co.I
Rigsby, J.W. GA 63rd Inf. Co.E
Rigsby, J.W. 7th Conf.Cav. Co.L
Rigsby, Kelly TX 30th Cav. Co.G
Rigsby, Larkin KY 5th Mtd.Inf. Co.K
Rigsby, Leb NC 1st Jr.Res. Co.D
Rigsby, Leroy NC 47th Inf. Co.I
Rigsby, Leroy G. NC 56th Inf. Co.E
Rigsby, Lewis H. AL Inf. 1st Regt. Co.A
Rigsby, Lewis H. GA 51st Inf. Co.K
Rigsby, Lewis J. GA 55th Inf. Co.G Sgt.
Rigsby, Lewis P. TN Inf. 1st Bn. (Colms') Co.C
Rigsby, Mattison VA 22nd Cav. Co.K
Rigsby, Nathaniel M. NC 24th Inf. Co.D
Rigsby, Philo D. AL 17th Inf. Co.B Cpl.
Rigsby, R.D. TN 5th Inf. Co.A
Rigsby, Richard MS 63rd Regt. Co.F
Rigsby, Richard TN 63rd Inf. Co.F
Rigsby, Robert TN 35th Inf. Co.E
Rigsby, Robert H. VA 44th Inf. Co.B 1st Sgt.
Rigsby, Robert M. VA 44th Inf. Co.B
Rigsby, Robert M. 1st Conf.Eng.Troops Co.G
Rigsby, Russel TN 23rd Inf. Co.E
Rigsby, Russell E. TX 26th Cav. Co.D
Rigsby, Samuel D. GA Inf. Cobb Guards Co.A
Rigsby, Samuel J. 7th Conf.Cav. Co.B
Rigsby, Samuel L. GA 51st Inf. Co.K Sgt.
Rigsby, Thomas KY 5th Mtd.Inf. Co.B
Rigsby, Thomas KY 5th Mtd.Inf. Co.K
Rigsby, Thomas KY 5th Mtd.Inf. 1st Co.K
Rigsby, Thomas NC 14th Inf. Co.E
Rigsby, Thomas TN Inf. 3rd Cons.Regt. Co.A
  Cpl.
Rigsby, Thomas TN 35th Inf. Co.E Sgt.
Rigsby, Thomas VA 16th Cav. Co.I
Rigsby, Thomas T. KY 5th Mtd.Inf. Co.K
Rigsby, Thomas W. GA Inf. Cobb Guards Co.A
Rigsby, W.H. AL Lt.Arty. 2nd Bn. Co.F
Rigsby, Wiley T. AL 36th Inf. Co.D
Rigsby, William GA 15th Inf. Co.I
Rigsby, William MS 1st (Percy's) Inf. Co.I
Rigsby, William TN 43rd Inf. Co.C Fifer
Rigsby, William H. AR 3rd Cav. Co.F Sgt.
Rigsby, William M. VA 16th Cav. Co.I
Rigsby, William R. AR Lt.Arty. Thrall's Btty.
Rigsby, William R. MS Inf. 2nd Bn. Co.C
Rigsby, William R. MS 48th Inf. Co.C
Rigsby, W.J. TN 23rd Inf. Co.C
Rigsby, W.J. TN 29th Inf. Co.C
Rigsby, W.L. AL Cp. of Instr. Talladega
Rigsby, W.L. TX 12th Cav. Co.B
Rigsby, Wright NC 47th Inf. Co.I

Rigsby, W.T. AL 13th Inf. Co.K
Rigsdell, George MS 28th Cav. Co.G
Rigsdell, H.N. MS 28th Cav. Co.G
Rigshar, W. KY Bowling Green
Rigsley, Samuel GA 5th Inf. Co.F Music.
Rigter, J. LA Mil. Borge's Co. (Garnet Rangers)
Rigu, William LA 22nd Inf. Co.D
Rigues, H.C. LA 2nd Cav. Co.A
Rigues, Leland LA 18th Inf. Co.F Sgt.
Rigues, L.F. LA Inf.Cons. 18th Regt. & Yellow
  Jacket Bn. Co.I
Rigues, Martin F. LA Arty. Green's Co. (LA
  Guard Btty.)
Rigues, M.F. LA 1st (Nelligan's) Inf. 1st Co.B
Rigues, M.F. LA Scouts Gordon's Co. 1st Lt.
Riguiton, J.H. AR 9th Inf.
Rigway, Desiah W. VA 8th Bn.Res. Co.A Capt.
Rigway, J.P. LA 1st Res. Co.E
Rikard, A.C. SC 13th Inf. Co.D
Rikard, A.J. AL 36th Inf. Co.F
Rikard, Charles MS 1st (Johnston's) Inf. Co.E
Rikard, Christian AL 53rd (Part.Rangers) Co.F
Rikard, D.B. AR Lt.Arty. Hart's Btty.
Rikard, Dennis B. AL 36th Inf. Co.G
Rikard, D. Franklin SC 20th Inf. Co.F Sgt.
Rikard, Garret AR Lt.Arty. Hart's Btty.
Rikard, George A. SC 2nd St.Troops Co.F
Rikard, George A. SC 13th Inf. Co.D
Rikard, G.W. SC Inf. Holcombe Legion Co.H
Rikard, Henry S. AL 36th Inf. Co.G
Rikard, J.A. SC 2nd Inf. Co.F
Rikard, J.A. SC 13th Inf. Co.G
Rikard, J. Adam SC 20th Inf. Co.F
Rikard, James P. SC 13th Inf. Co.D
Rikard, J.M. SC 13th Inf. Co.G
Rikard, John A. AL 36th Inf. Co.G
Rikard, John G. SC 13th Inf. Co.D Cpl.
Rikard, John J. AL Lt.Arty. 2nd Bn.
Rikard, L. MS Inf. 2nd St.Troops Co.B
Rikard, L.C. SC 3rd Inf. Co.H
Rikard, Levi SC Inf. Holcombe Legion Co.H
Rikard, L.H. AL 36th Inf. Co.G
Rikard, L.W. MS 18th Cav. Co.G
Rikard, Samuel W. AL 5th Cav. Co.A
Rikard, S.P. AL 36th Inf. Co.F
Rikard, Wiley SC Inf. Holcombe Legion Co.H
Rikard, W.M. SC 13th Inf. Co.D
Rikark, L. MS 1st Cav.Res. Co.H
Rike, Andrew J. AR 2nd Mtd.Rifles Co.H
Rike, Andrew J. NC 13th Inf. Co.E
Rike, Benjamin L. NC 13th Inf. Co.E Cpl.
Rike, Emanuel NC 13th Inf. Co.E
Rike, H.S. NC 7th Sr.Res. Bradshaw's Co.
Rike, J.H. NC 3rd Jr.Res. Co.B
Rike, Robert A. TX Inf. 3rd St.Troops Co.D
Rikens, J. SC 13th Inf. Co.G
Riker, A. TN 9th Inf. Co.I
Riker, David SC Cav. Walpole's Co.
Ri ke ty 1st Creek Mtd.Vol. 2nd Co.I
Riks, John TX 3rd Inf. Co.D
Riland, J.H. Gen. & Staff Asst.Surg.
Rilay, L.C. TN Holman's Bn.Part.Rangers Co.D
Rile, Arrington L. AL 39th Inf. Co.F
Rile, E.M. AL 2nd Cav. Co.B
Rile, V.H. Conf.Cav. Wood's Regt. 2nd Co.D
Rilee, Benjamin VA 24th Cav. Co.C
Rilee, Curtis VA 5th Cav. Co.A

Rilee, George D. VA 26th Inf. 2nd Co.B, Co.H
Rilee, Gideon R. VA Arty. Fleet's Co. Artif.
Rilee, Gideon R. VA Lt.Arty. Snead's Co. Artif.
Rilee, Gideon R. VA 55th Inf. Co.B
Rilee, James T. VA 26th Inf. Co.H
Rilee, John T. VA 26th Inf. 2nd Co.B, Co.H
  Music.
Rilee, Joshua VA 109th Mil. Co.B
Rilee, Joshua L. VA 26th Inf. 2nd Co.B, Co.H
  Cpl.
Rilee, Pascal D. VA 5th Cav. Co.A
Rilee, Philip S. VA 26th Inf. Co.H
Rilee, S. VA 26th Inf. Co.H
Rilee, William C. VA 24th Cav. Co.D
Rilee, William C. VA Cav. 40th Bn. Co.D
Riler, Louis AL 24th Inf. Co.I
Riles, C. GA 4th Inf. Co.C
Riles, Edmond LA 31st Inf. Co.B
Riles, George W. FL 9th Inf. Co.B
Riles, H. AL Lt.Arty. Goldthwaite's Btty.
Riles, Henry D. AL 1st Regt.Conscr. Co.B
Riles, J.B. LA 3rd (Wingfield's) Cav. Co.A
Riles, John AR 2nd Mtd.Rifles Co.I
Riles, John FL Lt.Arty. Perry's Co.
Riles, John MS 9th Cav. Co.D
Riles, Lewis FL 7th Inf. Co.I Cpl.
Riles, Marion MS 18th Cav. Co.K
Riles, R.L. NC 1st Jr.Res. Co.F
Riles, Thomas, Jr. AR 2nd Mtd.Rifles Co.I
Riles, Thomas, Sr. AR 2nd Mtd.Rifles Co.I
Riles, Thomas AR Cav. Gordon's Regt. Co.K
Riles, Thomas, Sr. AR Cav. Gordon's Regt.
  Co.K
Riles, William AL 38th Inf. Co.E
Riles, William AR 2nd Mtd.Rifles Co.I
Riles, William R. FL 7th Inf. Co.I Sgt.
Riley, --- AL 25th Inf. Co.H
Riley, --- SC 13th Inf.
Riley, --- TX 33rd Cav. Co.F
Riley, --- TX Cav. Bourland's Regt. Co.K
Riley, --- TX Cav. Mann's Regt. Co.K
Riley, --- TX Cav. McCord's Frontier Regt.
  Co.F
Riley, --- TX 8th Field Btty. Artif.
Riley, --- TX Lt.Arty. Dege's Bn. Artif.
Riley, --- TX Vol. Rainey's Co. Surg.
Riley, A. LA 9th Inf. Co.B
Riley, A. TX 25th Cav. Co.B
Riley, A. TX 14th Inf. Co.C
Riley, A. VA 7th Inf. Co.I
Riley, Able AR Inf. Cocke's Regt. Cons.Co.C,I
Riley, Abraham AL 7th Inf. Co.F
Riley, Abraham C. AL 30th Inf. Co.K
Riley, A.C. AL 20th Inf. Co.D
Riley, A.C. MO 1st & 4th Cons.Inf. Col.
Riley, Addison GA Inf. 25th Bn. (Prov.Guard)
  Co.C
Riley, A.J. TN 11th (Holman's) Cav. Co.B
Riley, A.J. TN Holman's Bn.Part.Rangers Co.A
Riley, A.J. TX 25th Cav. Co.A Sgt.
Riley, A.J. TX 11th (Spaight's) Bn.Vol. Co.D
Riley, A.J. TX 13th Vol. 1st Co.K
Riley, A.J. TX 15th Inf. 2nd Co.F
Riley, A.K. TN Lt.Arty. Winston's Co.
Riley, Albert O. GA 6th Cav. Co.F
Riley, Albert O. GA 1st (Ramsey's) Inf. Co.H
Riley, Alex NC 5th Cav. (63rd St.Troops) Co.K

Riley, Alex SC 6th Cav. Co.D
Riley, Alex SC Prov.Guard Hamilton's Co.
Riley, Alex VA 34th Mil. Co.A
Riley, Alexander VA 64th Mtd.Inf. Co.C
Riley, Alfred KY 4th Cav. Co.D
Riley, Alfred TN 45th Inf. Co.B
Riley, Alfred TX Inf. Griffin's Bn. Co.B
Riley, Allen NC 64th Inf. Co.M
Riley, Allen TN Cav. 16th Bn. (Neal's) Co.F
Riley, Allen VA 25th Cav. Co.B
Riley, Amos C. MO 1st Inf. Co.I Col.
Riley, And. J. VA Lt.Arty. Cayce's Co.
Riley, Anderson TN 9th Cav. Co.F
Riley, Andrew TN Sullivan Cty.Res.
  (Loc.Def.Troops) Witcher's Co.
Riley, Andrew F. TN 20th Cav.
Riley, Andrew F. VA Lt.Arty. W.H. Chapman's
  Co.
Riley, Andrew J. VA 27th Inf. 1st Co.H
Riley, Andrew Jackson MO 8th Inf. Co.E Sgt.
Riley, Andrew P. SC 1st (Orr's) Rifles Co.B
Riley, Andy TN 12th (Cons.) Inf. Co.H
Riley, Antony AL 40th Inf. Co.K
Riley, A.O. GA 65th Inf. Co.C
Riley, A.O. GA Smith's Legion Co.D Sgt.
Riley, A.R. SC 2nd Arty. Co.F
Riley, Austin AL 7th Inf. Co.K
Riley, Austin TN 9th Inf. Co.D
Riley, A.W. AL 25th Inf. Co.A
Riley, A.W. TN Inf. 2nd Cons.Regt. Co.D
Riley, A.W. TN 22nd Inf. Co.C
Riley, A.W. TX 15th Inf. 2nd Co.F
Riley, A.W. Brush Bn.
Riley, Bartholomew AL 12th Inf. Co.A
Riley, B.D. MS 28th Cav. Co.G
Riley, Benjamin LA 2nd Cav. Co.E
Riley, Benjamin LA 19th Inf. Co.H
Riley, Benjamin VA 15th Cav. Co.A Sgt.
Riley, Benjamin VA Cav. 40th Bn. Co.C
Riley, Benjamin F. VA 8th Cav. Co.H
Riley, Bernard LA Cav. Greenleaf's Co. (Orleans
  Lt.Horse)
Riley, Bernard Inf. School of Pract. Powell's
  Detach. Co.C
Riley, Berry L. VA 5th Inf. Co.L
Riley, B.F. AL 30th Inf. Co.B
Riley, B.F. MS 11th Inf. Co.B
Riley, Birt SC 5th Res. Co.B
Riley, B.M. SC 3rd Cav. Co.D
Riley, B.S. TN 47th Inf. Co.A
Riley, B.S. TX 13th Vol. 1st Co.K
Riley, B.S. TX 15th Inf. 2nd Co.F
Riley, Burgoin W. TX 6th Cav. Co.A
Riley, Burriss AR 23rd Inf. Co.E
Riley, C. AL 34th Inf. Co.E
Riley, C. KY 12th Cav. Co.E
Riley, C. LA Mil.Conf.Guards Regt. Co.I
Riley, Calvin P. NC 3rd Inf. Co.C
Riley, Carter MO 8th Inf. Co.D
Riley, C.B. AL 15th Inf. Co.D
Riley, C.C. KY 8th Mtd.Inf. Co.I 3rd Lt.
Riley, C.C. TX 1st Hvy.Arty. Co.H
Riley, Charles AL 2nd Cav. Co.E Bugler
Riley, Charles AL Inf. 2nd Regt. Co.E
Riley, Charles AL 9th Inf. Co.B
Riley, Charles MS 18th Inf. Co.E
Riley, Charles SC Ord.Guards Loc.Def.Troops

Riley, Charles TX Inf. Griffin's Bn. Co.B
Riley, Charles B. VA 11th Cav. Co.D
Riley, Charles H. VA 16th Cav. Co.B
Riley, Charles H. VA Cav. Caldwell's Bn. Gent's
  Co.
Riley, Charles H. VA 37th Inf. Co.I
Riley, C.J. SC 1st (Butler's) Inf. Co.G
Riley, Cornelius VA Hvy.Arty. Coleman's Co.
Riley, C.S. AL 15th Cav. Co.I
Riley, C.W. AL 33rd Inf. Co.D
Riley, C.W. SC 5th Inf. 2nd Co.A
Riley, D. GA 45th Inf. Co.A
Riley, D. MO 5th Cav. Co.K
Riley, D. NC 45th Inf. Co.C
Riley, D. TX 14th Inf. Co.C
Riley, D.A. GA 23rd Inf. Co.F
Riley, D.A. SC 2nd Arty. Co.I 1st Sgt.
Riley, Daniel AL 15th Inf. Co.G
Riley, Daniel GA 5th Res. Co.B
Riley, Daniel NC 2nd Arty. (36th St.Troops)
  Co.C,D
Riley, Daniel SC 1st Arty. Co.B
Riley, Daniel TX 33rd Cav. Co.G
Riley, Daniel TX 8th Inf. Co.C
Riley, David (Colored boy) GA 30th Inf. Co.D
  Music.
Riley, David NC 3rd Arty. (40th St.Troops)
  Co.G
Riley, David NC Lt.Arty. 13th Bn. Co.E
Riley, David NC 4th Bn.Jr.Res. Co.A
Riley, David TX 31st Cav. Co.F Sgt.
Riley, David A. SC 1st (Hagood's) Inf. 1st Co.A
Riley, David F. GA 53rd Inf. Co.H 1st Lt.
Riley, David L. AL 30th Inf. Co.I
Riley, David S. AL 42nd Inf. Co.E
Riley, David W. NC 31st Inf. Co.E
Riley, David W. TX 4th Inf. Co.F
Riley, D.E. GA Cav. 22nd Bn. (St.Guards) Co.D
Riley, D.E. GA 5th Res. Co.B
Riley, Dennis VA Inf. 1st Bn. Co.E
Riley, D.F. GA 13th Inf. Co.A
Riley, D.L. AL 20th Inf. Co.K
Riley, D.L. TX 33rd Cav. Co.B
Riley, Drury AL 43rd Inf. Co.H Cpl.
Riley, Dudley VA 21st Inf. Co.H
Riley, E. TN Inf. 4th Cons.Regt. Co.A
Riley, E. TX 2nd Cav. 2nd Co.F
Riley, E.B. FL Cav. 3rd Bn. Co.D
Riley, E.B. TX 12th Cav. Co.E
Riley, E.B. Dudley Gen. & Staff Maj.,Ord.Ch.
Riley, E.C. SC 2nd Arty. Co.I
Riley, E.C. SC 1st (Orr's) Rifles Co.B
Riley, Ed. TN 15th Inf. Music.
Riley, E.D. TX 7th Inf. Co.G
Riley, Edmond C. SC 2nd Inf. Co.F
Riley, Edward, Jr. AL 15th Inf. Co.G
Riley, Edward AL 51st (Part.Rangers) Co.K
Riley, Edward LA 1st (Strawbridge's) Inf. Co.K
Riley, Edward LA 21st (Patton's) Inf. Co.G Cpl.
Riley, Edward MS 17th Inf. Co.I
Riley, Edward SC 27th Inf. (Gaillard's Regt.)
  Co.B
Riley, Edward TN 10th Inf. Co.H
Riley, Edward TN 11th Inf. Co.C
Riley, Edward TX 26th Cav. 2nd Co.G
Riley, Edward TX 2nd Inf. Co.D Sgt.
Riley, Edward, Jr. AL 15th Inf. Co.G

Riley, Edward Gen. & Staff Sgt.
Riley, Edward B. TX 26th Cav. Co.D
Riley, Edward J. TX 13th Cav. Co.I Sgt.
Riley, Edward J. VA 30th Inf. Co.A
Riley, Edward O. GA 35th Inf. Co.E
Riley, E.G. AL 42nd Inf. Co.H Capt.
Riley, E.G. GA 16th Inf. Co.G
Riley, E.G. 15th Conf.Cav. Co.I
Riley, E.K. GA 20th Inf. Co.G
Riley, Eldred James SC 19th Inf. Co.D
Riley, Eldridge NC 54th Inf. Co.H
Riley, Eli GA 20th Inf. Co.I
Riley, Elias AL 33rd Inf. Co.B
Riley, Elias MO St.Guard W.H. Taylor's Co.
  4th Cpl.
Riley, Elijah VA 7th Inf. Co.B
Riley, Elsey NC 22nd Inf. Co.E
Riley, Ely H. AR 37th Inf. Co.I Jr.2nd Lt.
Riley, Elzy NC 56th Inf. Co.D
Riley, E.M. MS 39th Inf. Co.A
Riley, E.P. AL 5th Inf. New Co.C
Riley, E.S. SC 11th Res. Co.I Capt.
Riley, Eugene AL 32nd Inf. Co.C
Riley, E.W. GA Inf. 25th Bn.Loc.Def. Co.A
Riley, F.A. SC 2nd Rifles Co.B
Riley, F.D.N. AL 15th Bn.Part.Rangers Co.E
  1st Lt.
Riley, F.D.N. AL 56th Part.Rangers Co.E Capt.
Riley, Fincher NC 16th Inf. Co.B
Riley, F.M. MS 1st (King's) Inf. (St.Troops)
  Co.I Cpl.
Riley, F.M. VA 3rd Inf.Loc.Def. Co.D
Riley, Francis AL 1st Regt. Mobile Vol. British
  Guard Co.A
Riley, Francis MS Inf. 3rd Bn. Co.F
Riley, Francis E. TN 5th (McKenzie's) Cav.
  Co.G Sgt.
Riley, Francis M. AR 26th Inf. Co.D
Riley, Frank TX 2nd Cav. 1st Co.F
Riley, Frank VA 12th Cav. Co.F
Riley, Franklin L. MS 16th Inf. Co.B
Riley, G. AL 15th Inf. Co.G
Riley, G. Conf.Inf. 8th Bn. Co.D
Riley, Garnett M. KY 3rd Cav. Co.B Sgt.
Riley, Garnett M. KY Corbin's Men
Riley, G.B. SC 4th Bn.Res. Co.B
Riley, George AL 15th Inf. Co.G
Riley, George AL 21st Inf. Co.K
Riley, George AL 62nd Inf. Co.I,B
Riley, George LA 13th Inf. Co.C
Riley, George SC Hvy.Arty. 15th (Lucas') Bn.
  Co.A
Riley, George TN 5th (McKenzie's) Cav. Co.G
Riley, George TN 2nd (Walker's) Inf. Co.I
Riley, George TX 4th Cav. Co.B
Riley, George A. AL 61st Inf. Co.G
Riley, Geo. B. TN 33rd Inf. Co.K 2nd Lt.
Riley, George H. TX 3rd Cav. Co.I
Riley, George Hamilton NC 6th Inf. Co.C
Riley, George J. TX 6th Inf. Co.A
Riley, George S. SC 1st (McCreary's) Inf. Co.K
Riley, George T. AR 1st (Dobbin's) Cav. Co.C
Riley, George W. AL 3rd Cav. Co.A
Riley, George W. AL 8th (Hatch's) Cav. Co.K
Riley, George W. AL 17th Inf. Co.K 2nd Lt.
Riley, George W. AL 33rd Inf. Co.B
Riley, George W. AL 61st Inf. Co.G

Riley, George W. AL Rives' Supp.Force 9th Congr.Dist.
Riley, George W. FL 6th Inf. Co.K
Riley, George W. MS 3rd Inf. Co.G
Riley, George W. MO 6th Inf. Co.G
Riley, George W. NC 3rd Jr.Res. Co.A
Riley, George W. Conf.Cav. Wood's Regt. Co.C
Riley, Gerard NC 5th Cav. (63rd St.Troops) Co.B
Riley, G.F. GA 12th (Robinson's) Cav. (St.Guards) Co.D
Riley, G.H. AL 63rd Inf. Co.A
Riley, G.H. TN 15th (Cons.) Cav. Co.G
Riley, Gillum AL 15th Inf. Co.G
Riley, G.J. MS Inf. 2nd Bn. Co.F
Riley, G.J. MS 48th Inf. Co.F
Riley, G.M. KY 3rd Bn.Mtd.Rifles Co.B Sgt.
Riley, G.M. KY Jessee's Bn.Mtd.Riflemen Co.B Sgt.
Riley, G.O. SC 1st (Hagood's) Inf. 1st Co.I
Riley, Green B. TN 32nd Inf. Co.K Sgt.
Riley, Green W. NC 56th Inf. Co.D
Riley, G.S. SC 1st (Hagood's) Inf. 1st Co.F
Riley, G.W. AL 7th Cav. Co.G
Riley, G.W. AL 7th Inf. Co.K
Riley, G.W. AL 36th Inf. Co.B
Riley, G.W. AR Lt.Arty. 5th Btty. Artif.
Riley, G.W. AR 19th (Dockery's) Inf. Co.C
Riley, G.W. AR Inf. Hardy's Regt. Torbett's Co.
Riley, G.W. TX 25th Cav. Co.A Sgt.
Riley, H. KY 3rd Mtd.Inf. Co.C
Riley, H. MS 6th Inf. Co.C
Riley, H.A. AL 9th Inf. Co.I
Riley, Harrison 1st Cherokee Mtd.Vol. Co.I
Riley, Harrison A. AR 4th Inf. Co.D
Riley, Harrison T. GA 20th Inf. Co.G
Riley, Harrison W. TN 44th (Cons.) Inf. Co.F
Riley, H.C. NC 33rd Inf. Co.G
Riley, Henry GA Inf. Arsenal Bn. (Columbus) Co.B
Riley, Henry NC 3rd Inf. Co.A
Riley, Henry TN 2nd (Ashby's) Cav. Co.C
Riley, Henry TN Cav. 5th Bn. (McClellan's) Co.D
Riley, Henry TX Inf. Griffin's Bn. Co.B
Riley, Henry VA 28th Inf. Co.E
Riley, Henry G. VA 21st Mil. Co.D,E
Riley, Henry G. VA 34th Inf. Co.A
Riley, Henry H. LA 4th Inf. Co.D Cpl.
Riley, Henry T. VA 28th Inf. Co.E
Riley, H.F. FL 2nd Inf. Co.A 2nd Lt.
Riley, H.F. SC 10th Inf. 2nd Co.G
Riley, H.H. TN 5th Cav. Co.G
Riley, Hiram GA 20th Inf. Co.I
Riley, Hiram K. TN 5th (McKenzie's) Cav. Co.G
Riley, Hollis A. AL 6th Cav. Co.E,C Cpl.
Riley, Hugh NC 1st Cav. (9th St.Troops) Co.H Black.
Riley, Huston KY 3rd Cav. Co.C
Riley, H.W. GA Inf. 11th Bn. (St.Guards) Co.B
Riley, H.W., Jr. GA Phillips' Legion Co.E
Riley, I. LA 4th Cav. Co.B
Riley, I. TX 21st Inf. Co.G
Riley, Ike AL 43rd Inf. Co.F
Riley, Ira D. FL 9th Inf. Co.D Cpl.
Riley, Isaac AR 19th (Dockery's) Inf. Cons.Co.E,D

Riley, Isaac GA 11th Cav. Co.B
Riley, Isaac TX Inf. Griffin's Bn. Co.B
Riley, Isaac N. TN 24th Inf. 2nd Co.H 2nd Lt.
Riley, J. AL 12th Inf. Co.A
Riley, J. AL 63rd Inf. Co.C
Riley, J. GA 28th Inf. Co.G
Riley, J. LA 3rd (Wingfield's) Cav. Co.I
Riley, J. MS 8th Cav. Co.I
Riley, J. NC 27th Inf. Co.C 1st Sgt.
Riley, J. TX 25th Cav. Co.A
Riley, J. VA Cav. 41st Bn. Co.E
Riley, J. Conf.Inf. Tucker's Regt. Co.F Cpl.
Riley, J.A. MS Cav. Vivion's Co.
Riley, J.A. MS 1st (Johnston's) Inf. Co.I
Riley, J.A. TN 19th & 20th (Cons.) Cav. Co.D
Riley, J.A. TN Lt.Arty. Tobin's Co.
Riley, J.A. TN Inf. 12th Regt. Co.E
Riley, Jackson AL 33rd Inf. Co.B
Riley, Jackson GA 2nd Bn.S.S. Co.A
Riley, Jackson MS 15th Bn.S.S. Co.B
Riley, Jackson MO Searcy's Bn.S.S.
Riley, Jackson TX Cav. McCord's Frontier Regt. Co.E Cpl.
Riley, Jackson VA 21st Inf. Co.I
Riley, Jackson L. MS 6th Inf. Asst.Surg.
Riley, Jackson W. LA 2nd Inf. Co.B
Riley, Jacob TN 21st (Wilson's) Cav. Co.I
Riley, Jacob TX Inf. Griffin's Bn. Co.B
Riley, Jacob L. GA Lt.Arty. 14th Bn. Co.A
Riley, Jacob L. GA Lt.Arty. Havis' Btty.
Riley, James AL Seawell's Btty. (Mohawk Arty.)
Riley, James AL Inf. 2nd Regt. Co.I,E
Riley, James AL 21st Inf. Co.C
Riley, James AL 49th Inf. Co.C
Riley, James AR 18th (Marmaduke's) Inf. Co.D
Riley, James GA 20th Inf. Co.G
Riley, James GA Floyd Legion (St.Guards) Co.B
Riley, James KY 2nd (Duke's) Cav. Co.I
Riley, James KY 4th Cav. Co.D
Riley, James KY 3rd Mtd.Inf. Co.K
Riley, James KY 4th Cav. Co.K
Riley, James LA 1st Hvy.Arty. (Reg.) Co.G
Riley, James LA Inf. 1st Sp.Bn. (Wheat's) Co.B
Riley, James LA 7th Inf. Co.C
Riley, James LA 7th Inf. Co.E
Riley, James LA 13th Inf. Co.A
Riley, James LA 22nd Inf. D.H. Marks' Co.
Riley, James LA 22nd Inf. Wash. Marks' Co.
Riley, James MS 3rd Inf. Co.B
Riley, James MS 14th Inf. Co.I Ch.Music.
Riley, James MS 17th Inf. Co.I
Riley, James MO Cav. 3rd Bn. Co.A
Riley, James NC 1st Inf. Co.D
Riley, James NC 7th Inf. Co.F
Riley, James NC 12th Inf. Co.D,B
Riley, James NC 52nd Inf. Co.G
Riley, James NC 56th Inf. Co.D
Riley, James SC 1st (Butler's) Inf. Co.C Cpl.
Riley, James, 1st SC Inf. 1st (Charleston) Bn. Co.F
Riley, James, 2nd SC Inf. 1st (Charleston) Bn. Co.F Sgt.
Riley, James SC 7th Inf. Co.M,C
Riley, James SC 14th Inf. Co.K
Riley, James SC 27th Inf. Co.C 1st Sgt.
Riley, James SC 27th Inf. Co.C
Riley, James TN 5th (McKenzie's) Cav. Co.I

Riley, James TN 7th (Duckworth's) Cav. Co.H
Riley, James TN Cav. 9th Bn. (Gantt's) Co.F
Riley, James TN Cav. 12th Bn. (Day's) Co.C
Riley, James TN 5th Inf. Co.G
Riley, James TN 9th Inf. Co.I
Riley, James TN 13th Inf. Co.A
Riley, James TN 15th Inf. Co.A
Riley, James TN Sullivan Cty.Res. (Loc.Def. Troops) Witcher's Co.
Riley, James TX 21st Cav. Co.E
Riley, James TX 6th Inf. Co.K
Riley, James TX 8th Inf. Co.K
Riley, James VA Cav. 32nd Bn. Co.A
Riley, James VA Cav. 41st Bn. Co.G
Riley, James VA Hvy.Arty. 10th Bn. 3rd Co.C
Riley, James VA Lt.Arty. Carpenter's Co.
Riley, James VA 2nd Inf. Co.H
Riley, James VA Inf. 21st Bn. 2nd Co.C
Riley, James VA Inf. 22nd Bn. Co.D
Riley, James VA 27th Inf. Co.A
Riley, James VA 49th Inf. Co.C
Riley, James VA 64th Mtd.Inf. Co.C
Riley, James VA Lt.Arty. Jackson's Bn.St.Line Co.A
Riley, James 1st Conf.Cav. 2nd Co.F
Riley, James Conf.Inf. 1st Bn. 2nd Co.C
Riley, James Conf.Inf. Tucker's Regt. Co.C
Riley, James 1st Choctaw & Chickasaw Mtd.Rifles Co.G Lt.Col.
Riley, James A. MS 2nd Inf. Co.B
Riley, James Augustus AL 3rd Inf. Co.E
Riley, James B. GA 5th Inf. (St.Guards) Curley's Co. Sgt.
Riley, James B. TN 44th Inf. Co.I
Riley, James B. TN 44th (Cons.) Inf. Co.A
Riley, James C. GA 34th Inf. Co.A Cpl.
Riley, James E. FL 4th Inf. Co.H
Riley, James F. AL 3rd Cav. Co.A
Riley, James F. AL Lt.Arty. 2nd Bn.
Riley, James F. FL 7th Inf. Co.B
Riley, James F. FL 8th Inf. Co.K
Riley, James F. MS Cav. Jeff Davis Legion Co.D
Riley, James F. TX 7th Inf. Co.H
Riley, James F. Conf.Cav. Wood's Regt. Co.C
Riley, James G. TN 4th Inf. Co.I
Riley, James H. MS 28th Cav. Co.C
Riley, James H. MS 6th Inf. Co.I
Riley, James H. SC 2nd Rifles Co.K Sgt.
Riley, James H. TN 2nd Cav. Co.F
Riley, James H. VA Cav. 35th Bn. Co.A
Riley, James J. MO 6th Cav. Co.G
Riley, James M. FL 6th Inf. Co.D
Riley, James M. GA 44th Inf. Co.I
Riley, James M. MS 2nd Part.Rangers Co.E
Riley, James M. MS 3rd Inf. Co.D 1st Sgt.
Riley, James M. TX 32nd Cav. Co.G
Riley, James O. NC 3rd Arty. (40th St.Troops) Co.A
Riley, James P. MD 1st Cav. Co.G 2nd Lt.
Riley, James R. NC 17th Inf. (2nd Org.) Co.L
Riley, James S. MS 18th Inf. Co.D
Riley, James S. MS 43rd Inf. Co.C
Riley, Jas. T. AL 36th Inf. Co.D Sgt.
Riley, James T. TX 19th Inf. Co.H
Riley, James T.W. TN Detailed Conscr. Co.B Sgt.

Riley, James W. AL 3rd Res. Co.A
Riley, James W. MS 6th Cav. Co.C
Riley, James W. MS Inf. 2nd Bn. Co.D
Riley, James W. MS 48th Inf. Co.D
Riley, James W. NC 1st Inf. Co.D
Riley, James W. SC 1st (Hagood's) Inf. 1st
  Co.B, 2nd Co.B
Riley, James W. TX 18th Cav. Co.C
Riley, James W. VA 12th Cav. Co.I
Riley, James W. VA Cav. 39th Bn. Co.A
Riley, James Z. MS 17th Inf. Co.I
Riley, Jasper FL 8th Inf. Co.C
Riley, J.B. MO 10th Inf. Co.B
Riley, J.B. SC 2nd Arty. Co.F
Riley, J.B. SC 2nd Arty. Co.K
Riley, J.B. SC 1st (Hagood's) Inf. 1st Co.C
Riley, J.C. AL 18th Inf. Co.G
Riley, J.C. KY 9th Mtd.Inf. Co.F Cpl.
Riley, J.C. MS 3rd Inf. (St.Troops) Co.K
Riley, J.C. MS 32nd Inf. Co.D
Riley, J.C. TN 4th Inf. Co.C
Riley, J.C. TN Inf. 23rd Bn. Co.B
Riley, J.C. TX Cav. 2nd Regt.St.Troops Co.H
Riley, J.C. TX 4th Inf. (St.Troops) Co.D
Riley, J.D. AL 2nd Cav. Co.H Cpl.
Riley, J.E. KY 9th Mtd.Inf. Co.H
Riley, J.E. SC 2nd Arty. Co.I
Riley, J.E. TX 1st Hvy.Arty. 2nd Co.A 1st Sgt.
Riley, J.E. TX 15th Inf. 1st Co.E, Co.C
Riley, Jefferson AL Cav. Hardie's Bn.Res. Co.A
Riley, Jehu AR 9th Inf. Co.A
Riley, Jeremiah TX 19th Cav. Co.H
Riley, Jeremiah A. AL 17th Inf. Co.H,F
Riley, Jerry SC 1st (Hagood's) Inf.
Riley, Jesse AL Cav. Barbiere's Bn. Brown's Co.
Riley, Jesse MS Cav. Abbott's Co.
Riley, Jesse MO Searcy's Bn.S.S. Co.C
Riley, Jesse TX 14th Inf. Co.C
Riley, Jesse J. MS 14th Inf. Co.E
Riley, Jesse W. VA 33rd Inf. Co.H
Riley, J.F. AL 56th Part.Rangers Co.B
Riley, J.F. MS 2nd Part.Rangers Co.D
Riley, J.F. SC 2nd Arty. Co.I
Riley, J.F. Inf. Bailey's Cons.Regt. Co.A
Riley, J. Frank AL 15th Bn.Part.Rangers Co.B
Riley, J.G. MS 1st (Johnson's) Inf. Co.I
Riley, J.G. MS 1st (King's) Inf. (St.Troops)
  Co.H 1st Lt.
Riley, J.G. TN 7th Cav. Co.I Sgt.
Riley, J.H. MS 46th Inf. Co.D
Riley, J.H. SC 2nd Arty. Co.B
Riley, J.H. TN 21st & 22nd (Cons.) Cav. Co.C
Riley, J.H. TN 22nd (Barteau's) Cav. Co.K
Riley, J.H. TX 20th Inf. Co.E
Riley, J.H.F. NC 1st Inf. Sgt.Maj.
Riley, J.J. AL 5th Inf. New Co.C
Riley, J.J. AL Cav. Forrest's Regt.
Riley, J.J. GA Inf. 14th Bn. (St.Guards) Co.C
  2nd Lt.
Riley, J.J. TN 18th (Newsom's) Cav. Co.F
Riley, J.L. MS Cav. Vivion's Co.
Riley, J.L. NC 54th Inf. Co.H
Riley, J.L. TX 15th Inf. 2nd Co.F
Riley, J.M. AL 22nd Inf. Co.K
Riley, J.M. AL 40th Inf. Co.D
Riley, J.M. AL 63rd Inf. Co.E Sgt.
Riley, J.M. GA Inf. 25th Bn. (Prov.Guard) Co.D

Riley, J.M. GA 41st Inf. Co.C
Riley, J.M. KY 3rd Mtd.Inf. Co.G
Riley, J.M. MS Roach's Co. (Tippah Scouts)
Riley, J.M. SC 2nd Arty. Co.F
Riley, J.M. SC 1st (Hagood's) Inf. 1st Co.I
Riley, J.M. TX 32nd Cav. Co.G
Riley, J.M. 1st Conf.Cav. 1st Co.B
Riley, J.O. SC 2nd Rifles Co.B
Riley, Joe MS 1st Lt.Arty. Co.F
Riley, John AL Lt.Arty. 2nd Bn. Co.E
Riley, John AL 5th Bn.Vol. Co.A,D
Riley, John AL 15th Inf. Co.G
Riley, John AL 30th Inf. Co.I
Riley, John AL 36th Inf. Co.B Cpl.
Riley, John AL 40th Inf. Co.K
Riley, John GA 3rd Cav. Co.B
Riley, John GA 1st Inf.
Riley, John GA 1st (Olmstead's) Inf. Stiles' Co.
Riley, John GA 17th Inf. Co.G
Riley, John GA 20th Inf. Co.G
Riley, John GA 34th Inf.
Riley, John LA 1st Hvy.Arty. (Reg.) Co.C
Riley, John LA 1st Hvy.Arty. (Reg.) Co.G
Riley, John LA 1st (Strawbridge's) Inf. Co.G
Riley, John LA 3rd Inf. Co.E
Riley, John LA Inf. 4th Bn. Co.C
Riley, John (2) LA 5th Inf. Co.G
Riley, John LA 7th Inf. Co.C
Riley, John LA 13th Inf. Co.B
Riley, John LA 13th Inf. Co.C,K Sgt.
Riley, John LA 13th Inf. Co.H
Riley, John LA 14th Inf.
Riley, John MD 1st Inf. Co.E
Riley, John MS Lt.Arty. English's Co.
Riley, John MS 1st (King's) Inf. (St.Troops)
  Co.E 1st Sgt.
Riley, John MS Inf. 2nd Bn. Co.A
Riley, John MS Inf. 2nd Bn. (St.Troops) Co.B
Riley, John MS 9th Bn.S.S. Co.B
Riley, John MS 11th Inf. Co.D
Riley, John MS 16th Inf. Co.K
Riley, John MS 17th Inf. Co.I
Riley, John, Jr. MS 17th Inf. Co.I
Riley, John, Sr. MS 17th Inf. Co.I
Riley, John MS 39th Inf. Co.I
Riley, John MS 44th Inf. Co.B
Riley, John MS 48th Inf. Co.A
Riley, John MO 15th Cav. Co.F
Riley, John MO 8th Inf. Co.B
Riley, John MO 10th Inf. Co.C
Riley, John NC 2nd Arty. (36th St.Troops)
  Co.D,C
Riley, John NC Lt.Arty. Levi's Btty. Thomas'
  Legion
Riley, John NC 1st Inf. Co.A Music.
Riley, John NC 3rd Inf. Co.C
Riley, John NC 5th Inf. Co.E
Riley, John NC 56th Inf. Co.D
Riley, John SC 1st (Butler's) Inf. Co.A
Riley, John TN 4th (Murray's) Cav. Co.D 3rd
  Lt.
Riley, John TN 13th (Gore's) Cav. Co.E 2nd Lt.
Riley, John TN 1st Hvy.Arty. 3rd Co.A
Riley, John TN Arty. Bibb's Co.
Riley, John TN Arty. Marshall's Co.
Riley, John TN Inf. 2nd Cons.Regt. Co.D Cpl.
Riley, John TN 2nd (Walker's) Inf. Co.D

Riley, John TN 5th Inf. 1st Co.C
Riley, John TN 10th Inf. Co.H
Riley, John TN 12th Inf. Co.E
Riley, John TN 12th (Cons.) Inf. Co.H Cpl.
Riley, John TN 15th Inf. Co.B 1st Sgt.
Riley, John TN 22nd Inf. Co.C
Riley, John TN 44th (Cons.) Inf. Co.A
Riley, John TN Inf. 154th Sr.Regt. Co.D
Riley, John TX 1st (McCulloch's) Cav. Co.E
Riley, John TX Cav. 2nd Regt.St.Troops Co.D
  Sgt.
Riley, John TX 22nd Cav. Co.F
Riley, John TX 33rd Cav. Co.C
Riley, John TX 36th Cav. Co.G,I
Riley, John TX Vol. Duke's Co. Cpl.
Riley, John VA 11th Cav. Co.A
Riley, John VA 14th Cav. Co.D
Riley, John VA 21st Cav. Co.A
Riley, John VA Cav. 41st Bn. Co.G 1st Sgt.
Riley, John VA Mtd.Riflemen Balfour's Co.
Riley, John VA Hvy.Arty. 10th Bn. Co.C
Riley, John VA Hvy.Arty. 19th Bn. 3rd Co.C
  Cpl.
Riley, John VA Lt.Arty. Carrington's Co.
Riley, John VA 1st Inf. Co.G
Riley, John VA Inf. 4th Bn.Loc.Def. Co.C 1st
  Sgt.
Riley, John VA Inf. 4th Bn.Loc.Def. Co.F
Riley, John VA 15th Inf. Co.G
Riley, John VA 18th Inf. Co.E
Riley, John VA 27th Inf. Co.B
Riley, John VA 37th Inf. Co.A
Riley, John VA 45th Inf. Co.K
Riley, John VA 58th Mil. Co.E
Riley, John 1st Conf.Cav. 2nd Co.A
Riley, John 1st Conf.Cav. 2nd Co.C 3rd Lt.
Riley, John 4th Conf.Inf. Co.E
Riley, John 9th Conf.Inf. Co.E
Riley, John Conf.Inf. Tucker's Regt. Co.E
Riley, John 1st Cherokee Mtd.Rifles Co.B
Riley, John Sig.Corps,CSA
Riley, John A. AR 2nd Mtd.Rifles Co.A
Riley, John A. NC 42nd Inf. Co.G
Riley, John A. TN 24th Inf. Co.D
Riley, John B. AL St.Arty. Co.A Sgt.
Riley, John B. AR 36th Inf. Co.F
Riley, John B. LA 4th Inf. Co.D
Riley, John B. MO 1st Regt.St.Guards Co.C
  Cpl.
Riley, John C. GA 5th Inf. (St.Guards) Curley's
  Co. 2nd Lt.
Riley, John C. GA 46th Inf. Co.I
Riley, John C. LA Inf. 1st Sp.Bn. (Rightor's)
  Co.B
Riley, John C. LA 2nd Inf. Co.F
Riley, John E. AL 37th Inf. Co.A
Riley, John E. TN 5th (McKenzie's) Cav. Co.G
Riley, John E. VA 1st Cav. Co.A
Riley, John E. VA 8th Inf. Co.C
Riley, John F. AL Cav. Chisolm's Co.
Riley, John F. KY 1st Bn.Mtd.Rifles Co.B
Riley, John F. KY 3rd Bn.Mtd.Rifles Co.E
Riley, John F. MS 9th Inf. New Co.K
Riley, John F. VA 39th Inf. Co.L
Riley, John F. Gen. & Staff Asst.Comsy.
Riley, John G. NC 12th Inf. Co.C
Riley, John H. AL 33rd Inf. Co.C

Riley, John H. GA 1st (Ramsey's) Inf. Co.C
Riley, John H. KY 14th Cav. Co.D,C
Riley, John H. MS 6th Inf. Co.E
Riley, John H. NC 45th Inf. Co.B
Riley, John H. TN 24th Inf. 2nd Co.D
Riley, John H. VA Lt.Arty. Carrington's Co.
Riley, John H.F. NC Hvy.Arty. 1st Bn. Co.C
Riley, John J. AR Cav. Carlton's Regt. Co.A
Riley, John J. TX 9th Cav. Co.I
Riley, John J. SC Inf. Hampton Legion Co.D
Riley, John L. AL 16th Inf. Co.G
Riley, John M. KY 3rd Mtd.Inf. Co.L
Riley, John M. MO 3rd Inf. Co.I
Riley, John M. VA 23rd Inf. Co.A
Riley, John N. AL 15th Inf. Co.L
Riley, John P. MD 1st Cav. Co.C
Riley, John P. MS 43rd Inf. Co.H
Riley, John R. TX 18th Inf. Co.C
Riley, John S. TX Waul's Legion Co.A
Riley, Johnson 2nd Cherokee Mtd.Vol. Co.F
Riley, John T. GA Floyd Legion (St.Guards)
Co.A
Riley, John T. MS 4th Inf. Co.B
Riley, John T. MS 37th Inf. Co.B
Riley, John T. MO 1st Cav. Co.H 1st Sgt.
Riley, John T. MO 1st & 3rd Cons.Cav. Co.E
Sgt.
Riley, John T. VA 4th Cav. Co.H
Riley, John W. AL 16th Inf. Co.C
Riley, John W. AL 36th Inf. Co.D
Riley, John W. KY 2nd (Duke's) Cav. Co.B
Riley, John W. MO 1st Inf. Co.B
Riley, John W. NC 2nd Cav. (19th St.Troops)
Co.K
Riley, John W. NC 20th Inf. Co.A
Riley, John W. NC 28th Inf. Co.G
Riley, John W. NC 47th Inf. Co.B
Riley, John W. SC 1st (Hagood's) Inf. 1st Co.A
Riley, John W. SC 20th Inf. Co.B
Riley, John W. VA 4th Cav. Co.H
Riley, John William AL 32nd Inf. Co.C
Riley, Jonathan G. VA 19th Cav. Co.D
Riley, Joseph AL 1st Inf. Co.F
Riley, Joseph AL 8th Inf. Co.I
Riley, Joseph AR 18th Inf. Co.E
Riley, Joseph TN 11th (Holman's) Cav. Co.B
Riley, Joseph TN Holman's Bn.Part.Rangers
Co.A
Riley, Joseph TN 1st Hvy.Arty. Co.F, 2nd Co.D
Riley, Joseph TN 10th Inf.
Riley, Joseph TX Cav. Wells' Regt. Co.B
Riley, Joseph VA 7th Inf. Co.B
Riley, Joseph 2nd Cherokee Mtd.Vol. Co.I
Riley, Joseph C. MD Inf. 2nd Bn. Co.C,F
Riley, Joseph C. TN 33rd Inf. Co.E 2nd Lt.
Riley, Joseph E. TN 33rd Inf. Co.K Cpl.
Riley, Joseph E. TX Waul's Legion Co.H 1st
Sgt.
Riley, Joseph F. MS 11th Inf. Co.D Sgt.
Riley, Joseph L. MS 21st Inf. Co.I
Riley, Joshua MO 9th Inf. Co.K
Riley, J.P. SC 1st (McCreary's) Inf. Co.A Cpl.
Riley, J.R. AL 15th Bn.Part.Rangers Co.E
Riley, J.R. AL 56th Part.Rangers Co.E
Riley, J.R. AL 34th Inf. Co.E
Riley, J.R. MS 1st (King's) Inf. (St.Troops)
Co.H

Riley, J.R. TX 11th Cav. Co.H
Riley, J.S. MS 3rd Inf. Co.A
Riley, J.S. TX Inf. 1st St.Troops Wheat's Co.
Riley, J.T. GA Conscr.
Riley, J.T. TN Lt.Arty. Rice's Btty.
Riley, J.T. TX Cav. McCord's Frontier Regt.
Co.D
Riley, J.T. TX 1st Hvy.Arty. 2nd Co.A Capt.
Riley, J.T. TX 15th Inf. 1st Co.E, Co.C
Riley, J.T. 20th Conf.Cav. 2nd Co.I Jr.2nd Lt.
Riley, J.T. Conf.Cav. Wood's Regt. Co.K
Riley, Judson NC 54th Inf. Co.H
Riley, J.V. TX 1st Hvy.Arty. Co.B Capt.
Riley, J.W. AL 25th Inf. Co.H
Riley, J.W. AL Talladega Cty.Res. J. Hender-
son's Co.
Riley, J.W. AR 10th Inf. Co.C
Riley, J.W. GA Ind.Cav. (Res.) Humphrey's Co.
Riley, J.W. GA 59th Inf. Co.H
Riley, J.W. KY 2nd (Duke's) Cav. Co.K
Riley, J.W. KY 3rd Cav. Co.C
Riley, J.W. KY 3rd Mtd.Inf. Co.C
Riley, J.W. SC 1st Mtd.Mil. Evans' Co.
Riley, J.W. SC 1st (McCreary's) Inf. Co.A
Riley, J.W. TN 9th Inf. Co.D
Riley, J.W. TX 12th Cav. Co.H
Riley, J.W. TX Cav. Terry's Regt. Co.D
Riley, J.W.P. TN 60th Mtd.Inf. Co.G
Riley, L. AR 36th Inf.
Riley, L. KY 2nd (Duke's) Cav. Co.E
Riley, L. LA Mil. 4th Regt. 1st Brig. 1st Div.
Co.B
Riley, L. MS 48th Inf. Co.E
Riley, L. VA 2nd Inf. Co.C
Riley, Labon VA 77th Mil. Co.C
Riley, L.B. TX 3rd Cav. Co.I
Riley, L. Derick SC 2nd Arty. Co.B,K
Riley, Leven N. MO Searcy's Bn.S.S. Co.C
Riley, L.M. TX 29th Cav. Co.H
Riley, Louis MS Inf. 2nd Bn. Co.E
Riley, L.R. AL 17th Inf. Co.H
Riley, M. AL Cp. of Instr. Talladega Co.D
Riley, M. AR 15th (Josey's) Inf. 1st Co.C
Riley, M. KY 10th (Johnson's) Cav. New Co.F
Riley, M. KY 3rd Mtd.Inf. Co.G 1st Lt.
Riley, M. SC 2nd St.Troops Co.B
Riley, M.A. TN 2nd (Ashby's) Cav. Co.I
Riley, M.A. TN Cav. 4th Bn. (Branner's) Co.E
Riley, Marion MS 22nd Inf. Co.D
Riley, Marion TN Cav. Hay's Bn. Co.A
Riley, Mark R. VA 7th Inf. Co.C
Riley, Mark R. VA 49th Inf. 3rd Co.G
Riley, Martin AL 29th Inf. Co.A
Riley, Martin GA 2nd Bn.S.S. Co.A
Riley, Martin GA 5th Inf. Co.I,M
Riley, Martin H. GA 6th Inf. Co.G 1st Lt.
Riley, Martin V.B. AR 23rd Inf. Co.A
Riley, Maurice MS 46th Inf. Co.D Sgt.
Riley, M.B. KY 2nd (Duke's) Cav. Co.K
Riley, McD. LA 3rd (Wingfield's) Cav. Co.I
Riley, Michael GA Siege Arty. 28th Bn. Co.A
Riley, Michael GA 36th (Villepigue's) Inf. Co.I
Riley, Michael GA Inf. City Bn. (Columbus) Wil-
liams' Co.
Riley, Michael LA Hvy.Arty. 8th Bn. Co.A,I
Riley, Michael LA 1st (Strawbridge's) Inf. Co.H
Cpl.

Riley, Michael LA Mil. 4th Regt. 1st Brig. 1st
Div. Co.G
Riley, Michael LA 6th Inf. Co.F
Riley, Michael LA 21st (Patton's) Inf. Co.C
Riley, Michael MS Lt.Arty. English's Co.
Riley, Michael SC 6th Inf. Co.D
Riley, Michael TN Lt.Arty. Barry's Co.
Riley, Michael TN 11th Inf. Co.K
Riley, Michael TX 5th Inf.
Riley, Michael Inf. School of Pract. Co.A
Riley, Michael J. GA Inf. 2nd Bn. Co.A
Riley, M.L. AL 21st Inf. Co.A
Riley, M.L. AR 14th (McCarver's) Inf. Co.K
Riley, M.L. AR 21st Inf. Co.A
Riley, M.N. SC 2nd Arty. Co.F Sgt.
Riley, M.N. SC 1st (Hagood's) Inf. 1st Co.K
Riley, Morris MO 9th Inf. Co.K
Riley, M.S. AL 8th Inf. Co.F
Riley, M.T. KY 3rd Mtd.Inf. Co.K
Riley, M.W. TX 7th Inf. Co.B
Riley, Nathan MS 10th Cav. Co.K 1st Sgt.
Riley, Nathaniel NC 27th Inf. Co.A
Riley, Nathaniel NC 55th Inf. Co.K
Riley, N.B. KY 8th Mtd.Inf. Co.I Capt.
Riley, N.B. LA 2nd Inf. Co.I
Riley, Newton J. AL Inf. 1st Regt. Co.D Cpl.
Riley, Ningan AR 36th Inf. Co.D
Riley, N.P. MO 16th Inf. Co.D
Riley, O. TX 21st Inf. Co.B
Riley, O.D.A. SC 11th Res. Co.I 2nd Lt.
Riley, O.D.A. SC Post Guard Senn's Co.
Riley, Onan B. SC 20th Inf. Co.C
Riley, Owen MS 22nd Inf. Gaines' Co.
Riley, Owen SC 3rd Cav. Co.D
Riley, Owen TN 21st Inf. Co.I
Riley, Owen TX 11th (Spaight's) Bn.Vol. Co.E
Riley, Owen VA 7th Cav. Co.I
Riley, Owen 9th Conf.Inf. Co.G
Riley, P. AR 45th Cav. Co.K Sgt.
Riley, P. LA 14th Inf. Co.F
Riley, P. LA Mil. Chalmette Regt. Co.E
Riley, P. 2nd Conf.Eng.Troops Co.F
Riley, P.A. 1st Cherokee Mtd.Vol. 1st Co.C Cpl.
Riley, P.A. 2nd Cherokee Mtd.Vol. Co.I
Riley, Parker TN 13th Inf. Co.I
Riley, Paschal AR 38th Inf. Co.A
Riley, Pat LA Mil. 1st Regt. 3rd Brig. 1st Div.
Riley, Pat TX 11th (Spaight's) Bn.Vol. Co.G
Riley, Pat Conf.Inf. Tucker's Regt. Co.F
Riley, Patric VA 166th Mil. Co.A
Riley, Patrick GA 17th Inf. Co.G
Riley, Patrick GA 25th Inf. Co.C
Riley, Patrick MD Cav. 2nd Bn. Co.C Sgt.
Riley, Patrick MS 18th Inf. Co.D
Riley, Patrick MS 24th Inf. Co.G 1st Cpl.
Riley, Patrick TN 10th Inf. Co.D
Riley, Patrick TN 10th Inf. Co.K Cpl.
Riley, Patrick VA Hvy.Arty. 10th Bn. Co.C
Riley, Patrick VA Inf. 4th Bn.Loc.Def. Co.C
Riley, Patrick VA Inf. 25th Bn. Co.C
Riley, Patrick VA 27th Inf. Co.C
Riley, Patrick H. VA 52nd Inf. Co.E
Riley, Patrick R. LA 1st (Nelligan's) Inf. Co.A
Riley, P.C. AL 7th Cav. Co.G,K
Riley, Peter AR 2nd Inf. Co.B
Riley, Peter GA 66th Inf. Co.H
Riley, Peter NC 1st Arty. (10th St.Troops) Co.A

Riley, Peter VA 33rd Inf. Co.E
Riley, Peter J.O. LA Mil. Beauregard Bn.
   Frobus' Co.
Riley, P.H. VA 4th Cav. Co.K
Riley, Pharaoh TN 44th (Cons.) Inf. Co.A
Riley, Pharoah TN 44th Inf. Co.I
Riley, Pharoh TN Sullivan Cty.Res. (Loc.Def.
   Troops) Witcher's Co.
Riley, Phil TN Inf. Nashville Bn. Fulcher's Co.
Riley, Philip AL Seawell's Btty. (Mohawk Arty.)
Riley, Philip GA 26th Inf. Co.A
Riley, Philip LA 21st (Patton's) Inf. Co.G
Riley, Philip SC Inf. 1st (Charleston) Bn. Co.C
Riley, Philip TN Arty. Fisher's Co.
Riley, Philip N. SC 2nd Cav. Co.A
Riley, Philip S. VA 1st St.Res. Co.E
Riley, Phillip LA C.S. Zouave Bn. Co.D
Riley, Phillip G. NC 1st Cav. (9th St.Troops)
   Co.H
Riley, Phillips LA Pointe Coupee Arty.
Riley, Pinkney MO 9th Inf. Co.K
Riley, Pinkney B. FL 6th Inf. Co.K
Riley, P.J. SC 10th Inf. 1st Co.G
Riley, Presley NC 3rd Bn.Sr.Res. Durham's Co.
Riley, P.S. VA 2nd St.Res. Co.F
Riley, P.S. VA Inf. 2nd Bn.Loc.Def. Co.F
Riley, Quinten T. NC 8th Inf. Co.K
Riley, R. AL 1st Bn.Cadets Co.B
Riley, R. AL Mil. T. Hunt's Co.
Riley, R. AR 1st Inf. Co.I
Riley, R. FL 2nd Inf. Co.A
Riley, R. TN 19th & 20th (Cons.) Cav. Co.E
Riley, R.A. KY 1st Bn.Mtd.Rifles Co.E
Riley, R.A. KY Jessee's Bn.Mtd.Riflemen Co.B
Riley, Ralph FL 5th Inf. Co.H
Riley, Randolph 2nd Cherokee Mtd.Vol. Co.F
Riley, R.B. LA 3rd Inf. Co.B
Riley, R.D. MS Inf. 3rd Bn. (St.Troops) Co.D
Riley, R.F. AL 30th Inf. Co.B
Riley, R.F. MS 2nd Part.Rangers Co.E
Riley, R.H. LA Lt.Arty. 2nd Field Btty.
Riley, R.H. SC 2nd Arty. Co.F
Riley, Richard KY 5th Mtd.Inf. Co.D
Riley, Richard MS 19th Inf. Co.B Capt.
Riley, Richard VA 21st Mil. Co.D
Riley, Richmond AL 3rd Res. Co.G
Riley, Robert AL 1st Inf. Co.I,D
Riley, Robert AL Cp. of Instr. Talladega
Riley, Robert KY 4th Cav. Co.E
Riley, Robert TN 20th (Russell's) Cav. Co.I
Riley, Robert TN 21st Inf. Co.G Sgt.
Riley, Robert A. KY 3rd Bn.Mtd.Rifles Co.E
Riley, Robert F. AR 2nd Inf. Co.F
Riley, Robert H. AL Inf. 1st Regt. Co.G Capt.
Riley, Robert L. AL 36th Inf. Co.D
Riley, Robert R. SC 1st (Orr's) Rifles Co.B
Riley, Robert V. VA 12th Cav. Co.E
Riley, Robinson Ray AR 23rd Inf. Co.E
Riley, R.S. KY 12th Cav. Co.K
Riley, Rufus KY 9th Cav. Co.E
Riley, R.W. AL Inf. 1st Regt. Co.E
Riley, S. AR 10th Inf. Co.C
Riley, S. SC 23rd Inf. Co.C
Riley, S. SC Manigault's Bn.Vol. Co.B
Riley, S. TX Cav. McCord's Frontier Regt. Co.E
Riley, Sam AL 25th Inf. Co.I
Riley, Samuel AL 15th Inf. Co.G

Riley, Samuel KY 1st (Butler's) Cav. Co.F
Riley, Samuel SC Lt.Arty. Gaillard's Co. (Santee
   Lt.Arty.)
Riley, Samuel SC 10th Inf. 1st Co.G Cpl.
Riley, Samuel TN 9th Cav.
Riley, Samuel VA 7th Inf. Co.B
Riley, Samuel 1st Cherokee Mtd.Rifles Co.B
Riley, Samuel J. SC 2nd Arty. Co.B,K
Riley, Samuel W. TN 44th Inf. Co.G
Riley, Samuel W. TN 44th (Cons.) Inf. Co.F
Riley, Sanders C. NC 2nd Cav. (19th St.Troops)
   Co.K
Riley, S.G. TX 13th Vol. 2nd Co.D
Riley, S.H. MS 6th Cav. Co.E 1st Sgt.
Riley, S.H. MS 6th Inf. Co.E 1st Sgt.
Riley, Shepherd W. TN 19th Inf. Co.I
Riley, Simpson NC 56th Inf. Co.D
Riley, Sion LA Inf. 4th Bn. Co.F
Riley, S.J. LA 6th Inf. Co.D
Riley, Stephen NC 5th Inf. Co.I
Riley, Sylvester TX 23rd Cav. Co.F
Riley, T. MS Cav. Vivion's Co.
Riley, T.D. AL 45th Inf. Co.G Sgt.
Riley, T.D. GA Inf. Bard's Co. Sgt.
Riley, T.H. VA Horse Arty. D. Shanks' Co.
Riley, Thomas AL Lt.Arty. Goldthwaite's Btty.
Riley, Thomas AL 54th Inf. Co.D
Riley, Thomas AL 61st Inf. Co.A,H
Riley, Thomas AR Lt.Arty. Key's Btty.
Riley, Thomas GA 24th Inf. Co.A
Riley, Thomas GA Inf. 27th Bn. (NonConscr.)
   Co.C Sgt.
Riley, Thomas GA Loc.Bn. Co.B
Riley, Thomas KY 12th Cav. Co.E
Riley, Thomas KY 8th Mtd.Inf. Co.B
Riley, Thomas LA 1st (Strawbridge's) Inf. Co.B
Riley, Thomas LA 4th Inf. Co.D
Riley, Thomas LA 6th Inf. Co.D
Riley, Thomas LA 13th Inf. Co.C,B Cpl.
Riley, Thomas MD 1st Cav. Co.A
Riley, Thomas MS 18th Inf. Co.D
Riley, Thomas MO 8th Inf. Co.D
Riley, Thomas NC 31st Inf. Co.H
Riley, Thomas NC 45th Inf. Co.C Cpl.
Riley, Thomas SC 1st St.Troops Co.F Cpl.
Riley, Thomas SC 4th Bn.Res. Co.B
Riley, Thomas SC 5th Res. Co.B Cpl.
Riley, Thomas TN 10th Cav.
Riley, Thomas TN 13th (Gore's) Cav. Co.C
Riley, Thomas TN 1st Hvy.Arty. Co.G
Riley, Thomas, No.1 TN Arty. Fisher's Co.
Riley, Thomas, No.2 TN Arty. Fisher's Co.
Riley, Thomas TN 2nd (Walker's) Inf. Co.F
Riley, Thomas TN 10th Inf. Co.G
Riley, Thomas TN 15th Inf. 2nd Co.F
Riley, Thomas TN 21st Inf. Co.I
Riley, Thomas TN 27th Inf. Co.K
Riley, Thomas TX 34th Cav. Co.A
Riley, Thomas VA 15th Cav. Co.B
Riley, Thomas VA 7th Inf. Co.B
Riley, Thomas 4th Conf.Inf. Co.E
Riley, Thomas 9th Conf.Inf. Co.F
Riley, Thomas Inf. School of Pract. Co.A
Riley, Thomas C. TX 4th Field Btty.
Riley, Thomas D. GA 12th Cav. Co.E
Riley, Thomas D. GA 26th (Villepigue's) Inf.
   Co.B,F

Riley, Thomas E. TX 12th Inf. Co.I
Riley, Thomas F. SC 1st (Orr's) Rifles Co.B
Riley, Thomas H. VA Cav. Mosby's Regt.
   (Part.Rangers) Co.F
Riley, Thomas J. AL Lt.Arty. 2nd Bn. Co.E
   Ens.
Riley, Thomas J. AL St.Arty. Co.D
Riley, Thomas J. AL 63rd Inf. Co.H
Riley, Thomas J. AL 3rd Bn. Hilliard's Legion
   Vol. Co.F
Riley, Thomas J. GA 25th Inf. Co.C 2nd Lt.
Riley, Thomas J. MS 23rd Inf. Co.A
Riley, Thomas J. MS Nash's Co. (Leake
   Rangers)
Riley, Thomas J. NC Inf. 13th Bn. Co.A
Riley, Thomas J. NC 66th Inf. Co.A,E
Riley, Thomas J. SC 1st (McCreary's) Inf. Co.G
Riley, Thomas J. SC 11th Res. Co.I 3rd Lt.
Riley, Thomas L. VA Lt.Arty. 12th Bn. 1st Co.A
Riley, Thomas M. AL 5th Inf. New Co.C Capt.
Riley, Thomas P. TN 44th (Cons.) Inf. Co.A
   Sgt.
Riley, T.I. TN Inf. 2nd Cons.Regt. Co.D
Riley, Tillman TX Inf. Griffins' Bn. Co.B
Riley, Tillman T., Jr. MS 8th Inf. Co.G Jr.2nd
   Lt.
Riley, Timothy AR Lt.Arty. Key's Btty.
Riley, Timothy VA Arty. Bryan's Co.
Riley, T.J. AL 1st Regt. Mobile Vol. Co.E
Riley, T.J. AR 34th Inf. Co.G Cpl.
Riley, T.J. LA 4th Inf. Co.C
Riley, T.J. SC 3rd Cav. Co.F
Riley, T.J. TN Arty. Bibb's Co.
Riley, T.J.F. AL Mil. 3rd Vol. Co.C Sgt.
Riley, T.M. AL 2nd Cav. Co.K
Riley, T.O. TX 1st Hvy.Arty. Co.D
Riley, T.P. GA 5th Res. Co.B 1st Sgt.
Riley, Turner GA 64th Inf. Co.I
Riley, Turner L. AL 28th Inf. Co.H
Riley, T.W. AL 5th Inf. Capt.
Riley, T.W. NC 32nd Inf. Co.I
Riley, T.W. TX 6th Inf. Co.A
Riley, T.W. TX 12th Inf. Co.A
Riley, W. AL 7th Cav. Co.G
Riley, W. AL 9th Inf. Co.A
Riley, W. AL 63rd Inf. Co.K,G Cpl.
Riley, W. GA 1st Reg. Co.D
Riley, W. LA 4th Cav. Co.B
Riley, W. LA Lt.Arty. Holmes' Btty. Cpl.
Riley, W. LA 18th Inf. Co.H
Riley, W. LA Mil. Chalmette Regt. Co.G Sgt.
Riley, W. TN Cav. Nixon's Regt. Co.A
Riley, W.A. AL 2nd Cav. Co.H
Riley, Walter MS 8th Cav. Co.F
Riley, Walter MS Inf. 3rd Bn. (St.Troops) Co.F
Riley, Walter N. NC 33rd Inf. Co.F
Riley, Waymore J. MS Inf. 2nd Bn. Co.D
Riley, W.B. AL 1st Regt. Mobile Vol. Co.A
Riley, W.B. AL Mil. 2nd Regt.Vol. Co.D Cpl.
Riley, W.B. AR Inf. Cocke's Regt. Co.K
Riley, Wm. B. GA 63rd Inf. Co.B
Riley, W.B. SC 2nd Arty. Co.F
Riley, W.B. SC 1st (Hagood's) Inf. 1st Co.C
Riley, W.C. AL 33rd Inf. Co.D
Riley, W.C. TX 3rd Cav. Co.I
Riley, W.D. AR 2nd Mtd.Rifles Co.A
Riley, Wesley AL 33rd Inf. Co.B

Riley, Wesley NC 5th Sr.Res. Co.H
Riley, W.F. 15th Inf. Co.E
Riley, W.G. AL 5th Inf. New Co.C
Riley, W.H. GA 7th Inf. Co.I
Riley, W.H. GA 25th Inf. Co.C Cpl.
Riley, W.H. LA 3rd (Harrison's) Cav. Co.A
Riley, W.H. LA 4th Cav. Co.B
Riley, W.H. MS 10th Cav. Co.C
Riley, W.H. TX Cav. McCord's Frontier Regt. Co.D
Riley, Will H. KY 1st (Butler's) Cav. Co.D
Riley, William AL 51st (Part.Rangers) Co.G
Riley, William AL 53rd (Part.Rangers) Co.D
Riley, William AL Mil. 4th Vol. Co.H
Riley, William AL 9th Inf. Co.B
Riley, William AL 17th Inf. Co.D
Riley, William AL 33rd Inf. Co.B
Riley, William AL 36th Inf. Co.A Cpl.
Riley, William AL 39th Inf. Co.D Sgt.
Riley, William GA 1st Cav. Co.C
Riley, William GA 22nd Inf. Co.A
Riley, William KY 5th Cav. Co.E,F
Riley, Wm. KY 6th Mtd.Inf. Co.D 2nd Lt.
Riley, William LA 5th Inf. Co.G Cpl.
Riley, William LA 7th Inf. Co.D
Riley, William LA 11th Inf. Co.D
Riley, William LA C.S. Zouave Bn.
Riley, William MS Lt.Arty. (The Hudson Btty.) Hoole's Co.
Riley, William MS Inf. 2nd Bn. Co.A
Riley, William MS Inf. 5th Bn. Co.A
Riley, William MS 6th Inf. Co.B
Riley, William MS 9th Inf. Co.I
Riley, William MS 15th Inf. Co.C
Riley, William MS 19th Inf. Co.E Cpl.
Riley, William MS 36th Inf. Co.B,D
Riley, William MS 43rd Inf. Co.I
Riley, William MS 44th Inf. Co.L
Riley, William MS 48th Inf. Co.A
Riley, William MO 5th Cav. Co.H,K
Riley, William MO 8th Cav. Co.G,I 1st Lt.
Riley, William MO 1st Inf. Co.I,C Bvt.2nd Lt.
Riley, William MO 9th Inf. Co.K
Riley, William NC 2nd Arty. (36th St.Troops) Co.B,H
Riley, William NC 1st Inf. Co.D
Riley, William NC 7th Inf. Co.C
Riley, William NC 44th Inf. Co.C
Riley, William NC 47th Inf. Co.A
Riley, William NC 61st Inf. Co.C
Riley, William SC 7th Inf. 1st Co.B 2nd Co.B, Co.F Sgt.
Riley, William TN 5th (McKenzie's) Cav. Co.D
Riley, William TN Cav. 9th Bn. (Gantt's) Co.F,E Sgt.
Riley, William TN 15th (Cons.) Cav. Co.E
Riley, William TN Lt.Arty. McClung's Co.
Riley, William TN 39th Mtd.Inf. Co.I
Riley, William TN 40th Inf. Co.C
Riley, William TN 40th Inf. Co.I
Riley, William TN 42nd Inf. 2nd Co.E Cpl.
Riley, William TX 27th Cav. Co.D
Riley, William VA 20th Cav. Co.I
Riley, William VA Lt.Arty. 38th Bn. Co.A
Riley, William VA Inf. 5th Bn. Co.D
Riley, William VA Inf. 22nd Bn. Co.B
Riley, William VA 26th Inf. 1st Co.B

Riley, Wm. VA 46th Inf. Co.H
Riley, William VA 49th Inf. 1st Co.G
Riley, William VA 53rd Inf. Co.A
Riley, William Horse Arty. White's Btty.
Riley, William A. AL 5th Inf. New Co.C 2nd Lt.
Riley, William A. AR 2nd Inf.
Riley, William A. AR 34th Inf. Co.D
Riley, William B. GA 6th Inf. Co.H
Riley, William B. GA 51st Inf. Co.D
Riley, William Burt SC 1st (Orr's) Rifles Co.B
Riley, William D. TX 26th Cav. Co.D
Riley, William D. VA 45th Inf. Co.K
Riley, William Dudley NC 6th Inf. Co.C
Riley, William F. NC 16th Inf.
Riley, William H. AR 19th (Dawson's) Inf. Co.A
Riley, William H. GA 20th Inf. Co.C Cpl.
Riley, William H. GA Cherokee Legion (St.Guards) Co.B Cpl.
Riley, William H. MO 2nd Cav. Co.F
Riley, William H. NC 33rd Inf. Co.F
Riley, William H. NC 56th Inf. Co.D
Riley, William H. SC 4th Cav. Co.A
Riley, William H. SC Lt.Arty. Garden's Co. (Palmetto Lt.Btty.)
Riley, William H. TN 4th (McLemore's) Cav. Co.A
Riley, William H. TN 14th Inf. Co.B Sgt.
Riley, William H. TN 44th Inf. Co.G
Riley, William H. TN 55th (McKoin's) Inf. Co.F
Riley, William H. TX 1st (McCulloch's) Cav. Co.I
Riley, William H. TX Waul's Legion Co.C
Riley, William H. VA Lt.Arty. 38th Bn. Co.A
Riley, William H. VA 49th Inf. 1st Co.G
Riley, William H. VA 59th Inf. 2nd Co.A Cpl.
Riley, William L. KY 1st Inf. Co.B 1st Lt.
Riley, William L. MO 10th Inf. Co.B
Riley, William L. NC Inf. 13th Bn. Co.A
Riley, William L. NC 66th Inf. Co.A
Riley, William L. TN 16th (Logwood's) Cav. Co.G
Riley, William M. GA 22nd Inf. Co.K
Riley, William N. SC 2nd Inf. Co.F
Riley, William P. LA 18th Inf. Co.D
Riley, William S. GA 35th Inf. Co.E
Riley, William S. GA 45th Inf. Co.E Cpl.
Riley, William T. FL 6th Inf. Co.D
Riley, William T. LA 28th (Thomas') Inf. Co.B
Riley, William W. AL Mil. 4th Vol. Co.A
Riley, William W. AL 25th Inf.
Riley, Willie NC 56th Inf. Co.D
Riley, W.J. FL Cav. 3rd Bn. Co.C
Riley, W.J. FL Cav. 3rd Bn. Co.D
Riley, W.J. 15th Conf.Cav. Co.E
Riley, W.J. 15th Conf.Cav. Co.I
Riley, W.L. KY 14th Cav. Co.B
Riley, W.L.W. SC 5th Cav. Co.I
Riley, W.L.W. SC 2nd Arty. Co.C
Riley, W.M. GA Inf. 14th Bn. (St.Guards) Co.A 3rd Lt.
Riley, W.M. GA 25th Inf. Co.C
Riley, W.N. AL 42nd Inf. Co.H
Riley, W.P. NC 1st Jr.Res. Co.I
Riley, W.R. KY 3rd Cav. Co.E
Riley, W.S. AR 19th (Dawson's) Inf. Co.F Cpl.

Riley, W.S. AR Inf. Hardy's Regt. Co.I Cpl.
Riley, W.S. 4th Conf.Eng.Troops
Riley, W.T. AL Conscr.
Riley, W.T. TX 5th Inf. Co.A
Riley, W.W. AL 38th Inf. Co.H
Riley, W.W. AL 42nd Inf. Co.H 2nd Lt.
Riley, W.W. MS 38th Cav. Co.D
Riley, W.W. SC Mil.Arty. 1st Regt. Co.C Sgt.
Riley, W.W. SC Inf. 1st (Charleston) Bn. Co.E
Riley, W.W. SC 27th Inf. Co.A
Riley, Young Mead's Conf.Cav. Co.L
Riley, Zac VA 77th Mil. Co.C
Rilie, Benjamin VA 21st Mil. Co.E
Rilie, James Monroe VA 26th Inf. 2nd Co.B
Rilie, Robert L. VA 21st Mil. Co.E
Rilihan, Maurice GA 1st (Olmstead's) Inf. Guil-martin's Co.
Riling, William VA 22nd Inf. Co.E
Rill, Robert KY 5th Cav.
Rills, --- TX 24th Cav.
Rilley, James Gen. & Staff, QM Dept.
Rilley, Wm. F. AL 8th Inf. Co.H
Rillihan, Maurice VA 27th Inf. Co.F
Rillihan, Michael VA 27th Inf. Co.F
Rilling, D. TX 6th Field Btty.
Rilling, David TX 5th Field Btty.
Rilling, Joseph TX 3rd Inf. Co.B
Rillion, J.H. MO Cav. Coleman's Regt. Co.B
Rills, Edward H. LA 2nd Cav. Co.I Cpl.
Rills, J.B., Jr. LA 30th Inf. Co.I Band Music.
Rills, J.M. LA 16th Inf. Co.K
Rills, J.N. TX 1st Field Btty.
Rills, Narcisse LA 2nd Cav. Co.I Ch.Bugler
Rilly, H. VA 24th Cav. Co.G
Rils, J.B. LA 26th Inf. Co.D
Rils, John M. LA 11th Inf. Co.B Cpl.
Rils, Patrick E. LA 1st Cav. Co.A
Rily, A.R. TN 19th (Biffle's) Cav. Co.D
Rily, Daniel H. GA 45th Inf. Co.B
Rily, G. AL Mil. 3rd Vol. Co.G
Rily, James KY 4th Cav. Co.K
Rily, John TX 4th Cav. Co.B Capt.
Rily, John VA 67th Mil. Co.E
Rily, John H. SC 20th Inf. Co.A
Rily, Robert VA 11th Bn.Res. Co.B
Rily, Thomas GA 64th Inf. Co.A
Rily, W.H. AL 36th Inf. Co.D
Rilzon, G. MO 9th Bn.S.S. Co.D
Rimal, George W. VA 10th Inf. Co.B Cpl.
Rimare, Binion TX 11th Inf. Co.K
Rimassa Giovanni LA Mil. 6th Regt.Eur.Brig. (Italian Guards Bn.) Co.2
Rimboldt, --- LA Mil. 3rd Regt.Eur.Brig. (Garde Francaise) Co.5
Rime, --- LA Mil. 2nd Regt.French Brig. Co.3
Rime, Christian P. LA 21st (Pattons') Inf. Co.I
Rimel, Isaac MO 1st & 3rd Cons.Cav. Co.G 2nd Lt.
Rimel, Isaac MO Cav. 3rd Bn. Co.A 2nd Lt.
Rimel, Jacob VA 146th Mil. Co.A
Rimel, J.M. VA Lt.Arty. Carpenter's Co.
Rimel, John P. VA 46th Mil. Co.A
Rimel, J.W. VA 3rd (Chrisman's) Bn.Res. Co.A
Rimel, Pete VA 10th Inf. Co.E
Rimel, Philip F. VA 58th Mil. Co.B Sgt.
Rimer, Alexander FL 7th Inf. Co.E

Rimer, Alexander SC Inf. 7th Bn. (Enfield Rifles) Co.B Music.
Rimer, Andrew SC 3rd Bn.Res. Co.B
Rimer, David A. NC 42nd Inf. Co.B
Rimer, Eli NC 58th Inf. Co.G
Rimer, Gosper FL 7th Inf. Co.B
Rimer, Henry F. NC 7th Inf. Co.F
Rimer, H.F. NC 5th Inf. Co.K
Rimer, Hose MS Part.Rangers Smyth's Co.
Rimer, H.T. MS Part.Rangers Smyth's Co.
Rimer, H.T. Conf.Cav. Wood's Regt. 2nd Co.D
Rimer, Isaac NC 64th Inf. Co.M
Rimer, Isaac TN Cav. 16th Bn. (Neal's) Co.F
Rimer, John VA 6th Bn.Res. Co.A
Rimer, John A. SC 3rd Bn.Res. Co.B
Rimer, John L. NC 8th Inf. Co.K
Rimer, Leonard NC 8th Inf. Co.K
Rimer, Milton F. NC 8th Inf. Co.K
Rimer, Pulaski NC 25th Inf. Co.A
Rimer, Reuben H. NC 5th Inf. Co.K Cpl.
Rimer, S.M. NC 57th Inf. Co.C
Rimer, Stephen NC 64th Inf. Co.F
Rimes, A.L. MS Cav. 1st Bn. (McNair's) St.Troops Co.D Cpl.
Rimes, Andrew M. GA 61st Inf. Co.D Sgt.
Rimes, Benjamin F. MS 18th Inf. Co.H
Rimes, B.F. MS Cav. Powers' Regt. Co.A
Rimes, B.F. MS 1st Lt.Arty. Co.F
Rimes, B.W. TX 4th Inf. Co.C
Rimes, Cuyler A. GA 51st Inf. Co.E
Rimes, David A. FL 9th Inf. Co.D Sgt.
Rimes, E.F. MS 6th Inf. Co.F
Rimes, J. MS Cav. 1st Bn. (McNair's) St.Troops Co.D
Rimes, J.F. MS Cav. Powers' Regt. Co.A Capt.
Rimes, J.J. GA 25th Inf. Co.C
Rimes, J.L. GA Cav. 2nd Bn. Co.C
Rimes, J.L. GA 5th Cav. Co.E
Rimes, J.M. AL 53rd (Part.Rangers) Co.D
Rimes, J.M. FL 1st (Res.) Inf. Co.I Cpl.
Rimes, J.M. GA Cav. 2nd Bn. Co.C
Rimes, J.M. GA 5th Cav. Co.E
Rimes, J.M.C.D. GA 5th Cav. Co.E
Rimes, J. McD. GA Cav. 2nd Bn. Co.C
Rimes, John Conf.Inf. 8th Bn. Co.F
Rimes, John F. MS 18th Inf. Co.H Capt.
Rimes, Joseph MS Cav. Powers' Regt. Co.C
Rimes, J.P. GA 7th Cav. Co.H
Rimes, J.P. GA Hardwick Mtd.Rifles Co.B
Rimes, Malachia C. GA 12th Inf. Co.D
Rimes, Thomas W. AR 6th Inf. Co.H 1st Sgt.
Rimes, V.P. GA 51st Inf. Co.E
Rimes, William L. AR 12th Bn.S.S. Co.C Jr.2nd Lt.
Rimes, William S. FL 10th Inf. Co.F
Rimes, Willis J. TX 31st Cav. Co.C
Rimes, W.L. AR 18th Inf. Co.I 1st Sgt.
Rimey, Levi SC 1st Arty. Co.K
Rimicke, R. LA Mil. 1st Chasseurs a pied Co.A
Rimke, Bernard VA Inf. 6th Bn.Loc.Def. Co.B
Rimle, James MS 11th (Perrin's) Cav. Co.A
Rimmer, A. NC 50th Inf. Co.A
Rimmer, Calvin H. MS Lt.Arty. (Madison Lt.Arty.) Richards' Co.
Rimmer, F.M. TX 32nd Cav. Co.A
Rimmer, Hasten NC 50th Inf. Co.A

Rimmer, H.T. MS 1st (King's) Inf. (St.Troops) Co.F
Rimmer, H.W. MS 1st (King's) Inf. (St.Troops) Co.F
Rimmer, J. NC 8th Jr.Res. Co.C
Rimmer, James A. MS Lt.Arty. (Madison Lt.Arty.) Richards' Co.
Rimmer, J.B. MS 32nd Inf. Co.B
Rimmer, J.N. TX 1st Bn.S.S. Co.A,E
Rimmer, John VA 2nd Cav. Co.B
Rimmer, John H. TN Conscr. (Cp. of Instr.)
Rimmer, Joseph VA Inf. 23rd Bn. Co.E
Rimmer, J.W. NC 4th Bn.Jr.Res. Co.C
Rimmer, Merrell NC 24th Inf. Co.H
Rimmer, Samuel R. NC 50th Inf. Co.A Cpl.
Rimmer, S.P. MS 5th Cav. Co.E
Rimmer, S.P. MS 18th Cav. Co.I
Rimmer, W. MS 1st (King's) Inf. (St.Troops) D. Love's Co.
Rimmer, W.D. MS 18th Cav. Co.I
Rimmer, W.H. MS 5th Cav. Co.E
Rimmer, Wiley D. MS 20th Inf. Co.K
Rimmer, Wiley P. VA Inf. 23rd Bn. Co.E
Rimmer, William NC 50th Inf. Co.A
Rimmer, William VA 2nd Cav. Co.B
Rimmer, Wilson MS 3rd Cav. Co.B
Rimmier, Phillip MO 2nd Cav. Co.B,F
Rimner, John D. MS 2nd (Davidson's) Inf. Co.D
Rimon, P. FL 3rd Inf.
Rims, W. GA 26th Inf. Co.K
Rimsher, S. TX Cav. Baird's Regt. Co.F
Rin, --- LA C.S. Zouave Bn. Co.F
Rin, J. NC 2nd Arty. (36th St.Troops) Co.G
Rin, Joseph C. LA 26th Inf. Co.E 2nd Lt.
Rin, P.L. LA 26th Inf. Co.E Capt.
Rinach, E. AL Mil. 3rd Vol. Co.C
Rinaldi, Albert NC 2nd Arty. (36th St.Troops) Co.B Ord.Sgt.
Rinaldi, Albert NC 18th Inf. Co.K 1st Sgt.
Rinaldi, Benjamin F. NC 2nd Arty. (36th St.Troops) Co.B 1st Sgt.
Rinaldi, Benjamin F. NC 16th Inf. Co.K,A Capt.
Rinaldi, E.W. NC 3rd Arty. (40th St.Troops) Co.K
Rinaldi, H.C. AL 5th Inf. New Co.K Sgt.
Rinaldi, Henry C. AL 6th Inf. Co.M
Rinaldi, William S. AL 6th Inf. Co.M
Rinans, Robert AR 37th Inf. Co.K
Rinard, Elanson VA 136th Mil. Co.F
Rinauro, Girolamo LA Mil. 6th Regt.Eur.Brig. (Italian Guards Bn.) Co.3
Rinch, R.J. TN 17th Inf. Co.H
Rinck, Andrew NC 11th (Bethel Regt.) Inf. Co.I
Rinck, Christian R. NC 46th Inf. Co.K
Rinck, Daniel NC 22nd (Bethel Regt.) Inf. Co.I
Rinck, Noah NC 11th (Bethel Regt.) Inf. Co.I
Rincon, Jose TX Cav. Ragsdale's Bn. 1st Co.A
Rind, Henry G. AR 2nd Mtd.Rifles Co.G Capt.
Rind, J. LA Mil. Orleans Guards Regt. Co.K
Rind, James G. AR 2nd Mtd.Rifles Co.G Cpl.
Rind, James M. VA 3rd Inf.Loc.Def. Co.E Cpl.
Rind, John LA Mil. Bragg's Bn. Schwartz's Co. Cpl.
Rind, McNiel AR 33rd Inf. Co.H
Rind, R. VA 3rd Inf.Loc.Def. 1st Co.G Cpl.
Rind, R.G. VA 3rd Inf.Loc.Def. 2nd Co.G Sgt.

Rind, Seabrook, Jr. VA 1st Arty. 1st Co.C
Rind, Seabrook, Jr. VA 1st Inf. Co.F
Rind, S.S. VA 3rd Inf.Loc.Def. Co.D
Rind, W.A. VA 3rd Inf.Loc.Def. Co.E
Rind, W.M. GA 2nd Inf. Co.D
Rinderknecht, F. TX 4th Inf. Co.F
Rinderle, Bernard LA Mil. 1st Regt. 2nd Brig. 1st Div. Co.G
Rindet, --- AL 3rd Inf. Lt.
Rindey, John NC Currituck Guard J.W.F. Bank's Co.
Rindleman, J.B. AR Lt.Arty. Zimmerman's Btty.
Rindrick, D.J. MO 9th (Elliott's) Cav. Co.F
Rine, B.D. GA 43rd Inf. Co.A
Rine, Christopher C. TX 2nd Cav. Co.C
Rine, Ed MS 9th Inf. New Co.E 1st Lt.
Rine, Ed MS 10th Inf. Old Co.F Cpl.
Rine, Edward AL Lt.Arty. 2nd Bn. Co.E
Rine, G.C. TN 22nd (Barteau's) Cav. Co.H
Rine, J. GA 2nd Cav. Co.A
Rine, Jackson VA 8th Bn.Res. Co.C
Rine, John TN 63rd Inf. Co.G
Rine, John VA 42nd Inf. Co.I
Rine, John D. AL Lt.Arty. 2nd Bn. Co.E
Rine, John D. GA 36th (Villepigue's) Inf. Co.I 2nd Lt.
Rine, Joseph L. VA 14th Cav. Crawford's Co.
Rine, Joseph L. VA 17th Cav. Co.F
Rine, Ruff TN 27th Inf. Co.C
Rine, Samuel TN 27th Inf. Co.C
Rine, Thomas TX 20th Inf. Co.K
Rine, T.M. MO 11th Inf. Co.E
Rine, William H. VA Lt.Arty. Cooper's Co.
Rine, William H. Conf.Arty. Braxton's Bn. Co.A
Rineal, Everhart VA 2nd Inf. Co.D Cpl.
Rinehard, M.F. MO Robertson's Regt.St.Guard Co.13
Rinehardt, Abraham NC 23rd Inf. Co.F
Rinehardt, Daniel NC 34th Inf. Co.E
Rinehardt, Elias NC 23rd Inf. Co.F
Rinehardt, E.T. NC 23rd Inf. Co.F Cpl.
Rinehardt, Henry VA 10th Cav. Co.D
Rinehardt, Levi NC 23rd Inf. Co.F
Rinehardt, Michael C. NC 8th Inf. Co.H
Rinehart, Adam GA Cherokee Legion (St.Guards) Co.B
Rinehart, Algernon VA 58th Mil. Co.K
Rinehart, Anderson VA 45th Inf. Co.H
Rinehart, A.P. SC Inf. Holcombe Legion Co.H
Rinehart, C.A. SC Inf. Holcombe Legion Co.H
Rinehart, Caleb M. NC 1st Cav. (9th St.Troops) Co.F
Rinehart, C.M. MS Shields' Co.
Rinehart, Columbus AL 22nd Inf. Music.
Rinehart, D.A. MS 12th Cav. Co.K
Rinehart, E.C. VA 7th Cav. Co.F
Rinehart, Eli VA 20th Cav. Co.F
Rinehart, Elisha AL 41st Inf. Co.E
Rinehart, Elonza VA 2nd Cav. Co.C
Rinehart, Emanuel TN 43rd Inf. C.D Drum.
Rinehart, F.A. TX Waul's Legion Co.F Sgt.
Rinehart, F.E. SC 2nd Arty. Co.K
Rinehart, George MS 32nd Inf. Co.I
Rinehart, Giles MS 26th Inf. Co.B
Rinehart, Giles MS 32nd Inf. Co.I 1st Sgt.
Rinehart, James TN 42nd Inf. Co.G
Rinehart, James C. Inf. Thomas Legion Co.E

Rinehart, James H. AL 55th Vol. Co.B
Rinehart, Jeff MS 32nd Inf. Co.I
Rinehart, J.G.W. VA 190th Mil. Co.G
Rinehart, John MS 26th Inf. Co.B
Rinehart, John MS 32nd Inf. Co.I 2nd Lt.
Rinehart, John A. MS 32nd Inf. Co.I
Rinehart, John A. VA 33rd Inf. Co.A
Rinehart, Joseph NC 62nd Inf. Co.C
Rinehart, J.W. AL Cav. 5th Bn. Hilliard's
   Legion Co.E
Rinehart, J.W. NC 2nd Jr.Res. Co.E
Rinehart, Matthias NC 4th Sr.Res. Co.F
Rinehart, Michael MS 37th Inf.
Rinehart, M.L. TN 10th (DeMoss') Cav. Co.G
Rinehart, Nathan MO 2nd Inf. Co.D
Rinehart, Paul NC 4th Sr.Res. Co.F
Rinehart, S.D. SC 2nd Arty. Co.E
Rinehart, Thomas AL 55th Vol. Co.B
Rinehart, Thomas NC 4th Cav. (59th St.Troops)
   Co.E
Rinehart, Uriah MS 1st (Patton's) Inf. Co.E
Rinehart, W. SC 2nd St.Troops Co.B
Rinehart, West SC 2nd Arty. Co.K
Rinehart, William SC 6th Inf. Co.D
Rinehart, William D. NC 4th Cav. (59th
   St.Troops) Co.E
Rineheart, Caswell TN 3rd (Lillard's) Mtd.Inf.
   Co.I
Rineheart, E.L. AR Inf. Cocke's Regt. Co.I
Rineheart, Isaac M. NC 16th Inf. Co.A Drum.
Rineheart, Isaac M. NC 39th Inf. Co.K Drum.
Rineheart, Isaac M. NC Inf. Thomas Legion 1st
   Co.A Drum.
Rineheart, J.C. AR Inf. Cocke's Regt. Co.I
Rineheart, John NC 60th Inf. Co.B
Rineheart, John VA 146th Mil. Co.B
Rineheart, M.A. AR 45th Cav. Co.L
Rineheart, Thomas GA 6th Cav. Co.H
Rineheart, Thomas P. NC 16th Inf. Co.A
Rineheart, Thomas P. NC 39th Inf. Co.K
Rineheart, Thomas P. NC Inf. Thomas Legion
   1st Co.A
Rineheart, William TN 26th Inf. Co.E
Rineheat, J.W. AL 51st (Part.Rangers) Co.F
Rineke, F.A. VA 10th Cav. Co.D
Rinel, Henry LA Mil. 3rd Regt. 2nd Brig. 1st
   Div.
Rineman, Philip MO Cav. 1st Regt.St.Guard
   Co.C
Riner, Amos J. GA 48th Inf. Co.F
Riner, D. VA Wade's Regt.Loc.Def. Co.D
Riner, Daniel VA 11th Cav. Co.A
Riner, Daniel VA 67th Mil. Co.A
Riner, David VA Inf. 7th Bn.Loc.Def. Co.B
Riner, David J. GA 48th Inf. Co.F
Riner, George M. GA Crosby's Cav.
Riner, George W. VA 6th Bn.Res. Co.G
Riner, George W. VA 72nd Mil.
Riner, J. GA 6th Inf. Co.I
Riner, James VA 59th Inf. 2nd Co.D
Riner, James A. VA Inf. 26th Bn. Co.H Cpl.
Riner, James M. GA 48th Inf. Co.F Cpl.
Riner, James S. GA 48th Inf. Co.F
Riner, J.B. MS 35th Inf. Co.K
Riner, J.C. GA 10th Mil.
Riner, J.D. VA 1st Arty. Co.H
Riner, John VA 25th Cav. Co.K

Riner, John 1st Cherokee Mtd.Vol. 2nd Co.K
Riner, John D. VA Arty. C.F.Johnston's Co.
Riner, John T. VA 30th Bn.S.S. Co.C
Riner, John T. VA 166th Mil. Co.D,H Cpl.
Riner, L. GA 48th Inf. Co.F
Riner, Lawson Y. GA 48th Inf. Co.F
Riner, Lewis VA 166th Mil. Co.H Sgt.
Riner, Lewis S. VA 30th Bn.S.S. Co.C
Riner, Littleton J. GA 48th Inf. Co.F
Riner, Richard A. TX 11th Inf. Co.K
Riner, R.M. TX 32nd Cav. Co.D
Riner, R.P. FL Cav. 3rd Bn. Co.B Cpl.
Riner, R.P. 15th Conf.Cav. Co.D
Riner, Samuel W. VA 166th Mil. Co.H
Riner, T.E. MS 15th Inf. Co.H
Riner, V.E. GA 1st (Symons') Res. Co.H
Riner, Wiley Y. GA 48th Inf. Co.F
Riner, William, Jr. GA 48th Inf. Co.F
Riner, William MS 31st Inf. Co.E
Riner, William B. GA 32nd Inf. Co.G
Riner, William C. NC 15th Inf. Co.B
Riner, William C. VA 166th Mil. Co.H
Riner, Wilson GA 48th Inf. Co.F
Riner, Wilson Y. GA 48th Inf. Co.F Cpl.
Riners, W.J. AL Cav. Shockley's Co.
Rines, Ed TN 2nd Cav. 2nd Lt.
Rines, James H. VA 7th Cav. Co.F Black.
Rines, J.H. GA 12th Inf. Co.H
Rines, John NC 21st Inf. Co.K
Rines, John J. VA 7th Cav. Co.F
Rines, J.S. GA Lt.Arty. (Jackson Arty.) Massen-
   burg's Btty.
Rines, Samuel S. LA 25th Inf. Co.A
Rines, William MS 42nd Inf. Co.C
Rines, William VA 9th Inf. Co.F
Riney, Ben S. KY 1st (Butler's) Cav. Co.G Sgt.
Riney, Benjamin T. MO 1st Regt.St.Guards Co.F
Riney, Benjamin T. MO Inf. 8th Bn. Co.B
Riney, Benjamin T. MO 9th Inf. Co.F
Riney, Edward KY 8th Cav. Co.G
Riney, Frank X. KY 2nd Cav. Co.A
Riney, William MO 2nd N.E. Cav. (Franklin's
   Regt.) Co.B
Rinfro, J.S. AR 27th Inf. Co.C
Ring, Adam NC 28th Inf. Co.A
Ring, A.N. TN Cav. 1st Bn. (McNairy's) Co.D
Ring, Andrew AR 17th (Griffith's) Inf. Co.C
Ring, Andrew J. TN 4th (McLemore's) Cav.
   Co.A
Ring, Augustin NC 21st Inf. Co.H Sgt.
Ring, Austin VA 111th Mil. Co.2 1st Sgt.
Ring, B.G. TN 1st Hvy.Arty. 2nd Co.C
Ring, B.G. TN Hvy.Arty. Sterling's Co.
Ring, B.J. Conf.Cav. 6th Bn. Co.E
Ring, B.S. TN 8th (Smith's) Cav. Co.G
   Wagon M.
Ring, Charles TN 8th (Smith's) Cav. Co.G
Ring, David VA 2nd Inf.Loc.Def. Co.G
Ring, David VA Inf. 2nd Bn.Loc.Def. Co.A
Ring, David VA 63rd Inf. Co.G
Ring, David A. SC 12th Inf. Co.D
Ring, E. TX 9th (Nichols') Inf. Co.G
Ring, E. 4th Conf.Eng.Troops Co.E Cpl.
Ring, E.L. GA Cav. 1st Bn.Res. McKinney's
   Co.
Ring, Enoch NC Inf. 2nd Bn. Co.B
Ring, Enoch TX 26th Cav. Co.A,I

Ring, Fountain KY 13th Cav.
Ring, Fountain VA 63rd Inf. Co.G
Ring, G.E. KY 1st Inf. Co.A Cpl.
Ring, George AR 6th Inf. Co.A
Ring, George FL 9th Inf. Co.A
Ring, George P. LA 6th Inf. Co.K Capt.
Ring, H. LA 22nd Inf. Co.G
Ring, H.D. AR Inf. Cocke's Regt. Co.C
Ring, Henry TN 3rd (Forrest's) Cav. Co.C
Ring, Henry Inf. Bailey's Cons.Regt. Co.G
Ring, Henry J. TN 49th Inf. Co.A
Ring, H.J. TN Inf. 4th Cons.Regt. Co.G
Ring, Hugustin NC 2nd Inf. Co.A,B Sgt.
Ring, J.A. TX 2nd Cav. Co.B
Ring, Jack NC 1st Cav. (9th St.Troops) Co.G
Ring, Jacob P. TN 4th (McLemore's) Cav. Co.A
Ring, James LA 23rd Inf. D.H. Marks' Co.
Ring, James MO Cav. Snider's Bn. Co.C
Ring, James TN 15th (Cons.) Cav. Co.F Sgt.
Ring, James C. AR 14th (McCarver's) Inf. Co.F
   Cpl.
Ring, James C. AR 21st Inf. Co.B
Ring, James H. MO 5th Inf. Co.H
Ring, James H. MO 1st Div.St.Guards 1st Sgt.
Ring, Jeremiah MS Inf. 2nd Bn. Co.G
Ring, Jeremiah MS 48th Inf. Co.G
Ring, Jerry MS 21st Inf. Co.G
Ring, J.L. VA 4th Cav. Co.I,F
Ring, J.M. TN 8th (Smith's) Cav. Co.A
Ring, John LA 1st Cav. Co.C
Ring, John MS 1st Lt.Arty. Co.A
Ring, John SC 1st Inf. Co.M
Ring, John L. SC 1st (McCreary's) Inf. Co.I
Ring, John M. TN 4th (McLemore's) Cav. Co.A
Ring, John W. GA 40th Inf. Co.A
Ring, Joseph TN 23rd Inf. 1st Co.F,H
Ring, Joseph A. AZ Cav. Herbert's Bn. Helm's
   Co. Bvt.2nd Lt.
Ring, J.P. TN 8th (Smith's) Cav. Co.A
Ring, J.S. SC 4th Inf. Co.H Cpl.
Ring, J.W. KY 7th Cav. Co.G
Ring, J.W. KY 8th Mtd.Inf. Co.I
Ring, M. TX 8th Field Btty.
Ring, Marion MO 3rd Inf. Co.B
Ring, Martin AR 1st Vol. Co.G
Ring, Martin MO Cav. Freeman's Regt. Co.D
Ring, Martin NC 21st Inf. Co.H
Ring, Martin VA 63rd Inf. Co.G Sgt.
Ring, M.L. TN 8th (Smith's) Cav. Co.G
Ring, Peyton VA 8th Cav. Co.C
Ring, Robert S. VA 12th Inf. Co.E
Ring, R.S. MD Cav. 2nd Bn. Co.C 1st Lt.
Ring, Sanford NC 4th Bn.Jr.Res. Co.B
Ring, Shepard H. AR 14th (McCarver's) Inf.
   Co.F
Ring, Shepherd H. AR 21st Inf. Co.B
Ring, Stephen MO 6th Inf. Co.G
Ring, Stephen NC 28th Inf. Co.C
Ring, Taylor MO Cav. Freeman's Regt. Co.D
Ring, T.D. KY 7th Cav. Co.G
Ring, Thomas NC 9th Bn.S.S. Co.B
Ring, Thomas B. VA Cav. McFarlane's Co.
Ring, Thos. B. Conf.Cav. 6th Bn. Co.E
Ring, Timothy LA 11th Inf. Co.H
Ring, W.H.H. AR 38th Inf. New Co.I
Ring, William AR 38th Inf. Co.F

Ring, William MO Cav. Freeman's Regt. Co.G Sgt.
Ring, William MO 3rd Inf. Co.B
Ring, William NC 28th Inf. Co.A
Ring, William J. NC 1st Inf. Co.G
Ringdom, W.M. FL Kilcrease Lt.Arty. Cpl.
Ringell, Ernest SC Arty. Lee's Co.
Ringen, J.B. GA Cav. 29th Bn.
Ringer, C. AR Inf. Cocke's Regt. Co.A
Ringer, C. MO Cav. Woodson's Co.
Ringer, Charles AR Lt.Arty. Hart's Btty. 2nd Lt.
Ringer, Charles MO Lt.Arty. 1st Btty. Sgt.
Ringer, Charles Conf.Cav. Powers' Regt. Co.G
Ringer, Frederick H. MS 43rd Inf. Co.H
Ringer, Jacob E. GA Lt.Arty. (Jo Thompson Arty.) Hanleiter's Co.
Ringer, J.H. MS 5th Cav. Co.B Cpl.
Ringer, Joab VA 14th Cav. Co.I
Ringer, John TX 17th Inf. Co.D Sgt.
Ringer, J.S. TX 17th Inf. Co.B
Ringer, P.H. MS 5th Cav. Co.C
Ringer, P.H. MS 3rd Inf. (St.Troops) Co.C
Ringer, William MS 15th Inf. Co.K,E
Ringer, William H. MS 33rd Inf. Co.G
Ringer, William H. SC 9th Res. Co.G
Ringer, William J. GA 2nd Cav. (St.Guards) Co.K 2nd Lt.
Ringer, William N. GA 35th Inf. Co.D,B
Ringer, W.J. GA Mil. 57th Regt. Co.C Capt.
Ringerback, E. LA Mil. 3rd Regt. 1st Brig. 1st Div. Co.E
Ringet, Louis LA Inf.Cons. 18th Regt. & Yellow Jacket Bn. Co.A
Ringgold, Gardiner TX 20th Inf. Co.C
Ringgold, James G. GA Cobb's Legion Co.B
Ringgold, Joseph TN 27th Inf. Co.D 2nd Lt.
Ringgold, Lockett NC 3rd Inf. Co.D
Ringgold, Louis MS 25th Inf. Co.F Sgt.
Ringgold, R.M. TX 5th Inf. Co.E
Ringgold, Robert MS 28th Cav.
Ringgold, R.S. AL Lt.Arty. 2nd Bn. Co.A Asst.Surg.
Ringgold, R.S. MO Lt.Arty. 3rd Btty. Asst.Surg.
Ringgold, W. AR 36th Inf. Co.K
Ringgold, William H. LA 8th Inf. Co.H
Ringland, Oswell GA Inf. 26th Bn. Co.A Sgt.
Ringlehoff, Samuel AR Mil. Desha Cty.Bn.
Ringler, C. TX Inf. Timmons' Regt. Co.D
Ringler, C. TX Waul's Legion Co.F
Ringler, Melvin J. MO Cav. 3rd Bn. Ch.Bugler
Ringley, Jeriah D. VA 6th Bn.Res. Co.C
Ringner, H. TX 37th Cav. Gray's Co.
Ringner, H. TX 20th Inf. Co.B
Ringnet, Theophil LA Conscr.
Ringo, A.J. KY 5th Mtd.Inf. Co.H
Ringo, A. Jackson KY 10th (Diamond's) Cav. Co.E
Ringo, Benjamin R. TX 23rd Cav. Co.K
Ringo, Coleman KY 7th Mtd.Inf. Co.B
Ringo, D.W. AR 6th Inf. Co.A
Ringo, D.W. AR Mil. Borland's Regt. Peyton Rifles Capt.
Ringo, D.W. AR Inf. Cocke's Regt. Lt.Col.
Ringo, D.W. 3rd Conf.Inf. Co.D 2nd Lt.
Ringo, E. TX 10th Cav. Co.D

Ringo, E.V. MO 16th Inf. Co.A
Ringo, Everal F. TX 27th Cav. Co.L Cpl.
Ringo, Henry KY 12th Cav. Co.A
Ringo, Hervey MO 1st N.E. Cav. Co.K
Ringo, H.H. KY 7th Inf. Co.B
Ringo, I.E. GA 35th Inf. Co.D
Ringo, J.A. KY 7th Mtd.Inf. Co.B
Ringo, James MO 1st N.E. Cav. Co.K
Ringo, James F. KY 5th Mtd.Inf. Co.H
Ringo, John M. AR 3rd Inf. Co.C
Ringo, Joseph KY 7th Mtd.Inf. Co.B
Ringo, Joseph MO 1st N.E. Cav. Co.F
Ringo, Joseph MO 1st N.E. Cav. Co.K
Ringo, Joseph MO 9th Inf. Co.E
Ringo, Joseph MO Inf. Clark's Regt. Co.H
Ringo, Joseph H. FL 9th Inf. Co.F
Ringo, Joseph L. MO 1st N.E. Cav. Price's Co.M, White's Co. Sr.2nd Lt.
Ringo, L. AR 32nd Inf. Co.G
Ringo, Marvin A. AR 3rd Inf. Co.C
Ringo, Micajah AR 26th Inf. Co.E 1st Lt.
Ringo, Micajah AR Mil. Desha Cty.Bn.
Ringo, R. TX 10th Cav. Co.D
Ringo, R.C. TX 23rd Cav. Co.F
Ringo, Robert TX 29th Cav. Co.F
Ringo, Samuel TX 10th Cav. Co.D
Ringo, William MO 1st N.E. Cav. Co.K
Ringo, William E. MO 2nd Cav. 3rd Co.K
Ringo, William E. MO 3rd Inf. Co.C
Ringo, William E. MO 9th Inf. Co.G
Ringo, Willis L. KY 2nd Mtd.Inf. Co.A 2nd Lt.
Ringo, W.M. MS Mil. 4th Cav. Co.C 1st Lt.
Ringo, W.M. MS Stewart's Co. (Yalobusha Rangers) Sgt.
Ringold, --- MS 22nd Inf. Asst.Surg.
Ringold, Benjamin F. NC 8th Inf. Co.E
Ringold, Ernest SC Hvy.Arty. 15th (Lucas') Bn. Co.C
Ringold, Ernest SC Arty. Childs' Co.
Ringold, James MO 2nd Cav. Co.D
Ringold, James NC 27th Inf. Co.E
Ringold, James NC 67th Inf. Co.E Cpl.
Ringold, John NC 61st Inf. Co.B
Ringold, R.S. AR 12th Bn.S.S. Asst.Surg.
Ringold, R.S. Gen. & Staff Asst.Surg.
Ringold, Samuel AR 12th Bn.S.S. Co.A
Ringold, Thomas VA 23rd Cav. 1st Lt.
Ringold, William AR 50th Mil. Co.I
Ringold, William LA 14th Inf. Co.E
Ringold, W.R. TN 55th (Brown's) Inf. Co.E Sgt.
Ringold, Wyatt AR 50th Mil. Co.I
Ringole, Samuel AR 18th Inf. Co.A
Rings, John MO Lt.Arty. Von Phul's Co.
Ringstaff, G.W. AL 33rd Inf. Co.E
Ringstaff, Henry NC 43rd Inf. Co.B 1st Lt.
Ringstaff, J.C. NC 3rd Arty. (40th St.Troops) Co.G
Ringstaff, J.C. NC Lt.Arty. 13th Bn. Co.E
Ringstaff, Thomas NC 3rd Arty. (40th St.Troops) Co.G
Ringstaff, Thomas NC Lt.Arty. 13th Bn. Co.E
Ringstaff, W.H. AR 13th Mil. Co.E
Ringstaff, W.H. AR 13th Mil. Co.F
Ringuet, Joseph LA Inf. 10th Bn. Co.C
Ringuet, Louis LA Inf. 10th Bn. Co.C
Ringwald, Gustave A. LA 1st Cav. Co.A

Ringwald, William TN 15th Inf. Co.I Music.
Rinica, Andrew VA 33rd Inf. Co.H
Rinicke, A. TX 14th Inf. Co.A
Rinie, Joseph LA Mil. 1st Regt. French Brig. Co.6
Riniel, John P. VA 18th Cav. Co.I
Rink, Eli F. NC 23rd Inf. Co.F Cpl.
Rink, George F. NC 23rd Inf. Co.F
Rink, H.A. AR 3rd Cav. Co.G
Rink, Henry NC 28th Inf. Co.C
Rink, John F. AL 48th Inf. New Co.G
Rink, Lewis S. VA 15th Inf. Co.H
Rinka, Jacob AL 5th Inf. New Co.D
Rinkar, George VA Cav. 41st Bn. Co.A
Rinker, Benjamin VA 136th Mil. Co.C
Rinker, Benjamin F. VA 33rd Inf. Co.K
Rinker, Casper VA 51st Mil. Co.D
Rinker, C.F. SC Mil. 16th Regt. Triest's Co.
Rinker, Daniel VA 77th Mil. Co.A
Rinker, Dennis VA 18th Cav. 1st Co.G Sgt.
Rinker, Dennis VA Cav. 41st Bn. Co.A
Rinker, E.F. VA 12th Cav. Co.H
Rinker, Ephraim VA 136th Mil. Co.C
Rinker, Erasmus F. VA 136th Mil. Co.G Capt.
Rinker, Fenton S. VA Horse Arty. J.W. Carter's Co.
Rinker, Fenton T. VA 136th Mil. Co.H
Rinker, Frank VA 23rd Cav. Co.D
Rinker, Fred VA 23rd Cav. Co.D
Rinker, George VA 18th Cav. 1st Co.G
Rinker, George VA 23rd Cav. Co.A
Rinker, George VA 31st Mil. Co.F
Rinker, George VA 33rd Inf.
Rinker, I.P. VA Cav. 12th Regt. Co.K Capt.
Rinker, Israel C. VA 7th Cav. Co.K
Rinker, Jacob VA 31st Mil. Co.E
Rinker, Jacob G.S. VA 12th Cav. Co.K
Rinker, Jacob H. VA 136th Mil. Co.G
Rinker, Jacob M. VA 8th Bn.Res. Co.C
Rinker, Jacob Z. VA 10th Inf. 1st Co.C,F
Rinker, James VA 11th Cav. Co.E
Rinker, James F. VA 146th Mil. Co.K
Rinker, James G. VA 33rd Inf. Co.K
Rinker, J.F. VA 2nd Inf. Co.F
Rinker, Joel VA Cav. McNeill's Co.
Rinker, John A. VA Cav. 35th Bn. Co.A
Rinker, John G. VA 31st Mil. Co.F
Rinker, John W. VA 49th Inf. Co.D
Rinker, Jonathan VA 7th Cav. Co.C
Rinker, Jonathan H. VA 12th Cav. Co.K Sgt.
Rinker, Jonathan H. VA 10th Inf. 1st Co.C
Rinker, J.W. VA 2nd Inf. Co.F
Rinker, Lemuel H. VA 10th Inf. 1st Co.C Sgt.
Rinker, Michael F. VA 12th Cav. Co.K
Rinker, Michael F. VA 136th Mil. Co.F
Rinker, Moses VA 33rd Inf. Co.C
Rinker, Nathaniel B.F. VA Lt.Arty. Garber's Co.
Rinker, Noah VA 97th Mil. Co.G
Rinker, Noah F. VA 12th Cav. Co.K
Rinker, Noble B. VA Cav. Mosby's Regt. (Part.Rangers)
Rinker, Raphael H. VA Lt.Arty. B.Z. Price's Co.
Rinker, Raphael H. VA Lt.Arty. W.H. Rice's Co.
Rinker, Robert D. VA 7th Cav. Co.C
Rinker, Robert D. VA 12th Cav. Co.K

Rinker, Robert D. VA 10th Inf. 1st Co.C
Rinker, Romanus VA 17th Inf. Co.B
Rinker, Samuel VA 136th Mil. Co.G
Rinker, Samuel G. VA 8th Bn.Res. Co.C
Rinker, Samuel G. VA 97th Mil. Co.G
Rinker, S.D. VA 62nd Mtd.Inf. 2nd Co.M
Rinker, St.Dennis VA 33rd Inf. Co.K 1st Sgt.
Rinker, Thomas VA 18th Cav. Co.D
Rinker, Thomas J. VA 136th Mil. Co.E
Rinker, William VA 18th Cav. 1st Co.G
Rinker, William VA 23rd Cav. Co.A
Rinkle, H. TX 2nd Inf. Co.K
Rinkle, Jacob AL 18th Bn.Vol. Co.C
Rinkle, John AR Lt.Arty. Hart's Btty.
Rinn, J. TX Inf. Timmons' Regt. Co.B
Rinn, Jacob TX Waul's Legion Co.D
Rinn, John TX Waul's Legion Co.D
Rinn, L. TX Inf. Timmons' Regt. Co.B
Rinn, Louis TX Inf. Timmons' Regt. Co.B
Rinn, Ludwig TX Waul's Legion Co.D
Rinn, Ph. TX Inf. Timmons' Regt. Co.B
Rinn, Philip TX Waul's Legion Co.D
Rinn, Phillipp TX Inf. Timmon's Regt. Co.B
Rinn, Tim LA 14th Inf. Co.E
Rinnels, A.J. AR Lt.Arty. Zimmerman's Btty.
Rino, David TX 15th Inf. 2nd Co.E
Rino, Paul LA Mil. 3rd Regt. 3rd Brig. 1st Div.
  Co.H Sgt.
Rinor, William TN 53rd Inf. Co.D
Rinse, John W. NC 67th Inf. Co.B
Rinteln, Anton TX 17th Inf. Co.H
Rinter, E.T. VA Inf. 2nd Bn.Loc.Def. Co.A
Rinto, J. KY 5th Cav. Co.F
Rintoln, Anton TX 16th Inf. Co.H
Rints, Joseph TX 1st Inf. Co.A
Rinz, A.M. TX Cav. Benavides' Regt. Capt.
Rinz, Joseph VA Hvy.Arty. 20th Bn. Co.E
  Music.
Riodan, J. LA Mil. Orleans Fire Regt. Co.H
Rioden, William MS 18th Inf. Co.F
Riogell, J.D. SC Palmetto S.S. Co.F
Riojas, Jesus TX Cav. Benavides' Regt. Co.I
Riol, Jacob R. TN 53rd Inf. Co.F
Riola, Antonio LA 10th Inf. Co.G
Riols, A.T. SC 25th Inf. Co.A
Riols, John FL 1st Cav. Co.K Cpl.
Rion, Edward LA Inf. 4th Bn. Co.B
Rion, James H. SC Inf. 7th Bn. (Enfield Rifles)
  Co.B Lt.Col.
Rion, James H. SC 22nd Inf. Maj.
Rion, John D. VA 10th Inf. Co.I
Rion, Joseph T. TX Cav. Ragsdale's Bn. Co.A
Rion, Lastie TX Cav. Ragsdale's Bn. Co.A
Rion, Stephen TX Cav. Ragsdale's Bn. Co.A
Rion, Tyre TN 2nd (Smith's) Cav.
Rion, William TN 2nd (Smith's) Cav.
Riondel, Louis LA Mil. 1st Regt. French Brig.
  Co.8
Rions, J.R. TN 21st (Carter's) Cav. Co.A
Riooffe, Alexander LA 5th Inf. Co.B Capt.
Riordan, --- LA Mil. British Guard Bn. West's
  Co.
Riordan, Andrew FL 4th Inf. Co.B
Riordan, Daniel, 1st LA 6th Inf. Co.F
Riordan, Daniel, 2nd LA 6th Inf. Co.F
Riordan, Daniel LA Mil. Irish Regt. Co.G
Riordan, David LA 1st Hvy.Arty. (Reg.) Co.K

Riordan, Ed TX 26th Cav. Co.A Capt.
Riordan, Ed. TX Cav. Baird's Regt. Maj.
Riordan, Edward TX Cav. Hardeman's Regt.
  Lt.Col.
Riordan, James LA Mil.Conf.Guards Regt. Co.H
Riordan, John AL 1st Regt. Mobile Vol. British
  Guard Co.A
Riordan, John LA Mil. Irish Regt. Co.F
Riordan, John LA Mil. Brenan's Co. (Co.A,
  Shamrock Guards)
Riordan, John VA Lt.Arty. J.S. Brown's Co.
Riordan, Lafayette W. VA 56th Inf. Co.F
Riordan, Lafayette W. 1st Conf.Eng.Troops Co.E
Riordan, Michael LA 1st (Strawbridge's) Inf.
  Co.I
Riordan, Michael LA 21st (Patton's) Inf. Co.C
Riordan, Michael LA 22nd (Cons.) Inf. Co.K
Riordan, Michael TN 10th Inf. Co.D
Riordan, Michael 3rd Conf.Eng.Troops Co.F
Riordan, Patrick TN Lt.Arty. Tobin's Co.
Riordan, Thomas LA 13th Inf. Co.H
Riorden, Dan VA 3rd Inf.Loc.Def. Co.I
Riorden, Ed. TX 1st Hvy.Arty. Co.F
Riorden, John AR Lt.Arty. Wiggins' Btty.
Riordon, Daniel LA 21st (Kennedy's) Inf. Co.E
Riordon, Michael MS 18th Inf. Co.A,F
Riordon, Pat Henry GA 39th Inf. Co.A,H
Riordon, Thomas LA 1st (Nelligan's) Inf. Co.K
Riordon, Thomas J. LA 2nd Inf. Co.I
Rios, C. TX 4th Cav. Co.C
Rios, Demas TX 3rd Inf. Co.F
Rios, Vermin TX 3rd Inf. Co.H
Riosing, C. TX 3rd Inf. Co.B
Riost, Pierre LA Mil. 1st Regt. French Brig.
  Co.C
Riot, Thomas MO 6th Cav. Co.I 1st Sgt.
Rioux, H.G. LA Mil. Chalmette Regt. Co.H
Ripel, Joseph TX 17th Inf. Co.H
Riper, F.N.J. TN 1st Cav. Co.G
Ripert, Thomas W. LA 10th Inf. Co.H
Ripeto, John MO 9th Inf. Co.B
Ripetoe, J.M. TX 4th Inf. Co.B
Ripey, James KY Morgan's Men Co.D 1st Sgt.
Ripey, John LA 28th (Gray's) Inf. Co.A
Ripey, Thomas E. GA 18th Inf. Co.G Sgt.
Ripinsky, Chs. LA Mil. 4th Regt.Eur.Brig. Co.D
Ripka, D. TX 24th & 25th Cav. (Cons.) Co.H
Ripka, D. TX 25th Cav. Co.B,H
Ripke, D. TX Inf. 1st St.Troops Shield's Co.B
Ripkin, D. TX Conscr.
Riple, G.W. TX 14th Inf. Co.H
Riples, F. GA 48th Inf. Co.A
Ripley, A.J. VA Inf. 7th Bn.Loc.Def. Co.B
Ripley, Amberse TX 19th Inf. Co.G
Ripley, Adam SC 2nd Arty. Co.K
Ripley, Alexander LA 5th Cav. Co.H
Ripley, Andrew J. VA 61st Mil. Co.D
Ripley, Andrew S. VA Lt.Arty. Armistead's Co.
Ripley, Andrew S. Conf.Lt.Arty. Stark's Bn.
  Co.B
Ripley, B. AL 5th Inf. Co.B
Ripley, Charles P. VA 6th Cav. Co.A
Ripley, Demetrius B. TN 61st Mtd.Inf. Co.A
Ripley, Dwight Gen. & Staff QM Agent
Ripley, Edward SC 19th Inf. Co.B
Ripley, F.H. AL 9th Inf. Co.A Capt.
Ripley, F.H. AL 21st Inf. 1st Sgt.

Ripley, F.J. TN Lt.Arty. Rain's Co. Sgt.
Ripley, Francis M. AL 5th Bn.Vol. Co.B
Ripley, George GA 1st (Ramsey's) Inf.
Ripley, H.D. MS 3rd (St.Troops) Cav. Co.C
Ripley, Henry SC 2nd Arty. Co.B,K
Ripley, Hilleary Y. VA 28th Inf. 2nd Co.C
Ripley, I. TX Inf. Chambers' Bn.Res.Corps
  Co.D
Ripley, Irwin MO Parsons' Regt.
Ripley, J. MO Beck's Co.
Ripley, James AL 3rd Cav. Co.G
Ripley, James AL 9th (Malone's) Cav. Co.M
Ripley, James, Jr. VA 166th Mil. Co.A
Ripley, James, Sr. VA 166th Mil. Co.A
Ripley, James B. VA Inf. 23rd Bn. Co.E
Ripley, James L. VA Inf. 26th Bn. Co.E
Ripley, James M. VA 56th Inf. Co.D
Ripley, James R. VA 26th Inf. Co.D
Ripley, James R. VA Inf. 26th Bn. Co.E
Ripley, James W. NC 35th Inf. Co.G
Ripley, John SC 1st (Butler's) Inf. Co.A Cpl.
Ripley, John A. VA 166th Mil. Co.A
Ripley, John J. VA 61st Mil. Co.D
Ripley, John L. VA Inf. 26th Bn. Co.E Sgt.
Ripley, John Mc. VA Inf. 26th Bn. Co.E
Ripley, John S. VA Inf. 26th Bn. Co.E
Ripley, Joseph B. GA 1st (Olmstead's) Inf. Co.G
  1st Lt.
Ripley, J.P. VA 32nd Inf. Co.F
Ripley, J.R. VA Inf. 4th Bn.Loc.Def. Co.B
Ripley, J.W. TN 3rd (Forrest's) Cav. Co.C 1st
  Lt.
Ripley, J.W. TX 23rd Cav. Co.G
Ripley, L. GA 2nd Inf. Co.B
Ripley, Lemuel VA 32nd Inf. 1st Co.K
Ripley, Lorenzo D. GA Inf. 2nd Bn. Co.B 2nd
  Lt.
Ripley, Madison VA 11th Inf. Co.K
Ripley, Martin V.B. VA 57th Inf. Co.K Sgt.
Ripley, M.D. TX Inf. 1st St.Troops Co.F
Ripley, M.L. TN 63rd Inf. Co.D,K 1st Sgt.
Ripley, M.M. AR 35th Inf. Co.G
Ripley, N.N. TX 4th Inf. Co.E
Ripley, P. Lt.Arty. Dent's Btty.,CSA
Ripley, P.M. TX 4th Inf. Co.E 1st Sgt.
Ripley, Richard SC 2nd Arty. Co.K
Ripley, Roswell S. SC 1st Arty. Lt.Col.
Ripley, Roswell S. Gen. & Staff Brig.Gen.
Ripley, S. Gen. & Staff Brig.Gen.
Ripley, S.G. GA Lt.Arty. (Jackson Arty.) Mas-
  senburg's Btty.
Ripley, T.C. AR 30th Inf. Co.A Cpl.
Ripley, Thaddeus A. LA Inf. 1st Sp.Bn.
  (Wheat's) Co.C 1st Lt.
Ripley, Thomas B. VA 61st Mil. Co.D
Ripley, Thos. D. VA 61st Mil. Co.D
Ripley, Thomas J. VA 28th Inf. Co.D
Ripley, Thomas W. AL 5th Bn.Vol. Co.B
Ripley, T.R. GA Cav. Alexander's Co.
Ripley, Valentine VA 33rd Inf. Co.G 1st Lt.
Ripley, W.B. LA Ogden's Cav. 1st Lt.,Adj.
Ripley, Westly VA Lt.Arty. French's Co. Sgt.
Ripley, Wesley F. VA 61st Mil. Co.H
Ripley, William AL 5th Bn.Vol. Co.B
Ripley, William LA 28th (Gray's) Inf. Co.A
Ripley, William TN 39th Mtd.Inf. Co.G
Ripley, William VA 166th Mil. Co.A

Ripley, William B. MO 1st Inf. Co.A 1st Lt.

Ripley, William H. TN 61st Mtd.Inf. Co.F

Ripley, William J. GA 29th Inf. Co.E

Ripley, William P. LA 3rd (Harrison's) Cav. Lt.

Ripley, William R. VA Cav. Hounshell's Bn.
    Thurmons' Co.

Ripley, William R. VA Inf. 26th Bn. Co.E Cpl.

Ripley, William V. TX 2nd Field Btty.

Ripley, W.P. TN 7th (Duckworth's) Cav. Co.F

Riply, J.W. Gen. & Staff Hosp.Stew.

Ripoll, Franco LA Mil. 5th Regt.Eur.Brig.
    (Spanish Regt.) Co.5 Cpl.

Ripoll, Frank LA Mil. 5th Regt.Eur.Brig.
    (Spanish Regt.) Co.5

Rippe, --- TX 8th Field Btty.

Rippe, --- TX Lt.Arty. Dege's Bn.

Rippe, Christian TX 13th Vol. 2nd Co.G, Co.B

Rippe, Christien TX 35th (Brown's) Cav. Co.G

Rippe, H. TX 13th Vol. 2nd Co.B

Rippe, W. SC Mil.Arty. 1st Regt. Harms' Co.

Rippel, J. TX Inf. Timmons' Regt. Co.B

Rippel, Joseph TX 17th Inf. Co.H

Ripper, Joseph TX Sayle's Cav. Co.G

Rippeto, Abner AR 2nd Inf. Co.B,D

Rippeto, James P. VA 22nd Inf. Co.A

Rippeto, J.E. VA 88th Mil.

Rippeto, J.T. VA 88th Mil. Capt.

Rippeto, James T. VA Lt.Arty. 12th Bn. 2nd
    Co.A

Rippeto, O.H.P. MO 6th Inf. Co.A

Rippetoe, Andrew J. VA 22nd Inf. Co.A

Rippetoe, Carlisle VA 5th Inf. Co.D

Rippetoe, Dewitt VA 5th Inf. Co.K

Rippetoe, Dewitt C. VA Prov.Guard Avis' Co.

Rippetoe, James T. VA Lt.Arty. Sturdivant's Co.
    Sgt.

Rippetoe, John L. VA 22nd Inf. Co.A

Rippetoe, Joseph AR 3rd Cav. Co.F

Rippetoe, Lafayette VA 22nd Inf. Co.A

Rippetoe, P.H.P. MO Inf. 3rd Bn. Co.B

Rippetoe, William D. VA 33rd Inf. Co.H Capt.

Rippetoe, William F. VA 25th Inf. 2nd Co.D
    Sgt.

Rippett, E., Mrs. SC 1st (Orr's) Rifles

Rippey, Andrew TN 9th (Ward's) Cav. Co.E

Rippey, F.M. LA 3rd (Wingfield's) Cav. Co.C

Rippey, Henry NC IPG Co.I

Rippey, Isaac TN 6th (Wheeler's)Cav. Co.B,C

Rippey, J.A. TN 1st Cav.

Rippey, James NC 55th Inf. Co.D

Rippey, James A. NC 13th Inf. Co.E

Rippey, Jerry TN 9th (Ward's) Cav. Co.E

Rippey, Jesse TN 9th (Ward's) Cav. Co.E

Rippey, J.W. TN 9th (Ward's) Cav. Co.E

Rippey, L. NC 3rd Jr.Res. Co.B

Rippey, Moses MO 2nd Inf.

Rippey, S.L. TN 9th (Ward's) Cav. Co.E

Rippey, T.W. TN 9th (Ward's) Cav. Co.E Cpl.

Rippey, W. SC 1st Regt. Charleston Guard Co.G

Rippey, Wesley TN 9th (Ward's) Cav. Co.E
    Sgt.

Rippey, W.T. NC 3rd Jr.Res. Co.B

Rippi, W.C. SC 3rd Bn.Res. Co.D

Rippie, Edward TN Cav. 2nd Bn. (Biffle's) Co.F

Rippie, Isaac TN Cav. 2nd Bn. (Biffle's) Co.F

Ripple, Daniel AR 11th Inf. Co.D

Ripple, Elija AR 1st (Crawford's) Cav. Co.B

Ripple, Elijah AR 11th Inf. Co.D Sgt.

Ripple, Elijah AR 11th & 17th (Cons.) Inf. Co.D
    Color Cpl.

Ripple, E.M. AR 11th Inf. Co.D

Rippley, Thomas C. AR 1st (Dobbin's) Cav.
    Co.C

Rippon, John J. VA 2nd Inf. Co.I

Rippond, I. LA 3rd (Harrison's) Cav. Co.E

Rippstein, Clemens TX 3rd Inf. Co.H

Rippstein, J.K. KY 1st (Butler's) Cav. Co.F Sgt.

Rippstein, J.R. KY Cav. Thompson's Co.

Rippstein, Peter TX 3rd Inf. Co.H

Rippy, A.J. TN 17th Inf. Co.B

Rippy, Alford TN 20th Inf. Co.F

Rippy, Alfred TN 9th (Ward's) Cav. Co.E

Rippy, C. NC 57th Inf. Co.I

Rippy, Calvin TN 20th Inf. Co.F

Rippy, Calvin TX 9th Cav. Co.K

Rippy, C.G. NC 15th Inf. Co.C

Rippy, E. NC 57th Inf. Co.I

Rippy, E.R. NC 55th Inf. Co.D

Rippy, G.W. TX 12th Inf. Co.E

Rippy, Irvin MO 8th Inf. Co.A

Rippy, James KY 5th Cav. Co.H

Rippy, James NC 4th Sr.Res. Co.H

Rippy, Jesse TN 20th Inf. Co.F

Rippy, J.M. LA 9th Inf. Co.H

Rippy, Lewis NC 4th Bn.Jr.Res. Co.B

Rippy, R.H. NC Mallett's Bn. Co.A

Rippy, Richard LA 9th Inf. Co.H

Rippy, Samuel H. NC 15th Inf. Co.C Sgt.

Rippy, Simeon KY Morgan's Men Co.E Sgt.

Rippy, Simeon TN 9th (Ward's) Cav. Co.E Sgt.

Rippy, S.M. TN 2nd (Robison's) Inf.

Rippy, S.M. TN 20th Inf. Co.F Sgt.

Rippy, W.A. TN 20th Inf. Co.F

Rippy, William MO 8th Inf. Co.A

Rippy, William TX 9th Cav. Co.K

Rippy, William T. NC 4th Bn.Jr.Res. Co.B

Rippy, W.K. NC 57th Inf. Co.I

Rippy, W.W. TN 20th Inf. Co.F

Rips, George TX Conscr.

Riptoe, James MO Robertson's Regt.St.Guard
    Co.11

Ripton, S.E.A. AL 59th Inf. Co.F Cpl.

Riquer, Fco. LA Mil. 5th Regt.Eur.Brig.
    (Spanish Regt.) Co.2

Rirdel, Emil Conf.Inf. 8th Bn.

Rires, B.B. NC Nelsons' Co. (Loc.Def.)

Risbach, William LA Mil. 4th Regt. 2nd Brig. 1st
    Div. Co.C

Risbad, Murat AL 4th Inf.

Risbourg, Al LA Mil. 1st Regt. French Brig.
    Co.8 Sgt.

Risby, Benjamin 1st Conf.Eng.Troops Co.C

Risby, C.J. Conf.Arty. Lewis' Bn. Co.B

Risby, E. VA Hvy.Arty. 10th Bn. Co.D

Risby, John R. VA 8th Inf. Co.A

Risby, John R. VA 41st Inf. Co.C 2nd Lt.

Risby, J.R. AL 3rd Inf. Co.I,B

Risch, I. LA Mil. Orleans Fire Regt. Co.A

Risch, N.A. LA 20th Inf. Co.F

Rischard, Louis TX 8th Inf. Co.A

Rische, Edward TX Comal Res.

Risden, James TN 7th Inf. Co.A

Risden, W. AR 30th Inf. Co.K

Risdon, William J. VA 17th Inf. Co.K

Rise, H.E. GA 32nd Inf. Co.F

Rise, John H. VA 27th Inf. 1st Co.H

Rise, Samuel VA 5th Bn.Res. Co.C

Riseden, A.S. AR 30th Inf. Co.K

Riseden, Robert TN 37th Inf. Co.K

Riseden, William TN 2nd (Ashby's) Cav. Co.K

Risely, Joseph VA 2nd St.Res. Co.B

Riseman, G.W. FL 7th Inf.

Risen, James M. LA 1st Inf. Co.H

Risener, A. GA Cav. 24th Bn. Co.B

Risener, Charles H. AR 8th Inf. New Co.B

Risener, Christian AR 7th Inf. Co.H

Risener, Jackson 1st Choctaw & Chickasaw
    Mtd.Rifles 1st Co.E

Risener, James AR 27th Inf. Co.I

Risener, J. Newton GA 12th Cav. Co.F

Risener, M.J. GA 16th Inf. Co.C

Risener, Thomas J. GA 16th Inf. Co.C

Risenever, J.E. MS 9th Cav. Co.E

Risenger, John D. LA 28th (Gray's) Inf. Co.C

Risenhaver, Louis MS 30th Inf.

Risenhoover, James E. MS 15th Inf. Co.K Cpl.

Risenhoover, Jasper MO 1st & 4th Cons.Inf.
    Co.C

Risenhoover, Jasper MO 4th Inf. Co.C

Risenhoover, J.E. MS 10th Cav. Co.F

Risenhoover, J.E. TN Cav. 17th Bn. (Sanders')
    Co.B

Risenhoover, Joseph AR 33rd Inf. Co.I

Risenhoover, L. MS 8th Cav. Co.D

Risenhoover, L.H. MS 31st Inf. Co.B

Risenhoover, Robert P. AR 33rd Inf. Co.I

Risenhoover, William C. MO 3rd Cav. Co.G,K

Risenhoover, Young F. MS 15th Inf. Co.K
    Jr.2nd Lt.

Risenor, A. GA Arty. Maxwell's Reg.Lt.Btty.

Riser, Adam MS Cav. 3rd (St.Troops) Co.C

Riser, Adam MS 1st Lt.Arty. Co.A

Riser, A.H. LA 8th Cav. Co.E

Riser, David MS Inf. 1st Bn.St.Troops (30 days
    '64) Co.E

Riser, G. 2nd Conf.Eng.Troops Co.C

Riser, George MS 3rd (St.Troops) Cav. Co.C

Riser, George MS 1st (King's) Inf. (St.Troops)
    Co.C

Riser, George SC 3rd Inf. Co.E

Riser, H.A. LA 13th Bn. (Part.Rangers) Co.D,E

Riser, Henry H. SC Inf. Holcombe Legion Co.H

Riser, H.G. MS Cav. Powers' Regt. Co.H

Riser, H.G. 20th Conf.Cav. Co.A

Riser, H.H. SC 2nd St.Troops Co.B Sgt.

Riser, Isaac LA 31st Inf. Co.B

Riser, James A. SC Lt.Arty. 3rd (Palmetto) Bn.
    Co.F Cpl.

Riser, James M. LA 12th Inf. Co.H

Riser, J.F.W. SC 3rd Inf. Co.E,C Cpl.

Riser, John SC 2nd St.Troops Co.F

Riser, John F. SC 1st Inf. Co.L Cpl.

Riser, J.W. 20th Conf.Cav. Co.A

Riser, Lafayette M. MS 18th Inf. Co.H

Riser, Marion SC 14th Inf. Co.B

Riser, Martin VA Cav. 37th Bn. Co.K

Riser, M.B. LA 12th Inf. 2nd Co.M

Riser, M.D. Trans-MS Conf.Cav. 1st Bn. Co.C
    Cpl.

Riser, R.E. SC 3rd Inf. Co.H

Riser, R.E. VA Lt.Arty. W.P. Carter's Co.

Riser, R.W. SC 1st Cav. Co.E
Riser, Samuel MS 11th (Perrin's) Cav. Co.K
Riser, Stephen B. MS 20th Inf. Co.I
Riser, T.W. MS 15th Inf. Co.E
Riser, Thomas H. LA 12th Inf. Co.C Sgt.
Riser, T.M. AL 18th Inf. Co.E,K 2nd Lt.
Riser, W.A. AR 19th (Dawson's) Inf. Co.A
Riser, W.D. SC 4th Bn.Res. Co.A
Riser, William E. AL 10th Inf. Co.E
Riser, William E. AL 18th Inf. Co.K 2nd Lt.
Riser, William G. MS 3rd Inf. Co.C
Riser, William W. MS 18th Inf. Co.H
Riser, William Washington MS 1st Lt.Arty. Co.A
Riser, W.W. SC 1st Inf. Co.L
Riser, W.W. SC 3rd Inf. Co.E
Riser, W.W. SC 13th Inf. Co.D
Rish, A.J. GA Inf. 1st Loc.Troops (Augusta) Co.B
Rish, Andrew SC 2nd St.Troops Co.A Sgt.
Rish, George SC Hvy.Arty. Mathewes' Co.
Rish, G.F. GA 44th Inf. Co.K
Rish, H.A. GA 32nd Inf. Co.F Sgt.
Rish, J. SC 2nd St.Troops Co.A
Rish, J.A. SC 15th Inf. Co.I
Rish, John AL 24th Inf. Co.A
Rish, John GA 59th Inf. Co.E
Rish, John SC 20th Inf. Co.I
Rish, Lem E. GA 51st Inf. Co.I Cpl.
Rish, Michael SC 20th Inf. Co.H
Rish, N.H. 1st Conf.Cav. 1st Co.K Cpl.
Rish, Noah H. AL 4th Cav. 1st Sgt.
Rish, Samuel G. LA 21st (Pattons') Inf. Co.F Capt.
Rish, Wesley GA 51st Inf. Co.I
Rish, Wiley B. SC 20th Inf. Co.I
Rish, William SC 2nd St.Troops Co.F
Rish, William J. MS 31st Inf. Co.B
Rish, W.J. SC 15th Inf. Co.I
Risher, --- AR Lt.Arty. 5th Btty.
Risher, A.B. 7th Conf.Cav. Co.A
Risher, Alexander MS 1st Cav.Res. Co.A Cpl.
Risher, Andrew B. KY 1st Inf. Co.I
Risher, Andrew B. LA 1st (Nelligan's) Inf. Co.H
Risher, Asa W. MS 27th Inf. Co.H
Risher, B.B. SC 11th Inf. Sheridan's Co.
Risher, Benjamin SC Mil. 18th Regt. Co.F Sgt.
Risher, B.F. MS Cav. Garland's Bn. Co.B
Risher, B.F. 14th Conf.Cav. Co.B
Risher, B.L. SC 5th Cav. Co.C
Risher, B.L. SC Cav. 10th Bn. Co.C Sgt.
Risher, Christopher C. MS 27th Inf. Co.H
Risher, Derrick SC 2nd Cav. Co.D
Risher, Derrick SC Mil. 18th Regt. Co.F
Risher, E.C. MS Inf. 2nd St.Troops Co.E
Risher, F. LA 9th Inf. Co.G
Risher, George E. MS 40th Inf. Co.A
Risher, H.B. SC 1st (Hagood's) Inf. 1st Co.F, 2nd Co.B Sgt.
Risher, Hezekiah T. MS 37th Inf. Co.B
Risher, James N. MS 27th Inf. Co.H
Risher, J.B. MS 8th Inf. Co.A Sgt.
Risher, J.F. MS 8th Inf. Co.A
Risher, J.K. SC 24th Inf. Co.E Capt.
Risher, John AL 56th Part.Rangers Co.C
Risher, John MS 10th Cav. Co.F
Risher, John SC 1st Cav. Co.I
Risher, John SC 11th Inf. Sheridan's Co.

Risher, Michael R. MS 1st (Patton's) Inf. Co.K
Risher, Michael R. MS 14th Inf. Co.B
Risher, Michael R. MS 37th Inf. Co.B
Risher, R. SC 4th Cav. Co.G 1st Sgt.
Risher, R. SC Cav. 10th Bn. Co.C 1st Sgt.
Risher, R. SC Lt.Arty. 3rd (Palmetto) Bn. Co.D
Risher, Silas SC 1st Cav. Co.I
Risher, Silas SC 11th Inf. Sheridan's Co. Cpl.
Risher, Thomas SC Mil. 18th Regt. Co.F Cpl.
Risher, T.L. SC 3rd Cav. Co.B
Risher, T.R. LA 31st Inf. Co.F
Risher, W.B. SC 4th Cav. Co.G
Risher, Whitelock MS 27th Inf. Co.H
Risher, William MS 20th Inf. Co.I
Risher, William B. SC Cav. 10th Bn. Co.C Cpl.
Risin, Janett W.L. AR 18th (Marmaduke's) Inf. Co.G
Risin, J.W.S. AR Pine Bluff Arty.
Rising, Elias NC 2nd Arty. (36th St.Troops) Co.A
Rising, Elias NC Moseley's Co. (Sampson Arty.)
Rising, G.W. NC 34th Inf. Co.I
Rising, H.W. LA Cav. Nutt's Co. (Red River Rangers)
Rising, James NC 15th Inf. Co.F
Rising, Richard F. SC 10th Inf. Co.M
Risinger, David SC 15th Inf. Co.C
Risinger, David TX 24th Cav. Co.G
Risinger, G.D. SC 15th Inf. Co.C
Risinger, G.L. TX 10th Cav. Co.F
Risinger, Jackson TX 11th (Spaight's) Bn.Vol. Co.D
Risinger, J.B. TX 24th Cav. Co.G
Risinger, J.D. SC 7th Inf. Co.H
Risinger, J.G. TX 25th Cav. Co.A
Risinger, John C. AL 11th Inf. Co.F
Risinger, John C. AL 20th Inf. Co.B
Risinger, Jordan C. TX 28th Cav. Co.A
Risinger, Jordan J. TX 24th Cav. Co.G
Risinger, Jordan J. TX 25th Cav. Co.A
Risinger, Larkin LA Hvy.Arty. 2nd Bn. Co.A
Risinger, Leroy M. TX 28th Cav. Co.A
Risinger, L.J. TX 24th Cav. Co.G
Risinger, Mack TX 24th Cav. Co.G
Risinger, N. SC 15th Inf. Co.C
Risinger, N.T. TX 25th Cav. Co.A
Risinger, S. Alex VA 11th Bn.Res. Co.B
Risinger, T. SC 2nd St.Troops Co.A
Risinger, Tilman L. TX 28th Cav. Co.A
Risinger, W. SC 7th Inf. Co.H
Risinger, Wesley SC 15th Inf. Co.C
Risinger, William TX Waul's Legion Co.E
Risinger, Willis TX 24th Cav. Co.G
Risk, A.H. KY 2nd (Duke's) Cav. Co.F
Risk, A.H. KY 5th Cav. Co.E
Risk, D.L. MO 5th Cav. Co.D
Risk, D.L. MO Cav. Stallard's Co.
Risk, E.F. TN Inf. 3rd Bn. Co.A
Risk, George W. VA 7th Bn.Res. Co.D
Risk, Harvey VA 10th Bn.Res. Co.B
Risk, Harvey VA Rockbridge Cty.Res. Donald's Co.
Risk, J. LA Mil. Lewis Guards
Risk, J.A. MO 5th Cav. Co.D
Risk, James B. VA Horse Arty. Jackson's Co.
Risk, James Paxton VA Lt.Arty. Donald's Co.
Risk, James W. KY 2nd Mtd.Inf. Co.F Cpl.

Risk, John H. VA 5th Inf. Co.D
Risk, John W. VA Lt.Arty. Carrington's Co.
Risk, John W. VA Lt.Arty. Donald's Co.
Risk, J.R. LA Lt.Arty. Fenner's Btty.
Risk, Theodore AR 2nd Cav. 1st Co.A
Risk, T.T. KY 4th Cav. Co.D
Risk, W.H. KY 5th Cav.
Risk, W.H. KY 9th Cav. Co.E
Risland, Alvin SC 1st (Butler's) Inf. Co.F,H
Risler, Nathan TX 8th Inf. Co.I
Risley, Andrew AR 14th (Powers') Inf. Co.A
Risley, J.R. AL 3rd Cav. Co.I
Risley, Levi W. LA 14th (Austin's) Bn.S.S. Co.A
Risley, Levy LA 11th Inf. Co.E
Risley, William VA Hvy.Arty. Epes' Co.
Rismann, C.W. SC Mil.Arty. 1st Regt. Co.A
Risner, --- AL 25th Inf. Co.H Cpl.
Risner, A. GA 7th Cav. Co.C
Risner, Alford TN 54th Inf. Hollis' Co.
Risner, C.H. AR 32nd Inf. Co.I
Risner, Charles AR 45th Cav. Co.D
Risner, Ellert AR 1st Vol. Kelsey's Co.
Risner, F. AR Cav. McGehee's Regt. Co.G
Risner, G. AR Cav. McGehee's Regt. Co.G
Risner, George AR 32nd Inf. Co.I
Risner, George W. 1st Choctaw Mtd.Rifles Co.E 3rd Lt.
Risner, Jasper N. AL 4th Inf. Co.F
Risner, John AR 8th Inf. New Co.B
Risner, William TN 54th Inf. Hollis' Co. Cpl.
Riso, Seraffino LA Mil. 6th Regt.Eur.Brig. (Italian Guards Bn.) Co.1
Risomer, George N. GA 4th Res. Co.E
Rison, --- AL 4th (Russell's) Cav. Co.L 1st Lt.
Rison, D.W. SC 3rd Cav. Co.D
Rison, F.A. AL 17th Inf. Co.A
Rison, Henry C. TN 7th Inf. Co.B
Rison, M. KY 12th Cav. Co.E
Rison, M.T. TN 12th Inf. Co.F,C 1st Lt.
Rison, M.T. TN 12th (Cons.) Inf. Co.B 1st Lt.
Rison, Thomas W. TN 2nd (Smith's) Cav.
Rison, Thomas W. TN 4th (McLemore's) Cav. Co.G
Rison, William H. MD 1st Inf. Co.I Sgt.
Rison, Wilson B. AL 4th Inf. Co.F Lt.
Rison, W.M. KY 7th Cav. Co.C
Risor, Jacobs GA 2nd Bn.S.S. Co.E
Risor, J.M. LA 13th Bn. (Part.Rangers) Co.D
Risor, John LA 3rd Inf. Co.B
Risor, William E. AL 53rd (Part.Rangers) Co.K
Rispas, M.L. AL Talladega Cty.Res. D.M. Reid's Co. Cpl.
Rispess, Richard H. VA 61st Mil. Co.E
Rispiss, Edward J. VA 1st Arty. Co.E
Riss, Frederick VA Inf. 25th Bn. Co.E
Risscher, J.A. VA 2nd Inf. Co.E
Rissill, John SC Inf. 3rd Bn. Co.G
Risslad, Abram SC 1st (Butler's) Inf. Co.H
Rissland, W. SC 1st Regt. Charleston Guard Co.F Sgt.
Rissler, George L. VA 2nd Inf. Co.G
Rissler, Samuel J. VA 2nd Inf. Co.G,H
Risson, W.G. GA 27th Inf. Co.G
Rist, Charles A. LA 16th Inf. Co.A
Rist, Henry LA 16th Inf. Co.A
Rist, Henry LA 21st (Patton's) Inf. Co.C

Rist, Henry Conf.Cav. Powers' Regt. Co.A
Rist, John, Jr. LA 7th Inf. Co.B
Rist, William LA Miles' Legion Co.A
Rister, Charles TX 1st Hvy.Arty. Co.B
Rister, D.C. TX 17th Inf. Co.C
Rister, Edward R. MS 20th Inf. Co.E
Rister, Elias SC Lt.Arty. 3rd (Palmetto) Bn. Co.B
Rister, G.A. SC 15th Inf. Co.I
Rister, John A. SC 13th Inf. Co.K
Rister, L.S. SC 22nd Inf. Co.G
Rister, S. SC 15th Inf. Co.I
Rister, S.T. TX 17th Inf. Co.C 1st Lt.
Rister, William TX 4th Cav. Co.D
Rister, William M. TX 17th Inf. Co.C
Rister, William T. SC 13th Inf. Co.H
Ristig, W. SC 27th Inf. Co.C Sgt.
Ristig, William SC Inf. 1st (Charleston) Bn. Co.F Sgt.
Ristine, Charles E. TN Arty. Ramsey's Btty.
Ristine, John S. TN Arty. Ramsey's Btty. Sgt.
Riston, A.C. TX Cav. Hardeman's Regt. Co.D
Riswick, P. AR Inf. Sparks' Co.
Rit, John GA 59th Inf. Co.H
Ritch, A.C. GA 5th Inf. (St.Guards) Russell's Co.
Ritch, Andrew S. AL 60th Inf. Co.G
Ritch, Andrew S. AL 3rd Bn. Hilliard's Legion Vol. Co.E
Ritch, Burwell T. AL 62nd Inf. Co.E
Ritch, Daniel AL 13th Inf. Co.H
Ritch, E.A. AL 15th Inf. Co.L Sgt.
Ritch, Elias F. AL 62nd Inf. Co.E Cpl.
Ritch, Elijah M. AL 20th Inf. Co.C,G
Ritch, G.B. GA 54th Inf. Co.K 1st Lt.
Ritch, Green B. GA 4th (Clinch's) Cav. Co.I,K
Ritch, J. AL 8th (Livingston's) Cav. Co.D
Ritch, J. KY 3rd Mtd.Inf. 1st Co.F
Ritch, Jacob M. MS 46th Inf. Co.A
Ritch, J.A.M. GA 7th Inf. Co.D
Ritch, James MS 8th Cav. Co.A
Ritch, James NC 35th Inf. Co.F
Ritch, J.C. AR 1st Mtd.Rifles Co.K
Ritch, Jeremiah E. GA Cobb's Legion Co.C,H Capt.
Ritch, J.G. GA 54th Inf. Co.K
Ritch, J.L. NC 1st Inf. (6 mo. '61) Co.B
Ritch, J.N. GA Phillips' Legion Co.C
Ritch, John G. GA 4th (Clinch's) Cav. Co.A,K 2nd Lt.
Ritch, John L. NC 35th Inf. Co.F
Ritch, John P. NC Hvy.Arty. 10th Bn. Co.C
Ritch, John P. NC 20th Inf. Co.A
Ritch, Joseph E. NC Hvy.Arty. 10th Bn. Co.C
Ritch, Joseph M. AL Inf. 1st Regt. Co.C
Ritch, J.P. 2nd Conf.Eng.Troops Co.A Sgt.
Ritch, J.T. SC 1st Cav. Co.K
Ritch, L.F. AL 15th Inf. Co.L
Ritch, L.V. AL 36th Inf. Co.I
Ritch, M.F. AL 12th Cav. Co.G Cpl.
Ritch, Philemon M. NC 1st Cav. (9th St.Troops) Co.F
Ritch, S. GA 1st (Symons') Res. Co.F
Ritch, Thomas J. GA 12th (Robinson's) Cav. (St.Guards) Co.K Sgt.
Ritch, Thomas L. NC 1st Cav. (9th St.Troops) Co.F

Ritch, T.J. GA 54th Inf. Co.G Sgt.
Ritch, W.C. GA Inf. 4th Bn. (St.Guards) Co.B
Ritch, William LA 3rd Inf. Co.C
Ritch, William M. NC 35th Inf. Co.F
Ritch, William P. NC 35th Inf. Co.F
Ritch, William R. GA 2nd Inf. 1st Co.B
Ritch, William R. GA 26th Inf. Co.E
Ritch, W.P. MS 28th Cav. Co.F Cpl.
Ritchards, G.S. LA 4th Cav. Co.B
Ritchards, Leonard TX 34th Cav. Co.G
Ritchards, T.S. 8th (Wade's) Conf.Cav. Co.K
Ritchards, W. MS 8th Cav. Co.F
Ritchards, W.T. TX 34th Cav. Co.G
Ritchardson, Edmond MO 1st N.E. Cav. Co.H
Ritchardson, E.J. MO 11th Inf. Co.D
Ritchardson, Henry C. MO 10th Inf. Co.D
Ritchardson, I. LA 4th Cav. Co.B
Ritchardson, N.A. MO 11th Inf. Co.D
Ritchardson, R.L. AL Mil. 4th Vol. Co.E
Ritchardson, T. LA 4th Cav. Co.B
Ritchardson, Thomas J. AR Cav. 1st Bn. (Stirman's) Co.B
Ritchardson, W.S. AR Cav. 1st Bn. (Stirman's) Co.B Cpl.
Ritchason, David KY 13th Cav. Co.I Sgt.
Ritchbourg, W.D. AL 46th Inf. Co.C 1st Sgt.
Ritche, Charles KY 10th (Diamond's) Cav. Co.L
Ritchel, Otto TX Arty. 4th Bn. Co.A
Ritcher, David GA 5th Inf. (St.Guards) Brooks' Co.
Ritcherds, Jasper N. AR 17th (Lemoyne's) Inf. Co.G
Ritcherson, W.H. AR 32nd Inf. Co.E
Ritcherson, W.M. AR 15th (Johnson's) Inf. Co.A
Ritcheson, H.S. AL 35th Inf. Co.B
Ritcheson, J.R. GA 39th Inf. Co.E
Ritchey, Andrew AL 55th Vol. Co.J
Ritchey, Asa AL 49th Inf. Co.D
Ritchey, Benjamin MS 4th Inf. Co.A
Ritchey, B.H. Conf.Cav. Wood's Regt. Co.L
Ritchey, Caleb A. NC 1st Arty. (10th St.Troops) Co.C
Ritchey, C.D. TN 11th (Holman's) Cav. Co.E
Ritchey, D.B. TX Cav. Waller's Regt. Co.B Cpl.
Ritchey, D.L. 1st Conf.Cav. 2nd Co.K
Ritchey, D.P. TN 35th Inf. Co.E Chap.
Ritchey, Edmond NC 5th Inf. Co.F
Ritchey, Harvey F. VA Horse Arty. Shoemaker's Co.
Ritchey, H.N. 20th Conf.Cav. Co.M Cpl.
Ritchey, I.B. 3rd Conf.Eng.Troops AQM
Ritchey, Isaac MS 38th Cav. Co.B
Ritchey, Isaac H. AR 14th (McCarver's) Inf. Co.F
Ritchey, James Brown TN Inf. 16th Regt. AQM
Ritchey, James D.H. TX 9th Cav. Co.K Sgt.
Ritchey, James W. MS 4th Inf. Co.A
Ritchey, J.B. TN 16th Inf. Co.B AQM
Ritchey, J.M. MO 11th Inf. Co.D
Ritchey, J.M. TN 3rd (Forrest's) Cav. Co.D
Ritchey, John NC 46th Inf. Co.A
Ritchey, John A. TN 13th (Gore's) Cav. Co.C Sgt.
Ritchey, John D. NC 42nd Inf. Co.G
Ritchey, John L. LA 1st Cav.

Ritchey, John M. TX Cav. 2nd Regt.St.Troops Co.D
Ritchey, John R. NC 42nd Inf. Co.G
Ritchey, John R. TX 13th Cav. Co.B
Ritchey, John S. NC 1st Arty. (10th St.Troops) Co.C
Ritchey, John W. Conf.Cav. Wood's Regt. Co.L
Ritchey, Joseph AR 5th Inf. Co.C
Ritchey, Joseph TN 1st (Carter's) Cav. Co.K
Ritchey, Joseph 3rd Conf.Eng.Troops Co.A
Ritchey, J.R. MO 11th Inf. Co.D
Ritchey, J.T. 1st Conf.Cav. 2nd Co.K
Ritchey, Micajah TN 35th Inf. Co.E
Ritchey, Pleasant NC 5th Inf. Co.F
Ritchey, Robert AL 55th Vol. Co.J,K
Ritchey, Robert 1st Conf.Cav. 2nd Co.K
Ritchey, Samuel W. AR 14th (McCarver's) Inf. Co.F
Ritchey, S.W. Gen. & Staff Capt.,AQM
Ritchey, T.C. TX 15th Inf. Co.K
Ritchey, Thomas AR 5th Inf. Co.C
Ritchey, Thomas J. GA 12th Inf. Co.B
Ritchey, Thomas N. 3rd Conf.Eng.Troops Co.A
Ritchey, T.P. Conf.Cav. Wood's Regt. Co.L
Ritchey, W.F. GA Lt.Arty. (Arsenal Btty.) Hudson's Co.
Ritchey, W.F. GA Inf. Arsenal Bn. (Columbus) Co.A
Ritchey, William TX 9th Cav. Co.K
Ritchey, William 1st Conf.Cav. 2nd Co.K Cpl.
Ritchey, William C. GA 13th Cav. Co.G
Ritchey, William H. AR 5th Inf. Co.C
Ritchey, William H. GA 12th Inf. Co.B
Ritchey, William H. Conf.Cav. Wood's Regt. Co.L Cpl.
Ritchey, William M. SC 17th Inf. Co.D
Ritchey, William T. MS 38th Cav. Co.B
Ritchey, William W. AL 41st Inf. Co.F
Ritchey, William W. MS 4th Inf. Co.A
Ritchey, W.J. MS Inf. 2nd Bn. Co.L
Ritchey, W.L. TX Cav. Morgan's Regt. Co.G
Ritchie, --- TX 11th (Spaight's) Bn.Vol. Co.E
Ritchie, --- VA Inf. 4th Bn.Loc.Def. Co.F
Ritchie, A. SC Inf. 3rd Bn. Co.B
Ritchie, Abraham VA 58th Mil. Co.I
Ritchie, Absolom VA 146th Mil. Co.C
Ritchie, Adam VA 146th Mil. Co.C
Ritchie, Addison VA 10th Inf. Co.H
Ritchie, A.F. AR 4th Inf. Co.K
Ritchie, Alexander AR 1st Mtd.Rifles Co.G,B
Ritchie, Alexander GA 12th Cav. Co.E
Ritchie, Alexander VA Inf. 21st Bn. Co.A
Ritchie, Alfred AL Cp. of Instr. Talladega
Ritchie, Andrew KY 13th Cav. Co.C
Ritchie, Andrew KY 13th Cav. Co.I
Ritchie, Andrew TX 2nd Inf. Co.D Sgt.
Ritchie, Andrew Jackson AL Inf. 1st Regt. Co.D
Ritchie, Archy C. GA 45th Inf. Co.F
Ritchie, Austin KY 13th Cav. Co.C 2nd Lt.
Ritchie, Benjamin KY 13th Cav. Co.C
Ritchie, B.F. AL 40th Inf. Co.G
Ritchie, C. SC 11th Inf. Co.B
Ritchie, C.D. TN Holman's Bn.Part.Rangers Co.C
Ritchie, Charles LA Mil. 1st Regt. 2nd Brig. 1st Div.
Ritchie, Charles TX Waul's Legion Co.C

Ritchie, Charles R. VA Inf. 1st Bn.Loc.Def. Co.D
Ritchie, Crockett KY 13th Cav. Co.C
Ritchie, Curtis MS 4th Cav. Co.C
Ritchie, Curtis MS Cav. Hughes' Bn. Co.A
Ritchie, David AR 2nd (Cons.) Inf. Co.4
Ritchie, David LA 11th Inf. Co.E
Ritchie, David L. TN 28th Inf. Co.E
Ritchie, David P. Gen. & Staff Chap.
Ritchie, E.G. MS 7th Cav. Co.I
Ritchie, E.H. Conf.Cav. Wood's Regt. Co.I 2nd Lt.
Ritchie, E.J. GA 54th Inf. Co.A
Ritchie, Elias MO 9th (Elliott's) Cav.
Ritchie, Emanuel MS Cav. Garland's Bn. Co.C
Ritchie, Emanuell 14th Conf.Cav. Co.C
Ritchie, E.N. GA 27th Inf. Co.D
Ritchie, Ewell LA 11th Inf. Co.E
Ritchie, Finis E. KY 2nd (Duke's) Cav. Co.C,D
Ritchie, Francis H. VA 53rd Inf. Co.C Music.
Ritchie, Francis H. VA Inf. Montague's Bn. Co.D
Ritchie, Frank E. AL 41st Inf. Co.F
Ritchie, Frank J. VA 7th Cav. Co.B Cpl.
Ritchie, Gabriel KY 13th Cav. Co.C
Ritchie, Gabriel KY 13th Cav. Co.I
Ritchie, George E. NC 8th Inf. Co.H Bvt.2nd Lt.
Ritchie, George H. VA 20th Cav. Co.I Sgt.
Ritchie, George M. NC 49th Inf. Co.C
Ritchie, George M. Dallas VA 12th Cav. Co.H
Ritchie, George Q. AR 33rd Inf. Co.B
Ritchie, George W. VA 58th Mil. Co.K
Ritchie, G.W. AR 10th Inf. Co.G
Ritchie, G.W. AR 15th (Josey's) Inf. 1st Co.C
Ritchie, G.W. TX 2nd Inf. Co.I
Ritchie, Harvey F. VA Hvy.Arty. 10th Bn. Co.B
Ritchie, Harvey F. VA Hvy.Arty. 19th Bn. 3rd Co.C
Ritchie, H. Bain LA 6th Inf. Co.C Capt.
Ritchie, Henry KY 13th Cav. Co.I
Ritchie, Henry, Jr. MS 21st Inf. Co.A
Ritchie, Henry F. VA 52nd Inf. Co.D
Ritchie, G. MO 10th Inf. Co.F
Ritchie, Henry A. NC 20th Inf. Co.B
Ritchie, H.L. LA 25th Inf. Co.K
Ritchie, Isaac VA 7th Cav. Co.B Cpl.
Ritchie, Isaac H. AR 21st Inf. Co.B
Ritchie, Israel C. MS 16th Inf. Co.G
Ritchie, Ivy NC 14th Inf. Co.H Sgt.
Ritchie, J. AR 1st Mtd.Rifles Co.G
Ritchie, J.A. GA 2nd Inf. Co.A
Ritchie, J.A. TX 21st Inf. Co.F
Ritchie, Jacob MS Cav. Garland's Bn. Co.C
Ritchie, Jacob NC 5th Inf. Co.I
Ritchie, Jacob VA 11th Cav. Co.C
Ritchie, James AL 63rd Inf. Co.B,K
Ritchie, James MS Cav. 4th Bn. Sykes' Co.
Ritchie, James MS 2nd Inf.
Ritchie, James MS 12th Inf. Co.K
Ritchie, James VA 50th Inf. Co.H
Ritchie, James 8th (Wade's) Conf.Cav. Co.G
Ritchie, James B. Gen. & Staff AQM
Ritchie, James D. AR 51st Inf. Co.E
Ritchie, James J. AL 4th Inf. Co.E Cpl.
Ritchie, James K.P. VA 12th Cav. Co.H
Ritchie, James L. VA 1st Cav. 2nd Co.D

Ritchie, James M. GA 4th Cav. (St.Guards) Cannon's Co. 2nd Lt.
Ritchie, James R. AR 14th (Powers') Inf. Co.F
Ritchie, James T. VA 9th Inf. Co.F
Ritchie, Jefferson KY 9th Mtd.Inf. Co.G
Ritchie, Jeremiah VA 11th Cav. Co.C Sgt.
Ritchie, J.F. AR 6th Inf. Co.A
Ritchie, J.F. AR 8th Inf. New Co.B Capt.
Ritchie, J.F.M. MS 10th Inf. Co.I
Ritchie, J.J. MS 8th Inf. Co.H.
Ritchie, J.M. GA 11th Cav. Co.F
Ritchie, J.M. MS 5th Inf. (St.Troops) Co.C
Ritchie, J.M. TX Cav. Border's Regt. Co.D
Ritchie, John AL Cp. of Instr. Talladega
Ritchie, John KY 13th Cav. Co.I
Ritchie, John MS 12th Inf. Co.E
Ritchie, John MS 12th Inf. Co.K Cpl.
Ritchie, John SC 1st Arty. Co.F,C
Ritchie, John VA 9th Bn.Res. Co.A
Ritchie, John VA 58th Mil. Co.I
Ritchie, John VA 146th Mil. Co.C
Ritchie, John A. TX 11th (Spaight's) Bn.Vol. Co.F
Ritchie, John D. NC 20th Inf. Co.B
Ritchie, John M. MS Cav. Garland's Bn. Co.C
Ritchie, John R. AL 4th Inf. Co.E Sgt.
Ritchie, John S. VA 64th Mtd.Inf. Co.A
Ritchie, John V. KY 1st (Helm's) Cav. Co.B
Ritchie, John W. MS 10th Inf. Old Co.C, New Co.H
Ritchie, John W. MO 3rd Cav. Co.B
Ritchie, Joseph LA 1st Res. Co.I
Ritchie, Joseph C. VA 12th Cav. Co.H
Ritchie, Joseph W. MS 1st Cav. Co.I Bvt.2nd Lt.
Ritchie, Joseph W. MS Cav. 1st Bn. (Miller's) Cole's Co.
Ritchie, Josiah TN 63rd Inf. Co.H
Ritchie, J.S. SC 1st (Butler's) Inf.
Ritchie, J.S. TX 4th Cav. Co.E
Ritchie, J.W. MS 9th Inf. Co.D
Ritchie, J.W. MS 9th Bn.S.S. Co.C,D Cpl.
Ritchie, J.W. MS 13th Inf. Co.E
Ritchie, J.W. NC 35th Inf. Co.I
Ritchie, J.W. TN 31st Inf. Co.I
Ritchie, Kennedy LA Conscr.
Ritchie, Levi VA 146th Mil. Co.C
Ritchie, L.J. FL Cav. 3rd Bn. Co.D
Ritchie, L.J. 15th Conf.Cav. Co.I
Ritchie, L.V. AL Cp. of Instr. Talladega
Ritchie, M. AR 1st Mtd.Rifles Co.G
Ritchie, Manuel TX Part.Rangers Thomas' Co.
Ritchie, Marquis DeLafayette AL Inf. 1st Regt. Co.D
Ritchie, Martin KY 13th Cav. Co.C
Ritchie, Marvel NC 28th Inf. Co.D Sgt.
Ritchie, Moses TX 31st Cav. Co.F
Ritchie, Moses D. AR 18th Inf. Co.A Sgt.
Ritchie, Moses J. NC 42nd Inf. Co.B
Ritchie, Nelson AL City Troop (Mobile) Arrington's Co. Bugler
Ritchie, Nicholas KY 13th Cav. Co.C
Ritchie, P. VA 7th Cav. Co.H
Ritchie, Peter VA 9th Bn.Res. Co.D
Ritchie, Philip VA 62nd Mtd.Inf. 2nd Co.F,B
Ritchie, R.B. GA 11th Cav. Co.F
Ritchie, Robert AL Lt.Arty. 2nd Bn. Co.B

Ritchie, Robert GA 12th Cav. Co.C
Ritchie, Robert KY Horse Arty. Byrne's Co. Lt.
Ritchie, Robert LA Inf. 1st Sp.Bn. (Wheat's) Co.B Ord.Sgt.
Ritchie, Robert VA 3rd (Archer's) Bn.Res. Co.B 1st Lt.
Ritchie, Robert VA 9th Inf. 2nd Co.A
Ritchie, Robert VA 12th Inf. 1st Co.I
Ritchie, Robert G. MO 10th Inf. Co.F
Ritchie, Robt. R. Gen. & Staff AASurg.
Ritchie, Samuel KY 13th Cav. Co.C
Ritchie, Samuel KY 13th Cav. Co.I
Ritchie, Samuel MO 2nd Brig.St.Guard Comsy.Sgt.
Ritchie, Samuel W. AR 21st Inf. Co.B
Ritchie, S.N. MS Inf. 1st Bn. Co.A
Ritchie, Solomon VA 7th Cav. Co.B
Ritchie, Solomon VA 58th Mil. Co.I
Ritchie, Solomon VA 146th Mil. Co.C
Ritchie, S.P. TX 4th Cav. Co.E
Ritchie, Thomas MO 4th Cav. Co.E
Ritchie, Thomas VA 11th Cav. Co.C
Ritchie, Thomas B. AL 4th Inf. Co.E
Ritchie, Thos. M. MO 11th Inf. Co.E
Ritchie, Vincent LA 25th Inf. Co.A Sgt.
Ritchie, Warren W. MO 4th Cav. Co.E
Ritchie, W.H. LA 3rd (Harrison's) Cav. Co.K
Ritchie, William AR 12th Bn.S.S. Co.A
Ritchie, William MO 3rd Inf. Co.E
Ritchie, William TX Waul's Legion Co.C
Ritchie, William Conf.Lt.Arty. Richardson's Bn. Co.A
Ritchie, William B. AL Inf. 1st Regt. Co.C Cpl.
Ritchie, William B. VA 9th Inf. 2nd Co.A
Ritchie, William H. KY 1st (Butler's) Cav.
Ritchie, William N. NC 57th Inf. Co.F
Ritchie, William T. AR 18th Inf. Co.A
Ritchie, W.T. MO Cav. Ford's Bn. Co.D
Ritchie, W.W. MS 8th Inf. Co.H
Ritchie, Y.W. MS 10th Inf. New Co.I
Ritchison, David AR 18th Inf. Co.A
Rite, C. TN 50th Inf. Co.I
Rite, H.B. MS 3rd Inf. (St.Troops) Co.I
Rite, J.L. GA 18th Inf. Co.M
Rite, Solomon H. KY 10th (Diamond's) Cav. Co.C
Rite, William KY 2nd Bn.Mtd.Rifles Co.D Sgt.
Ritenhour, D.H. VA 11th Cav. Co.I
Ritenhour, Henry VA 146th Mil. Co.H
Ritenhour, Noah D. VA 2nd Inf. Co.E
Ritenour, Ambrose B. VA 7th Inf. Co.B
Ritenour, Andrew VA 33rd Inf. Co.B
Ritenour, Benton VA 17th Inf. Co.B
Ritenour, Calvin J. VA 33rd Inf. Co.C
Ritenour, Charles W. VA Lt.Arty. Carpenter's Co.
Ritenour, David VA 33rd Inf. Co.B
Ritenour, E.G. VA 33rd Inf. Co.G
Ritenour, George VA 33rd Inf. Co.B
Ritenour, George A. VA Cav. 41st Bn. Trayhern's Co.
Ritenour, George H. VA 13th Inf. Co.H
Ritenour, Hampson VA Cav. 35th Bn. Co.E
Ritenour, Harrison VA 146th Mil. Co.D
Ritenour, Hiram VA 33rd Inf. Co.B
Ritenour, Isaac VA 17th Inf. Co.B
Ritenour, Jacob VA 12th Cav. Co.I

Ritenour, Joel W. VA 33rd Inf. Co.B
Ritenour, John H. VA 146th Mil. Co.D
Ritenour, Jonathan VA 146th Mil. Co.K
Ritenour, Joseph W. VA Cav. 41st Bn. 1st
　Trayhern's Co.
Ritenour, Levi VA Cav. 41st Bn. Trayhern's Co.
Ritenour, Lewis C. VA 6th Cav. Co.B
Ritenour, Lewis C. VA 49th Inf. Co.E
Ritenour, Milton Gen. & Staff Surg.
Ritenour, M.N. VA Lt.Arty. Carpenter's Co.
Ritenour, Philip W. VA 33rd Inf. Co.C
Ritenour, Phillip VA 18th Cav. 1st Co.G
Riter, David MS 24th Inf. Co.A
Riter, F. KY 2nd (Woodward's) Cav. Co.F
Riter, J.E. TN 30th Inf. Co.E
Riter, Theophilus MO 3rd Inf. Co.G
Riter, William H. TN 14th Inf. Co.H
Riter, W.T. TN 30th Inf. Co.A
Ritesel, R. NC 3rd Jr.Res. Co.A
Riticor, Robert A. VA Cav. 35th Bn. Co.A
Ritings, Wm. T. Forrest's Cav. Lyon's Escort
Ritler, A.J. KY 7th Cav. Co.E
Ritley, B.F. AL Talladega Cty.Res. T.M.
　McClintick's Co.
Ritley, W.R. GA 64th Inf. Co.I
Ritly, J.B. AL Talladega Cty.Res. T.M. McClin-
　tick's Co.
Ritman, Henry VA 54th Mil. Co.E,F
Ritman, John AR Cav. 15th Bn. (Buster's Bn.)
　Co.D
Ritmun, J. SC Inf. 7th Bn. (Enfield Rifles) Co.D
Ritnour, Henry C. MS 6th Inf. Co.G Sgt.
Ritt, James VA 9th Inf. 2nd Co.A
Rittard, Davis NC 7th Sr.Res. Mitchell's Co.
Rittemann, John TX 3rd Inf. Co.K
Ritten, L.D. TN 7th Inf. Co.D
Ritten, W.R. AR 1st Inf. Co.I Sgt.
Rittenberg, J.F. TN 27th Inf. Co.C
Rittenberry, A. VA 72nd Mil.
Rittenberry, Isaac J. TN 53rd Inf. Co.K Capt.
Rittenberry, J.G. GA 3rd Res. Co.A
Rittenberry, J.W. AR 31st Inf. Co.E
Rittenberry, L.J. TN 22nd (Barteau's) Cav. Co.G
Rittenberry, L. Jack TN Cav. 7th Bn. (Bennett's)
　Co.E
Rittenberry, Marcellus G. GA Inf. 10th Bn. Co.E
Rittenberry, Romulus S. NC 7th Inf. Co.E
Rittenberry, Rual VA 51st Inf. Co.A
Rittenberry, Samuel L. GA Inf. 2nd Bn. Co.C
Rittenbery, N.B. TN 3rd (Clack's) Inf. Co.I
Rittenburg, D.M. TN 3rd (Clack's) Inf. Co.I
　Bvt.2nd Lt.
Rittenbury, Andrew J. GA 1st Reg. Co.M
Rittenbury, Andrew J. 1st Conf.Inf. 2nd Co.E
Rittenbury, James TN 18th Inf. Co.D
Rittenbury, William VA 21st Inf. Co.G
Rittenhour, W.H. VA 7th Cav. Co.G
Rittenhouse, Daniel MO 2nd Cav. Co.C
Rittenhouse, David W. VA 51st Inf. Co.E Cpl.
Rittenhouse, Henry J. VA 51st Inf. Co.E
Rittenour, Benton VA 12th Cav. Co.M
Rittenour, Calvin J. VA 12th Cav. Co.K
Rittenour, David H. VA 10th Inf. Co.G Music.
Rittenour, George H. VA 1st Cav. Co.A
Rittenour, Hampson VA 146th Mil. Co.G
Rittenour, Henry W. VA 58th Mil. Co.F 2nd Lt.
Rittenour, Jacob VA 33rd Inf. Co.G

Rittenour, John H. VA 12th Cav. Co.K
Rittenour, M. VA 82nd Mil. Co.A
Rittenour, Maffet VA 1st Cav. Co.A
Rittenour, Moffit N. VA Lt.Arty. Cutshaw's Co.
Rittenour, Noah D. VA 146th Mil. Co.G
Ritter, A. GA 1st (Olmstead's) Inf. Co.F
Ritter, A. GA 25th Inf. Pritchard's Co.
Ritter, A. TX 4th Inf. Co.C
Ritter, A.D. MS 1st (Johnston's) Inf. Co.H
Ritter, A.J. AR 11th Inf. Co.I
Ritter, A.J. AR 11th & 17th (Cons.) Inf. Co.C
Ritter, A.J. KY Cav. 2nd Bn. (Dortch's) Co.A,B
Ritter, Alfred VA 51st Mil. Co.C
Ritter, Anderson D. MS 43rd Inf. Co.H
Ritter, Andrew J. MO 2nd Cav. Co.A
Ritter, Anton TX 2nd Inf. Co.D
Ritter, Arthur J. MS 2nd Cav. Co.A
Ritter, August TX 1st Hvy.Arty. Co.G
Ritter, August TX Lt.Arty. Dege's Bn.
Ritter, A.W. MS 3rd Inf. Co.B
Ritter, B. TX Comal Res.
Ritter, Benjamin F. TX 37th Cav. Co.F 2nd Lt.
Ritter, B.F. TX 28th Cav. Co.C
Ritter, B.F. TX Cav. Terry's Regt. Co.A 2nd
　Lt.
Ritter, Birdine VA 54th Inf. Co.F
Ritter, Bruce KY 9th Cav. Co.I
Ritter, C. LA Mil. Fire Bn. Co.E
Ritter, C. MS 4th Cav. Co.G
Ritter, C. VA 7th Cav. Co.K
Ritter, Carter VA 5th Inf. Co.K
Ritter, Charles MS Cav. Hughes' Bn. Co.F
Ritter, Charles TN 1st Hvy.Arty. Co.K, 2nd
　Co.C Music.
Ritter, Charles H. NC 61st Inf. Co.G
Ritter, David H. VA 11th Cav. Co.A
Ritter, David H. VA Cav. Mosby's Regt.
　(Part.Rangers) Co.C
Ritter, David S. VA 54th Inf. Co.F
Ritter, E.B. FL 2nd Cav. Co.D
Ritter, E.B. MS 2nd St.Cav. 1st Co.C
Ritter, Edward VA 31st Mil. Co.F
Ritter, Edward B. FL 5th Inf. Co.C
Ritter, E.J. MS 3rd Inf. Co.C
Ritter, E.J. MS 23rd Inf. Co.C
Ritter, Everett B. AL 8th (Livingston's) Cav.
　Co.E 1st Sgt.
Ritter, Everett B. AL 16th Inf. Co.G
Ritter, Francis M. AR 33rd Inf. Co.K
Ritter, Frank S. TX Cav. Baird's Regt. Co.A
Ritter, George KY Cav. 2nd Bn. (Dortch's) Co.D
Ritter, George KY 14th Cav. Co.B
Ritter, George KY Morgan's Men Beck's Co.
Ritter, George MS Inf. 2nd Bn. Co.E
Ritter, George MS 12th Inf. Co.E
Ritter, George MS 48th Inf. Co.E Sgt.
Ritter, George S. VA 22nd Cav. Co.F
Ritter, George W. VA 6th Cav. Co.D
Ritter, H.C. SC 17th Inf. Co.G
Ritter, Henry VA 5th Inf. Co.K
Ritter, Henry P. NC 8th Inf. Surg.
Ritter, Henry P. Gen. & Staff Surg.
Ritter, Henry R. SC 24th Inf. Co.E
Ritter, Herman VA Cav. O'Ferrall's Bn. Co.B
Ritter, Hiram L. NC 51st Inf. Co.G
Ritter, H.R. SC 11th Inf. 1st Co.F
Ritter, Isaac A. AL 8th (Livingston's) Cav. Co.E

Ritter, Isaac A. AL Cp. of Instr. Talladega
Ritter, Isaac D. MO Cav. Freeman's Regt. Co.B
Ritter, Isaac W. MO 12th Inf. Co.B Cpl.
Ritter, I.W. MO 10th Inf. Co.F Cpl.
Ritter, J. AR Cav. McGehee's Regt. Co.F
Ritter, J. TX Cav. Well's Regt. Co.B
Ritter, J.A. MS Cav. 3rd Bn. (Ashcraft's) Co.F
Ritter, J.A. SC 2nd Inf. Co.K
Ritter, J.A. TN 3rd (Clack's) Inf. Co.E
Ritter, Jacob VA 2nd Inf. Co.C Fifer
Ritter, Jacob B. VA 1st Cav. Co.A
Ritter, James AR 31st Inf. Co.B
Ritter, James LA 6th Cav. Co.I
Ritter, James VA 12th Cav. Co.D
Ritter, James VA 4th Inf. Co.C
Ritter, James A. VA 41st Inf. Co.F
Ritter, James P. AR 15th (N.W.) Inf. Co.G
Ritter, James W. MO 12th Inf. Co.B
Ritter, James W. VA 11th Cav. Co.A
Ritter, James W. VA 51st Mil. Co.C
Ritter, Jasper N. AR 8th Inf. New Co.E
Ritter, J.C. SC 3rd Cav. Co.F
Ritter, J.D. AL 26th (O'Neal's) Inf. Co.B
Ritter, J.D. AR Inf. Hardy's Regt. Torbett's Co.
Ritter, J.E. FL 1st (Res.) Inf.
Ritter, J.F. SC Mil.Arty. 1st Regt. Werner's Co.
Ritter, J.H. TX 10th Cav. Co.F
Ritter, J.J. LA Arty. Huttons' Co. (Crescent
　Arty.,Co.A)
Ritter, John AL 27th Inf. Co.F
Ritter, John AR 34th Inf. Co.F Cpl.
Ritter, John GA Cav. 16th Regt. Co.C
Ritter, John NC 2nd Arty. (36th St.Troops) Co.D
　Cpl.
Ritter, John NC 6th Sr.Res. Co.H
Ritter, John NC 13th Inf. Co.G
Ritter, John A. VA 11th Cav. Co.A Cpl.
Ritter, John A. VA 51st Mil. Co.C
Ritter, John C. AR 23rd Inf. Co.C Sgt.
Ritter, John F. SC 1st Arty. Co.F
Ritter, John H. VA 22nd Inf. Swann's Co. Sgt.
Ritter, John N. AL 16th Inf. Co.G
Ritter, John S. NC 2nd Cav. (19th St.Troops)
　Co.I Jr.2nd Lt.
Ritter, John S. SC 1st Arty. Co.A
Ritter, John T. NC 2nd Bn.Loc.Def.Troops
　Co.A,B 2nd Lt.
Ritter, Jonathan C. KY 1st Inf. Co.G
Ritter, Joseph NC 8th Inf. Co.I
Ritter, Joseph VA 7th Cav. Co.K
Ritter, Joseph VA 5th Inf. Co.K
Ritter, Josiah SC 3rd Cav. Co.F
Ritter, J.W. SC 2nd St.Troops Co.E
Ritter, J.W. SC 8th Bn.Res. Co.C
Ritter, J.W. SC 11th Res. Co.E
Ritter, J.W. TN 1st Hvy.Arty. 2nd Co.C
Ritter, J.W. TN Hvy.Arty. Sterling's Co.
Ritter, Lewis MO Cav. 2nd Regt.St.Guard Co.G
Ritter, Lewis TX 5th Inf. Co.K
Ritter, Lewis H. MO Lt.Arty. 1st Btty.
Ritter, L.H. AR 19th (Dockery's) Inf.
　Cons.Co.E,D
Ritter, L.H. MO Lt.Arty. Walsh's Co.
Ritter, L.H. MO 6th Inf. Co.D
Ritter, L.T. AL 27th Inf. Co.E
Ritter, L.W. SC 3rd Cav. Co.A
Ritter, M. Conf.Inf. 8th Bn. Co.F

Ritter, Macom S. AR 11th Inf. Co.I
Ritter, Madison L. FL 5th Inf. Co.H
Ritter, Mark M. AR 7th Inf. Co.C
Ritter, Martin L. TX 34th Cav. Co.D Cpl.
Ritter, Moten SC 3rd Cav. Co.A
Ritter, M.S. AR 11th & 17th (Cons.) Inf. Co.C
Ritter, N. GA 3rd Inf. Co.I
Ritter, Obadiah KY 10th (Johnson's) Cav. New
    Co.C
Ritter, P. AR 11th & 17th (Cons.) Inf. Co.C,D
Ritter, Paul Conf.Reg.Inf. Brooks' Bn. Co.F
Ritter, Peter AR 15th (Josey's) Inf. Co.B
Ritter, Pierceall VA 51st Mil. Co.C
Ritter, Presley AR 11th Inf. Co.I
Ritter, R. SC 11th Inf. 1st Co.I
Ritter, Reddin SC 24th Inf. Co.E
Ritter, Richard C. VA Hvy.Arty. A.J. Jones' Co.
Ritter, Richard C. VA Inf. 5th Bn. Co.D Sgt.
Ritter, Riley MO 4th Cav. Co.D
Ritter, Robert T. MS 43rd Inf. Co.H
Ritter, Rudolph SC 11th Inf. 2nd Co.I
Ritter, Samuel MO Cav. Wood's Regt. Co.B
Ritter, Samuel VA 2nd Inf. Co.C
Ritter, S.J. TN 21st (Wilson's) Cav. Co.I
Ritter, Strother VA 51st Mil. Co.F
Ritter, T.H. AR 11th Inf. Co.F,I
Ritter, T.H. AR 11th & 17th (Cons.) Inf. Co.C
    1st Lt.
Ritter, T.Y. MS 2nd St.Cav. 1st Co.C,F Cpl.
Ritter, Vanburen TX 27th Cav. Co.K
Ritter, W.A. MS 2nd St.Cav. 1st Co.C
Ritter, W.A. Bradford's Corps Scouts & Guards
    Co.B
Ritter, Wade AL 5th Bn.Vol. Co.A Capt.
Ritter, Walker VA Cav. 39th Bn. Co.A
Ritter, Walker, Jr. VA 51st Mil. Co.F Cpl.
Ritter, Walker, Sr. VA 51st Mil. Co.F
Ritter, W.H. MS 3rd Inf. Co.C
Ritter, W.H. MS 23rd Inf. Co.C
Ritter, William AR 33rd Inf. Co.H
Ritter, William KY 4th Cav. Co.A
Ritter, William KY 8th Cav. Co.A
Ritter, William LA King's Sp.Bn. Cpl.
Ritter, William MD 1st Inf. Co.A
Ritter, William MD Inf. 2nd Bn. Co.C Sgt.
Ritter, William TX Cav. Martin's Regt. Co.C
Ritter, William TX Cav. Ragsdale's Bn. Co.A
Ritter, William VA Inf. 25th Bn. Co.E
Ritter, William 1st Conf.Eng.Troops Co.B
Ritter, William A. KY 3rd Mtd.Inf. Co.D 1st Lt.
Ritter, William A. TX 28th Cav. Co.C
Ritter, William B. VA 1st Arty. Co.I,E, 2nd
    Co.C Capt.
Ritter, William E. TX 22nd Cav. Co.H
Ritter, William H. AR 34th Inf. Co.K
Ritter, William H. FL 10th Inf. Co.F
Ritter, William H. VA 11th Cav. Co.A
Ritter, William H. VA 51st Mil. Co.F
Ritter, William L. GA Lt.Arty. Ritter's Co.
    Capt.
Ritter, William L. GA Lt.Arty. Van Den Cor-
    put's Co. Sr.2nd Lt.
Ritter, William L. MD Arty. 3rd Btty. 1st Lt.
Ritter, William P. TX Cav. Martin's Regt. Co.B
Ritter, William R. AR 15th (N.W.) Inf. Co.A
Ritter, William R.T. VA Hvy.Arty. 18th Bn.
    Co.A

Ritter, William Y. MS 43rd Inf. Co.H
Ritter, Wilson B. MO 12th Inf. Co.B
Ritter, W.J. AR 8th Inf. New Co.E
Ritter, W.J. NC 7th Bn.Jr.Res. Co.A
Ritter, W.P. TN 20th Inf. Co.E
Ritterath, Henry LA 1st Hvy.Arty. (Reg.) Co.E
Ritters, A.J. MO St.Guard
Ritters, L.M. TX Inf. 1st St.Troops White's
    Co.D
Rittershouse, J.C. NC Lt.Arty. 3rd Bn. Music.
Rittershouse, J.C. Post Band Cp.Lee,CSA Music.
Rittlebrand, J. FL 1st (Res.) Inf.
Rittler, Casimer LA 8th Inf. Co.B
Rittler, Clement LA 8th Inf. Co.B
Rittler, John H. AL 27th Inf. Co.E
Ritto, John AL 95th Mil. Co.D 3rd Sgt.
Rittonberry, Armstid VA 29th Inf. Co.A
Ritts, Benjamin SC 1st Mtd.Mil. Scott's Co.
Ritts, Edmund SC Lt.Arty. 3rd (Palmetto) Bn.
    Co.D
Ritts, J. GA 1st Inf. Co.I
Ritts, John W. SC 11th Inf. Co.B
Ritts, Thomas SC 11th Inf. Co.B
Ritz, Joseph LA Mil. Chalmette Regt. Co.I
Ritze, C.J. SC 4th St.Troops Co.A
Ritzell, A.A. NC 12th Inf. Co.A
Ritzell, Henry J. NC 12th Inf. Co.A
Ritzinger, Gustavus A. VA 25th Inf. 1st Co.K
    Asst.Fife Maj.
Ritzler, F. TX 9th (Nichols') Inf. Co.G
Ritzler, Jacob TX St.Troops Atkins' Co.
Ritzmann, Mike LA Mil. Chalmette Regt. Co.I
Rivailles, Ehibault Gen. & Staff Capt.
Rivans, Von LA 13th Inf. Co.F 1st Sgt.
Rivar, --- LA Mil. 1st Regt. 2nd Brig. 1st Div.
    Co.B
Rivard, Hippolite LA Mil. 2nd Regt. French
    Brig. Co.7
Rivard, John Conf.Inf. 8th Bn. Co.B
Rivarde, G. LA Lt.Arty. Holmes' Btty.
Rivarde, Gustav LA Arty. Castellanos' Btty. Cpl.
Rivas, Andrew TX 2nd Cav. Co.B
Rivas, Augustine TX 3rd Inf. 1st Co.A
Rivas, Edwards TX 8th Inf. Co.H
Rivas, Frank LA Mil. 5th Regt.Eur.Brig.
    (Spanish Regt.) Co.5
Rivas, Frank LA Inf. 9th Bn. Co.A Sgt.
Rivas, Fredirico TX 2nd Cav. Co.B
Rivas, Hilaire LA 8th Inf. Co.B 2nd Lt.
Rivas, Idalecio TX Cav. Benavides' Regt. Co.F
Rivas, John W. TN 4th (McLemore's) Cav. Co.A
Rivas, Jose TX Cav. Ragsdale's Bn. 1st Co.C
    Cpl.
Rivas, Juan Manuel TX 3rd Inf. 1st Co.A
Rivas, Manuel LA 30th Inf. Co.D Sgt.
Rivas, Seraphin L. LA 10th Inf. Co.G Capt.
Rivas, S.S. LA Arty. Green's Co. (LA Guard
    Btty.)
Rivas, S.S. Gen. & Staff Capt.,Comsy.
Rivas y Chinco, J. LA Mil. 5th Regt.Eur.Brig.
    (Spanish Regt.) Co.1 Sgt.
Rivas y Rivas, J. LA Mil. 5th Regt.Eur.Brig.
    (Spanish Regt.) Co.1 Sgt.
Rivault, Charles LA 4th Inf. Co.H
Riveau, Charles LA 13th Inf. Co.D
Rivecan J.M. LA Mil. Orleans Guards Regt.Co.C
Rivee, Samuel GA 4th (Clinch's) Cav.

Riveer, Abner VA 40th Inf. Co.D Cpl.
Rivegio, Jose LA Mil. 5th Regt.Eur.Brig.
    (Spanish Regt.) Co.3
Riveire, William C. GA Lt.Arty. Scogin's Btty.
    (Griffin Lt.Arty.)
Rivenack, P. TN Jackson's Cav. Music.
Rivenback, Charles NC 7th Bn.Jr.Res. Co.B
Rivenback, George T. NC 7th Bn.Jr.Res. Co.B
Rivenback, S.D. NC 67th Inf. Co.L Sgt.
Rivenbark, A.G. NC 61st Inf. Co.G
Rivenbark, Benjamin R. NC 51st Inf. Co.C
Rivenbark, Charles W. NC 1st Inf. Co.C Sgt.
Rivenbark, D.A. LA 9th Inf. Co.C
Rivenbark, Geo. NC Bass' Co.
Rivenbark, Henry D. NC 61st Inf. Co.G
Rivenbark, James NC 61st Inf. Co.G
Rivenbark, James T. NC 30th Inf. Co.E Cpl.
Rivenbark, John AL 39th Inf. Co.H
Rivenbark, John NC 8th Sr.Res. Broadhurst's
    Co.
Rivenbark, John N. NC 1st Arty. (10th
    St.Troops) Co.I Cpl.
Rivenbark, John N. NC 2nd Arty. (36th
    St.Troops) Co.A
Rivenbark, John V. NC 8th Inf. Co.F
Rivenbark, John W. NC 1st Inf. Co.C
Rivenbark, Joseph NC 30th Inf. Co.E
Rivenbark, Matthew J. NC Hvy.Arty. 1st Bn.
    Co.B Sgt.
Rivenbark, Owen J. NC 2nd Arty. (36th
    St.Troops) Co.E
Rivenbark, Robert FL 1st Inf. New Co.G
Rivenbark, Robert NC 3rd Inf. Co.K
Rivenbark, Robert NC 61st Inf. Co.G
Rivenbark, T.A. LA 17th Inf. Co.H Sgt.
Rivenbark, Teachey NC 30th Inf. Co.E 1st Sgt.
Rivenbark, Thomas E. NC 61st Inf. Co.G
Rivenbark, Washington L. NC 3rd Inf. Co.K
Rivenbark, William NC 30th Inf. Co.E Cpl.
Rivenbark, William G. NC 3rd Inf. Co.B
Rivenbark, William W. NC 20th Inf. Co.F
Rivenbarks, C. NC 3rd Jr.Res. Co.D
Rivenbarks, G. NC 3rd Jr.Res. Co.D
Rivenbarks, George FL 1st Inf. New Co.G
River, P. VA 5th Cav. Co.C
Rivera, John J. LA 6th Inf. Co.E Capt.
Rivera, Tito P. TX 1st (McCulloch's) Cav. Co.B
Rivera, T.P. TX 33rd Cav. Co.E Sgt.
Rivercomb, C.F. VA 11th Cav. Co.F
Rivercomb, G.B. VA 11th Cav. Co.F
Rivercomb, George L. VA 4th Cav. Co.C Cpl.
Rivercomb, Henry H. VA 162nd Mil. Co.A
Rivercomb, J.A. VA 11th Cav. Co.F
Rivercomb, Jacob VA 12th Cav. Co.G
Rivercomb, Jacob A. VA 34th Mil. Co.C
Rivercomb, John R. VA 162nd Mil. Co.A,C
Rivercomb, J.R. VA 11th Cav. Co.F
Rivercomb, Oliver VA 7th Inf. Co.G
Rivercomb, Richard VA 7th Inf. Co.G 1st Lt.
Rivercomb, Robert VA 7th Inf. Co.E
Rivercombs, J.A. VA 162nd Mil. Co.A Cpl.
Riverdam, J. LA 13th Inf.
Rivere, James GA 11th Mil. Co.K
Rivere, Richard GA Cav. 1st Bn.Res. Co.C
Rivere, Thomas VA 5th Cav. Co.E
Rivereau, E. LA Mil. 1st Native Guards

Rivero, J. LA Lt.Arty. LeGardeur, Jr.'s Co. (Orleans Guard Btty.

Rivero, M. TN 22nd Inf. Co.A

Rivero, M. TX Cav. Coopwood's Spy Co.

Rivers, --- TX 21st Cav. Ord.Sgt.

Rivers, --- TX Cav. Border's Regt. Co.K

Rivers, A. TX 20th Bn.St.Troops Co.A

Rivers, A.A. GA Arty. 11th Bn. (Sumter Arty.) Old Co.C, Co.B

Rivers, Abner E. AL Cav. Lenoir's Ind.Co.

Rivers, A.E. AL 4th (Russell's) Cav. Co.A

Rivers, A.J. AR 24th Inf. Co.A

Rivers, Andrew TN 63rd Inf. Co.E

Rivers, Andrew M. TN 61st Mtd.Inf. Co.K

Rivers, Avery TN 1st (Turney's) Inf. Co.F

Rivers, B. SC 2nd St.Troops Co.H

Rivers, Benjamin SC 11th Inf. Co.B

Rivers, B.R. GA Cav. 15th Bn. (St.Guards) Allen's Co.

Rivers, B.R. SC 8th Bn.Res. Fishburne's Co.

Rivers, Burrell G. GA 44th Inf. Co.H

Rivers, C. MS 28th Cav.

Rivers, C. SC Lt.Arty. Wagener's Co. (Co.A, German Arty.)

Rivers, C. TX 5th Cav. Co.K

Rivers, C.A. SC 23rd Inf. Co.A

Rivers, C.A. SC 25th Inf. Co.H

Rivers, Calvin SC 6th Cav. Co.D

Rivers, Capers M. SC Cav. 10th Bn. Surg.

Rivers, Capers M. SC Arty.Bn. Hampton Legion Co.A 1st Sgt.

Rivers, Capers M. Gen. & Staff Asst.Surg.

Rivers, C.H. SC Hvy.Arty. 15th (Lucas') Bn. Co.C

Rivers, C.H. SC 1st (Butler's) Inf. Co.D,E,K Capt.

Rivers, Charles MS Inf. 2nd Bn. Co.B Sgt.

Rivers, Charles MS 48th Inf. Co.B Sgt.

Rivers, Charles SC 23rd Inf. Co.A

Rivers, Charles H. SC 5th Bn.Res. Co.C

Rivers, C.J. AR 19th (Dawsons') Inf. Co.B

Rivers, C.M. SC 4th Cav. Asst.Surg.

Rivers, C.M. SC Cav. 19th Bn. Co.C

Rivers, C.M. SC Part.Rangers Kirk's Co.

Rivers, C.M. SC Lt.Arty. 3rd (Palmetto) Bn. Co.D Ord.Sgt.

Rivers, C.M. Gen. & Staff,PACS Asst.Surg.

Rivers, Cor. A. SC Simons' Co.

Rivers, C.P. KY 2nd Cav. Co.F

Rivers, C.T. LA Inf. 1st Sp.Bn. (Rightor's) Co.B

Rivers, D. SC 8th Inf. Co.B

Rivers, Daniel R. TN 24th Inf. Co.I Cpl.

Rivers, David T. SC Cav.Bn. Holcombe Legion Co.E

Rivers, Dempsey O. SC 8th Inf. Co.B

Rivers, D.J. AL 15th Bn.Part.Rangers Co.A

Rivers, D.J. AL 56th Part.Rangers Co.A

Rivers, D.J. AR Lt.Arty. Rivers' Btty.

Rivers, D.S. SC Mil. 1st Regt. (Charleston Res.) Co.F

Rivers, D.S. SC 23rd Inf. Co.D

Rivers, D.T. SC 7th Cav. Co.H

Rivers, E. AL 7th Cav. Co.G

Rivers, Edward M. AL Rives' Supp.Force 9th Congr.Dist.

Rivers, Elias L. SC 2nd Cav. Co.A QM

Rivers, Elias L. Gen. & Staff AQM

Rivers, Elisha F. MS 27th Inf. Co.C 2nd Lt.

Rivers, E.R. AL 1st Regt.Mobile Vol. Co.A

Rivers, E.R. AL 21st Inf. Co.K

Rivers, Eugene W. SC 5th Cav. Co.H

Rivers, E.W. SC Cav. 14th Bn. Co.A

Rivers, F. SC 8th Inf. Co.B

Rivers, F. SC 21st Inf. Co.E 2nd Lt.

Rivers, F.D. SC 11th Inf. Co.D

Rivers, F.F. SC 6th Cav. Co.D

Rivers, F.F. SC 2nd Res.

Rivers, F.J. VA 59th Inf. 2nd Co.E

Rivers, Francis LA 10th Inf. Co.I

Rivers, Frank AL 17th Inf. Co.F

Rivers, Frank LA 4th Inf. Co.A

Rivers, Frank 1st Squad. Cherokee Mtd.Vol. Co.A

Rivers, F.T. SC 11th Inf. Co.E

Rivers, George W. GA 38th Inf. Co.G

Rivers, George W. SC Cav. Walpole's Co.

Rivers, Geo. W. Gen. & Staff Asst.Surg.

Rivers, G.M. SC 11th Inf. Co.D

Rivers, G.W. GA 46th Inf. Co.E

Rivers, G.W. SC 3rd Cav. Co.I

Rivers, G.W. SC 10th Inf. 2nd Co.G

Rivers, G.W. TX 5th Cav. Co.D Bugler

Rivers, G.W. TX 14th Cav. Co.K

Rivers, H. SC Lt.Arty. Wagener's Co. (Co.A, German Arty.)

Rivers, Henry GA Inf. 1st Loc.Troops (Augusta) Co.B

Rivers, H.P. AL Cav. Murphy's Bn. Co.C

Rivers, H.P. MS 1st Lt.Arty. Co.D

Rivers, H.P. 15th Conf.Cav. Co.H

Rivers, H.S. GA 10th Inf. Co.I

Rivers, Hugh SC 5th Bn.Res. Co.C

Rivers, Isaac SC 26th Inf. Co.B

Rivers, J. SC 20th Inf. Co.D

Rivers, J.A. TN 24th Inf. Co.B

Rivers, Jacob SC 26th Inf. Co.B

Rivers, Jacob TN 43rd Inf. Co.H

Rivers, Jacob J. GA 12th Inf. Co.D

Rivers, James FL 1st (Res.) Inf. Co.G

Rivers, James GA 20th Inf. Co.I

Rivers, James LA 5th Inf. Co.A

Rivers, James SC 2nd Cav. Co.A

Rivers, James TN Cav. 11th Bn. (Gordon's) Co.A 3rd Lt.

Rivers, James TN Holman's Bn.Part.Rangers Co.D Capt.

Rivers, Jas. VA Inf. 26th Bn.

Rivers, James D. GA 26th Inf. Co.C

Rivers, James J. GA 10th Inf. Co.I

Rivers, James K. SC 6th Cav. Co.D

Rivers, James R. SC 14th Inf. Co.B

Rivers, James S. MS 36th Inf. Co.B

Rivers, James S. SC 6th Cav. Co.D

Rivers, James W. TN 11th (Holman's) Cav. Co.K Capt.

Rivers, James W. VA 61st Inf. Co.G

Rivers, Jasper TX 2nd Cav.

Rivers, J.B. TN 24th Inf. Co.B

Rivers, J.H. AR 19th (Dawson's) Inf. Co.B

Rivers, J.H. AR 24th Inf. Co.A

Rivers, J.H. GA 6th Inf. (St.Guards) Co.K

Rivers, J.H. SC 3rd Cav. Co.H

Rivers, J.H. SC Lt.Arty. J.T. Kanapaux's Co. (Lafayette Arty.)

Rivers, Jim TN 11th (Holman's) Cav. Co.K Capt.

Rivers, J.L. MS 41st Inf. Co.H 1st Lt.

Rivers, J.M. SC 11th Inf. Co.D

Rivers, J.M.M. Conf.Cav. Wood's Regt. Co.I

Rivers, Joel FL 6th Inf. Co.E

Rivers, Joel TN 24th Inf. Co.I

Rivers, Joel T. GA 57th Inf. Co.I

Rivers, John AL 1st Regt.Conscr. Co.D

Rivers, John AL 21st Inf. Co.D

Rivers, John AL 61st Inf. Co.A

Rivers, John NC 4th Inf. Co.E

Rivers, John NC 46th Inf. Co.C

Rivers, John SC 11th Inf. Co.F

Rivers, John B. SC 6th Cav. Co.D

Rivers, John D. AL 49th Inf. Co.H Lt.

Rivers, John D. SC 11th Inf. Co.E

Rivers, John F. SC 5th Cav. Co.B

Rivers, John F. SC Cav. 17th Bn. Co.C

Rivers, John H. GA Inf. 1st Conf.Bn. Co.D

Rivers, John H. GA 30th Inf. Co.F

Rivers, John M. GA Lt.Arty. Scogin's Btty. (Griffin Lt.Arty.)

Rivers, John M. SC 8th Inf. Co.B Sgt.

Rivers, John T. GA 10th Inf. Co.F

Rivers, John W. AR Lt.Arty. Rivers' Btty. Capt.

Rivers, Jonathan GA 8th Inf. Co.F Bvt.2nd Lt.

Rivers, Jonathan GA 49th Inf. Co.A Lt.Col.

Rivers, J.P. FL 2nd Cav. Co.H

Rivers, J.S. LA Inf. 16th Bn. (Conf.Guards Resp.Bn.) Co.A Cpl.

Rivers, J.S. MS 20th Inf. Co.E

Rivers, J.S. TN 19th (Biffle's) Cav. Co.H

Rivers, J.T. GA 29th Inf. Co.F

Rivers, J.T. SC 11th Inf. Co.D Cpl.

Rivers, J. Townsend SC Cav. Walpole's Co.

Rivers, J.W. GA 10th Inf. Co.I

Rivers, Kolb GA 1st Cav. Co.C

Rivers, L.B. SC 6th Cav. Co.D

Rivers, Lewis W. FL 1st Cav. Co.A Cpl.

Rivers, L.J. SC 26th Inf. Co.B

Rivers, Louis J. FL 6th Inf. Co.E Cpl.

Rivers, M. SC Cav. 19th Bn. Co.E

Rivers, M.A. GA 9th Inf. (St.Guards) Co.A Cpl.

Rivers, Mark SC Inf. 9th Bn. Co.B Cpl.

Rivers, Mark SC 20th Inf. Co.O

Rivers, Mark SC 26th Inf. Co.B

Rivers, Mark A. GA 12th Inf. Co.A

Rivers, Martin M. TN 24th Inf. Co.I

Rivers, M.C. LA Lt.Arty. LeGardeur, Jr.'s Co. (Orleans Guard Btty.) Asst.Surg.

Rivers, N.C. Gen. & Staff Asst.Surg.

Rivers, M.J. SC 26th Inf. Co.B Cpl.

Rivers, M.M. TN 19th (Biffle's) Cav. Co.H

Rivers, Nathaniel A. GA 44th Inf. Co.E

Rivers, N.H. GA 46th Inf. Co.E

Rivers, P.H. SC 1st Cav. Co.I

Rivers, P.H. 2nd Conf.Eng.Troops Co.F

Rivers, Philip SC 26th Inf. Co.B

Rivers, R. SC 2nd St.Troops Co.H

Rivers, R.A. GA 10th Inf. Co.I Cpl.

Rivers, R.B. AL Inf. 2nd Regt. Co.D Cpl.

Rivers, R.C. MS 27th Inf. Co.C

Rivers, R.C. MS 41st Inf. Co.H Sgt.

Rivers, R.E. LA Inf. 16th Bn. (Conf.Guards Resp.Bn.) Co.A Cpl.

Rivers, R.E. TN 51st (Cons.) Inf. Co.G

Rivers, R.H. SC 2nd Inf. Co.I Cpl.
Rivers, R.H. SC 11th Inf. Co.D
Rivers, Richard R. TX 1st (McCulloch's) Cav. Co.A
Rivers, R.J. SC 24th Inf. Co.D
Rivers, R.L. GA 3rd Inf. Co.F
Rivers, Robert MO 16th Inf. Co.K
Rivers, Robert TN 59th Mtd.Inf. Co.K
Rivers, Robert A. GA 53rd Inf. Co.C
Rivers, Robert B. AL 42nd Inf. Co.K 1st Lt.
Rivers, Robert L. MS Cav. Jeff Davis Legion Co.A
Rivers, R.P. SC 27th Inf. Co.D
Rivers, R.R. AL 58th Inf. Co.I
Rivers, R.S. SC Inf. Hampton Legion Co.G
Rivers, S. SC 5th Cav. Co.E
Rivers, S. SC 20th Inf. Co.O
Rivers, S. 3rd Conf.Eng.Troops Co.A Artif.
Rivers, Samuel SC Inf. 9th Bn. Co.B
Rivers, Samuel SC 26th Inf. Co.B
Rivers, Samuel TN 1st Btty.
Rivers, Seabron GA 2nd Res. Co.I
Rivers, Stikes SC Spark's Ind.Cav.
Rivers, Sylvester FL 7th Inf. Co.G Sgt.
Rivers, T. MO Inf. 4th Regt.St.Guard Asst.Surg.
Rivers, Thomas TN 31st Inf. Surg.
Rivers, Thomas TX 3rd Inf. Co.G
Rivers, Thomas Cheatham's Div. Surg.
Rivers, Thomas D. FL 9th Inf. Co.F
Rivers, Thomas H. TX 21st Cav. Co.B
Rivers, Thomas T. AL Inf. 1st Regt. Co.B
Rivers, T.N. GA 17th Inf. Co.H
Rivers, T.N. GA 46th Inf. Co.E Cpl.
Rivers, T.T. AL 45th Inf. Co.C
Rivers, T.W. NC 16th Inf. Co.G Cpl.
Rivers, W.A.J. MS Inf. 8th Bn. Co.C Sgt.
Rivers, W.A.J. MS 41st Inf. Co.C
Rivers, W.B. GA 10th Cav. (St.Guards) Co.K
Rivers, W.B. TN Inf. 2nd Cons.Regt. Co.B Cpl.
Rivers, W.B. TN 9th Inf. Co.C
Rivers, W.B. TN 51st Inf. Co.K Cpl.
Rivers, W.D. SC 10th Inf. 1st Co.G
Rivers, W.H. TN 17th Inf. Co.F
Rivers, William GA 10th Inf. Sgt.
Rivers, William SC 3rd Cav. Co.H
Rivers, William SC Lt.Arty. 3rd (Palmetto) Bn. Co.E
Rivers, William SC 2nd Inf. Co.I
Rivers, William TN 33rd Inf. Co.I
Rivers, William TX 17th Inf. Co.F
Rivers, William VA 94th Mil. Co.A
Rivers, William 15th Conf.Cav. Co.H
Rivers, William A. GA 39th Inf. Co.B,K
Rivers, William B. SC 8th Inf. Co.B
Rivers, William E. SC 3rd Cav. Co.C
Rivers, William E. SC Mil.Cav. 4th Regt. Howard's Co.
Rivers, William F. SC 8th Inf. Co.B 1st Sgt.
Rivers, William H. GA 26th Inf. Co.K,F
Rivers, William P. MS 3rd Inf. Co.E
Rivers, William R. VA 64th Mtd.Inf. Co.A
Rivers, William S. SC Cav. Walpole's Co.
Rivers, William W. GA Lt.Arty. Scogin's Btty. (Griffin Lt.Arty.)
Rivers, W.J. MO 16th Inf. Co.K
Rivers, W.J. SC Inf. 9th Bn. Co.B
Rivers, W.J. SC 26th Inf. Co.B

Rivers, W.L. LA 25th Inf. Co.G
Rivers, W.P. GA Cav. 22nd Bn. (St.Guards) Co.A
Rivers, W.P. MS Henley's Co. (Henley's Invinc.)
Rivers, W.W. AL 45th Inf. Co.C
Rivers, W.W. SC 14th Inf. Co.I
Rivers, W.W. SC 24th Inf. Co.D
Riverson, A.J. VA 50th Inf. Co.H
Riverville, J.J. NC 28th Inf. Co.G
Rives, A.A. AR 1st Mtd.Rifles Co.B
Rives, A.B.C. VA 2nd Arty. Co.E
Rives, Abram VA 38th Inf. Co.C
Rives, A.H. NC 3rd Jr.Res. Co.D
Rives, A.J. AL 43rd Inf. Co.F
Rives, A.L. Eng.,CSA Col.
Rives, Albert T. VA Inf. 5th Bn. Co.C
Rives, Albert T. VA 53rd Inf. Co.D
Rives, Alexander, Jr. AL 15th Inf. Asst.Surg.
Rives, Alexander NC 61st Inf. Surg.
Rives, Alexander VA 16th Inf. Co.F Cpl.
Rives, Alexander Gen. & Staff Surg.
Rives, Alfred L. Eng. Capt.
Rives, Barnwell E. GA 43rd Inf. Co.K 1st Sgt.
Rives, Bartlett S. AL 32nd Inf. Co.C
Rives, B.E. GA 4th Cav. (St.Guards) Armstrong's Co.
Rives, Benjamin A. MO 3rd Inf. Col.
Rives, Benjamin B. NC 27th Inf. Co.A Sgt.
Rives, Benjamin F. NC 2nd Bn.Loc.Def.Troops Co.A Laborer
Rives, Benjamin S. AL Rives' Supp.Force 9th Congr.Dist. Capt.
Rives, Benjamin T. FL 2nd Cav. Co.C,F
Rives, B.H. TN 8th Inf. Co.K
Rives, B.S. AL 17th Inf. Co.H
Rives, Burnell G. GA Cobb's Legion Co.H
Rives, Cadd SC 6th Inf. 1st Co.B
Rives, C.B. MS 42nd Inf. Co.A Cpl.
Rives, Charles M. VA 1st Arty. Co.H,G Jr.1st Lt.
Rives, Charles M. VA Arty. C.F. Johnston's Co. 1st Lt.
Rives, C.S. AL 34th Inf. Co.F
Rives, Daniel D. VA 38th Inf. Co.C
Rives, David FL 1st Cav. Co.F
Rives, D.E. NC 26th Inf. Co.E
Rives, D.N. TN 9th Inf. Co.D Sgt.
Rives, Edward VA 28th Inf. Surg.
Rives, Edward Pickett's Div. Surg.
Rives, Ephraim VA 38th Inf. Co.C
Rives, F.L. AL 15th Bn.Part.Rangers Co.A Ens.
Rives, F.L. AL 56th Part.Rangers Co.A
Rives, Franklin L. AL 6th Inf. Co.E
Rives, George, Jr. AL 15th Bn.Part.Rangers Co.A Lt.
Rives, George AL 56th Part.Rangers Co.A 1st Lt.
Rives, Geo. C. Gen. & Staff Capt.,AQM
Rives, George E. VA 5th Cav. (12 mo. '61-2) Co.C
Rives, George E. VA 13th Cav. Co.H
Rives, George M. TX Cav. Morgan's Regt. Co.I
Rives, George S. VA 5th Cav. (12 mo. '61-2) Co.C Cpl.
Rives, George S. VA 13th Cav. Co.K 1st Lt.
Rives, George S. Beale's Brig. Lt.,Prov.Marsh.

Rives, George W. NC 6th Sr.Res. Co.B
Rives, G. Tucker VA 46th Inf. 2nd Co.I Capt.
Rives, G. Tucker VA Inf. Hutter's Co.
Rives, G.W. Gen. & Staff Asst.Comsy.
Rives, H.B. Gen. & Staff Capt.,AQM
Rives, Henderson D. Cav. Murchison's Bn. Co.G
Rives, Henry J. MO 3rd Inf. Co.F
Rives, H.W. Gen. & Staff AQM
Rives, Ira O. TN 4th (McLemore's) Cav. Co.F
Rives, J. AL 5th Inf. Co.A
Rives, J.A. KY 2nd Mtd.Inf. Co.H
Rives, James A. VA 2nd Arty. Co.E
Rives, James B. AL 62nd Inf. Co.H
Rives, James H. MS 1st Cav. Co.F Capt.
Rives, James H. MS 1st Cav. Co.G
Rives, James H. MS 11th Inf. Co.F 1st Lt.
Rives, James Henry VA Lt.Arty. Rives' Co. Capt.
Rives, James M. AL Lt.Arty. 2nd Bn. Co.C
Rives, James M. MO 8th Inf. Co.B
Rives, James M. TN 8th Inf. Co.C
Rives, James P. TN 4th (McLemore's) Cav. Co.F
Rives, James P. TN 1st (Turney's) Inf. Co.E
Rives, James W. GA 2nd Bn.S.S. Co.C
Rives, J.E. NC 26th Inf. Co.E
Rives, Jefferson R. AL 44th Inf. Co.A Cpl.
Rives, Jesse AL 15th Inf. Co.E
Rives, J.F. MS 1st (King's) Inf. (St.Troops) Co.D
Rives, J.H. MD Cav. 2nd Bn. Co.C
Rives, J. Henry VA 4th Cav. Co.I
Rives, J. Henry Conf.Lt.Arty. Stark's Bn. Co.C Capt.
Rives, J.J. Gen. & Staff Surg.
Rives, J.M. MS 28th Cav. Co.D
Rives, J.M. MO St.Guard
Rives, Joel T. MS 11th Inf. Co.F
Rives, John C. AL 15th Bn.Part.Rangers Co.A
Rives, John C. AL 56th Part.Rangers Co.A
Rives, John C. AL 6th Inf. Co.E
Rives, John E. MS 14th Inf. Co.G
Rives, John F. GA 11th Cav. Co.B 2nd Lt.
Rives, John F. GA 43rd Inf. Co.K Capt.
Rives, John F.M. GA 4th Cav. (St.Guards) Robertson's Co. Sgt.
Rives, John G. TN 3rd (Forrest's) Cav. Co.A
Rives, John H. AL 17th Inf. Co.H
Rives, John H. TX 18th Inf. Co.D Sgt.
Rives, John H. VA 2nd Arty. Co.E
Rives, John J. VA Inf. 5th Bn. Co.A
Rives, John J. VA 53rd Inf. Co.H
Rives, John R. NC 2nd Bn.Loc.Def.Troops Co.F
Rives, J.S. TN 6th Inf. Co.D
Rives, J.T. AL 18th Inf. Co.G
Rives, Judson C. LA Inf. 11th Bn. Co.D
Rives, J.W.H. AL 2nd Cav. Co.K 2nd Lt.
Rives, Landon Gen. & Staff, Medical Dept. Surg.
Rives, Leonidas O. TN 4th Inf. Co.A Sgt.
Rives, L.F. MS 15th Bn.S.S. Co.A
Rives, L.W. TN 8th Inf. Co.C
Rives, M.L. MS 3rd Cav. Co.C,A Jr.2nd Lt.
Rives, Nat LA 4th Cav. Co.E
Rives, Nat F. TN Inf. 154th Sr.Regt. Co.G Cpl.
Rives, Nathaniel LA 2nd Inf. Co.F 1st Lt.

Rives, N.G. TN Lt.Arty. McClung's Co. 1st
  Gy.Sgt.
Rives, N.G. TN Inf. Nashville Bn.
Rives, Noah L. MO 3rd Cav. Co.K
Rives, O.R. AL Morris Scouts
Rives, Peter M. VA 3rd Cav. Co.H Cpl.
Rives, R. AL Inf. 2nd Regt. Co.D
Rives, R. LA 1st Cav. Co.F Cpl.
Rives, R.C. AL 1st Inf. Co.B
Rives, R.C. TN 24th Inf. Co.E
Rives, R.E. VA 1st (Farinholt's) Res. Co.D Sgt.
Rives, Reuben P. GA Cobb's Legion Co.H
Rives, R.F. KY Morgan's Men Co.E
Rives, R.G. AR 18th Inf. Co.D
Rives, R.G. MS 1st Cav. Co.F Sgt.
Rives, Richard W. NC 1st Inf. Co.H Capt.
Rives, Ro B. VA Cav. 37th Bn. Co.A
Rives, Robert AL Lt.Arty. 2nd Bn. Co.E
Rives, Robert AR 1st Mtd.Rifles Co.A
Rives, Robert MO 3rd Inf. Co.F 1st Lt.
Rives, Robert MO St.Guard Capt.
Rives, Robert TN 8th Inf. Co.C
Rives, Robert B. VA 10th Cav. Co.K
Rives, Robert D. AR 17th (Lemoyne's) Inf. Co.F
Rives, Robert D. AR 21st Inf. Co.E
Rives, Robert F. TN 14th Inf. Co.L
Rives, Robert G. MS 1st Cav. Co.G
Rives, Robert L. GA 13th Inf. Co.I Cpl.
Rives, Robert W. GA 43rd Inf. Co.K
Rives, R.R. AL 4th Res. Co.A
Rives, R.R. GA Mil.Res. Sgt.
Rives, R.S. AL 44th Inf. Co.C
Rives, R.T. GA 23rd Inf. Co.H
Rives, Samuel B. VA 41st Inf. 2nd Co.E
Rives, Samuel E. MS 11th (Perrin's) Cav. Co.H
Rives, Stephen T. TN 14th Inf. Co.L 3rd Lt.
Rives, S.W. SC 7th Cav. Co.G
Rives, S.W. SC 22nd Inf. Co.G
Rives, T.E. GA 20th Inf. Co.F
Rives, Thos. E. MS 12th Inf. Co.H
Rives, Thomas F. VA 3rd Cav. 2nd Co.I
Rives, Thomas J. AL 3rd Cav. Co.D
Rives, Thomas J. GA Cobb's Legion Co.C,H
Rives, Thomas L. MO 8th Inf. Co.B
Rives, Thomas V. GA 43rd Inf. Co.K
Rives, Thomas W. NC Cav. 12th Bn. Co.C Sgt.
Rives, Thomas W. NC Cav. 16th Bn. Co.G Sgt.
Rives, Thomas W. SC 12th Inf. Co.D
Rives, Timothy VA 3rd Inf. Capt.
Rives, Timothy Gen. & Staff Capt.,Comsy.
Rives, T.J. TN 8th Inf. Co.D
Rives, V.G. AL 2nd Cav. Co.K
Rives, Virgil A. VA 3rd Cav. 2nd Co.I
Rives, W.A. NC 26th Inf. Co.E
Rives, Wade H. SC 12th Inf. Co.D 1st Lt.
Rives, W.C. AL 26th Inf. Co.D
Rives, W.C. SC 5th Inf. 1st Co.I
Rives, W.G. TX 3rd Cav. Co.G
Rives, W.H. AL 2nd Cav. Co.K 2nd Lt.
Rives, W.H.G. AL Res. Belser's Co.
Rives, William AR 38th Inf. Co.A Cpl.
Rives, William TX 2nd Cav. Co.H
Rives, William VA 40th Inf.
Rives, William Mead's Conf.Cav. Co.D
Rives, William A. VA Hvy.Arty. 19th Bn. 3rd
  Co.C
Rives, William B. TX 8th Cav. Co.F

Rives, William C. SC 25th Inf. Co.G
Rives, William H. AL Montgomery Guards
Rives, William M. TN 14th Inf. Co.L
Rives, William T. MS 11th (Perrin's) Cav. Co.H
Rives, William T. MS 14th Inf. Co.G
Rives, William Thomas TX 8th Cav. Co.H
Rives, William W. VA 10th Cav. Co.K
Rives, Wilson AL 7th Cav. Co.C
Rives, W.J. GA 4th (Clinch's) Cav. Co.I
Rives, W.J. GA 11th Cav. (St.Guards) Johnson's
  Co.
Rives, W.J. GA Lt.Arty. Clinch's Btty. QMSgt.
Rives, W.J. GA Arty. Maxwell's Reg.Lt.Btty.
  Sgt.
Rives, W.M. KY 1st (Helm's) Cav. Co.A
Rives, W.M. VA Inf. 2nd Bn.Loc.Def. Co.B
Rives, W.P. MO 11th Inf. Co.D Sgt.
Rivet, Charles L. LA Mil. 1st Chasseurs a pied
  Co.5
Rivet, Chs. L. LA Mil. Jackson Rifle Bn. 1st Lt.
Rivet, Chs. L. LA Prov.Regt. Legion A.Adj.
Rivet, Cleophas LA 11th Inf. Co.B
Rivet, Ernest LA 30th Inf. Co.I,D
Rivet, H. LA Prov.Regt. Legion Co.1 Capt.
Rivet, H.J. LA Mil. Jackson Rifle Bn. Capt.
Rivet, James LA 2nd Cav. Co.I
Rivet, J.B. LA C.S. Zouave Bn.
Rivet, Joseph LA Mil.Cav.Squad. (Ind.Rangers
  Iberville)
Rivet, Joseph LA 30th Inf. Co.I,C Band Music.
Rivet, Joseph Gibson's Brig.Band,CSA
Rivet, Martin LA 28th (Thomas') Inf. Co.E
Rivet, S.O. LA 4th Inf. Co.H
Rivet, Transimond LA 11th Inf. Co.B
Rivet, Valier LA 28th (Thomas') Inf. Co.H
Rivet, Valmont LA Mil.Cav.Squad. (Ind.Rangers
  Iberville)
Rivetle, Francaios LA 26th Inf. Co.B
Rivett, Benjamin J. SC 1st (McCreary's) Inf.
  Co.K
Rivett, P.V. LA 2nd Cav. Co.I
Rivett, T. LA 20th Inf. New Co.E
Rivette, J. LA 13th & 20th Inf. Co.A
Riviere, A.M. GA 32nd Inf. Co.I
Riviere, Andrew G. TX 3rd Cav. Co.I Cpl.
Riviere, Elphege LA 3rd Inf. Co.A
Riviere, Emile LA 3rd Inf. Co.A
Riviere, Erasmus GA 4th Inf. Co.K
Riviere, Ernest LA Washington Arty.Bn. Co.3,1
Riviere, James F. MS Lt.Arty. (Jefferson Arty.)
  Darden's Co.
Riviere, J.G. LA 21st (Patton's) Inf. Co.A
Riviere, Joseph H. GA 4th Inf. Co.K 1st Lt.
Riviere, L. LA Mil. Orleans Guards Regt. Co.C
Riviere, Lange LA 30th Inf. Co.H,G
Riviere, Numa LA Mil. Orleans Guards Regt.
  Co.H
Riviere, P. LA Mil. Orleans Guards Regt. Co.A
Riviere, Richard MS Lt.Arty. (Jefferson Arty.)
  Darden's Co.
Riviere, Richard D. AL 37th Inf. Co.C
  Comsy.Sgt.
Riviere, R.J. AL 37th Inf. Co.C
Riviere, Talionis L. 15th Conf.Cav. Co.B
Riviere, Wesley GA Arty. 11th Bn. (Sumter
  Arty.) Co.B

Riviere, William A. 1st Conf.Eng.Troops Co.H
  Artif.
Riviere, William C. MS Lt.Arty. (Jefferson
  Arty.) Darden's Co.
Riviere, William J.I. GA Cav. 7th Bn.
  (St.Guards) Co.F Sgt.
Riville, P., Jr. LA Mil. Orleans Guards Regt.
  Co.G
Rivin, R.M. GA 44th Inf. Co.I
Rivinac, P. MS 28th Cav. Music.
Rivinac, Peter MS 10th Inf. Music.
Rivis, Edmond MO Cav. Hunter's Regt. Co.C
Rivis, J.R. TN 24th Bn.S.S. Co.B
Rivolta, F. LA Mil. 1st Chasseurs a pied Co.8
Rix, --- AL 12th Inf. Co.E
Rix, C.A. GA 62nd Cav. Co.L
Rix, H. LA 1st Cav. Co.C Sgt.
Rix, Henry J. AL Lt.Arty. Hurt's Btty. Sgt.
Rix, Henry J. AL 34th Inf. Co.F Capt.
Rix, Hiram AL 24th Inf. Co.G
Rix, J.D. VA 47th Mil.
Rix, John AL 25th Inf. Co.D
Rix, N.D. AL 11th Cav. Co.I
Rix, Richard L. GA 21st Inf. Co.I
Rix, Thomas GA Inf. Collier's Co.
Rix, William NC 37th Inf. Co.E
Rix, William H. NC 29th Inf. Co.A
Rixborn, S. MS 2nd (Quinn's St.Troops) Inf.
  Co.C
Rixey, James W. VA 9th Cav.
Rixey, John G. VA Lt.Arty. Carpenter's Co.
  QMSgt.
Rixey, John G. VA 27th Inf. Co.A Sgt.
Rixey, Richard VA Lt.Arty. Carpenter's Co.
Rixey, Richard H. MS 10th Inf. Old Co.E Cpl.
Rixey, Sam'l. R. Gen. & Staff Surg.
Rixread, H.A. VA 31st Inf. Co.E
Rixroad, Samuel VA 62nd Mtd.Inf. 2nd Co.C
Rixroad, Solomon VA 62nd Mtd.Inf. 2nd Co.C
Rixroad, Washington VA 62nd Mtd.Inf. 2nd
  Co.C
Rize, Zara NC 7th Sr.Res. Mitchell's Co.
Rizen, John F. VA 17th Inf. Co.F
Rizen, William KY 6th Cav. Co.K
Rizer, A. SC 3rd Cav. Co.D
Rizer, Cansford SC 3rd Cav. Co.G,F
Rizer, Charles FL Inf. 2nd Bn. Co.D
Rizer, Charles FL 10th Inf. Co.K
Rizer, George A. SC 1st Arty. Co.D
Rizer, George W. LA 31st Inf. Co.B
Rizer, Isaac MS 37th Inf. Co.H
Rizer, J.C. SC 11th Inf. Co.K
Rizer, J.L. TN 62nd Mtd.Inf. Co.G
Rizer, J.N. SC 3rd Cav.
Rizer, John E. VA 33rd Inf. Co.A
Rizer, L.A. VA 23rd Cav. Co.E
Rizer, L.A. VA Cav. 41st Bn. Co.E
Rizer, Thomas A. MS 1st Lt.Arty. Co.A
Rizer, T.P. SC 3rd Cav. Co.F
Rizer, T.P. SC 11th Inf. Co.K
Rizer, William LA Inf.Cons.Crescent Regt. Co.H
Rizer, William E. LA 3rd Inf. Co.B
Rizner, Andrew J. TN 54th Inf. Hollis' Co.
Rizo, Jos. LA Inf.Crescent Regt. Co.H,C
Rizor, J.G. MS 44th Inf. Co.G
Rizzo, Giuseppe LA Mil. 6th Regt.Eur.Brig.
  (Italian Guards Bn.) Co.2

Rizzotti, John LA Mil. Orleans Fire Regt. Co.F
Rlerll, G. Gen. & Staff Chap.
Ro, Fra M. AL Lt.Arty. 2nd Bn. Co.F
Roach, --- AL 1st Regt.Conscr. Co.I
Roach, A. LA Mil. Chalmette Regt. Co.E
Roach, A.A. TN 18th (Newsom's) Cav. Co.D
Roach, A.A. TN 31st Inf. Co.H
Roach, Abraham NC 8th Inf. Co.A Cook
Roach, Absolum TN Conscr. (Cp. of Instr.)
Roach, Agenan NC Walker's Bn. Thomas'
  Legion Co.G
Roach, Agenan TN 1st (Carter's) Cav. Co.H
Roach, A.J. AL 26th Inf. Co.F
Roach, A.J. GA Phillips' Legion Co.B
Roach, Alexander T. VA 41st Inf. Co.G
Roach, Alfred GA Cherokee Legion (St.Guards)
  Co.D
Roach, A.H. NC Walker's Bn. Thomas' Legion
  Co.G
Roach, Andrew LA 10th Inf. Co.B
Roach, Andrew E. VA Lt.Arty. Lowry's Co.
Roach, Andrew E. VA King's Bn.
Roach, Anthony LA Inf. 4th Bn. Co.C
Roach, A.P. TX 9th (Young's) Inf. Co.K Sgt.
Roach, Archibald NC 30th Inf. Co.C
Roach, Archibald VA 57th Inf. Co.H
Roach, Archibald VA 97th Mil. Co.H
Roach, Azra J. FL 7th Inf. Co.G,H
Roach, B. AR 30th Inf. Co.K
Roach, B. MS 20th Inf. Co.G
Roach, Baxter SC 22nd Inf. Co.D
Roach, B.C. MS 35th Inf. Co.A
Roach, Benjamin AR 38th Inf. Co.E
Roach, Benjamin GA 26th Inf. Co.G
Roach, Benjamin LA Conf.Regt. Co.A
Roach, Benjamin MO Cav. Freeman's Regt.
Roach, Benjamin A. MS 26th Inf. Co.C
Roach, Benjamin F. TX Cav. 6th Bn. Co.C Cpl.
Roach, Benjamin F. TX 1st Inf. Co.I
Roach, Benjamin F. VA Lt.Arty. Parker's Co.
Roach, Benjamin F. VA 52nd Mil. Co.A
Roach, Benjamin H. LA 6th Cav. Co.D,A
Roach, Benjamin U. AR
Roach, Berry SC 1st (Orr's) Rifles Co.E
Roach, B.F. SC 5th Inf. 2nd Co.E
Roach, B.F. SC 6th Inf. 1st Co.H
Roach, B.F. TX 7th Cav. Co.I
Roach, B.F. TX 25th Cav. Co.I
Roach, B.M. SC Mil. 16th Regt. Bancroft, Jr.'s
  Co.
Roach, B.T. TN 8th Inf. Co.C
Roach, C. NC 66th Inf. Co.D
Roach, C. VA 46th Inf. 2nd Co.K
Roach, Calvin NC Hvy.Arty. 10th Bn. Co.D,A
Roach, C.C. MS 44th Inf. Co.D
Roach, C.F. VA Lt.Arty. Lowry's Co.
Roach, Charles MO Cav. Slayback's Regt. Co.G
Roach, Charles TN 7th (Duckworth's) Cav. Co.C
Roach, Charles TX 1st (Yager's) Cav. Co.D
Roach, Charles TX 29th Cav. Co.I
Roach, Charles TX Part.Rangers Thomas' Co.
Roach, Charles TX 1st Hvy.Arty. Co.D
Roach, Charles 1st Choctaw & Chickasaw
  Mtd.Rifles 1st Co.I
Roach, Charles A. SC 2nd Cav. Co.C 2nd Lt.
Roach, Charles A. SC Cav. 4th Bn. Co.B Sgt.
Roach, Charles B. AL Cav. Bowie's Co.

Roach, Charles B. AL 3rd Inf. Co.F
Roach, Charles B. VA Inf. 26th Bn. Co.E
Roach, Charles B. 8th (Wade's) Conf.Cav. Co.A
Roach, Charles D. VA Lt.Arty. Pegram's Co.
Roach, Charles D. VA 12th Inf. Co.D,C Cpl.
Roach, Charles M. NC 44th Inf. Co.I Music.
Roach, Charles W. FL 5th Inf. Co.G
Roach, Charles W. GA 6th Inf. Co.D
Roach, Christopher MS 12th Inf. Co.B
Roach, Christopher VA 1st Arty. Co.F,E Cpl.
Roach, Christopher VA 32nd Inf. Co.G Cpl.
Roach, C.L. AL 8th Inf. Co.G
Roach, C.L. AR 8th Inf. New Co.I
Roach, C.M.K. GA 11th Inf. Co.I
Roach, C.T. TN 7th (Duckworth's) Cav. Co.C
Roach, C.W. FL 1st (Res.) Inf. Co.E Sgt.
Roach, D. TX 20th Inf. Co.B
Roach, Daniel LA 20th Inf. Co.I
Roach, Daniel TX 1st Hvy.Arty. 2nd Co.F
Roach, Daniel TX 2nd Inf. Odlum's Co.
Roach, Daniel H. TN Cav. Newsom's Regt.
  Co.G
Roach, David GA 1st Inf. (St.Guards) Co.I
Roach, David GA 4th Inf. Co.A,K
Roach, David GA Inf. 10th Bn. Co.C
Roach, David LA 14th Inf.
Roach, David LA 21st (Patton's) Inf. Co.A
Roach, David LA 22nd (Cons.) Inf. Co.I
Roach, David M. KY 5th Cav. Co.F Sgt.
Roach, David S. NC Coast Guards Galloway's
  Co. 1st Sgt.
Roach, D.C. AL 17th Inf. Co.K
Roach, D.D. FL Fernandez's Mtd.Co. (Supply
  Force)
Roach, D.K. GA Inf. (Jasper & Butts Cty.
  Guards) Lane's Co.
Roach, D.L. MS Cav. 1st Bn. (Montgomery's)
  St.Troops Hammond's Co. 2nd Lt.
Roach, D.L. MS Cav. Yerger's Regt. Co.A
Roach, D.M. TN 18th (Newsom's) Cav. Co.D
Roach, D.M. TN 1st (Feild's) & 27th Inf.
  (Cons.) Co.I
Roach, D.M. TN 27th Inf. Co.D
Roach, E. SC 5th Res. Co.C
Roach, E.B. AR 15th (Josey's) Inf. Co.G
Roach, E.C. LA Mil.Conf.Guards Regt. Co.D
Roach, E.D. TN 19th (Biffle's) Cav. Co.B
Roach, Edmond GA 31st Inf. Co.C Sgt.
Roach, Edmund AL 6th Inf. Co.B
Roach, Edward LA 22nd Inf. Jones' Co.
Roach, Edward SC Mil. 16th Regt. Bancroft,
  Jr.'s Co. Sgt.
Roach, Edward VA 33rd Inf. Co.E,A Cpl.
Roach, E.J. GA 18th Inf. Surg.
Roach, E.J. Gen. & Staff Surg.
Roach, E.L. SC Mil. 16th Regt. Bancroft, Jr.'s
  Co.
Roach, E.L. SC 27th Inf. Co.I
Roach, Elbert B. AR 18th Inf. Co.A
Roach, Elias GA Inf. 4th Bn. (St.Guards) Co.C
Roach, Elias GA 37th Inf. Co.F
Roach, Elias GA 54th Inf. Co.H
Roach, Elias MS 38th Cav. Co.I
Roach, Elias R. GA 52nd Inf. Co.A
Roach, Elijah VA 20th Inf. Co.B
Roach, Elijah VA Inf. 29th Bn. Co.B
Roach, Elijah T. VA 18th Inf. Co.K Cpl.

Roach, Elijah T. VA 38th Inf. Co.F
Roach, Elliot W. AL 13th Inf. Co.A Cpl.
Roach, E.M. AR 15th Mil. Maj.
Roach, E.M. AR Inf. Williamson's Bn. Maj.
  Commanding
Roach, Emanuel VA 34th Inf. Co.D
Roach, Emanuel VA 97th Mil. Co.H Sgt.
Roach, Erwin A. SC 14th Inf. Co.B 3rd Lt.
Roach, Eug. LA Mil. Chalmette Regt. Co.D
  Jr.2nd Lt.
Roach, Eugene LA Inf. 4th Bn. Co.E
Roach, Eugene LA 21st (Patton's) Inf. Co.A
Roach, Eugene LA 22nd (Cons.) Inf. Co.I
Roach, Ewing AR 7th Inf. Co.A
Roach, Farrow TN 19th (Biffle's) Cav. Co.I
Roach, F.E. TN 12th (Cons.) Inf. Co.H
Roach, F.E. TN 22nd Inf. Co.B
Roach, Finis TN 14th (Neely's) Cav. Co.E 1st
  Sgt.
Roach, Fisher TN 46th Inf. Co.D
Roach, F.M. MO Inf. 1st Bn. Co.C
Roach, F.M. Ord. Scouts & Guards Click's
  Co.,CSA
Roach, Forrester GA Inf. (Franklin Cty.Guards)
  Kay's Co.
Roach, F.P. TN 51st (Cons.) Inf. Co.F
Roach, Francis GA 1st (Olmstead's) Inf. Co.D
Roach, Francis TX 2nd Cav. Co.G
Roach, Francis M. AR 1st Vol. Simington's Co.
Roach, Francis M. MO 6th Inf. Co.K
Roach, Francis N. KY 2nd Cav. Co.B
Roach, Frank VA Lt.Arty. Clutter's Co.
Roach, Frank VA Arty. Fleet's Co.
Roach, Frank VA 55th Inf. Co.B
Roach, Franklin AR 7th Inf.
Roach, Franklin MS 29th Inf. Co.E Jr.2nd Lt.
Roach, Franklin A. GA 57th Inf. Co.I
Roach, Frederick VA Hvy.Arty. 10th Bn.
Roach, Frederick C. AL 4th Inf. Co.E Cpl.
Roach, G.B. NC 21st Inf. Co.L
Roach, George KY 3rd Mtd.Inf. Co.E
Roach, George TX 9th Cav. Co.A
Roach, George VA Cav. 34th Bn. Co.B
Roach, George VA 31st Mil. Co.D
Roach, George 1st Chicksaw Inf. McCord's Co.
Roach, George R. SC 12th Inf. Co.A Sgt.
Roach, George R. VA 21st Inf. Co.A 2nd Lt.
Roach, George R. VA Inf. 25th Bn. Co.D
Roach, George W. FL 5th Inf. Co.G
Roach, George W. GA 20th Inf. Co.D
Roach, George W. VA 8th Inf. Co.C
Roach, G.H. AL 4th (Russell's) Cav. Co.G
Roach, Gideon L. NC 5th Cav. (63rd St.Troops)
  Co.D
Roach, Glenn O. LA Cav. Cole's Co.
Roach, G.O. TN 7th (Duckworth's) Cav. Co.F
Roach, Green B. AL Arty. 4th Bn. Hilliard's
  Legion Co.A,D
Roach, G.W. GA 8th Inf. Co.H
Roach, H. VA 46th Inf. 2nd Co.K
Roach, Harrison FL 1st Cav. Co.G
Roach, Harvard TN 13th Inf. Co.D
Roach, H.C. TX 9th Cav. Co.I Sgt.
Roach, H.D. VA 13th Inf. Co.A
Roach, Henry AL Gorff's Co. (Mobile Pulaski
  Rifles) Sgt.
Roach, Henry AR Willett's Co.

Roach, Henry GA 36th (Broyles') Inf. Co.I
Roach, Henry LA 5th Inf. Co.G
Roach, Henry MS Inf. (Res.) Berry's Co.
Roach, Henry SC 22nd Inf. Co.D
Roach, Henry C. VA 30th Inf. Co.K
Roach, Henry H. VA 21st Inf. Co.K Capt.
Roach, Henry M. TN Cav. 2nd Bn. (Biffle's) Co.C
Roach, Henry O. MO 1st Regt.St.Guards
Roach, Henry P. VA 52nd Mil. Co.A
Roach, Henry T. AL 13th Inf. Co.G Sgt.
Roach, Hiram VA 4th Res. Co.B 2nd Lt.
Roach, H.O. MS 2nd St.Cav. Co.E
Roach, H.O. MS 10th Cav. Co.A
Roach, I. LA Mil. Borge's Co. (Garnet Rangers)
Roach, Ira B. AR 15th (Johnson's) Inf. Co.B
Roach, Isaac N. TX 5th Cav. Co.K 2nd Lt.
Roach, Isaac W. TN 12th (Cons.) Inf. Co.H
Roach, J. AL Mil. 2nd Regt.Vol. Co.F
Roach, J. GA 13th Inf. Co.C
Roach, J.A. TX Inf. 1st St.Troops Sheldon's Co.B
Roach, James AL Cav. Barbiere's Bn. Brown's Co. Cpl.
Roach, James AL 37th Inf. Co.C
Roach, James GA Arty. 11th Bn. (Sumter Arty.) Co.D,B Cpl.
Roach, James GA Lt.Arty. 12th Bn. Co.F
Roach, James GA 18th Inf. Co.G
Roach, James LA Mil. 3rd Regt. 1st Brig. 1st Div. Co.A
Roach, James LA 21st (Patton's) Inf. Co.E
Roach, James MS 20th Inf. Co.G
Roach, James MS Roach's Co. (Tippah Scouts)
Roach, James NC 1st Arty. (10th St.Troops) Co.E
Roach, James TN 19th (Biffle's) Cav. Co.A
Roach, James TX 20th Inf. Co.K
Roach, James VA 6th Cav. Co.I 2nd Lt.
Roach, James VA Cav. Hounshell's Bn. Gwinn's Co.
Roach, James VA 11th Bn.Res. Co.C
Roach, James VA 15th Inf. Co.D Drum.
Roach, James VA 23rd Inf. Co.H
Roach, James VA 27th Inf. Co.C
Roach, James VA 30th Inf. Co.K
Roach, James VA 50th Inf. Co.A
Roach, James VA 94th Mil. Co.A Sgt.
Roach, James VA 108th Mil. Co.G,E, Lemons' Co.
Roach, James A. GA 40th Inf. Co.C
Roach, James A. VA Lt.Arty. Parker's Co.
Roach, James A. VA 52nd Mil. Co.B
Roach, James B. FL 5th Inf. Co.G
Roach, James B. NC 44th Inf. Co.I
Roach, James E. GA 23rd Inf. Co.H
Roach, James E. GA 52nd Inf. Co.A
Roach, James H. GA 36th (Broyles') Inf. Co.G
Roach, James H. MS 31st Inf. Co.G
Roach, James H. VA 64th Mtd.Inf. Co.H
Roach, James I. AL 3rd Inf. Co.G Cpl.
Roach, James J. AL Lt.Arty. Lee's Btty. Cpl.
Roach, James L. VA 16th Cav. Co.I Cpl.
Roach, James M. AL 25th Inf. Co.C
Roach, James M. AL City Guards Lockett's Co.
Roach, James M. MS 2nd Part.Rangers Co.E
Roach, James P. NC 55th Inf. Co.C

Roach, James R. NC 6th Cav. Co.D,E
Roach, James R. NC Cav. 7th Bn. Co.E
Roach, James R. VA 56th Inf. Co.G
Roach, James S. GA 43rd Inf. Co.B
Roach, James T. NC 45th Inf. Co.G,C,E 1st Lt.
Roach, Jasper AR 15th (Josey's) Inf. 1st Co.G
Roach, J.B. GA Cav. Gartrell's Co.
Roach, J.B. GA 56th Inf. Co.D
Roach, J.B. TN 15th Inf. McCracken's Co. Guerrilla
Roach, J.B. VA 2nd Inf.Loc.Def. Co.A
Roach, J.B. VA Inf. 2nd Bn.Loc.Def. Co.C
Roach, J.B. 8th (Wade's) Conf.Cav. Co.A
Roach, J.D. GA 36th (Broyles') Inf. Co.L
Roach, J.D. TX 3rd Cav. Co.H
Roach, J.E. GA 1st Troops & Def. (Macon) Co.C
Roach, Jeremiah GA Inf. 9th Bn. Co.C
Roach, Jeremiah GA 87th Inf. Co.F
Roach, Jesse MS 38th Cav. Co.I
Roach, Jesse TN 42nd Inf. Co.D
Roach, Jesse VA 10th Cav. Co.G
Roach, Jesse 4th Conf.Inf. Co.K
Roach, Jesse P. AR 32nd Inf. Co.A
Roach, J.F. AR 7th Inf. Co.A
Roach, J.F.G. TX 9th Cav. Co.K
Roach, J.F.G. TX 9th (Young's) Inf. Co.K
Roach, J.G. KY 7th Cav. Co.C
Roach, J.H. AR 38th Inf. Co.E
Roach, J.H. TN Lt.Arty. Scott's Co.
Roach, J.I. TN 31st Inf. Co.H
Roach, J.J. SC 4th St.Troops Co.C
Roach, J.J. SC 23rd Inf. Co.A
Roach, J.K.P. TX 29th Cav. Co.F
Roach, J.L. SC 12th Inf. Co.H
Roach, J.L. VA 62nd Mtd.Inf. 1st Co.D
Roach, J.M. AL 31st Inf. Co.K
Roach, J.M. AL Loc.Def. & Sp.Serv. Toomer's Co.
Roach, J.M. AR Cav. Gordon's Regt. Co.H
Roach, J.M. KY 7th Mtd.Inf. Co.A
Roach, J.M. MS 12th Cav. Co.G
Roach, J.M. MS Cav. 24th Bn. Co.C
Roach, J.M. MS 9th Bn.S.S. Co.C
Roach, J.M. MS 10th Inf. New Co.K
Roach, J.M. MS 23rd Inf. Co.H
Roach, J.M. MS Roach's Co. (Tippah Scouts)
Roach, J.N.B. AL 10th Inf. Chap.
Roach, Joab GA 27th Inf. Co.B
Roach, John AL 9th (Malone's) Cav. Co.B
Roach, John AL 13th Inf. Co.D
Roach, John AL 38th Inf. Co.K
Roach, John AL 1st Bn. Hilliard's Legion Vol. Co.B
Roach, John AR 8th Inf. New Co.C
Roach, John AR 38th Inf. Co.H
Roach, John GA Cav. 21st Bn. Co.C
Roach, John KY 10th Cav. Co.E
Roach, John LA Inf. 1st Sp.Bn. (Rightor's) Co.E
Roach, John LA Mil. 4th Regt. 1st Brig. 1st Div. Co.G
Roach, John LA 10th Inf. Co.G Cpl.
Roach, John LA 20th Inf. Co.G
Roach, John, #1 LA 20th Inf. Co.G
Roach, John, #2 LA 20th Inf. Co.G
Roach, John, No.1 LA Herrick's Co. (Orleans Blues)

Roach, John, No.2 LA Herrick's Co. (Orleans Blues)
Roach, John LA Miles' Legion Co.F
Roach, John MS 18th Cav. Co.A
Roach, John MS 1st Lt.Arty. Co.E
Roach, John MS 21st Inf. Co.E
Roach, John NC 12th Inf. Co.C
Roach, John NC 54th Inf. Co.D
Roach, John NC 56th Inf. Co.C
Roach, John SC 1st (Butler's) Inf. Co.B
Roach, John SC 1st (Butler's) Inf. Co.D
Roach, John SC 1st St.Troops Co.E
Roach, John TN 32nd Inf. Co.A 1st Lt.
Roach, John TX Cav. Madison's Regt. Co.D
Roach, John TX Lt.Arty. Jones' Co.
Roach, John TX 4th Inf. Co.G 3rd Lt.
Roach, John TX 19th Inf. Co.E
Roach, John VA Cav. 46th Bn. Co.F
Roach, John VA 1st Lt.Arty. Co.B
Roach, John VA Lt.Arty. J.S. Brown's Co.
Roach, John VA Arty. Paris' Co.
Roach, John VA Lt.Arty. Taylor's Co.
Roach, John VA 17th Inf. Co.I
Roach, John A. NC 45th Inf. Co.E 1st Sgt.
Roach, John A. TN 14th (Neely's) Cav. Co.F
Roach, John A. VA 28th Cav. Co.G
Roach, John A. VA 52nd Mil. Co.A
Roach, John B. AL Cav. Bowie's Co.
Roach, John B. TN 4th (McLemore's) Cav. Co.K
Roach, John B. VA Lt.Arty. Parker's Co.
Roach, John B. VA 52nd Mil. Co.A
Roach, John C. AR 7th Inf. Co.A
Roach, John D. MS 1st Lt.Arty. Co.A
Roach, John D. MS 18th Inf. Co.E
Roach, John F. NC 45th Inf. Co.A
Roach, John G. KY 6th Cav. Co.E
Roach, John G. MS 1st Lt.Arty. Co.A
Roach, John H. AL 1st Inf. Co.B,D
Roach, John H. MS 26th Inf. Co.C
Roach, John H. NC 45th Inf. Co.A
Roach, John H. TN 48th (Voorhies') Inf. Co.K Sgt.
Roach, John H. VA 8th Cav. Co.F
Roach, John H. VA Lt.Arty. Parker's Co.
Roach, John H. VA 52nd Mil. Co.B
Roach, John J. MO 1st N.E. Cav. Co.D Surg.
Roach, John J. NC 23rd Inf. Co.A
Roach, John J. SC 1st Cav. Co.H
Roach, John J. Gen. & Staff Capt.,Comsy.
Roach, John M. SC 12th Inf. Co.H
Roach, John P. VA 8th Cav. Co.F
Roach, John R. NC 44th Inf. Co.I Capt.
Roach, John R. TX 11th (Spaight's) Bn.Vol. Co.C
Roach, John R. TX 21st Inf. Co.E
Roach, Johnson KY 6th Cav. Co.D
Roach, John W. MS 20th Inf. Co.G
Roach, John W. TN 23rd Inf. 1st Co.A, Co.B Cpl.
Roach, John W. VA 13th Inf. Co.F Cpl.
Roach, John W. VA 31st Mil. Co.E
Roach, Joseph FL 2nd Cav. Co.G
Roach, Joseph GA 31st Inf. Co.C
Roach, Joseph LA Mil. 3rd Regt. 1st Brig. 1st Div. Co.A
Roach, Joseph MS 23rd Inf. Co.I
Roach, Joseph E. VA Lt.Arty. Parker's Co.

Roach, Joseph E. VA 52nd Mil. Co.B
Roach, Joshua AL 19th Inf. Co.I
Roach, J.P. AR 15th (Josey's) Inf. 1st Co.G
Roach, J.P. GA 23rd Inf. Co.D
Roach, J.P. NC 2nd Home Guards Co.E
Roach, J.R. FL 1st (Res.) Inf. Co.K Cpl.
Roach, J.R. TN 47th Inf. Co.H
Roach, J.R. TX 29th Cav. Co.C Sgt.
Roach, J.S. AL Cp. of Instr. Talladega
Roach, J.S. AR Lt.Arty. Etter's Btty.
Roach, J.S. TN 23rd Inf. Co.E
Roach, J.W. AR 8th Inf. New Co.D
Roach, J.W. GA 7th Cav. Co.B
Roach, J.W. GA 60th Inf. Co.K
Roach, J.W. MS 28th Cav. Co.K
Roach, J.W. MS Scouts Montgomery's Co.
Roach, J.W. TN 22nd Inf. Co.B
Roach, J.W. TX Cav. Morgan's Regt. Co.K
Roach, L. GA 23rd Inf. Co.H
Roach, L. GA Cherokee Legion (St.Guards) Co.K
Roach, Larkin F. GA 43rd Inf. Co.B
Roach, Leonadas TN 35th Inf. 2nd Co.D
Roach, L.W. KY 12th Cav. Co.A Ord.Sgt.
Roach, L.W. TN 20th (Russell's) Cav. Co.H
Roach, L.W. TN 5th Inf. 2nd Co.K Cpl.
Roach, L. William VA 79th Mil. Co.4
Roach, M. AL 22nd Inf.
Roach, M. GA 19th Inf. Co.B
Roach, M. TX 24th Cav. Co.F
Roach, M. VA Conscr. Cp.Lee Co.B
Roach, M.A. Gen. & Staff A.Surg.
Roach, Marion TN 35th Inf. 2nd Co.D
Roach, Marshall MO 4th Cav. Co.C,B
Roach, Marshall N. MO Cav. Preston's Bn. Co.C
Roach, Mathew L. TX 27th Cav. Co.D
Roach, M.B. MS 1st (Patton's) Inf. Halfacre's Co.
Roach, M.B. Gen. & Staff Chap.
Roach, Merritt KY 6th Cav. Co.D Cpl.
Roach, Michael AR Unassign.
Roach, Michael LA 13th Inf. Co.I,F
Roach, Michael LA 22nd Inf. Co.A
Roach, Michael LA 22nd (Cons.) Inf. Co.A
Roach, Michael, Jr. MS 1st Lt.Arty. Co.E
Roach, Michael, Sr. MS 1st Lt.Arty. Co.E
Roach, Michael MS 21st Inf. Co.L
Roach, Michael TN 2nd (Walker's) Inf. Co.D
Roach, Michael TN 10th Inf. Co.I
Roach, Michael TN 14th Inf. Co.D
Roach, Michael TN Inf. 154th Sr.Regt. Co.H 2nd Lt.
Roach, Michael VA 13th Inf. Co.G
Roach, Mickle LA Inf.Cons. 18th Regt. & Yellow Jacket Bn. Co.K
Roach, Mickleberry VA 34th Inf. Co.D
Roach, Mike TN 83rd Inf. Co.E
Roach, Mike TX 15th Cav. Co.G
Roach, Miles SC 22nd Inf. Co.D
Roach, Milton A. AL 8th Inf. Co.D
Roach, Mineweather VA 15th Inf. Co.D
Roach, Montraville P. VA 22nd Inf. Co.G Capt.
Roach, Morris VA 8th Cav. Co.F
Roach, Morris VA 11th Bn.Res. Co.D
Roach, Morris VA 86th Mil. Co.C
Roach, N. LA 7th Inf. Co.E

Roach, N. MS 2nd Cav. Co.H
Roach, Napoleon B. MS 20th Inf. Co.G
Roach, Napoleon B. SC 12th Inf. Co.A
Roach, N.B. FL 2nd Cav. Co.G
Roach, N.B. SC 18th Inf. Co.G
Roach, N.E. TN 15th Inf. 2nd Co.F 1st Sgt.
Roach, Newton NC 55th Inf. Co.C
Roach, Newton W. MS 23rd Inf. Co.H 2nd Lt.
Roach, Nicholas FL 1st Inf. New Co.H
Roach, Nicholas TN 2nd (Robison's) Inf. Co.E
Roach, N.W. MS 2nd Part.Rangers Co.E Bvt.2nd Lt.
Roach, N.W. MS Roach's Co. (Tippah Scouts) Capt.
Roach, N.W. VA 3rd (Archer's) Bn.Res. Co.C
Roach, Oliver AL 1st Regt.Conscr. Co.F
Roach, P. TN Lt.Arty. Morton's Co.
Roach, P. VA Inf. 1st Bn. Co.D
Roach, Patrick LA 1st Hvy.Arty. (Reg.) Co.I Sgt.
Roach, Patrick LA 20th Inf. Co.H
Roach, Patrick SC 1st (McCreary's) Inf. Co.K
Roach, Patrick TN 10th Inf. Co.E
Roach, Patrick TN Inf. 154th Sr.Regt. Co.H
Roach, Patrick TX 1st Hvy.Arty. 2nd Co.F
Roach, Patrick TX 2nd Inf. Odlum's Co.
Roach, Peter J. GA 49th Inf. Co.A
Roach, Peyton AR 26th Inf. Co.I
Roach, Philip VA Cav. 35th Bn. Co.C
Roach, P.P. LA 6th Inf. Co.A
Roach, R. TN 51st Inf. Co.D
Roach, R.A. AR Lt.Arty. Etter's Btty.
Roach, R.A. VA 59th Inf. 3rd Co.G
Roach, Reuben GA 11th Inf. Co.I
Roach, Reuben VA 11th Bn.Res. Co.D
Roach, Reuben VA Cav. 34th Bn. Co.G
Roach, R.G. TN 19th (Biffle's) Cav. Co.B Cpl.
Roach, R.H. AL 3rd Inf. Co.C
Roach, R.H. VA Hvy.Arty. 18th Bn. Co.C
Roach, Richard LA 21st (Patton's) Inf. Co.F
Roach, Richard A. MS 17th Inf. Co.D
Roach, Richard H. VA 14th Inf. Co.K
Roach, R.J. TX 5th Inf. Surg.
Roach, R.J. VA Horse Arty. D. Shanks' Co.
Roach, R.M. TN 50th Inf. Co.E
Roach, Robert FL 6th Inf. Co.C
Roach, Robert VA 5th Cav. Co.G
Roach, Robert VA Lt.Arty. Parker's Co.
Roach, Robert VA 52nd Mil. Co.B
Roach, Robert A. VA 3rd Inf. 2nd Co.K
Roach, Robert E. TX 37th Cav. Co.A Cpl.
Roach, Robert H. AL 3rd Cav. Co.C
Roach, R.P. TN 21st (Wilson's) Cav. Co.I
Roach, R.P. TN 21st & 22nd (Cons.) Cav. Co.I
Roach, R.W. KY 1st (Helm's) Cav. Co.B
Roach, Samuel VA Cav. 34th Bn. Co.B Cpl.
Roach, Samuel VA Inf. 45th Bn. Co.E
Roach, Samuel E. GA 52nd Inf. Co.K Cpl.
Roach, S.D. TX 29th Cav. Co.C Sgt.
Roach, S.D. TX 1st Inf. Co.M Sgt.
Roach, S.D. VA 21st Inf. Co.K
Roach, S.H. TN 20th Inf. Co.B Sgt.
Roach, Sidney NC Inf. 3rd Bn. Co.F
Roach, Silas TN 4th Cav. Co.D
Roach, Silas TN Cav. 12th Bn. (Day's) Co.E
Roach, S.J. SC 1st (Butler's) Inf. Co.G
Roach, S.J. VA 19th Cav. Co.D,E

Roach, S.M. TN 21st & 22nd (Cons.) Cav. Co.C
Roach, S.M. TN 22nd (Barteau's) Cav. Co.K
Roach, S.M. TN 26th Inf. Co.G
Roach, S.M. TN 33rd Inf. Co.F
Roach, S.M. 1st Conf.Inf. 2nd Co.K
Roach, S.M. 3rd Conf.Eng.Troops Co.C
Roach, Solomon FL 2nd Cav. Co.G
Roach, Solomon B. AL 4th Inf. Co.C
Roach, Stephen A. AR 36th Inf. Co.H
Roach, T.A.B. AL 4th (Russell's) Cav. Co.G
Roach, T.B. TN 20th Inf. Co.B Color Cpl.
Roach, T.G. TX 11th Cav. Co.F
Roach, T.H. MS 3rd Inf. Co.H
Roach, Thomas AL Lt.Arty. 2nd Bn. Co.B
Roach, Thomas AR 1st Dobbins') Cav. Co.B
Roach, Thomas AR 23rd Inf. Co.B
Roach, Thomas GA 20th Inf. Co.A
Roach, Thomas GA 28th Inf. Co.D Cpl.
Roach, Thomas MS 16th Inf. Co.I
Roach, Thomas TN 7th (Duckworth's) Cav. Co.B
Roach, Thomas TN 1st Hvy.Arty. 2nd Co.D, 3rd Co.A
Roach, Thomas TN 10th Inf. Co.I
Roach, Thomas TN 50th Inf. Co.A
Roach, Thomas TX 4th Cav. Co.F
Roach, Thomas A. MS 2nd St.Cav. Co.A
Roach, Thomas B. KY 3rd Mtd.Inf. Co.E Sgt.
Roach, Thomas F. Gen. & Staff Lt.,AIG
Roach, Thomas H. MS 23rd Inf. Co.H
Roach, Thomas J. AR 25th Inf. Co.K
Roach, Thomas J. MS 1st Bn.S.S. Co.C
Roach, Thomas J. MS 11th Inf. Co.K Cpl.
Roach, Thomas J. SC 12th Inf. Co.H
Roach, Thomas N. GA 1st (Olmstead's) Inf. Davis' Co.
Roach, Thomas N. NC 5th Cav. (63rd St.Troops) Co.D
Roach, Thomas N. TX 18th Inf. Co.F
Roach, Thomas P. VA 60th Inf. Co.E
Roach, Thomas R. LA 22nd Inf. Co.A
Roach, Thomas R. LA 22nd (Cons.) Inf. Co.C,A
Roach, Thomas S. AL Inf. 1st Regt. Co.B
Roach, Thomas W. TX 14th Inf. Co.B
Roach, T.J. GA 23rd Inf. Co.E
Roach, T.J. MS 1st Cav. Sgt.
Roach, T.J. Conf.Cav. Raum's Co. Cpl.
Roach, T. Jefferson SC Inf. Hampton Legion Co.B
Roach, T.L. KY 7th Cav. Co.A
Roach, T.N. KY 7th Mtd.Inf. Co.A
Roach, T.P. VA 79th Mil. Co.1
Roach, T.S. GA Cav. 21st Bn. Co.C
Roach, Valentine VA 34th Inf. Co.D
Roach, Valentine VA 97th Mil. Co.H
Roach, W. GA 36th (Villepigue's) Inf. Co.F
Roach, W. LA 27th Inf. Co.K
Roach, W. MS Scouts Montgomery's Co.
Roach, W. MS Inf. 2nd St.Troops Co.G
Roach, W.A. NC Mallett's Bn. (Cp.Guard) Co.B
Roach, Wade H. TX 29th Cav. Co.F 1st Sgt.
Roach, W.F. TX Inf. Currie's Co.
Roach, W.H. KY 7th Mtd.Inf. Co.A
Roach, W.H. TN 7th Cav. Co.F
Roach, W.H. TN 12th (Cons.) Inf. Co.G
Roach, W.H. Hosp.Stew.

Roach, W.H.M. GA Inf. 25th Bn. (Prov.Guard) Co.A
Roach, W.H.M. 1st Conf.Inf. 2nd Co.C
Roach, Wiley H.M. GA 42nd Inf. Co.I
Roach, William AR 1st Mtd.Rifles Co.F,B
Roach, William AR 1st Vol. Kelsey's Co.
Roach, William GA 11th Cav. Co.G
Roach, William GA Lt.Arty. Pritchard's Co. (Washington Arty.)
Roach, William GA 1st Inf. (St.Guards) Co.I
Roach, William GA 5th Inf. Co.C
Roach, William GA 30th Inf. Co.G
Roach, William GA 39th Inf. Co.A
Roach, William MS Cav. Jeff Davis Legion Co.E
Roach, William MS 1st (Patton's) Inf. Halfacre's Co.
Roach, William MS 5th Inf. (St.Troops) Co.F 3rd Lt.
Roach, William MO 12th Inf. Co.G
Roach, William NC 1st Inf. Co.B
Roach, William NC 21st Inf. Co.L
Roach, William SC 1st Arty. Co.H
Roach, William SC Prov.Guard Hamilton's Co.
Roach, William TN 21st & 22nd (Cons.) Cav. Co.I
Roach, William TN 10th Inf. Co.D
Roach, William TN 46th Inf. Co.D
Roach, William TX 1st Inf. Co.M Sgt.
Roach, William VA Lt.Arty. Clutter's Co.
Roach, William VA Lt.Arty. Montgomery's Co. Artif.
Roach, William Lt.Arty. Dent's Btty.
Roach, William 9th Conf.Inf. Co.B Cpl.
Roach, William 1st Cherokee Mtd.Vol. 1st Co.B, 2nd Co.I
Roach, William 2nd Cherokee Mtd.Vol. Co.D
Roach, Wm. A. VA 8th Cav. Co.H
Roach, William B. GA 37th Inf. Co.F
Roach, William B. TN 33rd Inf. Co.B
Roach, William C. AL 44th Inf. Co.C
Roach, William C. TN 41st Inf. Co.G
Roach, William Cyrus AL 49th Inf. Co.C
Roach, William E. MS 2nd Part.Rangers Co.E
Roach, William E. MS 20th Inf. Co.G
Roach, William H. AR 1st (Colquitt's) Inf. Co.H
Roach, William H. AR 15th (N.W.) Inf. Co.H Cpl.
Roach, William H. GA Cobb's Legion Co.B Black.
Roach, William H. TN 22nd Inf. Co.G
Roach, William H. VA 17th Cav. Co.E
Roach, William H. VA 22nd Inf. Co.G Sgt.
Roach, William J. AR 1st Vol. Co.B
Roach, William J. VA 20th Inf. Co.B
Roach, William J. VA Inf. 22nd Bn. Co.B
Roach, William J.M. GA 66th Inf. Co.F,B
Roach, William L. VA 1st St.Res. Co.A
Roach, William M. AL 47th Inf. Co.E
Roach, William M. NC 45th Inf. Co.F
Roach, William M. VA 34th Inf. Co.D
Roach, William McD. LA 16th Inf. Co.C
Roach, William P. KY 6th Cav. Co.E
Roach, William P. VA 50th Inf. Cav.Co.B
Roach, William P. VA 64th Mtd.Inf. Co.H
Roach, William P. VA 94th Mil. Co.A
Roach, William R. GA 43rd Inf. Co.B
Roach, William R. GA 52nd Inf. Co.K

Roach, William S. NC 1st Arty. (10th St.Troops) Co.I
Roach, William S. TN 48th (Nixon's) Inf. Co.F
Roach, William S. TN 54th Inf. Co.A
Roach, William S. VA 18th Inf. Co.K Sgt.
Roach, William T. GA 33rd Inf.
Roach, William T. TN 33rd Inf.
Roach, W.J. KY 3rd Mtd.Inf. Co.G
Roach, W.J. SC 2nd Inf. Co.A
Roach, W.L. SC 12th Inf. Co.H Hosp.Stew.
Roach, W.L. TN 8th (Smith's) Cav. Co.G
Roach, W.L. Gen. & Staff Hosp.Stew.
Roach, W.M. GA 37th Inf. Co.F
Roach, W.P. KY 7th Cav. Co.C
Roach, W.W. AR 35th Inf. Co.C
Roach, W.W. AR 38th Inf. Co.E
Roache, A. VA 1st St.Res. Co.C
Roache, Edward SC 4th Bn.Res. Co.B
Roache, J. FL Sp.Cav. 1st Bn.
Roache, James VA Inf. 1st Bn. Co.D
Roache, Jeremiah GA 60th Inf. Co.F
Roache, J.H. 14th Conf.Cav. Co.H
Roache, M. TX Granbury's Cons.Brig. Co.I
Roache, Patrick LA 1st (Strawbridge's) Inf. Co.D
Roache, Thomas J. Conf.Cav. Wood's Regt. 1st Co.G
Roache, William KY 4th Mtd.Inf. Co.D
Roachel, J.S. TN 21st & 22nd (Cons.) Cav. Co.F Cpl.
Roachell, Edward AR 30th Inf. Co.K
Roachell, Isam A. TX 37th Cav. Co.B
Roachell, William AR 30th Inf. Co.K
Roachell, William NC Snead's Co. (Loc.Def.)
Roack, Meredith NC 44th Inf. Co.G
Road, Andrew M. VA 42nd Inf. Co.B
Road, G.H. TX 13th Vol. Co.C
Road, W.L. TX 13th Vol. Co.C
Roadcap, C. VA Conscr. Cp.Lee
Roadcap, David R. VA Inf. 4th Regt. Co.I
Roadcap, George R. VA 1st Cav. Co.I Cpl.
Roadcap, Harvey VA 11th Cav. Co.C
Roadcap, Jacob VA 10th Cav. Co.B
Roadcap, Jacob W. VA 11th Cav. Co.C Sgt.
Roadcap, James W. VA 10th Inf. Co.B
Roadcap, John of James VA 10th Inf. Co.B
Roadcap, John (of P.) VA 10th Inf. Co.B
Roadcap, Stephen VA 146th Mil. Co.C
Roaden, Marion D. TN 59th Mtd.Inf. Co.B Cpl.
Roader, J. LA Mil. 3rd Regt. 2nd Brig. 1st Div.
Roades, Aaron E. VA Lt.Arty. Kirkpatrick's Co.
Roades, Charles W. VA 19th Inf. Co.A
Roades, Edward A. VA 49th Inf. 3rd Co.G
Roades, John MD Cav. 2nd Bn.
Roades, Manuel NC 66th Inf. Co.C C.H.F.
Roades, William AR Cav. Gordon's Regt. Co.I
Roadlander, George AL 29th Inf. Co.D
Roadlander, G.W. LA 16th Inf. Co.H
Roadlander, R.L. AR 7th Inf. Co.A
Roadman, William C. VA 37th Inf. Co.K
Roads, A. AL 12th Cav. Co.D
Roads, A. AR 8th Cav. Co.C
Roads, Alexander TN 19th & 20th (Cons.) Cav. Co.B
Roads, Andrew J. TX Inf. W. Cameron's Co.
Roads, Bartley TN 46th Inf. Co.G
Roads, Benjamin NC 55th Inf. Co.B
Roads, Benjamin VA 146th Mil. Co.C

Roads, C.F. AR 27th Inf. Co.I
Roads, David AR 27th Inf. Co.H
Roads, Denton TN Inf. 1st Bn. (Colms') Co.E
Roads, E.W. MS 23rd Inf. Co.E
Roads, George W. VA 19th Cav. Co.E
Roads, J. AR 38th Inf. Co.E
Roads, Jacob C. VA 146th Mil. Co.C
Roads, James K.P. MO 10th Inf. Co.C
Roads, Jarvis TN 55th (McKoin's) Inf. Co.H
Roads, J.C. TN Inf. 1st Cons.Regt. Co.I
Roads, J.M. SC 1st (Hagood's) Inf. 1st Co.F, 2nd Co.G
Roads, J.M. TX 30th Cav. Co.D
Roads, J.N. MS 3rd Inf. Co.I
Roads, John R. VA 17th Cav. Co.H
Roads, M. AR 8th Inf. Old Co.E
Roads, N.B. SC 1st (Hagood's) Inf. 1st Co.F, 2nd Co.G
Roads, Perry VA 58th Mil. Co.H
Roads, R.L. SC 1st (Hagood's) Inf. 1st Co.F, 2nd Co.G
Roads, Robert A. TX 1st (McCulloch's) Cav. Co.E
Roads, William TX 20th Inf. Co.F
Roads, W.J. AR 10th Mil. Co.D Cpl.
Roads, W.N. MS 23rd Inf. Co.E
Roady, John AR 15th (N.W.) Inf. Co.D
Roady, Lorenzo D. AR 15th (N.W.) Inf. Co.D
Roady, Preston D. TN 5th (McKenzie's) Cav. Co.B Cpl.
Roah, John MS 2nd Cav. Co.G
Roahm, Gilbert Conf.Inf. 8th Bn. Co.E
Roahrbach, J.H. KY 8th Mtd.Inf. Co.E
Roak, J. Conf.Lt.Arty. Richardson's Bn. Co.A
Roak, Peter LA Mil. 3rd Regt. 3rd Brig. 1st Div. Co.E
Roake, John O. VA Inf. 4th Bn.Loc.Def. Co.A
Roalin, J.T. AL 10th Inf.
Roalts, Zac E Eng.,CSA
Roamack, Jacob VA 33rd Inf. Co.G
Roamack, John M. VA 33rd Inf. Co.G
Roamana, F. 1st Chickasaw Inf. Wallace's Co.
Roame, A.I. NC 5th Cav. (63rd St.Troops) Co.D
Roaminger, Jacob E. NC 15th Inf. Co.F
Roan, Addison E. AR 1st Bn. Co.B QMSgt.
Roan, Alexander F. KY 3rd Cav. Co.A
Roan, Benjamin S. GA 13th Inf. Co.I
Roan, C.P. KY 9th Cav. Co.E
Roan, Evan S. TN 48th (Voorhies') Inf. Co.A 2nd Lt.
Roan, Felix TX 5th Cav. Co.D 2nd Lt.
Roan, Felix TX Cav. Benavides' Regt. Co.G
Roan, Franklin TX 20th Inf. Co.I
Roan, George W. MS 16th Inf. Co.G
Roan, G.W. KY 2nd (Duke's) Cav. Co.L
Roan, J. MS 4th Inf. Co.G
Roan, James LA 18th & 20th Inf. Co.D
Roan, James TX 35th (Brown's) Cav. Co.F
Roan, James L. NC Cav. 12th Bn. Co.A
Roan, J.F. TN 6th (Wheeler's) Cav. Co.E
Roan, John AL 24th Inf. Co.E
Roan, John MO 2nd Inf. Co.A
Roan, John MO 11th Inf. Co.H
Roan, Joseph FL Milton Lt.Arty. Dunham's Co.
Roan, J.P. TX 20th Inf. Co.I
Roan, J.S. SC 12th Inf. Co.I
Roan, Leon GA 10th Cav. (St.Guards) Co.B

Roan, Marion TX 17tn Cav. Co.C
Roan, Martin VA 23rd Cav. 2nd Co.K
Roan, Martin VA 4th Inf. Co.D
Roan, Michael SC Inf.Loc.Def. Estill's Co.
Roan, Nathaniel K. NC 13th Inf. Co.A Sgt.
Roan, Newton AL 4th (Russell's) Cav. Co.D
Roan, Newton H. KY 3rd Mtd.Inf. Co.A
Roan, N.K. NC 56th Inf. Co.H
Roan, Patrick GA 1st (Ramsey's) Inf. Co.G
Roan, Preston Gen. & Staff Asst.Surg.
Roan, R.J. MO Cav. Freeman's Regt. Co.E
Roan, Robert MS 18th Cav. Co.K,L
Roan, Robert J. MO Cav. Wood's Regt. Co.A
Roan, Samuel H. TN 44th (Cons.) Inf. Co.B
Roan, Samuel M. NC Mallett's Bn. (Cp.Guard)
Co.B
Roan, Thomas J. TN 46th (Voorhies') Inf. Co.A
Roan, T.J. TN Inf. 4th Cons.Regt. Co.K
Roan, T.N. Gen. & Staff Surg.
Roan, Turner T. GA 2nd Bn. S.S. Co.A Sgt.
Roan, Turner T. GA 5th Inf. Co.H,M Sgt.
Roan, W.B. GA 11th Cav. (St.Guards) Johnson's
Co.
Roan, W.F. FL 1st (Res.) Inf. Co.D
Roan, Wiley NC 51st Inf. Co.A
Roan, William TN 1st (Feild's) Inf. Co.G
Roan, William B. TX Cav. Madison's Regt. Co.F
Bvt.2nd Lt.
Roan, William H. NC 1st Cav. (9th St.Troops)
Co.B
Roan, Winston 3rd Conf.Cav. Co.I Cpl.
Roan, W.T. TN 48th (Voorhies') Inf. Co.A
Roana, Anthony GA 36th (Villepigue's) Inf.
Co.G
Roane, --- AR Mil. Borland's Regt. Pulaski
Lancers
Roane, --- VA VMI Co.B
Roane, A. VA 3rd Inf.Loc.Def. Co.D
Roane, Addison M. VA Arty. Fleet's Co. Sgt.
Roane, Addison M. VA 55th Inf. Co.B Cpl.
Roane, A.F.M. KY 7th Cav. Co.A
Roane, A.H. TX 9th (Young's) Inf. Co.B
Roane, Allen A. VA 34th Inf. Co.A
Roane, Alonzo B. VA 9th Inf. Co.G
Roane, Archibald T. MS 17th Inf. Co.K 1st Lt.
Roane, A.T. MS 8th Cav. AQM
Roane, A.T. Gen. & Staff AQM
Roane, C.A. VA Res. Forces Thurston's Co.
Roane, Charles A. VA 26th Inf. Co.H
Roane, Claiborne VA Cav. 40th Bn. Co.C
Roane, C.T. VA 24th Cav. Co.C
Roane, Curtis AL 11th Inf. Co.D
Roane, David VA 3rd Cav. & Inf.St.Line Co.A
Roane, E.H. Gen. & Staff A.Surg.
Roane, Elijah LA 17th Inf. Co.C
Roane, Elmon M. VA 26th Inf. Co.C
Roane, Frank VA Cav. 40th Bn. Co.C
Roane, G.D. VA 14th Cav. Co.I
Roane, George A. VA 5th Cav. Co.A 1st Sgt.
Roane, George W. TN 1st Cav. Co.G
Roane, Harvey KY 2nd (Duke's) Cav. Co.G
Roane, Hastings AL 4th Cav. Co.E
Roane, J. VA 3rd Inf.Loc.Def. 1st Co.G
Roane, James MD Arty. 2nd Btty.
Roane, James A. VA 24th Cav. Co.C
Roane, James A. VA Cav. 40th Bn. Co.C
Roane, James E. Arty. Lightfoot's Bn.

Roane, James M. LA 3rd (Harrison's) Cav. Co.H
Roane, James M. NC 6th Cav. (65th St.Troops)
Co.A,E Sgt.
Roane, James M. NC Cav. 7th Bn. Co.A
Roane, James R. VA 9th Mil. Co.B
Roane, J.C. VA Cav. 1st Bn. Co.C
Roane, J.L. 8th (Dearing's) Conf.Cav. Co.A
Roane, John TX 19th Inf. Co.B
Roane, John C. Trans-MS Conf.Cav. 1st Bn.
Co.D
Roane, John J. AR 1st (Colquitt's) Inf. Co.D
Roane, John M. VA 55th Inf. Co.C
Roane, John R. NC 62nd Inf. Co.D
Roane, John Selden Gen. & Staff Brig.Gen.
Roane, Jonathan AR 31st Inf. Co.C 2nd Lt.
Roane, Joseph R. VA 1st St.Res. Co.C
Roane, Joseph R. VA 1st St.Res. Co.K
Roane, Joshua VA Cav. 40th Bn. Co.E
Roane, Joshua W. VA 24th Cav. Co.E Sgt.
Roane, Joshua W. VA 20th Inf. 2nd Co.B 2nd
Lt.
Roane, J.R. TN 31st Inf. Co.C
Roane, J.S. MS 13th Inf. Co.I
Roane, J.S. SC 4th St.Troops Co.B
Roane, J.S. VA Inf. 2nd Bn.Loc.Def. Co.A
Roane, J.T. GA 2nd Inf. Sgt.
Roane, Junius VA 2nd Cav. Surg.
Roane, Junius VA 3rd Cav. Co.D Asst.Surg.
Roane, Junius J. Gen. & Staff Surg.
Roane, J.W. TN 2nd (Ashby's) Cav. Co.K
Roane, J.W. TX 35th (Brown's) Cav. Co.F,C
Roane, Lawrence D. VA 55th Inf. Co.D Capt.
Roane, L.D. VA Inf. Hutter's Co.
Roane, L.D. Gen. & Staff R.F.B.D.
Roane, Lemuel T. VA 26th Inf. Co.C 1st Sgt.
Roane, Luther M. VA 26th Inf. Co.H Sgt.
Roane, M.L. TN 19th (Biffle's) Cav. Co.G
Roane, Patrick VA Lt.Arty. 38th Bn. Co.C
Roane, Patrick VA Lt.Arty. E.J. Anderson's Co.
Roane, Patrick H. NC Inf. Thomas Legion Co.I
1st Sgt.
Roane, P.H. NC 16th Inf. Co.H Cpl.
Roane, P.H. TN 62nd Mtd.Inf. Co.F
Roane, Preston VA Inf. 26th Bn. Asst.Surg.
Roane, R. Booker Gen. & Staff 2nd Lt.,Dr.M.
Roane, Richard VA Cav. 40th Bn. Co.C
Roane, Richard A. VA 24th Cav. Co.C
Roane, Rich B. VA 3rd Cav. Co.B
Roane, R. Upshur VA 24th Cav. Co.C
Roane, S.A. TX 9th (Young's) Inf. Co.B
Roane, Samuel F. VA 24th Cav. Co.C
Roane, Samuel H. VA 55th Inf. Co.C
Roane, S. Franklin VA 26th Inf. 2nd Co.B
Roane, S.R. MS Cav. Ham's Regt. Co.B
Roane, Thomas GA 10th Cav. (St.Guards) Co.I
Roane, Thomas R. NC 39th Inf. Co.B 2nd Lt.
Roane, Thomas R. VA 9th Cav. Co.F Cpl.
Roane, Thomas W. TN 51st Inf. Surg.
Roane, Thos. W. Gen. & Staff Surg.
Roane, Timothy R. VA Arty. Fleet's Co. Jr.1st
Lt.
Roane, Timothy R. VA 55th Inf. Co.B 1st Sgt.
Roane, T.L. VA Inf. Hutter's Co.
Roane, T.W. TN 51st (Cons.) Inf. Co.G 3rd Lt.
Roane, Warner P. VA 24th Cav. Co.C
Roane, Warner P. VA Cav. 40th Bn. Co.C
Roane, Warner P. VA 21st Mil. Co.E

Roane, Wilber NC 6th Cav. (65th St.Troops)
Co.E
Roane, Wilburn F. NC 39th Inf. Co.B
Roane, William TN Cav. 9th Bn. (Gantt's) Co.A
Cpl.
Roane, William E. VA 15th Inf. Co.E
Roane, William H. NC 1st Cav. (9th St.Troops)
Co.K 1st Lt.
Roane, William L. VA 5th Cav. Co.E
Roane, William L. VA 9th Mil. Co.B
Roane, William P. VA 5th Cav. Co.A
Roane, William P. VA 109th Mil. 2nd Co.A 1st
Sgt.
Roane, William S. VA 24th Cav. Co.C
Roane, William S. VA Cav. 40th Bn. Co.C
Roaney, William NC 1st Cav. (9th St.Troops)
Co.H
Roany, Auguste LA Mtd.Part.Rangers Bond's
Co.
Roany, Aurelian LA Mtd.Part.Rangers Bond's
Co.
Roany, Barnard AL 11th Inf. Co.D
Roap, John NC 2nd Cav. (19th St.Troops) Co.A
Roapatome, D. 1st Chickasaw Inf. Kesner's Co.
Roarax, Joseph GA Cav. (St.Guards) Bond's Co.
Roarer, Samuel S. TX 13th Vol. 2nd Co.I,B
Roarick, W.A. TN Cav. 12th Bn. (Day's) Co.D
Roarix, James H. TN 5th (McKenzie's) Cav.
Co.K
Roark, ---, Sr. KY Cav. 4th Bn. Co.C
Roark, A. TN 21st & 22nd (Cons.) Cav. Co.H
Roark, A. TX Cav. Lilley's Co.
Roark, A. TX 22nd Inf. Co.F
Roark, Absalom VA 21st Cav. Co.K
Roark, Adrian KY 5th Mtd.Inf. Co.E
Roark, Alex SC Inf. Hampton Legion Co.F
Roark, Alex VA 21st Cav. Co.K
Roark, Alfred TN 21st (Wilson's) Cav. Co.H
Roark, Alfred W. VA 8th Inf. Co.K
Roark, Alvin NC 52nd Inf. Co.H
Roark, Asa KY 2nd (Duke's) Cav. Co.K
Roark, A.W. AR 36th Inf. Co.E
Roark, Barney P. TX 10th Inf. Co.D
Roark, Booker VA 38th Inf. Co.F
Roark, B.P. TX Granbury's Cons.Brig. Co.E
Roark, C.H. GA 39th Inf. Co.E,G
Roark, Charles VA 21st Cav. Co.E
Roark, Charles H. TX 6th Cav. Co.K
Roark, Christopher VA 3rd Inf. 2nd Co.K
Roark, C.M. TX 3rd Cav. Co.C
Roark, C.T. 1st Conf.Cav. 2nd Co.A
Roark, Daniel AL 29th Inf. Co.E
Roark, Daniel AL 39th Inf. Co.E
Roark, David NC 52nd Inf. Co.H
Roark, D.L. KY 3rd Mtd.Inf. Co.F
Roark, D.L. 1st Conf.Cav. 1st Co.A
Roark, E. TN 18th (Newsom's) Cav. Co.K
Roark, E. TN 19th & 20th (Cons.) Cav. Co.H
Roark, Eli NC 2nd Inf. Co.A
Roark, Elijah TN Cav. Newsom's Regt. Co.H
Roark, Elisha VA 1st Arty. Co.K
Roark, Elisha VA Arty. L.F. Jones' Co.
Roark, Enoch NC 1st Arty. (10th St.Troops)
Co.H
Roark, Ephraim NC 37th Inf. Co.A
Roark, Ephraim VA 21st Cav. Co.K

Roark, F.R. TX 18th Inf. Co.A
Roark, Frank TN Arty. Bibb's Co.
Roark, Frank TN Lt.Arty. Winston's Co.
Roark, George R. VA 3rd Cav. Co.H
Roark, George W. AR 24th Inf. Co.G
Roark, Harvy J. NC 52nd Inf. Co.H
Roark, Henry AR 15th (Johnson's) Inf. Co.D
Roark, Henry C. TN Cav. 7th Bn. (Bennett's) Co.B
Roark, H.H. MS Cav. 1st Bn. (Montgomery's) St.Troops Hammond's Co.
Roark, H.H. MS Cav. Yerger's Regt. Co.A
Roark, Hiram VA 4th Inf. Co.F
Roark, H.M. VA 8th Inf. Co.H
Roark, Iredell L. TN 30th Inf. Co.D
Roark, Isaac NC 52nd Inf. Co.H
Roark, Isaac VA 21st Cav. Co.K
Roark, Isaac M. TX 14th Cav. Co.A
Roark, Isaac P. AR 34th Inf. Co.C 2nd Lt.
Roark, Isal AR 17th (Griffith's) Inf. Co.B Sgt.
Roark, Israel L. TN 30th Inf. Sgt.Maj.
Roark, J. TX Inf. Timmons' Regt. Co.A
Roark, James TN 1st (Carter's) Cav. Co.B
Roark, James TN 2nd Cav.
Roark, James TN 26th Inf. Co.A
Roark, James TX Cav. Benavides' Regt. Co.F
Roark, James, Jr. VA 4th Inf. Co.D
Roark, James VA 26th Inf. Co.K
Roark, James E. VA 56th Inf. Co.I
Roark, James M. TX 2nd Cav. Co.H Capt.
Roark, James R.A. TN Cav. 7th Bn. (Bennett's) Co.B
Roark, James T. VA Lt.Arty. Montgomery's Co.
Roark, James T. VA Lt.Arty. Wimbish's Co.
Roark, J.B. KY 3rd Mtd.Inf. Co.D
Roark, Jessee KY 5th Mtd.Inf. Co.E
Roark, Jesse L. TN 7th Inf. Co.E
Roark, J.H. TX 12th Cav. Co.K Cpl.
Roark, J.H. TX Cav. Benavide's Regt. Co.F
Roark, J.L. KY 7th Cav. Co.F Cpl.
Roark, J.L. TN 2nd Cav. Co.G
Roark, J.L. 1st Conf.Cav. 2nd Co.A Cpl.
Roark, J.M. TX Cav. Saufley's Scouting Bn. Co.F
Roark, Joel TN Cav. Newsom's Regt. Co.D 3rd Lt.
Roark, Joel G. TN Cav. 7th Bn. (Bennett's) Co.B
Roark, Joel Y. TN 22nd (Barteau's) Cav. Co.E
Roark, John FL 1st Inf. Old Co.A, New Co.B
Roark, John KY 10th (Johnson's) Cav. New Co.I,A
Roark, John KY Horse Arty. Byrne's Co.
Roark, John SC Inf. Hampton Legion Co.F
Roark, John TN 1st (Carter's) Cav. Co.B
Roark, John Inf. Bailey's Cons.Regt. Co.B
Roark, John TX 7th Inf. Co.G
Roark, John TX Waul's Legion Co.B
Roark, John A. TN Bennett's Cav.
Roark, John Quincy Adams AL 49th Inf. Co.C
Roark, Johnson VA 21st Cav. Co.K
Roark, Jonathan VA 21st Cav. Co.K
Roark, Joseph TN Lt.Arty. Barry's Co.
Roark, Joseph M. NC 42nd Inf. Co.D Capt.
Roark, Joshua NC 58th Inf. Co.L
Roark, Joshua VA 21st Cav. Co.K
Roark, Joshua VA Lt.Arty. Penick's Co.
Roark, J.P. AR Cav. 1st Bn. (Stirman's) Co.D

Roark, J.R.A. TN 22nd (Barteau's) Cav. Co.E
Roark, J.W. TN 31st Inf. Co.C
Roark, J.W. TX 26th Cav. Co.I Cpl.
Roark, Leonard TN 26th Inf. Co.K
Roark, Lewis Stanford AL 49th Inf. Co.C
Roark, M.B. TX 29th Cav. Co.A Cpl.
Roark, M.J. Gen. & Staff AASurg.
Roark, M.P. GA 11th Cav. Co.B
Roark, Nathaniel W. NC 52nd Inf. Co.H
Roark, Nathaniel W. VA 21st Cav. Co.K
Roark, Nath B. LA 9th Inf. Co.B
Roark, N.B. TX 26th Cav. Co.I
Roark, Page TX 16th Cav. Co.B
Roark, Page J. GA Cobb's Legion Co.H
Roark, Patrick TN Inf. 154th Sr.Regt. Co.C
Roark, P.W. MO Cav. 1st Regt.St.Guard Co.E 3rd Lt.
Roark, R.H. AL 17th Inf. Co.H
Roark, R.H. AL 32nd & 58th (Cons.) Inf. 2nd Lt.
Roark, R.H. AL 58th Inf. Co.H,F 2nd Lt.
Roark, R.J. TN 9th (Ward's) Cav. Co.G
Roark, R.M. NC 4th Sr.Res. Co.H
Roark, Ruffus R. NC 14th Inf. Co.D 1st Lt.
Roark, Rufus LA 8th Inf. Co.E
Roark, Samuel MO 6th Cav.
Roark, Samuel D. AR 18th Inf. Co.E
Roark, Samuel G. Houston TX 8th Cav. Co.H
Roark, Samuel Napoleon TX 20th Cav. Co.G Cpl.
Roark, Simeon S. MO Cav. Freeman's Regt. Co.F
Roark, S.N. TX Cav. Morgan's Regt. Co.F
Roark, Solomon NC 58th Inf. Co.L
Roark, Squire M. NC 21st Inf. Co.I
Roark, T. LA 3rd (Wingfield's) Cav. Co.I
Roark, T.J. LA 30th Inf. Co.F,G
Roark, V.T. 1st Conf.Cav. 2nd Co.A
Roark, V.Y. KY 7th Cav. Co.F
Roark, Walter AL 5th Inf. New Co.F
Roark, Wesley MO 6th Cav. Co.B
Roark, W.H. KY 2nd (Duke's) Cav. Co.K
Roark, W.H. TN 18th (Newsom's) Cav. Co.D
Roark, W.H. TN 19th & 20th (Cons.) Cav. Co.B 2nd Lt.
Roark, W.H. TN 31st Inf. Co.C
Roark, Wilburn VA 21st Cav. Co.K
Roark, Wiley Bransford MO 8th Inf. Co.G Sgt.
Roark, William AR 20th Inf. Co.I
Roark, William AR 33rd Inf. Co.C
Roark, William AR Inf. Adams' Regt. Moore's Co. 2nd Lt.
Roark, William MS 41st Inf. Co.A
Roark, William NC 2nd Cav. (19th St.Troops) Co.A
Roark, William NC 58th Inf. Co.L
Roark, William NC McMillan's Co.
Roark, William TN Cav. 7th Bn. (Bennett's) Co.B
Roark, William TN 26th Inf. Co.A
Roark, William B. NC 1st Cav. (9th St.Troops) Co.A
Roark, William B. TN 2nd Cav. Co.G
Roark, William H. MS Inf. 5th Bn. Co.C
Roark, William H. TN 18th (Newsom's) Cav. Co.G 3rd Lt.
Roark, William P. VA 38th Inf. Co.F Cpl.

Roark, Williamson TX 18th Cav. Co.E
Roark, Williamson R. TX 18th Cav. Witt's Co.
Roark, W.I.N. TX 2nd Cav. Co.H
Roark, W.M. AR 7th Cav. Co.G Cpl.
Roark, W.T. 1st Conf.Cav. 2nd Co.F
Roarke, A. KY Morgan's Men Co.E
Roarke, Edward MO 7th Cav. Co.E
Roarke, Elisha NC 44th Inf. Co.G
Roarke, John VA 14th Inf. Co.C
Roarke, John A. TN 2nd (Robison's) Inf. Co.K
Roarke, Patrick LA 15th Inf. Co.E Cpl.
Roarke, W.H. KY Morgan's Men Co.E
Roase, James MO 3rd Cav. Co.I
Roase, John NC 6th Sr.Res. Co.B
Roash, James 1st Conf.Inf. 2nd Co.G
Roash, Joseph LA Inf. 1st Sp.Bn. (Rightor's) Co.E
Roasmond, A. MS 5th Cav. Co.E
Roasmond, T.S. MS 5th Cav. Co.E
Roast, Joachin LA 28th (Thomas') Inf. Co.C
Roath, Alfred GA 1st Bn.S.S. Co.A
Roath, Alfred GA 25th Inf. Co.K
Roath, Clifford D. FL 5th Inf. Co.I Sgt.
Roath, James E. Eng.,CSA
Roath, J.C. SC Lt.Arty. 3rd (Palmetto) Bn. Co.B Ord.Comsy.Sgt.
Roath, W.F. SC 6th Cav. Co.B
Roath, William F. Milton's Staff 2nd Lt.
Roath, William T. LA Inf. 1st Sp.Bn. (Rightor's) Co.B Cpl.
Roatz, Julius TX 14th Field Btty. Bugler
Roax, R. LA 13th Bn. (Part.Rangers) Co.B
Rob, J.H. MS 12th Inf. Co.F
Robance, J.W. GA Arty. Lumpkin's Co.
Robara, W.H. AR 30th Inf. Co.D
Robard, Francis TN 2nd (Smith's) Cav.
Robard, R.D. NC 1st Jr.Res. Co.G
Robards, Alson J. KY 1st Bn.Mtd.Rifles Co.B
Robards, B.B. KY 2nd (Duke's) Cav. Co.A
Robards, C.L. TX Inf. Carter's Co.
Robards, D.L. NC Lt.Arty. Thomas' Legion Levi's Btty.
Robards, E. KY 2nd (Woodward's) Cav. Co.E Cpl.
Robards, E. TN 2nd (Forrest's) Cav. Co.A
Robards, G. AR 7th Inf. Co.F Capt.
Robards, George C. AR Cav. 1st Bn. (Stirman's) Co.E Capt.
Robards, George C. Stirman's Regt.S.S. Co.E Capt.
Robards, George W. AL 28th Inf. Co.K Sgt.
Robards, George W. AR 15th (N.W.) Inf. Asst.Surg.
Robards, G.W. LA 3rd Inf. Co.B
Robards, G.W. Gen. & Staff Surg.
Robards, H.C. AR Cav. 1st Bn. (Stirman's) Capt.,ACS
Robards, H.C. Gen. & Staff Capt.,AQM
Robards, Horace L. NC 38th Inf. Co.F AQM
Robards, Horace L. Gen. & Staff Capt.,QM
Robards, James NC 4th Cav. (59th St.Troops) Co.A
Robards, J.G. TN 3rd (Clack's) Inf. Co.I Cpl.
Robards, John GA 6th Cav. Co.G
Robards, John W. KY 4th Cav.

Robards, Joseph MS Inf. 3rd Bn. (St.Troops) Co.G Capt.

Robards, Joseph L. AR 2nd Inf. Co.F

Robards, J.W. NC 12th Inf. Co.B,D

Robards, J.W. NC 16th Inf. Co.D

Robards, S. TX 33rd Cav. Co.E

Robards, Thomas S. AL 4th Inf. Co.G 1st Sgt.

Robards, T.J. KY 13th Cav. Co.E

Robards, T.S. NC Mallett's Bn. (Cp.Guard) Co.D 1st Lt.

Robards, W.F. KY 2nd (Duke's) Cav. Co.E

Robards, William J. NC 7th Inf. Co.A 2nd Lt.

Robards, William J. NC 12th Inf. Co.B,D Sgt.Maj.

Robards, William L. AL 4th Inf. Co.G

Robards, Willis L. Gen. & Staff, Adj.Gen.Dept. Arty.Maj.

Robards, W.L. TN 13th Inf. Co.A

Robarts, Archibald NC 54th Inf. Co.C

Robarts, Edgar FL 2nd Inf. Co.G 2nd Lt.

Robarts, E.F. MO 1st & 4th Cons.Inf. Co.I

Robarts, James FL 2nd Inf. Co.G Cpl.

Robarts, James O.A. FL 1st Inf. Old Co.G Drum.

Robarts, J.J. GA Cav. 1st Bn. Walthour's Co.

Robarts, N. AL 35th Inf. Co.D

Robarts, Simpson MO Cav. Fristoe's Regt. Co.G

Robarts, W. MO Cav. Fristoe's Regt. Co.G

Robarts, William FL 10th Inf. Co.G Cpl.

Robason, Aaron NC 42nd Inf. Co.B

Robason, Aaron NC 61st Inf. Co.H Music.

Robason, Alfred NC 3rd Arty. (40th St.Troops) Co.B

Robason, Asa T. NC 61st Inf. Co.H

Robason, Benjamin F. NC 17th Inf. (1st Org.) Co.F

Robason, Eli S. NC 17th Inf. (1st Org.) Co.F

Robason, Harmon J. NC 61st Inf. Co.H

Robason, Henry, Jr. NC 42nd Inf. Co.B

Robason, Henry, Sr. NC 42nd Inf. Co.B

Robason, Henry, Jr. NC 61st Inf. Co.H

Robason, Henry, Sr. NC 61st Inf. Co.H

Robason, H.T. NC 17th Inf. (2nd Org.) Co.A

Robason, James B. NC 42nd Inf. Co.B Cpl.

Robason, James B. NC 61st Inf. Co.H Sgt.

Robason, James E. NC 42nd Inf. Co.B

Robason, James E. NC 61st Inf. Co.H

Robason, James T. NC 42nd Inf. Co.B

Robason, James T. NC 61st Inf. Co.H

Robason, Noah NC 42nd Inf. Co.B

Robason, Noah NC 61st Inf. Co.H Cpl.

Robason, R.T. NC 17th Inf. (2nd Org.) Co.A Cpl.

Robason, W. GA 8th Inf. Co.I

Robason, W.P. NC 17th Inf. (2nd Org.) Co.A

Robb, Alfred TN 49th Inf. Co.A Lt.Col.

Robb, Andrew AL 5th Bn.Vol. Co.A,D

Robb, Andy GA Cav. 29th Bn. Co.E

Robb, B.F. LA Inf. 4th Bn. Co.D

Robb, Braxton MO 2nd Inf. Co.A

Robb, Edward L. TX 4th Cav. Co.K 1st Lt.

Robb, Eugene A. MS 28th Cav. Co.D Sgt.

Robb, G. MO St.Guard Regt.Commander

Robb, George MO 6th Inf. Co.H

Robb, George Ord. Scouts & Guards Click's Co.,CSA

Robb, George F. NC Cav. McRae's Bn. Co.E 1st Lt.

Robb, George F. NC Mallett's Bn. (Cp.Guard) Co.B Sgt.

Robb, George W. NC 12th Inf. Co.A

Robb, G.F. Gen. & Staff 2nd Lt.,Dr.M.

Robb, Hugh MO 1st N.E. Cav. Co.I

Robb, J. MO 3rd & 5th Cons.Inf.

Robb, J.A. AR 2nd Cav. Co.E

Robb, J.A. TN 7th (Duckworth's) Cav. Co.C

Robb, James MS 6th Inf. Co.H

Robb, James SC 25th Inf. Co.B,A

Robb, James VA 9th Cav. Co.C

Robb, James VA 111th Mil. Co.8

Robb, James Gen. & Staff Surg.

Robb, James Calvin KY 9th Mtd.Inf. Co.K Bvt.2nd Lt.

Robb, J.C. KY 5th Mtd.Inf. Co.K 2nd Lt.

Robb, Jesse W. LA 1st (Strawbridge's) Inf. Co.I,E 1st Sgt.

Robb, J.H. TN Arty. Bibb's Co.

Robb, Joel MO Inf. 3rd Bn. Co.F

Robb, Joel MO 6th Inf. Co.H

Robb, John GA Brooks' Co. (Terrell Lt.Arty.)

Robb, John TX Cav. 3rd Regt.St.Troops Capt.

Robb, John A. LA 5th Cav. Co.A Sgt.

Robb, John F. MS 1st Lt.Arty. Co.A

Robb, Joseph MO Searcy's Bn.S.S. Green's Co.

Robb, Joseph H. KY 2nd (Duke's) Cav. Co.D

Robb, J.T. NC 4th Inf. Co.C

Robb, Julius LA Mil. Chalmette Regt. Co.K

Robb, J.W. SC 7th Inf. Co.E

Robb, L.I. AR 11th & 17th (Cons.) Inf. Co.G

Robb, Marion MO 1st N.E. Cav. Co.I

Robb, Martin R. AL Mil. 3rd Vol. Co.E

Robb, Peter MS Wilkinson Cty.Minute Men Co.B

Robb, Philip N. TN 2nd (Robison's) Inf. Co.C

Robb, Phillip L. VA 9th Cav. Co.B

Robb, R.J. KY Cav. 1st Bn. Co.E

Robb, R.J. KY 5th Cav. Co.A

Robb, R.J. KY Morgan's Men Beck's Co.

Robb, Robert L. VA 9th Cav. Co.F

Robb, Robert L. Gen. & Staff Capt.

Robb, Samuel C. TN Cav. 11th Bn. (Gordon's) Co.D

Robb, Samuel D. TX 2nd Inf. Co.K 2nd Lt.

Robb, Thomas B. TX 4th Cav. Co.K Cpl.

Robb, W.H. KY Cav. 2nd Bn. (Dortch's) Co.A,B

Robb, W.H. KY 7th Cav. Co.F

Robb, W.H. Gen. & Staff AQM

Robb, William AR Inf. 2nd Bn. Co.C

Robb, William KY 3rd Cav. Co.D Lt.

Robb, William KY 9th Mtd.Inf. Co.K

Robb, William SC Mil.Arty. 1st Regt. Co.C

Robb, William SC Mil. 1st Regt. (Charleston Res.) Co.C

Robb, William Guides Davis' Co.,CSA Guide

Robb, William H. AR 1st Mtd.Rifles Co.A

Robb, William H. TN 4th (McLemore's) Cav. Co.B

Robb, William H. TX 8th Cav.

Robb, William H. VA 9th Cav. Co.H

Robb, William M. KY 5th Mtd.Inf. Co.K

Robbard, Thomas G. Gen. & Staff 1st Lt.,Dr.M.

Robbards, H.H. MO 4th Cav. Co.I

Robbe, Charles A. GA 48th Inf. Co.C 2nd Lt.

Robber 1st Cherokee Mtd.Rifles Co.F

Robber, E.F. SC 12th Inf. Co.C

Robberd, Alfred MO 8th Inf. Co.B

Robberds, A.R. AR 16th Inf. Co.I

Robberds, W.R. AL Cav. Moreland's Regt. Co.E

Robberson, A. SC 4th Cav. Co.C

Robberson, Alxa AL 34th Inf. Co.I

Robberson, B.J. AR 10th (Witt's) Cav. Co.A

Robberson, Bryant TN 27th Inf. Co.G

Robberson, Charles MS 7th Cav. Co.I

Robberson, D.G. TX Cav. (Dismtd.) Chisum's Regt. Co.E

Robberson, G. AL Cav. Moreland's Regt. Co.E

Robberson, Gabriel S. TN 48th (Nixon's) Inf. Co.B

Robberson, H.D. TN 48th (Nixon's) Inf. Co.B

Robberson, James VA 22nd Inf. Co.E

Robberson, Jason SC Palmetto S.S. Co.B

Robberson, John MS Cav. 7th Regt. Co.A

Robberson, John W. MS 7th Cav. 1st Co.I

Robberson, J.R. AR 1st (Dobbin's) Cav. Co.K

Robberson, L.H. AR 10th (Witt's) Cav. Co.A

Robberson, M. AL 34th Inf. Co.H

Robberson, R.E. TN 27th Inf. Co.G

Robberson, T.G. MS 8th Inf. Co.B

Robberson, William AL 34th Inf. Co.I

Robberson, William GA 3rd Cav. Co.D

Robbert, C.D. LA Cav. 1st Regt. Co.I

Robbert, J.H. VA 59th Inf. 1st Co.B

Robbert, T.C. TX 1st Hvy.Arty. Co.I

Robberts, A. AR 10th Inf. Co.A

Robberts, A. NC 5th Sr.Res. Co.A

Robberts, Allison MS Part.Rangers Armistead's Co.

Robberts, B.G. GA Cav. 9th Bn. (St.Guards) Co.C

Robberts, B.J. GA Inf. 8th Bn. Co.F

Robberts, B.M. FL 11th Inf. Co.I

Robberts, C.C. SC Palmetto S.S. Co.G

Robberts, D.A. MO Cav. Freeman's Regt. Co.F

Robberts, E.J. TX Granbury's Cons.Brig. Co.C Sgt.

Robberts, E.R. AR Cav. McGehee's Regt. Co.I

Robberts, F.M. MO 11th Inf. Co.K

Robberts, Franklin N. NC 50th Inf. Co.H 2nd Lt.

Robberts, George MO 2nd N.E. Cav. (Franklin's Regt.) Co.B

Robberts, G.R. NC 2nd Jr.Res. Co.B

Robberts, Isah NC 58th Inf. Co.A Cpl.

Robberts, Jacob MS 6th Inf. Co.A

Robberts, James FL Sp.Cav. 1st Bn. Co.B Sgt.

Robberts, James H. AL 12th Cav. Co.D

Robberts, James R. TN 5th (McKenzie's) Cav. Co.C

Robberts, J.C. SC 4th Cav. Co.C Teamster

Robberts, J.K. AR 30th Inf. Co.G

Robberts, Joel C. MO Cav. Wood's Regt. Co.E

Robberts, John GA 1st Cav. Co.G,I

Robberts, John L. AL 55th Vol. Co.B

Robberts, John R. VA 10th Cav. Co.D

Robberts, John W. MS 6th Inf. Co.H

Robberts, J.W. AL 3rd Res. Co.F

Robberts, J.W. AR 37th Inf. Co.I Sgt.

Robberts, Louis TX 2nd Inf. Co.A

Robberts, P.A. MS 9th Cav. Co.E

Robberts, Philip MS 6th Inf. Co.H
Robberts, R.P. AR Inf. Hardy's Regt. Co.F
Robberts, S.D. GA Inf. Dozier's Co. Sgt.
Robberts, Sidney TN 25th Inf. Co.G
Robberts, Tilman MO 1st N.E. Cav. Co.A Cpl.
Robberts, T.P. AL 13th Bn.Part.Rangers Co.D
Robberts, W.A. NC 45th Inf. Co.H
Robberts, W.B. AL 47th Inf. Co.F
Robberts, W.B. AR 30th Inf. Co.G
Robberts, W.H. TN 31st Inf. Co.F
Robberts, William FL Sp.Cav. 1st Bn. Co.B
Robberts, William GA 1st Cav. Co.I
Robberts, William MO 2nd N.E. Cav. (Franklin's Regt.) Co.B
Robberts, William TN Lt.Arty. Scott's Co.
Robberts, W.S. TN 21st Inf. Co.A
Robberts, Young A. AL Vol. Meader's Co. Cpl.
Robbertson, Alfred C. SC 4th Inf. Co.F 2nd Lt.
Robbertson, D.S. MS 23rd Inf. Co.I
Robbertson, D.W. TX 29th Cav. Co.B
Robbertson, E.G. AL 51st (Part.Rangers) Co.D
Robbertson, Frank Conf.Cav. Clarkson's Bn. Ind.Rangers Co.B
Robbertson, George L. MO Cav. 3rd Bn. Co.C
Robbertson, George W. TN 7th Inf. Co.G
Robbertson, Henry W. GA Cav. 9th Bn. (St.Guards) Co.C
Robbertson, John W. GA 3rd Cav. Co.I 2nd Lt.
Robbertson, M.K. SC 16th & 24th (Cons.) Inf. Co.B Sgt.
Robbertson, N.R. AR 1st (Dobbin's) Cav. Co.K
Robbertson, W.B. AR 1st (Dobbin's) Cav. Co.D
Robbertson, W.E. VA 3rd Res. Co.I
Robbin, E.W. GA 26th Inf. Co.K
Robbin, George TN 30th Inf. Co.G
Robbin, J.F. AR 36th Inf. Co.E
Robbinett, Ira P. VA 48th Inf. Co.A Sgt.
Robbins, --- TX Cav. McCord's Frontier Regt. Co.F
Robbins, A. GA 1st (Symons') Res. Co.C
Robbins, A. NC Lt.Arty. 13th Bn. Co.C
Robbins, A. TX 2nd Cav. 2nd Co.F
Robbins, A. TX Waul's Legion Co.B
Robbins, A.A. GA 1st Reg. Co.F,B
Robbins, Absalom MS 2nd (Quinn's St.Troops) Inf. Co.A
Robbins, Absalom NC 22nd Inf. Co.I
Robbins, A.C. GA Inf. (Loc.Def.) Hamlet's Co.
Robbins, A.C. VA Cav. Hounshell's Bn. Gwinn's Co.
Robbins, A.G. NC 1st Jr.Res. Co.F
Robbins, Ahi C. NC 52nd Inf. Co.B
Robbins, A.J. TN 38th Inf. 2nd Co.H
Robbins, A.J.C. KY 6th Cav. Co.A Orderly Sgt.
Robbins, A. Jourdin TN 25th Inf. Co.C
Robbins, Albert A. AL 21st Inf. Co.E
Robbins, Alexander NC 2nd Arty. (36th St.Troops) Co.C
Robbins, Alexander 2nd Conf.Inf. Co.B
Robbins, Alex S. NC 52nd Inf. Co.B
Robbins, Algernon S. GA Lt.Arty. (Jo Thompson Arty.) Hanleiter's Co. Cpl.
Robbins, Algernon S. GA 38th Inf. Co.M Cpl.
Robbins, Allen M. TX 36th Cav. Co.D
Robbins, Almon P. NC 16th Inf. Co.D
Robbins, A.N. AR 38th Inf. Co.A
Robbins, Anderson NC 58th Inf. Co.F

Robbins, Andrew AR 16th Inf. Co.I
Robbins, Andrew AR 35th Inf. Co.K
Robbins, Andrew M. AL 28th Inf. Co.G,C
Robbins, Annanias D. VA 94th Mil. Co.A
Robbins, A.P. GA 5th Cav. Co.F
Robbins, Arthur NC 4th Inf. Co.I
Robbins, Arthur F. AL 3rd Inf. Co.B Capt.
Robbins, Asa TX 26th Cav. Co.F
Robbins, Asher C. VA Cav. Young's Co.
Robbins, Asher C. VA 39th Inf. Co.D Sgt.
Robbins, A.T. GA 5th Cav. Co.F
Robbins, Benjamin VA 52nd Mil. Co.B
Robbins, Benjamin C. TN Cav. Newsom's Regt. Co.F
Robbins, Benjamin F. NC Vol. Lawrence's Co.
Robbins, Benjamin F. 7th Conf.Cav. Co.H
Robbins, Benjamin L. TX 11th Inf. Co.K
Robbins, Benjamin W. LA 28th (Gray's) Inf. Co.G Sgt.
Robbins, B.R. TN 3rd (Forrest's) Cav. Co.G
Robbins, B.W. MS 6th Inf. Co.I Cpl.
Robbins, B.W. MS 14th (Cons.) Inf. Co.C Cpl.
Robbins, C. AR 51st Mil. Co.E
Robbins, C. MS 1st Cav.Res. Co.E
Robbins, C. NC 22nd Inf. Co.I
Robbins, Caleb W. KY 1st Bn.Mtd.Rifles Co.B 1st Lt.
Robbins, C.D. NC 2nd Jr.Res. Co.E Sgt.
Robbins, Charles TN 21st (Carter's) Cav. Co.A
Robbins, Chelsey SC 6th Res. Co.B Cpl.
Robbins, Clarkson NC 46th Inf. Co.F
Robbins, Clarkson NC 52nd Inf. Co.B
Robbins, Clarkson L. NC 52nd Inf. Co.B
Robbins, D. MS Inf. 1st Bn.St.Troops (30 days '64) Co.A
Robbins, Daniel AL 4th Res. Co.F
Robbins, Daniel VA 5th Cav. Co.G
Robbins, Daniel VA 4th Res. Co.B
Robbins, Daniel VA 53rd Inf. Co.E,B
Robbins, Daniel E. NC 1st Arty. (10th St.Troops) Co.E
Robbins, Daniel F. VA Mil. Grayson Cty.
Robbins, Daniel M. TX 11th Inf. Co.K
Robbins, Daniel S. VA 37th Inf. Co.G,I
Robbins, David AR 19th (Dockery's) Inf. Cons.Co.E,D
Robbins, David A. MS 42nd Inf. Co.F
Robbins, Demas GA 47th Inf. Co.D
Robbins, D.M. MS 6th Inf. Co.I
Robbins, D.M. 14th (Cons.) Inf. Co.C
Robbins, D.N. MS Mtd.Inf. (St.Troops) Maxey's Co.
Robbins, E. MS Inf. Lewis' Co.
Robbins, E.B. MS 38th Cav. Co.H Sgt.
Robbins, E.B. SC 6th Res. Co.B Cpl.
Robbins, E.C. Ross' Brig. 1st Lt.,Ord.Off.
Robbins, Edward AL 3rd Bn. Hilliard's Legion Vol. Co.D
Robbins, Edward C. MO Lt.Arty. Landis' Co. 1st Sgt.
Robbins, Edward G. AL 28th Inf. Co.C
Robbins, Edward J.M.C. NC 30th Inf. Co.I
Robbins, Edwin TX 8th Inf. Co.A
Robbins, E.F. SC 25th Inf. Co.B
Robbins, E.H. MS 8th Cav. Co.F
Robbins, E.K. AL 2nd Cav. Co.H Lt.
Robbins, Elam R. NC 8th Bn.Jr.Res. Co.A

Robbins, Elbert NC 1st Inf. Co.D
Robbins, Elias NC 52nd Inf. Co.B
Robbins, Elias S. NC 4th Cav. (59th St.Troops) Co.H
Robbins, Eli B. AL 28th Inf. Co.C
Robbins, Elijah NC 51st Inf. Co.G
Robbins, Elisha NC 34th Inf. Co.I Sgt.
Robbins, Ephraim D. NC 2nd Cav. (19th St.Troops) Co.E 1st Lt.
Robbins, E.R. AR 3rd Cav. Co.I
Robbins, E.V. AL 9th Inf. Co.K
Robbins, E.W. AL 60th Inf. Co.C,E
Robbins, F. SC 1st Regt. Charleston Guard Co.A Sgt.
Robbins, F. SC Mil. 1st Regt. (Charleston Res.) Co.D 1st Sgt.
Robbins, F.B. GA 5th Inf. Co.G
Robbins, Francis GA Cobb's Legion Co.A
Robbins, Frank LA 9th Inf. Co.E
Robbins, Frank C. AL 4th Inf. Co.C Capt.
Robbins, Farnk C. VA 18th Inf. Co.A
Robbins, Franklin W. NC 22nd Inf. Co.I Cpl.
Robbins, Frank M. VA 12th Inf. Co.E
Robbins, G. LA 9th Inf. Co.E
Robbins, G.A. MS 28th Cav. Co.G
Robbins, G.D. AR Inf. 4th Bn. Co.E
Robbins, George AR Cav. Gordon's Regt. Co.H
Robbins, George TX 9th (Nichols') Inf. Co.E
Robbins, George B. VA 6th Inf. Co.G
Robbins, George H. TX 5th Inf. Co.A
Robbins, George S. TX Cav. 6th Bn. Co.E
Robbins, George W. AL 3rd Bn. Hilliards Legion Vol. Co.C
Robbins, George W. MS 30th Inf. Co.F
Robbins, George W. NC 51st Inf. Co.G
Robbins, George W. TN 13th (Gore's) Cav. Co.E
Robbins, George W. VA 10th Cav. Co.C
Robbins, G.H. TN 30th Inf. Co.G
Robbins, G.L. TX 30th Cav. Co.B
Robbins, Green AL 28th Inf. Co.L
Robbins, G.W. AL 4th Res. 1st Co.D 1st Sgt.
Robbins, G.W. AL 23rd Inf. Co.D
Robbins, G.W. TX Cav. Johnson's Regt. Co.B
Robbins, G.W. TX 17th Inf. Co.D
Robbins, G.W. TX 19th Inf. Co.F
Robbins, G.W.L. MS 4th Inf. Co.C
Robbins, H. AL Res. Hancock's Co.
Robbins, Haman NC 22nd Inf. Co.I
Robbins, Hansel NC 17th Inf. (2nd Org.) Co.I
Robbins, Hardy H. NC 18th Inf. Co.B
Robbins, H.B. TX 2nd Inf. Co.I
Robbins, H.C. MO 5th Cav. Co.G
Robbins, Henry AL 54th Inf. Sgt.
Robbins, Henry AR 27th Inf. Co.B
Robbins, Henry MS 44th Inf. Co.G
Robbins, Henry SC 1st (Butler's) Inf. Co.D
Robbins, Henry SC 21st Inf. Co.D
Robbins, Henry S. TX Cav. Morgan's Regt. Co.A
Robbins, Henry T. NC 1st Inf. (6 mo. '61) Co.L
Robbins, Henry T. VA Hvy.Arty. 19th Bn. Co.B
Robbins, Hezekiah SC 7th Res. Co.C
Robbins, H.H. KY 2nd Cav. Co.I
Robbins, Hile AR 5th Inf. Co.I
Robbins, Hiram W. NC 7th Inf. Co.I
Robbins, H.W. MS 12th Inf. Co.C Cpl.

Robbins, Ira AL 13th Bn.Part.Rangers Co.B
Robbins, Iredell NC 22nd Inf. Co.I
Robbins, Isaac NC 46th Inf. Co.F
Robbins, Isaac C. NC 15th Inf. Co.K
Robbins, Isaac D. GA 25th Inf. Co.K
Robbins, Iassc E. AL 28th Inf. Co.G
Robbins, Isaiah S. NC 22nd Inf. Co.I 2nd Lt.
Robbins, J. GA Cav. 9th Bn. (St.Guards) Co.A
Robbins, J. TX Inf. Timmons' Regt. Co.G
  Music.
Robbins, J.A. GA 36th (Broyles') Inf. Co.C
Robbins, Jackson NC 34th Inf. Co.I Cpl.
Robbins, Jackson SC 13th Inf. Co.E
Robbins, Jacob J. GA 11th Inf. Co.C
Robbins, James AL 19th Inf. Co.C
Robbins, James KY 5th Mtd.Inf. Co.B
Robbins, James LA 19th Inf. Co.C
Robbins, James NC 6th Inf. Co.H
Robbins, James TN 12th (Green's) Cav. Co.F
Robbins, James TX Cav. Giddings' Bn. Car-
  rington's Co.
Robbins, James VA Lt.Arty. Armistead's Co.
Robbins, James VA 61st Mil. Co.G
Robbins, James Conf.Lt.Arty. Stark's Bn. Co.B
Robbins, James A. NC 8th Inf. Co.C
Robbins, James A. NC 51st Inf. Co.G
Robbins, James B. NC 58th Inf. Co.E
Robbins, James E. NC 34th Inf. Co.B
Robbins, James L. AL 4th Inf. Co.C
Robbins, James L. NC 58th Inf. Co.E
Robbins, James M. GA 1st (Symons') Res. Co.C
Robbins, James M. TX 12th Cav. Co.D
Robbins, James P. VA 53rd Inf. Co.B
Robbins, James P. VA Inf. Tomlin's Bn. Co.A
Robbins, James R. NC 4th Cav. (59th St.Troops)
  Co.H
Robbins, James R. NC 17th Inf. (2nd Org.) Co.I
Robbins, James W. GA Lt.Arty. (Jo Thompson
  Arty.) Hanleiter's Co.
Robbins, James W. GA 33rd Inf. Co.M
Robbins, James W. VA Lt.Arty. Moore's Co.
Robbins, J.B. AL Cp. of Instr. Talladega
Robbins, J.C. AR 12th Inf. Sr.2nd Lt.
Robbins, J.C. AR 35th Inf. Co.A
Robbins, J.C. TN 21st (Wilson's) Cav. Co.B
Robbins, J. Calvin MS 6th Inf. Co.D
Robbins, J.E. GA 12th Mil.
Robbins, Jefferson AR 19th (Dockery's) Inf.
  Cons.Co.E,D Cpl.
Robbins, Jessee E. AL 28th Inf. Co.G
Robbins, Jethro AL 60th Inf. Co.C Cpl.
Robbins, Jethro AL 3rd Bn. Hilliard's Legion
  Vol. Co.D Cpl.
Robbins, Jethro MS 7th Inf. Co.D
Robbins, J.H. TN 21st (Wilson's) Cav. Co.B
Robbins, J.H. TX 11th Inf. Co.K
Robbins, J.J. MS Hudson's Co. (Noxubee
  Guards)
Robbins, J.L. AR 26th Inf. Co.E
Robbins, J.L. KY 10th (Johnson's) Cav. New
  Co.H
Robbins, J.L. TN 3rd (Forrest's) Cav. Co.E,D
Robbins, J.M. AL 4th Inf. Co.H
Robbins, J.M. AR 36th Inf. Co.E
Robbins, J.M. AR Inf. Hardy's Regt. Co.E
Robbins, J.M. GA 19th Inf. Co.I
Robbins, J.M. MO 5th Cav. Co.G

Robbins, J.N. AR 24th Inf. Co.H
Robbins, Joel AR Mil. Louis' Co.
Robbins, Joel A. NC 51st Inf. Co.G
Robbins, John AL 51st (Part.Rangers) Co.I
  Capt.
Robbins, John AL 4th Inf. Co.A
Robbins, John AL 28th Inf. Co.C Cpl.
Robbins, John AL 55th Vol. Co.G 2nd Lt.
Robbins, John AR 51st Mil. Co.E
Robbins, John KY 4th Cav. Co.H
Robbins, John KY 5th Cav. Co.A Lt.
Robbins, John KY 5th Mtd.Inf. Co.B
Robbins, John LA Inf. 1st Sp.Bn. (Wheat's) New
  Co.E
Robbins, John LA 31st Inf. Co.C
Robbins, John MO 4th Cav. Co.B
Robbins, John MO Cav. Preston's Bn. Co.B
Robbins, John MO Lt.Arty. McDonald's Co.
Robbins, John MO 6th Inf. Co.D
Robbins, John NC Inf. 2nd Bn. Co.F
Robbins, John NC 6th Sr.Res. Co.F
Robbins, John NC 18th Inf. Co.I
Robbins, John NC 22nd Inf. Co.I
Robbins, John NC 34th Inf. Co.I
Robbins, John NC 42nd Inf. Co.D
Robbins, John NC 52nd Inf. Co.B
Robbins, John TN 16th Cav. Co.A
Robbins, John TN 42nd Inf. 1st Co.H
Robbins, John TX Cav. 6th Bn. Co.B
Robbins, John B. NC 56th Inf. Co.I Cpl.
Robbins, John B. SC 8th Inf. Co.I Cpl.
Robbins, John C. MS 23rd Inf. Co.I
Robbins, John C. NC 2nd Arty. (36th St.Troops)
  Co.G
Robbins, John C. 7th Conf.Cav. 2nd Co.I
Robbins, John D. AL 4th Inf. Co.E
Robbins, John D. TN Cav. Newsom's Regt.
  Co.F
Robbins, John D. 7th Conf.Cav. 2nd Co.I
Robbins, John G. TN Cross' Cav. Cross' Co.
Robbins, John H. AR 26th Inf. Co.F
Robbins, John H. TX 9th Field Btty.
Robbins, John J. MS 20th Inf. Co.D
Robbins, John J. NC 7th Sr.Res. Clinard's Co.
Robbins, John L. TN 53rd Inf. Co.I,C Sgt.
Robbins, John L. TX 35th (Brown's) Cav. Co.K
Robbins, John N. NC 1st Jr.Res. Co.F
Robbins, John Q. MS 12th Cav. Co.A
Robbins, John R. TX Cav. 2nd Bn.St.Troops
  Co.A
Robbins, John R. TX 16th Inf. Co.F
Robbins, John S. NC 20th Inf. Co.I 1st Lt.
Robbins, John T. GA 47th Inf. Co.D Sgt.
Robbins, John T. MS 19th Inf. Co.B
Robbins, John W. GA Lt.Arty. (Jo Thompson
  Arty.) Hanleiter's Co.
Robbins, John W. GA 38th Inf. Co.M
Robbins, John W. NC 2nd Jr.Res. Co.I
Robbins, John W. TN Cav. 12th Bn. (Day's)
  Co.B
Robbins, John W. TN 44th Inf. Co.D
Robbins, John W. TN 44th (Cons.) Inf. Co.D
Robbins, Jonathan NC 6th Sr.Res. Co.D
Robbins, Joseph TN 1st Hvy.Arty. Co.F Cpl.
Robbins, Joseph A. AL 44th Inf. Co.D
Robbins, Joseph N. NC 5th Inf. Co.G

Robbins, Joseph P. GA Lt.Arty. (Jo Thompson
  Arty.) Hanleiter's Co.
Robbins, Joseph P. GA 38th Inf. Co.M
Robbins, Joshua KY 5th Mtd.Inf. Co.B
Robbins, Josiah Y. MO 6th Cav. Co.G Jr.2nd
  Lt.
Robbins, J.R. MS 1st Cav. Co.F
Robbins, J.R. TN 42nd Inf. 2nd Co.E
Robbins, J.S. SC Palmetto S.S. Co.H
Robbins, J.T. TN 11th (Holman's) Cav. Co.E
Robbins, J.T. TN Holman's Bn.Part.Rangers
  Co.C
Robbins, Julius NC 44th Inf.
Robbins, Julius A. AL 8th Inf. Co.D AQM
Robbins, Julius A. Gen. & Staff Capt.,AQM
Robbins, J.W. AR Cav. McGehee's Regt. Co.A
Robbins, J.W. KY 2nd Bn.Mtd.Rifles Co.A
Robbins, J.W. TN 19th & 20th (Cons.) Cav.
  Co.K
Robbins, K.H. MS 32nd Inf. Co.D Cpl.
Robbins, L. AL 3rd Bn. Hilliard's Legion Vol.
  Co.D
Robbins, L.A. MS Inf. 2nd Bn. (St.Troops) Co.A
Robbins, Laft VA 54th Mil. Co.H
Robbins, Lansdon TN 13th (Gore's) Cav. Co.E,F
Robbins, Larken H. VA 94th Mil. Co.A
Robbins, Lemuel NC 22nd Inf. Co.I
Robbins, Lemuel R. TX Cav. Morgan's Regt.
  Co.A
Robbins, Lenard AL 60th Inf. Co.C
Robbins, Levi AL 13th Bn.Part.Rangers Co.B
Robbins, Levi MS 8th Cav. Co.A
Robbins, Levi MS 42nd Inf. Co.F
Robbins, Levi TN 55th (Brown's) Inf. Co.D
Robbins, Lewis AR 16th Inf. Co.I
Robbins, Lewis AR 35th Inf. Co.K
Robbins, Lewis TX 16th Inf. Co.I
Robbins, Lewis C. AL 4th (Roddey's) Cav. Co.D
Robbins, Lewis T. TN 1st (Turney's) Inf. Co.C
  Sgt.
Robbins, Luke A. GA 40th Inf. Co.F
Robbins, Madison C. AL 4th Inf. Co.G
Robbins, Martin G. AL 28th Inf. Co.C Sgt.
Robbins, M.C. AL 1st Bn.Cadets Co.A Cpl.
Robbins, M.C. LA 22nd (Cons.) Inf. Co.H
Robbins, McD. NC 17th Inf. (2nd Org.) Co.I
Robbins, M.E. VA Hvy.Arty. Allen's Co.
Robbins, Micajah NC 52nd Inf. Co.B
Robbins, Michael Gen. & Staff Chap.
Robbins, M.J. NC 2nd Jr.Res. Co.I
Robbins, Moses N. GA 25th Inf. Co.F
Robbins, M.R. AL 55th Vol. Co.D
Robbins, M.R. 2nd Conf.Inf. Co.B
Robbins, N. AL Cp. of Instr. Talladega
Robbins, Nathan NC 46th Inf. Co.F
Robbins, Nathaniel 3rd Conf.Eng.Troops Co.D
Robbins, Nathaniel B. AL 28th Inf. Co.C
Robbins, N.B. AR 8th Inf. New Co.D Cpl.
Robbins, Neilberry B. GA 1st Reg. Co.F,B
Robbins, Noah NC 2nd Arty. (36th St.Troops)
  Co.G
Robbins, Noah VA 61st Mil. Co.G
Robbins, Noah 2nd Conf.Eng.Troops Co.A
Robbins, Obediah SC 9th Inf. Co.I Cpl.
Robbins, Obediah SC 13th Inf. Co.E 1st Lt.
Robbins, Patrick H. NC 5th Inf. Co.G Cpl.
Robbins, Peter AL Cav. Forrest's Regt.

Robbins, Phillip NC 24th Inf. Co.B
Robbins, Phillip 3rd Conf.Cav. Co.D
Robbins, P.L. NC 56th Inf. Co.I
Robbins, P.V. AR 8th Inf. New Co.D
Robbins, R.B. GA Inf. 27th Bn. Co.D
Robbins, R.E. TX 9th (Young's) Inf. Co.C
Robbins, Reuben R. NC 58th Inf. Co.E
Robbins, R.G. SC 3rd Inf. Co.K
Robbins, R.H. AL 55th Vol. Co.D
Robbins, R.H. MS 25th Inf. Co.B
Robbins, R.H. 2nd Conf.Inf. Co.B
Robbins, Richard AL 6th Inf. Co.B
Robbins, Richard TX 4th Cav. Co.B
Robbins, R.J. AR 51st Mil. Co.E
Robbins, R.J. TX Lindell's Rangers
Robbins, R.M. SC 26th Inf. Co.C
Robbins, Robert C. GA 38th Inf. Co.G
Robbins, Robert F. NC 3rd Inf. Co.F
Robbins, Robert P. TN 41st Inf. Co.H 3rd Lt.
Robbins, Roswell W. NC 22nd Inf. Co.L Cpl.
Robbins, R.P. GA 2nd Inf. Co.G
Robbins, R.R. TX 12th Cav. Co.I Cpl.
Robbins, Rufus A. MS 17th Inf. Co.C Cpl.
Robbins, S. AR 37th Inf. Co.D
Robbins, S. MS 46th Inf. Co.B
Robbins, S. NC 61st Inf. Co.D Music.
Robbins, S.A. TX Inf. Timmons' Regt. Co.G
Robbins, Sampson R. AL 37th Inf. Co.F
Robbins, Samuel J. AL 43rd Inf. Co.G
Robbins, Samuel W. AL 48th Inf. Co.H
Robbins, S.D. MS 28th Cav. Co.G
Robbins, Seth NC 20th Inf. Co.G 1st Lt.
Robbins, S.F. MS Cav. Ham's Regt. Co.A
   Comsy.Sgt.
Robbins, S.F. SC 13th Inf. Co.E
Robbins, Sim MS 6th Inf. Co.A
Robbins, S.M. GA 37th Inf. Co.A
Robbins, S.M. NC 22nd Inf. Co.M
Robbins, Solomon NC 27th Inf. Co.A
Robbins, Solomon E. AL 17th Inf. Co.B
Robbins, Solomon E. LA 12th Inf. Co.D
Robbins, S.S. 14th Conf.Cav. Co.K
Robbins, Starkey NC 15th Inf. Co.K
Robbins, Stephen AL 17th Inf. Co.K
Robbins, Stephen AL 58th Inf. Co.E Cpl.
Robbins, Stephen M. GA 47th Inf. Co.D
Robbins, Stephen W. GA 21st Inf. Co.G
Robbins, Synonymus SC 9th Inf. Co.E,I
Robbins, T.A. NC Lt.Arty. 13th Bn. Co.C
   Ord.Sgt.
Robbins, T.B. TN 13th (Gore's) Cav. Co.E
Robbins, T.D. TN 3rd (Forrest's) Cav. Co.B
   Sgt.
Robbins, T.F. VA Mil. Scott Cty.
Robbins, Th. TN 1st (Carter's) Cav. Co.G
Robbins, Theo. MO St.Guard
Robbins, Thomas MO 5th Cav. Co.G
Robbins, Thomas NC 37th Inf. Co.B Cpl.
Robbins, Thomas NC 56th Inf. Co.I
Robbins, Thomas NC 64th Inf. Co.L
Robbins, Thomas TN 4th (Murray's) Cav. Co.D
Robbins, Thomas TN 32nd Inf. Co.E
Robbins, Thomas TN 45th Inf. Co.H 2nd Lt.
Robbins, Thomas 1st Conf.Cav. 2nd Co.C
Robbins, Thomas A. MO 8th Cav. Co.B,G,F
   Cpl.

Robbins, Thomas A. NC 1st Arty. (10th
   St.Troops) Co.K 1st Sgt.
Robbins, Thomas A. NC 2nd Arty. (36th
   St.Troops) Co.C
Robbins, Thomas B. GA 8th Inf. (St.Guards)
   Co.B
Robbins, Thomas C. AL 3rd Bn. Hilliard's
   Legion Vol. Co.C
Robbins, Thomas C. VA Inf. 6th Bn.Loc.Def.
   Co.A
Robbins, Thomas E. AL 4th Inf. Co.E
Robbins, Thomas E. NC 22nd Inf. Co.A
Robbins, Thomas G., Sr. SC Inf. Holcombe
   Legion Co.I Cpl.
Robbins, Thomas G., Jr. SC Inf. Holcombe
   Legion Co.I
Robbins, Thomas J. VA 10th Cav. Co.K
Robbins, Thomas R. NC Inf. 2nd Bn. Co.F
Robbins, Thomas S. GA 9th Inf. (St.Guards)
   Co.A 1st Sgt.
Robbins, T.J. AL 36th Inf. Co.F
Robbins, T.J. GA 4th Res. Co.I
Robbins, T.S. TX 13th Vol. 3rd Co.I
Robbins, T.S. Conf.Cav. Powers' Regt. Co.F
   Sr.2nd Lt.
Robbins, W. NC Allen's Co. (Loc.Def.)
Robbins, W. SC 21st Inf. Co.E
Robbins, W. VA Cav. Mosby's Regt. (Part.
   Rangers) Co.E
Robbins, W.A. AL 13th Cav. Co.G
Robbins, W.A. AR 27th Inf. Co.G
Robbins, W.A. MS Lt.Arty. 14th Bn. Co.C
Robbins, Wade SC Hvy.Arty. 15th (Lucas') Bn.
   Co.A
Robbins, Wallace VA 60th Inf. Co.A
Robbins, W.B. MS Lt.Arty. 14th Bn. Co.C
Robbins, W.B. VA Cav. 1st Bn. Co.C
Robbins, W.C. AR 35th Inf. Co.A
Robbins, W.D. MS 14th (Cons.) Inf. Co.C
Robbins, W.D.C. AR 50th Mil. Gleaves' Co.
Robbins, W.E. GA Phillips' Legion Co.B
Robbins, W.F. AL 48th Inf. Co.G Sgt.Maj.
Robbins, W.F. Gen. & Staff Capt.,Comsy.
Robbins, W.G. GA Inf. 27th Bn. Co.E 1st Lt.
Robbins, W.G. TN 27th Inf. Co.G
Robbins, W.H. GA 36th (Villepigue's) Inf. Co.H
   Sgt.
Robbins, W.H. KY 3rd Mtd.Inf. Co.A
Robbins, W.H. MS 20th Inf. Co.D
Robbins, W.H. TN 21st (Wilson's) Cav. Co.D
Robbins, W.H. 1st Conf.Inf. 1st Co.H Sgt.
Robbins, Wilbur J. LA 8th Inf. Co.D
Robbins, Wiley AL 36th Inf. Co.I
Robbins, Wiley AL 58th Inf. Co.E
Robbins, Wiley D. MS 6th Inf. Co.I
Robbins, Wiley F. KY 2nd Bn.Mtd.Rifles Co.A
   Bvt.2nd Lt.
Robbins, Willburn TN 4th (Murray's) Cav. Co.B
Robbins, William AL 44th Inf. Co.D
Robbins, William LA 13th Inf. Co.H
Robbins, William MO 5th Cav. Co.G
Robbins, William MO Lt.Arty. McDonald's Co.
Robbins, William MO 6th Inf. Co.D
Robbins, William NC 22nd Inf. Co.A
Robbins, William NC 23rd Inf.
Robbins, William SC 1st Cav. Co.D

Robbins, William SC Hvy.Arty. 15th (Lucas')
   Bn. Co.A
Robbins, William SC 5th Inf. 1st Co.C, 2nd
   Co.K
Robbins, William TN 12th (Green's) Cav. Co.I
Robbins, William TN 25th Inf. Co.C
Robbins, William VA Arty. C.F. Johnston's Co.
Robbins, William VA 53rd Inf. Co.B
Robbins, William VA Inf. Tomlin's Bn. Co.A
Robbins, William A. NC 1st Arty. (10th
   St.Troops) Co.E Cpl.
Robbins, William A.H. VA 54th Inf. Co.E Cpl.
Robbins, William B. AR 8th Inf. New Co.D
Robbins, William B. GA 25th Inf. Co.F
Robbins, William C. TN Cav. Wilson's Regt.
   3rd Lt.
Robbins, William E. 7th Conf.Cav. 2nd Co.I
Robbins, William F. AL 7th Inf. Co.C
Robbins, William F. NC 4th Inf. Co.E
Robbins, William G. KY 5th Mtd.Inf. Co.B
Robbins, William H. LA 1st Hvy Arty. (Reg.)
   Co.C
Robbins, William H. MS 1st Lt.Arty. Co.F
Robbins, William H. TN 7th Inf. Co.G 2nd Lt.
Robbins, William H. TX 16th Inf. Co.I
Robbins, William H. VA 40th Inf. Co.H Cpl.
Robbins, William J. LA 28th (Gray's) Inf. Co.G
   1st Lt.
Robbins, William J. TX 11th Inf. Co.K
Robbins, William J.A. MS 23rd Inf. Co.I Cpl.
Robbins, William M. AL 4th Inf. Co.G Maj.
Robbins, William O. AR 33rd Inf. Co.I
Robbins, William R. NC 37th Inf. Co.B
Robbins, William S. KY 10th Cav. Martin's Co.
Robbins, William T. (2) VA 9th Cav. Co.H Sgt.
Robbins, William W. NC 2nd Arty. (36th
   St.Troops) Co.G
Robbins, William W. NC 43rd Inf. Co.C
Robbins, Willie H. NC 30th Inf. Co.I
Robbins, Wilson Calloway TX Cav. McCord's
   Frontier Regt. Co.C
Robbins, Wilson L. MS 1st Lt.Arty. Co.D
Robbins, Winter W. MS 11th (Perrin's) Cav.
   Co.A
Robbins, W.J. SC 1st Cav. Co.F
Robbins, W.J. TN 12th (Green's) Cav. Co.A
Robbins, W.J. TX Cav. Terry's Regt. Co.A
Robbins, W.P. AL 24th Inf. Co.K Sgt.
Robbins, W.R. AR 7th Cav. Chap.
Robbins, W.R. TX 28th Cav. Co.L
Robbins, W.T. VA Cav. 40th Bn. Lt.Col.
Robbins, Zachariah NC 8th Inf. Co.K
Robbinson, D. AL 31st Inf. Co.D
Robbinson, Douglas MS Part.Rangers
   Armistead's Co.
Robbinson, Francis 1st Cherokee Mtd.Vol. 2nd
   Co.D
Robbinson, George AR Inf. Hardy's Regt. Co.D
Robbinson, Harrison KY 10th (Diamond's) Cav.
   Co.A
Robbinson, J.B. MS 15th (Cons.) Inf. Co.F
Robbinson, John KY 10th (Diamond's) Cav.
   Co.A
Robbinson, M.B. MO Robertson's Regt.St.Guard
   Co.3
Robbinson, Melbourn VA 6th Cav. Co.A
Robbinson, Newton NC 2nd Jr.Res. Co.C

Robbinson, S. NC 4th Cav. (59th St.Troops)
  Co.H Lt.
Robbinson, S.B. MS 6th Inf. Co.B
Robbinson, Thomas H. MO 16th Inf. Co.B
Robbinson, W. MS 2nd St.Cav. Co.K
Robbinson, W. MO 3rd Inf. Co.E
Robbinson, W.F. MS 6th Inf. Co.I
Robbinson, William A. GA Inf. 10th Bn. Co.A
Robbinson, W.T. MS 6th Cav. Co.F
Robbison, Elisha AL 44th Inf. Co.F
Robbison, Isaac AL 44th Inf. Co.H
Robbison, J. NC 6th Inf. Co.K
Robboth, W. GA 43rd Inf. Co.B Lt.
Robbs, Aaron GA 12th Cav. Co.D
Robbs, A.C. SC Palmetto S.S. Co.M Cpl.
Robbs, Andrew C. SC 5th Inf. 1st Co.G
Robbs, C.W. GA 12th Cav. Co.A
Robbs, Edward MO 6th Cav. Co.G
Robbs, E.W. AL 30th Inf. Co.F
Robbs, James GA 12th Cav. Co.A
Robbs, James SC 13th Inf. Co.I
Robbs, J. Cornelius SC 9th Inf. Co.I
Robbs, John AL 30th Inf.
Robbs, John TN Lt.Arty. Weller's Co.
Robbs, Johnson TX 14th Inf. Co.C
Robbs, J.W. AL 36th Inf. Co.F
Robbs, Robert J. KY 6th Cav.
Robbs, William A. GA 14th Inf. Co.E
Robbs, William F. KY 11th Cav. Co.B
Robbs, William H. AL Cav. Murphy's Bn. Co.C
  Teamster
Robbs, William H. 15th Conf.Cav. Co.H
Robburds, Aaron AR 10th Inf. Co.A Cpl.
Robburds, J.W. AR 10th Inf. Co.A
Robe, Andrew TX 14th Cav. Co.G
Robe, John W.T. TX 14th Cav. Co.G
Robear, Charles TN 1st Hvy.Arty. 2nd Co.D,
  3rd Co.B
Robeards, Pleasant A. TN Cav. 17th Bn.
  (Sanders') Co.B
Robeau, A. LA 18th Inf. Co.A
Robeau, P.A. LA 18th Inf. Co.A
Robeau, P.A. LA 22nd Inf. Co.E
Robechoux, O. LA Mil. LaFourche Regt.
Robeck, William MO Lt.Arty. 1st Btty.
Robecker, Henry LA 28th (Thomas') Inf. Co.A
Robedel, John VA 6th Inf. Co.C
Robedu, William TN 10th Inf. Co.D Drum.
Robeeson, James MS Condrey's Co. (Bull
  Mtn.Invinc.)
Robel, M.G. VA Mil. Scott Cty.
Robellard, John LA Pointe Coupee Arty.
Robelot, A. LA Mil. Orleans Guards Regt. Co.F
  Cpl.
Robelot, E. LA Pointe Coupee Arty.
Robelot, E.L. LA Cav. Greenleaf's Co. (Orleans
  Lt.Horse)
Robelot, E.S. LA Arty. Watson Btty.
Robelot, H.N. LA Cav. Greenleaf's Co. (Orleans
  Lt.Horse)
Robelot, Jules LA Cav. Greenleaf's Co. (Orleans
  Lt.Horse)
Robenet, Zachariah O. VA Inf. 21st Bn. 2nd
  Co.D Cpl.
Robenett, W.S. VA Cav. 37th Bn. Co.H
Robens, N. AL 28th Inf. Co.F
Robenson, David D. TX 2nd Cav. Co.G

Robenson, D.B. MS Inf. 3rd Bn. (St.Troops)
  Co.D
Robenson, D.S. AL 6th Cav. Co.A
Robenson, G.B. NC 15th Inf. Co.C
Robenson, John AL Jenk's Arty. Co.I
Robenson, Robert M. TX 2nd Cav. Co.G
Robenson, William AL 26th (O'Neal's) Inf. Co.C
Robenson, William H. AR 45th Cav. Co.E
Robenson, W.J. MS 11th (Cons.) Cav. Co.A
Robenson, W.L. GA Inf. 25th Bn. (Prov.Guard)
  Co.F
Rober, C. SC 1st Regt. Charleston Guard Co.G
Rober, C. SC Mil. 1st Regt. (Charleston Res.)
  Co.F
Rober, F.J. TN 21st & 22nd (Cons.) Cav. Co.F
Rober, T. GA 1st (Symons') Res. Co.A
Robera, Antonio TX 15th Field Btty. 1st Lt.
Roberd, K. AL 18th Inf. Co.G
Roberd, Thomas AL Cp. of Instr. Talladega
Roberdeau, J.D. TX 5th Inf. Co.B Capt.
Roberds, Absalom M. GA 61st Inf. Co.F
Roberds, A.C. AL 23rd Inf. Co.C Capt.
Roberds, A.C. GA Cav. 16th Bn. (St.Guards)
  Co.D
Roberds, A.J. AR 21st Inf. Co.I
Roberds, Alfred B. TX Inf. Griffin's Bn. Co.A
  Music.
Roberds, Andrew M. NC 25th Inf. Co.K
Roberds, Charley GA 1st Cav. Co.D
Roberds, D. AR 2nd Inf. Co.D
Roberds, David AR 32nd Inf. Co.B
Roberds, E. AR 1st (Dobbin's) Cav. Co.F
Roberds, Elbert G. GA 11th Inf. Co.D
Roberds, G.A. GA Cav. 16th Bn. Co.D 1st Sgt.
Roberds, G.H. MS 2nd St.Cav. Co.H Jr.2nd Lt.
Roberds, G.W. NC 64th Inf. Co.G,C
Roberds, Henry AR 27th Inf. New Co.B
Roberds, Jacob W. NC 25th Inf. Co.K Sgt.
Roberds, James H. GA 11th Inf. Co.D
Roberds, J.J. SC 1st Mtd.Mil. Smart's Co.
Roberds, J.L.B. AR 21st Inf. Co.I
Roberds, J.M. GA 12th (Wright's) Cav.
  (St.Guards) Brannen's Co.
Roberds, John GA 12th (Wright's) Cav.
  (St.Guards) Brannen's Co.
Roberds, John MO 10th Inf. Co.H
Roberds, John VA Inf. 21st Bn. 2nd Co.C
Roberds, John W. GA 61st Inf. Co.F
Roberds, L. TN 20th (Russell's) Cav. Co.K
Roberds, Martin NC Walker's Bn. Thomas'
  Legion Co.E
Roberds, Pierce A. GA 11th Inf. Co.D
Roberds, R.D. AR 10th (Witt's) Cav. Co.D
Roberds, Rila A. AL 43rd Inf. Co.A
Roberds, Robert J. GA 11th Inf. Co.D
Roberds, Robert Z. GA 11th Inf. Co.D
Roberds, R.T. GA 50th Inf. Co.D 1st Sgt.
Roberds, U.E. AL 23rd Inf. Co.C Sgt.
Roberds, Wes. SC 1st Cav. Co.A Lt.
Roberds, William G. SC 1st Cav. Co.A 2nd Lt.
Roberds, William R. AL 17th Inf. Co.I
Roberds, W.J. TN 12th (Green's) Cav. Co.H
Roberds, W.N. FL 2nd Cav. Co.H Cpl.
Roberds, W.T. AL 23rd Inf. Co.C 2nd Lt.
Robergen, Allen TX Cav. Wells' Regt. Co.G
Roberhoud, A. LA Inf.Cons.Crescent Regt.
  Ratcliffe's Co.

Roberre, Justin LA 5th (Wingfield's) Cav.
Roberre, Numa LA 5th (Wingfield's) Cav.
Roberry, I. GA 10th Inf.
Robers, Bears GA 27th Inf. Co.F
Robersen, Guilford AL Randolph Cty.Res. A.P.
  Hunter's Co.
Roberson, --- AL 32nd Inf. Co.I
Roberson, A. AL Cav. Moreland's Regt. Co.D
Roberson, A. MS 1st Cav. Co.B Cpl.
Roberson, A.A. MO Robertson's Regt.St.Guard
  Co.11
Roberson, A.B. AL 17th Inf. Co.A Sgt.
Roberson, Abram R. NC 62nd Inf. Co.C
Roberson, Absolum VA 129th Mil. Carter's Co.
Roberson, Ad T. TN Cav. 14th Bn. (Branner's)
  Co.F
Roberson, A.E. MO 6th Cav. Co.F
Roberson, A.F. KY 10th Cav. Co.D
Roberson, A.H. TX 8th Cav. Co.E
Roberson, A.J. MS Cav. Powers' Regt. Co.G
  Cpl.
Roberson, A. Judson MS Cav. Stockdale's Bn.
  Co.A,B
Roberson, Alexander NC 37th Inf. Co.F
Roberson, Alexander H. TN 43rd Inf. Co.C
  Capt.
Roberson, Alfred B. TX 31st Cav. Co.F 1st Lt.
Roberson, Allen GA 49th Inf. Co.E
Roberson, Allen TN 54th Inf. Ives' Co.
Roberson, Allen J. NC 44th Inf. Co.G Sgt.
Roberson, Allen R. AL 2nd Bn. Hilliard's Legion
  Vol. Co.F
Roberson, Alvius A. NC 62nd Inf. Co.C
Roberson, A.M. AL 11th Cav. Co.B Cpl.
Roberson, A.M. MS 1st (Johnston's) Inf. Co.F
Roberson, Amos NC 1st Inf. Co.H
Roberson, Amos VA 11th Cav. Co.D Sgt.
Roberson, Amos VA 77th Mil. Co.B Capt.
Roberson, Andrew VA 129th Mil. Carter's Co.
Roberson, Andrew A. TN Cav. 7th Bn. (Ben-
  nett's) Co.E
Roberson, Andrew J. AL Jeff Davis Arty.
Roberson, Andrew J. AR 45th Cav. Co.E
Roberson, Andrew J. NC 4th Inf. Co.F
Roberson, Andrew J. TX 12th Cav. Co.C
Roberson, Andrew J. VA 22nd Inf. Co.A
Roberson, A.O. GA 40th Inf. Co.K Sgt.
Roberson, A.P. VA Cav. 37th Bn. Co.B
Roberson, A.R. AL 59th Inf. Co.C
Roberson, A.S. GA Cav. Dorough's Bn.
Roberson, Asher E. TX 2nd Cav. Co.H
Roberson, A.T.M. TN 2nd (Ashby's) Cav. Co.F
Roberson, Austin C. MS 34th Inf. Co.E
Roberson, B.A. GA Inf. 8th Bn. Co.A
Roberson, Bayliss GA 23rd Inf. Co.C
Roberson, B.B. MS 8th Inf. Co.C
Roberson, B.D. MS Cav. Ham's Regt. Co.G
Roberson, Ben MS Hudson's Co. (Noxubee
  Guards)
Roberson, Benjamin MS 2nd Cav. Co.F
Roberson, Benjamin TN 3rd (Lillard's) Mtd.Inf.
  Co.F
Roberson, Benjamin TN 36th Inf. Co.B
Roberson, Benjamin TX 10th Inf. Co.I
Roberson, Benjamin F. GA 12th (Wright's) Cav.
  (St.Guards) Wright's Co. Adj.
Roberson, Benjamin F. TN 6th Inf. Co.H Cpl.

Roberson, Benjamin F. TN 27th Inf. Co.I
Roberson, Benjamin H. GA Lt.Arty. Scogin's
   Btty. (Griffin Lt.Arty.)
Roberson, Benjamin H. SC 7th Cav. Co.C
Roberson, Benjamin L. NC 1st Arty. (10th
   St.Troops) Co.H
Roberson, Benjamin S. VA 57th Inf. Co.C
Roberson, Berry MO Cav. Schnabel's Bn. Co.B
Roberson, B.F. KY 1st (Butler's) Cav. New
   Co.H
Roberson, B.J. AR 19th (Dawson's) Inf. Co.C
Roberson, B.S. GA 40th Inf. Co.K
Roberson, Bun AL 6th Inf. Co.H
Roberson, B.W. AL 53rd (Part.Rangers) Co.H
   Sgt.
Roberson, B.W. MS 39th Inf. Co.D
Roberson, C. AL 25th Inf. Co.H
Roberson, C. GA 27th Inf. Co.C
Roberson, C. TN 84th Inf. Co.D
Roberson, Caleb J. NC 32nd Inf. Co.E,F
Roberson, Calvin P. TN 2nd (Smith's) Cav.
Roberson, Carlos D. GA 20th Inf. Co.C
Roberson, Cason TN 16th Inf. Co.G Cpl.
Roberson, C.C. AR 7th Cav. Co.C
Roberson, C.F. AL 55th Vol. Co.C
Roberson, C.H. 1st Conf.Cav. 1st Co.C
Roberson, Charles NC 1st Inf. Co.H
Roberson, Charles A. FL 8th Inf. Co.G
Roberson, Charles H. NC 30th Inf. Co.G
Roberson, Charles W. TN 48th (Voorhies') Inf.
   Co.A
Roberson, C.L. AR 45th Mil. Co.B
Roberson, C.N. NC Inf. 2nd Bn. Co.A
Roberson, C.N. NC 4th Bn.Jr.Res. Co.B
Roberson, C.W. TX 8th Cav.
Roberson, C.W. 8th (Wade's) Conf.Cav. Co.H
Roberson, Cyrus KY 9th Cav. Co.H
Roberson, D. NC 7th Sr.Res. Watts' Co.
Roberson, Daniel AR 1st Mtd.Rifles Co.A
Roberson, David AR 14th (McCarver's) Inf.
   Co.B
Roberson, David NC 4th Bn.Jr.Res. Co.B
Roberson, David SC 7th Cav. Co.C
Roberson, David H. NC 29th Inf. Co.C
Roberson, David T. LA 12th Inf. Co.G
Roberson, D.D. GA 28th Inf. Co.I
Roberson, D.D. NC 1st Cav. (9th St.Troops)
   Co.E
Roberson, D.L. FL Cav. 3rd Bn. Co.D
Roberson, D.L. 15th Conf.Cav. Co.I
Roberson, Dock GA 55th Inf. Co.D
Roberson, D.W. MS Cav. Ham's Regt. Co.A
Roberson, E. AL 23rd Inf. Co.G
Roberson, E. AL Cp. of Instr. Talladega Co.D
Roberson, E. AR 1st Vol. Kelsey's Co.
Roberson, E. SC Manigault's Bn.Vol. Co.D
Roberson, E.D. MS Cav. Yerger's Regt. Co.A
Roberson, Edward NC 58th Inf. Co.C
Roberson, Edwin B. NC 3rd Inf. Co.G
Roberson, E.F. AR 15th (Johnson's) Inf. Co.C
Roberson, E.H. SC 2nd Inf. Co.G
Roberson, Eli J. NC 3rd Arty. (40th St.Troops)
   Co.D
Roberson, Elijah AL Mil. 4th Vol. Co.D
Roberson, Elijah N. GA 18th Inf. Co.A
Roberson, Elisha R. NC 2nd Inf. Co.K
Roberson, Ellis NC 23rd Inf. Co.G

Roberson, Ellison SC 26th Inf. Co.H Sgt.
Roberson, E.M. GA 45th Inf. Co.E 1st Lt.
Roberson, E.N. AR 15th Mil. Co.I Sgt.
Roberson, E.W. GA 11th Cav. Co.C
Roberson, F.A. VA Cav. 37th Bn. Co.F
Roberson, Felix TN 12th Inf. Co.A
Roberson, F.M. AL 34th Inf. Co.B
Roberson, Francis M. AL 18th Inf. Co.A
Roberson, Francis M. AR 3rd Cav. Co.K
Roberson, Francis M. GA Cobb's Legion Co.B
Roberson, Frank AL 17th Inf. Co.A
Roberson, Frank MS 34th Inf. Co.G
Roberson, Fulford NC 2nd Arty. (36th
   St.Troops) Co.G
Roberson, G. AL Cav. Moreland's Regt. Co.D
Roberson, G. GA Smith's Legion Co.G
Roberson, G. MS 3rd Inf. (A. of 10,000) Co.C
Roberson, G. MS 4th Inf. Co.E
Roberson, G. MS Condrey's Co. (Bull Mtn.
   Invinc.)
Roberson, G. NC 6th Inf. Co.K
Roberson, Garnetta TN 44th (Cons.) Inf. Co.A
Roberson, George AL 42nd Inf. Co.K
Roberson, George AR 1st Mtd Rifles Co.H
Roberson, George AR 20th Inf. Co.D Sgt.
Roberson, George FL 4th Inf. Co.K
Roberson, George GA 49th Inf. Co.B
Roberson, George MO 1st Cav. Co.I
Roberson, George MO 1st & 3rd Cons.Cav.
   Co.E
Roberson, George MO Cav. Schnabel's Bn. Co.B
Roberson, George NC 56th Inf. Co.C
Roberson, George C. NC 23rd Inf. Co.G
Roberson, George C. NC 29th Inf. Co.C
Roberson, George D. NC 17th Inf. (2nd Org.)
   Co.E
Roberson, George F. FL Cav. 3rd Bn. Co.D
Roberson, George P. NC 3rd Cav. (41st
   St.Troops) Co.K
Roberson, George W. MD Cav. 2nd Bn. Co.K
Roberson, George W. MS 23rd Inf. Co.B
Roberson, George W. NC 15th Inf. Co.E
Roberson, George W. TX 13th Cav. Co.H
Roberson, G.F. SC 6th Cav. Co.K,D Cpl.
Roberson, G.F. 15th Conf.Cav. Co.I
Roberson, Gilbert NC 29th Inf. Co.G
Roberson, Giorgio LA Mil. 6th Regt.Eur.Brig.
   (Italian Guards Bn.) Co.2
Roberson, G.M. SC 22nd Inf. Co.H
Roberson, Gordon MS Inf. 2nd Bn. (St.Troops)
   Co.C
Roberson, G.P. AL 8th Inf.
Roberson, Green B. NC 64th Inf. Co.D
Roberson, Griffen A. MS 40th Inf. Co.C
Roberson, G.S. NC 35th Inf. Co.E
Roberson, G.T. AL Cav. Moreland's Regt. Co.D
Roberson, G.W. AR Inf. Cocke's Regt. Co.G
Roberson, G.W. GA 8th Cav. Co.F Cpl.
Roberson, G.W. GA 62nd Cav. Co.F Cpl.
Roberson, G.W. GA Lt.Arty. Howell's Co.
Roberson, G.W. GA 2nd Inf. Co.H
Roberson, G.W. MS Cav. 2nd Bn.Res. Co.I
Roberson, G.W. MS 27th Inf. Co.C
Roberson, G.W. TN 15th (Stewart's) Cav. Co.B
Roberson, G.W. 3rd Conf.Cav. Co.G
Roberson, G.W.M. SC 15th Inf. Co.B
Roberson, H. AL 5th Cav. Co.B

Roberson, H. SC Palmetto S.S. Co.E
Roberson, H. TN 38th Inf. Co.L
Roberson, Harrison NC 17th Inf. (1st Org.) Co.F
Roberson, Harrison NC 17th Inf. (2nd Org.)
   Co.F
Roberson, Harry VA Mil. Washington Cty.
Roberson, Haston M. NC 28th Inf. Co.G Cpl.
Roberson, H.D. TN 34th Inf. Co.H
Roberson, H.E. SC 26th Inf. Co.H
Roberson, Henry FL 8th Inf. Co.G Sgt.
Roberson, Henry NC 5th Sr.Res. Co.H
Roberson, Henry NC 48th Inf. Co.D
Roberson, Henry TN 19th Inf. Co.H
Roberson, Henry VA 62nd Mtd.Inf. 2nd Co.C
Roberson, Henry B. NC 17th Inf. (2nd Org.)
   Co.D
Roberson, Henry C. AL 1st Bn. Hilliard's Legion
   Vol. Co.F
Roberson, Henry C. NC Inf. Thomas Legion
   Co.C
Roberson, Henry F. NC 4th Inf. Co.H
Roberson, Henry G. NC Inf. Thomas Legion
   Co.C
Roberson, Henry J. TN 48th (Voorhies') Inf.
   Co.H
Roberson, Herodotus F. NC 62nd Inf. Co.C
Roberson, Hezekiah VA 57th Inf. Co.G
Roberson, H.F. AR 15th (Johnson's) Inf. Co.D
   Comsy.Sgt.
Roberson, H.F. TN 18th (Newsom's) Cav. Co.I
   Cpl.
Roberson, Hickman D. TN 48th (Voorhies') Inf.
   Co.H
Roberson, Hillman NC 23rd Inf. Co.G
Roberson, Hiram NC 1st Bn.Jr.Res. Co.E
Roberson, Hiram R. TX 10th Inf. Co.I
Roberson, Hiram Russel TX 20th Cav. Co.E
Roberson, Hisukiah MO Cav. Schnabel's Bn.
   Co.B
Roberson, H.L. Inf. Bailey's Cons.Regt. Co.D
   2nd Lt.
Roberson, H.L. VA 2nd Inf.Loc.Def. Co.A
Roberson, H.P. GA 54th Inf. Co.K
Roberson, H.Q. AL 42nd Inf. Co.K
Roberson, H.W. GA 54th Inf. Co.K
Roberson, I.L. TN 2nd (Ashby's) Cav. Co.F
   Sgt.
Roberson, Isaac AL 8th (Livingston's) Cav.
   Co.A
Roberson, Isaac B. GA 49th Inf. Co.A
Roberson, Isaac J. TX 10th Inf. Co.I
Roberson, Isaac K.P. TN 43rd Inf. Co.C Sgt.
Roberson, Isaac L. TN Cav. 4th Bn. (Branner's)
   Co.F
Roberson, Isaac M. AL 13th Cav. Co.G
Roberson, Isaac W. NC 25th Inf. Co.F Cpl.
Roberson, Isaiah TN 7th Inf. Co.G
Roberson, Isham GA 4th (Clinch's) Cav. Co.A
Roberson, J. AL Lt.Arty. Kolb's Btty.
Roberson, J. FL 2nd Cav. Co.D
Roberson, J. GA Lt.Arty. 12th Bn.
Roberson, J. GA 46th Inf. Co.E
Roberson, J. MS 7th Cav. Co.A
Roberson, J. MO 9th Inf. Co.D
Roberson, J. NC 2nd Conscr. Co.E
Roberson, J. NC 7th Sr.Res. Johnston's Co.
Roberson, J. NC Mallett's Bn. Co.A

Roberson, J.A. AR 37th Inf. Co.E
Roberson, J.A. GA 8th Cav. Co.G
Roberson, J.A. GA 62nd Cav. Co.G
Roberson, J.A. NC 2nd Jr.Res. Co.F Cpl.
Roberson, J.A. TN 7th (Duckworth's) Cav. Co.F
Roberson, J.A. TN 20th (Russell's) Cav. Co.D
Roberson, J.A. TX 11th Cav. Co.B
Roberson, J.A. VA Cav. 37th Bn. Co.B
Roberson, J.A. VA 57th Inf. Co.A
Roberson, Jacob GA 4th (Clinch's) Cav. Co.A
Roberson, Jacob TX 10th Inf. Co.I
Roberson, Jacob VA Cav. 41st Bn. Trayhern's Co.
Roberson, Jacob W. SC 5th Cav. Co.A
Roberson, James AL 9th (Malone's) Cav. Co.F
Roberson, James AL 15th Inf. Co.A
Roberson, James AL 50th Inf. Co.D
Roberson, James AL 1st Bn. Hilliard's Legion Vol. Co.B
Roberson, James AR 8th Cav. Co.H
Roberson, James AR 14th (McCarver's) Inf. Co.B
Roberson, James AR Inf. Cocke's Regt. Co.I
Roberson, James FL 2nd Inf. Co.C
Roberson, James GA 52nd Inf. Co.H Sgt.
Roberson, James MS Cav. Ham's Regt. Co.G
Roberson, James MO Cav. Williams' Regt. Co.K
Roberson, James NC 5th Inf. Co.D
Roberson, James NC 5th Inf. Co.E
Roberson, James NC 6th Inf. Co.E
Roberson, James NC 30th Inf. Co.F
Roberson, James NC 45th Inf. Co.B
Roberson, James SC 7th Res. Co.E
Roberson, James TN 4th (Murray's) Cav. Co.K 1st Lt.
Roberson, James TN Inf. 22nd Bn. Co.F 1st Lt.
Roberson, James TN 30th Inf. Co.H
Roberson, James TX 25th Cav. Co.I
Roberson, James Morgan's Co.D,CSA
Roberson, James A. NC 5th Inf. Co.I
Roberson, James B. MS 2nd Inf. Co.E
Roberson, James B. VA 16th Inf. Co.G
Roberson, James C. AR 2nd Inf. Co.K
Roberson, James D. NC 29th Inf. Co.C
Roberson, James E. NC 5th Inf. Co.I Sgt.
Roberson, James E. TN 4th (Murray's) Cav. Co.K Sgt.
Roberson, James E. TX 10th Inf. Co.K
Roberson, James F. GA 48th Inf. Co.D
Roberson, James H. NC 1st Inf. Co.B
Roberson, James H. NC 26th Inf. Co.A
Roberson, James H. NC 58th Inf. Co.C
Roberson, James J. AL 6th Inf. Co.F
Roberson, James J. FL 5th Inf. Co.G
Roberson, James J. GA 50th Inf. Co.H
Roberson, James L. AR 34th Inf. Co.K Sgt.
Roberson, James M. MS Cav. Robertson's Unatt.Co.
Roberson, James M. MS 27th Inf. Co.E
Roberson, James M. TN 48th (Voorhies') Inf. Co.H
Roberson, James M.N. TX 10th Inf. Co.K
Roberson, James R. NC 3rd Inf. Co.H
Roberson, James R. NC 17th Inf. (2nd Org.) Co.E Sgt.
Roberson, James R.P. MS 2nd St.Cav. Co.A
Roberson, James T. AL Lt.Arty. Kolb's Btty.

Roberson, James T. NC Inf. Thomas Legion Co.C
Roberson, James W. GA 27th Inf. Co.C 2nd Lt.
Roberson, James W. LA 11th Inf. Co.E
Roberson, James William TX 21st Cav. Co.K
Roberson, J.A.P. GA 15th Inf. Co.K 1st Sgt.
Roberson, Jasper NC 1st Cav. (9th St.Troops) Co.D
Roberson, Jasper N. AR 45th Cav. Co.E
Roberson, J.B. AL 2nd Cav. Co.G
Roberson, J.B. AL 27th Inf. Co.E
Roberson, J.C. MS 14th Inf. Co.C
Roberson, J.D. TX 29th Cav. Co.C
Roberson, J.E. SC 5th St.Troops Co.E
Roberson, J.E. TN Inf. 22nd Bn. Co.F Sgt.
Roberson, Jesse NC 31st Inf. Co.F
Roberson, Jesse B. NC 1st Inf. (6 mo. '61) Co.A
Roberson, Jesse M. NC 62nd Inf. Co.C
Roberson, J.F. AL 11th Cav. Co.B Sgt.
Roberson, J.F. Conf.Cav. Clarkson's Bn. Ind. Rangers Co.A,G
Roberson, J.G. GA 55th Inf. Co.F
Roberson, J.H. AR 11th & 17th (Cons.) Inf. Co.F Drum.
Roberson, J.H. AR 19th (Dawson's) Inf. Co.C
Roberson, J.H. GA 59th Inf. Co.H
Roberson, J.H. GA Floyd Legion (St.Guards) Co.K
Roberson, J.H. LA 25th Inf. Co.E 1st Lt.
Roberson, J.H. MS Cav. Ham's Regt. Co.A
Roberson, J.H. MO Inf. Clark's Regt. Co.C
Roberson, J.H. NC Mallett's Bn. Co.A
Roberson, J.I. MS Graves' Co. (Copiah Horse Guards)
Roberson, J.J. AL 3rd Inf. Co.G
Roberson, J.K.P. GA 62nd Cav. Co.D
Roberson, J.L. AL 8th Inf. Co.A
Roberson, J.L. AL 17th Inf. Co.B 2nd Lt.
Roberson, J.L. GA 7th Inf. Co.F
Roberson, J.L. GA 59th Inf. Co.H
Roberson, J.L. MS 39th Inf. Co.D
Roberson, J.L. TN 21st (Wilson's) Cav. Co.B
Roberson, J.L. 7th Conf.Cav. Co.B
Roberson, J.M. AL 55th Vol. Co.C
Roberson, J.M. GA 60th Inf. Co.E Cpl.
Roberson, J.M. MS 1st (Johnston's) Inf. Co.D
Roberson, J.M. MS 8th Inf. Co.C
Roberson, J.M. SC 5th St.Troops Co.F
Roberson, J.M. TN 11th (Holman's) Cav. Co.B
Roberson, J.M. TX 11th Cav. Co.F
Roberson, J.N.P. GA Arty. St.Troops Pruden's Btty.
Roberson, Joe AL 27th Inf. Co.B
Roberson, Joel VA 11th Cav. Co.D
Roberson, Joel VA 18th Inf. Co.I
Roberson, John AL 18th Inf. Co.B
Roberson, John AR 7th Cav. Co.D
Roberson, John AR Inf. Cocke's Regt. Co.I
Roberson, John GA 1st (Symons') Res. Co.G
Roberson, John GA 41st Inf. Co.I
Roberson, John GA 65th Inf. Co.B
Roberson, John GA Smith's Legion Co.C
Roberson, John MS 2nd St.Cav. Co.A
Roberson, John MS 10th Cav. Co.E
Roberson, John MS Cav. Ham's Regt. Co.G
Roberson, John MS 2nd (Quinn's St.Troops) Inf. Co.E

Roberson, John MS 3rd Inf. Co.D
Roberson, John MS Condrey's Co. (Bull Mtn. Invinc.)
Roberson, John MO 9th (Elliott's) Cav. Co.A
Roberson, John MO Cav. Clardy's Bn. Co.A Sgt.
Roberson, John NC 2nd Cav. (19th St.Troops) Co.F
Roberson, John NC 1st Inf. Co.B
Roberson, John NC 2nd Inf. Co.G
Roberson, John NC 8th Inf. Co.D
Roberson, John NC 13th Inf. Co.K
Roberson, John NC 16th Inf. Co.G
Roberson, John NC 29th Inf. Co.B
Roberson, John NC 58th Inf. Co.C
Roberson, John NC 62nd Inf. Co.C
Roberson, John SC 4th Cav. Co.C
Roberson, John SC Cav. DeSausaure's Squad.
Roberson, John SC 2nd Arty. Co.D
Roberson, John SC Hvy.Arty. 15th (Lucas') Bn. Co.A
Roberson, John SC 5th St.Troops Co.E
Roberson, John SC 7th Res. Co.E
Roberson, John SC 19th Inf. Co.C
Roberson, John TN 15th Inf. Co.E
Roberson, John VA Cav. 32nd Bn. Co.A
Roberson, John VA 136th Mil. Co.D
Roberson, John A. NC 17th Inf. (2nd Org.) Co.K
Roberson, John A. NC 28th Inf. Co.G
Roberson, Johnathan MS 2nd St.Cav. Co.A
Roberson, Johnathan J. NC Cav. 16th Bn. Co.D
Roberson, John C. NC 58th Inf. Co.C
Roberson, John E. AR 14th (McCarver's) Inf. Co.B
Roberson, John E. MS 1st (Johnston's) Inf. Co.H
Roberson, John F. VA 18th Cav. Co.D
Roberson, John H. MS 2nd St.Cav. Co.A
Roberson, John H. VA Mil. Scott Cty.
Roberson, John L. NC 3rd Arty. (40th St.Troops) Co.G
Roberson, John M. MS 1st (Johnston's) Inf. Co.H
Roberson, John M. NC 7th Inf. Co.C
Roberson, John M. NC 44th Inf. Co.E
Roberson, John M. SC 2nd Inf. Co.F
Roberson, John N. GA 56th Inf. Co.C
Roberson, John P. NC Inf. Thomas Legion Co.C
Roberson, John P. TX 9th Field Btty.
Roberson, John R. TN 2nd (Ashby's) Cav. Co.F
Roberson, John R. VA 129th Mil. Carter's Co.
Roberson, Jno. S. NC Mallett's Bn. Co.A
Roberson, John W. AL Arty. 1st Bn. Co.E Cpl.
Roberson, John W. AL 2nd Bn. Hilliard's Legion Vol. Co.F
Roberson, John W. GA 20th Inf. Co.A
Roberson, John W. MS 1st (King's) Inf. (St.Troops) Co.E
Roberson, John W. MS 23rd Inf. Co.B
Roberson, John W. MS 34th Inf. Co.H Sgt.
Roberson, John W. NC 4th Inf. Co.H Cpl.
Roberson, John W. NC 6th Inf. Co.E
Roberson, John W. SC Hvy.Arty. 15th (Lucas') Bn. Co.A
Roberson, John W. TX 9th Field Btty.
Roberson, Joseph AL 12th Cav. Co.D
Roberson, Joseph GA 11th Inf. Co.G
Roberson, Joseph MS 2nd St.Cav. Co.L

Roberson, Joseph MS 37th Inf. Co.D
Roberson, Joseph NC 17th Inf. (2nd Org.) Co.F
Roberson, Joseph SC 9th Res. Co.H
Roberson, Joseph SC 26th Inf. Co.H
Roberson, Joseph VA 16th Cav. Co.E
Roberson, Joseph H. FL 1st Cav. Co.A
Roberson, Joseph J. AR 26th Inf. Co.B
Roberson, Joseph P. NC 1st Arty. (10th
    St.Troops) Co.H 1st Lt.
Roberson, Josiah AR Inf. Cocke's Regt. Co.I
Roberson, J.P. AR 34th Inf. Co.H
Roberson, J.P. MS 23rd Inf. Co.A
Roberson, J.R. GA 11th Cav. Co.H
Roberson, J.R. GA 8th Inf. Co.H
Roberson, J.R. TN 21st & 22nd (Cons.) Cav.
    Co.G,H
Roberson, J.S. AR 19th (Dawson's) Cav. Co.C
    RCO
Roberson, J.S. TN 19th (Biffle's) Cav. Co.G
Roberson, J.S. VA Lt.Arty. 13th Bn. Co.C
Roberson, J.T. GA 7th Inf. Co.G
Roberson, J.T. MS 3rd Inf. Co.A
Roberson, J.T. 3rd Conf.Eng.Troops Co.H
Roberson, J.T.C. GA 56th Inf. Co.C
Roberson, Julius AR 1st (Crawford's) Cav. Co.E
Roberson, Julius NC 58th Inf. Co.C Cpl.
Roberson, J.V. AL Cav. Moreland's Regt. Co.A
Roberson, J.V. AR Inf. Hardy's Regt. Co.C
Roberson, J.V. TN 10th Inf. Co.C
Roberson, J.W. AL 59th Inf. Co.C
Roberson, J.W. AR 1st Monroe's) Cav. Co.K
    Sgt.
Roberson, J.W. GA 8th Cav. Co.G
Roberson, J.W. GA 62nd Cav. Co.G
Roberson, J.W. MS 10th Cav. Co.B
Roberson, J.W. TN 21st (Wilson's) Cav. Co.B,D
Roberson, J.W. TN 21st & 22nd (Cons.) Cav.
    Co.G
Roberson, J. William NC 8th Inf. Co.D
Roberson, K. AR Cav. McGehee's Regt. Co.G
Roberson, K. LA Washington Arty.Bn. Co.5
Roberson, L. AL Cav. Moreland's Regt. Co.C
Roberson, L. NC Walker's Bn. Thomas' Legion
    Co.H
Roberson, L. TX Cav. Wells' Regt. Co.H
Roberson, Landon VA 51st Inf. Co.D
Roberson, L.B. GA Cav. 1st Bn.Res. Tufts' Co.
Roberson, L.B. NC 3rd Inf. Co.G
Roberson, L.D. SC Cav. 12th Bn. Co.D
Roberson, L.D. SC 2nd Inf. Co.G,H
Roberson, L.D. TN 84th Inf. Co.E
Roberson, Leander NC Walker's Bn. Thomas'
    Legion Co.E Sgt.
Roberson, Lemuel AL 6th Cav. Co.D,E
Roberson, Leroy 3rd Conf.Eng.Troops Co.A
    Artif.
Roberson, Lewis AR Inf. 4th Bn. Co.A
Roberson, Lewis NC 23rd Inf. Co.G
Roberson, Lewis SC 4th Bn.Res. Co.E
Roberson, L.G. AL Cav. Moreland's Regt. Co.A
Roberson, L.G. AL 27th Inf. Co.B
Roberson, L.J. AL 8th Inf. Co.A
Roberson, Lloyd AL 37th Inf. Co.I
Roberson, Logan A. 1st Conf.Inf. Co.B
Roberson, Luke S. TN 7th Inf. Co.G Sgt.
Roberson, M. AR 2nd Cav. Co.F
Roberson, M. AR 7th Cav. Co.C

Roberson, M. MS 1st (Johnson's) Inf. Co.F
Roberson, Marshall A. AL 24th Inf. Co.I
Roberson, Martin V.B. AL 61st Inf. Co.F
Roberson, Martin V.B. NC 6th Inf. Co.E
Roberson, Mason NC 2nd Arty. (36th St.Troops)
    Co.G
Roberson, Mathew MS Condrey's Co. (Bull
    Mtn.Invinc.)
Roberson, Mathew N. TX 10th Inf. Co.K
Roberson, McG. NC 17th Inf. (1st Org.) Co.F
Roberson, Merida GA 23rd Inf. Co.C
Roberson, Merritt M. NC 15th Inf. Co.H
Roberson, Michael SC 26th Inf. Co.H
Roberson, Miner GA 49th Inf. Co.B
Roberson, M.L. MS Inf. 7th Bn. Co.A
Roberson, M.M. AR 26th Inf. Co.C
Roberson, M.M. AR 30th Inf. Co.C
Roberson, M.M. GA 5th Res. Co.K Cpl.
Roberson, M.N. GA 1st Inf. (St.Guards) Co.C
Roberson, Monteville M. NC 62nd Inf. Co.C
Roberson, Moses AL Cav. 4th Bn. (Love's) Co.B
Roberson, M.R. LA 17th Inf. Co.D
Roberson, N. GA 28th Inf. Co.G
Roberson, Napoleon B. AL 10th Inf. Co.K
Roberson, Nathaniel AL 37th Inf. Co.I
Roberson, Nathaniel TN 22nd (Barteau's) Cav.
    Co.D Cpl.
Roberson, Natty NC 44th Inf. Co.G
Roberson, N.E. MO 6th Cav. Co.F
Roberson, Newton GA 11th Inf. Co.G
Roberson, N.F. AL 17th Inf. Co.B
Roberson, N.J. MS 12th Inf. Co.C
Roberson, N.M. AL 37th Inf. Co.G 2nd Lt.
Roberson, N.M. NC 6th Inf. Co.E
Roberson, Noah P. NC 1st Inf. Co.H
Roberson, N.Y. NC 23rd Inf. Co.G
Roberson, P. AL Cav. Moreland's Regt. Co.D
Roberson, P.A. NC 23rd Inf. Co.G
Roberson, Pleasant TN 84th Inf. Co.E Sgt.
Roberson, Posey A. NC 62nd Inf. Co.C
Roberson, Prior N. AL 30th Inf. Co.A
Roberson, P.W. AR 19th (Dockery's) Inf. Co.A
Roberson, P.W. TN 3rd (Lillard's) Mtd.Inf.
    Co.D Cpl.
Roberson, R. AL Cav. Moreland's Regt. Co.D
Roberson, R. AL 65th Inf. Co.B
Roberson, R. AR 24th Inf. Co.D
Roberson, R. AR Inf. Hardy's Regt. Co.C
Roberson, R. TN 19th (Biffle's) Cav. Co.G
Roberson, R. TN 19th & 22nd (Cons.) Cav. Co.B
Roberson, R. TN 20th (Russell's) Cav. Co.D
Roberson, R. TN 28th (Cons.) Inf. Co.H Capt.
Roberson, R.A. GA 1st (Ramsey's) Inf. Co.E
Roberson, Raymond AL 63rd Inf. Co.B
Roberson, R.D. AL 23rd Inf. Co.E
Roberson, R.D. SC 2nd Inf. Co.C Cpl.
Roberson, Richard MO 1st Cav. Co.I
Roberson, Richard, Jr. NC 62nd Inf. Co.C
Roberson, Richard, Sr. NC 62nd Inf. Co.A,C
Roberson, Richard VA 13th Inf. Co.I Sgt.
Roberson, Richard A. KY 8th Cav. Co.H
Roberson, Richard R. FL 7th Inf. Co.G
Roberson, Richmond GA 3rd Inf. Co.K
Roberson, R.J. KY 7th Mtd.Inf. Co.D
Roberson, R.J. NC 6th Inf. Co.F
Roberson, R.J.N. GA 46th Inf. Co.C
Roberson, Robert AR 19th (Dockery's) Inf. Co.A

Roberson, Robert A. NC 44th Inf. Co.E
Roberson, Robert D. SC 1st (Orr's) Rifles Co.C
Roberson, Robert F. GA 2nd Inf. Co.H Music.
Roberson, Roysdon TN 25th Inf. Co.K 2nd Lt.
Roberson, Roysdon TN 34th Inf. Co.D Capt.
Roberson, R.T.C. AL 34th Inf. Black's Co.
Roberson, Rufus KY 8th Cav. Co.E
Roberson, Rufus H. MO 3rd Cav. Co.C
Roberson, R.W. GA 5th Res. Co.H
Roberson, R.W. MS 23rd Inf. Co.A Sgt.
Roberson, S. GA 8th Cav. Co.G
Roberson, S. GA 62nd Cav. Co.G
Roberson, S. TX 20th Inf. Co.F
Roberson, Samuel AL 2nd Bn. Hilliard's Legion
    Vol. Co.F
Roberson, Samuel AL 59th Inf. Co.C
Roberson, Samuel GA 61st Inf. Co.F
Roberson, Samuel SC 5th Bn.Res. Co.F
Roberson, Samuel TX 11th Inf. Co.G
Roberson, Samuel A. AL Arty. 1st Bn. Co.E
Roberson, Samuel J. TN 2nd (Ashby's) Cav.
    Co.F Cpl.
Roberson, Samuel J. TN Cav. 4th Bn. (Bran-
    ner's) Co.F
Roberson, Samuel M. AR 9th Inf. Co.A
Roberson, Samuel M. LA 19th Inf. Co.E Cpl.
Roberson, Samuel P. KY 6th Cav. Co.E
Roberson, Sanford AL 2nd Bn. Hilliard's Legion
    Vol. Co.B
Roberson, S.B. FL Cav. 3rd Bn. Co.D
Roberson, S.B. 15th Conf.Cav. Co.I
Roberson, S.C. TN 51st (Cons.) Inf. Co.A
Roberson, S.H. MS 37th Inf. Co.D
Roberson, Silas GA 47th Inf. Co.F Sgt.
Roberson, Silas B. GA 52nd Inf. Co.A
Roberson, Simon P. TN 54th Inf. Ives' Co.
Roberson, Sirah H. MS 1st (Patton's) Inf. Co.K
Roberson, S.L. NC 2nd Jr.Res. Co.C 2nd Lt.
Roberson, Smith NC 50th Inf. Co.I
Roberson, Soverign G. TN 48th (Voorhies') Inf.
    Co.H
Roberson, S.T. MS Cav. Ham's Regt. Co.A
Roberson, Stephen M. NC 58th Inf. Co.C
Roberson, T. AL 12th Inf. Co.F
Roberson, T. TX 27th Cav. Co.D Sgt.
Roberson, T.C. GA 42nd Inf. Co.K
Roberson, T.C. TN 51st (Cons.) Inf. Co.A
Roberson, T.C. TN 52nd Inf. Co.A
Roberson, T.D. AL 7th Cav. Co.I,C
Roberson, T.H. AR 11th & 17th (Cons.) Inf.
    Co.F
Roberson, Tho F. TX 9th Cav. Co.D
Roberson, Thomas AL Mtd.Res. Logan's Co.
Roberson, Thomas AL Lt.Arty. 20th Bn. Co.B
Roberson, Thomas AL 3rd Bn.Res. Jackson's
    Co. Jr.2nd Lt.
Roberson, Thomas AR Cav. Wright's Regt. Co.I
Roberson, Thomas MS 39th Inf. Co.D
Roberson, Thomas NC 58th Inf. Co.K
Roberson, Thomas TN Cav. 4th Bn. (Branner's)
    Co.E
Roberson, Thomas TN 46th Inf. Co.A
Roberson, Thomas VA 62nd Mtd.Inf. 2nd Co.L
Roberson, Thomas C. NC 28th Inf. Co.E
Roberson, Thomas G. SC 26th Inf. Co.H Cpl.
Roberson, Thomas H. AR 11th Inf. Co.F Sgt.
Roberson, Thomas H. NC 28th Inf. Co.G

Roberson, Thomas H. TN 2nd (Robison's) Inf. Co.C

Roberson, Thomas J. MS 2nd Inf. Co.F Sgt.

Roberson, Thomas J. MS 34th Inf. Co.H 1st Lt.

Roberson, Thomas J. NC 28th Inf. Co.G

Roberson, Thomas M. AL Arty. 1st Bn. Co.E

Roberson, Thomas M. TN Cav. Newsom's Regt. Co.A

Roberson, Thomas N. TN 14th Inf. Co.L

Roberson, Thomas W. AL 10th Inf. Co.K

Roberson, Thomas W. NC 17th Inf. (2nd Org.) Co.E

Roberson, Thomas W. NC 18th Inf. Co.K 2nd Lt.

Roberson, Thomas W. VA 30th Inf. Co.B

Roberson, T.I. MS Cav. Yerger's Regt. Co.F

Roberson, T.J. GA 55th Inf. Co.F Capt.

Roberson, T.J. MS 3rd Inf. Co.D

Roberson, T.L. TX 12th Inf. Co.I

Roberson, T.M. AR 2nd Cav. Co.F

Roberson, T.P. MS 6th Cav. Co.A

Roberson, T.S. GA Smith's Legion Co.G

Roberson, V.A. TX Cav. (Dismtd.) Chisum's Regt. Co.E

Roberson, Valentine NC 2nd Arty. (36th St.Troops) Co.G

Roberson, W. AR 35th Inf. Co.F

Roberson, W. MO 15th Cav. Co.L

Roberson, W. VA 1st Cav. Co.A

Roberson, W. VA 4th Cav. Co.A

Roberson, W.A. GA Arty. St.Troops Pruden's Btty.

Roberson, W.A. TN 14th (Neely's) Cav. Co.D

Roberson, W.A. TX Cav. (Dismtd.) Chisum's Regt. Co.C

Roberson, Walter W. NC 26th Inf. Co.C

Roberson, W.B. VA Inf. 22nd Bn. Co.G

Roberson, W.C. GA Arty. Lumpkin's Co.

Roberson, W.D. TX 9th Field Btty.

Roberson, Westley AL 2nd Bn. Hilliard's Legion Vol. Co.F Sgt.

Roberson, W.F. GA 28th Inf. Co.I

Roberson, W.F. MS 31st Inf. Co.K

Roberson, W.F. SC 22nd Inf. Co.H

Roberson, W.G. AR 2nd Cav. Co.F

Roberson, W.G.S. MS 1st (Johnston's) Inf. Co.F

Roberson, W.H. GA Inf. 40th Bn. Co.F

Roberson, W.H. GA 54th Inf. Co.K

Roberson, W.H. MS 2nd St.Cav. Co.D

Roberson, W.H. NC 29th Inf. Co.C Sgt.

Roberson, Wilburn A. NC 6th Inf. Co.E Cpl.

Roberson, Wiley AR 2nd Mtd.Rifles Co.A

Roberson, Wiley NC 17th Inf. (1st Org.) Co.F

Roberson, William AL 25th Inf. Co.B

Roberson, William AL 34th Inf. Co.I Cpl.

Roberson, William AL 62nd Inf. Co.H

Roberson, William GA 1st Cav. Co.B

Roberson, William GA 8th Inf. (St.Guards) Co.A

Roberson, William GA 20th Inf. Co.H Cpl.

Roberson, William GA Inf. 25th Bn. (Prov. Guard) Co.A

Roberson, William GA 28th Inf. Co.I

Roberson, William GA Inf. (Anderson Guards) Anderson's Co.

Roberson, William GA Cherokee Legion (St.Guards) Co.E

Roberson, William LA 12th Inf. Co.G

Roberson, William LA 19th Inf. Co.C

Roberson, William LA 27th Inf. Co.D

Roberson, William LA Conscr.

Roberson, William MS 2nd St.Cav. Co.D

Roberson, William MS Cav. Yerger's Regt. Co.F

Roberson, William MS 1st (King's) Inf. (St.Troops) Co.E

Roberson, William MO Cav. Williams' Regt. Co.K

Roberson, William NC 17th Inf. (1st Org.) Co.K Music.

Roberson, William NC 18th Inf. Co.A

Roberson, William SC 7th Res. Co.F Cpl.

Roberson, William TN 31st Inf. Co.B

Roberson, William TX 29th Cav. Co.C

Roberson, William TX 10th Inf. Co.K

Roberson, William VA 3rd Cav. Co.E

Roberson, William VA 29th Inf. Co.D

Roberson, William VA 42nd Inf. Co.A

Roberson, William VA Mil. Scott Cty.

Roberson, William 10th Conf.Cav. Co.G

Roberson, William 3rd Conf.Eng.Troops Co.H

Roberson, William Lt.Arty. Dent's Btty.,CSA

Roberson, William A. MS St.Cav. Perrin's Bn. Co.B

Roberson, William A. NC 17th Inf. (2nd Org.) Co.D

Roberson, William A. SC 7th Res. Co.B

Roberson, William C. NC 58th Inf. Co.C

Roberson, William F. GA 15th Inf. Co.K Chap.

Roberson, William F. MS 21st Inf. Co.F

Roberson, William G. AL 44th Inf. Co.A

Roberson, William G. NC 15th Inf. Co.H

Roberson, William H. AL 3rd Inf. Co.F

Roberson, William H. AL 2nd Bn. Hilliard's Legion Vol. Co.C

Roberson, William H. GA 7th Inf. Co.F Cpl.

Roberson, William H. GA 27th Inf. Co.C 2nd Lt.

Roberson, William H. MS 27th Inf. Co.F

Roberson, William H. NC 1st Inf. Co.H

Roberson, William H. NC 17th Inf. (2nd Org.) Co.D

Roberson, William H. NC 22nd Inf. Co.B

Roberson, William H. TN 53rd Inf. Co.I 1st Lt.

Roberson, William Henry MS 34th Inf. Co.A

Roberson, William J. AL 28th Inf. Co.F

Roberson, William J. AL 43rd Inf. Co.B

Roberson, William J. MS 31st Inf. Co.E

Roberson, William J. VA 52nd Inf. Co.I Sgt.

Roberson, William K. MS 17th Inf. Co.H

Roberson, Wm. L. AL Cp. of Instr. Talladega

Roberson, William L. TN 32nd Inf. Co.H Sgt.

Roberson, William M. AL 2nd Bn. Hilliard's Legion Vol. Co.B Cpl.

Roberson, William M. NC 2nd Arty. (36th St.Troops) Co.G

Roberson, William M. NC 62nd Inf. Co.H Drum.

Roberson, William M. NC Inf. Thomas Legion Co.C

Roberson, William N. MS 37th Inf. Co.D

Roberson, William N. NC 29th Inf. Co.C

Roberson, William P. NC 3rd Cav. (41st St.Troops) Co.K Cpl.

Roberson, William R. MO Cav. Schnabel's Bn. Co.B

Roberson, William R. TN Cav. 7th Bn. (Bennett's) Co.E

Roberson, William R. TN 30th Inf. Co.G

Roberson, William S. NC 1st Arty. (10th St.Troops) Co.G

Roberson, William T. VA 22nd Inf. Co.C

Roberson, Willis H. AL 10th Inf. Co.F

Roberson, Wilton K. AL 33rd Inf. Co.B

Roberson, Wingfield GA 15th Inf. Co.K 1st Lt.

Roberson, W.J. AL 15th Inf. Co.D

Roberson, W.J. KY 12th Cav. Co.F

Roberson, W.J. MS 44th Inf. Co.D

Roberson, W.J. MS Shields' Co.

Roberson, W.J. TN Cav. Napier's Bn. Co.A 1st Lt.

Roberson, W.L. TN 51st Inf. Co.H

Roberson, W.M. AL 59th Inf. Co.K Cpl.

Roberson, W.M. MS 12th Cav. Co.G

Roberson, W.M. NC 5th Cav. (63rd St.Troops) Co.G

Roberson, W.M. TN 22nd (Barteau's) Cav.

Roberson, W.P. AR 37th Inf. Co.I

Roberson, W.R. TX Cav. McCord's Frontier Regt. Co.H Bugler

Roberson, W.R. Exch.Bn. 3rd Co.B,CSA

Roberson, W.S. SC 2nd Cav. Co.E

Roberson, W.T. AL 34th Inf. Co.B

Roberson, W.T. GA 16th Inf. Co.B

Roberson, W.T. GA 25th Inf. Co.C 1st Sgt.

Roberson, W.T. KY 2nd (Woodward's) Cav. Co.C

Roberson, W.T. MS 23rd Inf. Co.A

Roberson, W.T. TN 51st Inf. Co.H

Roberson, Wyatt NC 29th Inf. Co.B,K

Roberson, Wylie NC 31st Inf. Co.F

Roberson, Wyly D. GA 23rd Inf. Co.C Cpl.

Roberson, Y. GA 54th Inf. Co.B

Roberson, Y.L. GA 19th Inf. Co.K

Roberson, Young GA 4th Bn.S.S. Co.C

Roberson, Young NC 29th Inf. Co.B

Roberson, Z. NC 30th Inf. Co.G

Roberson, Z.H. GA 39th Inf. Co.E

Roberst, A. MS 4th Inf. Co.I

Robert VA Inf. 25th Bn. Co.G Cook

Robert 1st Choctaw & Chickasaw Mtd.Rifles 1st Co.E

Robert 1st Creek Mtd.Vol. Co.K

Robert, --- LA Mil. 2nd Regt. French Brig. Co.8 1st Lt.

Robert, A. MS 4th Inf. Co.G

Robert, A.J. AL 15th Inf. Co.K

Robert, Alexander C. GA 4th Inf. Co.E Cpl.

Robert, Alexander J. GA 4th Inf. Co.E Adj.

Robert, Alex J. Gen. & Staff 1st Lt.,Adj.

Robert, Alfred LA Mil. 2nd Regt. French Brig. Co.5

Robert, A.M. GA Inf. 18th Bn. (St.Guards) Adam's Co.

Robert, Augustus GA Inf. 1st Loc.Troops (Augusta) Co.A

Robert, Augustus M. GA 5th Inf. Co.A

Robert, Benjamin F. GA 4th Inf. Co.E

Robert, Bertrant LA Inf. 9th Bn. Co.D

Robert, B.F. SC 2nd Arty. Co.H

Robert, B.F. SC 12th Inf. Co.E

Robert, Bill LA Mil. 4th Regt. 1st Brig. 1st Div. Co.G

Robert, C. LA St.Mary's Regt. Co.A 2nd Lt.
Robert, Christopher GA Arty. (Chatham Arty.)
    Wheaton's Co.
Robert, Christopher GA 1st (Olmstead's) Inf.
    Claghorn's Co.
Robert, D.A. Conf.Cav. Wood's Regt. Co.B
    Cpl.
Robert, E. LA Mil. 1st Chasseurs a pied Co.2
Robert, Ed LA Mil. Orleans Guards Regt. Co.E
Robert, Edward Brush Bn.
Robert, Emile LA 1st Native Guards Sgt.
Robert, Edward J. LA 8th Inf. Co.H Cpl.
Robert, F.A. LA Bickham's Co. (Caddo Mil.)
Robert, F.R. GA Cav. 15th Bn. (St.Guards)
    Jones' Co.
Robert, Frank W. GA Cav. Nelson's Ind.Co.
Robert, Furman R. GA Cav. Nelson's Ind.Co.
Robert, G. LA 3rd (Wingfield's) Cav. Co.B
Robert, George E. MD Inf. 2nd Bn. Sgt.
Robert, Henry C. NC 3rd Arty. (40th St.Troops)
    Co.E
Robert, Hughes F. NC 54th Inf. Co.H Cpl.
Robert, J.A. GA Inf. 1st Loc.Troops (Augusta)
    Co.K
Robert, J.A. GA Inf. 18th Bn. (St.Guards)
    Adam's Co.
Robert, James GA 20th Inf. Co.H
Robert, James LA 8th Inf. Co.C
Robert, James LA Inf.Cons. 18th Regt. & Yellow
    Jacket Bn. Co.A
Robert, J.B. LA 22nd (Cons.) Inf. Co.E
Robert, J.B.J. LA Res.Corps Sgt.
Robert, J.B.P. LA Conscr.
Robert, J.E. LA 2nd Cav. Co.G
Robert, Jean Baptiste LA 10th Inf. Co.G
Robert, J.O. LA Mil. Orleans Guards Regt. Co.E
Robert, John LA 28th (Thomas') Inf. Co.G
Robert, John TN 6th Inf. Co.D
Robert, John B. LA 7th Inf. Co.E Music.
Robert, John F. LA 27th Inf. Co.C
Robert, John W. NC 39th Inf. Co.C
Robert, Joseph 1st Choctaw & Chickasaw
    Mtd.Rifles 2nd Co.K
Robert, Joseph C. GA 4th Inf. Co.E
Robert, Joseph S. LA 1st Cav. Co.D Cpl.
Robert, J.W. MS 24th Inf. Co.L
Robert, J.W. 3rd Conf.Inf. Co.F
Robert, L. LA 22nd Inf. Co.C
Robert, Lewis A. GA Inf. 2nd Bn. Co.A
Robert, Littleton J. MS Inf. 3rd Bn. Co.G Sgt.
Robert, Louis A. AL 39th Inf. Co.A 1st Lt.
Robert, M. LA 22nd Inf. Co.C,E
Robert, M. LA 22nd (Cons.) Inf. Co.E Cpl.
Robert, Martin NC Walker's Bn. Thomas'
    Legion Co.E
Robert, M.J. AL 11th Cav. Co.F
Robert, Moses AL Cav. Lewis' Bn. Co.B
Robert, N. LA 3rd (Wingfield's) Cav. Co.B
Robert, N.M. LA Arty. 1st Field Btty.
Robert, O. LA Mil.Cav. (Chasseurs Jefferson)
    Cagnolatti's Co.
Robert, O. LA Dreux's Cav. Co.A
Robert, P. SC 1st Arty. Co.F
Robert, Patrick LA C.S. Zouave Bn. Co.C
Robert, P.G. AL 2nd Inf. Chap.
Robert, P.G. Gen. & Staff Chap.
Robert, R.H. GA Siege Arty. 28th Bn. Co.K

Robert, R.M. KY 2nd Mtd.Inf. Co.H
Robert, Robert MS 18th Cav. Co.F
Robert, R.T. LA Inf.Crescent Regt. Co.H
Robert, Saathiel TX 28th Cav. Co.L
Robert, Samuel TN 16th (Logwood's) Cav. Co.I
Robert, Samuel H. LA 8th Inf. Co.H 1st Sgt.
Robert, S.J. GA Cav. 15th Bn. (St.Guards)
    Jones' Co.
Robert, T.H. TX 32nd Cav. Co.G
Robert, T.H. TX Cav. Wells' Regt. Co.K
Robert, Thomas W. FL Inf. 2nd Bn. Co.F Cpl.
Robert, T.W. LA Inf. Jeff Davis Regt. Co.F 1st
    Lt.
Robert, Ulysses M. GA 4th Inf. Co.E
Robert, Virgil GA Arty. 11th Bn. (Sumter Arty.)
    New Co.C
Robert, Virgil GA 9th Inf. Co.A
Robert, W. VA 46th Inf. Co.D
Robert, W.A. LA 18th Inf. 2nd Lt.
Robert, W.A. LA Inf.Cons. 18th Regt. & Yellow
    Jacket Bn. 2nd Lt.
Robert, W.C. GA Cav. 1st Bn.Res. Co.E
Robert, Whitmel P. MS 42nd Inf. Co.I Cpl.
Robert, William AL 8th Inf. Co.G
Robert, William LA Inf. 10th Bn. Co.H Capt.
Robert, William 1st Choctaw & Chickasaw
    Mtd.Rifles 2nd Co.C
Robert, William C. LA Hvy.Arty. 8th Bn. Co.3
Robert, William Arnaud LA 1st Cav. Co.A
Robert, William H. LA 39th Inf. Surg.
Robert, William H. VA 1st St.Res. Co.C
Robert, Wm. H. Gen. & Staff Surg.
Robert, William J. Stirman's Regt.S.S. Co.D 1st
    Lt.
Robert, W.S. LA Inf.Cons.Crescent Regt. Co.I
Robertes, Elijah L.J. MS 21st Inf. Co.K
Roberteson, J.H. AL 6th Cav. Co.E
Roberts, --- GA 8th Inf. Co.I
Roberts, --- LA 2nd Inf.
Roberts, --- MO St.Guard Capt.
Roberts, --- TX 33rd Cav. Co.G
Roberts, --- TX Cav. Baird's Regt. Co.E
Roberts, --- TX Cav. Good's Bn. Co.A
Roberts, --- TX Cav. McCord's Frontier Regt.
    Co.E
Roberts, --- TX Cav. McCord's Frontier Regt.
    Co.K
Roberts, A. AL 3rd Cav. Co.B
Roberts, A. AL 6th Inf. Co.I
Roberts, A. AL 8th Inf. Co.I
Roberts, A. AL 9th Inf. Co.G
Roberts, A. AL 21st Inf. Co.I
Roberts, A. AL Cp. of Instr. Talladega
Roberts, A. AR 3rd Cav. Co.E
Roberts, A. GA 59th Inf. Co.H
Roberts, A. LA 2nd Cav. Co.E
Roberts, A. LA 5th Cav. Co.C
Roberts, A. MS Arty. (Seven Stars.Arty.)
    Roberts' Co. 1st Sgt.
Roberts, A. MS Inf. 3rd Bn. (St.Troops) Co.H
Roberts, A. MS 26th Inf. Co.C
Roberts, A. MS 46th Inf. Co.F Cpl.
Roberts, A. MS 46th Inf. Co.G
Roberts, A. MS 46th Inf. Co.K 1st Sgt.
Roberts, A. MO Cav. Fristoe's Regt. Co.G
Roberts, A. MO Lt.Arty. Von Phul's Co.
Roberts, A. TX Cav. 3rd Regt.St.Troops Co.A

Roberts, A. TX 12th Cav. Co.A
Roberts, A. TX 29th Cav. Co.C Orderly
Roberts, A. VA 25th Cav. Co.B
Roberts, A. VA 59th Inf. 2nd Co.F
Roberts, A. Gillum's Regt. Co.F
Roberts, A.A. AR 15th Inf. Co.I Sgt.
Roberts, A.A. MS 18th Inf. Co.I Sgt.
Roberts, A.A. TN 48th (Nixon's) Inf. Co.F
Roberts, Aaron MO 1st Cav. Co.E
Roberts, Aaron MO 10th Cav. Co.B,A Lt.
Roberts, Aaron MO 1st & 4th Cons.Inf. Co.I
    Cpl.
Roberts, Aaron NC 6th Inf. Co.I
Roberts, Aaron A. MO 4th Inf. Co.D Cpl.
Roberts, Aaron K. GA 26th Inf. Co.A
Roberts, Aaron M. NC 64th Inf. Co.D
Roberts, A.B. GA 11th Inf. Co.F
Roberts, A.B. KY 13th Cav. Co.I
Roberts, A.B. TX 5th Inf. Co.F
Roberts, A.B. TX 21st Inf. Co.I Music.
Roberts, A.B. VA Cav. 36th Bn. Co.C
Roberts, Abel H. NC 50th Inf. Co.K
Roberts, Abell J. FL 4th Inf. Co.F
Roberts, Abner TX 4th Inf. Co.E
Roberts, Abner TX 20th Inf. Co.C
Roberts, Abner F. TN 14th Inf. Co.D
Roberts, Abraham MO 1st N.E. Cav. Co.M Sgt.
Roberts, Abraham VA 25th Cav. Co.B
Roberts, Abraham VA Mil. Scott Cty.
Roberts, Abram J. MS 44th Inf. Co.K
Roberts, Abram M. TX 1st (Yager's) Cav. Co.K
Roberts, Abram M. TX 6th Cav. Co.H
Roberts, Abram M. TX Cav. 8th (Taylor's) Bn.
    Co.B
Roberts, Absalom AL 38th Inf. Co.E
Roberts, Absalom TN Lt.Arty. Barry's Co.
Roberts, Absalum A. FL 6th Inf. Co.K
Roberts, Abselom V. GA 1st (Fannin's) Res.
    Co.H
Roberts, Absolum J. AL 19th Inf. Co.I
Roberts, A.C. FL 2nd Inf. Co.C Music.
Roberts, A.C. GA 11th Cav. Co.G
Roberts, A.C. MO 5th Cav. Co.I
Roberts, A.C. TN 53rd Inf. Co.D
Roberts, A. Clay MO Lt.Arty. 1st Field Btty.
Roberts, A.D. AR 36th Inf. Co.C
Roberts, A.D. AR 50th Mil. Co.A Sgt.
Roberts, Adam M. NC 16th Inf. Co.M 1st Lt.
Roberts, Adam N. VA Cav. 46th Bn. Co.B Cpl.
Roberts, A.E. AL 45th Inf. Co.K
Roberts, A.E. LA 2nd Cav. Co.E,K
Roberts, A.E. TX 12th Cav. Co.B
Roberts, A.G. GA Cav. 29th Bn. Co.G
Roberts, A.G. GA 55th Inf. Co.E
Roberts, A.G. TN 20th Inf. Co.G
Roberts, A.G. TX Cav. Border's Regt. Co.B
Roberts, Agrippa MS 5th Cav. Co.F
Roberts, Agrippa MS 4th Inf. Co.G
Roberts, Aggrippa P. GA 36th (Broyles') Inf.
    Co.H,A Capt.,ACS
Roberts, A.H. KY Franklin Cty. Adon's Co.
Roberts, A.H. MS 12th Inf.
Roberts, A.H. MO Cav. Fristoe's Regt. Co.C
Roberts, A.H. TX 20th Cav. Co.I Sgt.
Roberts, A.H. VA 34th Inf. Co.B
Roberts, A. Hance MO 8th Inf. Co.A
Roberts, A.J. AL 22nd Inf. Co.G

Roberts, A.J. AL 32nd Inf. Co.H
Roberts, A.J. AL 48th Inf. Co.I
Roberts, A.J. AR 17th (Lemoyne's) Inf. Co.E
Roberts, A.J. GA Arty. 11th Bn. (Sumter Arty.) Co.B Cpl.
Roberts, A.J. GA Lt.Arty. 12th Bn. Co.F
Roberts, A.J. GA 1st Inf. (St.Guards) Co.H Sgt.
Roberts, A.J. GA 3rd Res. Co.G Cpl.
Roberts, A.J. GA 5th Inf. Co.G
Roberts, A.J. GA Inf. 25th Bn. (Prov.Guard) Co.E
Roberts, A.J. GA 32nd Inf. Co.I
Roberts, A.J. GA 63rd Inf. Co.C
Roberts, A.J. KY 5th Mtd.Inf. Co.C
Roberts, A.J. LA 3rd (Wingfield's) Cav. Co.I
Roberts, A.J. LA 16th Inf. Co.A
Roberts, A.J. MS 2nd St.Cav. Co.E 1st Lt.
Roberts, A.J. MS 7th Cav. Co.E
Roberts, A.J. MS 22nd Inf. Hosp.Stew.
Roberts, A.J. SC 1st (Butler's) Inf. Co.A
Roberts, A.J. SC 17th Inf. Co.K
Roberts, A.J. TN 44th (Cons.) Inf. Co.G
Roberts, A.J. TX Cav. Martin's Regt. Co.H
Roberts, A.J. TX Inf. 2nd St.Troops Co.B
Roberts, A.J. Gen. & Staff Asst.Surg.
Roberts, A.L. AR Inf. Cocke's Regt. Co.H
Roberts, A.L. MS 3rd Cav. Co.H
Roberts, A.L. NC Hvy.Arty. 1st Bn. Co.A
Roberts, Albert GA Inf. Exempts Roberts' Co. Capt.
Roberts, Albert A. TN 54th Inf. Co.H
Roberts, Albert C. GA 35th Inf. Co.H Sgt.
Roberts, Albert C. TN 20th Inf. Co.A Capt.
Roberts, Albert G. FL 7th Inf. Co.F
Roberts, Albert G. VA 5th Inf. Co.E
Roberts, Alex. SC 17th Inf. Co.B
Roberts, Alex VA 1st (Farinholt's) Res. Co.G
Roberts, Alexander GA 3rd Res. Co.G
Roberts, Alexander LA 5th Cav. Co.B
Roberts, Alexander MS Arty. (Seven Stars Arty.) Roberts' Co. 1st Sgt.
Roberts, Alexander MS 16th Inf. Co.H
Roberts, Alexander C. MS 29th Inf. Co.G Lt.
Roberts, Alexander G. KY 5th Mtd.Inf. Co.A Capt.
Roberts, Alexander K. MO Cav. 3rd Bn. Co.D
Roberts, Alexander K. MO 10th Cav. Co.H
Roberts, Alex H. MS Cav. 24th Bn. Co.C
Roberts, Alford VA 8th Cav. Co.K
Roberts, Alfred AR 27th Inf. Co.E
Roberts, Alfred MS 9th Cav. Co.A
Roberts, Alfred MO 5th Cav. Co.C
Roberts, Alfred MO 6th Inf. Co.B
Roberts, Alfred NC 6th Cav. (65th St.Troops) Co.A,F
Roberts, Alfred TN 53rd Inf. Co.A
Roberts, Alfred TN 59th Mtd.Inf. Co.C
Roberts, Alfred TX 19th Cav. Co.G
Roberts, Alfred E. TN Lt.Arty. Kain's Co.
Roberts, Alfred E. TN 37th Inf. Co.F
Roberts, Alfred J. MS 1st (Johnston's) Inf. Co.I Hosp.Stew.
Roberts, Alfred R. MS 2nd Inf. Co.C
Roberts, Alfred W. TN 18th Inf. Co.H
Roberts, Allen AL 5th Inf. New Co.I
Roberts, Allen FL 9th Cav. Co.A
Roberts, Allen MS Inf. 3rd Bn. Co.G

Roberts, Allen NC 3rd Arty. (40th St.Troops) Co.H
Roberts, Allen NC Lt.Arty. 13th Bn. Co.F
Roberts, Allen G. TX Cav. Morgan's Regt. Co.A
Roberts, Allison KY 13th Cav. Co.G
Roberts, Alvin P. VA 19th Inf. Co.H
Roberts, A.M. MO 16th Inf. Co.E
Roberts, Amos, Jr. NC Inf. 2nd Bn. Co.H
Roberts, Amos J. NC Inf. 2nd Bn. Co.H
Roberts, Amsted D. KY 1st Bn.Mtd.Rifles Co.D
Roberts, Anderson FL 2nd Cav. Co.F
Roberts, Anderson GA Cav. 1st Bn.Res. McKinney's Co.
Roberts, Anderson NC 6th Inf. Co.K
Roberts, Anderson G. AL 12th Inf. Co.E
Roberts, Andrea J. FL 8th Inf. Co.I
Roberts, Andrew AR Cav. Harrell's Bn. Co.D
Roberts, Andrew GA 6th Inf. Co.A
Roberts, Andrew MS 2nd Part.Rangers Co.E
Roberts, Andrew J. GA 5th Res. Co.I
Roberts, Andrew J. MO 1st N.E. Cav. Co.H
Roberts, Andrew J. MO 4th Cav. Co.G
Roberts, Andrew J. NC 6th Inf. Co.B 1st Sgt.
Roberts, Andrew J. NC 16th Inf. Co.B
Roberts, Andrew J. NC 16th Inf. Co.C 1st Lt.
Roberts, Andrew J. TN 39th Mtd.Inf. Co.F
Roberts, Andrew J. TX 16th Cav. Co.H
Roberts, Andrew J. VA 3rd Cav. & Inf.St.Line Co.A
Roberts, Andrew S. FL 11th Inf. Co.I
Roberts, Anthony KY Lt.Arty. Cobb's Co.
Roberts, Anthony KY 4th Mtd.Inf. Co.C
Roberts, A.P. GA Inf. QM Dept.
Roberts, A.P. MS 4th Inf. Co.B
Roberts, A.P. TN 42nd Inf. 2nd Co.H
Roberts, A.P. TX 28th Cav. Co.E
Roberts, A.R. GA 8th Inf. (St.Guards) Co.E
Roberts, Arad F. VA Mil. Grayson Cty.
Roberts, Arch TX 3rd Cav. Co.H
Roberts, Armsted D. KY 3rd Bn.Mtd.Rifles Co.F
Roberts, Arthur AL 24th Inf. Co.H
Roberts, Arthur FL 1st Cav. Co.A Capt.
Roberts, Arthur GA 47th Inf. Co.D
Roberts, Arthurs L. VA 39th Inf. Co.D
Roberts, A.S. GA 54th Inf. Co.D Capt.
Roberts, A.S. MS 41st Inf. Co.I
Roberts, A.S. SC 4th Cav. Co.F
Roberts, A.S. SC Arty. Melchers' Co. (Co.B,German Arty.)
Roberts, A.S. SC Lt.Arty. M. Ward's Co. (Waccamaw Lt.Arty.)
Roberts, A.S. SC Manigault's Bn.Vol. Co.A
Roberts, A.S. TX 4th Inf. Co.B
Roberts, Asa J. AL 24th Inf. ACS
Roberts, Asa J. Gen. & Staff Capt.,Comsy.
Roberts, Asbury VA 31st Mil. Co.H
Roberts, Ashley AR Cav. 1st Bn. (Stirman's) Co.G
Roberts, Ashley G. GA 4th Inf. Co.G
Roberts, Ashwell NC 6th Inf. Co.I
Roberts, A.T. MS Cav. Gartley's Co. (Yazoo Rangers)
Roberts, A.T. TN 42nd Inf. Co.C
Roberts, A.T. 4th Conf.Inf. Co.H
Roberts, Atlas K. MS 2nd Inf. Co.H 2nd Lt.
Roberts, Augusta TN 2nd Cav. Co.A
Roberts, Augustus GA 22nd Inf. Co.F

Roberts, Augustus B. KY 4th Mtd.Inf. Co.D Sgt.
Roberts, Augustus F. VA 39th Inf. Co.K
Roberts, Augustus H. GA 25th Inf. Co.F
Roberts, Augustus M. GA Phillips' Legion Co.C Cpl.
Roberts, Austin MS Cav. 17th Bn. Co.E
Roberts, A.V. AR 23rd Inf. Co.K
Roberts, A.W. GA 11th Cav. Co.E
Roberts, A.W. GA Cherokee Legion (St.Guards) Co.E
Roberts, A.W. LA 13th Bn. (Part.Rangers) Co.B
Roberts, A.W. LA 4th Inf. Co.C 2nd Lt.
Roberts, A.W. MO St.Guard
Roberts, A.W. NC 28th Inf. Co.F
Roberts, Axom MS Cav. 24th Bn. Co.A
Roberts, B. AR 1st (Monroe's) Cav. Co.L
Roberts, B. MS Cav. 3rd Bn. (Ashcraft's) Co.C
Roberts, B. MO St.Guard
Roberts, B. MO St.Guard Col.,Comsy.
Roberts, Baker H. AL 28th Inf. Co.H
Roberts, Baker L. AL 5th Bn.Vol. Co.A Sgt.Maj.
Roberts, Barcley M. MS 17th Inf. Co.G Sgt.
Roberts, B.D. GA Cav. 29th Bn. Co.B
Roberts, Ben. NC Walker's Bn. Thomas' Legion Co.A
Roberts, Ben TX 3rd Cav. Co.E Jr.2nd Lt.
Roberts, Ben F. SC 1st (McCreary's) Inf. Co.E
Roberts, Benjamin AL 3rd Cav. Co.E
Roberts, Benjamin AL 3rd Res. Co.C
Roberts, Benjamin AL Talladega Cty.Res. I. Stone's Co.
Roberts, Benjamin MS Inf. (Res.) Berry's Co.
Roberts, Benjamin NC Inf. 2nd Bn. Co.H Cpl.
Roberts, Benjamin NC 14th Inf. Co.A
Roberts, Benjamin NC 64th Inf. Co.C
Roberts, Benjamin NC Walker's Bn. Thomas' Legion Co.A
Roberts, Benjamin TX 15th Cav. Co.G
Roberts, Benjamin TX 25th Cav. Co.H
Roberts, Benjamin A. VA 23rd Inf. Co.K Sgt.
Roberts, Benjamin C. GA Hvy.Arty. 22nd Bn. Co.D
Roberts, Benjamin C. VA 16th Inf. Co.D
Roberts, Benjamin D. MS 1st Lt.Arty. Co.E
Roberts, Benjamin D. VA 10th Cav. Co.A
Roberts, Benjamin D. VA 7th Inf. Co.K
Roberts, Benjamin F. FL 8th Inf. Co.I Capt.
Roberts, Benjamin F. GA Cav. 7th Bn. (St.Guards) Co.C
Roberts, Benjamin F. GA 4th Inf. Co.H
Roberts, Benjamin F. GA 27th Inf. Co.F
Roberts, Benjamin F. GA 43rd Inf. Co.I Lt.
Roberts, Benjamin F. MS 11th (Perrin's) Cav. Co.K
Roberts, Benjamin F. MO 16th Inf. Co.C
Roberts, Benjamin F. SC 5th Res. Co.B
Roberts, Benjamin F. TN 10th & 11th (Cons.) Cav. Co.B
Roberts, Benjamin F. VA 1st Bn.Res. Co.D
Roberts, Benjamin Franklin NC 22nd Inf. Co.E
Roberts, Benjamin G. MD Arty. 4th Btty. 2nd Lt.
Roberts, Benjamin J. GA 49th Inf. Co.I
Roberts, Benjamin L. VA 29th Inf. Co.A
Roberts, Benjamin M. FL 3rd Inf. Co.D

Roberts, Benjamin M. NC 2nd Arty. (36th
    St.Troops) Co.C
Roberts, Benjamin M. Inf. School of Pract.
    Powell's Command Powell's Detach.
Roberts, Ben. S. MO 1st Inf. Co.H 1st Lt.
Roberts, Benjamin W. GA 1st Reg. Co.L
Roberts, Bennett VA 49th Inf. Co.I
Roberts, Benton NC 6th Sr.Res. Co.E
Roberts, Benton NC 53rd Inf. Co.F
Roberts, Berry FL 4th Inf. Co.E Sgt.
Roberts, Berry TN 17th Inf. Co.I
Roberts, Berry H. TN 22nd (Barteau's) Cav.
    Co.F
Roberts, Bethel FL Inf. 2nd Bn. Co.F
Roberts, Beverly W. AL 41st Inf. Co.H
Roberts, B.F. AR 45th Cav. Co.D
Roberts, B.F. AR 13th Inf. Co.F
Roberts, B.F. AR Inf. Cocke's Regt. Co.E Cpl.
Roberts, B.F. GA Siege Arty. 28th Bn. Co.D
Roberts, B.F. GA 42nd Inf. Co.F
Roberts, B.F. GA 44th Inf. Co.D
Roberts, B.F. GA 65th Inf. Co.K
Roberts, B.F. GA Cherokee Legion (St.Guards)
    Co.K
Roberts, B.F. MS 36th Inf. Co.D
Roberts, B.F. MS 46th Inf. Co.I
Roberts, B.F. SC Lt.Arty. 3rd (Palmetto) Bn.
    Co.A,H Bugler
Roberts, B.F. SC 1st St.Troops Co.F
Roberts, B.F. TN 7th (Duckworth's) Cav. Co.I
Roberts, B.F. TN 12th Inf. Co.D
Roberts, B.F. TN 12th (Cons.) Inf. Co.E
Roberts, B.F. TN 24th Inf. Co.B
Roberts, B.F. TN 33rd Inf. Co.H
Roberts, B.F. VA 3rd Res. Co.C
Roberts, B.F. Eng.,CSA 1st Lt.
Roberts, B.F. 2nd Cherokee Mtd.Vol. Co.G
Roberts, B.H. TN Cav. 7th Bn. (Bennett's) Co.D
Roberts, Bird AL 18th Inf. Co.G
Roberts, B.J. GA Arty. Fraser's Btty.
Roberts, B.J. NC 28th Inf. Co.C
Roberts, B.J. TN 31st Inf. Co.A Capt.
Roberts, Bluford GA 13th Cav. Co.E
Roberts, Bluford MS 2nd St.Cav. Co.K,L
Roberts, B.M. AR Lt.Arty. 5th Btty.
Roberts, B.M. GA 11th Cav. Co.G Jr.2nd Lt.
Roberts, B.M. NC Lt.Arty. 13th Bn. Co.C
Roberts, B.M. NC 2nd Inf. Co.A
Roberts, Boas MO 9th (Elliott's) Cav. Co.G
Roberts, Bolin KY 14th Cav. Co.B Sgt.
Roberts, Bonaparte KY 5th Mtd.Inf. Co.I
Roberts, Bonaparte KY 9th Mtd.Inf. Co.I
Roberts, Bowlin Emory KY 6th Cav. Co.H
    Capt.
Roberts, B.P. MS Cav. 3rd Bn.Res. Co.C Jr.1st
    Lt.
Roberts, B.P. MO 1st Inf. Co.K
Roberts, B.P. MO 1st & 4th Cons.Inf. Co.K
Roberts, Bright NC 3rd Cav. (41st St.Troops)
    Co.E
Roberts, Bright NC 5th Cav. (63rd St.Troops)
    Co.E
Roberts, Brison GA 34th Inf. Co.A
Roberts, Bryan J. FL 4th Inf. Co.F
Roberts, B.S. 1st Conf.Inf. 2nd Co.H
Roberts, B. Thomas MS 13th Inf. Co.C
Roberts, Bud KY 2nd (Duke's) Cav. Co.H

Roberts, B.W. GA 11th Cav. Co.B
Roberts, B.W. GA Hvy.Arty. 22nd Bn. Co.A
    1st Lt.
Roberts, B.W. GA Lt.Arty. 14th Bn. Co.F Lt.
Roberts, B.W. GA 60th Inf. 1st Co.A Lt.
Roberts, B.W. KY 1st (Helm's) Cav. New Co.A
Roberts, B.W. Gen. & Staff 1st Lt.,Dr.M.
Roberts, Bynum MS 26th Inf. Co.C
Roberts, Bynum P. MS 35th Inf. Co.A Sgt.
Roberts, Byrd AL 43rd Inf. Co.K
Roberts, Byrd GA 41st Inf. Co.F
Roberts, C. AR 6th Inf. Co.E
Roberts, C. LA 5th Inf. Co.E
Roberts, C. MO 6th Cav. Co.C
Roberts, C. TX 15th Inf. 1st Co.E
Roberts, C. VA 30th Inf. Co.F
Roberts, C.A. AR 1st (Dobbin's) Cav. Co.A
Roberts, C.A. LA 4th Inf. Co.F Cpl.
Roberts, Caleb KY 13th Cav. Co.C Cpl.
Roberts, Caleb D. KY 5th Mtd.Inf. Co.D,F
Roberts, Callie GA Arty. 11th Bn. (Sumter Arty.)
    Co.D,B
Roberts, Calvin GA 62nd Cav. Co.L
Roberts, Calvin NC 15th Inf. Co.H
Roberts, Calvin VA 14th Inf. Co.A
Roberts, Calvin VA 59th Mil. Hunter's Co.
Roberts, Calvin E. GA 45th Inf. Co.C
Roberts, Calvit MS Cav. 24th Bn. Maj.
Roberts, Calvit MS Arty. (Seven Stars Arty.)
    Roberts' Co. Capt.
Roberts, Carl LA Inf. McLean's Co.
Roberts, Carter H. VA 25th Cav. Co.B
Roberts, Carter H. VA Inf. 21st Bn. 2nd Co.C
Roberts, Cary VA 115th Mil. Co.C
Roberts, C.B. AL 43rd Inf. Co.C
Roberts, C.B. GA 11th Inf. Co.G
Roberts, C.B. SC 1st St.Troops Co.K
Roberts, C.B. SC 3rd Res. Co.B 3rd Lt.
Roberts, C.C. KY 9th Cav. Co.G
Roberts, C.C. SC 5th Inf. 1st Co.I
Roberts, C.C. TX Cav. Terry's Regt. Co.B
Roberts, C.C.W. TX 35th (Brown's) Cav. Co.G
Roberts, C.E. GA 14th Inf. Co.C
Roberts, C.E. TX 1st Hvy.Arty. 2nd Co.A
Roberts, C.F. GA Inf. 27th Bn. Co.A
Roberts, C.F. MS 5th Cav. Co.G Sgt.
Roberts, C.F. TX Cav. Waller's Regt. Co.D
Roberts, C.H. GA 29th Inf. Co.B
Roberts, C.H. LA Cav. 1st Regt. Co.I
Roberts, C.H. MS 12th Inf.
Roberts, C.H. NC 18th Inf. Co.G
Roberts, Charles AL 18th Inf. 1st Lt.
Roberts, Charles LA 7th Inf. Co.D
Roberts, Charles MS Lt.Arty. Stanford's Co.
    Cpl.
Roberts, Charles NC 1st Arty. (10th St.Troops)
    Co.A
Roberts, Charles NC 32nd Inf. Co.B,C Cook
Roberts, Charles TN 50th Inf. Co.F
Roberts, Charles VA 2nd Cav. Co.D,G
Roberts, Charles VA 22nd Inf. Co.E Cpl.
Roberts, Charles VA 63rd Inf. Co.A
Roberts, Charles Morgan's Co.A,CSA
Roberts, Charles A. NC 3rd Cav. (41st
    St.Troops) Co.K
Roberts, Charles A. NC 17th Inf. (1st Org.)
    Co.K

Roberts, Charles B. GA 35th Inf. Co.G
Roberts, Charles B. LA 1st (Nelligan's) Inf.
    Co.G Cpl.
Roberts, Charles C. NC 26th Inf. Co.H Music.
Roberts, Charles E. NC 1st Inf. (6 mo. '61) Co.F
    Music.
Roberts, Charles E. NC 2nd Bn.Loc.Def.Troops
    Co.C 2nd Lt.
Roberts, Charles G. MS 5th Inf. (St.Troops)
    Co.D
Roberts, Charles J. TN 18th Inf. Co.C
Roberts, Charles M. GA Inf. 1st Loc.Troops
    (Augusta) Co.C
Roberts, Charles M. GA 57th Inf. Co.I
Roberts, Charles M. MS 12th Cav. Co.A,H
Roberts, Charles M. NC 25th Inf. Co.K Capt.
Roberts, Charles P. GA 1st (Ramsey's) Inf. Co.D
Roberts, Charles P. GA 2nd Bn.S.S. Co.C 1st
    Lt.,Adj.
Roberts, Charles P. GA 5th Inf. Co.N
Roberts, Charles R. VA 11th Inf. Co.E
Roberts, Charles T. MS 22nd Inf. Co.B
Roberts, Charles W. GA 41st Inf. Co.A
Roberts, Chris. C. AL Rives' Supp.Force 9th
    Congr.Dist.
Roberts, Christopher C. MS 1st Lt.Arty. Co.D
Roberts, Cicero AL 11th Cav. Co.I,K
Roberts, Claibourn VA 25th Cav. Co.B
Roberts, Clavin NC Unassign.Conscr.
Roberts, Clay AL 54th Inf. ACS,Sgt.
Roberts, C.M. MS 7th Inf. Co.G
Roberts, C.M. NC 1st Cav. Co.E,B 2nd Lt.
Roberts, C.M. NC Cav. 14th Bn. Maj.
Roberts, C.N. Gen. & Staff Capt.,Asst.Comsy.
Roberts, C.O. FL Fernandez's Mtd.Co. (Supply
    Force) Sgt.
Roberts, Columbus KY 4th Mtd.Inf. Co.E
Roberts, Columbus 1st Cherokee Mtd.Vol. 2nd
    Co.H
Roberts, Columbus W. TX 13th Vol. 2nd Co.G
Roberts, Connel MO Cav. Hicks' Co.
Roberts, Connell MO 1st N.E. Cav.
Roberts, Cornelious FL 11th Inf. Co.D
Roberts, Cornelius FL Inf. 2nd Bn. Co.F
Roberts, Cornelius B. TX 18th Cav. Co.D
Roberts, Cornelius H. GA 35th Inf. Co.H
Roberts, Cornelius H. TX 27th Cav. Co.C
    Bvt.2nd Lt.
Roberts, Cornelius L. GA 42nd Inf. Co.K,C
Roberts, Corner FL 8th Inf. Co.I
Roberts, C.P. GA Cav. 2nd Bn. Co.C
Roberts, C.P. GA 5th Cav. Co.E
Roberts, C.P. TX Cav. McCord's Frontier Regt.
    Co.E Cpl.
Roberts, C.R. AL 48th Inf.
Roberts, C.R. AR 3rd Inf. Co.K
Roberts, C.R. TN 38th Inf. Co.C
Roberts, C.R. TX 7th Inf. Co.H
Roberts, C.T. MS 5th Inf. Co.C Sgt.
Roberts, C.T. TX Cav. Terry's Regt. Co.F
Roberts, C.T. VA 59th Inf. 2nd Co.A
Roberts, C.W. TN 24th Inf. Co.E
Roberts, C.W. TX 11th Cav. Co.G
Roberts, C. Wesley MS 12th Inf. Co.B
Roberts, D. FL Res. Poe's Co.
Roberts, D. GA Arty. St.Troops Pruden's Btty.
Roberts, D. MS 3rd Cav. Co.H

Roberts, D. MO 9th Inf. Co.G
Roberts, D. SC 16th Inf. Co.C
Roberts, D. TN 19th & 20th (Cons.) Cav. Co.D
Roberts, D.A. AL 8th (Hatch's) Cav. Co.C
Roberts, D.A. SC 2nd Rifles Co.B
Roberts, Daniel AL 9th (Malone's) Cav. Co.D
Roberts, Daniel AL Cp. of Instr. Talladega
Roberts, Daniel GA Arty. Maxwell's Reg. Lt.Btty.
Roberts, Daniel GA 1st Reg. Co.D
Roberts, Daniel GA 50th Inf. Co.C
Roberts, Daniel GA 52nd Inf. Co.H
Roberts, Daniel NC 45th Inf. Co.A
Roberts, Daniel NC 62nd Inf. Co.A
Roberts, Daniel NC Inf. Thomas Legion Co.I
Roberts, Daniel TN Cav. 1st Bn. (McNairy's) Co.D
Roberts, Daniel TN Cav. 16th Bn. (Neal's) Co.F
Roberts, Daniel TN 22nd (Barteau's) Cav. Co.B
Roberts, Daniel TN 60th Mtd.Inf. Co.K
Roberts, Daniel VA Cav. 37th Bn. Co.I
Roberts, Daniel B. AL 6th Inf. Co.G
Roberts, Daniel B. VA 4th Inf. Co.E
Roberts, Daniel F. VA Mil. Grayson Cty.
Roberts, Daniel J. GA 7th Inf. Co.H Sgt.
Roberts, Daniel K. MS 20th Inf. Co.H
Roberts, Daniel L. FL 4th Inf. Co.G
Roberts, Daniel L. NC 2nd Arty. (36th St.Troops) Co.G Sgt.
Roberts, Daniel M. VA 1st Cav. Co.F
Roberts, Daniel W. TX 36th Cav. Co.K
Roberts, Darin H. GA 51st Inf. Co.G
Roberts, Darius SC 16th Inf. Co.K
Roberts, David AL Lt.Arty. Tarrant's Btty.
Roberts, David AL 30th Inf. Co.B
Roberts, David AL Pris.Guard Freeman's Co.
Roberts, David FL 1st Cav. Co.A
Roberts, David FL 1st Cav. Co.E
Roberts, David FL 11th Inf. Co.G
Roberts, David GA Arty. Lumpkin's Co.
Roberts, David MO 5th Cav. Co.A
Roberts, David NC Cav. 5th Bn. Co.A
Roberts, David NC 31st Inf. Co.D
Roberts, David NC 64th Inf. Co.A
Roberts, David SC 2nd Inf. Co.H
Roberts, David SC 4th St.Troops Co.G
Roberts, David SC 9th Inf. Co.B
Roberts, David 1st Creek Mtd.Vol. Co.F
Roberts, David A. AL 34th Inf. Co.B
Roberts, David A. FL 10th Inf. Co.C,I
Roberts, David B. FL 8th Inf. Co.F Sgt.
Roberts, David B. LA 21st (Kennedy's) Inf. Co.F
Roberts, David C. GA 23rd Inf. Co.I Cpl.
Roberts, David C. NC 6th Inf. Co.B Sgt.
Roberts, David C. TX 13th Vol. 1st Co.B Music.
Roberts, David C. VA 48th Inf. Co.I
Roberts, David F. GA 40th Inf. Co.E Sgt.
Roberts, David F. VA Mil. Grayson Cty.
Roberts, David H. NC 26th Inf. Co.I
Roberts, David J. VA 21st Inf. Co.C Cpl.
Roberts, David L. Conf.Cav. Wood's Regt. Co.I
Roberts, David M. GA Cav. 19th Bn. Co.B Sgt.
Roberts, David M. GA 10th Inf. Co.G
Roberts, David M. 10th Conf.Cav. Co.G 2nd Lt.
Roberts, David O. GA 44th Inf. Co.I
Roberts, David P. MO 8th Cav. Co.B,F

Roberts, David S. SC Inf. 7th Bn. (Enfield Rifles) Co.H
Roberts, David T. AL Cp. of Instr. Talladega
Roberts, David T. NC 64th Inf. Co.C
Roberts, David W. KY 5th Mtd.Inf. Co.C
Roberts, David W. NC 1st Arty. (10th St.Troops) Co.H
Roberts, D.B. AL 26th Inf. Co.C
Roberts, D.B. AL Cp. of Instr. Talladega
Roberts, D.B. GA Cav. 2nd Bn. Co.B
Roberts, D.B. GA 5th Cav. Co.F
Roberts, D.B. GA 2nd Inf. Co.D
Roberts, D.B. FL 1st (Res.) Inf. Co.I Cpl.
Roberts, D. Burwell GA 62nd Cav. Co.L
Roberts, D. Burwell VA 24th Cav. Co.I
Roberts, D. Burwell 8th (Dearing's) Conf.Cav. Co.D
Roberts, D.C. MS 3rd (St.Troops) Cav. Co.E
Roberts, D.C. MS 36th Inf. Co.E
Roberts, D.C. TX 24th Cav. Co.I
Roberts, D.C. TX 35th (Brown's) Cav. Co.A Music.
Roberts, D.C. TX Cav. Terry's Regt. Co.I
Roberts, D.E. GA 12th (Wright's) Cav. (St.Guards) Stubbs' Co. 1st Lt.
Roberts, D.E. TN 7th (Duckworth's) Cav. Co.F
Roberts, D.E. TN 37th Inf. Co.H
Roberts, D.E. TN 51st Inf. Co.H Sgt.
Roberts, D.E. TN 51st (Cons.) Inf. Co.D
Roberts, Dearing J. Gen. & Staff Surg.
Roberts, Deering J. TN 1st (Feild's) Inf. Co.C
Roberts, Deering J. TN 20th Inf. Asst.Surg.
Roberts, Dempsey GA 55th Inf. Co.F
Roberts, Dennis AL 49th Inf. Co.A
Roberts, D.H. AR 5th Inf.
Roberts, D.H. 3rd Conf.Inf. Co.E
Roberts, D.I. Cheatham's Div. Surg.
Roberts, Dixon H. MS 17th Inf. Co.C
Roberts, D.J. GA Phillips' Legion Co.B
Roberts, D.J. NC Lt.Arty. 13th Bn. Co.E
Roberts, D. Jasper MS Lt.Arty. Stanford's Co.
Roberts, D.K. MS 1st (King's) Inf. (St.Troops) Co.I
Roberts, D.K. MS Inf. 1st Bn.St.Trops (30 days '64) Co.B
Roberts, D.L. AL 33rd Inf. Co.K
Roberts, D.M. AL Cav. Hardie's Bn.Res. Co.F
Roberts, D.M. AL 55th Vol. Co.I 1st Sgt.
Roberts, D.M. GA Cav. 12th Bn. (St.Guards) Co.C
Roberts, D.M. GA 52nd Inf. Co.D Cpl.
Roberts, D.M. NC 1st Jr.Res. Co.B
Roberts, D.M. NC 8th Inf. Co.D
Roberts, D.M. VA 16th Cav. Co.D
Roberts, D.M. VA Cav. Ferguson's Bn. Morris' Co.
Roberts, D.O. GA 52nd Inf. Co.B
Roberts, Don C. MO 6th Inf. Surg.
Roberts, Don Carlos MS 31st Inf. Maj.,Surg.
Roberts, Don Carlos Gen. & Staff Surg.
Roberts, Dorcas NC 33rd Inf. Co.G Laundress
Roberts, D.P. AL 25th Inf. Co.I
Roberts, D.P. MO Inf. 5th Regt.St.Guard Co.A
Roberts, D.R. AL 13th Bn.Part.Rangers Co.A
Roberts, D.R. TN 22nd (Barteau's) Cav. 1st Co.H
Roberts, Drury H. GA 13th Cav. Co.I

Roberts, Drury H. GA 34th Inf. Co.E
Roberts, D.S.T. MO 11th Inf. Co.K
Roberts, D.T. TX Cav. Terry's Regt. Co.E
Roberts, Duke M. SC Arty. Gregg's Co. (McQueen Lt.Arty.)
Roberts, Duke M. SC Arty. Manigault's Bn. 1st Co.C
Roberts, Duncan MS 20th Inf. Co.I
Roberts, Duncan 15th Conf.Cav. Co.I
Roberts, D.W. SC 1st Regt. Charleston Guard Co.G
Roberts, D.W. TN 51st Inf. Co.H
Roberts, D.W. TX 34th Cav. Co.G
Roberts, D.W. VA 58th Inf. Co.B
Roberts, E. AL Cav. Murphy's Bn. Co.B
Roberts, E. AL Inf. 2nd Regt. Co.L
Roberts, E. AL 24th Inf. Co.K
Roberts, E. AL 31st Inf. Co.C
Roberts, E. AR 15th (Johnson's) Inf. Co.B
Roberts, E. AR Inf. Hardy's Regt. Co.I,A
Roberts, E. GA Lt.Arty. Croft's Btty. (Columbus Arty.)
Roberts, E. GA 8th Inf. Co.I
Roberts, E. KY 3rd Bn.Mtd.Rifles Co.B
Roberts, E. KY 5th Cav. Co.F
Roberts, E. MS 2nd Cav.Res. Co.A
Roberts, E. MS 3rd Inf. Co.E 2nd Lt.
Roberts, E. MS 23rd Inf. Co.E 2nd Lt.
Roberts, E. MS Cav. 24th Bn. Maj.
Roberts, E. TX Cav. Terry's Regt. Co.H
Roberts, E. TX 1st Hvy.Arty. Co.A
Roberts, E. TX 14th Inf. Co.H
Roberts, E. TX 15th Inf. 1st Co.E
Roberts, E. Trans-MS Conf.Cav. 1st Bn. Co.D
Roberts, E. 15th Conf.Cav. Co.G
Roberts, E.A. LA 1st Cav. Co.K
Roberts, E.B. MS Scouts Montgomery's Co.
Roberts, E.B. TX Waul's Legion Co.H
Roberts, E.B. Sig.Corps,CSA
Roberts, Ebenezer MO 1st N.E. Cav.
Roberts, Ebenezer TX 19th Cav. Co.D
Roberts, E.C. MS 2nd Cav.
Roberts, E.C. MS Cav. 4th Bn. Co.A Cpl.
Roberts, E.C. 8th (Wade's) Conf.Cav. Co.C
Roberts, E.D. MS 2nd Part.Rangers Co.L
Roberts, E.D. TN Inf. 154th Sr.Regt. Co.I
Roberts, Ed VA Cav. Mosby's Regt. (Part. Rangers) Co.E
Roberts, Edmond NC Walker's Bn. Thomas' Legion Co.A
Roberts, Edmond F. NC 54th Inf. Co.E 1st Sgt.
Roberts, Edmund NC 51st Inf. Co.G
Roberts, Edmund C. SC 2nd Rifles Co.A
Roberts, Ed. W. LA 7th Inf. Co.I
Roberts, Edward AL 1st Regt.Conscr. Co.A
Roberts, Edward AL Pris.Guard Freeman's Co. Drum Maj.
Roberts, Edward AL Conscr. Echols' Co.
Roberts, Edward KY 1st (Butler's) Cav. Co.G
Roberts, Edward LA 10th Inf. Co.E
Roberts, Edward LA 21st (Patton's) Inf. Co.F Cpl.
Roberts, Edward MS 3rd Inf. Co.E
Roberts, Edward MS 4th Inf. Co.E
Roberts, Edward TN Lt.Arty. Rice's Btty.
Roberts, Edward TX 22nd Cav. Co.E
Roberts, Edward TX 34th Cav. Co.G

Roberts, Edward 1st Conf.Inf. Co.A, 2nd Co.C
Roberts, Edward A. VA 44th Inf. Co.I 1st Lt.
Roberts, Edward B. NC 5th Cav. (63rd
  St.Troops) Co.B 1st Sgt.
Roberts, Edward B. NC 7th Inf. Co.I Capt.
Roberts, Edward B. NC 24th Inf. Co.A 2nd Lt.
Roberts, Edward G. SC 16th Inf. Co.I Capt.
Roberts, Edward L. VA 4th Inf. Co.D Sgt.
Roberts, Edward M. GA 15th Inf. Co.C
Roberts, Edward M. NC 14th Inf. Co.K Sgt.
Roberts, Edward T. MS 35th Inf. Co.B
Roberts, Edward W. MO 1st N.E. Cav. Co.A
Roberts, Edwin KY 7th Cav. Co.E
Roberts, Edwin NC Cav. 5th Bn. Co.A
Roberts, Edwin NC 6th Cav. (65th St.Troops)
  Co.A
Roberts, Edwin B. TX 19th Cav. Co.F
Roberts, Edwin W. KY 12th Cav. Co.C Cpl.
Roberts, E.F. MO 4th Inf. Co.D
Roberts, E.F. TX 9th Cav. Co.B
Roberts, E.G. SC 16th & 24th (Cons.) Inf. Co.D
  Capt.
Roberts, E.H. GA 51st Inf. Co.G
Roberts, E.H. TN 6th (Wheeler's) Cav. Co.D
Roberts, E.H. TX 3rd Cav. Co.E Cpl.
Roberts, E.J. AL 10th Inf. Co.F
Roberts, E.J. AL 25th Inf. Co.F
Roberts, E.J. AR 13th Inf. Co.F
Roberts, E.J. AR Inf. Cocke's Regt. Co.E
Roberts, E.J. MO 7th Cav. Co.K Cpl.
Roberts, E.K.S. TN 2nd (Ashby's) Cav. Co.A
Roberts, E.K.S. TN Cav. 5th Bn. (McClellan's)
  Co.A
Roberts, E.L. KY 2nd Mtd.Inf. Co.A
Roberts, Elberry GA Siege Arty. Campbell's
  Ind.Co.
Roberts, Elbert SC 5th St.Troops Co.A
Roberts, Elbert SC 6th Res. Co.B
Roberts, Elbert TN 43rd Inf. Co.H Drum.
Roberts, Elbert F. NC 29th Inf. Co.D
Roberts, Elbert H. VA 56th Inf. Co.G
Roberts, Eli AL 36th Inf. Co.H
Roberts, Eli NC 2nd Cav. (19th St.Troops) Co.A
Roberts, Eli TX 15th Cav. Co.H
Roberts, Eli A. NC 37th Inf. Co.F
Roberts, Eli A. SC 1st (Butler's) Inf. Co.C
Roberts, Elias AL 24th Inf. Co.G
Roberts, Elias GA 6th Inf. Co.A
Roberts, Elias GA 9th Inf. Co.H
Roberts, Elias LA 9th Inf.
Roberts, Elias E. MS Lt.Arty. Stanford's Co.
Roberts, Elias E. SC 16th Inf. Co.K
Roberts, Eli F. KY 3rd Mtd.Inf. Co.E
Roberts, Elijah KY 8th Cav. Co.F Cpl.
Roberts, Elijah MS 26th Inf. Co.I Jr.2nd Lt.
Roberts, Elijah TN 42nd Inf. 2nd Co.H
Roberts, Elijah TN 43rd Inf. Co.E
Roberts, Elijah TX 35th (Brown's) Cav. Co.D
Roberts, Elijah TX 13th Vol. 1st Co.I
Roberts, Elijah J. AL 10th Inf. Co.F Sgt.
Roberts, Eli M. AR 1st Mtd.Rifles Co.I
Roberts, Elisah AL 24th Inf. Co.E
Roberts, Elisha MS 23rd Inf. Co.H
Roberts, Elisha NC Walker's Bn. Thomas'
  Legion Co.C
Roberts, Elisha M. MO 3rd Cav. Co.A
Roberts, Elisha M. NC 60th Inf. Co.A Sgt.

Roberts, Elisha P. MS 18th Inf. Co.E
Roberts, Elisha R. LA 12th Inf. Co.C,K
Roberts, Elkanah NC 50th Inf. Co.E
Roberts, Elliot GA 26th Inf. Atkinson's Co.B
Roberts, Elliott R. GA 4th (Clinch's) Cav.
  Co.C,I
Roberts, Elsberry AR 3rd Cav. Co.I
Roberts, Elvis C. MS 2nd Inf. Co.H
Roberts, E.M. AL 17th Inf. Co.H
Roberts, E.M. NC 64th Inf. Co.D
Roberts, E.M. SC 1st Cav. Co.G
Roberts, E.M. SC Cav. 10th Bn. Co.B
Roberts, Emanuel M. Gen. & Staff Asst.Surg.
Roberts, Emsley TX 21st Cav. Co.D
Roberts, E.N. VA 51st Inf. Co.E
Roberts, Enoch B. GA 1st Inf. (St.Guards) Co.1
Roberts, E.R. GA Lt.Arty. Clinch's Btty.
Roberts, E.R. GA 1st (Olmstead's) Inf. Co.G
Roberts, E.R. GA 32nd Inf. Co.A
Roberts, Erastedes A. MS 15th Inf. Co.H
Roberts, Erastus TN 40th Inf. Co.D
Roberts, Ervin F. NC 29th Inf,. Co.D 2nd Lt.
Roberts, Ervin S. FL 2nd Cav. Co.B
Roberts, E.S. MS 2nd Inf. Co.H Lt.
Roberts, E.S. VA 1st Cav. Co.B
Roberts, Eugene J. TX 7th Inf. Co.K Sgt.
Roberts, E.W. AR 15th (Johnson's) Inf. Co.F
Roberts, E.W. GA 1st Bn.S.S. Co.B
Roberts, Ezra H. NC 61st Inf. Co.I
Roberts, Ezekiel M. GA 8th Inf. Co.F
Roberts, Ezekiel M. GA 35th Inf. Co.H Capt.
Roberts, Ezekiel W. GA 29th Inf. Co.G
Roberts, F. AL 4th Res. Co.E
Roberts, F. FL 1st Cav. Co.A
Roberts, F. LA Inf.Cons.Crescent Regt. Co.C
Roberts, F. TN Cav. Napier's Bn. Co.A
Roberts, F.A. MS 1st Cav.Res. Co.I
Roberts, F.A. TN 24th Inf. Co.I
Roberts, F.B. MS Inf. 3rd Bn. (St.Troops) Co.E
Roberts, F.C. NC 5th Cav. (63rd St.Troops)
  Co.B Capt.
Roberts, F.C. TX Cav. 2nd Regt.St.Troops Co.A
Roberts, F.D. TN 19th (Biffle's) Cav. Co.G
Roberts, Felix G. TN 1st (Turney's) Inf. Co.F
Roberts, F.H. Gillum's Regt. Co.F
Roberts, Finis H. MS 29th Inf. Co.K
Roberts, F.L. Gen. & Staff Capt.,AQM
Roberts, F.M. AL 8th (Livingston's) Cav. Co.B
Roberts, F.M. MS Cav. 24th Bn. Co.D
Roberts, F.M. MO 4th Inf. Co.D
Roberts, F.M. TN Lt.Arty. Barry's Co. Cpl.
Roberts, F.M. TN 16th Inf. Co.I
Roberts, F.N. VA 8th Cav. Co.G Sgt.
Roberts, F.R. AL 9th (Malone's) Cav. Co.K 2nd
  Lt.
Roberts, F.R. SC 2nd Arty. Co.F
Roberts, F.R. VA Loc.Def. Jordan's Co.
Roberts, Francis FL 9th Inf. Co.D
Roberts, Francis GA 12th (Robinson's) Cav.
  (St.Guards) Co.K Cpl.
Roberts, Francis GA 54th Inf. Co.G Sgt.
Roberts, Francis LA 1st (Strawbridge's) Inf.
  Co.B
Roberts, Francis SC 1st (Hagood's) Inf. 1st Co.D
Roberts, Francis B. VA 45th Inf. Co.C
Roberts, Francis C. VA 16th Inf. Co.D
Roberts, Francis M. FL 3rd Inf. Co.F Sgt.

Roberts, Francis M. FL 11th Inf. Co.K
Roberts, Francis M. GA 22nd Inf. Co.C
Roberts, Francis M. MS 15th Inf. Co.E
Roberts, Francis R. TX 13th Cav. Co.H
Roberts, Francis R. VA 6th Inf. Co.K
Roberts, Francis W. FL 4th Inf. Co.E
Roberts, Frank LA 8th (Wingfield's) Cav.
  Co.A,K 2nd Lt.
Roberts, Frank LA 8th Inf. Co.B
Roberts, Frank MD Inf. 2nd Bn. Co.E,B
Roberts, Frank MS Cav. Garland's Bn. Co.B
Roberts, Frank MS Moseley's Regt.
Roberts, Frank VA Lt.Arty. Brander's Co. Sgt.
Roberts, Frank VA 115th Mil. Co.C
Roberts, Frank B. VA 4th Inf. Co.F
Roberts, Frank G. TX 8th Inf. Co.K
Roberts, Franklin AR Lt.Arty. Wiggins' Btty.
  Capt.
Roberts, Franklin NC Inf. 2nd Bn. Co.H
Roberts, Franklin NC 24th Inf. Co.G
Roberts, Franklin NC 45th Inf. Co.I
Roberts, Franklin NC 56th Inf. Co.D
Roberts, Franklin VA Cav. Mosby's Regt.
  (Part.Rangers)
Roberts, Franklin 14th Conf.Cav. Co.B
Roberts, Franklin C. MS St.Cav. Perrin's Bn.
  Co.B
Roberts, Franklin E. TN 10th Inf. Co.F
Roberts, Frank M. FL Inf. 2nd Bn. Co.F
Roberts, Frank N. NC 2nd Arty. (36th
  St.Troops) Co.B
Roberts, Frank N. NC 1st Inf. (6 mo. '61) Co.F
  1st Lt.
Roberts, Frank N. NC 56th Inf. Co.B Capt.
Roberts, Frank S. GA 2nd Bn.S.S. Co.C
Roberts, F.S. GA 4th Res. Co.E 1st Lt.
Roberts, F.W. GA 10th Mil.
Roberts, F.W. SC Arty. Manigault's Bn. 1st
  Co.B
Roberts, F.W. TX Arty. 4th Bn. Co.A
Roberts, G. AL 50th Inf.
Roberts, G. GA Inf. 27th Bn. Co.C
Roberts, G. GA 29th Inf. Co.A
Roberts, G. GA Inf. (Loc.Def.) Whiteside's
  Nav.Bn. Co.B
Roberts, G. MS Cav. Powers' Regt. Co.B 1st
  Lt.
Roberts, G. NC 5th Sr.Res. Co.K
Roberts, G. SC Mil. 16th Regt. Jones' Co.
Roberts, G.A. AL Cav. 4th Bn. (Love's) Co.C
  Capt.
Roberts, G.A. AL 15th Inf. Co.K 1st Lt.
Roberts, G.A. TX 28th Cav. Co.F
Roberts, G.A. VA 20th Cav. Co.G
Roberts, Gale K. TN 39th Mtd.Inf. Co.K 2nd
  Lt.
Roberts, Garland VA 51st Inf. Co.G
Roberts, Garret NC 58th Inf. Co.C
Roberts, Garrett NC 6th Cav. (65th St.Troops)
  Co.C
Roberts, Garrett M. NC Cav. 5th Bn. Co.C
Roberts, Gaston NC 5th Cav. (63rd St.Troops)
  Co.K
Roberts, Gaston NC 56th Inf. Co.H Sgt.
Roberts, G.B. AL 50th Inf. Co.G
Roberts, G.B. GA Arty. 11th Bn. (Sumter Arty.)
  Co.D,B Cpl.

Roberts, G.B. GA 3rd Bn. (St.Guards) Co.A
Roberts, G.B. GA Inf. (Express Inf.) Witt's Co.
Roberts, G.B. MS 39th Inf. Co.F
Roberts, G.B. TX 14th Inf. Co.C 2nd Lt.
Roberts, G.C. AL 42nd Inf. Co.A
Roberts, G.C. VA Cav. 37th Bn. Co.D Cpl.
Roberts, G.C. VA Mil. Carroll Cty.
Roberts, G.D. GA 2nd Inf. Co.D Cpl.
Roberts, G.D. MO St.Guard
Roberts, G.D. TN 21st & 22nd (Cons.) Cav. Co.C
Roberts, G.D. TN 20th Inf. Co.C
Roberts, General J. TN 3rd (Lillard's) Mtd.Inf. Co.B Sgt.
Roberts, George AL 11th Inf. Co.E
Roberts, George FL 8th Inf. Co.B
Roberts, George GA Cav. 20th Bn. Co.D
Roberts, George GA 7th Inf. (St.Guards) Co.A Capt.
Roberts, George GA 36th (Villepigue's) Inf. Co.I
Roberts, George LA 3rd (Wingfield's) Cav. Co.A,K
Roberts, George LA 4th Cav. Co.H
Roberts, George LA 20th Inf. Co.H
Roberts, George LA 21st (Patton's) Inf.
Roberts, George MO 9th (Elliott's) Cav. Co.H
Roberts, George NC 7th Sr.Res. Fisher's Co.
Roberts, George NC 64th Inf. Co.G,C
Roberts, George TN 26th Inf. Co.C
Roberts, George TN 29th Inf. Co.H
Roberts, George TN 34th Inf. Co.H Color Cpl.
Roberts, George TN 45th Inf. Co.G
Roberts, George VA 25th Cav. Co.B
Roberts, George VA 6th Bn.Res. Co.E
Roberts, George VA 63rd Inf. Co.A
Roberts, George A. AL Hardy's Co. (Eufaula Minute Men) 1st Lt.
Roberts, George A. TX 12th Cav. Co.A
Roberts, George B. VA 6th Cav. Co.B Sgt.
Roberts, George B. VA 13th Inf. 1st Co.B
Roberts, George C. VA 29th Inf. 2nd Co.F
Roberts, George D. TN 22nd (Barteau's) Cav. Co.F
Roberts, George D. VA 1st Cav. Co.B
Roberts, George E. KY 6th Cav. Co.I
Roberts, George E. KY 8th Cav. Co.F Cpl.
Roberts, George E. KY 4th Mtd.Inf. Co.D,E
Roberts, George E. SC 5th Cav. Co.F
Roberts, George E. SC Cav. 14th Bn. Co.C
Roberts, George F. MO 1st Inf. Co.G
Roberts, George F. Shaver's Staff Lt.
Roberts, George G. TX 25th Cav. Co.K
Roberts, George H. AL 22nd Inf. Co.B 2nd Lt.
Roberts, George H. Gen. & Staff Surg.
Roberts, Geo. H. Gen. & Staff 2nd Lt.,Dr.M.
Roberts, George J. MS Cav. Garland's Bn. Co.A
Roberts, George J.W. VA 56th Inf. Co.G
Roberts, George K. MO 10th Cav.
Roberts, George L. AL Cav. Holloway's Co.
Roberts, George L. VA 39th Inf. Co.C
Roberts, George M. AL 47th Inf. Co.F
Roberts, George M. MO Lt.Arty. Landis' Co.
Roberts, George M. MO 5th Inf. Co.H
Roberts, George M. MO St.Guard
Roberts, George M. NC Cav. 5th Bn. Co.A
Roberts, George M.B. GA 19th Inf. Co.H
Roberts, George P. MO 10th Cav. Co.G 1st Lt.

Roberts, George P. TN 25th Inf. Co.H 1st Sgt.
Roberts, George R. VA 2nd Cav. Co.F
Roberts, George T. AL 6th Cav. Co.D
Roberts, George T. AL 6th Inf. Co.B
Roberts, George T. NC 60th Inf. Co.H
Roberts, George T. VA 14th Cav. Co.B Jr.2nd Lt.
Roberts, George W. FL 1st Cav. Co.A
Roberts, George W. GA 1st Inf. Co.D
Roberts, George W. GA Inf. 5th Bn. (St.Guards) Co.C Cpl.
Roberts, George W. GA 12th Inf. Co.H
Roberts, George W. GA Inf. 27th Bn. Co.C
Roberts, George W. GA 48th Inf. Co.B 1st Sgt.
Roberts, George W. GA Cobb's Legion Co.A
Roberts, George W. MS 5th Cav. Co.C
Roberts, George W. MS 11th (Perrin's) Cav. Co.B
Roberts, George W. MS 1st Lt.Arty. Co.B
Roberts, George W. MS 1st Lt.Arty. Co.E
Roberts, George W. MS 33rd Inf. Co.B
Roberts, George W. MO 5th Cav. Co.F
Roberts, George W. MO Inf. Perkins' Bn.
Roberts, George W. NC 51st Inf. Co.G
Roberts, George W. TN 34th Inf. Co.G
Roberts, George W. VA 22nd Cav. Co.H
Roberts, George W. 3rd Conf.Cav. Co.B
Roberts, George Washington AR 1st (Colquitt's) Inf. Co.G
Roberts, G.F. KY 10th (Johnson's) Cav. New Co.B
Roberts, G.G. TX 9th (Nichols') Inf. Co.E
Roberts, G.H. MS 5th Inf. Co.A
Roberts, G.H. VA 5th Cav. Co.G
Roberts, G.H. VA 15th Cav. Co.B
Roberts, G.H. 1st Bn.Res. Asst.Surg.
Roberts, Gideon AL 16th Inf. Co.C
Roberts, Gideon M. NC 2nd Inf. Co.C Capt.
Roberts, G.L. GA 26th Inf. Co.K Sgt.
Roberts, G.M. GA Arty. St.Troops Pruden's Btty.
Roberts, G.M. GA 13th Inf. Co.B
Roberts, G.M. MS 28th Cav. Co.I
Roberts, G.M. TN 5th (McKenzie's) Cav. Co.D
Roberts, G.M. Gen. & Staff Capt.,Comsy.
Roberts, Goodson M. NC 60th Inf. Co.F Capt.
Roberts, G.Q. MS 4th Inf. Co.G
Roberts, G.R. MS 2nd Inf. Co.B
Roberts, G.R. MS 23rd Inf. Co.B
Roberts, Green GA Cav. 8th Bn. (St.Guards) Co.A
Roberts, Green GA 13th Cav. Co.E
Roberts, Green KY 9th Mtd.Inf. Co.B
Roberts, Green NC 6th Inf. Co.B
Roberts, Green TX 26th Cav. Co.E
Roberts, Green B. MS 33rd Inf. Co.G
Roberts, Green B. MO 1st N.E. Cav. Co.M
Roberts, Green B. TN 38th Inf. 1st Co.H
Roberts, Greenbury KY 2nd (Duke's) Cav. Co.A
Roberts, Griffin MS Cav. 4th Bn. Co.C
Roberts, Griffin MS 20th Inf. Co.B
Roberts, Griffin 8th (Wade's) Conf.Cav. Co.E
Roberts, Griffin A. GA 1st (Fannin's) Res. Co.I
Roberts, G.S. AL 7th Cav. Co.H
Roberts, G.S. AL 8th (Livingston's) Cav. Co.A
Roberts, G.S. AL 37th Inf. Co.K
Roberts, G.S. TN 21st Inf. Co.H

Roberts, G.T. MS 2nd St.Cav. Co.H
Roberts, G.T. MS Inf. 3rd Bn. (St.Troops) Co.B
Roberts, G.T. TN 63rd Inf. Co.G
Roberts, G.T. VA 1st (Farinholt's) Res. Co.B
Roberts, Gustavus VA 50th Inf. Co.F
Roberts, G.W. AL 5th Inf. Co.C
Roberts, G.W. AL 28th Inf. Co.K
Roberts, G.W. AL Cp. of Instr. Talladega
Roberts, G.W. AR 1st Mtd.Rifles Co.G,B
Roberts, G.W. FL 1st (Res.) Inf. Co.B
Roberts, G.W. GA 6th Cav. Co.E 2nd Lt.
Roberts, G.W. GA Cav. 20th Bn. Co.A,D
Roberts, G.W. GA Cav. 29th Bn. Co.D
Roberts, G.W. GA 26th Inf. Co.K
Roberts, G.W. LA 1st Hvy.Arty. (Reg.) Co.D Cpl.
Roberts, G.W. MS 5th Inf. Co.B
Roberts, G.W. MS 13th Inf. Co.E
Roberts, G.W. NC 1st Cav. (9th St.Troops) Co.G
Roberts, G.W. NC 60th Inf. Co.F
Roberts, G.W. SC 10th Inf. 1st Co.G
Roberts, G.W. SC 23rd Inf. Co.B
Roberts, G.W. TN 1st (Carter's) Cav. Co.K
Roberts, G.W. TN 16th Inf. Co.G
Roberts, G.W. TN 28th (Cons.) Inf. Co.F Sgt.
Roberts, G.W. TN 84th Inf. Co.B Sgt.
Roberts, G.W. TX 24th & 25th Cav. (Cons.) Co.E
Roberts, G.W. TX 28th Cav. Co.C
Roberts, G.W. TX Jamison Res. Co.B
Roberts, G.W. TX 14th Inf. Co.H
Roberts, G.W. VA 15th Cav. Co.B
Roberts, G.W. 3rd Conf.Cav. Co.C
Roberts, G. Wade TX 1st (McCulloch's) Cav. Co.F
Roberts, G.W.G. TX 5th Cav. Co.A
Roberts, H. AL 5th Bn.Vol. Co.A
Roberts, H. AR 32nd Inf. Co.K
Roberts, H. FL 1st (Res.) Inf. Co.I
Roberts, H. GA 5th Cav. Co.C
Roberts, H. GA 26th Inf. Co.C Sgt.
Roberts, H. KY 3rd Bn.Mtd.Rifles Co.B
Roberts, H. MS 4th Inf. Co.G
Roberts, H. MO Cav. Freeman's Regt. Hain's Co.
Roberts, H. SC Arty. Manigault's Btty. 1st Co.B
Roberts, H. TN 9th Cav. Co.E
Roberts, H. TX Cav. Benavides' Regt. Co.H
Roberts, H. TX 2nd Inf. Co.K
Roberts, H. TX 3rd (Kirby's) Bn.Vol. Co.A
Roberts, H.A. MS 44th Inf. Co.K Cpl.
Roberts, H.A. TN 27th Inf. Co.B
Roberts, Hardin GA 35th Inf. Co.H
Roberts, Harris GA 12th Inf. Co.I Music.
Roberts, Harrison FL 11th Inf. Co.K
Roberts, Harrison MS 37th Inf. Co.H
Roberts, Harvey KY 10th (Diamond's) Cav. Co.H
Roberts, Harvey D. VA 50th Inf. Co.H
Roberts, Harvy C. NC 50th Inf. Co.K
Roberts, Hawood AL 41st Inf. Co.H
Roberts, Haywood AL St.Res. Palmer's Co.
Roberts, H.B. KY 5th Mtd.Inf. Co.K
Roberts, H.B. KY 9th Mtd.Inf. Co.K
Roberts, H.B. MS Cav. Part.Rangers Rhodes' Co.

Roberts, H.B. Conf.Cav. 7th Bn. Co.C Capt.
Roberts, H.B. 14th Conf.Cav. Co.F
Roberts, H.C. FL 1st (Res.) Inf. Co.B
Roberts, H.C. NC 29th Inf. Co.D
Roberts, H.C. TN 19th & 20th (Cons.) Cav. Co.E 1st Sgt.
Roberts, H.D. MS 9th Inf. Co.E
Roberts, H.D. TN 1st (Carter's) Cav. Co.B Cpl.
Roberts, H.E. TX 28th Cav. Co.F Sgt.
Roberts, Henderson KY 5th Mtd.Inf. Co.E
Roberts, Henry AL Cav. 4th Bn. (Love's) Co.B
Roberts, Henry AL Inf. 2nd Regt. Co.H
Roberts, Henry AR 27th Inf. Co.F
Roberts, Henry AR 27th Inf. Co.G
Roberts, Henry AR 30th Inf. Co.A
Roberts, Henry GA Cav. 2nd Bn. Co.E Cpl.
Roberts, Henry GA 11th Cav. Co.G
Roberts, Henry GA Cav. 29th Bn. Co.G Cpl.
Roberts, Henry GA Siege Arty. Campbell's Ind.Co.
Roberts, Henry GA 48th Inf. Co.I
Roberts, Henry GA 55th Inf. Co.E
Roberts, Henry LA 1st Hvy.Arty. (Reg.) Co.A
Roberts, Henry MS 9th Cav. Co.D
Roberts, Henry MS Cav. 17th Bn. Co.F
Roberts, Henry MS Cav. Jeff Davis Legion Co.I
Roberts, Henry MS Inf. 3rd Bn. (St.Troops) Co.A
Roberts, Henry MS 6th Inf. Co.E
Roberts, Henry MS 24th Inf. Co.A Capt.
Roberts, Henry NC 56th Inf. Co.D
Roberts, Henry TN 26th Inf. Co.K
Roberts, Henry TX 23rd Cav.
Roberts, Henry TX Inf. Cunningham's Co.
Roberts, Henry VA Cav. Young's Co. Sr.2nd Lt.
Roberts, Henry VA 48th Inf. Co.I
Roberts, Henry Conf.Cav. Clarkson's Bn. Ind. Rangers Teamster
Roberts, Henry 1st Chickasaw Inf. McConnell's Co. 1st Sgt.
Roberts, Henry B. GA 25th Inf. Co.F
Roberts, Henry B. VA 6th Bn.Res. Co.E Capt.
Roberts, Henry C. AL Cav. Roddey's Escort
Roberts, Henry C. AL 18th Inf. Co.A
Roberts, Henry C. FL 1st Cav. Co.A
Roberts, Henry C. FL 9th Inf. Co.E
Roberts, Henry C. TN 20th (Russell's) Cav. Co.I 1st Sgt.
Roberts, Henry C. VA Lt.Arty. Hankins' Co.
Roberts, Henry C. VA 3rd Inf. 1st Co.I
Roberts, Henry Clay GA 5th Inf. Co.D
Roberts, Henry D. MS 44th Inf. Co.K
Roberts, Henry E. NC Hvy.Arty. 1st Bn. Co.C Sgt.
Roberts, Henry G.B. AR Inf. 2nd Bn. Co.A
Roberts, Henry J. GA 2nd Res. Co.C
Roberts, Henry J. GA 50th Inf. Co.E
Roberts, Henry J. LA 9th Inf. Co.G Cpl.
Roberts, Henry J. MS 6th Inf. Co.F
Roberts, Henry J. MS 14th Inf. Co.D
Roberts, Henry J. MS 44th Inf. Co.K Cpl.
Roberts, Henry M. AL 16th Inf. Co.E
Roberts, Henry M. GA 50th Inf. Co.F
Roberts, Henry P. SC 5th Cav. Co.F
Roberts, Henry P. SC Cav. 14th Bn. Co.C Sgt.
Roberts, Henry P. TX 2nd Inf. Co.B

Roberts, Henry T.S. AL 3rd Bn.Res. Co.B
Roberts, Henry V. NC 6th Inf. Co.G
Roberts, Henry W. GA 38th Inf. Co.H
Roberts, Henry W. TN Cav. 7th Bn. (Bennett's) Co.D
Roberts, Henry W. TN 22nd (Barteau's) Cav. Co.F
Roberts, Henry W. TX 3rd Inf. Co.I
Roberts, Hezekiah GA 61st Inf. Co.C Sgt.
Roberts, Hezekiah MO 10th Inf. Co.D
Roberts, Hezekiah L.R. FL 1st Cav. Co.A Sgt.
Roberts, Hezekiah L.R. FL 4th Inf. Co.D Cpl.
Roberts, Hezekiah N. GA 7th Inf. Co.H
Roberts, Hezekiah R. MO 8th Inf. Co.B
Roberts, Hezekiah W. KY 5th Mtd.Inf. Co.A,K Sgt.
Roberts, H.G. TX 12th Cav. Co.B 1st Sgt.
Roberts, H.G. VA Lt.Arty. 13th Bn. Co.A
Roberts, H.H. MS Inf. 2nd St.Troops Co.K Sgt.
Roberts, H.H. MS Inf. 3rd Bn. Co.B
Roberts, H.H. TN 8th Inf. Co.G Cpl.
Roberts, H.H. TX 12th Cav. Co.G
Roberts, H.H. VA 1st (Farinholt's) Res. Co.B
Roberts, H.H. VA 3rd Res. Co.H
Roberts, Hilory KY 1st (Butler's) Cav. Co.G
Roberts, Hiram AL 42nd Inf. Co.E
Roberts, Hiram VA Inf. Mileham's Co.
Roberts, Hiram B. KY 5th Mtd.Inf. Co.A,K,G Sgt.
Roberts, Hiram C. VA 25th Cav. Co.I
Roberts, Hiram M. TX 15th Cav. Co.F Cpl.
Roberts, H.J. MS 7th Inf. Co.C
Roberts, H.J.S. LA Inf. 16th Bn.(Conf.Guards Resp.Bn.) Co.A
Roberts, H.K. NC 14th Inf. Co.D
Roberts, H.L. AR 7th Inf. Co.G
Roberts, H.L. MS 5th Cav. Co.H
Roberts, H.L. MS 18th Cav. Co.K
Roberts, H.L. TN Inf. 22nd Bn. Co.C
Roberts, H.M. GA 5th Res.
Roberts, H.M. TX 15th Inf. Co.A
Roberts, H.N. AR 58th Mil. Co.B
Roberts, H.N. GA Phillips' Legion Co.L
Roberts, Hope H. GA 35th Inf. Co.C 1st Lt.
Roberts, Horace AL 20th Inf. Co.F
Roberts, Horace E. VA 39th Inf. Co.I
Roberts, Houston TX 11th Cav. Co.E
Roberts, Houston W. AL 16th Inf. Co.F
Roberts, Howard D. AR 18th (Marmaduke's) Inf. Co.E
Roberts, Howel GA 29th Inf. Co.B
Roberts, Howell L. MO 2nd Cav. Co.G
Roberts, Hozea GA 1st Lt.Duty Men Co.A
Roberts, H.P. VA 2nd Cav. Co.B
Roberts, H.R. AL 3rd Res. Co.G
Roberts, H.R. AL 14th Inf. Co.H
Roberts, H.S. GA Cav. Newbern's Co. (Coffee Revengers)
Roberts, H.S. KY 1st (Butler's) Cav. Co.C
Roberts, H.S. KY 3rd Cav. Co.C
Roberts, H.S. Gen. & Staff Ord.Off.
Roberts, H.T. VA 2nd Cav. Co.B
Roberts, Hugh AL St.Arty. Co.A
Roberts, Hugh KY 7th Cav. Co.A
Roberts, Hugh TX Cav. Gano's Squad. Co.A
Roberts, Hugh VA 8th Cav. Co.C
Roberts, Hugh L. TN 1st Cav.

Roberts, Humphrey TX 14th Cav. Co.A
Roberts, Huston Gillum's Regt. Co.F 2nd Lt.
Roberts, H.W. MO 12th Cav. Co.G Cpl.
Roberts, I. KY 1st (Butler's) Cav. Co.F
Roberts, I. Brush Bn.
Roberts, I.B. MO Cav. Fristoe's Regt. Co.C
Roberts, I.C. AL Cav. Stuart's Bn. Co.F Sgt.
Roberts, I.C. LA 1st (Nelligan's) Inf. Co.B
Roberts, Icem TN 12th (Green's) Cav. Co.C
Roberts, I.L.G. MS 35th Inf. Co.D
Roberts, I.N. TX Cav. McCord's Frontier Regt. Co.E Sgt.
Roberts, Ira H. VA 29th Inf. 1st Co.F
Roberts, Ira H. VA Inf. French's Bn. Co.D
Roberts, Irvin MS 9th Cav. Co.A
Roberts, Irwin MS Cav. 17th Bn. Co.A
Roberts, Isaac AR 13th Inf. Co.I
Roberts, Isaac FL 1st (Res.) Inf. Co.A
Roberts, Isaac LA 3rd (Wingfield's) Cav. Co.K
Roberts, Isaac LA 16th Inf. Co.B 1st Lt.
Roberts, Isaac NC 3rd Cav. (41st St.Troops) Co.E 1st Lt.
Roberts, Isaac SC 3rd Bn.Res. Co.E
Roberts, Isaac SC 5th St.Troops Co.A
Roberts, Isaac SC 6th Res. Co.B
Roberts, Isaac TN 16th Inf. Co.G
Roberts, Isaac TN Conscr. (Cp. of Instr.)
Roberts, Isaac TX 27th Cav. Co.I Bvt.2nd Lt.
Roberts, Isaac TX Cav. Benavides' Regt. Co.A
Roberts, Isaac B. TN 1st (Turney's) Inf. Co.A
Roberts, Isaac M. GA 11th Inf. Co.E,H
Roberts, Isaac M. GA 39th Inf. Co.C
Roberts, Isaac N. AL 3rd Inf. Co.C
Roberts, Isaac N. NC 18th Inf. Co.G
Roberts, Isaac N. VA 10th Inf. Co.K
Roberts, Isaac T. TN 24th Inf. 2nd Co.G Capt.
Roberts, Isah MS Inf. 1st Bn.St.Troops (12 mo. '62-3) Co.D
Roberts, Isaiah AL 32nd Inf. Co.H
Roberts, Isaiah MS 3rd (St.Troops) Cav. Co.D
Roberts, Isaiah MS 8th Inf. Co.B
Roberts, Isaiah MS 13th Inf. Co.D
Roberts, Isaiah TX Cav. 6th Bn. Co.D
Roberts, Isaiah J. Gen. & Staff Surg.
Roberts, Isam GA 50th Inf. Co.G Cpl.
Roberts, Isham AR 34th Inf. Co.G
Roberts, Isham GA 47th Inf. Co.D
Roberts, Isham MS 1st (Percy's) Inf. Co.A
Roberts, Isham MS 39th Inf. Co.F
Roberts, Isham L. TN Lt.Arty. Baxter's Co.
Roberts, I.S.M. SC 23rd Inf. Co.F
Roberts, I.W. AL 63rd Inf. Co.E Sgt.
Roberts, I.W. GA 29th Inf. Co.F
Roberts, J. AL Cav. Hardie's Bn.Res. S.D. McClellan's Co.
Roberts, J. AL Lt.Arty. 20th Bn. Co.B
Roberts, J. AL 25th Inf. Co.I Cpl.
Roberts, J. AL 26th (O'Neal's) Inf. Co.E
Roberts, J. AL 53rd Inf. Co.C
Roberts, J. AR 13th Inf. Co.I
Roberts, J. GA Cav. 9th Bn. (St.Guards) Co.F
Roberts, J. GA Hvy.Arty. 22nd Bn. Co.F
Roberts, J. GA Inf. 19th Bn. (St.Guards) Co.F
Roberts, J. GA 54th Inf. Co.F,A
Roberts, J. GA Inf. Grubbs' Co.
Roberts, J. KY Cav. 2nd Bn. (Dortch's) Co.D
Roberts, J. LA 3rd (Wingfield's) Cav. Co.I,K

Roberts, J. LA Millaudon's Co. (Jefferson Mtd.Guards,Co.B)
Roberts, J. LA Mil. Fire Bn. Co.E
Roberts, J. LA Miles' Legion Co.C Sgt.
Roberts, J. MS 20th Inf. Co.K
Roberts, J. MO 12th Cav. Co.B
Roberts, J. SC Prov.Guard Hamilton's Co.
Roberts, J. TN 3rd (Forrest's) Cav. Co.D
Roberts, J. TN 14th (Neely's) Cav. Co.H
Roberts, J. TN Lt.Arty. Rice's Btty.
Roberts, J. TN 27th Inf. Co.H
Roberts, J. Inf. Bailey's Cons.Regt. Co.A
Roberts, J. TX 1st Hvy.Arty. Co.A
Roberts, J. TX 1st Hvy.Arty. 2nd Co.A
Roberts, J. VA Horse Arty. J.W. Carter's Co.
Roberts, J. VA 54th Mil. Co.G
Roberts, J. Trans-MS Conf.Cav. 1st Bn. Co.C
Roberts, J.A. AL 1st Inf. Co.G Sgt.
Roberts, J.A. AL 3rd Inf. Co.A
Roberts, J.A. AL 22nd Inf. Co.C 1st Sgt.
Roberts, J.A. AL 54th Inf. Comsy.Sgt.
Roberts, J.A. AR 6th Inf. Co.G
Roberts, J.A. AR 10th Mil. Co.E
Roberts, J.A. AR 11th Inf. Co.E
Roberts, J.A. AR 11th & 17th (Cons.) Inf. Co.E
Roberts, J.A. GA 6th Cav. Co.D
Roberts, J.A. GA Arty. Lumpkin's Co.
Roberts, J.A. GA 9th Inf. (St.Guards) Co.H
Roberts, J.A. GA 11th Inf. Co.F
Roberts, J.A. GA 18th Inf. Co.C
Roberts, J.A. GA 36th (Broyles') Inf. Co.F Sgt.
Roberts, J.A. KY 8th Cav. Co.B
Roberts, J.A. KY 10th (Johnson's) Cav. Co.E
Roberts, J.A. MO 10th Inf.
Roberts, J.A. MO Inf. Winston's Regt. Co.A
Roberts, J.A. SC Inf. Hampton Legion Co.F
Roberts, J.A. TN 4th (Murray's) Cav. Co.F
Roberts, J.A. TN 24th Inf. 1st Co.H
Roberts, J.A. 4th Conf.Inf. Co.B
Roberts, Jack AL 22nd Inf.
Roberts, Jack F. MO 11th Inf. Co.E
Roberts, Jackson AL 9th Inf. Co.B
Roberts, Jackson FL 8th Inf. Co.B
Roberts, Jackson FL 8th Inf. Co.H
Roberts, Jackson GA 6th Inf. (St.Guards) Co.H Sgt.
Roberts, Jackson KY 1st Bn.Mtd.Rifles Co.D
Roberts, Jackson SC Inf. Holcombe Legion Co.E
Roberts, Jackson TN Lt.Arty. Kain's Co.
Roberts, Jackson TN 19th Inf. Co.C
Roberts, Jackson Deneale's Regt. Choctaw Warriors Co.E
Roberts, Jackson A. MO 4th Cav. Co.I
Roberts, Jacob GA 55th Inf. Co.C 3rd Lt.
Roberts, Jacob MO 7th Cav. Ward's Co. Jr.2nd Lt.
Roberts, Jacob TN Cav. Nixon's Regt. Co.G
Roberts, Jacob A. MS 8th Inf. Co.E Cpl.
Roberts, Jacob J. NC 16th Inf. Co.M
Roberts, Jacob M. GA 19th Inf. Co.I
Roberts, Jacob T. VA 14th Inf. Co.A
Roberts, James AL 7th Cav. Co.M
Roberts, James AL 11th Cav. Co.A
Roberts, James AL Inf. 2nd Regt. Co.K
Roberts, James AL 18th Inf. Co.D
Roberts, James AL 39th Inf. Co.A
Roberts, James AL 50th Inf.

Roberts, Jas. AL 54th Inf. AACS,Sgt.
Roberts, James AR Cav. Gordon's Regt. Co.B
Roberts, James AR 8th Inf. Co.F
Roberts, James AR 19th (Dawson's) Inf. Co.D
Roberts, James AR 30th Inf. Co.H
Roberts, James AR 32nd Inf. Co.G
Roberts, James AR Inf. Hardy's Regt. Co.B
Roberts, James FL 1st Cav. Co.K
Roberts, James FL 2nd Cav. Co.G
Roberts, James FL 1st Inf. New Co.C
Roberts, James FL Inf. 2nd Bn. Co.A
Roberts, James FL 10th Inf. Co.I
Roberts, James GA 1st Cav. Co.H
Roberts, James GA 2nd Cav. Co.I
Roberts, James GA Arty. Maxwell's Reg.Lt.Btty.
Roberts, James GA 1st Reg. Co.D
Roberts, James GA 1st (Symons') Res. Co.B
Roberts, James GA Inf. 1st Conf.Bn. Co.E Music.
Roberts, James GA 7th Inf. Co.B
Roberts, James GA 18th Inf. Co.G
Roberts, James GA 21st Inf. Co.K
Roberts, James GA 26th Inf. Co.A
Roberts, James GA 49th Inf. Co.B
Roberts, James GA Phillips' Legion Co.E
Roberts, James KY 2nd (Woodward's) Cav. Co.A,E
Roberts, James KY 6th Cav. Co.I
Roberts, James KY 8th Cav. Co.B
Roberts, James KY 10th (Diamond's) Cav. Co.M
Roberts, James KY 5th Mtd.Inf. Co.D,F
Roberts, James LA 1st Hvy.Arty. (Reg.) Co.G Music.
Roberts, James LA 3rd Inf. Co.F
Roberts, James LA Inf. 10th Bn. Co.H
Roberts, James LA 18th Inf. Co.A
Roberts, James MS 9th Cav. Co.D
Roberts, James MS Cav. 17th Bn. Co.F
Roberts, James MS 20th Inf. Co.E
Roberts, James MS 23rd Inf. Co.C
Roberts, James MS 24th Inf. Co.G
Roberts, James MS 46th Inf. Co.E
Roberts, James MO 1st N.E. Cav. Co.M
Roberts, James MO 4th Cav. Co.I
Roberts, James MO Cav. Poindexter's Regt.
Roberts, James MO Inf. 3rd Bn. Co.C
Roberts, James MO 4th Inf. Co.I
Roberts, James MO 8th Inf. Co.A 1st Lt.
Roberts, James MO 16th Inf. Co.I
Roberts, James NC Cav. 5th Bn. Co.B
Roberts, James NC Inf. 13th Bn. Co.C
Roberts, James NC 21st Inf. Co.L
Roberts, James NC 33rd Inf. Co.G
Roberts, James NC 38th Inf. Co.K
Roberts, James NC 56th Inf. Co.D
Roberts, James NC 58th Inf. Co.A,K
Roberts, James NC 64th Inf. Co.C
Roberts, James NC Loc.Def. Griswold's Co.
Roberts, James NC Inf. Thomas Legion Co.G
Roberts, James SC 1st (Butler's) Inf. Co.A
Roberts, James SC 4th St.Troops Co.B
Roberts, James TN 19th (Biffle's) Cav. Co.D
Roberts, James TN 20th (Russell's) Cav. Co.I
Roberts, James TN 2nd (Robison's) Inf. Co.A
Roberts, James TN 16th Inf. Co.G Cpl.
Roberts, James TN 26th Inf. Co.E
Roberts, James TN 28th Inf. Co.G

Roberts, James TN 50th Inf. Co.F
Roberts, James TX 15th Cav. Co.B
Roberts, James TX 21st Cav. Co.C
Roberts, James TX 32nd Cav. Co.A
Roberts, James TX Cav. Martin's Regt. Co.H
Roberts, James TX 2nd Inf. Co.F
Roberts, James VA 8th Cav. Co.C
Roberts, James VA 12th Cav. Co.D
Roberts, James VA 20th Cav. Co.F
Roberts, James VA 22nd Cav. Co.C
Roberts, James VA Cav. 34th Bn. Co.B
Roberts, James VA Cav. 34th Bn. Co.D
Roberts, James VA Inf. 23rd Bn. Co.C
Roberts, James VA 57th Inf. Co.C
Roberts, James 15th Conf.Cav. Co.I
Roberts, James Conf.Cav. Baxter's Bn. 2nd Co.B
Roberts, James Horse Arty. White's Btty.
Roberts, James A. AR Cav. Harrell's Bn. Co.C
Roberts, James A. GA 45th Inf. Co.G
Roberts, James A. KY 1st Inf. Co.G
Roberts, James A. LA Lt.Arty. 6th Field Btty. (Grosse Tete Flying Arty.)
Roberts, James A. MS Cav. 3rd Bn.Res. Co.A Capt.
Roberts, James A. MS 6th Inf. Co.G
Roberts, James A. MS 10th Inf. Old Co.B, New Co.C
Roberts, James A. MS 15th Inf. Co.C,D 1st Sgt.
Roberts, James A. MS 16th Inf. Co.G
Roberts, James A. MS 20th Inf. Co.B 1st Lt.
Roberts, James A. MO 3rd Cav. Co.A
Roberts, James A. NC 64th Inf. Co.C
Roberts, James A. TN Cav. 9th Bn. (Gantt's) Co.D
Roberts, James A. TN 14th (Neely's) Cav.
Roberts, James A. TN 43rd Inf. Co.K
Roberts, James A. VA 37th Inf. Co.H
Roberts, James B. AR 3rd Inf. Co.L,A
Roberts, James B. FL 1st Inf. Old Co.K, Co.A Sgt.
Roberts, James B. GA 2nd Bn.S.S. Co.A
Roberts, James B. GA 5th Inf. Co.G
Roberts, James B. NC 27th Inf. Co.A Sgt.
Roberts, James B. NC 29th Inf. Co.D
Roberts, James B. TN 1st Cav. Co.C
Roberts, James B. TN 4th (Murray's) Cav. Co.D
Roberts, James B. 1st Conf.Cav. 2nd Co.C
Roberts, James C. NC 1st Inf. Co.E
Roberts, James C. NC 15th Inf. Co.H
Roberts, James C. SC Cav. 10th Bn. Co.B
Roberts, James C. TN 35th Inf. 3rd Co.F
Roberts, James D. MS 44th Inf. Co.K 3rd Lt.
Roberts, James D. NC 45th Inf. Co.A
Roberts, James D. NC Walker's Bn. Thomas' Legion Co.A
Roberts, James D. VA Cav. 35th Bn. Co.F
Roberts, James D. VA 14th Inf. Co.A
Roberts, James E. KY 10th (Diamond's) Cav. Co.L
Roberts, James E. MO 6th Inf. Co.B
Roberts, James E. VA 2nd Cav. Co.F
Roberts, James F. KY 4th Cav. Co.E Cpl.
Roberts, James F. MS Lt.Arty. Stanford's Co.
Roberts, James F. NC 25th Inf. Co.G
Roberts, James F. TN Cav. 1st Bn. (McNairy's) Co.B
Roberts, James F. TX 8th Cav. Co.A

Roberts, James G. FL Cav. (Marianna Drag.)
Smith's Co.
Roberts, James G. MS Inf. 3rd Bn. Co.G
Roberts, James G. NC 29th Inf. Co.D
Roberts, James G. 15th Conf.Cav. Co.B
Roberts, James Green MO 4th Cav. Co.I
Roberts, James H. AL 9th Inf. Co.K
Roberts, James H. AL St.Res. Palmer's Co.
Roberts, James H. AR 3rd Cav. Co.I
Roberts, James H. GA 6th Inf. Co.E Cpl.
Roberts, James H. GA 11th Inf. Co.G
Roberts, James H. MS 23rd Inf. Co.F 1st Sgt.
Roberts, James H. MO 10th Inf. Co.B
Roberts, James H. SC 8th Inf. Co.I
Roberts, James H. VA Goochland Lt.Arty. Cpl.
Roberts, James H. VA 24th Inf. Co.A
Roberts, James H. VA 56th Inf. Co.C
Roberts, James J. AL 11th Inf. Co.E
Roberts, James J. AL 13th Inf. Co.H
Roberts, James J. AL 46th Inf. Co.C
Roberts, James J. MO 5th Inf. Co.H
Roberts, James J. VA 34th Inf. Co.B
Roberts, James K.P. TN 5th Cav.
Roberts, James L. AL Inf. 6th (McClellan's) Bn.
Co.C 2nd Lt.
Roberts, James L. AL 22nd Inf. Sgt.
Roberts, James L. AL 50th Inf. Co.B
Roberts, James L. AL Cp. of Instr. Talladega
Roberts, James L. GA 55th Inf. Co.F
Roberts, James L. KY Cav. 1st Bn. Arnold's Co.
Roberts, James L. NC 14th Inf. Co.A
Roberts, James L. NC 35th Inf. Co.H
Roberts, James L. SC 23rd Inf. Co.F
Roberts, James L.A. AR 1st Cav.
Roberts, James M. AL Lt.Arty. Lee's Btty.
Roberts, James M. AL 16th Inf. Co.B
Roberts, James M. AL 50th Inf. Co.A
Roberts, James M. AL Randolph Cty.Res. J.
Orr's Co.
Roberts, James M. FL 2nd Inf. Co.E 1st Sgt.
Roberts, James M. GA Cav. 2nd Bn. Co.C
Roberts, James M. GA 8th Cav. New Co.D
Roberts, James M. GA Cav. 29th Bn. Co.B
Roberts, James M. GA Lt.Arty. Milledge's Co.
Secretary
Roberts, James M. GA Lt.Arty. Pritchard's Co.
(Washington Arty.) 2nd Lt.
Roberts, James M. GA Inf. 1st Loc.Troops
(Augusta) Barnes' Lt.Arty.Co. 1st Lt.
Roberts, James M. GA 6th Inf. Co.E
Roberts, James M. GA Inf. 25th Bn. (Prov.
Guard) Co.E
Roberts, James M. GA 30th Inf. Co.A Cpl.
Roberts, James M. GA 35th Inf. Co.H 2nd Lt.
Roberts, James M. GA 36th (Broyles') Inf. Co.H
Cpl.
Roberts, James M. GA Cobb's Legion Co.B
Roberts, James M. LA 28th (Gray's) Inf. Co.E
Roberts, James M. NC 45th Inf. Co.A
Roberts, James M. SC 16th Inf. Co.C 1st Lt.
Roberts, James M. TN Lt.Arty. Barry's Co.
Roberts, James M. TN 16th Inf. Co.G
Roberts, James M. TX 14th Cav. Co.A
Roberts, James M. VA Lt.Arty. Lowry's Co.
Bugler
Roberts, James M. VA 49th Inf. Co.H

Roberts, James M. VA 166th Mil. Taylor's Co.
Cpl.
Roberts, James N. AR 17th (Lemoyne's) Inf.
Co.F
Roberts, James N. AR 21st Inf. Co.E Cpl.
Roberts, James O. KY 8th Mtd.Inf. Co.G
Roberts, James O.A. Lt.Arty. Dent's Btty.,CSA
Sgt.
Roberts, James P. MS 24th Inf. Co.L
Roberts, James P. TN 19th Inf. Co.C
Roberts, James P. TX 3rd Cav. Co.B
Roberts, James R. GA 51st Inf. Co.F
Roberts, James R. VA 14th Inf. Co.B
Roberts, James S. FL 1st Cav. Co.G
Roberts, James S. FL 7th Inf. Co.H
Roberts, James S. GA 4th Inf. Co.H
Roberts, James S. GA 29th Inf. Co.G,K
Roberts, James S. GA 43rd Inf. Co.F
Roberts, James S. LA 5th Inf. New Co.A Sgt.
Roberts, James S. MS 1st Lt.Arty. Co.I Cpl.
Roberts, James S. TN 19th Inf. Co.H Sgt.
Roberts, James T. TX 18th Cav. Co.D
Roberts, James T. VA 21st Inf. Co.E Cpl.
Roberts, James T.A. AR 1st Cav. Co.H
Roberts, James W. AL 6th Inf. Co.L
Roberts, James W. AL 37th Inf. Co.H
Roberts, James W. AL 57th Inf. Co.I
Roberts, James W. AL 63rd Inf. Co.I
Roberts, James W. GA 29th Inf. Co.B
Roberts, James W. GA 42nd Inf. Co.A
Roberts, James W. GA 64th Inf. Co.E
Roberts, James W. MO Cav. Poindexter's Regt.
Roberts, James W. MO 4th Inf. Co.D Sgt.
Roberts, James W. NC 4th Inf. Co.K
Roberts, James W. NC 46th Inf. Co.C
Roberts, James W. SC 10th Inf. Co.B
Roberts, James W. TN 2nd (Smith's) Cav. Sgt.
Roberts, James W. VA Hvy.Arty. Coleman's Co.
Roberts, James W. VA 24th Inf. Co.F
Roberts, Jasper GA 29th Inf. Co.H Music.
Roberts, Jasper TN 16th Inf. Co.G
Roberts, Jasper M. GA 28th Inf. Co.G 2nd Lt.
Roberts, Jasper M. TN 39th Mtd.Inf. Co.F Sgt.
Roberts, Jasper N. AR Cav. Harrell's Bn. Co.C
Roberts, J.B. AL Randolph Cty.Res. Shepherd's
Co.
Roberts, J.B. GA Lt.Arty. 12th Bn. 3rd Co.E
Roberts, J.B. GA 15th Inf. Co.D
Roberts, J.B. KY 6th Mtd.Inf. Co.I
Roberts, J.B. MS 41st Inf. Co.I
Roberts, J.B. NC 18th Inf. Co.I
Roberts, J.B. SC 11th Inf. Co.D
Roberts, J.B. TN 7th (Duckworth's) Cav.
Co.K,C
Roberts, J.B. TN 8th Inf. Co.H
Roberts, J.B. TN 17th Inf. Co.I Cpl.
Roberts, J.B. TN 26th Inf. Co.B,H Cpl.
Roberts, J.B. TX 8th Cav. Co.E
Roberts, J.B. TX Cav. Baird's Regt. Co.G
Roberts, J.B. Conf.Lt.Arty. Richardson's Bn.
Co.C
Roberts, J.C. AL 5th Inf. New Co.D
Roberts, J.C. AL 48th Inf. Co.F Capt.
Roberts, J.C. GA 2nd Res. Co.G
Roberts, J.C. GA 7th Inf. Co.H
Roberts, J.C. KY 12th Cav. Co.H
Roberts, J.C. LA Inf. 9th Bn. Co.B

Roberts, J.C. MS 8th Cav. Co.F,B
Roberts, J.C. MS 28th Cav. Co.E
Roberts, J.C. MO Lt.Arty. 3rd Field Btty.
Roberts, J.C. MO 1st & 4th Cons.Inf. Co.E
Roberts, J.C. MO 4th Inf. Co.E,H
Roberts, J.C. MO St.Guard Cpl.
Roberts, J.C. SC Cav. 10th Bn. Co.B
Roberts, J.C. TX 20th Cav. Co.I 1st Lt.
Roberts, J.C. TX Cav. Benavides' Regt. Co.K
Roberts, J.C. TX Cav. Waller's Regt. Co.D
Roberts, J.C. TX 15th Inf. Co.I
Roberts, J.C. VA 17th Cav. Co.H
Roberts, J.C. VA Cav. 37th Bn. Co.I Cpl.
Roberts, J.C. VA Lt.Arty. 13th Bn. Co.A
Roberts, J.D. AL 12th Inf. Co.C
Roberts, J.D. LA 25th Inf. Co.I
Roberts, J.D. MS 2nd (Quinn's St.Troops) Inf.
Co.C
Roberts, J.D. SC 2nd Inf. Co.A,G
Roberts, J.D. TN Arty. Marshall's Co.
Roberts, J.D. TX Cav. Terry's Regt. Co.E
Jr.2nd Lt.
Roberts, J. DeB. SC Inf. Hampton Legion Co.G
Sgt.
Roberts, J.E. AL 7th Cav. Co.G
Roberts, J.E. AR Cav. McGehee's Regt. Co.A
Roberts, J.E. AR Cav. Gordon's Regt. Co.C
Roberts, J.E. AR 30th Inf. Co.B
Roberts, J.E. AR 35th Inf. Co.C
Roberts, J.E. AR 45th Mil. Co.C
Roberts, J.E. SC Lt.Arty. 3rd (Palmetto) Bn.
Co.A
Roberts, J.E. SC 1st (McCreary's) Inf.
Campbell's Co.
Roberts, J.E. TN 7th (Duckworth's) Cav. Co.A
Roberts, J.E. TN 62nd Mtd.Inf. Co.D
Roberts, J.E. TX 26th Cav. Co.H
Roberts, J.E. TX Cav. Baird's Regt. Co.G
Roberts, J.E. TX 20th Inf. Co.I
Roberts, J.E. 14th Conf.Cav. Co.G Sgt.
Roberts, J.E. Sig.Corps,CSA
Roberts, J.E. Gen. & Staff Capt.,QM
Roberts, J.E. Gen. & Staff Lt.,Ord.Off.
Roberts, J.E. Gen. & Staff Contr.Surg.
Roberts, J.E. Hosp.Stew.
Roberts, Jefferson GA 25th Inf. Co.C Capt.
Roberts, Jefferson, Jr. GA 25th Inf. Co.C Sgt.
Roberts, Jeremiah KY 5th Mtd.Inf. Co.D
Roberts, Jeremiah B. AR 12th Inf. Co.B
Roberts, Jesse LA 11th Inf. Co.I Cpl.
Roberts, Jesse MO 6th Inf. Co.G
Roberts, Jesse NC 2nd Cav. (19th St.Troops)
Co.K
Roberts, Jesse NC 60th Inf. Co.H
Roberts, Jesse NC 64th Inf. Co.C
Roberts, Jesse SC 16th Inf. Co.C
Roberts, Jesse TN 29th Inf. Co.K
Roberts, Jesse TX 30th Cav. Co.G
Roberts, Jesse TX 1st Hvy.Arty. Co.A
Roberts, Jesse VA 49th Inf. Co.I
Roberts, Jesse VA 50th Inf. Co.F
Roberts, Jesse VA 64th Mtd.Inf. Co.C
Roberts, Jesse A. AL 37th Inf. Co.F 1st Sgt.
Roberts, Jesse B. GA 51st Inf. Co.D
Roberts, Jessee C. GA 8th Inf. (St.Guards) Co.F
Roberts, Jessee H. GA 29th Inf. Co.B
Roberts, Jesse M. GA 37th Inf. Co.H

Roberts, Jesse W. VA 34th Inf. Co.B
Roberts, Jessey P. MO Inf. Perkins' Bn. Co.C
Roberts, J.F. FL 1st (Res.) Inf. Co.G
Roberts, J.F. GA 41st Inf. Co.H
Roberts, J.F. MS 7th Inf. Co.C
Roberts, J.F. SC 2nd Inf. Co.A
Roberts, J.F. SC 27th Inf. Co.D
Roberts, J.F. TN 21st & 22nd (Cons.) Cav. Co.K
Roberts, J.F. TN 22nd (Barteau's) Cav. Co.A
Roberts, J.F. TN 59th Mtd.Inf. Co.K
Roberts, J.F. TX 1st Bn.S.S. Co.E,A
Roberts, J.F. Brush Bn.
Roberts, J. Fred TX Inf. Whaley's Co.
Roberts, J.G. AL St.Arty. New Co.C
Roberts, J.G. AL 21st Inf. Co.K
Roberts, J.G. MS Cav. 17th Bn. Co.A
Roberts, J.G. MO 4th Inf. Co.C
Roberts, J.H. AL 4th Inf. Co.H
Roberts, J.H. AL 6th Inf. Co.F
Roberts, J.H. AL Cp. of Instr. Talladega Co.A
Roberts, J.H. AR 1st Mtd.Rifles Co.G
Roberts, J.H. FL Lt.Arty. Dyke's Co.
Roberts, J.H. GA 11th Cav. Co.G
Roberts, J.H. GA 9th Inf. (St.Guards) Co.H
Roberts, J.H. GA 1st (Olmstead's) Inf. Co.G
Roberts, J.H. GA Inf. 18th Bn. Co.B
Roberts, J.H. GA 32nd Inf. Co.K Cpl.
Roberts, J.H. GA Inf. (St.Guards) Hansell's Co.
Roberts, J.H. KY 1st (Butler's) Cav. New Co.H
Capt.
Roberts, J.H. LA Res.Corps Hatcher's Co.
Roberts, J.H. MS 11th (Perrin's) Cav. Co.C Sgt.
Roberts, J.H. MS 3rd Inf. Co.F
Roberts, J.H. MS 36th Inf. Co.D
Roberts, J.H. MS 41st Inf. Co.A
Roberts, J.H. NC 26th Inf. Co.G
Roberts, J.H. NC 64th Inf. Co.D
Roberts, J.H. NC Allen's Co. (Loc.Def.)
Roberts, J.H. SC 1st (Butler's) Inf. Co.K Music.
Roberts, J.H. TN 21st (Wilson's) Cav. Co.K
Roberts, J.H. TN 50th (Cons.) Inf. Co.H Sgt.
Roberts, J.H. TX Cav. McCord's Frontier Regt.
Co.E
Roberts, J.H. VA 15th Cav. Co.B
Roberts, J.H. VA Hvy.Arty. Allen's Co.
Roberts, J.H. VA 3rd Res. Co.G
Roberts, J.H. Conf.Inf. 1st Bn. Co.I, 2nd Co.B
Roberts, J.H.W. KY 12th Cav. Co.C Orderly
Sgt.
Roberts, J.H.W. TN 7th (Duckworth's) Cav.
Co.H
Roberts, J.I. MS Inf. 1st Bn.St.Troops (30 days
'64) Co.E
Roberts, Jiles J. MO Inf. Perkins' Bn.
Roberts, Jipthes W. AL 25th Inf. Co.H
Roberts, J.J. AL 6th Inf. Co.H
Roberts, J.J. AL 32nd Inf. Co.E
Roberts, J.J. AL 42nd Inf. Co.A
Roberts, J.J. FL 4th Inf. Co.F
Roberts, J.J. FL 9th Inf.
Roberts, J.J. GA 1st Cav. Co.G,I
Roberts, J.J. GA 5th Cav. Co.G
Roberts, J.J. GA 6th Cav. Co.D
Roberts, J.J. GA 11th Inf. Co.F
Roberts, J.J. GA 19th Inf. Co.H Sgt.
Roberts, J.J. KY Lt.Arty. Cobb's Co.
Roberts, J.J. MS 9th Cav. Co.K

Roberts, J.J. MS Inf. 1st Bn.St.Troops (30 days
'64) Co.C
Roberts, J.J. MS 24th Inf. Co.I
Roberts, J.J. MS 39th Inf. Co.F
Roberts, J.J. SC Cav. 17th Bn. Co.C
Roberts, J.J. TN 31st Inf. Co.A
Roberts, J.J. TX 27th Cav. Surg.
Roberts, J.J. TX 5th Inf. Co.E Asst.Surg.
Roberts, J.K. AL 37th Inf. Co.C
Roberts, J.K. GA 36th (Broyles') Inf. Co.K
Roberts, J.K. TN Inf. 22nd Bn. Co.B Sgt.
Roberts, J.K. TN 26th Inf. Co.G
Roberts, J.K. TN 35th Inf. 2nd Co.D Sgt.
Roberts, J.K. TN 63rd Inf. Co.H
Roberts, J.K. TX Cav. McCord's Frontier Regt.
Co.E
Roberts, J.K.P. AR 30th Inf. Co.B
Roberts, J.L. AL 25th Inf. Co.I 2nd Lt.
Roberts, J.L. AL 58th Inf. Co.C
Roberts, J.L. AL Cp. of Instr. Talladega
Roberts, J.L. AR Inf. 2nd Bn. Co.A
Roberts, J.L. AR 2nd Vol. Co.D Cpl.
Roberts, J.L. AR 37th Inf. Co.C
Roberts, J.L. FL 3rd Inf. Co.H
Roberts, J.L. GA Lt.Arty. 12th Bn. 3rd Co.C
Roberts, J.L. GA Inf. 1st Loc.Troops (Augusta)
Dearing's Cav.Co.
Roberts, J.L. GA 46th Inf. Co.C Cpl.
Roberts, J.L. GA 54th Inf. Co.A
Roberts, J.L. GA Phillips' Legion Co.B Cpl.
Roberts, J.L. MS Cav. Hughes' Bn. Co.F
Roberts, J.L. MO 1st Brig.St.Guard
Roberts, J.L. SC 26th Inf. Co.E Sgt.
Roberts, J.L. TN 33rd Inf. Co.H Cpl.
Roberts, J.L. TN 35th Inf. 1st Co.D
Roberts, J.L. VA 55th Inf. Co.D
Roberts, J.L.B. AR 17th (Lemoyne's) Inf. Co.E
Roberts, J.M. AL 1st Regt. Mobile Vol. Co.A
Sgt.
Roberts, J.M. AL Mil. 2nd Regt.Vol. Co.D 2nd
Lt.
Roberts, J.M. AL 11th Inf. Co.H
Roberts, J.M. AL 18th Inf. Co.K
Roberts, J.M. AL 22nd Inf. Co.G
Roberts, J.M. AL 25th Inf. Co.A
Roberts, J.M. AL 32nd Inf. Co.H
Roberts, J.M. AL 42nd Inf. Co.A
Roberts, J.M. AR Cav. Harrell's Bn. Co.D
Roberts, J.M. GA 11th Cav. Co.B,G Bvt.2nd
Lt.
Roberts, J.M. GA 11th Cav. Co.B
Roberts, J.M. GA Cav. 20th Bn. Co.A
Roberts, J.M. GA Hvy.Arty. 22nd Bn. Co.F
Roberts, J.M. GA Siege Arty. Campbell's
Ind.Co.
Roberts, J.M. GA 1st (Ramsey's) Inf. Co.D
Roberts, J.M. GA 5th Inf. Co.G 2nd Lt.
Roberts, J.M. GA Inf. 8th Bn. Co.C
Roberts, J.M. GA Inf. 9th Bn. Co.E
Roberts, J.M. GA 22nd Inf. Co.F
Roberts, J.M. GA 54th Inf. Co.D,F
Roberts, J.M. LA Siege Train Bn. Co.H
Roberts, J.M. MS Graves' Co. (Copiah Horse
Guards)
Roberts, J.M. MS 1st Lt.Arty. Co.F
Roberts, J.M. MS 6th Inf. Co.F
Roberts, J.M. MS 21st Inf. Co.C 2nd Lt.

Roberts, J.M. MS 32nd Inf. Co.G Comsy.
Roberts, J.M. MS 41st Inf. Co.A
Roberts, J.M. MS 43rd Inf. Co.C Cpl.
Roberts, J.M. NC 2nd Conscr. Co.B
Roberts, J.M. NC 4th Sr.Res. Co.G
Roberts, J.M. NC 18th Inf. Co.G
Roberts, J.M. SC Lt.Arty. 3rd (Palmetto) Bn.
Co.A
Roberts, J.M. SC Hvy.Arty. 15th (Lucas') Bn.
Co.A
Roberts, J.M. SC 18th Inf. Co.G 1st Lt.
Roberts, J.M. TN Inf. 22nd Bn. Co.B
Roberts, J.M. TN 26th Inf. Co.G
Roberts, J.M. TN 47th Inf. Co.I
Roberts, J.M. TX Cav. Giddings' Bn. Car-
rington's Co.
Roberts, J.M. TX 7th Inf. Co.I
Roberts, J.M. VA Lt.Arty. 13th Bn. Co.A
Roberts, J.M. 1st Conf.Inf. 2nd Co.K
Roberts, J.M. Gen. & Staff Hosp.Stew.
Roberts, J.N. AR 13th Mil. Co.A
Roberts, J.N. LA 6th Cav. Co.H
Roberts, J.N. NC 2nd Jr.Res. Co.D
Roberts, J.N. SC 3rd St.Troops Co.D
Roberts, J.N. TX 7th Cav. Co.E
Roberts, J.N. VA Inf. 31st Regt. Co.A 1st Sgt.
Roberts, J.N. Gen. & Staff Capt.,ACS
Roberts, J. Nathaniel SC 3rd Cav. Co.C
Roberts, J.O. AL 25th Inf. Co.H
Roberts, J.O. GA 2nd Cav. (St.Guards) Co.D
Roberts, J.O. GA Inf. 11th Bn. (St.Guards) Co.B
Roberts, J.O. GA Inf. (E. to W.Point Guards)
Matthews' Co.
Roberts, Joe KY 4th Cav. Co.F
Roberts, Joel AL 31st Inf. Co.H
Roberts, Joel AL 46th Inf. Co.K
Roberts, Joel GA 53rd Inf. Co.C
Roberts, Joel TX Cav. Hardeman's Regt. Co.A
Roberts, Joel TX Cav. Waller's Regt. Co.B
Roberts, Joel C. AR 31st Inf. Co.E
Roberts, Joel M. NC Walker's Bn. Thomas'
Legion Co.A
Roberts, John AL 13th Bn.Part.Rangers Co.B
Roberts, John AL 3rd Inf. Co.C
Roberts, John AL 8th Inf. Co.G
Roberts, John AL 24th Inf. Co.H,B
Roberts, John AL 34th Inf. Co.F
Roberts, John AL 39th Inf. Co.E
Roberts, John AL 40th Inf. Co.A
Roberts, John AL 3rd Bn. Hilliard's Legion Vol.
Co.C
Roberts, John AR Lt.Arty. Thrall's Btty.
Roberts, John AR 34th Inf. Co.D
Roberts, John FL Cav. Pickett's Co.
Roberts, John FL 4th Inf. Co.F
Roberts, John FL 7th Inf. Co.A
Roberts, John FL 9th Inf. Co.D
Roberts, John GA 8th Cav. New Co.I
Roberts, John GA 12th Cav. Co.L
Roberts, John GA Cav. 20th Bn. Co.A,D
Roberts, John GA Cav. Roswell Bn. Co.C,A
Sgt.
Roberts, John GA Lt.Arty. (Jo Thompson Arty.)
Hanleiter's Co.
Roberts, John GA 1st (Fannin's) Res. Co.H
Roberts, John GA 1st (Ramsey's) Inf. Co.E
Music.

Roberts, John GA 2nd Bn.S.S. Co.A
Roberts, John GA 3rd Bn. (St.Guards) Co.G
Roberts, John GA 5th Inf. Co.M
Roberts, John GA 7th Inf. (St.Guards) Co.A Cpl.
Roberts, John GA 25th Inf. Co.F
Roberts, John GA 26th Inf. Co.K
Roberts, John GA Inf. 26th Bn. Co.A
Roberts, John GA 40th Inf. Co.A
Roberts, John GA 45th Inf. Co.F
Roberts, John GA 50th Inf. Co.G
Roberts, John GA 59th Inf. Co.I
Roberts, John GA 61st Inf. Co.G
Roberts, John GA Inf. (Loc.Def.) Whiteside's Nav.Bn. Co.B
Roberts, John GA Res. Co.D
Roberts, John KY 7th Cav. Co.G
Roberts, John KY 13th Cav. Co.G
Roberts, John, Jr. KY Jessee's Bn.Mtd.Riflemen Co.A
Roberts, John KY Cav. Malone's Regt.
Roberts, John KY 5th Mtd.Inf. Co.K
Roberts, John KY 8th Mtd.Inf. Co.G
Roberts, John LA 1st Cav. Co.E
Roberts, John LA 1st (Nelligan's) Inf. Co.I
Roberts, John LA 3rd Inf. Co.F Sgt.
Roberts, John LA Mil. 3rd Regt. 1st Brig. 1st Div. Co.E
Roberts, John LA Inf. 9th Bn. Co.B
Roberts, John LA 15th Inf. Co.D,G
Roberts, John LA 16th Inf. Co.B
Roberts, John MS 1st Cav. Co.D
Roberts, John MS St.Cav. 2nd Bn. (Harris') Co.A,B Sgt.
Roberts, John MS 6th Cav. Co.H
Roberts, John MS 18th Cav. Co.A
Roberts, John MS 18th Cav. Co.K,L
Roberts, John MS 2nd (Davidson's) Inf. Co.E Sgt.
Roberts, John MS Inf. 3rd Bn. Co.G Cpl.
Roberts, John MS 5th Inf. Co.A
Roberts, John MS 10th Inf. Old Co.G, New Co.H
Roberts, John MS 20th Inf. Co.I
Roberts, John MS 21st Inf. Co.C
Roberts, John MS 29th Inf. Co.D
Roberts, John MO Lt.Arty. Landis' Co.
Roberts, John MO 8th Inf. Co.D
Roberts, John MO 8th Inf. Co.E
Roberts, John NC 6th Cav. (65th St.Troops) Co.I
Roberts, John NC Lt.Arty. 3rd Bn. Co.B
Roberts, John NC 1st Inf. Co.A
Roberts, John NC 5th Sr.Res. Co.K
Roberts, John NC 6th Inf. Co.I
Roberts, John NC 23rd Inf. Co.D
Roberts, John NC 42nd Inf. Co.A
Roberts, John NC 45th Inf. Co.A
Roberts, John NC 45th Inf. Co.I
Roberts, John NC 64th Inf. Co.D
Roberts, John NC Inf. Thomas Legion Co.I
Roberts, John SC 1st Arty. Co.D
Roberts, John SC 5th Inf. 2nd Co.B
Roberts, John SC 6th Inf. 1st Co.A
Roberts, John SC 16th Inf. Co.C
Roberts, John SC 23rd Inf. Co.H Lt.Col.
Roberts, John TN 12th (Green's) Cav. Co.E
Roberts, John TN 13th (Gore's) Cav. Co.A

Roberts, John TN 14th Cav. Co.B
Roberts, John TN 19th (Biffle's) Cav. Co.G
Roberts, John TN Douglass' Bn.Part.Rangers Perkins' Co.
Roberts, John TN Lt.Arty. Burrough's Co.
Roberts, John TN 7th Inf. Co.G
Roberts, John TN 13th Inf. Co.A
Roberts, John TN 16th Inf. Co.G
Roberts, John TN 29th Inf. Co.F
Roberts, John TN 35th Inf. 2nd Co.D
Roberts, John TN 37th Inf. Co.H
Roberts, John TN 47th Inf. Co.A
Roberts, John TN 48th (Voorhies') Inf. Co.D
Roberts, John TN 53rd Inf. Co.G
Roberts, John TN 61st Mtd.Inf. Co.I
Roberts, John TX 26th Cav. Co.E Cpl.
Roberts, John TX 30th Cav. Co.C
Roberts, John TX Cav. Giddings' Bn. Co.B
Roberts, John TX Cav. Morgan's Regt. Co.E
Roberts, John TX 4th Inf. Co.G
Roberts, John TX 9th (Young's) Inf. Co.G
Roberts, John TX 20th Inf. Co.D
Roberts, John VA 8th Cav. Co.C
Roberts, John VA 19th Cav. Co.A
Roberts, John VA 20th Cav. Co.F
Roberts, John VA Cav. 36th Bn. Co.B
Roberts, John VA Cav. Swann's Bn. Watkins' Co.
Roberts, John VA Inf. 1st Bn. Co.A
Roberts, John VA Inf. 21st Bn. Co.A
Roberts, John VA 23rd Inf. Co.H
Roberts, John VA 28th Inf. Co.G
Roberts, John VA Inf. 28th Bn. Co.D
Roberts, John VA 48th Inf. Co.I 1st Lt.
Roberts, John VA 63rd Inf. Co.A
Roberts, John VA 3rd Cav. & Inf.St.Line Co.A
Roberts, John 3rd Conf.Cav. Co.C
Roberts, John 14th Conf.Cav. Co.A
Roberts, John 14th Conf.Cav. Co.G
Roberts, John 2nd Cherokee Mtd.Vol. Co.A
Roberts, John Conf.Inf. Tucker's Regt. Co.F
Roberts, John A. AL 34th Inf. Co.B
Roberts, John A. AR 2nd Mtd.Rifles Co.B
Roberts, John A. AR 14th (Powers') Inf. Co.H
Roberts, John A. GA 9th Inf. Co.C
Roberts, John A. MS 12th Inf. Co.A
Roberts, John A. MO 1st N.E. Cav. Co.M Sgt.
Roberts, John A. MO Cav. Poindexter's Regt.
Roberts, John A. MO 1st Inf. Co.G Sgt.
Roberts, John A. MO 1st & 4th Cons.Inf. Co.G Sgt.
Roberts, John A. MO Inf. Perkins' Bn.
Roberts, John A. NC 23rd Inf. Co.B Sgt.
Roberts, John A. NC 34th Inf. Co.H Capt.
Roberts, John A. TN 8th (Smith's) Cav. Co.I
Roberts, John A. TN Inf. 22nd Bn. Co.A
Roberts, John A. TX 11th (Spaight's) Bn.Vol. Co.C Cpl.
Roberts, John A. VA 6th Cav. Co.I 2nd Lt.
Roberts, John A. VA Arty. Paris' Co. Sgt.
Roberts, John A. VA 3rd Res. Co.C
Roberts, John A.W. GA 11th Inf. Co.G
Roberts, John B. GA 20th Inf. Co.H
Roberts, John B. GA 49th Inf. Co.C,D Bvt.2nd Lt.
Roberts, John B. GA 55th Inf. Co.C 1st Sgt.
Roberts, John B. KY Cav. 1st Bn.

Roberts, John B. KY 3rd Cav. Co.B
Roberts, John B. KY Jessee's Bn.Mtd.Riflemen Co.A
Roberts, John B. LA Washington Arty.Bn. Co.2
Roberts, John B. MS 1st Cav.Res. Co.A
Roberts, John B. MS 17th Inf. Co.G Ens.
Roberts, John B. TN 25th Inf. Co.G
Roberts, John B. TX 19th Cav. Co.F
Roberts, John B. VA Lt.Arty. Grandy's Co.
Roberts, John B. VA 6th Inf. Vickery's Co.
Roberts, John B. VA 16th Inf. 1st Co.H
Roberts, John C. AL 18th Inf. 1st Lt.,Ens.
Roberts, John C. AL 37th Inf. Co.C
Roberts, John C. AL 38th Inf. Co.F
Roberts, John C. AR 6th Inf. New Co.D
Roberts, John C. AR 10th Inf. 1st Lt.
Roberts, John C. AR 12th Inf. 1st Lt.
Roberts, John C. GA Inf. 27th Bn. Co.B
Roberts, John C. GA 59th Inf. Co.F Cpl.
Roberts, John C. MS 41st Inf. Co.G
Roberts, John C. MS 42nd Inf. Co.G
Roberts, John C. SC Inf. 3rd Bn. Co.B 1st Lt.
Roberts, John C. TN Lt.Arty. Barry's Co.
Roberts, John C. TN 3rd (Lillard's) Mtd.Inf. Co.F 1st Lt.
Roberts, John C. TN 43rd Inf. Co.F
Roberts, John C. TX 6th Cav. Co.G
Roberts, John C. TX 14th Cav. Co.F 2nd Lt.
Roberts, John C. TX 17th Cav. Co.K
Roberts, John C. TX Cav. Border's Regt. Co.A
Roberts, John C. TX 4th Inf. Co.C Sgt.
Roberts, John C. VA 14th Inf. Co.A
Roberts, John D. FL 1st Cav. Co.A Cpl.
Roberts, John D. FL 3rd Inf. Co.K
Roberts, John D. NC 5th Cav. (63rd St.Troops) Co.D
Roberts, John D. TN 19th Inf. Co.K
Roberts, John D. TX 7th Inf. Co.A
Roberts, John D. VA Cav. 35th Bn. Co.C
Roberts, John E. AL Lt.Arty. Lee's Btty.
Roberts, John E. NC 1st Cav. (9th St.Troops) Co.D
Roberts, John E. NC 1st Cav. (9th St.Troops) Co.I
Roberts, John E. NC 49th Inf. Co.G
Roberts, John E. VA Horse Arty. Lurty's Co.
Roberts, John E. VA 4th Inf. Co.F Capt.
Roberts, John E. VA 59th Inf. 3rd Co.I
Roberts, John E. Gen. & Staff Hosp.Stew.
Roberts, John F. FL 1st Cav. Co.A
Roberts, John F. SC 1st (Butler's) Inf. Co.E
Roberts, John F. SC Inf. 1st (Charleston) Bn. Co.D
Roberts, John F. VA Cav. 39th Bn. Co.C
Roberts, John F. VA Hvy.Arty. 19th Bn. 3rd Co.C
Roberts, John F. VA 6th Bn.Res. Co.F
Roberts, John F. VA 51st Inf. Co.I
Roberts, John F. VA Mil. Grayson Cty.
Roberts, John G. GA 49th Inf. Co.F
Roberts, John G. MS 20th Inf. Co.K
Roberts, John H. AL 8th (Livingston's) Cav. Co.B
Roberts, John H. AR 1st Inf.
Roberts, John H. AR 11th Inf. Co.B
Roberts, John H. FL 3rd Inf. Co.D
Roberts, John H. FL 4th Inf. Co.H Cpl.

Roberts, John H. KY Cav. Buckner Guards 1st Lt.
Roberts, John H. LA Inf. 11th Bn. Co.D
Roberts, John H. MS Inf. 5th Bn. Co.C
Roberts, John H. MS 12th Inf. Co.C
Roberts, Jno. H. MO 2nd Inf. Co.F
Roberts, John H. NC 15th Inf. Co.M
Roberts, John H. NC 21st Inf. Co.F
Roberts, John H. NC 29th Inf.
Roberts, John H. NC 32nd Inf. Co.I
Roberts, John H. NC 37th Inf. Co.H 1st Lt.
Roberts, John H. SC 2nd St.Troops Co.D
Roberts, John H. SC 10th Inf. Co.B
Roberts, John H. TN 4th Inf. Co.A Cpl.
Roberts, John H. TN 19th Inf. Co.C
Roberts, John H. TN 24th Inf. Co.B Cpl.
Roberts, John H. TN 37th Inf. Co.D
Roberts, John H. TX 5th Inf. Co.E
Roberts, John H. VA 1st Cav. 2nd Co.D
Roberts, John H. VA 22nd Inf. Co.C
Roberts, John H. VA 34th Inf. Co.F 1st Lt.
Roberts, John Henry FL 1st Cav. Co.E
Roberts, John I. MS 30th Inf. Co.D 1st Lt.
Roberts, John J. AL Talladega Cty.Res. J. Hurst's Co.
Roberts, John J. AR 36th Inf. Co.H
Roberts, John J. FL 7th Inf. Co.A
Roberts, John J. FL 8th Inf. Co.H
Roberts, John J. GA 8th Cav.
Roberts, John J. GA 1st Inf. (St.Guards) Co.H
Roberts, John J. GA 36th (Broyles') Inf. Co.H
Roberts, John J. MO 1st N.E. Cav. Co.A
Roberts, John J. MO 15th Cav. Co.A
Roberts, John J. NC Lt.Arty. Thomas' Legion Levi's Btty.
Roberts, John J. SC 5th Cav. Co.B
Roberts, John J. SC 12th Inf. Co.E
Roberts, John J. VA Hvy.Arty. 19th Bn. Co.D
Roberts, John J. VA 8th Inf. Co.I
Roberts, Jno. J. Gen. & Staff Surg.
Roberts, John K. AL Mil. Jones' Co.
Roberts, John K. NC 39th Inf. Co.C
Roberts, John K. TN 2nd Cav. Co.B
Roberts, John L. AL 8th Cav. Co.B
Roberts, John L. AL 21st Inf. Co.C
Roberts, John L. AL 27th Inf. Co.B
Roberts, John L. AR 3rd Inf. Co.H
Roberts, John L. GA 50th Inf. Co.A
Roberts, John L. NC 8th Bn.Part.Rangers Co.F
Roberts, John L. NC 2nd Arty. (36th St.Troops) Co.G
Roberts, John L. NC 13th Inf. Co.A
Roberts, John L. NC 24th Inf. Co.B
Roberts, John L. NC 66th Inf. Co.I
Roberts, John L. TX Cav. Giddings' Bn. Onins' Co.
Roberts, John L. TX 5th Inf. Co.E
Roberts, John L. VA 9th Inf. 1st Co.H
Roberts, John L. VA Inf. 28th Bn. Co.C
Roberts, John L. VA 59th Inf. 2nd Co.H
Roberts, John Lynch VA 28th Inf. Co.E
Roberts, John M. AL Lt.Arty. Clanton's Btty.
Roberts, John M. GA 62nd Cav. Co.F,H 3rd Lt.
Roberts, John M. GA 1st (Olmstead's) Inf. Co.K
Roberts, John M. GA 2nd Inf. Co.G Sgt.
Roberts, John M. GA 14th Inf. Co.D
Roberts, John M. GA 20th Inf. Co.C

Roberts, John M. GA 21st Inf. Co.K
Roberts, John M. GA 39th Inf. Co.E
Roberts, John M. GA 45th Inf. Co.A Sgt.
Roberts, John M. MS 13th Inf. Co.C
Roberts, John M. MO 1st Cav. Co.H
Roberts, John M. MO 10th Cav. Co.G
Roberts, John M. MO Inf. Perkins' Bn.
Roberts, John M. NC 3rd Cav. (41st St.Troops) Co.E
Roberts, John M. SC 2nd Inf. Co.B Cpl.
Roberts, John M. VA 8th Cav. Co.B Sgt.
Roberts, John N. NC 16th Inf. Co.M Sgt.
Roberts, John N. SC Sea Fencibles Symons' Co.
Roberts, John Newton (1) SC 1st (Butler's) Inf. Co.E
Roberts, John P. AR 6th Inf. New Co.D
Roberts, John P. AR 14th (Powers') Inf. Co.B
Roberts, John P. FL 3rd Inf. Co.D 1st Sgt.
Roberts, John P. KY 13th Cav. Co.G
Roberts, John P. MS 10th Inf. New Co.I
Roberts, John P. NC 2nd Arty. (36th St.Troops) Co.G
Roberts, John P. VA 1st St.Res. Co.D
Roberts, John P. VA 12th Inf. Co.B
Roberts, John R. AR 20th Inf. Co.A
Roberts, John R. GA 12th (Robinson's) Cav. (St.Guards) Co.G
Roberts, John R. GA 6th Inf. (St.Guards) Co.D
Roberts, John R. GA 36th (Broyles') Inf. Co.B Cpl.
Roberts, John R. NC 6th Inf. Co.E
Roberts, John R. NC Inf. 13th Bn. Co.D
Roberts, John R. NC 51st Inf. Co.A
Roberts, John R. SC 12th Inf. Co.E
Roberts, John R. TX 12th Cav. Co.K
Roberts, John R. TX Cav. Baylor's Regt. Co.E
Roberts, John R. VA 3rd Inf. Co.C
Roberts, John R. VA Inf. 26th Bn. Co.A
Roberts, John R. VA 59th Inf. 2nd Co.K
Roberts, John S. AL 18th Inf. Co.E,K Cpl.
Roberts, John S. AR 27th Inf. New Co.B Sgt.
Roberts, John S. GA 12th Inf. Co.B
Roberts, John S. KY 8th Cav. Co.B,C
Roberts, John S. KY 9th Mtd.Inf. Co.K
Roberts, John S. MS Cav. 3rd Bn.Res. Co.A Cpl.
Roberts, John S. MS 12th Cav. Co.A,H
Roberts, John S. MO Cav. Freeman's Regt. Wolfe's Co.
Roberts, John S. MO Cav. Poindexter's Regt.
Roberts, John S. MO 2nd Inf. Co.F Sgt.
Roberts, John S. NC 2nd Arty. (36th St.Troops) Co.G Cpl.
Roberts, John S. NC 27th Inf. Co.G
Roberts, John S. SC 5th Cav. Co.F 3rd Lt.
Roberts, John S. SC Cav. 14th Bn. Co.C 3rd Lt.
Roberts, John S. TN 13th (Gore's) Cav. Co.E Capt.
Roberts, John S. TN 48th (Nixon's) Inf. Co.G
Roberts, John S. TN 54th Inf. Co.B
Roberts, John S. VA Hvy.Arty. 20th Bn. Co.D
Roberts, John T. AL Lt.Arty. Lee's Btty.
Roberts, John T. GA 2nd Cav. Co.C 1st Lt.
Roberts, John T. GA 13th Cav. Co.E
Roberts, John T. GA 38th Inf. Co.B
Roberts, John T. KY 1st Inf. Capt.,AQM
Roberts, John T. MS 10th Inf. Old Co.I

Roberts, John T. MO 5th Inf. Co.H
Roberts, John T. MO 10th Inf. Co.K
Roberts, John T. MO 11th Inf. Co.E
Roberts, John T. NC 2nd Arty. (36th St.Troops) Co.H
Roberts, John T. NC 27th Inf. Co.A
Roberts, John T. TN 43rd Inf. Co.K
Roberts, John T. VA 14th Cav. Co.B
Roberts, John T. VA Lt.Arty. Pollock's Co.
Roberts, John T. Cumming's Staff Maj.,QM
Roberts, John W. AL Loc.Guards Co.A
Roberts, John W. AL 42nd Inf. Co.A
Roberts, John W. AR 27th Inf. Co.A
Roberts, John W. GA Cav. 2nd Bn. Co.B
Roberts, John W. GA Cav. Roswell Bn. Co.C
Roberts, John W. GA 24th Inf. Co.B
Roberts, John W. GA 52nd Inf. Co.D Sr.2nd Lt.
Roberts, John W. GA Phillips' Legion Co.A
Roberts, John W. MS 12th Cav. Co.A,H
Roberts, John W. MO St.Guard 1st Lt.
Roberts, John W. NC 2nd Cav. (19th St.Troops) Co.K
Roberts, John W. NC 1st Arty. (10th St.Troops) Co.C
Roberts, John W. NC Moseley's Co. (Sampson Arty.)
Roberts, John W. NC 34th Inf. Co.H
Roberts, John W. VA 1st Cav. Co.F Cpl.
Roberts, John W. VA 2nd Cav. Co.F
Roberts, John W. VA 4th Cav. Co.B
Roberts, John W. VA Lt.Arty. Barr's Co.
Roberts, John W. VA 16th Inf. Co.D Sgt.
Roberts, John W. VA Inf. 25th Bn. Co.B
Roberts, John W.D. MO 10th Inf. Co.F
Roberts, John Wesley KY 2nd Cav. Co.H
Roberts, Jonathan KY 3rd Cav. Co.A Cpl.
Roberts, Jonathan MO 9th Inf. Co.B
Roberts, Jonathan MO Inf. Clark's Regt. Co.A
Roberts, Jonathan TN 17th Inf. Co.B
Roberts, Jonathan B. NC 39th Inf. Co.C
Roberts, Jonathan K. FL 1st Cav. Co.D Music.
Roberts, Jones C. MO 5th Inf. Co.K Cpl.
Roberts, Jones Calaway MO 1st Bn. Co.B
Roberts, Jones W. NC 45th Inf. Co.F 1st Lt.
Roberts, Jonithan K. FL 9th Inf. Co.E
Roberts, Joseph AL 6th Inf. Co.B Sgt.
Roberts, Joseph AL Randolph Cty.Res. A.P. Hunter's Co.
Roberts, Joseph GA 2nd Cav. Co.H
Roberts, Joseph GA 1st Reg. Co.F,B Cpl.
Roberts, Joseph GA 6th Inf. (St.Guards) Co.F
Roberts, Joseph GA 10th Inf. Co.I
Roberts, Joseph KY 10th (Diamond's) Cav. Co.H
Roberts, Joseph KY 5th Mtd.Inf. Co.E
Roberts, Joseph LA 2nd Cav. Co.G
Roberts, Joseph LA 6th Cav. Co.K
Roberts, Joseph LA 5th Inf. Co.H,B
Roberts, Joseph LA 15th Inf. Co.B Cpl.
Roberts, Joseph LA 17th Inf. Co.B
Roberts, Joseph LA 27th Inf. Co.D
Roberts, Joseph LA Inf. Jeff Davis Regt. Co.J
Roberts, Joseph MO 1st N.E. Cav. Co.M
Roberts, Joseph MO Cav. Hicks' Co.
Roberts, Joseph NC 7th Sr.Res. Fisher's Co.
Roberts, Joseph NC 64th Inf. Co.F
Roberts, Joseph SC 1st Arty. Co.A
Roberts, Joseph VA 21st Inf. Co.C

Roberts, Joseph VA 63rd Inf. Co.C
Roberts, Joseph 3rd Conf.Cav. Co.D
Roberts, Joseph Horse Arty. White's Btty.
Roberts, Joseph Gen. & Staff 2nd Lt.,Dr.M.
Roberts, Joseph A. AL 44th Inf. Co.A
Roberts, Joseph A. GA Inf. 1st City Bn.
  (Columbus) Co.F Capt.
Roberts, Joseph A. GA Inf. 19th Bn. (St.Guards)
  Co.A 1st Lt.
Roberts, Joseph A. MS 2nd Inf. Co.C
Roberts, Joseph A. VA Lt.Arty. Lowry's Co.
Roberts, Joseph A. VA W. Union Co.
Roberts, Joseph B. TN 1st Cav.
Roberts, Joseph B. VA 22nd Inf. Co.A QMSgt.
Roberts, Joseph C. GA 5th Inf. Co.A QMSgt.
Roberts, Joseph C. LA Inf. 11th Bn. Co.F
Roberts, Joseph C. TX 4th Cav. Co.A AQM
Roberts, Jos. C. Gen. & Staff Surg.
Roberts, Joseph D. MS 12th Inf. Co.A
Roberts, Joseph D. MO Cav. Poindexter's Regt.
Roberts, Joseph E. TX 26th Cav. Co.B Cpl.
Roberts, Joseph E. TX Cav. Martin's Regt. Co.H
Roberts, Joseph F. VA Mil. Grayson Cty.
Roberts, Joseph Gerrit FL 8th Inf. Co.I
Roberts, Joseph H. GA Inf. White's Co.
Roberts, Joseph H. MO 2nd Inf. Co.F
Roberts, Joseph H. TN Inf. 1st Bn. (Colms')
  Co.B Sgt.
Roberts, Joseph H. VA 44th Inf. Co.D
Roberts, Joseph K.J. MD 1st Cav. Co.E 3rd Lt.
Roberts, Joseph L. NC 3rd Arty. (40th
  St.Troops) Co.C
Roberts, Joseph M. AL 3rd Inf. Co.G
Roberts, Joseph M. GA 5th Inf. Co.D
Roberts, Joseph M. GA 48th Inf. Co.B Capt.
Roberts, Joseph M. MS 24th Inf. Co.L
Roberts, Joseph M. NC 64th Inf. Co.A
Roberts, Joseph P. TN 35th Inf. Co.L Sgt.
Roberts, Joseph R. AR 3rd Inf. Co.K
Roberts, Joseph T. TN 44th (Cons.) Inf. Co.C
Roberts, Joseph W. GA 1st (Olmstead's) Inf.
  Co.B
Roberts, Joseph W. GA 6th Inf. Co.E
Roberts, Joseph W. GA 42nd Inf. Co.A
Roberts, Joseph W. VA 4th Cav. Co.D
Roberts, Joseph W. VA 13th Inf. 1st Co.B
Roberts, Joshua GA 53rd Inf. Co.C
Roberts, Joshua GA Cherokee Legion
  (St.Guards) Co.D
Roberts, Joshua C. VA 39th Inf. Co.C
Roberts, Joshua J. NC 29th Inf. Co.D
Roberts, Joshua T. TN 1st (Turney's) Inf. Co.A
Roberts, Joshua T. TN 35th Inf. Co.D
Roberts, Josiah FL 8th Inf. Co.I Cpl.
Roberts, Josiah LA 1st Cav. Co.I
Roberts, Josiah MS 8th Cav. Co.B
Roberts, Josiah MS 3rd Inf. (St.Troops) Co.E
Roberts, Josiah SC 16th Inf. Co.C
Roberts, Josiah B. VA 2nd Cav. Co.F
Roberts, Josiah D. TN 20th (Russell's) Cav.
Roberts, Josiah L. SC Inf. 9th Bn. Co.D
Roberts, Josiah R. AR 1st (Colquitt's) Inf. Co.G
Roberts, J.P. AL 48th Inf. Co.F
Roberts, J.P. GA 12th Cav. Co.I Sgt.
Roberts, J.P. GA Cav. 1st Bn.Res. Co.E Cpl.
Roberts, J.P. MS 5th Cav. Co.D
Roberts, J.P. MO Cav. Jackman's Regt. Co.I

Roberts, J.P. TN 36th Inf. Co.L
Roberts, J.P. TX 7th Inf. Co.H
Roberts, J.P. VA 2nd Cav. Co.B 2nd Lt.
Roberts, J.P. VA 11th Inf. Co.B
Roberts, J.R. AL 6th Cav. Co.C,B
Roberts, J.R. AL 27th Inf. Co.D
Roberts, J.R. AR Lt.Arty. Key's Btty.
Roberts, J.R. AR 36th Inf. Co.C
Roberts, J.R. AR 50th Mil. Co.B
Roberts, J.R. GA 1st (Symons') Res. Co.D
Roberts, J.R. TX 12th Inf. Co.E Jr.2nd Lt.
Roberts, J.R. TX 22nd Inf. Co.B
Roberts, J.R. 3rd Conf.Eng.Troops Co.C
Roberts, J.S. AL 19th Inf. Co.H Sgt.
Roberts, J.S. AL Randolph Cty.Res. J. High-
  tower's Co. Sgt.
Roberts, J.S. AL Cp. of Instr. Talladega Co.B
Roberts, J.S. AR 10th (Witt's) Cav. Co.I
Roberts, J.S. FL 8th Inf. Co.I
Roberts, J.S. GA 11th Inf. Co.K
Roberts, J.S. GA 13th Inf. Co.K
Roberts, J.S. GA 18th Inf. Co.G
Roberts, J.S. GA 36th (Broyles') Inf. Co.K
Roberts, J.S. GA 56th Inf. Co.I
Roberts, J.S. GA 63rd Inf. Co.G
Roberts, J.S. LA 6th Cav. Co.K
Roberts, J.S. MS 6th Inf. Co.K
Roberts, J.S. NC 5th Inf. 2nd Co.G Cpl.
Roberts, J.S. TN 23rd Inf. Co.D
Roberts, J.S. TN 44th (Cons.) Inf. Co.K Sgt.
Roberts, J.S. TN 51st Inf. Co.H
Roberts, J.S. TN 51st (Cons.) Inf. Co.D
Roberts, J.S. Conf.Cav. 6th Bn. Co.A
Roberts, J.T. AL Lt.Arty. Kolb's Btty.
Roberts, J.T. AL 50th Inf. Co.K
Roberts, J.T. GA Cav. 1st Bn.Res. Tuft's Co.
Roberts, J.T. GA Lt.Arty. 12th Bn. 3rd Co.C
Roberts, J.T. GA Lt.Arty. 12th Bn. 2nd Co.D,F
Roberts, J.T. GA 23rd Inf. Co.I
Roberts, J.T. GA Inf. 25th Bn. (Prov.Guard)
  Co.G
Roberts, J.T. GA 46th Inf. Co.H
Roberts, J.T. KY 9th Mtd.Inf. Co.B
Roberts, J.T. SC Arty. Manigault's Bn. 1st Co.B
Roberts, J.T. SC Inf. 3rd Bn. Co.B
Roberts, J.T. SC 7th Inf. 1st Co.L, 2nd Co.L
  Cpl.
Roberts, J.T. TN 38th Inf. 1st Co.K
Roberts, J.T. TX Cav. 6th Bn. Co.F
Roberts, J.T. TX 28th Cav. Co.E
Roberts, J.T. TX Cav. Baird's Regt. Co.G
Roberts, J.T. TX Cav. McCord's Frontier Regt.
  Co.G
Roberts, J.T. TX Cav. Terry's Regt. Co.F
Roberts, J.T. TX 11th Inf. Co.H
Roberts, J.T. VA Hvy.Arty. 18th Bn. Co.C
Roberts, Judge C. AL 47th Inf. Co.H
Roberts, J.V. AR 34th Inf. Co.E
Roberts, J.V. MS 12th Inf. Co.I
Roberts, J.W. AL 4th (Roddey's) Cav. Co.B 2nd
  Lt.
Roberts, J.W. AL 15th Bn.Part.Rangers Co.A
Roberts, J.W. AL 56th Part.Rangers Co.A
Roberts, J.W. AL 48th Inf. Co.K
Roberts, J.W. AL 63rd Inf. Co.I
Roberts, J.W. AL Pris.Guard Freeman's Co.
Roberts, J.W. AR 18th (Marmaduke's) Inf. Co.F

Roberts, J.W. FL 1st (Res.) Inf. Co.E
Roberts, J.W. GA Cav. 12th Bn. (St.Guards)
  Co.B 1st Lt.
Roberts, J.W. GA Cav. 19th Bn. Co.D
Roberts, J.W. GA Cav. 20th Bn. Co.A
Roberts, J.W. GA 1st Inf. (St.Guards) Co.B
Roberts, J.W. GA Inf. 18th Bn. Co.B
Roberts, J.W. LA 3rd (Wingfield's) Cav. Co.E
Roberts, J.W. LA 4th Inf. Old Co.G
Roberts, J.W. MS Cav. Powers' Regt. Co.H
Roberts, J.W. MS Inf. 7th Bn. Co.F Sgt.
Roberts, J.W. SC Arty. Manigault's Bn. 1st
  Co.B,D, 2nd Co.B,D
Roberts, J.W. SC 14th Inf. Co.G
Roberts, J.W. TN 8th Inf. Co.C
Roberts, J.W. TN 22nd Inf. Co.F
Roberts, J.W. TN 35th Inf. Co.B
Roberts, J.W. TN 47th Inf. Co.H Cpl.
Roberts, J.W. TN 51st Inf. Co.H
Roberts, J.W. TN 51st (Cons.) Inf. Co.D
Roberts, J.W. TN Conscr. (Cp. of Instr.) Co.B
Roberts, J.W. TX 19th Cav. Co.F
Roberts, J.W. TX Arty. 4th Bn. Co.A
Roberts, J.W. TX 8th Inf. Co.A
Roberts, J.W. VA Cav. 37th Bn. Co.D
Roberts, J.W. VA Lt.Arty. W.P. Carter's Co.
Roberts, J.W. VA 1st Res.
Roberts, J.W. 10th Conf.Cav. Co.I
Roberts, Killis M. MS 2nd Inf. Co.H
Roberts, King H. NC 45th Inf. Co.A
Roberts, K.J. KY 10th Cav. Co.D,E
Roberts, K.L. TN Miller's Co. (Loc.Def.Troops)
  Cpl.
Roberts, K.M. MS 2nd Cav. Co.E Sgt.
Roberts, L. AL Cav. Murphy's Bn. Co.B
Roberts, L. AR 1st (Monroe's) Cav. Co.A
Roberts, L. FL 1st (Res.) Inf. Co.E
Roberts, L. GA 5th Cav. Co.C
Roberts, L. GA 26th Inf. Co.E
Roberts, L. KY 5th Cav. Co.H
Roberts, L. KY 8th Cav. Co.A
Roberts, L. LA Mil. Chalmette Regt. Co.C
Roberts, L. MS Cav. 17th Bn. Co.A
Roberts, L. MS Inf. 2nd St.Troops Co.D
Roberts, L. MS 29th Inf. Co.K
Roberts, L. SC 17th Inf. Co.B
Roberts, L. TX Granbury's Cons.Brig. Co.F
Roberts, L. TX 1st Mtd.Res. Co.C
Roberts, L.A. AL 4th Inf. Co.E
Roberts, L.A. GA 10th Cav. (St.Guards) Co.K
Roberts, L.A. GA 12th Cav. Co.A
Roberts, L.A. GA 4th Inf. Co.A
Roberts, Lafayette MO Cav. 4th Regt.St.Guard
  Co.C 2nd Lt.
Roberts, Langly H. NC 37th Inf. Co.F
Roberts, Larkin L. TN 60th Mtd.Inf. Co.I
Roberts, Larkin W. GA 5th Inf. Co.D
Roberts, Lawrence KY 1st (Butler's) Cav. Co.K
  Sgt.
Roberts, L.B. AL 32nd Inf. Co.D
Roberts, L.B. MO St.Guard
Roberts, L.B. VA 16th Inf. Co.D
Roberts, L.C. AL 37th Inf. Co.I
Roberts, L.C. MS 7th Cav. Co.E
Roberts, L.D. MO Inf. Winston's Regt. Co.A
  Capt.
Roberts, L.E. GA 10th Cav. Co.F

Roberts, L.E. GA Cav. 20th Bn. Co.A,F
Roberts, L.E. GA 27th Inf. Co.E
Roberts, Leander B. VA 48th Inf. Co.B Bvt.2nd Lt.
Roberts, L. Edward MD 1st Inf. Co.E
Roberts, Lee MO 8th Inf. Co.E
Roberts, Lee F. TN 25th Inf. Co.K Cpl.
Roberts, Leonard TX 15th Cav. Co.B
Roberts, Leroy AL 1st Bn.Cadets Co.A
Roberts, Leroy AL 38th Inf. Co.E
Roberts, Leroy MS 1st Lt.Arty. Co.I
Roberts, LeRoy SC 12th Inf. Co.E
Roberts, Leroy SC 23rd Inf. Co.F
Roberts, Leroy TN 54th Inf. Co.A
Roberts, Leroy D. MO 4th Cav. Co.I Capt.
Roberts, Levi AL 57th Inf. Co.K Sgt.
Roberts, Levi MS 9th Inf. Old Co.B, New Co.I Lt.
Roberts, Levi TX Inf. 3rd St.Troops Co.B
Roberts, Levi TX Inf. Rutherford's Co.
Roberts, Levy LA 28th (Gray's) Inf. Co.E
Roberts, Lewis AL Cav. Forrest's Regt.
Roberts, Lewis AL 32nd Inf. Co.H
Roberts, Lewis AR 15th (Johnson's) Inf. Co.A
Roberts, Lewis AR 34th Inf. Co.A
Roberts, Lewis FL Inf. 2nd Bn. Co.B
Roberts, Lewis FL 10th Inf. Co.G
Roberts, Lewis KY 4th Cav. Co.E
Roberts, Lewis MS 9th Cav. Co.A
Roberts, Lewis MS 2nd Inf.
Roberts, Lewis TN 18th (Newsom's) Cav. Co.F
Roberts, Lewis TN 40th Inf. Co.I
Roberts, Lewis 15th Conf.Cav. Co.G
Roberts, Lewis C. AL 4th (Roddey's) Cav. Co.D
Roberts, Lewis C. KY 1st Bn.Mtd.Rifles Co.D
Roberts, Lewis F. MO 2nd Inf. Co.H
Roberts, Lewis H. GA 29th Inf. Co.H 2nd Lt.
Roberts, Lewis N. AL 10th Cav. Co.B
Roberts, Lewis R. TN 6th Inf. Co.E Cpl.
Roberts, L.F. AL 48th Inf. Co.E
Roberts, L.F. TX Waul's Legion Co.C
Roberts, L.F. VA 32nd Inf. 2nd Co.I
Roberts, L.F. VA 115th Mil. Co.C
Roberts, L.H. GA 11th Cav. (St.Guards) Slaten's Co.
Roberts, L.H. GA 42nd Inf. Co.A
Roberts, Ligard TN 25th Inf. Co.K Cpl.
Roberts, Lindly M. VA 1st Cav. Co.H
Roberts, Littleton B. VA 25th Cav. Co.B
Roberts, Littleton T. GA 30th Inf. Co.I Jr.2nd Lt.
Roberts, L.M. GA 19th Inf. Co.H Sgt.
Roberts, L.M. TN 8th (Smith's) Cav. Co.G
Roberts, L.M. VA 6th Cav. Co.A
Roberts, L.M. VA 54th Mil. Co.A
Roberts, Logan VA 8th Cav. Co.C
Roberts, Louis AR 50th Mil. Co.D Sgt.
Roberts, Louis 2nd Cherokee Mtd.Vol. Co.B
Roberts, Louis A. TN 40th Inf. Co.I
Roberts, Louis J. TN 38th Inf.
Roberts, Lowery TN 50th Inf. Co.F
Roberts, Loyd B. TN 39th Mtd.Inf. Co.I
Roberts, L.P. AL 50th Inf. Co.I
Roberts, L.S. TN 10th (DeMoss') Cav. Co.B
Roberts, L.S. TN 19th & 20th (Cons.) Cav. Co.D
Roberts, L.S. TN 51st (Cons.) Inf. Co.A Sgt.

Roberts, L.T. GA 3rd Res. Co.G,H 1st Sgt.
Roberts, L.T. LA 8th Cav. Co.D
Roberts, L.T. LA Inf. 1st Bn. (St.Guards) Co.B
Roberts, L.T. TN 19th & 20th (Cons.) Cav. Co.K
Roberts, L.T. TN 33rd Inf. Co.H
Roberts, L.U. KY 2nd (Woodward's) Cav. Co.G
Roberts, L.U. KY 3rd Mtd.Inf. Co.G Sgt.
Roberts, Luke LA Inf. 4th Bn. Co.B
Roberts, Luke GA Inf. 25th Bn. (Prov.Guard) Co.F
Roberts, Luke MS 41st Inf. Co.K
Roberts, Luke A. GA 46th Inf. Co.F
Roberts, Luke R. AL 30th Inf. Co.B
Roberts, Luther AR 23rd Inf. Co.E
Roberts, Luther NC 34th Inf. Co.H Cpl.
Roberts, L.W. LA 19th Inf. Co.I
Roberts, L.W. VA 54th Mil. Co.E,F
Roberts, L. Wesley NC 60th Inf. Co.A,C,H
Roberts, M. AL 19th Inf. Co.I
Roberts, M. AL 24th Inf. Co.E
Roberts, M. AL 44th Inf. Co.K
Roberts, M. LA 2nd Cav. Co.C
Roberts, M. LA Inf.Crescent Regt. Co.A
Roberts, M. MS Cav. 3rd Bn. (Ashcraft's) Co.A Cpl.
Roberts, M. MS Inf. 1st Bn.St.Troops (12 mo. '62-3) Co.A
Roberts, M. MS 29th Inf. Co.G Lt.
Roberts, M. NC 2nd Conscr. Co.C
Roberts, M. SC 17th Inf. Co.B
Roberts, M. TN Inf. 4th Cons.Regt. Co.F Cpl.
Roberts, M. TX 1st Hvy.Arty. 2nd Co.A
Roberts, Mabrey SC 4th St.Troops Co.H
Roberts, Mack KY 11th Cav. Co.H
Roberts, Mack TN 53rd Inf. Co.D
Roberts, Mack C. TX 27th Cav. Co.L
Roberts, Madison NC 6th Sr.Res. Co.G
Roberts, Madison Conf.Arty. Marshall's Co.
Roberts, Major GA 43rd Inf. Co.F
Roberts, Malcomb M. GA 1st Inf. Co.H
Roberts, Malone M. MO 6th Cav.
Roberts, Manns L. MS 24th Inf. Co.I Cpl.
Roberts, Marcellus J. MS Inf. 5th Bn. Co.C
Roberts, Marcus VA 17th Inf. Co.B
Roberts, Marcus A. GA 30th Inf. Co.A
Roberts, Marcus Q. NC 29th Inf. Co.H,C Cpl.
Roberts, Marion LA 8th Inf. Co.G
Roberts, Marion MO Inf. Perkins' Bn.
Roberts, Marion NC 6th Inf. Co.H
Roberts, Marion F. MS 20th Inf. Co.I
Roberts, Mark GA 1st Bn.S.S. Co.B
Roberts, Mark GA 50th Inf. Co.G
Roberts, Mark R. TX 6th Cav. Co.D
Roberts, Marquis L. NC 29th Inf. Co.C,D
Roberts, Marshall TN 16th Inf. Co.G
Roberts, Marshall TN 35th Inf. 2nd Co.D
Roberts, Martial TN 4th (McLemore's) Cav. Co.I
Roberts, Martin AL 50th Inf. Co.G
Roberts, Martin GA 56th Inf. Co.I
Roberts, Martin GA 60th Inf. Co.E
Roberts, Martin NC 21st Inf. Co.L
Roberts, Martin NC 29th Inf. Co.D
Roberts, Martin NC 34th Inf. Co.H
Roberts, Martin TN 38th Inf. 1st Co.H
Roberts, Martin A. LA 4th Inf. Co.C
Roberts, Martin B. LA 14th Inf. Co.I

Roberts, Martin P. NC 1st Inf. (6 mo. '61) Co.E
Roberts, Martin P. NC 11th (Bethel Regt.) Inf. Co.K
Roberts, Martin P. TX 20th Cav. Co.B Capt.
Roberts, Martin V. TX 12th Cav. Co.C
Roberts, Martin V.B. AL 11th Inf. Co.B
Roberts, Martin V.B. GA 35th Inf. Co.H
Roberts, Mat TX 7th Field Btty.
Roberts, Mathew NC 6th Sr.Res. Co.K
Roberts, Mathew TN Inf. 23rd Bn. Co.C Cpl.
Roberts, Mathew TN 42nd Inf. 1st Co.I
Roberts, Matt G. TX 35th (Brown's) Cav. Co.A
Roberts, Matthew GA 29th Inf. Co.H,E 1st Lt.
Roberts, Matthew TN 5th (McKenzie's) Cav. Co.H
Roberts, Matthew Z. AL 35th Inf. Co.D Sgt.
Roberts, M.B. AL Randolph Cty.Res. Shepherd's Co.
Roberts, M.B. GA 5th Inf. (St.Guards) Johnston's Co.
Roberts, M.B. NC 60th Inf. Co.C Sgt.
Roberts, M.B. TX 23rd Cav. Co.K
Roberts, M.C. MS 7th Cav. Co.D,C
Roberts, McAfee GA 7th Cav. Co.G
Roberts, McAfee KY 7th Cav. Co.G
Roberts, McNeil TX 15th Cav. Co.D
Roberts, M.D. TN 11th (Holman's) Cav. Co.E
Roberts, M.D. TN 29th Inf. Co.K
Roberts, Melville C. GA 35th Inf. Co.C Cpl.
Roberts, Meredith LA 13th Bn. (Part.Rangers) Co.F
Roberts, Meredith MS Cav. Jeff Davis Legion Co.C
Roberts, Merill KY 11th Cav. Co.H
Roberts, Merrell KY 7th Cav. Co.G
Roberts, Merritt LA Inf.Cons.Crescent Regt. Co.C
Roberts, Merritt W. AR 9th Inf. Co.A
Roberts, M.G. TX 8th Cav. Co.B
Roberts, M.G. TX 13th Vol. 1st Co.B
Roberts, M.H. AR 1st (Monroe's) Cav. Co.K
Roberts, M.H. SC 1st Bn.S.S. Co.A
Roberts, M.H. 2nd Cherokee Mtd.Vol. Co.B
Roberts, Michael NC 4th Sr.Res. Co.E
Roberts, Mike LA 21st (Kennedy's) Inf. Co.C Sgt.
Roberts, Miles L. AL 28th Inf. Co.B
Roberts, Mills W. VA 16th Inf. Co.D 1st Sgt.
Roberts, Milton GA 18th Inf. Co.I Cpl.
Roberts, Milton TN 84th Inf. Co.G
Roberts, Milton M. 1st Conf.Inf. 2nd Co.H
Roberts, Mitchael FL 4th Inf. Co.F
Roberts, M.L. AL Cp. of Instr. Talladega
Roberts, M.L. GA 8th Inf. Co.F
Roberts, M.L. MS 8th Inf. Co.H Cpl.
Roberts, M.L. TN 6th Inf. Co.A
Roberts, M.M. AL 31st Inf. Co.A Cpl.
Roberts, M.M. AL 54th Inf. Co.C
Roberts, M.M. 4th Conf.Inf. Co.B
Roberts, M.O. MO Cav. 5th Regt.St.Guard Co.B 3rd Lt.
Roberts, Monroe TN 3rd (Clack's) Inf. Co.H
Roberts, Monroe TN 46th Inf. Co.C
Roberts, Moses GA 50th Inf. Co.G
Roberts, Moses MS 2nd (Quinn's St.Troops) Inf. Co.I
Roberts, Moses SC 3rd Bn.Res. Co.E Cpl.

Roberts, Moses SC 5th St.Troops Co.A
Roberts, Moses E. GA 29th Inf. Co.B
Roberts, Moses F. TX 27th Cav. Co.C
Roberts, Moses L.H. GA 24th Inf. Co.B
Roberts, Moses Oliver MO 8th Inf. Co.F,H
  Capt.
Roberts, Mountiville R. NC 39th Inf. Co.K
Roberts, M.P. AL 27th Inf. Co.F Capt.
Roberts, M.P. GA Cav. 24th Bn. Co.B Sgt.
Roberts, M.P. MS Inf. 3rd Bn. Co.H Capt.
Roberts, M.P. NC 64th Inf. Co.I 2nd Lt.
Roberts, M.P. TX 1st Hvy.Arty. Co.A
Roberts, M.R. NC 2nd Jr.Res. Co.E
Roberts, M.S. MS 3rd (St.Troops) Cav. Co.K
Roberts, M.S. MS 5th Inf. (St.Troops) Co.G
Roberts, M.V.B. GA 56th Inf. Co.D
Roberts, M.W. AR 1st Mtd.Rifles Co.H
Roberts, M.W. MO Inf. 4th Regt.St.Guard Co.E
Roberts, M.Y. MS Cav. Ham's Regt. Co.H
Roberts, M.Y. TN 8th (Smith's) Cav. Co.L Sgt.
Roberts, N. MS Cav. 8th Bn. (Ashcraft's) Co.C
Roberts, N. SC 1st (Butler's) Inf. Co.G
Roberts, N. TX 14th Inf. Co.C
Roberts, N. VA 2nd Cav. Co.I
Roberts, Napoleon B. GA 5th Inf. Co.A
Roberts, Napoleon B. TX 6th Cav. Co.D 1st
  Sgt.
Roberts, Nathan AL Cav. Lewis' Bn. Co.D Sgt.
Roberts, Nathan AL Mil. 4th Vol. Co.G 1st Sgt.
Roberts, Nathan AL 25th Inf. Co.I
Roberts, Nathan FL 9th Inf. Co.E
Roberts, Nathan MO Lt.Arty. 1st Field Btty.
Roberts, Nathan TN 17th Inf. Co.K Cpl.
Roberts, Nathan T. TX 30th Cav. Co.A
Roberts, Nathaniel AR 30th Inf. Co.D
Roberts, Nathaniel C. VA 16th Inf. Co.D
Roberts, Nathaniel H. VA 108th Mil. Co.D
Roberts, Nathaniel P. AL 23rd Bn.S.S. Co.G 1st
  Sgt.
Roberts, Nathan J. VA 31st Mil. Co.F
Roberts, Nathan W. NC Inf. 13th Bn. Co.D
Roberts, Nathan W. NC 27th Inf. Co.A
Roberts, Nathan W. NC 51st Inf. Co.A
Roberts, N.B. GA Cav. 20th Bn. Co.C Cpl.
Roberts, N.B. GA 2nd Inf. Co.G
Roberts, N.B. GA 54th Inf. Co.G 1st Lt.
Roberts, N.B. TN Holman's Bn.Part.Rangers
  Co.C
Roberts, N.C. GA 45th Inf. Co.G
Roberts, N.C. MS Inf. 1st Bn.St.Troops (30 days
  '64) Co.C
Roberts, N.E. FL 2nd Cav. Co.K,B
Roberts, Needham H. NC 38th Inf. Co.D
Roberts, Newton GA 56th Inf. Co.I
Roberts, Newton GA St. RR Guards
Roberts, Newton TN 16th (Logwood's) Cav.
  Co.B
Roberts, N.G. MS Cav. Jeff Davis Legion Co.E
Roberts, N.H. FL Inf. 2nd Bn. Co.C 1st Sgt.
Roberts, N. Hannibal FL 10th Inf. Co.H 1st Sgt.
Roberts, Nicholas O. AL 6th Inf. Co.L
Roberts, Nicholas W. TN 37th Inf. Co.I
Roberts, N.J. KY 3rd Mtd.Inf. Co.G
Roberts, N.J. SC 5th Inf. 2nd Co.G
Roberts, N.L. Inf. Bailey's Cons.Regt. Co.B
  Cpl.

Roberts, N.L. TX Granbury's Cons.Brig. Co.C
  1st Sgt.
Roberts, N.L. TX 7th Inf. Co.F 1st Sgt.
Roberts, N.O. SC 11th Inf. Co.E
Roberts, Noah NC 45th Inf. Co.A Sgt.
Roberts, Noah TN 3rd (Clack's) Inf. Co.H
Roberts, Noah TN Inf. 4th Cons.Regt. Co.C
Roberts, Noel G. TX 3rd Cav. Co.E
Roberts, Noel G. TX 27th Cav. Co.C
Roberts, Noel W. GA 60th Inf. Co.K
Roberts, N.P. AL 1st Bn. Hilliard's Legion Vol.
  Co.G Sgt.
Roberts, N.P. VA 8th Inf. Co.I
Roberts, N.T. AR 1st Mtd.Rifles Co.F Capt.
Roberts, N.T. AR Cav. Anderson's Unattach.Bn.
  Co.A Capt.
Roberts, N.T. Gen. & Staff 1st Lt.,Adj.
Roberts, N.W. NC 66th Inf. Co.K
Roberts, N.W. NC Snead's Co. (Loc.Def.)
Roberts, N.W. SC 9th Inf. Co.B
Roberts, O. AR 19th (Dawson's) Inf. Co.F
Roberts, O. GA 10th Inf. Co.B
Roberts, O. MS Cav. 17th Bn. Co.A
Roberts, O.B. GA 7th Cav. Co.I
Roberts, Oba TX 11th Inf. Co.G
Roberts, Oba TX Inf. Yarbrough's Co. (Smith
  Cty.Lt.Inf.)
Roberts, Oba E. TX 11th Inf. Co.K Capt.
Roberts, O.C. GA 10th Cav. (St.Guards) Co.K
Roberts, O.C. MS Inf. 3rd Bn. (St.Troops) Co.D
Roberts, O.D.T. TN 25th Inf. Co.B
Roberts, O.H. GA Conscr.
Roberts, Oliver C. AL 5th Cav. Co.D
Roberts, Oliver G. GA 3rd Inf. Co.H Sgt.
Roberts, Oliver W. TN Cav. Allison's Squad.
  Co.B
Roberts, Olney R. TN 59th Mtd.Inf. Co.D Sgt.
Roberts, O.M. FL 2nd Inf. Co.I
Roberts, O.M. GA 38th Inf. Co.H
Roberts, O.M. SC 21st Inf. Hosp.Stew.
Roberts, O.M. TN 11th Inf. Col.
Roberts, O.M. Gen. & Staff Hosp.Stew.
Roberts, O.P. GA 11th Cav. Co.E
Roberts, Orin H. GA 35th Inf. Co.D Cpl.
Roberts, Orlando A. AL 62nd Inf. Co.E Sgt.
Roberts, O.S. TN 12th (Cons.) Inf. Co.D
Roberts, O.S. TN 22nd Inf. Co.H
Roberts, Oston MS 9th Cav. Co.A
Roberts, P. AL Cav. Forrest's Regt.
Roberts, P. TN 18th (Newsom's) Cav. Co.F
Roberts, P.A. KY 12th Cav. Co.C
Roberts, P.A. MS 10th Cav. Co.F
Roberts, P.A. TN 2nd (Ashby's) Cav. Co.D
  Far.
Roberts, P.A. TN Cav. 4th Bn. (Branner's) Co.C
  Far.
Roberts, Paschal NC 42nd Inf. Co.F
Roberts, Paschal TX 15th Cav. Co.H
Roberts, Pat R. Gillum's Regt. Whitaker's Co.
Roberts, Patrick H. KY 5th Mtd.Inf. Co.A Cpl.
Roberts, Patrick H. VA 18th Inf. Co.H Sgt.
Roberts, P.B. TN 7th (Duckworth's) Cav. Co.C
Roberts, P.D. GA Inf. 1st Loc.Troops (Augusta)
  Dearing's Cav.Co.
Roberts, P.D. GA 5th Res. Co.E
Roberts, P.D. MO 9th (Elliott's) Cav. Co.H Sgt.
Roberts, P.D.T. NC 16th Inf. Co.G Hosp.Stew.

Roberts, Percy Gen. & Staff 1st Lt.,Adj.
Roberts, Perry GA 12th Cav. Co.I Sgt.
Roberts, Perry SC 16th Inf. Co.C
Roberts, Perry 14th Conf.Cav. Co.A
Roberts, Perry W. SC 16th Inf. Co.K
Roberts, Peter NC Walker's Bn. Thomas' Legion
  Co.C
Roberts, Peter C. SC Inf. Hampton Legion Co.E
Roberts, Peter E. TN 19th Inf. Co.C
Roberts, Peter E. TX Cav. Martin's Regt. Co.C
Roberts, Peyton NC 11th (Bethel Regt.) Inf.
  Co.A
Roberts, P.F. GA 23rd Inf. Co.D
Roberts, P.G. TN 5th (McKenzie's) Cav. Co.A
  2nd Lt.
Roberts, P.G. VA 34th Inf. Chap.
Roberts, P.H. GA 34th Inf. Co.E
Roberts, Phelix TX Cav. Hardeman's Regt. Co.F
Roberts, Philetus W. NC 14th Inf. Co.F Col.
Roberts, Philip VA 1st Cav. Co.I
Roberts, Philip VA 10th Inf. Co.K
Roberts, Philip A. NC 16th Inf. Co.H
Roberts, Philip H. MO 2nd N.E. Cav.
  (Franklin's Regt.)
Roberts, Philip H. TN 34th Inf. Co.G Capt.
Roberts, Philip L. TN 34th Inf. Co.G Cpl.
Roberts, Philip S. MO Cav. 3rd Bn. Co.D
Roberts, Philip S. VA 1st Inf. Co.B
Roberts, Phillip MO 1st N.E. Cav.
Roberts, Phillip TN 26th Inf. Co.C
Roberts, Phillip O. MS 18th Inf. Co.E 3rd Lt.
Roberts, Phillip S. MO 3rd Cav. Co.D
Roberts, Pierce NC 60th Inf. Co.F
Roberts, Pinckney J. SC 1st (McCreary's) Inf.
  Co.E
Roberts, Pinckney John FL 3rd Inf. Co.D
Roberts, Pinckney W. GA 36th (Broyles') Inf.
  Co.A
Roberts, Pink NC 5th Cav. (63rd St.Troops)
  Co.D
Roberts, P.J. NC 45th Inf. Co.F
Roberts, P.L. AL 55th Vol.Co.H
Roberts, P.L. TN 1st (Turney's) Inf. Co.A
Roberts, P.L. TN 42nd Inf. 1st Co.F
Roberts, Pleasant GA 7th Inf. Co.A
Roberts, Pleasant A. VA 11th Inf. Co.C
Roberts, Pleasant D. VA 21st Inf. Co.A
Roberts, Pleasant H. NC 28th Inf. Co.A
Roberts, Pleasant J. GA 34th Inf. Co.E
Roberts, P.M. NC 18th Inf. Co.G
Roberts, Polk AL 9th (Malone's) Cav. Co.C
Roberts, Posey TN Lt.Arty. Barry's Co.
Roberts, Presley NC 5th Inf. Co.A
Roberts, Preston KY 13th Cav. Co.H
Roberts, Preston TN 13th (Gore's) Cav. Co.F
Roberts, P.S. MS 29th Inf. Co.K 1st Sgt.
Roberts, Q. AL Talladega Cty.Res. W.Y.
  Hendrick's Co.
Roberts, Querlis W. GA Lt.Arty. (Jo Thompson
  Arty.) Hanleiter's Co.
Roberts, Quirles W. GA 38th Inf. Co.M
Roberts, R. AL 9th Inf. Co.H
Roberts, R. AR Cav. Crabtree's (46th) Regt.
  Co.A
Roberts, R. AR 11th Inf. Co.H
Roberts, R. AR 11th & 17th (Cons.) Inf. Co.C
Roberts, R. FL 4th Inf. Co.I

Roberts, R. GA 8th Cav. New Co.D
Roberts, R. GA Cav. 20th Bn. Co.A
Roberts, R. KY 12th Cav. Co.E
Roberts, R. MS Cav. 17th Bn. Co.A
Roberts, R. MS Horse Arty. Cook's Co.
Roberts, R. SC 6th Inf. 2nd Co.H
Roberts, R. TN 38th Inf. Co.G
Roberts, R. TX 3rd (Kirby's) Bn.Vol. Co.B
Roberts, R. TX Inf. Houston Bn. Co.D
Roberts, R. VA Lt.Arty. Barr's Co.
Roberts, R. VA 21st Inf. Co.F
Roberts, R.A. TN 10th (DeMoss') Cav. Co.A
Roberts, R.A. TN 31st Inf. Co.K Sgt.
Roberts, R.A. TX 8th Cav. Co.H
Roberts, Raleigh VA 29th Inf. 1st Co.F, Co.A
Roberts, Raleigh D. VA 64th Mtd.Inf. Co.H
Roberts, Raleigh D. VA Inf. French's Bn. Co.B,D
Roberts, Rankin KY 8th Cav. Co.B,A
Roberts, Ransom J. TX 2nd Inf. Co.E
Roberts, Raymond MS 2nd (Quinn's St.Troops) Inf. Co.E
Roberts, Raymon H. TX 15th Cav. Co.C
Roberts, R.B. TN 35th Inf. 2nd Co.D Lt.Col.
Roberts, R.C. AL 9th (Malone's) Cav. Co.C
Roberts, R.C. SC 3rd Cav. Co.D 2nd Lt.
Roberts, R.C. VA 7th Cav. Co.A
Roberts, R.C. VA 10th Cav. Co.F
Roberts, R.D. AR 7th Inf. Co.G
Roberts, Reason NC 13th Inf. Co.D
Roberts, Reason NC Walker's Bn. Thomas' Legion Co.A
Roberts, Redden AL 50th Inf.
Roberts, Redic R. AL Cav. 5th Bn. Hilliard's Legion Co.D
Roberts, Reece B. GA 17th Inf. Co.A
Roberts, Renbon GA Inf. 5th Bn. (St.Guards) Co.E
Roberts, Reuben GA 27th Inf. Co.B
Roberts, Reuben MS Cav. 1st Bn. (McNair's) St.Troops Co.D
Roberts, Reuben H. AL 1st Regt. Mobile Vol. Butt's Co.F 1st Lt.
Roberts, Reuben H. AL 4th Res. Co.A 2nd Lt.
Roberts, Reuben J. GA 54th Inf. Co.A
Roberts, Reuben M. MS 2nd Inf. Co.C Cpl.
Roberts, Reubin L. FL 9th Inf. Co.E,H
Roberts, R.F. GA 53rd Inf. Co.B
Roberts, R.F. SC 1st Mtd.Mil. Kirk's Co.
Roberts, R.F. SC 17th Inf. Co.F
Roberts, R.F. TN 7th (Duckworth's) Cav. Co.H
Roberts, R.F. TN 29th Inf. Co.F
Roberts, R.F.G. GA 66th Inf. Co.C Cpl.
Roberts, R.F.M. KY 12th Cav. Co.C
Roberts, R.G. AL 22nd Inf. Co.G Capt.
Roberts, R.G. AR 1st (Monroe's) Cav. Co.H
Roberts, R.G. NC 1st Jr.Res. Co.C Cpl.
Roberts, R.H. AL Mil. 2nd Regt.Vol. Co.A
Roberts, R.H. AR 30th Inf. Co.M
Roberts, R.H. GA Inf. 5th Bn. (St.Guards) Co.B
Roberts, R.H. NC 45th Inf. Co.K
Roberts, R.H. VA 34th Inf. Co.G
Roberts, Rheuben GA 12th (Wright's) Cav. (St.Guards) Stubb's Co.
Roberts, R.I. NC 5th Cav. (63rd St.Troops) Co.B
Roberts, Rich AL Mobile Fire Bn. Mullany's Co.
Roberts, Richar F. MS 1st Cav. Res. Co.H

Roberts, Richard AL 21st Inf. Co.I
Roberts, Richard FL 5th Inf. Co.C
Roberts, Richard FL 10th Inf. Co.B
Roberts, Richard GA Cobb's Legion Co.A
Roberts, Richard KY 9th Mtd.Inf. Co.G
Roberts, Richard MD 1st Cav. Co.E
Roberts, Richard MO 7th Cav. Ward's Co.
Roberts, Richard NC 2nd Arty. (36th St.Troops) Co.I
Roberts, Richard NC 3rd Arty. (40th St.Troops) Co.G
Roberts, Richard NC 7th Sr.Res. Fisher's Co.
Roberts, Richard NC 23rd Inf. Co.F
Roberts, Richard NC Currituck Guard J.W.F. Bank's Co.
Roberts, Richard TN 49th Inf. Co.F Capt.
Roberts, Richard Inf. Bailey's Cons.Regt. Co.C Capt.
Roberts, Richard VA Lt.Arty. 13th Bn. Co.C
Roberts, Richard VA 4th Inf. Co.F
Roberts, Richard VA 45th Inf. Co.K
Roberts, Richard B. TX 11th Inf. Co.H 1st Lt.
Roberts, Richard B. VA 21st Mil. Co.A
Roberts, Richard D. AL 51st (Part.Rangers) Co.A
Roberts, Richard D. AL 2nd Inf. Co.A
Roberts, Richard F. VA Lt.Arty. 38th Bn. Co.C
Roberts, Richd. H. GA 13th Inf. Co.G
Roberts, Richard L. VA Lt.Arty. Sturdivant's Co.
Roberts, Richard M. 1st Cherokee Mtd.Vol. 2nd Co.K
Roberts, Richard N. MS Lt.Arty. Stanford's Co.
Roberts, Richard R. GA Inf. 10th Bn. Co.E
Roberts, Richard R. NC 18th Inf. Co.B
Roberts, Riley KY 13th Cav. Co.B
Roberts, Riley B. TN 1st (Turney's) Inf. Co.A 1st Sgt.
Roberts, R.J. TX 25th Cav.
Roberts, R.J TX Cav. Waller's Regt. Menard's Co.
Roberts, R.J. TX 13th Vol. Co.C
Roberts, R.L. VA 7th Cav. Glenn's Co. Sgt.
Roberts, R.M. AR 3rd Inf. Co.K
Roberts, R.M. KY 12th Cav. Co.A
Roberts, R.M. MS 2nd Cav. Co.B
Roberts, R.M. MS 2nd Cav. Co.K
Roberts, R.M. MS 10th Cav. Co.C
Roberts, R.M. MS Inf. 1st Bn.St.Troops (12 mo. '62-3) Co.A Sgt.
Roberts, R.M. TN 51st Inf. Co.H
Roberts, R.M. TN 51st (Cons.) Inf. Co.D
Roberts, R.M. TX 1st Hvy.Arty. Co.K
Roberts, R.M. TX 20th Inf. Co.F
Roberts, R. Monterville NC 16th Inf. Co.A
Roberts, R. Mountiville NC Inf. Thomas Legion 1st Co.A
Roberts, R.N. VA 3rd Inf.Loc.Def. Co.I
Roberts, Robert GA 1st Bn.S.S. Co.B
Roberts, Robert KY 1st (Butler's) Cav. Co.F
Roberts, Robert LA 3rd (Harrison's) Cav. Co.C
Roberts, Robert LA 2nd Inf. Co.C Capt.
Roberts, Robert LA Inf. 4th Bn. Co.C
Roberts, Robert LA 19th Inf. Co.E Sgt.Maj.
Roberts, Robert LA Inf. Pelican Regt. Sgt.Maj.
Roberts, Robert MO 1st Cav. Co.G
Roberts, Robert MO 8th Inf. Co.E

Roberts, Robert NC 5th Cav. (63rd St.Troops) Co.D
Roberts, Robert TX 11th Inf. Co.K
Roberts, Robert TX 11th (Spaight's) Bn.Vol. Co.D
Roberts, Robert VA 1st St.Res. Co.A
Roberts, Robert VA 49th Inf. Co.I
Roberts, Robert VA 56th Inf. Co.H
Roberts, Robert A. TN Inf. 3rd Cons.Regt. Co.G
Roberts, Robert B. AL 57th Inf. Co.I
Roberts, Robert B. FL 1st Cav. Co.A
Roberts, Robert B. FL 9th Inf. Co.E Sgt.
Roberts, Robert C. TN 47th Inf. Co.E Sgt.Maj.
Roberts, Robert C. VA Cav. 35th Bn. Co.F
Roberts, Robert E. FL 5th Inf. Co.C
Roberts, Robert H. GA 11th Inf. Co.F
Roberts, Robert J. SC Simons' Co.
Roberts, Robert L. KY Cav. 1st Bn. Co.B
Roberts, Robert L. KY 4th Cav. Co.B
Roberts, Robert L. VA 12th Cav. Co.D
Roberts, Robert M. MS 2nd Inf. Co.C
Roberts, Robert M. NC 60th Inf. Co.F
Roberts, Robert N. NC 29th Inf.
Roberts, Robert P. VA 6th Cav. Co.B
Roberts, Robert R. VA 1st Arty. Co.D
Roberts, Robert R. VA Lt.Arty. 1st Bn. Co.D
Roberts, Robert R. VA Arty. B.H. Smith's Co. Cpl.
Roberts, Roberts AL 17th Inf. Co.G
Roberts, Robert S. NC 45th Inf. Co.A Cpl.
Roberts, Robert T. AL 13th Inf. Co.E
Roberts, Robert W. FL 7th Inf. Co.F
Roberts, Roger F. SC 3rd Cav. Co.C
Roberts, Roger F. SC Mil.Cav. 4th Regt. Howard's Co.
Roberts, Roger R. SC 1st (Orr's) Rifles Co.H
Roberts, Roland GA Inf. 1st Conf.Bn. Co.B
Roberts, Roland 1st Conf.Inf. 2nd Co.H
Roberts, Rolin Q. SC Arty. Manigault's Bn. 1st Co.C, 2nd Co.C
Roberts, R.P. AR 11th Inf. Co.E
Roberts, R.P. AR 24th Inf. Co.C
Roberts, R.P. TX 23rd Cav. Co.D
Roberts, R.R. FL 10th Inf. Co.E
Roberts, R.R. GA 4th (Clinch's) Cav. Co.E
Roberts, R.R. LA 2nd Inf. Co.C
Roberts, R.R. MS 2nd St.Cav. Co.E
Roberts, R.R. MS 3rd Inf. Co.G
Roberts, R.R. 10th Conf.Cav. Co.D
Roberts, R.R. Gen. & Staff Chap.
Roberts, R.S. AL 27th Inf. Co.H
Roberts, R.S. NC 4th Inf. Co.K
Roberts, R.S. TN 33rd Inf. Co.H
Roberts, R. Sidney NC 34th Inf. Co.H
Roberts, R.T.W. SC 11th Inf. Bellinger's Co.
Roberts, Ruben AR 1st (Dobbin's) Cav. Co.A
Roberts, Ruben Morgan's Co.A,CSA
Roberts, Ruffin A. MS 2nd Inf. Co.C Sgt.
Roberts, Rufus NC 49th Inf. Co.G Capt.
Roberts, Rufus A. MO 4th Cav. Co.I
Roberts, Rufus A. Gen. & Staff Asst.Surg.
Roberts, Rufus C. AL 4th (Russell's) Cav. Co.I Cpl.
Roberts, Rufus F. NC 37th Inf. Co.F
Roberts, Rufus L. NC 13th Inf. Co.A
Roberts, Russell MO 5th Inf. Co.H,E
Roberts, Rutledge FL 4th Inf. Co.I,G

Roberts, R.W. AR 15th Inf. Co.K
Roberts, R.W. FL 7th Inf. Co.F
Roberts, R.W. MS Wilkinson Cty. Minute Men Co.A 1st Sgt.
Roberts, R.W. TX 13th Vol. Co.F
Roberts, R.W. TX 14th Inf. Co.C Cpl.
Roberts, Ryal W. NC 55th Inf. Co.G
Roberts, S. GA 1st Troops & Def. (Macon) Co.B
Roberts, S. GA 4th Inf. Co.A
Roberts, S. GA 11th Inf. Co.D
Roberts, S. GA 16th Inf. Co.E
Roberts, S. GA 29th Inf. Co.A
Roberts, S. GA 54th Inf. Co.C
Roberts, S. MS 8th Inf. Co.K
Roberts, S. TN 52nd Inf. Co.A Cpl.
Roberts, S. TX 33rd Cav. Co.K
Roberts, S. TX 1st Hvy.Arty. 2nd Co.A
Roberts, S. TX 1st Hvy.Arty. Co.I
Roberts, S. TX 15th Inf. Co.B
Roberts, S.A. MS Cav. Jeff Davis Legion Co.K Capt.
Roberts, Samuel AL 3rd Res. Co.H
Roberts, Samuel AL Mil. 4th Vol. Co.H
Roberts, Samuel AR Cav. Harrell's Bn. Co.D
Roberts, Samuel AR Cav. McGehee's Regt. Co.I
Roberts, Samuel AR 17th (Lemoyne's) Inf. Co.H
Roberts, Samuel AR 21st Inf. Co.G
Roberts, Samuel FL Cav. 3rd Bn. Co.D
Roberts, Samuel GA 8th Inf. Co.E
Roberts, Samuel LA 15th Inf. Co.I
Roberts, Samuel LA 19th Inf. Co.E
Roberts, Samuel LA Inf. Pelican Regt. Co.A
Roberts, Samuel MS 12th Cav. Co.I
Roberts, Samuel SC 17th Inf. Co.F
Roberts, Samuel TN Inf. 1st Bn. (Colms') Co.C
Roberts, Samuel TN 19th Inf. Co.C
Roberts, Samuel TN 50th (Cons.) Inf. Co.K
Roberts, Samuel VA 7th Cav. Glenn's Co.
Roberts, Samuel VA 12th Cav. Co.A
Roberts, Samuel VA Inf. 1st Bn. Co.E
Roberts, Samuel VA 5th Inf. Co.L
Roberts, Samuel VA Inf. 26th Bn. Co.I
Roberts, Samuel 15th Conf.Cav. Co.I
Roberts, Samuel 1st Conf.Eng.Troops Co.A
Roberts, Samuel A. FL 8th Inf. Co.K
Roberts, Sam'l. A. Gen. & Staff, Adj.Gen.Dept. Lt.Col.
Roberts, Samuel B. TX 6th Cav. Co.D
Roberts, Samuel C. NC 2nd Arty. (36th St.Troops) Co.G
Roberts, Samuel D. TX 13th Cav. Co.H
Roberts, Samuel E. MS 22nd Inf. Co.I 1st Sgt.
Roberts, Samuel J. AR Cav. Poe's Bn. Co.A
Roberts, Samuel J. GA 43rd Inf. Co.G
Roberts, Samuel L. NC 35th Inf. Co.H
Roberts, Samuel M. AL 24th Inf. Co.F
Roberts, Samuel M. VA 1st Arty. Co.D
Roberts, Samuel N. VA Lt.Arty. W.P. Carter's Co.
Roberts, Samuel P. VA 38th Inf. Co.G
Roberts, Samuel R. AR 23rd Inf. Co.C
Roberts, Samuel S. MO 3rd Cav. Co.H
Roberts, Samuel S. TN 1st (Feild's) Inf. Co.B
Roberts, Samuel W. NC 18th Inf. Co.G
Roberts, Samuel W. NC 61st Inf. Co.G
Roberts, Sanford GA 42nd Inf. Co.A
Roberts, S.B. MS 31st Inf. Co.B

Roberts, S.C. MO Lt.Arty. Barret's Co.
Roberts, S.C. SC Arty. Manigault's Bn. 1st Co.A,B, 2nd Co.A,B
Roberts, S.C. SC 3rd Bn.Res. Co.E
Roberts, S.D. GA 19th Inf. Co.H
Roberts, S.D. TX Cav. Terry's Regt. Co.B
Roberts, S.D. TX 19th Inf. Co.K
Roberts, S.E. GA 4th (Clinch's) Cav. Co.H
Roberts, S.E. GA 11th Cav. (St.Guards) Smith's Co.
Roberts, S.E. LA Inf. 1st Sp.Bn. (Wheat's) Old Co.D
Roberts, S.E. LA Inf. 7th Bn. Co.B
Roberts, S.E. MS 2nd Cav. Co.E
Roberts, S.E. MS 33rd Inf. Co.B
Roberts, S.E. TN 44th (Cons.) Inf. Co.G Cpl.
Roberts, S.E. TN 55th (McKoin's) Inf. Bound's Co.
Roberts, Seaborn SC Inf. Holcombe Legion Co.E
Roberts, Seaborn J. GA 25th Inf. Co.F
Roberts, Sebron SC 5th St.Troops Co.E
Roberts, Seth W. AL St.Arty. Co.D
Roberts, Seth W. AL Mil. 2nd Regt.Vol. Co.C
Roberts, S.F. TN Inf. 1st Cons.Regt. Co.I Cpl.
Roberts, S.F. TN 34th Inf. Co.I Cpl.
Roberts, S.G. AL Cp. of Instr. Talladega Co.B,D
Roberts, S.H. GA 1st (Fannin's) Res. Co.C
Roberts, S.H. GA 32nd Inf. Co.K Cpl.
Roberts, S.H. GA 63rd Inf. Co.I
Roberts, S.H. TN 28th Cav. Co.A 2nd Lt.
Roberts, S.H. TX 15th Inf. Co.B
Roberts, Shadrach R. VA 29th Inf. 1st Co.F Jr.2nd Lt.
Roberts, Sherod E. GA 29th Inf. Co.H
Roberts, Sidney William MO 8th Inf. Co.A
Roberts, Silas F. TN 34th Inf. Co.G
Roberts, Silvester MO 1st N.E. Cav. Co.M
Roberts, Simeon FL 7th Inf. Co.A Sgt.
Roberts, Simeon GA 4th Inf. Co.H
Roberts, Simon TN 17th Inf. Co.K
Roberts, Simpson KY 2nd Cav. Co.C
Roberts, Simpson MS 8th Cav. Co.D
Roberts, Simpson MO 4th Inf. Co.I
Roberts, S.J. AR 2nd Inf. New Co.E
Roberts, S.J. AR 11th Inf. Co.E
Roberts, S.J. AR 11th & 17th (Cons.) Inf. Co.E
Roberts, S.J. GA 29th Inf. Co.H
Roberts, S.J. GA Mil.Inf. Detailed Man
Roberts, S.J. MO 6th Cav. Co.C
Roberts, S.L. AL 12th Inf. Co.F
Roberts, S.L. LA 27th Inf. Co.A
Roberts, S.L. TN 51st (Cons.) Inf. Co.A
Roberts, S.M. AL 22nd Inf. Co.E
Roberts, S.M. AR 34th Inf. Co.D
Roberts, S.M. GA 2nd St.Line Capt.
Roberts, S.M. GA 5th Res. Co.H 1st Sgt.
Roberts, S.M. GA 19th Inf. Co.H Sgt.
Roberts, S.M. LA Inf. 1st Sp.Bn. (Rightor's) Co.B
Roberts, S.M. SC Cav. 10th Bn. Co.A
Roberts, S.M. TX Cav. Hardeman's Regt. Co.A
Roberts, Smith MO 10th Cav. Co.I
Roberts, Solomon AL Lt.Arty. 2nd Bn. Co.A
Roberts, Solomon GA 54th Inf. Co.A
Roberts, Solomon NC 48th Inf. Co.K
Roberts, Solomon TX 18th Cav. Co.G
Roberts, Solomon TX Cav. Morgan's Regt. Co.D

Roberts, Solomon B. MO 11th Inf. Co.B Sgt.
Roberts, S.P. TN 7th (Duckworth's) Cav. Co.C
Roberts, S.P. VA Mil. Scott Cty.
Roberts, Squire KY 11th Cav. Co.H
Roberts, Squire MO 5th Inf. Co.H Sgt.
Roberts, Squire MO St.Guard 2nd Lt.
Roberts, S.R. AL 33rd Inf. Co.F
Roberts, S.T. GA 12th (Robinson's) Cav. (St.Guards) Co.F
Roberts, S.T. GA 1st (Fannin's) Res. Co.E
Roberts, S.T. GA 23rd Inf. Co.A
Roberts, S.T. TN 28th Cav. Co.C 1st Lt.
Roberts, Starling J. GA 41st Inf. Co.H Cpl.
Roberts, Step GA 23rd Inf. Co.I Sgt.
Roberts, Stephen AR 2nd Inf. Co.D Cpl.
Roberts, Stephen FL 4th Inf. Co.F Sgt.
Roberts, Stephen FL 9th Inf. Co.E Music.
Roberts, Stephen GA 13th Cav. Co.I
Roberts, Stephen GA 29th Inf. Co.H
Roberts, Stephen LA 1st Hvy.Arty. (Reg.) Co.I Cpl.
Roberts, Stephen MS 23rd Inf. Co.A Sgt.
Roberts, Stephen NC Lt.Arty. 13th Bn. Co.D
Roberts, Stephen TN 34th Inf. Co.I Cpl.
Roberts, Stephen TX 14th Cav. Co.F
Roberts, Stephen VA Horse Arty. J.W. Carter's Co.
Roberts, Stephen Inf. School of Pract. Co.D
Roberts, Stephen J. TX 14th Cav. Co.B
Roberts, Stephen N. GA 29th Inf. Co.G
Roberts, Stephen T. GA 18th Inf. Co.G
Roberts, Stephen T. GA 64th Inf. Co.E 2nd Lt.
Roberts, Stephen W. NC 1st Inf. (6 mo. '61) Co.M
Roberts, Stephen W. NC 11th (Bethel Regt.) Inf. Co.F 1st Lt.
Roberts, Sterling M. Cav. Murchison's Bn. Co.H,CSA
Roberts, Sterling W. GA 45th Inf. Co.G
Roberts, Steven J. TN 1st Inf. Co.H
Roberts, St.Francis C. VA 5th Inf. Co.F Capt.
Roberts, Strauther KY 4th Mtd.Inf. Co.D
Roberts, S.W. AL 22nd Inf. Co.A
Roberts, S.W. MS 9th Bn.S.S. Co.C
Roberts, S.W. NC 8th Inf. Co.D
Roberts, S.W. TX 13th Vol. Co.F
Roberts, S.W. 2nd Conf.Eng.Troops Co.G Artif.
Roberts, S. Warren MS 7th Inf. Co.H
Roberts, Sydney T. TN Cav. Shaw's Bn. Hamilton's Co.
Roberts, Sylvester J. VA 16th Inf. Co.D Cpl.
Roberts, T. AL 5th Inf. Co.C
Roberts, T. AL 23rd Inf. Co.I
Roberts, T. AL Cp. of Instr. Talladega
Roberts, T. GA 54th Inf. Co.C
Roberts, T. LA Lt.Arty. LeGardeur, Jr.'s Co. (Orleans Guard Btty.)
Roberts, T. MO 8th Inf. Co.E
Roberts, T. NC 6th Cav. Co.A,F
Roberts, T.A. AL 7th Cav. Co.K 2nd Lt.
Roberts, T.A. TN 49th Inf. Co.I
Roberts, Tabner G. GA Arty. 9th Bn. Co.D
Roberts, T.B. AL 23rd Inf. Co.D
Roberts, T.B. MS 2nd St.Cav. Co.K
Roberts, T.B. MS 7th Cav. Co.E
Roberts, T.B. TX Cav. Bourland's Regt. Co.F
Roberts, T.B. VA Cav. 37th Bn. Co.I Sgt.

Roberts, T.B. VA 1st Inf. Co.D
Roberts, T.C. GA 45th Inf. Co.C
Roberts, T.C. TX Cav. Bone's Co.
Roberts, T.E. GA 2nd Inf. Co.D
Roberts, T.E. GA 15th Inf. Co.E
Roberts, T.F. KY 7th Mtd.Inf. Co.F 2nd Lt.
Roberts, T.G. AL 45th Inf. Co.K
Roberts, T.G. GA 9th Inf. Co.C
Roberts, T.G. MS 7th Inf. Co.C
Roberts, T.G. Conf.Cav. Powers' Regt. Co.E
  Sgt.
Roberts, T.H. FL 4th Inf. Co.F
Roberts, T.H. MS 32nd Inf. Co.G
Roberts, T.H., Jr. VA 3rd Inf.Loc.Def. Co.K
Roberts, Tharp GA 11th Cav. (St.Guards)
  Slaten's Co. Sgt.
Roberts, Thomas AL 5th Cav. Co.H
Roberts, Thomas AL 3rd Bn.Res. Flemming's
  Co.
Roberts, Thomas AL 20th Inf. Co.F
Roberts, Thos. AL Cp. of Instr. Talladega
Roberts, Thomas AR Cav. 1st Bn. (Stirman's)
  Co.H
Roberts, Thomas AR Cav. Harrell's Bn. Co.C
Roberts, Thomas AR 34th Inf. Co.A
Roberts, Thomas GA Inf. 8th Bn. Co.B
Roberts, Thomas GA 26th Inf. Co.E
Roberts, Thomas GA 60th Inf. Co.E
Roberts, Thomas GA Cherokee Legion
  (St.Guards) Co.E
Roberts, Thomas MS Cav. Powers' Regt. Co.E
Roberts, Thomas MS 10th Inf. New Co.G
Roberts, Thomas NC 6th Cav. (65th St.Troops)
  Co.A,F
Roberts, Thomas NC 6th Inf. Co.H
Roberts, Thomas NC 23rd Inf. Co.G
Roberts, Thomas SC 5th St.Troops Co.A
Roberts, Thomas TN 3rd (Clack's) Inf. Co.H
Roberts, Thomas TN 35th Inf. 2nd Co.A
Roberts, Thomas TN 47th Inf. Co.K
Roberts, Thomas TX 16th Cav. Co.D
Roberts, Thomas TX 27th Cav. Co.B
Roberts, Thomas VA 21st Cav. 2nd Co.C
Roberts, Thomas VA 22nd Cav. Co.E
Roberts, Thomas VA 10th Inf. Co.E
Roberts, Thomas VA 36th Inf. 2nd Co.K
Roberts, Thomas VA 44th Inf. Co.C
Roberts, Thomas VA 63rd Inf. Co.F
Roberts, Thomas VA Mil. Washington Cty.
Roberts, Thomas 3rd Conf.Cav. Co.D
Roberts, Thomas A. SC Inf. 9th Bn. Co.D
Roberts, Thomas A. SC 26th Inf. Co.E
Roberts, Thomas A. VA 22nd Inf. Co.A
  Capt.,AQM
Roberts, Thos. A. Gen. & Staff Capt.,AQM
Roberts, Thomas B. FL 3rd Inf. Co.D
Roberts, Thomas B. MS 2nd (Davidson's) Inf.
  Co.D
Roberts, Thomas B. MS 3rd Inf. Co.I Cpl.
Roberts, Thomas B. MO 1st Cav. Co.H
Roberts, Thomas B. NC 38th Inf. Co.B 1st Sgt.
Roberts, Thomas B. SC 1st St.Troops Col.
Roberts, Thomas B. SC 3rd Res. Co.B Capt.
Roberts, Thomas B. SC 16th Inf. Co.A Capt.
Roberts, Thomas B. VA 61st Inf. Co.F
Roberts, Thomas C. AL 2nd Cav. Co.H
Roberts, Thomas C. NC 60th Inf. Co.F Sgt.

Roberts, Thomas E. AL 6th Inf. Co.F
Roberts, Thomas E. FL 3rd Inf. Co.F
Roberts, Thomas E. KY 7th Cav. Co.E
Roberts, Thomas E. NC 56th Inf. Co.D
Roberts, Thomas E. VA 5th Cav. (12 mo. '61-2)
  Co.I
Roberts, Thomas E. VA Cav. 14th Bn. Co.B
Roberts, Thomas E. VA 15th Cav. Co.I
Roberts, Thomas F. TN 1st Hvy.Arty. 2nd Co.C
Roberts, Thomas F. TN 19th Inf. Co.B
Roberts, Thomas F.B. GA 51st Inf. Co.D
Roberts, Thomas G. AL 3rd Bn.Res. Co.C
Roberts, Thomas H. AL 5th Inf. New Co.A 1st
  Lt.
Roberts, Thomas H. GA Inf. 1st Loc.Troops
  (Augusta) Co.A
Roberts, Thomas H. GA 22nd Inf. Co.F
Roberts, Thomas H. MS 11th Inf. Co.E Cpl.
Roberts, Thomas H. NC 34th Inf. Co.H
Roberts, Thomas H. VA 1st St.Res. Co.F Cpl.
Roberts, Thomas H. VA 4th Inf. Co.I
Roberts, Thomas H. VA 42nd Inf. Co.D
Roberts, Thomas H. VA Vol. Taylor's Co.
Roberts, Thomas H. Conf.Cav. Clarkson's Bn.
  Ind.Rangers Mitchell's Co.
Roberts, Thomas J. AL 3rd Inf. Co.C
Roberts, Thomas J. AL 25th Inf. Co.I Cpl.
Roberts, Thomas J. AR 1st (Crawford's) Cav.
  Co.H
Roberts, Thomas J. FL 6th Inf. Co.K
Roberts, Thomas J. GA 12th Inf. Co.I
Roberts, Thomas J. GA 29th Inf. Co.H
Roberts, Thomas J. MS 6th Inf. Co.F
Roberts, Thomas J. MS 18th Inf. Co.I
Roberts, Thomas J. MO 10th Cav. Co.G Cpl.
Roberts, Thomas J. SC 14th Inf. Co.G
Roberts, Thomas J. TN 33rd Inf. Co.D Cpl.
Roberts, Thos. L. TX Cav. Baird's Regt.
  Sgt.Maj.
Roberts, Thomas L. TX 10th Inf. Co.G
Roberts, Thomas L. VA 34th Inf. Co.F 2nd Lt.
Roberts, Thomas M. AR 35th Inf. Co.K
Roberts, Thomas M. AR 35th Inf. Co.K Cpl.
Roberts, Thomas M. LA 3rd Inf. Co.F
Roberts, Thomas M. MO 1st Cav. Co.F
Roberts, Thomas M. NC 37th Inf. Co.H
Roberts, Thomas R. AR 27th Inf. Co.A 1st Sgt.
Roberts, Thomas S. VA 20th Inf. Co.H Cpl.
Roberts, Thomas W. FL 3rd Inf. Co.F
Roberts, Thomas W. FL 11th Inf. Co.D Cpl.
Roberts, Thomas W. MS 15th Inf. Co.H
Roberts, Thomas W. VA 7th Inf. Co.E
Roberts, Tilford J. NC 29th Inf. Co.D
Roberts, Tillman MS Cav. Duncan's Co.
  (Tishomingo Rangers)
Roberts, T.J. AR Cav. Wright's Regt. Co.C
Roberts, T.J. FL Inf. 8th Regt. Co.B
Roberts, T.J. GA 11th Inf. Co.F
Roberts, T.J. GA 30th Inf. Co.K
Roberts, T.J. MD Cav. 2nd Bn. Co.D
Roberts, T.J. MS Graves' Co. (Copiah Horse
  Guards)
Roberts, T.J. MS Cav. Powers' Regt. Co.B Cpl.
Roberts, T.J. MS 39th Inf. Co.C
Roberts, T.J. TN Inf. 3rd Cons.Regt. Co.G Cpl.
Roberts, T.J. TX 9th Cav. Maj.
Roberts, T.J. TX 21st Cav. Co.A

Roberts, T.J. TX 35th (Brown's) Cav. Co.A,F
Roberts, T.J. TX Inf. 1st St.Troops Co.F
Roberts, T.J. TX 5th Inf. Co.B
Roberts, T.J. TX 14th Inf. Co.C Cpl.
Roberts, T.J. Conf.Cav. Powers' Regt. Co.E
Roberts, T.L. GA 29th Inf. Co.H,K
Roberts, T.L. Gen. & Staff Capt.,AQM
Roberts, T.M. AR 17th (Griffith's) Inf. Co.G
Roberts, T.M. LA 31st Inf. Co.F
Roberts, T.M. 3rd Conf.Cav. Co.G
Roberts, T.N. AL Pris.Guard Freeman's Co.
Roberts, T.O. TN 3rd (Lillard's) Mtd.Inf. Co.F
  Sgt.
Roberts, Toliver C. TX 26th Cav. Co.B
Roberts, T.P. AL 56th Part.Rangers Co.H
Roberts, T.P. AL 23rd Inf. Co.K
Roberts, Travis TX Cav. Morgan's Regt. Co.A
Roberts, T.T. MS 41st Inf. Co.B
Roberts, T.T. 15th Conf.Cav. Co.E
Roberts, T.W. AL 33rd Inf. Co.A
Roberts, T.W. MS 3rd Inf. (St.Troops) Co.A
Roberts, T.W. TX 3rd Cav. Co.C
Roberts, T.W. TX Cav. Hardeman's Regt. Co.A
Roberts, Ulysses M. FL 8th Inf. Co.I 1st Sgt.
Roberts, U.S. MS 13th Inf. Co.I
Roberts, Victor AL 3rd Bn.Res. Co.A
Roberts, Victor AL 18th Inf. Co.A
Roberts, V.L. GA 55th Inf. Co.I
Roberts, W. AL Mil. 2nd Regt.Vol. Co.E
Roberts, W. AR Cav. Davies' Bn. Co.C
Roberts, W. FL 10th Inf.
Roberts, W., Jr. GA 4th (Clinch's) Cav. Co.H
Roberts, W. GA 8th Cav. New Co.I
Roberts, W. GA Cav. 9th Bn. (St.Guards) Co.B
Roberts, W. GA Cobb's Legion Co.D
Roberts, W., Jr. LA Inf. 9th Bn. Co.B
Roberts, W. MO 1st & 3rd Cons.Cav. Co.C
Roberts, W. NC 2nd Conscr.
Roberts, W. SC 11th Inf. 2nd Co.F
Roberts, W. SC 21st Inf. Co.A
Roberts, W. TN 3rd (Forrest's) Cav. 3rd Co.D
Roberts, W. TN 19th & 20th (Cons.) Cav. Co.C
  Cpl.
Roberts, W. TN 13th Inf. Co.H
Roberts, W.A. AL 9th (Malone's) Cav. Co.K 1st
  Sgt.
Roberts, W.A. AL 14th Inf. Co.K Sgt.
Roberts, W.A. AL 24th Inf. Co.D
Roberts, W.A. GA Arty. Lumpkin's Co.
Roberts, W.A. MS 18th Cav. Co.C Sgt.
Roberts, W.A. NC 3rd Arty. (40th St.Troops)
  Co.G
Roberts, W.A. SC 24th Inf. Co.D
Roberts, W.A. TN 19th (Biffle's) Cav. Co.A
Roberts, W.A. TN 20th Inf. Co.G Cpl.
Roberts, W.A. VA 3rd Res. Co.H
Roberts, Wade G. TX 1st (Yager's) Cav. Co.K
Roberts, Wade G. TX Cav. 8th (Taylor's) Bn.
  Co.B
Roberts, W.A.E. NC 16th Inf. Co.G
Roberts, W.A.E. NC 50th Inf. Co.K 1st Sgt.
Roberts, Walter TX 18th Inf. Co.H
Roberts, Walter F. KY 4th Cav.
Roberts, Walter J. MS 39th Inf. Co.C Sgt.
Roberts, Walter N. VA 1st Res. Co.F
Roberts, Walter R. NC 34th Inf. Co.B
Roberts, Walter R. NC 45th Inf. Co.F

Roberts, Walton KY 2nd Cav. Co.E
Roberts, Warren GA Inf. 27th Bn. Co.B
Roberts, Warren B. TX 31st Cav. Co.C
Roberts, Washington H. MS 21st Inf. Co.A
Roberts, Washington L. MS 7th Inf. Co.A 2nd Lt.
Roberts, Washington P. NC 44th Inf. Co.G
Roberts, Wayne GA 12th Inf. Co.I
Roberts, W.B. AR 20th Inf. Co.C
Roberts, W.B. GA Cav. Gartrell's Co.
Roberts, W.B. GA 6th Mil. Sgt.
Roberts, W.B. GA 8th Inf. (St.Guards) Co.E
Roberts, W.B. GA 39th Inf. Co.E
Roberts, W.B. GA Inf. Fuller's Co.
Roberts, W.B. MS 39th Inf. Co.K Sgt.
Roberts, W.B. TN 19th (Biffle's) Cav. Co.E
Roberts, W.B. TN 28th (Cons.) Inf. Co.A 1st Lt.
Roberts, W.C. AL 58th Inf. Co.C
Roberts, W.C. AL Pris.Guard Freeman's Co.
Roberts, W.C. GA 11th Cav. Co.I
Roberts, W.C. MS 7th Cav. Co.D Sgt.
Roberts, W.C. MS 2nd (Davidson's) Inf. Co.C
Roberts, W.C. TN 22nd (Barteau's) Cav. Co.I 3rd Lt.
Roberts, W.C. TN 12th Inf. Co.F Sgt.
Roberts, W.C. TN 21st Inf. Co.C
Roberts, W.C. TX 13th Cav. Co.F
Roberts, W.C. TX Inf. Chambers' Bn.Res.Corps Co.C Capt.
Roberts, W.C. VA 2nd St.Res. Co.I
Roberts, W.D. AL 53rd (Part.Rangers) Co.D
Roberts, W.D. Inf. Bailey's Cons.Regt. Co.A Cpl.
Roberts, W.D. TX 12th Cav. Co.G
Roberts, W.D. TX 7th Inf. Co.H Cpl.
Roberts, W.D. TX 20th Inf. Co.I
Roberts, W.D. VA 7th Inf. Co.F
Roberts, W. David MS 7th Inf. Co.H
Roberts, W.E. AL 1st Cav. 2nd Co.B
Roberts, W.E. GA 25th Inf. Co.E
Roberts, W.E. TN 42nd Inf. 2nd Co.E
Roberts, W.E. TN Conscr. (Cp. of Instr.)
Roberts, W.E. TX 13th Vol. Co.B
Roberts, W.E. VA Second Class Mil. Hobson's Co.
Roberts, W.E. Brush Bn.
Roberts, Weightstile NC 18th Inf. Co.B
Roberts, Welcome H. AL 20th Inf. Co.F
Roberts, Wesley AR Inf. Cocke's Regt. Co.G
Roberts, Wesley TN Lt.Arty. Barry's Co.
Roberts, Wesley VA Cav. 37th Bn. Co.D
Roberts, Wessley AR 30th Inf. Co.F
Roberts, Westley MO Lt.Arty. 1st Field Btty. Capt.
Roberts, W.F. AL 48th Inf. Co.K Sgt.
Roberts, W.F. GA 11th Cav. Co.G 1st Sgt.
Roberts, W.F. GA Cav. 19th Bn. Co.D
Roberts, W.F. GA Inf. 3rd Bn. Co.C
Roberts, W.F. GA 44th Inf. Co.G
Roberts, W.F. KY 12th Cav. Co.C
Roberts, W.F. LA 1st (Nelligan's) Inf. Co.B Sgt.
Roberts, W.F. MS 28th Cav. Co.G
Roberts, W.F. MS Lt.Arty. (Warren Lt.Arty.) Swett's Co.
Roberts, W.F. MS 33rd Inf. Co.D

Roberts, W.F. TN 4th (McLemore's) Cav. Co.I
Roberts, W.F. TN Cav. Nixon's Regt. Co.K
Roberts, W.F. TN 11th Inf. Co.G
Roberts, W.F. TX 28th Cav. Co.G Capt.
Roberts, W.F. 10th Conf.Cav. Co.I
Roberts, W.G. LA 4th Cav. Co.H
Roberts, W.G. SC 7th Cav. Co.G
Roberts, W.G. SC Rutledge Mtd.Riflemen & Horse Arty. Trenholm's Co.
Roberts, W.G. TN 19th Inf. Co.H
Roberts, W.G. TX 7th Cav. Co.F
Roberts, W.H. AL Mil. 2nd Regt.Vol. Co.D
Roberts, W.H. AL 23rd Inf. Co.K
Roberts, W.H. AL 26th (O'Neal's) Inf. Co.E
Roberts, W.H. AR 17th (Lemoyne's) Inf. Co.E
Roberts, W.H. AR 20th Inf. Co.I
Roberts, W.H. AR 21st Inf. Co.I
Roberts, W.H. AR 24th Inf. Co.B
Roberts, W.H. GA 5th Cav. Co.A
Roberts, W.H. GA Cav. 20th Bn. Co.D
Roberts, W.H. GA 5th Inf. (St.Guards) Brooks' Co. 1st Sgt.
Roberts, W.H. GA Inf. 5th Bn. (St.Guards) Co.E
Roberts, W.H. GA 38th Inf. Co.H
Roberts, W.H. GA 52nd Inf. Co.B
Roberts, W.H. GA 55th Inf. Co.C
Roberts, W.H. GA Inf. City Bn. (Columbus) Co.A Sgt.
Roberts, W.H. GA Phillips' Legion Co.D
Roberts, W.H. KY 7th Mtd.Inf. Co.G Sgt.
Roberts, W.H. MS Cav. 24th Bn. Co.D
Roberts, W.H. MS 7th Inf. Co.G
Roberts, W.H. MS 22nd Inf. Co.I
Roberts, W.H. MS 36th Inf. Co.D
Roberts, W.H. NC 23rd Inf. Co.G
Roberts, W.H. SC Arty. Manigault's Bn. 1st Co.B,D, 2nd Co.B,D
Roberts, W.H. TN 20th Inf. Co.C
Roberts, W.H. TN 31st Inf. Co.K
Roberts, W.H. TX Inf. Rutherford's Co.
Roberts, W.H. VA 7th Cav. Glenn's Co.
Roberts, W.H. VA Lt.Arty. Lamkin's Co.
Roberts, W.H. 1st Conf.Eng.Troops Co.I Artif.
Roberts, Wiley GA 7th Cav. Co.I
Roberts, Wiley MS Cav. 17th Bn. Co.A
Roberts, Wiley MO 12th Cav. Co.H
Roberts, Wiley MO 2nd Inf.
Roberts, Wiley TX 11th (Spaight's) Bn.Vol. Co.D
Roberts, Wiley TX 21st Inf. Co.H
Roberts, Wiley H. AR Inf. Clayton's Co.
Roberts, Wiley M. AL 9th Inf. Co.H Cpl.
Roberts, Wiley P. GA 4th Inf. Co.B
Roberts, Wiley P. NC 46th Inf. Co.E
Roberts, Wiley S. NC 29th Inf. Co.D
Roberts, Wiley T. GA 34th Inf. Co.F
Roberts, Wiley W. SC 1st (McCreary's) Inf. Co.F 1st Sgt.
Roberts, Wiley W. VA Mil. Grayson Cty.
Roberts, Wilie T. GA 38th Inf. Co.H
Roberts, Wilkerson P. AL 16th Inf. Co.E 2nd Lt.
Roberts, William AL 9th (Malone's) Cav. Co.K
Roberts, William AL Cav. Hardie's Bn.Res. Co.C
Roberts, William AL Inf. 1st Regt. Co.F,A
Roberts, William AL 15th Inf. Co.A

Roberts, William AL 17th Inf. Co.G
Roberts, William AL 20th Inf. Co.K Cpl.
Roberts, William AL 24th Inf. Co.H,B
Roberts, William AL 26th (O'Neal's) Inf. Co.D
Roberts, William AL 30th Inf. Co.B
Roberts, William AL 32nd Inf. Co.E
Roberts, William AR 1st (Monroe's) Cav. Co.C
Roberts, William AR 1st Mtd.Rifles Co.B,A
Roberts, William AR 15th (N.W.) Inf. Co.G
Roberts, William AR 19th (Dawson's) Inf. Co.D
Roberts, William AR 38th Inf. Co.A
Roberts, William FL Inf. 2nd Bn. Co.B Cpl.
Roberts, William FL 5th Inf. Co.A
Roberts, William FL 5th Inf. Co.C
Roberts, William FL 9th Inf. Co.D
Roberts, William GA 4th (Clinch's) Cav. Co.H
Roberts, William GA Cav. 8th Bn. (St.Guards) Co.A
Roberts, William GA 13th Cav. Co.K
Roberts, William GA Cav. Dorough's Bn.
Roberts, William GA 1st Reg. Co.F
Roberts, William GA 1st (Olmstead's) Inf. Gordon's Co.
Roberts, William GA Inf. 1st Loc.Troops (Augusta) Dearing's Cav.Co.
Roberts, William GA 2nd Res. Co.A
Roberts, William GA 4th Inf. Co.H
Roberts, William GA 7th Mil.
Roberts, William GA 25th Inf. Co.F
Roberts, William GA 29th Inf. Co.B
Roberts, William GA 50th Inf. Co.D
Roberts, William GA 54th Inf. Co.F
Roberts, William GA 61st Inf. Co.I
Roberts, William GA 63rd Inf. Co.B
Roberts, Wm. GA Cobb's Legion Co.D
Roberts, William KY Lt.Arty. Green's Btty.
Roberts, William KY 2nd Mtd.Inf. Co.D
Roberts, William KY 5th Mtd.Inf. Co.E
Roberts, William LA Washington Arty.Bn. 2nd Co.B
Roberts, William LA Inf. 9th Bn. Co.B
Roberts, William LA 30th Inf. Co.E
Roberts, William LA Mil. Algiers Bn. Sgt.
Roberts, William MS Cav. 1st Bn. (Montgomery's) St.Troops Co.C
Roberts, William MS 2nd Cav. Co.A Cpl.
Roberts, William MS 3rd Cav.Res. Co.A
Roberts, Wm. MO 10th Cav. Co.A
Roberts, William MS Inf. 7th Bn. Co.D
Roberts, William MS 23rd Inf. Co.E
Roberts, William MO 1st Cav. Co.H
Roberts, William MO 4th Cav. Co.B
Roberts, William MO 8th Cav. Co.K
Roberts, William MO Lt.Arty. 1st Field Btty.
Roberts, William MO 1st & 4th Cons.Inf. Co.I
Roberts, William MO 4th Inf. Co.D
Roberts, William MO 8th Inf. Co.B
Roberts, William MO Inf. Perkins' Bn. Co.C
Roberts, Wm. MO St.Guard
Roberts, William NC 2nd Cav. (19th St.Troops) Co.K
Roberts, William NC 6th Cav. (65th St.Troops) Co.A
Roberts, William NC 6th Cav. (65th St.Troops) Co.A,F
Roberts, William NC 6th Cav. (65th St.Troops) Co.F

Roberts, William NC 3rd Arty. (40th St.Troops) Co.E

Roberts, William NC 6th Inf. Co.A

Roberts, William NC 7th Inf. Co.C

Roberts, William NC 8th Inf. Co.A

Roberts, William NC 15th Inf. Co.F

Roberts, William NC 21st Inf. Co.H

Roberts, William NC 21st Inf. Co.L

Roberts, William NC 26th Inf. Co.I

Roberts, William NC 32nd Inf. Co.B

Roberts, William NC 32nd Inf. Co.B,C Cook

Roberts, William NC 34th Inf. Co.B

Roberts, William NC Walker's Bn. Thomas' Legion Co.E

Roberts, William SC 1st Arty. Co.K

Roberts, William SC 3rd Res. Co.D Cpl.

Roberts, William SC 7th (Ward's) Bn.St.Res. Co.F

Roberts, William SC 16th Inf. Co.B

Roberts, William SC 16th Inf. Co.H,C

Roberts, William TN Cav. 1st Bn. (McNairy's) Co.A Sgt.

Roberts, William TN 4th (McLemore's) Cav. Co.I

Roberts, William TN 13th (Gore's) Cav. Co.A

Roberts, William TN 18th (Newsom's) Cav. Co.I Cpl.

Roberts, William TN Cav. Welcker's Bn. Co.A Sgt.

Roberts, William TN 3rd (Lillard's) Mtd.Inf. Co.G

Roberts, William TN 10th Inf. Co.D

Roberts, William TN 11th Inf. Co.C 2nd Lt.

Roberts, William TN 16th Inf. Co.K

Roberts, William TN 21st Inf. Co.F

Roberts, William TN 26th Inf. Co.D Cpl.

Roberts, William TN 35th Inf. Co.B

Roberts, William TN 39th Mtd.Inf. Co.D

Roberts, William TN 39th Mtd.Inf. Co.I

Roberts, William TN 55th (Brown's) Inf. Co.K

Roberts, William TN 62nd Mtd.Inf. Co.K

Roberts, William TX 10th Cav. Co.I 1st Lt.

Roberts, William TX 26th Cav. Co.F

Roberts, William TX 35th (Likens') Cav. Co.F 2nd Lt.

Roberts, William TX Cav. Morgan's Regt. Co.A

Roberts, William TX 22nd Inf. Co.B

Roberts, William VA 1st Cav. Co.B

Roberts, William VA 2nd Cav. Co.G

Roberts, William VA 8th Cav. Co.C

Roberts, William VA 25th Cav. Co.I

Roberts, William VA Lt.Arty. King's Co.

Roberts, William VA Inf. 1st Bn. Co.A

Roberts, William VA 2nd Inf. Co.D

Roberts, William VA Inf. 28th Bn. Co.D

Roberts, William VA 29th Inf. 1st Co.F

Roberts, William VA 59th Inf. 3rd Co.I

Roberts, William VA 63rd Inf. Co.A

Roberts, William VA 63rd Inf. Co.B

Roberts, William VA 64th Mtd.Inf. Co.B

Roberts, William VA 198th Mil.

Roberts, William Conf.Inf. 8th Bn.

Roberts, William 1st Cherokee Mtd.Vol. 1st Co.D

Roberts, William 2nd Cherokee Mtd.Vol. Co.A

Roberts, William Conf.Reg.Inf. Brooks' Bn. Co.B

Roberts, William A. AL 34th Inf. Co.D

Roberts, William A. AL 3rd Bn. Hilliard's Legion Vol. Co.C

Roberts, William A. GA 10th Cav. (St.Guards) Co.G

Roberts, William A. GA 1st (Olmstead's) Inf. Co.C

Roberts, William A. NC Lt.Arty. 13th Bn. Co.E Cpl.

Roberts, William A. NC 14th Inf. Co.A

Roberts, William A. NC 35th Inf. Co.H

Roberts, William A. NC 60th Inf. Co.A Sgt.

Roberts, William A. SC 2nd Rifles Co.A

Roberts, William A. SC Inf. 9th Bn. Co.D

Roberts, William A. SC 26th Inf. Co.E

Roberts, William A. TN Cav. 9th Bn. (Gantt's) Co.D

Roberts, William A.D. AL 41st Inf. Co.H

Roberts, William B. AL 50th Inf. Co.B 1st Sgt.

Roberts, William B. GA 34th Inf. Co.A

Roberts, William B. GA 49th Inf. Co.E Sgt.

Roberts, William B. TN 19th (Biffle's) Cav. Co.E

Roberts, William B. TN 28th Inf. Co.C 1st Lt.

Roberts, William B. VA 29th Inf. Co.A

Roberts, William C. AL Loc.Guards Co.A

Roberts, William C. AR 14th (Powers') Inf. Co.K

Roberts, William C. AR 15th (Josey's) Inf. Co.D

Roberts, William C. AR 25th Inf. Co.E

Roberts, William C. MS 4th Inf.

Roberts, William C. MS 20th Inf. Co.K Cpl.

Roberts, William C. SC 1st Arty. Co.I,A

Roberts, William C. SC Inf. 7th Bn. (Enfield Rifles) Co.H

Roberts, William C. SC 12th Inf. Co.E

Roberts, William C. TX 16th Cav. Co.B 1st Sgt.

Roberts, William C. VA 30th Inf. Co.C

Roberts, William C. VA 51st Inf. Co.E 1st Lt.

Roberts, William C. VA 54th Inf. Co.E Sgt.

Roberts, William C. 3rd Conf.Cav. Co.K

Roberts, William C. 1st Chickasaw Inf. Wallace's Co. 3rd Lt.

Roberts, Wm. C. Gen. & Staff Asst.Surg.

Roberts, Wm. C. Gen. & Staff Hosp.Stew.

Roberts, William D. TN 53rd Inf. Co.D

Roberts, William E. GA Lt.Arty. (Jo Thompson Arty.) Hanleiter's Co.

Roberts, William E. GA 25th Inf. Co.G,A

Roberts, William E. GA 38th Inf. Co.M

Roberts, William E. GA 57th Inf. Co.I

Roberts, William E. MO 5th Inf. Co.D

Roberts, William E. SC 12th Inf. Co.E

Roberts, William E. SC 16th Inf. Co.C

Roberts, William E. TN 53rd Inf. Co.G

Roberts, William E. VA 37th Inf. Co.B Cpl.

Roberts, William F. GA 37th Inf. Co.I

Roberts, William F. GA 52nd Inf. Co.K

Roberts, William F. MS 7th Inf. Co.C

Roberts, William F. MS 21st Inf. Co.E

Roberts, William F. MO 10th Cav. Co.G

Roberts, William F. NC Inf. 2nd Bn. Co.H

Roberts, William F. TN 16th Inf. Co.G Cpl.

Roberts, William G. GA 62nd Cav. Co.B

Roberts, William G. GA 35th Inf. Co.C Hosp.Stew.

Roberts, William G. GA 38th Inf. Co.H

Roberts, William G. SC Inf. Hampton Legion Co.F

Roberts, William G. TN Cav. Newsom's Regt. Co.F

Roberts, William G. TX 19th Cav. Co.F

Roberts, William G. TX 21st Cav. Co.C

Roberts, William G.B. NC 34th Inf. Co.C,H

Roberts, William H. AL Arty. 1st Bn. Co.A

Roberts, William H. AL 1st Regt. Mobile Vol. Butt's Co.

Roberts, William H. AL 4th Res. Co.A

Roberts, William H. AR 17th (Lemoyne's) Inf. Co.B

Roberts, William H. AR 21st Inf. Co.D

Roberts, William H. AR 50th Mil. Co.B Cpl.

Roberts, William H. GA Cav. 2nd Bn. Co.D

Roberts, William H. GA 11th Cav. Co.G

Roberts, William H. GA 12th (Robinson's) Cav. (St.Guards) Co.A

Roberts, William H. GA Hvy.Arty. 22nd Bn. Co.C

Roberts, William H. GA 5th Inf. Co.I

Roberts, William H. GA 15th Inf. Co.I

Roberts, William H. GA 23rd Inf. Co.H

Roberts, William H. GA 31st Inf. Co.E

Roberts, William H. GA 44th Inf. Co.I

Roberts, William H. GA 54th Inf. Co.A

Roberts, William H. MS 1st Lt.Arty. Co.D

Roberts, William H. MO Lt.Arty. 1st Field Btty.

Roberts, William H. NC 3rd Cav. (41st St.Troops) Co.K Cpl.

Roberts, William H. NC 13th Inf. Co.A Sgt.

Roberts, William H. NC 17th Inf. (1st Org.) Co.K

Roberts, William H. NC 43rd Inf. Co.I Music.

Roberts, William H. SC 15th Inf. Co.A

Roberts, William H. TX 8th Cav. Co.D

Roberts, William H. TX 37th Cav. Co.C Sgt.

Roberts, William H. TX 2nd Inf. Co.F

Roberts, William H. TX 3rd Inf. Co.D

Roberts, William H. VA 12th Cav. Co.A

Roberts, William H. VA 15th Cav. Co.B

Roberts, William H. VA 19th Cav. Co.A

Roberts, William H. VA 22nd Cav. Co.H

Roberts, William H. VA 1st Arty. Co.D

Roberts, William H. VA Lt.Arty. 1st Bn. Co.D

Roberts, William H. VA Arty. B.H. Smith's Co.

Roberts, William H. VA 14th Inf. Co.A

Roberts, William H. VA 34th Mil. Co.B

Roberts, William H.H. GA 6th Inf. Co.I Capt.

Roberts, William J. AL 51st (Part.Rangers) Co.A

Roberts, William J. AL 9th Inf. Co.C

Roberts, William J. AL 2nd Inf. Co.A

Roberts, William J. FL 1st Inf.

Roberts, William J. GA 9th Inf. Co.C

Roberts, William J. GA 25th Inf. Co.F Music.

Roberts, William J. GA 55th Inf. Co.D

Roberts, William J. LA Inf. 11th Bn. Co.E

Roberts, William J. LA Inf.Cons.Crescent Regt. Co.D

Roberts, William J. MO Cav. Poindexter's Regt.

Roberts, William J. MO Searcy's Bn.S.S. Co.E

Roberts, William J. NC Cav. 5th Bn. Co.A

Roberts, William J. NC 2nd Arty. (36th St.Troops) Co.G

Roberts, William J. NC 4th Inf. Co.D

Roberts, William J. NC 29th Inf. Co.D

Roberts, William J. NC 64th Inf. Co.D Cpl.
Roberts, William J. TN Lt.Arty. Palmer's Co.
Roberts, William J. TN 48th (Voorhies') Inf. Co.E
Roberts, William J. TX 17th Cav. Co.H
Roberts, William J. VA 12th Cav. Co.B Sgt.
Roberts, William J. VA 6th Inf. Co.H
Roberts, William J. VA 28th Inf. Co.G
Roberts, William J. VA 3rd Cav. & Inf.St.Line Co.A
Roberts, William K. NC 2nd Cav. (19th St.Troops) Co.K
Roberts, William K. NC 6th Inf. Co.B
Roberts, William L. AL 62nd Inf. Co.E
Roberts, William L. AL 3rd Bn. Hilliard's Legion Vol. Co.C 2nd Lt.
Roberts, William L. MS 9th Cav. Co.G
Roberts, William L. MO 8th Cav. Co.E
Roberts, William L. TN 34th Inf. Co.I 1st Sgt.
Roberts, William L. TX 36th Cav. Co.K
Roberts, William L. VA 61st Inf. Co.F
Roberts, William M. GA 12th Cav. Co.F
Roberts, William M. KY Cav. Bolen's Ind.Co.
Roberts, William M. MS 2nd (Davidson's) Inf. Co.D
Roberts, William M. TN 10th Inf. Co.I
Roberts, Wm. M. TX Cav. Bourland's Regt. Co.K
Roberts, William McB. NC 29th Inf. Co.H 1st Lt.
Roberts, William N. FL 2nd Inf. Co.E
Roberts, William N. GA 55th Inf. Co.F
Roberts, William N. VA 31st Inf. Co.A
Roberts, William P. AL 17th Inf. Co.D
Roberts, William P. GA 1st (Olmstead's) Inf. Co.C
Roberts, William P. GA 20th Inf. Co.A
Roberts, William P. KY 9th Cav. Co.I Capt.
Roberts, William P. NC 2nd Cav. (19th St.Troops) Co.C Col.
Roberts, William P. NC 15th Inf. Co.H
Roberts, William P. NC 45th Inf. Co.F Cpl.
Roberts, William P. TN Cav. Shaw's Bn. Hamilton's Co. 1st Sgt.
Roberts, William P. TX 3rd Cav. Co.F
Roberts, William P. TX 22nd Cav. Co.E
Roberts, William P. TX Inf. 3rd St.Troops Co.D
Roberts, William R. AL 4th (Russell's) Cav. Co.I
Roberts, William R. GA 1st (Olmstead's) Inf. Stiles' Co.
Roberts, William R. GA Inf. 18th Bn. Co.B
Roberts, William R. GA 36th (Villepigue's) Inf. Co.C Sgt.
Roberts, William R. GA Cobb's Legion Co.F Capt.
Roberts, William R. LA 19th Inf. Co.E Capt.
Roberts, William R. MO Cav. Poindexter's Regt.
Roberts, William R. TN 1st Cav. Co.B
Roberts, William R. TN 10th Inf. Co.I
Roberts, William R. TX 19th Cav. Co.B
Roberts, William R. VA 54th Mil. Co.A
Roberts, William Roy VA Hvy.Arty. 18th Bn. Co.B 1st Lt.
Roberts, William S. AR 31st Inf. Co.C
Roberts, William S. GA Cav. Roswell Bn. Co.A
Roberts, William S. LA 1st Cav. Co.C

Roberts, William S.P. NC 2nd Cav. (19th St.Troops) Co.A
Roberts, William T. AL 10th Inf. Co.F
Roberts, William T. AL 62nd Inf. Co.E
Roberts, William T. AR 3rd Cav. Co.I
Roberts, William T. GA Arty. Baker's Co.
Roberts, William T. GA 12th Inf. Co.K
Roberts, William T. GA 50th Inf. Co.G 2nd Lt.
Roberts, William T. MO 1st N.E. Cav. Co.M
Roberts, William T. MO Cav. Poindexter's Regt. Co.E
Roberts, William T. MO Lt.Arty. 3rd Btty.
Roberts, William T. NC 45th Inf. Co.F
Roberts, William T. TN 24th Inf. Co.B
Roberts, William T. TN 24th Inf. 2nd Co.H, Co.M Cpl.
Roberts, William T. TX 13th Cav. Co.H Lt.
Roberts, William T. TX 15th Cav. Co.A
Roberts, William T. TX 22nd Cav. Co.E
Roberts, William W. AL 7th Cav. Co.B Cpl.
Roberts, Wm. W. AL Cp. of Instr. Talladega
Roberts, William W. AR Inf. 1st Bn. Co.F
Roberts, William W. MS 26th Inf. Co.D
Roberts, William W. SC Inf. 9th Bn. Co.D
Roberts, William W. SC 26th Inf. Co.E
Roberts, William W. TX 6th Cav. Co.D
Roberts, William W. VA 48th Inf. Co.I
Roberts, William Y. GA 64th Inf. Co.K
Roberts, Willie GA 1st Inf. (St.Guards) Co.C Capt.
Roberts, Willie U. NC 6th Inf. Co.B
Roberts, Willis AL 15th Bn.Part.Rangers Co.B
Roberts, Willis AL 56th Part.Rangers Co.B
Roberts, Willis AL Cav. Murphy's Bn. Co.B
Roberts, Willis FL Cav. (Marianna Drag.) Smith's Co.
Roberts, Willis GA 41st Inf. Co.K
Roberts, Willis MO 10th Inf. Co.K
Roberts, Willis TN 16th Inf. Co.G
Roberts, Willis 15th Conf.Cav. Co.B
Roberts, Willis E. TN 53rd Inf. Co.D
Roberts, Willis R. GA Lt.Arty. (Jo Thompson Arty.) Hanleiter's Co.
Roberts, Willis S. KY 4th Mtd.Inf. Co.D Capt.
Roberts, Willis W. GA Cobb's Legion Co.A
Roberts, Wilson AL 2nd Cav. Co.A
Roberts, Wilson AR 19th (Dawson's) Inf. Co.F
Roberts, Wilson GA 42nd Inf. Co.A
Roberts, Wilson L. AR 1st Mtd.Rifles Co.K
Roberts, Wily MO 3rd Cav. Co.G
Roberts, Wingfield VA 61st Inf. Co.I,K
Roberts, Wingfield VA Inf. Cohoon's Bn. Co.C
Roberts, Winston H. VA Lt.Arty. Kirkpatrick's Co.
Roberts, Winston H. VA 58th Inf. Co.F
Roberts, W.J. AL 5th Cav.
Roberts, W.J. AL 37th Inf. Co.B
Roberts, W.J. AR Cav. 1st Bn. (Stirman's) Co.D 1st Lt.
Roberts, W.J. AR 2nd Cav. Co.C
Roberts, W.J. AR 15th (N.W.) Inf. Co.I
Roberts, W.J. GA Cav. 29th Bn. Co.D
Roberts, W.J. GA Inf. 1st Loc.Troops (Augusta) Co.F
Roberts, W.J. GA Inf. 8th Bn. Co.F
Roberts, W.J. GA Inf. 9th Bn. Co.D Sgt.
Roberts, W.J. GA 32nd Inf. Co.K

Roberts, W.J. GA 37th Inf. Co.C Cpl.
Roberts, W.J. NC 6th Cav. (65th St.Troops) Co.I,A
Roberts, W.J. NC 4th Inf. Co.B
Roberts, W.J. NC 26th Inf. Co.I
Roberts, W.J. SC 2nd Arty. Co.K
Roberts, W.J. SC 2nd Inf. Co.K
Roberts, W.J. TN 16th Inf. Co.G
Roberts, W.J. TN 31st Inf. Co.A Sgt.
Roberts, W.J. TX 7th Cav. Co.F
Roberts, W.J.C. SC 1st Cav. Co.D,F
Roberts, W.J.C. SC Inf. Holcombe Legion Co.A
Roberts, W.L. AL 23rd Inf. Co.H Sgt.
Roberts, W.L. AL 31st Inf. Co.B,C
Roberts, W.L. AL 60th Inf. Co.B 2nd Lt.
Roberts, W.L. TN Inf. 1st Cons.Regt. Co.I 1st Sgt.
Roberts, W.L. TX Cav. Mann's Regt. Co.I 1st Lt.
Roberts, W.M. GA 4th Res. Co.G
Roberts, W.M. GA Cherokee Legion (St.Guards) Co.F
Roberts, W.M. MS 2nd St.Cav. Co.K 1st Lt.
Roberts, W.M. MS 7th Cav. Co.E
Roberts, W.M. MS 43rd Inf. Co.C
Roberts, Woodfin TN 3rd (Forrest's) Cav. Co.D
Roberts, Woodfin TX 23rd Cav. Co.K
Roberts, W.P. FL 4th Inf. Co.F,D 2nd Lt.
Roberts, W.P. FL 9th Inf. Co.E Sgt.
Roberts, W.P. MS 3rd Inf. Co.G Sgt.
Roberts, W.P. TN Inf. 22nd Bn. Co.B
Roberts, W.P. TX Cav. (Dismtd.) Chisum's Regt. Co.K
Roberts, W.P. Brush Bn.
Roberts, W.P. Gen. & Staff Brig.Gen.
Roberts, W.R. GA 12th Cav. Co.G Cpl.
Roberts, W.R. MS 28th Cav. Co.H
Roberts, W.R. SC 2nd Rifles Co.B
Roberts, W.R. TN 23rd Inf. Co.D
Roberts, W.R. Gen. & Staff,PACS 1st Lt.
Roberts, W.S. AL Cav. Hardie's Bn.Res. Co.A
Roberts, W.S. AR Cav. Harrell's Bn. Co.D
Roberts, W.S. GA 11th Cav. (St.Guards) Slaten's Co. Cpl.
Roberts, W.S. GA Inf. 1st Loc.Troops (Augusta) Barnes' Lt.Arty.Co.
Roberts, W.S. NC 6th Inf. Co.D
Roberts, W.S. NC 64th Inf. Co.C
Roberts, W.T. GA 10th Inf. Co.E
Roberts, W.T. MS 2nd St.Cav. Co.H
Roberts, W.T. MO Inf. Clark's Regt. Co.C
Roberts, W.T. SC 23rd Inf. Co.F
Roberts, W.T., Jr. TX Inf. 1st St.Troops Saxton's Co.
Roberts, W.T. Conf.Cav. Wood's Regt. Co.I
Roberts, W.T. Brush Bn.
Roberts, W.V. MO 7th Cav. Ward's Co.
Roberts, W.V. TN Inf. 154th Sr.Regt. Co.L
Roberts, W.W. MS 2nd St.Cav. Co.K,L
Roberts, W.W. NC Lt.Arty. 13th Bn. Co.C
Roberts, W.W. SC 5th Cav. Co.I
Roberts, W.W. SC Cav. 14th Bn. Co.D
Roberts, W.W. SC Arty. Manigault's Bn. 1st Co.B
Roberts, W.W. TN 7th (Duckworth's) Cav. Co.F 2nd Lt.
Roberts, W.W. TN 4th Inf. Co.C

Roberts, W.W. TN 16th Inf. Co.C
Roberts, W.W. TX Cav. 2nd Regt.St.Troops Co.G
Roberts, W.W. TX 17th Field Btty.
Roberts, W.W. Gen. & Staff,PACS Capt.
Roberts, W.Y. GA 46th Inf. Co.K
Roberts, Young LA Watkins' Bn.Res.Corps Co.C
Roberts, Z. NC 5th Sr.Res. Co.K
Roberts, Zach NC 5th Sr.Res. Co.A
Roberts, Zachariah GA 61st Inf. Co.I
Roberts, Zachariah NC 6th Inf. Co.I
Roberts, Zachariah VA 49th Inf. Co.F
Roberts, Zachariah H. VA 38th Inf. Co.A
Roberts, Z.C. TN 23rd Inf. Co.D
Roberts, Zephania N. AR Cav. Harrell's Bn. Co.C
Roberts, Zephaniah AR Cav. Harrell's Bn. Co.D
Roberts, Zephaniah AR 27th Inf. Co.A
Roberts, Z.J. TN 60th Mtd.Inf. Co.I
Roberts, Z. Randall FL 3rd Inf. Co.F Cpl.
Robertsen, Daniel AL Randolph Cty.Res. D.A. Self's Co.
Robertsen, Ed. AL Talladega Cty.Res. R.N. Ware's Cav.Co.
Robertsen, H.B. AL Talladega Cty.Res. J. Hurst's Co.
Robertsen, William AL Talladega Cty.Res. R.N. Ware's Cav.Co.
Robertson, --- GA 8th Inf. Co.I
Robertson, --- KY 9th Mtd.Inf. Co.A
Robertson, --- MS 19th Inf. Co.B
Robertson, --- TX Cav. Border's Regt. Co.K
Robertson, --- TX Cav. Good's Bn. Co.C
Robertson, --- TX Cav. Mann's Regt. Co.K
Robertson, --- VA 4th Cav. Surg.
Robertson, --- VA 28th Inf. Co.B
Robertson, --- 8th (Wade's) Conf.Cav. Co.F Capt.
Robertson, A. AL 8th (Hatch's) Cav. Co.A
Robertson, A. GA Arty. (Macon Lt.Arty.) Slaten's Co.
Robertson, A. MS 10th Cav. Co.H
Robertson, A. MS 9th Inf. Co.C
Robertson, A. MS 35th Inf. Co.I
Robertson, A. NC 60th Inf. Co.C
Robertson, A. TN 2nd (Ashby's) Cav. Co.A
Robertson, A.A. TN 21st & 22nd (Cons.) Cav. Co.K
Robertson, A.A. TN 22nd (Barteau's) Cav. Co.G
Robertson, Aaron T. AR 3rd Inf. Co.C
Robertson, A.B. AL 18th Inf. Co.D
Robertson, A.B. AL 43rd Inf. Co.G Cpl.
Robertson, Abbott L. TN 6th Inf. Co.G
Robertson, Abbott L. Cheatham's Staff 1st Lt.,AAIG
Robertson, Abe TX 10th Inf. Co.D
Robertson, Abe TX 12th Inf. Co.L
Robertson, Abiah E. MS 11th Inf. Co.H
Robertson, Abner VA 18th Inf. Co.C
Robertson, Abner H. SC 1st (Orr's) Rifles Co.G
Robertson, Abner H. VA 18th Inf. Co.C
Robertson, Abraham SC 1st Arty. Co.D,F
Robertson, Abram VA 51st Inf. Co.D Cpl.
Robertson, A.C. AL 48th Inf. Co.K
Robertson, A.C. AL Pris.Guard Freeman's Co.
Robertson, A.C. LA 2nd Inf. Co.E

Robertson, A.C. TN 15th Inf. Co.E Cpl.
Robertson, A.C. Gen. & Staff Capt.,ACS
Robertson, A.D. AR 6th Inf. Co.K
Robertson, A.D. VA 51st Inf. Co.G
Robertson, Adams NC 57th Inf. Co.D
Robertson, Addison MS Bradford's Co. (Conf. Guards Arty.) Cpl.
Robertson, Adolphas MS 22nd Inf. Co.A
Robertson, Adoniram J. MS 27th Inf. Co.F Cpl.
Robertson, A.E. KY 4th Cav. Co.D
Robertson, A.E. SC Inf. 1st (Charleston) Bn. Co.E
Robertson, A.E. SC 27th Inf. Co.A
Robertson, A.F. Gen. & Staff Capt.,ACS
Robertson, A.F.E. AL 17th Inf. Co.F 1st Lt.
Robertson, A.G. AL Inf. 2nd Regt. Co.C
Robertson, A.G. AL 42nd Inf. Co.A
Robertson, A.G. MS Cav. Yerger's Regt. Co.B
Robertson, A.G. TN 36th Inf. Co.B 2nd Lt.
Robertson, A.G. VA Lt.Arty. 38th Bn. Co.C
Robertson, A.H. KY 3rd Cav. Co.B
Robertson, A.H. MS 8th Cav. Co.K
Robertson, A.H. NC 62nd Inf. Co.F
Robertson, A.H. TN 10th (DeMoss') Cav. Co.E
Robertson, A.H. VA Lt.Arty. Fry's Co.
Robertson, Ainzie SC 17th Inf. Co.K
Robertson, A.J. AR 34th Inf. Co.D Cpl.
Robertson, A.J. KY 7th Cav. Co.B
Robertson, A.J. MS 4th Cav. Co.B
Robertson, A.J. MS 1st Lt.Arty. Co.B
Robertson, A.J. MS 41st Inf. Co.D
Robertson, A.J. TN 11th Inf. Co.D
Robertson, A.J. TN 20th Inf. Co.E
Robertson, A.J. TX Cav. Gano's Squad. Co.B
Robertson, A.J. TX Cav. Morgan's Regt. Co.F
Robertson, A.J. VA Horse Arty. D. Shanks' Co.
Robertson, A.J. 20th Conf.Cav. Co.D
Robertson, A. Jackson AL 25th Inf. Co.C
Robertson, A.L. MS Cav. (St.Troops) Gamblin's Co.
Robertson, A.L. NC 5th Cav. (63rd St.Troops) Co.B
Robertson, A.L. TN 14th (Neely's) Cav. Co.H
Robertson, A.L. TN 16th (Logwood's) Cav. Co.F
Robertson, A.L. TX 24th Cav. Co.F
Robertson, A.L. TX 1st Hvy.Arty. Co.K
Robertson, A.L. VA 9th Cav. Co.G
Robertson, Albert KY 9th Mtd.Inf. Co.C
Robertson, Albert C. MO 10th Inf. Co.E 2nd Lt.
Robertson, Albert G. TX 34th Cav. Co.D
Robertson, Albert G. VA Hvy.Arty. Epes' Co.
Robertson, Alex SC 4th Cav. Co.K
Robertson, Alex SC Mil.Cav. Rutledge's Co.
Robertson, Alexander AR 15th (Josey's) Inf. Co.D Bvt.2nd Lt.
Robertson, Alexander KY 2nd (Woodward's) Cav. Co.G
Robertson, Alexander LA 11th Inf. Co.H
Robertson, Alexander MS 7th Cav. Co.K
Robertson, Alexander TN Inf. 22nd Bn. Co.D
Robertson, Alexander VA Arty. Bryan's Co.
Robertson, Alexander E. TN 2nd (Smith's) Cav.
Robertson, Alexander G. VA Cav. 1st Bn. (Loc.Def.Troops) Co.B Sgt.
Robertson, Alexander P. GA Cobb's Legion Co.C

Robertson, Alex W. TX 29th Cav. Co.A
Robertson, Alfred NC 2nd Cav. (19th St.Troops) Co.F
Robertson, Alfred NC 34th Inf. Co.C
Robertson, Alfred TN 13th Inf. Co.E
Robertson, Alfred B. 1st Conf.Eng.Troops Co.G Artif.
Robertson, Alfred C. AR Inf. Cocke's Regt. Co.A
Robertson, Alfred C. NC 56th Inf. Co.G 1st Sgt.
Robertson, Alfred G. NC 28th Inf. Co.G Sgt.
Robertson, Alfred L. GA 12th Inf. Co.D Sgt.
Robertson, Allen NC 2nd Cav. (19th St.Troops) Co.F
Robertson, Allen NC 25th Inf. Co.A Fifer
Robertson, Allen TN 48th (Nixon's) Inf. Co.I
Robertson, Allen H. NC 64th Inf. Co.F
Robertson, Allen J. AL 1st Regt.Conscr. Co.A
Robertson, Alonzo G. GA 44th Inf. Co.I
Robertson, Alsophus T. Gen. & Staff A.Surg.
Robertson, A.M. AL Cp. of Instr. Talladega
Robertson, A.M. KY 7th Cav. Co.K
Robertson, A.M. MO 3rd Inf. Co.D Sr.2nd Lt.
Robertson, A.M. NC 62nd Inf. Co.F
Robertson, A.M. SC Post Guard Senn's Co.
Robertson, A.M. Gen. & Staff Asst.Surg.
Robertson, Americus AR 27th Inf. Old Co.B, Co.D
Robertson, Americus AR 45th Mil. Co.B 2nd Lt.
Robertson, Amos T. AR 3rd Inf. Co.C
Robertson, A.N. AR 21st Inf. Co.F Sgt.
Robertson, Anderson VA 42nd Inf. Co.E
Robertson, Andrew GA Inf. 4th Bn. (St.Guards) Co.H
Robertson, Andrew NC 4th Sr.Res. Co.K
Robertson, Andrew C. GA 1st Reg. Co.I
Robertson, Andrew J. VA 25th Inf. 2nd Co.F
Robertson, Andrew P. AL 17th Inf. Co.E
Robertson, Anthony KY 3rd Cav. Co.B
Robertson, Anthony KY 7th Cav. Co.B
Robertson, Anthony TX Cav. Gano's Squad. Co.B
Robertson, Anthony P. GA Lt.Arty. 14th Bn. Co.C 1st Sgt.
Robertson, Anthony P. GA Lt.Arty. Ferrell's Btty. 1st Sgt.
Robertson, A.P. VA Cav. 47th Bn. Co.A
Robertson, Arch 1st Cherokee Mtd.Vol. 1st Co.F, 2nd Co.F,H
Robertson, Archelans J. VA 19th Inf. Co.K 1st Lt.
Robertson, Archer VA 18th Inf. Co.C
Robertson, Archer A. VA Hvy.Arty. 20th Bn. Co.A
Robertson, Archer A. VA 44th Inf. Co.A
Robertson, Archibald GA 1st Cav. Co.H
Robertson, Archibald T. VA 56th Inf. Co.D
Robertson, Arch.W. Gen. & Staff A.Surg.
Robertson, Arthur F. VA 51st Inf. Co.G
Robertson, A.S. AL 4th Res. Co.G
Robertson, A.S. AL 29th Inf. Co.A
Robertson, Asa MS Cav. 1st Bn. (Miller's) Bowles' Co.
Robertson, Asa MS 32nd Inf. Co.E
Robertson, Asa J. TX 34th Cav. Co.C
Robertson, A.T. AL 1st Cav. Co.G
Robertson, A.T. AL 12th Cav. Co.G

Robertson, A.T. AR 16th Inf. Asst.Surg.

Robertson, A.T. TN 22nd Inf. Co.B Lt.Col.

Robertson, A.T. VA Inf. 44th Bn. Co.C

Robertson, Atwell W. VA Lt.Arty. Jeffress' Co. 2nd Lt.

Robertson, Austin M. SC Inf. 3rd Bn. Co.C

Robertson, A.W. AR 7th Inf. Co.E 1st Lt.

Robertson, A.W. GA 38th Inf. Co.E 2nd Lt.

Robertson, A.W. MO 16th Inf. Co.D

Robertson, A.W. TN 46th Inf. Co.C

Robertson, A.W. TX 26th Cav. Co.F, 2nd Co.G

Robertson, B. KY 10th (Johnson's) Cav. Co.A

Robertson, B. TN 51st (Cons.) Inf. Co.B

Robertson, B. TX Inf. Carter's Co.

Robertson, B.A. NC 4th Cav. (59th St.Troops) Co.K

Robertson, B.A. NC Cav. 12th Bn. Co.A

Robertson, B.A. TX Inf. Timmons' Regt. Co.A

Robertson, B.A. 8th (Dearing's) Conf.Cav. Co.A

Robertson, Barnett SC 6th Cav. Co.E

Robertson, Battle TN 6th Inf. Co.G

Robertson, B.D. MS Cav. (St.Troops) Gamblin's Co.

Robertson, B.D. MS 20th Inf. Co.D

Robertson, Benjamin GA Inf. 4th Bn. (St.Guards) Co.H

Robertson, Benjamin GA 21st Inf. Co.F

Robertson, Benjamin KY 1st Bn.Mtd.Rifles Co.A

Robertson, Benjamin A. GA 21st Inf. Co.G

Robertson, Benjamin F. LA 7th Inf. Co.B

Robertson, Benjamin F. MS 27th Inf. Co.F

Robertson, Benjamin F. SC 1st (Orr's) Rifles Co.E

Robertson, Benjamin F. TX 18th Inf. Co.F

Robertson, Benjamin F. VA Lt.Arty. W.H. Chapman's Co.

Robertson, Benjamin F. VA 56th Inf. Co.C

Robertson, Benjamin F. VA 97th Mil. Co.H

Robertson, Benjamin L. VA 18th Inf. Co.C

Robertson, Benjamin P. AR 23rd Inf. Co.A Sr.2nd Lt.

Robertson, Benjamin P. NC 12th Inf. Co.C

Robertson, Benjamin P. TN 19th Inf. Co.I

Robertson, Benjamin S. VA 64th Mil. Hunley's Co.

Robertson, Benjamin T. KY 4th Cav. Co.I

Robertson, Benjamin W. GA 41st Inf. Co.C

Robertson, Benjamin W. SC 14th Inf. Co.C

Robertson, Bennett GA 1st Inf. (St.Guards) Co.E

Robertson, Bennett B. GA 22nd Inf. Co.K

Robertson, Benoni TX 6th Inf. Co.G

Robertson, Benoni M. AL 6th Inf. Co.M

Robertson, Berry SC 1st St.Troops Co.K

Robertson, Berry SC 3rd Res. Co.D

Robertson, Berry VA 6th Bn.Res. Co.G

Robertson, Berry W. SC 16th Inf. Co.I

Robertson, Beverly H. VA 4th Cav. Col.

Robertson, B.F. GA 36th (Broyles') Inf. Co.I

Robertson, B.F. MS 9th Inf. Co.E 1st Lt.

Robertson, B.F. MS 44th Inf. Co.A 2nd Lt.

Robertson, B.F. TN 27th Inf. Co.F

Robertson, B.F. TX 5th Inf. Co.I

Robertson, B.F. TX 20th Inf. Co.C

Robertson, B.H. MS 15th Inf. Co.K

Robertson, B.H. MS 35th Inf. Co.K

Robertson, B.H. SC 4th St.Troops Co.H

Robertson, B.H. SC 6th Res. Comsy.Sgt.

Robertson, B.H. TX 21st Cav. Co.C Sgt.

Robertson, B.H. VA Cav. Brig.Gen.

Robertson, Bird A. VA 157th Mil. Co.B

Robertson, B.L. VA Mtd.Guard 4th Congr.Dist.

Robertson, B.M. AL 5th Inf. Co.K

Robertson, Box SC 1st Arty. Co.D

Robertson, B.P. VA 46th Inf. 2nd Co.E

Robertson, B.P. Exch.Bn. 2nd Co.A,CSA 1st Lt.

Robertson, Branch M. VA 31st Inf. Co.F 1st Sgt.

Robertson, Bridge VA 23rd Inf. Co.C

Robertson, B.T. MS 5th Inf. Co.H

Robertson, Bunk VA 20th Cav. Co.I

Robertson, Burwell J. AL 43rd Inf. Co.F

Robertson, B.W. TN Park's Co. (Loc.Def. Troops)

Robertson, B.W. TX 9th (Nichols') Inf. Co.K Sgt.

Robertson, Byrd B. VA 3rd Res. Co.F

Robertson, C. KY 3rd Mtd.Inf. Co.H

Robertson, C. SC Palmetto S.S. Co.L

Robertson, Calvin AL Cav. Forrest's Regt.

Robertson, Calvin TN 18th (Newsom's) Cav. Co.F

Robertson, Calvin L. GA 53rd Inf. Co.K

Robertson, Calvin T. VA Hvy.Arty. 20th Bn. Co.A

Robertson, C.B. GA 27th Inf. Co.D

Robertson, C.C. AR 45th Mil. Co.B

Robertson, C.C. VA Lt.Arty. 13th Bn. Co.B

Robertson, C.F. NC 2nd Cav. (19th St.Troops) Co.G

Robertson, C.F. TX 15th Cav. Co.B

Robertson, C.F. VA 1st Cav. Co.G

Robertson, C. Franklin MS 33rd Inf. Co.I 1st Sgt.

Robertson, C.G. MS Bradford's Co. (Conf. Guards Arty.)

Robertson, C.H. AR 37th Inf. Co.H

Robertson, C.H. MS Cav. (St.Troops) Gamblin's Co.

Robertson, C.H. MS 27th Inf. Co.A Sgt.

Robertson, Charles AL 7th Inf. Co.I Music.

Robertson, Charles AL 18th Bn.Vol. Co.E

Robertson, Charles MS 18th Cav. Co.D Cpl.

Robertson, Charles TX 12th Inf. Co.I

Robertson, Charles TX 18th Inf. Co.H

Robertson, Charles VA 23rd Inf. Co.K 1st Lt.

Robertson, Charles VA 36th Inf. 3rd Co.I

Robertson, Charles VA 86th Mil. Co.F

Robertson, Charles H. MS 22nd Inf. Co.G

Robertson, Charles H. MS 29th Inf. Co.I Sgt.Maj.

Robertson, Charles H. VA 9th Cav. Co.K

Robertson, Charles H. VA 21st Inf. Co.K

Robertson, Charles S. TN 4th (McLemore's) Cav. Co.K

Robertson, Charles W. NC 14th Inf. Co.K Sgt.

Robertson, Charles W. VA 11th Bn.Res. Co.F

Robertson, Chastane VA 28th Inf. Co.K Capt.

Robertson, Chrispin D. VA 38th Inf. Co.D

Robertson, Christian NC 21st Inf. Co.K

Robertson, Christopher A. VA 21st Inf. Co.F

Robertson, Cincinatus AL 25th Inf. Co.H

Robertson, C.J. KY 10th (Johnson's) Cav. New Co.I Sgt.Maj.

Robertson, C.L. TN 18th Inf. Co.I

Robertson, Clay TN 14th Inf. Co.E Capt.

Robertson, Clay TX 12th Inf. Co.I Sr.2nd Lt.

Robertson, Colevis J. LA 28th (Gray's) Inf. Co.C

Robertson, Columbus F. AL 27th Inf. Co.A Cpl.

Robertson, C.P. GA 24th Inf. Co.G,E

Robertson, Creed T. VA Lt.Arty. French's Co.

Robertson, Creed T. VA 57th Inf. Co.F

Robertson, C.S. MO 9th Inf. Co.B

Robertson, C.S. 1st Conf.Cav. 2nd Co.G Lt.Col.

Robertson, C.T. MS Cav. (St.Troops) Gamblin's Co.

Robertson, C.T. VA 43rd Mil. Shaon's Co. Cpl.

Robertson, C.W. TN 14th (Neely's) Cav. Co.H Cpl.

Robertson, C.W. TN 15th Cav. Co.A

Robertson, C.W. TN 50th Inf. Co.A Maj.

Robertson, C.W. TX Inf. Timmons' Regt. Co.E

Robertson, C.W. TX Waul's Legion Co.D

Robertson, Cythe TX 3rd Cav. Co.C

Robertson, D. AL 25th Inf. Co.E

Robertson, D. AR 11th Inf. Co.K

Robertson, D. LA 3rd (Wingfield's) Cav. Co.G

Robertson, D. LA 13th Inf. Co.G

Robertson, D. MS 2nd St.Cav. Co.B

Robertson, D. MS Inf. 2nd Bn. (St.Troops) Co.B Sgt.

Robertson, D. NC 3rd Jr.Res. Co.B

Robertson, D. VA 7th Inf. Co.B

Robertson, D.A. TN 15th Cav. Co.D

Robertson, D.A. TN Inf. 154th Sr.Regt. Co.K

Robertson, D.A. VA Lt.Arty. Woolfolk's Co.

Robertson, D.A. VA 1st (Farinholt's) Res. Co.H

Robertson, Dan FL Harrison's Co. (Santa Rosa Guards)

Robertson, Daniel GA 18th Inf. Co.K

Robertson, Daniel NC 7th Sr.Res. Fisher's Co.

Robertson, Daniel NC 21st Inf. Co.G

Robertson, Daniel NC 23rd Inf. Co.I

Robertson, Daniel SC 6th Cav. Co.E

Robertson, Daniel SC 23rd Inf. Co.K

Robertson, Daniel TN Cav. Welcker's Bn. Co.A Cpl.

Robertson, Daniel A. VA 10th Cav. Co.K

Robertson, Daniel C. VA 38th Inf. Co.K

Robertson, Daniel H. VA 15th Inf. Co.B Sgt.

Robertson, Daniel J. TN Cav. 4th Bn. (Bran- ner's) Co.E

Robertson, Daniel S. AL 47th Inf. Co.D

Robertson, Daniel S. AL 63rd Inf. Co.B Sgt.

Robertson, David AL 43rd Inf. Co.E

Robertson, David AR 8th Inf. New Co.F

Robertson, David AR 27th Inf. Co.G

Robertson, David GA 36th (Broyles') Inf. Co.D

Robertson, David GA 65th Inf. Co.D,I

Robertson, David MS Moore's Co. (Palo Alto Guards) 2nd Lt.

Robertson, David SC 1st Arty. Co.G Cook

Robertson, David TN Cav. 7th Bn. (Bennett's) Co.E

Robertson, David TN 21st & 22nd (Cons.) Cav. Co.K

Robertson, David TN 22nd (Barteau's) Cav. Co.G

Robertson, David VA 14th Cav. Co.A

Robertson, David VA 52nd Inf. 2nd Co.B

Robertson, David A. NC 3rd Cav. (41st St.Troops) Co.I Capt.

Robertson, David C. NC 45th Inf. Co.K
Robertson, David F. MS 9th Inf. Old Co.E
Robertson, David G. TN Lt.Arty. Tobin's Co.
Robertson, David G. VA Lt.Arty. Hardwicke's Co.
Robertson, David L. MS 42nd Inf. Co.B
Robertson, David M. VA Cav. 1st Bn. (Loc.Def.Troops) Co.C
Robertson, David S. VA 61st Inf. Co.D 1st Sgt.
Robertson, David T. LA Cav. 18th Bn. Co.A 2nd Lt.
Robertson, David T. TN 1st (Turney's) Inf. Co.E Cpl.
Robertson, David W. AL 26th (O'Neal's) Inf. Co.D
Robertson, D.C. AL 31st Inf. Co.G
Robertson, D.C. SC Ind.Inf. Ind.Co.
Robertson, D.D. MO 2nd Inf. Asst.Ward M.
Robertson, D.F. FL 2nd Cav. Co.D
Robertson, D.G. AL 21st Inf. Co.I
Robertson, D.G. SC 7th Cav. Co.H
Robertson, D.G. TN 10th (DeMoss') Cav. Co.E
Robertson, D.G. TN Cav. Napier's Bn. Co.B
Robertson, D.G. VA 1st (Farinholt's) Res. Co.F
Robertson, D.H. LA Inf. 9th Bn. Co.D
Robertson, D.H. SC 6th Inf. 1st Co.D, 2nd Co.G
Robertson, D.H. TX 4th Inf. Co.C
Robertson, D.H. TX 5th Inf. Co.I
Robertson, D.J. GA Phillips' Legion Co.D
Robertson, D.J. TN 2nd (Ashby's) Cav. Co.I
Robertson, D.L. TN Cav. Napier's Bn. Co.B
Robertson, D.L. TN 11th Inf. Co.C
Robertson, D.M. MS 31st Inf. Co.H
Robertson, D.M. MO 7th Cav. Co.D
Robertson, D.M. VA 2nd Arty. Co.H
Robertson, D.M. VA Inf. 22nd Bn. Co.H
Robertson, D.N. GA Arty. Lumpkin's Co.
Robertson, Dobins D. NC 16th Inf. Co.D
Robertson, Doc F. TX 15th Cav. Co.A
Robertson, D.P. SC Mil. Charbonnier's Co.
Robertson, D.S. AL 18th Inf. Co.E
Robertson, D.S. TN Inf. 154th Sr.Regt. Adj.
Robertson, Dunbar P. SC Horse Arty. (Washington Arty.) Vol. Hart's Co.
Robertson, Duncan SC Lt.Arty. Garden's Co. (Palmetto Lt.Btty.)
Robertson, Duncan, Jr. VA 6th Inf. Co.G 1st Lt.
Robertson, Duncan C. SC Cav. Walpole's Co.
Robertson, E. AL 56th Part.Rangers Co.G
Robertson, E. MS 1st Cav. Lt.
Robertson, E. MS 1st Cav.Res. Co.H
Robertson, E. MS 5th Inf. (St.Troops) Co.C
Robertson, E. MS 40th Inf. Co.B
Robertson, E. VA 13th Cav. Co.C
Robertson, E. VA Conscr. Cp.Lee Co.A
Robertson, E.A. TN 1st Cav. Co.A
Robertson, E.A. VA 5th Cav. Co.D
Robertson, E.A. VA 28th Inf. 2nd Co.C
Robertson, E.B. TX 15th Inf. Co.I
Robertson, E.C. TX Jamison Res. Co.A
Robertson, E.C. 1st Seminole Mtd.Vol. ACS,Sgt.
Robertson, E.D. TX 18th Inf. Co.H
Robertson, Edgar W. VA 39th Inf. Co.L
Robertson, Edward AL 17th Inf. Co.F
Robertson, Edward NC 45th Inf. Co.F
Robertson, Edward TN 4th (McLemore's) Cav. Co.K

Robertson, Edward F. MS 7th Inf. Co.A Sgt.
Robertson, Edward F. VA 6th Inf. 2nd Co.E
Robertson, Edward G. TX 34th Cav. Co.A
Robertson, Edward G. VA 3rd Cav. Co.A
Robertson, Edward G. VA 56th Inf. Co.G
Robertson, Edward H. TN 56th (McKoin's) Inf. Dillehay's Co. Cpl.
Robertson, Edward S. VA 38th Inf. Co.H 2nd Lt.
Robertson, Edward S. VA 57th Inf. Co.D Lt.
Robertson, Edward T. VA Lt.Arty. Pegram's Co.
Robertson, Edwin F. GA 48th Inf. Co.D
Robertson, E.F. Conf.Cav. Powers' Regt. Co.E
Robertson, E.G. TN 4th Inf. Co.I Sgt.
Robertson, E.G. VA Inf. 44th Bn. Co.C 2nd Lt.
Robertson, E.H. NC 14th Inf. Co.G Cpl.
Robertson, E.H. SC Inf. Hampton Legion Co.I
Robertson, E.J. AL Morris' Co. (Mtd.)
Robertson, E.J. NC 4th Cav. (59th St.Troops) Co.F
Robertson, E.J. VA 3rd Arty. Co.H
Robertson, E.J. VA 10th Cav. Co.E
Robertson, Elam G. MS 3rd Inf. Co.C
Robertson, Elan G. MS 5th Inf. Co.C
Robertson, Elbridge C. VA Hvy.Arty. Kyle's Co.
Robertson, Eldridge C. VA Hvy.Arty. 19th Bn. Co.D
Robertson, Eldridge P. VA Lt.Arty. 38th Bn. Co.D
Robertson, Eli KY 1st Bn.Mtd.Rifles Co.B,E
Robertson, Eli KY 3rd Bn.Mtd.Rifles Co.E
Robertson, Eli MO 1st Cav. Co.G
Robertson, Eli MO 1st & 3rd Cons.Cav. Co.B
Robertson, Eli NC 33rd Inf. Co.K
Robertson, Elias AL 43rd Inf. Co.G
Robertson, Elias KY 2nd (Woodward's) Cav. Co.G Sgt.
Robertson, Elias KY 1st Inf. Co.F Cpl.
Robertson, Elias TX 34th Cav. Co.C
Robertson, Elifus MO 15th Cav. Co.C
Robertson, Elijah AL 31st Inf. Co.K
Robertson, Elijah AL 58th Inf. Co.K Cpl.
Robertson, Elijah GA 2nd Bn.S.S. Co.E
Robertson, Elijah A. TX 18th Cav. Co.A
Robertson, Elijah B. GA 22nd Inf. Co.A
Robertson, Elipus S. AR 8th Inf. New Co.A
Robertson, Elisha GA 4th Cav. (St.Guards) Robertson's Co.
Robertson, Elisha A. GA Carlton's Co. (Troup Cty.Arty.)
Robertson, Elisha G.S. MS 31st Inf. Co.H
Robertson, Elisha M. AL 1st Cav. Co.F 1st Lt.
Robertson, Elisha Z. VA 56th Inf. Co.D
Robertson, Elverton AR Inf. Cocke's Regt. Co.E
Robertson, E.M. MS 2nd Cav. Co.H
Robertson, Emmet VA 61st Inf. Co.H
Robertson, E.R. SC 4th Cav. Co.K
Robertson, E.S. AL 32nd Inf. Co.E
Robertson, E.S. NC 7th Sr.Res. Mitchell's Co.
Robertson, Esaw TN 1st (Carter's) Cav. Co.E Sgt.
Robertson, E. Sterling C. Gen. & Staff Vol.ADC
Robertson, E.T. TX Cav. Border's Regt. Co.B
Robertson, E.T. TX 19th Inf. Co.H
Robertson, Eugene VA Lt.Arty. 13th Bn. Co.B
Robertson, E.W. LA 27th Inf. Co.D Capt.

Robertson, E.W. TN Cav. Nixon's Regt. Co.C
Robertson, Ezra MS 1st Cav. Co.E
Robertson, F. AR 58th Mil. Co.E
Robertson, F. MS Lt.Arty. (Warren Lt.Arty.) Swett's Co.
Robertson, F. Gen. & Staff Maj.,AIG
Robertson, F.A. AR 7th Cav. Co.C Sgt.
Robertson, F.A. AR 15th Cav. Co.C 1st Sgt.
Robertson, F.A. MS 46th Inf. Co.B
Robertson, F.A. TX Cav. Hardeman's Regt. Co.A
Robertson, F.D. VA Arty. Bryan's Co.
Robertson, Felix H. Gen. & Staff Brig.Gen.
Robertson, Felix R. AR 18th Inf. Co.E Capt.
Robertson, Felix W. Gen. & Staff Capt.,ACS
Robertson, Fenwick Gen. & Staff AASurg.
Robertson, F.F. TX 12th Inf. Co.I
Robertson, F.G. TN 36th Inf. Co.B
Robertson, F.H. Lt.Arty. Dent's Btty.,CSA Capt.
Robertson, F.H. Conf.Arty. Palmer's Bn. Maj.
Robertson, Fitz O. VA Hvy.Arty. Epes' Co.
Robertson, F.J. AR 1st Mtd.Rifles Co.E
Robertson, F.J. GA 18th Inf. Co.A
Robertson, F.J. Gen. & Staff Surg.
Robertson, F.L. MO Robertson's Regt.St.Guard Col.
Robertson, F.L. SC 2nd Inf. Co.C
Robertson, Flavius J. AR 4th Inf. Co.B
Robertson, Fletcher S. KY 1st Bn.Mtd.Rifles Co.B
Robertson, F.M. AL 40th Inf. Co.H
Robertson, F.M. AR 7th Cav. Co.K
Robertson, F.M. GA 22nd Inf. Co.E
Robertson, F.M. MS Cav. Jeff Davis Legion Co.D Sgt.
Robertson, F.M. SC Mil. 1st Regt. (Charleston Res.) Surg.
Robertson, F.M. SC 12th Inf. Co.F
Robertson, F.M. TN 40th Inf. Co.I
Robertson, F.M. TX Conscr.
Robertson, F.M. Gen. & Staff Surg.
Robertson, F.N. AL 37th Inf. Co.A
Robertson, Francis AR 1st Mtd.Rifles Co.A N.C.S. Sgt.Maj.
Robertson, Francis AR 4th Inf. Co.B
Robertson, Francis NC 4th Bn.Jr.Res. Co.A Cpl.
Robertson, Francis GA 10th Inf. 1st Co.K Cpl.
Robertson, Francis H. GA Lt.Arty. Fraser's Btty. Sgt.
Robertson, Francis Lafayette TX 20th Cav. Co.A
Robertson, Francis M. AL 10th Inf. Co.G
Robertson, Francis M. AL 20th Inf. Co.C,G
Robertson, Francis M. AR Cav. 1st Bn. (Stirman's) Co.H
Robertson, Francis M. GA Arty. 9th Bn. Co.D
Robertson, Francis M. KY Cav. 1st Bn. Co.A
Robertson, Francis M. LA 16th Inf. Co.B
Robertson, Francis M. MO 3rd Cav. Co.A
Robertson, Francis M. TN 54th Inf. Hollis' Co.
Robertson, Francis M. TX 27th Cav. Co.B
Robertson, Francis Marion TN 40th Inf. Co.A
Robertson, Francis W. MS 1st Bn.S.S. Co.C Sgt.
Robertson, Frank MO Inf. Clark's Regt. Co.E
Robertson, Frank NC 21st Inf. Co.K
Robertson, Frank TX 4th Inf. Co.C

Robertson, Frank C. AL 17th Inf. Co.E
Robertson, Frank D. VA 108th Mil. Co.B
Robertson, Frank G. TX 2nd Cav. Co.B 2nd Lt.
Robertson, Franklin S. MO Inf. 8th Bn. Co.C
 Capt.
Robertson, Franklin S. Gen. & Staff Capt.,AIG
Robertson, Frank M. SC Inf. Hampton Legion
 Co.B
Robertson, Frank S. VA 48th Inf. Co.I 1st Lt.
Robertson, Fred E. KY 4th Mtd.Inf. Co.C Sgt.
Robertson, Frederick A. GA Lt.Arty. Scogin's
 Btty. (Griffin Lt.Arty.)
Robertson, Frederick D. LA 1st Cav. Co.A
Robertson, Frederick M. GA 13th Inf. Co.E
Robertson, F.S. AR Cav. 15th Bn. (Buster's Bn.)
 A.Adj.
Robertson, F.S. KY 1st (Butler's) Cav. Co.B
Robertson, F.S. MS 29th Inf. Co.F
Robertson, F.W. AR 45th Mil. Co.B 1st Lt.
Robertson, F.W. TN Inf. 154th Sr.Regt. Co.L
 1st Sgt.
Robertson, G. LA 1st Cav. Co.E, Robinson's
 Co.
Robertson, G. TN 12th (Green's) Cav. Co.F
Robertson, G. VA 43rd Mil. Shaon's Co.
Robertson, G.A. MS 7th Inf. Co.G Capt.
Robertson, Gabriel LA 28th (Thomas') Inf. Co.I
Robertson, G.A.C. MS 15th Inf. Co.C
Robertson, G.B. GA 54th Inf. Co.C
Robertson, G.B. NC 16th Inf. Co.D Cpl.
Robertson, G.C. AL 35th Inf. Co.G
Robertson, G.C. GA 15th Inf. Co.H
Robertson, G.D. KY 3rd Mtd.Inf. Co.H
Robertson, General T. TN 2nd Cav. Co.B
Robertson, George AL 4th Cav. Co.D
Robertson, George AL 17th Inf. Co.E
Robertson, George AL Randolph Cty.Res. J.
 Orr's Co.
Robertson, George GA Inf. 1st Loc.Troops
 (Augusta) Co.B
Robertson, George KY 9th Mtd.Inf. Co.H
Robertson, George LA Cav. Lott's Co. (Carroll
 Drag.)
Robertson, George LA Mil. 4th Regt. 1st Brig.
 1st Div. Co.H
Robertson, George MD Arty. 2nd Btty.
Robertson, George MS Inf. 2nd Bn. Co.H
Robertson, George MS 17th Inf. Co.B
Robertson, George MS 48th Inf. Co.H
Robertson, George NC 21st Inf. Co.K
Robertson, George SC 4th St.Troops Co.H
Robertson, George SC 6th Res. Co.I
Robertson, George SC 9th Res. Co.B
Robertson, George TN 4th Inf. Co.D
Robertson, George TX 25th Cav. Co.E Sgt.
Robertson, George TX Granbury's Cons.Brig.
 Co.K Sgt.
Robertson, George VA Lt.Arty. 38th Bn. Co.A
Robertson, George VA 3rd Res. Co.G
Robertson, George 20th Conf.Cav. Co.D
Robertson, George, Jr. Gen. & Staff Maj.,CS
Robertson, George A. MS 31st Inf. Co.E
Robertson, George A. VA Cav. Mosby's Regt.
 (Part.Rangers) Co.B
Robertson, George B. AL 19th Inf. Co.I
Robertson, George C. TN 14th Inf. Co.E
Robertson, George C. VA 9th Inf. 1st Co.H

Robertson, George C. VA 10th Inf. Co.K
Robertson, George C. VA Inf. 28th Bn. Co.C
Robertson, George C. VA 59th Inf. 2nd Co.H
Robertson, George E. VA 10th Cav. 2nd Co.E
 Cpl.
Robertson, George E. VA Horse Arty. E.
 Graham's Co.
Robertson, George E. VA 17th Inf. Co.G
Robertson, Geo. F. AL 19th Inf. Co.A
Robertson, George G. GA 6th Inf. Co.K
Robertson, George G. LA 9th Inf. Co.D
Robertson, George H. LA 1st Cav. Co.D
Robertson, George H. LA 2nd Inf. Co.B
Robertson, George H. MS 38th Cav. Co.H 1st
 Lt.
Robertson, George H. MS 1st (Percy's) Inf.
 Co.D Capt.
Robertson, George J. VA 38th Inf. Co.D
Robertson, George L. GA Cobb's Legion Co.C
Robertson, George L. TX Cav. Giddings' Bn.
 Carrington's Co.
Robertson, George L. TX 4th Inf. Co.B
Robertson, George M. AL 3rd Cav. Co.H
Robertson, George H. GA 54th Inf. Co.F Sgt.
Robertson, George R. MS 33rd Inf. Co.C
Robertson, George S. VA 23rd Inf. Co.C
Robertson, George S. VA 39th Inf. Co.A
Robertson, George W. AL 32nd Inf. Co.C Lt.
Robertson, Geo. W. AR Lt.Arty. 5th Btty.
Robertson, George W. AR 25th Inf. Co.D
Robertson, George W. GA 2nd Cav. (St.Guards)
 Co.H Sgt.
Robertson, George W. GA Lt.Arty. Scogin's
 Btty. (Griffin Lt.Arty.)
Robertson, George W. GA 41st Inf. Co.F
Robertson, George W. KY 9th Mtd.Inf. Co.H
Robertson, George W. LA 12th Inf. Co.F
Robertson, George W. MS 7th Inf. Co.F
Robertson, George W. MS 27th Inf. Co.F
Robertson, George W. MS 43rd Inf. Co.K
Robertson, George W. SC Inf. Hampton Legion
 Co.B
Robertson, George W. TN 13th Inf. Co.K
Robertson, George W. VA 19th Cav. Co.G 2nd
 Lt.
Robertson, George W. VA Horse Arty.
 McClanahan's Co.
Robertson, George W. VA Inf. 5th Bn. Co.A
Robertson, George W. VA 36th Inf. 3rd Co.I
Robertson, George W. VA 53rd Inf. Co.H
Robertson, George W.G. TX 8th Inf. Co.K
Robertson, George W.T. SC 16th Inf. Co.I
Robertson, G.F. KY 3rd Mtd.Inf. Co.H
Robertson, G.F. MS Cav. 1st Bn. (McNair's)
 St.Troops Co.B
Robertson, G.G. MS 46th Inf. Co.B
Robertson, G.H. MO Lt.Arty. Farris' Btty.
 (Clark Arty.)
Robertson, G.H. TX 3rd Cav. Co.D
Robertson, G.J. SC 3rd Cav. Co.A Saddler
Robertson, G.L. SC 11th Inf. 2nd Co.I
Robertson, G.L. TX Inf. Carter's Co.
Robertson, G.M. AL 4th (Russell's) Cav. Co.C
Robertson, G.M. AL 7th Inf. Co.D
Robertson, G.M. AL 25th Inf. Co.F
Robertson, G.M. NC 62nd Inf. Co.F
Robertson, G.M. VA Inf. 26th Bn. Co.I

Robertson, G.R. MS Lt.Arty. (Brookhaven
 Lt.Arty.) Hoskins' Btty.
Robertson, Granville VA Lt.Arty. Jeffress' Co.
Robertson, Granville W. VA 57th Inf. Co.F
Robertson, Green NC 3rd Cav. (41st St.Troops)
 Co.C
Robertson, Green B. AL Lt.Arty. Hurt's Btty.
Robertson, Green B. GA Lt.Arty. Scogin's Btty.
 (Griffin Lt.Arty.)
Robertson, Green B. TN 18th Inf. Co.G
Robertson, Green C. TN 53rd Inf. Co.A
Robertson, G.S. VA 23rd Inf. Co.C
Robertson, G.S. VA Conscr. Cp.Lee Co.B
Robertson, G.W. AL 2nd Cav. Co.D,C
Robertson, G.W. AL Cp. of Instr. Talladega
Robertson, G.W. AR 6th Inf. Co.D
Robertson, G.W. MO 1st & 4th Cons.Inf. Co.I
Robertson, G.W. MO 4th Inf. Co.I
Robertson, G.W. TN 15th (Cons.) Cav. Co.A
Robertson, G.W. TN 19th & 20th (Cons.) Cav.
 Co.F
Robertson, G.W. TN 20th (Russell's) Cav. Co.A
Robertson, G.W. TN 5th Inf. 2nd Co.D
Robertson, G.W. TX 11th Inf.
Robertson, G.W. VA 31st Inf. Co.D Cpl.
Robertson, G.W. 1st Conf.Eng.Troops Co.K
 Capt.
Robertson, G. Wilmer 1st Conf.Eng.Troops
 Co.G,K Sgt.
Robertson, H. AR Lt.Arty. Hart's Btty.
Robertson, H. FL 1st Cav. Co.A
Robertson, H. GA 40th Inf. Co.I
Robertson, H. LA 2nd Inf. Co.E
Robertson, H. LA 28th (Gray's) Inf. Co.H
Robertson, H. MO 6th Cav. Co.D
Robertson, H. NC 1st Arty. (10th St.Troops)
 Co.A
Robertson, H. SC 14th Inf. Co.E
Robertson, H. TN 13th Inf. Co.H
Robertson, H. TN 43rd Inf. Co.H
Robertson, H. TX Cav. 1st Regt.St.Troops Co.F
Robertson, H. TX Cav. Bourland's Regt. Co.K
Robertson, H. VA 54th Inf. Co.G
Robertson, H.A. AL 41st Inf. Co.F
Robertson, H.A. SC Inf.Bn. Co.D
Robertson, H.A. 15th Conf.Cav. Co.H
Robertson, H. Alexander SC 19th Inf. Co.C
Robertson, Han TX Cav. Giddings' Bn. Co.A
Robertson, Harison J. MO Inf. 3rd Bn. Co.A
Robertson, Harrison NC 1st Arty. (10th
 St.Troops) Co.K
Robertson, Harrison TX 22nd Cav. Co.A
Robertson, Harrison Gen. & Staff Capt.,QM
Robertson, Harrison J. MO 6th Inf. Co.E
Robertson, Hays H. TX Cav. Morgan's Regt.
 Co.E
Robertson, H.B. AL 6th Cav. Co.A
Robertson, H.C. AL Pris.Guard Freeman's Co.
Robertson, H.C. NC 8th Inf. Co.F
Robertson, H.C. SC 7th Cav. Co.B
Robertson, H.C. SC Lt.Arty. 3rd (Palmetto) Bn.
 Culpeper's Co.
Robertson, H.C. TN 13th (Gore's) Cav. Co.I
Robertson, H.C. Conf.Cav. Wood's Regt. 2nd
 Co.M
Robertson, H.E. VA 49th Inf. Co.H
Robertson, Henry AL 43rd Inf. Co.G

Robertson, Henry AL Pris.Guard Freeman's Co.
Robertson, Henry AR 14th (Powers') Inf. Co.B Sgt.
Robertson, Henry AR 20th Inf. Co.H
Robertson, Henry LA 9th Inf. Co.B
Robertson, Henry NC 2nd Inf. Co.E
Robertson, Henry SC 5th St.Troops Co.G
Robertson, Henry SC 7th Res. Co.C
Robertson, Henry SC 15th Inf. Co.K
Robertson, Henry TN 4th (McLemore's) Cav. Co.F
Robertson, Henry TN 19th (Biffle's) Cav. Co.B
Robertson, Henry TN 19th & 20th (Cons.) Cav. Co.F
Robertson, Henry TX 22nd Cav. Co.A
Robertson, Henry TX Cav. Giddings' Bn. Co.A
Robertson, Henry VA 3rd Cav. Co.A
Robertson, Henry A. TX 3rd Inf. Co.D
Robertson, Henry A. VA Lt.Arty. Jeffress' Co.
Robertson, Henry B. VA Arty. Dance's Co.
Robertson, Henry C. MS 18th Inf. Co.I,E
Robertson, Henry C. SC 1st Arty. Co.F
Robertson, Henry C. TN 1st (Turney's) Inf. Co.C Cpl.
Robertson, Henry F. NC 28th Inf. Co.G
Robertson, Henry G. MD Inf. 2nd Bn. Co.B
Robertson, Henry H. FL 6th Inf. Co.D
Robertson, Henry H. NC 28th Inf. Co.G
Robertson, Henry H. VA 27th Inf. Co.B Capt.
Robertson, Henry H. VA 38th Inf. Co.K
Robertson, Henry J. NC 1st Arty. (10th St.Troops) Co.A Sgt.
Robertson, Henry J. NC 17th Inf. (1st Org.) Co.H
Robertson, Henry J. NC 17th Inf. (2nd Org.) Co.G 2nd Lt.
Robertson, Henry J. VA 6th Inf. Co.A
Robertson, Henry M. TN 49th Inf. Co.I 1st Lt.
Robertson, Henry W. AL 13th Inf. Co.I
Robertson, Henry W. MS Cav. 24th Bn. Co.E
Robertson, Henry W. VA 18th Inf. Co.C
Robertson, Herbert GA Lt.Arty. Fraser's Btty. Sgt.
Robertson, Hewston SC 1st Arty. Co.E
Robertson, H.F. AR 6th Inf. Co.G
Robertson, H.G. AL 31st Inf. Co.E 1st Sgt.
Robertson, H.G. AR 20th Inf. Co.G Lt.Col.
Robertson, H.G. TN 29th Inf. Co.F
Robertson, H.G. TX 24th Cav. Co.F
Robertson, H.G. Gen. & Staff AQM
Robertson, H.H. AL Cav. Murphy's Bn. Co.C
Robertson, H.H. LA 22nd Inf. Wash. Marks' Co.
Robertson, H.H. MS 4th Inf. Co.G
Robertson, H.H. SC 6th Cav. Co.E
Robertson, H.H. TN 11th Inf. Co.B
Robertson, H.H. TN 11th Inf. Co.D
Robertson, H.H. TX 32nd Cav. Co.F
Robertson, H.H. TX 35th (Brown's) Cav. Co.E
Robertson, Hickman AL 55th Vol. Co.D
Robertson, Hickman 2nd Conf.Inf. Co.B
Robertson, Higdon SC 19th Inf. Co.C
Robertson, Higdon TN 1st Zouaves Co.H Capt.
Robertson, Hilliard W. GA 3rd Inf. Co.D
Robertson, H.J. AL 5th Inf. New Co.I
Robertson, H.J. GA 24th Inf. Co.F
Robertson, H.J. TN 1st (Carter's) Cav. Co.C

Robertson, H.J. VA 3rd Res. Co.D
Robertson, H.L. LA 2nd Inf. Co.B
Robertson, H.L. MS 7th Inf. Co.G
Robertson, H.L. TN 15th Inf. Co.D
Robertson, H.L. VA Inf. 2nd Bn.Loc.Def. Co.C
Robertson, H.O. TN 5th Inf. Co.I Sgt.
Robertson, Holcom TN 21st & 22nd (Cons.) Cav. Co.H
Robertson, Horace MO 6th Inf. Co.F
Robertson, Hosea SC 2nd Cav. Co.K
Robertson, Howard G. AR 3rd Cav. Co.B 2nd Lt.
Robertson, H.R. TX 20th Inf. Co.F
Robertson, Hubert AL 8th Inf. Co.H
Robertson, Hugh AL 1st Cav.
Robertson, Hugh AL 51st (Part.Rangers) Co.G
Robertson, Hugh B. MO St.Guards 1st Lt.
Robertson, Hugh L. VA Inf. 25th Bn. Co.B
Robertson, H.W. AL 12th Inf. Co.A Sgt.Maj.
Robertson, I. MS Post Guard at Enterprise
Robertson, I.B. MO Cav. Williams' Regt. Co.G
Robertson, I.H. NC McLean's Bn.Lt.Duty Men Co.A
Robertson, I.K. GA Phillips' Legion Co.M
Robertson, I.N. NC 2nd Inf. Co.C
Robertson, I.P. GA Phillips' Legion Co.M
Robertson, I.R. TX Cav. Co.B
Robertson, Ira G. AR Inf. 4th Bn. Co.D 1st Lt.
Robertson, Ira G. AR 18th (Marmaduke's) Inf. Co.K Capt.
Robertson, Ira G. TX 7th Inf. Co.K Sgt.
Robertson, Irvin AR 14th (Powers') Inf. Co.K 2nd Lt.
Robertson, I.S. GA 6th Res.
Robertson, Isaac AL Cp. of Instr. Talladega
Robertson, Isaac GA Cobb's Legion Co.K
Robertson, Isaac NC 16th Inf. Co.H
Robertson, Isaac TX 15th Cav. Co.B
Robertson, Isaac VA Horse Arty. D. Shanks' Co.
Robertson, Isaac A. AL 32nd Inf. Co.B 1st Sgt.
Robertson, Isaac D. MS Cav. 24th Bn. Co.A
Robertson, Isaac E. GA 44th Inf. Co.B
Robertson, Isaac W. TN 25th Inf. Co.A Sgt.
Robertson, Isham AL Cp. of Instr. Talladega
Robertson, Israel TN 49th Inf. Co.E
Robertson, I.T. AL 2nd Cav. Co.D
Robertson, J. AL 11th Inf. Co.E
Robertson, J. AR 58th Mil. Co.B
Robertson, J. LA Mil. British Guard Bn. Burrowes' Co.
Robertson, J. LA Hunt's Bn. Sgt.
Robertson, J. MS 5th Inf. (St.Troops) Co.F
Robertson, J. MS 35th Inf. Co.I
Robertson, J. MS T.P. Montgomery's Co.
Robertson, J. MO Cav. Ford's Bn. Co.F
Robertson, J. SC 1st (McCreary's) Inf. Campbell's Co.
Robertson, J. SC 2nd Bn.S.S. Co.C
Robertson, J. SC 11th Inf. Co.E
Robertson, J. TX 17th Cons.Dismtd.Cav. Co.E
Robertson, J. TX 35th (Brown's) Cav.
Robertson, J.A. AL 1st Cav. Co.G
Robertson, J.A. AL 12th Inf. Co.G
Robertson, J.A. GA 63rd Inf. Co.C Cpl.
Robertson, J.A. MS Cav. Ham's Regt. Co.B
Robertson, J.A. NC 2nd Inf. Co.G
Robertson, J.A. SC 12th Inf. Co.C

Robertson, J.A. TN Cav. 1st Bn. (McNairy's) Co.D
Robertson, J.A. TN 27th Inf. Co.B
Robertson, J.A. TN Inf. 154th Sr.Regt. Co.E,F
Robertson, J.A. TX 7th Cav. Co.I
Robertson, J.A. VA 2nd Cav. Surg.
Robertson, J.A. VA 3rd Inf.Loc.Def. Co.F
Robertson, J.A. Mead's Conf.Cav. Co.C Cpl.
Robertson, J.A. Gen. & Staff 1st Lt.,Adj.
Robertson, Jabez FL Lt.Arty. Perry's Co.
Robertson, Jacob TN 46th Inf. Co.C
Robertson, Jacob H.R. VA Cav. 35th Bn. Co.A
Robertson, J.A.G. GA Lt.Arty. Ritter's Co.
Robertson, Jairus G. AR 1st (Colquitt's) Inf. Co.B 2nd Lt.
Robertson, James AL St.Arty. Co.A
Robertson, James AL St.Arty. Co.C
Robertson, James AL 7th Inf. Co.D,I
Robertson, James AL 9th Inf. Co.I
Robertson, James AL 43rd Inf. Co.K
Robertson, James AR 16th Inf. Co.D
Robertson, James AR 35th Inf. Co.E
Robertson, James GA 1st (Olmstead's) Inf. Screven's Co.
Robertson, James GA Inf. 18th Bn. Co.A,C
Robertson, James GA 27th Inf. Co.B
Robertson, James LA 7th Inf. Co.B
Robertson, James LA 9th Inf. Co.D
Robertson, James LA 14th (Austin's) Bn.S.S. Co.A
Robertson, James LA Mil. Lewis Guards
Robertson, James MS 12th Cav. Co.F
Robertson, James MS 5th Inf. Co.F
Robertson, James MS 18th Inf. Co.I
Robertson, James MS 20th Inf. Co.D
Robertson, James MS 37th Inf. Co.D
Robertson, James MS Shields' Co.
Robertson, James MO Cav. Coffee's Regt. Co.C
Robertson, James MO Cav. Wood's Regt. Co.A
Robertson, James MO 3rd Inf. Co.B
Robertson, James MO Inf. 8th Bn. Co.F
Robertson, James MO 9th Inf. Co.K
Robertson, James NC 45th Inf. Co.D Cpl.
Robertson, James SC 19th Inf. Co.C
Robertson, James TN 1st (Carter's) Cav. Co.E
Robertson, James TN 20th Inf. Co.E
Robertson, James TN 35th Inf. 2nd Co.A
Robertson, James TN 49th Inf. Co.C
Robertson, James TN 53rd Inf. Co.A
Robertson, James Inf. Bailey's Cons.Regt. Co.F
Robertson, James TX 29th Cav. Co.A
Robertson, James TX 29th Cav. Co.I
Robertson, James TX 34th Cav. Co.C
Robertson, Jas. VA 4th Cav. Co.E Sgt.
Robertson, James VA Lt.Arty. Woolfolk's Co.
Robertson, James VA 2nd Inf.Loc.Def. Co.C
Robertson, James VA Inf. 2nd Bn.Loc.Def. Co.E
Robertson, James VA 38th Inf. Co.E
Robertson, James VA 46th Inf. Co.B
Robertson, James VA 48th Inf. Co.K
Robertson, James VA 58th Inf. Co.B
Robertson, James VA 72nd Mil.
Robertson, James VA 86th Mil. Co.F
Robertson, James Conf.Inf. 1st Bn. 2nd Co.E
Robertson, James 1st Choctaw Mtd.Rifles Co.G
Robertson, James A. GA 35th Inf. Co.A

Robertson, James A. MS 2nd Part.Rangers Co.K
  Cpl.
Robertson, James A. NC 6th Inf. Co.H
Robertson, James A. TX 6th Inf. Co.E Cpl.
Robertson, James A. VA Hvy.Arty. 19th Bn.
  Co.A
Robertson, James A. VA Lt.Arty. Hardwicke's
  Co.
Robertson, James A. VA Hvy.Arty. Kyle's Co.
Robertson, James A. VA 18th Inf. Co.C
Robertson, James A. VA Inf. 25th Bn. Co.A
Robertson, James A. VA 34th Inf. Co.F
Robertson, James A. VA 37th Inf. Co.B
Robertson, James B. AR 3rd Inf. Co.C
Robertson, James B. GA 1st Reg. Co.H
Robertson, James B. MO Cav. Slayback's Regt.
Robertson, James B. NC 24th Inf. Co.C 2nd Lt.
Robertson, James B. SC 15th Inf. Co.K
Robertson, James B. VA 12th Inf. Branch's Co.
Robertson, James B. VA 16th Inf. Co.K
Robertson, James C. AL Cav. Moses' Squad.
  Co.A
Robertson, James C. GA 22nd Inf. Co.E
Robertson, James C. MS 1st Lt.Arty. Co.A
Robertson, James C. VA 3rd Res. Co.K
Robertson, James C. VA 14th Inf. Co.I
Robertson, James C. VA 19th Inf. Co.K
Robertson, James C. VA 97th Mil. Co.F
Robertson, James E. TX 9th Cav. Surg.
Robertson, James E. VA Hvy.Arty. 20th Bn.
  Co.A Maj.
Robertson, James E. VA 44th Inf. Co.A Capt.
Robertson, James E. VA 46th Inf. 2nd Co.A
Robertson, James Edw. Gen. & Staff Surg.
Robertson, James F. AR 14th (Powers') Inf.
  Co.E
Robertson, James F. TX 15th Cav. Co.D
Robertson, James F. VA Cav. 41st Bn. Co.G
Robertson, James G. AL Mil. 2nd Regt.Vol.
  Co.D
Robertson, James H. KY 8th Mtd.Inf. Co.F Cpl.
Robertson, James H. SC 2nd Cav. Co.I
Robertson, James H. SC Cav.Bn. Hampton
  Legion Co.A
Robertson, James H. VA 157th Mil. Co.B
Robertson, James J. GA 51st Inf. Co.K Cpl.
Robertson, James K. MS 2nd Inf. (A. of 10,000)
  Co.A
Robertson, James L. AL Lt.Arty. 2nd Bn. Co.D
Robertson, James L. GA Lt.Arty. Scogin's Btty.
  (Griffin Lt.Arty.)
Robertson, James L. NC 16th Inf. Co.D
Robertson, James L. SC Lt.Arty. Parker's Co.
  (Marion Arty.) Cpl.
Robertson, James M. AL 25th Inf. Co.C
Robertson, James M. AR 3rd Inf. Co.I
Robertson, James M. GA 9th Inf. (St.Guards)
  Co.B
Robertson, James M. LA 1st Cav. Co.A Cpl.
Robertson, James M. MS 2nd Inf. Co.B
Robertson, James M. MO 9th Bn.S.S. Co.D
Robertson, James M. NC 3rd Cav. (41st
  St.Troops) Co.C
Robertson, James M. NC 14th Inf. Co.E
Robertson, James M. TN 8th Inf. Co.K
Robertson, James M. TN 14th Inf. Co.E
Robertson, James M. TN 39th Mtd.Inf. Co.C,A

Robertson, James M. TX 18th Inf. Co.I 1st Sgt.
Robertson, James M. VA Arty. Dance's Co.
Robertson, James M. VA 20th Inf. Co.D
Robertson, James M. VA 21st Inf. Co.E
Robertson, James M. VA 27th Inf. Co.G
Robertson, James M. VA 45th Inf. Co.G
Robertson, James O. MS 19th Inf. Co.G
Robertson, James P. AL 16th Inf.
Robertson, James P. KY 2nd Mtd.Inf. Co.E
Robertson, James Q. SC 6th Cav. Co.E
Robertson, James R. MO 9th (Elliott's) Cav.
  Co.D Sgt.
Robertson, James R. NC 37th Inf. Co.H
Robertson, James R. VA 6th Bn.Res. Co.I 2nd
  Lt.
Robertson, James R. VA 16th Inf. Co.F
Robertson, James R. VA 51st Inf. Co.D
Robertson, James R. VA 58th Inf. Co.E Sgt.
Robertson, James R. VA 97th Mil. Co.L
Robertson, James S. MS 30th Inf. Co.A
Robertson, James S. SC 23rd Inf. Co.F
Robertson, James S. TX Cav. Baylor's Regt.
  Co.H
Robertson, James S. VA Hvy.Arty. Allen's Co.
Robertson, James Townes SC 1st (Orr's) Rifles
  Co.B Lt.Col.
Robertson, James W. AL 17th Inf. Co.E
Robertson, James W. AL 37th Inf. Co.B Sgt.
Robertson, James W. GA 8th Inf. Co.E
Robertson, James W. GA 12th Inf. Co.D Cpl.
Robertson, James W. MO Searcy's Bn.S.S. Co.F
Robertson, James W. NC 7th Inf. Co.A
Robertson, James W. SC 19th Inf. Co.C
Robertson, James W. TN 5th Inf. 2nd Co.G
Robertson, Jas. W. Gen. & Staff Capt.
Robertson, James W.A. MS 24th Inf. Co.B
Robertson, Jason G. TX 16th Cav. Co.C Sgt.
Robertson, Jasper AR 9th Inf. Co.C 1st Sgt.
Robertson, J.B. FL 1st (Res.) Inf. Co.B
Robertson, J.B. GA 2nd Cav. (St.Guards) Co.H
Robertson, J.B. MS Cav. Hughes' Bn. Co.B
Robertson, J.B. MS 39th Inf. Co.C
Robertson, J.B. MS Mil. Hinds Cty. Col.
Robertson, J.B. SC 6th Inf. 1st Co.D
Robertson, J.B. SC 7th Inf. Co.A Sgt.
Robertson, J.B. SC Inf. 7th Bn. (Enfield Rifles)
  Co.H Cpl.
Robertson, J.B. TN 3rd (Forrest's) Cav. Co.E
Robertson, J.B. TN 10th (DeMoss') Cav. Co.H
Robertson, J.B. TN 12th (Green's) Cav. Co.H
Robertson, J.B. TN 14th (Neely's) Cav. Co.H
Robertson, J.B. TN 12th Inf. Co.I
Robertson, J.B. TN 31st Inf. Co.E Capt.
Robertson, J.B. TX 5th Inf. Co.I Col.
Robertson, J. Butler MS 1st Lt.Arty. Co.A
Robertson, J.C. AL 31st Inf. Co.G
Robertson, J.C. AR Inf. 8th Bn. Co.C 2nd Lt.
Robertson, J.C. MS 31st Inf. Co.H 1st Lt.
Robertson, J.C. MS 41st Inf. Co.L
Robertson, J.C. TN 45th Inf. Co.E
Robertson, J.C. TX 32nd Cav. Co.F
Robertson, J.C. TX 37th Cav. Co.I
Robertson, J.C. VA 4th Cav. Co.K
Robertson, J.D. AR 45th Cav. Co.I
Robertson, J.D. GA 3rd Cav. Co.D
Robertson, J.D. MS 2nd (Quinn's St.Troops) Inf.
  Co.G

Robertson, J.D. MS 23rd Inf. Co.H
Robertson, J.D. Gen. & Staff AASurg.
Robertson, J.E. AL 38th Inf. Co.A
Robertson, J.E. SC 6th Inf. 1st Co.D
Robertson, J.E. SC 22nd Inf. Co.C
Robertson, J.E. VA 21st Inf. Co.I
Robertson, J.E.F. MO 5th Cav. Co.H
Robertson, Jefferson KY 5th Mtd.Inf. Co.E
Robertson, Jefferson H. NC 12th Inf. Co.F
Robertson, Jeffrey MS 2nd (Quinn's St.Troops)
  Inf. Co.D
Robertson, Jeremiah TX 18th Inf. Co.I
Robertson, Jesse MS 35th Inf. Co.F
Robertson, Jesse NC 1st Jr.Res. Co.A Sgt.
Robertson, Jesse VA Horse Arty. D. Shanks' Co.
Robertson, Jesse VA 1st Bn.Res. Co.D
Robertson, Jesse VA 10th Bn.Res. Co.D
Robertson, Jesse VA 31st Inf. Co.B
Robertson, Jesse VA 44th Inf. Co.F Sgt.
Robertson, Jesse 8th (Wade's) Conf.Cav. Co.C
Robertson, Jesse B. GA 29th Inf. Co.B
Robertson, Jessee H. LA 28th (Gray's) Inf. Co.H
Robertson, Jesse J. AL 3rd Res. Co.I
Robertson, Jesse J. VA Lt.Arty. Montgomery's
  Co.
Robertson, Jesse P. VA Hvy.Arty. 20th Bn.
  Co.D
Robertson, Jesse R. TX 22nd Inf. Co.H
Robertson, Jessie J. AL 11th Inf. Co.F
Robertson, Jethro. H. NC 24th Inf. Co.F
Robertson, J.F. AR Mil. Desha Cty.Bn.
Robertson, J.F. GA 39th Inf. Co.K
Robertson, J.F. LA 3rd (Wingfield's) Cav. Co.D
Robertson, J.F. NC 3rd Jr.Res. Co.A Cpl.
Robertson, J.F. SC 26th Inf. Co.F Cpl.
Robertson, J.F. TX 9th (Nichols') Inf. Co.E
Robertson, J.F. TX 16th Inf. Co.K
Robertson, J.F. Gen. & Staff Surg.
Robertson, J.G. AL 1st Regt. Mobile Vol. Butt's
  Co. Sgt.
Robertson, J.G. AL 4th Res. Co.A Sgt.
Robertson, J.G. AR 1st Vol. Co.I
Robertson, J.G. AR 38th Inf. Co.K 2nd Lt.
Robertson, J.G. SC Cav. 14th Bn. Co.B
Robertson, J.G. VA Goochland Lt.Arty.
Robertson, J.H. AL 3rd Res. Co.G
Robertson, J.H. AR 30th Inf. Co.H
Robertson, J.H. AR 58th Mil. Co.E
Robertson, J.H. KY 10th (Johnson's) Cav. Co.K
Robertson, J.H. LA 3rd Inf. Co.K
Robertson, J.H. LA Inf. 7th Bn. Co.C
Robertson, J.H. LA 15th Inf. Co.K
Robertson, J.H. MS 28th Cav. Co.D
Robertson, J.H. MS 35th Inf. Co.I
Robertson, J.H. MS 41st Inf. Co.D
Robertson, J.H. MO 5th Cav. Co.H
Robertson, J.H. NC 33rd Inf. Co.F
Robertson, J.H. NC McLean's Bn.Lt.Duty Men
  Co.A
Robertson, J.H., Dr. TN 20th (Russell's) Cav.
  Co.A
Robertson, J.H. TX 3rd Cav. Co.B
Robertson, J.H. VA 2nd Cav. Co.G
Robertson, J.J. GA 13th Inf. Co.G,B
Robertson, J.J. GA Cherokee Legion (St.Guards)
  Co.K
Robertson, J.J. MS 4th Cav. Co.H Sgt.

Robertson, J.J. MS 38th Cav. Co.H
Robertson, J.J. MS 9th Inf. Co.A
Robertson, J.J. MS Conscr.
Robertson, J.J. TN 9th Inf. Co.H
Robertson, J.J. VA Lt.Arty. 38th Bn. Co.B
Robertson, J.J. VA Lt.Arty. Wimbish's Co.
Robertson, J.J. VA 43rd Mil. Shaon's Co.
Robertson, J.K. AR 30th Inf. Co.B
Robertson, J.K. MO 9th (Elliott's) Cav. Co.D
Robertson, J.K. MO Cav. Poindexter's Regt.
Robertson, J.K. SC 7th Res. Co.D 2nd Lt.
Robertson, J.K.P. TN 23rd Inf. Co.D
Robertson, J.L. AL 6th Cav. Co.H 1st Sgt.
Robertson, J.L. AL Inf. 2nd Regt. Co.C
Robertson, J.L. AL 23rd Inf. Co.H
Robertson, J.L. AL 42nd Inf. Co.A
Robertson, J.L. AR Inf. Cocke's Regt. Co.E
Robertson, J.L. MS 3rd (St.Troops) Cav. Co.E
Robertson, J.L. MS 34th Inf. Co.A
Robertson, J.L. MS 41st Inf. Co.L 1st Lt.
Robertson, J.L. SC 1st Arty. 2nd Lt.
Robertson, J.L. SC Mil.Arty. 1st Regt. Parker's Co.
Robertson, J.L. TN 4th Inf. Co.B
Robertson, J.L. VA 11th Bn.Res. Co.F
Robertson, J.M. AL 1st Cav. 2nd Co.B
Robertson, J.M. AL 12th Cav. Co.G
Robertson, J.M. AL 3rd Res. Co.K
Robertson, J.M. AL 31st Inf. Co.G
Robertson, J.M. AL 40th Inf. Co.D
Robertson, J.M. AL 62nd Inf. Co.F
Robertson, J.M. FL Cav. 5th Bn. Co.H
Robertson, J.M. GA 36th (Villepigue's) Inf. Co.F
Robertson, J.M. MS 1st Cav.
Robertson, J.M. MS 7th Cav. Co.E
Robertson, J.M. NC 1st Cav. (9th St.Troops) Co.E
Robertson, J.M. NC 2nd Inf. Co.E
Robertson, J.M. TN 10th (DeMoss') Cav. Co.E
Robertson, J.M. TN 20th Inf. Co.E
Robertson, J.M. TN 47th Inf. Co.F
Robertson, J.M. TN 50th Inf. Co.K Cpl.
Robertson, J.M. TX 7th Cav. Co.I
Robertson, J.M. TX 30th Cav. Co.H
Robertson, J.M. TX Cav. Hardeman's Regt. Co.E
Robertson, J.M. TX 15th Inf. 2nd Co.F
Robertson, J.M. VA 20th Cav. Co.C
Robertson, J.M. VA 10th Bn.Res. Co.D
Robertson, J.N. AR 5th Inf. Co.H
Robertson, J.N. AR 58th Mil. Co.D
Robertson, J.N. TN 1st Hvy.Arty. Co.L
Robertson, J.N. TN 35th Inf. Co.G
Robertson, J.N. TN 63rd Inf. Co.K Sgt.
Robertson, J.N. TX 9th Cav. Co.G
Robertson, Joab VA 57th Inf. Co.I
Robertson, Joe GA Inf. 27th Bn. Co.E Cpl.
Robertson, Joel GA 4th Bn.
Robertson, Joel T. VA 57th Inf. Co.D Cpl.
Robertson, John AL 8th Cav. Co.B
Robertson, John AL 4th Res. Co.G
Robertson, John AL 16th Inf. Co.H
Robertson, John AL 38th Inf. Co.K
Robertson, John AL 45th Inf. Co.B
Robertson, John AR Cav. Poe's Bn. Co.A
Robertson, John GA 40th Inf. Co.K

Robertson, John FL 5th Inf. Co.H
Robertson, John GA 1st Cav. Co.B
Robertson, John GA 2nd Cav. (St.Guards) Co.A
Robertson, John GA 2nd Bn.S.S. Co.D
Robertson, John GA Cherokee Legion (St.Guards) Co.C
Robertson, John LA 3rd (Harrison's) Cav. Co.H
Robertson, John LA 10th Inf. Co.H
Robertson, John LA Res.Corps Scott's Co.
Robertson, John MS 1st Cav. Co.C
Robertson, John MS 1st Cav. Co.I
Robertson, John MS 7th Cav. Co.E
Robertson, John MS Cav. Hughes' Bn. Co.B Cpl.
Robertson, John MS Inf. 3rd Bn. Co.I
Robertson, John MS 7th Inf. Co.K
Robertson, John MS 8th Inf. Co.F
Robertson, John MS 13th Inf. Co.B
Robertson, John MO Cav. Schnabel's Bn. Co.B 1st Lt.
Robertson, John MO Cav. Slayback's Regt. Co.F
Robertson, John MO Lt.Arty. 1st Field Btty.
Robertson, John, Jr. MO Robertson's Regt. St.Guard Co.1
Robertson, John MO 3rd Inf. Co.H
Robertson, John NC 2nd Cav. (19th St.Troops) Co.F
Robertson, John NC 2nd Inf.
Robertson, John NC 13th Inf. Co.A
Robertson, John NC 21st Inf. Co.K
Robertson, John NC 45th Inf. Co.F
Robertson, John NC 53rd Inf. Co.E
Robertson, John NC 55th Inf. Co.B Sgt.
Robertson, John SC 1st (Butler's) Inf. Co.A
Robertson, John SC Inf. 3rd Bn. Co.C
Robertson, John SC 4th St.Troops Co.D
Robertson, John SC 17th Inf. Co.D
Robertson, John SC 23rd Inf. Co.A,B Cpl.
Robertson, John SC Res. Co.B
Robertson, John TN 1st (Carter's) Cav. Co.E Capt.
Robertson, John TN 14th (Neely's) Cav. Co.I
Robertson, John TN Cav. Napier's Bn. Co.B
Robertson, John TN 7th Inf. Co.D
Robertson, John TN 20th Inf. Co.E
Robertson, John TN 39th Mtd.Inf. Co.K
Robertson, John TX 17th Cav. Co.B Cpl.
Robertson, John TX 14th Inf. Co.D
Robertson, John TX 15th Inf. 2nd Co.F
Robertson, John VA Hvy.Arty. Epes' Co.
Robertson, John VA Lt.Arty. Griffin's Co.
Robertson, John VA 4th Res. Co.A
Robertson, John VA 9th Inf. 1st Co.A
Robertson, John VA 9th Inf. Co.F
Robertson, John VA 23rd Inf. Co.K
Robertson, John 1st Choctaw Mtd.Rifles Co.G
Robertson, John A. AL 45th Inf. Co.I 1st Lt.
Robertson, John A. VA Inf. 5th Bn. Co.A
Robertson, John A. VA 21st Inf. Co.E Cpl.
Robertson, John A. VA Inf. 25th Bn. Co.B
Robertson, John A. VA 59th Inf. 2nd Co.B Hosp.Stew.
Robertson, John B. AL Cav. Moses' Squad. Co.A Cpl.
Robertson, John B. FL 5th Inf. Co.D Cpl.
Robertson, John B. Gen. & Staff Capt.,Ord.Ch.
Robertson, John C. AL 18th Inf. Co.E

Robertson, John C. GA Lt.Arty. Hamilton's Co. Sgt.
Robertson, John C. GA Lt.Arty. Milledge's Co. Cpl.
Robertson, John C. GA 1st Reg. Co.A Cpl.
Robertson, John C. NC 3rd Arty. (40th St.Troops) Co.F Capt.
Robertson, John C. TN 5th (McKenzie's) Cav. Co.H
Robertson, John C. TN 39th Mtd.Inf. Co.I
Robertson, John C. TX 17th Cav. Co.C Capt.
Robertson, John C. TX 37th Cav. Lt.Col.
Robertson, John D. AL 17th Inf. Co.E 1st Lt.
Robertson, John D. LA 21st (Patton's) Inf. Co.C 1st Sgt.
Robertson, John D. TN 14th Inf. Co.L
Robertson, John E. AR 8th Inf. New Co.F
Robertson, John E. GA Cobb's Legion Co.C
Robertson, John E. NC 13th Inf. Co.C Sgt.
Robertson, John E. VA 8th Cav. Co.E
Robertson, John E. VA 38th Inf. Co.K
Robertson, John F. MO 8th Cav. Co.A
Robertson, John F. NC 45th Inf. Co.D
Robertson, John F. TN 44th Inf. Co.I
Robertson, John F. TN 44th (Cons.) Inf. Co.A
Robertson, John F. VA 10th Inf. Co.K
Robertson, John F.M. NC 13th Inf. Co.H Cpl.
Robertson, John Franklin TN 2nd (Walker's) Inf. Co.E Sgt.
Robertson, John G. MO Inf. 8th Bn. Co.F
Robertson, John H. AL Cav. 5th Bn. Hilliard's Legion Co.A 1st Sgt.
Robertson, John H. AR 6th Inf. Co.H Cpl.
Robertson, John H. MS 29th Inf. Co.F
Robertson, John H. NC 3rd Cav. (41st St.Troops) Co.K
Robertson, John H. SC Lt.Arty. Kelly's Co. (Chesterfield Arty.)
Robertson, John H. SC 12th Inf. Co.I
Robertson, John H. TN 50th (Cons.) Inf. Sgt.Maj.
Robertson, John H. TX 31st Cav. Co.B
Robertson, John H. VA Arty. J.W. Drewry's Co. Sgt.
Robertson, John H. VA 38th Inf. Co.E
Robertson, John H. VA 46th Inf. 2nd Co.C Cpl.
Robertson, John H.W. VA 56th Inf. Co.E
Robertson, John J. AL 3rd Inf. Co.H,G Sgt.
Robertson, John J. FL 6th Inf. Co.D Sgt.
Robertson, John J. GA 7th Inf. (St.Guards) Co.E
Robertson, John J. GA 11th Inf. Co.E
Robertson, John J. MS Cav. 24th Bn. Co.C,E
Robertson, John J. MS Arty. (Seven Stars Arty.) Roberts' Co.
Robertson, John J. MS Inf. 2nd Bn. Co.C
Robertson, John J. MS 48th Inf. Co.C
Robertson, John J. MO 11th Inf. Co.D Music.
Robertson, John J. TN 34th Inf. 2nd Co.C
Robertson, John J. VA 12th Inf. Co.A
Robertson, John J. VA 46th Inf. 1st Co.G
Robertson, John J. VA 57th Inf. Co.F
Robertson, John J. Gen. & Staff Surg.
Robertson, John Jack TX 3rd Inf. Co.G
Robertson, John J.R. VA 12th Inf. Co.B
Robertson, John L. AL 8th Cav. Co.B 1st Sgt.
Robertson, John L. AL 31st Inf. Co.K

Robertson, John L. GA 1st (Olmstead's) Inf.
  Co.F
Robertson, John L. NC 15th Inf. Co.D
Robertson, John M. AL Cp. of Instr. Talladega
  Co.C
Robertson, John M. MS 11th (Perrin's) Cav.
  Co.A
Robertson, John M. MS 18th Cav. Co.D
Robertson, John M. TN 23rd Inf. Co.B Sgt.
Robertson, John M. TX 1st Bn.S.S. Co.A,E
Robertson, John M. TX 22nd Inf. Co.I
Robertson, John M. VA Lt.Arty. B.Z. Price's
  Co.
Robertson, John Martin TX 20th Cav. Co.E Cpl.
Robertson, John N. AL 8th Cav. Co.F
Robertson, John N. AL 5th Bn.Vol. Co.B
Robertson, John N. AR 8th Inf. Co.F
Robertson, John N. FL Lt.Arty. Perry's Co.
Robertson, John N. VA 47th Mil.
Robertson, John P. VA 2nd Cav. Co.B 2nd Lt.
Robertson, John R. MS 25th Inf. Co.B
Robertson, John R. MS 36th Inf. Co.A
Robertson, John R. SC 1st Arty. Co.D
Robertson, John R. SC 7th Res. Co.D
Robertson, John R. TN Cav. 4th Bn. (Branner's)
  Co.F Sgt.
Robertson, John R. TX 34th Cav. Co.C
Robertson, John R. VA 24th Cav. Co.H Maj.
Robertson, John R. VA Inf. 5th Bn. Co.A
Robertson, John R. VA 57th Inf. Co.E
Robertson, John S. AL 3rd Inf. Co.C
Robertson, John S. AL 17th Inf. Co.I
Robertson, John S. MS 2nd Cav. Co.E
Robertson, John S. MO Cav. 3rd Bn. Co.C
Robertson, John S. MO 9th Bn.S.S. Co.F 1st
  Sgt.
Robertson, John S. VA 19th Cav. Co.E
Robertson, John S. VA Hvy.Arty. 18th Bn. Co.D
Robertson, John S. VA 31st Inf. Co.E
Robertson, John S. VA 34th Inf. Norton's Co.
Robertson, John S. VA 38th Inf. Co.D
Robertson, John S.M. SC 23rd Inf. Co.F
Robertson, John T. MS Bradford's Co. (Conf.
  Guards Arty.)
Robertson, John T. MS 15th Inf. Co.H
Robertson, John T. MS 27th Inf. Co.A
Robertson, John T. NC 1st Inf. Co.I
Robertson, John T. NC 12th Inf. Co.G
Robertson, John T. NC 31st Inf. Co.H
Robertson, John T. TN 36th Inf. Co.A
Robertson, John T. VA 49th Inf. Co.A
Robertson, John T. VA 55th Inf. Co.L
Robertson, John T. VA 57th Inf. Co.D
Robertson, John T. VA 92nd Mil. Co.A
Robertson, John T. VA Conscr.Guard
Robertson, John Thompson VA 12th Inf. Co.E
Robertson, John W. GA 13th Cav. Co.C
Robertson, John W. GA 12th Inf. Co.D
Robertson, John W. GA 14th Inf. Co.K
Robertson, John W. LA 9th Inf. Co.G
Robertson, John W. MS 22nd Inf. Co.G
Robertson, John W. MS 23rd Inf. Co.H
Robertson, John W. NC 1st Cav. (9th St.Troops)
  Co.A
Robertson, John W. SC 11th Res. Co.K 2nd Lt.
Robertson, John W. TN 37th Inf. Co.C
Robertson, John W. TN 43rd Inf. Co.F 1st Lt.

Robertson, John W. TN 63rd Inf. Co.K Capt.
Robertson, John W. VA 1st Cav. Co.C
Robertson, John W. VA Lt.Arty. Arch. Graham's
  Co.
Robertson, John W. VA 46th Inf. 2nd Co.E Sgt.
Robertson, John W. VA 48th Inf. Co.C
Robertson, John W. VA 61st Inf. Co.F
Robertson, John W.F. VA 28th Inf. Co.K
Robertson, John W.T. MS 22nd Inf. Co.K 1st
  Sgt.
Robertson, Jordan J. TX Cav. Morgan's Regt.
  Co.A
Robertson, Joseph AL 4th Inf. Co.K
Robertson, Joseph AR 3rd Inf. Co.I
Robertson, Joseph AR 5th Inf. Co.D 1st Lt.
Robertson, Joseph AR 27th Inf.
Robertson, Joseph KY 10th (Johnson's) Cav.
  New Co.I
Robertson, Joseph MS Inf. 3rd Bn. Co.I
Robertson, Joseph MS 41st Inf. Co.K
Robertson, Joseph TX 36th Inf. Co.G Sgt.
Robertson, Joseph VA Cav. Ferguson's Bn.
  Spurlock's Co.
Robertson, Joseph VA 1st (Farinholt's) Res.
  Co.D
Robertson, Joseph 2nd Cherokee Mtd.Vol. Co.G
Robertson, Joseph A. AL 6th Cav. Co.A Adj.
Robertson, Joseph A. AL 4th Inf. Co.G
Robertson, Joseph C. MS 18th Inf. Co.I Sgt.
Robertson, Joseph C.G. NC 45th Inf. Co.D
Robertson, Joseph H. LA 7th Inf. Co.B 1st Sgt.
Robertson, Joseph H. VA 14th Inf. Co.D
Robertson, Joseph H. VA 19th Inf. Co.B
Robertson, Joseph H. VA 19th Inf. Co.K
Robertson, Joseph H. VA 21st Inf. Co.E
Robertson, Joseph H. VA Inf. 25th Bn. Co.C
Robertson, Joseph H. VA 34th Inf. Co.I
Robertson, Joseph L. KY 4th Mtd.Inf. Co.H
  Adj.
Robertson, Joseph L. MS 1st (Percy's) Inf. Co.A
Robertson, Jos. L. Gen. & Staff Capt.
Robertson, Joseph R. GA Inf. 4th Bn.
  (St.Guards) Co.H Cpl.
Robertson, Joseph R. MS 6th Inf. Co.I
Robertson, Joseph R. TN Lt.Arty. Scott's Co.
Robertson, Joseph R. VA Lt.Arty. 38th Bn. Co.C
Robertson, Joseph R. VA Lt.Arty. E.J. Ander-
  son's Co.
Robertson, Joseph S. VA Cav. 1st Bn.
  (Loc.Def.Troops) Co.B
Robertson, Joseph W. MS 11th Inf. Co.G
Robertson, Joseph W. MO 9th (Elliott's) Cav.
  Co.B
Robertson, Joseph W. VA 58th Inf. Co.D
Robertson, Joshua SC Lt.Arty. 3rd (Palmetto)
  Bn. Co.A,H Cpl.
Robertson, Joshua VA 52nd Inf. 2nd Co.B
Robertson, Josiah AL 2nd Cav. Co.G
Robertson, Josiah MS Conscr.
Robertson, Josiah W. MS 8th Inf. Co.K
Robertson, J.P. GA 1st Cav. Co.B
Robertson, J.P. NC Wallace's Co. (Wilmington
  RR Guard)
Robertson, J.P. SC 12th Inf. Co.I
Robertson, J.P. TN 3rd (Forrest's) Cav. Co.I
Robertson, J.P. TX 17th Cons.Dismtd.Cav.
  Co.H

Robertson, J.Q. SC Inf. 3rd Bn. Co.E
Robertson, J.R. AL 4th Res. Co.F
Robertson, J.R. AL 8th Inf. Co.K
Robertson, J.R. AL 48th Inf. Co.K
Robertson, J.R. AL 55th Vol. Co.F 2nd Lt.
Robertson, J.R. GA Phillips' Legion Co.D
Robertson, J.R. LA 1st Inf.
Robertson, J.R. MO Cav. Coffee's Regt. Co.C
Robertson, J.R. NC Lt.Arty. Thomas' Legion
  Levi's Btty.
Robertson, J.R. SC Inf. 1st (Charleston) Bn.
  Co.E Cpl.
Robertson, J.R. TN 2nd (Ashby's) Cav. Co.I
Robertson, J.R. TN 45th Inf. Co.G
Robertson, J.R. TX 4th Inf. Co.C
Robertson, J.R. TX 5th Inf. Co.D
Robertson, J.R. VA 10th Cav. Co.A
Robertson, J.R. VA Cav. 32nd Bn. Co.B Maj.
Robertson, J.R. VA Lt.Arty. Barr's Co.
Robertson, J.R. VA 3rd Bn. Valley Res. Co.A
Robertson, J.R. VA 53rd Inf. Hosp.Stew.
Robertson, J.R. 2nd Conf.Inf. Co.B
Robertson, J.R. Anderson's Div. Maj.,CS
Robertson, J.R. Gen. & Staff Maj.,CS
Robertson, J.R. Gen. & Staff A.Hosp.Stew.
Robertson, J. Russel TN Cav. 4th Bn. (Bran-
  ner's) Co.E
Robertson, J.S. AR 27th Inf. Co.G Sgt.
Robertson, J.S. GA 1st Inf. (St.Guards) Co.E
  Sgt.
Robertson, J.S. KY 7th Mtd.Inf. Co.G Cpl.
Robertson, J.S. MS 24th Inf. Co.B
Robertson, J.S. MS 46th Inf. Co.B
Robertson, J.S. MO 3rd Cav. Co.C
Robertson, J.S. MO Lt.Arty. Barret's Co.
Robertson, J.S. NC 6th Inf. Co.K
Robertson, J.S. NC 1st Jr.Res. Co.I
Robertson, J.S. TX 11th Inf. Co.A
Robertson, J.S. VA 13th Cav. Co.K
Robertson, J.S. VA 49th Inf. Co.F
Robertson, J.T. AL 6th Cav. Co.F 1st Sgt.
Robertson, J.T. AL 35th Inf. Co.A
Robertson, J.T. AR 27th Inf. Co.A
Robertson, J.T. GA Cav. 9th Bn. (St.Guards)
  Co.B 3rd Lt.
Robertson, J.T. GA Phillips' Legion Co.M 2nd
  Lt.
Robertson, J.T. MS Cav. 4th Bn. Co.A
Robertson, J.T. MS Rogers' Co. Sgt.
Robertson, J.T. NC 7th Sr.Res. Williams' Co.
Robertson, J.T. SC 6th Inf. 2nd Co.G
Robertson, J.T. SC 12th Inf. Co.C
Robertson, J.T. SC 16th Inf. Co.I
Robertson, J.T. TN 10th Cav. Co.D
Robertson, J.T. TX 14th Field Btty.
Robertson, J.T. VA Lt.Arty. Garber's Co.
Robertson, J.T. VA 21st Inf. Co.K
Robertson, J.T. VA 58th Inf. Co.D
Robertson, J. Tom TX 15th Inf. Co.C
Robertson, Julius LA 2nd Cav. Co.I
Robertson, June C. MS 11th Inf. Co.C 2nd Lt.
Robertson, J.V. TN 46th Inf. Co.C
Robertson, J.W. AL 19th Inf. Co.I
Robertson, J.W. AL 31st Inf. Co.G
Robertson, J.W. AL 35th Inf. Col.
Robertson, J.W. AR 15th (Johnson's) Inf. Co.B
Robertson, J.W. AR 38th Inf. Co.K

Robertson, J.W. GA Cav. 9th Bn. (St.Guards) Co.B

Robertson, J.W. GA Inf. 8th Bn. Co.C

Robertson, J.W. GA 9th Inf. (St.Guards) Co.G

Robertson, J.W. GA 16th Inf. Co.E Cpl.

Robertson, J.W. GA 28th Inf. Co.G

Robertson, J.W. KY 4th Cav. Co.C

Robertson, J.W. MS 3rd Inf. Co.C

Robertson, J.W. MO 16th Inf. Co.D

Robertson, J.W. NC 62nd Inf. Co.F

Robertson, J.W. SC 3rd Cav. Co.A

Robertson, J.W. TN 26th Cav. Co.A

Robertson, J.W. TN 47th Inf. Co.B

Robertson, J.W. TX 26th Cav. Co.H Cpl.

Robertson, J.W. TX Inf. Whaley's Co.

Robertson, J.W. VA 3rd Inf.Loc.Def. Co.F

Robertson, J.W. 1st Conf.Cav. 2nd Co.G

Robertson, J.W.B. VA 1st Cav. Co.G

Robertson, J.W.B. VA Hvy.Arty. 10th Bn. Co.C

Robertson, Kendrick H. VA 18th Inf. Co.C

Robertson, Kenneth AL 4th Cav. Co.K

Robertson, Lander LA 19th Inf. Co.B

Robertson, Larkin H. MO 6th Cav. Co.D

Robertson, L.B. TX 14th Inf. Co.D

Robertson, L.C. MS 35th Inf. Co.D

Robertson, L.C. SC 11th Inf. Bellinger's 2nd Co.I

Robertson, L.D. MS 37th Inf. Co.H

Robertson, L.D. SC 21st Inf. Co.L

Robertson, L.D. TN 49th Inf. Co.C

Robertson, L.D. Inf. Bailey's Cons.Regt. Co.F

Robertson, L.E. SC 14th Inf. Co.E Cpl.

Robertson, Lemuel P. VA Arty. Paris' Co.

Robertson, Len H. NC 12th Inf. Co.D,B

Robertson, Leonard B. AL 63rd Inf. Co.A

Robertson, Leonidas W. NC 47th Inf. Co.E 2nd Lt.

Robertson, Lewis AL 3rd Bn.Res. Appling's Co.

Robertson, Lewis AL 8th Inf. Co.G

Robertson, Lewis AR 16th Inf. Co.K

Robertson, Lewis FL 9th Inf. Co.I Cpl.

Robertson, Lewis SC 5th St.Troops Co.I

Robertson, Lewis, Jr. SC 9th Res. Co.C

Robertson, Lewis, Sr. SC 9th Res. Co.C

Robertson, Lewis TN 13th Inf. Co.I

Robertson, Lewis 1st Choctaw Mtd.Rifles Co.G

Robertson, Lewis E. MS 42nd Inf. Co.B

Robertson, Lewis G. VA 13th Inf. Co.C

Robertson, Lewis M. TX 3rd Inf. Co.D

Robertson, L.G. AR Lt.Arty. Zimmerman's Btty.

Robertson, L.G. MS Inf. 3rd Bn. Co.I Cpl.

Robertson, Littleton T. VA 18th Inf. Co.C

Robertson, L.J. GA 8th Inf. Co.A

Robertson, L.L. LA Inf. 11th Bn. Co.B Sgt.

Robertson, L.L. LA Inf.Cons.Crescent Regt. Co.K Sgt.

Robertson, Loderick KY 9th Mtd.Inf. Co.E

Robertson, Loderick TN Inf. 23rd Bn. Co.A

Robertson, Lodwick TX 29th Cav. Co.F

Robertson, Lorenzo B. AR 14th (Powers') Inf. Co.K 1st Lt.

Robertson, L.S. TN 20th Inf. Co.E

Robertson, L.T. GA 31st Inf. Co.H

Robertson, L.T. TX Waul's Legion Co.B

Robertson, Lucien K. SC 1st (Orr's) Rifles Co.G

Robertson, Lucius B. SC 1st Arty. Co.D

Robertson, Luther R. NC 16th Inf. Co.D

Robertson, Luther W. VA Hvy.Arty. 20th Bn. Co.A

Robertson, L.W. AR 45th Cav. Co.F

Robertson, L.W. AR 1st Vol. Co.K Capt.

Robertson, L.W. MS 4th Inf. Co.A Cpl.

Robertson, L.W. MO 9th Inf. Co.B

Robertson, L.W. MO Inf. Clark's Regt. Co.A

Robertson, Lycurgus TN Cav. 17th Bn. (Sanders') Co.A

Robertson, Lynch LA 8th Cav. Co.A

Robertson, M. AR Cav. Harrell's Bn. Co.D

Robertson, M. KY 2nd Cav. Co.D

Robertson, M. KY 2nd Bn.Mtd.Rifles Co.B

Robertson, M. NC 29th Inf. Co.B

Robertson, M. TN 47th Inf. Co.B

Robertson, M.A. AR 5th Inf. Co.I

Robertson, M.A. TX Cav. Saufley's Scouting Bn. Co.A

Robertson, M.A. Exch.Bn. 1st Co.C,CSA

Robertson, Madison F. VA 24th Inf. Co.I Sgt.

Robertson, Mad. M. VA 157th Mil. Co.B

Robertson, Manoah AL 43rd Inf. Co.G

Robertson, Marcellus VA 23rd Inf. Co.K 2nd Lt.

Robertson, Marian MS 44th Inf. Co.E Sgt.

Robertson, Marius G. VA 18th Inf. Co.C

Robertson, Masto AR 14th (Powers') Inf. Co.K 2nd Lt.

Robertson, Mathew MS Cav. 1st Bn. (McNair's) St.Troops Co.B

Robertson, Mathew H. NC 35th Inf. Co.B

Robertson, Matthew W. VA 5th Inf. Co.E

Robertson, M.B. MO Lt.Arty. Farris' Btty. (Clark Arty.)

Robertson, M.B. VA 1st (Farinholt's) Res. Co.I

Robertson, M.C. TX 17th Inf. Co.E

Robertson, M.G. VA Mtd.Guard 4th Congr.Dist.

Robertson, Michael NC 42nd Inf. Co.A

Robertson, Michael L. MD 1st Inf. Co.I Capt.

Robertson, Miller AR 33rd Inf. Co.D

Robertson, Mitchell A. TX Cav. Madison's Regt. Co.F

Robertson, M.K. AR 6th Inf. New Co.F

Robertson, M.K. AR 12th Inf. Co.C Cpl.

Robertson, M.K. SC 16th Inf. Co.H Sgt.

Robertson, M.L. LA 2nd Inf. Co.H Cpl.

Robertson, M.L. TN 30th Inf. Co.C Sgt.

Robertson, M.L. VA 24th Cav. Co.G

Robertson, M.L. Hosp.Stew.

Robertson, M.M. AL 31st Inf. Co.K Sgt.

Robertson, M.M. SC 4th St.Troops Co.D

Robertson, M.N. GA Cav. 1st Gordon Squad. (St.Guards) Co.A

Robertson, Monroe NC 13th Inf. Co.A

Robertson, Mortimore VA Lt.Arty. Parker's Co.

Robertson, Moses NC 17th Inf. (2nd Org.) Co.G

Robertson, Moses P. VA 54th Mil. Co.B

Robertson, M.S. Gen. & Staff Hosp.Stew.

Robertson, M.W. MS 9th Inf. New Co.I

Robertson, M.W. VA 10th Bn.Res. Co.B

Robertson, M.W. VA Rockbridge Cty.Res. Donald's Co.

Robertson, Myrtillo S.B. VA 2nd Inf. Co.A,H 1st Sgt.

Robertson, N. AL 4th Res. Co.G

Robertson, N. AL Loc.Def. & Sp.Serv. Toomer's Co.

Robertson, Nat TN 21st & 22nd (Cons.) Cav. Co.D Cpl.

Robertson, Nathan B. SC 1st (Orr's) Rifles Co.E

Robertson, Nathaniel GA 2nd Inf. Co.F Sgt.

Robertson, Nathaniel J. VA 50th Inf. Co.K

Robertson, Nathaniel T. VA 38th Inf. Co.D

Robertson, N.B. LA Cav. 18th Bn. Co.A Sgt.

Robertson, N.C. SC 6th Inf. 1st Co.D

Robertson, N.C. SC 12th Inf. Co.C Sgt.Maj.

Robertson, N.D. TN 18th Inf. Co.I

Robertson, N.D. TX 14th Inf. Co.C

Robertson, Newton AR 27th Inf. Co.G

Robertson, Newton J. VA 33rd Inf. Co.H

Robertson, N.F. AL 33rd Inf. Co.H

Robertson, N.F. AL 35th Inf. Co.D

Robertson, N.H. MS 7th Inf. Co.K

Robertson, Nicholas M. SC 1st Arty. Co.D

Robertson, N.J. VA 2nd Cav. Co.E 3rd Lt.

Robertson, N.L. MS Inf. 7th Bn. Co.G

Robertson, N.M. AL 37th Inf. Co.G 2nd Lt.

Robertson, N.M. SC 23rd Inf. Co.F

Robertson, Noah NC 47th Inf. Co.F

Robertson, Noah TN 18th (Newsom's) Cav. Co.F

Robertson, Nolvell R. GA 22nd Inf. Co.K

Robertson, N.P. GA Phillips' Legion Co.M Cpl.

Robertson, N.R. AL Cp. of Instr. Talladega

Robertson, N.R. MS Cav. 1st Bn. (McNair's) St.Troops Co.B

Robertson, N.T. AL 9th Inf. Co.F

Robertson, N.T. VA 13th Cav. Co.K

Robertson, N.W. GA Phillips' Legion Co.D

Robertson, O.B. TX 1st Bn.S.S. Co.A,E

Robertson, O. Hazard MS 39th Inf. Co.C Sgt.

Robertson, Oliver P. GA 60th Inf. Co.K Cpl.

Robertson, O.S. LA Inf.Cons.Crescent Regt. Co.N

Robertson, P.A. GA Cav. 9th Bn. (St.Guards) Co.B

Robertson, P.A. NC 33rd Inf. Co.K

Robertson, P.A. TN 44th (Cons.) Inf. Co.G

Robertson, Patrick H. VA Lt.Arty. Douthat's Co.

Robertson, Patton VA Lt.Arty. Cooper's Co. 2nd Lt.

Robertson, P.B. KY 4th Cav. Co.I

Robertson, P.D. KY 10th (Johnson's) Cav. New Co.C

Robertson, Pelham NC 24th Inf. Co.H

Robertson, Peter GA 4th Cav. (St.Guards) Robertson's Co. Capt.

Robertson, Peter SC Horse Arty. (Washington Arty.) Vol. Hart's Co.

Robertson, Peter TN 29th Inf. Co.F

Robertson, Peter D. NC 13th Inf. Co.H

Robertson, Peter E. NC 30th Inf. Co.B Cpl.

Robertson, P.F. AR 1st (Colquitt's) Inf. Co.C

Robertson, P.H. SC 3rd Cav. Co.A

Robertson, P.H. VA Arty. Bryan's Co.

Robertson, Pierson SC 4th Bn.Res. Co.D

Robertson, Pierson SC 9th Res. Co.B

Robertson, Pinckney H. TX 3rd Inf. Co.D

Robertson, Pink AL 16th Inf. Co.C

Robertson, Pinkney TX 15th Cav. Co.A

Robertson, P.J. GA 2nd Cav. (St.Guards) Co.A

Robertson, P.J. GA Hvy.Arty. 22nd Bn. Co.D

Robertson, Pleasant AR 7th Cav. Co.K 1st Sgt.

Robertson, Pleasant TN 45th Inf. Co.B

Robertson, P.M. AL 48th Inf. Co.K
Robertson, P.M. MS 29th Inf. Co.I
Robertson, P.P. GA Cav. Gartrell's Co.
Robertson, P.P. GA Tiller's Co. (Echols Lt.Arty.)
Robertson, P.P. GA 9th Inf. (St.Guards) Co.D
Robertson, P.P. TX 7th Inf. Co.I Sgt.
Robertson, P.P. TX 19th Inf. Co.I 1st Lt.
Robertson, P.W. AL 14th Inf. Co.B Sgt.
Robertson, R. AL 8th (Hatch's) Cav. Co.I
Robertson, R. AL Cp. of Instr. Talladega
Robertson, R. FL Cav. 5th Bn. Co.H
Robertson, R. GA 7th Inf. (St.Guards) Co.L
Robertson, R. KY 2nd Cav. Co.E
Robertson, R. MS 24th Inf. Co.A
Robertson, R. NC 7th Sr.Res. Watts' Co.
Robertson, R. SC 3rd Inf. Co.G Sgt.
Robertson, R. TN 1st (Carter's) Cav. Co.E
Robertson, R. TN 12th (Green's) Cav. Co.F
Robertson, R. TX 13th Vol. Co.H
Robertson, R. TX 14th Inf. Co.C
Robertson, R. TX 16th Inf. Co.K
Robertson, R.A. KY 3rd Cav. Co.H
Robertson, R.A. KY 4th Cav. Co.H
Robertson, R.A. SC 7th Inf. 1st Co.B
Robertson, Ralf TX 9th (Nichols') Inf. Co.K Cpl.
Robertson, Ransom MS 3rd (Quinn's St.Troops) Inf. Co.G
Robertson, R.B. MS 41st Inf. Co.K
Robertson, R.C. GA 1st Reg. Co.I
Robertson, R.C. SC 6th Res. Co.E
Robertson, R.C. SC 17th Inf. Co.K
Robertson, R.C. TN 44th (Cons.) Inf. Co.F
Robertson, R.C. Fort's Scouts,CSA
Robertson, R.D. GA 3rd Cav. Co.D
Robertson, R.E. AR 14th (McCarver's) Inf. Co.K
Robertson, R.E. MO 1st Cav. Co.I
Robertson, R.E. MO 1st Inf. Co.I
Robertson, Renyard E. VA 23rd Inf. Co.C
Robertson, Reuben SC 1st (McCreary's) Inf. Co.I
Robertson, Reuben SC 14th Inf. Co.E
Robertson, Reuben K. GA 52nd Inf. Co.A
Robertson, R.F. VA 9th Cav. Co.G
Robertson, R.F. VA 1st St.Res. Co.I
Robertson, R.G. MO Robertson's Regt.St.Guard Co.3
Robertson, R.H. AL 18th Inf. Co.E
Robertson, R.H. GA Hvy.Arty. 22nd Bn. Co.D
Robertson, R.H. NC 62nd Inf. Co.F
Robertson, R.H. TN 31st Inf. Co.E Asst.Surg.
Robertson, R.H. TX 12th Inf. Co.I
Robertson, R.H. VA Arty. (Loc.Def. & Sp.Serv.) Lanier's Co.
Robertson, R.H. VA Inf. 1st Bn.
Robertson, R.H. Gen. & Staff AASurg.
Robertson, Richard TN 2nd (Ashby's) Cav. Co.E
Robertson, Richard TN Cav. 4th Bn. (Branner's) Co.D
Robertson, Richard A. VA 21st Inf. Co.K
Robertson, Richard C. MO 10th Cav. Co.A
Robertson, Richard E. AR 21st Inf. Co.F Cpl.
Robertson, Richard E. VA 41st Inf. Co.D
Robertson, Richard G. MO 5th Cav. Co.E Sgt.
Robertson, Richard H. MS 9th Inf. Co.C
Robertson, Richard H. TN Greer's Regt. Part.Rangers Co.C

Robertson, Richard J. MO Cav. 12th Regt. St.Guard Maj.
Robertson, Richard J. VA 21st Inf. Co.E
Robertson, Richard P. TX Cav. Baylor's Regt. Co.C
Robertson, Richard T. KY 2nd (Woodward's) Cav. Co.E
Robertson, Richard W. TN 4th (McLemore's) Cav. Co.K
Robertson, Richard W. VA 21st Inf. Co.K
Robertson, Rich F. Gen. & Staff Capt.,Comsy.
Robertson, R.K. GA 24th Inf. Co.G
Robertson, R.L. AL 50th Inf.
Robertson, R.L., Jr. LA 21st (Patton's) Inf. Co.D Maj.
Robertson, R.L., Jr. Gen. & Staff Maj.,Ord.Off.
Robertson, R.M. AL 11th Inf. Co.D Comsy.
Robertson, R.M. LA 8th Cav. Co.A
Robertson, R.M. LA 2nd Inf. Co.B Cpl.
Robertson, R.M. Gen. & Staff Maj.,Comsy.
Robertson, R.O. VA 56th Inf. Co.G
Robertson, Robert AL 2nd Cav. Co.D
Robertson, Robert AL Lt.Arty. 2nd Bn. Co.E,A
Robertson, Robert AL 25th Inf. Co.C
Robertson, Robert AL 28th Inf. Co.C
Robertson, Robert AL St.Res. Palmer's Co.
Robertson, Robert KY 1st Inf. Co.C
Robertson, Robert LA 27th Inf. Co.D
Robertson, Robert NC 1st Inf. (6 mo. '61) Co.D
Robertson, Robert NC 14th Inf. Co.K
Robertson, Robert NC 30th Inf. Co.I
Robertson, Robert SC 5th St.Troops Co.B
Robertson, Robert VA Lt.Arty. Douthat's Co.
Robertson, Robert VA 3rd (Chrisman's) Bn.Res. Co.E
Robertson, Robert VA Rockbridge Cty.Res. Bacon's Co.
Robertson, Robert A. VA 18th Inf. Co.C Cpl.
Robertson, Robert B. MS 5th Inf. Co.H
Robertson, Robert E. MS 40th Inf. Co.K
Robertson, Robert F. NC 3rd Cav. (41st St.Troops) Co.I Sgt.
Robertson, Robert F. VA 2nd Cav. Co.F
Robertson, Robert H. AL 2nd Cav. Co.A
Robertson, Robert H. VA 16th Inf. Co.E
Robertson, Robert M. VA 32nd Inf. Co.F
Robertson, Robert P. FL 3rd Inf. Co.D Sgt.
Robertson, Robert R. TX 4th Cav. Co.D
Robertson, Robert S. VA 7th Cav. Co.K
Robertson, Robert S. VA 146th Mil. Co.D
Robertson, Robert W. GA 1st (Symons') Res. Co.I
Robertson, Robert W. TN 14th Cav. Co.E 3rd Lt.
Robertson, Robert W. TX 22nd Cav. Co.F 2nd Lt.
Robertson, Robert W. VA 21st Inf. Co.A
Robertson, Rowan TN 6th (Wheeler's) Cav. Co.G
Robertson, R.P. TX 9th Cav. Co.I
Robertson, R.Q. AL 26th (O'Neal's) Inf. Co.H
Robertson, R.R. TX 4th Inf. Co.B
Robertson, R.R. VA 59th Inf. 3rd Co.E
Robertson, R.R. VA Mil. 172nd Regt. Maj.
Robertson, R.S. VA 18th Inf. Co.E
Robertson, R.T. NC Lt.Arty. Thomas' Legion Levi's Btty.

Robertson, R.T. SC Inf. Hampton Legion Co.C
Robertson, R.T. VA Lt.Arty. Barr's Co.
Robertson, R. Thomas MS 11th (Perrin's) Cav. Co.K
Robertson, Rubin SC 9th Res. Co.E
Robertson, Rufus W. KY 6th Cav. Co.D 1st Sgt.
Robertson, R.W. GA 6th Res. Co.G
Robertson, R.W. MS 6th Cav. Co.G
Robertson, R.Y. GA 1st Inf. (St.Guards) Co.F
Robertson, S. AL 4th Cav. Co.G
Robertson, S. AR Lt.Arty. Hart's Btty.
Robertson, S. MS 24th Inf. Co.A
Robertson, S. MS 46th Inf. Co.B
Robertson, S. SC 4th St.Troops Music.
Robertson, S. Gen. & Staff Hosp.Stew.
Robertson, Sam MO 2nd Inf. Co.C
Robertson, Samuel AR 14th (Powers') Inf. Co.B
Robertson, Samuel KY 3rd Cav. Co.K
Robertson, Samuel KY 8th Mtd.Inf. Co.B
Robertson, Samuel SC 4th St.Troops Co.D
Robertson, Samuel SC Manigault's Bn.Vol. Co.D
Robertson, Samuel TN 18th (Newsom's) Cav. Co.F
Robertson, Samuel TN 1st (Feild's) Inf. Co.C
Robertson, Samuel TN 34th Inf. Co.B
Robertson, Samuel TX 14th Cav. Co.F
Robertson, Samuel TX 7th Inf. Co.C
Robertson, Samuel VA 33rd Inf. Co.B
Robertson, Samuel A. AL St.Arty. Co.A Cpl.
Robertson, Samuel A. SC 1st Arty. Co.D
Robertson, Samuel A. VA 57th Inf. Co.I
Robertson, Samuel B. MO Inf. 8th Bn. Co.D Capt.,ACS
Robertson, Samuel B. MO Robertson's Regt.St.Guard QM
Robertson, Samuel B. Gen. & Staff QM
Robertson, Samuel D. AL 43rd Inf. Co.E
Robertson, Samuel D. MS 12th Inf. Co.F
Robertson, Samuel D. MS 18th Inf. Co.I Capt.
Robertson, Samuel E. MO 3rd Inf. Co.C
Robertson, Samuel G. VA 58th Inf. Co.E Cpl.
Robertson, Samuel H. MO 2nd Cav. Co.I
Robertson, Samuel H. MO Inf. 8th Bn. Co.F
Robertson, Samuel H. MO 9th Inf. Co.K
Robertson, Samuel J. VA 3rd Res. Co.C
Robertson, Samuel L. AL 8th (Hatch's) Cav. Co.K 4th Cpl.
Robertson, Samuel L. AL 4th (Russell's) Cav. Co.F Sgt.
Robertson, Samuel P. SC 6th Cav. Co.K
Robertson, Samuel S. VA 38th Inf. Co.D
Robertson, Samuel T. VA 10th Cav. Co.K
Robertson, Samuel W. LA 12th Inf. Co.F
Robertson, Samuel W. NC 45th Inf. Co.D
Robertson, Sanford Morgan MS 24th Inf. Co.C
Robertson, S.B. Gen. & Staff 1st Lt.,EO
Robertson, S.C. AL 8th Cav. Co.F Cpl.
Robertson, S.C. LA 3rd (Wingfield's) Cav. Co.A,B
Robertson, S.C. Gen. & Staff Capt.,Vol.ADC
Robertson, S.D. KY 8th Mtd.Inf. Co.F
Robertson, S.D. MS Cav. 4th Bn. Co.H
Robertson, S.D. MS Lt.Arty. Yates' Btty.
Robertson, S.D. TN 3rd (Forrest's) Cav. Lt.
Robertson, Seaborn MS 37th Inf. Co.H
Robertson, Sevier C. GA 11th Inf. Co.E
Robertson, S.G. AR 18th Inf. Co.K

Robertson, S.G. AR 23rd Inf. Co.H
Robertson, S.G. GA 1st Reg. Co.F 1st Sgt.
Robertson, S.G. TX 10th Cav. Co.A
Robertson, S.H. SC 1st (Butler's) Inf. Co.F
Robertson, Shelby AL 3rd Res. Co.G
Robertson, Sidney A. LA 8th Inf. Co.A
Robertson, Sidney B. LA 2nd Inf. Co.A 2nd Lt.
Robertson, Silas GA 4th Res. Co.C Cpl.
Robertson, Simon P. TN 48th (Nixon's) Inf. Co.I
Robertson, S.J. MS 7th Cav. Co.H
Robertson, S.J. SC 7th Inf. 2nd Co.D
Robertson, S.J. TN 13th Inf. Co.E
Robertson, S.J. TX 3rd Cav. Co.H
Robertson, S.J. VA 1st (Farinholt's) Res. Co.F
Robertson, S.L. AL 7th Inf. Co.D
Robertson, S.L. SC 1st St.Troops Co.K
Robertson, Sledge M. AL 6th Inf. Co.L
Robertson, Sledge M. AL 37th Inf. Co.G Capt.
Robertson, S.M. AL 31st Inf. Co.G
Robertson, S.M. GA 39th Inf. Co.K
Robertson, S.M. MS 2nd Cav. Co.E 1st Lt.
Robertson, S.M. MS 2nd (Davidson's) Inf. Co.E 2nd Lt.
Robertson, S.N. AL 62nd Inf. Co.G
Robertson, Snowden GA 7th Inf. Co.D
Robertson, Solomon SC 3rd Res. Co.A
Robertson, S.P. AL 19th Inf. Co.A
Robertson, Squire TX 34th Cav. Co.F
Robertson, S.T. GA 49th Inf.
Robertson, Stanhope VA 12th Inf. Co.E
Robertson, Stephen MS 27th Inf. Co.A
Robertson, Stephen VA 4th Res. Co.K
Robertson, Stephen A. SC 1st Arty. Co.F
Robertson, Stephen G. FL 8th Inf. Co.I
Robertson, Struen MS 35th Inf. Co.F
Robertson, S.W. GA 7th Inf. (St.Guards) Co.C
Robertson, S.W. VA 7th Bn.Res. Co.D
Robertson, Sylas M. TN 4th (McLemore's) Cav. Co.K
Robertson, Sylvanus A. MS 19th Inf. Co.G
Robertson, T. FL 1st (Res.) Inf. Co.L
Robertson, T. KY 10th (Johnson's) Cav. Co.E Cpl.
Robertson, T. LA 31st Inf. Co.E
Robertson, T. LA Mil. British Guard Bn. Burrowes' Co.
Robertson, T. TN Lt.Arty. Scott's Co.
Robertson, T.A. MS St.Troops (Herndon Rangers) Montgomery's Ind.Co.
Robertson, T.A. MS 24th Inf. Co.A
Robertson, T.A. VA Inf. 44th Bn. Co.C
Robertson, Tapley J. GA 3rd Inf. Co.L
Robertson, T.B. MS Cav. Ham's Regt. Co.A,G
Robertson, T.B. NC 12th Inf. Co.K
Robertson, T.B. VA Cav. 37th Bn. Co.I
Robertson, T.B. VA VMI Co.D Capt.
Robertson, T.C. LA 4th Inf. Co.F
Robertson, T.C. VA 17th Inf. Co.G
Robertson, T.C.S. LA Ogden's Cav. Co.D Capt.
Robertson, T.C.S. LA 27th Inf. Co.H Capt.
Robertson, T.D. MO 9th Inf. Co.K Cpl.
Robertson, T.D. TN 19th (Biffle's) Cav. Co.B
Robertson, T.F. Exch.Bn. 1st Co.A,CSA
Robertson, T.G. MS 4th Cav. Co.I

Robertson, T.G. MS Wilkinson Cty. Minute Men Co.B Comsy.Sgt.
Robertson, T.G. SC 4th St.Troops Co.H
Robertson, T.G. Bradford's Corps Scouts & Guards Co.A
Robertson, T.H. GA Boddie's Co. (Troup Cty.Ind.Cav.)
Robertson, T.H. TN 19th (Biffle's) Cav. Co.A
Robertson, Theoderick J. VA 1st Inf. Co.D
Robertson, Theodore C. TN 54th Inf. Co.B
Robertson, Theodrick P. VA 18th Inf. Co.C
Robertson, Theofolus J. AL 30th Inf. Co.H
Robertson, Theophilus J. AL 39th Inf. Co.H
Robertson, Theophilus L. GA 11th Inf. Co.H
Robertson, Thomas AL 53rd (Part.Rangers) Co.D
Robertson, Thomas AR 20th Inf. Co.G
Robertson, Thomas GA 4th Inf. Co.C
Robertson, Thomas MS 1st Lt.Arty. Co.D
Robertson, Thomas MS 5th Inf. Co.H
Robertson, Thomas MS 11th Inf. Co.D
Robertson, Thomas MS 27th Inf. Co.A
Robertson, Thomas MO Cav. Snider's Bn. Co.A
Robertson, Thomas NC 12th Inf. Co.C
Robertson, Thomas NC 12th Inf. Co.D,B
Robertson, Thomas NC 42nd Inf. Co.E
Robertson, Thomas SC 1st St.Troops Co.F
Robertson, Thomas TN 2nd (Ashby's) Cav. Co.I
Robertson, Thomas TN 3rd (Forrest's) Cav. Co.B
Robertson, Thomas TN 29th Inf. Co.F
Robertson, Thomas VA 10th Bn.Res. Co.B
Robertson, Thomas VA 16th Inf. 2nd Co.H
Robertson, Thomas VA 21st Inf. Co.E
Robertson, Thomas VA 72nd Mil.
Robertson, Thomas VA 86th Mil. Co.F,A Fifer
Robertson, Thomas VA Rockbridge Cty.Res. Donald's Co.
Robertson, Thomas Conf.Inf. 8th Bn.
Robertson, Thomas A. VA 18th Inf. Co.C Cpl.
Robertson, Thomas Bird VA 2nd Cav. Co.D
Robertson, Thomas C. AL 41st Inf. Co.G
Robertson, Thomas C. MS 18th Inf. Co.I
Robertson, Thomas C. TN 48th (Nixon's) Inf. Co.G
Robertson, Thos. C. Gen. & Staff Capt.,AQM
Robertson, Thomas D. GA 42nd Inf. Co.E
Robertson, Thomas D. TX 15th Cav. Co.B 1st Lt.
Robertson, Thomas D. VA 11th Inf. Co.A
Robertson, Thomas D. VA 19th Inf. Co.C
Robertson, Thomas F. VA 17th Inf. Co.G
Robertson, Thomas F. Conf.Inf. 1st Bn. 2nd Co.E
Robertson, Thomas H. GA 53rd Inf. Co.E,G
Robertson, Thomas H. MO 6th Cav. Co.G 3rd Lt.
Robertson, Thomas H. NC 45th Inf. Co.D
Robertson, Thomas H. VA Hvy.Arty. 20th Bn. Co.C
Robertson, Thomas H. VA 42nd Inf. Co.C
Robertson, Thomas J. AL 13th Inf. Co.I
Robertson, Thomas J. GA 10th Cav. (St.Guards) Co.G
Robertson, Thomas J. GA 48th Inf. Co.G Capt.
Robertson, Thomas J. GA Cobb's Legion Co.C
Robertson, Thomas J. MO 15th Cav. Co.E 2nd Lt.

Robertson, Thomas J. TN 19th (Biffle's) Cav. Co.A
Robertson, Thomas J. TX 14th Cav. Co.E
Robertson, Thomas J. VA 2nd Cav. Co.F
Robertson, Thomas J. VA 13th Inf. Co.A
Robertson, Thomas J. VA 28th Inf. Co.G 2nd Lt.
Robertson, Thomas L. AL 6th Cav. Co.E
Robertson, Thomas L. AL 5th Bn.Vol. Co.A
Robertson, Thomas L. AL 22nd Inf.
Robertson, Thomas L. MS 9th Inf. Old Co.A, New Co.F Sgt.
Robertson, Thomas L. NC 15th Inf. Co.F
Robertson, Thomas L. SC 1st (Orr's) Rifles Co.E 1st Sgt.
Robertson, Thomas L. SC 14th Inf. Co.I
Robertson, Thomas M. GA 4th Inf. Co.F
Robertson, Thomas M. MS Cav. 24th Bn. Co.E
Robertson, Thomas M. MS Arty. (Seven Stars Arty.) Roberts' Co.
Robertson, Thomas M. MO 2nd Cav. Co.G
Robertson, Thomas M. SC 12th Inf. Co.F
Robertson, Thomas O. FL 6th Inf. Co.D
Robertson, Thomas S. VA 28th Inf. Co.F
Robertson, Thomas W. AL St.Res. 3rd Lt.
Robertson, Thomas W. AR 23rd Inf. Co.K
Robertson, Thomas W. MO Cav. Slayback's Regt. Co.C
Robertson, Thompson G. NC 22nd Inf. Co.G
Robertson, Timothy SC 27th Inf. Co.B
Robertson, T.J. AL 55th Vol. Co.D
Robertson, T.J. LA 17th Inf. Co.F
Robertson, T.J. MS Cav. 1st Bn. (Montgomery's) St.Troops Co.C
Robertson, T.J. MS 7th Cav. Co.G
Robertson, T.J. MS 3rd Inf. (St.Troops) Co.A Cpl.
Robertson, T.J. TN Cav. Jackson's Co.
Robertson, T.J. TN 59th Mtd.Inf. Co.I
Robertson, T.J. 3rd Conf.Inf. Co.B
Robertson, T.L. AL Lt.Arty. Tarrant's Btty.
Robertson, T.L. VA 3rd Res. Co.D
Robertson, T.M. AL 25th Inf. Co.F Sgt.
Robertson, T.N. MS 22nd Inf.
Robertson, T.N. NC 45th Inf. Co.K
Robertson, Tolivar SC 6th Cav. Co.E
Robertson, Toliver SC 9th Res. Co.E
Robertson, T.P. AL 4th (Russell's) Cav. Co.C
Robertson, T. Patrick SC 24th Inf. Co.I
Robertson, T.S. GA 36th (Broyles') Inf. Co.G Cpl.
Robertson, T.S. MS 29th Inf. Co.F
Robertson, T.S. Gen. & Staff Capt.,AQM
Robertson, Turner TN Lt.Arty. Barry's Co.
Robertson, T.W. GA 4th Inf. Co.A
Robertson, T.W. MO 10th Inf. Co.B
Robertson, Upson A. VA 18th Inf. Co.C
Robertson, U.R. SC 2nd Inf. Co.H Cpl.
Robertson, Urin MS 2nd Cav. Co.H
Robertson, V. 20th Conf.Cav. 2nd Co.I
Robertson, V.B. SC 3rd Inf. Co.A,I 1st Sgt.
Robertson, Vincent MS 41st Inf. Co.L
Robertson, Vincent R. TN 1st (Turney's) Inf. Co.F
Robertson, Virgil L. GA Carlton's Co. (Troup Cty.Arty.)

Robertson, W. AR Mil. Desha Cty.Bn.
Robertson, W. GA 1st (Fannin's) Res. Co.K
Robertson, W. GA 11th Inf. Co.E
Robertson, W. MO Robertson's Regt.St.Guard Secretary
Robertson, W. TN 1st (Carter's) Cav. Co.E
Robertson, W. TN 37th Inf. Co.E
Robertson, W. VA 5th Bn.Res.
Robertson, W.A. MS 11th (Perrin's) Cav. Co.H
Robertson, W.A. TN 49th Inf. Co.C
Robertson, W.A. Inf. Bailey's Cons.Regt. Co.F
Robertson, W.A. TX 10th Cav. Co.G
Robertson, W.A. Gen. & Staff Surg.
Robertson, W.A.J. GA Cav. 1st Gordon Squad. (St.Guards) Co.A
Robertson, Walter H. Gen. & Staff Rec. for ADC
Robertson, Walter S. GA 38th Inf. Co.E Sgt.Maj.
Robertson, Warren F. SC 1st (McCreary's) Inf. Co.B Hosp.Stew.
Robertson, Warren Y. GA 22nd Inf. Co.E
Robertson, Washington NC 24th Inf. Co.H
Robertson, Washington I. MS 40th Inf. Co.K Cpl.
Robertson, W.B. AR 38th Inf. Co.K
Robertson, W.B. MS 4th Inf. Co.F
Robertson, W.B. Gen. & Staff A.Surg.
Robertson, W.C. KY 3rd Mtd.Inf. Co.H
Robertson, W.C. MS 7th Cav. Co.D Sgt.
Robertson, W.C. MS 27th Inf. Co.A
Robertson, W.C. MS 46th Inf. Co.B
Robertson, W.C. TN 3rd (Forrest's) Cav. Co.I
Robertson, W.C. TN 12th (Green's) Cav. Co.H
Robertson, W.C. TN 20th Inf. Co.G
Robertson, W.C. TN 48th (Nixon's) Inf. Co.K
Robertson, W.C. Lt.Arty. Dent's Btty.,CSA
Robertson, W.C.A. AL 3rd Res. Co.F
Robertson, W.D. KY 5th Cav. Co.F
Robertson, W.D. MS 3rd Cav. Co.K
Robertson, W.D. MS 28th Cav. Co.F
Robertson, W.D. MS 3rd Inf. (St.Troops) Co.A 2nd Lt.
Robertson, W.D. TN 24th Inf. Co.A
Robertson, W.D. TN 30th Inf. Co.C
Robertson, W.E. AL 15th Inf. Co.L
Robertson, W.E. TN Lt.Arty. Tobin's Co.
Robertson, W.E. TN 4th Inf. Co.G
Robertson, W.E. VA Inf. 44th Bn. Co.B
Robertson, Welcher C. VA 58th Inf. Co.H
Robertson, Wesley SC 1st (Orr's) Rifles Co.G Cpl.
Robertson, Wesley SC 4th Bn.Res. Co.B,F Capt.
Robertson, W.F. FL Lt.Arty. Dyke's Co.
Robertson, W.F. GA 40th Inf. Co.K
Robertson, W.F. TN 51st (Cons.) Inf. Co.D
Robertson, W.F. TX 33rd Cav. Co.C
Robertson, W.F. Conf.Lt.Arty. Stark's Bn. Surg.
Robertson, W.F. Gen. & Staff Asst.Surg.
Robertson, W.F.X. TX Waul's Legion Co.F
Robertson, W.G. AL 18th Inf. Co.E 2nd Lt.
Robertson, W.G. AR 38th Inf. Co.K
Robertson, W.G. MS 18th Cav. Co.F
Robertson, W.G. MS 20th Inf. Co.D
Robertson, W.G. NC Currituck Guard J.W.F. Bank's Co.
Robertson, W.G. TN 18th Inf. Co.I 2nd Lt.

Robertson, W.G. VA Cav. Mosby's Regt. (Part.Rangers) Co.D
Robertson, W.G. Mead's Conf.Cav. Co.E
Robertson, W. Garrett TN 60th Mtd.Inf. Co.H
Robertson, W.H. AL 32nd Inf. Co.B
Robertson, W.H. GA 25th Inf. Co.I
Robertson, W.H. KY 2nd (Duke's) Cav. Co.K
Robertson, W.H. LA 2nd Inf. Co.E Sgt.
Robertson, W.H. MS 2nd St.Cav. Co.E
Robertson, W.H. MS Arty. (Seven Stars Arty.) Roberts' Co.
Robertson, W.H. MS 9th Inf. Co.A
Robertson, W.H. SC 1st St.Troops Co.F
Robertson, W.H. SC 4th Bn.Res. Co.B
Robertson, W.H. SC 5th Res. Co.A Cpl.
Robertson, W.H. TN 9th (Ward's) Cav. Co.E
Robertson, W.H. TN Inf. 3rd Cons.Regt. Co.B
Robertson, W.H. VA Cav. Mosby's Regt. (Part.Rangers) Co.E
Robertson, W.H. VA Inf. Montague's Bn. Co.B
Robertson, W.H. Gen. & Staff Asst.Surg.
Robertson, Wiley P. NC 13th Inf. Co.A Jr.2nd Lt.
Robertson, William AL 10th Inf. Co.I
Robertson, William AL 24th Inf. Co.B
Robertson, William AL 25th Inf. Co.F
Robertson, William AL 43rd Inf. Co.F Cpl.
Robertson, William AL 44th Inf. Co.D
Robertson, William AL Vol. Meador's Co.
Robertson, William AR 31st Inf. Co.D
Robertson, William AR 45th Mil. Co.A
Robertson, William GA Inf. 10th Bn. Co.E
Robertson, William GA 44th Inf.
Robertson, William GA 48th Inf. Co.C
Robertson, William KY 1st Cav. Co.F
Robertson, William KY 5th Mtd.Inf. Co.I
Robertson, William KY 9th Mtd.Inf. Co.I
Robertson, William LA 4th Inf. New Co.G
Robertson, William MS 11th (Perrin's) Cav. Co.E
Robertson, William MS Cav. 24th Bn. Co.F
Robertson, William MS Inf. 3rd Bn. (St.Troops) Co.F
Robertson, William MS 14th Inf. Co.G
Robertson, William MS 19th Inf. Co.D
Robertson, William MS 24th Inf. Co.A
Robertson, William MS 37th Inf. Co.H
Robertson, William MO 1st Cav. Co.G
Robertson, William MO Inf. 3rd Bn. Co.A
Robertson, William MO 6th Inf. Co.E Cpl.
Robertson, William MO Inf. Clark's Regt. Co.G
Robertson, William NC 8th Bn.Part.Rangers Co.A
Robertson, William NC 12th Inf. Co.K
Robertson, William NC 18th Inf. Co.A
Robertson, William NC 21st Inf. Co.K
Robertson, William NC 32nd Inf. QMSgt.
Robertson, William SC Cav. 4th Bn. Co.C
Robertson, William SC 1st St.Troops Co.F
Robertson, William SC 5th St.Troops Co.B
Robertson, William SC 5th Res. Co.F
Robertson, William SC 16th Inf. Co.H
Robertson, William TN 1st (Carter's) Cav. Co.E
Robertson, William TN 2nd Cav. Co.A
Robertson, William TN 5th (McKenzie's) Cav. Co.B

Robertson, William TN 12th (Green's) Cav. Co.A
Robertson, William TN 12th (Green's) Cav. Co.C
Robertson, William TN 21st (Carter's) Cav. Co.A
Robertson, William TN Cav. Jackson's Co.
Robertson, William TN 4th Inf. Co.C
Robertson, William TN 5th Inf. 2nd Co.F
Robertson, William TN 10th Inf. Co.B
Robertson, William TN 14th Inf. Co.I
Robertson, William TN 50th Inf. Co.D
Robertson, William TN 51st Inf. Co.E
Robertson, William TX Smith's Res.
Robertson, William VA 25th Cav. Co.C
Robertson, William VA Hvy.Arty. 18th Bn. Co.A
Robertson, William VA Lt.Arty. Cayce's Co.
Robertson, William VA 6th Inf. Co.G
Robertson, William VA 10th Inf. Co.A
Robertson, William VA 25th Inf. 2nd Co.F
Robertson, William VA 31st Inf. Co.E
Robertson, William VA 41st Inf. 1st Co.E
Robertson, William VA 42nd Inf. Co.H
Robertson, William Inf. School of Pract. Powell's Command Powell's Detach. Co.A
Robertson, William A. AL 6th Inf. Co.L 1st Sgt.
Robertson, William A. GA 4th Inf. Co.B
Robertson, William A. GA 22nd Inf. Co.C
Robertson, William A. LA 6th Inf. Co.C Surg.
Robertson, William A. MS 7th Cav. Co.E
Robertson, William A. MS 23rd Inf. Co.H 1st Lt.
Robertson, William A. MS 40th Inf. Co.K 2nd Lt.
Robertson, William A. TN 14th Cav.
Robertson, William A. TX 17th Cav. Co.F
Robertson, William A. VA Lt.Arty. Otey's Co.
Robertson, William B. GA 22nd Inf. Co.E
Robertson, William B. LA 1st Hvy.Arty. (Reg.) Co.B Capt.
Robertson, William B. LA Miles' Legion Co.C
Robertson, William B. MS 31st Inf. Co.D
Robertson, William B. NC 34th Inf. Co.I
Robertson, William B. VA 14th Inf. Co.I Sgt.
Robertson, William C. GA 36th (Villepigue's) Inf. Co.B
Robertson, William C. MS 7th Inf. Co.I
Robertson, William C. MO Inf. 8th Bn. Co.F
Robertson, William C. MO 9th Inf. Co.K
Robertson, William C. TN 54th Inf. Co.G
Robertson, William C. TX 11th Inf. Co.I Cpl.
Robertson, William C. VA 2nd Inf.Loc.Def. Co.C
Robertson, William C. 1st Conf.Inf. Co.B, 1st Co.F
Robertson, William D. VA 28th Inf. Co.D
Robertson, Wm. D. Gen. & Staff Hosp.Stew.
Robertson, William E. AL Lt.Arty. Ward's Btty.
Robertson, William E. VA 3rd Cav. Co.A
Robertson, William E.F. VA 38th Inf. Co.B Cpl.
Robertson, William F. MS Cav. Jeff Davis Legion Co.D
Robertson, William F. SC 6th Inf. Asst.Surg.
Robertson, Wm. F. Gen. & Staff Surg.
Robertson, William G. AL 18th Inf. Co.I

Robertson, William G. GA Inf. 27th Bn. Co.E
  1st Lt.
Robertson, William G. MO 2nd Cav. Co.G
Robertson, William H. AL 12th Inf. Co.A
Robertson, William H. AL 41st Inf. Co.F
Robertson, William H., Jr. AL 41st Inf. Co.F
Robertson, William H. AR 36th Inf. Co.A
Robertson, William H. FL 7th Inf. Co.C 2nd Lt.
Robertson, William H. GA 22nd Inf. Co.A
Robertson, William H. GA Cobb's Legion Co.A
  1st Sgt.
Robertson, William H. MO 6th Inf. Co.I Cpl.
Robertson, William H. MO 6th Inf. Co.I
Robertson, William H. MS 30th Inf. Co.E
Robertson, William H. NC 3rd Cav. (41st
  St.Troops) Co.K
Robertson, William H. NC 3rd Cav. (41st
  St.Troops) Co.K
Robertson, William H. NC 2nd Arty. (36th
  St.Troops) Co.G Music.
Robertson, William H. NC 64th Inf. Co.A
Robertson, William H. TN 37th Inf. Co.G
Robertson, William H. TN 55th (McKoin's) Inf.
  Dillehay's Co.
Robertson, William H., Jr. VA 5th Cav. (12 mo.
  '61-2) Co.D
Robertson, William H. VA 1st Arty. Co.F Cpl.
Robertson, William H. VA Arty. Dance's Co.
Robertson, William H. VA 23rd Inf. Co.C
Robertson, William H. VA 24th Inf. Co.I
Robertson, William H. VA 32nd Inf. Co.G
Robertson, William H. VA 86th Mil. Co.F
Robertson, William H. Cav. Robertson's Brig.
  Surg.
Robertson, William H. Conf.Cav. Wood's Regt.
  Co.E Cpl.
Robertson, Wm. H. Gen. & Staff Hosp.Stew.
Robertson, William Henry MO Lt.Arty. Parsons'
  Co. Cpl.
Robertson, William Henry TN 8th Inf. Co.K
  Cpl.
Robertson, William H.H. MS 8th Inf. Co.K
Robertson, William H.K. VA 18th Inf. Co.A
Robertson, William H.K. VA 21st Inf. Co.H
Robertson, William J. AL 37th Inf. Co.B
Robertson, William J. AL 48th Inf. New Co.G
Robertson, William J. MS 11th (Perrin's) Cav.
  Co.I
Robertson, William J. MS Inf. 1st St.Troops
  Co.F
Robertson, William J. NC 45th Inf. Co.F Sgt.
Robertson, William J. SC 14th Inf. Co.I 1st Lt.
Robertson, William J. VA 19th Inf. Co.B
Robertson, William J. VA 23rd Inf. Co.K
Robertson, William J. VA 56th Inf. Co.D Cpl.
Robertson, William K. NC 64th Inf. Co.F
Robertson, William K. SC 4th St.Troops Co.C
Robertson, William L. AR Inf. Clark's Regt.
  Foster's Co.
Robertson, William L. LA Inf. 9th Bn. Co.D
Robertson, William L. LA 14th Inf. Co.I
Robertson, William L. MS 7th Inf. Co.D Cpl.
Robertson, William L. MS 35th Inf. Co.G Sgt.
Robertson, William L. SC 6th Res. Co.E 1st Lt.
Robertson, William L. SC 24th Inf. Co.I
Robertson, William L. TX Inf. Whaley's Co.

Robertson, William L. Conf.Cav. Clarkson's Bn.
  Ind.Rangers Co.D
Robertson, William M. AL 17th Inf. Co.D
Robertson, William M. AL 43rd Inf. Co.D
Robertson, William M. AL 47th Inf. Co.D
Robertson, William M. GA 7th Inf. Co.E
Robertson, William M. GA 10th Inf. Co.D
Robertson, William M. GA Cobb's Legion Co.G
Robertson, William M. MS 38th Cav. Co.L Sgt.
Robertson, William M. MS 1st (Johnston's) Inf.
  Co.A
Robertson, William M. MS 17th Inf. Co.F
Robertson, William M. TN 38th Inf. Co.L Sgt.
Robertson, William M. TX Cav. Bourland's
  Regt. Co.K
Robertson, William N. MS 1st Cav. Co.B
Robertson, William O. AL 44th Inf. Co.I
Robertson, William O. VA Inf. 44th Bn. Co.E
Robertson, William P. GA 31st Inf. Co.H
Robertson, William P. MS Inf. 2nd Bn. Co.C
  Sgt.
Robertson, William P. MS 48th Inf. Co.C Sgt.
Robertson, William R. AL 41st Inf. Co.D
Robertson, William R. FL 6th Inf. Co.D Sgt.
Robertson, William R. TX 33rd Cav. Co.D 2nd
  Lt.
Robertson, William S. AL 36th Inf. Co.I
Robertson, William S. AR 1st Mtd.Rifles Co.H
Robertson, William S. AR 9th Inf. Old Co.B,
  Co.G,F
Robertson, William S. GA Cobb's Legion
  Co.B,G
Robertson, William S. SC 2nd Cav. Co.E
Robertson, William S. TN 63rd Inf. Co.D
Robertson, William S. VA 21st Inf. Co.F Sgt.
Robertson, William S. VA 27th Inf. Co.G Sgt.
Robertson, William S.B. SC 5th Cav. Co.K
Robertson, William T. MS Cav. Hughes' Bn.
  Co.B Sgt.
Robertson, William T. MS 30th Inf. Co.D
Robertson, William T. MO 2nd Inf. Co.C Cpl.
Robertson, William T. TN Cav. 7th Bn. (Ben-
  nett's) Co.C
Robertson, William T. SC 24th Inf. Co.K
Robertson, William T. TN Lt.Arty. Lynch's Co.
Robertson, William T. TN 60th Mtd.Inf.
Robertson, William T. VA 27th Inf. Co.G
Robertson, William T. VA 38th Inf. Co.K
Robertson, William T. VA 44th Inf. Co.H
  Sr.2nd Lt.
Robertson, William T. VA 49th Inf. Co.H
Robertson, William Thomas MO Inf. 3rd Bn.
  Co.D
Robertson, William W. MO Cav. Wood's Regt.
  Co.B Sgt.
Robertson, Willis MO 1st & 3rd Cons.Cav. Co.E
Robertson, Willis MO 10th Inf. Co.K Cpl.
Robertson, Willis H. AL 9th Inf.
Robertson, Willis M. GA Conscr.
Robertson, Wilson AR 14th (Powers') Inf. Co.C
Robertson, Wilson L. GA 44th Inf. Co.I
Robertson, Winchester TN Cav. 2nd Bn.
  (Biffle's) Co.B
Robertson, Winslow TN 21st (Wilson's) Cav.
  Co.D
Robertson, Winslow TN 21st & 22nd (Cons.)
  Cav. Co.H

Robertson, Winslow TN 13th Inf. Co.I
Robertson, W.J. AL Cav. Shockley's Co. Cpl.
Robertson, W.J. AR 6th Inf. Co.B
Robertson, W.J. GA 4th (Clinch's) Cav. Co.F
Robertson, W.J. MS 20th Inf. Co.D
Robertson, W.J. MS 41st Inf. Co.K
Robertson, W.J. NC 7th Sr.Res. Johnston's Co.
Robertson, W.J. NC 12th Inf. Co.K
Robertson, W.J. NC 62nd Inf. Co.F
Robertson, W.J. SC 2nd St.Troops Co.H
Robertson, W.J. SC 8th Bn.Res. Fishburne's Co.
Robertson, W.J. TX 15th Inf. Co.C
Robertson, W. Jabes B. GA Inf. 4th Bn.
  (St.Guards) Co.H 3rd Lt.
Robertson, W.J.B. GA 11th Cav. Co.H Cpl.
Robertson, W.L. MS 5th Cav. Co.E Cpl.
Robertson, W.L. MS 18th Cav. Co.I
Robertson, W.L. SC 17th Inf. Co.E 2nd Lt.
Robertson, W.L. TN 42nd Inf. Co.G
Robertson, W.L. TN 51st (Cons.) Inf. Co.D
Robertson, W.L. TX 9th (Nichols') Inf. Co.E
Robertson, W.L. TX 16th Inf. Co.K Sgt.
Robertson, W.M. AL Res.
Robertson, W.M. AR 19th (Dawson's) Inf. Co.C
  Cpl.
Robertson, W.M. GA 22nd Inf. Co.E
Robertson, W.M. MS 7th Inf. Co.G
Robertson, W.M. NC 33rd Inf. Co.F
Robertson, W.M. SC 7th Cav. Co.G,B
Robertson, W.M. SC Rutledge Mtd.Riflemen &
  Horse Arty. Trenholm's Co.
Robertson, W.M. SC 1st (Hagood's) Inf. 1st
  Co.C
Robertson, W.M. TN 28th (Cons.) Inf. Co.F
Robertson, W.M. TN 84th Inf. Co.B
Robertson, W.M. Conf.Cav. Powers' Regt. Co.A
Robertson, W.N. AL 4th (Russell's) Cav. Co.F
Robertson, W.N. MS 7th Inf. Co.G
Robertson, W.O. VA 58th Inf. Co.D
Robertson, W.P. AL 5th Inf.
Robertson, W.P. LA Mil. Chalmette Regt. Co.G
  Sgt.
Robertson, W.P. MS 7th Inf. Co.K
Robertson, W.P. TX 14th Inf. Co.D
Robertson, W.R. AL 25th Inf. Co.C
Robertson, W.R. TN 22nd (Barteau's) Cav. Co.G
Robertson, W.R. TX Inf. 3rd St.Troops Co.H
Robertson, W.R. Gen. & Staff Lt.
Robertson, W.S. AL 43rd Inf. Co.D
Robertson, W.S. GA 7th Inf. (St.Guards) Co.A
Robertson, W.S. KY 10th (Johnson's) Cav.
  Co.D,G
Robertson, W.S. VA 4th Cav. Co.D
Robertson, W.T. MS 11th Inf. Co.D
Robertson, W.T. SC 16th & 24th (Cons.) Inf.
  Co.H
Robertson, W.T. MS 4th Cav. Co.H Sgt.
Robertson, W.T. MS 5th Cav. Co.E
Robertson, W.T. MS 15th Inf. Co.K
Robertson, W.T. MS 35th Inf. Co.C
Robertson, W.T. TN 7th (Duckworth's) Cav.
  Co.F 1st Sgt.
Robertson, W.T. TN 21st & 22nd (Cons.) Cav.
  Co.D
Robertson, W.T. TN 22nd (Barteau's) Cav. Co.D
Robertson, W.T. TN 49th Inf. Co.E
Robertson, W.T. TN 84th Inf. Co.B

Robertson, W.T.L. GA 40th Inf. Co.A
Robertson, W.V. KY 7th Mtd.Inf. Co.G
Robertson, W.V. TN 3rd (Forrest's) Cav.
Robertson, W.W. MS 7th Inf. Co.K
Robertson, W.W. MS 24th Inf. Co.B
Robertson, W.W. MO 8th Inf. Co.E
Robertson, W.W. NC 43rd Inf. Co.F
Robertson, W.W. SC Inf. 3rd Bn. Co.G
Robertson, W.W. TX 13th Vol. 1st Co.K
Robertson, W.W. TX 15th Inf. 2nd Co.F Sgt.
Robertson, W.W. VA 1st (Farinholt's) Res. Co.D
Robertson, W.W. VA 53rd Inf. Co.A
Robertson, W.Y. MS 41st Inf. Co.L
Robertson, Wyatt NC Walker's Bn. Thomas'
    Legion Co.A
Robertson, Wyatt A. AL 37th Inf. Co.B
Robertson, Wyndham VA Lt.Arty. Jeffress' Co.
    Cpl.
Robertson, Y.A. TX Inf. 3rd St.Troops Co.H
Robertson, Y.H. SC 6th Inf. 1st Co.D, 2nd Co.G
Robertson, Young SC 9th Res. Co.K
Robertson, Z. SC 3rd Inf. Co.A
Robertson, Z.A. MS Inf. Comfort's Co.
Robertson, Zachariah TN 37th Inf. Co.D
Robertson, Zadoc TN 9th Cav. Co.E
Robertson, Zadock AL 3rd Res. Co.K
Robertson, Zadock TN 61st Mtd.Inf. Co.I
Robery, M. LA 2nd Res.Corps Co.A
Robes, McGarcia LA Mil. 5th Regt.Eur.Brig.
    (Spanish Regt.) Co.2
Robes, M.G. LA Mil. Fire Bn. Co.G
Robeson, A. NC 1st Jr.Res. Co.E
Robeson, Albert NC 2nd Arty. (36th St.Troops)
    Co.H
Robeson, Albert T. NC 51st Inf. Hosp.Stew.
Robeson, Alex AL 4th Cav.
Robeson, Alexander H. NC 2nd Arty. (36th
    St.Troops) Co.H
Robeson, A.M. MS 17th Inf. Co.G
Robeson, Cad. NC 2nd Arty. (36th St.Troops)
    Co.H
Robeson, Calvin C. TN 5th (McKenzie's) Cav.
    Co.I
Robeson, D. NC Cav. 16th Bn. Co.H
Robeson, David AR 7th Cav. Co.E
Robeson, David G. NC Hvy.Arty. 1st Bn. Co.A
    2nd Lt.
Robeson, D.J. SC 1st St.Troops Co.H
Robeson, E.A. SC 3rd Bn.Res. Co.D
Robeson, Eliphas NC 62nd Inf. Co.D
Robeson, E.N. NC 2nd Arty. (36th St.Troops)
    Co.B
Robeson, Evander N. NC 18th Inf. Co.K 1st Lt.
Robeson, E.W. SC Arty. Manigault's Bn. 2nd
    Co.C
Robeson, George SC 8th Inf. Co.C
Robeson, George M. SC 1st St.Troops Co.H
Robeson, H.C. NC 3rd Arty. (40th St.Troops)
    Co.I
Robeson, Jackson SC 1st (Butler's) Inf. Co.K,I
Robeson, James MS 1st Bn.S.S. Co.D
Robeson, Jas. 2nd Conf.Inf. Co.H
Robeson, James McK. NC 2nd Arty. (36th
    St.Troops) Co.H
Robeson, J.E. SC 6th Cav. Co.K,D
Robeson, J.K. NC 46th Inf. Co.B
Robeson, J. Madison TN 43rd Inf. Co.D

Robeson, John E. SC 5th Bn.Res. Co.C
Robeson, John H. AL 8th Inf. Co.D Bvt.2nd Lt.
Robeson, John W. NC 16th Inf. Co.L
Robeson, Joseph J.S. LA 31st Inf. Co.I
Robeson, J.P. NC Cav. 16th Bn. Co.H
Robeson, J.P. NC 60th Inf. Co.K
Robeson, M.A. NC 60th Inf. Co.K
Robeson, Malcolm NC 2nd Arty. (36th
    St.Troops) Co.H
Robeson, Matthew P. NC 2nd Arty. (36th
    St.Troops) Co.H
Robeson, M.W. NC 60th Inf. Co.K
Robeson, N. NC 3rd Jr.Res. Co.I
Robeson, Needham NC 4th Cav. (59th
    St.Troops) Co.C
Robeson, N.L. AL 8th Cav. Co.B
Robeson, Peter NC Hvy.Arty. 1st Bn. Co.C
Robeson, Peter L. GA 10th Inf. Co.F
Robeson, R.W. GA 1st (Fannin's) Res. Co.H
Robeson, Samuel H. SC 4th Cav. Co.A Sgt.
Robeson, Samuel H. SC Cav. 12th Bn. Co.A
    Sgt.
Robeson, S.H. SC 6th Cav. Co.D
Robeson, S.H. SC Arty. Manigault's Bn. 2nd
    Co.C
Robeson, T.F. NC 60th Inf. Co.K Ord.Sgt.
Robeson, Thomas NC Hvy.Arty. 1st Bn. Co.C
Robeson, Thomas W. NC 2nd Arty. (36th
    St.Troops) Co.B Sgt.
Robeson, T.Z. TN 50th Inf. Co.I
Robeson, W.A. SC 3rd Bn.Res. Co.D
Robeson, William AL 14th Inf.
Robeson, William NC 18th Inf. Co.G
Robeson, William A. TN 43rd Inf. Co.D Sgt.
Robeson, William B. AL 3rd Inf. Co.K
Robeson, William M. NC 25th Inf. Co.B
Robeson, William O. NC 18th Inf. Co.K,B 1st
    Lt.
Robeson, William R. NC 28th Inf. Co.H
Robeson, William T. NC 2nd Arty. (36th
    St.Troops) Co.B
Robeson, William T. NC 18th Inf. Co.K
Robeson, William W. MS Cav. Stockdale's Bn.
    Co.A,B Artif.
Robeson, W.O. NC 2nd Arty. (36th St.Troops)
    Co.B
Robeson, W.W. MS 4th Cav. Co.B Artif.
Robesson, Benjamin F. TX 37th Cav. Co.B
Robet, W.S. MS Cav. (St.Troops) Gamblin's Co.
Robetson, B.H. TN 84th Inf. Co.B
Robetson, M. TX 22nd Inf. Co.H
Robetson, McKager MO 8th Inf. Co.B
Robey, Archer N. VA 20th Inf. Co.B
Robey, Archer N. VA 59th Inf. 2nd Co.H Cpl.
Robey, Austin VA 38th Inf. Co.F
Robey, Charles F. VA 55th Inf. Co.M
Robey, C.O. VA 8th Inf. Co.G Cpl.
Robey, David A. TN 3rd (Lillard's) Mtd.Inf.
    Co.A
Robey, E. KY 8th & 12th (Cons.) Cav. Co.F
    2nd Lt.
Robey, E. KY 8th Mtd.Inf. Co.A
Robey, Francis E. VA Cav. Mosby's Regt.
    (Part.Rangers) Co.A
Robey, George D. KY 6th Mtd.Inf. Co.I
Robey, George H. MS Inf. 1st Bn.St.Troops
    (12 mo. '62-3) Co.C

Robey, George W. VA 38th Inf. Co.F
Robey, H.A. MD Arty. 2nd Btty.
Robey, James G. VA 6th Cav. Co.F
Robey, James S. KY 6th Mtd.Inf. Co.I Sgt.
Robey, J.H. GA 11th Inf. Co.G
Robey, John VA Hvy.Arty. 18th Bn. Co.E
Robey, John N. VA 2nd Inf. Co.A
Robey, John N. VA 60th Inf. Co.G
Robey, John W. KY Morgan's Men Co.G Sgt.
Robey, John W. VA Cav. Mosby's Regt.
    (Part.Rangers) Co.A
Robey, J.T. VA 1st (Farinholt's) Res. Co.D
Robey, J.W. VA 8th Inf. Co.E
Robey, L. VA 18th Cav. 2nd Co.E
Robey, Lucian R. GA 1st (Olmstead's) Inf. Co.C
Robey, Thomas VA Lt.Arty. W.H. Rice's Co.
Robey, Towney MD 1st Cav. Co.E 1st Sgt.
Robey, Townley VA 1st Cav. 2nd Co.K Sgt.
Robey, Townley VA 24th Cav. Co.F Sgt.
Robey, T.P. VA 56th Inf.
Robey, W.B. AL 47th Inf. Co.F
Robey, Wesley KY Cav. 2nd Bn. (Dortch's)
    Co.C
Robey, William MD Cav. 2nd Bn. Co.G
Robey, William VA Hvy.Arty. 19th Bn. 2nd
    Co.C Cpl.
Robey, William VA 17th Inf. Co.E
Robey, William VA 38th Inf. Co.F
Robey, William B. VA 9th Cav. Co.E
Robey, William B. VA 1st Inf. Co.I
Robey, William H. MD Inf. 2nd Bn. Co.G
Robey, William T. MD Arty. 1st Btty.
Robey, W.J. VA 8th Inf. Co.G
Robi, Charles LA 1st Inf.
Robi, M. LA Mil. 2nd Regt. French Brig. Co.1
Robic, Gustave LA Mil. Pointe Coupee Regt.
    Co.D Sgt.
Robich, Timothy LA Inf. (Conf.Guards
    Resp.Bn.) 16th Bn. Co.B Music.
Robichan, T. Exch.Bn. 1st Co.B,CSA
Robichand, A.E. LA Pointe Coupee Arty.
Robichand, Oscar LA Inf. 9th Bn. Co.C,A
Robichand, Thimon LA Inf. 10th Bn. Co.F
Robichaus, Theodule LA Inf.Cons. 18th Regt. &
    Yellow Jacket Bn. Co.F
Robichaux, Charles LA 1st Hvy.Arty. (Reg.)
    Co.C
Robichaux, Desire P. LA 4th Inf. Co.E
Robichaux, E. LA Mil. LaFourche Regt.
Robichaux, Edgar LA Mil. LaFourche Regt.
Robichaux, Joseph LA Mil. LaFourche Regt.
Robichaux, Leo LA 18th Inf. Co.G
Robichaux, Louis LA 26th Inf. Co.C
Robichaux, Theodule LA 18th Inf. Co.G,F Sgt.
Robichaux, Theophile P. LA 4th Inf. Co.E
Robichaux, Phiphole LA Mil. LaFourche Regt.
Robichaux, Pierre G. LA Mil. LaFourche Regt.
Robichaux, V. LA Mil. LaFourche Regt.
Robicheau, James LA Inf.Cons. 18th Regt. &
    Yellow Jacket Bn. Co.D
Robicheau, Lufroy LA Conscr.
Robicheau, Valery LA Conscr.
Robicheau, Valiere LA Conscr.
Robicheaux, Leo LA Inf.Cons. 18th Regt. & Yel-
    low Jacket Bn. Co.F
Robicheaux, Louis LA 26th Inf. Co.D
Robicheaux, Thephile LA 26th Inf. Co.D Sgt.

Robider, A. GA Inf. 18th Bn. Co.A
Robider, Anthony L. GA 1st (Olmstead's) Inf.
  Co.C, Gordon's Co.
Robider, Anthony L. GA 63rd Inf. Co.B
Robier, Leon Conf.Inf. Tucker's Regt. Co.D
Robier, Philip SC Lt.Arty. Beauregard's Co.
Robillard, Dorsin LA Pointe Coupee Arty.
  Bugler
Robillard, Emile LA 2nd Cav. Co.K
Robillard, Ludovic LA 2nd Cav. Co.K
Robillard, Maximillien LA 2nd Cav. Co.K
Robillard, Octave LA 2nd Cav. Co.K
Robillard, Ovide LA 2nd Cav. Co.K
Robillard, Savemen LA Mil. Knaps' Co. (Fausse
  River Guards)
Robillard, Savinien LA Pointe Coupee Arty.
Robilliard, Adamar LA Pointe Coupee Arty.
Robin, --- GA 1st Bn.S.S. Co.D Cook
Robin, --- 1st Cherokee Mtd.Rifles Co.H
Robin, A. LA 18th Inf. Co.H
Robin, A. LA Inf.Cons. 18th Regt. & Yellow
  Jacket Bn. Co.E
Robin, A.J. GA 17th Inf. Co.G
Robin, August N. LA 28th (Thomas') Inf. Co.K
  1st Lt.
Robin, Casimir LA 18th Inf. Co.B
Robin, Charles LA 1st (Nelligan's) Inf. Co.C
Robin, E. LA 7th Cav. Co.D Sgt.
Robin, E. LA Inf.Cons. 18th Regt. & Yellow
  Jacket Bn. Co.F
Robin, E. LA 30th Inf. Co.F
Robin, E. LA Mil. Orleans Guards Regt. Co.C
Robin, Emile LA 28th (Gray's) Inf. Co.K
Robin, Emile LA C.S. Zouave Bn.
Robin, Ernest LA Mil. Orleans Guards Regt.
  Co.C Capt.
Robin, Evariste LA 18th Inf. Co.B Cpl.
Robin, F. LA Mil. 4th Regt. 2nd Brig. 1st Div.
  Co.D 3rd Lt.
Robin, J. LA 18th Inf. Co.K
Robin, Jerome LA Inf.Cons. 18th Regt. & Yel-
  low Jacket Bn. Co.K
Robin, Joseph LA 28th (Thomas') Inf. Co.K
Robin, Louis LA 18th Inf. Co.B
Robin, Louis LA C.S. Zouave Bn.
Robin, Napoleon LA 28th (Thomas') Inf. Co.K
  Capt.
Robin, Numa LA Conscr.
Robin, Oscar LA Arty. 5th Field Btty. (Pelican
  Lt.Arty.) Capt.
Robin, Oscar LA Res.Corps 1st Lt.,ADC
Robin, P. LA Mil. 4th Regt. French Brig. Col.
Robin, Pierre LA Mil.Bn. French Vol. Co.10
  Capt.
Robin, Theodose S. LA 8th Inf. Co.F
Robin, Theodose S. LA 28th (Thomas') Inf.
  Co.K 2nd Lt.
Robin, W. Jackson's Co.,CSA
Robin, Wakin LA Miles' Legion Co.A Sgt.
Robin, William GA Inf. (Anderson Guards) An-
  derson's Co.
Robineau, William F. VA 52nd Mil. Co.B Sgt.
Robinet, Allen GA 34th Inf. Co.B
Robinet, A.M. GA Inf. Pool's Co.
Robinet, C.W. TN 12th (Green's) Cav. Co.K
Robinet, C.W. TN 21st Inf. Co.A
Robinet, Franklin J. VA 64th Mtd.Inf. Co.E

Robinet, James MO 4th Inf. Co.K
Robinet, James P. VA 23rd Cav. Co.H
Robinet, Louis N. LA Arty. 1st Field Btty.
Robinet, William M. VA Inf. 45th Bn. Co.B
Robinett, A.F.A. LA 16th Inf. Co.K
Robinett, Allen GA Cherokee Legion (St.Guards)
  Co.C
Robinett, Andrew J. GA 59th Inf. Co.H Sgt.
Robinett, Andrew J. MO 11th Inf. Co.B Cpl.
Robinett, Daniel GA 39th Inf. Co.E
Robinett, Daniel GA Cherokee Legion
  (St.Guards) Co.C
Robinett, Daniel J. GA Inf. 3rd Bn. Co.F Music.
Robinett, David VA 25th Cav. Co.B
Robinett, D.J. VA Mil. Scott Cty.
Robinett, Elisha GA 28th Inf. Co.D
Robinett, E.S. VA 64th Mtd.Inf. Co.C
Robinett, Francis M. VA 8th Cav. Co.F
Robinett, George VA 11th Bn.Res. Co.A
Robinett, George VA Mil. Stowers' Co.
Robinett, George W. VA 8th Cav. Co.F
Robinett, George W. VA 25th Cav. Co.B,H
Robinett, G.L. GA Inf. 19th Bn. (St.Guards)
  Co.D
Robinett, Hiram VA 11th Bn.Res. Co.A Sgt.
Robinett, Isaac VA Inf. 21st Bn. 2nd Co.C Cpl.
Robinett, Isaac W. VA 64th Mtd.Inf. Co.D
Robinett, J. VA 45th Inf. Co.F
Robinett, James TX 5th Inf. Co.H
Robinett, James VA Cav. Swann's Bn. Watkins'
  Co.
Robinett, James A. VA 25th Cav. Co.B
Robinett, James F. VA 16th Inf. Co.F Capt.
Robinett, James M. VA 25th Cav. Co.D
Robinett, James M. VA 48th Inf. Co.A
Robinett, James M. VA Mil. Scott Cty.
Robinett, James N. MO 3rd Cav. Co.F
Robinett, James S. VA 11th Bn.Res. Co.A 2nd
  Lt.
Robinett, Jasper J. MO 3rd Cav. Co.F
Robinett, Jefferson C. VA 25th Cav. Co.B
Robinett, Jesse F. VA 64th Mtd.Inf. Franklin's
  Co.
Robinett, J.F. TX 11th Cav. Co.F
Robinett, J.L. TX 10th Cav. Co.H 2nd Lt.
Robinett, John MS 1st Lt.Arty. Co.I
Robinett, John VA 51st Inf. Co.A
Robinett, John R. MS Inf. 3rd Bn. Co.K
Robinett, John W. TX Cav. 6th Bn. Co.C Cpl.
Robinett, John W. TX 20th Inf. Co.H
Robinett, Joseph Newton MO 8th Inf. Co.E
Robinett, J.R. AR 2nd Inf.Asst.Surg.
Robinett, J.R. Shelley's Staff Asst.Surg.
Robinett, J.S. VA Mil. Scott Cty.
Robinett, J.W. MS 2nd Part.Rangers Co.C
Robinett, Leander C. LA 4th Inf. Co.E
Robinett, L.G. Conf.Cav. Wood's Regt. Co.K
Robinett, M. GA 7th Inf. (St.Guards) Co.A
Robinett, Mardly L. GA 21st Inf. Co.G
Robinett, Marion VA 8th Cav. Co.F
Robinett, Marion VA Cav. 47th Bn. Co.B
Robinett, Martin J. VA 36th Inf. 2nd Co.G
Robinett, M.M. TX 10th Cav. Co.H Sgt.
Robinett, Nathan VA Cav. 34th Bn. Co.C
Robinett, Patin G. VA 198th Mil.
Robinett, Patton G. VA 22nd Cav. Co.F
Robinett, R.N. TN 48th (Nixon's) Inf. Co.F

Robinett, Samuel VA 25th Cav. Co.D,B,H
Robinett, Samuel VA 64th Mtd.Inf. Co.C
Robinett, Samuel E. VA Mil. Scott Cty.
Robinett, Samuel M. TX Cav. 6th Bn. Co.C
Robinett, Samuel R.T. VA 25th Cav. Co.B Cpl.
Robinett, S.R.T. VA Mil. Scott Cty.
Robinett, Stephen VA 16th Cav. Co.I
Robinett, Stephen VA 45th Inf. Co.H
Robinett, W.D. VA Burks' Regt.Loc.Def.
Robinett, W.H. AL 12th Cav. Co.B
Robinett, Wilbur VA 21st Cav. 2nd Co.E
Robinett, Wiley TX 20th Inf. Co.H
Robinett, William GA 28th Inf. Co.D
Robinett, William MS 1st Lt.Arty. Co.I
Robinett, William VA 25th Cav. Co.B,H
Robinett, William VA Inf. 21st Bn. 2nd Co.C
Robinett, William A. VA 45th Inf. Co.H
Robinett, William H. GA 12th Inf. Co.K Cpl.
Robinett, William S. VA 25th Cav. Co.D,B,H
Robinett, W.J. TX 20th Inf. Co.H
Robinett, W.W. LA 16th Inf. Co.K
Robinett, Wyley B. GA 21st Inf. Co.G,I
Robinett, Zachariah O. VA 64th Mtd.Inf. Co.D
  Sgt.
Robinette, Charles LA 1st (Strawbridge's) Inf.
  Co.B
Robinette, Jefferson VA 21st Cav. Co.B Cpl.
Robinette, Jefferson B. TX 18th Inf. Co.C
Robinette, W.C. MO 6th Cav. Co.K
Robinette, William VA 21st Cav. 2nd Co.E,
  Co.B
Robins, --- TX Cav. Mann's Regt. Co.C
Robins, A. GA 1st Inf. (St.Guards) Co.B
Robins, A. TX 9th (Young's) Inf. Co.I Sgt.
Robins, Aaron AR Cav. Gordon's Regt. Co.F
Robins, Abel AL Cav. Hardie's Bn.Res. Co.E
Robins, Abner NC 2nd Inf. Co.A
Robins, Albert H. VA 1st Inf. Co.A
Robins, Albert H. VA 12th Inf. Co.G
Robins, Alexander MS Cav. 1st Bn. (McNair's)
  St.Troops Co.C
Robins, Allen VA 1st Cav. Co.B
Robins, A.M. GA Phillips' Legion Co.A
Robins, A.M. TN 51st (Cons.) Inf. Co.B
Robins, Amos C. GA 40th Inf. Co.D
Robins, A.N. MO Cav. Coleman's Regt. Co.F
Robins, Andrew J. AR 33rd Inf. Co.I Bvt.2nd
  Lt.
Robins, Andy Mead's Conf.Cav. Co.A
Robins, Augustus AL 22nd Cav. Co.B
Robins, Augustus AL 27th Inf. Co.B
Robins, A. Warner VA 24th Cav. Co.D
Robins, B.C.T. VA Loc.Def. Sutherland's Co.
Robins, Benjamin 1st Cherokee Mtd.Vol. 2nd
  Co.G Cpl.
Robins, Benjamin F. VA 53rd Inf. Co.B
Robins, Benjamin L. TX 37th Cav. Co.K Cpl.
Robins, B.F. TN 18th (Newsom's) Cav. Co.I
Robins, B.R. TN 12th (Green's) Cav. Co.A
Robins, Carter AL 36th Inf. Co.H
Robins, C.W. TN 12th Inf. Co.F
Robins, C.W. TN 12th (Cons.) Inf. Co.B
Robins, Daniel MO 1st Cav. Co.A Black.
Robins, Daniel MO 12th Cav. Co.B
Robins, Daniel P. SC 1st (Orr's) Rifles Co.E
  Bvt.2nd Lt.
Robins, D.B. MS 10th Cav. Co.A Sgt.

Robins, D.D. GA 19th Inf. Co.I
Robins, D.H. VA 59th Inf. 1st Co.B Cpl.
Robins, D.H. VA 60th Inf. Co.A Cpl.
Robins, E. NC 8th Sr.Res. Williams' Co.
Robins, E.B. AL 28th Inf. Co.C
Robins, E.B. SC 5th St.Troops Co.A
Robins, Edley H. MO 8th Cav. Co.B,G 2nd Lt.
Robins, Edward C. MS 6th Cav. Co.B
Robins, Edward E. LA 19th Inf. Co.B 1st Lt.
Robins, E.H. MS 6th Cav. Co.B
Robins, E.K. NC 3rd Jr.Res. Co.F
Robins, E.L. MS 41st Inf. Co.B
Robins, Epperson VA 22nd Cav. Co.D
Robins, E.R. AL 31st Inf. Co.C
Robins, E.S. AL 50th Inf. Co.I
Robins, E.W. GA 6th Inf. (St.Guards) Co.I
Robins, F.F. SC Mil. Charbonnier's Co.
Robins, Francis TN 35th Inf. Co.L
Robins, Francis TN 36th Inf. Co.L
Robins, G. AL 20th Inf. Co.K
Robins, George W. AL 1st Bn. Hilliard's Legion
    Vol. Co.F
Robins, Gray MS 7th Cav. Co.F
Robins, Green D. AR 36th Inf. Co.B
Robins, H. AL 24th Inf. Co.G
Robins, H.A. GA Phillips' Legion Co.B
Robins, Henry S. LA 1st Cav. Co.E
Robins, H.F. GA 1st Inf. (St.Guards) Co.I
Robins, Hiram VA 22nd Cav. Co.D Cpl.
Robins, Hiram S. VA 37th Inf. Co.I
Robins, H.J. TN 25th Inf.
Robins, H.K. AR 24th Inf. Co.A
Robins, H.R. AL 42nd Inf. Co.E
Robins, Ira AL 56th Part.Rangers Co.F
Robins, Isaac VA Inf. 21st Bn. 2nd Co.D
Robins, Isaac VA 64th Mtd.Inf. Co.D
Robins, J. GA 12th (Robinson's) Cav.
    (St.Guards) Co.I
Robins, J. GA 13th Cav. Co.A
Robins, J. MO 1st Brig.St.Guard
Robins, J.A. TX 19th Inf. Co.E
Robins, James MS 1st Cav. Co.F
Robins, James MO Lt.Arty. 3rd Btty.
Robins, James A. MS 7th Cav. Co.C
Robins, James A. VA 9th Cav. Co.H
Robins, James B. GA 25th Inf. Co.E
Robins, James B. GA 28th Inf. Co.E Cpl.
Robins, James E. VA 37th Inf. Co.I
Robins, James H. AL 31st Cav. Co.I
Robins, James H. SC 1st (Orr's) Rifles Co.C
    2nd Lt.
Robins, James K. TN Conscr. (Cp. of Instr.)
Robins, James R. GA Phillips' Legion Co.A
Robins, James W. VA 21st Mil. Co.A
Robins, J.C. AR Lt.Arty. Rivers' Btty.
Robins, J.C. MS 7th Cav. Co.E
Robins, J.C. MO Inf. 5th Regt.St.Guard Co.D
Robins, J. Calvin AR 25th Inf. Co.K
Robins, Jefferson F. AR 4th Inf. Co.C
Robins, Jefferson F. AR 33rd Inf. Co.I Sgt.
Robins, J.H. TX 32nd Cav. Co.K
Robins, J.H. VA 5th Inf. Co.F
Robins, J.H. VA Mil. Scott Cty.
Robins, J.J. MS 1st Cav. Co.D
Robins, J.K. TN 62nd Mtd.Inf. Co.E
Robins, J.M. LA Ogden's Cav. Co.B
Robins, J.M. TN 31st Inf. Co.C 2nd Lt.

Robins, Joel VA 26th Inf. Co.E Cpl.
Robins, John AL 18th Inf. Co.G Cpl.
Robins, John AR Cav. Gordon's Regt. Co.K
Robins, John GA Inf. (Anderson Guards) Ander-
    son's Co.
Robins, John MS 38th Cav. Co.E
Robins, John NC 30th Inf. Co.C
Robins, John NC 39th Inf. Co.E
Robins, John TX Cav. Border's Regt. Co.A Cpl.
Robins, John VA 9th Cav. Co.D
Robins, John VA 21st Mil. Co.A
Robins, John VA 48th Inf. Co.A
Robins, John VA 92nd Mil. Co.A
Robins, John C. GA Hvy.Arty. 22nd Bn. Co.F
Robins, John C. MO 9th Inf. Co.D
Robins, John C. VA 24th Cav. Co.D
Robins, John C. VA Cav. 40th Bn. Co.D
Robins, John C. VA 21st Mil. Co.C
Robins, John E. VA 40th Inf. Co.D
Robins, John J. FL 7th Inf. Co.C
Robins, John L. GA 53rd Inf. Co.C
Robins, John M. NC 22nd Inf. Co.M 1st Lt.
Robins, John M. VA 55th Inf. Co.L
Robins, John V. VA 39th Inf. Co.D Drum.
Robins, John W. VA 26th Inf. Co.A
Robins, John W. VA 26th Inf. Co.F
Robins, Jonathan NC 30th Inf. Co.C
Robins, Joseph F. VA 26th Inf. Co.F Sgt.
Robins, Josiah AL 3rd Cav. Co.C Maj.
Robins, J.R. TN 45th Inf. Co.E
Robins, J.R. TX 37th Cav. Co.K
Robins, J.S. TX 19th Inf. Co.E
Robins, Julius M. AR 4th Inf. Co.C
Robins, J.W. AL 13th Inf. Co.E
Robins, J.W. AR 30th Inf. Co.I
Robins, J.W. MS Cp.Guard (Cp. of Instr. for
    Conscr.)
Robins, J.W. TN 32nd Inf. Co.G
Robins, J.W. TN 46th Inf. Co.A
Robins, J.W. TX 13th Vol. 2nd Co.D
Robins, L. NC 21st Inf. Co.C
Robins, Lansden TN 25th Inf. Co.H Cpl.
Robins, Lemuel M. GA Inf. 3rd Bn. Co.B
Robins, Levi AL 12th Cav. Co.B
Robins, Levi AL 56th Part.Rangers Co.F
Robins, Levi W. MS 26th Inf. Co.I Sgt.
Robins, Levi W. MS 31st Inf. Co.F
Robins, Lewis AR 34th Inf. Co.D
Robins, Logan S. GA 1st Inf. Co.B 1st Lt.
Robins, Louis TN 55th (Brown's) Inf. Co.F
Robins, M. NC 18th Inf. Co.E
Robins, Madison NC 14th Inf. Co.B
Robins, Madison NC 16th Inf. Co.D
Robins, Marmaduke NC 42nd Inf. Co.F
Robins, Martin G. AL 28th Inf. Co.C Cpl.
Robins, Mcfew A. AR 33rd Inf. Co.I Cpl.
Robins, M.H. MS 41st Inf. Co.B
Robins, Milton AL 12th Cav. Co.D,B
Robins, Milton TX Cav. Martin's Regt. Co.C
Robins, M.M. TN 31st Inf. Co.C Sgt.
Robins, Newton NC 39th Inf. Co.E
Robins, Obadiah SC 6th Inf. 1st Co.E, 2nd Co.I
    Cpl.
Robins, Oliver K. VA Hvy.Arty. 19th Bn. 3rd
    Co.E
Robins, Pleasant NC 14th Inf. Co.B
Robins, Pleasant M. GA 39th Inf. Co.F

Robins, R.C. VA Cav. 40th Bn. Co.D Sgt.
Robins, Richard NC 38th Inf. Co.G
Robins, Robert C. VA 24th Cav. Co.D Sgt.
Robins, Robert C., Jr. VA 21st Mil. Co.D,C
    2nd Lt.
Robins, Robert M. 2nd Conf.Eng.Troops Co.H
Robins, Robert P. GA 2nd Res. Co.G
Robins, S. MS 2nd Inf. (A. of !0,000) Co.G
Robins, Samuel GA Phillips' Legion Co.B
Robins, Samuel TN 30th Inf. Co.H
Robins, S.C. TN 5th Inf. 2nd Co.I
Robins, Seaborn GA Phillips' Legion Co.A
Robins, Shelton TX Cav. Martin's Regt. Co.K
Robins, S.L. TN 55th (Brown's) Inf. Co.F
Robins, S.M. GA 1st Inf. (St.Guards) Co.A
Robins, Sol T. MS 26th Inf. Co.D Sgt.
Robins, S.P. MS 2nd (Quinn's St.Troops) Inf.
    Co.D
Robins, Stephen MS 38th Cav. Co.E
Robins, Stephen A. SC 1st (Orr's) Rifles Co.C
    Cpl.
Robins, T. AL 26th (O'Neal's) Inf. Co.E
Robins, T.A. 15th Conf.Cav. Co.E
Robins, T.H. TN Cav. Williams' Co.
Robins, Thomas MO 10th Inf. Co.H Cpl.
Robins, Thomas TX Cav. Madison's Regt. Co.G
Robins, Thomas VA 26th Inf. Co.F 1st Sgt.
Robins, Thomas A. VA 34th Inf. Co.A 1st Lt.
Robins, Thomas C. VA 2nd Inf.Loc.Def. Co.D
Robins, Thomas D. TN 16th (Logwood's) Cav.
    Co.H Capt.
Robins, Thomas W. LA 3rd Cav. Co.I 2nd Lt.
Robins, T.S. LA 4th Inf. New Co.G
Robins, T. Sidney LA 5th Cav. Co.G 2nd Lt.
Robins, Victor AL 3rd Inf. Co.A
Robins, W. TX 7th Cav. Co.G 2nd Lt.
Robins, W.A. GA 1st Inf. (St.Guards) Co.B Sgt.
Robins, W.A. MS 1st Cav. Co.D
Robins, W.A. VA 5th Cav. Co.A
Robins, Waddy T. SC 1st (Orr's) Rifles Co.E
    Sgt.
Robins, Wade NC Inf. Luke's Bn. Co.A
Robins, Washington VA 26th Inf. Co.F
Robins, W.B. VA 5th Cav. AAQM
Robins, W.C. MO Inf. 5th Regt.St.Guard Co.D
Robins, W.F. MS Cav. 1st Bn. (McNair's)
    St.Troops Co.C
Robins, W.G. TN 14th (Neely's) Cav. Co.K
Robins, William AL 28th Inf. Co.L
Robins, William GA 6th Cav. Co.B
Robins, William MS 27th Inf. Co.C
Robins, William MO Lt.Arty. 3rd Btty.
Robins, William SC 6th Inf. 1st Co.E, 2nd Co.I
Robins, William TN Inf. 22nd Bn. Co.H
Robins, William TN 38th Inf. 1st Co.H
Robins, William VA Hvy.Arty. 19th Bn. 3rd
    Co.E
Robins, William VA 21st Mil. Co.D
Robins, William VA 26th Inf. Co.E
Robins, William Aug VA 24th Cav. Co.D
    QMSgt.
Robins, William B. AL 42nd Inf. Co.D
Robins, William D. MS 32nd Inf. Co.E
Robins, Wm. F. Gen. & Staff Chap.
Robins, William H. VA Lt.Arty. W.P. Carter's
    Co. Sgt.Maj.
Robins, William J. GA 36th (Broyles') Inf. Co.C

Robins, William J. VA 39th Inf. Co.C
Robins, William J. Conf.Cav. 6th Bn. Co.G
Robins, William M. AL 10th Cav.
Robins, William M. LA 11th Inf. Co.G
Robins, William T. NC 22nd Inf. Co.M
Robins, William T. (1) VA 9th Cav. Co.H
Robins, William T. VA 24th Cav. Col.
Robins, William T. VA 39th Inf. Co.K
Robins, Winter MS 1st Cav. Co.F
Robins, W.M. SC 1st Cav. Co.H
Robins, W.R. TX Cav. Morgan's Regt. Co.C
Robins, W.T. Gen. & Staff Capt.,AAG
Robinsen, D.T. AL Talladega Cty.Res. R.N.
  Ware's Cav.Co.
Robinson, --- AR 1st Cav. Co.B
Robinson, --- MS 2nd Inf. Co.C
Robinson, --- TX Cav. Border's Regt. Co.K
Robinson, A. LA 3rd (Wingfield's) Cav. Co.G
Robinson, A. LA 22nd Inf. Co.E
Robinson, A. MS 2nd Part.Rangers Co.C
Robinson, A. MS 46th Inf. Co.F
Robinson, A. NC Mallett's Bn. (Cp.Guard) Co.E
Robinson, A. SC Cav. 2nd Bn.Res. Co.B 2nd
  Lt.
Robinson, A. SC Cav. 17th Bn. Co.A
Robinson, A. SC 1st (Butler's) Inf. Co.G
Robinson, A. SC 3rd Inf. Co.A
Robinson, A. VA 4th Cav. Co.A
Robinson, A.A. AL 21st Inf. Co.F
Robinson, A.A. TN 7th Cav. Co.C
Robinson, A.A., Jr. VA 31st Mil. Co.E
Robinson, Aaron MS 10th Inf. Old Co.I
Robinson, Aaron B. NC 25th Inf. Co.C
Robinson, A.B. AL 42nd Inf. Co.H
Robinson, A.B. LA 19th Inf. Co.F
Robinson, A.B. MS 2nd Cav. 2nd Co.G
Robinson, A.B. MS 5th Cav. Co.B Sgt.
Robinson, A.B. MS 5th Inf. Co.B
Robinson, A.B. TN 10th & 11th (Cons.) Cav.
  Co.C
Robinson, A.B. TN 17th Inf. Co.F Music.
Robinson, Abel L. AL 7th Inf. Co.A
Robinson, Abner NC 2nd Bn.Loc.Def.Troops
  Co.B Cpl.
Robinson, Abner NC 7th Home Guards Co.D
Robinson, Abner C. MS 2nd Inf. Co.E
Robinson, Abraham T. AL 10th Inf. Co.C Sgt.
Robinson, Absalom TX 30th Cav. Co.H 1st Sgt.
Robinson, A.C. AL 42nd Inf. Co.H
Robinson, A.C. GA Inf. 1st Bn. (St.Guards)
  Co.B 1st Sgt.
Robinson, A.C. GA Inf. 17th Bn. (St.Guards)
  Fay's Co.
Robinson, A.C. SC 1st Cav. Co.G
Robinson, A.C. SC Hvy.Arty. 15th (Lucas') Bn.
  Co.B
Robinson, A.C. VA Arty. Dance's Co.
Robinson, A.D. VA 31st Inf. Co.H Cpl.
Robinson, Adam GA 24th Inf. Co.F 2nd Lt.
Robinson, Adam A. GA Arty. 11th Bn. (Sumter
  Arty.) Co.A
Robinson, Adam A. GA 1st (Ramsey's) Inf.
  Co.H
Robinson, Adam D. GA 55th Inf. Co.D Sgt.
Robinson, Adam P. NC 12th Inf. Co.A
Robinson, A.G. GA 6th Cav. Co.G Cpl.
Robinson, A.G. GA Smith's Legion Co.F

Robinson, A.J. AL 29th Inf. Co.A
Robinson, A.J. GA Phillips' Legion Co.D,K
Robinson, A.J. LA 22nd (Cons.) Inf. Co.A
Robinson, A.J. MS 12th Cav. Co.B
Robinson, A.J. MS 28th Cav. Co.G
Robinson, A.J. MO Cav. 3rd Bn. Co.E
Robinson, A.J. MO 4th Inf. Co.E
Robinson, A.J. SC 2nd Arty. Co.I
Robinson, A.J. SC Lt.Arty. J.T. Kanapaux's Co.
  (Lafayette Arty.) Teamster
Robinson, A.J. SC 5th Bn.Res. Co.D
Robinson, A.J. TN Lt.Arty. Polk's Btty.
Robinson, A.J. TN 23rd Inf. Co.B
Robinson, A.J. TN 24th Inf. Co.C
Robinson, A.J. TX 5th Cav. Co.E
Robinson, A.J. TX 12th Field Btty. Sgt.
Robinson, A.J. VA 2nd St.Res. Co.E
Robinson, A.L. AL 47th Inf. Co.I
Robinson, A.L. GA 56th Inf. Co.E
Robinson, A.L. KY 2nd (Woodward's) Cav.
  Co.E
Robinson, A.L. MS 35th Inf. Co.D
Robinson, A.L. TX 32nd Cav. Co.I Sgt.
Robinson, Albert LA 4th Cav. Co.E 1st Sgt.
Robinson, Albert LA 12th Inf. Co.H
Robinson, Albert NC 17th Inf. (2nd Org.) Co.E
Robinson, Albert VA Inf. 22nd Bn. Co.G
Robinson, Albert VA 53rd Inf. Co.D
Robinson, Albert B. MS 17th Inf. Co.I
Robinson, Albert B. SC Inf. Hampton Legion
  Co.D
Robinson, Albert G. MO 1st N.E. Cav. Co.F
Robinson, Albert M. TX 5th Cav. Co.K
Robinson, Albert R. LA 12th Inf. Co.D
Robinson, Albert T. NC 20th Inf. Faison's Co.
Robinson, Albert T. NC 61st Inf. Co.A Sgt.
Robinson, Alex SC 5th Cav. Co.D
Robinson, Alex SC 27th Inf. Co.C
Robinson, Alexander FL Cav. 3rd Bn. Co.B
Robinson, Alexander GA 1st (Fannin's) Res.
  Co.E
Robinson, Alexander MS 11th (Perrin's) Cav.
  Co.I
Robinson, Alexander MS 16th Inf. Co.F
Robinson, Alexander NC 23rd Inf. Co.G
Robinson, Alexander NC 31st Inf. Co.E
Robinson, Alexander TN 4th (McLemore's) Cav.
  Co.E
Robinson, Alexander TN 25th Inf. Co.E
Robinson, Alexander VA 8th Cav. Co.F Capt.
Robinson, Alexander VA 29th Inf. Co.C Capt.
Robinson, Alexander VA 60th Inf. Co.B
Robinson, Alexander VA 135th Mil. Co.D
Robinson, Alexander 15th Conf.Cav. Co.D
Robinson, Alexander 3rd Conf.Eng.Troops Co.E
  Artif.
Robinson, Alexander J. FL 6th Inf. Co.D Sgt.
Robinson, Alexander S. NC 30th Inf. Co.C Cpl.
Robinson, Alexander W. GA 38th Inf. Co.E
  Cpl.
Robinson, Alford G. NC 26th Inf. Co.I
Robinson, Alfred MS 2nd Inf. Co.K
Robinson, Alfred NC 32nd Inf. Co.E 2nd Lt.
Robinson, Alfred TX 33rd Cav. Co.D
Robinson, Alfred G. NC 2nd Cav. (19th
  St.Troops) Co.G

Robinson, Alfred G. VA Rockbridge Cty.Res.
  Bacon's Co.
Robinson, Alfred H. TX 13th Vol. 2nd Co.C
  Sgt.Maj.
Robinson, Alfred R. AR 2nd Mtd.Rifles Co.B
  Cpl.
Robinson, Allen SC 2nd Arty. Co.G
Robinson, Allen SC 3rd Res. Co.G Sgt.
Robinson, Allen SC 17th Inf. Co.I
Robinson, Allen H. TN 32nd Inf. Co.I Cpl.
Robinson, Allen H. TN 35th Inf. 2nd Co.F
Robinson, Alpheus VA 6th Cav. Co.H
Robinson, A.M. AL 8th Inf. Co.D
Robinson, A.M. AL 10th Inf. Co.E
Robinson, A.M. AR 16th Inf. Co.A
Robinson, A.M. NC 16th Inf. Co.I
Robinson, A.M. TN 9th Inf. Co.B 2nd Lt.
Robinson, A.M. TX Inf. Timmons' Regt. Co.I
Robinson, A.M. TX Waul's Legion Co.E Cpl.
Robinson, Ambrose MS 2nd Inf. Co.K
Robinson, Amon SC Cav. 10th Bn. Co.B
Robinson, Amon SC 1st (Butler's) Inf. Co.D
Robinson, Amos VA 29th Inf. Co.C, 2nd Co.F
Robinson, Amos 1st Choctaw & Chickasaw
  Mtd.Rifles 2nd Co.K
Robinson, Amos H. TX 2nd Cav. Co.I,K
Robinson, A.N. GA 16th Inf. Co.I
Robinson, Ancyl W. VA 47th Inf. 3rd Co.H
Robinson, And. J. NC 57th Inf. Co.E Sgt.
Robinson, Andrew AR Lt.Arty. Hart's Btty.
Robinson, Andrew AR 10th Inf. Co.C
Robinson, Andrew TN 1st (Carter's) Cav. Co.A
Robinson, Andrew VA 30th Bn.S.S. Co.E Cpl.
Robinson, Andrew D. VA 52nd Inf. Co.E
Robinson, Andrew J. GA 4th Inf. Co.B
Robinson, Andrew J. LA 12th Inf. Co.H
Robinson, Andrew J. LA 22nd Inf. Co.A
Robinson, Andrew J. VA 6th Bn.Res. Co.I
Robinson, Andrew J.M. GA 53rd Inf. Co.I
  Capt.
Robinson, Andrew L. VA 48th Inf. Co.F
Robinson, Andrew M. TX 13th Vol. 2nd Co.A
Robinson, Andrew M.C. TN 7th Inf. Co.A Cpl.
Robinson, Andrew R. VA Arty. L.F. Jones' Co.
Robinson, Andrew S. TN 5th (McKenzie's) Cav.
  Co.E
Robinson, Andy TX 13th Vol. Co.B
Robinson, Anson TX 17th Inf. Co.G
Robinson, Anthony G. TX 18th Cav. Co.G
Robinson, Antoney MO 2nd Inf.
Robinson, A.P. AL 8th Inf. Co.B
Robinson, A.R. GA 10th Inf. Co.E
Robinson, A.R. NC 46th Inf. Co.B
Robinson, A.R. TX 8th Cav. Co.A
Robinson, A.R. VA 25th Cav. Co.H Cpl.
Robinson, A.R. VA 1st Arty. Co.K
Robinson, Archibald P. MS 16th Inf. Co.F 3rd
  Cpl.
Robinson, Arcie C. AR 47th (Crandall's) Cav.
  Co.C
Robinson, Arthur AL 62nd Inf. Co.A
Robinson, Arthur AR 9th Inf. Co.D
Robinson, Arthur SC 4th Cav. Co.K Cpl.
Robinson, Arthur VA Lt.Arty. Arch. Graham's
  Co.
Robinson, Arthur R. MS 2nd Inf. Co.A
Robinson, A.S. AR Cav. McGehee's Regt. Co.I

Robinson, A.S. MS Cav. Drane's Co. (Choctaw Cty.Res.)
Robinson, A.S. MS 14th Inf. Co.K Cpl.
Robinson, A.S. TN 22nd Inf. Co.I
Robinson, Asa AR 1st Mtd.Rifles Co.D
Robinson, Asa AR 30th Inf. Co.D
Robinson, Asa TX 10th Inf. Co.H
Robinson, Asa B. MS 11th Inf. Co.F
Robinson, A.T. AL 29th Inf. Co.A
Robinson, A.T. NC 6th Sr.Res. Co.A Sgt.
Robinson, A.T. SC 2nd Cav. Co.B
Robinson, A.T. Gen. & Staff Hosp.Stew.
Robinson, Augustus NC 32nd Inf. Co.B
Robinson, Austin TX Rangers Co.A
Robinson, A.W. AR 1st (Dobbin's) Cav. Co.H,E
Robinson, A.W. GA 38th Inf. Co.K 2nd Lt.
Robinson, A.W. SC 12th Inf. Co.C
Robinson, A.W. TN 8th (Smith's) Cav. Co.G
Robinson, A.W. 7th Conf.Cav. Co.K
Robinson, A.Z. TX 11th Inf. Co.B
Robinson, B. MS Lt.Arty. Turner's Co.
Robinson, B. TN 12th (Cons.) Inf. Co.I
Robinson, B. TN 51st (Cons.) Inf. Co.K
Robinson, B.A. GA 1st Bn.S.S. Co.D
Robinson, B.A.K. GA 5th Cav. Co.G
Robinson, Bannister NC 23rd Inf. Co.I
Robinson, B.B. TN 21st (Wilson's) Cav. Co.B
Robinson, B.B TN 22nd (Barteau's) Cav. Co.H
Robinson, B.E. SC 9th Inf. Co.E
Robinson, B.E. SC Mil. 16th Regt. Sigwald's Co. Cpl.
Robinson, B.E. SC 24th Inf. Co.A 2nd Lt.
Robinson, Ben MO Inf. 5th Regt.St.Guard Co.D
Robinson, Benjamin AL 63rd Inf. Co.G 1st Lt.
Robinson, Benjamin KY 6th Cav. Co.G
Robinson, Benjamin MO Lt.Arty. 1st Btty.
Robinson, Benjamin MO Lt.Arty. Parsons' Co.
Robinson, Benjamin MO 6th Inf. Co.I
Robinson, Benjamin NC 5th Inf. Co.A Capt.
Robinson, Benjamin TN Cav. Allison's Squad. Co.A
Robinson, Benjamin TN 39th Mtd.Inf. Co.I
Robinson, Benjamin TX 24th Cav. Co.C
Robinson, Benjamin VA 21st Cav. Co.K
Robinson, Benjamin VA Lt.Arty. Cayce's Co.
Robinson, Benjamin D. MS 12th Inf. Co.H
Robinson, Benjamin D. MS 41st Inf. Co.D
Robinson, Benjamin F. AL 25th Inf. Co.C
Robinson, Benjamin F. AL 44th Inf. Co.E
Robinson, Benjamin F. FL 5th Inf. Co.I Cpl.
Robinson, Benjamin F. GA 30th Inf. Co.G
Robinson, Benjamin F. LA 28th (Gray's) Inf. Co.E
Robinson, Benjamin F. LA 31st Inf. Co.C
Robinson, Benjamin F. MS 16th Inf. Co.B 4th Cpl.
Robinson, Benjamin F. NC 18th Inf. Co.B
Robinson, Benjamin F. NC 58th Inf. Co.L
Robinson, Benjamin F. VA 6th Inf. Co.D
Robinson, Benjamin H. SC Cav.Bn. Holcombe Legion Co.D
Robinson, Benjamin H. VA 1st Arty. Co.I Sr.2nd Lt.
Robinson, Benjamin H. VA Lt.Arty. 38th Bn. Co.B Sr.2nd Lt.
Robinson, Benjamin H. VA 40th Inf. Co.I Capt.
Robinson, Benjamin K. MO 16th Inf. Co.H

Robinson, Benjamin R. VA 23rd Inf. Co.G
Robinson, Benjamin W. TX 26th Cav. Co.D
Robinson, Benoni D. KY 10th Cav. Co.C
Robinson, Berry GA Lt.Arty. Milledge's Co.
Robinson, Berry GA 3rd Inf. 1st Co.I
Robinson, Berry B. AR Cav. Harrell's Bn. Co.C
Robinson, B.F. AL 15th Bn.Part.Rangers Co.A
Robinson, B.F. AL 56th Part.Rangers Co.A
Robinson, B.F. AL 56th Inf. Co.L
Robinson, B.F. GA 56th Inf. Co.E
Robinson, B.F. LA 2nd Inf. Co.I
Robinson, B.F. MS 26th Inf. Co.A
Robinson, B.F. TN 19th (Biffle's) Cav. Co.L 1st Lt.
Robinson, B.F. TN 38th Inf. Co.E Jr.2nd Lt.
Robinson, B.F. TX 9th (Young's) Inf. Co.D
Robinson, B.H. TN 43rd Inf. Co.K
Robinson, B.J. MO Inf. 4th Regt.St.Guard Co.D Sgt.
Robinson, B.L. NC 17th Inf. (2nd Org.) Co.A
Robinson, B.M. AL 31st Inf. Co.K
Robinson, Bolling GA 13th Inf. Co.G 1st Lt.
Robinson, B.P. TN 20th Inf. Co.D
Robinson, B.P. TN 63rd Inf. Co.A Sgt.
Robinson, B.R. NC 2nd Jr.Res. Co.F 2nd Lt.
Robinson, B.R. TN 9th Cav. Co.L
Robinson, Bracy NC 27th Inf. Co.H
Robinson, Braxton TX 4th Cav. Co.D Bugler
Robinson, Bryant TN 27th Inf. Co.G
Robinson, B.W. MS 27th Inf. Co.C
Robinson, B.W. TX 25th Cav. Co.C
Robinson, B.W. Gen. & Staff AASurg.
Robinson, B.X. MS 36th Inf. Co.C
Robinson, C. GA Inf. 1st Loc.Troops (Augusta) Co.E
Robinson, C. MS 11th (Cons.) Cav. Co.I
Robinson, C. MS 20th Inf. Co.F
Robinson, C. SC 2nd Bn.S.S. Co.B
Robinson, C. TN Inf. Crews' Bn. Co.B
Robinson, C. TX 26th Cav. Co.C
Robinson, C. VA 2nd St.Res. Co.C
Robinson, C.A. AL 4th (Russell's) Cav. Co.C Sgt.
Robinson, C.A. MS 2nd Part. Co.A
Robinson, C.A. TN 3rd (Forrest's) Cav. 1st Co.F
Robinson, C.A. TN 8th (Smith's) Cav. Co.D
Robinson, C.A. VA 21st Inf. Co.F
Robinson, Callahill AR Inf. Cocke's Regt. Co.D
Robinson, Calvin GA Inf. 17th Bn. (St.Guards) McCarty's Co.
Robinson, Calvin KY 7th Mtd.Inf. Co.B
Robinson, Calvin NC 29th Inf. Co.H
Robinson, Calvin NC 39th Inf. Co.H
Robinson, Calvin TX 6th Cav. Co.F
Robinson, Calvin VA 56th Inf.
Robinson, Calvin F. TX 6th Inf. Co.E
Robinson, Calvin P. TN 4th (McLemore's) Cav. Co.G
Robinson, Campbell VA 1st St.Res. Co.D
Robinson, Cary VA 6th Inf. Co.G Sgt.Maj.
Robinson, C.B. AL 54th Inf.
Robinson, C.B. KY 9th Mtd.Inf. Co.B
Robinson, C.B. MS 46th Inf. Co.G
Robinson, C.C. AR 2nd Mtd.Rifles Co.H
Robinson, C.C. GA Inf. 2nd Bn. (St.Guards) New Co.D

Robinson, C.C. GA 3rd Inf. Co.H
Robinson, C.C. MS 2nd Part.Rangers Co.L
Robinson, C.C. MS Inf. 1st Bn.St.Troops (30 days '64) Co.D
Robinson, C.C. MS Inf. 2nd Bn. (St.Troops) Co.D
Robinson, C.C. VA Cav. 39th Bn.
Robinson, C.D. SC 18th Inf. Co.H
Robinson, C.F. AR Cav. Gordon's Regt. Co.A
Robinson, C.F. MS 32nd Inf. Co.D
Robinson, C.F. VA 46th Inf. Co.L
Robinson, C.F. Gen. & Staff A.Surg.
Robinson, C.H. AL 4th Cav. Co.B
Robinson, C.H. NC 31st Inf. Co.B QMSgt.
Robinson, C.H. VA 5th Cav. Co.D
Robinson, Chales SC 1st (Hagood's) Inf. 2nd Co.B
Robinson, Charles AL Arty. 1st Bn. Co.C,D
Robinson, Charles AL 8th Inf. Co.C Sgt.
Robinson, Charles AL 18th Bn.Vol. Co.C
Robinson, Charles AR 33rd Inf. Co.G
Robinson, Charles FL 2nd Cav. Co.D
Robinson, Charles GA Lt.Arty. Ritter's Co.
Robinson, Charles KY 10th Cav. Co.I
Robinson, Charles MS 34th Inf. Co.K
Robinson, Charles MS 37th Inf. Co.C
Robinson, Charles MO 1st Inf. 2nd Co.A
Robinson, Charles NC 3rd Arty. (40th St.Troops) Co.B
Robinson, Charles NC 1st Inf. (6 mo. '61) Co.M Cpl.
Robinson, Charles NC 52nd Inf. Co.E
Robinson, Charles SC 7th Inf. 1st Co.B, 2nd Co.B, Co.F
Robinson, Charles TN 9th (Ward's) Cav. Co.F
Robinson, Charles TX Lt.Arty. Jones' Co.
Robinson, Charles VA 4th Cav. Co.C Lt.
Robinson, Charles VA Lt.Arty. Garber's Co.
Robinson, Charles VA 9th Inf. Co.F
Robinson, Charles VA 9th 2nd Mil. Co.B
Robinson, Charles VA 54th Bn. Co.B
Robinson, Charles B. MS 31st Inf. Co.C
Robinson, Charles B. TN 48th (Voorhies') Inf.
Robinson, Charles C. AL Eufaula Lt.Arty. QMSgt.
Robinson, Charles C. AL Inf. 1st Regt. Co.B
Robinson, Charles C. AL 3rd Inf. Co.H
Robinson, Charles C. AL 6th Inf. Co.G
Robinson, Charles C. VA 9th Cav. Co.C Capt.
Robinson, Charles C. VA 16th Inf. Co.F Sgt.
Robinson, Charles E. NC 1st Inf. (6 mo. '61) Co.H
Robinson, Charles F. TX 2nd Inf. Co.D
Robinson, Charles H. MS 16th Inf. Co.B
Robinson, Charles H. VA Lt.Arty. Pollock's Co.
Robinson, Charles H. VA 15th Inf. Co.G
Robinson, Charles K. TX 1st (McCulloch's) Cav. Co.D
Robinson, Charles L. MS 6th Inf. Co.I
Robinson, Charles M. TN 44th (Cons.) Inf. Co.E
Robinson, Charles M. TX 18th Cav. Co.G 2nd Lt.
Robinson, Charles S. SC 2nd Rifles Co.F Comsy.Sgt.
Robinson, Charles S. SC 4th Inf. Co.B
Robinson, Charles T. MS Inf. 2nd Bn. Co.H
Robinson, Charles T. MS 48th Inf. Co.H

Robinson, Charles W. AL 25th Inf. Co.H Sgt.
Robinson, Charles W. LA 5th Inf. Co.E
Robinson, Charles W. NC Coast Guards Galloway's Co.
Robinson, Chesterfield G. FL 7th Inf. Co.F
Robinson, Chris SC 18th Inf. Co.B
Robinson, Christopher GA 34th Inf. Co.C N.C.S. QMSgt.
Robinson, Cicero F. NC Inf. 2nd Bn. Co.E Asst.Surg.
Robinson, C.J. GA 22nd Inf. Co.I
Robinson, C.J. LA 17th Inf. Co.D
Robinson, C.K. TX 23rd Cav. Co.H
Robinson, C.L. AL 56th Part.Rangers Co.H Cpl.
Robinson, C.L. GA 64th Inf. Co.B Sgt.
Robinson, C.L. LA 2nd Cav. Co.G
Robinson, C.L. NC 16th Inf. Co.H 1st Lt.
Robinson, Clarence SC 4th Inf.
Robinson, Clark VA Mil. Carroll Cty.
Robinson, Clark H. VA 29th Inf. Co.C
Robinson, Clark J. GA Hvy.Arty. 22nd Bn. Co.B
Robinson, Clark J. GA 25th Inf. 1st Co.K
Robinson, C.M. AR 32nd Inf. Co.C
Robinson, Coleman MS Cav. 3rd Bn. (Ashcraft's) Co.E Cpl.
Robinson, Coleman H. VA 53rd Inf. Co.I
Robinson, Columbus MS Cav. 3rd Bn. (Ashcraft's) Co.E
Robinson, Columbus MO 5th Cav. Co.F
Robinson, Columbus H. AL 6th Inf. Co.I
Robinson, Constantine H. VA 2nd Cav. Co.K
Robinson, Conway N. VA Hvy.Arty. 10th Bn. Co.E
Robinson, Cornelius, Jr. AL 3rd Inf. Co.H Capt.
Robinson, Cornelius MS 2nd Inf. Co.D,F
Robinson, Cornelius B. AL 3rd Inf. Co.H 2nd Lt.
Robinson, C.R. AL 15th Bn.Part.Rangers Co.E
Robinson, C.R. MS 2nd Part.Rangers Co.D
Robinson, C.R. TN Inf. 22nd Bn. Co.A
Robinson, C.S. MO Inf. Clark's Regt. Co.A
Robinson, C.S.D. SC Inf. Hampton Legion Co.H
Robinson, C. Stanley LA 21st (Patton's) Inf. Co.H
Robinson, C.T. KY 8th Mtd.Inf. Co.B
Robinson, C.T. SC 6th Inf. 1st Co.D, 2nd Co.G 1st Sgt.
Robinson, C.T. VA 59th Inf. 3rd Co.F
Robinson, Curtis FL Inf. 2nd Bn. Co.C
Robinson, Curtis FL 10th Inf. Co.H
Robinson, C.W. KY 9th Cav. Co.H
Robinson, C.W. LA 9th Inf. Co.H
Robinson, C.W. LA 21st (Patton's) Inf. 1st Lt.
Robinson, Cyrus A. MS 19th Inf. Co.F Sgt.
Robinson, D. AR 15th (N.W.) Inf. Co.D
Robinson, D. KY 3rd Mtd.Inf. Co.F,B
Robinson, D.A. MS 8th Inf. Co.A
Robinson, D.A. TN 14th Inf. Co.D
Robinson, D.A.J. TX Cav. Hardeman's Regt. Co.A
Robinson, Daniel FL 1st Inf. New Co.G
Robinson, Daniel NC 3rd Inf. Co.C
Robinson, Daniel SC 2nd Arty. Co.C
Robinson, Daniel SC 2nd Arty. Co.I
Robinson, Daniel VA 3rd Res. Co.C

Robinson, Daniel VA 37th Inf. Co.I
Robinson, Daniel VA Loc.Def. Scott's Co.
Robinson, Daniel C. AL 3rd Inf. Co.F
Robinson, Daniel C. NC 37th Inf. Co.I Sgt.
Robinson, Daniel F. GA 26th Inf. Co.C
Robinson, Daniel F. VA 49th Inf. Co.D
Robinson, Daniel G. MS 1st Cav. Co.H
Robinson, Daniel J. TN Inf. 154th Sr.Regt. Co.E
Robinson, Daniel W. AR 9th Inf. Co.E
Robinson, David AR 16th Inf. Co.A
Robinson, David KY 10th (Diamond's) Cav. Co.C
Robinson, David LA 17th Inf. Co.G
Robinson, David NC 16th Inf. Co.C Sgt.
Robinson, David NC 23rd Inf. Co.G
Robinson, David NC 24th Inf. Co.A
Robinson, David SC Cav.Bn. Holcombe Legion Co.D
Robinson, David VA 20th Cav. Co.K Cpl.
Robinson, David VA Inf. 21st Bn. 2nd Co.F
Robinson, David A. MO 10th Cav. Co.H
Robinson, David B. GA Siege Arty. 28th Bn. Co.E
Robinson, David C. TX 22nd Cav. Co.H Cpl.
Robinson, David C. VA Lt.Arty. French's Co.
Robinson, David C. VA Arty. Wise Legion
Robinson, David C. Conf.Lt.Arty. Stark's Bn. Co.D
Robinson, David F. VA Burks' Regt.Loc.Def. Beckner's Co.
Robinson, David H. GA 64th Inf. Co.H
Robinson, David M. NC 56th Inf. Co.D
Robinson, David N. TX 4th Cav. Co.D
Robinson, David O. AL 37th Inf. Co.D
Robinson, David O. GA 4th Inf. Co.D
Robinson, David O. NC 16th Inf. Co.H Sgt.
Robinson, David S. VA Cav. 39th Bn. Co.A
Robinson, David T. VA 4th Inf. Co.E 2nd Lt.
Robinson, D.C. AL Cav. 24th Bn. Co.C
Robinson, D.C. NC 5th Cav. (63rd St.Troops) Co.C
Robinson, D.C. TN 19th (Biffle's) Cav. Co.C
Robinson, D.C. TX 9th Cav. Co.C 2nd Lt.
Robinson, D.C. Gen. & Staff Agent
Robinson, Denton TN 11th Cav. Sgt.
Robinson, Derrick J. AR Inf. 1st Bn. Co.B
Robinson, Dewitt KY Cav. Malone's Regt. Co.D
Robinson, Dewitt C. TX 1st (McCulloch's) Cav. Co.B
Robinson, Dewitt C. TX 4th Cav. Co.D
Robinson, Dexter NC Coast Guards Galloway's Co.
Robinson, D.F. MS 9th Inf. New Co.I
Robinson, D.F. VA Cav. Mosby's Regt. (Part.Rangers) Co.E
Robinson, D.G. MS 7th Cav. Co.H
Robinson, D.G. MS 32nd Inf. Co.I,D
Robinson, D.G. VA 2nd Cav. Co.I
Robinson, D.H. AR 37th Inf. Co.K
Robinson, D.H. AR 50th Mil. Co.G
Robinson, D.H. VA 19th Cav. Co.E
Robinson, Dick M. LA Inf. 4th Bn. Co.A
Robinson, D.J. AL 23rd Inf. Co.G
Robinson, D.J. AL Cp. of Instr. Talladega
Robinson, D.J. NC 2nd Jr.Res. Co.G
Robinson, D.J. SC 3rd Res. Co.G
Robinson, D.J. Exch.Bn. 2nd Co.A,CSA

Robinson, D.L. AR 1st Mtd.Rifles Co.G
Robinson, D.L. NC 57th Inf. Co.E
Robinson, D.M. MS 2nd Cav.
Robinson, D.M. MS 22nd Inf.
Robinson, D.P. VA Lt.Arty. French's Co.
Robinson, D.S. GA 54th Inf. Co.E
Robinson, D.S. NC 32nd Inf. Co.D,E
Robinson, Dudley AL 3rd Inf. Co.H
Robinson, Dudley R. KY 4th Mtd.Inf. Co.I
Robinson, D.W. FL 2nd Inf. Co.B
Robinson, D.W. KY 9th Mtd.Inf. Co.B
Robinson, D.W. TX 35th (Brown's) Cav. Co.G
Robinson, E. AL 1st Bn.Cadets Co.B
Robinson, E. AL Cp. of Instr. Talladega Co.D
Robinson, E. AR 2nd Inf. Co.I
Robinson, E. AR 5th Mil. Co.I
Robinson, E. GA Phillips' Legion Co.A
Robinson, E. MS 3rd (St.Troops) Cav. Co.K
Robinson, E. NC 15th Inf. Co.C
Robinson, E. TN 37th Inf. Co.C
Robinson, E. VA 23rd Cav. Co.D
Robinson, E. VA Cav. Swann's Bn. Vincent's Co.
Robinson, E. 20th Conf.Cav. Co.E
Robinson, E.A. SC 18th Inf. Co.G
Robinson, E.A. TN 8th (Smith's) Cav. Co.D
Robinson, E.B. VA 45th Inf. Co.C
Robinson, E.C. LA 8th Cav. Co.C
Robinson, E.D. AL 4th (Russell's) Cav. Co.H
Robinson, E.D. GA 1st Bn.Cadets Co.A
Robinson, E.D. SC Mil.Arty. 1st Regt. Walter's Co.
Robinson, E.D. TN 55th (Brown's) Inf. Co.D Cpl.
Robinson, Edmond C. VA Lt.Arty. Moore's Co.
Robinson, Edmond C. Conf.Lt.Arty. Richardson's Bn. Co.D
Robinson, Edmund AR 27th Inf. Old Co.C, Co.D
Robinson, Edmund C., Jr. VA 6th Inf. Co.A Cpl.
Robinson, Edward MO St.Guard
Robinson, Edward TX 10th Field Btty.
Robinson, Edward VA 1st St.Res. Co.C
Robinson, Edward VA 13th Inf. Co.D
Robinson, Edward A. MS 16th Inf. Co.K Hosp.Stew.
Robinson, Edward B. LA 8th Inf. Co.E
Robinson, Edward C. AL 13th Inf. Co.A
Robinson, Edward C. LA Herrick's Co. (Orleans Blues)
Robinson, Edward D. GA 1st (Ramsey's) Inf. Co.H
Robinson, Edward D. GA 55th Inf. Co.D Cpl.
Robinson, Edward D. SC Lt.Arty. Walter's Co. (Washington Arty.) Sgt.Maj.
Robinson, Edward D. VA 3rd Res. Co.E
Robinson, Edward D. VA 18th Inf. Co.B
Robinson, Edward J. GA Inf. 2nd Bn. Co.C
Robinson, Edward M. AL 32nd Inf. Co.A
Robinson, Edward T. Gen. & Staff Hosp.Stew.
Robinson, Edward W. MD 1st Cav. Co.C
Robinson, Edwin LA 15th Inf. Co.A
Robinson, Edwin VA 1st Inf. Co.G
Robinson, Edwin W. VA 3rd Inf.Loc.Def. Co.A Cpl.
Robinson, E.E. VA 1st (Farinholt's) Res. Co.K

Robinson, E.F. SC 3rd Bn.Res. Co.E
Robinson, E.F. SC 5th St.Troops Co.A 1st Sgt.
Robinson, E.F. SC 6th Res. Co.B
Robinson, E.G. MS 32nd Inf. Co.I Cpl.
Robinson, E.G. SC Lt.Arty. 3rd (Palmetto) Bn. Co.E,G Sgt.
Robinson, E.H. AL 2nd Cav. Co.H
Robinson, E.H. TN 9th (Ward's) Cav. Co.F
Robinson, E.H. VA 28th Inf. Co.F Cpl.
Robinson, E.J. MS 23rd Inf. Co.I
Robinson, Elam NC 4th Sr.Res. Co.G,K
Robinson, Elam C. VA 20th Cav. Co.D Sgt.
Robinson, Elbert A. AL 44th Inf. Co.E
Robinson, Elbert E. TN 43rd Inf. Co.B 1st Sgt.
Robinson, Elbridge R. AR 15th (Josey's) Inf. Co.A Sgt.
Robinson, Eli KY 2nd Bn.Mtd.Rifles Co.E
Robinson, Elias KY 12th Cav. Co.G
Robinson, Elias L. VA Hvy.Arty. 10th Bn. Co.A
Robinson, Eli H. AL 44th Inf. Co.E Sgt.
Robinson, Elijah MS 1st Lt.Arty. Co.E
Robinson, Elijah NC 46th Inf. Co.C
Robinson, Elijah TN 6th Inf. Co.B
Robinson, Elisha AL 30th Inf. Co.A
Robinson, Elisha GA 24th Inf. Co.C
Robinson, Elisha H. TX 16th Cav. Co.E Sgt.
Robinson, Elisha Tarber TX 8th Cav. Co.H
Robinson, Ellison SC Inf. 6th Bn. Co.B
Robinson, E.M. AL 12th Cav. Co.D 1st Lt.
Robinson, E.M. AL 63rd Inf. Co.F
Robinson, E.M. GA 45th Inf. Co.E 1st Lt.
Robinson, E.M. 3rd Conf.Cav. Co.D Cpl.
Robinson, Emmet B. VA 12th Inf. Co.F
Robinson, E.N. GA Siege Arty. 28th Bn. Co.I
Robinson, Ephraim MO Cav. Freeman's Regt. Co.A
Robinson, Ephraim G. MS 26th Inf. Co.C Cpl.
Robinson, Erastus MS Inf. 2nd St.Troops Co.F
Robinson, E.S. MS 2nd (Quinn's St.Troops) Inf. Co.A
Robinson, E.T. LA Cav. Greenleaf's Co. (Orleans Lt.Horse)
Robinson, E.T. TN 18th Inf. Co.F
Robinson, Eugene C. MS 12th Cav. Co.B
Robinson, Eugene D. VA 53rd Inf. Co.D 1st Lt.
Robinson, Evan L. NC 1st Inf. Co.C Cpl.
Robinson, E.W. GA 13th Inf. Co.I Capt.
Robinson, E.W. TN Hvy.Arty. Johnston's Co.
Robinson, F. GA Inf. 23rd Bn.Loc.Def. Cook's Co.
Robinson, F. NC 2nd Arty. (36th St.Troops) Co.I
Robinson, F. TN Lt.Arty. Phillips' Co.
Robinson, F. 2nd Conf.Eng.Troops Co.C Artif.
Robinson, F.C. AR 36th Inf. Co.C
Robinson, F.C. TN 5th Inf. 2nd Co.F
Robinson, F.C. TN 22nd Inf. Co.C
Robinson, F.G. MS 36th Inf. Co.C
Robinson, F.G. NC 2nd Arty. (36th St.Troops) Co.C,F Sgt.
Robinson, F.H. TN Arty.Corps Co.5 3rd Lt.
Robinson, F.H. TN Inf. 154th Sr.Regt. 2nd Lt.,Adj.
Robinson, F.J. VA 54th Mil. Co.H
Robinson, Fleming W. VA 48th Inf. Co.H
Robinson, F.M. AR 36th Inf. Co.I Bvt.2nd Lt.
Robinson, F.M. AR 50th Mil. Co.B Ord.Sgt.

Robinson, F.M. GA 59th Inf. Co.H 1st Lt.
Robinson, F.M. TX 33rd Cav. Co.B
Robinson, F.M. Gen. & Staff Asst.Surg.
Robinson, Francis C. NC 52nd Inf. Co.G
Robinson, Francis E. GA 4th Inf. Co.I
Robinson, Francis M. KY 4th Cav. Co.D
Robinson, Francis M. KY 2nd Mtd.Inf. Co.I Sgt.
Robinson, Francis M. Wheeler's Scouts,CSA
Robinson, Francis O. NC 32nd Inf. Co.D,E
Robinson, Frank SC 18th Inf. Co.G
Robinson, Frank TN 10th Inf. Co.F Sgt.
Robinson, Frank TN 31st Inf. Co.B
Robinson, Frank TX 33rd Cav. Co.B 1st Lt.
Robinson, Franklin AL Inf. 1st Regt. Co.C
Robinson, Franklin AL 62nd Inf. Co.K
Robinson, Franklin AR 1st (Dobbin's) Cav. Co.B
Robinson, Franklin AR 1st Mtd.Rifles Co.B
Robinson, Franklin A. VA 5th Inf.
Robinson, Frederick G. NC 3rd Arty. (40th St.Troops) Co.K Sgt.
Robinson, Frederick G. NC 18th Inf. Co.I
Robinson, Frederick J. VA Arty. Kevill's Co.
Robinson, Frederick J. VA 41st Inf. 1st Co.E
Robinson, Frederick M. VA 2nd Inf. Co.G,H
Robinson, Fulford NC 3rd Arty. (40th St.Troops) Co.H
Robinson, Fulford NC Lt.Arty. 13th Bn. Co.F
Robinson, F.W. FL 2nd Cav. Co.D
Robinson, F.W. Conf.Cav. Clarkson's Bn. Ind.Rangers Sgt.Maj.
Robinson, G. AL 21st Inf. Co.H
Robinson, G. MS Cav. 2nd Bn.Res. Co.A
Robinson, G. MS Cav. Powers' Regt. Co.G
Robinson, G. MO Inf. Perkins' Bn.
Robinson, G. SC 12th Inf. Surg.
Robinson, G. TN Arty. Ramsey's Btty. Harness Maker
Robinson, G. TX 23rd Cav. Co.D
Robinson, G. TX Cav. Bourland's Regt. Co.H
Robinson, G. TX Inf. Timmons' Regt. Co.E
Robinson, G.A. AR 12th Inf. Co.E
Robinson, G.A. MS 3rd Inf. Co.H
Robinson, G.A. Conf.Cav. Powers' Regt. Co.G
Robinson, Gabriel A. NC 3rd Arty. (40th St.Troops) Co.C
Robinson, Gale C. AL 35th Inf. Co.C Sgt.
Robinson, G.B. AL 14th Inf. Co.I Cpl.
Robinson, G.B. MS Cav. 2nd Bn.Res. Co.B Cpl.
Robinson, G.B. TX Inf. Chambers' Bn. Res.Corps Co.C 1st Lt.
Robinson, G.C. 7th Conf.Cav. Co.C
Robinson, G.D. Trans-MS Conf.Cav. 1st Bn. Co.A
Robinson, G.E. SC 7th Cav. Co.B
Robinson, George AL Arty. 1st Bn. Co.C Drum.
Robinson, George AR 11th & 17th (Cons.) Inf. Co.I
Robinson, George AR 15th (Josey's) Inf. Co.D
Robinson, George FL 5th Inf. Co.B
Robinson, George FL 10th Inf. Co.C 1st Lt.
Robinson, George GA 1st Reg. Co.M
Robinson, George KY 2nd (Woodward's) Cav. Co.F

Robinson, George KY 10th (Johnson's) Cav. Co.A
Robinson, George LA Arty. Kean's Btty. (Orleans Ind.Arty.) 1st Sgt.
Robinson, George LA 3rd Inf.
Robinson, Geo. LA 7th Inf. Co.H
Robinson, George LA 13th Inf. Co.A
Robinson, George LA 16th Inf. Co.I
Robinson, George MS Cav. 24th Bn. Co.F
Robinson, George MS Lt.Arty. (Brookhaven Lt.Arty.) Hoskins' Btty.
Robinson, George NC 6th Cav. (65th St.Troops) Co.A,F
Robinson, George SC 2nd Inf. Co.C
Robinson, George SC 5th Res. Co.C
Robinson, George SC 8th Inf. Co.D
Robinson, George TN 16th (Logwood's) Cav. Co.E Sgt.
Robinson, George TN Lt.Arty. Morton's Co.
Robinson, George TX 24th & 25th Cav. (Cons.) Co.E Sgt.
Robinson, George TX 1st Inf. Co.C
Robinson, George TX 4th Inf. (St.Troops) Co.E
Robinson, George TX Waul's Legion Co.D Cpl.
Robinson, George VA Lt.Arty. G.B. Chapman's Co.
Robinson, George VA 67th Mil. Co.B
Robinson, George A. AL 28th Inf. Co.D
Robinson, George C. GA Arty. 11th Bn. (Sumter Arty.) Co.A
Robinson, George C. GA Inf. 1st Loc.Troops (Augusta) Dearing's Cav.Co.
Robinson, George D. LA Washington Arty.Bn. Co.3
Robinson, George D. LA Inf.Crescent Regt. Co.B
Robinson, George D. NC 27th Inf. Co.I
Robinson, George D. VA 11th Inf. Co.F
Robinson, George E. AL 42nd Inf. Co.K
Robinson, George E. GA 27th Inf. Co.D
Robinson, George E. SC Rutledge Mtd.Riflemen & Horse Arty. Trenholm's Co.
Robinson, George F. AR 14th (Powers') Inf. Co.H Sgt.
Robinson, George F. GA 4th Inf. Co.E
Robinson, George F. GA 38th Inf. Co.K Capt.
Robinson, George F. MO Cav. Fristoe's Regt. Co.F
Robinson, George H. AR 26th Inf. Co.F Sgt.
Robinson, George H. TX 22nd Cav. Co.K
Robinson, George H. VA 11th Cav. Co.A Cpl.
Robinson, George J. VA 47th Inf. Co.A
Robinson, George Julius TX 5th Inf. Co.A Sgt.
Robinson, George K. AR 32nd Inf. Co.A
Robinson, George M. AR Inf. 1st Bn. Co.B
Robinson, George M. GA 1st Cav. Co.H 1st Lt.
Robinson, George M. GA 1st Inf. Co.F
Robinson, George M. GA Phillips' Legion Co.D
Robinson, George M. TN 3rd (Forrest's) Cav. Co.C 2nd Lt.
Robinson, George M. TX 26th Cav. Co.D
Robinson, George M. 1st Conf.Inf. 2nd Co.F
Robinson, George M.B. SC 20th Inf. Co.E
Robinson, George O. GA Inf. 1st Loc.Troops (Augusta) Co.K
Robinson, George O. GA Inf. 18th Bn. (St.Guards) Adam's Co.

Robinson, George O. NC 17th Inf. (2nd Org.) Co.C

Robinson, George P. MS Hamer's Co. (Salem Cav.)

Robinson, George P. MS 34th Inf. Co.K Cpl.

Robinson, George R. VA 2nd Cav. Co.F

Robinson, George R. VA 7th Cav. Co.E

Robinson, George T. SC 5th Cav. Co.H Cpl.

Robinson, George T. VA Burks' Regt.Loc.Def. Sprinkle's Co.

Robinson, George W. AL 46th Inf. Co.G 2nd Lt.

Robinson, George W. AR 1st (Crawford's) Cav. Co.B

Robinson, George W. AR 16th Inf. Co.A

Robinson, George W. AR 16th Inf. Co.C

Robinson, George W. AR 17th (Griffith's) Inf. Co.F

Robinson, George W. AR 19th (Dockery's) Inf. Co.I

Robinson, George W. GA 7th Inf. (St.Guards) Co.D Sgt.

Robinson, George W. KY 4th Cav. Co.K

Robinson, George W. LA Mil.Cont.Regt. Mitchell's Co.

Robinson, George W. MD Arty. 1st Btty. Sgt.

Robinson, George W. MS 2nd Part.Rangers Co.B

Robinson, George W. MS 2nd Part.Rangers Co.C Sgt.

Robinson, George W. MS 2nd Inf. Co.K

Robinson, George W. MS 8th Inf. Co.C

Robinson, George W. MS 20th Inf. Co.B

Robinson, George W. MO Inf. 8th Bn. Co.A

Robinson, George W. NC 12th Inf. Co.A

Robinson, George W. NC 34th Inf. Co.E

Robinson, George W. TN 4th (McLemore's) Cav. Co.E Capt.

Robinson, George W. TN 14th (Neely's) Cav. Co.G Cpl.

Robinson, George W. TN 51st Inf. Co.B

Robinson, George W. TX 21st Cav. Co.K

Robinson, George W. TX 10th Field Btty.

Robinson, George W. VA 20th Cav. Co.D Cpl.

Robinson, George W. VA 2nd St.Res. Co.C

Robinson, George W. VA 31st Inf. Co.D Cpl.

Robinson, George W. Conf.Cav. Wood's Regt. Co.I 1st Lt.

Robinson, George Washington MS 33rd Inf. Co.K

Robinson, G.F. SC 7th Inf. Co.A

Robinson, G.H. AR 6th Inf. Co.C

Robinson, G.H. MD Arty. 2nd Btty.

Robinson, G.H. MS 10th Cav. Co.A 1st Sgt.

Robinson, Gideon S. MO Inf. Perkins' Bn.

Robinson, Gilbert M. AL 3rd Inf. Co.H

Robinson, G.L. GA 51st Inf. Co.K Cpl.

Robinson, G.L. LA 3rd Inf. Co.K

Robinson, G.L. TN 21st & 22nd (Cons.) Cav. Co.E

Robinson, G.L. Gen. & Staff Surg.

Robinson, G.M. AR Inf. 2nd Bn. Co.B

Robinson, G.N. AL Cav. Lewis' Bn. Co.C

Robinson, Goldsbury MS 12th Inf. Co.F

Robinson, G.R. AR 19th (Dawson's) Inf. Co.K

Robinson, G.R. GA 38th Inf. Co.I

Robinson, Granville MO Lt.Arty. Farris' Btty. (Clark Arty.)

Robinson, Greene GA Arty. 11th Bn. (Sumter Arty.) Co.D,A Cpl.

Robinson, Green M. VA 29th Inf. Co.E

Robinson, G.S. AL 8th Inf.

Robinson, G.S. MD Arty. 2nd Btty.

Robinson, G.S. MO 16th Inf. Co.G

Robinson, G.S. NC 25th Inf. Co.E

Robinson, G.T. AR 36th Inf. Co.C

Robinson, G.T. KY Cav.

Robinson, G.T. SC Cav. 14th Bn. Co.A Cpl.

Robinson, G.T. TN 42nd Inf. Co.C

Robinson, G.T. 4th Conf.Inf. Co.H

Robinson, Gutheridge L. TN 7th Inf. Surg.

Robinson, G.W. AL 1st Cav. Co.A

Robinson, G.W. AL 42nd Inf. Co.F

Robinson, G.W. AR 20th Inf. Co.G Sgt.

Robinson, G.W. KY 5th Mtd.Inf. Wag.

Robinson, G.W. MS 18th Cav. Co.A,C

Robinson, G.W. MS 23rd Inf. Co.K

Robinson, G.W. MO Cav. Freeman's Regt. Co.I

Robinson, G.W. NC 6th Cav. (65th St.Troops) Co.F

Robinson, G.W. TN 21st (Wilson's) Cav. Co.I

Robinson, G.W. TN Lt.Arty. Sparkman's Co.

Robinson, G.W. TN 6th Inf. Co.K

Robinson, G.W. TN 12th (Cons.) Inf. Co.F

Robinson, G.W. TN 22nd Inf. Co.I

Robinson, G.W. TN 31st Inf. Co.E 1st Lt.

Robinson, G.W. TN 55th (McKoin's) Inf. Bounds' Co.

Robinson, G.W. TX Inf. 1st St.Troops White's Co.D

Robinson, G.W. TX 7th Inf. Co.K

Robinson, G.W. TX Vol. Duke's Co.

Robinson, G.W. VA 7th Cav. Co.E

Robinson, H. AL 15th Inf. Co.E

Robinson, H. AL 29th Inf. Co.I

Robinson, H. FL Conscr.

Robinson, H. GA Lt.Arty. 14th Bn. Co.D

Robinson, H. GA Lt.Arty. King's Btty.

Robinson, H. SC Cav. 19th Bn. Co.B

Robinson, H. SC 20th Inf. Co.M

Robinson, H. VA Cav. Hounshell's Bn. Co.A

Robinson, H. VA 7th Inf. Co.H

Robinson, H. Brush Bn.

Robinson, Hanceford GA 26th Inf. Co.G

Robinson, Hardy SC 5th Bn.Res. Co.E Sgt.

Robinson, Harman R. NC 30th Inf. Co.A

Robinson, Harmon R. NC 20th Inf. Faison's Co.

Robinson, Harmond J. GA 9th Inf. Co.H

Robinson, Harris B. TX 1st (McCulloch's) Cav. Co.H

Robinson, Harris B. TX Cav. Morgan's Regt. Co.B

Robinson, Hartwell NC 46th Inf. Co.C

Robinson, Harvey NC 4th Sr.Res. Co.G

Robinson, Harvey SC 1st (Butler's) Inf. Co.E

Robinson, Harvy S. VA 63rd Inf. Co.F Sgt.

Robinson, H.B. LA 13th Bn. (Part.Rangers) Co.D

Robinson, H.C. AL 9th (Malone's) Cav. Co.G Cpl.

Robinson, H.C. MS 6th Cav. Co.C

Robinson, H.C. MS 8th Cav. Co.I

Robinson, H.C. MS Cav. Jeff Davis Legion Co.C 3rd Lt.

Robinson, H.C. MS 5th Inf. (St.Troops) Co.I Col.

Robinson, H.C. SC Mil.Arty. 1st Regt. Walter's Co. Sgt.

Robinson, H.C. SC 1st Regt. Charleston Guard Co.H

Robinson, H.D. SC Inf. 1st (Charleston) Bn. Co.E

Robinson, H.D. SC 27th Inf. Co.A

Robinson, Henry AR 20th Inf. Co.D

Robinson, Henry GA Hvy.Arty. 22nd Bn. Co.D

Robinson, Henry GA Lt.Arty. Daniell's Btty.

Robinson, Henry GA Arty. Maxwell's Reg. Lt.Btty.

Robinson, Henry GA 64th Inf. Co.E,A,I

Robinson, Henry KY 6th Cav. Co.G,I,D,B

Robinson, Henry LA Mil. Brenan's Co. (Co.A, Shamrock Guards)

Robinson, Henry MS 1st (Foote's) Inf. (St.Troops) Co.B

Robinson, Henry MO Cav. 3rd Regt.St.Guard Co.A

Robinson, Henry MO Inf. 4th Regt.St.Guard Co.C

Robinson, Henry MO Inf. 5th Regt.St.Guard Co.A

Robinson, Henry NC 1st Arty. (10th St.Troops) Co.F

Robinson, Henry NC 1st Inf. Co.E

Robinson, Henry NC 52nd Inf. Co.H

Robinson, Henry SC 6th Cav. Co.C

Robinson, Henry SC Inf. 3rd Bn. Co.C

Robinson, Henry SC Palmetto S.S. Co.E

Robinson, Henry TN 4th Cav. Co.K

Robinson, Henry TN 10th Inf. Co.F

Robinson, Henry TX 4th Inf. Co.F

Robinson, Henry TX 22nd Inf. Co.E

Robinson, Henry VA 1st Cav. Co.G

Robinson, Henry VA Cav. Mosby's Regt. (Part.Rangers) Co.D

Robinson, Henry VA Lt.Arty. Pollock's Co.

Robinson, Henry Gen. & Staff,PACS Asst.Surg.

Robinson, Henry Brush Bn.

Robinson, Henry Gen. & Staff Maj.,AAG

Robinson, Henry B. VA 1st Arty. Sgt.Maj.

Robinson, Henry B. VA Lt.Arty. 1st Bn. Sgt.Maj.

Robinson, Henry B. VA 12th Inf. Co.E

Robinson, Henry C. NC 25th Inf. Co.H

Robinson, Henry C. SC Lt.Arty. Walter's Co. (Washington Arty.) Sgt.

Robinson, Henry C. TN 44th (Cons.) Inf. Co.E

Robinson, Henry D. NC 11th (Bethel Regt.) Inf. Co.F

Robinson, Henry D. VA Cav. 39th Bn. Co.D

Robinson, Henry F. AL 30th Inf. Co.H

Robinson, Henry H. MS 41st Inf. Co.G

Robinson, Henry H. NC 46th Inf. Co.K

Robinson, Henry H. TN 20th Inf. Co.A

Robinson, Henry Hal NC 54th Inf. Co.K

Robinson, Henry J. FL 6th Inf. Co.D

Robinson, Henry J. KY 5th Mtd.Inf. Co.A,K Capt.

Robinson, Henry J. MS 32nd Inf. Co.E

Robinson, Henry J. NC 3rd Arty. (40th St.Troops) Co.C

Robinson, Henry J. VA 6th Inf. Co.A

Robinson, Henry L. LA Conscr.
Robinson, Henry L. NC Coast Guards Galloway's Co.
Robinson, Henry O. TN 5th (McKenzie's) Cav. Co.A
Robinson, Henry R. VA 1st Inf. Co.I
Robinson, Henry S. TX Cav. 6th Bn. Co.E Sgt.
Robinson, Henry W. GA 42nd Inf. Co.B
Robinson, Henry W. KY 2nd Mtd.Inf. Co.A Cpl.
Robinson, Henry W. NC 14th Inf. Co.C
Robinson, Hezekiah AR Cav. Harrell's Bn. Co.C
Robinson, H.F. TN 40th Inf. Co.G
Robinson, H.H. MS Inf. 1st Bn. Co.A
Robinson, H.H. MS 3rd Inf. Chap.
Robinson, H.H. TX 1st Inf. Co.A 1st Lt.
Robinson, High VA Richmond Guards
Robinson, Hilton SC Inf. 9th Bn. Co.E
Robinson, Hilton SC 26th Inf. Co.F
Robinson, Hiram F. VA Cav. McFarlane's Co.
Robinson, Hiram F. VA 72nd Mil.
Robinson, Hiram F. Conf.Cav. 6th Bn.
Robinson, H.J. KY 10th (Diamond's) Cav. Co.B
Robinson, H.J. NC 1st Btty. Co.A 2nd Lt.
Robinson, H.J. TN Lt.Arty. Sparkman's Co.
Robinson, H.M. TN 1st Hvy.Arty.
Robinson, H.O. MS 40th Inf. Co.H
Robinson, Holcram TN 21st (Wilson's) Cav. Co.D Comsy.Sgt.
Robinson, Horace MO Inf. 3rd Bn. Co.D Sgt.
Robinson, Horiot V. GA Cav. 1st Bn.Res. McKinney's Co.
Robinson, Horshoe TX 12th Cav. Co.E
Robinson, Hosea AR 15th (Johnson's) Inf. Co.D
Robinson, H.P. AL 1st Cav. 2nd Co.A
Robinson, H.P. VA 3rd (Chrisman's) Bn.Res. Co.E
Robinson, H.P. VA 10th Bn.Res. Co.C
Robinson, H.R. VA 54th Mil. Co.A
Robinson, H.S. MS 2nd (Davidson's) Inf. Co.H Sgt.
Robinson, Hubbard TX 13th Vol. 2nd Co.D
Robinson, Hugh AL 44th Inf. Co.E
Robinson, Hugh SC 12th Inf. Co.F
Robinson, Hugh SC 15th Inf. Co.E Sgt.
Robinson, Hugh SC 19th Inf. Co.I Capt.
Robinson, Hugh SC 22nd Inf. Co.G 2nd Lt.
Robinson, Hugh J. AL 40th Inf. Co.B
Robinson, H.W. AR 5th Inf. Co.I Capt.
Robinson, H.W. FL 9th Inf. Co.F
Robinson, H.W. GA Lt.Arty. Fraser's Btty. Sgt.
Robinson, I.A. TN 6th (Wheeler's) Cav. Co.A
Robinson, Icem MO Inf. 8th Bn. Co.A
Robinson, I.F. MO 3rd Cav. Co.D
Robinson, I.G. TN Lt.Arty. Sparkman's Co.
Robinson, I.I. AL 3rd Cav. Co.C
Robinson, Ike S. MS St.Troops (Herndon Rangers) Montgomery's Ind.Co. 1st Sgt.
Robinson, I.M. VA Hvy.Arty. 19th Bn. Co.B
Robinson, I.P. MS 35th Inf. Co.F
Robinson, I.R. MS 35th Inf. Co.G Sgt.
Robinson, Ira AL 35th Inf. Co.G Sgt.
Robinson, Ira TX 9th Cav. Co.D
Robinson, Ira G. 3rd Conf.Inf. Co.K Capt.
Robinson, Isaac MO 10th Inf. Co.H
Robinson, Isaac SC 19th Inf. Co.I
Robinson, Isaac VA 8th Cav. Co.C

Robinson, Isaac A. VA 2nd Cav. Co.C
Robinson, Isaac G. AL 6th Cav. Co.L
Robinson, Isaac H. MO 10th Inf. Co.G Cpl.
Robinson, Isaac H. SC 20th Inf. Co.E
Robinson, Isaac W. NC 16th Inf. Co.M
Robinson, Isaiah M. TX 21st Cav. Co.H
Robinson, Isam MO 9th Inf. Co.A
Robinson, Israel KY 2nd (Woodward's) Cav. Co.C
Robinson, Israel VA 67th Mil. Lt.Col.
Robinson, Israel L. NC 29th Inf. Co.F
Robinson, Ivey SC 1st (Butler's) Inf. Co.E
Robinson, J. AL 24th Inf. Co.K
Robinson, J. AL 36th Inf. Co.D
Robinson, J. FL 7th Inf. Co.H
Robinson, J. GA 8th Inf. (St.Guards) Co.K Cpl.
Robinson, J. GA 59th Inf. Co.G
Robinson, J. KY Morgan's Men Co.C
Robinson, J. KY 9th Mtd.Inf. Co.H
Robinson, J. LA 22nd (Cons.) Inf. Co.D
Robinson, J. MS 28th Cav. Music.
Robinson, J. MS 15th Inf. Co.I
Robinson, J. MS 46th Inf. Co.H
Robinson, J. NC 1st Arty. (10th St.Troops) Co.B
Robinson, J. SC 17th Inf. Co.B
Robinson, J. TX 6th Field Btty.
Robinson, J. TX Lt.Arty. Dege's Bn.
Robinson, J. VA Inf. 1st Bn.Loc.Def. Co.E
Robinson, J. Gen. & Staff Hosp.Stew.
Robinson, J.A. AL 1st Cav. 2nd Co.D
Robinson, J.A. AL 42nd Inf. Co.F
Robinson, J.A. AL 60th Inf. Co.B
Robinson, J.A. AL 3rd Bn. Hilliard's Legion Vol. Co.C
Robinson, J.A. FL 1st Inf. New Co.B
Robinson, J.A. GA 16th Inf. Co.I
Robinson, J.A. GA 36th (Broyles') Inf. Co.B
Robinson, J.A. KY 2nd (Woodward's) Cav. Co.E
Robinson, J.A. LA Mil. British Guard Bn. Kurczyn's Co.
Robinson, J.A. MS 7th Cav. Co.A
Robinson, J.A. MS 28th Cav. Co.H Cpl.
Robinson, J.A. MS Inf. 1st Bn.St.Troops (30 days '64) Co.H
Robinson, J.A. MS 8th Inf. Co.A
Robinson, J.A. MS 25th Inf. Co.G
Robinson, J.A. MS 44th Inf. Co.G
Robinson, J.A. SC 2nd Inf. Co.E
Robinson, J.A. SC 22nd Inf. Co.G
Robinson, J.A. TN 12th (Green's) Cav. Co.K
Robinson, J.A. TN 19th (Biffle's) Cav. Co.B
Robinson, J.A. TX 32nd Cav. Co.I
Robinson, J.A. TX 4th Inf. Co.E
Robinson, J.A. TX 22nd Inf. Co.I
Robinson, J.A. VA 2nd St.Res. Co.G Cpl.
Robinson, J.A. VA 3rd (Chrisman's) Bn.Res. Co.F
Robinson, J.A. VA Lt.Arty. Jackson's Bn. St.Line Co.A
Robinson, J.A. Conf.Cav. Wood's Regt. Co.I
Robinson, Jabez P. SC 7th Inf. 1st Co.C
Robinson, J.A.C. MS 1st (Percy's) Inf. Co.B
Robinson, J.A.C. NC 23rd Inf. Co.H
Robinson, J.A.C. TN 33rd Inf. Co.E
Robinson, Jack GA 1st (Fannin's) Res. Co.K
Robinson, Jack TN Cav. 12th Bn. (Day's) Co.F

Robinson, Jack TN 14th (Neely's) Cav. Co.E
Robinson, Jack VA Mil. Carroll Cty.
Robinson, Jackson TX 9th Cav. Co.G Cpl.
Robinson, Jackson TX Cav. Wells' Bn. Co.A
Robinson, Jackson VA 29th Inf. 2nd Co.F, Co.C
Robinson, Jackson Deneale's Regt. Choctaw's Warriors Co.D
Robinson, Jackson L. MS 44th Inf. Co.D
Robinson, Jackson V. TN 55th (Brown's) Inf. Co.G
Robinson, Jacob FL 10th Inf. Co.A
Robinson, Jacob MO 3rd Inf. Co.A
Robinson, Jacob NC 16th Inf. Co.C
Robinson, Jacob SC 1st (Orr's) Rifles Co.G,K
Robinson, Jacob VA 18th Cav. Co.D
Robinson, Jacob VA 146th Mil. Co.H
Robinson, Jacob N. TN 14th Inf. Co.B
Robinson, Jacob T. VA 53rd Inf. Co.G
Robinson, James AL 51st (Part.Rangers) Co.A
Robinson, James AL 2nd Inf. Co.A
Robinson, James AL 9th Inf. Co.E
Robinson, Jas. AL 18th Inf. Co.D
Robinson, James AL Home Guards
Robinson, James AR Cav. 1st Bn. (Stirman's) Co.C
Robinson, James AR 8th Inf. New Co.F
Robinson, James AR 10th Inf. Co.K
Robinson, James AR 23rd Inf. Co.C
Robinson, James AR 27th Inf. Co.D
Robinson, James AR 30th Inf. Co.D
Robinson, James AR Inf. Ballard's Co.
Robinson, James GA 2nd Inf. Co.D
Robinson, James GA 2nd Bn.S.S. Co.C
Robinson, James GA 20th Inf. Co.A
Robinson, James GA 26th Inf. Co.D
Robinson, James GA 31st Inf. Co.G
Robinson, James KY 2nd (Woodward's) Cav. Co.F
Robinson, James KY 6th Cav. Co.D
Robinson, James KY 6th Cav. Co.G Sgt.
Robinson, James LA Ogden's Cav. Co.E Cpl.
Robinson, James LA 14th Inf. Co.D Cpl.
Robinson, James LA 15th Inf. Co.H
Robinson, James LA 20th Inf. Co.K
Robinson, James LA Miles' Legion Co.A
Robinson, James LA Mil. Orleans Fire Regt. Co.F Ord.Sgt.
Robinson, James MS 13th Inf. Co.G
Robinson, James MS 25th Inf. Co.H
Robinson, James MS 40th Inf. Co.C
Robinson, James MO Cav. Fristoe's Regt. Co.F Sgt.
Robinson, James MO Inf. Clark's Regt. Co.D
Robinson, James NC 2nd Cav. (19th St.Troops) Co.C
Robinson, James NC 6th Cav. (65th St.Troops) Co.A,F
Robinson, James NC 22nd Inf. Co.H
Robinson, James NC 24th Inf. Co.A
Robinson, James NC Loc.Def. Griswold's Co.
Robinson, James SC 4th Cav. Co.B
Robinson, James SC Cav. 10th Bn. Co.A
Robinson, James SC Lt.Arty. 3rd (Palmetto) Bn. Co.G
Robinson, James SC 1st (Orr's) Rifles Co.K Cpl.
Robinson, James SC 3rd Bn.Res. Co.B
Robinson, James SC 5th St.Troops Co.M

Robinson, James SC Inf. 7th Bn. (Enfield Rifles) Co.F
Robinson, James SC 8th Res.
Robinson, James SC Inf. Hampton Legion Co.H
Robinson, James SC Inf. Hampton Legion Co.K
Robinson, James TN 1st (Carter's) Cav. Co.C
Robinson, James TN 1st (Carter's) Cav. Co.M
Robinson, James TN 2nd (Smith's) Cav.
Robinson, James TN 9th (Ward's) Cav. Co.F
Robinson, James TN Lt.Arty. Weller's Co.
Robinson, James TN 1st (Feild's) Inf. Co.H
Robinson, James TN 9th Inf. Co.B
Robinson, James TN 11th Inf. Co.B
Robinson, James TN 17th Inf. Co.K
Robinson, James TN 23rd Inf. Co.E
Robinson, James TX 5th Cav. Co.E
Robinson, James TX 17th Cav. Co.E
Robinson, James TX 4th Inf. Co.E
Robinson, James TX 7th Inf. Co.G
Robinson, James VA 1st Cav. Co.A
Robinson, James VA 5th Cav. 1st Co.F
Robinson, James VA 19th Cav. Co.C
Robinson, James VA 21st Cav. Co.A
Robinson, James VA Vol. Binford's Co.
Robinson, James VA Lt.Arty. W.P. Carter's Co.
Robinson, James VA 13th Inf. Co.D
Robinson, James VA 37th Mil. 2nd Co.B Sgt.
Robinson, James VA 52nd Mil. Co.B
Robinson, James VA 53rd Inf. Co.I
Robinson, James VA 64th Mtd.Inf. Co.K
Robinson, James VA 67th Mil. Co.B Capt.
Robinson, James 3rd Conf.Cav. Co.F
Robinson, James 14th Conf.Cav. Co.H Cpl.
Robinson, James Conf.Cav. Clarkson's Bn. Ind.Rangers Co.H
Robinson, James 1st Choctaw & Chickasaw Mtd.Rifles Co.A
Robinson, James A. AR 9th Inf. New Co.I, Co.K Sgt.
Robinson, James A. AR 16th Inf. Co.G
Robinson, James A. FL Cav. 5th Bn. Co.I
Robinson, James A. GA 3rd Inf. Co.G
Robinson, James A. GA 39th Inf. Co.C
Robinson, James A. MS 11th Inf. Co.H
Robinson, James A. NC 25th Inf. Co.C
Robinson, James A. NC 37th Inf. Co.I
Robinson, James A. SC 20th Inf. Co.E
Robinson, James A. TN Arty. Ramsey's Btty.
Robinson, James A. TN 63rd Inf. Co.A
Robinson, James A. TX 2nd Cav. Co.C 1st Lt.
Robinson, James A. TX 27th Cav. Co.C
Robinson, James A. VA 9th Cav. Co.K
Robinson, James A. 2nd Conf.Inf. Co.G Cpl.
Robinson, James B. AL 21st Inf. Co.K
Robinson, James B. LA 12th Inf. 1st Co.M, Co.C
Robinson, James B. MS 12th Cav. Co.A 2nd Lt.
Robinson, James B. SC 5th Inf. 1st Co.B, 2nd Co.F
Robinson, James B. TX 12th Cav. Co.D
Robinson, James B. VA 7th Cav. Co.G
Robinson, James B. VA 17th Cav. Co.B Sgt.
Robinson, James B. VA 2nd Inf. Co.H
Robinson, James C. LA 7th Inf. Co.K Sgt.
Robinson, James C. NC 5th Cav. (63rd St.Troops) Co.C

Robinson, James C. TN 55th (McKoin's) Inf. McEwen, Jr.'s Co. 1st Sgt.
Robinson, James C. VA 1st Arty. Co.I
Robinson, James C. VA Lt.Arty. 38th Bn. Co.B
Robinson, James C. VA 28th Inf. Co.A
Robinson, James D. AL 15th Bn.Part.Rangers Co.B Sgt.
Robinson, James D. AL 56th Part.Rangers Co.B 2nd Lt.
Robinson, James D. GA 42nd Inf. Co.I 2nd Lt.
Robinson, James D. MS 27th Inf. Co.C Sgt.
Robinson, James D. TN 59th Mtd.Inf. Co.B 1st Sgt.
Robinson, James D. 4th Conf.Inf. Co.B Bvt.2nd Lt.
Robinson, James E. SC 3rd Cav. Co.C Cpl.
Robinson, James E. SC Mil.Cav. 4th Regt. Howard's Co.
Robinson, James E. TX Cav. Baylor's Regt. Co.H 2nd Lt.
Robinson, James E. TX 2nd Inf. Co.D
Robinson, James E. VA 1st Inf. Co.I
Robinson, James F. AL 16th Inf. Co.H
Robinson, James F. AR 23rd Inf. Co.G Maj.
Robinson, James F. GA Cav. 22nd Bn. (St.Guards) Co.H
Robinson, James F. KY 1st Inf. Co.H Sgt.
Robinson, James F. MO Cav. 3rd Bn. Co.D
Robinson, James F. NC 12th Inf. Co.A
Robinson, James F. SC 7th Inf. 1st Co.H, 2nd Co.H 1st Sgt.
Robinson, James F. SC Inf. 9th Bn. Co.E
Robinson, James F. VA 10th Cav. Co.B
Robinson, James F. VA 12th Cav. Co.I
Robinson, James F. VA Inf. 26th Bn. Co.D
Robinson, James F. VA 59th Inf. 2nd Co.B Sgt.
Robinson, James G. AR 1st (Colquitt's) Inf. Co.A
Robinson, James G. TX 27th Cav. Co.D
Robinson, James G. VA Inf. 5th Bn.Loc.Def. Co.F
Robinson, James H. AL 51st (Part.Rangers) Co.F
Robinson, James H. AL Cav. Lewis' Bn. Co.D Cpl.
Robinson, James H. AL 6th Inf. Co.I Sgt.
Robinson, James H. AR 1st (Colquitt's) Inf. Co.C
Robinson, James H. MS 11th Inf. Co.C
Robinson, James H. MS 26th Inf. Co.F Sgt.
Robinson, James H. NC 17th Inf. (2nd Org.) Co.A
Robinson, James H. NC 20th Inf. Faison's Co.
Robinson, James H. NC 26th Inf. Co.B Sgt.
Robinson, James H. NC 26th Inf. Co.I,F
Robinson, James H. NC 61st Inf. Co.A Capt.
Robinson, James H. TN 13th Inf. Co.D,A 1st Lt.
Robinson, James H. TN 39th Mtd.Inf. Co.I 2nd Lt.
Robinson, James H. TN 60th Mtd.Inf.
Robinson, James H. VA 9th Inf. Co.K 2nd Lt.
Robinson, James H. 3rd Conf.Eng.Troops Co.F Artif.
Robinson, James I. MS 44th Inf. Co.C
Robinson, James J. AL Lt.Arty. 20th Bn. Co.A
Robinson, James J. GA 4th Inf. Co.D
Robinson, James J. GA 36th (Broyles') Inf. Co.E

Robinson, James J. TN 1st (Feild's) Inf. Co.D
Robinson, James J. TN 19th Inf.
Robinson, James J. VA 2nd Arty. Co.I
Robinson, James J. VA Inf. 22nd Bn. Co.G
Robinson, James K. SC 7th Inf. 2nd Co.H
Robinson, James K. TX Cav. Exempt Bn. Co.B
Robinson, James K.P. VA 38th Inf. Co.K
Robinson, Jas. L. AL 26th Inf. Co.H
Robinson, James L. AR 13th Inf. Co.B,G
Robinson, James L. MS 11th Inf. Co.H Sgt.
Robinson, James L. NC 3rd Arty. (40th St.Troops) Co.C
Robinson, James L. NC 16th Inf. Co.H Capt.
Robinson, James L. TN Holman's Bn.Part.Rangers Co.A
Robinson, James M. AL 7th Cav. Co.A 1st Lt.
Robinson, James M. AL 3rd Inf. Co.B,G
Robinson, James M. AL 4th Inf. Co.E Cpl.
Robinson, James M. AL 14th Inf. Co.C
Robinson, James M. AR 14th (Powers') Inf. Co.H
Robinson, James M. AR 27th Inf. Co.F
Robinson, James M. FL 8th Inf. Co.A 1st Lt.
Robinson, James M. GA Lt.Arty. Guerard's Btty. Cpl.
Robinson, James M. GA 5th Inf. Co.I
Robinson, James M. MS 6th Inf. Co.D
Robinson, James M. MS 35th Inf. Co.F
Robinson, James M. MS 36th Inf. Co.A
Robinson, James M. MO Cav. Poindexter's Regt.
Robinson, James M. NC 1st Inf. Co.C
Robinson, James M. SC 1st (Orr's) Rifles Co.K
Robinson, James M. SC 20th Inf. Co.E
Robinson, James M. TN Holman's Bn. Part.Rangers Co.A
Robinson, James M. TN 41st Inf. Co.F
Robinson, James M. TN 43rd Inf. Co.D
Robinson, James M. TN 43rd Inf. Co.H Cpl.
Robinson, James M. TX 1st Bn.RR
Robinson, James M. TX 12th Cav. Co.D
Robinson, James M. TX 11th Inf. Co.B
Robinson, James M. VA Lt.Arty. Donald's Co.
Robinson, James M. VA 29th Inf. Co.G
Robinson, James M. VA 46th Inf. 2nd Co.F
Robinson, James M. VA 60th Inf. Co.D
Robinson, James M. VA 72nd Mil.
Robinson, James M. 1st Choctaw & Chickasaw Mtd.Rifles 1st Co.I
Robinson, James Matt AL 4th Inf. Co.E
Robinson, James M.S. MS 44th Inf. Co.K
Robinson, James N. AL 32nd Inf. Co.D 3rd Lt.
Robinson, James N. GA 20th Inf. Co.B 1st Sgt.
Robinson, James N. TX 13th Vol. 1st Co.F Music.
Robinson, James N. TX 15th Inf. Co.D
Robinson, James O. VA 25th Cav. Co.B,H
Robinson, James Oscar TN 43rd Inf. Co.B
Robinson, James P. GA 36th (Broyles') Inf. Co.F Music.
Robinson, James P. NC 50th Inf. Co.E
Robinson, James P. VA Inf. 1st Bn. Co.A
Robinson, James R. AL 39th Inf. Co.F
Robinson, James R. FL 10th Inf. Co.A 1st Sgt.
Robinson, James R. GA 9th Inf. Co.H 1st Lt.
Robinson, James R. KY Horse Arty. Byrne's Co.
Robinson, James R. NC 30th Inf. Co.K
Robinson, James R. VA 34th Inf. Co.F Sgt.

Robinson, James R. VA Hood's Bn.Res. Tappey's Co.

Robinson, James S. MS 40th Inf. Co.H

Robinson, James S. SC 5th Res. Co.H Capt.

Robinson, James S. TX Cav. Morgan's Regt. Co.E

Robinson, James S. VA Lt.Arty. Garber's Co.

Robinson, James T. AL Lt.Arty. Kolb's Btty.

Robinson, James T. AL 37th Inf. Co.K

Robinson, James T. AL 3rd Bn. Hilliard's Legion Vol. Co.C

Robinson, James T. GA 57th Inf. Co.H

Robinson, James T. GA Phillips' Legion Co.K,D Cpl.

Robinson, James T. TX 10th Cav. Co.G

Robinson, James T. VA Lt.Arty. G.B. Chapman's Co.

Robinson, James V. VA 36th Inf. 2nd Co.C, 3rd Co.I

Robinson, James W. LA 8th Inf. Co.B

Robinson, James W. MO 16th Inf. Co.H Cpl.

Robinson, James W. SC 12th Inf. Co.C

Robinson, James W. TN 1st (Turney's) Inf. Co.E

Robinson, James W. TN 2nd (Robison's) Inf. Co.K 2nd Lt.

Robinson, James W. TX 29th Cav. Co.E 2nd Lt.

Robinson, James W. VA 7th Cav. Co.C,D

Robinson, James W.W. AL 43rd Inf. Co.A

Robinson, James Y. AR 19th (Dawson's) Inf. Co.F,K

Robinson, Jarvis Gen. & Staff Surg.

Robinson, Jason NC 39th Inf. Co.H

Robinson, Jasper GA Phillips' Legion Co.D

Robinson, Jasper D. GA 20th Inf. Co.B 2nd Lt.

Robinson, Jasper N. LA 12th Inf. Co.F

Robinson, J.B. AR 15th Mil. Co.D

Robinson, J.B. GA 10th Cav.

Robinson, J.B. GA Inf. 27th Bn. (NonConscr.) Co.A 2nd Lt.

Robinson, J.B. GA Inf. (NonConscr.) Howard's Co. Sgt.

Robinson, J.B. KY 7th Mtd.Inf. Co.I

Robinson, J.B. LA 13th Bn. (Part.Rangers) Co.A

Robinson, J.B. LA 27th Inf. Co.K

Robinson, J.B. MS Cav. Drane's Co. (Choctaw Cty.Res.)

Robinson, J.B. SC 2nd Bn.S.S. Co.B

Robinson, J.B. TN 8th (Smith's) Cav. Co.G

Robinson, J.B. VA Lt.Arty. Thornton's Co.

Robinson, J.B. 8th (Wade's) Conf.Cav. Co.K

Robinson, J.B.R. MS 1st (Patton's) Inf. Co.E

Robinson, J.C. FL Inf. 2nd Bn. Co.E

Robinson, J.C. GA 10th Cav. Co.D

Robinson, J.C. GA 1st (Fannin's) Res. Co.A

Robinson, J.C. LA 13th Bn. (Part.Rangers) Co.B

Robinson, J.C. MS Inf. 2nd Bn. Co.K

Robinson, J.C. MS 13th Inf. Co.K

Robinson, J.C. MS 44th Inf. Co.H

Robinson, J.C. MS 48th Inf. Co.K

Robinson, J.C. MO Cav. Williams' Regt. Co.C

Robinson, J.C. TN 3rd (Forrest's) Cav. Co.E

Robinson, J.C. TN Cav. Nixon's Regt. Co.D

Robinson, J.C. TN 38th Inf. Co.E 1st Lt.

Robinson, J.C. TN 44th (Cons.) Inf. Co.I

Robinson, J.C. TX 1st Inf. Co.D

Robinson, J.C. VA Cav. 1st Bn. (Loc.Def.Troops) Co.A

Robinson, J.C. VA Lt.Arty. W.P. Carter's Co.

Robinson, J.C. VA 3rd Inf.Loc.Def. Co.A

Robinson, J.C. 8th (Wade's) Conf.Cav. Co.F

Robinson, J.C.M. TN 28th (Cons.) Inf. Co.H

Robinson, J.D. LA 3rd (Harrison's) Cav. Co.C

Robinson, J.D. MS Cav. 2nd Bn.Res. Co.A Cpl.

Robinson, J.D. TN 18th (Newsom's) Cav. Co.K

Robinson, J.D. VA 8th Cav. Co.C

Robinson, J.D. Bradford's Corps Scouts & Guards Co.B

Robinson, J. DeW. MO Arty. Lowe's Co.

Robinson, J.E. AR 1st (Monroe's) Cav. Co.L Cpl.

Robinson, J.E. AR 6th Inf. Co.E

Robinson, J.E. AR 18th Inf. Co.K

Robinson, J.E. LA 28th (Gray's) Inf. Co.B Cpl.

Robinson, J.E. MS 2nd St.Cav. Co.K

Robinson, J.E. MS Cav. Ham's Regt. Co.G,K

Robinson, J.E. MO 10th Cav. Co.I 1st Lt.

Robinson, J.E. SC 1st (Butler's) Inf. Co.G

Robinson, J.E. SC 6th Inf. 1st Co.H, 2nd Co.F

Robinson, J.E. VA Mil. Washington Cty.

Robinson, J.E. Gen. & Staff Surg.

Robinson, Jeff. GA Inf. Hull's Co. Cpl.

Robinson, Jehiel F. TN 5th (McKenzie's) Cav. Co.G

Robinson, Jeremiah MS 21st Inf. Co.I,F

Robinson, Jeremiah NC 52nd Inf. Co.C

Robinson, Jeremiah SC Cav. 4th Bn. Co.A Sgt.

Robinson, Jeremiah Kirklin TX 24th Cav. Co.H

Robinson, Jervace W. VA 15th Inf. Co.G

Robinson, Jesse AL 11th Inf. Co.C Cpl.

Robinson, Jesse GA Inf. 23rd Bn.Loc.Def. Cook's Co.

Robinson, Jesse GA 26th Inf. Co.G

Robinson, Jesse NC 1st Arty. (10th St.Troops) Co.F

Robinson, Jesse SC 18th Inf. Co.B Sgt.

Robinson, Jesse SC 20th Inf. Co.E Cpl.

Robinson, Jesse TN 25th Inf. Co.C

Robinson, Jesse TN 26th Inf. Co.C

Robinson, Jesse TX 7th Cav. Co.G

Robinson, Jesse A. NC 29th Inf. Co.C

Robinson, Jesse A. VA 18th Inf. Co.F

Robinson, Jesse B. GA 31st Inf. Co.H

Robinson, Jessee GA 13th Cav. Co.I

Robinson, Jessee MO 8th Cav. Co.B

Robinson, Jesse I. GA 36th (Broyles') Inf. Co.F

Robinson, Jesse I. GA Cobb's Legion Co.C

Robinson, Jesse S. NC 6th Cav. (65th St.Troops) Co.A,E

Robinson, Jesse S. NC Cav. 7th Bn. Co.A Sgt.

Robinson, Jesse S. TN 13th Inf. Co.K

Robinson, Jesse W. VA 49th Inf. 3rd Co.G

Robinson, Jethro NC 32nd Inf. Co.D,E

Robinson, J.F. AL 4th Inf. Co.H

Robinson, J.F. AR 23rd Inf. Reason's Co.

Robinson, J.F. LA Res.Corps Scott's Co.

Robinson, J.F. TN 7th (Duckworth's) Cav. Co.D

Robinson, J.F. TN 8th Inf. Co.C

Robinson, J.F. TN 13th Inf. Co.G

Robinson, J.F. TX 33rd Cav. Co.A Capt.

Robinson, J.F. VA 25th Cav. Co.H

Robinson, J.F. 10th Conf.Cav. Co.K

Robinson, J. Frank MS 13th Inf. Co.C Sgt.

Robinson, J.G. AL Lt.Arty. Tarrant's Btty.

Robinson, J.G. LA Mil. Orleans Fire Regt. Pay M.

Robinson, J.G. MS 2nd Part. Co.A Cpl.

Robinson, J.G. MS 18th Cav. Co.G

Robinson, J.H. AL 3rd Cav. Co.C

Robinson, J.H. AL 5th Cav. Co.E

Robinson, J.H. AL 8th Cav. Co.D Cpl.

Robinson, J.H. AL 11th Cav. Co.A

Robinson, J.H. AL 14th Inf. Co.C

Robinson, J.H. AL 27th Inf. Co.G 2nd Lt.

Robinson, J.H. AL 33rd Inf. Co.K

Robinson, J.H. AL 46th Inf. Co.C

Robinson, J.H. AR 1st Mtd.Rifles Co.K

Robinson, J.H. AR Cav. Gordon's Regt. Co.A

Robinson, J.H. AR Cav. Gordon's Regt. Co.D

Robinson, J.H. AR 5th Inf. Co.I

Robinson, J.H. AR 10th Mil. Co.B

Robinson, J.H. AR 11th Inf. Co.C

Robinson, J.H. AR 11th Inf. Co.F Drum.

Robinson, J.H. AR 11th & 17th (Cons.) Inf. Co.C

Robinson, J.H. GA 36th (Villepigue's) Inf. Co.F

Robinson, J.H. GA 38th Inf. Co.N

Robinson, J.H. GA 64th Inf. Co.D Sgt.

Robinson, J.H. GA Phillips' Legion Co.D

Robinson, J.H. LA 17th Inf. Co.G

Robinson, J.H. MS 8th Inf. Co.A

Robinson, J.H. MS 32nd Inf. Co.G

Robinson, J.H. MS 46th Inf. Co.H

Robinson, J.H. MO 3rd Inf.

Robinson, J.H. MO St.Guard

Robinson, J.H. SC 2nd Inf. Co.E

Robinson, J.H. TN 4th Inf. Co.H

Robinson, J.H. TN 24th Inf. Co.C

Robinson, J.H. TN 61st Mtd.Inf. Co.G

Robinson, J.H. TX Cav. 1st Regt.St.Troops Co.F

Robinson, J.H. TX 30th Cav. Co.C

Robinson, J.H. TX 4th Inf. Co.E

Robinson, J.H. TX 13th Vol. Co.D

Robinson, J.H. TX 13th Vol. 2nd Co.D

Robinson, J.H. TX 15th Inf. Co.A Cpl.

Robinson, J.H. VA Cav. 36th Bn. Co.A

Robinson, J.H. VA 40th Inf. Co.F

Robinson, J.H. Conf.Cav. Baxter's Bn. 2nd Co.B

Robinson, J.H. Conf.Cav. Wood's Regt. 1st Co.G

Robinson, J.H. 1st Conf.Inf. 1st Co.F

Robinson, J.J. AL 5th Inf. New Co.A

Robinson, J.J. AR 5th Inf. Co.I

Robinson, J.J. FL 1st (Res.) Inf. Co.G

Robinson, J.J. GA 54th Inf. Co.B 2nd Lt.

Robinson, J.J. GA Smith's Legion Co.F

Robinson, J.J. LA 3rd (Harrison's) Cav. Co.H

Robinson, J.J. MS Cav. 3rd Bn.Res. Co.D

Robinson, J.J. MS Inf. 3rd Bn. (St.Troops) Co.E

Robinson, J.J. SC 26th Inf. Co.F

Robinson, J.J. TN 6th (Wheeler's) Cav. Co.A

Robinson, J.J. TN Hunley's Regt.

Robinson, J.J. VA 7th Inf. Co.K

Robinson, J.J. VA 29th Inf. Co.A

Robinson, J.K. SC 3rd Bn.Res. Co.A

Robinson, J.K. TX 7th Inf. Co.K

Robinson, J.K.P. TX 13th Vol. Co.D

Robinson, J.L. AL 21st Inf. Co.D

Robinson, J.L. GA 56th Inf. Co.E

Robinson, J.L. LA Inf. 4th Bn. Co.B

Robinson, J.L. LA Inf. Pelican Regt. Co.F

Robinson, J.L. NC 52nd Inf. Co.I

Robinson, J.L. NC Mallett's Bn. Co.F
Robinson, J.L. SC 14th Inf. Co.F
Robinson, J.L. TN 10th (DeMoss') Cav. Co.C
Robinson, J.L. TN 11th (Holman's) Cav. Co.B
Robinson, J.L. TN 13th Inf. Co.F Cpl.
Robinson, J.L. TX 33rd Cav. Co.B
Robinson, J.L. VA Mil. Washington Cty.
Robinson, J.L.B. LA Inf. 4th Bn. Co.B
Robinson, J.L.B. LA Inf. Pelican Regt. Co.F
Robinson, J.M. AL 25th Cav.
Robinson, J.M. AL 7th Inf. Co.D Cpl.
Robinson, J.M. AL 23rd Inf. Co.F
Robinson, J.M. AR Cav. Gordon's Regt. Co.K
Robinson, J.M. AR 20th Inf. Co.D
Robinson, J.M. AR 50th Mil. Gleaves' Co. Sgt.
Robinson, J.M. GA Arty. 11th Bn. (Sumter Arty.) Old Co.C
Robinson, J.M. GA Brooks' Co. (Terrell Lt.Arty.)
Robinson, J.M. GA Inf. 25th Bn. (Prov.Guard) Co.E
Robinson, J.M. KY 8th Cav. Co.B
Robinson, J.M. KY 10th (Johnson's) Cav. Co.D
Robinson, J.M. KY 12th Cav. Co.K
Robinson, J.M. KY Cav. Thompson's Co. Sgt.
Robinson, J.M. LA 17th Inf. Co.G
Robinson, J.M. MS 7th Cav. Co.A
Robinson, J.M. MS 1st (King's) Inf. (St.Troops) D. Love's Co.
Robinson, J.M. NC 5th Inf. Co.K
Robinson, J.M. SC 12th Inf. Co.F
Robinson, J.M. TN 3rd (Forrest's) Cav. 1st Co.F 3rd Lt.
Robinson, J.M. TN Arty. Bibb's Co.
Robinson, J.M. TN 34th Inf. Co.D
Robinson, J.M. TN 84th Inf. Co.D
Robinson, J.M. TX 30th Cav. Co.E 1st Sgt.
Robinson, J.M. TX Cav. Wells' Bn. Lt., Ord.Off.
Robinson, J.M. TX 18th Inf. Co.H
Robinson, J.M. VA 18th Inf. Co.F
Robinson, J.M. 1st Conf.Inf. 1st Co.F
Robinson, J.M. Eng.,CSA Capt.
Robinson, J.M.C. MS 26th Inf. Co.K,G
Robinson, J.N. AL 3rd Cav. Co.A
Robinson, J.N. AR Cav. Davies' Bn. Co.B
Robinson, J.N. AR 30th Inf. Co.F Cpl.
Robinson, J.N. GA 50th Inf. Co.B
Robinson, J.N. LA 13th Bn. (Part.Rangers) Co.D
Robinson, J.N. NC 34th Inf. Co.H
Robinson, J.N. TN Inf. 2nd Cons.Regt. Co.D
Robinson, J.N. TN 12th Inf. Co.F
Robinson, J.N. TN 12th (Cons.) Inf. Co.B
Robinson, J.N. TX 11th Cav. Co.K
Robinson, J.N. VA 3rd (Chrisman's) Bn.Res. Co.E
Robinson, J.N.P. GA Arty. St.Troops Pruden's Btty. Cpl.
Robinson, J.O. KY 2nd (Duke's) Cav. Co.A
Robinson, J.O. SC 1st (Butler's) Inf. Co.E
Robinson, J.O. SC 3rd Res. Co.K
Robinson, J.O. SC 4th Inf. Co.D
Robinson, Joel AR 34th Inf. Co.H
Robinson, Joel T. TX 15th Cav. Co.A
Robinson, Johiel VA 64th Mtd.Inf. 2nd Co.F
Robinson, John AL Jenks' Arty. Co.I

Robinson, John AL 1st Regt. Mobile Vol. British Guard Co.A
Robinson, John AL 6th Inf. Co.I
Robinson, John AL 16th Inf. Co.H
Robinson, John AL 18th Inf.
Robinson, John AL 27th Inf. Co.G
Robinson, John AL 30th Inf. Co.D
Robinson, John AL 32nd Inf. Co.I
Robinson, John AL 43rd Inf. Co.B
Robinson, John AL 47th Inf. Co.I
Robinson, John AL Montgomery Guards
Robinson, John AR 11th Inf. Co.A
Robinson, John AR 27th Inf. Co.I
Robinson, John AR 62nd Mil. Co.E
Robinson, John FL 9th Inf. Co.K
Robinson, John GA 6th Cav. Co.G
Robinson, John GA Cav. Roswell Bn. Co.C Cpl.
Robinson, John GA 2nd Res. Co.C
Robinson, John GA 3rd Res. Co.D
Robinson, John GA Inf. 5th Bn. (St.Guards) Co.D
Robinson, John GA 10th Inf. Co.K
Robinson, John GA Inf. 25th Bn. (Prov.Guard) Co.E
Robinson, John GA 27th Inf. Co.H
Robinson, John GA 30th Inf. Co.H
Robinson, John KY 4th Cav. Co.A
Robinson, John KY 4th Cav. Co.D
Robinson, John LA 1st Cav. Co.E
Robinson, John LA 1st Hvy.Arty. (Reg.) Co.G,K 1st Sgt.
Robinson, John LA 1st Hvy.Arty. (Reg.) Co.I,K
Robinson, John LA 4th Inf. Co.K
Robinson, John LA 5th Inf. Co.H
Robinson, John LA 8th Inf. Co.A
Robinson, John LA 9th Inf. Co.F
Robinson, John LA 22nd Inf. Co.C,D
Robinson, John LA 26th Inf. Co.C
Robinson, John LA Mil. British Guard Bn. Coburn's Co.
Robinson, John MS 2nd Cav. Co.A
Robinson, John MS 7th Cav. Co.A
Robinson, John MS Cav. Jeff Davis Legion Co.C Cpl.
Robinson, John MS 6th Inf. Co.B
Robinson, John MS 11th Inf. Co.E
Robinson, John MS 32nd Inf. Co.B
Robinson, John MS Terry's Co.
Robinson, John MO 3rd Cav. Co.C
Robinson, John MO Cav. Fristoe's Regt. Co.D
Robinson, John MO 5th Inf. Co.A
Robinson, John MO Inf. Clark's Regt. Co.I
Robinson, John NC 2nd Inf. Co.B
Robinson, John NC 2nd Inf. Co.I
Robinson, John NC 11th (Bethel Regt.) Inf. Co.F
Robinson, John NC 32nd Inf.
Robinson, John NC 50th Inf. Co.E
Robinson, John NC 64th Inf. Co.G
Robinson, John NC Coast Guards Galloway's Co.
Robinson, John NC Lt.Arty. Thomas' Legion Levi's Btty.
Robinson, John SC 4th Cav. Co.K
Robinson, John SC 7th Cav. Co.B
Robinson, John SC Mil.Cav. Rutledge's Co.
Robinson, John SC 2nd Arty. Co.C
Robinson, John SC 2nd Arty. Co.I

Robinson, John SC Lt.Arty. 3rd (Palmetto) Bn. Co.G
Robinson, John SC 1st (Butler's) Inf. Co.D
Robinson, John SC 5th Inf. 2nd Co.A
Robinson, John SC 5th St.Troops Co.M
Robinson, John SC 8th Res.
Robinson, John SC 18th Inf. Co.B
Robinson, John TN 5th (McKenzie's) Cav. Co.C
Robinson, John TN 7th (Duckworth's) Cav. Co.L
Robinson, John TN 13th (Gore's) Cav. Co.D
Robinson, John TN 14th (Neely's) Cav. Co.E
Robinson, John TN 14th (Neely's) Cav. Co.G 2nd Lt.
Robinson, John TN Cav. 16th Bn. (Neal's) Co.C
Robinson, John TN Cav. 16th Bn. (Neal's) Co.E
Robinson, John TN 12th (Cons.) Inf. Co.H
Robinson, John TN 17th Inf. Co.G,A,E
Robinson, John TN 26th Inf. Co.A Sgt.
Robinson, John TN 28th Inf. Co.H
Robinson, John TN 28th (Cons.) Inf. Co.C
Robinson, John TN 29th Inf. Co.H
Robinson, John Inf. Bailey's Cons.Regt. Co.B
Robinson, John, Jr. TX 5th Cav. Co.E
Robinson, John, Sr. TX 5th Cav. Co.E
Robinson, John TX Arty. 4th Bn. Co.A
Robinson, John TX 10th Field Btty. QMSgt.
Robinson, John TX 3rd Inf. Co.D
Robinson, John TX 13th Vol. Co.M
Robinson, John TX Vol. Rainey's Co. Cpl.
Robinson, John TX Waul's Legion Co.B
Robinson, John VA 7th Cav. Co.E
Robinson, John VA 7th Cav. Co.I
Robinson, John VA 18th Cav. Co.C Cpl.
Robinson, John VA 20th Cav. Co.I
Robinson, John VA 25th Cav. Co.K,I
Robinson, John VA Cav. 46th Bn. Co.F
Robinson, John VA Cav. Mosby's Regt. (Part.Rangers) Co.B
Robinson, John VA 3rd Lt.Arty. Co.F
Robinson, John VA Hvy.Arty. 10th Bn. Co.C
Robinson, John VA Hvy.Arty. 18th Bn. Co.E
Robinson, John VA Hvy.Arty. 19th Bn. 3rd Co.C
Robinson, John VA Lt.Arty. 38th Bn. Co.A
Robinson, John VA Lt.Arty. Barr's Co.
Robinson, John VA Lt.Arty. Grandy's Co. Music.
Robinson, John VA Inf. 1st Bn. Co.E
Robinson, John VA 2nd Inf. Co.H
Robinson, John VA 9th Inf. Co.F
Robinson, John VA 16th Inf. 1st Co.H Music.
Robinson, John VA 22nd Inf. Co.D
Robinson, John VA Inf. 26th Bn. Co.G
Robinson, John VA 27th Inf. Co.D
Robinson, John VA 49th Inf. 1st Co.G
Robinson, John VA 62nd Mtd.Inf. 1st Co.H Cpl.
Robinson, John VA 146th Mil. Co.H
Robinson, John Conf.Cav. Clarkson's Bn. Ind.Rangers Co.C
Robinson, John Forrest's Scouts T. Henderson's Co.,CSA
Robinson, John 1st Conf.Inf. 2nd Co.F
Robinson, John Conf.Inf. 8th Bn. Co.B
Robinson, John 1st Conf.Eng. Troops
Robinson, John 1st Choctaw Mtd.Rifles Co.H
Robinson, John A. AL 50th Inf.

Robinson, John A. GA 24th Inf. Co.C
Robinson, John A. GA 26th Inf. Co.G
Robinson, John A. MS 24th Inf. Co.B Cpl.
Robinson, John A. NC 6th Inf. Co.E,D
Robinson, John A. NC 32nd Inf. Co.D,E 2nd
   Lt.
Robinson, John A. NC Walker's Bn. Thomas'
   Legion Co.E 1st Lt.
Robinson, John A. SC 1st (McCreary's) Inf. Co.I
Robinson, John A. SC 12th Inf. Co.F
Robinson, John A. TN 3rd (Lillard's) Mtd.Inf.
   Co.A
Robinson, John A. TX Inf. Yarbrough's Co.
   (Smith Cty.Lt.Inf.) Cpl.
Robinson, John A. VA 5th Cav. Co.I
Robinson, John A. VA Inf. 9th Bn. Co.A Capt.
Robinson, John A. VA 19th Inf. Co.B
Robinson, John A. VA 25th Inf. 2nd Co.A Maj.
Robinson, John A. VA 53rd Inf. Co.H
Robinson, John A. VA 60th Inf. Co.I
Robinson, John A. Gen. & Staff Hosp.Stew.
Robinson, John B. AL 59th Inf. Co.I
Robinson, John B. AL Arty. 4th Bn. Hilliard's
   Legion Co.A
Robinson, John B. GA 4th (Clinch's) Cav. Co.B
Robinson, John B. GA 22nd Inf. Co.I
Robinson, John B. GA 26th Inf. Dent's Co.A
Robinson, John B. GA Inf. (Brunswick Rifles)
   Harris' Ind.Co.
Robinson, John B. LA 25th Inf. Co.C Sgt.
Robinson, John B. MS 20th Inf. Co.E
Robinson, John B. NC 1st Arty. (10th St.Troops)
   Co.G 1st Lt.
Robinson, John B. TX 15th Cav. Co.C
Robinson, John B. TX 35th (Brown's) Cav. Co.G
Robinson, John B. TX 13th Vol. 2nd Co.G
Robinson, John B. VA 3rd Res. Co.E
Robinson, John B. VA 55th Inf. Co.A
Robinson, John C. AR 32nd Inf. Co.H
Robinson, John C. GA 57th Inf. Co.H
Robinson, John C. MS 11th Inf. Co.G Jr.2nd Lt.
Robinson, John C. NC 25th Inf. Co.E ACS
Robinson, John C. NC 52nd Inf. Co.G
Robinson, John C. SC 9th Inf. Co.A
Robinson, John C. TX 7th Cav. Co.C Capt.
Robinson, John C. Gen. & Staff Capt.,Comsy.
Robinson, John D. GA 1st (Olmstead's) Inf.
   Co.B
Robinson, John D. MS 1st Inf. Co.A
Robinson, John D. TX 7th Cav. Co.I Sgt.
Robinson, John D. VA Cav. Mosby's Regt.
   (Part.Rangers) Co.A
Robinson, John D. VA 29th Inf. Co.A
Robinson, John D.W. MO Cav. Poindexter's
   Regt.
Robinson, John E. GA Lt.Arty. 12th Bn. 2nd
   Co.A
Robinson, John E. KY 2nd (Duke's) Cav. Co.B
Robinson, John E. NC 1st Jr.Res. Co.K
Robinson, John E. TN Cav. Allison's Squad.
   Co.A,D Sgt.
Robinson, John E. VA 21st Cav. Co.I
Robinson, John E.W. VA 28th Inf. Co.A
Robinson, John F. KY 9th Cav. Co.F
Robinson, John F. NC 2nd Arty. (36th
   St.Troops) Co.A
Robinson, John F. TX 7th Inf. Co.G

Robinson, John F. VA Hvy.Arty. 10th Bn. Co.B
Robinson, John G. AL 3rd Cav. Co.B Cpl.
Robinson, John G. AL 40th Inf. Co.B
Robinson, John G. VA 6th Cav. Co.A
Robinson, John G. VA 7th Cav. Co.I
Robinson, John G. VA Lt.Arty. Thornton's Co.
Robinson, John G. Conf.Cav. Wood's Regt. 1st
   Co.M Cpl.
Robinson, John H. AL 2nd Cav. Co.B
Robinson, John H. AL 4th (Russell's) Cav. Co.H
   1st Sgt.
Robinson, John H. AR 23rd Inf. Co.F
Robinson, John H. AR 25th Inf. Co.F
Robinson, John H. GA 12th (Robinson's) Cav.
   (St.Guards) Co.A
Robinson, John H. GA Lt.Arty. Pritchard's Co.
   (Washington Arty.)
Robinson, John H. GA 2nd Inf. Co.B
Robinson, John H. GA 5th Inf. Co.I
Robinson, John H. MS 2nd Cav. Co.B
Robinson, John H. MS 7th Cav. Co.A
Robinson, John H. MS 37th Inf. Co.K
Robinson, John H. MO Cav. 1st Regt.St.Guard
   Co.A
Robinson, John H. NC 2nd Arty. (36th
   St.Troops) Co.K
Robinson, John H. NC 1st Inf. (6 mo. '61) Co.H
   Sgt.
Robinson, John H. NC 29th Inf. Co.H Capt.
Robinson, John H. TN 8th (Smith's) Cav. Co.D
Robinson, John H. NC 52nd Inf. Co.B Adj.
Robinson, John H. NC 52nd Inf. Co.G Cpl.
Robinson, John H. TX Cav. 1st Regt.St.Troops
   Co.C
Robinson, John H. TX 26th Cav. Co.D
Robinson, John H. TX 33rd Cav. Co.C Maj.
Robinson, John H. TX 4th Inf. Co.G
Robinson, John H. TX 13th Vol. 2nd Co.C 1st
   Lt.,Adj.
Robinson, John H. VA 17th Cav. Co.E Sgt.
Robinson, John H. VA 24th Inf.
Robinson, John H. VA 38th Inf. Co.E Cpl.
Robinson, John H. VA 59th Inf. 2nd Co.I
Robinson, John H. VA 3rd Cav. & Inf.St.Line
   Co.A
Robinson, John H. Staff 1st Lt.,Adj.
Robinson, John H. Gen. & Staff A. of N.VA 1st
   Lt.,AAAG
Robinson, John H.W. VA Inf. 5th Bn. Co.A
Robinson, John J. AL 11th Inf. Co.E
Robinson, John J. AL 12th Cav.
Robinson, John J. AL Arty. 1st Bn. Co.D
Robinson, John J. GA 2nd Cav. Co.K
Robinson, John J. GA 1st (Olmstead's) Inf. Co.A
Robinson, John J. MS 1st Lt.Arty. Co.E
Robinson, John J. MS 23rd Inf. Co.E
Robinson, John J. TN 4th Cav. Co.A
Robinson, John J. TN 25th Inf. Co.E Cpl.
Robinson, John J. TX 7th Inf.
Robinson, John J. TX 8th Inf. Co.A
Robinson, John Jasper MS 1st Cav. Co.C
Robinson, John L. AL 6th Cav. Co.K
Robinson, John L. AL 44th Inf. Co.C Sgt.
Robinson, John L. GA 2nd Res. Co.K
Robinson, John L. GA 6th Inf. (St.Guards) Co.C
Robinson, John L. MS 2nd Part. Co.A
Robinson, John L. MS 13th Inf. Co.C

Robinson, John L. NC 28th Inf. Co.E
Robinson, John M. AR 8th Cav. Co.I
Robinson, John M. FL Milton Lt.Arty. Dun-
   ham's Co. Black.
Robinson, John M. MS 3rd Cav. Co.G Sgt.
Robinson, John M. MS Cav. 3rd Bn.Res. Co.C
   Sgt.
Robinson, John M. MS 34th Inf. Co.K
Robinson, John M. MO 8th Cav. Co.B
Robinson, John M. NC 18th Inf. Co.B
Robinson, John M. NC 20th Inf. Faison's Co.
Robinson, John M. NC 38th Inf. Co.D,B Capt.
Robinson, John M. NC 61st Inf. Co.A Sgt.
Robinson, John M. TN 6th Inf. Co.K Sgt.
Robinson, John M. TN 43rd Inf. Co.B
Robinson, John M. TX Cav. Hardeman's Regt.
   Co.E Cpl.
Robinson, John M. TX 5th Inf. Co.D Sgt.
Robinson, John M. TX 15th Inf. 2nd Co.D
Robinson, John M. VA Cav. 35th Bn. Co.B
Robinson, John M.M. SC Horse Arty.
   (Washington Arty.) Vol. Hart's Co.
Robinson, John N. VA 25th Cav. Co.H Sgt.
Robinson, John N. VA Inf. Mileham's Co.
Robinson, John O. GA Cobb's Legion Co.C
Robinson, John O. MS Inf. 5th Bn. Co.A
Robinson, John O. MS 43rd Inf. Co.I
Robinson, John P. NC 2nd Arty. (36th
   St.Troops) Co.G
Robinson, John P. NC 53rd Inf. Co.B
Robinson, John P. TN 41st Inf. Co.I
Robinson, John P. VA 4th Cav. Co.H
Robinson, John P. VA 5th Cav. Co.I
Robinson, John P. VA 17th Inf. Co.H
Robinson, John P. VA 22nd Inf. Co.F
Robinson, John P. VA 72nd Mil.
Robinson, John Patterson TX 20th Cav. Co.H
Robinson, John R. GA 3rd Inf. Co.G
Robinson, John R. GA 30th Inf. Co.G
Robinson, John R. VA 6th Inf. Ferguson's Co.
   Cpl.
Robinson, John R. VA 12th Inf. Co.H Sgt.
Robinson, John S. AL 3rd Res. Co.H
Robinson, John S. AR 19th (Dawson's) Inf.
   Co.F,K
Robinson, John S. KY 4th Mtd.Inf. Co.B
Robinson, John S. MS 3rd (St.Troops) Cav.
   Co.H
Robinson, John S. MS Lt.Arty. (Issaquena Arty.)
   Graves' Co.
Robinson, John S. MO Cav. Poindexter's Regt.
Robinson, John S. MO 5th Inf. Co.H
Robinson, John S. MO Robertson's Regt.
   St.Guard Co.1
Robinson, John S. NC 23rd Inf. Co.C
Robinson, John S. SC Inf. 3rd Bn. Co.G 1st Lt.
Robinson, John S. SC 25th Mil.
Robinson, John S. VA 1st Lt.Arty. Co.B Sgt.
Robinson, John S. VA 46th Inf. 2nd Co.A
Robinson, John S.E. AL 28th Inf. Co.D
Robinson, John S.E. AL 56th Inf. Co.G Cpl.
Robinson, John T. AL 13th Inf. Co.A
Robinson, John T. AL 18th Inf. Co.E Cpl.
Robinson, John T. AL 39th Inf. Co.F
Robinson, John T. GA Lt.Arty. Guerard's Btty.
Robinson, John T. GA 2nd Res. Co.K
Robinson, John T. GA Inf. 3rd Bn. Co.H

Robinson, John T. GA 4th Inf. Co.I
Robinson, John T. NC 52nd Inf. Co.I
Robinson, John T. SC 12th Inf. Co.C
Robinson, John T. VA 55th Inf. Co.L
Robinson, John W. AL Lt.Arty. 2nd Bn. Co.A
Robinson, John W. AL 3rd Inf. Co.H
Robinson, John W. AR 1st (Colquitt's) Inf. Co.G
Robinson, John W. AR 12th Inf. Co.E
Robinson, John W. AR 19th (Dawson's) Inf. Co.C,H Capt.
Robinson, John W. GA 27th Inf. Co.C Cpl.
Robinson, John W. GA 36th (Broyles') Inf. Co.F Music.
Robinson, John W. GA 57th Inf. Co.E
Robinson, John W. GA 59th Inf. Co.E
Robinson, John W. GA Phillips' Legion Co.A
Robinson, John W. KY 10th (Diamond's) Cav. Co.F Cpl.
Robinson, John W. LA 6th Inf. Co.E
Robinson, John W. LA 12th Inf. Co.B Sgt.
Robinson, John W. LA 28th (Gray's) Inf. Co.E 1st Lt.
Robinson, John W. MS 1st Cav. Co.F Cpl.
Robinson, John W. MS 7th Inf. Co.E
Robinson, John W. MS 27th Inf. Co.I
Robinson, John W. MS 36th Inf. Co.G
Robinson, John W. NC 5th Cav. (63rd St.Troops) Co.K
Robinson, John W. NC 1st Jr.Res. Co.K
Robinson, John W. NC 22nd Inf. Co.A
Robinson, John W. NC 57th Inf. Co.E
Robinson, John W. NC Inf. Thomas Legion Co.E
Robinson, John W. SC 5th Cav. Co.C
Robinson, John W. SC 25th Mil.
Robinson, John W. TN 2nd (Smith's) Cav.
Robinson, John W. TN 21st (Wilson's) Cav. Co.I
Robinson, John W. TN 13th Inf. Co.D,A
Robinson, John W. VA 2nd Cav. Co.C
Robinson, John W. VA 49th Inf. 3rd Co.G
Robinson, John W. VA 51st Inf. Co.B 2nd Lt.
Robinson, John W. VA 135th Mil. Co.I
Robinson, John W. Conf.Cav. Wood's Regt. Co.K
Robinson, John W. Gen. & Staff Capt.,Comsy.
Robinson, Jno. W. Gen. & Staff 1st Lt.,Adj.
Robinson, Jolly MS Inf. 1st Bn.St.Troops (30 days '64) Co.H Cpl.
Robinson, Jolly MS 5th Inf. (St.Troops) Co.G Cpl.
Robinson, Jolly H. GA Phillips' Legion Co.A,G
Robinson, Jonas AL Mil. 4th Vol. Co.A
Robinson, Jonathan FL 1st (Res.) Inf. Co.G
Robinson, Jonathan MS 7th Cav. Co.A
Robinson, Jonathan A. VA Lt.Arty. G.B. Chapman's Co.
Robinson, Jone R. AL 38th Inf. Co.F
Robinson, Jones TN 8th (Smith's) Cav. Co.G
Robinson, Jones Deneale's Regt. Choctaw Warriors Co.D
Robinson, Joseph GA Cav. 10th Bn. (St.Guards) Co.E
Robinson, Joseph GA 2nd Res. Co.C
Robinson, Joseph GA 45th Inf. Co.I
Robinson, Joseph GA 54th Inf. Co.B Sgt.
Robinson, Joseph LA 10th Inf. Co.D Sgt.
Robinson, Joseph LA 20th Inf. Co.K

Robinson, Joseph MD Inf. 2nd Bn. Co.H
Robinson, Joseph MS 8th Cav. Co.D Cpl.
Robinson, Joseph MS 12th Cav. Co.F
Robinson, Joseph MS 24th Inf. Co.G
Robinson, Joseph MS 27th Inf. Co.H Cpl.
Robinson, Joseph SC 5th St.Troops Co.H
Robinson, Joseph TX 15th Cav. Co.A
Robinson, Joseph TX 9th (Young's) Inf. Co.I
Robinson, Joseph VA 2nd Cav. Co.C
Robinson, Joseph VA Cav. 46th Bn. Co.F
Robinson, Joseph VA Hvy.Arty. 10th Bn. Co.E
Robinson, Joseph VA 5th Inf. Co.K
Robinson, Joseph VA 6th Bn.Res. Co.G
Robinson, Joseph VA 23rd Inf. Co.K 1st Lt.
Robinson, Joseph VA 42nd Inf. Co.A
Robinson, Joseph 3rd Conf.Cav. Co.D Capt.
Robinson, Joseph A. NC 43rd Inf. Co.G
Robinson, Joseph A. SC Inf. 7th Bn. (Enfield Rifles) Co.B
Robinson, Joseph B. FL 2nd Cav. Co.E
Robinson, Joseph B. LA 7th Inf. Co.K Drum.
Robinson, Joseph B. NC 52nd Inf. Co.G Cpl.
Robinson, Joseph B. TX Cav. Baird's Regt. Co.E
Robinson, Joseph B. VA Inf. 5th Bn. Co.F Cpl.
Robinson, Joseph B. VA 47th Inf. 3rd Co.H Cpl.
Robinson, Joseph C. TN 4th (McLemore's) Cav. Co.K
Robinson, Joseph C. VA 12th Inf. Co.C
Robinson, Joseph D. AL 37th Inf. Co.D,E Sgt.
Robinson, Joseph D. MS Inf. 3rd Bn. Co.A
Robinson, Joseph D. NC 15th Inf. Co.C
Robinson, Joseph E. GA 42nd Inf. Co.K
Robinson, Joseph F. SC 1st (Hagood's) Inf. 1st Co.B, 2nd Co.B Sgt.
Robinson, Joseph F. VA Burks' Regt.Loc.Def. Beckner's Co.
Robinson, Joseph G. SC 1st Arty. Co.G
Robinson, Joseph H. GA 40th Inf. Co.A
Robinson, Joseph H. VA 8th Inf.Loc.Def. Co.D
Robinson, Joseph H. FL Brig.Band,CSA Music.
Robinson, Joseph J. FL 7th Inf. Co.C Music.
Robinson, Joseph J. NC 25th Inf. Co.C Music.
Robinson, Joseph J. VA 3rd Cav. Co.G
Robinson, Joseph K. LA 5th Inf. Co.D
Robinson, Joseph L. AL 33rd Inf. Co.D 2nd Lt.
Robinson, Joseph L. NC Walker's Bn. Thomas' Legion Co.E Sgt.
Robinson, Joseph M. NC 5th Inf. Co.I 2nd Lt.
Robinson, Joseph M. NC 64th Inf. Co.D
Robinson, Joseph S. KY 2nd Mtd.Inf. Co.H Sgt.
Robinson, Joseph S. MS 15th Inf. Co.I
Robinson, Joseph S. NC 22nd Inf. Co.H
Robinson, Joseph S. VA Inf. 1st Bn.Loc.Def. Co.F
Robinson, Josephus NC 1st Arty. (10th St.Troops) Co.G
Robinson, Josephus VA Inf. 23rd Bn. Co.B Cpl.
Robinson, Josephus VA 36th Inf. 2nd Co.I
Robinson, Joseph William MS 5th Inf. Co.D
Robinson, Joshua MS 7th Cav. Co.A
Robinson, Josiah AL 17th Inf. Co.D
Robinson, Josiah NC 51st Inf. Co.C
Robinson, Josiah D. TX 18th Cav. Co.G
Robinson, J.P. AL 15th Bn.Part.Rangers Co.A
Robinson, J.P. AR 45th Cav. Co.L
Robinson, J.P. AR 10th Mil. Co.C

Robinson, J.P. MS 18th Cav. Co.K
Robinson, J.P. MS Cav. Ham's Regt. Co.G Lt.
Robinson, J.P. MS 2nd (Davidson's) Inf. Co.H Jr.2nd Lt.
Robinson, J.P. MS 6th Inf. Co.K
Robinson, J.P. MS 31st Inf. Co.K Sgt.
Robinson, J.P. MO 6th Cav. Co.F Cpl.
Robinson, J.P. MO 3rd Inf. Co.G
Robinson, J.P. NC 6th Sr.Res. Co.K
Robinson, J.P. SC 2nd Cav. Co.G
Robinson, J.P. TN 33rd Inf. Co.E Sgt.
Robinson, J.P. VA 9th Bn.Res. Co.A
Robinson, J.P. VA 157th Mil. Co.B
Robinson, J.P. 1st Conf.Cav. 1st Co.K
Robinson, J.Q. SC 12th Inf. Co.G
Robinson, J.R. AL 1st Inf. Co.K
Robinson, J.R. AL 17th Inf. Co.E
Robinson, J.R. AL 18th Inf. Co.K
Robinson, J.R. AL 22nd Inf. Co.F
Robinson, J.R. AR 10th Mil. Co.C
Robinson, J.R. GA 16th Inf. Co.I
Robinson, J.R. GA 53rd Inf. Co.F
Robinson, J.R. MS 36th Inf. Co.K,I
Robinson, J.R. SC 6th Cav. Co.C
Robinson, J.R. TN 21st (Wilson's) Cav. Co.D
Robinson, J.R. TX 2nd Inf. Co.E
Robinson, J.R. TX 20th Inf. Co.A
Robinson, J.R. Gen. & Staff Maj.,CS
Robinson, J. Reed AR 25th Inf. Co.I
Robinson, J.S. AL 8th Inf. Co.B
Robinson, J.S. AL 43rd Inf. Co.C
Robinson, J.S. GA 56th Inf. Co.E
Robinson, J.S. LA 3rd (Harrison's) Cav. Co.H
Robinson, J.S. MS 1st Cav. Co.D
Robinson, J.S. MS 2nd Cav. Co.B
Robinson, J.S. MS 36th Inf. Co.G
Robinson, J.S. MO Cav. Coffee's Regt. Co.A
Robinson, J.S. NC 3rd Jr.Res. Asst.Surg.
Robinson, J.S. SC Cav. 17th Bn. Co.A
Robinson, J.S. SC 2nd Arty. Co.C
Robinson, J.S. SC 6th Inf. 1st Co.D Sgt.
Robinson, J.S. SC 7th Inf. Co.A
Robinson, J.S. SC Inf. 7th Bn. (Enfield Rifles) Co.H Cpl.
Robinson, J.S. SC 15th Inf. Co.A
Robinson, J.S. SC 20th Inf. Co.D
Robinson, J.S. VA 1st St.Res. Co.F
Robinson, J.S. VA Loc.Def. Ezell's Co.
Robinson, J.S.E. AL 32nd & 58th (Cons.) Inf. Cpl.
Robinson, J.T. AR 7th Inf. Co.F Capt.
Robinson, J.T. AR 32nd Inf. Co.I 1st Lt.
Robinson, J.T. AR 1st Mtd.Rifles Co.D Cpl.
Robinson, J.T. AR 1st (Dobbin's) Cav. Co.H Capt.
Robinson, J.T. GA 5th Res. Co.D
Robinson, J.T. GA 31st Inf. Co.G
Robinson, J.T. SC 4th Inf. Co.H
Robinson, J.T. TX 9th Cav. Co.H Cpl.
Robinson, J.T. TX 12th Cav. Co.G 1st Sgt.
Robinson, J.T. TX 1st Inf. Co.E
Robinson, J.T. TX 14th Lt.Btty.
Robinson, J.T. TX 15th Inf. Co.A
Robinson, J.T. VA 19th Inf. Co.K
Robinson, J.T. Gen. & Staff Capt.,Enrolling Off.
Robinson, Jude SC 1st (Hagood's) Inf. 1st Co.A
Robinson, Jude SC 25th Inf. Co.G Cpl.

Robinson, Julius C. NC 2nd Arty. (36th St.Troops) Co.I,L
Robinson, Julius C. VA Cav. Mosby's Regt. (Part.Rangers) Co.C Sgt.
Robinson, Junius AL Inf. 1st Regt. Co.K
Robinson, J.W. AL Cav. Hardie's Bn.Res. Co.A
Robinson, J.W. AL Arty. 1st Bn. Co.B
Robinson, J.W. AL 9th Inf. Co.I
Robinson, J.W. AL 21st Inf. Co.D
Robinson, J.W. AL McCroskey's Bn. Co.B
Robinson, J.W. AR Cav. Gordon's Regt. Co.A
Robinson, J.W. AR 5th Mil. Co.I
Robinson, J.W. AR 10th Mil. Co.B
Robinson, J.W. AR 24th Inf. Co.C Capt.
Robinson, J.W. FL 1st Inf.
Robinson, J.W. GA 1st (Fannin's) Res. Co.E
Robinson, J.W. GA Inf. 26th Bn. Co.C
Robinson, J.W. KY 5th Cav. Co.B
Robinson, J.W. KY 12th Cav. Co.G
Robinson, J.W. LA 13th Bn. (Part.Rangers) Co.D
Robinson, J.W. MS 1st Lt.Arty. Co.B
Robinson, J.W. MS 2nd (Davidson's) Inf. Co.F
Robinson, J.W. MS 17th Inf.
Robinson, J.W. MO Lt.Arty. 3rd Btty.
Robinson, J.W. NC 23rd Inf. Co.B Cpl.
Robinson, J.W. SC 1st Cav. Co.A
Robinson, J.W. SC 6th Cav. Co.C
Robinson, J.W. SC Cav. 14th Bn. Co.B
Robinson, J.W. SC Inf. 3rd Bn. Co.G
Robinson, J.W., Jr. SC Inf. 3rd Bn. Co.G
Robinson, J.W., Sr. SC Inf. 3rd Bn. Co.G
Robinson, J.W. SC Inf. 7th Bn. (Enfield Rifles) Co.G
Robinson, J.W. SC Manigault's Bn.Vol. Co.C
Robinson, J.W. TN 14th (Neely's) Cav. Co.G
Robinson, J.W. TN 15th (Cons.) Cav. Co.A
Robinson, J.W. TN Lt.Arty. Sparkman's Co.
Robinson, J.W. TN 4th Inf. Co.B
Robinson, J.W. TN 16th Inf. Co.B
Robinson, J.W. TN 33rd Inf. Co.F
Robinson, J.W. TX 29th Cav. Co.B
Robinson, J.W. TX 7th Inf. Co.B
Robinson, J.W. TX 15th Inf. Co.C
Robinson, J.W. TX Inf. Timmons' Regt. Co.A
Robinson, J.W. VA 3rd Inf.
Robinson, J.W. VA 3rd Res. Co.H
Robinson, J.W. VA Inf. 26th Bn. Co.B Cpl.
Robinson, J.W. VA 26th Inf. Co.A
Robinson, J.W. VA 53rd Inf. Co.F
Robinson, J.W. Conf.Cav. Wood's Regt. Co.I
Robinson, J.Y. SC Inf. 3rd Bn. Co.G
Robinson, J.Y. SC 25th Mil.
Robinson, Kelly H. AL 4th (Roddey's) Cav. Co.D
Robinson, King D. GA 3rd Inf. Co.I
Robinson, L. GA Cav. 21st Bn. Co.C
Robinson, L. SC 20th Inf. Co.D
Robinson, L. TX 23rd Cav. Co.B
Robinson, L. TX Cav. Baird's Regt. Co.G
Robinson, Lafayette MS 15th Inf. Co.I
Robinson, Lafayette TX 18th Inf. Co.H 2nd Lt.
Robinson, Larkin FL 5th Inf. Co.C
Robinson, L.B. LA 2nd Inf. Co.I
Robinson, L.B. SC 6th Inf. 2nd Co.D
Robinson, L.B. TN 43rd Inf. Co.K
Robinson, L.B. Gen. & Staff Hosp.Stew.

Robinson, L.C. TX Cav. Giddings' Bn. Carrington's Co.
Robinson, L.D. AL 8th Inf. Co.B
Robinson, L.D. MS 1st Lt.Arty. Co.D
Robinson, L.D. SC 4th Cav. Co.F
Robinson, L.D. VA 5th Cav. Co.G
Robinson, L.D. Conf.Arty. R.C.M. Page's Bn. 2nd Lt.
Robinson, Leggert AL 1st Bn. Hilliard's Legion Vol. Co.C
Robinson, Legget AL 60th Inf. Co.K
Robinson, Leigh VA Lt.Arty. R.M. Anderson's Co.
Robinson, Lem TN Lt.Arty. Browne's Co. Cpl.
Robinson, Lemuel AL Lt.Arty. 2nd Bn. Co.D
Robinson, Lemuel GA Lt.Arty. Milledge's Co.
Robinson, Lemuel D. VA 5th Cav. (12 mo. '61-2) Co.B 1st Sgt.
Robinson, Lemuel D. VA Cav. 14th Bn. Co.A
Robinson, Lemuel D. VA 15th Cav. Co.F
Robinson, Lemuel H. SC 20th Inf. Co.F
Robinson, Lemuel W. TX 22nd Cav. Co.H
Robinson, Leper M. VA 9th Cav. Co.H
Robinson, Leroy GA Arty. 9th Bn. Co.D
Robinson, Leroy GA 22nd Inf. Co.I
Robinson, Levi LA 13th Inf. Co.G
Robinson, Levi B. LA 16th Inf. Co.B Cpl.
Robinson, Levi G. AR 1st Mtd.Rifles Co.C
Robinson, Levi J. TX 13th Vol. 2nd Co.F
Robinson, Levi T. TX Cav. Martin's Regt. Co.F
Robinson, Lewis MS 13th Inf. Co.G
Robinson, Lewis TX 2nd Inf. Co.I
Robinson, Lewis VA Cav. 37th Bn. Co.E
Robinson, Lewis C. TX 9th Bn. Co.B
Robinson, Lewis D. AL 12th Inf. Co.I
Robinson, L.F. MS 6th Cav. Co.F
Robinson, L.F. NC Mallett's Bn. (Cp.Guard) Co.D
Robinson, L.G. LA 25th Inf. Co.K Sgt.
Robinson, L.H. AR 10th Inf. Co.A
Robinson, Livingston NC 28th Inf. Co.E
Robinson, L.J. AR 38th Inf. Co.C
Robinson, L.J. TX Cav. 1st Regt.St.Troops Co.D 1st Lt.
Robinson, L.J. TX 11th Inf. Co.F
Robinson, Llewellyn GA Arty. 11th Bn. (Sumter Arty.) New Co.C
Robinson, Llewellyn GA 9th Inf. Co.A
Robinson, Logan H. VA 9th Cav. Co.F Sgt.
Robinson, Logan H. VA 40th Inf. Asst.Surg.
Robinson, Logan H. Gen. & Staff Asst.Surg.
Robinson, Lorimer B. VA 53rd Inf. Co.D
Robinson, Louis MS 4th Cav. Co.F Jr.2nd Lt.
Robinson, Louis MS Lt.Arty. (Brookhaven Lt.Arty.) Hoskins' Btty.
Robinson, L.S. AR 4th St.Inf. Co.C 3rd Lt.
Robinson, L.S. MO 12th Cav. Co.H
Robinson, Lt. VA Lt.Arty. Montgomery's Co. Lt.
Robinson, Lucian B. VA 28th Inf. Co.A Hosp.Stew.
Robinson, Lucian D. VA Lt.Arty. W.P. Carter's Co. 2nd Lt.
Robinson, L.W. AL 5th Cav. Co.I
Robinson, L.W. FL 1st (Res.) Inf. Co.I
Robinson, L.W. FL 10th Inf. Co.A
Robinson, L.W. MS 28th Cav. Co.G

Robinson, L.W. Gen. & Staff Asst.Surg.
Robinson, Lyman M. VA 9th Inf. Co.F
Robinson, M. AL 3rd Cav. Co.B
Robinson, M. AL 1st Regt. Mobile Vol. Baas' Co.
Robinson, M. AL 9th Inf. Co.I
Robinson, M. AL 21st Inf. Co.D
Robinson, M. LA Inf. Pelican Regt. Co.H
Robinson, M. MS Cav. Jeff Davis Legion Co.I Cpl.
Robinson, M. MS Cav. Ham's Regt. Co.C
Robinson, M. MS 20th Inf. Co.E
Robinson, M. SC 2nd Arty. Co.F
Robinson, M. SC 1st (Hagood's) Inf. 1st Co.C
Robinson, M. TN 15th (Stewart's) Cav. Co.B
Robinson, M. TX Waul's Legion Co.H
Robinson, M. VA Cav. Mosby's Regt. (Part. Rangers) Co.C
Robinson, M. Cherokee Regt. Miller's Co. Cpl.
Robinson, M.A. AL 89th Mil. Co.D 3rd Cpl.
Robinson, M.A. Brush Bn.
Robinson, Major NC 23rd Inf. Co.E
Robinson, Manliffe R. TN 13th Inf. Co.D,A Sgt.
Robinson, Marcellus VA Lt.Arty. Garber's Co.
Robinson, Marcellus VA 13th Inf. Co.A
Robinson, Marcus L. GA 30th Inf. Co.G
Robinson, Marcus L. MS 2nd Inf. Co.E Capt.
Robinson, Marcus L. MS Inf. 3rd Bn. Co.K
Robinson, Mark GA 26th Inf. Co.G Sgt.
Robinson, Marshal G. NC 2nd Cav. (19th St.Troops) Co.G
Robinson, Marshall VA 19th Cav. Co.H
Robinson, Mat. AR 5th Inf. Co.I
Robinson, Mat Conf.Cav. Raum's Co.
Robinson, Mat B. AL 12th Inf. Co.H Capt.
Robinson, Mathew AL 44th Inf. Co.H
Robinson, Mathew VA Wade's Regt.Loc.Def. Co.E
Robinson, Mathew D. MS 43rd Inf. Co.H
Robinson, Mathew H. Conf.Cav. Clarkson's Bn. Ind.Rangers Co.A AQM
Robinson, Mathew Mc. AL 4th Inf. Co.I
Robinson, Matthew GA 26th Inf. Co.G
Robinson, M.B. AR 32nd Inf. Co.C
Robinson, M.B. AL 5th Cav. Co.G 1st Lt.
Robinson, M.B. MS 33rd Inf. Co.K
Robinson, M.B. TN 11th (Holman's) Cav. Co.H
Robinson, M.B. VA 15th Inf. Co.A
Robinson, M.C. LA 2nd Inf. Co.B
Robinson, M.C. SC 1st Cav. Co.D Cpl.
Robinson, M.D. AL 15th Bn.Part.Rangers Co.E
Robinson, M.D. LA 3rd (Wingfield's) Cav. Co.F
Robinson, M.D. TX St.Troops Teel's Co.
Robinson, M.E. AL 1st Bn.Cadets Co.A
Robinson, M.F. TN 20th Cav. Co.I
Robinson, M.H. AR 36th Inf. Co.H
Robinson, M.H. MS 18th Cav. Co.C
Robinson, Michael AL Lt.Arty. 2nd Bn. Co.E
Robinson, Michael AL Recruits
Robinson, Michael MS 2nd Inf. Co.F
Robinson, Michael MO 8th Cav. Co.G
Robinson, Michael NC 2nd Arty. (36th St.Troops) Co.H
Robinson, Michael NC 111th Regt.St.Troops Co.E
Robinson, Michael SC Inf. 9th Bn. Co.E

Robinson, Michael SC 26th Inf. Co.F
Robinson, Michael VA 30th Inf. Co.D Cpl.
Robinson, Michael J. TX 18th Cav. Co.G
Robinson, Milas AL 22nd Inf. Co.C
Robinson, Milas B. NC 43rd Inf. Co.B
Robinson, Miles J. VA Hvy.Arty. 10th Bn. Co.E
Robinson, Milton VA 8th Inf. Co.B
Robinson, Milton K. AL 33rd Inf. Co.B
Robinson, Milus J. AL 25th Inf. Co.E
Robinson, Mitchell GA Inf. White's Co.
Robinson, Mitchell E. NC 29th Inf. Co.D
Robinson, M.J. AL 34th Inf. Co.B
Robinson, M.J. AL Cp. of Instr. Talladega
Robinson, M.J. NC 39th Inf. Co.H
Robinson, M.J. SC 18th Inf. Co.B
Robinson, M.L. AR Cypert's Cav. Co.B
Robinson, M.L. GA 56th Inf. Co.B
Robinson, M.L. KY Cav. Sypert's Regt. Co.B
Robinson, M.L. LA 11th Inf. Co.I
Robinson, M.L. MS Inf. 7th Bn. Co.D
Robinson, M.L. NC 57th Inf. Co.G
Robinson, M.L. TX 9th Cav. Co.C
Robinson, M.L. VA Inf. 25th Bn. Co.C
Robinson, M.M. TX Cav. Hardeman's Regt. Co.C Sgt.
Robinson, M. McC. AL 9th Cav. Co.A 2nd Lt.
Robinson, M. McD. TX 21st Cav. Co.K
Robinson, M. McD. TX 24th Cav. Co.C
Robinson, M.N. LA 19th Inf. Co.I
Robinson, Monroe TN 4th Inf. Co.A
Robinson, Mortimer VA Inf. 1st Bn.Loc.Def. Co.E
Robinson, Moses TN 26th Inf. Co.K Sgt.
Robinson, Moses TN 63rd Inf. Co.F
Robinson, Moses 1st Choctaw & Chickasaw Mtd.Rifles 2nd Co.D
Robinson, Moses E. TX Cav. 6th Bn. Co.E 2nd Lt.
Robinson, Moses L. LA 20th Inf. Co.D
Robinson, M.R. AL 1st Cav. Co.A
Robinson, M.R. TN 18th Inf. Co.A
Robinson, M.S. MO Cav. 5th Regt.St.Guard Co.D 1st Lt.
Robinson, Munroe M. NC 43rd Inf. Co.B
Robinson, Murry SC 1st (Hagood's) Inf. 1st Co.A
Robinson, Murry SC 25th Inf. Co.G
Robinson, M.W. TN 7th (Duckworth's) Cav. Co.D
Robinson, N. AL 3rd Inf. Co.E
Robinson, N. GA Inf. 25th Bn. (Prov.Guard) Co.D
Robinson, N. NC 7th Bn.Jr.Res. Co.C
Robinson, N. TN 19th & 20th (Cons.) Cav. Co.D
Robinson, N.A. LA Maddox's Regt.Res.Corps Co.B
Robinson, Napoleon A. NC 3rd Arty. (40th St.Troops) Co.G
Robinson, Nathaniel GA Cav. 1st Gordon Squad. (St.Guards) Reeves' Co.
Robinson, Nathaniel TN 2nd (Robison's) Inf. Co.H
Robinson, Nathaniel VA 3rd Res. Co.C
Robinson, Nathaniel T. AL 9th Inf. Co.F
Robinson, N.B. TX 23rd Cav. Co.K
Robinson, N.C. 3rd Conf.Eng.Troops Co.B

Robinson, N.D. LA 1st Cav. Co.F
Robinson, Nelson LA 15th Inf. Co.F
Robinson, Nelson VA 25th Cav. Co.I Sgt.
Robinson, Newman SC 5th Inf. 2nd Co.A
Robinson, Newton NC 32nd Inf. Co.F
Robinson, Newton J. TN 24th Inf. Co.D,I
Robinson, N.F. GA 6th Cav. Co.I
Robinson, N.G. VA 30th Bn.S.S. Chap.
Robinson, N.G. VA 60th Inf. Co.I 2nd Lt.
Robinson, N.G. Gen. & Staff Chap.
Robinson, N.G.R. GA Lt.Arty. 12th Bn. 3rd Co.E
Robinson, N.H. AR 1st Mtd.Rifles Co.B
Robinson, Nimrod A. LA Inf. 11th Bn. Co.G
Robinson, N.J. AL 17th Inf. Co.H
Robinson, Noah AL Cav. Forrest's Regt.
Robinson, Noah GA 26th Inf. Co.G 2nd Lt.
Robinson, Noah A. AL 50th Inf. Co.C
Robinson, N.T.N. LA 1st Cav. Robinson's Co. Capt.,ACS
Robinson, N.T.N. LA Inf. 1st Sp.Bn. (Rightor's) Co.B 2nd Lt.
Robinson, N.T.N. Hodge's Staff Capt.,AAG
Robinson, O. MS 37th Inf. Co.B,F
Robinson, O. MS Cp.Guard (Cp. of Instr. for Conscr.)
Robinson, O. MO 2nd Cav. Co.D
Robinson, O. MO 12th Cav. Co.D
Robinson, O.D. Wheeler's Scouts,CSA
Robinson, O.E. NC Snead's Co. (Loc.Def.)
Robinson, O.J. MS Cav. 1st Bn. (McNair's) St.Troops Co.A 1st Sgt.
Robinson, O.J. MS Cav. Gibson's Co.
Robinson, O.J. MS Cav. Stockdale's Bn. Co.A
Robinson, Oliver P. NC 3rd Inf. Co.B,D
Robinson, O.P. NC Mallett's Bn. (Cp.Guard) Co.B
Robinson, O.P. TN 21st Inf. Co.G Sgt.
Robinson, O.P. Conf.Cav. Raum's Co.
Robinson, O.S. AL 32nd Inf. Co.D
Robinson, Oscar NC Lt.Arty. Thomas' Legion Levi's Btty.
Robinson, Oscar VA Lt.Arty. Barr's Co.
Robinson, Oscar VA 6th Bn.Res. Co.I
Robinson, Oscar VA 16th Inf. Co.F
Robinson, Oscar F. AR 32nd Inf. Co.B
Robinson, Owen B. NC Part.Rangers Swindell's Co.
Robinson, P. SC 5th Bn.Res. Co.E
Robinson, P. TN 19th & 20th (Cons.) Cav. Co.E
Robinson, P. TX 19th Cav. Co.F
Robinson, P. VA 3rd Inf.Loc.Def. 2nd Co.G
Robinson, P.A. TN 55th (McKoin's) Inf. Bounds' Co.
Robinson, Parker S. VA 63rd Inf. Co.F
Robinson, Patrick AR 1st (Colquitt's) Inf. Co.K
Robinson, Patrick GA 1st (Olmstead's) Inf. Co.A,E
Robinson, Patrick KY 10th (Diamond's) Cav. Co.A
Robinson, Patrick H. VA 5th Cav. (12 mo. '61-2) Winfield's Co.
Robinson, Patrick H. VA 13th Cav. Co.D Sgt.
Robinson, Patrick H. VA 28th Inf. Co.H
Robinson, Paxton VA Burks' Regt.Loc.Def. Beckner's Co.
Robinson, P.B. Gen. & Staff Capt.,QM

Robinson, P.C. LA 13th Bn. (Part.Rangers) Co.D
Robinson, Peter AL Arty. 1st Bn. Co.F Drum.
Robinson, Peter AR Inf. Cocke's Regt. Co.K
Robinson, Peter MS 5th Inf. (St.Troops) Co.D
Robinson, Peter TN 4th Inf. Co.B
Robinson, Peter TX 18th Cav. Co.F
Robinson, Peter VA Inf. 5th Bn. Co.D
Robinson, Peter VA 53rd Inf. Co.A
Robinson, Peyton AL Cav. Forrest's Regt.
Robinson, Peyton A. NC 20th Inf. Co.F
Robinson, P.G. AL 3rd Inf. Asst.Surg.
Robinson, P.G. NC 22nd Inf. Surg.
Robinson, P. Gervais SC 1st (McCreary's) Inf. Surg.
Robinson, P. Gervais Gen. & Staff Surg.
Robinson, P.H. FL Adv.Board Member
Robinson, P.H. SC 7th Inf. 1st Co.C, 2nd Co.C
Robinson, P.H. VA Burks' Regt.Loc.Def. Allen's Co.
Robinson, Philamon SC 4th St.Troops Co.B
Robinson, Philip B. GA Phillips' Legion Co.A Capt.
Robinson, Philip R. AR 32nd Inf. Co.B
Robinson, Philo NC 52nd Inf. Co.H
Robinson, Pinckney AL 46th Inf. Co.G
Robinson, P.L. FL Lt.Arty. Dyke's Co.
Robinson, Pleasant TN 28th (Cons.) Inf. Co.I Sgt.
Robinson, P.M. MS 18th Cav. Co.C
Robinson, P.O. TN 45th Inf. Co.C
Robinson, Powhatan Eng.,CSA Capt.
Robinson, P.P. AR Cav. Gordon's Regt. Co.E
Robinson, Pulk GA 64th Inf. Co.D Capt.
Robinson, P.W. AL Cav. Lewis' Bn. Co.C
Robinson, P.W. GA 9th Inf. Co.E
Robinson, R. AL 12th Inf. Co.B
Robinson, R. AL 15th Inf. Co.A
Robinson, R. AL 21st Inf. Co.D
Robinson, R. AL 24th Inf. Co.K
Robinson, R. AR 1st (Monroe's) Cav. Co.L
Robinson, R. AR 2nd Inf. Co.B
Robinson, R. AR 18th (Marmaduke's) Inf. Co.H
Robinson, R. GA 22nd Inf.
Robinson, R. GA Phillips' Legion Co.K
Robinson, R. KY 5th Cav. Co.H
Robinson, R. KY 8th Mtd.Inf.
Robinson, R. MS Lt.Arty. Turner's Co.
Robinson, R. SC Mil. 18th Regt. Co.E
Robinson, R. TN 14th Cav. Co.F
Robinson, R. TX 8th Cav. Co.L
Robinson, R. TX Inf. 1st St.Troops Biehler's Co.A
Robinson, R. VA 7th Cav. Co.K
Robinson, R.A. KY 2nd Mtd.Inf. Co.K
Robinson, R.A. TN 20th Inf. Co.D
Robinson, R.A. TN 23rd Inf. 2nd Co.F
Robinson, Ransom TN 63rd Inf. Co.A
Robinson, Rasha TX 13th Vol. 1st Co.H 1st Lt.
Robinson, R.B. AL 4th Cav. Co.E
Robinson, R.B. AL 6th Cav. Co.G
Robinson, R.B. KY 6th Mtd.Inf. Co.I
Robinson, R.B. SC 2nd Inf. Co.E
Robinson, R.B. TX 9th Cav. Co.I
Robinson, R.B. TX Cav. Benavides' Regt. Co.C
Robinson, R.C. TX Cav. Mann's Regt. Co.D
Robinson, R.D. SC 6th Inf. 2nd Co.C

Robinson, R.D. TN 49th Inf. Co.E
Robinson, R.E. TN 27th Inf. Co.G
Robinson, R.E. VA 6th Cav. Co.A
Robinson, Reily AL 49th Inf. Co.I
Robinson, Reuben B. NC 25th Inf. Co.C
Robinson, Reubene AL Mtd.Inf. J. Oden's Co.
Robinson, Reuben R. TN Cav. 4th Bn. (Branner's) Co.E
Robinson, Reuben W. GA 44th Inf. Co.E 1st Lt.
Robinson, R.F. VA 18th Cav. Co.C
Robinson, R.F. VA Lt.Arty. Parker's Co.
Robinson, R.G. MS Cav. 2nd Bn.Res. Co.A
Robinson, R.H. MS 2nd Part.Rangers Co.C
Robinson, R.H. NC 2nd Jr.Res. Co.F
Robinson, R.H. TX Cav. Benavides' Regt. Co.G Sgt.
Robinson, R.H. TX 2nd Inf. Co.E
Robinson, R.H.P. VA 3rd Inf.Loc.Def. Co.A 2nd Lt.
Robinson, R.H.P. VA 17th Inf. Co.A
Robinson, Rich TN 45th Inf. Co.C
Robinson, Rich. F. VA 9th Inf. Co.D
Robinson, Richard AL Cav. McCrosker's Bn. Co.D
Robinson, Richard AR 13th Mil. Co.F
Robinson, Richard GA 20th Inf. Co.G,E
Robinson, Richard KY 8th Cav. Co.I
Robinson, Richard SC 1st (Orr's) Rifles Co.K
Robinson, Richard TN 2nd (Ashby's) Cav. Co.E
Robinson, Richard TN Cav. Wilson's Regt.
Robinson, Richard TN 26th Inf. Co.C
Robinson, Richard VA 7th Cav. Co.I
Robinson, Richard VA 20th Cav. Co.I
Robinson, Richard VA 29th Inf. Co.C, 2nd Co.F
Robinson, Richard 1st Cherokee Mtd.Rifles Co.H
Robinson, Richard B. SC 20th Inf. Co.E
Robinson, Richard B.A. SC 20th Inf. Co.E
Robinson, Richard C. VA Lt.Arty. W.P. Carter's Co. Sgt.
Robinson, Richard F. VA 21st Inf. Co.F
Robinson, Richard F. VA 62nd Mtd.Inf. 1st Co.H
Robinson, Richard K. AL 30th Inf. Co.H
Robinson, Richard L. GA Arty. 11th Bn. (Sumter Arty.) Co.A
Robinson, Richard L. MS 35th Inf. Co.G
Robinson, Richard M. VA Inf. 5th Bn. Co.F
Robinson, Richard R. TN 44th (Cons.) Inf. Co.D
Robinson, Richard S. MS 34th Inf. Co.K Sgt.
Robinson, Richard W. VA 49th Inf. 3rd Co.G
Robinson, Richmond AR 24th Inf. Co.D
Robinson, Richmond C. VA Hvy.Arty. 10th Bn. Co.E
Robinson, Richmond L. AL 35th Inf. Co.G
Robinson, Riley AL 44th Inf. Co.G
Robinson, R.J. MS 8th Inf. Co.H Cpl.
Robinson, R.J. SC 1st (Butler's) Inf. Co.G Capt.
Robinson, R.J. TX 1st Hvy.Arty. 2nd Co.A
Robinson, R.L. AL 59th Inf. Co.I
Robinson, R.L. MS 1st (Patton's) Inf. Co.E
Robinson, R.L. TX 2nd Inf. Co.G Sgt.
Robinson, R.M. MS 10th Inf. Co.D
Robinson, R.M. MS 12th Inf. Co.D
Robinson, R.M. NC McLean's Bn.Lt.Duty Men Co.B
Robinson, R.M. VA Loc.Def. Scott's Co.
Robinson, R.N. AL 21st Inf. Co.C

Robinson, R.N. GA 16th Inf. Co.I
Robinson, R.N. TX 33rd Cav. Co.A
Robinson, R.O. TX 37th Cav. Co.G
Robinson, Rob VA 14th Cav. Co.D
Robinson, Robert AL 3rd Bn.Res. Co.C
Robinson, Robert AL Mobile City Troop Sgt.
Robinson, Robert GA 26th Inf. Co.G Sgt.
Robinson, Robert KY Miners Bn. Co.C
Robinson, Robert LA 6th Inf. Co.E
Robinson, Robert LA 21st (Patton's) Inf. Co.A
Robinson, Robert MS 18th Cav. Co.H
Robinson, Robert NC 23rd Inf. Co.G
Robinson, Robert NC 26th Inf. Co.B
Robinson, Robert SC 5th Inf. 1st Co.B, 2nd Co.F Cpl.
Robinson, Robert SC Mil. 22nd Regt. Co.E
Robinson, Robert VA 16th Cav. Co.D
Robinson, Robert VA Inf. 26th Bn. Co.D,G
Robinson, Robert VA 135th Mil. Co.C
Robinson, Robert VA 135th Mil. Co.I
Robinson, Robert A. NC 38th Inf. Co.E Bvt.2nd Lt.
Robinson, Robert B. VA 22nd Inf. Co.D
Robinson, Robert E. VA Cav. 39th Bn. Co.D
Robinson, Robert H. VA 6th Inf. Co.G
Robinson, Robert H. VA 47th Inf. Co.F
Robinson, Robert H. VA 59th Inf. 2nd Co.B
Robinson, Robert J. NC 46th Inf. Co.C
Robinson, Robert J. TN 41st Inf. Co.F Cpl.
Robinson, Robert J. TX 5th Cav. Co.I 2nd Lt.
Robinson, Robert L. KY 2nd (Duke's) Cav. Co.G
Robinson, Robert M. GA 38th Inf. Co.A Sgt.
Robinson, Robert R. VA 37th Mil. Co.D
Robinson, Robert S. TX 1st Inf. Co.L Cpl.
Robinson, Robert S. VA 2nd Arty. Co.I
Robinson, Robert S. VA Lt.Arty. Parker's Co.
Robinson, Robert S. VA Inf. 22nd Bn. Co.G
Robinson, Robert W. MS 42nd Inf. Co.B
Robinson, Robert W. VA 1st St.Res. Co.E
Robinson, Robert W. VA 34th Inf. Co.F
Robinson, Royal VA 2nd Inf.Loc.Def. Co.F
Robinson, Royal VA Inf. 6th Bn.Loc.Def. Co.C
Robinson, R.R. SC 5th Inf. 1st Co.I
Robinson, R.R. TN 2nd (Ashby's) Cav. Co.I
Robinson, R.R. TX Cav. 6th Bn. Co.A
Robinson, R.S. MS 18th Cav. Co.A
Robinson, R.S. TN 7th (Duckworth's) Cav. Co.D
Robinson, R.S. VA 18th Inf. Co.E
Robinson, R.T. KY 2nd Cav. Co.E
Robinson, R.T. SC Cav. 10th Bn. Co.D
Robinson, R.T.C. AL Inf. 1st Regt. Co.B Cpl.
Robinson, R.T.C. AL 45th Inf. Co.D
Robinson, Rufus AR 50th Mil. Gleaves' Co. Cpl.
Robinson, Rufus A. TN 41st Inf. Co.F
Robinson, Rufus A. VA 59th Inf. 2nd Co.I
Robinson, Rufus M. MO 3rd Cav. Co.C
Robinson, Rufus N. MS 11th Inf. Co.C
Robinson, Rufus P. GA Inf. 2nd Bn. Co.A
Robinson, Rufus W. VA 19th Inf. Co.B
Robinson, Rusell VA 25th Cav. Co.H Cpl.
Robinson, R.W. GA 46th Inf. Co.E 1st Lt.
Robinson, R.W. MS 6th Cav. Co.G
Robinson, R.W. MS 5th Inf. (St.Troops) Co.C
Robinson, R.W. MS 15th Inf. Co.I

Robinson, R.W. VA 2nd Inf.Loc.Def. Co.F
Robinson, R.W. VA Inf. 6th Bn.Loc.Def. Co.C Cpl.
Robinson, S. AR 51st Mil. Co.D
Robinson, S. KY 5th Cav. Co.F
Robinson, S. SC 6th Inf. 2nd Co.F
Robinson, S. TN Lt.Arty. Kain's Co.
Robinson, S. TN Inf. Nashville Bn. Fulcher's Co.
Robinson, S. TX Cav. Benavides' Regt. Co.C
Robinson, S.A. SC Mil. 16th Regt. Robinson's Co. Capt.
Robinson, S.A. SC 25th Inf. Co.B,A
Robinson, S.A. TN 8th (Smith's) Cav. Co.G
Robinson, S.A. TN 55th (Brown's) Inf. Co.G Sgt.
Robinson, S.A. TX 4th Inf. Co.E
Robinson, Sam TN Inf. 1st Cons.Regt. Co.H
Robinson, Sam 1st Choctaw Mtd.Rifles Co.D
Robinson, Sampson B. LA 7th Inf. Co.A
Robinson, Samuel AL Cav. Forrest's Regt.
Robinson, Samuel AL 32nd Inf. Co.I
Robinson, Samuel AL 40th Inf. Co.B
Robinson, Samuel AR 2nd Vol. Co.B 1st Sgt.
Robinson, Samuel AR 9th Inf. Co.D
Robinson, Samuel AR 31st Inf. Co.A
Robinson, Samuel GA 27th Inf. Co.B
Robinson, Samuel GA 29th Inf. Co.D,I
Robinson, Samuel KY Jessee's Bn.Mtd.Riflemen Co.A
Robinson, Samuel LA Cav. Cole's Co.
Robinson, Samuel MS Inf. 3rd Bn. (St.Troops) Co.D
Robinson, Samuel MS 4th Inf. Co.A Cpl.
Robinson, Samuel MO Cav. Jackman's Regt. Co.G
Robinson, Samuel MO Lt.Arty. Landis' Co.
Robinson, Samuel MO 11th Inf. Co.C,G
Robinson, Samuel NC 23rd Inf. Co.K
Robinson, Samuel SC 1st Cav. Co.G
Robinson, Samuel SC Arty. Fickling's Co. (Brooks Lt.Arty.)
Robinson, Samuel SC 2nd Inf. Co.I 2nd Lt.
Robinson, Samuel SC 2nd Rifles Co.A
Robinson, Samuel SC 8th Inf. Co.D
Robinson, Samuel SC 14th Inf. Co.A
Robinson, Samuel TN 2nd Cav. Co.F
Robinson, Samuel TN 7th (Duckworth's) Cav. Co.F
Robinson, Samuel TN 2nd (Robison's) Inf. Co.D
Robinson, Samuel TX 37th Cav. Co.G
Robinson, Samuel VA Hvy.Arty. 10th Bn. Co.E
Robinson, Samuel VA Hvy.Arty. 20th Bn. Co.E
Robinson, Samuel VA 36th Inf. Co.F
Robinson, Samuel VA 37th Inf. Co.F
Robinson, Samuel VA 63rd Inf. 2nd Co.I Jr.2nd Lt.
Robinson, Samuel VA Mil. Carroll Cty.
Robinson, Sam'l. A. Gen. & Staff Maj.,QM
Robinson, Samuel B. MS 9th Inf. Old Co.C, New Co.B
Robinson, Samuel B. MS 30th Inf. Co.B
Robinson, Samuel C. GA 36th (Villepigue's) Inf. Co.D Cpl.
Robinson, Samuel C. 1st Conf.Inf. 2nd Co.C Sgt.
Robinson, Samuel E. AL 6th Cav.

Robinson, Samuel E. GA 53rd Inf. Co.F
Robinson, Samuel E. SC 20th Inf. Co.E
Robinson, Samuel F. NC Coast Guards Galloway's Co. Sgt.
Robinson, Samuel G. LA 7th Inf. Co.H
Robinson, Samuel G. TX 22nd Cav. Co.H
Robinson, Samuel H. MS 31st Inf. Co.G 1st Sgt.
Robinson, Samuel H. VA Lt.Arty. G.B. Chapman's Co.
Robinson, Samuel J. NC 43rd Inf. Co.B
Robinson, Samuel L. AL 8th Cav. Co.K Cpl.
Robinson, Samuel McB. FL 7th Inf. Co.C Music.
Robinson, Samuel McF. FL Brig.Band,CSA Music.
Robinson, Samuel N. MS 26th Inf. Co.F
Robinson, Samuel N. SC 12th Inf. Co.E
Robinson, Samuel N.C. TN 28th Inf. Co.G
Robinson, Samuel P. KY 6th Mtd.Inf. Co.E
Robinson, Samuel S. GA 20th Inf. Co.B
Robinson, Samuel S. NC 16th Inf. Co.C
Robinson, Sam'l. T. AR 1st (Colquitt's) Inf.
Robinson, Samuel T. LA 9th Inf. Co.C 1st Lt.
Robinson, Samuel T. VA 5th Cav.
Robinson, Samuel W. AL 51st (Part.Rangers) Co.H
Robinson, Samuel W. AL 38th Inf. Co.K 1st Lt.
Robinson, Samuel W. KY 7th Cav. Co.H Sgt.
Robinson, Samuel W. NC 7th Inf. Co.F Sgt.
Robinson, Sandford AL 59th Inf. Co.K
Robinson, Sanford KY 5th Cav. Co.B
Robinson, S.B. AL 50th Inf. Co.G
Robinson, S.B. MS 24th Inf. Co.B
Robinson, S.B. NC 2nd Jr.Res. Co.F Cpl.
Robinson, S.B. SC Inf. Holcombe Legion Co.D Sgt.
Robinson, S.C. AR 2nd Inf. Co.K
Robinson, S.C. TN 17th Inf. Co.E
Robinson, S.C. TN 28th (Cons.) Inf. Co.A
Robinson, S.D. FL 1st (Res.) Inf. Co.I
Robinson, S.D. MS Cav. Gibson's Co. 1st Lt.
Robinson, S.D. MS Lt.Arty. 14th Bn. Co.A
Robinson, S.D. TN 6th (Wheeler's) Cav. Co.A
Robinson, S.D. TX Cav. Hardeman's Regt. Co.C Sr.2nd Lt.
Robinson, S.D. VA 31st Inf. Co.A
Robinson, S.E. SC 2nd Inf. Co.E
Robinson, S.F. TN 9th Inf. Co.H
Robinson, S.G. GA 7th Cav. Co.G
Robinson, S.G. GA Cav. 24th Bn. Co.A
Robinson, S.G. TN 5th (McKenzie's) Cav. Co.A
Robinson, S.H. MS 28th Cav. Co.G
Robinson, S.H. MO 12th Cav. Co.I
Robinson, S.H. TX Granbury's Cons.Brig. Co.E
Robinson, Shelly D. MS 16th Inf. Co.B Cpl.
Robinson, Sherod T. AL 43rd Inf. Co.B
Robinson, Sidney NC 6th Inf. Co.D
Robinson, Sidney J. AL 1st Bn. Hilliard's Legion Vol. Co.C
Robinson, Silas AL 35th Inf.
Robinson, Simeon B. MS 21st Inf. Co.G
Robinson, Simon A. AL 51st (Part.Rangers) Co.G
Robinson, Sion NC 2nd Arty. (36th St.Troops) Co.I
Robinson, Sion NC 38th Inf. Co.D
Robinson, S.J. AL 60th Inf. Co.K

Robinson, S.J. SC 3rd Inf. Co.B
Robinson, S.L. AL 5th Cav. Co.E
Robinson, S.L. SC 2nd Inf. Co.K
Robinson, S.L. SC 4th Inf. Co.H
Robinson, S.M. NC 49th Inf. Co.H
Robinson, S.M. TX Cav.St.Troops Doughty's Co.
Robinson, Smith VA 19th Cav. Co.D
Robinson, S.N. LA 14th Inf. Co.E
Robinson, S.N.C. TN 28th (Cons.) Inf. Co.A
Robinson, Sol. GA Cav. 21st Bn. Co.A 2nd Lt.
Robinson, Sol GA 1st (Symons') Res. Co.K 1st Lt.
Robinson, Sol GA Inf. 18th Bn. (St.Guards) Co.C Sgt.
Robinson, Solomon C. TN 28th Inf. Co.G
Robinson, Solomon H. TX 10th Inf. Co.H
Robinson, S.P. KY 7th Cav. Co.C
Robinson, S.P. MS 1st (King's) Inf. (St.Troops) Co.D
Robinson, S.P.C. TN Cav. 16th Bn. (Neal's) Co.C
Robinson, S.S. MS 2nd Part. Co.A
Robinson, S.S. MS 18th Cav. Co.F
Robinson, S.S. MS 19th Inf. Co.A
Robinson, S.S. MS 37th Inf. Co.H
Robinson, S.T. TX Cav. Mann's Regt. Co.K
Robinson, Starkie VA Lt.Arty. Douthat's Co.
Robinson, Starling L. GA Inf. Cobb Guards Co.A
Robinson, Stephen MO 5th Cav. Co.F
Robinson, Stephen SC 24th Inf. Co.A Drum.
Robinson, Stephen VA 19th Inf. Co.C
Robinson, Stephen M. NC 15th Inf. Co.H 2nd Lt.
Robinson, S.U. SC 5th Bn.Res. Co.E
Robinson, S.W. KY 5th Cav. Co.H
Robinson, S.W. LA Inf. 4th Bn. Co.B
Robinson, S.W. LA 17th Inf. Co.G
Robinson, S.X. MS 8th Inf. Co.H
Robinson, Sylvaneous G. AL Inf. 1st Regt. Co.A
Robinson, Sylvanus G. GA 47th Inf. Co.B
Robinson, T. AR 3rd Inf. (St.Troops) Co.C
Robinson, T. LA 2nd Inf. Co.D
Robinson, T. MS Cav. Hughes' Bn. Co.E 2nd Lt.
Robinson, T. SC Hvy.Arty. Mathewes' Co.
Robinson, T. Conf.Cav. Wood's Regt. 1st Co.A
Robinson, T.A. SC 14th Inf. Co.G
Robinson, T.A.J. AL 14th Inf. Co.D 2nd Lt.
Robinson, T.B. NC 1st Jr.Res. Co.A
Robinson, T.B. VA VMI Co.D Capt.
Robinson, T.B. 20th Conf.Cav. 2nd Co.H
Robinson, T.C. GA 56th Inf. Co.E
Robinson, T.C. NC 1st Jr.Res. Co.E
Robinson, T.D. TN 28th (Cons.) Inf. Co.I
Robinson, T.F. TX 24th Cav. Co.A
Robinson, T.G. GA Cav. 20th Bn. Co.A,F
Robinson, T.G. KY 4th Mtd.Inf. Co.E
Robinson, T.G. LA Mil. British Guard Bn. Coburn's Co.
Robinson, T.G. TX 6th Cav. Co.F
Robinson, T.H. AR 23rd Cav. Co.A 1st Sgt.
Robinson, T.H. AR 2nd Inf. New Co.E
Robinson, T.H. MS 2nd Inf. (A. of 10,000) Co.A Capt.
Robinson, T.H. MO 9th Bn.S.S. Co.C

Robinson, Thaddeus NC 2nd Jr.Res. Co.A
Robinson, Thaddeus K. MS 9th Inf. Old Co.E, New Co.K Cpl.
Robinson, Thaddeus P. AL Jeff Davis Arty. Hosp.Stew.
Robinson, Thad P. Gen. & Staff Hosp.Stew.
Robinson, Theodore LA 19th Inf. Co.H
Robinson, Theodore TX 16th Inf. Co.I
Robinson, Theodore VA 7th Inf. Co.H
Robinson, Thomas AR 1st Mtd.Rifles Co.D
Robinson, Thomas AR Mtd.Vol. (St.Troops) Abraham's Co.
Robinson, Thomas GA Cav. Corbin's Co.
Robinson, Thomas GA 57th Inf. Co.H
Robinson, Thomas GA Inf. (Express Inf.) Witt's Co. 2nd Lt.
Robinson, Thomas KY 9th Mtd.Inf. Co.H
Robinson, Thomas LA Mtd.Rifles Miller's Ind.Co. Sgt.
Robinson, Thomas LA 2nd Res.Corps Co.I
Robinson, Thomas LA 7th Inf. Co.G
Robinson, Thomas LA O'Hara's Co. (Pelican Guards,Co.B)
Robinson, Thomas LA Red River S.S. Co.B
Robinson, Thomas MS Lt.Arty. Turner's Co.
Robinson, Thomas MS 3rd Inf. Co.C 3rd Lt.
Robinson, Thomas MS 40th Inf. Co.H
Robinson, Thomas MS Terry's Co.
Robinson, Thomas MO 2nd Inf. Co.G Cpl.
Robinson, Thomas NC 2nd Arty. (36th St.Troops) Co.G
Robinson, Thomas NC 3rd Arty. (40th St.Troops) Co.H
Robinson, Thomas NC Lt.Arty. 13th Bn. Co.F
Robinson, Thomas NC 34th Inf. Co.C
Robinson, Thomas SC 11th Res. Co.G
Robinson, Thomas TN 1st (Carter's) Cav. Co.A Sgt.
Robinson, Thomas TN 14th (Neely's) Cav. Co.E
Robinson, Thomas TX Cav. Morgan's Regt. Co.B
Robinson, Thomas TX 9th (Nichols') Inf. Co.A
Robinson, Thomas VA 16th Cav. Co.A
Robinson, Thomas VA Inf. 1st Bn. Co.C
Robinson, Thomas VA 6th Inf. 1st Co.B
Robinson, Thomas VA 29th Inf. Co.G
Robinson, Thomas VA 59th Inf. 2nd Co.B
Robinson, Thos. Gen. & Staff Maj.,Comsy.
Robinson, Thomas A. MS Cav. Powers' Regt. Co.G
Robinson, Thomas A. MS 33rd Inf. Co.B,K
Robinson, Thomas A. MS 36th Inf. Co.A
Robinson, Thomas A. NC 3rd Cav. (41st St.Troops) Co.G
Robinson, Thomas A. NC 18th Inf. Co.K,B 1st Sgt.
Robinson, Thomas A. SC 2nd Rifles Co.E
Robinson, Thomas A. TX 27th Cav. Co.D
Robinson, Thomas B. NC Coast Guards Galloway's Co.
Robinson, Thomas B. VA 21st Inf. Co.G Capt.
Robinson, Thomas C. GA 1st Bn.S.S. Co.B Cpl.
Robinson, Thomas C. GA 5th Inf. Co.I
Robinson, Thomas C. GA Phillips' Legion Co.A
Robinson, Thomas C. VA 9th Cav. Co.K
Robinson, Thomas D. AL 44th Inf. Co.E Cpl.
Robinson, Thomas D. TN 41st Inf. Co.F

Robinson, Thomas E. SC 2nd Cav. Co.D
Robinson, Thomas E. TX 5th Cav. Co.I
Robinson, Thomas E.H. MS 8th Inf. Co.K Cpl.
Robinson, Thomas F. AL 51st (Part.Rangers) Co.A
Robinson, Thomas F. AL 2nd Inf. Co.A
Robinson, Thomas G. MS 15th Inf. Co.I
Robinson, Thomas G. VA 40th Inf. Co.I
Robinson, Thomas H. AL 35th Inf. Co.A
Robinson, Thomas H. KY 9th Cav. Co.E
Robinson, Thomas H., Jr. MS 2nd Inf. (A. of 10,000) Co.A
Robinson, Thomas H. MS 11th Inf. Co.G
Robinson, Thomas H. MS 30th Inf. Co.B Capt.
Robinson, Thomas H. MO 1st Inf. Co.B
Robinson, Thomas H. TX 1st (McCulloch's) Cav. Co.H
Robinson, Thomas H. VA 49th Inf. Co.C
Robinson, Thomas H.B. MS 2nd Inf. Co.D
Robinson, Thomas H.P. MS 11th Inf. Co.A
Robinson, Thomas J. AL 4th Inf. Co.E
Robinson, Thomas J. AL 29th Inf. Co.D
Robinson, Thomas J. AL 39th Inf. Co.D
Robinson, Thomas J. AL Cav. 5th Bn. Hilliard's Legion Co.D
Robinson, Thomas J. AR 32nd Inf. Co.I 1st Lt.
Robinson, Thomas J. GA 10th Cav. (St.Guards) Co.F
Robinson, Thomas J. GA 44th Inf. Co.H
Robinson, Thomas J. MD Cav. 2nd Bn. Co.A
Robinson, Thomas J. MS 20th Inf. Co.B
Robinson, Thomas J. MO 5th Inf. Co.F
Robinson, Thomas J. NC 2nd Bn.Loc.Def. Troops Co.C
Robinson, Thomas J. TN 19th Inf. Co.A
Robinson, Thomas J. TN 23rd Inf. Co.E Sgt.
Robinson, Thomas J. TX 15th Inf. 2nd Co.E
Robinson, Thomas J.S. MS 2nd Inf. Co.L
Robinson, Thomas L. VA Lt.Arty. Thornton's Co.
Robinson, Thomas L. VA 18th Inf. Co.F
Robinson, Thomas L. VA 55th Inf. Co.M
Robinson, Thomas M. NC 2nd Arty. (36th St.Troops) Co.A Cpl.
Robinson, Thomas M. NC 20th Inf. Faison's Co.
Robinson, Thomas M. NC 30th Inf. Co.A
Robinson, Thomas M. NC 52nd Inf. Co.G
Robinson, Thomas M. NC 67th Inf. Capt.
Robinson, Thomas M. TN 21st (Wilson's) Cav. Co.E
Robinson, Thomas M. Gen. & Staff, QM Dept. Capt.,AQM
Robinson, Thomas N. MS 20th Inf. Co.H
Robinson, Thomas P. VA Inf. 5th Bn. Co.F
Robinson, Thomas P. VA 53rd Inf. Co.F
Robinson, Thomas P. 8th (Dearing's) Conf.Cav. Co.E
Robinson, Thomas R. NC 23rd Inf. Co.G
Robinson, Thomas R. VA 45th Inf. Co.D Cpl.
Robinson, Thomas S. GA 6th Cav. Co.G Sgt.
Robinson, Thomas S. GA 21st Inf. Old Co.E
Robinson, Thomas S. VA 12th Inf. Co.H
Robinson, Thomas U. TX 18th Cav. Co.D Cpl.
Robinson, Thomas V. VA 1st Arty. Co.K
Robinson, Thomas V. VA Arty. L.F. Jones' Co.
Robinson, Thomas V. VA 34th Inf. Co.A Ord.Sgt.

Robinson, Thomas W. VA Lt.Arty. Brander's Co.
Robinson, Thompson NC 53rd Inf. Co.B
Robinson, Tho. P. VA 24th Cav. Co.K
Robinson, Timothy GA 27th Inf. Co.C
Robinson, T.J. AL 10th Cav. Co.D
Robinson, T.J. AR Cav. 1st Bn. (Stirman's) Co.D
Robinson, T.J. MS Inf. 1st Bn.St.Troops (30 days '64) Co.E
Robinson, T.J. MS Inf. 3rd Bn. (St.Troops) Co.E
Robinson, T.J. SC 9th Inf. Co.D
Robinson, T.J. SC Palmetto S.S. Co.E
Robinson, T.J. TN 14th (Neely's) Cav. Co.G
Robinson, T.J. TN 4th Inf. Co.B
Robinson, T.J. TN 8th Inf. Co.D 1st Sgt.
Robinson, T.J. VA 10th Cav. Co.D
Robinson, T.J. VA 40th Inf. Co.F
Robinson, T.J. 10th Conf.Cav. Co.D
Robinson, T.J. Nitre & Min. Bureau War Dept.,CSA
Robinson, T.L. GA 2nd Cav. Co.D
Robinson, T.L. MD Inf. 2nd Bn.
Robinson, T.L. VA 1st Bn.Res. Co.G,E 1st Lt.
Robinson, T.L. Gen. & Staff Asst.Surg.
Robinson, T.M. TN 63rd Inf. Co.G
Robinson, T.M. TX 8th Cav.
Robinson, T.M. TX Cav. Morgan's Regt. Co.F
Robinson, T.M. TX 5th Inf. Co.C
Robinson, T.M. Hodge's Staff Capt.
Robinson, T.N. AL 55th Vol. Co.I
Robinson, T.N. MS 2nd Cav. Co.K
Robinson, T.N. TN 42nd Inf. 1st Co.I
Robinson, Tod C. GA 1st Inf. (St.Guards) Co.K
Robinson, Todd MO Cav. Wood's Regt. Co.C
Robinson, Toddy LA 19th Inf. Co.E 1st Lt.
Robinson, Tom MS 4th Cav. Co.F 2nd Lt.
Robinson, T.P. GA 62nd Cav. Co.L
Robinson, T.P. MS 6th Cav. Co.A
Robinson, T.R. MS 15th Inf. Co.H
Robinson, T.T. VA 3rd Res. Co.B Capt.
Robinson, Turner MS 18th Cav. Co.D
Robinson, T.V. VA Hvy.Arty. Allen's Co. Ord.Sgt.
Robinson, T.W. AR 7th Inf. Co.F 2nd Lt.
Robinson, T.W. GA 9th Inf. (St.Guards) Co.C 1st Sgt.
Robinson, T.W. LA 9th Inf. Co.K
Robinson, T.W. MS 2nd Cav. Co.G,A Sgt.
Robinson, T.W. TN 23rd Inf. Co.C
Robinson, T.W. TX 17th Cons.Dismtd.Cav. 1st Co.G, Co.E Cpl.
Robinson, U.A. TN 26th Inf. Co.C
Robinson, Valentine MO 4th Cav. Co.K
Robinson, Van MS Cav. Powers' Regt. Co.G Cpl.
Robinson, V.D. MS 9th Inf. Co.E
Robinson, Vincent G. TX 5th Cav. Co.I Sgt.
Robinson, W. AL 62nd Inf. Co.C
Robinson, W. AL Cp. of Instr. Talladega Co.C Sgt.
Robinson, W. AR 26th Inf. Co.F
Robinson, W. GA 64th Inf. Co.B
Robinson, W. KY 12th Regt. Co.B
Robinson, W. LA Inf. 1st Sp.Bn. (Rightor's) Co.B
Robinson, W. LA Inf. 4th Bn. Co.D

Robinson, W. LA Inf.Cons. 18th Regt. & Yellow Jacket Bn. Co.H,C
Robinson, W. LA 19th Inf. Co.F
Robinson, W. LA Mil. Chalmette Regt. Co.G
Robinson, W. LA Mil. Fire Bn. Co.B Lt.
Robinson, W. MS 2nd St.Cav. Co.G
Robinson, W. MS 7th Cav. Co.F
Robinson, W. MO Inf. 5th Regt.St.Guard Co.B
Robinson, W. SC 3rd Bn.Res. Co.D Cpl.
Robinson, W. SC 5th Bn.Res. Co.E
Robinson, W. SC 11th Res. Co.G
Robinson, W. TN 1st (Carter's) Cav. Co.C
Robinson, W. TN Patterson's Regt. Co.A
Robinson, W. TN Inf. Harman's Regt. Co.A Cpl.
Robinson, W. VA Cav. Hounshell's Bn. Co.C
Robinson, W. VA 11th Bn.Res. Co.F
Robinson, W. Exch.Bn. 2nd Co.C,CSA
Robinson, W. Gen. & Staff Asst.Surg.
Robinson, W.A. AL 41st Inf. Co.K
Robinson, W.A. AL 62nd Inf. Co.D
Robinson, W.A. AR 18th Inf. Co.F Sgt.
Robinson, W.A. GA Arty. St.Troops Pruden's Btty.
Robinson, W.A. GA Lt.Arty. Ritter's Co.
Robinson, W.A. GA Inf. (Express Inf.) Witt's Co. Sgt.
Robinson, W.A. KY 2nd (Duke's) Cav. Co.F
Robinson, W.A. KY 12th Cav. Co.H
Robinson, W.A. MS Inf. 1st Bn.St.Troops (30 days '64) Co.H
Robinson, W.A. MS 35th Inf. Co.A
Robinson, W.A. TN 3rd (Forrest's) Cav. Co.D
Robinson, W.A. TN 18th Inf. Co.F
Robinson, W.A. TN 62nd Mtd.Inf. Co.I 1st Lt.
Robinson, W.A. TX 30th Cav. Co.E
Robinson, W.A. TX 16th Inf. Co.D
Robinson, Wade M. TX Cav. Madison's Regt. Co.C
Robinson, Walker MO Inf. 3rd Bn. Co.D Cpl.
Robinson, Walker L. MO 6th Inf. Co.F Cpl.
Robinson, Wallace A. GA Inf. 1st Loc.Troops (Augusta) Co.F
Robinson, Walter LA 3rd (Harrison's) Cav. Co.G
Robinson, Walter MS Cav. 3rd Bn. (Ashcraft's) Co.E
Robinson, Walter NC 6th Sr.Res. Co.A
Robinson, Walter Calvin AR 36th Inf. Co.C Lt.Col.
Robinson, Walter J. FL Inf. 2nd Bn. Co.E Capt.
Robinson, Walter J. FL 11th Inf. Co.A Capt.
Robinson, Walter L. MO 2nd Cav. Co.C
Robinson, Walter M. TX 1st Inf. Co.L
Robinson, Walton TX 18th Inf. Co.H Sgt.
Robinson, Warren SC 5th Inf. 2nd Co.A
Robinson, Warren SC 9th Inf. Co.A
Robinson, Warren A. GA Inf. 8th Bn. Co.B
Robinson, Washington NC 6th Sr.Res. Co.A Sgt.
Robinson, Washington C. NC 23rd Inf. Co.C
Robinson, Watkins Leigh VA 1st Arty. Co.K
Robinson, W.B. AL 1st Cav. 2nd Co.E
Robinson, W.B. AL 48th Inf. Co.E
Robinson, W.B. AL Cp. of Instr. Talladega
Robinson, W.B. AL University Cadet
Robinson, W.B. GA 1st Cav. Co.K
Robinson, W.B. GA 13th Cav. Co.C

Robinson, W.B. GA Arty. 11th Bn. (Sumter Arty.) Old Co.C

262

Robinson, W.B. GA Arty. 11th Bn. (Sumter Arty.) Old Co.C
Robinson, W.B. LA 18th Inf. Co.K Cpl.
Robinson, W.B. LA Inf.Crescent Regt. Co.F Cpl.
Robinson, W.B. LA Inf.Cons.Crescent Regt. Co.G
Robinson, W.B. SC 1st Cav. Co.D 1st Sgt.
Robinson, W.B. TN Patterson's Regt. Co.F
Robinson, W.B. VA Inf. 25th Bn. Co.G
Robinson, W.B. Eng.Dept. Polk's Corps A. of TN Sap. & Min. Co.,CSA
Robinson, W.C. AR Inf. 4th Bn. Co.B 1st Lt.
Robinson, W.C. AR 6th Inf. Co.C
Robinson, W.C. AR 19th (Dawson's) Inf. Co.K
Robinson, W.C. GA Lt.Arty. Pritchard's Co. (Washington Arty.)
Robinson, W.C. MS 11th Inf. Co.D
Robinson, W.C. TN 38th Inf. Co.E Capt.
Robinson, W.C. Gen. & Staff, QM Dept. Capt.,AQM
Robinson, W.D. AL 1st Cav.
Robinson, W.D. AR 10th Mil. Co.B
Robinson, W.D. MS Cav. 1st Bn. (McNair's) St.Troops Co.C Cpl.
Robinson, W.D. SC 2nd Arty. Co.I
Robinson, W.D. SC 2nd Inf. Co.C
Robinson, W.D. TN 4th (McLemore's) Cav. Co.E
Robinson, W.D. TN 19th (Biffle's) Cav. Co.C
Robinson, W.D. TN 2nd (Robison's) Inf. Sgt.
Robinson, W.D. TN 11th Inf. Co.G
Robinson, W.D. TX 21st Cav. Co.B
Robinson, W.D. 1st Conf.Cav. 2nd Co.G 1st Sgt.
Robinson, W.E. AL 12th Inf. Co.I
Robinson, W.E. FL 10th Inf. Davidson's Co.
Robinson, W.E. MS 28th Cav. Co.K
Robinson, W.E. MS 15th Inf. Co.F
Robinson, W.E. NC 49th Inf. Co.H
Robinson, Wesley AL Mil. 4th Vol. Co.E
Robinson, Wesley AR 10th Inf. Co.A
Robinson, Wesly Conf.Cav. Wood's Regt. Co.I
Robinson, Westley NC 52nd Inf. Co.H
Robinson, W.F. GA 7th Inf. Co.I Sgt.
Robinson, W.F. LA 19th Inf. Co.F
Robinson, W.F. SC 12th Inf. Co.I
Robinson, W.F. TX Cav. Giddings' Bn. Carrington's Co. Sgt.
Robinson, W.F. Gen. & Staff Chap.
Robinson, W.G. AL 47th Inf. Co.A
Robinson, W.G. FL Conscr.
Robinson, W.G. GA Conscr.
Robinson, W.G. MS Inf. 2nd St.Troops Co.A
Robinson, W.H. AL 60th Inf. Co.E
Robinson, W.H. AR 1st (Dobbin's) Cav. Co.B Bvt.2nd Lt.
Robinson, W.H. AR 1st Vol. Co.I
Robinson, W.H. AR 5th Inf. Co.I
Robinson, W.H. GA 4th (Clinch's) Cav. Co.A
Robinson, W.H. GA Inf. 1st Loc.Troops (Augusta) Dearing's Cav.Co.
Robinson, W.H. GA 16th Inf. Co.I
Robinson, W.H. GA Inf. 25th Bn. (Prov.Guard) Co.E
Robinson, W.H. KY 2nd (Woodward's) Cav. Co.H

Robinson, W.H. LA 28th (Gray's) Inf. Co.H
Robinson, W.H. MS 44th Inf. Co.H
Robinson, W.H. MS Hudson's Co. (Noxubee Guards)
Robinson, W.H. MO St.Guard
Robinson, W.H. SC Inf. 3rd Bn. Co.G Sgt.
Robinson, W.H. TN 38th Inf. Co.C Cpl.
Robinson, W.H. TX Cav. 3rd Bn.St.Troops Co.E 1st Lt.
Robinson, W.H. TX 12th Cav. Co.G
Robinson, W.H. TX Cav. McCord's Fronter Regt. Asst.Surg.
Robinson, W.H. TX 1st Inf. Co.D
Robinson, W.H. TX 15th Inf. 2nd Co.G
Robinson, W.H. Gen. & Staff Surg.
Robinson, Whig E. MS 9th Inf. Old Co.I
Robinson, W.I. MS 31st Inf. Co.K
Robinson, Wiley GA 1st (Symons') Res. Co.B
Robinson, Wiley NC 17th Inf. (2nd Org.) Co.A
Robinson, Wiley TX 10th Field Btty.
Robinson, Wiley W. LA 12th Inf. 2nd Co.M
Robinson, Wilkin 1st Choctaw Mtd.Rifles Co.D Cpl.
Robinson, William AL 3rd Cav. Co.B 1st Sgt.
Robinson, William AL 53rd (Part.Rangers) Co.A,G
Robinson, William AL Cav.Res. Brooks' Co.
Robinson, William AL Lt.Arty. 2nd Bn. Co.C
Robinson, William AL 9th Inf. Co.K Cpl.
Robinson, Wm. AL 18th Inf. Co.D
Robinson, William AL 21st Inf. Co.F Cpl.
Robinson, William AL 22nd Inf. Co.D
Robinson, William AL 23rd Inf. Co.D
Robinson, William AL 24th Inf. Co.B
Robinson, William AL 25th Inf. Co.C
Robinson, William AL 31st Inf. Co.E
Robinson, William AL 44th Inf. Co.F
Robinson, William AL 61st Inf. Co.A
Robinson, William AL 62nd Inf. Co.H
Robinson, William AR 1st (Monroe's) Cav. Co.L
Robinson, William AR Cav. Gordon's Regt. Co.H
Robinson, William AR 19th (Dawson's) Inf. Co.C
Robinson, William AR Inf. Ballard's Co.
Robinson, William FL 2nd Cav. Co.E
Robinson, William FL 8th Inf. Co.H
Robinson, William FL 8th Inf. Co.I
Robinson, William GA 1st Cav. Co.G
Robinson, William GA Cav. 9th Bn. (St.Guards) Co.E Ens.
Robinson, William GA Cav. 19th Bn. Co.A
Robinson, William GA Cav. 19th Bn. Co.B
Robinson, William GA 1st (Fannin's) Res. Co.G
Robinson, William KY 3rd Bn.Mtd.Rifles Co.G
Robinson, William LA 2nd Cav. Co.B
Robinson, William LA 1st Inf. Co.I
Robinson, William LA 1st (Strawbridge's) Inf. Co.A
Robinson, William LA 1st (Strawbridge's) Inf. Co.F
Robinson, William LA Inf. 4th Bn. Co.A
Robinson, William LA 17th Inf. Co.A,H
Robinson, William LA 18th Inf. Co.C Cpl.
Robinson, William, Jr. MS 2nd Cav. Co.D
Robinson, William, Sr. MS 2nd Cav. Co.D
Robinson, William MS 3rd Cav. Co.F

Robinson, William MS 6th Cav. Co.E
Robinson, William MS St.Cav. Perrin's Bn. Co.F
Robinson, William MS Cav. Powers' Regt. Co.A Sgt.
Robinson, William MS Inf. 1st Bn.St.Troops (12 mo. '62-3) Co.C
Robinson, William MS 2nd Inf. Co.L
Robinson, William MS Inf. 2nd Bn. (St.Troops) Co.F
Robinson, William MS 5th Inf. (St.Troops) Co.D
Robinson, William MS 10th Inf. Co.F,K
Robinson, William MS 11th Inf. Co.H
Robinson, William MS 23rd Inf. Co.A
Robinson, William MS 26th Inf. Co.K,B
Robinson, William MS 27th Inf. Co.E
Robinson, William MS 32nd Inf. Co.I
Robinson, William MS 41st Inf. Co.G
Robinson, William MS 42nd Inf. Co.I
Robinson, William MO 1st N.E. Cav. Co.K
Robinson, William MO 10th Cav. Co.K
Robinson, William MO Cav. Fristoe's Regt. Co.D
Robinson, Wm. MO Lt.Arty. 1st Btty. Cpl.
Robinson, William MO Lt.Arty. Walsh's Co. 2nd Lt.
Robinson, William MO 1st & 4th Cons.Inf. Co.B
Robinson, William MO 4th Inf. Co.G
Robinson, William NC 1st Arty. (10th St.Troops) Co.F
Robinson, William NC 1st Inf. (6 mo. '61) Co.M
Robinson, William NC 24th Inf. Co.A
Robinson, William NC Nelson's Co. (Loc.Def.)
Robinson, William SC 6th Cav. Co.D
Robinson, William SC Hvy.Arty. 15th (Lucas') Bn. Co.C
Robinson, William SC Arty. Childs' Co.
Robinson, William SC 5th Res. Co.A
Robinson, William SC 12th Inf. Co.E
Robinson, William SC 24th Inf. Co.A
Robinson, William SC Inf. Hampton Legion Co.H
Robinson, William TN 15th (Stewart's) Cav. Co.K
Robinson, William TN 4th Inf. Co.D
Robinson, William TN 15th Inf. Co.H
Robinson, William TN 21st Inf. Co.F
Robinson, William TN 22nd Inf.
Robinson, William TN 55th (Brown's) Inf. Co.G
Robinson, William TN Inf. Harman's Regt. Co.K
Robinson, William TX Cav. 2nd Regt.St.Troops Co.B
Robinson, William TX 12th Cav.
Robinson, William TX 17th Cav. Co.E
Robinson, William TX 23rd Cav. Co.D
Robinson, William TX 26th Cav. Co.D
Robinson, William TX Cav. Baird's Regt. Co.B
Robinson, William TX Arty. 4th Bn. Co.A
Robinson, William TX 4th Inf. (St.Troops) Co.E
Robinson, William TX 5th Inf. Co.H 1st Lt.
Robinson, William TX 6th Inf. Co.B
Robinson, William TX 13th Vol. 2nd Co.D
Robinson, William TX 20th Inf. Co.H
Robinson, William TX Waul's Legion Co.B
Robinson, William VA 6th Cav. Co.A
Robinson, William VA 7th Cav. Co.E
Robinson, William VA 7th Cav. Co.I
Robinson, William VA 8th Cav. Co.C

Robinson, William VA Cav. McNeill's Co.
Robinson, William VA Hvy.Arty. 20th Bn. Co.B
Robinson, William VA 1st Inf. Co.D
Robinson, William VA 1st Inf. Co.E
Robinson, William VA 3rd Inf.Loc.Def. Co.A 1st Sgt.
Robinson, William VA Inf. 4th Bn.Loc.Def. Co.B
Robinson, William VA 11th Inf. Co.D
Robinson, William VA 27th Inf. Co.E
Robinson, William VA 36th Inf. 1st Co.B, 2nd Co.D
Robinson, William VA 45th Inf. Co.I
Robinson, William VA 62nd Mtd.Inf. 2nd Co.D
Robinson, William VA 63rd Inf. 2nd Co.I
Robinson, William VA 67th Mil. Co.D
Robinson, William VA 92nd Mil. Co.B
Robinson, William VA 136th Mil. Co.B
Robinson, William VA 146th Mil. Co.H
Robinson, William VA Mil. Carroll Cty.
Robinson, William 10th Conf.Cav. Co.F
Robinson, William 14th Conf.Cav. Co.H
Robinson, William Wheeler's Scouts, CSA
Robinson, William Conf.Cav. Wood's Regt. 1st Co.M 1st Sgt.
Robinson, William Conf.Inf. 1st Bn. 2nd Co.A
Robinson, William 1st Seminole Mtd.Vol. Capt.
Robinson, William A. AL 7th Cav. Co.A 2nd Lt.
Robinson, William A. AL 7th Inf. Co.D Sgt.
Robinson, William A. AL 38th Inf. Co.F
Robinson, William A. GA 1st (Ramsey's) Inf. Co.G
Robinson, William A. GA 4th Inf. Co.I
Robinson, William A. GA Inf. 17th Bn. (St.Guards) Fay's Co. Sgt.
Robinson, William A. GA 26th Inf. Co.C
Robinson, William A. GA 54th Inf. Co.H
Robinson, William A. GA Phillips' Legion Co.A
Robinson, William A. MS 11th Inf. Co.C
Robinson, William A. MS 26th Inf. Co.A
Robinson, William A. MS 32nd Inf. Co.H Sgt.
Robinson, William A. NC 3rd Cav. (41st St.Troops) Co.G
Robinson, William A. NC 12th Inf. Co.C
Robinson, William A. TX 15th Cav. Co.A 2nd Lt.
Robinson, William A. VA Inf. 1st Bn.Loc.Def. Co.F
Robinson, William A. VA 56th Inf. Co.C
Robinson, William A.M. VA Inf. Mileham's Co.
Robinson, William B. AL 16th Inf. Co.K
Robinson, William B. AR 8th Inf. New Co.H Sgt.
Robinson, William B. KY 2nd Mtd.Inf. Co.H
Robinson, William B. TX 1st Inf. Co.L Sgt.
Robinson, William B. VA 2nd Arty. Co.I
Robinson, William B. VA Inf. 22nd Bn. Co.G
Robinson, William B. 3rd Conf.Eng.Troops Co.B Artif.
Robinson, William Booker VA 15th Inf. Co.A Cpl.
Robinson, Wm. C. AL 15th Inf. Co.E
Robinson, William C. GA 4th Inf. Co.I
Robinson, William C. GA 14th Inf. Co.H
Robinson, William C. MS 13th Inf. Co.A
Robinson, William C. SC 14th Inf. Co.G

Robinson, William C. TN 41st Inf. Co.H
Robinson, William C. TX Cav. Martin's Regt. Co.F
Robinson, William C. VA 21st Cav. Co.K
Robinson, William C. VA Hvy.Arty. 10th Bn. Co.C
Robinson, William C. VA Inf. 2nd Bn.Loc.Def. Co.E
Robinson, William C. VA 6th Inf. Co.G
Robinson, William C. VA Inf. 25th Bn. Co.G
Robinson, William C. VA 55th Inf. Co.H 2nd Lt.
Robinson, Wm. D. AL Cp. of Instr. Talladega Co.C Sgt.
Robinson, William D. GA 25th Inf. Co.I
Robinson, William D. SC Horse Arty. (Washington Arty.) Vol. Hart's Co.
Robinson, William D. SC Arty.Bn. Hampton Legion Co.A
Robinson, William D. TX 18th Cav. Co.H
Robinson, William D. Conf.Inf. 1st Bn. Co.F Sgt.
Robinson, William D. 1st Conf.Eng.Troops Co.H Artif.
Robinson, William E. AL 2nd Cav. Co.B
Robinson, William E. AL 61st Inf. Co.I
Robinson, William E. FL 6th Inf. Co.A
Robinson, William E. GA 38th Inf. Co.N Cpl.
Robinson, William E. GA Phillips' Legion Co.A
Robinson, William E. MS 8th Cav. Co.C Sgt.
Robinson, William E. NC 1st Jr.Res. Co.K
Robinson, William E. NC 25th Inf. Co.H
Robinson, William E. NC 26th Inf. Co.B
Robinson, William E. NC 31st Inf. Co.F
Robinson, William E. NC 51st Inf. Co.C
Robinson, William E. VA 47th Inf. Co.A
Robinson, William F. AL 2nd Bn. Hilliard's Legion Vol. Co.D
Robinson, William F. GA 27th Inf. Co.H 3rd Cpl.
Robinson, William F. MS 38th Cav. Co.D
Robinson, William F. NC 1st Cav. (9th St.Troops) Co.H
Robinson, William F. NC 5th Cav. (63rd St.Troops) Co.K Cpl.
Robinson, William F. TX 21st Cav. Co.B
Robinson, William F. VA 23rd Inf. Co.F
Robinson, William G. MS 3rd Cav. Co.F
Robinson, William G. MO 10th Cav. Co.H
Robinson, William G. NC 2nd Cav. (19th St.Troops) Col.
Robinson, William G. NC 7th Inf. Co.K Sgt.Maj.
Robinson, William G. Gen. & Staff, Post QM Dept.
Robinson, William H. AL 8th Cav. Co.I
Robinson, William H. AL 4th Inf. Co.K Capt.
Robinson, William H. AL 49th Inf. Co.D
Robinson, William H. GA 12th (Robinson's) Cav. (St.Guards) Co.A Col.
Robinson, William H. GA 4th Inf. Co.H Cpl.
Robinson, William H. GA 8th Inf. Co.I
Robinson, William H. GA 41st Inf. Co.D
Robinson, William H. LA 16th Inf. Co.D
Robinson, William H. MD 1st Cav. Co.C
Robinson, William H. MD Cav.Bn. Co.C
Robinson, William H. MD 1st Inf. Co.D

Robinson, William H. MS Inf. 5th Bn. Co.A
Robinson, William H. MS 43rd Inf. Co.I
Robinson, William H. MO 10th Cav. Co.A
Robinson, William H. NC 30th Inf. Co.K
Robinson, William H. NC 53rd Inf. Co.F
Robinson, William H. TX 2nd Cav. Co.B
Robinson, William H. TX 15th Cav. Co.D
Robinson, William H. TX 19th Cav. Co.I
Robinson, William H. TX 27th Cav. Co.D Cpl.
Robinson, William H. TX 22nd Inf. Co.E,H
Robinson, William H. VA 1st Arty. Co.I
Robinson, William H. VA Lt.Arty. 38th Bn. Co.B
Robinson, William H. VA Hvy.Arty. Patteson's Co.
Robinson, William H. VA 36th Inf. 2nd Co.C, 3rd Co.I
Robinson, William H. Cheatham's Div. Asst.Surg.
Robinson, William H.H. NC 23rd Inf. Co.C
Robinson, William H.H. VA 24th Inf. Co.K
Robinson, William J. AL 24th Inf. Co.H
Robinson, William J. FL 7th Inf. Co.F
Robinson, William J. GA 16th Inf. Co.I
Robinson, William J. MS Griffin's Co. (Madison Guards)
Robinson, William J. MO 3rd Cav. Co.F
Robinson, William J. MO 6th Cav. Co.F Sgt.
Robinson, William J. MO 10th Cav. White's Co.
Robinson, William J. SC 1st Mtd.Mil. Screven's Co. Sgt.
Robinson, William J. SC 3rd Cav. Co.C Cpl.
Robinson, William J. SC Mil.Cav. 4th Regt. Howard's Co. Cpl.
Robinson, William J. TN 13th Inf. Co.D,A Ord.Sgt.
Robinson, William J. TN 20th Inf. Co.A Sgt.
Robinson, William J. VA 26th Cav. Co.A Lt.
Robinson, William J. VA Cav. 46th Bn. Co.A 2nd Lt.
Robinson, William J. VA Inf. 9th Bn. Co.A 2nd Lt.
Robinson, William J. VA 25th Inf. 2nd Co.A 1st Lt.
Robinson, William J. VA 57th Inf. Co.B
Robinson, William J. VA Loc.Def. Scott's Co.
Robinson, William K. NC 16th Inf. Co.C
Robinson, William L. AL 6th Inf. Co.I
Robinson, William L. FL 2nd Cav. Co.E
Robinson, William L. FL Cav. (Marianna Drag.) Smith's Co.
Robinson, William L. GA 12th Inf. Co.E 1st Lt.
Robinson, William L. GA 13th Inf. Co.I
Robinson, William L. LA Lt.Arty. Holmes' Btty. Sgt.
Robinson, William L. LA 7th Inf. Co.A Cpl.
Robinson, William L. LA Inf.Crescent Regt. Co.B
Robinson, William L. NC 29th Inf. Co.B,K
Robinson, William L. VA 3rd Cav. Co.G
Robinson, William L. VA 18th Inf. Co.A
Robinson, William L. 15th Conf.Cav. Co.B
Robinson, William M. AL 28th Inf. Co.D
Robinson, William M. MS 33rd Inf. Co.H
Robinson, William M. MO 2nd N.E. Cav. (Franklin's Regt.)
Robinson, William M. MO Cav. Hicks' Co.

Robinson, William M. MO Lt.Arty. Landis' Co.
Robinson, William M. MO 5th Inf. Co.H
Robinson, William M. NC Hvy.Arty. 10th Bn.
  Co.D
Robinson, William M. TN 4th (McLemore's)
  Cav. Co.D Capt.
Robinson, William M. TN 2nd (Robison's) Inf.
  Co.D Sgt.
Robinson, William M. TN 17th Inf. Co.K
Robinson, William M. TX 9th Cav. Co.A
Robinson, William M. VA Lt.Arty. G.B. Chap-
  man's Co. Cpl.
Robinson, William M. VA 37th Inf. Co.E
Robinson, William N. AR 32nd Inf. Co.A
Robinson, William N. TN 41st Inf. Co.I
Robinson, William N. VA 4th Cav. Co.H
Robinson, William P. AL 6th Inf. Co.M
Robinson, William P. AR Lt.Arty. Thrall's Btty.
Robinson, William P. SC 1st (Orr's) Rifles Co.D
Robinson, William P. VA 9th Cav. Co.F
Robinson, William P. VA Lt.Arty. 13th Bn.
  Co.B Sr.1st Lt.
Robinson, William R. AL 29th Inf. Co.D
Robinson, William R. AR Cav. Harrell's Bn.
  Co.C
Robinson, William R. MS Terry's Co.
Robinson, William R. TX 6th Cav. Co.F
Robinson, William R. TX 13th Vol. 1st Co.F
Robinson, William R. TX 15th Inf. 2nd Co.D
Robinson, William R. TX 16th Inf. Co.C
Robinson, William R. TX 18th Inf. Co.E
Robinson, William R. VA 3rd Inf. Co.G
Robinson, Wm. R. Gen. & Staff Surg.
Robinson, William Rilley NC 16th Inf. Co.C
Robinson, William S. GA Cav. 19th Bn. Co.D,E
  Cpl.
Robinson, William S. GA Siege Arty. 28th Bn.
  Co.A
Robinson, William S. GA Inf. 2nd Bn. Co.A
  Lt.,Adj.
Robinson, William S. NC 23rd Inf. Co.C
Robinson, William S. SC 1st (Orr's) Rifles Co.C
Robinson, William S. TN 27th Inf. Co.A
Robinson, Williams TX 8th Cav. Co.K
Robinson, William S. VA 44th Inf. Co.G
Robinson, William S.B. SC 18th Inf. Co.A
Robinson, William T. GA 24th Inf. Co.F
Robinson, William T. LA Mil. 1st Regt. 2nd
  Brig. 1st Div. Col.
Robinson, William T. MS 39th Inf. Co.C Sgt.
Robinson, William T. NC 66th Inf. Co.D Capt.
Robinson, William T. TN 15th Cav.
Robinson, William T. TX 13th Vol. 2nd Co.C
Robinson, William T. VA Lt.Arty. Pollock's Co.
Robinson, William T. VA 1st Regt.Rangers Co.K
Robinson, William T. VA 13th Inf. Co.D
Robinson, William T. VA 61st Inf. Co.D Sgt.
Robinson, William Thomas MO 6th Inf. Co.F
  Cpl.
Robinson, William Thomas VA 15th Inf. Co.H
  1st Sgt.
Robinson, William U. FL 6th Inf. Co.A
Robinson, William W. MS 20th Inf. Co.A
  QMSgt.
Robinson, William W. MS 24th Inf. Co.B 1st Lt.
Robinson, William W. MS 30th Inf. Co.B
Robinson, William W. NC 13th Inf. Co.B Capt.

Robinson, William W. NC 17th Inf. (2nd Org.)
  Co.C
Robinson, William W. NC 22nd Inf. Co.H
Robinson, William W. NC 25th Inf. Co.C
Robinson, William W. SC 20th Inf. Co.A
Robinson, William Wirt VA Inf. Hutter's Co.
Robinson, William Y. VA 40th Inf. Co.G
Robinson, Willis LA Inf.Cons.Crescent Regt.
  Co.B
Robinson, Willis W. VA 24th Cav. Co.A Sgt.
Robinson, Willis W. VA Cav. 40th Bn. Co.A
  Cpl.
Robinson, Willis W. VA Inf. 5th Bn. Co.D Sgt.
Robinson, Willoby C. MS Inf. 3rd Bn. Co.F
Robinson, Wills NC 68th Inf.
Robinson, Wilson AR 1st (Monroe's) Cav. Co.E
Robinson, Winchester TN 6th (Wheeler's) Cav.
  Co.G
Robinson, Windal T. NC 8th Bn.Part.Rangers
  Co.B,C Capt.
Robinson, Winslow LA 1st Cav. Robinson's Co.
  1st Lt.
Robinson, Winslow LA 15th Inf. Co.F Sgt.Maj.
Robinson, Winslow Gen. & Staff 1st Lt.,Dr.M.
Robinson, W.J. AL 46th Inf. Co.K
Robinson, W.J. AR 1st (Monroe's) Cav. Co.E
  Cpl.
Robinson, W.J. GA 59th Inf. Co.G
Robinson, W.J. LA 13th Bn. (Part.Rangers)
  Co.C
Robinson, W.J. MS 28th Cav. Co.C
Robinson, W.J. MS 9th Inf. Co.E
Robinson, W.J. MS 12th Inf. Co.K
Robinson, W.J. NC 2nd Jr.Res. Co.B
Robinson, W.J. SC Mil.Arty. 1st Regt. Parker's
  Co.
Robinson, W.J. SC Mil. 16th Regt. Sigwald's
  Co.
Robinson, W.J. SC 17th Inf. Co.I
Robinson, W.J. TN 10th (DeMoss') Cav. Co.D
  Capt.
Robinson, W.J. TN 21st (Wilson's) Cav. Co.I
Robinson, W.J. TN 21st & 22nd (Cons.) Cav.
  Co.I
Robinson, W.J. TN 17th Inf. Co.F
Robinson, W.J. TN 38th Inf. Co.F
Robinson, W.J. TN 38th Inf. Co.G
Robinson, W.L. AL 21st Inf. Co.D
Robinson, W.L. AL 32nd Inf. Co.E
Robinson, W.L. AL Cp. of Instr. Talladega
Robinson, W.L. AR 8th Cav. Co.D
Robinson, W.L. AR 1st Vol. Co.I Cpl.
Robinson, W.L. AR 2nd Vol. Co.A
Robinson, W.L. AR 32nd Inf. Co.C
Robinson, W.L. FL Cav. 5th Bn. Sgt.
Robinson, W.L. LA 7th Inf. Capt.
Robinson, W.L., Jr. LA Inf.Cons.Crescent Regt.
  Co.C
Robinson, W.L. NC 2nd Jr.Res. Co.H
Robinson, W.L. SC 5th St.Troops Co.K 2nd Lt.
Robinson, W.L. TX 28th Cav. Co.G Sgt.
Robinson, W.L. TX Inf. 2nd St.Troops Co.C
Robinson, W.L. Gen. & Staff Capt.,QM
Robinson, W.M. AL 9th Cav. Co.I
Robinson, W.M. TX 20th Bn.St.Troops Co.A
Robinson, W.N. AL 35th Inf. Co.G
Robinson, W.N. MS 8th Inf. Co.A

Robinson, W.N. MS 16th Inf. Co.C
Robinson, W.O. GA 10th Cav. (St.Guards) Co.I
  Ord.Sgt.
Robinson, W.O. SC Inf. 3rd Bn. Co.G
Robinson, Woodard MO Inf. 8th Bn. Co.A
Robinson, W.P. AL 5th Inf. Co.K
Robinson, W.P. GA Inf. 1st Loc.Troops
  (Augusta) Co.F
Robinson, W.P. GA Inf. 2nd Bn. (St.Guards)
  Co.C
Robinson, W.P. GA 53rd Inf. Co.F
Robinson, W.P. MS 23rd Inf. Co.D Capt.
Robinson, W.P. TX 37th Cav. Co.K
Robinson, W.P. VA Inf. 44th Bn. Co.B
Robinson, W.P. 2nd Cherokee Mtd.Vol. Co.H
Robinson, W.R. AR Cav. Gordon's Regt. Co.A
Robinson, W.R. MS 37th Inf. Co.H
Robinson, W.R. MO 1st Inf. Co.K,H
Robinson, W.R. MO 1st & 4th Cons.Inf. Co.K
Robinson, W.R. VA Hvy.Arty. 10th Bn. Co.E
Robinson, W.R. Conf.Cav. Clarkson's Bn.
  Ind.Rangers Co.D
Robinson, W.S. AL 3rd Res. Co.G
Robinson, W.S. AR 38th Inf. Old Co.I, Co.H
Robinson, W.S. GA 10th Cav. Sgt.
Robinson, W.S. KY 2nd Bn.Mtd.Rifles Co.A
Robinson, W.S. LA 18th Inf. Co.K
Robinson, W.S. MS 16th Inf. Co.G
Robinson, W.S. SC 1st Cav. Co.G
Robinson, W.S. SC 6th Cav. Co.C
Robinson, W.S. TX Cav. Terry's Regt. Co.I
Robinson, W.S. TX 4th Inf. Co.E
Robinson, W.S. VA 7th Cav. Co.A
Robinson, W.S. 10th Conf.Cav. Co.K Sgt.
Robinson, W.T. GA 10th Cav. (St.Guards) Co.C
Robinson, W.T. GA 9th Inf. (St.Guards) Co.F
Robinson, W.T. MS 8th Inf. Co.A Cpl.
Robinson, W.T. MS 14th (Cons.) Inf. Co.C
Robinson, W.T. MO Inf. 3rd Bn. Co.B
Robinson, W.T. SC 6th Inf. 1st Co.H Cpl.
Robinson, W.T. TN 4th Inf. Co.B
Robinson, W.T. TX Cav. Terry's Regt. AQM
Robinson, W.T. Gen. & Staff Asst.Surg.
Robinson, W.T.N. 20th Conf.Cav. AAAG
Robinson, W.T.N. Gen. & Staff Capt.,AAAG
Robinson, W.U. FL 10th Inf. Davidson's Co.
Robinson, W.W. AR 27th Inf. Co.I
Robinson, W.W. KY Lt.Arty. Green's Btty.
Robinson, W.W. MS 6th Cav. Co.C Capt.
Robinson, W.W. MS 8th Cav. Co.I Capt.
Robinson, W.W. MS 1st Lt.Arty. Co.B
Robinson, W.W. MS 6th Inf. Co.I Cpl.
Robinson, W.W. MS 15th (Cons.) Inf. QMSgt.
Robinson, W.W. SC Cav. 4th Bn. Co.A Bvt.2nd
  Lt.
Robinson, W.W. SC 24th Mil.
Robinson, W.W. 7th Conf.Cav. Co.L
Robinson, W.W. Stewart's Arty. Ord.Off.
Robinson, W.W.C. AL 47th Inf. Co.I 2nd Lt.
Robinson, W. Wirt MD Arty. 2nd Btty. Ord.Sgt.
Robinson, Wyatt E. KY 2nd Mtd.Inf. Co.F
Robinson, W.Z. AL 45th Inf. Co.B
Robinson, Yancy TX 18th Cav. Co.I
Robinson, Young MS 36th Inf. Co.K
Robinson, Zachariah W. TX 14th Cav. Co.D
Robinson, Zack KY 7th Mtd.Inf. Co.I
Robinson, Z.D. AL 63rd Inf. Co.I

Robinson, Zedock TN Cav. 16th Bn. (Neal's)
Co.E
Robinson, Zekiah NC Mallett's Bn. (Cp.Guard)
Co.E
Robinson, Zoraster TX Cav. Baylor's Regt. Co.E
Robintson, J.H. LA 13th Bn. (Part.Rangers)
Co.B
Robin Young Duck 1st Cherokee Mtd.Rifles Co.G
Robion, G. Sidney FL 3rd Inf. Co.A
Robira, A. LA Inf. 7th Bn. Co.A
Robira, Anto. LA Mil. 5th Regt.Eur.Brig.
(Spanish Regt.) Co.4 1st Lt.
Robira, Antonio LA Arty. Kean's Btty. (Orleans
Ind.Arty.) 2nd Lt.
Robira, Antonio LA C.S. Zouave Bn. Co.E 2nd
Lt.
Robira, Isidore LA Mil. 1st Chasseurs a pied
Co.5
Robira, J. LA Mil. Jackson Rifle Bn.
Robischeau, Dorville LA 2nd Cav. Co.H
Robisen, J.K. MS 18th Cav. Co.E
Robisho, F.R. LA 7th Cav. Co.I
Robiso, T. LA 18th Inf. Co.G
Robiso, T. LA Inf.Cons. 18th Regt. & Yellow
Jacket Bn. Co.G
Robison 1st Choctaw Mtd.Rifles Co.F
Robison, A. MS Cav. 1st Bn. (McNair's)
St.Troops Co.E
Robison, A. NC 2nd Arty. (36th St.Troops)
Co.H
Robison, A. NC 45th Inf. Co.C
Robison, A. SC Inf. 1st (Charleston) Bn. Co.F
Robison, Abel TX 29th Cav. Co.K
Robison, Abslam VA 1st Cav.St.Line Co.A
Robison, A.C.V. AR 13th Inf. Co.F 1st Sgt.
Robison, A.D. VA 19th Cav. Co.D
Robison, A.E. SC 5th St.Troops Co.B
Robison, A.K. AL 21st Inf. Co.C Cpl.
Robison, A.L. TN Lt.Arty. Phillips' Co.
Robison, Alfred G. VA Rockbridge Cty.Res.
Miller's Co.
Robison, Andrew VA 1st Cav.St.Line Co.A
Robison, And. W. TX 19th Inf. Co.D
Robison, Archer LA 1st Cav. Co.H
Robison, B.F. Inf. Bailey's Cons.Regt. Co.A
Robison, B.F. TX 7th Inf. Co.B
Robison, C.F. AL 56th Part.Rangers Co.C Cpl.
Robison, C.H. MS Inf. 4th St.Troops Co.A
Robison, Chapman E. MO Inf. Perkins' Bn.
Co.F
Robison, Charles H. TN 7th Inf. Co.I
Robison, Christopher GA 1st (Ramsey's) Inf.
Co.A
Robison, Columbus AL 55th Vol. Co.C
Robison, Columbus W. AL 6th Cav. Co.E
Robison, D. GA 8th Cav. Old Co.D
Robison, David GA 62nd Cav. Co.D
Robison, David H. VA 14th Cav. Co.M
Robison, D.G. VA 1st (Farinholt's) Res. Co.F
Robison, D.J. AL 22nd Inf. Co.F
Robison, D.S. AL Cav. (St.Res.) Young's Co.
Robison, Edward C. LA 20th Inf. Co.G Cpl.
Robison, Elbert A. GA 49th Inf. Co.H
Robison, Elijah J. MS 31st Inf. Co.K
Robison, Felix G. TN 36th Inf. Co.B
Robison, Felix W. TN 3rd (Lillard's) Mtd.Inf.
Co.D

Robison, George LA 9th Inf. Co.K
Robison, George SC 5th St.Troops Co.D
Robison, George T. LA 12th Inf. 2nd Co.M
Robison, G.M. TN 3rd (Lillard's) Mtd.Inf. Co.D
Robison, G.T.L. AL 8th Inf. Co.B Capt.
Robison, G.W. AL 1st Btty. Co.A
Robison, G.W. TN 3rd (Forrest's) Cav. Co.F
Sgt.
Robison, G.W. 8th (Wade's) Conf.Cav. Co.H
Robison, H. MS St.Mil. Ruth's Co.
Robison, H. Gen. & Staff,PACS Asst.Surg.
Robison, H.D. GA 11th Cav. (St.Guards)
Bruce's Co.
Robison, Hiram Ford MS 8th Cav. Co.A
Robison, Hiram R. AR 2nd Inf. Co.F
Robison, Horatio H. AL 3rd Inf. Co.I
Robison, Isaac H. GA 56th Inf. Co.C Cpl.
Robison, Israel VA 8th Cav. Co.I Cpl.
Robison, J. LA 10th Inf. Co.E
Robison, J. NC 2nd Jr.Res. Co.C
Robison, J. SC Inf. 1st (Charleston) Bn. Co.F
Robison, J. TN 9th Inf. Co.C
Robison, Jacob A. VA 1st Cav. Co.C
Robison, James VA 3rd Cav. & Inf.St.Line Co.D
Robison, James A. TN 38th Inf. 1st Co.H Cpl.
Robison, James C. MO Inf. Perkins' Bn. Co.F
Robison, James H. NC 49th Inf. Co.C
Robison, James M. AR 2nd Inf. Co.F
Robison, James M. AR 25th Inf. Co.H 2nd Lt.
Robison, James M. LA 12th Inf. 2nd Co.M
Robison, James M. TN 7th Inf. Co.B
Robison, James W. MO Lt.Arty. 1st Field Btty.
Robison, James W. TN Cav. Newsom's Regt.
Co.E 1st Lt.
Robison, J.B. GA 5th Res. Co.F 2nd Lt.
Robison, J.B. LA 27th Inf. Co.G
Robison, J.C. AL 23rd Inf. Co.D
Robison, J.D. TN 19th & 20th (Cons.) Cav.
Co.H
Robison, J.D. TN Lt.Arty. Phillips' Co.
Robison, Jeff. F. MS 15th Inf. Co.H
Robison, J.H. AL 14th Inf. Co.D
Robison, J.H. GA Phillips' Legion Co.F Cpl.
Robison, J.H. SC 18th Inf. Co.G
Robison, J.J. 10th Conf.Cav. Co.K
Robison, J.K. SC 27th Inf. Co.K,I
Robison, J.K.P. GA 8th Cav. Old Co.D
Robison, J.L. AR 13th Mil. Co.G
Robison, J.L. AR 36th Inf. Co.K
Robison, J.M. AL 30th Inf. Co.H Sgt.
Robison, J.M. LA 9th Inf. Co.K
Robison, J.M. MO 12th Cav. Co.I
Robison, John AL 30th Inf. Co.H
Robison, John AR 2nd Inf. Co.F
Robison, John AR 25th Inf. Co.H
Robison, John SC 9th Res. Co.A
Robison, John TX 2nd Cav. Co.I
Robison, John VA 8th Bn.Res. Co.D
Robison, John VA 114th Mil. Co.F Sgt.
Robison, John 1st Choctaw & Chickasaw
Mtd.Rifles 3rd Co.K 1st Sgt.
Robison, John A. MS 31st Inf. Co.K
Robison, John D.H. AL 13th Inf. Co.E 1st Lt.
Robison, John D. Howell AL 13th Inf. Co.E 1st
Lt.
Robison, John F. MO 8th Cav. Co.A
Robison, John J. MS 1st (Percy's) Inf. Co.A

Robison, John M. MS Hamer's Co. (Salem Cav.)
Robison, John R. AR 20th Inf. Co.A
Robison, John R. VA 1st Cav.St.Line Co.A
Robison, John S. GA Inf. Taylor's Co.
Robison, John S., Jr. GA Inf. Taylor's Co.
Robison, John Thomas GA 37th Inf. Co.K
Robison, John W. GA 1st (Ramsey's) Inf. Co.G
Robison, John W. GA 22nd Inf. Co.I
Robison, Jno. W. Gen. & Staff Adj.
Robison, Joseph VA 28th Inf. 2nd Co.C
Robison, Joseph A. NC 1st Inf. Co.H
Robison, Joseph E. GA 43rd Inf. Co.B
Robison, Joseph M. 8th (Wade's) Conf.Cav.
Co.H Cpl.
Robison, Joseph R. TN 18th (Newsom's) Cav.
Co.B
Robison, Joseph R. TN Cav. Newsom's Regt.
Co.E
Robison, Joshua S. GA 49th Inf. Co.H
Robison, J.P. AR 6th Inf.
Robison, J.R. SC 5th St.Troops Co.E
Robison, J.R. TX 33rd Cav. Co.C
Robison, J.S. GA 28th Inf. Co.A Sgt.
Robison, J.W. GA 3rd Cav. Co.I 2nd Lt.
Robison, J.W. GA 32nd Inf. Co.E
Robison, J.W. GA 49th Inf. Co.H
Robison, J.W. MS Cav. 3rd Bn. (Ashcraft's)
Co.C
Robison, J.W. MS 27th Inf. Co.B
Robison, L. GA 7th Cav. Co.B
Robison, Lewellen TX Cav. Ragsdale's Bn. Co.B
Capt.
Robison, Lewellyn TX 2nd Cav. Co.I
Robison, Lewis Deneale's Regt. Choctaw War-
riors Co.B 1st Lt.
Robison, L.M. MO Quantrill's Co.
Robison, Lucas VA 62nd Mtd.Inf. 2nd Co.L
Robison, M.A. NC 5th Sr.Res. Co.E
Robison, Manoah D. AL 13th Inf. Co.E Capt.
Robison, Mathew M. GA Cav. 7th Bn.
(St.Guards) Co.B
Robison, Milton NC 58th Inf. Co.F
Robison, Milus F. TN 18th (Newsom's) Cav.
Co.I
Robison, Nathan B. NC 62nd Inf. Co.C
Robison, Neil AL 36th Inf. Co.E
Robison, Newton GA Inf. (Muscogee Guards)
Thornton's Co.
Robison, Pearson SC 5th St.Troops Co.D
Robison, P.K. MS 18th Inf. Co.E
Robison, P.P. TN 7th (Duckworth's) Cav.
White's Co.
Robison, R.A. NC 4th Inf. Co.K
Robison, R.A. SC 2nd Inf. Co.E
Robison, R.B.F. 8th (Wade's) Conf.Cav. Co.H
Robison, R.C. SC 5th St.Troops Co.K
Robison, Richard TN 6th Inf. Co.I
Robison, Richard S. MS Hamer's Co. (Salem
Cav.)
Robison, Robert MS 28th Cav. Co.H
Robison, Robert SC 1st Arty. Co.B
Robison, Robert B. MS 19th Inf. Co.G
Robison, Robert J. AL 6th Cav. Co.E Cpl.
Robison, R.R. SC Palmetto S.S. Co.G Cpl.
Robison, Rufus MS Inf. 5th Bn. Co.C
Robison, Rufus MS 41st Inf. Co.A

Robison, S. SC Hvy.Arty. Gilchrist's Co. (Gist Guard) Music.
Robison, Samuel AR 50th Mil. Co.C
Robison, Samuel GA 49th Inf. Co.H
Robison, Samuel B. TN 38th Inf. 1st Co.H
Robison, Samuel E. GA 17th Inf. Co.C Adj.
Robison, S.B. TX Inf. 1st Bn. (St.Troops) Co.F
Robison, Simpson W. SC 12th Inf. Co.A
Robison, S.J. LA 3rd (Wingfield's) Cav. Co.F
Robison, Smith NC 56th Inf. Co.I
Robison, S.O. VA Cav. 37th Bn. Co.H
Robison, Stephen NC 68th Inf.
Robison, S.W. NC 27th Inf. Co.I
Robison, Thomas A. MS 1st (Percy's) Inf. Co.A
Robison, Thomas G. AL 12th Inf. Co.B
Robison, Thomas T. NC 49th Inf. Co.C Sgt.
Robison, Thomas W. LA 12th Inf. 2nd Co.M Cpl.
Robison, T.R. FL 2nd Cav. Co.D
Robison, W. GA 26th Inf. Co.D
Robison, Wallace MS 1st Arty. Co.C Cpl.
Robison, W.B. TN 4th Inf. Co.D
Robison, W.H. 1st Chickasaw Inf. McCord's Co. Cpl.
Robison, W.H.H. GA 46th Inf. Co.C
Robison, Wilborn C. NC 58th Inf. Co.L
Robison, William AR Cav. Poe's Bn. Dismuks' Co.
Robison, William MS 15th Inf. Co.G
Robison, William MO 7th Cav. Co.F
Robison, William NC 30th Inf. Co.F
Robison, William SC Simons' Co.
Robison, William VA 11th Bn.Res. Co.B
Robison, William Conf.Lt.Arty. 1st Reg.Btty.
Robison, William A. GA 44th Inf. Co.C
Robison, William A. TN 3rd (Lillard's) Mtd.Inf. Co.D
Robison, William A. TN 59th Mtd.Inf. Co.A
Robison, William A. TN Inf. 154th Sr.Regt. 2nd Co.B
Robison, William A.M. VA 25th Cav. Co.H Cpl.
Robison, William C. NC 48th Inf. Co.C
Robison, William D. TN 2nd (Robison's) Inf. Co.F Col.
Robison, William L. TN 18th (Newsom's) Cav. Co.B
Robison, William L. TN 35th Inf. 2nd Co.F 1st Sgt.
Robison, William M. MO 1st Cav. Co.B
Robison, William R. AL 5th Inf. Co.B
Robison, William R. GA 57th Inf. Co.G
Robison, William R. TN 3rd (Clack's) Inf. Co.D
Robison, William S. NC 62nd Inf. Co.C
Robison, William Stevenson LA 28th (Gray's) Inf. Co.F 1st Lt.
Robison, W.J. AL Inf. 2nd Regt. Co.C 2nd Lt.
Robison, W.J. AL 17th Inf. Co.H 2nd Lt.
Robison, W.J. AL 42nd Inf. Co.A
Robison, W.J. MS Corps
Robison, W.L. TX 7th Cav. Co.I
Robison, W.R. AR 14th (Powers') Inf. Co.I
Robison, W.R. GA 1st (Ramsey's) Inf. Co.E
Robison, W.S. GA 12th Mil.
Robison, W.S. TX 18th Inf. Co.K
Robison, Wyatt TN 6th Inf. Co.I
Robison, Wyatt E. MS 17th Inf. Co.B

Robitzsch, John E. NC 1st Inf. Co.C
Robitzsch, Richard F. NC 1st Inf. Co.C Sgt.
Robitzsch, Robert B. NC 1st Inf. Co.C
Robitzsch, William E. MS 2nd Part.Rangers Co.I
Robjohn, R. MS 22nd Inf. Co.A
Robke, Frederick TX 15th Field Btty.
Robke, John TX 1st Hvy.Arty. Co.D
Robkie, Frederick TX 1st Hvy.Arty. Co.D
Roblais, Philibert LA 18th Inf. Co.C
Roble, George LA Mil.Conf.Guards Regt. Co.G
Robleau, Elwa LA 19th Inf. Co.H
Robleau, S. LA Inf. Pelican Regt. Co.E
Robleau, Sebastian LA 19th Inf. Co.H
Roblero, Fusto TX Cav. Benavides' Regt. Co.I
Robles, Dolores TX Cav. Ragsdale's Bn. 1st Co.A
Robles, John G. FL 9th Inf. Co.C
Robles, Juan TX Cav. Benavides' Regt. Co.B
Robles, Michael F. FL 4th Inf. Co.K
Robles, Punciano TX Cav. Ragsdale's Bn. 1st Co.A
Roblet, J.H. AL 21st Inf. Co.C
Roblett, W.J. GA 11th Inf. Co.E Lt.
Robley, A. TN 14th (Neely's) Cav. Co.F
Robley, C.B. TN 31st Inf. Co.B
Robley, C.B. TN 51st Inf. Co.E Sgt.
Robley, C.B. TN 51st (Cons.) Inf. Co.F
Robley, F.A. TN Lt.Arty. Polk's Btty.
Robley, J.B. TN 14th (Neely's) Cav. Co.F
Robley, John TN 18th (Newsom's) Cav. Co.B
Robley, John TX 12th Inf. Co.F
Robley, John R. TN 51st Inf. Co.E Cpl.
Robley, J.R. TN 51st (Cons.) Inf. Co.I,F
Robley, Thomas P. AR 15th (Josey's) Inf. Co.A Sgt.
Robley, W.D. TN 14th (Neely's) Cav. Co.F
Robley, W.H. TN 51st (Cons.) Inf. Co.I,F
Robley, William H. TN 51st Inf. Co.E
Robline, Bernard VA 5th Cav. Co.B
Roblins, E.H. MS Wilson's Co. (Ponticola Guards)
Robned, J.H. AR 30th Inf. Co.B
Robner, Marion VA Cav. 47th Bn. Aldredge's Co.
Robnet, G.M. NC 39th Inf. Co.E
Robnett, Abner E. NC 37th Inf. Co.G
Robnett, A.L. NC 5th Sr.Res. Co.D 1st Sgt.
Robnett, B.F. TX 15th Inf. Co.C
Robnett, Elisha L. NC 37th Inf. Co.G
Robnett, George W. MO 11th Inf. Co.B
Robnett, G.M. NC Mallett's Co.
Robnett, Isaac TX 10th Cav. Co.I
Robnett, James MO 1st & 4th Cons.Inf. Co.H
Robnett, James W. NC 37th Inf. Co.G Sgt.
Robnett, Jesse A. NC 37th Inf. Co.G Sgt.
Robnett, Jesse F. NC 37th Inf. Co.G Sgt.
Robnett, J.N. MO Cav. Coleman's Regt. Co.K 2nd Lt.
Robnett, Joel B. NC 37th Inf. Co.G
Robnett, John C. NC 37th Inf. Co.G
Robnett, J.P. TX 15th Inf. Co.C
Robnett, Lawson C. NC 37th Inf. Co.G 1st Sgt.
Robnett, W.H. AR 7th Cav. Co.I
Robnett, W.H. AR 38th Inf. Co.D
Robnett, W.H. TX 30th Cav. Co.K Ord.Sgt.
Robnett, William VA 51st Inf. Co.I

Robnett, William A., Jr. NC 37th Inf. Co.G Music.
Robnett, William A., Sr. NC 37th Inf. Co.G Cpl.
Robnett, William P. NC 37th Inf. Co.G
Robnett, William W. NC 37th Inf. Co.G
Robniet, Henry L. LA Hvy.Arty. 8th Bn. Co.3
Robnol, R.W. VA 4th Cav. Co.K
Robonett, Amos VA 48th Inf. Co.G
Roborg, S.A. GA Inf. (GA RR Guards) Porter's Co. Surg.
Robosson, B.S. VA 2nd St.Res. Co.E
Robotham, Jonathan GA 1st (Olmstead's) Inf. Gordon's Co.
Robotham, Jonathan GA 63rd Inf. Co.B
Robothem, B.H. AR 7th Cav. Co.B Sgt.
Robothom, Henry LA Mil. St.John the Baptist Res.Guards
Robron, T.J. TN 25th Inf. Co.G
Robrts, T. AL 55th Vol. Co.C
Robry, Thomas VA 18th Cav. Co.E
Robs, J. AL Talladega Cty.Res. W.Y. Hendrick's Co.
Robson, A.P. GA 32nd Inf. Co.D
Robson, Cornelius R. GA 3rd Bn. (St.Guards) Co.C
Robson, D. VA Cav. Mosby's Regt. (Part. Rangers) Co.E
Robson, Francis M. SC 1st Arty. Co.G
Robson, George MS 18th Cav. Co.L
Robson, George Inf. School of Pract. Powell's Detach. Co.C
Robson, George M. NC 1st Cav. (9th St.Troops) Co.C Sgt.
Robson, H.T. GA Lt.Arty. 12th Bn. 3rd Co.B 1st Lt.
Robson, H.T. GA 1st (Ramsey's) Inf. Co.E
Robson, I.B. TN 7th (Duckworth's) Cav. Co.C
Robson, J.A. GA Lt.Arty. 12th Bn. 3rd Co.B Sgt.
Robson, Jacob TN 10th Inf. Co.B
Robson, James FL 1st Cav. Co.E
Robson, James MO St.Guards
Robson, James F. GA Lt.Arty. Guerard's Btty.
Robson, James W. KY 2nd Mtd.Inf. Co.E Sgt.
Robson, J.A.P. GA 6th Inf. (St.Guards) Co.F 2nd Lt.
Robson, Jesse A. GA 1st (Ramsey's) Inf. Co.E
Robson, J.M. SC 1st Regt. Charleston Guard Co.A
Robson, John GA Cav. 1st Bn. Hopkins' Co. Cpl.
Robson, John KY 13th Cav. Co.H
Robson, John S. VA 52nd Inf. Co.D Cpl.
Robson, Lewis LA 28th (Gray's) Inf. Co.H
Robson, L.Q.C. AR 3rd Cav. Co.H
Robson, Milton B. NC 27th Inf. Co.G
Robson, Robert MS 29th Inf. Co.B Capt.
Robson, Robert MS A. of 10,000 Col.
Robson, S.B. GA 3rd Bn. (St.Guards) Co.C 3rd Lt.
Robson, S.B. GA Capt.,ACS
Robson, W.A. GA 5th Cav. Co.H
Robson, W.G. GA Lt.Arty. Howell's Co. 1st Lt.
Robson, W.G. GA 1st (Ramsey's) Inf. Co.E,B
Robson, W.G. NC Lt.Arty. 13th Bn. Co.E Sgt.
Robson, W.G. TN 7th Cav.

Robson, Wiley FL 1st Cav. Co.E Cpl.
Robson, Wiley GA Cav. Rumph's Co. (Wayne Cav.Guards) Cpl.
Robson, William LA 25th Inf. Co.A Capt.
Robson, William NC 1st Inf. (6 mo. '61) Co.D
Robson, William A. GA Cav. 1st Bn. Hopkins' Co., Brailsford's Co.
Robson, William G. NC 3rd Arty. (40th St.Troops) Co.G 1st Sgt.
Robson, William H. VA 59th Inf. 1st Co.F
Robson, William H. VA 60th Inf. Co.C
Robson, William J. MS 33rd Inf. Co.H Sgt.
Robson, William T. VA 12th Cav. Co.G
Robson, W.J. GA Cav. Rumph's Co. (Wayne Cav.Guards)
Robson, W.J. MS 18th Cav. Co.K,L
Robts, John R. VA 22nd Inf. Swann's Co.
Robuck, A.H. GA 1st Mil. Co.C Sgt.
Robuck, A.M. MO 5th Inf. Co.H
Robuck, A.W. MS 14th Inf. Co.F
Robuck, B.F. SC 3rd Inf. Co.K
Robuck, Elias SC Inf. Holcombe Legion Co.G
Robuck, Ephraim 1st Choctaw & Chickasaw Mtd.Rifles 2nd Co.D
Robuck, George N. AL 20th Inf. Co.C,A
Robuck, George W. NC 17th Inf. (2nd Org.) Co.K Cpl.
Robuck, Hillory FL 2nd Cav. Co.I
Robuck, Isaac M. SC Inf. Holcombe Legion Co.E Cpl.
Robuck, James FL 3rd Inf. Co.I
Robuck, James MS 6th Cav. Co.B
Robuck, James MS Cav. Davenport's Bn. (St.Troops) Co.A
Robuck, James H. FL Lt.Arty. Abell's Co.
Robuck, J.B. AL 16th Inf. Co.A Sgt.
Robuck, Jesse J. SC 3rd Inf. Co.K
Robuck, J.H. SC Inf. Holcombe Legion Co.E
Robuck, J.M. SC Inf. Holcombe Legion Co.E
Robuck, John SC 3rd Inf. Co.K
Robuck, John E. MS 29th Inf. Co.A
Robuck, J.P. GA 55th Inf. Co.I
Robuck, J.P. SC 3rd Inf. Co.K Capt.
Robuck, J.S. GA 55th Inf. Co.I
Robuck, J.W. AL 29th Inf. Co.D Sgt.
Robuck, Oliver P. GA 1st Reg. Co.F
Robuck, P.C. GA 4th (Clinch's) Cav. Co.A,K
Robuck, Robert W. AL 16th Inf. Co.G 1st Lt.
Robuck, Samuel B. AL 16th Inf. Co.G Sgt.
Robuck, S.G. FL 2nd Cav. Co.I
Robuck, S.S. SC 5th St.Troops Co.H Sgt.
Robuck, S.S. SC 9th Res. Co.I Sgt.
Robuck, W.B. MS 5th Inf. Co.E Cpl.
Robuck, W.E. TX 12th Cav. Co.B
Robuck, William B. MS 29th Inf. Co.A Cpl.
Robuck, William E. GA 35th Inf. Co.H
Robuck, William H. GA 49th Inf. Co.K
Robuck, William P. AL 11th Inf. Co.B
Robuck, William R. MS 26th Inf. Co.G
Robuck, William R. MS 32nd Inf. Co.K
Robuck, W.N. MS 44th Inf. Co.F
Robuck, W.P. MS 35th Inf. Co.D
Robuck, W.P. SC 3rd Inf. Co.K
Robuck, W.P. SC Inf. Holcombe Legion Co.E Capt.
Robuck, W.W. TX 17th Inf. Co.K Cpl.
Robun, Charles P. LA 31st Inf. Co.I

Robush, J.S. VA 12th Cav. Co.H
Robuson, J.W. AR 19th (Dockery's) Inf. Co.A
Roby, A.G. MS Burt's Ind.Co. (Dixie Guards)
Roby, A.J. VA 41st Inf. Co.I
Roby, Archer N. VA 9th Inf. 1st Co.H Cpl.
Roby, Archer N. VA Inf. 28th Bn. Co.C Cpl.
Roby, Benedic S. KY Cav. 22nd Regt.
Roby, C.F. AR 21st Inf. Co.D
Roby, Charles F. AR 17th (Lemoyne's) Inf. Co.B
Roby, Christopher C. MO 10th Inf. Co.D,B
Roby, D. AR 45th Cav. Co.B
Roby, David A. AR 1st (Colquitt's) Inf. Co.G
Roby, David A. AR 30th Inf. Co.D
Roby, Edwin KY 1st (Butler's) Cav. Co.D
Roby, E.P. MS 15th Inf. Co.A Asst.Surg.
Roby, E.P. Gen. & Staff A.Surg.
Roby, E.W. KY 4th Cav. Co.D
Roby, E.W. KY 3rd Bn.Mtd.Rifles Co.D
Roby, F.M. MS 44th Inf. Co.A
Roby, F.M. MS Burt's Ind.Co. (Dixie Guards)
Roby, F.M. Gen. & Staff 1st Lt.,Ord.Off.
Roby, Frank M. MS 35th Inf. Co.F
Roby, George H. MS 3rd Cav. Co.B
Roby, George N. MS Lt.Arty. (Brookhaven Lt.Arty.) Hoskins' Btty.
Roby, George W. KY 8th Cav. Co.A
Roby, G.W. GA Inf. 17th Bn. (St.Guards) Jefferson's Co. 1st Sgt.
Roby, H.A. MD Cav. 2nd Bn. Co.B Sgt.
Roby, Henry KY 8th Cav. Co.G
Roby, Henry TX Inf. Griffin's Bn. Co.C
Roby, Henry W. GA 3rd Inf. Co.B
Roby, Isaac R. VA 18th Inf. Co.A
Roby, James AR 8th Cav. Co.G
Roby, James G. TX 22nd Cav. Co.D
Roby, James L. GA 55th Inf. Co.A
Roby, James L. VA 9th Inf. 2nd Co.A
Roby, James R. GA 3rd Inf. Co.B
Roby, James R. MS 30th Inf. Co.G 2nd Lt.
Roby, Jefferson R. GA 44th Inf. Co.F
Roby, J.K. 10th Conf.Cav. Co.F
Roby, John TX 4th Inf. (St.Troops) Co.C
Roby, John W. KY 10th (Johnson's) Cav. Co.A,F Sgt.
Roby, Joseph TX Cav. Martin's Regt. Co.H Sgt.
Roby, Joseph VA Cav. 41st Bn. Trayhern's Co.
Roby, J.R. SC 2nd Arty. Co.A
Roby, J.W. MO 1st & 4th Cons.Inf. Co.C,K
Roby, Lafayette MS 21st Inf. Co.G
Roby, Lewis VA 9th Inf. 2nd Co.A
Roby, Lewis H. VA 8th Inf. Co.G Sgt.
Roby, Lucius LA C.S. Zouave Bn. Co.E
Roby, M.J. VA 17th Cav. Co.K
Roby, M.T. MS 3rd Cav. Co.B Sgt.
Roby, M.T. MS 1st (King's) Inf. (St.Troops) Co.F
Roby, M.T. MS 2nd Inf. (A. of 10,000) Co.F
Roby, Robert GA 46th Inf. Co.G
Roby, R.P. TX 12th Cav. Co.A
Roby, R.R. LA Res.Corps Doyle's Co.
Roby, S.H. GA 8th Cav.
Roby, Singleton TX 15th Cav. Co.E Cpl.
Roby, S.S. VA 17th Cav. Co.C
Roby, Theodore VA Hood's Bn.Res. Tappey's Co.
Roby, Thomas GA Inf. 27th Bn. Co.F

Roby, Thomas G. AR Lt.Arty. Thrall's Btty.
Roby, Thomas G. AR 30th Inf. Co.D
Roby, Thomas M. MO 10th Inf. Co.E
Roby, Thomas S. MS 11th Inf. Co.F
Roby, Tim K. LA 9th Inf. Co.D
Roby, T.J. AR 45th Cav. Co.B Sgt.
Roby, T.S. LA 1st Hvy.Arty. (Reg.) Co.D
Roby, W.A. GA 9th Inf. (St.Guards) Co.A
Roby, W.A. MS 11th (Perrin's) Cav. Co.H
Roby, W.A. MS Burt's Ind.Co. (Dixie Guards)
Roby, Walter A. VA 25th Inf. 2nd Co.I,D Music.
Roby, William GA 2nd Inf. Co.C Sgt.
Roby, William MO Lt.Arty. Walsh's Co.
Roby, William VA Cav. 15th Bn. Co.C
Roby, William C. GA 44th Inf. Co.F Cpl.
Roby, William E. GA 45th Inf. Co.D
Roby, William W. TX Cav. Martin's Regt. Co.H
Roby, W.S. MS Shields' Co.
Roby, Z.D. GA Inf. (Loc.Def.) Whiteside's Nav.Bn. Co.A
Roca, Augustin LA Mil. 5th Regt.Eur.Brig. (Spanish Regt.) Co.3
Roca, Federico LA Mil. 5th Regt.Eur.Brig. (Spanish Regt.) Co.3
Roca, John LA Mil. 5th Regt.Eur.Brig. (Spanish Regt.) Co.5
Roca, Juan LA Mil. 5th Regt.Eur.Brig. (Spanish Regt.) Co.6
Roca, L. LA Mil. Cazadores Espanoles Regt. Co.3,4 1st Lt.
Roca, Mateo LA Mil. 5th Regt.Eur.Brig. (Spanish Regt.) Co.3
Roca, P. LA Mil. 4th Regt. 2nd Brig. 1st Div. Co.E
Rocca, Francisco MS 12th Inf. Co.G
Rocca, J. LA Mil. 1st Regt. French Brig. Co.9
Rocca, Jean LA Mil. 1st Regt. French Brig. Co.8
Rocco, Batista LA Mil. 4th Regt.Eur.Brig. Cognevich's Co.
Rocco, Laste LA Miles' Legion Co.G
Rocco, Lucchin LA 1st (Strawbridge's) Inf. Co.H
Rocford, Keveir NC Nelson's Co. (Loc.Def.)
Roch, Ch. Celestin LA Mil. 2nd Regt. French Brig. Co.5 Cpl.
Roch, E.J. GA Cobb's Legion Co.B
Roch, F.M. LA 22nd Inf. Co.K
Roch, Guillaume LA Mil. 2nd Regt. French Brig. Co.5
Roch, Jean Eugene LA Mil. 2nd Regt. French Brig. Co.5 Cpl.
Roch, John LA Mil. 4th Regt. 2nd Brig. 1st Div. Co.G
Rochal, R.S. AR 21st Inf. Co.E Sgt.
Rochan, I.B. LA 3rd (Harrison's) Cav. Co.I
Rochard, J.H. GA 13th Cav. Co.I
Rochbacher, --- LA Mil. 2nd Regt. French Brig. Co.3
Roche, A. GA 22nd Inf. Co.B
Roche, A. LA Mil. 1st Native Guards
Roche, A. LA 18th Inf. Co.H
Roche, Auguste LA Mil. Orleans Guards Regt. Co.C Capt.
Roche, Charles LA Inf. 9th Bn. Co.C
Roche, Daniel GA 1st (Olmstead's) Inf. Co.A,B Sgt.

Roche, Denis LA Mil. Orleans Guards Regt.
    Co.D
Roche, Dennis LA Pointe Coupee Arty.
Roche, Edward SC 1st St.Troops Co.I
Roche, Edward SC 5th Res. Co.I Cpl.
Roche, E.L. SC Inf. 1st (Charleston) Bn. Co.A
Roche, Francis Y. Gen. & Staff, QM Dept. Clerk
Roche, Frank T. VA 32nd Inf. Co.A
Roche, Frederick VA 32nd Inf. 2nd Co.I
Roche, H.P. LA 26th Inf.
Roche, J. LA Mil. 3rd Regt. French Brig. Co.8
Roche, James VA Lt.Arty. Hardwicke's Co.
Roche, James VA Hvy.Arty. Read's Co.
Roche, James R. VA 40th Inf. Co.K
Roche, J.E. MS 4th Inf. Co.C
Roché, J.H. LA Ogden's Cav. Co.E
Roche, J.J. LA 30th Inf. Co.F
Roche, J.J. VA 21st Cav. Co.A
Roche, John LA Inf. 7th Bn. Co.C
Roche, John LA Inf.Crescent Regt. Co.F
Roche, John MS 6th Cav. Co.H
Roche, John SC 22nd Inf. Co.D
Roche, John F. GA 1st (Olmstead's) Inf. Co.A
Roche, John J. GA 47th Inf. Co.A Sgt.
Roche, Julian TX 33rd Cav. 1st Co.I
Roche, Julian LA Mil. 1st Native Guards Cpl.
Roche, Lawrence N. LA Pointe Coupee Arty.
Roche, L.N. LA Mil. 1st Chasseurs a pied Co.2
Roche, Marcus TX 4th Field Btty. Sgt.
Roche, Michael GA 48th Inf. Co.B
Roche, Nicholas TN Inf. 154th Sr.Regt. Co.C
    Cpl.
Roche, Patrick GA Siege Arty. 28th Bn. Co.F
Roche, Patrick GA Inf. 1st Loc.Troops (Augusta)
    Co.A
Roche, Patrick LA Inf. 9th Bn. Co.C Sgt.
Roche, Peter GA 1st (Olmstead's) Inf. Co.A,K
Roche, Q. LA Mil. 3rd Regt. French Brig. Co.3
Roche, Richard W. TX 2nd Inf. Co.A 2nd Lt.
Roche, Robert VA Arty. Wise Legion
Roche, Samuel D. VA 20th Cav. Co.K
Roche, Theodore GA Cav. Roswell Bn. Co.A
Roche, Thomas TN 2nd (Walker's) Inf. Co.H
Roche, Thomas TX 2nd Cav. Co.E
Roche, Thomas F. MD Weston's Bn. Co.B
Roche, Thomas F. VA 21st Inf. Co.B
Roche, Thomas F. VA 30th Bn.S.S. Adj.
Roche, Thomas F. Gen. & Staff 1st Lt.,Adj.
Roche, Thomas M. GA 1st (Olmstead's) Inf.
    Co.A
Roche, Thomas T. MS 16th Inf. Co.K
Roche, T.W. SC 22nd Inf. Co.I Cpl.
Roche, W. 1st Conf.Inf. 1st Co.F
Roche, William SC 22nd Inf. Co.D
Roche, William TN 21st Inf. Co.B
Rochefort, Charles LA 13th Inf. Co.F
Rochel, E.S. AL 35th Inf. Co.H
Rochel, James MS Adair's Co. (Lodi Co.)
Rochel, Littleton H. VA 48th Inf. Co.B
Rochel, R. MS 3rd Cav. Co.E
Rochell, A.H. NC 47th Inf. Co.I
Rochell, E.B. TX 29th Cav. Asst.Surg.
Rochell, E.G. NC 3rd Cav. (41st St.Troops)
    Co.A
Rochell, Franklin R. MS 15th Inf. Co.D
Rochell, George W. GA 59th Inf. Co.B
Rochell, G.W. NC 47th Inf. Co.I

Rochell, Henderson B. TN 32nd Inf. Co.C
Rochell, Henry MS 2nd Cav. Co.H
Rochell, Henry G. MS 14th Inf. Co.F
Rochell, J.A. TX 32nd Cav. Co.A
Rochell, J.E. TX 32nd Cav. Co.A
Rochell, J.L.B. TX Cav. 2nd Regt.St.Troops
    Co.E Cpl.
Rochell, John S. TN 21st (Wilson's) Cav. Co.E
    Cpl.
Rochell, John S. TN Cav. Newsom's Regt. Co.C
Rochell, Jno. T. MS 30th Inf. Co.B
Rochell, J.W. TN 21st (Wilson's) Cav. Co.K
Rochell, S. TN 14th (Neely's) Cav. Co.C
Rochell, T. AL 1st Cav.
Rochell, T.B. NC 11th (Bethel Regt.) Inf. Co.H
Rochell, Thomas J. TN 11th Inf. Co.H
Rochell, Thomas W. LA 19th Inf. Surg.
Rochell, T.W. TN 48th (Nixon's) Inf. Co.D
Rochell, T.W. TN 48th (Voorhies') Inf. Co.D
Rochell, William MS 3rd Cav. Co.I
Rochell, William P. AL 10th Cav.
Rochell, W.P. MS 18th Cav. Co.F
Rochelle, Benjamin NC 38th Inf. Co.A
Rochelle, Benjamin H. VA Lt.Arty. Clutter's Co.
Rochelle, Blaney J. NC 3rd Inf. Co.K
Rochelle, Charles TX 29th Cav. Co.I
Rochelle, Charles M. TX Cav. 2nd Bn.St.Troops
    Hubbard's Co.
Rochelle, D.C. TX 1st (Yager's) Cav. Co.M
Rochelle, D.N. MS 1st (Johnston's) Inf. Co.F
Rochelle, Edward G. NC 3rd Inf. Co.K
Rochelle, Eli S. TN 53rd Inf. Co.A
Rochelle, Ephraim J. NC 3rd Inf. Co.K
Rochelle, Eugene B. Gen. & Staff Asst.Surg.
Rochelle, G.E. AL 2nd Cav. Co.I Sr.2nd Lt.
Rochelle, G.E. 10th Conf.Cav. Co.D 1st Lt.
Rochelle, Isaac NC 3rd Inf. Co.K
Rochelle, J. AL Cav. Callaway's Co.
Rochelle, J. LA 26th Inf. Co.G
Rochelle, J.A. SC 24th Inf. Co.I
Rochelle, James E. MS 15th Inf. Co.K
Rochelle, James J. TN Inf. 154th Sr.Regt. Co.E
Rochelle, Jasper TN Lt.Arty. McClung's Co.
Rochelle, J.B. LA Lt.Arty. LeGardeur, Jr.'s Co.
    (Orleans Guard Btty.)
Rochelle, J.B. MO Lt.Arty. Barret's Co.
Rochelle, J.L. MS 30th Inf. Co.B
Rochelle, John AL 4th Res. Co.H
Rochelle, John KY 3rd Mtd.Inf. Co.D
Rochelle, John F. AL 1st Regt. Mobile Vol.
    Co.K 1st Lt.
Rochelle, John G.W. TN 42nd Inf. Co.B
Rochelle, John R. TX Cav. 2nd Bn.St.Troops
    Hubbard's Co.
Rochelle, John T. NC 3rd Inf. Co.D
Rochelle, John W. SC 5th Res. Co.E Cpl.
Rochelle, John W. SC Inf. Hampton Legion
    Co.B
Rochelle, J.P. LA 27th Inf. Co.G
Rochelle, J.W. TX 6th Inf. Co.E
Rochelle, Marcellus R. TN 32nd Inf. Co.C Cpl.
Rochelle, M.S. NC 3rd Cav. (41st St.Troops)
    Co.B
Rochelle, Napoleon B. NC 3rd Inf. Co.D
Rochelle, Quincey V.B. NC 1st Cav. (9th
    St.Troops) Co.I
Rochelle, Robert H. NC 3rd Inf. Co.K

Rochelle, S. TN Lt.Arty. Phillips' Co.
Rochelle, T.B. NC 3rd Cav. (41st St.Troops)
    Co.B
Rochelle, T.W. Gen. & Staff Surg.
Rochelle, Wiley G.W. TN 32nd Inf. Co.C
Rochelle, William MS 42nd Inf. Co.I
Rochelle, William TN 19th (Biffle's) Cav. Co.H
Rochelle, William J. SC 24th Inf. Co.I
Rochelle, W.J. SC 16th & 24th (Cons.) Inf.
    Co.G Music.
Rochelle, W. Wallace TN Inf. 154th Sr.Regt.
    Co.E
Rochelle, Z.A. NC 2nd Jr.Res. Co.A
Rochenbaugh, C. AR 58th Mil. Co.D
Rochereau, Albin LA Mil. 1st Regt. French Brig.
    Col.
Rochester, A.M. SC Inf. Hampton Legion Co.F
Rochester, Edwin T. KY 6th Cav. Capt.
Rochester, George SC 5th Cav. Co.K
Rochester, George SC Cav.Bn. Holcombe Legion
    Co.D
Rochester, George W. SC 5th Inf. 2nd Co.D
Rochester, H.D. SC 2nd Rifles Co.C
Rochester, J. SC Lt.Arty. 3rd (Palmetto) Bn.
    Co.H
Rochester, James SC 12th Inf. Co.K
Rochester, James SC 22nd Inf. Co.H
Rochester, James H. SC 1st (Orr's) Rifles Co.A
Rochester, J.H. SC 1st St.Troops Co.E Cpl.
Rochester, J.L. SC 7th Inf. 2nd Co.L Cpl.
Rochester, John SC 16th Inf. Co.H
Rochester, John SC 22nd Inf. Co.H
Rochester, John M. KY 3rd Cav. Co.I
Rochester, John M. KY 7th Cav. Co.I
Rochester, John M. TN 3rd (Forrest's) Cav. 1st
    Co.G
Rochester, Jonathan A. SC 1st (Orr's) Rifles
    Co.A
Rochester, Lewis NC 3rd Inf.
Rochester, N.A. SC 1st (Orr's) Rifles Co.A
Rochester, Reuben S. GA 41st Inf. Co.D Artif.
Rochester, R.S. GA Inf. 17th Bn. (St.Guards)
    Jefferson's Co. 1st Lt.
Rochester, Samuel LA 19th Inf. Co.D 1st Sgt.
Rochester, Samuel N. LA Inf.Crescent Regt.
    Co.A Cpl.
Rochester, S.M. LA Inf.Cons.Crescent Regt.
    Co.C
Rochester, S.M. Sig.Corps,CSA
Rochester, S.N. LA 18th Inf. Co.K
Rochester, W.A. SC 25th Inf. Co.H Cpl.
Rochester, W.D. SC 2nd Inf. Co.C
Rochester, W.D. SC Palmetto S.S. Co.B
Rochester, W.F. MS 7th Cav. Co.B
Rochester, William LA 28th (Gray's) Inf. Co.A
Rochester, William NC 15th Inf. Co.I
Rochester, William SC 2nd Inf. Co.A
Rochester, William A. SC Simons' Co.
Rochester, William Asberry Alton SC 4th Inf.
    Co.C
Rochester, William E. SC 16th Inf. Co.A,K
Rochester, William T. SC 20th Inf. Co.A
Rochew, W.P. LA Arty. 5th Field Btty. (Pelican
    Lt.Arty.)
Rochill, John Thomas MS 3rd Cav. Co.A
Rochoo, William TX 2nd Cav. Co.G, 2nd Co.F
Rochotch, M.H. AL St.Arty. Co.C

Rochotsh, Magnus H. AL 12th Inf. Co.C
Rochou, Adolph LA Mil. 1st Native Guards
Rochow, George W. TX Arty. 4th Bn. Co.B
Rochow, George W. TX 8th Inf. Co.B Sgt.
Rochtean, Henry Trans-MS Conf.Cav. 1st Bn. Co.B
Rock, --- TX 3rd Inf. Co.H
Rock, Adolphus VA 109th Mil. Co.B
Rock, Adolphus S. VA 55th Inf. Co.H
Rock, Anderson A. VA 36th Inf. Beckett's Co.
Rock, Andrew J. VA 40th Inf. Co.C
Rock, Benjamin E. VA 40th Inf. Co.B
Rock, B.G. VA 21st Cav. Co.F
Rock, Carlos VA 40th Inf. Co.F
Rock, Cromwell M. VA Lt.Arty. Pollock's Co. Lance Sgt.
Rock, Edward TX 21st Cav. Co.K Music.
Rock, Edward TX 25th Cav. Co.D Cpl.
Rock, George W. VA 3rd Inf.Loc.Def. Co.E
Rock, George W. VA 22nd Inf. Co.C
Rock, G.W. VA Hvy.Arty. 20th Bn. Co.C
Rock, Harry GA 1st (Symons') Res. Co.B
Rock, Harvey O. VA 28th Inf. Co.K
Rock, H.C. VA 40th Inf. Co.C
Rock, Henry GA 1st (Symons') Res. Co.B
Rock, Henry VA 25th Cav. Co.G
Rock, Hezekiah VA Lt.Arty. Garber's Co.
Rock, James A. VA 5th Cav. Co.H
Rock, James A. VA 15th Cav. Co.D
Rock, James F. VA 45th Inf. Co.H
Rock, James M. VA 4th Res. Co.D
Rock, John VA Hvy.Arty. 20th Bn. Co.C
Rock, John VA 36th Inf. 2nd Co.H
Rock, John VA 86th Mil. Co.D
Rock, John H. VA 15th Inf. Co.G
Rock, John J. VA Lt.Arty. Hardwicke's Co. Sgt.
Rock, John James VA 2nd Cav. Co.C Sgt.
Rock, John W. MO Conscr.
Rock, Joseph A. VA 37th Mil. Co.D
Rock, Joseph A. VA 55th Inf. Co.K
Rock, Josie LA 28th (Thomas') Inf. Co.B
Rock, J.W. MO 5th Cav. Co.D
Rock, Martin TN 1st Hvy.Arty. Co.F, 2nd Co.D
Rock, Michael VA 54th Mil. Co.C,D
Rock, Owen GA 47th Inf. Co.A
Rock, P.H. VA Loc.Def. Durrett's Co.
Rock, Phillip H. VA 15th Inf. Co.G
Rock, Rosser S. VA Goochland Lt.Arty.
Rock, Samuel J. VA Goochland Lt.Arty.
Rock, Samuel J. VA 56th Inf. Co.B
Rock, S.J. TX 1st Inf. Co.F
Rock, Sosthene LA Mil. 1st Native Guards 1st Lt.
Rock, T.D. TX 1st Inf. Co.F Bvt.2nd Lt.
Rock, Thomas TX 25th Cav. Co.I Ord.Sgt.
Rock, Thomas VA 7th Cav. Co.H
Rock, Thomas VA Cav. 36th Bn. Co.C
Rock, Thomas VA Cav. 39th Bn. Co.B
Rock, Thomas VA 86th Mil. Co.F
Rock, Thomas 1st Conf.Inf. Co.B
Rock, Thomas J. VA 37th Inf. Co.B
Rock, Walter P. VA 37th Mil. Co.A
Rock, Walter R. VA 40th Inf. Co.C
Rock, W.H. AL 11th Inf. Co.D
Rock, William TX Cav. Benavides' Regt. Co.K
Rock, William VA Lt.Arty. E.J. Anderson's Co.

Rock, William B. VA Goochland Lt.Arty.
Rock, William C. VA 37th Mil. Co.D
Rock, William C. VA 55th Inf. Co.K
Rock, William D. VA Inf. 4th Bn.Loc.Def. Co.D
Rock, William N. VA 15th Inf. Co.H,G
Rock, William R. VA 4th Cav. Co.F
Rock, William S. TX 36th Cav. Co.A
Rock, William S. VA 52nd Mil. Co.A
Rock, William S. VA 53rd Inf. Co.K
Rock, W.L. VA 1st St.Res. Co.C
Rock, W.R. GA 52nd Inf. Co.K Sgt.
Rock, Zephamah VA 40th Inf. Co.C
Rock, Zephaniah VA 37th Mil. Co.E
Rockanback, L. LA 18th Inf. Co.E
Rockanback, L. LA Inf.Cons. 18th Regt. & Yellow Jacket Bn. Co.E
Rocke, A.A. VA 8th Cav. Co.G Capt.
Rocke, F.G. VA 19th Cav. Capt.,AQM
Rocke, F.G. Gen. & Staff Capt.,AQM
Rocke, Floyd G. VA 28th Inf. Co.E Capt.
Rocke, J.B. TX 21st Cav. Co.L Capt.
Rocke, John J. VA 11th Inf. Co.A
Rocke, William B. VA 26th Cav. Co.A
Rockecharlie, Vincent VA 11th Inf. Co.E
Rockel, F. LA Mil. Fire Bn. Co.C Ord.Sgt.
Rockel, T.W. TN Inf. Sowell's Detach.
Rockell, Frank M. MS 15th (Cons.) Inf. Co.D
Rockell, W. LA 1st (Strawbody's) Inf. Co.E
Rockell, William LA 21st (Kennedy's) Inf. Co.F
Rockelt, R.J. TX 4th Inf. (St.Troops) Co.H
Rockenbach, Frank J. VA 34th Inf. Co.C 2nd Lt.
Rockenbaugh, J.H. GA Cav. 1st Bn. Winn's Co., Walthour's Co.
Rocker, Andrew GA Cav. 7th Bn. (St.Guards) Co.A
Rocker, Charles J. GA 15th Inf. Co.K Sgt.
Rocker, Henry LA Mil.Cont.Regt. Roder's Co.
Rocker, Jacob GA 5th Inf. Co.D Sgt.
Rocker, J.W. 20th Conf.Cav. 1st Co.H
Rocker, Peter C. AL 38th Inf. Co.A
Rocker, P.W. AL Inf. Co.E
Rocker, William GA 48th Inf. Co.B
Rocker, William E. AL 38th Inf. Co.A
Rocket, A.D. LA 11th Inf. Co.A
Rocket, E.D. TN Lt.Arty. Winston's Co.
Rocket, Jo. D. AR 8th Cav. Co.I
Rocket, Richard B. GA 49th Inf. Co.H
Rockett, A.C. NC 35th Inf. Co.K
Rockett, A.D. AL 40th Inf. Co.A
Rockett, B.A. AL 18th Inf. Co.K
Rockett, C. NC 3rd Jr.Res. Co.E
Rockett, E.B. AR 1st (Monroe's) Cav. Co.D
Rockett, Edward LA 11th Inf. Co.A
Rockett, Elam M. NC 1st Arty. (10th St.Troops) Co.C
Rockett, E.M. AR 11th Inf. Co.E
Rockett, Harman J. TX 14th Cav. Co.I 1st Lt.
Rockett, H.B. AL Cp. of Instr. Talladega
Rockett, H. DeL. AL Cp. of Instr. Talladega
Rockett, Horace B. AL Cp. of Instr. Talladega
Rockett, Hosea H. LA 31st Inf. Co.I
Rockett, Hosea H. MS 19th Inf. Co.G
Rockett, J.A. NC 35th Inf. Co.K
Rockett, J.B. MS Standefer's Co. 1st Lt.
Rockett, J. Monroe NC 35th Inf. Co.K 2nd Lt.
Rockett, J.R. AL 18th Inf. Co.G 1st Sgt.

Rockett, J.R. AR 11th Inf. Co.E
Rockett, J.R. AR 11th & 17th (Cons.) Inf. Co.E
Rockett, Julius W. AR 33rd Inf. Co.K
Rockett, M.R. AL 2nd Cav. Co.B
Rockett, M.R. AL Inf. 2nd Regt. Co.B
Rockett, M.R. AL Cp. of Instr. Talladega Co.D
Rockett, Peter Conf.Inf. Tucker's Regt. Co.I
Rockett, R.C. AL Cp. of Instr. Talladege Co.D
Rockett, R.C. 2nd Conf.Eng.Troops Co.B
Rockett, R.D. AL 30th Inf. Co.K
Rockett, R.D. AL Cp. of Instr. Talladega
Rockett, Rich. D. AL Cp. of Instr. Talladega
Rockett, R.P. NC 35th Inf. Co.K
Rockett, Squire A. TX 14th Cav. Co.I
Rockett, T.J. AR 37th Inf. Co.I
Rockett, T.W. AL 18th Inf. Co.G
Rockett, W.H. MS 28th Cav. Co.A
Rockett, William H. MS 19th Inf. Co.G
Rockett, William H. NC McCorkle's Bn.Sr.Res. Co.D 1st Lt.
Rockhold, D.C. MO 1st Cav. Co.E
Rockhold, Frank TN 43rd Inf. Co.D
Rockhold, J.W. MS Inf. Lewis' Co.
Rockhold, Richard L. MO 1st Inf. Co.C
Rockhold, R.L. MO Cav. Poindexter's Regt.
Rockhold, T. MO Todd's Co.
Rockhold, Thomas TN 43rd Inf. Co.D
Rockhold, Toba MO Dorsey's Regt.
Rockhole, R.L. MO Inf. Clark's Regt. Co.C
Rockholt, F. AL 3rd Cav. Co.I 1st Lt.
Rockholt, Francis 3rd Conf.Cav. Co.I 1st Lt.
Rockholt, Franklin TN 1st (Carter's) Cav. Co.D Bugler
Rockholt, Jason GA 6th Inf. Co.B
Rockholt, J.H. TN 12th (Green's) Cav. Co.A
Rockholt, John E. KY 9th Mtd.Inf. Co.H
Rockley, W.B. VA Cav. 37th Bn. Co.B
Rockman, J.W. VA 19th Cav. Co.I
Rockmore, C.A. GA Cav. 1st Bn.Res. Co.C
Rockmore, John J. GA 12th (Robinson's) Cav. (St.Guards) Co.K
Rockmore, J.R. TX 32nd Cav. Co.C
Rockmore, J.T. GA 54th Inf. Co.A
Rockmore, J.W. TX Cav. Wells' Regt. Co.D
Rockmore, Peter GA Cav. Arnold's Co.
Rockmore, S. GA Cav. 1st Bn.Res. Tufts' Co.
Rockmore, Thomas J. 1st Choctaw & Chickasaw Mtd.Rifles 1st Co.K
Rockner, Julious C. FL 4th Inf. Co.K 1st Sgt.
Rocks, Lloyd VA 19th Cav. Asst.QM
Rocks, Thomas LA Inf. 1st Sp.Bn. (Wheat's) New Co.D
Rockshirt 1st Cherokee Mtd.Vol. 1st Co.E, 2nd Co.C Cpl.
Rockward, J.C. AR 34th Inf. Co.D
Rockwell, --- GA 8th Inf. Co.B
Rockwell, --- TX 33rd Cav. Co.I
Rockwell, A.H. GA 1st (Olmstead's) Inf. Gordon's Co.
Rockwell, Augustus H. GA 63rd Inf. Co.F,D
Rockwell, C.F. MO 3rd Inf. Co.D
Rockwell, Charles S. GA Inf. (St.Guards) Hansell's Co.
Rockwell, C.S. GA Cav. 29th Bn.
Rockwell, C.S. GA 29th Inf. Co.F Capt.
Rockwell, E.C. VA 53rd Inf. Co.H
Rockwell, E.C. Conf.Inf. 1st Bn. 2nd Co.C

Rockwell, Edward VA 89th Mil. Co.H 1st Lt.

Rockwell, Edward Conf.Reg.Inf. Brooks' Bn. Co.C

Rockwell, Edward G. Conf.Reg.Inf. Brooks' Bn. Co.C

Rockwell, Edward J. VA 11th Cav. Co.A Sgt.

Rockwell, Elias VA 89th Mil. Co.H

Rockwell, Ellis C. AL Inf. 2nd Regt. Co.H,E

Rockwell, Geo. F. VA 12th Cav. Co.F

Rockwell, George F. VA 2nd Inf. Co.E 3rd Lt.

Rockwell, George M. GA Lt.Arty. Scogin's Btty. (Griffin Lt.Arty.) 2nd Lt.

Rockwell, George W. LA 21st (Patton's) Inf. Co.A

Rockwell, G.W. LA Washington Arty.Bn. Co.2

Rockwell, H.C. Clingman's Brig. Capt.

Rockwell, Henry C. NC 51st Inf. Co.H QM

Rockwell, Henry L. GA 2nd Inf. Co.K 1st Lt.

Rockwell, Jacob MO Robertson's Regt.St.Guard Co.1

Rockwell, Jacob H. MO 5th Cav. Co.E Cpl.

Rockwell, James R. VA 41st Inf. Co.C

Rockwell, John VA 67th Mil. Co.B

Rockwell, Joseph E. VA 12th Inf. Co.A Sgt.

Rockwell, Seth VA 40th Inf. Co.B

Rockwell, Seth, Jr. VA 41st Mil. Co.B Capt.

Rockwell, Simeon B. AR 25th Inf. Co.A

Rockwell, Ste. MO Lt.Arty. Von Phul's Co.

Rockwell, Stephen MO 3rd Inf. Co.D

Rockwell, Stephen MO Inf. Clark's Regt. Co.G

Rockwell, Stephen W. MO 1st Inf. Co.A

Rockwell, Wash. TX 1st Inf. Co.G

Rockwell, William VA 9th Cav. Co.K Sgt.

Rockwell, William VA 41st Mil. Co.B 1st Sgt.

Rockwell, William VA 89th Mil. Co.H

Rockwell, William C. LA 8th Inf. Co.G Jr.2nd Lt.

Rockwell, William H. NC 18th Inf. Co.H

Rockwell, William S., Jr. GA Hvy.Arty. 22nd Bn. Co.F,E 1st Lt.

Rockwell, William S. GA 1st (Olmstead's) Inf. Lt.Col.

Rockwell, Winfield J. VA 12th Inf. Co.F

Rockwell, W.S., Jr. GA 1st (Olmstead's) Inf. Bonaud's Co. Lt.

Roco, Adolphus G. TX 21st Cav. Co.H

Roco, A.G. TX 24th Cav. Co.A Music.

Roco, A.G. TX Granbury's Cons.Brig. Music.

Roco, Albert C. TX 4th Inf. Co.G

Roco, Rufus H. TX 21st Cav. Co.H

Roco, Rufus H. TX 24th Cav. Co.A Music.

Rocquemore, James GA 12th (Robinson's) Cav. (St.Guards) Co.H Sgt.

Rocquet, A. LA Lt.Arty. Bridges' Btty. Cpl.

Rocquet, A. LA Mil. Orleans Guards Regt. Co.A,G

Rocquet, Adolph SC Arty. Manigault's Bn. 1st Co.A,D Cpl.

Rocquet, L. LA Lt.Arty. Bridges' Btty.

Rocquet, L. LA Mil. Orleans Guards Regt. Co.A

Rocquet, L. SC Arty. Manigault's Bn. 1st Co.A,D

Rocus, Henry MO 10th Inf. Co.I

Rod, --- LA Mil. 3rd Regt.Eur.Brig. (Garde Francaise) Euler's Co.

Rod, J.M. GA 11th Cav. Co.E

Roda, Preston D. TN 43rd Inf. Co.F

Rodabaugh, Joshua VA 31st Inf. Co.C Capt.

Rodaham, John GA 19th Inf. Co.F N.C.S. Comsy.Sgt.

Rodahan, John GA 7th Inf. (St.Guards) Co.I

Rodahoeffer, George VA 33rd Inf. Co.I,A

Rodan, E. TX 8th Inf. Co.G

Rodan, J.H. AR 7th Inf. Co.K

Rodan, John TN 59th Mtd.Inf. Co.D

Rodan, John D. SC 5th Inf. 2nd Co.E,B

Rodan, William GA 12th Inf. Co.H

Rodarmel, George TX 35th (Brown's) Cav. Co.C Sgt.

Roday, Philip D. TX 35th (Browns') Cav. Co.K

Rodcap, D.S. VA 4th Inf. Co.I

Rodcliffe, Thomas D. TX Cav. Co.A

Rodd, J.E. VA 3rd Inf.Loc.Def. Co.C

Rodd, J.H. VA 3rd Res. Co.D

Rodd, John E. LA Washington Arty.Bn. Co.1

Rodda, William TX 28th Cav. Co.B

Roddam, James A. AL 44th Inf. Co.K

Roddam, John A. AL 44th Inf. Co.K,I

Roddam, John A. AL Cp. of Instr. Talladega

Roddam, John B. AL 31st Inf. Co.D

Rodden, Andrew TN 59th Mtd.Inf. Co.D

Rodden, Andrew J. TN 42nd Inf. 1st Co.F

Rodden, B. GA 7th Inf.

Rodden, Henry E. VA 23rd Inf. Co.E Sgt.

Rodden, James TN 59th Mtd.Inf. Co.A

Rodden, James J. NC 34th Inf. Co.G

Rodden, James W. VA 1st Arty. 3rd Co.C Sgt.

Rodden, James W. VA Lt.Arty. 1st Bn. Co.C Sgt.

Rodden, James W. VA 14th Inf. 1st Co.G

Rodden, J.F. MO Cav. Slayback's Regt. Co.A

Rodden, J.H. TX 22nd Inf. Co.C

Rodden, J.M. TX 3rd Cav. Co.B

Rodden, John TN 42nd Inf. 1st Co.F

Rodden, John TN 59th Mtd.Inf. Co.D

Rodden, J.T. TX 22nd Inf. Co.C

Rodden, J.W. VA Arty. Young's Co. Sgt.

Rodden, N.B. NC 53rd Inf. Co.B

Rodden, R.R. LA 2nd Inf. Co.H

Rodden, R.R. TX Cav. Crump's Regt. Co.H

Rodden, T.B. NC 1st Arty. (10th St.Troops) Co.C

Rodden, Thomas J. GA 7th Inf. Co.A

Rodden, William Lory 1st Conf.Eng.Troops Co.F

Rodden, William S. VA 23rd Inf. Co.E

Rodden, W.J. TN 19th Inf. Co.H

Rodden, W.J. TX 3rd Cav. Co.B

Rodden, W.R. NC 53rd Inf. Co.B

Roddenberry, Allen FL 1st (Res.) Inf. Co.E

Roddenberry, Archibald FL 3rd Inf. Co.E

Roddenberry, G. FL 10th Inf. Co.K

Roddenberry, George FL Inf. 2nd Bn. Co.D

Roddenberry, George FL 5th Inf. Co.I

Roddenberry, H. FL 3rd Inf. Co.E

Roddenberry, John GA Mil. Camden Cty. (Mtd.)

Roddenberry, M. FL 1st Inf. New Co.C

Roddenberry, Richard FL 1st (Res.) Inf. Co.E

Roddenberry, Sampson FL 2nd Inf. Co.F

Roddenberry, Sampson FL 11th Inf. Co.H

Roddenberry, William FL 1st Cav. Co.I

Roddenbery, John GA Cav. 1st Bn. Brailsford's Co.

Roddenbury, A. FL 5th Inf. Co.I

Roddenbury, G. GA 4th (Clinch's) Cav. Co.C

Roddenbury, Henry J. GA 26th Inf. Co.D 2nd Lt.

Roddenbury, John GA 4th (Clinch's) Cav. Co.A,K,E Cpl.

Roddenbury, Sampson FL 1st (Res.) Inf. Co.E Sgt.

Roddenburg, S.A. GA Conscr.

Roddenbury, W.A. FL 1st Inf. New Co.G

Roddenbury, W.J. FL 1st (Res.) Inf. Co.E

Roddey, David SC 6th Inf. 1st Co.B, 2nd Co.A

Roddey, P.D. AL 4th (Roddey's) Cav. Col.

Roddey, P.D. Gen. & Staff Brig.Gen.

Roddey, R. GA Inf. 27th Bn. Co.D

Roddey, R.L. GA 14th Inf. Surg.

Roddey, Robt. L. Gen. & Staff Surg.

Roddey, Thomas E. SC 12th Inf. Co.H 1st Sgt.

Roddey, W. Lyle SC 24th Inf. Co.H Capt.

Roddie, --- GA 45th Inf. Lt.,Ens.

Roddie, James W. KY 4th Cav.

Roddie, James W. TN Blair's Co. (Loc.Def. Troops)

Roddie, Reuben TN 37th Inf. Co.F Capt.

Roddie, Reuben TN Vol. (Loc.Def.Troops) McLin's Co.

Roddie, William L. TN 19th Inf. Co.B 1st Sgt.

Roddie, William L. TN 37th Inf. Co.F Capt.

Roddin, B. SC Mil.Cav. Rutledge's Co.

Roddin, J.J. VA Inf. 2nd Bn.Loc.Def. Co.B

Roddin, William SC Mil.Cav. Rutledge's Co.

Roddin, William D. MS St.Cav. Perrin's Bn. Co.B

Roddon, A.C. TX 28th Cav. Co.D

Roddon, William AR 1st (Colquitt's) Inf. Co.D

Roddon, William B. MS 24th Inf. Co.B

Roddy, A. TX 18th Inf. Co.G

Roddy, Albert D. TN 24th Inf. Co.L

Roddy, Alexander GA 42nd Inf. Co.C

Roddy, Benjamin F. TN 24th Inf. 2nd Co.G, Co.L

Roddy, Blackburn TN 5th (McKenzie's) Cav. Co.A

Roddy, D.S. AR 2nd Inf. Co.I

Roddy, Erwin TN 2nd (Ashby's) Cav. Co.K

Roddy, F.W. Gen. & Staff Surg.

Roddy, George AL Lt.Arty. Goldthwaite's Btty.

Roddy, George GA 31st Inf. Co.A Sgt.

Roddy, George P. TN 26th Inf. Co.E 2nd Lt.

Roddy, G.W. TX Cav. W.H. Randolph's Co.

Roddy, Henderson NC Walker's Bn. Thomas' Legion Co.F

Roddy, Henderson TN 5th (McKenzie's) Cav. Co.K

Roddy, Holston NC Walker's Bn. Thomas' Legion Co.C

Roddy, Irvin TN Cav. 5th Bn. (McClellan's) Co.E

Roddy, J.A. AR 1st (Dobbin's) Cav. Co.H Sgt.

Roddy, J.A. AR 14th (McCarver's) Inf. Co.K 1st Sgt.

Roddy, J.A. AR 21st Inf. Co.F 2nd Lt.

Roddy, James GA 39th Inf. Co.F

Roddy, James LA 3rd Inf. Co.K

Roddy, James LA 22nd (Cons.) Inf. Co.H Sgt.

Roddy, James TN 1st (Carter's) Cav. Co.B

Roddy, James TX 3rd Cav. Co.E

Roddy, James 1st Conf.Cav. 2nd Co.K Lt.

Roddy, James 1st Conf.Inf. 2nd Co.D

Roddy, James A. AR 2nd Vol. Co.D
Roddy, James H. TN 44th Inf. Co.D
Roddy, James H. TN 44th (Cons.) Inf. Co.D
Roddy, James M. AR 37th Inf. Co.C Sgt.
Roddy, James M. TN 43rd Inf. Co.B Sgt.
Roddy, James V. GA 42nd Inf. Co.C,H
Roddy, J.B. SC 1st Cav. Co.H
Roddy, J.B. TX Cav. Morgan's Regt. Co.A
Roddy, J.H. 3rd Conf.Eng.Troops Ramsey's Co.
Roddy, J.J. LA Ogden's Cav. Co.C Cpl.
Roddy, J.J. SC 16th Inf. Co.F
Roddy, J.J. SC 16th & 24th (Cons.) Inf. Co.A
Roddy, J.J. 14th Conf.Cav. Co.G Cpl.
Roddy, J.L. TN 43rd Inf. Co.B
Roddy, John GA 1st Reg. Co.C
Roddy, John LA Inf. 9th Bn. Co.A
Roddy, John SC 13th Inf. Co.F
Roddy, John VA 59th Inf. 3rd Co.E
Roddy, John H. LA Inf. 1st Sp.Bn. (Rightor's)
    Co.E
Roddy, John L. GA 43rd Inf. Co.B
Roddy, John T. TN 19th Inf. Co.D
Roddy, Joseph B. TX 17th Inf. Co.A
Roddy, Joseph G. TN 24th Inf. 2nd Co.G, Co.L
    2nd Lt.
Roddy, J.P. TN Cav. Welcker's Bn. Co.A
Roddy, J.T. TN Cav. 16th Bn. (Neal's) Co.C
Roddy, Ladson NC 18th Inf. Co.E
Roddy, Levi TN 44th (Cons.) Inf. Co.K
Roddy, Levy TN 44th Inf. Co.C
Roddy, M. GA Inf. 18th Bn. (St.Guards) Co.E
Roddy, M. MS 7th Inf. Co.K
Roddy, Murty GA 1st (Olmstead's) Inf. Co.A
Roddy, Nathaniel SC 13th Inf. Co.I,F
Roddy, Nimrod B. SC 13th Inf. Co.B
Roddy, Patrick NC 3rd Inf. Co.F
Roddy, P.D. 8th (Wade's) Conf.Cav. Maj.
Roddy, Perry 1st Conf.Eng.Troops Co.K
Roddy, Philip D. MS Cav. 4th Bn. Roddy's Co.
    Capt.
Roddy, Philip D. TX 13th Vol. 3rd Co.I
Roddy, Preston NC Walker's Bn. Thomas'
    Legion 1st Co.D
Roddy, Preston TN 1st (Carter's) Cav. Co.I
Roddy, Robert GA Hvy.Arty. 22nd Bn. Co.D
Roddy, S.C. GA 39th Inf. Co.F 2nd Lt.
Roddy, Taylor LA Inf. 1st Sp.Bn. (Rightor's)
    Co.E
Roddy, Thomas LA Inf. 1st Sp.Bn. (Rightor's)
    Co.E
Roddy, Thomas MS 21st Inf. Co.E
Roddy, Thomas TN 43rd Inf. Co.B Cpl.
Roddy, Thomas VA 10th Cav. 1st Co.E
Roddy, T.W. SC 5th St.Troops Co.L
Roddy, William AR 1st (Crawford's) Cav. Co.G
Roddy, Wm. AR 1st (Colquitt's) Inf. Co.I
Roddy, William LA 4th Inf. Co.E
Roddy, William MS 13th Inf. Co.F
Roddy, William SC 1st Cav. Co.D
Roddy, William M. TX 17th Cav. 1st Co.I
Roddy, William T. GA 42nd Inf. Co.C
Roddy, W.M. AR 1st (Monroe's) Cav. Co.H
Roddy, W.P. SC 16th Inf. Co.F
Roddy, W.P. SC 16th & 24th (Cons.) Inf. Co.A
Roddy, W.S. TN 43rd Inf. Co.B
Roddy, W.T. SC 17th Inf. Co.A
Rode, Casper LA 30th Inf. Co.I,B

Rode, Frederick TX Arty. 4th Bn. Co.B
Rode, Frederick TX 8th Inf. Co.B
Rode, M.D.L. GA Cav. 1st Bn.Res. McKinney's
    Co.
Rodebaugh, Jacob VA Horse Arty. Lurty's Co.
Rodefeld, Frank TX 1st Hvy.Arty. Co.B
Rodefeld, Friedrich William TX 3rd Inf. Co.D
    Cpl.
Rodefeld, Heinrich TX 3rd Inf. Co.D
Rodefeld, Henry TX 1st Hvy.Arty. Co.B
Rodefeld, William TX 1st Hvy.Arty. Co.B,C
Rodefer, Chas. P. Gen. & Staff Chap.
Rodefer, Emanuel KY Williams' Btty.
Rodefer, Emanuel VA 48th Inf. Co.I Bvt.2nd Lt.
Rodefer, Joseph A. VA 1st Cav. 2nd Co.D
    Bugler
Rodefer, Joseph Alexander VA 37th Inf. Co.B
Rodefer, Wm. Gen. & Staff Capt.,QM
Rodeffar, George VA 18th Inf. Co.I
Rodeffer, David VA 10th Inf. Co.F
Rodeffer, Edward VA 33rd Inf. Co.C,A
Rodeffer, George VA 14th Mil. Co.A
Rodeffer, James H. VA Horse Arty. J.W. Car-
    ter's Co.
Rodeffer, James H. VA 10th Inf. Co.F Cpl.
Rodeffer, John W. VA Horse Arty. J.W. Carter's
    Co.
Rodeffer, John W. VA 136th Mil. Co.E
Rodeffer, Jonathan VA 14th Mil. Co.A
Rodeffer, Marcus VA Horse Arty. J.W. Carter's
    Co. Cpl.
Rodeffer, M.M. MS 10th Inf. Old Co.A
Rodeffer, Philip VA 33rd Inf. Co.K
Rodeffer, Philip VA 146th Mil. Co.D
Rodeffer, Philip D. VA 33rd Inf. Co.C
Rodeffer, S. VA Horse Arty. J.W. Carter's Co.
Rodeffer, Samuel VA 2nd Inf. Co.B
Rodeffer, T. VA Horse Arty. J.W. Carter's Co.
Rodeffer, William H. VA 10th Inf. Co.G Music.
Rodegers, J.H. AR 32nd Inf. Co.A
Rodehaver, George MO Lt.Arty. Walsh's Co.
Rodehaffer, Alexander VA 2nd Inf. Co.A
Rodeheffer, Alexander VA 58th Mil. Co.C Cpl.
Rodeheffer, George TN Detailed Conscr. Co.B
Rodeheffer, John VA 2nd Inf. Co.A
Rodeheffer, John VA 58th Mil. Co.C
Rodeillat, Ferdinand LA Mil. French Co. of
    St.James
Rodelsperger, P. SC 3rd Inf. Co.E
Rodemann, Henry LA Mil. Chalmette Regt. Co.I
Rodemllanor, D. TN 59th Mtd.Inf. Co.B
Roden, A. MS 12th Cav. Co.D
Roden, Aiken AL 7th Cav. Co.I,C
Roden, A.J. AL 11th Cav. Co.D Sgt.
Roden, A.J. AL 55th Vol. Co.H
Roden, Albine C. TN 32nd Inf. Co.I
Roden, A.P. AL 9th Inf. Co.K
Roden, Benjamin F. AL 49th Inf. Co.G
Roden, Bennett H. AL 49th Inf. Co.E
Roden, B.M. TX 22nd Inf. Co.F
Roden, Calvin AR Lt.Arty. Wiggins' Btty.
Roden, Carroll AL 16th Inf. Co.I
Roden, Clement C. TX 13th Cav. Co.A
Roden, Elias TX 5th Inf. Co.B
Roden, Emry AL 48th Inf. Co.E
Roden, Epps T. AL 51st (Part.Rangers) Co.A
Roden, Epps T. AL 2nd Inf. Co.A

Roden, F. MO Cav. Schnabel's Bn. Co.C
Roden, Felix M. AL 4th (Russell's) Cav. Co.G
Roden, Frank AL 46th Inf. Co.E
Roden, Frank AL 48th Inf. Co.G,E
Roden, G. AL 63rd Inf. Co.K,G Cpl.
Roden, George MS 1st Cav. Co.H
Roden, George MS Cav. 1st Bn. (Miller's) Co.A
Roden, George O. TX Cav. Ragsdale's Bn. Co.E
Roden, G.O. TX Inf. 1st St.Troops Whitehead's
    Co.
Roden, G.W. MS Scouts Montgomery's Co.
Roden, Henry GA Inf. 1st Loc.Troops (Augusta)
    Co.H
Roden, Isaac N. AL 10th Inf. Co.G Cpl.
Roden, James AL 55th Vol. Co.E
Roden, James AL 56th Part.Rangers Co.E
Roden, James 3rd Conf.Cav. Co.C
Roden, James B. TN 32nd Inf. Co.I
Roden, James B. TN 44th Inf. Co.K Cpl.
Roden, James H. AR Inf. Cocke's Regt. Co.I
    Drum.
Roden, James W. AL 2nd Inf. Co.A Cpl.
Roden, James W. AL 51st (Part.Rangers) Co.A
Roden, J.C. AR Arty. 2nd Btty. Co.A
Roden, J. Carter AL Cav. Holloway's Co.
Roden, J.E. MS Inf. 7th Bn. Co.C
Roden, J.H. AR 8th Cav. Co.E
Roden, J.H. TN 11th (Holman's) Cav. Co.E
Roden, J.N. AL 16th Inf. Co.C Cpl.
Roden, J.N. AL 49th Inf. Co.B
Roden, Jacob AL 55th Vol. Co.E
Roden, John AL 16th Inf. Co.B
Roden, John AL 48th Inf. Co.E
Roden, John AL 55th Vol. Co.H
Roden, John AR 45th Cav. Co.L
Roden, John MS 15th Bn.S.S. Co.A
Roden, John 3rd Conf.Cav. Co.C
Roden, John B. LA 7th Inf. Co.E
Roden, John D. SC 6th Inf. 1st Co.A
Roden, John H. TN 32nd Inf. Co.I
Roden, John W. AL 16th Inf. Co.I
Roden, Joseph MO 11th Inf. Co.H
Roden, Joseph H. AR Inf. Cocke's Regt. Co.I
Roden, J.P. AL 13th Bn.Part.Rangers Co.D
Roden, J.P. AL 56th Part.Rangers Co.K Bugler
Roden, J.S. AL 48th Inf. Co.A Sgt.
Roden, L. MO Lt.Arty. 3rd Field Btty.
Roden, L.C. AL 9th Inf. Co.F
Roden, Lee AL 4th (Russell's) Cav. Co.G 1st
    Sgt.
Roden, Levi TN 2nd Bn. (Biffle's) Co.C
Roden, Martin M. AL Cav. Lewis' Bn. Co.E
Roden, M.E. AL 48th Inf. Co.G
Roden, Moses AR 13th Inf. Co.E
Roden, M.P. TX 22nd Inf. Co.F
Roden, Philip LA 15th Inf. Co.F 1st Sgt.
Roden, Portland AL 49th Inf. Co.E
Roden, Samuel 1st Conf.Cav. Co.G
Roden, T. AL Cav. Barbiere's Bn. Bowie's Co.
    Cpl.
Roden, Thomas AL 4th Cav.
Roden, Thomas F. NC 39th Inf. Co.H
Roden, T.M. AL Cav. Barbiere's Bn. Co.C
Roden, T.R. LA 2nd Inf. Co.C
Roden, T.R. LA 25th Inf. Co.C
Roden, W.A. AL 62nd Inf. Co.E
Roden, Warren W. AL 16th Inf. Co.B

Roden, W.C. AL 16th Inf. Co.I Cpl.
Roden, W.F. 3rd Conf.Cav. Co.K Sgt.
Roden, Wiley SC 5th Res. Co.K Sgt.
Roden, William H. AR Inf. Cocke's Regt. Co.I
Roden, William M. TN 32nd Inf. Co.I Sgt.
Roden, William N. AL 43rd Inf. Co.H
Roden, William W. AL 10th Cav. Co.B
Roden, W.J. AL 31st Inf. Co.D,G
Roden, W.M. AL 48th Inf. Co.G
Roden, W.W. MS 15th Bn.S.S. Co.A
Roden, Y.R. LA Inf. Pelican Regt. Co.C Sgt.
Roden, Zealous AL 48th Inf. Co.B
Rodena, J. LA Mil. 3rd Regt. 3rd Brig. 1st Div.
  Co.E
Rodenberg, Albert G. LA 7th Inf. Co.H Cpl.
Rodenberry, John K. GA 5th Cav. Co.H,B
Rodenberry, John M. FL 6th Inf. Co.K
Rodenburg, Christopher TN 5th (McKenzie's)
  Cav. Co.E
Rodenburg, John SC 17th Inf. Co.G
Rodenheiser, J.C. VA Arty. L.F. Jones' Co.
Rodenheiser, John C. VA 1st Arty. Co.K
Rodenhizer, George VA 19th Inf. Co.C
Rodenhizer, George C. VA Lt.Arty. (Loc.Def.)
  Otey's Co.
Rodenhizer, George C. VA 14th Inf. Co.H Sgt.
Rodenhizer, Henry W. VA 14th Inf. Co.H Cpl.
Rodenhizer, John W. VA 14th Inf. Co.H
Rodenhizer, R.R. VA Lt.Arty. (Loc.Def.) Otey's
  Co.
Rodenilin, P. LA Mil. 2nd Regt. 3rd Brig. 1st
  Div.
Rodenkirch, H. LA Inf.Cons. 18th Regt. & Yel-
  low Jacket Bn. Co.G
Rodenmeyer, George TN Hvy.Arty. Sterling's
  Co.
Rodens, Levi MO 3rd Cav. Co.D
Roder, Antoine LA 14th Inf. Co.D
Roder, Frank LA Mil.Cont.Regt. Roder's Co.
  Capt.
Roder, Isaac N. AL 49th Inf. Co.B
Roder, James TN 49th Inf. Co.C
Roder, John H. MO 11th Inf. Co.H
Roder, J.T. NC 29th Inf. Sgt.
Roderer, Andres LA 21st (Patton's) Inf. Co.I
Roderfer, James W. MO Cav. Snider's Bn. Co.C
Roderic, E.A. NC 2nd Jr.Res. Co.C
Roderick, A.M. TN 29th Inf. Co.A Cpl.
Roderick, C.D. NC Cav. McRae's Bn. Co.E
Roderick, Cephus NC 57th Inf. Co.E
Roderick, Charles D. NC 22nd Inf. Co.K
Roderick, Daniel VA 33rd Inf. Co.F
Roderick, E.W. TN 29th Inf. Co.A,H
Roderick, J. MD Cav. 2nd Bn. Co.B
Roderick, Jacob MD Cav. 2nd Bn. Co.D
Roderick, J.H. TX 34th Cav. Co.I Capt.
Roderick, John AL Inf. 1st Regt. Co.A
Roderick, John AL 40th Inf. Co.K
Roderick, John MD Cav. 2nd Bn. Co.D
Roderick, John SC 1st (Butler's) Inf. Co.K
Roderick, Philip VA Horse Arty. J.W. Carter's
  Co.
Roderick, Sidney M. NC 3rd Cav. (41st
  St.Troops) Co.F
Roderick, Thomas VA 12th Cav. Co.C
Roderick, William TN 43rd Inf. Co.I
Roderick, William F. SC 2nd Inf. Co.F

Roderick, Z. GA Inf. 1st Bn. (St.Guards) Co.A
Roderickerr, William LA Mil. 2nd Regt. 3rd
  Brig. 1st Div. Co.A
Roderigo, G. AR Mil. Borland's Regt. Pulaski
  Lancers Co.
Roderigues, C. Conf.Lt.Arty. 1st Reg.Btty.
Roderigues, McGriel TX Cav. 3rd (Yager's) Bn.
  Co.A
Rodriguez, Joseph AL Mil. 2nd Regt.Vol. Co.B
Rodriguez, Rosalle LA 3rd Inf. Co.D
Roderka, August LA 21st (Patton's) Inf. Co.B
Roderus, John M. LA Arty. Green's Co. (LA
  Guard Btty.)
Roderus, John M. LA Inf. 1st Sp.Bn. (Wheat's)
  Co.A
Rodery, W.J.B. MS 24th Inf. Co.D Sgt.
Rodes, B.C. KY 6th Cav. Co.A
Rodes, Byant S. GA 12th (Robinson's) Cav.
  (St.Guards) Co.A
Rodes, C. Dallas VA Lt.Arty. Carrington's Co.
Rodes, Charles C. GA 3rd Bn. (St.Guards) Co.B
  Sgt.
Rodes, D.M. AR 11th Inf. Co.K
Rodes, Fayette VA Cav. Mosby's Regt.
  (Part.Rangers)
Rodes, George R. MO 1st N.E. Cav. Co.F
Rodes, Greene VA Cav. Hounshell's Bn. Thur-
  mond's Co. Sgt.
Rodes, J.A. VA 2nd Inf. Co.I
Rodes, J.A. VA 13th Inf. Co.C
Rodes, Jacob Conf.Inf. 8th Bn. Co.D
Rodes, James Munroe AL 1st Cav. Co.E
Rodes, James W. VA 8th Cav. Co.B Sgt.
Rodes, James Y. VA Cav. Hounshell's Bn. Thur-
  mond's Co.
Rodes, J.M. GA Arty. 11th Bn. (Sumter Arty.)
Rodes, Joel Y. VA Cav. Hounshell's Bn. Thur-
  mond's Co.
Rodes, John NC 8th Bn.Part.Rangers Co.E
Rodes, John TX 4th Cav. Co.K
Rodes, John 2nd Conf.Eng.Troops Co.C Artif.
Rodes, John A. VA 62nd Mtd.Inf. 2nd Co.I
Rodes, John Q. VA 47th Mil.
Rodes, John W. VA 7th Inf. Co.I 1st Lt.
Rodes, Joseph VA Inf. 26th Bn. Co.G
Rodes, Joseph B. KY 8th Cav. Co.A,K
Rodes, King J. NC 1st Inf. (6 mo. '61) Co.H
Rodes, Lewis GA Inf. 1st Loc.Troops (Augusta)
Rodes, R.E. VA VMI Maj.Gen.
Rodes, R.E. Gen. & Staff Maj.Gen.
Rodes, Robert E. AL 5th Inf. Col.
Rodes, Robert Walker VA 19th Inf. Co.B
Rodes, R. Walker VA 46th Inf. 2nd Co.D
Rodes, S. AL 23rd Inf. Co.I
Rodes, Solomon MO 8th Inf. Co.H,K
Rodes, T. AL 5th Inf. Co.E
Rodes, Thomas L. VA Cav. 39th Bn. Co.C
Rodes, T.W. AL Lt.Arty. Clanton's Btty.
Rodes, V.H. Gen. & Staff 1st Lt.,ADC
Rodes, W.H. VA 49th Inf. Co.F
Rodes, Wiley NC 30th Inf. Co.H
Rodes, William VA 16th Cav. Co.G
Rodes, William Lee GA 8th Inf. Co.D Capt.
Rodes, W.R. VA 15th Cav. Co.B
Rodewald, H. LA Mil.Conf.Guards Regt. Co.A
Rodewald, John AL Conscr.
Rodey, Thomas A. NC 35th Inf. Co.H

Rodge, Clemir LA Conscr.
Rodge, E.M. GA 14th Inf.
Rodge, Louis M. LA Conscr.
Rodge, W.A. AL 31st Inf. Co.E
Rodger, John SC Lt.Arty. Jeter's Co. (Macbeth
  Lt.Arty.) Bugler
Rodger, John SC 3rd Bn.Res. Co.A
Rodger, Sumpter SC 7th Cav. Co.E
Rodgers, --- AR 30th Inf. Co.I Bvt.2nd Lt.
Rodgers, --- FL 1st Inf. Co.D
Rodgers, --- LA 22nd (Cons.) Inf. Co.H
Rodgers, --- TX 1st Hvy.Arty. Co.H
Rodgers, A. AL 48th Inf. Co.C
Rodgers, A. AL 58th Inf. Co.A
Rodgers, A. GA 26th Inf. Co.B
Rodgers, A. SC 2nd St.Troops Co.B
Rodgers, A. TN 3rd (Forrest's) Cav. Co.C
Rodgers, A.B. AR 37th Inf. Co.C
Rodgers, A.B. TN 10th Inf. Co.C
Rodgers, A.B. TN 30th Inf. Co.E Cpl.
Rodgers, Abel M. MS 8th Inf. Co.E
Rodgers, Abner NC 1st Jr.Res. Co.A
Rodgers, Abner NC 48th Inf. Co.D
Rodgers, Absalom NC 24th Inf. Co.K
Rodgers, A.C. GA 54th Inf. Co.H
Rodgers, A.C. LA 25th Inf. Co.K
Rodgers, A.C. MS 33rd Inf. Co.E
Rodgers, A.D. AL 1st Cav. 1st Co.K
Rodgers, A.D. AL 5th Inf. Co.H
Rodgers, Adolphus A. GA 39th Inf. Co.I
Rodgers, A.F. LA Jr.2nd Lt.
Rodgers, A.F. TN 3rd (Forrest's) Cav. Co.G
Rodgers, A.H. AL 38th Inf. Co.D 2nd Lt.
Rodgers, A.H. SC 2nd Rifles Co.F
Rodgers, A.J. TX 20th Cav. Co.K
Rodgers, A.J. VA 5th Inf. Co.C
Rodgers, Albert AR 8th Inf. New Co.A
Rodgers, Albert TN 31st Inf. Co.C
Rodgers, Albert G. VA 23rd Inf. Co.I
Rodgers, Albert S. MS 34th Inf. Co.E
Rodgers, Albert W. AR 3rd Inf. Co.D 2nd Lt.
Rodgers, Alex NC 21st Inf. Co.C
Rodgers, Alexander AR 14th (Powers') Inf. Co.D
  1st Lt.
Rodgers, Alexander GA Cav. 21st Bn. Co.C
Rodgers, Alexander TN 48th (Voorhies') Inf.
  Co.D Cpl.
Rodgers, Alexander A. GA 38th Inf. Co.G
Rodgers, Alexander M. KY 4th Cav. Co.B
Rodgers, Alexander W. AL Lt.Arty. Ward's
  Btty.
Rodgers, Alpheus M. GA Burke Cty. 1st Lt.
Rodgers, A.M. GA Lt.Arty. 12th Bn. Co.A
  QMSgt.
Rodgers, A.M. GA Cobb's Legion Co.L Capt.
Rodgers, A.M. SC 1st Bn.S.S. Co.C
Rodgers, A.M. SC 9th Res. Co.E
Rodgers, Amos GA Inf. 10th Bn. Co.A
Rodgers, And. NC 7th Sr.Res. Bradshaw's Co.
Rodgers, Anderson TN 18th (Newsom's) Cav.
  Co.G,B
Rodgers, Anderson TN 19th & 20th (Cons.) Cav.
  Co.B
Rodgers, Anderson TN Cav. Newsom's Regt.
  Co.A Sgt.
Rodgers, Andrew TN 2nd (Walker's) Inf. Co.H
Rodgers, Andrew TN 5th Inf. Co.F

Rodgers, Andrew J. TX 29th Cav. Co.E,K
Rodgers, Andrew J. VA 24th Cav. Co.G Capt.
Rodgers, Andrew J. VA Cav. 32nd Bn. Co.A Capt.
Rodgers, Anthony AL 9th Inf. Co.B
Rodgers, Anthony LA 14th Inf. Co.F
Rodgers, Ar. VA 79th Mil. Co.4
Rodgers, Arthur NC 67th Inf. Co.C
Rodgers, Arthur M. SC 27th Inf. Co.G
Rodgers, Artman SC Rutledge Mtd.Riflemen & Horse Arty. Trenholm's Co.
Rodgers, Asa NC 2nd Cav. (19th St.Troops) Co.G Bugler
Rodgers, Asa C. GA 14th Inf. Co.G
Rodgers, A.T. SC 7th Cav. Co.A
Rodgers, A.T. SC Cav. Tucker's Co.
Rodgers, A.W. AR 7th Cav. Co.G Capt.
Rodgers, A.W. SC 18th Inf. Co.G Sgt.
Rodgers, B. GA 5th Res. Co.C
Rodgers, B. MS 46th Inf. Co.B
Rodgers, B.A. AL 21st Inf. Co.D
Rodgers, Baine M. AL 63rd Inf. Co.G
Rodgers, B.A.L. KY 12th Cav. Co.C
Rodgers, Ballard VA 14th Cav. Co.L
Rodgers, Barney TN 2nd (Walker's) Inf. Co.H
Rodgers, B.C. MS Wilkinson Cty. Minute Men
Rodgers, Benjamin AR 36th Inf. Co.A
Rodgers, Benjamin MS 2nd Inf. Co.G
Rodgers, Benjamin TN 84th Inf. Co.B
Rodgers, Benjamin F. MS 26th Inf. Co.C
Rodgers, Benjamin F. TN 18th Inf. Co.A
Rodgers, Benjamin R. MS 42nd Inf. Co.D
Rodgers, Benjamin S. AL Cav. Holloway's Co.
Rodgers, Bernard MS 20th Inf. Co.C
Rodgers, Bernard MS 42nd Inf. Co.A
Rodgers, B.F. AR 10th (Witt's) Cav. Co.G 2nd Lt.
Rodgers, B.F. KY 5th Mtd.Inf. Co.K Sgt.
Rodgers, B.F. NC 60th Inf. Co.F Cpl.
Rodgers, B.F. TN 18th (Newsom's) Cav. Co.D
Rodgers, B.M. MO Lt.Arty. 13th Btty. Cpl.
Rodgers, B.P. 1st Conf.Cav. 1st Co.B
Rodgers, Branch A. VA Inf. 25th Bn. Co.C
Rodgers, Bruce TN Inf. 154th Sr.Regt. Co.L
Rodgers, B.T. NC 1st Jr.Res. Co.H
Rodgers, Buckner NC 3rd Arty. (40th St.Troops) Co.G Cpl.
Rodgers, Buckner NC 1st Inf. (6 mo. '61) Co.A
Rodgers, Burl MS 26th Inf. Co.A
Rodgers, Burrell MS 27th Inf. Co.H
Rodgers, B.W. AR Lt.Arty. Etter's Btty.
Rodgers, C. SC 2nd St.Troops Co.B
Rodgers, C.A. TN 42nd Inf. Co.C
Rodgers, Cader P. MS 10th Inf. Old Co.G, New Co.H
Rodgers, Caleb M. SC 20th Inf. Co.G
Rodgers, Casper VA 27th Inf. 1st Co.H
Rodgers, C.B. AL 7th Cav. Co.K
Rodgers, C.B. AL 5th Inf. New Co.K
Rodgers, C.B. GA Lt.Arty. Croft's Btty. (Columbus Arty.)
Rodgers, C.B. MS Scouts Morphis' Ind.Co.
Rodgers, C.B. TN 31st Inf. Co.G
Rodgers, C.C. AR 10th (Witt's) Cav. Co.G
Rodgers, C.C. GA 3rd Res. Co.F
Rodgers, C.C. SC 10th Inf. Co.D
Rodgers, C.E. SC 7th Inf. 1st Co.H

Rodgers, C.F. AL Lt.Arty. Ward's Btty.
Rodgers, C.G. AR 38th Inf. Co.C
Rodgers, Charles AL 17th Inf. Co.H
Rodgers, Charles AR 15th (Johnson's) Inf. Co.C
Rodgers, Charles AR 19th (Dawson's) Inf. Co.B
Rodgers, Charles AR 26th Inf. Co.D Sgt.
Rodgers, Charles KY 2nd (Duke's) Cav. Co.C
Rodgers, Charles A. MO 1st Cav. Co.K Capt.
Rodgers, Charles E. GA 48th Inf. Co.C
Rodgers, Charles E. GA Cobb's Legion Co.L
Rodgers, Charles F. AR 6th Inf. Co.G N.C.S.
Rodgers, Charles H. VA 58th Mil. Co.E
Rodgers, Charles K. SC Mil.Arty. 1st Regt. Tupper's Co. Cpl.
Rodgers, Charles N. AR Cav. Wright's Regt. Co.B
Rodgers, Charles R. VA Lt.Arty. Carpenter's Co. Cpl.
Rodgers, Charles R. VA Lt.Arty. Cutshaw's Co.
Rodgers, Charles S. TN 50th Inf. Co.F
Rodgers, Charles W. NC 46th Inf. Co.C Music.
Rodgers, Charles W. VA 30th Inf. Co.K
Rodgers, Chesly VA 14th Cav. Co.D
Rodgers, C.L. AR 10th (Witt's) Cav. Co.G
Rodgers, C.L. AR 12th Inf. Co.G
Rodgers, Clark A. NC 25th Inf. Co.G
Rodgers, C.M. GA 49th Inf. Co.C
Rodgers, C.M. TN 31st Inf. Co.I
Rodgers, Comadore J. AR 6th Inf. Co.I
Rodgers, Council NC 1st Inf. (6 mo. '61) Co.A
Rodgers, C.R. AR 10th Inf. Co.C Bvt.2nd Lt.
Rodgers, Crawford G. AR 8th Inf. New Co.A
Rodgers, Curtis NC 3rd Arty. (40th St.Troops) Co.H
Rodgers, D. AL 48th Inf. Co.C
Rodgers, D. GA 2nd Inf. Co.B,G Cpl.
Rodgers, D. GA 10th Inf. Co.D
Rodgers, D. SC 2nd Bn.S.S. Co.B
Rodgers, D. TX 33rd Cav. Co.H
Rodgers, D.A. GA 39th Inf. Co.I
Rodgers, D.A. Forrest's Cav. Lyon's Escort,CSA
Rodgers, Daniel LA 21st (Patton's) Inf. Co.F
Rodgers, Daniel 1st Conf.Inf. 2nd Co.E
Rodgers, Daniel D. FL 3rd Inf. Co.K Cpl.
Rodgers, David AR 35th Inf. Co.K
Rodgers, David MS Cav. Ham's Regt. Co.G
Rodgers, David SC 16th Inf. Co.B
Rodgers, David TN 2nd (Smith's) Cav.
Rodgers, David TN 14th Inf. Co.C
Rodgers, David TX 29th Cav. Co.F
Rodgers, David C. GA 3rd Inf. Co.E
Rodgers, David C. GA Inf. 10th Bn. Co.A
Rodgers, David C. MS 27th Inf. Co.F
Rodgers, David C. VA 2nd Cav. Co.E,H
Rodgers, David C. VA Hvy.Arty. 20th Bn. Co.A
Rodgers, David C.C. MS 11th Inf. Co.A 2nd Lt.
Rodgers, David G. AR 33rd Inf. Co.B
Rodgers, David J. NC 3rd Inf. Co.B
Rodgers, David L. VA 58th Mil. Co.D
Rodgers, David W. MS 32nd Inf. Co.A 2nd Lt.
Rodgers, D.C. TN 30th Inf. Co.E
Rodgers, D.D. TN C. Levy's Co.
Rodgers, Dennis AL 57th Inf. Co.A,F
Rodgers, Dennis H. MS 44th Inf. Co.K
Rodgers, D.F. KY 1st (Helm's) Cav. Co.B
Rodgers, D.F. KY 3rd Mtd.Inf. Co.C
Rodgers, D.G. GA 3rd Mil.

Rodgers, D.H. MS 31st Inf. Co.K
Rodgers, Dinsey MS 8th Inf. Co.H
Rodgers, D.L. 7th Conf.Cav. Co.L Sgt.
Rodgers, D.M. MS 6th Cav. Co.E
Rodgers, Douglas J. LA 19th Inf. Co.F 1st Sgt.
Rodgers, D.P. AR 38th Inf. Co.C
Rodgers, D.S. MS Cav. Ham's Regt. Co.H
Rodgers, D.S. NC 3rd Cav. (41st St.Troops) Co.B Cpl.
Rodgers, D.T. AR Cav. Nave's Bn. Co.B
Rodgers, E. Conf.Cav. Wood's Regt. Co.I
Rodgers, E.A. SC 6th Cav. Co.G
Rodgers, E.A. TN 3rd (Clack's) Inf. Co.A
Rodgers, E.B. AR Inf. Sparks' Co.
Rodgers, Ed VA 12th Cav. Co.F
Rodgers, Edward VA 10th Inf. Co.E
Rodgers, Edward J. AL 8th Inf. Co.C,I
Rodgers, E.E. GA 59th Inf.
Rodgers, E.F. GA Siege Arty. 28th Bn. Co.G
Rodgers, E.H. SC 23rd Inf. Co.A
Rodgers, E.H. SC Mil. Charbonnier's Co.
Rodgers, E.J. AR 20th Inf. Co.K
Rodgers, E.J. SC Macbeth Lt.Arty. Boyce's Co.
Rodgers, E.L. SC 2nd Cav. Co.D
Rodgers, Elbert S. NC 25th Inf. Co.G
Rodgers, Elemuel AR 15th (Josey's) Inf. Co.F
Rodgers, Eli NC 2nd Cav. (19th St.Troops) Co.I
Rodgers, Elijah AR 26th Inf. Co.A
Rodgers, Elijah GA 30th Inf. Co.C
Rodgers, Elijah TX Conscr.
Rodgers, Elijah Y. AR Cav. Wright's Regt. Co.D
Rodgers, Elisha AL 48th Inf. Co.D Cpl.
Rodgers, E.M. TN 31st Inf. Co.G
Rodgers, Emanuel C. VA Res. Keyser's Co.
Rodgers, Ephraim L. AR 36th Inf. Co.A
Rodgers, Erasmus C. NC 23rd Inf. Co.K
Rodgers, Ervin SC 21st Inf. Co.C
Rodgers, Ervin SC 25th Inf. Co.I
Rodgers, E.S. TN 55th (Brown's) Inf. Ford's Co.
Rodgers, E.W. TX 23rd Cav. Co.D
Rodgers, Ezekiel H. VA 9th Inf. Co.B
Rodgers, Ezekiel J. NC 2nd Arty. (36th St.Troops) Co.G
Rodgers, F. GA Cav. 1st Bn.Res. Tufts' Co.
Rodgers, F. LA Mil. Lafayette Arty.
Rodgers, F.A. TX Inf. (St.Troops) 24th Bn. Co.B
Rodgers, F.B. TN 7th (Duckworth's) Cav. Co.A
Rodgers, F.B. TN Inf. 154th Sr.Regt. Co.L
Rodgers, F.B. Gen. & Staff 1st Lt.,ADC
Rodgers, F.E. SC 7th Cav. Co.A
Rodgers, F.E. SC Cav. Tucker's Co.
Rodgers, F.M. NC Lt.Arty. Thomas' Legion Levi's Btty.
Rodgers, F.M. SC 7th Inf. 1st Co.E, 2nd Co.E
Rodgers, F.M. TX 10th Cav. Co.B
Rodgers, F.M. Horse Arty. White's Btty.
Rodgers, Fountain AR 38th Inf. Co.F
Rodgers, Fountain AR Inf. Clayton's Co.
Rodgers, Fountin MO Cav. Freeman's Regt. Co.D
Rodgers, Francis D. VA Lt.Arty. Thompson's Co.
Rodgers, Francis M. GA 50th Inf. Co.E
Rodgers, Francis M. TN 1st (Turney's) Inf. Co.F
Rodgers, Francis M. VA Horse Arty. Jackson's Co.

Rodgers, Francis M. Sap. & Min.,CSA
Rodgers, Frank MS 3rd Inf. Co.A Sgt.
Rodgers, Frank MO 8th Inf. Co.F
Rodgers, Frank TN 3rd (Forrest's) Cav. Co.C
Rodgers, Fred MS Inf. 1st Bn.St.Troops (30 days
  '64) Co.F
Rodgers, Frederick R. GA 31st Inf. Co.B
Rodgers, F.W. AL 21st Inf. Co.D
Rodgers, G. MS 1st (Percy's) Inf. Co.F
Rodgers, G.A. AL 33rd Inf. Co.K
Rodgers, G.A. SC Cav. 14th Bn. Co.B
Rodgers, G.C. AR 11th & 17th (Cons.) Inf. Co.I
Rodgers, G.C. NC 2nd Inf. Co.H
Rodgers, G.C. TX 15th Cav. Co.G
Rodgers, G.D. FL 7th Inf. Co.K
Rodgers, G.D.B. TN 20th (Russell's) Cav. Co.F
Rodgers, George AL 3rd Inf. Co.C
Rodgers, George KY Cav. 2nd Bn. (Dortch's)
  Co.B
Rodgers, George LA 4th Inf. Co.D
Rodgers, George MD 1st Cav. Co.C
Rodgers, George MO Cav. Fristoe's Regt. Co.C
Rodgers, George TN 2nd (Ashby's) Cav. Co.D
Rodgers, George TN 16th (Logwood's) Cav.
  Co.H
Rodgers, George VA 27th Inf. Co.C
Rodgers, George VA 29th Inf. Co.A
Rodgers, George A. GA 38th Inf. Co.G
Rodgers, George A. SC Mil. Trenholm's Co.
Rodgers, George H. NC 17th Inf. (2nd Org.)
  Co.H Sgt.
Rodgers, George H. SC 4th St.Troops
Rodgers, George J. TN 19th Inf. Co.G
Rodgers, George L. Gen. & Staff, Ord.Dept.
Rodgers, George N. NC 3rd Cav. (41st
  St.Troops) Co.D
Rodgers, George R. NC 42nd Inf. Co.G
Rodgers, George T. FL 1st Inf. Old Co.I, New
  Co.C
Rodgers, George W. AL Inf. 1st Regt. Co.A
Rodgers, George W. AL 38th Inf. Co.B
Rodgers, George W. AR Inf. Clayton's Co.
Rodgers, George W. LA 15th Inf. Co.G Cpl.
Rodgers, George W. SC Inf. Hampton Legion
  Co.F
Rodgers, George W. VA Inf. 1st Bn.Loc.Def.
  Co.D
Rodgers, George W. VA 13th Inf. Co.G
Rodgers, George W. VA 36th Inf. Co.A
Rodgers, G.F. AR 2nd Cav. Co.B
Rodgers, G.H. GA Lt.Arty. 12th Bn. 3rd Co.E
Rodgers, G.H. KY 1st (Butler's) Cav. Co.D
Rodgers, Gillis GA 26th Inf. Co.D
Rodgers, G.J. GA 11th Cav. Co.H
Rodgers, G.M. NC 6th Cav. (65th St.Troops)
  Co.E
Rodgers, G.R. VA 21st Cav. Dobin's Co.
Rodgers, Green MS 31st Inf. Co.B
Rodgers, Green E. TX Cav. Morgan's Regt.
  Co.E
Rodgers, G.T. AR 10th Inf. Co.C
Rodgers, G.W. GA Inf. 17th Bn. (St.Guards)
  Stocks' Co.
Rodgers, G.W. MO Cav. Freeman's Regt. Co.D
Rodgers, G.W. MO 3rd Inf. Chap.
Rodgers, G.W. AR 35th Inf. Co.K
Rodgers, G.W.H. NC 6th Inf. Co.I

Rodgers, H. MS 1st Cav.Res. Co.B
Rodgers, H. MS 41st Inf. Co.C
Rodgers, H. SC 14th Inf. Nurse
Rodgers, H. TX 25th Cav. Co.H
Rodgers, H.A. SC Cav. 14th Bn. Co.A
Rodgers, Hardin F. KY 2nd Mtd.Inf. Co.H Sgt.
Rodgers, Harrison AR 8th Inf. New Co.A
Rodgers, Harrison B. KY 2nd Mtd.Inf. Co.D
  Capt.
Rodgers, H.B. AR Lt.Arty. Zimmerman's Btty.
Rodgers, H.C. AL 6th Cav. Co.D
Rodgers, Henry AR 6th Inf. 1st Co.B
Rodgers, Henry NC 2nd Arty. (36th St.Troops)
  Co.F
Rodgers, Henry NC 2nd Inf. Co.A
Rodgers, Henry NC 18th Inf. Co.A
Rodgers, Henry A. SC 5th Cav. Co.H
Rodgers, Henry C. GA 12th (Wright's) Cav.
  (St.Guards) Wright's Co.
Rodgers, Henry C. VA 5th Cav. Co.C
Rodgers, Henry H. NC 49th Inf. Co.C
Rodgers, Henry L. AL 11th Inf. Co.I Cpl.
Rodgers, Henry P. AR 11th Inf. Co.I
Rodgers, Henry W. NC 20th Inf. Co.E
Rodgers, H.F. NC 3rd Arty. (40th St.Troops)
  Co.H
Rodgers, H.H. TN 13th (Gore's) Cav. Co.C
Rodgers, H.H. TN 18th Inf. Co.A
Rodgers, Hiram G. VA 42nd Inf. Co.A
Rodgers, Hiram R. TX 5th Inf. Co.A
Rodgers, H.P. NC 17th Inf. (2nd Org.) Co.L
Rodgers, H.Q. SC 7th Inf. Co.F
Rodgers, H.R. AL 46th Inf. Co.C
Rodgers, H.R. MS Cav. Street's Bn.
Rodgers, H.S. MS 2nd Part. Co.E 2nd Lt.
Rodgers, H.T. GA Hvy.Arty. 22nd Bn. Co.F
Rodgers, H.T. TN Cav. 16th Bn. (Neal's) Co.C
  Cpl.
Rodgers, Hugh LA 20th Inf. Co.H
Rodgers, Hugh SC Inf. 9th Bn. Co.G
Rodgers, Hugh SC 20th Inf. Co.F
Rodgers, Hugh SC 26th Inf. Co.K
Rodgers, Hugh A. TN 39th Mtd.Inf. Co.E Sgt.
Rodgers, Hugh C. TX 37th Cav. Co.H
Rodgers, H.W. AR 3rd Cav. Co.A Cpl.
Rodgers, H.W. AR 6th Inf. Co.C
Rodgers, H.W. AR 15th (Johnson's) Inf. Co.D
Rodgers, H.W.C. AR 12th Inf. Co.I
Rodgers, Hypolite LA 1st Inf.
Rodgers, I. Brush Bn.
Rodgers, I.F. MS Cav. Powers' Regt. Co.I
Rodgers, I.J. AR 26th Inf. Co.K
Rodgers, I.L. SC Post Guard Senn's Co.
Rodgers, I.S. MS Cav. 2nd Bn.Res. Co.D
Rodgers, Isaac TN Inf. 4th Cons.Regt. Co.A
Rodgers, Isaac TN 37th Inf. Co.K
Rodgers, Isaac TX Cav. 1st Bn.St.Troops Co.A
Rodgers, Isaac TX 11th Inf. Co.I
Rodgers, Isaac TX 15th Inf. Co.E
Rodgers, Isaac C. MO Cav. Williams' Regt.
  Co.B
Rodgers, Isaac L. AR 36th Inf. Co.A
Rodgers, Isaac N. MO Inf. 1st Regt.St.Guard
  Co.N Capt.
Rodgers, Isaac T. KY 2nd Bn.Mtd.Rifles Co.E,A
Rodgers, Israel LA 28th (Gray's) Inf. Co.B
Rodgers, J. AL 15th Inf. Co.F

Rodgers, J. FL 7th Inf. Co.E
Rodgers, J. MS 10th Cav. Co.G
Rodgers, J. MS Inf. 1st Bn.St.Troops (12 mo.
  '62-3) Co.A
Rodgers, J. MS 12th Inf. Cpl.
Rodgers, J. NC 1st Bn.Jr.Res. Co.B
Rodgers, J. SC 4th St.Troops Co.I
Rodgers, J. TN 22nd (Barteau's) Cav. Co.F
Rodgers, J.A. AR 12th Inf. Co.I
Rodgers, J.A. GA 1st (Fannin's) Res. Co.E
Rodgers, J.A. GA Inf. 8th Bn. Co.C
Rodgers, J.A., No.1 GA 18th Inf. Co.C
Rodgers, J.A., No.2 GA 18th Inf. Co.C
Rodgers, J.A. SC 1st (Orr's) Rifles Co.F
Rodgers, J.A. SC 17th Inf. Co.D
Rodgers, J.A. TN 5th Inf. 2nd Co.F
Rodgers, J.A. VA 7th Cav. Co.D
Rodgers, J.A.C. MS 32nd Inf. Co.G
Rodgers, Jackson GA Cav. Lee's Bn. Co.I
Rodgers, Jackson GA Inf. 40th Bn. Co.B
Rodgers, Jackson TN 48th (Voorhies') Inf. Co.G
Rodgers, Jackson W. MS 15th Inf. Co.E
Rodgers, Jacob MS 2nd Part.Rangers Co.G
Rodgers, Jacob TN 34th Inf. Co.H
Rodgers, James AL Cav. 4th Bn. (Love's) Co.C
Rodgers, James AL 55th Vol. Co.B
Rodgers, James AL 57th Inf. Co.B
Rodgers, James AR 15th (N.W.) Inf. Co.I Cpl.
Rodgers, James GA Lt.Arty. 14th Bn. Co.B
Rodgers, James GA Lt.Arty. Anderson's Btty.
Rodgers, James GA 53rd Inf. Co.F
Rodgers, James LA 8th Inf. Co.B
Rodgers, James MS 2nd Inf. Co.B
Rodgers, James MS 8th Inf. Co.H
Rodgers, James MS 36th Inf. Co.F
Rodgers, James MS 39th Inf. Co.G,C
Rodgers, James MO 1st N.E. Cav. Co.K Sgt.
Rodgers, James MO 4th Cav. Co.A
Rodgers, James MO 6th Cav. Co.D
Rodgers, James MO 12th Cav. Co.I
Rodgers, James NC 7th Inf.
Rodgers, James NC 43rd Inf. Co.B
Rodgers, James SC 5th Cav. Co.K
Rodgers, James SC Inf. 1st (Charleston) Bn.
  Co.B,G
Rodgers, James SC 14th Inf. Co.B
Rodgers, James SC 16th Inf. Co.B
Rodgers, James SC 26th Inf. Co.F
Rodgers, James TN 13th (Gore's) Cav. Co.G
Rodgers, James TN 18th Inf. Co.A
Rodgers, James TN 19th Inf. Co.F
Rodgers, James 30th Bn.S.S. Co.A
Rodgers, James 1st Conf.Reg.Cav. Co.A
Rodgers, James A. AR 31st Inf. Co.D
Rodgers, James A. VA Lt.Arty. Carpenter's Co.
Rodgers, James B. GA Lt.Arty. 12th Bn. 1st
  Co.A
Rodgers, James B. GA 63rd Inf. Co.A
Rodgers, James B. MS 2nd Inf. Co.C
Rodgers, James B. VA 47th Inf. Co.A Sgt.
Rodgers, James C. AL Arty. 1st Bn. Co.D Cpl.
Rodgers, James C. GA 40th Inf.
Rodgers, James C. TX 30th Cav. Co.A
Rodgers, James D. AL 13th Inf. Co.E
Rodgers, James D. SC 20th Inf. Co.G
Rodgers, James E. GA 6th Inf. (St.Guards) Co.K
Rodgers, James F. FL 3rd Inf. Co.K

Rodgers, James F. SC 2nd Rifles Co.G
Rodgers, James G. GA 12th Inf. Co.H Capt.
Rodgers, James G. KY 2nd Bn.Mtd.Rifles Co.A
   Cpl.
Rodgers, James H. AR 12th Inf. Co.I
Rodgers, James H. AR 26th Inf. Co.B
Rodgers, James H. GA 39th Inf. Co.I
Rodgers, James H. TX 1st Rangers Co.C
Rodgers, James Henry AL 2nd Bn. Hilliard's
   Legion Vol. Co.A
Rodgers, James Irwin TX 20th Cav. Co.A
Rodgers, James J. NC 8th Inf. Co.B
Rodgers, James K.P. TN Cav. Newsom's Regt.
   Co.C
Rodgers, James L. AL 33rd Inf. Co.C
Rodgers, James L. FL 1st Inf. Old Co.F
Rodgers, James L. SC 20th Inf. Co.G
Rodgers, James L. VA 19th Cav. Co.F
Rodgers, James L. VA 2nd Cav.St.Line
   McNeel's Co.
Rodgers, James M. FL 7th Inf.
Rodgers, James M. FL 10th Inf. Co.K
Rodgers, James M. GA 4th Inf. Co.I Cpl.
Rodgers, James M. LA 5th Cav. Co.I
Rodgers, James M. NC 1st Cav. (9th St.Troops)
   Co.F
Rodgers, James M. NC 2nd Inf. Co.D
Rodgers, James M. NC 29th Inf. Co.E
Rodgers, James M. NC 52nd Inf. Co.A
Rodgers, James M. VA 64th Mtd.Inf. Co.D
Rodgers, James P. AL Mil. 4th Vol. Co.B
Rodgers, James P. GA 63rd Inf. Co.G
Rodgers, James R. AL 13th Inf. Co.C
Rodgers, James R. NC 2nd Inf. Co.C
Rodgers, James R. SC 3rd Res. Co.A
Rodgers, James W. GA Lt.Arty. (Jo Thompson
   Arty.) Hanleiter's Co.
Rodgers, James W. GA Inf. 25th Bn. (Prov.
   Guard) Co.C
Rodgers, James W. GA 38th Inf. Co.G
Rodgers, James W. MS 9th Inf. Old Co.D
Rodgers, James W. MS 34th Inf. Co.E Capt.
Rodgers, James W. TX 9th Field Btty. Sgt.
Rodgers, James W. VA 8th Cav. Co.G
Rodgers, James W. VA 5th Inf. Co.I Cpl.
Rodgers, James W. 8th (Wade's) Conf.Cav. Co.I
Rodgers, Jasper TN 51st (Cons.) Inf. Co.D
Rodgers, Jasper N. VA 24th Cav. Co.G
Rodgers, J.B. AR 19th (Dockery's) Inf. Co.G
Rodgers, J.B. KY 4th Cav. Co.G
Rodgers, J.B. MS 1st (Patton's) Inf. Co.E
Rodgers, J.B. MS 3rd Inf. Co.K
Rodgers, J.B. MO 1st Cav.
Rodgers, J.B. SC 12th Inf. Co.H
Rodgers, J.B. TN 3rd (Clack's) Inf. Co.H Sgt.
Rodgers, J.B. TN Inf. 4th Cons.Regt. Co.C
Rodgers, J.C. GA Hvy.Arty. 22nd Bn. Co.B
Rodgers, J.C. GA 15th Inf. Co.E
Rodgers, J.C. GA 44th Inf. Co.H
Rodgers, J.C. KY Cav. 2nd Bn. (Dortch's) Co.B
Rodgers, J.C. LA Ogden's Cav. Co.C
Rodgers, J.C. LA 1st Hvy.Arty. (Reg.) Co.D
Rodgers, J.C. LA Washington Arty.Bn. Co.6
   Can.
Rodgers, J.C. MS 28th Cav. Co.C
Rodgers, J.C. MS 2nd (Davidson's) Inf. Potts'
   Co.

Rodgers, J.C. MS 8th Inf. Co.E
Rodgers, J.C. MS 41st Inf. Co.B
Rodgers, J.C. NC 6th Cav. (65th St.Troops)
   Co.E
Rodgers, J.C. NC 7th Inf. Co.D
Rodgers, J.C. VA Cav. 37th Bn. Co.B
Rodgers, J.D. GA 4th Inf. Co.B
Rodgers, J.D. SC 1st Arty. Co.E
Rodgers, J.D. SC Inf. 7th Bn. (Enfield Rifles)
   Co.A
Rodgers, J.D. SC 27th Inf. Co.K
Rodgers, J.D. SC Inf.Bn. Co.B Cpl.
Rodgers, J.D. TN 47th Inf. Co.C
Rodgers, J.D.S.A. SC Cav. 19th Bn. Co.D
Rodgers, J.E. NC 51st Inf. Co.C
Rodgers, Jefferson VA 10th Inf. Co.E
Rodgers, Jeramiah D., Jr. AR Inf. Clayton's Co.
Rodgers, Jeramiah D., Sr. AR Inf. Clayton's Co.
Rodgers, Jeremiah MO Cav. Freeman's Regt.
   Co.D Sr.2nd Lt.
Rodgers, Jeremiah NC 42nd Inf. Co.G
Rodgers, Jerry 1st Conf.Cav. 2nd Co.K 1st Sgt.
Rodgers, Jesse GA Lt.Arty. 14th Bn. Co.B
Rodgers, Jesse GA Lt.Arty. Anderson's Btty.
Rodgers, Jesse SC 4th St.Troops Co.E
Rodgers, Jesse SC Inf. 9th Bn. Co.G
Rodgers, Jesse SC 26th Inf. Co.K Sgt.
Rodgers, Jesse B. AL 38th Inf. Co.K
Rodgers, Jessee AL 16th Inf. Co.I
Rodgers, Jesse N. NC 25th Inf. Co.D
Rodgers, Jesse P. MS 15th Inf. Co.K
Rodgers, Jesse R. FL 1st Inf. New Co.E
Rodgers, Jesse S. AR Cav. Gordon's Regt. Co.K
   Sgt.
Rodgers, Jesse S. TN 44th (Cons.) Inf. Co.E
   Cpl.
Rodgers, J.F. GA 36th (Villepigue's) Inf. Co.K
Rodgers, J.F. LA 22nd (Cons.) Inf. Co.E
Rodgers, J.F. SC 7th Cav. Co.A
Rodgers, J.F. SC Cav. Tucker's Co.
Rodgers, J.F. TN 7th (Duckworth's) Cav. Co.A
Rodgers, J.F. TN 20th (Russell's) Cav. Co.F
Rodgers, J.F. TN 13th Inf. Co.F
Rodgers, J. Ferd. TN 3rd (Forrest's) Cav. Co.F
   Capt.
Rodgers, J.G. TX Cav. Waller's Regt. Dunn's
   Co.
Rodgers, J.H. AL 50th Inf. Co.F
Rodgers, J.H. AR 45th Cav. Co.G
Rodgers, J.H. AR 26th Inf. Co.G
Rodgers, J.H. GA Cav. 8th Bn. (St.Guards)
   Co.C
Rodgers, J.H. KY 1st (Helm's) Cav. Old Co.G
Rodgers, J.H. TN 13th Inf. Co.C Ens.
Rodgers, J.H. TX 17th Cons.Dismtd.Cav. Co.B
Rodgers, J.H.C. KY 1st (Helm's) Cav. Old Co.G
Rodgers, J.H.M. AL 57th Inf. Co.A,F
Rodgers, Jiddian S. AR 11th Inf. Co.I Cpl.
Rodgers, J.J. AR Inf. Cocke's Regt. Co.C
Rodgers, J.J. MS 1st Cav.Res. Co.I
Rodgers, J.J. VA Lt.Arty. Nelson's Co.
Rodgers, J.J. 1st Conf.Cav. 2nd Co.K
Rodgers, J.J.F. GA 31st Inf. Co.A 2nd Lt.
Rodgers, J.K. TX Cav. Border's Regt. Co.D
Rodgers, J.L. SC 3rd St.Troops Co.A
Rodgers, J.L. SC 10th Inf. Co.D
Rodgers, J.L. SC 21st Inf. Co.C

Rodgers, J.L. SC 25th Inf. Co.I
Rodgers, J.M. AR 12th Inf. Co.G
Rodgers, J.M. AR 35th Inf. Co.K
Rodgers, J.M. GA 3rd Res. Co.F
Rodgers, J.M. MS 4th Cav. Co.C
Rodgers, J.M. MS Cav. Hughes' Bn. Co.A
Rodgers, J.M. MS 1st Lt.Arty. Co.C
Rodgers, J.M. MS Shields' Co.
Rodgers, J.M. MO 5th Inf. Co.C
Rodgers, J.M. SC 7th Cav. Co.A
Rodgers, J.M. SC 14th Inf. Co.E
Rodgers, J.M. SC 21st Inf. Co.C
Rodgers, J.M. TN 13th (Gore's) Cav. Co.I
Rodgers, J.M. 1st Conf.Cav. 2nd Co.K
Rodgers, J.M. Gen. & Staff Surg.
Rodgers, J.Mc. GA 54th Inf. Co.H
Rodgers, J.N. KY 3rd Mtd.Inf. Co.M Sgt.
Rodgers, J.N. MS 9th Bn.S.S. Co.C
Rodgers, J.N. 1st Conf.Cav. 2nd Co.K
Rodgers, Job GA 12th Cav. Co.C
Rodgers, John AL Cav. Lewis' Bn. Co.D
Rodgers, John AL 12th Inf. Co.D
Rodgers, John AL 16th Inf. Co.H
Rodgers, John AL 21st Inf. Co.C,A
Rodgers, John AR 27th Inf. New Co.B
Rodgers, John AR 30th Inf. Co.H
Rodgers, John AR 32nd Inf. Co.I
Rodgers, John GA 22nd Inf. Co.C
Rodgers, John GA 41st Inf. Co.D
Rodgers, John KY 2nd Cav. Co.A
Rodgers, John LA 4th Inf. Co.B
Rodgers, John LA 21st (Kennedy's) Inf. Co.D
Rodgers, John LA 28th (Gray's) Inf.
Rodgers, John MS Cav. 2nd Bn.Res. Co.B
Rodgers, John MS 2nd Part.Rangers Co.G
Rodgers, John MS 3rd (St.Troops) Cav. Co.I
Rodgers, John MS Cav. Yerger's Regt. Co.F
Rodgers, John MS 9th Inf. Old Co.F
Rodgers, John MS 24th Inf. Co.E
Rodgers, John MS 46th Inf. Co.C
Rodgers, John MO 7th Cav. Co.B
Rodgers, John MO 9th Inf. Co.E
Rodgers, John MO Inf. Clark's Regt. Co.H
Rodgers, John NC 37th Inf. Co.C
Rodgers, John NC 52nd Inf. Co.B
Rodgers, John SC 1st (Butler's) Inf. Co.F
Rodgers, John SC 5th Inf. 1st Co.D,A, 2nd Co.C
   Band Music.
Rodgers, John SC Inf. 9th Bn. Co.E
Rodgers, John SC 23rd Inf. Co.H
Rodgers, John SC 25th Inf. Co.C
Rodgers, John SC 26th Inf. Co.F
Rodgers, John TN 31st Inf. Co.C
Rodgers, John TX Cav. Benavides' Regt. Co.K
Rodgers, John VA 1st Cav. Co.A
Rodgers, John VA Inf. 1st Bn. Co.E
Rodgers, John VA Inf. 4th Bn.Loc.Def. Co.E
Rodgers, John VA 28th Inf. 2nd Co.C
Rodgers, John VA 46th Mil. Co.A
Rodgers, John VA 58th Mil. Co.H
Rodgers, John VA 59th Inf. 3rd Co.C
Rodgers, John VA 62nd Mtd.Inf. 1st Co.A
Rodgers, John Conf.Cav. Wood's Regt. Co.K
Rodgers, John Conf.Reg.Inf. Brooks' Bn. Co.B
Rodgers, John A. MS 27th Inf. Co.H
Rodgers, John A. MO Inf. 5th Regt.St.Guard
   Co.D Cpl.

Rodgers, John C. GA 12th (Robinson's) Cav. (St.Guards) Co.A
Rodgers, John C. NC 22nd Inf. Co.L
Rodgers, John C. TN 60th Mtd.Inf. Co.C 1st Lt.
Rodgers, John C. 1st Cherokee Mtd.Vol. 1st Co.K Sgt.
Rodgers, John D. GA 1st Inf. Co.D
Rodgers, John D. GA 30th Inf. Co.B 1st Sgt.
Rodgers, John D. MS 16th Inf. Co.B
Rodgers, John D. SC 10th Inf. Co.L
Rodgers, John D. VA Horse Arty. Jackson's Co.
Rodgers, John D.R. AL 1st Regt.Conscr. Co.K
Rodgers, John E. NC 14th Inf. Co.A
Rodgers, John E. TX 31st Cav. Co.C
Rodgers, John F. TX Inf. Griffin's Bn.
Rodgers, John F. VA 13th Inf. 2nd Co.E
Rodgers, John G. GA 3rd Inf. Co.K
Rodgers, John G. TN 11th (Holman's) Cav. Co.G
Rodgers, John G. TN Holman's Bn.Part.Rangers Co.B
Rodgers, John G. TX 35th (Brown's) Cav. Co.I
Rodgers, John G. TX 13th Vol. 3rd Co.I
Rodgers, John H. MS 26th Inf. Co.E
Rodgers, John H. NC 2nd Jr.Res. Co.A
Rodgers, John H. NC 22nd Inf. Co.G
Rodgers, John H. VA 6th Cav. Co.C
Rodgers, John H. VA 6th Cav. Co.G
Rodgers, John H. VA 5th Inf. Co.F
Rodgers, John H.C. KY Morgan's Men Co.D
Rodgers, John J. AL 3rd Inf. Co.I
Rodgers, John L. AL 43rd Inf. Co.H
Rodgers, John L. MO Cav. Snider's Bn. Co.A
Rodgers, John M. GA 1st Inf. Co.F
Rodgers, John M. MS 1st Lt.Arty. Co.E
Rodgers, John M. TX 2nd Cav. Co.G
Rodgers, John M. VA Hvy.Arty. 20th Bn. Co.D
Rodgers, John N. TX 8th Cav. Co.I
Rodgers, John N.G. NC 7th Inf. Co.H
Rodgers, John P. AR 8th Inf. New Co.G
Rodgers, John R. GA 12th Inf. Co.F
Rodgers, John R. MS 31st Inf. Co.A
Rodgers, John R. VA 6th Cav. Co.G
Rodgers, John S. GA 38th Inf. Co.G
Rodgers, John S. SC 14th Inf. Co.F Sgt.
Rodgers, John S. TX 30th Cav. Co.D Cpl.
Rodgers, John T. GA Lt.Arty. Milledge's Co. Cpl.
Rodgers, John T. MS Cav. 3rd Bn.Res. Co.E
Rodgers, John T. TN Cav. Newsom's Regt. Co.C
Rodgers, John T. TN 1st (Turney's) Inf. Co.K
Rodgers, John T. TX 4th Inf. Co.A
Rodgers, John T. Conf.Arty. Nelson's Bn. Co.I Sr.1st Lt.
Rodgers, John V.L. NC 42nd Inf. ACS
Rodgers, John W. AL 28th Inf. Co.K Sgt.
Rodgers, John W. MS 16th Inf. Co.H
Rodgers, John W. NC 29th Inf. Co.C
Rodgers, John W. VA 23rd Inf. Co.C
Rodgers, Jonathan AR 1st Cav. (St.) Co.D
Rodgers, Jonathan B. VA 5th Inf. Co.H
Rodgers, Jonathan S. AR 36th Inf. Co.A
Rodgers, Joseph AL 1st Cav. Co.H,E
Rodgers, Joseph AL 16th Inf. Co.I
Rodgers, Joseph AR Inf. Cocke's Regt. Co.A Cpl.

Rodgers, Joseph GA Inf. 17th Bn. (St.Guards) Stocks' Co.
Rodgers, Joseph GA 21st Inf. Co.F
Rodgers, Joseph GA 48th Inf. Co.G Cpl.
Rodgers, Joseph LA 5th Cav. Co.K
Rodgers, Joseph NC 31st Inf. Co.K
Rodgers, Joseph NC 43rd Inf. Co.D
Rodgers, Joseph SC 2nd Inf. Co.D
Rodgers, Joseph TN 35th Inf. 2nd Co.D Sgt.
Rodgers, Joseph TX 25th Cav. Co.A
Rodgers, Joseph TX 3rd Inf. Co.I
Rodgers, Joseph VA 7th Cav. Co.D
Rodgers, Joseph VA 12th Cav. Co.H
Rodgers, Joseph B. FL 10th Inf. Co.K
Rodgers, Joseph B. MS 23rd Inf. Co.K
Rodgers, Joseph D. SC 7th Res. Co.E
Rodgers, Joseph M. TN Holman's Bn. Part.Rangers Co.D
Rodgers, Joseph N. TX 13th Cav. Co.C
Rodgers, Joseph R. AL 4th (Russell's) Cav. Co.I
Rodgers, Joseph T. GA 61st Inf. Co.D
Rodgers, Joseph W. MS Lt.Arty. Turner's Co.
Rodgers, Joshua AR 8th Inf. New Co.A
Rodgers, Joshua H. NC 22nd Inf. Co.G
Rodgers, Josiah MS 46th Inf. Co.B
Rodgers, Josiah MO 8th Inf. Co.G,K 1st Lt.
Rodgers, Josiah SC 1st (Hagood's) Inf. 2nd Co.K
Rodgers, Josiah SC 19th Inf. Co.D
Rodgers, Josiah TN Inf. 22nd Bn. Co.B
Rodgers, Josiah M. NC 2nd Cav. (19th St.Troops) Co.I
Rodgers, J.P. VA 30th Inf. Co.B
Rodgers, J.R. AL 50th Inf. Co.F
Rodgers, J.R. AR 11th Inf. Co.F
Rodgers, J.R. AR 11th & 17th (Cons.) Inf. Co.F
Rodgers, J.R. GA 32nd Inf. Co.H
Rodgers, J.R. SC 12th Inf. Co.H
Rodgers, J.R. SC 23rd Inf. Co.H
Rodgers, J.R. TX Cav. Baird's Regt. Co.E
Rodgers, J.S. AL 48th Inf. Co.C
Rodgers, J.S. AR 20th Inf. Co.K
Rodgers, J.S. 20th Conf.Cav. Co.M
Rodgers, J.S.B. LA 15th Inf. Co.G
Rodgers, J.T. AR 10th (Witt's) Cav. Co.G
Rodgers, J.T. KY 7th Cav. Co.B
Rodgers, J.T. TN 3rd (Clack's) Inf. Co.H
Rodgers, Julius D. 3rd Conf.Eng.Troops Co.A Cpl.
Rodgers, J.V. TX 7th Cav. Co.I
Rodgers, J.V.L. Gen. & Staff Capt.,Insp.
Rodgers, J.W. AL 4th (Russell's) Cav. Co.K
Rodgers, J.W. AL 33rd Inf. Co.F
Rodgers, J.W. AL 57th Inf. Co.I Sgt.
Rodgers, J.W. AR 8th Inf. New Co.E
Rodgers, J.W. AR 9th Inf. Co.I
Rodgers, J.W. GA 12th Cav. Co.D
Rodgers, J.W. MS 1st Cav. Co.C Artif.
Rodgers, J.W. MS Cav. Ham's Regt. Co.G 2nd Lt.
Rodgers, J.W. MS 5th Inf. (St.Troops) Co.I
Rodgers, J.W. MS 6th Inf. Co.E
Rodgers, J.W. MS 41st Inf. Co.C 1st Sgt.
Rodgers, J.W. MS T. Williams' Co.
Rodgers, J.W. MO Cav. Freeman's Regt. Co.D
Rodgers, J.W. NC 2nd Jr.Res. Co.E
Rodgers, J.W. SC 2nd Bn.S.S. Co.C

Rodgers, J.W. TN 7th (Duckworth's) Cav. White's Co.
Rodgers, J.W. TN 13th Inf. Co.C Sgt.
Rodgers, J.W. TX 25th Cav. Co.A
Rodgers, J.W. TX 19th Inf. Co.E
Rodgers, J.W. 20th Conf.Cav. 1st Co.H
Rodgers, Kimberly NC 8th Inf. Co.B
Rodgers, L. MS Cav. Ham's Regt. Co.G
Rodgers, L. SC Inf. 3rd Bn. Co.E
Rodgers, Lafayette TX 7th Cav. Co.C
Rodgers, Larkin SC 1st St.Troops Co.C
Rodgers, L.D. GA 65th Inf. Co.H Sgt.
Rodgers, Lemuel, Jr. GA 13th Inf. Co.A
Rodgers, Letcher NC 14th Inf. Co.A
Rodgers, Levi TN 55th (McKoin's) Inf. James' Co.
Rodgers, Lewis AR 7th Inf. Co.I
Rodgers, Lewis TN Cav. 32nd Regt.
Rodgers, Lewis 2nd Cherokee Mtd.Vol. Co.G 2nd Lt.
Rodgers, L.F. NC 57th Inf. Co.B
Rodgers, L.H. TX 18th Cav. Co.G
Rodgers, L.H. TX 13th Vol. 3rd Co.I
Rodgers, L.L. KY 2nd Bn.Mtd.Rifles Co.A
Rodgers, Lord TN 10th Inf. Co.G,E
Rodgers, L.P. SC 5th St.Troops Co.I
Rodgers, L.P. SC 9th Res. Co.C
Rodgers, L.P. SC 27th Inf. Co.G
Rodgers, L.T. MS 26th Inf. Co.G
Rodgers, L.T. VA 2nd Inf. Co.B
Rodgers, L.W.T. MS 1st Cav.Res. Co.B
Rodgers, M. AL 12th Cav. Co.D
Rodgers, M. GA 22nd Inf. Co.F Sgt.
Rodgers, M. LA 21st (Kennedy's) Inf. Co.D
Rodgers, M. MS Cav. Yerger's Regt. Co.A
Rodgers, M. SC 9th Inf. Co.E
Rodgers, M. SC 23rd Inf. Co.H
Rodgers, M. TX 25th Cav. Co.H
Rodgers, M.A. AL 6th Cav. Co.C,B
Rodgers, Marcus NC 48th Inf. Co.E
Rodgers, Marcus D.L. LA 12th Inf. Co.F
Rodgers, Marion MO 1st N.E. Cav. Co.K
Rodgers, Marion D. MS 26th Inf. Co.C
Rodgers, Marion D. SC 12th Inf. Co.H
Rodgers, Mark AL 57th Inf. Co.A,H
Rodgers, Martin SC 14th Inf. Co.K
Rodgers, Martin TX 6th Inf. Co.D
Rodgers, Martin A. SC 14th Inf. Co.B
Rodgers, Martin J. GA 14th Inf. Co.G
Rodgers, Martin V. MS 9th Inf. Old Co.F
Rodgers, Mathew W. AL 3rd Inf. Co.I
Rodgers, Matthew AL Cav. Barbiere's Bn. Brown's Co. Cpl.
Rodgers, McDonald AR 20th Inf. Co.I
Rodgers, M.E. GA Lt.Arty. 12th Bn. 3rd Co.E Sgt.
Rodgers, M.H. GA Inf. 9th Bn. Co.A
Rodgers, Micajah SC 6th Inf. 1st Co.B
Rodgers, Mike MS 27th Inf. Co.H 1st Lt.
Rodgers, Millington SC 8th Inf. Co.H
Rodgers, Mills, Jr. VA 41st Inf. Co.I Sgt.
Rodgers, Mills VA 59th Mil. Riddick's Co.
Rodgers, Milton L. AL Cav. Lewis' Bn. Co.D
Rodgers, M.J. AL 54th Inf. Co.H
Rodgers, M.J. FL 2nd Cav. Co.D
Rodgers, M.L. AL Inf. 2nd Regt. Co.C
Rodgers, M.M. MS 7th Cav. Co.H

Rodgers, M.M. MS Cav. Street's Bn.
Rodgers, M.M. TN 42nd Inf. Co.D
Rodgers, M.M. Gen. & Staff 2nd Lt.,Dr.M.
Rodgers, M.N. MS 42nd Inf. Co.E
Rodgers, M.N. TX 1st Hvy.Arty. Co.F
Rodgers, Moses AL 17th Inf. Co.G
Rodgers, Moses G. MS 37th Inf. Co.K
Rodgers, Moses H. Conf.Cav. Wood's Regt. Co.K
Rodgers, Moses K. AR 12th Inf. Co.I
Rodgers, M.P. AL 9th Inf. Co.C
Rodgers, M.P. AL 17th Inf. Co.G
Rodgers, M.P. GA Cav. 6th Bn. (St.Guards) Co.A
Rodgers, M.R. GA 45th Inf. Co.A Maj.
Rodgers, M.T. MS 2nd Cav.Res. Co.C
Rodgers, M.T. TX 26th Cav. Co.E
Rodgers, Munroe Conf.Reg.Inf. Brooks' Bn. Co.C
Rodgers, M.V. GA 11th Cav. Co.I
Rodgers, M.V. KY 7th Cav. Co.G,I
Rodgers, M.W. NC 60th Inf. Co.F
Rodgers, M.W. TN 31st Inf. Co.I
Rodgers, N. AL 59th Inf. Co.H
Rodgers, N. AR 26th Inf. Co.G Cpl.
Rodgers, N. MS 1st Cav.Res. Co.B
Rodgers, N. MS 46th Inf. Co.B
Rodgers, Nap. B. LA 15th Inf. Co.G
Rodgers, Nathaniel AL 10th Inf. Co.H
Rodgers, Nathaniel B. GA 26th Inf. Co.C 2nd Lt.
Rodgers, Nathaniel B. KY 4th Cav. Co.C
Rodgers, Newton V. AR 24th Inf. Co.F
Rodgers, Newton V. AR Inf. Hardy's Regt. Co.D
Rodgers, N.H. NC 8th Sr.Res. Callihan's Co.
Rodgers, N.J. NC 1st Inf. Co.H
Rodgers, N.J. SC Inf. 7th Bn. (Enfield Rifles) Co.A
Rodgers, N.P. VA 14th Cav. Co.E Cpl.
Rodgers, N.P. VA Cav. Hounshell's Bn. Co.B 2nd Lt.
Rodgers, N.P. VA Inf. 26th Bn. Co.D
Rodgers, N.R. LA 1st Hvy.Arty. (Reg.) Co.I
Rodgers, N.R. TN 1st Hvy.Arty.
Rodgers, N.R. TN 18th Inf. Co.A
Rodgers, O. MS Lt.Arty. (Jefferson Arty.) Darden's Co.
Rodgers, Oliver AR 38th Inf. Co.F
Rodgers, P. AL 12th Cav. Co.D
Rodgers, P. SC 1st Bn.S.S. Co.A
Rodgers, P.A. SC 14th Inf. Co.K
Rodgers, Patrick LA 1st Hvy.Arty. (Reg.) Co.D Sgt.
Rodgers, Patrick TN Inf. 2nd Cons.Regt. Co.B
Rodgers, Patrick TN 15th Inf. Co.F
Rodgers, Patrick TN Inf. 154th Sr.Regt. Co.H
Rodgers, Patrick VA 2nd Inf. Co.C
Rodgers, Patterson LA 31st Inf. Co.G
Rodgers, Paul SC 24th Inf. Co.D Teamster
Rodgers, Peter TN 8th Cav. Co.I
Rodgers, Peter H. AR 12th Inf. Co.I
Rodgers, Philip MD 1st Cav. Co.C
Rodgers, Philip VA 16th Inf. Co.B Cpl.
Rodgers, Pinckney SC 8th Inf. Co.B
Rodgers, P.J. AL 5th Inf. Co.C
Rodgers, P.J. TX 13th Vol. Co.E

Rodgers, P.J. VA 5th Cav. Co.G
Rodgers, P.K. GA 6th Cav. Co.E Cpl.
Rodgers, Pleasant H. AL 33rd Inf. Co.C Sgt.
Rodgers, Preston W.C.P. FL 5th Inf. Co.E
Rodgers, R. SC 16th Inf. Co.K
Rodgers, R. VA 10th Cav. Co.B
Rodgers, R. VA 1st St.Res. Co.B
Rodgers, R. 20th Conf.Cav. Co.M
Rodgers, R.A. MS 18th Cav. Co.G
Rodgers, R.A. MS 31st Inf. Co.I
Rodgers, R.A. MS Moseley's Regt.
Rodgers, Ransom MS 2nd Inf. Co.G
Rodgers, R.C. AL 27th Inf. Co.F
Rodgers, R.D. TN 16th (Logwood's) Cav. Co.H
Rodgers, R.E. TN 12th Inf. Co.D Capt.
Rodgers, Redick C. MS 8th Inf. Co.E
Rodgers, Reuben B. TX 9th Cav. Co.A
Rodgers, R.H. GA Lt.Arty. 12th Bn. 3rd Co.E
Rodgers, R.H. GA Inf. 19th Bn. (St.Guards) Co.C
Rodgers, R.H. SC Manigault's Bn.Vol. Co.D 2nd Lt.
Rodgers, R.H. TN 18th Inf. Co.A
Rodgers, Richard MO 3rd Cav. Co.C
Rodgers, Richard H. MO 6th Inf. Co.B QMSgt.
Rodgers, Richard H. VA 41st Inf. Co.I
Rodgers, R.J. TX Cav. Waller's Regt. Dunn's Co.
Rodgers, R.M. SC Cav. 14th Bn. Co.A
Rodgers, R.N. TX 26th Cav. Co.A Sgt.
Rodgers, Robert AL 24th Inf. Co.B
Rodgers, Robert GA Lt.Arty. 14th Bn. Co.B
Rodgers, Robert GA Lt.Arty. Anderson's Btty.
Rodgers, Robert GA 7th Inf. (St.Guards) Co.C
Rodgers, Robert GA 54th Inf. Co.H
Rodgers, Robert LA 5th Cav. Co.I
Rodgers, Robert MS 7th Inf. Co.A
Rodgers, Robert MS 36th Inf. Co.F
Rodgers, Robert SC 3rd St.Troops Co.A
Rodgers, Robert SC Inf. Hampton Legion Co.E
Rodgers, Robert TN 3rd (Forrest's) Cav. 1st Co.B
Rodgers, Robert TN 51st (Cons.) Inf. Co.D
Rodgers, Robert TN 62nd Mtd.Inf. Co.G Sgt.
Rodgers, Robert VA 27th Inf. 1st Co.H
Rodgers, Robert Brewster MO 8th Inf. Co.H Sgt.
Rodgers, Robert C. NC 12th Inf. Co.G
Rodgers, Robert D. MS 11th Inf. Co.C,I
Rodgers, Robert H. AL 10th Inf. Co.H
Rodgers, Robert J. TX 35th (Brown's) Cav. Co.I
Rodgers, Robert J. TX 13th Vol. 3rd Co.I
Rodgers, Robert L. AL 63rd Inf. Co.G Sgt.
Rodgers, Robert L. GA 43rd Inf. Co.K
Rodgers, Robert M. AL 10th Inf. Co.B
Rodgers, Robert M. SC 5th Cav. Co.H
Rodgers, Robert M. TN Holman's Bn. Part.Rangers Co.B
Rodgers, Robert M. TX 31st Cav. Co.D
Rodgers, Robert R. MS 9th Inf. Old Co.F
Rodgers, Rodrick E. VA 38th Inf. 2nd Co.I
Rodgers, Romulus S. NC 22nd Inf. Co.G Sgt.
Rodgers, Ross TX 27th Cav. Co.K
Rodgers, R.R. AR 10th (Witt's) Cav. Co.G
Rodgers, Ruben B. AR 1st Cav. Co.I
Rodgers, Rufus AL 31st Inf. Co.I
Rodgers, Rufus AR 26th Inf. Co.A

Rodgers, Rufus H. AR 36th Inf. Co.A
Rodgers, R.W. GA Lt.Arty. Van Den Corput's Co.
Rodgers, R.W. SC 23rd Inf. Co.H
Rodgers, R.W. TN Inf. 3rd Cons.Regt. Co.D
Rodgers, S. LA 18th Inf.
Rodgers, S.A. MS Hall's Co.
Rodgers, Sampson TX 31st Cav. Co.D
Rodgers, Samuel AL Cp. of Instr. Talladega
Rodgers, Samuel AR Cav. Davies' Bn. Co.D
Rodgers, Samuel KY 4th Cav.
Rodgers, Samuel KY 7th Mtd.Inf. Co.G
Rodgers, Samuel TN Lt.Arty. Palmer's Co.
Rodgers, Samuel VA 22nd Inf. Chap.
Rodgers, Samuel Gen. & Staff Chap.
Rodgers, Samuel H. VA 30th Inf. Co.B Sgt.
Rodgers, Samuel L. GA 36th (Broyles') Inf. Co.G 1st Sgt.
Rodgers, Samuel R. GA 42nd Inf. Co.F
Rodgers, Samuel T. VA 46th Inf. 2nd Co.F
Rodgers, S.B. MS 7th Cav. Co.H Cpl.
Rodgers, S.B. SC 7th Inf. Co.G
Rodgers, S.C. GA 54th Inf. Co.H
Rodgers, S.C. SC Inf. 7th Bn. (Enfield Rifles) Co.A
Rodgers, S.D. GA Lt.Arty. Scogin's Btty. (Griffin Lt.Arty.)
Rodgers, S.H. AR 32nd Inf. Co.G
Rodgers, S.H. SC 23rd Inf. Co.A
Rodgers, Shade MS 46th Inf. Co.B
Rodgers, Silas D. MS 37th Inf. Co.A
Rodgers, Simpson MS Moseley's Regt. 3rd Lt.
Rodgers, S.J. AL 15th Inf. Co.F
Rodgers, S.J. MS Inf. 2nd St.Troops Co.D
Rodgers, S.L. AL 12th Inf. Co.G
Rodgers, S.L. GA Cav. 19th Bn. Co.E
Rodgers, S.L. SC 7th Cav. Co.A
Rodgers, S.L. SC Cav. Tucker's Co.
Rodgers, S.L. SC Inf. 6th Bn. Co.C
Rodgers, S.L. SC Manigault's Bn.Vol. Co.E Cpl.
Rodgers, S.L. 10th Conf.Cav. Co.K
Rodgers, S.M. GA 1st (Fannin's) Res. Co.E
Rodgers, S.M. LA 12th Inf. Co.F
Rodgers, S.M.N. TN 12th (Green's) Cav. Co.E
Rodgers, Solomon AR 8th Inf. New Co.A
Rodgers, Spyrous A. AR 12th Inf. Co.I
Rodgers, S.R. AL 50th Inf.
Rodgers, S.R. SC Cav. 19th Bn. Co.D
Rodgers, S.R. SC Cav. Rodgers' Co. Sgt.
Rodgers, Stephen GA 4th Inf. Co.C
Rodgers, Stephen TN 19th Inf. Co.F
Rodgers, Stephen G. LA 5th Cav. Co.C
Rodgers, Stephen H. AL 50th Inf. Co.B
Rodgers, Stephen T. VA 6th Cav. Co.G
Rodgers, T. AR Lt.Arty. 5th Btty.
Rodgers, T. AR 15th (Josey's) Inf. Co.F Cpl.
Rodgers, T. GA Inf. 1st City Bn. (Columbus) Co.C Sgt.
Rodgers, T. SC 2nd St.Troops Co.B
Rodgers, T.A. KY 8th Cav. Co.I
Rodgers, T.A. GA Inf. 10th Bn. Co.D
Rodgers, Taylor KY 1st (Helm's) Cav. Co.B
Rodgers, T.C. MO 9th Inf. Co.F
Rodgers, T.C. TX Cav. 1st Regt.St.Troops Co.F
Rodgers, T.D. SC Cav. 14th Bn. Co.A
Rodgers, T.F. AL 26th Inf. Co.H

Rodgers, Thad B. LA 9th Inf. Co.K
Rodgers, Thomas AL 4th (Roddey's) Cav. Co.F
Rodgers, Thomas AL 26th (O'Neal's) Inf. Co.E
Rodgers, Thomas GA 21st Inf. Co.G
Rodgers, Thomas GA 48th Inf. Co.G
Rodgers, Thomas MS Cav. 1st Bn. (McNair's) St.Troops Co.D
Rodgers, Thomas MS 28th Cav. Co.C
Rodgers, Thomas MS 4th Inf. Co.G
Rodgers, Thomas MO 1st N.E. Cav. Co.K
Rodgers, Thomas MO Lt.Arty. H.M. Bledsoe's Co. Cpl.
Rodgers, Thomas NC 1st Inf. Co.H
Rodgers, Thomas SC 1st Arty. Co.I
Rodgers, Thomas SC 5th Res. Co.F
Rodgers, Thomas SC 23rd Inf. Co.H
Rodgers, Thomas TN 4th (McLemore's) Cav. Co.I
Rodgers, Thomas TX 20th Cav. Co.A
Rodgers, Thomas TX 34th Cav. Co.A
Rodgers, Thomas VA 1st Cav. Co.F
Rodgers, Thomas VA Loc.Def. Morehead's Co.
Rodgers, Thomas A. AL Inf. 1st Regt. Co.G
Rodgers, Thomas A. AL 3rd Bn. Hilliard's Legion Vol. Co.B Sgt.
Rodgers, Thomas A. FL 3rd Inf. Co.G Sgt.
Rodgers, Thomas C. MO 6th Cav. Co.K
Rodgers, Thomas D. NC 1st Cav. (9th St.Troops) Co.K
Rodgers, Thomas D. NC 27th Inf. Co.A
Rodgers, Thomas D. SC 5th Cav. Co.H
Rodgers, Thomas G. TX 31st Cav. Co.E
Rodgers, Thomas H. AL 1st Inf. Sgt.Maj.
Rodgers, Thomas H. VA 23rd Inf. Co.I
Rodgers, Thomas J. AL 21st Inf. Co.A
Rodgers, Thomas O. AL 3rd Bn. Hilliard's Legion Vol. Co.D
Rodgers, Thomas P.P. NC 35th Inf. Co.H
Rodgers, Thomas R. TX 29th Cav. Co.F
Rodgers, Thomas S. NC 7th Inf. Co.H
Rodgers, Timothy MS 41st Inf. Co.C
Rodgers, Timothy MS 46th Inf. Co.B
Rodgers, Timothy SC 23rd Inf. Co.H
Rodgers, Timothy M. AL 39th Inf. Co.H
Rodgers, T.J. AR 10th (Witt's) Cav. Co.G
Rodgers, T.J. GA 54th Inf. Co.H
Rodgers, T.J. MS 9th Inf. Co.I
Rodgers, T.J. MS 41st Inf. Co.B
Rodgers, T.J. TN 4th (McLemore's) Cav. Co.I
Rodgers, T.J. TN 16th Inf. Co.D
Rodgers, T.M. LA 2nd Inf. Co.E Sgt.
Rodgers, T.M. MS 3rd (St.Troops) Cav. Co.D
Rodgers, T.M. MS 6th Inf. Co.E
Rodgers, T.R. SC 6th Inf. Co.D
Rodgers, Tristram MS Inf. 1st Bn.St.Troops (30 days '64) Co.A
Rodgers, Turner D. AR 36th Inf. Co.A
Rodgers, T.W. TX Inf. Timmons' Regt. Co.G N.C.S. Comsy.Sgt.
Rodgers, T.W. TX Waul's Legion Co.A
Rodgers, V. LA Mil. LaFourche Regt.
Rodgers, V.A. TN 20th (Russell's) Cav. Co.B
Rodgers, V.B. TN 42nd Inf. Co.C
Rodgers, Vine A. NC 27th Inf. Co.K
Rodgers, Viney A. NC 27th Inf. Co.A
Rodgers, V.P. AR 1st (Dobbin's) Cav. Co.F
Rodgers, V.W. TX 26th Cav. Co.E

Rodgers, W. MS 8th Cav. Co.K
Rodgers, W. SC 7th Res. Co.L
Rodgers, W. TX 25th Cav.
Rodgers, W.A. SC 4th Bn.Res. Co.E
Rodgers, W.A. SC 9th Res. Co.C Cpl.
Rodgers, W.A. TN 51st (Cons.) Inf. Co.B
Rodgers, W.A. TX Inf. Houston Bn.Loc.Def.Troops Co.D 1st Lt.
Rodgers, Wade SC 23rd Inf. Co.H
Rodgers, W.A.J. MS 32nd Inf. Co.F
Rodgers, Washington K. MS 42nd Inf. Co.B
Rodgers, W.B. AL 6th Inf. Co.C
Rodgers, W.B. MS 3rd Cav. Co.K
Rodgers, W.B. MS 26th Inf. Co.F
Rodgers, W.C. GA 2nd Cav. Co.B
Rodgers, W.C. MS Blythe's Bn. (St.Troops) Co.B
Rodgers, W.C. TN 13th (Gore's) Cav. Co.I
Rodgers, W.C. TN 20th (Russell's) Cav. Co.F Cpl.
Rodgers, W.D. AL 19th Inf. Co.D
Rodgers, W.D. AR 12th Inf. Co.G
Rodgers, W.D. AR 24th Inf. Co.E Ord.Sgt.
Rodgers, W.D. MS 2nd (Davidson's) Inf. Co.K
Rodgers, W.D. TX 7th Cav. Co.K
Rodgers, W.D. VA Horse Arty. McClanahan's Co.
Rodgers, W.E. SC 16th & 24th (Cons.) Inf. Co.G Sgt.
Rodgers, Wesley D. AL 17th Inf. Co.C
Rodgers, Wesly MS 20th Inf. Co.I
Rodgers, Western VA 30th Inf. 1st Co.I
Rodgers, W.F. GA 6th Inf. (St.Guards) Co.A
Rodgers, W.F. MS Inf. 1st Bn.St.Troops (12 mo. '62-3) Co.E
Rodgers, W.F. MS 46th Inf. Co.B
Rodgers, W.F. SC Cav. 12th Bn. Co.B
Rodgers, W.G.B. TX 25th Cav. Co.H
Rodgers, W.H. GA 59th Inf. Co.G
Rodgers, W.H. MS 3rd (St.Troops) Cav. Co.D
Rodgers, W.H. MS 16th Inf. Co.D
Rodgers, W.H. SC Manigault's Bn.Vol. Co.D
Rodgers, W.H. TN 3rd (Forrest's) Cav. Co.C
Rodgers, W.H. TX 17th Cons.Dismtd.Cav. Co.B
Rodgers, W.H. TX 25th Cav. Co.A
Rodgers, W.H. 2nd Conf.Eng.Troops Co.D
Rodgers, W.H.H. FL 2nd Inf. Co.L Capt.
Rodgers, W.H.H. LA 2nd Inf. Co.E
Rodgers, Wiley MS 30th Inf. Co.D
Rodgers, William AL 4th (Russell's) Cav. Co.I
Rodgers, William AL 12th Cav. Co.D Cpl.
Rodgers, William AL Lt.Arty. Hurt's Btty.
Rodgers, William AL 10th Inf. Co.K
Rodgers, William AL 17th Inf. Co.H
Rodgers, William AR 7th Inf. Co.F
Rodgers, William AR 35th Inf. Co.K
Rodgers, William GA 8th Inf. Co.A
Rodgers, William GA 1st Bn.S.S.
Rodgers, William GA Inf. 17th Bn. (St.Guards) Stocks' Co.
Rodgers, William GA 25th Inf. Co.K
Rodgers, William GA 27th Inf. Co.A
Rodgers, William GA 54th Inf. Co.H Cpl.
Rodgers, William GA 64th Inf. Co.B
Rodgers, William KY 2nd Bn.Mtd.Rifles Co.A
Rodgers, William KY 4th Cav. Co.B
Rodgers, William LA 8th Cav. Co.D

Rodgers, William MS 1st Cav.Res. Co.B
Rodgers, William MS 3rd Cav. Co.G
Rodgers, William MS 6th Inf. Co.K
Rodgers, William MS 8th Inf. Co.A
Rodgers, William MS 8th Inf. Co.E Sgt.
Rodgers, William MS 36th Inf. Co.F
Rodgers, William MO 1st N.E. Cav. Co.K
Rodgers, William MO Cav. Fristoe's Regt. Co.F
Rodgers, William NC 5th Cav. (63rd St.Troops) Co.K
Rodgers, William NC 7th Sr.Res. Bradshaw's Co.
Rodgers, William NC 7th Sr.Res. Fisher's Co.
Rodgers, William NC 24th Inf. Co.K
Rodgers, William NC 43rd Inf. Co.D
Rodgers, William NC 46th Inf. Co.B
Rodgers, William NC 60th Inf. Co.F Music.
Rodgers, William SC 4th Cav. Co.D
Rodgers, William SC 1st Arty. Co.G,E
Rodgers, William SC 21st Inf. Co.C
Rodgers, William SC 25th Inf. Co.I
Rodgers, William SC Manigault's Bn.Vol. Co.A
Rodgers, William TN 2nd (Ashby's) Cav. Co.D
Rodgers, William TN 1st Hvy.Arty. Co.K, 2nd Co.C 1st Lt.
Rodgers, William TN Arty.Corps Co.7 2nd Lt.
Rodgers, William TN 2nd (Robison's) Inf. Co.E
Rodgers, William TN 18th Inf. Co.A
Rodgers, William TN 21st Inf. Co.I
Rodgers, William TN 30th Inf. Co.H
Rodgers, William TN 37th Inf. Co.B
Rodgers, William TX Cav. Waller's Regt. Menard's Co.
Rodgers, William VA Lt.Arty. 12th Bn. Co.B
Rodgers, William VA Lt.Arty. Brander's Co.
Rodgers, William VA 4th Res. Co.A
Rodgers, William VA 22nd Inf. Co.K
Rodgers, William Brush Bn.
Rodgers, William A. AR 36th Inf. Co.A
Rodgers, William A. Sig.Corps,CSA
Rodgers, William B. NC Hvy.Arty. 1st Bn. Co.C
Rodgers, William C. SC 1st Arty. Co.C
Rodgers, William C. SC 1st (Butler's) Inf. Co.H
Rodgers, William C. SC 1st (Orr's) Rifles Co.H
Rodgers, William C. TX 37th Cav. Co.H
Rodgers, William C. VA 61st Inf. Co.D
Rodgers, William C. 15th Conf.Cav. Co.A
Rodgers, William D. AR Inf. Hardy's Regt. N.C.S. Ord.Sgt.
Rodgers, William D. FL 1st Inf. Old Co.K, New Co.K
Rodgers, William D. GA 12th Inf. Co.C
Rodgers, William D. TX Inf. Griffin's Bn. Co.B
Rodgers, William D. VA 62nd Mtd.Inf. 1st Co.A
Rodgers, William D. VA 97th Mil. Co.D
Rodgers, William E. MS 2nd Inf. Co.F 1st Lt.
Rodgers, William E. MS 18th Inf. Maj.
Rodgers, William E. MS 23rd Inf. Maj.
Rodgers, William E. TX 11th (Spaight's) Bn.Vol.
Rodgers, William Edward SC 24th Inf. Co.I Sgt.
Rodgers, William G.S. GA 20th Inf. Co.D Cpl.
Rodgers, William H. AL 4th Cav. Co.D
Rodgers, William H. AL 1st Regt.Conscr. Co.C
Rodgers, William H. AL 61st Inf. Co.I,G Sgt.
Rodgers, William H. AR 24th Inf. Co.B
Rodgers, William H. LA 1st (Strawbridge's) Inf. Co.B

Rodgers, William H. TX 2nd Cav. Co.C Sgt.
Rodgers, William H. VA 24th Cav. Co.G
Rodgers, William H. VA Cav. 32nd Bn. Co.A
Rodgers, William H., Jr. VA Cav. 32nd Bn. Co.A
Rodgers, William H. VA Lt.Arty. Cooper's Co.
Rodgers, William H. VA 5th Inf. Co.F
Rodgers, William Henry TX 20th Cav. Co.A Cpl.
Rodgers, William H.R. TN 30th Inf. Co.B
Rodgers, William J. GA 12th Cav. Co.D Capt.
Rodgers, William J.J. NC 2nd Arty. (36th St.Troops) Co.F
Rodgers, William M. MS 16th Inf. Co.D
Rodgers, William M. TX 17th Cav. Co.B
Rodgers, William O. FL 3rd Inf. Co.G
Rodgers, William P. FL 7th Inf. Co.E
Rodgers, William R. NC 27th Inf. Co.A
Rodgers, William R. NC 52nd Inf. Co.F
Rodgers, William R. SC Inf. Hampton Legion Co.F
Rodgers, William S. AR 26th Inf. Co.A
Rodgers, William S. MS Lt.Arty. (Jefferson Arty.) Darden's Co.
Rodgers, William S. NC 51st Inf. Co.F
Rodgers, Wm. T. AL 5th Inf. Co.E
Rodgers, William T. AL 9th Inf. Co.D
Rodgers, William T. FL 5th Inf. Co.E
Rodgers, William T. TN 48th (Voorhies') Inf. Co.D
Rodgers, William W. AL 6th Inf. Co.M
Rodgers, William W. NC 20th Inf. Faison's Co.
Rodgers, William W. TN 44th (Cons.) Inf. Co.E
Rodgers, William W. VA Lt.Arty. Turner's Co.
Rodgers, William W. VA Arty. Wise Legion
Rodgers, William Wallace MO 8th Inf. Co.H Cpl.
Rodgers, Willis SC 23rd Inf. Co.H
Rodgers, Wilson MS 41st Inf. Co.C
Rodgers, W.J. AL 12th Inf. Co.G
Rodgers, W.J. AL 27th Inf. Co.F
Rodgers, W.J. AL 59th Inf. Co.H
Rodgers, W.J. AR 8th Inf. New Co.E
Rodgers, W.J. KY 7th Mtd.Inf. Co.H
Rodgers, W.J. MS Inf. 3rd Bn. Co.H
Rodgers, W.J. SC 23rd Inf. Co.H
Rodgers, W.J. TN 13th Inf. Co.G,E 2nd Lt.
Rodgers, W.J. VA 12th Cav. Co.F
Rodgers, W.M. AR 45th Cav. Co.G
Rodgers, W.M. MS 1st (Percy's) Inf. Co.B
Rodgers, W.M. TN 23rd Inf. Co.E
Rodgers, W.N. SC 1st Cav. Co.F
Rodgers, W.N.G. SC Cav. (St.Troops) Rodgers' Co. Capt.
Rodgers, W.O. LA Mil.Conf.Guards Regt. Co.D
Rodgers, Wood M. NC 1st Cav. (9th St.Troops) Co.F
Rodgers, Woodson M. NC 1st Inf. (6 mo. '61) Co.K
Rodgers, W.P. AR Cav. McGehee's Regt. Co.I
Rodgers, W.P. TN 63rd Inf. Co.G
Rodgers, W.R. AR 8th Inf. New Co.D
Rodgers, W.S. AR 6th Inf. Old Co.F
Rodgers, W.S. SC Arty. Manigault's Bn. 2nd Co.C
Rodgers, W.S. SC Arty. Zimmerman's Co. (Pee Dee Arty.)

Rodgers, W.S. SC 3rd Inf. Co.A
Rodgers, W.S. SC 23rd Inf. Co.H
Rodgers, W.S. TN 6th (Wheeler's) Cav. Co.K
Rodgers, W.S. TN 20th (Russell's) Cav. Co.D
Rodgers, W.T. KY 1st (Helm's) Cav. Old Co.G
Rodgers, W.T. NC 11th (Bethel Regt.) Inf. Co.G
Rodgers, W.W. AL 8th Inf. Co.H
Rodgers, W.W. AL Cp. of Instr. Talladega Co.A
Rodgers, W.W. MS 4th Inf. Co.G
Rodgers, W.W. MS 7th Inf. Co.G Cpl.
Rodgers, W.W. NC 2nd Jr.Res. Co.E
Rodgers, W.W. TN 13th Inf. Co.H
Rodgers, W.Z. TN 20th (Russell's) Cav. Co.F
Rodgers, Y. FL 1st (Res.) Inf.
Rodgers, Z. AL 5th Inf. New Co.K
Rodgers, Zachariah AL 13th Inf. Co.E
Rodgers, Zachariah AL 23rd Inf. Co.B
Rodgers, Zachariah J. GA Lt.Arty. Milledge's Co.
Rodgers, Zachariah J. GA 3rd Inf. 1st Co.I
Rodgers, Zacheriah AL 61st Inf. Co.H
Rodgers, Z.M. MS 46th Inf. Co.B
Rodgers, Zodoc GA 43rd Inf. Co.L,C
Rodgers, Z.T. GA 64th Inf. Co.B
Rodgerson, A.D. TN 9th Inf. Co.B
Rodgerson, James A. NC 17th Inf. (2nd Org.) Co.E
Rodgerson, J.C. NC 4th Cav. (59th St.Troops) Co.I
Rodgerson, Job C. NC Cav. 12th Bn. Co.A,B
Rodgerson, John LA Mil. British Guard Bn. Hamilton's Co. 1st Lt.
Rodgerson, W. TX 4th Inf. (St.Troops) Co.D
Rodgerson, William A. NC 17th Inf. (2nd Org.) Co.H
Rodgerson, William O. NC 4th Cav. (59th St.Troops) Co.I
Rodgerson, William O. NC Cav. 12th Bn. Co.B Sgt.
Rodgerson, William O. NC 17th Inf. (1st Org.) Co.D
Rodgerson, William O. 8th (Dearing's) Conf.Cav. Co.B Sgt.
Rodges, James MS 38th Cav. Co.E
Rodges, James J. TX Cav. Terry's Regt. Co.C
Rodges, James W. MS 5th Inf. Co.G
Rodges, J.T. VA 53rd Inf.
Rodifer, E. KY Williams' Btty.
Rodig, Charles AL 1st Regt. Mobile Vol. Co.E
Rodigan, John VA 2nd Inf.Loc.Def. Co.G
Rodiger, H. AL 48th Mil. Co.D
Rodiger, Francisco MD Arty. 3rd Btty.
Rodigues, Oscar LA Arty. Castellanos' Btty. Lt.
Rodiheifer, George VA 62nd Mtd.Inf. 1st Co.D
Rodin, E. TX Cav. 3rd (Yager's) Bn. Co.D
Rodin, F.M. LA Bienville Res.
Rodin, M. KY 7th Mtd.Inf. 1st Co.K
Rodin, Vincent LA 6th Inf. Co.G
Rodiregres, Antonio TX 35th (Brown's) Cav. Co.D
Rodisk, Henry LA Mil. 4th Regt. 3rd Brig. 1st Div. Co.G
Rodius, John VA 1st Inf. Co.K
Rodjers, Joseph TX 3rd Cav.
Rodlett, G.E. GA 10th Inf.
Rodley, Edward SC Simons' Co.
Rodley, Edward S. MD Cav. 2nd Bn. Co.D,B

Rodley, Edward S. SC Hvy.Arty. 15th (Lucas') Bn. Co.C
Rodley, Edward S. SC Arty. Childs' Co.
Rodlinski, A. LA 18th Inf. Co.H
Rodman, A.T. AR 36th Inf. Co.K
Rodman, A.T. AR 50th Mil. Co.I
Rodman, Benjamin F. TX 22nd Cav. Co.H
Rodman, Charles E. SC Hvy.Arty. 15th (Lucas') Bn. Co.C
Rodman, Charles E. SC Arty. Childs' Co.
Rodman, Charles E. SC Arty. Lee's Co.
Rodman, E.M. Gen. & Staff Chap.
Rodman, Hardy NC 2nd Inf. Co.K
Rodman, H.M. TX 12th Cav. Co.A
Rodman, J.C. AR 10th Inf. Co.D
Rodman, J.F. AR 5th Inf. Co.I
Rodman, J.L. AR 27th Inf. Co.G Capt.
Rodman, John F. AR 25th Inf. Co.I
Rodman, John F. NC 5th Inf. Co.E,K 1st Sgt.
Rodman, Pearson VA 41st Inf. Co.G
Rodman, Robert C. VA 9th Inf. Co.K
Rodman, Thomas AR Cav. Wright's Regt. Co.B
Rodman, Thomas AR 9th Inf. Co.K
Rodman, Thomas J. LA Cav. Cole's Co.
Rodman, T.J. TN 7th (Duckworth's) Cav. Co.F
Rodman, T.W. TN 22nd (Barteau's) Cav. Co.H
Rodman, W.D. MS 22nd Inf. Co.C Capt.
Rodman, Will B. Anderson's Corps Col.
Rodman, William MS 33rd Inf. Co.H
Rodman, William B. NC 3rd Arty. (40th St.Troops) Co.C Capt.
Rodman, William D. MS 1st (Johnston's) Inf. Co.A Sgt.Maj.
Rodman, William H. MO Cav. Wood's Regt. Co.K
Rodman, William J. TX Cav. Martin's Regt. Co.K
Rodmand, B.B. AR 36th Inf. Co.K
Rodmann, Michael LA 28th (Thomas') Inf. Co.D
Rodmend, Thomas MS 3rd Inf. Co.H
Rodmon, Steven D. AR 27th Inf. New Co.B, Co.G Sgt.
Rodmon, Thomas AR 2nd Cav.
Rodmond, --- TN 21st & 22nd (Cons.) Cav. Co.C
Rodney, A.P. MS Wilkinson Cty. Minute Men Harris' Co. 3rd Lt.
Rodney, Atchison VA 33rd Inf. Co.E
Rodney, J. GA 32nd Inf. Co.K
Rodney, J.F. GA Lt.Arty. Howell's Co.
Rodney, J.M. LA Lt.Arty. 2nd Field Btty.
Rodney, J.M. MO Inf. 1st Bn. Co.C
Rodney, Jno. C. MO 6th Inf. Co.K 2nd Lt.
Rodney, John M. MO 6th Inf. Co.K
Rodney, John P. MO 6th Inf. Co.K Lt.
Rodney, J.P. MO Inf. 1st Bn. Co.C
Rodney, Louis L. MO 8th Cav. Co.B,F
Rodney, M. LA 8th Inf. Co.D
Rodney, Michael LA 28th (Thomas') Inf. Co.D,G
Rodney, M.V. MO Inf. 5th Regt.St.Guard Co.D
Rodney, Thomas MO Lt.Arty. 1st Btty.
Rodney, Thomas MO Inf. 5th Regt.St.Guard Co.D Ord.Sgt.
Rodney, Thomas MO 6th Inf. Co.D
Rodolph, F. TX 21st Cav. Co.E
Rodolph, John LA 20th Inf. Co.A Music.

Rodolph, John S. AL Montgomery Lt.Arty.
Rodomel, George TX 13th Vol. 1st Co.H
Rodrecus, Jose M. TX 18th Cav. Co.D
Rodregues, Remond LA Res.Corps
Rodrey, J.B. MS 28th Cav. Co.C
Rodrey, J.G. AR 18th (Marmaduke's) Inf. Co.F
Rodrick, John R. VA Mil. 55th Regt. Co.C
Rodrico, Emanuel AR 2nd Cav. Co.C
Rodridge, George AR 1st Mtd.Rifles Co.F
  Bugler
Rodriges, Antone Conf.Inf. Tucker's Regt. Co.D
Rodriges, E. TX Cav. Benavides' Regt. Co.G
Rodriges, Jose Ma. TX Cav. Benavides' Regt.
  Co.E Cpl.
Rodriges, Mariano TX Cav. Benavides' Regt.
  Co.E Sgt.
Rodriges, Rafal TX Cav. Benavides' Regt. Co.A
Rodrigez, F. GA Lt.Arty. Ritter's Co.
Rodrignez, Theo. LA 2nd Cav. Co.H
Rodrigo, Charles Conf.Reg.Inf. Brooks' Bn.
  Co.D
Rodriguas, E. TX Inf. 24th Bn. (St.Troops)
Rodrigue, David LA 18th Inf. Co.E
Rodrigue, Dupreville LA 30th Inf. Co.H
Rodrigue, Edgar LA 30th Inf. Co.G
Rodrigue, Faustin LA 30th Inf. Co.G
Rodrigue, Honorat LA 30th Inf. Co.G Sgt.
Rodrigue, Louis LA 26th Inf. Co.D
Rodrigue, M. LA Mil. 2nd Regt. 2nd Brig. 1st
  Div. Co.F
Rodrigue, Obtime LA 30th Inf. Co.G
Rodrigue, T.V. LA Inf.Cons. 18th Regt. & Yel-
  low Jacket Bn. Co.F
Rodrigue, Ursin LA 18th Inf. Co.E
Rodrigues, A.B. TX 15th Field Btty.
Rodrigues, Anto. LA Mil. 5th Regt.Eur.Brig.
  (Spanish Regt.) Co.4 Music.
Rodrigues, Checacio TX 2nd Cav. Co.B
Rodrigues, D. LA Mil. Chalmette Regt. Co.K
Rodrigues, Damacio TX Cav. Ragsdale's Bn.
  Co.B
Rodrigues, Eugene LA Mil. St.James Regt. Co.F
Rodrigues, Felix MS 3rd Inf. Co.A
Rodrigues, Francisco TX Cav. Ragsdale's Bn.
  Co.B
Rodrigues, Frank TX 26th Cav. Co.A 1st Bugler
Rodrigues, J. LA Mil.Cont.Cadets
Rodrigues, J.C. 14th Conf.Cav. Co.G
Rodrigues, Jose AZ Cav. Herbert's Bn. Oury's
  Co.
Rodrigues, Jose LA Mil. 5th Regt.Eur.Brig.
  (Spanish Regt.) Co.A,2,3,10
Rodrigues, Joseph LA Inf. 10th Bn. Co.E
Rodrigues, Joseph 14th Conf.Cav. Co.G Cpl.
Rodrigues, Juan TX 3rd Inf. 1st Co.C Recruit
Rodrigues, Manuel TX 8th Inf. Co.C
Rodrigues, Miguel TX 2nd Cav. Co.B
Rodrigues, N. TX Cav. (Dismtd.) Chisum's
  Regt. Co.B
Rodrigues, Narciso TX 18th Cav. Co.H Cpl.
Rodrigues, Oscar LA Arty. Castellanos' Btty.
  Lt.
Rodrigues, Philip AL 8th Inf. Co.E Cpl.
Rodrigues, R. LA Inf. Pelican Regt. Co.H
Rodrigues, Rafael TX 3rd Inf. Co.D
Rodrigues, Revara TX 8th Inf. Co.I
Rodrigues, Rigardo TX 8th Inf. Co.E

Rodrigues, U. LA Inf.Cons. 18th Regt. & Yellow
  Jacket Bn. Co.B
Rodrigues, Ventura TX Cav. Ragsdale's Bn.
  Co.B
Rodrigues, Victoriano LA Mil. 5th Regt.
  Eur.Brig. (Spanish Regt.) Co.A
Rodrigues, Zenon LA 26th Inf. Co.K Cpl.
Rodriguez, A. Conf.Lt.Arty. Richardson's Bn.
  Co.B
Rodriguez, Adam LA Arty. Landry's Co.
  (Donaldsonville Arty.)
Rodriguez, Alcario TX 8th Inf. Co.C
Rodriguez, Anastacio TX 8th Inf. Co.C
Rodriguez, Andreas TX 8th Inf. Co.C
Rodriguez, Antonio TX 3rd Inf. 1st Co.C
Rodriguez, Auguste LA 30th Inf. Co.D
Rodriguez, Benito TX 8th Field Btty.
Rodriguez, Berdo. LA Mil. 5th Regt.Eur.Brig.
  (Spanish Regt.) Co.8 3rd Lt.
Rodriguez, Cayetanio TX 3rd Inf. 1st Co.C
Rodriguez, Cesario TX 33rd Cav. 1st Co.I
Rodriguez, Cesario TX Cav. Benavides' Regt.
  Co.B Cpl.
Rodriguez, Charles Conf.Reg.Inf. Brooks' Bn.
  Co.D
Rodriguez, Esperion TX 8th Inf. Co.C
Rodriguez, Espinosa TX Cav. Benavides' Regt.
  Co.C
Rodriguez, Evaristo TX 33rd Cav. 1st Co.I
Rodriguez, Francisco TX 3rd Inf. Co.G
Rodriguez, Franco. LA Mil. Cazadores Es-
  panoles Regt. Co.2
Rodriguez, Franco LA Mil. Cazadores Espanoles
  Regt. Co.5
Rodriguez, Guadalupe TX 3rd Inf. 1st Co.C
Rodriguez, Gumecindo TX 8th Inf. Co.H Cpl.
Rodriguez, Isidro TX 3rd Inf. Co.F
Rodriguez, Jesus TX 33rd Cav. 1st Co.I
Rodriguez, Jesus TX Cav. Benavides' Regt.
  Co.C
Rodriguez, Jesus TX Cav. L. Trevinio's Co. 1st
  Sgt.
Rodriguez, Jesus TX 3rd Inf. 1st Co.C
Rodriguez, Jesus TX 3rd Inf. Co.F
Rodriguez, Jesus TX 3rd Inf. Co.H Music.
Rodriguez, Jesus TX 8th Inf. Co.C Cpl.
Rodriguez, Jose LA 30th Inf. Co.D
Rodriguez, Jose TX 2nd Cav. Co.B
Rodriguez, Jose Ma. TX 8th Inf. Co.C Cpl.
Rodriguez, Jose Ma. TX 8th Inf. Co.H
Rodriguez, Jose Maria TX 3rd Inf. Co.F 1st Sgt.
Rodriguez, Joseph LA 7th Inf. Co.B
Rodriguez, Joseph LA Conscr.
Rodriguez, Juan TX Cav. 3rd (Yager's) Bn.
  Rhodes' Co. Sgt.
Rodriguez, Juan TX 8th Inf. Co.C
Rodriguez, Juan Antonio LA 30th Inf. Co.D
Rodriguez, Manuel LA Mil. 5th Regt.Eur.Brig.
  (Spanish Regt.) Co.6
Rodriguez, Marcel 14th Conf.Cav. Co.D
Rodriguez, Mariano TX 8th Inf. Co.H
Rodriguez, Martiniano TX 3rd Inf. Co.F
Rodriguez, Mateo LA Mil. Cazadores Espanoles
  Regt. Co.1
Rodriguez, P. TX Cav. L. Trevinio's Co.
Rodriguez, Pedro TX 3rd Inf. 1st Co.C
Rodriguez, Rafael TX 33rd Cav. 1st Co.H

Rodriguez, Ramon LA Mil. 5th Regt.Eur.Brig.
  (Spanish Regt.) Co.6
Rodriguez, Raymond LA 8th Inf. Co.G
Rodriguez, S. TX St.Troops Teel's Co.
Rodriguez, Salvador TX 8th Inf. Co.C
Rodriguez, Thomas LA 30th Inf. Co.D
Rodriguez, Thomas A. TX Cav. Benavides'
  Regt. Capt.
Rodriguez, Thomas A. TX 8th Inf. Co.H 2nd
  Lt.
Rodriguez, Timoteo TX Cav. Benavides' Regt.
  Co.B
Rodriguez, William GA 1st (Olmstead's) Inf.
  Gordon's Co.
Rodriguez, William GA 63rd Inf. Co.B,D
Rodriguez, Ysabel TX 8th Inf. Co.H
Rodrigus, Frank TX 1st Hvy.Arty. Co.E
Rodrigus, Roque TX 33rd Cav. 1st Co.I
Rodrique, D.L. LA 27th Inf. Co.K
Rodrique, Philip LA 18th Inf.
Rodrique, T.V. LA 18th Inf. Co.F
Rodriques, Andrew LA 1st Hvy.Arty. (Reg.)
  Co.D
Rodriques, J. LA Mil. 5th Regt.Eur.Brig.
  (Spanish Regt.) Co.1
Rodriques, J.A. LA Ogden's Cav. Co.C Cpl.
Rodriques, John LA Mil. LaFourche Regt.
Rodriques, Raphael LA Mil. LaFourche Regt.
Rodriquez, J. TX Cav. L. Trevinio's Co.
Rodriquez, Juan TX Cav. Benavides' Regt. Co.C
Rodriquez, Marcel LA Ogden's Cav. Co.A
Rodriquez, P. LA Inf.Crescent Regt. Co.A
Rodriquez, Prudencio LA Mil. 5th Regt.
  Eur.Brig. (Spanish Regt.) Co.3 Sgt.
Rodriquez, R. LA Inf.Crescent Regt. Co.A
Rodriquez, S. TX Cav. L. Trevinio's Co.
Rodriquez, Thomas TX Cav. Benavides' Regt.
  Co.D
Rodriques, Trinidad TX Cav. Benavides' Regt.
  Co.I
Rodruff, J.H. NC 3rd Jr.Res. Co.B Sgt.
Rodsdale, J. TN 18th Inf. Co.I
Rodsore, F. LA 30th Inf.
Rodt, Martin H. SC 17th Inf. Co.G,I 1st Lt.
Rodt, M.H. SC 1st (Hagood's) Inf. 1st Co.I
Rodus, J.G. SC 4th St.Troops Co.D
Rodus, J.J. LA 26th Inf. Co.G
Rodus, T.H. AL 9th Inf. Co.F
Rodwell, Joseph L. NC 43rd Inf. Co.G
Rodwell, T.D. NC 1st Cav. (9th St.Troops) Co.E
Rodwell, Thomas D. NC 12th Inf. Co.C
Rodwell, Thomas H. AL 51st (Part.Rangers)
  Co.G
Rodwell, Thomas H. MS Cav. 4th Bn. Sykes'
  Co.
Rodwell, Thomas H. 8th (Wade's) Conf.Cav.
  Co.G
Rodwell, William H. GA 66th Inf. Co.K
Rody, C.E. GA 42nd Inf. Co.C
Rody, David VA Cav. Hounshell's Bn. Thur-
  man's Co.
Rody, G. SC 1st Mtd.Mil. Christopher's Co.
Rody, George W. TN 1st (Turney's) Inf. Co.A
Rody, Lee W. TN Inf. 1st Bn. (Colms') Co.A
Rody, William L. TN Inf. 1st Bn. (Colms') Co.A
Roe, Abraham SC 5th Mil. Beat Co.3

Roe, Absalom T. NC 3rd Arty. (40th St.Troops)
  Co.B
Roe, Absolom SC Inf. 7th Bn. (Enfield Rifles)
  Co.D
Roe, Albert TN 19th Inf. Co.B
Roe, Alfred TX 27th Cav. Co.A
Roe, Allen TX 19th Cav. Co.A
Roe, Amos B. SC Inf. 9th Bn. Co.D
Roe, Amos B. SC 26th Inf. Co.E Cpl.
Roe, Andrew A. GA 40th Inf. Co.D Sgt.
Roe, Andrew J. AL 55th Vol.
Roe, Anthony E. VA Lt.Arty. 12th Bn. 2nd
  Co.A
Roe, Anthony E. VA Lt.Arty. Sturdivant's Co.
Roe, Ben VA Mil. Washington Cty.
Roe, Benjamin NC 47th Inf. Co.D
Roe, Benjamin F. Horse Arty. White's Btty.
Roe, Benjamin H. VA 63rd Inf. Co.F
Roe, Benjamin J. VA 37th Inf. Co.F
Roe, Benjamin J. VA 63rd Inf. Co.F
Roe, Benjamin T. KY 2nd (Duke's) Cav. Co.C
Roe, Ben. T. TN 4th (McLemore's) Cav. Co.G
Roe, Berry GA Cav. 1st Gordon Squad.
  (St.Guards) Co.A
Roe, B.F. AL 12th Inf. Co.E
Roe, B.F. TN 47th Inf. Co.F 1st Lt.
Roe, B.F. 3rd Conf.Cav. Co.A
Roe, Bony GA 29th Inf. Co.G
Roe, Carter SC 2nd Rifles Co.E
Roe, C.G. AR 30th Inf. Co.I
Roe, Charles A. NC 2nd Bn.Loc.Def.Troops
  Co.B Music.
Roe, Charles Y. AL Lt.Arty. Goldthwaite's Btty.
  Sgt.
Roe, C.J. AR 19th (Dawson's) Inf. Co.B
Roe, Columbus B. GA 36th (Broyles') Inf. Co.L
Roe, C.W.G. GA 15th Inf. Co.H Cpl.
Roe, Daniel LA 15th Inf. Co.F Sgt.
Roe, David GA 24th Inf. Co.C
Roe, David KY 10th Cav. Co.C
Roe, David VA Horse Arty. D. Shanks' Co.
Roe, David S. NC 4th Inf. Co.I
Roe, D.D. KY 4th Mtd.Inf.
Roe, D.J. AL 7th Cav. Co.G
Roe, D.J. GA Cav. Russell's Co. 1st Sgt.
Roe, D.R. VA Lt.Arty. Barr's Co.
Roe, Edward GA 1st (Olmstead's) Inf. Co.A
Roe, Edward LA 22nd Inf. Jones' Co.
Roe, Edward LA Inf.Crescent Regt. Co.C
Roe, Edward LA Inf.Cons.Crescent Regt. Co.G
Roe, Edward SC 4th St.Troops Co.G
Roe, Edward TX Arty. Douglas' Co.
Roe, Edward T. LA 5th Cav. Co.E
Roe, Edward W. VA 37th Inf. Co.H
Roe, E.J. TX 22nd Inf. Co.F
Roe, Elisha VA 37th Inf. Co.B
Roe, Elisha VA 63rd Inf. Co.E
Roe, Ezekiel GA 50th Inf. Co.I
Roe, F.M. AR 45th Cav. Co.C
Roe, F.M. AR 38th Inf. Co.B
Roe, Francis M. TX 12th Cav. Co.D,I
Roe, Fred GA 5th Cav. Co.K
Roe, Frederic GA Cav. 1st Bn. Hopkins' Co.
Roe, F.W. AR 1st Vol. Co.E
Roe, Gaston NC 8th Bn.Part.Rangers Co.D,E
Roe, Gaston NC 66th Inf. Co.H
Roe, G.E. AL 6th Inf.

Roe, George SC 7th Inf. Co.K
Roe, George VA 6th Inf.
Roe, George C. LA 31st Inf. Co.G
Roe, George R. NC 4th Inf. Co.I
Roe, George W. GA 26th Inf. Co.B
Roe, George W. NC 4th Inf. Co.I
Roe, George W. VA 12th Cav. Co.D Black.
Roe, G.J. MS 5th Inf. Co.D
Roe, G.T. 8th (Wade's) Conf.Cav. Co.D
Roe, H. AR 30th Inf. Co.K
Roe, H. GA 5th Res. Co.A
Roe, H. LA Inf.Cons.Crescent Regt. Co.O
Roe, H. VA Cav. Swann's Bn. Vincent's Co.
Roe, H.D. SC 2nd Inf. Co.B
Roe, Hiram VA 51st Mil. Co.D
Roe, Hiram C. MS Lt.Arty. (Brookhaven
  Lt.Arty.) Hoskins' Btty.
Roe, Hough J. SC 1st Arty. Co.A
Roe, Isaac T. TN Lt.Arty. Barry's Co.
Roe, J. AL Cp. of Instr. Talladega
Roe, J. SC Manigault's Bn.Vol. Co.C
Roe, J. TN 42nd Inf. 2nd Co.E
Roe, J.A. GA 13th Inf. Co.G
Roe, J.A. GA 19th Inf. Co.K Capt.
Roe, J.A. TX 22nd Inf. Co.F
Roe, Jackson SC 14th Inf. Co.B
Roe, James AL 42nd Inf. Co.K
Roe, James GA 10th Inf. Co.A
Roe, James GA Cherokee Legion (St.Guards)
  Co.I
Roe, James MO 10th Inf. Co.G
Roe, James SC 1st Arty. Co.C
Roe, James TN Lt.Arty. Barry's Co.
Roe, James VA 115th Mil. Co.B
Roe, James VA Inf. Mileham's Co.
Roe, James B. AR 13th Inf. Co.I
Roe, James D. TX Cav. Baylor's Regt. Co.D
Roe, James E. FL Inf. 2nd Bn. Co.B
Roe, James E. FL 10th Inf. Co.G
Roe, James H. AL 19th Inf. Co.H
Roe, J.B. MS 15th Cav. Co.F
Roe, J.B. TN 9th Inf. Co.K
Roe, J.C. TN 12th Inf. Co.K Jr.2nd Lt.
Roe, J.C. VA 17th Cav. Co.G
Roe, J.E. GA Detailed Banks Cty. Tanney
Roe, Jesse M. GA 19th Inf. Co.K
Roe, J.G. AL 1st Cav. 1st Co.K
Roe, J.H. GA 13th Inf. Co.G
Roe, J.J. AL 12th Cav. Co.G
Roe, J.J. GA 23rd Inf. Co.D
Roe, J.L. GA 19th Inf. Co.K
Roe, J.M. GA Inf. Arsenal Bn. (Columbus) Co.A
Roe, J.O. VA 30th Bn.S.S. Co.E
Roe, John AL 48th Inf. Co.H Cpl.
Roe, John AL 55th Vol. Co.B
Roe, John AZ Cav. Herbert's Bn. Oury's Co.
Roe, John FL 8th Inf. Co.F
Roe, John FL 10th Inf. Co.E
Roe, John GA 1st (Olmstead's) Inf. Co.A
Roe, John GA 50th Inf. Co.I
Roe, John MS 22nd Inf. Co.C Cpl.
Roe, John SC 1st Arty. Co.K
Roe, John SC 2nd Inf. Co.G
Roe, John VA Tuttle's Bn.Loc.Def. Co.A 1st
  Sgt.
Roe, John E. GA 43rd Inf. Co.D 1st Lt.
Roe, John F. TX Cav. Baylor's Regt. Co.D

Roe, John G. NC 4th Inf. Co.I
Roe, John K. AL 48th Inf. Co.E
Roe, John O. TN 3rd (Lillard's) Mtd.Inf. Co.F
  Sgt.
Roe, John T. MS Inf. 3rd Bn. (St.Troops) Co.A
Roe, John W. AL 36th Inf. Co.F
Roe, John W. GA 36th (Broyles') Inf. Co.L,F
Roe, Josiah GA 50th Inf. Co.I
Roe, Jourdane GA 50th Inf. Co.I
Roe, J.P. TX Cav. Terry's Regt. Co.K
Roe, J.P. TX 4th Inf. (St.Troops) Co.D
Roe, J.T. MS 8th Cav. Co.F
Roe, K. VA Cav. Swann's Bn. Vincent's Co.
Roe, Lawrence SC 7th Inf. Co.E
Roe, Leander C. TN 12th (Cons.) Inf. Co.C
Roe, Leander C. TN 22nd Inf. Co.A
Roe, Martin TX 1st Bn.S.S. Co.D
Roe, Matthew GA 50th Inf. Co.I
Roe, M.G. MS 46th Inf. Co.F Cpl.
Roe, Noah GA 1st (Olmstead's) Inf. Co.C
Roe, Noah GA 54th Inf. Co.E
Roe, Noah D. NC 4th Inf. Co.I
Roe, P. LA 3rd Inf. Co.E Cpl.
Roe, Patrick LA 6th Inf. Co.F
Roe, Patrick LA 16th Inf. Co.H
Roe, Peter FL Inf. 2nd Bn. Co.B
Roe, Peter FL 10th Inf. Co.G
Roe, Pleasant LA 12th Inf. Co.D
Roe, Pleasant LA Res.Corps Sgt.
Roe, Pleasant B. TN Hvy.Arty. Caruthers' Btty.
  Jr.1st Lt.
Roe, R. VA Mil. Washington Cty.
Roe, R.A. TN 12th (Green's) Cav. Co.G
Roe, R.A. TN Cav. Nixon's Regt. Co.D
Roe, R.A. TN 47th Inf. Co.F
Roe, Richard GA 22nd Inf. Co.E
Roe, Richard GA 54th Inf. Co.C
Roe, Richard SC Lt.Arty. 3rd (Palmetto) Bn.
  Co.F
Roe, Robert H. VA 5th Cav. (12 mo. '61-2)
  Winfield's Co.
Roe, Robert S. VA 63rd Inf. Co.F
Roe, Robert W. VA 13th Cav. Co.D
Roe, Rowan GA Cav. 1st Bn. Hopkins' Co.
Roe, Rowan GA 5th Cav. Co.K
Roe, Samuel MD 1st Cav. Co.E Sgt.
Roe, Samuel TN 7th (Duckworth's) Cav. Co.I
Roe, Samuel TN 4th Inf. Co.I
Roe, Samuel B. GA 50th Inf. Co.E
Roe, Samuel B. VA 40th Inf. Co.E Cpl.
Roe, Samuel L. GA 15th Inf. Co.H Cpl.
Roe, Shadrick LA 9th Inf. Co.A
Roe, Sidney M. VA 6th Bn.Res. Co.I
Roe, S.M. TX 12th Cav. Co.D
Roe, Soloman TX Inf. 2nd St.Troops Co.H
Roe, Solomon AL 48th Inf. Co.H
Roe, T. TX 4th Cav. Co.F
Roe, T. TX 15th Field Btty.
Roe, Taylor AL 34th Inf. Co.H
Roe, T.G. AL 1st Inf. Co.C
Roe, Thomas MO Inf. 5th Regt.St.Guard Co.F
Roe, Thomas E. GA Inf. 26th Bn. Co.A Sgt.
Roe, Thomas J. VA 37th Inf. Co.H
Roe, Thomas N. SC 26th Inf. Co.E
Roe, T.S. MS 6th Cav. Co.F
Roe, T.T. LA Mil. British Guard Bn. Burrowes'
  Co.

Roe, W. MO 5th Cav. Co.K
Roe, W. TX Cav. Bourland's Regt. Co.K
Roe, Wallace GA 1st (Olmstead's) Inf. Co.C
Roe, W.C. TX 4th Inf. (St.Troops) Co.E
Roe, W.F. AL Cav. 5th Bn. Hilliard's Legion Co.E
Roe, W.F. SC Manigault's Bn.Vol. Co.C
Roe, W.G. TN Co.G
Roe, Wiley TN Cav. 12th Bn. (Day's) Co.C
Roe, William AL 48th Inf. Co.H
Roe, William MS 1st Lt.Arty. Co.L,E
Roe, William MO 5th Inf. Co.F
Roe, William NC 2nd Inf. Co.B
Roe, William TX 20th Cav. Co.D,C
Roe, William VA 15th Cav. Co.B
Roe, William VA Arty. Wise Legion
Roe, William VA 48th Inf. Co.D
Roe, William H. VA 40th Inf. Co.A
Roe, William P. AL 27th Inf. Co.E
Roe, William R. GA 36th (Broyles') Inf. Co.L
Roe, Williams AR Lt.Arty. 5th Btty.
Roe, Wilson SC Lt.Arty. 3rd (Palmetto) Bn. Co.F
Roe, W.J. TN 1st Hvy.Arty. 1st Co.C, 2nd Co.A
Roeber, A. TX 5th Field Btty.
Roeber, A. TX 3rd Inf. 2nd Co.A
Roeber, A. TX Inf. 4th Bn. (Oswald's) Co.A
Roeber, Achilles TX 5th Field Btty.
Roeblitz, A. SC Mil.Arty. 1st Regt. Harms' Co.
Roeblitz, A. SC Arty. Melchers' Co. (Co.B,German Arty.)
Roebuck, A.H. GA 1st (Fannin's) Res. Co.D Sgt.
Roebuck, A.J. AL 8th (Hatch's) Cav. Co.A
Roebuck, A.J. MS 37th Inf. Co.I
Roebuck, Andrew J. FL Cav. (Marianna Drag.) Smith's Co.
Roebuck, Andrew J. 15th Conf.Cav. Co.B
Roebuck, A.W. AL 5th Cav. Co.G
Roebuck, Benjamin 1st Choctaw & Chickasaw Mtd.Rifles Maytubby's Co.
Roebuck, Eppy W. MS 3rd (St.Troops) Cav. Co.B Sgt.
Roebuck, George L. NC 33rd Inf. Co.B
Roebuck, George W. AL 2nd Cav. Co.I
Roebuck, George W. MO Cav. Poindexter's Regt.
Roebuck, G.W. AL 62nd Inf. Co.I Sgt.
Roebuck, Henry A. GA Cobb's Legion Co.C
Roebuck, H.L. NC 1st Inf. Co.H
Roebuck, Hylary FL 10th Inf. Co.B
Roebuck, James FL Cav. (Marianna Drag.) Smith's Co.
Roebuck, James FL Campbellton Boys
Roebuck, James A. AL 8th Cav. Co.H
Roebuck, James A. AL 10th Inf. Co.B
Roebuck, James A. AL Cp. of Instr. Talladega
Roebuck, James H. FL 5th Inf. Co.F Music.
Roebuck, James H. GA 24th Inf. Co.B
Roebuck, James V. SC 1st (McCreary's) Inf. Co.B Cpl.
Roebuck, James Z. GA 1st (Ramsey's) Inf. Co.D
Roebuck, James Z. GA 63rd Inf. Co.A
Roebuck, J.H. AL 2nd Cav. Co.D
Roebuck, John R. FL 8th Inf. Co.C
Roebuck, J.P. AL 2nd Cav. Co.D
Roebuck, J.S. MS 1st Cav. Co.F Sgt.

Roebuck, J.T. FL 10th Inf. Co.E
Roebuck, J.Z. GA Lt.Arty. 12th Bn. 1st Co.A
Roebuck, K. MS 3rd Inf. (St.Troops) Co.K
Roebuck, P.T.A. GA 5th Res. Co.I Sgt.
Roebuck, R. TX 6th Inf. Co.C
Roebuck, Robert AL 62nd Inf. Co.D
Roebuck, Robert C.C. GA 15th Inf. Co.F
Roebuck, R.W. GA Inf. 2nd Bn. (St.Guards) Co.C QMSgt.
Roebuck, Samuel H. NC 1st Inf. Co.H Cpl.
Roebuck, Simon NC 17th Inf. (2nd Org.) Co.H
Roebuck, S.N. AL 2nd Cav. Co.G
Roebuck, Thomas L. MO 6th Inf. Co.G
Roebuck, W.E. GA 11th Cav. Co.G
Roebuck, William MS 42nd Inf. Co.K
Roebuck, William 1st Chickasaw Inf. McCord's Co. 1st Sgt.
Roebuck, William L. NC 17th Inf. (2nd Org.) Co.C
Roebuck, William P. SC Inf. Hampton Legion Co.D
Roebuck, William T. FL 8th Inf. Co.E Sgt.
Roebuck, Willis R. FL 10th Inf. Co.B
Roebuck, W.J. MS 8th Inf. Co.B Ens.
Roebuck, Z.J. GA 1st (Ramsey's) Inf. Co.D
Roeckner, H.W. GA 1st (Olmstead's) Inf. Co.I 1st Sgt.
Roedel, J.F. TN Hvy.Arty. Sterling's Co.
Roeder, Charles H. AL Arty. 1st Bn. Co.B
Roeder, H. TX 4th Cav. Co.G
Roeder, J. TX Lt.Arty. Dege's Bn.
Roeder, Jacob TX 6th Field Btty.
Roeder, L. LA Mil. 4th Regt.Eur.Brig. Co.C
Roeder, Ludwig Van TX 4th Cav. Co.C 1st Lt.
Roeder, L. Van TX St.Troops Hampton's Co. Sgt.
Roeder, O.W. TX St.Troops Hampton's Co.
Roeder, W.H. AR 31st Inf. Co.E Sgt.
Roehin, A.W. TN Arty. Stewart's Co.
Roehl, H. LA Mil. 4th Regt.Eur.Brig. Co.C 3rd Lt.
Roehl, Robert TX Arty. 4th Bn. Co.B
Roehl, Robert TX 8th Inf. Co.B
Roellnits, J.R. Gen. & Staff AASurg.
Roemer, Adolph AL Arty. 1st Bn. Co.F
Roemer, Bernard VA Arty. Wise Legion Capt.
Roemer, Bernard Gen. & Staff Surg.
Roemer, C.G. TX Inf. 1st St.Troops Shields' Co.B
Roemer, Charles LA Mil. German Guards Capt.
Roemer, E.F. AL 60th Inf. Co.F Cpl.
Roemer, E.F. AL 1st Bn. Hilliard's Legion Vol. Co.A Cpl.
Roemer, T.J.B. Gen. & Staff Surg.
Roemis, John Conf.Inf. 8th Bn.
Roemmell, Henry TX 6th Inf. Co.E
Roempke, A.F. SC Mil.Arty. 1st Regt. Tupper's Co.
Roen, John AR 35th Inf. Old Co.F
Roensly, --- TX Cav. Good's Bn. Co.B
Roeoe, David 1st Cherokee Mtd.Rifles Co.A
Roeper, Jacob TX QM Dept.
Roerth, C.J. TX Cav. Benavides' Regt. Co.F
Roesch, Charles TX 4th Cav. Co.C
Roesch, Louis LA Washington Arty.Bn. Co.2,4
Roesel, August GA 36th (Villepigue's) Inf. Co.F
Roesel, August 1st Conf.Inf. 1st Co.F

Roesel, Herman GA Cobb's Legion Co.H
Roeser, George LA 20th Inf. Old Co.B
Roesh, J. AL Mil. 4th Vol. Co.G
Roesh, Joseph LA 21st (Kennedy's) Inf. Co.C
Roesing, Ernest G. TX Cav. 8th (Taylor's) Bn. Co.C
Roesing, Ernst TX 1st (Yager's) Cav. Co.E 1st Sgt.
Roessler, Julius NC 13th Inf. Co.F Capt.
Roestel, Julius LA 21st (Patton's) Inf. Co.H Sgt.
Roeth, Conrad VA 15th Inf. Co.K
Roeve, Ambrose MS Inf. 111th Regt. Co.D
Roever, William B. TX 17th Inf. Co.H Sr.2nd Lt.
Rofe, John GA 2nd Mil. Co.D
Rofer, W.J. TX 6th Cav. Co.A
Roff, A. TX Cav. Bourland's Regt. Co.A
Roff, Alvin B. TX 11th Cav. Co.A
Roff, C.L. TX Cav. Bourland's Regt. Co.A Maj.
Roff, Edmund G. MS 21st Inf. Co.F
Roff, Edward G. GA 3rd Cav. Co.A
Roff, Freeman T. GA 2nd Cav. Co.A
Roff, F.S. TX 21st Cav. Co.F
Roff, F.T. GA Hvy.Arty. 22nd Bn. Co.D
Roff, H.J. AL 1st Regt. Mobile Vol. Co.E
Roff, James KY 9th Cav. Co.H
Roff, James F. KY 14th Cav. Co.D
Roff, J.E. AL Talladega Cty.Res. R.N. Ware's Cav.Co.
Roff, J.O. MS 34th Inf. Co.G
Roff, J.T. GA 10th Inf. Co.B
Roff, Michael F.B. GA 10th Inf. Co.B 2nd Lt.
Roff, N.B. MO 2nd Cav. Co.I Capt.
Roff, N.B. TX 5th Cav. Co.E
Roff, N.B. TX 12th Field Btty.
Roff, N.B. TX Waul's Legion Co.G Capt.
Roff, N.B. Exch.Bn. 1st Co.B,CSA Capt.
Roff, S.F. AL 62nd Inf. Co.H,D
Roff, Thomas GA 10th Inf. Co.K
Roff, William TX 17th Inf. Co.C
Roffe, Charles S. VA 38th Inf. Co.G
Roffe, Edward E. VA 38th Inf. Co.G
Roffe, J.A.J. MS 7th Cav. Co.A Cpl.
Roffe, James KY 12th Cav. Co.A Cpl.
Roffe, J.C. TN 31st Inf. Co.K
Roffe, John VA 34th Inf. Co.B
Roffe, John R. VA 41st Inf. 2nd Co.E
Roffe, Lewis J. VA 38th Inf. Co.G Cpl.
Roffe, Thomas VA 22nd Inf. Co.H
Roffe, Thomas L. TX 14th Cav. Co.C
Roffe, W. TN 5th Inf. 2nd Co.K
Roffe, W.F. TN 31st Inf. Co.K
Roffe, William VA 22nd Inf. Co.H
Roffe, William S. VA 3rd Inf. Co.C
Roffey, Henry TX 2nd Inf. Co.C
Roffield, J.A. MS 3rd Cav. Co.C
Roffrey, Volcey LA Inf. 16th Bn. (Conf.Guards Resp.Bn.) Co.B
Roffy, Harvey VA 14th Mil. Co.D
Roftery, Thomas LA 10th Inf. Co.H
Rogan, Alex TN 9th (Ward's) Cav. Co.I
Rogan, Amos L. AL 4th Inf. Co.A
Rogan, Andrew AL 5th Cav. Co.L
Rogan, C.B. TN Inf. 4th Cons.Regt. Co.I 1st Lt.
Rogan, C.F. AR Lt.Arty. 5th Btty. Cpl.

Rogan, Charles B. TN 2nd (Robison's) Inf. Co.K
  1st Lt.
Rogan, D. GA 19th Inf. Co.B Cpl.
Rogan, Daniel J. AL 53rd (Part.Rangers) Co.D
Rogan, David NC 35th Inf. Co.E
Rogan, Ed. TN 6th (Wheeler's) Cav. Co.G
Rogan, Edgar H. TX 17th Inf. Co.K Sr.2nd Lt.
Rogan, Edward TN 63rd Inf. Co.D
Rogan, George W. AL 44th Inf. Co.D Cpl.
Rogan, James TN 3rd (Forrest's) Cav. Co.D
Rogan, James TX 1st Hvy.Arty. Co.D
Rogan, James A. TN Cav. 12th Bn. (Day's)
  Co.A Cpl.
Rogan, James W. AR 30th Inf. Col.
Rogan, John KY 3rd Cav. Capt.
Rogan, John LA 10th Inf. Co.C
Rogan, John TX 1st Field Btty. Cpl.
Rogan, John M. TN 2nd (Robison's) Inf. Co.K
Rogan, John N. TX 17th Inf. Co.A
Rogan, John W. TN Cav. 12th Bn. (Day's) Co.A
  1st Lt.
Rogan, J.W. TN 15th Inf. Co.C Capt.
Rogan, Lafayette MS 34th Inf. Co.B 2nd Lt.
Rogan, L.C. GA Inf. Hull's Co.
Rogan, Leonidas TX 26th Cav. Co.B QMSgt.
Rogan, L.H. MS 2nd (Davidson's) Inf. Co.C
Rogan, L.H. MS 34th Inf. Co.B
Rogan, Lloyd W. MS 18th Inf. Co.H
Rogan, L.W. Conf.Cav. Wood's Regt. Co.L
Rogan, M. GA 3rd Bn. (St.Guards) Co.A
Rogan, Norman TN Cav. 12th Bn. (Day's) Co.E
Rogan, Owen AL 5th Inf. New Co.F
Rogan, Pat. MO St.Guard
Rogan, R. TX 24th Cav. Co.F
Rogan, Richard C. AL 10th Inf. Co.D Capt.
Rogan, Thomas Conf.Inf. 1st Bn. Co.I
Rogan, Thomas G. MS 18th Inf. Co.H
Rogan, T.J. GA 38th Inf. Co.B
Rogan, William MS 3rd (St.Troops) Cav. Co.C
Rogan, William TN 9th (Ward's) Cav. Co.G
Rogan, William W. GA 56th Inf. Co.C
Rogan, W.R. TN 30th Inf. Co.C
Rogannie, W.S. VA 2nd Inf.Loc.Def. Co.D
Rogannie, W.S. VA Inf. 6th Bn.Loc.Def. Co.A
Roge, J. TX 1st Hvy.Arty. Co.G
Roge, Nicolas LA Mil. 1st Regt. French Brig.
  Co.6
Rogelat, Alfred LA 26th Inf.
Rogen, R. MS Cav. 1st Bn. (McNair's)
  St.Troops Co.E
Rogen, S.T. LA 2nd Cav. Co.E
Rogens, F.M. 1st Chickasaw Inf. Kesner's Co.
Roger, --- LA 30th Inf. Co.H 1st Lt.
Roger, --- LA 30th Inf. Co.I 1st Lt.
Roger, Adrien LA 4th Inf. Co.E
Roger, Alexander LA 26th Inf. Co.F
Roger, Augustin LA 26th Inf. Co.D
Roger, B.T. MO 5th Inf. Co.H Sgt.
Roger, E. LA Mil. 1st Regt. French Brig. Co.1
  1st Lt.
Roger, E.E. AL 7th Cav. Co.I
Roger, Francois LA 18th Inf. Co.G,B
Roger, Francois LA 26th Inf. Co.D
Roger, G.A. LA 26th Inf. Co.I
Roger, Jacob W. AL 13th Inf.
Roger, James MS 42nd Inf. Co.G
Roger, John MO 9th (Elliott's) Cav. Co.B

Roger, John W. TN 23rd Inf. Co.C
Roger, Joseph LA 26th Inf. Co.D
Roger, Joseph H. VA 42nd Inf. Co.H Sgt.
Roger, L. LA Mil. Chalmette Regt. Co.H Jr.2nd
  Lt.
Roger, L. 14th Conf.Cav. Co.H
Roger, Louis LA 30th Inf. Co.A Cpl.
Roger, Maurice Sap. & Min. Gallimard's
  Co.,CSA 2nd Sap.
Roger, M.W. VA 42nd Inf. Co.G Sgt.
Roger, R.C. KY 8th Cav. Co.K Sgt.
Rogero, John FL Inf. 2nd Bn. Co.A
Rogero, Manuel FL 8th Inf. Co.D
Rogero, Manuel H. FL 9th Inf. Co.F 2nd Lt.
Rogers 1st Cherokee Mtd.Rifles Co.D
Rogers, --- AL Lt.Arty. Clanton's Btty.
Rogers, --- TX Cav. Border's Regt. Co.K
Rogers, --- TX Cav. Good's Bn. Co.C
Rogers, --- TX Cav. Good's Bn. Co.D
Rogers, --- TX Cav. Mann's Regt. Co.G Cpl.
Rogers, --- Hill's Staff Lt.
Rogers, A. AL Lt.Arty. Goldthwaite's Btty.
Rogers, A. AL 43rd Inf. Co.C
Rogers, A. AR 2nd Cav. Co.F
Rogers, A. AR 19th (Dawson's) Inf. Co.C
Rogers, A. GA Arty. (Macon Lt.Arty.) Slaten's
  Co.
Rogers, A. KY 9th Cav. Co.A
Rogers, A. MS 1st Cav. Co.E
Rogers, A. MS Cav. 24th Bn. Co.I
Rogers, A. NC 8th Inf. Co.F
Rogers, A., Sr. SC Arty. Manigault's Bn. 1st
  Co.C
Rogers, A. TX 35th (Brown's) Cav. Co.F
Rogers, A. TX Cav. Terry's Regt. Co.A
Rogers, A. VA 8th Inf. Co.D
Rogers, A.A. AR 11th Inf. Co.E
Rogers, A.A. MS Cav. 1st Bn. (McNair's)
  St.Troops Co.A
Rogers, A.A. MS 39th Inf. Co.A Cpl.
Rogers, Aaron NC 28th Inf. Co.K
Rogers, Aaron B. LA 28th (Gray's) Inf. Co.K
Rogers, Aaron P. LA Inf. 11th Bn. Co.D
Rogers, Aaron P. LA Inf.Cons.Crescent Regt.
  Co.B
Rogers, A.B. NC 17th Inf. (2nd Org.) Co.C
Rogers, Abel L. SC 2nd Arty. Co.D
Rogers, Abram D. NC 58th Inf. Co.G
Rogers, Absalom T. MS 3rd (St.Troops) Cav.
  Co.G Cpl.
Rogers, A.C. FL 2nd Cav. Co.H
Rogers, A.C. GA 7th Cav. Co.B Cpl.
Rogers, A.C. GA 6th Inf. (St.Guards) Co.D
Rogers, A.C. TN 2nd (Ashby's) Cav. Co.H
Rogers, A.C. TX 35th (Likens') Cav. Jr.2nd Lt.
Rogers, A.C. TX 7th Inf. Co.B Cpl.
Rogers, A.D. AR 20th Inf. Co.H 1st Lt.
Rogers, A.D. SC Arty. Gregg's Co. (McQueen
  Lt.Arty.)
Rogers, A.D. SC Arty. Manigault's Bn. 1st Co.C
Rogers, A.D. 10th Conf.Cav. Co.D
Rogers, Adam VA 11th Cav. Co.G
Rogers, Adam F. GA 23rd Inf. Co.K
Rogers, A.E. MS 46th Inf. Co.H
Rogers, A.F. AL 45th Inf. Co.F 1st Lt.
Rogers, A.F. FL Cav. 5th Bn. Co.C
Rogers, A.G. GA 12th Cav. Co.L

Rogers, A.G. GA 19th Inf. Co.K
Rogers, A.G. Inf. Bailey's Cons.Regt. Co.A
Rogers, A.G. TX 7th Inf. Co.C
Rogers, A.H. TX 4th Inf. Co.K
Rogers, A.H. TX 14th Inf. Co.F Maj.
Rogers, A.H. Gen. & Staff Lt.,ADC
Rogers, A.J. GA 2nd Inf. Co.I
Rogers, A.J. MS 46th Inf. Co.H
Rogers, A.J. NC 8th Inf. Co.D Maj.
Rogers, A.J. TN 24th Bn.S.S. Co.B Cpl.
Rogers, A.J. TX 21st Inf. Co.K
Rogers, A.J. Gen. & Staff Surg.
Rogers, A.L. GA 1st (Ramsey's) Inf. Co.E
Rogers, A.L. SC 2nd Res.
Rogers, A.L. TX 3rd Cav. Co.G Sgt.Maj.
Rogers, A.L. 2nd Conf.Eng.Troops Co.C Cpl.
Rogers, Albert NC 15th Inf. Co.A Sgt.
Rogers, Albert NC 54th Inf. Co.D 1st Lt.
Rogers, Albert SC 19th Inf. Co.E
Rogers, Albert TN 60th Inf. Co.F
Rogers, Albert VA 5th Cav. 1st Co.F
Rogers, Albert VA 10th Inf. Co.D
Rogers, Albert F. KY 1st Inf. Co.A
Rogers, Albert G. TX Cav. 6th Bn. Co.E Capt.
Rogers, Albert R. TN 28th Inf. Co.G,I
Rogers, Albert T. VA Lt.Arty. Kirkpatrick's Co.
Rogers, Alex AL 42nd Inf. Co.B Sgt.
Rogers, Alex AR 10th Mil. Co.C
Rogers, Alex TX Cav. 2nd Bn.St.Troops Nel-
  son's Co.
Rogers, Alexander AL Inf. 2nd Regt. Co.B
Rogers, Alexander GA 56th Inf. Co.A Sgt.
Rogers, Alexander LA 16th Inf. Co.D
Rogers, Alexander NC 2nd Inf. Co.C
Rogers, Alexander NC 31st Inf. Co.C
Rogers, Alexander NC 33rd Inf. Co.E
Rogers, Alexander SC Arty. Gregg's Co.
  (McQueen Lt.Arty.)
Rogers, Alexander SC Arty. Manigault's Bn. 1st
  Co.C
Rogers, Alexander TN 63rd Inf. Co.I
Rogers, Alexander TX 22nd Inf. Co.C
Rogers, Alexander VA 8th Bn.Res. Co.B
Rogers, Alexander 1st Cherokee Mtd.Rifles Co.C
  Cpl.
Rogers, Alexander R. AR 7th Cav. Co.B
Rogers, Alexander S. SC 1st (Orr's) Rifles Co.C
Rogers, Alfa AR 1st (Crawford's) Cav. Co.E
Rogers, Alfred AR 7th Cav. Co.B
Rogers, Alfred MO 1st N.E. Cav. Co.A
Rogers, Alfred F. KY 2nd Cav. Co.B
Rogers, Alfred M. AR 15th Cav. Co.B,D
Rogers, Allen NC 16th Inf. Co.D
Rogers, Allen NC 47th Inf. Co.E
Rogers, Allen SC 1st (McCreary's) Inf. Co.E
Rogers, Allen SC 8th Inf. Co.I
Rogers, Allen TX 7th Inf. Co.C
Rogers, Allen R. NC 3rd Cav. (41st St.Troops)
  Co.I 2nd Lt.
Rogers, Allen T. NC 29th Inf. Co.E
Rogers, Alphonso B. GA 22nd Inf. Co.B Capt.
Rogers, Alvin LA 4th Cav. Co.E
Rogers, Alvis NC 14th Inf. Co.K
Rogers, A.M. GA 56th Inf. Co.A
Rogers, A.M. GA 63rd Inf. Co.A
Rogers, A.M. LA 28th (Gray's) Inf. Co.B
Rogers, A.M. SC 3rd Inf. Co.G Cpl.

Rogers, A.M. TX 11th (Spaight's) Bn.Vol. Co.B
Rogers, A.M. TX 13th Vol. 4th Co.I
Rogers, A.M. TX Loc.Def.Troops Merriman's
Co. (Orange Cty.Coast Guard)
Rogers, Amariah NC 24th Inf. Co.B
Rogers, Amos TX 11th Inf. Co.A
Rogers, A.N. NC 60th Inf. Co.E
Rogers, Ancel SC 1st (Orr's) Rifles Co.H
Rogers, Anderson GA Smith's Legion
Standridge's Co. 1st Sgt.
Rogers, Anderson NC 26th Inf. Co.B
Rogers, Anderson SC 22nd Inf. Co.C
Rogers, Anderson SC Post Guard Senn's Co.
Rogers, Andrew KY 1st Inf. 2nd Lt.
Rogers, Andrew KY 6th Mtd.Inf. Co.A 2nd Lt.
Rogers, Andrew TN 14th Inf. Co.F
Rogers, Andrew TN 39th Mtd.Inf. Co.K
Rogers, Andrew Lt.Arty. Dent's Btty.,CSA
Rogers, Andrew 9th Conf.Inf. Co.F
Rogers, Andrew A. AR 1st (Crawford's) Cav.
Co.E Cpl.
Rogers, Andrew J. AL Lt.Arty. 2nd Bn. Co.C
Cpl.
Rogers, Andrew J. TN 3rd (Lillard's) Mtd.Inf.
Co.H
Rogers, Andrew J. TX Cav. 6th Bn. Co.E Sgt.
Rogers, Andrew J. 1st Choctaw & Chickasaw
Mtd.Rifles 1st Co.I
Rogers, Andrew Jackson GA 27th Inf. Co.A
Rogers, Andrew S. TN 32nd Inf. Co.B
Rogers, Ansel NC 39th Inf. Co.A 1st Lt.
Rogers, A.P. MS 7th Cav. Co.C
Rogers, A.P. TX 19th Inf. Co.G
Rogers, A.R. NC 1st Jr.Res. Co.K
Rogers, A.R. NC 47th Inf.
Rogers, A.R. TN 28th (Cons.) Inf. Co.A
Rogers, Arch VA Inf. 26th Bn. Co.B
Rogers, Arch. F. TN 3rd (Lillard's) Mtd.Inf.
Co.G
Rogers, Arthur NC 61st Inf. Co.F
Rogers, Arthur TN Cav. 4th Bn. (Branner's)
Co.A
Rogers, Arthur VA Hvy.Arty. 20th Bn. Co.E
Rogers, Arthur VA Inf. 21st Bn. 2nd Co.C
Rogers, Arthur VA 64th Mtd.Inf. Co.C
Rogers, Arthur L. VA Lt.Arty. Rogers' Co.
Capt.
Rogers, Arthur L. Gen. & Staff Maj.
Rogers, Arthur M. AL 9th Inf. Co.F
Rogers, Asa, Jr. VA 1st Cav. Co.H Capt.
Rogers, Asa VA 5th Cav. (12 mo. '61-2) Co.G
Rogers, Asa VA Lt.Arty. Hankins' Co.
Rogers, Asberry G. GA 6th Cav. Co.A
Rogers, Asbury G. GA Smith's Legion
Standridge's Co.
Rogers, Asbury T. NC 62nd Inf. Co.A Capt.
Rogers, Asher MS 5th Inf. Co.H Sgt.
Rogers, A. Sidney VA Cav. 14th Bn. Co.D
Rogers, A. Sidney VA 15th Cav. Co.K
Hosp.Stew.
Rogers, A.T. AL 48th Inf. Co.A
Rogers, A.T. MS 1st Cav. Co.E
Rogers, A.T. TX Cav. (Loc.Def.) Durant's Co.
Rogers, A.T. TX Cav. Madison's Regt. Co.B
Rogers, Augustus C. GA Inf. 2nd Bn. Co.B
Rogers, Augustus F. VA 1st Inf. Co.A
Rogers, Augustus F. VA 12th Inf. Co.G

Rogers, Augustus L. GA 28th Inf. Co.H
Rogers, Augustus W. TX 17th Cav. Co.H
Rogers, Austin MS 41st Inf. Co.D
Rogers, Austin P. AL 5th Inf. Co.B
Rogers, Avery AL 6th Inf. Co.D
Rogers, A.W. MS 43rd Inf. Co.C
Rogers, B. MS Cav. Ham's Regt. Co.G
Rogers, B. MO Cav. Ford's Bn. Co.C
Rogers, B. SC 26th Inf. Co.C Cpl.
Rogers, B.A. SC 3rd Inf. Co.G Capt.
Rogers, B.A. SC 8th Inf. Co.K Capt.
Rogers, B.A. VA Loc.Def. Ezell's Co.
Rogers, Ballard VA 17th Cav. Co.I
Rogers, Barney NC Walker's Bn. Thomas'
Legion Co.E
Rogers, Barney 9th Conf.Inf. Co.F Cpl.
Rogers, Bartholomew AR 1st (Colquitt's) Inf.
Co.F
Rogers, Bartholomew TN 4th (McLemore's)
Cav. Co.H
Rogers, Barton H. AR Cav. Wright's Regt. Co.D
Rogers, B.B. TN Lt.Arty. Phillips' Co. Cpl.
Rogers, B.C. MS Part.Rangers Smyth's Co.
Rogers, B.C. Conf.Cav. Wood's Regt. 2nd Co.D
Rogers, B.D. AL 21st Inf. Co.C
Rogers, B.D. TN 4th (McLemore's) Cav. Co.B
Rogers, Ben FL McGee Mil.
Rogers, Ben. James VA Hvy.Arty. Coleman's
Co. Ord.Sgt.
Rogers, Benjamin MS Inf. 3rd Bn. (St.Troops)
Co.C
Rogers, Benjamin MO 3rd Inf. Co.C
Rogers, Benjamin SC 3rd St.Troops Co.B
Rogers, Benjamin TN 28th (Cons.) Inf. Co.F
Rogers, Benjamin TX 9th Cav. Co.I
Rogers, Benjamin F. AR 15th (Josey's) Inf. Co.A
Rogers, Benjamin F. GA 55th Inf. Co.F
Rogers, Benjamin F. MO 1st Inf. Co.C,E
Rogers, Benjamin F. NC 17th Inf. (1st Org.)
Co.F
Rogers, Benjamin F. NC 17th Inf. (2nd Org.)
Co.A Sgt.
Rogers, Benjamin F. VA 10th Cav. Co.F
Rogers, Benjamin L. KY 2nd Cav. Co.D
Rogers, Benjamin N. SC 4th St.Troops Co.F
Rogers, Berriman AL 6th Inf. Co.D Sgt.
Rogers, Bethel SC 4th Cav. Co.F
Rogers, Bethel SC 21st Inf. Co.L
Rogers, Bettis AR 17th (Griffith's) Inf. Co.F
Cpl.
Rogers, Beverly GA Inf. 1st Loc.Troops
(Augusta) Co.F,B Cpl.
Rogers, B.F. AL 18th Inf. Co.G
Rogers, B.F. AR 8th Cav. Co.A Sgt.
Rogers, B.F. AR 2nd Vol. Co.C
Rogers, B.F. GA 1st (Symons') Res. Co.I
Rogers, B.F. GA 2nd Inf. Co.D 1st Lt.
Rogers, B.F. GA 19th Inf. Co.H Lt.
Rogers, B.F. GA 44th Inf. Co.F
Rogers, B.F. KY 5th Cav. Co.B
Rogers, B.F. KY 9th Mtd.Inf. Co.K Sgt.
Rogers, B.F. LA 22nd Inf. QMSgt.
Rogers, B.F. LA 22nd (Cons.) Inf. QMSgt.
Rogers, B.F. MO 1st & 4th Cons.Inf. Co.F
Rogers, B.F. NC 2nd Jr.Res. Co.E 2nd Lt.
Rogers, B.F. NC 54th Inf. Co.K
Rogers, B.F. SC 22nd Inf. Co.E

Rogers, B.F. TN 1st Hvy.Arty. Co.B
Rogers, B.F. TX 7th Inf. Co.B 1st Sgt.
Rogers, B.F. VA 13th Inf. Co.C
Rogers, B.H. MS 7th Cav. Co.K
Rogers, B.H. MS 2nd (Davidson's) Inf. Co.I
Rogers, B.H. MS 26th Inf. Co.C
Rogers, B.L. AR 24th Inf. Co.E
Rogers, B.L. MS Lt.Arty. Turner's Co.
Rogers, B.R. TX Cav. 1st Regt.St.Troops Co.F
Rogers, Bradford FL Lt.Arty. Abell's Co.
Rogers, B.S. FL 1st (Res.) Inf. Co.F
Rogers, Buckner NC 1st Arty. (10th St.Troops)
Co.A
Rogers, Burlasque P. GA Cav. 29th Bn. Co.E
Rogers, Burrell LA 19th Inf. Co.F
Rogers, Burwel MS 1st (Patton's) Inf. Co.K
Rogers, Burwell MS 11th (Perrin's) Cav. Co.F
Rogers, B.W. SC Inf. Hampton Legion Co.K
Rogers, Byrd R. VA 3rd Cav. Co.C
Rogers, C. GA 46th Inf. Co.A
Rogers, C. MS 16th Inf. Co.A
Rogers, C. SC Cav. 12th Bn. Co.D
Rogers, C. SC Mil. 2nd Regt. Co.B
Rogers, C. SC 3rd Inf. Co.B
Rogers, C. SC 21st Inf. Co.L
Rogers, C. TN Inf. 1st Cons.Regt. Co.G
Rogers, C. TN 28th (Cons.) Inf. Co.F
Rogers, C.A. 4th Conf.Inf. Co.H
Rogers, Cade SC Arty. Gregg's Co. (McQueen
Lt.Arty.)
Rogers, Cade SC Arty. Manigault's Bn. 1st Co.C
Rogers, Calloway TN Cav. 16th Bn. (Neal's)
Co.F
Rogers, Caloway VA 64th Mtd.Inf. Co.C
Rogers, Calvin GA 45th Inf. Co.B
Rogers, Calvin MO 8th Cav. Co.H
Rogers, Calvin NC 4th Sr.Res. Co.I 2nd Lt.
Rogers, Calvin TN 19th & 20th (Cons.) Cav.
Co.E
Rogers, Calvin J. NC 43rd Inf. Co.A
Rogers, Calvin N. AR 9th Inf. Old Co.B, Co.F
Rogers, Carrol TN 3rd (Forrest's) Cav. Co.D
Rogers, C.B. AR 3rd Inf. Co.K
Rogers, C.B. AR 11th Inf. Co.G
Rogers, C.B. AR 11th & 17th (Cons.) Inf. Co.G
Rogers, C.C. AL 32nd Inf. Co.F
Rogers, C.C. AR 8th Cav. Co.A
Rogers, C.C. AR 17th (Griffith's) Inf. Co.B
Rogers, C.C. MO 11th Inf. Co.F
Rogers, C.C. TN 20th (Russell's) Cav. Co.D
Rogers, C.D. MS 1st Cav.Res. Co.B
Rogers, C.F. AR Cav. 1st Bn. (Stirman's) Co.E
Rogers, C.G. Gen. & Staff, A. of TN Lt.Col.
Rogers, C.H. AR 6th Inf. Co.I
Rogers, C.H. GA Inf. 14th Bn. (St.Guards) Co.C
Rogers, Ch. LA Mil.Cont.Regt. Roder's Co.
Jr.2nd Lt.
Rogers, Charles AL 2nd Cav. Co.K
Rogers, Charles AR 1st Mtd.Rifles Co.C
Rogers, Charles LA 5th Inf. Co.I
Rogers, Charles NC 8th Sr.Res. Broadhurst's Co.
Rogers, Charles VA 24th Cav. Co.E
Rogers, Charles VA Lt.Arty. Moore's Co. Cpl.
Rogers, Charles VA 6th Inf. Vickery's Co.
Rogers, Charles 2nd Cherokee Mtd.Vol. Co.F
Rogers, Charles A. MS 18th Inf. Co.H
Rogers, Charles A. TN 61st Mtd.Inf. Co.G

Rogers, Charles A. VA 50th Inf. Co.F
Rogers, Charles B. AL 6th Inf. Co.M
Rogers, Charles C. TN Eng.Corps Capt.
Rogers, Charles E. VA 61st Inf. Co.B
Rogers, Charles H. GA Inf. 2nd Bn. Co.B
  Asst.Comsy.
Rogers, Charles H. GA Cobb's Legion Co.I
  Cpl.
Rogers, Charles H. SC 18th Inf. Co.A Cpl.
Rogers, Chas. H. Gen. & Staff Capt.,ACS
Rogers, Charles L. MO 2nd Brig.St.Guard Adj.
Rogers, Charles M. NC 30th Inf. Co.D 2nd Lt.
Rogers, Charles M.A. AL 42nd Inf. Co.D
Rogers, Charles P. AL 37th Inf. Capt.
Rogers, Charles P. VA 57th Inf. Co.H Sgt.
Rogers, Charles P. Gen. & Staff, QM Dept.
  Capt.,AQM
Rogers, Charles R. LA 1st (Nelligan's) Inf. Co.I
Rogers, Charles S. Conf.Cav. Wood's Regt. 2nd
  Co.G 2nd Lt.
Rogers, Charles W. KY 9th Cav. Co.C
Rogers, Charles W. NC 15th Inf. Co.K
Rogers, Charles W. VA 24th Cav. Co.G Sgt.
Rogers, Charley B. AR Cav. Poe's Bn. Co.A
Rogers, Christopher C. MO Lt.Arty. 1st Field
  Btty.
Rogers, Cicero NC 20th Inf. Co.E
Rogers, C.J. LA 13th Bn. (Part.Rangers) Co.A
Rogers, C.J. TX Cav. 1st Bn.St.Troops Co.F
Rogers, C.K. AL 50th Inf. Co.H
Rogers, C.L. AR 10th Inf. Co.D
Rogers, C.L. GA Hvy.Arty. 22nd Bn. Co.E
Rogers, C.L. TX 20th Inf. Co.G
Rogers, C.M. KY 7th Cav. Co.A
Rogers, C.M. NC 2nd Jr.Res. Co.F
Rogers, C.M. TX Cav. Gano's Squad. Co.A
Rogers, C.M.A. MS 2nd Cav. Co.C
Rogers, Columbus GA Lt.Arty. Ferrell's Btty.
Rogers, Columbus TX 15th Cav. Co.B
Rogers, Columbus M. NC 37th Inf. Co.E
Rogers, Cooper VA 60th Inf. Co.D
Rogers, Cornelius FL 2nd Cav. Co.A Sgt.
Rogers, Cornelius D. GA 1st (Olmstead's) Inf.
  Co.K,G Jr.2nd Lt.
Rogers, C.P. MS Moore's Vol. Capt.
Rogers, C.P. SC 1st St.Troops Co.A Cpl.
Rogers, C.S. SC 6th Inf. Co.H
Rogers, C.S. VA Lt.Arty. Grandy's Co. Cpl.
Rogers, C.S. Conf.Lt.Arty. Richardson's Bn.
  Co.C Cpl.
Rogers, C.T. GA Inf. (Loc.Def.) Whiteside's
  Nav.Bn. Co.B
Rogers, Cullen L. GA 5th Inf. Co.B
Rogers, Cullen L. GA 6th Inf. (St.Guards) Co.I
Rogers, Cunningham MS 33rd Inf. Co.G
Rogers, Cuthbert B. VA 8th Inf. Co.D Cpl.
Rogers, C.V. 1st Cherokee Mtd.Vol. 2nd Co.G
  Lt.
Rogers, C.W. GA Cav. 2nd Bn. Co.D
Rogers, C.W. GA 5th Cav. Co.A
Rogers, C.W. TX 8th Cav. Co.A
Rogers, Cyrus A. NC 15th Inf. Co.B
Rogers, D. AL 59th Inf. Co.D
Rogers, D. TX Cav. Wells' Regt. Co.K Jr.2nd
  Lt.
Rogers, D.A. KY 12th Cav. Co.A
Rogers, Daniel AL Inf. 2nd Regt. Co.B

Rogers, Daniel AL 37th Inf. Co.C
Rogers, Daniel AL 42nd Inf. Co.B
Rogers, Daniel GA 12th Cav. Co.B
Rogers, Daniel LA 17th Inf. Co.E
Rogers, Daniel LA 28th (Gray's) Inf. Co.F
Rogers, Daniel SC 5th St.Troops Co.E
Rogers, Daniel TX 17th Cav. Co.E Sgt.
Rogers, Daniel TX Granbury's Cons.Brig. Co.G
Rogers, Daniel C. GA Siege Arty. 28th Bn.
  Co.D
Rogers, Daniel D. NC 48th Inf. Co.E
Rogers, Daniel L. TN 14th Inf. Co.I
Rogers, Daniel M. SC Lt.Arty. 3rd (Palmetto)
  Bn. Co.E,G Sr.1st Lt.
Rogers, Daniel M. SC 2nd Rifles Co.G
Rogers, Daniel S. MO Cav. Poindexter's Regt.
Rogers, David AL 6th Inf. Co.I
Rogers, David AL 31st Inf. Co.I
Rogers, David FL 4th Inf. Co.D
Rogers, David FL 6th Inf. Co.D Sgt.
Rogers, David GA Brooks' Co. (Terrell Lt.Arty.)
Rogers, David GA Lt.Arty. (Jackson Arty.) Mas-
  senburg's Btty.
Rogers, David LA 2nd Cav. Co.E
Rogers, David LA 14th Inf. Co.C
Rogers, David MS 37th Inf. Co.E Sgt.
Rogers, David MO 5th Cav. Co.G
Rogers, David NC 25th Inf. Co.B Capt.
Rogers, David NC 32nd Inf. Co.I
Rogers, David NC 43rd Inf. Co.F
Rogers, David SC Arty. Gregg's Co. (McQueen
  Lt.Arty.)
Rogers, David SC Arty. Manigault's Bn. 1st
  Co.C
Rogers, David, Jr. SC Inf. Hampton Legion
  Co.D
Rogers, David TN 61st Mtd.Inf. Co.E
Rogers, David TX Cav. Good's Bn. Co.A 2nd
  Lt.
Rogers, David C. FL 2nd Inf. Co.M
Rogers, David C. GA 59th Inf. Co.G
Rogers, David C.C. MS 1st (Johnston's) Inf.
  Co.A 3rd Lt.
Rogers, David D. LA 1st Cav. Co.D
Rogers, David D. NC 52nd Inf. Co.I Cpl.
Rogers, David F. NC 51st Inf. Co.K
Rogers, David G. AR 10th Mil. Co.D
Rogers, David J. MS 34th Inf. Co.D
Rogers, David J. NC 6th Cav. (65th St.Troops)
  Co.C
Rogers, David J. NC Cav. 7th Bn. Co.C
Rogers, David L. GA 42nd Inf. Co.E
Rogers, David M. GA 8th Inf. (St.Guards) Co.F
Rogers, David P. MS 26th Inf. Co.C Sgt.
Rogers, David P. MS 32nd Inf. Co.I Capt.
Rogers, David R. GA 6th Cav. Co.A
Rogers, David R. GA Smith's Legion
  Standridge's Co.
Rogers, David T. MO 5th Inf. Co.H Sgt.
Rogers, David W. NC 28th Inf. Co.K
Rogers, D.C. KY 7th Cav. Co.A
Rogers, D.C. TX Cav. Gano's Squad. Co.A
Rogers, D.D. LA Lt.Arty. Bridges' Btty.
Rogers, D.D. LA Mil. Orleans Guards Regt.
  Co.D
Rogers, D.D. SC Arty. Manigault's Bn. 1st
  Co.B,D

Rogers, Dennis B. SC 1st (McCreary's) Inf.
  Co.E
Rogers, Dennis B. SC 1st Inf. Co.K
Rogers, DeWitt W. GA Inf. 27th Bn. Co.A
Rogers, D.F. MS Cav. 2nd Bn.Res. Co.A
Rogers, D.F. TN Cav. Woodward's Co.
Rogers, D.G. AR 7th Cav. Co.B
Rogers, D.L. MS 4th Inf. Co.G N.C.S. QMSgt.
Rogers, D.M. MS 32nd Inf. Co.A 2nd Lt.
Rogers, D.M. MS 32nd Inf. Co.I
Rogers, D.M. MS Rogers' Co. Capt.
Rogers, D.M. Gen. & Staff QM,Insp.
Rogers, D.O. AL 37th Inf. Co.G
Rogers, Doctor F. GA 49th Inf. Co.I
Rogers, Dominick LA 10th Inf. Co.D
Rogers, Dorn MS 6th Cav. Co.C Cpl.
Rogers, D.P. AR 8th Cav. Co.G
Rogers, D.P. Gen. & Staff Capt.,Comsy.
Rogers, Drury F. KY 3rd Cav. Co.C
Rogers, Drury W. GA Cav. 7th Bn. (St.Guards)
  Co.F
Rogers, D.S. SC 6th Cav. Co.E
Rogers, D.S. 1st Conf.Cav. 2nd Co.E
Rogers, D.T. MS 1st (Johnston's) Inf. Co.G Sgt.
Rogers, D.T. MS 14th Inf. Co.E
Rogers, D.W.W. GA 63rd Inf. Co.G Cpl.
Rogers, E. AR 58th Mil. Co.E
Rogers, E. GA 5th Res. Co.A
Rogers, E. SC 21st Inf. Co.H
Rogers, E. TN 60th Mtd.Inf. Co.K
Rogers, E. TX 14th Inf. Co.G
Rogers, E. VA 5th Cav. Co.K
Rogers, E.A. KY 1st (Butler's) Cav. Co.D
Rogers, E.A. TX 25th Cav. Co.C
Rogers, E.B. AR 11th & 17th (Cons.) Inf. Co.I
  Cpl.
Rogers, E.B. AR 35th Inf. Co.A
Rogers, E.B. GA 27th Inf. Co.F
Rogers, E.B. Inf. Bailey's Cons.Regt. Co.A
Rogers, E.B. TX 7th Inf. Co.B
Rogers, E.B. Trans-MS Conf.Cav. 1st Bn. Co.B
Rogers, Eben SC 6th Cav. Co.E
Rogers, Ebenezer SC Arty. Gregg's Co.
  (McQueen Lt.Arty.)
Rogers, Ebenezer SC Arty. Manigault's Bn. 1st
  Co.C
Rogers, Ebz. SC 8th Inf. Co.L,I Sgt.
Rogers, E.C. GA Inf. (Mell Scouts) Wyly's Co.
Rogers, E.C. LA 17th Inf. Co.E Sgt.
Rogers, E.D. SC Mil. 17th Regt. Rogers' Co.
  Capt.
Rogers, E. Dawkins SC 18th Inf. Co.A
Rogers, Ed J. TX 17th Cons.Dismtd.Cav. Co.K
  Hosp.Stew.
Rogers, Edmond J. AL 12t Inf. Co.F
Rogers, Edward VA 97th Mil. Co.H
Rogers, Edward VA Vol. Taylor's Co.
Rogers, Edward G. VA 21st Inf. Co.B
Rogers, Edward J. TX 17th Cav. Co.K Sgt.
Rogers, Edward J. MD Cav. 2nd Bn. Co.A
Rogers, Edward R. SC 1st (Orr's) Rifles Co.H
Rogers, Edward T. AL 21st Inf. Co.K
Rogers, Edward T. SC 10th Inf. Co.M
Rogers, Edwin SC 2nd Arty. Co.D
Rogers, Edwin SC 4th St.Troops Co.E Sgt.
Rogers, Edwin SC 8th Inf. Co.A 2nd Lt.
Rogers, Edwin A. MS 27th Inf. Co.K

Rogers, Edwin C. GA 1st (Olmstead's) Inf. Co.G
Rogers, Edwin C. GA Inf. 2nd Bn. Co.B
Rogers, Edwin M. GA 38th Inf. Co.G
Rogers, Edwin P., Jr. NC 2nd Cav. (19th St.Troops) Co.B
Rogers, Edwin P., Sr. NC 2nd Cav. (19th St.Troops) Co.B Black.
Rogers, E.F. GA 46th Inf. Co.C
Rogers, E.F. LA 9th Inf. Co.F
Rogers, E.G. MD Weston's Bn. Co.B
Rogers, E.G. Bradford's Corps Scouts & Guards Co.B
Rogers, E.H. GA Conscr.
Rogers, E.H. NC 47th Inf. Co.C
Rogers, E.H., Jr. SC 27th Inf. Co.B
Rogers, E.H. TX 21st Cav. Co.B
Rogers, E.H. TX 22nd Inf. Co.A
Rogers, E.J. AL 18th Inf. Co.B 1st Lt.
Rogers, E.J. AR 7th Inf. Co.I 3rd Lt.
Rogers, E.J. MO Cav. Fristoe's Regt. Co.B
Rogers, E.J. SC Lt.Arty. Jeter's Co. (Macbeth Lt.Arty.)
Rogers, Elbert MS Inf. 1st Bn. Co.C 3rd Lt.
Rogers, Elbert H. Government Agent,CSA
Rogers, Elbert W. MS 48th Inf. Co.L
Rogers, Eli GA 3rd Cav. Co.G
Rogers, Eli MO Cav. Freeman's Regt. Co.G
Rogers, Eli NC 31st Inf. Co.C
Rogers, Elias SC 3rd Inf. Co.D,K
Rogers, Elias J. MS 10th Inf. New Co.H
Rogers, Elijah AR 8th Cav. Co.D
Rogers, Elijah GA 7th Inf. Co.D
Rogers, Elijah GA 26th Inf. Co.E
Rogers, Elijah TN 16th Inf. Parks' Co.
Rogers, Elijah TN 27th Inf. Co.A
Rogers, Elijah S. TX Cav. Morgan's Regt. Co.E
Rogers, Elisha GA 13th Inf. Co.A
Rogers, Elisha GA 41st Inf. Co.K
Rogers, Elisha KY 12th Cav. Co.D
Rogers, Elisha 3rd Conf.Eng.Troops Co.D Artif.
Rogers, Elisha H. GA Inf. 1st Loc.Troops (Augusta) Co.A 1st Sgt.
Rogers, Elly B. TX 13th Cav. Co.G Sgt.
Rogers, E.M. SC 21st Inf. Co.H Sgt.
Rogers, E.M. Inf. Bailey's Cons.Regt. Co.A
Rogers, E.M. TX 7th Inf. Co.C
Rogers, Emanuel C. VA Cav. 35th Bn. Co.E
Rogers, E.N. Gen. & Staff Asst.Surg.
Rogers, Enoch GA 25th Inf. Co.I
Rogers, Enoch SC 4th Cav. Co.F
Rogers, Enoch SC Cav. 12th Bn. Co.D
Rogers, Enoch TN 43rd Inf. Co.C
Rogers, Enoch M. NC 38th Inf. Co.G
Rogers, Enoch P. GA 3rd Cav. Co.F Sgt.
Rogers, Enoch R. GA 14th Inf. Co.A
Rogers, Enos AL 8th Cav. Co.B
Rogers, Enos AL Mil. 4th Vol. Modawell's Co. 3rd Lt.
Rogers, E.O. AR Lt.Arty. Wiggins' Btty.
Rogers, Ephraim SC 19th Inf. Co.C
Rogers, Ephraim M. MS 2nd Cav. Co.I
Rogers, Ephraim T. GA 34th Inf. Co.F Capt.
Rogers, E.R. FL Cav. 5th Bn. Co.G
Rogers, E.R. GA 5th Res. Co.B
Rogers, Ervin SC 1st (McCreary's) Inf. Co.E
Rogers, Ervin SC 1st Inf. Co.K
Rogers, Ervin SC 8th Inf. Co.I

Rogers, E.S. TN 6th Inf. Co.L
Rogers, E.T. AR Lt.Arty. Wiggins' Btty.
Rogers, E.T. GA 25th Inf. Co.I
Rogers, E.T. Gen. & Staff Hosp.Stew.
Rogers, Eugene W. FL Milton Lt.Arty. Dunham's Co.
Rogers, E.W. MS Inf. 2nd Bn. Co.L
Rogers, E.W. TX 12th Cav. Co.F Maj.
Rogers, E. William KY Cav. Buckner Guards
Rogers, Ezekiel NC 31st Inf. Co.C
Rogers, Ezra T. GA 1st (Olmstead's) Inf. Co.D Sgt.
Rogers, F. AL 46th Inf. Co.I
Rogers, F. MS Cav. 3rd Bn. (Ashcraft's) Co.C
Rogers, F.A. MO 2nd Regt.St.Guards Co.C Capt.
Rogers, F.A. SC 8th Inf. Co.K
Rogers, F.A. SC Bn.St.Cadets Co.B
Rogers, F.B. TX 22nd Inf. Co.B 2nd Lt.
Rogers, F.E. AL Cp. of Instr. Talladega
Rogers, Felix G. TN 53rd Inf.
Rogers, Ferdinand G. SC 4th Cav. Co.F
Rogers, F.G. SC 21st Inf. Co.L
Rogers, F.L. AL 50th Inf. Co.H
Rogers, F.L. LA 17th Inf. Co.E Sgt.
Rogers, Fleet AR 15th (N.W.) Inf.
Rogers, F.M. AL 25th Inf. Co.H
Rogers, F.M. GA 12th Cav. Co.E
Rogers, F.M. GA 46th Inf. Co.E
Rogers, F.M. MS 4th Cav. Co.B
Rogers, F.M. MS 9th Inf. New Co.G
Rogers, F.M. MS 14th Inf. Co.E Capt.
Rogers, F.M. MS 15th (Cons.) Inf. Co.G
Rogers, F.M. MS 27th Inf. Co.A
Rogers, F.M. NC 60th Inf. Co.I
Rogers, F.M. NC Lt.Arty. Thomas' Legion Levi's Btty.
Rogers, F.M. SC 2nd Arty. Co.D
Rogers, F.M. SC 21st Inf. Co.I
Rogers, F.M. TN 14th (Neely's) Cav. Co.K
Rogers, F.M. TX 17th Cav. Co.B
Rogers, F.M. TX Inf. 3rd St.Troops Co.E
Rogers, F.M. TX 12th Inf. Co.K
Rogers, Fountain VA 9th Bn.Res. Co.B
Rogers, F.P. AR 36th Inf. Co.B
Rogers, Francis SC Arty. Gregg's Co. (McQueen Lt.Arty.)
Rogers, Francis SC Arty. Manigualt's Bn. 1st Co.C
Rogers, Francis TN 12th (Green's) Cav. Co.I
Rogers, Francis D. VA Lt.Arty. Moore's Co.
Rogers, Francis E. TX 18th Inf. Co.B
Rogers, Francis M. AL 11th Inf. Co.A
Rogers, Francis M. FL 6th Inf. Co.D
Rogers, Francis M. GA 26th Inf. Co.C Cpl.
Rogers, Francis M. MS 43rd Inf. Co.C
Rogers, Francis M. TX 11th Inf. Co.K
Rogers, Francois LA Mil. LaFourche Regt. Co.D
Rogers, Frank AR 7th Cav. Co.B
Rogers, Frank AR 7th Inf. Co.F
Rogers, Frank KY 7th Cav. Co.I
Rogers, Frank LA 1st (Strawbridge's) Inf. Co.B
Rogers, Frank LA Mil. 4th Regt. 1st Brig. 1st Div. Co.C
Rogers, Frank MS 10th Inf. New Co.G
Rogers, Frank NC 1st Inf. Co.K
Rogers, Frank 3rd Conf.Eng.Troops Co.D

Rogers, Frank J. AR 1st (Monroe's) Cav. Co.C
Rogers, Franklin NC 17th Inf. (1st Org.) Co.C
Rogers, Franklin NC 55th Inf. Co.E
Rogers, Franklin SC 1st Arty. Co.K
Rogers, Franklin J. GA Inf. 2nd Bn. (St.Guards) Co.B
Rogers, Franklin L. LA 31st Inf. Co.K
Rogers, Franklin L. NC 15th Inf. Co.B 1st Lt.
Rogers, Frank M. MS Cav. Stockdale's Bn. Co.B
Rogers, Frank M. MS 20th Inf. Co.B
Rogers, Frank N. MS 41st Inf. Co.D
Rogers, Frederick C. AL 24th Inf. Co.G
Rogers, Frederick H. AL 12th Inf. Co.A Capt.
Rogers, Friend O. GA 41st Inf. Co.E
Rogers, F.T. MS 14th Inf. Co.E
Rogers, G. NC 21st Inf. Co.I
Rogers, G. TN 12th Cav. Co.B
Rogers, G.B. AR Cav. Gordon's Regt. Co.K
Rogers, G.B. AR 58th Mil. Co.E
Rogers, G.B. NC 1st Inf. Co.I
Rogers, G.C. GA Cav. Alexander's Co.
Rogers, G.D. AL 4th (Russell's) Cav. Co.C
Rogers, G.D. GA 11th Mil.
Rogers, G.D.B. TN 19th & 20th (Cons.) Cav. Co.K
Rogers, G.E. TN 11th Inf. Co.C
Rogers, George AL 5th Inf. New Co.C
Rogers, George AL 7th Inf. Co.G
Rogers, George AL 18th Bn.Vol. Co.C Capt.
Rogers, George GA 1st (Olmstead's) Inf. Co.I
Rogers, George MO 3rd Inf. Co.G
Rogers, George NC 67th Inf. Co.D
Rogers, George TX 1st Inf. Co.L
Rogers, George VA 16th Cav. Co.K
Rogers, George VA Hvy.Arty. 18th Bn. Co.C
Rogers, George VA Hvy.Arty. 19th Bn. 3rd Co.C
Rogers, George VA 2nd Inf.Loc.Def. Co.H
Rogers, George VA Inf. 2nd Bn.Loc.Def. Co.F
Rogers, George Conf.Reg.Inf. Brooks' Bn. Co.C
Rogers, George A. GA 20th Inf. Co.C
Rogers, George F. GA 1st (Olmstead's) Inf. Co.D
Rogers, George F. GA Inf. 2nd Bn. Co.B
Rogers, George G. AL 23rd Inf. Co.B
Rogers, George H. MS Inf. 3rd Bn. Co.C
Rogers, George J. VA 41st Inf. Co.A Lt.,AQM
Rogers, George L. MS 2nd Part.Rangers Co.C
Rogers, George L. NC 14th Inf. Co.C
Rogers, George M. GA 9th Inf. Co.C
Rogers, George M. NC 62nd Inf. Co.E
Rogers, George N. NC 16th Inf. Co.L Lt.
Rogers, George N. NC 29th Inf. Co.E Cpl.
Rogers, George N. VA 52nd Inf. Co.C
Rogers, George O. LA 9th Inf. Co.A
Rogers, Georges LA 28th (Thomas') Inf. Co.D
Rogers, George S. NC 14th Inf. Co.E Cpl.
Rogers, George T. MS Inf. 3rd Bn. Co.C
Rogers, George T. VA 6th Inf. Co.F Col.
Rogers, George W. AL 5th Cav. Co.F
Rogers, George W. AL 58th Inf. Co.F
Rogers, George W. AR 15th (N.W.) Inf. Co.G
Rogers, George W. AR 38th Inf. Co.M
Rogers, George W. GA 12th Inf. Co.D
Rogers, George W. GA 40th Inf. Sgt.
Rogers, George W. KY 1st (Butler's) Cav. Co.E
Rogers, George W. KY 7th Cav. Co.A

Rogers, George W. KY 1st Bn.Mtd.Rifles Co.B
 1st Sgt.
Rogers, George W. KY 3rd Bn.Mtd.Rifles Co.E
Rogers, George W. KY 2nd Mtd.Inf. Co.H Cpl.
Rogers, George W. KY 4th Mtd.Inf. Co.A Cpl.
Rogers, George W. KY 4th Mtd.Inf. Co.K 2nd
 Lt.
Rogers, George W. LA 4th Inf. New Co.G
Rogers, George W. MS 8th Cav. Co.C
Rogers, George W. MS 1st Lt.Arty. Co.L
Rogers, George W. MS 3rd Inf. Co.H
Rogers, George W. MS 19th Inf. Co.K
Rogers, George W. MO 1st N.E. Cav. Co.M
Rogers, George W. MO 3rd Cav. Co.D
Rogers, George W. MO 3rd Inf. Co.I Chap.
Rogers, George W. MO 10th Inf. Co.F Cpl.
Rogers, George W. NC 24th Inf. Co.H 2nd Lt.
Rogers, George W. NC 43rd Inf. Co.F
Rogers, George W. NC Walker's Bn. Thomas'
 Legion Co.B
Rogers, George W. SC Arty. Manigault's Bn. 1st
 Co.C
Rogers, George W. TN Cav. 4th Bn. (Branner's)
 Co.F
Rogers, George W. TN Cav. 9th Bn. (Gantt's)
 Co.C
Rogers, George W. TX 15th Cav. Co.B 1st Sgt.
Rogers, George W. TX Cav. Gano's Squad.
 Co.A
Rogers, George W. VA 7th Cav. Co.A
Rogers, George W. VA Lt.Arty. 13th Bn. Co.C
Rogers, George W. VA 11th Inf. Co.H
Rogers, George W. VA 20th Inf. Co.H
Rogers, George W. VA Inf. 21st Bn. 1st Co.D
Rogers, G.F. TN Inf. 23rd Bn. Co.D Sgt.
Rogers, G.H. MS 9th Bn.S.S. Co.B
Rogers, G.H. MS 41st Inf. Co.D
Rogers, Gilbert W. VA Lt.Arty. Hankins' Co.
Rogers, Gilbert W. VA 3rd Inf. 1st Co.I
Rogers, Giles NC 67th Inf. Co.L
Rogers, G.J. Kirkland's Brig. Capt.,AQM
Rogers, G.L. TN 4th Inf. Co.C
Rogers, G.L. TX 24th & 25th Cav. (Cons.) Co.F
Rogers, G.L. TX 1st Inf. Co.A
Rogers, G.M. AL 26th (O'Neal's) Inf. Co.C
Rogers, G.M. NC Cav. 7th Bn. Co.E
Rogers, G.N. NC 60th Inf. Co.B
Rogers, G.N. TX Cav. Martin's Regt. Co.A Sgt.
Rogers, Gordon T. MS 20th Inf. Co.D
Rogers, G.P. TN 14th (Neely's) Cav. Co.K
Rogers, G.R. MS 4th Inf. Co.G
Rogers, Gracen GA 6th Cav. Co.B
Rogers, Granberry AR 1st Mtd.Rifles Co.B
Rogers, Grandison M. VA 4th Inf. Co.H
Rogers, Greenville B. TN 3rd (Lillard's) Mtd.Inf.
 Co.H
Rogers, Green W. Conf.Cav. Clarkson's Bn.
 Ind.Rangers Co.H
Rogers, G.W. AL 15th Inf. Co.L
Rogers, G.W. AL 41st Inf. Co.G
Rogers, G.W. AR 2nd Cav. Co.D
Rogers, G.W. AR 7th Cav. Co.B
Rogers, G.W. AR 17th (Griffith's) Inf. Co.G
Rogers, G.W. GA 46th Inf. Co.C
Rogers, G.W. GA 46th Inf. Co.F
Rogers, G.W. KY 12th Cav. Co.D

Rogers, G.W. LA 1st Cav. Co.E, Robinson's
 Co. Cpl.
Rogers, G.W. LA 17th Inf. Co.E
Rogers, G.W. MS 2nd St.Cav. Co.K
Rogers, G.W. MS 10th Cav. Co.B,E Cpl.
Rogers, G.W. MS 12th Cav. Co.A,H
Rogers, G.W. MS 28th Cav. Co.K
Rogers, G.W. MS 2nd (Quinn's St.Troops) Inf.
 Co.D
Rogers, G.W. MS 15th Inf. Co.C
Rogers, G.W. MS 19th Inf. Co.A
Rogers, G.W. MO 5th Inf. Co.H
Rogers, G.W. NC 4th Cav. (59th St.Troops)
 Co.C
Rogers, G.W. TN 2nd (Ashby's) Cav. Co.F Sgt.
Rogers, G.W. TN 15th (Cons.) Cav. Co.G
Rogers, G.W. TN 15th (Stewart's) Cav. Co.E
 Sgt.
Rogers, G.W. TN Arty. Ramsey's Btty. Cpl.
Rogers, G.W. TN 9th Inf. Co.K Cpl.
Rogers, G.W. TN 55th (Brown's) Inf. Co.H
Rogers, G.W. TX 19th Inf. Co.F
Rogers, G.W. VA 40th Inf. Co.B
Rogers, G.W. 1st Conf.Inf. 2nd Co.E
Rogers, G.W. Gen. & Staff Chap.
Rogers, H. AR 2nd Cav. Co.D
Rogers, H. GA 8th Cav. Co.F
Rogers, H. GA 12th Cav. Co.I
Rogers, H. GA 62nd Cav. Co.F
Rogers, H. LA 2nd Cav. Co.G
Rogers, H. LA Mil. 2nd Regt. 3rd Brig. 1st Div.
Rogers, H. LA Mil. LaFourche Regt.
Rogers, H. MS 1st Cav. Co.B
Rogers, H. NC 2nd Jr.Res. Co.A
Rogers, H. SC Inf. 6th Bn. Co.A
Rogers, H. TN 14th (Neely's) Cav. Co.A Cpl.
Rogers, H.A. LA 3rd (Wingfield's) Cav. Co.A,K
Rogers, H.A. TN 9th Inf. Co.I Maj.
Rogers, Hamilton VA 18th Cav. Co.F
Rogers, Hanibal C. MS 15th Inf. Co.C,F
Rogers, Harbert TN 28th Inf. Co.K Sgt.
Rogers, Harmon H. MS 15th Inf. Co.C
Rogers, Harry H. TN Cav. 16th Bn. (Neal's)
 Co.F
Rogers, Harvey GA 11th Inf. Co.F,C
Rogers, Harvey J. AR 15th (N.W.) Inf. Co.B
 2nd Lt.
Rogers, Harvey P. AL 12th Inf. Co.I
Rogers, Haywood GA 1st (Symons') Res. Co.E
Rogers, Hazel AR 2nd Inf. Co.G
Rogers, H.B. GA 1st Inf. (St.Guards) Co.I
Rogers, H.B. GA Inf. Alexander's Co.
Rogers, H.B. SC 6th Cav. Co.E,C
Rogers, H.B. TX 4th Inf. Co.E
Rogers, H.C. AL Lt.Arty. Goldthwaite's Btty.
Rogers, H.C. AL 17th Inf. Co.H
Rogers, H.C. GA Cav. 21st Bn. Co.A
Rogers, H.C. GA 1st (Ramsey's) Inf. Co.I
Rogers, H.C. GA 3rd Inf. Co.B
Rogers, H.C. GA Inf. 18th Bn. (St.Guards) Co.E
Rogers, H.C. MS 5th Cav. Co.H
Rogers, H.C. VA Lt.Arty. Hankins' Co.
Rogers, H.C. VA 3rd Inf.Loc.Def. Co.H
Rogers, H.C. Conf.Cav. Powers' Regt. Co.A
Rogers, H.C. Gen. & Staff A.Surg.
Rogers, H.D. SC 6th Cav. Co.C
Rogers, H.E.A. TX 1st (Yager's) Cav. Co.D

Rogers, H.E.A. TX Cav. 3rd (Yager's) Bn.
 Co.D
Rogers, Henderson VA 50th Inf. Co.A
Rogers, Henderson H. GA Cobb's Legion Co.G
 Cpl.
Rogers, Henderson W.C. AR 6th Inf. New Co.D
Rogers, Henry FL 2nd Cav. Co.A
Rogers, Henry FL Cav. 5th Bn. Co.B
Rogers, Henry GA Inf. 18th Bn. (St.Guards)
 Co.E
Rogers, Henry KY Cav. 1st Bn.
Rogers, Henry LA 11th Inf. Co.F
Rogers, Henry LA 14th (Austin's) Bn.S.S. Co.B
Rogers, Henry NC 17th Inf. (2nd Org.) Co.K
Rogers, Henry NC 44th Inf. Co.D
Rogers, Henry NC 44th Inf. Co.K
Rogers, Henry NC 61st Inf. Co.F
Rogers, Henry, Jr. SC 3rd St.Troops Co.B
Rogers, Henry TN 3rd (Clack's) Inf. Co.G
Rogers, Henry TN 62nd Mtd.Inf. Co.B
Rogers, Henry VA Inf. 2nd Bn.Loc.Def. Co.B
Rogers, Henry A. AR 15th (N.W.) Inf. Co.F
Rogers, Henry A. NC 13th Inf. Co.D Lt.Col.
Rogers, Henry C. GA Cherokee Legion
 (St.Guards) Co.B Staff Ord.Sgt.
Rogers, Henry C. MS 7th Inf. Co.C
Rogers, Henry C. VA 15th Inf. Co.H
Rogers, Henry Clay MD 1st Inf. Co.I
Rogers, Henry Clay VA Cav. 15th Bn. Co.C
Rogers, Henry D. TN 3rd (Lillard's) Mtd.Inf.
 Co.C
Rogers, Henry F. MS 26th Inf. Co.I
Rogers, Henry H. GA 3rd Cav. Co.G
Rogers, Henry H. GA Phillips' Legion Co.C
Rogers, Henry H. TX 14th Cav. Co.K
Rogers, Henry J. FL 1st Inf. Old Co.E
Rogers, Henry J. Eng.,CSA 1st Lt.
Rogers, Henry K. KY Cav. Co.B
Rogers, Henry L. AL 1st Cav. 1st Co.K
Rogers, Henry L. AL 45th Inf. Co.K Sgt.
Rogers, Henry M. NC 26th Inf. Co.E
Rogers, Henry M. TN 19th Inf. Co.B
Rogers, Henry N. NC 56th Inf. Co.G
Rogers, Henry R. GA 49th Inf. Co.I
Rogers, Henry R. TX 9th Cav. Co.H
Rogers, Henry T. GA Arty. 11th Bn. (Sumter
 Arty.) Co.A
Rogers, Herod VA 24th Cav. Co.E
Rogers, Herod VA Cav. 40th Bn. Co.E
Rogers, Hewey NC 6th Cav. (65th St.Troops)
 Co.C
Rogers, Hezekiah R. 1st Choctaw & Chickasaw
 Mtd.Rifles 1st Co.K
Rogers, H.G. GA 40th Inf.
Rogers, H.G. NC 6th Sr.Res. Co.K
Rogers, H.G. 1st Conf.Cav. 1st Co.C
Rogers, H.H. GA Inf. 8th Bn. Co.C
Rogers, H.H. MS 4th Inf. Co.C
Rogers, Hickory AR 35th Inf. Co.C
Rogers, Hilliard NC 47th Inf. Co.C
Rogers, Hily J.C. TX 17th Cav. Co.K
Rogers, Hiram NC 29th Inf. Co.E Capt.
Rogers, Hiram VA 10th Inf. 2nd Co.C
Rogers, Hiram VA 97th Mil. Co.H
Rogers, Hiram C. KY 2nd Cav.
Rogers, Hiram C. KY 9th Cav. Co.C
Rogers, Hiram C. MO 11th Inf. Co.B

Rogers, Hiram Runnels TX 24th Cav. Co.H

Rogers, H.J. MS Cav. 1st Bn. (McNair's)
St.Troops Co.C

Rogers, H.J. MS 38th Cav. Co.E

Rogers, H.J. SC Cav. 19th Bn. Co.E

Rogers, H.J. SC 20th Inf. Co.N

Rogers, H.J. TN 4th (McLemore's) Cav. Co.B

Rogers, H.J.C. TX 7th Inf. Co.H

Rogers, H.L. GA 40th Inf. Co.K

Rogers, H.M. LA Inf. Crescent Regt. Co.K

Rogers, H.M. MS 41st Inf. Co.F

Rogers, H.M. NC 62nd Inf. Asst.Surg.

Rogers, H.N. GA 65th Inf. Co.B,E

Rogers, H.N. GA Smith's Legion Co.C

Rogers, Hosea M. GA 53rd Inf. Co.C

Rogers, Housten NC 29th Inf. Co.A

Rogers, Houston NC Walker's Bn. Thomas'
Legion Co.B

Rogers, Howell N. TN 39th Mtd.Inf. Co.F Sgt.

Rogers, H.P. VA Lt.Arty. R.M. Anderson's Co.

Rogers, H.R. MS Cav. Davenport's Bn.
(St.Troops) Co.B

Rogers, H.R. MS 10th Inf. New Co.C, Co.L

Rogers, H.R. TN 9th Inf. Co.F

Rogers, H.R. TX Cav. Well's Regt. Co.C

Rogers, H.S. MS 3rd Cav. Co.A Jr.2nd Lt.

Rogers, H.T. AR 1st (Colquitt's) Inf. Co.D Cpl.

Rogers, H.T. GA Lt.Arty. (Jo Thompson Arty.)
Hanleiter's Co.

Rogers, Huger SC 1st (Orr's) Rifles Co.H 1st
Lt.

Rogers, Hugh GA 1st Inf. (St.Guards) Co.K

Rogers, Hugh LA Mil. British Guard Bn. West's
Co.

Rogers, Hugh LA Mil. Irish Regt. Laughlin's Co.

Rogers, Hugh SC 6th Cav. Co.E

Rogers, Hugh TN 3rd (Lillard's) Mtd.Inf. Co.E
Sgt.

Rogers, Hugh 3rd Conf.Cav. Co.G

Rogers, Hugh C. TX 13th Vol. 1st Co.F, 2nd
Co.D

Rogers, Hugh H. AL 11th Inf. Co.A

Rogers, Hugh H. VA 8th Inf. Co.F

Rogers, Hugh H. Sig.Corps,CSA

Rogers, Hugh Hamilton Gen. & Staff 1st
Lt.,ADC

Rogers, Hugh M. Gen. & Staff Surg.

Rogers, Hugh W. KY 13th Cav. Co.D

Rogers, Hugh W. NC 39th Inf. Co.C,G 2nd Lt.

Rogers, H.W. AL 17th Inf. Co.C

Rogers, H.W. GA 11th Cav. Co.A

Rogers, H.W. TN 40th Inf. Co.G

Rogers, H.W. VA Lt.Arty. Hankins' Co.

Rogers, Hynard SC 26th Inf. Co.C

Rogers, I.C. GA 8th Inf.

Rogers, I.D. MS 8th Inf. Co.H

Rogers, I.E. GA 51st Inf.

Rogers, I.J. AL 27th Inf. Co.B Capt.

Rogers, I.J. TX 12th Inf. Co.G

Rogers, Iley NC 47th Inf. Co.C

Rogers, I.R. TX 14th Cav. Co.B

Rogers, Ira 1st Cherokee Mtd.Vol. 1st Co.C

Rogers, Irvin VA 5th Cav. Co.B

Rogers, Isaac AL Arty. 4th Bn. Hilliard's Legion
Co.D

Rogers, Isaac AR 27th Inf. Co.H 1st Sgt.

Rogers, Isaac TX 15th Inf. Co.E

Rogers, Isaac D. AL Cav. Hardie's Bn.Res.
Co.E

Rogers, Isaac H. LA 1st Cav. Co.B

Rogers, Isaac M. AL 3rd Res. Co.H

Rogers, Isaac N. TN Lt.Arty. Barry's Co.

Rogers, Isaac N. TX 7th Cav. Co.I

Rogers, Isaac N. TX 22nd Inf. Co.K

Rogers, Isaac T. KY 2nd Cav. Co.E

Rogers, Isaac T. NC 5th Cav. (63rd St.Troops)
Co.C

Rogers, Isaiah TN 35th Inf. 1st Co.A

Rogers, Isam MS St.Cav. 3rd Bn. (Cooper's) 1st
Co.A

Rogers, Israel MS 22nd Inf. Co.E

Rogers, J. AL Cav. 24th Bn. Co.C

Rogers, J. AL 1st Bn.Cadets Co.B

Rogers, J. AL 1st Regt. Mobile Vol. Baas' Co.

Rogers, J. AR 58th Mil. Co.E

Rogers, J. AR 62nd Mil. Co.C Sgt.

Rogers, J. GA 5th Res. Co.E

Rogers, J. GA 10th Mil. Sgt.

Rogers, J. GA Inf. (E. to W.Point Guards)
Matthews' Co.

Rogers, J. LA 25th Inf. Co.K

Rogers, J. LA Mil. Chalmette Regt. Co.B

Rogers, J. MS 6th Cav. Co.E

Rogers, J. MO 2nd Inf. Co.I

Rogers, J. SC Lt.Arty. 3rd (Palmetto) Bn. Co.G

Rogers, J. TX 3rd Cav.

Rogers, J. TX 24th & 25th Cav. (Cons.) Co.B

Rogers, J. VA Cav. 32nd Bn.

Rogers, J.A. AL 37th Inf. Co.K

Rogers, J.A. AR 2nd Inf. Co.H

Rogers, J.A. AR 36th Inf. Co.D

Rogers, J.A. GA 7th Cav. Co.D

Rogers, J.A. GA 8th Cav.

Rogers, J.A. GA Cav. 24th Bn. Co.A,C

Rogers, J.A. GA 1st Inf. (St.Guards) Co.D

Rogers, J.A. GA 32nd Inf. Co.F

Rogers, J.A. GA Inf. (Mitchell Home Guards)
Brooks' Co.

Rogers, J.A. LA 27th Inf. Co.F

Rogers, J.A. MS Cav. 1st Bn. (McNair's)
St.Troops Co.B

Rogers, J.A. TN 8th (Smith's) Cav. Co.F

Rogers, J.A. TN 38th Inf. 2nd Co.H Sgt.

Rogers, J.A. VA 1st Cav. Co.A

Rogers, J.A. Gen. & Staff Chap.

Rogers, Jackson GA 1st Inf. (St.Guards) Co.B

Rogers, Jackson J. NC 62nd Inf. Co.I Cpl.

Rogers, Jacob MS 5th Inf. (St.Troops) Co.H,B

Rogers, Jacob MO 1st & 4th Cons.Inf. Co.B

Rogers, Jacob MO 4th Inf. Co.G Cpl.

Rogers, Jacob TN 61st Mtd.Inf. Co.E Cpl.

Rogers, Jacob VA Cav. 46th Bn. Co.A

Rogers, Jacob D. SC 6th Cav. Co.E Far.

Rogers, Jacob H. AR 16th Inf. Co.C

Rogers, Jacob H. VA Lt.Arty. French's Co.

Rogers, Jacob J. AL 12th Inf. Co.E

Rogers, Jacob M. NC 14th Inf. Co.K

Rogers, Jacob W. MS 2nd St.Cav. Co.D Sgt.

Rogers, Jacob W. MS 11th (Perrin's) Cav. Co.A

Rogers, Jacob W. MS 9th Inf. Old Co.F

Rogers, James AL 6th Cav. Co.A

Rogers, James AL Inf. 1st Regt. Co.E

Rogers, James AL Inf. 1st Regt. Co.G

Rogers, James AL 19th Inf. Co.G

Rogers, James AL 42nd Inf. Co.B

Rogers, James AR 5th Inf. Co.D

Rogers, James AR 15th (N.W.) Inf. Co.K

Rogers, James FL Inf. 2nd Bn. Co.D

Rogers, James FL 5th Inf. Co.A

Rogers, James GA Cav. 1st Gordon Squad.
(St.Guards) Reeves' Co. 1st Lt.

Rogers, James GA Cav. 1st Bn. Hughes' Co.

Rogers, James GA 5th Cav. Co.D

Rogers, James GA 12th Cav. Co.I Cpl.

Rogers, James GA Hvy.Arty. 22nd Bn. Co.E

Rogers, James GA 1st (Olmstead's) Inf. Co.A

Rogers, James GA Inf. 6th Bn. ACS

Rogers, James GA 60th Inf. Co.D

Rogers, James GA 64th Inf. Co.A

Rogers, James KY 13th Cav. Co.D Capt.

Rogers, James LA 10th Inf. Co.C

Rogers, James LA 15th Inf. Co.B

Rogers, James LA 19th Inf. Co.K

Rogers, James LA 28th (Gray's) Inf. Co.H

Rogers, James LA 28th (Thomas') Inf. Co.C

Rogers, James LA Conscr.

Rogers, James MS 1st Cav. Co.F

Rogers, James MS 9th Cav. Co.G

Rogers, James MS 38th Cav. Co.E

Rogers, James MS Cav. Garland's Bn. Co.C

Rogers, James MS Inf. 2nd Bn. (St.Troops) Co.C

Rogers, James MS 10th Inf. New Co.G 1st Lt.

Rogers, James MS 26th Inf. Co.F

Rogers, James MS 41st Inf. Co.F Sgt.

Rogers, James MO Inf. 3rd Bn. Co.E

Rogers, James MO 4th Inf. Co.G

Rogers, James MO 6th Inf. Co.C

Rogers, James NC 5th Inf. Co.F

Rogers, James NC 13th Inf. Co.D

Rogers, James NC 13th Inf. Co.I

Rogers, James NC 24th Inf. Co.E

Rogers, James NC 26th Inf. Co.B

Rogers, James NC 30th Inf. Co.H

Rogers, James NC 44th Inf. Co.B

Rogers, James SC Arty. Gregg's Co. (McQueen
Lt.Arty.)

Rogers, James SC Arty. Manigault's Bn. 1st
Co.C

Rogers, James SC 1st (McCreary's) Inf. Co.E

Rogers, James SC 1st Inf. Co.K

Rogers, James SC 3rd St.Troops Co.C

Rogers, James SC 5th Inf. 2nd Co.H

Rogers, James SC 22nd Inf. Co.C

Rogers, James TN 3rd (Forrest's) Cav. Co.A

Rogers, James TN 4th (Murray's) Cav. Co.B

Rogers, James TN Cav. Welcker's Bn. Co.A

Rogers, James TN 12th (Cons.) Inf. Co.H

Rogers, James TN 17th Inf. Co.K

Rogers, James TN 22nd Inf. Co.B

Rogers, James TN Inf. 22nd Bn. Co.H

Rogers, James TN 41st Inf. Co.G

Rogers, James TN 42nd Inf. Co.D 1st Lt.

Rogers, James TN 43rd Inf. Co.A

Rogers, James TN Detailed Conscr. Co.A

Rogers, James TX Cav. 3rd (Yager's) Bn. Co.A

Rogers, James TX 21st Cav. Co.C

Rogers, James TX 27th Cav. Co.I,N

Rogers, James TX Cav. Mann's Regt. Co.C

Rogers, James TX 2nd Inf. Co.F

Rogers, James VA 1st Cav. Co.A

Rogers, James VA 5th Cav. (12 mo. '61-2) Co.G

Rogers, James VA 13th Cav. Co.I
Rogers, James VA 19th Cav. Co.H Cpl.
Rogers, James VA 20th Cav. Co.I
Rogers, James VA Cav. Mosby's Regt. (Part.Rangers)
Rogers, James VA 2nd Inf.Loc.Def. Co.C
Rogers, James VA Inf. 2nd Bn.Loc.Def. Co.E
Rogers, James VA 36th Inf. 2nd Co.C
Rogers, James VA 48th Inf. Co.A
Rogers, James VA 54th Inf. Co.F
Rogers, James VA Inf. 54th Bn. Co.G
Rogers, James VA Wade's Regt.Loc.Def. Co.A
Rogers, James 1st Conf.Cav. 2nd Co.E Cpl.
Rogers, James 4th Conf.Inf. Co.K 1st Lt.
Rogers, James 1st Cherokee Mtd.Vol. 2nd Co.C
Rogers, James 2nd Cherokee Mtd.Vol. Co.F
Rogers, James Gen. & Staff Capt.,QM
Rogers, James A. AL Arty. 1st Bn. Co.B
Rogers, James A. AR 6th Inf. New Co.D
Rogers, James A. GA Lt.Arty. 14th Bn. Co.D Sgt.
Rogers, James A. GA Lt.Arty. (Jo Thompson Arty.) Hanleiter's Co.
Rogers, James A. GA Lt.Arty. King's Btty. Sgt.
Rogers, James A. GA 56th Inf. Co.A
Rogers, James A. KY 13th Cav. Co.C
Rogers, James A. MS 2nd (Quinn's St.Troops) Inf. Co.D
Rogers, James A. NC 15th Inf. Co.A
Rogers, James A. NC 54th Inf. Co.D Maj.
Rogers, James A. TN 1st (Carter's) Cav. Co.K
Rogers, James A. TN 8th Cav.
Rogers, James A. TX 32nd Cav. Co.G Cpl.
Rogers, James A. VA 27th Inf. Co.A
Rogers, James A. VA 31st Mil. Co.F
Rogers, James B. MO 4th Cav. Co.G
Rogers, James B. NC 29th Inf. Co.G,B
Rogers, James B. TN 61st Mtd.Inf. Co.A
Rogers, James B. TX 2nd Inf. Co.H
Rogers, James B. TX 17th Inf. Co.B
Rogers, James B. VA 11th Inf. Co.A
Rogers, James C. AL Arty. 1st Bn. Co.C
Rogers, James C. AL Inf. 1st Regt. Co.K
Rogers, James C. AR 9th Inf. Co.K
Rogers, James C. GA 12th Cav. Co.D 1st 2nd Lt.
Rogers, James E. MS 21st Inf. Co.C Cpl.
Rogers, James E. TX 17th Cav. Co.K
Rogers, James E. VA 9th Cav. Co.I
Rogers, James F. TN 22nd Cav.
Rogers, James G. AL 19th Inf. Co.C Sgt.
Rogers, James G. KY 5th Mtd.Inf. Co.C
Rogers, James G. VA 41st Inf. Co.I
Rogers, James H. GA Cav. 16th Bn. (St.Guards) Co.F
Rogers, James H. GA 5th Inf. Co.K,E Capt.
Rogers, James H. GA 6th Inf. Co.A Sgt.
Rogers, James H. GA 14th Inf. Co.F
Rogers, James H. GA Cobb's Legion Co.G
Rogers, James H. MS 7th Inf. Co.D
Rogers, James H. NC Hvy.Arty. 10th Bn. Co.D
Rogers, James H. NC 3rd Inf. Co.E
Rogers, James H. NC 6th Inf. Co.K
Rogers, James H. TN 31st Inf. Co.G
Rogers, James H. TX 1st Inf. Co.C
Rogers, Jas. H. VA 8th Inf. Co.D
Rogers, James H. Gen. & Staff 1st Lt.,Adj.

Rogers, James I. NC 57th Inf. Co.C
Rogers, James J. GA 14th Inf. Co.B
Rogers, James J. SC Arty. Manigault's Bn. 1st Co.B,C
Rogers, James K. AL 18th Bn.Vol. Co.B
Rogers, James K. TN 35th Inf. Co.L
Rogers, James K.P. TN 43rd Inf. Co.A Sgt.
Rogers, James L. AL 15th Bn.Part.Rangers Co.D Cpl.
Rogers, James L. GA 11th Inf. Co.C Drum.
Rogers, James L. LA 9th Inf. Co.I
Rogers, James L.W. NC Inf. Thomas Legion Co.K
Rogers, James M. AL 3rd Res. Co.H
Rogers, James M. AL 28th Inf. Co.H
Rogers, James M. AR 9th Inf. Old Co.B, Co.F
Rogers, James M. FL 6th Inf. Co.B Sgt.
Rogers, James M. GA 1st Reg. Co.F
Rogers, James M. GA 9th Inf. Co.C
Rogers, James M. GA 48th Inf. Co.G
Rogers, James M. GA 60th Inf. Co.F Sgt.
Rogers, James M. LA 3rd (Harrison's) Cav. Co.H
Rogers, James M. LA 12th Inf. 2nd Co.M
Rogers, James M. MS 16th Inf. Co.H Sgt.
Rogers, James M. MO 19th Cav. Co.F
Rogers, James M. NC Hvy.Arty. 1st Bn. Co.B
Rogers, James M. SC 4th Cav. Co.E
Rogers, James M. TN 2nd (Smith's) Cav. Rankin's Co.
Rogers, James M. TN 4th (McLemore's) Cav. Co.H Bvt.2nd Lt.
Rogers, James M. TN 1st (Turney's) Inf. Co.D
Rogers, James M. TN 3rd (Lillard's) Mtd.Inf. Co.G Cpl.
Rogers, James M. TN 43rd Inf. Co.G Cpl.
Rogers, James M. TX Cav. 1st Bn.St.Troops Co.A
Rogers, James M. TX 19th Cav. Co.A
Rogers, James M. TX 19th Cav. Co.G
Rogers, James M. TX 21st Cav. Co.A
Rogers, James M. VA 10th Cav. Co.G
Rogers, James M. VA 20th Cav. Co.H 2nd Lt.
Rogers, James M. VA Inf. 21st Bn. 2nd Co.D
Rogers, James M. Gen. & Staff Asst.Surg.
Rogers, James M.L. NC 37th Inf. Co.F,C
Rogers, James P. AL 4th Inf. Co.G
Rogers, James P. LA 4th Inf. Co.G
Rogers, James P. LA 6th Inf. Co.G
Rogers, James P. MD 1st Cav. Co.C
Rogers, James P. MD Weston's Bn. Co.B
Rogers, James P. MS 15th Inf. Co.C
Rogers, James P. TX 14th Cav. Co.B
Rogers, James P. VA 21st Inf. Co.B
Rogers, James P. Sig.Corps,CSA
Rogers, James R. KY 1st Bn.Mtd.Rifles Co.C
Rogers, James R. KY 3rd Bn.Mtd.Rifles Adj.
Rogers, James R. MS Lt.Arty. Turner's Co.
Rogers, James R. NC 29th Inf. Co.E
Rogers, James R. TX 11th (Spaight's) Bn.Vol. Co.C,D,B,E Cpl.
Rogers, James R. Sig.Corps,CSA
Rogers, Jas. R. Gen. & Staff 1st Lt.,Adj.
Rogers, James T. GA 34th Inf. Co.E
Rogers, James T. KY 1st Bn.Mtd.Rifles Co.C 3rd Lt.
Rogers, James T. KY 13th Cav. Co.D Capt.

Rogers, James T. MS Cav. Stockdale's Bn. Co.B
Rogers, James T. NC 13th Inf. Co.H
Rogers, James T. NC 15th Inf. Co.M 2nd Lt.
Rogers, James T. NC 32nd Inf. Co.I 2nd Lt.
Rogers, James T. TN Cav. Cooper's Regt. Co.B,D
Rogers, James T. TN 32nd Inf. Co.C
Rogers, James T. TN 48th (Nixon's) Inf. Co.G
Rogers, James W. AL 18th Inf. Co.H
Rogers, James W. AL 25th Inf. Co.A
Rogers, James W. AL 48th Inf. Co.C
Rogers, James W. GA Cav. 16th Bn. (St.Guards) Co.F
Rogers, James W. GA 25th Inf. Co.K
Rogers, James W. KY 2nd Bn.Mtd.Rifles Co.E
Rogers, James W. KY 5th Mtd.Inf. Co.C
Rogers, James W. MS 1st Cav. Co.H
Rogers, James W. MS 1st Lt.Arty. Co.C
Rogers, James W. MS 1st (Patton's) Inf. Co.B
Rogers, James W. NC 33rd Inf. Co.C
Rogers, James W. NC 35th Inf. Co.H
Rogers, James W. TN Cav. 16th Bn. (Neal's) Co.A 1st Lt.
Rogers, James Warren AL 18th Inf. Co.B
Rogers, Jared VA 19th Cav. Co.D
Rogers, Jared VA 20th Cav. Co.A
Rogers, Jasper AL 12th Inf. Co.E
Rogers, Jasper AL 37th Inf. Co.F
Rogers, Jasper NC 26th Inf. Co.G
Rogers, Jasper SC Inf. 7th Bn. (Enfield Rifles) Co.H
Rogers, Jasper TN 51st Inf. Co.H
Rogers, Jasper N. AR 23rd Inf. Co.I
Rogers, Jasper N. GA 1st (Olmstead's) Inf. Co.H
Rogers, Jasper N.W. NC 64th Inf. Co.C
Rogers, J.B. AL 9th (Malone's) Cav. Co.I
Rogers, J.B. AL 40th Inf. Co.G
Rogers, J.B. AR 15th Inf. Co.A 1st Lt.
Rogers, J.B. AR 37th Inf. Co.B
Rogers, J.B. GA 12th Cav. Co.D
Rogers, J.B. GA 8th Inf. Co.H
Rogers, J.B. GA 46th Inf. Co.D
Rogers, J.B. GA Cobb's Legion Co.C
Rogers, J.B. LA Inf.Crescent Regt. Co.C
Rogers, J.B. MS 2nd St.Cav. Co.B
Rogers, J.B. MS 3rd (St.Troops) Cav. Co.K
Rogers, J.B. MS 8th Cav. Co.G
Rogers, J.B. MS 25th Inf.
Rogers, J.B. MS 41st Inf. Co.D
Rogers, J.B. NC Lt.Arty. 13th Bn. Co.D
Rogers, J.B. NC 62nd Inf.
Rogers, J.B. SC Cav. 12th Bn. Co.D
Rogers, J.B. SC 21st Inf. Co.L
Rogers, J.B. TN 40th Inf. Co.D 1st Lt.
Rogers, J.B. TX 4th Inf. Co.B
Rogers, J.B. VA 10th Cav. Co.G
Rogers, J.B. 3rd Conf.Cav. Co.G 1st Lt.
Rogers, J.B.S. NC 3rd Cav. (41st St.Troops) Co.I
Rogers, J.C. AL 9th Inf. Co.I
Rogers, J.C. AL Talladega Guards
Rogers, J.C. GA 7th Cav. Co.D
Rogers, J.C. GA 16th Inf. Co.H
Rogers, J.C. GA 20th Inf. Co.A
Rogers, J.C. GA 36th (Broyles') Inf. Co.E
Rogers, J.C. KY 2nd Mtd.Inf. Co.D
Rogers, J.C. MS Inf. 1st Bn. Co.C Capt.

Rogers, J.C. MS 34th Inf. Co.K
Rogers, J.C. NC 6th Cav. (65th St.Troops)
  Co.C,D
Rogers, J.C. NC 12th Inf. Co.K
Rogers, J.C. SC Inf. 13th Bn. Co.A
Rogers, J.C. SC Inf. Hampton Legion Co.K
Rogers, J.C. TN 10th (DeMoss') Cav. Co.F
Rogers, J.C. TN Cav. Napier's Bn. Co.C
Rogers, J.C. TN Inf. 4th Cons.Regt. Co.H
Rogers, J.C. TN 5th Inf. 2nd Co.H
Rogers, J.C. TN 16th Inf. Co.I
Rogers, J.C. TN 48th (Nixon's) Inf. Co.G
Rogers, J.C. TX 12th Inf. Co.C
Rogers, J.D. AL 1st Regt.Conscr. Co.F
Rogers, J.D. AL 59th Inf. Co.H
Rogers, J.D. GA 6th Cav. Co.B 1st Sgt.
Rogers, J.D. MS 7th Cav. Co.E Capt.
Rogers, J.D. MS 4th Inf. Co.G,H
Rogers, J.D. MS 23rd Inf. Co.H
Rogers, J.D. TX Cav. Terry's Regt. Surg.
Rogers, J.D. VA Cav. 41st Bn. Co.C
Rogers, J.D. Trans-MS Conf.Cav. 1st Bn. Co.B
Rogers, J.E. AL 8th Inf. Co.C
Rogers, J.E. AL 33rd Inf. Co.F Cpl.
Rogers, J.E. GA 4th (Clinch's) Cav. Co.A
Rogers, J.E. TN 4th Inf. Co.C Cpl.
Rogers, J.E. TN 5th Inf. 2nd Co.D
Rogers, Jeff KY 1st (Butler's) Cav. Co.D Capt.
Rogers, Jeff KY 3rd Cav. Co.E 2nd Lt.
Rogers, Jeff MS 20th Inf. Co.D
Rogers, Jeff NC 6th Inf. Co.K
Rogers, Jefferson VA 25th Cav. Co.B
Rogers, Jefferson VA Inf. 21st Bn. 1st Co.D
Rogers, Jefferson C. TX 5th Inf. Co.G Maj.
Rogers, Jeff J. TX 3rd Cav. Co.G
Rogers, Jeff W. AR 9th Inf. Co.F 1st Lt.
Rogers, Jeremiah TN 35th Inf. Co.L Sgt.
Rogers, Jeremiah TN 36th Inf. Co.L
Rogers, Jeremiah D. AR 38th Inf. Co.M
Rogers, Jeremiah D. MO 10th Inf. Co.F
Rogers, Jeremiah M. TX 27th Cav. Co.D
Rogers, Jeremiah S. NC Inf. Thomas Legion
  Co.H
Rogers, Jerome B. AR 15th (Johnson's) Inf.
  Co.B 1st Lt.
Rogers, Jerret I. TX 21st Inf. Co.E
Rogers, Jesse AR 16th Inf. Co.C Cpl.
Rogers, Jesse MS 37th Inf. Co.A
Rogers, Jesse NC 48th Inf. Co.F
Rogers, Jesse SC Arty. Gregg's Co. (McQueen
  Lt.Arty.)
Rogers, Jesse SC Arty. Manigault's Bn. 1st
  Co.B,C
Rogers, Jesse SC 1st (Orr's) Rifles Co.H
Rogers, Jesse B. TX 13th Cav. Co.G 2nd Lt.
Rogers, Jesse C. AL 43rd Inf. Co.A
Rogers, Jesse E. TX 9th Cav. Co.A
Rogers, Jessee Henderson MO 8th Inf. Co.H
Rogers, Jesse F. MS 1st Lt.Arty. Co.L
Rogers, Jesse F. NC 29th Inf. Co.E
Rogers, Jesse J.S. NC 60th Inf. Co.I Fifer
Rogers, Jesse M. TN 39th Mtd.Inf. Co.C
Rogers, Jesse M. VA Hvy.Arty. 20th Bn. Co.E
Rogers, Jesse R. NC 29th Inf. Co.E
Rogers, Jesse R. TN 60th Mtd.Inf. Co.G
Rogers, Jesse S. TN 55th (McKoin's) Inf. Co.H
Rogers, Jesse S. VA 17th Inf. Co.F 1st Sgt.

Rogers, Jesse T. AL 42nd Inf. Co.B
Rogers, Jesse W. AL 4th (Russell's) Cav. Co.D
Rogers, Jesse W. MS 5th Inf. Co.K
Rogers, Jesse W. VA 14th Inf. Co.D
Rogers, Jesse W. VA 59th Mil. Hunter's Co.
Rogers, Jethro W. GA Cobb's Legion Co.F
Rogers, Jewett G. VA 10th Inf. Co.G Music.
Rogers, J.F. FL Cav. 3rd Bn. Co.C
Rogers, J.F. GA Cav. 1st Bn.Res. Tufts' Co.
Rogers, J.F. GA Cav. 6th Bn. (St.Guards) Co.D
Rogers, J.F. GA Lt.Arty. Howell's Co.
Rogers, J.F. LA 2nd Cav. Co.G
Rogers, J.F. LA 25th Inf. Co.E
Rogers, J.F. MS St.Cav. 2nd Bn. (Harris') Co.B
Rogers, J.F. TN 19th & 20th (Cons.) Cav. Co.K
Rogers, J.F. TN 59th Mtd.Inf. Co.K
Rogers, J.F. TX 8th Cav. Co.A
Rogers, J.F. TX 7th Inf. Co.A
Rogers, J.F. Inf. Bailey's Cons.Regt. Co.B
Rogers, J.F. TX 21st Inf. Co.G
Rogers, J.F. 3rd Conf.Cav. Co.A
Rogers, J.F. 15th Conf.Cav. Co.E
Rogers, J.F. 1st Conf.Inf. 1st Co.K
Rogers, J.G. GA 55th Inf. Co.C
Rogers, J.G. TN Inf. 1st Cons.Regt. Co.H
Rogers, J.G. TN 28th (Cons.) Inf. Co.D 1st Lt.
Rogers, J.G. TX Cav. Gano's Squad. Co.B
Rogers, J.G. VA 7th Cav. Co.G
Rogers, J.G. 3rd Conf.Cav. Co.G
Rogers, J. Green SC 8th Inf. Co.K
Rogers, J.H. AL 14th Inf. Co.H
Rogers, J.H. AL 17th Inf. Co.H
Rogers, J.H. AR 7th Cav. Co.B
Rogers, J.H. AR 38th Inf. Co.E
Rogers, J.H. AR 38th Inf. Co.G
Rogers, J.H. GA 8th Cav. Co.F
Rogers, J.H. GA Cav. 20th Bn. Co.D
Rogers, J.H. GA 62nd Cav. Co.F
Rogers, J.H. GA 66th Inf. Co.G,A 2nd Lt.
Rogers, J.H. MS 9th Inf. New Co.H, Co.F 1st
  Lt.
Rogers, J.H. MS 31st Inf. Co.I 1st Sgt.
Rogers, J.H. NC 5th Inf. Co.B
Rogers, J.H. NC 17th Inf. (2nd Org.) Co.I
Rogers, J.H. NC Snead's Co. (Loc.Def.)
Rogers, J.H. TN 3rd (Forrest's) Cav. Co.G
Rogers, J.H. TN 12th (Green's) Cav. Co.A
Rogers, J.H. TN Inf. 3rd Bn. Co.C
Rogers, J.H. TN 13th Inf. Co.H
Rogers, J.H. TN 45th Inf. Co.H
Rogers, J.H. TX 28th Cav. Co.C
Rogers, J. Henry AL 59th Inf. Co.I,F
Rogers, Jim 1st Creek Mtd.Vol. Co.F
Rogers, J.J. AL 8th Cav. Co.F
Rogers, J.J. AR 62nd Mil. Co.C 1st Sgt.
Rogers, J.J. GA Cav. 20th Bn. Co.A,D,E
Rogers, J.J. GA 1st (Symons') Res. Co.E
Rogers, J.J. KY 7th Cav. Co.A
Rogers, J.J. MS 38th Cav. Co.E
Rogers, J.J. MS 3rd Inf. (St.Troops) Co.G
Rogers, J.J. MS 41st Inf. Co.L Sgt.
Rogers, J.J. NC 6th Sr.Res. Co.E
Rogers, J.J. SC Arty. Gregg's Co. (McQueen
  Lt.Arty.)
Rogers, J.J. TN 28th (Cons.) Inf. Co.F
Rogers, J.J. TN 55th (Brown's) Inf. Co.F
Rogers, J.J. TX 11th Cav. Co.E

Rogers, J.J. TX Cav. Gano's Squad. Co.A
Rogers, J.J. TX 11th (Spaight's) Bn.Vol. Co.C
Rogers, J.J. VA Mil. Scott Cty.
Rogers, J.L. AL 56th Part.Rangers Co.D 1st
  Sgt.
Rogers, J.L. AL Cav. Moreland's Regt. Co.H
Rogers, J.L. AL 27th Inf. Co.B Cpl.
Rogers, J.L. AR 37th Inf. Co.E Cpl.
Rogers, J.L. GA Cav. 10th Bn. (St.Guards) Co.C
Rogers, J.L. KY 5th Cav. Co.F
Rogers, J.L. SC 20th Inf. Co.M
Rogers, J.L. TN 39th Inf. Co.B
Rogers, J.L. TX 4th Inf. Co.E Cpl.
Rogers, J.L. TX 15th Inf. 2nd Co.E
Rogers, J.L. VA Inf. 2nd Bn.Loc.Def. Co.B
Rogers, J.L. 2nd Cherokee Mtd.Vol. Co.G
Rogers, J.M. AL 34th Inf. Co.B
Rogers, J.M. AR 2nd Cav. Co.G
Rogers, J.M. AR Lt.Arty. Marshall's Btty.
Rogers, J.M. AR 17th (Griffith's) Inf. Co.G
Rogers, J.M. AR 37th Inf. Co.E
Rogers, J.M. GA 4th (Clinch's) Cav. Co.F
Rogers, J.M. GA 11th Cav. Co.G
Rogers, J.M. GA 36th (Broyles') Inf. Co.G 2nd
  Lt.
Rogers, J.M. GA Inf. (Anderson Guards) Ander-
  son's Co. Sgt.
Rogers, J.M. LA Inf.Cons.Crescent Regt. Co.H
Rogers, J.M. MS 2nd St.Cav. Co.A
Rogers, J.M. MS 3rd Inf. (A. of 10,000) Co.G
Rogers, J.M. MS 14th Inf. Co.C
Rogers, J.M. MS 35th Inf. Surg.
Rogers, J.M. MS 41st Inf. Co.D
Rogers, J.M. MS 46th Inf. Co.H
Rogers, J.M. MS Yerger's Co. (St.Troops) Sgt.
Rogers, J.M. MO 1st & 4th Cons.Inf. Co.B
Rogers, J.M. MO 9th Inf. Co.H
Rogers, J.M. MO Inf. Clark's Regt. Co.C
Rogers, J.M. NC 1st Cav. (9th St.Troops) Co.F
Rogers, J.M. NC 62nd Inf.
Rogers, J.M. SC Lt.Arty. M. Ward's Co. (Wac-
  camaw Lt.Arty.)
Rogers, J.M. SC Bn.St.Cadets Co.A
Rogers, J.M. TN 11th (Holman's) Cav. Co.K
Rogers, J.M. TN Inf. 3rd Cons.Regt. Co.A
Rogers, J.M. TN 4th Inf. Co.C
Rogers, J.M. TN 11th Inf. Co.C
Rogers, J.M. TN Inf. 23rd Bn. Co.D
Rogers, J.M. TN 27th Inf. Co.E Drum.
Rogers, J.M. TN 33rd Inf. Co.I
Rogers, J.M. TN Conscr. (Cp. of Instr.) Co.B
Rogers, J.M. TX 4th Cav. Co.E
Rogers, J.M. TX 8th Cav. Co.C
Rogers, J.M. TX 15th Cav. Co.B
Rogers, J.M. TX Cav. Border's Regt. Co.C
Rogers, J.M. VA 5th Cav. Co.B
Rogers, J.M. VA Lt.Arty. Jackson's Bn.St.Line
  Co.A
Rogers, J.M. Gen. & Staff Surg.
Rogers, J.N. AL Cav. Barbiere's Bn. Truss' Co.
Rogers, J.N. TN 22nd Inf. Co.F Cpl.
Rogers, J.N. TX 30th Cav. Co.H Cpl.
Rogers, J.N. TX Cav. Terry's Regt. Co.K
Rogers, J.N. VA Lt.Arty. Fry's Co.
Rogers, J. Newton SC 7th Inf. 1st Co.C
Rogers, J.N.W. NC 60th Inf. Co.A
Rogers, J.O. MS 41st Inf. Co.L

Rogers, Jobe NC 30th Inf. Co.E
Rogers, Joe B. TX 8th Cav. Co.D Sgt.
Rogers, Joe C. MS 5th Inf. Co.K Capt.
Rogers, Joel P. MS 48th Inf. Co.L Capt.
Rogers, John AL 6th Inf. Co.I
Rogers, John AL 9th Inf. Co.G
Rogers, John AL 12th Inf. Co.A 1st Lt.
Rogers, John AL 12th Inf. Co.A
Rogers, John AL 12th Inf. Co.E Capt.
Rogers, John AL 18th Inf. Co.G
Rogers, John AL 45th Inf. Co.I
Rogers, John AL 58th Inf. Co.G
Rogers, John AL 61st Inf. Co.B
Rogers, John AR Cav. Gordon's Regt. Co.H
Rogers, John AR Cav. Wright's Regt. Co.I
Rogers, John AR 5th Inf. Co.D
Rogers, John AR 62nd Mil. Co.C
Rogers, John AR Inf. Adams' Regt. Moore's Co.
Rogers, John FL 2nd Cav. Co.A Sgt.
Rogers, John FL 2nd Cav. Co.H
Rogers, John FL Milton Lt.Arty. Dunham's Co.
Rogers, John FL 1st (Res.) Inf. Co.C
Rogers, Jno. FL Res. Poe's Co.
Rogers, John GA Cav. 20th Bn. Co.A,E
Rogers, John GA Lt.Arty. Croft's Btty.
    (Columbus Arty.) Cpl.
Rogers, John GA Lt.Arty. Scogin's Btty. (Griffin
    Lt.Arty.)
Rogers, John GA 6th Inf. Co.I
Rogers, John GA 7th Inf. Co.K
Rogers, John GA 9th Inf. (St.Guards) Co.E
Rogers, John GA 11th Inf. Co.E
Rogers, John GA 30th Inf. Co.F
Rogers, John GA 40th Inf. Co.B
Rogers, John GA 49th Inf. Co.A
Rogers, John KY 4th Cav. Co.G,B
Rogers, John KY 7th Cav. Co.B
Rogers, John KY 7th Mtd.Inf. Co.C
Rogers, John LA 1st (Strawbridge's) Inf. Co.C
Rogers, John LA 7th Inf. Co.D Cpl.
Rogers, John LA 12th Inf. 2nd Co.M
Rogers, John MS 2nd St.Cav. Co.D Cpl.
Rogers, John MS Cav. Ham's Regt. Co.B,D
Rogers, John MS 5th Inf. (St.Troops) Co.H
Rogers, John MS 8th Inf. Co.F
Rogers, John MS 19th Inf. Co.K
Rogers, John MS 21st Inf. Co.D
Rogers, John MS 34th Inf. Co.A
Rogers, John MS 37th Inf. Co.G
Rogers, John MS 42nd Inf. Co.H
Rogers, John MS 44th Inf. Co.L
Rogers, John MO 7th Cav. Co.B
Rogers, John MO 10th Cav. Co.B
Rogers, John MO 8th Inf. Co.H Sgt.
Rogers, John NC 4th Inf. Co.B
Rogers, John NC 35th Inf. Co.E
Rogers, John NC 57th Inf. Co.I Cpl.
Rogers, John SC 6th Cav. Co.E
Rogers, John SC Arty. Gregg's Co. (McQueen
    Lt.Arty.)
Rogers, John SC Arty. Manigault's Bn. 1st Co.C
Rogers, John SC 5th Bn.Res. Co.B
Rogers, John SC 10th Inf. 2nd Co.G
Rogers, John SC 13th Inf. Co.B
Rogers, John SC 18th Inf. Co.G
Rogers, John SC 21st Inf. Co.A
Rogers, John TN Cav. 1st Bn. (McNairy's) Co.B

Rogers, John TN 16th (Logwood's) Cav. Co.G
Rogers, John TN Lt.Arty. Winston's Co.
Rogers, John TN 4th Inf.
Rogers, John TN 14th Inf. Co.I
Rogers, John TN 20th Inf. Co.I
Rogers, John TN 23rd Inf. Co.D,F
Rogers, John TN 39th Mtd.Inf. Co.K
Rogers, John TN 62nd Mtd.Inf. Co.K
Rogers, John TX 7th Cav. Co.I
Rogers, John TX 20th Cav. Co.A
Rogers, John TX 4th Inf. Co.D
Rogers, John TX 20th Inf. Co.D
Rogers, John TX 22nd Inf. Co.K
Rogers, John TX Home Guards Killough's Co.
Rogers, John TX Inf. Yarbrough's Co. (Smith
    Cty.Lt.Inf.)
Rogers, John VA 8th Cav. Co.E
Rogers, John VA Cav. 36th Bn. Co.D 1st Sgt.
Rogers, John VA Lt.Arty. 38th Bn. Co.C
Rogers, John VA Lt.Arty. E.J. Anderson's Co.
Rogers, John VA Arty. Curtis' Co.
Rogers, John VA 1st Res. Co.G
Rogers, John VA 10th Inf. Co.G
Rogers, John VA 12th Inf. Co.D
Rogers, John VA 27th Inf. Co.G
Rogers, John Conf.Cav. Clarkson's Bn. Ind.
    Rangers Co.H
Rogers, John Conf.Reg.Inf. Brooks' Bn. Co.B
Rogers, John 1st Cherokee Mtd.Rifles Co.A Sgt.
Rogers, John 1st Cherokee Mtd.Rifles Co.H
    Bugler
Rogers, John 1st Cherokee Mtd.Vol. 2nd Co.F
Rogers, John 2nd Cherokee Mtd.Vol. Co.F
Rogers, John Sig.Corps,CSA
Rogers, John A. AL Inf. 2nd Regt. Co.B
Rogers, John A. AL 57th Inf. Co.B
Rogers, John A. NC 48th Inf. Co.E
Rogers, John A. SC 14th Inf. Co.H
Rogers, John A. SC 22nd Inf. Co.C
Rogers, John A. TN 53rd Inf. Co.F
Rogers, John A. TX 2nd Inf. Co.K
Rogers, John A. VA 2nd Cav. Co.K
Rogers, John A. VA 9th Cav. Co.D
Rogers, John A. VA 15th Cav. Co.B Sgt.
Rogers, Johnathan W. VA Inf. Cohoon's Bn.
    Co.D Cpl.
Rogers, John B. AL Cav. Hardie's Bn.Res. Co.E
    Capt.
Rogers, John B. GA Cav. 6th Bn. (St.Guards)
    Co.B Capt.
Rogers, John B. MS 20th Inf. Co.K
Rogers, John B. NC 43rd Inf. Co.A
Rogers, John B. SC 21st Inf. Co.I
Rogers, John B. TN 37th Inf. Co.D
Rogers, John B. 1st Conf.Inf. 2nd Co.H
Rogers, John B.F. AL 32nd Inf.
Rogers, John Bird KY 4th Mtd.Inf. Co.A Maj.
Rogers, John C. AL 3rd Res. Co.H 1st Sgt.
Rogers, John C. AR 2nd Inf. Co.K
Rogers, John C. AR 17th (Lemoyne's) Inf. Co.C
Rogers, John C. GA Cav. 24th Bn. Co.B,C
Rogers, John C. GA 26th Inf. Co.C
Rogers, John C. GA 47th Inf. Co.K
Rogers, John C. LA 9th Inf. Co.A
Rogers, John C. LA 9th Inf. Co.I
Rogers, John C. MD 1st Inf. Co.C
Rogers, John C. MO 1st N.E. Cav. Co.A

Rogers, John C. NC Cav. 7th Bn. Co.E
Rogers, John C. NC 12th Inf. Co.L
Rogers, John C. NC 25th Inf. Co.F
Rogers, John C. NC 39th Inf. Co.A Sgt.
Rogers, John C. NC 62nd Inf. Co.E
Rogers, John C. VA Lt.Arty. Grandy's Co.
Rogers, John Columbus SC 4th Inf. Co.D
Rogers, John D. GA 3rd Inf. Co.B
Rogers, John D. LA 9th Inf. Co.F
Rogers, John D. MS 1st Lt.Arty. Co.D
Rogers, John D. MS 12th Inf. Co.I
Rogers, John D. TN Cav. 12th Bn. (Day's) Co.E
Rogers, John D. TX 5th Inf. Co.E Capt.
Rogers, John D. VA 4th Inf. Co.A
Rogers, John D. VA 11th Inf. Co.E
Rogers, Jno. D. Gen. & Staff Maj.,QM
Rogers, John D. Gen. & Staff Surg.
Rogers, John Dew SC 1st (McCreary's) Inf.
    Co.E
Rogers, John D.R. AL 45th Inf. Co.H
Rogers, John E. VA 30th Inf. Co.F
Rogers, John F. AL 19th Inf. Co.C
Rogers, John F., Sr. AL 19th Inf. Co.C
Rogers, John F. AR 33rd Inf. Co.B
Rogers, John F. TN 5th (McKenzie's) Cav. Col.
Rogers, John F. VA 24th Inf. Co.I
Rogers, John G. TN 11th Inf. Co.A Cpl.
Rogers, John G. TN 14th Inf. Co.A
Rogers, John H. AL 8th (Livingston's) Cav.
    Co.E
Rogers, John H. AL 14th Cav. Co.A
Rogers, John H. AL Cav. Moreland's Regt.
    Co.H
Rogers, John H. AR 1st (Dobbins') Cav. Co.B
    2nd Lt.
Rogers, John H. MO Inf. 3rd Regt.St.Guard
    Co.D 2nd Lt.
Rogers, John H. NC 1st Cav. (9th St.Troops)
    Co.K
Rogers, John H. NC 30th Inf. Co.D
Rogers, John H. NC 52nd Inf. Co.I
Rogers, John H. TX 2nd Field Btty.
Rogers, John H. VA 23rd Cav. Co.H
Rogers, John H. VA 22nd Inf. Co.D
Rogers, John H. VA Inf. 25th Bn. Co.A
    Sgt.Maj.
Rogers, John H.C. KY 5th Cav. Co.K
Rogers, John J. GA 49th Inf. Co.I
Rogers, John J. GA Cobb's Legion Co.B,G
Rogers, John J. MS 22nd Inf. Co.G,I
Rogers, John J. MS 31st Inf. Co.K
Rogers, John J. MS 42nd Inf. Co.A
Rogers, John J. MO 4th Cav. Co.G
Rogers, John J. NC 2nd Cav. (19th St.Troops)
    Co.D
Rogers, John J. SC 8th Inf. Co.I
Rogers, John J. Sig.Corps,CSA
Rogers, John K. VA 48th Inf. Co.B
Rogers, John L. KY 6th Mtd.Inf. Co.E
Rogers, John L. LA Conscr.
Rogers, John L. MO 10th Cav. Co.G 2nd Lt.
Rogers, John L. NC 16th Inf. Co.L Sgt.
Rogers, John L. TN 1st (Turney's) Inf. Co.D
Rogers, John L. VA 1st Cav. Co.H
Rogers, John L. VA 8th Inf. Co.D
Rogers, John L. VA 57th Inf. Co.I Cpl.
Rogers, John M. AL 3rd Inf. Co.B

Rogers, John M. GA 25th Inf. Co.K Jr.2nd Lt.
Rogers, John M. GA 36th (Broyles') Inf. Co.A
Rogers, John M. GA Cobb's Legion Co.E
Rogers, John M. KY 5th Mtd.Inf. Co.I
Rogers, John M. KY 9th Mtd.Inf. Co.I
Rogers, John M. LA Inf. 11th Bn. Co.G Sgt.
Rogers, John M. LA Inf.Cons.Crescent Regt. Co.D
Rogers, John M. MS 13th Inf. Co.K
Rogers, John M. MS 15th Inf. Co.K
Rogers, John M. MO 2nd Cav. Co.C Sgt.
Rogers, John M. TN 7th Inf. Co.D
Rogers, John M. TX Cav. Morgan's Regt. Co.I
Rogers, John M. VA 12th Inf. Co.H
Rogers, John M.C. AR 1st (Colquitt's) Inf. Co.G
Rogers, John N. AL 38th Inf. Co.B
Rogers, John N. GA 35th Inf. Co.B
Rogers, John N. MS 10th Inf. New Co.H, Old Co.G
Rogers, John Nichols MS 34th Inf. Co.A
Rogers, John P. AR 1st (Crawford's) Cav. Co.D
Rogers, John P. AR 14th (McCarver's) Inf. Co.A
Rogers, John P. TX 4th Inf. Co.H
Rogers, John R. AL 33rd Inf.
Rogers, John R. NC 35th Inf. Co.H
Rogers, John R. SC Lt.Arty. Walter's Co. (Washington Arty.)
Rogers, John R. TN 2nd (Ashby's) Cav. Co.B Capt.
Rogers, John R. TN Cav. 5th Bn. (McClellan's) Co.C 1st Lt.
Rogers, John R. VA 55th Inf. Co.G
Rogers, John S. GA 12th Inf. Co.D
Rogers, John S. SC 5th St.Troops Co.H
Rogers, John S. SC 9th Res. Co.I
Rogers, John S. TN Inf. 23rd Bn. Co.D Sgt.
Rogers, John S. VA 3rd Cav. Co.C
Rogers, John S.K. VA 32nd Inf. Co.A
Rogers, Johnson SC Arty. Manigault's Bn. 1st Co.B,C
Rogers, Johnson J. KY 3rd Bn.Mtd.Rifles Co.D
Rogers, John T. AL 7th Cav. Co.E
Rogers, John T. GA 3rd Inf. 1st Co.I
Rogers, John T. GA 35th Inf. Co.B
Rogers, John T. GA 46th Inf. Co.C
Rogers, John T. NC 13th Inf. Co.G
Rogers, John T. NC 29th Inf. Co.A
Rogers, John T. NC Walker's Bn. Thomas' Legion Co.B
Rogers, John T. TN 21st (Wilson's) Cav. Co.E
Rogers, John T. TN 14th Inf. Co.K
Rogers, John T. VA 2nd Cav. Co.K
Rogers, John T. VA 2nd St.Res. Co.F Sr.1st Lt.
Rogers, John T. VA 40th Inf. Co.I
Rogers, John Tait VA 1st Inf. Co.I 1st Lt.
Rogers, John V.B. NC 2nd Cav. (19th St.Troops) Co.A Maj.
Rogers, Jno. V.L. Gen. & Staff Capt.,Comsy.
Rogers, John W. AL Arty. 1st Bn. Co.E
Rogers, John W. AL 12th Inf. Co.H
Rogers, John W. AL 32nd Inf. Co.B
Rogers, John W. AL 52nd Inf. Co.I
Rogers, John W. AL Cav. 5th Bn. Hilliard's Legion Co.C
Rogers, John W. AR 1st (Colquitt's) Inf. Co.E
Rogers, John W. AR 9th Inf. Co.F
Rogers, John W. AR 36th Inf. Co.A

Rogers, John W. GA 14th Inf. Co.E
Rogers, John W. GA 36th (Broyles') Inf. Co.B
Rogers, John W. KY 4th Cav. Co.A,H
Rogers, John W. KY 2nd Mtd.Inf. Co.C 2nd Lt.
Rogers, John W. MS 1st Cav.Res. Co.A
Rogers, John W. MS 10th Inf. Old Co.B, New Co.G
Rogers, John W. MS 17th Inf. Co.C
Rogers, John W. MO Lt.Arty. 1st Field Btty.
Rogers, John W. NC 2nd Cav. (19th St.Troops) Co.C
Rogers, John W. NC 28th Inf. Co.K Sgt.
Rogers, John W. NC 43rd Inf. Co.C
Rogers, John W. SC 1st (Orr's) Rifles Co.C Sgt.
Rogers, John W. TN 20th (Russell's) Cav. Co.I
Rogers, John W. TX Cav. Sutton's Co.
Rogers, John W. VA 9th Cav. Co.I
Rogers, John W. VA 20th Cav. Co.I
Rogers, John W. VA 1st Arty. Co.B
Rogers, John W. VA Lt.Arty. 1st Bn. Co.B
Rogers, John W. VA Arty. Richardson's Co.
Rogers, John W. VA 1st Inf.
Rogers, John W. VA 25th Mil. Co.A
Rogers, John W. VA 25th Mil. Co.C
Rogers, John W. 10th Conf.Cav. Co.C
Rogers, John Walter VA 1st Arty. Co.F,E
Rogers, John Walter VA 32nd Inf. Co.G
Rogers, Jonah C. AL 43rd Inf. Co.A
Rogers, Jonah M. AL 43rd Inf. Co.E
Rogers, Jonathan LA 2nd Cav. Co.E
Rogers, Jonathan NC 29th Inf. Co.A
Rogers, Jonathan TN 43rd Inf. Co.I
Rogers, Jonathan TX 33rd Cav. Co.C Cpl.
Rogers, Jonathan G. TN 28th Inf. Co.E 1st Sgt.
Rogers, Jonathan K. NC 1st Inf.
Rogers, Jonathan K. NC Walker's Bn. Thomas' Legion Co.B
Rogers, Jonathan R. AL 58th Inf. Co.K Cpl.
Rogers, Jonathan R. GA 2nd Bn.S.S. Co.E
Rogers, Jones AR Cav. Gordon's Regt. Co.K
Rogers, Jones V. AR 15th (N.W.) Inf. Co.B 1st Sgt.
Rogers, Jonithan A. NC 60th Inf. Co.I
Rogers, Joseph AL Lt.Arty. 2nd Bn. Co.C
Rogers, Joseph AL 9th Inf. Co.E
Rogers, Joseph FL 5th Inf. Co.H
Rogers, Joseph FL 9th Inf. Co.D
Rogers, Joseph GA 11th Cav. Co.C
Rogers, Joseph GA 1st Reg. Co.B
Rogers, Joseph KY Cav. Buckner Guards
Rogers, Joseph LA 1st Hvy.Arty. (Reg.) Co.H
Rogers, Joseph LA 18th Inf. Co.G
Rogers, Joseph LA Inf.Cons. 18th Regt. & Yellow Jacket Bn. Co.F
Rogers, Joseph MS 5th Inf. Co.I
Rogers, Joseph MS 41st Inf. Co.K
Rogers, Joseph MO 12th Cav. Co.H Cpl.
Rogers, Joseph MO Arty. Jos. Bledsoe's Co.
Rogers, Joseph MO 3rd Inf. Co.G
Rogers, Joseph NC 13th Inf. Co.D
Rogers, Joseph NC 18th Inf. Co.F
Rogers, Joseph NC 26th Inf. Co.H
Rogers, Joseph NC 51st Inf. Co.K
Rogers, Joseph NC Walker's Bn. Thomas' Legion Co.B
Rogers, Joseph SC 1st Arty. Co.K
Rogers, Joseph SC 1st (Orr's) Rifles Co.H

Rogers, Joseph SC 3rd Inf. Co.K
Rogers, Joseph TN 17th Inf. Co.K
Rogers, Joseph TN 25th Inf. Co.C
Rogers, Joseph TN 50th Inf. Co.H
Rogers, Joseph TN 63rd Inf. Co.F
Rogers, Joseph VA 5th Cav. Co.K Cpl.
Rogers, Joseph 1st Cherokee Mtd.Vol. 1st Co.D, 2nd Co.D
Rogers, Joseph 2nd Cherokee Mtd.Vol. Co.D
Rogers, Joseph 2nd Cherokee Mtd.Vol. Co.G
Rogers, Jos. Gen. & Staff AQM
Rogers, Joseph A. AL 43rd Inf. Co.E
Rogers, Joseph A. GA 45th Inf. Co.B
Rogers, Joseph A. TN 28th Inf. Co.F
Rogers, Joseph A. TN 28th (Cons.) Inf. Co.B Hosp.Stew.
Rogers, Joseph A. VA 3rd (Archer's) Bn.Res. Co.D Capt.
Rogers, Joseph A. VA 16th Inf. Co.E
Rogers, Joseph A. VA Second Class Mil. Wolff's Co. Cpl.
Rogers, Joseph B. SC 1st (Orr's) Rifles Co.H Sgt.
Rogers, Joseph C. MS 18th Inf. Co.H
Rogers, Joseph C. TX 4th Cav. Co.H
Rogers, Joseph C. VA 42nd Inf. Co.A Cpl.
Rogers, Joseph C.H. TN 32nd Inf. Co.C
Rogers, Joseph D. GA Smith's Legion 1st Sgt.
Rogers, Joseph E. MS 7th Cav. AQM
Rogers, Joseph E. VA 39th Inf. Co.D
Rogers, Joseph E. Gen. & Staff Capt.,AQM
Rogers, Joseph F. GA 12th Cav. Co.F
Rogers, Joseph F. TN 45th Inf.
Rogers, Joseph G. MS 3rd Inf. Co.A Cpl.
Rogers, Joseph J. GA 26th Inf. Co.C
Rogers, Joseph L. VA 59th Inf. 1st Co.G Sgt.
Rogers, Joseph L. VA 60th Inf. Co.D
Rogers, Joseph N. TX Cav. 6th Bn. Co.A
Rogers, Joseph S. AR 2nd Cav. Co.D
Rogers, Joseph S. GA 12th Cav. Co.I
Rogers, Joseph S. GA 23rd Inf. Co.K
Rogers, Joseph S. TN 34th Inf. 2nd Co.C
Rogers, Joseph T. NC 14th Inf. Co.E Ens.
Rogers, Joseph T. NC 29th Inf. Co.E
Rogers, Joseph T. 1st Conf.Inf. Co.B
Rogers, Josephus KY 4th Mtd.Inf. Co.D
Rogers, Joseph W. AL 34th Inf. Co.C
Rogers, Joseph W. VA 19th Cav. Co.H
Rogers, Joseph W. VA 20th Cav. Co.I
Rogers, Joshua TX 14th Inf. Co.F
Rogers, Josiah MS 2nd (Quinn's St.Troops) Inf. Co.D
Rogers, Josiah TN 35th Inf. 1st Co.A
Rogers, Josiah B. GA 49th Inf. Co.I
Rogers, Josiah C. NC 44th Inf. Co.A
Rogers, Josiah R. MS 5th Inf. Co.I
Rogers, Josiah S. TN 45th Inf.
Rogers, Josiah W. NC 20th Inf. Co.A Cpl.
Rogers, J.P. AL 40th Inf. Co.H Ord.Sgt.
Rogers, J.P. AR Lt.Arty. Owen's Btty.
Rogers, J.P. AR 21st Mil. Co.H
Rogers, J.P. MD Arty. 3rd Btty.
Rogers, J.P. MS Cav. (St.Troops) Gamblin's Co.
Rogers, J.P. MS Inf. 2nd Bn. Co.L Capt.
Rogers, J.P. MS Inf. 3rd Bn. (St.Troops) Co.C
Rogers, J.P. MS 14th Inf. Co.C Capt.
Rogers, J.P. MS 44th Inf. Co.G

Rogers, J.P. SC 1st St.Troops Co.C
Rogers, J.P. SC Inf. Hampton Legion Co.D
Rogers, J.P. TX 35th (Brown's) Cav. Co.C
Rogers, J.P. TX Cav. Ragsdale's Bn. Co.B Sgt.
Rogers, J.P. TX 17th Inf. Co.C
Rogers, J.P. 3rd Conf.Cav. Co.K
Rogers, J. Pendleton 1st Conf.Eng.Troops Co.F
   Sgt.
Rogers, J.P.G. VA 2nd Inf. Co.D
Rogers, J.R. AR Mil. Desha Cty.Bn.
Rogers, J.R. GA 4th (Clinch's) Cav. Co.A
Rogers, J.R. GA Cav. 8th Bn. (St.Guards) Co.A
Rogers, J.R. GA 2nd Inf. Co.E
Rogers, J.R. MS 1st Inf. Co.F
Rogers, J.R. MS 11th Inf. Co.I
Rogers, J.R. TN 46th Inf. Co.H
Rogers, J.R. TX Arty. Douglas' Co.
Rogers, J. Rice SC 15th Inf. Co.B 1st Lt.
Rogers, J.S. AL 8th (Livingston's) Cav. Co.C
Rogers, J.S. AR Cav. Gordon's Regt. Co.K Sgt.
Rogers, J.S. AR 10th Mil. Co.A Sgt.
Rogers, J.S. AR 58th Mil. Co.D Cpl.
Rogers, J.S. GA 6th Cav. Co.B
Rogers, J.S. GA 1st Inf. (St.Guards) Co.D Cpl.
Rogers, J.S. MS 3rd Inf. (St.Troops) Co.K
Rogers, J.S. NC 1st Cav. (9th St.Troops) Co.K
Rogers, J.S. SC 3rd Inf. Co.K
Rogers, J.S. TN 14th (Neely's) Cav. Co.K
Rogers, J.S. TN Inf. 23rd Bn. Co.D
Rogers, J.S. TX 23rd Cav. Co.C
Rogers, J. Stewart MS 13th Inf. Co.K
Rogers, J.T. AL 37th Inf. Co.G
Rogers, J.T. AR 27th Inf. Co.I
Rogers, J.T. GA 4th Cav. (St.Guards)
   Robertson's Co. 1st Sgt.
Rogers, J.T. GA 5th Inf. (St.Guards) Allums'
   Co.
Rogers, J.T. GA 46th Inf. Co.E
Rogers, J.T. MS 4th Cav. Co.B
Rogers, J.T. NC 37th Inf. Co.G
Rogers, J.T. SC 22nd Inf. Co.E
Rogers, J.T. TN 1st (Feild's) & 27th Inf. (Cons.)
   Co.I
Rogers, J.T. TN 9th Inf. Co.F
Rogers, J.T. TN 27th Inf. Co.E Sgt.
Rogers, J.T. TN 47th Inf. Co.F Cpl.
Rogers, J.T. TX 17th Cons.Dismtd.Cav. Co.I
Rogers, J.T. TX 17th Inf. Co.C
Rogers, J.T. Gen. & Staff Capt.,Comsy.
Rogers, Judge C. LA 28th (Gray's) Inf. Co.E
   Cpl.
Rogers, Judson J. KY 3rd Cav. Co.A
Rogers, Julius D. FL 7th Inf. Co.B
Rogers, Julius R. NC 47th Inf. Co.I 2nd Lt.
Rogers, J.V. TN 19th & 20th (Cons.) Cav.
   Co.E,D
Rogers, J.V. TN 20th (Russell's) Cav. Co.I
Rogers, J.V. TN Cav. Williams' Co.
Rogers, J.W. AL 4th Cav. Co.G
Rogers, J.W. AL Cav. Moreland's Regt. Co.H,C
Rogers, J.W. AL 40th Inf. Co.G
Rogers, J.W. AL 59th Inf. Co.K
Rogers, J.W. AL 2nd Bn. Hilliard's Legion Vol.
   Co.B
Rogers, J.W. AR 7th Cav. Co.B
Rogers, J.W. AR 9th Inf. Lt.Col.
Rogers, J.W. AR 25th Inf. Co.H

Rogers, J.W. GA 60th Inf. Co.F
Rogers, J.W. KY 1st (Helm's) Cav. New Co.G
Rogers, J.W. KY 9th Cav. Co.A
Rogers, J.W. LA 17th Inf. Co.E
Rogers, J.W. LA 27th Inf. Co.G
Rogers, J.W. MS 1st Cav.Res. Co.F
Rogers, J.W. MS Cav. Ham's Regt. Co.H
Rogers, J.W. MS 1st Inf. Co.D
Rogers, J.W. MS 39th Inf. Co.B
Rogers, J.W. MS Inf. (Res.) Berry's Co.
Rogers, J.W. NC 1st Cav. (9th St.Troops) Co.F
Rogers, J.W. NC 4th Cav. (59th St.Troops)
   Co.C
Rogers, J.W. NC 31st Inf. Co.C
Rogers, J.W. NC 57th Inf. Co.K
Rogers, J.W. SC 21st Inf. Co.L Cpl.
Rogers, J.W. TN 15th (Cons.) Cav. Co.G
Rogers, J.W. TN 19th & 20th (Cons.) Cav. Co.E
Rogers, J.W. TN 9th Inf. Co.C,F
Rogers, J.W. TN 31st Inf. Asst.Surg.
Rogers, J.W. TX 8th Cav. Co.K
Rogers, J.W. TX 29th Cav. Co.I
Rogers, J.W. TX Cav. Waller's Regt. Co.B
Rogers, J.W. TX 6th Field Btty.
Rogers, J.W. TX Lt.Arty. Dege's Bn.
Rogers, J.W. TX 7th Inf. Co.H Cpl.
Rogers, J.W. VA 3rd (Archer's) Bn.Res, Co.A
Rogers, J.W. Gen. & Staff Chap.
Rogers, J.Y. TX 12th Inf. Co.H
Rogers, Kelley TN 14th Inf. Co.K
Rogers, L. AR 15th Mil. Co.C
Rogers, L.A. GA 39th Inf. Co.E
Rogers, Lafayette D. GA 6th Cav. Co.A 2nd
   Bvt.
Rogers, Lafayette D. GA Smith's Legion Co.A
   3rd Lt.
Rogers, Lafayette R. AR 7th Cav. Co.M
Rogers, Larkin A. TN 1st (Turney's) Inf. Co.D
   Sgt.
Rogers, Larkin J. MS Inf. 3rd Bn. Co.B
Rogers, L.B. MS 7th Cav. Co.G
Rogers, L.B. SC 3rd St.Troops Co.B
Rogers, L.B. SC 8th Inf. Co.L
Rogers, L.B. TN 16th Inf. Co.H
Rogers, L.C. AR 9th Inf. New Co.I
Rogers, L.C. MS 25th Inf. Co.G
Rogers, L.C. 2nd Conf.Inf. Co.G
Rogers, L.C.L. MS 5th Inf. Co.C
Rogers, L.D. GA 9th Inf. (St.Guards) Co.A
Rogers, L.D. GA Inf.Bn. Smith's Legion Co.A
   3rd Sgt.
Rogers, L.D. TX 19th Inf. Co.G
Rogers, Leander S. MS 34th Inf. Co.B QMSgt.
Rogers, Leander Sylvester MS Inf. 1st Bn. Co.D
   Sgt.
Rogers, Lemuel M. TN 12th (Green's) Cav. Co.I
Rogers, Leonard SC 1st (Orr's) Rifles Co.C
   Capt.
Rogers, Leroy M. VA 50th Inf. Co.F
Rogers, Levi AR 1st (Crawford's) Cav. Co.I 2nd
   Lt.
Rogers, Levi MS Cav. Ham's Regt. Co.C,A
Rogers, Levi MS 19th Inf. Co.K
Rogers, Levi NC 15th Inf. Co.M
Rogers, Levi NC 32nd Inf. Co.I
Rogers, Levi TN Inf. 23rd Bn. Co.D
Rogers, Levi TX Cav. Good's Bn. Co.C 1st Lt.

Rogers, Levi TX Cav. Well's Regt. Co.H 1st Lt.
Rogers, Levi B. MS 9th Inf. Old Co.A
Rogers, Levi L. TX 24th Cav. Co.C
Rogers, Levi T. VA 41st Inf. Co.I
Rogers, Levy C. Lee MS 27th Inf. Co.F
Rogers, Lewis MS 5th Inf. Co.I Cpl.
Rogers, Lewis SC Inf. Hampton Legion Co.D
Rogers, Lewis TX 19th Cav. Co.H
Rogers, Lewis 1st Cherokee Mtd.Vol. Co.J
Rogers, Lewis M. 1st Conf.Eng.Troops Co.H
Rogers, Lewis B. MS Inf. (Red Rebels) D.J.
   Red's Co. Cpl.
Rogers, Lewis B. VA 86th Mil. Co.F,A
Rogers, Lewis L. NC 1st Inf. Co.K
Rogers, Lewis W. AR 7th Inf. Co.I 2nd Lt.
Rogers, L.F. MS 3rd Inf. Co.C
Rogers, L.H. MO 16th Inf. Co.C
Rogers, L.H. MO St.Guard
Rogers, L.H. TN Cav. Napier's Bn. Co.C
Rogers, L.H. TN 5th Inf. 2nd Co.H
Rogers, L.H. Gen. & Staff Ord.Off.
Rogers, Lindsay L. SC 1st (Orr's) Rifles Co.H
Rogers, Little H. TX 4th Cav. Co.I
Rogers, L.J. MS 1st (Johnston's) Inf. Co.I
Rogers, L.J.W. TN 20th (Russell's) Cav. Co.I
Rogers, L.J.W. TX 7th Inf. Co.H
Rogers, L.L. AR 10th Inf. Co.D
Rogers, L.L. VA 5th Inf. Co.C
Rogers, L.L. 8th (Wade's) Conf.Cav. Co.B
Rogers, L.M. AR 2nd Inf. Old Co.E, Co.D Sgt.
Rogers, L.M. TN 14th (Neely's) Cav. Co.K
Rogers, L.M. TX Cav. 3rd Regt.St.Troops Maj.
Rogers, Louis LA 18th Inf. Co.H
Rogers, Louis LA Inf.Cons. 18th Regt. & Yellow
   Jacket Bn. Co.H
Rogers, Louis L. AL 38th Inf. Co.B
Rogers, Louis M. VA 46th Inf. 4th Co.F Ens.
Rogers, Lovel A. TN 37th Inf. Co.C
Rogers, L.P. VA 3rd Inf.Loc.Def. Co.C
Rogers, L.R. AL 20th Inf. Co.G
Rogers, L.R. VA 9th Bn.Res. Co.B
Rogers, L.S. MS 24th Inf. Co.H
Rogers, L.S. 1st Conf.Cav. 2nd Co.F Capt.
Rogers, Lucious G. AR 26th Inf. Co.A
Rogers, Ludford L. AL 38th Inf. Co.B
Rogers, L.W. LA 4th Inf. New Co.G Sgt.
Rogers, L.W. MS 37th Inf. Co.D
Rogers, Lwd. L. KY 5th Mtd.Inf. Co.C
Rogers, M. GA Cav. 20th Bn. Co.E
Rogers, M. LA Mil. 3rd Regt. 1st Brig. 1st Div.
   Co.B 1st Lt.
Rogers, M. LA 15th Inf. Co.F
Rogers, M. LA 17th Inf. Co.E Lt.Col.
Rogers, M. SC 3rd Inf. Co.K
Rogers, M. VA Cav. 34th Bn. Co.C
Rogers, M.A. AR 16th Inf. Co.I
Rogers, M.A. LA Mil.Conf.Guards Regt. Co.C
Rogers, M.A. TX 27th Cav. Co.E
Rogers, Madison TN Cav. 4th Bn. (Branner's)
   Co.A
Rogers, Madison M. NC 28th Inf. Co.D
Rogers, Major J. AR 9th Inf. Co.H Sgt.
Rogers, Marcus VA Lt.Arty. Cooper's Co.
Rogers, Marion P. NC 48th Inf. Co.C
Rogers, Mark TN 2nd (Ashby's) Cav. Co.H
Rogers, Mark D. LA 9th Inf. Co.C
Rogers, Martin MS Inf. 3rd Bn. Co.C

Rogers, Martin TX 4th Cav. Co.A
Rogers, Martin VA 31st Mil. Co.F
Rogers, Martin E. GA Cav. 20th Bn. Co.E
Rogers, Martin E. TX 14th Cav. Co.E
Rogers, Martin J. GA 61st Inf. Co.H
Rogers, Martin L.V. NC 30th Inf. Co.D Bvt.2nd Lt.
Rogers, Martin T. MS Cav. Ham's Regt. Co.I
Rogers, Martin T. MS 20th Inf. Co.D
Rogers, Martin V. GA 65th Inf. Co.G
Rogers, Martin V. TN 41st Inf. Co.K
Rogers, Massingale MS 1st Lt.Arty. Co.L
Rogers, Mat TN 2nd (Ashby's) Cav. Co.H Black.
Rogers, Mat TX Waul's Legion Co.H
Rogers, Mathew LA Miles' Legion
Rogers, Mathew TN 8th Inf. Co.G
Rogers, Mathew McA. NC 25th Inf. Co.F
Rogers, Matthew TN 8th Cav. Co.G
Rogers, Mattison NC 62nd Inf. Co.A
Rogers, M.B. AL 50th Inf. Co.H
Rogers, M.D.L. TX 22nd Inf. Co.G
Rogers, M.E. VA 5th Cav. Co.K
Rogers, Merritt C. NC 62nd Inf. Co.I Cpl.
Rogers, M.H. FL Cav. 5th Bn. Co.H
Rogers, M.H. GA Cav. 1st Bn. Brailsford's Co.
Rogers, M.H. GA 5th Cav. Co.H
Rogers, Micajah GA Hvy.Arty. 22nd Bn. Co.F
Rogers, Michael KY 2nd Mtd.Inf. Co.F
Rogers, Michael KY 4th Mtd.Inf. Co.I,G
Rogers, Michael TX 4th Inf. Co.D
Rogers, Middleton D. FL 8th Inf. Co.G
Rogers, Mike GA Inf. 27th Bn. Co.C
Rogers, Mills B. AL 5th Inf. Co.C
Rogers, Milton VA Inf. 21st Bn.
Rogers, Milton M. VA 17th Inf. Co.C
Rogers, Milton P. SC Inf. Hampton Legion Co.D
Rogers, Milton S. NC 62nd Inf. Co.B
Rogers, Mitchel A. GA 26th Inf. Co.C Cpl.
Rogers, Mitchell NC Walker's Bn. Thomas' Legion Co.H
Rogers, M.J. FL Cav. 5th Bn. Co.C
Rogers, M.L. AL Mil. 4th Vol. Co.G
Rogers, M.L. TX 13th Cav. Co.D
Rogers, M.L. TX 22nd Inf. Co.K
Rogers, M.L. Gen. & Staff Physician
Rogers, M.M. GA Phillips' Legion Co.D
Rogers, M.M. MS Lt.Arty. Turner's Co.
Rogers, M.M. TN 14th (Neely's) Cav. Co.A
Rogers, M.M. VA 1st Cav. Co.H
Rogers, M.M. VA Lt.Arty. 38th Bn. Co.A 1st Lt.
Rogers, M.M. 4th Conf.Inf. Co.K
Rogers, Monroe Conf.Reg.Inf. Brooks' Bn. Co.C
Rogers, Mort. M. Gen. & Staff Ord.Sgt.
Rogers, Moseley NC Hvy.Arty. 10th Bn. Co.C
Rogers, Moses AL 58th Inf. Co.C Sgt.
Rogers, Moses LA 4th Inf. New Co.G
Rogers, Moses MO Lt.Arty. 12th Btty.
Rogers, Moses TN 60th Mtd.Inf. Co.B
Rogers, Moses TX 24th Cav. Co.C
Rogers, Moses Columbus TX 15th Cav. Co.F
Rogers, Moses K. AR 6th Inf. New Co.D
Rogers, M.P. AL 58th Inf. Co.C Sgt.
Rogers, M.P. SC 4th Cav. Co.C Sgt.
Rogers, M.P. SC Cav. 10th Bn. Co.B Sgt.
Rogers, M.R. GA 5th Res. Co.A,D 2nd Lt.

Rogers, M.R. GA 27th Inf. Co.A
Rogers, M.R. VA Burks' Regt.Loc.Def.
Rogers, M.S. TX 3rd Cav. Co.H
Rogers, M.T. AR 19th (Dockery's) Inf. Co.H Sgt.
Rogers, M.T. GA 5th Inf. Co.D
Rogers, M.V. TN 14th Inf. Co.K
Rogers, M.W. AL 63rd Inf. Co.G,B
Rogers, N. AR 9th Inf. Co.I
Rogers, N. 1st Cherokee Mtd.Vol. 1st Co.D
Rogers, Napoleon 2nd Cherokee Mtd.Vol. Co.D
Rogers, Nathan MS 38th Cav. Co.E
Rogers, Nathan MS 8th Inf. Co.A
Rogers, Nathan VA 31st Mil. Co.F
Rogers, Nathan A. NC 44th Inf. Co.E
Rogers, Nathaniel AL Arty. 4th Bn. Hilliard's Legion Co.D
Rogers, Nathaniel SC 18th Inf. Co.A
Rogers, Nathan L. TX 11th (Spaight's) Bn.Vol. Co.A,G
Rogers, N.C. Sig.Corps,CSA
Rogers, N.E. AL 26th Inf. Co.G
Rogers, Needham R. GA 57th Inf. Co.G
Rogers, Nelson 2nd Cherokee Mtd.Vol. Co.D
Rogers, Newton TN 23rd Inf. Co.D
Rogers, Newton J. GA 6th Inf. (St.Guards) Co.F Sgt.
Rogers, Newton T. NC 6th Cav. (65th St.Troops) Co.C
Rogers, Newton T. NC Cav. 7th Bn. Co.C
Rogers, N.F. TX Cav. Waller's Regt. Co.B
Rogers, N.H. TX 3rd Cav. Co.H
Rogers, Nic MS 1st Cav. Co.F
Rogers, Nicodemus NC 3rd Cav. (41st St.Troops) Co.A
Rogers, N.L. TX 21st Inf. Co.K
Rogers, M.M. TN 17th Inf. Co.K
Rogers, Noah NC 61st Inf. Co.F
Rogers, N.R. MS 8th Cav. Co.G
Rogers, N.R. TN Inf. 1st Bn. (Colms') Co.E
Rogers, N.R. TN 23rd Inf. Co.H
Rogers, N.T. TN 26th Inf. Co.K
Rogers, O.B. AR Cav. Wright's Regt. Co.I
Rogers, O.B. SC 6th Cav. Co.C
Rogers, Obediah L. MS 33rd Inf. Co.G
Rogers, Oliver SC 1st Arty. Co.K
Rogers, Oliver G. LA 12th Inf. Co.C
Rogers, Oliver G. SC 7th Cav. Co.C 2nd Lt.
Rogers, Oliver G. SC Cav.Bn. Holcombe Legion Co.D 3rd Lt.
Rogers, O.M. SC 21st Inf. Co.L Sgt.
Rogers, Osborne MS Cp.Guard (Cp. of Instr. for Conscr.)
Rogers, Osburn MS Conscr.
Rogers, Oscar MS 27th Inf. Co.K
Rogers, O.T. GA 10th Cav. (St.Guards) Co.K 3rd Lt.
Rogers, P. MS 8th Cav. Co.D
Rogers, P. SC Inf. Hampton Legion Co.C
Rogers, P. TN 12th (Green's) Cav. Co.K
Rogers, P. Inf. Bailey's Cons.Regt. Co.A
Rogers, P. TX Cav. Terry's Regt. Co.A
Rogers, P. TX 7th Inf. Co.C
Rogers, P.A. AL 18th Bn.Vol. Co.A
Rogers, P.A. SC 15th Inf. Co.K
Rogers, Pat KY 2nd (Duke's) Cav. Co.H
Rogers, Patrick TN 2nd (Walker's) Inf. Co.I

Rogers, Patrick 9th Conf.Inf. Co.D Cpl.
Rogers, Patten SC 20th Inf. Co.A
Rogers, Paul H. MS Inf. (Red Rebels) D.J. Red's Co.
Rogers, P.C. LA 2nd Cav. Co.C
Rogers, Pearson D. VA Inf. 9th Bn. Co.A
Rogers, Peleg T. LA 12th Inf. Co.C
Rogers, Perry GA 52nd Inf. Co.E Sgt.
Rogers, Perry NC Cav. 5th Bn. Co.A
Rogers, Perry NC 64th Inf. Co.D
Rogers, Peter AR 6th Inf. New Co.D
Rogers, Peter GA 6th Inf. Co.I
Rogers, Peter MS 15th Inf. Co.C
Rogers, Peter A. AL 5th Bn.Vol. Co.A
Rogers, Peter A. MS 2nd Cav. Co.C
Rogers, Peter L. FL 6th Inf. Co.D
Rogers, Peyton W. MS 7th Inf. Co.I
Rogers, P.G. LA 27th Inf. Co.G
Rogers, P.H. AL 2nd Bn. Hilliard's Legion Vol. Co.B
Rogers, P.H. SC 6th Cav. Co.C
Rogers, P.H. SC 15th Inf. Co.K
Rogers, P.H. TX 8th Cav. Co.A
Rogers, P.H. TX 5th Inf. Co.E
Rogers, Philip SC Arty. Manigault's Bn. 2nd Co.C
Rogers, Philip R. AL 27th Inf. Co.H
Rogers, Philip R. AL 57th Inf. Co.F
Rogers, Phillip L. AL 41st Inf. Co.G
Rogers, Pinckney SC Arty. Gregg's Co. (McQueen Lt.Arty.)
Rogers, Pinckney SC Arty. Manigault's Bn. 1st Co.B,C
Rogers, Pinckney Trans-MS Conf.Cav. 1st Bn. Co.E
Rogers, Pitt M. AR 1st Mtd.Rifles Co.A
Rogers, P.L. Gen. & Staff Maj.,QM
Rogers, Pleasant TX 3rd Inf. Co.E
Rogers, Pleasant Madison MS 34th Inf. Co.A Cpl.
Rogers, Pleasant W.M. TX 36th Cav. Co.D
Rogers, Pleasant W.W. GA 61st Inf. Co.B Cpl.
Rogers, P.M.C. VA Inf. 21st Bn. 2nd Co.C Music.
Rogers, P.M.C. VA 64th Mtd.Inf. Co.C
Rogers, Posey AL 19th Inf. Co.G
Rogers, P.R. MS 7th Cav. Co.K
Rogers, P.R. MS 2nd (Davidson's) Inf. Co.I
Rogers, Prear G. MO 10th Cav. Co.G
Rogers, Pryor G. LA 9th Inf. Co.F
Rogers, P.S. GA 42nd Inf. Co.H
Rogers, Purvis SC 4th St.Troops Co.D
Rogers, P.W. TN Inf. 1st Bn. (Colms') Co.E
Rogers, R. AL 50th Inf.
Rogers, R. GA 5th Inf. (St.Guards) Miller's Co.
Rogers, R. KY 7th Cav. Co.G
Rogers, R. SC Cav. 12th Bn. Co.D
Rogers, R. TX 5th Cav. Co.I
Rogers, R.A. AR 26th Inf. Co.H
Rogers, R.A. GA 54th Inf. Co.H
Rogers, Radford TX 15th Inf. Co.A
Rogers, Ralph TX 9th (Young's) Inf. Co.I
Rogers, Ralph Lewis VA 57th Inf. Co.H Capt.
Rogers, Rasmon R. GA 2nd Cav. (St.Guards) Co.E
Rogers, R.B. AR 15th Inf. Co.A
Rogers, R.B. MO 12th Cav. Co.F

Rogers, R.B. TN 3rd (Lillard's) Mtd.Inf. 1st
Co.K
Rogers, R.B. TN 63rd Inf. Co.E
Rogers, R.C. AL Cav. Moreland's Regt. Co.H
2nd Lt.
Rogers, R.C. MS Inf. 3rd Bn. Co.H
Rogers, R.C. NC 39th Inf. Co.A
Rogers, R.C. TN 5th Inf. 2nd Co.D
Rogers, R.C. TX 8th Cav.
Rogers, R.C. TX 12th Cav. Co.D
Rogers, R.C. TX 17th Inf. Co.C
Rogers, R.C. VA Goochland Lt.Arty.
Rogers, R.E. SC 3rd Inf. Co.B
Rogers, R.E. TN 7th (Duckworth's) Cav. Co.B
Rogers, R.E. TN 12th (Cons.) Inf. Co.E 1st Lt.
Rogers, Reuben KY 7th Mtd.Inf. Co.G
Rogers, Reuben NC 47th Inf. Co.B
Rogers, Reuben TN Cav. 12th Bn. (Day's) Co.D
Rogers, Reuben TN 37th Inf. Co.F
Rogers, Reuben VA Hvy.Arty. 10th Bn. Co.B
Rogers, Reuben C. NC 27th Inf. Co.D
Rogers, Reuben W. GA 3rd Inf. Co.B
Rogers, Reubin AL 6th Inf. Co.B
Rogers, Reubin TN Cav. 16th Bn. (Neal's) Co.A
Rogers, R.F. FL 1st (Res.) Inf. Co.G Sgt.
Rogers, R.F. TN 42nd Inf. Co.D Cpl.
Rogers, R.H. MS 22nd Inf. Co.D
Rogers, R.H. MO 2nd Cav. Co.C
Rogers, R.H. SC Inf. 6th Bn. Co.A 2nd Lt.
Rogers, R.H. SC 8th Inf. Co.I 2nd Lt.
Rogers, R.H. SC 26th Inf. Co.C 1st Lt.
Rogers, R.H. TN Inf. 4th Cons.Regt. Co.F
Rogers, R.H. VA 50th Inf. Co.F
Rogers, Richard LA 14th Inf. Co.I
Rogers, Richard TX Vol. Benton's Co.
Rogers, Richard H. MO Inf. 3rd Bn. Co.C
Rogers, Richard H. VA 6th Cav. Co.K Sgt.
Rogers, Richard J. MS 33rd Inf. Co.F Cpl.
Rogers, Richard T. VA 59th Mil. Riddick's Co.
1st Lt.
Rogers, Richard W. AL 19th Inf. Co.C
Rogers, Richmond GA 26th Inf. Co.C
Rogers, Riley TN 62nd Mtd.Inf. Co.K Sgt.
Rogers, R.J. AL 59th Inf. Co.H
Rogers, R.J. MS 22nd Inf. Co.E
Rogers, R.J. MS 27th Inf. Co.E
Rogers, R.J. TN 10th (DeMoss') Cav. Co.F
Rogers, R.J. 4th Conf.Inf. Co.K
Rogers, R.L. GA Cav. 10th Bn. (St.Guards)
Co.C
Rogers, R.M. AL 1st Bn.Cadets Co.A Cpl.
Rogers, R.M. AL Capt.,Asst.Ord.Off.
Rogers, R.M. MS Inf. 1st Bn. Johnston's Co.
Rogers, R.M. SC Arty. Manigault's Bn. 2nd
Co.C
Rogers, R.M. SC Arty. Zimmerman's Co. (Pee
Dee Arty.)
Rogers, R.M. SC 1st Inf. Co.B Sgt.
Rogers, R.M. TN 51st Inf. Co.H
Rogers, R.N. TX 1st Hvy.Arty. Co.F
Rogers, Robbin SC Arty. Manigault's Bn. 1st
Co.C
Rogers, Robert AL 19th Inf. Co.C
Rogers, Robert AR 36th Inf. Co.D Cpl.
Rogers, Robert GA 43rd Inf. Co.I Cpl.
Rogers, Robert LA C.S. Zouave Bn. Co.A
Rogers, Robert MO 1st N.E. Cav. Co.L,M

Rogers, Robert NC 6th Cav. (65th St.Troops)
Co.C,G
Rogers, Robert NC Cav. 7th Bn. Co.C
Rogers, Robert NC 26th Inf. Co.B
Rogers, Robert SC 4th Inf. Co.D
Rogers, Robert SC Inf. 13th Bn. Co.A
Rogers, Robert TN 20th Inf. Co.I
Rogers, Robert TX Cav. 6th Bn. Co.B
Rogers, Robert TX 11th Inf. Co.A
Rogers, Robert VA 13th Inf. Co.A
Rogers, Robert VA 50th Inf. Co.A
Rogers, Robert VA 54th Inf. Co.F
Rogers, Robert Wheeler's Scouts,CSA
Rogers, Robert 1st Creek Mtd.Vol. Co.H
Rogers, Robert A. AL 4th Inf. Co.I
Rogers, Robert A.J. MS 12th Inf. Co.I
Rogers, Robert B. NC 16th Inf. Co.L
Rogers, Robert B. NC 62nd Inf. Co.C
Rogers, Robert C. KY 8th Cav. Co.A Cpl.
Rogers, Robert C. SC Arty. Gregg's Co.
(McQueen Lt.Arty.) Sgt.
Rogers, Robert C. SC Arty. Manigault's Bn. 1st
Co.C Sgt.
Rogers, Robert C. TN 21st Inf.
Rogers, Robert C.C. TX 18th Cav. Co.A
Rogers, Robert F. FL 5th Inf. Co.B
Rogers, Robert F. MS 1st (Johnston's) Inf. Co.I
Rogers, Robert H. SC 4th Cav. Co.F
Rogers, Robert H. VA 13th Inf. Co.A
Rogers, Robert J. AL Arty. 4th Bn. Hilliard's
Legion Co.A,D
Rogers, Robert L. MS 10th Cav. Co.G
Rogers, Robert M. SC 1st (McCreary's) Inf.
Co.D 2nd Lt.
Rogers, Robert M. TN 11th (Holman's) Cav.
Co.G
Rogers, Robert M. VA 19th Cav. Co.A
Rogers, Robert M. VA 20th Cav. Co.H
Rogers, Robert M. VA 3rd Cav. & Inf.St.Line
Co.A
Rogers, Robert N. GA 14th Inf. Co.E Capt.
Rogers, Robert R. GA 21st Inf. Co.C
Rogers, Robert R. TN 53rd Inf. Co.F Sgt.
Rogers, Robert T. GA 18th Inf. Co.C
Rogers, Robert W. NC 29th Inf. Co.E
Rogers, Robert W. SC 1st (Butler's) Inf. Co.D
Rogers, Robert W. TN 1st (Turney's) Inf. Co.I
Rogers, Robert W. VA 8th Inf. Co.E
Rogers, Roderick VA Hvy.Arty. 20th Bn. Co.B
Rogers, R.P. VA 46th Inf. 2nd Co.E
Rogers, R.Q. MS 38th Cav. Co.D
Rogers, R.R. AR 2nd Cav. Co.F
Rogers, R.R. AR 27th Inf. Co.I
Rogers, R.R. GA 43rd Inf. Co.I
Rogers, R.R. MS 18th Cav. Co.C
Rogers, R.R. MS 34th Inf. Co.D
Rogers, R.S. GA 11th Inf.
Rogers, R.T. AR Inf. Hardy's Regt. Co.G
Rogers, R.T. MS 1st Lt.Arty. Co.K
Rogers, R.T. MS 43rd Inf. Co.C
Rogers, R.T. VA 14th Inf. Co.I
Rogers, Russell B. TN 37th Inf. Co.B
Rogers, R.W. GA Inf. 3rd Bn. Co.A
Rogers, R.W. MS 16th Inf. Co.A
Rogers, R.W. TN 39th Mtd.Inf. Co.C
Rogers, R.W. TN 61st Mtd.Inf. Co.G
Rogers, S. GA 60th Inf. Co.B

Rogers, S. KY 7th Cav. Co.A
Rogers, S. LA 7th Cav. Co.C
Rogers, S. TX Cav. Wells' Bn. Co.H
Rogers, S. Aden VA 8th Inf. Co.D
Rogers, Sam M. TX 11th Inf. Co.C
Rogers, Sampson TN 12th (Green's) Cav. Co.K
Rogers, Samuel AL 7th Cav. Co.E
Rogers, Samuel AL 21st Inf. Co.K
Rogers, Samuel AR 1st Vol. Anderson's Co.
Rogers, Samuel KY Jessee's Bn.Mtd.Riflemen
Co.A
Rogers, Samuel MS Cav. Ham's Regt. Co.G
Rogers, Samuel MS Inf. 3rd Bn.
Rogers, Samuel MO 11th Inf. Co.H
Rogers, Samuel NC 18th Inf. Co.G
Rogers, Samuel TN 60th Mtd.Inf. Co.A
Rogers, Samuel TX 37th Cav. Co.A
Rogers, Samuel VA 6th Cav. Co.K
Rogers, Samuel B. GA 61st Inf. Co.H Cpl.
Rogers, Samuel B. MD 1st Cav. Co.C
Rogers, Samuel B. MD 1st Inf. Co.H
Rogers, Samuel B. TN 3rd (Lillard's) Mtd.Inf.
Co.H
Rogers, Samuel C. KY 4th Mtd.Inf. Co.E
Rogers, Samuel E. KY 1st Inf. Cpl.
Rogers, Samuel E. VA Cav. Mosby's Regt.
(Part.Rangers)
Rogers, Samuel H. AL 41st Inf. Co.A Sgt.
Rogers, Samuel J. TX 18th Cav. Co.C
Rogers, Samuel M.C. VA 45th Inf. Co.K
Rogers, Samuel P. AL 18th Bn.Vol. Co.B Sgt.
Rogers, Samuel P. TX Cav. Baylor's Regt. Co.A
Black.
Rogers, Samuel R. VA 146th Mil. Co.K Sgt.
Rogers, Samuel S. NC 15th Inf. Co.B
Rogers, Samuel S. TX 4th Inf. Co.K
Rogers, Samuel S. VA Cav. Mosby's Regt.
(Part.Rangers) Co.A
Rogers, Samuel T. GA 5th Inf. Co.A
Rogers, Samuel T. VA 6th Inf. Co.K
Rogers, Sanford V. SC 22nd Inf. Co.C
Rogers, S.B. GA 5th Inf. Co.A
Rogers, S.B. TN 14th (Neely's) Cav. Co.A
Rogers, S.B.M. TN 34th Inf. Co.A
Rogers, S.C. FL 5th Inf. Co.B
Rogers, S.C. MS 15th (Cons.) Inf. Co.F
Rogers, S.D. GA 59th Inf. Co.C Sgt.
Rogers, S.D. MO 6th Cav. Co.D
Rogers, S.E. LA 25th Inf. Co.K
Rogers, S.E. MO 1st & 4th Cons.Inf. Co.H
Rogers, S.E. MO 4th Inf. Co.K
Rogers, Seaborn FL 6th Inf. Co.E,D
Rogers, Seaborne J. FL Cav. (Marianna Drag.)
Smith's Co.
Rogers, Seaborn J. FL 11th Inf. Co.H
Rogers, Seborn T. NC 16th Inf. Co.L Drum.
Rogers, Seborn T. NC Inf. Thomas Legion Co.E
Drum.
Rogers, Seth GA Inf. 14th Bn. (St.Guards) Co.H
Rogers, Seth MS 1st Lt.Arty. Co.L
Rogers, Seth VA 11th Regt.Rangers Co.A
Rogers, Seth VA 3rd Cav. & Inf.St.Line Co.A
Rogers, Seth F. MS 16th Inf. Co.F
Rogers, S.G. AR 34th Inf. Co.A
Rogers, S.G. LA 2nd Inf. Cpl.
Rogers, S.G. LA 17th Inf. Co.E
Rogers, S.G. TN Inf. 23rd Bn. Co.D

Rogers, S.H. AR Cav. McGehee's Regt. Co.G
  Cpl.
Rogers, S.H. AR 35th Inf. Co.C
Rogers, S.H. AR 62nd Mil. Co.A Drum.
Rogers, S.H. GA 2nd Inf. Co.E
Rogers, S.H. VA 2nd Inf.Loc.Def. Co.K
Rogers, S.H. VA Inf. 2nd Bn.Loc.Def. Co.B
Rogers, S.H. 1st Conf.Cav. 1st Co.C
Rogers, Shadrach J. TX 13th Cav. Co.G
Rogers, Sidney R. AR 20th Inf. Co.G Sgt.
Rogers, Silas KY Arnold Creek Ghent Cty.
Rogers, Silas D. MS 8th Inf. Co.H
Rogers, Silas D. 1st Conf.Eng.Troops Co.A
Rogers, Silk 1st Cherokee Mtd.Rifles Co.K Far.
Rogers, Simeon MS 5th Inf. (St.Troops) Co.B
  Sgt.
Rogers, Simeon TX 12th Inf. Co.D
Rogers, Simeon TX 22nd Inf. Co.B
Rogers, Simeon A. NC 50th Inf. Co.A
Rogers, Simeon D. GA 6th Inf. Co.A Band
  Music.
Rogers, Simeon D. GA 30th Inf. Co.F
Rogers, Simeon W. GA Inf. 2nd Bn. Co.B
Rogers, Simeon W. GA 5th Inf. Co.K
Rogers, Sim R. TN 14th Inf. Co.H
Rogers, Sion H. NC 14th Inf. Co.K 1st Lt.
Rogers, Sion H. NC 47th Inf. Col.
Rogers, Sion M. MS 17th Inf. Co.B
Rogers, Sion M. MS 34th Inf. Co.B
Rogers, S.J. MS 5th Inf. (St.Troops) Co.H Sgt.
Rogers, S.J. SC 6th Cav. Co.I
Rogers, S.J. TN 18th Inf. Co.C
Rogers, S.J. TN 42nd Inf. 2nd Co.H
Rogers, S.K. NC 4th Sr.Res. Co.F
Rogers, S.L. AR 10th (Witt's) Cav. Co.C
Rogers, S.L. AR 16th Inf. Co.F
Rogers, S.L. MS St.Cav. 2nd Bn. (Harris') Co.B
Rogers, Solomon L. AL 6th Inf. Co.G
Rogers, S.P. AL 7th Inf. Co.G
Rogers, S.P. SC 2nd Inf. Co.F
Rogers, Spencer A. NC 48th Inf. Co.G
Rogers, Spirus A. AR 6th Inf. New Co.D
Rogers, S.S. VA 8th Inf. Co.E
Rogers, S. St.George FL 2nd Inf. Lt.Col.
Rogers, S. St.George Gen. & Staff, Cav. Col.
Rogers, Stephen AL 57th Inf. Co.F
Rogers, Stephen GA 6th Inf. Co.I
Rogers, Stephen NC 61st Inf. Co.F
Rogers, Stephen TX 1st (Yager's) Cav. Co.E
Rogers, Stephen B. VA 6th Bn.Res. Co.C,E
Rogers, Stephen S. GA Inf. 2nd Bn. Co.D
Rogers, S.W. AR 2nd Cav. Co.D
Rogers, Sydney L. AL 15th Inf. Co.K
Rogers, Sylvester P. LA Inf. 11th Bn. Co.D
Rogers, T. MS Cav. 3rd Bn. (Ashcraft's) Co.C
  Cpl.
Rogers, T. MS 25th Inf. Co.C
Rogers, T. VA 46th Inf. Co.L
Rogers, T.A. SC 5th Res. Co.H Bvt.2nd Lt.
Rogers, Tavner MS 19th Inf. Co.K
Rogers, Taylor MS Inf. 3rd Bn. Co.F
Rogers, Taylor NC Inf. Thomas Legion Co.I
Rogers, T.B. MS St.Cav. 3rd Bn. (Cooper's) 1st
  Co.A
Rogers, T.C. NC 44th Inf. Hosp.Stew.
Rogers, T.C. TX 14th Inf. Co.F
Rogers, T.E. GA 7th Cav. Co.B

Rogers, T.E. GA Cav. 21st Bn. Co.C
Rogers, T.F. GA 1st (Symons') Res. Co.E
Rogers, T.F. VA Lt.Arty. Grandy's Co.
Rogers, T.F. Conf.Lt.Arty. Richardson's Bn.
  Co.C
Rogers, T.G. LA 2nd Inf. Co.E
Rogers, T.G. SC 21st Inf. Co.I Sgt.
Rogers, T.G. TN 2nd (Ashby's) Cav. Co.I Far.
Rogers, T. Gwinn TN Cav. 4th Bn. (Branner's)
  Co.E
Rogers, T.H. GA 1st (Symons') Res. Co.E
Rogers, Thacker VA 25th Mil. Comsy.
Rogers, Thacker Gen. & Staff Capt.,Comsy.
Rogers, Theodore VA Vol. Taylor's Co.
Rogers, Theopholus A. SC 7th Inf. 1st Co.C
  Bvt.2nd Lt.
Rogers, Thomas AL 19th Inf. Co.C
Rogers, Thomas AL 21st Inf. Co.E
Rogers, Thomas AL 3rd Bn. Hilliard's Legion
  Vol. Co.F
Rogers, Thomas AL Cp. of Instr. Talladega
Rogers, Thomas AR Inf. Cocke's Regt. Co.K
Rogers, Thomas GA 2nd Inf. Co.E
Rogers, Thomas GA 6th Inf. (St.Guards) Co.D
Rogers, Thomas GA 42nd Inf. Co.G
Rogers, Thomas GA 46th Inf. Co.A
Rogers, Thomas KY 5th Cav. Co.D
Rogers, Thomas MS 21st Inf. Co.C
Rogers, Thomas MO 8th Inf. Co.H
Rogers, Thomas NC 8th Sr.Res. Broadhurst's
  Co.
Rogers, Thomas SC 6th Cav. Co.E
Rogers, Thomas SC 17th Inf. Co.A
Rogers, Thomas SC 21st Inf. Co.I Sgt.
Rogers, Thomas TN Cav. 16th Bn. (Neal's) Co.F
Rogers, Thomas TN 43rd Inf. Co.H
Rogers, Thomas VA 54th Inf. Co.F
Rogers, Thomas Gen. & Staff,PACS Asst.Surg.
Rogers, Thomas A. AR 9th Inf. Old Co.B
Rogers, Thomas A. GA Cobb's Legion Co.C
Rogers, Thomas A. NC 37th Inf. Co.D
Rogers, Thomas A. SC 5th Mil. Beat Co.3
Rogers, Thomas A. TN 5th (McKenzie's) Cav.
  Co.H
Rogers, Thomas B. GA Cherokee Legion
  (St.Guards) Co.K
Rogers, Thomas B. LA 2nd Inf. Co.B
Rogers, Thomas B. LA 12th Inf. 2nd Co.M
Rogers, Thomas C. MS 20th Inf. Co.D
Rogers, Thomas C. NC 14th Inf. Co.C
Rogers, Thomas E. GA 57th Inf. Co.G
Rogers, Thomas F. TX 14th Cav. Co.I
Rogers, Thomas H. GA 51st Inf. Co.E 1st Lt.
Rogers, Thomas H. KY Lt.Arty. Green's Btty.
Rogers, Thomas H. TN 11th (Holman's) Cav.
  Co.I Cpl.
Rogers, Thomas H. TN 63rd Inf. Co.A
Rogers, Thomas J. GA Lt.Arty. Ritter's Co.
  Asst.Surg.
Rogers, Thomas J. GA 53rd Inf. Co.F Cpl.
Rogers, Thomas J. KY 4th Cav. Co.A
Rogers, Thomas J. KY 4th Mtd.Inf. Co.H
Rogers, Thomas J. MD Arty. 3rd Btty.
  Asst.Surg.
Rogers, Thomas J. MS Cav. Jeff Davis Legion
  Co.E Cpl.
Rogers, Thomas J. MS 15th Inf. Co.K

Rogers, Thomas J. MS 26th Inf. Co.I
Rogers, Thomas J. MO 4th Cav. Co.G
Rogers, Thomas J. NC 6th Inf. Co.K
Rogers, Thomas J. NC 29th Inf. Co.E
Rogers, Thomas J. SC 1st (Orr's) Rifles Co.H
Rogers, Thomas J. TX 3rd Cav. Co.H
Rogers, Thos. J. Gen. & Staff Asst.Surg.
Rogers, Thomas Jefferson TX 18th Inf. Co.D
  Capt.
Rogers, Thomas L. FL 6th Inf. Co.D
Rogers, Thos. L. GA Mil. 6th Regt. Co.D
Rogers, Thomas L. GA 60th Inf. Co.F 2nd Lt.
Rogers, Thomas L. SC 7th Cav. Co.C
Rogers, Thomas L. SC Cav.Bn. Holcombe
  Legion Co.D
Rogers, Thomas N. GA 38th Inf. Co.B
Rogers, Thomas P. GA 18th Inf. Co.I
Rogers, Thomas P. MS 26th Inf. Co.F,G
Rogers, Thomas S. TN 1st (Turney's) Inf. Co.D
  Sgt.
Rogers, Thomas S. VA 1st Inf. Co.G
Rogers, Thompson SC 8th Inf. Co.L,I
Rogers, Thourman TN Cav. 16th Bn. (Neal's)
  Co.F
Rogers, Tillman MS 37th Inf. Co.I Sgt.
Rogers, Tim L. MS 17th Inf. Co.A Capt.
Rogers, Timothy MS 22nd Inf. Co.E
Rogers, Timothy H. NC Hvy.Arty. 1st Bn.
  Co.B,D
Rogers, Timothy L. MS 16th Inf. Co.H
Rogers, T.J. AL 53rd (Part.Rangers) Co.G
Rogers, T.J. AL 12th Inf. Co.G Cpl.
Rogers, T.J. AL 62nd Inf. Co.K,E
Rogers, T.J. GA 50th Inf. Co.D
Rogers, T.J. LA 27th Inf. Co.A
Rogers, T.J. MS 3rd Inf. (A. of 10,000) Co.A
  Capt.
Rogers, T.J. MS 15th Bn.S.S. Co.A Cpl.
Rogers, T.J. MS 32nd Inf. Co.K Cpl.
Rogers, T.J. MO Lt.Arty. 4th (Harris') Field
  Btty.
Rogers, T.J. TN 4th (McLemore's) Cav. Co.I
Rogers, T.J. TX 12th Cav. Co.G
Rogers, T.J. VA 45th Inf. Co.B
Rogers, T.K. AL 5th Inf. New Co.C
Rogers, T.L. GA 5th Inf. (St.Guards) Miller's
  Co.
Rogers, T.L. TN 9th Inf. Co.I
Rogers, T.L. 1st Cherokee Mtd.Vol. 2nd Co.G
Rogers, T.L. 2nd Cherokee Mtd.Vol. Co.F
Rogers, Tobias TN 51st (Cons.) Inf. Co.K
Rogers, Toliver SC 1st Arty. Co.K
Rogers, T.R. AR 2nd Cav. Co.D
Rogers, Trasimond LA 2nd Cav. Co.G
Rogers, Tristam B. SC Arty. Manigault's Bn. 1st
  Co.C
Rogers, T.S. AR 1st (Dobbins') Cav. Co.C
Rogers, T.S. TX 3rd Cav. Co.G Sgt.
Rogers, T.T. AL 60th Inf. Co.D
Rogers, T.W. AL 21st Inf. Co.C 1st Lt.
Rogers, T.W. AL 21st Inf. Co.C
Rogers, T.W. GA Cav. 22nd Bn. (St.Guards)
  Co.B Capt.
Rogers, T.W. LA 11th Inf. Co.I
Rogers, T.W. TX 12th Cav. Co.H
Rogers, T.W. TX 3rd (Kirby's) Bn.Vol. Co.A
  Cpl.

Rogers, T.W.S. TX 3rd (Kirby's) Bn.Vol. Co.C
Rogers, Tyrance VA 22nd Inf. Co.D
Rogers, Uriah J. GA 26th Inf. Co.C Capt.
Rogers, Vincent AR 2nd Cav. Co.D
Rogers, V. AR 2nd Cav. Co.D
Rogers, V.A. TN 19th & 20th (Cons.) Cav. Co.B
Rogers, V.B. 4th Conf.Inf. Co.H
Rogers, Virgil M. SC 18th Inf. Co.E
Rogers, Vit TN 19th & 20th (Cons.) Cav. Co.E
Rogers, V.W. TX 8th Cav. Co.B
Rogers, W. FL 11th Inf.
Rogers, W. GA Lt.Arty. Ritter's Co.
Rogers, W. KY 7th Cav. Co.A
Rogers, W. MD Arty. 3rd Btty.
Rogers, W. MS 1st Cav. Co.B
Rogers, W. MS 6th Cav. Co.D
Rogers, W. MS 8th Cav. Co.I
Rogers, W. MS 12th Cav. Co.H
Rogers, W. MO Arty.
Rogers, W. VA 10th Cav. Co.K
Rogers, W. 1st Conf.Cav. 1st Co.C
Rogers, W.A. AL 15th Bn.Part.Rangers Co.B
Rogers, W.A. AL 56th Part.Rangers Co.B
Rogers, W.A., Jr. GA 6th Inf. (St.Guards) Co.I
Rogers, W.A. GA 9th Inf. Co.C
Rogers, W.A. LA 1st Res. Co.D
Rogers, W.A. MS 26th Inf. Co.B
Rogers, W.A. SC Inf. 3rd Bn. Co.E
Rogers, W.A. SC 7th (Ward's) Bn.St.Res. Adj.
Rogers, W.A. TN 19th (Biffle's) Cav. Co.I
Rogers, W.A. VA 7th Cav. Co.E
Rogers, Walter VA 12th Inf. Co.B
Rogers, Walter H. VA 1st Arty. Co.B
Rogers, Warren KY 8th Cav. Co.A Sgt.
Rogers, Warren NC 3rd Arty. (40th St.Troops) Co.D
Rogers, Warren A. GA Inf. 2nd Bn. Co.B Cpl.
Rogers, Warren H. TN 30th Inf. Co.K
Rogers, Warrenton GA 9th Inf. Co.C
Rogers, Washington SC 5th St.Troops Co.E
Rogers, Washington TN 14th Inf. Co.F
Rogers, Washington J. TN 53rd Inf. Co.A 1st Lt.
Rogers, W.B. AL 5th Inf. New Co.C
Rogers, W.B. GA 27th Inf. Co.F Sgt.
Rogers, W.B. KY 9th Cav. Co.A
Rogers, W.B. NC Snead's Co. (Loc.Def.)
Rogers, W.B. TN 5th (McKenzie's) Cav. Co.D,E
Rogers, W.B. TN 16th Inf. Co.H
Rogers, W.B. 2nd Creek Mtd.Vol. N.C.S. Ord.Sgt.
Rogers, W.C. AL 9th (Malone's) Cav. Co.B 2nd Lt.
Rogers, W.C. MS 7th Cav. Co.K
Rogers, W.C. MS 2nd (Davidson's) Inf. Co.I
Rogers, W.C. MS Inf. (Res.) Berry's Co.
Rogers, W.C. TN 3rd (Lillard's) Mtd.Inf. Co.I
Rogers, W.D. AL 40th Inf. Co.G
Rogers, W.D. SC 4th Cav. Co.D
Rogers, W.D. SC 8th Inf. Co.L
Rogers, W.D. TN 12th (Cons.) Inf. Co.G
Rogers, W.D. TN 22nd Inf. Co.E
Rogers, W.D. TX 24th Cav. Co.B
Rogers, W.D. TX 4th Inf. Co.E
Rogers, W.D. TX 16th Inf. Co.B
Rogers, W.D. TX 21st Inf. Co.G
Rogers, W.D. 15th Conf.Cav. Co.E

Rogers, W.D. Gen. & Staff Contr.Surg.
Rogers, W.E. GA 8th Inf. (St.Guards) Co.F
Rogers, W.E. GA 63rd Inf. Co.G
Rogers, W.E. Inf. Bailey's Cons.Regt. Co.A 2nd Lt.
Rogers, W.E. TX 11th Cav. Co.I
Rogers, W.E. TX 21st Inf. Co.A
Rogers, W.E. Gen. & Staff Surg.
Rogers, W.E. Gen. & Staff Dr.M.
Rogers, W. Edgar SC Palmetto S.S. Co.H
Rogers, Wesley AL 3rd Regt.St.Troops Co.D
Rogers, Wesley J. NC 23rd Inf. Co.E 1st Sgt.
Rogers, Weston NC 47th Inf. Co.C
Rogers, Weston VA 47th Inf. 3rd Co.I
Rogers, W.F. AL Auburn Home Guards Vol. Darby's Co.
Rogers, W.F. SC 18th Inf. Co.F
Rogers, W.G. TX Arty. Douglas' Co.
Rogers, W.H. AR 37th Inf. Co.A
Rogers, W.H. AR Inf. Hardy's Inf. Co.B
Rogers, W.H. GA 4th (Clinch's) Cav. Co.F
Rogers, W.H. GA Lt.Arty. Croft's Btty. (Columbus Arty.)
Rogers, W.H. GA 32nd Inf. Co.K
Rogers, W.H. LA Lt.Arty. Fenner's Btty.
Rogers, W.H. LA Inf. 1st Sp.Bn. (Rightor's) Co.F
Rogers, W.H. LA Inf.Cons. 18th Regt. & Yellow Jacket Bn. Co.I Jr.2nd Lt.
Rogers, W.H. LA Inf.Crescent Regt. Co.K,E Lt.
Rogers, W.H. MS 3rd Inf. (A. of 10,000) Co.G
Rogers, W.H. MS 4th Inf. Co.E
Rogers, W.H. SC Arty. Gregg's Co. (McQueen Lt.Arty.)
Rogers, W.H. SC Inf. 6th Bn. Co.A
Rogers, W.H. SC 26th Inf. Co.C
Rogers, W.H. TN 10th (DeMoss') Cav. Co.F
Rogers, W.H. TN Cav. Napier's Bn. Co.C
Rogers, W.H. TX 24th & 25th Cav. (Cons.) Co.B
Rogers, W.H. VA 5th Cav. Co.F
Rogers, W.H. VA 14th Inf. 2nd Co.G
Rogers, W.H. VA Inf. 25th Bn. Co.D
Rogers, W.H. Gen. & Staff 1st Lt.,ADC
Rogers, W.H.H. MS 36th Inf. Co.K
Rogers, W.H.P. AL Lt.Arty. Tarrant's Btty.
Rogers, Wilburn TN 4th Cav.
Rogers, Wiley MS 8th Inf. Co.F
Rogers, Wiley MS 37th Inf. Co.E
Rogers, Wiley NC 48th Inf. Co.F
Rogers, Wiley M. AR 1st (Crawford's) Cav. Co.A
Rogers, Wiley P. TX 1st (McCulloch's) Cav. Co.K
Rogers, Wiley P. TX 1st (Yager's) Cav. Co.I
Rogers, Wiley P. TX Cav. 8th (Taylor's) Bn. Co.D
Rogers, Wiley Wesley NC Inf. 13th Bn. Co.D
Rogers, Wilford L. TN 42nd Inf. Co.B
Rogers, William AL 12th Cav. Co.G
Rogers, William AL 18th Bn.Vol. Co.A
Rogers, William AL 33rd Inf. Co.D
Rogers, Wm. AL 35th Inf. Co.D
Rogers, William AL 50th Inf. Co.G
Rogers, William AR 7th Inf. Co.M
Rogers, William AR 10th Mil. Co.A
Rogers, William AR 10th Mil. Co.D

Rogers, William AR 26th Inf. Co.H
Rogers, Wm. AR 27th Inf. Co.B
Rogers, William AR 38th Inf. Co.G
Rogers, William AR Inf. Adams' Regt. Moore's Co.
Rogers, William FL 9th Inf. Co.D
Rogers, William GA 4th Cav. (St.Guards) Robertson's Co.
Rogers, William GA 12th Cav. Co.D
Rogers, Wm. GA 13th Cav. Co.E
Rogers, William GA 62nd Cav. Co.A
Rogers, William GA Arty. 9th Bn. Co.A,E
Rogers, William GA Lt.Arty. Croft's Btty. (Columbus Arty.)
Rogers, William GA Arty. St.Troops Pruden's Btty.
Rogers, William GA 1st Inf. (St.Guards)
Rogers, William GA 1st (Olmstead's) Inf. Gallie's Co.
Rogers, William GA 1st (Symons') Res. Co.B Lt.
Rogers, William GA 3rd Inf. Co.B
Rogers, William GA 5th Res. Co.I
Rogers, William GA 5th Inf. (St.Guards) Rucker's Co.
Rogers, William GA 8th Inf. (St.Guards) Co.F 1st Lt.
Rogers, William GA 15th Inf.
Rogers, Wm. GA 19th Inf. Co.H
Rogers, William GA 48th Inf. Co.A
Rogers, William LA Cav. Greenleaf's Co. (Orleans Lt.Horse)
Rogers, William LA Lt.Arty. Bridges' Btty.
Rogers, William LA 5th Inf. Co.E 1st Sgt.
Rogers, William LA 12th Inf. Co.K
Rogers, William LA 21st (Patton's) Inf. Co.A
Rogers, William MS 7th Cav. Co.I
Rogers, William MS 8th Cav. Co.C
Rogers, William MS 9th Cav. Co.B
Rogers, William MS Cav. 17th Bn. Co.D
Rogers, William MS 1st (King's) Inf. (St.Troops) Co.C
Rogers, William MS 14th Inf. Co.A
Rogers, William MS 32nd Inf. Co.F 1st Sgt.
Rogers, William MS 41st Inf. Co.F
Rogers, William MO 2nd Cav. Co.A,C
Rogers, William MO Cav. Wood's Regt. Co.D
Rogers, William NC Cav. 5th Bn. Co.A Cpl.
Rogers, William NC Inf. 2nd Bn. Co.H
Rogers, William NC 29th Inf. Co.A
Rogers, William NC 30th Inf. Co.A
Rogers, William NC 34th Inf. Co.B
Rogers, William NC 34th Inf. Co.H
Rogers, William NC 64th Inf. Co.D
Rogers, William SC 4th Cav. Co.D
Rogers, William SC Arty. Manigault's Bn. Co.D
Rogers, William SC 15th Inf. Co.F
Rogers, William SC Inf. Holcombe Legion Co.K
Rogers, William TN Cav. 4th Bn. (Branner's) Co.C
Rogers, William TN 4th (McLemore's) Cav. Co.H
Rogers, William TN 23rd Inf. Co.H
Rogers, William TX 4th Cav. Co.I
Rogers, William TX 17th Cons.Dismtd.Cav. Co.C
Rogers, William TX 31st Cav. Co.E Music.

Rogers, William TX 32nd Cav. Co.C,H
Rogers, William TX Cav. Baird's Regt. Co.F 2nd Lt.
Rogers, William TX 3rd (Kirby's) Bn.Vol. Co.A,C
Rogers, William TX 12th Inf. Co.G
Rogers, William TX 22nd Inf. Co.A
Rogers, William VA 2nd Cav. Co.K
Rogers, William VA Cav. 15th Bn. Co.C
Rogers, William VA 19th Cav. Co.B,K
Rogers, William VA Hvy.Arty. 19th Bn. 3rd Co.C
Rogers, William VA Lt.Arty. Cayce's Co.
Rogers, William VA 30th Inf. Co.C
Rogers, William VA 36th Inf. 2nd Co.C
Rogers, William, Jr. 1st Cherokee Mtd.Vol. 1st Co.E, 2nd Co.C
Rogers, William, Sr. 1st Cherokee Mtd.Vol. 1st Co.E, 2nd Co.C
Rogers, William 1st Chickasaw Inf. Kesner's Co.
Rogers, William Conf.Reg.Inf. Brooks' Bn. Co.C
Rogers, William A. AL 62nd Inf. Co.A,D
Rogers, William A. AR 3rd Inf. Co.B
Rogers, William A. FL Cav. 5th Bn. Co.A
Rogers, William A. GA 31st Inf. Co.H
Rogers, William A. MS 2nd Cav. Co.C Capt.
Rogers, William A. MS Bradford's Co. (Conf. Guards Arty.) Cpl.
Rogers, William A. NC 1st Jr.Res. Co.K
Rogers, William A. NC 29th Inf. Co.E
Rogers, William A. SC Inf. Hampton Legion Co.B
Rogers, William A. TN 34th Inf. Co.A
Rogers, William A. VA 20th Inf. Co.H
Rogers, William B. LA 9th Inf. Co.I
Rogers, William B. VA 54th Mil. Co.B
Rogers, William C. AL Arty. 1st Bn. Co.E
Rogers, William C. GA 52nd Inf. Co.E Sgt.
Rogers, William C. LA 9th Inf. Co.F
Rogers, William C. MD Arty. 2nd Btty.
Rogers, William C. MO Cav. Poindexter's Regt.
Rogers, William C. NC 18th Inf. Co.I
Rogers, William C. NC 26th Inf. Co.D
Rogers, William C. NC 35th Inf. Co.E Cpl.
Rogers, William C. NC 43rd Inf. Co.H
Rogers, William C. SC 6th Cav. Co.E Sgt.
Rogers, William C. TN 5th (McKenzie's) Cav. Co.C
Rogers, William C. TX 35th (Brown's) Cav. Co.G
Rogers, William C. TX 13th Vol. 1st Co.K, 2nd Co.C,G
Rogers, William C. VA 26th Inf. Co.E Cpl.
Rogers, Wm. C. Gen. & Staff Capt.,ACS
Rogers, William D. MS Cav. Jeff Davis Legion Co.E
Rogers, William D. SC 5th Inf. 1st Co.H, 2nd Co.B
Rogers, William D. VA 5th Cav. (12 mo. '61-2) Co.G Cpl.
Rogers, William D. VA 13th Cav. Co.I Sgt.
Rogers, William Diver SC 1st (Orr's) Rifles Co.C
Rogers, William E. GA Cav. Hendry's Co. (Atlantic & Gulf Guards)
Rogers, William E. GA 14th Inf. Co.E
Rogers, William E. TX 24th Cav. Co.C
Rogers, William E. TX 7th Inf. Co.A 1st Lt.

Rogers, William E. VA 92nd Mil. Co.C 2nd Lt.
Rogers, William F. AL 28th Inf. Co.H
Rogers, William F. MS 4th Cav. Co.A
Rogers, William F. MS 20th Inf. Co.C
Rogers, William F. TN 7th Inf. Co.D
Rogers, William F. TX 15th Cav. Co.F 1st Lt.
Rogers, William F. VA 51st Mil. Co.B
Rogers, William G. GA 18th Inf. Co.I 1st Lt.
Rogers, William G. MS 27th Inf. Co.B
Rogers, William G. TX 32nd Cav. Co.G Sgt.
Rogers, William H. AL 11th Inf. Co.A
Rogers, William H. AL 32nd Inf. Co.B
Rogers, William H. AR 38th Inf. Co.M
Rogers, William H. GA 12th Cav. Co.F
Rogers, William H. MD 1st Inf. Co.C
Rogers, William H. MD Weston's Bn. Co.A 1st Sgt.
Rogers, William H. MS 4th Cav. Co.E
Rogers, William H. MS Cav. Hughes' Bn. Co.D
Rogers, William H. MS 10th Inf. New Co.C, Old Co.B 2nd Lt.
Rogers, William H. MS 15th Inf. Co.F
Rogers, William H. MO 10th Inf. Co.F
Rogers, William H. NC 27th Inf. Co.G
Rogers, William H. SC 10th Inf. Co.L
Rogers, William H. TN 19th Inf. Co.I
Rogers, Wm. H. TX 19th Cav. Co.E
Rogers, William H. VA 7th Cav. Co.D
Rogers, William H. VA 15th Cav. Co.E
Rogers, William H. VA Cav. 35th Bn. Co.E
Rogers, William H. VA 1st Arty. Co.I
Rogers, William H. VA Hvy.Arty. 19th Bn. 3rd Co.E
Rogers, William H. VA Lt.Arty. 38th Bn. Co.B
Rogers, William H. VA 4th Inf. Co.H
Rogers, William H. VA 39th Inf. Co.A,K Sgt.
Rogers, William H. VA 59th Inf. 3rd Co.F
Rogers, William H. 1st Creek Mtd.Vol. Co.H
Rogers, Wm. H. Gen. & Staff AQM
Rogers, William H.H. GA 9th Inf. Co.G
Rogers, William H.H. GA 43rd Inf. Co.I
Rogers, William H.H. GA 56th Inf. Co.A Sgt.
Rogers, William H.H. MS 1st (Johnston's) Inf. Co.G
Rogers, William H.H. Anderson's Brig. Ord.Sgt.
Rogers, William H.R. VA Lt.Arty. Grandy's Co. Sgt.
Rogers, William H.R. VA 6th Inf. Vickery's Co. Cpl.
Rogers, William H.R. VA 16th Inf. 1st Co.H Sgt.
Rogers, William J. AL 17th Inf. Co.K
Rogers, William J. AL 57th Inf. Co.K
Rogers, William J. AR 1st (Colquitt's) Inf. Co.C
Rogers, William J. AR 25th Inf. Co.H Capt.
Rogers, William J. GA 1st (Symons') Res. Co.E
Rogers, William J. GA 51st Inf. Co.E
Rogers, William J. MS 26th Inf. Asst.Surg.
Rogers, William J. NC Lt.Arty. 3rd Bn. Co.A Sr.1st Lt.
Rogers, William J. NC Hvy.Arty. 10th Bn. Co.D
Rogers, William J. NC 16th Inf. Co.L
Rogers, William J. NC 25th Inf. Co.D
Rogers, William J. NC Inf. Thomas Legion Co.E Sgt.
Rogers, William J. TN 12th (Green's) Cav. Co.I
Rogers, William J. TX 28th Cav. Co.K

Rogers, William J. VA 5th Cav. Co.H
Rogers, William J. VA 6th Cav. Co.G
Rogers, William J. VA 15th Cav. Co.E
Rogers, William J. VA 58th Mil. Co.B
Rogers, William K. TX 2nd Inf. Co.H
Rogers, William L. AL 18th Bn.Vol. Co.C 2nd Lt.
Rogers, William L. GA Cav. 22nd Bn. (St.Guards) Co.I 1st Sgt.
Rogers, William L. GA 20th Inf. Co.K 1st Sgt.
Rogers, William L. KY 4th Mtd.Inf. Co.A
Rogers, William L. NC Cav. 7th Bn. Co.D,E
Rogers, William L. VA 3rd Cav. Co.C
Rogers, William L. VA 62nd Mtd.Inf. 2nd Co.E
Rogers, William M. GA 6th Inf. Co.B
Rogers, William M. MS 1st Lt.Arty. Co.D
Rogers, William M. MS 4th Inf. Co.G
Rogers, William M. MS 42nd Inf. Co.A Sgt.
Rogers, William M. NC 64th Inf. Co.C
Rogers, William M. SC 15th Inf. Co.K 1st Lt.
Rogers, William M. TN 27th Inf. Co.E
Rogers, William M. TX 3rd Inf. Co.I
Rogers, William O. AR 19th (Dockery's) Inf. Co.B
Rogers, William P. AR 33rd Inf. Co.D
Rogers, William P. TX 2nd Inf. Col.
Rogers, William P. VA Inf. 23rd Bn. Co.B
Rogers, William P. VA 151st Mil. Co.A
Rogers, William P.D. NC 3rd Inf. Co.B
Rogers, William P.D. NC 43rd Inf. Co.A,K
Rogers, William R. AR Cav. Harrell's Bn. Co.B
Rogers, William R. GA 13th Cav. Co.E
Rogers, William R. GA 1st (Olmstead's) Inf. Co.G Cpl.
Rogers, William R. GA 2nd Bn.S.S. Co.B
Rogers, William R. MO 2nd Inf. Co.A
Rogers, William R. TN 1st (Turney's) Inf. Co.I
Rogers, William R. TN 3rd (Lillard's) Mtd.Inf. Co.H
Rogers, William R. TN 44th Inf. Co.G
Rogers, William R. TX 27th Cav. Co.L,N
Rogers, William S. AL Cav. Hardie's Bn.Res. Co.E
Rogers, William S. AR 3rd Cav. 3rd Co.E
Rogers, William S. AR Cav. 6th Bn. Co.C
Rogers, William S. KY 1st Bn.Mtd.Rifles Co.C
Rogers, William S. KY 5th Mtd.Inf. Capt.
Rogers, William S. NC 4th Inf. Co.A
Rogers, William S. SC 1st (Orr's) Rifles Co.H
Rogers, William S.C. GA 12th Inf. Co.H
Rogers, Williamson AL 63rd Inf. Co.C Capt.
Rogers, William T. AL 24th Inf. Co.F
Rogers, William T. AL 28th Inf. Co.K
Rogers, William T. AR 9th Inf. Co.E Cpl.
Rogers, William T. GA 6th Inf. Co.A
Rogers, William T. MS 26th Inf. Co.C
Rogers, William T. TX 19th Cav. Co.A
Rogers, William T. TX 27th Cav. Co.A 2nd Lt.
Rogers, William T. TX 35th (Brown's) Cav. 2nd Co.B
Rogers, William T. TX 2nd Field Btty.
Rogers, William T. VA 59th Inf. 3rd Co.F
Rogers, William W. GA Arty. 9th Bn. Co.A,E
Rogers, William W. GA 61st Inf. Co.B Sgt.
Rogers, William W. LA 12th Inf. Co.D
Rogers, William W. MS 15th Inf. Co.C Sgt.
Rogers, William W. MS 23rd Inf. Co.I

Rogers, William W. NC 1st Inf. Co.I
Rogers, William W. NC 5th Inf. Co.D Music.
Rogers, William W. NC 61st Inf. Co.A Cpl.
Rogers, William W. NC 62nd Inf. Co.A
Rogers, William W. SC 1st (Orr's) Rifles Co.H
Rogers, William Walker MS 4th Cav. Co.G
Rogers, Willis NC Jones' Co. (Supp.Force)
Rogers, Willis W. VA 8th Bn.Res. Co.B
Rogers, Willis W. VA 97th Mil. Co.L Capt.
Rogers, Wilson GA Arty. 9th Bn. Co.A,E
Rogers, Wilson TX 2nd Inf. Co.H Sgt.
Rogers, Wilson VA 16th Cav. Co.K
Rogers, Winston VA 1st Inf. Co.A
Rogers, Winston VA 12th Inf. Co.G
Rogers, W.J. AL 6th Cav. Co.A
Rogers, W.J. AL 6th Cav. Co.I Sgt.
Rogers, W.J. AR Lt.Arty. Owen's Btty. Cpl.
Rogers, W.J. AR 2nd Vol. Co.B Sgt.Maj.
Rogers, W.J. AL 3rd Inf. Co.K
Rogers, W.J. AR 23rd Inf. Co.K
Rogers, W.J. AR 37th Inf. Co.K
Rogers, W.J. GA 62nd Cav. Co.F 2nd Lt.
Rogers, W.J. GA 2nd Inf. Co.G
Rogers, W.J. GA 20th Inf. Co.C
Rogers, W.J. GA 32nd Inf. Co.F
Rogers, W.J. GA 43rd Inf. Co.I
Rogers, W.J. LA 17th Inf. Co.E
Rogers, W.J. LA 26th Inf. Co.F
Rogers, W.J. MS 1st Cav. Co.E 1st Sgt.
Rogers, W.J. MS Cav. 3rd Bn. (Ashcraft's) Co.C Sgt.
Rogers, W.J. MS 9th Inf. New Co.H
Rogers, W.J. MS 41st Inf. Co.F
Rogers, W.J. NC Snead's Co. (Loc.Def.)
Rogers, W.J. TN 14th (Neely's) Cav. Co.K
Rogers, W.J. TN Cav. Napier's Bn. Co.C
Rogers, W.J., Jr. TN Cav. Napier's Bn. Co.C
Rogers, W.J. TX Inf. Griffin's Bn. Co.B
Rogers, W.J. Gen. & Staff Surg.
Rogers, W.J.C. TX 2nd Cav. Surg.
Rogers, W.J.C. Gen. & Staff Surg.
Rogers, W.J.T. MS 46th Inf. Co.F Cpl.
Rogers, W.L. AR Inf. Hardy's Regt. Co.B
Rogers, W.L. MS 3rd Inf. (St.Troops) Co.G
Rogers, W.L. NC 4th Cav. (59th St.Troops) Co.C
Rogers, W.L. NC 6th Cav. (65th St.Troops) Co.D,C
Rogers, W.L. NC 57th Inf. Co.I Cpl.
Rogers, W.L. TN 1st (Carter's) Cav. Co.K
Rogers, W.L. VA 25th Inf. 2nd Co.A
Rogers, W.M. AL Cav. Moreland's Regt. Co.H
Rogers, W.M. AL 40th Inf. Co.H
Rogers, W.M. TN 1st (Feild's) & 27th Inf. (Cons.) Co.I,E
Rogers, W.M. TN 61st Mtd.Inf. Co.F Cpl.
Rogers, W.M. TX 3rd Cav. Co.H
Rogers, W.M. TX 9th (Young's) Inf. Co.C
Rogers, W.N. AL 43rd Inf. Co.C
Rogers, W.P. AL 53rd (Part.Rangers) Co.F
Rogers, W.P. AL 5th Inf. New Co.C
Rogers, W.P. MS St.Cav. 2nd Bn. (Harris') Co.B
Rogers, W.P. MS 7th Cav. Co.C
Rogers, W.P. MS 32nd Inf. Co.G
Rogers, W.P. NC 4th Sr.Res. Co.F

Rogers, W.P. TX Cav. Terry's Regt. Co.E 2nd Lt.
Rogers, W.P. TX 20th Inf. Co.E
Rogers, W.Q. AR 50th Mil. Co.G
Rogers, W.R. AL 32nd Inf. Co.I
Rogers, W.R. AR 7th Cav. Co.L Sgt.
Rogers, W.R. SC 2nd Arty. Co.E
Rogers, W.R. SC 3rd Inf. Co.K
Rogers, W.R. TX 32nd Cav. Co.K
Rogers, W.R. TX 22nd Inf. Co.I
Rogers, W. Rom TX 1st Inf. Co.A,M
Rogers, W.S. AR 2nd Cav. 1st Co.A
Rogers, W.S. KY 2nd (Duke's) Cav. Co.E 1st Lt.
Rogers, W.S. KY 1st Inf. Co.C 1st Lt.
Rogers, W.S. TN 19th & 20th (Cons.) Cav. Co.B
Rogers, W.S. TX 12th Cav. Co.K
Rogers, W.S. VA 5th Cav. Co.I
Rogers, W.S. VA 1st St.Res. Co.D
Rogers, W.S. Gen. & Staff Capt.,QM
Rogers, W. Simpson SC 18th Inf. Co.E
Rogers, W.S.V. MS Cav. Ham's Regt. Co.A
Rogers, W.T. AR 2nd Mtd.Rifles Hawkins' Co.
Rogers, W.T. AR Cav. Gordon's Regt. Co.H
Rogers, W.T. GA Lt.Arty. (Jackson Arty.) Massenburg's Btty.
Rogers, W.T. GA Inf. 25th Bn. (Prov.Guard) Co.D Sgt.
Rogers, W.T. MS 26th Inf. Co.G
Rogers, W.T. MS 32nd Inf. Co.I
Rogers, W.T. SC 8th Inf. Co.K 2nd Lt.
Rogers, W.T. TX 1st Inf. Co.A
Rogers, W.T. TX St.Troops Teel's Co.
Rogers, W.T. Sig.Corps,CSA Sgt.
Rogers, W.T.H. NC Snead's Co. (Loc.Def.) Sgt.
Rogers, W.V.P. AL Mil. 2nd Regt.Vol. Co.F
Rogers, W.V.S. MS 7th Cav. Co.G
Rogers, W.W. FL 5th Inf. Co.B
Rogers, W.W. MS 39th Inf. Co.D
Rogers, W.W. NC 1st Arty. (10th St.Troops) Co.B
Rogers, W.W. NC 1st Arty. (10th St.Troops) Co.D 1st Lt.
Rogers, W.W. NC 66th Inf. Co.K
Rogers, W.W. TN 8th (Smith's) Cav. Co.G
Rogers, W.W. TN 20th Inf. Co.D
Rogers, W.W. VA Lt.Arty. Fry's Co.
Rogers, W.W. 3rd Conf.Eng.Troops Co.C
Rogers, W.W. Eng.Dept. Polk's Corps A. of TN Sap. & Min. Co.,CSA
Rogers, W.Z. TN 19th & 20th (Cons.) Cav. Co.K
Rogers, Young A. SC 1st (Butler's) Inf. Co.D Sgt.
Rogers, Young C. AR Cav. Carlton's Regt. Co.B
Rogers, Y.W. LA 27th Inf. Co.G
Rogers, Z. AL 7th Cav. Co.C,G
Rogers, Z. MS 5th Inf. (St.Troops) Co.H
Rogers, Z. MO 7th Cav. Co.C
Rogers, Zach AL Rives' Supp.Force 9th Congr. Dist.
Rogers, Zachariah TX 27th Cav. Co.I
Rogers, Zadock SC 22nd Inf. Co.C
Rogers, Z.M. SC Lt.Arty. Jeter's Co. (Macbeth Lt.Arty.)

Rogers, Z.T. MO Lt.Arty. Barret's Co.
Rogerson, A. SC Lt.Arty. M. Ward's Co. (Waccamaw Lt.Arty.)
Rogerson, Arden NC 1st Inf. Co.H
Rogerson, Calvin NC 31st Inf. Co.F
Rogerson, David NC 17th Inf. (1st Org.) Co.F
Rogerson, David NC 17th Inf. (2nd Org.) Co.A
Rogerson, David L. NC 17th Inf. (1st Org.) Co.F
Rogerson, Edward FL 2nd Inf. Co.C Sgt.
Rogerson, Godfrey NC 42nd Inf. Co.B
Rogerson, Godfrey NC 61st Inf. Co.H
Rogerson, H. SC Lt.Arty. M. Ward's Co. (Waccamaw Lt.Arty.) Cpl.
Rogerson, Harrison NC 42nd Inf. Co.B
Rogerson, Harrison NC 61st Inf. Co.H
Rogerson, H.E. NC 17th Inf. (1st Org.) Co.F
Rogerson, J. TN 15th (Stewart's) Cav. Co.D
Rogerson, J.E. SC Lt.Arty. M. Ward's Co. (Waccamaw Lt.Arty.) Cpl.
Rogerson, Jeremiah NC 1st Inf. Co.A
Rogerson, Jesse NC 68th Inf.
Rogerson, Jesse W. NC 1st Inf. Co.A
Rogerson, John NC 66th Inf.
Rogerson, John TX 4th Inf. Co.G
Rogerson, McG. NC 17th Inf. (1st Org.) Co.F
Rogerson, McG. NC 17th Inf. (2nd Org.) Co.A
Rogerson, M.O. NC 31st Inf. Co.G
Rogerson, Nathan NC 17th Inf. (1st Org.) Co.F
Rogerson, Nathan NC 17th Inf. (2nd Org.) Co.A Cpl.
Rogerson, Ransom S. NC 42nd Inf. Co.B
Rogerson, Ransom S. NC 61st Inf. Co.H
Rogerson, Reuben S. NC 17th Inf. (2nd Org.) Co.A
Rogerson, Samuel NC 1st Arty. (10th St.Troops) Co.K
Rogerson, Slade NC 17th Inf. (1st Org.) Co.F Cpl.
Rogerson, Slade NC 17th Inf. (2nd Org.) Co.A
Rogerson, Solomon NC 68th Inf.
Rogerson, Thomas NC 1st Inf. Co.H
Rogerson, W.D. SC 7th (Ward's) Bn.St.Res. Co.F
Rogerson, William NC 17th Inf. (1st Org.) Co.F
Rogerson, William NC 17th Inf. (2nd Org.) Co.A
Rogerson, William B. NC 17th Inf. (2nd Org.) Co.A
Rogerson, William H. VA 3rd Cav. 2nd Co.I 2nd Lt.
Rogerson, William H. VA 12th Inf. Co.E
Rogert, Ernest LA 30th Inf. Co.H 1st Lt.
Roges, James G. VA 14th Inf. Co.A
Rogester, John MS 1st Cav. Co.B
Rogester, W.J. MS 1st Cav. Co.B
Roget, Avelino LA Mil. 5th Regt.Eur.Brig. (Spanish Regt.) Co.9 Cpl.
Roget, Joaqin LA Mil. Cazadores Espanoles Regt. Co.5
Rogge, C. TX 4th Inf. (St.Troops) Co.F
Roggen, Frederic LA C.S.Zouave Bn. Co.A
Roggentine, H. GA 1st (Symons') Res. Co.A
Roggers, A.C. AL 54th Inf.
Roggers, C. TX 84th Inf. Co.B
Roggers, Charles VA 19th Cav. Co.K
Roggers, Erastus T. AR 37th Inf. Co.H
Roggers, G.E. TN Inf. 2nd Cons.Regt. Co.F
Roggers, G.W. MS 3rd Inf. (St.Troops) Co.I

Roggers, G.W. TN 47th Inf. Co.C
Roggers, H.B. MS 6th Cav. Co.C Cpl.
Roggers, Hiram AR 11th Inf. Co.F Teamster
Roggers, Hiram MS 7th Cav. 2nd Co.G
Roggers, Hugh Y. GA 52nd Inf. Co.H
Roggers, James GA 52nd Inf. Co.B
Roggers, James B. AR 37th Inf. Co.H
Roggers, James C. GA 1st (Ramsey's) Inf. Co.F
Roggers, J.C. AR 11th Inf. Co.F
Roggers, Jessee P. MS 15th Inf. Co.K
Roggers, J.F. MS 11th (Cons.) Cav. Co.G
Roggers, J.J. TN 84th Inf. Co.B
Roggers, John GA 17th Inf. Co.E
Roggers, John C. AR 21st Inf. Co.C
Roggers, John J. TX 8th Inf. Co.A
Roggers, John S. TX Cav. Baylor's Regt. Co.H
  Sgt.
Roggers, John W. NC 29th Inf. Co.B
Roggers, Leroy W. TN 53rd Inf. Co.C
Roggers, McQueen NC 1st Bn.Jr.Res. Co.C
Roggers, Nathaniel A. TX 37th Cav. Co.F Cpl.
Roggers, Nathan W. AL 16th Inf. Co.A
Roggers, R. MS 8th Cav. Co.D
Roggers, R.C. MS 7th Cav. Co.K
Roggers, Richard TX 36th Cav. Co.B
Roggers, Robert TN Inf. 23rd Bn. Co.A
Roggers, S.L. MS 11th (Cons.) Cav. Co.G
Roggers, W. GA Inf. 27th Bn. Co.E
Roggers, Wiley AR 37th Inf. Co.H
Roggers, William NC 50th Inf. Co.I
Roggers, William TX 9th (Young's) Inf. Co.B
Roggers, William R. TN 28th Inf. Co.F Sgt.
Roggers, William S. AL 34th Inf. Black's Co.
Roggers, W.P. MS 11th (Cons.) Cav. Co.G
Roggers, W.T. AR 11th Inf. Co.F
Roggers, W.W. MS 15th (Cons.) Inf. Co.C
Rogginsbury, S.A. VA Cav. 40th Bn. Co.E
Rogie, C.W. Gen. & Staff Hosp.Stew.
Rogiero, R. SC 1st Regt. Charleston Guard Co.D
Rogiers, Edward Conf.Lt.Arty. 1st Reg.Btty.
  Sgt.
Rogiers, Edward Julian Inf. School of Pract.
  Powell's Detach. Co.D 1st Sgt.
Rogillio, Benjamin F. MS 16th Inf. Co.G 3rd
  Sgt.
Rogillio, C.B. LA 4th Inf. New Co.G Cpl.
Rogillio, C.E. MS Cav. Hughes' Bn. Co.C
Rogillio, Elias MS Lt.Arty. (Jefferson Arty.)
  Darden's Co.
Rogillio, E.R. MS Inf. 2nd Bn. Co.F
Rogillio, E.R. MS 48th Inf. Co.F
Rogillio, G.W. LA 4th Inf. Co.K
Rogillio, H.S. LA 4th Inf. New Co.G Cpl.
Rogillio, John 20th Conf.Cav. Co.D Sgt.
Rogillio, John G. LA 4th Inf. Co.K
Rogillio, John W. MS 38th Cav. Co.B
Rogillio, Martin LA 1st Cav. Co.E
Rogillio, Robert J. LA 1st Cav. Co.E
Rogillio, W.H. LA 4th Inf. Co.K
Rogillio, William F. MS Inf. 2nd Bn. Co.F
Rogillio, William F. MS 48th Inf. Co.F Sgt.
Rogin, T.E. SC 4th Cav. Co.I
Rogin, W.R. AL 18th Inf. Co.H
Roginbert, L. LA Mil. French Co. of St.James
Rogins, J.H. MS Lt.Arty. Yates' Btty.
Rogister, James NC 30th Inf. Co.A
Roglan, C.J. GA 16th Inf. Co.E

Rogland, C.Q. TX 8th Inf. Co.F
Rogles, Juan TX 33rd Cav. 1st Co.I
Rogsdale, Jack AR 8th Inf. Old Co.A
Rogton, W.J. AR 15th Mil. Co.C
Roguemon, J.D. AL 7th Cav. Co.F
Rogues, E. LA Mil. 3rd Regt.Eur.Brig. (Garde
  Francaise) Co.1
Roguigny, E. LA Mil. St.John the Baptist Res.
  Guards
Rogus, W.C. VA Inf. 26th Regt. Co.E Cpl.
Roh, Charles AL 8th Inf. Co.G Sgt.
Roh, M. AL Mil. West's Co.
Rohan, John A. VA 27th Inf. Co.G
Rohan, Thomas AL 13th Inf. Co.B
Rohan, Thomas MO 8th Cav. Co.E
Rohan, William VA 31st Inf. Co.I
Rohbecker, G. TX 1st Hvy.Arty. Co.C
Rohbock, J.M. LA Washington Arty.Bn. Co.4
Rohde, Charles AL 1st Bn. Hilliard's Legion
  Vol. Co.A
Rohde, George F. SC Arty. Bachman's Co.
  (German Lt.Arty.)
Rohde, George F. SC Arty.Bn. Hampton Legion
  Co.B
Rohde, H. SC Mil.Arty. 1st Regt. Werner's Co.
  Cpl.
Rohde, H.B. SC Lt.Arty. Wagener's Co. (Co.A,
  German Arty.)
Rohde, J. TX 4th Inf. (St.Troops) Co.A
Rohdefelde, Henry TX Lt.Arty. Jones' Co.
Rohden, Edward LA 21st (Kennedy's) Inf. Co.C
Rohdie, Calvin VA Hvy.Arty. 10th Bn. Co.C
Rohe, John SC Inf. 3rd Bn.
Rohe, M. AL St.Arty. Co.D
Rohe, Michael AL 1st Regt. Mobile Vol. Co.E
Rohed, B. NC 3rd Jr.Res. Co.B
Rohen, M. LA Mil.Conf.Guards Regt. Band
Rohenbach, R. LA Mil. 2nd Regt. 3rd Brig. 1st
  Div. Co.H
Roher, A. MS 38th Cav. Co.B
Roher, J.M. AL 47th Inf. Co.E
Rohie, Louis TX 13th Vol. 3rd Co.K
Rohier, Louis TX Inf. Griffin's Bn. Co.F
Rohit, S.C. VA 19th Cav. Co.D
Rohl, Julius Inf. School of Pract. Co.B
Rohl, T. LA Mil. 1st Chasseurs a pied Co.7
Rohlink, Henry FL 4th Inf. Co.B
Rohlins, L.K. NC 2nd Jr.Res. Co.D
Rohlter, Joseph SC 20th Inf. Co.A
Rohm, David NC 4th Sr.Res. Co.E
Rohm, Isaac NC 6th Inf. Co.E
Rohmann, V. LA Mil. 4th Regt.Eur.Brig. Co.F
Rohmer, F. LA Mil. 2nd Regt. 3rd Brig. 1st Div.
  Co.G
Rohmer, John B. TN 1st Hvy.Arty. Co.K
Rohmick, Max LA 6th Inf. Co.H
Rohn, J.D. TN 3rd (Clack's) Inf. Co.B Teamster
Rohner, John VA Hvy.Arty. 20th Bn. Co.B
Rohner, John VA 9th Inf. Co.B
Rohner, John VA 61st Inf. Co.C
Rohner, John VA Inf. Cohoon's Bn. Co.A Cpl.
Rohon, Andrew GA 3rd Res. Co.G
Rohr, C. VA 1st St.Res. Co.B
Rohr, Charles VA Cav. 40th Bn. Wren's Co.
Rohr, Charles W. VA 10th Cav. Co.G
Rohr, David E. Gen. & Staff, Ord.Dept.
Rohr, F.F. VA Inf. 2nd Bn.Loc.Def. Co.D

Rohr, F.J. VA 2nd Inf.Loc.Def. Co.B
Rohr, F.J. VA Inf. 2nd Bn.Loc.Def. Co.D
Rohr, George TN 21st Inf. Co.D Cpl.
Rohr, George E. 9th Conf.Inf. Co.G
Rohr, J.A. LA Arty. Hutton's Co. (Crescent
  Arty.,Co.A)
Rohr, Jacob VA Lt.Arty. Garber's Co. Artif.
Rohr, Jacob VA 3rd Bn. Valley Res. Co.B
Rohr, J.E. TN 21st Inf. Co.D
Rohr, John 9th Conf.Inf. Co.G
Rohr, Stansberry VA 10th Inf. Co.D
Rohr, William S. VA 10th Inf. Co.G
Rohr, W.S. MO Cav. Woodson's Co. Sgt.
Rohrbacher, John KY 8th Mtd.Inf. Co.D Cpl.
Rohrbacher, M. LA Mil. 3rd Regt.Eur.Brig.
  (Garde Francaise) Co.4
Rohrbacker, J.S. MS 12th Inf. Co.E
Rohrbaugh, James VA Lt.Arty. 38th Bn. Co.B
Rohrbough, A.E. Conf.Inf. 8th Bn.
Rohrburg, A. TN 15th Inf. Co.I
Rohrebacker, C.A. LA 5th Inf. Co.E
Rohrer, E.A. GA 1st (Olmstead's) Inf. Stiles' Co.
Rohrer, E.A. GA Inf. 18th Bn. Co.B
Rohrer, E.A. VA 6th Cav. 1st Co.E
Rohrer, Edward A. MS Cav. Jeff Davis Legion
  Co.F
Rohrer, John KY 4th Cav. Co.K,C
Rohus, Peter L. TX 28th Cav. Co.A Cpl.
Roi, Clement LA 2nd Cav. Co.D
Roi, Etienne LA 2nd Cav. Co.D
Roi, Fostin LA 2nd Cav. Co.D
Roi, J. LA Mil. 4th Regt. French Brig. Co.6
Roice, Owen MS Cav. 1st Bn. (Montgomery's)
  St.Troops Hammond's Co.
Roig, J. LA Mil. 5th Regt.Eur.Brig. (Spanish
  Regt.) Co.1
Roig, Jose Rivas LA Mil. 5th Regt.Eur.Brig.
  (Spanish Regt.) Co.3
Roig, Juan LA Mil. 5th Regt.Eur.Brig. (Spanish
  Regt.) Co.4,10
Roise, A.W. MO 6th Cav. Co.H
Roise, O. MS Cav. Yerger's Regt. Co.A
Roister, Madison MS 19th Inf. Co.C Music.
Roiston, Benjamin TN 61st Mtd.Inf. Co.B
Roiston, Thomas TN 61st Mtd.Inf. Co.B
Rojair, A. LA 18th Inf. Co.I
Rojair, A. LA Inf.Cons. 18th Regt. & Yellow
  Jacket Bn. Co.H
Rojas, Joseph LA Mil. 5th Regt.Eur.Brig.
  (Spanish Regt.) Co.5
Roke, Patrick O. TN 38th Inf. Co.F
Roke, Peter VA Inf. 5th Bn. Co.D
Rokenbaugh, J.H. GA 5th Cav. Co.G
Rokenbaugh, J.H. GA Cav. 20th Bn. Co.F
Roker, A. VA 13th Cav. Co.G
Rokes, F. LA 28th (Thomas') Inf. Co.G
Rolack, J.B. FL Norwood's Co. (Home Guards)
Rolades, J.G. AL 48th Inf. Co.K
Rolain, Samuel T. AL 10th Inf. Co.B
Rolan, James, Dr. KY Hopkinsville Lt.
Rolan, James G. AR Inf. 4th Bn. Co.B
Rolan, Joseph B. LA 9th Inf.
Rolan, Pleasant H. MO Cav. 2nd Bn.St.Guard
  Co.B
Rolan, Robert J. GA 27th Inf. Co.C
Rolan, S.W. GA 13th Inf. Co.G
Roland, A. MO Cav. Slayback's Regt. Co.A

Roland, A. TN 19th & 20th (Cons.) Cav. Co.K
Roland, A. TX Cav. Saufley's Scouting Bn. Co.F
Roland, A.A. LA Arty. Watson Btty.
Roland, A.A. LA 5th Inf. Co.E
Roland, Abner S. NC 1st Cav. (9th St.Troops) Co.D
Roland, A.F. MS 3rd (St.Troops) Cav. Co.B
Roland, A.J. AR 27th Inf. Co.E
Roland, A.J. TN 8th (Smith's) Cav. Co.C
Roland, A.J. TN 20th Inf. Co.G
Roland, Alfred AR Inf. Cocke's Regt. Co.E
Roland, A.M. GA Inf. 9th Bn. Co.A
Roland, A.M. GA 37th Inf. Co.D
Roland, Andrew Jackson GA 12th Inf. Co.E
Roland, Anthony VA 10th Cav. 1st Co.E
Roland, A.R. AR 5th Inf. Co.D
Roland, A.S. MS 3rd Inf. (St.Troops) Co.B
Roland, Asa FL 9th Inf. Co.G
Roland, Austin SC Inf. 3rd Bn. Co.D
Roland, Baswell GA Inf. 2nd Bn. Co.C
Roland, Benjamin TN Inf. 1st Bn. (Colms') Co.C
Roland, B.F. SC 1st (Butler's) Inf. Co.I
Roland, B.M. TX 35th (Brown's) Cav.
Roland, B.S. TX 9th (Young's) Inf. Co.K Sgt.
Roland, C.H. MS 12th Inf. Co.G
Roland, Charles LA Mil. 1st Native Guards Cpl.
Roland, Charles NC 38th Inf. Co.K
Roland, Chesley H. NC 8th Inf. Co.C
Roland, Christopher C. TX 22nd Cav. Co.E
Roland, Clark AR 25th Inf. Co.D
Roland, C.R. SC 9th Res. Co.E
Roland, David GA 12th Inf. Co.E
Roland, David LA Mil. 1st Regt. 3rd Brig. 1st Div. Co.E
Roland, David TN 44th (Cons.) Inf. Co.C Sgt.
Roland, David TN 45th Inf. Co.H 3rd Lt.
Roland, Denton TX 27th Cav. Co.H
Roland, D.G. TN Cav. Jackson's Co.
Roland, D.W. GA Siege Arty. Campbell's Ind.Co.
Roland, E. GA Inf. (GA Defenders) Chapman's Co.
Roland, Edward TN 14th Inf. Co.B
Roland, Eli MO 11th Inf. Co.F
Roland, Eli C. TN Inf. 1st Bn. (Colms') Co.C
Roland, Elijah AR 19th (Dawson's) Inf. Co.H
Roland, Ezekiel AL 37th Inf. Co.F
Roland, F.D. TX 7th Cav. Co.K
Roland, George GA 32nd Inf. Co.E
Roland, George F. TN 2nd Cav. Co.A
Roland, George T. KY 2nd (Duke's) Cav. Co.E,H
Roland, George W. AR 3rd Inf. Co.F
Roland, George W. NC 54th Inf. Co.B
Roland, Green FL 4th Inf. Co.G
Roland, Greene FL 7th Inf. Co.G
Roland, H. TX Inf. 4th Bn. (Oswald's) Co.A Pioneer
Roland, H.D. KY Lt.Arty. Cobb's Co.
Roland, H.E. AR 27th Inf. Co.E
Roland, Henry TX Waul's Legion Co.E
Roland, Henry VA 2nd Inf.Loc.Def. Co.E Sgt.
Roland, Henry H. AL 43rd Inf. Co.I
Roland, Henry H. VA 89th Mil. Co.H
Roland, Henry M. AL 61st Inf. Co.K
Roland, Henry M. GA 25th Inf. Co.E

Roland, Henry T. LA 28th (Gray's) Inf. Co.I Cpl.
Roland, H.G. MS 1st Cav.
Roland, Hiram M. AL 43rd Inf. Co.I
Roland, H.M. GA 38th Inf. 2nd Co.I
Roland, H.M. GA 60th Inf. 2nd Co.A
Roland, J.A. AL 6th Inf. Co.H
Roland, J.A. GA 28th Inf. Co.D
Roland, J.A. NC 1st Jr.Res. Co.D Cpl.
Roland, Jackson AR 16th Inf. Co.B
Roland, Jacob KY 3rd Bn.Mtd.Rifles Co.E
Roland, Jacob NC Cav. 5th Bn. Co.D
Roland, James AR 5th Inf. Co.D
Roland, James AR 25th Inf. Co.D
Roland, James AR 30th Inf. Co.C
Roland, James GA 60th Inf. Co.G
Roland, James TX 19th Cav. Co.F
Roland, James E. MS 15th (Cons.) Inf. Co.H
Roland, James E. VA 12th Inf. Co.F
Roland, James F. LA Siege Train Bn. Co.E
Roland, James F. LA 3rd Inf. Co.B,H
Roland, James J. TX 30th Cav. Co.A
Roland, James K. TN 24th Inf. Co.A
Roland, James N. TN 7th Inf. Co.C
Roland, James P. AR 3rd Cav. Co.G 2nd Lt.
Roland, James R. GA 12th (Wright's) Cav. (St.Guards) Wright's Co.
Roland, James T. AR 2nd Inf.
Roland, James T. GA Phillips' Legion Co.D
Roland, James W. NC 39th Inf. Co.E
Roland, J.B. MS 1st (Johnston's) Inf. Co.E
Roland, J.E. MS 7th Cav. Co.I
Roland, J.E. TN 51st (Cons.) Inf. Co.E
Roland, Jeremiah SC 6th Cav. Co.E
Roland, Jeremiah SC 18th Inf. Co.D
Roland, J.G. SC 1st St.Troops Co.E
Roland, J.H. TN 51st (Cons.) Inf. Co.E
Roland, J.J. SC Cav.
Roland, J.K. AR 24th Inf. Co.A
Roland, J.M. MO Cav. Poindexter's Regt.
Roland, Jo A. TN 51st (Cons.) Inf. Co.E Sgt.
Roland, John AR 18th Inf. Co.C
Roland, John GA 2nd Bn. Troops & Def. (Macon) Co.D
Roland, John KY 6th Cav. Co.K
Roland, John LA 13th Inf. Co.H
Roland, John MS Lt.Arty. 14th Bn. Co.C
Roland, John MS Wilkinson Cty. Minute Men Co.A Cpl.
Roland, John MO 1st N.E. Cav. Co.M Cpl.
Roland, John TN 2nd (Ashby's) Cav. Co.A
Roland, John TN Holman's Bn.Part.Rangers Co.B
Roland, John VA 21st Cav. 2nd Co.E
Roland, John C. TN Holman's Bn.Part.Rangers Co.D
Roland, John E. KY 6th Mtd.Inf. Co.A
Roland, John E. LA 28th (Gray's) Inf. Co.I
Roland, John S. MS 15th (Cons.) Inf. Co.H
Roland, John W. NC 14th Inf. Co.I
Roland, Jonas TN 54th Inf. Co.C
Roland, Joseph G. TX 5th Inf. (St.Troops) Co.B
Roland, Joshua T. VA Lt.Arty. Pegram's Co.
Roland, Josiah MS Rogers' Co.
Roland, J.S. AL 17th Inf. Co.G
Roland, J.S. SC 9th Res. Co.E
Roland, J.T. AR 34th Inf. Co.D

Roland, J.T. KY 2nd (Duke's) Cav. Co.H
Roland, J.T. TN 15th Inf. Co.G
Roland, J.W. NC 1st Jr.Res. Co.D
Roland, L. GA 32nd Inf. Co.E
Roland, Leston GA 37th Inf. Co.D
Roland, L.J. TN 8th (Smith's) Cav. Co.C
Roland, L.T. TN 55th (Brown's) Inf. Co.H
Roland, Luther MO 12th Cav. Co.G
Roland, Malchigah R. TX 6th Cav. Co.D
Roland, Martin TX Arty. 4th Bn. Co.A
Roland, Martin TX 8th Inf. Co.A
Roland, Mat AR 27th Inf. Co.D
Roland, Michael TN 37th Inf. Co.I
Roland, M.M. MO Inf. Perkins' Bn. Co.F Sgt.
Roland, M.O. SC 1st Cav. Co.K
Roland, Moore MO Cav. Preston's Bn. Co.B
Roland, N. NC 6th Sr.Res. Co.G
Roland, Neat KY 4th Cav. Co.G
Roland, N.R. NC Mallett's Bn. (Cp.Guard) Co.E
Roland, P. Gen. & Staff Maj.,AAG
Roland, Preston AR 27th Inf. Co.E
Roland, Rayburn NC 29th Inf. Co.B
Roland, R.G. VA Loc.Def. Durrett's Co.
Roland, Richard AL 38th Inf. Co.K
Roland, Richard N. VA 17th Inf. Co.E Sgt.
Roland, Richard P. GA 41st Inf. Co.D Cpl.
Roland, Robert AL Cav. Moreland's Regt. Co.G
Roland, R.P. TX 32nd Cav. Co.G
Roland, S.A. GA Cav. 22nd Bn. (St.Guards) Co.A
Roland, Samuel VA 5th Inf. Co.A
Roland, S.D. GA 12th Inf. Co.K
Roland, Shedrick TX 5th Cav. Co.C
Roland, Sherod TX 16th Cav. Co.I Cpl.
Roland, Silas NC 29th Inf. Co.D
Roland, T. 1st Conf.Eng.Troops Co.C
Roland, T.A. AR 11th Inf. Co.B
Roland, T.A. AR 11th & 17th (Cons.) Inf. Co.A
Roland, T.E. MS 38th Cav. Co.G
Roland, Thomas MO Lt.Arty. 1st Field Btty.
Roland, Thomas VA 6th Bn.Res. Co.A
Roland, Thomas B. AR 25th Inf. Co.D
Roland, Thomas L. VA 41st Inf. Co.B
Roland, Thomas W. MS 16th Inf. Co.K
Roland, T.J. SC 1st Cav. Co.F,K
Roland, T.M. SC 1st (Butler's) Inf. Co.I
Roland, T.R. KY 2nd (Duke's) Cav. Co.B
Roland, W.B. GA 4th Inf. Co.K
Roland, W.D. GA 32nd Inf. Co.F
Roland, W.H. TX 9th (Young's) Inf. Co.K 2nd Lt.
Roland, William AR 27th Inf. Co.D
Roland, William GA 11th Cav. Co.K
Roland, William GA 5th Inf. Co.B
Roland, William GA 23rd Inf. Co.D
Roland, William MS 38th Cav. Co.G
Roland, William MO 1st N.E. Cav. Co.M Cpl.
Roland, William MO 4th Cav. Co.G
Roland, William NC Cav. 5th Bn. Co.D
Roland, William TN Lt.Arty. Huggins' Co.
Roland, William TN 61st Mtd.Inf. Co.I
Roland, William TX 30th Cav. Co.A Cpl.
Roland, William A. AR 33rd Inf. Co.I
Roland, William A. TN 11th Inf. Co.F
Roland, William C. TN 54th Inf. Co.G
Roland, William F. MO Lt.Arty. 1st Field Btty.
Roland, William H. GA 15th Inf. Co.H

Roland, William H. NC 58th Inf. Co.G
Roland, William James GA 57th Inf. Co.A
Roland, William R. AR 25th Inf. Co.E
Roland, Willis MS 36th Inf. Co.F
Roland, Willis L. NC 5th Cav. (63rd St.Troops) Co.A
Roland, W.J. MS 46th Inf. Co.H
Roland, W.L. NC 6th Cav. (65th St.Troops) Co.E
Roland, W.M. TN 38th Inf. Co.E
Roland, Zack MO 9th Inf. Co.G
Roland, Zeno LA 12th Inf. Co.H
Rolands, John R. VA Cav. 27th Regt. Co.G
Rolans, John W. NC Cav. 14th Bn. Co.E
Rolater, Edmond M. AL 19th Inf. Co.G
Rolber, John VA 7th Cav. Co.I
Roleman, G.J. TN Inf. 23rd Bn. Co.D
Roleman, Harry TN Inf. 23rd Bn. Co.D
Rolen, D. AR Cav. Gordon's Regt. Co.I
Rolen, James AL 43rd Inf. Co.A
Rolen, James MO 6th Cav. Co.G
Rolen, James VA 63rd Inf. Co.K
Rolen, James 1st Conf.Cav. 2nd Co.F
Rolen, John GA 18th Inf. Co.F 2nd Lt.
Rolen, John NC 28th Inf. Co.I
Rolen, John TN Cav. Newsom's Regt. Co.B
Rolen, J.W. AL 17th Inf. Co.H
Rolen, L.J. AR Cav. Gordon's Regt. Co.I
Rolen, Marion VA 26th Cav. Co.H
Rolen, M.S. Mead's Conf.Cav. Co.H
Rolen, Philip J. VA 63rd Inf. Co.K
Rolen, W.H. GA 26th Inf. Co.K
Rolen, William T. VA 63rd Inf. Co.K
Rolen, Zachariah A. AL 44th Inf. Co.A Cpl.
Rolents, G. TX Inf. Houston's Bn. Co.D
Roler, Addison B. VA Lt.Arty. Carrington's Co.
Roler, C.A. VA 1st Cav. Co.E
Roler, C.A. VA 5th Inf. Co.M Sgt.
Roler, Charles S. VA 1st Cav. Co.E
Roler, David TN 19th Inf. Co.G
Roler, George AL 42nd Inf. Co.K
Roler, George TN 8th (Smith's) Cav. Co.B
Roler, George S. VA Lt.Arty. Carrington's Co.
Roler, James TN 8th (Smith's) Cav. Co.B Cpl.
Roler, James V. TN 19th Inf. Co.G
Roler, John, Jr. MO 11th Inf. Co.B
Roler, John H. VA 5th Inf. Co.L Sgt.
Roler, Noah TN 19th Inf. Co.G
Roler, S.P. TN 8th (Smith's) Cav. Co.B
Roler, William MS 5th Inf. (St.Troops) Co.E
Roler, William MS 10th Inf. New Co.F
Roler, William SC 18th Inf. Co.C
Rolerson, Berry FL 9th Inf. Co.E,H
Rolerson, Jacob FL 9th Inf. Co.H
Rolerson, John FL 9th Inf. Co.H
Roles, --- AR Cav. Wright's Regt. Co.H
Roles, A.J. GA 53rd Inf. Co.H
Roles, Andrew VA Mil. 184th Regt.
Roles, Christopher VA 36th Inf. 2nd Co.C Capt.
Roles, Christopher C. VA 36th Inf. 2nd Co.C
Roles, C.J. VA 36th Inf. Co.C
Roles, Green VA 166th Mil. W. Lively's Co., Taylor's Co.
Roles, Hansberry B. VA 36th Inf. 2nd Co.C
Roles, Henry VA Cav. Hounshell's Bn. Thurmond's Co.
Roles, James VA Inf. 23rd Bn. Thurman's Co.

Roles, John VA 36th Inf. 2nd Co.C
Roles, Leonidas T. NC 47th Inf. Co.E
Roles, William N. TN 50th Inf. Co.A
Roles, W.N. KY 7th Cav. Co.G
Roleson, B. AR 30th Inf. Co.D Sgt.
Rolether, Pruno AR 34th Inf. Co.D
Roley, John MO 16th Inf. Co.H
Roley, Marshal VA 49th Inf. Co.C
Rolf, Adolphus Conf.Inf. Tucker's Regt. Co.I
Rolf, Calvin H. TX 5th Cav. Co.B
Rolf, Charles MO Inf. 1st Bn. Co.C
Rolf, Charles G. MO 2nd Inf. Co.C
Rolf, H. TX Inf. Timmons' Regt. Co.E
Rolf, M. GA 9th Inf. Co.H
Rolf, Thomas LA Inf.Crescent Regt. Co.H,F,C
Rolf, T.M. LA 18th Inf. Co.H
Rolf, W.C. AL 5th Inf. Co.C
Rolf, William LA 14th Inf. Co.C
Rolf, W.S. MS 6th Inf. Co.I
Rolfe, A.V. AR 30th Inf. Co.D Cpl.
Rolfe, E.H. AL 11th Cav. Co.I,K
Rolfe, Henry TX 13th Vol. Co.C
Rolfe, James Conf.Inf. Tucker's Regt. Co.F
Rolfe, John J. VA 3rd Cav. Co.A
Rolfe, L.W. Gen. & Staff, Ord.Dept.
Rolfe, Phocean VA 12th Cav. Co.E Cpl.
Rolfe, W.G. AR Inf. 1st Bn. Co.F Capt.
Rolfe, William E. VA 3rd Cav. Co.A
Rolfes, F. LA Mil. 3rd Regt. 3rd Brig. 1st Div. Co.F
Rolfes, J.D. LA Mil. 4th Regt.Eur.Brig. Co.F
Rolffs, Theodore AL Inf. 1st Regt. Co.D Cpl.
Rolffs, Theodore MS 9th Inf. New Co.F
Roliff, John VA 25th Cav. Co.H
Rolin, A. LA Mil. 2nd Regt. French Brig. Co.4
Rolin, Charles AL 61st Inf. Co.A Sgt.
Rolin, Everett TX 37th Cav. Co.H
Rolin, Henry TX 9th (Nichols') Inf. Co.K
Rolin, J.A. MS Cav. Polk's Ind.Co. (Polk Rangers)
Rolin, James VA 45th Inf. Co.F
Rolin, J.K. MS 3rd Inf. Co.C
Rolin, Joseph 1st Conf.Cav. 2nd Co.F
Rolin, Richard J. GA 12th Inf. Co.C
Rolin, Shad TX 9th (Nichols') Inf. Co.K
Rolin, T. GA 12th Mil.
Rolin, T. TX Cav. Hardeman's Regt. Co.A
Rolin, T.C. AR 58th Mil. Co.A
Rolin, Wesley R. NC 39th Inf. Co.E
Rolin, William GA 10th Inf. Co.G
Rolin, William TN 12th (Cons.) Inf. Co.K
Roling, C.B. AL 1st Conscr. Co.H
Roling, J. MS Inf. 1st Bn.St.Troops (12 mo. '62-3) Co.D
Roling, Marion VA Cav. 47th Bn. Co.B Cpl.
Roling, P.R. MS 2nd (Davidson's) Inf. Co.A
Roling, S.F. TN 34th Inf. 2nd Co.C
Roling, T.J. SC 1st (Butler's) Inf. Co.G
Rolings, A.J. GA Inf. 10th Bn. Co.E
Rolins, J. AL 62nd Inf. Co.A
Rolins, John Forrest's Scouts T.N. Kizer's Co.,CSA
Rolins, Napoleon AL Lt.Arty. 2nd Bn. Co.A
Rolins, William TN 35th Inf. Co.L
Rolinson, Fred F. LA 9th Inf. Co.C
Rolinson, George SC 3rd Inf. Co.G Cpl.
Rolinson, G.R. AR Inf. Hardy's Regt. Co.K

Rolinson, James W. TN 2nd (Smith's) Cav. Sgt.
Rolinson, S.P. MS 3rd (St.Troops) Cav. Co.C
Rolinson, William AR Inf. Hardy's Regt. Co.K
Rolison, Benjamin G. SC 1st (Orr's) Rifles Co.K Bvt.2nd Lt.
Rolison, B.F. TX 12th Inf. Co.B Cpl.
Rolison, H.B. TX 12th Inf. Co.B
Rolison, John TX 12th Inf. Co.B
Rolison, John VA 151st Mil. Co.E
Rolison, Joseph H. VA 14th Inf. Co.I
Rolison, L.L. TX 12th Inf. Co.B
Rolison, Paterson VA 166th Mil. Taylor's Co.
Rolison, Peter VA 36th Inf. 2nd Co.I
Rolison, Simeon AL 20th Inf. Co.A
Rolison, William TX 12th Inf. Co.B
Rolison, W.L. TX 12th Inf. Co.B
Roll, Edward J. VA 8th Cav. Co.K
Roll, James H. KY 9th Mtd.Inf. Co.C Cpl.
Roll, John W. MS 8th Cav. Co.H
Roll, John W. MS 28th Cav. Co.L Cpl.
Roll, John W. TN 7th (Duckworth's) Cav. Co.C
Roll, Robert T. GA Hvy.Arty. 22nd Bn. Co.C Sgt.
Roll, R.T. GA 1st (Ramsey's) Inf. Co.D
Roll, W.A. GA 1st (Ramsey's) Inf. Co.D
Rolla, Addison VA Cav. Mosby's Regt. (Part. Rangers) Co.B
Rolla, John A. TN 10th Inf.
Rolla, L.J. FL 1st Inf. New Co.G, Co.K Sgt.
Rolla, William A. GA 7th Inf. Co.I
Rollan, John TN 2nd (Ashby's) Cav. Co.D
Rollan, J.W. GA 13th Inf. Co.G Sgt.
Rolland, A.C. AL 38th Inf. Co.K
Rolland, Archibald AR 15th (N.W.) Inf. Co.D
Rolland, Charles B. LA 21st (Patton's) Inf. Co.A
Rolland, D.E. MS 18th Inf.
Rolland, Edward VA 54th Mil. Co.E,F
Rolland, Edward L. VA Hvy.Arty. 18th Bn. Co.B Cpl.
Rolland, Edward L. VA 6th Inf. Co.H
Rolland, Frank VA 54th Mil. Co.E,F
Rolland, Henry F. VA Hvy.Arty. 18th Bn. Co.B
Rolland, H.F. VA 6th Inf. Co.D Sgt.
Rolland, J. VA 5th Inf. Co.A
Rolland, J.A. TN 3rd (Forrest's) Cav. Co.D
Rolland, James TN 50th Inf. Co.B
Rolland, J.C. TN 11th (Holman's) Cav. Co.K
Rolland, Lynch B. 4th Conf.Eng.Troops Co.H Sgt.
Rolland, Wiley M. AL City Guards Lockett's Co.
Rollands, Andrew VA 17th Cav. Co.H
Rollangs, Robert AL 3rd Inf. Co.F
Rollans, H.N. AR 8th Cav. Co.E
Rollans, John A. TN 2nd (Ashby's) Cav. Co.D
Rollds, Creighton VA 46th Inf. 2nd Co.C
Rolle, L. LA Mil. 1st Regt. French Brig. Co.3
Rollen, David TN 55th (McKoin's) Inf. James' Co.
Rollen, George AR 2nd Mtd.Rifles Co.A
Rollen, J.H. MO 1st & 4th Cons.Inf. Co.I
Rollen, John Stuart Horse Arty.,CSA
Rollens, J. NC 6th Inf. Co.A
Rollens, William GA 66th Inf. Co.F
Roller, VA VMI Co.C
Roller, A.J. AL 17th Inf. Co.H
Roller, Albert H. VA 28th Inf. Co.I 1st Sgt.
Roller, Allen MO 3rd Inf. Co.B

Roller, Allen MO 11th Inf. Co.B
Roller, Amos VA 25th Cav. Co.B
Roller, Andrew NC 64th Inf. Co.M
Roller, Andrew TN Cav. 16th Bn. (Neal's) Co.F
Roller, Andrew J. VA 64th Mtd.Inf. Co.B
Roller, Austin MO 3rd Cav. Co.I
Roller, Austin MO 3rd Inf. Co.B
Roller, Austin MO 11th Inf. Co.B
Roller, Benjamin SC 1st (Butler's) Inf. Co.E
Roller, Benjamin SC Inf. 9th Bn. Co.C
Roller, Benjamin SC 26th Inf. Co.D
Roller, Daniel MO 11th Inf. Co.B
Roller, David TN Detailed Conscr. Co.B
Roller, Elisha MO 11th Inf. Co.B
Roller, Emanuel VA 12th Cav. Co.H
Roller, Emanuel VA 58th Mil. Co.D
Roller, F. TN Hvy.Arty. Sterling's Co.
Roller, G. MS Condrey's Co. (Bull Mtn.Invinc.)
Roller, George MO 11th Inf. Co.B
Roller, George TN Cav. 11th Bn. (Gordon's) Co.D
Roller, George W. MO 11th Inf. Co.B
Roller, George W. TN 19th Inf. Co.G
Roller, Granville MO 11th Inf. Co.B
Roller, G.W. TN Inf. 3rd Cons.Regt. Co.C
Roller, Harvey J. VA Inf. 21st Bn. 2nd Co.C 1st Sgt.
Roller, Henry SC Inf. 9th Bn. Co.C
Roller, Henry T. SC 26th Inf. Co.D
Roller, Henry W. VA 12th Cav. Co.H
Roller, Henry W. VA 25th Inf. 1st Co.I
Roller, Hiram P. VA 48th Inf. Co.B Sgt.
Roller, Hiram P. VA 64th Mtd.Inf.
Roller, H.P. NC 64th Inf. Co.M 1st Sgt.
Roller, H.P. TN Cav. 16th Bn. (Neal's) Co.F 1st Sgt.
Roller, I.B. VA 1st Cav. Band
Roller, J. LA Arty. Watson Btty. Artif.
Roller, Jacob AR 4th Inf. Kelley's Co.
Roller, Jacob AR 16th Inf. Co.H
Roller, Jacob, Jr. MO 11th Inf. Co.B
Roller, Jacob, Sr. MO 11th Inf. Co.B
Roller, Jacob TN 60th Mtd.Inf.
Roller, Jacob VA 33rd Inf. Co.C
Roller, Jacob VA 146th Mil. Co.D Cpl.
Roller, James AL 41st Inf. Co.B Cpl.
Roller, James TN Cav. 5th Bn. (McClellan's) Co.F
Roller, Jesse Deneale's Regt. Choctaw Warriors Co.E
Roller, John GA Inf. 1st Loc.Troops (Augusta) Dearing's Cav.Co.
Roller, John GA 36th (Villepigue's) Inf. Co.F
Roller, John, Sr. MO 11th Inf. Co.B
Roller, John SC Inf. 9th Bn. Co.C Cpl.
Roller, John TN Cav. 16th Bn. (Neal's) Co.F
Roller, John VA 10th Cav. Co.H
Roller, John VA Mil. Scott Cty.
Roller, John 1st Conf.Inf. 1st Co.F
Roller, John B. AL Cav. Holloway's Co.
Roller, John B. VA 25th Inf. 1st Co.I Cpl.
Roller, John J. VA 58th Mil. Co.D
Roller, Joshua MO 11th Inf. Co.B
Roller, Joshua TN Inf. 154th Sr.Regt. Co.I
Roller, Levi MO 12th Cav. Co.A
Roller, Martin L. TN 59th Mtd.Inf. Co.F
Roller, Martin L. TN 60th Mtd.Inf.

Roller, M.H. VA Cav. Mosby's Regt. (Part. Rangers) Co.H
Roller, M.H. VA 3rd (Chrisman's) Bn.Res. Co.A
Roller, M.L. TN Detailed Conscr. Co.B
Roller, Noah MO 11th Inf. Co.B
Roller, Peter F. VA 10th Inf. Co.H
Roller, Phillip MO 11th Inf. Co.B
Roller, S. TN Inf. 3rd Cons.Regt. Co.C Cpl.
Roller, Samuel P. TN Cav. 5th Bn. (McClellan's) Co.F
Roller, Solomon TN 19th Inf. Co.G Cpl.
Roller, T.D. AL 24th Inf. Co.H
Roller, William MS St.Cav. Perrin's Bn. Co.C
Roller, William MO 11th Inf. Co.B
Roller, William NC 64th Inf. Co.M Cpl.
Roller, William SC Inf. 9th Bn. Co.C
Roller, William SC 21st Inf. Co.D
Roller, William SC Post Guard Senn's Co.
Roller, William TN Cav. 16th Bn. (Neal's) Co.F Cpl.
Roller, William VA Inf. 21st Bn. 2nd Co.C
Roller, William E. MO Robertson's Regt. St.Guard Co.1
Roller, William H. TN 19th Inf. Co.G
Rollerson, Benjamin F. VA 1st Arty. Co.B
Rollerson, Benjamin F. VA 32nd Inf. 1st Co.H
Rollerson, George VA Inf. 4th Bn.Loc.Def. Co.D
Rollerson, John FL 9th Inf. Co.I
Rollerson, John A. AL 61st Inf. Co.I
Rollerson, Mathew FL 2nd Cav. Co.B
Rolles, John MS 26th Inf. Co.B
Rolles, J.P. MO 11th Inf. Co.F
Rollet, Philip VA 9th Cav. Co.I
Rolley, G. AR Inf. Cocke's Regt. Co.A
Rolley, J.W. TN 9th Cav. Co.D
Rolley, Thomas TX 4th Cav. Co.C
Rolley, Thomas H. MD 1st Cav. Co.D
Rollfing, William TX 2nd Inf. Co.F Sgt.
Rollilliard, Sarion LA Mil. Pointe Coupee Regt. Co.D Sgt.
Rollims, Jonathan AR Inf. Hardy's Regt. Torbett's Co.
Rollims, S.W. AR Inf. Hardy's Regt. Torbett's Co.
Rollin, A.B. TX 13th Vol. Co.B
Rollin, Benjamin F. TN Cav. Newsom's Regt. Co.F
Rollin, H. LA 13th Inf. Co.I
Rollin, James TN Inf. 23rd Bn. Co.E
Rollin, J.E. 2nd Conf.Eng.Troops Co.G 1st Lt.
Rollin, John AL 63rd Inf. Co.G
Rollin, Luther MO 2nd Cav. Co.C,G
Rollin, M.M. MO Inf. Perkins' Bn. 1st Lt.,Ens.
Rollin, Samuel MS 2nd Inf. Co.C
Rollin, Theophilus R. AL 1st Regt.Conscr. Co.H
Rollin, T.R. TN Inf. 23rd Bn. Co.E
Rollin, W. VA Lt.Arty. B.H. Smith's Co.
Rollin, William GA 31st Inf. Co.F
Rolling, Benjamin F. TN 34th Inf. Co.A
Rolling, C. LA Mil. Orleans Fire Regt. Co.H
Rolling, Charles B. AL 1st Regt.Conscr. Co.H
Rolling, E.H. TN 45th Inf. Co.D
Rolling, H. LA Mil. 1st Regt. French Brig. Band 1st Ch.Music.
Rolling, Henry LA Mil. Orleans Guards Regt. Co.B

Rolling, J. LA Mil. Orleans Fire Regt. Co.A
Rolling, John F. AL 57th Inf. Co.I
Rolling, John L. FL 6th Inf. Co.H
Rolling, John R. AL Conscr.
Rolling, John W. TX 15th Cav. Co.H
Rolling, T.R. AL 33rd Inf. Co.F
Rollings, A.J. TN 34th Inf. Co.A
Rollings, Albert SC Inf. 9th Bn. Co.E
Rollings, Austin VA Cav. 39th Bn. Co.A
Rollings, Daniel TN 13th (Gore's) Cav. Co.A
Rollings, Evan S. SC Lt.Arty. Kelly's Co. (Chesterfield Arty.)
Rollings, G.T. SC 9th Inf. Co.D
Rollings, H.C. VA 10th Cav. Co.G
Rollings, Jackson SC Lt.Arty. Kelly's Co. (Chesterfield Arty.)
Rollings, James SC Inf. 9th Bn. Co.E
Rollings, James S. TN 1st (Turney's) Inf. Co.B Cpl.
Rollings, James W. VA 10th Inf. Co.K
Rollings, Jesse NC 43rd Inf. Co.E
Rollings, John NC 43rd Inf. Co.E
Rollings, John H. VA 6th Cav. Co.K Sgt.
Rollings, John W. VA Cav. 39th Bn. Co.A
Rollings, Joseph D. VA 41st Inf. Co.A
Rollings, Joshua VA 6th Cav. Co.K
Rollings, L.P. SC 24th Inf. Co.G
Rollings, M. KY 7th Mtd.Inf. Co.C
Rollings, Pleasant L. AL 49th Inf. Co.E 1st Lt.
Rollings, R.B. SC Arty. Zimmerman's Co. (Pee Dee Arty.)
Rollings, Richard SC Lt.Arty. Kelly's Co. (Chesterfield Arty.)
Rollings, R.J. SC Lt.Arty. 3rd (Palmetto) Bn. Co.C
Rollings, R.J. SC 2nd Bn.S.S. Co.C
Rollings, R. John SC Lt.Arty. Kelly's Co. (Chesterfield Arty.)
Rollings, Robert SC 2nd Inf. Co.H Music.
Rollings, Robert TN 17th Inf. Co.D 2nd Lt.
Rollings, Robert B. VA 46th Inf. 2nd Co.F
Rollings, Thomas SC 1st (Butler's) Inf. Co.C
Rollings, William TN 16th Inf. Co.B
Rollings, William H. GA 39th Inf. Co.A
Rollins, A. SC 23rd Inf. Co.A
Rollins, A.J. MS Inf. 2nd Bn. Co.L
Rollins, A.J. MS 48th Inf. Co.L Cpl.
Rollins, A.L. GA 12th Cav. Co.I
Rollins, A.L. GA Lt.Arty. Scogin's Btty. (Griffin Lt.Arty.)
Rollins, Albert SC 1st (Butler's) Inf. Co.H
Rollins, Alfred SC 4th St.Troops Co.K
Rollins, Alfred B. VA 9th Cav. Co.B Sgt.
Rollins, Alfred D. NC 48th Inf. Co.E
Rollins, Alfred F. VA 8th Inf. Co.A
Rollins, Allen VA 29th Inf. Co.I
Rollins, Amon TN 24th Inf. Co.F Cpl.
Rollins, Amos GA Inf. 1st Loc.Troops (Augusta) Co.H
Rollins, Amos D. NC 38th Inf. Co.I
Rollins, Andrew J. GA 2nd Res. Co.K
Rollins, Andrew J. MS 14th Inf. Co.G Cpl.
Rollins, Andrew J. MS 14th (Cons.) Inf. Co.F Cpl.
Rollins, A.P. GA Inf. Fuller's Co.
Rollins, B.A. GA 12th Cav. Co.C
Rollins, Benjamin KY 2nd Cav. Co.I

Rollins, Benjamin TN 2nd (Robison's) Inf. Co.F
Rollins, Benjamin F. GA 20th Inf. Co.C
Rollins, Benjamin F. TN 18th (Newsom's) Cav. Co.I 3rd Lt.
Rollins, B.F. GA Inf. 2nd Bn. (St.Guards) Co.A Sgt.
Rollins, B.F. MO Lt.Arty. Farris' Btty. (Clark Arty.)
Rollins, B.F. MO Inf. 3rd Bn. Co.C
Rollins, B.F. TN 38th Inf. Co.E
Rollins, Butler VA 25th Mil. Co.A
Rollins, Butler R. VA 9th Cav. Co.I
Rollins, Carolus VA 47th Inf. Co.B
Rollins, C.G. AL 2nd Cav. Co.I
Rollins, C.G. MS 12th Cav. Co.G
Rollins, C.G. MS 43rd Inf. Co.G
Rollins, Charles AL 49th Inf. Co.E Sgt.
Rollins, Charles A. VA 5th Inf. Co.B
Rollins, Charles A. VA 27th Inf. Co.H Sgt.
Rollins, Charles H. NC 25th Inf. Co.I
Rollins, Christopher C. MS 38th Cav. Co.K
Rollins, C.J. NC 1st Arty. (10th St.Troops) Co.H
Rollins, Columbus VA 20th Cav. Co.E
Rollins, Cornelius V. VA 7th Inf. Co.G
Rollins, David SC 1st (Butler's) Inf. Co.A
Rollins, David VA Inf. 23rd Bn. Co.D
Rollins, David VA 29th Inf. Co.I
Rollins, D.D. NC 28th Inf. Co.H 2nd Lt.
Rollins, D.H. TN 14th Inf. Co.L
Rollins, D.L. TN 34th Inf. Co.K
Rollins, Dock O. NC 34th Inf. Co.I
Rollins, Doctor O. NC 28th Inf. Co.H
Rollins, Drury D. NC 34th Inf. Co.I
Rollins, E. TN Cav. 12th Bn. (Day's) Co.C
Rollins, E. TX Cav. Terry's Regt. Co.D
Rollins, Ed KY 10th (Johnson's) Cav. New Co.B
Rollins, Edward T. VA 9th Cav. Co.K
Rollins, Eliphalus B. TX Cav. Martin's Regt. Co.I
Rollins, Emsley VA Inf. 23rd Bn. Co.D
Rollins, Enoch TN Cav. 12th Bn. (Day's) Co.B
Rollins, Enoch TN 29th Inf. Co.H
Rollins, Francis M. AR 19th (Dawson's) Inf. Co.A
Rollins, G.B. GA 12th (Robinson's) Cav. (St.Guards) Co.F
Rollins, G.B. GA Conscr.
Rollins, George NC 64th Inf. Co.I
Rollins, George TN Inf. 23rd Bn. Co.E
Rollins, George VA 9th Cav. Co.I
Rollins, George VA 19th Cav. Co.H
Rollins, George VA 25th Mil. Co.A
Rollins, George B. TN 15th (Cons.) Cav. Co.K
Rollins, George M. VA 5th Cav. Co.G,D
Rollins, George M. VA 49th Inf. 3rd Co.G
Rollins, George W. MO 10th Inf. Co.K
Rollins, George W. VA 17th Inf. Co.F
Rollins, Gibson S. NC 24th Inf. Co.F
Rollins, G.T. SC Inf. 9th Bn. Co.F
Rollins, G.T. SC 26th Inf. Co.G
Rollins, G.W. AL Cav. 4th Bn. (Love's) Co.C
Rollins, G.W. LA 16th Inf. Co.A
Rollins, G.W. MS Cav. Jeff Davis Legion Co.K
Rollins, G.W. MS 3rd Inf. Co.C
Rollins, G.W. MS 7th Inf. Co.D
Rollins, H. VA 2nd St.Res. Co.I
Rollins, H.A. GA 5th Res. Co.C

Rollins, Hanson C. VA 3rd Cav. & Inf.St.Line Co.A
Rollins, Harrison VA 26th Cav. Co.D Capt.
Rollins, Harrison C. VA 19th Cav. Co.A
Rollins, Harrison C. VA Cav. 46th Bn. Co.D 1st Lt.
Rollins, Harrison C. VA 3rd Cav. & Inf.St.Line Co.A
Rollins, Harrison H. NC 22nd Inf. Co.I
Rollins, Hay AR 16th Inf. Co.G
Rollins, Henry VA 19th Cav. Co.H
Rollins, Henry G. NC 47th Inf. Co.H
Rollins, Henry M. MS 14th Inf. Co.G
Rollins, H.J. TX 23rd Cav. Co.I
Rollins, H.J. TX 32nd Cav. Co.B
Rollins, Hugh SC 1st (Butler's) Inf. Co.H
Rollins, I.E. NC 55th Inf. Co.D
Rollins, Isaac NC 62nd Inf. Co.E
Rollins, Isaac L. AR 1st Vol. Co.B
Rollins, Isaac M. AL 4th Inf. Co.A
Rollins, Isaac N. NC 46th Inf. Co.G
Rollins, Isham GA Lt.Arty. Milledge's Co.
Rollins, Isham GA Inf. 1st Loc.Troops (Augusta) Co.H
Rollins, J. AR 19th (Dawson's) Inf. Co.C
Rollins, J.A. AL 59th Inf. Co.F
Rollins, Jackson FL 1st (Res.) Inf. Co.B
Rollins, James LA 3rd Inf. Co.H
Rollins, James LA 21st (Kennedy's) Inf. Co.B Music.
Rollins, James MS 5th Inf. (St.Troops) Co.C
Rollins, James MO 4th Cav. Co.D
Rollins, James MO 12th Cav. Co.A
Rollins, James MO Lt.Arty. Farris' Btty. (Clark Arty.)
Rollins, James MO Inf. 3rd Bn. Co.C
Rollins, James MO 6th Inf. Co.B
Rollins, James NC 2nd Inf. Co.H
Rollins, James SC Lt.Arty. Garden's Co. (Palmetto Lt.Btty.)
Rollins, James SC 4th St.Troops Co.K
Rollins, James TX 20th Inf. Co.K
Rollins, James VA 25th Cav. Co.G
Rollins, James VA 29th Inf. Co.I
Rollins, James A. AL 2nd Bn. Hilliard's Legion Vol. Co.A
Rollins, James A. GA 36th (Broyles') Inf. Co.C
Rollins, James A. TN 50th Inf. Co.F
Rollins, James C. TX 9th Cav. Co.K
Rollins, James D. VA 17th Inf. Co.F
Rollins, James E. MS 21st Inf. Co.E
Rollins, James G. MS 12th Inf. Co.K
Rollins, James J. NC 28th Inf. Co.H Sgt.
Rollins, James M. TN 29th Inf. Co.H
Rollins, James T. FL 5th Inf. Co.I Cpl.
Rollins, James V. GA 34th Inf. Co.B Sgt.
Rollins, James W. AR 27th Inf. Co.K
Rollins, James W. KY 7th Mtd.Inf. Co.C Sgt.
Rollins, James W. MO Cav. Freeman's Regt. Ford's Co.G
Rollins, J.B. AL Inf. 1st Regt. Co.H
Rollins, Jefferson AL Cav. Lewis' Bn. Co.C
Rollins, J.F. GA 13th Inf. Co.B
Rollins, J.F. GA 60th Inf. Co.D Cpl.
Rollins, J.H. MO Inf. Clark's Regt. Co.C
Rollins, J.H. TX 9th Cav. Co.K Cpl.
Rollins, J.J. AR 7th Inf. Co.E

Rollins, J.J. GA Lt.Arty. Howell's Co.
Rollins, John AL 59th Inf. Co.F
Rollins, John AL 2nd Bn. Hilliard's Legion Vol. Co.A
Rollins, John AL 2nd Bn. Hilliard's Legion Vol. Co.E
Rollins, John FL 1st Cav. Co.B
Rollins, John LA 3rd (Harrison's) Cav. Co.A
Rollins, John LA 12th Inf. Co.C
Rollins, John LA 19th Inf. Co.K
Rollins, John LA 21st (Patton's) Inf. Co.E
Rollins, John LA 27th Inf. Co.F
Rollins, John MS 1st Lt.Arty. Co.F
Rollins, John MS Horse Arty. Cook's Co.
Rollins, John MS 21st Inf. Co.C
Rollins, John MS 33rd Inf. Co.H
Rollins, John MO Lt.Arty. 1st Btty.
Rollins, John TN 6th Inf. Co.E
Rollins, John VA 17th Cav. Co.K
Rollins, John Forrest's Scouts T. Henderson's Co.,CSA
Rollins, John A. TN Cav. 4th Bn. (Branner's) Co.C
Rollins, John C. VA 4th Inf. Co.F
Rollins, Jno. D. GA 1st St.Line Co.I
Rollins, John D. NC 26th Inf. Co.B
Rollins, John F. MS 31st Inf. Co.B
Rollins, John F. NC 25th Inf. Co.I
Rollins, John H. AR 23rd Inf. Co.D
Rollins, John H. VA 5th Cav. Co.H
Rollins, John H. VA 15th Cav. Co.E
Rollins, John H. VA 25th Mil. Co.C
Rollins, John H. Conf.Inf. 8th Bn. Co.E
Rollins, John M. MS 14th Inf. Co.G 2nd Lt.
Rollins, John P. NC 34th Inf. Co.I,B
Rollins, John P. TN 2nd (Robison's) Inf. Co.F
Rollins, John R. AL Inf. 1st Regt. Co.B,F
Rollins, John R. NC 27th Inf. Co.H 1st Sgt.
Rollins, John S. GA 39th Inf. Co.A
Rollins, John W. GA 7th Inf. Co.C Cpl.
Rollins, John W. VA 47th Inf. Co.E 1st Lt.
Rollins, Jonathan A. VA 16th Cav. Co.I
Rollins, Jonathan J. NC 22nd Inf. Co.I
Rollins, Joseph VA 115th Mil. Co.C
Rollins, Joseph E. VA 30th Inf. Co.B Cpl.
Rollins, Joseph M. NC 62nd Inf. Co.E
Rollins, Joseph V. VA 22nd Inf. Co.A
Rollins, Joseph V. VA 166th Mil. Co.A
Rollins, Joseph W. GA 49th Inf. Co.E
Rollins, Joseph W. LA 16th Inf. Co.D Cpl.
Rollins, J.R. TN 21st & 22nd (Cons.) Cav. Co.I Cpl.
Rollins, J. Richard GA Lt.Arty. 14th Bn. Co.A
Rollins, J. Richard GA Lt.Arty. Havis' Btty.
Rollins, J.S. MO 12th Inf. Co.I
Rollins, J.S. VA 17th Cav. Co.G
Rollins, J.T. MO 5th Cav. Co.D
Rollins, J.T. MO Cav. Stallard's Co. Cpl.
Rollins, J.W. KY 7th Cav. Co.C,K
Rollins, L.A. TN 24th Inf. Co.F
Rollins, Lawson R. NC 34th Inf. Co.I
Rollins, L.B. VA 25th Mil. Co.A
Rollins, Louis H. MO St.Guard
Rollins, L.R. TX Cav. Morgan's Regt. Co.G
Rollins, L.R. VA Cav. Mosby's Regt. (Part. Rangers) Co.F
Rollins, L.W.P. SC Inf. 9th Bn. Co.F Sgt.Maj.

Rollins, M. GA 8th Inf. (St.Guards) Co.H
Rollins, Madison SC 5th Inf. 1st Co.C, 3rd Co.K
Rollins, Madison F. VA 25th Mil. Co.C Cpl.
Rollins, Mathew SC 4th St.Troops Co.K
Rollins, M.B. LA Inf. 4th Bn. Co.D 1st Sgt.
Rollins, Moses VA 20th Cav. Co.H Cpl.
Rollins, M.W. GA 12th Cav. Co.E Cpl.
Rollins, Nathan AR 16th Inf. Co.D
Rollins, N.C. SC Hvy.Arty. Gilchrist's Co. (Gist
    Guard)
Rollins, N.C. SC Arty. Manigault's Bn. Co.E
Rollins, N.L.W. AR 7th Inf. Co.B
Rollins, N.L.W. AR 30th Inf. Co.K
Rollins, Noah J. NC 28th Inf. Co.H
Rollins, O. SC 18th Inf. Co.I
Rollins, O.F. MO Inf. Clark's Regt. Co.C
Rollins, Peter FL 1st Cav. Co.C
Rollins, R. FL 2nd Cav. Co.K
Rollins, Ransom R. VA 37th Inf. Co.D Sgt.
Rollins, R.B. SC 1st (McCreary's) Inf. Co.D
Rollins, R.D. SC 26th Inf. Co.G
Rollins, R.D.F. SC 4th St.Troops Co.E
Rollins, R.D.F. SC 8th Inf. Co.E
Rollins, R.D.F. SC Inf. 9th Bn. Co.F Capt.
Rollins, R.D.F. SC 26th Inf. Co.G Capt.
Rollins, R.E. SC 14th Inf. Co.F
Rollins, Richard NC 2nd Inf. Co.H Cpl.
Rollins, Riley MO Inf. Perkins' Bn. Co.F
Rollins, R.J. SC Lt.Arty. 3rd (Palmetto) Bn.
    Co.C
Rollins, Robert AL Talladega Cty.Res. Breed's
    Co. Cpl.
Rollins, Robert AR 35th Inf. Co.C
Rollins, Robert MS 1st Lt.Arty. Co.E
Rollins, Robert NC 26th Inf. Co.D
Rollins, Robert VA 25th Cav. Co.G
Rollins, Robert A. KY 2nd Mtd.Inf. Co.E 2nd
    Lt.
Rollins, Robert M. AR Cav. Wright's Regt. Co.G
    Cpl.
Rollins, Robert S. GA Inf. 3rd Bn. Co.B
Rollins, Robert S. GA 37th Inf. Co.A
Rollins, Robert W. VA 7th Inf. Co.G
Rollins, Roderick TX 6th Cav. Co.F
Rollins, R.P.B. GA 12th Cav. Co.E
Rollins, R.S. KY 4th Cav. Co.D
Rollins, Samuel GA Cav. Allen's Co.
Rollins, Samuel VA 30th Inf. Co.K
Rollins, Samuel W. MO Dorsey's Regt. Co.A
Rollins, S.C. GA 49th Inf. Co.K
Rollins, S.F. GA 35th Inf. Co.F
Rollins, Shadrick AL 12th Cav. Co.A
Rollins, S.R. NC 49th Inf. Co.B
Rollins, Stephen B. VA 47th Inf. Co.E Jr.2nd
    Lt.
Rollins, S.W. AL 46th Inf. Co.A
Rollins, S.W. MO 12th Cav. Co.F
Rollins, T.B. NC 11th (Bethel Regt.) Inf. Co.G
Rollins, T.F. TX Waul's Legion Co.H
Rollins, Thomas GA 8th Inf. Co.K
Rollins, Thomas GA Cobb's Legion Co.C
Rollins, Thomas TN 18th (Newsom's) Cav. Co.I
Rollins, Thomas TN 38th Inf. Co.E
Rollins, Thomas B. NC 5th Cav. (63rd
    St.Troops) Co.G 3rd Lt.
Rollins, Thomas C. MO St.Guard
Rollins, Thomas J. GA 60th Inf. Co.K

Rollins, Thomas J. NC 62nd Inf. Co.E
Rollins, Thomas L. VA 4th Inf. Co.I
Rollins, Thomas W. FL 2nd Inf. Co.K
Rollins, T.J. MS 2nd St.Cav. 2nd Co.C
Rollins, T.J. SC 5th Inf. 1st Co.C, 2nd Co.K
Rollins, W. FL 2nd Cav. Co.K
Rollins, W. TN 15th (Cons.) Cav. Co.K
Rollins, Wallace NC 29th Inf. Co.D Capt.
Rollins, Washington MO 12th Cav. Co.F
Rollins, W.D. SC Inf. 9th Bn. Co.F Cpl.
Rollins, W.D. SC 26th Inf. Co.G
Rollins, W.D.R. SC Inf. 9th Bn. Co.F Music.
Rollins, W.F. LA 16th Inf. Co.A,I
Rollins, W.G. SC Lt.Arty. 3rd (Palmetto) Bn.
    Co.E
Rollins, W.H. LA 27th Inf. Co.D
Rollins, W.H. TN 7th (Duckworth's) Cav. Co.A
    Sgt.
Rollins, William AL Cav. Lewis' Bn. Co.C
Rollins, William AL 16th Inf. Co.E Sgt.
Rollins, William AL 59th Inf. Co.D
Rollins, William FL 1st Cav. Co.B
Rollins, William GA 63rd Inf. Co.C
Rollins, William LA 1st Cav. Co.A
Rollins, William MS 35th Inf. Co.A
Rollins, William MO 12th Cav. Co.F Cpl.
Rollins, William SC 5th Inf. 2nd Co.K
Rollins, William TN Cav. Allison's Squad. Co.C
Rollins, William TN 61st Mtd.Inf. Bundren's Co.
Rollins, William TX 19th Inf. Co.A
Rollins, William VA 16th Cav. Co.I
Rollins, William VA 20th Cav. Co.H
Rollins, William 2nd Conf.Eng.Troops Co.D
Rollins, William A. GA 20th Inf. Co.C
Rollins, William A. GA 27th Inf. Co.H
Rollins, William A. NC 33rd Inf. Co.F Cpl.
Rollins, William H. MO Searcy's Bn.S.S. Co.A
Rollins, William H. TN 18th (Newsom's) Cav.
    Co.I
Rollins, William H. VA 4th Inf. Co.I
Rollins, William H. VA 30th Inf. Co.A
Rollins, William L.D. SC 9th Inf. Co.I
Rollins, William L.D. SC Inf. Hampton Legion
    Co.C
Rollins, William L.D. SC Palmetto S.S. Co.H
Rollins, William P. NC 62nd Inf. Co.E
Rollins, William P. SC 18th Inf. Co.K
Rollins, William R. MS 2nd Inf. Co.A
Rollins, Williams MS 46th Inf. Co.C
Rollins, William S. VA 64th Mtd.Inf. Co.K Cpl.
Rollins, William W. NC 16th Inf. Co.F Cpl.
Rollins, Wilson VA 20th Cav. Co.H Cpl.
Rollins, W.L. GA 1st Cav. Co.D
Rollins, W.T. MS 4th Cav. Co.I
Rollins, Wyatt NC 8th Bn.Part.Rangers Co.A
Rollins, Wyatt P. NC 61st Inf. Co.D
Rollins, Z.D. LA 16th Inf. Co.A
Rollinski, William SC Simons' Co.
Rollinson, A.J.B. AL Lt.Arty. Goldthwaite's
    Btty.
Rollinson, B.F. VA Lt.Arty. 1st Bn. Co.B
Rollinson, B.F. VA Arty. Richardson's Co.
Rollinson, F.C. AL Cav. Hardie's Bn.Res.
Rollinson, J.E. AL Lt.Arty. Goldthwaite's Btty.
Rollinson, John R. NC 17th Inf. (1st Org.) Co.E
Rollinson, John R. NC 32nd Inf. Co.B

Rollinson, Silas AL Lt.Arty. Goldthwaite's Btty.
    Artif.
Rollinson, Thomas H. TX 16th Inf. Co.H Sgt.
Rollinson, William M. MS 48th Inf. Co.H
Rollison, George W. VA 52nd Mil. Co.B Cpl.
Rollison, James H. VA Cav. 32nd Bn. Co.A
Rollison, John TX 11th Cav. Co.B
Rollison, John VA 61st Inf. Co.C
Rollison, L. GA 24th Inf. Co.G Cpl.
Rollison, William M. MS Inf. 2nd Bn. Co.H
Rollman, J.L. TN 17th Inf. Co.K
Rollo, Benjamin L. AL 1st Regt.Conscr. Co.H
Rollo, Benjamin L. AL 18th Inf. Co.H
Rollo, Benjamin L. AL 61st Inf. Co.A Cpl.
Rollo, Jesse V. AL 1st Regt.Conscr. Co.H
Rollo, Jesse V. AL 61st Inf. Co.A
Rollo, Jesse W. AL 34th Inf. Co.H
Rollo, J.J. AL 8th Inf. Co.F
Rollo, J.K.T. MO 2nd Cav. Co.D
Rollo, John AL 34th Inf. Co.H
Rollo, John Eng.Dept. Polk's Corps A. of TN
    Sap. & Min. Co.,CSA
Rollo, Miles J. AL 1st Regt.Conscr. Co.H
Rollo, Thomas H. AL 1st Regt.Conscr. Co.H
Rollo, Thomas H. AL 61st Inf. Co.A
Rollo, William LA Miles' Legion Co.A
Rollo, William A. AL 1st Regt.Conscr. Co.H
Rollons, Washington AR 19th (Dawson's) Inf.
    Co.A
Rollosson, J.A. AL 61st Inf. Co.I
Rollow, A. AR 8th Cav. Co.E
Rollow, Arch AR 10th Inf. Co.A
Rollow, Charles VA 30th Inf. Co.B
Rollow, J.P., Sr. AR 10th (Witt's) Cav. Co.A
Rollow, P.J. AR 8th Cav. Co.E Capt.
Rollow, P.J. AR 10th Inf. Co.K
Rolls, A.H. GA Inf. 19th Bn. (St.Guards) Co.C
Rolls, Allen AR 30th Inf. Co.L
Rolls, Allen MO 7th Cav. Co.B
Rolls, Benjamin AL 33rd Inf. Co.F
Rolls, Charles VA 49th Inf. Co.B
Rolls, C.J. MO 6th Inf. Co.K
Rolls, E.E. TN 5th Inf. 1st Co.F
Rolls, Frank TN 5th Inf. 2nd Co.G
Rolls, Franklin E. VA 49th Inf. Co.E
Rolls, Gabriel MS 16th Inf. Co.D
Rolls, George TN 21st Inf. Co.H
Rolls, George VA 8th Inf. Co.I
Rolls, Green VA Cav. Thurmond's Co.
Rolls, Henry NC 23rd Inf. Co.A
Rolls, Henry NC 31st Inf. Co.C
Rolls, J.H. AR Inf. Hardy's Regt. Co.K Cpl.
Rolls, J.H. AR 1st (Symons') Res. Co.G
Rolls, John AR Inf. 2nd Bn. Co.A
Rolls, Landin VA 49th Inf. Co.B
Rolls, McGwilbert NC 2nd Jr.Res. Co.I
Rolls, Robert TN 50th Inf. Co.H Sgt.
Rolls, Robert TN 50th (Cons.) Inf. Comsy.Sgt.
Rolls, Thomas J. FL 4th Inf. Co.G Capt.
Rolls, W.J. TN 16th Inf. Co.I
Rolls, W.M. AR 2nd Mtd.Rifles Co.E
Rolls, W.M. TN 46th Inf. Co.B
Rolls, W.N. AR Inf. Hardy's Regt. Co.K
Rollyson, John VA 22nd Inf. Co.K
Rolman, J.L. TN Inf. 23rd Bn. Co.D
Rolman, John L. TN 41st Inf. Co.G
Rolnell, R. AR 30th Inf. Co.B

Roloan, B.P. MO Cav. Coleman's Regt. Co.A
Rolodo, James TX Cav. Baird's Regt. Co.C
Rolong, Jacob SC Manigault's Bn.Vol. Co.D
Roloph, William FL 1st Inf. Old Co.B
Roloph, William GA 3rd Cav. Co.A
Rolph, Charles MO 6th Inf. Co.K
Rolph, George W. MD 1st Cav. Co.E
Rolph, J.T. AR Cav. McGehee's Regt. Co.A
Rolph, Wilbert F. MD 1st Cav. Co.F Sgt.
Rols, George W. TX 4th Cav. Co.D
Rolson, Andrew VA 62nd Mtd.Inf. 2nd Co.D
Rolstan, Samuel VA 162nd Mil. Co.C
Rolston, Aaron S. MS 15th Inf. Co.C Sgt.
Rolston, Abraham VA 146th Mil. Co.C
Rolston, Almoth TN 22nd Inf. Co.B
Rolston, B. AL 3rd Cav. Co.E
Rolston, David MO Lt.Arty. 1st Field Btty. Cpl.
Rolston, David H. VA 10th Inf. Co.H
Rolston, James TN Cav. 31st Regt. Co.B
Rolston, James P. VA 7th Bn.Res. AQM
Rolston, James P. VA 10th Inf. Co.H Capt.
Rolston, J.H. VA 3rd (Chrisman's) Bn.Res. Co.B 1st Lt.
Rolston, J.L. KY 1st Inf. Co.B
Rolston, J.N. MS 19th Cav. Co.I
Rolston, John MS 18th Inf. Co.G
Rolston, John TN 2nd (Walker's) Inf. Co.G
Rolston, John H. VA 10th Inf. Co.H Capt.
Rolston, Joseph KY 5th Mtd.Inf. Co.A
Rolston, Joseph C. MO 4th Cav. Co.I
Rolston, J.W. AR 19th (Dockery's) Inf. Cons.Co.E,D
Rolston, L. MO 6th Cav. Co.B
Rolston, Michael H. VA 10th Inf. Co.H Jr.2nd Lt.
Rolston, Robert S. MS 21st Inf. Co.G
Rolston, Wallace NC 64th Inf. Co.L
Rolston, William VA 3rd (Chrisman's) Bn.Res. Co.B Sgt.
Rolston, William VA 10th Inf. Co.H
Rolston, William C. KY 3rd Cav. Co.B
Rolston, William M. MS 17th Inf. Co.E
Rolton, S.L. AL 34th Inf. Co.B
Rolton, William W. TX 17th Cons.Dismtd.Cav. Co.D
Rolum, T.R. GA 48th Inf. Co.B
Roly, F.M. MS 11th Inf. Co.E
Roly, H. TX 21st Inf. Co.C
Roma, Nicholas TX 1st (Yager's) Cav. Co.C
Roma, Nicholas TX Cav. 3rd (Yager's) Bn. Co.C
Romack, James AR 6th Inf. Co.B
Romack, Joseph R. AR 33rd Inf. Co.E
Romack, William AR 26th Inf. Co.C
Romagosa, L.F. LA Inf.Cons. 18th Regt. & Yellow Jacket Bn. Co.F
Romaguera, Frank LA Mil. 5th Regt.Eur.Brig. (Spanish Regt.) Co.5
Romaguera, J. LA Mil. 5th Regt.Eur.Brig. (Spanish Regt.) Co.5
Romaguera, S. LA Mil. 5th Regt.Eur.Brig. (Spanish Regt.) Co.2
Romain, A. LA Mil. 1st Native Guards
Romain, A.G. LA Mil. Orleans Guards Regt. Co.D
Romain, Alexander VA Horse Arty. G.W. Brown's Co. Cpl.
Romain, Alexandre LA 10th Inf. Co.G Sgt.

Romain, F. LA Arty. Watson Btty.
Romain, Gre. LA Mil. 3rd Regt.Eur.Brig. (Garde Francaise) Frois' Co. Sgt.Maj.
Romain, Henry Sap. & Min. Gallimard's Co.,CSA Sgt.
Romain, Jean LA Inf.Cons.Crescent Regt. Co.P
Romain, Pleasant C. MS 21st Inf. Co.H Cpl.
Romain, Semon MS 3rd Inf. Co.E
Romaine, --- TX 33rd Cav. Co.O
Roman, A. LA 22nd Inf. Gomez's Co.
Roman, Alfred LA 18th Inf. Lt.Col.
Roman, Alfred Beauregard's Staff Lt.Col.,AIG
Roman, Andrew J. TX Inf. Griffin's Bn. Co.D
Roman, Anthony LA 8th Inf. Co.B
Roman, Arthur J. LA 4th Inf. Co.E 1st Sgt.
Roman, Charles LA Mil. Orleans Guards Regt. Co.A Capt.
Roman, Ed LA Lt.Arty. LeGardeur, Jr.'s Co. (Orleans Guard Btty.)
Roman, Felix LA 18th Inf. Co.E
Roman, G.F. LA 20th Inf. Co.C Lt.
Roman, H. LA Mil. St.James Regt. Gaudet's Co.
Roman, Jacob LA 14th Inf. Co.F Cpl.
Roman, J.G. TN 21st Cav. Co.A Cpl.
Roman, L. GA 38th Inf. Co.E
Roman, Lilburn VA Cav. 34th Bn. Co.G
Roman, Lilburn J. VA Cav. McFarlane's Co.
Roman, L.J. VA 72nd Mil.
Roman, L.J. Conf.Cav. 6th Bn.
Roman, Michael LA 2nd Inf. Co.F
Roman, P. LA Dreux's Cav. Co.A Cpl.
Roman, Paul LA Lt.Arty. LeGardeur, Jr.'s Co. (Orleans Guard Btty.)
Roman, P.B. GA 1st Inf. Co,E
Roman, P.B. GA Inf. (Loc.Def.) Whiteside's Nav.Bn. Co.A
Roman, R.S. TX 21st Cav. Co.A Cpl.
Roman, Thomas J. GA Phillips' Legion Co.C
Roman, W.B. SC Inf. Holcombe Legion Co.F Sgt.
Roman, William MS Gage's Co. (Wigfall Guards)
Roman, William B. SC 1st St.Troops Co.F Sgt.
Romane, Aut. KY Part.Rangers Rowan's Co.
Romanet, L. LA Mil. 1st Regt. French Brig. Co.4
Romanger, C. AL 29th Inf. Co.H
Romanger, L. AL 29th Inf. Co.H
Romaniski, T. SC 1st Cav. Co.E
Romano, Ant. KY Jessee's Bn.Mtd.Riflemen Co.C
Romano, Augustus B. NC 38th Inf. Co.F
Romano, Jose LA Mil. 5th Regt.Eur.Brig. (Spanish Regt.) Co.10
Romano, Raffaele LA Mil. 6th Regt.Eur.Brig. (Italian Guards Bn.) Co.4
Romano, Rovusto TX Ford's Cav. Co.B
Romanole, A. AR Inf. Sparks' Co.
Romans, A.J. TX 13th Vol. Co.A
Romans, Daniel S. TX 18th Inf. Co.I
Romans, James H.H. VA 4th Inf. Co.D
Romans, James J.H. AR 33rd Inf. Co.E
Romans, J.H. AR 12th Inf. Co.A
Romans, J.J. TX 22nd Inf. Co.A Cpl.
Romans, John VA 36th Inf. 1st Co.B, 2nd Co.D
Romans, J.W. KY 3rd Cav. Co.C
Romans, J.W. KY 3rd Cav. Grant's Co.

Romans, Richard TN 34th Inf. Co.D
Romans, Richard M. GA 47th Inf. Co.F
Romans, Samuel L. KY 4th Cav. Co.A
Romans, Silas J. AL 4th (Russell's) Cav. Co.G
Romans, Stephen MS 19th Inf. Co.B
Romans, William AL 4th (Russell's) Cav. Co.G
Romanstine, George C. SC 2nd Cav. Co.C
Romare, Paul SC 6th Inf. 1st Co.F QMSgt.
Romare, Paul VA 3rd Inf.Loc.Def. Co.A
Romaro, Adolphe LA 7th Cav. Co.G
Romaro, Prosper LA 7th Cav. Co.G
Romaro, Savaira LA 7th Cav. Co.G
Romaro, U. LA 7th Cav. Co.I Sgt.
Romaur, Omaur LA 2nd Cav. Co.F
Rombach, Benedict LA Arty. 1st Field Btty.
Romberg, Frederick MO 2nd Inf. Co.G
Romberg, Fredrick Conf.Inf. 8th Bn.
Rombley, A.J. SC 20th Inf. Co.F
Rome, A. LA Mil. St.James Regt. Co.G Cpl.
Rome, Adrien LA 30th Inf. Locoul's Co.
Rome, A.L. LA Inf.Cons. 18th Regt. & Yellow Jacket Bn. Co.B Cpl.
Rome, Andre LA 28th (Thomas') Inf. Co.E
Rome, Augustin LA 18th Inf. Co.A
Rome, Augustin LA 28th (Thomas') Inf. Co.E
Rome, Charles Conf.Lt.Arty. 1st Reg.Btty.
Rome, C.O. AL Inf. 1st Regt.
Rome, Donat LA 18th Inf. Co.A
Rome, F. LA Mil. St.James Regt. Co.G
Rome, Florestan LA 2nd Cav. Co.K
Rome, Florestan LA 30th Inf. Locoul's Co. 1st Sgt.
Rome, Florian LA 30th Inf. Co.F
Rome, Florian LA Mil. St.James Regt. Gaudet's Co.
Rome, Francis TX 8th Cav. Co.G
Rome, Harvey R. KY 2nd Mtd.Inf. Co.G
Rome, Joseph LA 18th Inf. Co.A
Rome, Joseph LA Inf.Cons. 18th Regt. & Yellow Jacket Bn. Co.C
Rome, Laurent LA 18th Inf. Co.E
Rome, Laurent. LA Inf.Cons. 18th Regt. & Yellow Jacket Bn. Co.B
Rome, Laurent. LA 30th Inf. Locoul's Co. 2nd Lt.
Rome, Lovincy LA 18th Inf. Co.E
Rome, Lovincy LA Inf.Cons. 18th Regt. & Yellow Jacket Bn. Co.B
Rome, Lovincy LA 30th Inf. Locoul's Co.
Rome, Lovinsky LA Mil. St.James Regt. Co.F
Rome, M. LA Mil. LaFourche Regt.
Rome, M. LA Mil. St.James Regt. Co.G
Rome, R.H. LA 1st Inf. Co.I
Rome, Sebastien LA 18th Inf. Co.A
Rome, S.R. TN 1st Hvy.Arty. Co.B
Rome, T.B. TX 1st Hvy.Arty.
Rome, Thomas NC Mil. Clark's Sp.Bn. D.N. Bridger's Co.
Rome, T.L. LA Mil. St.James Regt. Co.F 2nd Lt.
Rome, T.W. Gen. & Staff Maj.,Surg.
Rome, V. LA Mil. St.James Regt. Co.G
Rome, Vasseur LA 30th Inf. Locoul's Co.
Rome, Victor LA 18th Inf. Co.E
Rome, Victor LA 28th (Thomas') Inf. Co.E
Rome, W.B. TX 5th Inf. Co.D
Romed, M. LA Mil. 3rd Regt. French Brig. Co.8

Romeo, W.T. VA 23rd Cav. 2nd Co.K
Romer, Dan'l AL 26th Inf. Co.I
Romer, Daniel LA 6th Inf. Co.E
Romer, F.J.D. Gen. & Staff Surg.
Romer, G.R. LA 22nd Inf. Co.C Cpl.
Romer, J.A. LA Mil. 4th Regt. 2nd Brig. 1st Div. Co.B Capt.
Romer, J.A. LA 22nd Inf. Co.C Cpl.
Romer, J.A. LA 22nd (Cons.) Inf. Co.C Sgt.
Romer, Jacob LA 20th Inf. Co.G
Romer, Jacob LA Herrick's Co. (Orleans Blues)
Romer, J.B. LA Mil. Col.,Surg.Gen.
Romer, P. AL St.Arty. Co.C Sgt.
Romer, W.B. Gen. & Staff Hosp.Stew.
Romer, William AL 3rd Inf. Co.A
Romero, Adolphe LA Conscr.
Romero, Aladin LA Inf. 10th Bn. Co.C
Romero, Alexandre LA Inf.Cons. 18th Regt. & Yellow Jacket Bn. Co.A
Romero, Aurelien LA Conscr.
Romero, C. LA 7th Cav. Co.H Sgt.
Romero, Cleveland LA Inf.Cons. 18th Regt. & Yellow Jacket Bn. Co.A
Romero, Dominigue LA Conscr.
Romero, Dorséle LA Conscr.
Romero, Duplexis LA Inf.Cons. 18th Regt. & Yellow Jacket Bn. Co.A
Romero, Dupré LA Conscr.
Romero, E.L. LA Inf.Cons. 18th Regt. & Yellow Jacket Bn. Co.A
Romero, Emile LA Conscr.
Romero, Eutimo Conf.Lt.Arty. Davis' Co.
Romero, F. LA Inf. 10th Bn. Co.C
Romero, Ferdinand LA Inf.Cons. 18th Regt. & Yellow Jacket Bn. Co.A
Romero, Filipe TX Cav. Ragsdale's Bn. Co.B
Romero, Francisco TX Cav. Ragsdale's Bn. Co.B
Roméro, Gerard LA Conscr.
Romero, Girard LA Inf. 10th Bn. Co.C
Romero, G.V. LA Conscr.
Romero, Jose LA Mil. 5th Regt.Eur.Brig. (Spanish Regt.) Co.9
Romero, Jose LA Mil. Cazadores Espanoles Regt. Co.5
Romero, Joseph LA Inf.Cons. 18th Regt. & Yellow Jacket Bn. Co.A
Roméro, Joseph LA Conscr.
Romero, Joseph D. LA Inf. 10th Bn. Co.C
Romero, J.S. LA Conscr.
Romero, Leon LA Inf. 10th Bn. Co.C
Romero, Lewis TX Granbury's Cons.Brig. Co.A
Roméro, L.F. LA Conscr.
Romero, Louis LA 7th Cav. Co.I
Romero, Louis TX 6th Inf. Co.H
Roméro, Moleon LA Conscr.
Romero, O. LA Inf. 10th Bn. Co.C
Roméro, Ozeme LA Conscr.
Romero, Ozime LA Inf.Cons. 18th Regt. & Yellow Jacket Bn. Co.A
Romero, P. LA Mil. 3rd Regt. 2nd Brig. 1st Div.
Romero, Pedro LA Mil. 5th Regt.Eur.Brig. (Spanish Regt.) Co.6
Romero, S. LA Inf. 10th Bn. Co.E
Romero, Severin LA Conscr.
Romero, Theogine LA Conscr.
Romero, V. LA Inf. 10th Bn. Co.C

Romero, Vilmont LA Conscr.
Romgel, Presentario TX Cav. Benavides' Regt. Co.I
Romilly, C. SC 2nd Inf. Co.B
Romine, A.D. AL 13th Bn.Part.Rangers Co.D
Romine, A.D. AL 56th Part.Rangers Co.H
Romine, Allen AL 10th Cav. Co.B
Romine, Andrew MO 10th Inf. Co.E Cpl.
Romine, Benjamin F. VA 12th Cav. Co.G
Romine, B.F. VA 17th Cav. Co.B
Romine, C.F. VA Cav. 37th Bn. Co.E
Romine, Christopher AL Lt.Arty. 2nd Bn. Co.D
Romine, George TN 36th Inf. Co.A
Romine, George R. VA 17th Cav. Co.F
Romine, George W. VA 49th Inf. 3rd Co.G
Romine, Hiram VA 10th Cav. Co.G
Romine, James A. VA 17th Cav. Co.B,K
Romine, J.B. AL 13th Bn.Part.Rangers Co.A 2nd Lt.
Romine, J.B. AL 56th Part.Rangers Co.L 2nd Lt.
Romine, J.B. TN 22nd (Barteau's) Cav. 1st Co.H Bvt.2nd Lt.
Romine, J.L. TN 22nd (Barteau's) Cav. 1st Co.H
Romine, Joe MO 8th Cav. Phillips' Co.
Romine, John MO 1st Inf. Co.I
Romine, John MO 1st & 4th Cons.Inf. Co.K
Romine, John VA 17th Cav. Co.C
Romine, John VA Cav. 46th Bn. Co.D
Romine, Jose Maria TX 8th Inf. Co.E
Romine, Joseph B. VA 7th Inf. Co.G Cpl.
Romine, Mathew VA 19th Cav. Co.H
Romine, M.F. MO Walker's Regt.St.Guard Crisp's Co.
Romine, Miledge F. MO Walker's Regt.St.Guard Crisp's Co.
Romine, Milledge MO Thompson's Command
Romine, N. AL 13th Bn.Part.Rangers Co.D Cpl.
Romine, R.N. AL 56th Part.Rangers Co.H Cpl.
Romine, Smith VA 14th Cav. Crawford's Co.
Romine, Smith VA 17th Cav. Co.F
Romine, Thomas AL 48th Inf. Co.D
Romine, W. AL 35th Inf. Co.B
Romine, William VA Cav. 46th Bn. Co.D
Romines, Bey F. VA 34th Mil. Co.C
Romines, Calvin AL 4th (Russell's) Cav. Co.D
Romines, Christopher TN Lt.Arty. Browne's Co.
Romines, Henry MO 2nd Cav. Co.G
Romines, H.J. TX Conscr.
Romines, Isaac TN 13th (Gores') Cav. Co.C
Romines, James AR 18th (Marmaduke's) Inf. Co.F
Romines, James GA 21st Inf. Co.K
Romines, James TN 36th Inf. Co.A
Romines, J.L. MO 7th Cav. Co.C
Romines, John TN 39th Mtd.Inf. Co.A
Romines, John TX 32nd Cav. Co.B
Romines, John M. TN 19th Inf. Co.I
Romines, John S.M. AL 12th Inf. Co.H
Romines, Joseph TN 36th Inf. Co.A
Romines, J.S. 3rd Conf.Inf. Co.F
Romines, Laton TN 39th Mtd.Inf. Co.C
Romines, Levi MS 2nd St.Cav. Co.A
Romines, Martin TN 26th Inf. Co.B,H
Romines, Martin TN 61st Mtd.Inf. Bundren's Co. Cpl.
Romines, Mathew AL 12th Inf. Co.H

Romines, Noah TN 39th Mtd.Inf. Co.A
Romines, Peter AL 27th Inf. Co.I
Romines, Reuben TX 9th Cav. Co.G
Romines, Samuel L. TN 39th Mtd.Inf. Co.G,A
Romines, Thomas TX 18th Cav. Co.B
Romines, Wane AL Cav. Hardie's Bn.Res. Co.E
Romines, W.C. TX 9th Cav. Co.G
Romines, W.C. TX 32nd Cav. Co.B
Romines, W.S. TN 21st (Wilson's) Cav. Co.A Sgt.
Romines, W.T. MO 7th Cav. Co.H
Rominger, A. NC 6th Sr.Res. Co.C
Rominger, Charles AL 12th Inf. Co.A 4th Sgt.
Rominger, David NC 7th Sr.Res. Holland's Co.
Rominger, E.A. NC 1st Cav. (9th St.Troops) Co.G
Rominger, Frank NC 6th Cav. (65th St.Troops) Co.F,G
Rominger, Franklin J. NC 15th Inf. Co.C
Rominger, H.A. NC 1st Arty. (10th St.Troops) Co.H
Rominger, James A. NC 33rd Inf. Co.G
Rominger, John NC 3rd Jr.Res. Co.B
Rominger, John NC 4th Bn.Jr.Res. Co.B
Rominger, Leander M. NC 63rd Inf. Co.D,E
Rominger, Moses NC 48th Inf. Co.K
Rominger, Reuben NC Inf. 2nd Bn. Co.G
Rominger, Wesley J. NC 21st Inf. Co.K
Rominger, William J. NC 1st Jr.Res. Co.C
Romingh, E.F. AL 7th Inf. Co.B
Rominson, J.H. MS 1st Inf. Co.F
Romley, Israel NC 5th Cav. (63rd St.Troops) Co.I
Romley, Marshall NC 5th Cav. (63rd St.Troops) Co.I
Romley, Patrick TX Waul's Legion Co.B
Rommel, Francis GA 36th (Villepigue's) Inf. Co.F Cpl.
Rommel, Francis 1st Conf.Inf. 1st Co.F Cpl.
Rommel, John A. VA 1st Inf. Co.K
Rommel, William TN Inf. 3rd Bn. Co.G
Rommell, C.C. LA 25th Inf. Co.D
Rommerkirchen, Frank LA 10th Inf. Co.K
Rommines, W.C. MO Cav. Slayback's Regt. Co.B
Rommines, W.J. MO Cav. Slayback's Regt. Co.B
Rompel, Victor TX 3rd Inf. Co.K
Romph, Adolphus GA 25th Inf. Co.D
Romsey, William T. VA 135th Mil. Co.I
Romstree, John W. SC Mil. 7th Regt. Lt.
Romthom, F. TX Waul's Legion Co.E
Romulatt, A.J.A. SC 2nd Inf. Co.I
Romules, D. LA 1st Inf. Co.A
Ron, Stephen GA 34th Inf. Co.H
Ronald, Charles A. VA 4th Inf. Co.E Col.
Ronald, James E. VA 24th Inf. Co.A 2nd Lt.
Ronalds, George W. VA 25th Cav. Co.F
Ronalds, Hiram FL 5th Inf. Co.I
Ronalds, Hugh NC 12th Inf. Co.F
Ronalds, Hy H. VA 36th Inf. 3rd Co.I
Ronalds, J.W. MS 9th Inf. Co.K
Ronan, Charles MS 13th Inf. Co.B
Ronan, F. Marion SC Mil. 16th Regt. 1st Lt.,Adj.
Ronan, J. SC Inf. 1st (Charleston) Bn. Co.B

Ronan, James GA Inf. 1st Loc.Troops (Augusta) Co.I

Ronan, Martin MD Cav. 2nd Bn. Co.B

Ronan, Martin SC 1st (Butler's) Inf. Co.G,H

Ronan, Michael SC 13th Inf. Co.H

Ronan, Morris SC Lt.Arty. 3rd (Palmetto) Bn. Co.D

Ronan, Patrick SC 1st Arty. Co.D

Ronan, P.F. SC Lt.Arty. 3rd (Palmetto) Bn. Co.B

Ronan, P.F. SC Simons' Co.

Ronan, Robert T. KY 7th Cav. Co.F

Ronan, W. SC Mil. 16th Regt. Sigwald's Co.

Ronayne, Thomas LA 22nd Inf. Wash. Marks' Co.

Ronbion, A. LA Mil. 1st Regt. French Brig. Co.1

Ronbion, P. LA Mil. 1st Regt. French Brig. Co.1

Ronblanc, Francis Conf.Inf. Tucker's Regt. Co.C

Ronce, Pulcer TN 61st Mtd.Inf. Co.K

Rond, Antoine LA 2nd Cav. Co.C Cpl.

Rond, Charles VA Inf. 4th Bn.Loc.Def. Co.C

Rond, Charles A. VA 3rd Inf. Co.H

Rond, Henry VA 129th Mil. Buchanon's Co.

Rond, J.B. LA 2nd Cav. Co.C

Rondabush, Alexander VA 5th Inf. Co.F

Rondabush, Noah D. VA 7th Cav.

Rondal, Marco LA Mil. 5th Regt.Eur.Brig. (Spanish Regt.) Co.A

Ronde, E. TX Inf. 1st St.Troops Martin's Co.A

Rondeau, Albert AL 1st Bn.Cadets Co.A,B

Rondeau, Edward AL 24th Inf. Co.G,C

Rondeau, Henry W. AL 3rd Inf. Co.B

Rondeau, John AL Lt.Arty. 2nd Bn. Co.E

Rondeau, J.P. LA 5th Inf. Co.E

Rondeau, J.P. 14th Conf.Cav. Co.H

Rondeau, W.A.S. LA Cav. Greenleaf's Co. (Orleans Lt.Horse)

Rondeau, William A.S. MS Lt.Arty. Stanford's Co. Cpl.

Roudet, P.C. 20th Conf.Cav. Roudet's Co. Capt.

Rondle, G.R. LA 3rd Inf. Co.I

Rondol, J.A. MS 24th Inf.

Rondon, James 1st Choctaw & Chickasaw Mtd.Rifles 3rd Co.B

Rondot, Julius Smith's Staff Maj.

Rondot, St.Jules Gen. & Staff,PACS Capt.

Ronds, Richard TN 1st (Turney's) Inf.

Rondtree, John NC 31st Inf. Co.G

Rone, C.T. MS Scouts Morphis' Ind.Co.

Rone, Ed. FL 2nd Inf. Co.D

Rone, Edwin G. NC 62nd Inf. Co.D

Rone, George B. MO 1st Inf. Co.G

Rone, George B. MO 1st & 4th Cons.Inf. Co.G

Rone, George Washington 1st Conf.Cav. 2nd Co.G

Rone, Green L. AL 48th Inf. New Co.G

Rone, Hugh GA Inf. 26th Bn. Co.C

Rone, Jacob AL Mobile City Troop

Rone, James TX 13th Vol. 1st Co.H

Rone, Jerry TX 5th Inf. Co.K

Rone, John AL 1st Regt. Mobile Vol. British Guard Co.B

Rone, John MS 1st Lt.Arty. Co.D

Rone, John MS 1st Lt.Arty. Co.K

Rone, John TN 53rd Inf. Co.B

Rone, John T. AR 5th Inf. Co.E 1st Sgt.

Rone, J.T. SC Hvy.Arty. 15th (Lucas') Bn. Co.C

Rone, Loyd K. NC 4th Sr.Res. Co.I Capt.

Rone, O. MS 9th Cav. Co.B

Rone, Rodolph GA Inf. 1st Loc.Troops (Augusta) Co.H

Rone, Samuel N. AL Mil. 2nd Regt.Vol. Co.B

Rone, S.M. NC 39th Inf. Co.A

Rone, S.M. NC Mallett's Bn. Co.B

Rone, S.N. AL 4th Res. Co.A

Rone, Thomas GA Inf. 26th Bn. Co.C

Rone, Thomas J. TX 11th Cav. Co.A Capt.

Rone, Thomas J. TX Cav. Martin's Regt. Co.E Capt.

Rone, Thomas T. GA 3rd Cav. Co.D

Rone, W.H. TN 17th Inf. Co.H

Rone, William M. TN 53rd Inf. Co.B 1st Sgt.

Rone, W.M. TN 10th & 11th (Cons.) Cav. Co.C

Ronebac, I.H. KY 7th Cav. Co.A

Ronels, J. AR Pine Bluff Arty.

Ronemous, George M. VA 12th Cav. Co.D

Ronemous, J.M. VA 7th Cav. Glenn's Co.

Ronemous, John H. VA 1st Cav. Co.F

Ronemous, John M. VA 12th Cav. Co.A 1st Sgt.

Ronemouse, Lewis VA 2nd Inf. Co.H

Ronemouse, William VA 2nd Inf. Co.H

Ronen, Charles AL 1st Regt. Mobile Vol. British Guard Co.B

Rones, Charles Conf.Cav. Clarkson's Bn. Ind. Rangers Co.H

Roney, A.A. AL 15th Inf. Co.G

Roney, A.H. TN 30th Inf. Co.E

Roney, Amos L. NC 57th Inf. Co.I 1st Sgt.

Roney, Benjamin F. VA 36th Inf. 2nd Co.B

Roney, Calvin N. NC 6th Inf. Co.I 2nd Lt.

Roney, Charles VA 30th Inf. Co.B

Roney, Daniel M. NC 13th Inf. Co.E Cpl.

Roney, E. AR 15th Inf. Co.E

Roney, Ed. AR 31st Inf. Co.A

Roney, Elmore L. TN 7th Inf. Co.C

Roney, E.M. TN 30th Inf. Co.C

Roney, Ezekiel TN 40th Inf. Co.F

Roney, George W. FL Cav. 3rd Bn. Co.A

Roney, G.H. TN 30th Inf. Co.K

Roney, Henry C. GA 22nd Inf. Co.H

Roney, Henry P. VA 3rd Cav. 2nd Co.I

Roney, Hugh AR Cav. 6th Bn. Co.C

Roney, Hugh FL 11th Inf. Co.C

Roney, I.C. MD Arty. 2nd Btty.

Roney, J.A. AL 57th Inf. Co.H

Roney, James AL 15th Inf. Co.G

Roney, James AL 37th Inf. Co.H

Roney, James GA 25th Inf. Co.B

Roney, James N. VA 3rd Cav. 2nd Co.I

Roney, J.C. MD Cav. 2nd Bn. Co.A

Roney, J.F. TN 30th Inf. Co.K

Roney, J.H. TN 30th Inf. Co.K

Roney, J.N. NC 3rd Arty. (40th St.Troops) Co.C

Roney, Joab GA 3rd Inf. Co.G

Roney, John GA 25th Inf. Co.E

Roney, John LA Mil.Cav.Squad. (Ind.Rangers Iberville)

Roney, John NC 15th Inf. Co.H 2nd Lt.

Roney, John NC 57th Inf. Co.I

Roney, John SC 1st (Butler's) Inf. Co.G Cpl.

Roney, John A. GA 25th Inf. Co.E

Roney, John A. NC 1st Inf. (6 mo. '61) Co.K

Roney, John C. TN Arty. Stewart's Co.

Roney, John W. AL 15th Inf. Co.G

Roney, Joseph AL 15th Inf. Co.G

Roney, Joseph C. GA 1st Mil. Co.E Cpl.

Roney, L.H. NC 57th Inf. Co.I Lt.

Roney, M. GA 19th Inf. Co.B

Roney, Michael J. FL 2nd Inf. Co.M

Roney, Morris J. AL 6th Cav. Co.D

Roney, Morris L. AL 15th Inf. Co.G

Roney, Newton SC 1st (McCreary's) Inf. Co.A

Roney, Nicholas GA 19th Inf. Co.D

Roney, Patrick SC 17th Inf. Co.A

Roney, Peter GA Inf. 9th Bn. Co.E

Roney, Peter GA 37th Inf. Co.H

Roney, R. LA Mil. Lewis Guards

Roney, Robert SC 6th Inf. 1st Co.A

Roney, Thomas GA 44th Inf. Co.B

Roney, Thomas SC 17th Inf. Co.A Cpl.

Roney, W. TN 30th Inf. Co.K

Roney, W.H.L. TN 30th Inf. Co.K

Roney, William AL 6th Cav. Co.D,E

Roney, William NC 57th Inf. Co.I

Roney, William P. NC 8th Bn.Jr.Res. Co.B

Roney, William T. VA 46th Inf. 2nd Co.F

Roney, W.T. SC 1st Cav. Co.D

Roney, W.T. SC 17th Inf. Co.A

Ronie, A.J. NC 23rd Inf. Co.A

Ronie, Solomon M. AL 3rd Bn. Hilliard's Legion Vol. Co.A

Ronie, Thomas B. AL 3rd Bn.Res. Appling's Co., Co.I

Ronie, William L. AL 3rd Bn. Hilliard's Legion Vol. Co.A

Ronir, Sol. M. AL 60th Inf. Co.E

Ronits, A.H. LA Mil. 2nd Regt. 3rd Brig. 1st Div. Co.B

Ronk, Andrew J. VA 22nd Inf. Co.A

Ronk, Benjamin VA 51st Inf. Co.I

Ronk, D. VA 22nd Inf. Co.F

Ronk, David VA 157th Mil. Co.B

Ronk, Jacob D. VA 22nd Inf. Co.A

Ronk, James M. VA 22nd Inf. Co.A Sgt.

Ronk, Joseph VA 51st Inf. Co.I

Ronk, Samuel VA 22nd Inf. Co.A

Ronk, Samuel VA 28th Inf. Co.E

Ronk, William VA 157th Mil. Co.B

Ronkey, John LA Mil. Chalmette Regt. Co.G Cpl.

Ronkins, D.V. MS 6th Inf. Co.H

Ronlain, M.O. AL 9th Inf.

Ronlain, Theodore AL 10th Inf. Co.B

Ronlain, Thomas AL 10th Inf. Co.B

Ronneke, F. TX Waul's Legion Co.B

Ronnie, T.B. AL 3rd Res.

Ronnsavall, Isaac M. TX 4th Inf. Co.K

Ronnsavall, John A. TX 4th Inf. Co.K Cpl.

Ronnsavall, William D. TX 4th Inf. Co.K 2nd Lt.

Ronquillo, A. LA Mil. Chalmette Regt. Co.K

Ronquillo, Anselme LA 28th (Thomas') Inf. Co.G Cpl.

Ronquist, A. Francis VA Lt.Arty. Kirkpatrick's Co.

Ronselkope LA Mil. 2nd Regt. 3rd Brig. 1st Div. Co.K

Ronsephano, E. 1st Chickasaw Inf. Haynes' Co.

Ronsey, J. AL 16th Inf. Co.H

Ronsick, Henry AR 38th Inf. Co.F Cpl.
Ronsin, Leon MO Cav. 3rd Regt.St.Guard Co.D
    2nd Lt.
Ronsley, William NC 26th Inf. Co.G
Ronsselot, Aug. LA Mil. 1st Regt. French Brig.
    Co.8
Ronssin, Theodule L. MO Cav. 3rd Regt.
    St.Guard Co.C Cpl.
Ront, Francis MO Cav. 3rd Regt.St.Guard Co.E
Ronte, George LA Mil. 1st Regt. 2nd Brig. 1st
    Div. Co.F
Ronton, John W. AL 33rd Inf. Co.C
Rontree, Elijah GA 44th Inf. Co.D
Rony, J.H. AL 7th Cav. Co.F
Rony, Joseph A.J. FL Lt.Arty. Dyke's Co.
Ronzan, G.M. LA Lt.Arty. 2nd Field Btty.
Roocksby, James W. KY 3rd Cav. Co.C
Rood, Bailey AR 50th Mil. Co.A Ord.Sgt.
Rood, H. GA 28th Inf.
Rood, John Conf.Inf. Tucker's Regt. Co.D
Rood, J.S. AL Mobile City Troop
Roodes, Benjamin VA 7th Cav. Co.H
Roody, J.C. GA 29th Inf. Co.D
Roodye, Edward W. GA 8th Inf.
Roof, Benjamin J. SC 20th Inf. Co.H
Roof, Daniel J. SC 20th Inf. Co.H Cpl.
Roof, Daniel M. VA 10th Inf. Co.H
Roof, Edwin J. SC 5th Cav. Co.F
Roof, Edwin J. SC Cav. 14th Bn. Co.C
Roof, George SC 4th Cav. Co.B
Roof, George SC Cav. 10th Bn. Co.A
Roof, George SC Inf. Hampton Legion Co.I
Roof, George W. VA 52nd Inf. Co.D
Roof, Henry J. SC 20th Inf. Co.H Sgt.
Roof, H.J. SC 2nd Inf. Co.B
Roof, J. SC 2nd St.Troops Co.A Cpl.
Roof, Jacob L. SC 20th Inf. Co.H
Roof, Jesse SC 20th Inf. Co.H
Roof, Jesse M. SC 20th Inf. Co.H Cpl.
Roof, J.L. SC 2nd Inf. Co.B
Roof, John SC 5th Cav. Co.F
Roof, John SC Cav. 14th Bn. Co.C
Roof, John SC 22nd Inf. Co.I
Roof, John C. SC 5th Cav. Co.F
Roof, John C. SC Cav. 14th Bn. Co.C
Roof, John F. VA 10th Inf. Co.G
Roof, John N. SC 20th Inf. Co.K
Roof, Joseph VA 58th Mil. Co.E
Roof, Joseph W. SC 20th Inf. Co.H
Roof, Martin SC 20th Inf. Co.H
Roof, Martin VA 58th Mil. Co.F Cpl.
Roof, Reuben SC 20th Inf. Co.K
Roof, Samuel D. GA 32nd Inf. Co.F
Roof, Samuel M. SC 20th Inf. Co.H Capt.
Roof, S.G.J. SC 2nd Inf. Co.K
Roof, Simeon G.J. SC 20th Inf. Co.K
Roof, Simeon W. SC 5th Cav. Co.F
Roof, Simeon W. SC Cav. 14th Bn. Co.C
Roof, T.E. SC 15th Inf. Co.K
Roof, Thomas E. SC 20th Inf. Co.H
Roof, Thomas J. SC 20th Inf. Co.H
Roof, W. SC 2nd Inf. Co.K
Roof, William TN 4th Inf. Co.G
Roof, Z. SC Inf. Hampton Legion Co.I
Roof, Zachariah SC Cav. 10th Bn. Co.A
Roof, Zack SC 4th Cav. Co.B
Rooff, Samuel D. SC Mil. 15th Regt. Co.D

Rook, Alfred TN 21st Cav. Co.H
Rook, Benjamin MS 29th Inf. Co.H
Rook, Benjamin E. NC Lt.Arty. 3rd Bn. Co.C,A
Rook, Benjamin E. VA 61st Inf. Co.G
Rook, Benjamin F. MS 2nd Inf. Co.H Sgt.
Rook, Benjamin N. MS 30th Inf. Co.G
Rook, Benjamin S. MS 12th Inf. 2nd Co.I Sgt.
Rook, B.F. MS 2nd Cav. Co.E
Rook, B.T. MS 8th Cav. Co.H
Rook, B.T. MS 28th Cav. Co.L
Rook, Charles TX 2nd Cav. Co.I
Rook, Daniel M. MS 17th Inf. Co.F
Rook, Dennis GA 5th Inf. Co.I
Rook, E.C. SC 25th Inf. Co.F
Rook, F.M. MS 5th Cav. Co.I
Rook, F.M. MS 40th Inf. Co.K
Rook, Francis W. MS 20th Inf. Co.C
Rook, Franklin SC 15th Inf. Co.B
Rook, George W. TX Cav. 6th Bn. Co.A
Rook, Green B. SC 18th Inf. Co.E
Rook, G.W. TX 7th Cav. Co.E
Rook, G.W. TX Cav. Ragsdale's Bn. 2nd Co.F
Rook, H. 2nd Conf.Eng.Troops Co.B
Rook, Henry 1st Conf.Eng.Troops Co.C
Rook, H.T. MS 4th Inf. Co.K
Rook, James AL 18th Inf. Co.B
Rook, James SC 15th Inf. Co.B
Rook, James L. NC 12th Inf. Co.N
Rook, James L. NC 32nd Inf. Co.B,C
Rook, James M. VA 12th Inf. 2nd Co.I Cpl.
Rook, J.B. SC 2nd Bn.S.S. Co.C
Rook, J.F. MS 5th Cav. Co.I 2nd Lt.
Rook, J.F. MS 20th Inf. Co.K
Rook, John 3rd Conf.Cav. Co.K,I
Rook, John C. TX 8th Inf. Co.A
Rook, John D. MS 17th Inf. Co.F
Rook, John H. MS Cav. 3rd Bn. (Ashcraft's)
    Co.B
Rook, John H. MS 7th Cav. Co.I Sgt.
Rook, John W. VA 24th Cav. Co.I
Rook, John W. 8th (Dearing's) Conf.Cav. Co.D
Rook, Joseph MS 13th Inf. Co.G
Rook, Joseph TN 50th Inf. Co.D
Rook, Joseph H. VA 12th Inf. Co.F
Rook, J.R. MS 1st Cav.Res. Co.E
Rook, J.S. MS 8th Cav. Co.H
Rook, J.S. TN 15th (Cons.) Cav. Co.F
Rook, J.W. SC 20th Inf. Co.F
Rook, Martin V. VA 5th Bn.Inf. Co.F
Rook, Patrick AL 2nd Inf. Co.A
Rook, R. GA 10th Inf. Co.A
Rook, Samuel G. SC 20th Inf. Co.F
Rook, Samuel L. GA 27th Inf. Co.A
Rook, S.G. SC 2nd Inf. Co.F
Rook, S.H. TX 20th Inf. Co.E Cpl.
Rook, S.L. SC Inf. 3rd Bn. Co.D
Rook, S.L. SC 5th St.Troops Co.I
Rook, S.L. SC 27th Inf. Co.A
Rook, S.L. SC Inf. Holcombe Legion Co.H
Rook, Thomas G. TN Lt.Arty. McClung's Co.
Rook, Thomas J. SC 20th Inf. Co.F
Rook, Thomas J. VA 12th Inf. Co.F
Rook, Thomas P. SC 15th Inf. Co.A
Rook, W.D. VA 24th Cav. Co.G
Rook, W.D. VA Cav. 32nd Bn. Co.A
Rook, William B. NC 12th Inf. Co.G
Rook, William J. SC 13th Inf. Co.A 2nd Lt.

Rooke, A.B. VA 8th Cav. Co.I Sgt.
Rooke, Artemus SC 1st Bn.S.S. Co.C
Rooke, Artemus SC 27th Inf. Co.G
Rooke, B.T. MS 2nd Part.Rangers Co.D
Rooke, Calvin E. SC 1st (Hagood's) Inf. 1st
    Co.D
Rooke, J.D. MS 2nd Part.Rangers Co.D
Rooke, John TX Arty. 4th Bn. Co.A
Rooke, John B. VA Inf. 4th Bn.Loc.Def. Co.A
Rooke, Martin V. VA 53rd Inf. Co.F
Rooke, Thomas J. VA Inf. 4th Bn.Loc.Def.
    Co.A Sgt.
Rooker, David T. NC 14th Inf. Co.A
Rooker, E.T. TN 14th (Neely's) Cav. Co.E,B
Rooker, F.M. AL 18th Inf. Co.I
Rooker, F.M. AL 58th Inf. Co.A
Rooker, George W. NC 14th Inf. Co.A Cpl.
Rooker, George W. TN 25th Inf. Co.H
Rooker, G.W. TN 14th (Neely's) Cav. Co.E,B
    1st Sgt.
Rooker, Henry FL Sp.Cav. 1st Bn. Co.A
Rooker, H.F. GA Arty. St.Troops Pruden's Btty.
Rooker, James TN 11th Inf. Co.K
Rooker, James TN 24th Inf. Co.D
Rooker, James B. TN 11th Inf. Co.E
Rooker, J.L. AL 16th Inf. Co.I
Rooker, J.M. AL 3rd Res. Co.I
Rooker, J.M. MS 46th Inf. Co.G Sgt.
Rooker, John TN 12th (Green's) Cav. Co.I
Rooker, John TX Inf. Griffin's Bn. Co.E
Rooker, John A. GA 36th (Broyles') Inf. Co.A
Rooker, John C. MS 2nd Inf. Co.D
Rooker, John W. TN 11th Inf. Co.E Cpl.
Rooker, J.P. MS 34th Inf. Co.H
Rooker, J.P. NC 12th Inf. Co.I
Rooker, J.P. 3rd Conf.Eng.Troops Co.G Artif.
Rooker, Marcellus B. MS 19th Inf. Co.E
Rooker, Moses F. TX 21st Cav. Co.L
Rooker, N.B. MS 19th Inf. Co.E
Rooker, P.B. GA 36th (Broyles') Inf. Co.A
Rooker, Samuel VA 22nd Inf. Co.I
Rooker, W. GA 12th Cav. Co.A
Rooker, W.B. MS 19th Inf. Co.E
Rooker, William GA 1st Inf. (St.Guards) Co.K
Rooker, William T. NC 14th Inf. Co.A Cpl.
Rooker, W.J. TN 14th (Neely's) Cav. Co.E
Rooks, A.B. KY 8th Mtd.Inf. Sgt.
Rooks, Abel GA 16th Inf. Co.I
Rooks, A.J. GA 7th Inf. Co.G
Rooks, A.J. GA 9th Inf. Co.B
Rooks, Andrew J. GA 9th Inf. Co.C Sgt.
Rooks, Archibald B. GA 18th Inf. Co.E
Rooks, Archibald B. NC 18th Inf. Co.E
Rooks, Archibald P. NC 18th Inf. Co.E
Rooks, Charles SC 8th Bn.Res. Co.C
Rooks, Christopher GA 2nd Res. Co.H
Rooks, Columbus C. AL 23rd Bn.S.S. Co.F
Rooks, Columbus C. AL 1st Bn. Hilliard's
    Legion Vol. Co.F
Rooks, Daniel W. TX 35th (Brown's) Cav. Co.E
Rooks, Dempsey AR 30th Inf. Co.D
Rooks, Dennis S. GA 41st Inf. Co.I
Rooks, D.W. TX 13th Vol. 2nd Co.D
Rooks, Eli AR 23rd Inf. Co.K
Rooks, Elijah GA 30th Inf. Co.D
Rooks, E.R. TN 19th & 20th (Cons.) Cav. Co.E
Rooks, E.R. TN 20th (Russell's) Cav. Co.H

Rooks, F.N. GA 29th Inf. Co.G
Rooks, F.M. GA 56th Inf. Co.H
Rooks, F.M. MO 6th Cav. Co.A
Rooks, F.M. TN 12th Inf. Co.I
Rooks, Frank M. TN 12th (Cons.) Inf. Co.I
Rooks, George AL 6th Cav. Co.K Cpl.
Rooks, George W. TN 7th (Duckworth's) Cav. Co.L
Rooks, Green GA 11th Inf. Co.K
Rooks, G.W. TN 6th Inf. Co.A
Rooks, G.W. TN 38th Inf. Co.F
Rooks, Hezekiah GA 16th Inf. Co.K
Rooks, Hiram GA Cav. Rumph's Co. (Wayne Cav.Guards)
Rooks, J. AL 31st Inf. Co.I
Rooks, J. GA 55th Inf. Co.H
Rooks, J.A. TX 13th Vol. Co.D
Rooks, James FL 3rd Inf. Co.C
Rooks, James GA 4th (Clinch's) Cav. Co.A
Rooks, James GA Cav. 24th Bn. Co.A,C
Rooks, James GA Inf. 26th Bn. Co.A Cpl.
Rooks, James GA 51st Inf. Co.H
Rooks, James F. FL 7th Inf. Co.D
Rooks, James K. AR 5th Inf. Co.F
Rooks, James M. MO 6th Cav. Co.A 1st Lt.
Rooks, James M. TX 1st Bn.S.S. Co.C
Rooks, James R. TN 5th Inf. Co.F
Rooks, James R. TN 6th Inf. Co.G
Rooks, J.E. GA 7th Inf. Co.G
Rooks, Jeremiah GA 63rd Inf. Co.A
Rooks, Jesse FL 1st Inf. New Co.D Music.
Rooks, Jessee GA Lt.Arty. 12th Bn. 1st Co.A
Rooks, J.F. 3rd Conf.Cav. Co.I
Rooks, J.J. TN Inf. 3rd Cons.Regt. Co.G
Rooks, J.J. TN 31st Inf. Co.F
Rooks, J.J. 3rd Conf.Cav. Co.B
Rooks, J.M. TX 9th (Young's) Inf. Co.B Cpl.
Rooks, J.M. TX St.Troops Gould's Co. (Clarksville Lt.Inf.)
Rooks, John GA 62nd Cav. Co.B
Rooks, John GA 49th Inf. Co.C
Rooks, John MS 12th Cav. Co.F
Rooks, John J. FL Cav. Smith's Co. (Marianna Drag.)
Rooks, John J. NC 18th Inf. Co.E
Rooks, John J. 15th Conf.Cav. Co.B
Rooks, John T. GA 3rd Inf. Co.I,L
Rooks, John T. GA 26th Inf. Co.D
Rooks, John W. GA 41st Inf. Co.I
Rooks, Joseph W. AR 23rd Inf. Co.K
Rooks, J.P.M. 3rd Conf.Cav. Co.I
Rooks, J.S. GA Lt.Arty. Fraser's Btty.
Rooks, J.W. AR 30th Inf. Co.D
Rooks, J.W. NC 3rd Jr.Res. Co.D
Rooks, Malichi GA Inf. 27th Bn. Co.C
Rooks, N. GA 10th Inf. Co.B
Rooks, Napoleon B. AL 12th Inf. Co.E
Rooks, Nathaniel R. GA Sieg Arty. 28th Bn. Co.C
Rooks, Noah TX 1st Inf. Co.L
Rooks, Noah TX 9th (Nichols') Inf. Co.E
Rooks, N.R. GA Arty. 11th Bn. (Sumter Arty.) Co.B,K
Rooks, Obediah GA Lt.Arty. 12th Bn. 1st Co.A
Rooks, Obediah GA 63rd Inf. Co.A
Rooks, P.B. TX 27th Cav. Co.G
Rooks, P.R. TX 2nd Inf. Co.F

Rooks, Reason R. GA 14th Inf. Co.A
Rooks, S.H. TX 19th Inf. Co.C Cpl.
Rooks, Simeon L. NC 53rd Inf. Co.D
Rooks, S.J. SC 1st (Hagood's) Inf. 2nd Co.G
Rooks, Thomas 3rd Conf.Cav. Co.C
Rooks, Thomas E. TN 7th (Duckworth's) Cav. Co.L Sgt.
Rooks, Thomas F. FL 1st Inf. New Co.D
Rooks, Timothy GA Arty. 11th Bn. (Sumter Arty.) Co.B
Rooks, W.H. GA 56th Inf. Co.H
Rooks, William FL 1st Inf. New Co.D
Rooks, William GA 7th Inf. Co.G Sgt.
Rooks, William GA 56th Inf. Co.H
Rooks, William TN 10th (DeMoss') Cav. Co.C
Rooks, William E. GA 26th Inf. Co.D
Rooks, William J. GA 48th Inf. Co.G
Rooks, William J. GA 53rd Inf. Co.B
Rooks, William S. NC 3rd Inf. Co.K
Rooks, William W. GA Arty. 11th Bn. (Sumter Arty.) Co.B
Rooks, W.L. MO 6th Cav. Co.A
Rooks, W.R. TN 6th Inf. Co.B
Rooks, W.T. TN 31st Inf. Co.F
Rooks, Z. GA 62nd Cav. Co.B 3rd Lt.
Rooks, Z. GA 54th Inf. Co.E
Rooks, Z. GA 55th Inf. Co.H
Rooksby, J.M. KY 7th Cav. Co.K
Rookstool, Harvey VA 135th Mil. Co.D
Rookstool, John VA 79th Mil. Co.5
Rool, J.C. NC Mallett's Bn. (Cp.Guard) Co.C
Rool, S.D. NC 7th Sr.Res. Mitchell's Co.
Rool, W.M. AL 5th Inf. Co.K
Roolen, George AL 46th Inf. Co.B
Roolen, George TN 60th Mtd.Inf. Co.L 1st Sgt.
Roome, Charles LA Herrick's Co. (Orleans Blues) 1st Sgt.
Roome, Charles VA 10th Cav. Co.K 3rd Lt.
Roome, Edward MS 25th Inf. Co.F
Roome, Edward MO 1st Inf. Co.C
Roome, Edward MO 1st & 4th Cons.Inf. Co.G
Roomer, P. Gen. & Staff,PACS Surg.
Roon, J.H. SC Inf. Hampton Legion Co.F
Roon, J.R. VA 6th Inf.
Roonan, Martin SC Inf. 1st (Charleston) Bn. Co.F
Roonan, Patrick AL 21st Inf. Co.B
Roonen, J. LA Mil. 2nd Regt. 3rd Brig. 1st Div. Co.C
Rooney, Arthur J. VA 1st Inf. Co.B
Rooney, B. AL 17th Inf. Co.F
Rooney, Barnard GA 25th Inf. Co.A
Rooney, B.R. GA 25th Inf. Co.A
Rooney, Edward E. LA 1st (Nelligan's) Inf. Co.F
Rooney, Edward L. Sig.Corps,CSA Sgt.
Rooney, J. AR 18th (Marmaduke's) Inf. Co.A
Rooney, James AL 8th Inf. Co.H
Rooney, James AL 21st Inf. Co.B Sgt.
Rooney, James AL 42nd Inf. Co.I
Rooney, James GA Inf. (RR Guards) Preston's Co.
Rooney, James MO 5th Inf. Co.F Cpl.
Rooney, James SC Lt.Arty. 3rd (Palmetto) Bn. Co.D
Rooney, James TX 26th Cav. Co.B, 2nd Co.G
Rooney, J.C. SC Inf. 1st (Charleston) Bn. Co.C

Rooney, J.C. SC 27th Inf. Co.H
Rooney, John LA 1st Hvy.Arty. (Reg.) Co.H
Rooney, John LA 5th Inf. Old Co.A
Rooney, John LA 22nd Inf. Co.A
Rooney, John LA 22nd (Cons.) Inf. Co.A
Rooney, John, Jr. MS 24th Inf. Co.G,B Cpl.
Rooney, John, Sr. MS 24th Inf. Co.G Sgt.
Rooney, John TN Lt.Arty. Scott's Co.
Rooney, Lawrence GA 20th Inf. Co.C
Rooney, Mark GA Hvy.Arty. 22nd Bn. Co.E
Rooney, Mark GA 1st (Olmstead's) Inf. Guilmartin's Co.
Rooney, Martin LA 10th Inf. Co.C
Rooney, Matt. GA 47th Inf. Co.A
Rooney, Michael LA 6th Inf. Co.I Color-bearer
Rooney, Michael LA 15th Inf. Co.F
Rooney, Michael NC 37th Inf. Co.E
Rooney, Michael SC 27th Inf. Co.B
Rooney, Owen LA 10th Inf. Co.B
Rooney, Patrick AL Inf. 2nd Regt. Co.F
Rooney, Patrick LA Mil. 4th Regt. 1st Brig. 1st Div. Co.F
Rooney, Patrick LA 20th Inf. Co.K
Rooney, Patrick TN 15th Inf. Co.B
Rooney, Peter LA Mil.Cont.Regt. Kirk's Co.
Rooney, Rose, Mrs. LA 15th Inf. Co.K Laundress
Rooney, Thomas GA 5th Cav. Co.C
Rooney, Thomas GA Inf. 18th Bn. (St.Guards) Co.D
Rooney, Thomas LA 1st Hvy.Arty. (Reg.) Co.I
Rooney, Thomas SC 6th Cav. Co.B
Rooney, Thomas VA 11th Cav. Co.C
Rooney, Thomas Inf. School of Pract. Powell's Command Co.A
Rooney, Thomas S. SC Cav.Bn. Hampton Legion Co.C
Rooney, T.M. KY 4th Cav. Co.B
Rooney, William GA Arty. 11th Bn. (Sumter Arty.) New Co.C
Rooney, William GA 9th Inf. Co.A
Rooney, William MS 22nd Inf. Gaines' Co.
Rooney, William TN 21st Inf. Co.D
Rooney, William J. LA 1st (Strawbridge's) Inf. Co.A
Rooney, William P. GA 13th Cav. Co.B 1st Lt.
Rooney, William W. LA 12th Inf. Co.H
Roony, Thomas KY 11th Cav. Co.D
Roony, Thomas SC 1st Arty. Co.G
Roony, W. LA Mil. British Guard Bn. Coburn's Co.
Roop, Asa G. VA 64th Mtd.Inf. Co.G
Roop, B. VA 21st Cav. 2nd Co.D
Roop, Bluford VA 11th Inf. Co.F
Roop, C. VA Wade's Regt.Loc.Def. Co.D
Roop, Charles VA 64th Mtd.Inf. Co.B
Roop, Christian NC 52nd Inf. Co.F
Roop, Crockett VA 4th Res. Co.A 2nd Lt.
Roop, Fleming S. VA 11th Inf. Co.F Cpl.
Roop, Floyd VA 54th Inf. Co.A
Roop, F.S. VA 21st Cav. 2nd Co.D Cpl.
Roop, George G. AL 16th Inf. Co.A
Roop, George W.C. VA 54th Inf. Co.C
Roop, Giles H. VA 54th Inf. Co.A
Roop, Gordon VA 54th Inf. Co.A
Roop, Harvey VA 22nd Cav. Co.K
Roop, Harmon VA 17th Inf. Co.G

Roop, Harrison VA 17th Inf. Co.G
Roop, Henry R. VA 25th Cav. Co.F
Roop, H.R. VA 21st Cav. 2nd Co.D
Roop, H.R. VA 11th Inf. Co.F
Roop, J. VA 21st Cav. 2nd Co.D
Roop, Jacob VA 22nd Cav. Co.K Cpl.
Roop, Jacob A. VA 64th Mtd.Inf. Co.K 1st Sgt.
Roop, Jacob C. NC 37th Inf. Co.K
Roop, James R. VA 17th Inf. Co.G
Roop, J.C. VA Cav. 36th Bn. Co.D
Roop, J.K. GA Phillips' Legion Co.F 1st Sgt.
Roop, J.R. VA Wade's Regt.Loc.Def. Co.D
Roop, J.W. AL 9th (Malone's) Cav. Co.D 2nd Lt.
Roop, L. NC 3rd Jr.Res. Co.E
Roop, Linzy C. VA 64th Mtd.Inf. Co.G
Roop, M.W. VA 21st Cav. 2nd Co.D
Roop, R.H. GA Phillips' Legion Co.F
Roop, Samuel D. VA 63rd Inf. Co.D
Roop, William VA 25th Cav. Co.F
Roop, William VA 54th Inf. Co.A
Roop, William T. VA 64th Mtd.Inf. Co.G
Roop, W.W. GA Phillips' Legion Co.F Cpl.
Roope, D.S. MS 15th Inf. Co.F Music.
Roope, Henry TN 8th (Smith's) Cav. Co.L
Roope, J. AR 51st Mil. Co.H
Roope, James MO 5th Inf. Co.H
Roope, John NC 34th Inf. Co.A
Roope, John T. MS 15th Inf. Co.F
Roope, Martin VA Inf. 23rd Bn. Co.H
Roope, R. AR 51st Mil. Co.H
Roope, S. AR 51st Mil. Co.H
Rooper, M. VA Cav. 37th Bn. Co.B
Rooper, T.L. VA Cav. 37th Bn. Co.B
Roops, Bird VA Inf. 1st Bn. Co.A
Roork, Charles NC 2nd Arty. (36th St.Troops) Co.B
Roos, Adolphe LA 3rd (Harrison's) Cav. Co.K Music.
Roos, C.R. LA Mil. 2nd Regt. 2nd Brig. 1st Div. Co.D Jr.2nd Lt.
Roos, C.R. LA Inf.Crescent Regt. Co.A Cpl.
Roos, D. GA 63rd Inf. Co.F
Roos, Henry TX Cav. 8th (Taylor's) Bn. Co.C
Roose, D. TX Inf. Timmons' Regt. Co.E
Roose, Frederick LA 6th Inf. Co.H Cpl.
Root, --- TX Cav. Ragsdale's Bn. Co.C
Root, Alexander P. TX 35th (Brown's) Cav. Co.E Sgt.
Root, A.P. TX 15th Field Btty. 1st Lt.
Root, B.F. MO 2nd Inf. Co.D
Root, Buel T. MO 2nd Inf. Co.D
Root, C.S. TX Conscr.
Root, Daniel E. MO 3rd Inf. Co.F
Root, Erastus C. VA Lt.Arty. Arch. Graham's Co.
Root, E.W. KY 3rd Cav. Co.D
Root, George W. MS 16th Inf. Co.E
Root, Irving TX 11th Cav. Co.C Jr.2nd Lt.
Root, Irving Gen. & Staff 1st Lt.,Adj.
Root, Iverson L. VA 1st Cav. Co.C
Root, James LA Inf.Cons. 18th Regt. & Yellow Jacket Bn. Co.A
Root, James L. GA 1st (Olmstead's) Inf. Co.G
Root, Jerome Mead's Conf.Cav. Co.L Capt.
Root, Jesse H. VA 38th Inf. Co.B Cpl.
Root, J.L. SC 1st Inf. Co.A

Root, John AL 21st Inf. Co.C
Root, John L. SC 1st (McCreary's) Inf. Co.C
Root, Joseph LA Mil. British Guard Bn. Burrowes' Co.
Root, Junius F. VA 1st Cav. Co.E
Root, Martin 1st Cherokee Mtd.Vol. 1st Co.B, 2nd Co.D
Root, R.A. LA Inf.Crescent Regt. Co.G Cpl.
Root, R.A. LA Inf.Cons.Crescent Regt. Co.C
Root, Robert P. AL 9th Inf. Co.B 2nd Lt.
Root, S. GA Inf. (Collier Guards) Collier's Co.
Root, S. SC 1st Regt. Charleston Guard Co.H
Root, Samuel VA 6th Cav. Co.C
Root, Sidney S. GA 2nd Res. Co.A
Root, Thomas A. 1st Cherokee Mtd.Vol. 1st Co.G, 2nd Co.D Ord.Sgt.
Root, Thomas J. MS 1st Cav. Co.I
Root, Thomas J. MS Cav. 1st Bn. (Miller's) Cole's Co.
Root, W.E. LA Dreux's Cav. Co.A
Root, William A. MO 3rd Inf. Co.F
Root, William D. VA 4th Inf. Co.B Cpl.
Rootch, Charles Conf.Lt.Arty. 1st Reg.Btty.
Roote, Eugenius M. VA Prov.Guard Avis' Co.
Roote, William D. VA Cav. 41st Bn. Co.B Jr.2nd Lt.
Rootes, George F. MO Lt.Arty. 3rd Field Btty.
Rootes, George F., Jr. Shafer's Staff 1st Lt.
Rootes, Lawrence VA Vol. Taylor's Co.
Rootes, William S. VA 23rd Cav. Co.B 2nd Lt.
Rooth, Joh LA Mil. Orleans Fire Regt. Co.C Cpl.
Roots, G.F., Jr. MO Lt.Arty. 1st Btty.
Roots, John L. VA 14th Mil. Co.C Sgt.
Roots, John W. GA 42nd Inf. Co.I
Roots, Martin V. VA 2nd Inf. Co.D
Roots, Thomas R. TX 4th Cav. Co.C Sgt.
Roots, Thomas R., Jr. VA 4th Cav.
Roots, Thomas R. VA Lt.Arty. Pollock's Co.
Roots, William TX Cav. Martin's Regt. Co.B
Roots, W.R. TX Cav. Giddings' Bn. Weisiger's Co.
Roovy, John TX 6th Inf. Co.H
Rope, R.D. TN 4th Inf. Co.B
Rope, Thomas A. GA 1st Cav.
Rope, W. GA 4th Res. Co.F
Rope, W.S. AL 5th Inf. Co.A
Rope, W.W. MS 15th Inf. Co.K
Rope Camroe 1st Cherokee Mtd.Rifles Co.A
Ropen, H. AL 4th Inf. Co.F
Ropen, S.A. GA 8th Inf. Co.D
Roper, A. GA Cav. Logan's Co. (White Cty. Old Men's Home Guards)
Roper, A. KY 7th Mtd.Inf. Co.B
Roper, Absalom SC 3rd Res. Co.I
Roper, A.C. GA Inf. (Loc.Def.) Whiteside's Nav.Bn. Co.C
Roper, A.J. GA 3rd Res. Co.E
Roper, A.M. GA Inf. 3rd Bn. Co.H
Roper, A.M. GA 10th Inf. Co.A 1st Sgt.
Roper, A.M. Inf. Bailey's Cons.Regt. Co.B
Roper, A.M. TX 7th Inf. Co.A
Roper, Amos L. SC 2nd Rifles Co.H Cpl.
Roper, Amos W. NC 18th Inf. Co.F Cpl.
Roper, Anderson SC Cav. 4th Bn. Co.A
Roper, Anderson SC 2nd Rifles Co.E
Roper, Andrew J. GA 51st Inf. Co.H

Roper, Andrew J. VA Hvy.Arty. 10th Bn. Co.E
Roper, Asa AL 25th Inf. Co.I
Roper, A.W. SC Inf. Hampton Legion Co.D
Roper, Barney NC 6th Inf. Co.A
Roper, Bartlett VA 5th Cav. (12 mo. '61-2) Co.D
Roper, Benjamin AR 27th Inf. Co.E
Roper, Benjamin GA 4th Res. Co.A
Roper, Benjamin MO Cav. Coffee's Regt. Co.F
Roper, Benjamin SC 7th Inf. 1st Co.I, 2nd Co.I Capt.
Roper, Benjamin F. AL 3rd Inf. Co.K
Roper, Beverly GA 64th Inf. Co.E Sgt.
Roper, B.J. AR 14th (Powers') Inf. Co.D
Roper, B.N. GA 1st (Fannin's) Res. Co.E Sgt.
Roper, C. SC 2nd Res.
Roper, Caswell SC 4th Cav. Co.E
Roper, C.B. SC 6th Cav. Co.B
Roper, C.F. AL Cp. of Instr. Talladega
Roper, Charles GA 39th Inf. Co.A
Roper, Charles GA 43rd Inf. Co.I
Roper, Charles SC 5th Mil. Beat Co.3
Roper, Charles J. AR 27th Inf. Co.E
Roper, C.J. AR 45th Mil. Co.A
Roper, D. TX 24th Cav. Co.F
Roper, Daniel LA 14th Inf. Co.H
Roper, Daniel NC 6th Cav. (65th St.Troops) Co.A,E
Roper, Daniel NC Cav. 7th Bn. Co.A
Roper, David GA 52nd Inf. Co.F
Roper, David MS 6th Inf. Co.I
Roper, David NC 34th Inf. Co.I
Roper, David SC Cav. 4th Bn. Co.A
Roper, David SC 2nd Rifles Co.K Cpl.
Roper, David SC 3rd Res. Co.H
Roper, David SC Inf. Hampton Legion Co.F
Roper, David F. SC 7th Inf. 2nd Co.H
Roper, David H. SC 1st Arty. Co.D
Roper, David M. LA 12th Inf. Co.I,E
Roper, David R. NC 16th Inf. Co.M Sgt.
Roper, D.H. SC Cav. 2nd Bn.Res. Co.F Lt.
Roper, D.H. SC Inf. Hampton Legion Co.D Cpl.
Roper, Dick AL 1st Bn.Cadets Co.A 1st Lt.
Roper, Dick A. AL 21st Inf. Co.E
Roper, D.P. AL 29th Inf.
Roper, D.S. GA 46th Inf. Co.K
Roper, E. AL 4th Cav. Co.E
Roper, E. SC 22nd Inf. Co.F
Roper, E.A. GA 65th Inf. Co.K
Roper, Earl A. GA Smith's Legion Co.K
Roper, E.B. LA 18th Inf. Co.C Sgt.
Roper, E.C. AL 41st Inf. Co.D Cpl.
Roper, E.C. VA Hvy.Arty. Coffin's Co. Cpl.
Roper, Edward C. VA Hvy.Arty. A.J. Jones' Co.
Roper, Edward E. TX 20th Inf. Co.H
Roper, Edwin VA Lt.Arty. 38th Bn. Co.B
Roper, Edwin A. VA 1st Arty. Co.I
Roper, E.E. TX 35th (Brown's) Cav. 2nd Co.B
Roper, E.E. TX 12th Inf. Co.A
Roper, E.E. TX 20th Inf. Co.H
Roper, E.F. GA Inf. 1st City Bn. (Columbus) Co.B
Roper, E.H. AL 3rd Cav. Co.E
Roper, E.H. LA Inf.Crescent Regt. Co.B
Roper, Elisha GA 36th (Broyles') Inf. Co.L

Roper, E.M. AL Arty. 1st Bn. Co.F
Roper, Emmet VA 12th Inf. Co.E Hosp.Stew.
Roper, Emsley M. AL 33rd Inf. Co.H
Roper, F.A. AL 32nd Inf. Co.G
Roper, Fleming VA Hvy.Arty. 10th Bn. Co.E Drum.
Roper, Francis TX Lt.Arty. Hughes' Co.
Roper, Frederick M. AL 42nd Inf. Co.K
Roper, F.S. NC Gibbs' Co. (Loc.Def.)
Roper, F.W. AL 1st Bn. Hilliard's Legion Vol. Co.D
Roper, G.B. AL 32nd Inf. Co.F
Roper, G.C. GA Cav. Russell's Co.
Roper, George AR 7th Cav. Co.D
Roper, George TN 44th Inf. Co.G
Roper, George C. GA 52nd Inf. Co.I
Roper, George K. VA Lt.Arty. 1st Bn. Co.D
Roper, George K. VA Lt.Arty. B.H. Smith's Co.
Roper, George T. TN 44th (Cons.) Inf. Co.F
Roper, George W. SC Inf. Hampton Legion Co.A
Roper, G.M. AL 1st Bn.Cadets Co.A
Roper, G.W. AR 14th (Powers') Inf. Co.D
Roper, G.W. GA 3rd Res. Co.E
Roper, G.W. TX 37th Cav. Co.K
Roper, H. AR 1st (Monroe's) Cav. Co.L
Roper, H. MS 2nd Inf. Co.E
Roper, Hardee AL 4th (Russell's) Cav. Co.I
Roper, Hardy MS 9th Inf. Old Co.I
Roper, Harman S. AL 31st Inf. Co.K
Roper, Harrison H. GA Inf. 25th Bn. (Prov. Guard) Co.E
Roper, Harvey A. NC 1st Inf. Co.D
Roper, Henry A. NC 17th Inf. (1st Org.) Co.I
Roper, Henry B. AL 4th Inf. Co.I 2nd Lt.
Roper, Henry C. GA Phillips' Legion Co.C
Roper, Henry C. VA 13th Cav. Co.B
Roper, Henry C. VA 12th Inf. Co.E
Roper, H.F. GA Cherokee Legion (St.Guards) Co.E Sgt.
Roper, H.H. GA 12th Cav. Co.G
Roper, Hilliard AR 26th Inf. Co.B
Roper, Hiram GA Floyd Legion (St.Guards) Co.G Cpl.
Roper, Hiram W. TX 35th (Brown's) Cav. Co.D
Roper, I.B. AL 6th Cav. Co.I Cpl.
Roper, Isaac SC Arty. Fickling's Co. (Brooks Lt.Arty.)
Roper, J. AL 25th Inf. Co.I
Roper, Jacob R. TN 43rd Inf. Co.K 2nd Lt.
Roper, James GA 52nd Inf. Co.F
Roper, James GA Cobb's Legion Co.K
Roper, James NC Cav. 7th Bn. Co.C
Roper, James TX 11th Inf. Co.D
Roper, James B. TN 48th (Nixon's) Inf. Co.G Sgt.
Roper, James B. TN 54th Inf. Co.B Sgt.
Roper, James D. AR 37th Inf. Co.G
Roper, James M. GA 1st Inf. Co.G
Roper, James M. NC 6th Cav. (65th St.Troops) Co.C
Roper, James M. VA 6th Inf. Co.I Sgt.
Roper, James P. AR 1st Mtd.Rifles Co.E 1st Lt.
Roper, James R. VA Hvy.Arty. A.J. Jones' Co.
Roper, Jas. R. VA Inf. 5th Bn. Co.D
Roper, James T. Gen. & Staff 2nd Lt.,Dr.M.

Roper, James W. NC 6th Cav. (65th St.Troops) Co.H,G
Roper, J.B. AL 1st Bn. Hilliard's Legion Vol. Co.D Sgt.
Roper, J.B. AL Talladega Cty.Res. D.M. Reid's Co.
Roper, J.B. GA Inf. (Loc.Def.) Whiteside's Nav.Bn. Co.A
Roper, J.B. NC 43rd Inf. Co.C
Roper, J.C. MO 3rd Cav. Co.E
Roper, J.C. NC 39th Inf. Co.C
Roper, J.D. SC 7th Inf. 2nd Co.I
Roper, J.D. SC 14th Inf. Co.D Cpl.
Roper, J.E. AL 1st Bn. Hilliard's Legion Vol. Co.D Cpl.
Roper, Jesse E. SC 2nd Rifles Co.H
Roper, J.F. AL 42nd Inf. Co.K
Roper, J.H. GA Cav. 9th Bn. (St.Guards) Co.D
Roper, J.H. GA 36th (Broyles') Inf. Co.A
Roper, J.H. LA 27th Inf. Co.G
Roper, J.H. MS 7th Cav. Co.F,I
Roper, J.H. MS Blythe's Bn. (St.Troops) Co.B
Roper, J.H. TX 15th Cav. Co.C
Roper, J.J. AR 1st (Monroe's) Cav. Co.L
Roper, J.L. GA 1st Inf. (St.Guards) Co.H
Roper, J.L. VA 11th Cav. Co.F
Roper, J.M. AR 13th Inf. Co.A
Roper, J.M. GA Inf. 8th Bn. Co.F
Roper, J.M. TX 2nd Cav. Co.D
Roper, J.N. VA Second Class Mil. Wolff's Co.
Roper, Joel C. GA 18th Inf. Co.F Capt.
Roper, Joel D. TN 4th (McLemore's) Cav. Co.F
Roper, John AL 40th Inf. Co.H
Roper, John MO Cav. 1st Regt.St.Guard Co.A
Roper, John NC 2nd Inf. Co.D
Roper, John VA 41st Inf. 2nd Co.E
Roper, John B. GA 12th (Robinson's) Cav. (St.Guards) Co.F Sgt.
Roper, John E. AL Arty. 1st Bn. Co.F
Roper, John H. AL 25th Inf. Co.I
Roper, John H. TX 17th Cav. Co.E
Roper, John L. AL 3rd Res. Co.B
Roper, John T. AL Arty. 1st Bn. Co.E,C
Roper, John T. LA 22nd (Cons.) Inf. Co.D
Roper, John T. TX 14th Cav. Co.G Cpl.
Roper, John W. FL 2nd Cav. Co.C Cpl.
Roper, John W. NC 18th Inf. Co.F 2nd Lt.
Roper, John W. NC 26th Inf. Co.E
Roper, John W. NC 46th Inf. Co.D 2nd Lt.
Roper, John W. SC 19th Inf. Co.B
Roper, John W. VA 38th Inf. Co.F
Roper, Jordan Sig.Corps,CSA
Roper, Joseph GA 11th Inf. Co.E
Roper, Joseph LA 12th Inf. Co.D Sgt.
Roper, Joseph TX Cav. Baird's Regt. Co.A
Roper, Joseph A. TN 32nd Inf. Co.C
Roper, Joseph M. AL 44th Inf. Co.E
Roper, Joseph T. GA 21st Inf. Co.D Sgt.
Roper, Joshua S. GA 20th Inf. Co.G Sgt.
Roper, Joshua W. NC Cav. 7th Bn. Co.C
Roper, J.P. AL 31st Inf.
Roper, J.R. GA Cav. 6th Bn. (St.Guards) Co.G
Roper, J.R. VA Hvy.Arty. Coffin's Co.
Roper, J.S. GA 4th Cav. (St.Guards) McDonald's Co.
Roper, J.S. GA 46th Inf. Co.K Sgt.

Roper, J.T. MS Condrey's Co. (Bull Mtn. Invinc.)
Roper, J.Y. TN 6th Inf. Co.E
Roper, L. TN Lt.Arty. Scott's Co. Artif.
Roper, Levi NC Cav. 7th Bn. Co.A
Roper, L.H. SC Inf. Hampton Legion Co.D
Roper, M. AL 4th Inf. Co.I
Roper, M. AL 25th Inf. Co.I Sgt.
Roper, Marcus SC 3rd Res. Co.H
Roper, Marcus SC 4th Inf. Co.H
Roper, Marion LA 28th (Gray's) Inf. Co.G Cpl.
Roper, Martin V. GA 11th Inf. Co.C
Roper, M.H. NC 5th Inf. Co.C
Roper, Miles LA 12th Inf. Co.D
Roper, Monroe L. NC 8th Bn.Jr.Res. Co.C
Roper, M.P. AL Arty. 1st Bn. Co.F
Roper, M.P. AL 1st Bn. Hilliard's Legion Vol. Co.D
Roper, N.C. SC 1st (Butler's) Inf. Co.G
Roper, N.C. SC 5th Mil. Beat Co.3
Roper, Newman SC 1st Cav. Co.F
Roper, Patrick LA Miles' Legion Co.G
Roper, P.H. GA 36th (Broyles') Inf. Co.A
Roper, Pinkney H. NC 5th Cav. (63rd St.Troops) Co.F,D
Roper, Pleasant G. AR 2nd Inf. Old Co.E, Co.D 1st Lt.
Roper, Pleasant G. AR Inf. Cocke's Regt. Co.A Capt.
Roper, P.W. AL 60th Inf. Co.I
Roper, P.W. AL 1st Bn. Hilliard's Legion Vol. Co.D
Roper, R. SC 1st Mtd.Mil. Heyward's Co.
Roper, R. VA 3rd (Archer's) Bn.Res. Co.E
Roper, R. VA Second Class Mil. Wolff's Co.
Roper, Richard SC 8th Bn.Res. Co.A
Roper, Richard W. LA 21st (Patton's) Inf. Co.D
Roper, Robert A. VA 10th Cav. Co.I N.C.S. Hosp.Stew.
Roper, Robinson NC 2nd Inf. Co.D
Roper, R.P. GA 43rd Inf. Co.I
Roper, S. MS 2nd Inf. Co.E
Roper, Samuel NC 6th Cav. (65th St.Troops) Co.A,E
Roper, Samuel NC Cav. 7th Bn. Co.A
Roper, Samuel SC 2nd Rifles Co.H Sgt.
Roper, Samuel B. AL 2nd Cav. Co.B
Roper, Samuel L. SC 2nd Cav. Co.I
Roper, Samuel L. SC Cav.Bn. Hampton Legion Co.A
Roper, S.H. AL Randolph Cty.Res. B.C. Raney's Co.
Roper, Simeon L. GA 2nd Bn.S.S. Co.A
Roper, Simeon L. GA 5th Inf. Co.F,M
Roper, Solomon D. GA 36th (Broyles') Inf. Co.L Sgt.
Roper, T. TX 9th Cav. Co.C
Roper, T. TX Cav. Terry's Regt. Co.I
Roper, T.A. AL 13th Inf. Co.G
Roper, T.A. AR 37th Inf. Co.G
Roper, Taliafero SC Palmetto S.S. Co.I
Roper, Thomas KY 12th Cav. Co.C
Roper, Thomas A. AR Cav. Wright's Regt. Co.G Sgt.
Roper, Thomas E. TN 32nd Inf. Co.C
Roper, Thomas F. AL 11th Inf. Co.F
Roper, Thomas J. LA Cav. Cole's Co.

Roper, T.J. AL 25th Inf. Co.I
Roper, T.J. AR 1st (Monroe's) Cav. Co.L
Roper, T.J. TN 7th (Duckworth's) Cav. Co.F
Roper, T.L. TX Cav. Hardeman's Regt. Co.A
Roper, Toliver SC 4th Inf. Co.H
Roper, T.R. TX 13th Cav. Co.C
Roper, T.W. MS Cav. Williams' Co.
Roper, V.B. AL 17th Inf. Co.F
Roper, V.B. AL 58th Inf. Co.C
Roper, W.A. AL 5th Inf. Co.I
Roper, W.A. GA Inf. 1st City Bn. (Columbus)
    Co.B
Roper, W.A. GA Inf. 8th Bn. Co.F
Roper, W.A. MS 35th Inf. Co.E
Roper, Warren D. GA 4th Cav. (St.Guards)
    McDonald's Co.
Roper, Washington GA 1st Inf. (St.Guards) Co.I
    Cpl.
Roper, Watson C. AL 42nd Inf. Co.K
Roper, W.B. TX Cav. 2nd Regt.St.Troops Co.B
Roper, W.C. MS Condrey's Co. (Bull Mtn.
    Invinc.)
Roper, W.D. GA 4th Regt.St.Line Co.I Cpl.
Roper, W.E. TN 7th (Duckworth's) Cav. Co.F
Roper, W.H. GA 5th Inf. Co.G
Roper, W.H. MS 10th Cav. Co.I
Roper, W.H. SC 2nd Cav. Co.F
Roper, W.H. SC Cav. 4th Bn. Co.A
Roper, W.H. SC Arty. Fickling's Co. (Brooks
    Lt.Arty.) Bugler
Roper, Wm. AL 25th Inf. Co.G
Roper, William MO Cav. 1st Regt.St.Guard
    Co.A
Roper, William NC 17th Inf. (1st Org.) Co.E
Roper, William NC 32nd Inf. Co.B
Roper, William SC Cav. Walpole's Co. 1st Sgt.
Roper, William B. 3rd Conf.Cav. Co.F
Roper, William C. NC 16th Inf. Co.F
Roper, William F. MS 14th Inf. Co.A Cpl.
Roper, William J. LA 12th Inf. Co.E
Roper, William M. AL 4th Inf. Co.I
Roper, William R. AL 3rd Cav. Co.H
Roper, William S. NC 8th Bn.Jr.Res. Co.C
Roper, William T. KY 2nd (Woodward's) Cav.
    Co.A,G
Roper, William T. NC 52nd Inf. Co.E Cpl.
Roper, William W. GA 6th Cav. Co.F
Roper, Wilson TX Cav. Morgan's Regt. Co.K
    1st Sgt.
Roper, W.M. AL Cp. of Instr. Talladega
Roper, W.P. FL Cav. 5th Bn. Co.H
Roper, W.R. AL Arty. 1st Bn. Co.F
Roper, W.R. AL 1st Bn. Hilliard's Legion Vol.
    Co.D
Roper, W.T. AL 32nd Inf. Co.F
Roper, W.Z. MS 5th Inf. Co.B
Ropey, John E. VA 30th Inf.
Ropka, Orney H. MO 1st Inf. 2nd Co.A
Ropke, C.K. MO 1st Inf. 2nd Co.A
Ropp, A.S. SC 20th Inf. Co.F
Ropp, George H. VA 67th Mil. Co.B Cpl.
Ropp, G.S. SC Inf. Hampton Legion Co.G
Ropp, Henry P. VA 37th Inf. Co.K
Ropp, J.L. SC Inf. 3rd Bn. Co.E
Ropp, J.L. SC 5th St.Troops Co.I
Ropp, J.L. SC 9th Res. Co.E
Ropp, J.S. VA 67th Mil. Co.B

Ropp, J.W. SC 9th Res. Co.F
Ropp, William H. VA 37th Inf. Co.K
Ropper, J. AL Cav. Moreland's Regt. Co.E
Roque, Franco. LA Mil. 5th Regt.Eur.Brig.
    (Spanish Regt.) Co.4
Roquemire, J.A. AL Cav. 4th Bn. (Love's) Co.C
Roquemore, Benjamin W. AL 43rd Inf. Co.H
    2nd Lt.
Roquemore, C.F. AL 34th Inf. Black's Co.
Roquemore, Frank L. GA 8th Inf. (St.Guards)
    Co.D
Roquemore, H.A.D. TX 7th Inf. Co.I
Roquemore, H.A.D. TX 11th Inf. Co.E 2nd Lt.
Roquemore, Henry G. TX 14th Cav. Co.G
    Capt.
Roquemore, H.P. TX Cav. 1st Bn.St.Troops
    Co.C
Roquemore, H.P. TX 11th Inf. Co.E
Roquemore, J.A. GA 12th (Robinson's) Cav.
    (St.Guards) Co.D
Roquemore, J.A. GA Lt.Arty. Havis' Btty.
Roquemore, James A. AL Lt.Arty. Kolb's Btty.
Roquemore, James A. AL Hardy's Co. (Eufaula
    Minute Men)
Roquemore, James A. GA 11th Inf. Co.K
Roquemore, J.B. AL 36th Inf. Co.C
Roquemore, J.H. TX 11th Inf. Co.E
Roquemore, J.W. AL 17th Inf. Co.G
Roquemore, John GA Cobb's Legion Co.A
Roquemore, John M. GA 35th Inf. Co.G
Roquemore, Joseph GA Cobb's Legion Co.A
Roquemire, Joseph H. President's Guard,CSA
Roquemore, P.W. AL Lt.Arty. 20th Bn. Co.B
Roquemore, T.C. TX 11th Inf. Co.E
Roques, F. LA Mil. 3rd Regt.Eur.Brig. (Garde
    Francaise) Co.5
Roques, F. LA Mil. 3rd Regt.Eur.Brig. (Garde
    Francaise) Co.7
Roques, P. LA Mil. 3rd Regt.Eur.Brig. (Garde
    Francaise) Co.5 Cpl.
Roques, P. LA Mil. 3rd Regt.Eur.Brig. (Garde
    Francaise) Co.7
Roquet, Victor LA Mil. 2nd Regt. French Brig.
    Co.5
Roquimore, John T. AL Inf. 1st Regt. Co.A
Rorax, J.W. AL 27th Inf. Co.E
Rorax, W.D. TN Inf. Spencer's Co.
Rorax, William D. TN 44th Inf. Co.E
Rorax, William D. TN 44th (Cons.) Inf. Co.B
Rorch, F. VA 6th Cav. Co.E
Rorden, Henry GA Inf. (Muscogee Guards)
    Thornton's Co.
Rordy, O. MS Inf. 1st Bn.St.Troops (12 mo.
    '62-3) Co.D
Rore, John LA 22nd Inf. Wash. Marks' Co.
Rorer, Binney C. VA 57th Inf. Co.E 1st Lt.
Rorer, Charles H. VA 57th Inf. Co.D
Rorer, John H. VA 22nd Inf. Co.K
Rorer, John Q. VA Hvy.Arty. 10th Bn. Co.B
Rorer, Peter F. VA 22nd Inf. Co.K
Rorer, W.A. VA Lt.Arty. Fry's Co.
Rorer, Walter A. MS 20th Inf. Co.B Lt.Col.
Rorer, William E. MO 11th Inf. Co.C Sgt.
Rorer, William R. VA 51st Inf. Co.D
Rorex, James William AL 49th Inf. Co.C
Rorex, J.P. AL 6th Inf. Co.K
Rorex, J.T. GA 60th Inf. Co.E Sgt.

Rorex, J.W. Exch.Bn. Co.E,CSA
Rorex, Samuel TN 60th Mtd.Inf. Co.I Sgt.
Rorex, William P. TX 19th Cav. Co.A
Rorgers, J.W. TN 84th Inf. Co.C
Rorgers, P.W. TN 50th (Cons.) Inf. Co.H
Rorick, Branson O. VA 10th Cav. Co.H
Rorick, M. TX Cav. Morgan's Regt. Co.E
    Bugler
Rorie, Absalom AR 14th (Powers') Inf. Co.H
Rorie, A.E. GA Inf. 1st Loc.Troops (Augusta)
    Co.G
Rorie, A.J. MO Cav. Fristoe's Regt. Co.D
Rorie, David GA 35th Inf. Co.K Cpl.
Rorie, E.B. MS 32nd Inf. Co.D Cpl.
Rorie, G.B. GA Inf. 9th Bn. Co.E
Rorie, G.B. GA 37th Inf. Co.H
Rorie, J.A. AR 27th Inf. Co.F
Rorie, J.G. AR 27th Inf. Co.F
Rorie, John A. AR 45th Mil. Co.A
Rorie, John B. MO Cav. Fristoe's Regt. Co.D
Rorie, John G. AR 14th (Powers') Inf. Co.H
Rorie, John Howard TX 8th Cav. Co.H
Rorie, Samuel Jackson B. TX 8th Cav. Co.H
    Sgt.
Rorie, Thomas NC 23rd Inf. Co.A
Rorie, W.A. GA 37th Inf. Co.H
Rorie, W.A. GA 54th Inf. Co.K
Rorie, William H. GA 35th Inf.
Rorie, William H. MS 26th Inf. Co.B
Rorie, W.W. MS Cav. Ham's Regt. Co.A
Rorie, Z.T. SC Inf. 9th Bn. Co.E Cpl.
Rorie, Z.T. SC 26th Inf. Co.F
Rorison, A.C. TX 3rd Cav. Co.B 1st Lt.
Rorix, James A. NC Walker's Bn. Thomas'
    Legion Co.F
Rork, Francis TN 12th Inf. Co.E
Rork, Patrick AL Brooks' Home Guards
Rork, W.O. SC 15th Inf. Co.A 2nd Lt.
Rorke, Charles K.S. VA 52nd Inf. Co.K
Rorke, George VA 32nd Inf. Co.C
Rorke, Henry VA Hvy.Arty. 19th Bn. 1st Co.E
Rorke, John TN 15th Inf. Co.B
Rorke, M.O. LA 3rd (Wingfield's) Cav. Co.C
    1st Lt.
Rorks, William J. GA 6th Inf. Co.I
Roroboch, George B. LA 1st Hvy.Arty. (Reg.)
    Co.A Sgt.
Rorok, D.L. KY 7th Cav. Co.D
Rorrer, John W. VA 51st Inf. Co.H
Rorrer, Samuel G. VA 51st Inf. Co.H Sgt.
Rory, S. MO Cav. Wood's Regt. Co.A
Ros, Louis LA Mil. 1st Regt. French Brig. Co.8
Rosa, Alceste LA 1st Hvy.Arty. (Reg.) Co.G
Rosa, Antonio LA Mil. 5th Regt.Eur.Brig.
    (Spanish Regt.) Co.A,4
Rosa, Antonio LA 10th Inf. Co.F
Rosa, Frederick LA 17th Inf. Co.I
Rosa, Lastin LA 1st Hvy.Arty. (Reg.) Co.B
Rosa, Ramondela TX 3rd Inf. 1st Co.C
Rosado, Antonio LA Mil. 5th Regt.Eur.Brig.
    (Spanish Regt.) Co.10 Sgt.
Rosado, Jose LA Mil. 5th Regt.Eur.Brig.
    (Spanish Regt.) Co.6
Rosaint, Joseph Inf. School of Pract. Powell's
    Detach. Co.D
Rosales, Bidal TX Cav. Ragsdale's Bn. 1st Co.C
Rosales, Pedro TX 8th Inf. Co.C

Rosalie, Pierre LA Maddox's Regt.Res.Corps Co.B
Rosalles, Vidal TX Cav. Madison's Regt. Co.E
Rosaman, B.V. MS Cav. 1st Bn. (Montgomery's) St.Troops Hammond's Co.
Rosaman, C.S. MS Cav. 1st Bn. (Montgomery's) St.Troops Hammond's Co.
Rosaman, James MS Cav. 1st Bn. (Montgomery's) St.Troops Hammond's Co.
Rosamand, T.A. MS Inf. (Choctaw Silver Grays) Drane's Co.
Rosamon, Thomas C. MS Lt.Arty. Stanford's Co.
Rosamon, V.R. MS 11th (Perrin's) Cav. Co.C
Rosamon, William N. SC 16th Inf. Co.C Sgt.
Rosamond, Benjamin C. MS 29th Inf. Co.G
Rosamond, James F. SC 4th Inf. Co.G
Rosamond, J.C. AL 10th Cav. Sgt.Maj.
Rosamond, J.F. SC Inf. 13th Bn. Co.B 3rd Lt.
Rosamond, John C. MS 15th Inf. Co.D
Rosamond, Joseph GA Inf. 1st Loc.Troops (Augusta) Co.C
Rosamond, J.R. MS 40th Inf. Co.D
Rosamond, J.S. MS 4th Inf. Co.G Cpl.
Rosamond, Ried B. MS 31st Inf. Co.E
Rosamond, Samuel G. TX 6th Cav. Co.D Capt.
Rosamond, Theo. C. MS K. Williams' Co. (Gray's Port Greys)
Rosamond, V.B. MS 15th Inf. Co.D
Rosamond, William C. AL 56th Part.Rangers Asst.Surg.
Rosamond, Wm. Capers Gen. & Staff A.Surg.
Rosan, Charles W. MD 1st Cav. Co.D
Rosan, Sterling MD 1st Cav. Co.F
Rosanan, Ed TX 20th Inf. Co.B
Rosanbalm, W.H. TN Inf. 4th Conf.Regt. Co.A Sgt.
Rosans, Andreas TX 8th Inf. Co.I
Rosas, E.A. TN Cav. Jackson's Co.
Rosas, Eugene LA 18th Inf. Co.E Drum Maj.
Rosberg, G.H. VA Lt.Arty. Waters' Co.
Rosberry, James W. MO 16th Inf. Co.E Lt.
Rosberry, John Conf.Lt.Arty. 1st Reg.Btty.
Rosberry, John D. AR 37th Inf. Co.G
Rosboro, E.K. SC 3rd Bn.Res. Co.B
Rosboro, F.F. SC Manigault's Bn.Vol. Co.C
Rosboro, J.T. TX Cav. 6th Bn. Co.F Jr.2nd Lt.
Rosboro, R.A. SC Maniguailt's Bn.Vol. Co.C
Rosboro, Samuel SC Manigault's Bn.Vol. Co.C
Rosborough, C.B. LA 9th Inf. Co.D
Rosborough, D.D. TX 17th Inf. Co.I AQM
Rosborough, D.D. Gen. & Staff Capt.,AQM
Rosborough, Edward F. SC 12th Inf. Co.C
Rosborough, James F. SC Inf. 7th Bn. (Enfield Rifles) Co.B Sgt.
Rosborough, James L. SC 12th Inf. Co.F,C
Rosborough, James T. NC 6th Inf. Co.G 1st Lt.
Rosborough, John A. SC 12th Inf. Co.C Sgt.
Rosborough, R.A. SC 6th Cav. Co.C Sgt.
Rosborough, R.R. SC 6th Res. Co.H Capt.
Rosborough, Samuel SC 6th Cav. Co.C
Rosborough, Samuel Y. SC 12th Inf. Co.C 1st Lt.
Rosborough, Thomas G. TN 1st (Turney's) Inf. Co.F
Rosborough, Thomas L. SC 6th Cav. Co.C Sgt.

Rosborough, William Y. TX 17th Cons. Dismtd.Cav. Co.K
Rosborough, W.L. SC 6th Res. Co.H
Rosborough, W.M. TN 8th Inf. Co.C
Rosborrough, John SC 5th Inf. 2nd Co.E Sgt.
Rosborrough, W.J. TX 17th Inf. Co.K
Rosby, William C. SC 5th Inf. 2nd Co.E 2nd Lt.
Rosch, Frederick LA 6th Inf. Co.E
Roscher, A. VA 1st St.Res. Co.B
Roscher, David TX Lt.Arty. Hughes' Co.
Roscher, David TN Inf. Griffin's Bn. Co.F
Rosco, I. LA Inf.Cons.Crescent Regt. Co.G Color Cpl.
Rosco, John W. AL 35th Inf. Co.I
Rosco, T.J. KY 3rd Mtd.Inf. Co.L
Roscoe, Alex H. VA Lt.Arty. 1st Bn. Surg.
Roscoe, Alexander H. VA 1st Arty. Surg.
Roscoe, Alex. H. Gen. & Staff Surg.
Roscoe, G.W. AL 46th Inf. Co.G
Roscoe, James W. TN 18th Inf. Co.B Capt.
Roscoe, Joseph KY 3rd Mtd.Inf. Co.L
Roscoe, Martin L. TN 2nd (Robison's) Inf. Co.C
Roscoe, Martin Luther TN 2nd Cav. Co.C
Roscoe, Oliver SC 1st (Butler's) Inf. Co.C
Roscoe, S.H. KY 3rd Mtd.Inf. Co.L
Roscoe, T.L. LA Inf. 1st Bn. (St.Guards) Co.B
Roscoe, W.S. TN 18th Inf. Co.B
Roscr, Joseph LA 19th Inf. Co.F
Rose, --- GA 1st (Olmstead's) Inf. 1st Co.A
Rose, --- GA 1st Bn.S.S. Co.B
Rose, --- TX 24th & 25th Cav. (Cons.) Co.H
Rose, --- VA Horse Arty. G.W. Brown's Co.
Rose, --- VA VMI Co.C
Rose, A. KY 12th Cav. Co.G
Rose, A. NC 7th Sr.Res. Co.H
Rose, A. SC 25th Inf. Co.E
Rose, A. TX 3rd Inf. Co.B
Rose, A. VA Loc.Def. Jordan's Co.
Rose, A.B. SC 3rd Bn.Res. Co.D
Rose, Absalom KY 1st Inf. Co.B 3rd Lt.
Rose, A.G. TN 1st Cav. Co.B
Rose, A.H. NC 5th Inf. Co.D
Rose, A.H. NC Mil. Clark's Sp.Bn. Co.L
Rose, Ahigha Pinking TX Cav. Benavides' Regt. Gibson's Co.
Rose, A.J. TN 21st (Wilson's) Cav. Co.I
Rose, A.L. TN Inf. 4th Cons.Regt. Co.A
Rose, Albert MO 8th Cav. Co.F
Rose, Alex SC 4th Cav. Co.K
Rose, Alex SC Mil.Cav. Rutledge's Co.
Rose, Alexander AR 1st Mtd.Rifles Co.C
Rose, Alexander AR Cav. Gordon's Regt. Co.D
Rose, Alexander NC 37th Inf. Co.A
Rose, Alexander Gen. & Staff Capt.
Rose, Alexander L. TN 37th Inf. Co.G
Rose, Alfred MO Cav. Poindexter's Regt.
Rose, Alfred MO Inf. Clark's Regt. Co.C
Rose, Alfred NC 39th Inf. Co.E
Rose, Alfred A. AL 16th Inf. Co.C
Rose, Aligah Pinking TX Cav. Benavides' Regt. Gibson's Co.
Rose, Allen S. AR 25th Inf. Co.H
Rose, Amaleck NC 33rd Inf. Co.F
Rose, Amanuel GA Cav. 16th Bn. (St.Guards) Co.B
Rose, Anderson TN 7th (Duckworth's) Cav. Co.M

Rose, Andrew MO Cav. 3rd Bn. Co.E
Rose, Andrew J. GA 15th Inf. Co.C
Rose, Anthony B. KY Cav. Malone's Regt. Co.H
Rose, A.P. MS 7th Cav. Co.I
Rose, A.P. MS 18th Cav. Co.D
Rose, Archibald O. AR 14th (Powers') Inf. Co.G
Rose, Ardell NC 20th Inf. Co.C
Rose, Armstead KY 10th (Diamond's) Cav. Co.A
Rose, Arthur VA Lt.Arty. Clutter's Co.
Rose, A.S. AR 1st Mtd.Rifles Co.K
Rose, Asa S. TX Cav. Waller's Regt. Co.A
Rose, Asa S. TX 6th Inf. Co.E
Rose, Asbury MO St.Guard
Rose, Augustus SC 25th Inf. Co.E
Rose, Augustus C. MS 15th Inf. Co.B
Rose, Augustus P. VA 1st Lt.Arty. Co.B
Rose, Augustus P. VA 18th Inf. Co.B
Rose, A.W. SC 11th Inf. Co.B Music.
Rose, A.W. TN 39th Mtd.Inf. Co.A
Rose, B. GA 8th Cav. Old Co.I
Rose, B. VA 51st Inf. Co.K
Rose, Barney NC Lt.Arty. 3rd Bn. Co.B
Rose, Bazill AR 19th (Dawson's) Inf. Co.H
Rose, B.D. GA 19th Inf. Co.H
Rose, Benjamin GA 62nd Cav. Co.I
Rose, Benjamin F. AL 16th Inf. Co.A Cpl.
Rose, Benjamin F. AL 33rd Inf. Co.B
Rose, Benjamin F. AR 8th Inf. New Co.G Sgt.
Rose, Benjamin F. AR 14th (McCarver's) Inf. Co.H Sgt.
Rose, Benjamin F. TX Waul's Legion Co.E
Rose, Benjamin L. NC 54th Inf. Co.H
Rose, Benjamin O.W. GA 13th Cav. Co.G Cpl.
Rose, Benjamin O.W. GA Inf. White's Co.
Rose, Bennett B. AL 16th Inf. Co.C
Rose, Beuford C. TX 9th (Nichols') Inf. Co.C
Rose, B.F. KY 10th (Diamond's) Cav. Co.E Cpl.
Rose, B.F. TX Waul's Legion Co.E
Rose, B.F. VA 4th Cav. Co.C
Rose, Bill SC 1st Inf. Band
Rose, B.K. MO Cav. Freeman's Regt. Co.H
Rose, Bluford C. TX Lt.Arty. H. Van Buren's Co. Sgt.
Rose, Brunett TN Cav. 16th Bn. (Neal's) Co.E
Rose, Bunyan NC 43rd Inf. Co.C
Rose, C. SC 19th Inf. Co.D
Rose, C.A. TN 15th Inf. Co.D Capt.
Rose, C.A. TN Inf. 154th Sr.Regt. Co.L 2nd Lt.
Rose, C.A. VA 3rd Inf.Loc.Def. Co.F
Rose, Calvin SC 4th St.Troops Co.C
Rose, Calvin TN 54th Inf. Co.H
Rose, Carroll TX Cav. Ragsdale's Co.
Rose, C.C. AR 12th Inf. Lt.
Rose, C.C. TX 8th Cav. Co.B
Rose, C.C. TX 35th (Brown's) Cav. Co.A
Rose, C.G. TN 4th Cav. Co.B
Rose, C.G. TN Arty. Fisher's Co.
Rose, C.H. TX Cav. Waller's Regt. Co.A
Rose, Charles AR 25th Inf. Co.H
Rose, Charles VA 2nd St.Res. Co.B
Rose, Charles B. AR 15th (N.W.) Inf. Co.B
Rose, Charles B. VA 54th Inf. Co.C
Rose, Chesley H. TX Cav. McCord's Frontier Regt. Co.H Sgt.
Rose, Christ. C. MO 6th Cav. Co.G
Rose, Claiborne C. AR 1st Mtd.Rifles Co.I

Rose, Clinton G. KY 11th Cav. Co.A
Rose, Cornelius C. VA 47th Inf. Co.E
Rose, Cuthbert O. VA 6th Cav. Co.A
Rose, C.W. TX Cav. Giddings' Bn. Maddox's
 Co.
Rose, D. LA Dreux's Cav. Co.A
Rose, D. LA Mil. Lewis Guards
Rose, D. Brush Bn.
Rose, Dallas TN 42nd Inf. 1st Co.E
Rose, Daniel AR 26th Inf. Co.I
Rose, Daniel LA Inf. 16th Bn. (Conf.Guards
 Resp.Bn.) Co.B
Rose, Daniel MO Cav. Wood's Regt. Co.F
Rose, Daniel E. AR 13th Inf. Co.E Cpl.
Rose, Daniel E. KY 7th Mtd.Inf. 1st Co.K Cpl.
Rose, Daniel M. NC 15th Inf. Co.B Sgt.
Rose, David LA 1st Cav. Co.D
Rose, David LA 16th Inf. Co.G 1st Sgt.
Rose, David TX 10th Cav. Co.H Bugler
Rose, David A. NC 47th Inf. Co.K Cpl.
Rose, David D. MS 12th Cav. Co.E
Rose, David J. TN 13th (Gore's) Cav. Co.G
Rose, Dempsey NC 5th Inf. Co.G
Rose, D.H. Inf. Bailey's Cons.Regt. Co.A
Rose, D.H. TX 7th Inf. Co.C
Rose, Dorset E. NC 22nd Inf. Co.L
Rose, D.R. MO 16th Inf. Co.G Cpl.
Rose, D. William NC 17th Inf. (2nd Org.) Co.I
Rose, E. LA 7th Cav. Co.A
Rose, E. MO 3rd & 5th Cons.Inf.
Rose, E. TX 7th Cav. Co.G
Rose, E. Sap. & Min. Flynn's Co.,CSA
Rose, E.A. TX 7th Cav. Co.G
Rose, E.D. NC 1st Cav. (9th St.Troops) Co.B
Rose, Edmond TN 34th Inf. 2nd Co.C
Rose, Edmund GA 3rd Res. Co.K Sgt.
Rose, Edward GA 4th Inf. Co.B
Rose, Edward NC 55th Inf. Co.B
Rose, Edward VA 22nd Cav. Co.G
Rose, Edward VA 22nd Inf. Co.G
Rose, Edward L. TX 16th Cav. Co.H
Rose, Edward W. VA 51st Inf. Co.B
Rose, Edwin NC 47th Inf. Co.D
Rose, Eli VA 16th Cav. Co.F
Rose, Eli VA Cav. 34th Bn. Co.C
Rose, Elias NC 50th Inf. Co.C
Rose, Elias VA 21st Cav. 1st Co.E
Rose, Elias P. VA 17th Cav. Co.H
Rose, Elijah VA 51st Inf. Co.F
Rose, Elisha NC 35th Inf. Co.C
Rose, E.M. KY 13th Cav. Co.K Sgt.
Rose, E.M. SC 1st Cav. Co.K
Rose, E.M. SC 5th Inf. 1st Co.I
Rose, E.M. SC Palmetto S.S. Co.G
Rose, Emanuel LA 27th Inf. Co.H
Rose, Emanuel NC 29th Inf. Co.I
Rose, Enoch GA Cav. 16th Bn. (St.Guards) Co.B
 Sgt.
Rose, Enoch GA Cav. 16th Bn. (St.Guards) Co.C
Rose, Ephraim TN Cav. 12th Bn. (Day's) Co.B
Rose, E. Porter MD 1st Cav. Co.C
Rose, E.W. GA 5th Inf. Co.K Sgt.
Rose, F. VA 17th Inf. Co.E
Rose, F.G. AR 1st (Dobbin's) Cav. Co.C
Rose, F.G. AR 13th Inf. Co.K
Rose, F.H. TN Hvy.Arty. Johnston's Co. Cpl.
Rose, Fielding AR 16th Inf. Co.F

Rose, Fielding NC 47th Inf. Co.K
Rose, Fielding VA 17th Cav. Co.I
Rose, Fielding VA Inf.
Rose, Fleming VA Cav. 36th Bn. Co.C
Rose, Francis M. MS 2nd Inf. Co.I
Rose, Francis M. TN 43rd Inf. Co.H
Rose, Frank AL 12th Inf. Co.C
Rose, Frank AL 42nd Inf. Co.I
Rose, Franklin AL 18th Bn.Vol. Co.B
Rose, Franklin NC 29th Inf. Co.G
Rose, Franklin NC 29th Inf. Co.I
Rose, Franklin VA 22nd Inf. Co.G
Rose, Frank R. NC 5th Cav. (63rd St.Troops)
 Co.A Ch.Bugler
Rose, F.W. GA 1st (Olmstead's) Inf. Screven's
 Co.
Rose, F.W. GA Inf. 18th Bn. Co.A,C
Rose, F.W. TN 4th Inf. Co.B
Rose, G. MS 7th Cav. 2nd Co.G
Rose, G. TN 14th (Neely's) Cav. Co.A
Rose, Ganiss TN 9th Inf. Co.F
Rose, G.B. Exch.Bn. 1st Co.B,CSA
Rose, G.C. TN 19th (Biffle's) Cav. Co.D
Rose, George GA 54th Inf. Co.F
Rose, George TX Cav. Waller's Regt. Co.E
Rose, George TX 6th Inf. Co.A
Rose, George VA Cav. 46th Bn. Co.A
Rose, George H. VA Cav. 46th Bn. Co.D
Rose, George H. VA 12th Inf. 2nd Co.I
Rose, George H. VA 41st Inf. Co.A 1st Sgt.
Rose, George J. AR Inf. Clear Lake Ind.Guards
Rose, George J. TX 4th Cav. Co.I
Rose, George J. TX Cav. Ragsdale's Bn. 2nd
 Co.C
Rose, George M. NC 66th Inf. Adj.
Rose, George R. VA 26th Cav. Co.A
Rose, George T. NC 15th Inf. Co.A
Rose, George T. TN 9th (Ward's) Cav. Co.D
Rose, George W. AL 6th Inf. Co.L Sgt.
Rose, George W. GA 39th Inf. Co.H
Rose, George W. TN 5th Inf. 1st Co.C
Rose, George W. TX Cav. Giddings' Bn. Car-
 rington's Co.
Rose, George W. TX 9th (Nichols') Inf. Co.H
 1st Lt.
Rose, George W. VA 10th Cav. Co.G
Rose, George W. VA 25th Cav. Co.A
Rose, George W. VA 48th Inf.
Rose, G.I. VA Inf. 1st Bn. Co.B
Rose, G.M.D. AL 56th Part.Rangers Co.F
Rose, G.M.D. AL 55th Vol. Co.F
Rose, G.P. NC Mil. Clark's Sp.Bn. Co.L
Rose, Granby B. MO 3rd Cav. Co.G
Rose, Grantham AR 1st (Crawford's) Cav. Co.E
Rose, Green NC 60th Inf. Co.H
Rose, Gustin AR 27th Inf. New Co.C
Rose, G.W. AR 5th Inf. Co.A
Rose, G.W. NC 2nd Cav. (19th St.Troops) Co.H
Rose, G.W. TX 35th (Likens') Cav. Co.E Jr.2nd
 Lt.
Rose, G.W. TX 4th Inf. Co.B
Rose, H. GA Arty. St.Troops Pruden's Btty.
Rose, Hardin M. TN 1st (Feild's) Inf. Co.K
Rose, Harmon H. TX 15th Inf. Co.B
Rose, Harris NC Alex. Brown's Co.
Rose, Harry J. VA 51st Inf. Co.G 2nd Lt.
Rose, Harvey TX 5th Inf. Co.H

Rose, Haywood NC 2nd Inf. Co.B,K
Rose, H.B. NC 30th Inf. Co.H Sgt.
Rose, H.C. NC 1st Jr.Res. Co.A
Rose, H.C. NC 50th Inf. Co.C
Rose, Heistin VA Lt.Arty. Cayce's Co.
Rose, Henry LA Inf. 1st Sp.Bn. (Wheat's) New
 Co.D
Rose, Henry SC Manigault's Bn.Vol. Co.A
Rose, Henry TN Cav. 7th Bn. (Bennett's) Co.F
 Music.
Rose, Henry TN 22nd (Barteau's) Cav. Co.G
Rose, Henry TX Cav. 2nd Regt. Co.C Ord.Sgt.
Rose, Henry VA 6th Inf. Ferguson's Co.
Rose, Henry C. TN 19th Inf. Co.K Sgt.
Rose, Henry C. TN 29th Inf. Co.I
Rose, Henry E. MO Cav. Wood's Regt. Co.C
Rose, Henry J. VA Horse Arty. Shoemaker's Co.
Rose, Henry L. MS 30th Inf. Co.H
Rose, Henry M. TN 5th Inf. 1st Co.C, Co.A
Rose, Henry M. VA 6th Bn.Res. Co.D
Rose, Herman LA Inf. 1st Sp.Bn. (Wheat's)
 Co.C
Rose, Herman VA Hvy.Arty. 19th Bn. 3rd Co.C
Rose, Hesekiah AR 14th (Powers') Inf. Co.H
 Cpl.
Rose, Hezekiah TX 27th Cav. Co.K
Rose, H.F. GA 18th Inf. Co.C
Rose, H.F. GA Inf. Fuller's Co.
Rose, H.F. TN 1st Hvy.Arty. Co.L
Rose, Hiram MO Cav. 3rd Bn. Co.E
Rose, Hiram MO 10th Inf. Co.D
Rose, H.J. TX 19th Inf. Co.G
Rose, H.L. AL 18th Bn.Vol. Co.B 2nd Lt.
Rose, H.L. MS 24th Inf. Co.C
Rose, H.M. TN 10th (DeMoss') Cav. Co.I Cpl.
Rose, H.M. TN Cav. Napier's Bn. Co.E
Rose, Howard E. VA Lt.Arty. Cayce's Co.
Rose, Howell M. GA Cav. 7th Bn. (St.Guards)
 Co.C Sgt.
Rose, H. Robert MO 8th Inf. Co.A
Rose, Hugh F. Sig.Corps,CSA
Rose, Ira VA 48th Inf. Co.A
Rose, Ira P. VA 48th Inf. Co.A
Rose, Isaac AR 14th (Powers') Inf. Co.H
Rose, Isaac VA Inf. 45th Bn. Co.C
Rose, Isaac T. NC Walker's Bn. Thomas' Legion
 Co.F
Rose, Isaac T. TN 5th (McKenzie's) Cav. Co.K
Rose, Isaac W. NC 28th Inf. Co.I Music.
Rose, Isaah AL 9th Inf. Co.E
Rose, Isaiah TN 60th Mtd.Inf. Co.A
Rose, J. AR 58th Mil. Co.A
Rose, J. AR Inf. (Loc.Def.) Ernest's Co.
Rose, J. LA Mil. 3rd Regt.Eur.Brig. (Garde
 Francaise) Co.1 1st Sgt.
Rose, J. MO 5th Cav. Co.K
Rose, J. TN 22nd Cav. Co.H
Rose, J. TX 27th Cav. Co.K
Rose, J.A. AL 17th Inf. Co.C
Rose, J.A. GA 39th Inf. Co.H
Rose, J.A. VA 4th Cav. Co.C
Rose, Jack AL Cav. Lewis' Bn. Co.C
Rose, Jackson TN 1st (Carter's) Cav. Co.M
Rose, Jackson VA 108th Mil. Co.G,E
Rose, Jacob VA 50th Inf. Co.K
Rose, Jacob M. NC 1st Cav. (9th St.Troops)
 Co.K Cpl.

Rose, James AL 4th (Roddey's) Cav. Co.F
Rose, James AR 7th Inf. Co.K
Rose, James GA Cav. 16th Bn. (St.Guards) Co.B
Rose, James KY 8th Cav. Co.D
Rose, James NC Walker's Bn. Thomas' Legion Co.A Sgt.
Rose, James TN Cav. Welcker's Bn. Co.A
Rose, James TN 55th (Brown's) Inf. Co.B
Rose, James TX 10th Cav. Co.H
Rose, James TX Cav. Benavides' Regt. Gibson's Co.D
Rose, James TX 20th Inf. Co.H
Rose, James VA Lt.Arty. 38th Bn. Co.C
Rose, James VA 7th Inf. Co.K
Rose, James VA 8th Inf. Co.H
Rose, James VA 37th Inf. Co.E
Rose, James VA 60th Inf. Co.A
Rose, James VA 108th Mil. Co.E
Rose, James A. AR 36th Inf. Co.A
Rose, James A. VA 151st Mil. Co.B
Rose, James D. AR 17th (Lemoyne's) Inf. Co.D
Rose, James D. AR 21st Inf. Co.H
Rose, James E. AR 2nd Inf. New Co.C
Rose, James E. VA Lt.Arty. Carpenter's Co. Cpl.
Rose, James E. VA 27th Inf. Co.A Cpl.
Rose, James G. TN 29th Inf. Co.D Capt.
Rose, James G. TN 61st Mtd.Inf. Col.
Rose, James H. MS 15th Inf. Co.E
Rose, James H. TN 30th Inf. Co.B
Rose, James H. TX 1st (Yager's) Cav. Co.D
Rose, James H. TX Cav. Benavides' Regt. Gibson's Co.
Rose, James H. TX Lt.Arty. H. Van Buren's Co.
Rose, James H. TX 9th (Nichols') Inf. Co.C
Rose, James H. TX Inf. Griffin's Bn. Co.D Music.
Rose, James H. VA Lt.Arty. E.J. Anderson's Co. Cpl.
Rose, James Henry H. TN 14th Inf. Co.L
Rose, James M. MS 34th Inf. Co.E
Rose, James M. TX 12th Cav. Co.A
Rose, James N. TX Cav. Martin's Regt. Co.B
Rose, James P. TN 13th (Gore's) Cav. Co.G
Rose, James T. GA 13th Inf. Co.D
Rose, James T. NC 1st Cav. (9th St.Troops) Co.H
Rose, James T. NC 5th Cav. (63rd St.Troops) Co.A Sgt.
Rose, James T. NC 1st Inf. (6 mo. '61) Co.F Sgt.
Rose, J.B. AR 51st Mil. Co.B
Rose, J.C. KY 3rd Mtd.Inf. Co.G
Rose, J.C. LA Mil.Conf.Guards Regt. Co.B
Rose, J.C. NC 2nd Conscr. Co.C
Rose, J.C. NC 59th Inf. Co.C
Rose, J.C. NC Alex. Brown's Co.
Rose, J.C. NC Mil. Clark's Sp.Bn. Co.K
Rose, J.D. AR 16th Inf. Co.G
Rose, J.D. TX 5th Inf. Co.D
Rose, J.D. Conf.Cav. 6th Bn.
Rose, J.E. TN 22nd Inf. Co.C Cpl.
Rose, Jeff. AL 18th Bn.Vol. Co.B
Rose, Jeff. TN 17th Inf. Co.I
Rose, Jefferson L. AR Cav. Gordon's Regt. Co.E
Rose, Jeremiah MO St.Guard QMSgt.
Rose, Jerry TN 35th Inf. Co.L

Rose, Jerry TN 36th Inf. Co.L
Rose, Jesse KY Fields' Co. (Part.Rangers)
Rose, Jesse KY 1st Bn.Mtd.Rifles Co.E
Rose, Jesse KY 5th Mtd.Inf. Co.D
Rose, Jesse MD 1st Cav. Co.F
Rose, Jesse VA 16th Cav. Co.F
Rose, Jesse VA Cav. Caldwell's Bn. Taylor's Co.
Rose, Jesse VA Horse Arty. D. Shanks' Co.
Rose, Jesse C. SC 2nd Inf. Co.A
Rose, Jesse F. LA 19th Inf. Co.K Cpl.
Rose, J.F. AR 1st Mtd.Rifles Co.A Sgt.
Rose, J.G. MO 16th Inf. Co.E
Rose, J.H. VA Lt.Arty. 38th Bn. Co.C
Rose, J.J. AR 16th Inf. Co.F
Rose, J.J. MS 22nd Inf. Co.I
Rose, J.J. NC 57th Inf. Co.A Cpl.
Rose, J.J. SC Mil.Arty. 1st Regt. Walter's Co., Co.C
Rose, J.J. TX 27th Cav. Co.E
Rose, J.L. TX 26th Cav. 1st Co.G
Rose, J.L. TX Waul's Legion Co.D
Rose, J.M. AR 38th Inf. Old Co.I, Co.H Cpl.
Rose, J.M. VA Mtd.Guard 8th Congr.Dist.
Rose, J. Minor VA Inf. 25th Bn. Co.A
Rose, J.N. AR 1st (Dobbin's) Cav. Co.C
Rose, Joel NC Cav. 5th Bn. Co.B
Rose, Joel NC 58th Inf. Co.A
Rose, Joel VA Cav. 34th Bn. Co.C Sgt.
Rose, John AL 25th Mil. Co.G
Rose, John AL 48th Inf. Co.E 2nd Lt.
Rose, John AR 5th Inf. Co.G
Rose, John AR 14th (Powers') Inf. Co.G
Rose, John, Jr. AR 27th Inf. Co.A
Rose, John AR 27th Inf. Co.F
Rose, John GA 39th Inf. Co.B
Rose, John KY 10th (Johnson's) Cav. New Co.B
Rose, John KY 2nd Bn.Mtd.Rifles Co.D
Rose, John KY 5th Mtd.Inf. Co.K
Rose, John LA 1st Cav. Co.I
Rose, John MS Cav. 1st Bn. (Miller's) Co.A
Rose, John MO Cav. Wood's Regt. Co.A
Rose, John MO 1st Inf. Co.K
Rose, John MO 3rd & 5th Cons.Inf. Sgt.
Rose, John NC 39th Inf. Co.E
Rose, John NC 47th Inf. Co.D
Rose, John SC Hvy.Arty. 15th (Lucas') Bn. Co.A
Rose, John SC 14th Inf. Co.A
Rose, John TN 2nd (Ashby's) Cav. Co.G,E Sgt.
Rose, John TN Cav. 4th Bn. (Branner's) Co.B
Rose, John TN 8th Cav. Co.E
Rose, John TN 8th (Smith's) Cav. Co.L
Rose, John, Jr. TN 13th (Gore's) Cav. Co.G Sgt.
Rose, John TN 1st (Turney's) Inf. Co.A
Rose, John TN 19th Inf. Co.A
Rose, John TN 35th Inf. Co.L Cpl.
Rose, John TN 36th Inf. Co.L Cpl.
Rose, John TX 2nd Cav. Co.A,H
Rose, John TX Cav. Hardeman's Regt. Co.H
Rose, John TX 6th Inf. Co.A
Rose, John TX 10th Inf. Co.I
Rose, John VA 16th Cav. Co.C
Rose, John VA 16th Cav. Co.H
Rose, John VA 21st Cav. 1st Co.E

Rose, John VA Cav. Caldwell's Bn. Hankins' Co.
Rose, John VA Cav. Ferguson's Bn. Ferguson's Co.
Rose, John VA Lt.Arty. Pollock's Co.
Rose, John VA 30th Inf. Co.B
Rose, John VA 36th Inf. 2nd Co.B
Rose, John VA 64th Mtd.Inf. 2nd Co.F
Rose, John Mead's Conf.Cav. Co.I Cpl.
Rose, John A. FL 3rd Inf. Co.B Sgt.
Rose, John A. NC 5th Inf. Co.K
Rose, John A. NC 42nd Inf. Co.G
Rose, John A. SC Inf. 7th Bn. (Enfield Rifles) Co.B
Rose, John B. MO Searcy's Bn.S.S. Co.B Cpl.
Rose, John B. TN 29th Inf. Co.B
Rose, John C. NC 4th Inf. Co.I
Rose, John C. VA 63rd Inf. Co.A
Rose, John D. KY 2nd Mtd.Inf. Co.C
Rose, John D. VA 6th Bn.Res. Co.E
Rose, John E. AR 47th (Crandall's) Cav. Co.H
Rose, John E. NC 44th Inf. Co.A
Rose, John E. VA 21st Cav. 1st Co.E
Rose, John F. TX 13th Vol. Co.F
Rose, John H. KY Jessee's Bn.Mtd.Riflemen Co.A
Rose, John H. TX Cav. 3rd (Yager's) Bn. Co.D
Rose, John H. TX 17th Cav. Co.D
Rose, John H. TX 17th Cons.Dismtd.Cav. Co.C
Rose, John H. VA 12th Inf. Co.H
Rose, John J. AR 6th Inf. Co.G
Rose, John M. AL 36th Inf. Co.D
Rose, John M. AR 1st Mtd.Rifles Co.C 1st Lt.
Rose, John M. VA Lt.Arty. Thornton's Co.
Rose, John M. Churchill's Brig. 1st Lt.,Ord.Off.
Rose, John N. VA 3rd Inf.Loc.Def. Co.D
Rose, John P. MS 2nd Inf. Co.A
Rose, John P. MO Inf. 1st Bn. Co.B
Rose, John P. TN 55th (Brown's) Inf. Co.E
Rose, John R. NC 2nd Cav. (19th St.Troops) Co.C
Rose, John R. NC Cav. 12th Bn. Co.A
Rose, John W. AR 14th (Powers') Inf. Co.H
Rose, John W. GA 22nd Inf. Co.C
Rose, John W. LA 27th Inf. Co.F
Rose, John W. MO 3rd Cav. Co.H
Rose, John W. TN 5th (McKenzie's) Cav. Co.C,D
Rose, John W. TX 19th Cav. Co.K
Rose, John W. TX Inf. Griffin's Bn. Co.D
Rose, John W. VA 15th Cav. Co.G
Rose, John W. VA 25th Mil. Co.C
Rose, John W. VA 51st Inf. Co.A
Rose, John W. VA 64th Mtd.Inf. Co.C
Rose, Jonathan MO 1st & 4th Cons.Inf. Co.K Sgt.
Rose, Joseph NC 2nd Arty. (36th St.Troops) Co.G
Rose, Joseph NC 2nd Inf. Co.I
Rose, Joseph SC 12th Inf. Co.C
Rose, Joseph TX 36th Cav. Co.C
Rose, Joseph TX 5th Inf. Co.C
Rose, Joseph VA Cav. 34th Bn. Co.D
Rose, Joseph VA 51st Inf. Co.A
Rose, Joseph B. AR 35th Inf. Co.B
Rose, Joseph M. VA 29th Inf. Co.I
Rose, Joseph P. NC 20th Inf. Co.G

Rose, Joseph P. TN 34th Inf. 2nd Co.C
Rose, Joseph T. TX Cav. Martin's Regt. Co.B
Rose, Joseph W. VA 108th Mil. Lemons' Co.
Rose, Joshua TX 6th Inf. Co.E Music.
Rose, Joshua VA 16th Cav. Co.C
Rose, Joshua VA 4th Res. Co.I
Rose, Joshua VA 29th Inf. Co.H
Rose, J.P. LA 1st (Nelligan's) Inf. Co.B
Rose, J.P. TN Cav. Napier's Bn. Co.E
Rose, J.R. AR 1st (Dobbin's) Cav. Co.C
Rose, J.R. AR 15th (Johnson's) Inf. Co.A
Rose, J.S. AR 30th Inf. Co.B
Rose, J.S. MO 3rd Inf. Co.G
Rose, J.T. KY Jessee's Bn.Mtd.Riflemen Co.A
Rose, J.T. MS 1st (Patton's) Inf. Co.H
Rose, J.T. MS 30th Inf. Co.D Cpl.
Rose, Julius LA Mil. 4th Regt. 1st Brig. 1st Div. Co.I
Rose, J.W. AR 16th Inf. Co.I Sgt.
Rose, J.W. LA 25th Inf. Co.F
Rose, J.W. NC 57th Inf. Co.F
Rose, J.W. SC 12th Inf. Co.C
Rose, J.W. TN 24th Inf. Co.C 2nd Lt.
Rose, J.W. TX 5th Cav. Co.G
Rose, J.W. TX 12th Field Btty.
Rose, J.W.A. NC 57th Inf. Co.C Sgt.
Rose, K. KY 12th Cav. Co.C
Rose, Kenneth R. KY 2nd (Woodward's) Cav. Co.A,B Sgt.
Rose, Kernelias VA 51st Inf. Co.F
Rose, L. SC 1st Mtd.Mil. Heyward's Co.
Rose, L. TN 7th (Duckworth's) Cav. Co.I
Rose, L. TN 12th (Green's) Cav. Co.G
Rose, L.B. Gen. & Staff A.Surg.
Rose, L.C. AL 22nd Inf. Co.F
Rose, L.C. AL 39th Inf. Co.A
Rose, L.C. NC 13th Inf. Co.A
Rose, L.D. AR Cav. Gordon's Regt. Co.H
Rose, Levi GA 8th Cav. Old Co.I, Co.H
Rose, Levi GA 62nd Cav. Co.I
Rose, Levi NC 6th Inf. Co.E
Rose, Levi VA 11th Cav. Co.C
Rose, Lewis TN Cav. 12th Bn. (Day's) Co.B
Rose, Lewis VA Lt.Arty. Moore's Co.
Rose, Lewis Conf.Lt.Arty. Richardson's Bn. Co.D
Rose, Lewis D. NC 12th Inf. Co.C
Rose, Lewis D. NC 30th Inf. Co.B
Rose, Lewis H. AL Inf. 1st Regt. Co.D 1st Sgt.
Rose, Lewis W. VA 27th Inf. Co.C
Rose, L.H. LA 25th Inf. Co.F 1st Sgt.
Rose, Littlebury R. NC 33rd Inf. Co.C 2nd Lt.
Rose, Louis TX 15th Cav. Co.D
Rose, Louis TX 19th Cav. Co.K
Rose, Louis C. NC 5th Cav. (63rd St.Troops) Co.A
Rose, Lovell VA Lt.Arty. Cayce's Co.
Rose, L.R. NC 20th Inf. Co.B Cpl.
Rose, L. Rowan NC 1st Cav. (9th St.Troops) Co.F
Rose, L.W. Mead's Conf.Cav. Co.I 2nd Lt.
Rose, M. AR 35th Inf.
Rose, M. MO Cav. Wood's Regt. Co.A Cpl.
Rose, Major KY 3rd Bn.Mtd.Rifles Co.B
Rose, Manon TN Cav. 12th Bn. (Day's) Co.B
Rose, Marcus GA 1st Reg. Co.B
Rose, Marcus MS 24th Inf. Co.G Cpl.

Rose, Marcus A. VA 1st Inf. Co.H
Rose, Marshall VA 22nd Inf. Co.E
Rose, Marshall J. MS 33rd Inf. Co.G Capt.
Rose, Martin AL 18th Bn.Vol. Co.B
Rose, Martin MO 1st & 4th Cons.Inf. Co.B
Rose, Martin MO 4th Inf. Co.G
Rose, Martin D. SC 12th Inf. Co.D Sgt.
Rose, Martin H. MS 15th Inf. Co.K 4th Cpl.
Rose, Martin V. TN 1st (Turney's) Inf. Co.H
Rose, Martin V. TN 24th Inf. Co.L
Rose, Mathew MS 18th Inf. Co.C
Rose, Mathew NC 43rd Inf. Co.C
Rose, Mathew 7th Conf.Cav. 2nd Co.I
Rose, Mathias NC 12th Inf. Co.O
Rose, Mathias NC 32nd Inf. Co.C,D
Rose, M.B. GA 46th Inf. Co.A
Rose, M.C. LA 13th Bn. (Part.Rangers) Co.F
Rose, M.F. MS 2nd Cav. Co.G
Rose, M.F. MS 5th Cav. Co.B
Rose, Michael FL 8th Inf. Co.F
Rose, Miles W. MS 15th Inf. Co.K Capt.
Rose, Miller F. MS 15th Inf. Co.K
Rose, M.M. TN 51st (Cons.) Inf. Co.C
Rose, Monterville MO Inf. Clark's Regt. Co.C
Rose, Montgomery B. MO 10th Inf. Co.G
Rose, Morris Alexis MS 15th Inf. Co.G
Rose, Mortimer TN Arty. Bibb's Co.
Rose, M.W. VA 3rd (Archer's) Bn.Res. Co.A
Rose, N. AL 11th Cav. Co.D
Rose, Nathan NC 1st Cav. (9th St.Troops) Co.B
Rose, Nathaniel A. MS 15th Inf. Co.B
Rose, Newton TX 11th Cav. Co.C Sgt.
Rose, Newton C. TX Cav. Benavides' Regt. Co.F
Rose, Newton C. TX Lt.Arty. H. Van Buren's Co.
Rose, Newton C. TX 9th (Nichols') Inf. Co.C
Rose, Newton C. TX Inf. Griffin's Bn. Co.D
Rose, Nicholas C. TN 14th Inf. Co.C Cpl.
Rose, Noah NC Part.Rangers Swindell's Co.
Rose, O. LA Mil. Lewis Guards
Rose, O.A.V. GA 49th Inf. Co.K Capt.
Rose, Oscar TX 1st Hvy.Arty. Co.I
Rose, Oscar TX 15th Inf. Co.B
Rose, P. AR 45th Mil. Co.A
Rose, P.A.B. AR 50th Mil. Co.G
Rose, Paul AR 27th Inf. Co.F
Rose, Payton R. GA Inf. 1st Loc.Troops (Augusta) Co.A
Rose, Permenius T. AR 14th (Powers') Inf. Co.G
Rose, Peter MO 10th Inf. Co.C
Rose, Philip M. VA 47th Inf. Co.E
Rose, Pickett L. NC 5th Cav. (63rd St.Troops) Co.A
Rose, P.K. AR 15th (Johnson's) Inf. Co.A Sgt.
Rose, P.L. NC Lt.Arty. 13th Bn. Co.C
Rose, Pompey S. NC 4th Inf. Co.G
Rose, P.R. GA Inf. 18th Bn. (St.Guards) Adam's Co.
Rose, Q.L. NC Lt.Arty. Thomas' Legion Levi's Btty.
Rose, Q.L. VA Lt.Arty. Barr's Co.
Rose, Quilla L. NC 1st Cav. (9th St.Troops) Co.K
Rose, Quillan L. NC 29th Inf. Co.F
Rose, R.A. NC 5th Inf. Co.K
Rose, R.A. SC 12th Inf. Co.C

Rose, R.A. TN 7th (Duckworth's) Cav. Co.H Cpl.
Rose, R.D. TN 4th Inf. Co.B
Rose, Reuben GA 34th Inf. Co.H
Rose, Reuben NC 33rd Inf. Co.B
Rose, R.H. AR 1st Inf. Co.K
Rose, R.H. TN 7th (Duckworth's) Cav.
Rose, R.H. TN 16th (Logwood's) Cav. Co.I
Rose, Richard MO 3rd Cav. Co.E
Rose, Richard TN 62nd Mtd.Inf. Dodd's Co.
Rose, Richard VA Mil. Grayson Cty.
Rose, Richard Exch.Bn. 1st Co.B,CSA
Rose, Richard R. VA 55th Inf. Co.L
Rose, Richard R. VA 92nd Mil. Co.A Sgt.
Rose, R.M. AR 30th Inf. Co.A
Rose, R.M. GA Cav. 22nd Bn. (St.Guards) Co.F
Rose, R.M. SC Cav.Bn. Holcombe Legion Co.A
Rose, Robbin NC 12th Inf. Co.H
Rose, Robbin NC 32nd Inf. Co.H
Rose, Robert, Jr. KY 5th Mtd.Inf. Co.D
Rose, Robert, Sr. KY 5th Mtd.Inf. Co.D
Rose, Robert NC 1st Cav. (9th St.Troops) Co.F
Rose, Robert TN Cav. Jackson's Regt.
Rose, Robert TX Cav. Hardeman's Regt. Co.F Sgt.
Rose, Robert TX 13th Vol. Co.F
Rose, Robert VA Lt.Arty. Brander's Co.
Rose, Robert VA Hvy.Arty. Wilkinson's Co.
Rose, Robert VA 3rd Arty. Co.H
Rose, Robert VA 51st Inf. Co.A
Rose, Robert A. TN 7th (Duckworth's) Cav. Co.I
Rose, Robert C. TN 5th Inf. 1st Co.C
Rose, Robert F. NC 46th Inf. Co.C
Rose, Robert H. AL 4th Inf. Co.E
Rose, Robert L. KY 5th Mtd.Inf. Co.D
Rose, Robert M. VA 10th Cav. Co.G
Rose, Robert T. MS 1st (Patton's) Inf. Co.A 2nd Lt.
Rose, Robert W. VA 54th Mil. Co.B
Rose, R.R. AR 51st Mil. Co.F
Rose, Ruffin NC 55th Inf. Co.A
Rose, Rufus M. GA 10th Inf. Co.G Cpl.
Rose, Rupt VA 2nd St.Res. Co.B
Rose, Russell C. VA 45th Inf. Co.K
Rose, S. TN Lt.Arty. Scott's Co.
Rose, S. TX 7th Cav. Co.G
Rose, Sampson W. NC 33rd Inf. Co.H
Rose, Samuel AR 15th (N.W.) Inf. Co.A
Rose, Samuel AR 16th Inf. Co.G
Rose, Samuel KY 10th (Diamond's) Cav. Co.A
Rose, Samuel MS Lt.Arty. (Warren Lt.Arty.) Swett's Co.
Rose, Samuel VA Cav. 36th Bn.
Rose, Samuel NC 39th Inf. Co.C
Rose, Samuel NC 58th Inf. Co.K,A
Rose, Samuel SC 12th Inf. Co.C
Rose, Samuel TN Hvy.Arty. Johnston's Co.
Rose, Samuel VA 16th Cav. Co.C
Rose, Samuel VA Cav. Caldwell's Bn. Hankins' Co.
Rose, Samuel Sig.Corps,CSA
Rose, Samuel A. NC 5th Inf. Co.A Sgt.
Rose, Samuel L. MS 30th Inf. Co.H Sgt.
Rose, Samuel S. VA Inf. 21st Bn. 1st Co.D 2nd Lt.
Rose, Samuel W. NC 4th Inf. Co.G

Rose, Sandy TX Waul's Legion Co.B
Rose, S.B. AR 58th Mil. Co.E
Rose, S.H. MS 16th Inf. Co.K
Rose, Sheldon H. Gen. & Staff Chap.
Rose, Sidney GA 52nd Inf. Co.H
Rose, Silas AR 45th Mil. Co.A Sgt.
Rose, Silas NC 39th Inf. Co.C,G
Rose, Singleton C. GA Inf. 3rd Bn. Co.C 1st Lt.
Rose, S.J. TN 14th Cav. Co.K
Rose, S.L. MS 24th Inf. Co.C
Rose, Solomon TN 32nd Inf. Co.K
Rose, Solomon VA 8th Cav. Co.H
Rose, Solomon VA 188th Mil. Co.C
Rose, Solomon T. VA 22nd Cav. Co.D
Rose, S.P. TN 9th Inf. Co.I 2nd Lt.
Rose, Stephen TN 17th Inf. Co.I
Rose, Stephen VA Lt.Arty. Cayce's Co.
Rose, Stephen VA 42nd Inf. Co.B
Rose, Stephen C. TN 1st (Turney's) Inf. Co.A
Rose, Swinfield VA 51st Inf. Co.A
Rose, T.A. TX 9th (Nichols') Inf. Co.H 1st Sgt.
Rose, Temple KY 10th (Diamond's) Cav. Co.A
Rose, Theodore Conf.Inf. 8th Bn. Co.D
Rose, Theophilus NC 2nd Jr.Res. Co.H
Rose, Thomas AL 4th Cav.
Rose, Thomas AL 18th Bn.Vol. Co.B
Rose, Thomas NC 8th Sr.Res. Gardner's Co.
  Cpl.
Rose, Thomas NC 29th Inf. Co.L
Rose, Thomas NC 42nd Inf. Co.C
Rose, Thomas TN 2nd (Ashby's) Cav. Co.D
Rose, Thomas TN Cav. 4th Bn. (Branner's) Co.C
Rose, Thomas TN 13th Cav. Co.D
Rose, Thomas TN 7th Inf. Co.C
Rose, Thomas VA 6th Inf. 1st Co.B
Rose, Thomas A. NC 28th Inf. Co.I
Rose, Thomas E. AL 30th Inf. Co.B
Rose, Thomas E. TN 30th Inf. Co.B
Rose, Thomas E. VA Hvy.Arty. 20th Bn. Co.C
Rose, Thomas J. TX 27th Cav. Co.E
Rose, Thomas J. TX 1st Inf. Co.G 2nd Lt.
Rose, Thomas L. VA Inf. 45th Bn. Co.E
Rose, Thomas N. AL 13th Bn.Part.Rangers Co.C
Rose, Thomas N. AL 56th Part.Rangers Co.G
Rose, Thomas R. AR 14th (Powers') Inf. Co.G
Rose, Thomas T. AR 8th Inf. New Co.F
Rose, Thomas W. NC Mil. Clark's Sp.Bn. Co.H
Rose, Thomas W. NC 8th Sr.Res. Daniel's Co.
Rose, Thomas W. TN 61st Mtd.Inf. Co.H
Rose, Thomas W. VA 27th Inf. Co.C Sgt.
Rose, Tilman F. NC 2nd Arty. (36th St.Troops)
  Co.G
Rose, Timothy NC 15th Inf. Co.I
Rose, Tobias NC 3rd Arty. (40th St.Troops)
  Co.H
Rose, Tobias VA 19th Cav. Co.C,F
Rose, T.P. AR 15th (Johnson's) Inf. Co.A
Rose, Uriah VA 4th Inf. Co.A
Rose, V.B. AR 5th Inf. Co.A
Rose, Victor M. TX 3rd Cav. Co.A Sgt.
Rose, V.J. TX St.Troops Hampton's Co. 1st
  Sgt.
Rose, Volney J. TX 4th Cav. Co.C
Rose, W. NC Mallett's Bn. Co.A
Rose, W. SC 20th Inf. Co.O
Rose, W. TN 2nd Cav. Co.G

Rose, W.A. AL 5th Inf. New Co.E Cpl.
Rose, W.A. NC 12th Inf. Co.C
Rose, W.A. SC 4th Bn.Res. Co.E 1st Lt.
Rose, W.A. SC 5th St.Troops Co.I
Rose, W.A. SC 9th Res. Co.D
Rose, Waimen L. TN 1st (Turney's) Inf. Co.H
Rose, Wallace NC 2nd Arty. (36th St.Troops)
  Co.G
Rose, Walter L. NC 5th Cav. (63rd St.Troops)
  Co.A Ord.Sgt.
Rose, Walter L. NC 1st Inf. (6 mo. '61) Co.F
Rose, Washington LA 6th Inf. Co.C
Rose, Washington W. TN 1st (Feild's) Inf. Co.K
Rose, W.B. AR 27th Inf. Co.D
Rose, W.E. LA 3rd Inf. Co.F
Rose, W.E. TN 14th (Neely's) Cav. Co.A
Rose, W.E. TN 9th Inf. Co.F
Rose, W.F. AR 1st (Monroe's) Cav. Co.E
Rose, W.F. TN 62nd Mtd.Inf. Co.G
Rose, W.G. MO 16th Inf. Co.E
Rose, W.H. AR 1st (Monroe's) Cav. Co.K
Rose, W.H. AR 10th Inf. Co.D Sgt.
Rose, W.H. KY 3rd Mtd.Inf. Co.A
Rose, W.H. MS 7th Cav. 2nd Co.G
Rose, W.H. TN 14th (Neely's) Cav. Co.A
Rose, W.H. VA 2nd Cav. Co.D
Rose, Wiley NC 3rd Arty. (40th St.Troops) Co.G
Rose, William AL 43rd Inf. Co.K
Rose, William AR Cav. Gordon's Regt. Co.E
Rose, William AR 15th (Josey's) Inf. Co.D
Rose, William AR 27th Inf. New Co.C
Rose, William AR Mil. Desha Cty Bn.
Rose, William GA 1st Cav. Co.H
Rose, William GA 8th Cav. Old Co.I
Rose, William GA 62nd Cav. Co.I
Rose, William GA 1st (Olmstead's) Inf. Stiles'
  Co. Music.
Rose, William GA Inf. 18th Bn. Co.B Music.
Rose, William KY 5th Mtd.Inf. Co.K
Rose, William LA 12th Inf. Co.F
Rose, William LA 13th Inf. Co.G
Rose, William LA Inf. 16th Bn. (Conf.Guards
  Resp.Bn.) Co.B
Rose, William MS 28th Cav. Co.B 2nd Lt.
Rose, William MO Cav. Coffee's Regt. Co.F
Rose, William NC Cav. 16th Bn. QMSgt.
Rose, William NC 5th Inf. Co.D
Rose, William NC 44th Inf. Co.B
Rose, William NC 55th Inf. Co.B
Rose, William NC Walker's Bn. Thomas' Legion
  Co.A
Rose, William SC 5th Cav. Co.E
Rose, William SC 1st (McCreary's) Inf. Co.C
  Music.
Rose, William SC 27th Inf. Co.E
Rose, William SC Manigault's Bn.Vol. Co.A
Rose, William TN 4th (Murray's) Cav. Co.H
Rose, William TN 8th (Smith's) Cav. Co.C
Rose, William TN 17th Inf. Co.I
Rose, William TN 40th Inf. Co.I
Rose, William TN 48th (Nixon's) Inf. Co.F
Rose, William TN 54th Inf. Co.H
Rose, William VA 6th Cav.
Rose, William VA Hvy.Arty. Coffin's Co.
Rose, William VA 22nd Inf. Co.E
Rose, William VA 36th Inf. 1st Co.C
Rose, William A. NC 1st Inf. (6 mo. '61) Co.F

Rose, William A. NC 7th Inf. Co.I
Rose, William A. SC 12th Inf. Co.C
Rose, William B. AR 14th (Powers') Inf. Co.G
Rose, William B. GA 45th Inf. Co.E
Rose, William B. MS Lt.Arty. Stanford's Co.
Rose, William B. TX 2nd Cav. Co.A
Rose, William C. NC 32nd Inf. Co.H
Rose, William C. NC 43rd Inf. Co.E
Rose, William D. KY 8th Cav. Co.B
Rose, William E. VA 47th Inf. Co.B
Rose, William G. AR 14th (Powers') Inf. Co.G
Rose, William G. TN 13th (Gore's) Cav. Co.G
  2nd Lt.
Rose, William H. AL 3rd Inf. Co.E
Rose, William H. GA 1st (Olmstead's) Inf. Co.H
  Cpl.
Rose, William H. NC 2nd Cav. (19th St.Troops)
  Co.G
Rose, William H. NC 17th Inf. (1st Org.) Co.L
Rose, William H. TN 32nd Inf. Co.K 2nd Lt.
Rose, William H. TX 31st Cav. Co.A
Rose, William H. VA 42nd Inf. Co.C Cpl.
Rose, William H. VA 51st Inf. Co.C Cpl.
Rose, William J. NC 46th Inf. Co.C
Rose, William J. TX 14th Cav. Co.B 1st Bugler
Rose, William J. TX Cav. Martin's Regt. Co.B
Rose, Wm. J. VA Mtd.Res. Rappahannock Dist.
  Sale's Co.
Rose, William L. VA Courtney Arty.
Rose, William M. AL Arty. 1st Bn. Co.C Cpl.
Rose, William N. NC 24th Inf. Co.E Sgt.
Rose, William N. NC Mil. Clark's Sp.Bn. D.H.
  Bridger's Co. Cpl.
Rose, William N. SC 16th Inf. Co.K Adj.
Rose, William N. Wheeler's Scouts,CSA
Rose, Wm. N. Gen. & Staff 1st Lt.,Adj.
Rose, William P. Inf. Hampton Legion Co.G
Rose, William S. VA 22nd Inf. Co.C
Rose, William S. VA 166th Mil. W. Lively's Co.
Rose, William T. KY 8th Cav. Co.K
Rose, William T. NC 2nd Inf. Co.B
Rose, William T. TN 46th Inf. Co.D
Rose, William W. KY 5th Mtd.Inf. Co.D
Rose, William W. VA 9th Cav. Co.C,I
Rose, William W. VA 60th Inf. Co.D
Rose, Willis MO Searcy's Bn.S.S. Co.F
Rose, Willoughby C. SC Inf. 7th Bn. (Enfield
  Rifles) Co.B
Rose, Willoughby C. 2nd Conf.Eng.Troops Co.G
  Artif.
Rose, Wilson AR 34th Inf. Co.E
Rose, Wilson A. KY 8th Cav. Co.B
Rose, W.J. GA 10th Inf. Co.A
Rose, W.L. LA 3rd (Wingfield's) Cav. Co.H
Rose, W.N., Sr. NC 24th Inf. Co.E
Rose, W.P. SC 23rd Inf. Co.A
Rose, W.R. KY 6th Cav. Co.A
Rose, W.R. TN Cav. Nixon's Regt. Co.B
Rose, W.T. SC 9th Inf. Co.A
Rose, W.T. TX Inf. Griffin's Bn. Co.B
Rose, W.W. SC Cav. 4th Bn. Co.B Cpl.
Rose, Wyatt NC 58th Inf. Co.L
Rose, Wyatt W. SC 2nd Cav. Co.C Sgt.
Rose, W.Z. VA Courtney Arty.
Rose, Zachariah KY Jessee's Bn.Mtd.Riflemen
Rose, Zachariah M. TX 17th Cav. Co.D
Rose, Zachariah P. MS 15th Inf. Co.E

Rose, Zachariah P. MS 30th Inf. Co.C Cpl.
Rose, Z.B. KY 7th Cav. Co.F
Rose, Z.B. 1st Conf.Cav. 2nd Co.A
Rosebalm, John VA 8th Inf. Co.A
Rosebaud, Able LA Mil. 6th Regt.Eur.Brig.
   (Italian Guards Bn.)
Rosebaugh, Jesse L. VA 33rd Inf. Co.A
Roseberry, --- MO St.Guard Lt.
Roseberry, Absolem AR 35th Inf. Co.F
Roseberry, Calvin VA 4th Res. Co.F
Roseberry, Calvin VA Mil. Scott Cty.
Roseberry, Charles AR 35th Inf. Co.F
Roseberry, Charles MS Inf. (Res.) Berry's Co.
Roseberry, G.W. VA Cav. 37th Bn. Co.H
Roseberry, Isham A. AR 15th (N.W.) Inf. Co.A
Roseberry, James AR Inf. Hardy's Regt. Co.A
Roseberry, James LA Lt.Arty. 6th Field Btty.
   (Grosse Tete Flying Arty.)
Roseberry, James MS Lt.Arty. (Brookhaven
   Lt.Arty.) Hoskins' Btty.
Roseberry, James W. AR 15th (N.W.) Inf. Co.A
Roseberry, James W. MO 16th Inf. Co.E Lt.
Roseberry, Jesse VA Mil. Scott Cty.
Roseberry, John MO Inf. 3rd Bn. Co.F Lt.
Roseberry, John MO 6th Inf. Co.H Lt.
Roseberry, J.S. VA Hvy.Arty. 18th Bn. Co.D
Roseberry, R.B. MO 16th Inf. Co.E
Roseberry, R.L. AL 1st Cav. 2nd Co.A
Roseberry, R.L. AL 8th Cav. Co.G
Roseberry, Samuel VA 4th Res. Co.F
Roseberry, Thomas J. TN Cav. 17th Bn. (San-
   ders') Co.A
Roseberry, W.J.D. AR 37th Inf. Co.I
Roseboro, Rufus W. TN 4th (McLemore's) Cav.
   Co.K
Roseborogh, Samuel L. TX 20th Inf. Co.H
Roseborough, --- SC Mil. 17th Regt. Rogers' Co.
Roseborough, B.W. Mead's Conf.Cav. Co.H 3rd
   Lt.
Roseborough, Cyrus A. TX 6th Cav. Co.H
Roseborough, J. GA 27th Inf. Co.H
Roseborough, James Inf. School of Pract.
   Powell's Command Powell's Detach. Co.A
Roseborough, James S. TX 9th (Nichols') Inf.
   Co.E
Roseborough, J.D. MO 6th Cav. Co.G
Roseborough, John SC 6th Inf. 1st Co.H
Roseborough, J.T. Gen. & Staff 1st Lt.,ADC
Roseborough, Samuel L. TX 9th (Nichols') Inf.
   Co.E
Roseborough, W.G. AR 1st (Dobbin's) Cav.
   Co.H
Roseborough, William D. TN 44th Inf. Co.E
Roseborough, William Y. TX 17th Cav. Co.K
Rosebourough, --- Fort's Scouts,CSA
Rosebourough, Robert D. MO 6th Cav. Co.G
Rosebrock, Charles VA 18th Cav. Co.H Sgt.
Rosebrock, H.J. VA 18th Cav. Co.H
Rosebrooks, Lathrop D. MS 18th Inf. Co.A
Rosebrough, C.D. VA 114th Mil. Co.G
Rosebrough, D.R.S. AR 1st (Dobbin's) Cav.
   Co.C
Rosebrough, Jesse L. VA 114th Mil. Co.G Cpl.
Rosebrough, S.F. VA 114th Mil. Co.G
Rosebury, Calvin VA 25th Cav. Co.A
Rosebury, Jesse VA 25th Cav. Co.A
Rosebury, Thomas MO 8th Cav. Reed's Co.

Rosecrans, William TN 1st Cav.
Rosel, A.K. TX St.Troops Hampton's Co.
Roselius, C. LA Millaudon's Co. (Jefferson
   Mtd.Guards,Co.B)
Rosell, A.K. TX Cav. Waller's Regt. Co.A Cpl.
Rosell, A.R. TX Cav. Waller's Regt. Co.A Cpl.
Rosell, C.C. TX Cav. Mann's Bn. Cox's Co.
Rosell, C.C. TX Cav. Waller's Regt. Co.A
Rosell, E.H. MO Cav. Snider's Bn. Co.B
Rosell, F. LA Mil. 5th Regt.Eur.Brig. (Spanish
   Regt.) Co.8
Rosell, George W. TX 11th Cav. Co.B
Rosell, James A. MS 44th Inf. Co.I
Rosell, John KY 9th Cav. Co.A
Rosell, John MO Cav. Snider's Bn. Co.B
Rosell, Joseph W. KY Mt.Zion Ghent Cty.
Rosell, William M. KY 8th Cav. Co.F
Roselle, Alfred K. TX 8th Cav. Co.G
Roselle, Edward T. TX 22nd Inf. Co.C 3rd Cpl.
Roselle, F.M. TX 18th Inf. Co.A
Roselle, Lafayette TX 8th Cav. Co.A
Rosellini, Louis Sap. & Min. Gallimard's
   Co.,CSA 1st Sap.
Rosellis, Henry MO 10th Cav. Co.C Cpl.
Rosello, Jose LA Mil. 5th Regt.Eur.Brig.
   (Spanish Regt.) Co.9
Rosello, Miguel LA Mil. 5th Regt.Eur.Brig.
   (Spanish Regt.) Co.9
Roselus, George G. LA Mil. 4th Regt. 3rd Brig.
   1st Div. Co.H
Roseman, A. MS 5th Cav. Co.I
Roseman, A. MS 18th Cav. Co.I
Roseman, Benjamin F. MS 12th Inf. Co.I
Roseman, B.F. MS 5th Cav. Co.A
Roseman, Cyrus P. NC 38th Inf. Co.F
Roseman, Cyrus P. NC 49th Inf. Co.E
Roseman, Daniel F. NC 38th Inf. Co.F Capt.
Roseman, E.H. NC 5th Inf. Co.H
Roseman, Elphonso A. NC 7th Inf. Co.A
Roseman, G.M. TN 47th Inf. Co.B
Roseman, G.N. MS 41st Inf. Co.F
Roseman, G.W. NC 1st Bn.Jr.Res. Co.D Cpl.
Roseman, H. LA 3rd Inf. Co.H
Roseman, Henry NC 6th Inf. Co.D
Roseman, Isaac GA 4th Inf. Co.K
Roseman, James O. NC 4th Sr.Res. Co.B
Roseman, John B. AR 33rd Inf. Co.B
Roseman, John B. MS Bradford's Co. (Conf.
   Guards Arty.)
Roseman, J.R. MS 18th Cav. Co.F
Roseman, J.R.W. MS 3rd Inf. (St.Troops) Co.D
Roseman, M. NC McLean's Bn.Lt.Duty Men
   Co.B
Roseman, Maury I. NC Co.F 1st Sgt.
Roseman, Robert M. NC 11th (Bethel Regt.) Inf.
   Co.I
Roseman, T. MS 3rd Inf. (St.Troops) Co.D
Roseman, T.A. NC 49th Inf. Co.E
Roseman, T.A.P. NC 66th Inf. Co.G
Roseman, W.N. SC Inf. Hampton Legion Co.F
Roseman, W.R. AL Arty. 1st Bn.
Rosemary, Phillip VA 5th Cav. (12 mo. '61-2)
   Co.E
Rosemon, George W. FL 7th Inf. Co.C
Rosemon, G.W. TN 14th (Neely's) Cav. Co.E
Rosemon, J.W. TN 14th (Neely's) Cav. Co.E
Rosemond, G.W. MS 3rd Cav. Co.K

Rosemond, James S. MS 15th Inf. Co.D
Rosemond, Joseph GA 10th Mil.
Rosemond, T. MS 3rd Cav. Co.K
Rosemond, T.A. MS Hall's Co.
Rosemond, Thomas J. MS 1st Lt.Arty. Co.C
Rosemond, V.B. MS Cav. Dunn's Co. (MS
   Rangers)
Rosemond, W.E. AR 26th Inf. Co.C
Rosen, Andrew J. VA 31st Inf. Co.H
Rosen, David F. VA 52nd Inf. Co.I
Rosen, David H. VA 4th Inf. Co.I
Rosen, George VA 5th Inf. Co.D
Rosen, Jacob VA 52nd Inf. Co.I
Rosen, James A. VA 25th Inf. 2nd Co.D
Rosen, John H. VA 5th Inf. Co.D
Rosen, John M. VA 5th Inf. Co.D
Rosen, Thomas M. VA 5th Inf. Co.D
Rosen, William LA Mil. 3rd Regt. 3rd Brig. 1st
   Div. Co.C
Rosen, Wm. MO St.Guard W.H. Taylor's Co.
Rosen, William H. VA 5th Inf. Co.D
Rosen, William T. VA 25th Inf. 2nd Co.H
Rosenan, Edward 4th Conf.Eng.Troops Co.E
   Artif.
Rosenan, Herman AL 10th Inf. Co.C
Rosenand, Adolphe LA C.S. Zouave Bn. Co.A
Rosenau, E. LA C.S. Zouave Bn. Co.B
Rosenau, Ed TX 26th Cav. Co.E
Rosenau, Edward Central Div. KY Sap. &
   Min.,CSA
Rosenau, Seekmond TX 6th Cav. Co.I
Rosenbach, John TX 1st (Yager's) Cav. Co.E
Rosenbach, John TX Cav. 8th (Taylor's) Bn.
   Co.C
Rosenbalm, A. VA 63rd Inf. Co.F 1st Sgt.
Rosenbalm, A. VA Mil. Washington Cty.
Rosenbalm, Aaron VA Mil. Washington Cty.
Rosenbalm, A.D. VA 1st Cav. 2nd Co.D
Rosenbalm, A.J. VA 8th Cav. Co.A
Rosenbalm, Andrew D. VA 50th Inf. 1st Co.G
Rosenbalm, Asa VA 30th Bn.S.S. Co.E
Rosenbalm, David VA 37th Inf. Co.H
Rosenbalm, Drewry H. TN 37th Inf. Co.K
Rosenbalm, Eli A. VA 37th Inf. Co.H 3rd Lt.
Rosenbalm, George W. VA 37th Inf. Co.H
Rosenbalm, Isaac VA 37th Inf. Co.H
Rosenbalm, James VA 37th Inf. Co.H
Rosenbalm, James H. VA 63rd Inf. Co.E
Rosenbalm, John S. VA 63rd Inf. Co.F
Rosenbalm, John S. VA Mil. Washington Cty.
Rosenbalm, Mathias VA 37th Inf. Co.H
Rosenbalm, Parker S. VA 37th Inf. Co.H
Rosenbalm, Parker S. VA 48th Inf. Co.F
Rosenbalm, Russell R. VA 37th Inf. Co.F
Rosenbalm, Samuel TN 5th (McKenzie's) Cav.
   Co.G
Rosenbalm, Thomas M. VA 8th Cav. Co.A Cpl.
Rosenbalm, William H. TN 37th Inf. Co.K Sgt.
Rosenbam, A. 1st Chickasaw Inf. Wallace's Co.
Rosenbam, Hamilton TN Cav. 12th Bn. (Day's)
   Co.C
Rosenbam, Jacob TN Cav. 12th Bn. (Day's)
   Co.C
Rosenbarger, Adam VA Cav. 41st Bn.
   Trayhern's Co.
Rosenbarger, Elijah VA Cav. 41st Bn.
   Trayhern's Co.

Rosenbarger, Isaac VA 23rd Cav. Co.I
Rosenbarger, J.B. VA 62nd Mtd.Inf. 2nd Lt.
Rosenbarger, Joseph VA 8th Bn.Res. Co.D
Rosenbarger, Joseph VA 136th Mil. Co.E
Rosenbarger, Levi VA 8th Bn.Res. Co.C
Rosenbaulm, William H. VA 25th Cav. Co.I
Rosenbaum, --- LA Mil. 1st Regt. 2nd Brig. 1st Div. Co.A
Rosenbaum, Aaron MS 35th Inf. Co.B
Rosenbaum, Aaron VA 30th Bn.S.S. Co.E 1st Sgt.
Rosenbaum, Alexander AR Lt.Arty. Etter's Btty.
Rosenbaum, Alexander TX 22nd Inf. Co.I
Rosenbaum, Alfred J. VA 1st Inf. Co.K
Rosenbaum, Auguste Lt.Arty. Dent's Btty.,CSA
Rosenbaum, David MS 5th Inf. (St.Troops) Co.C
Rosenbaum, David MS 13th Inf. Co.C
Rosenbaum, F. AR 13th Mil. Co.G
Rosenbaum, G. LA Mil. 2nd Regt. 3rd Brig. 1st Div. Co.G
Rosenbaum, George W. AR 4th Inf. Co.E
Rosenbaum, G.W. AR 1st Mtd.Rifles Co.E
Rosenbaum, H. TX 11th (Spaight's) Bn.Vol. Co.A,F
Rosenbaum, H. TX 21st Inf. Co.F
Rosenbaum, H.A. VA Loc.Def. Neff's Co.
Rosenbaum, Henry AR 2nd Mtd.Rifles Co.H
Rosenbaum, Henry TX 21st Cav. Co.G Artif.
Rosenbaum, Hezekiah VA 45th Inf. Co.D
Rosenbaum, Isaac MS 5th Inf. (St.Troops) Co.C
Rosenbaum, J. Lt.Arty. Dent's Btty.,CSA
Rosenbaum, Jacob MS 13th Inf. Co.C
Rosenbaum, John TN 45th Inf.
Rosenbaum, John VA 8th Cav. Co.A
Rosenbaum, John VA 6th Bn.Res. Co.F
Rosenbaum, Jonas M. GA Inf. 10th Bn. Co.C
Rosenbaum, Joseph VA 1st St.Res. Co.F Cpl.
Rosenbaum, L. AR 15th (Johnson's) Inf. Co.A
Rosenbaum, Louis LA 20th Inf. Co.A 1st Lt.
Rosenbaum, M. MS 5th Inf. (St.Troops) Co.I
Rosenbaum, M. MS Rogers' Co.
Rosenbaum, Michael VA 1st St.Res. Co.F
Rosenbaum, Peter VA 45th Inf. Co.D
Rosenbaum, P.S. VA Loc.Def. Jordan's Co.
Rosenbaum, S.A. VA 8th Cav. Co.A
Rosenbaum, Sam. LA Ogden's Cav. Co.E
Rosenbaum, Samuel 14th Conf.Cav. Co.B,I
Rosenbaum, Samuel M. VA 1st St.Res. Co.A
Rosenbaum, Stephen VA 45th Inf. Co.D
Rosenberg, A.S. AR 37th Inf. Co.K
Rosenberg, Bernhart TX 14th Cav. Co.G
Rosenberg, Charles SC 1st Arty. Co.H
Rosenberg, Eugene V. TX Waul's Legion Co.E Sgt.
Rosenberg, F. LA Mil. 4th Regt.Eur.Brig. Co.A
Rosenberg, Jacob R. TX 3rd Inf. Co.D
Rosenberg, L. LA Mil. 2nd Regt. 3rd Brig. 1st Div. Co.B
Rosenberg, Louis LA Mil. 4th Regt.Eur.Brig. Co.C
Rosenberg, M. LA Mil. 4th Regt.Eur.Brig. Co.E
Rosenberg, M. VA 3rd Inf.Loc.Def. Co.I
Rosenberg, Michael VA 6th Inf. Co.G
Rosenberg, N.S. AR 50th Mil. Gleaves' Co.
Rosenberg, Raphael GA 3rd Inf. Co.F
Rosenberg, Samuel GA 3rd Inf. Co.I Sgt.
Rosenberg, Solomon Gen. & Staff Hosp.Stew.

Rosenberge, Lewis TX 5th Cav. Co.E
Rosenberger, Adam VA 18th Cav. Co.D
Rosenberger, Adam VA 97th Mil. Co.G
Rosenberger, Andrew VA 7th Cav. Co.I
Rosenberger, C. MS 9th Inf. Music.
Rosenberger, Calvin VA 18th Cav. Co.D
Rosenberger, Calvin VA 146th Mil. Co.G
Rosenberger, Calvin G. VA Cav. 41st Bn. Trayhern's Co.
Rosenberger, Christopher VA 7th Cav. Co.C Sgt.
Rosenberger, Daniel MO Arty. Lowe's Co.
Rosenberger, David VA 136th Mil. Co.A
Rosenberger, David W. VA 1st Cav. Co.A 1st Lt.
Rosenberger, Elijah VA 18th Cav. Co.D
Rosenberger, Erasmus VA 7th Cav. Co.C 1st Lt.
Rosenberger, George W. VA 10th Cav. Co.H
Rosenberger, George W. VA 58th Mil. Co.H 2nd Lt.
Rosenberger, George W. VA 97th Mil. 2nd Lt.
Rosenberger, George W. VA 146th Mil. Co.B 2nd Lt.
Rosenberger, Gideon VA 146th Mil. Co.B
Rosenberger, Gustav GA 1st (Ramsey's) Inf. Co.K
Rosenberger, Harvey VA Lt.Arty. B.Z. Price's Co.
Rosenberger, Harvey VA Lt.Arty. W.H. Rice's Co.
Rosenberger, Harvey J. VA 58th Mil. Co.H Capt.
Rosenberger, Henry TN 34th Inf. 2nd Co.C, Co.F
Rosenberger, H.J. VA 7th Bn.Res. Co.A
Rosenberger, J.A. VA 10th Cav. Co.D
Rosenberger, J.A. Post Band Cp.Lee,CSA Music.
Rosenberger, Jacob B. VA 18th Cav. Co.D 1st Lt.
Rosenberger, Jacob B. VA 5th Inf. Co.L
Rosenberger, James VA 136th Mil. Co.E
Rosenberger, James H. VA 33rd Inf. Co.B,K 2nd Lt.
Rosenberger, John A. VA 1st Inf. Co.I
Rosenberger, John A. VA 10th Inf. Co.D
Rosenberger, John W. VA 10th Cav. Co.H
Rosenberger, John W. VA 33rd Inf. Co.D
Rosenberger, John W. VA 33rd Inf. Co.H Sgt.
Rosenberger, John W. VA 51st Mil. Co.E
Rosenberger, John W. VA 97th Mil. Co.I
Rosenberger, L. Post Band Cp.Lee,CSA Music.
Rosenberger, Lawrence VA 1st Inf. Co.I
Rosenberger, Levi VA 136th Mil. Co.B
Rosenberger, Philip VA 1st Inf. Co.I
Rosenberger, Samuel MS 13th Inf. Co.E,D
Rosenbergh, Henry LA 6th Inf. Co.B
Rosenbery, S.J. AR 50th Mil. Gleaves' Co.
Rosenblat, A. LA Lewis' Regt. Co.B
Rosenblat, F. LA Lewis' Regt. Co.B
Rosenblut, Anton TX Lt.Arty. Jones' Co.
Rosenbom, F.A. AR 30th Inf. Co.F
Rosenbom, Joseph AR 30th Inf. Co.F
Rosenboro, A.J. VA 7th Cav. Co.I
Rosenbower, Cond. TX Cav. McCord's Frontier Regt. Co.I

Rosenbum, Henry M. TN 26th Inf. Co.K
Rosenbum, John TN Inf. 23rd Bn. Co.B
Rosenbum, Samuel TN 26th Inf. Co.K
Rosenbum, Timothy TN Inf. 23rd Bn. Co.B
Rosenbumb, William MO 7th Cav. Ward's Co.
Rosenburg, A.S. AR Lt.Arty. Zimmerman's Btty.
Rosenburg, August TX 21st Cav. Co.F
Rosenburg, E. Von TX Inf. Timmons' Regt. Co.B
Rosenburg, Louis MS 12th Inf. Co.B
Rosenburg, Michael VA 54th Mil. Co.E,F
Rosenburg, R. MO Cav. Clardy's Bn. Co.B
Rosenburg, S.J. AR 37th Inf. Co.K
Rosenburger, H.J. VA 3rd (Chrisman's) Bn.Res. Co.A
Rosenburger, J.A. VA Inf. 25th Bn. Co.C Music.
Rosenburger, Joseph VA 3rd (Chrisman's) Bn. Co.C
Rosenburger, Lawrence VA Inf. 25th Bn. Co.C Music.
Rosenby, Louis MS Wilkinson Cty. Minute Men Co.A
Rosencrantz, J. GA 29th Inf. Co.I
Rosencrantz, O.F. KY 3rd Mtd.Inf. Co.D Sgt.
Rosencrantz, T. GA 29th Inf. Co.I
Rosencranz, Leonidas VA 19th Cav. Co.K
Rosencranz, O.F. KY 7th Cav. Co.B
Rosendez, Faustino LA Mil. 5th Regt.Eur.Brig. (Spanish Regt.) Co.7
Rosendorff, M.J. SC 1st Cav. Co.K,C
Rosenfeld, Ferdnand LA Mil. Bragg's Bn. Schwartz's Co.
Rosenfeld, H. A 1st St.Res. Co.A
Rosenfeld, Jacob GA Inf. 2nd Bn. Co.C
Rosenfeld, L. GA Inf. 18th Bn. (St.Guards) Co.B
Rosenfels, J. VA Inf. 28th Bn. Co.D Sgt.
Rosenfels, Jacob VA 59th Inf. Co.K Sgt.
Rosenfels, Simon VA 1st Inf. Co.A
Rosenfels, Simon VA 12th Inf. Co.G
Rosenfelt, E. GA Inf. 18th Bn. (St.Guards) Co.E
Rosenfield, A. LA 22nd Inf. Co.B
Rosenfield, A. LA 22nd (Cons.) Inf. Co.B
Rosenfield, Alex TX 26th Cav. Co.A
Rosenfield, Henry TX 26th Cav. Co.A
Rosenfield, Henry Gen. & Staff, QM Dept.
Rosenfield, J. LA Mil. 1st Regt. 2nd Brig. 1st Div. Co.B
Rosenfield, J. LA 21st (Kennedy's) Inf. Co.D Bvt.2nd Lt.
Rosenfield, J.J. TX 2nd Inf. Co.H
Rosenfield, J.J. TX Inf. Houston Bn. Co.A Cpl.
Rosenfield, Julius LA 22nd (Cons.) Inf. Co.A,B Cpl.
Rosenfield, L. LA Mil.Conf.Guards Regt. Co.H
Rosenfield, L. LA Mil. Jackson Rifle Bn. 1st Lt.
Rosenfield, M. TX 26th Cav. Co.A
Rosenfield, Michael GA 26th Inf. 1st Co.G
Rosenfield, Michael GA 29th Inf. Co.E
Rosenheim, Sigmund VA 37th Inf. Co.A
Rosenheimer, John R. TX 3rd Inf. Co.F Capt.
Rosenhorn, Ed LA Arty. Guyol's Co. (Orleans Arty.)
Rosens, J. GA 21st Inf. Co.K
Rosenschein, M. LA Mil. 4th Regt.Eur.Brig. Co.C

Rosensteal, A. LA 27th Inf. Co.H
Rosensteel, James N. MD 1st Inf. Co.A
Rosensteil, A. LA 4th Inf. Co.D
Rosensteil, Charles GA Inf. 1st Bn. (St.Guards) Co.D 1st Lt.
Rosensteil, William GA Inf. 1st Bn. (St.Guards) Co.D Sgt.
Rosenstihl, C. GA Inf. City Bn. (Columbus) Co.C Capt.
Rosenstihl, Charles AL 3rd Inf. Co.D
Rosenstihl, William GA Inf. City Bn. (Columbus) Co.C
Rosenstine, Rudolph TN 29th Inf. Co.B 1st Lt.
Rosentall, B.L. MS 3rd Inf. (St.Troops) Co.I 1st Cpl.
Rosenthal, A. GA 38th Inf. Co.D
Rosenthal, A. LA 13th Bn. (Part.Rangers) Co.E
Rosenthal, A. TX 33rd Cav. Co.E Hosp.Stew.
Rosenthal, Abraham GA 49th Inf. Co.G
Rosenthal, A.L. MS 10th Inf. Old Co.K
Rosenthal, B.L. MS 2nd Cav. Co.A
Rosenthal, E. SC Mil.Arty. 1st Regt. Harms' Co.
Rosenthal, Gustav NC 18th Inf. Co.A
Rosenthal, H. TN Inf. 3rd Bn. Co.F
Rosenthal, Isaac LA Cav. Benjamin's Co.
Rosenthal, Jonas LA 3rd (Harrison's) Cav. Co.K Cpl.
Rosenthal, L. AR 18th (Marmaduke's) Inf. Co.A
Rosenthal, L. LA 3rd Inf. Co.K
Rosenthal, L.J. LA Mil. 4th Regt.Eur.Brig. Co.C
Rosenthal, M. LA Inf.Crescent Regt. Co.K
Rosenthal, Marx GA 10th Inf. Co.G
Rosenthal, Morris LA Mil. Mooney's Co. (Saddlers Guards)
Rosenthal, Moses LA 3rd (Harrison's) Cav. Co.K 1st Sgt.
Rosenthal, Phillipp LA Arty. 1st Field Btty.
Rosenthal, S. LA Mil. 4th Regt.Eur.Brig. Co.C
Rosenthal, Solomon LA 1st (Strawbridge's) Inf. Co.H
Rosenthal, T. LA Mil. 1st Chasseurs a pied Co.7
Rosenthal, Theodore LA Arty. 1st Field Btty.
Rosenthal, W. TN Inf. Nashville Bn. Cattles' Co.
Rosenthal, William LA Mil. 4th Regt.Eur.Brig. Co.D Cpl.
Rosenthaler, Samuel LA 1st (Strawbridge's) Inf. Co.I Fifer
Rosenthall, Abram Conf.Cav. Wood's Regt. Co.K
Rosenthall, Isaac VA 61st Inf. Co.D Cpl.
Rosenthall, L.J. LA Mil.Cont.Regt. Mitchell's Co.
Rosenthall, M. LA Cav. Benjamin's Co.
Rosenthall, Mires LA 2nd Inf. Co.B
Rosenthall, P. MS Lt.Arty. English's Co.
Rosenthall, R. LA 2nd Inf. Co.B
Rosenthall, S. LA Mil.Cont.Regt. Mitchell's Co.
Rosenwald, Isaac GA 4th Inf. Co.K
Rosenwald, M. GA Inf. 14th Bn. (St.Guards) Co.B Cpl.
Rosenward, J.E. LA 3rd (Harrison's) Cav.
Rosenwhite, L. LA Mil. 1st Chasseurs a pied Co.4
Rosenwick, George SC 5th Res. Co.I
Rooser, A. LA Mil. Fire Bn. Co.E
Roser, Andrew VA 11th Cav. Co.C
Roser, Charles TX 12th Field Btty.

Roser, Christopher AL Vol. Rabby's Coast Guard Co. No.1
Roser, Peter D. VA 8th Cav. Co.K
Roser, Peter D. VA Horse Arty. Jackson's Co.
Roser, W. LA 2nd Inf. Co.B
Rosern, S.T. VA Cav. Mosby's Regt. (Part. Rangers)
Roses, Thms. MO Cav. Fristoe's Regt. Co.D
Roseter, George VA Lt.Arty. Clutter's Co.
Rosette, --- LA Mil. 3rd Regt. French Brig. Co.1 Sap.
Rosette, George W. GA Inf. City Bn. (Columbus) Williams' Co. 2nd Lt.
Rosette, James B. MS 44th Inf. Co.L Sgt.
Rosette, John AL 21st Inf. Co.A Sgt.
Rosette, John LA 1st Cav. Co.A
Rosetto, George W. GA 5th Inf. (St.Guards) Everitt's Co.
Rosetto, Jose LA Mil. Cazadores Espanoles Regt. Co.2
Rosetto, Pedro LA Mil. 3rd Regt.Eur.Brig. (Spanish Regt.) Co.3
Rosey, J.W. GA 60th Inf. Co.E
Rosh, F. AL 6th Inf. Co.E
Roshal, Robert AR 17th (Lemoyne's) Inf. Co.F Sgt.
Rosham, C. VA Lt.Arty. Pegram's Co.
Rosham, M. LA Mil. 1st Regt. French Brig. Co.2
Rosia, J.L. LA 6th Cav. Co.I
Rosich, George W. NC 34th Inf. Co.G
Rosier, A. GA 45th Inf. Co.G
Rosier, Charles MD 1st Cav. Co.A
Rosier, C. Henry FL 10th Inf. Co.D,H
Rosier, C.R. FL 10th Inf. Co.A
Rosier, E.L. MS 3rd Inf. (St.Troops) Co.C
Rosier, Finley LA Inf. 9th Bn. Co.A
Rosier, H. FL Conscr.
Rosier, Henry FL 10th Inf. Co.D
Rosier, Isham 1st Conf.Eng.Troops Co.B
Rosier, J. GA 3rd Cav. Co.C
Rosier, James W. GA Lt.Arty. Anderson's Btty.
Rosier, John GA Mayer's Co. (Appling Cav.)
Rosier, John GA 5th Res. Co.A,I
Rosier, John SC 2nd St.Troops Co.K
Rosier, John C. SC 1st Inf. Co.M
Rosier, J.R. SC Inf. Hampton Legion Co.C
Rosier, Luke FL Inf. 2nd Bn. Co.C
Rosier, Luke FL 10th Inf. Co.H
Rosier, Luke M. FL Inf. 2nd Bn. Co.C
Rosier, Luke M. FL 10th Inf. Co.H
Rosier, Milton TN Inf. 23rd Bn. Co.A
Rosier, R. GA 5th Res. Co.I
Rosier, R.A. SC 11th Inf. 2nd Co.F
Rosier, S. SC Mil. 16th Regt. Stiles' Co.
Rosier, Solomon FL Inf. 2nd Bn. Co.C
Rosier, Solomon FL 10th Inf. Co.H
Rosier, Stephen W. GA 20th Inf. Co.C
Rosier, William GA Inf. (Richmond Factory Guards) Barney's Co.
Rosiere, E. LA 30th Inf. Co.F Sgt.
Rosiere, E. LA Mil. Orleans Guards Regt. Co.C
Rosiere, G. LA Mil. Orleans Guards Regt. Co.C
Rosiere, George LA Pointe Coupee Arty.
Rosin 1st Cherokee Mtd.Rifles Co.F
Rosin, A. GA 2nd (Stapleton's) St.Troops Co.A
Rosin, Edward TN Conscr. (Cp. of Instr.)

Rosin, Mike TN 55th (Brown's) Inf. Co.D Sgt.
Rosinbalm, John TN Cav. 12th Bn. (Day's) Co.G
Rosinbum, James TX 18th Cav. Co.K
Rosis, J. SC 25th Inf. Co.E
Rosis, Joseph SC Inf.Loc.Def. Estill's Co.
Rosis, Juan LA Mil. 5th Regt.Eur.Brig. Co.9
Rosjon, James AR Cav. Gordon's Regt. Co.A
Roska, Albert TX 21st Cav. Co.H
Roska, Andrew TX 13th Vol. 2nd Co.C Principal Music.
Roskelly, J.H. TN Lt.Arty. Rice's Btty. Cpl.
Rosler, C. SC 1st Regt. Charleston Guard Co.G
Rosler, George MO Cav. Slayback's Regt. Co.C 3rd Lt.
Rosler, J.A. NC 1st Arty. (10th St.Troops) Co.K
Rosman, D.R. MS 1st (Percy's) Inf. Co.I
Rosman, S. MS 1st Cav.Res. Co.C
Rosmann, Theo. J. AL 37th Inf. Co.B
Rosmarich, Georgio LA Mil. 4th Regt.Eur.Brig. Cognevich's Co.
Rosmary, P. VA 2nd St.Res. Co.M Cpl.
Rosmino, J. LA Mil. 2nd Regt. French Brig. Co.8
Rosmond, Joseph GA Hvy.Arty. 22nd Bn. Co.C
Rosmond, S.W. GA 20th Inf. Co.C
Rosolis, F. TX Cav. Border's Regt. Co.E
Roson, G.W. TX 34th Cav. Co.G
Roson, John H., Jr. TN 21st Inf. Co.C 1st Lt.
Rosonbalm, Isaac D. VA 37th Inf. Co.F,K
Rosonbalm, James VA 37th Inf. Co.F
Rosrell, W. TX Cav. Bourland's Regt. Co.F
Ross, --- SC Inf. 1st Charleston Bn. Co.A
Ross, --- TX 24th & 25th Cav. (Cons.) Co.F
Ross, A. GA Arty. Maxwell's Reg.Lt.Btty.
Ross, A. GA Arty. (Macon Lt.Arty.) Slaten's Co.
Ross, A. GA 1st Reg. Co.D
Ross, A. GA Inf. (Anderson Guards) Anderson's Co.
Ross, A. LA Mil. 1st Regt. 2nd Brig. 1st Div.
Ross, A. MS 5th Inf. Co.C
Ross, A. TX 8th Inf. Co.E
Ross, A.A. SC 1st Cav. Co.H
Ross, A.B. MS 6th Inf. Co.A
Ross, A.B. SC 3rd Inf. Co.E
Ross, A.B. TX 11th Inf. Co.E Jr.2nd Lt.
Ross, Abijah J. AR 16th Inf. Co.E
Ross, Abraham TX 13th Vol. 1st Co.H Jr.2nd Lt.
Ross, Abram TX 35th (Brown's) Cav. Co.C 2nd Lt.
Ross, Abram L. FL 7th Inf. Co.H
Ross, Absalom R. VA 52nd Inf. 2nd Co.B
Ross, A.C. AR Cav. Harrell's Bn. Co.D
Ross, A.C. AR 3rd Inf. Co.E
Ross, Adam NC 3rd Inf. Co.K
Ross, Adolphus A. FL 5th Inf. Co.B
Ross, Adolphus E. GA 3rd Cav. Co.H
Ross, Adolphus E. GA Floyd Legion (St.Guards) Co.C
Ross, A.E. AR 20th Inf. Co.D
Ross, A.E. AR Inf. Cocke's Regt. Co.I
Ross, A.E. GA 8th Inf. Co.A
Ross, A.E. TX 4th Inf. Co.E
Ross, A.G. MS 13th Inf. Co.I Cpl.
Ross, A.H. TN 19th (Biffle's) Cav. Co.F 2nd Lt.
Ross, A.H. TN 33rd Inf. Co.H Sgt.

Ross, A.J. LA 28th (Gray's) Inf. Co.A
Ross, A.J. MS 3rd Inf. Co.F
Ross, A.J. MS 15th (Cons.) Inf. Co.K
Ross, A.J. SC 6th Cav. Co.H
Ross, A.J. TN 3rd (Forrest's) Cav. Co.H
Ross, A.J. TX 22nd Inf. Adj.
Ross, A.J. Conf.Cav. Clarkson's Bn. Ind.Rangers Co.H
Ross, Albert B. GA 20th Inf. Co.A Maj.
Ross, Albert R. NC 3rd Cav. (41st St.Troops) Co.F
Ross, Alec AL 8th (Hatch's) Cav. Co.H
Ross, Alex AL 42nd Inf. Co.H
Ross, Alex KY 6th Cav. Co.G
Ross, Alex VA 5th Bn.Res. Co.D Cpl.
Ross, Alexander AL 53rd (Part.Rangers) Co.D
Ross, Alexander AR 15th (Josey's) Inf. Co.H
Ross, Alexander AR 17th (Griffith's) Inf. Co.B
Ross, Alexander AR 33rd Inf. Co.A
Ross, Alexander KY 2nd (Duke's) Cav. Co.G
Ross, Alexander LA 1st (Nelligan's) Inf. Co.K
Ross, Alexander MD Line
Ross, Alexander MS 29th Inf. Co.K
Ross, Alexander SC Inf. 3rd Bn. Co.C
Ross, Alexander TN Lt.Arty. Tobin's Co.
Ross, Alexander VA 7th Bn.Res. Co.D
Ross, Alexander VA 44th Inf. Co.C
Ross, Alexander VA 48th Inf. Co.E
Ross, Alexander C. KY Cav. 1st Bn. Co.B
Ross, Alexander C. KY 4th Cav. Co.B Sgt.
Ross, Allen NC 1st Cav. (9th St.Troops) Co.I
Ross, Allen 1st Cherokee Mtd.Rifles Co.H Sgt.
Ross, Allen A. SC 5th Inf. 1st Co.G, 2nd Co.C
Ross, Allen G. AL 13th Inf. Co.B
Ross, Alpheus A. NC 22nd Inf. Co.E
Ross, A.M. MS 4th Inf. Co.G
Ross, Amos S. MS 13th Inf. Co.E
Ross, Andrew AL 43rd Inf. Co.G
Ross, Andrew MS Inf. 2nd Bn. Co.A
Ross, Andrew MS 48th Inf. Co.A
Ross, Andrew VA 26th Inf. 1st Co.B
Ross, Andrew VA 33rd Inf. Co.B
Ross, Andrew VA 136th Mil. Co.E
Ross, Andrew Mtd.Spies & Guides Madison's Co.
Ross, Andrew 1st Cherokee Mtd.Vol. 2nd Co.H
Ross, Andrew 2nd Cherokee Mtd.Vol. Co.B
Ross, Andrew B. TN 1st (Turney's) Inf. Co.I
Ross, Andrew D. AL 3rd Res. Co.I
Ross, Andrew J. GA 21st Inf. Old Co.E
Ross, Andrew J. MS 23rd Inf. Co.F Sgt.
Ross, Andrew Jackson MO 8th Inf. Co.E
Ross, Angus AR 14th (Powers') Inf. Co.E Capt.
Ross, Anthony P. MD Arty. 2nd Btty.
Ross, A.P. VA 4th Cav. Co.D
Ross, Armistead VA 166th Mil. Co.E
Ross, A.S. NC 48th Inf. Co.E
Ross, A.S. 1st Cherokee Mtd.Vol. 1st Co.D
Ross, Asa AL 8th Inf. Co.F Sgt.
Ross, Asa NC Coast Guards Galloway's Co.
Ross, Augustus V. TN 14th Inf. Co.F,E
Ross, Austin LA 5th Inf. Co.E
Ross, Austin SC 6th Inf. 2nd Co.D
Ross, A.W. AR 1st (Monroe's) Cav. Co.A Cpl.
Ross, A.W. AR 5th Inf. Co.I
Ross, A.W. SC 6th Cav. Co.I Sgt.
Ross, A.W. SC 8th Inf. Co.I
Ross, B. VA Inf. 1st Bn.Loc.Def. Co.C

Ross, B.A. NC 66th Inf. Co.G
Ross, B.A. TN 21st & 22nd (Cons.) Cav. Co.E
Ross, B.C. SC 6th Cav. Co.C
Ross, Benjamin MO Cav. Ford's Bn. Recruit
Ross, Benjamin TN 63rd Inf. Co.C
Ross, Benjamin B. NC 4th Inf. Co.I Cpl.
Ross, Benjamin F. NC 6th Inf. Co.F Cpl.
Ross, Benjamin F. TN Cav. 17th Bn. (Sanders') Co.A
Ross, Benjamin F. TX 24th & 25th Cav. Co.B Capt.
Ross, Benjamin Suthards MS Inf. 1st St.Troops Co.E Sgt.
Ross, Benjamin W. MS 42nd Inf. Co.B
Ross, Bernard VA Hvy.Arty. 18th Bn. Co.C
Ross, Beth KY 7th Cav. Co.G
Ross, Beth KY Lt.Arty. Cobb's Co. Cpl.
Ross, Beverly G. VA 56th Inf. Co.E
Ross, B.F. AL 3rd Inf. Co.I
Ross, B.F. AL 27th Inf. Co.E
Ross, B.F. MO Robertson's Regt.St.Guard Co.9
Ross, B.F. TX 25th Cav. Co.A,B Capt.
Ross, B.F. TX 9th (Nichols') Inf. Co.H
Ross, B.G. VA 3rd Lt.Arty. (Loc.Def.) Co.D
Ross, Birel VA Cav. Swann's Bn. Lilly's Co.
Ross, B.J. KY 3rd Mtd.Inf. 1st Co.F
Ross, B.K. TN 40th Inf. Co.I
Ross, B.M. LA 7th Inf. Co.I
Ross, Bony TX Cav. Baylor's Regt. Co.B
Ross, B.S. MS 5th Inf. (St.Troops) Co.I
Ross, Caleb VA 9th Cav. Co.H
Ross, Canada AR Lt.Arty. Key's Btty.
Ross, Canida AR 15th (Josey's) Inf. Co.C
Ross, Carl TX 1st (Yager's) Cav. Co.A Bugler
Ross, C.C. GA 42nd Inf. Co.K
Ross, C.C. MO 11th Inf. Co.A
Ross, C.C. TX 25th Cav. Co.E Sgt.
Ross, C.H. NC 1st Jr.Res. Co.B
Ross, Charles GA 53rd Inf. Co.F
Ross, Charles LA 10th Inf. Co.F
Ross, Charles LA 14th Inf. Co.F Cpl.
Ross, Charles LA Mil. Chalmette Regt. Co.I
Ross, Charles MO 2nd Cav. Co.C
Ross, Charles NC 2nd Arty. (36th St.Troops) Co.H
Ross, Charles VA Hvy.Arty. 18th Bn. Co.B
Ross, Charles A. KY 13th Cav. N.C.S. Comsy.Sgt.
Ross, Charles C. SC Hvy.Arty. 15th (Lucas') Bn. Co.C Sgt.
Ross, Charles C. SC Arty. Childs' Co.
Ross, Charles D. FL 1st Inf.
Ross, Charles G. GA 36th (Villepigue's) Inf. Co.C 1st Sgt.
Ross, Charles E. 1st Conf.Inf. 2nd Co.E 1st Lt.,Adj.
Ross, Charles F. VA 51st Inf. Co.D 2nd Lt.
Ross, Charles G. NC 33rd Inf.
Ross, Charles H. FL 3rd Inf. Co.I Capt.
Ross, Charles L. GA Inf. 2nd Bn. Co.C Cpl.
Ross, Charles L. MS 19th Inf. Co.E
Ross, Charles M. KY 1st (Butler's) Cav. Co.E Cpl.
Ross, Charles Melvin TN Greer's Regt.Part.# Rangers Co.C,F
Ross, Charles R. GA 41st Inf. Co.C
Ross, Charles S. TX 37th Cav. Co.A

Ross, Christopher C. GA 34th Inf. Co.F
Ross, Christopher C. TX 4th Inf. Co.K
Ross, Cincinnati MS 4th Inf.
Ross, C.L. MS Inf. 3rd Bn. (St.Troops) Co.B
Ross, Clinton J. NC 3rd Bn.Sr.Res. Co.A
Ross, C.M. TN 15th (Stewart's) Cav. Co.C
Ross, C.M. TN 22nd Inf. Co.E
Ross, Commador 2nd Cherokee Mtd.Vol. Co.B
Ross, Cortes E. GA 42nd Inf. Co.A,K
Ross, C.P. VA Lt.Arty. Lowry's Co. Sgt.
Ross, C.P. VA 51st Inf. Co.C
Ross, C.R. AL 11th Inf. Co.D
Ross, C.S. TX 35th (Brown's) Cav. Co.I
Ross, C.S. TX 1st Hvy.Arty. Co.E
Ross, C.W. TN 6th Inf. Co.A Cpl.
Ross, Cyrus W. GA Arty. 11th Bn. (Sumter Arty.) Co.A
Ross, D. AR Lt.Arty. Zimmerman's Btty.
Ross, D. AR 27th Inf. Co.E
Ross, D. MS 3rd Cav. Co.H Sgt.
Ross, D. SC 1st Cav. Co.E
Ross, D. TN 1st (Feild's) & 27th Inf. (Cons.) Co.I
Ross, D. VA 12th Cav. Co.K
Ross, D.A. GA Inf. Co.C
Ross, D.A. MS 41st Inf. Co.F
Ross, D.A.G. 8th (Wade's) Conf.Cav. Co.B
Ross, Daniel AL 42nd Inf. Co.H Cpl.
Ross, Daniel LA 1st Hvy.Arty. (Reg.) Co.C
Ross, Daniel LA Inf. 1st Sp.Bn. (Wheat's) New Co.D Sgt.
Ross, Daniel LA Miles' Legion Co.H
Ross, Daniel MS 9th Inf. New Co.B, Old Co.B Sgt.
Ross, Daniel MO 2nd Cav. Co.D
Ross, Daniel MO 8th Cav. Co.K
Ross, Daniel TN 27th Inf. Co.F
Ross, Daniel 1st Cherokee Mtd.Vol. 2nd Co.H
Ross, Daniel O. MS 11th Inf. Co.K
Ross, Daniel W. TX 14th Cav. Co.C 2nd Lt.
Ross, David AL 24th Inf. Co.H Music.
Ross, David LA Mil. Fire Bn. Co.G Jr. 2nd Lt.
Ross, David MS Inf. 1st Bn.St.Troops (30 days '64) Co.B
Ross, David MO 12th Inf. Co.K
Ross, David TN Cav. 12th Bn. (Day's) Co.B
Ross, David VA 7th Cav. Co.C
Ross, David VA Horse Arty. McClanahan's Co.
Ross, David VA 10th Inf. Co.F,A
Ross, David VA Inf. 25th Bn. Co.A
Ross, David A. SC 1st (Orr's) Rifles Co.E
Ross, David B. VA 97th Mil. Co.D
Ross, David C. AR 3rd Inf. Co.I
Ross, David C. NC 47th Inf. Co.K
Ross, David H. GA 8th Inf. Co.C Sgt.
Ross, Davidson C. VA 17th Cav. Co.E
Ross, Davidson C. VA 36th Inf. 2nd Co.I
Ross, David Y. NC 4th Inf. Co.F
Ross, D.B. AL Cp. of Instr. Talladega Co.A
Ross, D.C. NC Mallett's Bn. Co.B
Ross, D.C. TX 5th Inf. Co.G Cpl.
Ross, D.C. VA Inf. 23rd Bn. Co.B
Ross, D.D. AR 1st Mtd.Rifles Co.B Cpl.
Ross, D.D. MO Collins' Cav.
Ross, Denis K. TN 5th (McKenzie's) Cav. Co.E
Ross, D.J. GA 27th Inf. Co.C
Ross, D.L. VA 21st Cav. 2nd Co.G

323

Ross, D.L. VA 51st Inf. Co.C Capt.
Ross, D.M. MD Cav. 2nd Bn. Capt.
Ross, D.M.A. Sap. & Min.,CSA 1st Lt.
Ross, D.M.N. AL 89th Mil. Co.B Capt.
Ross, D.M.N. 2nd Conf.Eng.Troops Co.C 1st Lt.
Ross, Dock TX 20th Inf. Co.G
Ross, Doctor M. NC 26th Inf. Co.K Sgt.
Ross, Drury H. AR 2nd Mtd.Rifles Co.E
Ross, D.T. AR Lt.Arty. Wiggins' Btty.
Ross, D.T. TX 18th Cav. Co.I
Ross, D.W. MD Cav. 2nd Bn. Capt.
Ross, E. AR 30th Inf. Co.G
Ross, E. MO 1st & 4th Cons.Inf. Co.E,C
Ross, E. NC Hvy.Arty. 10th Bn. Co.C
Ross, E. TX Inf. 1st St.Troops Whitehead's Co.
Ross, E. TX 20th Inf. Co.G
Ross, E.A. NC 1st Inf. (6 mo. '61) Co.C Capt.
Ross, Eaton NC 8th Inf. Co.H
Ross, E.B. KY 3rd Mtd.Inf. Co.K 1st Lt.
Ross, Edmund J. GA 45th Inf. Co.B
Ross, Edward KY 3rd Cav. Co.K 1st Lt.
Ross, Edward LA 1st Cav. Co.E
Ross, Edward NC 47th Inf. Co.K
Ross, Edward TN 31st Inf. Co.D
Ross, Edward VA Hvy.Arty. 20th Bn. Co.B
Ross, Edward H. TX 8th Cav. Co.A Cpl.
Ross, Edwin NC 35th Inf.
Ross, Edwin Conf.Inf. Tucker's Regt. Co.G
Ross, Egbert A. NC 11th (Bethel Regt.) Inf. Co.A Maj.
Ross, E.J. LA 9th Inf. Co.H
Ross, E.J. MS 41st Inf. Co.F
Ross, E.L. LA Lt.Arty. Fenner's Btty.
Ross, E.L. LA Inf. 1st Sp.Bn. (Rightor's) Co.B
Ross, Elias AL Inf. 1st Regt. Co.E
Ross, Elias AL 3rd Bn.Res. Co.H
Ross, Elias MO 1st Cav. Co.E
Ross, Elias MO 4th Inf. Co.E
Ross, Elijah AR 34th Inf. Co.G
Ross, Elisha NC 22nd Inf. Co.K Cpl.
Ross, E.M. LA Mil. British Guard Bn. Burrowes' Co.
Ross, E.M. TN Hvy.Arty. Johnston's Co. Sgt.
Ross, E.M. Gen. & Staff 2nd Lt.,Dr.M.
Ross, E. McE. Gen. & Staff, Inf. 2nd Lt.
Ross, Emmett L. LA 20th Inf. Co.K 1st Lt.
Ross, E.P. SC Mil. 15th Regt.
Ross, Erasmus NC 47th Inf. Co.I
Ross, Erastus B. TX 16th Cav. Co.C Cpl.
Ross, Erskine VA VMI Co.A Ord.Sgt.
Ross, Erskine M. VA Bn.Cadets Co.A Capt.
Ross, Erskine R. MS 11th Inf. Co.D
Ross, E.S. LA Lt.Arty. Fenner's Btty.
Ross, E.S. LA Mil. Beauregard Bn. Co.C
Ross, E.T. AL 46th Inf. Co.D Sgt.
Ross, E.T.M. AL 46th Inf. Co.D Sgt.
Ross, Eugene A. MS 11th Inf. Co.D
Ross, E.W. GA 24th Inf. Co.D
Ross, E. Wilds LA 3rd (Harrison's) Cav. Co.A
Ross, Ewler H. TX 7th Inf. Co.C
Ross, F. KY 10th (Johnson's) Cav. New Co.H
Ross, F. LA 9th Inf. Co.H
Ross, F. LA 12th Inf. Co.H
Ross, F.A. Gen. & Staff Surg.
Ross, F.C. TN 33rd Inf. Co.H Sgt.
Ross, F.E. GA 3rd Bn.S.S. Co.D Capt.

Ross, F.G. GA 7th Inf. (St.Guards) Co.C Cpl.
Ross, F.M. AL Cav. Lewis' Bn. Co.C
Ross, F.M. AL 12th Inf. Co.G
Ross, F.M. AL 48th Inf. Co.E Capt.
Ross, F.M. LA 13th Bn. (Part.Rangers) Co.B
Ross, F.M. LA 2nd Inf. Co.G
Ross, F.M. MS 1st Cav. Co.K
Ross, F.M., Jr. MS Cav. Jeff Davis Legion Co.E
Ross, F.M., Sr. MS Cav. Jeff Davis Legion Co.E
Ross, F.M. TN 7th (Duckworth's) Cav. Co.I
Ross, F.M. TX Cav. Martin's Regt. Co.G
Ross, F.M. TX 14th Inf. Co.H
Ross, F.M. TX 19th Inf. Co.F Sgt.
Ross, F. Mathew GA 2nd Res. Co.B
Ross, F.N. MS Inf. 1st Bn. Co.A
Ross, Fountain P. AR 4th Inf. Co.A
Ross, Fountain P. TN 45th Inf. Co.F Cpl.
Ross, Francis LA 20th Inf. Co.G Cpl.
Ross, Francis SC 5th St.Troops Co.A
Ross, Francis SC 6th Res. Co.B
Ross, Francis B. MS 11th Inf. Co.D
Ross, Francis C. TN 27th Inf. Co.I
Ross, Francis H. AR 33rd Inf. Co.B
Ross, Francis M. LA 15th Inf. Co.G
Ross, Francis M. MS 24th Inf. Co.H,I
Ross, Francis P. MS 20th Inf. Co.B
Ross, Frank AL 32nd Inf. Co.G Drum.
Ross, Frank KY 11th Cav. Co.A
Ross, Frank SC 3rd Bn.Res. Co.E
Ross, Frank SC 6th Inf. 1st Co.A
Ross, Frank TN 19th Inf. Co.A
Ross, Frank A. AL 4th Inf. Co.I
Ross, Frank C. AL 32nd Inf. Co.I
Ross, Frank C. AL 32nd & 58th (Cons.) Inf.
Ross, Frank D. TX 14th Cav. Co.B 1st Lt.
Ross, Franklin A. SC 5th Inf. 2nd Co.B Sgt.
Ross, Franklin C. GA 1st Reg. Co.B 2nd Lt.
Ross, Franklin C. GA Inf. 2nd Bn. Co.C
Ross, Franklin S. TX 17th Cav. Co.D
Ross, Frank M. MS 13th Inf. Co.I Sgt.
Ross, Frank S. MS 17th Inf. Co.B
Ross, Frank W. AR 3rd Cav. Co.G
Ross, Frank W. FL 3rd Inf. Co.I 1st Lt.
Ross, Frederick A. MS 11th Inf. Co.B Sgt.
Ross, Frederick E. GA Cobb's Legion Co.B 1st Lt.
Ross, Fredrick W. GA 14th Inf. Co.D
Ross, French S. NC 24th Inf. Co.K
Ross, F.S. TX 11th Inf. Co.C Sgt.
Ross, F.W. 2nd Conf.Eng.Troops Co.C
Ross, G. AR 50th Mil. Co.I
Ross, G. SC Lt.Arty. 3rd (Palmetto) Bn. Co.H,I
Ross, G.A. AR 2nd Inf. Co.I Capt.
Ross, G.A. MO 10th Cav. Co.I
Ross, G.A. MO Cav. Coleman's Regt. Co.C
Ross, G.A. MO 1st & 4th Cons.Inf. Co.E
Ross, G.A. MO 4th Inf. Co.E
Ross, Gabriel NC 44th Inf. Co.D
Ross, Gaines F. SC 2nd Inf. Co.F
Ross, G.B. TN Inf. Nashville Bn. Cattles' Co.
Ross, G.D. VA Cav. 47th Bn. Co.A
Ross, George AL 1st Regt. Mobile Vol. Co.E
Ross, George AL 4th Res. Co.B
Ross, George AL 18th Inf. Co.I
Ross, George AL 94th Mil. Co.A
Ross, George AR 11th & 17th (Cons.) Inf. Co.C

Ross, George GA Cav. 15th Bn. (St.Guards) Wooten's Co.
Ross, George MD Cadet Corps
Ross, George MS 18th Cav.
Ross, George MS 14th Inf. Co.E
Ross, George MS 16th Inf. Co.C
Ross, George NC 39th Inf. Co.F
Ross, George TN 49th Inf. Co.H Cpl.
Ross, George TN Inf. Nashville Bn. Felts' Co.
Ross, George TX 29th Cav. Co.I
Ross, George TX Granbury's Cons.Brig. Co.F
Ross, George TX 4th Inf.
Ross, George VA Inf. 4th Bn.Loc.Def. Co.E
Ross, George VA 61st Inf. Co.H Cpl.
Ross, George VA Inf. Hutter's Co. 1st Lt.
Ross, Geo. VA VMI Asst.Surg.
Ross, George Conf.Cav. Wood's Regt. Co.L
Ross, George Gen. & Staff A.Surg.
Ross, George F. GA Siege Arty. 28th Bn. Co.C Sgt.
Ross, George F. SC 20th Inf. Co.A
Ross, George H. AR 9th Inf. Co.K
Ross, George H. LA 13th Bn. (Part.Rangers) Co.A
Ross, George H. NC Walker's Bn. Thomas' Legion Co.H
Ross, George H. TN 3rd (Lillard's) Mtd.Inf. Co.A Capt.
Ross, George L. MD 1st Inf. Co.G Cpl.
Ross, George L. MD Inf. 2nd Bn. Co.E Sgt.
Ross, George M. GA 4th Bn.S.S. Co.B
Ross, George P. NC 28th Inf. Co.K
Ross, George W. AR 1st Inf. Co.A
Ross, George W. GA Inf. 2nd Bn. Co.C Maj.
Ross, George W. GA 6th Inf. (St.Guards) Co.B 1st Sgt.
Ross, George W. MS 11th Inf. Co.D
Ross, George W. MS 17th Inf. Co.K
Ross, George W. MO 1st Cav. Co.F
Ross, George W. MO 5th Inf. Co.H
Ross, George W. NC 1st Bn.Jr.Res. Co.A
Ross, George W. NC 3rd Inf. Co.I
Ross, George W. TX 4th Cav. Co.D
Ross, George W. TX 15th Cav. Co.G
Ross, George W. TX Cav. Mann's Regt. Co.A
Ross, George W. VA Hvy.Arty. 10th Bn. Co.C 1st Sgt.
Ross, George W. VA 6th Inf. Co.A
Ross, George W. 1st Cherokee Mtd.Rifles Co.H 2nd Lt.
Ross, George W. 1st Cherokee Mtd.Rifles 2nd Co.K Cpl.
Ross, Gerhard VA Inf. 4th Bn.Loc.Def. Co.C
Ross, G.F. AR 24th Inf. Co.A
Ross, G.F. AR Inf. Hardy's Regt. Co.H
Ross, G.F. GA 1st Reg. Co.I
Ross, G.F.H. MS 9th Inf. New Co.F
Ross, G.H.H. MS 3rd Inf. Co.F
Ross, G.H.H. MS 15th (Cons.) Inf. Co.K
Ross, G.I. TX 15th Inf. 1st Co.E
Ross, G.J. FL 1st (Res.) Inf. Co.K
Ross, G.J. MS Cp.Guard (Cp. of Instr. for Conscr.)
Ross, G.J. TX 1st Hvy.Arty. 2nd Co.A
Ross, G.L. TN 13th Inf. Co.I Capt.
Ross, G.M.D. TN 19th & 20th (Cons.) Cav. Co.D

Ross, G.M.D. TN 20th (Russell's) Cav. Co.K
Ross, G.M.D. TN 33rd Inf. Co.H
Ross, Granville H.H. MS 23rd Inf. Co.F
Ross, Green B. FL 8th Inf. Co.A
Ross, Griffin MS 27th Inf. Co.D
Ross, Griffin W. MS 29th Inf. Co.B
Ross, G.W. AL 3rd Inf. Co.I
Ross, G.W. GA 9th Inf. (St.Guards) Co.A
Ross, G.W. GA 54th Inf. Co.B
Ross, G.W. MS 2nd Cav. Co.I,B
Ross, G.W. MS St.Cav. 3rd Bn. (Cooper's) Little's Co.
Ross, G.W. MO Cav. 3rd Bn.
Ross, G.W. VA 8th Cav. Co.C
Ross, H. MS 18th Cav. Wimberly's Co.
Ross, H. NC 27th Inf. Co.I
Ross, H. TX 25th Cav. Co.E
Ross, H.A. AL 32nd & 58th (Cons.) Inf.
Ross, H.A. AL 58th Inf. Co.H,D
Ross, Harman NC 3rd Arty. (40th St.Troops) Co.B
Ross, Harvy D. VA 54th Inf. Co.F
Ross, Havey B. VA 46th Inf. 2nd Co.K
Ross, Henry AR 19th (Dockery's) Inf. Cons.Co. E,D
Ross, Henry GA 6th Cav. Co.I
Ross, Henry LA 1st (Strawbridge's) Inf. Co.E
Ross, Henry NC 1st Inf. Co.E
Ross, Henry TX 1st (Yager's) Cav. Co.E
Ross, Henry VA 6th Cav. Co.D
Ross, Henry VA 5th Inf. Co.E 2nd Lt.
Ross, Henry VA Prov.Guard Avis' Co.
Ross, Henry F. VA 19th Cav. Co.H
Ross, Henry W. SC 2nd Arty. Co.B
Ross, Henry W. SC 2nd St.Troops Co.K
Ross, H.G. GA Arty. (Macon Lt.Arty.) Slaten's Co.
Ross, H.H. TX 12th Cav. Co.B
Ross, Hilliard J. NC 48th Inf. Co.A
Ross, Hilliard L. AL 3rd Inf. Co.K
Ross, H.J. GA 9th Inf. Co.H
Ross, H.J. TX 11th Inf. Co.H
Ross, H.J. TX 18th Inf. Co.I
Ross, H.M. TN 27th Inf. Co.I
Ross, Horace C. TN Lt.Arty. Morton's Co. Sgt.
Ross, Horace E. Gen. & Staff, Arty. 1st Lt.
Ross, Hosea T. NC Hvy.Arty. 10th Bn. Co.C
Ross, H.P. TN 5th (McKenzie's) Cav. Co.D
Ross, H.T. MS St.Cav. 3rd Bn. (Cooper's) 2nd Co.A
Ross, H.T. MS Cav. Terrell's Unatt.Co.
Ross, Hugh AR 5th Inf. Co.I Capt.
Ross, Hugh AR 18th Inf. Co.B
Ross, Hugh, Jr. AR 36th Inf. Co.C 2nd Lt.
Ross, Hugh FL 4th Inf. Co.G
Ross, Hugh D. NC 48th Inf. Co.F
Ross, Hugh D. NC 52nd Inf. Co.A
Ross, Hugh M. GA Arty. 11th Bn. (Sumter Arty.) Co.A Maj.
Ross, Hugh R. AR Lt.Arty. Thrall's Btty.
Ross, H.W. MS 2nd St.Cav. Co.K
Ross, H.W. MS Cav. Ham's Regt. Co.K
Ross, H. William AL 21st Inf. Co.H
Ross, I.A. MO Cav. Clardy's Bn. Co.B
Ross, Isaac A. LA 3rd (Harrison's) Cav. Co.A
Ross, Isaac A. Conf.Cav. Wood's Regt. 1st Co.A
Ross, Isaac A. Beall's Staff Capt.

Ross, J. AL 6th Cav. Co.F
Ross, J. FL 1st (Res.) Inf. Co.E
Ross, J. FL 5th Inf. Co.B
Ross, J. GA 22nd Inf. Co.E
Ross, J. LA 15th Inf. Co.D
Ross, J. MS 4th Cav. Co.F
Ross, J. SC 1st (Butler's) Inf. Co.K
Ross, J. SC 4th St.Troops Co.C
Ross, J.A. AR Inf. 4th Bn. Co.C Maj.
Ross, J.A. LA 25th Inf. Co.K Cpl.
Ross, J.A. LA Inf.Cons.Crescent Regt. Co.I
Ross, J.A. MS 1st (King's) Inf. (St.Troops) Co.F
Ross, J.A. TN 7th (Duckworth's) Cav. Co.H
Ross, Jackson GA 8th Inf. (St.Guards) Co.D
Ross, Jackson 1st Choctaw & Chickasaw Mtd.Rifles 2nd Co.B
Ross, Jacob AL 48th Inf. Co.G
Ross, Jacob AR 26th Inf. Co.C 1st Lt.
Ross, James AZ Cav. Herbert's Bn. Oury's Co.
Ross, James AR 18th Inf. Co.K
Ross, James GA Inf. 1st Loc.Troops (Augusta) Co.H
Ross, James GA 7th Inf. (St.Guards) Co.C
Ross, James GA 21st Inf. Co.C
Ross, James GA 32nd Inf. Co.H
Ross, James GA 57th Inf. Co.H
Ross, James KY 6th Mtd.Inf. Co.H
Ross, James LA 15th Inf. Co.D
Ross, James LA 16th Inf. Co.D,A
Ross, James LA 20th Inf. Co.G Cpl.
Ross, James LA Mil.Conf.Guards Regt. Co.B
Ross, James MS 6th Inf. Co.H
Ross, James MS 14th Inf. Co.A
Ross, James MS 39th Inf. Co.G
Ross, Jas. MS 48th Inf. Co.I
Ross, James MO 1st Inf. Co.C
Ross, James MO 1st & 4th Cons.Inf. Co.G
Ross, James NC 39th Inf. Co.F,A
Ross, James NC 5th Inf. Co.G Cpl.
Ross, James NC 54th Inf. Co.E
Ross, James NC 56th Inf. Co.F
Ross, James NC 64th Inf. Co.N
Ross, James SC Inf. 7th Bn. (Enfield Rifles) Co.E 1st Lt.
Ross, James TN Cav. 12th Bn. (Day's) Co.B,D
Ross, James TN Cav. 12th Bn. (Day's) Co.C
Ross, James TN 17th Cav. Co.C
Ross, James TN 21st Cav.
Ross, James TN Lt.Arty. Phillips' Co.
Ross, James TN 1st (Feild's) Inf. Co.L
Ross, James TN 44th Inf. Co.F Cpl.
Ross, James TN 44th (Cons.) Inf. Co.D
Ross, James TX 1st (Yager's) Cav. Co.A
Ross, James TX 20th Bn.St.Troops Co.G
Ross, James VA Inf. 4th Bn.Loc.Def. Co.B
Ross, James VA 60th Inf. Co.F
Ross, James Conf.Reg.Inf. Brooks' Bn. Co.E
Ross, James A. AL 24th Inf. Hosp.Stew.
Ross, James A. AR 15th (Josey's) Inf. Co.C
Ross, James A. GA 4th (Clinch's) Cav. Co.H
Ross, James A. GA Cav. 7th Bn. (St.Guards) Co.E
Ross, James A. GA Inf. 10th Bn. Co.B
Ross, James A. MO 8th Cav. Co.D
Ross, James A. NC 2nd Arty. (36th St.Troops) Co.C

Ross, James A. SC 25th Inf. Co.A 2nd Lt.
Ross, James A. TN 12th (Green's) Cav. Co.E
Ross, James A. TN 6th Inf. Co.E Cpl.
Ross, James A. TN 16th Inf. Co.F
Ross, James A. TN 27th Inf. Co.D
Ross, James B. VA 11th Bn.Res. Co.D
Ross, James C. AL 33rd Inf. Co.I
Ross, James C. GA Cav. 29th Bn. Co.B Sgt.
Ross, James C. GA Siege Arty. Campbell's Ind.Co. Sgt.
Ross, James C. GA 26th Inf. 1st Co.G
Ross, James C. GA 29th Inf. Co.E 2nd Lt.
Ross, James C. Conf.Cav. Wood's Regt. Co.L Sgt.
Ross, James E. LA 28th (Gray's) Inf. Co.K Cpl.
Ross, James E. VA 1st Bn.Mtd.Rangers Co.B
Ross, James E. VA Horse Arty. Lurty's Co.
Ross, James E. VA 14th Inf. Co.C
Ross, James E. VA 27th Inf. Co.C
Ross, James F. GA Arty. 11th Bn. (Sumter Arty.) Co.A Sgt.Maj.
Ross, James F. MS 31st Inf. Co.D Cpl.
Ross, James H. AR Cav. Gordon's Regt. Co.F Cpl.
Ross, James H. AR 12th Inf. Co.E
Ross, James H. NC 47th Inf. Co.K Sgt.
Ross, James H. SC 2nd Cav. Co.I
Ross, James H. SC Cav.Bn. Hampton Legion Co.A
Ross, James H. TN Cav. 9th Bn. (Gantt's) Co.F Sgt.
Ross, James H. TX 13th Vol. Co.E
Ross, James H. TX 15th Inf. 2nd Co.G Cpl.
Ross, James Hunter KY 2nd (Woodward's) Cav. Co.G
Ross, James J. AR 1st Vol. Co.F
Ross, James J. MS Cav. 4th Bn. Roddy's Co.
Ross, James J. NC 53rd Inf. Co.I
Ross, James L. MS 24th Inf. Co.E
Ross, James M. AL 18th Bn.Vol. Co.A Cpl.
Ross, James M. MS 10th Inf. New Co.F, Old Co.C
Ross, James M. MS 14th Inf. Co.C
Ross, James M. MS 46th Inf. Co.D
Ross, James M. NC 8th Inf. Co.I Cpl.
Ross, James M. TN 53rd Inf. Co.K Sgt.
Ross, James M. VA 16th Inf. Co.B
Ross, James M. 1st Cherokee Mtd.Vol. 2nd Co.K
Ross, James N. AL 11th Inf. Co. H
Ross, James P. AL 6th Inf. Co.K
Ross, James P. GA 12th Inf. Co.H Cpl.
Ross, James P. KY 13th Cav. Co.B
Ross, James P. MS 9th Inf.
Ross, James P. NC 30th Inf. Co.G
Ross, James P. TN 17th Inf. Co.H
Ross, James P. VA 4th Cav. Co.D
Ross, James P. VA 13th Inf. 1st Co.E
Ross, James R. AR 9th Inf. Co.G
Ross, James S. AR 15th Mil. Co.C
Ross, James S. SC 5th Inf. 1st Co.H, 2nd Co.B
Ross, James S. VA 1st Arty. Co.H QMSgt.
Ross, James V. TX 1st (McCulloch's) Cav. Co.B Sgt.
Ross, James V. TX 16th Inf. Co.G
Ross, James W. FL 8th Inf. Co.A Sgt.
Ross, James W. TN 19th (Biffle's) Cav. Co.A
Ross, James W. TN 1st (Feild's) Inf. Co.I

Ross, James W. VA 41st Inf. 2nd Co.E
Ross, James W. VA 51st Inf. Co.D
Ross, James W.W. KY 11th Cav. Co.B
Ross, Jasper N. NC 22nd Inf. Co.K
Ross, Jasper W. TN 28th Inf. Co.H Cpl.
Ross, Jasper Z. MS 15th Inf. Co.F
Ross, J.B. AL Lt.Arty. Goldthwaite's Btty.
Ross, J.B. GA Hvy.Arty. 22nd Bn. Co.E
Ross, J.B. MS 1st (King's) Inf. (St.Troops) Co.E
Ross, J.B. TX 10th Cav. Co.F
Ross, J.B. TX 5th Inf. Co.H Cpl.
Ross, J.C. MS 1st (King's) Inf. (St.Troops) Co.D
Ross, J.C. NC 4th Sr.Res. Co.G
Ross, J.C. TX 5th Inf. Co.F
Ross, J.D. AL Cp. of Instr. Talladega Co.A
Ross, J.D. KY 3rd Mtd.Inf. Co.H
Ross, J.D. KY 7th Mtd.Inf. Co.D
Ross, J.D. SC 2nd Inf. Co.D
Ross, J.D.H. VA VMI Lt.Col.
Ross, J.E. AL Gid Nelson Lt.Arty.
Ross, J.E. AL Mil. 2nd Regt.Vol. Co.E
Ross, J.E. AL 48th Inf. Co.B 2nd Lt.
Ross, J.E. AR 7th Inf. Co.B
Ross, J.E. GA 9th Inf. (St.Guards) Culp's Co.
Ross, J.E. TN 3rd (Lillard's) Mtd.Inf. Co.C
Ross, J. Edward Conf.Cav. Wood's Regt. Co.L
Ross, Jefferson AR 2nd Mtd.Rifles Co.B
Ross, Jehue AL Lt.Arty. Clanton's Btty.
Ross, Jess SC 1st (McCreary's) Inf. Campbell's Co.
Ross, Jesse AR 3rd St.Inf. AQM
Ross, Jesse MS Cav. Hughes' Bn. Co.E
Ross, Jesse MS 6th Inf. Co.H
Ross, Jesse NC Inf. Thomas Legion Co.B
Ross, Jesse SC Lt.Arty. 3rd (Palmetto) Bn. Co.A,H Cpl.
Ross, Jesse TN 21st (Wilson's) Cav. Co.H Sgt.
Ross, Jesse TN 21st & 22nd (Cons.) Cav. Co.H
Ross, Jesse TN 27th Inf. Co.I
Ross, Jesse TN 50th Inf. Co.F
Ross, Jesse VA Cav. 37th Bn. Co.D
Ross, Jesse G. LA 9th Inf. Co.F 2nd Lt.
Ross, Jesse H. SC 19th Inf. Co.D
Ross, Jesse M. MS 1st (Patton's) Inf. Co.K
Ross, Jesse R. SC 1st (Orr's) Rifles Co.C
Ross, Jeter AL Lt.Arty. Kolb's Btty.
Ross, J.F. AR 1st Vol. Co.F
Ross, J.F. AR Cav. 15th Bn. (Buster's Bn.) Co.D Capt.
Ross, J.F. GA Cav. 19th Bn. Co.A Sgt.
Ross, J.F. MS 2nd Inf. (A. of 10,000) Co.G
Ross, J.F. MO 1st Inf. Co.K
Ross, J.F. TN 6th (Wheeler's) Cav. Co.K
Ross, J.F. 10th Conf.Cav. Co.F Sgt.
Ross, J.F.H. MS Inf. 1st Bn. Polk's Co.
Ross, J.G. AR 2nd Cav. Co.E Cpl.
Ross, J.G. NC 57th Inf. Co.I
Ross, J.H. AL 8th (Livingston's) Cav. Co.D
Ross, J.H. GA 11th Cav. Co.C 1st Sgt.
Ross, J.H. SC 5th St.Troops Co.F
Ross, J.H. TN 12th Inf. Co.G
Ross, J.H. TN 12th (Cons.) Inf. Co.E
Ross, J.H. 4th Conf.Inf. Co.I
Ross, J.J. AL 11th Cav. Co.I
Ross, J.J. AR 27th Inf. New Co.C
Ross, J.J. GA Cav. 20th Bn. Co.D
Ross, J.J. MS Cav. 1st Bn. (Miller's) Co.A

Ross, J.J. MS 3rd Inf. (St.Troops) Co.E
Ross, J.J. SC 5th Bn.Res. Co.D
Ross, J.K.P. TN 18th Inf. Co.F
Ross, J.L. AL 14th Inf. Co.H
Ross, J.L. KY 2nd (Woodward's) Cav. Co.C
Ross, J.L. TX 12th Inf. Co.G Sgt.
Ross, J.M. AL 14th Inf. Co.A Sgt.
Ross, J.M. AL 43rd Inf. Co.G
Ross, J.M. AR 45th Cav. Co.B 1st Lt.
Ross, J.M. MS 9th Inf. Co.I
Ross, J.M. MS 14th (Cons.) Inf. Co.F
Ross, J.M. MS 41st Inf. Co.C
Ross, J.M. MO 9th Bn.S.S. Co.B
Ross, J.M. MO 2nd N.E. Cav. (Franklin's Regt.) Co.B
Ross, J.M. NC 7th Sr.Res. Boon's Co.
Ross, J.M. TN 6th (Wheeler's) Cav. Co.K
Ross, J.M. TN 2nd (Walker's) Inf. Co.H
Ross, J.M. TN 22nd Inf. Co.E Cpl.
Ross, J.M. TX 20th Inf. Co.C
Ross, J.N. GA Inf. 1st Bn. (St.Guards) Co.A
Ross, J.N. NC 23rd Inf.
Ross, J.N. NC 30th Inf. Co.K
Ross, J.N. VA Cav. 37th Bn. Co.D
Ross, J.N. VA Conscr.
Ross, J.O. FL Fernandez's Mtd.Co. (Supply Force)
Ross, John AL 3rd Inf. Co.C
Ross, John AL 4th Res. Co.F
Ross, John AL 23rd Inf. Co.G Capt.
Ross, John AL 29th Inf. Co.D
Ross, John AL 31st Inf. Co.D 1st Lt.
Ross, John AL 34th Inf. Co.D
Ross, John AR 10th (Witt's) Cav. Co.A
Ross, John AR 7th Inf. Co.F
Ross, John AR 12th Inf. Co.E
Ross, John GA 1st Reg. Co.A 1st Sgt.
Ross, John GA 10th Inf. Co.G Sgt.
Ross, John GA 29th Inf. Co.A Music.
Ross, John GA 36th (Villepigue's) Inf. Co.I
Ross, John GA 51st Inf. Co.H
Ross, John GA Cobb's Legion Co.A
Ross, John KY 2nd (Duke's) Cav. Co.F
Ross, John KY 10th (Diamond's) Cav. Co.D,B
Ross, John KY 5th Mtd.Inf. Co.H
Ross, John KY 7th Mtd.Inf. Co.B,D
Ross, John LA 1st (Strawbridge's) Inf. Co.I
Ross, John LA 5th Inf.
Ross, John LA 17th Inf. Co.K
Ross, John LA 22nd (Cons.) Inf. Co.G Hosp.Stew.
Ross, John MS 7th Cav. Co.F
Ross, John MS 28th Cav. Co.I
Ross, John MS 4th Inf.
Ross, John MS 15th (Cons.) Inf. Co.F
Ross, John MS 44th Inf. Co.L
Ross, John MO St.Guard
Ross, John NC 3rd Bn.Sr.Res. Co.C
Ross, John NC 37th Inf. Co.K Capt.
Ross, John NC Inf. Thomas Legion Co.B Sgt.
Ross, John SC 1st (Butler's) Inf. Co.B
Ross, John SC 2nd Inf. Co.F
Ross, John SC 4th St.Troops Co.G
Ross, John SC 5th Inf. 2nd Co.B
Ross, John SC 6th Inf. 1st Co.A
Ross, John SC 14th Inf. Co.G
Ross, John SC 20th Inf. Co.A

Ross, John, Jr. TN 2nd (Smith's) Cav. Rankin's Co.
Ross, John, Jr. TN 4th (McLemore's) Cav. Co.H Wag.
Ross, John TN 4th Cav. Co.I
Ross, John TN 8th (Smith's) Cav. Co.H
Ross, John TN 21st (Wilson's) Cav. Co.D
Ross, John TN 4th Inf. Co.E
Ross, John TN 12th (Cons.) Inf. Co.G
Ross, John TN Inf. 154th Sr.Regt. Co.H
Ross, John TX Cav. Border's Regt. Co.D
Ross, John TX Arty. 4th Bn. Co.A
Ross, John TX Inf. 1st St.Troops Co.F
Ross, John TX 2nd Inf. Co.A
Ross, John TX 8th Inf. Co.A Ens.
Ross, John VA 10th Cav. Co.I
Ross, John VA 24th Cav. Co.E
Ross, John VA 3rd Res. Co.K
Ross, John VA 6th Inf. Co.A Sgt.
Ross, John VA 54th Inf. Co.F
Ross, John VA Burks' Regt.Loc.Def.
Ross, John 1st Chickasaw Inf. Gregg's Co.
Ross, John 1st Creek Mtd.Vol. 2nd Co.C
Ross, John 2nd Cherokee Mtd.Vol. Co.G
Ross, John A. AL Inf. 1st Regt. Co.E
Ross, John A. AL 23rd Bn.S.S. Co.G
Ross, John A. AL 59th Inf. Co.B
Ross, John A. AL 1st Bn. Hilliard's Legion Vol. Co.G
Ross, John A. AL 2nd Bn. Hilliard's Legion Vol. Co.E
Ross, John A. AL 3rd Bn. Hilliard's Legion Vol. Co.B
Ross, John A. AR 9th Inf. Co.G
Ross, John A. AR 27th Inf. Co.G
Ross, John A. KY Lt.Arty. Cobb's Co.
Ross, John A. LA 1st Hvy.Arty. (Reg.) Co.A
Ross, John A. MO 8th Cav. Co.D
Ross, John A. NC 2nd Arty. (36th St.Troops) Co.C,E
Ross, John A. TN Cav. 12th Bn. (Day's) Co.B
Ross, John A. TX Cav. Mann's Regt. Co.C
Ross, John A. VA 31st Inf. 2nd Co.B
Ross, John A. Gen. & Staff Hosp.Stew.
Ross, John A.J. GA 6th Inf. Co.G 2nd Lt.
Ross, John B. AL Auburn Home Guards Vol. Darby's Co. Bvt.2nd Lt.
Ross, John B. KY 2nd (Woodward's) Cav. Co.G
Ross, John B. MO 12th Inf. Co.D 1st Lt.
Ross, John B. VA 28th Inf. Co.B
Ross, John C. AL Inf. 1st Regt. Co.B Cpl.
Ross, John C. AL 39th Inf. Co.K 2nd Lt.
Ross, John C. AR 16th Inf. Co.E Cpl.
Ross, John C. AR 31st Inf. Co.E
Ross, John C. GA Siege Arty. 28th Bn. Co.F Sgt.
Ross, John C. GA 49th Inf. Co.H
Ross, John C. MS 24th Inf. Co.I,D
Ross, John C. MS 35th Inf. Co.B
Ross, John C. 1st Conf.Cav. 2nd Co.G
Ross, John Crossett LA 19th Inf. Co.D
Ross, John D. AR Lt.Arty. Wiggins' Btty.
Ross, John D. KY 5th Cav. Co.H
Ross, John D. MS 36th Inf. Co.K Cpl.
Ross, John D. VA Cav. Ferguson's Bn. Ferguson's Co., Parks' Co.
Ross, John E. AL 42nd Inf. Co.I

Ross, John E. GA 11th Cav. Co.B Sgt.
Ross, John E. TN 5th (McKenzie's) Cav. Co.E
Ross, John E. VA 38th Inf. 2nd Co.I Cpl.
Ross, John F. GA Inf. 2nd Bn. Co.C
Ross, John F. MS 18th Cav. Co.A
Ross, John F. MO Inf. Clark's Regt. Co.D Capt.
Ross, John F. NC Snead's Co. (Loc.Def.)
Ross, John F. TN 34th Inf. Co.I Capt.
Ross, John F. Conf.Cav. Clarkson's Bn. Ind.
  Rangers Co.H Capt.
Ross, John F. 1st Cherokee Mtd.Vol. 1st Co.K
  1st Lt.
Ross, John F.M. NC 45th Inf. Co.B
Ross, John H. AR 27th Inf. Co.H Cpl.
Ross, John H. SC 7th Res. Co.M
Ross, John H. TX 11th Inf. Co.E 1st Sgt.
Ross, John H. VA Cav. 34th Bn. Co.A
  Hosp.Stew.
Ross, John H. VA Horse Arty. Lurty's Co.
Ross, John H.D. VA 52nd Inf. Lt.Col.
Ross, John J. AL 9th Inf. Co.A 1st Sgt.
Ross, John J. AR 33rd Inf. Co.B
Ross, John J. GA 14th Inf. Co.G Sgt.
Ross, John J. MO 5th Inf. Co.C
Ross, John L. AR 18th Inf. Co.B
Ross, John L. LA 5th Inf. Co.I 1st Sgt.
Ross, John L. LA 8th Inf. Co.E
Ross, John L. LA 17th Inf. Co.C
Ross, John L. MS Inf. 2nd Bn. Co.F
Ross, John L. MS 48th Inf. Co.F
Ross, John L. NC 17th Inf. (2nd Org.) Co.K
Ross, John M. FL 9th Inf. Co.K,I
Ross, John M. KY 3rd Mtd.Inf. Co.F Sgt.
Ross, John M. KY 4th Mtd.Inf. Co.C
Ross, John M. MS Bradford's Co. (Conf.Guards
  Arty.)
Ross, John M. MS 19th Inf. Co.E
Ross, John M. MO 10th Cav. Co.E 1st Lt.
Ross, John M. MO 11th Inf. Co.F
Ross, John M. NC 14th Inf. Co.H
Ross, John M. TN Cav. 11th Bn. (Gordon's)
  Co.A
Ross, John O. AR 18th Inf. Co.D
Ross, John O. FL 1st (Res.) Inf.
Ross, John P. VA 166th Mil. Co.E
Ross, John R. GA 45th Inf. Co.D
Ross, John R. NC 3rd Arty. (40th St.Troops)
  Co.B Sgt.
Ross, John R. VA 6th Inf. Co.H
Ross, John R. 1st Conf.Inf. 2nd Co.G
Ross, John Robert TN Greer's Regt.Part.Rangers
  Co.C
Ross, Johnson AR Inf. Hardy's Regt. Co.I
Ross, Johnston VA 60th Inf. Co.F
Ross, John T. AL 1st Regt.Conscr. Co.H
Ross, John T. AL Conscr. Echols' Co.
Ross, John T. KY 7th Mtd.Inf. Co.F
Ross, John T. NC 35th Inf. Co.F
Ross, John T. NC 48th Inf. Co.A
Ross, John T. VA Cav. Hounshell's Bn. Thur-
  mond's Co. Jr. 2nd Lt.
Ross, John T. VA 22nd Inf. Co.C
Ross, John T. VA 51st Inf. Co.D Cpl.
Ross, John W. AR 9th Inf. Co.K
Ross, John W. LA 13th Inf. Co.G
Ross, John W. MS 20th Inf. Co.A Cpl.
Ross, Jno. W. MO St.Guard Adj.

Ross, John W. TX 21st Cav. Co.H
Ross, John W. TX 11th Inf. Co.H
Ross, John W. VA 4th Cav. Co.B
Ross, John W. VA 1st Arty. Co.B
Ross, John W. VA Lt.Arty. 1st Bn. Co.B
Ross, John W. VA Arty. Richardson's Co.
Ross, Jonah J. 1st Cherokee Mtd.Rifles Co.G
Ross, Jonathan E. GA 45th Inf. Co.K
Ross, Jonathan R. VA 24th Cav. Co.D
Ross, Jonathan R. VA Cav. 40th Bn. Co.D
Ross, Jonathan T. SC 22nd Inf. Co.E
Ross, Jose LA Mil. 5th Regt.Eur.Brig. (Spanish
  Regt.) Co.8
Ross, Jos. E. AL 8th (Hatch's) Cav. Co.E
Ross, Joseph GA 4th Inf. Co.F
Ross, Joseph SC 16th Inf.
Ross, Joseph TN 27th Inf. Co.F
Ross, Joseph TN Conscr. (Cp. of Instr.)
Ross, Joseph TX 1st Field Btty. Artif.
Ross, Joseph VA 23rd Inf. Co.C
Ross, Joseph 1st Conf.Eng.Troops Co.F
Ross, Joseph E. VA 22nd Inf. Co.I
Ross, Joseph G. NC 1st Inf. Co.E
Ross, Joseph L. TX 5th Inf. Co.C
Ross, Joseph N. AL 11th Inf. Co.D
Ross, Joseph N. AR 35th Inf. Co.B
Ross, Joseph S. MS 12th Inf. Co.F Sgt.
Ross, Joseph S. VA 62nd Mtd.Inf. 2nd Co.K
Ross, Joseph W. VA 51st Inf. Co.D
Ross, Joshua VA 8th Bn.Res. Co.D
Ross, Joshua VA 136th Mil. Co.F
Ross, Joshua H. VA Horse Arty. Lurty's Co.
Ross, Josiah T. AL 1st Cav. Co.A
Ross, J.R. AR 2nd Inf. Co.B
Ross, J.R. GA 32nd Inf. Co.H
Ross, J.R. TX 18th Inf. Co.K
Ross, J.R. VA 1st Inf. Co.D
Ross, J.R.M. TN 5th Inf. 2nd Co.F
Ross, J.S. AL 51st (Part.Rangers) Co.D Sgt.
Ross, J.S. AR 21st Mil. Co.A
Ross, J.S. MS 40th Inf. Co.C
Ross, J.S. TN 9th (Ward's) Cav. Co.E
Ross, J.T. AL 21st Inf. Co.H
Ross, J.T. TN 20th Inf. Co.G Cpl.
Ross, J.T. VA 8th Cav. Co.C Sgt.
Ross, Julius N. SC 8th Inf. Co.I 1st Lt.
Ross, J.W. AR 46th (Crabtree's) Cav. Co.B
Ross, J.W. GA 54th Inf. Co.A Cpl.
Ross, J.W. GA 64th Inf. Co.K
Ross, J.W. MS 23rd Inf. Co.E
Ross, J.W. MO Cav. Coleman's Regt. Co.E
Ross, J.W. MO 2nd Inf. Co.D
Ross, J.W. SC 18th Inf. Co.K
Ross, J.W. TN 28th (Cons.) Inf. Co.C Cpl.
Ross, J.W.N. 1st Conf.Cav. 1st Co.A
Ross, Kolvin MO Cav. Fristoe's Regt. Co.L
Ross, Larkin GA Cav. 8th Bn. (St.Guards) Co.B
Ross, Lawrence S. Gen. & Staff Brig.Gen.
Ross, Lawrence Sullivan TX 6th Cav. Co.G Col.
Ross, L.C. GA Cav. 29th Bn.
Ross, L.D. MS 5th Inf. Co.B
Ross, L.E. AR 5th Inf. Co.I
Ross, Leander AR 8th Cav. Co.A
Ross, Lemuel E. GA 14th Inf. Co.D
Ross, Leonidas D. MS 11th Inf. Co.D
Ross, Levin B. NC 4th Inf. Co.E
Ross, Levy TN 3rd (Clack's) Inf. Co.D

Ross, Lewis NC 5th Sr.Res. Co.B
Ross, Lewis T. VA 24th Inf. Co.I
Ross, Lewis W. TX 9th (Young's) Inf. Co.A
Ross, L.F. AR 10th (Witt's) Cav. Co.G
Ross, L.F. TN 19th (Biffle's) Cav. Co.F
Ross, L.G. MS 1st Lt.Arty. Co.I
Ross, Lightfoot AL 22nd Inf. Co.H 2nd Lt.
Ross, L.O. AR Inf. 8th Bn.
Ross, Lorenzo D. FL 7th Inf. Co.B Sgt.
Ross, Lott GA Inf. 10th Bn. Co.B
Ross, L.S. NC St.Mil. Lt.
Ross, L.S. Gen. & Staff, Cav. Col.
Ross, L.T. TN 19th Inf. Co.E
Ross, Luico R. NC 14th Inf. Co.E
Ross, Luke MO 8th Inf. Co.E
Ross, Luke W. NC 3rd Inf. Co.K
Ross, L.W. AR 10th Inf. Co.E
Ross, M. AR 51st Mil. Co.F Cpl.
Ross, M. GA Arty. Lumpkin's Co.
Ross, M. MO 5th Cav. Co.C
Ross, M. MO Cav. Slayback's Regt. Co.A
Ross, M. NC 1st Jr.Res. Co.B
Ross, M. TN 1st (Feild's) Inf. Co.F 3rd Lt.
Ross, M.A. GA 3rd Cav. Co.H 1st Sgt.
Ross, M.A. GA 8th Inf. Co.A
Ross, Madison TX 5th Inf. Co.H Sgt.
Ross, Marion MO Cav. 1st Regt.St.Guard Co.C
Ross, Martin MS 27th Inf. Co.D
Ross, Mass AR 2nd Inf.
Ross, Mathew NC 4th Sr.Res. Co.H
Ross, Mathew F. GA 45th Inf. Co.D
Ross, M.B. TX 11th Inf. Co.B
Ross, M.C. AR 1st Mtd.Rifles Co.D
Ross, M.C. AR 37th Inf. Co.D
Ross, M.C. SC 12th Inf. Co.A
Ross, M.C. TN 33rd Inf. Co.F
Ross, McDaniel VA 6th Inf. Co.K
Ross, McGilbert NC Inf. 13th Bn. Co.C
Ross, Miles N. MO 15th Cav. Co.A,B
Ross, Milton NC 8th Inf. Co.I
Ross, M.L. SC 18th Inf. Co.K
Ross, M.M. AR 10th Inf. Co.E
Ross, Morgan O. LA 31st Inf. Co.B
Ross, M.V. SC 23rd Inf. Co.B Cpl.
Ross, M.V. TX 10th Cav. Co.C
Ross, Napoleon B. GA 41st Inf. Co.H,B
Ross, Nate KY 9th Cav. Co.H Cpl.
Ross, Nathaniel W. VA 14th Inf. Co.C
Ross, N.B. GA 22nd Inf. Co.F Cpl.
Ross, N.B TN Inf. 154th Sr.Regt. 2nd Co.B
Ross, Newton B. VA Lt.Arty. Lowry's Co. Cpl.
Ross, Newton J. GA 41st Inf. Co.H Capt.
Ross, N.H. AL Cav. Barbiere's Bn. Truss' Co.
Ross, N.H.C. TN 63rd Inf. Co.A Cpl.
Ross, Nicholas VA 25th Cav. Co.K
Ross, N.M. AL 29th Inf. Co.C
Ross, Noah W. NC 56th Inf. Co.F
Ross, O.G. TX 9th (Nichols') Inf. Co.E
Ross, O.G. TX 9th (Nichols') Inf. Co.I
Ross, O.G. TX 20th Inf. Co.H
Ross, Oliver 1st Cherokee Mtd.Rifles Co.K
Ross, Oliver C. NC 64th Inf. Co.E
Ross, Oliver H.P. MS 40th Inf. Co.G 1st Cpl.
Ross, Osborn NC 56th Inf. Co.F
Ross, Oscar TN 45th Inf. Co.C
Ross, Oscar G. TX 35th (Brown's) Cav. Co.I
Ross, P. LA Mil. Irish Regt. Co.B

Ross, Patrick GA Inf. 1st Loc.Troops (Augusta) Co.H

Ross, P.E. KY 8th Mtd.Inf. Co.F

Ross, Perry MO 6th Cav. Co.F

Ross, Perry NC 56th Inf. Co.F

Ross, Perryman GA Cobb's Legion Co.K

Ross, Peter LA 5th Inf. Co.D,C

Ross, Peter F. TX 6th Cav. Co.G Capt.

Ross, Peyton N. TN 50th Inf. Co.F

Ross, P.H. GA 36th (Broyles') Inf. Co.K

Ross, P.J. MD 2nd Cav. Co.F

Ross, P.J. TN 5th (McKenzie's) Cav. Co.A

Ross, Polemon D. AL 12th Inf. Co.G Capt.

Ross, P.W. MO 6th Cav. Co.B Sgt.

Ross, Quitman D. MS 11th (Perrin's) Cav. Co.C

Ross, R. MO 9th Inf. Co.D

Ross, R. MO Inf. Clark's Regt. Co.C

Ross, R.A. AL 6th Cav. Co.A,G

Ross, R.A. AL 21st Inf. Co.C

Ross, R.B. VA 50th Inf. Co.D

Ross, R.D. AL 19th Inf. Co.D

Ross, R.D. AL Cp. of Instr. Talladega Co.A

Ross, R.E. AR 1st (Crawford's) Cav. Co.G

Ross, R.E. AR Inf. Cocke's Regt. Co.I

Ross, R.E. TX 12th Cav. Co.I

Ross, Reuben C. VA 4th Res. Co.B

Ross, Reuben R. Humes' Staff Lt.,Insp.Gen.

Ross, Reuel H. VA Lt.Arty. 12th Bn. 1st Co.A

Ross, R.F. MS 4th Cav. Co.G Sgt.

Ross, R.F. MS Cav. Hughes' Bn. Co.F Sgt.

Ross, Rhadamanthus M. AL 61st Inf. Co.E

Ross, Rice F. MS 9th Inf. Old Co.B

Ross, Richard J. 1st Creek Mtd.Vol. Sgt.Maj.

Ross, Richard P. MS 27th Inf. Co.D

Ross, Richard S. NC 14th Inf. Co.E

Ross, Richard S. NC 30th Inf. Co.D

Ross, R.J. SC 6th Cav. Co.C

Ross, R.J. SC Manigault's Bn.Vol. Co.C

Ross, R.L. AL 11th Cav. Co.H

Ross, R.L. AR 1st Cav. Co.H

Ross, R.L. TN 50th Inf. Co.I

Ross, R.L. TX 25th Cav. Co.B

Ross, R.M. AL 35th Inf. Co.I

Ross, R.M., Jr. MS Mtd.Men (Neshoba Rangers) Wilson's Ind.Co.

Ross, R.M., Sr. MS Mtd.Men (Neshoba Rangers) Wilson's Ind.Co.

Ross, R.M. VA Inf. 4th Bn.Loc.Def. Co.C

Ross, R.N. AL 42nd Inf. Co.D

Ross, R.N. AR 2nd Mtd.Rifles Co.C

Ross, Robert AR 6th Inf. Co.C 3rd Lt.

Ross, Robert MS 28th Cav. Co.E Cpl.

Ross, Robert MO 8th Cav. Co.I

Ross, Robert MO 1st Inf. Co.I

Ross, Robert MO 1st & 4th Cons.Inf. Co.K

Ross, Robert SC 6th Res. Co.H

Ross, Robert TN 62nd Mtd.Inf. Co.C

Ross, Robert TX Cav. Sutton's Co.

Ross, Robert VA 10th Cav. 1st Co.E

Ross, Robert VA 16th Cav. Co.H Sgt.

Ross, Robert VA Cav. Ferguson's Bn. Ferguson's Co.

Ross, Robert VA 27th Inf. Co.C

Ross, Robert 2nd Conf.Eng.Troops Co.C

Ross, Robert A. MS 15th Inf. Co.E

Ross, Robert A. MO 10th Inf. Co.F

Ross, Robert A. NC 11th (Bethel Regt.) Inf. Co.H,A

Ross, Robert Budds VA Lt.Arty. 38th Bn. Co.D

Ross, Robert H. GA 27th Inf. Co.G

Ross, Robert J. MS 11th (Perrin's) Cav. Co.D

Ross, Robert J. MO 1st Cav. Co.E

Ross, Robert K. TN 17th Inf. Co.H

Ross, Robert N. MS 2nd Inf. Co.D

Ross, Robert S. AR 1st Cav. Co.H

Ross, Robert S. MS 2nd Cav. Co.F 1st Sgt.

Ross, Robert S. TX 14th Cav. Co.B

Ross, Robeson VA Cav. Hounshell's Bn. Co.B

Ross, Robison VA 166th Mil. Co.E

Ross, Roderick M. LA 7th Inf. Co.G

Ross, Roland T. GA 6th Inf. (St.Guards) Co.H Capt.

Ross, R.P. MS 1st Cav. Co.D

Ross, R.R. TN Lt.Arty. Sparkman's Co. Capt.

Ross, R.R. TN Arty.Corps Co.8 Capt.

Ross, R.R. TX 3rd Cav. Co.E

Ross, R.S. TX 6th Cav. Sgt.

Ross, Ruel H. VA Lt.Arty. Utterback's Co.

Ross, Russell GA 27th Inf. Co.G

Ross, R.W. AR 27th Inf. New Co.C

Ross, R.W. KY 2nd Mtd.Inf. Co.B

Ross, R.W. MS Cav. Davenport's Bn. (St.Troops) Co.C

Ross, R.W. Morgan's Co.D,CSA Sgt.

Ross, S. 2nd Cherokee Mtd.Vol. Co.B

Ross, S.A. NC 11th (Bethel Regt.) Inf. Co.D

Ross, S.A. TX 21st Cav. Co.A Cpl.

Ross, S.A. VA 51st Inf. Co.C,D

Ross, Samuel AL 55th Vol. Co.C

Ross, Samuel MS 3rd Cav.Res. Co.F

Ross, Samuel MO 6th Cav. Co.F

Ross, Samuel MO Cav. Wood's Regt. Co.E

Ross, Samuel MO 2nd Inf. Co.K 1st Lt.

Ross, Samuel MO 12th Inf. Co.D

Ross, Samuel Carter MS Inf. 1st St.Troops Co.E

Ross, Samuel H. MO 4th Regt.St.Guards Co.A

Ross, Samuel H. Gen. & Staff Capt.,AQM

Ross, Samuel N. TN 50th Inf. Co.F

Ross, Samuel P. AL 32nd Inf. Co.K

Ross, Samuel R. NC 17th Inf. (2nd Org.) Co.K Cpl.

Ross, Samuel S. SC 5th Inf. 1st Co.G 3rd Lt.

Ross, Samuel S. VA 30th Bn.S.S. Co.A Sgt.

Ross, S.B. MO Inf. Clark's Regt. Co.D

Ross, S.B. TX 35th (Likens') Cav. Co.A

Ross, S.E. LA 2nd Inf. Co.D

Ross, S.G. NC 42nd Inf. Co.D

Ross, S.H. TX Home Guards Killough's Co.

Ross, Sherwood TN 17th Inf. (2nd Org.) Co.L

Ross, Silas M. TN 34th Inf. Co.I

Ross, Silas M. TN 44th Inf. Co.C 2nd Lt.

Ross, S.M. MO 1st Inf. Co.K Sgt.

Ross, S.M. MO 1st & 4th Cons.Inf. Co.K Cpl.

Ross, S.M. TN 44th (Cons.) Inf. Co.K 1st Lt.

Ross, S.M. Sig.Corps,CSA

Ross, Solomon VA 7th Cav. Co.C

Ross, Spencer NC 49th Inf. Co.A Cpl.

Ross, S.T. TX 5th Inf. Co.D

Ross, Stanfield MO Inf. 8th Bn. Co.E

Ross, Stanfield MO 9th Inf. Co.I

Ross, Stephen KY 5th Mtd.Inf. Co.F,D

Ross, Stephen B. Conf.Cav. Clarkson's Bn. Ind.Rangers Co.H

Ross, Stephen B. 1st Cherokee Mtd.Vol. 1st Co.K 1st Sgt.

Ross, Stephen D. TX 34th Cav. Co.C Capt.

Ross, Stephen M. SC 1st (McCreary's) Inf. Co.G

Ross, T. GA Lt.Arty. 12th Bn.

Ross, T. TX Conscr.

Ross, T.A. GA Arty. Maxwell's Reg.Lt.Btty.

Ross, Talmage S. GA 22nd Inf. Co.F

Ross, T.C. SC Lt.Arty. 3rd (Palmetto) Bn. Co.H

Ross, T.C. SC 16th Inf. Co.F

Ross, Tecumpseh B. TX Cav. 6th Bn. Co.C

Ross, Theodore A. TX 16th Cav. Co.C

Ross, Thomas GA Arty. Maxwell's Reg.Lt.Btty.

Ross, Thomas KY 10th (Diamond's) Cav. Co.B

Ross, Thomas KY 5th Mtd.Inf. Co.C

Ross, Thomas LA 14th Inf. Co.D

Ross, Thomas MO 6th Cav. Co.B 2nd Lt.

Ross, Thomas MO Inf. Clark's Regt. Co.A

Ross, Thomas NC 2nd Arty. (36th St.Troops) Co.C,H

Ross, Thomas NC 39th Inf. Co.A

Ross, Thomas NC 47th Inf. Co.I

Ross, Thomas NC Jones' Co. (Supp.Force)

Ross, Thomas SC Inf. 3rd Bn. Co.C

Ross, Thomas SC Inf. 3rd Bn. Co.F

Ross, Thomas TN 55th (McKoin's) Inf. Co.F

Ross, Thomas TN 60th Mtd.Inf. Co.B

Ross, Thomas 1st Cherokee Mtd.Rifles Co.K 1st Sgt.

Ross, Thomas A. MS 19th Inf. Co.E

Ross, Thomas Alston MS Bradford's Co. (Conf.Guards Arty.)

Ross, Thomas B. TX 10th Inf. Co.H Sgt.

Ross, Thomas E. NC 42nd Inf. Co.D

Ross, Thomas E. NC Pris.Guard Howard's Co.

Ross, Thomas F. AL 11th Inf. Co.A

Ross, Thomas H. VA Lt.Arty. 38th Bn. Co.D

Ross, Thomas J. AL 20th Inf. Co.I

Ross, Thomas J. AR 10th (Witt's) Cav. Co.F

Ross, Thomas J. GA Arty. 11th Bn. (Sumter Arty.) Co.A

Ross, Thomas J. MS 1st Lt.Arty. Co.B

Ross, Thomas J. MS 34th Inf. Co.F

Ross, Thomas J. VA Cav. 37th Bn. Co.A

Ross, Thomas J. 1st Cherokee Mtd.Vol. 1st Co.D, 2nd Co.K

Ross, Thomas K. NC 14th Inf. Co.H

Ross, Thomas L. GA 16th Inf. Co.G Capt.

Ross, Thomas L. TX 12th Cav. Co.H

Ross, Thomas M. SC 2nd Inf. Co.F

Ross, Thomas R. TN 44th (Cons.) Inf. Co.E

Ross, Thomas S. AL 21st Inf. Co.E

Ross, Thomas T. AR 14th (McCarver's) Inf. Co.E

Ross, Thomas W. GA Inf. 1st Bn. (St.Guards) Co.B

Ross, Thomas W. MO Searcy's Bn.S.S. Co.B

Ross, Thomas W. NC 6th Sr.Res. Co.K

Ross, Thomas W. VA 13th Inf. 2nd Co.B Sgt.

Ross, Tilman N. MS 31st Inf. Co.H

Ross, T.J. AR 35th Inf. Co.I

Ross, T.J. AR 1st (Monroe's) Cav. Co.A

Ross, T.J. AR Lt.Arty. Zimmerman's Btty.

Ross, T.J. AR 9th Inf. Co.K

Ross, T.J. AR 10th Inf. Co.H

Ross, T.J. KY 2nd Cav. Co.F

Ross, T.J. MS Cav. 1st Bn. (McNair's) St.Troops Co.C
Ross, T.J. MS 3rd Inf. (A. of 10,000) Co.C Cpl.
Ross, T.J. MO 9th Inf. Co.B,D
Ross, T.J. SC 16th Inf. Co.F
Ross, T.J. TN 36th Inf. Co.A
Ross, T.J. Exch.Bn. 2nd Co.A, 3rd Co.B,CSA
Ross, T. John NC 1st Bn.Jr.Res. Co.C
Ross, T.L. NC 14th Inf. Co.C 1st Lt.
Ross, T.M. AL 21st Inf. Co.C
Ross, T.M. NC 66th Inf. Co.E
Ross, T.M. TN 3rd (Lillard's) Mtd.Inf. Co.D
Ross, T.N. GA 28th Inf. Co.C Cpl.
Ross, T.W. MO 3rd Inf. Co.I
Ross, T.W. TN 7th (Duckworth's) Cav. Co.K
Ross, Vardaman KY 9th Mtd.Inf. Co.K Sgt.
Ross, Virgil A. AR Cav. Gordon's Regt. Co.F Sgt.
Ross, Virgil A. AR 16th Inf. Co.G Jr.2nd Lt.
Ross, W. LA Mil. 4th Regt. 1st Brig. 1st Div. Co.E
Ross, W. MD 1st Inf. Co.G Sgt.
Ross, W. SC 6th Cav. Co.F
Ross, W. TN 12th (Cons.) Inf. Co.G
Ross, W. TX 24th & 25th Cav. (Cons.) Co.E
Ross, W.A. AL 13th Bn.Part.Rangers Co.C
Ross, W.A. AL 56th Part.Rangers Co.G Cpl.
Ross, W.A. AR 1st (Monroe's) Cav. Co.A
Ross, W.A. LA 1st Cav. Co.K
Ross, W.A. NC 3rd Jr.Res. Co.G Sgt.
Ross, W.A. SC Inf. 7th Bn. (Enfield Rifles) Co.E Sgt.
Ross, Wainberry SC 11th Res. Co.B
Ross, Walker AL 25th Inf. Co.D
Ross, Walter MO 2nd Inf. Co.D
Ross, Walter B. AR 36th Inf. Co.G
Ross, Warren 1st Conf.Cav. 2nd Co.F
Ross, Washington L. AR Cav. 1st Bn. (Stirman's) Co.A
Ross, Washington L. MS 44th Inf. Co.C
Ross, W.B. AR Lt.Arty. Zimmerman's Btty.
Ross, W.B. AR 18th (Marmaduke's) Inf. Co.C
Ross, W.B. AR 31st Inf. Co.G Cpl.
Ross, W.B. GA Inf. 1st Loc.Troops (Augusta) Co.G
Ross, W.B. KY 8th Cav. Co.H
Ross, W.B. MS Lt.Arty. Turner's Co.
Ross, W.B. TN 2nd (Walker's) Inf. Lt.Col.
Ross, W.B. TN Inf. 22nd Bn. Co.E
Ross, W.B. TX 24th Cav. Co.I
Ross, W.C. AL 5th Inf. New Co.C
Ross, W.C. AR 17th (Lemoyne's) Inf. Co.E
Ross, W.C. GA Inf. 1st Loc.Troops (Augusta) Co.B
Ross, W.C. GA 5th Res. Co.A
Ross, W.C. MS 20th Inf. Co.K
Ross, W.C. TN 12th (Cons.) Inf. Co.G
Ross, W.C. TN 22nd Inf. Co.G
Ross, W.D. TX 7th Cav. Co.K
Ross, W.E. AL 18th Inf. Co.G 1st Sgt.
Ross, W.E. AR 1st Mtd.Rifles Co.I 1st Lt.
Ross, W.E. GA 42nd Inf. Co.A
Ross, W.E. LA Inf.Cons.Crescent Regt. Co.I
Ross, W.E. MS 1st (Patton's) Inf. Co.E Capt.
Ross, Wesley TX 20th Inf. Co.G 2nd Lt.
Ross, W.F. AL 7th Cav. Co.G

Ross, W.F. AR 1st Mtd.Rifles Co.K
Ross, W.F. AR 3rd Inf. Co.E
Ross, W.F. MS 11th (Cons.) Cav. Co.I
Ross, W.F. MS Inf. 3rd Bn. (St.Troops) Co.C Sgt.
Ross, W. Frame AR 25th Inf. Co.I
Ross, W.G. AL 1st Bn.Cadets Co.B
Ross, W.G. TX Cav. Border's Regt. Co.A
Ross, W.H. AL 11th Cav. Co.I
Ross, W.H. AR 2nd Inf. New Co.E
Ross, W.H. Hardee's Corps Capt.,AAIG
Ross, Wiley F. MS 15th Inf. Co.G
Ross, Wiley N. SC 2nd Inf. Co.F
Ross, Wiley W. SC 3rd Res. Co.E 3rd Lt.
Ross, William AL Cav. Moreland's Regt. Co.G
Ross, William AL Lt.Arty. 2nd Bn. Co.E
Ross, William AR 1st (Crawford's) Cav. Co.B
Ross, William AR 1st (Crawford's) Cav. Co.H
Ross, William AR 19th (Dawson's) Inf. Co.G
Ross, William AR 50th Mil. Co.H
Ross, William GA Inf. 3rd Bn. Co.B
Ross, William GA 37th Inf. Co.A
Ross, William GA 50th Inf. Co.K
Ross, William KY 5th Cav. Co.C
Ross, William KY 10th (Diamond's) Cav. Co.D
Ross, William KY 11th Cav. Co.G
Ross, William KY 4th Mtd.Inf. Co.C Music.
Ross, William LA Mil. 3rd Regt. 1st Brig. 1st Div. Co.G
Ross, William LA Mil.Cont.Regt. Kirk's Co. Sgt.
Ross, William MS Cav. 3rd Bn. (Ashcraft's) Co.E
Ross, William MS Inf. 2nd Bn. Co.L
Ross, William MS 18th Inf. Co.B
Ross, William MS 48th Inf. Co.L
Ross, William MO 9th Inf. Co.H
Ross, William MO 12th Inf. Co.H
Ross, William NC 6th Inf. Co.A
Ross, William NC 62nd Inf. Co.F
Ross, Wm. SC Hvy.Arty. 14th (Lucas') Bn. Co.C
Ross, William SC 4th St.Troops Co.C
Ross, William SC 5th Bn.Res. Co.D
Ross, William TN 1st (Feild's) Inf. Co.L
Ross, William TN 11th Inf. Co.E
Ross, William TN 20th Inf. Co.G
Ross, William TN 42nd Inf. Co.A
Ross, William TN 44th (Cons.) Inf. Co.C
Ross, William TN 47th Inf. Co.A
Ross, William TN 62nd Mtd.Inf. Co.C
Ross, William TN Inf. Nashville Bn. Cattles' Co.
Ross, William TX 13th Cav. Co.G
Ross, William TX Inf. 2nd St.Troops Co.G
Ross, William VA 1st Res. Co.E
Ross, William Conf.Reg.Inf. Brooks' Bn. Co.B
Ross, William A. AL 34th Inf. Co.G
Ross, William A. AL Conscr. Echols' Co.
Ross, William A. AR 34th Inf. Co.K
Ross, William A. FL 9th Inf. Co.G
Ross, William A. KY 4th Cav. Co.G
Ross, William A. MO 6th Cav. Co.F
Ross, William A. NC 8th Bn.Jr.Res. Co.C
Ross, William A. NC 49th Inf. Co.F
Ross, William A. VA 52nd Inf. Co.C 2nd Lt.
Ross, William A. VA Inf. Hutter's Co. Cpl.
Ross, William A. 2nd Conf.Eng.Troops Co.H

Ross, William B. AR 37th Inf. Co.F
Ross, William B. TN 1st (Feild's) Inf. Co.A Cpl.
Ross, William B. TX Inf. 25th Regt.
Ross, William C. AL 11th Inf. Co.A
Ross, William C. AL 39th Inf. Co.H
Ross, William C. GA 32nd Inf. Co.H
Ross, William C. LA 2nd Cav. Co.F
Ross, William C. MS 18th Cav.
Ross, William C. MS 2nd Inf. Co.D
Ross, William C. MS 18th Inf. Co.F
Ross, William C. NC 1st Inf. (6 mo. '61) Co.B
Ross, William C. NC 42nd Inf. Co.D 1st Sgt.
Ross, William C. VA 50th Inf. Co.D
Ross, William D. GA 61st Inf. Co.A Sgt.
Ross, William D. MS 13th Inf. Co.I
Ross, William D. VA 14th Inf. Co.C
Ross, William E. AR 9th Inf. Co.K,G 1st Lt.
Ross, William E. MS 39th Inf. Co.I Lt.Col.
Ross, William F. AR 3rd Cav. 2nd Co.E
Ross, William F. VA Inf. 5th Bn. Co.F
Ross, William G. AL Lt.Arty. 2nd Bn. Co.A
Ross, William G. AL 11th Inf. Co.G
Ross, William G. AR Lt.Arty. Thrall's Btty.
Ross, William G. GA 4th Bn.S.S. Co.B
Ross, William G. VA 30th Bn.S.S. Co.E
Ross, William H., Jr. AL Corps Cadets Co.C Cadet Capt.
Ross, William H. AR 11th Inf. Co.B
Ross, William H. AR 11th & 17th (Cons.) Inf. Co.A,B
Ross, William H. FL 3rd Inf. Co.I 2nd Lt.
Ross, William H. FL 9th Inf. Co.I
Ross, William H. GA 1st Bn.S.S. Co.C Capt.
Ross, William H. GA Inf. 2nd Bn. Co.C 1st Lt.
Ross, William H. KY 2nd (Duke's) Cav. Co.H
Ross, William H. MS 3rd Inf. Co.C Music.
Ross, William H. MS 10th Inf. Old Co.G, New Co.H
Ross, William H. MS 26th Inf. Co.B Cpl.
Ross, William H. NC 45th Inf. Co.B
Ross, William H. SC 6th Inf. 1st Co.A, 2nd Co.I Cpl.
Ross, William H. TN 9th (Ward's) Cav. Co.D Cpl.
Ross, William H. VA Mtd.Riflemen Balfour's Co.
Ross, William H. VA 9th Inf. 2nd Co.A
Ross, William H. VA 19th Inf. Co.F
Ross, Wm. H. Gen. & Staff Maj.,Comsy.
Ross, William Henry MO 8th Inf. Co.A
Ross, William J. AL 6th Inf. Co.G
Ross, William J. GA 13th Cav. Co.E,A Sgt.
Ross, William J. LA Mtd.Part.Rangers Bond's Co.
Ross, William J. NC 28th Inf. Co.K Sgt.
Ross, William J. NC 30th Inf. Co.K
Ross, William J. TX 30th Cav. Co.I Sgt.
Ross, William J.F. GA Inf. 2nd Bn. Co.C 2nd Lt.
Ross, William L. MS 20th Inf. Co.B
Ross, William L. TN 2nd (Smith's) Cav. Lea's Co. Cpl.
Ross, William L. TN 55th (McKoin's) Inf. Dillehay's Co.
Ross, William M. AL Cav. Moreland's Regt. Co.G

Ross, William M. AR 26th Inf. Co.D
Ross, William M. AR 35th Inf. Co.I
Ross, William M. GA 27th Inf. Co.C 1st Lt.
Ross, William M. GA 45th Inf. Co.D
Ross, William M. MS 19th Inf. Co.G
Ross, William M. SC 18th Inf. Co.K
Ross, William M. TN 37th Inf. Co.H
Ross, William M. TX 11th Inf. Co.B
  Capt.,AQM
Ross, William N. NC 37th Inf. Co.K 2nd Lt.
Ross, William Newton MS 23rd Inf. Co.F
Ross, William P. AL 33rd Inf. Co.I
Ross, William P. AR Inf. 4th Bn. Co.C
Ross, William P. AR 15th (N.W.) Inf. Co.C
Ross, William P. AR 18th Inf. Co.B
Ross, William P. GA Inf. 3rd Bn. Co.D
Ross, William P. GA 4th Bn.S.S. Co.B
Ross, William P. VA Hvy.Arty. A.J. Jones' Co.
Ross, William P. 10th Conf.Cav. Co.C
Ross, William P. 1st Cherokee Mtd.Rifles
  Lt.Col.
Ross, William R. AR 26th Inf. Co.D
Ross, William R. GA Inf. 2nd Bn. Co.C
Ross, William R. GA 47th Inf. Co.A
Ross, William S. MO 12th Inf. Co.E
Ross, William T. TN 1st (Turney's) Inf. Co.G
Ross, William T. VA 30th Bn.S.S. Co.A
Ross, William T. VA 51st Inf. Co.D
Ross, William W. MS 35th Inf. Co.A Sgt.
Ross, William W. VA 8th Inf. Co.F
Ross, William Y. AR 6th Inf. Co.E
Ross, William Y. TN 1st Cav.
Ross, Willis VA Hvy.Arty. 19th Bn. Co.A
Ross, W.J. AR 15th Mil. Co.E
Ross, W.J. GA 12th Cav. Co.G
Ross, W.J. KY 12th Cav. Co.C
Ross, W.J. LA 30th Inf. Co.I,E Cpl.
Ross, W.J. MS 43rd Inf. Co.F
Ross, W.J. NC 4th Inf. Co.E
Ross, W.J. TN 2nd (Ashby's) Cav. Co.A
Ross, W.J. TN Cav. 5th Bn. (McClellan's) Co.A
Ross, W.J. TN 8th Inf. Co.E
Ross, W.J.M. TX 6th Inf. Co.H
Ross, W.L. MS 5th Inf. Co.B
Ross, W.L. MO Cav. 3rd Bn.
Ross, W.L. TX 2nd Cav. Co.E
Ross, W.L. 3rd Conf.Cav. Co.A
Ross, W.M. AL 28th Inf. Co.C
Ross, W.M. AR 15th Mil. Co.D
Ross, W.M. SC 5th Inf. 2nd Co.D
Ross, W.M. SC 16th Inf. Co.F
Ross, W.M. SC 16th & 24th (Cons.) Inf. Co.A
Ross, W.M. TN 22nd Inf. Co.E
Ross, W.M. TN 31st Inf. Co.A
Ross, W.M. TX 4th Inf. Co.E
Ross, W.M.G. SC 27th Inf. Co.I
Ross, W.N. MS 3rd Inf. Co.F
Ross, W.N. MS 15th (Cons.) Inf. Co.K
Ross, W.P. GA 6th Res.
Ross, W.P. MO 3rd Inf. Co.I
Ross, W.R. AR 30th Inf. Co.D
Ross, W.R. GA 5th Res. Co.A 1st Sgt.
Ross, W.R. GA 66th Inf. Co.D Lt.
Ross, W.R. MO 11th Inf. Co.G
Ross, W.R. NC 4th Inf. Co.E
Ross, W.R. TN 40th Inf. Co.D

Ross, W.S. MS 2nd Inf. (A. of 10,000) Co.G
  Sgt.
Ross, W.S. TN 16th Inf. Co.C 1st Sgt.
Ross, W. Stuart MS 30th Inf. Co.H Cpl.
Ross, W.T. GA 29th Inf. Co.E
Ross, W.T. MS 8th Cav. Co.D
Ross, W.T. MS 5th Inf. Co.B
Ross, W.T. MS 31st Inf. Co.H
Ross, W.T. MO 2nd Inf. Co.B
Ross, W.T. TN 16th (Logwood's) Cav. Co.H
Ross, W.T. TN Lt.Arty. Huggins' Co. Cpl.
Ross, W.W. SC 1st St.Troops Co.H
Ross, W.W. SC 16th Inf. Co.F
Ross, W.W. SC 16th Inf. Co.F Bvt.2nd Lt.
Ross, W.W. TX 9th Cav. Co.B
Ross, W.W. 8th (Wade's) Conf.Cav. Co.I
Ross, Wyatt NC 43rd Inf. Co.D
Ross, Wyett TN 2nd (Smith's) Cav. Lea's Co.
  Cpl.
Ross, Wyett 3rd Conf.Cav. Co.A Cpl.
Ross, Z.A. MS 11th (Perrin's) Cav. Co.B
Ross, Zaddock H. MS 26th Inf. Co.I
Ross, Zenas N. MO 8th Cav. Co.D
Ross, Zeph T. VA 13th Inf. 1st Co.B, 2nd Co.B
  Capt.
Rossa, S.A. SC Lt.Arty. 3rd (Palmetto) Bn.
  Co.G
Rossan, Elijah MS Cav. 24th Bn. Co.B
Rossan, L. MO Cav. 1st Bn.St.Guard Co.D 2nd
  Lt.
Rossan, R.G. TN 41st Inf. Co.H
Rossan, William VA 54th Mil. Co.E,F
Rossan, W.M. TN Cav. Napier's Bn. Co.D
Rossas, Santos TX 5th Inf. Co.F
Rossatubba G. 1st Chickasaw Inf. Haynes' Co.
Rosse, Ambroise LA 30th Inf. Co.H
Rosse, George TN 61st Mtd.Inf. Co.C
Rosse, John LA Mil. LaFourche Regt.
Rosse, John A. MO 1st Inf. 2nd Co.A
Rosse, John W. LA 28th (Gray's) Inf. Co.C
Rosse, Joseph GA 1st (Olmstead's) Inf. Co.G
Rosse, Lewis Conf.Inf. Tucker's Regt. Co.C
Rosse, Louis GA Inf. 18th Bn. Co.C Music.
Rosse, William John VA Courtney Arty.
Rossea, William SC 1st Arty. Co.K Cpl.
Rosseau, F.L. AL 5th Inf. New Co.F
Rosseau, G.W. TX 1st Inf. Co.C Sgt.
Rosseau, James GA 26th Inf. Co.B
Rosseau, J.L. KY 10th (Diamond's) Cav. Co.F
  Sgt.
Rosseau, John MO 1st Inf. 2nd Co.A
Rosseau, John L. GA 29th Inf. Co.D
Rosseau, Louis LA 30th Inf. Co.D
Rosseau, P. LA 2nd Cav. Co.C
Rosseau, W.J. MS Inf. 1st Bn. Co.C 1st Sgt.
Rossee, J.F. 2nd Conf.Eng.Troops Co.C Artif.
Rossee, L.D. GA 66th Inf. Co.F
Rossee, M.D. SC 3rd Cav. Co.D
Rossee, Thomas GA 36th (Villepigue's) Inf.
  Co.A
Rossee, Thomas J. 1st Conf.Inf. Co.A Cpl.
Rossel, E.T. KY 4th Cav. Co.C
Rossel, J.C. AL 4th (Russell's) Cav. Co.E
Rossel, Marion J. MS 42nd Inf. Co.C Surg.
Rossell, Alexander KY 11th Cav. Co.B
Rossell, B. TN 1st (Feild's) & 27th Inf. (Cons.)
  Co.C,G

Rossell, Euphrates P. MS 17th Inf. Co.B
Rossell, J.L.D. AL 4th (Russell's) Cav. Co.E
Rossell, J.N. TX 29th Cav. Co.K
Rossell, John M. MS 17th Inf. Co.B Sgt.
Rossell, Samuel VA 9th Inf. 1st Co.A
Rossell, Tolman D. MS 17th Inf. Co.B
Rosselle, O. TN 4th Inf. Co.H
Rosselle, O. 3rd Conf.Eng.Troops Co.B
Rosselle, O. Eng.Dept. Polk's Corps A. of TN
  Sap. & Min.Co.,CSA
Rossen, A. MS 25th Inf.
Rossen, Abner 2nd Conf.Inf. Co.B
Rossen, E.C. TX Cav. Baird's Regt. Co.D
Rossen, E.R. VA 13th Inf. 2nd Co.B
Rossen, James MS 18th Inf. Co.D
Rossen, John TN 20th Inf. Co.G Cpl.
Rossen, Thomas GA Inf. Dozier's Co. Cpl.
Rossen, W.C. TN 3rd (Forrest's) Cav.
Rossen, W.H. MO 11th Inf. Co.F
Rossen, Wm. AR 4th St.Inf. Co.E 3rd Lt.
Rossen, William GA Inf. Dozier's Co.
Rossen, William TX 28th Cav. Co.G
Rossen, W.M. TN 10th (DeMoss') Cav. Co.G
Rosser, --- GA 31st Inf. Co.C
Rosser, A.F. AR 6th Inf. Co.B
Rosser, A.G. VA 3rd Res. Co.F
Rosser, Alexander J. GA 17th Inf. Co.I
Rosser, Alfred S. VA 11th Inf. Co.C
Rosser, Benjamin TX 2nd Cav. Co.K
Rosser, Benjamin F. GA 55th Inf. Co.K
Rosser, Benjamin H. AL Mil. 4th Vol. Co.C
Rosser, B.F. TX 23rd Cav. Co.D
Rosser, B.H. AL Cp. of Instr. Talladega Co.A
Rosser, B.H. GA 2nd Cav. (St.Guards) Co.A
Rosser, B.H., Jr. GA 1st (Fannin's) Res. Co.E
Rosser, B.H., Sr. GA 1st (Fannin's) Res. Co.E
Rosser, Burel H. GA Lt.Arty. 14th Bn. Co.C
  Cpl.
Rosser, Calvin L. VA Inf. 25th Bn. Co.E Cpl.
Rosser, Charles F. VA 41st Inf. 2nd Co.E
Rosser, Charles H. VA 2nd Cav. Co.I
Rosser, Cincinnattus VA Goochland Lt.Arty.
Rosser, D.F. SC 7th Inf. Co.F
Rosser, E. GA 10th Cav. (St.Guards) Co.K
Rosser, E.A. GA 10th Inf. Co.C
Rosser, E.B. Hosp.Stew.
Rosser, E.D. GA 42nd Inf. Sgt.Maj.
Rosser, Edward B. VA Horse Arty. Shoemaker's
  Co.
Rosser, Edward L. VA 23rd Inf. Co.K
Rosser, Edwin VA 7th Inf. Co.K
Rosser, Egbert B. GA 42nd Inf. Co.F
Rosser, Egbert B. Gen. & Staff Hosp.Stew.
Rosser, E.H. AL 2nd Cav. Co.D
Rosser, Elijah TX 23rd Cav. Co.D 1st Lt.
Rosser, Elisha TX 23rd Cav. Co.D 1st Lt.
Rosser, F.A. AL 32nd Inf. Co.B
Rosser, F.A. GA 9th Inf. Co.B
Rosser, F.R. VA Burks' Regt.Loc.Def. Shield's
  Co.
Rosser, Francis M. AL 11th Inf. Co.G
Rosser, Francis M. MS 6th Cav. Co.K
Rosser, G.C. AR 37th Inf. Co.I 1st Sgt.
Rosser, George G. VA 6th Cav. 2nd Co.E Sgt.
Rosser, George S. GA 17th Inf. Co.A 1st Lt.
Rosser, George T. VA 11th Inf. Co.C Cpl.
Rosser, G.F. AL Cp. of Instr. Talladega Co.D

Rosser, G.G. VA 10th Cav. Co.E Sgt.
Rosser, G.H. VA 34th Inf. Co.D
Rosser, G.M. AL 1st Bn.Cadets Co.A
Rosser, Granville D. VA 11th Inf. Co.C
Rosser, G.S. GA 53rd Inf. Co.A Sgt.
Rosser, H. AL 7th Cav. Co.D
Rosser, Henry N. MS 12th Cav. Co.A 1st Sgt.
Rosser, H.P. AL Cav. Shockley's Co.
Rosser, H.S. NC 48th Inf. Co.G
Rosser, I.P. GA 13th Inf. Co.C
Rosser, Isaac TN Hvy.Arty. Johnston's Co.
Rosser, Isaac TN Lt.Arty. Tobin's Co. 2nd Lt.
Rosser, J. GA 3rd Res. Co.H
Rosser, J. MS 3rd Cav. Co.F,K
Rosser, Jabez R. VA 11th Inf. Co.C 1st Lt.
Rosser, James GA Phillips' Legion Co.D
Rosser, James B. LA Inf.Crescent Regt. Co.B 2nd Lt.
Rosser, James H. LA 3rd Inf. Co.F
Rosser, James M. VA 7th Inf. Co.K Jr.2nd Lt.
Rosser, James T. GA Floyd Legion (St.Guards) Co.G Sgt.
Rosser, James W. GA 12th Inf. Co.K Sgt.
Rosser, J.B. LA Inf.Cons. 18th Regt. & Yellow Jacket Bn. Adj.
Rosser, J.C. TX 11th Cav. Co.K
Rosser, J.G. TX 18th Inf. Co.C
Rosser, J.H. MS 38th Cav. Co.C
Rosser, J.H. NC 1st Jr.Res. Co.H
Rosser, J.H. TN 38th Inf. Co.C
Rosser, J.H. TX 7th Cav. Co.C
Rosser, J.M. GA 64th Inf. Co.E
Rosser, J.N. TN 12th (Cons.) Inf. Co.G
Rosser, J.N. TN 22nd Inf. Co.G Cpl.
Rosser, John AL 40th Inf. Co.H
Rosser, John GA 64th Inf. Co.E Sgt.
Rosser, John TN 13th Inf. Co.E
Rosser, John TX 36th Cav. Co.E Far.
Rosser, John A. GA 44th Inf. Co.A
Rosser, John A. VA Conscr. Cp.Lee
Rosser, John B. NC 48th Inf. Co.G
Rosser, John C. TX 28th Cav. Co.C A.Surg.
Rosser, John G. VA 3rd Res. Co.B
Rosser, John K. VA 1st Bn.Res. Co.H
Rosser, John M. GA Inf. 27th Inf. Co.A
Rosser, John O. GA 66th Inf. Co.F Jr.2nd Lt.
Rosser, John W. VA 11th Inf. Co.C
Rosser, Joseph F. MO Lt.Arty. 3rd Btty.
Rosser, Joseph F. MO Arty. Lowe's Co. (Jackson Btty.)
Rosser, J.P. NC 35th Inf. Co.D
Rosser, J.P. Gen. & Staff,PACS Maj.,Surg.
Rosser, J. Travis VA 10th Cav. Co.K Maj.
Rosser, L.C.V. AR 20th Inf. Co.C Sgt.
Rosser, L.D.F. GA 2nd Cav. (St.Guards) Co.A
Rosser, L.D.F. GA Inf. 26th Bn. Co.B Cpl.
Rosser, Leroy J. VA Hvy.Arty. 19th Bn. Co.A
Rosser, Leroy J. VA Hvy.Arty. Kyle's Co.
Rosser, Lewis W. TX 18th Inf. Co.F
Rosser, L.J. VA 3rd Res. Co.I
Rosser, Loren H. AL Lt.Arty. 2nd Bn. Co.F
Rosser, M.F. GA Inf. 40th Bn. Chap.
Rosser, M.F. Gen. & Staff Chap.
Rosser, Montgomery GA 10th Inf. Co.E
Rosser, M.R. AL 4th Inf. Co.K
Rosser, M.R. AL 18th Inf. Co.E,G
Rosser, N. TN 12th (Cons.) Inf. Co.G

Rosser, N. TN 22nd Inf. Co.G
Rosser, R. TN 38th Inf. Co.C Cpl.
Rosser, R.F. VA 19th Inf. Co.B
Rosser, R.L. GA 10th Inf. Co.C
Rosser, Robert VA Cav. McNeill's Co.
Rosser, Robert P. GA 2nd Inf. Co.B
Rosser, Robert S. AR 1st (Crawford's) Cav. Co.F 1st Lt.
Rosser, R.P. GA Inf. 26th Bn. Co.B
Rosser, R.S. Gen. & Staff AQM
Rosser, Rufus, M. AL Lt.Arty. 2nd Bn. Co.F
Rosser, Samuel VA Lt.Arty. Brander's Co.
Rosser, Samuel A. Cav.Bn. Holcombe Legion Co.E
Rosser, Silas M. MO 2nd Inf. Co.A Sgt.
Rosser, Simpson A. GA 8th Inf. Co.D
Rosser, Th. H. AL 62nd Inf. Col.
Rosser, Thomas A. MO Lt.Arty. 3rd Btty.
Rosser, Thomas A. MO Inf. 1st Regt.St.Guards QM
Rosser, Thomas Allen MO Arty. Lowe's Co.
Rosser, Thomas H. MO Inf. 1st Regt.St.Guard Col.
Rosser, Thomas H. MO Inf. 3rd Bn. Co.C
Rosser, Thomas J. AL Lt.Arty. Phelan's Co.
Rosser, Thomas L. LA Washington Arty.Bn. Co.2 Capt.
Rosser, Thomas L. VA 5th Cav. Col.
Rosser, Thomas L. Conf.Lt.Arty. Stark's Bn. Lt.Col.
Rosser, Thos. L. Gen. & Staff Brig.Gen.
Rosser, Thomas W. VA Lt.Arty. Carpenter's Co. Sgt.
Rosser, Thomas W. VA 11th Inf. Co.C
Rosser, Thomas W. VA 27th Inf. Co.A Sgt.
Rosser, T.M. GA 41st Inf. Chap.
Rosser, W. TX 26th Cav. Co.D
Rosser, Walter C. VA 11th Inf. Co.C
Rosser, W.B. TN 13th Inf. Co.E
Rosser, W.D. GA 6th Cav. Co.E
Rosser, W.H. Gen. & Staff Chap.
Rosser, William TN 14th (Neely's) Cav. Co.E
Rosser, William TN 38th Inf. Co.C
Rosser, William VA Hvy.Arty. 18th Bn. Co.D
Rosser, William VA Inf. 1st Bn.Loc.Def. Co.B
Rosser, William 1st Choctaw & Chickasaw Mtd.Rifles QMSgt.
Rosser, William A. VA Hvy.Arty. Patteson's Co.
Rosser, William E. 1st Choctaw & Chickasaw Mtd.Rifles 1st Co.K 1st Cpl.
Rosser, William G. AL Lt.Arty. Phelan's Co.
Rosser, William J.R. AR 37th Inf. Co.G Cpl.
Rosser, William S. GA 21st Inf. Co.C
Rosser, Willis D. GA 2nd Inf. Co.B
Rosser, W.L. TN 4th (McLemore's) Cav. Co.C
Rosser, W.L. TN 8th Cav. Adj.
Rosser, W.M. TN 31st Inf. Co.F
Rosser, W.S. GA Inf. 25th Bn. (Prov.Guard) Co.G
Rosser, W.Z. MS 5th Inf. Co.B
Rossers, J.E. LA 3rd (Wingfield's) Cav. Co.A
Rosseter, James FL 4th Inf. Co.A
Rossetto, Peter MS 3rd Inf. Co.F
Rossey, D.E. TX Cav. Hardeman's Regt. Co.C
Rossey, John MO 1st Inf. Co.K
Rossi, Augustine LA Mil. LaFourche Regt.
Rossi, Edward LA Mil. LaFourche Regt.

Rossi, Francesco LA Mil. 6th Regt.Eur.Brig. (Italian Guards Bn.) Co.3
Rossi, Giov. Batta LA Mil. Cazadores Espanoles Regt. Co.F Cpl.
Rossier, R.F. GA 3rd Res. Co.A
Rossignol, Adolphe LA 4th Inf. Co.E
Rossignol, Henry Gen. & Staff A.Surg.
Rossignol, J. LA Mil. 4th Regt. French Brig. Co.6 Cpl.
Rossignol, James L. GA Inf. 1st Loc.Troops (Augusta) Co.A,H
Rossignol, Lewis H. GA Arty. (Chatham Arty.) Wheaton's Co.
Rossignol, Lewis H. GA 1st (Olmstead's) Inf. Claghorn's Co.
Rossignol, Louis H. FL 2nd Cav. Co.C
Rossin, Abraham AR 30th Inf. Co.K
Rossin, G.W. TN 43rd Inf. Co.I
Rossin, Jerry MS 1st Cav.Res. Co.E
Rossin, N.B. VA 7th Inf. Co.K Sgt.
Rossin, William MS 1st Cav.Res. Co.E
Rossin, William TN 19th (Biffle's) Cav. Co.D
Rossini, F. Stuart Horse Arty.,CSA
Rossiter, Charles LA Washington Arty.Bn. Co.1
Rossiter, Jefferson B. LA 19th Inf. Co.E Sgt.
Rossiter, John GA Hvy.Arty. 22nd Bn. Co.D
Rossiter, John GA 25th Inf. Co.A
Rossiter, Patrick GA 1st (Olmstead's) Inf. Co.A
Rossiter, T.D. AL 3rd Res. Co.G
Rossiter, Thomas AL 3rd Res. Co.H
Rossler, August TX 20th Inf. Co.A
Rossler, Ernst TX 20th Inf. Co.A
Rossler, Henry TX 20th Inf. Co.A
Rossman, M. TX St.Troops Edgar's Co.
Rossman, Mathew TX 1st Field Btty.
Rossman, R.S. Conf.Cav. Wood's Regt. Co.L
Rossmeyer, P. LA Mil. 4th Regt. 1st Brig. 1st Div. Co.A Cpl.
Rossmissick, --- MD 1st Inf. Co.G
Rossner, Charles LA Inf.Cons.Crescent Regt. Co.A Cpl.
Rossner, Charles W. LA Inf. 16th Bn. (Conf. Guards Resp.Bn.) Co.B 1st Sgt.
Rosso, Joseph AL 21st Inf. Co.G
Rosso, Leonardo LA Mil. Cazadores Espanoles Regt. Co.F
Rosson, Abner AL 55th Vol. Co.D
Rosson, A.F. KY 7th Cav. Co.G
Rosson, A.J. TX 28th Cav. Co.G Sgt.
Rosson, Andrew J. TN 53rd Inf. Co.D
Rosson, Anthony F. KY 3rd Cav. Co.G
Rosson, A.P. TN 42nd Inf. Co.A
Rosson, A.P. 4th Conf.Inf. Co.G
Rosson, Barnett M. VA 34th Inf. Fray's Co.D
Rosson, B.F. TX 22nd Inf. Co.K
Rosson, C.F. VA Inf. 2nd Bn.Loc.Def. Co.B Sgt.
Rosson, Charles F. NC 26th Inf. Co.G
Rosson, Daniel MO Searcy's Bn.S.S. Co.F
Rosson, E.B. TX 7th Inf. Co.A Lt.
Rosson, Emanuel B. VA 7th Inf. Co.K
Rosson, F. LA Washington Arty.Bn. Co.3
Rosson, Franklin VA 47th Inf. 3rd Co.H
Rosson, George VA 6th Inf. 1st Co.B
Rosson, George L. AL 8th Inf. Co.E
Rosson, George T. KY 3rd Cav. Co.G
Rosson, George W. VA 7th Inf. Co.G Cpl.

Rosson, G.T. KY 7th Cav. Co.G
Rosson, Henry H. VA Lt.Arty. 12th Bn. 1st Co.A
Rosson, Henry H. VA Lt.Arty. Utterback's Co.
Rosson, J.A. KY 6th Mtd.Inf. Co.C
Rosson, J.A. VA 54th Mil. Co.G
Rosson, James MS 1st Lt.Arty. Co.B
Rosson, James MO 9th Inf. Co.B
Rosson, James MO Inf. Clark's Regt. Co.A
Rosson, James C. TN 14th Inf. Co.K
Rosson, James F. NC 26th Inf. Co.G
Rosson, James M. LA 6th Inf. Co.D
Rosson, James S. VA 82nd Mil. Co.A
Rosson, James W. NC 6th Inf. Co.C
Rosson, J.E. MS Scouts Morphis' Ind.Co.
Rosson, J.H. MS 10th Cav. Co.H
Rosson, J.M. MS 46th Inf. Co.A
Rosson, J.M. TX 28th Cav. Co.D Cpl.
Rosson, Joel F. VA Lt.Arty. Brander's Co.
Rosson, Joel F. VA 82nd Mil. Co.A
Rosson, Joel F. 1st Conf.Eng.Troops Co.F Artif.
Rosson, John AR Cav. Harrell's Bn. Co.A 1st Lt.
Rosson, John TX 35th (Brown's) Cav. Co.I Bugler
Rosson, John TX 13th Vol. 3rd Co.I
Rosson, John VA 34th Mil. Co.D
Rosson, John A. VA Cav. Mosby's Regt. (Part.Rangers) Co.A
Rosson, John C. MO Inf. 3rd Bn. Co.E
Rosson, John C. MO 6th Inf. Co.C
Rosson, John D.E. VA Lt.Arty. Utterback's Co.
Rosson, John E. AR 25th Inf. Co.K 2nd Lt.
Rosson, John H. TN 21st Inf. Co.C Lt.
Rosson, John W. VA 12th Cav. Co.G Cpl.
Rosson, Joseph G. TN 23rd Inf. Co.B
Rosson, Joseph G. TN 41st Inf. Co.H Cpl.
Rosson, Joseph J. MO Searcy's Bn.S.S. Co.F
Rosson, Joseph S. TN 11th Inf. Co.F Sgt.
Rosson, J.S. KY 7th Cav. Co.G
Rosson, J.S. VA 7th Inf. Co.G
Rosson, L. LA 1st Cav. Co.I
Rosson, M. TN 22nd (Barteau's) Cav. Co.I Sgt.
Rosson, Martin V. VA 10th Inf. Co.L
Rosson, Martin V. VA 82nd Mil. Co.A
Rosson, M.C. TX 3rd Cav. Co.G
Rosson, M.D. AL 8th Inf. Co.H Cpl.
Rosson, Merritt NC 26th Inf. Co.G
Rosson, Morgan C. TX 37th Cav. Co.A
Rosson, S. TN 21st & 22nd (Cons.) Cav. Co.C
Rosson, Samuel TN 22nd (Barteau's) Cav. Co.I
Rosson, Tecumseh R. TN 17th Inf. Co.C
Rosson, Thomas J. FL 1st Inf. New Co.C
Rosson, Thomas J. TX 10th Cav. Co.G
Rosson, Thomas T. AR 1st Mtd.Rifles Co.F
Rosson, T.M. FL 2nd Inf. Co.A Cpl.
Rosson, U.B. VA 7th Inf. Co.K Sgt.
Rosson, W. TX Conscr.
Rosson, William AR 7th Mil. Co.A
Rosson, William AR 34th Inf. Co.I
Rosson, William A. VA Lt.Arty. 12th Bn. 1st Co.A Cpl.
Rosson, William A. VA Lt.Arty. Utterback's Co. Cpl.
Rosson, William A. VA 82nd Mil. Co.A
Rosson, William H. AR 27th Inf. Co.I 1st Lt.
Rosson, William H. VA 10th Inf. Co.L

Rosson, William M. TX 22nd Inf. Co.K
Rosson, William P. VA 34th Inf. Fray's Co.D
Rosson, William R. MS 11th Inf. Co.C
Rosson, Wilson B. VA 47th Inf. 2nd Co.K
Rosson, W.R. TN 42nd Inf. Co.G
Rosson, Yancey P. VA Lt.Arty. Brander's Co.
Rosson, Yancy Powell 1st Conf.Eng.Troops Co.F Artif.
Rossor, James S. VA 82nd Mil. Co.A
Rossvally, M.L. Gen. & Staff Asst.Surg.
Rossy, Emil TX 31st Cav. Co.C
Rossy, William E. TX Cav. Hardeman's Regt. Co.C
Rost, A. AL 17th Inf. Ch.Music.
Rost, A. LA Washington Arty.Bn. Co.5
Rost, August AL Gorff's Co. (Mobile Pulaski Rifles)
Rost, D.W. SC Inf. 9th Bn. Co.D,F 2nd Lt.
Rost, F.C. AR 2nd Cav. Co.C
Rost, Fred AR 2nd Inf. Co.C
Rost, Henry TX 1st Hvy.Arty. Co.E
Rost, Henry TX Lt.Arty. Jones' Co.
Rost, J. TX 4th Inf. (St.Troops) Co.F
Rost, J.G. TX 1st Hvy.Arty. Co.A Ord.Sgt.
Rost, Joachim LA 1st Hvy.Arty. (Reg.) Co.A
Rost, John LA Mil. 3rd Regt. 1st Brig. 1st Div. Co.H
Rost, John TX 1st Hvy.Arty. Co.E
Rost, John TX Res.Corps
Rost, John C. AL 4th Inf. Co.A Cpl.
Rost, M. NC 49th Inf.
Rosteet, Miguel J. TX Cav. Ragsdale's Bn. Co.A Lt.
Rosten, William MO 6th Cav. Co.D
Roster, George MO St.Guard 3rd Lt.
Rosto, B. LA Cav. Benjamin's Co.
Roston, S.W. GA Inf. 9th Bn. Co.C
Rostrum, Oliver FL 1st (Res.) Inf. Co.C
Rostrup, James LA Mil. Fire Bn. Co.G
Rosua, F. AR 17th (Griffith's) Inf. Co.A
Rosvally, Dr. LA Mil. 4th Regt. 1st Brig. 1st Div. Co.G
Roswald, Simon AL 12th Inf. Co.C
Roswalt, J. AL 1st Regt.Conscr. Co.B
Roswell, A.B. AL 27th Inf. Co.F
Roswell, A.B. AL 49th Inf.
Roswell, B. NC 37th Inf.
Roswell, Elijah H. MO Cav. Poindexter's Regt.
Roswell, J.M. TN 3rd (Forrest's) Cav. Co.B
Roswell, John T. MO Cav. Poindexter's Regt.
Roswell, John W. AL Inf. 1st Regt. Co.D
Roswell, J.T. NC 66th Inf. Co.K
Roswell, R. AR 11th Inf. Co.D
Roswell, Simon B. AR 33rd Inf. Co.D
Roswell, S.T. AL Cav. Hardie's Bn.Res. Co.A
Roswell, T.L. TN 27th Inf. Co.A
Roswell, William TN 49th Inf. Co.I
Roswell, William Inf. Bailey's Cons.Regt. Co.D
Roswell, William R. AR 33rd Inf. Co.D Sgt.
Roswell, W.W. LA 1st Hvy.Arty. (Reg.) Co.G
Roswood, H.F. TX Cav. Martin's Regt. Co.A
Roszel, Stephen G. VA Cav. 35th Bn. Co.C
Roszell, Dulany D. VA 6th Cav. Co.A
Roszell, Samuel S. VA Lt.Arty. Griffin's Co.
Rotan, David NC 37th Inf. Co.A
Rotan, Eli C. NC 42nd Inf. Co.D
Rotan, George W. MO 1st Cav.

Rotan, James E. TN 16th Inf. Co.K 2nd Lt.
Rotan, James M. TX 25th Cav. Co.F
Rotan, James M. TX 3rd (Kirby's) Bn.Vol. Co.C Sgt.
Rotan, J.M. TX 24th & 25th Cav. (Cons.) Co.B
Rotan, J.M. TX Granbury's Cons.Brig. Co.K 1st Lt.
Rotan, W.T. TX 4th Inf. Co.E
Rotch, Gideon W. MS Lt.Arty. (Madison Lt.Arty.) Richards' Co.
Rotch, Jacob MS 9th Inf. New Co.E
Rotch, John GA Hvy.Arty. 22nd Bn. Co.C
Rotch, W.W. AL 45th Inf. Co.E
Rotchford, Edward GA 29th Inf. Co.E
Rotchford, James LA Inf. 10th Bn. Co.H,B
Rotchford, James W. LA Mil.Conf.Guards Regt. Co.C
Rotchford, John GA Hvy.Arty. 22nd Bn. Co.C
Rotchford, R.L. VA Lt.Arty. Otey's Co.
Rote, M. GA 1st (Ramsey's) Inf. Co.F Music.
Roten, Ashley NC 26th Inf. Co.A
Roten, J.A.B. MO 1st Brig.St.Guard
Roten, Jacob NC Cav. 5th Bn. Co.D
Roten, Jacob NC 6th Cav. (65th St.Troops) Co.D,B
Roten, James NC 58th Inf. Co.L
Roten, J.B. TN 35th Inf. Co.E
Roten, J.M. MS 2nd (Davidson's) Inf. Co.G
Roten, John H. MO 16th Inf. Co.A Asst.Surg.
Roten, John L. NC Cav. 5th Bn. Co.D
Roten, Jonathan NC 26th Inf. Co.A
Roten, Josiah G. NC 37th Inf. Co.A
Roten, J.T. MS 6th Cav. Co.C Sgt.
Roten, L.C. TN 42nd Inf. Co.A
Roten, L.C. 4th Conf.Inf. Co.G
Roten, M. MS 22nd Inf. Co.F
Roten, M.A. MS 2nd (Davidson's) Inf. Co.G
Roten, M.A. TN 15th (Cons.) Cav. Co.E
Roten, Solomon NC 26th Inf. Co.A
Roten, W.C. MS 7th Cav. Co.A
Roten, W.G. LA 17th Inf. Co.B
Roten, W.H.H. TN 42nd Inf. Co.A Sgt.
Roten, W.H.H. 4th Conf.Inf. Co.G Sgt.
Roten, William C. MS 2nd St.Cav. Co.A
Roten, William S. NC 37th Inf. Co.A
Rotenberry, Columbus L. AL 20th Inf. Co.D
Rotenberry, James VA 37th Inf. Co.F
Rotenberry, James J. AL 20th Inf. Co.D
Rotenberry, William GA 20th Inf. Co.G
Rotgs, Dominique LA Mil. 1st Regt. French Brig. Co.7
Roth, A. LA Mil. 3rd Regt. 1st Brig. 1st Div. Co.H
Roth, A. LA 30th Inf. Co.I Band Music.
Roth, Ant. LA Mil. Chalmette Regt. Co.C
Roth, Alphonso LA Mil.Cav.Squad. (Ind.Rangers Iberville)
Roth, Amadeo LA 2nd Cav. Co.I Sgt.
Roth, Amadeo LA Mil.Cav.Squad. (Ind.Rangers Iberville) 1st Lt.
Roth, Armand LA Arty. Kean's Btty. (Orleans Ind.Arty.)
Roth, Benjamin LA 4th Inf. Co.B
Roth, C.A. LA 27th Inf. Co.D 2nd Lt.
Roth, Charles MS 22nd Inf. Co.I 2nd Lt.
Roth, David LA 1st (Strawbridge's) Inf. Co.A

Roth, Edward LA Mil. 3rd Regt. 2nd Brig. 1st Div. Co.I

Roth, E.N. LA 30th Inf. Co.I Band Music.

Roth, E.N. Gibson's Brig.Band,CSA

Roth, F. LA 21st (Patton's) Inf. Co.A

Roth, F. TX 4th Cav. Co.C Sgt.

Roth, Felix LA 3rd Inf. Co.A Sgt.

Roth, Frank LA 1st Hvy.Arty. (Reg.) Co.G

Roth, Frank LA Arty. Kean's Btty. (Orleans Ind.Arty.)

Roth, George Conf.Reg.Inf. Brooks' Bn. Co.B

Roth, Gustave LA 3rd Inf. Co.A Cpl.

Roth, Gustave LA 21st (Patton's) Inf. Co.A

Roth, Gustavus A. MS 21st Inf. Co.F

Roth, H. TX 2nd Inf. Co.G,D

Roth, J. AL 12th Inf. Co.B

Roth, J. LA Mil. 3rd Regt. 2nd Brig. 1st Div.

Roth, J. LA Mil. Orleans Guards Regt. Co.K

Roth, J.A. TX 2nd Inf. Co.C

Roth, Jacob MS 1st (King's) Inf. (St.Troops) Co.E

Roth, Jacob MS Inf. 2nd Bn. Co.E Cpl.

Roth, Jacob MS 48th Inf. Co.E Capt.

Roth, James LA 15th Inf. Co.H

Roth, James MS 1st Lt.Arty. Co.H M.Black.

Roth, J.N. GA 9th Inf.

Roth, John LA 3rd (Harrison's) Cav. Co.G

Roth, John LA Ogden's Cav. Co.I

Roth, John LA 4th Inf. Co.B Band Music.

Roth, John LA 19th Inf. Co.A

Roth, John TX Cav. McCord's Frontier Regt. 2nd Co.A

Roth, Joseph AL 22nd Inf. Co.H

Roth, Joseph AR 1st Mtd.Rifles Co.H

Roth, Joseph AR 9th Inf. Co.H Sgt.

Roth, Joseph LA 30th Inf. Co.E

Roth, Joseph I. AL 40th Inf. Co.K

Roth, K. LA Mil. 4th Regt. 3rd Brig. 1st Div. Co.B

Roth, L. Gerard LA 27th Inf. Co.D

Roth, M. LA Mil. 2nd Regt. 3rd Brig. 1st Div. Co.I

Roth, Martin B. LA Mil. Chalmette Regt. Co.C

Roth, Matthew LA 8th Inf. Co.B

Roth, Morris GA 9th Inf. Co.B

Roth, Nicholas MS 9th Inf. Old Co.I, New Co.F

Roth, Nicholas MS 12th Inf. Co.C

Roth, Nicholas 3rd Conf.Eng.Troops Co.G

Roth, Nick Eng.Dept. Polk's Corps A. of TN Sap. & Min.Co.,CSA

Roth, Omer LA 2nd Cav. Co.I

Roth, Philip LA 2nd Cav. Co.I

Roth, R. SC Arty. Manigault's Bn. Co.E

Roth, Richard SC Hvy.Arty. Gilchrist's Co. (Gist Guard)

Roth, T. LA Mil. Orleans Guards Regt. Co.K

Roth, Tilghman F. LA 1st (Strawbridge's) Inf. Co.D

Roth, William LA Washington Arty.Bn. Co.2

Rothaas, J.F., Jr. LA Mil. Orleans Fire Bn. Co.H Sgt.

Rothacker, J. AL 17th Inf. Co.H

Rotham, F. LA Mil. 1st Regt. French Brig. Co.7

Rothbod, George E. VA Res. Keyser's Co.

Rothchild, F. GA Inf. (GA Defend.) Chapman's Co.

Rothchild, G.W. GA 5th Inf. (St.Guards) Brooks' Co.

Rothchild, S. GA Inf. (GA Defend.) Chapman's Co.

Rothchilds, Henry M. FL Lt.Arty. Perry's Co.

Rothchilds, Jacob TN 26th Inf. Co.F Sgt.

Rothe, Benjamin LA Inf. 9th Bn. Co.C

Rothe, F., 1st TX 3rd Inf. Co.B

Rothe, H., 2nd TX 3rd Inf. Co.B

Rothel, James SC 12th Inf. Co.K

Rothel, Samuel H. SC 12th Inf. Co.K

Rothell, Andrew W. GA 24th Inf. Co.C Sgt.

Rothell, B.C. SC 2nd Rifles Co.C

Rothell, J.J. GA 24th Inf. Co.C

Rothell, W.D. AL 9th Inf. Co.E

Rothell, William SC 22nd Inf. Co.D

Rother, A.T. GA 3rd Res.

Rothermel, A. TX Inf. 1st St.Troops Martin's Co.

Rothermel, Adolphus VA 36th Inf. 1st Co.H, 2nd Co.D

Rothermell, Adolphe VA Lt.Arty. Jeffress' Co.

Rothery, William LA Inf.Crescent Regt. Co.C

Rothery, W.M. LA 18th Inf. Co.B

Rothgeb, Abraham J. VA Lt.Arty. W.H. Chapman's Co.

Rothgeb, Abram J. VA Cav. 39th Bn. Co.C

Rothgeb, Alexander VA 97th Mil. Co.I Sgt.

Rothgeb, Ambrose B. VA 97th Mil. Co.I Sgt.

Rothgeb, Edmond J. VA 97th Mil. Co.E Sgt.

Rothgeb, Edmund J. VA 33rd Inf. Co.H Sgt.

Rothgeb, Emanuel VA 33rd Inf. Co.H

Rothgeb, Emanuel VA 97th Mil. Co.I

Rothgeb, Franklin VA 33rd Inf. Co.H

Rothgeb, Franklin VA 97th Mil. Co.I

Rothgeb, George VA 97th Mil. Co.H

Rothgeb, John W. VA Cav. 39th Bn. Co.C

Rothgeb, John W. VA Lt.Arty. W.H. Chapman's Co. Cpl.

Rothgeb, Martin VA 97th Mil. Co.E Cpl.

Rothgeb, Samuel VA 33rd Inf. Co.H

Rothgeb, Samuel VA 97th Mil. Co.E

Rothgeb, S.D. VA 10th Inf. Co.K

Rothgeb, Solomon D. VA 97th Mil. Co.I

Rothget, George VA 33rd Inf. Co.A,H

Rothman, William TX 2nd Inf. Co.B

Rothmier, T. AR 34th Inf. Co.D

Rothrick, John SC 1st St.Troops Co.F

Rothrock, Champ T. VA 8th Inf. Co.K Sgt.

Rothrock, Charles NC 33rd Inf. Co.I

Rothrock, Charles W. KY 9th Mtd.Inf. Co.C

Rothrock, D.B. SC 1st Cav. Co.K

Rothrock, D.B. SC 6th Res. Co.A

Rothrock, Edward C. MS Lt.Arty. (Brookhaven Lt.Arty.) Hoskins' Btty. Cpl.

Rothrock, George TN Holman's Bn.Part.Rangers Co.C Cpl.

Rothrock, George T. MO 1st Cav. Co.D 1st Sgt.

Rothrock, George T. MO 1st & 3rd Cons.Cav. Co.A Sgt.

Rothrock, G.M. TN 10th & 11th (Cons.) Cav. Co.E Lt.

Rothrock, G.M. TN 11th (Holman's) Cav. Co.E Cpl.

Rothrock, G.M. TN 3rd (Clack's) Inf. Co.H

Rothrock, Henry NC 48th Inf. Co.K

Rothrock, J.H. SC Inf. Holcombe Legion Co.F

Rothrock, John NC 4th Bn.Jr.Res. Co.B Sgt.

Rothrock, John SC 5th Res. Co.A

Rothrock, John M. NC 9th Bn.S.S. Co.B

Rothrock, John M. NC 21st Inf. Co.E

Rothrock, John T. TN 6th (Wheeler's) Cav. Co.H

Rothrock, Joseph B. AR 1st Vol. Simington's Co. 2nd Lt.

Rothrock, J.R. KY 12th Cav. Co.D

Rothrock, J.S. SC 1st Cav. Co.K Black.

Rothrock, J.T. TN 11th (Holman's) Cav. Co.E

Rothrock, J.T. TN Holman's Bn.Part.Rangers Co.C

Rothrock, Lewis H. LA 6th Inf. Co.G 1st Lt.

Rothrock, Lewis H. NC 6th Inf. Co.G 1st Lt.

Rothrock, Noah D. 3rd Conf.Cav. Adj.

Rothrock, Orvil B. AR 9th Inf. Co.E

Rothrock, P.H. KY 3rd Mtd.Inf. Co.L

Rothrock, P.H. TN 12th Inf. Co.E

Rothrock, R.G. TN 50th Inf. Asst.Surg.

Rothrock, R.G. TN 50th (Cons.) Inf. Asst.Surg.

Rothrock, Robert G. KY 2nd Mtd.Inf. Asst.Surg.

Rothrock, Robert G. TN Inf. 2nd Cons.Regt. Asst.Surg.

Rothrock, Robert G. TN 53rd Inf. Co.E

Rothrock, Robt. G. Gen. & Staff Asst.Surg.

Rothrock, W. TN 12th (Cons.) Inf. Co.G

Rothrock, W. VA 3rd Inf.Loc.Def. Co.D

Rothrock, W. Gen. & Staff Hosp.Stew.

Rothrock, Weller MS 21st Inf. Co.A

Rothrock, W.F. SC Inf. Holcombe Legion Co.F 1st Sgt.

Rothrock, W.H. TN 22nd Inf. Co.G

Rothrum, Edward TX 9th Cav. Co.B

Rothschild, A. 8th Inf. Co.G Cpl.

Rothschild, Benjamin SC 1st (Orr's) Rifles Co.B Music.

Rothwal, John B. VA 88th Mil. Capt.

Rothwell, Benjamin SC 1st (McCreary's) Inf. Co.H

Rothwell, Calvin M. TN 39th Mtd.Inf. Co.F

Rothwell, Ebenezer KY 5th Mtd.Inf. Co.H

Rothwell, F.E. VA 19th Inf. Co.K

Rothwell, George MO Cav. Wood's Regt. Co.I

Rothwell, G.W. 1st Conf.Cav. 2nd Co.A Sgt.

Rothwell, H. TX 3rd Cav. Co.K

Rothwell, J. GA 1st (Olmstead's) Inf. Gordon's Co.

Rothwell, James W. VA 56th Inf. Co.D

Rothwell, J.B. VA 15th Cav. Co.B

Rothwell, J.G. KY 3rd Mtd.Inf. Co.A

Rothwell, J.O. VA Arty. C.F. Johnston's Co.

Rothwell, John GA 63rd Inf. Co.B

Rothwell, John H. MO 1st N.E. Cav.

Rothwell, John H. MO Cav. Poindexter's Regt.

Rothwell, John H. MO 5th Inf. Co.G,H

Rothwell, John M. TN 39th Mtd.Inf. Co.F

Rothwell, John W. MO 2nd Inf. Co.H

Rothwell, J.W. VA 2nd Cav. Co.K

Rothwell, Richard AL 54th Inf.

Rothwell, Solomon KY 5th Mtd.Inf. Co.H

Rothwell, T.H. VA Inf. 1st Bn.Loc.Def. Co.F

Rothwell, W.B. TN 43rd Inf. Co.D

Rothwell, William KY 5th Mtd.Inf. Co.H

Rothwell, William J. NC 18th Inf. Co.G

Rotin, Josiah VA 21st Cav. 2nd Co.C

Rotin, William VA 21st Cav. 2nd Co.C
Rotka, George TX Lt.Arty. Hughes' Co.
Rotkamm, M. LA Mil. 1st Regt. French Brig. Co.2
Rotling, James TN Lt.Arty. Weller's Co.
Rotmann, William TX 1st (Yager's) Cav. Co.A
Roton, Archie AL 27th Inf. Co.K
Roton, Dutton VA Mil. Scott Cty.
Roton, George W. MO Cav. 3rd Bn. Co.A
Roton, Jacob VA 21st Cav. 2nd Co.C
Roton, P.B. AR 26th Inf. Co.G Cpl.
Roton, Zach MS 4th Cav. Co.D
Rotonberry, William F. TN 53rd Inf. Co.A
Rotramble, A.J. 1st Cherokee Mtd.Vol. 1st Co.H
Rotston, James P. VA Invalid Corps Capt.
Rott, Heinrich LA 20th Inf. Co.C Drum.
Rott, R.C. MS Cav. 17th Bn. Co.F 1st Sgt.
Rotten, D.E. TX 9th (Nichol's) Inf. Co.I
Rotten, D.E. TX 20th Inf. Co.K Cpl.
Rotten, John P. AL 63rd Inf. Co.G
Rotten, L.J. TX 24th Cav. Co.B
Rotten, William J. AL City Guards Lockett's Co.
Rotten, Wm. O. AL 17th Inf. Co.I
Rotten, William S. SC Inf. Hampton Legion Co.B
Rotten, W.W. AL Cp. of Instr. Talladega
Rotten, W.W. TX 24th Cav. Co.B
Rottenberg, James AL 26th Inf. Co.B
Rottenberry, Henry F. AL 44th Inf. Co.H 1st Lt.
Rottenberry, James A. MS 33rd Inf. Co.A
Rottenberry, J.M. AL 29th Inf. Co.H
Rottenberry, R.J. AL Cp. of Instr. Talladega Co.A
Rottenburg, John NC 21st Inf. Co.I
Rottenbury, Harris NC 2nd Inf. Co.A Fifer
Rottenbury, William NC 21st Inf. Co.I
Rottenbury, William A. NC 46th Inf. Co.E
Rottenman 1st Cherokee Mtd.Vol. 2nd Co.C
Rottenstein, Frank S. TX 1st Hvy.Arty. Co.G 1st Lt.
Rottenstein, F.S. TX 17th Field Btty. 1st Lt.
Rottenstein, George E. TX Cav. Baylor's Regt. Co.F 1st Lt.
Rottenstein, George E. TX 1st Hvy.Arty. Co.C 1st Lt.
Rotteroun, J. SC Mil. 1st Regt. (Charleston Res.) Co.B
Rottman, William GA Inf. 1st Loc.Troops (Augusta) Co.G
Rottman, William 1st Conf.Reg.Cav. Co.A Far.
Rotto, --- TX Cav. McCord's Frontier Regt. Co.A
Rottolf, Jacob LA 20th Inf. Old Co.B
Rotton, Augustus C. AL 3rd Bn. Hilliard's Legion Vol. Co.E
Rotton, David C. AL 60th Inf. Co.G
Rotton, David C. AL 3rd Bn. Hilliard's Legion Vol. Co.E
Rotton, D.L. AL 15th Inf. Co.I
Rotton, D.L. SC 2nd St.Troops Co.B
Rotton, F.L. SC 22nd Inf. Co.A
Rotton, Frank MS 27th Inf. Co.E
Rotton, H.P. SC 22nd Inf. Co.A
Rotton, James SC 7th Inf. 1st Co.G, Co.M
Rotton, John C. AL 6th Cav. Co.D
Rotton, J.T. SC 7th Inf. Co.K

Rotton, M.B. AL 22nd Inf. Co.K
Rotton, W.C. AL 3rd Inf. Co.L
Rotton, William G. AL 22nd Inf. Co.H
Rotton, William O. AL Cav. 4th Bn. (Love's) Co.B
Rotton, William T. AL 63rd Inf. Co.G
Rotton, W.W. TN 50th Inf. Co.C 1st Sgt.
Rotton, W.W. TN 50th (Cons.) Inf. Co.C 1st Sgt.
Rottschaffer, Adolph TX 1st Hvy.Arty. Co.C
Rou, A.B. FL Cav. 5th Bn. Co.G
Rou, Adam B. FL 2nd Cav. Co.C,F Sgt.
Rou, Michael H. FL 2nd Cav. Co.F Sgt.
Rou, S. GA 11th Inf. Co.H
Rou, Samuel F. FL 2nd Cav. Co.C,F Capt.
Rouah, John VA 11th Inf. Co.E
Rouan, Wyatt LA 26th Inf. Co.E
Rouark, C.C. AR Cav. Harrell's Bn. Co.D
Rouark, J.N. TN 19th (Biffle's) Cav. Co.G
Rouark, John NC 61st Inf. Co.C Sgt.
Rouark, Michael MD 1st Inf. Co.E
Rouark, Olsey D. TN Cav. Newsom's Regt.
Rouark, Thomas 9th Conf.Inf. Co.F
Rouay, A. LA Mil. Chalmette Regt. Co.H
Rouay, J.T. LA Mil. Chalmette Regt. Co.H Cpl.
Roubaltham, Joseph LA 26th Inf. Co.C
Roubiac, B. LA Mil. 4th Regt. French Brig. Co.5
Roubidoux, Felix TX 3rd Cav. Co.F
Roubien, P. LA Mil. 1st Chasseurs a pied Co.2 Sgt.
Roubillac, --- LA Mil. 2nd Regt. French Brig. Co.6
Roubillac, N. LA Mil. 3rd Regt. French Brig. Co.7
Roubion, A. LA Mil. 3rd Regt.Eur.Brig. (Garde Francaise) Co.3
Roubion, P. LA Mil. 3rd Regt.Eur.Brig. (Garde Francaise) Co.3
Roubion, V. LA Mil. 3rd Regt.Eur.Brig. (Garde Francaise) Co.4
Rouble, D.E. TN 36th Inf. Co.G Cpl.
Roubleau, Emile LA 10th Inf. Co.H Sgt.
Roubrough, Koratio J. VA 7th Cav. Co.A
Rouby, --- LA Mil. 2nd Regt. French Brig. Co.3
Rouby, Maseumain LA 7th Cav. Co.A
Roucaw, Paul LA Mil. French Co. of St.James
Rouce, James GA 23rd Inf. Co.A
Rouce, Marion GA 23rd Inf. Co.A
Rouce, Samuel VA 25th Cav. Co.H
Rouch, D.L. MS 3rd Inf. (St.Troops) Co.H
Rouch, Henry VA 42nd Inf. Co.D
Rouch, J.M. MS 8th Inf. Co.C
Rouch, John KY 10th (Johnson's) Cav. New Co.F
Rouch, Joseph VA 162nd Mil. Co.B
Rouch, W.A.C. MS 8th Inf. Co.C
Rouch, William VA 1st (Farinholt's) Res. Co.B
Rouche, J.S. LA 4th Cav. Co.C
Rouchon, Gilbert LA Mil. 1st Regt. French Brig. Co.6
Rouchot, Lewis AL 2nd Cav. Co.I
Roucke, M. LA 28th (Thomas') Inf. Co.G
Roudabush, D.B. VA 20th Cav. Co.C
Roudabush, John VA 14th Cav. Co.I
Roudabush, William R. VA 7th Cav. Co.I Sgt.
Roudenboush, S.D. VA Lt.Arty. Ellett's Co.
Roudet, Pete C. AL 3rd Inf. Co.A,I

Roueche, Richard F. NC 29th Inf. Co.D
Rouede, J.P. LA Mil. 3rd Regt.Eur.Brig. (Garde Francaise) Co.7
Rouel, D.J. SC 3rd St.Troops Co.C 1st Lt.
Rouer, William AL 42nd Inf. Co.D
Rouevens, Eugene LA Mil. 6th Regt.Eur.Brig. (Italian Guards Bn.) Co.5
Rouff, Charles A. LA C.S. Zouave Bn. Co.B Music.
Rouff, Joseph LA 1st Hvy.Arty. (Reg.) Co.G
Rouga, A.W. TN 62nd Mtd.Inf. Co.G Sgt.
Rougean, A. LA Miles' Legion Co.H
Rougeau, A. LA Mil. French Co. of St.James
Rougeau, Adolphe LA Arty. Landry's Co. (Donaldsonville Arty.)
Rougeau, Ignace LA Arty. Landry's Co. (Donaldsonville Arty.)
Rougeau, T. LA 21st (Kennedy's) Inf. Co.D
Rougement, Edward KY 2nd Mtd.Inf. Co.E
Rougeon, A. LA 15th Bn.S.S. (Weatherly's) Co.B
Rougeon, J.L. LA 15th Bn.S.S. (Weatherly's) Co.B
Rougeor, Loy LA 2nd Res.Corps Co.B
Rouger, Florian LA Inf.Cons. 18th Regt. & Yellow Jacket Bn. Co.F
Rouger, M. LA 22nd Inf. Co.C
Rougest, C. LA Res.Corps
Rough, Alpheus VA 20th Cav. Co.I
Rough, B. VA 6th Cav. Co.C
Rough, Franklin NC 42nd Inf. Co.I Music.
Rough, John W. VA 25th Inf. 1st Co.E
Rough, John W. VA 62nd Mtd.Inf. 2nd Co.I
Rough, J.W. LA 6th Cav. Co.H
Rough, P. LA Bienville Res.
Rough, William C. NC 42nd Inf. Co.I
Rough, William M. NC 42nd Inf. Co.I Music.
Roughen, William TX Inf. 24th Bn. (St.Troops)
Roughenberger, Christian GA 36th (Villepigue's) Inf. Co.I
Roughman, John LA Inf. 9th Bn. Co.B
Roughton, A.L. GA 6th Inf. (St.Guards) Co.G
Roughton, C.D. KY 9th Mtd.Inf. Co.E
Roughton, Charles H. NC 32nd Inf. Co.F,A
Roughton, Daniel NC 12th Inf. Co.L
Roughton, Daniel NC 32nd Inf. Co.F,A
Roughton, Eli F.A. GA 3rd Inf. Co.B
Roughton, Eliza A. NC 32nd Inf. Nurse
Roughton, George W. GA 49th Inf. Co.H 1st Lt.
Roughton, Hezekiah NC 12th Inf. Co.L Cpl.
Roughton, Hezekiah G. NC 32nd Inf. Co.F,A Cpl.
Roughton, James L. NC 28th Inf. Co.I
Roughton, James M. TN 1st (Turney's) Inf. Co.E
Roughton, James R. AR 15th (N.W.) Inf. Co.A Sgt.
Roughton, J.F. TN Inf. 23rd Bn. Co.E
Roughton, J.M. TN Inf. 23rd Bn. Co.E
Roughton, Thomas AR Cav. Gordon's Regt. Co.G
Roughton, Thomas H., Jr. AR 15th (N.W.) Inf. Co.A
Roughton, Thomas H., Sr. AR 15th (N.W.) Inf. Co.A
Roughton, Thomas T. MO 6th Cav. Co.D
Roughton, Thomas T. TN 45th Inf. Co.E
Roughton, T.T. KY 9th Mtd.Inf. Co.E

Roughton, W.B. KY 9th Mtd.Inf. Co.E
Roughton, Zachariah NC 12th Inf. Co.L Sgt.
Roughton, Zachariah NC 32nd Inf. Co.F,A Sgt.
Roughton, Z.H. GA Conscr.
Rougott, J.W. LA 6th Cav. Co.I Cpl.
Rougrulle, E. LA 7th Cav.
Rouillet, A. LA 22nd (Cons.) Inf. Co.G
Rouillet, Arestide LA 28th (Thomas') Inf. Co.E
Rouillet, Esteve LA 22nd (Cons.) Inf. Co.G
Rouillet, Esteve LA 28th (Thomas') Inf. Co.E
Rouillon, A. LA Mil. 3rd Regt. French Brig.
　Co.7 Sgt.
Rouis, Rofine LA 7th Inf. Co.G
Rouis, Solomon GA 61st Inf. Co.K
Rouis, T. GA Inf. 1st Loc.Troops (Augusta)
　Co.K
Rouis, Thomas GA 1st (Symons') Res. Co.K
Rouk, David VA 129th Mil. Buchanon's Co.
Rouk, George W. VA Inf. 26th Bn. Co.E
Rouk, George W. VA 135th Mil. Co.I
Rouk, Jesse NC 4th Sr.Res. Co.K
Rouk, L.S. AL 31st Inf. Co.C
Rouke, Bernard VA 6th Inf. 1st Co.E
Rouke, John VA 1st Arty. Co.I
Rouke, John T. SC Ord.Guards
Rouke, Miles AR 18th (Marmaduke's) Inf. Co.D
Rouke, Patrick H. VA 11th Inf. Co.H Cpl.
Rouke, William O. VA Lt.Arty. 12th Bn. Co.C
Roulain, M.O. AL 10th Inf. Co.B
Roulain, Robert SC Horse Arty. (Washington
　Arty.) Vol. Hart's Co.
Roulain, Robert SC Arty.Bn. Hampton Legion
　Co.A
Rouland, P.M. 8th (Wade's) Conf.Cav. Co.B 1st
　Lt.
Roulant, Adolphe LA Mil. 2nd Regt. French
　Brig. Co.5
Roule, A.C. LA Cav. Dubecq's Co. Cpl.
Roulean, Frank MS 48th Inf. Co.C Cpl.
Rouleau, Frank MS Inf. 2nd Bn. Co.C Cpl.
Roulen, J.M. AL 8th Cav. Co.F
Roulet, O. LA Mil. 3rd Regt. French Brig. Co.6
Roulett, B.A. LA 2nd Cav. Co.C
Roulett, Michael GA 2nd Bn.S.S. Co.C Cpl.
Rouley, D.D. LA Mil.Cav. (Jeff Davis Rangers)
　Norwood's Co.
Roulhac, C.H. KY 7th Mtd.Inf. Adj.
Roulhac, C.H. Gen. & Staff 1st Lt.,Adj.
Roulhac, J.B. Gen. & Staff Lt.,AAQM
Roulhac, Joseph KY 1st Inf. Co.E,C Bvt.2nd Lt.
Roulhac, Joseph B. FL Cav. (Marianna Drag.)
　Smith's Co. 1st Lt.
Roulhac, Thomas R. NC 49th Inf. Co.D 1st Lt.
Roulhac, T.R. NC 1st Arty. (10th St.Troops)
　Co.A
Roulhag, Thomas R. NC 29th Inf. Dr.M.
Rouliss, S. LA Arty. Watson Btty.
Roulof, John LA Mil. 3rd Regt. 1st Brig. 1st
　Div. Co.F
Roulston, A.G. TN 16th Inf. Co.K 1st Sgt.
Roulston, James L. KY 3rd Cav. Co.A
Rouluff, John AL Mil. 2nd Regt.Vol. Co.C
Rouly, J.W. TX 24th Cav. Co.I
Rouma, A. LA 15th Inf. Co.E
Roumillac, Ch. LA Mil. 3rd Regt. French Brig.
　Co.1 Cantinier

Roumillat, A. SC Mil. 1st Regt. (Charleston
　Res.) Co.D
Roumillat, A.J. SC Inf. 1st (Charleston) Bn.
　Co.D
Roumillat, A.T. SC 27th Inf. Co.D
Roumillat, Jacques E. SC Arty. Manigault's Bn.
　1st Co.A
Rounceville, A.A. MO 8th Cav. Co.G
Rounceville, J.R. TX 10th Cav. Co.B
Rounceville, Wesley MS 3rd Inf. (St.Troops)
　Co.D
Round, George F. SC 5th Inf. 1st Co.K, 2nd
　Co.K
Round, G.H. AR 19th (Dawson's) Inf. Co.E
Round, Joe NC Inf. Thomas' Legion
Round, Major 1st Cherokee Mtd.Rifles Co.F
Round, W.B. VA Cav. 36th Bn. Co.A
Round, William C. SC 1st (Orr's) Rifles Co.B
Roundabush, William VA 11th Cav. Co.C
Rounder 1st Cherokee Mtd.Rifles Co.D
Rounder, G.B. KY 9th Cav. Co.G
Rounder, Thomas NC Cav. 16th Bn. Co.F
Rounds, B.T. LA Cav. 18th Bn. Co.G
Rounds, B.T. LA 16th Inf. Co.F
Rounds, D.A. MO 2nd N.E. Cav. (Franklin's
　Regt.) Co.B
Rounds, J.J. LA 16th Inf. Co.F
Rounds, J.M. MO Lt.Arty. H.M. Bledsoe's Co.
Rounds, John MO Lt.Arty. H.M. Bledsoe's Co.
Rounds, W. LA 20th Inf. New Co.E
Rounds, William LA 5th Cav. Co.D
Rounds, William LA 11th Inf. Co.B
Rounds, W.L. AR 24th Inf. Co.K
Roundtree, Abner J. NC 4th Cav. (59th
　St.Troops) Co.D
Roundtree, Abram VA 59th Mil. Hunter's Co.
Roundtree, Adam W. AL 17th Inf. Co.K
Roundtree, Alexander VA 6th Inf. Weisiger's Co.
Roundtree, Alexander VA 16th Inf. Co.I
Roundtree, Alexander W. VA Lt.Arty.
　Weisiger's Co. Sgt.
Roundtree, A.M. SC 1st (Hagood's) Inf. 1st
　Co.G
Roundtree, Benjamin F. AL 51st (Part.Rangers)
　Co.B
Roundtree, B.F. TN 3rd (Clack's) Inf. Co.F
Roundtree, E. GA 11th Inf. Co.I
Roundtree, E.A. NC Music.
Roundtree, Elias L. MS 40th Inf. Co.I
Roundtree, F.M. AL 15th Inf. Co.F
Roundtree, Francis TX 16th Cav. Co.E
Roundtree, Franklin NC 2nd Inf. Co.D,B
Roundtree, George W. TN Holman's Bn.
　Part.Rangers Co.B
Roundtree, G.W. AL 51st Part.Rangers Co.A
Roundtree, Hampton FL 7th Inf. Co.I
Roundtree, H.C. TX 6th Inf. Co.G Cpl.
Roundtree, Henry MO 16th Inf. Co.A
Roundtree, Henry TX 32nd Cav. Co.K
Roundtree, Isaac FL 7th Inf. Co.I
Roundtree, James AL 6th Cav. Co.H
Roundtree, James SC 18th Inf. Co.F
Roundtree, James L. GA 1st (Olmstead's) Inf.
　Co.H
Roundtree, James R. MS 5th Inf. Co.I 1st Lt.
Roundtree, James S. 1st Conf.Eng.Troops Co.K
Roundtree, J.B. TX Cav. Morgan's Regt. Co.E

Roundtree, Jehu NC Cav. 16th Bn. Co.F
Roundtree, J.H. TX 32nd Cav. Co.K
Roundtree, J.M. MO 9th Inf. Co.B
Roundtree, John AL 57th Inf. Co.A
Roundtree, John VA 1st St.Res. Co.B
Roundtree, John A. FL Sp.Cav. 1st Bn. Co.B
Roundtree, John D. MS 20th Inf. Co.I
Roundtree, John J. AL 57th Inf. Co.B
Roundtree, John M. AL 61st Inf. Co.A
Roundtree, J.R. AL 13th Inf. Co.B
Roundtree, J.R. SC 1st (Hagood's) Inf. 2nd Co.E
Roundtree, J.T. TX 11th Inf. Co.C Asst.Surg.
Roundtree, Leander TN 22nd (Barteau's) Cav.
　Co.F
Roundtree, Leonidas A. TX 36th Cav. Co.K
Roundtree, M. GA 1st Reg. Co.B
Roundtree, Martin V. MS 40th Inf. Co.I
Roundtree, Mills GA Siege Arty. 28th Bn. Co.C
Roundtree, Moses FL Lt.Arty. Abell's Co.
Roundtree, Moses A. SC 8th Inf. Co.G
Roundtree, M.V. VA 59th Inf. 2nd Co.F Cpl.
Roundtree, Nathan AR Inf. 4th Bn. Co.C
Roundtree, Newson NC 33rd Inf. Co.E
Roundtree, R.A. MO 16th Inf. Co.G
Roundtree, Reddick NC 33rd Inf. Co.H
Roundtree, Reuben LA 28th (Gray's) Inf. Co.D
Roundtree, R.J. SC Cav. 19th Bn. Co.C
Roundtree, R.J. SC Part.Rangers Kirk's Co.
Roundtree, Robert B. VA 15th Inf. Co.D
Roundtree, Robert M. 37th Inf. Co.F
Roundtree, R.R. AR Inf. Cocke's Regt. Co.A
Roundtree, Scott L. Gen. & Staff Asst.Surg.
Roundtree, S.D. TX 1st Inf. Co.G
Roundtree, T.B. MO 16th Inf. Co.G
Roundtree, Thaddeus NC 2nd Inf. Co.B
Roundtree, Thomas LA 26th Inf. Co.H
Roundtree, Thomas J. TN Holman's Bn.
　Part.Rangers Co.B
Roundtree, Thomas J. TX Cav. Martin's Regt.
　Co.C,I 2nd Lt.
Roundtree, W.A. TX 1st Inf. Co.F Cpl.
Roundtree, W.C. SC 1st (Hagood's) Inf. 1st
　Co.G
Roundtree, W.D. SC 6th Cav. Co.B Cpl.
Roundtree, W.F. KY 12th Cav. Co.E
Roundtree, W.H. SC 2nd Arty. Co.H
Roundtree, William TN Cav. 11th Bn. (Gor-
　don's) Co.E Capt.
Roundtree, William TN 19th (Biffle's) Cav. Co.C
Roundtree, William VA Inf. 1st Bn.Loc.Def.
　Co.F Sgt.
Roundtree, William G. TX 16th Inf. Co.G
Roundtree, William J. AL 4th Inf. Co.A
Roundtree, William J. AL 28th Inf. Co.I
Roundtree, W.J. FL Sp.Cav. 1st Bn. Co.B
Roundy, George LA Mil. Bragg's Bn. Schwartz's
　Co.
Roune, H. TX 1st Inf. Co.K
Rouner, H.H. MO 10th Inf. Co.A
Rouney, John A. NC 33rd Inf. Co.I
Rouney, Patrick Conf.Inf. 1st Bn. 2nd Co.E
Rounquist, William P. VA Lt.Arty. Kirkpatrick's
　Co.
Rounquist, William P. VA Lt.Arty. Nelson's Co.
Rounsaval, W.A. TX Cav. Sutton's Co.
Rounsavall, A.M. TX 18th Cav. Co.K
Rounsavall, David M. GA 39th Inf. Co.H

Rounsavall, J.D. TN 34th Inf. Co.K
Rounsavall, J.E. LA Inf. 4th Bn. Co.F
Rounsavall, Wessley MS 48th Inf. Co.D
Rounsavall, William MS 48th Inf. Co.D
Rounsavill, Robert TX 22nd Inf. Co.E
Rounsavill, Wesley MS Inf. 2nd Bn. Co.D
Rounsaville, A.A. AR 18th (Marmaduke's) Inf. Co.C
Rounsaville, A.F. TN 34th Inf. Co.K
Rounsaville, D.H. LA 16th Inf. Co.A
Rounsaville, Elias MS 24th Inf. Co.A
Rounsaville, Ellis MS 24th Inf. Co.A
Rounsaville, Emzi G. TX 27th Cav. Co.B
Rounsaville, Enizi G. AR Cav. 1st Bn. (Stirman's) Co.H Sgt.
Rounsaville, H.T. AR 18th (Marmaduke's) Inf. Co.C
Rounsaville, H.T. 3rd Conf.Inf. Co.C
Rounsaville, James AR 18th (Marmaduke's) Inf. Co.C
Rounsaville, James 3rd Conf.Inf. Co.C
Rounsaville, James B. TX 13th Cav. Co.C,E Capt.
Rounsaville, J.K. TX 22nd Inf. Co.E Sgt.
Rounsaville, John L. AR 31st Inf. Co.K 1st Sgt.
Rounsaville, John W. AL 19th Inf. Co.G
Rounsaville, Peter K. AR 1st (Crawford's) Cav. Co.D
Rounsaville, Thomas J. TX 13th Cav. Co.C 2nd Lt.
Rounsaville, Thomas J. TX Lt.Arty. H. Van Buren's Co.
Rounsaville, William MS Inf. 2nd Bn. Co.D
Rounsaville, W.R. MS 8th Cav. Co.I
Rounseville, John L. TN 34th Inf. Co.D
Rounsileatt, J. SC Mil. 17th Regt. Buist's Co.
Rountre, William VA Inf. 2nd Bn.Loc.Def. Co.B
Rountree, --- TX 11th Inf. Co.A
Rountree, Abram VA Inf. Cohoon's Bn. Co.B,A
Rountree, Adam W. AL 1st Inf. Co.C
Rountree, Alex. W. VA Inf. 25th Bn. Co.A
Rountree, Allen GA Inf. (Emanuel Troops) Moring's Co.
Rountree, A.M. SC 2nd Arty. Co.G,H
Rountree, Andrew J. SC 1st St.Troops Co.D
Rountree, Andrew J. SC 5th Res. Co.F
Rountree, A.R. AL 15th Inf. Co.E
Rountree, Asa W. AL Cav. 8th Regt. (Livingston's) Co.I Cpl.
Rountree, Asa W. AL Cav. Moses' Squad. Co.A Cpl.
Rountree, Asa W. AL 61st Inf. Co.F
Rountree, A.W. LA Cav. Greenleaf's Co. (Orleans Lt.Horse)
Rountree, A.W. MS 9th Inf. Co.I
Rountree, Benjamin F. TN 48th (Voorhies') Inf. Co.A
Rountree, B.M. AR 3rd Cav. Co.H
Rountree, Burrell F. AL Inf. 1st Regt. Co.B
Rountree, B.W. AL Randolph Cty.Res. J. Hightower's Co. Sgt.
Rountree, Charles D. NC 8th Inf. Co.G 1st Lt.
Rountree, Charles N. GA 45th Inf. Co.H Capt.
Rountree, Charles W. TN 1st (Feild's) Inf. Co.G Sgt.
Rountree, C.L. SC 2nd Arty. Co.H
Rountree, C.L. SC 11th Res. Co.A Cpl.

Rountree, Daniel R. VA Lt.Arty. 38th Bn. Co.C
Rountree, E. TX Cav. Morgan's Regt. Co.G
Rountree, Edward SC 2nd St.Troops Co.K
Rountree, Ephraim GA 27th Inf. Co.E
Rountree, Ephraim R. GA 44th Inf. Co.D
Rountree, E.R. MS 39th Inf. Co.H
Rountree, Erastus NC 27th Inf. Co.H
Rountree, Erastus A. 7th Conf.Cav. 1st Co.I, Co.H
Rountree, Frank AL 30th Inf. Co.E
Rountree, George S. GA Inf. (Emanuel Troops) Moring's Co. 1st Lt.
Rountree, George W. TN 48th (Voorhies') Inf. Co.A
Rountree, G.F. SC Inf. Holcombe Legion Co.D
Rountree, Gordon NC 55th Inf. Co.A
Rountree, H.S. AL 4th (Russell's) Cav. Co.K 1st Sgt.
Rountree, J. FL 9th Inf. Co.F
Rountree, J. NC 4th Cav. Co.F
Rountree, J.A. TN 3rd (Clack's) Inf. Co.F
Rountree, Jackson NC 1st Inf. (6 mo. '61) Co.L Sgt.
Rountree, Jackson NC 66th Inf. Co.F
Rountree, James A. GA Cobb's Legion Co.F 1st Sgt.
Rountree, James H. VA Inf. Cohoon's Bn. Co.D
Rountree, J.B. SC 2nd Arty. Co.H
Rountree, J.D. SC 2nd St.Troops Co.K 1st Sgt.
Rountree, Jehu NC Vol. Lawrence's Co.
Rountree, Jehu 7th Conf.Cav. 1st Co.I, Co.H
Rountree, J.H. TX 10th Cav. Co.E
Rountree, J.J. TX 22nd Inf. Co.D
Rountree, J.M. TX 3rd Cav. Co.B
Rountree, J.M. TX Lt.Arty. Hughes' Co.
Rountree, Job SC 2nd St.Troops Co.K
Rountree, John NC 17th Inf. (2nd Org.) Co.D
Rountree, John SC 2nd St.Troops Co.K
Rountree, John SC 8th Bn.Res. Co.C
Rountree, John SC 11th Res. Co.B
Rountree, John Mead's Conf.Cav. Co.L
Rountree, John I. AL 27th Inf. Co.G
Rountree, John M. GA 3rd Inf. Co.E Cpl.
Rountree, John M. GA 48th Inf. Co.H
Rountree, John R. TN 48th (Voorhies') Inf. Co.A
Rountree, J.R. SC 2nd Arty. Co.H
Rountree, J.R. SC 3rd Inf. Co.K Cpl.
Rountree, J.R. SC 11th Res. Co.A
Rountree, J.S. SC 3rd Inf. Co.K
Rountree, Judson SC 3rd Cav. Co.K Sgt.
Rountree, J.W. GA 12th (Robinson's) Cav. (St.Guards) Co.D
Rountree, J.W. TX Inf. 1st St.Troops Wheat's Co.A
Rountree, L.C. TX 35th (Brown's) Cav. Maj.
Rountree, Leonidas C. NC 3rd Arty. (40th St.Troops) Co.B
Rountree, Leonidas C. TX 13th Vol. 3rd Co.I Maj.
Rountree, M.A. SC 3rd Cav. Co.K Lt.
Rountree, Miles VA 59th Mil. Riddick's Co.
Rountree, M.M. GA 59th Inf. Co.D 1st Sgt.
Rountree, Noah NC 11th (Bethel Regt.) Inf. Co.F
Rountree, Orange NC 2nd Cav. (19th St.Troops) Co.C
Rountree, P.C. TX 12th Inf. Co.A
Rountree, R.D. TX 7th Cav. Co.I

Rountree, Reuben GA 61st Inf. Co.A
Rountree, Reuben LA 12th Inf. Co.K
Rountree, R.J. SC 2nd St.Troops Co.K
Rountree, R.J. SC 11th Res. Co.B
Rountree, R.M. TX 30th Cav. Co.C
Rountree, R.M. TX 7th Field Btty.
Rountree, R.R. TX 11th Cav. Co.I
Rountree, R.R. TX 11th Inf. Co.D
Rountree, Sam'l H. NC Mil. Clark's Sp.Bn. Rountree's Co. Capt.
Rountree, S.C. MS Inf. 3rd Bn. Co.E
Rountree, Simeon J. NC 5th Inf. Co.B Lt.
Rountree, S.J. TX 11th Cav. Co.I Sgt.
Rountree, S.L. AL 4th (Russell's) Cav. Co.C,K
Rountree, Thomas NC Vol. Lawrence's Co.
Rountree, Thomas 7th Conf.Cav. Co.H
Rountree, Thomas C. NC 56th Inf. Co.D Sgt.
Rountree, Thomas H. TX 11th Inf. Co.D Maj.
Rountree, Thomas P. TX Cav. Giddings' Bn. Carrington's Co. Cpl.
Rountree, Thomas W. AR 37th Inf. Co.A
Rountree, T.J. SC 7th Inf. 1st Co.K, 2nd Co.K
Rountree, T.J. TN 3rd (Clack's) Inf. Co.F
Rountree, W. SC 11th Res. Co.A
Rountree, W.B. TX 19th Inf. Co.B,K 2nd Lt.
Rountree, W.C. SC 2nd Arty. Co.G
Rountree, W.C. SC 2nd Arty. Co.H
Rountree, W.D. SC 19th Inf. Co.C 2nd Lt.
Rountree, W.D. TN 3rd (Clack's) Inf. Co.F 1st Sgt.
Rountree, W.H. SC 11th Res. Co.A
Rountree, W.H. 8th (Wade's) Conf.Cav. Co.K Cpl.
Rountree, William AL 22nd Inf. Co.G
Rountree, William SC 2nd Arty. Co.H
Rountree, William TX Cav. Hardeman's Regt. Co.E Cpl.
Rountree, William A. TN 1st (Feild's) Inf. Co.G
Rountree, William F. KY 8th Cav.
Rountree, William F. NC 27th Inf. Co.H
Rountree, William H. SC 2nd Arty. Co.H
Rountree, William P. GA 5th Cav. Co.E 1st Lt.
Rountree, William R. GA Cobb's Legion Co.F
Rountree, William R. VA 1st St.Res. Co.K
Rountree, W.J. FL 1st Cav.
Rountree, W.P. GA Cav. 2nd Bn. Co.C Sgt.
Roup, Abram VA Mil. Grayson Cty.
Roup, Elihu VA Inf. 26th Bn. Co.C
Roupbe, D.S. LA 4th Cav. Co.B
Roupe, Daniel AR 51st Mil. Co.H
Roupe, L. AR 51st Mil. Co.H
Roupe, Oliver LA Inf.Crescent Regt. Co.G
Roupe, Samuel NC 34th Inf. Co.I
Roupin, T.L. MO Cav. Clardy's Bn. Co.B 2nd Lt.
Rouquet, I.B.O. LA Maddox's Regt.Res.Corps Co.B
Rouquette, A. LA Mil. Orleans Guards Regt. Co.K
Rouquette, Armand LA Pointe Coupee Arty.
Rouquette, W. LA 22nd Inf. Co.B
Rouquie, S.W. SC Arty. Melchers' Co. (Co.B,German Arty.)
Rouquie, S.W. SC 10th Inf. Co.A 1st Lt.
Rouquier, Alphonse LA 3rd Inf. Co.D
Rouquier, Edward TN 53rd Inf. Co.F
Rouquillo, E. Conf.Lt.Arty. 1st Reg.Btty.

Rour, William NC Nelson's Co. (Loc.Def.)
Roure, Juan LA Mil. 5th Regt.Eur.Brig. (Spanish Regt.) Co.3
Rourk, Asa KY 2nd Cav.
Rourk, Benjamin NC 33rd Inf. Co.F
Rourk, Jacob L. SC Lt.Arty. 3rd (Palmetto) Bn. Co.D
Rourk, James AL Inf. 2nd Regt. Co.F
Rourk, James J. SC 1st (McCreary's) Inf. Co.H Cpl.
Rourk, John NC 1st Inf. Co.E
Rourk, John E. SC 1st (McCreary's) Inf. Co.H
Rourk, Owen VA 13th Inf. Co.F
Rourk, William H. KY 2nd Cav.
Rourke, D. TN 42nd Inf. 2nd Co.I
Rourke, Daniel LA 28th (Thomas') Inf. Co.E
Rourke, Daniel MS 38th Cav. Co.H
Rourke, Daniel 4th Conf.Inf. Co.A
Rourke, Edward MO 1st N.E. Cav.
Rourke, George VA Inf. 1st Bn. Co.A
Rourke, Gilbie AL Inf. 1st Regt. Co.D
Rourke, Henry S. AL 21st Inf. Co.E
Rourke, Henry S. MS 10th Inf. Old Co.E
Rourke, Hugh VA Hvy.Arty. 19th Bn. 3rd Co.C Cpl.
Rourke, J. LA 1st (Strawbridge's) Inf. Co.E
Rourke, Jack LA 11th Inf. Co.K
Rourke, James LA 1st (Strawbridge's) Inf. Co.B
Rourke, James LA 7th Inf. Co.I
Rourke, James LA Miles' Legion Co.F
Rourke, James VA Hvy.Arty. 18th Bn. Co.B
Rourke, James Conf.Inf. 1st Bn. Co.I
Rourke, J.E. MS 1st Lt.Arty. Co.H
Rourke, John GA Inf. 1st Loc.Troops (Augusta) Co.E Cpl.
Rourke, John GA 1st (Olmstead's) Inf. Co.B
Rourke, John MS Cav. 4th Bn. Sykes' Co.
Rourke, John TX 1st Hvy.Arty. 2nd Co.F
Rourke, John TX 2nd Inf. Odlum's Co.
Rourke, John VA Lt.Arty. 38th Bn. Co.B
Rourke, John 8th (Wade's) Conf.Cav. Co.G
Rourke, John A. AL 1st Cav. 1st Co.K
Rourke, John O. TX 1st Inf. Co.L
Rourke, Joseph LA 21st (Kennedy's) Inf. Co.F
Rourke, P. GA 63rd Inf. Co.B
Rourke, P. SC Mil. 16th Regt. Bancroft, Jr.'s Co.
Rourke, Patrick VA Arty. Bryan's Co.
Rourke, Philip LA 1st Hvy.Arty. (Reg.) Co.I,H
Rourke, Thomas AL 18th Inf. Co.K
Rourke, Thos. LA 1st (Strawbridge's) Inf. Co.F
Rourke, Thomas TN 2nd (Walker's) Inf. Co.F
Rourke, Thomas VA 2nd St.Res. Co.A Cpl.
Rourke, Timothy A. AL 20th Inf. Co.K
Rourke, William J. SC 1st (Butler's) Inf. Co.E,G
Rous, C.B. VA 1st St.Res. Co.I
Rousca, Joseph LA Inf. 11th Bn. Co.B
Rousca, Joseph LA Inf.Cons.Crescent Regt. Co.K
Rousch, J. TX 24th Cav. Co.I
Rouse, --- AL Inf. 1st (Loomis') Bn. Co.B
Rouse, A.E. AL 1st Regt. Mobile Vol. Baas' Co.
Rouse, A. Jackson NC 3rd Cav. (41st St.Troops) Co.E
Rouse, Alexander NC 1st Arty. (10th St.Troops) Co.I
Rouse, Alexander NC 66th Inf. Co.E

Rouse, Alexandre NC 67th Inf. Co.A Sgt.
Rouse, Alex E. NC Inf. 3rd Bn. Co.C Sgt.
Rouse, Alfred MO Mtd.Inf. Boone's Regt.
Rouse, Alfred MO 12th Inf. Co.F
Rouse, Allen AL 39th Inf. Co.I
Rouse, Alonzo D. AL 63rd Inf. Co.B
Rouse, Amos AL 33rd Inf. Co.E
Rouse, Andrew VA Inf. 23rd Bn. Co.A Sgt.
Rouse, Andrew VA 37th Inf. Co.E
Rouse, Asa NC 3rd Inf. Co.D
Rouse, Augustus MO 1st N.E. Cav. White's Co.
Rouse, Austin J. MO 1st N.E. Cav.
Rouse, Barnet NC 30th Inf. Co.E
Rouse, Benjamin NC 61st Inf. Co.E Cpl.
Rouse, Benjamin B. NC Loc.Def. Griswold's Co.
Rouse, Benjamin F. MO 1st N.E. Cav. Co.L
Rouse, Benjamin F. MO 9th Bn.S.S. Co.D
Rouse, Benjamin F. NC 2nd Inf. Co.F
Rouse, Benjamin P. FL 2nd Cav. Co.C
Rouse, Benjamin S. NC Loc.Def. Griswold's Co.
Rouse, B.J. GA Inf. 18th Bn. Co.C
Rouse, B.O.W. GA 18th Inf. Co.C
Rouse, B.S. AL 3rd Bn.Res. Co.H Cpl.
Rouse, Burrell MS 38th Cav. Co.I
Rouse, C.A. GA 3rd Res. Co.E
Rouse, Calvin D. GA Inf. 10th Bn. Co.B
Rouse, C.D. AL 3rd Inf. Co.I Cpl.
Rouse, Charles E. Gen. & Staff,PACS Surg.
Rouse, C.J. SC Lt.Arty. J.T. Kanapaux's Co. (Lafayette Arty.)
Rouse, D. SC Mil. 16th Regt. Robinson's Co.
Rouse, Daniel TN 7th Inf.
Rouse, Daniel H. GA 48th Inf. Co.I
Rouse, David NC 8th Sr.Res. Broadhurst's Co.
Rouse, Edward A. AL 13th Inf. Co.C
Rouse, Edward J. NC 2nd Inf. Co.F
Rouse, Eli AL 10th Inf. Co.B
Rouse, Elias GA 18th Inf. Co.C
Rouse, Enoch NC 48th Inf. Co.D
Rouse, Ephraim VA 82nd Mil. Co.A
Rouse, Gaustavus MO 1st N.E. Cav. Price's Co.M
Rouse, George AL 13th Inf. Co.K
Rouse, George J.C. AL 13th Inf. Co.C
Rouse, George W. MO 1st N.E. Cav. Co.L
Rouse, George W. NC 3rd Arty. (40th St.Troops) Co.A
Rouse, George W. NC 3rd Inf. Co.D
Rouse, George W. NC 32nd Inf. Lenoir Braves 1st Co.K
Rouse, G.W. SC 1st Regt.Charleston Guard Co.I
Rouse, G.W. TX Cav. Mann's Regt. Co.F
Rouse, H. MS Cav. 17th Bn. Co.E
Rouse, Hayden VA 47th Inf. 2nd Co.G
Rouse, Henry VA 25th Cav. Co.H
Rouse, Henry VA 37th Inf. Co.E
Rouse, Henry H. GA 59th Inf. Co.F
Rouse, Hezekieh MS 3rd Inf. Co.H
Rouse, Ira S. FL 2nd Inf. Co.I Cpl.
Rouse, Ira S. FL 11th Inf. Co.G 1st Lt.
Rouse, Irving T. AL Inf. 1st Regt. Co.F,E
Rouse, J.A. KY 8th Mtd.Inf. Co.C Sgt.
Rouse, Jacob MO 2nd Inf. Co.A Sgt.
Rouse, Jacob NC 8th Sr.Res. Broadhurst's Co.
Rouse, Jacob R. GA 1st Reg. Co.L
Rouse, Jame GA 5th Inf.
Rouse, James KY 4th Mtd.Inf. Co.C

Rouse, James VA 48th Inf. Co.D
Rouse, James 14th Conf.Cav. Co.G
Rouse, James B. NC 5th Cav. (63rd St.Troops) Co.B
Rouse, James M. GA 59th Inf. Co.F Capt.
Rouse, James M. VA 47th Inf. 2nd Co.G
Rouse, James N. AL 18th Inf. Co.D
Rouse, James N. GA 17th Inf. Co.B
Rouse, James W. AL 19th Inf. Co.C 2nd Lt.
Rouse, J.E. NC Lt.Arty. 13th Bn. Co.C
Rouse, Jefferson W. 3rd Cav. (41st St.Troops) Co.E
Rouse, Jefferson W. NC Mil. Clark's Sp.Bn. Rountree's Co. 1st Cpl.
Rouse, J.H. TX 12th Inf. Co.C Cpl.
Rouse, J.J. TN 7th Inf.
Rouse, J.M. LA Mil. French Co. of St.James
Rouse, J.M. TX Cav. Baird's Regt. Co.H
Rouse, J.N. GA 46th Inf. Co.B
Rouse, John GA 8th Cav. Co.A
Rouse, John GA Hvy.Arty. 22nd Bn.
Rouse, John GA Siege Arty. 28th Bn. Co.D
Rouse, John GA 2nd Inf. Co.G
Rouse, John TN 7th Inf.
Rouse, John VA 25th Cav. Co.H
Rouse, John VA Inf. 21st Bn. Co.C
Rouse, John VA Inf. 23rd Bn. Co.A
Rouse, John VA 48th Inf. Co.D
Rouse, John VA Inf. Mileham's Co.
Rouse, John A. GA 49th Inf. Co.I
Rouse, John G. NC 27th Inf. Co.C
Rouse, John H. VA Hvy.Arty. A.J. Jones' Co. Cpl.
Rouse, John J. SC 8th Inf. Co.A 1st Lt.
Rouse, John L. NC 1st Cav. (9th St.Troops) Co.H
Rouse, John L. NC 3rd Cav. (41st St.Troops) Co.E
Rouse, John M. GA 2nd Bn.S.S. Co.D
Rouse, John M. TX 17th Inf. Co.A
Rouse, John Q. FL 3rd Inf. Co.H
Rouse, John W. GA 14th Inf. Co.G
Rouse, John W. NC 1st Arty. (10th St.Troops) Co.I
Rouse, John W. NC 2nd Bn.Loc.Def.Troops Co.A
Rouse, John W. NC 3rd Inf. Co.C
Rouse, John W. NC 61st Inf. Co.E
Rouse, John W. NC Mil. Clark's Sp.Bn. Rountree's Co., Co.C
Rouse, John W. VA Mil. Washington Cty.
Rouse, Joseph GA 12th Cav. Co.G
Rouse, Joseph GA Inf. 11th Bn. (St.Guards) Co.C
Rouse, Joseph B. GA Arty. 11th Bn. (Sumter Arty.) Co.A
Rouse, Joseph T. LA 7th Inf. Co.B
Rouse, Joshua NC 3rd Inf. Co.C,E
Rouse, Joshua NC Mil. Clark's Sp.Bn. Co.C
Rouse, Joshua L. NC 27th Inf. Co.C
Rouse, J.T. NC 2nd Jr.Res. Co.G
Rouse, J.W. GA Inf. 17th Bn. (St.Guards) Stocks' Co.
Rouse, J.W. GA 27th Inf. Co.D
Rouse, J.W. GA Inf. Collier's Co.
Rouse, J.W. NC 8th Bn.Part.Rangers Co.B,E
Rouse, J.W. NC 7th Bn.Jr.Res. Co.B

Rouse, J.W. NC 66th Inf. Co.H
Rouse, J.W. NC Mil. Clark's Sp.Bn. Co.C
Rouse, Lee MO 1st N.E. Cav. Price's Co.M
Rouse, Leegrand MO 1st N.E. Cav. White's Co. Sgt.
Rouse, Lemuel G. NC 3rd Inf. Co.A
Rouse, Lewis H. AL Inf. 1st Regt. Co.F
Rouse, Lewis H. AL 40th Inf. Co.C
Rouse, L.H. AL 46th Inf. Co.C Music.
Rouse, Marcellous NC 67th Inf. Co.D
Rouse, Marian GA Inf. 17th Bn. (St.Guards) Stock's Co.
Rouse, Maurice AR 1st Mtd.Rifles Co.G
Rouse, Michael VA 25th Cav. Co.H Cpl.
Rouse, Milton VA 12th Cav. Co.B 1st Lt.
Rouse, M.J. VA 7th Cav. 1st Lt.
Rouse, Mordecai B. VA Hvy.Arty. A.J. Jones' Co. Sgt.
Rouse, Napoleon B. AL 22nd Inf. Lt.Col.
Rouse, N.B. AL 25th Inf. Co.B Capt.
Rouse, Noah NC 3rd Arty. (40th St.Troops) Co.K
Rouse, Noah NC 18th Inf. Co.H
Rouse, Noah NC 51st Inf. Co.H
Rouse, Oliver P. SC 1st (McCreary's) Inf. Co.I Cpl.
Rouse, Paulser VA Inf. 23rd Bn. Co.A
Rouse, Philip VA Mil. Washington Cty.
Rouse, Pleasant F. MS 24th Inf. Co.F
Rouse, R.A. GA Cav. 19th Bn. Co.D
Rouse, R.A. SC 3rd St.Troops Co.C Lt.Col.
Rouse, Redden T. AL Vol. Lee, Jr.'s Co. Sgt.
Rouse, Redding T. GA 12th Inf. Co.C
Rouse, R.J. VA 8th Cav. Co.C
Rouse, R.M. MO 12th Inf. Co.F
Rouse, Robert GA 50th Inf. Co.I
Rouse, Robert A. 10th Conf.Cav. Co.I
Rouse, Robert Emmett LA 7th Inf. Co.B
Rouse, R.S. AL 3rd Res. Co.E Cpl.
Rouse, R.T. AL 1st Bn. Hilliard's Legion Vol. Co.E
Rouse, R.T. GA Inf. 1st Conf.Bn. Co.B
Rouse, R.T. 1st Conf.Inf. 2nd Co.E
Rouse, S. FL 1st (Res.) Inf. Co.B 1st Lt.
Rouse, S. Fauntleroy VA 47th Inf. 2nd Co.G
Rouse, Simon B. NC 27th Inf. Co.C
Rouse, Solomon H. AL Inf. 1st Regt. Co.F
Rouse, Solomon W. GA 59th Inf. Co.F
Rouse, Stephen GA 62nd Cav. Co.A
Rouse, Stephen GA 5th Mil.
Rouse, Stephen GA 59th Inf. Co.F
Rouse, Stephen VA Inf. 23rd Bn. Co.A Sgt.
Rouse, Tazwell A. VA 26th Inf. Co.I
Rouse, Theodore A. AL 13th Inf. Co.C
Rouse, Thomas NC 8th Sr.Res. Gardner's Co.
Rouse, Thomas A. NC 27th Inf. Co.D Sgt.
Rouse, Thomas B. NC 2nd Inf. Co.F
Rouse, Thomas B. VA 26th Inf. Co.I
Rouse, Thomas W. NC 27th Inf. Co.C 2nd Lt.
Rouse, W. AR Mil. Desha Cty.Bn.
Rouse, W. FL Lt.Arty. Dyke's Co.
Rouse, W. NC Mil. Clark's Sp.Bn. Co.C
Rouse, W.A. FL 2nd Cav. Co.K
Rouse, W.A. FL Lt.Arty. Dyke's Co.
Rouse, W.A. GA Cav. 22nd Bn. (St.Guards) Co.G
Rouse, W.D. AL 25th Inf. Co.B Sgt.

Rouse, W.H. GA Inf. 2nd Bn. (St.Guards) Co.C
Rouse, W.H. TX 5th Cav. Co.C
Rouse, Wiley GA 27th Inf. Co.D Sgt.
Rouse, Wiley J. NC Mil. Clark's Sp.Bn. Rountree's Co., Co.G
Rouse, William AL 1st Regt. Mobile Vol. Baas' Co.
Rouse, William GA 8th Cav. Co.A
Rouse, William GA 62nd Cav. Co.A
Rouse, William GA 40th Inf. Co.B
Rouse, William GA 59th Inf. Co.F
Rouse, William NC 3rd Inf. Co.H
Rouse, William VA 21st Cav. 1st Co.E
Rouse, William VA 2nd Inf.Loc.Def. Co.A
Rouse, William VA Inf. 2n Bn.Loc.Def. Co.A
Rouse, William VA 48th Inf. Co.D
Rouse, William A. FL Cav. Pickett's Co.
Rouse, William B. TX 12th Inf. Co.D
Rouse, William G. VA Hvy.Arty. 19th Bn. Co.A Sgt.
Rouse, William H. NC 27th Inf. Co.C Cpl.
Rouse, William J. NC 2nd Inf. Co.H
Rouse, William N. GA 2nd Bn.S.S. Co.D Cpl.
Rouse, William N. GA 5th Inf. Co.G,I,M
Rouse, W.M. SC Mil. 1st Regt. (Charleston Res.) Co.D
Rouse, W.R. SC 1st Mtd.Mil. Screven's Co.
Rouse, W.R. SC 24th Inf. Co.D Cpl.
Rouseau, Daniel MS 3rd Inf. Co.E
Rouseau, Sabien MS 3rd Inf. Co.E
Rouseau, W.L. LA Miles' Legion Co.C
Rousell, Abner AL 1st Regt.Conscr. Co.F
Rousell, James LA Ogden's Cav. Co.E
Rousell, Joseph MS 3rd Inf. Co.E
Rouselle, Edward T. TX 22nd Inf. Co.C Cpl.
Rouselly, J. LA Mil. 4th Regt. French Brig. Co.6
Rousey, A. GA 38th Inf. Co.H
Rousey, H.C. MS 22nd Inf. Co.H
Rousey, Henry GA 20th Inf. Co.A
Rousey, Henry VA 20th Cav. Co.K
Rousey, J. GA 38th Inf. Co.H
Rousey, James H. VA 58th Inf. Co.C
Rousey, J.W. TN 51st (Cons.) Inf. Co.E 1st Sgt.
Rousey, Marion VA 58th Inf. Co.G
Rousey, M.G. GA 38th Inf. Co.H
Rousey, Thomas George MS 7th Cav. Co.E Sgt.
Rousey, W. GA 38th Inf. Co.H
Roush, Charles M. VA 1st Cav. Co.B
Roush, H.B. KY 7th Mtd.Inf. Co.B
Roush, Levi VA 30th Inf. Co.A
Roushe, H.L. VA Cav. 37th Bn. Co.E
Rousherbourg, Frederick A. GA 39th Inf. Co.B
Rousie, G.W. TX Cav. Giddings' Btty. Co.B
Rousin, T.L. MO 1st & 4th Cons.Inf. Co.I Cpl.
Rousine, J. LA Mil.Cont.Cadets
Rousley, W.R. NC 4th Inf. Co.E
Rousow, Raynee LA Inf. 11th Bn. Co.C
Rousow, Raynee LA Inf.Cons.Crescent Regt. Co.F
Rouss, C.B. VA 12th Cav. Co.B
Roussan, Adolph NC 5th Sr.Res. Co.K Capt.
Roussan, L. TN 40th Inf. Co.C Capt.
Roussan, L. TN 42nd Inf. 2nd Co.E 2nd Lt.
Rousse, Bertrand LA Mil. 2nd Regt. French Brig. Co.4
Rousse, Dominique LA Mil. 6th Regt.Eur.Brig. (Italian Guards Bn.) Co.5

Roussea, William LA Mil. LaFourche Regt.
Rousseau, A. GA 18th Inf. Co.A
Rousseau, Aaron GA 57th Inf. Co.F
Rousseau, Adolph LA 28th (Thomas') Inf. Co.H Cpl.
Rousseau, Adolphus LA Inf. 9th Bn. Co.C Sgt.
Rousseau, David AL Nitre & Min.Corps Young's Co.
Rousseau, David T. AL 1st Cav.
Rousseau, David T. AL Nitre & Min.Corps Young's Co. Sgt.
Rousseau, Dufossard LA 28th (Thomas') Inf. Co.H
Rousseau, Edmond LA 26th Inf. Co.C
Rousseau, George W. GA 46th Inf. Co.G
Rousseau, Hibbard L. TN 4th Inf. Co.E
Rousseau, J. LA Mil. 3rd Regt. French Brig. Co.7
Rousseau, J.A.A. LA Mil. Orleans Guards Regt. Co.E Cpl.
Rousseau, James P. AL 42nd Inf. Co.E 1st Lt.
Rousseau, J.C. LA Mil. Chalmette Regt. Co.H 1st Sgt.
Rousseau, J.L. FL Cav. 5th Bn. Co.G
Rousseau, John L. MS Lt.Arty. (Issaquena Arty.) Graves' Co. Cpl.
Rousseau, John Lovell KY 4th Mtd.Inf. Co.B 2nd Lt.
Rousseau, Jonathan AL 50th Inf. Co.C
Rousseau, Joseph LA Pointe Coupee Arty.
Rousseau, Joseph F. TX 2nd Inf. Ch.Bugler
Rousseau, Jules A.A. LA Washington Arty.Bn. Co.3
Rousseau, L., Jr. LA Mil. 3rd Regt. 2nd Brig. 1st Div. Co.K
Rousseau, Louis LA 8th Inf. Co.F
Rousseau, O. LA Arty. Watson Btty.
Rousseau, O. LA 22nd Inf. Co.E
Rousseau, Paul LA Pointe Coupee Arty.
Rousseau, Paul LA Mil. 1st Chasseurs a pied Co.3
Rousseau, Pierre LA Mil. LaFourche Regt.
Rousseau, Pink W. TX 11th Inf. Co.G
Rousseau, Reuben AL 25th Cav.
Rousseau, Samuel LA Washington Arty.Bn. Co.3
Rousseau, Samuel LA Inf. 7th Bn. Co.C
Rousseau, Samuel LA 15th Inf. Co.K
Rousseau, W.H. FL 1st (Res.) Inf. Co.B 2nd Lt.
Rousseau, William J. MS 48th Inf. Co.L,K 2nd Lt.
Rousseau, William T. AL Inf. 1st Regt. Co.A Music.
Rousseau, William T. GA 3rd Cav. Co.A
Rousseau, W.J. MS Inf. 2nd Bn. Co.L Sgt.
Rousseaux, S. LA Inf. 9th Bn. Co.C
Rousseaux, William LA 3rd (Wingfield's) Cav. Co.B
Rousseaux, William LA Ogden's Cav.
Rousseaux, William LA Miles' Legion Co.A
Roussel, A. LA Inf.Cons. 18th Regt. & Yellow Jacket Bn. Co.C
Roussel, Charles LA 10th Inf. Co.H 1st Lt.
Roussel, Charles LA Inf.Cons. 18th & Yellow Jacket Bn. Co.C
Roussel, Chas. Gen. & Staff 2nd Lt.,Dr.M.
Roussel, Edgar LA 30th Inf. Co.G
Roussel, Edouard LA 18th Inf. Co.A Bugler

Roussel, Emile LA 30th Inf. Co.G
Roussel, Felix LA 18th Inf. Co.E Sgt.
Roussel, G. LA Lt.Arty. 6th Field Btty. (Grosse Tete Flying Arty.)
Roussel, J. Abel LA 4th Inf. Co.E
Roussel, J.L. LA Inf.Cons.18th Regt. & Yellow Jacket Bn. Co.B
Roussel, Joseph, Jr. LA 18th Inf. Co.E,B
Roussel, Joseph, Jr. LA Inf.Cons. 18th Regt. & Yellow Jacket Bn. Co.B
Roussel, Joseph Louis LA 18th Inf. Co.E
Roussel, L. LA 18th Inf. Co.E
Roussel, L. LA Inf.Cons. 18th Regt. & Yellow Jacket Bn. Co.B
Roussel, L. Amos LA 4th Inf. Co.E
Roussel, Marcelius LA 30th Inf. Co.G
Roussel, Octave LA 30th Inf. Co.G 1st Sgt.
Roussel, P. LA Lt.Arty. 6th Field Btty. (Grosse Tete Flying Arty.)
Roussel, P. LA 18th Inf. Co.E
Roussel, P. LA Inf.Cons. 18th Regt. & Yellow Jacket Bn. Co.B
Roussel, Prudent LA 30th Inf. Locoul's Co.
Roussel, T.F. LA 26th Inf. Co.I
Roussel, Valery LA 30th Inf. Co.G
Roussel, Z. LA Inf.Cons. 18th Regt. & Yellow Jacket Bn. Co.B
Roussel, Zephirin LA 18th Inf. Co.E
Rousselet, A.J. LA Mil. 1st Regt. French Brig. Co.6
Rousselin, H. LA Mil. 3rd Regt.Eur.Brig. (Garde Francaise) Co.3
Rousselin, H. LA 30th Inf. Co.F
Rousselin, H. LA Mil. Orleans Guards Regt. Co.A
Roussell, Abner AL 32nd Inf. Co.I
Roussell, Alf AL 18th Inf. Co.A
Roussell, Augustus LA 18th Inf. Co.A
Roussell, Charles LA 18th Inf. Co.A
Roussell, E.C. AL 32nd Inf.
Roussell, J. LA 30th Inf. Co.A
Roussell, J.A. Conf.Cav. Wood's Regt. 2nd Co.F
Roussell, Joseph LA 18th Inf. Co.A
Roussell, O. LA 18th Inf. Co.A
Roussell, Thomas LA 4th Inf. Co.E
Rousselle, John W. AL 24th Inf. Co.F,B
Rousselle, William J. AL 24th Inf. Co.F
Rousselot, C.A. MD Cav. 2nd Bn. Co.D 2nd Lt.
Rousselot, George LA C.S. Zouave Bn. Co.B
Rousselot, Joseph LA Mil. 2nd Regt. French Brig. Co.6
Rousselot, R. LA Mil. 1st Regt. French Brig. Co.4
Rousset, E. LA Arty. Guyol's Co. (Orleans Arty.)
Roussett, Alfred LA Mil. Orleans Guards Regt. Co.A
Roussett, Amedee LA Mil. 5th Regt.Eur.Brig. (Spanish Regt.) Co.8
Roussette, B. LA Mil. 4th Regt. French Brig. Co.2
Roussin, T.L. MO 4th Inf. Co.I Cpl.
Roussy, Francois LA Mil. 2nd Regt. French Brig. Co.6
Roust, J.W. NC 3rd Jr.Res. Co.D
Roustan, Louis A. LA 4th Inf. Co.E Sgt.

Rout, George A. KY 3rd Bn.Mtd.Rifles Co.A 2nd Lt.
Rout, George T. KY 4th Cav. Co.D Cpl.
Rout, James KY 2nd Bn.Mtd.Rifles Co.B
Rout, James M. KY 3rd Bn.Mtd.Rifles Co.A 1st Sgt.
Rout, Richard VA 15th Cav. Co.D
Rout, Richard G. KY 6th Mtd.Inf. Co.G
Rout, Samuel 1st Chickasaw Inf. Milam's Co.
Rout, S.T. KY 3rd Bn.Mtd.Rifles Co.A
Rout, T.D. KY 3rd Bn.Mtd.Rifles Co.A
Rout, Thornton D. KY 4th Cav. Co.D
Rout, Wesley L. KY 6th Mtd.Inf. Co.G
Rout, William P. KY 6th Mtd.Inf. Co.G
Routan, Thos. J. AL 22nd Inf. Co.I
Routch, Henry M. AL 61st Inf. Co.E
Route, Richard J. VA Cav. 15th Bn. Co.B
Route, Richard J. VA 37th Mil. Co.A Cpl.
Routen, Andrew J. GA 55th Inf. Co.K
Routen, A.R. GA 55th Inf. Co.K
Routen, John A. VA Hvy.Arty. Kyle's Co.
Routen, Samuel B. VA Hvy.Arty. 19th Bn. Co.A
Routen, Samuel B. VA Hvy.Arty. Kyle's Co.
Routen, Samuel B. VA 28th Inf. Co.A
Router, C. TX Inf. Timmons' Regt. Co.D
Router, C. TX Waul's Legion Co.F
Router, E.T. VA 2nd Inf.Loc.Def. Co.G
Routh, --- LA Catahoula Bn. Capt.
Routh, Aaron NC 22nd Inf. Co.M
Routh, Alexander NC 46th Inf. Co.K 1st Lt.
Routh, Alfred NC 6th Sr.Res. Co.D
Routh, A.M. TX 11th Cav. Co.G
Routh, Andrew S. Conf.Cav. Wood's Regt. 1st Co.A
Routh, A.S. LA 3rd (Harrison's) Cav. Co.A
Routh, Charles B. MS 4th Cav. Co.C
Routh, F.M. TN 36th Inf. Co.E
Routh, Francis M. TN 43rd Inf. Co.K
Routh, George C. TX 19th Cav. Co.K
Routh, George E. NC 22nd Inf. Co.M
Routh, George W. TN 63rd Inf. Co.H 2nd Lt.
Routh, G.W. TN 5th (McKenzie's) Cav. Co.C Sgt.
Routh, Horatio S. Conf.Cav. Wood's Regt. 1st Co.A
Routh, Horatio S. Gen. & Staff Maj.,Depot QM
Routh, Hugh L. AR Cav. 1st Bn. (Stirman's) Co.E Sgt.
Routh, Isaac TX 31st Cav. Co.E
Routh, Isum TX 11th Cav. Co.G
Routh, J. LA Mil. Bragg's Bn. Fowler's Co.
Routh, James C. GA 39th Inf. Co.C 2nd Lt.
Routh, James E. VA 9th Inf. 2nd Co.A 2nd Lt.
Routh, James M. NC 22nd Inf. Co.M Cpl.
Routh, James M. NC Hahr's Bn. Co.K
Routh, J.C. TN 36th Inf. Co.E
Routh, J.C. TN 43rd Inf. Co.K 1st Sgt.
Routh, J.E. GA 1st Lt.Duty Men Co.A
Routh, Jesse NC 22nd Inf. Co.M
Routh, J.H. TX 9th (Nichlos') Inf. Co.A
Routh, J.H. TX Inf. Timmons' Regt. Co.E
Routh, J.H. TX Waul's Legion Co.D Sgt.
Routh, J.K. Conf.Cav. Wood's Regt. 1st Co.A Sgt.
Routh, Job MS 16th Inf. Co.G Adj.
Routh, Job Conf.Cav. Wood's Regt. 1st Co.A Cornet

Routh, Job Gen. & Staff 1st Lt.,Adj.
Routh, John TX Cav. Madison's Regt. Co.F
Routh, John A. VA Prov.Guard Avis' Co.
Routh, Jonathan TX 11th Cav. Co.G
Routh, Joseph A. NC 22nd Inf. Co.M
Routh, Joshua M. NC 22nd Inf. Co.M
Routh, J.W. TN 36th Inf. Co.E
Routh, Kinney GA 60th Inf. Co.E
Routh, Levi W. NC 46th Inf. Co.K Sgt.
Routh, M.H. AR 15th (Josey's) Inf. 1st Co.C Sgt.
Routh, Moses NC 6th Sr.Res. Co.D
Routh, Oct. Gen. & Staff, Arty. Lt.,Ord.Off.
Routh, Octavus Conf.Cav. Wood's Regt. 1st Co.A
Routh, R.F. GA 1st Lt.Duty Men Co.A
Routh, Rice I. GA 34th Inf. Co.A
Routh, R.J. GA 39th Inf. Co.E 1st Sgt.
Routh, S.F. LA 11th Inf. Co.G 2nd Lt.
Routh, S.F. LA 31st Inf. Co.F Capt.
Routh, Stephen M. MS Cav. Jeff Davis Legion Co.A
Routh, Stephen M. Conf.Cav. Wood's Regt. 1st Co.A
Routh, Stephen M. Sig.Corps,CSA Capt.
Routh, Wesley P. NC 22nd Inf. Co.M
Routh, W.F. GA 39th Inf. Co.E 1st Lt.
Routh, William A. TX 11th Field Btty. 1st Lt.
Routh, William C. NC 22nd Inf. Co.M
Routh, William F. GA 34th Inf. Co.A 1st Sgt.
Routh, William M. NC 3rd Arty. (40th St.Troops) Co.I
Routh, William R. FL 1st Inf. Old Co.A Sgt.
Routh, William R. NC 22nd Inf. Co.M
Routh, W.J. TN 43rd Inf. Co.K
Routh, Z.M. TX 9th (Nichols') Inf. Co.A
Routh, Z.M. TX Waul's Legion Co.G
Routi, August LA Conscr.
Routin, William H. 1st Seminole Mtd.Vol. AQMSgt.
Routon, George D. VA Hvy.Arty. 20th Bn. Co.A
Routon, George D. VA 44th Inf. Co.A
Routon, James AR 17th (Griffith's) Inf. Co.D
Routon, James H. AR 11th & 17th Cons.Inf. Co.K
Routon, J.B. TX Cav. Baird's Regt. Co.H
Routon, J.M. AL 37th Inf. Co.K
Routon, John A. VA Hvy.Arty. 19th Bn. Co.A
Routon, John H. VA Hvy.Arty. 20th Bn. Co.A
Routon, John P. LA 8th Inf. Co.H Cpl.
Routon, John W. 1st Conf.Inf. 2nd Co.H
Routon, Peter H. VA Hvy.Arty. 20th Bn. Co.A
Routon, Peter H. VA 44th Inf. Co.A Cpl.
Routon, R.J. TN Lt.Arty. Huggins' Co.
Routon, S.W. TX 20th Inf. Co.F
Routon, Thomas T. TN 45th Inf. Co.E
Routon, Washington AR 1st (Crawford's) Cav. Co.E Sgt.
Routon, William AL 18th Inf. Co.H
Routt, Bryan KY Cav. 2nd Bn. (Dortch's) Co.D
Routt, Byron M. KY 11th Cav. Co.C
Routt, Elbert M. VA 47th Inf. Co.F
Routt, George KY 1st Bn.Mtd.Rifles Co.A
Routt, George A. KY 1st Bn.Mtd.Rifles Co.A
Routt, G.W. TX 8th Cav. Co.K
Routt, Hudson TN 41st Inf. Co.C

Routt, Hudson TN 44th (Cons.) Inf. Co.B
Routt, Isham T. KY Cav. Jenkins' Co.
Routt, Isham T. KY 1st Bn.Mtd.Rifles Co.A Sgt.
Routt, James KY 2nd Cav. Co.B
Routt, James KY 9th Cav.
Routt, James M. KY 1st Bn.Mtd.Rifles Co.A
Routt, James R. TN 44th Inf. Co.E
Routt, James R. TN 44th (Cons.) Inf. Co.B
Routt, John M. TN 44th (Cons.) Inf. Co.B 1st
    Sgt.
Routt, J.W. TX 8th Cav. Co.K
Routt, Peter A. VA Lt.Arty. 12th Bn. 1st Co.A
Routt, Peter A. VA Lt.Arty. Utterback's Co.
Routt, Richard TN 1st (Turney's) Inf. Co.G
    Capt.
Routt, S.R. TX 8th Cav. Co.K
Routt, Thomas LA 4th Cav. Co.G
Routt, Thornton D. KY 1st Bn.Mtd.Rifles Co.A
Routt, W. AR 1st (Dobbin's) Cav. Co.K
Routt, William VA 157th Mil. Co.A
Routt, William H. VA Lt.Arty. J.S. Brown's Co.
Routt, William H. VA Lt.Arty. Taylor's Co.
Routt, William H. VA Mil. Greene Cty.
Routten, E. LA 1st Cav. Robinson's Co. Sgt.
Routten, Edward TN Arty. Ramsey's Btty.
    Sgt.Maj.
Routten, Joseph VA 115th Mil. Co.A
Routter, L. TX Inf. Timmons' Regt. Co.D
Routzhan, Nat VA 31st Mil. Co.C
Rouvert, Edmond LA 18th Inf. Co.G
Rouvette, A. LA Inf. 10th Bn. Co.G
Roux, A. LA Mil. 1st Chasseurs a pied Co.1
    Sgt.
Roux, A. LA Mil. 3rd Regt. French Brig. Co.5
Roux, A. MO Lt.Arty. Barret's Co.
Roux, A.L. MS 1st (King's) Inf. (St.Troops)
    Co.C
Roux, Aml. LA Mil. Orleans Guards Regt. Co.A
Roux, Arthur LA Lt.Arty. LeGardeur, Jr.'s Co.
    (Orleans Guard Btty.)
Roux, B. LA Mil. 1st Regt. French Brig. Co.8
Roux, Charles LA Mil. St.James Regt. Co.F
Roux, Edwin T. FL 7th Inf. Co.G 2nd Lt.
Roux, Emile LA Mil. 2nd Regt. French Brig.
    Co.1,6
Roux, E.T. FL 2nd Inf. Co.K
Roux, Eugene LA Lt.Arty. LeGardeur, Jr.'s Co.
    (Orleans Guard Btty.)
Roux, Eugene LA Mil. 4th Regt. 2nd Brig. 1st
    Div. Co.F 3rd Lt.
Roux, F. LA Mil. 4th Regt. French Brig. Co.6
Roux, F.C. MO 2nd Cav. Co.E Sgt.
Roux, F.L. GA Loc.Inf.
Roux, F.L. SC 10th Inf. 1st Co.G
Roux, Foster LA 2nd Cav.
Roux, F.S. FL 2nd Cav. Co.K
Roux, Henry SC Inf. Hampton Legion Co.A
Roux, H.S. SC 10th Inf. 1st Co.G
Roux, J. LA Mil. 1st Chasseurs a pied Co.1
Roux, J. LA Mil. 3rd Regt. French Brig. Co.4
Roux, J. MS Cav. Hughes' Bn. Co.E
Roux, Joseph AL Mil. 3rd Vol. Co.E
Roux, Leoport LA Mil. 2nd Regt. 2nd Brig. 1st
    Div. Co.K
Roux, L.F. Gen. & Staff Capt.,ACS
Roux, Louis FL 2nd Cav. Co.K Capt.
Roux, Louis LA Inf.Crescent Regt. Co.G

Roux, Louis LA Mil. Orleans Guards Regt. Co.H
Roux, M. LA Mil. 1st Regt. French Brig. Co.1
Roux, T. LA Arty. 1st Field Btty.
Rouya, O. LA 7th Cav. Co.D
Rouyer, Florian LA 18th Inf. Co.G
Rouyie, Simon LA Ogden's Cav. Co.A Sgt.
Rouzan, Martin LA Mil. 1st Native Guards
Rouzee, James H. VA 146th Mil. Co.K
Rouzee, J.B. VA 7th Cav. Co.E
Rouzee, John R. MS 41st Inf. Co.F Sgt.
Rouzee, John W. VA 146th Mil. Co.K
Rouzee, Thomas E. VA 7th Inf. Co.A
Rouzet, Simon LA 1st Cav. Co.H
Rouzie, A.R. Gen. & Staff A.Surg.
Rouzie, Edward VA 19th Cav. Co.F
Rouzie, Edward J. VA Lt.Arty. Nelson's Co.
    Sgt.
Rouzie, E.J. VA Cav. 38th Bn. Co.A
Rouzie, R.R. VA 9th Cav. Co.F
Rouzie, Simon 14th Conf.Cav. Co.D
Rouzie, William B. VA Res.
Rovax, Joshua AL 58th Inf. Co.L
Rove, John VA Cav. 32nd Bn. Co.A
Rovello, Candellore LA Mil. Cazadores
    Espanoles Regt. Co.F
Rovels, F.M. TN 23rd Inf. Co.F
Roven, J. TN Cav. 9th Bn. (Gantt's) Co.E
Rovenstein, William GA 5th Inf. (St.Guards)
    Russell's Co.
Rover, Armistead D. VA 14th Inf. Co.B Sgt.
Rover, George MO 8th Inf. Co.B
Rover, James R. AL Lt.Arty. Ward's Btty.
Rover, John D. AR 1st Inf.
Rover, Peter T. VA Lt.Arty. Brander's Co.
Rover, Samuel T. VA 46th Inf. 2nd Co.C
Rover, S.T. VA 34th Inf. Co.C
Rovert, William GA Inf.St.Line
Rovett, W.S. SC 7th Cav.
Rovie, James MO 12th Cav.
Row, A.E. NC 3rd Jr.Res. Co.E
Row, A.J. AR 31st Inf. Co.D 3rd Lt.
Row, Alex MO Cav. 1st Regt.St.Guard Co.A
Row, Benjamin MS Wilkinson Cty. Minute Men
    Harris' Co.
Row, Carlton VA 9th Cav. Co.B Sgt.
Row, Charles B. GA 9th Inf. Co.C
Row, David GA 9th Inf. Co.C
Row, David NC 6th Cav. (65th St.Troops)
    Co.K,B
Row, David S. VA 7th Cav. Co.D
Row, Ed TX Cav. Bourland's Regt. Co.H,K
Row, E.L. LA 3rd (Wingfield's) Cav. Co.I
Row, Frederick TX 13th Vol. 2nd Co.C
Row, H. AR Cav. McGehee's Regt.
Row, Henry NC 48th Inf. Co.B
Row, Jacob MO 8th Cav. Co.A
Row, Jacob A. LA 3rd (Wingfield's) Cav. Co.I
Row, James H. GA 1st (Ramsey's) Inf. Co.H
Row, Jared O. VA 7th Cav. Co.C
Row, J.H. GA 21st Inf. Co.H
Row, John LA 11th Inf. Co.E
Row, John MO Inf. 4th Regt.St.Guard Co.E Sgt.
Row, John VA 2nd Inf. Co.B
Row, John D. AL 18th Inf. Co.D
Row, John E. SC 24th Inf. Co.G
Row, John S. VA 6th Cav. Co.I Capt.
Row, John W. NC 42nd Inf. Co.D Music.

Row, John W. VA 20th Cav. Co.D
Row, J.S. MO 6th Cav. Co.I
Row, L. LA 3rd (Wingfield's) Cav. Co.I
    AASurg.
Row, L.C. LA 27th Inf. Co.I
Row, Lewis J. SC 15th Inf. Co.A
Row, Michael Conf.Cav. Wood's Regt. 1st Co.G
Row, Noah D. VA 12th Cav. Co.K
Row, Noah D. VA 136th Mil. Co.B Sgt.
Row, Peter VA 3rd Bn.Valley Res. Co.D
Row, R.F. GA 9th Inf. Co.C
Row, Richard MS Lt.Arty. (Brookhaven
    Lt.Arty.) Hoskins' Btty.
Row, Seaborn GA 7th Inf. Co.E
Row, Stephen A. NC 1st Arty. (10th St.Troops)
    Co.D
Row, Vincent MS Cav. Semple's Co.
Row, W.H. VA 7th Cav. Co.D
Row, William FL 3rd Inf. Co.C
Row, William MO Inf. 4th Regt.St.Guard Co.E
Row, William SC 14th Inf. Co.C
Row, William TX 18th Cav. Witt's Co.E
Row, William TX Cav. Wells' Bn. Co.B Cpl.
Row, William D. VA 5th Inf. Co.D
Row, William H. MO 6th Cav. Co.F
Row, William T. LA 16th Inf. Co.I Sgt.
Row, W.M. GA 21st Inf. Co.H
Row, W.T. LA Mil. Chalmette Regt. Co.F 1st
    Sgt.
Rowald, Albert M. AL 12th Inf. Co.C
Rowall, W.J. FL 2nd Inf. Co.K
Rowan, --- VA Wise's Bn.Vol. Lt.
Rowan, Aaron VA 31st Inf. Co.I
Rowan, Abraham A. GA 19th Inf. Co.G
Rowan, Allan C. VA 22nd Inf. Co.C 2nd Lt.
Rowan, Allen C. VA 189th Mil. Co.C Capt.
Rowan, Baily D. AL 27th Inf. Co.B
Rowan, B.D. AL 55th Vol. Co.E Sgt.
Rowan, B.D. TN 42nd Inf. 1st Co.K Sgt.
Rowan, C. MS 14th Inf. Co.C
Rowan, C.C. MO 1st Brig.St.Guard
Rowan, C.H. VA 59th Inf. 1st Co.B Sgt.
Rowan, Charles LA 1st Hvy.Arty. (Reg.) Co.D
Rowan, C.L. VA 14th Cav. Co.E Cpl.
Rowan, C.L. VA 60th Inf. Co.A Sgt.
Rowan, Cleveland MS Inf. 2nd Bn. Co.F
Rowan, Cleveland MS 48th Inf. Co.F
Rowan, Crockett TN Cav. 4th Bn. (Branner's)
    Co.B
Rowan, C.T. LA Cav. Nutt's Co. (Red River
    Rangers)
Rowan, E.A. MS 6th Inf. Co.G Capt.
Rowan, Elias A. MS 12th Inf. Co.D
Rowan, Elijah MS 14th Inf. Co.D
Rowan, Elisha AL 55th Vol. Co.E
Rowan, E.M. NC 21st Inf. Co.D
Rowan, E.S. TN Inf. 1st Cons.Regt. Co.K
Rowan, E.S. TN 16th Inf. Co.C
Rowan, General M. MS 26th Inf. Co.I
Rowan, George AR 5th Inf. Co.A
Rowan, George W. GA 8th Inf. Co.F
Rowan, George W. NC 2nd Cav. (19th
    St.Troops) Co.A
Rowan, George W. VA 31st Inf. Co.F Cpl.
Rowan, G.W. TX 27th Cav. Co.K Sgt.
Rowan, Hezekiah VA 19th Cav. Co.C

Rowan, Hezekiah VA 3rd Cav. & Inf.St.Line
  Co.D
Rowan, Jacob TN 29th Inf. Co.E Sgt.
Rowan, Jacob B. TN Inf. 2nd Cons.Regt. Co.H
  Sgt.
Rowan, James AR 1st (Monroe's) Cav. Co.B
Rowan, James MS 12th Inf. Co.B
Rowan, James MS 32nd Inf. Co.B
Rowan, James H. VA 28th Inf. Co.B
Rowan, James H. VA 60th Inf. Co.A
Rowan, James M. TN 35th Inf. Co.B
Rowan, James R. MS 1st (Johnston's) Inf. Co.C
Rowan, James W. SC 6th Inf. 1st Co.K
Rowan, James W. VA 22nd Inf. Co.C
Rowan, J.B. MS 32nd Inf. Co.B
Rowan, J.C. TN 3rd (Forrest's) Cav. Co.K
Rowan, J.C., Jr. TN 3rd (Lillard's) Mtd.Inf.
  Co.H
Rowan, J.C. TN 3rd (Lillard's) Mtd.Inf. Co.H,
  2nd Co.K
Rowan, J.C. TN 59th Mtd.Inf. Music.
Rowan, J.C. Brass Band Vaughn's Brig.,CSA
  Music.
Rowan, J. Crocket TN 2nd (Ashby's) Cav. Co.G
Rowan, J. Crockett NC 62nd Mtd.Inf.
  Capt.,ACS
Rowan, J.D. VA 14th Cav. Co.I
Rowan, J.H. AR 1st (Monroe's) Cav. Co.H
Rowan, J.J. FL Cav. 5th Bn. Co.D Cpl.
Rowan, J.K. TN 62nd Mtd.Inf. Co.D 2nd Lt.
Rowan, J.M. GA 2nd Cav. Co.F
Rowan, John AR 24th Inf. Co.G
Rowan, John LA 1st Hvy.Arty. (Reg.) Co.G
Rowan, John LA 7th Inf. Co.G 1st Lt.
Rowan, John VA 1st Arty. 2nd Co.C, Co.H
Rowan, John VA Arty. C.F. Johnston's Co.
Rowan, John A. FL 9th Inf. Co.E
Rowan, John A. TN 2nd (Ashby's) Cav. Co.G
  Capt.
Rowan, John A. TN Cav. 4th Bn. (Branner's)
  Co.B Capt.
Rowan, John A. TN 62nd Mtd.Inf. Col.
Rowan, John B. AL 18th Inf. Co.L
Rowan, John B. GA Lt.Arty. Ritter's Co. Capt.
Rowan, John Brown MD Arty. 3rd Btty. Capt.
Rowan, John C. AR Inf. Clayton's Co.
Rowan, John D. Nitre & Min. Bureau War
  Dept.,CSA
Rowan, John F. GA 30th Inf. Co.A,B
Rowan, John J. NC 2nd Arty. (36th St.Troops)
  Co.B
Rowan, John M. VA 108th Mil. Col.
Rowan, John W. VA 2nd Inf. Co.A Capt.
Rowan, John W. VA 189th Mil. Co.C
Rowan, Joseph B. MS 19th Inf. Co.K
Rowan, J.P. AR 1st (Monroe's) Cav. Co.A
Rowan, J.W. TN 16th Inf. Co.G
Rowan, J.W. TN 43rd Inf. Co.H
Rowan, J.W. VA 14th Cav. Co.E
Rowan, Lytle KY 2nd Cav. Co.C 1st Lt.
Rowan, Lytle KY 4th Cav. Co.C 1st Lt.
Rowan, Lytle TN 5th (McKenzie's) Cav. Co.I
Rowan, Martin VA 31st Inf. Co.I
Rowan, Michael SC Mil. 1st Regt. (Charleston
  Res.) Co.A
Rowan, Montgomery M. MS 24th Inf. Co.D
  Capt.

Rowan, Nicholas VA 31st Inf. Co.I
Rowan, O.M. AL St.Arty. Co.D
Rowan, Phillips TX 17th Cons.Dismtd.Cav.
  Co.D
Rowan, Richard AL 24th Inf. Co.E 1st Lt.
Rowan, Richard AL 28th Inf. Co.D Sgt.
Rowan, Robert C. TN 62nd Mtd.Inf. Co.D
  Capt.
Rowan, Samuel AR 7th Inf. Co.D
Rowan, Samuel MS St.Cav. 2nd Bn. (Harris')
  Co.A,B Cpl.
Rowan, Samuel MS 11th (Perrin's) Cav. Co.G
  Sgt.
Rowan, Samuel MO Cav. Ford's Bn. Co.E
Rowan, Samuel J. NC 2nd Arty. (36th St.Troops)
  Co.B
Rowan, Samuel T. FL 6th Inf. Co.C
Rowan, S.J. NC McIlhenny's Co.
Rowan, Stephen W. KY 9th Mtd.Inf. Co.C Sgt.
Rowan, S.W. SC 2nd Inf. Co.A
Rowan, T. VA 11th Bn.Res. Co.F
Rowan, Taylor VA Cav. Swann's Bn. Watkins'
  Co.
Rowan, Thomas AL Arty. 1st Bn. Co.A
Rowan, Thos. AL Cp. of Instr. Talladega
Rowan, Thomas TN 21st Inf. Co.E
Rowan, Thomas TX 26th Cav. Co.A 1st Lt.
Rowan, Thomas VA Hvy.Arty. 19th Bn. 3rd
  Co.C
Rowan, Thomas G. AR 1st (Colquitt's) Inf. Co.E
Rowan, Thomas J. MS 19th Inf. Co.K Capt.
Rowan, Thomas N. MS 26th Inf. Co.I Cpl.
Rowan, Thomas N. MS 31st Inf. Co.K
Rowan, T.Y.S. SC Mil. 16th Regt. Jones' Co.
Rowan, W.C. FL Cav. 5th Bn. Co.D
Rowan, W.F. MS 2nd (Davidson's) Inf. Co.K
Rowan, W.F. MS 32nd Inf. Co.B
Rowan, W.H. KY 3rd Cav. Co.A Capt.
Rowan, W.H. SC 27th Inf. Co.I
Rowan, William FL 9th Inf. Co.H,E
Rowan, William GA 11th Cav. Co.I
Rowan, William H. AL 15th Bn.Part.Rangers
  Co.B
Rowan, William H. AR 1st (Colquitt's) Inf. Co.E
Rowan, William H. GA 6th Cav. 1st Co.K Capt.
Rowan, William H. KY 3rd Bn.Mtd.Rifles Co.C
  Capt.
Rowan, William H. KY Jessee's Bn.Mtd.Rif-
  lemen Co.C Capt.
Rowan, William H. KY Part.Rangers Rowan's
  Co. Capt.
Rowan, William H. KY 1st Inf. Co.D Capt.
Rowan, William H. VA 3rd Inf. Co.H
Rowan, William H. Conf. Cav. 6th Bn. Co.C
  Capt.
Rowan, William S. FL 4th Inf. Co.A
Rowan, William S. VA 60th Inf. Co.A Maj.
Rowan, W.M. AR 11th Inf. Co.B
Rowan, W.P. NC 2nd Arty. (36th St.Troops)
  Co.G
Rowan, W.S. VA 59th Inf. 1st Co.B 1st Lt.
Rowand, C.E. SC 25th Inf. Co.A
Rowand, Robert SC Inf. 1st (Charleston) Bn.
  Co.A Sgt.
Rowand, Robert SC 27th Inf. Co.I Sgt.
Rowand, W.H. SC 3rd Cav. Co.H
Rowans, T. VA Lt.Arty. Fry's Co.

Roward, W.F. FL 1st (Res.) Inf.
Rowark, A. TN 12th (Green's) Cav. Co.K
Rowark, E. TN 14th (Neely's) Cav. Co.C
Rowark, Samuel MO St.Guard
Rowark, William H. TN Cav. Newsom's Regt.
  Co.A
Rowbish, Jacob VA 9th Bn.Res. Co.A
Rowbothen, J.W. AR 7th Cav. Co.B
Rowbottom, John LA 3rd (Harrison's) Cav. Co.K
Rowbottom, John LA Lt.Arty. 2nd Field Btty.
  Sgt.
Rowbottom, John LA 2nd Inf. Co.E
Rowden, ---, 1st TX Cav. Mann's Regt. Co.F
Rowden, ---, 2nd TX Cav. Mann's Regt. Co.F
Rowden, A.C. GA 8th Inf. Co.A
Rowden, A.M. GA 42nd Inf. Co.F
Rowden, B.F. GA 53rd Inf. Co.B
Rowden, C.G. GA 42nd Inf. Co.A
Rowden, Crockett A. GA 36th (Broyles') Inf.
  Co.K
Rowden, E.A. GA 19th Inf. Co.G
Rowden, Edmund D. GA 20th Inf. Co.F
Rowden, E.L. MO 7th Cav. Co.H
Rowden, Ezekiel TX 10th Inf. Co.E
Rowden, H. FL Cav. 5th Bn. Sgt.
Rowden, James W. TX 36th Cav. Co.A
Rowden, John A. AL 24th Inf. Co.E
Rowden, John H. MO 11th Inf. Co.I
Rowden, John M. MO 11th Inf. Co.I
Rowden, L. GA Smith's Legion Co.F
Rowden, Laban GA 65th Inf. Co.D,I
Rowden, P.H. GA 63rd Inf. Co.C
Rowden, Samuel G. MO 11th Inf. Co.I
Rowden, T.D. TN 45th Inf. Co.K
Rowden, Thomas J. MS 26th Inf. Co.C Cpl.
Rowden, William A. 11th Inf. Co.I
Rowden, William C. TX 36th Cav. Co.A
Rowden, William M. GA 42nd Inf. Co.F,B Sgt.
Rowdon, John VA 12th Cav. Co.D
Rowdon, W.A. MO 2nd Cav. Co.D
Rowdon, W.M. TN 15th (Cons.) Cav. Co.A
Rowdy, John Conf.Inf. Tucker's Regt. Co.K
Rowdybah, Samuel VA 10th Bn.Res. Co.E
Rowe, A. Eng.,CSA Asst.Eng.
Rowe, A.B. MS 12th Inf. Co.I
Rowe, Achilles VA 26th Inf. Co.F 1st Lt.
Rowe, Adolphus E. NC 6th Bn.Jr.Res. Co.B
Rowe, A.G. SC 20th Inf. Co.B
Rowe, A. Govan SC 1st (Hagood's) Inf. 1st
  Co.A
Rowe, A.H. LA 3rd Inf. Co.G
Rowe, A.J. GA 1st Cav. Co.B
Rowe, A.J. GA 3rd Res. Co.G
Rowe, A.J. GA 5th Res. Co.C,A
Rowe, A.J. MS Inf. 2nd St.Troops Co.G
Rowe, A.J. SC Cav. 19th Bn. Co.E Cpl.
Rowe, A.J. SC 5th Res. Co.K
Rowe, A.J. SC 20th Inf. Co.L
Rowe, A.J. TX 7th Cav. Co.F
Rowe, A.J. TX 14th Inf. Co.H
Rowe, A.K. NC 48th Inf. Co.G
Rowe, Albert VA 21st Mil. Co.A
Rowe, Albert VA 26th Inf. Co.E
Rowe, Alexander TX 17th Inf. Co.B
Rowe, Alexander M. NC 2nd Arty. (36th
  St.Troops) Co.C
Rowe, Alfred TX 27th Cav. Co.A

Rowe, Allen M. NC 2nd Cav. (19th St.Troops) Co.I
Rowe, Alonzo H. NC 46th Inf. Co.K
Rowe, Alpheus J. VA Cav. 46th Bn. Co.C
Rowe, A.M. NC Lt.Arty. 13th Bn. Co.C
Rowe, Ambrose MS Inf. Cooper's Co.
Rowe, Ambroze L. MS 6th Inf. Co.I
Rowe, Amos VA 2nd Inf. Co.G
Rowe, Andrew J. GA 7th Inf. Co.F 1st Lt.
Rowe, Andrew P. VA 34th Inf. Co.A
Rowe, Andrew P. Conf.Hvy.Arty. Montague's Bn. Co.A
Rowe, Andrew T. GA 49th Inf. Co.I
Rowe, Andrew T. Gen. & Staff Asst.Surg.
Rowe, Aug. H. GA Inf. 1st Loc.Troops (Augusta) Co.A
Rowe, A.V. MS 28th Cav. Co.A
Rowe, A.V. VA 1st St.Res. Co.K
Rowe, A.V. Gen. & Staff Surg.
Rowe, A.W. AL 50th Inf. Co.C
Rowe, A.W. TN 9th (Ward's) Cav. Co.F Capt.
Rowe, A.W. TN 1st Hvy.Arty. 2nd Co.C 2nd Lt.
Rowe, A.W. TN Arty. Marshall's Co. 1st Sgt.
Rowe, Azel FL 1st Cav. Co.B
Rowe, Barney H. NC 31st Inf. Co.K
Rowe, Benjamin VA 21st Mil. Co.A
Rowe, Benjamin VA 26th Inf. Co.E
Rowe, Benjamin A. VA 21st Mil. Co.A
Rowe, Benjamin A. VA 34th Inf. Co.A
Rowe, Benjamin C. NC 1st Arty. (10th St.Troops) Co.D
Rowe, Benjamin F. TN 19th Inf. Co.A Sgt.
Rowe, Benjamin F. VA 32nd Inf. 2nd Co.I
Rowe, Benjamin T. VA 21st Mil. Co.A
Rowe, Benjamin T. VA 28th Inf. Co.F
Rowe, B.F. TX 35th (Brown's) Cav. Co.C
Rowe, B.H. TX 10th Cav. Co.F
Rowe, C.B. SC 4th Cav. Co.D
Rowe, C.B. SC 5th Cav. Co.E
Rowe, Charles MO 10th Inf. Co.L
Rowe, Charles NC 42nd Inf. Co.D
Rowe, Charles TN 19th Inf. Co.I
Rowe, Charles D. MO 12th Inf. Co.E
Rowe, Clack VA Lt.Arty. Thornton's Co.
Rowe, C.M. LA 31st Inf. Co.E
Rowe, Conradrado NC 58th Inf. Co.K
Rowe, Cornelius SC 19th Inf. Co.D
Rowe, Cullen SC 14th Inf. Co.D
Rowe, D. SC 1st (Hagood's) Inf. 1st Co.G
Rowe, Daniel J. TX 3rd Cav. Co.K
Rowe, David AL Inf. 1st Regt. Co.G
Rowe, David GA 66th Inf. Co.G
Rowe, David NC 1st Arty. (10th St.Troops) Co.H
Rowe, David TN 60th Mtd.Inf. Co.D
Rowe, David A. NC Cav. 5th Bn. Co.B
Rowe, David M. GA 11th Inf. Co.A
Rowe, David Pinkney NC 12th Inf. Co.A Maj.
Rowe, David S. VA 97th Mil. Co.F Sgt.
Rowe, Dennis TX 5th Inf. Co.K
Rowe, D.G. GA Cav. 20th Bn. Co.B
Rowe, D. Lafayette NC 12th Inf. Co.A
Rowe, Donald J. SC 1st (Hagood's) Inf. 1st Co.A QMSgt.
Rowe, E. SC 3rd St.Troops Co.A
Rowe, E. TX Cav. 1st Bn.St.Troops Co.A Cpl.

Rowe, E. TX 33rd Cav. Co.F
Rowe, E. TX 12th Inf. Co.B
Rowe, Earley H. LA 31st Inf. Co.E
Rowe, E.B. SC 4th Cav. Co.D
Rowe, E.B. SC Manigault's Bn.Vol. Co.B
Rowe, Eben SC 4th Cav. Co.D
Rowe, Edgar C. VA 55th Inf. Co.M
Rowe, Edward GA 1st (Olmstead's) Inf. Co.A
Rowe, Edward VA 21st Cav. Co.F
Rowe, Edward VA 2nd Inf. Co.H
Rowe, Edward D. AL Lt.Arty. Phelan's Co.
Rowe, Edw. H. VA 24th Cav. Co.D
Rowe, Edward H. VA 26th Inf. Co.F Capt.,ACS
Rowe, Edward H., Jr. VA 26th Inf. Co.F
Rowe, Edward H., Sr. VA 26th Inf. Co.F
Rowe, Edward H. Gen. & Staff, Comsy.Dept. Capt.
Rowe, Edward J. VA 26th Inf. Co.F Sgt.
Rowe, E.L. Bradford's Corps Scouts & Guards Co.A
Rowe, Eldridge VA 26th Inf. Co.F Cpl.
Rowe, Eleasar TN 32nd Inf. Co.I
Rowe, Elhannon W. VA 6th Cav. Co.I
Rowe, Eli AL 20th Inf. Co.I
Rowe, Elisha D. AL Cav. Falkner's Co.
Rowe, E.S. VA Inf. 1st Bn.Loc.Def. Co.C
Rowe, Ethanon W. Gen. & Staff Surg.
Rowe, Ethelbert VA 26th Inf. Co.I
Rowe, E.W. NC 5th Sr.Res. Co.D
Rowe, E.W. VA 14th Cav. Surg.
Rowe, Fletcher AL 8th Inf. Co.A
Rowe, Fletcher GA 31st Inf. Co.A
Rowe, F.M. LA Inf. 16th Bn. (Conf.Guards Resp.Bn.) Co.B Sgt.
Rowe, F.M. LA Hatcher's Res.Corps
Rowe, Frederick TX 15th Inf. 3rd Co.H
Rowe, French 1st Cherokee Mtd.Rifles Co.E
Rowe, Gale AL 6th Inf. Co.D
Rowe, G.B. GA Cav. 20th Bn. Co.B
Rowe, George VA 26th Inf. Co.F
Rowe, George A. 3rd Conf.Eng.Troops Co.D
Rowe, Geo. T. AL 8th Inf. Co.D
Rowe, George W. AL Lt.Arty. Phelan's Co.
Rowe, George W. MS 35th Inf. Co.B
Rowe, George W. VA 6th Cav. Co.I
Rowe, George W. VA Lt.Arty. 38th Bn. Co.C
Rowe, George W. VA Lt.Arty. E.J. Anderson's Co.
Rowe, George W. VA 55th Inf. Co.E
Rowe, George Washington AL 5th Inf. Old Co.H
Rowe, George W.E. VA 9th Cav. Co.E Cpl.
Rowe, G.G. AL 1st Cav. Co.G
Rowe, Granbury NC 47th Inf. Co.D
Rowe, Green H. AL 61st Inf. Co.C
Rowe, G.T. MS Cav. 4th Bn. Co.B
Rowe, G.T. VA 2nd Bn.Res.
Rowe, G.W. AL 19th Inf. Co.H
Rowe, G.W. AL 22nd Inf. Co.A
Rowe, H. TX 22nd Inf. Co.F
Rowe, H.A. GA Smith's Legion Co.F
Rowe, Hamilton F. AR 13th Inf. Co.A Cpl.
Rowe, Henry KY 8th Cav. Co.D
Rowe, Henry SC 11th Res. Co.G Cpl.
Rowe, Henry Clay VA 9th Cav. Co.B
Rowe, Hezekiah VA Lt.Arty. Garber's Co.
Rowe, H.H. TX 5th Inf. Co.G

Rowe, Hiram A. GA 65th Inf. Co.D
Rowe, Hiram C. LA 1st (Strawbridge's) Inf. Co.F
Rowe, H.T. TX 4th Inf. Co.G
Rowe, I. 2nd Conf.Eng.Troops Co.F
Rowe, Irvin M. SC 13th Inf. Co.B
Rowe, J. LA 22nd Inf. Co.B
Rowe, J. VA 1st St.Res. Co.B
Rowe, J.A. TN 6th (Wheeler's) Cav. Co.K
Rowe, Jack 1st Cherokee Mtd.Rifles Co.C
Rowe, Jackson AR Cav. Davies' Bn. Co.D
Rowe, Jacob LA 28th (Gray's) Inf. Co.K Sgt.
Rowe, James GA Lt.Arty. 12th Bn. 2nd Co.D
Rowe, James LA Mil. Irish Regt. Laughlin's Co.
Rowe, James SC 7th Cav. Co.A
Rowe, James SC Cav. Tucker's Co.
Rowe, James SC 21st Inf. Co.A
Rowe, James TN 6th (Wheeler's) Cav. Co.K
Rowe, James TN 19th Inf. Co.I Sgt.
Rowe, James TX 13th Vol. Co.H
Rowe, James TX 22nd Inf. Co.F Cpl.
Rowe, James VA 21st Mil. Co.A
Rowe, James 1st Cherokee Mtd.Vol. 2nd Co.F
Rowe, James A. GA 28th Inf. Co.E Capt.
Rowe, James C. AL 40th Inf. Co.G
Rowe, James C. GA 20th Inf. Co.E Sgt.
Rowe, James C. 1st Conf.Eng.Troops Co.H
Rowe, James E.D. MS 1st Lt.Arty. Co.B Lt.
Rowe, James F. VA 5th Cav. Co.E Sgt.
Rowe, James H. VA 5th Cav. Co.A
Rowe, James J. GA 1st Reg. Co.G
Rowe, James J. GA 47th Inf. Co.H
Rowe, James M. NC 2nd Arty. (36th St.Troops) Co.C 1st Lt.
Rowe, James M. NC Lt.Arty. 13th Bn. Co.C 1st Lt.
Rowe, James M. VA 26th Inf. Co.E
Rowe, James M. VA 41st Inf. Co.A
Rowe, James N. SC 10th Inf. Co.A
Rowe, James P. FL 5th Inf. Co.D
Rowe, James P. GA 3rd Cav. (St.Guards) Co.G
Rowe, James P. MS 44th Inf. Co.G,I
Rowe, James R. TX 17th Cav. 1st Co.I 2nd Lt.
Rowe, James V. TX 17th Inf. Co.B
Rowe, James W. SC Inf. 7th Bn. (Enfield Rifles) Co.G
Rowe, James W. VA 9th Cav. Co.B
Rowe, James W. VA 26th Inf. Co.F 2nd Lt.
Rowe, Jason E. VA 3rd Inf. Co.D
Rowe, Jasper VA 26th Inf. Co.F
Rowe, Jasper C. VA 5th Cav. Co.A
Rowe, Jasper L. VA 1st St.Res. Co.F
Rowe, J. Dallas NC 46th Inf. Co.K 1st Sgt.
Rowe, J. Dobson VA 26th Inf. Co.E
Rowe, J.E. AL 12th Cav. Co.C
Rowe, J.E. FL 1st Cav. Co.B
Rowe, J.E. GA 3rd Cav. Co.D
Rowe, J.E. SC 5th Cav. Co.I
Rowe, J.E. TX 14th Inf. Co.C
Rowe, Jesse B. TX 8th Cav. Co.D
Rowe, Jesse J. GA 1st Reg. Co.G
Rowe, Jesse J. GA 47th Inf. Co.H
Rowe, Jesse M. MS 35th Inf. Co.B
Rowe, J.F. AL 34th Inf. Co.D 1st Lt.
Rowe, J.F. TX 10th Cav. Co.F
Rowe, J.H. AR Inf. Cocke's Regt. Co.E
Rowe, J.H. FL 2nd Cav. Co.I

Rowe, J.H. SC 24th Inf. Co.B
Rowe, J.H. TN 3rd (Clack's) Inf. Co.K
Rowe, J.L. NC 37th Inf. Co.F
Rowe, J.L. SC 4th St.Troops Co.D
Rowe, J.L. SC 23rd Inf. Co.I
Rowe, J.M. FL 2nd Cav. Co.K
Rowe, J.M. VA Inf. 1st Bn.Loc.Def. Co.C
Rowe, J.M. VA Inf. 25th Bn. Co.G
Rowe, J. Milton VA Inf. 1st Bn.Loc.Def. Co.C
    1st Sgt.
Rowe, Joel M. VA 26th Inf. Co.F
Rowe, John AL 34th Inf. Co.C
Rowe, John AR Cav. Davies' Bn. Co.D
Rowe, John AR 1st Mtd.Rifles Co.G
Rowe, John FL 1st Cav. Co.B
Rowe, John FL 2nd Cav. Co.A
Rowe, John GA Cav. 6th Bn. (St.Guards) Co.G
Rowe, John GA 1st (Olmstead's) Inf. Co.A
Rowe, John KY 5th Cav.
Rowe, John LA 14th (Austin's) Bn.S.S. Co.A
Rowe, John SC 19th Inf. Co.K
Rowe, John SC Inf.Bn. Co.D
Rowe, John TX 1st Field Btty.
Rowe, John TX Loc.Def.Troops McNeel's Co.
    (McNeel Coast Guards)
Rowe, John VA Hvy.Arty. 18th Bn. Co.A
Rowe, John A. GA 6th Inf. Co.D
Rowe, John E. AL 1st Cav. Co.I
Rowe, John F. VA 21st Mil. Co.A Sgt.
Rowe, John G. AR 33rd Inf. Co.D
Rowe, John G. NC Inf. 13th Bn. Co.D Cpl.
Rowe, John G. NC 66th Inf. Co.K Cpl.
Rowe, John G. TX 11th Inf. Co.F
Rowe, John H. GA 45th Inf. Co.G
Rowe, John H. VA 24th Cav. Co.D
Rowe, John H. VA Cav. 40th Bn. Co.D
Rowe, John H. VA 26th Inf. Co.F Music.
Rowe, John J. VA 30th Inf. Co.B
Rowe, John L. GA 20th Inf. Co.D
Rowe, John M. SC 5th Cav. Co.H
Rowe, John M. SC Cav. 14th Bn. Co.A
Rowe, John M. TX 19th Cav. Co.K
Rowe, John R. MS 18th Inf. Co.B
Rowe, John S. LA 4th Inf. Co.C
Rowe, John S. VA 51st Inf. Co.G
Rowe, John T. FL 10th Inf. Co.D Cpl.
Rowe, John T. VA Mtd.Riflesmen Balfour's Co.
Rowe, John T. VA Lt.Arty. Thornton's Co. 1st
    Sgt.
Rowe, John U. GA Cav. 2nd Bn. Co.C Music.
Rowe, John W. AL Cp. of Instr. Talladega
Rowe, John W. NC 2nd Cav. (19th St.Troops)
    Co.I
Rowe, John W. NC 3rd Inf. Co.K Sgt.
Rowe, John W. NC 7th Inf. Co.F Drum.
Rowe, John W. NC 37th Inf. Co.F
Rowe, John W. SC 14th Inf. Co.K
Rowe, John W. VA 26th Inf. Co.F
Rowe, John W. VA 31st Inf. Co.B
Rowe, John W. VA 47th Inf. Co.A
Rowe, John W. VA Vol. Taylor's Co.
Rowe, Joseph TX Fird's Cav. Doe's Co.
Rowe, Joseph F. AL 3rd Inf. Co.D
Rowe, Joseph H. SC 8th Inf. Co.G
Rowe, Joseph J. SC 4th St.Troops Co.F
Rowe, Joseph S. TN 32nd Inf. Co.I
Rowe, Joseph W. NC 4th Inf. Co.F

Rowe, Joshua TX 7th Cav. Co.F
Rowe, J.P. AL 24th Inf. Co.K
Rowe, J.R. TX 18th Cav. Co.B
Rowe, J.R. TX 28th Cav. Co.B 2nd Lt.
Rowe, J.R. TX 22nd Inf. Co.F
Rowe, J.S. AR Cav. Davies' Bn. Co.D
Rowe, J.S. AR Inf. Cocke's Regt. Co.E
Rowe, J.T. TX 35th (Brown's) Cav. Co.C
Rowe, J.U. GA 5th Cav. Co.E Music.
Rowe, Judson A. FL 2nd Inf. Co.E
Rowe, Judson A. FL 9th Inf. Co.K
Rowe, Junius M. VA 41st Inf. Co.A
Rowe, J.V. GA 1st Reg. Co.H
Rowe, J.V. GA 47th Inf. Co.C Cpl.
Rowe, J.W. AL 34th Inf. Co.A
Rowe, J.W. AR 8th Inf. New Co.C
Rowe, J.W. GA 20th Inf. Co.D
Rowe, J.W. GA 47th Inf. Co.C
Rowe, J.W. TN 3rd (Forrest's) Cav. 1st Co.F
Rowe, J.W. VA 32nd Inf. Co.A
Rowe, Kinion NC Inf. 2nd Bn. Co.E
Rowe, L. SC 4th St.Troops Co.A
Rowe, L.D. TN 60th Mtd.Inf. Co.K
Rowe, Legrande KY 4th Mtd.Inf. Co.C
Rowe, Leroy VA 21st Mil. Co.A
Rowe, Levi LA 16th Inf. Co.H
Rowe, Levi 1st Cherokee Mtd.Rifles Co.E
Rowe, Levi F. NC 27th Inf. Co.I Sgt.
Rowe, Lewis AL 51st (Part.Rangers) Co.F
Rowe, Lewis TN 19th Inf. Co.A Sgt.
Rowe, Lorenzo VA 21st Mil. Co.B
Rowe, Lorenzo VA 26th Inf. Co.F
Rowe, M. AR 1st Mtd.Rifles Co.G
Rowe, M.A. AL 5th Inf. New Co.B
Rowe, Madison TN 19th Inf. Co.I Cpl.
Rowe, Marcellus VA 26th Inf. Co.F
Rowe, Marcus D.L. GA 20th Inf. Co.E 2nd Lt.
Rowe, Marion TX 12th Cav. Co.D
Rowe, Mark GA 60th Inf. Co.A
Rowe, Mark NC Inf. 2nd Bn. Co.E
Rowe, Marion KY 10th (Diamond's) Cav. Co.G
Rowe, Martin GA Inf. 18th Bn. Co.A
Rowe, Mastin A. SC 14th Inf. Co.B
Rowe, Mathew TX Cav. Waller's Regt. Co.E
Rowe, Mathew F. AL Cav. 5th Bn. Hilliard's
    Legion Co.C
Rowe, Matthew F. 10th Conf.Cav. Co.C Black.
Rowe, M.D.L. GA 3rd Cav. Co.D
Rowe, Michael Conf.Cav. Raum's Co.
Rowe, Miles Epison KY 10th (Diamond's) Cav.
    Co.G
Rowe, M.W. TN 7th (Duckworth's) Cav. Co.G
Rowe, N. GA Inf. 26th Bn. Co.B
Rowe, Napoleon B. NC 3rd Arty. (40th
    St.Troops) Co.D
Rowe, Napoleon B. VA 55th Inf. Co.E
Rowe, Nathaniel SC 7th Cav. Co.A
Rowe, Nathaniel SC Cav. Tucker's Co.
Rowe, N.B. TX 35th (Brown's) Cav. Co.C
Rowe, Noah D. VA 7th Cav. Co.C
Rowe, Noah J. NC 12th Inf. Co.A
Rowe, O.C. Gen. & Staff Asst.Surg.
Rowe, Oliver J. VA 2nd Inf. Co.F
Rowe, O.P. GA 28th Inf. Co.E 2nd Lt.
Rowe, Osburn AL 62nd Inf. Co.G
Rowe, O.T. MO 1st N.E. Cav.
Rowe, P.A. AL 34th Inf. Co.D

Rowe, Patrick LA 20th Inf. Co.G
Rowe, P.B. TN 1st Hvy.Arty. 1st Lt.
Rowe, Peter NC 7th Inf. Co.F
Rowe, P.R. TX 20th Inf. Co.E
Rowe, Prince A. AL Inf. 1st Regt. Co.A
Rowe, Ralph VA 21st Mil. Co.A Corp.
Rowe, Ralph VA 26th Inf. Co.F
Rowe, Randolph GA 9th Inf. Co.I
Rowe, R.B. VA 30th Inf. Co.F
Rowe, R.D. VA 40th Inf. Co.K
Rowe, R.F. GA 16th Inf. Co.F
Rowe, R.H. NC Conscr.
Rowe, Richard Lt.Arty. Dent's Btty.,CSA Cpl.
Rowe, R.J. TX 20th Inf. Co.E
Rowe, R.L. FL 2nd Cav. Co.K Sgt.
Rowe, R.L. GA 10th Cav. (St.Guards) Co.D
Rowe, Robert TN 2nd (Ashby's) Cav. Co.H
Rowe, Robert TN Cav. 4th Bn. (Branner's) Co.A
Rowe, Robert A. LA 8th Inf. Co.F Capt.
Rowe, Robert R. VA 34rd Inf. Co.A
Rowe, S. AL Chas. A. Herts' Co.
Rowe, S. GA Cav. 20th Bn. Co.B
Rowe, Samuel TN 8th Inf. Co.K
Rowe, Samuel TX 22nd Inf. Co.I
Rowe, Samuel M. VA 26th Inf. Co.F Cpl.
Rowe, S.D. GA 10th Inf. Asst.Surg.
Rowe, S.D. VA 5th Cav. Co.A
Rowe, Seborn GA 16th Inf. Co.H
Rowe, S.F. TX 32nd Cav. Co.B
Rowe, S.H. NC 12th Inf. Co.A Cpl.
Rowe, S.H. SC Cav. 19th Bn. Co.E
Rowe, Sidney H. NC 23rd Inf. Co.F Sgt.
Rowe, Simpson SC 14th Inf. Co.D
Rowe, S.M. TX 35th (Brown's) Cav. Co.C
Rowe, S.N. TX Cav. Border's Regt. Co.C
Rowe, Solomon KY 10th (Diamond's) Cav. Co.G
Rowe, Solomon TN 33rd Inf. Co.K
Rowe, Solomon E. KY 10th (Diamond's) Cav.
    Co.G
Rowe, Stephen GA 3rd Cav. (St.Guards) Co.G
Rowe, Stephen KY 10th (Diamond's) Cav. Co.G
Rowe, Stephen SC 21st Inf. Co.A
Rowe, Stephen D. GA Inf. 10th Bn.
    Capt.,Asst.Surg.
Rowe, Stephen D. TX 3rd Cav. Co.K 2nd Lt.
Rowe, Stephen D. VA 6th Inf. Co.G
Rowe, Stephen D. Gen. & Staff Asst.Surg.
Rowe, S.W. MS 41st Inf. Co.F
Rowe, T.E. GA Cav. 20th Bn. Co.D
Rowe, Thomas GA 62nd Cav. Co.E
Rowe, Thomas TN 60th Mtd.Inf. Co.K
Rowe, Thomas TX 21st Cav. Co.A
Rowe, Thomas A. NC 3rd Cav. (41st St.Troops)
    Co.E
Rowe, Thomas B. TX 1st Hvy.Arty. Co.D
Rowe, Thomas B. VA 5th Cav. Co.A
Rowe, Thomas H. GA Cav. 22nd Bn.
    (St.Guards) Co.H 1st Lt.
Rowe, Thomas H. GA 14th Inf. Co.H 1st Lt.
Rowe, Thomas I. GA Conscr.
Rowe, Thomas J. GA 8th Cav. Old Co.E 1st
    Sgt.
Rowe, Thomas J. GA Cav. 12th Bn. (St.Guards)
    Co.C Cpl.
Rowe, Thomas J. GA 5th Inf. Co.I
Rowe, Thomas J. LA 13th Bn. (Part.Rangers)
    Co.C

Rowe, Thomas J. NC 43rd Inf. Co.C Sgt.
Rowe, Thomas J. VA 26th Inf. Co.F Cpl.
Rowe, Thomas L. VA 5th Cav. Co.E Cpl.
Rowe, Thomas W. TN 1st (Turney's) Inf. Co.A
Rowe, T.J. GA Inf. 25th Bn. (Prov.Guard) Co.D
Rowe, T.J. NC Cav. 16th Bn. Co.A 1st Sgt.
Rowe, T.R. GA 2nd Cav. (St.Guards) Co.A Sgt.
Rowe, W. NC 6th Sr.Res. Co.C
Rowe, W. SC Manigault's Bn.Vol. Co.A
Rowe, W. TX 25th Cav. Co.A
Rowe, W.A. AL 8th (Hatch's) Cav. Co.D
Rowe, W.A. MS 14th (Cons.) Inf. Co.E
Rowe, Washington P. MS 29th Inf. Co.H
Rowe, W.F. SC Inf. 7th Bn. (Enfield Rifles) Co.G
Rowe, W.F. TN 5th Inf. 2nd Co.K
Rowe, W.G. GA 5th Inf. Co.E
Rowe, W.H. VA 2nd Arty. Co.G
Rowe, Wiley NC 8th Bn.Part.Rangers
Rowe, Wiley NC 11th (Bethel Regt.) Inf. Co.B Sgt.
Rowe, Wiley A. NC 1st Arty. (10th St.Troops) Co.I
Rowe, Wiley A. NC 67th Inf. Co.B
Rowe, William AL 1st Regt.Conscr. Co.H
Rowe, William AL 3rd Inf. Co.H Cpl.
Rowe, William FL 1st Cav. Co.B
Rowe, William SC Hvy.Arty. 15th (Lucas') Bn. Co.B,C
Rowe, William SC 12th Inf. Co.F
Rowe, William TN 3rd (Forrest's) Cav. 1st Co.E
Rowe, William TX Cav. Wells' Regt. Co.B
Rowe, William VA 9th Mil. Co.A
Rowe, William VA 21st Mil. Co.A
Rowe, William A. MS 14th Inf. Co.F
Rowe, William A., Jr. VA 21st Mil. Co.A 2nd Lt.
Rowe, William B. NC 2nd Cav. (19th St.Troops) Co.I 2nd Lt.
Rowe, William D. AL 33rd Inf. Co.A
Rowe, William D. SC 24th Inf. Co.B
Rowe, William D. VA Arty. Curtis' Co.
Rowe, William D. VA 26th Inf. Co.E
Rowe, William F. NC 43rd Inf. Co.C
Rowe, William F. NC 51st Inf. Co.A
Rowe, William F. VA Hvy.Arty. 18th Bn. Co.A
Rowe, William G. AL 4th (Russell's) Cav. Co.K
Rowe, William G. TN 3rd (Forrest's) Cav. 1st Co.F Sgt.
Rowe, William H. GA 31st Inf. Co.H
Rowe, William H. MS 31st Inf. Co.F
Rowe, William H. TN Lt.Arty. Winston's Co.
Rowe, William H. TX 19th Cav. Co.K
Rowe, William H. TX 13th Vol. 1st Co.H, 2nd Co.G
Rowe, William J. AR 37th Inf. Co.H 1st Lt.
Rowe, William L. AL 6th Inf. Co.L Capt.
Rowe, William L. NC 3rd Inf. Co.F
Rowe, William L. VA 5th Cav. Co.E
Rowe, William M. TN 16th Inf. Co.E
Rowe, William R. VA Cav. Young's Co.
Rowe, William T. AL 6th Inf. Co.L
Rowe, William T. MS 41st Inf. Co.F
Rowe, William T. SC Cav. Tucker's Co.
Rowe, William T. VA 26th Inf. Co.E
Rowe, William T.J. AL 22nd Inf. Co.I
Rowe, William W. AL 19th Inf. Co.C

Rowe, William W. VA 1st St.Res. Co.F
Rowe, William W. VA 15th Inf. Co.D 2nd Lt.
Rowe, Wilson VA 55th Inf. Co.G
Rowe, W.J. AR 2nd Mtd.Rifles Co.E 3rd Lt.
Rowe, W.J. SC 16th Inf. Co.F
Rowe, W.M. AR Bell's Regt.
Rowe, W.P. MS 12th Inf. Co.B
Rowe, W.R. GA Cav. 20th Bn. Co.B
Rowe, W.R. VA 54th Mil. Co.E,F
Rowe, W.S. NC 2nd Jr.Res. Co.K
Rowe, W.T. SC 7th Cav. Co.A
Rowe, W.T. SC 6th Inf. 2nd Co.G
Rowe, W.T. 8th (Wade's) Conf.Cav. Co.B
Rowe, W.W. TX 37th Cav. Co.G
Rowe, W.W. VA 3rd Inf.Loc.Def. Co.B
Rowel, Benjamin GA 26th Inf. Co.K
Rowel, Charles W. GA 41st Inf. Co.I
Rowel, David GA 54th Inf. Co.B
Rowel, John MS 2nd (Quinn's St.Troops) Inf. Co.G
Rowel, John NC 32nd Inf. Co.B,C
Rowel, John L. AL 34th Inf. Co.E
Rowel, J.V. MS 36th Inf. Co.C
Rowel, J.W. AL 8th (Livingston's) Cav. Co.A
Rowel, J.W. MS 32nd Inf. Co.E
Rowel, T.L. SC Inf. Holcombe Legion Co.D
Rowel, William J. GA 26th Inf. Co.K
Rowell, --- VA 13th Cav. Co.F
Rowell, A. SC 1st Mtd.Mil. Screven's Co.
Rowell, Abraham MS 8th Inf. Co.F
Rowell, Abraham J. MS 24th Inf. Co.G
Rowell, Abraham J. MS 27th Inf. Co.H
Rowell, Adolphus D. GA 35th Inf. Co.A
Rowell, Alexander GA 35th Inf. Co.A
Rowell, Alfred SC Mil.Cav. 4th Regt. Howards' Co.
Rowell, Andrew J. AL 16th Inf. Co.A
Rowell, Andrew J. AL 36th Inf. Co.E
Rowell, Andrew J. AL 62nd Inf. Co.D
Rowell, Andrew J. Sap. & Min. G.W. Maxson's Co.
Rowell, B.A.W. SC 5th Cav. Co.I
Rowell, B.A.W. SC Cav. 14th Bn. Co.D
Rowell, Benjamin F. MS Inf. 2nd Bn. Co.B Sgt.
Rowell, Benjamin F. MS 23rd Inf. Co.G
Rowell, B.F. AR Inf. Cocke's Regt. Co.C
Rowell, B.F. MS 7th Cav. Co.C,A
Rowell, B.F. MS 48th Inf. Co.B Sgt.
Rowell, B.M. GA 4th (Clinch's) Cav. Co.F
Rowell, C. AR 1st (Monroe's) Cav. Co.L
Rowell, C. AR 24th Inf. Co.D
Rowell, C. AR Inf. Hardy's Regt. Co.C
Rowell, C. TX 3rd Inf. 2nd Co.A
Rowell, Caleb M. LA Inf. 11th Bn. Co.C
Rowell, Caleb M. LA Inf.Cons.Crescent Regt. Co.F
Rowell, C.D. SC Inf. 6th Bn. Co.A Capt.
Rowell, C.D. SC 26th Inf. Co.C Maj.
Rowell, C.D. SC Manigault's Bn.Vol. Co.D Capt.
Rowell, Charles M. GA 2nd Cav. Co.G
Rowell, Charles M. GA Arty. 11th Bn. Co.A
Rowell, Christopher AL 4th Inf. Co.H
Rowell, C.M. GA 12th (Robinson's) Cav. (St.Guards) Co.E
Rowell, D. FL 1st (Res.) Inf. Co.E
Rowell, D. GA Lt.Arty. Clinch's Btty.

Rowell, D. GA 4th Inf.
Rowell, D. SC 5th Cav. Co.I
Rowell, D. SC 23rd Inf. Co.E
Rowell, D.A. SC 10th Inf. Co.F
Rowell, D.A. SC 21st Inf. Co.I
Rowell, Daniel SC Cav. 14th Bn. Co.D
Rowell, Darling FL Inf. 2nd Bn. Co.D
Rowell, David FL 4th Inf. Co.E
Rowell, David GA 4th (Clinch's) Cav. Co.G
Rowell, David GA Cav. 24th Bn. Co.A,C Sr.2nd Lt.
Rowell, David GA Cav. Hendry's Co. (Atlantic & Gulf Guards) Sgt.
Rowell, David GA Mtd.Inf. (Pierce Mtd.Vol.) Hendry's Co.
Rowell, David SC 23rd Inf. Co.H
Rowell, David A. FL 5th Inf. Co.D
Rowell, David H. MS 27th Inf. Co.H
Rowell, David J. MS 9th Cav. Co.G
Rowell, David R. FL 5th Inf. Co.A
Rowell, D.F. LA 1st Hvy.Arty. (Reg.) Co.D
Rowell, D.J. MS 27th Inf. Co.H
Rowell, D.J. MS Cp.Guard (Cp. of Instr. for Conscr.)
Rowell, Doctor Floyd MS 32nd Inf. Co.E
Rowell, Durham G. LA 9th Inf. Co.A
Rowell, E.A. VA 4th Cav.
Rowell, E.L. SC 9th Bn.Res. Co.C
Rowell, Elihu MS 27th Inf. Co.H
Rowell, Elihu SC 22nd Inf. Co.E
Rowell, Elihu E. MS 24th Inf. Co.G
Rowell, Eliphus MS 27th Inf. Co.H
Rowell, Eliphus D. MS 24th Inf. Co.G
Rowell, Ezekiel AL 12th Inf. Co.K Capt.
Rowell, Floyd MS 23rd Inf. Co.G
Rowell, Francis AL Cav. Holloway's Co.
Rowell, Frank KY Morehead's Regt. (Part. Rangers) Co.A
Rowell, Frank KY 1st Inf. Co.I
Rowell, Frank KY 9th Mtd.Inf. Co.H
Rowell, Frank LA 1st (Nelligan's) Inf. Co.H
Rowell, G.B. AL 15th Bn.Part.Rangers Co.E
Rowell, G.B. AL 56th Part.Rangers Co.E 2nd Lt.
Rowell, George A. VA 13th Cav. Co.G
Rowell, George A. VA 3rd Inf. 1st Co.I
Rowell, George C. GA 35th Inf. Co.A
Rowell, George W. AL Cav. Holloway's Co.
Rowell, George W. AR 3rd Inf. Co.D
Rowell, George W. LA 9th Inf. Co.I
Rowell, G.R. SC 1st Cav. Co.C
Rowell, G.W. AR Cav. Carlton's Regt. Co.B Bvt.2nd Lt.
Rowell, H.B. MS 3rd Inf. Co.G
Rowell, H.B. MS 23rd Inf. Co.G
Rowell, Henry GA 59th Inf. Co.A Cpl.
Rowell, Henry SC 1st (Butler's) Inf. Co.A
Rowell, Henry A. FL 5th Inf. Co.D
Rowell, Henry G. GA 48th Inf. Co.H
Rowell, H.H. AL 18th Inf. Co.B
Rowell, Hilliard MS 8th Inf. Co.F
Rowell, H.L. MS 5th Inf. (St.Troops) Co.B
Rowell, H.M. AL 34th Inf. Co.E
Rowell, Hugh P. TN 41st Inf. Co.D
Rowell, I.B. MS 27th Inf. Co.H
Rowell, I.W. SC Inf. Hampton Legion Co.I
Rowell, J. GA 8th Inf.

Rowell, J. GA 16th Inf. Co.H
Rowell, J. SC 23rd Inf. Co.E
Rowell, J.A. AR Cav. Gordon's Regt. Co.B
Rowell, J.A. AR Inf. Cocke's Regt. Co.G
Rowell, J.A.C. AL 22nd Inf. Co.D
Rowell, Jackson GA 9th Inf. Co.K
Rowell, James AL 42nd Inf. Co.E Sgt.
Rowell, James GA 7th Cav. Co.D
Rowell, James GA Cav. 24th Bn. Co.A,C
Rowell, James GA Cav. 29th Bn. Co.C
Rowell, James GA 49th Inf. Co.F
Rowell, James A. GA 12th Inf. Co.F
Rowell, James A. TN 1st (Turney's) Inf. Co.F
    Cpl.
Rowell, James A.C. AL 25th Inf. Co.K
Rowell, James C. MS 2nd Inf. Co.B
Rowell, James D. MS 27th Inf. Co.H
Rowell, James E. AL 18th Inf. Co.B Sgt.
Rowell, James G. SC 6th Cav. Co.K
Rowell, James G. VA 5th Cav. (12 mo. '61-2)
    Co.E Cpl.
Rowell, James G. VA 13th Cav. Co.G Sgt.
Rowell, James H. MS 42nd Inf. Co.E
Rowell, James H. VA Lt.Arty. Hankins' Co.
Rowell, James H. VA 3rd Inf. 1st Co.I
Rowell, James J. LA 9th Inf. Co.I
Rowell, James J. TN 41st Inf. Co.D
Rowell, James S. MS 1st Cav.Res. Co.H,C
Rowell, James S. MS Inf. 2nd Bn. Co.B Cpl.
Rowell, James T. TN 41st Inf. Co.D
Rowell, James V. SC 1st Arty. Co.D Sgt.
Rowell, James V. SC 23rd Inf. Co.H Cpl.
Rowell, James W. GA 6th Inf. Co.E Cpl.
Rowell, J.C. AR 17th Cav. Co.E 1st Lt.
Rowell, J.C. AR Inf. Hardy's Regt. Co.C
Rowell, J.C. VA 3rd (Archer's) Bn.Res. Co.F
    Sgt.
Rowell, J.D. GA Inf. Clemons' Co. Cpl.
Rowell, J.D. MS 8th Inf. Co.F
Rowell, J.D. VA Lt.Arty. 12th Bn. Co.B
Rowell, J. Edmund AL 42nd Inf. Co.E
Rowell, Jehu V. MS 9th Cav. Co.G
Rowell, Jeremiah SC Hvy.Arty. 15th (Lucas')
    Bn. Co.A
Rowell, Jesey GA 40th Inf. Co.K
Rowell, Jesse SC 23rd Inf. Co.H
Rowell, J.F. AL 31st Inf. Co.I
Rowell, J.L. MS 48th Inf. Co.B Cpl.
Rowell, John AL 1st Regt.Conscr. Co.E
Rowell, John FL 2nd Cav. Co.I
Rowell, John FL 5th Inf. Co.A
Rowell, John LA 5th Inf. Co.F
Rowell, John MS 23rd Inf. Co.G
Rowell, John NC 12th Inf. Co.N
Rowell, John A. AL 12th Inf. Co.K
Rowell, John B. AL 36th Inf. Co.E
Rowell, John E. SC 22nd Inf. Co.E
Rowell, John H. AL 6th Cav. Co.A
Rowell, John H. SC 6th Cav. Co.K
Rowell, John H. SC 23rd Inf. Co.H
Rowell, John J. GA 6th Inf. Co.E
Rowell, John P. AL 38th Inf. Co.K
Rowell, John P. KY 6th Cav. Hines' Co.
Rowell, Johnson GA 44th Inf. Co.D
Rowell, Jonas SC 3rd Cav. Co.C Sgt.
Rowell, Jonas SC Mil.Cav. 4th Regt. Howards'
    Co. Sgt.

Rowell, Joseph AL 21st Inf. Co.F Music.
Rowell, Joseph MS 46th Inf. Co.B
Rowell, Joseph SC 1st Arty. Co.E
Rowell, Joseph H. AL 6th Inf. Co.L,B
Rowell, Joseph R. FL 11th Inf. Co.E
Rowell, Josiah LA 9th Inf. Co.I
Rowell, J.R. FL 2nd Inf. Co.L
Rowell, J.R. GA Inf. 5th Bn. (St.Guards) Co.E
Rowell, J.R. GA 26th Inf. Co.K
Rowell, J.W. SC 21st Inf. Co.I
Rowell, Lewis J. MS 9th Cav. Co.G
Rowell, L.H. SC 1st (Butler's) Inf. Co.A
Rowell, Manson E. TN 41st Inf. Co.D
Rowell, Milton N. TN 41st Inf. Co.D
Rowell, M.N. TN 10th & 11th (Cons.) Cav.
    Co.E
Rowell, N.W. MS 5th Inf. (St.Troops) Co.B
Rowell, N. Westley MS 1st Cav.Res. Co.H
Rowell, Patrick H. VA Lt.Arty. Hankins' Co.
Rowell, Patrick H. VA 3rd Inf. 1st Co.I
Rowell, Perry SC 24th Inf. Co.D
Rowell, Pleasant A. TN 41st Inf. Co.D
Rowell, R. GA 1st (Symons') Res. Co.F,E
Rowell, R. NC 2nd Jr.Res. Co.K
Rowell, R. SC Cav. 12th Bn. Co.D
Rowell, R. TX 26th Cav. Co.C
Rowell, R.F. AL 2nd Cav. Co.I
Rowell, Richard F. SC 4th Cav. Co.F
Rowell, Richard F. VA 5th Cav. (12 mo. '61-2)
    Co.E
Rowell, R.N. AL 17th Inf. Co.I Cpl.
Rowell, Robert E. TX 18th Inf. Co.D Surg.
Rowell, Robert E. Gen. & Staff Surg.
Rowell, Robert H. AL 42nd Inf. Co.C
Rowell, Robert N. AL 53rd (Part.Rangers) Co.B
    Sgt.
Rowell, Robert W. AL 63rd Inf. Co.A Sgt.
Rowell, R.W. AL 15th Inf. Co.L
Rowell, S. MS 27th Inf. Co.H
Rowell, Samuel B. MS 42nd Inf. Co.B
Rowell, Samuel J. NC 48th Inf. Co.I
Rowell, Samuel T. VA Hvy.Arty. 18th Bn. Co.A
Rowell, S.G. MS 17th Inf. Co.F
Rowell, Simple VA 3rd (Archer's) Bn.Res. Co.F
    Sgt.
Rowell, S.J. AR 19th (Dockery's) Inf. Co.C
Rowell, Thomas MS 6th Inf. Co.D
Rowell, Thomas TN 1st (Turney's) Inf. Co.F
Rowell, Thomas E. GA 6th Inf. Co.E
Rowell, Thomas J. VA 3rd Inf. 1st Co.I
Rowell, Thomas M. TN 41st Inf. Co.D
Rowell, Tillman MS 8th Inf. Co.F Cpl.
Rowell, T.K. GA 40th Inf. Co.K
Rowell, V. SC 21st Inf. Co.L
Rowell, V.C. SC 21st Inf. Co.I
Rowell, W. GA 4th (Clinch's) Cav. Co.F
Rowell, W.A. LA 13th Bn. (Part.Rangers) Co.C
Rowell, W.A. MS 2nd Cav. Co.D Cpl.
Rowell, W.B. MS 5th Inf. (St.Troops) Co.B
Rowell, W.B. MS 27th Inf. Co.H
Rowell, W.C. AR 5th Inf. Co.A Cpl.
Rowell, Wesley GA 41st Inf. Co.I
Rowell, W.H. AL St.Arty. Co.C
Rowell, W.H. AL Mil. 2nd Regt.Vol. Co.B
Rowell, William GA Lt.Arty. Clinch's Btty.
Rowell, William MS 1st Cav.Res. Co.B

Rowell, William MS Inf. 1st Bn.St.Troops (30
    days '64) Co.D
Rowell, William MS 46th Inf. Co.B
Rowell, William SC 22nd Inf. Co.E
Rowell, William SC 24th Inf. Co.D
Rowell, William VA Inf. 4th Bn.Loc.Def. Co.C
Rowell, William A. LA 28th (Gray's) Inf. Co.D
Rowell, William B. TN 41st Inf. Co.D
Rowell, William D. AL 46th Inf. Co.F
Rowell, William E. VA Lt.Arty. 12th Bn. Co.B
Rowell, William J. FL 1st Inf.
Rowell, William J. SC 3rd Cav. Co.C
Rowell, William J. SC Mil.Cav. 4th Regt.
    Howards' Co.
Rowell, William R. MS 23rd Inf. Co.G
Rowell, William T. AL 43rd Inf. Co.E
Rowell, Wilson SC 22nd Inf. Co.E
Rowell, W.J. MS 5th Cav. Co.K
Rowell, W.J. MS 18th Cav. Co.G
Rowell, W.P. SC 21st Inf. Co.L
Rowell, W.R. GA 6th Inf. Co.E
Rowell, W.S. AL 4th (Russell's) Cav. Co.A
Rowell, W.T. AL 8th Cav. Co.C
Rowell, W.T. SC 25th Inf. Co.K
Rowell, W.W. AL 15th Bn.Part.Rangers Co.C
Rowell, W.W. AL 56th Part.Rangers Co.C
    Bugler
Rowell, W.W. MS 10th Cav. Co.F Bugler
Rowels, E. AL Inf. 1st Regt. Co.H
Rowen, E.C. AL 32nd Inf. Co.G
Rowen, Hezekiah VA 20th Cav. Co.F
Rowen, Hiram AR 7th Cav. Co.K
Rowen, Hugh GA 3rd Inf. Co.G
Rowen, James AL 61st Inf. Co.E
Rowen, James LA 11th Inf. Co.H
Rowen, James LA 20th Inf. Co.C
Rowen, J.D. AL 5th Cav. Co.E
Rowen, John B. AL Cav. Lewis' Bn. Co.E
Rowen, Michael MS 29th Inf. Co.H
Rowen, Philip H. TX 15th Cav. Co.I
Rowen, Samuel C. NC 25th Inf. Co.D
Rowen, Tim LA 14th Inf. Co.G Cpl.
Rowen, W. AL 11th Inf. Co.F
Rowen, Washington LA 7th Cav. Co.G
Rowen, William TN Arty. Ramsey's Btty.
Rowers, J. AL 9th Inf.
Rowes, A.F. GA 10th Inf. Co.I
Rowhough, Leonard MO 1st Cav. Co.G
Rowin, Abraham TX 12th Inf. Co.G
Rowin, T. AL 43rd Inf. Co.D
Rowin, T.G. AR Mil. Borland's Regt. Peyton
    Rifles
Rowin, T.M. AR Cav. Harrell's Bn. Co.D 3rd
    Lt.
Rowlan, W. MS 6th Inf. Co.E
Rowland, --- TX Cav. Steele's Command Co.A
    Capt.
Rowland, A. AR Cav. Davies' Bn. Co.C
Rowland, A. TN 20th (Russell's) Cav. Co.F
Rowland, A. TX Cav. 4th Regt.St.Troops Co.F
    2nd Lt.
Rowland, A. TX Cav. Giddings' Bn. Carr's Co.
Rowland, A. VA 17th Inf. Co.A
Rowland, A.A. Gen. & Staff Surg.
Rowland, A.C. NC 3rd Arty. (40th St.Troops)
    Co.G
Rowland, A.C. NC Lt.Arty. 13th Bn. Co.E

Rowland, A.E. NC 1st Arty. (10th St.Troops) Co.G

Rowland, A.F. NC 12th Inf. Co.H

Rowland, A.J. KY 1st (Helm's) Cav. Old Co.G

Rowland, A.J. TN 4th (Murray's) Cav. Co.H

Rowland, Alexander E. AR 3rd Cav. Co.C

Rowland, Alex W. NC 5th Cav. (63rd St.Troops) Co.G

Rowland, Alfred NC 18th Inf. Co.D 2nd Lt.

Rowland, A.M. AL 4th Inf. Co.I 1st Lt.

Rowland, A.M. GA 6th Inf. 1st Lt.

Rowland, A.M. GA Rowland's Bn.Conscr. Maj.

Rowland, A.M. Gen. & Staff Maj.

Rowland, Amos L. GA 57th Inf. Co.B

Rowland, Anak H. Gen. & Staff Surg.

Rowland, Anthony KY 1st Inf. Co.I

Rowland, Anthony LA 1st (Nelligan's) Inf. Co.H

Rowland, A.S. MS 4th Inf. Co.E,G

Rowland, A.W. KY 3rd Mtd.Inf. Co.B

Rowland, A.W. NC 12th Inf. Co.B,D Sgt.

Rowland, A.W.B. LA Lt.Arty. Tarrant's Btty.

Rowland, B. TN 16th Inf. Co.A

Rowland, Benjamin TN Inf. 22nd Bn. Co.B

Rowland, Benjamin TN 50th (Cons.) Inf. Co.K

Rowland, Benjamin F. GA Lt.Arty. 12th Bn. 2nd Co.A

Rowland, Benjamin F. GA 2nd Inf. Co.A

Rowland, Benjamin W. NC 2nd Arty. (36th St.Troops) Co.F

Rowland, Bethel B. TN 53rd Inf. Co.F

Rowland, B.F. GA Lt.Arty. 12th Bn. 1st Co.A

Rowland, B.F. GA 63rd Inf. Co.A

Rowland, B.G. SC Lt.Arty. 3rd (Palmetto) Bn. Co.B Jr.1st Lt.

Rowland, Birch AR 30th Inf. Co.C

Rowland, B.J. MS 32nd Inf. Co.A

Rowland, B.M. TN 16th Inf. Co.D

Rowland, Bowlin R. GA 59th Inf. Co.E Sgt.

Rowland, C.A. GA Inf. 40th Bn. Co.C

Rowland, C.A. GA 43rd Inf. Co.I

Rowland, Calvin NC 2nd Cav. (19th St.Troops) Co.A

Rowland, Carlas A. SC 1st (Orr's) Rifles Co.E

Rowland, C.D. AR Cav. Davies' Bn. Co.C

Rowland, C.F. TX Inf. Timmons' Regt. Co.A

Rowland, C.F. TX Waul's Legion Co.B

Rowland, Charles GA Lt.Arty. Pritchard's Co. (Washington Arty.)

Rowland, Charles GA Inf. 1st St.Troops (Augusta) Co.G

Rowland, Charles GA 5th Inf. Co.C Music.

Rowland, Charles A. GA Inf. 1st Loc.Troops (Augusta) Co.B Sgt.

Rowland, Charles P. GA 1st (Olmstead's) Inf. Davis' Co.

Rowland, Charles W. VA 16th Inf. Co.E

Rowland, Columbus W. NC 28th Inf. Co.D

Rowland, C.P. AR 35th Inf. Co.F

Rowland, C.R. SC 5th St.Troops Co.I

Rowland, D. GA 5th Res. Co.G

Rowland, Daniel GA 18th Inf. Co.I

Rowland, David GA 66th Inf. Co.A Sgt.

Rowland, David Conf.Cav. Wood's Regt. Co.M

Rowland, David C. MS 18th Inf. Co.B Sgt.

Rowland, David C. MS Griffin's Co. (Madison Guards)

Rowland, David G. TX 17th Cav. Co.F 1st Sgt.

Rowland, David R. GA Inf. 27th Bn. Co.C Sgt.

Rowland, Doctor F. MO Cav. Snider's Bn. Co.B

Rowland, D.P. GA Lt.Arty. Ritter's Co.

Rowland, D.T. NC 12th Inf. Co.H

Rowland, D.T. NC Mallett's Bn. Co.A

Rowland, E. GA 5th Inf. (St.Guards) Everitt's Co., Allums' Co.

Rowland, E. TN Lt.Arty. Lynch's Co.

Rowland, Eason GA 18th Inf. Co.I

Rowland, Ed TN 50th Inf. Co.B

Rowland, E.F. AR 1st Mtd.Rifles Co.I

Rowland, E.F.T. GA Inf. 18th Bn. Co.B

Rowland, Eli MO 4th Inf. Co.C,A

Rowland, Eli C. TN 50th (Cons.) Inf. Co.K

Rowland, E.S. GA Conscr.

Rowland, Eugene F. AR 9th Inf. Co.G

Rowland, F.A. MS 5th Cav. Co.H

Rowland, Franklin F. MS 15th Inf. Co.B 4th Cpl.

Rowland, George VA 12th Cav. Co.B 2nd Lt.

Rowland, George M. TN 31st Inf. Co.F 1st Sgt.

Rowland, George T. VA 32nd Inf. Co.E

Rowland, George W. GA 14th Inf. Co.H

Rowland, George W. MO Inf. Perkins' Bn. Co.F Capt.

Rowland, George W. TN 9th (Ward's) Cav. Co.D

Rowland, George W. VA 7th Cav. Baylor's Co. 2nd Lt.

Rowland, G.F. TN 7th Cav. Co.D

Rowland, G.F. TN 8th Inf. Co.A

Rowland, G.M. GA 15th Inf. Co.H

Rowland, Goliah 1st Creek Mtd.Vol. Co.E

Rowland, Grattan VA Lt.Arty. R.M. Anderson's Co.

Rowland, G.W. AR 27th Inf. Co.E

Rowland, G.W. MS 28th Cav. Co.D

Rowland, G.W. TN 49th Inf. Co.E

Rowland, G.W. VA 54th Mil. Co.A

Rowland, H. KY 12th Cav. Co.D

Rowland, Harris C. AR 1st (Colquitt's) Inf. Co.E 2nd Lt.

Rowland, Hawkins G. AR Cav. 1st Bn. (Stirman's) Co.A

Rowland, Henry VA Inf. 6th Bn.Loc.Def. Co.B Sgt.

Rowland, Henry D. SC 1st (Orr's) Rifles Co.L Cpl.

Rowland, Henry M. MS 2nd Inf. Co.K

Rowland, Henry R. LA 5th Inf. New Co.A

Rowland, Henry T. KY 8th Mtd.Inf. Co.H Jr.2nd Lt.

Rowland, H.G. AR 13th Inf. Co.E Sgt.

Rowland, H.G. KY 7th Cav. Co.G

Rowland, H.G. KY 7th Mtd.Inf. 1st Co.K Sgt.

Rowland, Hinton NC 1st Inf. Co.I

Rowland, H.J. AL 33rd Inf. Co.K

Rowland, H.P. MS 43rd Inf. Co.G

Rowland, H.R. MD 1st Cav. Co.A

Rowland, Hugh B. AL 6th Inf. Co.H

Rowland, H. Young MS 13th Inf. Co.A Cpl.

Rowland, I.N. MO Cav. Snider's Bn. Co.B 1st Sgt.

Rowland, Isaac M. MS 34th Inf. Co.G

Rowland, Isaac N. MO Cav. Poindexter's Regt.

Rowland, J. GA 2nd Brig. Capt.

Rowland, J. GA 5th Res. Co.I

Rowland, J., Jr. GA 54th Inf. Co.K

Rowland, J. MS 25th Inf. Co.F

Rowland, J. SC Mil. 18th Regt. Lawrences' Co.

Rowland, J. VA 122nd Mil. Co.B

Rowland, J.A. SC 15th Inf. Co.F 1st Sgt.

Rowland, J.A. VA 53rd Inf.

Rowland, Jackson GA 48th Inf. Co.I

Rowland, Jacob MS Inf. 3rd Bn. (St.Troops) Co.A

Rowland, Jacob NC 6th Cav. (65th St.Troops) Co.D

Rowland, James GA 30th Inf. Co.A Sgt.

Rowland, James GA 63rd Inf. Co.D

Rowland, James GA Inf. (Loc.Def.) Hamlet's Co.

Rowland, James MS Cav. 2nd Bn.Res. Co.G

Rowland, James NC 8th Inf. Co.D

Rowland, James TN 16th Inf. Co.D

Rowland, James VA 12th Cav. Co.B

Rowland, James A. GA 4th Res. Co.E

Rowland, James A. MO Inf. Perkins' Bn. Co.F 1st Sgt.

Rowland, James A. VA 1st Arty. 3rd Co.C

Rowland, James A. VA Lt.Arty. 1st Bn. Co.C

Rowland, James A. VA Arty. Young's Co.

Rowland, James A. VA 14th Inf. 1st Co.G

Rowland, James B. GA Inf. 2nd Bn. Co.C

Rowland, James B. GA 49th Inf. Co.G

Rowland, James C. TX Cav. Sutton's Co.

Rowland, James C. TX 11th Inf. Co.D

Rowland, James D. GA 12th Inf. Co.B

Rowland, James D. MS 34th Inf. Co.G

Rowland, James E. MS 20th Inf. Co.G

Rowland, James F. AL 10th Inf. Co.F

Rowland, James F. TX 6th Cav. Co.C

Rowland, James H. NC 23rd Inf. Co.E

Rowland, James H. VA 7th Cav. Baylor's Co.

Rowland, James M. GA 7th Inf. Co.H

Rowland, James M. MO Cav. Snider's Bn. Co.B

Rowland, James O. TX 16th Cav. Co.A

Rowland, James R. GA Inf. 27th Bn. Co.B

Rowland, James R. KY 2nd (Duke's) Cav. Co.K

Rowland, James R. VA 52nd Mil. Co.B 1st Lt.

Rowland, James S. GA 48th Inf. Co.F

Rowland, James S. VA 23rd Cav. 2nd Co.K

Rowland, James T. MO Cav. Snider's Bn. Co.B

Rowland, James W. GA 26th Inf. Co.D

Rowland, J.B. AL 12th Inf. Co.I Sgt.

Rowland, J.B. KY 7th Mtd.Inf. Co.G

Rowland, J.B. SC 1st St.Troops Co.A

Rowland, J.C. AR 5th Inf. Co.H

Rowland, J.C. TX 2nd Inf. Co.G 2nd Lt.

Rowland, J.D. TX 27th Cav. Co.K 1st Lt.

Rowland, J.D. 1st Conf.Cav. 2nd Co.F

Rowland, J.E. KY 1st (Helm's) Cav. Old Co.G

Rowland, Jefferson TX 14th Cav. Co.I

Rowland, Jeremiah AR 11th Inf. Co.A

Rowland, Jeremiah AR 11th & 17th Cons.Inf. Co.A

Rowland, Jeremiah W. GA 13th Inf. Co.G 5th Sgt.

Rowland, J.G. TX 6th Inf. Co.H

Rowland, J.H. MS 3rd Cav. Co.C,D 2nd Lt.

Rowland, J.H. MO 4th Inf. Co.I

Rowland, J.H. TX Cav. Hardeman's Regt. Co.A

Rowland, J. Hamilton VA Hvy.Arty. 20th Bn. Sgt.Maj.

Rowland, J.J. AR 20th Inf. Co.G
Rowland, J.J. SC 9th Res. Co.D
Rowland, J.K.P. AR 7th Cav. Co.B
Rowland, J.K.P. TN 24th Inf. Co.A
Rowland, J.L. GA Cav. 10th Bn. (St.Guards) Co.C
Rowland, J.L. TN 50th Inf. Co.B
Rowland, J.L. TX 2nd Cav. Co.I
Rowland, J.M. GA 2nd Mil. Co.E
Rowland, J.M. GA Inf. (Jones Hussars) Jones' Co.
Rowland, J.M. TN Inf. 22nd Bn. Co.B
Rowland, J.N. TN 25th Inf. Co.C
Rowland, Joe MO 1st Inf. Co.C
Rowland, John AR 14th (Powers') Inf. Co.E
Rowland, John GA 24th Inf. Co.K
Rowland, John KY 2nd (Duke's) Cav. Co.B
Rowland, John KY 5th Mtd.Inf. Co.E
Rowland, John LA 1st Hvy.Arty. (Reg.) Co.G
Rowland, John LA 4th Inf. Co.D
Rowland, John LA C.S. Zouave Bn. Co.B
Rowland, John MS 4th Inf. Co.E
Rowland, John TN 50th Inf. Co.B
Rowland, John B. MO Inf. Perkins' Bn. Co.F
Rowland, John B. NC 18th Inf. Co.D 2nd Lt.
Rowland, John B. SC Lt.Arty. 3rd (Palmetto) Bn. Co.B Cpl.
Rowland, John C. GA 1st (Olmstead's) Inf. Co.K 1st Lt.
Rowland, John D. AL 1st Cav. Co.E 2nd Lt.
Rowland, John D. VA 38th Inf. Co.H Sgt.
Rowland, John F. NC 37th Inf. Co.D
Rowland, John F. SC 20th Inf. Co.H
Rowland, John G. LA Mil.Conf.Guards Regt. Co.K
Rowland, John G. NC 57th Inf. Co.H
Rowland, John H. NC Mallett's Bn.
Rowland, John H. VA 6th Inf. Co.G
Rowland, John J. GA 7th Cav. Co.F
Rowland, John J. GA Cav. 21st Bn. Co.B,E
Rowland, John J. VA 21st Inf. Co.H
Rowland, John L. AR 1st (Dobbin's) Cav. Co.C Sgt.
Rowland, John L. TN 25th Inf. Co.C
Rowland, John M. NC 3rd Cav. (41st St.Troops) Co.I
Rowland, John S. MS 20th Inf. Co.G
Rowland, John W. GA 26th Inf. Co.D
Rowland, John W. MS 1st Cav. Co.D
Rowland, John W. NC 16th Inf. Co.C
Rowland, John W. SC 2nd Rifles Co.F Sgt.
Rowland, John W. TX 16th Cav. Co.B
Rowland, Jordan GA 34th Inf. Co.C Capt.
Rowland, Joseph GA 63rd Inf. Co.H
Rowland, Joseph KY 9th Mtd.Inf. Co.I
Rowland, Joseph MS 10th Inf. Old Co.A, New Co.D Cpl.
Rowland, Joseph MS 34th Inf. Co.G
Rowland, Joseph A. MS 34th Inf. Co.G
Rowland, Joseph B. MS 42nd Inf. Co.I
Rowland, Joseph C. TX Waul's Legion Co.A Capt.
Rowland, Joseph E. MS 18th Cav. Co.D
Rowland, Joseph N. NC 1st Inf. Co.I
Rowland, Joseph T. VA 41st Inf. Co.A
Rowland, Josf. 1st Conf.Cav. 1st Co.G
Rowland, Joshua M. MO Cav. Poindexter's Regt.

Rowland, J.P. GA 1st Inf. Co.C
Rowland, J.Q. KY 2nd (Woodward's) Cav. Co.A,B
Rowland, J.R. GA 21st Inf. Co.B
Rowland, J.R. KY Horse Arty. Byrne's Co. Sgt.Maj.
Rowland, J.R. MS 3rd Cav. Co.K
Rowland, J.R. TX 10th Cav. Co.A Sgt.
Rowland, J.R. VA Lt.Arty. Ellett's Co.
Rowland, J.S. SC 5th St.Troops Co.I
Rowland, J.T. GA Cav. 1st Bn. Walthour's Co.
Rowland, J.T., Jr. GA 5th Cav. Co.G
Rowland, J.T. MO 8th Inf. Co.I
Rowland, J.T. TX Cav. McCord's Frontier Regt. Co.D Capt.
Rowland, J.W. AL 10th Inf. Co.F
Rowland, J.W. AR 30th Inf. Co.E
Rowland, J.W. GA 4th Res. Co.K
Rowland, J.W. KY 2nd (Duke's) Cav. Co.B
Rowland, Kinzie VA 17th Cav. Co.E 2nd Lt.
Rowland, Kinzie VA 59th Inf. 2nd Co.I
Rowland, Lafayette MO Inf. Perkin's Bn. Co.F
Rowland, L.B. TX 28th Cav. Co.D 1st Sgt.
Rowland, L.C. TN Lt.Arty. Lynch's Co.
Rowland, Lewis A. MS 30th Inf. Co.C
Rowland, Littleberry GA 21st Inf. Co.F
Rowland, L.J. TN 4th (Murray's) Cav. Co.H
Rowland, Lloyd A. AR 1st (Colquitt's) Inf. Co.E Sgt.
Rowland, L.R. GA 55th Inf. Co.A
Rowland, Marel LA 9th Inf. Co.A 2nd Lt.
Rowland, Mathias NC 28th Inf. Co.D
Rowland, Meritt R. GA Cobb's Legion Co.E
Rowland, M.H. AR Cav. Harrell's Bn. Co.D
Rowland, Michael NC 58th Inf. Co.D
Rowland, Michael VA Inf. 6th Bn.Loc.Def. Co.A
Rowland, Michael W. NC 4th Inf. Co.K
Rowland, Miles B. VA 8th Cav. Co.F
Rowland, M.O. SC 5th Inf. 1st Co.C Sgt.
Rowland, Moor MO 4th Cav. Co.B
Rowland, N. GA 32nd Inf. Co.E
Rowland, Nathan TN 49th Inf. Co.E
Rowland, Nathan TN 50th Inf. Co.B
Rowland, Nathan Inf. Bailey's Cons.Regt. Co.F
Rowland, Nathaniel P. VA 16th Inf. Co.E
Rowland, Pat TN 2nd (Walker's) Inf. Co.I
Rowland, Peter M. AL Cav. Falkner's Co. 1st Lt.
Rowland, Peter M. AL Cav. 5th Bn. Hilliard's Legion Co.A Capt.
Rowland, Peter M. 10th Conf.Cav. Co.A Capt.
Rowland, Peter W. MS 11th Inf. Co.H
Rowland, Pleasant AL 49th Inf. Co.A
Rowland, P.R. MS 43rd Inf. Co.G
Rowland, P. Stark MS 13th Inf. Co.A
Rowland, R. TN 16th Inf. Co.A
Rowland, Rederick GA 12th Inf. Co.I
Rowland, Reuben TN 4th Inf. Co.A Cpl.
Rowland, R.F. TN 13th Inf. Co.L
Rowland, R.G. VA Lt.Arty. R.M. Anderson's Co.
Rowland, R.H. GA 2nd Brig.St.Troops Capt.
Rowland, R.H. MS Lt.Arty. 14th Bn. Co.C
Rowland, R.H. MS Lt.Arty. Merrin's Btty.
Rowland, Richard LA 7th Inf. Co.G Artif.
Rowland, Richard L. GA 50th Inf. Co.B

Rowland, R.L. KY 1st (Helm's) Cav. Old Co.G
Rowland, R.M. TN 8th Inf. Co.B
Rowland, R.M. VA 14th Cav. Co.C
Rowland, Robert AL 8th Inf. Co.C
Rowland, Robert GA Mil. Camden Cty. (Mtd.)
Rowland, Robert GA 26th Inf. Co.D
Rowland, Robert GA 50th Inf. Co.B
Rowland, Robert GA Cherokee Legion (St.Guards) Co.I
Rowland, Robert VA 1st Arty. 3rd Co.C
Rowland, Robert VA Lt.Arty. 1st Bn. Co.C
Rowland, Robert VA Arty. Young's Co.
Rowland, Robert VA 14th Inf. 1st Co.G
Rowland, Robert A. MO Cav. Poindexter's Regt. Lt.
Rowland, Robert A. MO Cav. Snider's Bn. Co.B 1st Lt.
Rowland, Robert A. MO Inf. Perkins' Bn. Co.F
Rowland, Robert E. SC 14th Inf. Co.F
Rowland, Robert H. MS 29th Inf. Co.B
Rowland, Robert H. NC 58th Inf. Co.C
Rowland, Robert M. VA 28th Inf. Co.A
Rowland, Robert R. NC 44th Inf. Co.A
Rowland, Robert T. TX Waul's Legion Co.A Bugler
Rowland, Robert W. LA 28th (Gray's) Inf. Co.I
Rowland, R.P. TN 35th Inf. 2nd Co.A 2nd Lt.
Rowland, R.R. KY 8th Mtd.Inf. Co.H Capt.
Rowland, Rufus E.J. VA 16th Inf. Co.E
Rowland, Rufus F. VA 24th Inf. Co.G 1st Lt.
Rowland, S. TX 20th Cav. Co.K
Rowland, S. VA 122nd Mil. Co.B Sgt.
Rowland, Samuel GA 4th Inf. Co.B
Rowland, Samuel C. SC 1st (Orr's) Rifles Co.E
Rowland, Samuel H. GA 5th Inf. Co.A Capt.
Rowland, Samuel J. GA 21st Inf. Co.F Ord.Sgt.
Rowland, S.B. AR 7th Cav. Co.B
Rowland, S.H. Gen. & Staff 1st Lt.,A.Ord.Off.
Rowland, Sherwood P. NC 57th Inf. Co.H Sgt.
Rowland, Silas NC 58th Inf. Co.C
Rowland, S.M.W. GA 31st Inf. Co.G
Rowland, Stephen FL 2nd Cav. Co.E
Rowland, Sumter AR 3rd Inf. Co.C
Rowland, T.B. AL 5th Inf. New Co.D
Rowland, T.B. SC 5th Inf. Co.D
Rowland, T.C. TN 2nd (Walker's) Inf. Co.C 1st Sgt.
Rowland, T.C. 9th Conf.Inf. Co.E,F Capt.
Rowland, Thad P. NC 12th Inf. Co.D,B
Rowland, Thomas AR Cav. Wright's Regt. Co.E
Rowland, Thomas GA Inf. 25th Bn. (Prov. Guard) Co.E
Rowland, Thomas GA 50th Inf. Co.H
Rowland, Thomas NC 2nd Arty. (36th St.Troops) Adj.
Rowland, Thomas TX 16th Cav. Co.A
Rowland, Thomas VA 7th Cav. Baylor's Co.
Rowland, Thomas VA 122nd Mil. Co.B
Rowland, Thomas Gen. & Staff Maj.,AAG
Rowland, Thomas VA 54th Mil. Co.E,F
Rowland, Thomas C. MO Inf. Perkins' Bn. Co.F
Rowland, Thomas C. NC 2nd Jr.Res. Co.F Capt.
Rowland, Thomas H. NC 7th Inf. Co.B
Rowland, Thomas J. GA 48th Inf. Co.F Cpl.
Rowland, Thomas M. 3rd Conf.Cav. Co.E
Rowland, Thomas R. AL 10th Inf. Co.G Sgt.

Rowland, Thomas W. MS 34th Inf. Co.G Cpl.
Rowland, T.J. NC 12th Inf. Co.B,D
Rowland, T.J. TX 14th Cav. Co.I
Rowland, T.R. AR 23rd Inf. Co.F
Rowland, T.T. AL 4th (Roddey's) Cav. Julian's Co.
Rowland, T.T. AL Inf. 2nd Regt. Co.E
Rowland, T.T. GA 5th Res. Co.I
Rowland, T.T. NC 43rd Inf. Co.G
Rowland, T.W. GA Inf. 18th Bn. Co.B
Rowland, T.Y. MS 20th Inf. Co.G
Rowland, W. GA 15th Inf. Co.B
Rowland, W. KY 6th Cav. Co.K
Rowland, Waddy T. TN 1st (Turney's) Inf. Co.B
Rowland, W.B. GA Inf. Pool's Co.
Rowland, W.B. TX 2nd Cav. Co.I
Rowland, W.C. GA 27th Inf. Co.D Sgt.
Rowland, W.C. TN 35th Inf. 2nd Co.A
Rowland, Wesley A. AR 9th Inf. Co.G Jr.2nd Lt.
Rowland, W.F. MS 32nd Inf. Co.A
Rowland, W.H. GA 15th Inf. Co.H
Rowland, W.H. GA Inf. 18th Bn. Co.C,A
Rowland, W.H. KY 3rd Mtd.Inf. Co.D
Rowland, W.H. TX 6th Cav. Co.C
Rowland, W.H. TX Cav. Sutton's Co.
Rowland, Wiley B. GA 4th Inf. Co.B
Rowland, William AR Cav. 1st Bn. (Stirman's) Co.B
Rowland, William AR 2nd Cav. Co.G
Rowland, William AR 30th Inf. Co.C
Rowland, William GA 3rd Inf. Co.E
Rowland, William GA 3rd Res. Co.A
Rowland, William GA 15th Inf. Co.H
Rowland, William GA 31st Inf. Co.F
Rowland, William KY 2nd (Duke's) Cav. Co.B Sgt.
Rowland, William MS Cav. Ham's Regt. Co.G
Rowland, William MS 31st Inf. Co.K
Rowland, William NC 6th Cav. (65th St.Troops) Co.D,B
Rowland, William A. GA 44th Inf. Co.K Surg.
Rowland, William D. GA 44th Inf. Co.K
Rowland, William E. NC 53rd Inf. Co.I
Rowland, William F. SC 1st Arty. Co.A
Rowland, William G. FL Cav. 5th Bn. Co.H Cpl.
Rowland, William G. GA 1st Reg. Co.K Cpl.
Rowland, William H. AR 31st Inf. Co.E
Rowland, William H. GA 1st (Olmstead's) Inf. Co.C
Rowland, William H. GA 26th Inf. Co.D
Rowland, William H. KY 9th Mtd.Inf. Co.D
Rowland, William H. NC 55th Inf. Co.G Music.
Rowland, William Henry GA 21st Inf. Co.F Sgt.
Rowland, William J. GA 48th Inf. Co.F
Rowland, William J. MO Cav. Poindexter's Regt.
Rowland, William J. MO Cav. Snider's Bn. Co.B
Rowland, William L. AR 9th Inf. Co.G Ord.Sgt.
Rowland, William N. GA 50th Inf. Co.B
Rowland, William P. NC 7th Inf. Co.B
Rowland, William P. VA 57th Inf. Co.K Sgt.
Rowland, William R. SC 5th Inf. 1st Co.G, 2nd Co.C Sgt.
Rowland, Williamson GA 48th Inf. Co.F Cpl.
Rowland, William T. AR 15th (Josey's) Inf. Co.A

Rowland, Willis F. NC 12th Inf. Co.H 1st Lt.
Rowland, Willis W. GA 57th Inf. Co.E
Rowland, W.J. GA 13th Inf. Co.I
Rowland, W.L. AR 1st Mtd.Rifles Co.I
Rowland, W.L. GA Cav. 10th Bn. (St.Guards) Co.C
Rowland, W.L. KY 7th Mtd.Inf. Co.G
Rowland, W.P. MS Cav.Res. Mitchell's Co.
Rowland, W.R. SC 22nd Inf. Co.G
Rowland, W.T. MS 18th Cav. Co.D
Rowland, W.T. TN 13th Inf. Co.E,L
Rowland, Z.C. TX Inf. Timmons' Regt. Co.A
Rowland, Z.C. TX Waul's Legion Co.B
Rowle, George W. AL 36th Inf. Co.G
Rowle, John MS 19th Inf. Co.C
Rowlean, Alf MO 7th Cav. Co.I
Rowlen, A.L. AL 8th (Livingston's) Cav. Co.A
Rowlen, J.V. AL 7th Cav. Co.D
Rowlenn, R. FL Cav. 5th Bn. Co.H
Rowler, James V. AL 7th Inf. Co.C
Rowles, Benjamin F. VA 7th Inf. Co.C
Rowles, Crayton VA 46th Inf. 2nd Co.G
Rowles, Crayton VA 57th Inf. Co.D
Rowles, David J. TN 61st Mtd.Inf. Co.A
Rowles, George TN 19th & 20th (Cons.) Cav. Co.E
Rowles, George H. AR 9th Inf. Old Co.I, Co.E
Rowles, George W. VA 13th Inf. 2nd Co.B
Rowles, G. Warren GA 23rd Inf. Co.H
Rowles, John LA 13th Bn. (Part.Rangers) Co.F
Rowles, John A. AR 4th Inf. Co.E Capt.
Rowles, John F. VA 6th Cav. Co.B
Rowles, Joseph S. VA 6th Cav. Co.B
Rowles, Marshall NC 1st Cav. (9th St.Troops) Co.H
Rowles, Richard M. VA 51st Inf. Co.C
Rowles, Samuel B. VA 13th Inf. 2nd Co.B
Rowles, Wilford G. VA 57th Inf. Co.D 1st Lt.
Rowles, William VA Lt.Arty. Clutter's Co. Artif.
Rowles, William VA 57th Inf. Co.D,E
Rowles, William J. AR 1st (Colquitt's) Inf. Co.A
Rowles, W.J. AR 37th Inf. Co.D Capt.
Rowlet, Daniel FL Milton Lt.Arty. Dunham's Co. Cpl.
Rowlet, H. TN 45th Inf. Co.K
Rowlet, J.D. TN 20th (Russell's) Cav. Co.F
Rowlet, Joseph W. TN 45th Inf. Co.K
Rowlett, Alexander W. VA Inf. 25th Bn. Co.F Sgt.
Rowlett, Augustus M. VA 41st Inf. 2nd Co.E
Rowlett, Aurelius E. VA 9th Cav. Co.G
Rowlett, B.F. TN 11th (Holman's) Cav. Co.B
Rowlett, B.F. TN 24th Inf. 1st Co.G 2nd Lt.
Rowlett, B.F. TN 45th Inf. Co.K
Rowlett, Charles W. NC Walker's Bn. Thomas' Legion Co.C
Rowlett, C.J. TN 45th Inf. Co.K
Rowlett, Daniel A. KY 5th Mtd.Inf. Co.E
Rowlett, Daniel L. MO 4th Inf. Co.D
Rowlett, D.L. MO 1st & 4th Cons.Inf. Co.I
Rowlett, Donnel MO Cav. Freeman's Regt. Co.I
Rowlett, E. AR Lt.Arty. Marshall's Btty.
Rowlett, E.J. VA 1st (Farinholt's) Res. Co.G Sgt.
Rowlett, Ewing AR 14th (Powers') Inf. Co.G Cpl.

Rowlett, Frank AR 8th Cav. Co.A
Rowlett, George TN 46th Inf. Co.A Sgt.
Rowlett, George E. VA Inf. 25th Bn. Co.A
Rowlett, George E. VA 44th Inf. Co.H
Rowlett, G.W. TN 20th (Russell's) Cav. Co.I
Rowlett, J. TX 3rd (Kirby's) Bn.Vol. Co.B
Rowlett, James TN 46th Inf. Co.A
Rowlett, James TX 17th Inf. Co.F
Rowlett, James Chap. VA 3rd Cav. Co.K
Rowlett, James E. VA 36th Inf. 2nd Co.H Cpl.
Rowlett, James E. VA 86th Mil. Co.B
Rowlett, James T. VA 9th Inf. Co.C
Rowlett, Jasper MO 4th Inf. Co.D
Rowlett, J.M. TX Cav. 6th Bn. Co.F
Rowlett, J.N. VA 20th Inf. Co.G
Rowlett, John B. AR 14th (Powers') Inf. Co.I
Rowlett, John F. VA 14th Inf. Co.D
Rowlett, John W. KY 4th Cav. Co.A
Rowlett, Joseph H. VA 9th Inf. Co.C
Rowlett, Junius VA 53rd Inf. Co.C
Rowlett, Junius C. VA 3rd Cav. Co.K
Rowlett, J.W. TN 13th Inf. Co.C Sgt.
Rowlett, Peter A. VA 9th Inf. Co.C
Rowlett, Peter F. VA 18th Inf. Co.G Capt.
Rowlett, P.T. VA Mtd.Guard 4th Congr.Dist.
Rowlett, R. Cobbs VA 12th Inf. Co.E
Rowlett, R.D. AR Lt.Arty. Owen's Btty.
Rowlett, Richard C. VA 5th Cav. (12 mo. '61-2) Co.D
Rowlett, Richard C. VA 13th Cav. Co.B
Rowlett, Samuel S. VA 3rd Cav. Co.K
Rowlett, S.M. MO 1st & 4th Cons.Inf. Co.I
Rowlett, S.M. MO 4th Inf. Co.D
Rowlett, T.B. AR 30th Inf. Co.K
Rowlett, Thomas VA 1st (Farinholt's) Res. Co.G
Rowlett, Thomas M. VA 6th Cav. Co.G Sgt.
Rowlett, Thomas M. VA 2nd Arty. Co.I
Rowlett, T.M. VA Inf. 25th Bn. Co.A
Rowlett, W. TX Cav. Giddings' Bn. White's Co.
Rowlett, Waverly GA 62nd Cav. Co.L
Rowlett, Waverly VA 24th Cav. Co.I
Rowlett, Waverly VA 3rd Inf. Co.E Sgt.Maj.
Rowlett, Waverly 8th (Dearing's) Conf.Cav. Co.D
Rowlett, W.E. TN Inf. 2nd Cons.Regt. Co.B
Rowlett, W.E. TN 51st Inf. Co.I 1st Sgt.
Rowlett, W.E. TN 51st (Cons.) Inf. Co.D
Rowlett, William KY 3rd Mtd.Inf. Co.I
Rowlett, William TX Cav. Baylor's Regt. Co.D
Rowlett, William VA 1st St.Res. Co.I
Rowlett, William M. VA 5th Cav. (12 mo. '61-2) Co.D
Rowlett, William M. VA 13th Cav. Co.B
Rowlett, William M. VA 9th Inf. Co.C
Rowlett, W.J. MO 1st & 4th Cons.Inf. Co.I
Rowlett, W.J. MO 4th Inf. Co.D
Rowlette, Benjamin F. AR 14th (McCarver's) Inf. Co.F
Rowlette, B.F. AR 21st Inf. Co.B
Rowlette, B.F. TN Holman's Bn.Part.Rangers Co.A
Rowlette, Calvin W. VA 21st Inf. Co.K 2nd Lt.
Rowlette, Thomas J. AR 14th (McCarver's) Inf. Co.F
Rowlette, T.J. AR 21st Inf. Co.B
Rowley, Charles N. LA Mil. Brig.Gen.
Rowley, Charles P. TX 4th Field Btty. Sgt.

Rowley, C.S. AL Cp. of Instr. Talladega

348

Rowley, C.S. AL Cp. of Instr. Talladega
Rowley, Edward GA 9th Inf. Co.F
Rowley, Elbert F.S. SC 2nd Inf. Co.B
Rowley, E.R. TN Inf. 154th Sr.Regt. Co.D
Rowley, F.H. TX Cav. Madison's Regt. Co.C
    1st Sgt.
Rowley, George GA Cav. 21st Bn. Co.A
Rowley, George H. TX 11th (Spaight's) Bn.Vol.
    Co.E
Rowley, H.T. LA 3rd (Wingfield's) Cav. Co.A
Rowley, J.B. MO Lt.Arty. Barret's Co. QMSgt.
Rowley, J.F. TX 1st Hvy.Arty. Co.E
Rowley, John MO 1st Cav. Co.I
Rowley, John VA 9th Cav. Co.I
Rowley, John VA 25th Mil. Co.A
Rowley, John Sig.Corps,CSA
Rowley, John F. AR 12th Inf. Co.B
Rowley, J.W. TX 24th & 25th Cav. (Cons.) Co.I
Rowley, Major VA 47th Inf. Co.B
Rowley, Peter F. TX 7th Cav. Co.A Sgt.
Rowley, R.D. LA 1st Cav. Co.E
Rowley, Robert VA 15th Cav. Co.E
Rowley, Robert P. TN 4th Inf. Co.A
Rowley, R.P. 4th Conf.Eng.Troops Capt.
Rowley, R.P. Eng.,CSA 1st Lt.
Rowley, W. GA Cav. 21st Bn. Co.A
Rowley, William TX Waul's Legion Co.F
Rowley, William VA 15th Cav. Co.E
Rowley, William VA 25th Mil. Co.A
Rowley, Wm. Conf.Inf. Tucker's Regt. Co.A
Rowley, William H. KY 2nd Mtd.Inf. Co.C Cpl.
Rowlin, T.J. AL 6th Cav. Co.F Cpl.
Rowling, George F. TN 9th (Ward's) Cav. Co.D
Rowling, J. GA 48th Inf. Co.F
Rowling, John FL 5th Inf. Co.B
Rowling, J.T. NC 12th Inf. Co.H
Rowling, Thomas TX 1st (Yager's) Cav. Co.E
Rowlings, James A. VA 3rd Lt.Arty. Co.D
Rowlins, Wiley M. AL 50th Inf. Co.H
Rowlinski, William SC 24th Inf. Co.A
Rowlison, John VA 14th Cav. Co.D
Rowlison, John S. VA 27th Inf. Co.F Cpl.
Rowll, William MS 1st Cav.Res. Co.K
Rowls, Milton A. AR 1st (Colquitt's) Inf. Co.C
Rowls, Richard H. TX 18th Cav. Co.F
Rowls, Thomas GA 53rd Inf. Co.F
Rowly, Sewell VA 20th Inf. Co.A
Rowman, R.M. KY 7th Cav. Co.G Sgt.
Rowmer, J.M. AR 3rd Cav. Co.E
Rownan, James TN 15th Inf. Co.C
Rownan, Robert KY 11th Cav. Co.F
Rowntree, John A. FL 1st Cav.
Rowoldt, A. AL 12th Inf. Co.C
Roworth, Joseph G. AR 23rd Inf. Co.B Adj.
Rowper, James H. GA 1st Cav. Co.K
Rowrie, John B. GA Inf. 1st City Bn.
    (Columbus) Co.C
Rows, M.V.H. AL 46th Inf. Co.C
Rowse, A.B. SC 3rd Cav. Co.D
Rowse, A.B. SC 11th Inf. Co.E
Rowse, J.T. SC 3rd Cav. Co.D
Rowse, M.D. SC 3rd Cav. Co.D
Rowse, William H. LA 11th Inf. Co.F
Rowse, William R. SC 2nd Bn.S.S. Co.A
Rowse, W.R. SC 3rd Cav. Co.D
Rowse, W.R. SC 11th Inf. Co.E
Rowse, W.T. SC 3rd Cav. Co.D

Rowsee, John W. VA 4th Cav. Co.C
Rowsel, William S. TX 17th Cav. Co.K
Rowser, M.G. TN Inf. Harman's Regt. Co.K
Rowsey, Archibald VA 1st Cav. Co.F
Rowsey, Archibald VA 8th Cav. Co.G
Rowsey, Edmond GA 37th Inf. Co.G
Rowsey, Edmund GA Inf. 9th Bn. Co.D
Rowsey, G.D. MS 3rd Inf. Co.F
Rowsey, G.D. MS 23rd Inf. Co.F
Rowsey, George P. VA 49th Inf. Co.I Sgt.
Rowsey, George W.H. AR 18th Inf. Co.E
Rowsey, G.W.W. MS 18th Cav. Co.E
Rowsey, Henry A. VA 58th Inf. Co.C
Rowsey, Henry C. MS 23rd Inf. Co.F
Rowsey, James L. VA 58th Inf. Co.F
Rowsey, J.M. MS 1st Cav. Co.C
Rowsey, John VA 8th Cav. Co.G
Rowsey, John VA 38th Inf. Co.C
Rowsey, Joseph VA 146th Mil. Co.H
Rowsey, J.W. AR 6th Inf. Co.E
Rowsey, Lafayette VA 4th Inf. Co.I
Rowsey, Louis S. MS 42nd Inf. Co.E
Rowsey, Thomas MS 41st Inf. Co.H
Rowsey, Thomas VA 8th Cav. Co.I
Rowsey, W.F. TN 51st (Cons.) Inf. Co.E 1st
    Sgt.
Rowsey, W.F. TN 52nd Inf. Co.H 1st Lt.
Rowsey, W.H. MS 10th Cav. Co.H
Rowsey, W.H. Conf.Cav. Baxter's Bn. Co.A
Rowsey, William H. AR 18th Inf. Co.E
Rowsy, J.H. TN 1st (Feild's) & 27th Inf. (Cons.)
    Co.I
Rowsy, J.H. TN 27th Inf. Co.E
Rowtan, James H. VA 4th Cav. Co.K
Rowtan, J.J. VA 4th Cav. Co.K
Rowten, J.J. AL 22nd Inf. Co.I
Rowton, Chillochtor AR 4th Inf. Co.C
Rowton, F.D. AR 19th (Dockery's) Inf. Co.C
    1st Lt.
Rowton, John TX 20th Inf. Co.F
Rowton, Quintus C. AR 33rd Inf. Co.I Sgt.
Rowton, Washington TN 1st Hvy.Arty. 2nd
    Co.A
Rowton, William R. AR 33rd Inf. Co.I
Rowton, W.P. TX 17th Inf. Co.F
Rowzee, Allison H. NC 4th Inf. Co.K
Rowzee, Alonzo L. MS 12th Inf. Co.F
Rowzee, Benjamin VA 12th Cav. Co.E
Rowzee, Claudius W. NC 8th Inf. Co.K Music.
Rowzee, George A. VA Cav. Mosby's Regt.
    (Part.Rangers) Co.A
Rowzee, J.H. MS 11th (Cons.) Cav. Co.G
Rowzee, J.H. MS 41st Inf. Co.F Sgt.
Rowzee, John MS Cav. 1st Bn. (Miller's) Cole's
    Co. 1st Sgt.
Rowzee, John B. VA 97th Mil. Co.L Sgt.
Rowzee, John E. VA Cav. Mosby's Regt.
    (Part.Rangers) Co.A
Rowzee, J.W. VA Cav. Mosby's Regt. (Part.
    Rangers) Co.A Sgt.
Rowzee, Theodore F. GA 15th Inf. Co.F Sgt.
Rowzee, Thomas E. VA 1st Bn.Res. Co.H 1st
    Lt.
Rowzee, W.C. MS 2nd Cav. Co.B
Rowzee, W.W. MS 2nd Cav. Co.B
Rowzell, C.A. TN 55th (McKoin's) Inf. Co.H
Rowzer, Martin Conf.Inf. 1st Bn. Co.F

Rowzie, Archibald R. Gen. & Staff Asst.Surg.
Rowzie, E.J. VA Lt.Arty. Woolfolk's Co.
Rowzie, Henry S. VA 55th Inf. Co.F
Rowzie, John S., Jr. VA 55th Inf. Co.A
Rowzie, John S., Jr. Gen. & Staff, QM Dept.
    Capt.,AQM
Rowzie, Richard, Jr. VA 55th Inf. Co.A,F
    Ord.Sgt.
Rowzie, Robert R. VA 55th Inf. Co.A 2nd Lt.
Rowzie, William D. VA Mtd.Res. Rappahannock
    Dist. Sale's Co.
Rowzie, William D. VA Res. Forces Thurston's
    Co.
Rowzie, William E. VA 40th Inf. Co.K
Rowzie, William H. VA 49th Inf. Co.H Sgt.
Rowzie, William W. VA 55th Inf. Co.F
    Sgt.Maj.
Rowzle, John MS 1st Cav. Co.I
Roxburo, Tho. AL 41st Inf. Co.I
Roxbury, Edward VA 17th Inf. Co.H
Roxling, J.R. MS 3rd Inf. (St.Troops) Co.E
Roxo, Jose Maria TX Cav. L. Trevinio's Co.
Roxrhodes, James VA Cav. 47th Bn. Co.A
Roxx, D. TX Waul's Legion Co.D
Roy, --- LA Mil. 1st Regt. French Brig. Co.6
Roy, --- LA Mil. 2nd Regt. French Brig. Co.2
Roy, --- TX Cav. Ragsdale's Bn. Co.D
Roy, A. LA Mil. 1st Chasseurs a pied Co.2
Roy, A. LA 28th (Gray's) Inf. Co.A Sgt.
Roy, A.A. VA 1st Inf. Co.H
Roy, Adam AR 2nd Inf. Old Co.C, Co.B
Roy, Adolph LA 22nd Inf. Co.D
Roy, A.H. TX 7th Cav. Co.K
Roy, A.J. AR 35th Inf. Old Co.F
Roy, A.J. MO 11th Inf. Co.H
Roy, Alexander LA 18th Inf. Co.B,F
Roy, Alexander LA Inf.Cons. 18th Regt. & Yel-
    low Jacket Bn. Co.F
Roy, Alfred LA Res.Corps William's Co.
Roy, Andre LA 1st Hvy.Arty. (Reg.) Co.G
Roy, Andrew AR 32nd Inf. Co.C
Roy, Andrew V.B. TX 19th Cav. Co.A
Roy, Archd. Gen. & Staff Capt.,Asst.Comsy.
Roy, Atien LA Inf. 10th Bn. Co.H
Roy, August LA 7th Cav. Co.D
Roy, Benjamin P. Brown's Div. Maj.,QM
Roy, Ben P. TN 3rd (Clack's) Inf. QM
Roy, C.C. TN 3rd (Forrest's) Cav. 1st Co.B
Roy, Cevennes LA 26th Inf. Co.E
Roy, C.H. AR 21st Inf. Surg.
Roy, Charles A. LA 28th (Gray's) Inf. Co.A
Roy, Charles C. VA 55th Inf. Co.D 1st Lt.
Roy, Christopher C. VA 22nd Inf. Swann's Co.
    1st Lt.
Roy, Christopher C. VA 59th Inf. 2nd Co.K 1st
    Lt.
Roy, Churchill B. VA 46th Inf. 2nd Co.A
Roy, Clement LA Mil. Knaps' Co. (Fausee River
    Guards)
Roy, Clement E. LA Pointe Coupee Arty. Sgt.
Roy, C.S. TN 3rd (Forrest's) Cav. 1st Co.B
Roy, C.S. Gen. & Staff Asst.Surg.
Roy, David AL 59th Inf. Co.B
Roy, David AL 2nd Bn. Hilliard's Legion Vol.
    Co.E
Roy, David LA 26th Inf. Co.F
Roy, D.E. LA 8th Cav. Co.A Sgt.

Roy, D.J. AR 24th Inf. Co.I
Roy, D.L. TX 32nd Cav. Co.D
Roy, E. LA 18th Inf. Co.C
Roy, E.L. LA Mil. French Co. of St.James
Roy, Elijah B. VA 58th Mil. Co.K
Roy, Elisha VA 23rd Cav. Co.D
Roy, Felix 1st Choctaw & Chickasaw Mtd.Rifles 1st Co.K
Roy, Ferney L. NC 2nd Cav. (19th St.Troops) Co.G
Roy, F.F. LA 2nd Inf. Co.E
Roy, Fountain P. TX 19th Cav. Co.A
Roy, Francis M. TX 19th Cav. Co.A
Roy, Frederick AR 1st (Colquitt's) Inf. Co.G
Roy, Frederick TX 3rd Cav. Co.I Bugler
Roy, Frosin LA Inf.Cons. 18th Regt. & Yellow Jacket Bn. Co.A
Roy, F.S. SC 1st Cav. Co.H
Roy, Garnett VA Inf. 55th Regt. Co.D Capt.
Roy, George J. TN 4th (Murray's) Cav. Co.E
Roy, G.L. NC 23rd Inf. Co.F
Roy, Gustavus G. VA 55th Inf. Co.D Capt.
Roy, Gustavus G. Gen. & Staff Asst.Surg.
Roy, G.W. AR 10th Mil. Co.B
Roy, G.W. MO Cav. Fristoe's Regt. Co.G
Roy, Hansford D. AL 2nd Bn. Hilliard's Legion Vol. Co.E
Roy, Henderson H. TN 3rd (Lillard's)Mtd.Inf. Co.F
Roy, Henry AR Inf. Hardy's Regt. Co.D
Roy, Henry MO 1st Brig.St.Guard
Roy, Henry S. MO 9th (Elliott's) Cav. Co.B
Roy, H.H. TN Hvy.Arty. Caruthers' Btty.
Roy, Hicks MO Cav. Wood's Regt. Co.C
Roy, Hill W. TN Holman's Bn.Part.Rangers Co.B
Roy, Hiram L. TX 6th Cav. Co.C
Roy, Hix AR 38th Inf. Co.C
Roy, H.L. AR 2nd Cav. Co.E
Roy, Isaac A.L. AL 30th Inf. Co.K
Roy, Isaac L. TN 10th Cav.
Roy, J.A. TN 21st Inf. Co.A
Roy, J.A. 9th Conf.Inf. Co.H
Roy, Jacob AL 63rd Inf. Co.D,A
Roy, Jacob TX Cav. Morgan's Regt. Co.C
Roy, James C. VA 15th Inf. Co.B
Roy, James H. Gen. & Staff Hosp.Stew.
Roy, J.B. LA 18th Inf. Co.C
Roy, J.C. Hosp.Stew.
Roy, Jean Bte. LA 28th (Thomas') Inf. Co.K
Roy, Jeff W. LA Watkins' Bn.Res.Corps Co.C
Roy, Jesse AR 30th Inf. Co.H Capt.
Roy, J.G. MS 7th Inf. Co.H
Roy, J.H. AL 7th Cav. Co.K
Roy, J.H. Hosp.Stew.
Roy, J.M. AL 55th Vol. Co.C
Roy, Joel TX 15th Cav. Co.C
Roy, John AL 2nd Cav.
Roy, John LA 22nd (Cons.) Inf. Co.G
Roy, John MO 2nd Cav. Co.A
Roy, John MO Cav. Fristoe's Regt. Co.G
Roy, John TN 1st (Feild's) Inf. Co.D
Roy, John TN Inf. Nashville Bn. Cattles' Co.
Roy, John C. TX Cav. 8th (Taylor's) Bn. Co.E
Roy, John W. AL 59th Inf. Co.B Cpl.
Roy, John W. AL 2nd Bn. Hilliard's Legion Vol. Co.E

Roy, Jonathan NC Walker's Bn. Thomas' Legion Co.H
Roy, Joseph AL 59th Inf. Co.B
Roy, Joseph AL 2nd Bn. Hilliard's Legion Vol. Co.E
Roy, Joseph LA 2nd Cav. Co.A
Roy, Joseph LA 3rd (Harrison's) Cav. Co.C
Roy, Joseph LA 2nd Res.Corps Co.B Cpl.
Roy, Joseph LA 17th Inf. Co.D
Roy, Joseph LA Inf.Cons. 18th Regt. & Yellow Jacket Bn. Co.F
Roy, Joseph NC Walker's Bn. Thomas' Legion Co.H
Roy, Joseph C. VA Horse Arty. Shoemaker's Co.
Roy, Joseph W. LA 18th Inf. Co.B Sgt.
Roy, J.P. LA 2nd Res.Corps Co.A
Roy, J.T. TN 12th (Green's) Cav. Co.D
Roy, Jule LA Inf. 10th Bn. Co.B
Roy, L. LA 2nd Cav. Co.F
Roy, L. MS 7th Inf. Co.I
Roy, Larkin C. VA 10th Cav. Co.D
Roy, Larkin C., Jr. VA 22nd Inf. Swann's Co.
Roy, Larkin C., Sr. VA 22nd Inf. Swann's Co.
Roy, Larkin C. VA 59th Inf. 2nd Co.K
Roy, Leando F. LA 18th Inf. Co.F
Roy, L.F. LA Inf.Cons. 18th Regt. & Yellow Jacket Bn. Co.I
Roy, L.N. AL 30th Inf. Co.K Sgt.
Roy, Louis LA 8th Inf. Co.F Cpl.
Roy, Louis LA 22nd Inf. Co.B
Roy, L.V. AL Cp. of Instr. Talladega
Roy, M.D. VA 11th Cav. Co.A
Roy, Michael AL Gorff's Co. (Mobile Pulaski Rifles)
Roy, Milton LA 27th Inf. Co.F Cpl.
Roy, N. LA 2nd Res.Corps Co.A
Roy, Nelson TN 3rd (Lillard's) Mtd.Inf. Co.F
Roy, O.B. MS 44th Inf. Co.B
Roy, Oct LA 2nd Res.Corps Co.A Sgt.
Roy, P. LA Mil. 1st Chasseurs a pied Co.2
Roy, P. LA Mil. 3rd Regt. French Brig. Co.7
Roy, P.B. LA 8th Cav. Co.A Sgt.
Roy, P.B. LA Inf. 10th Bn. Co.F 2nd Lt.
Roy, Peirre LA Inf. 10th Bn. Co.H
Roy, P.H. AL 1st Regt.Conscr. Co.F
Roy, Phelix TX Cav. Wells' Regt. Co.C
Roy, Pierre LA 2nd Res.Corps Co.A
Roy, Pierre LA Conscr.
Roy, Pleasant AR 5th Inf.
Roy, Richard R. VA 2nd Inf. Co.I
Roy, Robert SC Inf. Hampton Legion Co.A 2nd Lt.
Roy, Robert B. VA 26th Inf. Co.G 1st Lt.
Roy, Romulus LA 1st (Strawbridge's) Inf. Co.I
Roy, Russel AL 34th Inf. Breedlove's Co.
Roy, Russel AL 45th Inf. Co.H
Roy, S.M. TN 15th (Cons.) Cav. Co.F
Roy, S.M. TN Cav. Nixon's Regt. Co.A
Roy, S.R. AR 16th Inf. Co.I
Roy, Stanilis LA Mil. Mooney's Co. (Saddlers Guards)
Roy, T.A. MS 1st (Percy's) Inf. Co.I Sgt.
Roy, T.A. MS 15th Inf. Co.A
Roy, T.A. TN 15th (Cons.) Cav. Co.F
Roy, T.B. Hardee's Corps Lt.Col.,AAG
Roy, Thomas KY 4th Cav. Co.F

Roy, Thomas KY 5th Mtd.Inf. Co.E
Roy, Thomas LA Arty. Kean's Btty. (Orleans Ind.Arty.)
Roy, Thomas SC 1st Mtd.Mil. Earnest's Co.
Roy, Thomas SC Hvy.Arty. Gilchrist's Co. (Gist Guard)
Roy, Thomas B. VA 17th Inf. Co.B
Roy, Thomas L. AL 1st Regt. Mobile Vol. British Guard Co.B
Roy, Thomas L. NC 2nd Inf. Co.H
Roy, Thomas M. VA 7th Cav. Co.E Cpl.
Roy, Thomas S. VA 55th Inf. Co.A
Roy, T.M. NC 1st Arty. (10th St.Troops) Co.F
Roy, Ulger LA 7th Cav. Co.B
Roy, U.P., Jr. LA 1st Cav. Co.H
Roy, V. LA Res.Corps Co.A
Roy, W.A. AR 45th Cav. Co.I
Roy, Walter S. VA 17th Inf. Co.B 2nd Lt.
Roy, W.B. TN 2nd Cav. Co.B
Roy, Wesley TN 24th Bn.S.S. Co.C
Roy, W.H. TN Inf. 154th Sr.Regt. 1st Co.B
Roy, W.H. TX Cav. McCord's Frontier Regt. Co.G
Roy, William AL 53rd (Part.Rangers) Co.K
Roy, William AZ Cav. Herbert's Bn. Helm's Co.
Roy, William LA 18th Inf. Co.H
Roy, William LA Inf.Cons. 18th Regt. & Yellow Jacket Bn. Co.H
Roy, William SC Mil.Arty. 1st Regt. Walter's Co. Sgt.
Roy, William SC Lt.Arty. Walter's Co. (Washington Arty.) Sgt.
Roy, William TN 10th Cav.
Roy, William TN 3rd (Lillard's) Mtd.Inf. Co.F
Roy, William TN 11th Inf. Co.I
Roy, William VA 2nd Cav. Co.G
Roy, William B. VA Cav. 40th Bn. Co.C 1st Sgt.
Roy, William H. TN 3rd (Forrest's) Cav. Co.A
Roy, William R. AL 6th Inf. Co.G
Roy, W.M. TX 25th Cav. Co.G
Roy, W.W. AL 30th Inf. Co.K
Royal, A.J. Inf. Bailey's Cons.Regt. Co.B
Royal, Albert NC 2nd Inf. Co.E,C Sgt.
Royal, Albert H. VA 9th Inf. 1st Co.H
Royal, Alexander NC 20th Inf. Co.F
Royal, Archibald NC 46th Inf. Co.I Cpl.
Royal, Asa A. GA Arty. 11th Bn. (Sumter Arty.) Co.A Sgt.
Royal, Benjamin F. GA Cobb's Legion Co.E
Royal, Berry GA 32nd Inf. Co.K
Royal, Charles LA Mil. 3rd Regt. 1st Brig. 1st Div. Co.K
Royal, C.J. AL 18th Inf. Co.B
Royal, D. MS 28th Cav. Co.A
Royal, D. MS 3rd Inf. (St.Troops) Co.C
Royal, Daniel N. GA 6th Inf. Co.F
Royal, Dickerson MS 28th Cav. Co.A
Royal, E.B. GA Cav. 22nd Bn. (St.Guards) Co.D
Royal, E.J. AL Inf. 1st Regt. Co.B
Royal, Elias F. AR 1st (Colquitt's) Inf. Co.I
Royal, Elias F. Gen. & Staff 2nd Lt.,Dr.M.
Royal, Evans E. AL Eufaula Lt.Arty.
Royal, F.A. AL 8th Cav. Co.F
Royal, Franklin NC 34th Inf. Co.A
Royal, George AL 9th (Malone's) Cav. Co.E
Royal, George B. VA 9th Inf. 2nd Co.H

Royal, Gideon MS 19th Inf. Co.G
Royal, Gilford GA 32nd Inf. Co.C
Royal, H.A. NC 9th Bn.S.S. Co.B
Royal, Hardy AL 17th Inf. Co.F
Royal, Hardy NC 46th Inf. Co.I
Royal, Hardy D. GA 45th Inf. Co.C 1st Sgt.
Royal, Hardy D. GA 59th Inf. Co.F
Royal, Hardy S. NC 20th Inf. Faison's Co.
Royal, Hardy S. NC 30th Inf. Co.A Sgt.
Royal, Henry NC 21st Inf. Co.E
Royal, Henry S. GA Arty. 11th Bn. (Sumter Arty.) Co.A
Royal, Herman GA Hvy.Arty. 22nd Bn. Co.E
Royal, H.G. NC 53rd Inf. Co.A
Royal, H.J. GA Cav. Floyd's Co.
Royal, Hollin B. AR 14th (McCarver's) Inf. Co.I
Royal, Isaac NC 9th Bn.S.S. Co.A
Royal, Isham NC 46th Inf. Co.I
Royal, J. FL Cav. 5th Bn. Co.H
Royal, J.A. NC Cav. 16th Bn. Co.C
Royal, Jacob AL 57th Inf. Co.G
Royal, James D. GA 6th Inf. Co.G
Royal, James G. GA 3rd Inf. Co.E Capt.
Royal, James P. SC 2nd Inf. Co.I
Royal, James R. GA 18th Inf. Co.D
Royal, J.B. GA 1st Troops & Def. (Macon) Co.E
Royal, J.C. NC 3rd Jr.Res. Co.H
Royal, J.C. NC 9th Bn.S.S. Co.A Sgt.
Royal, Jesse TX 12th Cav. Co.D
Royal, Jesse TX 6th Inf. Co.F
Royal, John NC 9th Bn.S.S. Co.B
Royal, John NC 34th Inf. Co.A
Royal, John NC 46th Inf. Co.I
Royal, John B. GA 3rd Inf. Co.E
Royal, John B. VA Hvy.Arty. 10th Bn. Co.D
Royal, John C. NC 21st Inf. Co.B Cpl.
Royal, John O. NC 37th Inf. Co.K
Royal, John P. VA 3rd Cav. Co.D
Royal, Jordon C. GA 32nd Inf. Co.C Sgt.
Royal, J.T. VA Inf. 23rd Bn. Co.H
Royal, J.W. GA 32nd Inf. Co.C Cpl.
Royal, L. GA 32nd Inf. Co.C Sgt.
Royal, L.B. TN 35th Inf. 2nd Co.D
Royal, Marshall NC 30th Inf. Co.A
Royal, Martin NC 20th Inf. Faison's Co.
Royal, Martin NC 30th Inf. Co.A
Royal, Matthew NC 46th Inf. Co.I
Royal, Michael NC 20th Inf. Co.I
Royal, Molton NC 2nd Arty. (36th St.Troops) Co.C
Royal, Moses A. GA Inf. 27th Bn. Co.D Cpl.
Royal, Nevill NC 30th Inf. Co.A
Royal, Nevils GA 35th Inf. Co.E
Royal, Noah GA 3rd Inf. Co.A
Royal, Noah GA Cobb's Legion Co.E
Royal, O.B. AR 21st Inf. Co.B
Royal, Ollin NC 2nd Arty. (36th St.Troops) Co.A
Royal, Peter VA 12th Inf. Co.C,D
Royal, Peter J. VA Lt.Arty. Pegram's Co. Sgt.
Royal, Raiford NC 20th Inf. Co.I Music.
Royal, Richard F. VA Inf. 22nd Bn. Co.B
Royal, Richard H. TX 6th Cav. Co.I 2nd Lt.
Royal, Robert GA 50th Inf. Co.H
Royal, R.W. NC 6th Cav. (65th St.Troops) Co.H
Royal, S.A. GA 46th Inf. Co.B Bvt.2nd Lt.
Royal, Sherman NC 30th Inf. Co.A

Royal, Simon MS 19th Inf. Co.G
Royal, S.L. GA 32nd Inf. Co.C
Royal, Stephen GA 12th Inf. Co.D
Royal, T.A. GA 5th Inf. Co.H
Royal, Thomas NC 1st Cav. (9th St.Troops) Co.A
Royal, Thomas A. GA 50th Inf. Co.H
Royal, Thomas P. GA Arty. 11th Bn. (Sumter Arty.) Co.A
Royal, Timothy C. Conf.Inf. Tucker's Regt. Co.H
Royal, Tolbert P. NC 51st Inf. Co.K
Royal, T.T. MS 18th Cav. Co.D
Royal, W.A. AR 21st Inf. Co.B
Royal, W.A. AR 26th Inf. Co.I
Royal, W.A.H. GA Arty. St.Troops Pruden's Btty.
Royal, W.A.H. GA 5th Inf. (St.Guards) Rucker's Co.
Royal, Whitney NC 5th Cav. (63rd St.Troops) Co.C Sgt.
Royal, William LA 14th Inf. Co.H
Royal, William NC 33rd Inf. Co.D
Royal, William NC 37th Inf. Co.A
Royal, William NC 38th Inf. Co.B
Royal, William A. AR 14th (McCarver's) Inf. Co.I
Royal, William B. NC 38th Inf. Co.C Sgt.
Royal, William H. GA 5th Inf. Co.D
Royal, William M. GA 32nd Inf. Co.C
Royal, William R. NC 20th Inf. Co.F
Royal, William R. TX Cav. Martin's Regt. Co.B
Royal, Willie D. NC 28th Inf. Co.I Music.
Royal, Wilson NC 61st Inf. Co.I
Royal, W.M. AL Inf. 1st Regt. Co.B
Royal, W.P. GA Inf. 1st Loc.Troops (Augusta) Barnes' Lt.Arty.Co.
Royal, W.S. GA Inf. 1st Loc.Troops (Augusta) Co.B
Royald, Albert H. VA Inf. 28th Bn. Co.C
Royalds, Moss MS 6th Inf. Co.K
Royale, Gabriel NC 2nd Jr.Res. Co.A
Royale, Hardy NC 2nd Jr.Res. Co.A
Royale, L. LA Mil. 1st Regt. 2nd Brig. 1st Div. Co.A
Royall, A.J. TX 7th Inf. Co.A
Royall, A.P. Hosp.Stew.
Royall, Croskey GA 26th Inf. Dent's Co. Cpl.
Royall, Croskeys GA 4th (Clinch's) Cav. Co.B Sgt.
Royall, Edward M. Gen. & Staff A.Surg.
Royall, E.M. SC Lt.Arty. Galliard's Co. (Santee Lt.Arty.) 2nd Lt.
Royall, E.M. SC 10th Inf. 1st Co.G
Royall, E.M. SC Manigault's Bn.Vol. Co.B Sgt.
Royall, E.M. VA Lt.Arty. 13th Bn. Asst.Surg.
Royall, E.M. Conf.Arty. Haskell's Bn. Asst.Surg.
Royall, F.L. VA 4th Cav. Co.I
Royall, George VA Hvy.Arty. Epes' Co.
Royall, George VA Lt.Arty. Cayce's Co.
Royall, George B. VA 12th Inf. 1st Co.I
Royall, George H. VA 23rd Inf. Co.C
Royall, George K. VA 11th Inf. Co.G
Royall, Henry C. MS 11th Inf. Co.K
Royall, James B. VA 23rd Inf. Co.C
Royall, J.B. VA Lt.Arty. R.M. Anderson's Co.

Royall, J.C. VA 25th Cav.
Royall, John B. GA 26th Inf. Dent's Co.
Royall, John B. VA 1st Arty. Co.D
Royall, John C. VA 38th Inf. Co.D Sgt.
Royall, John H. AR 2nd Inf. Co.A Sgt.
Royall, John M. VA 1st St.Res. Co.E
Royall, John Thomas AL 9th Inf. Co.C
Royall, J.T. VA 1st (Farinholt's) Res. Co.H
Royall, Junius E. VA Inf. 25th Bn. Co.F
Royall, M.A. TX 2nd Cav. Co.E
Royall, Marcus A. TX Waul's Legion Co.E
Royall, Richard J. VA 38th Inf. Co.D
Royall, Richard Jesse VA 57th Inf. Co.F Sgt.Maj.
Royall, Richard Kendal VA 4th Cav. Co.B
Royall, Robert AR 4th Inf. Co.F
Royall, Robert R. VA 23rd Inf. Co.C
Royall, R.W. VA Lt.Arty. R.M. Anderson's Co.
Royall, S.H. VA 4th Cav. Co.E
Royall, T.F. MS Cav. Gartley's Co. (Yazoo Rangers)
Royall, Thomas E. VA Lt.Arty. Parker's Co. Sgt.
Royall, Thos. H. VA Arty. (Loc.Def. & Sp.Serv.) Lanier's Co.
Royall, Thomas H. VA 18th Inf. Co.B QMSgt.
Royall, Thos. H. Gen. & Staff 2nd Lt.,Dr.M.
Royall, T.J. TX 12th Cav. Co.D
Royall, T.M. VA Lt.Arty. Parker's Co.
Royall, W. GA 4th (Clinch's) Cav. Co.E
Royall, W.A.H. GA Arty. St.Troops Pruden's Btty.
Royall, W.B. NC 55th Inf. Co.I Comsy.Sgt.
Royall, W.B. SC Lt.Arty. Gaillard's Co. (Santee Lt.Arty.) Cpl.
Royall, W.B. TX 20th Inf. Co.B
Royall, W.H. AL 45th Inf. Co.B
Royall, William AR 4th Inf. Co.F
Royall, William NC Cav. Co.H
Royall, William SC Manigault's Bn.Vol. Co.B
Royall, William Gen. & Staff Chap.
Royall, William H. VA 41st Inf. 2nd Co.E
Royall, William L. VA 9th Cav. Co.A
Royall, William P. VA 23rd Inf. Co.C
Royall, William S. GA 5th Cav. Co.C
Royall, William S. NC 27th Inf. Co.A Sgt.
Royall, William W. GA Inf. Taylor's Co.
Royall, William W. TX 18th Cav. Co.K
Royall, W.S.A. VA Inf. 4th Bn.Loc.Def. Co.F
Royals, Adam NC 2nd Cav. (19th St.Troops) Co.F
Royals, A.H. NC Conscr.
Royals, Alexander FL 5th Inf. Co.F
Royals, Asa SC 7th Cav. Co.F
Royals, Asa SC Cav. Tucker's Co.
Royals, Benjamin B. AL Arty. 1st Bn. Co.F Cpl.
Royals, C.H. MS 44th Inf. Co.G
Royals, Charles H. AL Inf. 1st Regt. Co.K Sgt.
Royals, Daniel GA 61st Inf. Co.C 1st Lt.
Royals, Daniel A. SC 1st (McCreary's) Inf. Co.F
Royals, General H. AL Inf. 1st Regt. Co.K Cpl.
Royals, George L. SC 1st (McCreary's) Inf. Co.F
Royals, G.H. AL 21st Inf. Co.E Sgt.
Royals, Hardy GA 5th Inf. (St.Guards) Allums' Co.

Royals, Hardy NC Mil. Clark's Sp.Bn. D.N. Bridgers' Co.
Royals, Isaac GA 61st Inf. Co.C
Royals, J. GA 32nd Inf. Co.K
Royals, James GA 5th Inf. (St.Guards) Allums' Co.
Royals, J.C. GA 55th Inf. Co.C
Royals, J.M. AL 21st Inf. Co.D
Royals, John GA 10th Inf. Co.C
Royals, John A. 7th Conf.Cav. Co.F
Royals, John A. 8th (Dearing's) Conf.Cav. Co.G
Royals, John B. GA 59th Inf. Co.F
Royals, John C. GA Siege Arty. 28th Bn. Co.H
Royals, Joseph GA Siege Arty. 28th Bn. Co.A
Royals, J.P. GA 12th Inf. Co.F
Royals, J.R. MS 37th Inf. Co.G
Royals, J.W. SC 26th Inf. Co.A
Royals, L.G. MS 16th Inf. Co.H
Royals, M. MS 36th Inf. Co.F
Royals, Peleg GA 55th Inf. Co.C
Royals, R. MS 3rd (St.Troops) Cav. Co.K
Royals, R.K. MS 16th Inf. Co.H
Royals, Robert D. NC 51st Inf. Co.I
Royals, Walter D. MS 16th Inf. Co.H
Royals, W.H.H. MS 1st Cav. Co.C
Royals, William FL 6th Inf. Co.I,E
Royals, William B. GA 64th Inf. Co.H
Royals, William B. NC 24th Inf. Co.I Cpl.
Royals, William R. SC 1st (McCreary's) Inf. Co.F
Royals, William W. SC 26th Inf. Co.A
Royals, Z. MS 16th Inf. Co.H
Royalston, W.A. GA 4th Inf. Co.B
Royalty, George W. VA 34th Inf. Co.H
Royalty, James H. VA Hvy.Arty. 20th Bn. Co.D
Royalty, John W. VA 34th Inf. Co.H
Royalty, T. VA Conscr.
Royalty, Theodore VA Lt.Arty. 13th Bn. Co.C
Royce, A.J. KY 5th Mtd.Inf. Co.C,E
Royce, A.W.W. 1st Creek Mtd.Vol. 2nd Co.D
Royce, Isaac E. TX St.Mil. Hunter's Regt.
Royce, John VA 5th Inf. Co.A
Royce, John T. VA 21st Inf. Co.D
Royce, M.S. TN Starnes' Escort Capt.
Royce, William VA 11th Cav. Co.A
Royce, William VA 89th Mil. Co.A
Roycraft, John C. MS Lt.Arty. Stanford's Co.
Roycroft, Anson C. AL 41st Inf. Co.A 2nd Lt.
Roycroft, C.C. TX Cav. 2nd Regt.St.Troops Co.F
Roycroft, H.D. AL St.Res. Palmer's Co. Cpl.
Roycroft, J.A.J. GA Cav. 22nd Bn. (St.Guards) Co.I
Roycroft, J.A.J. GA 60th Inf. Co.G
Roycroft, James M. AL Lt.Arty. Phelan's Co.
Roycroft, N.W. AR 1st (Dobbin's) Cav. Co.A
Roycroft, Robert Wesley TN 13th Inf. Co.K Cpl.
Royde, S.C. LA 27th Inf. Co.K
Royder, Adam TX 20th Inf. Co.C
Royds, William GA Lt.Arty. Milledge's Co.
Royds, William GA 3rd Inf. 1st Co.I
Roye, A. LA Lt.Arty. 2nd Field Btty.
Roye, David LA 3rd (Harrison's) Cav. Co.K
Roye, E. LA Lt.Arty. 2nd Field Btty.
Roye, F. LA Lt.Arty. 2nd Field Btty.
Roye, F.L. NC 17th Inf. (1st Org.) Co.C

Roye, Henry J. AL 4th Inf. Co.B
Roye, Jacob TX 28th Cav. Co.L
Roye, John VA 10th Cav. Co.A Music.
Roye, Joseph G. MS 1st (Johnston's) Inf. Co.C
Roye, Joseph P. TX 5th Cav. Co.B
Roye, Lemuel AL 4th Inf. Co.B
Roye, Samuel VA 16th Cav.
Royel, A.J. TX 8th Cav. Co.A
Royell, W.S. TN 3rd (Forrest's) Cav. 1st Co.B
Royels, William TN Arty. Co.C
Royer, Adison VA 9th Bn.Res. Co.B,A Cpl.
Royer, A.J. TN 13th Inf. Co.F
Royer, Auguste LA 18th Inf. Co.G
Royer, Auguste LA Inf.Cons. 18th Regt. & Yellow Jacket Bn. Co.F
Royer, Aurelien LA 18th Inf. Co.G
Royer, Charles E. LA Dreux's Cav. Co.A
Royer, Claude LA Mil. 3rd Regt. French Brig. Co.1
Royer, David VA Conscr.
Royer, E. VA 9th Bn.Res. Co.C Sgt.
Royer, Eli LA 2nd Cav. Co.A
Royer, Emanuel VA 58th Mil. Co.F
Royer, J. LA Inf. 10th Bn. Co.G Cpl.
Royer, James VA 6th Cav. Co.C
Royer, John VA Cav. McNeill's Co.
Royer, John H. VA 1st Cav. 1st Co.K Sgt.
Royer, John H. VA 6th Cav. Co.C 1st Lt.
Royer, Joseph L. VA 10th Inf. Co.E
Royer, Joseph R. VA 7th Bn.Res. Co.A Sgt.
Royer, Julis TX 18th Cav. Co.C
Royer, L. LA Mil. Mooney's Co. (Saddlers Guards)
Royer, Noah VA 58th Mil. Co.B
Royer, Noah A. VA 10th Inf. Co.E
Royer, Volentine LA 2nd Cav. Co.A
Royes, M. LA Mil.Cont.Cadets
Royes, William NC 15th Inf. Co.B
Royet, C. LA Inf. 10th Bn.
Royiston, S.W. GA 54th Inf. Co.H
Roylds, Davis AL 45th Inf. Co.F
Roylds, Ethel AL 45th Inf. Co.F
Royle, Dan Rip TN 15th (Stewart's) Cav. Co.G
Royle, T. NC 7th Sr.Res. Johnston's Co.
Royles, A.M. NC 32nd Inf. Co.H
Royles, John GA 17th Inf. Co.C
Royls, Thomas A. SC 10th Inf. 2nd Co.G
Royn, Y. AL 44th Inf. Co.C
Royne, L.B. GA 39th Inf. Chap.
Royne, Robert LA 26th Inf. Co.D
Roys, W. Henry H. TN 1st (Feilds's) Inf. Co.A
Roysdon, A.W. LA 3rd Inf. Co.K
Royse, Albert MO 9th Inf. Co.I
Royse, Burgess G. MO Inf. 8th Bn. Co.E
Royse, Burgess G. MO 9th Inf. Co.I
Royse, Campbell KY 2nd Bn.Mtd.Rifles Co.A
Royse, Campbell KY 5th Mtd.Inf. Co.H
Royse, James F. KY 9th Cav. Co.B Sgt.
Royse, Southwell MS 28th Cav. Co.G
Royse, Southwell MS 10th Inf. Old Co.I
Royster, --- VA 1st Bn.Res. Co.H
Royster, --- VA VMI Co.A,B Sgt.
Royster, A.D. NC 47th Inf. Co.H 1st Sgt.
Royster, Amos B. NC 47th Inf. Co.H Cpl.
Royster, A.S. VA 11th Cav.
Royster, Charles TN 17th Inf. Co.F
Royster, Charles E. TN 23rd Inf. 2nd Co.A Sgt.

Royster, Charles E. TN 24th Inf. 2nd Co.H, Co.M
Royster, Clark VA 14th Inf. Co.F
Royster, C.M. VA 1st (Farinholt's) Res. Co.E
Royster, David W. NC 14th Inf. Co.K
Royster, D.R. TN 13th Inf. Co.H
Royster, E.D. TN 11th (Holman's) Cav. Co.C
Royster, E.D. TN 17th Inf. Co.F
Royster, Elmus GA 44th Inf. Co.C
Royster, F.M. 3rd Conf.Cav. Co.H
Royster, George D. VA 20th Inf. Co.K
Royster, George D. VA 59th Inf. 3rd Co.C
Royster, George W. NC 55th Inf. Co.K
Royster, Granville VA 38th Inf. Co.F Cpl.
Royster, G.W. NC 12th Inf. Co.D
Royster, H. NC Lt.Arty. Thomas' Legion Levi's Btty.
Royster, H.T. NC 1st Cav. (9th St.Troops) Co.E Cpl.
Royster, Hunter NC Lt.Arty. Thomas' Legion Levi's Btty.
Royster, Hunter VA Lt.Arty. Jackson's Bn. St.Line Co.A
Royster, I.M. NC 1st Cav. (9th St.Troops) Co.E Sgt.
Royster, Iowa NC 37th Inf. Co.G 2nd Lt.
Royster, Ira E. TN 7th Inf. Co.B
Royster, J.A.G. MS 1st Cav. Co.B
Royster, James AL Randolph Cty.Res. A.P. Hunter's Co.
Royster, Jas. AL Cp. of Instr. Talladega
Royster, James NC 12th Inf. Co.B,D
Royster, James VA Lt.Arty. B.Z. Price's Co. Cpl.
Royster, James A. VA 1st Inf. Co.G
Royster, James B. VA 1st St.Res. Co.D
Royster, James E. GA 44th Inf. Co.C
Royster, James H. NC 38th Inf. Co.I Sgt.
Royster, James M. NC 14th Inf. Co.E 2nd Lt.
Royster, James M. NC 47th Inf. Co.C
Royster, Jay Conf.Cav. Wood's Regt. Co.K
Royster, J.C. AR 18th (Marmaduke's) Inf. Co.C
Royster, J.J. VA 3rd Cav. Co.F Sgt.
Royster, J.L. VA 34th Inf. Co.B
Royster, John MS 1st Cav. Co.B
Royster, John VA Inf. 25th Bn. Co.A
Royster, John P. NC 35th Inf. Co.E
Royster, Joseph VA Lt.Arty. B.Z. Price's Co.
Royster, J.W. TN 11th (Holman's) Cav. Co.C
Royster, L. VA VMI Co.B Sgt.
Royster, L. Conf.Inf. Tucker's Regt. Co.H 2nd Lt.
Royster, Lawrence VA Cav. Mosby's Regt. (Part.Rangers) Co.G
Royster, Lawrence VA 1st Inf. Co.A
Royster, Lawrence VA 12th Inf. Co.G
Royster, Littleton VA 3rd Cav. Co.F Cpl.
Royster, Littleton VA 24th Cav. Co.C
Royster, M. TN 12th Inf. Co.D
Royster, M. TN 12th (Cons.) Inf. Co.E
Royster, M.D. NC 23rd Inf. Co.I
Royster, Norborne L. VA 1st Inf. Co.G
Royster, Parker C. VA 1st St.Res. Co.K
Royster, P.C. VA Cav. 1st Bn. Co.C
Royster, R.D. NC 35th Inf. Co.E 2nd Lt.
Royster, Reuben M. NC 55th Inf. Co.K 2nd Lt.
Royster, Robert D. NC 24th Inf. Co.H Cpl.

Royster, Robert D. NC 55th Inf. Co.K
Royster, S. NC 50th Inf. Co.A
Royster, T.E. KY 8th Cav. Co.H
Royster, T.F. LA 4th Inf. Co.K
Royster, Thomas KY 1st (Butler's) Cav. Co.A
Royster, Thomas VA Lt.Arty. B.Z. Price's Co.
Royster, Thomas D. NC 12th Inf. Co.B,D
Royster, Thomas E. KY 4th Mtd.Inf. Co.B
Royster, Thomas E. MS Lt.Arty. (Issaquena
    Arty.) Graves' Co.
Royster, Thomas J. LA 21st (Patton's) Inf. Co.H
    2nd Lt.
Royster, Thomas J. Sap. & Min.,CSA 2nd Lt.
Royster, Thomas M. AR 36th Inf. Co.A
Royster, T.J. LA 22nd (Cons.) Inf. Co.K 1st Lt.
Royster, W. TN 15th (Stewart's) Cav. Co.D Sgt.
Royster, W.B. NC 1st Jr.Res. Co.B Cpl.
Royster, W.G. NC 35th Inf. Co.E
Royster, William LA 17th Inf. Co.A
Royster, William VA 3rd Inf.Loc.Def. 1st Co.G
Royster, William A. MD Cav. 2nd Bn. Co.B
Royster, William B. NC 56th Inf. Co.C Music.
Royster, William B. VA Inf. Cohoon's Bn. Co.A
    Cpl.
Royster, William David NC 12th Inf. Co.D,B
Royster, William E. NC 55th Inf. Co.K Cpl.
Royster, William G. MS Cav. 1st Bn. (Miller's)
    Bowles' Co.
Royster, William H. TN 14th (Neely's) Cav.
    Co.I
Royster, William H. VA 3rd Cav. Co.A
Royster, William J. VA 59th Mil. Riddick's Co.
Royster, William L. NC 44th Inf. Co.A
Royster, William S. VA 14th Inf. Co.I
Royster, William S. VA Inf. 25th Bn. Co.A
Royster, Willis NC 23rd Inf. Co.I
Royster, Willis T. NC 24th Inf. Co.A
Royston, --- 8th (Wade's) Conf.Cav. Co.K
Royston, Benjamin AL 61st Inf. Co.F
Royston, C.B. AL 14th Inf. Co.D
Royston, C.B. Gen. & Staff 2nd Lt.,ADC
Royston, C.W. LA Inf. 11th Bn. Co.B
Royston, Elcany TN 61st Mtd.Inf. Co.K
Royston, George R. VA 1st Cav. 1st Co.D
Royston, George R. VA 6th Cav. Co.D
Royston, George W. SC 5th St.Troops Co.F
Royston, G.W. SC 5th Inf. 1st Co.C, 2nd Co.K
    Sgt.
Royston, G.W. SC 7th Res. Co.M Sgt.
Royston, James TN 61st Mtd.Inf. Co.H Sgt.
Royston, James W. VA Cav. Mosby's Regt.
    (Part.Rangers) Co.F
Royston, J.D. TN 61st Mtd.Inf. Co.H Sgt.
Royston, J.M. TX 17th Inf. Co.F
Royston, Joel E. SC 5th Inf. 2nd Co.K
Royston, John C. LA 12th Inf. 1st Co.M
Royston, John R. VA Cav. O'Ferrall's Bn. Co.B
Royston, John W. VA Cav. Mosby's Regt. (Part.
    Rangers) Co.G
Royston, Jo. M. TX 8th Cav. Co.D
Royston, Joseph AL 61st Inf. Co.F
Royston, Joseph LA Arty. Green's Co. (LA
    Guard Btty.)
Royston, Joseph LA 1st (Nelligan's) Inf. Co.K
Royston, Joseph TN 61st Mtd.Inf. Co.K
Royston, J.R. MO 6th Cav. Co.B
Royston, J.R. VA 23rd Cav. Co.D

Royston, J.W. KY 7th Cav. Co.E Cpl.
Royston, L.W. VA 8th Inf. Co.B
Royston, Martin H. TX 8th Cav. Co.K Adj.
Royston, Mathew VA 2nd Inf. Co.C
Royston, Mathew T. VA 11th Cav. Co.A
Royston, M.H. Gen. & Staff Maj.
Royston, P.K. VA 129th Mil. Co.E
Royston, R.C. TX 8th Cav. Co.D
Royston, Richard C. TX 36th Cav. Co.A
Royston, Robert Gen. & Staff Surg.
Royston, Robert T. AL 8th Inf. Co.A Surg.
Royston, Samuel TN 61st Mtd.Inf. Co.K Cpl.
Royston, Solomon W. GA 4th Bn.S.S. Co.C
    Sgt.
Royston, S.W. GA 37th Inf. Co.F
Royston, Theodore F. VA 7th Cav. Co.E
Royston, Thomas T. MS Hamer's Co. (Salem
    Cav.)
Royston, Thomas W. MO Cav. 2nd Regt.
    St.Guard Co.A Capt.
Royston, Thomas W. MO 10th Cav. Co.H
Royston, T.W. VA 5th Cav. Co.K
Royston, T.W. VA Loc.Def. Durrett's Co.
Royston, W.A. GA 3rd Cav. (St.Guards) Co.B
Royston, William SC 5th Inf. 1st Co.C, 2nd
    Co.K
Royston, William P. VA 2nd Inf. Co.C
Royston, W.V. TX 5th Inf. Co.I
Royston, Young L. AL 8th Inf. Co.A Col.
Royston, Zachariah VA 8th Inf. Co.B
Roza, Hardeman MS 10th Inf.
Rozals, R.K. MS 46th Inf. Co.G
Rozar, Benjamin GA 26th Inf. Co.B
Rozar, David GA 26th Inf. Co.B
Rozar, E.J. GA 6th Inf. (St.Guards) Co.A Sgt.
Rozar, I.J. GA Cav. 22nd Bn. (St.Guards) Co.G
    3rd Lt.
Rozar, James GA 26th Inf. Co.B
Rozar, James D. GA 26th Inf. Co.B
Rozar, John D. GA 49th Inf. Co.K
Rozar, Jonathan GA 26th Inf. Co.B
Rozar, Luke GA 26th Inf. Co.B
Rozar, Luke A. GA 26th Inf. Co.B
Rozar, Nelson GA 26th Inf. Co.B
Rozar, Robert GA Cav. 22nd Bn. (St.Guards)
    Co.G Cpl.
Rozar, Robert F. GA 49th Inf. Co.G Cpl.
Rozar, Shadrack GA 49th Inf. Co.K
Rozar, Wiley L. FL 5th Inf. Co.F
Rozar, William GA 49th Inf. Co.K
Rozar, William A. GA 49th Inf. Co.G
Rozar, William F. GA 49th Inf. Co.K
Rozar, William H. GA 5th Inf. Co.B
Roze, J. LA Mil. 3rd Regt.Eur.Brig. (Garde
    Francaise) Co.7
Roze, P.L. TN 62nd Mtd.Inf. Co.B
Rozel, Peter Cherokee Regt. Miller's Co.
Rozel, W.C. Cherokee Regt. Miller's Co.
Rozel, W.W. MS 27th Inf. Co.A
Rozell, A.B. AL Cav. Forrest's Regt.
Rozell, A.B. TN 18th (Newsom's) Cav. Co.F
Rozell, Ashley B. TN 1st (Feild's) Inf. Co.D
    Color Cpl.
Rozell, B.L. MS 3rd Regt. Col.
Rozell, G.W. TX 10th Cav. Co.B Bugler
Rozell, Jacob F.W. TX 15th Cav. Co.A
Rozell, James TX 10th Cav. Co.B Jr.2nd Lt.

Rozell, James TX 15th Cav. Co.A
Rozell, James P. TX 15th Cav. Co.B,A Cpl.
Rozell, John Conf.Cav. Clarkson's Bn. Ind.
    Rangers Co.C
Rozell, John W. AL Inf. 1st Regt. Co.D,G
Rozell, John W. TX 10th Cav. Co.B
Rozell, J.W. KY Cav. Jenkins' Co.
Rozell, Logan D. TN 1st Cav.
Rozell, Luther Calvin TX 20th Cav. Co.C
Rozell, Milton J. AL Inf. 1st Regt. Co.D
Rozell, Peter TX 10th Cav. Co.B
Rozell, R.B. TN Inf. 1st Cons.Regt. Co.H 1st
    Sgt.
Rozell, Ruford B. TN 1st (Feild's) Inf. Co.C 1st
    Sgt.
Rozell, Solomon B. TN 11th (Holman's) Cav.
    Co.I 2nd Lt.
Rozell, Solomon B. TN 1st (Feild's) Inf. Co.C
Rozell, S.R. TN Douglass' Bn.Part.Rangers Per-
    kins' Co. 2nd Lt.
Rozell, Stephen N. MO 1st & 4th Cons.Inf. Co.B
    Sgt.
Rozell, Stephen N. MO 4th Inf. Co.A,F 1st Sgt.
Rozell, William G. TX 15th Cav. Co.A
Rozell, W.W. TX 7th Inf. Co.A
Rozelle, --- TX Cav. Mann's Regt. Co.H
Rozelle, Newton MO 3rd Inf. Co.D
Rozenberger, F. MS 38th Cav. Co.D
Rozenburg, Charles AR 5th Inf. Co.A
Rozenburg, John AR 5th Inf. Co.A,C
Rozenburg, Louis AR 5th Inf. Co.A,C
Rozer, T. 10th Conf.Cav. Co.H
Rozier, Ad. LA Mil. 1st Regt. 3rd Brig. 1st Div.
    Co.A
Rozier, Adolphus GA 6th Inf. (St.Guards) Co.F
    Cpl.
Rozier, Amos L. NC 51st Inf. Co.D
Rozier, B.B. GA 5th Cav. Co.K Sgt.
Rozier, Benjamin B. GA Cav. 1st Bn. Hopkins'
    Co.
Rozier, C.H. FL 2nd Cav. Co.H
Rozier, C.H. FL Inf. 2nd Bn. Co.C
Rozier, Charles H. FL 1st Cav. Co.C
Rozier, Charles R. FL 1st Cav. Co.C
Rozier, David LA Hvy.Arty. 8th Bn. Co.3
Rozier, Earel L. MS 30th Inf. Co.K
Rozier, E.L. MS 3rd Cav. Co.A
Rozier, E.L. MS 24th Inf. Co.C
Rozier, Evander C. NC 51st Inf. Co.D
Rozier, H.D. NC Hvy.Arty. 1st Bn. Co.A
Rozier, Henient FL 11th Inf. Co.H
Rozier, Henry GA Cav. 1st Bn. Hopkins' Co.
Rozier, Henry GA 5th Cav. Co.K
Rozier, Isham GA Cav. 1st Bn. Hopkins' Co.
Rozier, Isham GA 5th Cav. Co.K
Rozier, Isham SC 3rd Cav. Co.K
Rozier, Isham SC Mtd.Mil. Johnson's Co.
Rozier, James SC 5th Res. Co.K
Rozier, James H. FL 1st Cav. Co.C
Rozier, James W. GA Lt.Arty. 14th Bn. Co.B
    Artif.
Rozier, J.C. SC 5th Res. Co.K
Rozier, J.C. SC Mil. 16th Regt. Sigwalds' Co.
Rozier, Joel GA 5th Cav. Co.K
Rozier, John SC 3rd Cav. Co.D
Rozier, John C. SC Arty.Bn. Hampton Legion
    Co.A

Rozier, John L.B. AL 17th Inf. Co.K
Rozier, Lewis M. GA 47th Inf. Co.B
Rozier, Luke GA Cav. 1st Bn. Hopkins' Co.
Rozier, Luke GA 5th Cav. Co.K
Rozier, Meada GA Cav. 19th Bn. Co.C
Rozier, Meada 10th Conf.Cav. Co.H
Rozier, Meady GA Lt.Arty. Anderson's Btty.
Rozier, Milby NC 31st Inf. Co.A
Rozier, Nat GA 5th Cav. Co.K
Rozier, Nathaniel GA Cav. 1st Bn. Hopkins' Co.
Rozier, Nathaniel KY 4th Cav. Co.G
Rozier, N. Russel NC 51st Inf. Co.A
Rozier, Oliver NC 51st Inf. Co.A
Rozier, Reuben NC 3rd Arty. (40th St.Troops)
    Co.K
Rozier, Reuben 1st Conf.Inf. Co.A
Rozier, Robert A. NC 51st Inf. Co.D
Rozier, Robert S. GA Inf. 3rd Bn. Co.G Cpl.
Rozier, Robert S. GA 4th Bn.S.S. Co.A Cpl.
Rozier, Samuel GA Cav. 1st Bn. Hopkins' Co.
Rozier, Solomon J. FL 1st Cav. Co.C
Rozier, Theophilus GA Cav. 19th Bn. Co.C
Rozier, William D. TN 41st Inf. Co.K
Rozier, Williamson MS 5th Cav. Co.C
Rozillio, E. LA 3rd Inf. Co.I
Rozin, Gustave LA Pointe Coupee Arty.
Rozin, L.M. GA 1st Reg. Co.F
Rozles, Wiley N. GA 17th Inf. Co.C Cpl.
Rozzell, James A. NC 20th Inf. Surg.
Rozzell, James M. AL 3rd Res. Co.I
Rozzell, James T. NC 11th (Bethel Regt.) Inf.
    Co.E Sgt.
Rozzell, J.T. NC 1st Inf. (6 mo. '61) Co.B
Rozzell, W.F. NC 1st Inf. (6 mo. '61) Co.B
Rozzell, William F. NC 11th (Bethel Regt.) Inf.
    Co.E Ord.Sgt.
Rozzelle, M. KY 9th Cav. Co.A
Rozzelle, William J. AL 19th Inf. Co.A,B 2nd
    Lt.
Rozzer, J.T. AL 10th Cav. Co.K Capt.
Rrollan, J.D. MO Cav. Coleman's Regt. Co.A
Rualcada, Antonio TX 3rd Inf. 1st Co.A
Ruallo, C. KY 8th Mtd.Inf. Co.C
Ruan, William R. FL Lt.Arty. Abell's Co. 1st
    Sgt.
Ruan, William R. FL Milton Lt.Arty. Dunham's
    Co. Sgt.
Ruane, Anthony 1st Conf.Inf. 2nd Co.G
Ruark, Edward R. NC 30th Inf. Co.C 2nd Lt.
Ruark, Joel J. GA 7th Cav. Co.F Cpl.
Ruark, John H. NC 2nd Bn.Loc.Def.Troops
    Co.D Sgt.
Ruark, John H. NC Wallace's Co. (Wilmington
    RR Guard)
Ruark, Robert M. NC Coast Guards Galloway's
    Co.
Ruark, S. LA 27th Inf. Co.F
Ruark, Samuel B. LA 28th (Gray's) Inf. Co.K
Ruark, T.J. GA Conscr.
Ruark, W.A. TX 5th Inf. Co.E
Ruarks, William C. GA Cobb's Legion Co.G
Rub, G. LA Mil.Squad. Guides d'Orleans
    Cavalier
Rub, George 4th Conf.Eng.Troops Co.E Cpl.
Rub, George Kellersberg's Corps Sap. & Min.
    Cpl.

Rub, Louis M. LA Arty. Kean's Btty. (Orleans
    Ind.Arty.) 1st Lt.
Ruba, John NC 17th Inf. (2nd Org.) Co.E
Ruba, John C. NC 42nd Inf. Co.G
Ruban, Thomas AL 95th Mil. Co.D
Ruban, W. MS 32nd Inf. Co.K Cpl.
Rubbottom, Thomas P. MO 15th Cav. Co.M
Rubel, Emanuel MS 19th Inf. Co.D
Rubel, Joseph VA 22nd Cav. Co.C
Ruben, John SC Arty. Bachman's Co. (German
    Lt.Arty.)
Ruben, John SC Arty.Bn. Hampton Legion Co.B
Ruben, W.L. VA 1st Inf.
Rubens, Joseph SC 1st Arty. Co.B
Rubenstein, Alex VA 2nd St.Res. Co.L
Rubenstein, Julius VA 2nd St.Res. Co.L
Rubenthall, Henry VA 89th Mil. Co.B
Ruber, Frank LA Mil. 4th Regt. 2nd Brig. 1st
    Div. Co.H
Rubert, --- LA C.S. Zouave Bn. Co.C
Rubey, Charles MS 25th Inf. Co.D
Rubey, Conrad AL 50th Inf. Co.C Music.
Rubic, Gus LA 30th Inf. Co.A
Rubin, F. LA Mil. Mech.Guard
Rubio, Adriano TX Cav. Benavides' Regt. Co.C
Rubio, Adriano TX 8th Inf. Co.C
Rubio, Francisco TX 2nd Cav. Co.B
Rubio, Francisco TX Cav. Benavides' Regt.
    Co.F
Rubio, Juan TX 8th Inf. Co.E
Rubio, Manuel LA Mil. 5th Regt.Eur.Brig.
    (Spanish Regt.) Co.3 Sgt.
Rubio, Miguel LA Miles' Legion Co.H
Rubio, Salama TX 33rd Cav. 1st Co.H
Rubira, P. LA Mil. 5th Regt.Eur.Brig. (Spanish
    Regt.) Co.1
Rubitshek, I. GA 1st Mil.
Rublddys, L.M. AL 62nd Inf. Co.A
Ruble, Christopher VA 22nd Cav. Co.F
Ruble, H.C. MS 37th Inf. Co.H 1st Sgt.
Ruble, J.A. TN Lt.Arty. Barry's Co.
Ruble, Jacob LA 5th Inf. Co.G
Ruble, Jacob NC 3rd Inf. Co.A
Ruble, James VA 11th Bn.Res. Co.B
Ruble, James VA Mil. Washington Cty.
Ruble, John J. TX 14th Cav. Co.A
Ruble, John M. TN 25th Inf. Co.B
Ruble, John M. VA 14th Cav. Crawford's Co.
Ruble, John M. VA 17th Cav. Co.F
Ruble, J.O.R. AR Cav. Harrell's Bn. Co.D
Ruble, J.O.R. AR 27th Inf. Old Co.C Capt.
Ruble, Lewis LA 1st (Strawbridge's) Inf. Co.D
Ruble, M.A. VA Cav. Caldwell's Bn. Graham's
    Co.
Ruble, Martin VA 136th Mil. Co.C
Ruble, Oliver H.P. TX 30th Cav. Co.I Sgt.
Ruble, V.E. AR 27th Inf. Old Co.C, Co.D Sgt.
Ruble, W.H.H. TN Inf. 22nd Bn. Co.G
Ruble, William VA 6th Bn.Res. Co.B
Rubler, J. MS 1st Lt.Arty. Co.A
Rublert, Eugene Conf.Inf. Tucker's Regt. Co.K
Rubles, F. TX 1st Hvy.Arty. Co.K
Rubles, John AZ Cav. Herbert's Bn. Oury's Co.
Rubles, W.L. MS 29th Inf. Co.I
Rubottom, John AR Cav. Crabtree's (46th) Regt.
    Co.B
Rubottom, J.R. AR 2nd Inf. Co.K

Rubottom, J.W. AR 30th Inf. Co.K
Rubottom, Lafayette MO 15th Cav. Co.A,M 1st
    Lt.
Rubottom, Lafayette MO 12th Inf. Co.E
Rubottom, T.S. AR 8th Inf. New Co.C
Rubracht, Antonio TX Cav. Martin's Regt. Co.D
Rubush, Abraham C. VA 5th Inf. Co.E,H
Rubush, Christian VA 5th Inf. Co.E 1st Sgt.
Rubush, John C. VA 5th Inf. Co.E
Rubush, Matthew H. VA 5th Inf. Co.E
Rubush, Samuel J. VA 37th Inf. Co.D
Rubush, Silas VA 14th Cav. Co.I
Rubush, William H. VA 5th Inf. Co.I
Ruby, --- TX 8th Field Btty.
Ruby, --- TX Lt.Arty. Dege's Bn.
Ruby, Benjamin VA 14th Inf. Co.A
Ruby, Charles AL 56th Vol. Co.G
Ruby, Charles MO 2nd Inf.
Ruby, Charles 2nd Conf.Inf. Co.D
Ruby, Charles W. MS 42nd Inf. Co.D
Ruby, Conrad AL 11th Cav. Co.A
Ruby, Conrad Conf.Cav. Baxter's Bn. 2nd Co.B
Ruby, David TX 17th Inf. Co.K
Ruby, D.T. MO 11th Inf. Co.D
Ruby, Ed L. VA 16th Cav. Co.K
Ruby, Ed L. VA Inf. 26th Bn. Co.B 2nd Lt.
Ruby, Edward VA 22nd Inf. Co.H
Ruby, E.L. TX 4th Cav. Co.K
Ruby, G. TX 20th Inf. Co.C,A
Ruby, Henry Conf.Cav. 6th Bn. Co.E
Ruby, J.H. VA 11th Cav. Co.G
Ruby, John VA 136th Mil. Co.G Sgt.
Ruby, John C. VA 12th Cav. Co.K
Ruby, John C. VA 22nd Inf. Co.H ACS
Ruby, Jno. C. Gen. & Staff Capt.,ACS
Ruby, Joseph H. VA 12th Cav. Co.K
Ruby, Joseph H. VA 33rd Inf. Co.G
Ruby, J.R. MS 9th Inf. New Co.A
Ruby, J.W. TX 4th Cav. Co.K
Ruby, Matthew MO 15th Cav. Co.C
Ruby, M.S. AR 8th Cav. Co.I Sgt.
Ruby, Robert VA 146th Mil. Co.E
Ruby, Robert C. VA Lt.Arty. B.Z. Price's Co.
Ruby, Thomas VA 58th Inf. Co.K
Ruby, William KY 7th Cav. Co.D
Ruby, William H. VA 7th Cav. Co.C
Ruby, William H. VA 12th Cav. Co.K
Ruby, William Homer VA 136th Mil. Co.G
Ruby, William T. TX 36th Cav. Co.A
Rucempt, W.B. Gen. & Staff Asst.Surg.
Ruch, A.A. LA Lt.Arty. LeGardeur, Jr.'s Co.
    (Orleans Guard Btty.) Cpl.
Ruch, A.A. MO Lt.Arty. Barret's Co.
Ruch, J. AL Mil. Gueringer's Co.
Ruch, Phillip LA 20th Inf. Co.A
Ruche, --- LA Mil. 1st Chasseurs a pied Co.1
Rucher, G.W. VA 4th Res. Co.A
Rucher, J.R. KY 1st (Butler's) Cav.
Rucher, J.T. LA 4th Cav. Co.K
Ruck, F. SC 1st Regt. Charleston Guard Co.G
Ruck, J.C. MS 4th Cav. Co.H
Ruck, J.C. MS Cav. Hughes' Bn. Co.B
Ruck, S.W. SC Mil.Arty. 1st Regt. Co.A
Ruck, W. AL 47th Inf. Co.B
Rucker, --- TX Cav. Border's Regt. Co.A
Rucker, Abbott C. MS 2nd Inf. Co.F 2nd Lt.

Rucker, Abbott C. MS 2nd (Davidson's) Inf.
  Co.C Capt.
Rucker, Abe KY 8th Cav. Co.C
Rucker, Abner TN 37th Inf. Co.K
Rucker, A.C. MS 34th Inf. Co.B Capt.
Rucker, A.C. Gen. & Staff Dr.M.
Rucker, A.D. TN 20th Inf. Co.D 2nd Lt.
Rucker, A.E. SC 1st (Hagood's) Inf. 1st Co.B
Rucker, A.E. SC 20th Inf. Co.D
Rucker, A.J. AR 12th Inf. Co.E
Rucker, A.J. TX 15th Cav. Co.K 1st Lt.
Rucker, A.L. NC 62nd Inf. Co.F Hosp.Stew.
Rucker, Alexander GA 15th Inf. Co.I
Rucker, Alexander C. TN 2nd (Robison's) Inf.
  Co.K
Rucker, Alexander R. GA Cobb's Legion Co.A
  2nd Lt.
Rucker, Alfred TX 12th Cav. Co.E
Rucker, Alfred R. VA 14th Inf. Co.A
Rucker, Ambrose VA 46th Inf. Co.C
Rucker, Ambrose 1st Chickasaw Inf. Milam's Co.
Rucker, A.M.D. VA 28th Inf. Co.F
Rucker, Armer GA 4th Cav. (St.Guards)
  McDonald's Co.
Rucker, Armor M. GA 24th Inf. Co.A,K 1st
  Sgt.
Rucker, Andrew J. VA Inf. 26th Bn. Co.E
Rucker, Andrew J. VA 28th Inf. Co.D
Rucker, Arthur A. GA 14th Inf. Co.A
Rucker, Atterson W. MO 16th Inf.
Rucker, A.W. AL 15th Bn.Part.Rangers Co.A
Rucker, A.W. AL 56th Part.Rangers Co.A
Rucker, Ballard VA 62nd Mtd.Inf. 2nd Co.A
  Color Cpl.
Rucker, Benjamin TN 9th (Ward's) Cav. Co.G
Rucker, Benjamin TN 21st (Carter's) Cav. Co.A
Rucker, Benjamin L. VA 19th Inf. Co.H
Rucker, Burton GA 13th Cav. Co.G
Rucker, Calvin MS 1st Lt.Arty. Co.L,C
Rucker, Caswell GA 1st (Fannin's) Res. Co.B
Rucker, C.C., Jr. MS 7th Cav. Co.B
Rucker, C.D. VA 1st Cav. Co.A
Rucker, C.H. VA 3rd Res. Co.A 1st Lt.
Rucker, C.H. VA 11th Inf. Co.A
Rucker, Charles KY 6th Mtd.Inf. Co.H Music.
Rucker, Christian VA Cav. 36th Bn. Co.E
Rucker, Clifton H. VA 16th Inf. Co.I Sgt.
Rucker, C.N. AR 10th Inf. Co.D
Rucker, Daniel B. KY 4th Mtd.Inf. Co.F
Rucker, David MO 1st Brig.St.Guard
Rucker, David B.F. MS 18th Inf. Co.A
Rucker, D.B. KY 3rd Mtd.Inf. Co.C
Rucker, D.J. SC Cav.Bn. Holcombe Legion
  Co.B
Rucker, D.O. TN 45th Inf. Co.G
Rucker, E. MS Lt.Arty. (Warren Lt.Arty.)
  Swett's Co.
Rucker, Ed TX 21st Cav. Co.F
Rucker, Edmond T. TX 10th Inf. Co.G Sgt.
Rucker, Edmund W. Rucker's Brig. Brig.Gen.
Rucker, Ed. T. MS S.W. Red's Co. (St.Troops)
  Cpl.
Rucker, Edward MO 5th Cav. Co.D
Rucker, Edward MO 10th Cav. Co.A
Rucker, Edward L. VA 2nd Cav. Co.E
Rucker, Edward P. VA 11th Inf. Co.A
Rucker, E.H. MS 1st Cav.Res. Co.G

Rucker, E.M. GA 3rd Mil. Co.K
Rucker, Enoch A. GA 24th Inf. Co.A Sgt.
Rucker, E.T. MS 12th Cav. Co.E
Rucker, E.W. TN Cav. 16th Bn. (Neal's) Maj.
Rucker, E.W. TN 1st Hvy.Arty. 2nd Co.D
  Capt.
Rucker, E.W. TN Eng.Corps 1st Lt.
Rucker, E.W. Sap. & Min. Flynn's Co.,CSA 2nd
  Lt.
Rucker, F.M. MS 2nd (Davidson's) Inf. Co.H
Rucker, F.P. AL 15th Inf. Co.A
Rucker, Franklin AR 1st (Crawford's) Cav. Co.B
Rucker, Franklin VA 97th Mil. Co.H 1st Sgt.
Rucker, F.S. GA Arty. St.Troops Pruden's Btty.
  Orderly Sgt.
Rucker, F.S. GA 5th Inf. (St.Guards) Rucker's
  Co. Capt.
Rucker, G. KY 3rd Cav. Co.D
Rucker, G.A. TX Cav. Hardeman's Regt. Co.D
Rucker, G.A. VA Wade's Regt.Loc.Def. Co.A
Rucker, George AL 27th Inf. Co.K Sgt.
Rucker, George KY 1st (Butler's) Cav. Co.E
Rucker, George A. VA 24th Inf. Co.D
Rucker, George E. GA 8th Inf. (St.Guards) Co.F
  Capt.
Rucker, George G. TX 17th Inf. Co.C 2nd Lt.
Rucker, George M. GA 22nd Inf. Co.E
Rucker, George M. TX 19th Cav. Co.E
Rucker, George M. VA 3rd Res.
Rucker, George W. TX 10th Inf. Co.B
Rucker, George W. VA 11th Inf. Co.H
Rucker, Gerhard SC 1st (Hagood's) Inf. 1st
  Co.B, 2nd Co.B
Rucker, G.F. TX 24th Cav. Co.E
Rucker, G.G. GA 2nd Inf. Co.G
Rucker, Godfrey J. VA 2nd Cav. Co.E
Rucker, G.W. TN 31st Inf. Co.K
Rucker, G.W. TX 24th Cav. Co.E
Rucker, H.C. MS 1st (Percy's) Inf. Co.B
Rucker, Henry AL 4th Inf. Co.C
Rucker, Henry T. MS 23rd Inf. Co.G
Rucker, H.L. SC 1st (Hagood's) Inf. 1st Co.B,
  2nd Co.B
Rucker, H.L. SC 25th Inf. Co.F
Rucker, Houston VA 2nd Cav. Co.I
Rucker, Houston VA 3rd Cav. Co.G
Rucker, Houston VA Horse Arty. Shoemaker's
  Co.
Rucker, H.P. KY 12th Cav. Co.A,B
Rucker, H.T. GA Arty. St.Troops Pruden's Btty.
Rucker, H.W. KY Fields' Co. (Part.Rangers)
Rucker, Hymen K. NC 16th Inf. Co.I Sgt.
Rucker, I.C. Sig.Corps,CSA
Rucker, I.M. Gillum's Regt. Co.H Capt.
Rucker, Isaac TN 45th Inf. Co.C
Rucker, Isaac Henry VA 2nd Cav. Co.E
Rucker, Isaac W. VA Lt.Arty. Kirkpatrick's Co.
Rucker, J. LA 2nd Cav. Co.E
Rucker, J.A. KY 7th Mtd.Inf. Co.H Lt.
Rucker, J.A. TX 12th Inf. Co.C
Rucker, Jackson VA 11th Inf. Co.E Cpl.
Rucker, James AL 25th Inf. Co.K
Rucker, James FL 7th Inf. Co.C
Rucker, James KY 8th Cav. Co.C
Rucker, James MO 5th Cav. Co.D
Rucker, James TX 23rd Cav. Co.E 1st Lt.
Rucker, James 1st Chickasaw Inf. Milam's Co.

Rucker, James A. GA 6th Inf. Co.G 1st Sgt.
Rucker, James A. VA 51st Inf. Co.G
Rucker, James E. MO 10th Cav. Co.A
Rucker, James E. TX 14th Cav. Co.B Capt.
Rucker, James E. TX 9th Bn.Res.Corps Co.L
  Capt.
Rucker, James F. MO 10th Cav. Co.K
Rucker, James G. VA 2nd Cav. Co.B
Rucker, James G. VA Horse Arty. Shoemaker's
  Co.
Rucker, James H. LA 31st Inf. Co.A
Rucker, James H. TX 10th Cav. Co.C Capt.
Rucker, James K.P. MS 23rd Inf. Co.C Cpl.
Rucker, James L. NC 16th Inf. Co.D Asst.Surg.
Rucker, Jas. L. Gen. & Staff Asst.Surg.
Rucker, James M. TX 24th Cav. Co.E Sgt.
Rucker, James R. GA Cav. 1st Bn.Res. McKin-
  ney's Co.
Rucker, James S. VA Horse Arty. Shoemaker's
  Co.
Rucker, James T. GA 37th Inf. Co.G
Rucker, J.B. LA 17th Inf. Co.I
Rucker, J.C. Sig.Corps,CSA
Rucker, J.E. TN 11th (Holman's) Cav. Co.B
  Cpl.
Rucker, J.E. TN Holman's Bn.Part.Rangers
  Co.A Cpl.
Rucker, J.E. TX 20th Inf. Co.C,B
Rucker, Jeremiah T. TX 10th Inf. Co.K
Rucker, Jerry MO Staff St.Guard Wagon M.
Rucker, Jesse TN 36th Inf. Co.F Sgt.
Rucker, Jesse G. GA 21st Inf. Co.C 1st Lt.
Rucker, J.F. MO Inf. 1st Regt.St.Guard 2nd
  Co.D
Rucker, J.H. GA 1st Inf. Co.A Cpl.
Rucker, J.H. TN 45th Inf. Co.G
Rucker, J.H. TX Cav. Terry's Regt. Co.G Capt.
Rucker, J.K.P. LA 6th Cav. Co.C
Rucker, J.K.P. MS 7th Cav. Co.B
Rucker, J.L. MO 6th Cav. Co.B,C
Rucker, J.L. TN Cav. 12th Bn. (Day's) Co.C
  1st Lt.
Rucker, J.M. AR 12th Inf. Co.E
Rucker, J.M. GA 27th Inf. Co.G
Rucker, J.M. MS 1st Cav.Res. Co.F
Rucker, J.M. TN 31st Inf. Co.K
Rucker, J.N. MO St.Guard Comsy.Sgt.
Rucker, Jo TN 21st (Carter's) Cav. Co.A
Rucker, Joel C. TN 2nd (Robison's) Inf. Co.A
Rucker, John GA 22nd Inf. Co.E
Rucker, John KY 2nd Bn.Mtd.Rifles Co.D
Rucker, John A. GA 40th Inf. Co.E
Rucker, John A. GA 48th Inf. Co.E
Rucker, John A. KY 2nd Mtd.Inf. Co.H Sgt.
Rucker, John C. VA 28th Inf. Co.F Sgt.
Rucker, John E. TN 24th Inf. Co.B
Rucker, John F. MO 7th Cav. Co.D
Rucker, John F. MO 1st Inf. Maj.
Rucker, John F. MO St.Guard Maj.
Rucker, John H. MO 1st Inf. Co.B Sgt.
Rucker, John H. TN 10th Inf.
Rucker, John H. VA 1st Cav. Co.G
Rucker, John H. VA 2nd Arty. Co.I
Rucker, John P. AR 6th Inf. New Co.D
Rucker, John S. TN 4th (McLemore's) Cav.
  Co.F
Rucker, John T. GA 7th Inf. Co.K

Rucker, John W. GA 24th Inf. Co.A
Rucker, John W. MS 2nd Inf. Co.H
Rucker, John W. TN 55th (McKoin's) Inf. Dug-
gan's Co. Cpl.
Rucker, John W. VA 51st Inf. Co.G
Rucker, Joseph B. KY 2nd Mtd.Inf. Co.H
Rucker, Joseph H. VA 2nd Cav. Co.D
Rucker, Joseph T. GA 22nd Inf. Co.E
Rucker, Joshua T. VA Lt.Arty. Kirkpatrick's Co.
2nd Lt.
Rucker, J.P. AR 12th Inf. Co.B
Rucker, J.P. TN 45th Inf. Co.G
Rucker, J.P.M. Mead's Conf.Cav. Co.A
Rucker, J.R. GA 64th Inf. Co.I Cpl.
Rucker, J.R. MS 48th Inf. Co.B Cpl.
Rucker, J.S. TN 20th Inf. Co.D
Rucker, J.T. GA Arty. 9th Bn. Co.A
Rucker, J.T. GA Inf. 9th Bn. Co.D
Rucker, J.W. GA 3rd Bn. (St.Guards) Co.E Cpl.
Rucker, J.W. GA Conscr.
Rucker, J.W. MO Lt.Arty. H.M. Bledsoe's Co.
Cpl.
Rucker, J.W. SC 25th Inf. Co.F
Rucker, J.W. TX Conscr.
Rucker, L. AR 12th Inf. Co.B
Rucker, L. VA 1st Bn.Res. Co.G 2nd Lt.
Rucker, L.B. TN 45th Inf. Co.G
Rucker, L.C. GA Inf. 27th Bn. (NonConscr.)
Co.E
Rucker, L.C. TN 60th Mtd.Inf. Co.H
Rucker, L.C. VA 23rd Cav. Co.C
Rucker, Leonidas KY Jessee's Bn.Mtd.Riflemen
Co.A
Rucker, Leroy AL 14th Inf. Co.C
Rucker, L.H. TX Cav. 1st Bn.St.Troops Capt.
Rucker, Lindsay AL 4th Inf. Co.C
Rucker, Linza AR 6th Inf. New Co.D
Rucker, M. TN 45th Inf. Co.D
Rucker, Marcelus P. VA 2nd Cav. Co.E
Rucker, Mark P. KY 2nd Mtd.Inf. Co.C
Rucker, Minor B. VA Cav. 35th Bn. Co.F
Rucker, Moses GA 24th Inf. Co.A
Rucker, Moses P. VA 2nd Cav. Co.F
Rucker, N.A. AL 4th (Roddey's) Cav. Co.K
Rucker, N.A. TX 24th Cav. Co.A
Rucker, N.A. 1st Conf.Cav. 1st Co.K
Rucker, N.B. TX 35th (Brown's) Cav. Co.A
Rucker, N.B. TX 13th Vol. 2nd Co.B, 1st Co.B
Rucker, O.T. KY 2nd (Woodward's) Cav. Co.A
Rucker, Paul B. VA 2nd Cav. Co.E
Rucker, Paulus G. VA 11th Inf. Co.H
Rucker, P.E. Hvy.Arty. DeGournay's Bn. Co.D
Rucker, Pinkney MO 11th Inf. Co.C Cpl.
Rucker, R. TX 6th Cav. Co.K
Rucker, R. VA 2nd St.Res. Co.H
Rucker, R.B. GA 13th Inf. Co.A
Rucker, R.D. TX 20th Inf. Co.F
Rucker, R.D.P. SC 25th Inf. Co.D
Rucker, R.E. TN Douglass' Bn.Part.Rangers
Lytle's Co.
Rucker, Reuben S. KY 12th Cav. Co.B
Rucker, R.H. GA Inf. 2nd Bn. Co.A
Rucker, Richard Z. GA Inf. 2nd Bn. Co.A
Rucker, Riley MO 11th Inf. Co.C
Rucker, R.J. GA 22nd Inf. Co.E
Rucker, R.J. MS Inf. 2nd Bn. Co.B
Rucker, Robert MO 3rd Inf. Co.K Cpl.

Rucker, Robert E. TN 1st (Feild's) Inf. Co.I
Rucker, Robert M. TN 2nd (Robison's) Inf.
Co.A
Rucker, Robert T. AL 62nd Inf. Co.K
Rucker, Samuel TN Cav. 12th Bn. (Day's) Co.G
Rucker, Samuel VA 12th Cav. Co.E
Rucker, Samuel J. Gen. & Staff,PACS Capt.
Rucker, S.B. VA 6th Cav. Co.F
Rucker, Simeon G. KY 4th Mtd.Inf. Co.F
Rucker, Simeon L. GA 22nd Inf. Co.E
Rucker, S.J. TN Inf. 4th Cons.Regt. Co.C
Rucker, S.J. TN 45th Inf. Co.C
Rucker, Sterling B. TN 7th Inf. Co.G
Rucker, T. MO 9th (Elliott's) Cav. Co.E
Rucker, Tandy KY 4th Cav. Co.A
Rucker, Tandy C. KY 5th Cav. Co.A
Rucker, T.C. KY 6th Cav. Co.A
Rucker, Thomas MO Lt.Arty. H.M. Bledsoe's
Co.
Rucker, Thomas VA 28th Inf. Co.K
Rucker, Thomas A. MO Inf. 2nd Regt.St.Guard
Co.G
Rucker, Thomas R. Nitre & Min. Bureau War
Dept.,CSA
Rucker, Thomas W. TX Cav. Mann's Regt.
Co.A
Rucker, Thomas W. TX Cav. Mann's Bn. Co.A
Rucker, Thomas W.A. TN 7th Inf. Co.G
Rucker, Tinsley S. VA Lt.Arty. Griffin's Co.
Rucker, Tinsley S. VA 58th Inf. Co.K
Rucker, U.S.L. SC 1st (Hagood's) Inf. 1st Co.B,
2nd Co.B 2nd Lt.
Rucker, Valentine H. VA 2nd Cav. Co.E 2nd
Lt.
Rucker, W. MS 2nd Cav. 2nd Co.G
Rucker, W. TX 35th (Brown's) Cav. 2nd Co.B
Sgt.
Rucker, W. VA 1st Res. Co.E
Rucker, W. 1st Conf.Inf. 2nd Co.C
Rucker, W.A. MS 2nd Cav.Res. Co.I
Rucker, W.A. SC 3rd Inf. Co.H
Rucker, W.A. SC 20th Inf. Co.D
Rucker, Washington J. VA 2nd Cav. Co.E
Rucker, Western T. TN 2nd (Robison's) Inf.
Co.A
Rucker, Wiley GA 2nd Inf. Co.A
Rucker, William AL 27th Inf. Co.K
Rucker, William AR 19th (Dockery's) Inf.
Cons.Co.E,D
Rucker, William MD Arty. 2nd Btty.
Rucker, William MS 4th Cav. Co.D
Rucker, William MS 5th Cav. Co.B
Rucker, William MS Part.Rangers Armistead's
Co.
Rucker, William MS 1st Lt.Arty. Co.L
Rucker, William MO 15th Cav. Co.C
Rucker, William TN 26th Inf. Co.B,H Sgt.
Rucker, William TN 61st Mtd.Inf. Bundren's Co.
Sgt.
Rucker, William VA 25th Inf. 1st Co.G
Rucker, William VA 62nd Mtd.Inf. 2nd Co.A
Rucker, William VA 146th Mil. Co.E
Rucker, William A. VA 2nd Cav. Co.E
Rucker, William B. GA 38th Inf. Co.F 1st Lt.
Rucker, William D. GA 8th Inf. (St.Guards)
Co.F
Rucker, William F. MO 2nd Cav. 2nd Co.K

Rucker, William J. AR 36th Inf. Co.A
Rucker, William J. TN 45th Inf. Co.I
Rucker, William J. TX 14th Cav. Co.B
Rucker, William L. VA 58th Inf. Co.F
Rucker, William M. 1st Conf.Cav. 2nd Co.E
Rucker, William N. AL 47th Inf. Co.D
Rucker, William Pleasant VA 2nd Cav. Co.G
Rucker, William R. TN 2nd (Robison's) Inf.
Co.A
Rucker, William R. VA 19th Inf. Co.H
Rucker, William Richard VA 2nd Cav. Co.E
Rucker, William T. TX 20th Inf. Co.C
Rucker, William T. VA 24th Inf. Co.D
Rucker, William W. MS 18th Inf. Co.C ACS
Rucker, William W. Gen. & Staff 1st Lt.,Dr.M.
Rucker, Willis AL 62nd Inf. Co.D
Rucker, Willis L. LA 19th Inf. Co.H
Rucker, Winston KY 3rd Mtd.Inf. Co.C 1st Lt.
Rucker, W.J. AR 21st Mil. Dollar's Co.
Rucker, W.J. VA Cav. Mosby's Regt. (Part.
Rangers) Co.C
Rucker, W.L. TX Inf. Rutherford's Co.
Rucker, W.M. TN 15th (Cons.) Cav. Co.F
Rucker, Wooster B. VA 58th Inf. Co.H 2nd Lt.
Rucker, W.P. TN 20th Inf. Co.D Capt.
Rucker, W.T. TX 8th Cav. Co.D
Rucker, W.T. TX Cav. Ragsdale's Bn. Co.F 1st
Lt.
Rucker, Z.G. GA 2nd Inf. Co.G
Ruckert, --- GA Arty. (Macon Lt.Arty.) Slaten's
Co.
Ruckert, Charles LA C.S. Zouave Bn. Co.F
Rucket, John T. MS 44th Inf. Co.D
Ruckh, F.J. SC Inf. 1st (Charleston) Bn. Co.F
Ruckle, John TN 7th (Duckworth's) Cav. Co.L
Ruckles, Lawrence L. VA Hvy.Arty. A.J. Jones'
Co. 1st Lt.
Ruckley, Homer GA 6th Inf. Co.F
Ruckley, J.S. SC 20th Inf. 2nd Lt.
Rucklins, J.W. TX Cav. Giddings' Bn. Carr's
Co.
Ruckly, Shade AR 19th (Dockery's) Inf. Co.B
Ruckman, Amos R. MO Cav. 3rd Bn. Co.E
Ruckman, A.R. MO 3rd Cav. Co.E
Ruckman, Charles B. VA 19th Cav. Co.F
Ruckman, Charles B. VA Cav. McNeill's Co.
Ruckman, Charles B. VA 31st Inf. Co.G 1st Lt.
Ruckman, Charles B. VA 2nd Cav.St.Line
McNeel's Co.
Ruckman, David VA Cav. 46th Bn. Co.E
Ruckman, D.B. VA Cav. 36th Bn. Co.A
Ruckman, D.V. VA 26th Cav. Co.E
Ruckman, Elias MO 3rd Cav. Co.I
Ruckman, George W. VA 13th Inf. Co.I
Ruckman, James VA 33rd Inf. Co.F
Ruckman, James F. VA 33rd Inf. Co.A
Ruckman, James J. VA 114th Mil. Co.B Cpl.
Ruckman, James T. VA 18th Cav. Co.K Cpl.
Ruckman, James T. VA 114th Mil. Co.B Sgt.
Ruckman, James W. VA 19th Cav. Co.F
Ruckman, J.J. VA 18th Cav. Co.K
Ruckman, John TX 36th Cav. Co.E 1st Lt.
Ruckman, John G. VA 33rd Inf. Co.F
Ruckman, John G. VA 114th Mil. Co.B
Ruckman, John L. MO Cav. 3rd Bn. Co.E
Ruckman, John W. VA 33rd Inf. Co.F
Ruckman, John W. VA 114th Mil. Co.B

Ruckman, Joseph MO Cav. 3rd Bn. Co.E
Ruckman, J.W. VA 18th Cav. Co.C
Ruckman, J.W. VA 18th Cav. Co.K
Ruckman, J.W. VA 62nd Mtd.Inf. 1st Co.H
Ruckman, Lewis TX 11th Inf. Co.D
Ruckman, Moses MS Inf. 2nd Bn. Co.F
Ruckman, Moses MS 48th Inf. Co.F
Ruckman, Moses VA 20th Cav. Co.G
Ruckman, Sam. TN Inf. 2nd Cons.Regt. Co.D
Ruckman, Samuel TN 12th Inf. Co.C
Ruckman, Samuel TN 12th (Cons.) Inf. Co.B
Ruckman, Samuel VA 20th Cav. Co.G
Ruckman, Samuel VA 31st Inf. Co.G
Ruckman, Shepd. VA 14th Cav. Co.E
Ruckman, Sidney VA 19th Cav. Co.F
Ruckman, Sidney B. VA 31st Inf. Co.G 1st Lt.
Ruckman, Thomas VA 20th Cav. Co.G
Ruckman, Thomas J. VA Cav. 39th Bn. Co.D
Ruckman, Thomas M. VA 18th Cav. Co.K
Ruckman, Thomas W. VA 2nd Arty. Co.A
Ruckman, V. VA 18th Cav. Co.K
Ruckman, Valentine VA 14th Mil. Co.C Cpl.
Ruckman, Valentine VA 62nd Mtd.Inf. 1st Co.G
Ruckman, William MO Cav. 3rd Bn. Co.E
Ruckman, William VA 19th Cav. Co.C
Ruckmen, Samuel TN 2nd (Robison's) Inf. Co.D
Ruckner, Wm. MO St.Guard
Rucks, --- AR 12th Inf. Co.D 2nd Lt.
Rucks, Ambrose KY 3rd Mtd.Inf. Co.B
Rucks, Andrew J. VA Cav. 1st Bn. Co.A
Rucks, B.F. AR 6th Inf. Co.C
Rucks, B.F. MS 6th Inf. Co.E
Rucks, Ed AR 3rd Cav. Co.A
Rucks, Edward AR 1st (Colquitt's) Inf. Co.C 1st Sgt.
Rucks, Elisha AL Cp. of Instr. Talladega Co.D
Rucks, Elisha Parks AL 49th Inf. Co.B Sgt.
Rucks, E.P. Exch.Bn. Co.D,CSA Sgt.
Rucks, George AL 3rd Cav. Co.E
Rucks, G.W. AL 48th Inf. Co.G,E
Rucks, H.C. AR 37th Inf. Co.E
Rucks, Howell F. TN 9th (Ward's) Cav. Co.D Bvt.2nd Lt.
Rucks, Howell T. TN 7th Inf. Co.B,K
Rucks, James Patton McGee AL 49th Inf. Co.B
Rucks, L. Taylor MS 18th Inf. Co.K
Rucks, S.C. VA Inf. 28th Bn. Co.D
Rucks, S.C. VA 59th Inf. 3rd Co.I
Rucks, William TN 2nd Cav.
Rucks, William Emerson AL 49th Inf. Co.B
Rucks, William George Washington AL 49th Inf. Co.B
Rucks, W.J. AR 12th Inf. Co.D 2nd Lt.
Rucks, W.R. KY 3rd Mtd.Inf. Co.G
Ruckward, Robert TX Waul's Legion Co.B
Ruckwarth, R. TX Inf. Timmons' Regt. Co.K
Ruclex, M. LA Mil. 2nd Regt. 2nd Brig. 1st Div. Co.E Sgt.
Rud, --- TX Cav. 4th Regt.St.Troops Co.H
Rud, G.F. GA Inf. 40th Bn. Co.A Cpl.
Rud, J.J. NC 8th Inf. Co.F
Rud, J.P. TN 3rd (Forrest's) Cav. Co.E
Rud, Nicholas VA 33rd Inf. Co.B
Rud, Samuel AR 19th (Dockery's) Inf. Co.A
Rudacil, Henry SC 7th Res. Co.G
Rudacile, Eli SC 1st Arty. Co.C
Rudacilla, Jacob VA 146th Mil. Co.H

Rudacilla, John W. VA 146th Mil. Co.H
Rudacilla, Samuel H. VA 146th Mil. Co.H
Rudacillar, George VA 49th Inf. Co.D
Rudacille, James E. GA Phillips' Legion Co.C
Rudaciller, Isaac VA 49th Inf. Co.D
Rudaciller, Jacob VA Cav. 35th Bn. Co.E
Rudaciller, Jacob VA Cav. 41st Bn. Trayhern's Co.
Rudaciller, Jacob F. VA Cav. 35th Bn. Co.E
Rudaciller, Jacob F. VA Cav. 41st Bn. Trayhern's Co.
Rudaciller, John W. VA Cav. 35th Bn. Co.E
Rudaciller, Philip VA Cav. 41st Bn. Trayhern's Co.
Rudaciller, Phillip VA Cav. 35th Bn. Co.E
Rudaciller, Thomas VA Cav. 35th Bn. Co.E,D
Rudaneler, John VA 4th Inf. Co.I
Rudasel, A. AL 5th Cav. Co.B
Rudasil, Jonas NC 4th Sr.Res. Co.G
Rudasil, Wiley M. NC 16th Inf. Co.M Cpl.
Rudasill, Alpaus VA 34th Mil. Co.D
Rudasill, Andrew C. VA 7th Inf. Co.B Sgt.
Rudasill, Cephas M. Conf.Cav. Raum's Co.
Rudasill, Emanuel NC 16th Inf. Co.M Color Sgt.
Rudasill, J.A. VA Cav. Mosby's Regt. (Part. Rangers) Co.C
Rudasill, James M. VA 6th Cav. Co.B
Rudasill, John NC 28th Inf. Co.D
Rudasill, John W. VA 6th Cav. Co.B
Rudasill, J.T. NC 28th Inf. Co.B
Rudasill, Levi L. Conf.Cav. Wood's Regt. 2nd Co.G 1st Sgt.
Rudasill, Philip H. MO 1st N.W. Cav. Co.C Cpl.
Rudasill, Philip H. MO 4th Cav. Co.G
Rudasill, Samuel Conf.Cav. Wood's Regt. 2nd Co.G
Rudasill, Thaddeus A. VA 6th Cav. Co.B
Rudasill, William G. VA 6th Cav. Co.B
Rudasill, William K. VA 6th Cav. Co.B
Rudasill, William K. VA 16th Cav. Co.B
Rudasillar, John W. VA 49th Inf. Co.D
Rudasiller, P. VA 23rd Cav. Co.A
Rudd, A. AR Mil. Desha Cty.Bn.
Rudd, A. VA 32nd Inf. 2nd Co.K Sgt.
Rudd, A.A. AR 2nd Inf. New Co.E
Rudd, A.A. AR 11th Inf. Co.H,G
Rudd, A.A. AR 11th & 17th Cons.Inf. Co.G
Rudd, A.A. VA 2nd Inf.Loc.Def. Co.B
Rudd, A.A. VA Inf. 2nd Bn.Loc.Def. Co.D
Rudd, Acastus C. VA 32nd Inf. Co.A
Rudd, Alexander B. NC 12th Inf. Co.F
Rudd, Alfred A. VA 6th Inf. Co.K Cpl.
Rudd, Allen F. Conf.Inf. Tucker's Regt. Co.D
Rudd, A.M. AL 9th Inf. Co.F
Rudd, A.M. AR Cav. Harrell's Bn. Co.A
Rudd, A.M. TN 19th Inf. Co.D
Rudd, Anderson P. NC 6th Inf. Co.H Sgt.
Rudd, Archd. VA 45th Inf. Co.A
Rudd, Augustus S. VA 9th Inf. Co.I
Rudd, Aurelius VA 1st Inf. Co.I
Rudd, Barnett NC 47th Inf. Co.F
Rudd, Ben MO 5th Cav. Co.C
Rudd, Benjamin VA 1st Inf. Co.I
Rudd, Benjamin F. VA Inf. 4th Bn. Co.C 2nd Lt.

Rudd, Benjamin F. VA 9th Inf. Co.K
Rudd, Berry TN Inf. 23rd Bn. Co.B
Rudd, B.S. VA 1st (Farinholt's) Res. Co.G
Rudd, Burrell AL 3rd Bn.Res. Flemming's Co. Cpl.
Rudd, Charles AL 8th Inf. Co.E
Rudd, Charles D. VA 17th Inf. Co.E
Rudd, David LA 5th Inf. Co.H
Rudd, David NC 7th Sr.Res. Mitchell's Co.
Rudd, D.M. GA 40th Inf. Co.H
Rudd, E. VA 54th Mil. Co.H
Rudd, Edmund P. KY 4th Mtd.Inf. Co.F Cpl.
Rudd, Edw. AR 15th (Johnson's) Inf. Co.F 3rd Lt.
Rudd, Edward AR 1st (Crawford's) Cav. Co.C
Rudd, Edward VA Inf. 4th Bn.Loc.Def. Co.C
Rudd, Elias FL 1st (Res.) Inf. Co.L
Rudd, Elijah KY 2nd Bn.Mtd.Rifles Co.A
Rudd, Elijah KY 5th Mtd.Inf. Co.A
Rudd, Elijah L. TN 1st (Carter's) Cav. Co.D
Rudd, Elijah L. TN 3rd (Forrest's) Cav.
Rudd, Elisha W. NC 6th Inf. Co.H Cpl.
Rudd, Elison FL 1st (Res.) Inf. Co.L
Rudd, F.J. VA 3rd Arty.Loc.Def. Co.A
Rudd, Francis Marion AL 15th Inf. Co.F
Rudd, Frederick J. VA 15th Inf. Co.B
Rudd, George KY Morgan's Men Co.D
Rudd, George B. KY Cav. 2nd Bn. (Dortch's) Co.C
Rudd, George W. KY Cav. 1st Bn.
Rudd, George W. KY 10th (Johnson's) Cav. Co.D
Rudd, George W. SC Lt.Arty. 3rd (Palmetto) Bn. Co.D
Rudd, George W. VA 1st St.Res. Co.B Sgt.
Rudd, George W. VA 14th Inf. Co.F
Rudd, George W. VA 41st Inf. Co.D
Rudd, Guilford NC 15th Inf. Co.E
Rudd, G.W. TN Inf. 23rd Bn. Co.B
Rudd, H. SC 5th Cav. Co.G
Rudd, H.C. AL 14th Inf. Co.I
Rudd, H.C. AL 30th Inf. Co.F
Rudd, Henry FL 6th Inf. Co.G
Rudd, Henry B. VA 32nd Inf. Co.C
Rudd, H.H. TN Cav. 16th Bn. (Neal's) Co.B
Rudd, Hiram SC Mil. 18th Regt. Co.F Cpl.
Rudd, Hortensceus GA 40th Inf. Co.H
Rudd, Isaac W. VA 17th Inf. Co.E
Rudd, J. SC 2nd Bn.S.S. Co.B
Rudd, J. VA 1st (Farinholt's) Res. Co.E
Rudd, James AR Cav. Harrell's Bn. Co.A
Rudd, James AR 1st (Colquitt's) Inf. Co.H
Rudd, James MO 5th Cav. Co.A
Rudd, James SC 1st Mtd.Mil. Earnest's Co.
Rudd, James SC Cav. 17th Bn. Co.B
Rudd, James SC Lt.Arty. 3rd (Palmetto) Bn. Co.D
Rudd, James VA 3rd Lt.Arty. Co.A 2nd Lt.
Rudd, James VA Burks' Regt.Loc.Def. Miller's Co.
Rudd, James C. NC 3rd Cav. (41st St.Troops) Co.C
Rudd, James D. AL 27th Inf.
Rudd, James D. AL 57th Inf. Co.G
Rudd, James E. AL 11th Inf. Co.H
Rudd, James E. AL 31st Inf. Co.G
Rudd, James H. TX 14th Cav. Co.G

Rudd, James N. VA 17th Inf. Co.H
Rudd, J.B. AR 26th Inf. Co.G Jr.2nd Lt.
Rudd, J.D. LA 3rd Cav. Co.G
Rudd, J.D. LA 3rd (Harrison's) Cav. Co.G
Rudd, J.D. TN 40th Inf. Co.H
Rudd, J.E. AL 15th Inf. Co.F
Rudd, J.E. VA 1st (Farinholt's) Res. Co.G
Rudd, Jefferson FL 6th Inf. Co.G
Rudd, Jerry FL 6th Inf. Co.A
Rudd, Jesse FL 6th Inf. Co.G
Rudd, J.F. AR 30th Inf. Co.C
Rudd, J.F. TX 1st Inf. Co.E
Rudd, J.F. TX 7th Inf.
Rudd, J.H. TX 1st Inf. Co.H
Rudd, J.J. SC 11th Inf. Co.B
Rudd, J.L. NC 34th Inf. Co.B
Rudd, J.M. VA Inf. Montague's Bn. Co.B
Rudd, John FL 6th Inf. Co.G
Rudd, John A.M. MO 5th Cav. Co.C
Rudd, John D. VA 11th Bn.Res. Co.C
Rudd, John F. VA Inf. 25th Bn. Co.E
Rudd, John M. VA 53rd Inf. Co.I
Rudd, John S. VA Cav. 46th Bn. Co.A
Rudd, John S. VA Horse Arty. Lurty's Co.
Rudd, John Speed Gen. & Staff, Inf. 2nd Lt.
Rudd, John T. VA 9th Cav. Co.G
Rudd, John W. MO 1st N.E. Cav.
Rudd, Jonathan D. TX 14th Cav. Co.G Cpl.
Rudd, Joseph TN 9th Inf. Co.D,L
Rudd, Joseph VA 6th Bn.Res. Co.B
Rudd, Joseph R.R. FL Cav. 8th Bn. Co.A
  Music.
Rudd, Joseph T. KY 4th Cav. Co.B
Rudd, J.R. TN 37th Inf. Co.G
Rudd, J.R.R. 15th Conf.Cav. Co.A Music.
Rudd, J.S. TX 1st Inf. Co.H
Rudd, Leon AL 21st Inf.
Rudd, Lorenzo D. NC 4th Cav. (59th St.Troops)
  Co.B
Rudd, L.P. VA 1st Cav. Co.G Cpl.
Rudd, Luther Y. NC 6th Inf. Co.H
Rudd, M. AR Mil. Desha Cty.Bn.
Rudd, M.V.B. AL 15th Inf. Co.F
Rudd, Pleasant G. MO 5th Inf. Co.C
Rudd, P.W. VA Conscr. Cp.Lee
Rudd, Raymond GA 11th Cav. (St.Guards)
  Bruce's Co.
Rudd, Reuben A. VA 34th Inf. Co.B
Rudd, R.L. GA Rowland's Bn.Conscr.
Rudd, Robert VA 17th Inf. Co.E
Rudd, Robert W. VA 6th Inf. Co.K 1st Sgt.
Rudd, Royal S. VA Cav. Mosby's Regt.
  (Part.Rangers) Co.A
Rudd, Samuel FL 6th Inf. Co.A
Rudd, Samuel FL 10th Inf. Davidson's Co.
Rudd, Samuel GA 46th Inf. Co.F
Rudd, Samuel MO 2nd N.E. Cav. (Franklin's
  Regt.) Co.B
Rudd, Samuel W. VA 6th Inf. Co.K
Rudd, Sandy KY 4th Mtd.Inf. Co.B
Rudd, Sandy MS Lt.Arty. (Issaquena Arty.)
  Graves' Co.
Rudd, S.H. MO Cav. Slayback's Regt. Co.H
Rudd, Sidney 1st Conf.Eng.Troops Co.K
Rudd, St.Clair TN 37th Inf. Co.I
Rudd, Stephen W. VA 19th Inf. Co.D

Rudd, T.A. SC 9th Res. Co.K Cpl.
Rudd, Thomas VA 32nd Inf. Co.E
Rudd, Thomas H. NC 1st Cav. (9th St.Troops)
  Co.H
Rudd, Thomas H. NC 12th Inf. Co.C
Rudd, Thomas J. LA 5th Inf. Co.H
Rudd, Thomas S. NC 34th Inf. Co.B
Rudd, T.J. TN 17th Inf. Co.A
Rudd, W. MO 9th Inf. Co.G
Rudd, W. VA 3rd Arty. Co.A
Rudd, W.A. SC 12th Inf. Co.A
Rudd, W.B. TN Inf. 23rd Bn. Co.E
Rudd, W.E. AL 15th Inf. Co.F Cpl.
Rudd, W.G. TN 20th (Russell's) Cav. Co.I
Rudd, W.H. AR 2nd Inf. New Co.E Sgt.
Rudd, W.H. AR 11th Inf. Co.H
Rudd, W.H. GA 23rd Inf. Co.I
Rudd, William NC 5th Cav. (63rd St.Troops)
  Co.E Cook
Rudd, William TN 19th & 20th (Cons.) Cav.
  Co.E
Rudd, William VA 1st Inf. Co.I
Rudd, William A. FL 5th Inf. Co.F
Rudd, William A. VA 6th Inf. Co.K
Rudd, William C. AL 47th Inf. Co.D Cpl.
Rudd, William D. VA 61st Inf. Co.E
Rudd, William G. TX 14th Cav. Co.G
Rudd, William H. TN 3rd (Lillard's) Mtd.Inf.
  Co.H Capt.
Rudd, William H. VA 14th Inf. Co.F
Rudd, William S. VA 2nd Arty. Co.A
Rudd, William W. NC 46th Inf. Co.C
Rudd, W.J. KY 3rd Mtd.Inf. Co.B
Rudd, W.S. VA 44th Inf. Co.H
Ruddel, James H. GA 62nd Inf. Co.F
Ruddell, Alfred MS 19th Inf. Co.B
Ruddell, George M. GA Lt.Arty. Pritchard's Co.
  (Washington Arty.) Ord.Sgt.
Ruddell, George M. GA 36th (Villepigue's) Inf.
  Co.F
Ruddell, George M. 1st Conf.Inf. 1st Co.F
Ruddell, George W. VA 28th Inf. Co.I
Ruddell, Isaac TX Inf. Cotton's Co.
Ruddell, Isaac N. TX 1st Inf. 2nd Co.K Sgt.
Ruddell, James C. KY Cav. 1st Bn. Co.A
Ruddell, James F. 3rd Conf.Inf. Co.C
Ruddell, James H. VA 28th Inf. Co.I
Ruddell, James N. GA 1st Inf. (St.Guards)
Ruddell, J.F. AR 18th (Marmaduke's) Inf. Co.C
  1st Sgt.
Ruddell, J.H. GA Cav. 24th Bn. Co.B
Ruddell, John H. Gen. & Staff Surg.
Ruddell, John L. AR 1st Mtd.Rifles Co.K
Ruddell, John L. TX 15th Cav. Co.A
Ruddell, Joseph KY 4th Cav. Revill's Co.
Ruddell, Joseph KY Jessee's Bn.Mtd.Riflemen
  Co.B
Ruddell, Michael VA 28th Inf. Co.I
Ruddell, Richard VA 28th Inf. Co.I
Ruddell, Steven W. VA Lt.Arty. G.B. Chap-
  man's Co.
Ruddell, T. TX 14th Inf. Co.G
Ruddell, William G. VA 28th Inf. Co.I Cpl.
Rudden, S.G. AL Randolph Cty.Res. B.C.
  Raney's Co.
Rudden, Thomas MD 1st Inf. Co.F

Rudden, Thomas VA Horse Arty. D. Shanks'
  Co.
Rudder, Albert G. MO 10th Inf. Co.I Cpl.
Rudder, Alfred VA 16th Inf. Co.G
Rudder, A.P. TX 22nd Inf. Co.D Sgt.
Rudder, A.V. AR 5th Inf. Co.B
Rudder, Benjamin F. MO 10th Inf. Co.I
Rudder, B.J. LA 6th Cav. Co.D,A
Rudder, C.F. AL 54th Inf. Co.F
Rudder, Charles M. VA 45th Inf. Co.F
Rudder, C.T. AL 22nd Inf. Co.C
Rudder, D.J. TN 4th Inf. Co.K
Rudder, Edward NC 45th Inf. Co.I
Rudder, Edward V. NC 45th Inf. Co.I
Rudder, George W. VA 6th Cav. Co.G
Rudder, Jarrett TN 15th (Stewart's) Cav. Co.C
Rudder, J.F. AR 1st (Dobbin's) Cav. Co.F Cpl.
Rudder, J.M. AL 22nd Inf. Co.C
Rudder, J.M. AL 54th Inf. Comsy.Sgt.
Rudder, John VA 3rd Inf. 2nd Co.K
Rudder, John T. VA Lt.Arty. Penick's Co.
Rudder, John W. VA 9th Inf. 1st Co.H
Rudder, John W. VA Inf. 28th Bn. Co.C
Rudder, John W. VA 59th Inf. 2nd Co.H
Rudder, Jonathan M. AL 37th Inf. Co.F 2nd Lt.
Rudder, Joseph C. NC 12th Inf. Co.M Fifer
Rudder, Joseph C. NC 32nd Inf. Co.B Capt.
Rudder, M. NC 35th Inf. Co.E
Rudder, Marshall C. MO 1st Cav. Co.F Jr.2nd
  Lt.
Rudder, Mumford TN 2nd (Ashby's) Cav. Co.B
Rudder, Mumford TN Cav. 5th Bn. (McClel-
  lan's) Co.C
Rudder, R.A. TN 19th Inf. Co.B
Rudder, Robert TN Lt.Arty. McClung's Co.
Rudder, Robert Alexander Lafayette AL 49th Inf.
  Co.C
Rudder, S. TN 61st Mtd.Inf. Co.C
Rudder, Samuel H. AL 18th Bn.Vol. Co.A
Rudder, S.D. 53rd (Part.Rangers) Co.G
Rudder, T. TN 61st Mtd.Inf. Co.C
Rudder, W. TN 61st Mtd.Inf. Co.C
Rudder, W.C. AL 1st Cav. 1st Co.B
Rudder, William TN Lt.Arty. McClung's Co.
Rudder, William E. LA 1st (Nelligan's) Inf.
  Co.A
Rudder, William H. AL Lt.Arty. Clanton's Btty.
Rudder, William H. NC 24th Inf. Co.A
Rudder, William H. NC 45th Inf. Co.I
Rudder, William H. TN 63rd Inf. Co.B
Ruddick, --- MS Arty. Byrne's Btty.
Ruddick, D.C. TX 5th Cav. Co.K
Ruddick, D.C. TX 12th Field Btty.
Ruddick, Joseph AR 35th Inf. Co.F Cpl.
Ruddick, R. KY 3rd & 7th (Cons.) Cav. Co.G
  2nd Lt.
Ruddick, Ranson MO 8th Inf. Co.E
Ruddick, S.D.C. AR 35th Inf. Co.F
Ruddick, Thomas MS 28th Cav. Co.D
Ruddick, William AR 35th Inf. Co.F Sgt.
Ruddie, R. KY Lt.Arty. Cobb's Co. Sgt.
Ruddin, James SC 2nd Arty. Co.A
Ruddisill, S.A. AR Arty. 2nd Btty.
Ruddissill, John R. MO 2nd Inf. Co.A
Ruddle, Abel M. VA 62nd Mtd.Inf. 2nd Co.F
Ruddle, Able VA 25th Inf. 1st Co.F
Ruddle, Edmond D. VA 25th Inf. 1st Co.F

Ruddle, Edward D. VA 62nd Mtd.Inf. 2nd Co.F
Ruddle, George A. TX 11th Inf. Co.F
Ruddle, G.W. MO 1st Inf. Co.K
Ruddle, G.W. MO 1st & 4th Cons.Inf. Co.K
Ruddle, G.W. MO 4th Inf. Co.C
Ruddle, Hiram AL 4th Inf. Co.B
Ruddle, Isaac C. VA 25th Inf. 1st Co.F Jr.2nd
Lt.
Ruddle, Isaac C. VA 62nd Mtd.Inf. 2nd Co.F
2nd 2nd Lt.
Ruddle, James C. VA 14th Cav. Co.I
Ruddle, James H. VA 25th Inf. 1st 2nd Co.E
Ruddle, James H. VA 46th Mil. Co.A
Ruddle, James H. VA 62nd Mtd.Inf. 2nd Co.F
Ruddle, J.C. KY Corbin's Men
Ruddle, J.D. MO 1st Inf. Co.H
Ruddle, John VA 23rd Cav. Co.M
Ruddle, John M. VA 25th Inf. 1st Co.F
Ruddle, John M. VA 46th Mil. Co.A
Ruddle, John M. VA 62nd Mtd.Inf. 2nd Co.F
Cpl.
Ruddle, John M. VA 62nd Mtd.Inf. 2nd Co.K
Ruddle, John S. MO 1st Inf. Co.H
Ruddle, John T. VA 5th Inf. Co.H
Ruddle, Salathiel B. AR 36th Inf. Co.A
Ruddle, S.B. AR 21st Mil. Dollar's Co.
Ruddle, S.L. VA 3rd Bn. Valley Res. Co.B
Ruddle, S.T. AR 35th Inf. Co.D
Ruddle, S.T. AR 51st Mil. Co.E
Ruddle, Stephen L. VA 5th Inf. Co.H
Ruddle, Theodoric TX 3rd Cav. Co.B
Ruddle, Thomas MO Cav. 3rd Bn. Co.K
Ruddle, Thomas MO 1st Inf. Co.K
Ruddle, Thomas MO 1st & 4th Cons.Inf. Co.K
Ruddle, William G. VA 25th Inf. 1st Co.F
Ruddle, William G. VA 62nd Mtd.Inf. 2nd Co.F
Sgt.
Ruddock, B.M. NC 11th (Bethel Regt.) Inf.
Co.A
Ruddock, B.W. NC 11th (Bethel Regt.) Inf.
Co.A
Ruddock, T.C. NC 1st Inf. (6 mo. '61) Co.C
Ruddock, Theo C. NC 11th (Bethel Regt.) Inf.
Co.A Cpl.
Ruddock, William O. NC 23rd Inf. Co.K
Ruddock, W.O. AL 4th Inf. Co.F
Rudduck, S.W. GA 1st Res. Co.B
Ruddy, A. GA 26th Inf. Co.B
Ruddy, Isaac VA 11th Cav. Co.E
Ruddy, P.H. AR Mil. Desha Cty.Bn.
Ruddy, Taylor LA 28th (Gray's) Inf.
Rude, George SC 3rd Cav. Co.G
Rude, Isaac J. TX Cav. Martin's Regt. Co.F
Rude, Thomas P. TX Cav. Martin's Regt. Co.F
Rude, William MO 6th Cav. Co.D
Rude, William S. VA 7th Cav. Co.K
Rudeau, A. LA Mil. 3rd Regt. French Brig. Co.7
Rudeau, J. Eng.,CSA
Rudeau, Joseph LA 1st Hvy.Arty. (Reg.) Co.G
Rudeau, Joseph LA Arty. Castellanos' Btty.
Rudeau, Pierre LA 13th Inf. Co.D
Rudeau, T. 2nd Conf.Eng.Troops Co.A
Rudecilla, Jacob VA 146th Mil. Co.K
Rudecilla, Philip VA 146th Mil. Co.K
Rudecilla, Thomas VA 146th Mil. Co.K
Rudeger, A. MS Lt.Arty. English's Co.
Rudel, E. AR 51st Mil. Co.E

Ruden, J.M. AL 48th Inf. Co.G Sgt.
Ruddell, B. AL 8th (Hatch's) Cav. Co.D
Rudensholz, --- LA C.S. Zouave Bn. Co.C
Ruder, H. AR 3rd Cav. Co.E
Ruder, M.H. AL 33rd Inf. Co.F Cpl.
Ruderhill, E.S. MS 1st (King's) Inf. (St.Troops)
Co.E
Rudersil, J.G. MO 9th Inf. Co.B Sgt.
Rudersville, P.A. NC 2nd Conscr. Co.G
Rudesell, J.C. AR 5th Inf. Co.G
Rudesell, P.C. AR 50th Mil. Co.G
Rudesell, W.K. AR 50th Mil. Co.G
Rudesill, James Y. VA 10th Cav. Co.F
Rudesill, John G. VA Burks' Regt.Loc.Def.
Rudesills, George E. VA Burks' Regt.Loc.Def.
Price's Co. 2nd Lt.
Rudesol, William F. MO 7th Cav. Co.I
Rudford, Calvin VA 5th Inf. Co.B
Rudge, John SC 16th Inf. Co.K Music.
Rudgely, R.D. GA 36th (Villepigue's) Inf. Co.K
Rudicil, A. SC 5th Inf. 2nd Co.D
Rudicil, Anderson NC 5th Inf. Co.G
Rudicil, E. GA 38th Inf. Co.I
Rudicil, H.F. NC 4th Inf. Co.G
Rudicil, Jacob NC 54th Inf. Co.B
Rudicil, John NC 42nd Inf. Co.F
Rudicil, Joseph TX 1st Inf. Co.I
Rudicil, M.R. LA 1st Eng.Corps Co.F
Rudicil, R.Y. GA 6th Cav. Surg.
Rudicil, Solomon NC 54th Inf. Co.B
Rudicil, William A. TX Conscr.
Rudicill, David SC 13th Inf. Co.F Sgt.
Rudicill, Philip NC 23rd Inf. Co.K
Ruding, Charles LA Inf.Crescent Regt. Co.G
Rudinger, Joseph TX 3rd Inf. Co.B
Rudisail, Alex SC 6th Cav. Co.H
Rudisail, G.A. SC 6th Cav. Co.H Cpl.
Rudisail, J.M. SC 6th Cav. Co.H
Rudisail, Marcus SC 6th Cav. Co.H
Rudisail, Marion SC 6th Cav. Co.H
Rudisal, Martin SC 6th Cav. Co.H
Rudiseal, Ezra GA 52nd Inf. Co.A
Rudiseal, John B. GA 52nd Inf. Co.A
Rudisee, John GA 32nd Inf. Co.A
Rudisel, J.C. TX 9th (Youngs') Inf. Co.K
Rudisell, A.L. AL Mil. 4th Vol. Modawell's Co.
Rudisell, C. NC 3rd Jr.Res. Co.E
Rudisell, Charles W. VA 60th Inf. Co.K
Rudisell, Eli NC 37th Inf. Co.H
Rudisell, H.I. GA 12th Inf. Co.A 2nd Lt.
Rudisell, Johnathan GA Inf. 4th Bn. (St.Guards)
Co.D Sgt.
Rudisell, Jonas G. NC 1st Inf. (6 mo. '61) Co.K
Cpl.
Rudish, D.L. GA 4th (Clinch's) Cav. Co.G
Rudisil, J.G. MO Inf. Clark's Regt. Co.A Sgt.
Rudisil, W.K. AR 37th Inf. Co.K Cpl.
Rudisil, Wylie V. SC 17th Inf. Co.B Cpl.
Rudisill, Abel L. 3rd Conf.Eng.Troops Co.A
Sgt.
Rudisill, Absalom NC 11th (Bethel Regt.) Inf.
Co.D
Rudisill, Absalom NC 44th Inf. Co.D
Rudisill, A.L. AL 43rd Inf. Co.A
Rudisill, A.W. TN 4th Inf. Co.A
Rudisill, Benj. F. Gen. & Staff Asst.Surg.
Rudisill, B.F. GA Lt.Arty. 12th Bn. Asst.Surg.

Rudisill, B.F. GA 1st (Ramsey's) Inf. Co.E
Rudisill, C. NC 8th Bn.Jr.Res. Co.B
Rudisill, Charles VA Burks' Regt.Loc.Def.
Price's Co.
Rudisill, D.R. NC 57th Inf. Co.G
Rudisill, E.D. GA 28th Inf. Co.B Sgt.
Rudisill, George E. TN 4th Inf. Co.A
Rudisill, H.A. NC 57th Inf. Co.G
Rudisill, Henry P. NC 12th Inf. Co.A Bvt.2nd
Lt.
Rudisill, Jacob NC 37th Inf. Co.I
Rudisill, Jacob F. NC 32nd Inf. Co.D,E Cpl.
Rudisill, Jacob R. VA 56th Inf. Co.D 1st Lt.
Rudisill, James GA Lt.Arty. 12th Bn. 3rd Co.B
Cpl.
Rudisill, J.H. LA 13th Bn. (Part.Rangers) Co.D
Rudisill, John W. GA Lt.Arty. 12th Bn. 3rd
Co.B Capt.
Rudisill, John W. GA 1st (Ramsey's) Inf. Co.E
1st Lt.
Rudisill, Jonas E. NC 37th Inf. Co.D
Rudisill, J.P. NC 57th Inf. Co.G
Rudisill, Marcus GA 3rd Cav. Co.F
Rudisill, Martin NC 23rd Inf. Co.B
Rudisill, M.C. NC 57th Inf. Co.G
Rudisill, Michael R. LA Inf. 11th Bn. Co.D
Rudisill, P.C. NC 32nd Inf. Co.E
Rudisill, Samuel A. AR Lt.Arty. Wiggins' Btty.
Rudisill, W.T. TN 12th (Green's) Cav. Co.E
Rudisol, William F. MO 8th Cav. Co.G
Rudlage, William AL 30th Inf. Co.B
Rudlehuber, Peter Lt.Arty. Bent's Btty.,CSA
Rudler, A.F. GA 37th Inf. Col.
Rudler, Anthony F. GA Inf. 3rd Bn. Co.G Maj.
Rudleton, J.M. TX 28th Cav. Co.K
Rudley, --- TX 24th & 25th Cav. (Cons.) Co.B
Rudley, John VA Lt.Arty. Lamkin's Co.
Rudley, W.A. AR Inf. Crawford's Bn. Co.B
Sgt.
Rudloff, C.H. TX 2nd Inf. Co.F
Rudloff, Chr. TX 4th Inf. Co.A
Rudnell, W. NC 2nd Conscr.
Rudney, James GA 2nd Inf. Co.B Sgt.
Rudolph, Adam VA 33rd Inf. Co.C
Rudolph, Amzi GA 65th Inf. Co.C,F Capt.
Rudolph, Amzi GA Smith's Legion Co.D 1st Lt.
Rudolph, Benjamin W. KY Cav. 37th Regt.
Rudolph, C.J. TN 14th Inf. Co.K
Rudolph, C.J. TN 49th Inf. Co.F Sgt.
Rudolph, C.J. Inf. Bailey's Cons.Regt. Co.C Sgt.
Rudolph, Daniel R. AL Mil. 4th Vol. Gantt's Co.
Sgt.
Rudolph, D.R. AL 40th Inf. Co.I 2nd Lt.
Rudolph, E.C. KY 12th Cav. Co.G
Rudolph, Eli TN 49th Inf. Co.F
Rudolph, Eli Inf. Bailey's Cons.Regt. Co.C
Rudolph, Emmett KY 2nd (Woodward's) Cav.
Co.G
Rudolph, F. GA 4th (Clinch's) Cav. Co.D Cpl.
Rudolph, F.G. TX 20th Inf. Co.H
Rudolph, Fr. TX 20th Inf. Co.I
Rudolph, George VA 33rd Inf. Co.C
Rudolph, Gustav TX 1st Hvy.Arty. Co.C
Rudolph, Horace W. VA 1st Arty. Co.D
Rudolph, Hugo AL St.Arty. Co.A Music.
Rudolph, J. VA 54th Mil. Co.G
Rudolph, J.A. TN 49th Inf. Co.F

Rudolph, J.A. Inf. Bailey's Cons.Regt. Co.C
Rudolph, Jacob LA 20th Inf. Co.A
Rudolph, Jacob VA 10th Inf. Co.A
Rudolph, James A. TN 29th Inf.
Rudolph, James M. AL 6th Inf. Co.M
Rudolph, J.C. VA 18th Cav. Co.I
Rudolph, J.C. VA 62nd Mtd.Inf. 1st Co.D
Rudolph, J.J. GA 4th (Clinch's) Cav. Co.D 2nd Lt.
Rudolph, J.L. KY 3rd Mtd.Inf. Co.F
Rudolph, John LA 22nd Inf. Co.B
Rudolph, John LA 22nd (Cons.) Inf. Co.B
Rudolph, John TN Inf. 3rd Bn. Co.E
Rudolph, John E. AR 8th Inf. New Co.F
Rudolph, John E. AR 14th (McCarver's) Inf. Co.B
Rudolph, John W. VA 11th Cav. Co.D
Rudolph, John W. VA 77th Mil. Co.A 1st Sgt.
Rudolph, John W. VA 146th Mil. Co.G
Rudolph, Joseph S. VA 12th Cav. Co.C Cpl.
Rudolph, J.W. KY 3rd Mtd.Inf. Co.F,B
Rudolph, J.W. TN 14th Inf. Co.K
Rudolph, L.A. SC Arty. Fickling's Co. (Brooks Lt.Arty.)
Rudolph, L. Adolphus SC 2nd Inf. Co.K
Rudolph, Martin Conf.Inf. Tucker's Regt. Co.C
Rudolph, Moritz LA Lewis Regt. Co.C
Rudolph, Nashvill VA 136th Mil. Co.A
Rudolph, Nashville D. VA 12th Cav. Co.C
Rudolph, P. KY 7th Mtd.Inf. Co.D
Rudolph, Peter R. TN 14th Inf. Co.K
Rudolph, R. GA 4th (Clinchs's) Cav. Co.D Cpl.
Rudolph, Samuel AL Lt.Arty. Lee's Btty.
Rudolph, Samuel Braxton's Bn.,CSA
Rudolph, Silas AR 14th (McCarver's) Inf. Co.B
Rudolph, Silas T. AR 8th Inf. New Co.F Cpl.
Rudolph, Simon VA 11th Cav. Co.D
Rudolph, Simons VA 77th Mil. Co.A
Rudolph, Thadeus L. TX Cav. Martin's Regt. Co.K 2nd Lt.
Rudolph, V. LA Mil. 2nd Regt. 2nd Brig. 1st Div. Co.I
Rudolph, W.A., Jr. KY 3rd Mtd.Inf. Co.F
Rudolph, W.A., Sr. KY 3rd Mtd.Inf. Co.F
Rudolph, W.H. KY 3rd Mtd.Inf. Co.F
Rudolph, W.H. Inf. Bailey's Cons.Regt. Co.C 1st Lt.
Rudolph, William D. AR 8th Cav. Co.H,D Chap.
Rudolph, William H. TN 49th Inf. Co.F 1st Lt.
Rudolph, W.M. GA Inf. 23rd Bn.Loc.Def. Sims' Co.
Rudolph, W.R. KY 12th Cav. Co.D
Rudolphe, Hugo AL 5th Inf.
Rudsil, E. AR 3rd Cav. Co.E
Rudsle, M.P. SC Inf. 37th Regt.
Rudspethe, William MS 18th Cav. Co.E
Rudte, A.W.A. FL 3rd Inf. Co.H
Rudulph, Burrell AL Lt.Arty. Lee's Btty.
Rudulph, Burrell AL 3rd Inf. Co.G
Rudulph, D.R. AL 9th Inf. Co.G
Rudulph, J.M. AL 5th Inf. New Co.K
Rudulph, John B. AL Cav. 5th Bn. Hilliard's Legion Co.D Capt.
Rudulph, John B. 10th Conf.Cav. Co.D Maj.
Rudulph, John D. GA 26th Inf. Co.A 2nd Lt.
Rudulph, John S. AL Lt.Arty. Lee's Btty.

Rudulph, John S. AL 3rd Inf. Co.G
Rudulph, Julius A. GA 26th Inf. Co.A Sgt.
Rudulph, Samuel AL 9th Inf. Co.G
Rudulph, Z.J. AL Lowndes Rangers Vol. Fagg's Co.
Rudulph, Z.J. Conf.Cav. Wood's Regt. Co.H
Rudy, B.G. GA Inf. 1st City Bn. (Columbus) Co.D
Rudy, B.H. AL 9th Inf. Co.B
Rudy, Daniel VA 10th Inf. Co.F
Rudy, David VA 5th Inf. Co.K
Rudy, D.C. VA 10th Cav. Co.F
Rudy, Elias VA 63rd Inf. Co.E
Rudy, F.O. KY 9th Cav. Co.G 2nd Lt.
Rudy, Frederick VA 37th Inf. Co.K
Rudy, George VA 33rd Inf. Co.K
Rudy, George VA 45th Inf. Co.G
Rudy, George VA 136th Mil. Co.C
Rudy, George H. AR Cav. 15th Bn. (Buster's Bn.) Co.A 1st Lt.
Rudy, George H. MO Inf. Clark's Regt. Co.I 3rd Lt.
Rudy, George H. Conf.Cav. Clarkson's Bn. Ind.Rangers Co.C 1st Lt.
Rudy, I.T. KY Cav.
Rudy, James H. KY 14th Cav. Co.B 1st Lt.
Rudy, J.H. KY 2nd (Duke's) Cav. Co.B Lt.
Rudy, J.H. KY 9th Cav. Co.G Sgt.
Rudy, John M. VA 37th Inf. Co.K
Rudy, Joseph VA 136th Mil. Co.C
Rudy, Levi KY 4th Mtd.Inf. Co.B Cpl.
Rudy, Levi TN 3rd (Forrest's) Cav. Co.D
Rudy, Rufus TN 29th Inf. Co.D
Rudy, S.G. GA 22nd Inf. Co.G Sgt.
Rudy, T. AL 9th Inf. Co.G
Rudy, Thomas C. TX 22nd Cav. Co.D QMSgt.
Rudy, William VA 37th Inf. Co.H
Rue, Abraham NC 8th Bn.Part.Rangers Co.C
Rue, Alexander M. NC 2nd Cav. (19th St.Troops) Co.G Cpl.
Rue, Allen KY 2nd (Duke's) Cav. Co.H
Rue, B.L. TX 29th Cav. Co.H
Rue, Edgar E. NC 2nd Cav. (19th St.Troops) Co.G
Rue, F.M. KY 9th Cav. Co.H Sgt.
Rue, Francis M. KY 2nd (Duke's) Cav. Co.H Sgt.
Rue, Henry NC 61st Inf. Co.B
Rue, John B. TX 14th Cav. Co.H
Rue, John G. NC 2nd Cav. (19th St.Troops) Co.G
Rue, John T. NC 33rd Inf. Co.H
Rue, P. NC 3rd Arty. (40th St.Troops) Co.G
Rue, Peter LA 1st Hvy.Arty. (Reg.) Co.E
Rue, Precinth NC 2nd Arty. (36th St.Troops) Co.I
Rue, Precinth NC 3rd Arty. (40th St.Troops) Co.G
Rue, R.H. TX Cav. Bourland's Regt. Co.G
Rue, Richard W. TX 14th Cav. Co.H
Rue, Robert MO 9th Inf. Co.H
Rue, William B. TX 14th Cav. Co.H
Rueben, W. GA 1st Bn.S.S. Co.C
Ruebush, James K. VA 5th Inf. Co.M
Ruebush, J.C. VA 5th Cav. Co.E
Ruebush, John C. VA Prov.Guard Avis' Co.
Ruedas, Clandio TX 3rd Inf. 1st Co.C

Ruede, William E. GA Phillips' Legion Co.L Cpl.
Rueff, Frederick H. MS Cav. 1st Bn. (Miller's) Bowles' Co. 3rd Lt.
Rueger, Henry VA 12th Inf. Co.C
Rueger, Henry VA 39th Mil. Co.B
Ruel, J. LA Mil. 3rd Regt.Eur.Brig. (Garde Francaise) Co.2
Ruel, O.F. AR 1st (Dobbin's) Cav. Co.A
Ruel, P. LA Mil. 3rd Regt.Eur.Brig. (Garde Francaise) Co.2
Ruelberg, E. LA Mil. Otero's Co. (Titterton's Guards) Ord.Sgt.
Ruell, Frank LA Mil. 5th Regt.Eur.Brig. (Spanish Regt.) Co.5
Ruenbuhl, Henry TX Cav. Waller's Regt. Menard's Co.
Ruenbuhl, J.E. TX Lt.Arty. Jones' Co.
Ruennbuhl, J.E.J. TX 6th Field Btty.
Ruennbuhl, J.E.J. TX Lt.Arty. Dege's Bn.
Ruens, E.F. LA 3rd Inf. Co.D
Rueper, W.P. LA 2nd Cav. Co.A
Ruer, Daniel SC Lt.Arty. 3rd (Palmetto) Bn. Culpeper's Co.
Ruer, G.D. SC 8th Inf.
Rues, Jues LA 26th Inf. Co.G
Rues, Jose TX Cav. L. Trevinio's Co.
Ruess, Jean LA Mil. 4th Regt. 2nd Brig. 1st Div. Co.G
Ruet, Jacob LA Arty. Castellanos' Btty.
Ruez, Pedro TX 17th Field Btty.
Ruez, Thomas AL 21st Inf.
Rufa, H. 1st Chickasaw Inf. Hansell's Co.
Ruff, --- FL Cav. 5th Bn. Co.G
Ruff, --- VA 16th Cav. Co.K
Ruff, A.F. SC 12th Inf. Co.D Sgt.
Ruff, Allen TX 5th Inf. Co.H
Ruff, Andrew W. VA Rockbridge Cty.Res. Bacon's Co.
Ruff, Augustus MS Lt.Arty. (Brookhaven Lt.Arty.) Hoskins' Btty.
Ruff, A.V. AR Cav. Witherspoon's Bn. Lt.Col.
Ruff, Benjamin TX Inf. Griffin's Bn. Co.A
Ruff, Benjamin A. NC 3rd Inf. Co.A
Ruff, Benjamin H. VA 37th Inf. Co.A
Ruff, C.H. TX 2nd Inf. Co.G Capt.,AQM
Ruff, Charles N. LA 19th Inf. Co.A
Ruff, C.T. MS Cav. 4th Bn. Co.B 1st Sgt.
Ruff, C.T. 8th (Wade's) Conf.Cav. Co.D 1st Sgt.
Ruff, C.W. AR 36th Inf. Co.E
Ruff, D. MS Cav. 1st Bn. (Montgomery's) St.Troops Hammond's Co.
Ruff, D. MS 3rd Inf. (St.Troops) Co.I
Ruff, Daniel VA 1st Cav. Co.I
Ruff, David MS 26th Inf. Co.G
Ruff, David A. SC 13th Inf. Co.D
Ruff, David E. VA 4th Inf. Co.I Sgt.
Ruff, David F. FL 9th Inf. Co.E
Ruff, David H. MS Inf. 3rd Bn. Co.B
Ruff, D.G. SC 2nd Cav. Co.F
Ruff, D.N. AL 42nd Inf. Co.K
Ruff, D.W. SC Cav. 4th Bn. Co.B Bvt.2nd Lt.
Ruff, D.W. SC 12th Inf. Co.F
Ruff, D.W. SC 25th Mil.
Ruff, D. Walter SC 2nd Cav. Co.C 2nd Lt.
Ruff, Fletcher A. SC 2nd Cav. Co.C
Ruff, F.M. MS 1st Cav. Co.G Cpl.

Ruff, Frank SC 13th Inf. Co.K
Ruff, Franklin SC 24th Inf. Co.G
Ruff, G. MS 8th Cav. Co.I
Ruff, G. NC 1st Bn.Jr.Res. Co.C
Ruff, George AL 51st (Part.Rangers) Co.H
Ruff, George C.W. FL 2nd Cav. Co.C
Ruff, George F. MD 1st Inf. Co.D 1st Sgt.
Ruff, George W. AR 5th Inf. Co.C
Ruff, George W. LA 3rd Inf. Co.F
Ruff, George W. MS Inf. 3rd Bn. Co.B
Ruff, George W. MS 13th Inf. Co.I
Ruff, G.R. MS 18th Cav. Wimberly's Co.A
Ruff, G.W. KY 12th Cav. Co.E Cpl.
Ruff, H. AL 24th Inf. Co.G
Ruff, H.B. FL Inf. 2nd Bn. Co.C
Ruff, H.C. GA Cav. 1st Bn.Res. Co.E
Ruff, H.C. GA 7th Inf. (St.Guards) Co.L Sgt.
Ruff, Henry MS Cav. Ham's Regt. Co.I
Ruff, Henry H. MS Inf. 3rd Bn. Co.B
Ruff, Henry L. MO Cav. Wood's Regt. Co.E
Ruff, H.L. AR 15th Mil. Co.H 1st Sgt.
Ruff, H.L. SC 4th Bn.Res. Co.C
Ruff, Hosea NC 25th Inf. Co.A
Ruff, J.A. LA 8th Cav. Co.K
Ruff, J.A. MS Inf. 3rd Bn. (St.Troops) Co.C
Ruff, Jacob LA 28th (Thomas') Inf. Co.C
Ruff, James MS 40th Inf. Co.K
Ruff, James C. GA 15th Inf. Co.C
Ruff, James C. NC 42nd Inf. Co.B
Ruff, James E. MS 4th Inf.
Ruff, James H. GA Arty. 9th Bn. Co.E Sgt.
Ruff, James M. GA 22nd Inf. Co.C
Ruff, James R. NC 61st Inf. Co.F Music.
Ruff, James R. SC 13th Inf. Co.K Ord.Sgt.
Ruff, James S.L. AL 13th Inf. Co.G
Ruff, James W. VA 1st Cav. Co.C
Ruff, J.H. SC 3rd Inf. Co.E
Ruff, J.J. SC 13th Inf. Co.D
Ruff, J.M.H. GA 26th Inf. Asst.Surg.
Ruff, J.M.H. SC 3rd Inf. Co.E Sgt.
Ruff, J.M.H. Gen. & Staff Asst.Surg.
Ruff, John AR Cav. Woosley's Bn. Co.G
Ruff, John GA 61st Inf. Co.I
Ruff, John NC 3rd Inf. Co.A
Ruff, John VA 1st Cav. Co.I
Ruff, John A. SC 2nd Cav. Co.H
Ruff, John A. SC Cav.Bn. Hampton Legion
Co.D
Ruff, John A. VA 1st Cav. Co.C
Ruff, John F. MS 7th Cav. Co.B
Ruff, John F. MS Inf. 3rd Bn. Co.F
Ruff, John H. SC 13th Inf. Co.D 2nd Lt.
Ruff, John H. TX 11th (Spaight's) Bn.Vol. Co.C
Ruff, John H. TX 21st Inf. Co.E
Ruff, John J. MS 24th Inf. Co.C
Ruff, John J. SC 1st (McCreary's) Inf. Co.B
Cpl.
Ruff, John S. SC 3rd Inf. Co.E Sgt.
Ruff, John W. MS Inf. 3rd Bn. Co.B
Ruff, Joseph H. FL 2nd Cav. Co.C
Ruff, J.R. AL 51st (Part.Rangers) Co.H
Ruff, J.S. SC 2nd Cav. Co.G
Ruff, J.T. AL 3rd Inf. Co.G
Ruff, J.W. AR 45th Mil. Co.B
Ruff, J.W. GA 33rd Regt. Co.E
Ruff, J.W. NC 64th Inf. Co.H
Ruff, Martin GA 3rd Cav. (St.Guards) Co.H

Ruff, Martin L. GA 15th Inf. Co.C
Ruff, Maximillian SC 9th Res. Co.G
Ruff, Minor NC 29th Inf. Co.E
Ruff, M.L. GA Cav. 1st Bn.Res. Co.E
Ruff, M.L. GA 7th Inf. (St.Guards) Co.L
Ruff, Moorman SC 3rd Inf. Co.E
Ruff, Nathaniel GA 1st Reg. Co.L
Ruff, N.B. MS 5th Inf. Co.E
Ruff, Newton F. MS 17th Inf. Co.D
Ruff, Paul M. SC 1st (McCreary's) Inf. Co.C
Ruff, P.M. SC 1st Inf. Co.O Cpl.
Ruff, P.M. Gen. & Staff QM Agent
Ruff, R. MS McLelland's Co. (Noxubee Home
Guards)
Ruff, R. TX 21st Inf. Co.B
Ruff, Reuben NC 64th Inf. Co.E
Ruff, Reuben L. SC 1st (McCreary's) Inf. Co.B
Ruff, R.F. SC 3rd Inf. Co.E
Ruff, R.L. SC 1st Inf. Co.L
Ruff, Robert TX 11th (Spaight's) Bn.Vol. Co.E
Ruff, Robert R. VA 14th Cav. Co.I 1st Lt.
Ruff, R.R. 1st Conf.Cav. 1st Co.G
Ruff, S.A. FL Inf. 2nd Bn. Co.C
Ruff, Samuel A. FL 10th Inf. Co.H
Ruff, Samuel W. VA 5th Inf. Co.B Cpl.
Ruff, Samuel W. VA 27th Inf. 2nd Co.H Cpl.
Ruff, Silas P. NC 62nd Inf. Co.A
Ruff, Silas W. SC 12th Inf. Co.F
Ruff, S.Z. GA 18th Inf. Col.
Ruff, T.G. MS Cav. 1st Bn. (Montgomery's)
St.Troops Hammond's Co.
Ruff, Thomas FL 4th Inf. Co.F
Ruff, Thomas LA 9th Inf. Co.H
Ruff, Thomas A. MS Inf. 2nd Bn. Co.D
Ruff, Thomas A. MS 48th Inf. Co.D
Ruff, Thomas E. SC 13th Inf. Co.K
Ruff, T.L. MS 41st Inf. Co.H
Ruff, W.A. NC 3rd Arty. (40th St.Troops) Co.I
Ruff, Walter G. SC 1st (McCreary's) Inf. Co.C
Sgt.
Ruff, W.C. GA 8th Cav. Co.F Sgt.
Ruff, W.D. MS 4th Inf. Co.K Cpl.
Ruff, W.E. NC 62nd Inf. Co.F
Ruff, W.F. MS 15th Inf. Co.D
Ruff, W.G. SC 1st Inf. Co.O
Ruff, W.H. SC 3rd Bn.Res. Co.B
Ruff, Wiley E. NC 6th Cav. (65th St.Troops)
Co.D,E
Ruff, William AL 53rd (Part.Rangers) Co.G
Ruff, William NC 64th Inf. Co.E
Ruff, William A. SC 2nd Cav. Co.C
Ruff, William C. GA 62nd Cav. Co.H Sgt.
Ruff, William D. NC 61st Inf. Co.F Cpl.
Ruff, William G. MS Inf. 2nd Bn. Co.D
Ruff, William G. MS 48th Inf. Co.D
Ruff, William M. AL Cav. Lewis Bn. Co.D
Ruff, William W. SC 3rd Inf. Co.E
Ruff, W.J. MS St.Cav. 2nd Bn. (Harris') Co.B
Ruff, W.P. GA Inf. 9th Bn. Co.D
Ruffan, M. SC 11th Inf.
Ruffat, J. LA Mil. 1st Chasseurs a pied Co.8
Ruffe, Newman R. AL 3rd Inf. Co.H Sgt.
Ruffe, Zachariah SC 6th Inf. 1st Co.E
Ruffea, Lewis TX 6th Cav. Co.E
Ruffen, George E. LA 1st Inf. Co.E
Ruffer, E. LA Mil.Conf.Guards Regt. Co.H
Ruffey, E. LA Mil. 2nd Regt. 2nd Brig. 1st Div.

Ruffian, Philip MS 17th Inf. Co.E
Ruffie, S. LA Mil. Chalmette Regt. Co.H
Ruffield, George NC 4th Sr.Res. Co.K
Ruffier, Charles LA 1st Hvy.Arty. (Reg.) Co.A
Ruffier, Chs. LA Arty. Castellanos' Btty.
Ruffier, Charles LA Inf.Crescent Regt. Co.D
Sgt.
Ruffier, Charles LA Inf.Cons.Crescent Regt.
Co.G Sgt.
Ruffier, E. LA Washington Arty.Bn. Co.5 Cpl.
Ruffier, Edward LA Mil. 1st Chasseurs a pied
Co.3
Ruffier, H. LA Arty. Guyol's Co. (Orleans
Arty.)
Ruffier, James G. LA Arty. Watson Btty.
Ruffin, A. NC 8th Sr.Res. Co.F
Ruffin, A.G. GA Inf. 1st Loc.Troops (Augusta)
Barnes' Lt.Arty.Co.
Ruffin, A.G. GA 1st (Symons') Res. Co.I Cpl.
Ruffin, A.G. NC 66th Inf. Co.K
Ruffin, A. Gray NC Inf. 13th Bn. Co.D
Ruffin, A.J. AL 34th Inf. Co.K
Ruffin, A.J. GA Siege Arty. 26th Bn. Co.H
Ruffin, Algernon M. VA Inf. 5th Bn. Co.C
Ruffin, Algernon M. VA 53rd Inf. Co.C
Ruffin, Andrew J. NC 2nd Arty. (36th St.Troops)
Co.F
Ruffin, C.H. TN Cav. Jackson's Co.
Ruffin, Charles H. NC 30th Inf. Co.I
Ruffin, Charles L. Sig.Corps,CSA
Ruffin, Charles M. GA 41st Inf. Co.G
Ruffin, C.L. LA 17th Inf. Co.D Cpl.
Ruffin, C.L. SC 2nd Inf. Co.I
Ruffin, D. NC 8th Sr.Res. Co.C
Ruffin, David C. NC 3rd Arty. (40th St.Troops)
Co.F
Ruffin, Davis NC 61st Inf. Co.F
Ruffin, D.C. NC 8th Inf. Co.C
Ruffin, E. AL Cav. Musgrove's Bn. Co.E
Ruffin, E. MS 35th Inf. Co.E
Ruffin, Edmund, Jr. VA 5th Cav. (12 mo. '61-2)
Co.F Capt.
Ruffin, E.F. MS 10th Inf. Old Co.D Cpl.
Ruffin, E.T. Sig.Corps,CSA 2nd Lt.
Ruffin, Etheldred F. NC 1st Cav. (9th St.Troops)
Co.H Ord.Sgt.
Ruffin, F.L. MS Inf. 3rd Bn. (St.Troops) Co.E
Cpl.
Ruffin, Frank G. Gen. & Staff Lt.Col.
Ruffin, Fullen GA 20th Inf. Co.K
Ruffin, G. NC 67th Inf. Co.G
Ruffin, George C. VA Lt.Arty. 12th Bn. Co.B
Cpl.
Ruffin, George E. VA Inf. 1st Bn.Loc.Def. Co.E
Ruffin, Gray NC 17th Inf. (2nd Org.) Co.I
Ruffin, Gray NC Mallett's Bn. Co.F
Ruffin, H.J. AL 60th Inf. Co.D
Ruffin, H.J. AL 3rd Bn. Hilliard's Legion Vol.
Co.F
Ruffin, H.J. TN 49th Inf. Co.C
Ruffin, James FL 11th Inf.
Ruffin, James GA 13th Inf. Co.D
Ruffin, James GA Inf. 19th Bn. (St.Guards) Co.A
Ruffin, James MS 2nd Cav. Co.D,B Capt.
Ruffin, James Conf.Cav. Wood's Regt. Co.B
Ruffin, James G. LA Pointe Coupee Arty. Sgt.

Ruffin, James H. NC 2nd Cav. (19th St.Troops)
Co.E
Ruffin, J.C. VA Lt.Arty. 12th Bn. Co.B Sgt.
Ruffin, J.E. TN 50th Inf. Co.E 1st Lt.
Ruffin, J.E. TN 50th (Cons.) Inf. Co.E 1st Lt.
Ruffin, Jefferson R. VA Lt.Arty. Arch. Graham's
Co.
Ruffin, J.L. AL 2nd Cav. Co.G
Ruffin, J.M. AR 12th Inf. Co.A Capt.
Ruffin, John MS 14th Inf. Co.C
Ruffin, John A. AL 13th Inf. Co.G
Ruffin, John D. NC 55th Inf. Co.A
Ruffin, John E. AL Gid Nelson Lt.Arty.
Ruffin, John E. AL 11th Inf. Co.D
Ruffin, John K. NC 5th Inf. Asst.Surg.
Ruffin, John K. NC 49th Inf. Surg.
Ruffin, John K. Gen. & Staff Surg.
Ruffin, John R. NC 33rd Inf. Co.B
Ruffin, John R. VA 13th Cav. Co.G
Ruffin, Jonathan NC 5th Inf. Co.G
Ruffin, Joseph VA 3rd Inf. Co.E Jr.2nd Lt.
Ruffin, J.R. TN 7th (Duckworth's) Cav. Co.E
Sgt.
Ruffin, J.R. VA Lt.Arty. Ellett's Co. Cpl.
Ruffin, K.D. GA 46th Inf. Co.A
Ruffin, Laman NC 6th Cav. (65th St.Troops)
Co.K,B
Ruffin, Lamon KY 2nd Cav. Co.B
Ruffin, Layman NC Cav. 5th Bn. Co.B
Ruffin, Leander TN Cav. Newsom's Regt. Co.C
Ruffin, O.S. NC 1st Cav. (9th St.Troops)
Ruffin, P.F. VA 13th Cav. Co.E
Ruffin, Reuben VA 9th Cav. 2nd Co.A Sgt.
Ruffin, Richard AR 12th Inf. Co.I
Ruffin, Robert E. TN 11th Inf. Co.F
Ruffin, Robert R. NC 17th Inf. (2nd Org.) Co.I
Ruffin, Samuel MS 5th Inf. (St.Troops) Co.B
Ruffin, Samuel H. NC 3rd Arty. (40th St.Troops)
Co.G
Ruffin, Samuel W. MS 12th Cav. Co.H
Ruffin, Shep AL 18th Inf. Co.H Capt.
Ruffin, S.S. 7th Conf.Cav. Co.G
Ruffin, Theoderic B. VA 12th Inf. Co.B,K
Ruffin, Thomas MS 2nd Part. Co.F 2nd Lt.
Ruffin, Thomas MS 3rd Cav. Co.F
Ruffin, Thomas NC 1st Cav. (9th St.Troops)
Co.H Lt.Col.
Ruffin, Thomas NC 4th Cav. (59th St.Troops)
Co.D 1st Lt.
Ruffin, Thomas NC Lt.Arty. 3rd Bn. Co.C,A
Ruffin, Thomas NC 1st Inf. (6 mo. '61) Co.L
Sgt.
Ruffin, Thomas NC 2nd Jr.Res. Co.G Cpl.
Ruffin, Thomas, Jr. NC 6th Inf. Co.H Capt.
Ruffin, Thomas, Jr. NC 13th Inf. Co.E Lt.Col.
Ruffin, Thomas TN 50th Inf. Co.C
Ruffin, Thomas Conf.Cav. Wood's Regt. Co.B
Ruffin, Thomas Gen. & Staff, A. of TN Capt.
Ruffin, Thomas D. 1st Conf.Cav. 1st Co.E
Ruffin, Thomas J. TN Cav. Newsom's Regt.
Co.H Capt.
Ruffin, Thomas S. VA 5th Cav. (12 mo. '61-2)
Co.F Cpl.
Ruffin, Thomas W. VA 3rd Inf. 1st Co.I Capt.
Ruffin, T.J. TN 7th (Duckworth's) Cav. Co.E
Cpl.

Ruffin, T.J. Forrest's Scouts T.N. Kizer's
Co.,CSA Cpl.
Ruffin, T.P. AR Inf. 4th Bn. Co.B Sgt.
Ruffin, V.F. TN 7th (Duckworth's) Cav. Co.E
Cpl.
Ruffin, Vinson MS 14th Inf. Co.C
Ruffin, W. GA Inf. 1st Loc.Troops (Augusta)
Co.B
Ruffin, W.D. MS St.Troops (Peach Creek
Rangers) Maxwell's Co.
Ruffin, W.D. TN Inf. 154th Sr.Regt. Co.G
Ruffin, William AL 46th Inf. Co.D
Ruffin, William Conf.Cav. Wood's Regt. Co.B
Comsy.
Ruffin, Wm. Gen. & Staff Capt.,Comsy.
Ruffin, Wm. F. GA Inf. 1st Loc.Troops
(Augusta) Co.B
Ruffin, William H. MS 14th Inf. Co.C
Ruffin, William H. NC 17th Inf. (2nd Org.) Co.I
Ruffin, William J. VA 5th Cav. (12 mo. '61-2)
Co.E
Ruffin, William J. VA 13th Cav. Co.G
Ruffin, William R. Conf.Arty. McIntosh's Bn.
2nd Lt.
Ruffin, William R. 1st Conf.Eng.Troops Sgt.Maj.
Ruffin, W.R. VA Lt.Arty. 13th Bn. Co.C Order-
ly Sgt.
Ruffner, Andrew AR 45th Cav. Co.D Sgt.
Ruffner, Andrew VA 8th Cav. Co.I Sgt.Maj.
Ruffner, Andrew L. VA 22nd Inf. Co.H
Ruffner, Andy AR 38th Inf. Co.A
Ruffner, Augustus AR 1st (Colquitt's) Inf. Co.D
1st Lt.
Ruffner, Benjamin F. VA 12th Cav. Co.I
Ruffner, Daniel VA 8th Cav. Co.E 1st Sgt.
Ruffner, David L. VA 22nd Inf. Co.H Capt.
Ruffner, H.D. VA Cav. 46th Bn. Maj.
Ruffner, Henry D. VA 19th Cav. Co.G Capt.
Ruffner, Henry D. VA 26th Cav. Lt.Col.
Ruffner, Henry D. VA 22nd Inf. Co.H 3rd Lt.
Ruffner, James W. VA 62nd Mtd.Inf. 2nd Co.K
Ruffner, Jesse A.J. VA 62nd Mtd.Inf. 2nd Co.K
Ruffner, Joel VA 22nd Inf. Co.E 1st Lt.
Ruffner, John H. VA 13th Inf. Co.D
Ruffner, Joseph AR 45th Cav. Co.D
Ruffner, Joseph AR 38th Inf. Co.A
Ruffner, Joshua VA 97th Mil. Co.F
Ruffner, Lewis AR 45th Cav. Co.D 2nd Lt.
Ruffner, Lewis AR 38th Inf. Co.A Bvt.2nd Lt.
Ruffner, Martin VA 7th Cav. Co.D Cpl.
Ruffner, Meredith P. VA 22nd Inf. Co.H
Ruffner, M.M. MO 1st & 4th Cons.Inf. Co.H
Ruffner, M.M. MO 4th Inf. Co.K
Ruffner, Morton MO 4th Cav. Co.H
Ruffner, Oscar VA 8th Cav. Co.E
Ruffner, P. Harrison VA 7th Inf. Co.C
Ruffner, Philip VA Cav. 39th Bn. Co.C Cpl.
Ruffner, Philip VA 97th Mil. Co.F
Ruffner, Robert M. VA 10th Cav. Co.H
Ruffner, R.S. VA Lt.Arty. 13th Bn. Co.A
Ruffner, Rubin VA 97th Mil. Co.F
Ruffner, S. AR 45th Cav. Co.L Bvt.2nd Lt.
Ruffner, Samuel L. VA 19th Cav. Co.G 2nd Lt.
Ruffner, Samuel T. MO Lt.Arty. 1st Field Btty.
Capt.
Ruffner, Silas AR 38th Inf. Co.A
Rufford, E.M. GA 44th Inf.

Ruffta, H. 1st Chickasaw Inf. Kesner's Co.
Ruffunack, John MS 48th Inf. Co.E Sgt.
Ruffunnach, J.B. MS Inf. 2nd Bn. Co.E
Rufner, Philip VA 4th Cav. Co.B
Rufner, William C. LA Mil. Orleans Fire Regt.
Ruford, R. GA 29th Inf.
Ruford, S. GA 54th Inf. Co.H
Rufton, Samuel R. NC 7th Inf. Co.F
Rufty, E. NC 37th Inf. Co.G
Rufty, George W. AR 11th Inf. Co.I
Rufty, George W. NC 5th Inf. Co.E
Rufty, James F. TX 11th Inf. Co.D
Rufty, James R. NC 6th Inf. Co.K
Rufty, J.H. NC 37th Inf. Co.G
Rufty, John NC 5th Sr.Res. Co.D
Rufty, Michael NC 49th Inf. Co.I
Rufty, Milas A. NC 1st Arty. (10th St.Troops)
Co.D
Rufty, Rufus NC 7th Inf. Co.F
Rufty, W.E. AR 20th Inf. Co.G
Rufty, William NC 57th Inf. Co.A
Rufus, C.W. GA 13th Inf. Co.F
Rufus, Daniel AL 59th Inf.
Rufus, H. TX 19th Inf. Co.F
Rugby, W.J.H. NC 22nd Inf. Co.A Lt.
Rugel, --- TX Cav. Baird's Regt. Co.G
Rugel, A.J. LA Mil.Conf.Guards Regt. Co.B
Rugeley, Alexander F. TX 13th Vol. 1st Co.I
1st Lt.
Rugeley, Edward S. TX 35th (Brown's) Cav.
Co.D Capt.
Rugeley, Edward S. TX 13th Vol. 1st Co.I Capt.
Rugeley, H. AL Res. Belser's Co.
Rugeley, Henry L. TX 35th (Brown's) Cav.
Co.D
Rugeley, Henry L. TX 13th Vol. 1st Co.I
Rugeley, Henry L. Gen. & Staff Asst.Surg.
Rugeley, J.D. TX 8th Cav. Co.B
Rugeley, R.D. FL Cav. 3rd Bn. Co.C Sgt.Maj.
Rugeley, R.D. 15th Conf.Cav. Co.E
Rugeley, R.D. 1st Conf.Inf. 1st Co.K Bugler
Rugeley, Robert TX 8th Cav. Co.B
Rugeley, William C. AL 3rd Inf. Co.G
Rugely, A. SC 6th Cav. Co.C
Rugely, Henry L. TX 26th Cav. A.Surg.
Rugely, H.L. TX 1st Hvy.Arty. Asst.Surg.
Rugely, H.R. AL Rebels
Ruger, James Allen AL 33rd Inf. Co.F
Ruger, M.D. AL 33rd Inf. Co.A
Ruger, Stephen G. LA 2nd Cav. Co.F
Ruger, W.F. SC 25th Inf. Co.E
Rugers, Andrew D. AL 6th Inf. Co.M
Rugg, A.J. SC Arty. Zimmerman's Co. (PeeDee
Arty.)
Rugg, A.J. SC 1st Inf. Co.B Sgt.
Rugg, A.J. SC 21st Inf. Co.B Sgt.Maj.
Rugg, C. LA 21st (Kennedy's) Inf. Co.D
Rugg, Edward T. SC 21st Inf. Co.G
Rugg, Francis D. AL 33rd Inf. Co.A
Rugg, Hiram AL 6th Inf. Co.M
Rugg, H.N. TX 29th Cav. Co.C
Rugg, N.J. AR 2nd Cav. Co.G
Rugg, R.P. SC 21st Inf. Co.B
Rugg, Zachariah C. LA 31st Inf. Co.G
Ruggett, James AL 25th Inf. Co.C
Ruggiero, M. VA 2nd St.Res. Co.K Sgt.
Ruggle, G. AL 9th Inf. Co.C

Ruggles, Daniel Gen. & Staff Maj.Gen.
Ruggles, Edward Leyman Sig.Corps,CSA Lt.
Ruggles, E.S. Gen. & Staff Maj.,Comsy.
Ruggles, Frank D. LA Washington Arty.Bn.
 Co.1 Cpl.
Ruggles, J. VA 20th Cav. Co.A
Ruggles, Mortimer B. Gen. & Staff ADC
Ruggles, S. GA 22nd Inf. Co.I
Ruggles, Thomas C. NC 1st Cav. (9th St.Troops)
 Co.H
Ruggs, Alex C. TX 3rd Inf. Co.E Sgt.
Ruggs, Charles H. LA 8th Inf. Co.B
Rugheimer, J. SC Mil.Arty. 1st Regt. Co.A
Rugher, J.W. GA 41st Inf. Co.K
Rugle, Charles F. TN 39th Mtd.Inf. Co.C Cpl.
Rugle, J.M. MS 4th Inf. Co.B
Rugsley, W.C. AL Cp. Watts
Ruh, Christian LA 20th Inf. Co.C
Ruhe, Herman TN Arty. Marshall's Co. Artif.
Ruhe, William Conf.Inf. Tucker's Regt. Co.B
Ruhfeldt, Charles LA 15th Inf. Co.K
Ruhfus, H. TX Cav. 2nd Regt. Co.B
Ruhl, August LA 21st (Pattons') Inf. Co.I
Ruhl, C.E. VA 24th Cav. Co.B
Ruhl, Frederich LA 21st (Kennedy's) Inf. Co.C
Ruhl, Peter LA 20th Inf. Co.B 1st Lt.
Ruhl, Wiegand VA 136th Mil. Co.B
Ruhle, W. TX Inf. 1st St.Troops Shield's Co.B
Ruhlege, J.W. AL 60th Inf. Co.H
Ruhlman, Ed C. LA 22nd Inf. Co.A Sgt.
Ruhlman, John B. LA 8th Inf. Co.A
Ruhlmann, Philippe LA Mil. 1st Regt. French
 Brig. Co.6 Cpl.
Ruhmann, Philip TX 17th Inf. Co.H
Ruide, A.D. GA Inf. 2nd Bn. (St.Guards) Old
 Co.D
Ruin, J.W. AL 9th Inf. Co.K
Ruis, Alfred GA 1st (Symons') Res.
Ruis, Calvin GA 50th Inf. Co.C
Ruis, Carpio TX 3rd Inf. 1st Co.C
Ruis, Eugene TX 2nd Cav. Co.B
Ruis, Graviel TX Cav. Ragsdale's Bn. Co.B
Ruis, James J. GA 50th Inf. Co.C
Ruis, Malikiah GA 50th Inf. Co.B
Ruis, Manning GA 50th Inf. Co.B
Ruis, R.R. GA Inf. 1st Loc.Troops (Augusta)
 Co.B
Ruis, William GA 1st (Symons') Res. Co.F,E
Ruitt, J.E. AL 28th Inf. Co.E
Ruitz, J.F. AL 12th Inf. Co.H
Ruiz, A. LA Mil. Orleans Fire Regt. Co.H
Ruiz, A.J. LA 30th Inf. Co.A
Ruiz, Alejo TX 8th Inf. Co.H
Ruiz, Alex M. TX 3rd Inf. 1st Co.A Capt.
Ruiz, Antonio LA 10th Inf. Co.F
Ruiz, Armand LA 30th Inf. Co.A 2nd Lt.
Ruiz, Emile LA Mil. 4th Regt. 1st Brig. 1st Div.
 Co.I Capt.
Ruiz, Eugene TX Cav. Benavides' Regt. Co.F
Ruiz, Fausto LA 30th Inf. Co.D 1st Sgt.
Ruiz, Fausto LA C.S. Zouave Bn. Co.F Sgt.
Ruiz, Francisco TX Cav. 3rd (Yager's) Bn.
 Rhode's Co. Cpl.
Ruiz, Frank A. LA 21st (Patton's) Inf. Co.D
 Sgt.
Ruiz, Inez LA 28th (Thomas') Inf. Co.G
Ruiz, Jose Maria TX 3rd Inf. 1st Co.A

Ruiz, Manuel LA 28th (Thomas') Inf. Co.H
Ruiz, Marcelino TX 8th Inf. Co.C
Ruiz, Paul LA 21st (Pattons') Inf. Co.D
Ruiz, Paul LA Mil. Chalmette Regt. Co.H,K
Ruiz, Pedro TX 3rd Inf. 1st Co.A
Ruiz, R. LA Mil. Orleans Fire Regt. Co.H
Ruiz, T.A. LA 30th Inf. Co.A
Ruize, Jessus TX 2nd Cav. Co.F
Ruke, J.W. GA 62nd Cav. Co.L
Ruker, H.F. GA Cav. 12th Bn. (St.Guards) Co.A
Ruker, Joseph T. GA 55th Inf. Co.G
Ruks, W.J. AL 48th Inf. Co.G
Rulberg, Ernest LA Mil. 1st Regt. 3rd Brig. 1st
 Div. Co.E Sgt.
Rule, Adam VA Burks' Regt.Loc.Def. Shield's
 Co.
Rule, Anthony VA 22nd Inf. Co.C
Rule, Barnett O. VA Hvy.Arty. 19th Bn. Co.A
Rule, Barnett O. VA Hvy.Arty. Kyle's Co.
Rule, Boston B. VA 2nd Cav. Co.H Black.
Rule, C. NC 64th Inf. Co.L
Rule, Caleb B. VA 2nd Cav. Co.H
Rule, Caleb B. VA Hvy.Arty. 19th Bn. Co.A
Rule, Cary VA 22nd Inf. Co.C
Rule, C.C. KY 5th Cav. Co.C 1st Sgt.
Rule, C.C. KY Kirkpatrick's Bn. Co.C 1st Sgt.
Rule, Charles C. KY 11th Cav. Co.G Ord.Sgt.
Rule, Christian C. VA 2nd Cav. Co.H
Rule, David VA 6th Cav. Co.F
Rule, George R. KY 4th Cav. Co.D
Rule, G.F. MO 12th Cav. Co.E
Rule, G.W. KY 9th Mtd.Inf. Co.I
Rule, James MS 6th Inf. Co.I
Rule, J.B. MS 10th Cav. Co.I
Rule, J.B. MS 1st (Patton's) Inf. Co.K
Rule, Jefferson TN 13th (Gore's) Cav. Co.G
Rule, Jesse D. MS 1st (Patton's) Inf. Co.K
Rule, John AR Cav. Crabtree's (46th) Regt. Co.I
Rule, Madison MS 6th Inf. Co.I
Rule, Nathaniel LA Inf. 4th Bn. Co.A
Rule, Peter A. MS 6th Inf. Co.I
Rule, Peter H. VA Lt.Arty. Hardwicke's Co.
Rule, Ransum AR 8th Cav. Co.L
Rule, Richard F. VA Hvy.Arty. 19th Bn. Co.A
Rule, T.B. MS 6th Inf. Co.I
Rule, Thad MS 12th Cav. Co.E
Rule, W.A. MO 10th Cav. Co.I
Ruleau, Felix LA Washington Arty.Bn. Co.3
Ruleff, George, Jr. LA 7th Inf. Co.A
Ruleman, Henry D. VA 62nd Mtd.Inf. 2nd Co.K
Ruleman, William C. VA 62nd Mtd.Inf. Co.E
Ruleman, W.J. TN 7th (Duckworth's) Cav.
 White's Co.
Ruley, B. Oscar TX 9th Cav. Co.A Ord.Sgt.
Ruley, B.W. 3rd Conf.Eng.Troops Co.E
Ruley, D.H. VA 23rd Cav. Co.H
Ruley, Henry H. VA Cav. McFarlane's Co.
Ruley, H.F. MO 5th Cav. Co.C
Ruley, James M. MD 1st Inf. Co.D Music.
Ruley, James M. VA 12th Cav. Co.I
Ruley, James P. TN 63rd Inf. Co.D Cpl.
Ruley, John F. VA 52nd Inf. Co.E Sgt.
Ruley, T.J. VA 72nd Mil.
Ruley, William A. VA 12th Cav. Co.I
Rulhman, J. LA Mil. 3rd Regt.Eur.Brig. (Garde
 Francaise) Frois' Co.

Rulhman, P. LA Mil. 1st Regt. French Brig.
 Co.9
Rulhmann, Louis LA Mil. 3rd Regt.Eur.Brig.
 (Garde Francaise) Co.4
Ruling, James M. VA 5th Cav. Co.K
Ruling, L.B. TN 1st (Feild's) Inf.
Rulisle, Benjamin AR 1st (Dobbin's) Cav. Co.D
Rulkenberg, C. LA Mil. 3rd Regt. 3rd Brig. 1st
 Div. Co.E
Rulle, John TN 2nd (Walker's) Inf. Co.K
Rulle, John 9th Conf.Inf. Co.A
Rullens, N.C. SC Prov.Guard Hamilton's Co.
Rullman, William LA Mil. 4th Regt. 2nd Brig.
 1st Div. Co.B
Rulls, J.F. GA 17th Inf. Co.E
Rulo, J. KY 3rd Mtd.Inf. 1st Co.F
Rulo, James KY Lt.Arty. Cobb's Co. Cpl.
Rulo, N. KY Lt.Arty. Cobb's Co. Cpl.
Rulong, Chs. LA 8th Inf. Co.B
Rulottone, LaFayette 4th Conf.Eng.Troops
Rulphen, H. MS 2nd (Quinn's St.Troops) Inf.
 Co.H
Rulter, L. KY 3rd Mtd.Inf. Co.K
Ruly, J.W. TX 10th Field Btty.
Ruly, Robert VA 58th Inf. Co.G Cpl.
Ruly, William VA Cav. 46th Bn. Co.E
Rum, James AR 37th Inf.
Rumag, J.L. TN Holman's Bn.Part.Rangers
 Co.A
Rumage, A.J. TN 3rd (Clack's) Inf. Co.F
Rumage, E.R. NC 42nd Inf. Co.C
Rumage, Franklin NC 42nd Inf. Co.C
Rumage, George W. NC 42nd Inf. Co.C
Rumage, Harris NC 52nd Inf. Co.I Cpl.
Rumage, Henry A. NC 33rd Inf. Co.C
Rumage, J.B. KY 10th (Johnson's) Cav. Co.E
Rumage, J.B. KY Lt.Arty. Cobb's Co.
Rumage, John M. NC 42nd Inf. Co.C
Rumage, Joseph A. TN 48th (Voorhies') Inf.
 Co.H
Rumage, J.T.H. MS 1st (Johnston's) Inf. Co.I
 Bvt.2nd Lt.
Rumage, J.W. SC 13th Inf. Co.A
Rumage, Lindsay NC 37th Inf. Co.I
Rumage, Nathan NC 42nd Inf. Co.C
Rumage, Nathaniel NC 5th Inf. Co.F
Rumage, T.A. NC 1st Jr.Res. Co.G
Rumage, Tilman NC 42nd Inf. Co.C
Rumage, William TN 62nd Mtd.Inf. Co.C
Rumage, William R. NC 14th Inf. Co.H
Rumage, W.F. AL 9th Inf.
Rumaie, A.J. AR 19th (Dawson's) Inf. Co.F
 Sgt.
Rumans, Andrew J. MO 6th Inf.
Rumble, S.E. MS 7th Inf. Capt.,AQM
Rumble, Steven E. Gen. & Staff Capt.,AQM
Rumble, T. GA 5th Res. Co.A
Rumble, William GA 5th Res. Co.A Sgt.
Rumble, Woodbridge GA 45th Inf. Co.B
Rumbles, Urban GA 14th Inf. Co.A
Rumbley, Enoch TN Detailed Conscr. Co.B
Rumbley, E. Wash. TN 5th Inf. 2nd Co.G
Rumbley, H.C. MS 4th Cav. Co.H
Rumbley, Henry AL 3rd Cav. Co.B Sgt.

Rumbley, Henry Conf.Cav. Wood's Regt. 1st
Co.M Sgt.
Rumbley, H.M. AL 17th Inf. Co.H,G 1st Sgt.
Rumbley, J.D. SC 1st Cav. Co.C
Rumbley, John S. NC 13th Inf. Co.E
Rumbley, John W. AL 42nd Inf. Co.A Sgt.
Rumbley, J.W. AL Inf. 2nd Regt. Co.C
Rumbley, Nathan NC 44th Inf. Co.G
Rumbley, T.A. AL 17th Inf. Co.H
Rumbley, Thomas SC 1st Cav. Co.C
Rumbley, William L. TN 5th Inf. 2nd Co.G
Rumbley, William R. GA 15th Inf. Co.G
Rumbly, A.J. SC 1st Bn.S.S. Co.A
Rumbly, A.J. SC 27th Inf. Co.E
Rumbly, H.M. AL 32nd & 58th (Cons.) Inf. 1st
Lt.
Rumbly, H.M. AL 58th Inf. Co.C,F 1st Lt.
Rumbly, Julius Caesar NC 64th Inf. Co.F
Rumbo, James C. KY Cav. Bolen's Ind.Co.
Rumbo, James C. TN 10th Inf. Co.I
Rumbo, John GA 11th Cav. (St.Guards) Smith's
Co.
Rumbo, John F. KY Cav. Bolen's Ind.Co.
Rumbo, John K. TN 10th Inf. Co.I
Rumbo, Samuel Gen. & Staff Contr.Surg.
Rumbo, T.I. TN 6th (Wheeler's) Cav. Co.A
Rumbo, W.L. TN 6th (Wheeler's) Cav. Co.A
Rumbo, W.L. TN Lt.Arty. Sparkman's Co.
Rumbok, A. TX 2nd Inf. Co.B
Rumbough, G.P.C. 1st Conf.Eng.Troops Co.K
1st Lt.
Rumbough, Jacob E. VA 19th Inf. Co.A
Rumbough, Lemuel D. 1st Conf.Eng.Troops
Co.A Sgt.
Rumbough, Thomas S. TN Cav. 16th Bn.
(Neal's) Co.E Capt.
Rumbough, Thomas S. TN 29th Inf. Co.H Capt.
Rumburg, James D. TX Cav. Martin's Regt.
Co.B
Rumburg, William J. VA Inf. 23rd Bn. Co.B
Rumburge, George MS 10th Inf. Old Co.G
Rumby, --- TX Cav. Good's Bn. Co.C
Rumby, --- TX Cav. Wells' Regt. Co.H
Rumell, John J. AL Inf. 1st Regt. Co.D Cpl.
Rumfelt, Columbus MO 8th Cav. Co.H
Rumfelt, Hugh J. TN 50th Inf. Co.H
Rumfelt, James S. NC 49th Inf. Co.A
Rumfelt, J.F. NC 43rd Inf. Co.B
Rumfelt, John L. NC 49th Inf. Co.A
Rumfelt, John L. NC 49th Inf. Co.H
Rumfelt, Martin L. NC 43rd Inf. Co.B
Rumfelt, William H. NC 1st Arty. (10th
St.Troops) Co.C Artif.
Rumfelt, William H. TN 50th Inf. Co.H
Rumff, David J. SC Mil. 15th Regt. Col.
Rumfield, Henry TX Lt.Arty. Hughes' Co. Cpl.
Rumfield, S. TX 16th Inf. Co.K
Rumford, Jackson VA 49th Inf. Co.E
Rumford, James AL 4th Res. Co.D
Ruminer, David AR 27th Inf. Co.I
Rumlee, H.A. TN 2nd Cav.
Rumless, Jack GA Inf. 18th Bn. Co.C Music.
Rumley, A. NC 7th Sr.Res. Bradshaw's Co.
Rumley, Benjamin AR 32nd Inf. Co.C
Rumley, Benjamin W. AR 31st Inf. Co.A
Rumley, Charles F. TX 26th Cav. Co.K
Rumley, Christian TX 2nd Cav. Co.E

Rumley, E. NC 7th Sr.Res. Bradshaw's Co.
Rumley, Elijah GA 10th Inf. Co.D
Rumley, Elijah GA 48th Inf. Co.C
Rumley, Enoch TN Sullivan Cty.Res.
(Loc.Def.Troops) White's Co.
Rumley, Fred C. AL 24th Inf. Co.I Cpl.
Rumley, George NC 7th Sr.Res. Watts' Co.
Rumley, George W. VA 48th Inf. Co.F
Rumley, H.A. TN 5th Cav. Co.A
Rumley, Harvey 1st Conf.Cav. 2nd Co.F
Rumley, Israel NC 45th Inf. Co.F
Rumley, Jacob NC 21st Inf. Co.F
Rumley, J.M. TN 5th Inf. 2nd Co.G
Rumley, Joseph J. TX 4th Inf. Co.F
Rumley, N. NC Mallett's Bn. Co.A
Rumley, Oregon NC 1st Arty. (10th St.Troops)
Co.G
Rumley, R. AR Cav. Gordon's Regt. Co.F Sgt.
Rumley, Samuel D. NC 1st Arty. (10th
St.Troops) Co.G Sgt.
Rumley, Thomas NC 54th Inf. Co.F
Rumley, William NC 2nd Arty. (36th St.Troops)
Co.G 2nd Lt.
Rumley, William F. AR 31st Inf. Co.A Sgt.
Rumley, William W. NC 1st Arty. (10th
St.Troops) Co.G
Rumley, Willis GA Cav. 21st Bn. Co.A
Rumley, Willis GA 10th Inf. Co.D
Rumley, Willis GA 36th (Villepigue's) Inf. Co.F
Rumley, Willis 1st Conf.Inf. Co.F
Rumly, J.D. SC 1st Cav. Co.C
Rummage, Andrew J. AR Inf. Crawford's Bn.
Co.A Sgt.
Rummage, George TN 24th Inf. 1st Co.G, Co.B
Sgt.
Rummage, James TN 9th Inf. Co.H
Rummage, James K. TN 2nd Cav.
Rummage, J.K. TN 3rd (Forrest's) Cav. Co.D
Rummage, J.L. TN 11th (Holman's) Cav. Co.B
Rummage, John L. TN 2nd Cav.
Rummage, Samuel M. TN 2nd Cav.
Rummage, S.M. TN 3rd (Forrest's) Cav. Co.D
Rummage, W.C. TN 3rd (Forrest's) Cav. Do.D
Rummel, Andrew VA 5th Inf. Co.I
Rummel, Ernst TX 3rd Inf. Co.H
Rummel, F. TX 6th Inf. Co.I
Rummel, George TX Inf. 1st St.Troops Co.F
Rummel, J.M. LA 1st Res. Co.D
Rummel, John LA Mil. 1st Regt. 2nd Brig. 1st
Div. Co.F
Rummel, Vendolin LA 20th Inf. Co.B
Rummel, W. TX Waul's Legion Co.F
Rummell, Black VA 20th Cav. Co.C
Rummell, T. GA Inf. 1st Loc.Troops (Augusta)
Barnes' Lt.Arty.Co. 1st Sgt.
Rummell, Thomas B. VA 31st Inf. Co.C
Rummell, W. TX Inf. Timmons' Regt. Co.D
Rummins, A.S. MO 10th Inf. Co.E
Rummons, James MO Inf. Perkins' Bn. Co.F
Sgt.
Rummons, John W. MO Inf. Perkins' Bn. Co.F
Cpl.
Rummons, J.W. MO Inf. Clark's Regt. Co.C
Rummons, Landon A. MO 2nd Inf. Co.C
Rumnel, Justis LA 14th Inf. Co.E
Rumney, Ben F. GA 3rd Cav. (St.Guards) Co.F
Rumney, B.F. GA Phillips' Legion Co.E

Rumney, B.W. GA 9th Inf. (St.Guards) Co.H
Rumney, J.A. GA Cobb's Legion Co.D
Rumney, James E. GA 5th Inf. Co.K
Rumney, J.E. GA Lt.Arty. Pritchard's Co.
(Washington Arty.)
Rumney, J.E. GA 36th (Villepiegue's) Inf. Co.F
Rumney, J.E. Lt.Arty. Dent's Btty.,CSA
Rumney, J.E. 1st Conf.Inf. 1st Co.F
Rumney, Joseph E. GA 8th Inf. Co.K
Rumny, S.J. AR 37th Inf. Co.C
Rumond, J. LA Mil. 2nd Regt. French Brig.
Co.8
Rumons, Franklin MO Cav. Williams' Regt.
Co.K
Rumpel, William TX Conscr.
Rumpell, August TX 8th Field Btty.
Rumpelt, John NC 2nd Arty. (36th St.Troops)
Co.I
Rumpey, E.R. MS Cav. 2nd Bn.Res. Co.A
Rumpff, Joseph MO 5th Inf. Co.F Sgt.
Rumpff, Jos. D. MO 5th Inf. Co.F Sgt.
Rumph, A.W. SC 1st Cav. Co.I 1st Sgt.
Rumph, A.W. SC 1st Mtd.Mil. Smith's Co. 1st
Lt.
Rumph, Charles S. GA 6th Inf. Co.C
Rumph, Christian W. AL 51st (Part.Rangers)
Co.B
Rumph, Christian W. AL Inf. 1st Regt. Co.G
Rumph, D. AL 23rd Inf. Co.B,I 1st Sgt.
Rumph, D.A. SC 11th Inf. Co.B Sgt.
Rumph, D.M. GA 3rd Res. Co.E 2nd Lt.
Rumph, George SC 6th Cav. Co.B,G
Rumph, George W. GA 4th (Clinch's) Cav. Co.A
Cpl.
Rumph, Hazard P. SC Lt.Arty. 3rd (Palmetto)
Bn. Co.D Cpl.
Rumph, Irvin SC Lt.Arty. 3rd (Palmetto) Bn.
Co.D
Rumph, Jacob C. MS 6th Inf. Co.F
Rumph, James C. MS 16th Inf. Co.C 2nd Lt.
Rumph, James L. GA Vol.
Rumph, J.C. MS Cav. 24th Bn. Co.D
Rumph, J.D. GA 4th (Clinch's) Cav. Co.A 3rd
Lt.
Rumph, John SC 3rd Res. Co.A
Rumph, John D. GA Cav. 24th Bn. Co.A 1st Lt.
Rumph, John D. GA Cav. (Wayne Cav.Guards)
Rumph's Co. Capt.
Rumph, John G. GA Phillips' Legion Co.C
Rumph, John J. GA 6th Inf. Co.C
Rumph, John W. MS 36th Inf. Co.G Sgt.
Rumph, J.T. MS 1st Lt.Arty. Co.F
Rumph, Langdon L. AL Inf. 1st Regt. Co.G
Rumph, Louis D. GA 6th Inf. Co.C
Rumph, S.C. GA 12th (Robinson's) Cav.
(St.Guards) Co.B
Rumph, Thomas E. AL 3rd Cav. Co.D
Rumph, William J. AL Cav. Lenoir's Ind.Co.
Rumph, W.V. GA 13th Inf. Co.E
Rumple, C.S. TX Lt.Arty. Dege's Bn.
Rumple, Eli C. NC 4th Inf. Co.A
Rumple, Henry J.C. NC 8th Bn.Jr.Res. Co.A
Rumple, James F. NC 42nd Inf. Co.G Cpl.
Rumple, James M. NC 7th Inf. Co.I
Rumple, James M. NC 42nd Inf. Co.G
Rumple, J.C. NC 4th Inf. Co.A
Rumple, J.E. AL 3rd Cav. Co.D

Rumple, J.L. NC 3rd Jr.Res. Co.F
Rumple, J.M. NC 17th Inf. (2nd Org.) Co.L
Rumple, J.N. NC 23rd Inf. Co.C
Rumple, John W. NC 42nd Inf. Co.G Music.
Rumple, P.A. NC 46th Inf. Co.B
Rumple, P.C. NC 4th Inf. Co.A
Rumple, R. NC 42nd Inf. Co.B
Rumple, T.D. TN Cav. 16th Bn. (Neal's) Co.B
Rumple, W.A. TX 5th Cav. Co.E Sgt.
Rumple, William Aug. NC 7th Inf. Co.B
Rumple, William M. NC 42nd Inf. Co.G
Rumple, William N. NC 2nd Cav. (19th St.Troops) Co.B
Rumples, Robert A. NC 29th Inf. Co.B
Rumpley, J.Berry SC 5th St.Troops Co.H
Rumpp, L. LA Mil. 4th Regt.Eur.Brig. Co.F Sgt.
Rumpt, W.P. MS 1st (Percy's) Inf. Co.H Cpl.
Rumril, Joseph VA 54th Mil. Co.E,F
Rumsam, Ed TX Inf. Rutherford's Co.
Rumsay, James GA Inf. 1st City Bn. (Columbus) Co.F
Rumsay, L.B. GA Lt.Arty. Van Den Corput's Co.
Rumsburg, Joseph VA 23rd Cav. Co.C
Rumsey, Andrew M. TX 12th Cav. Co.I
Rumsey, B.F. TN St.Troops Davis' Co.
Rumsey, C. KY 5th Cav. Co.F
Rumsey, D.G. TN 19th Inf. Co.E Cpl.
Rumsey, Fields GA 64th Inf. Co.F,A
Rumsey, Fields 1st Conf.Inf. 2nd Co.C
Rumsey, Floyd 1st Conf.Inf. 2nd Co.C
Rumsey, F.M. 1st Conf.Inf. 1st Co.D, 2nd Co.C
Rumsey, Francis M. GA 36th (Villepigue's) Inf. Co.D
Rumsey, George W. VA 33rd Inf. Co.I
Rumsey, Harris M. GA 16th Inf. Co.C
Rumsey, Henry W. GA Lt.Arty. Van Den Corput's Co.
Rumsey, Henry W. GA Inf. 3rd Bn. Co.A
Rumsey, H.F. TX 18th Inf. Co.H
Rumsey, James GA 16th Inf. Co.C
Rumsey, James A. GA Inf. 9th Bn. Co.D Sgt.
Rumsey, John GA 52nd Inf. Co.A
Rumsey, John W. GA 4th Bn.S.S. Co.C
Rumsey, John W. GA Inf. 9th Bn. Co.A
Rumsey, Jordan GA Inf. 9th Bn. Co.C
Rumsey, Joseph F. GA 4th Bn.S.S. Co.C
Rumsey, J.W. GA 54th Inf. Co.B
Rumsey, L. MO 2nd Inf. Co.D
Rumsey, L. MO 16th Inf. Co.K
Rumsey, Lafayette AR Inf. Cocke's Regt. Co.B Sgt.
Rumsey, Larkin D. AL 10th Inf. Co.I
Rumsey, Matthew J. GA 4th Bn.S.S. Co.C
Rumsey, M.J. GA Inf. 9th Bn. Co.C
Rumsey, R. GA Inf. 25th Bn. (Prov.Guard) Co.D
Rumsey, Shaderick R. GA 4th Res. Co.E
Rumsey, Singleton B. GA Lt.Arty. Van Den Corput's Co.
Rumsey, Singleton B. GA Inf. 3rd Bn. Co.A
Rumsey, S.N. TN 24th Bn.S.S. Co.C
Rumsey, W.F. LA Mil. Irish Regt. O'Brien's Co.
Rumsey, William VA 6th Inf. Co.H
Rumsey, William A. GA 52nd Inf. Co.A
Rumsey, William M. VA Cav. 36th Bn. Co.D
Rumsour, W.H. TX 11th Cav. Co.G

Rumsy, G.T. LA 21st (Kennedy's) Inf. Co.B
Rumville, Joseph VA 6th Inf. 1st Co.B
Runabout 1st Cherokee Mtd.Rifles Co.A
Runabout 1st Cherokee Mtd.Rifles Co.F
Runabout 1st Cherokee Mtd.Rifles Co.H
Runabout 1st Cherokee Mtd.Vol. 1st Co.F, 2nd Co.E
Runagan, N.B. VA 24th Bn.Part.Rangers Cropper's Co.
Runalden, John VA 54th Mil. Co.A
Runalds, Calvin AR 2nd Mtd.Rifles Co.I
Runalls, Francis TX 22nd Cav. Co.C
Runals, Charles R. AR 2nd Inf. Co.B
Runaway, Frank 1st Cherokee Mtd.Vol. 1st Co.D, 2nd Co.F
Runaway, James AL Talladega Cty.Res. T.M. McClintick's Co.
Runaway Person 1st Cherokee Mtd.Rifles Co.D
Runaway Samuel 1st Cherokee Mtd.Rifles Co.D 2nd Lt.
Runban, F.M. AR 15th Inf. Co.G
Runbo, James C. TN 3rd (Clack's) Inf.
Runch, Lewis SC 1st Regt. Pioneers Co.B
Runciman, John W. NC 3rd Inf. Co.F 2nd Lt.
Rund, J.M. LA Mil.Conf.Guards Regt. Co.B
Rund, W. LA Mil.Cont.Regt. Mitchell's Co.
Rund, William LA Mil. 1st Regt. 3rd Brig. 1st Div. Co.B
Rundal, John TX 25th Cav. Co.A
Rundel, Joseph Gillum's Regt. Whitaker's Co.
Rundell, Chas. H. Gen. & Staff 1st Lt.,ADC
Rundell, E. MS Inf. 2nd Bn. (St.Troops) Co.D
Rundell, Ed TX 21st Cav. Co.F 1st Sgt.
Rundell, Ezra MS Inf. 1st Bn.St.Troops (30 days '64) Co.D
Rundell, F.M. TX 2nd Inf. Co.C 1st Sgt.
Rundell, F.M. TX St.Troops Hampton's Co.
Rundell, Francis M. TX 1st (Yager's) Cav. Co.B Lt.,Adj.
Rundell, Francis M. TX Cav. 3rd (Yager's) Bn. Co.B Ch.Bugler
Rundell, George W. LA 31st Inf. Co.C
Rundell, George W. MS 28th Cav. Co.C
Rundell, G.J.B. MS Cav. Hughes' Bn. Co.A
Rundell, J. MS Cav. Hughes' Bn. Co.A
Rundell, John TX 24th Cav. Co.F,I
Rundell, Thomas MS 4th Cav. Co.D
Runderburg, John J. MS 16th Inf. Co.G
Rundle, D.B. LA Lt.Arty. Fenner's Btty. Cpl.
Rundle, D.B. LA Mil.Conf.Guards Regt. Co.E
Rundle, G.K. LA 22nd (Cons.) Inf. Co.H
Rundle, John VA 36th Inf. 2nd Co.B 1st Lt.
Rundle, Jonathan VA 36th Inf. 2nd Co.B
Rundle, T.J. LA 9th Inf. Co.B
Rundles, W.W. MS 3rd Inf. (St.Troops) Co.H
Rundy, B.F. NC 38th Inf.
Runells, J.J. AR 19th (Dawson's) Inf. Co.I Cpl.
Runels, Andrew NC 33rd Inf. Co.G
Runels, John MS 15th Inf. Co.A
Runels, Mathew J. NC 33rd Inf. Co.G
Runels, Perry TX 1st Inf. Co.F 2nd Lt.
Runels, W.M. TN 17th Inf. Co.K
Runey, Jasper SC 16th Inf. Co.C
Runge, Gerhard H.W. NC 18th Inf. Co.A 2nd Lt.
Runge, Gustav VA 15th Inf. Co.K
Runge, J. TX 8th Inf. Co.G

Runge, John TX 17th Inf. Co.H
Runge, L.A. MS 6th Inf. Co.B Capt.
Runge, William H. VA 49th Inf. Co.A
Runger, G. VA 2nd St.Res. Co.H 1st Lt.
Rungnor, F. TN Inf. 154th Sr.Regt. Music.
Runians, William TN 10th (DeMoss') Cav. Co.C
Runick, John LA Mil. Mech.Guard
Runion, Abraham MO 8th Inf. Co.I
Runion, A.M. SC Lt.Arty. 3rd (Palmetto) Bn. Co.I
Runion, Andrew VA Cav. 37th Bn. Co.B
Runion, Andrew J. NC 64th Inf. Co.C Sgt.
Runion, Andrew M. SC Inf. Hampton Legion Co.F
Runion, Benjamin W. MO 7th Cav. Co.I
Runion, B.M. NC 64th Inf. Co.K
Runion, B.O. NC 64th Inf. Co.K
Runion, Christian VA 146th Mil. Co.C
Runion, C.P. SC Lt.Arty. 3rd (Palmetto) Bn. Co.H,I
Runion, Dudley TN 48th (Voorhies') Inf. Co.C
Runion, F. VA 7th Bn.Res. Co.B
Runion, George W. TX 11th Inf. Co.F
Runion, George Washington MO 8th Inf. Co.I
Runion, J. VA 7th Bn.Res. Co.B
Runion, James MO Cav. Hunter's Regt.
Runion, James M. SC Inf. Hampton Legion Co.F
Runion, John KY 12th Cav. Co.B
Runion, John TN 48th (Voorhies') Inf. Co.C
Runion, John VA 151st Mil. Co.D
Runion, Joseph TN 39th Mtd.Inf. Co.B,F Music.
Runion, J.S. VA 60th Inf. Co.G
Runion, J.W. MS 6th Cav. Co.K
Runion, Levi TN 3rd (Lillard's) Mtd.Inf. Co.E Music.
Runion, L.P. NC 64th Inf. Co.K
Runion, Moses VA 58th Mil. Co.I
Runion, Philip VA Cav. 37th Bn. Co.B
Runion, Silas VA 18th Cav. Co.K
Runion, Thomas G. NC 64th Inf. Co.F
Runion, W.F. NC 64th Inf. Co.C
Runion, William VA 58th Mil. Co.I
Runion, William VA 86th Mil. Co.E,C
Runion, William E. TN Cav. 16th Bn. (Neal's) Co.B
Runions, James M. VA Inf. 21st Bn. 2nd Co.F
Runions, James R. TN 63rd Inf. Co.A
Runions, Joseph TN 5th (McKenzie's) Cav. Co.E
Runions, J. Stewart TN 62nd Mtd.Inf. Co.B
Runions, S.O. TN 26th Inf. Co.B Fifer
Runions, William GA Inf. 17th Bn. (St.Guards) McCarty's Co.
Runions, W.J. GA 11th Cav. Co.E
Runison, W. TN Cav. Cox's Bn. Co.B
Runk, Benjamin M. VA 11th Cav. Co.A Sgt.
Runk, Benton VA 67th Mil. Co.B
Runk, George W. LA Arty. 1st Field Btty. Artif.
Runkle, B.P. VA Mil. Greene Cty.
Runkle, Charles E. VA 2nd Inf. Co.F Cpl.
Runkle, Christopher VA 5th Inf. Co.D
Runkle, David VA 52nd Inf. Co.I
Runkle, George W. VA 34th Inf. Co.D
Runkle, George W. VA Mil. Greene Cty.
Runkle, H. TN 15th Inf. Co.I
Runkle, J.A. TX 17th Inf. Co.A
Runkle, Jacob VA 5th Inf. Co.D

Runkle, James A. TX 2nd Inf. Co.H
Runkle, James E. VA 34th Inf. Co.D Sgt.
Runkle, James T. TX 2nd Inf. Co.H
Runkle, J.W. VA 2nd Inf. Co.F
Runkle, Milton D.L. VA 34th Inf. Co.D 2nd Lt.
Runkle, Nimrod VA 34th Inf. Co.D
Runkle, Noble VA Cav. Mosby's Regt. (Part.
  Rangers) Co.C
Runkles, F. AR 13th Inf. Co.D
Runkles, Joseph TX 17th Inf. Co.A
Runkwitz, Otto VA Lt.Arty. Brander's Co.
Runkwitz, Otto VA 15th Inf. Co.K
Runley, Harvey TN 5th Inf. 2nd Co.H
Runls, Martin TX Inf. 3rd St.Troops Co.F
Runnals, Daniel NC Unassign.Conscr.
Runnals, Samuel TN Cav. 1st Bn. (McNairy's)
  Co.B
Runnell, Reuben AL 41st Inf. Co.C
Runnell, W. MS 14th (Cons.) Inf. Co.C
Runnells, E.J. MS 5th Inf. (St.Troops) QM
Runnells, G.W. TN Holman's Bn.Part.Rangers
  Co.A Sgt.
Runnells, James VA Cav. 41st Bn. 2nd Co.H
Runnells, James Brush Bn.
Runnells, James B. TX 1st (Yager's) Cav. Co.B
Runnells, James E. TN 41st Inf. Co.A Cpl.
Runnells, J.F. MS 39th Inf. Co.F
Runnells, J.H. TN 11th (Holman's) Cav. Co.L
  Cpl.
Runnells, John NC 1st Inf. Co.G
Runnells, John NC 6th Sr.Res. Co.I
Runnells, John SC Inf. 3rd Bn. Co.D
Runnells, John TX 8th Inf. Co.E
Runnells, John C. TX 16th Inf. Co.D
Runnells, Larkin TX Cav. Hardeman's Regt.
  Co.B
Runnells, Major SC 2nd Rifles Co.H
Runnells, Patrick TN 10th Inf.
Runnells, Patrick TN 10th Inf. Co.K
Runnells, P.M. GA Inf. 26th Bn. Co.B
Runnells, S. SC 6th (Merriwether's) Bn.St.Res.
  Co.D
Runnells, Stephen VA 23rd Cav. Co.C Cpl.
Runnells, Stephen VA Cav. 41st Bn. 2nd Co.H
  Cpl.
Runnels, --- SC Inf. Hampton Legion Co.I
Runnels, --- TX Cav. Border's Regt. Co.K
Runnels, A. MS 15th Inf. Co.K
Runnels, A. TX 9th (Nichols') Inf. Co.D
Runnels, A.J. TX 25th Cav. Co.B
Runnels, Alexander TX 25th Cav. Co.B
Runnels, A.S. AR 19th (Dockery's) Inf. Co.E
Runnels, Asberry 14th Conf.Cav. Co.D
Runnels, Benjamin F. AR 14th (McCarver's) Inf.
  Co.A
Runnels, Charles GA 4th Res. Co.K
Runnels, C.W. AR Inf. Adams' Regt. Moore's
  Co.
Runnels, Danforth SC 6th Cav. Co.B
Runnels, David GA 59th Inf. Co.E
Runnels, David TX 4th Field Btty.
Runnels, Drury M. MS 46th Inf. Co.A
Runnels, E. MS Inf. 1st Bn.St.Troops (12 mo.
  '62-3) Co.E Cpl.
Runnels, E.J. MS 6th Cav. Co.G Maj.
Runnels, E.J. MS 6th Inf. Co.A Capt.
Runnels, Elijah KY 5th Mtd.Inf. Co.A

Runnels, F.M. TX 25th Cav. Co.B
Runnels, F.M. TX Cav. Border's Regt.
Runnels, G.B. MS Cav. Hughes' Bn. Co.E Sgt.
Runnels, G.B. TX 25th Cav. Co.B
Runnels, G.B. TX 9th (Nichols') Inf. Co.D
Runnels, George M. AR 1st Vol. Co.B
Runnels, George W. GA 59th Inf. Co.E
Runnels, Gid 2nd Cherokee Mtd.Vol. Co.I
Runnels, G.W. MS 6th Inf. Co.H
Runnels, H. MS 4th Cav. Co.D
Runnels, Hal G. TX 2nd Inf. Co.A Maj.
Runnels, Hal G. Moore's Staff Maj.,Vol.ADC
Runnels, Harvey TX 15th Cav. Co.D
Runnels, H.H. TX 28th Cav. Co.A
Runnels, I.S. TX 32nd Cav. Co.F
Runnels, Isham AR Inf. Adams' Regt. Moore's
  Co.
Runnels, Isham MS 1st Cav.Res. Co.H
Runnels, J. NC 1st Bn.Jr.Res. Co.D
Runnels, J. TN 1st Hvy.Arty. 2nd Co.B
Runnels, J. TX Cav. Border's Regt. Co.F
Runnels, James TN 23rd Inf.1st Co.F, Co.H
Runnels, James Mead's Conf.Cav. Co.K
Runnels, James A. MS 24th Inf. Co.B
Runnels, James A. TX 15th Cav. Co.F
Runnels, James H. MS 16th Inf. Co.H
Runnels, James L. VA 14th Cav. Co.H
Runnels, J.B. TX Cav. 3rd (Yager's) Bn. Co.B
Runnels, Jesse TX 25th Cav. Co.B
Runnels, J.F. TX Cav. Hardeman's Regt. Co.A
Runnels, J. Floyd MS 1st Cav.Res. Co.H
Runnels, J.H. MS 8th Cav. Co.C
Runnels, John TX 22nd Cav. Co.E
Runnels, John TX 34th Cav. Co.G
Runnels, John TX Cav. Border's Regt. Co.H
Runnels, Jordan SC 18th Inf. Co.C
Runnels, Joseph GA 31st Inf. Co.F
Runnels, Joseph B. TX 28th Cav. Co.A
Runnels, J.R. FL 1st (Res.) Inf.
Runnels, L. TN 33rd Inf. Co.E
Runnels, Lewis TX 20th Inf. Co.K
Runnels, Mansfield AL 12th Inf. Co.H
Runnels, Michael MS 29th Inf. Co.H
Runnels, M.N. AL 34th Inf. Co.F
Runnels, P.R. TN 4th (McLemore's) Cav. Co.E
Runnels, R.H. LA 18th Inf. Co.K
Runnels, R.H. TX 7th Cav. Co.K
Runnels, R.H. TX 11th Inf. Co.H
Runnels, Richard VA 10th Cav.
Runnels, Richard VA 10th Inf. 2nd Co.C
Runnels, Riley TX Cav. Martin's Regt. Co.E
Runnels, Samuel VA 11th Bn.Res. Co.B
Runnels, Samuel VA 57th Inf. Co.K
Runnels, S.M. AL 34th Inf. Co.F
Runnels, Wiley AL 9th Inf. Co.F
Runnels, William SC 2nd Rifles Co.B
Runnels, William D. VA 14th Cav. Co.H
Runnels, W.J. TX 19th Inf. Co.B
Runner, Ben KY 2nd (Duke's) Cav. Co.L
Runner, George W. MO 5th Cav. Co.F
Runner, G.W. TX Conscr.
Runner, Henry VA 6th Cav. Co.H
Runner, S.D. VA 10th Cav. Co.G Sgt.
Runner, S.H. KY 6th Mtd.Inf. Co.H
Runner, William VA 2nd St.Res. Co.A
Runner Chekele 1st Cherokee Mtd.Rifles Co.G
Runnion, Christian VA 33rd Inf. Co.E

Runnion, Elihu VA 60th Inf. Co.G
Runnion, George W. TN 19th Inf. Co.H
Runnion, Isaac VA 60th Inf. Co.G
Runnion, John TN 48th (Nixon's) Inf. Co.A
Runnion, M.K. AR 24th Inf. Co.I
Runnion, Moses VA 33rd Inf. Co.E
Runnion, Noah W. TN 3rd (Lillard's) Mtd.Inf.
  Co.D
Runnion, Wiley J. NC 25th Inf. Co.G
Runnion, William VA 33rd Inf. Co.E
Runnion, Wilson MO 7th Cav. Co.F
Runnions, Abraham MO 11th Inf. Co.I
Runnions, B. TN Cav. Cox's Bn. Co.B
Runnions, George MO 11th Inf. Co.I
Runnions, Hiram H. TN 3rd (Lillard's) Mtd.Inf.
  Co.D
Runnions, James MO 11th Inf. Co.I
Runnions, James SC 1st Arty. Co.K
Runnions, Joseph TN 3rd (Lillard's) Mtd.Inf.
  Co.D
Runnions, Joseph TN 29th Inf. Co.B
Runnions, L. TN 1st (Carter's) Cav. Co.C
Runnions, Lewis P. NC 25th Inf. Co.K
Runnions, Timothy J. NC 12th Inf. Co.E
Runnions, William J. TN 3rd (Lillard's) Mtd.Inf.
  Co.D
Runnolds, John AL Cav. Moses' Squad. Co.B
Runnolds, N.D. AL Cav. Moses' Squad. Co.B
Runnolds, Samuel H. VA 5th Inf. Co.D
Runnolds, Thomas MO 5th Cav.
Runnols, John O. TX 23rd Cav. Co.B
Runnols, William R. VA Mil. Washington Cty.
Runnyan, J.N. AR 1st (Monroe's) Cav. Co.K
  Cpl.
Runo, Giovanni LA Mil. 6th Regt.Eur.Brig.
  (Italian Guards Bn.) Co.2
Runolds, Malekiah AR 27th Inf. Co.G
Runolds, Malikiah AR 8th Inf. New Co.F
Runson, C.R. LA 15th Inf. Co.I
Runte, John LA Mil. 1st Regt. 2nd Brig. 1st Div.
  Co.F
Runty, James VA 5th Cav. Co.C
Runuls, J. TX 7th Cav. Co.D
Runy, Sidney O. MS 7th Cav. Co.E
Runyan, Aldolphus D. NC 55th Inf. Co.D
Runyan, A.J. TN 40th Inf. Co.G Cpl.
Runyan, Daniel F. GA 40th Inf. Co.B Sgt.
Runyan, Daniel F. GA 43rd Inf. Co.B Sgt.
Runyan, D.N. MO Cav. Hunter's Regt. Co.C
Runyan, George KY 7th Cav. Co.F
Runyan, George TN 60th Mtd.Inf. Co.I
Runyan, H. GA 2nd Inf. Co.N,B Lt.
Runyan, H.C. TN 5th (McKenzie's) Cav. Co.C
Runyan, Henry TN 60th Mtd.Inf. Co.I
Runyan, H. Franklin Trans-MS Conf.Cav. 1st Bn.
  Co.E
Runyan, Hiram AL 24th Inf. Co.K
Runyan, Hiram AL Cav. 5th Bn. Hilliard's
  Legion Co.C
Runyan, Ike L. TN 14th Inf. Co.E
Runyan, Jacob NC 55th Inf. Co.D
Runyan, James H. NC 29th Inf. Co.D
Runyan, James L. VA Mil. Stowers' Co.
Runyan, James M. NC 55th Inf. Co.D Cpl.
Runyan, J.C. TN 5th (McKenzie's) Cav. Co.C
Runyan, J.L. TN 5th (McKenzie's) Cav. Co.C

Runyan, John H. AR 17th (Lemoyne's) Inf. Co.D
Runyan, John H. AR 21st Inf. Co.H
Runyan, Joseph KY 10th (Diamond's) Cav. Co.I Sgt.
Runyan, Joseph M. TN Lt.Arty. Lynch's Co.
Runyan, J.P. NC 49th Inf. Co.G
Runyan, Silas S. TX 6th Cav. Co.F Cpl.
Runyan, T.A.J. MO Cav. Ford's Bn. Co.A
Runyan, Thomas J. TN 40th Inf. Co.G Cpl.
Runyan, T.P. TN 40th Inf. Co.G
Runyan, T.T. TN 3rd (Lillard's) Mtd.Inf. Co.G
Runyan, Vincent TN 4th Inf. Co.C
Runyan, William AR 1st (Crawford's) Cav. Co.E
Runyan, William B. FL 1st Inf. Old Co.K, New Co.A 2nd Lt.
Runyan, William B. TN 5th (McKenzie's) Cav. Co.C
Runyan, William B. TN 3rd (Lillard's) Mtd.Inf. Co.I
Runyan, William B. Gen. & Staff A.Pay M.
Runyan, William C. VA 129th Mil. Baisden's Co.
Runyan, William J. TN 40th Inf. Co.G Bvt.2nd Lt.
Runyon, A.G. TX 7th Cav. Co.K Cpl.
Runyon, Alexander C. VA 24th Inf. Co.E
Runyon, Cephas VA Loc.Def. Morehead's Co.
Runyon, Ceph C. VA Lt.Arty. Lowry's Co.
Runyon, Conrad VA Inf. 45th Bn. Co.E
Runyon, Conrad VA 1st Cav.St.Line Co.A
Runyon, George J. KY 3rd Cav. Co.F
Runyon, Henry VA 36th Inf. 1st Co.B, 2nd Co.D
Runyon, Jacob VA 31st Inf. Co.C
Runyon, James VA 8th Cav. Co.F
Runyon, Jefferson B. TX 13th Vol. 2nd Co.C Sgt.
Runyon, John VA 60th Inf. 2nd Co.H
Runyon, Loss AR 15th (Josey's) Inf. Co.F
Runyon, Richard VA 60th Inf. 2nd Co.H
Runyon, T.H. LA 1st Cav. Co.F Jr.2nd Lt.
Runyon, Thomas KY 5th Mtd.Inf. Co.G
Runyon, William VA 1st Cav. Co.A
Runyon, William VA 36th Inf. 1st Co.B, 2nd Co.D
Runyon, William VA 1st Cav.St.Line Co.A Sgt.
Runyon, William B. VA 24th Inf. Co.E
Runyon, William R. VA 8th Cav. Co.F Bugler
Runyons, H.J. GA 36th (Broyles') Inf. Co.D
Runyons, John GA 36th (Broyles') Inf. Co.D
Runyoon, L. AR 15th (Josey's) Inf. 1st Co.G
Ruoff, M. MS 1st Lt.Arty. Co.H
Rupard, Caleb NC 26th Inf. Co.C
Rupard, Elkana NC 4th Inf. Co.D
Rupard, Hampton NC 54th Inf. Co.E
Rupaw, J. GA 5th Res. Co.B
Rupaw, T. GA 5th Res. Co.B
Rupe, Daniel P. VA 24th Inf. Co.E
Rupe, David M. TX 21st Cav. Co.K
Rupe, David M. TX Cav. Benavides' Regt. Co.G
Rupe, E. TN 63rd Inf. Co.D
Rupe, George VA 5th Inf. Co.C
Rupe, George W. MO 10th Cav. Co.D
Rupe, George W. MO 16th Inf. Co.C
Rupe, Harvey MO 2nd Cav. Co.G
Rupe, Harvy O. MO 3rd Inf. Co.I Jr.2nd Lt.

Rupe, Henry MO 16th Inf. Co.C
Rupe, Jackson TX Cav. Border's Regt.
Rupe, James MO 11th Inf. Co.H
Rupe, James MO Thompsons' Command
Rupe, James MO St.Guard
Rupe, James T. TX 25th Cav. Co.D
Rupe, John SC Inf. Holcombe Legion Co.A
Rupe, John H. VA 24th Inf. Co.K
Rupe, Lewis VA 4th Res. Co.C
Rupe, M.C. MS 3rd Cav. Co.G,K Cpl.
Rupe, Oscar W. MO Cav. 2nd Regt.St.Guard Co.G
Rupe, Thomas VA 8th Cav. Co.G
Rupe, Thomas VA Loc.Def. Morehead's Co.
Rupe, William SC Inf. Holcombe Legion Co.A
Rupe, William H. KY 2nd Mtd.Inf. Co.E Cpl.
Rupe, William H. VA 24th Inf. Co.K Cpl.
Rupean, W.J. GA 44th Inf. Co.F
Rupee, Charles MO 6th Cav. Co.G
Rupel, E.C. AL 5th Inf. Co.I
Rupel, George W. GA Smith's Legion Co.D Sgt.
Ruper, George R. AR 33rd Inf. Co.H
Ruper, W.A. VA 10th Inf. Co.D
Rupersburg, J. TX Cav. Baird's Regt. Co.F
Rupert, Jacob C. VA 97th Mil. Co.B
Rupert, James MO Cav. Snider's Bn. Co.E
Rupert, James MO Inf. Clark's Regt. Co.H
Rupert, John AL 62nd Inf. Co.B
Rupert, J.P. AR 38th Inf. Co.E
Rupert, Samuel VA 2nd Inf. Co.G
Rupert, S.H. TX Cav. Border's Regt. Co.C Sgt.
Rupert, Siram P. VA 136th Mil. Co.G
Rupert, William H. TN Arty. Bibb's Co. 2nd Lt.
Ruph, J.W. TN 4th Inf. Co.G Sgt.
Ruph, J.W. TN 4th Inf. Co.G
Ruple, A.J. SC 2nd Arty. Co.F
Ruple, A.J. SC 11th Res. Co.H
Ruple, J.L. MS 40th Inf. Co.I
Ruple, J.L. 10th Conf.Cav. Co.D
Ruple, Joseph H. SC 1st Arty. Co.H
Ruple, J.R. MS Cav. Garland's Bn. Co.B
Ruple, S.H. TN 40th Inf. Co.H
Ruple, William C. AL Cav. 5th Bn. Hilliard's Legion Co.D
Ruple, William C. 10th Conf.Cav. Co.D
Ruples, J. LA 4th Cav. Co.F
Rupley, James A. TX 6th Inf. Co.B Capt.
Rupp, George VA 2nd Inf.Loc.Def. Co.D
Rupp, George VA Inf. 6th Bn.Loc.Def. Co.A
Rupp, Harry LA Mil. Chalmette Regt. Co.G
Rupp, Jack LA Mil. Chalmette Regt. Co.G
Rupp, P. LA Mil. Squad.Guides d'Orleans
Rupp, William F. VA 136th Mil. Co.B
Ruppe, H.E. SC Inf. Holcombe Legion Co.K
Ruppe, James SC 5th Inf. 2nd Co.C
Ruppe, J.D. SC Inf. Holcombe Legion Co.K Cpl.
Ruppe, J.V. SC Inf. Holcombe Legion Co.K
Ruppe, Thomas M. NC 34th Inf. Co.I
Ruppe, W.J. NC 2nd Jr.Res. Co.D
Ruppe, W.W. SC Inf. Holcombe Legion Co.K Cpl.
Ruppenthal, J. AL Res. Belser's Co.
Ruppenthal, J. AL Rebels
Ruppersberger, Lewis TN 10th Inf. Co.B
Ruppert, A. VA 2nd St.Res. Co.H

Ruppert, H. TX Inf. Timmons' Regt. Co.B Sgt.
Ruppert, Henry TX Inf. Timmon's Regt. Co.B Sgt.
Ruppert, Henry TX Waul's Legion Co.D Cpl.
Ruppier, C. LA 18th Inf. Co.B
Ruppins, H. LA Mil. 4th Regt.Eur.Brig.
Ruppins, T. LA Mil. 4th Regt.Eur.Brig. Co.E
Rupprich, Simon LA Mil.Bn. French Vol. Co.3 1st Lt.
Ruprecht, F. VA 1st St.Res. Co.B
Rupton, W.J. AR 24th Inf. Co.E
Rurk, G.W. LA 2nd Cav. Co.C
Rurts, R.H. TN 12th (Green's) Cav. Co.G Sgt.
Rus, Isaac TN Cav. 12th Bn. (Day's) Co.F
Rus, Jr. LA Mil. 3rd Regt.Eur.Brig. (Garde Francaise)
Rusbush, Samuel VA 2nd Inf. Co.G
Rusby, B. SC 14th Inf. Co.B
Rusby, E. LA Mil. British Guard Bn. Kurczyn's Co.
Rusca, John LA Conscr.
Rusca, Joseph LA 18th Inf. Co.C
Rusch, C. SC Mil.Arty. 1st Regt. Co.A
Rusch, John L. SC 3rd Cav. Co.A
Rusch, Leopold A. SC 1st Arty. Co.D
Rusch, Louis TX 2nd Inf. Co.F
Rusche, Francis TX Inf. 2nd St.Troops Co.C
Rusche, Henry TX 12th Inf. Co.G Music.
Rusche, John VA 1st St.Res. Co.A
Rusco, Charles G. AR 26th Inf. Co.E
Rusco, John W. TN Inf. Tackitt's Co.
Ruscol, Alexander B.S. NC 43rd Inf. Co.H
Rusdule, E.B. AR 38th Inf. Co.E
Rusdule, Wiley AR 38th Inf. Co.E
Rusdule, William AR 38th Inf. Co.E
Ruse, A.F. AR Inf. 8th Bn. Co.F
Ruse, Charles C. GA 48th Inf. Co.B
Ruse, Charles J. LA 1st Hvy.Arty. (Reg.) Co.E
Ruse, G.A. GA Arty. 11th Bn. (Sumter Arty.) New Co.C
Ruse, George GA Hvy.Arty. 22nd Bn. Co.D
Ruse, Jacob I. MS 11th Inf. Co.B
Ruse, James O. MS 2nd Inf. Co.A
Ruse, J.J. GA 2nd Inf.
Ruse, J.M. NC 3rd Jr.Res. Co.F
Ruse, Joel Brown MO Inf. 1st Bn. Co.A 2nd Lt.
Ruse, John NC Inf. Thomas Legion
Ruse, W.B. NC McLean's Bn.Lt.Duty Men Co.A
Ruse, W.J.R. AL 42nd Inf. Co.K
Ruse, W.P. TX 9th (Young's) Inf. Co.D
Rusel, --- AR 21st Mil. Dollar's Co.
Rusel, Freeman 1st Choctaw Mtd.Rifles Co.D
Rusell, James TX Cav. Wells' Regt. Co.E
Rusell, James W. FL 9th Inf. Co.E
Rusell, J.L. TX 17th Cons.Dismtd.Cav. Co.G
Rusell, J. William AL 12th Inf. Co.A
Rusell, L.A. AL Cav. 4th Bn. (Love's) Co.C
Rusell, P.M. TX Cav. Wells' Regt. Co.E
Rusell, S.M. AR 32nd Inf. Co.E
Rusell, William W. GA 3rd Inf.
Rusels, H.H. TX 4th Cav. Co.B
Rusey, N.I. FL Kilcrease Lt.Arty.
Rush, --- LA Mil. 2nd Regt. 3rd Brig. 1st Div.
Rush, Abner NC 14th Inf. Co.I
Rush, A.C. SC Lt.Arty. 3rd (Palmetto) Bn. Co.G
Rush, A.G. NC 27th Inf. Co.F

Rush, A.J. SC 1st (Butler's) Inf. Co.A
Rush, A.J. TX Cav. Mann's Regt. Co.A
Rush, A.J. TX 19th Inf. Co.H,I
Rush, Alexander MO 15th Cav. Co.H
Rush, Alexander TN 4th Inf. Co.G
Rush, Alexander S. MS 13th Inf. Co.C Sgt.
Rush, Alfred AL 41st Inf. Co.K
Rush, Alfred C. NC 54th Inf. Co.K
Rush, Alson J. NC 52nd Inf. Co.B 1st Sgt.
Rush, Andrew J. VA 63rd Inf. Co.E Sgt.
Rush, Andrew W. GA 21st Inf. Co.C
Rush, Archibald F. NC 52nd Inf. Co.B
Rush, Atlas F. MS 24th Inf. Co.H,I 2nd Lt.
Rush, A.W. SC 1st Arty. Co.E
Rush, A.W. SC 3rd Inf. Co.I
Rush, A.W. SC 4th St.Troops Co.D Cpl.
Rush, A.W. SC Inf. 6th Bn. Co.B
Rush, A.W. SC Manigault's Bn.Vol. Co.D
Rush, A.W. 1st Conf.Cav. 1st Co.A
Rush, Azel G. NC 52nd Inf. Co.B
Rush, B. SC 1st Cav. Co.E
Rush, B.E. VA 4th Cav. Co.K
Rush, B.E. 1st Conf.Eng.Troops Co.D
Rush, Benjamin AL 45th Inf. Co.B,D
Rush, Benjamin AL 46th Inf. Co.B
Rush, Benjamin NC 5th Cav. (63rd St.Troops) Co.A
Rush, Benjamin NC 2nd Arty. (36th St.Troops) Co.B 2nd Lt.
Rush, Benjamin NC Lt.Arty. 13th Bn. Co.B 1st Lt.
Rush, Benjamin NC 1st Inf. (6 mo. '61) Co.F 1st Sgt.
Rush, Benjamin NC 6th Sr.Res. Co.F
Rush, Benjamin 7th Conf.Cav. Co.A
Rush, Benjamin 1st Conf.Eng.Troops Co.D
Rush, Benjamin A. AL 15th Bn.Part.Rangers Co.A 1st Sgt.
Rush, Benjamin F. AL Inf. 1st Regt. Co.A,C
Rush, Benjamin F. AL 39th Inf. Co.H
Rush, Benjamin F. MS 35th Inf. Co.A Capt.
Rush, Benjamin F. TN 50th Inf. Co.C
Rush, Benj. F. VA 146th Mil. Comsy.
Rush, Benjamin T. MS 35th Inf. Co.B Cpl.
Rush, B.F. NC 17th Inf. (2nd Org.) Co.L Sgt.
Rush, C. SC 11th Inf. Co.B
Rush, Calvin SC Lt.Arty. 3rd (Palmetto) Bn. Co.F
Rush, Calvin J. NC 52nd Inf. Co.B 1st Sgt.
Rush, C.C. SC 2nd Arty. Co.G 1st Lt.
Rush, C.C. SC 1st (Hagood's) Inf. 1st Co.F Cpl.
Rush, C.G. GA Inf. 1st Bn. (St.Guards) Co.A
Rush, Charles AL 45th Inf. Co.B
Rush, Charles LA 1st Hvy.Arty. (Reg.) Co.F
Rush, Charles LA Washington Arty.Bn. Co.1 Driver
Rush, Charles MO 16th Inf. Co.D
Rush, Charles SC Inf.Loc.Def. Estill's Co.
Rush, Charles A. TX 7th Cav. Co.D
Rush, Charles C. SC 2nd Arty. Co.G Lt.
Rush, Charles G. GA Siege Arty. 28th Bn. Co.H
Rush, Charles O. GA 3rd Cav. Co.C,H Cpl.
Rush, Cicero TX Inf. Riflemen Arnold's Co.
Rush, C.J. KY Cav.
Rush, Claiborn MO Cav. 3rd Regt.St.Guard Co.D

Rush, Clemons 1st Cherokee Mtd.Vol. 1st Co.K
Rush, Columbus G. GA 21st Inf. Co.C
Rush, C.R. VA 97th Mil. 1st Lt.
Rush, C.W. GA 8th Inf. Co.A
Rush, C.W. GA Floyd Legion (St.Guards) Co.E
Rush, C.W. GA Smith's Legion Co.F
Rush, D. MS Inf. 1st St.Troops Co.I Cpl.
Rush, D. MS 5th Inf. (St.Troops) Co.E
Rush, David KY 2nd Bn.Mtd.Rifles Co.C
Rush, David SC 1st St.Troops Co.D
Rush, David SC 5th Res. Co.F
Rush, David SC 6th (Merriwether's) Bn.St.Res. Co.E
Rush, David C. MS St.Cav. Perrins' Bn. Co.F
Rush, David C. MS 48th Inf. Co.C
Rush, David Charles MS Inf. 1st St.Troops Co.D
Rush, David H. SC Inf. Hampton Legion Co.E
Rush, David M. AL 41st Inf. Co.G
Rush, David O. VA 50th Inf. 1st Co.G Sgt.
Rush, David O. VA 63rd Inf. Co.E Capt.
Rush, D.C. TX 22nd Inf. Co.H
Rush, D.O. VA Inf. 54th Bn. Capt.,A.Maj.
Rush, Doctor MO 1st N.E. Cav. Price's Co.M
Rush, D.R. NC 6th Sr.Res. Co.I
Rush, E. GA 2nd Cav. Co.F
Rush, E.B. SC 2nd Cav. Co.E
Rush, E.B. VA Mil. Washington Cty.
Rush, Ellison GA 7th Inf. (St.Guards) Co.F
Rush, Emmett B. VA 63rd Inf. Co.E 2nd Lt.
Rush, E.W. SC 1st (Hagood's) Inf. 1st Co.E
Rush, E.W. SC 25th Inf. Co.C,H 2nd Lt.
Rush, F. AL 26th (O'Neal's) Inf. Co.K 1st Sgt.
Rush, F.D. SC 2nd Inf. Co.K Cpl.
Rush, Felix GA Phillips' Legion Co.F
Rush, Felix D. MS 2nd Inf. (A. of 10,000) Co.H
Rush, F.M. TX 22nd Inf. Co.E Sgt.
Rush, F.P. SC 7th Inf. 1st Co.K, 2nd Co.K
Rush, George NC 52nd Inf. Co.B
Rush, George G. AL 16th Inf. Co.A
Rush, George H. VA 60th Inf. Co.E
Rush, George H. VA 135th Mil. Co.C
Rush, George M.D. VA 63rd Inf. Co.E
Rush, George W. AL 17th Inf. Co.D
Rush, George W. GA 22nd Inf. Co.A Capt.
Rush, Girard AL 5th Inf. Co.K
Rush, Girard AL 6th Inf. Co.M
Rush, G.L. AL 41st Inf. Co.G
Rush, G.T. MS 4th Cav. Co.G
Rush, G.T. MS 5th Inf. (St.Troops) Co.I Cpl.
Rush, G.W. AR 51st Mil. Co.D
Rush, H. MS Inf. 1st Bn.St.Troops (30 days '64) Co.H
Rush, H.A. GA 21st Inf. Co.C
Rush, Harman M. SC 1st (Hagood's) Inf. 1st Co.A
Rush, Harrison K. AL 22nd Inf. Co.G
Rush, H.C. AR 1st (Monroe's) Cav. Co.C
Rush, H.C. GA Floyd Legion (St.Guards) Co.E
Rush, N.C. TX Arty. Douglas' Co.
Rush, Henry MO 6th Cav. Co.G
Rush, Henry NC 58th Inf. Co.E
Rush, Henry SC Inf. 7th Bn. (Enfield Rifles) Co.H
Rush, Henry B. NC 22nd Inf. Co.I Sgt.
Rush, H.H. VA 56th Inf. Co.G
Rush, H.J. SC 24th Inf. Co.K
Rush, H.K. AL 29th Inf. Co.G

Rush, H.L. AL 34th Inf. Co.C
Rush, H.M. SC 6th Cav. Co.H 1st Lt.
Rush, H.S. GA 31st Inf. Co.B 1st Lt.
Rush, Isaac N. MO 3rd Cav. Co.D
Rush, Isaiah MS 10th Inf. Old Co.C
Rush, Isaih MS 38th Cav. Co.B
Rush, J. GA 8th Inf.
Rush, J. GA 16th Inf. Co.H
Rush, J.A. GA Inf. Ezzard's Co.
Rush, Jackson AL 28th Inf. Co.A
Rush, Jackson MO 12th Inf. Co.A
Rush, Jackson TN 28th (Cons.) Inf.
Rush, Jacob SC Inf. 7th Bn. (Enfield Rifles) Co.H
Rush, Jacob VA 1st Cav. Co.F
Rush, Jacob VA 7th Bn.Res. Co.A Sgt.
Rush, Jacob VA 67th Mil. Co.D
Rush, James AL 59th Inf. Co.C
Rush, James SC 11th Inf. Co.B
Rush, James TN 4th (Murray's) Cav. Co.E
Rush, James TN Cav. 12th Bn. (Day's) Co.B
Rush, James TN Inf. 22nd Bn. Co.K
Rush, James TN 25th Inf. Co.G Cpl.
Rush, James TN 39th Mtd.Inf. Co.E
Rush, James TX 26th Cav. Co.A
Rush, James TX 1st Hvy.Arty. Co.D
Rush, James TX Waul's Legion Co.A
Rush, James VA 63rd Inf. Co.E
Rush, James VA Mil. Washington Cty.
Rush, James C. MS 24th Inf. Co.I,H
Rush, James C. VA 7th Inf. Co.A
Rush, James E. TN 25th Inf. Co.G
Rush, James F. AL 2nd Bn.Hilliard's Legion Vol. Co.F
Rush, James F. MS 7th Inf. Co.A
Rush, James H. MS 24th Inf. Co.H,I
Rush, James H. MS 35th Inf. Co.A Sgt.
Rush, James H. SC Inf. 7th Bn. (Enfield Rifles) Co.H
Rush, James J. GA 44th Inf. Co.G Sgt.
Rush, James J. VA Lt.Arty. 12th Bn. 1st Co.A
Rush, James J. VA Lt.Arty. Utterback's Co.
Rush, James J. VA 82nd Mil. Co.A
Rush, James M. MO 12th Inf. Co.K Cpl.
Rush, James W. TN 2nd (Ashby's) Cav.
Rush, James W. VA Conscr.
Rush, Jasper SC 7th Inf. 1st Co.K
Rush, Jasper N. SC Inf. 7th Bn. (Enfield Rifles) Co.H
Rush, J.B. MS 2nd (Quinn's St.Troops) Inf. Co.A
Rush, J.C. SC 2nd Arty. Co.I
Rush, Jeremiah VA Inf. 23rd Bn. Co.H
Rush, Jeremiah C. VA 1st Cav. 2nd Co.D
Rush, Jeremiah R. VA 10th Inf. Co.L
Rush, Jesse Conf.Cav. Clarkson's Bn. Ind. Rangers Co.H
Rush, J.H. AR Inf. Cocke's Regt. Co.G Sgt.
Rush, J.H.F. VA 6th Cav. Co.C
Rush, J.J. GA 54th Inf. Co.F
Rush, J.J. MO 16th Inf. Co.D
Rush, J.J. SC 1st Inf. Co.N
Rush, J.J. SC Inf. 7th Bn. (Enfield Rifles) Co.D
Rush, J.K. Inf. Bailey's Cons.Regt. Co.A Sgt.
Rush, J.K. TX 7th Inf. Co.H Sgt.
Rush, J.L. SC 5th Cav. Co.A
Rush, J.M. NC 6th Sr.Res. Co.G Sgt.

Rush, J.M. SC 9th Inf. Co.C
Rush, J.M. TX Cav. Bourland's Regt. Co.H,K
Rush, J.N.N. AR 51st Mil. Co.E
Rush, Joel G. MO Inf. Clark's Regt. Co.G
Rush, Joel G. Conf.Cav. Clarkson's Bn. Ind. Rangers Co.E
Rush, J.O.H. AL Inf. 2nd Regt. Co.B
Rush, John MS 33rd Inf. Co.D
Rush, John NC 64th Inf. Co.H
Rush, John SC 1st Cav. Co.I
Rush, John SC 1st Mtd.Mil. Scott's Co.
Rush, John SC 4th St.Troops Co.C
Rush, John SC 5th Bn.Res. Co.D
Rush, John TN 26th Inf. Co.G
Rush, John TX Inf. 1st Bn. Co.F
Rush, John VA Lt.Arty. Utterback's Co.
Rush, John VA 82nd Mil. Co.A
Rush, John VA 86th Mil. Co.D
Rush, John 14th Conf.Cav. Co.I
Rush, John B. AL 12th Inf. Co.B
Rush, John D. MO 6th Cav. Co.B
Rush, John G. AL 41st Inf. Co.G
Rush, John H. AR 14th (Powers') Inf. Co.G
Rush, John H. VA 5th Inf. Co.D
Rush, John L. VA 18th Cav. Co.D, 1st Co.G Sgt.
Rush, John L. VA Cav. 41st Bn. Trayhern's Co.
Rush, John M. SC Palmetto S.S. Co.E
Rush, John O.H. AL 2nd Cav. Co.B
Rush, John P. AR 1st Mtd.Rifles Co.H
Rush, John P. MS 33rd Inf. Co.C
Rush, John R. SC 5th Cav. Co.A
Rush, John S. VA Hvy.Arty. 20th Bn. Co.A
Rush, John S. VA 44th Inf. Co.A
Rush, John S. 1st Conf.Eng.Troops Co.D Artif.
Rush, John T. MS 35th Inf. Co.G 2nd Lt.
Rush, John W. MS Inf. 7th Bn. Co.B Sgt.
Rush, John W. MS 8th Inf. Co.K
Rush, John W. VA 36th Inf. 2nd Co.H
Rush, Jon D. MO 5th Inf. Co.B
Rush, Joseph SC 10th Inf. Co.K
Rush, Joseph SC 11th Inf. Co.B
Rush, Joseph TN 19th Inf. Co.D
Rush, Joseph VA 18th Cav. Co.D
Rush, Joseph VA Cav. 41st Bn. Co.A
Rush, Joseph B. VA 10th Inf. Co.E 1st Sgt.
Rush, Joseph H. NC 22nd Inf. Co.L Sgt.
Rush, Joseph M. MO 3rd Cav. Co.D
Rush, J.R. SC Cav. 14th Bn. Co.B
Rush, J.T. AL 32nd Inf. Co.E
Rush, J.T. MS 3rd Regt.Res. Co.F 1st Lt.
Rush, J.W. MS 27th Inf. Co.B
Rush, J.W. MO 1st N.E. Cav. White's Co.
Rush, J.W. SC 5th Bn.Res. Co.D
Rush, J.W. 4th Conf.Inf. Co.C Capt.
Rush, L. GA 3rd Cav. Chap.
Rush, L.B. SC 2nd Arty. Co.A,G
Rush, L.D. AR Inf. Cocke's Regt. Co.G
Rush, Leonard Gen. & Staff Chap.
Rush, Levi NC 5th Sr.Res. Co.K
Rush, Lewis B. SC 2nd Arty. Co.A
Rush, Lewis F. SC 25th Inf. Co.G
Rush, L.F. SC 2nd Arty. Co.C
Rush, L.J. TX 7th Inf. Co.I
Rush, Martais LA Miles' Legion
Rush, Martin MO Inf. 3rd Bn. Co.C
Rush, Martin NC 34th Inf. Co.K

Rush, Martin E. MO 6th Inf. Co.B
Rush, Massie D. VA 34th Mil. Co.D
Rush, Mathew D. SC 10th Inf. Co.K
Rush, M.D. 3rd Conf.Eng.Troops Co.G Sgt.
Rush, M.D. Eng.Dept. Polk's Corps A. of TN Sap. & Min. Co.,CSA
Rush, M.E. LA 22nd (Cons.) Inf. Co.A
Rush, M.G. AL 29th Inf. Co.G
Rush, M.J. MS Inf. 2nd St.Troops Co.H Sgt.
Rush, N. LA Mil. 3rd Regt. 3rd Brig. 1st Div. Co.D
Rush, Noah NC 38th Inf. Co.H Capt.
Rush, Otis TX 26th Cav. Co.C
Rush, P.D. SC 5th Cav. Co.A 1st Lt.
Rush, P.D. SC Cav. 14th Bn. Co.B 1st Lt.
Rush, Peter MD 1st Inf. Co.F,B
Rush, Peter MD Inf. 2nd Bn. Co.E
Rush, Peter MS 5th Inf. Co.B
Rush, Pleasant KY Horse Arty. Byrne's Co.
Rush, Preston AR 7th Cav. Co.K Sgt.
Rush, R.C. GA Inf. 9th Bn. Co.A
Rush, R.F. VA 10th Inf. Co.L
Rush, R.G. AL Inf. 1st Regt. Co.A
Rush, R.H. AL Mobile City Troop
Rush, R.H. 15th Conf.Cav. Co.I
Rush, Richard H. VA 13th Inf. 1st Co.B
Rush, Robert MO Cav. Hobb's Co.
Rush, Robert TN Cav. 12th Bn. (Day's) Co.G
Rush, Robert VA 1st Bn.Res. Co.H
Rush, Robert VA 82nd Mil. Co.A Cpl.
Rush, Robert A. VA 59th Inf. 2nd Co.H
Rush, Robert M. LA 25th Inf. Co.A
Rush, Robert T. NC 3rd Arty. (40th St.Troops) Co.G
Rush, Robert W. VA 48th Inf. Co.I
Rush, S. GA 46th Inf. Co.A
Rush, Samuel GA 46th Inf. Co.A
Rush, Samuel SC 11th Inf. Co.B
Rush, Samuel R. MS 13th Inf. Co.D
Rush, Sashel A. TX 18th Cav. Co.C Sgt.
Rush, S.G. SC 1st (Butler's) Inf. Co.G
Rush, S.H. AR 34th Inf. Co.E
Rush, S.H. SC 8th Res.
Rush, S.H. SC 17th Inf. Co.G
Rush, Shady AR Inf. Hardy's Regt. Co.B
Rush, Shederick C. AR 3rd Inf. Co.G
Rush, Simeon H. MS 33rd Inf. Co.A Sgt.
Rush, Simon KY 1st Inf. Co.I
Rush, Singleton LA 31st Inf. Co.I
Rush, S.N. SC Lt.Arty. 3rd (Palmetto) Bn. Co.E,G
Rush, S.R. MS 36th Inf. Co.C
Rush, S.W. AL 45th Inf. Co.B Sgt.
Rush, Thomas TN 10th Inf. Co.K
Rush, Thomas 2nd Conf.Inf. Co.D
Rush, Thomas A. VA 59th Inf. 2nd Co.H
Rush, Thomas C. AL 60th Inf. Co.G
Rush, Thomas N. KY 7th Mtd.Inf. Co.A
Rush, T.L. MS 38th Cav. Co.B
Rush, Toliver Terrel LA 28th (Gray's) Inf. Co.F
Rush, T.T. MS 4th Cav. Co.G
Rush, U.W. Inf. Bailey's Cons.Regt. Co.A
Rush, U.W. TX 7th Inf. Co.I
Rush, W.A. SC Inf. 7th Bn. (Enfield Rifles) Co.H
Rush, Warren R. AL 17th Inf. Co.D 2nd Lt.
Rush, W.D. MS Cav. Garland's Bn. Co.B

Rush, W.D. 14th Conf.Cav. Co.B
Rush, W.F. AR Mil. Borland's Regt. Pulaski Lancers
Rush, W.H. GA 31st Inf. Co.B 1st Lt.
Rush, W.H. MS Cav. Williams' Co. Cpl.
Rush, W.H. MO 16th Inf. Co.D
Rush, W.H. SC 7th Inf. 1st Co.K
Rush, W.H. TX 4th Cav. Co.B
Rush, Willey W. MS 26th Inf. Co.F
Rush, William AR 19th (Dockery's) Inf. Co.I
Rush, William KY 1st Inf. Co.I
Rush, William LA 1st (Nelligan's) Inf. Co.H
Rush, William LA Inf. 1st Sp.Bn. (Wheat's) Co.B
Rush, William MS 25th Inf. Co.B
Rush, William SC Inf. 7th Bn. (Enfield Rifles) Co.B,C
Rush, William SC 12th Inf. Co.C
Rush, William TN 4th Cav. Co.A
Rush, William TN Inf. 1st Bn. (Colms') Co.D
Rush, William TN 19th Inf. Co.D
Rush, William TN 39th Mtd.Inf. Co.E
Rush, William VA 34th Mil. Co.D
Rush, William 2nd Conf.Inf. Co.B
Rush, William A. AL 47th Inf. Co.D
Rush, William B. GA Lt.Arty. Scogin's Btty. (Griffin Lt.Arty.)
Rush, William B. TN 1st (Carter's) Cav. Co.D
Rush, William C. VA 63rd Inf. Co.E Cpl.
Rush, William C. 3rd Conf.Eng.Troops Co.E Cpl.
Rush, William H. SC Inf. 7th Bn. (Enfield Rifles) Co.H Sgt.
Rush, William H.H. TX 2nd Cav. Co.G Cpl.
Rush, William L. 1st Conf.Cav. 2nd Co.E
Rush, William M. SC 7th Inf. Co.C
Rush, William P. TN Inf. 22nd Bn. Co.K Cpl.
Rush, William P. VA 19th Cav. Co.I
Rush, William Pleasant TN 4th (Murray's) Cav. Co.E Cpl.
Rush, William S. LA 12th Inf. 1st Co.M
Rush, William S. NC 1st Inf. (6 mo. '61) Co.K
Rush, William S. TX 22nd Inf. Co.H
Rush, William V. MS 3rd Cav.Res. Co.F Sgt.
Rush, William W. AR 16th Inf. Co.D 2nd Lt.
Rush, William W. TN 13th Inf. Co.K
Rush, William W. VA 46th Inf.2nd Co.A
Rush, W.L. SC Inf. Holcombe Legion Co.B Music.
Rush, W.R. SC 22nd Inf. Co.G
Rush, Z.F. NC 1st Jr.Res. Co.F 2nd Lt.
Rusha, Edward W. LA 6th Inf. Co.E Cpl.
Rusha, E.M. LA Mil.Cont.Regt. Mitchell's Co. 2nd Lt.
Rusha, H. LA 11th Inf. Co.D
Rusha, Henry LA 14th (Austin's) Bn.S.S. Co.B
Rusha, John A. LA 5th Inf. New Co.A
Rusha, John A. LA Mil. Orleans Fire Regt.
Rushan, Abel MS 10th Cav. Co.B
Rushan, J.C. LA 31st Inf. Co.D
Rushbenburg, E. GA Inf. Bard's Co.
Rushbrook, Charles W. VA 6th Inf. Co.I
Rushbrook, Joseph W. VA Courtney Arty.
Rushbrook, Joseph W. VA Lt.Arty. Weisiger's Co.
Rushbrook, Joseph W. VA 6th Inf. Weisiger's Co.

Rushbrook, Joseph W. VA 16th Inf. Co.I
Rushbrook, Samuel LA Inf. 4th Bn. Co.D Music.
Rushen, David TN 50th Inf. Co.B
Rushen, James M. TN 50th Inf. Co.B
Rushen, L. MS Inf. 1st Bn.St.Troops (30 days '64) Co.C
Rushen, Richard B. MO 8th Cav. Co.B,F
Rushens, Mat. AR 45th Cav. Co.B
Rusher, A.J. KY 1st Inf. Co.I
Rusher, Andrew B. VA 2nd Cav. Co.A
Rusher, A.W. NC 57th Inf. Co.A Sgt.
Rusher, Edward A. NC 42nd Inf. Co.D 2nd Lt.
Rusher, F.J. VA 16th Inf. Co.D
Rusher, G.A. NC 42nd Inf. Co.D
Rusher, George A. NC Lt.Arty. 3rd Bn. Co.C
Rusher, Henry Conf.Cav. Raum's Co.
Rusher, Jesse T. VA 2nd Cav. Co.A
Rusher, Milas NC 4th Sr.Res. Co.B,D Sgt.
Rushien, D.W. TN 46th Inf. Co.H
Rushin, Alonzo M. GA 26th Inf. Co.H 1st Lt.
Rushin, A.P. GA 8th Cav. Co.K Cpl.
Rushin, A.P. GA 62nd Cav. Co.K Cpl.
Rushin, D.C. MS 30th Inf. Co.A
Rushin, Dempsy B. MS 7th Inf. Co.E
Rushin, George W. GA 3rd Cav. Co.A
Rushin, I.M. GA 1st Res.
Rushin, I.M. GA 29th Inf.
Rushin, James M. FL 5th Inf. Co.K
Rushin, James M. GA 8th Cav.
Rushin, James M. GA 26th Inf. Co.C 2nd Lt.
Rushin, James M. MS 7th Inf. Co.E
Rushin, James R. MS 7th Inf. Co.E
Rushin, J.C. GA 15th Inf. Co.E
Rushin, J.M. GA Cav. 20th Bn. Co.A Ord.Sgt.
Rushin, John GA Cobb's Legion Co.H
Rushin, John R. GA 2nd Inf. Co.I Sgt.
Rushin, John R. GA 46th Inf. Co.H 2nd Lt.
Rushin, Joseph A. GA Cobb's Legion Co.C
Rushin, J.T. GA 8th Cav. Co.K
Rushin, J.T. GA 62nd Cav. Co.K
Rushin, R. LA 17th Inf. Co.F
Rushin, Solm TN 55th (Brown's) Inf. Co.A
Rushin, Thomas MO 12th Inf. Co.I
Rushin, William AL 54th Inf. Co.H
Rushin, William GA 3rd Res. Co.D
Rushin, William 4th Conf.Inf. Co.I
Rushing, --- TX Cav. Good's Bn. Co.A
Rushing, A. SC 1st (McCreary's) Inf. Co.E
Rushing, Abel TN 6th Inf. Co.B
Rushing, Abraham D. NC 53rd Inf. Co.I
Rushing, A.J. AL 40th Inf. Co.C
Rushing, A.J. LA 2nd Cav. Co.F
Rushing, A.J. TN 50th Inf. Co.I Cpl.
Rushing, A.J. 20th Conf.Cav. Co.G
Rushing, Albert J. MS 38th Cav. Co.B
Rushing, Alfred TN 5th Inf. 2nd Co.C 1st Lt.
Rushing, Alx. J. NC 2nd Jr.Res. Co.F 2nd Lt.
Rushing, A.M. MS 1st (Foote's) Inf. (St.Troops) Hobart's Co.
Rushing, Andrew J. LA 16th Inf. Co.I
Rushing, Andrew J. MS 38th Cav. Co.B
Rushing, Andrew J. MS 34th Inf. Co.D
Rushing, Andrew J. SC Hvy.Arty. 10th Bn. Co.D,C
Rushing, Andrew P. NC 23rd Inf. Co.A
Rushing, A.R. SC 11th Inf. Co.E

Rushing, Archibald FL 1st Inf. New Co.G
Rushing, A.W. MS 5th Cav. Co.A
Rushing, A.W. MS 3rd Inf. (St.Troops) Co.H Sgt.
Rushing, Baron D. AL 33rd Inf. Co.A 1st Sgt.
Rushing, Ben TX 10th Cav. Co.E Sgt.
Rushing, Benjamin G. SC 3rd Cav. Co.E
Rushing, Berry AR 4th Inf. Co.D Cpl.
Rushing, B.F. AL 5th Inf. New Co.E
Rushing, B.G. SC 6th Inf. 1st Co.I Cadet
Rushing, Burne LA 2nd Cav. Co.F Cpl.
Rushing, Burrill Philip TX 20th Cav. Co.G
Rushing, C. TX 7th Field Btty.
Rushing, C. TX Lt.Arty. Jones' Co.
Rushing, Calvin GA 25th Inf. Co.H
Rushing, Calvin TN 5th Inf. 2nd Co.C 2nd Lt.
Rushing, Calvin TX 19th Cav. Co.I
Rushing, C.C. AL 5th Inf. New Co.E
Rushing, C.C. MS 37th Inf. Co.I
Rushing, C.C. TN 14th (Neely's) Cav. Co.C
Rushing, C.C. TN 21st (Wilson's) Cav. Co.I
Rushing, C.E. MS 5th Inf. (St.Troops) Co.C
Rushing, Clinton TN 10th (DeMoss') Cav. Co.G
Rushing, Clinton TN 11th Inf. Co.A
Rushing, Darling B. AR 1st (Crawford's) Cav. Co.D
Rushing, Darling B. AR 33rd Inf. Co.D
Rushing, David TX Cav. Baylor's Regt. Co.H
Rushing, David H. AR 17th (Lemoyne's) Inf. Co.E Cpl.
Rushing, David H. AR 21st Inf. Co.I 1st Lt.
Rushing, David M. TX 6th Cav. Co.I Sgt.
Rushing, David S. MS 16th Inf. Co.B
Rushing, D.D. AR 8th Inf. New Co.C Sgt.
Rushing, Dennis TX 14th Cav. Co.H
Rushing, Dennis TX Cav. Wells' Regt. Co.E
Rushing, E. MS 39th Inf. Co.G
Rushing, E. SC 21st Inf. Co.D
Rushing, E. TX Cav. Wells' Regt. Co.K
Rushing, E.B. TN 31st Inf. Co.H
Rushing, E.C. MS 22nd Inf. Co.G
Rushing, E.D. AL 8th (Livingston's) Cav. Co.C
Rushing, E.D. AL 11th Inf. Co.G
Rushing, Edward E. MS 37th Inf. Co.A 2nd Lt.
Rushing, E.H. LA 3rd (Wingfield's) Cav. Co.A
Rushing, E.J. NC 3rd Arty. (40th St.Troops) Co.H
Rushing, E.J. TX 11th Inf. Co.H Cpl.
Rushing, Eli F. MS 8th Inf. Co.K Sgt.
Rushing, Elijah J. TX 4th Field Btty.
Rushing, Elijah P. GA 25th Inf. Co.G
Rushing, Elijah W. TX 18th Cav. Co.H
Rushing, Elisha T. MS 16th Inf. Co.E
Rushing, Ephraim MS 33rd Inf. Co.H
Rushing, E. Pinkney NC 48th Inf. Co.A
Rushing, E.R. TN 31st Inf. Co.H Sgt.
Rushing, E.T. MS Cav. Co.D,K Sgt.
Rushing, Evan C. MS 33rd Inf. Co.E
Rushing, E.W. TX Cav. Morgan's Regt. Co.F
Rushing, Felix TX 13th Cav. Co.E
Rushing, Felix G. NC 37th Inf. Co.D
Rushing, Felix P. MS 48th Inf. Co.L
Rushing, F.M. AL 25th Inf. Co.K
Rushing, F.M. LA Inf. 16th Bn. (Conf.Guards Resp.Bn.) Co.B
Rushing, F.M. MS 38th Cav. Co.H
Rushing, F.P. MS Inf. 2nd Bn. Co.L

Rushing, Francis M. AL Cav. Barbiere's Bn. Brown's Co. 1st Lt.
Rushing, G.B.D. TX 28th Cav. Co.A
Rushing, G.E. Conf.Cav. Raum's Co.
Rushing, George M. NC 37th Inf. Co.D Cpl.
Rushing, George U. SC 3rd Cav. Co.E
Rushing, George W. TN 14th Inf. Co.B,F
Rushing, G.H. TN 5th Inf. 2nd Co.C
Rushing, Green B. NC 4th Sr.Res. Co.I
Rushing, G.U. SC 1st Mtd.Mil. Martin's Co.
Rushing, G.W. TN 24th Bn.S.S. Co.B
Rushing, H. MS Cav. 14th Regt. Co.C
Rushing, H. MS 4th Inf. Co.E
Rushing, Hampton MS 29th Inf. Co.G Cpl.
Rushing, Henry MS Cav. 14th Regt. Co.C
Rushing, Henry 14th Conf.Cav. Co.B,I
Rushing, Henry L. SC 1st Inf. Co.K
Rushing, Henry L. SC 1st (McCreary's) Inf. Co.E
Rushing, Henry T. MS 1st Lt.Arty. Co.C
Rushing, Horace F. NC 23rd Inf. Co.A
Rushing, I.H. MS 27th Inf. Co.E
Rushing, J. MS 2nd (Quinn's St.Troops) Inf. Co.B
Rushing, J.A. MS Inf. 1st Bn.St.Troops (12 mo. '62-3) Co.D
Rushing, Jackson 14th Conf.Cav. Co.B,I
Rushing, Jacob MS 33rd Inf. Co.D
Rushing, James LA 16th Inf. Co.I
Rushing, James NC 6th Sr.Res. Co.G
Rushing, James SC 25th Inf. Co.D
Rushing, James B. SC 25th Inf. Co.D
Rushing, James C. NC 48th Inf. Co.I
Rushing, James D. AR 16th Inf. Co.A
Rushing, James H. TX 4th Inf. Co.K
Rushing, James K.P. AL 8th Cav. Co.G
Rushing, James K.P. AL 28th Inf. Co.L
Rushing, James T. MS 14th Inf. Co.G
Rushing, James T. SC 26th Inf. Co.F Cpl.
Rushing, James W. MS 24th Inf. Co.E
Rushing, Jasper LA Inf.Cons.Crescent Regt. Co.F
Rushing, Jasper N. LA Inf. 16th Bn. Co.B
Rushing, Jasper N., Sr. LA Inf.Cons.Crescent Regt. Co.A
Rushing, J.B. GA Hvy.Arty. 22nd Bn. Co.F
Rushing, J.C. AL 3rd Res. Co.G
Rushing, J.C. MS 38th Cav. Co.H
Rushing, J.C. MS 2nd (Quinn's St.Troops) Inf. Co.H
Rushing, J.E. MS Part.Rangers Smyth's Co.
Rushing, J.E. Conf.Cav. Wood's Regt. 2nd Co.D
Rushing, Jesse TN 14th Inf. Co.F
Rushing, J.F. TN 5th Inf. 1st Co.F
Rushing, J.H. SC 11th Inf. Co.E
Rushing, J.H. SC 11th Inf. Co.E
Rushing, J.H. TN 5th Inf. 2nd Co.C 2nd Lt.
Rushing, J.J. SC 1st Mtd.Mil. Blakewood's Co.
Rushing, J.K. TN 8th (Smith's) Cav. Co.E
Rushing, J.M. AL 33rd Inf. Co.C
Rushing, J.M. GA 25th Inf. Co.B
Rushing, J.M. TN 50th (Cons.) Inf. Co.A
Rushing, J.N. TX 13th Vol. Co.E
Rushing, John GA 9th Inf. Co.I
Rushing, John GA 49th Inf. Co.B
Rushing, John MD 1st Cav. Co.F
Rushing, John SC 8th Inf. Co.B Cpl.

Rushing, John TN 11th Inf.
Rushing, John 20th Conf.Cav. Co.G
Rushing, John B. TX 11th Inf. Co.H
Rushing, John C. TX 10th Cav. Co.A
Rushing, John D. AR Cav. 1st Bn. (Stirman's) Co.A
Rushing, John E.A.H. AL 53rd (Part.Rangers) Co.B
Rushing, John K. TN 18th Inf. Co.A
Rushing, John R. TN 18th Inf. Co.A Sgt.
Rushing, John W. AL 25th Inf. Co.K
Rushing, Joseph C. MS St.Cav. Perrin's Bn. Co.A
Rushing, Joseph D. MS 14th Inf. Co.G
Rushing, Joseph E. TN 18th Inf. Co.A
Rushing, Joseph H. SC 1st Mtd.Mil. Martin's Co.
Rushing, Joseph J. SC 3rd Cav. Co.E
Rushing, Joseph J. TN 41st Inf. Co.K Cpl.
Rushing, Joseph L. MS 11th (Perrin's) Cav. Co.A
Rushing, J.R. AR 8th Inf. New Co.C 1st Lt.
Rushing, J.R. SC 26th Inf. Co.F
Rushing, J.S. 1st Conf.Cav. 2nd Co.G
Rushing, J.T. AL 15th Inf. Co.I
Rushing, J.T. TN 6th Inf. Co.B
Rushing, J.T. TX 13th Vol. 1st Co.K Cpl.
Rushing, J.W. MS 6th Inf. Co.C
Rushing, L. AL 2nd Cav. Co.C
Rushing, L. MS Inf. 1st Bn.St.Troops (12 mo. '62-3) Co.D
Rushing, L. TN 30th Inf.
Rushing, Leonidas TN 31st Inf. Co.H
Rushing, Levander T. NC 53rd Inf. Co.I Cpl.
Rushing, Mathew M. AL 33rd Inf. Co.A
Rushing, Matthew GA 47th Inf. Co.C
Rushing, Matthew SC 3rd Inf. Co.C
Rushing, Matthew M. MS 33rd Inf. Co.E
Rushing, M.F. MS 33rd Inf. Co.D
Rushing, M.G. TN 38th Inf. Co.E
Rushing, Miles GA 25th Inf. Co.G
Rushing, Milton R. TN 18th Inf. Co.A Capt.
Rushing, M.R. GA 29th Inf.
Rushing, Nerval E. MS 33rd Inf. Co.E
Rushing, N.R. MS 27th Inf. Co.E
Rushing, O.H.P. AL 33rd Inf. Co.E Sgt.
Rushing, O.P. TX 13th Vol. 1st Co.K
Rushing, O.P. TX 15th Inf. 2nd Co.F
Rushing, Peter TN Lt.Arty. Weller's Co.
Rushing, Philander TN 4th Inf.
Rushing, Philander TN 24th Bn.S.S. Co.B
Rushing, Philip MO Inf. 5th Regt.St.Guard Co.D
Rushing, Phillip TN 27th Inf. Co.E
Rushing, P.R. TN 50th Inf. Co.G
Rushing, P.V. TN 50th Inf. Co.D
Rushing, P.V. TN 50th (Cons.) Inf. Co.D
Rushing, R.C. TN 50th Inf. Co.I Sgt.
Rushing, R.E. SC 1st Mtd.Mil. Blakewood's Co.
Rushing, Reuben D. NC 53rd Inf. Co.I 2nd Lt.
Rushing, R.G. AR Inf. 1st Bn. Co.G Ord.Sgt.
Rushing, R.G. MO Cav. Coleman's Regt. Co.F Ord.Sgt.
Rushing, Richard E. SC 3rd Cav. Co.E
Rushing, R.L. MS Inf. 1st Bn.St.Troops (12 mo. '62-3) Co.D
Rushing, Ruben LA 1st Hvy.Arty. (Reg.) Co.H
Rushing, Samuel AL 2nd Cav. Co.E

Rushing, S.D. 8th (Wade's) Conf.Cav. Co.C
Rushing, S.H. FL 6th Inf. Surg.
Rushing, S.H. LA 16th Inf. Co.H
Rushing, S.H. Taylor Corps,PACS Surg.
Rushing, Shepard S. NC 48th Inf. Co.I
Rushing, Silas C. MS 33rd Inf. Co.E
Rushing, Silas E. GA 25th Inf. Co.G
Rushing, S.J. AL 60th Inf. Co.C
Rushing, S.J. AL 3rd Bn. Hilliard's Legion Vol. Co.D
Rushing, S.R. SC 1st Mtd.Mil. Martin's Co.
Rushing, S.R. SC 3rd Cav. Co.E
Rushing, S.S. AR 1st Mtd.Rifles Co.K
Rushing, S.S. AR 25th Inf. Co.E
Rushing, S.T. TN Cav. Nixon's Regt. Co.E
Rushing, S.T. TN Cav. Williams' Co.
Rushing, Steven D. AL 8th (Livingston's) Cav. Co.C Cpl.
Rushing, T.A. AL 60th Inf. Co.C
Rushing, T.A. AL 3rd Bn. Hilliard's Legion Vol. Co.D
Rushing, T.E. MS 38th Cav. Co.H
Rushing, Theophilus H. FL 1st Cav. Co.K
Rushing, Theoplous H. FL 7th Inf. Co.B
Rushing, Thomas MS 22nd Inf. Co.D
Rushing, Thomas NC 23rd Inf. Co.A Cpl.
Rushing, Thomas SC Inf. 9th Inf. Co.E
Rushing, Thomas TN 5th Inf. 2nd Co.C
Rushing, Thomas TX 10th Cav. Co.E
Rushing, Thomas E. AL 8th Cav. Co.G
Rushing, Thomas J. AL 3rd Bn. Hilliard's Legion Vol. Co.D 1st Lt.
Rushing, Thomas J. GA 12th Inf. Co.K Sgt.
Rushing, Thomas J. MS 24th Inf. Co.K
Rushing, Thomas J. MS 33rd Inf. Co.D
Rushing, T.J. AL 60th Inf. Co.C 1st Lt.
Rushing, T.M. AR 37th Inf. Co.D
Rushing, T.O. SC 1st Mtd.Mil. Screven's Co.
Rushing, T.O. SC 16th & 24th (Cons.) Inf. Co.I Cpl.
Rushing, T.O. SC 24th Inf. Co.D
Rushing, U.K. MS 22nd Inf. Co.G
Rushing, Uriah K. MS 33rd Inf. Co.E
Rushing, Van Buren LA 16th Inf. Co.I
Rushing, W. MS 2nd (Quinn's St.Troops) Inf. Co.H Sgt.
Rushing, W.A. TN 8th (Smith's) Cav. Co.E Sgt.Maj.
Rushing, W.B. TX 35th (Likens') Cav. Co.C
Rushing, W.F. MS 5th Cav. Co.A
Rushing, W.F. MS 3rd Inf. (St.Troops) Co.H
Rushing, W.F. TN 55th (Brown's) Inf. Co.F Sgt.
Rushing, W.G. AL 2nd Cav. Co.B
Rushing, W.H. AR 15th (Johnson's) Inf. Co.B
Rushing, W.H. GA 1st (Symons') Res. Co.C
Rushing, W.H.H. TN 31st Inf. Co.H 1st Ord.Sgt.
Rushing, Wiley MS 7th Inf. Co.E
Rushing, Wiley MS 33rd Inf. Co.E
Rushing, Wiley MS 33rd Inf. Co.H
Rushing, William AR 27th Inf. Co.F
Rushing, William LA Inf.Cons.Crescent Regt. Co.E
Rushing, William SC 1st (McCreary's) Inf. Co.E
Rushing, William SC 26th Inf. Co.F
Rushing, William TN 11th Inf. Co.I

Rushing, William TX 7th Field Btty.
Rushing, William TX 13th Vol. 1st Co.K
Rushing, William TX 15th Inf. 2nd Co.F
Rushing, William H. AR Cav. 1st Bn. (Stirman's) Co.A
Rushing, William H. GA 61st Inf. Co.D
Rushing, William J. GA 47th Inf. Co.G
Rushing, William R. GA 1st (Olmstead's) Inf. Co.K
Rushing, William R. TX 13th Cav. Co.E Sgt.
Rushing, W.K. AL Cp. of Instr. Talladega Co.D
Rushing, W.K. MS 44th Inf. Co.I 1st Lt.
Rushing, W.O. TN 8th (Smith's) Cav. Co.E AQM
Rushing, W.O. TX 35th (Brown's) Cav. Co.G
Rushing, W.P. TX Cav. McCord's Frontier Regt. Co.H
Rushing, W.R. AL Cp. of Instr. Talladega Co.D
Rushing, W.R. TX Cav. 2nd Regt.St.Troops Co.G
Rushing, W.T. MS 2nd (Quinn's St.Troops) Inf. Co.H
Rushing, W.T. MS 16th Inf. Co.E
Rushing, W.T. TN 31st Inf. Co.H Cpl.
Rushing, W.T. TX Vol. Rainey's Co.
Rushins, Philip AR 32nd Inf. Co.E
Rushion, William N.J. MS 26th Inf. Co.H
Rushmore, H. VA 3rd (Archer's) Bn.Res. Co.D
Rushmore, H. VA Second Class Mil. Wolff's Co.
Rushmore, Thomas VA 3rd (Archer's) Bn.Res. Co.C
Rushon, Augustus AL 24th Inf. Co.D
Rushton, B.J. MS 5th Inf. (St.Troops) Co.H
Rushton, B.N. AL 17th Inf. Co.F
Rushton, C.H. TX Inf. Carter's Co.
Rushton, Charles H. TX 4th Inf. Co.B
Rushton, Davis SC 7th Inf. 1st Co.G, Co.M,C
Rushton, George W. TN 48th (Voorhies') Inf. Co.K 2nd Lt.
Rushton, H.D. SC 7th Inf. 1st Co.G, Co.M Cpl.
Rushton, Henry T. MS 34th Inf. Co.I
Rushton, H.F. SC 7th Inf. 1st Co.G
Rushton, James C. AL 60th Inf. Co.G Cpl.
Rushton, James C. AL 3rd Bn. Hilliard's Legion Vol. Co.E
Rushton, James L. MS 15th Inf. Co.E
Rushton, James R. TN 48th (Voorhies') Inf. Co.K Cpl.
Rushton, J.C. GA Lt.Arty. Ferrell's Btty.
Rushton, J.D. SC 7th Inf. 1st Co.G
Rushton, J.E. SC 1st (Butler's) Inf. Co.E
Rushton, Jesse SC 7th Inf. Co.M
Rushton, Jesse G. TN 48th (Voorhies') Inf. Co.K
Rushton, J.G. AL 33rd Inf. Co.E
Rushton, J.H. AL 17th Inf. Co.F Sgt.
Rushton, J.H. AL 33rd Inf. Co.E
Rushton, John AL 39th Inf. Co.E
Rushton, John SC 7th Inf. Co.M,C
Rushton, John SC 19th Inf. Co.D
Rushton, John A. AL 39th Inf. Co.A
Rushton, Joseph GA Lt.Arty. 14th Bn. Co.C
Rushton, J.R. TN 38th (Nixon's) Inf. Co.C
Rushton, Martin SC 7th Inf. 1st Co.G, Co.M Sgt.
Rushton, Moses AL 3rd Bn. Hilliard's Legion Vol. Co.D
Rushton, Obelus E. MS 37th Inf. Co.K

Rushton, O.C. AL Res.

Rushton, Thomas MS 3rd Cav. Co.D

Rushton, W. LA Mil.Conf.Guards Regt. Surg.

Rushton, W.H.P. AL 17th Inf. Co.F

Rushton, William GA Inf. (RR Guards) Porter's Co.

Rushton, William LA Inf. 11th Bn. Co.B

Rushton, William LA Inf.Cons.Crescent Regt. Co.K

Rushton, William SC 19th Inf. Co.D

Rushton, William M., Jr. SC 7th Inf. 2nd Co.G, Co.D

Rushton, William M., Sr. SC 7th Inf. 2nd Co.G

Rusin, I.F. SC 2nd Rifles Co.H

Rusing, R.L. TX 24th Cav. Co.I

Rusk, Benjamin L. TX 4th Cav. Co.H Capt.

Rusk, Benjamin L. TX 17th Cons.Dismtd.Cav. Co.A

Rusk, Benjamin L. TX Inf.Riflemen Arnold's Co. Cpl.

Rusk, Cicero TX 4th Cav. Co.H

Rusk, Cicero TX 17th Cons.Dismtd.Cav. Co.A

Rusk, David GA Cobb's Legion Co.E Bugler

Rusk, Dempsy P. GA Cobb's Legion Co.E

Rusk, Dorsey LA Pointe Coupee Arty.

Rusk, E. MO 9th Bn.S.S. Co.A

Rusk, E.S. LA 2nd Cav. Co.E

Rusk, Henry C. AL 22nd Inf. Co.F

Rusk, J. MD 1st Cav. Co.D

Rusk, J.A. GA 2nd Res. Co.E

Rusk, James E. GA Cherokee Legion (St.Guards) Col.

Rusk, James E. GA Phillips' Legion Co.C

Rusk, James M. GA Phillips' Legion Co.C

Rusk, James W. VA 22nd Inf. Co.F

Rusk, J.L. AL Cp. of Instr. Talladega

Rusk, John MS 21st Inf. Co.C

Rusk, John TX 17th Cons.Dismtd.Cav. Co.A

Rusk, John TX 12th Inf. Co.G

Rusk, John C. TX 17th Cav. Co.A

Rusk, John C. TX 37th Cav. Co.G

Rusk, John C. TX Inf.Riflemen Arnold's Co.

Rusk, John C. VA Arty. Bryan's Co. Cpl.

Rusk, John H. VA 22nd Inf. Co.F

Rusk, John J. VA 8th Inf. Co.I

Rusk, Mason VA 135th Mil. Co.D

Rusk, M.M. VA Arty. Bryan's Co. Cpl.

Rusk, R.A. TX 35th (Brown's) Cav. Co.F

Rusk, Reuben MO Cav. 11th Regt.St.Guard Co.D 2nd Lt.

Rusk, Thomas D. TX 17th Cav. Co.A

Rusk, Thomas D. TX 17th Cons.Dismtd.Cav. Co.A Sr.2nd Lt.

Rusk, Thomas D. TX Inf.Riflemen Arnold's Co.

Rusk, Thomas J. GA 20th Inf. Co.F

Rusk, William AL 6th Inf. Co.H

Rusk, William LA 18th Inf. Co.B

Rusk, William LA Inf.Cons. 18th Regt. & Yellow Jacket Bn. Co.B

Rusk, William D. GA Phillips' Legion Co.C

Rusk, William H. AL Lt.Arty. 20th Bn. Co.A,B

Rusk, W.J. LA 2nd Cav. Co.E

Ruskell, George VA Cav. 1st Bn. Co.B Lt.

Ruskell, George VA Inf. 25th Bn. Co.E

Ruskell, Thomas VA Cav. 1st Bn. Co.A 2nd Lt.

Ruskell, Thomas VA Inf. 2nd Bn.Loc.Def. Co.D 1st Sgt.

Ruskell, W. Sig.Corps,CSA

Ruskell, William VA 46th Inf. 2nd Co.A

Ruskin, J.K. Gen. & Staff Surg.

Ruskin, M.D.L. TX 4th Inf. Co.I

Ruskin, W.T. AL 29th Inf. Co.C

Ruskin, W.W. AL 46th Inf. Co.B

Rusking, J. GA Mil. Coast Guard Bn. Co.A

Rusking, J.M. AR 1st Cav. Co.A

Rusking, W.R. AL Inf. 2nd Regt. Co.B

Rusler, Jacob VA Inf. 22nd Bn. Co.G

Rusler, John TX 8th Inf. Co.G

Rusmisell, G.B. VA 2nd Inf. Co.C

Rusmisell, George S. VA 52nd Inf. Co.C

Rusmisell, James A. VA Cav. 47th Bn. Co.A

Rusmisell, William H.H. VA 52nd Inf. Co.C Sgt.

Rusmisle, A.S. VA 62nd Mtd.Inf.

Rusmisle, John I. VA 25th Inf. 2nd Co.F Sgt.

Rusmun, George TX 16th Inf. Co.I

Rusnasell, J.A. VA 26th Cav. Co.G

Rusnor, R. AL 31st Inf. Co.H Sgt.

Russ, A.J. MS Inf. 1st Bn. Polk's Co.

Russ, Anderson NC 2nd Arty. (36th St.Troops) Co.I,E

Russ, Andrew TN Inf. 23rd Bn. Co.C

Russ, Archibald NC 2nd Arty. (36th St.Troops) Co.B

Russ, Asa W. TX 11th Inf. Co.K

Russ, Berry AR 7th Cav. Co.C

Russ, C. NC 21st Inf. Co.D

Russ, Caswell C. AL 13th Inf. Co.C

Russ, C.E. AL 7th Cav. Co.H,D

Russ, Charles D. NC 8th Inf. Co.C 2nd Lt.

Russ, D.P. SC 3rd St.Troops Co.A

Russ, Edward NC 2nd Arty. (36th St.Troops) Co.I,E

Russ, Edward J. NC 8th Inf. Co.C

Russ, E.H. MS Cav. 17th Bn. Co.B Sgt.

Russ, Ellis NC 20th Inf. Co.G Sgt.

Russ, Ely SC 10th Inf. Co.B Cpl.

Russ, Francis VA Lt.Arty. Thompson's Co. 2nd Lt.

Russ, Franklin NC 3rd Inf. Co.H

Russ, G.A. AL 19th Inf. Co.K

Russ, G.A. AL 31st Inf. Co.A

Russ, George W. NC 18th Inf. Co.A

Russ, Hamden NC 31st Inf. Co.A

Russ, Hugh NC 2nd Arty. (36th St.Troops) Co.B

Russ, I. AL 62nd Inf. Co.B

Russ, Isham NC 23rd Inf. Co.D

Russ, Isham SC 6th Cav. Co.D

Russ, Isham SC 26th Inf. Co.D

Russ, J. GA 32nd Inf. Co.I

Russ, J.A. LA 25th Inf. Co.G

Russ, Jacob FL 1st Inf. New Co.G

Russ, James L. FL 2nd Cav. Co.G

Russ, James L. FL 4th Inf. Co.H

Russ, James L. NC 8th Inf. Co.C

Russ, James L. TN 41st Inf. Co.F Sgt.

Russ, James S. NC 2nd Arty. (36th St.Troops) Co.B

Russ, James W. AL 2nd Bn. Hilliard's Legion Vol. Co.B

Russ, Jasper LA Inf.Crescent Regt. Co.H

Russ, Jasper NC 20th Inf. Co.G

Russ, J.D. GA 32nd Inf. Co.I 2nd Lt.

Russ, J.G. GA 8th Cav. Co.C Sgt.

Russ, J.G. GA 62nd Cav. Co.C Sgt.

Russ, J.H. TN 19th (Biffle's) Cav. Co.I

Russ, J.L. LA Mil. Beauregard Bn. Co.C Sgt.

Russ, J.L. LA Red River S.S. Co.A

Russ, John NC 3rd Inf. Co.F

Russ, John A. MS Cav. 17th Bn. Co.D

Russ, John A. NC 2nd Arty. (36th St.Troops) Co.K

Russ, John C. AL 19th Inf. Co.D Cpl.

Russ, John C. SC 1st Inf. Co.K

Russ, John C. SC 1st (Orr's) Rifles Co.H

Russ, John G. FL Cav. 5th Bn. Co.I

Russ, John J. FL 4th Inf. Co.H

Russ, John J. FL 11th Inf. Co.K

Russ, John J. NC 18th Inf. Co.D

Russ, John L. FL Cav. 5th Bn. Co.A

Russ, John R. FL 4th Inf. Co.H Cpl.

Russ, John R. MS 3rd Inf. Co.E

Russ, John R. NC 15th Inf. Co.C

Russ, Jonah D. NC 8th Inf. Co.C Cpl.

Russ, Jonas MO 7th Cav. Co.F

Russ, Jonathan NC 53rd Inf. Co.F

Russ, Josiah NC 20th Inf. Co.G

Russ, J.W. AL 15th Inf. Co.H

Russ, J.W. AL 59th Inf. Co.K

Russ, J.W. AL 1st Bn. Hilliard's Legion Vol. Co.G

Russ, J.W. TN 19th (Biffle's) Cav. Co.I 1st Sgt.

Russ, L.H. TN Cav. Jackson's Co.

Russ, Matthew NC 18th Inf. Co.D

Russ, Miles T. NC 43rd Inf. Co.K

Russ, Morgan NC 24th Inf. Co.G

Russ, Olin M. NC 3rd Inf. Co.H

Russ, Porter NC 8th Inf. Co.C

Russ, P.R. NC 15th Inf. Co.C

Russ, R.H. FL 2nd Cav. Co.G

Russ, Robert H. FL 6th Inf. Co.K 1st Lt.

Russ, Samuel NC 2nd Arty. (36th St.Troops) Co.K Sgt.

Russ, Samuel P. VA Lt.Arty. Moore's Co. Cpl.

Russ, Samuel P. VA Lt.Arty. Thompson's Co.

Russ, S.E. LA 2nd Inf. Co.D

Russ, Simeon S. AL 38th Inf. Co.G

Russ, Simpson NC Hvy.Arty. 10th Bn. Asst.Surg.

Russ, Simpson NC 18th Inf. Co.K Asst.Surg.

Russ, Simpson NC 46th Inf. Co.F 3rd Lt.

Russ, Simpson Gen. & Staff, A. of N.VA Asst.Surg.

Russ, S.P. LA 3rd Inf. Co.K Cpl.

Russ, Stewart NC 30th Inf. Co.C Sgt.

Russ, T. SC Inf. 9th Bn. Co.A

Russ, T. SC 26th Inf. Co.A

Russ, Thomas GA Cav. 29th Bn. Co.H

Russ, Thomas B. SC 10th Inf. Co.L 2nd Lt.

Russ, Thomas C. GA 40th Inf. Co.H 1st Lt.

Russ, Thomas D. NC 61st Inf. Co.B

Russ, Thomas J. FL 4th Inf. Co.H 1st Lt.

Russ, Thomas J. NC 3rd Arty. (40th St.Troops) Co.K

Russ, T.J. GA 47th Inf. Co.H Lt.

Russ, T.J. NC 2nd Arty. (36th St.Troops) Co.A

Russ, Travers NC 20th Inf. Co.G

Russ, Troy M. NC 18th Inf. Co.B Cpl.

Russ, V.C. LA 3rd Inf. Co.K

Russ, W. SC Inf. 9th Bn. Co.A

Russ, W.H. SC Inf. Hampton Legion Co.G Sgt.
Russ, Whiteford S. AL 19th Inf. Co.D,K
Russ, William NC 2nd Arty. (36th St.Troops) Co.K
Russ, William NC 3rd Arty. (40th St.Troops) Co.G
Russ, William NC 8th Inf. Co.C Cpl.
Russ, William NC 17th Inf. (2nd Org.) Co.B
Russ, William SC 26th Inf. Co.A
Russ, William A. NC 35th Inf. Co.H
Russ, William C. NC 1st Inf. Co.H
Russ, William H. NC Hvy.Arty. 1st Bn. Co.C
Russ, William H. NC 2nd Arty. (36th St.Troops) Co.A Sgt.
Russ, William H. NC 2nd Arty. (36th St.Troops) Co.G Music.
Russ, William H. NC 3rd Inf. Co.H
Russ, W.J. GA 46th Inf. Co.H
Russ, W.O. GA 32nd Inf. Co.I
Russ, W.S. AL 10th Inf. Co.H
Russ, Zachariah SC 1st (Orr's) Rifles Co.H
Russama, L. 1st Chickasaw Inf. Kesner's Co.
Russau, Abner GA 12th Inf. Co.B
Russau, Ezekiel GA 12th Inf. Co.B
Russau, R.H.V.B. GA 18th Inf. Co.E
Russaw, John MS 8th Inf. Co.E
Russaw, John SC 2nd St.Troops Co.I
Russay, James AL 15th Inf. Co.F
Russeau, Adolphus NC 2nd Detailed Men Co.H 2nd Lt.
Russeau, D.T. Mead's Conf.Cav. Co.A
Russeau, John M. GA 21st Inf. Co.I
Russeau, Robert R. FL 1st Inf. Old Co.H
Russel, --- MO St.Guard Capt.
Russel, A. AL 7th Inf. Co.D
Russel, A. LA Inf.Cons.Crescent Regt. Co.I
Russel, Alex MS Inf. 1st Bn.St.Troops (30 days '64) Co.E
Russel, Alexander K. VA Inf. 21st Bn. Co.B Capt.
Russel, Alfred MS 34th Inf. Co.B
Russel, Allen J. MS Graves' Co. (Copiah Horse Guards)
Russel, Andrew J. AL 58th Inf. Co.A,H
Russel, Calvin VA Cav. 37th Bn. Co.D Cpl.
Russel, Charles GA 12th (Wright's) Cav. (St.Guards) Stapleton's Co.
Russel, Daniel TN 44th Inf. Co.D
Russel, David NC 62nd Inf. Co.A
Russel, David G. NC 48th Inf. Co.I
Russel, David S. AL 4th Inf. Co.E
Russel, David W. AL 28th Inf. Co.I Cpl.
Russel, D.L. TN Inf. 22nd Bn. Co.F
Russel, D.W. GA 62nd Cav. Co.L
Russel, E. AR 10th Inf. Co.C
Russel, E. KY 8th Mtd.Inf. Co.I
Russel, E. MS 1st (King's) Inf. (St.Troops) Co.I
Russel, Ebenezer MS 13th Inf. Co.B
Russel, Edmond NC 8th Bn.Part.Rangers Co.C
Russel, Edward VA 64th Mtd.Inf. Co.F
Russel, Edward Nitre & Min. Bureau War Dept.,CSA
Russel, E.L. TN 30th Inf. Co.G
Russel, Elam MS 36th Inf. Co.C
Russel, Elijah GA Smith's Legion Co.B 3rd Lt.
Russel, Elijah E. NC 39th Inf. Co.A Cpl.
Russel, Elisha MO Inf. 8th Bn. Co.F

Russel, Elisha 1st Cherokee Mtd.Vol. 1st Co.H
Russel, Erastus MS Inf. 1st Bn.St.Troops (30 days '64) Co.E
Russel, Fletcher LA 1st Res. Co.D
Russel, F.M. AR 1st Vol. Simington's Co. 1st Sgt.
Russel, Francis H. MS Cav. 24th Bn. Co.A
Russel, Franklin M. TX 30th Cav. Co.D Cpl.
Russel, G.A. AL Mil. 2nd Regt.Vol. Co.E
Russel, Gabriel D. MO 8th Cav. Co.E
Russel, Gabriel H. AL 25th Inf. Co.H Sgt.
Russel, G.D. TX 22nd Inf. Co.D
Russel, George N. GA 34th Inf. Co.H
Russel, George S. VA 46th Inf. 4th Co.F
Russel, George W. MO Inf. 8th Bn. Co.F
Russel, George W. VA 64th Mtd.Inf. Co.C
Russel, Gideon B. MS 33rd Inf. Co.A
Russel, G.S. LA Lt.Arty. LeGardeur, Jr.'s Co. (Orleans Guard Btty.)
Russel, G.W. MO 1st Inf. Co.K
Russel, H. MO Cav. Ford's Bn. Co.F
Russel, H.F. SC 19th Inf. Co.H
Russel, H.H. TN 20th Inf. Co.D
Russel, H.W. TX Granbury's Cons.Brig. Co.G
Russel, Isaac P. NC 57th Inf. Co.H
Russel, J. MS 10th Cav. Co.B
Russel, J. NC 23rd Inf.
Russel, J. TX 11th Inf. Co.K
Russel, J.A. SC 19th Inf. Co.H
Russel, Jacob P. LA 1st (Nelligan's) Inf. Howell's Co.
Russel, James AL 14th Inf. Co.D
Russel, James LA 1st Res. Co.D
Russel, James TN 3rd (Forrest's) Cav.
Russel, James TN 84th Inf. Co.D
Russel, James A. TX Waul's Legion Co.H
Russel, James C. AL 1st Inf. Co.I
Russel, James H. NC 25th Inf. Co.C
Russel, James K.P. GA 65th Inf. Co.A
Russel, James M. LA 26th (Gray's) Inf. Co.B
Russel, James P. GA 7th Inf. Co.A
Russel, James W. NC 6th Inf. Co.G
Russel, J.C. AL 12th Inf. Co.I
Russel, J.C. TX Inf. 1st St.Troops Sheldon's Co.B
Russel, J.E. MS Cav. Powers' Regt. Co.H
Russel, J.E. 20th Conf.Cav. Co.A
Russel, J.E.M. GA Inf. 9th Bn. Co.B
Russel, J.E.M. GA 37th Inf. Co.E
Russel, Jesse D. AR 3rd Inf. Co.G
Russel, J.G. AR 35th Inf. Surg.
Russel, J.H. AL 6th Inf. Co.B
Russel, J.H. TX 7th Cav. Co.C
Russel, J.N. AL 8th Inf. Co.K
Russel, John AL Cav. Moreland's Regt. Co.H
Russel, John FL 8th Inf. Co.I
Russel, John GA 4th (Clinch's) Cav. Co.E
Russel, John GA Inf. 9th Bn. Co.B
Russel, John GA 37th Inf. Co.E
Russel, John GA 65th Inf. Co.A Sgt.
Russel, John GA Smith's Legion Co.B
Russel, John LA Mil. 4th Regt. 1st Brig. 1st Div. Co.I
Russel, John MS 2nd Cav. Co.E
Russel, John MS 3rd (St.Troops) Cav. Co.K
Russel, John MS 46th Inf. Co.G
Russel, John MO Cav. Ford's Bn. Co.F

Russel, John 1st Conf.Inf. 1st Co.F
Russel, John A. NC 62nd Inf. Co.A Sgt.
Russel, John P. NC 33rd Inf. Co.D
Russel, John P. NC 56th Inf. Co.A
Russel, John R. NC 20th Inf. Co.A
Russel, John S. TN 12th (Green's) Cav. Co.I Cpl.
Russel, John T. AL 5th Cav. Co.E,F
Russel, John T. AL 46th Inf. Co.H
Russel, Joseph LA 26th (Gray's) Inf. Co.E Sgt.
Russel, Joseph 1st Cherokee Mtd.Vol. 1st Co.G, 2nd Co.K Cpl.
Russel, Joseph S. AR Inf. Hardy's Regt. Co.F
Russel, Josiah Thompson SC 19th Inf. Co.I
Russel, J.R. MS Cav. Ham's Regt. Co.G
Russel, J.R. TN 15th Cav.
Russel, J.R. TX 10th Cav. Co.G
Russel, J.S. Trans-MS Conf.Cav. 1st Bn. Co.C
Russel, J.T. GA Inf. 9th Bn. Co.B
Russel, J.W. AL 5th Bn. (Blount's) Vol. Co.B 2nd Lt.
Russel, J.W. MS 39th Inf. Co.E
Russel, J.W. TN 33rd Inf. Co.E,F
Russel, L.M. AL 40th Inf. Co.D
Russel, Loransy D. VA 64th Mtd.Inf. Co.G
Russel, Madison NC 64th Inf. Co.E
Russel, Martin W. TN 50th Inf. Co.H Sgt.
Russel, McKenzie NC 57th Inf. Co.H
Russel, Michael J. NC 3rd Arty. (40th St.Troops) Co.K
Russel, Monroe TN 84th Inf. Co.B 3rd Lt.
Russel, Nelson AR 17th (Lemoyne's) Inf. Co.H
Russel, Nelson AR 21st Inf. Co.G
Russel, Oliver AR 11th Inf. Co.A
Russel, Osamus MS 3rd Inf. (St.Troops) Co.E
Russel, Pryor AL Cav. Moreland's Regt. Co.H
Russel, Rec. T. GA 37th Inf. Co.E
Russel, Reuben R. TX 1st Inf. Co.I
Russel, R.F. VA 51st Inf. Co.I
Russel, R.M. AL 15th Inf. Co.C
Russel, Robert AL 9th Inf. Co.E
Russel, Robert, Jr. KY 6th Cav. Co.A
Russel, R.T. GA Inf. 9th Bn. Co.B
Russel, Rubin NC 6th Cav. (65th St.Troops) Co.C Saddler
Russel, S. NC 8th Jr.Res. Co.C
Russel, S.A. NC 1st Bn.Jr.Res. Co.C
Russel, Samuel A. TX 25th Cav. Co.F
Russel, Samuel E. GA Inf. 26th Bn. Co.A
Russel, Sanders V. FL 11th Inf. Co.F
Russel, S.M. MO 3rd Brig. Capt.
Russel, Stephen AL 33rd Inf. Co.E
Russel, Stephen AR 8th Cav. Co.G
Russel, Stephen MO 4th Cav. Co.I
Russel, T.G. TX Inf. 2nd St.Troops Co.A Cpl.
Russel, Thomas GA Inf. (Anderson Guards) Anderson's Co.
Russel, Thomas B. TX 1st Inf. Co.I
Russel, Thomas F. AL 10th Inf. Co.K 1st Sgt.
Russel, Thomas J. AL 62nd Inf. Co.C 2nd Lt.
Russel, Thomas R. VA 5th Cav. Co.G
Russel, Thomas R. VA Cav. 14th Bn. Co.A
Russel, T.J. AL 17th Inf. Co.F
Russel, T.J. TX Cav. Bourland's Regt. Co.C
Russel, T.M. TX Cav. 3rd Regt.St.Troops Co.A
Russel, W. AL 19th Inf. Co.D
Russel, W.D. AL 23rd Inf. Co.F

Russel, Wesley MS 2nd (Quinn's St.Troops) Inf. Co.D
Russel, Wesley S. NC 51st Inf. Co.D
Russel, W.H. TN 5th Inf. 2nd Co.I
Russel, William AL 19th Inf. Co.B
Russel, William AL 40th Inf. Co.G
Russel, William AR 33rd Inf. Co.H
Russel, William AR 38th Inf. Old Co.I, Co.H Sgt.
Russel, William FL Lt.Arty. Dyke's Co.
Russel, William GA Inf. 11th Bn. (St.Guards) Co.A
Russel, William B. MS 6th Cav. Surg.
Russel, William B. MS 23rd Inf. Surg.
Russel, William D. TX 25th Cav. Co.F
Russel, William H. NC 28th Inf. Co.K
Russel, William H. VA 8th Cav. Co.F
Russel, Wm. J. AL 30th Inf. Co.A
Russel, William J. AR 1st Vol. Simington's Co.
Russel, William R. MS 33rd Inf. Co.F
Russel, William T. SC Inf. Holcombe Legion Surg.
Russel, W.J. GA Inf. 9th Bn. Co.B
Russel, W.J. GA 37th Inf. Co.E
Russel, W.J. GA 54th Inf. Co.I
Russel, W.M. AR 2nd Mtd.Rifles Hawkins' Co.
Russel, W.M. AR 8th Cav. Co.K
Russel, W.S. TX 9th (Young's) Inf. Co.D
Russel, W.W. TN 31st Inf. Co.C
Russell, --- AL 35th Inf. Co.D
Russell, --- GA 20th Inf. Co.C
Russell, --- TX Cav. Good's Bn. Co.D
Russell, ---, 1st TX Cav. McCord's Frontier Regt. Co.K
Russell, ---, 2nd TX Cav. McCord's Frontier Regt. Co.K
Russell, --- (Dr.) TX 16th Bn.St.Troops
Russell, --- VA 6th Cav. Co.K
Russell, A. AL 3rd Bn.Res. Flemming's Co.
Russell, A. AR 11th Inf. Co.A
Russell, A. AR 11th & 17th Cons.Inf. Co.A
Russell, A. GA Inf. 1st Loc.Troops (Augusta) Co.E
Russell, A. MS 37th Inf. Co.G
Russell, A. VA 46th Inf. 2nd Co.H
Russell, A.A. AL 4th (Russell's) Cav. Col.
Russell, A.A. SC Manigault's Bn.Vol. Co.A
Russell, Aaron NC 54th Inf. Co.H
Russell, Aaron TN 29th Inf. Co.K
Russell, Aaron TN 29th Inf. Co.K Laborer
Russell, Aaron TX Inf. Griffin's Bn. Co.A
Russell, A.B. GA 66th Inf. Co.F
Russell, Abednego 53rd Inf. Co.K
Russell, Abin GA 42nd Inf. Co.E
Russell, Abner J. MS 3rd Inf. Co.I 2nd Lt.
Russell, Abraham MO Cav. 2nd Regt.St.Guard Co.A
Russell, Abraham MO 15th Cav. Co.A
Russell, Absalom C. KY 5th Mtd.Inf. Co.D
Russell, Absolem AR 2nd Mtd.Rifles Co.F
Russell, A.C. AL 19th Inf. Co.H
Russell, A.C. AR 37th Inf. Co.H
Russell, A.C. TN 42nd Inf. Co.A
Russell, A.C. 4th Conf.Inf. Co.G
Russell, Adam GA 3rd Inf. Co.G
Russell, A.E. MS 1st Cav. Co.E Sgt.
Russell, A.E. MS 1st (Percy's) Inf. Co.D

Russell, A.G. AL 4th (Russell's) Cav. Co.H
Russell, A.G. AL 4th Res. 2nd Co.D
Russell, A.G. KY 9th Mtd.Inf. Co.E Sgt.
Russell, A.G. 3rd Conf.Cav. Co.K
Russell, A.H. TN Inf. Harman's Regt. Co.K
Russell, A.J. AL 5th Inf. New Co.K Cpl.
Russell, A.J. AR 7th Inf. Co.K
Russell, A.J. AR 32nd Inf. Co.H
Russell, A.J. LA 13th Bn. (Part.Rangers) Co.E
Russell; A.J. MS 6th Cav. Co.A
Russell, A.J. MS 41st Inf. Co.H
Russell, A.J. TN 11th (Holman's) Cav. Co.D
Russell, A.J. Gen. & Staff 1st Lt.,Dr.M.
Russell, A.L. AR 37th Inf. Co.E
Russell, A.L. MO 3rd Cav. Co.F
Russell, A.L. NC 14th Inf. Co.K
Russell, A.L. TN 62nd Mtd.Inf. Co.C
Russell, Alanson G. TN Inf. 23rd Bn. Co.A Sgt.
Russell, Albert AR 35th Inf. Co.I Sgt.
Russell, Albert GA Cav. 24th Bn.
Russell, Albert B. GA 24th Inf. Co.D
Russell, Albert G. MS 37th Inf. Co.C
Russell, Albert G. VA 8th Cav. Co.E
Russell, Albert J. FL 2nd Inf. Co.G 2nd Lt.
Russell, Albert K. VA 59th Mil. Riddick's Co.
Russell, Alberto AL 20th Inf. Co.C
Russell, Alex AR 2nd Inf. New Co.E 1st Lt.
Russell, Alexander MO 8th Inf. Co.H
Russell, Alexander NC 48th Inf. Co.G
Russell, Alexander SC Lt.Arty. 3rd (Palmetto) Bn. Co.F
Russell, Alexander M. NC 44th Inf. Co.F 2nd Lt.
Russell, Alexander R. VA 64th Mtd.Inf. 2nd Co.F
Russell, Alex W.L. AR Cav. Poe's Bn. Co.A
Russell, Alfred LA Miles' Legion Co.A
Russell, Alfred MS 1st Lt.Arty. Co.F
Russell, Alfred MS 1st (Percy's) Inf. Co.I
Russell, Alfred A. AL 7th Inf. Co.G Maj.
Russell, Alfred G. TN 3rd (Forrest's) Cav.
Russell, Alkani VA 136th Mil. Co.D
Russell, Allen J. MS 12th Inf. Co.D
Russell, Allen W. FL 10th Inf. Co.F
Russell, Alonzo G. TX 2nd Cav. Co.C Bugler
Russell, Alva J. MS 15th Inf. Co.H
Russell, A.M. AR 1st (Dobbin's) Cav. Co.D
Russell, A.M. AR Inf. 8th Bn. Co.C
Russell, A.M. GA Inf. 11th Bn. (St.Guards) Co.B
Russell, A.M. MS 1st (King's) Inf. (St.Troops) D. Love's Co.
Russell, A.M. TN 33rd Inf. Co.F
Russell, A.Mc. 2nd Cherokee Mtd.Vol. Co.C Sgt.
Russell, Anderson P. NC 39th Inf. Co.B Fifer
Russell, Andrew D. GA 52nd Inf. Co.E Sgt.
Russell, Andrew J. AL 41st Inf. Co.E
Russell, Andrew J. AR 15th (N.W.) Inf. Floyd's Co.
Russell, Andrew J. KY 4th Mtd.Inf. Co.F
Russell, Andrew J. TX 14th Cav. Co.I
Russell, Andrew K. KY 4th Mtd.Inf. Co.F Sgt.
Russell, Andrew W. AL 28th Inf. Co.A
Russell, Anthony P. MS 18th Inf. Co.K
Russell, A.P. TN 19th Inf. Co.E
Russell, A.R. AL St.Arty. Co.C Sgt.Maj.

Russell, A.R. AL 23rd Inf. Co.C Sgt.
Russell, A.R. GA Lt.Arty. Van Den Corput's Co.
Russell, A.R. GA Inf. 3rd Bn. Co.A
Russell, A.R. TN 31st Inf. Co.B
Russell, Arch B. NC 2nd Arty. (36th St.Troops) Co.B
Russell, Archibald B. NC Lt.Arty. 13th Bn. Co.B
Russell, Archibald B. NC 1st Inf. (6 mo. '61) Co.H
Russell, Arnold J. AL 6th Inf. Co.M
Russell, Arthur L. MO 1st Inf.
Russell, Arthur Lee MO Cav. 3rd Bn. Co.F
Russell, A.S. AR 37th Inf. Co.E 1st Lt.
Russell, Asberry C. AL 40th Inf. Co.B
Russell, Augustus E. MS 33rd Inf. Co.A
Russell, Augustus H. GA 45th Inf. Co.G
Russell, Aulsey NC 23rd Inf. Co.C
Russell, Aurelius A. SC 5th Cav. Co.E
Russell, A.W. TN Cav. Williams' Co. Bvt.2nd Lt.
Russell, A.W.L. AR 11th Inf. Co.D
Russell, A.W.L. AR 11th & 17th Cons.Inf. Co.D
Russell, B. AR Inf. Adams' Regt. Moore's Co.
Russell, B.A. AL Mil. 4th Vol. Co.K
Russell, B.A. AL Cp. of Instr. Talladega
Russell, B.A. TN 41st Inf. Co.E
Russell, Baxter S. TN 53rd Inf. Co.G
Russell, Beng R. NC 1st Inf. (6 mo. '61) Co.H
Russell, Benjamin AL Cav. Barbiere's Bn. Goldsby's Co. Cpl.
Russell, Benjamin AL 62nd Inf. Co.D
Russell, Benjamin GA 57th Inf. Co.H
Russell, Benjamin A. FL 5th Inf. Co.K
Russell, Benjamin B. GA Inf. 1st Loc.Troops (Augusta) Co.C 1st Sgt.
Russell, Benjamin E. FL 8th Inf. Co.B 2nd Lt.
Russell, Benjamin E. GA 1st (Ramsey's) Inf. Co.G
Russell, Benjamin E. LA 19th Inf. Co.F
Russell, Benjamin F. NC 3rd Inf. Co.F Cpl.
Russell, Benjamin F. TN 1st Cav.
Russell, Benjamin F. TX 11th Inf. Co.I
Russell, Benjamin F.C. AL 47th Inf. Co.C
Russell, Benjamin H. AL 16th Inf. Co.H 2nd Lt.
Russell, Benjamin J. FL Cav. 3rd Bn. Co.A
Russell, Benjamin J. GA 6th Inf. Co.H Capt.
Russell, Benjamin P. TX 31st Cav. Co.E Cpl.
Russell, Benjamin R. NC 2nd Bn.Loc.Def. Troops Co.A Laborer
Russell, Benjamin T. MS 24th Inf. Co.I
Russell, Bennett NC 14th Inf. Co.H Sgt.
Russell, Bennett TX 11th Cav. Co.C
Russell, Bennett VA 1st Cav. 1st Co.D
Russell, Bennett VA 6th Cav. Co.D
Russell, Berry TN 20th Inf. Co.B
Russell, B.F. AR 27th Inf. New Co.B
Russell, B.F. LA 25th Inf. Co.B 1st Lt.
Russell, B.F. MS 33rd Inf. Co.A
Russell, B.F. MS Rogers' Co.
Russell, B.F. MO Lt.Arty. Walsh's Co.
Russell, B.F. SC 1st (Butler's) Inf. Co.G
Russell, B.G. AR 19th (Dawson's) Inf. Co.K Sgt.
Russell, B.H. AL 26th (O'Neal's) Inf. Co.F
Russell, B.J. GA 4th Inf. Capt.
Russell, Bluford TN 29th Inf. Co.I

Russell, B.S. TN 23rd Inf. 2nd Co.F
Russell, B.T. AL Cp. of Instr. Talladega
Russell, C. SC Mil. 1st Regt. (Charleston Res.)
Co.F
Russell, C.A. 3rd Conf.Cav. Co.K 1st Sgt.
Russell, Call TX 19th Inf. Co.F
Russell, C.B. MS 6th Cav. Co.A
Russell, C.B. TN 11th (Holman's) Cav. Co.D
Cpl.
Russell, C.B. TN Douglass' Bn.Part.Rangers
Lytle's Co. Cpl.
Russell, C.B. TX 14th Inf. Co.D 1st Lt.
Russell, C.C. MS 12th Cav. Co.L
Russell, C.F. AL 17th Inf. Co.I
Russell, C.F. VA 7th Cav. Co.G
Russell, C.G. AL 5th Inf. Co.K
Russell, C.H. LA Mil. British Guard Bn.
Coburn's Co. Sgt.
Russell, Charles AL 32nd Inf. Co.K
Russell, Charles MS 3rd Inf. Co.C
Russell, Charles MS 21st Inf. Co.A
Russell, Charles MO 2nd Cav. Co.D
Russell, Charles NC 42nd Inf. Co.D
Russell, Charles Gen. & Staff Maj.,QM
Russell, Charles A. KY 2nd Cav.
Russell, Charles B. FL Inf. 2nd Bn. Co.B
Russell, Charles B. FL 10th Inf. Co.G
Russell, Charles F. VA 11th Cav. Hosp.Stew.
Russell, Charles G. AL 6th Inf. Co.M
Russell, Charles H. AL 17th Inf. Co.H
Russell, Charles H. GA 5th Inf. Co.B
Russell, Charles M. GA 20th Inf. Co.G
Russell, Charles M. TN 34th Inf. Co.G
Russell, Charles P. LA Washington Arty.Bn.
Co.3
Russell, Charles P. LA 7th Inf. Co.G
Russell, Charles R. GA 54th Inf. Co.H Capt.
Russell, Charles T. MS 18th Inf. Co.K 2nd Cpl.
Russell, Charles W. AL 5th Bn.Vol. Co.A Cpl.
Russell, Chist VA 2nd St.Res. Co.L
Russell, Christopher GA Inf. 18th Bn. Co.A
Russell, Christopher VA 10th Cav. Co.D
Russell, Christopher VA 20th Inf. Co.A
Russell, C.J. MS 4th Inf. Co.I Cpl.
Russell, C.M. AR 37th Inf. Co.E
Russell, C.M. TN 2nd (Robison's) Inf. Cpl.
Russell, C.M. VA 5th Cav. Co.G Cpl.
Russell, Columbus NC 52nd Inf. Co.G
Russell, Coriolanus VA 12th Inf. Co.E
Russell, C.P. GA 4th (Clinch's) Cav. Co.D
Russell, C.R. GA 2nd Inf. Co.G
Russell, C.R. TX 14th Inf. Co.F
Russell, Crue C. TX 10th Cav. Co.G
Russell, Crue S. TX 14th Cav. Co.C
Russell, C.S. SC 17th Inf. Co.K
Russell, C.T. TN Inf. 154th Sr.Regt. Co.A
Russell, C.W. KY 12th Cav. Co.A
Russell, C.W. KY 8th Mtd.Inf. Co.C
Russell, C.W. TN 10th Inf. Co.D
Russell, Cyrus AL 28th Inf. Co.A
Russell, D. AR 5th Mil. Co.E
Russell, D. FL 1st Cav.
Russell, D. Conf.Cav. Raum's Co.
Russell, D.A. TN 48th (Nixon's) Inf. Co.K
Russell, D.A. TN 51st (Cons.) Inf. Co.B
Russell, D.A. TX Cav. Wells' Regt. Co.I
Russell, Daniel GA Inf. 3rd Bn. Co.E Ch.Music.

Russell, Daniel MS 3rd Inf. Co.A
Russell, Daniel NC 1st Arty. (10th St.Troops)
Co.G
Russell, Daniel NC 38th Inf. Co.H
Russell, Daniel NC 52nd Inf. Co.B
Russell, Daniel Conf.Cav. Baxter's Bn. Co.C
Russell, Daniel A. TN 54th Inf. Co.E
Russell, Daniel C. GA Siege Arty. 28th Bn.
Co.C 1st Sgt.
Russell, Daniel L., Jr. NC 2nd Arty. (36th
St.Troops) Co.G Capt.
Russell, Daniel L. TX 8th Cav. Co.C Sgt.
Russell, Daniel R. MS 20th Inf. Co.C Col.
Russell, Daniel W. FL 5th Inf. Co.C
Russell, Daniel W. MS 33rd Inf. Co.A 1st Sgt.
Russell, David AL Mil. 2nd Regt.Vol. Co.B
Russell, David AR 35th Inf. Co.B
Russell, David FL 1st Inf.
Russell, David KY 13th Cav. Co.G
Russell, David KY 5th Mtd.Inf. Co.I
Russell, David MO Inf. Clark's Regt. Co.I
Russell, David NC 6th Sr.Res. Co.E
Russell, David NC 22nd Inf. Co.E
Russell, David TN 11th (Holman's) Cav. Co.K
Russell, David TN Holman's Bn.Part.Rangers
Co.D
Russell, David TX 10th Cav. Co.H 2nd Lt.
Russell, David TX 18th Inf. Co.E
Russell, David Conf.Cav. Clarkson's Bn. Ind.
Rangers Co.C
Russell, David 9th Conf.Inf. Co.G
Russell, David A. GA 15th Inf. Co.A
Russell, David A. MS 1st Lt.Arty. Co.K
Russell, David A. TN 52nd Inf. Co.B Sgt.
Russell, David A. TN 53rd Inf. Co.B Sgt.
Russell, David H. TX 31st Cav. Co.G Bvt.2nd
Lt.
Russell, David L. TN Lt.Arty. Lynch's Co.
Russell, David M. NC 25th Inf. Co.D
Russell, David M. NC 48th Inf. Co.I
Russell, David M. NC Inf. Thomas Legion Co.E
Russell, David Marion SC 4th Inf. Co.E
Russell, David P. NC Part.Rangers Swindell's
Co.
Russell, David S. NC 23rd Inf. Asst.Surg.
Russell, David T. LA 31st Inf. Capt.,ACS
Russell, David T. 3rd Conf.Eng.Troops Co.D
Russell, David T. Gen. & Staff Capt.,Comsy.
Russell, David W. MS 24th Inf. Co.I
Russell, David W. NC 1st Arty. (10th St.Troops)
Co.C
Russell, David W. TN Cav. 31st Regt. Co.H
Russell, David W. TX 11th Inf. Co.G
Russell, David Y. FL 1st (Res.) Inf. Co.A
Russell, David Y. NC 18th Inf. Co.I Cpl.
Russell, D.C. TX Cav. 2nd Bn.St.Troops Co.A
Cpl.
Russell, D.D. NC 21st Inf. Co.H
Russell, Dd. TN 21st Inf. Co.D
Russell, Decatur TX 6th Field Btty.
Russell, Dewitt C. Conf.Cav. Wood's Regt. Co.E
Sgt.
Russell, D.F. TX 12th Cav. Co.A
Russell, D.G. GA 54th Inf. Co.H
Russell, D.G. NC 4th Sr.Res. Co.I
Russell, D.G. 10th Conf.Cav. Co.F
Russell, D.H. SC 1st Cav. Co.F

Russell, D.H. SC 4th Inf. Co.B
Russell, D.H. TN 31st Inf. Co.E
Russell, Dickson H. VA 64th Mtd.Inf. Co.G
Russell, D.J. AL 16th Inf. Co.D Sgt.
Russell, D.L. MS 28th Cav. Co.F
Russell, D.L. TN 4th (Murray's) Cav. Co.K
Russell, D.L. TN Cav. Allison's Squad. Co.A
Russell, D.M. AL 40th Inf. Co.G
Russell, D.M. KY 8th Mtd.Inf. Co.C
Russell, D.M. SC Palmetto S.S. Co.B Capt.
Russell, D.M. TN 8th Inf. Co.E
Russell, Drayton P. GA 66th Inf. Co.H
Russell, D.S. AL 2nd Cav. Co.E
Russell, D.S. NC 27th Inf. Co.I Cpl.
Russell, D.S. SC 6th Inf. 2nd Co.I
Russell, D.S. Gen. & Staff Asst.Surg.
Russell, D.W. TN 1st Hvy.Arty. 2nd Co.B
Russell, E. MS 3rd (St.Troops) Cav. Co.A
Russell, E. MS 12th Cav. Co.F
Russell, E. TN 2nd (Ashby's) Cav. Co.A
Russell, E. TX 15th Cav. Co.E
Russell, E. TX 5th Inf. Co.D
Russell, E.A. KY 4th Cav. Co.C
Russell, E.A. SC Cav. 2nd Bn.Res. Co.H
Bvt.2nd Lt.
Russell, E.A. TN Inf. 3rd Cons.Regt. Co.E
Russell, Earl A. NC Inf. 2nd Bn. Co.H Ord.Sgt.
Russell, E.B. MS Cav. 4th Bn. Co.C
Russell, E.B. MS 5th Inf. Co.K
Russell, E.B. MO 6th Cav. Co.E
Russell, E.B. SC 17th Inf. Co.K Sgt.
Russell, E.B. 8th (Wade's) Conf.Cav. Co.E
Russell, Ebenezer MS 37th Inf. Co.C
Russell, E.D. AR 37th Inf. Co.E
Russell, Edmond AR 4th Inf. Co.C
Russell, Edmond TN 43rd Inf. Co.C
Russell, Edmund LA Pointe Coupee Arty.
Russell, Edward TN 28th Inf. Co.H
Russell, Edward 4th Conf.Inf. Co.A
Russell, Edward A. FL Inf. 2nd Bn. Co.B
Russell, Edward A. FL 10th Inf. Co.G
Russell, Edward A. TN 1st (Feild's) Inf. Co.G
Russell, Edward S. VA 11th Inf. Co.B
Russell, Edward P. NC 16th Inf. Co.L
Russell, Edward P. NC Inf. Thomas Legion Co.E
Russell, Edwin TN 5th Cav.
Russell, Edwin H. NC 12th Inf. Co.C 1st Sgt.
Russell, Edwin H. NC 37th Inf. Co.I 1st Lt.
Russell, E.E. TN 5th (McKenzie's) Cav. Co.D
Sgt.
Russell, E.E. TN Cav. 5th Bn. (McClellan's)
Co.A
Russell, E.F. LA 22nd (Cons.) Inf. Co.F 1st Lt.
Russell, E.F. LA 27th Inf. Co.H Bvt.2nd Lt.
Russell, E.F. TN 17th Inf. Co.A Cpl.
Russell, E.G. SC 5th Inf. 1st Co.I
Russell, E.J. AL 9th Cav. Adj.
Russell, E.L. MS 41st Inf. Co.E Cpl.
Russell, Elem TN 28th Inf. Co.H
Russell, Elem P. TN 28th Inf. Co.H
Russell, Eli NC 34th Inf. Co.K
Russell, Eli TX 12th Inf. Co.B,I
Russell, Elias G. NC 7th Inf. Co.F
Russell, Elijah AR 4th Inf. Co.H Cpl.
Russell, Elijah AR 15th (Josey's) Inf. Co.E
Russell, Elijah GA 65th Inf. Co.A 2nd Lt.
Russell, Elijah NC 16th Inf. Co.H

Russell, Elijah A. NC 34th Inf. Co.K
Russell, Elijah Allen TN 41st Inf. Co.F
Russell, Elijah J. TN 50th (Cons.) Inf. Co.H
Russell, Elisha MO 8th Inf. Co.I
Russell, Elisha MO 9th Inf. Co.K
Russell, Elisha MO 11th Inf. Co.C
Russell, Elisha L. NC 44th Inf. Co.F Sgt.
Russell, Elisha T. MD 1st Inf. Co.H
Russell, Eli W. MS 48th Inf. Co.H
Russell, Eli W. VA 27th Inf. Co.G Sgt.
Russell, E.M. AR 15th Inf.
Russell, E.M. GA 37th Inf. Co.E
Russell, E.M. VA 6th Cav. Co.G
Russell, E.P. KY 2nd (Woodward's) Cav. Co.D
  2nd Lt.
Russell, E.R. TN Lt.Arty. McClung's Co.
Russell, E. Tarleton VA Horse Arty. D. Shank's
  Co. Cpl.
Russell, E.W. GA Cav. 1st Bn. Winn's Co.,
  Walthour's Co.
Russell, E.W. GA 5th Cav. Co.G Sgt.
Russell, E.W. MS Inf. 2nd Bn. Co.H
Russell, E.Y. MO 16th Inf. Co.E
Russell, E.Z. MS 8th Cav. Co.B
Russell, E.Z. MS 28th Cav. Co.E
Russell, Ezekiel 1st Cherokee Mtd.Rifles Co.D
  2nd Lt.
Russell, F.B. MS 1st Lt.Arty. Co.G
Russell, F.B. MS 9th Inf. Old Co.H
Russell, F.B. TX 5th Cav. Co.G
Russell, F.C. TN 45th Inf. Co.A
Russell, F.G. TN 5th (McKenzie's) Cav. Co.I
  Sgt.
Russell, Fletcher H. VA Inf. Cohoon's Bn. Co.B
Russell, F.M. AL 27th Inf. Co.H
Russell, F.M. AR 38th Inf. Co.E
Russell, F.M. GA 4th Inf. Co.H
Russell, F.M. GA 52nd Inf. Co.D
Russell, F.M. LA 1st Cav. Co.F
Russell, F.M. TN 40th Inf. Co.E
Russell, F.M. TX 1st Inf. Co.I
Russell, Fountain F. AL 16th Cav. Co.K
Russell, Francis FL Cav. 3rd Bn. Co.A
Russell, Francis VA 12th Cav. Co.I
Russell, Francis R. VA 13th Cav. Co.F
Russell, Francis R. VA 12th Inf. Co.E
Russell, Frank AL 1st Regt.Mobile Vol. Co.A
Russell, Frank AL 4th Res. Co.C
Russell, Frank MS 29th Inf. Co.F
Russell, Frank SC 1st (McCreary's) Inf. Co.I
Russell, Frank TX 3rd Cav. Co.E Sgt.
Russell, Frank 15th Conf.Cav. Co.A
Russell, Frank D. LA 1st Hvy.Arty. (Reg.) Co.I
Russell, Frank D. Inf. School of Pract. Co.C
Russell, Franklin MS 39th Inf. Co.D
Russell, Franklin TX 22nd Cav. Co.F
Russell, Franklin M. AL 54th Inf. Co.I
Russell, F.S. KY 7th Mtd.Inf. Co.H
Russell, F. Stanley VA 13th Inf. Co.H Sgt.
Russell, F.W. MS Cav. Lake's Unatt.Co. 1st Lt.
Russell, F.W. MS 14th Inf. Co.C
Russell, F.W. MS 35th Inf. Co.C
Russell, G. FL 1st (Res.) Inf. Co.E
Russell, Gabriel NC 28th Inf. Co.K
Russell, G.C. AL 21st Inf. Co.K
Russell, G.D. AL 35th Inf. Co.B
Russell, G.D. MS 12th Cav. Co.F

Russell, George AL Mil. 2nd Regt.Vol. Co.F
Russell, George AL 21st Inf. Co.K
Russell, George GA Inf. 3rd Bn. Co.D
Russell, George GA 3rd Inf. Co.H
Russell, George GA 4th Bn.S.S. Co.B
Russell, George GA 23rd Inf. Co.A
Russell, George GA Inf. Bard's Co. Cpl.
Russell, George GA Inf. (Madison Cty. Home
  Guard) Milner's Co.
Russell, George KY 3rd Bn.Mtd.Rifles Co.B 1st
  Sgt.
Russell, George LA 15th Inf. Co.B
Russell, George MS 22nd Inf. Gaines' Co.
Russell, George NC 29th Inf. Co.E
Russell, George TN 21st Inf. Co.H
Russell, George VA 6th Cav. Co.F
Russell, George VA 37th Inf. Co.K
Russell, George Gen. & Staff Chap.
Russell, George B. VA Cav. 39th Bn. Co.A
Russell, George C. LA 6th Inf. Co.K
Russell, George D. MO 8th Cav.
Russell, George E. KY 1st (Butler's) Cav. Co.B
  Sgt.
Russell, George E. KY 4th Cav. Co.B 2nd Lt.
Russell, George F. MS 14th Inf. Co.D
Russell, George F. NC 22nd Inf. Co.L
Russell, George Henderson MO 5th Inf. Co.C
Russell, George M. AL 3rd Inf. Co.F
Russell, George S. TN 15th Cav.
Russell, George S. VA 39th Inf. Co.G
Russell, George T. AR 34th Inf. Co.B
Russell, George W. AL Cav. Murphy's Bn. Co.C
Russell, George W. AL 1st Regt.Mobile Vol.
  Butt's Co.F 2nd Lt.
Russell, George W. AL 4th Res. Co.A 2nd Lt.
Russell, George W. AR 1st (Crawford's) Cav.
  Co.C
Russell, George W. AR 14th (McCarver's) Inf.
  Co.C
Russell, George W. GA 65th Inf. Co.C
Russell, George W. GA 65th Inf. Co.G,E
Russell, George W. MS 13th Inf. Co.D
Russell, George W. MS 26th Inf. Co.H
Russell, George W. MS 32nd Inf. Co.K
Russell, George W. MO 1st Cav. Co.K
Russell, George W. MO Cav. Wood's Regt.
  Co.A
Russell, George W. MO 9th Inf. Co.K Cpl.
Russell, George W. NC 13th Inf. Co.H
Russell, George W. TN 8th Inf. Co.I
Russell, George W. TN 28th Inf. Co.C Capt.
Russell, George W. TX 18th Inf. Co.C
Russell, George W. VA 8th Cav. Co.E
Russell, George W. 15th Conf.Cav. Co.H
Russell, G.F. NC 5th Cav. (63rd St.Troops)
  Co.H
Russell, G.H. MO St.Guard
Russell, Gilbert NC 44th Inf. Co.F Sgt.
Russell, G.L. NC 22nd Inf. Ord.Sgt.
Russell, G.T. VA Horse Arty. G.W. Brown's
  Co.
Russell, G.W. AL Mil. 2nd Regt.Vol. Co.D
Russell, G.W. AL 15th Inf. Co.D
Russell, G.W. AR 15th (N.W.) Inf. Co.I
Russell, G.W. AR 21st Inf. Co.A
Russell, G.W. GA 10th Cav. (St.Guards) Co.H
Russell, G.W. GA 11th Inf. Co.B

Russell, G.W. KY 12th Cav. Co.B
Russell, G.W. KY 8th Mtd.Inf. Co.A
Russell, G.W. MS 41st Inf. Co.D
Russell, G.W. TN Cav. 9th Bn. (Gantt's) Co.G
Russell, G.W. TN 3rd (Clack's) Inf. Co.E
Russell, G.W. TX 14th Cav. Co.A,H
Russell, H. GA 28th Inf. Co.F
Russell, H. NC 1st Jr.Res. Co.E
Russell, H. TN 20th Inf. Co.C
Russell, H. TX Cav. Wells' Regt. Co.I
Russell, H. TX 21st Inf. Co.C
Russell, H.A. GA 5th Cav. Co.G
Russell, H.A. GA 11th Inf. Co.G Sgt.
Russell, Hardin T. TN 20th Cav.
Russell, Hardy A. NC 60th Inf. Co.D
Russell, Harris NC 22nd Inf. Co.L
Russell, Harris NC 38th Inf. Co.H
Russell, Harvey GA 60th Inf. Co.H
Russell, Harvey T. NC 53rd Inf. Co.B
Russell, Haywood NC 44th Inf. Co.F
Russell, H.B. VA Arty. Young's Co.
Russell, H.C. AL 17th Inf. Co.H
Russell, H.C. NC 18th Inf. Co.G
Russell, H.C. VA Cav. Mosby's Regt. (Part.
  Rangers) Co.C
Russell, H.D. SC 1st Cav. Co.A
Russell, Henry FL 2nd Cav. Co.A
Russell, Henry FL Cav. 5th Bn. Co.E
Russell, Henry FL 9th Inf. Co.I
Russell, Henry GA 21st Inf. Co.H
Russell, Henry GA 57th Inf. Co.H
Russell, Henry MD Arty. 4th Btty.
Russell, Henry NC 28th Inf. Co.K
Russell, Henry SC 1st (Butler's) Inf. Co.D
Russell, Henry TN 40th Inf. Co.F
Russell, Henry TX Cav. 2nd Regt.St.Troops.
  Co.I
Russell, Henry TX Cav. Baylor's Regt. Co.K
Russell, Henry VA 1st Cav. Co.H
Russell, Henry VA Cav. Mosby's Regt. (Part.
  Rangers) Co.B
Russell, Henry Mead's Conf.Cav. Co.E
Russell, Henry B. VA 1st Arty. 3rd Co.C
Russell, Henry B. VA Lt.Arty. 1st Bn. Co.C
Russell, Henry B. VA 14th Inf. 1st Co.G
Russell, Henry C. AL 4th (Russell's) Cav. Co.H
Russell, Henry C. AL Lt.Arty. 2nd Bn. Co.C
  Music.
Russell, Henry C. AL Eufaula Lt.Arty.
Russell, Henry C. AL 17th Inf. Co.C
Russell, Henry C. AL 32nd Inf. Co.B
Russell, Henry C. AL 57th Inf. Co.B Sgt.
Russell, Henry C. NC 23rd Inf. Co.E
Russell, Henry C. VA 10th Cav.
Russell, Henry D. VA Lt.Arty. Utterback's Co.
Russell, Henry F. GA Inf. 1st Loc.Troops
  (Augusta) Co.A
Russell, Henry H. AR 25th Inf. Co.I
Russell, Henry J. VA 6th Bn.Res. Co.A
Russell, Henry W. TX 17th Cav. 2nd Co.I
Russell, Henry W. TX 18th Inf. Co.L
Russell, Hezekiah AR 27th Inf. Co.H
Russell, Hezekiah NC 64th Inf. Co.I
Russell, Hezekiah TX Inf. Griffin's Bn. Co.C
Russell, H.F. SC Inf.Bn. Co.F
Russell, H.H. AL 10th Inf. Co.K Cpl.
Russell, H.H. MO 1st & 4th Cons.Inf. Co.B

Russell, H.H. TX Cav. Border's Regt. Co.H
Russell, Hillary SC 44th Inf. Co.F
Russell, Hiram MS Nash's Co. (Leake Rangers)
Russell, Hiram H. MO 4th Inf. Co.A
Russell, Hiram R. TX 34th Cav. Co.C
Russell, H.J. MS 4th Inf. Co.H,G
Russell, H.L. GA Phillips' Legion Co.B
Russell, H.M. GA Ind.Cav. (Res.) Humphrey's Co.
Russell, H.M. TX 12th Cav. Co.A
Russell, H.N. MS Cav. 24th Bn. Co.A
Russell, Houson G. VA 38th Inf. Co.C Sgt.
Russell, H.R. SC 14th Inf. Co.G
Russell, H.R. TX 14th Inf. Co.D
Russell, H.T. KY Cav. 2nd Bn. (Dortch's) Co.B
Russell, H.T. KY 7th Cav. Co.B
Russell, H.T. TN 20th Inf. Co.C
Russell, H.T. TN 24th Inf. 2nd Co.H
Russell, Hugh H. MS 43rd Inf. Co.E
Russell, H.W. KY 8th Mtd.Inf. Co.K
Russell, H.W. TN 3rd (Clack's) Inf. Co.F
Russell, H.W. TX 14th Inf. 1st Co.K
Russell, I.A. SC Inf.Bn. Co.F
Russell, Ichabud C. FL 4th Inf. Co.G
Russell, Ignitius AL Cav. 5th Bn. Hilliard's Legion Co.E
Russell, Ira A. MS 11th Inf. Co.F
Russell, Irby R. GA Cav. 1st Bn.Res.
Russell, Irvin AR 10th Inf. Co.H
Russell, Isaac AL 2nd Cav. Co.E
Russell, Isaac FL 1st Inf. New Co.H
Russell, Isaac GA 1st (Olmstead's) Inf. Gordon's Co.
Russell, Isaac GA 63rd Inf. Co.B
Russell, Isaac GA Mil. Capt.,AIG
Russell, Isaac NC 5th Sr.Res. Co.D
Russell, Isaac TN 59th Mtd.Inf. Co.E
Russell, Isaac A. MS 39th Inf. Co.E Sgt.
Russell, Isaac B. NC 64th Inf. Co.I
Russell, Isaac Newton GA Cav. 21st Bn. Co.B,E
Russell, Isaac W. TN 18th Inf. Co.E
Russell, Isaiah NC 5th Inf. Co.F
Russell, I.W. NC 34th Inf. Co.K
Russell, I.W. 2nd Corps A.Hosp.Stew.
Russell, J. AL 1st Inf. Co.B
Russell, J. AL 1st Bn. Hilliard's Legion Vol. Co.D
Russell, J. MS Cav. 1st Bn. (McNair's) Co.E
Russell, J. MS Cav. 2nd Bn.Res. Co.F
Russell, J. MO Cav. Schnabel's Bn. Co.C
Russell, J. TN 19th & 20th (Cons.)Cav. Co.C
Russell, J. TX 3rd Cav. Co.H
Russell, J. TX 23rd Cav. Co.D
Russell, J. Conf.Reg.Inf. Brooks' Bn. Co.A
Russell, J.A. AL 21st Inf. Co.C
Russell, J.A. GA Inf. (Newton Factory Employees) Russell's Co. Sgt.
Russell, J.A. KY 6th Mtd.Inf. Co.I
Russell, J.A. LA 3rd (Wingfield's) Cav. Co.D
Russell, J.A. LA 6th Cav. Co.A
Russell, J.A. LA 5th Inf. Co.H
Russell, J.A. MS Inf. 1st Bn.St.Troops (30 days '64) Co.F
Russell, J.A. MS 3rd Inf. (St.Troops) Co.D 1st Cpl.
Russell, J.A. MS 25th Inf. Co.D
Russell, J.A. MO 2nd Inf. Co.B

Russell, J.A. TN 21st (Wilson's) Cav. Co.A
Russell, J.A. TN 21st & 22nd (Cons.) Cav. Co.E
Russell, J.A. TN 31st Inf. Co.B
Russell, J.A. TN 51st (Cons.) Inf. Co.B Capt.
Russell, J.A. TN 51st (Cons.) Inf. Co.B
Russell, J.A. TN 52nd Inf. Co.B Capt.
Russell, J.A. TX Cav. 2nd Bn.St.Troops Co.A
Russell, J.A. TX 9th (Young's) Inf. Co.H
Russell, J.A. 2nd Conf.Inf. Co.D Sgt.
Russell, Jack TN 29th Inf. Co.E
Russell, Jacob LA 2nd Inf. Co.H
Russell, Jacob P. VA 9th Inf. Co.E Sgt.
Russell, James AL Lt.Arty. 2nd Bn. Co.A
Russell, James AL Mil. 4th Vol. Moore's Co. Sgt.
Russell, James AL 27th Inf. Co.G
Russell, James AL 28th Inf. Co.E
Russell, Jas. AL Mil. Bligh's Co.
Russell, James AL Mobile Fire Bn. Mullany's Co.
Russell, James FL 2nd Inf. Co.F
Russell, James FL 5th Inf. Co.B
Russell, James FL 11th Inf. Co.C
Russell, James GA Cav. 1st Gordon Squad. (St.Guards) Co.A
Russell, James GA Cav. 21st Bn. Co.A
Russell, James GA Cav. 24th Bn. Co.A
Russell, James GA 57th Inf. Co.H
Russell, James KY 6th Cav. Co.A
Russell, James KY 9th Cav. Co.G
Russell, James KY 5th Mtd.Inf. Co.I
Russell, James LA Inf. 1st Sp.Bn. (Wheat's) New Co.E Music.
Russell, James LA 6th Inf. Co.K Music.
Russell, James LA Mil.St.Guards Co.B
Russell, James MS St.Cav. 2nd Bn. (Harris') Co.A
Russell, James MS 9th Inf. Old Co.K, New Co.B 1st Lt.
Russell, James MS 16th Inf. Co.H
Russell, James MS 30th Inf. Co.D,B,G
Russell, James MO 5th Cav. Co.A
Russell, James MO 10th Cav. Co.B
Russell, James MO 16th Inf. Co.E
Russell, James NC 6th Sr.Res. Co.A
Russell, James NC 43rd Inf. Co.K
Russell, James SC 9th Inf. Co.E,I
Russell, James SC 24th Inf. Co.C Cook
Russell, James TN 5th (McKenzie's) Cav. Co.G
Russell, James TN 12th (Green's) Cav. Co.K
Russell, James TN 21st (Wilson's) Cav. Co.A
Russell, James TN 2nd (Walker's) Inf. Co.E
Russell, James TN 19th Inf. Co.K
Russell, James TN 29th Inf. Co.K Laborer
Russell, James TN 33rd Inf. Co.H
Russell, James TN 39th Mtd.Inf. Co.B
Russell, James TN 51st (Cons.) Inf. Co.B
Russell, James TN 59th Mtd.Inf. Co.K
Russell, James TX 29th Cav. Co.I
Russell, James TX Cav. Border's Regt. Co.B
Russell, James VA 23rd Cav. 2nd Co.K
Russell, James, Jr. VA Hvy.Arty. 18th Bn. Co.D 2nd Lt.
Russell, James VA Hvy.Arty. Patteson's Co.
Russell, James Conf.Cav. Baxter's Bn. Co.C
Russell, James Conf.Reg.Inf. Brooks' Bn. Co.A
Russell, James Gen. & Staff Capt.,AQM

Russell, James A. FL 2nd Inf. Co.H
Russell, James A. MS 1st (King's) Inf. (St.Troops) Co.C
Russell, James A. MS 22nd Inf. Co.B
Russell, James A. MS 43rd Inf. Co.E
Russell, James A. NC 57th Inf. Co.H
Russell, James A. VA 51st Mil. Co.G
Russell, James B. AR 15th (N.W.) Inf.
Russell, James B. LA Washington Arty.Bn.
Russell, James B. NC Hvy.Arty. 10th Bn. Co.C,B
Russell, James B. NC 56th Inf. Co.C
Russell, James B. SC 1st (Orr's) Rifles Co.A
Russell, James B. TN 29th Inf. Co.B
Russell, James B. VA Cav. Mosby's Regt. (Part.Rangers) Co.B
Russell, James B. VA 13th Inf. Co.H
Russell, James B. VA 10th Inf. Co.G
Russell, James B. VA 48th Inf. Co.E
Russell, James B. Walker's Brig. AADC
Russell, James C. AL 51st Part.Rangers Co.I
Russell, James C. TN 41st Inf. Co.B
Russell, James D. NC 25th Inf. Co.D 1st Sgt.
Russell, James E. NC 25th Inf. Co.H Sgt.
Russell, James E. VA 51st Inf. Co.I
Russell, James F. GA Inf. 2nd Bn. Co.C
Russell, James F. GA Inf. 3rd Bn. Co.A
Russell, James F. TN 28th Inf. Co.H Sgt.
Russell, James F. VA 15th Inf. Co.F
Russell, James F. VA 45th Inf. Co.C
Russell, James Fuller AL 14th Inf. Co.H Sgt.
Russell, James G. MO Inf. 5th Regt.St.Guard Surg.
Russell, James G. MO Inf. 6th Regt.St.Guard 1st Lt.,Regt.Surg.
Russell, James G. NC 25th Inf. Co.D Cpl.
Russell, James G. NC Walker's Bn. Thomas' Legion Co.C
Russell, James H. AL Eufaula Lt.Arty. Cpl.
Russell, James H. NC 12th Inf. Co.C
Russell, James H. VA 30th Bn.S.S. Co.B Sgt.
Russell, James H.N. NC 17th Inf. (2nd Org.) Co.F Sgt.
Russell, James J. GA 63rd Inf. Co.A Cpl.
Russell, James J. MS 30th Inf. Co.G Cpl.
Russell, James J. TX 34th Cav. Co.H
Russell, James J. Conf.Inf. Tucker's Regt. Co.C Jr.2nd Lt.
Russell, James K.P. NC 33rd Inf. Co.G
Russell, James K.P. NC 39th Inf. Co.B Cpl.
Russell, James K.P. TN 4th Inf. Co.B
Russell, James K.P. TX 16th Cav. Co.E 1st Lt.
Russell, James L. AR 27th Inf. Co.H Sgt.
Russell, James L. TN 44th Inf. Co.H Cpl.
Russell, James L. TN 44th (Cons.) Inf. Co.A
Russell, James L.S. TN 2nd (Robison's) Inf. Co.B,D
Russell, James M. AL Cav. Murphy's Bn. Co.D
Russell, James M. AR 8th Cav. Co.H
Russell, James M. AR 14th (Powers') Inf. Co.G Cpl.
Russell, James M. AR 34th Inf. Co.B
Russell, James M. GA Arty. 9th Bn. Co.C
Russell, James M. GA 5th Inf. (St.Guards) Russell's Co. Capt.
Russell, James M. GA 31st Inf. AQM
Russell, James M. MS Inf. 3rd Bn. Co.C

Russell, James M. MS 26th Inf. Co.D
Russell, James M. MS 26th Inf. Co.H
Russell, James M. TX 13th Inf. 3rd Co.A
Russell, James M. TX Inf. Griffin's Bn. Co.D
Cpl.
Russell, James M. Gen. & Staff Capt.,QM
Russell, James M. Gen. & Staff Chap.
Russell, James Madison TX 13th Vol. 3rd Co.A
Russell, James Maxwell AL 49th Inf. Co.C 1st
Lt.
Russell, James P. GA 20th Inf. Co.I Sgt.
Russell, James P. TN 7th (Duckworth's) Cav.
Co.B Capt.
Russell, James R. AL Cav. 5th Bn. Hilliard's
Legion Co.A
Russell, James R. GA 40th Inf. Co.D
Russell, James R. NC 29th Inf. Co.D
Russell, James R. TX 14th Cav. Co.D
Russell, James S. AR 4th Inf. Co.H
Russell, James S. NC 7th Inf. Co.H
Russell, James S. NC 42nd Inf. Co.C Sgt.
Russell, James S. SC Palmetto S.S. Co.H
Russell, James T. AL Cav. 5th Bn. Hilliard's
Legion Co.C
Russell, James T. NC 4th Cav. (59th St.Troops)
Co.D
Russell, James T. TN 24th Inf. 2nd Co.H, Co.M
Russell, James T. TX 17th Cav. Co.F Adj.
Russell, James T. 10th Conf.Cav. Co.C
Russell, James V. GA Inf. 3rd Bn. Co.A
Russell, James V. TX 16th Cav. Co.B Cpl.
Russell, James W. AL 30th Inf. Co.A
Russell, James W. AR Cav. 1st Bn. (Stirman's)
Co.F Capt.
Russell, James W. AR 7th Inf. Co.K Sgt.
Russell, James W. AR Inf. Williamson's Bn.
Co.D 2nd Lt.
Russell, James W. GA 45th Inf. Co.G
Russell, James W. TN 53rd Inf. Co.A
Russell, James W. VA 8th Inf. Co.A
Russell, James W. 1st Conf.Eng.Troops Co.C
Russell, James W. Stirman's Regt.S.S. Co.C 1st
Lt.
Russell, Jason NC 28th Inf. Co.E
Russell, Jasper A. LA 14th Inf. Co.I
Russell, J.B. AL Inf. 2nd Regt. Co.K
Russell, J.B. FL 2nd Cav. Co.D
Russell, J.B. FL Cav. 5th Bn. Co.C
Russell, J.B. GA Cav. 21st Bn. Co.B
Russell, J.B. MS 8th Inf. Co.C
Russell, J.B. NC 27th Inf. Co.C
Russell, J.B. TN 11th (Holman's) Cav. Co.B
Russell, J.B. TN Holman's Bn.Part.Rangers
Co.A
Russell, J.B. TX 32nd Cav. Co.E
Russell, J.B. VA 31st Mil. Co.B
Russell, J.B. 2nd Cherokee Mtd.Vol. Co.C
Russell, J.B. Gen. & Staff Capt.,Ord.Off.
Russell, J. Bill NC 22nd Inf. Co.L
Russell, J.C. FL 1st (Res.) Inf. Co.K
Russell, J.C. LA 13th Bn. (Part.Rangers) Co.E
Russell, J.C. MS 8th Cav. Co.F
Russell, J.C. TX 1st Hvy.Arty. Co.D
Russell, J.C. Morgan's,CSA
Russell, J.D. AL 4th Inf. Co.D
Russell, J.D. AL 5th Inf. Co.I
Russell, J.D. MO 9th Cav.

Russell, J.E. AL 35th Inf. Co.D
Russell, J.E. AL Mtd.Inf. Oden's Co.
Russell, J.E. KY Corbin's Men
Russell, J.E. LA 27th Inf. Co.B
Russell, J.E. TX Inf. 2nd St.Troops Co.B
Russell, Jefferson TN Inf. 1st Bn. (Colms') Co.B
Russell, Jerre P. MS 6th Inf. Co.I
Russell, Jerry LA 13th Inf. Co.G
Russell, Jerry MD Arty. 4th Btty.
Russell, Jesse GA 57th Inf. Co.H
Russell, Jesse MS 32nd Inf. Co.C
Russell, Jesse MS 43rd Inf. Co.E
Russell, Jesse TN 18th (Newsom's) Cav. Co.K
Russell, Jesse 1st Cherokee Mtd.Vol. 2nd Co.E
Russell, Jessee D. FL 5th Inf. Co.C
Russell, Jesse G. TX 16th Cav. Co.C
Russell, Jesse H. AR 27th Inf. Co.E,H
Russell, Jesse J. MO Cav. Wood's Regt. Co.A
Russell, Jesse M. VA 1st Cav. 1st Co.D Cpl.
Russell, Jesse M. VA 6th Cav. Co.D Cpl.
Russell, Jesse S. AL 61st Inf. Co.I
Russell, J.F. AL Loc.Def. & Sp.Serv. Toomer's
Co.
Russell, J.F. GA Lt.Arty. Van Den Corput's Co.
Russell, J.F. GA Inf. 14th Bn. (St.Guards) Co.C
Cpl.
Russell, J.F. GA 19th Inf. Co.D Sgt.
Russell, J.F. VA Inf. 2nd Bn.Loc.Def. Co.C
Russell, J.G. AL 1st Regt.Conscr. Co.D
Russell, J.G. AR 37th Inf. Co.E
Russell, J.G. GA 27th Inf. QMSgt.
Russell, J.G. NC 1st Cav. (9th St.Troops) Co.K
Russell, J.G. NC 38th Inf. Co.H
Russell, J.G. MO 1st Brig.St.Guard Surg.
Russell, J.G. Conf.Cav. Clarkson's Bn. Ind.
Rangers Surg.
Russell, J.G. Gen. & Staff Surg.
Russell, J.H. AL 5th Cav. Co.A 2nd Lt.
Russell, J.H. AL 10th Cav. Co.D 2nd Lt.
Russell, J.H. AL 1st Regt.Mobile Vol. Co.A
Sgt.
Russell, J.H. AL 5th Bn. (Blount's) Vol. Co.B
2nd Lt.
Russell, J.H. AR Cav. 6th Bn. Co.C
Russell, J.H. GA Floyd Legion (St.Guards) Co.B
Drum.
Russell, J.H. KY 12th Cav. Co.G
Russell, J.H. MS 5th Inf. (St.Troops) Co.B
Russell, J.H. NC 62nd Inf. Co.K
Russell, J.H. TN 12th Cav. Co.F
Russell, J.H. TN 5th Inf. 2nd Co.F
Russell, J.H. TN 21st Inf. Co.C
Russell, J.H. TN 28th (Cons.) Inf. Co.B
Russell, J.H. TN 55th (Brown's) Inf. Co.D
Russell, J.J. AL 17th Inf. Co.I
Russell, J.J. GA 7th Cav. Co.A
Russell, J.J. GA Lt.Arty. 12th Bn. 1st Co.A
Russell, J.J. MS 5th Cav. Co.E
Russell, J.J. NC 1st Jr.Res. Co.I
Russell, J.J. NC 7th Inf. Co.C
Russell, J.J. SC 1st Mtd.Mil. Martin's Co.
Russell, J.J. VA Arty. Young's Co. Bvt.2nd Lt.
Russell, J.L. AL 20th Inf. Co.A Cpl.
Russell, J.L. AL 40th Inf. Co.G Sgt.
Russell, J.L. AR 12th Inf. Co.I
Russell, J.L. AR 35th Inf. Co.I
Russell, J.L. MS 6th Inf. Co.A

Russell, J.L. MO Cav. Schnabel's Bn. Co.A
Russell, J.L. NC 15th Inf. Co.G
Russell, J.L. TN 17th Inf. Co.A
Russell, J.L. TX Cav. Wells' Regt. Co.C
Russell, J.L. TX 19th Inf. Co.C
Russell, J.M. AL 9th Cav. QMSgt.
Russell, J.M. AL 15th Bn.Part.Rangers Co.C
Russell, J.M. AL 56th Part.Rangers Co.C
Russell, J.M. AL Cp. of Instr. Talladega
Russell, J.M. AR 1st (Dobbin's) Cav. Co.C
Russell, J.M. AR 15th (N.W.) Inf. Co.I
Russell, J.M. AR 36th Inf. Co.E
Russell, J.M. AR 36th Inf. Co.I
Russell, J.M. AR 36th Inf. Co.K
Russell, J.M. LA 3rd Inf.
Russell, J.M. MS Cav. 3rd Bn.Res. Co.C
Russell, J.M. MS 10th Cav. Co.F
Russell, J.M. MS 11th (Perrin's) Cav. Co.H
Russell, J.M. MS 8th Inf. Co.H
Russell, J.M. MS 22nd Inf. Co.H
Russell, J.M. TN 2nd (Ashby's) Cav. Co.I
Russell, J.M. TN Cav. 9th Bn. (Gantt's) Co.G
Russell, J.M. TN 19th & 20th (Cons.) Cav. Co.E
Russell, J.M. TX Cav. Hardeman's Regt. Co.F
Russell, J.M. TX 6th Field Btty. Cpl.
Russell, J.M. TX Lt.Arty. Dege's Bn. Cpl.
Russell, J.M. 15th Conf.Cav. Co.K
Russell, J.N. GA 5th Cav. Co.G
Russell, J.N. KY 2nd Mtd.Inf. Co.A
Russell, J.N. MS Scouts Morphis' Ind.Co.
Russell, J.N. VA 8th Cav. Co.E
Russell, J.N. VA 94th Mil.
Russell, J.N.B. MS 1st (King's) Inf. (St.Troops)
Co.I
Russell, J.N.B. MS 39th Inf. Co.G
Russell, Jo AL 55th Vol. Co.A
Russell, J.O. GA Cav. Russell's Co. 3rd Lt.
Russell, Joab A. 1st Conf.Cav. 2nd Co.G
Russell, Job GA 3rd Inf. Co.H
Russell, Job GA Inf. (Newton Factory
Employees) Russell's Co. Capt.
Russell, Jo C. TN 63rd Inf. Co.A
Russell, Joel NC 5th Inf. Co.B
Russell, Joel B. GA Phillips' Legion Co.A
Russell, Joel C. TN 41st Inf. Co.B Capt.
Russell, Joel H. VA 9th Cav. Co.G
Russell, John AL 2nd Cav. Co.E
Russell, John AL Cav. Murphy's Bn. Co.C
Bugler
Russell, John, Jr. AR Cav. Wright's Regt. Co.H
Russell, John AR 15th (Josey's) Inf. Co.E
Russell, John AR 19th (Dawson's) Inf. Co.I
Russell, John FL 7th Inf. Co.K
Russell, John GA 12th (Wright's) Cav.
(St.Guards) Stapleton's Co. Cpl.
Russell, John GA Lt.Arty. 14th Bn. Co.A
Russell, John GA Lt.Arty. Havis' Btty.
Russell, John GA 27th Inf. Co.K
Russell, John GA 32nd Inf. Co.A
Russell, John GA 36th (Villepigue's) Inf. Co.I,F
Russell, John GA 54th Inf. Co.I
Russell, John KY 2nd Cav. Co.B
Russell, John LA 1st Hvy.Arty. (Reg.) Co.A
Sgt.
Russell, John LA 1st (Strawbridge's) Inf. Co.C
Russell, John LA Inf.Cons.Crescent Regt. Co.E
Russell, John MS 3rd (St.Troops) Cav. Co.A

Russell, John MS Lt.Arty. Lomax's Co.
Russell, John MS 8th Inf. Co.C
Russell, John MS 16th Inf. Co.H
Russell, John MS 16th Inf. Co.I 1st Lt.
Russell, John MS Inf. Cooper's Co.
Russell, John MO 6th Cav. Co.I
Russell, John MO 10th Cav. Co.B
Russell, John NC 3rd Arty. (40th St.Troops) Co.G
Russell, John NC 5th Sr.Res. Co.H
Russell, John NC 23rd Inf. Co.E
Russell, John NC 53rd Inf. Co.K
Russell, John NC 64th Inf.
Russell, John SC Mil. 1st Regt. (Charleston Res.) Co.E 2nd Lt.
Russell, John SC 1st (McCreary's) Inf. Co.I
Russell, John TN 3rd (Forrest's) Cav. Co.A
Russell, John TN 10th & 11th (Cons.) Cav. Co.I
Russell, John TN 9th Inf. Co.B
Russell, John TN 13th Inf. Co.H
Russell, John TN 17th Inf. Co.I
Russell, John TN 19th Inf. Co.H
Russell, John TN 21st Inf. Co.D
Russell, John TN 27th Inf. Co.A
Russell, John TN Inf. 154th Sr.Regt. 1st Co.B
Russell, John TN Conscr. (Cp.of Instr.) Co.B
Russell, John TX 12th Cav. Co.A
Russell, John TX 20th Cav. Co.C Sgt.
Russell, John TX 23rd Cav. Co.F
Russell, John TX 36th Cav. Co.B
Russell, John VA 23rd Cav. Co.D
Russell, John VA Cav. 41st Bn. Co.F
Russell, John VA 2nd Inf. Co.G
Russell, John VA Inf. 4th Bn.Loc.Def. Co.B
Russell, John VA 18th Inf. Co.B
Russell, John VA 59th Mil. Hunter's Co.
Russell, John VA Vol. Taylor's Co.
Russell, John 15th Conf.Cav. Co.H Ch.Bugler
Russell, John Conf.Lt.Arty. 1st Reg.Btty.
Russell, John Inf. School of Pract. Powell's Detach. Co.D
Russell, John Conf.Inf. Tucker's Regt. Co.K
Russell, John A. AL 40th Inf. Co.B Cpl.
Russell, John A. AR 18th Inf. Co.B
Russell, John A. GA 13th Cav. Co.B
Russell, John A. LA 5th Inf. Co.C Capt.
Russell, John A. MS Bradford's Co. (Conf.Guards Arty.)
Russell, John A. MS Inf. 5th Bn. Co.C
Russell, John A. MS 41st Inf. Co.A
Russell, John A. MO 1st & 4th Cons.Inf. Co.B
Russell, John A. MO 4th Inf. Co.A
Russell, John A. TN 59th Mtd.Inf. Co.K Capt.
Russell, John A.J. TN 24th Inf.
Russell, John A.J. TN 34th Inf. Co.H Sgt.
Russell, John B. GA Lt.Arty. Havis' Btty.
Russell, John B. MO 12th Inf. Co.K
Russell, John B. NC 1st Arty. (10th St.Troops) Co.H
Russell, John B. SC Inf. Hampton Legion Co.A
Russell, John C. GA 36th (Villepigue's) Inf. Co.B
Russell, John C. LA 5th Cav. Co.I
Russell, John C. MS Part.Rangers Smythe's Co. 1st Lt.
Russell, John C. MS 18th Inf. Co.C 2nd Lt.

Russell, John C. NC Moseley's Co. (Sampson Arty.) Cpl.
Russell, John C. NC 11th (Bethel Regt.) Inf. Co.H
Russell, John C. NC 35th Inf. Co.E
Russell, John C. NC 46th Inf. Co.E 2nd Lt.
Russell, John C. TX 8th Inf. Co.I Jr.1st Lt.
Russell, John C. 1st Conf.Inf. Co.B Sgt.
Russell, John D. AL 29th Inf. Co.F
Russell, John E. MO St.Guard
Russell, John E. VA 39th Inf. Co.G
Russell, John E.S. TX 11th Cav. Co.G Capt.
Russell, John F. AR 33rd Inf. Co.A
Russell, John F. NC 22nd Inf. Co.L
Russell, John G. AL 19th Inf. Co.H Sgt.
Russell, John G. LA 27th Inf. Co.C,H
Russell, John G. MS 43rd Inf. Co.E
Russell, John H. GA Inf. 3rd Bn. Co.A
Russell, John H. MS 5th Cav. Co.A
Russell, John H. MS 15th Inf. Co.C
Russell, John H. MS 20th Inf. Co.C
Russell, John H. MS 26th Inf. Co.H 1st Lt.
Russell, John H. MO Arty. Lowe's Co.
Russell, John H. MO 1st Inf. Co.C
Russell, John H. MO 12th Inf. Co.C
Russell, John H. NC 44th Inf. Co.F
Russell, John H. TN 8th Inf. Co.I Ord.Sgt.
Russell, John H. TN 20th Inf. Co.A Sgt.
Russell, John H. TN 28th Inf. Co.F
Russell, John H. VA 37th Inf. Co.D
Russell, John J. AL 1st Regt.Conscr. Co.C
Russell, John J. AL 61st Inf. Co.I Sgt.
Russell, John J. MS Cav. 6th Bn. Prince's Co.
Russell, John J. MS 21st Inf. Co.G
Russell, John J. MO 5th Inf. Co.G
Russell, John J. NC 37th Inf. Co.G Sgt.
Russell, John J. TX Cav. Good's Bn. Surg.
Russell, John J. VA 1st Arty. 3rd Co.C 2nd Lt.
Russell, John J. VA Lt.Arty. 1st Bn. Co.C 2nd Lt.
Russell, John J. VA 14th Inf. 1st Co.G 1st Sgt.
Russell, John J. Gen. & Staff Asst.Surg.
Russell, John L. AR 6th Inf. Co.C
Russell, John L. AR 15th Mil. Co.E
Russell, John L. MO 15th Cav. Co.A
Russell, John L. SC 14th Inf. Co.K
Russell, John L. 10th Conf.Cav. Co.E
Russell, John M. AL 6th Inf. Co.L
Russell, John M. AL 16th Inf. Co.K
Russell, John M. AL Arty. 4th Bn. Hilliard's Legion Co.A
Russell, John M. MS 31st Inf. Co.G Sgt.
Russell, John M. NC 39th Inf. Co.B
Russell, John M. NC 52nd Inf. Co.F
Russell, John M. TN 19th Inf. Co.C
Russell, John McK. NC 6th Sr.Res. Co.D,F
Russell, John O. MS 11th Inf. Co.F
Russell, John P. VA 40th Inf. Co.F Cpl.
Russell, John R. AR Cav. Wright's Regt. Co.H
Russell, John R. GA 52nd Inf. Co.I Capt.
Russell, John R. MS 22nd Inf. Co.B Capt.
Russell, John R. NC 61st Inf. Co.G Cpl.
Russell, John R. TN 19th Inf. Co.B
Russell, John R. TX 14th Cav. Co.C
Russell, John R. TX 19th Cav. Co.F
Russell, John R. VA 1st Cav. 2nd Co.D
Russell, John R. VA 39th Inf. Co.D

Russell, John R. 1st Conf.Inf. 2nd Co.D
Russell, John S. AL 15th Inf. Co.C
Russell, John S. NC 33rd Inf. Co.E
Russell, John S. TN 9th Inf. Co.B Bvt.2nd Lt.
Russell, John S. VA Cav. Mosby's Regt. (Part.Rangers) Co.C Lt.
Russell, Johnsey NC 33rd Inf. Co.E
Russell, Johnson NC 6th Sr.Res. Co.E
Russell, Johnsy VA Inf. Cohoon's Bn. Co.D
Russell, John T. AL 4th Inf. Co.A
Russell, John T. GA 4th Bn.S.S. Co.A
Russell, John T. MS 33rd Inf. Co.F
Russell, John T. TN 3rd (Lillard's) Mtd. Inf. Co.I
Russell, John V. GA 52nd Inf. Co.F Sgt.
Russell, John W. KY 1st (Butler's) Cav.
Russell, John W. LA 31st Inf. Co.I
Russell, John W. NC 26th Inf. Co.E
Russell, John W. VA 6th Cav. Co.H
Russell, John W. VA 1st Arty. Co.B
Russell, John W. VA Lt.Arty. 1st Bn. Co.B
Russell, John W. VA Arty. Richardson's Co.
Russell, John W. VA 122nd Mil. Co.A
Russell, John William VA 32nd Inf. 1st Co.H
Russell, Jonas D. GA Arty. 9th Bn. Co.C
Russell, Jonathan TX 3rd Cav. Co.H Capt.
Russell, Jonathan A. MO 1st Brig.St.Guard
Russell, Jordan F. NC 60th Inf. Co.D
Russell, Jordan J. SC 3rd Cav. Co.E
Russell, Joseph FL 2nd Cav. Co.E
Russell, Joseph GA 16th Inf. Co.I Music.
Russell, Joseph GA 54th Inf. Co.H
Russell, Joseph GA 57th Inf. Co.H
Russell, Joseph KY 2nd (Woodward's) Cav. Co.D
Russell, Joseph MO 1st Cav. Co.E
Russell, Joseph NC 16th Inf. Co.L
Russell, Joseph NC 29th Inf. Co.E
Russell, Joseph SC 19th Inf. Co.H
Russell, Joseph TN 63rd Inf. Co.C
Russell, Joseph VA 3rd Lt.Arty. Co.D
Russell, Joseph A. NC Cav. 14th Bn. Co.E Capt.
Russell, Joseph C. MS 1st Lt.Arty. Co.E Artif.
Russell, Joseph C. MS 36th Inf. Co.K
Russell, Joseph C. NC 28th Inf. Co.E
Russell, Joseph H. AL 6th Inf. Co.D Capt.
Russell, Joseph H. AL 24th Inf. Co.F 2nd Lt.
Russell, Joseph H. GA 20th Inf. Co.K 2nd Lt.
Russell, Joseph L. NC 60th Inf. Co.D
Russell, Joseph M. TN Cav. 4th Bn. (Branner's) Co.E
Russell, Joseph M. TN 34th Inf. Co.G
Russell, Joseph P. AL 44th Inf. Co.D
Russell, Joseph R. AL Inf. 1st Regt. Co.F
Russell, Joseph S. AR 24th Inf. Co.G
Russell, Joseph S. GA 56th Inf. Co.E
Russell, Joseph T. AL 47th Inf. Co.C Capt.
Russell, Joseph W. TX 9th (Young's) Inf. Co.I
Russell, Joshua J. TX 18th Inf. Co.C
Russell, Josiah J. TN 28th Inf. Co.F
Russell, Josiah Q. MO 3rd Cav. Co.H
Russell, J.P. AL 62nd Inf. Co.K
Russell, J.P. KY Cav. 2nd Bn. (Dortch's) Co.B
Russell, J.P. KY 7th Cav.
Russell, J.P. MS 14th (Cons.) Inf. Co.C Cpl.
Russell, J.P. 10th Conf.Cav. Co.F

Russell, J.R. AL Lt.Arty. Kolb's Btty. Sgt.
Russell, J.R. AL 8th Inf. Co.K
Russell, J.R. AR 15th (N.W.) Inf. Co.I
Russell, J.R. GA Inf. 25th Bn. (Prov.Guard)
  Co.E
Russell, J.R. GA Inf. 40th Bn. Co.A Cpl.
Russell, J.R. MS 10th Cav. Co.H
Russell, J.R. MS St.Troops (Herndon Rangers)
  Montgomery's Ind.Co. Cpl.
Russell, J.R. MS Cav. Russell's Co. Capt.
Russell, J.R. MS Inf. 1st Bn.St.Troops (12 mo.
  '62-3) Co.B 3rd Lt.
Russell, J.R. MS 2nd (Davidson's) Inf. Co.I
Russell, J.R. MS 4th Inf. Co.H
Russell, J.R. MS 39th Inf. Co.K
Russell, J.R. TN 62nd Mtd.Inf. Co.D
Russell, J.R. TX 34th Cav. Lt.Col.
Russell, J.R. 10th Conf.Cav. Co.A
Russell, J.R. Conf.Cav. Baxter's Bn. Co.A
Russell, J.S. KY 12th Cav. Co.C
Russell, J.S. MD 1st Cav. Co.E,C
Russell, J.S. SC 2nd Inf.
Russell, J.S. SC Palmetto S.S. Co.C
Russell, J.S. TN Inf. 154th Sr.Regt.
Russell, J.S. TX 12th Inf. Co.I
Russell, J. Samuel AR 8th Cav. Co.F
Russell, J.T. AL 23rd Inf. AASurg.
Russell, J.T. LA Mil.Conf.Guards Regt. Co.C
Russell, J.T. TN 5th (McKenzie's) Cav. Co.D
Russell, J.V. GA Lt.Arty. Van Den Corput's Co.
Russell, J.W. AL 1st Inf. Co.F
Russell, J.W. AL 49th Inf. Co.G
Russell, J.W. AL 62nd Inf. Co.C
Russell, J.W. AL Cp. of Instr. Talladega
Russell, J.W. AR Cav. Gordon's Regt. Co.D
Russell, J.W. AR 10th Mil. Co.I Capt.
Russell, J.W. AR 37th Inf. Co.A
Russell, J.W. AR 37th Inf. Co.K
Russell, J.W. AR 50th Mil. Co.G
Russell, J.W. AR 50th Mil. Co.I
Russell, J.W. MS 4th Inf. Co.H,A Cpl.
Russell, J.W. TN 20th (Russell's) Cav. Co.H
Russell, J.W. TN 51st (Cons.) Inf. Co.B Sgt.
Russell, J.W. VA 34th Inf. Co.B
Russell, J.W. Morgan's,CSA
Russell, J.W. Gen. & Staff Capt.,AQM
Russell, J.W.H. GA Phillips' Legion Co.D
Russell, L. AL Cav. 24th Bn.
Russell, L. MS 3rd (St.Troops) Cav. Co.A Cpl.
Russell, L. MS 3rd (St.Troops) Cav. Co.A
Russell, Larkin NC 22nd Inf. Co.A
Russell, Larkin TN 28th Inf. Co.H
Russell, Larkin TX 16th Cav. Co.H
Russell, L.E. AR 19th (Dockery's) Inf. Co.K
Russell, L.E. LA 31st Inf. Co.E
Russell, Leander NC 64th Inf. Co.F,I
Russell, Leander TN 29th Inf. Co.D
Russell, Lee NC 22nd Inf. Co.L Maj.
Russell, Leo MO 12th Inf. Co.A
Russell, Leonard F. NC 34th Inf. Co.K
Russell, Leroy TN 3rd (Lillard's) Mtd.Inf. Co.F
Russell, Leroy Conf.Cav. Baxter's Bn. Co.C
Russell, Levi MS 38th Cav. Co.E
Russell, Levi NC 27th Inf. Co.C
Russell, Levi TX 12th Inf. Co.B,I
Russell, Levi M. AL 20th Inf. Co.D
Russell, Levi S. GA 29th Inf. Co.B Capt.

Russell, Levy SC 24th Inf. Co.C Cook
Russell, Lewis AL 18th Inf. Co.A
Russell, Lewis GA 2nd Bn.S.S. Co.D Sgt.
Russell, Lewis C. MO 3rd Inf. Co.A
Russell, Lewis F. AR 13th Inf. Co.I
Russell, Lewis K. AL 44th Inf. Co.F
Russell, Lewis R. AR Cav. Wright's Regt. Co.H
Russell, Lewis W. VA Inf. 22nd Bn. Co.B
Russell, L.F. SC 3rd Inf. Co.H
Russell, L.H. SC 1st Cav. Co.A 1st Lt.
Russell, L.H. TX 12th Inf. Co.B
Russell, L.H. Gen. & Staff Dr.M.
Russell, Liberty C. KY 6th Cav. Co.A
Russell, Littleton N. MS 13th Inf. Co.G
Russell, L.N. TX 30th Cav. Co.C
Russell, Lorenzo Newton MS Bradford's Co.
  (Conf.Guards Arty.)
Russell, Louis AR Inf. Cocke's Regt. Co.A
Russell, Louis F. GA 57th Inf. Co.A
Russell, Louis T. AR 15th (N.W.) Inf. Co.I
Russell, Lovelace NC 38th Inf. Co.H
Russell, L.S. GA 29th Inf. Co.B Capt.
Russell, L.S. TN 49th Inf. Co.D
Russell, L.S. Inf. Bailey's Cons.Regt. Co.L
Russell, L.W. GA 27th Inf. Co.H Music.
Russell, L.W. NC 18th Inf. Co.G
Russell, M. KY 2nd Mtd.Inf. Co.K
Russell, M. LA Cav. Greenleaf's Co. (Orleans
  Lt.Horse)
Russell, M. LA Inf.Crescent Regt. Co.K
Russell, M. MS 39th Inf. Co.D
Russell, M. NC 1st Jr.Res. Co.F
Russell, M. TX Cav. Steele's Command Co.B
  2nd Lt.
Russell, M. VA 2nd St.Res. Co.E
Russell, M.A. MS 8th Inf. Co.C
Russell, Macum TX 9th Cav. Co.G 2nd Lt.
Russell, Madison AL 53rd Part.Rangers Co.D
Russell, M.A.H. SC 1st Cav. Co.D
Russell, Major NC 27th Inf. Co.I 1st Lt.
Russell, Manson D. NC 16th Inf. Co.L
Russell, Marcus AR 2nd Vol. Co.C Sgt.
Russell, Marion TX 4th Cav. Co.H
Russell, Mark AL 46th Inf. Co.E
Russell, Mark N. TX 19th Cav. Co.H
Russell, Martin GA Inf. 26th Bn. Co.A
Russell, Martin NC 64th Inf. Co.F
Russell, Mathew TN 29th Inf. Co.K Laborer
Russell, Mathew N. NC 62nd Inf. Co.D Sgt.
Russell, Mathew S. MS 31st Inf. Co.G
Russell, M.B. SC 12th Inf. Co.F
Russell, M.C. AL Cav. Holloway's Co.
Russell, M.C. MS 2nd Cav. Co.A
Russell, M.C. SC 17th Inf. Co.K
Russell, M.C. Gen. & Staff A.Surg.
Russell, M.D. AR 32nd Inf. Co.H Cpl.
Russell, Merrill GA Inf. Bard's Co. 1st Lt.
Russell, M.F. AR 2nd Cav. Co.E Sgt.
Russell, M.F. AR 6th Inf. Co.C
Russell, M.F. TN 37th Inf. Co.C Sgt.
Russell, M.H. AL 7th Cav. Co.A
Russell, M.H. NC 32nd Inf. Co.A 1st Lt.
Russell, Michael AR 37th Inf. Co.G
Russell, Michael NC 2nd Inf. Co.A
Russell, Milby NC 38th Inf. Co.H
Russell, Milton GA 60th Inf. Co.C Capt.
Russell, M.J. AL 12th Inf. Co.A

Russell, M.J. Gen. & Staff Surg.
Russell, M.L. AR 1st Cav. Stirman's Co.E
Russell, M.M. AL 29th Inf. Co.F Capt.
Russell, M.N. NC 16th Inf. Co.H Sgt.
Russell, Monroe AL 9th (Malone's) Cav. Co.C
  Cpl.
Russell, Monroe SC 7th Res. Co.M
Russell, Monroe TN 28th (Cons.) Inf. Co.F 2nd
  Lt.
Russell, Monroe TX 6th Cav. Co.G Cpl.
Russell, Monteville VA 7th Cav. Co.C
Russell, Morton NC 14th Inf. Co.E
Russell, Moses GA 28th Inf. Co.I
Russell, Moses R. AL 17th Inf. Co.D
Russell, Moses W. TX 4th Cav. Co.H
Russell, M.P. TN 5th Inf. 2nd Co.F
Russell, M.W. TN 11th (Holman's) Cav. Co.H
Russell, M.W. TN 51st Inf. Co.F Capt.
Russell, M.W. TN 51st (Cons.) Inf. Co.F
Russell, N. LA 22nd (Cons.) Inf. Co.G Sgt.
Russell, Nace, Jr. AL 53rd (Part.Rangers) Co.H
Russell, Nace AL 3rd Inf. Co.E
Russell, Nathaniel GA 6th Inf. (St.Guards) Sims'
  Co.
Russell, Nathaniel P. MS 21st Inf. Co.K
Russell, Nathaniel S. GA 57th Inf. Co.H
Russell, N.B. LA 4th Inf. Co.C Sgt.
Russell, N.E. NC 38th Inf. Co.H
Russell, Ned LA Mil. 4th Regt. 1st Brig. 1st Div.
  Co.F
Russell, Newton TX 17th Cav. Co.H
Russell, Newton TX 12th Inf. Co.I
Russell, Nicholas LA 28th (Thomas') Inf. Co.D
  Sgt.
Russell, Nicholas NC 2nd Inf. Co.A
Russell, Nicholas VA 59th Inf. 3rd Co.D
Russell, Nicholas A. NC 3rd Arty. (40th
  St.Troops) Co.H
Russell, Nicholson LA 1st (Strawbridge's) Inf.
  Co.A
Russell, Noah NC 26th Inf. Co.I
Russell, N.P. MS 3rd Cav. Co.F
Russell, O. MS 25th Inf. Co.C
Russell, O.F. AR 1st (Dobbins') Cav. Co.G
Russell, Oliver R. Hunter's Staff Capt.,AAG
Russell, O.R. GA Cav. 21st Bn. Co.D
Russell, O.R. SC Cav. 14th Bn. Co.D
Russell, O.W.D. SC Hvy.Arty. 15th (Lucas') Bn.
  Co.B
Russell, P. MO Cav. Williams' Regt. Co.H
Russell, Palesteen TX 7th Inf. Co.H
Russell, Patrick F. VA 23rd Inf. Co.A
Russell, Patrick J. GA Arty. Maxwell's Reg.
  Lt.Btty. Cpl.
Russell, Patrick J. GA 1st Reg. Co.D
Russell, Perry AR 8th Inf. New Co.G
Russell, Perry AR 14th (McCarver's) Inf. Co.H
Russell, Perry W. AR 27th Inf. Co.H
Russell, Peter, Jr. AR Inf. Hardy's Regt. Co.F
Russell, Peter VA Inf. 1st Bn. Co.A
Russell, P.G. MS 41st Inf. Co.D
Russell, P.H. TN 14th Inf. Co.I
Russell, Philip F. VA 45th Inf. Co.C
Russell, Philip M., Jr. GA 1st (Olmstead's) Inf.
  Davis' Co.
Russell, Phillip TX 37th Cav. Co.F
Russell, Phillip TX Cav. Terry's Regt. Co.A

Russell, Phillip J. NC 5th Cav. (63rd St.Troops) Co.F

Russell, Piram NC 1st Arty. (10th St.Troops) Co.H

Russell, P.J. AR 24th Inf. Co.C

Russell, P.L. AR 10th Inf. Co.I,K 1st Lt.

Russell, Pleasant NC 38th Inf. Co.C

Russell, Pleasant J. MO 3rd Cav. Co.I

Russell, Pleasant M. TX Inf. Griffin's Bn. Co.C

Russell, Pleasant N. TN Cav. 2nd Bn. (Biffle's) Co.D

Russell, P.Q. TX Cav. Bourland's Regt. Co.C

Russell, Prince A. MS 33rd Inf. Co.A Cpl.

Russell, R. AL Cav. Barbiere's Bn. Co.E

Russell, R. MS 3rd Inf. Co.C

Russell, R. TN 14th (Neely's) Cav. Co.I

Russell, R. TN 19th & 20th (Cons.) Cav. Co.D

Russell, R.A. AL Cp. of Instr. Talladega

Russell, R.A. NC Mil. Clark's Sp.Bn. Co.A Capt.

Russell, R.A. TN 51st (Cons.) Inf. Co.B Sgt.

Russell, Ransom AL 2nd Cav. Co.E Sgt.

Russell, Ransom B. TX 9th Cav. Co.A

Russell, Rayford MS 38th Cav. Co.E

Russell, R.B. MS 28th Cav. Co.F

Russell, R.B. TN 5th Inf. 2nd Co.K

Russell, R.B. TN 15th Inf. Co.A

Russell, R.C. GA Inf. 27th Bn. (NonConscr.) Co.B

Russell, R.C. TX Cav. Border's Regt. Co.H

Russell, R.D. MO Cav. 2nd Regt.St.Guard Co.A

Russell, Reuben NC Cav. 7th Bn. Co.C

Russell, R.H. FL 2nd Inf. Co.K

Russell, R.H. GA 54th Inf. Co.H

Russell, R.H. NC 36th Inf. Co.H

Russell, R.H. VA 30th Inf. Co.A

Russell, Richard FL 2nd Cav. Co.H Cpl.

Russell, Richard D. NC 38th Inf. Co.B

Russell, Richard H. NC 55th Inf. Co.K Cpl.

Russell, Richard J. TN Cav. 17th Bn. (Sanders') Co.A

Russell, Richard M. NC 2nd Arty. (36th St.Troops) Co.B

Russell, Richard M. VA Inf. 22nd Bn. Co.B

Russell, Riley TN 19th Inf. Co.G

Russell, R.J. AL 32nd & 58th (Cons.) Inf.

Russell, R.J. NC 64th Inf. Co.L

Russell, R.J. SC 7th Inf. 2nd Co.C, Co.G

Russell, R.J. TN 46th Inf. Co.B

Russell, R.J. TN 59th Mtd.Inf. Co.K

Russell, R.L. MS Conscr.

Russell, R.M. AL 40th Inf. Co.G

Russell, R.M. TN 19th & 20th (Cons.) Cav. Col.

Russell, R.M. TN 20th (Russell's) Cav. Col.

Russell, R.M. TN Arty.Corps Capt.

Russell, R.M. TN 12th Inf. Co.E Col.

Russell, R.M. TX 9th (Nichols') Inf. Co.A

Russell, Robert AL 3rd Cav. Co.H

Russell, Robert AL Mtd.Inf. J. Oden's Co.

Russell, Robert LA 13th Bn. (Part.Rangers) Co.A

Russell, Robert NC 1st Cav. (9th St.Troops) Co.B

Russell, Robert TN 51st (Cons.) Inf. Co.B 1st Lt.

Russell, Robert VA Hvy.Arty. 19th Bn. Co.B

Russell, Robert 1st Conf.Cav. Co.G

Russell, Robert A. AR 17th (Lemoyne's) Inf. Co.B

Russell, Robert A. AR 21st Inf. Co.D 1st Sgt.

Russell, Robert B. AR 31st Inf. Co.E

Russell, Robert B. MO 8th Inf. Co.G,K

Russell, Robert C. TN 48th (Voorhies') Inf. Co.K

Russell, Robert D. MO 15th Cav. Co.A 1st Sgt.

Russell, Robert E. NC 20th Inf. Co.A

Russell, Robert F. TN 5th (McKenzie's) Cav. Co.H

Russell, Robert G. NC 12th Inf. Co.D,B

Russell, Robert G. NC 54th Inf. Co.E 2nd Lt.

Russell, Robert G. SC 14th Inf. Co.G

Russell, Robert H. VA 6th Inf. Co.C

Russell, Robert J. AR 15th (Josey's) Inf. Co.E

Russell, Robert J. TN 19th Inf. Co.H Sgt.

Russell, Robert L. KY 4th Mtd.Inf. Co.E Capt.

Russell, Robert M. AR 15th (N.W.) Inf. Co.I

Russell, Robert M. TX 35th (Likens') Cav. Sgt.Maj.

Russell, Robert M. TX Waul's Legion Co.C

Russell, Robert N. GA 10th Cav. (St.Guards) Co.D

Russell, Robert P. TN 8th (Smith's) Cav. Co.L 1st Lt.

Russell, Robert P. TX 27th Cav. Co.D

Russell, Robert R. MO Cav. 3rd Bn. Co.B Jr.2nd Lt.

Russell, Robert R. MO 8th Cav. Co.B 1st Lt.

Russell, Robert S. VA Inf. 21st Bn. 2nd Co.C

Russell, Robert Y. SC 17th Inf. Co.K

Russell, Rodolph GA Hvy.Arty. 22nd Bn. Co.D

Russell, Roland A. GA 64th Inf. Co.F 2nd Lt.

Russell, Rolin A. GA 31st Inf. Co.I 3rd Lt.

Russell, R.R. AR 3rd Cav. Co.D Cpl.

Russell, R.R. FL 2nd Inf. Co.K

Russell, R.R. MO Cav. 1st Regt.St.Guard Co.C

Russell, R.S. AL Supp.Force 2nd Congr.Dist. 1st Lt.

Russell, R.S. TN 9th Inf. Co.B Capt.

Russell, R.S. TX 23rd Cav. Co.D

Russell, R.T. NC 64th Inf. Co.L

Russell, Ruben J. AL 17th Inf. Co.I

Russell, R.W. LA 13th Bn. (Part.Rangers) Co.A

Russell, R.W. NC 5th Cav. (63rd St.Troops) Co.F

Russell, R.W. Gen. & Staff, ICAVD Hosp.Stew.

Russell, R.Y. SC 5th Inf. 1st Co.I, 2nd Co.E Cpl.

Russell, S. AL 42nd Inf. Co.H

Russell, S. SC 5th Cav. Co.E

Russell, S. TN 9th Cav. Co.E

Russell, S. VA Loc.Def. Chappell's Co.

Russell, Samuel AR 2nd Mtd.Rifles Co.E

Russell, Samuel AR 4th Inf. Co.I

Russell, Samuel AR 37th Inf. Co.H

Russell, Samuel FL 1st Cav. Co.B Cpl.

Russell, Samuel GA 4th (Clinch's) Cav. Co.F

Russell, Samuel GA 57th Inf. Co.H

Russell, Samuel MO 11th Inf. Co.K

Russell, Samuel NC 7th Inf. Co.H

Russell, Samuel TN 8th (Smith's) Cav. Co.A

Russell, Samuel TN Lt.Arty. Lynch's Co.

Russell, Samuel TN 51st (Cons.) Inf. Co.B

Russell, Samuel B. TX 16th Inf. Co.G

Russell, Samuel C. TN 39th Mtd.Inf.

Russell, Samuel C. VA 9th Inf. Co.C

Russell, Samuel D. LA 3rd Inf. Co.D Col.

Russell, Samuel D. MS 22nd Inf. Co.D Capt.

Russell, Samuel H. AL 4th (Russell's) Cav. Co.I Sgt.

Russell, Samuel J. MS 15th Inf. Co.A

Russell, Samuel L. AL 19th Inf. Co.H,E 2nd Lt.

Russell, Samuel L. Gen. & Staff Chap.

Russell, Samuel P. AR 34th Inf. Co.B

Russell, Samuel P. AR Brooks' Inf. Buchanan's Co.B

Russell, Samuel R. TN 61st Mtd.Inf. Co.B

Russell, Samuel T. AL 33rd Inf. Co.E

Russell, Samuel T. TX Waul's Legion Co.E

Russell, Samuel Y. AR 9th Inf. Co.D

Russell, S.B. TX 20th Bn.St.Troops Co.A Lt.

Russell, S.B. TX Inf. Houston Bn. Co.A 1st Lt.

Russell, S.C. KY 5th Cav. Co.G

Russell, S.C. KY 9th Mtd.Inf. Co.G

Russell, S.C. TN 28th (Cons.) Inf. Co.C

Russell, S.C. TN Inf. 154th Sr.Regt. 2nd Co.B, Co.G

Russell, Scott TX 14th Cav. Co.C

Russell, S.D. AR 33rd Inf. Co.G

Russell, S.D. SC 2nd Arty. Co.I Jr.2nd Lt.

Russell, S.E. TX 24th & 25th Cav. (Cons.) Co.B

Russell, Sebron D. MS 15th Inf. Co.A

Russell, S.H. GA 7th Cav. Co.A

Russell, S.H. GA Cav. 21st Bn. Co.A

Russell, S.H. TX 25th Cav. Smith's Co.

Russell, S.H. TX 11th Inf. Co.G 1st Sgt.

Russell, Sidney MO 11th Inf. Co.C

Russell, Silas C. TN 28th Inf. Co.H

Russell, Simeon LA Mil. British Guard Bn. Kurczyn's Co. Cpl.

Russell, Simeon D. MO 4th Inf. Co.A

Russell, Simeon J.M. AL 3rd Inf. Co.B

Russell, Simon H. GA Inf. 1st Loc.Troops (Augusta) Co.B

Russell, S.J. AR 37th Inf. Co.E

Russell, S.J. MS 1st (Percy's) Inf. Co.I

Russell, S.L. SC 1St Cav. Co.A

Russell, S.L. TX 12th Inf. Co.I Sgt.

Russell, S.M. AL 45th Inf. Co.D

Russell, S.M. AL 62nd Inf. Co.H

Russell, S.M. MO 7th Cav. 1st Lt.

Russell, S.M. TX 14th Inf. Co.D

Russell, S.M. TX 20th Inf. Co.G

Russell, Smith J. NC 17th Inf. (2nd Org.) Co.B

Russell, S.O. AL 4th Res. Co.G

Russell, S.O. SC 1st Cav. Co.A

Russell, S.O. SC Lt.Arty. Gaillard's Co. (Santee Lt.Arty.)

Russell, S. Oliver SC 1st (Hagood's) Inf. 1st Co.D

Russell, Squire H. SC 1st (Orr's) Rifles Co.E

Russell, S.R. SC 1st (McCreary's) Inf. 3rd Lt.

Russell, S.T. AL 17th Inf. Co.C

Russell, S.T. LA Washington Arty.Bn. Co.5

Russell, S.T. TN Cav. 31st Regt. Co.H

Russell, S.T. TX 15th Cav. Co.E

Russell, S.T. TX 26th Cav. 1st Co.G

Russell, S.T. TX 9th (Nichols') Inf. Atchison's Co.

Russell, Stapleton GA 45th Inf. Co.F

Russell, Stephen GA 22nd Inf. Co.B

Russell, Stephen GA Inf. Cobb Guards Co.B

Russell, Stephen NC 2nd Arty. (36th St.Troops) Co.B

Russell, Stephen NC Lt.Arty. 13th Bn. Co.D

Russell, Stephen NC 1st Inf. (6 mo. '61) Co.H

Russell, Stephen TN 18th (Newsom's) Cav. Co.D,G

Russell, Stephen TN 19th & 20th (Cons.) Cav. Co.B

Russell, Stephen C. VA 45th Inf. Co.C

Russell, Stephen E. NC 51st Inf. Co.I

Russell, Stephen H. TN 32nd Inf. Co.F

Russell, Stephen H. TN 35th Inf. 2nd Co.F

Russell, Sterling H. NC 37th Inf. Co.I

Russell, Sturdevant O. TX Cav. Benavides' Regt. Co.F

Russell, S.W. AL Talladega Cty.Res. G. M. Gamble's Co.

Russell, S.Y. AR 1st (Monroe's) Cav. Co.B

Russell, Sylvester AL Mil. 3rd Vol. Co.B

Russell, Sylvester AL 8th Inf. Co.I

Russell, T. SC 14th Inf. Co.G

Russell, T.A. MS 20th Inf. Co.D

Russell, Tandy AR 10th Mil. Co.B

Russell, T.B. TX 32nd Cav. Co.F

Russell, T.B. TX Inf. Currie's Co.

Russell, T.C. GA Inf. 27th Bn. (NonConscr.) Co.A

Russell, T.D. LA 11th Inf. Co.G

Russell, T.D. MS 8th Inf. Co.H 1st Sgt.

Russell, T.D. TX Cav. Waller's Regt. Co.F

Russell, Thomas AR 33rd Inf. Co.C

Russell, Thomas FL Cav. 3rd Bn. Co.A

Russell, Thomas FL 1st Inf. Co.K

Russell, Thomas FL 7th Inf. Co.K

Russell, Thomas GA 5th Inf. Co.A

Russell, Thomas GA Inf. 18th Bn. (St.Guards) Co.E

Russell, Thomas KY 2nd (Duke's) Cav. Co.D

Russell, Thomas LA 13th Inf. Co.I

Russell, Thomas MS Inf. 3rd Bn. (St.Troops) Co.C

Russell, Thomas MS 21st Inf. Co.A Music.

Russell, Thomas MO 7th Cav. Co.E

Russell, Thomas MO 12th Cav. Co.H,E

Russell, Thomas MO 11th Inf. Co.C

Russell, Thomas NC 46th Inf. Co.F

Russell, Thomas NC 64th Inf. Co.F

Russell, Thomas TN 29th Inf. Co.K Laborer

Russell, Thomas TN 37th Inf. Co.C

Russell, Thomas TN 69th Mtd.Inf. Co.K

Russell, Thomas TX 30th Cav. Co.H

Russell, Thomas VA Hvy.Arty. 10th Bn. Co.A Jr.2nd Lt.

Russell, Thomas VA Lt.Arty. 38th Bn. Co.A

Russell, Thomas VA 30th Inf. Co.I

Russell, Thomas A. GA 36th (Villepigue's) Inf. Co.B

Russell, Thomas A. MD 1st Inf. Co.H

Russell, Thomas A. MS 15th Inf. Co.K,D

Russell, Thomas A. TX Inf. Griffin's Bn. Co.A

Russell, Thomas A. VA Cav. Mosby's Regt. (Part.Rangers) Co.F Sgt.

Russell, Thomas A. VA Horse Arty. D. Shank's Co. Sgt.

Russell, Thomas A. 1st Conf.Inf. Co.B

Russell, Thomas B. NC 12th Inf. Co.G

Russell, Thomas C. AR 27th Inf. New Co.B

Russell, Thomas C. AR Flannigan's Regt. St.Troops Co.B

Russell, Thomas C. GA 27th Inf. Co.E Cpl.

Russell, Thomas C. LA Hvy.Arty. 2nd Bn. Co.C

Russell, Thomas C. NC 46th Inf. Co.G

Russell, Thomas D. TN 34th Inf. Co.B

Russell, Thomas E. TN 4th (McLemore's) Cav. Co.D

Russell, Thomas E. TN 8th Inf. Co.I Ord.Sgt.

Russell, Thomas F. TN 41st Inf. Co.F

Russell, Thomas G. VA 49th Inf. 1st Co.G

Russell, Thomas H. SC 1st St.Troops Co.A Capt.

Russell, Thomas J. AL 28th Inf. Co.E Sgt.

Russell, Thomas J. LA 5th Inf. Co.C

Russell, Thomas J. MO Lt.Arty. 3rd Btty.

Russell, Thomas J. MO Arty. Lowe's Co.

Russell, Thomas J. TN 3rd (Lillard's) Mtd.Inf. Co.I

Russell, Thomas J. VA 1st Cav. 1st Co.D

Russell, Thomas J. VA 6th Cav. Co.D

Russell, Thomas K. VA 15th Cav. Co.F

Russell, Thomas L. MS Bradford's Co. (Conf. Guards Arty.) Cpl.

Russell, Thomas P. VA 64th Mtd.Inf. Co.G

Russell, Thomas R. TN 59th Mtd.Inf. Co.K Sgt.

Russell, Thomas R. VA 5th Cav. (12 mo. '61-2) Co.B

Russell, Thomas T. VA Loc.Def. Chappell's Co.

Russell, Thomas Wallace SC 4th Inf. Co.D Cpl.

Russell, Tipton MO 1st Cav. Co.E

Russell, T.J. AL 33rd Inf. Co.E

Russell, T.J. MS 1st Cav. Co.C

Russell, T.J. NC 61st Inf. Co.D

Russell, T.L. GA 27th Inf. Co.H

Russell, T.L. NC 38th Inf. Co.H

Russell, T.L. Gen. & Staff Capt.,Comsy.

Russell, T.M. AL 14th Inf. Co.H 2nd Lt.

Russell, T.M. TN 19th & 20th (Cons.) Cav. Co.E

Russell, T.M. TN 20th (Russell's) Cav. Co.H

Russell, T.M. TN 21st (Wilson's) Cav. Co.A

Russell, T.P. AL 55th Vol. Co.F

Russell, T.R. MS 7th Cav. Co.K

Russell, T.S. FL 2nd Inf. Co.D

Russell, T.W. MS 31st Inf. Co.C

Russell, T.W. SC 1st Cav. Co.F 2nd Lt.

Russell, T.W. TX 28th Cav. Co.D

Russell, V. Inf. Bailey's Cons.Regt. Co.A

Russell, Valentine TX 7th Inf. Co.H

Russell, Valentine VA 7th Cav. Co.C

Russell, Valentine VA 136th Mil. Co.F

Russell, W. AL 6th Cav. Co.I

Russell, W. LA 1st (Nelligan's) Inf. Co.H

Russell, W. SC Lt.Arty. 8th (Palmetto) Bn. Co.I

Russell, W. SC 1st (Hagood's) Inf. 2nd Co.F

Russell, W.A. AR 6th Inf. Co.H, 1st Co.B Sgt.

Russell, W.A. AR 19th (Dockery's) Inf. Co.K

Russell, W.A. LA 13th Bn. (Part.Rangers) Co.B

Russell, W.A. MS 1st Lt.Arty. Co.F Cpl.

Russell, W.A. MS Horse Arty. Cook's Co.

Russell, W.A. MS 36th Inf. Co.D Sgt.

Russell, Wafford AL 49th Inf. Co.G

Russell, Wallace R.C. GA 55th Inf. Co.I 3rd Lt.

Russell, Walter A. AR 23rd Inf. Co.E Cpl.

Russell, Walter B. NC 17th Inf. (1st Org.) Co.L

Russell, Walter R. NC 52nd Inf. Co.C QMSgt.

Russell, Walter S. MS 31st Inf. Co.D

Russell, Warren VA 3rd (Archer's) Bn.Res. Co.A

Russell, Washington H. AL 53rd (Part.Rangers) Co.B

Russell, W.B. TX 3rd Cav. Co.G

Russell, W.B. Wheeler's Scouts,CSA

Russell, W.C. TN Arty. Bibb's Co.

Russell, W.C. TX 26th Cav. Co.E

Russell, W.D. GA 7th Cav. Co.A Capt.

Russell, W.D. GA Cav. 21st Bn. Co.A Capt.

Russell, W.D. GA 1st (Ramsey's) Inf. Co.I 1st Lt.

Russell, W.D. MS Cav. 2nd Bn.Res. Co.A

Russell, W.D. MS 28th Cav. Co.F

Russell, W.D. MS 1st Lt.Arty. Co.F Cpl.

Russell, W.D. TX 24th & 25th Cav. (Cons.) Co.B

Russell, W.E. KY 1st (Helm's) Cav. QMSgt.

Russell, W.E. MS Bradford's Co. (Conf.Guards Arty.)

Russell, W.E. MS 39th Inf. Co.G

Russell, W.E. NC Allen's Co. (Loc.Def.)

Russell, Wellington S. NC 17th Inf. (1st Org.) Co.B Sgt.

Russell, Wesley MS 7th Inf. Co.I

Russell, W.F. AL 1st Regt. Mobile Vol. British Guards Co.A

Russell, W.F. SC 7th Cav. Co.K

Russell, W.F. TN 17th Inf. Co.A

Russell, W.G. GA Cav. Russell's Co. Capt.

Russell, W.G. TN 41st Inf. Co.F

Russell, W.G. VA 9th Cav. Co.G

Russell, W.G. VA Inf. 44th Bn. Co.C Cpl.

Russell, W.H. AR 7th Mil. Co.E

Russell, W.H. AR 10th Inf. Co.I 2nd Lt.

Russell, W.H. FL 1st (Res.) Inf. Sgt.

Russell, W.H. MS Cav. 3rd Bn. (Ashcraft's) Co.B

Russell, W.H. MS Lt.Arty. Stanford's Co.

Russell, W.H. MS 46th Inf. Co.E 1st Lt.

Russell, W.H. MO St.Guard

Russell, W.H. NC 42nd Inf. Co.C

Russell, W.H. TN 16th Inf. Co.H Sgt.

Russell, W.H. TX 24th Cav. Co.F

Russell, W.H. TX 9th (Nichols') Inf. Co.A

Russell, Wheeler TN 5th Cav.

Russell, Whitmill S. TX 14th Cav. Co.I Capt.

Russell, Whitson NC 5th Cav. (63rd St.Troops) Co.K Cpl.

Russell, Whitson A. GA 7th Inf. Co.F

Russell, Wilbern NC 5th Inf. Co.I

Russell, Wiley MS 18th Cav. Co.G

Russell, Wiley MS 7th Inf. Co.I

Russell, Wiley J. NC 44th Inf. Co.F

Russell, Wiley W. NC 34th Inf. Co.K

Russell, William AL Pris.Guard Freeman's Co.

Russell, William AR 2nd Mtd.Rifles Hawkins' Co.

Russell, William AR Cav. Gordon's Regt. Co.A

Russell, William AR 1st Vol. Co.I

Russell, William AR 4th Inf. Co.I

Russell, William AR 7th Inf. Co.G

Russell, William AR 7th Inf. Co.H

Russell, William AR Inf. 8th Bn. Co.D

Russell, William AR 15th (N.W.) Inf. Co.I

Russell, William AR 27th Inf. Co.H Capt.

Russell, William FL 8th Inf. Co.I
Russell, William GA 6th Inf. (St.Guards) Co.B
Russell, William GA 12th Mil.
Russell, William GA 36th (Villepigue's) Inf. Co.D
Russell, William GA 44th Inf. Co.F
Russell, William GA 46th Inf. Co.C
Russell, William KY 6th Cav. Co.B
Russell, William KY Fields' Co. (Part.Rangers)
Russell, William KY 5th Mtd.Inf. Co.D
Russell, William LA 6th Cav. Co.K
Russell, William LA 1st Hvy.Arty. (Reg.) Co.H
Russell, William LA Inf. 1st Sp.Bn. (Rightor's) Co.D
Russell, William LA 2nd Inf. Co.A
Russell, William LA 2nd Inf. Co.K
Russell, William MS 9th Inf. New Co.G
Russell, William MS 24th Inf. Co.F
Russell, William MS 35th Inf. Co.C 2nd Lt.
Russell, William MO 1st Cav. Co.E,A
Russell, William MO Cav. Fristoe's Regt. Co.G
Russell, Wm. MO St.Guard
Russell, William NC 1st Arty. (10th St.Troops) Co.G
Russell, William NC Inf. 2nd Bn. Co.H
Russell, William NC 23rd Inf. Co.E Cpl.
Russell, William NC 44th Inf. Co.F
Russell, William NC 53rd Inf. Co.F Cpl.
Russell, William NC 55th Inf. Co.H
Russell, William NC Loc.Def. Groom's Co.
Russell, William NC Inf. Thomas Legion Co.I
Russell, William SC Lt.Arty. Beauregard's Co.
Russell, William SC 11th Inf. Co.E
Russell, William SC 16th Inf. Co.G
Russell, William SC 17th Inf. Co.K
Russell, William TN 2nd (Ashby's) Cav. Co.E
Russell, William TN Cav. 4th Bn. (Branner's) Co.D
Russell, William TN 5th Inf. Co.B
Russell, William TN Inf. 23rd Bn. Co.C
Russell, William TN 24th Inf. Co.A
Russell, William TN 28th (Cons.) Inf. Co.C Capt.
Russell, William TN 39th Mtd.Inf. Co.C
Russell, William TN 46th Inf. Co.K
Russell, William TX 29th Cav. Co.I
Russell, William TX 36th Cav. Co.B
Russell, William TX Inf. 2nd St.Troops Co.H
Russell, William TX 4th Inf. Co.D
Russell, William TX Vol. Benton's Co.
Russell, William VA Goochland Lt.Arty.
Russell, William VA Lt.Arty. Lamkin's Co.
Russell, William VA 1st (Farinholt's) Res. Co.E
Russell, William VA 6th Bn.Res. Co.H
Russell, William VA 10th Inf.
Russell, William VA 11th Inf. Co.H
Russell, William VA 26th Inf. 2nd Co.B
Russell, William VA 26th Inf. Co.H Sgt.
Russell, William VA 28th Inf. Co.K
Russell, William VA 30th Bn.S.S. Co.B
Russell, William VA 39th Inf. Co.G
Russell, William VA 51st Mil. Co.G
Russell, William VA 56th Inf. Co.A 2nd Lt.
Russell, William 1st Cherokee Mtd.Vol. 2nd Co.A
Russell, William A. AL 4th Cav. Co.D 1st Lt.
Russell, William A. AL 39th Inf. Co.B

Russell, William A. AL Vol. Lee, Jr.'s Co.
Russell, William A. FL 9th Inf. Co.G
Russell, William A. GA Lt.Arty. Van Den Corput's Co. 2nd Lt.
Russell, William A. GA Inf. 3rd Bn. Co.A Sgt.
Russell, William A. MS Cav. Jeff Davis Legion Co.B
Russell, William A. NC 22nd Inf. Co.L
Russell, William A. NC 25th Inf. Co.D
Russell, William A. TN 3rd (Clack's) Inf. Co.G
Russell, William A. TN 19th Inf. Co.B
Russell, William A. TX 3rd Cav. Co.G
Russell, William B. AL 25th Inf. Co.A
Russell, William B. AR 14th (Powers') Inf. Surg.
Russell, William B. TN 28th Inf. Co.H
Russell, William B.T. TX 28th Cav. Co.I
Russell, William C. AL 4th (Russell's) Cav. Co.G
Russell, William C. AL 19th Inf. Co.H
Russell, William C. MS 21st Inf. Co.F
Russell, William C. TN 39th Mtd.Inf. Co.H
Russell, William C. TX 18th Inf. Co.C
Russell, Wm. D. AL 3rd Inf. Co.F
Russell, William D. AL 5th Inf. New Co.I
Russell, William D. FL 1st Inf. Old Co.I
Russell, William D. NC 11th (Bethel Regt.) Inf. Co.F
Russell, William D. NC 30th Inf. Co.K Sgt.
Russell, Wm D. VA 50th Inf. Co.H
Russell, William E. FL 3rd Inf. Co.H Cpl.
Russell, William E. LA 3rd Inf. Co.D Capt.
Russell, William F. AR 27th Inf. Co.H
Russell, William F. NC 34th Inf. Co.K
Russell, William F. TX 11th Inf. Co.G
Russell, William G. KY 2nd Cav.
Russell, William G. TN 14th Inf. Co.B Capt.
Russell, William G. 2nd Corps Hosp.Stew.
Russell, William H. AL Lt.Arty. 2nd Bn. Co.E
Russell, William H. GA Boddie's Co. (Troup Cty.Ind.Cav.)
Russell, William H. GA Lt.Arty. Scogin's Btty. (Griffin Lt.Arty.)
Russell, William H. GA 3rd Bn. (St.Guards) Co.H
Russell, William H. GA 41st Inf. Co.E
Russell, William H. KY 6th Cav. Co.A
Russell, William H. NC 12th Inf. Co.B,D
Russell, William H. NC 29th Inf. Co.E
Russell, William H. NC 54th Inf. Co.I
Russell, William H. NC 67th Inf. Co.A
Russell, William H. SC 7th Inf. 1st Co.D, 2nd Co.D
Russell, William H. TN 62nd Mtd.Inf. Co.D
Russell, William H. TX 13th Vol. AAdj.
Russell, William H. VA Inf. Cohoon's Bn. Co.D
Russell, Wm. H. Gen. & Staff Capt.,AAG
Russell, William H.H. MS 21st Inf. Co.K
Russell, William H.H. MS 43rd Inf. Co.E
Russell, William J. AL Cav. Holloway's Co.
Russell, William J. AR 2nd Cav. Co.G
Russell, William J. AR 27th Inf. New Co.B Sgt.
Russell, William J. AR 31st Inf. Co.E
Russell, William J. GA 3rd Inf. Co.C
Russell, William J. GA 7th Inf. (St.Guards) Co.D Comsy.Sgt.
Russell, William J. MS 3rd Inf. Co.I Cpl.

Russell, William L. KY 1st (Butler's) Cav. Co.C,A
Russell, William L. LA 3rd (Wingfield's) Cav. Co.E Cpl.
Russell, William M. AL 6th Cav. Co.A Sgt.
Russell, William M. AL 28th Inf. Co.A
Russell, William M. AL Cp. of Instr. Talladega
Russell, William M. GA 21st Inf. Co.G
Russell, William M. GA 40th Inf. Co.D 1st Sgt.
Russell, William M. KY 1st (Butler's) Cav. Co.B
Russell, William M. MS 1st (Percy's) Inf. Co.B
Russell, William M. MS 15th Inf. Co.A
Russell, William M. NC 34th Inf. Co.K
Russell, William M. TN 49th Inf. Co.D 2nd Lt.
Russell, William M. (No.1) TX 27th Cav. Co.A
Russell, William M., No.2 TX 27th Cav. Co.A
Russell, William N. GA 11th Inf. Co.G 2nd Lt.
Russell, William P. GA 5th Inf. (St.Guards) Russell's Co.
Russell, William P. VA 32nd Inf. Co.E
Russell, William R. AR 38th Inf. Co.A
Russell, William R. GA 36th (Broyles') Inf. Co.I 1st Lt.
Russell, William R. NC 43rd Inf. Co.K
Russell, William R. TX 2nd Cav. Co.C
Russell, William R. TX 11th Cav. Co.A
Russell, William S. TN 24th Inf. Co.D,M
Russell, William S.D. GA Lt.Arty. Van Den Corput's Co.
Russell, Williamson M. NC 7th Inf. Co.H
Russell, William T. AR 18th (Marmaduke's) Inf. Co.G
Russell, William T. NC 33rd Inf. Co.E
Russell, William T. TN 5th Inf. 2nd Co.H
Russell, William T. VA 14th Inf. Co.A
Russell, William T. VA 59th Mil. Hunter's Co.
Russell, Wm. T. Gen. & Staff Surg.
Russell, William W. GA Inf. 3rd Bn. Co.A
Russell, William W. GA 3rd Res. Co.I Sgt.
Russell, William W. GA Inf. 10th Bn. Co.D 1st Lt.
Russell, William W. GA 42nd Inf. Co.B Sgt.
Russell, William W. MS 30th Inf. Co.I Cpl.
Russell, William W. MO Arty. Jos. Bledsoe's Co.
Russell, Willis KY 4th Cav. Co.G
Russell, Willis NC 1st Cav. (9th St.Troops) Co.A Black.
Russell, Willis P. TN Cav. 2nd Bn. (Biffle's) Co.D
Russell, Wilson W. 10th Conf.Cav. Co.E
Russell, W.J. AL 1st Inf. Co.F
Russell, W.J. AL Pris.Guard Freeman's Co.
Russell, W.J. FL Kilcrease Lt.Arty.
Russell, W.J. GA Cav. 9th Bn. (St.Guards) Co.B
Russell, W.J. KY 12th Cav. Co.C
Russell, W.J. MS Inf. 1st Bn.St.Troops (30 days '64) Co.G
Russell, W.J. TN 24th Inf. Co.D Fifer
Russell, W.J. TX Vol. Teague's Co. (So.Rights Guards)
Russell, W.J.F. AL 62nd Inf. Co.H
Russell, W.J.F. AL Loc.Def. & Sp.Serv. Toomer's Co.
Russell, W.L. AR Cav. 1st Bn. (Stirman's) Co.E Driver
Russell, W.L. AL 55th Vol. Co.I Sgt.

Russell, W.L. LA 4th Inf. Old Co.G
Russell, W.L. TN 42nd Inf. 1st Co.I
Russell, W.L. TN Inf. 154th Sr.Regt. Co.F
Russell, W. Linsay MS 30th Inf. Co.H Cpl.
Russell, W.M. AL 22nd Inf. Co.H
Russell, W.M. AL 47th Inf. Co.C
Russell, W.M. AR 7th Mil. Co.E
Russell, W.M. GA Inf. 1st Loc.Troops (Augusta) Co.K
Russell, W.M. GA Inf. 18th Bn. (St.Guards) Adam's Co.
Russell, W.M. MS 40th Inf. Co.D
Russell, W.M. TN 3rd (Forrest's) Cav.
Russell, W.M. TN 11th (Holman's) Cav. Co.E
Russell, W.M. TN Cav. 16th Bn. (Neal's) Co.C
Russell, W.M. TN Inf. 1st Cons.Regt. Co.G
Russell, W.M. TN 28th (Cons.) Inf. Co.G Sgt.Maj.
Russell, W.M. TN 84th Inf. Co.C
Russell, W. McN. MS Inf. 2nd Bn. (St.Troops) Co.D
Russell, W.N. TN 16th Inf. Co.H
Russell, W.N. TN 43rd Inf. Co.H Sgt.
Russell, W.P. GA 1st (Fannin's) Res. Co.I
Russell, W.P. MS 8th Cav. Co.I Sgt.
Russell, W.P. MS T.P. Montgomery's Co.
Russell, W.P. TN 2nd (Ashby's) Cav. Co.E
Russell, W.P. TN 6th (Wheeler's) Cav. Co.A Cpl.
Russell, W.P. VA 54th Mil. Co.C,D
Russell, W.R. GA 4th Res. Co.C
Russell, W.R. TN 3rd (Forrest's) Cav. Co.C
Russell, W.R. VA 22nd Cav. Co.E
Russell, W.S. TX 7th Inf. Co.H Sgt.
Russell, W.T. AR 5th Inf.
Russell, W.T. TN 11th (Holman's) Cav. Co.D
Russell, W.T. TX Granbury's Cons.Brig. Co.C Sgt.
Russell, W.T. VA 72nd Mil.
Russell, W.V. AR Cav. Gordon's Regt. Co.F 3rd Lt.
Russell, W.W. AL Cav. 5th Bn. Hilliard's Legion Co.E
Russell, W.W. MS 4th Inf. Co.H
Russell, W.W. SC 1st Cav. Co.F
Russell, Zachariah MS 13th Inf. Co.B
Russell, Zachariah MS 37th Inf. Co.C Cpl.
Russell, Zachariah NC 14th Inf. Co.B
Russell, Zachariah NC 14th Inf. Co.E
Russell, Z.M. MS 16th Inf. Co.H
Russell, Z.T. Conf.Cav. Wood's Regt. Co.K
Russells, J.C. AL 51st (Part.Rangers) Co.I
Russels, Edward LA 2nd Cav.
Russer, M.D. NC 2nd Jr.Res. Co.F
Russey, A.W. GA Inf. 2nd Bn. (St.Guards) Co.C Sgt.
Russey, B.G. AR 19th (Dawson's) Inf. Co.K
Russey, C.C. AL 4th (Russell's) Cav. Co.K Cpl.
Russey, C.C. TN 3rd (Forrest's) Cav. 1st Co.F
Russey, Columbus Mead's Conf.Cav. Co.G
Russey, James J. AR 2nd Mtd.Rifles Hawkins' Co. Sgt.
Russey, James J. TX 27th Cav. Co.A Sgt.
Russey, J.W. TN 17th Inf. Co.D
Russey, W.P. GA Lt.Arty. Scogins' Btty. (Griffin Lt.Arty.)
Russhing, C. TN Cav. Napier's Bn. Co.D

Russi, David TX 3rd Inf. Co.H 1st Lt.
Russian, Charles C. GA 37th Inf. Co.I
Russian, L. GA 5th Res. Co.I
Russian, L.T. GA Cav. 1st Bn.Res. Tufts' Co.
Russian, Phillip AL Cav. Forrest's Regt.
Russian, Phillip TN 18th (Newsom's) Cav. Co.F
Russian, William AL Cav. Forrest's Regt.
Russian, William TN 18th (Newsom's) Cav. Co.F
Russian, William J. MS 10th Inf. New Co.C, Old Co.B
Russill, C.W. AL 40th Inf. Co.B
Russim, B.A. GA 41st Inf. Co.C
Russing, J.L. LA 4th Cav. Co.C
Russion, W.P. NC 26th Inf. Co.B
Russle, James NC 1st Jr.Res. Co.E
Russle, J.H. MO Parsons' Regt.
Russle, J.M. AR 21st Mil. Co.D
Russle, Joseph S. MS 22nd Inf. Co.D
Russle, S.M. AL Cav. Moreland's Regt. Co.D
Russman, Charles AL 20th Inf. Co.E
Russo, Agostino LA Mil. 6th Regt.Eur.Brig. (Italian Guards Bn.) Co.4
Russo, Agostno. LA Mil. 6th Regt.Eur.Brig. (Italian Guards Bn.) Co.3
Russo, Saverio LA Mil. 6th Regt.Eur.Brig. (Italian Guards Bn.) Co.4
Russoe, George AL 18th Inf.
Russom, George MS 19th Inf. Co.H
Russom, Henry C. TN 18th (Newsom's) Cav. Co.B,G
Russom, Henry C. TN Cav. Newsom's Regt. Co.A Cpl.
Russom, John Bradford's Corps Scouts & Guards Co.A
Russom, John M. TN 18th (Newsom's) Cav. Co.B Sgt.
Russom, John M. TN Cav. Newsom's Regt. Co.A
Russom, John P. GA Phillips' Legion Co.C
Russom, J.P. GA Cav. 6th Bn. (St.Guards) Co.G
Russom, J.W. MS Inf. 1st Bn.St.Troops (12 mo. '62-3) Co.D
Russom, M.Y. MS 44th Inf. Co.H
Russom, O.M. GA 22nd Inf. Co.C 1st Lt.
Russom, T.A. MS Inf. 1st Bn.St.Troops (12 mo. '62-3) Co.D
Russom, Thomas A. MS 3rd (St.Troops) Cav. Co.I
Russom, William GA 24th Inf. Co.B
Russom, William A. GA Phillips' Legion Co.C
Russon, H.C. TN 19th & 20th (Cons.) Cav. Co.H
Russon, John GA 2nd Inf. Co.I
Russum, B.A. MS 6th Inf. Co.K
Russum, Elihu NC 21st Inf. Co.M
Russum, Frank MS 6th Inf. Co.K
Russum, Henry B. MS 19th Inf. Co.H
Russum, J.I. MS 6th Inf. Co.K
Russum, J.J. MS Cav. 24th Bn. Co.F Sgt.
Russum, John MS 6th Inf. Co.K
Russum, John J. MS Cav. Hughes Bn. Co.B
Russum, S.W. MS Cav. 24th Bn. Co.F 1st Lt.
Russum, S.W. MS 16th Inf. Co.G
Russum, Thomas R. TX Cav. Wells' Bn.
Russum, W. AL 5th Inf. New Co.F
Russum, W. MS Cav. Hughes' Bn. Co.A

Russum, W. MS 5th Inf. (St.Troops) Co.A
Russum, William H. MS 4th Cav. Co.C
Russum, William H. MS Cav. Yerger's Regt. Co.C
Russworm, George R. TX 36th Cav. Co.G Sgt.
Russwurm, Samuel C. MS 17th Inf. Co.I Capt.
Russwurm, T.E.S. TN 9th (Ward's) Cav. Co.B 1st Lt.
Russy, Michael TX Conscr.
Rust, --- TN 21st & 22nd (Cons.) Cav. Co.C
Rust, A. TN 21st & 22nd (Cons.) Cav. Co.C
Rust, A. Gen. & Staff,PACS Brig.Gen.
Rust, A.C. TN 19th (Biffle's) Cav. Co.K Sgt.
Rust, A.G. AL Randolph Cty.Res. Shepherd's Co.
Rust, Albert AR 3rd Inf. Col.
Rust, Armistead T.K. VA Mil. 57th Regt. Col.
Rust, A.T.M. VA 19th Inf. Col.
Rust, A.T.M. Gen. & Staff, Military Court Dept. SW VA Col.
Rust, August TX 3rd Inf. Co.K
Rust, B.D. VA 17th Cav. Co.G
Rust, Benjamin D. VA 22nd Inf. Co.B
Rust, Benjamin F. LA Inf. 11th Bn. Co.F
Rust, B.F. LA 4th Inf. Co.C
Rust, B.F. LA 25th Inf. Co.K
Rust, B.F. Gen. & Staff Capt.,Comsy.
Rust, Bushrod VA 7th Cav. Co.E
Rust, Bushrod VA 12th Cav. Co.I Cpl.
Rust, Bushrod VA 17th Inf. Co.B
Rust, Charles P. VA 9th Cav. Co.C,H
Rust, Clay VA 12th Cav. Co.I Bvt.2nd Lt.
Rust, D.A. GA 10th Inf. Co.K
Rust, Edwin TX 8th Inf. Co.K
Rust, G.E. TN 12th Inf. Co.F 1st Sgt.
Rust, George B. VA 22nd Inf. Co.A 2nd Lt.
Rust, George H. VA 15th Cav. Co.G
Rust, George H. VA Cav. 15th Bn. Co.D
Rust, George H. VA 41st Mil. Co.C
Rust, George T. TN 12th (Cons.) Inf. Co.K
Rust, George W. AR 35th Inf. Co.D
Rust, Geo. W. Gen. & Staff AASurg.
Rust, G.M. TN 19th (Biffle's) Cav. Co.K
Rust, G.M. TN 31st Inf. Co.E
Rust, G.T. TN 47th Inf. Co.F Sgt.
Rust, G.W. AR 27th Inf. Co.I
Rust, G.W. KY 8th Mtd.Inf. Co.C
Rust, G.W. TN 31st Inf. Co.A
Rust, Henry D. VA 2nd Inf. Co.A Sgt.
Rust, Ira MO Inf. 5th Regt.St.Guard Co.D
Rust, J. AR 8th Cav. Co.F
Rust, J.A. AL 10th Inf. Co.H
Rust, J.A. TN 22nd (Barteau's) Cav. Co.I
Rust, J.A. TN 47th Inf. Co.H
Rust, Jacob VA 63rd Inf. Co.B
Rust, James AR 27th Inf. Co.I Music.
Rust, James VA 6th Cav. Co.H Cpl.
Rust, James A. AR 3rd Inf. Co.C AQM
Rust, James A. Gen. & Staff, A. of N.VA Capt.,AQM
Rust, James W. KY 8th Mtd.Inf. Co.A Sgt.
Rust, James W. VA 6th Cav. Co.H
Rust, James W. VA 22nd Inf. Co.A
Rust, J.C. Mead's Conf.Cav. Co.I Cpl.
Rust, Jeremiah VA 6th Bn.Res. Co.C
Rust, Jerry T. AR 35th Inf. Co.D
Rust, J.F.M. TN 12th Inf. Co.K

Rust, J.H. KY 3rd Mtd.Inf. Co.B
Rust, J.M. TN Douglass' Bn.Part.Rangers Bruster's Co. 2nd Lt.
Rust, J.M. VA 34th Mil. Co.D
Rust, J.M. Gen. & Staff A.Surg.
Rust, J.N. KY 3rd Mtd.Inf. Co.B
Rust, J.N. TN 19th (Biffle's) Cav. Co.K Cpl.
Rust, John AR 27th Inf. Co.I Music.
Rust, John AR Inf. Hardy's Regt. Co.A
Rust, John MO 3rd Inf. Co.I
Rust, John C. TN 34th Inf. Co.G
Rust, John C. VA 9th Cav. Co.C
Rust, John L. KY 1st Inf. Co.K
Rust, John L. TN 60th Mtd.Inf. Co.C
Rust, John M. TN 10th & 11th (Cons.) Cav. Co.A Capt.
Rust, John M. TN 11th (Holman's) Cav. Co.L 1st Lt.
Rust, John R. VA 12th Cav. Co.I Lt.
Rust, John T. MS 30th Inf. Co.G 2nd Lt.
Rust, John W. GA 32nd Inf. Co.D 1st Lt.
Rust, John W. KY 1st Inf. Co.K
Rust, J.R. MO Inf. 4th Regt.St.Guard Co.E
Rust, J.W. TN 19th (Biffle's) Cav. Co.K Sgt.
Rust, J.W. TN 31st Inf. Co.E Sgt.
Rust, Lemuel W. AR 35th Inf. Co.D
Rust, Leroy T. TN 14th Inf. Co.K
Rust, Lewis TN 11th Inf. Co.F
Rust, Lind T. KY Cav. 2nd Bn. (Dortch's) Co.C
Rust, L.T. KY 10th (Johnson's) Cav. Co.A,C
Rust, L.T. KY Morgan's Men Co.G
Rust, Martin V. AR 17th (Griffith's) Inf. Co.C
Rust, Moris LA 1st Hvy.Arty. (Reg.) Co.K
Rust, M.V. AR 11th & 17th Cons.Inf. Co.I
Rust, M.V. AR 35th Inf. Co.A Cpl.
Rust, Newton H. MS 29th Inf. Co.D
Rust, Nimrod A. VA 6th Cav. Co.H
Rust, Oscar L. GA 34th Inf. Co.G
Rust, P.E. GA 4th Res. Co.K
Rust, P.J. AL 3rd Inf. Co.H
Rust, R.L. KY 9th Mtd.Inf. Co.A
Rust, R.L.B. VA 2nd St.Res. Co.F
Rust, Robert S. AR 3rd Inf. Co.C
Rust, Robert S. VA 6th Cav. Co.H
Rust, R.S. TX 4th Inf. Co.B Sgt.
Rust, S.A. TN 22nd (Barteau's) Cav. Co.I
Rust, S.R.M. Mead's Conf.Cav. Co.I
Rust, T.B. KY 7th Mtd.Inf. Co.F
Rust, Thomas KY 5th Cav. Co.D
Rust, Thomas VA Cav. Mosby's Regt. (Part. Rangers)
Rust, Thomas B. TN 35th Inf. Co.B Capt.
Rust, Thomas G. VA 2nd Inf. Co.A
Rust, Valentine C. VA 63rd Inf. Co.B 1st Lt.
Rust, V.C. VA 21st Cav. 2nd Co.C
Rust, V.G. TN Inf. 154th Sr.Regt. Co.F
Rust, W. AR 8th Cav. Co.F
Rust, W.B. NC McLean's Bn.Lt.Duty Men Co.A
Rust, W.H. KY 9th Mtd.Inf. Co.A
Rust, W.H. TN 19th (Biffle's) Cav. Co.K
Rust, W.H. TX 13th Vol. 1st Co.H
Rust, William AR 1st Vol. Co.G
Rust, William KY 7th Mtd.Inf. Co.F Cpl.
Rust, William LA Inf. 10th Bn. Co.H
Rust, William VA 2nd Inf. Co.D
Rust, William H. TN 11th Inf. Co.F

Rust, William H. TX 35th (Brown's) Cav. Co.C Jr.2nd Lt.
Rust, William J. KY 1st Inf. Co.K
Rust, William M. TX 21st Cav. Co.B Capt.
Rust, William M. VA 12th Cav. Co.I
Rust, William O. VA 17th Inf. Co.B
Rust, William R. VA 9th Cav. Co.C
Rust, William S. AL 10th Inf. Co.H
Rust, W.J. AR 27th Inf. Co.I
Rust, W.J. TN 47th Inf. Co.F 1st Sgt.
Rust, W.W. TN 5th Inf. 1st Co.C
Rust, Y.G. GA Cav. 15th Bn. (St.Guards) Jones' Co.
Rust, Youel G. GA 4th Inf. Co.E Capt.
Rustan, John TN Cav. 12th Bn. (Day's) Co.B
Rustenbach, Adolph LA 13th Inf. Co.D
Rustin, Benjamin W. GA Cav. 1st Bn. Hughes' Co.
Rustin, B.W. GA 7th Cav. Co.H
Rustin, B.W. GA Hardwick Mtd.Rifles Co.B
Rustin, H. TN Cav. Cox's Bn. Co.A
Rustin, J. TX Inf. 1st St.Troops Whitehead's Co.
Rustin, John GA Cav. 1st Bn. Hughes' Co.
Rustin, John M. MS 36th Inf. Co.I
Rustin, J.P. GA 5th Cav. Co.D
Rustin, S.B. GA 5th Cav. Co.D 2nd Lt.
Rustin, Seaborn B. GA Cav. 1st Bn. Hughes' Co. 3rd Lt.
Rustin, W.B. GA 5th Cav. Co.K
Ruston, --- TX Cav. Mann's Regt. Co.C
Ruston, Andrew J. TN 61st Mtd.Inf. Co.A
Ruston, Elijah TN 48th (Voorhies') Inf. Co.G
Ruston, H. TN 21st (Carter's) Cav. Co.G
Ruston, Hiram TN 37th Inf. Co.D
Ruston, J.E. MS 39th Inf. Co.D
Ruston, J.J. TN 37th Inf. Co.D
Ruston, J.M. TN 19th & 20th (Cons.) Cav. Co.B Sgt.
Ruston, John M. TX 24th Cav. Co.K
Ruston, Joseph TN 61st Mtd.Inf. Co.A
Ruston, William TN Cav. 12th Bn. (Day's) Co.F
Rustworm, George A. TX 16th Inf. Co.I
Rutcher, John TX Cav. Bourland's Regt. Co.B
Ruter, J.M. GA 3rd Inf. Co.D
Ruth, Abraham J. GA 2nd Inf. 1st Co.B
Ruth, Abraham J. GA 26th Inf. Co.E
Ruth, Abraham M. SC 2nd Cav. Co.B Capt.
Ruth, Abraham M. SC Cav.Bn. Hampton Legion Co.C Sgt.
Ruth, Adam LA Mil. Fire Bn. Co.F
Ruth, A.J. GA Cav. 20th Bn. Co.C
Ruth, A.J. SC 11th Inf. Co.E
Ruth, A.L. AL 28th Inf. Co.H
Ruth, Ambrose D. MO 1st Cav. Co.H
Ruth, Ambrose D. MO Cav. 3rd Bn. Co.B
Ruth, Andrew J. MS 31st Inf. Co.A
Ruth, Andrew J. NC 1st Arty. (10th St.Troops) Co.D
Ruth, Benjamin GA 10th Inf. 1st Co.K
Ruth, Benjamin H. GA Lt.Arty. Fraser's Btty.
Ruth, B.H. NC 18th Inf. Co.K
Ruth, Braxton R. NC 25th Inf. Co.H
Ruth, C.E. AL Herron's Regt. Home Guards Co.B Sgt.
Ruth, Charles L. Gen. & Staff, Medical Dept. Hosp.Stew.
Ruth, C.L. TN 23rd Inf. Co.D

Ruth, Edward W. KY 3rd Cav. Co.D
Ruth, Edward W. KY 7th Cav. Co.F
Ruth, E.J. GA 12th (Wright's) Cav. (St.Guards) Longstreet's Co. Cpl.
Ruth, E.J. SC 3rd Cav. Co.F
Ruth, E.W. KY Cav. 2nd Bn. (Dortch's) Co.A
Ruth, Ferd MO Inf. 3rd Regt.St.Guard Co.E Maj.
Ruth, Hopkins D. GA 65th Inf. Co.G
Ruth, I.L. NC Harr's Bn. Co.B
Ruth, James GA 52nd Inf. Co.A
Ruth, James A. TN 62nd Inf. Co.A
Ruth, James M. TX 16th Cav. Co.E
Ruth, J.H. AR 7th Mil. Co.A
Ruth, Joab TN 51st (Cons.) Inf. Co.C
Ruth, John AR 6th Inf. Co.H
Ruth, John GA 52nd Inf. Co.A
Ruth, John NC 16th Inf. Co.F
Ruth, John VA 30th Bn.S.S. Co.E
Ruth, John VA Mil. Scott Cty.
Ruth, John C. TN 41st Inf. Co.F Sgt.
Ruth, John W. MO Cav. 3rd Bn. Co.B
Ruth, Jonathan H. TX 34th Cav. Co.F
Ruth, Joseph B. TN 39th Mtd.Inf. Co.G
Ruth, Lorenzo D. NC 1st Arty. (10th St.Troops) Co.D
Ruth, M.H. AR 2nd Cav. Co.F
Ruth, M.H. TN 9th Inf. Co.A
Ruth, M.L. TN 32nd Inf. Co.A
Ruth, N.A. GA 11th Inf. Co.B Cpl.
Ruth, R. TN Inf. Nashville Bn. Fulcher's Co.
Ruth, R.G. SC 5th Cav. Co.B
Ruth, R.M. NC 3rd Bn. Co.K
Ruth, Robert GA 16th Inf. Co.E
Ruth, Rufus TX 19th Inf. Co.B Comsy.
Ruth, Rufus Gen. & Staff Capt.,Comsy.
Ruth, Rufus H. NC 14th Inf. Co.K
Ruth, Samuel VA 2nd St.Res. Co.G Capt.
Ruth, S.D. MS 28th Cav. Co.E
Ruth, S.D. TN 32nd Inf. Co.A
Ruth, Sevier W. NC 56th Inf. Co.G
Ruth, Simpson GA 1st Reg. Co.K Cpl.
Ruth, Solomon NC 53rd Inf. Co.B
Ruth, Solomon VA 53rd Inf. Co.B
Ruth, Starling D. MS 42nd Inf. Co.G
Ruth, Thomas GA 45th Inf. Co.A
Ruth, Thomas VA 25th Cav. Co.K
Ruth, Thomas VA Mil. Scott Cty.
Ruth, Walter VA Cav. 1st Bn. (Loc.Def.Troops) Co.A
Ruth, W.H. VA 2nd St.Res. Co.G Cpl.
Ruth, William NC 66th Inf. Co.G
Ruth, William C. NC 56th Inf. Co.G
Ruth, William J. GA 52nd Inf. Co.A
Ruth, Wilson A. NC 60th Inf. Co.D
Ruth, W.M. NC 42nd Inf. Co.D
Ruthe, S.D. MS 8th Cav. Co.F,B
Ruthe, Solomon TN Cav. Newsom's Regt. Co.F
Ruther, A. LA Mil. 4th Regt. 2nd Brig. 1st Div. Co.D
Ruther, F. AL 4th Res. Co.B
Ruther, F.M. AL 1st Regt. Mobile Vol. Baas' Co.
Rutherferd, A.S. GA 3rd Mil. Capt.
Rutherferd, W.B. TX Cav. Giddings' Bn. Onins' Co.
Rutherford, --- TX Cav. Bourland's Regt. Co.G

Rutherford, --- TX Coopwood's Spy Co.
Rutherford, --- TX Cav. Mann's Regt. Co.D
Rutherford, --- VA VMI Co.C
Rutherford, A. AR 5th Mil. Co.I
Rutherford, A. MS 15th Inf. Co.A
Rutherford, A. 3rd Conf.Cav. Co.D
Rutherford, A.A. TX Inf. 1st Bn. (St.Troops) Co.F
Rutherford, A.A. TX Inf. Rutherford's Co. Capt.
Rutherford, A.C. KY 7th Cav. Co.H
Rutherford, Adolphus S. GA 6th Inf. (St.Guards) Co.F Sgt.
Rutherford, A.H. GA 2nd Inf. Co.G
Rutherford, A.H. VA 67th Mil. Co.E
Rutherford, Albert S. TN 28th Cav. Co.A
Rutherford, Alex VA 63rd Inf. 1st Co.I
Rutherford, Alexander SC 2nd Cav. Co.I
Rutherford, Alexander SC Cav.Bn. Hampton Legion Co.A Far.
Rutherford, Alexander TN 19th Inf. Co.I
Rutherford, Alexander C. KY 3rd Cav. Co.H
Rutherford, Alexander H. VA 1st St.Res. Co.F
Rutherford, Alexander L. VA 50th Inf. 1st Co.G
Rutherford, Alex E. VA 50th Inf. Co.B,D Cpl.
Rutherford, Alfred Conf.Cav. Clarkson's Bn. Ind.Rangers Co.C
Rutherford, Andrew NC 37th Inf. Co.K
Rutherford, Antine G. FL 7th Inf. Co.H Bvt.2nd Lt.
Rutherford, Archibald VA 11th Cav. Co.C
Rutherford, A.S. VA 10th Inf. 2nd Co.C
Rutherford, A. Sidney TN 24th Inf. 2nd Co.G, Co.L
Rutherford, Augustus H. GA 1st Reg. Co.L,A,K 1st Lt.
Rutherford, B. AR 11th & 17th Cons.Inf. Co.I
Rutherford, Benjamin AR 17th (Griffith's) Inf. Co.C
Rutherford, Benjamin O. TN 7th Inf. Co.E,C
Rutherford, B.F. VA 4th Res. Co.E
Rutherford, B.H. GA 23rd Inf. Co.F Cpl.
Rutherford, C.C. MS 35th Inf. Co.F
Rutherford, C.C. TX 16th Inf. Co.F Cpl.
Rutherford, Charles H. TN 59th Mtd.Inf. Co.A Sgt.
Rutherford, Charlton MO 11th Inf. Co.I
Rutherford, Cheseldon C. TN 4th (McLemore's) Cav. Co.B 1st Lt.
Rutherford, C.L. AR 34th Inf. Co.D
Rutherford, Clark AL 29th Inf. Co.C
Rutherford, Clinton TX 36th Cav. Co.E Cpl.
Rutherford, Clinton TX Cav. Benavides' Regt. Co.G
Rutherford, C.T. AL 29th Inf. Co.F,I Cpl.
Rutherford, David F. MS 23rd Inf. Co.G
Rutherford, D.C. TX 12th Inf. Co.I Cpl.
Rutherford, Dionicious VA 146th Mil. Co.H
Rutherford, D.M. VA 51st Inf. Co.I
Rutherford, D.N. VA Mil. Grayson Cty.
Rutherford, E. SC 2nd St.Troops Co.B
Rutherford, E.H. GA Arty. (Macon Lt.Arty.) Slaten's Co. Sgt.
Rutherford, E.L. GA 5th Res. Co.F
Rutherford, Elbert GA 57th Inf. Co.D
Rutherford, Elijah SC 22nd Inf. Co.A
Rutherford, Eli S. AL 63rd Inf. Co.C 1st Sgt.

Rutherford, Elliott TN 24th Inf. 2nd Co.G
Rutherford, E.S. GA Inf. 27th Bn. (NonConscr.) Co.C
Rutherford, Eugenius H. GA 1st (Ramsey's) Inf. Co.C
Rutherford, F. MO Lt.Arty. 3rd Field Btty.
Rutherford, F.A. AL 23rd Inf. Co.B 1st Lt.
Rutherford, F.C. GA 6th Inf. (St.Guards) Co.A
Rutherford, Fielding TN 26th Inf. Co.C
Rutherford, F.M. TN Cav. 16th Bn. (Neal's) Co.D
Rutherford, Francis S. AL 4th Inf. Co.B
Rutherford, Frank Gillum's Regt. Co.G
Rutherford, Franklin AL 3rd Inf. Co.D Color Sgt.
Rutherford, Franklin W. MS 15th Inf. Co.A
Rutherford, G. TX Cav. Benavides' Regt. Co.H Sgt.
Rutherford, George AL 18th Bn.Vol. Co.A
Rutherford, George AL 32nd Inf. Co.A
Rutherford, George GA 48th Inf. Co.A
Rutherford, George MS Standefer's Co.
Rutherford, George W. FL 11th Inf. Co.K
Rutherford, George W. KY 2nd Bn.Mtd.Rifles Co.D Sgt.
Rutherford, George W. VA 48th Inf. Co.G
Rutherford, Gerard D. VA 2nd Inf. Co.A
Rutherford, Gideon M. TN 7th Inf. Co.I
Rutherford, G.J. MS 40th Inf. Co.A
Rutherford, G.M.T. AL 39th Inf. Co.A
Rutherford, Granville TN 34th Inf. Co.F
Rutherford, Griffith TX 1st (McCulloch's) Cav. Co.K
Rutherford, Griffith TX 1st (Yager's) Cav. Co.I 2nd Lt.
Rutherford, Griffith TX Cav. 8th (Taylor's) Bn. Co.D Sgt.
Rutherford, G.S. MS 10th Inf. New Co.K Sr.2nd Lt.
Rutherford, G.W. AR 1st (Dobbin's) Cav. Co.D Capt.
Rutherford, G.W. AR Lt.Arty. Key's Btty.
Rutherford, G.W. MS 2nd St.Cav. Co.G
Rutherford, H. AL St.Arty. Co.C
Rutherford, H. AR Lt.Arty. Marshall's Btty.
Rutherford, H. VA 7th Bn.Res. Co.D
Rutherford, H. 1st Chickasaw Inf. Gregg's Co. Cpl.
Rutherford, H.C. KY 9th Mtd.Inf. Co.G
Rutherford, Henry AL 19th Inf. Co.K
Rutherford, Henry AL Mil. Bligh's Co. 1st Lt.
Rutherford, Henry AR 1st Inf. Co.A
Rutherford, Henry TN 50th Inf. Co.E
Rutherford, Henry R. AR 15th (N.W.) Inf. Co.A
Rutherford, H.J. GA Cav. 6th Bn. (St.Guards) Co.B
Rutherford, Horace M. LA 16th Inf. Co.C
Rutherford, Hubbard GA Cav. Nelson's Ind.Co.
Rutherford, Hudson KY 5th Mtd.Inf. Surg.
Rutherford, Hudson Gen. & Staff Surg.
Rutherford, Ira AL 19th Inf. Co.K,I
Rutherford, Isaac TN Inf. 3rd Cons.Regt. Co.H Cpl.
Rutherford, Isaac TN 19th Inf. Co.E Cpl.
Rutherford, J. GA Arty. Maxwell's Reg.Lt.Btty.
Rutherford, J. GA 8th Inf.
Rutherford, J. GA 16th Inf. Co.H

Rutherford, J. LA Cav. Benjamin's Co.
Rutherford, J. MO Lt.Arty. Von Phul's Co.
Rutherford, J. TX 33rd Cav. Co.K
Rutherford, J.A. AL 12th Cav. Co.D
Rutherford, J.A. AL 53rd (Part.Rangers) Co.D
Rutherford, J.A.H. MS Lt.Arty. 14th Bn.
Rutherford, James AL 1st Regt. Mobile Vol. Co.C Sgt.
Rutherford, James AL 33rd Inf. Co.F
Rutherford, James AL Mil. Bligh's Co.
Rutherford, James AR Cav. Crabtree's (46th) Regt. Capt.,AQM
Rutherford, James AR 7th Inf. Co.E Lt.Col.
Rutherford, James GA 34th Inf. Co.B
Rutherford, James GA 35th Inf. Co.I
Rutherford, James MO 8th Cav. Co.H
Rutherford, James TN Lt.Arty. Burroughs' Co.
Rutherford, James TN 59th Mtd.Inf. Co.A
Rutherford, James 1st Conf.Reg.Cav. Co.A Sgt.
Rutherford, James A. MO 5th Cav. Co.E
Rutherford, James A. TN 40th Inf. Co.D
Rutherford, James C. Gen. & Staff Capt.,AA,IG
Rutherford, James E. TN 2nd (Ashby's) Cav. Co.G
Rutherford, James E. TN Cav. 4th Bn. (Branner's) Co.B
Rutherford, James E. TX 11th (Spaight's) Bn.Vol. Co.C
Rutherford, James F. SC 14th Inf. Co.B
Rutherford, James M. MS 34th Inf. Co.A Jr.2nd Lt.
Rutherford, James M. TN 37th Inf. Co.A
Rutherford, James M. TN 59th Mtd.Inf.
Rutherford, James R. NC 25th Inf. Co.I
Rutherford, James R. VA 63rd Inf. Co.A
Rutherford, James S. GA 30th Inf. Co.C Sgt.
Rutherford, James S. GA 31st Inf. Co.C Sgt.
Rutherford, James W. AR 35th Inf. Co.B
Rutherford, James W. TX 18th Inf. Co.F
Rutherford, Jasper G. TX 11th (Spaight's) Bn.Vol. Co.G
Rutherford, J.B. MS 6th Inf. Co.B
Rutherford, J.B. MS 46th Inf. Co.D
Rutherford, J.B. TN 29th Inf. Co.F
Rutherford, J.C. TN 1st (Carter's) Cav. Co.K
Rutherford, J.C. VA 10th Cav. 2nd Co.E
Rutherford, Jefferson VA Mil. Grayson Cty.
Rutherford, J.G. TX 12th Cav. Co.A Cpl.
Rutherford, J.H. AL 4th (Russell's) Cav. Co.F 1st Sgt.
Rutherford, J.H. GA 12th (Robinson's) Cav. (St.Guards) Co.D
Rutherford, J.H. MS 32nd Inf. Co.G
Rutherford, J.H. TN 63rd Inf. Co.K
Rutherford, J.J. AL 17th Inf. Co.H
Rutherford, J.J. GA Lt.Arty. Daniell's Btty. Cpl.
Rutherford, J.J. 2nd Conf.Eng.Troops Co.A
Rutherford, J. Jordan FL 11th Inf. Co.E
Rutherford, J.K. TX 3rd Cav. Co.H
Rutherford, J.L. MS 2nd St.Cav. Co.A
Rutherford, J.L. MS 1st (King's) Inf. (St.Troops) Co.E
Rutherford, J.L. MS 23rd Inf. Co.G
Rutherford, J.L. MS 34th Inf. Co.A
Rutherford, J.M. MS 24th Inf. Co.H 2nd Lt.
Rutherford, J.M. TN 1st (Carter's) Cav. Co.C
Rutherford, J.O. AL 24th Inf. Co.E

Rutherford, John GA 3rd Cav. (St.Guards) Co.A
Rutherford, John GA Hvy.Arty. 22nd Bn. Co.D
Rutherford, John GA 1st (Fannin's) Res. Co.D Cpl.
Rutherford, John GA Inf. 14th Bn. (St.Guards) Co.B
Rutherford, John GA 35th Inf. Co.I
Rutherford, John GA 60th Inf. Co.C
Rutherford, John TN Lt.Arty. Burroughs' Co.
Rutherford, John TN Arty. Ramsey's Btty.
Rutherford, John TX 1st Hvy.Arty. Co.H
Rutherford, John, Jr. VA 34th Mil. Co.A
Rutherford, John VA 50th Inf. Co.B Sgt.
Rutherford, John VA 64th Mtd.Inf. Co.K
Rutherford, John A. TN 4th (McLemore's) Cav. Co.B
Rutherford, John A. VA 11th Cav. Co.E Cpl.
Rutherford, John A. VA 2nd Inf. Co.H
Rutherford, John B. MS 12th Inf. Co.D
Rutherford, John C. GA Cobb's Legion Co.C Adj.
Rutherford, John C. VA 52nd Inf. Co.F Cpl.
Rutherford, John C. Gen. & Staff,PACS Capt.,AAG
Rutherford, John D. VA 6th Bn.Res. Co.B 1st Lt.
Rutherford, John E. VA 31st Inf. Co.A
Rutherford, John F. TN 5th (McKenzie's) Cav. Co.B
Rutherford, John H. AL 17th Bn.S.S. Co.A
Rutherford, John H. AL 19th Inf. Co.K
Rutherford, John H. TN 5th Inf. Co.A
Rutherford, John J. TN 63rd Inf. Co.E
Rutherford, John J. VA Mtd.Guard 4th Congr.Dist.
Rutherford, John R. AL 29th Inf. Co.C
Rutherford, John R. MS Inf. 3rd Bn. Co.F 1st Lt.
Rutherford, John S. AL 3rd Inf. Co.E
Rutherford, John T. VA 11th Cav. Co.E
Rutherford, John W. TN 59th Mtd.Inf. Co.F Cpl.
Rutherford, John William VA 49th Inf. Co.E
Rutherford, John W.P. AL 16th Inf. Co.F Sgt.
Rutherford, Joseph AL 18th Bn.Vol. Co.A
Rutherford, Joseph FL 6th Inf. Co.H Cpl.
Rutherford, Joseph TN 17th Inf.
Rutherford, Joseph TN Sullivan Cty.Res. (Loc.Def.Troops) White's Co.
Rutherford, Joseph D. MS 1st Lt.Arty. Co.C
Rutherford, J.P. TN Conscr. (Cp. of Instr.)
Rutherford, J.R. MS 7th Cav. Co.D
Rutherford, J.R. MO 9th Inf. Co.D
Rutherford, J.R. MO Inf. Clark's Regt. Co.C
Rutherford, J.R. TN 3rd (Lillard's) Mtd.Inf. Co.A
Rutherford, J.T. AL 22nd Inf. Co.F
Rutherford, J.W. AR 15th (N.W.) Inf. Co.D
Rutherford, J.W. TN 45th Inf. Co.F
Rutherford, J. Wesley FL 11th Inf. Co.E
Rutherford, L. AR Cav. Crabtree's (46th) Regt. Co.A
Rutherford, Lewis GA 6th Cav. Co.H
Rutherford, L.I. MS 3rd Cav.Res. Co.B
Rutherford, Lorenzo TX 17th Cav. Co.E
Rutherford, Lorenzo M. TX 17th Cons. Dismtd.Cav. Co.K

Rutherford, M.A. AL Cav. Chisolm's Co. 1st Sgt.
Rutherford, Maberry VA 36th Inf. 2nd Co.B
Rutherford, Marcus S. VA 31st Inf. Co.A
Rutherford, M.B. TX 9th (Young's) Inf. Co.A
Rutherford, Meloin A. FL Cav. 5th Bn. Co.I 2nd Lt.
Rutherford, Melvin A. FL 6th Inf. Co.D Music.
Rutherford, Middleton B. VA 31st Inf. Co.A
Rutherford, M.M. MS Lt.Arty. Yates' Btty.
Rutherford, Moses Brush Bn.
Rutherford, M.S. TX 18th Cav. Co.H
Rutherford, Nathaniel VA 36th Inf. Co.B
Rutherford, N.D. MO 1st & 4th Cons.Inf. Co.H
Rutherford, N.D. MO 4th Inf. Co.K
Rutherford, Newton F. TX 1st Bn.S.S. Co.C
Rutherford, N.R. TX 35th (Brown's) Cav. Co.C
Rutherford, O.A. GA 12th (Robinson's) Cav. (St.Guards) Co.E Cpl.
Rutherford, Patrick H. AL 61st Inf. Co.I
Rutherford, Preston TN 25th Inf. Co.E
Rutherford, R. TN 7th (Duckworth's) Cav. Co.I
Rutherford, R. TN 14th (Neely's) Cav. Co.F
Rutherford, R. TX Inf. Griffin's Bn. Co.F
Rutherford, R.A. AR 34th Inf. Co.K
Rutherford, R.A. GA 10th Cav. Co.D
Rutherford, R.A. GA 17th Inf. Co.C
Rutherford, R.A. 7th Conf.Cav. Co.D
Rutherford, Ralph W. TX 13th Vol. 3rd Co.K
Rutherford, Randolph TN Sullivan Cty.Res. (Loc.Def.Troops) White's Co.
Rutherford, R.B. AR 6th Inf. Old Co.F 1st Lt.
Rutherford, R.B. Gen. & Staff, Comsy.Subs. Agent
Rutherford, R.C. TX 4th Inf. Co.C
Rutherford, R.D. LA 27th Inf. Co.G
Rutherford, R.H.L. Gen. & Staff Asst.Surg.
Rutherford, Richard TX 19th Cav. Co.B
Rutherford, Richmond TN 4th Inf. Co.I
Rutherford, R.M. GA 2nd Inf. Co.G
Rutherford, R.M. TN 55th (Brown's) Inf. Co.C Sgt.
Rutherford, R.M. TX Cav. 6th Bn. Co.B Cpl.
Rutherford, Robert KY 3rd Cav. Co.H
Rutherford, Robert KY 7th Cav. Co.H
Rutherford, Robert TN 61st Mtd.Inf. Co.C
Rutherford, Robert VA 3rd Cav. Co.G
Rutherford, Robert VA 49th Inf. Co.E
Rutherford, Robert C. TX Inf. Townsend's Co. (Robertson Five S.)
Rutherford, Robert M. GA Cav. Nelson's Ind.Co. 1st Sgt.
Rutherford, Robert N. KY 3rd Cav.
Rutherford, Robert R. GA 1st Reg. Co.K,D 2nd Lt.
Rutherford, Robert R. GA Cobb's Legion Co.L
Rutherford, Robert T. AL 3rd Inf. Co.D,L 1st Lt.
Rutherford, Robert W. GA 3rd Inf. Co.E
Rutherford, Robert Walker MS 34th Inf. Co.A
Rutherford, R.R. GA Arty. Maxwell's Reg. Lt.Btty. Lt.
Rutherford, R.R. GA Inf. 27th Bn. (NonConscr.) Co.D 2nd Lt.
Rutherford, Rufus, Jr. KY 1st Inf. Co.A
Rutherford, Rufus TN 2nd (Ashby's) Cav. Co.G Cpl.

Rutherford, R.W. GA Arty. (Macon Lt.Arty.) Slaten's Co. Cpl.
Rutherford, R.W. GA Inf. 2nd Bn. Co.B
Rutherford, Samuel AL 17th Inf. Co.D
Rutherford, Samuel AL 33rd Inf. Co.F
Rutherford, Samuel FL 4th Inf. Co.C
Rutherford, Samuel VA 31st Inf. Co.A 1st Sgt.
Rutherford, Samuel VA 36th Inf. 2nd Co.B
Rutherford, S.F. MS 18th Inf. Co.K
Rutherford, S.M. AR 7th Mil. Asst.Surg.
Rutherford, Stephen LA Res.Corps
Rutherford, T.A. AR Inf. Sparks' Co. 2nd Lt.
Rutherford, T.B. GA Lt.Arty. King's Btty. QMSgt.
Rutherford, T.B. Conf.Arty. Palmer's Bn. QMSgt.
Rutherford, T.F. TN 24th Inf. Co.F Sgt.
Rutherford, T.H. KY 2nd (Duke's) Cav. Co.E
Rutherford, T.H. TN 7th (Duckworth's) Cav. Co.I
Rutherford, Thomas AR Cav. Gordon's Regt. Co.A
Rutherford, Thomas GA Lt.Arty. Havis' Btty.
Rutherford, Thomas NC 26th Inf. Co.A Cpl.
Rutherford, Thomas TN 4th Inf. Co.I
Rutherford, Thomas TX 35th (Brown's) Cav. Co.C
Rutherford, Thomas VA 12th Cav. Co.D
Rutherford, Thomas VA 21st Cav. 2nd Co.I
Rutherford, Thomas VA Lt.Arty. 13th Bn. Co.A
Rutherford, Thomas A. AR 35th Inf. Co.C Sgt.
Rutherford, Thomas A. TX 1st (Yager's) Cav. Co.I
Rutherford, Thomas B. GA Lt.Arty. 14th Bn. Co.B,F Sgt.
Rutherford, Thomas B. GA Lt.Arty. Anderson's Btty.
Rutherford, Thomas B. GA 1st Reg. Co.A
Rutherford, Thomas Franklin MS 34th Inf. Co.A Sgt.
Rutherford, Thomas H. VA 11th Cav. Co.E
Rutherford, Thomas J. AL 8th Inf. Co.A
Rutherford, Thomas J. VA 4th Cav. Co.F
Rutherford, Thomas J. VA 56th Inf. Co.F
Rutherford, Thomas M. GA 41st Inf. Co.C
Rutherford, Thomas W. VA 2nd Inf. Co.H
Rutherford, Timothy VA Inf. 23rd Bn. Co.C
Rutherford, T.J. MS 40th Inf. Co.K
Rutherford, T.M. VA 3rd Inf.Loc.Def. 1st Co.G
Rutherford, T.R. GA 23rd Inf. Co.F
Rutherford, V.H. MS 6th Inf. Co.H
Rutherford, W. GA 1st (Olmstead's) Inf. Gordon's Co.
Rutherford, W. MS 3rd Inf. (St.Troops) Co.C
Rutherford, W. TX 7th Cav. Co.A
Rutherford, W.C. AL 8th Inf. Co.A
Rutherford, W.C. AL 20th Inf. Co.H
Rutherford, W.C. AL 29th Inf. Co.C
Rutherford, W.E. MS Cav. 17th Bn. Co.E
Rutherford, W.E. 1st Conf.Inf. Post Comsy.
Rutherford, W.H. VA 9th Bn.Res. Co.A
Rutherford, Wm. AL 30th Inf. Co.K 1st Lt.
Rutherford, William GA 2nd Cav. (St.Guards) Co.D
Rutherford, William GA 3rd (Johnson's) St.Troops Co.A
Rutherford, William GA 63rd Inf. Co.K Sgt.

Rutherford, William NC 25th Inf. Co.I
Rutherford, William SC Inf. Holcombe Legion Co.G
Rutherford, William TN 21st (Wilson's) Cav. Co.G
Rutherford, William TN 21st & 22nd (Cons.) Cav. Co.K,I
Rutherford, William TN 26th Inf. Co.C Sgt.
Rutherford, William TN Detailed Conscr. Co.B
Rutherford, William VA Cav. 1st Bn. (Loc.Def.Troops) Co.A
Rutherford, William VA 49th Inf. Co.E
Rutherford, William 15th Conf.Cav. Co.H
Rutherford, William A.R. TN 5th (McKenzie's) Cav. Co.B
Rutherford, William B. AL 6th Inf. Co.G
Rutherford, William D. SC 3rd Inf. Col.
Rutherford, William E. LA Inf. 2nd Regt. Co.I 1st Lt.
Rutherford, William E. VA Cav. 1st Bn. Co.A
Rutherford, Wm. E. Gen. & Staff, Comsy.Dept. Capt.
Rutherford, William F. VA 50th Inf. 1st Co.G 2nd Lt.
Rutherford, William F. VA 63rd Inf. Co.A Sgt.
Rutherford, William J. GA Lt.Arty. Milledge's Co.
Rutherford, Wm. J. GA Conscr.
Rutherford, William P. TN 59th Mtd.Inf. Co.E
Rutherford, Williams GA 9th Inf. (St.Guards) Co.H
Rutherford, Williams GA 45th Inf. Co.K Capt.
Rutherford, William T. TX 35th (Likens') Cav. Co.D
Rutherford, William W. GA 23rd Inf. Co.F
Rutherford, William W. MS 2nd St.Cav. Co.A Capt.
Rutherford, W.J. GA Inf. 1st Loc.Troops (Augusta) Barnes' Lt.Arty.Co.
Rutherford, Wm. MS Lt.Arty. 14th Bn. Co.A
Rutherford, W.P. GA 5th Inf. Co.H
Rutherford, W.P. TN 2nd (Smith's) Cav. Lea's Co.
Rutherford, W.P. 3rd Conf.Cav. Co.A
Rutherford, W.W. GA 29th Inf. Co.G
Rutherford, Zebulon B. TX 18th Inf. Co.F
Rutherfourd, J.A.H. MS Lt.Arty. Yates' Btty.
Ruthers, M. LA 15th Inf. Co.K
Ruthledge, Absalom F. VA 6th Inf. Co.D
Ruthler, --- TX 8th Field Btty.
Ruthler, --- TX Lt.Arty. Dege's Bn.
Ruthley, --- TX 8th Inf. Co.A
Ruths, Adam LA Mil. 1st Regt. 3rd Brig. 1st Div.
Ruthven, A.G. MS Cav. (St.Troops) Gamblin's Co. Cpl.
Ruthven, Cornelius G. SC 2nd Arty. Co.D
Ruthven, H.G. SC 2nd Arty. Co.D
Ruthven, John B. Parson's Brig. Maj.,ACS
Ruthven, John G. MS 26th Inf. Co.E
Ruthven, William C. MS 40th Inf. Co.I Cpl.
Rutlage, F.M. TN 12th Inf. Co.F
Rutlage, James TN 45th Inf. Co.B
Rutlage, John GA 6th Cav. Co.G
Rutlage, J.T. TN 12th Inf. Co.F
Rutlage, R.N. AR 30th Inf. Co.H
Rutlage, Sanford AL 42nd Inf. Co.G

Rutland, --- AL 1st Regt.Conscr. Co.I
Rutland, A. MS 46th Inf. Co.B
Rutland, A.B. AL Cav. Roddey's Escort Sgt.
Rutland, Abram W. SC 19th Inf. Co.A 1st Sgt.
Rutland, A.E. SC 20th Inf. Co.B
Rutland, Anderson MS Inf. 7th Bn. Co.G
Rutland, Aulcy AL 18th Inf. Co.D
Rutland, Benjamin H. MS 30th Inf. Co.F 2nd Lt.
Rutland, Benjamin H. Cheatham's Div. Surg.
Rutland, B.H. AL 18th Inf. Surg.
Rutland, Calvin SC 11th Res. Co.G
Rutland, Cephus SC 2nd St.Troops Co.G
Rutland, C.S. SC 2nd Inf. Co.A,G
Rutland, C.S. SC 6th Inf. 1st Co.D
Rutland, Cullen E. MS 7th Inf. Co.H
Rutland, D.W. GA 6th Inf. (St.Guards) Co.A
Rutland, E. SC 2nd Arty. Co.E
Rutland, E. SC 2nd St.Troops Co.C
Rutland, E. SC 27th Inf. Co.F
Rutland, Edmond J. MS 29th Inf. Co.I
Rutland, Emanuel AL 39th Inf. Co.I
Rutland, E.W. SC 14th Inf. Co.B 1st Lt.
Rutland, Ezekiel SC 1st Bn.S.S. Co.B
Rutland, Ezekiel SC 19th Inf. Co.A
Rutland, George SC 2nd Arty. Co.I
Rutland, George SC 1st (McCreary's) Inf. Co.K,L
Rutland, H. SC Mil. 14th Regt. Co.B
Rutland, H.A. SC 20th Inf. Co.B
Rutland, Henry F. GA 57th Inf. Co.D Cpl.
Rutland, H.W. AL Inf. 2nd Regt. Co.E
Rutland, H.W. AL 16th Inf. Co.A
Rutland, I.P. GA 64th Inf.
Rutland, Isaac A. KY Kirkpatrick's Bn. Co.A
Rutland, Isaac A. TN 7th Inf. Co.K
Rutland, J.A. GA 64th Inf.
Rutland, J.A. TN 9th (Ward's) Cav. Co.A
Rutland, James MS Lt.Arty. (Brookhaven Lt.Arty.) Hoskins' Btty.
Rutland, James SC 2nd Arty. Co.E
Rutland, James A. TN 20th Inf. Co.A
Rutland, James M. SC 3rd Bn.Res. Co.B
Rutland, James R. AL 39th Inf. Co.I
Rutland, J.B. LA Inf. 11th Bn. Co.G Cpl.
Rutland, J.B. LA Inf.Cons.Crescent Regt. Co.D 1st Sgt.
Rutland, J.H. LA Ogden's Cav. Co.F Sgt.
Rutland, J.H. LA 2nd Inf. Co.A Sgt.
Rutland, J.J. FL 1st (Res.) Inf. Co.H
Rutland, J.M. Forrest's Scouts T. Henderson's Co.,CSA
Rutland, John A. AL 16th Inf. Co.A
Rutland, John B. TN 7th Inf. Co.H
Rutland, John D. GA 64th Inf. Co.D
Rutland, John H. GA 64th Inf. Co.D Cpl.
Rutland, John R. MS Inf. 7th Bn. Co.G
Rutland, John W. MS 2nd Part. Co.A
Rutland, J.W. GA 12th Inf. Co.F
Rutland, J.W. SC Lt.Arty. Jeter's Co. (Macbeth Lt.Arty.) Sgt.
Rutland, J.W. SC Rhett's Co.
Rutland, J.W. TN 45th Inf. Co.F
Rutland, L.D. GA Arty. 11th Bn. (Sumter Arty.) New Co.C
Rutland, L.P. TN Cav. Allison's Squad. Co.B 3rd Lt.

Rutland, Michael SC 19th Inf. Co.A
Rutland, Moses H. AL 57th Inf. Co.B
Rutland, N.G. MS 28th Cav. Co.D
Rutland, Reddick P. TX Cav. Crump's Regt. Co.E
Rutland, R.F. MS 29th Inf. Co.I Cpl.
Rutland, R.G. AL 11th Inf.
Rutland, Robert F. MS 1st (Johnston's) Inf. Co.D Sgt.
Rutland, R.P. TX 3rd Cav. Co.I 3rd Lt.
Rutland, R.W. FL 1st (Res.) Inf. Co.H
Rutland, Thomas C. KY 8th Mtd.Inf. Co.G
Rutland, Thomas W.H. GA 57th Inf. Co.D Sgt.
Rutland, W.C. MS 2nd Cav.
Rutland, W.C. MS 2nd Part. Co.A
Rutland, W.E. SC 2nd Arty. Co.H
Rutland, W.H. MS 1st (King's) Inf. (St.Troops) Co.K
Rutland, William AL 8th Inf.
Rutland, William SC 11th Res. Co.C
Rutland, William SC 11th Res. Co.G
Rutland, William A. SC 7th Inf. 1st Co.E, 2nd Co.E 1st Lt.
Rutland, William H. NC 2nd Arty. (36th St.Troops) Co.C Artif.
Rutland, William H. TX 3rd Cav. Co.I 2nd Lt.
Rutland, William P. TN 4th Cav.
Rutland, William P. TN 1st (Feild's) Inf. Co.B
Rutland, William P. Wheeler's Scouts,CSA
Rutland, Wm. R. AL 14th Inf. Co.C
Rutland, William R. LA Inf. 11th Bn. Co.G 1st Lt.
Rutland, William T. GA 12th Inf. Co.F
Rutland, William W. AL 39th Inf. Co.I
Rutland, W.M. SC 2nd St.Troops Co.K
Rutland, W.R. MS Rogers' Co.
Rutland, W.W. SC 2nd Arty. Co.H
Rutland, W.W. SC 20th Inf. Co.B
Rutland, Z.T. AL 63rd Inf. Co.D
Rutledg, Martin VA Inf. 23rd Bn. Co.H
Rutledg, W.L. GA 3rd Res. Co.H
Rutledge, --- LA 1st Cav. Co.C
Rutledge, A. AR 12th Inf. Co.I
Rutledge, A. MS 14th Inf. Co.E
Rutledge, A. TX 35th (Brown's) Cav. Co.C
Rutledge, A. TX 13th Vol. 1st Co.H
Rutledge, A.B. AL 62nd Inf. Co.A Cpl.
Rutledge, Abner D. VA 44th Inf. Co.I
Rutledge, Abraham TX Part.Rangers Thomas' Co.
Rutledge, Adney NC 21st Inf. Co.F
Rutledge, A.H. TX 11th Cav. Co.C
Rutledge, A.H. TX 4th Inf. Co.D
Rutledge, A.J. GA 54th Inf. Co.D
Rutledge, A.J. Exch.Bn. Co.E,CSA
Rutledge, Alexander AR 6th Inf. New Co.D
Rutledge, Alf AL Part.Rangers 13th Bn. Co.C Sgt.
Rutledge, Alfred AL 28th Inf. Co.E Cpl.
Rutledge, Alfred MS 10th Inf. New Co.G, Co.P Cpl.
Rutledge, Allen MS Cav. Davenport's Bn. (St.Troops) Co.C
Rutledge, A.M. Gen. & Staff Maj.,Staff Off.
Rutledge, Amos P. KY 4th Mtd.Inf. Co.G
Rutledge, Andrew J. AL 5th Cav. Co.G Sgt.
Rutledge, Andrew J. GA 1st Bn.S.S. Co.C

Rutledge, Andrew Jackson MS 34th Inf. Co.C
Rutledge, Anthony VA 9th Inf. Co.I
Rutledge, Arthur M. TN Arty.Corps Co.1 Capt.
Rutledge, Augustus AL Inf. 1st Regt. Co.B
Rutledge, Augustus AL 59th Inf. Co.H
Rutledge, Augustus AL Arty. 4th Bn. Hilliard's
  Legion Co.D
Rutledge, B. GA 7th Inf. (St.Guards) Co.B
Rutledge, Barney SC 2nd Rifles Co.A
Rutledge, Barney C. SC Inf. Hampton Legion
  Co.B
Rutledge, Baxter TN Cav. 12th Bn. (Day's) Co.A
Rutledge, Baxter TN 29th Inf. Co.K Drum.
Rutledge, B.C. SC 2nd Rifles Co.A
Rutledge, Benjamin F. MO Inf. 1st Bn. Co.A
Rutledge, B.H. SC 4th Cav. Co.K Col.
Rutledge, B.H. SC Mil.Cav. Rutledge's Co.
  Capt.
Rutledge, Bird E. TN 9th (Ward's) Cav. Co.C
Rutledge, B.M. AR 35th Inf. Co.E Sgt.
Rutledge, B.S. NC 57th Inf. Co.D
Rutledge, B.S. SC 1st Arty. Co.F 2nd Lt.
Rutledge, B.W. AL 43rd Inf. Co.E
Rutledge, B.W. 2nd Conf.Eng.Troops Co.H
Rutledge, C.A. TN 63rd Inf. Co.E
Rutledge, Caleb W. TN 39th Mtd.Inf. Co.F Sgt.
Rutledge, Calvin S. AR 14th (Powers') Inf. Co.G
Rutledge, Calvin W. LA 1st Hvy.Arty. (Reg.)
  Co.K
Rutledge, C.C. MO 11th Inf. Co.K
Rutledge, C.E. TX Cav. Morgan's Regt. Co.H
Rutledge, C.E. Conf.Lt.Arty. Stark's Bn. Co.B
Rutledge, Charles AL 9th Inf. Co.G
Rutledge, Charles AL 94th Mil. Co.A
Rutledge, Charles A. VA Lt.Arty. Arch.
  Graham's Co.
Rutledge, Charles Abram Gen. & Staff, Medical
  Dept. Asst.Surg.
Rutledge, Charles B. GA 9th Inf. Co.G
Rutledge, Charles E. VA Arty. Wise Legion
Rutledge, Charles J.K. AL 23rd Inf. Co.K
Rutledge, Charles J.K.P. AL 38th Inf. Co.K
Rutledge, C.K.P. AR 8th Cav. Co.C
Rutledge, C.M. TN 1st (Turney's) Inf. Co.G
Rutledge, C.M. TN 16th Inf. Co.H 1st Sgt.
Rutledge, C.S. MS 6th Cav. Co.B,G
Rutledge, D. MO Lt.Arty. Von Phul's Co.
Rutledge, D. TN 16th (Logwood's) Cav. Co.D
Rutledge, D. TN 42nd Inf. Co.C
Rutledge, D. 4th Conf.Inf. Co.H
Rutledge, D.A. AL 59th Inf. Co.H Sgt.
Rutledge, Daniel AR Arty. Hughey's Btty.
Rutledge, David AL 13th Bn.Part.Rangers Co.C
Rutledge, David AL 56th Part.Rangers Co.G
Rutledge, David MO 5th Cav. Co.B
Rutledge, David W. GA 52nd Inf. Co.H
Rutledge, D.J. NC 21st Inf. Co.G
Rutledge, Doley H. MO 3rd Cav. Co.B Lt.
Rutledge, Dudley LA 16th Inf. Co.K
Rutledge, Dudley A. AL Arty. 4th Bn. Hilliard's
  Legion Co.A,D
Rutledge, D.W. LA 8th Cav. Co.B
Rutledge, E. TN Cav. 12th Bn. (Day's) Co.C
Rutledge, E.B. KY Morgan's Men Co.C
Rutledge, E.B. TX 24th Cav. Co.I
Rutledge, Edward MO 6th Cav. Co.E

Rutledge, Edward J. VA 22nd Inf. Co.D
  Ord.Sgt.
Rutledge, Edward S. GA 3rd Inf. Co.L
Rutledge, Edward S. GA 42nd Inf. Co.G
Rutledge, E.H. MS 1st Cav.Res. Co.D
Rutledge, E.H. MS 25th Inf. Co.I
Rutledge, E.H. MO 10th Inf. Co.E
Rutledge, Elijah W.P. TN Cav. 7th Bn. (Ben-
  nett's) Co.F Black.
Rutledge, Elisha C. TX Cav. Ragsdale's Bn.
  Co.D
Rutledge, E.P. NC 61st Inf. Co.E
Rutledge, E.P. NC Mil. Clark's Sp.Bn. Co.C
Rutledge, E.W.P. TN 22nd (Barteau's) Cav.
  Co.G Black.
Rutledge, F. GA 64th Inf. Co.I
Rutledge, F.E. NC 1st Inf. Co.G
Rutledge, Festus LA 7th Inf. Co.F
Rutledge, F.M. TN 12th (Cons.) Inf. Co.B
Rutledge, Fountain TN Cav. 7th Bn. (Bennett's)
  Co.A
Rutledge, Francis M. AR 8th Inf. New Co.B
  Cpl.
Rutledge, Gabriel T. TN 53rd Inf. Co.E
Rutledge, G.B. TN 35th Inf. 2nd Co.D Cpl.
Rutledge, G.C. AR 8th Cav. Co.C Sgt.
Rutledge, G.C. AR 2nd Vol. Co.C
Rutledge, George AL 43rd Inf. Co.G
Rutledge, George LA 9th Inf. Co.E
Rutledge, George Q. GA 66th Inf. Co.G
Rutledge, George W. GA 10th Cav. Co.I
Rutledge, George W. MS 1st (King's) Inf.
  (St.Troops) Co.A
Rutledge, George W. VA 4th Inf. Co.E
Rutledge, George W. VA 4th Inf. Co.L
Rutledge, George W. 10th Conf.Cav. Co.I Far.
Rutledge, G.G. NC 64th Inf. Co.I,H Sgt.
Rutledge, G.G. TN 63rd Inf. Co.H
Rutledge, Granville H. VA 24th Inf. Co.F
Rutledge, G.W. AR 38th Inf. New Co.I Sgt.
Rutledge, G.W. GA Cav. 19th Bn. Co.D
Rutledge, Hamilton J. VA Inf. 23rd Bn. Co.H
Rutledge, Henry AL Inf. 1st Regt. Co.B
Rutledge, Henry H. AL Arty. 4th Bn. Hilliard's
  Legion Co.A,D Capt.
Rutledge, Henry M. NC 25th Inf. Col.
Rutledge, H.F. Forrest's Scouts T. Henderson's
  Co.,CSA
Rutledge, H.H. AL 59th Inf. Co.H Capt.
Rutledge, H.M. GA 2nd Cav. Co.D
Rutledge, Hughes NC 53rd Inf. Co.D
Rutledge, I. 15th Conf.Cav. Co.F
Rutledge, I.A. AL 6th Cav. Co.D Sgt.
Rutledge, I.G. TX 2nd Inf. Co.G
Rutledge, Isaac KY 9th Mtd.Inf. Co.E
Rutledge, I.W. KY 1st (Butler's) Cav. Co.G,A
Rutledge, J. AL Cav. Hardie's Bn.Res. Co.E
Rutledge, J. AL 8th Inf.
Rutledge, J. MS 18th Cav. Co.H
Rutledge, J.A. AL Cav. Moreland's Regt. Co.I
  1st Sgt.
Rutledge, J.A. AL 22nd Inf. Co.E
Rutledge, J.A. GA 68th Regt. Co.H
Rutledge, J. Allen MS 26th Inf. Co.A Sgt.
Rutledge, James AL 3rd Cav. Co.F
Rutledge, James AL 15th Inf. Co.K
Rutledge, James AL 20th Inf. Co.E,A

Rutledge, James AL 28th Inf. Co.E
Rutledge, James GA 46th Inf. Co.G
Rutledge, James KY 7th Cav. Co.A
Rutledge, James KY 11th Cav. Co.A
Rutledge, James MO 6th Cav. Co.E
Rutledge, James TN 4th (McLemore's) Cav.
  Co.D
Rutledge, James TN 8th (Smith's) Cav. Co.F
  Cpl.
Rutledge, James TN 12th Inf. Co.I
Rutledge, James TN 25th Inf. Co.C
Rutledge, James VA 51st Inf. Co.D
Rutledge, James A. GA 6th Cav. Co.G
Rutledge, James C. AR 2nd Mtd.Rifles Co.F
Rutledge, James H. MS 31st Inf. Co.A
Rutledge, James H. SC 2nd Rifles Co.A Sgt.
Rutledge, James H. VA 22nd Inf. Swann's Co.
Rutledge, James H. VA 50th Inf. Co.K
Rutledge, James J. AL 3rd Inf. Co.C Sgt.
Rutledge, James M. GA 42nd Inf. Co.D
Rutledge, James N. AL 24th Inf. Co.I
Rutledge, James R. SC Lt.Arty. Parker's Co.
  (Marion Arty.)
Rutledge, James S. MO St.Guard
Rutledge, James W. GA 55th Inf. Co.I
Rutledge, James W. TN Cav. 7th Bn. (Bennett's)
  Co.A Trump.
Rutledge, James W. TN 13th (Gore's) Cav. Co.B
Rutledge, James W. TN 22nd (Barteau's) Cav.
  Co.D
Rutledge, Jamison C. TX 15th Cav. Co.A
Rutledge, J.B. SC Palmetto S.S. Co.B Sgt.
Rutledge, J.C. AR 1st Mtd.Rifles Co.D
Rutledge, J.C. TN 33rd Inf. Co.A Sgt.
Rutledge, J.D. TN 3rd (Clack's) Inf. Co.B
Rutledge, J.E. GA 16th Inf. Co.H
Rutledge, J.E. LA 8th Cav. Co.B
Rutledge, J.E. SC Inf. 7th Bn. (Enfield Rifles)
  Co.D
Rutledge, J.E. SC 27th Inf. Co.D
Rutledge, Jeff J. TX 2nd Cav. Co.B
Rutledge, Jes. MO Dismtd.Cav. Lawther's Tem-
  porary Regt.
Rutledge, J.F. MO 11th Inf. Co.G
Rutledge, J.F. TN 22nd (Barteau's) Cav. Co.G
  Black.
Rutledge, J.F. TN Inf. 3rd Cons.Regt. Co.B
Rutledge, J.F. TN 38th Inf. Co.F
Rutledge, J.G. MO 10th Inf. Co.E
Rutledge, J.H. AL 12th Cav. Co.E
Rutledge, J.H. GA Inf. 25th Bn. (Prov.Guard)
  Co.B
Rutledge, J.H. GA 60th Inf. Co.C
Rutledge, J.H. GA 60th Inf. Co.H
Rutledge, J.H. SC 7th Inf. Co.K
Rutledge, J.H. VA 1st (Farinholt's) Res. Co.K
Rutledge, J.H. VA Inf. 44th Bn. Co.C
Rutledge, J.J. AL 13th Bn.Part.Rangers Co.A
  Sgt.
Rutledge, J.J. GA 3rd Inf. Co.G
Rutledge, J.J. MS 26th Inf. Co.A Cpl.
Rutledge, J.J. TN 22nd (Barteau's) Cav. 1st
  Co.H Sgt.
Rutledge, J.J. VA 1st (Farinholt's) Res. Co.K
Rutledge, J.K. AL 50th Inf. Co.G
Rutledge, J.L. TX 24th & 25th Cav. (Cons.) Co.I
Rutledge, J.M. NC 57th Inf. Co.D

Rutledge, J.M. TN 12th (Cons.) Inf. Co.I
Rutledge, J.N. AL Cp. of Instr. Talladega
Rutledge, John AL 4th Res. Co.F
Rutledge, John AL 22nd Inf. Co.C
Rutledge, John AL 25th Inf. Co.C
Rutledge, John AL 30th Inf. Co.B,H
Rutledge, John AL 36th Inf. Co.K,H
Rutledge, John AL 49th Inf. Co.A
Rutledge, John AL 50th Inf. Co.G
Rutledge, John AR 45th Cav. Co.E Sgt.
Rutledge, John AR 38th Inf. New Co.I
Rutledge, John GA 64th Inf. Co.I
Rutledge, John KY 2nd (Duke's) Cav. Co.A,B
Rutledge, John MS 34th Inf. Co.C
Rutledge, John MO Lt.Arty. Von Phul's Co.
Rutledge, John MO Inf. 8th Bn. Co.B
Rutledge, John MO 9th Inf. Co.F
Rutledge, John TN 9th (Ward's) Cav. Co.G
Rutledge, John TN 16th Inf. Co.C Bvt.2nd Lt.
Rutledge, John TN 53rd Inf. Co.I
Rutledge, John TX 24th Cav. Co.I Sgt.
Rutledge, John GA 16th Inf. Co.H
Rutledge, John A. VA 19th Cav. Co.I
Rutledge, John B. TX 13th Cav. Co.H
Rutledge, John Berry SC 4th Inf. Co.E
Rutledge, John F. GA 46th Inf. Co.C
Rutledge, John H. VA 44th Inf. Co.I 1st Lt.
Rutledge, John J. AL 56th Part.Rangers
Rutledge, John J. MS 3rd Inf. (St.Troops) Co.C
Rutledge, John J. MS 12th Inf. Co.F
Rutledge, John J. TX 22nd Cav. Co.A Cpl.
Rutledge, John J. TX 36th Cav. Co.C
Rutledge, John L. AL 24th Inf. Co.I
Rutledge, John O. AL 27th Inf. Co.H
Rutledge, John R. VA Cav. 39th Bn. Co.C
Rutledge, John S. MS Lt.Arty. (Issaquena Arty.) Graves' Co.
Rutledge, John T. AL 37th Inf. Co.G
Rutledge, John T. AR Inf. Ballard's Co.
Rutledge, John T. FL 1st (Res.) Inf. Co.G
Rutledge, John T. FL 9th Inf. Co.D
Rutledge, John W. AL 19th Inf. Co.G
Rutledge, John W. TN Cav. 7th Bn. (Bennett's) Co.A
Rutledge, John W. TN 22nd (Barteau's) Cav. Co.D
Rutledge, Joseph AL 18th Inf. Co.G Sgt.
Rutledge, Joseph AR 2nd Inf. Co.D
Rutledge, Joseph KY 6th Cav. Co.H
Rutledge, Joseph MS 4th Cav. Co.E
Rutledge, Joseph MS Cav. Hughes' Bn. Co.D
Rutledge, Joseph MS 1st (King's) Inf. (St.Troops) Co.B
Rutledge, Joseph VA 4th Inf. Co.L
Rutledge, Joseph E. TN 54th Inf. Co.B
Rutledge, Joseph I. GA 7th Inf. Co.K
Rutledge, Joseph M. GA 16th Inf. Co.H
Rutledge, Joseph N. GA 55th Inf. Co.I
Rutledge, Joseph R. LA 8th Inf. Co.H
Rutledge, Joseph S. GA 36th (Broyles') Inf. Co.F
Rutledge, Joshua MS 12th Inf. Co.F
Rutledge, Joshua B. VA 4th Inf. Co.L
Rutledge, J.R. SC Mil.Arty. 1st Regt. Parker's Co.
Rutledge, J.S. AL 50th Inf. Co.G
Rutledge, J.S. GA 7th Inf. Co.D
Rutledge, J.T. MS 21st Inf. Co.E

Rutledge, J.T. MO 4th Inf. Co.I
Rutledge, J.T. TN 12th (Cons.) Inf. Co.B
Rutledge, Junius P. MS 66th Inf. Co.B
Rutledge, J.W. MS 12th Cav. Co.G
Rutledge, J.W. MS Inf. 3rd Bn. (St.Troops) Co.A
Rutledge, L.A. AL 13th Bn.Part.Rangers Co.A Cpl.
Rutledge, L.A. TN 22nd (Barteau's) Cav. 1st Co.H
Rutledge, Lafayette AL Lt.Arty. 2nd Bn. Co.E
Rutledge, L.B. VA 21st Inf. Co.K
Rutledge, Little B. 2nd Cherokee Mtd.Vol. Co.A
Rutledge, M. TN 15th (Cons.) Cav. Co.I
Rutledge, M. TN 16th (Logwood's) Cav. Co.D
Rutledge, M. TN 42nd Inf. Co.C
Rutledge, M. VA 30th Bn.S.S. Co.E
Rutledge, M. 4th Conf.Inf. Co.H
Rutledge, Manlas TX Part.Rangers Thomas' Co.
Rutledge, Marion TN 36th Inf. Co.A
Rutledge, Mathias A. GA 21st Inf. Co.C
Rutledge, Matt VA Mil. Washington Cty.
Rutledge, McHenry VA 36th Inf. 2nd Co.H
Rutledge, McHenry VA 86th Mil. Co.B
Rutledge, Michael VA 22nd Inf. Co.I
Rutledge, Michael VA 36th Inf. Co.F
Rutledge, M.J. GA 16th Inf. Co.H
Rutledge, N.F. AR 38th Inf. New Co.I
Rutledge, Obediah MS 40th Inf. Co.B
Rutledge, O.C. TX 2nd Inf. Co.G
Rutledge, P. TN Inf. 1st Cons.Regt. Co.H
Rutledge, Paul AL 25th Inf. Co.C 2nd Lt.
Rutledge, Paul A. AL 4th Inf. Co.G
Rutledge, Peter VA 5th Inf. Co.F
Rutledge, Peter VA 6th Bn.Res. Co.F
Rutledge, Peter B. GA 41st Inf. Co.B Sgt.
Rutledge, P.H. VA 1st (Farinholt's) Res. Co.B
Rutledge, Philip W. VA 5th Inf. Co.F
Rutledge, Pleasant TN 1st (Feild's) Inf. Co.H
Rutledge, P.S. SC 5th Res. Co.I
Rutledge, R.A. AL 25th Inf. Co.K
Rutledge, R.A. MS 12th Cav. Co.G
Rutledge, R.A. TN 5th (McKenzie's) Cav. Co.C 1st Sgt.
Rutledge, R.A. TX Conscr.
Rutledge, R.A. VA 21st Inf. Co.K
Rutledge, R. Alax TN 63rd Inf. Co.H Capt.
Rutledge, R.F. AL 27th Inf. Co.H
Rutledge, R.H. TN 18th Inf. Co.C
Rutledge, Richard H. TN Cav. 12th Bn. (Day's) Co.A
Rutledge, Richard J. TN 7th Inf. Co.C Sgt.
Rutledge, Robert TN Cav. 12th Bn. (Day's) Co.A
Rutledge, Robert NC 4th Sr.Res. Co.E
Rutledge, Robert SC 1st (Butler's) Inf. Co.F
Rutledge, Robert SC Holcombe Legion Sgt.Maj.
Rutledge, Robert M. TX 2nd Cav. Co.H
Rutledge, Robert M. TX 37th Cav. Adj.
Rutledge, Robert M. TX Inf. Griffin's Bn. Adj.
Rutledge, Robert S. SC 1st (Orr's) Rifles Co.C Cpl.
Rutledge, R.R. VA 30th Bn.S.S. Co.E
Rutledge, Ruburtus G. NC 28th Inf. Co.B
Rutledge, Russell J. AL 24th Inf. Co.I
Rutledge, R.W. TX 2nd Cav. Co.B
Rutledge, S. AL 5th Inf. New Co.I

Rutledge, S. AL 50th Inf.
Rutledge, S. TX 35th (Brown's) Cav.
Rutledge, S. TX Cav. Mann's Regt. Co.B
Rutledge, Samuel KY 9th Mtd.Inf. Co.E
Rutledge, Samuel MS Arty. (Seven Stars Arty.) Roberts' Co.
Rutledge, Samuel VA Arty. Wise Legion
Rutledge, Samuel C. TN Cav. 12th Bn. (Day's) Co.A
Rutledge, Samuel R. AL 22nd Inf. Co.A
Rutledge, Samuel T. VA Inf. 23rd Bn. Co.B
Rutledge, S.C. VA Mil. Scott Cty.
Rutledge, S.H. AL 3rd Res. Co.C
Rutledge, S.H. TX Cav. Giddings' Bn. Pickerell's Co. Sgt.
Rutledge, S.R. AL Cp. of Instr. Talladega
Rutledge, Stephen W. TN 32nd Inf. Co.H
Rutledge, St.John VA Inf. 28th Bn. Co.C
Rutledge, T. VA 4th Cav. & Inf.St.Line 1st Co.I
Rutledge, Thomas H. AL 43rd Inf. Co.G 1st Lt.
Rutledge, Thomas J. AL 3rd Inf. Chap.
Rutledge, Thomas J. GA 43rd Inf. Co.C
Rutledge, Thos. J. Gen. & Staff Chap.
Rutledge, Thomas K. TN Cav. 12th Bn. (Day's) Co.A 1st Sgt.
Rutledge, Thomas T. GA 1st Reg. Co.H
Rutledge, T.J. GA 60th Inf. Co.C,E
Rutledge, T.P. VA 4th Inf. Co.E
Rutledge, T.R. AL City Troop (Mobile) Arrington's Co.A
Rutledge, T.R. 15th Conf.Cav. Co.F
Rutledge, U.C. AL 59th Inf. Co.H
Rutledge, Ulysses AL Arty. 4th Bn. Hilliard's Legion Co.A,D
Rutledge, W. GA 43rd Inf. Co.C
Rutledge, W. TN Inf. 4th Cons.Regt. Co.E
Rutledge, W.A. MS St.Cav. 2nd Bn. (Harris') Co.B
Rutledge, W.A. MS 11th (Cons.) Cav. Co.G
Rutledge, W.A. NC 21st Inf. Co.G
Rutledge, W.A.E. TN Cav. Jackson's Co. Cpl.
Rutledge, Wallace W. TN 3rd (Clack's) Inf. Co.G 2nd Lt.
Rutledge, Walter G. MS 2nd Inf. Co.B Sgt.Maj.
Rutledge, W.B. VA 9th Cav.
Rutledge, W.B. VA Inf. 44th Bn. Co.C
Rutledge, W.C. NC 1st Arty. (10th St.Troops) Co.H
Rutledge, W.C. TN 24th Inf. Co.A
Rutledge, W.D. AR 7th Inf. Co.E
Rutledge, W.D. TN Conscr. (Cp. of Instr.)
Rutledge, W.G. NC 21st Inf. Co.C
Rutledge, W.H. GA 60th Inf. Co.C
Rutledge, W.H. VA Cav. Mosby's Regt. (Part.Rangers)
Rutledge, Wiley MO 6th Inf. Co.C
Rutledge, William AL 22nd Inf. Co.A
Rutledge, Wm. AL Cp. of Instr. Talladega
Rutledge, William AR 5th Inf. Co.C
Rutledge, William AR 23rd Inf. Co.E
Rutledge, William GA 60th Inf. Co.B
Rutledge, William MS 3rd Inf. Co.D 2nd Lt.
Rutledge, William MS 5th Inf. (St.Troops) Co.E Cpl.
Rutledge, William MS 7th Inf. Co.I
Rutledge, William MS 25th Inf. Co.I
Rutledge, William TN 2nd Cav. Co.G

Rutledge, William TX 13th Cav. Co.H
Rutledge, William VA Hvy.Arty. Epes' Co.
Rutledge, William VA 21st Inf. Co.F
Rutledge, William VA Inf. 23rd Bn. Co.B
Rutledge, William VA 36th Mil. Co.F
Rutledge, William A. GA 3rd Inf. Co.L
Rutledge, William A. NC 21st Inf. Co.F Fifer
Rutledge, William A. TN 8th Inf. Co.K 3rd Lt.
Rutledge, William C. VA 20th Inf. Co.B
Rutledge, William D. TN 26th Inf. Co.K
Rutledge, William E. TX 22nd Cav. Co.A Cpl.
Rutledge, William E. VA 22nd Inf. Co.K
Rutledge, William F. SC Inf. 7th Bn. (Enfield
    Rifles) Co.D
Rutledge, William F. SC 9th Inf. Music.
Rutledge, William G. NC 52nd Inf. Co.H 1st
    Sgt.
Rutledge, William G. TN Lt.Arty. Burroughs'
    Co. Far.
Rutledge, William H. AL 29th Inf. Co.A
Rutledge, William H. VA Inf. 28th Bn. Co.C
Rutledge, William J. TX 31st Cav. Co.C
Rutledge, William P. GA Phillips' Legion Co.O
    Cpl.
Rutledge, William R. NC 2nd Inf. Co.K
Rutledge, William R. TX 2nd Cav. Co.B
Rutledge, William T. MO 12th Inf. Co.C
Rutledge, William W. NC 38th Inf. Co.B
Rutledge, W.M. AL City Troop (Mobile) Ar-
    rington's Co.A
Rutledge, W.M. 15th Conf.Cav. Co.F
Rutledge, W.P. MO 5th Cav. Co.B
Rutledge, W.P. TN 19th Inf. Co.G
Rutledge, W.P. TX 6th Inf. Co.G
Rutledge, W.W. TN 6th Inf. Co.A Bvt.2nd Lt.
Rutlege, --- AL Talladega Cty.Res. Cunning-
    ham's Co.
Rutlege, A. MS 6th Cav. Co.D
Rutlege, B.F. NC 21st Inf. Co.C
Rutlege, Charles E. VA Lt.Arty. French's Co.
Rutlege, D.A. AL 4th Inf. Co.G Sgt.
Rutlege, Francis E. NC 21st Inf. Co.G
Rutlege, George W. MS 3rd Cav. Co.B
Rutlege, Greenville A. VA 27th Inf. Co.D
Rutlege, Irvin A. NC 21st Inf. Co.F
Rutlege, J. AL 59th Inf. Co.H Cpl.
Rutlege, Jerry D. MS 21st Inf. Co.E
Rutlege, J.M. TX Cav. Hardeman's Regt. Co.G
Rutlege, John MS Cav. Davenport's Bn.
    (St.Troops) Co.C
Rutlege, Martin NC 21st Inf. Co.F
Rutlege, M.B. GA Cherokee Legion (St.Guards)
    Co.I
Rutlege, Roburtus NC 37th Inf. Co.H
Rutlege, Samuel S. GA 35th Inf. Co.I
Rutlege, St.John VA 59th Inf. 2nd Co.H
Rutlege, W. 4th Conf.Inf. Co.H
Rutlege, William NC 7th Sr.Res. Fisher's Co.
Rutlege, William H. VA 59th Inf. 2nd Co.H
Rutlegg, H.P. TX Cav. Mann's Regt. Co.B
Rutley, A.H. NC Inf. 2nd Bn. Co.A
Rutlidg, G.T. TN Inf. Sowell's Detach.
Rutlidge, Benjamin W. AL 8th Inf. Co.A
Rutlidge, C.M. TN 19th (Biffle's) Cav. Co.H
Rutlidge, David S. GA 16th Inf. Co.H
Rutlidge, D.H. MO 6th Cav. Co.B 1st Lt.
Rutlidge, Isaac TN Inf. 23rd Bn. Co.A

Rutlidge, James LA Mil. British Guard Bn.
    Kurczyn's Co.
Rutlidge, John MS 6th Cav. Co.I
Rutlidge, John MO 6th Cav. Co.B
Rutlidge, Joshua AL 5th Inf. New Co.E
Rutlidge, J.P. TN 15th (Cons.) Cav. Co.G
Rutlidge, R. SC 9th Inf. Co.A
Rutlidge, Robert G. TN Cav. 9th Bn. (Gantt's)
    Co.F Cpl.
Rutlidge, Samuel TN Inf. 23rd Bn. Co.A
Rutlidge, William NC 7th Sr.Res. Watts' Co.
Rutlidge, William TX Cav. Martin's Regt. Co.E
Rutlidge, William A. AL 10th Inf. Co.G
Rutlin, C. SC Kemp's Inf. Co.D
Rutlin, J.R. AL 15th Bn.Part.Rangers Co.D
Rutlin, J.R. AL 56th Part.Rangers Co.D
Rutling, Asa MS 38th Cav. Co.I
Rutllegge, John H. SC 22nd Inf. Co.D
Rutrough, Jacob W. VA 54th Inf. Co.I
Ruts, Fred. AR Mil. Desha Cty.Bn.
Ruts, Jacob H. VA 14th Mil. Co.C
Rutt, Samuel MO 1st N.E. Cav.
Rutter, --- VA 1st Bn.Res. Co.H
Rutter, Bartholomew VA 1st Res. Co.D
Rutter, C. KY 12th Cav. Co.E
Rutter, E.D. AR 34th Inf. Co.I
Rutter, E.D. MO 9th Bn.S.S. Co.A
Rutter, Edwin M. VA 2nd Inf. Co.I,C
Rutter, E.J. TX Inf. Timmons' Regt. Co.H Sgt.
Rutter, E.J. TX Waul's Legion Co.A Sgt.
Rutter, Elias VA 146th Mil. Co.H
Rutter, Elisha MD Inf. 2nd Bn. Co.E,D
Rutter, E.V. NC 48th Inf. Co.I
Rutter, F. MS 28th Cav. Co.E
Rutter, Felix G. MO 3rd Inf. Co.K
Rutter, Felix Grandy AR 36th Inf. Co.G Cpl.
Rutter, F.G. MO 11th Inf. Co.H
Rutter, Frank TX 1st Hvy.Arty. Co.C
Rutter, George W. TN 63rd Inf. Co.E
Rutter, George W. VA 2nd Inf. Co.C Drum.
Rutter, G.W. VA 5th Cav. 2nd Co.F
Rutter, G.W. VA 11th Cav. Co.I
Rutter, H. VA Cav. Mosby's Regt. (Part.
    Rangers) Co.E
Rutter, James MO 3rd Inf. Co.K Capt.
Rutter, James W. VA Cav. Mosby's Regt.
    (Part.Rangers) Co.A
Rutter, J.R. KY 2nd Mtd.Inf. Co.A
Rutter, J.W. VA Cav. 36th Bn. Co.F
Rutter, J.W. VA Cav. 41st Bn.
Rutter, P. SC Rhett's Co.
Rutter, R. KY 12th Cav. Co.E
Rutter, Samuel VA 2nd Inf. Co.C
Rutter, Tharian T. NC 17th Inf. (1st Org.) Co.L
    Drum.
Rutter, T.W. TN 21st Inf. Co.G
Rutter, Wilbur MD Inf. 2nd Bn. Co.E Sgt.
Rutter, William F. MD Walters' Co. (Zarvona
    Zouaves)
Rutter, William F. VA Inf. 25th Bn. Co.B
Rutter, William T. VA 1st Cav. Co.H
Rutter, W.J. NC 3rd Jr.Res. Co.H
Rutterford, Benjamin R.F. VA Loc.Def. Neff's
    Co.
Ruttley, Edward LA 28th (Thomas') Inf. Co.G
Rutton, John LA 11th Inf. Co.K

Ruty, H. LA Mil. 3rd Regt.Eur.Brig. (Garde
    Francaise) Co.2
Ruty, Henry LA Mil. 1st Regt. French Brig.
    Co.2
Ruty, J. LA Mil. 3rd Regt.Eur.Brig. (Garde
    Francaise) Co.2
Ruty, J.H. LA Mil. 3rd Regt.Eur.Brig. (Garde
    Francaise) Co.6
Rutyell, Joseph LA 3rd (Harrison's) Cav. Co.C
Rutz, George H. VA 146th Mil. Co.G
Rutzel, Caspar AR 51st Mil. Co.B
Rutzler, J.F. GA 1st (Olmstead's) Inf. Co.I
Ruwald, Charles TX 2nd Inf. Co.F
Rux, A.J. VA 9th Cav. Co.G
Rux, J.J. KY 7th Mtd.Inf. Co.F
Rux, Thomas TN 2nd (Smith's) Cav.
    Thomason's Co.
Rux, Wiley W. TN 2nd (Smith's) Cav.
    Thomason's Co.
Rux, W.W. 3rd Conf.Cav. Co.C
Ruxton, Robert MO Cav. Fristoe's Regt.
    Capt.,ACS
Ruxton, Robert MO 8th Inf. Comsy.
Ruyan, S.S. TX 12th Inf. Co.E
Ruyer, David AL 21st Inf. Co.B
Ruyhaw, W.M. AL 3rd Inf. Co.H
Ruyle, Alfred TX Cav. Hardeman's Regt. Co.A
Ruyle, William A. MO 5th Inf. Co.C Sgt.
Ruyle, William A. Inf. Bailey's Cons.Regt. Co.B
Ruyle, William A. TX 7th Inf. Co.A
Ruyle, William M. MO 11th Inf. Co.G
Ruynols, M. MO Cav. Fristoe's Regt. Co.D
Ruzes, Frank MS 26th Inf. Co.F
Ruzes, J.H. MS 26th Inf. Co.F
Ryal, H. AL 63rd Inf. Co.F
Ryal, H. AL 2nd Bn. Hilliard's Legion Vol.
    Co.D
Ryal, James LA 1st (Nelligan's) Inf. Co.F
Ryal, J.C. VA Loc.Def. Ezell's Co.
Ryal, John LA 20th Inf. New Co.B Sgt.
Ryal, John LA 21st (Kennedy's) Inf. Co.F
Ryal, J.R. TN Cav. Cox's Bn.
Ryal, J.R. Morgan's,CSA
Ryal, Lem TN Cav. 5th Bn. (McClellan's) Co.B
Ryal, Peter LA 15th Inf. Co.A
Ryal, Wade H. KY 4th Cav.
Ryal, William F. KY Cav. 2nd Bn. (Dortch's)
Ryalas, J. MS 1st (King's) Inf. (St.Troops) Co.H
Ryalds, Joseph MS 5th Cav. Co.I
Ryales, Charles MS 20th Inf. Co.K
Ryales, J. AL 8th Inf. Co.G
Ryall, A.P. Gen. & Staff Hosp.Stew.
Ryall, H.C. LA Cav. Greenleaf's Co. (Orleans
    Lt.Horse)
Ryall, J. LA Cav. Greenleaf's Co. (Orleans
    Lt.Horse)
Ryall, John E. AL Gid Nelson Lt.Arty.
Ryall, J.S. TN Cav. Jackson's Co.
Ryall, Peter M. VA Inf. 25th Bn. Co.E
Ryall, Thomas C. TN 41st Inf. Co.F
Ryall, Walter S. TN 1st (Feild's) Inf. Co.B
Ryall, Walter S. Sig.Corps,CSA
Ryall, W.R. FL Sp.Cav. 1st Bn. Co.B
Ryalls, Charles W. GA 37th Inf. Co.K
Ryalls, Charles W. GA 47th Inf. Co.K
Ryalls, James M. AL Inf. 1st Regt. Co.A
Ryalls, J.B. AL Archie Cadets 1st Lt.

Ryalls, J.H. MS 7th Cav. Co.G
Ryalls, John H.M. TX 1st (Yager's) Cav. Co.F
Ryalls, John J. GA 1st Bn.S.S. Co.C
Ryalls, Jordan L. GA 26th Inf. Atkinson's Co.B
Ryalls, Luke E. GA 26th Inf. Co.B
Ryalls, Richard B. AL Cav. 4th Bn. (Love's) Co.B
Ryalls, R.K. TN 45th Inf. Co.C
Ryals, Alfred TN 20th Inf. Co.G
Ryals, A.M. 1st Conf.Eng.Troops Co.E
Ryals, Asa M. VA 14th Inf. Co.C
Ryals, B. GA 5th Cav. Co.K
Ryals, Benjamin GA Cav. 1st Bn. Hopkins' Co.
Ryals, Britton NC 24th Inf. Co.I 2nd Lt.
Ryals, Bryan S. NC 24th Inf. Co.I
Ryals, Bryant H. GA 61st Inf. Co.E Cpl.
Ryals, Calvin MS 7th Inf. Co.F
Ryals, Charles GA Cav. 1st Bn. Hopkins' Co.
Ryals, Charles GA 8th Cav. New Co.I
Ryals, Charles GA Cav. 20th Bn. Co.D
Ryals, Charles H. TN 27th Inf. Co.I
Ryals, C.W. GA Inf. 3rd Bn. Co.H
Ryals, Daniel W. NC Loc.Def. Griswold's Co.
Ryals, David GA Cav. 19th Bn. Co.B
Ryals, David 10th Conf.Cav. Co.G
Ryals, D.W. AR 9th Inf. Co.K
Ryals, E.C. GA 5th Cav. Co.H
Ryals, Elijah MS 7th Inf. Co.F
Ryals, Elisha G. MS 7th Inf. Co.F
Ryals, Erwin MS 7th Inf. Co.F
Ryals, Evans MS 7th Inf. Co.F
Ryals, Felix MS 7th Inf. Co.F
Ryals, Ferdinand GA 51st Inf. Co.K
Ryals, Garland M. VA 3rd Cav. Co.G Sgt.
Ryals, Geo. AL 42nd Inf. Co.H
Ryals, G.F. MS 39th Inf. Co.E
Ryals, G.M. Gen. & Staff, A. of N.VA Maj.
Ryals, H. MS 2nd (Quinn's St.Troops) Inf. Co.H
Ryals, Harlow H. GA 4th (Clinch's) Cav. Co.I
Ryals, H.E. SC Inf. 9th Bn. Co.F
Ryals, Henry GA 47th Inf. Co.G Cpl.
Ryals, Henry J. NC 50th Inf. Co.D Maj.
Ryals, H.J. AR 9th Inf. Co.K
Ryals, Hugh J. MS 7th Inf. Co.F
Ryals, Isaac GA Cav. 1st Bn. Hopkins' Co.
Ryals, J. GA 5th Cav. Co.K
Ryals, Jabez GA Cav. 1st Bn. Hopkins' Co.
Ryals, Jabez GA 5th Cav. Co.K
Ryals, James GA Cav. 22nd Bn. (St.Guards) Co.B
Ryals, James GA 45th Inf. Co.A
Ryals, James A. NC 24th Inf. Co.I
Ryals, James D. VA 18th Inf. Co.E
Ryals, James G. GA Cav. 10th Bn. (St.Guards) Co.C 2nd Lt.
Ryals, James M. AL Eufaula Lt.Arty.
Ryals, James M. FL 1st Inf. Old Co.E
Ryals, J.B. MS 4th Inf. Co.B
Ryals, Jesse MS 7th Inf. Co.D
Ryals, Jesse MS 30th Inf. Co.G
Ryals, J.G. MS 4th Inf. Co.B
Ryals, J.J. GA 4th (Clinch's) Cav. Co.D Comsy.
Ryals, J.J. GA Cav. 21st Bn. Co.D 1st Lt.
Ryals, J.M. GA Cav. 20th Bn. Co.B
Ryals, J.M. TN 21st & 22nd (Cons.) Cav. Co.H
Ryals, Joel MS 4th Inf. Co.B

Ryals, John MS 30th Inf. Co.G
Ryals, John H. GA 49th Inf. Co.B
Ryals, John J. GA 61st Inf. Co.K
Ryals, John L. NC Hvy.Arty. 10th Bn. Co.B
Ryals, John V. VA 3rd Cav. Co.G
Ryals, John V. VA Inf. 25th Bn. Co.G
Ryals, John W. NC 50th Inf. Co.D
Ryals, Joseph NC 1st Inf. Co.I
Ryals, Joseph H. NC 24th Inf. Co.I
Ryals, Joseph J. MS 14th Inf. Co.B
Ryals, Joshua C. GA 61st Inf. Co.K,E
Ryals, J.R. GA Lt.Arty. Clinch's Btty.
Ryals, J.W. GA 5th Cav. Co.K
Ryals, Lewit W. NC 51st Inf. Co.K
Ryals, L.J. GA 4th (Clinch's) Cav. Co.E
Ryals, Luke E. GA 5th Cav. Co.K,H
Ryals, M. TN 21st (Wilson's) Cav. Co.H
Ryals, Madison GA 47th Inf. Co.G
Ryals, Nathaniel GA Siege Arty. Campbell's Ind.Co. Sgt.
Ryals, P. AL 4th Res. Co.G
Ryals, Perry AL 8th Inf. Co.H
Ryals, Richard B. NC 50th Inf. Co.D Cpl.
Ryals, Richard H. NC 3rd Cav. (41st St.Troops) Co.D
Ryals, Samuel AL 23rd Inf. Co.F
Ryals, Samuel S. VA 44th Inf. Co.F
Ryals, S.M. GA 47th Inf. Co.H Cpl.
Ryals, Thomas GA 10th Inf. Co.C
Ryals, Thomas GA 45th Inf. Co.A Cpl.
Ryals, Thomas GA 49th Inf. Co.B
Ryals, Thomas TN 7th (Duckworth's) Cav. Co.H
Ryals, T.J. GA 1st Reg. Co.M
Ryals, W.A. TX 4th Cav. Co.C 1st Lt.
Ryals, W.A. TX 21st Cav. Co.C 3rd Lt.
Ryals, W.B. VA 14th Inf. Co.C 2nd Lt.
Ryals, William GA 50th Inf. Co.G
Ryals, William TN 20th Inf. Co.G
Ryals, William B. MO 1st Inf. Co.D 2nd Lt.
Ryals, William B. VA 1st Bn.Res. Co.D 2nd Lt.
Ryals, William J. VA 14th Inf. Co.C
Ryals, Will R. GA Cav. 22nd Bn. (St.Guards) Co.B Sgt.
Ryals, W.J. MS 38th Cav. Co.I
Ryals, W.J. MS 20th Inf. Co.K
Ryals, W. Jordan GA Cav. 1st Bn. Hopkins' Co. Cpl.
Ryals, W.M. AR Lt.Arty. Wiggins' Btty.
Ryals, W.M. NC 50th Inf. Co.D
Ryals, W.N. TN 51st (Cons.) Inf. Co.C
Ryals, Wright NC 24th Inf. Co.I
Ryals, W.W. TN 21st (Wilson's) Cav. Co.H
Ryan, --- LA Washington Arty.Bn. Co.5
Ryan, --- MO Cav. 10th Regt.St.Guard Co.D
Ryan, --- SC Inf. 1st (Charleston) Bn. Co.A
Ryan, A. AL Cav. Murphy's Bn. Co.B
Ryan, A. AR 21st Inf. Co.F
Ryan, A. LA 3rd (Harrison's) Cav. Co.C
Ryan, A. TN Lt.Arty. Winston's Co.
Ryan, A. TX Cav. McCord's Frontier Regt. Co.B
Ryan, A. 15th Conf.Cav. Co.G
Ryan, Abram M. TX 27th Cav. Co.A
Ryan, A.G. VA 4th Cav. Co.D
Ryan, A.H. MS Conscr.
Ryan, A.K. 1st Conf.Cav. Co.I
Ryan, A.L. AL 9th (Malone's) Cav. Co.B

Ryan, A.L. GA Inf. 1st City Bn. (Columbus) Co.A
Ryan, Albert VA Cav. Mosby's Regt. (Part. Rangers) Co.B
Ryan, Alfred MS 3rd Inf. Co.A
Ryan, Alfred T. VA Cav. 35th Bn. Co.A
Ryan, Alvis P. TX Cav. Good's Bn. Co.D Capt.
Ryan, A.M. AR 2nd Mtd.Rifles Hawkins' Co.
Ryan, Ambrose TX Waul's Legion Co.A
Ryan, Amos VA 97th Mil. Co.C
Ryan, Amos Lafayette AL 49th Inf. Co.B
Ryan, Andrew AR 13th Inf. Co.A
Ryan, Andrew LA 7th Inf. Co.G
Ryan, Andrew MS Griffin's Co. (Madison Guards)
Ryan, Andrew MO Lt.Arty. Parsons' Co.
Ryan, Andrew MO 6th Inf. Co.I
Ryan, Andrew Conf.Inf. Tucker's Regt. Co.C
Ryan, Andy AR 13th Inf. Co.C
Ryan, Anthony LA 6th Inf. Co.G
Ryan, Antonia MS 3rd Inf. Co.A
Ryan, A.P. TX Cav. Wells' Regt. Co.I Capt.
Ryan, A.P. TX 9th (Young's) Inf. Co.A
Ryan, A.P. TX Lt.Inf. & Riflemen Maxey's Co. (Lamar Rifles)
Ryan, A.S. TX 25th Cav. Co.D
Ryan, Asa LA 10th Inf. Co.K
Ryan, A.T. TX 9th (Nichols') Inf. Atchison's Co.
Ryan, B. AL 24th Inf. Co.H Cpl.
Ryan, B.B. Gen. & Staff AASurg.
Ryan, B.C. MO 1st & 4th Cons.Inf. Co.H
Ryan, B.C. MO 4th Inf. Co.K
Ryan, Benjamin AL Jeff Davis Arty.
Ryan, Benjamin G. SC 7th Inf. 1st Co.H, Co.A Sgt.
Ryan, Benjamin L. AL 15th Inf. Co.A
Ryan, Benjamin L. AR Lt.Arty. Wiggins' Btty.
Ryan, Boman G. VA 60th Inf. Co.I Cpl.
Ryan, C. KY 2nd (Woodward's) Cav. Co.E
Ryan, Carroll AL 12th Inf. Co.H
Ryan, C.D. 24th & 25th Cav. (Cons.) Co.G
Ryan, C.E. GA 1st Symons' Res. Sgt.
Ryan, Charles LA Mil. 4th Regt. 1st Brig. 1st Div. Co.D
Ryan, Charles TX 1st Inf.
Ryan, Charles S. LA 1st Hvy.Arty. (Reg.) Co.A
Ryan, C.M. AR 7th Inf. Co.H
Ryan, Cornelius LA 10th Inf. Co.B
Ryan, Cornelius NC 6th Inf. Co.D
Ryan, Daniel AL 24th Inf. Co.H
Ryan, Daniel AR Mil. Borland's Regt. King's Co.
Ryan, Daniel LA 1st Hvy.Arty. (Reg.) Co.I
Ryan, Daniel LA Mil. 1st Regt. 2nd Brig. 1st Div. Co.G
Ryan, Daniel LA Inf. 1st Sp.Bn. (Wheat's) Co.B
Ryan, Daniel LA 5th Inf. Old Co.A
Ryan, Daniel LA 6th Inf. Co.K Sgt.
Ryan, Daniel LA 8th Inf. Co.I
Ryan, Daniel LA 11th Inf. Co.F
Ryan, Daniel LA 14th (Austin's) Bn.S.S. Co.A
Ryan, Daniel MO 6th Inf. Co.I
Ryan, Daniel TN 6th Inf. Co.F
Ryan, Daniel TX Granbury's Cons.Brig. Co.D
Ryan, Daniel TX 9th Field Btty.
Ryan, Daniel TX 10th Inf. Co.F

Ryan, Daniel B. MS Graves' Co. (Copiah Horse Guards)
Ryan, Daniel B. MS 3rd Inf. Co.K 2nd Lt.
Ryan, Daniel C. VA 48th Inf. Co.F
Ryan, Daniel C. Sap. & Min. Flynn's Co.,CSA Sgt.
Ryan, David KY 8th Cav. Co.K
Ryan, David TX 17th Inf. Co.A
Ryan, David S. NC 1st Cav. (9th St.Troops) Co.H
Ryan, D.B. MS Cav. 3rd Bn.Res. Co.D 1st Sgt.
Ryan, D.B. MS Cav. Hughes' Bn. Co.D
Ryan, D.D. AL 25th Inf. Co.K
Ryan, D.D. TX 25th Cav. Co.E
Ryan, Denis LA 6th Inf. Co.I
Ryan, Denis LA 22nd Inf. Jones' Co.
Ryan, Dennis AL 21st Inf. Co.B
Ryan, Dennis LA Inf. 1st Sp.Bn. (Wheat's) Co.C
Ryan, Dennis MS 25th Inf. Co.K
Ryan, Dennis MO 1st Inf. Co.C
Ryan, Dennis MO 1st & 4th Cons.Inf. Co.G
Ryan, Dennis MO 16th Inf. Co.A
Ryan, Dennis TN 1st (Feild's) Inf. Co.F
Ryan, Dennis L. GA 3rd Inf. Co.B
Ryan, D.R. SC 2nd Inf. Co.E Sgt.
Ryan, D.S. TX 24th & 25th Cav. (Cons.) Co.F
Ryan, E. AL 8th Cav. Co.E
Ryan, Ed MS 2nd Inf.
Ryan, Ed TN 27th Inf. Co.H
Ryan, E.D. TX 4th Inf. Co.E Capt.
Ryan, Edward GA 4th (Clinch's) Cav. Co.B
Ryan, Edward GA 3rd Mil.
Ryan, Edward LA Arty. Moody's Co. (Madison Lt.Arty.)
Ryan, Edward LA 1st (Nelligan's) Inf. Co.D
Ryan, Edward LA 5th Inf. Old Co.A, Co.K
Ryan, Edward LA 7th Inf. Co.G Jr.2nd Lt.
Ryan, Edward MS Cav. 4th Bn. Sykes' Co.
Ryan, Edward MS 1st Lt.Arty. Co.G
Ryan, Edward MS Davis' Bn. 1st Lt.
Ryan, Edward TN 5th Inf.
Ryan, Edward TN 10th Inf. Co.E 2nd Lt.
Ryan, Edward TN 21st Inf. Co.B
Ryan, Edward TX 1st Field Btty.
Ryan, Edward VA 6th Inf. Co.I
Ryan, Edward 8th (Wade's) Conf.Cav. Co.G
Ryan, Edward 9th Conf.Inf. Co.B
Ryan, Edward 9th Conf.Inf. Co.F
Ryan, Edward C. SC 1st Arty. Co.F
Ryan, Edward M. VA 60th Inf. Co.I
Ryan, Edward M. VA 151st Mil. Co.E Cpl.
Ryan, E.H. AL 43rd Inf. Co.E
Ryan, E.J. VA 1st (Farinholt's) Res. Co.D
Ryan, Elbert L. SC Inf.Bn. Co.C Cpl.
Ryan, Elijah F. AL 12th Inf. Co.H 2nd Lt.
Ryan, E.N. SC Mil. 16th Regt. Jones' Co.
Ryan, Ephraim VA 136th Mil. Co.F
Ryan, F. LA 3rd (Harrison's) Cav. Co.C
Ryan, F. LA 1st Hvy.Arty. (Reg.) Co.G
Ryan, F.M. AL 18th Inf. Co.C
Ryan, Francis M. VA 17th Cav. Co.C
Ryan, Frank H. LA 31st Inf. Co.B
Ryan, Frank T. AR 1st Mtd.Rifles Co.B
Ryan, F.T. AR 15th (Josey's) Inf. Co.H
Ryan, G.C. VA 3rd Cav. Co.C
Ryan, George LA 7th Cav. Co.A
Ryan, George LA 10th Inf. Co.D

Ryan, George A. AL 3rd Res. Co.H
Ryan, George A. GA Arty. 9th Bn. Co.A
Ryan, George K. SC 11th Inf. Co.I 2nd Lt.
Ryan, George W. MS 8th Inf. Co.G Capt.
Ryan, George W. VA Lt.Arty. Rogers' Co.
Ryan, G.H. TN 26th Inf. Co.E
Ryan, G.K. SC Inf. 7th Bn. (Enfield Rifles) Co.D
Ryan, G.K. SC Bn.St.Cadets Co.A
Ryan, G.W. MS Inf. 2nd St.Troops Co.E
Ryan, G.W. VA Cav. Mosby's Regt. (Part. Rangers) Co.C
Ryan, H. LA 21st (Kennedy's) Inf. Co.D
Ryan, Harris TX 27th Cav. Co.D,M
Ryan, Harris TX Cav. Good's Bn. Co.D 2nd Lt.
Ryan, Harvey TN Arty. Ramsey's Btty.
Ryan, Harvey VA 36th Inf. Co.A
Ryan, Harvey VA 157th Mil. Co.A
Ryan, H.C. AL 17th Inf. Co.E
Ryan, Henry AL 27th Inf. Co.H 1st Lt.
Ryan, Henry VA 9th Inf. 1st Co.A
Ryan, Henry C. TX 1st (Yager's) Cav. Co.F
Ryan, Henry C. VA Lt.Arty. Griffin's Co.
Ryan, Henry C. VA 157th Mil. Co.A
Ryan, Henry F. AR 14th (McCarver's) Inf. Co.H
Ryan, Hillary TX 17th Inf. Co.D Capt.
Ryan, H.J. AL 9th (Malone's) Cav. Co.B
Ryan, H.J. SC Mil. 16th Regt. Triest's Co.
Ryan, H.J. SC 24th Inf. Co.A
Ryan, Hugh LA Mil. Bonnabel Guards
Ryan, I. GA 20th Inf. Music.
Ryan, I.N. MS 32nd Inf. Co.F
Ryan, Isaac AL 27th Inf. Co.H
Ryan, Isaac AL 41st Inf. Co.E
Ryan, Isaac LA 10th Inf. Co.K 2nd Lt.
Ryan, Isaac MS 1st (King's) Inf. (St.Troops) Co.A
Ryan, Isaac VA 2nd Inf. Co.F Cpl.
Ryan, Isaac M. AR 33rd Inf. Co.F
Ryan, J. GA Inf. City Bn. (Columbus) Co.B
Ryan, J. LA 1st Cav. Co.F
Ryan, J. LA 1st (Nelligan's) Inf. Co.E
Ryan, J. LA Mil. 3rd Regt. 1st Brig. 1st Div. Co.K
Ryan, J. MD Inf. 2nd Bn. Co.E
Ryan, J. MS Inf. 1st St.Troops Co.I
Ryan, J. MS 35th Inf. Co.I
Ryan, J. SC 23rd Inf. Co.C
Ryan, J. 3rd Conf.Eng.Troops Co.F
Ryan, J. Conf.Reg.Inf. Brooks' Bn. Co.A
Ryan, J.A. NC Mallett's Bn. Co.A
Ryan, J.A. VA Inf. 1st Bn. Co.C Sgt.
Ryan, Jabez B. SC Cav.Bn. Hampton Legion Co.A Sgt.
Ryan, Jack GA 10th Inf. Co.C Sgt.
Ryan, Jacob J. KY 4th Mtd.Inf. Co.I
Ryan, James AL 51st Part.Rangers Co.K
Ryan, James AL City Troop (Mobile) Arrington's Co.A
Ryan, James AL Arty. 1st Bn. Co.B
Ryan, James AL 8th Inf. Co.I Cpl.
Ryan, James AL 12th Inf. Co.A
Ryan, James AL 18th Inf. Co.C
Ryan, James AL 18th Bn.Vol. Co.C
Ryan, James GA 19th Inf. Co.A
Ryan, James GA 25th Inf. Co.A
Ryan, James KY 2nd (Woodward's) Cav. Co.F
Ryan, James KY 1st Inf. Co.B

Ryan, James LA 1st Hvy.Arty. (Reg.) Co.K
Ryan, James LA Hvy.Arty. 8th Bn. Co.E
Ryan, James LA 1st (Strawbridge's) Inf. Co.F
Ryan, James LA 2nd Inf. Co.G
Ryan, James LA Mil. 4th Regt. 1st Brig. 1st Div. Co.G
Ryan, James LA 6th Inf. Co.B Cpl.
Ryan, James LA 11th Inf. Co.H
Ryan, James LA 13th Inf. Co.B
Ryan, James LA 14th Inf. Co.K
Ryan, James LA 20th Inf. Co.C
Ryan, James LA 21st (Kennedy's) Inf. Co.C
Ryan, James LA 21st (Patton's) Inf. Co.H Capt.
Ryan, James LA Mil. Irish Regt. O'Brien's Co.
Ryan, James MD 1st Inf. Co.G
Ryan, James MS 18th Inf. Co.D
Ryan, James MS 21st Inf. Co.G
Ryan, James MS 21st Inf. Co.L,I
Ryan, James MS 42nd Inf. Co.C
Ryan, James MS Griffin's Co. (Madison Guards)
Ryan, James MO Lt.Arty. Barret's Co.
Ryan, James MO 1st Inf. Co.C
Ryan, James NC 8th Inf. Co.D
Ryan, James SC 1st Arty. Co.E
Ryan, James SC Mil. 1st Regt. (Charleston Res.) Co.A
Ryan, James TN Cav. 7th Bn. (Bennett's) Co.A
Ryan, James TN 21st & 22nd (Cons.) Cav. Co.D
Ryan, James TN 22nd (Barteau's) Cav. Co.D
Ryan, James TN Inf. 4th Cons.Regt. Co.A Sgt.
Ryan, James TN 10th Inf. Co.E
Ryan, James TN 10th Inf. Co.G
Ryan, James TN 15th Inf. Co.D Sgt.
Ryan, James TN 21st Inf. Co.B
Ryan, James TN 21st Inf. Co.B
Ryan, James TN 61st Mtd.Inf. Co.E
Ryan, James TX 1st Hvy.Arty. 2nd Co.F
Ryan, James TX 2nd Inf. Odlum's Co.
Ryan, James TX 5th Inf. Co.F
Ryan, James TX 20th Inf. Co.C
Ryan, James VA 12th Cav. Co.F
Ryan, James VA Lt.Arty. Jeffress' Co.
Ryan, James VA 2nd St.Res. Co.L
Ryan, James VA Inf. 4th Bn.Loc.Def. Co.E
Ryan, James VA 6th Inf. Co.C
Ryan, James VA 8th Bn.Res. Co.E
Ryan, James VA 9th Inf. Co.F
Ryan, James VA 15th Inf. Co.D
Ryan, James VA 33rd Inf. Co.E
Ryan, James VA 53rd Inf. Co.A
Ryan, James VA 53rd Inf. Co.G
Ryan, James 9th Conf.Inf. Co.F
Ryan, James Conf.Reg.Inf. Brooks' Bn. Co.A
Ryan, James Sap. & Min.,CSA Capt.
Ryan, James A. MD 1st Inf. Co.H
Ryan, James A. VA Horse Arty. D. Shanks' Co.
Ryan, James B. KY 14th Cav. Capt.
Ryan, James B. LA 27th Inf. 1st Lt.,Adj.
Ryan, James C. VA 3rd Cav. Co.C
Ryan, James D. TX 9th Cav. Co.K
Ryan, James G. AL 28th Inf. Co.E
Ryan, James H. AL 12th Inf. Co.H
Ryan, James H. NC Hvy.Arty. 1st B. Co.C 1st Lt.
Ryan, James H. VA 8th Inf. Co.H
Ryan, James H. Gen. & Staff Capt.,AQM
Ryan, James L. AL 2nd Cav. Co.C QMSgt.

Ryan, James L. TX 1st Bn.S.S. Co.D
Ryan, James L. VA 54th Inf. Co.E Capt.
Ryan, James M. TN Douglass' Bn.Part.Rangers
  Co.A
Ryan, James P. GA Inf. 2nd Bn. Co.A
Ryan, James P. LA 1st Hvy.Arty. Co.I
Ryan, James P. SC 1st Arty. Co.C
Ryan, James P. Inf. School of Pract. Powell's
  Command Co.A
Ryan, James S. VA 3rd Inf. Co.E Sgt.
Ryan, James T. AL 62nd Inf. Co.D
Ryan, James T. NC 2nd Arty. (36th St.Troops)
  Co.F
Ryan, James W. GA 2nd Inf. Co.I Prin.Music.
Ryan, James W. GA 10th Inf. Co.C
Ryan, James W. GA 20th Inf.
Ryan, J.B. TN Cav. 1st Bn. (McNairy's) Co.D
  2nd Lt.
Ryan, J.C. AL 56th Part.Rangers Co.G,H
Ryan, J.C. NC 16th Inf. Co.L
Ryan, Jefferson K. VA 10th Inf. Co.B
Ryan, Jeremiah VA Hvy.Arty. Wilkinson's Co.
Ryan, Jerry AR Lt.Arty. Rivers' Btty. Cpl.
Ryan, Jerry GA Hvy.Arty. 22nd Bn. Co.D
Ryan, Jerry TX Waul's Legion Co.A
Ryan, J.G. AR 1st (Crawford's) Cav. Co.G Cpl.
Ryan, J.G. AR 18th Inf. Co.K
Ryan, J.G. TN 49th Inf. Co.F 2nd Lt.
Ryan, J.G. Inf. Bailey's Cons.Regt. Co.C 2nd
  Lt.
Ryan, J.H. AL Lt.Arty. Goldthwaite's Btty.
Ryan, J.H. MO 12th Cav. Co.D
Ryan, J.H. TX 2nd Inf. Co.G
Ryan, J.J. AL 5th Bn.Vol. Co.F
Ryan, J.J. LA 21st (Kennedy's) Inf. Co.A
Ryan, J.J. SC 11th Res. Col.
Ryan, J.J. TX Cav. Hardeman's Regt. Co.C
Ryan, J.J. TX 2nd Inf. Co.G
Ryan, J.M. AR 1st Inf. Co.I
Ryan, J.M. TN 45th Inf. Co.A
Ryan, J.M. TX Cav. Baird's Regt. Co.F
Ryan, J.M. VA 48th Inf. Co.D
Ryan, Job LA 31st Inf. Co.D
Ryan, John AL 3rd Cav. Co.E
Ryan, John, Jr. AL 12th Cav. Co.E 1st Lt.
Ryan, John AL 15th Bn.Part.Rangers Co.D
Ryan, John AL 56th Part.Rangers Co.D
Ryan, John AL Arty. 1st Bn. Co.D
Ryan, John AL Lt.Arty. 2nd Bn. Co.B
Ryan, John AL 4th Res. Co.A
Ryan, John AL 5th Bn.Vol. Co.D
Ryan, John AL 8th Inf. Co.H
Ryan, John AL 8th Inf. Co.I,C
Ryan, John AL 12th Inf. Co.A
Ryan, John AL 17th Inf. Lt.Col.
Ryan, John AL 32nd Inf. Co.K
Ryan, John AL 40th Inf. Co.F
Ryan, John AL 57th Inf. Co.H
Ryan, John AL Vol. Rabby's Coast Guard Co.
  No.1
Ryan, John AR Lt.Arty. 5th Btty.
Ryan, John AR Lt.Arty. Key's Btty.
Ryan, John AR 1st (Colquitt's) Inf. Co.F
Ryan, John AR 11th Inf. Co.A
Ryan, John AR 13th Inf. Co.A
Ryan, John GA Siege Arty. Campbell's Ind.Co.
Ryan, John GA Inf. 3rd Bn. Co.D

Ryan, John GA 4th Bn.S.S. Co.B
Ryan, John GA Inf. 19th Bn. (St.Guards) Co.F
Ryan, John GA 36th (Villepigue's) Inf. Co.I
Ryan, John GA 64th Inf. Co.F
Ryan, John KY 7th Cav. Co.G Cpl.
Ryan, John KY 10th Cav. Co.D,B
Ryan, John KY 11th Cav. Co.H
Ryan, John KY Morgan's Men Co.D
Ryan, John KY 7th Mtd.Inf. Co.A
Ryan, John LA 1st Hvy.Arty. (Reg.) Co.A
Ryan, John LA 1st Hvy.Arty. (Reg.) Co.B
Ryan, John LA 1st Hvy.Arty. (Reg.) Co.C
Ryan, John LA 1st Hvy.Arty. (Reg.) Co.E
Ryan, John LA 1st Hvy.Arty. (Reg.) Co.F
Ryan, John LA 1st Hvy.Arty. (Reg.) Co.G
Ryan, John (No.1) LA Arty. Moody's Co.
  (Madison Lt.Arty.)
Ryan, John (No.2) LA Arty. Moody's Co.
  (Madison Lt.Arty.)
Ryan, John LA 1st (Nelligan's) Inf. Co.C
Ryan, John LA 1st (Nelligan's) Inf. Co.D Sgt.
Ryan, John LA Inf. 1st Sp.Bn. (Wheat's) New
  Co.E
Ryan, John LA Mil. 3rd Regt. 1st Brig. 1st Div.
  Co.I
Ryan, John LA 4th Inf. Co.C
Ryan, John LA 5th Inf. Old Co.A, Co.K 1st Lt.
Ryan, John LA 5th Inf. Co.C
Ryan, John LA 6th Inf. Co.F
Ryan, John LA 7th Inf. Co.K
Ryan, John LA 8th Inf. Co.I Sgt.
Ryan, John LA 9th Inf. Co.A,E
Ryan, John LA 11th Inf. Co.A
Ryan, John, No.1 LA 11th Inf. Co.H
Ryan, John, No.2 LA 11th Inf. Co.H
Ryan, John LA 14th Inf. Co.D
Ryan, John LA 15th Inf. Co.B,D
Ryan, John LA 20th Inf. Co.F Cpl.
Ryan, John LA 22nd Inf. Co.B
Ryan, John LA 22nd (Cons.) Inf. Co.B
Ryan, John LA Mil. Leeds' Guards Regt. Co.D
Ryan, John LA Miles' Legion Co.A
Ryan, John, Jr. LA Miles' Legion Co.A
Ryan, John LA
Ryan, John MD 1st Inf. Co.F Cpl.
Ryan, John MS Inf. 2nd Bn. Co.G
Ryan, John MD Inf. 2nd Bn. Co.H
Ryan, John MS 3rd Inf. Co.A
Ryan, John MS 3rd Inf. Co.B
Ryan, John MS 15th Inf. Co.B,E
Ryan, John MS 18th Inf. Co.B
Ryan, John MS 19th Inf. Co.F
Ryan, John MS 21st Inf. Co.B
Ryan, John MS 48th Inf. Co.G
Ryan, John MO 11th Inf. Co.D
Ryan, John SC 1st Arty. Co.B
Ryan, John SC 1st Arty. Co.D
Ryan, John SC 1st Arty. Co.H Cpl.
Ryan, John SC Lt.Arty. Garden's Co. (Palmetto
  Lt.Btty.)
Ryan, John SC 1st (Butler's) Inf. Co.K
Ryan, John SC 27th Inf. Co.I
Ryan, John TN 2nd (Walker's) Inf. Co.A
Ryan, John TN 2nd (Walker's) Inf. Co.B
Ryan, John TN 2nd (Walker's) Inf. Co.F
Ryan, John TN 2nd (Walker's) Inf. Co.G
Ryan, John TN 2nd (Walker's) Inf. Co.K

Ryan, John TN Inf. 3rd Cons.Regt. Co.I
Ryan, John TN 5th Inf.
Ryan, John TN 10th Inf. Co.D
Ryan, John TN 19th Inf. Co.E
Ryan, John TN 21st Inf. Co.B Cpl.
Ryan, John TN 37th Inf. Co.C
Ryan, John TX 16th Cav. Co.I
Ryan, John TX 17th Cons.Dismtd.Cav. Co.C
Ryan, John TX Cav. Terry's Regt. Co.K
Ryan, John TX 7th Inf. Co.K
Ryan, John TX Waul's Legion Co.A Sgt.
Ryan, John VA 1st Cav. Co.A
Ryan, John VA 11th Cav. Co.E
Ryan, John VA 24th Cav. Co.G
Ryan, John VA Cav. 32nd Bn. Co.A
Ryan, John VA Cav. O'Ferrall's Bn. Co.B Cpl.
Ryan, John VA Arty. Wise Legion
Ryan, John VA 3rd Res. Co.G
Ryan, John VA 11th Bn.Res. Co.C 2nd Lt.
Ryan, John VA 17th Inf. Co.I
Ryan, John VA Inf. 25th Bn. Co.A
Ryan, John VA Inf. 25th Bn. Co.H
Ryan, John VA 27th Inf. Co.B
Ryan, John VA 52nd Inf. Co.G
Ryan, John VA 166th Mil. W. Lively's Co.E
Ryan, John Conf.Inf. 8th Bn. Co.A
Ryan, John Conf.Inf. 8th Bn. Co.B
Ryan, John 9th Conf.Inf. Co.A
Ryan, John 9th Conf.Inf. Co.B Sgt.
Ryan, John 9th Conf.Inf. Co.C
Ryan, John Conf.Reg.Inf. Brooks' Bn. Co.B
Ryan, John Conf.Reg.Inf. Brooks' Bn. Co.C
Ryan, John Conf.Reg.Inf. Brooks' Bn. Co.E
Ryan, John Sap. & Min. G.W. Maxson's
  Co.,CSA
Ryan, John Gen. & Staff Maj.,QM
Ryan, John Gen. & Staff, Adj.Gen.Dept. Capt.
Ryan, John A. VA Conscr. Cp.Lee Co.A Cpl.
Ryan, John C. AL 13th Bn.Part.Rangers Co.C
Ryan, John C. LA 6th Inf. Co.F
Ryan, John E. AL Inf. 1st Regt. Co.D
Ryan, John E. AL 9th Inf.
Ryan, John E. AL 10th Inf. Co.E,G
Ryan, John F. VA Lt.Arty. Garber's Co.
Ryan, John G. GA Cav. 1st Bn. Hughes' Co.
Ryan, John G. MS 12th Cav. Co.B Capt.
Ryan, John H. VA 15th Inf. Co.D
Ryan, John H. VA 28th Inf. Co.D
Ryan, John J. AL Mil. 3rd Vol. Co.E Cpl.
Ryan, John J. LA 1st (Strawbridge's) Inf.
  Co.A,C Sgt.
Ryan, John J. MS 1st (Percy's) Inf. Co.A
Ryan, John J. MS 18th Inf. Co.D Cpl.
Ryan, John J. TN 2nd (Walker's) Inf. Co.A
Ryan, John J. VA Lt.Arty. Brander's Co. Sgt.
Ryan, John J. Conf.Inf. 1st Bn. Co.F Sgt.
Ryan, John James TX Arty. 4th Bn. Co.B
Ryan, John James TX 8th Inf. Co.B
Ryan, John L. TN 34th Inf. Co.F Bvt.2nd Lt.
Ryan, John M. MO 1st N.E. Cav.
Ryan, John M. MO 5th Inf. Co.C,H
Ryan, John O. VA 51st Inf. Co.A
Ryan, John R. AL Lt.Arty. 2nd Bn. Co.E
Ryan, John R. AL Mil. Bligh's Co. 1st Cpl.
Ryan, John R. AL 4th Res. Co.A
Ryan, John R. TN 37th Inf. Co.C
Ryan, John R. VA 17th Cav. Co.C Sgt.

Ryan, John S. SC 1st (McCreary's) Inf. Asst.CS
Ryan, Jno. S. Gen. & Staff Capt.,Comsy.
Ryan, John T. LA 19th Inf. Co.G Cpl.
Ryan, John T. SC 1st Inf. Co.M
Ryan, John T. SC 1st (McCreary's) Inf. Co.L
Ryan, John T. VA Inf. 1st Bn. Co.A Sgt.
Ryan, John T. VA 2nd St.Res. Co.I
Ryan, John T. VA 6th Inf. Co.I
Ryan, John V. TX 9th (Young's) Inf. Co.A
Ryan, John W. VA 6th Cav. Co.B
Ryan, John W. VA 23rd Cav. Co.G Cpl.
Ryan, Joseph MD 1st Inf. Co.F
Ryan, Joseph MD 1st Inf. Co.G
Ryan, Joseph MS 3rd Inf. Co.A
Ryan, Joseph SC Inf. 1st (Charleston) Bn. Co.C
Ryan, Joseph TN 2nd (Walker's) Inf. Co.K
Ryan, Joseph TN 10th Inf. Co.E 1st Lt.
Ryan, Joseph TN 61st Mtd.Inf. Co.E
Ryan, Joseph TX 9th (Young's) Inf. Co.E
Ryan, Joseph 9th Conf.Inf. Co.A
Ryan, Joseph F. VA Mil. Maj.
Ryan, Joseph H. AL Lt.Arty. Tarrant's Btty.
Ryan, Joseph L. LA 10th Inf. Co.K
Ryan, Joseph N. VA 5th Inf. Co.L 1st Lt.
Ryan, Joseph W. SC Inf.Bn. Co.C
Ryan, Joseph W. VA 60th Inf. Co.I 2nd Lt.
Ryan, Joshua GA 14th Inf. Co.G
Ryan, J.P. LA 11th Inf. Co.D
Ryan, J.R. TX 2nd Inf. Co.G
Ryan, J.S. TX 2nd Inf. Co.G
Ryan, J.T. MS 5th Inf. Co.E
Ryan, J.W. TX Cav. 3rd Regt.St.Troops Co.A
Ryan, J.W. TX 9th (Young's) Inf. Co.C
Ryan, J.W. VA 7th Cav. Co.I
Ryan, Kennedy GA Hvy.Arty. 22nd Bn. Co.F
Ryan, Kennedy GA 1st (Olmstead's) Inf. Read's
    Co., Bonaud's Co.
Ryan, Lanty TN 15th Inf. Co.D
Ryan, Lawrence GA Hvy.Arty. 22nd Bn. Co.A
Ryan, Lawrence LA 8th Inf. Co.D
Ryan, Lawrence MS 11th Inf. Co.C
Ryan, Lawrence VA Cav. 37th Bn. Co.D,E
Ryan, Lawrence VA Cav. Mosby's Regt.
    (Part.Rangers) Co.C
Ryan, Lawrence VA 146th Mil. Co.H
Ryan, L.C. GA 5th Res. Co.E
Ryan, Lemon J. AL Hardy's Co. (Eufaula
    Minute Men)
Ryan, L.J. AL Cav. 4th Bn. (Love's) Co.C Sgt.
Ryan, Louis MS 3rd Inf. Co.A
Ryan, M. LA Mil. 2nd Regt. 3rd Brig. 1st Div.
Ryan, M. LA Mil. Lewis Guards
Ryan, M. MS 1st Lt.Arty. Co.I
Ryan, M. MS Packer's Co. (Pope Guards)
Ryan, M. SC 1st Cav. Co.C,K
Ryan, M. TN 12th Inf. Co.E
Ryan, M. TN 12th (Cons.) Inf. Co.E
Ryan, M. VA 2nd St.Res. Co.D
Ryan, M. 3rd Conf.Inf. Co.E Sgt.
Ryan, M.A. MS 20th Inf. Co.I
Ryan, Mack AR 1st (Crawford's) Cav. Co.K
Ryan, Madison AL 19th Inf. Co.F
Ryan, Malachi TN 10th Inf. Co.H Cpl.
Ryan, Marcus R. TX Cav. Benavides' Regt.
Ryan, Martin MS 3rd Inf. Co.A
Ryan, Martin MS 44th Inf. Co.L
Ryan, Matthew SC 2nd Arty. Co.B

Ryan, Michael AL Lt.Arty. 2nd Bn. Co.B
Ryan, Michael AL Seawell's Btty. (Mohawk
    Arty.)
Ryan, Michael GA Cav. 20th Bn. Co.G
Ryan, Michael GA Cav. 21st Bn. Co.D
Ryan, Michael GA 1st (Olmstead's) Inf. Read's
    Co., Gordon's Co.
Ryan, Michael GA 20th Inf. Co.K
Ryan, Michael GA 36th (Villepigue's) Inf. Co.I
Ryan, Michael GA 61st Inf. Co.F
Ryan, Michael GA 63rd Inf. Co.B
Ryan, Michael LA 1st Hvy.Arty. (Reg.) Co.G
Ryan, Michael LA 1st Hvy.Arty. (Reg.) Co.K
Ryan, Michael (No.1) LA Arty. Moody's Co.
    (Madison Lt.Arty.)
Ryan, Michael (No.2) LA Arty. Moody's Co.
    (Madison Lt.Arty.)
Ryan, Michael LA Mil. 4th Regt. 3rd Brig. 1st
    Div. Co.A,H
Ryan, Michael LA 10th Inf. Co.K
Ryan, Michael LA 14th Inf. Co.E
Ryan, Michael LA O'Hara's Co. (Pelican
    Guards,Co.B)
Ryan, Michael MD Arty. 3rd Btty.
Ryan, Michael MS Lt.Arty. (Jefferson Arty.)
    Darden's Co.
Ryan, Michael MS Lt.Arty. (Madison Lt.Arty.)
    Richards' Co.
Ryan, Michael SC 1st Arty. Co.A
Ryan, Michael SC 1st Regt. Charleston Guard
    Co.F
Ryan, Michael VA Cav. 1st Bn. Co.B
Ryan, Michael VA Cav. 32nd Bn.
Ryan, Michael VA Hvy.Arty. 19th Bn. 3rd Co.C
    Sgt.
Ryan, Michael VA 24th Inf. Co.H
Ryan, Michael VA 45th Inf. Co.C
Ryan, Michael G. AL Mil. 3rd Vol. Co.E
Ryan, Michael G. AL 40th Inf. Co.F
Ryan, Mike LA Mil. 4th Regt. 1st Brig. 1st Div.
    Co.B
Ryan, Mike TN 10th Inf. Co.E
Ryan, Mike TN 10th Inf. Co.F
Ryan, Milton A. MS 14th Inf. Co.B Cpl.
Ryan, M.J. LA Washington Arty.Bn. Co.4
Ryan, M.J. VA 54th Mil. Co.A
Ryan, M.L. AL 8th Inf. Co.I
Ryan, M.R. TN 12th (Green's) Cav. Co.E
Ryan, M.R. TX 2nd Inf. Co.G
Ryan, M.S. TN Inf. 3rd Bn. Co.A
Ryan, N. TN 45th Inf. Co.K
Ryan, N.B. GA 48th Inf. Co.K
Ryan, N.J. LA 21st (Patton's) Inf. Co.H
Ryan, Obediah VA 28th Inf. Co.D
Ryan, Owen TN 10th Inf. Co.A
Ryan, P. LA Mil. British Guard Bn. Coburn's
    Co.
Ryan, P. SC Hvy.Arty. 15th (Lucas') Bn. Co.B
Ryan, P. SC 23rd Inf. Co.C
Ryan, P. TN 12th Inf. Co.D
Ryan, P. TN 12th (Cons.) Inf. Co.E
Ryan, P. VA Lt.Arty. Barr's Co.
Ryan, P. 3rd Conf.Inf. Co.D
Ryan, P. 4th Conf.Inf. Co.A
Ryan, Pat TN Inf. Nashville Bn. Fulcher's Co.
Ryan, Pat Conf.Cav. Raum's Co.
Ryan, Patrick AR 2nd Inf. Co.B Sgt.

Ryan, Patrick AR 18th (Marmaduke's) Inf. Co.D
Ryan, Patrick GA Hvy.Arty. 22nd Bn. Co.E
Ryan, Patrick GA Arty. Maxwell's Reg.Lt.Btty.
Ryan, Patrick GA 1st Inf. Co.F
Ryan, Patrick GA 1st (Olmstead's) Inf. Guilmar-
    tin's Co.
Ryan, Patrick GA 61st Inf. Co.F
Ryan, Patrick (1) LA 1st Hvy.Arty. (Reg.) Co.H
Ryan, Patrick (2) LA 1st Hvy.Arty. (Reg.) Co.H
Ryan, Patrick LA 1st (Nelligan's) Inf. Co.D
Ryan, Patrick LA 1st (Strawbridge's) Inf. Co.D
Ryan, Patrick LA 1st (Strawbridge's) Inf. Co.G
Ryan, Patrick LA Inf. 1st Sp.Bn. (Wheat's) Co.C
Ryan, Patrick LA 7th Inf. Co.F
Ryan, Patrick LA 11th Inf. Co.B
Ryan, Patrick LA 13th Inf. Co.A
Ryan, Patrick LA 14th Inf. Co.H
Ryan, Patrick LA 20th Inf. New Co.E
Ryan, Patrick LA 20th Inf. Co.H
Ryan, Patrick LA 22nd Inf. Wash. Marks' Co.
Ryan, Patrick MD 1st Inf. Co.B
Ryan, Patrick MS Inf. 2nd Bn. Co.G
Ryan, Patrick MS 12th Inf. Co.E
Ryan, Patrick MS 18th Inf. Co.B
Ryan, Patrick MS 19th Inf. Co.C
Ryan, Patrick MS 21st Inf. Co.B
Ryan, Patrick MS 22nd Inf. Co.C
Ryan, Patrick MS 48th Inf. Co.G
Ryan, Patrick NC Lt.Arty. Thomas' Legion
    Levi's Btty.
Ryan, Patrick NC 1st Inf. Co.E
Ryan, Patrick SC 1st Arty. Co.F
Ryan, Patrick SC 1st (Butler's) Inf. Co.F
Ryan, Patrick SC Inf.Loc.Def. Estill's Co.
Ryan, Patrick TN Lt.Arty. Winston's Co.
Ryan, Patrick TN 2nd (Robison's) Inf. Co.E
Ryan, Patrick TN 2nd (Walker's) Inf. Co.F
Ryan, Patrick TN 38th Inf. Co.E
Ryan, Patrick VA Lt.Arty. Brander's Co.
Ryan, Patrick VA 2nd Inf. Co.G
Ryan, Patrick VA 2nd Inf. Co.K Cpl.
Ryan, Patrick VA 4th Res. Co.E,G
Ryan, Patrick VA 9th Inf. Co.B
Ryan, Patrick 3rd Conf.Eng.Troops Co.D
Ryan, Patrick Gen. & Staff Chap.
Ryan, Patrick J. AL Inf. 1st Regt. Co.A Lt.
Ryan, Patrick P. VA Lt.Arty. Penick's Co.
    Bugler
Ryan, Patrick P. VA 14th Inf. Co.K Music.
Ryan, P.B.E. SC 14th Inf. Co.D
Ryan, P.E. MS Cav. Buck's Co.
Ryan, Peter GA 61st Inf. Co.F
Ryan, Peter SC 1st Arty. Co.F
Ryan, Peter SC Lt.Arty. 3rd (Palmetto) Bn. Co.B
Ryan, Peter TX 2nd Inf. Co.B
Ryan, Peter C. AL 3rd Inf. Co.G
Ryan, P.F. AR 5th Inf. Co.D
Ryan, P.H. SC 2nd Inf. Co.E Cpl.
Ryan, P.K. AL 5th Inf. Co.C
Ryan, Philip AL Cp. of Instr. Talladega
Ryan, Philip GA 1st (Olmstead's) Inf. Gordon's
    Co.
Ryan, Philip GA 63rd Inf. Co.B
Ryan, Philip LA Arty. Kean's Btty. (Orleans
    Ind.Arty.)
Ryan, Philip LA Mil. Leeds' Guards Regt. Co.D
Ryan, Phillip LA 10th Inf. Co.B

Ryan, Phillip MS 1st (King's) Inf. (St.Troops) Co.E
Ryan, Phillip H. VA Hvy.Arty. 20th Bn. Co.D
Ryan, Pierre MS 3rd Inf. Co.A
Ryan, P.W. TX 9th (Young's) Inf. Co.A
Ryan, R.B. AL 16th Inf. Co.I
Ryan, R.B. AL Metropolitan Guards Sgt.
Ryan, R.B. Eng.,CSA 1st Lt.
Ryan, R.C. AR 18th Inf. Co.C
Ryan, Redman R. AR 21st Inf. Co.C
Ryan, Redmon R. AR 17th (Lemoyne's) Inf. Co.C
Ryan, Reyne MS 3rd Inf. Co.A
Ryan, Richard GA 1st (Olmstead's) Inf. Co.A
Ryan, Richard KY 8th Cav. Co.K
Ryan, Richard VA 6th Inf. 1st Co.B
Ryan, Richard D. VA Horse Arty. McClanahan's Co.
Ryan, Richard D. VA Prov.Guard Avis' Co. Sgt.
Ryan, R.J. TX 10th Cav. Co.E
Ryan, Robert AR 8th Inf. New Co.D
Ryan, Robert AR 15th (Josey's) Inf. 1st Co.G
Ryan, Robert TN 2nd (Walker's) Inf. Co.B
Ryan, Robert 9th Conf.Inf. Co.F Cpl.
Ryan, Robert E.J. VA Hvy.Arty. 10th Bn. Co.A
Ryan, Robert E.J. VA 23rd Inf. Co.H
Ryan, Robert F. NC 2nd Inf. Co.E Cpl.
Ryan, Robert S. MD 1st Inf. Co.D
Ryan, Rody MO 1st Inf. Co.F
Ryan, R.P. GA 2nd Cav. Co.A
Ryan, R.R. AR 1st (Monroe's) Cav. Co.H
Ryan, Rubin J. GA Inf. 1st Loc.Troops (Augusta) Co.C
Ryan, Rufus B. GA 10th Inf. Co.C
Ryan, Samuel AL 4th Res. Co.G
Ryan, Samuel KY 4th Cav. Co.B Sgt.
Ryan, Samuel TN 61st Mtd.Inf. Co.E
Ryan, Samuel VA Cav. 35th Bn. Co.B
Ryan, Samuel VA 8th Inf. Co.H
Ryan, Samuel B. KY 2nd Cav. Co.B
Ryan, Samuel B. KY 3rd Cav. Co.H
Ryan, Samuel B. KY 9th Mtd.Inf. Co.A
Ryan, Samuel G. NC 28th Inf. Co.G Sgt.
Ryan, Samuel L. KY 9th Cav. Co.A
Ryan, Samuel L. KY 9th Mtd.Inf. Co.A Cpl.
Ryan, S.B. SC 5th Cav. Co.D
Ryan, S.B. SC Cav. 17th Bn. Co.A
Ryan, S.B. SC 7th Inf. 1st Co.H
Ryan, S.B. SC 22nd Inf. Co.A
Ryan, S.D. AR Inf. Cocke's Regt. Co.K
Ryan, Simpson S. LA 21st (Kennedy's) Inf. Co.A
Ryan, S.S. LA 1st (Strawbridge's) Inf. Co.C
Ryan, S. Seabrook VA 17th Inf. Co.A
Ryan, S.W. GA Hvy.Arty. 22nd Bn. Co.F
Ryan, T. SC Mil. 1st Regt.Rifles Chichester's Co.
Ryan, T. TN 21st Inf. Co.H
Ryan, T.A. SC Arty. Fickling's Co. (Brooks Lt.Arty.)
Ryan, T.A. SC 3rd Bn.Res. Co.A
Ryan, T.A. SC 25th Inf. Co.E
Ryan, T.C. LA 1st Cav. Co.A
Ryan, T.C. SC Lt.Arty. J.T. Kanapaux's Co. (Lafayette Arty.) Sgt.

Ryan, T.D.L. GA Cav. 22nd Bn. (St.Guards) Co.G
Ryan, T.D.L. GA 8th Inf. Co.G Capt.
Ryan, T.E. GA Inf. (Wright Loc.Guards) Holmes' Co.
Ryan, Thomas AL 3rd Cav. Co.F
Ryan, Thomas AL Seawell's Btty. (Mohawk Arty.)
Ryan, Thomas AL 42nd Inf. Co.I
Ryan, Thomas AR Cav. Gordon's Regt. Co.B
Ryan, Thomas AR 10th Inf. Lt.
Ryan, Thomas GA Cav. 1st Bn. Hopkins' Co.
Ryan, Thomas GA 5th Cav. Co.K
Ryan, Thomas GA 1st (Olmstead's) Inf. Co.B
Ryan, Thomas GA 10th Inf. Co.C
Ryan, Thomas GA 14th Inf.
Ryan, Thomas LA 1st Hvy.Arty. (Reg.) Co.G Cpl.
Ryan, Thomas LA 1st (Strawbridge's) Inf. Co.D
Ryan, Thomas LA Inf. 1st Sp.Bn. (Wheat's) Co.A
Ryan, Thomas LA Mil. 3rd Regt. 1st Brig. 1st Div. Co.A
Ryan, Thomas LA 8th Inf. Co.I
Ryan, Thomas LA 10th Inf. Co.D
Ryan, Thomas LA 20th Inf. Co.H
Ryan, Thomas LA Miles' Legion Co.G
Ryan, Thomas MS Inf. 2nd Bn. (St.Troops) Co.D
Ryan, Thomas MS 7th Inf. Co.A
Ryan, Thomas MS 16th Inf. Co.I
Ryan, Thomas MS 21st Inf. Co.E,L
Ryan, Thomas MO Lt.Arty. 3rd Field Btty.
Ryan, Thomas MO 1st Inf. Co.F
Ryan, Thomas MO 10th Inf. Lt.
Ryan, Thos. MO St.Guard Maj.
Ryan, Thomas NC 2nd Inf. Co.A
Ryan, Thomas NC 4th Inf. Co.K
Ryan, Thomas NC 8th Inf. Co.F
Ryan, Thomas SC Hvy.Arty. 15th (Lucas') Bn. Co.B
Ryan, Thomas SC Hvy.Arty. Gilchrist's Co. (Gist Guard)
Ryan, Thomas SC Lt.Arty. J.T. Kanapaux's Co. (Lafayette Arty.)
Ryan, Thomas SC 1st (McCreary's) Inf. Co.K
Ryan, Thomas SC 27th Inf. Co.H
Ryan, Thomas TN Douglass' Bn.Part.Rangers Perkins'
Ryan, Thomas TN 1st (Feild's) Inf. Co.K
Ryan, Thomas TN 2nd (Walker's) Inf. Co.C
Ryan, Thomas TX Cav. Waller's Regt. Menard's Co. Teamster
Ryan, Thomas TX 20th Inf. Co.K
Ryan, Thomas VA 17th Cav. Co.C
Ryan, Thomas VA Lt.Arty. 18th Bn. Co.A
Ryan, Thomas VA 1st Inf. Co.C
Ryan, Thomas VA 7th Inf. Gibson's Co.
Ryan, Thomas VA Inf. 25th Bn. Co.A
Ryan, Thomas VA 136th Mil. Co.F
Ryan, Thomas 1st Conf.Reg.Cav. Co.A
Ryan, Thomas Conf.Inf. 8th Bn. Co.A
Ryan, Thomas 3rd Conf.Eng.Troops Co.G Artif.
Ryan, Thomas A. SC 2nd Inf. Co.K
Ryan, Thomas C. AL 12th Cav. Co.E
Ryan, Thomas C. AL 27th Inf. Co.H
Ryan, Thomas E. AL 62nd Inf. Co.G

Ryan, Thomas H. VA 49th Inf. Co.K
Ryan, Thomas M. LA Inf. 1st Sp.Bn. (Rightor's) Co.B
Ryan, Thomas M. LA 20th Inf. Co.G Capt.
Ryan, Thomas P. SC 1st (McCreary's) Inf. Co.K 2nd Lt.
Ryan, Thomas P. SC 23rd Inf. Co.A,C Capt.
Ryan, Thomas P.B. LA Arty. Green's Co. (LA Guard Btty.) Cpl.
Ryan, Thomas P.B. LA 1st (Nelligan's) Inf. 1st Co.B
Ryan, Thomas S. AL 8th Inf. Co.E
Ryan, Timothy AL 8th Inf. Co.E
Ryan, Timothy MS 44th Inf. Co.L
Ryan, Timothy VA Hvy.Arty. 19th Bn. 3rd Co.C
Ryan, Timothy VA 17th Inf. Co.I
Ryan, T.M. LA Inf.Crescent Regt. Co.E
Ryan, T.P.B. LA 1st Hvy.Arty. (Reg.) Co.A,D,G,H,B,I 1st Lt.
Ryan, T.W. AL 41st Inf. Co.E
Ryan, Van AR Mil. Desha Cty.Bn.
Ryan, Van R. AR 1st (Colquitt's) Inf. Co.D
Ryan, Victor AR 2nd Inf. Old Co.C, Co.B Cpl.
Ryan, Victor LA 18th Inf. Co.H,E
Ryan, Victor MS 3rd Inf. Co.A
Ryan, W. GA 47th Inf. Co.C
Ryan, W. LA 1st Hvy.Arty. (Reg.) Co.B
Ryan, W. SC 1st Regt. Charleston Guard Co.A,F
Ryan, W. SC 23rd Inf. Co.C
Ryan, W. TX Cav. Giddings' Bn. Co.A
Ryan, W.A. TX 17th Cons.Dismtd.Cav. Maj.
Ryan, W.A. TX Granbury's Cons.Brig. Lt.Col.
Ryan, W.B. SC 3rd Cav. Co.H
Ryan, W.D. GA Lt.Arty. (Arsenal Btty.) Hudson's Co.
Ryan, W.F. VA Inf. 26th Bn. Co.F
Ryan, W.G. AL 10th Inf. Co.E
Ryan, W.G. VA Horse Arty. G.W. Brown's Co.
Ryan, W.H. GA 10th Inf. Co.C
Ryan, W.H. SC 3rd Arty. Co.H
Ryan, W.H. SC 27th Inf. Co.H Capt.
Ryan, White G. VA 4th Res. Co.A Capt.
Ryan, White G. VA 60th Inf. Co.I Capt.
Ryan, William AL 51st (Part.Rangers) Co.K
Ryan, William AL 7th Inf. Co.C
Ryan, William AL Gorff's Co. (Mobile Pulaski Rifles)
Ryan, William GA 11th Inf. Co.D
Ryan, William GA 50th Inf. Co.B
Ryan, William LA 6th Inf. Co.H
Ryan, William LA 15th Inf. Co.H
Ryan, William LA 21st (Patton's) Inf. Co.H
Ryan, William, Jr. LA 31st Inf. Co.B
Ryan, William LA Miles' Legion Co.D
Ryan, William MS Inf. 2nd Bn. Co.G
Ryan, William MS 12th Inf. Co.E
Ryan, William MS 19th Inf. Co.C
Ryan, William MS 48th Inf. Co.G
Ryan, William SC 1st Arty. Co.A
Ryan, William SC 1st (Butler's) Inf. Co.F
Ryan, William SC Inf. 1st (Charleston) Bn. Co.C
Ryan, William SC Inf. 1st (Charleston) Bn. Co.F
Ryan, William SC Ord.Scouts Loc.Def.Troops
Ryan, William TN 2nd (Walker's) Inf. Co.K Sgt.
Ryan, William TN 10th Inf.
Ryan, William TN 15th Inf. Co.D

Ryan, William TX 3rd Cav. Co.F
Ryan, William TX 8th Cav. Co.L
Ryan, William TX 5th Inf. Co.B
Ryan, William TX 12th Inf. Co.A
Ryan, William VA 9th Cav. Co.H
Ryan, William VA Btty.
Ryan, William VA 1st Inf. Co.C Cpl.
Ryan, William VA Inf. 1st Bn. Co.D
Ryan, William VA 2nd St.Res. Co.B
Ryan, William VA 14th Inf. Co.B
Ryan, William VA Inf. 22nd Bn. Co.E
Ryan, William VA 36th Inf. Co.A
Ryan, William VA 59th Inf. 3rd Co.F
Ryan, William VA 60th Inf. 1st Co.H
Ryan, William VA 108th Mil. Co.G
Ryan, William VA 157th Mil. Co.A
Ryan, William Conf.Cav. Wood's Regt. Co.B
Ryan, William 9th Conf.Inf. Co.A
Ryan, William A. AL 8th Inf. Co.E 2nd Lt.
Ryan, William A. TX 18th Cav. Lt.Col.
Ryan, William A. Gen. & Staff 1st Lt.,Adj.
Ryan, William F. VA 11th Bn.Res. Co.C
Ryan, William H. GA 31st Inf. Co.G
Ryan, William H. MD Cav. 2nd Bn. Co.C
Ryan, William H. SC Inf. 1st (Charleston) Bn.
  Co.C Capt.
Ryan, William H. VA 2nd Cav. Co.E
Ryan, William H. VA Lt.Arty. Lamkin's Co.
Ryan, William H. VA 51st Inf. Co.A
Ryan, William J. AL Cav. Holloway's Co.
Ryan, William K. SC 2nd Arty. Co.D 1st Lt.
Ryan, William M. AL 18th Inf. Co.C
Ryan, William M. AR 21st Inf. Co.H
Ryan, William M. SC Lt.Arty. 3rd (Palmetto)
  Bn. Co.D
Ryan, William N. AR 17th (Lemoyne's) Inf.
  Co.D
Ryan, William O. VA 14th Inf. Co.K
Ryan, William P. MO Cav. 3rd Bn. Co.B
Ryan, William P. NC 14th Inf. Co.D
Ryan, William P. TN 24th Inf. Co.D
Ryan, William R. VA 3rd Cav. Co.A
Ryan, William S. AL 3rd Inf. Co.A
Ryan, William T. LA 5th Inf. Co.C Cpl.
Ryan, William V. VA Lt.Arty. Garber's Co.
Ryan, William W. KY 4th Mtd.Inf. Co.G
Ryan, W.K. SC 2nd Arty. Co.H
Ryan, W.O. SC Rhett's Co.
Ryan, W.P. SC Mil. 16th Regt. Jones' Co.
Ryan, W.P. SC 24th Inf. Co.A
Ryan, W.P. SC Charleston Arsenal Bn. Co.A 1st
  Lt.
Ryan, W.R. VA 47th Inf. Co.H
Ryan, W.S. LA 18th Inf. Co.H
Ryan, W.S. LA Mil. Chalmette Regt. Co.G
Ryan, W.S. LA Inf.Crescent Regt. Co.E
Ryan, W.S. TX 9th Cav. Co.K
Ryan, W. Stone LA Lt.Arty. Holmes' Btty.
Ryan, W.W. LA Mil. 3rd Regt. 3rd Brig. 1st
  Div. Co.F
Ryan, Z.J. MS 4th Inf. Co.F 2nd Lt.
Ryans, Bowling G. GA 10th Inf. Co.D
Ryans, James GA 2nd Bn.S.S. Co.D
Ryans, James NC 33rd Inf. Co.H
Ryans, John GA 46th Inf. Co.E
Ryans, John LA 1st (Strawbridge's) Inf. Co.A
Ryans, John LA Miles' Legion Co.F

Ryans, John SC 2nd St.Troops Co.H
Ryans, John SC 11th Res. Co.D
Ryans, Joseph SC 19th Inf. Co.B
Ryans, K. TN 21st & 22nd (Cons.) Cav. Co.C
Ryans, M.M. AL 1st Cav. Co.B
Ryans, Samuel VA Horse Arty. G.W. Brown's
  Co.
Ryans, Thomas GA 12th Inf. Co.I
Ryas, Levi NC 32nd Inf. Co.I
Rybischi, Caesar LA Arty. Landry's Co.
  (Donaldsonville Arty.)
Rybon, Peter Gen. & Staff Chap.
Ryburn, David B. VA 1st Cav. 2nd Co.D
Ryburn, Frank M. LA 11th Inf. Co.D
Ryburn, James O. VA 6th Bn.Res. Co.I
Ryburn, John VA 6th Bn.Res. Co.C
Ryburn, Joseph A. KY 2nd Mtd.Inf. Co.D Sgt.
Ryburn, J.P.S. TN 8th (Smith's) Cav. Co.B
Ryburn, W.D. KY 12th Cav. Co.H Cpl.
Ryburn, William B. VA 37th Inf. Co.F
Ryce, Francis W. MD 1st Inf. Co.H
Ryche, J.M. NC 15th Inf. Co.B
Ryckley, Charles GA Inf. (Loc.Def.) Whiteside's
  Nav.Bn. Co.C
Rycroft, J.A.J. GA 4th (Clinch's) Cav.
Rycroft, Rufus T. NC 3rd Bn.Sr.Res. Co.C
Rycroft, T.R.D. GA 4th (Clinch's) Cav. Co.K
Ryder, Albert T. VA 10th Inf. Co.L
Ryder, Alexander TX 19th Cav. Co.E
Ryder, Bernard AL 1st Regt. Mobile Vol. British
  Guard Co.B
Ryder, Bernard AL Mil. 3rd Vol. Co.B
Ryder, B.H. GA 46th Inf. Co.K
Ryder, Charles AL Arty. 1st Bn. Co.D,B
Ryder, Corbet A. AL 3rd Inf. Co.K
Ryder, George LA 22nd Inf. Co.B
Ryder, G.V.M. TX 9th (Nichols') Inf. Co.C
  Music.
Ryder, G.V.M. TX Waul's Legion Co.C Music.
Ryder, G.W. GA 11th Inf. Co.C
Ryder, James AL St.Arty. Co.A
Ryder, James GA 11th Inf. Co.C
Ryder, James LA 22nd (Cons.) Inf. Co.F,A
Ryder, James B. LA 27th Inf. Co.E Lt.,Adj.
Ryder, Jesse GA 66th Inf. Co.K
Ryder, John AL Mil. 3rd Vol. Co.B
Ryder, John AL 36th Inf. Co.E
Ryder, John AR 50th Mil. Co.C
Ryder, John LA Lt.Arty. 6th Field Btty. (Grosse
  Tete Flying Arty.)
Ryder, John TX Arty. 4th Bn. Co.A
Ryder, John TX 8th Inf. Co.A
Ryder, Joseph KY 2nd Mtd.Inf. Co.E
Ryder, L.F. SC Inf. 7th Bn. (Enfield Rifles)
  Co.D,G
Ryder, Marshall MO Robertson's Regt.St.Guard
  Co.1
Ryder, Martin V. GA 56th Inf. Co.H
Ryder, Michael AL 26th Inf. Co.G
Ryder, Richard G. MS 27th Inf. Co.L Sgt.
Ryder, Samuel GA 30th Inf. Co.E
Ryder, Thomas LA Mil. 4th Regt. 1st Brig. 1st
  Div. Co.E
Ryder, W. GA 7th Mil. Co.D
Ryder, William GA 7th Res. Co.K
Ryder, William GA Inf. 14th Bn. (St.Guards)
  Co.C

Ryder, William TN Inf. 154th Sr.Regt. Co.C
  Cpl.
Rydner, A.W. TX Inf. 1st Bn. Co.F
Rye, A.H. AL 26th (O'Neal's) Inf. Co.B
Rye, Alex. B. TN 14th Inf. Co.D,F
Rye, Ambrose GA 66th Inf. Co.D
Rye, Benjamin F. TX 18th Inf. Co.E
Rye, Bennet L. TX 37th Cav. Surg.
Rye, B.L. TX Cav. 1st Bn.St.Troops Co.C
Rye, B.L. TX 10th Cav. Co.F
Rye, B.L. Gen. & Staff AASurg.
Rye, Blakney NC 43rd Inf. Co.I
Rye, D.A. AR Cav. Gordon's Regt. Co.E Capt.
Rye, D.W. MS 1st Cav. Co.F
Rye, D.W. MS 2nd St.Cav. Co.H,F Cpl.
Rye, Erasmus FL 7th Inf. Co.B
Rye, Frank D. AL Cav. Murphy's Bn. Co.D
Rye, George W. VA 45th Inf. Co.H
Rye, H. FL Lt.Arty. Dyke's Co.
Rye, H.C. TN 50th Inf. Co.B Sgt.
Rye, H.F. FL Lt.Arty. Dyke's Co.
Rye, H.F. FL 11th Inf. Co.G
Rye, H.F. GA Cav. 29th Bn.
Rye, Hiram VA 86th Mil. Co.E
Rye, Hosea FL Kilcrease Lt.Arty.
Rye, James MO 9th Inf. Co.C
Rye, James TN 38th Inf. 2nd Co.H
Rye, James D. GA Lt.Arty. Guerard's Btty.
Rye, James G. AR Cav. 1st Bn. (Stirman's) Co.A
  Music.
Rye, James M. TN 45th Inf. Co.B
Rye, J.C. MS 2nd St.Cav. Co.F
Rye, J.C. MS 14th Inf. Co.E
Rye, J.C. MS 43rd Inf. Co.C
Rye, J.E. SC 14th Inf. Co.E
Rye, J.F. GA 63rd Inf. Co.D
Rye, J.F. TN 50th Inf. Co.B Sgt.
Rye, J.F. TN 50th (Cons.) Inf. Co.A
Rye, J.J. AL 26th (O'Neal's) Inf. Co.B
Rye, J.M. MS 1st Cav. Co.F
Rye, J.M. MS 2nd St.Cav. Co.H,F
Rye, J.M. MS 4th Inf. Co.E
Rye, John VA 16th Cav. Co.F
Rye, John VA Cav. Caldwell's Bn. Taylor's Co.
Rye, John VA Arty. Curtis' Co.
Rye, John C. AR Cav. 1st Bn. (Stirman's) Co.A
Rye, John J. AR Cav. 1st Bn. (Stirman's) Co.F
Rye, John K. GA 45th Inf. Co.A
Rye, John M. MD Arty. 1st Btty.
Rye, John M. MS 43rd Inf. Co.L
Rye, John R.D. AR Inf. Cocke's Regt. Co.I 1st
  Lt.
Rye, John S. VA 6th Inf. Co.I
Rye, John W. MS 2nd St.Cav. Co.F
Rye, Joseph D. GA Lt.Arty. Guerard's Btty.
Rye, J.R. TN 49th Inf. Co.B
Rye, J.R. Inf. Bailey's Cons.Regt. Co.D
Rye, J.R.D. AR 11th Inf. Co.D 3rd Lt.
Rye, M.H. MS 14th Inf. Co.E
Rye, Morgan TX 28th Cav. Co.I 2nd Lt.
Rye, Moses H. MS 43rd Inf. Co.A Sgt.
Rye, O.B. TX 18th Inf. Co.E
Rye, Richard VA Lt.Arty. Moore's Co.
Rye, S.P. AL 1st Cav. Co.B 1st Lt.
Rye, Stephen M. AR Cav. 1st Bn. (Stirman's)
  Co.A
Rye, S.W. MS 2nd St.Cav. Co.H,F 1st Lt.

Rye, T.F. TN 24th Bn.S.S. Co.B
Rye, Thomas MS 11th (Perrin's) Cav. Co.I Capt.
Rye, Thomas TN 11th Inf. Co.C
Rye, Thomas J. MS St.Cav. 2nd Bn. (Harris') Co.A,C Capt.
Rye, Thomas J. MS 2nd Inf. Co.G Sgt.
Rye, W. TN 3rd (Forrest's) Cav. Co.D
Rye, W.G. GA 54th Inf. Co.A
Rye, W.H. GA Inf. Clemons' Co. Cpl.
Rye, W.H. TN 45th Inf. Co.B
Rye, William GA Cav. 12th Bn. (St.Guards) Co.B Cpl.
Rye, William GA 1st Bn.S.S. Co.C
Rye, William GA 31st Inf. Co.G
Rye, William SC 26th Inf. Co.D
Rye, William G. GA Lt.Arty. (Jackson Arty.) Massenburg's Btty.
Rye, William G. GA 63rd Inf. Co.B
Rye, William T. AR 35th Inf. Co.B 1st Lt.
Rye, William W. FL 3rd Inf. Co.G Sgt.
Rye, William W. GA Lt.Arty. Guerard's Btty.
Rye, William W. NC 14th Inf. Co.C
Rye, W.R. AR Cav. Gordon's Regt. Co.E Cpl.
Rye, W.W. AL 8th (Livingston's) Cav. Co.C
Rye, W.W. SC 21st Inf. Co.D
Ryehard, B.F. MS 36th Inf. Co.G
Ryels, M. MS Cav.Res. Mitchell's Co.
Ryen, Andrew TN 62nd Mtd.Inf. Co.G
Ryen, John MO Lt.Arty. 3rd Field Btty.
Ryen, William Q. VA Hvy.Arty. 18th Bn. Co.C
Ryene, Pat VA 27th Inf. Co.E
Ryens, Peter TN Sullivan Cty.Res. (Loc.Def.Troops) Trevitt's Co.
Ryer, Charles C. TN 3rd (Forrest's) Cav. Hensel's Co.
Ryer, G.H. GA 38th Inf. Co.H
Ryerson, Peter LA Washington Arty.Bn. Co.1
Ryerson, William F. SC 2nd Cav. Co.C
Ryfield, Marion SC 5th Inf. 2nd Co.G
Ryfield, R.L. SC 5th Inf. 2nd Co.G
Rygan, A.J. AL Lt.Arty. 20th Bn.
Ryhburn, D.C.H. MO 15th Cav. Co.A
Ryions, Bauxton MS 39th Inf. Co.C
Rykard, Edmund C. FL 4th Inf. Co.C 1st Sgt.
Rykard, Fed SC Post Guard Senn's Co.
Rykard, James D. NC 62nd Inf. Co.K
Rykard, J.H. SC 6th Cav. Co.C
Rykard, J.W. NC 62nd Inf. Co.K
Rykard, Levi H. SC 2nd Inf. Co.F
Rykard, Levi H. SC 5th Res. Co.B 3rd Lt.
Rykard, L.H. SC 4th Bn.Res. Co.B 2nd Lt.
Rykard, Robert FL 5th Inf. Co.D
Rykard, Robert H. NC 62nd Inf. Co.K
Rykard, S.P. SC 4th Bn.Res. Co.B
Rykard, Thomas J. SC 2nd Inf. Co.F
Ryker, William MS 16th Inf. Co.I
Rylan, William R. AR 3rd Cav. Co.D
Ryland, A.G. VA 9th Inf. 2nd Co.A Sgt.
Ryland, A.W. LA 18th Inf. Co.D
Ryland, C.H. Gen. & Staff Hosp.Stew.
Ryland, George TN 63rd Inf. Co.D
Ryland, James J. AL 36th Inf. Co.F Cpl.
Ryland, J.G. VA 34th Inf. Co.B
Ryland, J.H. MS 44th Inf. Co.A Asst.Surg.
Ryland, J.H. Gen. & Staff A.Surg.
Ryland, John S. VA 21st Inf. Co.C

Ryland, John William VA 34th Inf. Co.K Sgt.
Ryland, Joseph H. AL Lt.Arty. 2nd Bn. Co.F
Ryland, Joseph H. MS 11th (Perrin's) Cav. Co.H
Ryland, Josiah VA 9th Cav. Co.H
Ryland, Josiah, Jr. VA 34th Inf. Co.K 1st Lt.
Ryland, Josiah, Sr. VA 34th Inf. Co.K 1st Lt.
Ryland, Josiah Conf.Hvy.Arty. Montague's Bn. Co.B 2nd Lt.
Ryland, J.T. VA 1st (Farinholt's) Res. Co.K
Ryland, Kinchen NC 3rd Inf. Co.A
Ryland, Noah NC 3rd Arty. (40th St.Troops) Co.F
Ryland, Norvell VA 34th Inf. Co.K
Ryland, Norvell Conf.Hvy.Arty. Montague's Bn. Co.B
Ryland, O.G.M. AL 22nd Inf. Co.D Teamster
Ryland, O.G.M. AL 25th Inf. Co.K
Ryland, Richard 15th Conf.Cav. Co.I
Ryland, Robert NC 2nd Arty. (36th St.Troops) Co.E
Ryland, Robert SC Inf. 9th Bn. Co.G
Ryland, Robert S. VA 9th Cav. Co.H
Ryland, Robert S. VA Lt.Arty. W.P. Carter's Co. 2nd Lt.
Ryland, R.S. Conf.Arty. R.C.M. Page's Bn. 2nd Lt.
Ryland, Samuel VA 34th Inf. Co.K
Ryland, Talbot TN 63rd Inf. Co.D Sgt.
Ryland, Thomas M. VA Lt.Arty. Pollock's Co.
Ryland, William TN 3rd (Lillard's) Mtd.Inf. Co.H
Ryland, William H. VA 2nd Arty. Co.D
Ryland, William H. VA Inf. 22nd Bn. Co.D
Ryland, W.S. VA 13th Inf. Chap.
Ryland, W.S. Gen. & Staff Chap.
Rylander, Edw. P. AL Arty. 4th Bn. Hilliard's Legion Co.A
Rylander, J.A. GA 12th (Robinson's) Cav. (St.Guards) Co.E
Rylander, J.B. AL 1st Cav. 2nd Co.B Sgt.
Rylander, J.D.P. AL Arty. 1st Bn. Co.A Sgt.
Rylander, Joel F. AL Arty. 1st Bn. Co.A
Rylander, John E. GA Inf. 10th Bn. Maj.
Rylander, John E. GA 12th Inf. Co.A 1st Sgt.
Rylander, Joseph B. GA Inf. 10th Bn. Co.E
Rylands, William AL Logan's Res.
Rylant, B.F. AL 2nd Cav. Co.G
Rylant, H.D. AL 2nd Cav. Co.I
Rylant, H.J. AL 2nd Cav. Co.G
Rylant, William AL 2nd Cav. Co.G Sgt.
Ryle, Adam F. GA 14th Inf. Co.B
Ryle, Adam J. GA 14th Inf. Co.B Cpl.
Ryle, Benjamin KY 5th Cav. Co.G
Ryle, Coates GA 4th Inf. Co.C
Ryle, Daniel J. GA 4th Inf. Co.C
Ryle, Daniel J. GA 14th Inf. Co.B
Ryle, F.M. GA 54th Inf. Co.A
Ryle, James MS 6th Inf. Co.C
Ryle, Jasper N. GA 34th Inf. Co.B
Ryle, J.F. GA 66th Inf. Co.A
Ryle, J.K. GA 14th Inf. Co.B Cpl.
Ryle, John C. GA 6th Inf. (St.Guards) Co.F
Ryle, John C. KY 1st (Butler's) Cav. Co.G Sgt.
Ryle, John F. GA 10th Inf. Co.H
Ryle, John R. KY 2nd Cav. Co.I
Ryle, John W. KY 2nd (Duke's) Cav. Co.I,A
Ryle, Oscar J. KY 2nd (Duke's) Cav. Co.I

Ryle, Pembroke S. MO 11th Inf. Co.I
Ryle, W.B. GA Cav. 22nd Bn. (St.Guards) Co.A
Ryle, William KY 2nd (Duke's) Cav. Co.I
Ryle, William H. KY 10th (Johnson's) Cav. Co.C
Ryle, William L. KY 8th Cav. Co.F
Ryle, William N. GA 14th Inf. Co.B Capt.
Ryle, William T. GA 3rd Inf. Co.F
Rylee, Andrew J. GA Cobb's Legion Co.C
Rylee, Benjamin F. GA 24th Inf. Co.I
Rylee, Isaac GA 4th Cav. (St.Guards) Armstrong's Co.
Rylee, J. GA 19th Inf. Co.C
Rylee, James B. GA Cobb's Legion Co.C
Ryles, A.A. AR Cav. Gordon's Regt. Co.B
Ryles, A.A. AR 34th Inf. Co.D
Ryles, C.H. TN Inf. 1st Cons.Regt. Co.I
Ryles, Charles G. MO 2nd Inf. Co.E
Ryles, Eli J. GA 13th Cav. Co.E,G
Ryles, H.E. SC 26th Inf. Co.G
Ryles, J. GA Inf. (NonConscr.) Howard's Co.
Ryles, J. Bently MO 3rd Inf. Co.K
Ryles, J.H. TN Inf. 1st Cons.Regt. Co.I
Ryles, Joel GA Inf. 27th Bn. (NonConscr.) Co.B
Ryles, John MS Cav. 17th Bn. Co.F
Ryles, John G. GA 14th Inf. Co.B
Ryles, Larkin M. NC 5th Cav. (63rd St.Troops) Co.D
Ryles, R.B. MS Cav. Jeff Davis Legion Co.I
Ryles, Thomas, Jr. AR Cav. Gordon's Regt. Co.K
Ryles, Thomas E. GA 10th Cav. Co.C
Ryles, Thomas E. GA 16th Inf. Co.C
Ryles, W.F. AL 38th Inf. Co.E
Ryles, William AR Cav. Gordon's Regt. Co.I
Ryles, William GA 13th Cav. Co.G
Ryles, Willis AL Inf. 1st Regt. Co.I
Ryles, W.T. AL 38th Inf.
Ryley, A.B. AR 15th (Josey's) Inf. Co.F
Ryley, Bennett GA 4th Cav. (St.Guards) McDonald's Co. Sgt.
Ryley, James NC 15th Inf. Co.D
Ryley, James SC 1st Arty. Co.D
Ryley, Jo B. AR 8th Cav. Co.L
Ryley, Joel GA Inf. 27th Bn. (NonConscr.) Co.D
Ryley, John NC 1st Inf. (6 mo. '61) Co.M
Ryley, John TN 11th Inf. Co.B
Ryley, P. LA Mil. 4th Regt. 1st Brig. 1st Div. Co.D Sgt.
Ryley, Patrick NC 23rd Inf. Co.G
Ryley, Thomas VA Lt.Arty. 13th Bn. Co.C
Ryley, William TN Conscr. (Cp. of Instr.)
Rylie, J.N. GA 30th Inf.
Rylir, J.A. TX 30th Cav. Co.K
Rylis, William GA 13th Cav. Co.G
Ryman, A.H. TX St.Troops Teel's Co.
Ryman, Allison TX 3rd Inf. Co.G 1st Lt.
Ryman, Charles LA 22nd Inf. Co.A
Ryman, Daniel VA 12th Cav. Co.K
Ryman, Daniel VA 136th Mil. Co.F
Ryman, David VA 7th Cav. Co.K
Ryman, David VA 136th Mil. Co.G Cpl.
Ryman, George VA 12th Cav. Co.E
Ryman, George H. VA 136th Mil. Co.C
Ryman, H.A. TX 2nd Cav. Co.B
Ryman, Hugh VA 136th Mil. Co.G
Ryman, Isaac VA 12th Cav. Co.E

Ryman, Isaac VA 136th Mil. Co.D
Ryman, Jacob VA 136th Mil. Co.F
Ryman, John VA Cav. 35th Bn. Co.A
Ryman, John VA 2nd Inf. Co.C
Ryman, John (of Joseph) VA 97th Mil. Co.C
Ryman, John of David VA 136th Mil. Co.G
Ryman, John L. VA 33rd Inf. Co.K
Ryman, Joseph M. VA 22nd Cav. Co.I
Ryman, Levi H. VA 58th Mil. Co.I 1st Sgt.
Ryman, Moses VA 2nd Inf. Co.G
Ryman, Moses VA 136th Mil. Co.G
Ryman, Samuel A. VA 12th Cav. Co.H
Ryman, Samuel A. VA 146th Mil. Co.C Cpl.
Ryman, Thomas J. VA 7th Cav. Co.K
Ryme, Francis MS 20th Inf. Co.D
Rymel, John T. VA 146th Mil. Co.B
Rymer, Allison TN 62nd Mtd.Inf. Co.B
Rymer, Alson TN 29th Inf. Co.B
Rymer, Caleb NC 4th Sr.Res. Co.B
Rymer, David TN 3rd (Lillard's) Mtd.Inf. Co.D
Rymer, David TN 3rd (Lillard's) Mtd.Inf. Co.G
Rymer, David P. NC 60th Inf. Co.A
Rymer, David W. TN 3rd (Forrest's) Cav. Co.D
Rymer, Eli TN 3rd (Lillard's) Mtd.Inf. Co.D
Rymer, F. NC Mallett's Co.
Rymer, George L. VA 62nd Mtd.Inf. 2nd Co.D
Rymer, George L. VA 162nd Mil. Co.A
Rymer, J.A. TN 3rd (Lillard's) Mtd.Inf. Co.D
Rymer, Jacob M. TN 3rd (Lillard's) Mtd.Inf. Co.D
Rymer, James AL 13th Inf. Co.G
Rymer, James TN 3rd (Forrest's) Cav.
Rymer, James H. TN 3rd (Lillard's) Mtd.Inf. Co.D
Rymer, J.C. NC 64th Inf. Co.C
Rymer, Jesse TN 62nd Mtd.Inf. Co.B Sgt.
Rymer, John TN 3rd (Lillard's) Mtd.Inf. Co.D
Rymer, John W. TN 3rd (Lillard's) Mtd.Inf. Co.D 2nd Lt.
Rymer, J.W. NC 3rd Arty. (40th St.Troops) Co.H
Rymer, Leroy TN 3rd (Lillard's) Mtd.Inf. Co.D
Rymer, Mitchel NC 64th Inf. Co.C
Rymer, Silas G. VA 62nd Mtd.Inf. 2nd Co.D
Rymer, Solomon E.A. TN 3rd (Lillard's) Mtd.Inf. Co.G
Rymer, Solomon G. TN 3rd (Lillard's) Mtd.Inf. Co.D
Rymer, T.B. NC 60th Inf. Co.K
Rymer, Thomas J. VA 62nd Mtd.Inf. 2nd Co.D
Rymer, Thomas J. VA 162nd Mil. Co.A
Rymer, W.D. TN 3rd (Lillard's) Mtd.Inf. Co.D Cpl.
Rymer, W.G.B. TN 3rd (Lillard's) Mtd.Inf. Co.D
Rymer, William E. NC 39th Inf. Co.D
Rymes, Canada J. NC 29th Inf. Co.H
Rymes, J.F. Conf.Cav. Powers' Regt. Co.A 1st Lt.
Rymes, John C. TX 2nd Cav. Co.I
Rymes, John F. MS 1st (King's) Inf. (St.Troops) Co.C
Rymes, L.J. MS 4th Cav. Co.F
Rymore, J.C. TN 6th Inf. Co.K
Ryn, Thomas TN 2nd (Walker's) Inf. Co.F Cpl.
Rynard, Jackson VA 136th Mil. Co.G
Ryne, Andrew MO Inf. 4th Regt.St.Guard Co.A

Ryne, C. GA 10th Inf. Co.B
Ryne, J.J. MO 1st & 3rd Cons.Cav. Co.C Sgt.
Ryne, John MS 39th Inf. Co.I
Ryne, Pat. MS 39th Inf. Co.I
Ryne, T. LA Mil. Fire Bn. Co.B Cpl.
Ryne, Thomas W. GA Hvy.Arty. 22nd Bn. Co.F
Ryne, William MO 3rd Cav. Co.F
Rynehart, D.D. NC 21st Inf. Co.A
Rynehart, H. VA 10th Bn.Res. Co.C
Ryneheart, Alfred NC 6th Inf. Co.K
Ryner, A.N. TN 17th Inf. Co.H
Ryner, David W. VA 52nd Inf. Co.G
Ryner, J.E. VA 13th Inf. Co.C
Ryner, Mitchel NC 64th Inf. Co.C
Ryner, W. TX 11th (Spaight's) Bn.Vol. Co.E
Rynes, Jacob MS 24th Inf. Co.A
Rynes, John NC 21st Inf. Co.K
Rynes, William TN 62nd Mtd.Inf. Co.G
Ryneson, --- TX Cav. Good's Bn. Co.D
Rynings, G.W. LA 25th Inf. Co.D 2nd Lt.
Rynold, George MS 8th Cav. Co.H
Rynolds, Peter VA 2nd Inf.Loc.Def. Co.E
Rynord, James H. GA 1st (Olmstead's) Inf. Co.G
Ryols, T. MO Inf. Clark's Regt. Co.C
Ryon, A. AR 14th (McCarver's) Inf. Co.K
Ryon, Albion T. TX Waul's Legion Co.E 1st Lt.
Ryon, A.T. TX 26th Cav. 1st Co.G
Ryon, D.S. TX 24th Cav. Co.F
Ryon, Edward Darnaby TX 8th Cav. Co.H
Ryon, F. MS Cav. 3rd Bn. (Ashcraft's) Co.A
Ryon, George W. KY 8th Cav. Co.A
Ryon, Henry TN Lt.Arty. Kain's Co.
Ryon, Henry C. VA Cav. 35th Bn. Co.A
Ryon, Henry F. AR 8th Inf. New Co.G
Ryon, J. TX 8th Cav. Co.H
Ryon, James MS 15th Inf. Co.C
Ryon, James H. VA Cav. 41st Bn. Co.A
Ryon, James W. VA Cav. 35th Bn. Co.A
Ryon, James W. VA 7th Inf. Co.I
Ryon, J.D. LA 21st (Kennedy's) Inf. Co.E
Ryon, John AL Lt.Arty. 2nd Bn. Co.C
Ryon, John MS 1st (Percy's) Inf. Co.K
Ryon, John G. GA 5th Cav. Co.D
Ryon, John W. VA 48th Inf. Co.D
Ryon, Matt TN 16th (Logwood's) Cav. Co.C
Ryon, Pat LA Mil. 4th Regt. 1st Brig. 1st Div. Co.E
Ryon, Robert AL 3rd Bn.Res. Co.C
Ryon, T. LA 10th Inf. Co.E
Ryon, Thomas A.B. AL 1st Cav. Co.D
Ryon, William LA Mil. 4th Regt. 1st Brig. 1st Div. Co.E
Ryon, William H. GA 25th Inf. Co.H Sgt.
Ryons, Philip TN 62nd Mtd.Inf. Co.G Cpl.
Ryor, Martin VA 79th Mil. Co.4
Ryppel, Franz TX Waul's Legion Co.E,D
Rysinger, J.M. LA 28th (Gray's) Inf. Co.C
Rystol, L. AR 15th (Josey's) Inf. 1st Co.C
Ryston, R.T. Gen. & Staff, A. of N.VA Surg.
Ryth, C.N. SC 3rd Cav. Co.C

S

S., K.H. VA 9th Cav. Lt.
S., Ney 1st Cherokee Mtd.Rifles McDaniel's Co.
S., W. AR 1st Mtd.Rifles Co.B
S., W.B. MS 21st Inf. Co.K
S---her, J.R. FL 9th Inf. Co.F
Saage, William TX Waul's Legion Co.D
Saal, H. VA 1st St.Res. Co.B Cpl.
Saal, Robert F. TN 9th Inf. Co.B
Saary, James LA 14th Inf. Co.I
Saary, Patrick LA 20th Inf. Co.E
Saba, Mateo LA Mil. 5th Regt.Eur.Brig.
  (Spanish Regt.) Co.8
Sabal, A.M. Gen. & Staff AASurg.
Sabal, E.T. FL 2nd Inf. Co.K
Saballo, S. LA 5th Inf. Co.G
Sabalos, Auguste LA Mil. 2nd Regt. French
  Brig. Co.5
Sabalot, J.M. VA 2nd Inf.Loc.Def. Co.K
Sabalot, J.M. VA Inf. 2nd Bn.Loc.Def. Co.B
Sabalot, John M. LA 5th Inf. Co.G
Saban, J.L. GA 43rd Inf. Co.C
Sabastan, D. LA 8th Cav. Co.B
Sabastian, William W. 3rd Conf.Cav. Co.F
Sabate, P. FL 2nd Cav. Co.H
Sabate, Robert P. GA 63rd Inf. Co.B,D
Sabate, R.P. GA 1st (Olmstead's) Inf. Gordon's
  Co.
Sabaten, S. LA 18th Inf. Co.H
Sabates, Jose LA Mil. 5th Regt.Eur.Brig.
  (Spanish Regt.) Co.4
Sabath, C.A. TX 17th Inf. Co.H Capt.
Sabath, C.A. TX Inf. Houston Bn. Co.D
Sabathe, D. LA Mil. 4th Regt. French Brig. Co.2
Sabatier, Dorsin LA Mil. 1st Native Guards
Sabatier, E. Gen. & Staff Surg.
Sabatier, J. LA Mil. 4th Regt. French Brig. Co.3
  Sgt.
Sabatier, L. LA Mil. 2nd Regt. French Brig.
  Co.4
Sabatier, Paul LA Mil. 1st Native Guards
Sabatin, W.L. KY 5th Mtd.Inf. Sgt.
Sabatini, Giovanni LA Mil. 6th Regt.Eur.Brig.
  (Italian Guards Bn.) Co.3
Sabatki, William LA 1st (Strawbridge's) Inf.
  Co.G
Sabbadini, G.C. LA Mil. Cazadores Espanoles
  Regt. Co.1
Sabedra, Rafel TX Cav. Mann's Regt. Co.A
Sabedray, Rafell TX Cav. Mann's Bn. Co.A
Sabell, Nicholas S. MS 12th Inf. Co.D
Sabil, J.H. NC 6th Inf.
Sabin, Anson J. AR 3rd Cav. Co.F 1st Sgt.
Sabin, D.G. TX Conscr.
Sabin, John LA Res.Corps Oliver's Co.
Sabine, Melvin L. TX 1st (McCulloch's) Cav.
  Co.K
Sabine, Melvin L. TX 1st (Yager's) Cav. Co.I

Sabine, Melvin L. TX Cav. 8th (Taylor's) Bn.
  Co.D Bugler
Sabine, P. LA Mil. 4th Regt. French Brig. Co.5
Sabins, Thomas MO 12th Cav. Co.A
Sabio, J. LA 1st Cav. Co.B
Sabiston, Joseph W. NC 1st Arty. (10th
  St.Troops) Co.H Cpl.
Sable, Zack TX 1st Inf. Co.L
Sablett, --- MO Cav. 10th Regt.St.Guard Co.F
Sablow, R.E. LA Mil. 1st Regt. French Brig.
  Co.4
Sabon, M. GA 3rd Inf. Co.E
Sabot, P. LA Mil. 2nd Regt. French Brig. Co.2
  2nd Lt.
Saboular, F.J. LA Mil. 2nd Regt. 2nd Brig. 1st
  Div. Co.B
Saboulard, Isidore LA 2nd Regt. French Brig.
  Co.6
Sabree, T.J. KY 5th Cav. Co.B
Sabrey, Rufus SC 17th Inf. Co.I Cpl.
Sabrier, R. LA Mil. 1st Regt. French Brig. Co.4
Sacerdotte, A. LA Mil. 1st Chasseurs a pied Co.4
Sacertir, Santago LA 26th Inf. Co.G
Sacherar, Emil TX 2nd Cav. 2nd Co.F Sgt.
Sa chik larf ka 1st Creek Mtd.Vol. Co.A
Sachoo thla nay 1st Creek Mtd.Vol. Co.E
Sachre, John W. NC 1st Arty. (10th St.Troops)
  Co.E
Sachre, John W. NC 2nd Arty. (36th St.Troops)
  Co.A
Sachtleben, A.H. TX 16th Inf. Co.C
Sachtleben, August TX 16th Inf. Co.C
Sachtleben, Charles TX 16th Inf. Co.C
Sa chum kah 1st Creek Mtd.Vol. Co.A
Sack, Cordon TN 50th Inf. Co.C
Sack, Henry GA 63rd Inf. Co.F
Sack, Henry SC 18th Inf. Co.I
Sack, P. AL 47th Inf. Co.E
Sack, Richard AL 8th Inf. Co.A
Sacket, E. Conf.Reg.Inf. Brooks' Bn. Co.A
Sacket, John AR 3rd Inf. Co.C
Sackett, A. MS Inf. 2nd Bn. Co.F
Sackett, A. MS 48th Inf. Co.F
Sackett, Charles H. TN 63rd Inf. Co.I 2nd Lt.
Sackett, Charles H. VA Hvy.Arty. 19th Bn.
  Co.D
Sackett, Charles H. VA Hvy.Arty. Kyle's Co.
  Sgt.
Sackett, Edward A. GA 1st (Ramsey's) Inf. Co.A
  Cpl.
Sackett, George Conf.Reg.Inf. Brooks' Bn. Co.E
Sackett, George W. Conf.Reg.Inf. Brooks' Bn.
  Co.E
Sackett, James AR 9th Inf. New Co.B
Sackett, James GA 2nd Bn.S.S. Co.E
Sackett, J.M. AR Lt.Arty. 5th Btty. 1st Sgt.
Sackett, John AR 26th Inf. Co.A
Sackett, Larkin AR 26th Inf. Co.A

Sackett, S.D. TX 12th Inf. Co.E
Sackett, William AR Cav. Wright's Regt. Co.C
Sackey, S. AL Cav. Barbiere's Bn. Co.C
Sackford, J.M. GA Arty. Lumpkin's Co.
Sackhoff, C. AL 1st Regt. Mobile Vol. Co.C 1st
  Sgt.
Sackhoff, John C. AL 21st Inf. Co.A
Sackinger, J.G. GA 47th Inf. Co.I
Sackinger, L.A. GA 47th Inf. Co.I
Sackman, Benjamin VA 67th Mil. Co.A
Sackman, David VA 67th Mil. Co.A
Sackman, Henry LA 2nd Cav. Co.A Bugler
Sackman, William MO 5th Cav.
Sacks, E.C. MO 15th Cav. 1st Lt.,Adj.
Sacks, John R. VA 6th Bn.Res. Co.A
Sacks, Michael LA 2nd Cav. Co.D Cpl.
Sackser, R.N. GA 3rd Res.
Sackson, W. MS Cav. Powers' Regt. Co.G Sgt.
Sackwell, David NC 21st Inf. Co.M
Sackwell, Robert M. NC 21st Inf. Co.M
Sackwell, S.S. Gen. & Staff Surg.
Sackwell, T. AR 15th Inf. Co.C
Sacoon 1st Seminole Mtd.Vol.
Sa cot che 1st Creek Mtd.Vol. Co.M
Sacott, John AR 13th Mil. Co.E
Sacra, Benjamin VA 47th Inf. 3rd Co.H
Sacra, C.H. VA Loc.Def. Tayloe's Co.
Sacra, Charles H. VA 30th Inf. Co.C
Sacra, C.M. VA 2nd Bn.Res. Co.B
Sacra, Edmund VA 13th Inf. Co.D
Sacra, George H. VA 55th Inf. Co.M
Sacra, Henry S. TN Cav. 7th Bn. (Bennett's)
  Co.B Black.
Sacra, Henry S. TN 22nd (Barteau's) Cav. Co.E
  Black.
Sacra, H.S. TN 21st & 22nd (Cons.) Cav. Co.B
Sacra, James R. VA 55th Inf. Co.M
Sacra, James T. VA 47th Inf. 2nd Co.K
Sacra, Jefferson M. VA Lt.Arty. Montgomery's
  Co.
Sacra, John S. VA 30th Inf. Co.D
Sacra, Thomas KY 2nd Cav. Co.B,D
Sacra, William J. VA 2nd Cav. Co.B
Sacrae, Francis M. GA Inf. 2nd Bn. Co.C
Sacre, Elias B. VA 40th Inf. Co.D
Sacre, F.M. GA 2nd Inf. Co.C
Sacre, James MO Cav. Snider's Bn. Co.A
Sacre, Jerry M. MO Cav. Wood's Regt. Co.K
Sacre, Thomas KY 8th Cav. Co.B
Sacre, William MO Cav. Wood's Regt. Co.K
Sacrey, Andrew J. VA Lt.Arty. Cayce's Co.
Sacrey, Andrew J. VA Arty. Curtis' Co.
Sacrey, Charles H. GA 10th Inf. 1st Co.K
Sacrey, John VA 30th Inf. Co.A
Sacrey, Joseph B. VA 1st Inf. Co.A
Sacrey, Joseph B. VA 12th Inf. Co.G
Sacriste, J.D. LA Mil. 1st Native Guards
Sacry, Charles P. GA Lt.Arty. Fraser's Btty.

Sacvir, Benjamin FL 1st (Res.) Inf.
Sadawhite, J.P. NC 1st Jr.Res. Co.B
Sadberry, J. NC 3rd Jr.Res. Co.I
Sadberry, James NC 34th Inf. Co.K Cpl.
Sadberry, Samuel AL 44th Inf. Co.E
Sadberry, Webster M. Wheeler's Scouts,CSA 3rd Lt.
Sadburry, James NC 7th Bn.Jr.Res. Co.C
Sadbury, William AR 11th Inf. Co.B Cpl.
Sadbury, William AR 11th & 17th Cons.Inf. Co.A
Saddawhite, R. AL 63rd Inf. Co.H
Saddeler, S.F.H. AL 3rd Inf. Co.F
Sadderwight, C. LA Washington Arty.Bn. Co.1
Saddle, --- TX Cav. Ragsdale's Bn. Co.B
Saddle, John H. TX 4th Cav. Co.D
Saddlemier, Jacob VA 24th Cav. Co.E
Saddler, A. VA Inf. 28th Bn. Co.D
Saddler, A.D. MS 3rd Inf. Co.E 2nd Lt.
Saddler, Adolphus VA 3rd Lt.Arty. Co.D
Saddler, Adolphus H. VA 12th Inf. 2nd Co.I
Saddler, A.E. VA 59th Inf. 3rd Co.I
Saddler, Albert A. VA 14th Inf. Co.E
Saddler, Archer C. VA 14th Inf. Co.E
Saddler, Arthur B. VA 55th Inf. Co.H
Saddler, A.S. SC Inf. Hampton Legion Co.I
Saddler, Augustine A. VA 61st Mil. Co.G
Saddler, B. TN 16th (Logwood's) Cav. Co.G
Saddler, Benjamin MO Cav. Preston's Bn. Co.A
Saddler, B.H. AR 36th Inf. Co.C
Saddler, C. LA Mil. 1st Regt. 2nd Brig. 1st Div. Co.E
Saddler, C.G. AR 2nd Mtd.Rifles Co.A
Saddler, Charles VA 34th Inf. Co.F
Saddler, Charles VA 56th Inf. Co.G
Saddler, Cyrus TX 2nd Field Btty.
Saddler, D.M. TX 11th Cav. Co.C
Saddler, D.W. MS 10th Cav. Co.A
Saddler, E.A. AL 53rd (Part.Rangers)
Saddler, E.A. AL Auburn Home Guards Vol. Darby's Co.
Saddler, Elijah TN 9th (Ward's) Cav. Co.A
Saddler, Elijah TN 15th Cav. Co.A
Saddler, Flem TN 23rd Inf. 1st Co.F, Co.H
Saddler, Frank A. MO 8th Cav. Co.A,B
Saddler, F.W. AL 3rd Cav. Co.H
Saddler, G. TN 14th (Neely's) Cav. Co.G
Saddler, George MO Cav. Fristoe's Regt. Co.B
Saddler, George VA 111th Mil. Co.4,2
Saddler, George W. 14th Conf.Cav. Co.H
Saddler, G.M. SC 3rd Inf. Co.F
Saddler, Green AL 14th Inf. Co.E
Saddler, Green TX Cav. Wells' Bn. Co.A
Saddler, G.T. AL 12th Inf. Co.G Music.
Saddler, G.W. KY 7th Cav. Co.D
Saddler, G.W. SC 3rd Inf. Co.B
Saddler, Henry MO Cav. Preston's Bn. Co.A
Saddler, Henry TX 12th Cav. Co.K
Saddler, Henry J. VA Horse Arty. Jackson's Co.
Saddler, Hollas MO Lt.Arty. Parsons' Co.
Saddler, Hollis MO 2nd Cav.
Saddler, Hollis MO 6th Inf. Co.I
Saddler, I.B. Inf. Bailey's Cons.Regt. Co.B
Saddler, J.A. AR 51st Mil. Co.E
Saddler, James NC 33rd Inf. Co.H
Saddler, James SC 7th Inf. Co.M
Saddler, James VA Cav. McFarlane's Co.

Saddler, James Conf.Cav. 6th Bn. Co.E
Saddler, James H. VA 55th Inf. Co.H
Saddler, James M. MO 7th Cav. Co.I
Saddler, J.F.W. VA Cav. Swann's Bn. Watkins' Co.
Saddler, J.L. TX 11th Cav. Co.C
Saddler, John GA 3rd Res. Co.C
Saddler, John LA Inf. 7th Bn. Co.C
Saddler, John TN 2nd (Ashby's) Cav. Co.A
Saddler, John TN Cav. 5th Bn. (McClellan's) Co.A
Saddler, John VA Mil. Washington Cty.
Saddler, John F.W. VA Cav. McFarlane's Co.
Saddler, John J. GA Inf. Cobb Guards Co.A
Saddler, Joseph A. MO 8th Cav. Co.K
Saddler, J.W. TN 16th (Logwood's) Cav. Co.G
Saddler, J.W. VA Inf. 44th Bn. Co.B
Saddler, J.W. 1st Conf.Eng.Troops Co.E
Saddler, Leonard L. VA 12th Cav. Co.B
Saddler, Merit VA Arty. Paris' Co.
Saddler, M.J. MO 7th Cav. Co.B Cpl.
Saddler, Nathaniel F. TX Cav. 6th Bn. Co.C
Saddler, N.D. AR 7th Mil. Co.E
Saddler, N.P. AR 4th St.Inf. Co.E 1st Lt.
Saddler, O.R. MS 10th Inf. Old Co.K
Saddler, Pleasant R. VA Arty. Paris' Co.
Saddler, P.R. VA 14th Inf. Co.K
Saddler, R.F. TN 40th Inf. Co.I Sgt.
Saddler, Richard FL 1st (Res.) Inf.
Saddler, Richard B. VA Horse Arty. E. Graham's Co.
Saddler, Richard L. VA Hvy.Arty. 18th Bn. Co.A
Saddler, Richard S. VA 55th Inf. Co.C,I 2nd Lt.
Saddler, Robert Alexander 1st Conf.Eng.Troops Co.F
Saddler, Robert B. VA Courtney Arty.
Saddler, Robert H. VA Hvy.Arty. 20th Bn. Co.B Sgt.
Saddler, Samuel TX 12th Cav. Co.K
Saddler, T. LA Miles' Legion Co.C Cpl.
Saddler, T.A. AL 63rd Inf. Co.H Sgt.
Saddler, T.C. TX Cav. 1st Regt.St.Troops Co.F
Saddler, Thomas TN 30th Inf. Co.I
Saddler, Thomas VA 4th Cav. Co.G
Saddler, Thomas A. VA Lt.Arty. B.Z. Price's Co.
Saddler, Thomas J. AL 13th Inf. Co.A
Saddler, Thomas J. MS 2nd (Davidson's) Inf. Co.D 1st Sgt.
Saddler, Thomas M. TN 2nd (Smith's) Cav.
Saddler, Thomas R. TX 11th Cav. Co.C
Saddler, W. KY 12th Cav. Co.E
Saddler, W. VA 13th Cav. Co.K
Saddler, W.C. GA Inf. 1st Loc.Troops (Augusta) Dearing's Cav.Co.
Saddler, W.C. TN 22nd (Barteau's) Cav. Co.G
Saddler, W.E. VA 5th Cav. Co.K,E Sgt.
Saddler, Wellington VA 5th Cav. (12 mo. '61-2) Winfield's Co.
Saddler, Wesley MO Lt.Arty. McDonald's Co.
Saddler, William AL 3rd Bn.Res. Appling's Co.
Saddler, Wm. KY Cav. 2nd Bn. (Dortch's) Co.E
Saddler, Wm. KY 3rd Bn. Co.A
Saddler, William LA 5th Inf. Co.B
Saddler, William MS Roach's Co. (Tippah Scouts)

Saddler, William MO Lt.Arty. Walsh's Co.
Saddler, William SC 7th Inf. 1st Co.E, Co.M Cpl.
Saddler, William TN 6th (Wheeler's) Cav. Co.C
Saddler, William VA 6th Cav. Co.G
Saddler, William Conf.Inf. 8th Bn. Co.C
Saddler, William B. VA 14th Inf. Co.D
Saddler, William C. TN Cav. 7th Bn. (Bennett's) Co.E
Saddler, William J. TN Cav. 11th Bn. (Gordon's) Co.C
Saddler, William R. TN Cav. 17th Bn. (Sanders') Co.B 2nd Lt.
Saddler, W.J. MS 2nd St.Cav. Co.K
Saddler, W.J. MS 5th Inf. (St.Troops) Co.E 2nd Lt.
Saddler, W.P. TN 21st & 22nd (Cons.) Cav. Co.K
Saderfield, James A. MS 37th Inf. Co.K
Sadey, John AL 3rd Inf. Co.D
Sadirs, B.F. AR 37th Inf. Co.D
Sadlen, O.N.B. AL Cp. of Instr. Talladega
Sadler, A. MS 2nd Cav. Co.D
Sadler, A. MS 1st (Patton's) Inf. Co.H 1st Lt.
Sadler, A. NC 14th Inf. Co.E
Sadler, A. SC Cav. A.C. Earle's Co. 1st Sgt.
Sadler, A. SC 4th Regt. Co.E
Sadler, Absalom VA 24th Cav. Co.E
Sadler, Absalom VA Cav. 40th Bn. Co.E
Sadler, Absalom VA 61st Mil. Co.F
Sadler, Absalom M. VA 26th Inf. Co.D
Sadler, A.C. AR 11th & 17th Cons.Inf. Co.I
Sadler, A.C. AR Inf. Cocke's Regt. Co.F
Sadler, A.D. MS 23rd Inf. Co.E Capt.
Sadler, A.D. MO 15th Cav. Co.I Cpl.
Sadler, A.D. VA 61st Mil. Co.C
Sadler, Addison J. VA 16th Inf. Co.F Sgt.
Sadler, A.E. VA 21st Inf. Co.G Sgt.
Sadler, A.J. TN 3rd (Forrest's) Cav. Co.C
Sadler, Alfred D. MO 4th Inf. Co.D
Sadler, Alfred H. AR 26th Inf. Co.D Cpl.
Sadler, Andrew VA Lt.Arty. Armistead's Co.
Sadler, Andrew VA 61st Mil. Co.A
Sadler, Archibald S. SC 4th Inf. Co.B
Sadler, A.S. SC Inf. 13th Bn. Co.E
Sadler, A.S. VA Cav. 37th Bn. Co.B
Sadler, August Conf.Lt.Arty. Stark's Bn. Co.B
Sadler, Augustus D. MS 21st Inf. Co.G 2nd Sgt.
Sadler, A.W. MS 11th Cav. Co.D
Sadler, Benjamin MO 4th Cav. Co.A
Sadler, Benjamin NC 33rd Inf. Co.F
Sadler, Benjamin F. AL 5th Inf. New Co.D
Sadler, Beverly O. VA 14th Inf. Co.A Cpl.
Sadler, B.F. LA 3rd (Wingfield's) Cav. Co.B
Sadler, B.H. AR Inf. 4th Bn. Co.B Music.
Sadler, Birton TX 22nd Cav. Co.G Bugler
Sadler, B.O. NC Mallett's Bn. Co.A
Sadler, B.R. TN 1st (Turney's) Inf. Co.B
Sadler, C. LA 3rd (Wingfield's) Cav. Co.B
Sadler, C. LA 18th Inf. Co.F
Sadler, C.A. LA Arty. Hutton's Co. (Crescent Arty.,Co.A)
Sadler, Calhoun C. TX 19th Cav. Co.H
Sadler, C.D. MS 2nd Cav. Co.D
Sadler, C.E. AL 17th Inf. Co.A Capt.
Sadler, Charles LA Inf.Crescent Regt. Co.D
Sadler, Charles A. VA 56th Inf. Co.E

Sadler, C.R. VA Inf. 26th Bn. Co.I
Sadler, C.W. TN 17th Inf. Co.K
Sadler, David G. NC 3rd Arty. (40th St.Troops) Co.D,B
Sadler, Drury MS 17th Inf. Co.F
Sadler, D.W. MS 9th Cav. Co.F Sgt.
Sadler, D.W. MS Inf. 3rd Bn. (St.Troops) Co.A
Sadler, D.W. TN Cav. 17th Bn. (Sanders') Co.C Sgt.Maj.
Sadler, Edward M. VA 14th Inf. Co.A
Sadler, Edward W. VA 14th Inf. Co.A
Sadler, E.M. MS Patton's Co. (St.Troops)
Sadler, Ewing F. TX 19th Cav. Co.H
Sadler, Francis W. AL Lt.Arty. Clanton's Btty. QMSgt.
Sadler, G.B. 8th (Wade's) Conf.Cav. Co.I
Sadler, G.D. VA 19th Inf. Co.C
Sadler, George AL 61st Inf. Co.I
Sadler, George E. VA 1st St.Res. Co.K Cpl.
Sadler, George H. VA Cav. Young's Co. Cpl.
Sadler, Geo. W. AL 37th Inf. Co.G
Sadler, George W. LA 5th Inf. Co.E
Sadler, George W. MS 3rd Cav. Co.F 2nd Lt.
Sadler, George W. MS 17th Inf. Co.K
Sadler, George W. VA 109th Mil. Co.B
Sadler, Gordan VA 54th Inf. Co.F Cpl.
Sadler, Green TX Cav. Wells' Regt. Co.A
Sadler, G.T. TN 3rd (Forrest's) Cav. Co.D
Sadler, Gustav TX 36th Cav. Music.
Sadler, G.W. LA Ogden's Cav. Co.E
Sadler, H. TX 3rd Inf. Co.B
Sadler, Hartwell S. MS 19th Inf. Co.H,A
Sadler, Henry MO 4th Cav. Co.A
Sadler, Henry TN 30th Inf. Co.E
Sadler, Henry TX 2nd Cav. 2nd Co.F
Sadler, Henry A. AR 2nd Mtd.Rifles Co.A
Sadler, Henry P. MS 17th Inf. Co.K Sgt.
Sadler, Henry W. TX 19th Cav. Co.H
Sadler, Henry W. VA 2nd Arty. Co.H Sgt.
Sadler, Henry W. VA Inf. 22nd Bn. Co.H Sgt.
Sadler, H.M. GA Lt.Arty. 12th Bn. 3rd Co.C
Sadler, H.M. GA Arty. Siege Train (Buist) QMSgt.
Sadler, H.M. GA Inf. 18th Bn. Co.C
Sadler, H.M. SC Arty. Manigault's Bn. 1st Co.A
Sadler, Hollis MO Cav. 1st Regt.St.Guard Co.C
Sadler, Ira B. TX 7th Inf. Co.A 1st Lt.
Sadler, Isaac SC 20th Inf. Co.E
Sadler, Isaac L. VA Lt.Arty. Armistead's Co.
Sadler, Isaac L. VA 61st Mil. Co.C Cpl.
Sadler, Isaiah S. NC 17th Inf. (2nd Org.) Co.B
Sadler, I.W. VA Inf. 44th Bn. Co.C
Sadler, J.A. Gen. & Staff Maj.,Comsy.
Sadler, James FL 6th Inf. Co.C
Sadler, James MS 2nd Cav.
Sadler, James NC 17th Inf. (1st Org.) Co.B
Sadler, James NC 17th Inf. (2nd Org.) Co.B
Sadler, James NC Part.Rangers Swindell's Co.
Sadler, James TX 22nd Cav. Co.G
Sadler, James TX Cav. Baylor's Regt. Co.E
Sadler, James VA 60th Inf. 2nd Co.H
Sadler, James A. TX 19th Cav. Co.H
Sadler, James C. VA 61st Mil. Co.C
Sadler, James D. MO 1st Inf. Co.H,C
Sadler, James O. AR 1st Mtd.Rifles Co.C Capt.
Sadler, James O. AR Cav. Gordon's Regt. Co.C Capt.

Sadler, James R. TX 19th Cav. Co.H
Sadler, J.B. MS 2nd Part.Rangers Co.D
Sadler, J.C. VA 19th Inf. Co.C
Sadler, J.F.W. Conf.Cav. 6th Bn. Co.E
Sadler, J.H. MS 35th Inf. Co.E
Sadler, J.H. SC 2nd Inf. Co.D Sgt.
Sadler, J.H. SC 24th Inf. Co.F Sgt.
Sadler, J.L. TN 7th (Duckworth's) Cav. Co.H
Sadler, J. Milton SC 9th Inf. Co.A
Sadler, John FL 6th Inf. Co.C
Sadler, John LA Ogden's Cav. Co.B
Sadler, John NC 23rd Inf. Co.I
Sadler, John SC 5th Res. Co.B
Sadler, John TN 18th Inf. Co.G
Sadler, John TX 11th Cav. Co.F
Sadler, John TX Cav. Bourland's Regt. Co.C
Sadler, John VA 4th Res. Co.C
Sadler, John VA 61st Mil. Co.C
Sadler, John A. LA Miles' Legion Co.A Sgt.
Sadler, John A. SC 7th Inf. 2nd Co.D
Sadler, John A. VA Lt.Arty. Armistead's Co.
Sadler, John A. VA Res.Forces Thurston's Co. 1st Lt.
Sadler, John C. VA Lt.Arty. Armistead's Co.
Sadler, John C. VA 61st Mil. Co.C
Sadler, John E. SC 1st (Orr's) Rifles Co.D Sgt.
Sadler, John F. VA 55th Inf. Co.G QMSgt.
Sadler, John F. VA 56th Inf. Co.E
Sadler, John H. SC 2nd Inf. Co.F,D
Sadler, John J. VA 44th Inf. Co.H
Sadler, John M. LA 19th Inf. Co.A
Sadler, John N. VA 2nd Inf. Co.G
Sadler, John R. AL 42nd Inf. Co.C Sgt.
Sadler, John S. SC 5th Cav. Co.K
Sadler, John T. LA 19th Inf. Co.A
Sadler, John W. FL 6th Inf. Co.C
Sadler, John W. LA Arty. Moody's Co. (Madison Lt.Arty.)
Sadler, John W. MS 11th Inf. Co.D
Sadler, John W. VA Lt.Arty. Armistead's Co.
Sadler, John W. VA 16th Inf. Co.F Sgt.
Sadler, John W. VA 44th Inf. Co.F Cpl.
Sadler, John W. VA 46th Inf. 4th Co.F
Sadler, John W. VA 61st Mil. Co.B
Sadler, Joseph MS Cav. 2nd Bn.Res. Co.G
Sadler, Joseph MS 3rd (St.Troops) Cav. Co.A
Sadler, Joseph A. AL Lt.Arty. 2nd Bn. Co.F
Sadler, Joseph A. VA 23rd Inf. Co.F
Sadler, Joseph L. MS 14th Inf. Co.I Cpl.
Sadler, Joseph R. SC 1st (Orr's) Rifles Co.D 2nd Lt.
Sadler, J.P. TN 3rd (Forrest's) Cav. Co.D,C
Sadler, J.T. MO 15th Cav. Co.I
Sadler, Julius NC 1st Inf. (6 mo. '61) Co.B
Sadler, J.W. TN 3rd (Forrest's) Cav. Co.E
Sadler, J.W. TN 30th Inf. Co.E
Sadler, J.W. VA Inf. 44th Bn. Co.C
Sadler, K.H. SC 5th Cav. Co.K
Sadler, K.H. SC 6th Inf. 1st Co.H
Sadler, L.A. MS 2nd Part.Rangers Co.L
Sadler, Lee TN 8th Inf. Co.G
Sadler, Leonard L. VA 2nd Inf. Co.A
Sadler, Leonidas TN 17th Inf. Co.K
Sadler, Leonidas Y. AL Inf. 1st Regt. Co.B Sgt.
Sadler, Lewis VA 61st Mil. Co.E
Sadler, Lewis F. TX 11th Cav. Co.F 2nd Lt.
Sadler, Lewis M. AR 2nd Inf. Co.F

Sadler, Lewis W. VA 61st Mil. Co.B
Sadler, L.P. SC 17th Inf. Co.K Capt.
Sadler, Lucian P. SC 5th St.Troops Co.K Maj.
Sadler, L.Y. AL 4th Inf. Co.A Sgt.
Sadler, Marion B. VA Hvy.Arty. Coleman's Co. Music.
Sadler, Napoleon D. AR Cav. Gordon's Regt. Co.K 1st Lt.
Sadler, N.B. FL 2nd Inf. Co.H
Sadler, N.B. GA Arty. (Chatham Arty.) Wheaton's Co.
Sadler, N.B. GA 1st (Olmstead's) Inf. Claghorn's Co.
Sadler, N. Bayard GA 1st Bn.S.S. Co.C 2nd Lt.
Sadler, N.F. TX 37th Cav. Co.E
Sadler, O.M. NC 1st Inf. (6 mo. '61) Co.B
Sadler, O.R. MS 28th Cav. Co.G
Sadler, O.W. SC 17th Inf. Co.K
Sadler, P.C. TX 13th Vol. 2nd Co.D
Sadler, Phelem TN 8th Cav.
Sadler, Price Harris AL 3rd Inf. Co.H
Sadler, R. SC 5th St.Troops Co.K Cpl.
Sadler, R.B. NC 3rd Inf. Co.I
Sadler, R.B. VA Conscr. Cp.Lee Co.B
Sadler, R.C. VA 2nd Inf.Loc.Def. Co.G
Sadler, R.C. VA Inf. 2nd Bn.Loc.Def. Co.A
Sadler, R.D. AR Inf. (St.Troops) Lawrence's Co.5
Sadler, Richard B. TX 6th Cav. Co.G Asst.Surg.
Sadler, Richard E. VA 12th Inf. Co.A
Sadler, Riley B. NC 3rd Arty. (40th St.Troops) Co.H Cpl.
Sadler, Riley B. NC Lt.Arty. 13th Bn. Co.F Sgt.
Sadler, Riley B. NC 17th Inf. (1st Org.) Co.B
Sadler, R.J. VA 19th Inf. Co.C
Sadler, Roarer D. AR 17th (Lemoyne's) Inf. Co.F
Sadler, Roarer D. AR 21st Inf. Co.E
Sadler, Robert NC 6th Inf. Co.C
Sadler, Robert NC 23rd Inf. Co.I
Sadler, Robert VA 61st Mil. Co.C,F
Sadler, Robert H. VA 38th Inf. 2nd Co.I Sgt.
Sadler, Robert J. VA 6th Inf. Co.I
Sadler, R.T. NC Gibbs' Co. (Loc.Def.)
Sadler, S.A.M. MS 9th Inf. New Co.G 2nd Lt.
Sadler, Samuel NC Part.Rangers Swindell's Co.
Sadler, Samuel A.M. MS 20th Inf. Co.B 2nd Lt.
Sadler, Samuel C. VA 56th Inf. Co.E
Sadler, Sam'l R. KY 4th Cav. Co.B
Sadler, Samuel R. NC 17th Inf. (1st Org.) Co.B
Sadler, Samuel R. NC 17th Inf. (2nd Org.) Co.B 1st Sgt.
Sadler, S.C. SC 5th Inf. 1st Co.I Sgt.
Sadler, S.C. SC 12th Inf. Co.B Adj.
Sadler, S.C. SC Palmetto S.S. Co.G
Sadler, S.M. NC 1st Arty. (10th St.Troops) Co.F
Sadler, S.N. SC 5th Cav. Co.K
Sadler, S.O. MS 2nd Cav. Co.D
Sadler, S.R. NC 3rd Inf. Co.I
Sadler, S.R. TN 51st Inf. Co.K
Sadler, S.R. TN 51st (Cons.) Inf. Co.G Cpl.
Sadler, S.T.H. AL 28th Inf. Co.E
Sadler, Sylvester NC 33rd Inf. Co.I,H
Sadler, T. AL 37th Inf. Co.G
Sadler, T.H. MS 19th Inf. Co.H
Sadler, Thaddeus W. NC 43rd Inf. Co.G,B
Sadler, Thomas VA 61st Mil. Co.E

Sadler, Thomas A. LA 5th Inf. Co.E
Sadler, Thomas B. VA Arty. J.W. Drewry's Co.
Sadler, Tho. J. MS A. of 10,000 Maj.
Sadler, Thomas R. MS 10th Cav. Co.C
Sadler, T.R. MS 44th Inf. Co.B 1st Lt.
Sadler, W. NC 2nd Jr.Res. Co.K
Sadler, Wallace W. NC 33rd Inf. Co.F
Sadler, W.B. SC 5th Cav. Co.F
Sadler, W.B. SC 5th Inf. 1st Co.I
Sadler, W.B. SC Palmetto S.S. Co.G
Sadler, W.C. SC 5th Res. Co.B
Sadler, W.E. NC 33rd Inf. Co.F
Sadler, Weightman E. NC 3rd Arty. (40th St.Troops) Co.D,B
Sadler, Wesley MO 6th Inf. Co.D
Sadler, W.H. AL 1st Regt. Mobile Vol. Baas' Co.
Sadler, W.H. FL 1st (Res.) Inf. Co.K
Sadler, W.H. LA 3rd (Harrison's) Cav. Co.K
Sadler, W.I. KY 12th Cav. Co.E
Sadler, William AR 21st Inf. Co.E
Sadler, William KY 7th Cav. Co.K
Sadler, William MS 35th Inf. Co.E
Sadler, William SC 20th Inf. Co.E
Sadler, William TN 8th Inf. Co.G Capt.
Sadler, William TN 46th Inf. Co.A
Sadler, William A. AL Inf. 1st Regt. Co.B
Sadler, William A. MO 8th Cav. Co.G
Sadler, William B. NC 43rd Inf. Co.B Sgt.
Sadler, William B. VA Hvy.Arty. Epes' Co.
Sadler, William C. TN 21st & 22nd (Cons.) Cav.
Sadler, William E. NC 3rd Arty. (40th St.Troops) Co.D
Sadler, William H. VA 61st Mil. Co.E
Sadler, William J. MS 11th Inf. Co.D
Sadler, William M. NC 45th Inf. Co.H
Sadler, William T. VA 22nd Inf. Co.D
Sadler, William W. AR 17th (Lemoyne's) Inf. Co.G
Sadler, Willis SC 2nd Inf. Co.F
Sadler, Willis A. VA 12th Inf. Co.F
Sadler, W.J. MS 6th Cav. Co.G
Sadler, W.J. MS Cav. Ham's Regt. Co.K
Sadler, W.K. TN 16th Inf. Co.K 1st Lt.
Sadler, W.M. AL 46th Inf. Co.K
Sadler, W.R. MS 9th Cav. Co.E 2nd Lt.
Sadler, W.R. MS 10th Cav. Co.F 3rd Lt.
Sadler, W.T. GA Cav. 15th Bn. (St.Guards) Allen's Co.
Sadler, W.T. GA Arty. 11th Bn. (Sumter Arty.) Co.D 2nd Lt.
Sadler, W.T. GA 10th Mil. Sgt.
Sadler, W.W. AR Inf. Cocke's Regt. Co.F Sgt.
Sadlier, Kate TN 34th Inf. Co.F Off.'s Cook
Saedtler, Charles A. TX Waul's Legion Co.B
Saes, E. LA Mil. Chalmette Regt. Co.H
Saettler, Ernest TX 1st Hvy.Arty. Co.C
Safe, John AL 1st Cav. Co.F
Saferight, C. NC 7th Sr.Res. Boon's Co.
Saferight, Emsley NC 6th Inf. Co.B
Saffarans, G.L. TN 3rd (Forrest's) Cav. Co.A
Saffarans, G.L. TN Inf. 154th Sr.Regt. 1st Co.B
Saffarans, Isaac TN 2nd (Walker's) Inf. QM
Saffarans, John L. TN 2nd (Walker's) Inf. Co.I Capt.
Saffarans, Thomas TN Cav. 1st Bn. (McNairy's) Co.A

Saffarrans, J. Gen. & Staff Capt.,QM
Saffarrans, R.R. TN Cav. Nixon's Regt. Co.K Sgt.
Saffarraus, Daniel KY 2nd (Woodward's) Cav. Co.D
Saffel, H.N. TN 37th Inf. Co.G
Saffel, John AR 14th (McCarver's) Inf. Co.G
Saffel, Stephen TN 37th Inf. Co.G
Saffell, A.J. TN 20th Inf. Co.I
Saffell, Edwin M. VA 17th Inf. Co.B
Saffell, James T. TN 10th Inf. Co.K
Saffell, J.F. AR Lt.Arty. Rivers' Btty.
Saffell, John AR 21st Inf. Co.F
Saffell, John A. AR 45th Cav. Co.H
Saffell, Richard M. TN 26th Inf. Co.F 1st Lt.
Saffell, Samuel TN 63rd Inf. Co.B 1st Lt.
Saffer, B.F. GA 1st Reg. Civilian
Saffer, John W. VA 5th Cav. 2nd Co.F
Saffer, J.W. VA 11th Cav. Co.I
Saffer, Thornton VA 6th Cav. Co.K
Saffernaus, Daniel KY 9th Mtd.Inf. Co.A Sgt.
Saffier, B. LA 1st (Nelligan's) Inf. Co.G
Saffill, Andrew J. TX 19th Cav. Co.C
Saffin, William TN Inf. Nashville Bn. Fulcher's Co., Cattles' Co. 2nd Lt.
Saffir, Benjamin F. VA Cav. 35th Bn. Co.A
Saffle, John D.F. AR 4th Inf. Co.B
Saffles, E.H. TN 3rd (Lillard's) Mtd.Inf. Co.K
Saffles, Stephen TN 3rd (Lillard's) Mtd.Inf. Co.H
Saffles, Thomas TN 3rd (Lillard's) Mtd.Inf. Co.F
Saffley, Jasper TN 35th Inf. Co.B
Saffold, A.G.K. GA Cav. 24th Bn. Co.A
Saffold, Albert V. MS 15th Inf. Co.K
Saffold, B.F. AL Mil. 4th Vol. Co.K
Saffold, Daniel AL 14th Inf. Co.G
Saffold, Daniel P. FL 1st Cav. Co.E
Saffold, D.W. AR 2nd Inf. New Co.C
Saffold, Eli C. AR 2nd Inf. New Co.C
Saffold, Hiram AR 45th Cav. Co.H
Saffold, James AL Mil. 4th Vol. Co.G 2nd Lt.
Saffold, James AL First Class Mil.
Saffold, J.E. AR 30th Inf. Co.H
Saffold, J.H. GA Conscr.
Saffold, John D. AR 15th Inf. Co.I
Saffold, M.J. AL 53rd (Part.Rangers) Co.H Capt.
Saffold, R.B. GA 37th Inf. Co.H
Saffold, R.B. GA 54th Inf. Co.H
Saffold, R.B. GA 61st Inf. Band Music.
Saffold, Reubin S. GA 9th Inf. (St.Guards) Co.B
Saffold, Robert 10th Conf.Cav. Co.C
Saffold, Robert C. MS Cav. 24th Bn. Co.C
Saffold, Robert S. AL 46th Inf. Co.D
Saffold, S.J. GA 2nd Regt. (Storey's) St.Line Co.K Capt.
Saffold, S.W. AL 46th Inf. Co.D
Saffold, Thomas P. GA 9th Inf. (St.Guards) Co.B
Saffold, W.C. MS 3rd Inf. (St.Troops) Co.F 2nd Lt.
Saffold, William TX 8th Inf. Co.K
Saffold, William TX Vol. Benton's Co.
Saffold, William C. MS 5th Inf. Co.F
Saffold, William S. AL 14th Inf. Co.G
Safford, A. GA 8th Cav. 1st Sgt.
Safford, A.J. GA 23rd Inf. Co.B
Safford, A.P. AL 1st Inf. Co.B

Safford, B. AL 16th Inf. Co.F
Safford, D.F. TN 1st (Feild's) & 27th Inf. (Cons.) Co.I
Safford, H. LA Cav. Greenleaf's Co. (Orleans Lt.Horse)
Safford, Henry LA 2nd Cav. Co.E
Safford, Henry S. LA 6th Inf. Co.H
Safford, J. GA Inf. Co.A
Safford, J.W. GA 2nd Inf. Co.A
Safford, R.D. TX 4th Inf. Co.H
Safford, W.B.T. GA Brooks' Co. (Terrell Lt.Arty.) Guidon
Safford, William C. MS Inf. (Red Rebels) D.J. Red's Co.
Saffrit, John NC 18th Inf. Co.H
Safler, John AR Lt.Arty. (Helena Arty.) Clarkson's Btty.
Safley, George W. NC 5th Inf. Co.F
Safley, Hall NC 1st Jr.Res. Co.G
Safley, Jerome TN 16th Inf. Co.H Cpl.
Safley, Jesse A. TN 35th Inf. Co.B 2nd Lt.
Safley, R.M. TN Inf. 1st Cons.Regt. Co.F
Safley, Robert TN 16th Inf. Co.H Sgt.
Safley, T.F. NC 60th Inf. Co.K
Safley, W.B. TN 62nd Mtd.Inf. Co.I
Safley, William TN 16th Inf. Co.H
Safley, William W. NC 28th Inf. Co.D
Safly, P. NC 1st Jr.Res. Co.G
Safort, Peter NC 4th Inf. Co.B
Safreit, James A. NC 49th Inf. Co.C
Safret, M.A. NC 2nd Inf. Co.E
Safriet, Alexander NC 8th Inf. Co.H
Safriet, Daniel NC 42nd Inf. Co.F
Safriet, J.M. NC 8th Inf. Co.H
Safriet, Wiley NC 42nd Inf. Co.F
Safriett, John M. NC 57th Inf. Co.F
Safrit, Eli NC 5th Inf. Co.K
Safrit, Jacob Monroe NC 6th Inf. Co.G
Safrit, M.A. NC 2nd Jr.Res. Co.E
Safrit, Moses NC 5th Inf. Co.K
Safrit, Paul NC 7th Inf. Co.B
Safrit, Powell NC 5th Inf. Co.H
Safrit, R.A. NC 22nd Inf. Co.A Cpl.
Safrit, Rufus A. NC 52nd Inf. Co.A Cpl.
Safrit, Tobias M. NC 8th Inf. Co.H
Safrit, W.C. NC 5th Inf. Co.H
Safrit, William NC 57th Inf. Co.C
Safrit, William W. NC 8th Inf. Co.H Cpl.
Saften, R.T. NC Inf. Co.B
Sagar, Samuel 1st Cherokee Mtd.Vol. 2nd Co.A
Sagar, William LA 1st Hvy.Arty. (Reg.) Co.A
Sagar, William LA Miles' Legion Co.H Sgt.
Sagarra, Ramon LA Mil. Cazadores Espanoles Regt. Co.5
Sagarras, Antoine LA 13th Inf. Co.D
Sagas, James VA 14th Mil. Co.E
Sage, Andrew J. VA 4th Inf. Co.F
Sage, A.P. TN 21st Inf. Co.A 2nd Lt.
Sage, C.C. TX 4th Cav. Co.E
Sage, Edward AL 1st Bn.Cadets Co.A Cpl.
Sage, Elisha W. TN 2nd (Robison's) Inf. Co.A
Sage, E.W. TN Inf. 4th Cons.Regt. Co.I
Sage, G.E. TN Lt.Arty. Tobin's Co.
Sage, George TX 13th Cav. Co.C Sgt.
Sage, George 1st Seminole Mtd.Vol.
Sage, George W. VA 4th Inf. Co.F
Sage, H.K. MS 12th Inf. Co.B

Sage, I.V. VA 63rd Inf. Co.C
Sage, James M. MS 17th Inf. Co.F
Sage, J.C. MS 12th Inf. Co.B
Sage, Jeff MS 9th Bn.S.S. Co.C
Sage, Jeff. MS 29th Inf. Co.H
Sage, Jefferson AR 36th Inf. Co.A
Sage, John NC 64th Inf. Co.F
Sage, John NC 6th Cav. (65th St.Troops) Co.A
Sage, John Deneale's Regt. Choctaw Warriors
    Co.B
Sage, John B. NC Cav. 5th Bn. Co.A
Sage, John M. AR Cav. 1st Bn. (Stirman's) Co.G
Sage, John W. TN 2nd (Robison's) Inf. Co.F
Sage, John W. VA 50th Inf. Co.D
Sage, Jonathan NC Mil. 66th Bn. J.H. Whitman's
    Co.
Sage, J.W. Shecoe's Chickasaw Mtd.Vol. Co.A
Sage, M. TX Inf. 1st Bn. (St.Troops) Co.B
Sage, Oliver TN 24th Inf. Co.B
Sage, Patrick Inf. School of Pract. Powell's
    Detach Powell's Command, Co.A
Sage, P.J. GA Cherokee Legion (St.Guards)
    Co.A
Sage, Robert V. NC 39th Inf. Co.A
Sage, S. AR 38th Inf. Co.E
Sage, Thomas AR 25th Inf. Co.A
Sage, Van Buren VA 4th Inf. Co.F
Sage, William TX Inf. Timmons' Regt. Co.B
Sage, William TX Waul's Legion Co.D
Sage, William H. GA Inf. (Madison Cty. Home
    Guard) Milner's Co. 1st Lt.
Sage, William M. SC Holcombe Legion AQM
Sage, William M. Gen. & Staff Capt.,AQM
Sage, William W. MS 9th Inf. Old Co.B
Sage, William Wallace MS 2nd Part.Rangers
    Co.G
Sagebiel, August TX 1st (Yager's) Cav. Co.E
    Sgt.
Sagebiel, August TX Cav. 8th (Taylor's) Bn.
    Co.C
Sagee, Frank LA Washington Arty.Bn. Co.1
Sagee, Frank LA 1st (Nelligan's) Inf. Co.C
Sagee, Frank LA Inf. 1st Sp.Bn. (Rightor's) New
    Co.C
Sagel, W.C. MS Inf. Lewis' Co.
Sageley, Joseph AR 35th Inf. Co.G
Sagely, J.C. AL 22nd Inf. Co.F Cpl.
Sagely, John TN 18th Inf. Co.H Sgt.
Sageman, P. SC 14th Inf.
Sager, Abraham VA 8th Bn.Res. Co.C
Sager, Abraham VA 136th Mil. Co.F
Sager, A.C. AR 15th (N.W.) Inf. Co.H Sgt.
Sager, Allmon VA 18th Cav. Co.B
Sager, Alman VA 14th Mil. Co.F
Sager, Conrad VA 18th Cav. Co.I
Sager, Conrad VA 14th Mil. Co.F
Sager, Conrad VA 62nd Mtd.Inf. 1st Co.D
Sager, F. VA 1st St.Res. Co.B
Sager, Harvie W. VA 14th Mil. Co.F
Sager, Henry VA 62nd Mtd.Inf. Co.B
Sager, Henry VA 136th Mil. Co.F Drum.
Sager, Isaac VA 12th Cav. Co.K
Sager, Isaac VA 136th Mil. Co.F
Sager, Jacob VA 11th Cav. Co.B
Sager, Jacob VA 14th Mil. Co.E Cpl.
Sager, James AL Mil. 4th Vol. Co.D

Sager, James VA 18th Cav. Co.H
Sager, James VA Cav. 41st Bn. 2nd Co.H
Sager, Jeremiah VA 11th Cav. Co.B
Sager, Jeremiah VA 14th Mil. Co.E
Sager, J.F. AR 15th (N.W.) Inf. Co.H
Sager, J.H. VA 18th Cav. Co.H
Sager, J.H. VA 62nd Mtd.Inf. 1st Co.D
Sager, John VA 8th Bn.Res. Co.D 1st Sgt.
Sager, John VA 14th Mil. Co.E
Sager, John A. TX 19th Inf. Co.D Sgt.
Sager, John T. VA 10th Inf. Co.F
Sager, Joseph LA O'Hara's Co. (Pelican
    Guards,Co.B)
Sager, Joseph G. VA 10th Inf. Co.F
Sager, Levi VA 11th Cav. Co.C Cpl.
Sager, M. TX 5th Cav. Co.D
Sager, M. VA 23rd Cav. Co.C
Sager, Michael VA 14th Mil. Co.E 1st Lt.
Sager, Mike VA Cav. 41st Bn. 2nd Co.H
Sager, Morris VA 2nd Inf. Co.H
Sager, Morris VA 136th Mil. Co.F
Sager, P. TX 4th Cav. Co.C
Sager, William C. AL Mil. 4th Vol. Co.D
Sager, William D. VA 10th Inf. Co.F Sgt.
Sagers, A.S. AL 3rd Inf. Co.F
Sagers, Samuel VA 23rd Cav. Co.M
Saggee, Allman VA 62nd Mtd.Inf. 1st Co.G
Saggerty, Michael AL 24th Inf. Co.B
Saggs, Hinton J. TN Inf. 22nd Bn. Co.H 2nd Lt.
Saggus, Stephen S. GA Phillips' Legion Co.O,I
Sagimga 1st Seminole Mtd.Vol.
Sagister, Amos MO 3rd Inf. Co.C
Sagley, B.L. TN 8th (Smith's) Cav. Co.G
Sagley, J.A. TN 8th (Smith's) Cav. Co.G 2nd
    Lt.
Sagory, Charles LA Mil. Orleans Guards Regt.
    Co.D Sgt.
Sagur, A. MS 10th Inf. Old Co.C Band Music.
Sagure, G.D. LA 7th Cav. Co.I
Sagurs, Charles A. GA 1st (Olmstead's) Inf.
    Co.C
Sagurs, James H. GA 1st (Olmstead's) Inf. Co.C
    Cpl.
Sagurs, William H. GA 1st (Olmstead's) Inf.
    Co.C
Sahbiker, --- TX 1st Hvy.Arty. Co.C
Sah Co Choctaw Inf. Wilkins' Co.
Sah con thlon nay 1st Creek Mtd.Vol. Co.E
Sah co win nay 1st Creek Mtd.Vol. Co.E
Sah ge yah NC Inf. Thomas Legion Co.D,B
Sah hin thli chee 1st Creek Mtd.Vol. 2nd Co.C
Sa hin thle 1st Creek Mtd.Vol. Co.A
Sahjimechee 1st Seminole Mtd.Vol.
Sahlman, Bernard SC Inf.Loc.Def. Estills' Co.
Sahlman, L. SC 5th Cav. Co.D
Sahlman, Luder SC 3rd Cav. Co.G
Sahlmann, L. SC Mil.Cav. Theo. Cordes' Co.
Sahlmann, L. SC Mil. 1st Regt.Rifles Chiches-
    ter's Co.
Sahlmann, Luder SC Cav. 17th Bn. Co.A
Sahlmon, C. SC Mil. 1st Regt. (Charleston Res.)
    Co.B
Sahm, Adolph TX 7th Cav. Co.B Cpl.
Sahm, August TX 3rd Inf. Co.K
Sahm, George TX Inf. 4th Bn. (Oswald's) Co.B
Sahm, George 4th Conf.Eng.Troops Co.E

Sahm, George Kellersberg's Corps Sap. &
    Min.,CSA
Sahm, Joseph MD 1st Inf. Co.G
Sahms, John NC 16th Inf. Co.M
Sah Nah Ne 1st Cherokee Mtd.Rifles Co.K
Sah ne Te kin Nie 1st Cherokee Mtd.Rifles Co.E
Sahr, Simon LA 10th Inf. Co.F
Sai ille tubbee 1st Choctaw & Chickasaw
    Mtd.Rifles 2nd Co.C
Sail, Booth E. Wheeler's Scouts,CSA
Sail, James S. KY 10th Cav. Co.E 1st Lt.
Sailens, William S. GA 34th Inf. Co.E
Sailer, Charles GA 1st Bn.S.S. Co.B
Sailer, Peter R. VA 8th Cav. Co.F
Sailers, James MO St.Guard
Sailers, John J. AL 13th Inf. Co.D
Sailes, Harrison H. TN 26th Inf. Co.A
Sailes, William NC 58th Inf. Co.G
Sailesberry, Newman VA 162nd Mil. Co.B Cpl.
Sailhorst, Albert TN Lt.Arty. Scott's Co. Sgt.
Sailitabee Rias 1st Choctaw & Chickasaw
    Mtd.Rifles 2nd Co.C
Saillas, Esteve LA Mil. 4th Regt. 1st Brig. 1st
    Div. Co.G
Sailler, W.S. GA 2nd Cav. Co.C
Sailor, Alfred VA 45th Inf. Co.D
Sailor, Andrew 1st Chickasaw Inf. Hansell's Co.
    Cpl.
Sailor, David Conf.Inf. Tucker's Regt. Co.K
    Cpl.
Sailor, Enoch M. TN 61st Mtd.Inf. Co.A
Sailor, J. KY 2nd (Woodward's) Cav. Co.F
Sailor, Jany KY 2nd (Duke's) Cav. Co.E
Sailor, Jerry KY 1st Inf. Co.B
Sailor, John W. VA 10th Inf. Co.K
Sailor, Joseph NC 48th Inf. Co.K
Sailor, Lewis W. VA 63rd Inf. Co.A
Sailor, William NC 7th Sr.Res. Holland's Co.,
    Clinard's Co.
Sailors, A. GA 4th Cav. (St.Guards) Deadwyler's
    Co. Cpl.
Sailors, A.J. GA 37th Inf. Co.E
Sailors, A.J. GA 54th Inf. Co.I
Sailors, Andy GA 34th Inf. Co.E
Sailors, Crawford GA Inf. 9th Bn. Co.B
Sailors, Crawford GA 37th Inf. Co.E
Sailors, Daniel W. AR 27th Inf. Co.K Cpl.
Sailors, George GA 34th Inf. Co.E
Sailors, George LA Cav. 12th Regt. Co.L
Sailors, H. MO 2nd Cav. Co.F
Sailors, Henry GA 4th Res. Co.C
Sailors, Isham GA 34th Inf. Co.E
Sailors, James MO 2nd Cav. Co.D,F Sgt.
Sailors, James M. GA 34th Inf. Co.E
Sailors, J.B. GA 55th Inf. Co.D
Sailors, John GA 4th Res. Co.C
Sailors, John, Jr. GA 16th Inf. Co.D
Sailors, John, Sr. GA 16th Inf. Co.D
Sailors, John GA 40th Inf. Co.A
Sailors, John KY 9th Cav. Co.A
Sailors, John N. AL 5th Inf. New Co.C
Sailors, M. AL 3rd Inf. Co.C
Sailors, M. AL Talladega Cty.Res. J. Lucius'
    Co.
Sailors, M. GA Lt.Arty. Ritter's Co.
Sailors, M.D. MD Arty. 3rd Btty.

Sailors, M.J. GA 4th Cav. (St.Guards) Gower's
Co.
Sailors, Monroe TN 28th (Cons.) Inf. Co.K 2nd
Lt.
Sailors, Thornton GA 4th Res. Co.C
Sailors, W.C. GA Inf. 9th Bn. Co.B
Sailors, William GA 4th Res. Co.C
Sailors, William GA 28th Inf. Co.G
Sailors, William M. SC 1st (Butler's) Inf.
Co.A,H
Sails, William TN 18th (Newsom's) Cav. Co.E
Sailton, Thomas AR 9th Inf.
Saimey, William NC 74th Bn.
Sain, A. TN 14th (Neely's) Cav. Co.A
Sain, Andrew NC 13th Inf. Co.F
Sain, A.T. 7th Conf.Cav. Co.G
Sain, Basil 7th Conf.Cav. Co.G
Sain, C. MS 7th Cav. 2nd Co.G
Sain, C. TN 14th (Neely's) Cav. Co.A
Sain, Cheshire NC 13th Inf. Co.F 3rd Lt.
Sain, Chesire NC 4th Sr.Res. Co.A Capt.
Sain, D.D. TN 14th (Neely's) Cav. Co.F
Sain, D.D. TN 22nd Inf. Co.C
Sain, E. TN 14th (Neely's) Cav. Co.F
Sain, Elam NC 23rd Inf. Co.B
Sain, George M. TN 16th Inf. Co.E
Sain, G.W. NC 1st Bn.Jr.Res. Co.E 2nd Lt.
Sain, Henry MS 44th Inf. Co.E
Sain, Isham D. TN 35th Inf. 2nd Co.D
Sain, J.A. 3rd Conf.Eng.Troops Co.C
Sain, Jacob NC 4th Sr.Res. Co.K
Sain, Jacob NC 13th Inf. Co.F
Sain, John A. NC 42nd Inf. Co.F
Sain, John A. TN 12th (Cons.) Inf. Co.B
Sain, Joseph NC 5th Sr.Res. Co.E
Sain, Joseph NC 13th Inf. Co.F
Sain, Lawrence AR Mil. Desha Cty.Bn.
Sain, Nathan NC 42nd Inf. Co.D
Sain, Nimrod B. NC 13th Inf. Co.F 2nd Lt.
Sain, Philip B. TX 16th Inf. Co.I
Sain, Thomas MS 6th Cav. Co.H
Sain, Thomas TN 35th Inf. 2nd Co.D Sgt.
Sain, Thomas M. NC 42nd Inf. Co.F Cpl.
Sain, W.H. MS 43rd Inf. Co.F
Sain, William AR 15th (Josey's) Inf. Co.A
Sain, William MS 6th Cav. Co.H
Sain, William NC 13th Inf. Co.F
Sain, William F. MS 34th Inf. Co.E
Sain, William M. NC 42nd Inf. Co.F Cpl.
Sain, W.M. TN 35th Inf. 2nd Co.D
Saine, Andrew NC 1st Cav. (9th St.Troops)
Co.K
Saine, Elisha Reynolds MS Inf. 1st St.Troops
Co.G
Saine, Joseph TN 4th (McLemore's) Cav. Co.I
Saine, W.H. MS 6th Cav. Co.K
Saines, William KY 7th Mtd.Inf. 1st Co.K
Sainey, John VA 17th Inf. Co.B
Sainsimon, J. GA Inf. 1st Loc.Troops (Augusta)
Barnes' Lt.Arty.Co.
Saint, Benjamin TN 31st Inf. Co.H
Saint, George W. AL 32nd Inf. Co.A 2nd Lt.
Saint, G.Z. GA 59th Inf. Co.L
Saint, Isham TN 31st Inf. Co.H
Saint, Jack AL 11th Cav. Co.C
Saint, James L. LA 2nd Inf. Co.K Cpl.
Saint, John B. AL 49th Inf. Co.D Music.

Saint, Reuben TX 13th Vol. Co.E Cpl.
Saint, Reuben TX 15th Inf. 2nd Co.G
Saint, T.B. AL 42nd Inf. Co.F 1st Sgt.
Saint, Thomas B. AL Inf. 2nd Regt. Co.D
Saint, William AL 49th Inf. Co.D,B
Saintaignan, A. LA 22nd (Cons.) Inf. Co.C
Saintclair, James NC 52rd Inf. Co.F
Saint Clair, J.O. AL 9th Inf. Co.A
Saintclair, John NC 52nd Inf. Co.F
Saintes, Jean LA Arty. 1st Field Btty.
Saintgermes, S. LA Mil. 3rd Regt. French Brig.
Co.4
Saintignan, A. LA 22nd Inf. Co.C
Saintigraw, A. LA Mil. 1st Chasseurs a pied
Co.4
Saintjohn, Leonidas NC 55th Inf. Co.B
Saint Martin, Emile LA 8th Inf. Co.K 1st Sgt.
Saint Martin, Victor LA 8th Inf. Co.K Capt.
Saint Paul 1st Choctaw & Chickasaw Mtd.Rifles
3rd Co.E
Saintsing, George W. NC 15th Inf. Co.F
Saintsing, George W. NC 43rd Inf. Co.G
Saintsing, James, Jr. NC 43rd Inf. Co.G
Saintsing, John A. NC 30th Inf. Co.B
Saintsing, Somerville NC 43rd Inf. Co.G
Saintsing, Wilie NC 34th Inf.
Saint William Exch.Bn. Co.E,CSA
Sair, A. VA 22nd Cav. Co.E
Sairbaugh, C. MO Cav. Williams' Regt. Co.G
Sais, Guadalupe TX 3rd Inf. 1st Co.C
Sais, Jose TX 8th Inf. Co.I
Sais, M. TX 1st (Yager's) Cav. Co.A
Sais, Manuel TX 8th Inf. Co.E Drum.
Sais, Martain TX Cav. 3rd (Yager's) Bn. Co.A
Saisan, Louis LA 4th Inf. Co.B
Saiser, Eli NC 24th Inf. Co.I
Saitigee 1st Seminole Mtd.Vol.
Saiver, George MO 4th Cav. Co.A
Saiz, Abbino TX Part.Rangers Thomas' Co.
Saiz, Guadalupe TX Res.Corps Co.B
Saizan, Auguste LA 2nd Cav. Co.K
Saizan, Hippolite LA 2nd Cav. Co.K
Saizan, Hippolyte LA Mil. Knaps' Co. (Fausse
River Guards)
Saizan, Ovide LA 2nd Cav. Co.K
Saizan, Paul LA Pointe Coupee Arty.
Saizan, Paul F. LA 2nd Cav. Co.K
Sajoux, J. Marie LA Mil. 2nd Regt. French Brig.
Co.6
Sakers, John MD 1st Cav. Co.K
Sakers, John T. VA 1st Cav. 2nd Co.K
Sakers, Samuel VA 7th Cav. Co.G
Sakes, Jacob LA 1st Hvy.Arty. (Reg.) Co.C,G
Sakes, Jacob LA Miles' Legion Co.H
Sakes, John J. LA 22nd Inf. Co.A Cpl.
Sala, Aug. LA 30th Inf. Co.D
Sala, Levi TX 2nd Inf. Co.A
Sa la like 1st Creek Mtd.Vol. Co.A Cpl.
Sala, Publo LA Mil. 5th Regt.Eur.Brig. (Spanish
Regt.) Co.2
Sala, Ramon LA Mil. 5th Regt.Eur.Brig.
(Spanish Regt.) Co.9
Salagar, T. TX 5th Cav. Co.D
Salaman, H.D. TN 49th Inf. Co.C
Salaman, S.F. TN 49th Inf. Co.C
Salasan, Jesus TX Cav. 3rd (Yager's) Bn. Co.A
Salasar, Crecencio TX 3rd Inf. 1st Co.C

Salasar, Petashio TX 8th Inf. Co.E
Salasar, Santiago TX 8th Inf. Co.E
Salasse, J.S. LA Inf. 9th Bn. Co.D
Salatan, Casimiro TX 2nd Field Btty.
Salathial, Robert TX Cav. Morgan's Regt.
Salaun, A. LA Mil. Orleans Guards Regt. Co.A
Salaun, O. LA Mil. Orleans Guards Regt. Co.H
Salazar, Diego LA Mil. 5th Regt.Eur.Brig.
(Spanish Regt.) Co.A
Salazar, Fernando TX Cav. 3rd (Yager's) Bn.
Rhodes' Co.
Salazar, Griserto TX Cav. 3rd (Yager's) Bn.
Rhodes' Co.
Salazar, Jose TX Cav. Ragsdale's Bn. 1st Co.C
Salazar, Juan TX Cav. Ragsdale's Bn. 1st Co.C
Salazar, Margarito TX 1st (Yager's) Cav. Co.F
Salazar, Narcisso TX Cav. Benavides' Regt.
Co.D
Salazar, Natividad TX 3rd Inf. Co.F
Salbe, E. LA Inf. 10th Bn. Co.C 2nd Lt.
Salberg, Joseph J. TX 2nd Inf. Co.F 1st Sgt.
Salberry, John LA Mil. British Guard Bn.
Kurczyn's Co.
Salbite, M. GA Arty. Baker's Co.
Salbreath, F.S. MO St.Guard
Salcido, Mariano TX Cav. Madison's Regt. Co.E
Saldania, Antoine LA Pointe Coupee Arty.
Salder, F.M. GA 38th Inf. Co.I
Salding, W.D. GA Cav. Dorough's Bn.
Saldiva, Vicenta TX 8th Inf. Co.I
Sale,--- VA Mtd.Res. Rappahannock Dist. Sale's
Co. Capt.
Sale, A. VA 13th Inf. 2nd Co.E
Sale, Alfred A. NC 54th Inf. Co.G 1st Sgt.
Sale, Andrew J. VA 5th Cav. Co.A
Sale, Anthony J. VA 26th Inf. Co.I
Sale, Austin KY 4th Cav. Co.G
Sale, Austin KY 9th Cav. Co.E
Sale, Benjamin L. VA 9th Cav. Co.F
Sale, Benjamin P. VA 34th Inf. Co.K
Sale, B.P. VA 5th Cav. Co.D
Sale, Charles C. AL 4th Inf. Co.I 2nd Lt.
Sale, Charles M. KY 1st Bn.Mtd.Rifles Co.D
Sale, Charles W. VA Lt.Arty. Douthat's Co.
Sale, Edmond W. VA 28th Inf. 1st Co.C Cpl.
Sale, Edmund W. VA Lt.Arty. J.R. Johnson's
Co. Cpl.
Sale, E.P. AL 4th (Roddey's) Cav. Sgt.Maj.
Sale, Eugene Paul MS 43rd Inf. Co.C Sgt.Maj.
Sale, E.W. AL 9th Inf. Co.C
Sale, E.W. Gen. & Staff Surg.
Sale, Finley NC 5th Cav. (63rd St.Troops) Co.D
1st Cpl.
Sale, F.O. TN 7th (Duckworth's) Cav. Co.B
Sale, Francis M. NC 37th Inf. Co.F Sgt.
Sale, G.B. TN 7th (Duckworth's) Cav. Co.B
Sale, George L. VA Conscr. Cp.Lee
Sale, George O. KY 9th Cav. Co.C
Sale, George T. VA 58th Inf. Co.F
Sale, George W. AR 15th (Josey's) Inf. Co.C
Sale, George W. MS 2nd Part.Rangers Co.D
Sale, George W. NC 37th Inf. Co.F Sgt.
Sale, George W. VA 11th Inf. Co.K
Sale, Granville S. VA 51st Inf. Co.G
Sale, Granville T. VA 50th Inf. Co.F 1st Lt.
Sale, G.W. NC 64th Inf. Co.H Lt.
Sale, G.W. TN Inf. 3rd Bn. Co.A

Sale, H. LA Mil. Orleans Fire Regt. Co.A
Sale, Henry A. AR 15th (Josey's) Inf. Co.C
Sale, Henry A. NC 64th Inf. Co.H 1st Lt.
Sale, Henry G. VA 9th Inf. Co.D
Sale, Henry T. TN 7th (Duckworth's) Cav. Co.B
  1st Lt.
Sale, Hickerson M. GA 15th Inf. Co.G Sgt.
Sale, Hugh NC 54th Inf. Co.H
Sale, James KY 8th Cav. Co.H
Sale, James VA 17th Inf. Co.A
Sale, James D. AL 1st Regt.Conscr. Co.I
Sale, James D. AL Conscr. Echols' Co.
Sale, James E. VA 2nd Cav. Co.B
Sale, James E. VA 22nd Inf. Co.B
Sale, James H. VA 55th Inf. Co.A
Sale, James I. VA 53rd Inf. Co.H 1st Lt.
Sale, James Judson VA 9th Cav. Co.B
Sale, James M. KY 2nd (Duke's) Cav. Co.E
  Capt.
Sale, James M. KY 1st Inf. Co.K 5th Sgt.
Sale, James M. VA 3rd Res. Co.F
Sale, James P. NC 54th Inf. Co.G
Sale, James P. VA 11th Inf. Co.G Cpl.
Sale, John B. MS Inf. 5th Bn. Co.B Capt.
Sale, John B. MS 27th Inf. Co.K Capt.
Sale, Jno. B. Gen. & Staff Col.,AAG
Sale, Jno. B. Gen. & Staff, Cav. Col.
Sale, John C. VA 34th Inf. Co.K
Sale, John D. KY 2nd Mtd.Inf. Co.I
Sale, John E. VA 9th Inf. Co.G
Sale, John F. VA 6th Inf. Ferguson's Co.
Sale, John F. VA 12th Inf. Co.H 2nd Lt.
Sale, John H. VA Hvy.Arty. 18th Bn. Co.B 2nd
  Lt.
Sale, John M. VA 13th Inf. Co.A
Sale, John S. VA 6th Cav. Co.I 2nd Lt.
Sale, John T. NC 54th Inf. Co.G
Sale, J.P. LA Mil. Claiborne Regt. Co.A
Sale, L.A. Conf.Hvy.Arty. Montague's Bn. Co.D
  1st Lt.
Sale, Lauriston A. VA 34th Inf. Co.I Capt.
Sale, Louis A. VA 51st Inf. Co.G
Sale, Lucius TX 2nd Inf. Co.H
Sale, Matthew G. VA 19th Inf. Co.A Sgt.
Sale, Melville W. AL Cav. 11th Bn. Maj.
Sale, Melville W. AR 15th (Josey's) Inf. Co.C
  Cpl.
Sale, Miles Sedden VA 30th Inf. Co.H
Sale, M.W. Lee's Corps Capt.
Sale, Noah NC 54th Inf. Co.H
Sale, P.B. VA 14th Cav. Co.H
Sale, Philip VA Lt.Arty. W.P. Carter's Co.
Sale, Philip VA 17th Inf. Co.I
Sale, R.A. AL 21st Inf. Co.G
Sale, R.D. LA 27th Inf. Co.I
Sale, R.D.M. VA Lt.Arty. Cayce's Co.
Sale, Richard LA Inf. 1st Sp.Bn. (Rightor's)
  Co.E
Sale, Richard C.M. VA Lt.Arty. J.R. Johnson's
  Co.
Sale, Richard C.M. VA 28th Inf. 1st Co.C
Sale, Richard C.M. VA 34th Inf. Co.I Capt.
Sale, Richard D.M. VA Lt.Arty. J.R. Johnson's
  Co.
Sale, Richard D.M. VA 28th Inf. 1st Co.C
Sale, Robert NC 54th Inf. Co.G

Sale, Robert F. AR 1st (Colquitt's) Inf. Co.A
  Sgt.
Sale, Samuel S. VA Inf. 5th Bn. Co.F
Sale, S.B. KY 4th Cav. Co.G
Sale, Sidney B. VA 51st Inf. Co.G
Sale, Thomas KY 1st (Butler's) Cav. Co.G 1st
  Sgt.
Sale, Thomas KY 1st Inf. Co.G
Sale, Thomas E. VA 54th Mil. Co.E,F
Sale, Thomas L. VA Lt.Arty. Douthat's Co.
Sale, Thomas S. GA 15th Inf. Co.G Sgt.
Sale, T. Sanders TN Lt.Arty. Morton's Co.
  Sr.1st Lt.
Sale, W. LA Inf. 1st Sp.Bn. (Rightor's) Co.A
Sale, W. VA Inf. 25th Bn. Co.D
Sale, W.B. KY 9th Cav. Co.E
Sale, W. Charles NC 5th Cav. (63rd St.Troops)
  Co.D
Sale, W.D. Gen. & Staff, A. of TN Asst.Surg.
Sale, W.F. AR 1st (Dobbin's) Cav. Co.A
Sale, W.H. TN Inf. 3rd Bn. Co.E 2nd Lt.
Sale, W.H. Gen. & Staff Asst.Comsy.
Sale, William AL Cav. Forrest's Regt.
Sale, William A. AR 6th Inf. Co.K
Sale, William Augustus SC 1st (McCreary's) Inf.
  Co.G
Sale, William H. VA 1st Cav. Co.C Capt.,ACS
Sale, William J. VA 26th Inf. Co.A Sgt.
Sale, W.V. KY 4th Cav. Co.G Sgt.
Sale, W.W. SC Mil. 1st Regt. (Charleston Res.)
  Co.G 1st Lt.
Salee, Martin L. MO 1st N.E. Cav. Co.E
Salem, Giuliano LA Mil. 6th Regt.Eur.Brig.
  (Italian Guards Bn.) Co.3
Salen, G. TN Inf. 3rd Bn. Co.B
Salen, G.S. AL 18th Inf.
Salen, H.C. AR 19th (Dockery's) Inf. Cons.
  Co.E,D
Salens, Jenkins GA 47th Inf. Co.H
Salent, J.M. GA Inf. Athens Reserved Corps
Saler, John AL 54th Inf.
Saler, John AR Cav. McGehee's Regt. Co.C
Saler, John AR 1st Mtd.Rifles Co.F Black.
Saler, Layman M. KY 1st (Butler's) Cav. Co.C
Salers, C.C. AL 14th Inf. Co.D
Salers, George W. AL 25th Inf. Co.F
Salers, James AL 23rd Inf. Co.B
Salers, James AL 25th Inf. Co.F
Salers, J.F. GA 2nd Inf. Co.B
Salers, William GA 4th Inf. Co.A
Sales, A. VA Arty. C.F. Johnston's Co.
Sales, A. VA Inf. 2nd Bn.Loc.Def. Co.G Cpl.
Sales, Alexander VA 2nd Cav. Co.B
Sales, Anthony VA Courtney Arty. Sgt.
Sales, Anthony VA 2nd Inf.Loc.Def. Co.I
Sales, B.S. VA 1st Cav. Co.F
Sales, George VA Inf. Cohoon's Bn. Co.B
  Hosp.Stew.
Sales, Henry MO 8th Inf. Co.F
Sales, J. TN 27th Inf. Co.F
Sales, J.A. AL 22nd Inf. Co.I
Sales, James KY 1st (Helm's) Cav. New Co.A
Sales, James S. AR 2nd Mtd.Rifles Co.A
Sales, J.G. TN 27th Inf. Co.H
Sales, John AL 21st Inf. Co.D Cpl.
Sales, John MO Cav. Fristoe's Regt. Co.E Sgt.
Sales, John MO 8th Inf. Co.F

Sales, John TX 4th Field Btty.
Sales, John D. KY 6th Mtd.Inf. Co.G
Sales, John H. VA 54th Mil. Co.E,F
Sales, John M. VA 1st Cav. Co.E
Sales, John T. NC 1st Inf. (6 mo. '61) Co.E
Sales, John T. NC 58th Inf. Co.C 1st Lt.
Sales, John T. NC 60th Inf. Co.K 2nd Lt.
Sales, Joseph B. NC 1st Inf. (6 mo. '61) Co.E
Sales, Joseph B. NC 58th Inf. Co.C
Sales, Joseph B. NC 60th Inf. Co.K
Sales, J.P. LA 4th Cav. Co.F Sgt.
Sales, J.T. TN 27th Inf. Co.H
Sales, J.W. TX Cav. Baird's Regt. Co.H
Sales, L. GA 3rd Cav. Co.C
Sales, Lanson AR 2nd Mtd.Rifles Co.A
Sales, Phillip AR 34th Inf. Co.G
Sales, P.L. KY 7th Cav. Co.G
Sales, Richard VA 2nd Inf. Co.D
Sales, Robert F. NC 60th Inf. Co.K
Sales, S.A. LA 17th Inf. Co.H
Sales, S.B. GA Floyd Legion (St.Guards) Co.F
  Sgt.
Sales, Thomas VA Inf. 1st Bn.Loc.Def. Co.A
Sales, Thomas L. VA 28th Inf. Co.H Cpl.
Sales, W.C. NC 60th Inf. Co.K
Sales, W.E. AR Inf. Adams' Regt. Moore's Co.
Sales, W.H. NC 60th Inf. Co.K
Sales, William AL Cav. Forrest's Regt.
Sales, William TN 18th (Newsom's) Cav. Co.E
Sales, William H. VA 13th Inf. 2nd Co.B
Sales, William M. VA 14th Cav. Co.H
Salesberry, S.C. VA 20th Cav. Co.C Sgt.
Salesberry, Walter D. NC 25th Inf. Co.A
Salesberry, W.L. GA Lt.Arty. Croft's Btty.
  (Columbus Arty.)
Salescox, D. AL 11th Inf. Co.A
Salettes, --- LA Mil. French Co. of St.James
Salfner, George M. MS Cav. Jeff Davis Legion
  Co.F
Salgee, Henry VA Hvy.Arty. 10th Bn. Co.C
Saliba, Charles S. LA 7th Inf. Co.E
Salier, Anselm LA 2nd Cav. Co.A
Saliers, Archibald AR 35th Inf. Co.G
Salina, Rafael TX Cav. Benavides' Regt. Co.D
Salinas, Andres TX Part.Rangers Thomas' Co.
  1st Sgt.
Salinas, Carlos TX Cav. Benavides' Regt. Co.B
Salinas, Carlos M. TX 33rd Cav. 1st Co.I Cpl.
Salinas, Celestino TX 3rd Inf. 1st Co.C
Salinas, F.E. SC 23rd Inf. Co.A Sgt.
Salinas, Francisco TX Part.Rangers Thomas' Co.
Salinas, Jacobo TX 33rd Cav. 1st Co.I 2nd Lt.
Salinas, Jose TX Cav. Baylor's Regt. Co.B
Salinas, Manuel TX Cav. Benavides' Regt. Co.B
Salinas, Manuel TX Cav. Ragsdale's Bn. 1st
  Co.C
Salinas, Martin TX 3rd Inf. 1st Co.C
Salinas, Monico TX 33rd Cav. Co.H
Salinas, Pablo TX 2nd Field Btty.
Salinas, Rafael TX Cav. Ragsdale's Bn. Co.D
Salinas, Ramon TX Part.Rangers Thomas' Co.
  Cpl.
Salinas, Vincente TX 3rd Inf. Co.F Cpl.
Salinas, Ynes TX Cav. Ragsdale's Bn. 1st Co.C
Salines, J.C. TN 19th (Biffle's) Cav. Co.I
Saling, James S. MO 1st N.E. Cav.

Saling, James S. MO 5th Inf. Co.H
Saling, James S. MO 9th Bn.S.S. Co.D Sgt.
Saling, James W. MO 3rd Cav. Co.B
Salinger, C.D. AL Cav. Moreland's Regt. Co.E
Salinger, S. TN 3rd (Clack's) Inf. Co.A
Salinger, William H. NC 1st Inf. Co.H
Salinos, Jose TX 17th Field Btty.
Salis, Asa N. FL 4th Inf. Co.C
Salisa, Eugene LA 25th Inf. Co.F
Salisair, Thomas TX 36th Cav. Co.C
Salisar, Narciso TX Cav. Ragsdale's Bn. 1st
     Co.A
Salisberry, A.S. TX Cav. Bourland's Regt. Co.D
Salisberry, J.S. SC Mil. 18th Regt. Co.F
Salisbery, James VA 25th Inf. 2nd Co.C
Salisbury, Francis M. TN 15th (Stewart's) Cav.
     Co.D
Salisbury, George W. VA 31st Inf. Co.F 2nd Lt.
Salisbury, George W. VA 62nd Mtd.Inf. 2nd
     Co.A,D 2nd Lt.
Salisbury, Henry LA Mil. Orleans Fire Regt.
     2nd Lt.
Salisbury, Henry MS 1st Cav. Co.K
Salisbury, Herman L. TX 22nd Cav. Co.H
Salisbury, Hy LA Inf. 1st Sp.Bn. (Rightor's)
     Co.F Cpl.
Salisbury, J. GA Inf. 23rd Bn.Loc.Def. Sims'
     Co. 2nd Lt.
Salisbury, J. SC Cav. 17th Bn. Co.A
Salisbury, J.E. SC 5th Cav. Co.D
Salisbury, John SC 5th Cav. Co.D
Salisbury, John SC Cav. 17th Bn. Co.A
Salisbury, J.S. SC 5th Cav. Co.G
Salisbury, J.S. SC Cav. 17th Bn. Co.B
Salisbury, N.B. TN 15th (Cons.) Cav. Co.G
Salisbury, T.W. SC 5th Cav. Co.D
Salisbury, T.W. SC Cav. 17th Bn. Co.A
Salisbury, W.F. TN 15th (Cons.) Cav. Co.G
Salisbury, William 3rd Conf.Eng.Troops Co.G
     Sgt.
Salisbury, William H. MS 27th Inf. Co.L
Salisbury, William L. GA 5th Inf. Co.B Maj.
Salisbury, W.L. GA 5th Inf. (St.Guards) Col.
Salius, D.H. MS 1st Cav. Co.A
Salker, W.M. AL 44th Inf. Co.I
Sall, C. KY 1st Inf. Co.A
Sallager, M.P. VA 5th Cav. Co.I
Sallapo, F. 1st Chickasaw Inf. Hansell's Co.
Sallas, A.S. GA 54th Inf. Co.A Cpl.
Sallas, David GA 54th Inf. Co.H
Sallas, E.L. AL 34th Inf. Co.I
Sallas, Ephraim GA 54th Inf. Co.H Cpl.
Sallas, Gomocindo FL 1st Cav. Co.D Cpl.
Sallas, J.J. AL 34th Inf. Co.I
Sallas, John GA 27th Inf. Co.F
Sallas, Solomon J. GA Inf. 27th Bn. Co.B
Sallassi, Joseph S. AL St.Arty. Co.A
Sallatt, M. SC 2nd St.Troops Co.I
Salle, George F. TN Cav. 17th Bn. (Sanders')
     Co.A
Salle, Marcus A. MS 44th Inf. Co.H
Salle, R.C. VA 1st (Farinholt's) Res. Co.G 2nd
     Lt.
Salle, R.E. TN Cav. 17th Bn. (Sanders') Co.A
Sallee, Christian KY 4th Mtd.Inf. Co.H
Sallee, D.D. TX 17th Inf. Co.E
Sallee, George G. KY 4th Cav. Co.B

Sallee, George W. AR 1st (Colquitt's) Inf. Co.C
Sallee, G.W. AR 3rd Cav. Co.A
Sallee, I. MO Cav. Fristoe's Regt. Co.G
Sallee, J. VA 1st St.Res. Co.B
Sallee, J.W. AL 1st Bn.Cadets Co.B
Sallee, Lycurgus A. AR 1st (Colquitt's) Inf.
     Co.C
Sallee, William MO Cav. Snider's Bn. Co.A
Sallee, William MO Inf. Clark's Regt. Co.H
Sallee, William H. MO Lt.Arty. H.M. Bledsoe's
     Co.
Sallen, Michael LA 14th Inf. Co.B Music.
Sallen, P. LA Mil. 3rd Regt. 3rd Brig. 1st Div.
     Co.F
Sallenger, David P. NC 1st Inf. Co.H Sgt.
Saller, Adam LA 14th Inf. Co.E
Saller, J. TN Inf. 3rd Bn. Co.D
Sallerfield, Jesse B. AL 22nd Inf. Co.D
Sallers, Jesse GA 17th Inf. Co.E
Sallers, Lemuel GA 4th (Clinch's) Cav. Co.A,K
Sallerwhite, N.M. TN 3rd (Forrest's) Cav. Co.L
Salles, --- LA Mil. 2nd Regt. French Brig. Co.2
Salles, B.A. LA Arty. Landry's Co. (Donaldson-
     ville Arty.)
Salles, B.A. TX 5th Inf. Co.K
Salles, B.A. Conf.Lt.Arty. Richardson's Bn. Co.B
Salles, F.H. LA Inf.Crescent Regt. Co.E
Salles, J.A. AL 10th Cav. Co.F
Salles, John NC 5th Sr.Res. Co.A
Salles, L.E. TX 17th Inf. Co.A
Salles, M. LA 2nd Cav.
Salles, Mortimer LA Arty. 1st Field Btty.
Salles, William NC 5th Sr.Res. Co.A
Sallet, J.R. GA Lt.Arty. Guerard's Btty.
Sallett, William H. GA Cav. 1st Bn. Hopkins'
     Co.
Sallett, William H. GA 5th Cav. Co.K,D
Sallette, P. Oscar LA 30th Inf. Co.E
Salley, A.G. SC 4th Cav. Co.B
Salley, A.G. SC Cav. 10th Bn. Co.A
Salley, A.G. SC Cav. 14th Bn. Co.B
Salley, Alexander Gen. & Staff Surg.
Salley, A.S. SC 20th Inf. Surg.
Salley, B.F. AL 2nd Cav. Co.I
Salley, D.D. SC 2nd St.Troops Co.C
Salley, F.H. TN 7th Cav. Co.A
Salley, Franklin B. AL Cav. 5th Bn. Hilliard's
     Legion Co.D
Salley, G.B. SC 2nd Arty. Co.I
Salley, Henry J. MS 15th Inf. Co.E
Salley, H.U.A. AR 1st (Monroe's) Cav. Co.L
Salley, James W. MS Inf. 3rd Bn. Co.D
Salley, James W. MS 15th Inf. Co.K
Salley, John A. MS 15th Inf. Co.E
Salley, J.S. SC 1st (McCreary's) Inf. Co.A
Salley, J.T. SC 6th Cav. Co.F
Salley, J.T. TX 14th Cav. Co.I
Salley, J.W. AR Cav. Gordon's Regt. Co.I
Salley, N.A. VA 50th Inf. Co.A
Salley, Robert S. FL 4th Inf. Co.B Sgt.
Salley, T.B. SC 3rd Cav. Co.I
Salley, Thomas VA 94th Mil. Co.A
Salley, Thomas J. AL Cav. 5th Bn. Hilliard's
     Legion Co.D
Salley, T.J. AL 2nd Cav. Co.I
Salley, W.B. SC 2nd Arty. Co.I
Salley, Wm. VA 48th Inf. Co.H

Sallie, B.M. NC 35th Inf. Co.E
Sallie, B.M. VA 59th Inf. 3rd Co.G
Sallie, George F. AR Mil. Desha Cty.Bn.
Sallie, George W. KY 8th Cav. Co.B
Sallie, James NC 7th Sr.Res. Davie's Co.
Sallie, J.H. KY 8th Cav. Co.B
Sallie, John VA Inf. 1st Bn.Loc.Def. Co.A
Sallie, John B. MO 9th Inf. Co.I
Sallie, Phillip KY 8th Cav. Co.B
Sallie, R.B. NC 35th Inf. Co.E
Sallie, T.G.W. MO 12th Cav. Co.H 1st Lt.
Sallie, Thomas NC 35th Inf. Co.E
Sallie, William MO 9th Inf. Co.E
Sallie, William NC 7th Sr.Res. Davie's Co.
Sallie, William NC 35th Inf. Co.E
Sallie, William VA Conscr. Cp.Lee Co.A
Sallie, William E. MO 12th Cav. Co.F
Sallie, William G. VA Inf. 1st Bn.Loc.Def. Co.B
Sallier, Arsene TX Cav. Ragsdale's Bn. Co.A
Sallier, Louis LA King's Sp.Bn.
Sallier, Louis TX Cav. Ragsdale's Bn. Co.A
Salliers, Andrew AR 20th Inf. Co.B
Salliers, John KY 1st (Helm's) Cav. Old Co.G
Salliers, Samuel AR 9th Inf. Co.C
Sallines, Jose Conf.Lt.Arty. Davis' Co.
Salling, Creed T. KY Mtd.Rifles 1st Bn. Co.B
Salling, George W. VA 2nd Cav. Co.C Cpl.
Salling, G.W. VA Mil. Scott Cty.
Salling, James H. AR Cav. 1st Bn. (Stirman's)
     Co.C 1st Sgt.
Salling, Mitchel M. VA 25th Cav. Co.C
Salling, Mitchel M. VA 48th Inf. Co.C
Salling, William L. AR Cav. 1st Bn. (Stirman's)
     Co.C Sgt.
Salling, W.W. TX Inf. 1st St.Troops Lawrence's
     Co.D Cpl.
Sallinger, James NC 1st Inf. Co.H
Sallinger, Kenneth NC 1st Jr.Res. Co.K
Sallinger, S. AR 18th (Marmaduke's) Inf. Co.A
Sallinger, Thomas NC 1st Inf. Co.G
Sallins, D. Jenkins GA 26th Inf. Co.A
Sallins, D. Jenkins GA Inf. (Brunswick Rifles)
     Harris' Ind.Co.
Sallins, William J. GA 4th (Clinch's) Cav. Co.B
Sallins, William J. GA Inf. (Brunswick Rifles)
     Harris' Ind.Co.
Sallis, A.M. Conf.Lt.Arty. 1st Reg.Btty.
Sallis, Asa N. FL 1st Inf. Old Co.F
Sallis, David FL 1st Cav. Co.F
Sallis, David FL 5th Inf. Co.D
Sallis, D.E. TX 20th Inf. Co.B
Sallis, Elias D. MS 1st (Johnston's) Inf. Co.H
     Sgt.
Sallis, F.M. MS 3rd Cav. Co.F
Sallis, F.M. MS 9th Bn.S.S. Co.B
Sallis, Jacob MS Inf. 2nd St.Troops Co.A
Sallis, James MS 3rd Cav. Co.C
Sallis, James Conf.Cav. Wood's Regt. 2nd Co.M
Sallis, J.E. TN 20th (Russell's) Cav. Co.H
Sallis, J.F. FL 1st (Res.) Inf.
Sallis, J.H. LA Cav. Benjamin's Co.
Sallis, J.M. MS 3rd Cav. Co.C
Sallis, J.M. MS 1st (King's) Inf. (St.Troops) D.
     Love's Co.
Sallis, John F. FL 1st Inf. Old Co.F, New Co.B
Sallis, John M. MS Cav. 3rd Bn. (Ashcraft's)
     Co.F Capt.

Sallis, John M. MS 1st (Johnston's) Inf. Co.H
2nd Lt.
Sallis, Joseph M. MS 11th (Perrin's) Cav. Co.C
Sallis, J.W. MS 1st (King's) Inf. (St.Troops) D.
Love's Co.
Sallis, Luke TN 20th (Russell's) Cav. Co.H
Sallis, Robert J. MS 11th (Perrin's) Cav. Co.C
Sallis, Robert J. MS 15th Inf. Co.A 2nd Lt.
Sallis, S.S. MS Cav. 3rd Bn. (Ashcraft's) Co.F
Sallis, S.S. MS 11th (Perrin's) Cav. Co.K
Sallis, Thomas D. MS 15th Inf. Co.A Cpl.
Sallis, T.M. AL 7th Cav. Co.I
Sallis, William J. MS 11th (Perrin's) Cav. Co.C
QMSgt.
Sallis, William J. MS 1st (Johnston's) Inf. Co.H
Sgt.
Sallis, W.J. MS Cav. 3rd Bn. (Ashcraft's) Co.F
Sallis, W.J. MS 30th Inf. Co.D
Sallisbery, J.M. MS 9th Cav. QMSgt.
Salliver, Charles E. TN 12th Cav. Co.C
Sallon, Mark R. AL 32nd Inf. Co.A
Salls, R. LA Mil. 4th Regt. French Brig. Co.1
Sgt.
Sallus, Domatio FL 3rd Inf. Co.A
Sallus, Fibian FL 3rd Inf. Co.A Cpl.
Sallus, Joseph AL Vol. Rabby's Coast Guard
No.1
Sally, A.G. SC Cav. 19th Bn. Co.A
Sally, Ahart VA 50th Inf. Co.A
Sally, Beriah KY 13th Cav. Co.D
Sally, D.D. SC 11th Res. Co.G 2nd Lt.
Sally, Dempsey SC Arty.Bn. Hampton Legion
Co.A
Sally, Dempsey H. SC Horse Arty. (Washington
Arty.) Vol. Hart's Co.
Sally, D.J. MS 15th Inf. Co.E
Sally, George NC 35th Inf. Co.E
Sally, George G. SC 20th Inf. Co.I
Sally, G.F. AR Sanders' Cav. Co.A
Sally, H.A. SC 22nd Inf. Co.I Cpl.
Sally, H.H. SC 22nd Inf. Co.I Capt.
Sally, Henry F. SC Arty.Bn. Hampton Legion
Co.A
Sally, Howell A. SC 2nd Cav. Co.D
Sally, Isaac VA 50th Inf. Co.A
Sally, J.A. NC 35th Inf. Co.E
Sally, James K. VA 50th Inf. Co.A
Sally, J.J. SC 22nd Inf. Co.I 2nd Lt.
Sally, J.M. SC 22nd Inf. Co.I 2nd Lt.
Sally, John AL 21st Inf. Co.C,D Cpl.
Sally, John F. VA 50th Inf. Co.A
Sally, John J. SC 22nd Inf. Co.I Lt.
Sally, Mastin VA 64th Mtd.Inf. Co.I
Sally, Nathaniel M. SC Horse Arty. (Washington
Arty.) Vol. Hart's Co.
Sally, N.W. SC 1st (Butler's) Inf. Co.A
Sally, Peter AL 4th Res. Co.B
Sally, Peter LA 1st Hvy.Arty. (Reg.) Co.I
Sally, Thomas VA 64th Mtd.Inf. Co.H
Sally, Thomas VA 64th Mtd.Inf. Co.I
Sally, W.M. KY 7th Mtd.Inf. Co.F
Sallyads, Green B. VA 14th Mil. Co.D 1st Lt.
Sallyer, Joseph VA 48th Inf. Co.C
Sallyers, Daniel TX 15th Cav. Co.G
Salman, A. AL 34th Inf. Co.A
Salman, Charles M. MS 10th Inf. Old Co.I
Salmanowitz, A. MS 28th Cav. Co.A

Salmen, James H. TX Cav. Border's Regt. Co.K
2nd Lt.
Salmes, F. VA 2nd Inf. Co.I
Salmon, A.J. GA Inf. 8th Bn. Co.A
Salmon, Benjamin F. VA Arty. Dance's Co.
Salmon, B.L. LA Siege Train Bn. Co.D
Salmon, Charles F. VA Arty. Dance's Co.
Salmon, Charles M. MS Lt.Arty. (Madison
Lt.Arty.) Richards' Co.
Salmon, D.A. NC 62nd Inf. Co.F
Salmon, David D. NC 3rd Arty. (40th St.Troops)
Co.E
Salmon, Edward MS 48th Inf. Co.E
Salmon, Edward A. NC 50th Inf. Co.H
Salmon, E.E. GA 2nd Mil. Co.E
Salmon, E.J. VA 5th Bn.Res. Co.A 2nd Lt.
Salmon, E.L. MS 38th Cav. Co.H
Salmon, Elisha NC 4th Sr.Res. Co.D
Salmon, E.Y. Gen. & Staff Surg.
Salmon, Ezekiel Y. TN 1st (Turney's) Inf. Co.E
Capt.
Salmon, F.M. NC 38th Inf. Co.D
Salmon, George VA 1st St.Res. Co.I
Salmon, George P. VA 2nd St.Res. Co.A
Salmon, G.W. LA 26th Inf. Co.K
Salmon, G.W. MS 39th Inf. Co.I
Salmon, Henry NC 30th Inf. Co.B
Salmon, Hezekiah AR 30th Inf. Co.I
Salmon, H.T. MS 38th Cav. Co.H
Salmon, H.W. MO 1st Cav. Capt.
Salmon, H.W. MO 1st Regt.St.Guards Capt.
Salmon, J. TX Cav. McCord's Frontier Regt.
Co.H
Salmon, Jacob VA 1st St.Res. Co.D
Salmon, Jacob L. AL Cav. 5th Bn. Hilliard's
Legion Co.A
Salmon, James TX 28th Cav. Co.L
Salmon, James TX Cav. Morgan's Regt. Co.C
Salmon, James VA 19th Inf. Co.E Lt.
Salmon, James B. MO 2nd Inf. Co.D Sgt.Maj.
Salmon, James C. LA Cav. Cole's Co. Cpl.
Salmon, James H. AL 50th Inf. Co.C
Salmon, James P. NC 50th Inf. Co.H
Salmon, James T. NC 44th Inf. Co.E
Salmon, James W. TX 9th (Nichols') Inf. Co.F
Salmon, James W. TX 13th Vol. 2nd Co.F 1st
Sgt.
Salmon, J.B. MO 11th Inf. Co.G
Salmon, Jefferson D. GA 6th Inf. Co.A
Salmon, Jefferson Dix AL 5th Inf. New Co.B
Salmon, J.H. AL 34th Inf. Co.G
Salmon, J.H. TX 9th (Young's) Inf. Co.D
Salmon, J.H. VA 2nd Cav. Co.K
Salmon, J.H. VA 88th Mil.
Salmon, J.L. 10th Conf.Cav. Co.A
Salmon, J.N. TN 51st Inf. Co.B
Salmon, J.N. TN 51st (Cons.) Inf. Co.H
Salmon, John AL Inf. 1st Regt. Co.F,A
Salmon, John AL 9th Inf. Co.E
Salmon, John NC 56th Inf. Co.B
Salmon, John TX 1st (McCulloch's) Cav. Co.C
Salmon, John TX 20th Cav. Co.B
Salmon, John H. MS 9th Inf. New Co.H
Salmon, John H. TX 19th Inf. Co.F
Salmon, John H. VA Lt.Arty. 12th Bn. 2nd Co.A
Salmon, John H. VA Lt.Arty. Sturdivant's Co.

Salmon, John H. Conf.Cav. Wood's Regt. 2nd
Co.M
Salmon, John M. TX Cav. Chisum's Regt. Co.D
3rd Lt.
Salmon, John W. NC 24th Inf. Co.I
Salmon, Joseph NC 56th Inf. Co.B
Salmon, Joseph M. SC 1st (Orr's) Rifles Co.H
Salmon, J.T. NC 38th Inf. Co.D
Salmon, J.W.P. GA Inf. 8th Bn. Co.A
Salmon, Kilby NC 8th Sr.Res. Broadhurst's Co.
Salmon, Kilby NC 30th Inf. Co.E
Salmon, L.M. VA Lt.Arty. Sturdivant's Co.
Salmon, L.M. VA 88th Mil.
Salmon, Lucien B. VA Arty. Dance's Co. Cpl.
Salmon, Michael Conf.Inf. 8th Bn.
Salmon, Milton Jasper TX 20th Cav. Co.B
Salmon, M.J. TX Cav. Morgan's Regt. Co.C
Salmon, R. NC 3rd Jr.Res. Co.H
Salmon, Randal NC 7th Bn.Jr.Res. Co.A
Salmon, R.B. GA Inf. 8th Bn. Co.A 2nd Lt.
Salmon, Reuben NC 44th Inf. Co.E
Salmon, R.G. TX Brazoria Cty. Minute Men
Physician
Salmon, Richard NC 24th Inf. Co.F Drum Maj.
Salmon, Richard T. MS 2nd Inf. Co.I
Salmon, R.M. TX 20th Cav. Co.D
Salmon, Robert MO 5th Inf. Co.F 2nd Lt.
Salmon, Robert VA 59th Inf. 3rd Co.D
Salmon, R.V. 8th (Wade's) Conf.Cav. Co.I
Salmon, Samuel B. LA Cav. Cole's Co.
Salmon, Samuel J. SC 1st (Orr's) Rifles Co.H
Sgt.
Salmon, Sidney NC 3rd Arty. (40th St.Troops)
Co.G
Salmon, Thaddeus, Jr. VA 24th Inf. Co.H
Salmon, Tho. A. MS 34th Inf. Co.E
Salmon, Thomas B. VA 19th Inf. Co.E
Salmon, Thos. H. VA 44th Bn. Co.D
Salmon, Walter NC 62nd Inf. Co.F
Salmon, W.B. KY Cav. 2nd Bn. (Dortch's) Co.D
Salmon, W.B. TX 19th Inf. Co.F
Salmon, W.D. TX Waul's Legion Co.F Cpl.
Salmon, W.F. MO 6th Cav. Co.B
Salmon, W.H. LA 1st Hvy.Arty. (Reg.) Co.D
Salmon, William B. KY 3rd Cav. Co.D
Salmon, William B. KY 5th Cav. Co.D
Salmon, William T. AL 36th Inf. Co.B
Salmond, B.B. AL Inf. 2nd Regt. Co.B 1st Sgt.
Salmond, B.B. 8th (Wade's) Conf.Cav. 2nd Lt.
Salmond, E. Martin's Escort,CSA 5th Cpl.
Salmond, E.A. SC 2nd Inf. Surg.
Salmond, H.C. SC 7th Cav. Co.H Cpl.
Salmond, Henry C. SC Cav.Bn. Holcombe
Legion Co.E Cpl.
Salmond, Jabez TN 1st (Feild's) Inf. Co.A
Salmond, Jabez TN Inf. 1st Cons.Regt. Co.H
Salmond, S.G. LA 13th Inf. Sgt.
Salmond, Thomas W. SC 2nd Inf. Surg.
Salmond, T.W. Gen. & Staff Surg.
Salmonds, B.B. AL 8th Inf. Co.D
Salmonds, James T. VA 21st Inf. Co.A
Salmonds, John R. VA 24th Cav. Co.H 2nd Lt.
Salmonds, Richard NC 5th Sr.Res. Co.H
Salmonds, William L. MO 5th Inf. Co.G Jr.2nd
Lt.
Salmons, Allie KY 6th Mtd.Inf. Co.I 1st Sgt.
Salmons, A.W. GA 19th Inf. Co.A

Salmons, B.F. VA 46th Inf. 2nd Co.H
Salmons, Calvin VA 54th Mil. Co.E,F
Salmons, David KY 5th Mtd.Inf. Co.E
Salmons, David N. VA 44th Inf. Co.B
Salmons, D.M. SC 23rd Inf. Co.F
Salmons, Elbert B. NC 55th Inf. Co.I 1st Lt.
Salmons, Ellis SC 4th Inf. Co.G Sgt.
Salmons, Frank Y. SC 2nd Cav. Co.K
Salmons, Frank Y. SC Cav.Bn. Hampton Legion Co.B
Salmons, Granville J. VA 11th Inf. Co.G
Salmons, Henry H. VA 44th Inf. Co.B
Salmons, Hesekiah AR 23rd Inf. Co.I 1st Cpl.
Salmons, H.H. VA 46th Inf. 2nd Co.H
Salmons, Jackson B. VA 46th Inf. Co.H
Salmons, John VA 51st Inf. Co.D
Salmons, John L. VA Hvy.Arty. 10th Bn. Co.B
Salmons, John N. VA 44th Inf. Co.B
Salmons, John R. VA Cav. 32nd Bn. Co.B 2nd Lt.
Salmons, John R. VA Cav. 47th Bn. Co.C
Salmons, John R. VA 29th Inf. Co.D
Salmons, John W. KY 6th Mtd.Inf. Co.I Cpl.
Salmons, Jonathan VA 51st Inf. Co.D
Salmons, L.A. VA 34th Inf. Co.E
Salmons, L.B. VA 1st (Farinholt's) Res. Co.I 2nd Lt.
Salmons, L.S. GA 3rd Bn. (St.Guards) Co.E
Salmons, Luis J. AL 19th Inf. Co.H
Salmons, Nelson AL 19th Inf. Co.H
Salmons, Nelson LA 12th Inf. Co.C
Salmons, Robert KY 2nd Bn.Mtd.Rifles Co.C
Salmons, Robert KY 5th Mtd.Inf. Co.E
Salmons, S. AL 19th Inf. Co.H
Salmons, W.H. SC Lt.Arty. 3rd (Palmetto) Bn. Co.H
Salmons, Wiley G. GA 49th Inf. Co.C
Salmons, William MO 2nd & 6th Cons.Inf.
Salmons, William VA 3rd Inf. 2nd Co.K
Salmons, William D. SC 23rd Inf. Co.F
Salmons, William E. VA Lt.Arty. 13th Bn. Co.B
Salmons, Willis J. AL 19th Inf. Co.H
Salms, E. NC 21st Inf. Co.H
Salnary, J.H. GA 43rd Inf. Co.E
Saloi, Peter TX 5th Inf. Co.A
Saloi, Peter M. TX 1st (Yager's) Cav. Co.C
Saloi, Peter M. TX Cav. 3rd (Yager's) Bn. Co.C
Saloi, P.M. TX 9th Cav. Co.A Capt.
Salois, Alfred LA Inf. 7th Bn. Co.C
Salois, Alfred LA 15th Inf. Co.K Cpl.
Salome, Bacilio TX 33rd Cav. 1st Co.H
Salome, Thomas TX 37th Cav. Co.K
Salomon, --- LA Mil. 3rd Regt.Eur.Brig. (Garde Francaise) Co.5 Cpl.
Salomon, A. LA Mil. 4th Regt. French Brig. Co.2
Salomon, Fredric TX 12th Cav. Co.E
Salomon, J. LA Mil. 3rd Regt. French Brig. Co.2
Salomon, John VA Inf. 25th Bn. Co.A
Salomon, L.J. LA Inf.Crescent Regt. Co.E
Salomon, William LA Mil. 1st Regt. 3rd Brig. 1st Div. Co.C Capt.
Salomone, Antonis LA Mil. 6th Regt.Eur.Brig. (Italian Guards Bn.) Co.1
Salomone, Lorenzo LA Mil. 6th Regt.Eur.Brig. (Italian Guards Bn.) Co.1

Salone, Isaac MO 4th Cav. Co.F
Salonicho, Christopholo LA 10th Inf. Co.I
Salopa, E. 1st Chickasaw Inf. Minnis' Co.
Salor, Jose LA Mil. 5th Regt.Eur.Brig. (Spanish Regt.) Co.10 3rd Lt.
Salors, David GA 55th Inf. Co.D
Salors, Michael GA 55th Inf. Co.D
Salors, Wm. GA 11th Cav. Co.A
Saloshm, M. GA 3rd Bn. (St.Guards) Co.D
Saloskin, G. LA Mil. 4th Regt.Eur.Brig. Co.B
Salousky, Frederick FL 2nd Cav. Co.B Band Music.
Salridge, John J. AR 34th Inf. Co.D
Salsberry, Elias TN 3rd (Lillard's) Mtd.Inf. Co.A
Salsberry, Green KY 10th (Diamond's) Cav. Co.A Black.
Salsberry, H. LA 1st Cav. Co.F
Salsberry, Jacob S. VA 20th Cav. Co.C
Salsberry, James 3rd Conf.Eng.Troops Co.H
Salsburg, David KY 9th Mtd.Inf. Co.C
Salsburg, Samuel S. VA 37th Inf. Co.A
Salsbury, Albert LA Cav. 13th Regt.
Salsbury, A.W. NC 17th Inf. (2nd Org.) Co.H Sgt.
Salsbury, James O. NC 17th Inf. (2nd Org.) Co.H
Salsbury, John O. NC 17th Inf. (2nd Org.) Co.H
Salsbury, Richard MO 1st Inf. Co.D
Salsbury, Richard B. NC 3rd Cav. (41st St.Troops) Co.G Cpl.
Salsbury, Thomas LA 1st Hvy.Arty. (Reg.) Co.C Cpl.
Salsbury, W. VA 8th Cav. Co.C
Salsby, John B.F. GA 52nd Inf. Co.K
Salser, Elemuel AL 29th Inf. Co.E
Salser, Emanuel AL 25th Inf.
Salser, George AL 29th Inf. Co.E
Salser, Jacob AL 29th Inf. Co.E
Salser, Jacob AL 58th Inf. Co.E
Salser, James AL 29th Inf. Co.E
Salser, P.M. AL 29th Inf. Co.E,A
Salser, Robert AL 29th Inf. Co.E
Salser, William AL 29th Inf. Co.E
Salser, William J. AL 29th Inf. Co.E
Salset, Daniel AL 31st Inf. Co.K
Salsman, George W. MO Cav. Wood's Regt. Co.D Sgt.
Salsman, Moses AR 8th Inf. Co.H
Salsmons, John KY 8th Cav. Co.E
Salster, Manuel AL Cp. of Instr. Talladega
Salstonstall, --- MO St.Guard
Salt 1st Cherokee Mtd.Rifles Co.F
Salt, J.M. SC Lt.Arty. Parker's Co. (Marion Arty.)
Saltar, William AR 1st Mtd.Rifles Co.I Music.
Saltenstall, G.F. MO 5th Cav. Co.E
Saltenstall, G.F. MO 9th Inf. Co.B
Saltenstall, Girdle MO Inf. Clark's Regt. Co.A
Salter, A. TN 10th Cav. Co.H
Salter, Abner M. AL 23rd Bn.S.S. Co.F
Salter, Abner M. AL 1st Bn. Hilliard's Legion Vol. Co.F
Salter, Abram W. AL 36th Inf. Co.G
Salter, A.J. AL 14th Inf. Co.H
Salter, A.L. AL 6th Inf. Co.H
Salter, A.L. LA Inf. 1st Bn. (St.Guards) Co.B Cpl.

Salter, B. GA 3rd Inf.
Salter, B. GA 3rd Res. Co.D
Salter, C. FL 1st Inf. New Co.I 1st Lt.
Salter, C. 15th Conf.Cav. Co.A
Salter, C. Eng.,CSA
Salter, C.C. AL 60th Inf. Co.B
Salter, C.C. FL 1st Inf. New Co.I 2nd Lt.
Salter, Charles P. LA 18th Inf. Co.I
Salter, Charles V. TX 35th (Likens') Cav. Co.E
Salter, Columbus C. AL 3rd Bn. Hilliard's Legion Vol. Co.C
Salter, C.P. TX Cav. Morgan's Regt. Co.E
Salter, C.P. TX Inf. Townsend's Co. (Robertson Five S.)
Salter, David AL 36th Inf. Co.F Cpl.
Salter, David H. MS 14th Inf. Co.F
Salter, David S. MS 40th Inf. Co.G 1st Sgt.
Salter, D.E. LA Inf.Cons.Crescent Regt. Co.G
Salter, D.W. AL Cav. (St.Res.) Young's Co.
Salter, E.A. LA 17th Inf. Co.B Cpl.
Salter, E.A. LA Inf. Jeff Davis Regt. Co.J
Salter, Edward H. NC 2nd Inf. Co.I Sgt.
Salter, Eli AL 3rd Cav. Co.B
Salter, Eli MS 4th Cav. Co.K
Salter, Eli Conf.Cav. Wood's Regt. 1st Co.M
Salter, Enoch P. AL 3rd Bn. Hilliard's Legion Vol. Co.E Sgt.
Salter, F. GA 28th Inf. Co.B
Salter, Francis M. GA 3rd Inf. Co.I
Salter, George W. AL 3rd Cav. Co.B
Salter, George W. AL 17th Inf. Co.H
Salter, George W. AL 36th Inf. Co.F Cpl.
Salter, George W. Conf.Cav. Wood's Regt. 1st Co.M
Salter, G.L.C. VA 1st St.Res. Co.B
Salter, G.L.C. Gen. & Staff Hosp.Stew.
Salter, G.M. MS Inf. 2nd St.Troops Co.K
Salter, G.W. GA 28th Inf. Co.B 1st Lt.
Salter, Henry NC 1st Arty. (10th St.Troops) Co.G
Salter, Henry W. AL 33rd Inf. Co.I
Salter, Isaac B. GA 55th Inf. Co.H
Salter, J. GA Cav. 29th Bn. Co.C
Salter, Jackson J. AL 6th Inf. Co.G
Salter, James AL 5th Inf. New Co.C
Salter, James GA 10th Mil.
Salter, James SC 7th Inf. 2nd Co.E
Salter, James Day TX 28th Cav. Co.A,K Cpl.
Salter, James E. GA 55th Inf. Co.K
Salter, James L. GA 28th Inf. Co.H
Salter, James M. AL 3rd Bn. Hilliard's Legion Vol. Co.E Sgt.
Salter, James M. VA Lt.Arty. Clutter's Co.
Salter, James W. AL 33rd Inf. Co.I,K
Salter, J.C. AL 23rd Inf. Co.F
Salter, J.D. AL 23rd Inf. Co.E
Salter, Jefferson AL 1st Bn. Hilliard's Legion Vol. Co.F
Salter, Jesse GA 3rd Field Arty.
Salter, Jesse GA Siege Arty. 28th Bn. Co.C
Salter, Jesse C. AL 23rd Bn.S.S. Co.F
Salter, Jesse C. AL 1st Bn. Hilliard's Legion Vol. Co.F
Salter, J.F. AL 2nd Cav. Co.H
Salter, J.F. AL 4th (Russell's) Cav. Co.A
Salter, J.F. GA 48th Inf. Co.E
Salter, J.G. AL 60th Inf. Co.B

Salter, J.G. AL 3rd Bn. Hilliard's Legion Vol. Co.C

Salter, J.M. AL 8th Cav. Co.I

Salter, J.M. AL 1st Mil. Co.B 3rd Lt.

Salter, J.M. SC 2nd Arty. Co.E,A

Salter, J.M. SC Arty. Manigault's Bn. 2nd Co.C

Salter, J.M. SC 14th Inf. Co.B

Salter, J.M. TX 1st Field Btty. Capt.

Salter, J.M. TX 1st Inf. Co.C

Salter, J.M. 8th (Wade's) Conf.Cav. Co.I

Salter, J.N. GA Cav. 22nd Bn. (St.Guards) Co.A

Salter, Joel AL 4th Inf. Co.E

Salter, John AL 23rd Inf. Co.E

Salter, John AL 24th Inf. Co.K

Salter, John AL 36th Inf. Co.F

Salter, John GA Lt.Arty. Howell's Co.

Salter, John KY Cav. 3rd Bn.

Salter, John MS 37th Inf. Co.I

Salter, John C. SC 19th Inf. Co.D

Salter, John F. GA 3rd Inf. Co.F

Salter, John H. NC 1st Arty. (10th St.Troops) Co.G

Salter, John J. GA 51st Inf. Co.B Sgt.

Salter, John R. AL Mil. 4th Vol. Gantt's Co. 2nd Lt.

Salter, John Russell SC 19th Inf. Co.D

Salter, John S. KY 6th Cav. Co.A,B

Salter, John S. MS 14th Inf. Co.F

Salter, John W. NC 2nd Arty. (36th St.Troops) Co.G

Salter, John W. NC 3rd Arty. (40th St.Troops) Co.H

Salter, John W. NC Lt.Arty. 13th Bn. Co.F Cpl.

Salter, Joseph A. GA 59th Inf. Co.D

Salter, Joseph E. NC 2nd Arty. (36th St.Troops) Co.G

Salter, Joseph E. NC 3rd Arty. (40th St.Troops) Co.H

Salter, Joseph E. NC Lt.Arty. 13th Bn. Co.F

Salter, Joseph S. GA 2nd Cav. Co.C

Salter, J.P. GA Smith's Legion Co.F

Salter, J.R. AL 2nd Cav. Co.E

Salter, J.R. SC 7th Inf. 1st Co.H

Salter, J.R. SC Inf.Bn. Co.D

Salter, J.R. TN 50th Inf. Co.C

Salter, J.R. TN 50th (Cons.) Inf. Co.C

Salter, J.T. GA Lt.Arty. Howell's Co.

Salter, J.W. AL 12th Inf. Co.F

Salter, J.W. AL 34th Inf. Co.C

Salter, J.W. AL 63rd Inf. Co.F

Salter, J.W. AL Inf. Echols' Bn. Co.C 1st Lt.

Salter, K. AL 42nd Inf. Co.H

Salter, Kit SC 18th Inf. Co.C

Salter, L. SC 1st (Butler's) Inf. Co.E

Salter, L. SC 2nd St.Troops Co.B

Salter, L. SC 19th Inf. Co.D

Salter, Larkin SC 7th Inf. 1st Co.H

Salter, Lawrence Gideon SC 19th Inf. Co.D

Salter, Leroy J. AL Cav. Falkner's Co.

Salter, Leroy J. 8th (Wade's) Conf.Cav. Co.B Cpl.

Salter, L.G. SC 2nd Arty. Co.K,A

Salter, M. GA 3rd Mil.

Salter, Mathew GA 2nd Res. Co.B

Salter, Michael KY 7th Cav. Co.E Capt.

Salter, Michael KY 7th Cav. Co.I

Salter, Michael TN 3rd (Forrest's) Cav. 1st Co.G

Salter, Mike KY 2nd (Duke's) Cav. Co.C Bvt.2nd Lt.

Salter, Mitchell B. AL 4th Inf. Co.E

Salter, Neill AL 23rd Inf. Co.E Cpl.

Salter, Pleasant GA 3rd Res. Co.D

Salter, P.P. GA 3rd Inf.

Salter, Richard TN 40th Inf. Co.H

Salter, Richard R. AL 23rd Bn.S.S. Co.F Sgt.

Salter, Richard R. AL 1st Bn. Hilliard's Legion Vol. Co.F Cpl.

Salter, Robert TX Inf. 1st St.Troops Sheldon's Co.B

Salter, Robert Y. AL 3rd Bn. Hilliard's Legion Vol. Co.C

Salter, R.P. LA 2nd Cav. Co.K Lt.

Salter, R.P. LA 3rd (Harrison's) Cav. Co.K

Salter, R.P. AL Washington Arty.Bn. Co.5

Salter, R.Y. AL 60th Inf. Co.B

Salter, S. SC 1st (Butler's) Inf. Co.E

Salter, S.A.J. AR 32nd Inf. Co.K

Salter, Samuel AL 23rd Bn.S.S. Co.F Capt.

Salter, Samuel AL 1st Bn. Hilliard's Legion Vol. Co.F 1st Sgt.

Salter, Samuel A. MS 40th Inf. Co.G

Salter, Samuel W. MS 8th Inf. Co.I

Salter, S.G. MS Cav. Hughes' Bn. Co.D

Salter, S.H. GA 59th Inf. Co.A

Salter, Simeon Jackson SC 19th Inf. Co.D

Salter, Simon AL 17th Inf. Co.H

Salter, Simpson G. MS 4th Cav. Co.E

Salter, Simpson G. MS 36th Inf. Co.E

Salter, Sion D. GA 3rd Res. Co.K

Salter, S.J. SC 17th Inf. Co.D

Salter, Sugar AL 5th Inf. New Co.C

Salter, T. MS Cav. Hughes' Bn. Co.C

Salter, T.F. TN 3rd (Forrest's) Cav. 1st Co.B

Salter, Thomas Trans-MS Conf.Cav. 1st Bn. Co.E

Salter, Thomas C. LA 3rd (Harrison's) Cav. Co.K

Salter, Thomas C. LA Inf. 1st Sp.Bn. (Rightor's) Co.B

Salter, Thomas J. AL 16th Inf. Co.D Bvt.2nd Lt.

Salter, Thomas J. AL 23rd Inf. Co.F Cpl.

Salter, Thos. Jefferson AL 23rd Bn.S.S. Co.F Cpl.

Salter, Thomas W. GA Cobb's Legion Co.H Sgt.

Salter, T.J. GA Cav. 29th Bn. Co.H

Salter, T.S. LA 5th Inf. Co.E

Salter, T.S. MS 4th Cav. Co.D

Salter, Wallace R. NC 2nd Arty. (36th St.Troops) Co.G

Salter, Warren NC 3rd Arty. (40th St.Troops) Co.H

Salter, Warren NC Lt.Arty. 13th Bn. Co.F

Salter, W.D. AL 62nd Inf. Co.F

Salter, William GA 44th Inf. Co.A

Salter, William GA 49th Inf. Co.G

Salter, William GA 61st Inf. Co.B,C

Salter, William GA Inf. (Emanuel Troops) Moring's Co.

Salter, William MS 25th Inf. Co.G

Salter, William 2nd Conf.Inf. Co.G Drum Maj.

Salter, William H. GA 3rd Inf. Co.I Cpl.

Salter, William J. LA Lt.Arty. Fenner's Btty. Cpl.

Salter, William J. LA Inf. 1st Sp.Bn. (Rightor's) Co.F

Salter, William T. GA Lt.Arty. 12th Bn. 3rd Co.B

Salter, William Y. TX 1st Inf. Co.I

Salter, Wilson NC 1st Arty. (10th St.Troops) Co.G

Salter, Wilson L. GA Inf. Cobb Guards Co.A Cpl.

Salter, W.J. LA Inf. Jeff Davis Regt. Co.J

Salter, W.L. GA 18th Inf. Co.D

Salter, W.R. SC 2nd Arty. Co.K,A

Salter, Zion GA Arty. 9th Bn. Co.B

Salter, Z.W. AL 21st Inf. Co.F

Saltero, D. SC 1st Regt. Charleston Guard Co.I

Salters, J.A. SC 4th Cav. Co.I

Salters, J.A. SC Cav. 12th Bn. Co.B Cpl.

Salters, J.A. SC 3rd St.Troops Co.A

Salters, J.C. SC 27th Inf. Co.I 1st Lt.

Salters, John A. SC 25th Inf. Co.K

Salters, Philip SC 25th Inf. Music.

Salters, Samuel M. MO Cav. 2nd Regt.St.Guard Co.G

Salters, William AR 9th Inf. New Co.I Ch.Music.

Salters, William SC 25th Inf. Co.K 2nd Lt.

Saltes, E.P. AL Mil.Cav. 1st Regt. Co.B Sgt.

Saltes, I.R. AL Mil.Cav. 1st Regt. Co.B

Saltes, W.J. TN 21st Cav. Co.E

Salt Face 1st Cherokee Mtd.Vol. 1st Co.E, 2nd Co.C Cpl.

Saltin, James Gen. & Staff, QM Dept. Lt.

Saltmarsh, Joseph H. AL 28th Inf. Co.I

Saltmarsh, William L. AL Cav. Lewis' Bn. Co.D

Saltmarsh, W.L. AL Mil. 4th Vol. Co.G

Saltmarsh, W.L. AL 28th Inf. Co.I

Saltonstall, W.C. AL 8th Inf. Co.H

Saltonstall, William C. MS 14th Inf. Co.K

Saltonstall, William G. FL 5th Inf. Co.G

Salts, Davis B. TN Lt.Arty. Lynch's Co.

Salts, John TN 19th Inf. Co.B

Salts, John TN 60th Mtd.Inf. Co.F Cpl.

Salts, Nicholas TN 60th Mtd.Inf. Co.A

Salts, Reese TN 29th Inf. Co.F

Salts, William GA 13th Cav.

Saltskiver, William MS 17th Inf. Co.D

Saltsman, Fleming F. LA 1st Hvy.Arty. (Reg.) Co.A

Saltsman, Frederick L. AL 14th Inf. Co.G

Saltsman, John W. AR 23rd Inf. Co.B

Saltus, James C. SC Mil.Arty. 1st Regt. Tupper's Co. Sgt.

Saltus, James C. SC Inf. 1st (Charleston) Bn. Co.A 2nd Lt.

Saltus, Samuel SC 25th Inf. Co.B

Saltzer, Samuel AL 28th Inf. Co.E

Saltzgiver, O.P. TN Lt.Arty. Weller's Co.

Saltzman, John W. AR 1st (Dobbins') Cav. Co.B

Saltzman, N. LA Mil. Orleans Fire Regt. Co.G

Saltzman, T. LA Mil. Orleans Fire Regt. Co.G

Saltzman, Thn. LA Mil. Orleans Fire Regt. Co.G

Salusbury, William Eng.Dept. Polk's Corps A. of TN Sap. & Min.Co.,CSA

Sa lut ke 1st Creek Mtd.Vol. 2nd Co.C

Salvador, F. AL 12th Inf. Co.A

Salvador, Gaspard LA Mil. 1st Native Guards

Salvador, J. Ferro LA Mil. 5th Regt.Eur.Brig. (Spanish Regt.) Co.1

Salvador, Juan LA Mil. 5th Regt.Eur.Brig. (Spanish Regt.) Co.3

Salvador, Manuel LA Mil. 5th Regt.Eur.Brig. (Spanish Regt.) Co.A Sgt.

Salvador, Pedro LA Mil. 5th Regt.Eur.Brig. (Spanish Regt.) Co.A

Salvage, B.G. GA Floyd Legion (St.Guards) Co.I Cpl.

Salvage, H.H. MO 1st Brig.St.Guard

Salvant, E.A. LA Inf. 7th Bn. Co.A

Salvant, Joseph D. LA 15th Inf. Co.D

Salvater, Theodore AR 19th (Dawson's) Inf. Co.H

Salvator, John AR 5th Inf. Co.K

Salvatory, E. LA Mil. 4th Regt. 1st Brig. 1st Div. Co.G Jr.2nd Lt.

Salvensky, J. FL Cav. Co.I

Salvidge, J.J. AR 3rd (Cons.) Inf. Co.K

Salvo, Christopher GA Inf. (GA Defend.) Chapman's Co.

Salvo, F. SC Mil.Arty. 1st Regt. Walter's Co.

Salvo, James SC Mil.Arty. 1st Regt. Walter's Co. 2nd Lt.

Salvo, James SC Lt.Arty. Walter's Co. (Washington Arty.) 1st Lt.

Salvo, J.F. SC Mil. 1st Regt.Rifles Palmer's Co.

Salvo, J.F. SC 25th Inf. Co.A,B

Salvo, Peter A. SC Lt.Arty. Walter's Co. (Washington Arty.)

Salvo, T.A. MS 20th Inf. Co.A Music.

Salvo, V.M. SC Mil.Arty. 1st Regt. Walter's Co.C

Salvo, V.M. SC Lt.Arty. J.T. Kanapaux's Co. (Lafayette Arty.)

Salvona, L. SC Mil. 1st Regt. (Charleston Res.) Co.B

Saly, Peter Inf. School of Pract. Powell's Command Co.B

Salyards, George W. VA 10th Inf. Co.B 2nd Lt.

Salyards, James H. VA 97th Mil. Co.D

Salyer, A. VA Mil. Scott Cty.

Salyer, Abram VA 72nd Mil.

Salyer, A.J. KY 5th Mtd.Inf. Co.C

Salyer, Ananias VA 22nd Cav. Co.A Sgt.

Salyer, Andrew J. KY 10th Cav. Co.B

Salyer, Benjamin KY 5th Mtd.Inf. Co.F

Salyer, Carroll DeKalb KY 1st (Helm's) Cav. Co.B

Salyer, Carroll DeKalb KY 1st Inf. Co.B

Salyer, Daniel KY 5th Mtd.Inf. Co.C

Salyer, Daniel NC 37th Inf. Co.F

Salyer, David J. VA 22nd Cav.

Salyer, D.J. KY 10th (Diamond's) Cav. Co.B

Salyer, D.J. VA 72nd Mil.

Salyer, D.R. KY 3rd Mtd.Inf. Co.A

Salyer, Elisha M. KY 5th Mtd.Inf. Co.C

Salyer, Elisha M. VA 22nd Cav. Co.A

Salyer, F.N. TX 30th Cav. Co.B

Salyer, Henry VA 72nd Mil.

Salyer, Henry M. VA 22nd Cav.

Salyer, H.H. KY Fields' Co. (Part.Rangers)

Salyer, Isaiah KY 5th Mtd.Inf. Co.A,C,H

Salyer, J. VA 72nd Mil.

Salyer, James VA 6th Bn.Res. Co.H

Salyer, James VA 50th Inf. Co.H

Salyer, Jeremiah VA 22nd Cav. Co.A

Salyer, Jery VA 72nd Mil.

Salyer, Jesse KY 5th Mtd.Inf. Co.C Cpl.

Salyer, Jesse NC 37th Inf. Co.F

Salyer, J.H. VA 72nd Mil.

Salyer, John KY 5th Mtd.Inf. Co.C

Salyer, John H. VA 22nd Cav. Co.A

Salyer, Joseph VA 22nd Cav. Co.A

Salyer, Joseph N. VA Mil. Scott Cty.

Salyer, L.H.N. Gen. & Staff Lt.Col.

Salyer, Logan H.N. VA 50th Inf. Co.H Lt.Col.

Salyer, M. KY 3rd Mtd.Inf. Co.A

Salyer, Mathew KY 5th Mtd.Inf. Co.C

Salyer, M.L. KY Fields' Co. (Part.Rangers)

Salyer, Peter KY 3rd Mtd.Inf. Co.A

Salyer, Riley KY 5th Mtd.Inf. Co.F

Salyer, Roan KY 50th Inf. Co.H

Salyer, Ruben KY 5th Mtd.Inf. Co.C

Salyer, Rufus KY 10th (Diamond's) Cav. Co.B

Salyer, S. TX 9th (Young's) Inf. Co.C

Salyer, Samuel NC 17th Inf. (1st Org.) Co.L

Salyer, Samuel VA 50th Inf. Co.H 1st Sgt.

Salyer, Samuel P. VA 22nd Cav. Co.A

Salyer, Shanklin VA 50th Inf. Co.H 2nd Lt.

Salyer, Thomas VA 48th Inf. Co.E

Salyer, Thomas VA Mil. Scott Cty.

Salyer, Tyree T. VA 50th Inf. Co.H 2nd Lt.

Salyer, William KY 2nd (Woodward's) Cav. Co.G

Salyer, William VA 6th Bn.Res. Co.H

Salyer, William, Jr. VA 72nd Mil.

Salyer, William, Sr. VA 72nd Mil.

Salyer, W.W. KY 10th (Diamond's) Cav. Co.B

Salyers, Ananias VA Inf. 23rd Bn. Co.C

Salyers, Bradford S. KY 13th Cav. Co.A

Salyers, Cambridge C. KY 3rd Cav. Co.B

Salyers, Carroll D. KY 1st (Butler's) Cav. Co.B

Salyers, C.C. KY 5th Cav. Co.B

Salyers, David AR 1st (Crawford's) Cav. Co.H

Salyers, Erastus AR Inf. 2nd Bn. Co.C

Salyers, Erastus AR 3rd Inf. Co.E

Salyers, Hanson VA Mil. Scott Cty.

Salyers, H.M. VA Inf. 23rd Bn. Co.C

Salyers, Jefferson W. AR 2nd Mtd.Rifles Co.C

Salyers, J.H. VA Inf. 23rd Bn. Co.C

Salyers, Joseph AR 24th Inf. Co.C

Salyers, Joseph A. AR Inf. Hardy's Regt. Co.F

Salyers, Martin P. AR 33rd Inf. Co.I 2nd Lt.

Salyers, Philip T. AR 33rd Inf. Co.I Cpl.

Salyers, S. KY 3rd Mtd.Inf. 1st Co.F

Salyers, Samuel KY Lt.Arty. Cobb's Co.

Salyers, W.J. KY 5th Mtd.Inf. Co.F

Salyers, W.W. AL 12th Cav. Co.C

Salyey, Samuel NC 68th Inf. Co.B

Salylen, J.H. MO Cav. Coleman's Regt. Co.C

Salzedo, Benjamin L. MS 18th Inf. Co.C

Salzeger, Godfried TX 6th Inf. Co.D

Salzer, --- LA Mil. Mech.Guard

Salzer, Adam AL 36th Inf. Co.E

Salzig, John VA 9th Cav. Co.K

Salzig, John VA 41st Mil. Co.B

Salzijer, Godfrey TX Granbury's Cons.Brig. Co.A

Salzman, Frank TX 8th Field Btty.

Salznex, J. LA Mil. Chalmette Regt. Co.G

Sam KY 3rd Mtd.Inf. Co.M Co.Cook (Negro)

Sam LA 1st Hvy.Arty. (Reg.) Co.G Negro

Sam MS 3rd Inf. (St.Troops) Co.F Cook

Sam (Boy) MS 23rd Inf. Co.I Cook

Sam MS 31st Inf. Co.K Cook

Sam SC Cav.Bn. Holcombe Legion Co.A Cook

Sam (Negro) TX 23rd Cav. Co.E

Sam (Contraband) TX 7th Inf. Co.H

Sam 1st Choctaw & Chickasaw Mtd.Rifles 2nd Co.C, 3rd Co.H

Sam 1st Seminole Mtd.Vol. Cpl.

Sam Deneale's Regt. Choctaw Warriors Co.C

Sam, --- TX 24th Cav. Co.G

Sam, Anderson NC 60th Inf. Co.H

Sam, Jack 1st Cherokee Mtd.Rifles McDaniel's Co.

Sam, James 1st Choctaw & Chickasaw Mtd.Rifles 2nd Co.B

Sam, S.W. KY 12th Cav. Co.I

Sam, William 1st Choctaw & Chickasaw Mtd.Rifles 3rd Co.D

Sam, William 1st Choctaw & Chickasaw Mtd.Rifles 2nd Co.H

Sam Charles Deneale's Regt. Choctaw Warriors Co.E

Sam Charley 1st Seminole Mtd.Vol. Sgt.

Sam Isaac 1st Choctaw & Chickasaw Mtd.Rifles 2nd Co.I

Sam Jackson 1st Choctaw & Chickasaw Mtd.Rifles 3rd Co.F

Sam Jackson Choctaw Inf. Wilkins' Co. Cpl.

Samain, --- LA Mil. 2nd Regt. French Brig. Co.3

Samani, A. VA 1st St.Res. Co.I

Samamie, Anto. VA 26th Inf. Co.D

Samanni, Francis R. VA 1st Inf. Co.D

Samanni, L.P. MS 9th Inf. Old Co.K, New Co.K

Samanni, Thomas VA 6th Inf. Co.I

Samannin, A. VA 23rd Inf. Co.E

Samaron, M. LA Mil. 4th Regt. French Brig. Co.3

Sambert, Josephus MO Cav. 1st Regt.St.Guard Co.C

Sambins, Adolphe VA Lt.Arty. Jackson's Btty. St.Line Co.A

Samble, Cowan Blake's Scouts,CSA

Sambless, Joseph GA 8th Cav.

Sambo, --- SC 23rd Inf. Co.A Music.

Sambo, Alfred VA Mtd.Riflemen St.Martin's Co. Sgt.

Sambo, Charles MS 24th Inf. Co.G,B

Sambo, John VA Mtd.Riflemen St.Martin's Co. Cpl.

Sambola, Anthony LA Washington Arty.Bn. Co.5

Sambola, Francisco LA Mil. Cazadores Espanoles Regt. Co.2 Lt.

Sambola, Franco. LA Mil. 5th Regt.Eur.Brig. (Spanish Regt.) Co.5

Sambos, Joseph LA Mil. 1st Regt. 3rd Brig. 1st Div. Co.F

Sambre, P. LA Mil. 3rd Regt. French Brig. Co.2

Sambs, Obediah TN 8th (Smith's) Cav. Co.B

Sambs, Robert W. VA 27th Inf. Co.D

Sambuis, Adolph LA C.S. Zouave Bn. Co.B,D Cpl.

Samby, J. GA 48th Inf.

Samby, William NC 5th Sr.Res. Co.A

Same, Mathias AR 1st Inf. Co.K Music.

Samee 1st Creek Mtd.Vol. 2nd Co.C

Sameek, J.H. AL Conscr. & Res.Bn. Cpl.
Samelson, L. TN Inf. 3rd Bn. Co.F
Sameno, T. 1st Chickasaw Inf. Hansell's Co.
Sames, Benjamin F. VA 108th Mil. Co.F,
  Lemons' Co.
Sames, Berry NC 6th Cav. Co.A,I Sgt.
Sames, Edmond NC Inf. 2nd Bn. Co.H
Sames, Edward NC 64th Inf. Co.D
Sames, Elsbury R. NC Cav. 5th Bn. Co.A Sgt.
Sames, E.R. NC 64th Inf. Co.F
Sames, F.M. AR Cav. Gordon's Regt. Co.A
Sames, Francis FL 8th Inf. Co.F
Sames, James W. NC 64th Inf. Co.D
Sames, J.E. AR Cav. Gordon's Regt. Co.A
Sames, Jeremiah NC 64th Inf. Co.F
Sames, John NC 64th Inf. Co.K Cpl.
Sames, Richard KY 3rd Mtd.Inf. Co.C
Sames, R.W. KY 9th Cav. Co.I
Samford, Elbridge H. TN 48th (Nixon's) Inf.
  Co.H
Samford, Elbridge H. TN 54th Inf. Co.C Sgt.
Samford, Joab TX 28th Cav. Co.A
Samford, Marshall A. TN 5th Inf. 2nd Co.G
Samford, Paul W. VA 12th Inf. Co.B
Samford, Paul W. VA Inf. Cohoon's Bn. Co.C
  Sgt.
Samford, T.C. TX 28th Cav. Co.A
Samford, Thomas L. AL 37th Inf. Adj.
Samford, Thomas P. TX 1st Inf. Co.I
Samford, Willer AL 46th Inf.
Samford, William A. TX 28th Cav. Co.A
Samford, William J. AL Inf. 46th Regt. Co.G
  1st Lt.
Samford, William J. TX 28th Cav. Co.A
Samials, James AR 11th & 17th Cons.Inf. Co.I
Samie, August AL 40th Inf. Co.E
Sa Mille 1st Creek Mtd.Vol. Co.A
Saminton, N. GA 45th Inf. Co.A
Saminton, William TN 12th (Green's) Cav. Co.C
  Sgt.
Samlers, J.P. Forrest's Scouts T. Henderson's
  Co.,CSA
Samme, Auguste LA C.S. Zouave Bn. Co.C,D,F
  1st Sgt.
Samme Chupco 1st Creek Mtd.Vol. Co.A
Sammerell, William S. NC 5th Cav. (63rd
  St.Troops) Co.B
Sammert, George A. LA 4th Cav. Co.H Bugler
Sammih, Nedda NC Inf. Thomas Legion 2nd
  Co.A
Sammill, G.W. MS 3rd Inf. Co.H
Sammis, N. MO 1st Inf. 2nd Co.A
Sammis, Nelson M. TN 10th Inf. Co.B
Sammon, E.D. GA 16th Inf. Co.I
Sammon, James B. AR 36th Inf. Co.G
Sammon, T.D.H. TX 32nd Cav. Co.C
Sammond, Benjamin F. GA 15th Inf. Co.B
Sammonds, Jerry NC 33rd Inf. Co.D
Sammonds, Thomas KY 13th Cav. Co.F
Sammonds, W.F. AL Talladega Cty.Res. I.
  Stone's Co.
Sammonds, William NC 3rd Inf. Co.H
Sammons, A.B. AL Inf. 2nd Regt. Co.K
Sammons, A.B. AL 38th Inf. Co.I
Sammons, A.J. AR 1st (Crawford's) Cav. Co.G
Sammons, A.L. GA 54th Inf. Co.F,C
Sammons, Allen VA 61st Inf. Co.G

Sammons, Allen VA 135th Mil. Co.A
Sammons, Alvin H. GA 22nd Inf. Co.B
Sammons, Andrew B. TN 37th Inf. Co.E
Sammons, B.B. GA 54th Inf. Co.C 1st Sgt.
Sammons, Benjamin AL 27th Inf. Co.D
Sammons, Benjamin AL 29th Inf. Co.D
Sammons, Benjamin F. GA 3rd Inf. Co.D
Sammons, Benjamin F.W. GA 48th Inf. Co.A
Sammons, Benjamin M. AR 25th Inf. Co.A
Sammons, Charles VA 14th Cav. Co.A
Sammons, Charles B. VA 22nd Inf. Co.A
Sammons, Charles B. VA 135th Mil. Co.F Capt.
Sammons, Daniel SC 6th Res. Co.B
Sammons, D.M. SC 1st Cav. Co.D
Sammons, E.G. AL 18th Inf. Co.I
Sammons, Eli MS 48th Inf. Co.E
Sammons, Ellis W. GA 1st (Olmstead's) Inf.
  Co.C
Sammons, Francis AL 2nd Cav. Co.C
Sammons, G.W. GA Inf. 27th Bn. Co.A
Sammons, Harvey VA 8th Cav. Co.L
Sammons, Harvey VA 14th Cav. Co.A
Sammons, Harvey VA 135th Mil. Co.C,I
Sammons, Henry GA Inf. 27th Bn. Co.A
Sammons, Henry L. GA 22nd Inf. Co.B
Sammons, Howell AL 29th Inf. Co.D
Sammons, Howell TN Inf. 154th Sr.Regt. 2nd
  Co.B
Sammons, Jacob AR 38th Inf. Co.H
Sammons, James AR 45th Cav. Co.K
Sammons, James AR 25th Inf. Co.A
Sammons, James KY 8th Cav. Co.E
Sammons, James A. GA 13th Inf. Co.H
Sammons, James H. VA 12th Inf. 1st Co.I
Sammons, James L. VA 12th Inf. 2nd Co.I
Sammons, J.B. GA 55th Inf. Co.I
Sammons, J.J. GA Arty. St.Troops Pruden's
  Btty.
Sammons, John AR 3rd Cav. Co.F
Sammons, John GA 54th Inf. Co.C
Sammons, John KY 8th Cav. Co.D
Sammons, John MS 13th Inf. Co.B
Sammons, John TN 14th (Neely's) Cav. Co.F
Sammons, John H. GA Inf. 27th Bn. Co.A
Sammons, John L. GA Inf. 10th Bn. Co.C Sgt.
Sammons, Joseph KY 8th Cav. Co.E
Sammons, Joseph MS Cav. Jeff Davis Legion
  Co.E
Sammons, J.W. AL 18th Inf. Co.I
Sammons, J.W. GA 5th Res. Co.E
Sammons, J.W. KY 3rd Mtd.Inf. Co.N,F
Sammons, J.W. TN 14th (Neely's) Cav. Co.F
  Cpl.
Sammons, J.W. TN 9th Inf. Co.D
Sammons, L.A. VA Hvy.Arty. 20th Bn. Co.C
Sammons, Leroy AL 29th Inf. Co.D
Sammons, L.M. GA 34th Inf. Co.F
Sammons, Louis GA 48th Inf. Co.A
Sammons, M.L. GA 10th Cav. (St.Guards) Co.C
Sammons, Richard LA 3rd (Harrison's) Cav.
  Co.E
Sammons, Richard E. VA 3rd Inf. 2nd Co.K
Sammons, Richard J. GA 1st (Olmstead's) Inf.
  Co.C
Sammons, Robert AR 3rd Cav. Co.F
Sammons, Rolan VA Cav. 34th Bn. Co.B
Sammons, Samuel J. VA Hvy.Arty. Epes' Co.

Sammons, T.C. TX 25th Cav. Co.E
Sammons, Tench C. AL 24th Inf. Co.K
Sammons, Thomas KY 2nd Bn.Mtd.Rifles Co.E
Sammons, W.E. LA 8th Inf. Co.F
Sammons, W.F. AL 39th Inf. Co.C
Sammons, W.G. GA 54th Inf. Co.C
Sammons, Wiley G., Jr. GA 48th Inf. Co.A
Sammons, Wiley G., Sr. GA 48th Inf. Co.A
Sammons, William LA 3rd (Harrison's) Cav.
  Co.B
Sammons, William C. VA 23rd Inf. Co.B
Sammons, William J. AR Inf. Ballard's Co.
Sammons, William J. GA 21st Inf. Co.H Sgt.
Sammons, Willoughby NC 32nd Inf. Co.B
Sammons, W.W. AR 1st (Crawford's) Cav. Co.G
Samms, Add KY 3rd Mtd.Inf. Co.N,F
Samms, Creed KY Jessee's Bn.Mtd.Riflemen
  Co.A
Samms, Frank W. FL 3rd Inf. Co.B
Samms, G.W. KY 4th Cav. Co.E
Sammy, No.1 1st Seminole Mtd.Vol.
Sammy, No.2 1st Seminole Mtd.Vol.
Samns, Columbus C. GA 2nd Cav. (St.Guards)
  Co.E
Samonds, Thomas K. NC 37th Inf. Co.I 1st Lt.
Samonds, T.K. NC 4th Cav. (59th St.Troops)
  Co.E 2nd Lt.
Samons, John TX 20th Inf. Co.B
Samons, Shade A. AR 3rd Cav. Co.F
Samonzet, J. LA Mil. 3rd Regt. French Brig.
  Co.4
Samor, J. GA 23rd Inf. Co.B 1st Lt.
Samora, Gregorio TX 8th Inf. Co.C
Samow, William TX 26th Cav. Co.A
Sampayrae, I.A. LA 3rd Inf. Co.G
Sampel, Henry Conf.Cav. Raum's Co.
Sampels, Fielding NC Walker's Bn. Thomas'
  Legion Co.G
Sampels, Fielding TN 1st (Carter's) Cav. Co.H
Sampey, Francis M. AL 4th Inf. Co.E
Sampey, Greenberry G. AL 4th Inf. Co.E
Sampite, A. LA 26th Inf. Co.G
Sample, A.D. MS S.W. Red's Co. (St.Troops)
Sample, A.H. TX 8th Cav. Co.E
Sample, Alex Conf.Reg.Inf. Brooks' Bn. Co.D
Sample, Alexander TX Cav. Morgan's Regt.
  Co.I
Sample, A.W. TX 35th (Brown's) Cav. Co.H
Sample, Benjamin TX 2nd Inf. Co.E
Sample, Bethelua TN 5th (McKenzie's) Cav.
  Co.F
Sample, Bethuel TN 26th Inf. Co.C
Sample, B.F. SC 2nd Arty. Co.K
Sample, B.F. SC 7th Inf. 1st Co.E, Co.M 2nd
  Lt.
Sample, Caleb L. Gen. & Staff Asst.Surg.
Sample, C.G. AR Lt.Arty. Wiggins' Btty.
Sample, C.G. AL 1st Cav. 2nd Co.B
Sample, Charles GA 1st (Olmstead's) Inf. Co.I
Sample, C.L. FL 10th Inf. Asst.Surg.
Sample, C.L. FL 11th Inf. Asst.Surg.
Sample, C.L. GA Cav. 2nd Bn. Co.C Stew.
Sample, Clark J. AR 9th Inf. Co.B
Sample, Daniel J. MS Part.Rangers Smyth's Co.
Sample, David I. NC 53rd Inf. Co.B Cpl.
Sample, D.I. NC 1st Inf. (6 mo. '61) Co.C
Sample, D.J. Conf.Cav. Wood's Regt. 2nd Co.D

Sample, Drury R.M. TX 2nd Inf. Co.E
Sample, Elam A. NC 37th Inf. Co.C
Sample, Felix AL 63rd Inf. Co.B
Sample, George AL 44th Inf. Co.G
Sample, George I. MS 12th Cav. Co.E
Sample, George Washington LA Inf. 11th Bn.
  Co.D
Sample, H. LA Inf. 7th Bn. Co.B Sgt.
Sample, Harvey MS 18th Inf. Co.K
Sample, Henry LA 11th Inf. Co.D
Sample, Henry LA 14th (Austin's) Bn.S.S. Co.B
Sample, Henry W. AL 16th Inf. Co.C 1st Lt.
Sample, H.H. LA 2nd Cav. Co.E
Sample, H.H. LA 1st (Nelligan's) Inf. Co.A,H
Sample, H.H. LA Inf. 1st Sp.Bn. (Rightor's)
  Co.D
Sample, Hiram LA Inf. 1st Sp.Bn. (Wheat's) Old
  Co.D Sgt.
Sample, Hiram LA 15th Inf. Co.I 1st Sgt.
Sample, H.M. MS 2nd Cav. Co.E,B
Sample, Hugh B. NC 53rd Inf. Co.B Sgt.
Sample, Isaac W. NC 37th Inf. Co.C Sgt.
Sample, I.W. NC 1st Inf. (6 mo. '61) Co.C
Sample, J.A. AL 27th Inf. Co.H
Sample, J.A. MS 2nd Part.Rangers Co.C
Sample, J.A. MS Adams' Co. (Holmes Cty.Ind.)
Sample, J.A. TN Inf. 3rd Bn. Co.D Lt.
Sample, Jacob LA Inf. 16th Bn. (Conf.Guards
  Resp.Bn.) Co.A
Sample, Jacob R. MS 7th Inf. Co.A Hosp.Stew.
Sample, James AR 9th Inf. Co.G
Sample, James TN 2nd (Ashby's) Cav. Co.G
  Sgt.
Sample, James TN 62nd Mtd.Inf. Co.D 1st Sgt.
Sample, James A. AL 6th Inf. Co.L
Sample, James A. AL 44th Inf. Co.G
Sample, James A. GA 21st Inf. Co.F
Sample, James A. TN 5th (McKenzie's) Cav.
  Co.F
Sample, James M. GA 17th Inf. Co.F
Sample, James Mc. NC 53rd Inf. Co.B QMSgt.
Sample, J.B. MS Conscr.
Sample, J.E. LA 27th Inf. Co.G
Sample, J.E. Trans-MS Conf.Cav. 1st Bn. Co.B
Sample, J.H. AR Lt.Arty. Marshall's Btty.
Sample, J.H. MS 4th Inf. Co.G
Sample, J.J. TX 21st Cav. Co.I
Sample, J.J. TX Home Guards Killough's Co.
Sample, J.M. TX 8th Cav. Co.E
Sample, J.N. TX 12th Inf. Co.F
Sample, John A. MS 7th Inf. Co.A
Sample, John A. 14th Conf.Cav. Co.B
Sample, John B. SC Inf. Holcombe Legion Co.F
  2nd Lt.
Sample, John C. LA 16th Inf. Co.C
Sample, John F. GA 44th Inf. Co.F
Sample, John H. LA 9th Inf. Co.F Cpl.
Sample, John H. TN 26th Inf. Co.C
Sample, John M. LA 16th Inf. Co.A
Sample, John N. LA 27th Inf. Co.G
Sample, John N. GA 56th Inf. Co.K
Sample, John W. NC 37th Inf. Co.C 2nd Lt.
Sample, John W. NC 53rd Inf. Co.B
Sample, John W. TX 35th (Brown's) Cav. Co.H
Sample, John W. TX 13th Vol. 2nd Co.A
Sample, Joseph AL Lt.Arty. 2nd Bn. Co.F
Sample, Joseph AL 5th Inf. New Co.D

Sample, Joseph TN 62nd Mtd.Inf. Co.D
Sample, Joshua AR 1st (Colquitt's) Inf. Co.G
Sample, J.P. MS 44th Inf. Co.B Sgt.
Sample, J.R. MS 9th Inf. Co.A
Sample, J.W. AR 1st Mtd.Rifles Co.K
Sample, J.W. AR 25th Inf. Co.E
Sample, J.W. AR 36th Inf. Co.E
Sample, J.W. NC 1st Inf. (6 mo. '61) Co.C
Sample, Larken J. VA Cav. Caldwell's Bn.
  Gent's Co.
Sample, Larkin J. VA Cav. Ferguson's Bn. Mor-
  ris' Co.
Sample, Leroy TX 35th (Brown's) Cav. Co.H
Sample, Leroy W. TX 35th (Brown's) Cav. Co.H
Sample, Leroy W. TX 13th Vol. 2nd Co.A
Sample, Marcus L. AL 28th Inf. Co.I
Sample, M.M. TX 28th Cav. Co.K 2nd Lt.
Sample, N.E. GA 5th Cav. Co.E
Sample, O.P. MS Conscr.
Sample, R. TX Inf. Timmons' Regt. Co.E Sgt.
Sample, Reece TN 26th Inf. Co.C
Sample, R.M. AL 13th Bn.Part.Rangers Co.D
Sample, Robert TX 9th (Nichols') Inf. Co.A
Sample, Robert TX Waul's Legion Co.D Sgt.
Sample, Robert W. AL 28th Inf. Co.I
Sample, Samuel W. SC 1st (McCreary's) Inf.
  Co.B
Sample, T. TN 12th (Green's) Cav. Co.G
Sample, T.D. TN 47th Inf. Co.G
Sample, Thomas J. GA 21st Inf. Co.F Cpl.
Sample, Thomas M. AL 62nd Inf. Co.D
Sample, T.J. AL 53rd (Part.Rangers) Co.C
Sample, W.A. MS 4th Inf. Co.G
Sample, W.E. SC 2nd Cav. Co.G
Sample, Wellington TX Cav. 3rd (Yager's) Bn.
  Co.D
Sample, W.H. AR Mil. Desha Cty.Bn.
Sample, William AL 2nd Bn. Hilliard's Legion
  Vol. Co.F
Sample, William LA Res.Corps
Sample, William NC 30th Inf. Co.K
Sample, William A. MS 15th Inf. Co.B
Sample, William E. SC 7th Inf. 1st Co.E
Sample, William J. AL 44th Inf. Co.G
Sample, William L. NC 37th Inf. Co.C Sgt.
Sample, William M. TX 2nd Inf. Co.E
Sample, William Neely KY 14th Cav. Co.G
Sample, William P. LA 9th Inf. Co.F
Sample, William T. TN 30th Inf. Co.F Capt.
Sample, William W. AR Cav. Wright's Regt.
  Co.I
Sample, Willis AL Mil. 4th Vol. Co.I
Sample, W.M. AR 11th Inf. Co.A
Sample, W.R. MS Inf. 3rd Bn. (St.Troops) Co.C
Sampler, B.F. AR 30th Inf. Co.K
Sampler, Thomas G. GA 23rd Inf. Co.C
Sampler, W.W. GA 23rd Inf. Co.C
Samples, Anderson G. GA Arty. 9th Bn. Co.D
Samples, Augustus F. GA Lt.Arty. Scogin's Btty.
  (Griffin Lt.Arty.)
Samples, David AL 4th Inf. Co.K
Samples, David GA 6th Inf. Co.B
Samples, Elijah MS 10th Inf. Old Co.B, New
  Co.H
Samples, Elisha MS 41st Inf. Co.I 3rd Lt.
Samples, F.C. AR 3rd Cav. Co.C
Samples, George W. GA 6th Inf. Co.B

Samples, George W. LA Inf.Cons.Crescent Regt.
  Co.B
Samples, Green TN 35th Inf. Co.H
Samples, Harison VA 19th Cav. Co.G
Samples, Henry J. MS 10th Inf. Old Co.B, New
  Co.C
Samples, I.B. GA 19th Inf. Co.E
Samples, Isaac P. MS 34th Inf. Co.G
Samples, J.A. TN 34th Inf. Co.K
Samples, James AR 30th Inf. Co.I
Samples, James GA 36th (Broyles') Inf. Co.A
Samples, James GA 36th (Broyles') Inf. Co.C
Samples, James KY 10th (Diamond's) Cav. Co.G
Samples, James TN Cav. 4th Bn. (Branner's)
  Co.B Sgt.
Samples, James TN Inf. 2nd Cons.Regt. Co.H
Samples, James TN 29th Inf. Co.A
Samples, James A. AL 28th Inf. Co.C
Samples, James G. TN 35th Inf. 3rd Co.F 1st
  Lt.
Samples, James M. AR 23rd Inf. Co.I
Samples, Jesse TN 34th Inf. Co.K
Samples, Jesse F. GA 22nd Inf. Co.E
Samples, J.F. AL Inf. 2nd Regt. Co.K
Samples, J.M. GA 7th Inf. Co.G
Samples, J.Mc. GA 8th Cav. Co.F
Samples, J.N. GA 4th Cav. (St.Guards) Pirkle's
  Co.
Samples, John MS 9th Inf. Co.F
Samples, John MS 10th Inf. Old Co.B, New
  Co.C
Samples, John MS 41st Inf. Co.I
Samples, John TN 34th Inf. Co.K
Samples, John TN 35th Inf. Co.H
Samples, John C. AL Cav. Lewis' Bn. Co.C
  Cpl.
Samples, John C. GA 43rd Inf. Co.I
Samples, John G. GA 22nd Inf. Co.E
Samples, John H. AR 23rd Inf. Co.I
Samples, John H. TN 16th (Logwood's) Cav.
  Co.I
Samples, John J. MO 2nd Cav. Co.C
Samples, John L. LA Inf. 11th Bn. Co.D
Samples, John L. LA Inf.Cons.Crescent Regt.
  Co.B
Samples, John L. MO Cav. 3rd Bn. Co.B
Samples, John N. GA 4th Inf. Co.B
Samples, John T. GA 60th Inf. Co.B
Samples, John W. GA Phillips' Legion Co.B
Samples, John W. TX 1st (McCulloch's) Cav.
  Co.A
Samples, Joshua VA 72nd Mil.
Samples, J.W. KY 10th (Diamond's) Cav.
  Co.B,D,G
Samples, J.W. VA Inf. 26th Bn. Co.B
Samples, Larkin VA Cav. McFarlane's Co.
Samples, Larkin J. VA 22nd Cav. Co.I 2nd Lt.
Samples, Larkin J. VA 37th Inf. Co.I
Samples, Levi GA 6th Inf. Co.B
Samples, Levi MS 41st Inf. Co.I
Samples, M. GA 1st Inf. (St.Guards) Co.D
Samples, Marion AL 28th Inf. Co.C
Samples, R.C. GA 19th Inf. Co.E
Samples, Reuben M. AL 28th Inf. Co.C
Samples, R.M. AL 56th Part.Rangers Co.H
Samples, Robert TN 3rd (Lillard's) Mtd.Inf.
  Co.F Sgt.

Samples, Robert M. GA 1st Lt.Duty Men Co.A
Samples, Robert M. GA 63rd Inf. Co.H
Samples, Thomas S. AL 18th Inf. Co.D
Samples, U.C. GA 1st (Cons.) Inf. Co.C
Samples, W. TN 1st (Feild's) Inf. Co.C
Samples, W.H. TN 2nd (Ashby's) Cav. Co.A
Samples, William AR 2nd Inf. Old Co.E
Samples, William AR 7th Mil. Co.C
Samples, William TN 3rd (Lillard's) Mtd.Inf. Co.F
Samples, William TN 36th Inf. Co.B
Samples, William C. GA 36th (Broyles') Inf. Co.A
Samples, William D. GA 63rd Inf. Co.H
Samples, William H. AL 62nd Inf. Co.D
Samples, William M. AR Cav. Poe's Bn. Co.A Cpl.
Samples, William M. VA 79th Mil. Co.3 Capt.
Samples, William P. AL 62nd Inf. Co.E Cpl.
Samples, William P. VA 22nd Cav. Co.I Capt.
Samples, William P. VA 37th Inf. Co.I 2nd Lt.
Samples, W.M. AR 11th & 17th Cons.Inf. Co.A
Samples, W.V. GA 43rd Inf. Co.E
Sampley, A.J. TN 11th (Holman's) Cav. Co.L
Sampley, A.J. TN 35th Inf. Co.L
Sampley, A.J. TN 36th Inf. Co.I
Sampley, A.T. TN 42nd Inf. 1st Co.E
Sampley, George W. TN 42nd Inf. 1st Co.E
Sampley, James H. AL Inf. 1st Regt. Co.C
Sampley, J.B. AR 10th Inf. Co.B
Sampley, Jesse 3rd Conf.Cav. Co.G
Sampley, Jesse C. TN 42nd Inf. 1st Co.E
Sampley, Jesse S. AL Inf. 1st Regt. Co.C,D
Sampley, John AL 23rd Inf. Co.F Cpl.
Sampley, J.S. 3rd Conf.Cav. Co.G
Sampley, Martin V. TN 35th Inf. 3rd Co.F Cpl.
Sampley, Martin V. TN 42nd Inf. 1st Co.E
Sampley, M.V. TN Conscr. (Cp. of Instr.)
Sampley, Oliver Miller AL 49th Inf. Co.B
Sampley, Thomas A. AL 55th Vol. Co.F
Samplin, S.A. AL 1st Inf. Co.C
Sampsell, George TN Hvy.Arty. Caruthers' Btty.
Sampsell, Henry G. VA Cav. 35th Bn. Co.A
Samp sey 1st Creek Mtd.Vol. Co.F
Sampson (Slave) MS 23rd Inf. Co.A,B Cook
Sampson 1st Choctaw & Chickasaw Mtd.Rifles 2nd Co.I
Sampson 1st Creek Mtd.Vol. Co.B
Sampson, 1st 1st Seminole Mtd.Vol.
Sampson, 2nd 1st Seminole Mtd.Vol.
Sampson Deneale's Regt. Choctaw Warriors Co.B
Sampson Deneale's Regt. Choctaw Warriors Co.D
Sampson, --- TX Cav. 4th Regt.St.Troops Co.D
Sampson, Allmon GA Mayer's Co. (Appling Cav.)
Sampson, Bedford C. TN 3rd (Lillard's) Mtd.Inf. Co.A
Sampson, B.F. VA Inf. 26th Bn. Co.B
Sampson, B.F. VA 108th Mil. Lemons' Co.
Sampson, Billy TX 24th Cav. Co.G
Sampson, C.C. GA 13th Cav. Co.I
Sampson, C.E. LA Mil. British Guard Bn. Kurczyn's Co.
Sampson, Charles MS 22nd Inf. Co.I
Sampson, C.N. TN Detailed Conscr. Co.B
Sampson, C.N. TN Sullivan Cty.Res. (Loc.Def.Troops) Witcher's Co.

Sampson, Creed KY Corbin's Men
Sampson, E. TN Cav. Allison's Squad. Co.C
Sampson, E. Gen. & Staff Capt.,AQM
Sampson, Ed TX Inf. Cunningham's Co. Cpl.
Sampson, Edwin J. TX 4th Inf. Co.F Sgt.
Sampson, Ely NC 2nd Arty. (36th St.Troops) Co.H
Sampson, F. TN 50th Inf. Co.C
Sampson, F.J. VA Inf. 4th Bn.Loc.Def. Co.F 1st Sgt.
Sampson, F.M. GA 18th Inf. Co.E
Sampson, F.M. GA 23rd Inf. Co.H
Sampson, Franc G. TN 13th Inf. Co.K Sgt.
Sampson, Franc G. TN 47th Inf. Co.E Capt.
Sampson, Franklin VA 1st Bn.Res. Co.A
Sampson, G. TX Inf. 1st Bn. (St.Troops) Co.D
Sampson, G.A. KY 12th Cav. Co.I
Sampson, George KY 1st Bn.Mtd.Rifles Co.D
Sampson, George KY 3rd Bn.Mtd.Rifles Co.F
Sampson, George VA 10th Cav. Co.C
Sampson, George T. VA 10th Cav. Co.C
Sampson, G.W. Gen. & Staff Asst.Comsy.
Sampson, George W. GA 11th Inf. Co.G
Sampson, George W. TX 6th Inf. Co.G 1st Lt.
Sampson, George W. VA 40th Inf. Co.A 1st Sgt.
Sampson, G.L. TX 3rd Cav. Co.D
Sampson, G.W. KY 3rd Bn.Mtd.Rifles
Sampson, G.W. MS 2nd Inf. Co.I
Sampson, G.W. TX Inf. Carter's Co.
Sampson, G.W. VA 19th Inf. Co.E
Sampson, Henry AL 1st Regt. Mobile Vol. Co.E Cpl.
Sampson, Henry VA Inf. 4th Bn.Loc.Def. Co.F
Sampson, Henry VA 97th Mil. Co.H
Sampson, Isaac Deneale's Regt. Choctaw Warriors Co.E
Sampson, Isaac E. TN 5th (McKenzie's) Cav. Co.H
Sampson, J. AL 48th Inf. Co.E
Sampson, J. LA 21st (Kennedy's) Inf. Co.A
Sampson, J. TX 1st Hvy.Arty. Co.I
Sampson, James AL 48th Inf. Co.C
Sampson, James KY 5th Mtd.Inf. Co.K
Sampson, James KY 9th Mtd.Inf. Co.K
Sampson, James MS 12th Cav. Co.F
Sampson, James MS Inf. 2nd St.Troops Co.A
Sampson, James TN Cav. Allison's Squad. Co.C
Sampson, James TN 28th (Cons.) Inf. Co.C
Sampson, James TN Conscr. (Cp. of Instr.)
Sampson, James A. TX 6th Inf. Co.H Sgt.
Sampson, James N. TX Cav. 2nd Regt.St.Troops Co.D
Sampson, James W. AL St.Arty. Co.A
Sampson, James W. AL Inf. 2nd Regt. Co.F
Sampson, James W. TN 28th Inf. Co.H Cpl.
Sampson, James W. TX 22nd Cav. Co.D Far.
Sampson, J.D. AL 11th Inf. Co.G
Sampson, Jesse NC 2nd Cav. (19th St.Troops)
Sampson, Joel 1st Choctaw & Chickasaw Mtd.Rifles 3rd Co.E Sgt.
Sampson, John GA 4th Inf. Co.A
Sampson, John MO Cav. Wood's Regt. Co.K
Sampson, John 1st Choctaw & Chickasaw Mtd.Rifles 2nd Co.K
Sampson, John F. GA 19th Inf. Co.I
Sampson, John J. MS 12th Cav. Co.F

Sampson, John R. VA Inf. 4th Bn.Loc.Def. Co.E Sgt.
Sampson, John R. VA 6th Inf. Co.H
Sampson, Johnson TN 22nd (Barteau's) Cav. Co.G
Sampson, John W. NC 3rd Inf. Co.F
Sampson, Joseph SC 21st Inf. Co.I
Sampson, Joseph VA 2nd Bn.Res. QMSgt.
Sampson, Joseph B. GA 40th Inf.
Sampson, Joseph W. VA 40th Inf. Co.A
Sampson, J.P. TX 3rd Cav. Co.D
Sampson, J.P. TX 32nd Cav. Co.D
Sampson, J.W. TX 3rd Cav. Co.D
Sampson, Laton VA 7th Bn.Res. Co.D
Sampson, Lawrence NC Mil. Clark's Sp.Bn. A.R. Davis' Co. Cook
Sampson, Lemuel H. AR Lt.Arty. Thrall's Btty. Cpl.
Sampson, Leroy VA 9th Cav. Co.K
Sampson, Leroy I. VA 40th Inf. Co.A
Sampson, Lorenzo D. TN 19th Inf. Co.I
Sampson, M.A. TN 12th (Cons.) Inf. Co.G
Sampson, M.A. TN 22nd Inf. Co.G
Sampson, Mitchel A. VA 52nd Inf. Co.K Cpl.
Sampson, Mitchell VA 25th Inf. 1st Co.G
Sampson, M.T. NC 20th Inf. Co.H
Sampson, N.A. GA 52nd Inf. Co.I
Sampson, Oliver Conf.Inf. Tucker's Regt. Co.H
Sampson, Paton TN Cav. Allison's Squad. Co.C
Sampson, P.C. MO 1st Inf. Co.I
Sampson, P.C. MO 1st & 4th Cons.Inf. Co.K
Sampson, Peter FL 1st Inf. New Co.I
Sampson, Phillip GA 65th Inf. Co.G
Sampson, P.H.S. NC 5th Sr.Res. Co.A
Sampson, R.B. VA 8th Inf. Co.A
Sampson, Richard B. VA 40th Inf. Co.A
Sampson, Robert AR 23rd Inf. Co.A
Sampson, Robert VA Lt.Arty. Carrington's Co.
Sampson, R.P. NC 5th Cav. (63rd St.Troops) Co.A
Sampson, S. SC 4th St.Troops Co.G
Sampson, Samuel SC 21st Inf. Co.I
Sampson, So. SC Mil. 16th Regt. Steinmeyer, Jr.'s Co.
Sampson, S.S. TN 19th Inf. Co.D
Sampson, T.D. GA 11th Inf. Co.G
Sampson, Thomas TN 10th Inf. Co.G
Sampson, Thomas B. AR 20th Inf. Co.H
Sampson, Thornton VA 37th Mil. Co.A
Sampson, Thornton T. VA 9th Cav. Co.D,K
Sampson, Titus TN 44th (Cons.) Inf. Co.I Sgt.
Sampson, Titus TN 55th (McKoin's) Inf. Dillehay's Co.
Sampson, W.H. VA Mil. Scott Cty.
Sampson, William AL 4th (Russell's) Cav. Co.H 4th Cpl.
Sampson, William GA 40th Inf. Co.G
Sampson, William TN 60th Mtd.Inf. Co.D
Sampson, William VA 40th Inf. Co.A
Sampson, William H. VA Inf. 21st Bn. 2nd Co.D
Sampson, William H. VA 64th Mtd.Inf. Co.D
Sampson, William H.A. AL St.Arty. Co.A Sgt.
Sampson, William J. VA 2nd Inf. Co.A
Sampson, William J. VA 97th Mil. Co.H
Sampy, Joseph H.R. AL 23rd Inf. Co.E
Sampy, R.H.J. AL 25th Inf.
Sams, A.A. VA 22nd Inf. Co.B

Sams, A.L. TN Cav. 16th Bn. (Neal's) Co.F
Sams, Andrew A. VA Lt.Arty. G.B. Chapman's Co.
Sams, Andrew J. VA 108th Mil. Co.F, Lemons' Co. 2nd Lt.
Sams, Andrew J.W. VA Lt.Arty. G.B. Chapman's Co.
Sams, Anson M. NC 29th Inf. Co.C
Sams, Asa W. NC 64th Inf. Co.A
Sams, B. AL 46th Inf. Co.H
Sams, Benjamin F. VA Lt.Arty. G.B. Chapman's Co.
Sams, B.S. SC Cav. 10th Bn. Co.A
Sams, C. SC 1st Cav. Asst.Surg.
Sams, C.A. SC 20th Inf. Co.O Sgt.
Sams, C.A. SC Manigault's Bn.Vol. Co.A
Sams, Calhoun SC 11th Inf. Co.A
Sams, Calhoun Gen. & Staff Surg.
Sams, C.C. Rhett's Brig. Comsy.Sgt.
Sams, C.E. MS 22nd Inf. Co.I Music.
Sams, Christopher C. GA Inf. 2nd Bn. Co.D
Sams, Cornelius A. SC 5th Cav. Co.E
Sams, D.A. VA 6th Cav. Co.I
Sams, David K. AL Cav. Lenoir's Ind.Co.
Sams, D.K. AL Cav. Lewis' Bn. Co.A
Sams, D.K. AL 5th Inf. New Co.F
Sams, D.R. AL 12th Inf. Co.H 2nd Lt.
Sams, E.B.H. NC 60th Inf. Co.B
Sams, E.B.H. NC 64th Inf. Co.G
Sams, Edmund W. NC 52nd Inf. Co.K
Sams, E.L. TN 60th Mtd.Inf. Co.L
Sams, Elbert E. NC 64th Inf. Co.G
Sams, Elijah NC Inf. 2nd Bn. Co.A
Sams, Elijah TN Cav. 12th Bn. (Day's) Co.A
Sams, Elijah VA Inf. 23rd Bn. Co.H Sgt.
Sams, F.F. SC Arty. Stuart's Co. (Beaufort Vol.Arty.)
Sams, F.M. 3rd Conf.Cav. Co.E
Sams, F.W. FL 1st (Res.) Inf. Co.A,H
Sams, Gabriel NC 64th Inf. Co.K
Sams, George W. NC 45th Inf. Co.F
Sams, George W. TN 63rd Inf. Co.F
Sams, Green L. NC Inf. 2nd Bn. Co.A
Sams, H.C. VA 135th Mil. Co.A
Sams, Henry B. TN 10th Inf.
Sams, H.H. AL Inf. 2nd Regt. Co.E
Sams, H.H. SC 11th Inf. ACS
Sams, H.H. Conf.Inf. 1st Bn. Co.I
Sams, H.H. Elliott's Brig. CS
Sams, Hiram TN 63rd Inf. Co.F Fifer
Sams, Hiram K. AL 28th Inf. Co.D
Sams, Hugh C. VA Lt.Arty. G.B. Chapman's Co.
Sams, Jackson TN 59th Mtd.Inf. Co.C
Sams, James NC Inf. 2nd Bn. Co.A
Sams, James TN 26th Inf. Co.B,H
Sams, James E. AR 2nd Mtd.Rifles Co.K Sgt.
Sams, James G. GA Smith's Legion Ralston's Co.
Sams, James K. AR 20th Inf. Co.K
Sams, James K. KY 7th Cav. Co.F
Sams, James R. KY 4th Cav. Co.E
Sams, James R. NC 64th Inf. Co.A
Sams, Jeremiah B. NC Cav. 5th Bn. Co.A
Sams, Jeremiah B. NC 64th Inf. Co.A,F
Sams, J.G. GA 12th Cav. Co.B 2nd Lt.
Sams, J.G. SC 1st Mtd.Mil. Fripp's Co.

Sams, J.G. SC Arty. Stuart's Co. (Beaufort Vol.Arty.)
Sams, J. Graham SC 11th Inf. Co.A
Sams, J.K. AR 12th Bn.S.S. Co.C
Sams, J.K. KY 11th Cav. Co.F Sgt.
Sams, J.K. TN 38th Inf. 2nd Co.A
Sams, John AR 20th Inf. Co.K Cpl.
Sams, John TN Cav. Shaw's Bn. Hamilton's Co.
Sams, John C. AL 27th Inf. Co.H
Sams, John E. GA 20th Inf. Co.F
Sams, John H. SC 3rd Cav. Co.I
Sams, John H. TN Cav. Welcker's Bn. Kincaid's Co.
Sams, John K. GA 42nd Inf. Co.E 1st Sgt.
Sams, John R. TN 29th Inf. Co.K
Sams, Joseph L. NC 29th Inf. Co.D
Sams, J.V. SC Arty. Stuart's Co. (Beaufort Vol.Arty.)
Sams, L.A. GA 43rd Inf. Co.I
Sams, L.B. TN Sullivan Cty.Res. (Loc.Def. Troops) Witcher's Co.
Sams, L.G. NC 21st Inf. Co.H
Sams, L.R. SC Arty. Stuart's Co. (Beaufort Vol.Arty.)
Sams, L.R. SC 11th Inf. Co.A
Sams, L.R. SC Mil. 17th Regt. Buist's Co.
Sams, Martin L. AR 14th (McCarver's) Inf. Co.D 1st Lt.
Sams, M.M. Gen. & Staff AASurg.
Sams, M.W. SC Cav. 19th Bn. Co.A Sgt.
Sams, M.W. SC Part.Rangers Kirk's Co. Cpl.
Sams, Obediah TN Cav. 5th Bn. (McClellan's) Co.F
Sams, Obediar TN 59th Mtd.Inf. Co.C
Sams, Owen TN Cav. 5th Bn. (McClellan's) Co.F
Sams, Owen TN Detailed Conscr. Co.B Cpl.
Sams, Reuben NC 64th Inf. Co.A
Sams, Reuben W. GA 20th Inf. Co.F
Sams, R.F. SC Arty. Stuart's Co. (Beaufort Vol.Arty.)
Sams, R.F. SC 11th Inf. Co.A
Sams, Rice TN 63rd Inf. Co.D
Sams, Richard KY 5th Cav.
Sams, Rich'd F. Gen. & Staff Asst.Surg.
Sams, Riley AL 25th Inf. Co.I
Sams, R.J. GA Lt.Arty. Ritter's Co.
Sams, R.J. MD Arty. 3rd Btty.
Sams, R.J. NC 60th Inf. Co.B Sgt.
Sams, R.O. SC Bn.St.Cadets Co.B 2nd Lt.
Sams, Robert NC 64th Inf. Co.K
Sams, Robert VA Lt.Arty. 12th Bn. Co.B
Sams, R.R. SC Arty. Stuart's Co. (Beaufort Vol.Arty.)
Sams, S.A. SC Arty. Stuart's Co. (Beaufort Vol.Arty.)
Sams, S.A. SC 11th Inf. Co.A
Sams, Samuel S. AR 14th (McCarver's) Inf. Co.H
Sams, S.S. AR 8th Inf. New Co.G
Sams, T.F. SC Arty. Stuart's Co. (Beaufort Vol.Arty.)
Sams, Thomas F. SC 11th Inf. Co.A
Sams, V. SC 11th Inf. Co.A
Sams, Washington TN 59th Mtd.Inf. Co.C
Sams, Washington TN 63rd Inf. Co.F Drum.
Sams, W.B. MO 1st N.E. Cav.

Sams, W.B. SC 3rd Cav.
Sams, W.B. SC 1st (Butler's) Inf. Co.K
Sams, William TN 59th Mtd.Inf. Co.C
Sams, William A. NC Inf. 2nd Bn. Co.A
Sams, William E. NC 64th Inf. Co.C
Sams, William J. GA 20th Inf. Co.F Cpl.
Sams, William J. GA 27th Inf. Co.E 1st Lt.
Sams, William W. NC 64th Inf. Co.A
Sams, Wilson TN 3rd (Lillard's) Mtd.Inf. Co.K
Sams, Wilson TN 61st Mtd.Inf. Co.K Sgt.
Sams, Wilson TN 63rd Inf. Co.E
Sams, W.N. GA 56th Inf. Co.D
Sams, Zeph NC 64th Inf. Co.D
Sams, Zephaniah NC Inf. 2nd Bn. Co.H
Samsel, James TN 14th Inf. Co.D
Samsell, David VA 5th Inf. Co.K
Samson 1st Creek Mtd.Vol. Co.A
Samson 1st Creek Mtd.Vol. 2nd Co.I
Samson 1st Creek Mtd.Vol. Co.M
Samson, Abraham J. SC 1st (McCreary's) Inf. Co.L
Samson, Clement LA Mil. Knaps' Co. (Fausse River Guards)
Samson, Field 1st Choctaw Mtd.Rifles Ward's Co.
Samson, Francois V. LA 2nd Cav. Co.K Sgt.
Samson, F.V. LA Mil. Knaps' Co. (Fausse River Guards)
Samson, George W. VA Mil. Greene Cty.
Samson, Harvey G. VA 3rd Cav. & Inf.St.Line Co.A 1st Sgt.
Samson, James SC Mil. 1st Regt. (Charleston Res.) Co.H Cpl.
Samson, James TX 16th Cav. Co.E
Samson, John KY 2nd Bn.Mtd.Rifles Co.D Cpl.
Samson, Johnson TN Cav. 7th Bn. (Bennett's) Co.E
Samson, L.B. TN 5th Inf. Co.C
Samson, Marcel LA 2nd Cav. Co.K 1st Lt.
Samson, Marcel LA Mil. Knaps' Co. (Fausse River Guards)
Samson, Omer LA Pointe Coupee Arty.
Samson, Omer LA 4th Inf. Co.D
Samson, W.C. MS 19th Inf. Co.G
Samson, William LA Inf. 1st Sp.Bn. (Rightor's) Co.E
Samson, William VA 4th Inf. Co.B
Samson, William J. VA Mil. Greene Cty.
Samson, W.S. FL 1st (Res.) Inf.
Samtsing, W. NC 34th Inf.
Samuel MS 3rd Inf. Co.G Cook
Samuel VA Goochland Lt.Arty. Cook
Samuel 1st Cherokee Mtd.Rifles Co.F
Samuel 1st Choctaw & Chickasaw Mtd.Rifles 2nd Co.K
Samuel, --- VA 6th Cav. Co.H
Samuel, --- VA 55th Inf. Co.K
Samuel, Albert H. NC 21st Inf. Co.G
Samuel, Albert T. VA Lt.Arty. Parker's Co.
Samuel, Albert W. NC 21st Inf. Co.G
Samuel, Almar VA 30th Inf. Co.E
Samuel, Andrew J. VA 55th Inf. Co.A
Samuel, Anthony VA 7th Inf. Co.F
Samuel, Archer T. TN 14th Inf. Co.C
Samuel, Archibald VA 30th Inf. Co.E
Samuel, Aurelius E. MO 3rd Inf. Co.K Capt.
Samuel, Ben F. AL 10th Inf. Co.E Sgt.

Samuel, Benjamin GA 3rd Cav. (St.Guards) Co.I
Samuel, Benjamin F. AL 30th Inf. Co.D Capt.
Samuel, B.H. AL 18th Inf. Co.I 1st Sgt.
Samuel, C.G. AL 30th Inf. Co.D Capt.
Samuel, C.W. SC 19th Inf. Co.K
Samuel, D.B. TX 1st Inf. Co.C 1st Sgt.
Samuel, D.T. MO St.Guard
Samuel, D. Todd MO Cav. 3rd Bn. Lt.Col.
Samuel, E. VA Lt.Arty. 12th Bn. Co.B
Samuel, Edmund W. MO 3rd Inf. Co.K Cpl.
Samuel, E.F. GA Inf. 1st Loc.Troops (Augusta) Co.I
Samuel, Elijah F. GA 5th Inf. Co.C
Samuel, Emanuel TN Cav. 12th Bn. (Day's) Co.D
Samuel, Ethelburt S. TN 6th (Wheeler's) Cav. Co.H
Samuel, George W. VA 55th Inf. Co.A
Samuel, H. MS Inf. 1st Bn.St.Troops (30 days '64) Co.A
Samuel, Henley A. AL 18th Inf. Co.I Cpl.
Samuel, Henry VA 47th Inf. 3rd Co.H
Samuel, H.J. VA 59th Inf. 2nd Co.F
Samuel, J. LA Mil. 3rd Regt.Eur.Brig. (Garde Francaise) Co.3
Samuel, J. TX Cav. Waller's Regt. Co.F
Samuel, James VA 47th Inf. 3rd Co.H
Samuel, James M. MO Cav. 3rd Regt.St.Guard Co.C
Samuel, J.M. MO Lt.Arty. 3rd Field Btty.
Samuel, Joe N. SC 7th Inf. 1st Co.H
Samuel, John AR 2nd Inf. Co.A
Samuel, John MO 16th Inf. Co.H
Samuel, John L. MO 3rd Inf. Co.E Sgt.
Samuel, John P., Jr. VA 30th Inf. Co.E Sgt.
Samuel, John R. AL 8th Cav.
Samuel, J.T. MS 14th (Cons.) Inf. Co.E Cpl.
Samuel, J.W. NC 2nd Inf. Co.I 1st Lt.
Samuel, Landon VA 30th Inf. Co.H
Samuel, Lis TN 51st (Cons.) Inf. Co.A
Samuel, M. SC 1st Regt. Charleston Guard Co.F
Samuel, M. VA 21st Cav. Co.A Cpl.
Samuel, Meyer LA 2nd Inf. Co.F
Samuel, Micajah VA 30th Inf. Co.H
Samuel, N. AL 17th Inf. Co.E
Samuel, Nathan VA Mtd.Riflemen Balfour's Co.
Samuel, N.G. NC 21st Inf. Co.G
Samuel, Oscar LA Mil. 1st Native Guards
Samuel, Paul T. VA 9th Cav. Co.B
Samuel, Philip, Jr. VA 30th Inf. Co.E 1st Lt.
Samuel, Philip VA 30th Inf. Co.H
Samuel, R.D. KY 3rd Mtd.Inf. Co.E
Samuel, Richard H. VA 55th Inf. Co.E
Samuel, R.J. TX 20th Inf. Co.I 2nd Lt.
Samuel, Robert G. VA 30th Inf. Co.E
Samuel, S.P. TX Arty. (St.Troops) Good's Co.
Samuel, Snowden D. TX 18th Cav. Co.F
Samuel, T. NC 7th Sr.Res. Watts' Co.
Samuel, T.E. LA 27th Inf. Co.I
Samuel, Theodore H. VA 30th Inf. Co.H
Samuel, Thomas VA 30th Inf. Co.H
Samuel, Thomas H. VA Lt.Arty. B.Z. Price's Co.
Samuel, Thomas T. NC 21st Inf. Co.G
Samuel, Wade SC 7th Inf. 1st Co.H
Samuel, W.G.M. Gen. & Staff Capt.,Ord.Ch.
Samuel, William MS 6th Cav. Co.G Sgt.

Samuel, William VA 30th Inf. Co.H
Samuel, William B. VA 9th Cav. Co.B,F
Samuel, William C. AL 20th Inf. Co.K Sgt.
Samuel, William H. VA 30th Inf. Co.E Cpl.
Samuel, William J. SC 22nd Inf. Co.A
Samuel, William M. MS 5th Inf. (St.Troops) Co.E 1st Sgt.
Samuel, William N. VA 30th Inf. Co.E
Samuel, William P. NC 21st Inf. Co.G
Samuel, William R. MO 2nd Cav. Co.G
Samuel, William S. VA 55th Inf. Co.A
Samuel, William W. VA Lt.Arty. B.Z. Price's Co. Cpl.
Samuele, William AL 24th Inf. Co.H
Samuell, Humphry B. VA 30th Inf. Co.H
Samuell, W.T. AL 42nd Inf. Co.B
Samuels, A. LA Inf.Crescent Regt. Co.G
Samuels, Abraham AL 5th Bn.Vol. Co.A Cpl.
Samuels, Abraham LA 6th Inf. Co.C
Samuels, Abraham VA 36th Inf. Co.A
Samuels, Abraham B. VA 30th Bn.S.S. Co.B 2nd Lt.
Samuels, Abram B. VA Cav. 36th Bn. Co.B Lt.
Samuels, A.F. Gen. & Staff Hosp.Stew.
Samuels, Alexander Cheatam's Div. Asst.Surg.
Samuels, Alexander H. VA 8th Cav. Co.E 1st Lt.
Samuels, Archibald VA 15th Inf. Co.B
Samuels, A.S. VA 4th Cav. Co.I,E
Samuels, B. TX 6th Inf. Co.A
Samuels, Benj. F. VA Horse Arty. Pelham's Co. 1st Lt.
Samuels, Benno TX 17th Cons.Dismtd.Cav. Co.H
Samuels, Daniel N. VA 36th Inf. Co.A
Samuels, DeSoto AR 2nd Cav. Co.E
Samuels, E.A. VA 1st Cav. Co.I
Samuels, E.L. LA Mil.Conf.Guards Regt. Co.H
Samuels, E.R. SC 7th Inf. 1st Co.G
Samuels, E.R. SC 22nd Inf. Co.A
Samuels, Erasmus A. VA 52nd Inf. Co.D 1st Sgt.
Samuels, Ethelbert S. TN Cav. 11th Bn. (Gordon's) Co.B
Samuels, Ezekiel GA 22nd Inf. Co.G Sgt.
Samuels, F. AL 15th Inf. Co.A
Samuels, Fielding TX 12th Inf. Co.F Cpl.
Samuels, G. TX 17th Cons.Dismtd.Cav. 1st Co.G 2nd Lt.
Samuels, Gabe TX 18th Cav. Co.I 2nd Lt.
Samuels, G.B. VA 22nd Inf. Co.E
Samuels, G.B. VA 36th Inf. Co.A
Samuels, George KY 3rd Cav. Co.H
Samuels, George VA 5th Cav. 1st Co.F
Samuels, George VA Hvy.Arty. 10th Bn. Co.C Drum.
Samuels, George S. MO 10th Inf. Co.A Music.
Samuels, George W. SC 5th Res. Co.C
Samuels, Green B. VA 10th Inf. Co.F 1st Lt.
Samuels, Green B. 3rd Conf.Eng.Troops Co.E Cpl.
Samuels, G.W. SC 1st Cav. Co.C Cpl.
Samuels, Harry S. TX 9th Field Btty.
Samuels, Harry T. AR 26th Inf. Co.F
Samuels, H.C. KY 3rd Mtd.Inf. Co.B
Samuels, H.C. KY 7th Mtd.Inf. Co.C
Samuels, Hiram G. VA 52nd Inf. Co.D Cpl.

Samuels, Hugh P. VA 36th Inf. Co.A
Samuels, James AR 17th (Griffith's) Inf. Co.A
Samuels, James A. NC 21st Inf. Co.D
Samuels, James E. VA Lt.Arty. 13th Bn. Co.B
Samuels, J.B. LA 10th Inf. Co.F 1st Lt.
Samuels, J.D. GA Inf. 9th Bn. Co.E
Samuels, J.M. MO 2nd Cav. Co.E
Samuels, John AR Inf. 2nd Bn. Co.A
Samuels, John GA Siege Arty. 28th Bn. Co.C Sgt.
Samuels, John KY 4th Mtd.Inf. Co.B
Samuels, John TN Inf. Nashville Bn. Cattles' Co.
Samuels, John J. AL 4th Inf. Co.A
Samuels, John J. AR 18th Inf. Co.A
Samuels, Joseph VA 8th Bn.Res. Co.D
Samuels, Joseph G. VA 136th Mil. Co.E
Samuels, Joseph H. VA 97th Mil. Co.E
Samuels, Joseph M. VA 5th Inf. Co.I
Samuels, Joseph M. VA 52nd Inf. Co.D Sgt.
Samuels, Joseph T. VA 97th Mil. Co.E 1st Sgt.
Samuels, J.P. AR 18th (Marmaduke's) Inf. Co.B
Samuels, J.P. TN Cav. 11th Bn. (Gordon's) Co.E
Samuels, J.P. TN Inf. 154th Sr.Regt. Co.L
Samuels, J.S. KY 8th Cav. Co.G
Samuels, J.S. KY 2nd Mtd.Inf. Co.G
Samuels, J.W. GA Inf. 9th Bn. Co.E
Samuels, Lafayette VA 16th Cav. Co.K 1st Lt.
Samuels, Lafayette VA Cav. Ferguson's Bn. Nounnan's Co. Jr.2nd Lt.
Samuels, Libbens MS 6th Inf. Co.I
Samuels, L.P. GA Inf. 2nd Bn. (St.Guards) Old Co.D
Samuels, M. VA 7th Inf. Co.F
Samuels, N. TX 20th Inf. Co.H
Samuels, Nathan AR 19th (Dawson's) Inf. Co.B
Samuels, Nathan AR Inf. Hardy's Regt. Co.G
Samuels, Patterson M. AL 4th Inf. Co.A 2nd Lt.
Samuels, Robert KY 11th Cav. Co.B Sgt.
Samuels, Robert SC 5th Res. Co.D
Samuels, Robert N. KY 7th Cav. Co.B Sgt.
Samuels, Samuel C. VA 10th Inf. Co.F
Samuels, Stephen S. TX 17th Inf. Co.K
Samuels, T.D. AL Cp. of Instr. Talladega Co.C
Samuels, T.E. LA 22nd (Cons.) Inf. Co.F
Samuels, Temple VA Hvy.Arty. 10th Bn. Co.C
Samuels, Temple VA Hvy.Arty. Wilkinson's Co.
Samuels, Thomas VA 5th Cav. 1st Co.F
Samuels, Thomas VA 24th Cav. Co.G
Samuels, Thomas VA Cav. 32nd Bn. Co.A
Samuels, Thomas L. AL 4th Inf. Co.A 2nd Lt.
Samuels, T.R. AL 47th Inf. Co.I
Samuels, W.C. SC 2nd Arty. Co.E
Samuels, William AL 34th Inf. Co.B
Samuels, William KY 9th Mtd.Inf. Co.B
Samuels, William SC 5th Res. Co.C
Samuels, William VA 36th Inf. Co.A
Samuels, William VA Mil. Greene Cty.
Samuels, William G. LA 7th Inf. Co.B
Samuels, William J. AL 28th Inf. Co.B Sgt.
Samuels, William J. TN 1st (Feild's) Inf. Co.K
Samuels, Wm. R. Gen. & Staff Capt.
Samuels, W.L. LA Inf.Crescent Regt. Co.B
Samuels, W.N. VA 34th Inf. Co.D
Samuels, Wolff GA 2nd Bn.S.S. Co.C
Samuels, W.R. AL Lt.Arty. Goldthwaite's Btty.
Samuels, W.R. SC 1st Cav. Co.C

Samusch, Isaac TX 12th Inf. Co.A
San, Domingo TX 17th Cav. Co.H
Sanan, F.D. NC 3rd Arty. (40th St.Troops)
Sanangle, George VA 62nd Mtd.Inf.
Sanareins, J. Bste. LA Mil. 3rd Regt. French Brig. Co.1 Cpl.
Sanarens, L. LA Mil. 3rd Regt.Eur.Brig. (Garde Francaise) Co.3
Sanat, J. MS 12th Inf. Co.H
Sanazin, J.P. LA Mil. Orleans Guards Regt. Co.C Sgt.
Sanazu, Paul LA Mil. Orleans Guards Regt. Co.C
Sanazu, V.E. LA Mil. Orleans Guards Regt. Co.C
Sanbach, L.D. AR 2nd Cav. Co.B
Sanberry, W.L. AL 6th Inf. Co.I
Sanborn, Ira W. FL 2nd Cav. Co.E
Sanborn, John J. VA 2nd Inf. Co.G
Sanborn, Lorenzo VA 54th Mil. Co.B
Sanborn, S.H. AL 15th Bn.Part.Rangers Co.E
Sanborn, S.H. AL 56th Part.Rangers Co.E
Sanborn, William VA 20th Inf. Co.H
Sanborn, William H. AL 7th Cav. Co.B
Sanbower, Adam NC 17th Inf. (1st Org.) Co.G
Sanbower, J.H. NC 17th Inf. (1st Org.) Co.G
Sanbrain, Eliz TX Cav. Ragsdale's Bn. 1st Co.C
Sanbun, John P. LA 1st (Nelligan's) Inf. Co.C Sgt.
Sanburn, Lorenzo VA Hvy.Arty. 20th Bn. Co.B
Sanceda, Albino TX 3rd Inf. Co.G
Sanceda, Juan TX 8th Inf. Co.C Jr.2nd Lt.
Sancedo, Severiano TX 8th Inf. Co.H
Sancedo, Umecindo TX 8th Inf. Co.C Sgt.
Sanceman, D.L. MS 7th Cav. Co.I
Sanceman, John MS Lt.Arty. Turner's Co.
Sancer, John NC 61st Inf. Co.C
Sanch, Joseph H. TX 29th Cav. Co.A
Sancher, Brigido TX Cav. Benavides' Regt. Co.I
Sancher, Dionino LA Mil. 5th Regt.Eur.Brig. (Spanish Regt.) Co.4 Cpl.
Sanches, Agapitto Conf.Lt.Arty. Davis' Co.
Sanches, Antonio TX 33rd Cav. 1st Co.H
Sanches, Carlos LA Mil. Cazadores Espanoles Regt. Co.1
Sanches, Cimon TX 8th Inf. Co.I
Sanches, Clemente TX 33rd Cav. 1st Co.H
Sanches, D. TX St.Troops Teel's Co.
Sanches, Demetris TX Part.Mtd.Vol. Trevino's Squad.
Sanches, Felix TX Part.Mtd.Vol. Trevino's Squad.
Sanches, Francisco TX 33rd Cav. 1st Co.H
Sanches, Francisco TX Cav. Benavides' Regt. Co.A
Sanches, George FL 9th Inf. Co.A
Sanches, Ijinio TX 33rd Cav. 1st Co.H
Sanches, John FL Inf. 2nd Bn. Co.D Music.
Sanches, Justo TX Cav. Ragsdale's Bn. 1st Co.C
Sanches, Leon TX 33rd Cav. 1st Co.H
Sanches, M. LA Inf.Cons. 18th Regt. & Yellow Jacket Bn. Co.H
Sanches, M. TX Inf. 1st St.Troops Whitehead's Co.
Sanches, Mariano TX 3rd Inf. 1st Co.C
Sanches, State SC 1st Regt. Charleston Guard Co.G

Sanches, U. LA 5th Inf. Co.K
Sanchez, A. LA Ogden's Cav. Co.I
Sanchez, A. LA Miles' Legion Co.A
Sanchez, A. SC Mil. 16th Regt. Bancroft, Jr.'s Co.
Sanchez, A. Conf.Lt.Arty. Richardson's Bn. Co.B 2nd Lt.
Sanchez, Anthony LA Inf. 9th Bn. Co.B
Sanchez, Anto. LA Mil. 5th Regt.Eur.Brig. (Spanish Regt.) Co.7
Sanchez, Antoine LA Arty. Landry's Co. (Donaldsonville Arty.) Jr.2nd Lt.
Sanchez, Antonio TX Cav. 6th Bn. Co.D
Sanchez, Antonio TX 8th Field Btty.
Sanchez, B. GA Lt.Arty. Ritter's Co. Cpl.
Sanchez, B. MD Arty. 3rd Btty. Cpl.
Sanchez, Barnardino S. GA Arty. (Chatham Arty.) Wheaton's Co. Jr.2nd Lt.
Sanchez, Bernard LA 28th (Thomas') Inf. Co.B
Sanchez, Bernardio S. Gen. & Staff Maj.
Sanchez, B.S. GA 1st (Olmstead's) Inf. Claghorn's Co. Jr.2nd Lt.
Sanchez, Cayetano LA Mil. Cazadores Espanoles Regt. Co.5
Sanchez, Daniel FL 3rd Inf. Co.F Music.
Sanchez, Desiderca TX 8th Inf. Co.I
Sanchez, E. FL 2nd Inf. Co.H
Sanchez, E. LA 2nd Cav.
Sanchez, E. LA 4th Inf. Co.F
Sanchez, E. LA Mil. Orleans Fire Regt.
Sanchez, E. LA Mil. Orleans Guards Regt. Co.I
Sanchez, Eugene LA 8th Inf. Co.K
Sanchez, F. LA 22nd Inf. Co.D
Sanchez, F. LA 22nd (Cons.) Inf. Co.B,D
Sanchez, F. LA Mil. Orleans Guards Regt. Co.H
Sanchez, F.N. LA 3rd Inf. Co.G Sgt.
Sanchez, F.P. FL 1st (Res.) Inf. Co.H
Sanchez, Franco. LA Mil. 5th Regt.Eur.Brig. (Spanish Regt.) Co.8
Sanchez, Francisco TX 3rd Inf. 1st Co.C
Sanchez, Francisco P. AL Lt.Arty. 2nd Bn. Co.C Artif.
Sanchez, Francis R. FL 10th Inf. Co.F
Sanchez, Frank LA 2nd Cav. Co.H
Sanchez, Frank X. FL 1st Cav. Co.G
Sanchez, Gad H. FL 1st Inf. New Co.K Cpl.
Sanchez, G.W. FL 1st (Res.) Inf. Co.A
Sanchez, Henry C. FL 10th Inf. Co.F
Sanchez, Herman LA 8th Inf. Co.I
Sanchez, J. LA Ogden's Cav. Co.I
Sanchez, J. LA 3rd Inf. Co.K
Sanchez, J. LA Miles' Legion Co.A
Sanchez, James LA 1st Cav. Co.A
Sanchez, James P. FL 3rd Inf. Co.B
Sanchez, Jesus TX 3rd Inf. 1st Co.A
Sanchez, John LA 18th Inf.
Sanchez, John LA 22nd Inf. Durrive, Jr.'s Co.
Sanchez, John Y. FL 10th Inf. Co.F
Sanchez, Jose LA Mil. 5th Regt.Eur.Brig. (Spanish Regt.) Co.2
Sanchez, Jose TX 2nd Inf. Co.K
Sanchez, Joseph LA 4th Inf. Co.E
Sanchez, J.P. FL 1st (Res.) Inf. Co.A
Sanchez, Juan TX 2nd Inf. Co.G
Sanchez, Juan Esteban TX 3rd Inf. Co.F
Sanchez, Julian TX 8th Inf. Co.H

Sanchez, M. LA Lt.Arty. 6th Field Btty. (Grosse Tete Flying Arty.)
Sanchez, M. LA 18th Inf. Co.I
Sanchez, M. LA 22nd Inf. Co.E Sgt.
Sanchez, Manuel FL 2nd Inf. Co.H
Sanchez, Manuel LA 7th Inf. Co.B
Sanchez, Marcos LA Mil. 5th Regt.Eur.Brig. (Spanish Regt.) Co.2
Sanchez, Marion TX 6th Inf. Co.H
Sanchez, Martin LA Maddox's Regt.Res.Corps Co.B
Sanchez, Massaline TX 17th Cav. Co.H
Sanchez, N. LA 2nd Cav.
Sanchez, Nestor TX 8th Inf. Co.C
Sanchez, Pedro TX 1st (Yager's) Cav. Co.F
Sanchez, Pedro Conf.Inf. Tucker's Regt. Co.C
Sanchez, Placides TX 2nd Inf. Co.G,H
Sanchez, R. LA Ogden's Cav. Co.I
Sanchez, Rafeel LA 3rd (Wingfield's) Cav. Co.D,G
Sanchez, Ricardo LA Mil. 5th Regt.Eur.Brig. (Spanish Regt.) Co.7
Sanchez, Roman FL 10th Inf. Co.F
Sanchez, Rufino TX 8th Inf. Co.H
Sanchez, S.J. FL 2nd Inf. Co.B Sgt.
Sanchez, Stephen TX 17th Cav. Co.H
Sanchez, William LA 18th Inf. Co.A Capt.
Sanchez, William LA Inf.Cons. 18th Regt. & Yellow Jacket Bn. Co.C Capt.
Sanchez, W.J. FL 1st Mil.
Sanchis, Manuel TX 4th Cav. Co.H
Sancho, Francisco LA Mil. Cazadores Espanoles Regt.
Sanchos, Thomas TX Cav. Ragsdale's Bn. Co.B
Sancius, Manuel TX 11th Inf. Co.A
Sanclair, J. TX Cav. Bourland's Regt. Co.D
Sancoat, R.J. Eng.,CSA Capt.
Sand, A.S. Gen. & Staff Maj.,QM
Sand, B. LA Mil. Beauregard Regt. Co.C
Sand, D. AL 1st Inf. Co.E
Sand, J.S. AR Pine Bluff Arty.
Sand, Phillip LA Mil. 3rd Regt. 3rd Brig. 1st Div. Co.A
Sandage, James G. LA 6th Cav. Co.B,C
Sandage, J.M. LA 6th Cav. Co.C
Sandak, Charles LA Mil. 3rd Regt. 3rd Brig. 1st Div. Co.A 1st Lt.
Sandal, E.E. TX 20th Inf. Co.H
Sandal, F.M. MS 7th Inf. Co.H
Sandal, H.J. TX 20th Inf. Co.H
Sandal, J.J. SC 2nd St.Troops Co.C
Sandal, J.J. SC 11th Res. Co.H
Sandal, J.M. TX 20th Inf. Co.K
Sandal, J.W. TX 20th Inf. Co.H Cpl.
Sandal, William SC 2nd St.Troops Co.C
Sandalin, William NC Hvy.Arty. 1st Bn. Co.C
Sandall, E.E. 4th Conf.Eng.Troops
Sandall, Henry MS Inf. 2nd St.Troops Co.E
Sandall, H.J. 4th Conf.Eng.Troops Artif.
Sandall, J.D. LA Inf.Cons.Crescent Regt. Co.D
Sandall, J.M. 4th Conf.Eng.Troops
Sandall, J.W. 4th Conf.Eng.Troops Artif.
Sandall, W. TX 1st Inf. Co.B
Sandals, Jno. Gen. & Staff Chap.
Sandaval, Tomas TX Part.Mtd.Vol. Trevino's Squad.

Sanday, Howard T. NC 5th Cav. (63rd St.Troops) Co.B
Sandbach, W. AR Conscr.
Sandback, W.S. AR Mil. Desha Cty.Bn.
Sandbatch, William S. AR Brandenburch's Cav.
Sandberg, Theodore Conf.Reg.Inf. Brooks' Bn. Co.B Cpl.
Sandbower, John VA 7th Inf. Co.B
Sandcliff, --- TX Inf. Houston Bn. Lt.
Sandcliffe, Edward TX 2nd Field Btty.
Sandcliffe, Edward 4th Conf.Eng.Troops Co.E 2nd Lt.
Sandclitf, Gustavus TX Cav. Madison's Regt. Co.E
Sandeck, S.J. VA 2nd St.Res. Co.L 1st Sgt.
Sandedge, T.J. MS 4th Inf. Co.E
Sandefer, A.D. KY 10th (Johnson's) Cav. Co.E
Sandefer, Daniel LA Hvy.Arty. 8th Bn. Co.3 Sgt.
Sandefer, Edward L. AL 10th Inf. Co.B
Sandefer, E.W. AR 19th (Dockery's) Inf. Co.B
Sandefer, J.K. MS 3rd Cav. Co.B
Sandefer, J.M. MS 6th Cav. Co.K
Sandefer, J.M. MS Inf. 3rd Bn. (St.Troops) Co.D
Sandefer, John MS 2nd (Quinn's St.Troops) Inf. Co.A
Sandefer, John W. GA 45th Inf. Co.K
Sandefer, Joseph J. AR 24th Inf. Co.B
Sandefer, J.P. TX 9th (Nichols') Inf. Co.C
Sandefer, J.P. TX Inf. Timmons' Regt. Co.F 2nd Lt.
Sandefer, Philo KY 10th (Johnson's) Cav. New Co.G
Sandefer, Samuel T. NC 21st Inf. Co.C 1st Sgt.
Sandefer, S.S. VA Mil. Washington Cty.
Sandefer, W.B. AR 1st Vol. Co.E
Sandefer, W.B. AR 38th Inf. Co.B
Sandefer, William L. MS 25th Inf. Co.A
Sandefers, John T. KY 7th Cav. Co.G
Sandeford, J.D. LA Inf.Crescent Regt. Co.C
Sandeford, B.H. TN 12th Inf. Co.H Capt.
Sandeford, Elliot NC 2nd Inf. Co.G
Sandeford, J.M. SC 24th Inf. Co.D Sgt.
Sandeford, John W. GA 3rd Inf. Co.A
Sandeford, John W. NC 47th Inf. Co.E,F
Sandeford, William E. GA 5th Inf. Co.I 1st Lt.
Sandefur, A.H. KY 10th (Johnson's) Cav. Co.B
Sandefur, Archibald KY 10th (Johnson's) Cav. New Co.G
Sandefur, Benj. KY Lt.Arty. Cobb's Co.
Sandefur, Benjamin M. MS Lt.Arty. (Issaquena Arty.) Graves' Co.
Sandefur, Charles H. KY 4th Mtd.Inf. Co.B
Sandefur, Charles H. MS Lt.Arty. (Issaquena Arty.) Graves' Co.
Sandefur, E.P. AR 20th Inf. Co.C
Sandefur, George W. MS 25th Inf. Co.C
Sandefur, G.W. AR 1st (Monroe's) Cav. Co.D Sgt.Maj.
Sandefur, James C. MS 1st Lt.Arty. Co.D
Sandefur, J.O. AR 1st Mtd.Rifles Co.D
Sandefur, J.O. AR 2nd Mtd.Rifles Co.H
Sandefur, John T. MS Lt.Arty. (Issaquena Arty.) Graves' Co. Bugler
Sandefur, John W. LA 8th Inf. Co.F
Sandefur, J.P. TX Waul's Legion Co.C 1st Sgt.

Sandefur, R.M. LA Siege Train Bn. Co.D
Sandefur, R.P. LA 19th Inf. Co.I
Sandefur, Samuel M. VA Lt.Arty. King's Co.
Sandefur, T. KY 10th (Johnson's) Cav. Co.B
Sandefur, T.B. AL 35th Inf. Co.D
Sandefur, T.H. KY 10th (Johnson's) Cav. Co.B
Sandefur, Thomas B. AL 9th Inf. Co.F
Sandefur, W.N. LA 19th Inf. Co.I
Sandege, P.S. MO 8th Inf. Co.A QMSgt.
Sandege, Z.A.E. VA 79th Mil. Co.1 Sgt.
Sandek, Jacob MS 18th Inf. Co.D
Sandek, S.J. MS 18th Inf.
Sandel, Caleb LA 1st Cav.
Sandel, Dewitt C. TX Waul's Legion Co.E Sgt.
Sandel, D.W. MS 1st (Percy's) Inf. Co.F Cpl.
Sandel, M.L. TX 24th & 25th Cav. (Cons.) Co.A
Sandel, Samuel L. MS 16th Inf. Co.E
Sandeliff, Edward Eng.Troops,CSA Lt.
Sandelin, E.T. TN Cav. Nixon's Regt. Co.A
Sandell, Charles LA 3rd (Wingfield's) Cav. Co.I
Sandell, E.E. TX 9th (Nichols') Inf. Co.I
Sandell, Henry C.P. TX 10th Inf. Co.A
Sandell, J.M. TX 9th (Nichols') Inf. Co.I Cpl.
Sandell, J.W. MS 39th Inf. Co.K 1st Lt.
Sandell, Oliver TX 24th Cav. Co.B
Sandell, Peter TX 24th Cav. Co.B
Sandell, Peter TX 9th (Nichols') Inf. Co.I
Sandell, Peter W. LA Inf. 11th Bn. Co.C
Sandell, P.T. TX Granbury's Cons.Brig. Co.I
Sandell, Silas D. LA Inf.Cons.Crescent Regt. Co.D
Sandell, W.S. TX 5th Inf. Co.K Music.
Sandels, M.T. AR 17th (Griffith's) Inf. Co.C Sgt.
Sandenacque, J. LA Mil. 3rd Regt. French Brig. Co.2
Sander, A. TX Waul's Legion Co.C
Sander, B.L. TN 19th (Biffle's) Cav. Co.A
Sander, Christian MO Inf. 4th Regt.St.Guard Co.A
Sander, F. LA Mil.Cont.Regt. Lang's Co.
Sander, F. TX 16th Inf. Co.E
Sander, I.M. KY 7th Cav. Co.K
Sander, J. SC Mil. 1st Regt. (Charleston Res.) Co.C
Sander, John MS 1st Cav. Co.L
Sander, O. TX 4th Inf. (St.Troops) Co.F
Sander, Peter MO 5th Cav. Co.G
Sander, P.J. LA Mil. Fire Bn. Co.E
Sander, Samuel AL 6th Cav. Co.E
Sander, William TX Inf. Timmons' Regt. Co.K
Sanderdal, James A. AL 57th Inf. Co.C
Sanderfer, D. LA Siege Train Bn. Co.D
Sanderfer, Franklin G. MS 1st Lt.Arty. Co.D
Sanderfer, G.W. SC 5th Cav. Co.I
Sanderfer, H.C. LA Inf. 1st Bn. (St.Guards) Co.B
Sanderfer, J.C. MS Inf. 3rd Bn. (St.Troops) Co.C
Sanderfer, John S. AR Inf. Hardy's Regt. Co.F
Sanderfer, J.S. AR 1st (Monroe's) Cav. Co.K
Sanderfer, J.T. GA Lt.Arty. 14th Bn. Co.A
Sanderfer, J.W. MS Hall's Co.
Sanderfer, Preston TN Cav. 9th Bn. (Gantt's) Co.G
Sanderfer, Thomas AL 9th Inf. Co.H
Sanderfer, William M. NC 61st Inf. Co.C

Sanderford, A.A. NC Mallett' Bn. (Cp.Guard) Co.C Cpl.
Sanderford, Alexander A. NC 24th Inf. Co.K
Sanderford, B.A. MS 41st Inf. Co.C Cpl.
Sanderford, B.H. TN 12th (Cons.) Inf. Capt.
Sanderford, E.D. NC 31st Inf. Co.G
Sanderford, Edward D. NC 17th Inf. (1st Org.) Co.D
Sanderford, H.S. MS Cav. Jeff Davis Legion Co.D
Sanderford, James GA 1st (Olmstead's) Inf. Co.C
Sanderford, James NC 31st Inf. Co.I
Sanderford, James SC 11th Inf. Co.E
Sanderford, James O. NC 37th Inf. Co.I
Sanderford, J.J. NC 31st Inf. Co.H
Sanderford, John AL 40th Inf. Co.E
Sanderford, John MS 20th Inf. Co.H
Sanderford, John M. MS 39th Inf. Co.C
Sanderford, J.R. MS 9th Inf. Co.I Sgt.
Sanderford, J.R. MS 41st Inf. Co.C Cpl.
Sanderford, Luther NC 33rd Inf. Co.H
Sanderford, N. Green NC 1st Inf. Co.I
Sanderford, R.N. LA Hvy.Arty. 8th Bn.
Sanderford, Samuel MS 20th Inf. Co.H
Sanderford, Samuel MS 20th Inf. Co.H
Sandford, Sidney MS 20th Inf. Co.H
Sanderford, T.H. NC Mallett's Bn. (Cp.Guard) Co.C
Sanderford, Thomas FL 6th Inf. Co.F
Sanderford, Thomas H. NC 24th Inf. Co.K
Sanderford, W.E. MS 9th Inf. Co.I
Sanderford, W.E. MS 41st Inf. Co.C
Sanderford, William AR 21st Mil. Co.F Cpl.
Sanderford, W.T. MS 12th Cav. Co.L
Sanderlain, W.L. AR 1st (Monroe's) Cav. Co.B
Sanderland, Elbert F. AR 3rd Inf. Co.E Sgt.
Sanderlin, Andrew P. GA Arty. 9th Bn.
Sanderlin, Caleb NC 32nd Inf. Co.I Drum.
Sanderlin, D.M. TN 13th Inf. Co.B
Sanderlin, Dorsey NC 4th Cav. (59th St.Troops) Co.G Cpl.
Sanderlin, Dorsey NC 32nd Inf. Co.I
Sanderlin, E.D. GA 51st Inf. Co.I
Sanderlin, Enoch G. NC 32nd Inf. Co.H
Sanderlin, E.T. TN 15th (Cons.) Cav. Co.I
Sanderlin, George W. NC 3rd Inf. Co.E Capt.
Sanderlin, George W. NC 33rd Inf. Co.E,H,I Capt.
Sanderlin, Griffin S. GA 11th Inf. Co.I
Sanderlin, H.B. AR Inf. Hardy's Regt. Co.B
Sanderlin, Jacob E. SC 4th Inf. Co.F
Sanderlin, James B. GA Arty. 9th Bn. Co.C
Sanderlin, James T. GA 2nd Res. Co.C Sgt.
Sanderlin, J.E. SC Inf. 13th Bn. Co.D
Sanderlin, J.E. SC Inf. Hampton Legion Co.I
Sanderlin, Jerry NC 8th Bn.Part.Rangers Co.B,E
Sanderlin, J.M. TX 4th Inf. Co.H
Sanderlin, John GA Hardwick Mtd.Rifles Co.B
Sanderlin, John GA Inf. 18th Bn. Co.C
Sanderlin, John VA Cav. 14th Bn. Co.A
Sanderlin, John A. GA 11th Inf. Co.I Cpl.
Sanderlin, John A. GA 25th Inf. Co.B Cpl.
Sanderlin, John M. TN 3rd (Forrest's) Cav. Co.C
Sanderlin, John W. NC 4th Cav. (59th St.Troops) Co.G

Sanderlin, John W. VA 5th Cav. (12 mo. '61-2)
Co.B
Sanderlin, J.S. GA Cav. 12th Bn. (St.Guards)
Co.A Sgt.
Sanderlin, J.W. MS 2nd Part.Rangers Co.K
Sanderlin, J.W. TN 13th Inf. Co.B
Sanderlin, Lemuel GA 47th Inf. Co.B
Sanderlin, Lemuel NC 2nd Cav. (19th St.Troops)
Co.G
Sanderlin, L.M. GA 3rd Res. Co.C
Sanderlin, Noah GA 36th (Villepigue's) Inf.
Co.C
Sanderlin, Noah GA 45th Inf. Co.A
Sanderlin, Robert GA Siege Arty. 28th Bn. Co.B
Sanderlin, Thomas TN 16th (Logwood's) Cav.
Co.G
Sanderlin, W.G. GA 11th Inf. Co.I
Sanderlin, Willis B. NC Inf. 66th Regt. Co.B
Capt.
Sanderlin, Willis B. NC 68th Inf. Co.F Capt.
Sanderlin, W.W. TN Cav. 17th Bn. (Sanders')
Co.A
Sanderline, J.M. MS 7th Cav. Co.F
Sanders, --- TX Cav. 4th Regt.St.Troops Co.L
Sanders, --- TX Cav. Border's Regt. Co.B
Sanders, --- TX Cav. Border's Regt. Co.K Cpl.
Sanders, --- TX Cav. Mann's Regt. Co.F
Sanders, --- TX Cav. Mann's Regt. Co.H
Sanders, --- TX Cav. Steele's Command Co.D
Sanders, --- TX 21st Inf. Co.D
Sanders, A. AL 8th (Hatch's) Cav. Co.A
Sanders, A. AL 2nd Cav. Co.A
Sanders, A. AL 6th Cav. Co.E
Sanders, A. AL 24th Inf.
Sanders, A. AR Cav. Gordon's Regt. Co.F
Sanders, A. AR 2nd Inf. Co.K
Sanders, A. GA 3rd Inf. Co.I
Sanders, A. LA 26th Inf. Co.B
Sanders, A. MS Cav. Jeff Davis Legion Co.I
Sanders, A. MS 5th Inf. (St.Troops) Co.E
Sanders, A. MS 33rd Inf. Co.A
Sanders, A. SC 2nd Inf. Co.F
Sanders, A. TN 28th Cav. Co.C Capt.
Sanders, A. TN 9th Inf. Co.B
Sanders, A. TX 35th (Likens') Cav. Co.A
Sanders, A. TX 5th Inf. Co.D
Sanders, A. TX Inf. Timmons' Regt. Co.K
Sanders, A.A. MS 46th Inf. Co.H
Sanders, A.A. NC 1st Jr.Res. Co.E
Sanders, A.A. SC Inf. 9th Bn. Co.B
Sanders, Aaron AR Inf. (Loc.Def.) Ernest's Co.
Ord.Sgt.
Sanders, Aaron AR 4th Inf. Co.F
Sanders, Aaron NC 5th Sr.Res. Co.A
Sanders, Aaron C. GA 24th Inf. Co.A
Sanders, A.B. MS 38th Cav. Co.E
Sanders, A.B. TN Lt.Arty. Huggins' Co.
Sanders, Abe TN Detailed Conscr. Co.B
Sanders, Abijah NC 43rd Inf. Co.I
Sanders, Abram N. GA 25th Inf. Co.E
Sanders, A.C. GA 1st Cav. Co.D
Sanders, A.C. GA 5th Res. Co.M Cpl.
Sanders, A.C. SC 2nd Inf. Co.I
Sanders, A. Campbell SC Lt.Arty. Walter's Co.
(Washington Arty.)
Sanders, Acy D. AL 3rd Res. Co.G 1st Sgt.
Sanders, A.D. FL Inf. 2nd Bn. Co.C

Sanders, A.D. MS 9th Inf. Co.K
Sanders, A.D. MS 41st Inf. Co.K
Sanders, Adam GA 1st Reg. Co.F
Sanders, Adams TX 6th Inf. Co.E Sgt.
Sanders, A. Edward NC 34th Inf. Co.K
Sanders, A.F. AL 15th Inf. Co.I Sgt.
Sanders, A.F. AL 30th Inf. Co.C
Sanders, A.F. AR 1st (Dobbin's) Cav. Co.B
Sanders, A.F. TN 18th Inf. Co.C
Sanders, A.G. TX 24th & 25th Cav. (Cons.)
Co.A
Sanders, A.G. TX Cav. Mann's Regt. Co.A
Sanders, A.H. MS 7th Cav. Co.B
Sanders, A.I. MO Cav. Fristoe's Regt. Co.G
Sanders, A.J. AL 5th Inf. New Co.H
Sanders, A.J. AL 5th Inf. New Co.I
Sanders, A.J. AL 40th Inf. Co.C
Sanders, A.J. AR Mtd.Vol. Baker's Co.
Sanders, A.J. GA 24th Inf. Co.A Cpl.
Sanders, A.J. GA 28th Inf. Co.F
Sanders, A.J. GA 41st Inf. Co.H
Sanders, A.J. LA 9th Inf. Co.D Band
Sanders, A.J. MS Inf. 7th Bn. Co.F
Sanders, A.J. MS 33rd Inf. Co.C
Sanders, A.J. MO 1st & 4th Cons.Inf. Co.I
Sanders, A.J. MO 4th Inf. Co.D
Sanders, A.J. SC 7th Inf. Co.I
Sanders, A.J. SC 15th Inf. Co.F
Sanders, A.J. TN 18th Inf. Co.E
Sanders, A.J. TN 25th Inf. Co.A
Sanders, A.L. GA 2nd Res. Co.I
Sanders, A.L. MS 33rd Inf. Co.A
Sanders, A.L. MO 6th Cav. Co.G
Sanders, Alberry GA Inf. 9th Bn. Co.A
Sanders, Alberry GA 37th Inf. Co.D
Sanders, Alberry GA 54th Inf. Co.H
Sanders, Albert AR Lt.Arty. Thrall's Btty.
Sanders, Albert H. MO 8th Cav. Co.A
Sanders, Albert W. TN 10th Cav.
Sanders, Alex MS 41st Inf. Co.F
Sanders, Alex NC 2nd Cav. (19th St.Troops)
Co.C
Sanders, Alexander MS Inf. 3rd Bn. Co.F
Sanders, Alexander NC 26th Inf. Co.A
Sanders, Alexander NC 47th Inf. Co.H
Sanders, Alexander VA 77th Mil. Co.B
Sanders, Alexander F. NC 23rd Inf. Co.C 1st
Lt.
Sanders, Alexander H. TN 1st (Turney's) Inf.
Co.A Cpl.
Sanders, Alexander P. Green MS 34th Inf. Co.A
Sanders, Alexander T. SC 2nd Cav. Co.A
Sanders, Alfred GA Conscr.
Sanders, Alfred MO 8th Inf. Co.A
Sanders, Alfred NC 45th Inf. Co.G
Sanders, Alfred NC 62nd Inf. Co.D
Sanders, Alfred TN 20th Inf. Co.B
Sanders, Alfred G. TX 13th Cav. Co.K Sgt.
Sanders, Alfred M. VA 51st Inf. Co.K
Sanders, Alic H. Mead's Conf.Cav. Co.I 1st Lt.
Sanders, Allen AL 6th Cav. Co.K
Sanders, Allen AL 48th Inf. Co.C
Sanders, Allen GA 23rd Inf. Co.A
Sanders, Allen J. NC 15th Inf. Co.C
Sanders, Allen J. VA 40th Inf. Co.D
Sanders, Allen N. AR 38th Inf. Adams' Co.
Sanders, Allen N. TX 6th Cav. Co.K

Sanders, Allen P. GA 30th Inf. Co.D
Sanders, Allison C. GA 5th Inf. Co.H,E Sgt.
Sanders, Almond MS Nash's Co. (Leake
Rangers)
Sanders, A.M. AL 30th Inf. Co.E
Sanders, Amas A. AL 27th Inf. Co.I Sgt.
Sanders, Ambros GA Cherokee Legion
(St.Guards) Co.H
Sanders, Ambrose GA 4th Res. Co.G Sgt.
Sanders, A.N. SC 1st (Butler's) Inf. Co.I
Sanders, Anderson AR Lt.Arty. Thrall's Btty.
Sanders, Andrew AL Cav. 4th Bn. (Love's) Co.B
Sanders, Andrew NC Inf. 2nd Bn. Co.G
Sanders, Andrew NC 6th Inf. Co.B
Sanders, Andrew TX 11th Inf. Co.F
Sanders, Andrew J. MS 5th Inf. Co.K
Sanders, Andrew J. TN 15th Inf. Co.I 1st Sgt.
Sanders, Andrew J. TN 37th Inf. Co.I 1st Sgt.
Sanders, Andrew J. TN 44th Inf. Co.B
Sanders, Andrew P. SC 6th Inf. 1st Co.E 2nd
Lt.
Sanders, Andrew S. TN 45th Inf.
Sanders, Andrew T. VA 4th Inf. Co.D
Sanders, A.P. MS 3rd Cav. Co.A
Sanders, A.P. TX 22nd Inf. Co.D
Sanders, A.R. MS 3rd Cav. Co.K,G
Sanders, A.R. MS 3rd Inf. (St.Troops) Co.K
Sgt.
Sanders, A.R. NC 22nd Inf. Co.I
Sanders, A.R. TX 17th Cons.Dismtd.Cav. Co.D
Sanders, A.S. TN 38th Inf. Co.G
Sanders, Asa KY 5th Mtd.Inf. Co.B Cpl.
Sanders, Asa C. GA Inf. 9th Bn. Co.A
Sanders, Asa C. GA 37th Inf. Co.D
Sanders, Asa L. TX Cav. Baylor's Regt. Co.D
Sanders, Asberry GA Cherokee Legion
(St.Guards) Co.B
Sanders, Ashford FL Cav. Pickett's Co.
Sanders, Ashford D. FL 10th Inf. Co.H
Sanders, Ashford G. FL 8th Inf. Co.H
Sanders, Ashley A. LA 31st Inf. Co.C
Sanders, Ashley S. NC 50th Inf. Co.D
Sanders, A.T. GA 54th Inf. Co.A
Sanders, A.T. SC 1st Inf. Co.L
Sanders, Augustus A. SC 26th Inf. Co.B Cpl.
Sanders, Augustus O. VA 4th Inf. Co.D
Sanders, A.V. TN Inf. 154th Sr.Regt. Co.G
Cpl.
Sanders, A.W. AL Cav. Lewis' Bn. Co.A
Sanders, A.W. AR 2nd Inf. Co.A
Sanders, A.W. AR 32nd Inf. Co.K
Sanders, A.W. NC 1st Jr.Res. Co.F
Sanders, B. AR 8th Cav. Co.I
Sanders, B. KY 7th Mtd.Inf. Co.H
Sanders, B. MS 30th Inf. Co.K
Sanders, B.A. LA 14th Inf. Co.D
Sanders, Barney TN 27th Inf. Co.F
Sanders, Bartlet GA 48th Inf. Co.I
Sanders, Bartlett VA 3rd Res. Co.E
Sanders, B.B. AL 3rd Res. Co.C
Sanders, B.B. AL 3rd Bn.Res. Jackson's Co.
Sanders, B.B. AL Mil. 4th Vol. Co.F Sgt.
Sanders, B.B. AL 40th Inf. Co.K 2nd Lt.
Sanders, B.B. AR 50th Mil. Co.I
Sanders, B.B. TX 4th Cav. Co.I
Sanders, B.E. TX Cav. Border's Regt. Co.F
Sanders, Benjamin AR 1st Mtd.Rifles Co.F

Sanders, Benjamin AR 4th Inf. Co.F
Sanders, Benjamin KY Guerrilla Mead Cty.
  Rangers
Sanders, Benjamin TX Inf. 1st Bn. (St.Troops)
  Co.B
Sanders, Benjamin VA 30th Inf. Co.C
Sanders, Benjamin F. AL Inf. 1st Regt. Co.B
Sanders, Benjamin F. AL 11th Inf. Co.K
Sanders, Benjamin F. GA 1st Reg. Co.L,D
Sanders, Benjamin F. MO 2nd Inf. Co.A
Sanders, Benjamin F. TX 11th Inf. Co.D
Sanders, Benjamin H. SC 25th Inf. Co.G
Sanders, Benjamin J. FL Lt.Arty. Perry's Co.
Sanders, Benjamin T. TX Cav. Baylor's Regt.
  Co.D Cpl.
Sanders, Berry GA 3rd Res. Co.A
Sanders, B.F. AR 6th Inf. New Co.F
Sanders, B.F. AR 12th Inf. Co.A
Sanders, B.F. GA 3rd Cav. Co.I
Sanders, B.F. GA 18th Inf. Co.E
Sanders, B.F. KY 2nd (Duke's) Cav. Co.G
Sanders, B.F. MS 41st Inf. Co.E Cpl.
Sanders, B.F. MO 8th Cav. Co.E
Sanders, B.F. TN 12th Inf. Co.F
Sanders, B.F. TN 12th (Cons.) Inf. Co.B
Sanders, B.F.G. SC 5th Inf. 1st Co.E
Sanders, B.F.G. SC 18th Inf. Co.F
Sanders, B.H. AR 10th Inf. Co.A
Sanders, B.H. SC 1st (Hagood's) Inf. 1st Co.A
Sanders, B.J. MS Inf. 1st Bn.St.Troops (12 mo.
  '62-3) Co.B
Sanders, Blake MO Cav. Ford's Bn. Co.E
Sanders, Blake S. MO Cav. Ford's Bn. Co.E
Sanders, B.M. GA 22nd Inf. Co.D
Sanders, B.O. SC 2nd Arty. Co.G
Sanders, B.O. SC 1st (Hagood's) Inf. 1st Co.G
Sanders, B.R. GA 9th Inf. Co.K 1st Sgt.
Sanders, Briton A. NC 5th Cav. (63rd St.Troops)
  Co.E
Sanders, Britton AR 2nd Inf.
Sanders, Britton E. GA 16th Inf. Co.D 2nd Lt.
Sanders, B.T. GA 16th Inf. Co.C
Sanders, B.T. MS Cav. 1st Bn. (McNair's)
  St.Troops Co.C
Sanders, B.T. MS 2nd Part. Co.A
Sanders, Buford MS 26th Inf. Co.A,E
Sanders, B.W. SC Part.Rangers Kirk's Co.
Sanders, C. GA 32nd Inf. Co.D
Sanders, C. KY 3rd Cav. Co.E
Sanders, C. LA 2nd Cav. Co.E
Sanders, C. TN 12th (Green's) Cav. Co.F
Sanders, C. TX 4th Cav. Co.B
Sanders, C. TX 26th Cav. Co.E
Sanders, C. TX 29th Cav. Co.B
Sanders, C. 2nd Cherokee Mtd.Vol. Co.K
Sanders, C.A. MS 18th Cav. Co.G
Sanders, C.A. TX Cav. Waller's Regt. Co.F
Sanders, Cader P. LA 12th Inf. Co.C
Sanders, Calvin 1st Cherokee Mtd.Vol. 2nd Co.H
Sanders, Calvin F. KY Cav. Buckner Guards
  Capt.
Sanders, Carrell LA 28th (Gray's) Inf. Co.I Cpl.
Sanders, C.B. TX 4th Inf. Co.H
Sanders, C.C. GA 24th Inf. Col.
Sanders, C.C. MS 33rd Inf. Co.F
Sanders, C.D. TN 33rd Inf. Co.F
Sanders, C.H. GA 38th Inf. Co.H

Sanders, Chapman D. TN 32nd Inf. Co.K
Sanders, Charles AL 41st Inf. Co.D
Sanders, Charles AL 63rd Inf. Co.G
Sanders, Charles GA 44th Inf. Co.C
Sanders, Charles LA 1st Cav. Co.C
Sanders, Charles LA 20th Inf. Co.I,G 1st Lt.
Sanders, Charles MO 12th Cav. Co.E
Sanders, Charles SC 22nd Inf. Co.D
Sanders, Charles TN 44th Inf. Co.D Cpl.
Sanders, Chas. Gen. & Staff 1st Lt.,Adj.
Sanders, Charles A. VA 14th Cav. Crawford's
  Co.
Sanders, Charles E. GA 23rd Inf. Adj.
Sanders, Charles E. TN 44th (Cons.) Inf. Co.F
Sanders, Charles H. GA Cobb's Legion Co.A
  Capt.
Sanders, Charles H. TX Waul's Legion Co.C
Sanders, Charles M. GA 3rd Inf. Co.C
Sanders, Charles R. TN 20th Inf. Co.C
Sanders, Charles W. AL 11th Inf. Co.C Music.
Sanders, Charles W. AR 18th Inf. Co.H
Sanders, Charles W. SC 6th Inf. 1st Co.E Capt.
Sanders, Charnel TX 22nd Cav. Co.H
Sanders, Christian MO 8th Cav. Co.A
Sanders, Clark TX Cav. Baird's Regt. Co.B
Sanders, Clow KY 2nd Cav. Co.B
Sanders, C.M. AL Lt.Arty. Kolb's Btty.
Sanders, Conelius 2nd Cherokee Mtd.Vol. Co.B
Sanders, C.R. TX Cav. 2nd Regt.St.Troops
  Co.G
Sanders, C.W. AR 12th Bn.S.S. Co.A
Sanders, C.W. AR 11th Inf. Co.C
Sanders, C.W. LA 25th Inf. Co.B
Sanders, C.W. SC 4th Cav. Co.B
Sanders, C.W. SC Cav. 10th Bn. Co.A
Sanders, C.W. SC 5th Inf. 2nd Co.E 1st Lt.
Sanders, C.W. TN 31st Inf. Co.G 2nd Lt.
Sanders, D. GA 5th Res. Co.I
Sanders, D. GA 54th Inf. Co.D
Sanders, D. MS 44th Inf. Co.F
Sanders, D. TX Cav. Hardeman's Regt. Co.C
Sanders, Daniel AR 34th Inf. Co.E
Sanders, Daniel FL Cav. Pickett's Co.
Sanders, Daniel GA Cav. 29th Bn. Co.B
Sanders, Daniel GA Siege Arty. Campbell's
  Ind.Co.
Sanders, Daniel GA Inf. 25th Bn. (Prov.Guard)
  Co.B
Sanders, Daniel GA 51st Inf. Co.C
Sanders, Daniel MS 27th Inf. Co.E
Sanders, Daniel C. AR 8th Inf. New Co.B Sgt.
Sanders, Daniel C. FL 1st Cav. Co.H 2nd Lt.
Sanders, Daniel W. GA 57th Inf. Co.F Cpl.
Sanders, Dave 1st Cherokee Mtd.Rifles Co.B
Sanders, David AL 17th Inf. Co.E
Sanders, David AR 8th Cav. Co.K Sgt.
Sanders, David AR 10th (Witt's) Cav. Co.C
Sanders, David AR 21st Inf. Co.E 2nd Lt.
Sanders, David MS 41st Inf. Co.F
Sanders, David MO Inf. 3rd Bn. Co.A
Sanders, David MO 6th Inf. Co.E
Sanders, David MO 12th Inf. Co.A Cpl.
Sanders, David NC 55th Inf. Co.B
Sanders, David SC 2nd Rifles Co.C Sgt.
Sanders, David TN 15th (Cons.) Cav. Co.K
Sanders, David TN 17th Inf. Co.H Bvt.2nd Lt.

Sanders, David 1st Cherokee Mtd.Vol. 1st Co.I,
  2nd Co.I Cpl.
Sanders, David H. NC 53rd Inf. Co.C
Sanders, David H. SC 10th Inf. Co.K
Sanders, David L. NC 13th Inf. Co.K
Sanders, David M. AL Jeff Davis Arty.
Sanders, David M. MS 10th Inf. Old Co.I
Sanders, David M. TN 41st Inf.
Sanders, David M. Gen. & Staff Hosp.Stew.
Sanders, David N. 15th Conf.Cav. Co.B
Sanders, David S. NC 1st Arty. (10th St.Troops)
  Co.H
Sanders, David W. SC 2nd Cav. Co.B
Sanders, David W. SC Cav.Bn. Hampton Legion
  Co.C
Sanders, D.B. Brush Bn.
Sanders, D.C. AL Mil. 4th Vol. Co.H
Sanders, D.C. NC 49th Inf. Co.G
Sanders, D.D. AL Inf. 1st Regt. Co.G
Sanders, Dennis N. GA 3rd Inf. Co.C Capt.
Sanders, D.H. SC Inf.Bn. Co.B
Sanders, Dickenson H. GA 2nd Cav. Co.C
  Ord.Sgt.
Sanders, D.J. TN 45th Inf. Co.C
Sanders, D.L. MS 3rd Cav. Co.K,H
Sanders, D.L. MS 12th Cav. Co.A
Sanders, D.L. MS 1st (King's) Inf. (St.Troops)
  D. Love's Co. Cpl.
Sanders, D.M. AR 4th Inf. Co.H
Sanders, D.M. Forrest's Scouts T.N. Kizer's
  Co.,CSA
Sanders, D.M. Hosp.Stew.
Sanders, D.P. AL 4th Res. Cpl.
Sanders, D.R. MS 19th Inf. Co.A
Sanders, Drury TX 3rd (Kirby's) Bn.Vol. Co.A
Sanders, D.T. GA Arty. Lumpkin's Co.
Sanders, Dudley LA 28th (Gray's) Inf. Co.K
  Cpl.
Sanders, D.W. FL 1st (Res.) Inf. Co.F
Sanders, D.W. GA 4th Inf. Co.F
Sanders, D.W. TN 35th Inf. 2nd Co.A Sgt.
Sanders, D.W. Gen. & Staff Maj.,AAG
Sanders, D.W.T. MS 1st (Percy's) Inf. Co.I
  Cpl.
Sanders, E. LA 3rd Inf. Co.C
Sanders, E. MS 41st Inf. Co.F Sgt.
Sanders, E. SC 21st Inf. Co.A
Sanders, E. TN Patterson's Regt.
Sanders, E. VA 12th Cav.
Sanders, E.A. LA 3rd (Wingfield's) Cav. Co.C
Sanders, E.A. TN 20th Inf. Co.C
Sanders, Earby TX 10th Inf. Co.H
Sanders, E.A.T. TN 45th Inf. Co.E Sgt.
Sanders, E.B. LA Lt.Arty. 3rd Btty. (Benton's)
Sanders, E.B. LA 17th Inf. Co.E
Sanders, E.B. MS 6th Cav. Co.F
Sanders, E.B. NC 35th Inf. Co.A Sgt.
Sanders, E.B. SC 3rd Cav. Co.B
Sanders, E.B. SC 2nd Arty. Co.G
Sanders, E.B. SC 1st (Hagood's) Inf. 1st Co.G
Sanders, E.C. AL 40th Inf. Co.K
Sanders, E.D. MS 1st Cav.Res. Co.E 1st Lt.
Sanders, E.D. MS 6th Inf. Co.C 1st Sgt.
Sanders, E.D. MS 9th Bn.S.S. Co.A
Sanders, E.D. MS 35th Inf. Co.K
Sanders, E.D. MS 41st Inf. Co.F
Sanders, Edward AL 20th Inf. Co.E

Sanders, Edward LA 31st Inf. Co.E 1st Sgt.
Sanders, Edward MS 2nd St.Cav. Co.A
Sanders, Edward NC 3rd Cav. (41st St.Troops)
    Co.D
Sanders, Edward NC 58th Inf. Co.B
Sanders, Edward SC 6th Inf. 1st Co.A
Sanders, Edward VA 5th Cav. Co.K
Sanders, Edward VA 23rd Cav. Co.M
Sanders, Edward E. KY 1st Bn.Mtd.Rifles Co.E
    1st Lt.
Sanders, Edward H. VA 6th Bn.Res. Co.D
Sanders, Edward H. VA 26th Inf. Co.K Music.
Sanders, Edward J. KY 2nd Mtd.Inf. Co.H
Sanders, Edward J. TN Cav. 17th Bn. (Sanders')
    Co.A Maj.
Sanders, Edward L. GA Cobb's Legion Co.D
    1st Lt.
Sanders, Edward L. TN 21st (Wilson's) Cav.
    Co.E Sgt.
Sanders, Edwin 7th Conf.Cav. 1st Co.I, Co.H
Sanders, Edwin S. NC 3rd Cav. (41st St.Troops)
    Co.D
Sanders, E.H. GA 16th Inf. Co.C
Sanders, E.H. MS 33rd Inf. Co.F
Sanders, E.H. VA 21st Cav. Co.A 1st Lt.
Sanders, E.J. AL 41st Inf. Co.D
Sanders, E.J. KY 4th Cav. Co.C 1st Lt.
Sanders, E.J. MS 9th Cav. Maj.
Sanders, E.L. AL 2nd Cav. Co.D
Sanders, E.L. AL 18th Inf. Co.E
Sanders, E.L. AL 25th Inf. Co.D
Sanders, E.L. TN Inf. 154th Sr.Regt. Co.I
Sanders, E.L. 4th Conf.Inf. Co.G
Sanders, Elam AL 47th Inf. Co.K
Sanders, Elbert TN Cav. 12th Bn. (Day's) Co.C
Sanders, Eli VA 62nd Mtd.Inf. 2nd Co.G
Sanders, Elias GA 3rd Cav. Co.B
Sanders, Elias, Jr. GA Inf. 9th Bn. Co.A
Sanders, Elias MO Cav. Wood's Regt. Co.C
Sanders, Elias SC 1st (Butler's) Inf. Co.I
Sanders, Elias SC 1st St.Troops Co.C
Sanders, Elias O. MS 22nd Inf. Co.A,H
Sanders, Eli B. GA Inf. Cobb Guards Co.B
Sanders, Elijah AL 5th Cav. Co.K
Sanders, Elijah AL Arty. 1st Bn. Co.B
Sanders, Elijah AL 26th (O'Neal's) Inf. Co.C
Sanders, Elijah LA 28th (Gray's) Inf. Co.K
Sanders, Elijah MO 6th Cav. Co.G Sgt.
Sanders, Elijah NC 25th Inf. Co.B
Sanders, Elijah SC 4th St.Troops Co.F
Sanders, Elijah SC 20th Inf. Co.A
Sanders, Elijah TN 32nd Inf. Co.K
Sanders, Elijah F. MS Bradford's Co.
    (Conf.Guards Arty.)
Sanders, Elijah O. GA 41st Inf. Co.A
Sanders, Elijah W. GA 1st Cav. Co.C
Sanders, Elijah W. NC 34th Inf. Co.K Sgt.
Sanders, Elim GA Inf. 27th Bn. (NonConscr.)
    Co.D
Sanders, Elisha AR 8th Inf. Old Co.I
Sanders, Elisha AR 38th Inf. New Co.I
Sanders, Elisha C. NC 34th Inf. Co.K
Sanders, Elisha H. AR 33rd Inf. Co.I
Sanders, Ellis 1st Cherokee Mtd.Vol. 1st Co.I,
    2nd Co.I 1st Sgt.
Sanders, Ellison TX 18th Cav. Co.B 2nd Lt.
Sanders, Emanuel SC 5th Res. Co.K

Sanders, Emanuel SC 20th Inf. Co.I
Sanders, Ennis AL 3rd Res. Co.G
Sanders, E.P. MS Graves' Co. (Copiah Horse
    Guards)
Sanders, E.P. MS Arty. (Seven Stars Arty.)
    Roberts' Co. Artif.
Sanders, Ephraim TN 62nd Mtd.Inf. Co.F
Sanders, Ephraim F. GA 4th Inf. Co.G
Sanders, E.R. SC 7th Cav. Co.K
Sanders, Erasmus J. AR 1st Mtd.Rifles Co.A
    Cpl.
Sanders, Ervin SC 5th St.Troops Co.G
Sanders, Ervin SC 7th Res. Co.H
Sanders, E.S. GA 18th Inf. Co.D
Sanders, E.S. MS 41st Inf. Co.L,A
Sanders, Evermoth J. KY 4th Mtd.Inf. Co.A
Sanders, E.W. AR Lt.Arty. Etter's Btty.
Sanders, E.W. MS 41st Inf. Co.F
Sanders, E.W. SC 3rd Cav. Co.G
Sanders, E.W. SC 5th Inf. 2nd Co.E
Sanders, Ewell P. MS 12th Inf. Co.H
Sanders, F. AL Cav. Moreland's Regt. Co.C
Sanders, F. AR Cav. Anderson's Unatt.Bn. Co.A
    2nd Lt.
Sanders, F. FL 2nd Cav. Co.K
Sanders, F. SC 21st Inf. Co.A
Sanders, F.A. TX 2nd Cav. Co.D Sgt.
Sanders, F.A. 3rd Conf.Cav. Co.I
Sanders, F.E. NC 3rd Arty. (40th St.Troops)
    Co.F
Sanders, Felix G. TX 14th Cav. Co.K
Sanders, F.F. TN 44th Inf. Co.C
Sanders, F.H. TN 18th (Newsom's) Cav. Co.E
Sanders, Fielding C. VA 37th Inf. Co.I
Sanders, F.J. AL 15th Inf. Co.E
Sanders, F.J. AR 27th Inf. Co.E
Sanders, F.J. SC 1st (Hagood's) Inf. 1st Co.G
    1st Lt.
Sanders, F.J. TX 22nd Inf. Co.A
Sanders, Fleming AR 11th & 17th Cons.Inf.
    Co.H
Sanders, Flemming VA 166th Mil. Co.B
Sanders, Flemon AR 17th (Griffith's) Inf. Co.H
    1st Sgt.
Sanders, F.M. AL 1st Cav. 2nd Co.C
Sanders, F.M. AR Cav. Gordon's Regt. Co.F
Sanders, F.M. AR 19th (Dawson's) Inf. Co.E
Sanders, F.M. GA 28th Inf. Co.E
Sanders, F.M. 2nd Conf.Inf. Co.B
Sanders, Francis AR 34th Inf. Co.H
Sanders, Francis A. TX 27th Cav. Co.C Cpl.
Sanders, Francis M. AR 1st Cav. Co.F
Sanders, Francis M. GA 65th Inf. Co.I
Sanders, Francis M. MS 22nd Inf. Co.A
Sanders, Francis M. TN Cav. 9th Bn. (Gantt's)
    Co.C
Sanders, Frank GA 3rd Res. Co.D Cpl.
Sanders, Frank TN 14th (Neely's) Cav. Co.I
Sanders, Frank VA Cav. Mosby's Regt.
    (Part.Rangers)
Sanders, Franklin GA Inf. 9th Bn. Co.A
Sanders, Franklin GA 37th Inf. Co.D
Sanders, Franklin M. MS 33rd Inf. Co.A
Sanders, Fred. MS Lt.Arty. (Issaquena Arty.)
    Graves' Co.
Sanders, Frederick AR 16th Inf. Co.H
Sanders, Frederick FL 9th Inf. Co.B 1st Sgt.

Sanders, Frederick KY 4th Mtd.Inf. Co.B
Sanders, Frederick TX 1st Field Btty.
Sanders, Frederick VA 6th Bn.Res. Co.H
Sanders, Fredrick S. MO Cav. Williams' Regt.
    Co.C
Sanders, F.T. SC 10th Inf. Co.K
Sanders, Furney W. AL 3rd Res. Co.H
Sanders, F.W. TX 1st Hvy.Arty. Co.H
Sanders, G. TN 20th Inf. Co.E
Sanders, Gabrel MO Inf. 3rd Bn. Co.A
Sanders, Gabriel MO 6th Inf. Co.E
Sanders, Gainer SC 23rd Inf. Co.K
Sanders, Garner SC Inf. 7th Bn. (Enfield Rifles)
    Co.E
Sanders, Garrison GA 22nd Inf. Co.C
Sanders, G.B. AL 33rd Inf. Co.K
Sanders, G.B. TN 24th Bn.S.S. Co.C Cpl.
Sanders, G.C. SC 3rd Cav. Co.F
Sanders, G.C. SC 1st (Hagood's) Inf. 1st Co.I
Sanders, George AL 8th Cav. Co.B
Sanders, George AL 9th (Malone's) Cav. Co.L
Sanders, George FL 8th Inf. Co.H
Sanders, Geo. GA Inf. 3rd Bn. Co.H
Sanders, George GA 46th Inf. Co.I
Sanders, George KY 4th Cav. Co.A
Sanders, George NC 6th Inf. Co.G
Sanders, George SC 21st Inf. Co.A
Sanders, George TN Inf. 2nd Cons.Regt. Co.I
Sanders, George TN 14th Inf. Co.D
Sanders, George TN 41st Inf. Co.C
Sanders, George TN 45th Inf. Co.E
Sanders, George TX Cav. Benavides' Regt. Co.G
Sanders, George TX 1st Hvy.Arty. Co.G
Sanders, George VA 41st Mil. Co.E
Sanders, George 2nd Cherokee Mtd.Vol. Co.B
Sanders, George A. GA 34th Inf. Co.E,F
Sanders, George A. VA 45th Inf. Co.D
Sanders, George C. FL 2nd Inf. Co.D Music.
Sanders, George C. SC 2nd Arty. Co.G
Sanders, George E. AL 3rd Inf. Co.I
Sanders, George F. GA 37th Inf. Music.
Sanders, George G. MS 13th Inf. Co.H
Sanders, George G. MS 31st Inf. Co.C 2nd Lt.
Sanders, George G. TX 1st (Yager's) Cav. Co.A
Sanders, George G. TX Cav. 3rd (Yager's) Bn.
    Co.A
Sanders, George H. AL 41st Inf. Co.G
Sanders, George H. MO 9th Inf. Co.F
Sanders, George J. MS 28th Cav. Co.H
Sanders, George L. VA 40th Inf. Co.D
Sanders, George M. GA 45th Inf. Co.K
Sanders, George O. 1st Cherokee Mtd.Rifles
    Co.B 2nd Lt.
Sanders, George P. TX 10th Inf. Co.G
Sanders, George W. AL 1st Bn.Cadets Co.A
    Cpl.
Sanders, George W. AL 41st Inf. Co.D
Sanders, George W. AL 44th Inf. Co.D
Sanders, George W. FL 2nd Inf. Co.D 2nd Lt.
Sanders, George W. GA 47th Inf. Co.B
Sanders, George W. KY 1st (Butler's) Cav. Co.D
Sanders, George W. MS 5th Inf. Co.K
Sanders, George W. MS 11th Inf. Co.C
Sanders, George W. MS 11th Inf. Co.F
Sanders, George W. MS 26th Inf. Co.D Sgt.
Sanders, George W. MS 36th Inf. Co.D Sgt.
Sanders, George W. MO 16th Inf. Co.D

Sanders, George W. SC 1st (McCreary's) Inf. Co.C
Sanders, George W. TN 1st (Turney's) Inf. Co.D
Sanders, George W. TN 32nd Inf. Co.K
Sanders, George W. TN 34th Inf. Co.G
Sanders, George W. TN 44th (Cons.) Inf. Co.E
Sanders, George W. TN 55th (McKoin's) Inf. Co.H Cpl.
Sanders, George W. TX Cav. 6th Bn. Co.A
Sanders, George W. VA 15th Cav. Co.G 2nd Lt.
Sanders, George W. VA Cav. 15th Bn. Co.D 2nd Lt.
Sanders, Geo. W. VA Hvy.Arty. 20th Bn.
Sanders, George W. VA 40th Inf. Co.D
Sanders, George W. VA 40th Inf. Co.H Sgt.
Sanders, G.F. GA 54th Inf. Co.K Music.
Sanders, G.F. GA 61st Inf. Band Music.
Sanders, G.G. SC 11th Inf. 2nd Co.I Sgt.
Sanders, G.H. GA 10th Cav. Co.D
Sanders, G.H. GA 30th Inf. Co.E
Sanders, G.H. 7th Conf.Cav. Co.D
Sanders, G.M. AL 22nd Inf. Co.E
Sanders, Gordon VA 8th Cav. Co.F
Sanders, Gosley KY 4th Cav. Co.A
Sanders, Govey B. GA 14th Inf. Co.B
Sanders, G.R. NC 32nd Inf. Co.K
Sanders, Granville A. GA 34th Inf. Sgt.
Sanders, Green AL 7th Cav. Co.E
Sanders, Green AR 25th Inf. Co.K
Sanders, Green B. NC 38th Inf. Co.E
Sanders, Green E. GA 27th Inf. Co.D
Sanders, Greenville VA Cav. 36th Bn. Co.A
Sanders, Greenville AR 16th Inf. Co.H
Sanders, Green W. AL 38th Inf. Co.A
Sanders, Griffin NC 56th Inf. Co.F
Sanders, Griffin VA Cav. 15th Bn. Co.D
Sanders, Griffin VA 41st Mil. Co.E
Sanders, G.S. KY 1st Inf. Co.F Sgt.
Sanders, G.T. GA Cav. 29th Bn. Co.G
Sanders, G.T. GA 16th Inf. Co.C
Sanders, G.T. GA 16th Inf. Co.D
Sanders, G.T. GA 32nd Inf. Co.E
Sanders, G.T. TX Cav. (Dismtd.) Chisum's Regt. Co.H
Sanders, G.W. AL 18th Bn.Vol. Co.C Sgt.
Sanders, G.W. KY 3rd Cav. Co.E Sgt.
Sanders, G.W. MS 13th Inf. Co.I
Sanders, G.W. TN 12th (Cons.) Inf. Co.D Sgt.
Sanders, G.W. TN 22nd Inf. Co.H Sgt.
Sanders, G.W. TN 33rd Inf. Co.A
Sanders, G.W. TN 50th Inf. Co.D
Sanders, G.W. TN 50th (Cons.) Inf. Co.D
Sanders, G.W. TX 32nd Cav. Co.C Cpl.
Sanders, G.W. VA 1st Cav. Co.B
Sanders, G.W. VA Lt.Arty. King's Co.
Sanders, G.W. VA Post Guards (Abingdon) Martin's Co.
Sanders, G.W. 2nd Conf.Eng.Troops Co.D
Sanders, G.W.C. MS Inf. 3rd Bn. (St.Troops) Co.D
Sanders, H. AL 1st Bn.Cadets Co.A
Sanders, H. AL 25th Inf. Co.K
Sanders, H. AL 40th Inf. Co.G
Sanders, H. AR 30th Inf. Co.B
Sanders, H. KY 2nd Mtd.Inf. Co.C Sgt.
Sanders, H. LA 22nd Inf. Co.E

Sanders, H. MS Cav. 4th Bn. Co.B
Sanders, H. MS Cav. Ham's Regt. Co.G
Sanders, H. SC 17th Inf. Co.B
Sanders, H. TN 15th (Cons.) Cav. Co.G
Sanders, H.A. TN 21st & 22nd (Cons.) Cav. Co.E
Sanders, Hamilton MO Cav. Coffee's Regt. Co.F
Sanders, Hamlin AR 1st (Crawford's) Cav. Co.B
Sanders, Hampton LA Inf. 11th Bn. Co.D
Sanders, Hampton S. TX 15th Cav. Co.F
Sanders, Hardy T. GA 3rd Cav. (St.Guards) Co.G
Sanders, Harmon NC 16th Inf. Co.H Sgt.Maj.
Sanders, Harris NC 38th Inf. Co.H
Sanders, Harrison 8th (Wade's) Conf.Cav. Co.D
Sanders, Harrison S. GA 24th Inf. Co.D Sgt.
Sanders, Harry B. TN 22nd Cav.
Sanders, Harvy AL 41st Inf. Co.G
Sanders, Hasten TN 32nd Inf. Co.K
Sanders, H.B. AR 7th Inf. Co.H Capt.
Sanders, H.C. MS 7th Cav. Co.B
Sanders, H.C. TX Cav. Hardeman's Regt. Co.C
Sanders, H.C. Brush Bn.
Sanders, H.D. TX 15th Cav. Co.B
Sanders, H.E. MS 1st Lt.Arty. Co.B
Sanders, Henderson Mead's Conf.Cav. Co.I
Sanders, Henderson L. NC Cav. 7th Bn. Co.C
Sanders, Henry AL 1st Cav. 1st Co.K
Sanders, Henry AL 2nd Cav. Co.K
Sanders, Henry AL Cav. Lewis' Bn. Co.A
Sanders, Henry AL 45th Inf. Co.K
Sanders, Henry AR Inf. 4th Bn. Co.C
Sanders, Henry KY 4th Cav. Co.F
Sanders, Henry KY Lt.Arty. Cobb's Co.
Sanders, Henry LA 3rd (Wingfield's) Cav. Co.K
Sanders, Henry LA 1st (Strawbridge's) Inf. Co.B
Sanders, Henry MS 44th Inf. Co.I,G
Sanders, Henry MO Cav. Poindexter's Regt.
Sanders, Henry MO Inf. Clark's Regt. Co.D,H
Sanders, Henry NC 4th Bn.Jr.Res. Co.B
Sanders, Henry TN 40th Inf. Co.H
Sanders, Henry TN 41st Inf. Co.A
Sanders, Henry TN 41st Inf. Co.D
Sanders, Henry TX Arty. 4th Bn. Co.B
Sanders, Henry TX 8th Inf. Co.B
Sanders, Henry VA Cav. 15th Bn. Co.D
Sanders, Henry VA 22nd Cav. Co.B
Sanders, Henry VA 41st Mil. Co.E
Sanders, Henry 1st Conf.Cav. 2nd Co.E
Sanders, Henry 3rd Conf.Cav. Co.D
Sanders, Henry Conf.Cav. Clarkson's Bn. Ind. Rangers Co.H
Sanders, Henry A. 1st Cherokee Mtd.Vol. 1st Co.K
Sanders, Henry C. GA 6th Inf. Co.E 1st Lt.
Sanders, Henry C. MS 26th Inf. Co.I
Sanders, Henry C. TN 41st Inf. Co.F
Sanders, Henry F. MS 14th Inf. Co.A
Sanders, Henry G. TX 15th Cav. Co.F
Sanders, Henry H. MO 4th Inf. Co.H
Sanders, Henry J. NC Hvy.Arty. 10th Bn. Co.B
Sanders, Henry J. VA Cav. 34th Bn. Co.A
Sanders, Henry L. TN 1st (Feild's) Inf. Co.K
Sanders, Henry P. MS 48th Inf. Co.L
Sanders, Henry S. MS 2nd Inf. (A. of 10,000) Co.H
Sanders, Henry S. MS 11th Inf. Co.K

Sanders, Henry W. GA 36th (Villepigue's) Inf. Co.C
Sanders, Henson C. NC 13th Inf. Co.K
Sanders, H.E.P. SC 21st Inf. Co.B QMSgt.
Sanders, Herman LA 1st Hvy.Arty. (Reg.) Co.G
Sanders, Hermann TX 1st Hvy.Arty. Co.B
Sanders, H.F. GA 37th Inf. Co.E
Sanders, H.G. TX 17th Cons.Dismtd.Cav. Co.H
Sanders, H.H. AL 40th Inf. Co.B
Sanders, H.H. AL 41st Inf. Co.D
Sanders, H.H. MO 10th Cav. Co.I
Sanders, H.H. MO 1st & 4th Cons.Inf. Co.E
Sanders, H.H. NC 6th Inf. Co.D
Sanders, Hinton Jones TX 21st Cav. Co.H Cpl.
Sanders, Hiram AR 10th Inf. Co.C,F
Sanders, Hiram SC 7th Res. Co.A
Sanders, Hiram TX 9th (Nichols') Inf. Co.H Cpl.
Sanders, Hiram J. VA 4th Inf. Co.C
Sanders, H.J. SC Inf. Hampton Legion Co.H Cpl.
Sanders, H.L. LA 6th Cav. Co.I
Sanders, H.L. KY 4th Cav.
Sanders, H.L. NC 6th Cav. (65th St.Troops) Co.G
Sanders, H.L. TN 11th (Holman's) Cav. Co.K
Sanders, H.L. TN Holman's Bn.Part.Rangers Co.D
Sanders, H.L.T. TN 16th Inf. Co.G
Sanders, H.P. MS Inf. 2nd Bn. Co.L
Sanders, H.R. TX 17th Inf. Co.I
Sanders, H.S. AR 6th Inf. Co.B Sgt.
Sanders, H.S. MS 28th Cav. Co.B Sgt.
Sanders, H.S. TX 26th Cav. 2nd Co.G
Sanders, H.S. TX 20th Inf. Co.I
Sanders, H.T. MS Bn.Vol. Co.F Sgt.
Sanders, H.T. TX 11th Cav. Co.I
Sanders, H.T. TX Waul's Legion Co.E
Sanders, H.T. TX Waul's Legion Co.F Sgt.
Sanders, Hugh MS 9th Inf. New Co.H
Sanders, Hugh L. LA 27th Inf. Co.C Cpl.
Sanders, H.W. TN 6th (Wheeler's) Cav. Co.E
Sanders, I. MO Cav. Fristoe's Regt. Co.G
Sanders, I.B. MO Cav. Williams' Regt. Co.C
Sanders, Icck AL Cav. Moreland's Regt. Co.C
Sanders, Ignatius SC Inf. Holcombe Legion Co.A
Sanders, I.H. GA 13th Inf.
Sanders, I.J. GA Cav. 12th Bn. (St.Guards) Co.C
Sanders, I.N. AL 2nd Cav. Co.H
Sanders, I.N. TN 18th Inf. Co.C
Sanders, Ira AR 1st (Monroe's) Cav. Co.G
Sanders, Isaac, Jr. AR 4th Inf. Co.F
Sanders, Isaac, Sr. AR 4th Inf. Co.F
Sanders, Isaac AR Inf. (Loc.Def.) Ernest's Co.
Sanders, Isaac MS 12th Cav. Co.F
Sanders, Isaac SC 24th Inf. Co.B
Sanders, Isaac TN 15th (Stewart's) Cav. Co.A
Sanders, Isaac TX Cav. Hardeman's Regt. Co.H
Sanders, Isaac 1st Cherokee Mtd.Vol. 1st Co.I, 2nd Co.I
Sanders, Isaac, Sr. 1st Cherokee Mtd.Vol. 2nd Co.I
Sanders, Isaac B. NC 39th Inf. Co.B
Sanders, Isaac H. AL 26th (O'Neal's) Inf. Co.D
Sanders, Isaac H. MS Cav. 18th Regt. Co.B
Sanders, Isaac M. TX 17th Cav. 1st Co.I
Sanders, Isaac T. LA 28th (Gray's) Inf. Co.K

Sanders, Isaiah MS 41st Inf. Co.D
Sanders, Isham LA 9th Inf. Co.K
Sanders, Isiah AL 43rd Inf. Co.D
Sanders, Isom AR 1st Cav. Co.D Sgt.
Sanders, Iverson GA 5th Res. Co.I
Sanders, Ivory AL 50th Inf. Co.C
Sanders, I. Young LA 26th Inf. Co.B 1st Lt.
Sanders, J. AL 3rd Cav. Co.B
Sanders, J. AL 7th Cav. Co.C
Sanders, J. AL 2nd Bn. Hilliard's Legion Vol. Co.D
Sanders, J. AR Inf. (Loc.Def.) Ernest's Co.
Sanders, J. FL 1st (Res.) Inf. Co.I
Sanders, J. FL 4th Inf. Co.D
Sanders, J. GA 23rd Inf. Co.F
Sanders, J. LA Miles' Legion Co.E
Sanders, J. MS 3rd Cav. Co.I
Sanders, J. MS Cav. Davenport's Bn. (St.Troops) Co.B
Sanders, J. MS 9th Bn.S.S. Co.B
Sanders, J. SC 2nd Res.
Sanders, J. SC 16th & 24th (Cons.) Inf. Co.K
Sanders, J. TN Cav. Nixon's Regt. Co.C
Sanders, J. TX 1st (Yager's) Cav. Co.D
Sanders, J. TX 6th Inf. Co.B
Sanders, J. TX 21st Inf. Co.G
Sanders, J. 1st Cherokee Mtd.Vol. Co.J Cpl.
Sanders, J. Hosp.Stew.
Sanders, J.A. AL 48th Inf. Co.E
Sanders, J.A. AR Inf. Cocke's Regt. Co.D
Sanders, J.A. KY 9th Cav. Co.A
Sanders, J.A. GA 3rd Cav. Co.A
Sanders, J.A. MS 12th Cav. Co.K
Sanders, J.A. SC Mil. 1st Regt. (Charleston Res.) Co.I 2nd Lt.
Sanders, J.A. TN 20th Inf. Co.E
Sanders, J.A. TN Inf. 23rd Bn. Co.E
Sanders, J.A. TN 33rd Inf. Co.F
Sanders, J.A. TN Inf. Sowell's Detach.
Sanders, J.A. TX 11th Cav. Co.K
Sanders, Jack TX Cav. 3rd (Yager's) Bn. Co.D
Sanders, Jackson AL 8th Cav. Co.B
Sanders, Jackson SC 22nd Inf. Co.I
Sanders, Jackson TN Cav. 9th Bn. (Gantt's) Co.C
Sanders, Jacob AL Cav. 4th Bn. (Love's) Co.B
Sanders, Jacob NC 2nd Jr.Res. Co.F
Sanders, Jacob NC 11th (Bethel Regt.) Inf. Co.H
Sanders, Jacob NC 14th Inf. Co.K
Sanders, Jacob Conf.Cav. 7th Bn. Co.C 1st Lt.
Sanders, Jacob B. MO Cav. Williams' Regt. Co.C
Sanders, Jacob F. GA 55th Inf. Co.D,E
Sanders, Jacob W. MS 32nd Inf. Co.I
Sanders, James AL 3rd Bn.Res. Co.H
Sanders, James AL 41st Inf. Co.D
Sanders, James AL Arty. 4th Bn. Hilliard's Legion Co.D
Sanders, James AR 8th Cav. Co.F
Sanders, James FL 2nd Inf. Co.D
Sanders, James FL Rangers
Sanders, James GA Cav. 6th Bn. (St.Guards) Co.F
Sanders, James GA 1st Inf. (St.Guards) Co.F
Sanders, James GA 1st (Olmstead's) Inf. Co.D
Sanders, James GA 2nd Inf. Co.H
Sanders, James GA 9th Inf. Co.F

Sanders, James GA Inf. 9th Bn. Co.A
Sanders, James GA 37th Inf. Co.D
Sanders, James GA Inf. Alexander's Co.
Sanders, James LA 5th Inf. Co.G Cpl.
Sanders, James LA 20th Inf. Co.G,H Cpl.
Sanders, James MS 9th Inf. New Co.H
Sanders, James MS 25th Inf. Co.B
Sanders, James MO Cav. Clardy's Bn. Farris' Co.
Sanders, James MO Lt.Arty. 3rd Btty.
Sanders, James MO Arty. Lowe's Co. (Jackson Btty.)
Sanders, James NC 6th Sr.Res. Co.H
Sanders, James NC 17th Inf. (2nd Org.) Co.D
Sanders, James NC 47th Inf. Co.B
Sanders, James NC 62nd Inf. Co.D
Sanders, James SC Lt.Arty. Beauregard's Co.
Sanders, James SC 5th Inf. 2nd Co.E
Sanders, James SC 6th Inf. 1st Co.H
Sanders, James SC Inf. 7th Bn. (Enfield Rifles) Co.E Cpl.
Sanders, James SC 10th Inf. Co.D
Sanders, James SC 22nd Inf. Co.I
Sanders, James SC Manigault's Bn.Vol. Co.B
Sanders, James TN 21st (Wilson's) Cav. Co.E
Sanders, James TN 25th Inf. Co.C
Sanders, James TN 34th Inf. Co.K
Sanders, James TX 21st Cav. Co.G
Sanders, James TX 20th Inf. Co.K
Sanders, James TX Inf. Griffin's Bn. Co.B
Sanders, James VA Arty. Wise Legion
Sanders, James Mead's Conf.Cav. Co.I
Sanders, James 2nd Conf.Inf. Co.B
Sanders, James 1st Cherokee Mtd.Rifles Co.H
Sanders, James 1st Choctaw & Chickasaw Mtd.Rifles 3rd Co.D
Sanders, James Gen. & Staff Hosp.Stew.
Sanders, James A. AL 40th Inf. Co.F
Sanders, James A. GA Inf. 9th Bn. Co.D 2nd Lt.
Sanders, James A. GA 37th Inf. Co.G Capt.
Sanders, James A. GA 54th Inf. Co.C Capt.
Sanders, James A. MS 15th Inf. Co.K
Sanders, James A. MS 31st Inf. Co.H
Sanders, James A. MS 37th Inf. Co.K
Sanders, James A. NC McDugald's Co.
Sanders, James A. SC 5th Inf. 2nd Co.E Sgt.
Sanders, James A. SC 6th Inf. 1st Co.E Sgt.
Sanders, James A. TN 1st (Feild's) Inf. Co.G
Sanders, James A. TN 1st (Turney's) Inf. Co.D
Sanders, James A. VA 4th Inf. Co.C
Sanders, James A.B. VA 41st Mil. Co.E
Sanders, James B. VA 6th Bn.Res. Co.D
Sanders, James C. AR 36th Inf. Co.H
Sanders, James C. SC Lt.Arty. Kelly's Co. (Chesterfield Arty.) Sgt.
Sanders, James C. TN 8th Inf. Co.I
Sanders, James D. AL 13th Inf. Co.I
Sanders, James D. MO Cav. Coffee's Regt. Co.K
Sanders, James E. MS 11th Inf. Co.C
Sanders, James E. NC 6th Inf. Co.B
Sanders, James E. SC 13th Inf. Co.I
Sanders, James E. VA 40th Inf. Co.H
Sanders, James F. TX 6th Cav. Co.A
Sanders, James F. VA 108th Mil. Co.F
Sanders, James G. AL 42nd Inf. Co.B
Sanders, James G. KY 4th Cav. Co.A

Sanders, James H. MS 15th Inf. Co.F
Sanders, James H. SC 2nd Rifles Co.H
Sanders, James H. SC 11th Inf. 2nd Co.I
Sanders, James H. TX 11th Inf. Co.D
Sanders, James H.L. AL Inf. 1st Regt. Co.F
Sanders, James H.L. AL 29th Inf. Co.K
Sanders, James J. GA 2nd Bn.S.S. Co.E Cpl.
Sanders, James K. VA 166th Mil. Co.B 2nd Lt.
Sanders, James L. AL 3rd Cav. Co.F
Sanders, James L. AL 59th Inf. Co.H
Sanders, James L. MO 12th Cav. Co.H
Sanders, James L. TX 11th Inf. Co.D
Sanders, James M. AL 11th Cav. Co.C
Sanders, James M. AL 17th Inf. Co.E
Sanders, James M. GA 4th Res. Co.E
Sanders, James M. GA Inf. 9th Bn. Co.A
Sanders, James M. GA 37th Inf. Co.D
Sanders, James M. GA 41st Inf. Co.E Sgt.
Sanders, James M. MS 37th Inf. Co.C
Sanders, James M. MS 41st Inf. Co.D
Sanders, James M. MO 15th Cav. Co.A
Sanders, James M. NC Cav. 7th Bn. Co.C
Sanders, James M. NC 6th Inf. Co.B
Sanders, James M. NC 34th Inf. Co.K
Sanders, James M. NC 43rd Inf. Co.H
Sanders, James M. SC 20th Inf. Co.F
Sanders, James M. TN 1st (Turney's) Inf. Co.A
Sanders, James M. TN 48th (Nixon's) Inf. Co.G Cpl.
Sanders, James M. TN 54th Inf. Co.B
Sanders, James M. TX 10th Inf. Co.H
Sanders, James M. VA 51st Inf. Co.C
Sanders, James Marion TX 20th Cav. Co.A
Sanders, James N. AL Cav. 4th Bn. (Love's) Co.A Sgt.
Sanders, James N. AL 3rd Bn. Hilliard's Legion Vol. Co.A
Sanders, James N. LA 31st Inf. Co.A
Sanders, James N. SC 2nd Cav. Co.A
Sanders, James O. MS 15th Inf. Asst.Surg.
Sanders, James O.S. MS 11th Inf. Co.K
Sanders, James R. AL 60th Inf. Co.G
Sanders, James R. AL 3rd Bn. Hilliard's Legion Vol. Co.E
Sanders, James R. GA 3rd Inf. Co.C 1st Lt.
Sanders, James R. TN 41st Inf. Co.F
Sanders, James R. VA Rockbridge Cty.Res. Miller's Co.
Sanders, James S. AR 9th Inf. Co.C
Sanders, James S. TN 7th Inf. Co.E
Sanders, James S. TN 9th Inf. Co.D
Sanders, James T. GA 30th Inf. Co.D
Sanders, James T. MO 16th Inf. Co.D
Sanders, James W. AL 2nd Cav. Co.D 1st Sgt.
Sanders, James W. AR 1st (Crawford's) Cav. Co.D
Sanders, James W. GA 14th Inf. Co.B
Sanders, James W. LA 3rd Inf. Co.B Sgt.
Sanders, James W. MO 1st & 4th Cons.Inf. Co.E
Sanders, James W. MO 4th Inf. Co.H
Sanders, James W. SC 1st (Butler's) Inf. Co.A
Sanders, James W. SC 1st (McCreary's) Inf. Co.B
Sanders, James W. TN 11th Cav.
Sanders, James W. TX 25th Cav. Co.C 1st Sgt.
Sanders, James W. TX 31st Cav. Co.E

Sanders, James William AL 5th Inf. Old Co.H
 1st Sgt.
Sanders, Jason L. KY 2nd Mtd.Inf. Co.G
Sanders, Jasper MO 4th Cav. Co.E
Sanders, Jasper D. AL 47th Inf. Co.I 1st Sgt.
Sanders, J.B. AR 2nd Cav. 1st Co.A
Sanders, J.B. GA 10th Inf. Co.C
Sanders, J.B. MS Inf. 1st St.Troops Co.I Sgt.
Sanders, J.B. SC 4th Cav. Co.G
Sanders, J.B. SC 5th Cav. Co.C
Sanders, J.B. SC Cav. 10th Bn. Co.C
Sanders, J.B. SC Cav. 17th Bn. Co.D
Sanders, J.B. SC Lt.Arty. M. Ward's Co. (Wac-
 camaw Lt.Arty.)
Sanders, J.B. SC 2nd Inf. Co.I
Sanders, J.B. SC 2nd Rifles Co.C
Sanders, J.B. TN 16th (Logwood's) Cav. Co.H
Sanders, J.B. TX 11th Cav. Co.I
Sanders, J.B. TX 13th Cav. Co.K
Sanders, J.B. TX 5th Inf. Co.F Music.
Sanders, J.C. AR 10th (Witt's) Cav. Co.C
Sanders, J.C. GA 3rd Cav. Co.I
Sanders, J.C. GA 27th Inf. Co.D
Sanders, J.C. MS Inf. 3rd Bn. (St.Troops) Co.D
Sanders, J.C. MS 5th Inf. Co.H
Sanders, J.C. SC 7th Cav. Co.H
Sanders, J.C. SC Lt.Arty. Gaillard's Co. (Santee
 Lt.Arty.)
Sanders, J.C. SC 1st (Hagood's) Inf. 1st Co.E
 Cpl.
Sanders, J.C. SC 22nd Inf. Co.D
Sanders, J.C. SC Conscr. (Cp. of Instr.)
Sanders, J.C. TN 21st (Carter's) Cav. Co.A
Sanders, J.C. TN Lt.Arty. Rice's Btty.
Sanders, J.C. TN 38th Inf. 2nd Co.H 1st Lt.
Sanders, J.C.A. GA 5th Res. Co.C
Sanders, J.D. AL 3rd Inf. Co.D
Sanders, J.D. AL 26th (O'Neal's) Inf. Co.H
Sanders, J.D. MS 2nd Cav. Co.I
Sanders, J.D. MS 10th Cav. Co.B Cpl.
Sanders, J.D. SC Arty. Stuart's Co. (Beaufort
 Vol.Arty.)
Sanders, J.D. SC 2nd St.Troops Co.D
Sanders, J.D.D. SC 2nd Arty. Co.C
Sanders, J.E. AL 40th Inf. Co.C
Sanders, J.E. GA 16th Inf. Co.D Sgt.
Sanders, J.E. GA 38th Inf. Co.H
Sanders, J.E. MS 41st Inf. Co.F
Sanders, J.E. SC 1st Bn.S.S. Co.B
Sanders, J.E. TN 5th Inf. 2nd Co.E
Sanders, Jeff GA Phillips' Legion Co.E,N
Sanders, Jeff. MS 6th Inf. Co.C
Sanders, Jefferson TX 24th Cav. Co.H Far.
Sanders, Jeremiah GA 4th Inf. Co.C Capt.
Sanders, Jeremiah GA 44th Inf. Co.F
Sanders, Jeremiah C. SC 1st (Butler's) Inf. Co.H
Sanders, Jerry AL 3rd Bn.Res. Co.H
Sanders, Jerry GA 43rd Inf. Co.G
Sanders, Jesse AR 33rd Inf. Co.H
Sanders, Jesse MS 8th Cav. Co.G
Sanders, Jesse TN Arty. Fisher's Co. Cpl.
Sanders, Jesse A. GA 30th Inf. Co.D
Sanders, Jesse A. NC 34th Inf. Co.K 1st Lt.
Sanders, Jessee MS Inf. 3rd Bn. (St.Troops)
 Co.F
Sanders, Jesse H. NC Cav. 7th Bn. Co.C
Sanders, Jesse M. SC 2nd Arty. Co.G

Sanders, Jesse M. SC 1st (Hagood's) Inf. 1st
 Co.G
Sanders, Jesse R. MS 20th Inf. Co.I Cpl.
Sanders, Jesse T. GA 30th Inf. Co.E
Sanders, Jessy MS 30th Inf. Co.I
Sanders, J.F. GA 4th Cav. McDonald's Co.
Sanders, J.F. MS 6th Inf. Co.D
Sanders, J.F. MS 46th Inf. Co.C
Sanders, J.F. MO Cav. Williams' Regt. Co.C
 Cpl.
Sanders, J.F. SC 1st (Hagood's) Inf. 1st Co.I
 Cpl.
Sanders, J.F. TX Cav. Terry's Regt. Co.K
Sanders, J.F. TX 1st Inf. 2nd Co.K
Sanders, J.F. TX 4th Inf. (St.Troops) Co.D
Sanders, J.G. AL 6th Cav. Co.E
Sanders, J.G. AL Inf. 2nd Regt. Co.B
Sanders, J.G. FL 1st Inf. New Co.D
Sanders, J.G. GA 5th Res. Co.B Sgt.
Sanders, J.G. TX Cav. 6th Bn. Co.B
Sanders, J.G. VA 8th Cav. Co.A
Sanders, J.H. AL 19th Inf. Co.D
Sanders, J.H. AL 31st Inf. Co.C
Sanders, J.H. AL 40th Inf. Co.G
Sanders, J.H. AL 47th Inf. Co.I
Sanders, J.H. AR Cav. 1st Bn. (Stirman's) Co.D
Sanders, J.H. AR 8th Cav. Co.A
Sanders, J.H. GA 2nd Inf. Co.G Music.
Sanders, J.H. GA 4th Res. Co.A
Sanders, J.H. MS 2nd Cav. Co.F
Sanders, J.H. MS 33rd Inf. Co.A 2nd Lt.
Sanders, J.H. SC 1st Mtd.Mil. Anderson's Co.
Sanders, J.H. SC 2nd Arty. Co.G
Sanders, J.H. SC Lt.Arty. 3rd (Palmetto) Bn.
 Co.D
Sanders, J.H. SC Lt.Arty. Gaillard's Co. (Santee
 Lt.Arty.)
Sanders, J.H. TN 12th (Cons.) Inf. Co.F
Sanders, J.H. TX Cav. Baird's Regt. Co.D
Sanders, J.H. Conf.Cav. Wood's Regt. 1st Co.A
Sanders, J.J. AL 53rd (Part.Rangers) Co.D
Sanders, J.J. AL 15th Inf. Co.E
Sanders, J.J. AR 1st (Dobbin's) Cav. Co.A
Sanders, J.J. GA 3rd Inf. Co.I
Sanders, J.J. GA 38th Inf. Co.H
Sanders, J.J. MS Inf. 3rd Bn. Co.D
Sanders, J.J. NC 6th Sr.Res. Co.K
Sanders, J.J. SC 2nd Arty. Co.G
Sanders, J.J. TN 49th Inf. Co.D 2nd Lt.
Sanders, J.J. Inf. Bailey's Cons.Regt. Co.L Cpl.
Sanders, J.J. 9th Conf.Inf. Co.E
Sanders, J.J.T. AL 23rd Inf. Co.H
Sanders, J.K. TX 13th Cav. Co.B
Sanders, J.L. MS 8th Cav. Co.C
Sanders, J.L. MS Graves' Co. (Copiah Horse
 Guards)
Sanders, J.L. MS 34th Inf. Co.D
Sanders, J.L. NC 39th Inf. Co.B
Sanders, J.L. TN 14th (Neely's) Cav. Co.F
Sanders, J.L. TN Inf. 4th Cons.Regt. Co.F
Sanders, J.L. TN 45th Inf. Co.I
Sanders, J.M. AL 3rd Res. Co.A
Sanders, J.M. AL 3rd Res. Co.F
Sanders, J.M. AL 20th Inf.
Sanders, J.M. AL 21st Inf. Co.H Sgt.
Sanders, J.M. AL 45th Inf. Co.K
Sanders, J.M. AL St.Res. Co.I

Sanders, J.M. AR 11th Inf. Co.C Capt.
Sanders, J.M. GA Arty. (Macon Lt.Arty.)
 Slaten's Co.
Sanders, J.M. GA 1st Troops & Def. (Macon)
 Co.C
Sanders, J.M. GA 4th Res. Co.E Sgt.
Sanders, J.M. GA 5th Res. Co.I
Sanders, J.M. GA 16th Inf. Co.C
Sanders, J.M. LA 4th Cav. Co.A
Sanders, J.M. MS 20th Inf. Co.H
Sanders, J.M. SC 3rd Cav. Co.A
Sanders, J.M., Jr. SC 1st Bn.S.S. Co.B
Sanders, J.M., Sr. SC 1st Bn.S.S. Co.B
Sanders, J.M. SC 2nd Inf. Co.F
Sanders, J.M., Jr. SC 22nd Inf. Co.D
Sanders, J.M. TN 12th (Cons.) Inf. Co.K
Sanders, J.M. TN 41st Inf. Co.C
Sanders, J.M. TX 11th Cav. Co.K
Sanders, J.M. TX 28th Cav. Co.B
Sanders, J.M. TX Granbury's Cons.Brig. Co.E
Sanders, J.M. TX 9th (Nichols') Inf. Co.I
Sanders, J.N. AL 1st Inf. Co.A
Sanders, J.N. GA 25th Inf. Co.C
Sanders, J.N. GA 32nd Inf. Co.F
Sanders, J.N. MS Cav. Jeff Davis Legion Co.H
 Sgt.
Sanders, J.N. SC 21st Inf. Co.B
Sanders, J.N. TN 12th Inf. Co.H
Sanders, J.N. 2nd Conf.Eng.Troops Co.D Cpl.
Sanders, J.N.B. GA 3rd Cav. Co.I
Sanders, J.O. MS 1st Bn.S.S. Asst.Surg.
Sanders, J.O. SC 1st St.Troops Co.E Cpl.
Sanders, J.O. SC Bn.St.Cadets Co.B
Sanders, Jo. A. TX 17th Cav. Co.E
Sanders, Joel FL 5th Inf. Co.F
Sanders, J. O'Hear SC Cav. Walpole's Co. Cpl.
Sanders, John AL 1st Cav. 2nd Co.B
Sanders, John AL 2nd Cav. Co.C
Sanders, John AL 15th Bn.Part.Rangers Co.E
Sanders, John AL Inf. 1st Regt. Co.E
Sanders, John AL 19th Inf. Co.I
Sanders, John AL 26th (O'Neal's) Inf. Co.D
Sanders, John AL 41st Inf. Co.D
Sanders, John AL 41st Inf. Co.G
Sanders, John AL 48th Inf. Co.D
Sanders, John AL 95th Mil. Co.D
Sanders, John AL 3rd Bn. Hilliard's Legion Vol.
 Co.A
Sanders, John AZ Cav. Herbert's Bn. Helm's
 Co.
Sanders, John GA 12th Cav. Co.C
Sanders, John GA 12th Cav. Co.I
Sanders, John GA 1st (Ramsey's) Inf. Co.F
Sanders, John GA 3rd Inf.
Sanders, John GA Inf. 9th Bn. Co.A
Sanders, John GA 14th Inf. Co.B
Sanders, John GA 48th Inf. Co.I
Sanders, John LA 1st (Nelligan's) Inf. Co.A
Sanders, John LA 15th Inf. Co.D
Sanders, John LA 17th Inf. Co.D
Sanders, John LA 26th Inf. Co.K Cpl.
Sanders, John MD 1st Inf. Co.G
Sanders, John MS 10th Cav. Co.K
Sanders, John MS Cav. 24th Bn. Co.C
Sanders, John MS Inf. 1st St.Troops Co.F
Sanders, John MS 21st Inf. Co.E
Sanders, John MS 25th Inf. Co.E

Sanders, John MS 36th Inf. Co.A
Sanders, John MO 4th Cav. Co.E
Sanders, John MO 4th Inf. Co.C
Sanders, John NC Cav. 15th Bn. Co.A
Sanders, John NC 6th Inf. Co.C
Sanders, John NC 22nd Inf. Co.G
Sanders, John NC 43rd Inf. Co.I
Sanders, John NC 45th Inf. Co.G
Sanders, John NC 53rd Inf. Co.C
Sanders, John NC Inf. Thomas Legion 2nd Co.A
Sanders, John SC 3rd Bn.Res. Co.A Capt.
Sanders, John SC 5th St.Troops Co.M 1st Lt.
Sanders, John SC 7th Res. Co.K Bvt.2nd Lt.
Sanders, John SC Inf. 7th Bn. (Enfield Rifles) Co.E
Sanders, John SC 8th Bn.Res. Co.C
Sanders, John SC 12th Inf. Co.D
Sanders, John SC 13th Inf. Co.I
Sanders, John SC 18th Inf. Co.C 2nd Lt.
Sanders, John SC 20th Inf. Co.I
Sanders, John SC 24th Inf. Co.H
Sanders, John TN 14th (Neely's) Cav. Co.D
Sanders, John TN 22nd (Barteau's) Cav. Co.F
Sanders, John TN 15th Inf. Co.D 1st Sgt.
Sanders, John TN 34th Inf. Co.A
Sanders, John TN 38th Inf. Co.G
Sanders, John TN 38th Inf. Co.I
Sanders, John TN 41st Inf. Co.D
Sanders, John TN 45th Inf. Co.I
Sanders, John TN 60th Mtd.Inf. Co.F
Sanders, John TX 7th Cav. Co.G
Sanders, John TX 13th Cav. Co.I
Sanders, John TX 15th Cav. Co.F
Sanders, John TX 32nd Cav. Co.C,H Sgt.
Sanders, John TX Cav. Border's Regt. Co.G
Sanders, John TX Cav. Terry's Regt. Co.H
Sanders, John TX 9th (Nichols') Inf. Co.I
Sanders, John TX 20th Inf. Co.K Sgt.
Sanders, John VA Cav. 34th Bn. Co.F
Sanders, John VA Lt.Arty. Huckstep's Co.
Sanders, John VA Inf. 1st Bn. Co.C
Sanders, John VA 9th Inf. Co.B
Sanders, John VA 41st Mil. Co.E
Sanders, John VA 51st Inf. Co.C
Sanders, John Mead's Conf.Cav. Co.I
Sanders, John 1st Cherokee Mtd.Rifles Co.C
Sanders, John 2nd Cherokee Mtd.Vol. Co.I
Sanders, John A. AL 3rd Bn. Hilliard's Legion Vol. Co.B
Sanders, John A. MS 2nd Inf. Co.C,H
Sanders, John A. TN Cav. 2nd Bn. (Biffle's) Co.D
Sanders, John A. TN 48th (Nixon's) Inf. Co.E
Sanders, John A.T. NC Cav. 7th Bn. Co.C
Sanders, Johnathan AL 3rd Bn.Res. Co.A
Sanders, John B. AR 10th Inf. Co.D Sgt.
Sanders, John B. MS 7th Inf. Co.A
Sanders, John B. MS 13th Inf. Co.I
Sanders, John C. NC 26th Inf. Co.K
Sanders, John C. SC 17th Inf. Co.C 2nd Lt.
Sanders, John C. TN Cav. 7th Bn. (Bennett's) Co.E
Sanders, John C. TN 22nd (Barteau's) Cav. Co.G
Sanders, John C. VA 51st Inf. Co.B
Sanders, John C.C. AL 11th Inf. Co.C Capt.
Sanders, John C.C. Gen. & Staff Brig.Gen.

Sanders, John D. AL 11th Inf. Co.H
Sanders, John D. FL Milton Lt.Arty. Dunham's Co.
Sanders, John D. GA 14th Inf. Co.B
Sanders, John D. GA 16th Inf. Co.H
Sanders, John D. TX 13th Vol. 3rd Co.K
Sanders, John E. VA Inf. 25th Bn. Co.B
Sanders, John F. TX 22nd Cav. Co.B Cpl.
Sanders, John F. VA 14th Cav. Crawford's Co.
Sanders, John F. VA Lt.Arty. Fry's Co. Cpl.
Sanders, John G. FL 7th Inf. Co.I
Sanders, John G. 1st Cherokee Mtd.Rifles Co.C
Sanders, John H. AL 17th Inf. Co.I
Sanders, John H. LA 19th Inf. Co.B
Sanders, John H. LA 22nd Inf. Co.B
Sanders, John H. TN 1st (Turney's) Inf. Co.D
Sanders, John H. TN 60th Mtd.Inf. Co.F
Sanders, John H. VA Cav. 34th Bn. Co.F
Sanders, John H. VA Cav. Mosby's Regt. (Part.Rangers) Co.A
Sanders, John Henry Durant NC 14th Inf. Co.C
Sanders, John J. GA 14th Inf. Co.B
Sanders, John J. GA 23rd Inf. Co.H
Sanders, John K. LA 16th Inf. Co.I
Sanders, John L. AR 18th (Marmaduke's) Inf. Co.I 1st Sgt.
Sanders, John L. AR 32nd Inf. Co.F 1st Sgt.
Sanders, John L. GA 2nd Cav. Co.K
Sanders, John L. GA Arty. 9th Bn. Co.A,E,B
Sanders, John L. MS Cav. 24th Bn. Co.C
Sanders, John L. MS 20th Inf. Co.E
Sanders, John L. MO 8th Cav. Co.H
Sanders, John Lawson MS Arty. (Seven Stars Arty.) Roberts' Co.
Sanders, John M. AL 41st Inf. Co.I
Sanders, John M. AR 8th Inf. New Co.D
Sanders, John M. GA 6th Inf. Co.E
Sanders, John M. SC 22nd Inf. Co.D
Sanders, John M. TN 1st (Turney's) Inf. Co.K Cpl.
Sanders, John N. SC Inf. 9th Bn. Co.B Cpl.
Sanders, John N. SC 26th Inf. Co.B Cpl.
Sanders, John P. AR 3rd Inf. Co.L,A
Sanders, John P. LA 14th Inf. Co.B
Sanders, John P. TN 23rd Inf. Co.E
Sanders, John P. TN
Sanders, John R. AL 27th Inf. Co.H
Sanders, John R. AL 37th Inf. Co.K 2nd Lt.
Sanders, John R. AL 57th Inf. Co.F
Sanders, John R. GA Cav. Pemberton's Co. 1st Sgt.
Sanders, John R. GA 44th Inf. Co.H
Sanders, John R. GA 57th Inf. Co.F
Sanders, John R. KY 4th Cav. Co.A Bvt.2nd Lt.
Sanders, John R. TN 6th (Wheeler's) Cav. Co.B
Sanders, John R. TN 7th Inf. Co.F
Sanders, John R. TN 44th Inf. Co.B
Sanders, John R. TN 44th (Cons.) Inf. Co.K
Sanders, John R. TX 34th Cav. Co.E
Sanders, John S. AL 7th Inf. Co.E,G
Sanders, John S. AL 17th Bn.S.S. Co.B Sgt.
Sanders, John S. GA 24th Inf. Co.D Sgt.
Sanders, John S. MO Burress' Cav. Co.K
Sanders, John S. NC 2nd Inf. Co.G
Sanders, Johnson B. TX Cav. 3rd (Yager's) Bn. Co.A
Sanders, John Steward MS 34th Inf. Co.A

Sanders, John T. AL 8th Cav. Co.B
Sanders, John T. AL 32nd Inf. Co.H
Sanders, John T. AL 33rd Inf. Co.H
Sanders, John T. GA 46th Inf. Co.I
Sanders, John T. MS 13th Inf. Co.C
Sanders, John T. MS 41st Inf. Co.E
Sanders, John T. TX 17th Cav. Co.A
Sanders, John Turner Brig.Band B.R. Johnson's Brig.,CSA Music.
Sanders, John V. GA 11th Inf. Co.A Sgt.
Sanders, John W. AL 11th Inf. Co.H Sgt.
Sanders, John W. AL 20th Inf. Co.A
Sanders, John W. AL 40th Inf. Co.B Sgt.
Sanders, John W. AR 3rd Inf. Co.B
Sanders, John W. GA Arty. 11th Bn. (Sumter Arty.) New Co.C Cpl.
Sanders, John W. GA 2nd Inf. Co.A
Sanders, John W. LA 12th Inf. Co.B
Sanders, John W. MS 15th Inf. Co.A
Sanders, John W. MS 26th Inf. Co.D
Sanders, John W. MS Conscr.
Sanders, John W. MO Searcy's Bn.S.S. Co.B Cpl.
Sanders, John W. NC 1st Arty. (10th St.Troops) Co.H 1st Lt.
Sanders, John W. SC 3rd Cav. Co.K
Sanders, John W. SC 7th Inf. 1st Co.D, 2nd Co.D, Co.G
Sanders, John W. TN 45th Inf. Co.I Sgt.
Sanders, John W. TX 4th Inf. Co.K
Sanders, John W. VA Cav. 15th Bn. Co.D
Sanders, John W. VA 55th Inf. Co.L Cpl.
Sanders, John W. VA 92nd Mil. Co.A Cpl.
Sanders, John Wesley TX 20th Cav. Co.F
Sanders, John W.S. VA 1st Cav. 2nd Co.D
Sanders, Jonathan AL 2nd Bn. Hilliard's Legion Vol. Co.F
Sanders, Jonathan VA 48th Inf. Co.H
Sanders, Jones M. SC 2nd Arty. Co.G
Sanders, Jones M. SC 1st (Hagood's) Inf. 1st Co.G
Sanders, Joseph AL Lt.Arty. Kolb's Btty.
Sanders, Joseph AL 42nd Inf. Co.C
Sanders, Joseph AL 47th Inf. Co.E
Sanders, Joseph AL 3rd Bn. Hilliard's Legion Vol. Co.A
Sanders, Joseph AR 1st Vol. Co.G
Sanders, Joseph AR 4th Inf. Co.F
Sanders, Joseph AR 38th Inf. Co.D
Sanders, Joseph GA 8th Cav. Co.H
Sanders, Joseph GA 12th Cav. Co.L
Sanders, Joseph GA 62nd Cav. Co.H
Sanders, Joseph GA 48th Inf. Co.I
Sanders, Joseph GA Floyd Legion (St.Guards) Co.B
Sanders, Joseph LA 2nd Cav. Co.E
Sanders, Joseph LA 28th (Thomas') Inf. Co.I
Sanders, Joseph MD 1st Inf. Co.I
Sanders, Joseph MS 14th Inf. Co.F
Sanders, Joseph MO 4th Cav. Co.C
Sanders, Joseph MO Cav. Preston's Bn. Co.C
Sanders, Joseph SC 3rd Cav. Co.D
Sanders, Joseph SC 2nd St.Troops Co.I
Sanders, Joseph TN 9th (Ward's) Cav. Co.G
Sanders, Joseph TN 16th (Logwood's) Cav. Co.B
Sanders, Joseph TN 5th Inf. 2nd Co.H
Sanders, Joseph TX 32nd Cav. Co.H

Sanders, Joseph VA 23rd Cav. Co.M
Sanders, Joseph VA Lt.Arty. Brander's Co.
Sanders, Joseph Mead's Conf.Cav. Co.I
Sanders, Joseph 1st Cherokee Mtd.Rifles Co.I
Sanders, Joseph A. LA 15th Inf. Co.K 2nd Lt.
Sanders, Joseph B. MS 37th Inf. Co.H Sgt.
Sanders, Joseph D. MS 24th Inf. Co.I,H
Sanders, Joseph F. TN 41st Inf. Co.F
Sanders, Joseph F. VA Cav. 15th Bn. Co.D
Sanders, Joseph F. VA 41st Mil. Co.E
Sanders, Joseph G. GA 31st Inf. Co.C Capt.
Sanders, Joseph G. VA 9th Inf. Co.E
Sanders, Joseph H. GA Inf. Cobb Guards Co.A
Sanders, Joseph H. KY 5th Cav. Co.A
Sanders, Joseph H. LA Inf. 7th Bn. Co.C 2nd Lt.
Sanders, Joseph H. MS 41st Inf. Co.E
Sanders, Joseph L. TN Lt.Arty. Morton's Co.
Sanders, Joseph M. GA 44th Inf. Co.F
Sanders, Joseph S. VA 9th Cav. Co.D
Sanders, Joseph S. VA Cav. 15th Bn. Co.D
Sanders, Joseph W. SC 11th Inf. Bellinger's Co., 2nd Co.I Sgt.
Sanders, Joshua 2nd Cherokee Mtd.Vol. Co.B
Sanders, Josiah MS Cav. Yerger's Regt. Co.C
Sanders, Josiah SC 5th Res. Co.K
Sanders, Josiah TN 3rd (Forrest's) Cav. Co.G
Sanders, J.P. AL 40th Inf. Co.H
Sanders, J.P. AR 7th Inf. Co.D 1st Sgt.
Sanders, J.P. GA 13th Inf. Co.B
Sanders, J.P. MS 5th Inf. Co.K
Sanders, J.P. SC 1st (Hagood's) Inf. 1st Co.G
Sanders, J.P. TN 1st (Carter's) Cav. Co.E Cpl.
Sanders, J.P. TN Cav. 12th Bn. (Day's) Co.C
Sanders, J.P. TN 20th Inf. Co.E
Sanders, J.P. TX Cav. Hardeman's Regt. Co.C
Sanders, J.P. VA 166th Mil. Taylor's Co.
Sanders, J.R. AL Cav. Moreland's Regt. Co.F
Sanders, J.R. AL 23rd Inf. Co.A Sgt.
Sanders, J.R. AR 5th Inf. Co.I Sgt.
Sanders, J.R. GA 2nd Inf. Co.G Sgt.
Sanders, J.R. GA 9th Inf. (St.Guards) Co.C
Sanders, J.R. MS 28th Cav. Co.H,I 1st Lt.
Sanders, J.R. MO 1st & 4th Cons.Inf. Co.C
Sanders, J.R. SC 6th Cav. Co.C
Sanders, J.R. SC 2nd Arty. Co.F,C
Sanders, J.R. SC 2nd St.Troops Co.E
Sanders, J.R. TN Arty. Marshall's Co.
Sanders, J.R. TN 35th Inf. 2nd Co.A Cpl.
Sanders, J.R. TX 17th Inf. Co.I
Sanders, J.R. 2nd Conf.Eng.Troops Co.D Artif.
Sanders, J.S. AL 7th Cav. Co.C,G
Sanders, J.S. AR Inf. Cocke's Regt. Co.F
Sanders, J.S. GA 13th Inf. Co.K
Sanders, J.S. NC 60th Inf. Co.B
Sanders, J.S. TN 61st Mtd.Inf. Co.H 2nd Lt.
Sanders, J.S. VA 4th Res. Co.E,G Sgt.
Sanders, J.T. AL 15th Bn.Part.Rangers Co.C
Sanders, J.T. AL 56th Part.Rangers Co.C
Sanders, J.T. MS 9th Inf. Co.K
Sanders, J.T. MS 37th Inf. Co.B
Sanders, J.T. MS 41st Inf. Co.F
Sanders, J.T. SC 25th Inf. Co.E Sgt.
Sanders, J.T. TN 17th Inf. Co.E
Sanders, J.T. TX Inf. 1st St.Troops Wheat's Co.A
Sanders, Julius Caesar GA 45th Inf. Co.F

Sanders, J.V. MS 3rd (St.Troops) Cav. Co.B
Sanders, J.W. AL Cav. Moreland's Regt. Co.C
Sanders, J.W. AL 1st Inf. 3rd Co.G
Sanders, J.W. AL 19th Inf. Co.H,E Sgt.
Sanders, J.W. AR 2nd (Cons.) Inf. Co.I
Sanders, J.W. AR 36th Inf. Co.C Sgt.
Sanders, J.W. AR 50th Mil. Co.A Sgt.
Sanders, J.W. FL Sp.Cav. 1st Bn. Co.B
Sanders, J.W. FL Cav. 5th Bn. Co.H
Sanders, J.W. FL 7th Inf. Co.B Sgt.
Sanders, J.W. GA 2nd Inf. Co.H
Sanders, J.W. MS 10th Cav. Co.B
Sanders, J.W. MS Inf. 2nd Bn. (St.Troops) Co.B
Sanders, J.W. MS 6th Inf. Co.C
Sanders, J.W. MS 15th Inf. Co.K Music.
Sanders, J.W. MS 27th Inf. Co.A
Sanders, J.W. MS 35th Inf. Co.K
Sanders, J.W. MS 41st Inf. Co.F
Sanders, J.W. MS Rogers' Co.
Sanders, J.W. MO 1st & 4th Cons.Inf. Co.E
Sanders, J.W. NC 61st Inf. Co.D
Sanders, J.W. SC 2nd Arty. Co.B Sgt.
Sanders, J.W. SC 1st St.Troops Co.E
Sanders, J.W. SC 5th Inf. 1st Co.C, 2nd Co.K
Sanders, J.W. TN 1st (Feild's) Inf. Co.A
Sanders, J.W. TN 9th Inf. Co.D
Sanders, J.W. TN 12th Inf. Co.B 1st Lt.
Sanders, J.W. TN 12th (Cons.) Inf. Co.A 1st Lt.
Sanders, J.W. TX 9th (Nichols') Inf. Co.H Sgt.
Sanders, J. Welssley AR Inf. 8th Bn. Co.A
Sanders, J.W.S. VA Cav. Mosby's Regt. (Part.Rangers)
Sanders, Kelly AL Pris.Guard Freeman's Co.
Sanders, K.H. AR Cav. McGehee's Regt. Co.G
Sanders, K.H. AR Lt.Arty. Zimmerman's Btty.
Sanders, King TN 33rd Inf. Co.K
Sanders, L. AL 1st Cav. 1st Co.K
Sanders, L. AL Cav. Forrest's Regt.
Sanders, L. AL Talladega Cty.Res. T.M. McClintock's Co.
Sanders, L. MS 12th Inf. Co.I
Sanders, L. TN 18th (Newsom's) Cav. Co.F
Sanders, L. TX Cav. Bone's Co.
Sanders, L. TX Inf. Timmons' Regt. Co.E
Sanders, L.A. MS 12th Cav. Co.D
Sanders, L.A. SC 1st Bn.S.S. Co.B
Sanders, Lafayette AR 8th Inf. New Co.F
Sanders, Lafayette AR 14th (McCarver's) Inf. Co.E
Sanders, Larkin TN 16th (Logwood's) Cav. Co.H
Sanders, Larkin F. KY Rebel A. Gallatin Cty. 2nd Lt.
Sanders, Lawrence SC 11th Inf. Bellinger's 2nd Co.I
Sanders, Lawrence W. AL Cav. Roddey's Escort
Sanders, L.B. AL Auburn Home Guards Vol. Darby's Co.
Sanders, L.B. AR 2nd Cav. Co.F 1st Lt.
Sanders, L.B. GA 5th Res. Co.E
Sanders, L.D. MS Cav. 4th Bn. Co.A
Sanders, L.D. MS Inf. 2nd St.Troops Co.K
Sanders, L.D.S. NC 15th Inf. Co.C
Sanders, Leander J. NC 64th Inf. Co.D
Sanders, Lee TX 7th Inf. Co.D
Sanders, Lemuel VA 41st Mil. Co.D
Sanders, Lemuel A. MS 1st (Patton's) Inf. Co.C

Sanders, Lemuel D. TX 21st Cav. Co.G Sgt.
Sanders, Lemuel S. NC 39th Inf. Co.G
Sanders, Levi L. TX 6th Cav. Co.I Sgt.
Sanders, Levis AR 8th Inf. Co.I
Sanders, Lewis GA Inf. 9th Bn. Co.A
Sanders, Lewis KY 2nd (Woodward's) Cav. Co.E
Sanders, Lewis KY Lt.Arty. Cobb's Co.
Sanders, Lewis KY 2nd Bn.Mtd.Rifles Co.C
Sanders, Lewis MS 28th Cav. Co.K
Sanders, Lewis TN 3rd (Forrest's) Cav. Co.A
Sanders, Lewis TN 44th Inf. Co.B
Sanders, Lewis TN 44th (Cons.) Inf. Co.K
Sanders, Lewis TX 22nd Inf. Co.D
Sanders, Lewis G. MS Part.Rangers Smyth's Co.
Sanders, Lewis H. NC Hvy.Arty. 1st Bn. Co.B
Sanders, Lewis M. KY 5th Mtd.Inf. Co.B,C
Sanders, Lewis N. AL 41st Inf. Co.K
Sanders, Lewis R. LA Inf.Crescent Regt. Co.F
Sanders, Lewis W. VA 166th Mil. Co.B Capt.
Sanders, L.H. SC 22nd Inf. Co.D
Sanders, Lindsay TN 33rd Inf. Co.H
Sanders, L.J. KY 10th (Johnson's) Cav. Co.D
Sanders, L.J. TN Inf. 4th Cons.Regt. Co.I
Sanders, L.K. Gen. & Staff Asst.Surg.
Sanders, L.M. GA 37th Inf. Co.G
Sanders, L.M. MS 40th Inf. Co.H
Sanders, L.N. TN 20th Inf. Co.E
Sanders, L.N. Gen. & Staff A.Surg.
Sanders, Lovel MS 1st Inf. Co.D
Sanders, Loyd P. TX Cav. 8th (Taylor's) Bn. Co.E
Sanders, Loyed P. TX 1st (Yager's) Cav. Co.H
Sanders, L.P. TX 1st (McCulloch's) Cav. Co.C
Sanders, L.S. GA 11th Cav. Co.C
Sanders, L.T. AR 16th Inf. Co.G Sgt.
Sanders, L.T. AR 32nd Inf. Co.B Cpl.
Sanders, Luke S. AL 22nd Inf. Co.D
Sanders, L.V. VA 23rd Cav. Co.H Sgt.
Sanders, L.W. MS 18th Inf. Co.C Cpl.
Sanders, L.W. SC Bn.St.Cadets Co.B,A
Sanders, M. LA 2nd Cav. Co.F
Sanders, M. LA Pointe Coupee Arty.
Sanders, M. LA Inf. 1st Bn. (St.Guards) Co.B
Sanders, M. MS 2nd St.Cav. Co.H
Sanders, M. MS Inf. 1st Bn.St.Troops (12 mo. '62-3) Co.B Sgt.
Sanders, M. MS Inf. 1st Bn.St.Troops (30 days '64) Co.G Sgt.
Sanders, M. MO Cav. Slayback's Regt. Co.B
Sanders, M. TN 21st & 22nd (Cons.) Cav. Co.K Sgt.
Sanders, M.A. AL Mil. 3rd Vol. Co.A
Sanders, Madell TN 9th (Ward's) Cav. Co.C
Sanders, Madison TX 25th Cav. Co.D,C
Sanders, Madison J. AR 23rd Inf. Co.H
Sanders, Major H. AR 38th Inf. Co.D 2nd Lt.
Sanders, Malichi M. GA 14th Inf. Co.B
Sanders, Malichi M., Sr. GA 14th Inf. Co.B
Sanders, Manuel W. TX 15th Cav. Co.H
Sanders, Marcus TN 21st & 22nd (Cons.) Cav. Sgt.
Sanders, Marion GA 8th Inf. Co.G
Sanders, Mark TN Cav. 1st Bn. (McNairy's) Co.C
Sanders, Mark TN 22nd (Barteau's) Cav. Co.B
Sanders, Mark L. SC 12th Inf. Co.B

Sanders, Marshall R. MS 44th Inf. Co.D
Sanders, Marshall R. MS 9th Inf. Co.K
Sanders, Marshall R. Conf.Cav. Wood's Regt. 2nd Co.G
Sanders, Martin AL 37th Inf. Co.K Sgt.
Sanders, Martin GA 43rd Inf. Co.D
Sanders, Martin MS 1st Cav. Co.K
Sanders, Martin S. GA Inf. (St.Guards) Co.H
Sanders, Martin S. MS Inf. 3rd Bn. Co.F
Sanders, Mathew GA 34th Inf. Co.H
Sanders, Mathew Mead's Conf.Cav. Co.I
Sanders, Mathew S. GA 1st Reg. Co.H
Sanders, Mathy V. GA 4th Cav. (St.Guards) McDonald's Co.
Sanders, Matthew NC 62nd Inf. Co.D
Sanders, May SC 1st (Butler's) Inf. Co.E
Sanders, M.C. MS 22nd Inf. Co.E 2nd Lt.
Sanders, M.C. SC Inf. Hampton Legion Co.G 1st Sgt.
Sanders, M.J. Gen. & Staff, Ord. 1st Lt.
Sanders, McCager C. MS 33rd Inf. Co.A
Sanders, M.D. NC 56th Inf. Co.F
Sanders, M.D.L. AL 29th Inf. Co.G Cpl.
Sanders, M.D.L. 2nd Conf.Eng.Troops Co.C Sgt.
Sanders, M.E. MS 2nd Cav. Co.B Forage M.
Sanders, Meedy AR 30th Inf. Co.A
Sanders, M.F. AR 15th (Josey's) Inf. Co.C
Sanders, M.H. AR Inf. 4th Bn. Co.B Sgt.
Sanders, M.H. AR 7th Inf. Co.D
Sanders, M.H. AR 38th Inf. Co.D 2nd Lt.
Sanders, M.H. GA 24th Inf. Co.A
Sanders, M.H. GA 43rd Inf. Co.D
Sanders, M.H. GA 46th Inf. Co.D
Sanders, M.H. TX 8th Cav. Co.F
Sanders, Micager MS 40th Inf. Co.B
Sanders, Michael MS 15th Inf. Co.C
Sanders, Michael S. VA 4th Inf. Co.C,D
Sanders, Miles NC 62nd Inf. Co.D
Sanders, Milford MO 15th Cav. Co.A
Sanders, Milton AL Calhoun Cty.Res. A. Bryant's Co.
Sanders, Milton P. TN 1st (Turney's) Inf. Co.A
Sanders, Miniard M. GA 34th Inf. Co.E 3rd Lt.
Sanders, Miskel VA 40th Inf. Co.D
Sanders, Mitchell Mead's Conf.Cav. Co.I
Sanders, Mitchell 1st Cherokee Mtd.Rifles Co.G
Sanders, M.J. MS 18th Inf. Co.K
Sanders, M.L. GA 8th Inf. Co.A
Sanders, M.M. GA 1st Inf. Co.G
Sanders, M.M. TN 20th Inf. Co.E 1st Lt.
Sanders, M.N. SC 3rd Cav. Co.F
Sanders, Monroe AL 10th Inf. Co.D
Sanders, Monroe GA Inf. 9th Bn. Co.A
Sanders, Monroe MS 1st Cav. Co.D
Sanders, Morton GA Inf. (Mell Scouts) Wyly's Co.
Sanders, Moses AL 13th Bn.Part.Rangers Co.B
Sanders, Moses AL 56th Part.Rangers Co.F
Sanders, Moses AL 39th Inf. Co.G
Sanders, Moses KY 2nd Bn.Mtd.Rifles Co.C
Sanders, Moses LA 28th (Gray's) Inf. Co.I
Sanders, Moses MS Cav. 24th Bn. Co.C
Sanders, Moses SC Cav. 12th Bn. Co.C
Sanders, Moses SC 20th Inf. Co.H
Sanders, Moses Conf.Cav. Powers' Regt. Co.A

Sanders, Moses A. AL 1st Regt. Mobile Vol. Co.E
Sanders, Moses H.O. GA 34th Inf. Co.H
Sanders, Moses M. AR 1st (Colquitt's) Inf. Co.B 2nd Lt.
Sanders, Moses P. SC 4th Cav. Co.E
Sanders, Moses S. KY 5th Mtd.Inf. Co.B,C
Sanders, Moses W. GA Cherokee Legion (St.Guards) Co.D
Sanders, M.P. SC Inf. Hampton Legion Co.C
Sanders, M.R. MS 1st (Johnston's) Inf. Co.D
Sanders, M.R. MS 1st (Percy's) Inf. Co.D
Sanders, M.R. SC 2nd Cav. Co.A
Sanders, M.R. SC Arty. Melchers' Co. (Co.B,German Arty.)
Sanders, M.S. MS 41st Inf. Co.F
Sanders, M.V.B. SC 2nd Arty. Co.B
Sanders, M.W. TX Cav. 2nd Regt.St.Troops Co.C
Sanders, N. AL 13th Bn.Part.Rangers Co.B
Sanders, N. 1st Cherokee Mtd.Vol. Co.J
Sanders, Napoleon B. MS Inf. 1st St.Troops Co.F
Sanders, Nathan SC 4th St.Troops Co.F
Sanders, Nathaniel LA 6th Cav. Co.I 2nd Lt.
Sanders, Nathaniel LA 9th Inf. Co.D
Sanders, N.B. SC Cav. 19th Bn. Co.C
Sanders, N.B. TN 61st Mtd.Inf. Co.F
Sanders, Needham AL 19th Inf. Co.E
Sanders, Newton MO Cav. Wood's Regt. Co.I
Sanders, Newton TX 5th Inf. Co.B
Sanders, N.H. NC 39th Inf. Co.B
Sanders, N.I. GA 1st Res.
Sanders, Nicholas AL 19th Inf. Co.C
Sanders, Nicholas B. 1st Cherokee Mtd.Rifles Co.B Capt.
Sanders, N.J. AR 2nd Cav. Co.G
Sanders, N.J. GA 12th Cav. Co.B
Sanders, N.J. MS 38th Cav. Co.E
Sanders, N.M. KY 4th Cav. Co.K,C 1st Lt.
Sanders, N.M. MS 18th Inf. Co.C
Sanders, Noah B. VA 16th Cav. Co.B
Sanders, Noah C. NC 48th Inf. Co.F
Sanders, Noah H. VA 29th Inf. Co.G
Sanders, Noah R. NC 26th Inf. Co.E
Sanders, Norval MS 18th Inf. Co.C
Sanders, N.T. AL 56th Part.Rangers Co.F Cpl.
Sanders, O. SC 5th Bn.Res. Co.B
Sanders, Obadiah GA 1st (Fannin's) Res. Co.K
Sanders, Orren LA 9th Inf. Co.I
Sanders, Owen MS Nash's Co. (Leake Rangers)
Sanders, P. LA Mil. 4th Regt. French Brig. Co.6
Sanders, P. SC 5th Cav. Co.C
Sanders, P. TX 8th Field Btty. 2nd Lt.
Sanders, P. TX 11th (Spaight's) Bn.Vol. Co.A
Sanders, Paschal NC 43rd Inf. Co.H
Sanders, Patrick GA 2nd Inf. Co.E
Sanders, Patrick SC Inf. 7th Bn. (Enfield Rifles) Co.D
Sanders, P.B. AR 34th Inf. Co.H
Sanders, P.B. TX 17th Cav. Co.H
Sanders, P.B. TX 14th Inf. 1st Co.K
Sanders, P.D. TX Cav. 1st Bn.St.Troops Co.A Sgt.
Sanders, P.D. TX 12th Inf. Co.H
Sanders, Percival F. LA 31st Inf. Co.A
Sanders, Perry AL Inf. 1st Regt. Co.A

Sanders, Peter MO 4th Cav. Co.E Lt.
Sanders, Peter TX 13th Cav. Co.K
Sanders, Peter T. SC 1st (Orr's) Rifles Co.H
Sanders, P.H. AR 37th Inf. Co.D
Sanders, Philip NC Inf. 2nd Bn. Co.G
Sanders, P.K. TX 29th Cav. Co.C
Sanders, P.L. TN Lt.Arty. Huggins' Co.
Sanders, Pleasant J. TX 36th Cav. Co.E
Sanders, Plunk TN 29th Inf. Co.E
Sanders, Plutarch SC Cav. 17th Bn. Co.D
Sanders, P.M. GA 38th Inf. Co.H Cpl.
Sanders, Presley P. AL 3rd Res. Co.H
Sanders, P.W. NC 44th Inf. Co.H
Sanders, Q.C. TN 4th (Murray's) Cav. Co.H Capt.
Sanders, R. AL 4th Res. Co.H
Sanders, R. AL Talladega Cty.Res. J.T. Smith's Co. Cpl.
Sanders, R. GA 3rd Inf. Co.G
Sanders, R. NC 5th Sr.Res. Co.F
Sanders, R. TN 1st (Carter's) Cav. Co.E
Sanders, R. TX 5th Cav. Co.F
Sanders, R.A. MS 1st Cav.Res. Co.E Cpl.
Sanders, R.A. TN 45th Inf. Co.E
Sanders, R.A. Gillum's Regt. Co.F
Sanders, Randle NC Inf. 2nd Bn. Co.G
Sanders, Ransom NC 53rd Inf. Co.C
Sanders, R.B. AL 8th (Livingston's) Cav. Co.C
Sanders, R.B. GA 54th Inf. Co.F
Sanders, R.C. TN 28th (Cons.) Inf. AQM
Sanders, R.C. TN 84th Inf. Co.A
Sanders, R.C. TX 17th Cav. Co.F
Sanders, R.C. TX 17th Cons.Dismtd.Cav. Co.F
Sanders, Reid Hawes' Staff Maj.,Brig.Comsy.
Sanders, Reuben GA 10th Inf. Co.K Cpl.
Sanders, Reuben MS Inf. 3rd Bn. (St.Troops) Co.B
Sanders, Reuben A. GA 51st Inf. Co.G Cpl.
Sanders, Reuben E. TX 19th Cav. Co.E Capt.
Sanders, R.F. 8th (Wade's) Conf.Cav. Co.I Cpl.
Sanders, R.G. AL 37th Inf. Co.A
Sanders, R.G. MS 1st Cav. Co.I 2nd Lt.
Sanders, R.G. TN 12th Inf. Co.B
Sanders, R.G. TN 12th (Cons.) Inf. Co.A
Sanders, R.G. TX 3rd Cav. Co.F
Sanders, R.H. AR 4th St.Inf. Co.A Capt.
Sanders, R.H. MS Inf. 2nd Bn. (St.Troops) Co.C Capt.
Sanders, R.H. TN 38th Inf. 2nd Co.H Cpl.
Sanders, R.H. VA 1st Cav. Co.B
Sanders, Richard AL 4th Res. Co.I
Sanders, Richard GA 38th Inf. Co.H
Sanders, Richard GA Phillips' Legion Co.M
Sanders, Richard MO 3rd St.Guards
Sanders, Richard NC 13th Inf. Co.K
Sanders, Richard VA 21st Cav. 2nd Co.C
Sanders, Richard C. TN 25th Inf. Co.F Lt.Col.
Sanders, Richard E. TX 8th Inf. Co.K
Sanders, Richard H. TX 17th Cav. Co.G
Sanders, Richard J. MS 31st Inf. Co.C
Sanders, Richard J. MS 26th Inf. Co.E
Sanders, Richard M. TX 27th Cav. Co.E
Sanders, Richard S. MO Cav. Hancock Regt. Jackman's Co.
Sanders, Richard T. SC 2nd Arty. Co.G 1st Lt.
Sanders, Riley P. NC 22nd Inf. Co.F
Sanders, R.J. AL 40th Inf. Co.C

Sanders, R.J. MS 11th (Cons.) Cav. Co.E Cpl.
Sanders, R.J. MS 3rd Inf. (St.Troops) Co.C
Sanders, R.J. MS 5th Inf. (St.Troops) Co.I
Sanders, R.J. MO 12th Cav. Co.I Cpl.
Sanders, R.K. LA 3rd (Wingfield's) Cav. Co.A
Sanders, R.L. MS Cav. 4th Bn. Co.B
Sanders, R.L. 8th (Wade's) Conf.Cav. Co.D
Sanders, R.M. TX 9th (Nichols') Inf. Co.H
Sanders, Roberson C. NC 13th Inf. Co.K
Sanders, Robert AL 43rd Inf. Co.D
Sanders, Robert AL 44th Inf. Co.D
Sanders, Robert AR 1st (Crawford's) Cav. Co.H
Sanders, Robert AR Cav. Gordon's Regt. Co.A
Sanders, Robert LA 1st (Nelligan's) Inf. Co.G
Sanders, Robert MS 38th Cav. Co.G
Sanders, Robert MS 1st (Percy's) Inf. Co.I
Sanders, Robert MS 9th Inf. New Co.K
Sanders, Robert MS 34th Inf. Co.A
Sanders, Robert MO Cav. Slayback's Regt. Co.E
Cpl.
Sanders, Robert NC 22nd Inf. Co.G
Sanders, Robert SC Lt.Arty. Gaillard's Co.
(Santee Lt.Arty.)
Sanders, Robert TN 33rd Inf. Co.C
Sanders, Robert VA 22nd Cav. Co.G
Sanders, Robert VA 51st Inf. Co.B
Sanders, Robert 2nd Cherokee Mtd.Vol. Co.B
Sanders, Robert A. VA 57th Inf. Co.G
Sanders, Robert B. MS 30th Inf. Co.G
Sanders, Robert D. MS 11th Inf. Co.F
Sanders, Robert D. VA 9th Inf. Co.E
Sanders, Robert G. MS Cav. 1st Bn. (Miller's)
Cole's Co.
Sanders, Robert G. NC 21st Inf. Co.C
Sanders, Robert H. MO 2nd Bn.St.Guards Co.B
Capt.
Sanders, Robert H. VA Inf. 5th Bn. Co.C
Sanders, Robert J. MS St.Cav. 2nd Bn. (Harris')
Co.A
Sanders, Robert J. VA 1st Cav. 2nd Co.D
Sanders, Robert L. KY 4th Cav. Co.B Cpl.
Sanders, Robert M. MS 40th Inf. Co.A
Sanders, Robert N. KY 6th Mtd.Inf. Co.D
Sanders, Robert S. MS 34th Inf. Co.I,K
Sanders, Robert T. NC 3rd Inf. Co.K Sgt.
Sanders, Robert W. AL 8th Inf. Co.A Capt.
Sanders, Robert W. VA 51st Inf. Co.F Capt.
Sanders, Rolling J. AR 9th Inf. Co.G
Sanders, Romulous F. NC 23rd Inf. Co.C
Sanders, Romulus AR 2nd Mtd.Rifles Co.G
Sanders, R.P. MO 6th Cav. Co.D
Sanders, R.S. AR Cav. McGehee's Regt. Co.G
Sanders, R.S. MS 5th Cav. Co.H
Sanders, R.S. MS 1st (Johnston's) Inf. Co.E
Sanders, R.S. MO 11th Inf. Co.A
Sanders, R.T. AL 41st Inf. Co.D
Sanders, R.T. AR Cav. McGehee's Regt. Co.A
Sanders, R.T. GA 8th Cav. Co.D
Sanders, R.T. GA 62nd Cav. Co.G
Sanders, R.T. GA 32nd Inf. Co.E
Sanders, Rufus LA 1st Res. Co.D
Sanders, Rufus NC 47th Inf. Co.C Cpl.
Sanders, Rufus F. AL 7th Inf. Co.A
Sanders, Rufus R. NC 39th Inf. Co.K
Sanders, Rufus R. AL 26th Inf. Co.H
Sanders, R.W. LA 18th Inf. Co.D 1st Lt.
Sanders, R.W. MS 1st (Johnston's) Inf. Co.E

Sanders, R.W. NC 52nd Inf. Co.I
Sanders, R.W. SC 2nd Arty. Co.H
Sanders, R.W. SC Lt.Arty. M. Ward's Co.
(Waccamaw Lt.Arty.)
Sanders, R.W. SC 10th Inf. Co.E
Sanders, R.W. TX 33rd Cav. Co.B
Sanders, R.W. Taylor's Corps Maj.,AQM
Sanders, S. AL Lt.Arty. Tarrant's Btty.
Sanders, S. AL Inf. 1st Regt. Co.G
Sanders, S. GA Inf. (Milledgeville Guards)
Caraker's Co.
Sanders, S. KY Morgan's Men. Co.E
Sanders, S. LA Pointe Coupee Arty.
Sanders, S. SC 17th Inf. Co.C Cpl.
Sanders, S.A. SC 3rd Cav. Co.F
Sanders, S.A. SC 11th Inf. Co.C
Sanders, S.A. TX 13th Cav. Co.B
Sanders, S.A. Gen. & Staff Asst.Surg.
Sanders, Sames W. TN 32nd Inf.
Sanders, Samuel AL Cav. 8th Regt.
(Livingston's) Co.G Sgt.
Sanders, Samuel GA 28th Inf. Co.B
Sanders, Samuel TX 18th Inf. Co.F
Sanders, Samuel TX 22nd Inf. Co.A
Sanders, Samuel B. AL 13th Inf. Co.I
Sanders, Samuel B. AR Inf. Clayton's Co.
Sanders, Samuel D. SC 6th Inf. 1st Co.I
Sanders, Samuel D. SC 21st Inf. Co.D 1st Lt.
Sanders, Samuel E. KY 4th Mtd.Inf. Co.I
Sanders, Samuel Guy VA 4th Inf. Co.A 2nd Lt.
Sanders, Samuel H. GA 24th Inf. Co.A
Sanders, Samuel H. TN 33rd Inf. Co.D
Sanders, Samuel M. VA 40th Inf. Co.D Sgt.
Sanders, Samuel R. LA 28th (Gray's) Inf. Co.I
Sanders, Samuel T. NC 26th Inf. Co.K
Sanders, Samuel W. MS 20th Inf. Co.K 2nd Lt.
Sanders, Sar Ke Yah 1st Cherokee Mtd.Rifles
Co.H
Sanders, S.D. GA 11th Inf. Co.I
Sanders, S.D. SC 5th Inf. 2nd Co.I
Sanders, S.D. VA 1st Cav. 2nd Co.D, Co.B
Sanders, S.E. NC 3rd Bn.Sr.Res. Williams' Co.
Sanders, Seaborn GA 10th Inf. Co.G
Sanders, S.F. MS 8th Inf. Co.G
Sanders, S.F. TX 11th Inf. Co.F
Sanders, S.F. Gen. & Staff Asst.Surg.
Sanders, S.G. MO 3rd Cav. Co.C
Sanders, S.H. GA 16th Inf. Co.C Cpl.
Sanders, S.H. GA Phillips' Legion Co.D
Sanders, S.H. MS 6th Cav. Co.C
Sanders, S.H. MS 46th Inf. Co.C
Sanders, S.H. TN 9th Inf. Co.D
Sanders, S.H. TN 24th Inf. Co.C
Sanders, S.H. TN 40th Inf. Co.I
Sanders, S.H. TX Cav. 1st Bn.St.Troops Co.B
Sgt.
Sanders, S.H. TX 15th Cav. Co.B
Sanders, S.I. GA 54th Inf.
Sanders, Sidney GA Cav. 7th Bn. (St.Guards)
Co.E
Sanders, Sidney W. LA 3rd Inf. Co.B
Sanders, Silas D. MS 12th Cav. Co.A
Sanders, Silas J. GA 14th Inf. Co.B
Sanders, Simeon MS 22nd Inf. Co.A
Sanders, Simeon L. AR 1st (Colquitt's) Inf. Co.B
Cpl.
Sanders, Simon NC 48th Inf. Co.D

Sanders, Simon P. AL Cav. 4th Bn. (Love's)
Co.B
Sanders, Simpson AR 36th Inf. Co.H
Sanders, Simpson NC 4th Sr.Res. Co.E
Sanders, Simpson SC 5th St.Troops Co.G
Sanders, Simpson SC 13th Inf. Co.I
Sanders, S.J. GA Cav. 22nd Bn. (St.Guards)
Co.A
Sanders, S.J. SC 2nd Rifles Co.K
Sanders, S.L. MS Inf. 7th Bn. Co.F
Sanders, S.L. MS Clayton's Co. (Jasper Defend.)
Sanders, S.L. SC 2nd Arty. Co.G
Sanders, S.L. SC 1st (Hagood's) Inf. 1st Co.I
Sanders, S.L. TN 15th (Cons.) Cav. Co.A
Sanders, S.M. GA 1st Cav. Co.A
Sanders, S.M. SC 2nd Arty. Co.G Sgt.
Sanders, S.M. SC 1st (Hagood's) Inf. 1st Co.G
Sanders, Smith SC 6th Inf. 1st Co.H
Sanders, Smith SC 17th Inf. Co.F
Sanders, Smith VA 72nd Mil.
Sanders, S.N. AR 35th Inf. Co.H
Sanders, Solomon GA 22nd Inf. Co.C
Sanders, Solomon GA Phillips' Legion Co.L
Sanders, Solomon MS 39th Inf. Co.C Cpl.
Sanders, Solomon TN 34th Inf. Co.G
Sanders, S.P. AL Cav. Forrest's Regt.
Sanders, S.P. MO 12th Cav. Co.H
Sanders, S.P. TN 18th (Newsom's) Cav. Co.E
Bugler
Sanders, S.P. TN 19th & 20th (Cons.) Cav. Co.E
Sanders, S.T. AL 1st Cav. Co.A
Sanders, Stephen TN 23rd Inf. 2nd Co.F
Sanders, Stephen TX 29th Cav. Co.B
Sanders, Stephen VA 45th Inf. Co.D Cpl.
Sanders, Stephen A. SC 1st (McCreary's) Inf.
Co.C,H
Sanders, Stephen C. VA 4th Inf. Co.A
Sanders, Sterling MS 8th Cav. Co.C
Sanders, Stewart TX 6th Inf. Co.E
Sanders, S.W. GA 46th Inf. Co.F
Sanders, T. GA 5th Res. Co.D
Sanders, T. MS 10th Cav. Co.D
Sanders, T. MS Cav. Ham's Regt. Co.D
Sanders, T.A. KY 1st (Butler's) Cav. Co.C Sgt.
Sanders, T.A. KY 3rd Cav. Co.C
Sanders, T.A. Exch.Bn. 3rd Co.B,CSA
Sanders, T.B. LA 17th Inf. Co.H
Sanders, T.B. MS 6th Cav. Co.H
Sanders, T.B. MS 4th Inf. Co.I
Sanders, T.B. MS 29th Inf. Co.D
Sanders, T.B. MS 40th Inf. Co.B
Sanders, T.C. AL 38th Inf. Co.G
Sanders, T.C. SC 2nd St.Troops Co.H
Sanders, T.C. TN 8th (Smith's) Cav. Co.C
Sanders, T.C. TX Lt.Arty. Hughes' Co.
Sanders, T.D. NC 68th Inf.
Sanders, T.D. TN 47th Inf. Co.F
Sanders, T.D. TX Cav. Baird's Regt. Co.H
Capt.
Sanders, T.D. TX 1st Inf. Co.F
Sanders, T.D. 2nd Cherokee Mtd.Vol. Co.I
Sanders, T.F. TN 21st (Wilson's) Cav. Co.A
Sgt.
Sanders, T.H. GA 16th Inf. Co.C
Sanders, T.H. MS Cav. Powers' Regt. Co.A,C
Sanders, T.H. TN 33rd Inf. Co.C Sgt.
Sanders, T.H. Conf.Cav. Powers' Regt. Co.A

Sanders, Thadeus C. LA 31st Inf. Co.A Sgt.
Sanders, Theodore MO St.Guard QM
Sanders, Theodore Gen. & Staff Lt.Col.,AQM
Sanders, Theodore A. SC 2nd Cav. Co.A 2nd
   Lt.
Sanders, T. Hillen MD 1st Cav. Co.C Cpl.
Sanders, T. Hilton VA 1st Cav. Co.L
Sanders, Thomas AL 61st Inf. Co.A
Sanders, Thomas AR 24th Inf. Co.A
Sanders, Thomas AR 34th Inf. Co.H
Sanders, Thomas GA 1st (Olmstead's) Inf. Co.F
   2nd Lt.
Sanders, Thomas, Sr. GA Inf. 9th Bn. Co.A
Sanders, Thomas GA 26th Inf. Co.I
Sanders, Thomas GA 37th Inf. Co.D
Sanders, Thomas KY 2nd Bn.Mtd.Rifles Co.C
Sanders, Thomas LA 1st (Nelligan's) Inf. Co.A
Sanders, Thomas MS 12th Cav. Co.E
Sanders, Thomas MO Cav. Slayback's Regt.
   Co.B
Sanders, Thomas MO Inf. 3rd Bn. Co.A
Sanders, Thomas MO 6th Inf. Co.E
Sanders, Thomas NC 25th Inf. Co.E
Sanders, Thomas NC 39th Inf. Co.I
Sanders, Thomas SC 1st Cav. Co.D Cpl.
Sanders, Thomas SC Cav. 17th Bn. Co.A
Sanders, Thomas TN 4th Cav. Co.C
Sanders, Thomas VA Cav. 15th Bn. Co.C
Sanders, Thomas VA 49th Inf. Co.B
Sanders, Thomas 1st Cherokee Mtd.Vol. 2nd
   Co.E,I
Sanders, Thomas Gillum's Regt. Co.H
Sanders, Thomas A. Trans-MS Conf.Cav. 1st Bn.
Sanders, Thos. A. Gen. & Staff, Comsy.Dept.
Sanders, Thomas B. MS 1st (Johnston's) Inf.
   Co.D
Sanders, Thomas B. Conf.Cav. Wood's Regt. 2nd
   Co.G
Sanders, Thomas D. GA 2nd Cav. Co.K Sgt.
Sanders, Thomas D. TN 10th Inf. Co.K
Sanders, Thomas D. TN 12th (Cons.) Inf. Co.K
Sanders, Thomas D. TX 8th Cav. Co.A
Sanders, Thomas F. AL 1st Regt. Mobile Vol.
   Co.B
Sanders, Thomas F. MO 4th Cav. Co.E
Sanders, Thomas F. TN 44th Inf. Co.B
Sanders, Thomas G. TX 8th Cav. Co.C
Sanders, Thomas H. NC 6th Cav. (65th
   St.Troops) Co.G
Sanders, Thomas H. NC Cav. 7th Bn. Co.C
Sanders, Thomas H. TN 15th (Stewart's) Cav.
   Co.A Sgt.
Sanders, Thomas H. TX 17th Cav. Co.K
Sanders, Thomas J. AR 8th Inf. New Co.B
Sanders, Thomas J. GA 4th Bn.S.S. Co.C
Sanders, Thomas J. LA 9th Inf. Co.C
Sanders, Thomas J. MS 14th Inf. Co.F
Sanders, Thomas J. MS 14th Inf. Co.K
Sanders, Thomas J. MS 17th Inf. Co.H
Sanders, Thomas J. MS 27th Inf. Co.E Cpl.
Sanders, Thomas J. MS 41st Inf. Co.F
Sanders, Thomas J. TX 12th Cav. Co.F
Sanders, Thomas J. TX 23rd Cav. Co.K
Sanders, Thomas J. TX 9th (Nichols') Inf. Co.C
Sanders, Thomas L. MO Cav. Schnabel's Bn.
   Co.F 2nd Lt.
Sanders, Thomas L. NC 28th Inf. Co.B

Sanders, Thomas L. SC 3rd Cav. Co.H
Sanders, Thomas L. VA 56th Inf. Co.E
Sanders, Thomas M. TN 45th Inf. Co.E 1st Sgt.
Sanders, Thomas O. LA 28th (Gray's) Inf. Co.E
Sanders, Thomas P. MO 4th Cav. Co.E Cpl.
Sanders, Thomas P. SC Cav.Bn. Holcombe
   Legion Co.E
Sanders, Thomas R. AL Inf. 1st Regt. Co.B
Sanders, Thomas R. FL 8th Inf. Co.C
Sanders, Thomas R. SC 1st (Hagood's) Inf. 1st
   Co.H Sgt.
Sanders, Thomas S. AL 19th Inf. Co.A
Sanders, Thomas W. GA 11th Inf. Co.I
Sanders, Thomas W. TX 15th Cav. Co.A
Sanders, Thomas W. VA 6th Cav. Co.I
Sanders, Thomas W.H. VA 62nd Mtd.Inf. 2nd
   Co.G
Sanders, Thompson KY 10th Cav.
Sanders, Thornton GA Inf. 9th Bn. Co.A
Sanders, Thornton GA 37th Inf. Co.D
Sanders, Thornton VA 40th Inf. Co.D
Sanders, Tilman J. MO Lt.Arty. 1st Field Btty.
Sanders, Tilman J. MO 11th Inf. Co.B
Sanders, Timothy AR 1st Inf.
Sanders, T.J. GA Inf. 9th Bn. Co.A
Sanders, T.J. GA 25th Inf. Pritchard's Co. Sgt.
Sanders, T.J. MS 7th Cav. Co.E
Sanders, T.J. MS 38th Cav. Co.E
Sanders, T.J. MS 41st Inf. Co.B
Sanders, T.L. SC 3rd Cav. Co.H
Sanders, T.M. MS 5th Inf. Co.A
Sanders, T.M. MS 25th Inf. Co.B
Sanders, T.M. TN Inf. 4th Cons.Regt. Co.B
Sanders, T.N. GA 16th Inf. Co.H
Sanders, T.O. SC 8th Res.
Sanders, T.P. KY 1st (Butler's) Cav. Co.F
Sanders, T.P. MO St.Guard
Sanders, T.P. SC 7th Cav. Co.H Cpl.
Sanders, T.P. SC Inf. Hampton Legion Co.G
Sanders, T.S. MS 2nd Cav. Co.E
Sanders, T.W. FL 2nd Inf. Co.K
Sanders, T.W. TN 23rd Inf. 2nd Co.F
Sanders, T.W. TX 26th Cav. Co.H
Sanders, T.W. VA Loc.Def. Durrett's Co.
Sanders, Valerius P. TX 15th Cav. Co.A Maj.
Sanders, V.P. TX 6th & 15th (Cons.) Vol. Maj.
Sanders, W. AL 26th (O'Neal's) Inf. Co.D
Sanders, W. AR Inf. (Loc.Def.) Ernest's Co.
Sanders, W. GA 8th Inf. Co.G
Sanders, W. GA 32nd Inf. Co.F
Sanders, W. LA Mil.Squad. Guides d'Orleans
   Cavalier
Sanders, W. MS 2nd Cav.Res. Co.B,L
Sanders, W. MS 10th Cav. Co.C
Sanders, W. SC 2nd Bn.S.S. Co.B
Sanders, W. TN 17th Inf. Co.E
Sanders, W. TN 42nd Inf. 2nd Co.E
Sanders, W. TN 45th Inf. Co.K
Sanders, W. TX 17th Cav. Co.H
Sanders, W. TX Cav. Bone's Co.
Sanders, W.A. AL 9th Inf. Co.A
Sanders, W.A. AR 19th (Dawson's) Inf. Co.I
Sanders, W.A. GA 23rd Inf. Co.B
Sanders, W.A. GA Inf. 23rd Bn.Loc.Def. Pen-
   dergrass' Co.
Sanders, W.A. GA 40th Inf. Co.G
Sanders, W.A. MS 12th Cav. Co.F

Sanders, W.A. MS 6th Inf. Co.C
Sanders, W.A. TN 17th Inf. Capt.
Sanders, W.A. TX 32nd Cav. Co.F
Sanders, Walton Gen. & Staff Asst.Surg.
Sanders, Wash AL 18th Bn.Vol. Co.B
Sanders, Washington NC 58th Inf. Co.E
Sanders, Washington J. AR Cav. Harrell's Bn.
   Co.B Sgt.
Sanders, Watson 1st Cherokee Mtd.Vol. 1st
   Co.G, 2nd Co.H
Sanders, Watson T. GA 1st (Olmstead's) Inf.
   Co.A
Sanders, W.B. AL 23rd Inf. Co.A
Sanders, W.B. AR 10th Mil. Co.I
Sanders, W.B. AR 50th Mil. Co.D
Sanders, W.B. GA 1st Reg. Co.F Sgt.
Sanders, W.B. GA 32nd Inf. Co.D
Sanders, W.B. MS 15th Inf. Co.A
Sanders, W.B. SC 2nd Arty. Co.B
Sanders, W.B. SC 1st (Butler's) Inf. Co.G
Sanders, W.B. SC 2nd St.Troops Co.E
Sanders, W.B. SC 3rd Bn.Res. Co.B
Sanders, W.B. SC 17th Inf. Co.H
Sanders, W.B. TN 20th Inf. Co.E
Sanders, W.B. TN 40th Inf. Co.H
Sanders, W.C. AR 5th Inf. Co.F
Sanders, W.C. AR 32nd Inf. Co.B
Sanders, W.C. GA 46th Inf. Co.D
Sanders, W.C. TN 49th Inf. Co.K
Sanders, W.C. Inf. Bailey's Cons.Regt. Co.E
Sanders, W.C. TX 20th Cav. Co.K
Sanders, W.C. TX 2nd Inf. Co.F
Sanders, W.C. Jackson's Co.,CSA
Sanders, W.D. AR 5th Inf. Co.I
Sanders, W.D. GA 14th Inf. Co.B
Sanders, W.D. TX Cav. Terry's Regt. Co.G
Sanders, W.E. AL 20th Inf. Co.E,A
Sanders, W.E. SC 17th Inf. Co.C
Sanders, W.E. SC 17th Inf. Co.K
Sanders, Wesley Mead's Conf.Cav. Co.I Sgt.
Sanders, Wesley M. TN Cav. 35th Regt.
Sanders, Wesley S. GA 40th Inf. Co.E
Sanders, W.F. AL 2nd Bn. Hilliard's Legion
   Vol. Co.D
Sanders, W.F. MO 9th Inf. Co.C
Sanders, W.F. MO Inf. Clark's Regt. Co.B
Sanders, W.F. SC 1st Mtd.Mil. Screven's Co.
Sanders, W.F. SC 15th Inf. Co.C
Sanders, W.F. TX 20th Inf. Co.K
Sanders, W.F. VA 13th Cav. Co.D
Sanders, W.G. Conf.Cav. Powers' Regt. Co.A
Sanders, W.H. AL Cav. 24th Bn. Co.B
Sanders, W.H. AL 26th (O'Neal's) Inf. Co.K
Sanders, W.H. AR 5th Inf. Co.A
Sanders, W.H. FL 2nd Inf. Co.K
Sanders, W.H. FL 7th Inf. Co.I Cpl.
Sanders, W.H. LA 9th Inf. Co.K
Sanders, W.H. MS 6th Cav. Co.A
Sanders, W.H. MS 11th (Cons.) Cav. Co.E
Sanders, W.H. MS 34th Inf. Co.A
Sanders, W.H. MS 35th Inf. Co.D
Sanders, W.H. MS 41st Inf. Co.E
Sanders, W.H. MS Wilson's Co. (Ponticola
   Guards) 2nd Lt.
Sanders, W.H. MO 10th Cav. Co.I
Sanders, W.H. MO 2nd Inf. Co.I

Sanders, W.H. NC 1st Cav. (9th St.Troops) Co.C
Sanders, W.H. SC Cav.Bn. Holcombe Legion Co.D
Sanders, W.H. TN 13th Cav. Co.K
Sanders, W.H. Gen. & Staff Hosp.Stew.
Sanders, W.H.H. AL 2nd Cav. Co.D
Sanders, Whitfield KY 4th Cav. Co.K,C
Sanders, Whitfield KY 5th Mtd.Inf. Co.E
Sanders, Wiley AL 1st Inf. Co.A
Sanders, Wiley AL 47th Inf. Co.F
Sanders, Wiley TN 16th Inf. Co.G
Sanders, Wiley Brig.Band B.R. Johnson's Brig.,CSA Music.
Sanders, Wiley M. TN 10th (DeMoss') Cav.
Sanders, Wiley M. TN 24th Inf. Co.I Drum.
Sanders, Wiley W. AL 55th Vol. Co.D Comsy.Sgt.
Sanders, William AL Inf. 1st Regt. Co.G
Sanders, William AL 16th Inf. Co.I
Sanders, William AL 28th Inf. Co.A
Sanders, William AL 41st Inf. Co.G
Sanders, William AL 42nd Inf. Co.F
Sanders, William AR 19th (Dawson's) Inf. Co.G
Sanders, William AR 21st Inf. Co.E Sgt.
Sanders, William AR 27th Inf. Co.I
Sanders, William AR 45th Mil. Co.C
Sanders, William GA 1st (Symons') Res. Co.A
Sanders, William GA 2nd Inf. Co.D
Sanders, William GA 7th Inf. (St.Guards) Co.F
Sanders, William GA Inf. 9th Bn. Co.D
Sanders, William KY Cav. 2nd Bn. (Dortch's) Co.D
Sanders, William KY 3rd Cav. Co.D
Sanders, William KY 4th Cav. Co.K
Sanders, William MS 28th Cav. Co.I
Sanders, William MS Inf. 3rd Bn. (St.Troops) Co.F
Sanders, William MO Inf. Clark's Regt. Co.I
Sanders, William NC 5th Sr.Res. Co.F
Sanders, William NC 22nd Inf. Co.F
Sanders, William NC 22nd Inf. Co.G
Sanders, William NC 56th Inf. Co.C
Sanders, William NC 61st Inf. Co.K
Sanders, William SC 6th Cav. Co.E
Sanders, William SC 6th Inf. 2nd Co.I
Sanders, William SC 7th Res. Co.K
Sanders, William SC Inf. 7th Bn. (Enfield Rifles) Co.G
Sanders, William SC 11th Inf. 1st Co.I, 2nd Co.I
Sanders, William SC 14th Inf. Co.A
Sanders, William SC 18th Inf. Co.A
Sanders, William SC 18th Inf. Co.H
Sanders, William TN Douglass' Bn.Part.Rangers Coffee's Co.
Sanders, William TN 8th Inf. Co.C
Sanders, William TN 13th Inf. Co.F
Sanders, William TN 20th Inf. Co.B
Sanders, William TN 34th Inf. Co.G
Sanders, William TN 44th Inf. Co.B
Sanders, William TN 61st Mtd.Inf. Co.C Sgt.
Sanders, William TX 1st (Yager's) Cav. Co.M
Sanders, William TX Cav. Giddings' Bn. White's Co.
Sanders, William TX 11th Inf. Co.F
Sanders, William TX 12th Inf. Co.H
Sanders, William VA 20th Inf. Co.H

Sanders, William VA 40th Inf. Co.D
Sanders, William VA 51st Inf. Co.B
Sanders, William Mead's Conf.Cav. Co.I
Sanders, William Forrest's Scouts,CSA
Sanders, William 1st Cherokee Mtd.Vol. Co.J, 2nd Co.H
Sanders, William Bradford's Corps Scouts & Guards Co.A
Sanders, William Gillum's Regt. Co.H
Sanders, William A. AL 45th Inf. Co.K
Sanders, William A. FL 1st Inf. Old Co.E
Sanders, William A. AR Cav. 1st Bn. (Stirman's) Co.H
Sanders, William A. NC 53rd Inf. Co.K
Sanders, William A. TX 27th Cav. Co.B Cpl.
Sanders, William B. GA 1st Cav. Co.C
Sanders, William B. MS Lt.Arty. Stanford's Co.
Sanders, William C. GA Inf. Fuller's Co.
Sanders, William C. LA 16th Inf. Co.B
Sanders, William C. MS 18th Inf. Co.K Cpl.
Sanders, William C. TX 37th Cav. Co.C Sgt.
Sanders, William C. VA 45th Inf. Co.D Capt.
Sanders, William E. GA Inf. 10th Bn. Co.E
Sanders, William E. TX 11th Cav. 1st Lt.
Sanders, Wm. E. Gen. & Staff Asst.Surg.
Sanders, William F. NC 22nd Inf. Co.G
Sanders, William F. SC 3rd Cav. Co.C
Sanders, William F. SC Mil.Cav. 4th Regt. Howard's Co.
Sanders, William F. Conf.Cav. Clarkson's Bn. Ind.Rangers Co.E
Sanders, William Freeman NC 26th Inf. Co.K
Sanders, William G. GA 3rd Inf. Co.I
Sanders, William G. MS 35th Inf. Co.B
Sanders, William H. AL 4th Inf. Co.I
Sanders, William H. AL 11th Inf. Co.E Surg.
Sanders, William H. AL 62nd Inf. Co.D
Sanders, William H. AR Inf. Hardy's Regt. Co.F
Sanders, William H. AR 24th Inf. Co.G
Sanders, William H. LA 12th Inf. 2nd Co.M 2nd Lt.
Sanders, William H. MS St.Cav. 2nd Bn. (Harris') Co.A
Sanders, William H. MS Cav. Jeff Davis Legion Co.B
Sanders, William H. MO Inf. 3rd Bn. Co.A Sgt.
Sanders, William H. MO 6th Inf. Co.E Sgt.
Sanders, William H. SC 7th Cav. Co.C
Sanders, William H. SC 1st (Orr's) Rifles Co.F
Sanders, William H. SC 5th Inf. Co.A
Sanders, William H. SC Palmetto S.S. Co.A
Sanders, William H. TN Lt.Arty. Winston's Co.
Sanders, Wm. H. Gen. & Staff Surg.
Sanders, William Henry Harrison AL 5th Inf. Old Co.H
Sanders, William H.H. AL 11th Inf. Co.C
Sanders, William H.H. AL 11th Inf. Co.H
Sanders, William H.H. TX 9th Cav. Co.I
Sanders, William J. AL 38th Inf. Co.A
Sanders, William J. AL 39th Inf. Co.A
Sanders, William J. AL Nitre & Min. Corps Young's Co.
Sanders, William J. AR 1st Mtd.Rifles Co.E Cpl.
Sanders, William J. AR 2nd Mtd.Rifles Co.G
Sanders, William J. AR 38th Inf. Co.D Capt.
Sanders, William J. GA 14th Inf. Co.B

Sanders, William J. MS 15th Inf. Co.A
Sanders, William J. SC 2nd Arty. Co.G
Sanders, William J. TX 17th Cav. 1st Co.I
Sanders, William J. TX Cav. Martin's Regt. Co.D
Sanders, William J. Conf.Cav. Clarkson's Bn. Ind.Rangers Co.C Cpl.
Sanders, William K. TX 13th Cav. Co.E
Sanders, William L. MS 14th Inf. Co.C
Sanders, William L. MO Inf. Perkins' Bn. Cpl.
Sanders, William Lafayette LA 28th (Gray's) Inf. Co.F Sgt.
Sanders, William M. AR 38th Inf. Co.D Sgt.
Sanders, William M. FL 5th Inf. Co.F Cpl.
Sanders, William M. GA 2nd Bn.S.S. Co.E
Sanders, William M. MS Cav. 27th Regt. Co.A Sgt.
Sanders, William M. MS 15th Inf. Co.A
Sanders, William Mc. MS Cav. 4th Bn. Co.B
Sanders, William N. MS 41st Inf. Co.E
Sanders, William O. VA 40th Inf. Co.D
Sanders, William O. VA 41st Mil. Co.E
Sanders, William P. AL 6th Cav. Co.K
Sanders, William P. AL Inf. 1st Regt. Co.F
Sanders, William P. MS 26th Inf. Co.D Sgt.
Sanders, William P. TX 7th Inf. Co.D 1st Sgt.
Sanders, William R. AL 10th Inf. Co.D Music.
Sanders, William R. AR 4th Inf. Co.D
Sanders, William R. GA Lt.Arty. 14th Bn. Co.B
Sanders, William R. GA Lt.Arty. Anderson's Btty.
Sanders, William R. GA 41st Inf. Co.K
Sanders, William R. MS 8th Inf. Co.G
Sanders, William R. SC 4th Inf. Co.E
Sanders, William T. AR 1st Field Btty.
Sanders, William T. AL Inf. 1st Regt. Co.E
Sanders, William T. AL 3rd Bn. Hilliard's Legion Vol. Co.B
Sanders, William T. NC 47th Inf. Co.C
Sanders, William T. TX 10th Inf. Co.H
Sanders, William T. VA 15th Inf. Co.G
Sanders, William V. TN 24th Inf. 2nd Co.H Music.
Sanders, William W. NC 39th Inf. Co.H Fifer
Sanders, William W. VA 4th Inf. Co.D
Sanders, Willis AR 20th Inf. Co.H
Sanders, Willis AR 25th Inf. Co.K
Sanders, Willis MS 8th Cav. Co.D
Sanders, Willis J. MS 16th Inf. Co.D
Sanders, Willis S. MS 31st Inf. Co.B
Sanders, Wilson SC 5th Res. Co.K
Sanders, Wilson 2nd Cherokee Mtd.Vol. Co.B
Sanders, Wilson L. GA 14th Inf. Co.B
Sanders, Winfrey B. TX 14th Cav. Co.K
Sanders, W.J. AL 3rd Inf. Co.G
Sanders, W.J. AL 17th Inf. Co.K
Sanders, W.J. GA 6th Cav. Co.E
Sanders, W.J. GA 11th Inf.
Sanders, W.J. LA 9th Inf. Co.G
Sanders, W.J. MS Cav. 24th Bn. Co.C
Sanders, W.J. MS 6th Inf. Co.C
Sanders, W.J. MS 27th Inf. Co.E
Sanders, W.J. NC 4th Cav. (59th St.Troops) Co.C
Sanders, W.J. SC 1st (Hagood's) Inf. 1st Co.G
Sanders, W.J. SC 2nd Inf. Co.D
Sanders, W.J. TN 17th Inf. Co.E

Sanders, W.J. TN Inf. 23rd Bn. Co.E
Sanders, W.J. TX 5th Cav. Co.E
Sanders, W.J. TX Cav. Crump's Regt. Co.D
Sanders, W.J. TX 12th Field Btty.
Sanders, W.J. TX Arty. Douglas' Co. 2nd Lt.
Sanders, W.J. TX 14th Inf. Co.E
Sanders, W.J. TX Inf. Griffin's Bn. Co.E
Sanders, W.J. Jackson's Co.,CSA
Sanders, W.L. TN 47th Inf. Co.B
Sanders, W.L. TX Cav. (Dismtd.) Chisum's Regt. Co.D
Sanders, W.M. AL 41st Inf. Co.D
Sanders, W.M. AR 7th Inf. Co.D
Sanders, W.M. MS 1st (King's) Inf. (St.Troops) D. Love's Co.
Sanders, W.M. TN Inf. 23rd Bn. Co.E
Sanders, W.M. TN 45th Inf. Co.E
Sanders, W.M. TN 47th Inf. Co.I
Sanders, W.M. VA Cav. 37th Bn. Co.B
Sanders, W. McQueen FL 2nd Cav. Co.H 2nd Lt.
Sanders, W.N. MS Cav. Powers' Regt. Co.C
Sanders, W.O. TX 16th Inf. Co.B
Sanders, W.P. MS 12th Cav. Co.B
Sanders, W.P. MS 46th Inf. Co.K
Sanders, W.P. Inf. Bailey's Cons.Regt. Co.B
Sanders, W.P. VA 6th Cav. Co.I
Sanders, W.R. AL Cav. Moreland's Regt. Co.G
Sanders, W.R. GA 16th Inf. Co.C
Sanders, W.R. MS Inf. 3rd Bn. (St.Troops) Co.F
Sanders, W.R. SC Cav. 8th Regt. Co.I
Sanders, W.R. SC 8th Bn.Res. Co.C
Sanders, W.R. TX 1st Inf. Co.M
Sanders, W.R. TX 20th Inf. Co.C
Sanders, Wright GA Cav. 29th Bn. Co.F
Sanders, Wright TX 11th Inf. Co.K
Sanders, W.S. AL 23rd Inf. Co.A
Sanders, W.S. MS Morgan's Co. (Morgan Riflemen)
Sanders, W.T. AL 35th Inf. Co.D Capt.
Sanders, W.T. AL 60th Inf. Co.A
Sanders, W.T. FL Cav. 5th Bn. Co.C
Sanders, W.T. MS 8th Cav. Co.B
Sanders, W.T. MS 1st (Johnston's) Inf. Co.D Sgt.
Sanders, W.T. SC 1st Mtd.Mil. Heyward's Co. Sgt.
Sanders, W.T. SC 3rd Cav. Co.H Sgt.
Sanders, W.T. SC 1st Regt. Charleston Guard Co.H Sgt.
Sanders, W.T. SC 17th Inf. Co.H Capt.
Sanders, W.T. TN 12th Inf. Co.F
Sanders, W.T. TN Inf. Nashville Bn. Cattles' Co.
Sanders, W.T. TX 22nd Inf. Co.A Cpl.
Sanders, W.W. AL 4th (Russell's) Cav. Co.B
Sanders, W.W. MS 25th Inf. Co.B
Sanders, W.W. SC 2nd Arty. Co.G
Sanders, W.W. SC 1st (Butler's) Inf. Co.K
Sanders, W.W. TN Inf. 1st Cons.Regt. Co.B Cpl.
Sanders, W.W. TN 1st (Feild's) Inf. Co.G Cpl.
Sanders, W.W. 2nd Conf.Inf. Co.B Cpl.
Sanders, Wyatt E. GA 36th (Villepigue's) Inf. Co.C
Sanders, Wyatt E. 1st Conf.Inf. 2nd Co.E 2nd Lt.

Sanders, Zachariah MS 20th Inf. Co.K
Sanders, Zachariah VA 15th Cav. Co.A Sgt.
Sanders, Zack MS 40th Inf. Co.K
Sanders, Zadoc M. FL 9th Inf. Co.F
Sanders, Zedick M. FL 7th Inf. Co.I
Sanders, Z.F. GA 2nd St.Line Capt.
Sandersalls, J. LA Arty. Catellanos' Btty.
Sanderslin, G.W. GA 45th Inf. Co.H
Sanderson, Abygilbia AL 23rd Inf. Co.E
Sanderson, A.D. TX 1st Inf. Co.B Sgt.
Sanderson, Albert T. MS 40th Inf. Co.F
Sanderson, Alexander LA 5th Cav. Co.E
Sanderson, Alexander LA 13th Bn. (Part. Rangers) Co.F Cpl.
Sanderson, Alexander J. MS 1st Lt.Arty. Co.L 1st Lt.
Sanderson, Anderson NC 7th Inf. Co.C
Sanderson, A.W.B. MS Inf. 7th Bn. Co.B
Sanderson, B.C. 3rd Conf.Eng.Troops Co.F Artif.
Sanderson, B.C. Sap. & Min. G.W. Maxson's Co.,CSA
Sanderson, Benjamin C. AL 33rd Inf. Co.A
Sanderson, Benjamin C. AR Inf. 2nd Bn. Co.C
Sanderson, Benjamin M. LA 19th Inf. Co.B,A
Sanderson, Blaney AL 6th Cav. Co.E
Sanderson, B.O. TN 49th Inf. Co.H
Sanderson, B.P. LA 2nd Cav. Co.B
Sanderson, Calvin NC 3rd Inf. Co.B
Sanderson, C.C. AL 7th Cav. Co.C
Sanderson, Christopher C. AL 36th Inf. Co.G
Sanderson, D. SC 23rd Inf. Co.E Cpl.
Sanderson, Dan AL 50th Inf. Co.B
Sanderson, Daniel MS Bradford's Co. (Conf. Guards Arty.)
Sanderson, Daniel B. MS 42nd Inf. Co.H
Sanderson, Daniel S. AL 10th Cav. Co.H
Sanderson, David Conf.Reg.Inf. Brooks' Bn. Co.D Cpl.
Sanderson, David Conf.Reg.Inf. Brooks' Bn. Co.D
Sanderson, Douglas AL 27th Inf. Co.K
Sanderson, E. MS 1st Cav.Res. Co.C
Sanderson, E. MS Inf. 3rd Bn. (St.Troops) Co.D Sgt.
Sanderson, E. MS 27th Inf. Co.B
Sanderson, E.L. AL 53rd (Part.Rangers) Co.I Capt.
Sanderson, E.L. AL 37th Inf. Co.D
Sanderson, Elijah MS Inf. 1st St.Troops Co.G Cpl.
Sanderson, Ellison G. AL 4th Inf. Co.I
Sanderson, E.S. LA 6th Cav. Co.C
Sanderson, Eugene TX 1st Hvy.Arty. Co.E
Sanderson, F. MS 37th Inf. Co.F
Sanderson, F.M. AL 23rd Inf. Co.G
Sanderson, G.B. TX 7th Cav. Co.K
Sanderson, George KY 1st Inf. Co.D
Sanderson, George C. LA 14th Inf. Co.G
Sanderson, George F. MS 1st Lt.Arty. Co.E Capt.
Sanderson, George L. VA 1st Cav. Co.G
Sanderson, George W. AL 28th Inf. Co.I
Sanderson, George W. LA 28th (Gray's) Inf. Co.H Cpl.
Sanderson, George W. NC 2nd Cav. (19th St.Troops) Co.A 1st Sgt.

Sanderson, G. Frederick MS Cav. Jeff Davis Legion Co.A
Sanderson, G.H. NC 38th Inf. Co.A
Sanderson, Green MS 1st (Johnston's) Inf. Co.F
Sanderson, H. LA 17th Inf. Co.G
Sanderson, H.C. AL 2nd Cav. Co.K
Sanderson, Henry LA 6th Inf. Co.I
Sanderson, Henry NC 3rd Arty. (40th St.Troops) Co.A
Sanderson, Henry NC 32nd Inf. Lenoir Braves 1st Co.K
Sanderson, Henry R. LA 12th Inf. Co.A
Sanderson, H.F. LA 2nd Inf. Co.F
Sanderson, Hiram J. TN 54th Inf. Co.A
Sanderson, H.S. MS 2nd Inf. Co.K
Sanderson, Hugh Burr MS 24th Inf. Co.C
Sanderson, Isaac NC 8th Bn.Part.Rangers Co.B
Sanderson, Isaac NC 51st Inf. Co.B
Sanderson, Isaac NC 66th Inf. Co.C
Sanderson, Ivey NC Hvy.Arty. 1st Bn. Co.A
Sanderson, J. AL 25th Inf. Co.B
Sanderson, J. AR 11th & 17th Cons.Inf. Co.I
Sanderson, J. TN 14th Cav. Co.D
Sanderson, J. TN 27th Inf. Co.B
Sanderson, J. TX Inf. 1st St.Troops Stevenson's Co.F
Sanderson, J. 1st Chickasaw Inf. Kesner's Co. Cpl.
Sanderson, J.A. AL Cav. 24th Bn. Co.C 2nd Lt.
Sanderson, James GA 39th Inf. Co.A
Sanderson, James NC 4th Inf. Co.D
Sanderson, James TN 14th (Neely's) Cav. Co.G
Sanderson, James TN 14th (Neely's) Cav. Co.I
Sanderson, James TN Cav. Newsom's Regt. Co.H
Sanderson, James Horse Arty. White's Btty.
Sanderson, James M. TN 25th Inf. Co.C 1st Sgt.
Sanderson, James T. MS 42nd Inf. Co.H
Sanderson, J.B. AL 38th Inf. Co.D
Sanderson, J.C. LA 5th Cav. Co.E
Sanderson, J.C. LA 13th Bn. (Part.Rangers) Co.F
Sanderson, J.C. SC Palmetto S.S. Co.M
Sanderson, Jesse VA 2nd Arty. Co.I
Sanderson, Jesse S. NC 38th Inf. Co.C
Sanderson, J.F. 1st Conf.Cav. 2nd Co.A
Sanderson, J.H. MS 1st (Johnston's) Inf. Co.F Sgt.
Sanderson, J.H. MS 2nd Inf. Co.B
Sanderson, J.H. MS 27th Inf. Co.B Sgt.
Sanderson, John AL 11th Cav. Co.A
Sanderson, John LA 6th Cav. Co.I
Sanderson, John NC 8th Bn.Part.Rangers Co.E
Sanderson, John NC 3rd Inf. Co.C
Sanderson, John NC 66th Inf. Co.H
Sanderson, John TX 3rd Cav. Co.I 1st Sgt.
Sanderson, John VA 3rd Bn. Valley Res. Co.B
Sanderson, John A. AL 45th Inf. Co.I
Sanderson, John A. VA 2nd Cav. Co.D
Sanderson, John B. VA 1st Cav. Co.G
Sanderson, John F. VA 44th Inf. Co.D
Sanderson, John H. MS Inf. 7th Bn. Co.B
Sanderson, John H. MS 8th Inf. Co.K
Sanderson, John L. LA 28th (Gray's) Inf. Co.I
Sanderson, John P. NC 2nd Cav. (19th St.Troops) Co.A Cpl.

Sanderson, John W. AR 18th (Marmaduke's) Inf.
  Co.E
Sanderson, John W. NC 2nd Inf. Co.H
Sanderson, John W. VA 15th Cav. Co.F
Sanderson, Joseph VA 24th Cav. Co.I
Sanderson, Joseph B. AL 10th Cav. Co.H
Sanderson, J.P. AR 23rd Cav.
Sanderson, J.P. FL Detailed Res.Conscr.Dept.
Sanderson, J.R. LA 3rd (Harrison's) Cav. Co.H
Sanderson, Julius C. LA 28th (Gray's) Inf. Co.I
Sanderson, J.W. AR 5th Inf.
Sanderson, J.W. MS 5th Inf. (St.Troops) Co.I
Sanderson, J.W. SC Inf. 6th Bn. Co.A
Sanderson, J.W. SC 26th Inf. Co.C Cpl.
Sanderson, J.W. SC Manigault's Bn.Vol. Co.D
Sanderson, J.W. VA 5th Cav. Co.G
Sanderson, L. AL 7th Cav. Co.K
Sanderson, L. GA 43rd Inf. Co.C
Sanderson, L.D. MS 18th Cav. Co.F
Sanderson, Leford DeKalb MS 24th Inf. Co.C
Sanderson, Levi NC 8th Bn.Part.Rangers Co.B
Sanderson, Levi NC 66th Inf. Co.H
Sanderson, Lewis NC 8th Bn.Part.Rangers
  Co.B,E
Sanderson, Lewis NC 66th Inf. Co.H
Sanderson, Lewis Nelson TN 40th Inf. Co.A
Sanderson, Lipe AR 62nd Mil. Co.C Fifer
Sanderson, L.M. AL 54th Inf. Co.G,B
Sanderson, Major NC 32nd Inf. Lenoir Braves
  1st Co.K
Sanderson, Major F. NC 3rd Arty. (40th
  St.Troops) Co.A
Sanderson, Marion AL 42nd Inf. Co.K
Sanderson, M.C. AL 23rd Inf. Co.K,E
Sanderson, M.J. AR 17th (Griffith's) Inf. Co.C
Sanderson, M.J. AR 35th Inf. Co.A
Sanderson, Morris MO 9th Inf. Co.I
Sanderson, Olin VA 1st Cav. Co.G
Sanderson, Oliver TX 1st Hvy.Arty. Co.E
Sanderson, Pleasant S. AR Cav. 1st Bn. (Stir-
  man's) Co.F
Sanderson, P.S. AR Cav. McGehee's Regt. Co.G
Sanderson, R. TN 7th (Duckworth's) Cav.
  White's Co.
Sanderson, R.B. TX 4th Inf. (St.Troops) Co.E
Sanderson, R.C. MS Inf. 3rd Bn. (St.Troops)
  Co.D
Sanderson, Richard Carroll MS Inf. 1st St.Troops
  Co.G 1st Lt.
Sanderson, Robert MS 12th Inf. Co.B
Sanderson, S. TX 21st Inf. Co.F
Sanderson, Samuel AL Arty. 1st Bn. Co.E
Sanderson, Samuel TX 11th (Spaight's) Bn.Vol.
  Co.F
Sanderson, S.E. LA 2nd Cav. Co.B
Sanderson, Solomon A. SC 1st (McCreary's) Inf.
  Co.E
Sanderson, Thomas AL 29th Inf. Co.I
Sanderson, Thomas NC 4th Cav. (59th
  St.Troops) Co.G
Sanderson, Thomas NC 46th Inf. Co.A Sgt.
Sanderson, Thomas H. NC Part.Rangers Swin-
  dell's Co.
Sanderson, Thomas H. NC 17th Inf. (1st Org.)
  Co.B
Sanderson, Thomas J. MS 1st (Patton's) Inf.
  Co.C

Sanderson, Thomas J. MS 35th Inf. Co.H
Sanderson, Thomas P. NC 17th Inf. (2nd Org.)
  Co.G
Sanderson, Thomas P. VA 1st Cav. Co.G
Sanderson, Thomas P. VA Horse Arty. E.
  Graham's Co.
Sanderson, V.P. MS 1st (Johnston's) Inf. Co.F
Sanderson, W. AR 11th & 17th Cons.Inf. Co.I
Sanderson, W. AR 35th Inf. Co.A
Sanderson, Wesley AL Inf. 1st Regt. Co.G,E
Sanderson, W.F. AR 20th Inf. Co.K
Sanderson, W.G. MS 18th Cav.
Sanderson, W.G. VA 10th Cav. Co.I
Sanderson, W.H. AR 23rd Cav. Co.I
Sanderson, W.H. AR 13th Inf. Co.F Cpl.
Sanderson, W.H. MO 7th Cav. Co.B
Sanderson, William AR 17th (Griffith's) Inf.
  Co.C
Sanderson, William LA 6th Cav. Co.I
Sanderson, William MS Cav. Buck's Co.
Sanderson, William MS 35th Inf. Co.G
Sanderson, William MS 46th Inf. Co.A Sgt.
Sanderson, William TN 3rd (Forrest's) Cav.
  Co.C Cpl.
Sanderson, William D. VA 1st Cav. Co.G
Sanderson, William H. KY 4th Cav. Co.F,H
Sanderson, Willis G. VA 2nd Arty. Co.I
Sanderson, W.J. 1st Conf.Cav. 2nd Co.A
Sanderson, W.J. Horse Arty. White's Btty.
Sanderson, W.L. TX 20th Inf. Co.I
Sanderson, Woodson T. MS 2nd Part.Rangers
  Co.K,H
Sanderson, Zack T. VA 2nd Arty. Co.A
Sanderson, Zed. T. VA Inf. 22nd Bn. Co.A
Sandes, J. AL 1st Cav. 2nd Co.D
Sandes, L.B. AR 2nd Cav. Co.F 1st Lt.
Sandex, S.J. MS 18th Inf. Co.D
Sandey, H. TN Cav. Nixon's Regt. Co.E Sgt.
Sandfer, W.N. AR 11th & 17th Cons.Inf. Co.C
Sandford, --- GA 19th Inf. Co.D
Sandford, --- KY 9th Mtd.Inf. Co.D
Sandford, --- MS St.Cav. 3rd Bn. (Cooper's) Lit-
  tle's Co. Sgt.
Sandford, --- TX Cav. 4th Regt.St.Troops Co.E
Sandford, A.J. NC 1st Jr.Res. Co.B
Sandford, Albert GA 5th Inf. (St.Guards)
  Johnston's Co.
Sandford, Alexander NC 1st Arty. (10th
  St.Troops) Co.C
Sandford, Alfred VA 9th Cav. Sandford's Co.
Sandford, Alfred VA 111th Mil. Co.4 Cpl.
Sandford, Asbury NC 23rd Inf. Co.D
Sandford, A.W. Conf.Cav. Wood's Regt. Co.F
  1st Lt.
Sandford, Benjamin F. AL 20th Inf. Co.B
Sandford, B.F. AL 47th Inf. Co.H
Sandford, Caswell B. GA 3rd Inf. Co.G Sgt.
Sandford, C.H. AR 1st (Dobbin's) Cav. Co.A
Sandford, Charles H. LA 1st Hvy.Arty. (Reg.)
  Co.F 2nd Lt.
Sandford, C.R. AL 51st (Part.Rangers) Co.G
Sandford, David K. TN 1st (Feild's) Inf. Co.C
Sandford, Derrell MS 2nd (Quinn's St.Troops)
  Inf. Co.A
Sandford, E.C. VA 15th Cav. Co.A
Sandford, E.D. NC 2nd Arty. (36th St.Troops)
  Co.B

Sandford, E.D. NC Lt.Arty. 13th Bn. Co.B
Sandford, Emanuel G. AL 13th Inf. Co.C
Sandford, F.M. AL 4th (Russell's) Cav. Co.C
Sandford, George L. VA 47th Inf. Co.C Cpl.
Sandford, George M. AL 3rd Inf. Co.G
Sandford, George W. MS 29th Inf. Co.C
Sandford, G.R. VA 9th Cav. Sandford's Co.
Sandford, G.W. AL Lt.Arty. Lee's Btty.
Sandford, G.W. AL 59th Inf. Co.K
Sandford, G.W. TN 21st & 22nd (Cons.) Cav.
  Co.D
Sandford, Hamlet KY 1st (Butler's) Cav. Co.C
  1st Lt.
Sandford, Hamlett KY 3rd Cav. Co.C 2nd Lt.
Sandford, Hiram M. AL 9th (Malone's) Cav.
  Co.I
Sandford, Hugh W. AL 3rd Cav. Co.D
Sandford, Isac GA 3rd Inf. Co.G
Sandford, James AL Cav. Forrest's Regt.
Sandford, James AR 1st (Monroe's) Cav. Co.C
Sandford, James MO 4th Inf. Co.H
Sandford, James NC 44th Inf. Co.H
Sandford, James NC Mallett's Bn. Co.A
Sandford, James TN 18th (Newsom's) Cav. Co.A
Sandford, James VA Lt.Arty. Arch. Graham's
  Co.
Sandford, James VA Conscr. Cp.Lee Co.A
Sandford, James Exch.Bn. Co.D,F,CSA Sgt.
Sandford, James B. VA 9th Cav. Sandford's Co.
Sandford, James B. VA Cav. 15th Bn. Co.A
Sandford, James F. NC 44th Inf. Co.A
Sandford, James M. GA 40th Inf. Co.C
Sandford, J.B. AL 4th (Russell's) Cav. Co.C
Sandford, Jeremiah NC 1st Jr.Res. Co.B
Sandford, Jesse SC 11th Res. Co.G
Sandford, Jesse SC 25th Inf. Co.G
Sandford, Jesse H. MS 46th Inf. Co.K
Sandford, Jesse L. AR 3rd Inf. Co.B
Sandford, J.H. AL 13th Inf. Co.F
Sandford, J.H. AL 59th Inf. Co.K
Sandford, J.L. AR 2nd Cav. Co.E 2nd Lt.
Sandford, J.M. AL 24th Inf. Co.D
Sandford, John AL 8th Cav. Co.C
Sandford, John FL 5th Inf. Co.E
Sandford, John MO 1st Inf. Co.D
Sandford, John B. VA 47th Inf. Co.D Cpl.
Sandford, John H. AL 2nd Bn. Hilliard's Legion
  Vol. Co.B
Sandford, John H. GA Lt.Arty. Hamilton's Co.
Sandford, John L. Echols' Staff Capt.
Sandford, John T. AL Lt.Arty. 2nd Bn. Co.E
Sandford, John W. MO 1st Inf. Co.D
Sandford, Joseph AL Cav. Forrest's Regt.
Sandford, Joseph MS 17th Inf. Co.C
Sandford, Joseph NC 23rd Inf. Co.E
Sandford, Joseph TN 18th (Newsom's) Cav.
  Co.A
Sandford, J.R. NC 1st Jr.Res. Co.B
Sandford, J.S. AL 13th Inf. Co.F
Sandford, J.T. NC 23rd Inf. Co.I
Sandford, Kelita NC 52nd Inf. Co.E
Sandford, L.A. LA Inf.Cons.Crescent Regt. Co.I
Sandford, Lucius E. VA 9th Cav. Sandford's Co.
  Capt.
Sandford, Lucius E. VA 15th Cav. Co.A Capt.
Sandford, Lucius E. VA Cav. 15th Bn. Co.A
  Capt.

Sandford, Lucius E. VA 111th Mil. Co.5 Capt.
Sandford, M. AL 28th Inf. Co.D
Sandford, Mark W. AL 13th Inf. Co.C
Sandford, Matthew NC 62nd Inf. Co.A
Sandford, M.M. LA Inf.Cons.Crescent Regt. Co.A
Sandford, O.P. GA Inf. City Bn. (Columbus) Co.C Cpl.
Sandford, P. GA 5th Res. Co.D
Sandford, P.C. Sig.Corps,CSA
Sandford, R. MS Rogers' Co. Cpl.
Sandford, R.A. AL St.Arty. Co.D
Sandford, R.A. TN 38th Inf. Co.L 1st Lt.
Sandford, Robert Gen. & Staff Maj.,ADC
Sandford, Robert F. NC 55th Inf. Co.K
Sandford, Robert H. NC 2nd Arty. (36th St.Troops) Co.B Cpl.
Sandford, Robert H. NC Lt.Arty. 13th Bn. Co.B Cpl.
Sandford, Robert H. NC 1st Inf. (6 mo. '61) Co.C
Sandford, Robert P. KY 4th Mtd.Inf. Co.G,I Sgt.
Sandford, S. SC 2nd Arty. Co.C
Sandford, Samuel D. AL 13th Inf. Co.C Sgt.
Sandford, Samuel W. AL 4th (Russell's) Cav. Co.K
Sandford, S.B. AL 34th Inf. Co.C
Sandford, Stephen H. NC 55th Inf. Co.K
Sandford, T.B. MO Cav. 1st Bn.St.Guard Co.A 2nd Lt.
Sandford, T.B. MO St.Guard Capt., Asst.Div.Comsy.
Sandford, Theodore G. GA Cav. 7th Bn. (St.Guards) Co.B Cpl.
Sandford, Thomas TX Conscr.
Sandford, Thomas B. MO 12th Inf. Maj.
Sandford, Thomas D. GA 66th Inf. Co.G
Sandford, Thomas H. NC 55th Inf. Co.K Cpl.
Sandford, Thomas V. VA 47th Inf. Co.C AQM
Sandford, W. GA 5th Res. Co.G
Sandford, W.D. AL 13th Inf. Co.H
Sandford, W.E. GA Inf. 19th Bn. (St.Guards) Co.F 3rd Lt.
Sandford, W.E. VA 15th Cav.
Sandford, W.F. Gen. & Staff Chap.
Sandford, W.G. SC 2nd Arty. Co.C
Sandford, William MS Inf. 3rd Bn. Co.A
Sandford, William SC 1st (Hagood's) Inf. 2nd Co.A
Sandford, William A. AL 20th Inf. Co.B Lt.
Sandford, William E. VA 9th Cav. Sandford's Co.
Sandford, William H. NC 7th Inf. Comsy.
Sandford, William P. VA 47th Inf. Co.C
Sandford, William S. MS Cav. 4th Bn. Sykes' Co.
Sandford, W.J. VA 10th Cav. 2nd Co.E
Sandford, W.L. KY 7th Cav. Co.G
Sandford, W.T. MS Cav. Yerger's Regt. Co.A
Sandford, W.T. NC 23rd Inf. Co.E
Sandfur, J.K.P. MS 1st (Percy's) Inf. Co.B
Sandheer, H.J. AR 1st (Monroe's) Cav. Co.H
Sandidge, A.J. TX Cav. 1st Bn.St.Troops Co.D
Sandidge, A.J. TX 3rd Cav. Co.A
Sandidge, Alexander M. VA Lt.Arty. Kirkpatrick's Co.

Sandidge, Alexander M. VA 58th Inf. Co.F
Sandidge, C.C. MS 9th Inf. New Co.A
Sandidge, C.F. MS St.Cav. Perrin's Bn. Co.H
Sandidge, Dabney S. MO 3rd Inf. Co.H
Sandidge, E.M. MS 9th Inf. New Co.A
Sandidge, George M. LA 6th Cav. Co.C,B 1st Lt.
Sandidge, George R. MS 22nd Inf. Co.F Cpl.
Sandidge, G.M. VA 88th Mil.
Sandidge, G.W. VA 88th Mil.
Sandidge, James MS 1st Cav.Res. Co.I
Sandidge, James G. LA 6th Cav. Co.B
Sandidge, J.D. VA 88th Mil.
Sandidge, John M. Gen. & Staff, Ord. Maj.,Ord.Ch.
Sandidge, Mathew P. MS 22nd Inf. Co.A,F
Sandidge, M.C. MO 5th Cav. Co.D
Sandidge, M.C. MO Cav. Stallard's Co.
Sandidge, Pleasant S. MO 5th Cav. Co.E 1st Sgt.
Sandidge, Richard P. VA 51st Inf. Co.G
Sandidge, Robert E. MS 18th Inf. Co.I
Sandidge, Thomas H. MS 1st Lt.Arty. Co.A
Sandidge, V.F. VA 51st Inf. Co.G
Sandidge, William D. VA 51st Inf. Co.G
Sandifee, W. MS 1st Cav.Res. Co.F
Sandifer, Abram MS 36th Inf. Co.B
Sandifer, A.J. SC Inf. Hampton Legion Co.G
Sandifer, Alex. F. VA 11th Inf. Co.B
Sandifer, Amos MS 33rd Inf. Co.E
Sandifer, Benj. J. VA Inf. 44th Bn. Co.E
Sandifer, B.F. VA Inf. 44th Bn. Co.E
Sandifer, B.T. MS 5th Inf. Co.A 2nd Lt.
Sandifer, C.F. KY 8th Mtd.Inf. Co.H
Sandifer, D.W. SC 17th Inf. Co.H
Sandifer, E. Cobb MS 16th Inf. Co.B 4th Sgt.
Sandifer, Ethaniel MS Cav. Gibson's Co.
Sandifer, F.J. SC Cav. 14th Bn. Co.D
Sandifer, F.J. SC 2nd Inf. Co.K,H
Sandifer, Frank AR 11th & 17th Cons.Inf. Co.C
Sandifer, George P. VA 11th Inf. Co.B
Sandifer, G.M. GA 3rd Cav. QMSgt.
Sandifer, G.W. SC Cav. 14th Bn. Co.D
Sandifer, H.A. SC 5th Cav. Co.I
Sandifer, H.A. SC 11th Res. Co.E
Sandifer, Hansford D. MS 16th Inf. Co.E
Sandifer, Hansf. T. MS 36th Inf. Co.B
Sandifer, Henry J. MS 36th Inf. Co.A
Sandifer, H.T. MS 1st (Percy's) Inf. Co.A
Sandifer, J. MS 1st (Percy's) Inf. Co.F
Sandifer, J.A. MS 5th Inf. Co.A
Sandifer, James GA 3rd Res. Co.A
Sandifer, James J. AR Inf. Hardy's Regt. Co.B
Sandifer, James K. MS 36th Inf. Co.A
Sandifer, James M. GA Lt.Arty. Scogin's Btty. (Griffin Lt.Arty.)
Sandifer, James S. SC 12th Inf. Co.H Sgt.
Sandifer, James W. MS 38th Cav. Co.K Cpl.
Sandifer, J.D. MS 5th Inf. Co.A
Sandifer, Jesse W. MS 1st (Percy's) Inf. Co.A
Sandifer, Jesse W. MS 36th Inf. Co.A
Sandifer, J.J. MS Cav. Part.Rangers Rhodes' Co.
Sandifer, J.J. SC 2nd St.Troops Co.E
Sandifer, J.J. SC 11th Res. Co.E
Sandifer, J.J. 14th Conf.Cav. Co.F

Sandifer, J.K. MS 1st (King's) Inf. (St.Troops) Co.B
Sandifer, J.M. MS 11th (Perrin's) Cav. Co.H
Sandifer, John H. VA 32nd Inf. 2nd Co.H
Sandifer, John J. MS 38th Cav. Co.K
Sandifer, John M. TX 4th Inf. Co.A
Sandifer, Johnson MS Inf. 1st Bn.St.Troops (12 mo. '62-3) Co.F
Sandifer, Johnson MS Inf. 3rd Bn. Co.A
Sandifer, Johnson MS 16th Inf. Co.B
Sandifer, John T. KY Lt.Arty. Cobb's Co. Ord.Sgt.
Sandifer, John W. MS 36th Inf. Co.G
Sandifer, J.O.J. LA 6th Cav. Co.C
Sandifer, Joseph MS 16th Inf. Co.B
Sandifer, Joseph F. MS 33rd Inf. Co.E
Sandifer, Joseph W. MO 4th Cav.
Sandifer, J.T. GA Lt.Arty. Havis' Btty.
Sandifer, J.W. MS Cav. Part.Rangers Rhodes' Co. Sgt.
Sandifer, J.W. MS 38th Cav. Co.F
Sandifer, J.W. MS 2nd (Quinn's St.Troops) Inf. Co.H
Sandifer, J.W. SC 1st (Hagood's) Inf. 1st Co.K
Sandifer, J.W. 14th Conf.Cav. Co.F
Sandifer, Levi J. MS 33rd Inf. Co.B,D
Sandifer, Levi W. MS 33rd Inf. Co.E
Sandifer, L.G. TX 4th Inf. Co.E
Sandifer, L.G. TX Inf. Houston Bn.Loc.Def. Troops Co.D 1st Sgt.
Sandifer, L.G. VA 3rd Inf.Loc.Def. Co.A
Sandifer, L.J. MS Graves' Co. (Copiah Horse Guards)
Sandifer, L.J. SC 5th Cav. Co.I
Sandifer, L.J. SC 11th Res. Co.E
Sandifer, L.W. MS 22nd Inf. Co.G
Sandifer, Nathaniel M. SC 12th Inf. Co.A
Sandifer, P.C. TN 8th (Smith's) Cav. Co.A
Sandifer, P.R. SC 17th Inf. Co.K
Sandifer, R.M. MS 2nd (Quinn's St.Troops) Inf. Co.H
Sandifer, R.M. 14th Conf.Cav. Co.F
Sandifer, Robert T. VA 11th Inf. Co.B
Sandifer, R.P. MS 38th Cav. Co.F
Sandifer, R.W. MS Cav. Part.Rangers Rhodes' Co.
Sandifer, Samuel B. AR 38th Inf. Co.M Sgt.
Sandifer, Seaborn J. LA 28th (Gray's) Inf. Co.G
Sandifer, S.L. AR 18th Inf. Co.K
Sandifer, S.N. MS 28th Cav. Co.G
Sandifer, T. MS 1st (Percy's) Inf. Co.F
Sandifer, Thomas KY Morgan's Men Co.D
Sandifer, Thomas J. VA 11th Inf. Co.B
Sandifer, Thomas P. VA 32nd Inf. 2nd Co.H
Sandifer, Thomas R. KY 4th Cav. Co.H,K
Sandifer, T.J. AR 11th Inf. Co.H
Sandifer, T.J. AR 11th & 17th Cons.Inf. Co.C
Sandifer, T.J. KY Lt.Arty. Cobb's Co. Ord.Sgt.
Sandifer, W. 20th Conf.Cav. 1st Co.H
Sandifer, W.B. SC Cav. 14th Bn. Co.D
Sandifer, W.C. MS 38th Cav. Co.F
Sandifer, W.C. MS 1st (Percy's) Inf. Co.F
Sandifer, W.D. VA 3rd (Archer's) Bn.Res. Co.B
Sandifer, W.E. MS 2nd (Quinn's St.Troops) Inf. Co.H
Sandifer, W.E. 14th Conf.Cav. Co.F

Sandifer, W.G. SC 1st (Hagood's) Inf. 1st Co.K,
  2nd Co.A
Sandifer, William MS Cav. Gibson's Co.
Sandifer, William MS 1st Bn.S.S. Co.B
Sandifer, William MS 3rd Inf. Co.K
Sandifer, William A. VA 11th Inf. Co.B Cpl.
Sandifer, William A. VA 39th Mil. Co.B
Sandifer, William C. MS 38th Cav. Co.K
Sandifer, William E. VA 41st Inf. Co.C
Sandifer, William V. MS 36th Inf. Co.A
Sandifer, W.L. MS 4th Inf. Co.C
Sandifer, W.N. AR 11th Inf. Co.H
Sandifer, W.R. MS 1st Lt.Arty. Co.F
Sandifer, W.R. MS 1st (Percy's) Inf. Co.A
Sandifer, W.R. SC 1st (Hagood's) Inf. 1st Co.K,
  2nd Co.A
Sandifer, W.V. MS 1st (Percy's) Inf. Co.A
Sandiffer, Anderson MS 21st Inf. Co.C
Sandiffer, William V. MS 21st Inf. Co.C
Sandiford, Emery S. AL 43rd Inf. Co.F
Sandiford, F. KY 3rd Cav. Co.E Sgt.
Sandiford, George W. GA 6th Inf. Co.I Sgt.
Sandiford, G.W. KY 7th Mtd.Inf. Co.K
Sandiford, Henry J. GA 6th Inf. Co.I
Sandiford, James SC 3rd Cav. Co.F
Sandiford, James SC 5th Cav. Co.B
Sandiford, James A. GA 6th Inf. Co.I
Sandiford, James M. SC Cav. 17th Bn. Co.C
Sandiford, James W. LA 12th Inf. Co.A 1st Lt.
Sandiford, James W. 1st Conf.Eng.Troops Co.K
Sandiford, Jas. W. Gen. & Staff 1st Lt.,Adj.
Sandiford, J.C. GA 1st (Olmstead's) Inf. Co.F
  Sgt.
Sandiford, J.C. GA 25th Inf. Pritchard's Co.
Sandiford, J.E. GA 1st (Olmstead's) Inf. Co.F
Sandiford, J.E. GA 25th Inf. Pritchard's Co.
Sandiford, J.M. SC 3rd Cav. Co.F
Sandiford, John B. AL 36th Inf. Co.A
Sandiford, John N. AL 24th Inf. Co.F
Sandiford, Joseph J. GA 6th Inf. Co.I
Sandiford, J.T. AL 4th Res. Co.B
Sandiford, R.B. GA 8th Inf. Co.B
Sandiford, Robert C. GA 25th Inf. Co.I
Sandiford, Thomas GA Cav. 19th Bn. Co.C
Sandiford, W. GA Mil. Camden Cty. (Mtd.)
Sandiford, W.E. LA 3rd (Wingfield's) Cav. Co.C
Sandiford, W.F. GA 4th (Clinch's) Cav. Co.D
Sandiford, W.P. SC 8th Bn.Res. Co.C
Sandifur, J.T. KY Lt.Arty. Cobb's Co.
Sandifur, Robert GA 8th Inf. (St.Guards) Co.K
  Capt.
Sandifur, Tandy KY Lt.Arty. Cobb's Co.
Sandifure, G.W. 2nd Conf.Inf. Co.C
Sandige, Alfred L. VA 3rd Lt.Arty. (Loc.Def.)
  Co.C
Sandige, Benjamin L. MS 1st Lt.Arty. Co.B Sgt.
Sandige, F.M. MO Robertson's Regt.St.Guard
  Co.12
Sandige, F.M. TN 17th Inf. Co.E
Sandige, Henry A. VA 1st Bn.Res. Co.A
Sandige, J.M. LA 3rd Inf. Co.I
Sandige, Joseph E. VA 23rd Inf. Co.G 2nd Lt.
Sandige, L.D. Gen. & Staff, Arty. 2nd Lt.
Sandige, N. LA 3rd Inf. Co.I
Sandige, P.S. MO Robertson's Regt.St.Guard
  Co.12

Sandige, Thomas O. VA 3rd Lt.Arty. (Loc.Def.)
  Co.C
Sandige, V.F. VA 13th Inf. 2nd Co.E
Sandige, William H. VA 22nd Inf. Co.K Sgt.
Sandige, W.P. TN 17th Inf. Co.E
Sandige, Z.A.E. VA Inf. 26th Bn. Co.B
Sandipher, Thomas KY Cav. 2nd Bn. (Dortch's)
  Co.C
Sandirfer, W. Gillum's Regt. Co.F
Sandize, Jiles MS 25th Inf. Co.D
Sandland, Lewis TN 41st Inf. Co.D
Sandland, William AR 46th Inf.
Sandle, C.A. MS 36th Inf. Co.C
Sandle, S.D. LA Inf. 11th Bn. Co.E
Sandleben, Christian TX 3rd Inf. Co.H
Sandlen, J.A. SC 17th Inf. Co.K
Sandler, Isaac N. TN Cav. Allison's Squad. Co.E
Sandler, John W. MO 1st Inf.
Sandler, William MD 1st Inf. Co.E
Sandles, M.T. AR 11th & 17th Cons.Inf. Co.I
  Sgt.
Sandlin, A. TN 14th (Neely's) Cav. Co.I,G Sgt.
Sandlin, A.D. AL 26th (O'Neal's) Inf. Co.H
Sandlin, A.J. MS 10th Inf. Co.L, New Co.C
Sandlin, Albert Conf.Inf. 1st Bn. 2nd Co.B
Sandlin, Alexander LA 1st Cav. Co.I
Sandlin, Alexander K. TX 13th Cav. Co.K
Sandlin, Alfred W. MS 1st (Johnston's) Inf. Co.B
  2nd Lt.
Sandlin, Alfred W. MS 43rd Inf. Co.H 1st Sgt.
Sandlin, Anderson AL 26th (O'Neal's) Inf. Co.H
Sandlin, Andrew D. SC 17th Inf. Co.H
Sandlin, Ben W. AL 59th Inf. Co.C
Sandlin, B.J. AL 2nd Bn. Hilliard's Legion Vol.
  Co.F
Sandlin, B.W. AL 9th (Malone's) Cav. Co.K
Sandlin, Crawford NC 66th Inf. Co.D
Sandlin, Curtis NC 3rd Inf. Co.B Cpl.
Sandlin, Daniel S. NC 12th Inf. Co.L
Sandlin, Daniel S. NC 32nd Inf. Co.F,A Sgt.
Sandlin, D.J. 3rd Conf.Cav. Co.D
Sandlin, D.M. SC 16th Inf. Co.F
Sandlin, E. LA 2nd Cav. Co.G
Sandlin, Elijah LA 9th Inf. Co.D Cpl.
Sandlin, G.E. AL 5th Cav. Co.I 1st Lt.
Sandlin, Geordon AL 5th Cav. Co.L
Sandlin, G.F. MS 10th Inf. Co.L, New Co.C
Sandlin, H. TN 12th (Green's) Cav. Co.I
Sandlin, H. TN 14th (Neely's) Cav. Co.K
Sandlin, Henry L. NC 1st Arty. (10th St.Troops)
  Co.I
Sandlin, Henry W. FL 4th Inf. Co.D Sgt.
Sandlin, Hiram L. NC 12th Inf. Co.C
Sandlin, Hiram S. NC 51st Inf. Co.B Sgt.
Sandlin, H.R. AL 7th Cav. Co.I
Sandlin, H.R. MS 2nd Cav. Co.I
Sandlin, Isaac TN 7th Inf. Co.A
Sandlin, J. AL 12th Cav. Co.D
Sandlin, J. AR 1st (Colquitt's) Inf. Co.B
Sandlin, J.A. Conf.Inf. 1st Bn. 2nd Co.B
Sandlin, James AR 11th & 17th Cons.Inf.
  Co.H,K
Sandlin, James M. AR 17th (Griffith's) Inf. Co.H
Sandlin, James W. AL 35th Inf. Co.C
Sandlin, J.B. AL 3rd Inf. Co.I
Sandlin, J.B. LA 28th (Gray's) Inf. Co.K
Sandlin, J.E. SC 16th Inf. Co.F

Sandlin, Jesse MS 10th Cav. Co.I
Sandlin, Jesse NC 12th Inf. Co.C
Sandlin, Jesse NC 38th Inf. Co.A
Sandlin, Jesse G. LA 9th Inf. Co.D
Sandlin, Jesse R. FL 9th Inf. Co.D 1st Sgt.
Sandlin, J.F. TN 8th Inf. Co.E
Sandlin, J.H. AL 9th (Malone's) Cav. Co.D
Sandlin, J.H. LA Inf.Crescent Regt. Co.K
Sandlin, J.H. LA Inf.Cons.Crescent Regt. Co.E
Sandlin, J.M. AL 5th Cav. Co.I
Sandlin, John TN 3rd (Forrest's) Cav. Co.D
Sandlin, John 3rd Conf.Cav. Co.D
Sandlin, John I. 3rd Conf.Cav. Co.D
Sandlin, John J. MS 1st (Patton's) Inf. Co.C
Sandlin, John R. MS Cav. Ham's Regt. Co.E
Sandlin, Jno. R. MS Inf. 4th St.Troops Co.E
Sandlin, John W. GA 45th Inf.
Sandlin, Joseph AL 29th Inf. Co.C
Sandlin, Joseph H. LA 9th Inf. Co.D
Sandlin, J.S. AL 1st Cav. 1st Co.C
Sandlin, J.S. AL 5th Cav. Co.D
Sandlin, J.W. AL 9th (Malone's) Cav. Co.K
Sandlin, J.W. TN 40th Inf. Co.E
Sandlin, L. AL 42nd Inf. Co.F
Sandlin, Lewis GA 51st Inf. Co.H Cpl.
Sandlin, M. NC 32nd Inf. Co.F
Sandlin, M.A. AL 5th Cav. Co.I
Sandlin, Marion J.O. AR Lt.Arty. Thrall's Btty.
Sandlin, N. AL 12th Cav. Co.C
Sandlin, Nicholas AL 28th Inf. Co.L
Sandlin, Nicholas TN 38th Inf. 1st Co.H
Sandlin, Nicholas J. LA 8th Inf. Co.G 1st Lt.
Sandlin, O. TN 12th (Green's) Cav. Co.I
Sandlin, O. TN 27th Inf. Co.G
Sandlin, Obediah AL 29th Inf. Co.C
Sandlin, O.N.B. AL Cp. of Instr. Talladega
Sandlin, P.H. AL 28th Inf. Co.L
Sandlin, Ran 3rd Conf.Cav. Co.D
Sandlin, Randolph AL Morgan Defend. Orr's
  Co.
Sandlin, Robert AL 7th Cav. Co.D
Sandlin, Robert AL 12th Cav. Co.C
Sandlin, Robert NC 3rd Inf. Co.G
Sandlin, Robert NC 66th Inf. Co.I
Sandlin, Robert W. GA 51st Inf. Co.H
Sandlin, S.S. AL 5th Cav. Co.I
Sandlin, Thomas R. MS 18th Cav. Co.A
Sandlin, T.P. AL 9th (Malone's) Cav. Co.K
  Cpl.
Sandlin, W.A. AL Cav. Roddey's Escort
Sandlin, W.A. LA 2nd Cav. Co.G
Sandlin, Wasil NC 8th Sr.Res. Broadhurst's Co.
Sandlin, W.D. FL 4th Inf. Co.D
Sandlin, W.E. SC 16th Inf. Co.F
Sandlin, W.E. TN 12th (Green's) Cav. Co.I
Sandlin, W.E. TN 9th Inf. Co.B
Sandlin, Wiley D. FL 9th Inf. Co.D Sgt.
Sandlin, William AR 17th (Griffith's) Inf. Co.H
Sandlin, William LA 5th Cav. Co.E
Sandlin, William LA 13th Bn. (Part.Rangers)
  Co.F
Sandlin, William NC 1st Cav. (9th St.Troops)
  Co.I Sgt.
Sandlin, William NC 15th Inf. Co.E
Sandlin, William H. NC 18th Inf. Co.I
Sandlin, William H. NC 32nd Inf. Co.F
Sandlin, William H. TX 13th Cav. Co.C

Sandlin, William J. NC 1st Arty. (10th
 St.Troops) Co.I
Sandlin, William J. NC 2nd Arty. (36th
 St.Troops) Co.A
Sandlin, William J. NC 38th Inf. Co.A
Sandling, Franklin MS 30th Inf. Co.E
Sandling, Gordon M. TN 2nd (Robison's) Inf.
 Co.G,C
Sandling, H.K. NC 55th Inf. Co.I
Sandling, J.A. TN 21st & 22nd (Cons.) Cav.
 Co.C
Sandling, John TN 22nd (Barteau's) Cav. Co.K
Sandling, John TN 27th Inf. Co.C
Sandling, L.C. AR 21st Mil. Co.F
Sandling, Robert AL Cav. Lewis' Bn. Co.E
Sandmann, Christ. TX 1st Hvy.Arty. Co.C
Sandmeyer, J. TX Inf. 1st St.Troops Martin's
 Co.A
Sandmyre, Julian TX 13th Vol. 2nd Co.C
Sandoe, David P. VA 1st Cav. 2nd Co.D
Sandoe, John GA Cherokee Legion (St.Guards)
 Co.A
Sandoe, M.A. AL St.Arty. Co.D
Sandofer, William R. MS Horse Arty. Cook's
 Co.
Sandon, William M. AR 8th Inf. Co.F Sgt.
Sandoval, Carlos TX Cav. L. Trevinio's Co. 1st
 Cpl.
Sandoval, Gregario TX 3rd Inf. 1st Co.C
Sandoval, Ignacio TX 3rd Inf. Co.F
Sandoval, Jesus TX Cav. Benavides' Regt. Co.C
Sandoval, Jesus TX Cav. Ragsdale's Bn. 1st
 Co.C Sgt.
Sandoval, Rilar TX Cav. Ragsdale's Bn. 1st
 Co.A
Sandoz, Ami LA Conscr.
Sandoz, Charles LA 7th Cav. Co.C
Sandoz, Leonce LA 8th Inf. Co.F
Sandoz, Leonce LA Inf.Cons.Crescent Regt.
 Co.H
Sandrean, Lewis Conf.Inf. Tucker's Regt. Co.C
Sandres, Absalum NC 38th Inf. Co.H
Sandress, Correa VA 54th Mil. Co.A
Sandridge, --- TX Cav. Good's Bn. Co.B
Sandridge, Alfred L. VA Hvy.Arty. 10th Bn.
 Co.A
Sandridge, Alfred L. VA Hvy.Arty. Wilkinson's
 Co.
Sandridge, C.F. MS 8th Cav. Co.E
Sandridge, C.F. MS Inf. 3rd Bn. (St.Troops)
 Co.F
Sandridge, Charles VA Cav. 39th Bn. Co.C
Sandridge, Frederick VA 31st Inf. Co.H
Sandridge, George M. VA Lt.Arty. 12th Bn. 2nd
 Co.A
Sandridge, George M. VA Lt.Arty. Sturdivant's
 Co.
Sandridge, G.W. VA 56th Inf. Co.H Cpl.
Sandridge, Henry KY 2nd Bn.Mtd.Rifles Co.B
Sandridge, Ira L. VA Lt.Arty. 12th Bn. 2nd
 Co.A
Sandridge, Ira L. VA Lt.Arty. Sturdivant's Co.
Sandridge, James D. VA Lt.Arty. Sturdivant's
 Co.
Sandridge, James J. VA 19th Inf. Co.E Cpl.
Sandridge, John KY 2nd Bn.Mtd.Rifles Co.B
Sandridge, Mordica B. VA 56th Inf. Co.F

Sandridge, Perry KY 2nd Bn.Mtd.Rifles Co.B
Sandridge, Pleasant W. KY 6th Cav. Co.E
Sandridge, P.S. MO Cav. Wood's Regt. Co.H
Sandridge, Thomas O. VA Hvy.Arty. 10th Bn.
 Co.A
Sandridge, Thomas O. VA Hvy.Arty. Wilkin-
 son's Co.
Sandridge, William VA 56th Inf. Co.H
Sandridge, William A. VA 14th Cav. Co.H
Sandridge, William P. TN 41st Inf. Co.G
Sandridge, W.O. VA 7th Inf. Co.I
Sandridge, W.R. VA 7th Inf. Co.I
Sandridge, Zachariah VA 7th Inf. Co.I
Sandrige, William Mead's Conf.Cav. Co.F
Sandrin, H. 1st Cherokee Mtd.Vol. Co.E 1st Lt.
Sandro, Condy H. GA Inf. 3rd Bn. Co.E
Sandrue, Fred J. SC Mil.Arty. 1st Regt.
Sandry, B. LA Inf.Cons. 18th Regt. & Yellow
 Jacket Bn.
Sands, --- VA 46th Inf. Co.E
Sands, A.C. GA 46th Inf. Co.E
Sands, Alexander AR 13th Inf. Co.H
Sands, Anderson NC Inf. 2nd Bn. Co.A
Sands, Andrew TX Arty. 4th Bn. Co.B Cpl.
Sands, Andrew TX 8th Inf. Co.B Cpl.
Sands, C.F. AL 8th Inf. Co.A
Sands, C.F.S. AL Cons. & Res.Bn. Co.E 2nd
 Lt.
Sands, C.F.S Gen. & Staff 2nd Lt.,Dr.M.
Sands, C.G. GA 46th Inf.
Sands, Charles TX 1st Field Btty. Sgt.
Sands, Columbus C. NC 22nd Inf. Co.H
Sands, Constantine MO 10th Inf. Co.H
Sands, Eli VA 23rd Cav.
Sands, F.M. AL 48th Inf. Co.G
Sands, F.M. TX 1st Hvy.Arty. Co.H
Sands, G.T. TN 4th (McLemore's) Cav. Co.B
Sands, G.V. FL 7th Inf. Co.K
Sands, H. TN 8th (Smith's) Cav. Co.B
Sands, H.B. TX 2nd Inf. Co.I
Sands, J. 1st Chickasaw Inf. Wallace's Co.
Sands, Jack AR 1st (Dobbin's) Cav. McGehee's
 Co.
Sands, Jack TX 8th Inf. Co.I
Sands, James AR Cav. Chrisman's Bn. Co.A
Sands, James KY 10th (Johnson's) Cav. Co.E
Sands, James LA 9th Inf. Co.G
Sands, James MS 8th Cav. Co.K
Sands, James MS 12th Cav. Co.I
Sands, James NC Inf. 2nd Bn. Co.A
Sands, James D. TN 4th (McLemore's) Cav.
 Co.B
Sands, James R.H. VA 36th Inf. 3rd Co.I
Sands, Jasper N. TX 19th Cav. Co.F 1st Sgt.
Sands, J.E. TN 3rd (Clack's) Inf. Co.B
Sands, J.G. AR 1st Cav. Co.B
Sands, J.H. GA 46th Inf. Co.E
Sands, J.H. LA Mil. Leeds' Guards Regt. Co.F
Sands, J.M. MS 22nd Inf. Co.F
Sands, John AL 16th Inf. Co.I
Sands, John AL 48th Inf. Co.G
Sands, John AR 1st (Colquitt's) Inf. Co.D 1st
 Lt.
Sands, John LA Mil.Conf.Guards Regt. Co.G
 Cpl.
Sands, John NC 53rd Inf. Co.H
Sands, John TN Conscr. (Cp. of Instr.)

Sands, John B. FL 7th Inf. Co.K
Sands, John M. MS 33rd Inf. Co.K
Sands, John M. VA 37th Inf. Co.I
Sands, Johnson VA 3rd Inf.Loc.Def. Co.C
Sands, Johnson H. VA 1st Arty. 2nd Co.C Capt.
Sands, Joseph TN Lt.Arty. Lynch's Co.
Sands, Joseph M. VA 6th Bn.Res. Co.I
Sands, J.T. GA 46th Inf. Co.E
Sands, L.G. NC 21st Inf. Co.H
Sands, N. MS 35th Inf. Co.K
Sands, R. LA Inf. 16th Bn. (Conf.Guards
 Resp.Bn.) Co.A
Sands, R.G. TX 1st Inf. Co.E
Sands, Riley G. LA Inf. 1st Sp.Bn. (Wheat's)
 New Co.D Sgt.
Sands, R.J. MO Lt.Arty. 3rd Btty.
Sands, R.N. MS 35th Inf. Co.K
Sands, Robert M. AL 3rd Inf. Co.A Lt.Col.
Sands, Robt. M. Gen. & Staff Lt.Col.
Sands, Samuel S. VA 62nd Mtd.Inf. 2nd Co.G
Sands, S.F. TN 3rd (Clack's) Inf. Co.B Cpl.
Sands, S.W. GA 15th Inf.
Sands, Thomas TN 4th Cav.
Sands, Thomas D. MS 23rd Inf. Co.H
Sands, W.A. GA 22nd Inf.
Sands, W.B. AL 5th Cav. Co.L
Sands, William LA 18th Inf. Co.I
Sands, William TN 4th (McLemore's) Cav. Co.B
Sands, William TN 8th (Smith's) Cav. Co.B
Sands, William TN Cav. 12th Bn. (Day's) Co.A
Sands, William VA 8th Cav. Co.K
Sands, William J. VA Horse Arty. Jackson's Co.
Sands, William T. LA 5th Inf. Co.B
Sands, W.P. TN 3rd (Clack's) Inf. Co.B
Sandsberry, J.G. TX 9th (Young's) Inf. Co.A
 Cpl.
Sandsbury, J.M. SC 4th St.Troops Co.E
Sandsbury, W.A. SC 6th Cav. Co.I
Sandsford, F.M. TN 3rd (Forrest's) Cav. Co.H
Sandsing, Albert H. LA 14th Inf. Co.I Music.
Sandstrom, James KY Jessee's Bn.Mtd.Riflemen
 Co.C
Sandt, Edmond Conf.Inf. 8th Bn. Co.E Cpl.
Sandum, Thomas AL 3rd Res. Co.I
Sandurs, Solomon N. AR Inf. Hardy's Regt.
 Co.A
Sanduskey, Isaac N. AR 27th Inf. Co.D Cpl.
Sanduskey, John J. TN 53rd Inf. Co.G
Sandusky, C. KY 9th Cav. Co.C
Sandusky, Chitton KY 5th Mtd.Inf. Co.F
Sandusky, Dudley KY 5th Mtd.Inf. Co.F
Sandusky, E. AR Cav. 1st Bn.Res. Co.F Lt.
Sandusky, G.C. 3rd Conf.Cav. Co.H Capt.
Sandusky, George W. MO 2nd Inf. Co.K Capt.
Sandusky, Jacob KY 5th Mtd.Inf. Co.F Cpl.
Sandusky, James TX 26th Cav. Co.F, 2nd Co.G
 Cpl.
Sandusky, J.M. MS Inf. Lewis' Co.
Sandusky, Lewis E. KY 5th Mtd.Inf. Co.F
Sanduval, Vivian TX Cav. 3rd (Yager's) Bn.
 Co.A
Sandvan, Franz GA Lt.Arty. Daniell's Btty.
Sandwich, William O. GA 2nd Bn.S.S. Co.B
 Sr.2nd Lt.
Sandwich, William O. GA 5th Inf. Co.K,L 2nd
 Lt.
Sandwich, W.O. GA 2nd Inf. Co.B Lt.

Sandwich, W.T. GA Mil. 7th Regt. Co.A
Sandy GA 1st (Olmstead's) Inf. Co.C Cook
Sandy, No.1 1st Creek Mtd.Vol. Co.A
Sandy, No.2 1st Creek Mtd.Vol. Co.A
Sandy 1st Creek Mtd.Vol. Co.F
Sandy, A. VA Mil. Grayson Cty.
Sandy, Andrew J.M. TN 32nd Inf. Co.C
Sandy, Bane AL Randolph Cty.Res. D.A. Self's
  Co. 1st Sgt.
Sandy, Ellison P. VA 15th Cav. Co.G
Sandy, Ellison P. VA Cav. 15th Bn. Co.D
Sandy, Ellison P. VA 41st Mil. Co.E
Sandy, E.P. VA 5th Cav.
Sandy, George H. VA 37th Mil. Co.E
Sandy, George H. VA 40th Inf.
Sandy, George W. TX 3rd Cav. Co.H
Sandy, George W. VA 9th Cav. Sandford's Co.
Sandy, George W. VA 15th Cav. Co.A Sgt.
Sandy, George W. VA Cav. 15th Bn. Co.A
Sandy, G.W. VA 5th Cav.
Sandy, Hiram M. VA 40th Inf. Co.D
Sandy, J.E. VA 5th Cav.
Sandy, John NC 16th Inf. Co.I
Sandy, John VA 58th Mil. Co.D
Sandy, John A.W. NC 51st Inf. Co.I
Sandy, John E. VA 15th Cav. Co.G Sgt.
Sandy, John E. VA Cav. 15th Bn. Co.D Sgt.
Sandy, John E. VA 41st Mil. Co.E Cpl.
Sandy, John H. VA 2nd Inf. Co.B
Sandy, John S. VA 15th Cav. Co.A
Sandy, John S. VA 47th Inf. Co.C
Sandy, John S. VA 55th Inf. Co.E
Sandy, John W. VA 23rd Cav. Co.B
Sandy, Joseph N. TN 20th Cav.
Sandy, J.S. VA 5th Cav.
Sandy, Lorenzo VA 9th Bn.Res. Co.B
Sandy, Marion TN 32nd Inf. Co.C
Sandy, Mart W. VA Mil. Grayson Cty.
Sandy, P.A. Gen. & Staff Capt.,AQM
Sandy, Phillip A. VA 55th Inf. Co.F Capt.
Sandy, Reuben W. VA 10th Inf. Co.D
Sandy, Samuel VA 6th Cav. Co.C
Sandy, Samuel VA 58th Mil. Co.D
Sandy, Samuel VA 58th Mil. Co.G
Sandy, Thomas AL 95th Mil. Co.D
Sandy, Thomas TN 21st (Wilson's) Cav. Co.F
Sandy, Thomas W. TN 54th Inf. Ives' Co.
Sandy, Tilman VA 58th Mil. Co.D
Sandy, Tilmon VA 2nd Inf. Co.B
Sandy, T.W. TN 48th (Nixon's) Inf. Co.I
Sandy, W. VA Cav. 41st Bn. Co.B
Sandy, W.H. TN 48th (Nixon's) Inf. Co.G
Sandy, William VA 7th Cav. Co.H
Sandy, William VA 62nd Mtd.Inf. 2nd Co.A
Sandy, William H. VA 40th Inf. Co.D
Sandy, William J. NC 8th Inf. Co.E
Sandyford, W.G. AR 36th Inf. Co.B
Sandz, Ferdinando LA 28th (Thomas') Inf. Co.F
Sane, Andrew NC 57th Inf. Co.G
Sane, Andrew TN 1st (Feild's) Inf.
Sane, A.W. AL 21st Inf. Co.K
Sane, Conrad TX Inf. Timmons' Regt. Co.K
Sane, Conrad TX Waul's Legion Co.B
Sane, Daniel NC 34th Inf. Co.E
Sane, Daniel NC 57th Inf. Co.G
Sane, D.F. KY 3rd Mtd.Inf. Co.L Cpl.
Sane, D.F. TN 12th Inf. Co.E

Sane, Elijah NC 34th Inf. Co.C
Sane, G.W. TN 34th Inf. Co.I
Sane, J.A. 3rd Conf.Eng.Troops Co.C
Sane, Jacob, Jr. NC 34th Inf. Co.E
Sane, Jacob, Sr. NC 34th Inf. Co.E
Sane, John NC 57th Inf. Co.G
Sane, John TN 12th Inf. Co.C
Sane, Joseph NC 57th Inf. Co.G
Sane, Levi NC 57th Inf. Co.G
Sane, Nathan NC 66th Inf. Co.G
Sane, Nathan NC Pris.Guards Howard's Co.
Sane, Noah NC 57th Inf. Co.G
Sane, Samuel GA 52nd Inf. Co.D
Sane, Solomon NC 16th Inf. Co.D
Sane, Thomas GA 52nd Inf. Co.D
Sane, W. GA 15th Inf.
Sanellin, Daniel AL 36th Inf. Co.D
Saner, John F. AR 20th Inf. Co.A 2nd Lt.
Sanerbry, Adolph Conf.Lt.Arty. 1st Reg.Btty.
Sanes, A.J. TN 4th (McLemore's) Cav. Co.I
Sanes, J.F. AR 3rd Inf. Co.A
Sanes, L. AR 3rd Inf. Co.A
Sanfer, James VA 1st Arty. Co.F
Sanfer, James VA Arty. Dance's Co.
Sanfer, James VA 32nd Inf. Co.G
Sanferd, W.G.L. VA 79th Mil. Co.2
Sanfield, Hender AR 1st (Crawford's) Cav. Co.B
Sanfield, J.O. NC 4th Inf. Co.B
Sanfley, James VA 6th Cav. Co.C
Sanfley, J.C. TX Cav. Crump's Regt. Co.B
Sanfley, John C. TX 2nd Cav. Co.F
Sanfley, Mike C. KY 6th Cav. Co.H 2nd Lt.
Sanfley, Thomas J. TX 9th (Young's) Inf. Co.A
  ACS
Sanfley, Thos. J. Gen. & Staff Capt.,
  Asst.Comsy.
Sanfly, John VA 6th Cav. Co.C
Sanford, --- TX Cav. 4th Regt.St.Troops Co.I
Sanford, --- TX 33rd Cav. Co.B Sgt.
Sanford, --- TX Cav. Bourland's Regt. Co.G
Sanford, A. AL 34th Inf. Co.A
Sanford, Absolem B. AL 41st Inf. Co.A
Sanford, Adolphus S. VA 40th Inf. Co.K
Sanford, Alexander M. TX 14th Cav. Co.G
  Capt.
Sanford, Alfred VA Westmoreland Cty.Res.
Sanford, Allen GA Cobb's Legion
Sanford, Alvin VA 40th Inf. Co.E
Sanford, A.M. TN 4th Cav. Co.G Capt.
Sanford, A.P. AL 14th Inf. Co.A
Sanford, A.W. GA 22nd Inf. Co.H
Sanford, A.W.H. TX 33rd Cav. Co.A Sgt.
Sanford, A.W.H. TX Greer's Rocket Btty.
Sanford, B. AL 51st (Part.Rangers) Co.D
Sanford, B. GA Cav. 9th Bn. (St.Guards) Co.E
Sanford, B. VA 9th Cav. Co.D
Sanford, B.A. LA 13th Bn. (Part.Rangers) Co.D
Sanford, Bailey TN 7th (Duckworth's) Cav.
  Co.B,F
Sanford, B.D. TN 10th (DeMoss') Cav. Co.A
Sanford, Ben TN 45th Inf. Co.C
Sanford, Ben J. TX 35th (Brown's) Cav. Co.C
Sanford, Benjamin GA Arty. St.Troops Pruden's
  Btty.
Sanford, Benjamin B. GA Floyd Legion
  (St.Guards) Co.G

Sanford, Benjamin B. 8th (Wade's) Conf.Cav.
  Co.G
Sanford, Benjamin F. AL 11th Inf. Co.F Cpl.
Sanford, Benjamin H. AL 38th Inf. Co.C Cpl.
Sanford, Benjamin J. TX 8th Cav. Co.L Sgt.
Sanford, Benjamin W. GA 57th Inf. Co.E Sgt.
Sanford, B.J. TX Cav. Ragsdale's Bn. Co.B 2nd
  Lt.
Sanford, B.O. MS 46th Inf. Co.K
Sanford, B.O. VA 59th Inf. 2nd Co.F Sgt.
Sanford, B.R. NC 26th Inf. Co.F
Sanford, Calvin C. NC 42nd Inf. Co.F 3rd Lt.
Sanford, C.B. AL 1st Regt. Mobile Vol. Co.E
Sanford, C.B. AL 4th Res. Co.B
Sanford, C.H. VA 5th Cav.
Sanford, C.H. VA 15th Cav. Co.A
Sanford, Charles GA Smith's Legion Co.B
Sanford, Charles TN 34th Inf. Co.F
Sanford, Charles R. GA 44th Inf. Co.F 1st Sgt.
Sanford, Charles W. AL 1st Regt.Conscr. Co.F
Sanford, C.K. AL 40th Inf. Co.B
Sanford, C.V. GA Arty. 11th Bn. (Sumter Arty.)
  New Co.C
Sanford, C.W. AL 34th Inf. Co.A
Sanford, C.W. GA 65th Inf. Co.A
Sanford, D. VA 3rd Arty. Co.H
Sanford, D.A. VA 2nd Inf.Loc.Def. Co.F
Sanford, D.A. VA Inf. 6th Bn.Loc.Def. Co.C
Sanford, Daniel B. GA Phillips' Legion Co.A
  Capt.
Sanford, Daniel M. GA 14th Inf. Co.A
Sanford, Dennis B. NC 52nd Inf. Co.E
Sanford, Derrel MS Cav. 1st Bn. (McNair's)
  St.Troops Co.C Sgt.
Sanford, Douglas NC 1st Arty. (10th St.Troops)
  Co.C
Sanford, E. GA 2nd Inf.
Sanford, E. MS Inf. 1st Bn.St.Troops (12 mo.
  '62-3) Co.D
Sanford, E.C. MO Lt.Arty. 1st Btty.
Sanford, E.C. MO Lt.Arty. H.M. Bledsoe's Co.
Sanford, E.C. VA 47th Inf. Co.C
Sanford, Edouard LA C.S. Zouave Bn. Co.B
Sanford, Edward MD Arty. 1st Btty.
Sanford, Edward MO Lt.Arty. H.M. Bledsoe's
  Co.
Sanford, E.Q. VA 7th Bn.Res. Co.B
Sanford, Ezekiel AL 4th Cav.
Sanford, F. AL 32nd Inf. Co.E
Sanford, Felix P. AL 47th Inf. Co.K
Sanford, F.F. MS 11th (Perrin's) Cav. Co.C
Sanford, F.J. AL 34th Inf. Co.A
Sanford, F.M. AR Inf. Cocke's Regt. Co.D
Sanford, Francis M. AL Lt.Arty. Ward's Btty.
Sanford, G.B. VA 59th Inf. 2nd Co.F
Sanford, George AL 12th Inf. Co.A
Sanford, George AL 34th Inf. Co.A
Sanford, George GA Hvy.Arty. 22nd Bn. Co.D
Sanford, George VA 41st Mil. Co.B
Sanford, George P. VA 2nd Cav. Co.F Sgt.
Sanford, George W. AL 13th Inf. Co.F
Sanford, George W. MS 23rd Inf. Co.B
Sanford, Gerard VA 111th Mil. Co.4
Sanford, Gerrord VA Cav. 15th Bn. Co.A
Sanford, G.K. GA 8th Inf. Co.A Jr.2nd Lt.
Sanford, G.P. MS 46th Inf. Co.K
Sanford, Green W. AL 3rd Bn.Res. Co.C Sgt.

Sanford, G.W. AL 2nd Bn. Hilliard's Legion
  Vol. Co.B
Sanford, G.W. MS 7th Cav. Co.B
Sanford, H. AL 8th (Hatch's) Cav. Co.I
Sanford, H. AL 56th Part.Rangers Co.B
Sanford, H. MS 46th Inf. Co.K
Sanford, H. TX Cav. Border's Regt. Co.D
Sanford, H.C. AL 5th Bn.Vol. Co.C
Sanford, Henderson VA 27th Inf. Co.E Sgt.
Sanford, Henry AL 15th Bn.Part.Rangers Co.B
Sanford, Henry GA 19th Inf. Co.H
Sanford, Henry GA 44th Inf. Co.I
Sanford, Henry TN 51st Inf. Capt.,AQM
Sanford, Henry TN 51st (Cons.) Inf. Co.G
  Ord.Sgt.
Sanford, Henry 1st Conf.Cav. 2nd Co.E Cpl.
Sanford, Henry Hardee's Corps AQM
Sanford, Henry F. VA 34th Inf. Co.K
Sanford, Henry F. VA 40th Inf. Co.I
Sanford, Henry H. GA 23rd Inf. Co.E
Sanford, Henry H. GA 26th Inf. 1st Co.G
Sanford, Henry H. GA 29th Inf. Co.E
Sanford, Henry H. VA 55th Inf. Co.E
Sanford, H.H. SC 5th Cav. Co.I
Sanford, H.H. SC Cav. 14th Bn. Co.D
Sanford, Hilard NC Inf. 2nd Bn. Co.G
Sanford, Holman H. AL 13th Inf. Co.C
Sanford, H.P. AL 41st Inf. Co.E
Sanford, H.P. AL 47th Inf. Co.E
Sanford, H.W. AL 2nd Cav. Co.C
Sanford, J. AL 44th Inf. Co.A
Sanford, J. AR Lt.Arty. Hart's Btty.
Sanford, J. MO 1st & 4th Cons.Inf. Co.E
Sanford, J.A. GA 48th Inf. Co.E
Sanford, James AL Mil. 2nd Regt.Vol. Co.A
Sanford, James AL 3rd Inf. Co.G
Sanford, James AL 31st Inf. Co.K Sgt.
Sanford, James GA Cav. 9th Bn. (St.Guards)
  Co.E
Sanford, James GA 19th Inf. Co.H
Sanford, James LA Hvy.Arty. 2nd Bn. Co.A
Sanford, James MS 10th Cav. Co.H
Sanford, James MS 2nd (Davidson's) Inf. Co.H
  Sgt.
Sanford, James MS 15th (Cons.) Inf. Co.K Cpl.
Sanford, James MO Cav. Hicks' Co.
Sanford, James VA 47th Inf. Co.C
Sanford, James VA 92nd Mil. Co.C
Sanford, James Conf.Cav. Baxter's Bn. Co.A
Sanford, James Conf.Inf. Tucker's Regt. Co.F
Sanford, James A. AL Inf. 1st Regt. Co.A Sgt.
Sanford, James A. AL 47th Inf. Co.K Capt.
Sanford, James A. LA 31st Inf. Co.B
Sanford, James B. VA 111th Mil. Co.4,2
Sanford, James G. TN 32nd Inf. Co.G Bvt.2nd
  Lt.
Sanford, James H. NC 62nd Inf. Co.A Sgt.
Sanford, James H. TX 13th Vol. 2nd Co.F Capt.
Sanford, James L. VA 55th Inf. Co.E
Sanford, James N. VA 40th Inf. Co.I
Sanford, James O. NC 34th Inf. Co.G
Sanford, James R. MS 23rd Inf. Co.B Sgt.
Sanford, James R. TN 2nd (Robison's) Inf. Co.I
  Sgt.
Sanford, James Robt. Gen. & Staff AASurg.
Sanford, J.B. GA 28th Inf. Co.G
Sanford, J.B. VA Lt.Arty. 12th Bn. Co.B

Sanford, J.B. Mead's Conf.Cav. Co.F
Sanford, Jeptha TX 9th (Nichols') Inf. Co.D
Sanford, Jerrie GA 9th Inf. Co.F
Sanford, Jesse AL 31st Inf. Co.C
Sanford, Jesse AL 58th Inf. Co.E
Sanford, Jesse SC 2nd Arty. Co.C
Sanford, Jesse J.R. LA 31st Inf. Co.I
Sanford, J.G. TN 35th Inf. 2nd Co.I Cpl.
Sanford, J.H. AL 53rd (Part.Rangers) Co.C
Sanford, J.H. AR 24th Inf. Co.H
Sanford, J.H. MS 2nd (Quinn's St.Troops) Inf.
  Co.D
Sanford, J.H. TN 45th Inf. Co.H
Sanford, J.H. TX Cav. Benavides' Regt. 1st Lt.
Sanford, J.L. LA 5th Cav. Co.C
Sanford, J.L. TX 2nd Inf. Co.I
Sanford, J.M. AL 14th Inf. Co.H
Sanford, J.M. AL 18th Inf. Co.B
Sanford, J.M. TX 12th Inf. Co.K
Sanford, John AL Lt.Arty. Ward's Btty.
Sanford, John GA Cav. 19th Bn. Co.A
Sanford, John GA Cav. 20th Bn. Co.C
Sanford, John LA 9th Inf. Co.B
Sanford, John MS Inf. 3rd Bn. Co.A
Sanford, John MS Inf. Perkins' Bn. Co.D
Sanford, John VA 55th Inf. Co.E
Sanford, John 10th Conf.Cav. Co.F
Sanford, John A. GA Lt.Arty. 12th Bn. 2nd
  Co.D
Sanford, John A. TX 2nd Inf. Co.K Cpl.
Sanford, John B. AL 10th Inf. Co.B
Sanford, John C. KY 6th Cav.
Sanford, John D. MS 9th Cav. Co.B
Sanford, John D. MS Cav. 17th Bn. Co.B,D
Sanford, John H. AL Inf. 1st Regt. Co.A 2nd
  Lt.
Sanford, John H. AL 13th Inf. Co.F
Sanford, John H. GA Lt.Arty. Millege's Co.
Sanford, John H. GA 1st Reg. Co.A
Sanford, John L. NC 1st Arty. (10th St.Troops)
  Co.K
Sanford, John L. NC 17th Inf. (1st Org.) Co.H
Sanford, John M. NC 34th Inf. Co.G
Sanford, John R. AL 41st Inf. Co.H
Sanford, John R. TX 28th Cav. Co.A,K
Sanford, John S. AL 13th Inf. Co.F
Sanford, John T. MS 1st (Patton's) Inf. Co.E
Sanford, John W. AL 41st Inf. Co.H
Sanford, John W. MO Lt.Arty. 1st Btty. 1st Sgt.
Sanford, John W.A. AL 3rd Inf. Co.F QM
Sanford, John W.A. AL 60th Inf. Col.
Sanford, John W.A. GA 4th Inf. Co.H
Sanford, Jno. W.A. Gen. & Staff Col.
Sanford, Joseph AR 2nd Inf. Co.G
Sanford, Joseph MS 11th (Cons.) Cav. Co.E
Sanford, Joseph TN 45th Inf. Co.C
Sanford, Joseph VA Lt.Arty. Pollock's Co.
Sanford, Joseph Lt.Arty. Dent's Btty.,CSA
Sanford, Joseph B., Jr. VA 9th Cav. Co.E
Sanford, Josephus H. TX 14th Cav. Co.B
Sanford, J.R. TN 7th (Duckworth's) Cav. Co.I
Sanford, J.R. TN 24th Inf. Co.E Cpl.
Sanford, J.R. TN 51st Inf. Co.G 3rd Lt.
Sanford, J.S. LA 13th Bn. (Part.Rangers) Co.D
Sanford, J.T. TX Cav. Saufley's Scouting Bn.
  Co.C
Sanford, J.W. AL 26th Inf. Co.H

Sanford, J.W. SC 12th Inf. Co.G
Sanford, J.W.A. AL 3rd Bn. Hilliard's Legion
  Vol. Lt.Col.
Sanford, J.Y. AR 27th Inf. Co.D
Sanford, Larkin L. AL 41st Inf. Co.A
Sanford, Lawrence VA Lt.Arty. Pollock's Co.
Sanford, L.C. LA Cav. Benjamin's Co.
Sanford, L.H. AL 31st Inf. Co.A
Sanford, M.A. AL Inf. 1st Regt. Co.A
Sanford, Marion TN 20th Inf. Co.B
Sanford, Martin V. GA 35th Inf. Co.A
Sanford, M.J. FL Cav. 5th Bn. Co.G
Sanford, Moses LA 28th (Gray's) Inf. Co.F
Sanford, Nathan C. GA 3rd Inf. Co.C
Sanford, Nathaniel MS 33rd Inf. Co.C
Sanford, N.G. VA Inf. 3rd Regt. Co.I
Sanford, N.J. AL 24th Inf. Co.G Cpl.
Sanford, N.J. AL 34th Inf. Co.A Cpl.
Sanford, O.P. GA Inf. 1st Bn. (St.Guards) Co.A
Sanford, Perry LA 1st Cav. Asst.Surg.
Sanford, Presley KY 9th Mtd.Inf. Co.K
Sanford, R. TN 15th (Stewart's) Cav. Co.D
Sanford, R.A. TN 3rd (Forrest's) Cav. Maj.
Sanford, R.A. Gen. & Staff 1st Lt.,Adj.
Sanford, Raymond B. GA 38th Inf. Co.N
Sanford, R.B. GA 5th Inf. Co.G
Sanford, R.B. GA Inf. 25th Bn. (Prov.Guard)
  Co.E Sgt.
Sanford, R.H. TN 47th Inf. Co.A
Sanford, R.H. TX 21st Cav. Co.D
Sanford, R.H. TX 25th Cav. Co.A
Sanford, Richard TN 12th (Green's) Cav. Co.C
Sanford, Richard TN 45th Inf. Co.C Capt.
Sanford, Richard H. VA 41st Mil. Co.C
Sanford, Rob AL 89th Mil. Co.B
Sanford, Robert LA 30th Inf. Co.D
Sanford, Robert MS Inf. 2nd St.Troops Co.C
Sanford, Robert TN 15th (Cons.) Cav. Co.H
Sanford, Robert VA 55th Inf. Co.E
Sanford, Robert A. VA 9th Cav. Co.C
Sanford, Robert J. VA 111th Mil. Co.2 Capt.
Sanford, Samuel SC 15th Inf. Co.C
Sanford, Samuel TX Cav. Crump's Regt. Co.G
  1st Lt.
Sanford, Samuel VA 37th Mil. Co.E
Sanford, Samuel VA 40th Inf. Co.C
Sanford, Samuel G. AL 63rd Inf. Co.B
Sanford, Samuel H. LA 19th Inf. Co.A,E
Sanford, Sam'l. W. TN 3rd (Forrest's) Cav.
  Co.F
Sanford, S.B. LA 17th Inf. Co.B Cpl.
Sanford, S.H. TN 1st Cav.
Sanford, S.J. Conf.Inf. Tucker's Regt. Co.G
Sanford, S.P. SC 2nd Rifles Co.D 1st Lt.
Sanford, Stephen TN 27th Inf. Co.C Capt.
Sanford, S.W. TN 3rd (Forrest's) Cav. Co.F
Sanford, Taylor MS 9th Cav. Co.B
Sanford, T.G. GA Arty. St.Troops Pruden's Btty.
Sanford, T.H. GA 4th Cav. (St.Guards)
  Armstrong's Co.
Sanford, T.H. GA Inf. 25th Bn. (Prov.Guard)
  Co.E QMSgt.
Sanford, Thad., Jr. AL 8th Inf. Co.C
Sanford, Theodore G. GA Lt.Arty. 12th Bn.
Sanford, Theodore G. GA 4th Inf. Co.H
Sanford, Thomas FL 1st Inf.
Sanford, Thomas KY 10th Cav.

Sanford, Thomas MS 9th Inf. Old Co.C, New
Co.A
Sanford, Thomas B. LA Watkins' Bn.Res.Corps
Co.C
Sanford, Thomas J. GA Phillips' Legion Co.A
Sanford, Thomas L. AL 7th Inf. Co.A
Sanford, Thos. L. Gen. & Staff 1st Lt.,Adj.
Sanford, Thomas P. TX 1st Inf. Co.M 1st Lt.
Sanford, Thomas S. GA 14th Inf. Co.A
Sanford, Thos. S.J. Gen. & Staff Capt.,Comsy.
Sanford, T.J. AL Cp. of Instr. Talladega
Sanford, T.J.J. AR 15th (Johnson's) Inf. Co.B
Sanford, T.J.S. AL 28th Inf. Comsy.
Sanford, Truman H. GA 38th Inf. Co.N 1st Lt.
Sanford, Tully C. GA Inf. 27th Bn. Co.A
Sanford, Turley G. KY 2nd (Woodward's) Cav.
Co.B
Sanford, T.V. Field's Staff Capt.,Pay M.
Sanford, T.W. AL 4th Cav. Co.B Sgt.
Sanford, T.W. SC 22nd Inf. Co.D Cpl.
Sanford, V. TN 3rd (Forrest's) Cav. Co.H
Sanford, Val TN 12th (Green's) Cav. Co.C
Sanford, Van. VA 8th Cav. Co.G
Sanford, Van B. VA 36th Inf. Beckett's Co.
Sanford, Van Linden VA 1st Cav. Co.F 1st Lt.
Sanford, Vinson H. AL Inf. 1st Regt. Co.H
Sanford, W. GA Lt.Arty. Barnwell's Btty. Artif.
Sanford, Wade SC 15th Inf. Co.C,I
Sanford, Wade F. GA 57th Inf. Co.A,G
Sanford, W.B. VA 8th Cav. Co.H
Sanford, W.C. TN 45th Inf. Co.K Cpl.
Sanford, W.D. AL 24th Inf. Co.H
Sanford, W.D. LA Inf. 4th Bn. Co.F Sr.2nd Lt.
Sanford, W. Daniel TX 2nd Cav. 1st Co.F
Sanford, W. Daniel TX Cav. Morgan's Regt.
Co.I
Sanford, W.E. VA 5th Cav.
Sanford, W.F. GA Conscr.
Sanford, W.G. SC 1st (Hagood's) Inf. 1st Co.C
Sanford, W.H. Gen. & Staff, QM Dept. Capt.
Sanford, William AL 7th Cav. Co.I Sgt.
Sanford, William AR 13th Inf. Co.E Sgt.
Sanford, William GA 12th Cav. Co.L
Sanford, William GA 8th Inf. Co.G
Sanford, William GA 65th Inf. Co.A
Sanford, William GA Smith's Legion Co.B
Sanford, William KY 7th Mtd.Inf. 1st Co.K Sgt.
Sanford, William LA 15th Inf. Co.E
Sanford, William NC 33rd Inf. Co.D
Sanford, William TN 7th (Duckworth's) Cav.
Co.I
Sanford, William TX 28th Cav. Co.A,K
Sanford, William TX 17th Inf. Co.E
Sanford, William Conf.Inf. Tucker's Regt. Co.C
Sanford, William B. MO 3rd Regt.St.Guards
Sanford, William D. SC 12th Inf. Co.G
Sanford, William E. VA Murphy's Co.
Sanford, William F. MO 2nd Cav. Co.B
Sanford, William Frank NC 52nd Inf. Co.E
Sanford, William H. LA 31st Inf. Co.B
Sanford, William J. AL 13th Inf. Co.F
Sanford, William J. AL 46th Inf. Co.G 1st Lt.
Sanford, William L. AL Inf. 1st Regt. Co.H,K
Sgt.
Sanford, William M. GA 35th Inf. Co.A
Sanford, William N. AR 4th Inf. Co.G
Sanford, William P. AL 61st Inf. Co.E

Sanford, William R. VA 5th Cav. (12 mo. '61-2)
Co.A,I
Sanford, William R. VA Cav. 14th Bn. Co.B
Sanford, William R. VA 15th Cav. Co.I
Sanford, William S. 8th (Wade's) Conf.Cav.
Co.G
Sanford, William T. VA 1st Cav. Co.F
Sanford, W.L. SC Inf. Hampton Legion Co.H
Sanford, W.M. AR 1st Mtd.Rifles Co.F
Sanford, W.M. TX 33rd Cav. Co.K
Sanford, W.S. GA Lt.Arty. Van Den Corput's
Co.
Sanford, W.S. GA 43rd Inf. Co.I
Sanford, W.S. GA Floyd Legion (St.Guards)
Co.I
Sanford, W.T. AL 39th Inf. Co.H
Sanford, W.W. AL 1st Cav. Co.C
Sanford, Zacchariah C. LA Inf. 11th Bn. Co.C
Sanford, Z.C. LA Inf.Cons.Crescent Regt. Co.F
Sanforien, S. LA 21st (Kennedy's) Inf. Co.D
Sangaver, V.M. VA Cav. 40th Bn.
Sanger, Daniel VA 58th Mil. Co.G
Sanger, E.E. 2nd Creek Mtd.Vol. Capt.,ACS
Sanger, F. AR 3rd St.Inf. 1st Lt.
Sanger, F.M. Gen. & Staff Capt.,AQM
Sanger, H.H. TX 2nd Inf. Co.B
Sanger, I. TX Cav. McCord's Frontier Regt.
Co.G
Sanger, Jacob VA 58th Mil. Co.K
Sanger, Joseph VA Cav. Hounshell's Bn. Thur-
mond's Co. Cpl.
Sanger, L. TX 21st Inf. Co.I
Sanger, Lehman TX Inf. Griffin's Bn. Co.A
Sanger, Phillip GA 32nd Inf. Co.G
Sanger, Stephen S. 2nd Creek Mtd.Vol. QMSgt.
Sanger, W.F.M. AR 3rd Inf. (St.Troops) Stuart's
Co.
Sanger, William H. VA 22nd Inf. Co.K
Sanges, John R. GA 7th Inf. (St.Guards) Co.E
Sanginna, J.B. GA 30th Inf. Co.B
Sangpo, H. 1st Chickasaw Inf. McCord's Co.
Sangroevber, A. AL Inf. 1st Regt. Co.F
Sangrouber, Edwin AL 43rd Inf. Co.A Music.
Sangruber, Albert LA 1st (Strawbridge's) Inf.
Co.F
Sangsing, J.D. AL Lt.Arty. Tarrant's Btty.
Sangster, A.E. TN 6th Inf. Co.A
Sangster, D.J. GA 55th Inf. Co.C
Sangster, E. VA 3rd Inf.Loc.Def. Co.D
Sangster, F.M. TN 9th Inf. Co.B Cpl.
Sangster, G.A. TN 22nd Inf. Co.B 2nd Lt.
Sangster, George TN 7th (Duckworth's) Cav.
Co.E
Sangster, H.C. TN 7th (Duckworth's) Cav. Co.L
Sangster, J. VA 3rd Inf.Loc.Def. Co.K
Sangster, James M. AR 1st (Monroe's) Cav.
Co.G
Sangster, J.H.L. VA 17th Inf. Co.A Cpl.
Sangster, John TN 7th (Duckworth's) Cav. Co.L
Sangster, J.W. TN 15th (Stewart's) Cav. Co.F
Sangster, M.W. TN 9th Inf. Co.B
Sangster, Robert GA 8th Cav. Co.K
Sangster, Robert GA 62nd Cav. Co.K
Sangster, S.O. TN 7th (Duckworth's) Cav. Co.A
Cpl.
Sangster, Thomas R. VA 17th Inf. Co.A
Sangster, William GA Inf. 26th Bn. Co.A

Sangston, H.W. SC 8th Rifles
Sangton, M.H. VA 1st Cav. Co.A
Sanguinet, John LA 18th Inf. Co.A
Sanguinette, John MS 11th Inf. Co.B
Sanguinetti, S. VA 2nd St.Res. Co.E
Sanguinnette, John SC 19th Inf. Co.F
Saniford, W.S. FL 2nd Inf. Co.F
Sanines, S.S. LA Inf.Cons.Crescent Regt. Co.C
Sanis, W. AR Mil. Desha Cty.Bn.
Sanit, George W. AL 17th Inf. Co.E
Sankey, G.T. AL 15th Bn.Part.Rangers Co.A
Sankey, G.T. AL 56th Part.Rangers Co.A
Sankey, H.L. GA Cav. Ragland's Co.
Sankey, Hugh L. GA Cav. Nelson's Ind.Co.
Sankey, R.O. AL 15th Bn.Part.Rangers Co.A
Sgt.
Sankey, R.O. AL 56th Part.Rangers Co.A Sgt.
Sankey, S.L. AL 22nd Inf. Co.K
Sankey, William J. AL 39th Inf. Co.E 2nd Lt.
Sankins, J.J. GA 1st Inf. Co.D
Sankit, J.W. KY Hall's Guerrillas
Sanks, George M. FL Cav. 3rd Bn. Co.D
Sanks, George M. 15th Conf.Cav. Co.I
Sanks, George W. VA 61st Mil. Co.D Music.
Sanks, John W. 15th Conf.Cav. Co.I
Sanks, J.W. FL Cav. 3rd Bn. Co.D
Sanksley, H. GA 16th Inf. Co.H
Sanlar, Joseph AL 5th Inf. Co.D
Sanley, William A. NC 32nd Inf. Co.F
Sanlin, --- TX Cav. Baird's Regt. Co.G
Sanlin, Benjamin W. AL 7th Inf. Co.K
Sanlin, George L. NC 49th Inf. Co.A
Sanlin, J.H. LA 16th Inf. Co.E
Sanlin, Joseph N. AL 4th Cav. Co.A Sgt.
Sanlis, P. LA 3rd Inf. Co.G
Sanlon, Lewis AL 19th Inf. Co.K
Sanly, John H. NC Cav. 5th Bn. Co.A
San Migel, Domingo TX Cav. Benavides' Regt.
Co.A
San Migel, Nabor TX Cav. Benavides' Regt.
Co.A
San Migel, Rafael TX Cav. Benavides' Regt.
Co.A
San Migual, Blas TX Cav. Benavides' Regt.
Co.D
San Miguel, Alejandro TX 33rd Cav. 1st Co.I
San Miguel, Alejandro TX Cav. Benavides' Regt.
Co.B
San Miguel, Andrew TX 6th Inf. Co.K
San Miguel, D. TX Cav. L. Trevinio's Co.
San Miguel, George TX 3rd Inf. 1st Co.A, Co.G
San Miguel, Jacinto TX 17th Field Btty.
San Miguel, Nabor TX 33rd Cav. 1st Co.H
San Miguel, Rafel TX Cav. Ragsdale's Bn. 1st
Co.A
San Miguil, Domingo TX 33rd Cav. 1st Co.H
San Miguil, Filipe TX 33rd Cav. Co.H
Sannders, Thomas J. LA Inf. 11th Bn. Co.F
Sannduels, J. NC 5th Inf. Co.E
Sanner, Abraham VA 136th Mil. Co.H
Sanner, Alex. O. VA Lt.Arty. (Loc.Def.) Otey's
Co.
Sanner, C. VA 17th Cav. Co.H
Sanner, Charles H. VA 13th Inf. Co.D
Sanner, J.M. Gen. & Staff Maj.,QM
Sanner, John C. VA 13th Inf. Co.D
Sanner, Joseph C. VA Inf. 4th Bn.Loc.Def. Co.E

Sanner, Joseph C. VA 16th Inf. Co.C 1st Sgt.
Sanner, Joseph H. VA 13th Inf. Co.D,B
Sanner, V. SC 17th Inf. Co.B
Sanner, William H. MS 2nd (Davidson's) Inf. Potts' Co. 2nd Lt.
Sannichson, Nicholas H. MS 27th Inf. Co.L
Sannitt, Michael LA 20th Inf. Co.C
Sannon, --- NC 14th Inf. Co.B
Sannon, Theophiles LA Mil. 1st Native Guards Sgt.
Sannoner, F.J. GA 23rd Inf. (Loc.Def.) Cook's Co. Adj.
Sannoner, F.J. TN Inf. 3rd Bn. Co.E
Sannoner, Frank GA Inf. 23rd Bn.Loc.Def. Cook's Co.
Sannoner, James H. TN 4th Inf. Co.H Capt.
Sannoner, Samuel LA 20th Inf. Co.I 2nd Lt.
Sannoner, Samuel TN 4th Inf. Co.H Bvt.2nd Lt.
Sanorige, William TX 9th Cav. Co.F
Sanpilipo, D.P. AL 21st Inf. Co.G
San Romain, Gustave LA Inf.Cons.Crescent Regt. Co.E
Sans, Diego LA Mil. 5th Regt.Eur.Brig. (Spanish Regt.) Co.5
Sans, H. TX 13th Vol. Co.C
Sans, Robert NC 29th Inf. Co.D
Sansberry, J.H. SC 8th Inf. Co.A
Sansberry, J.W. TX Loc.Def. Perry's Co. (Fort Bend Scouts) Sgt.
Sansbery, William SC Inf. Hampton Legion Co.G
Sansbey, Robert GA 41st Inf. Co.C
Sansbuery, John TN 7th (Duckworth's) Cav. Co.M
Sansburg, John N. AL 27th Inf. Co.F Sgt.
Sansbury, Burdell SC 21st Inf. Co.K
Sansbury, Cowen L. SC 21st Inf. Co.K 1st Lt.
Sansbury, Daniel SC 21st Inf. Co.G
Sansbury, E.F. SC Inf. 9th Bn. Co.F Cpl.
Sansbury, E.F. SC 26th Inf. Co.G Cpl.
Sansbury, E.T. SC Inf. 9th Bn. Co.F
Sansbury, E.T. SC 26th Inf. Co.G
Sansbury, J.D. SC Lt.Arty. 3rd (Palmetto) Bn. Co.E
Sansbury, J.D. SC Inf. 9th Bn. Co.F
Sansbury, J.D. SC 26th Inf. Co.G
Sansbury, J.L. SC Inf. 9th Bn. Co.F
Sansbury, J.L. SC 26th Inf. Co.G 2nd Lt.
Sansbury, John N. AL 57th Inf. Co.D Sgt.
Sansbury, J.W. TX Cav. 3rd Regt.St.Troops Co.A
Sansbury, J.W. TX Cav. Waller's Regt. Goode's Co. Cpl.
Sansbury, T.J. SC Inf. 9th Bn. Co.F
Sansbury, T.J. SC 26th Inf. Co.G Sgt.
Sansbury, W. SC Lt.Arty. 3rd (Palmetto) Bn. Co.E
Sansbury, W.A.E. TX 29th Cav. Co.C
Sansbury, W.W. SC Inf. 9th Bn. Co.F
Sansbury, W.W. SC 26th Inf. Co.G
Sansero, Germasinto TX Cav. Benavides' Regt. Co.C Sgt.
Sansibaugh, Thomas VA 25th Inf. 1st Co.H
Sansibaugh, Thomas VA 62nd Mtd.Inf. 2nd Co.B
Sansibough, David VA 53rd Inf.
Sansing, F.M. LA 9th Inf. Co.A

Sansing, Francis MS 1st Cav.Res. Co.D
Sansing, Francis MS 5th Inf. (St.Troops) Co.E 2nd Lt.
Sansing, G.P.C. MS 1st Cav.Res. Co.D
Sansing, James H. MS 27th Inf. Co.A
Sansing, J.D. MS 35th Inf. Co.K
Sansing, J.D. MS 44th Inf. Co.F
Sansing, J.H. MS 8th Inf. Co.B
Sansing, John TX 19th Cav. Co.G
Sansing, Martin MS 27th Inf. Co.A
Sansing, N.N. MS 44th Inf. Co.F
Sansing, P.W. MS 8th Inf. Co.B
Sansing, R. MS Inf. 2nd St.Troops Co.G
Sansing, Robert MS Inf. 3rd Bn. (St.Troops) Co.F 1st Cpl.
Sansing, R.P.M. SC 5th Inf. 2nd Co.K
Sansing, R.R. MS 1st (Foote's) Inf. (St.Troops) Hobart's Co.
Sansing, W.A. MS 8th Inf. Co.B Sgt.
Sansing, William NC 38th Inf. Co.I
Sansing, William H. MS 13th Inf. Co.H
Sansing, William J. AL 36th Inf. Co.K
Sansing, Z.B. LA 2nd Inf. Co.I
Sansom, --- TX Cav. Morgan's Regt. Co.K
Sansom, A.B. MS 1st (Johnston's) Inf. Co.G
Sansom, Alfred B. MS 19th Inf. Co.G
Sansom, Andrew VA 16th Cav. Co.E Sgt.
Sansom, Bennet T. FL 5th Inf. Co.H Sgt.
Sansom, Bennett T. FL 1st Inf. Old Co.E
Sansom, F.M. TX Cav. Morgan's Regt. Co.K 1st Lt.
Sansom, F.M. TX 20th Inf. Co.E
Sansom, G.H. AL 51st (Part.Rangers) Co.E
Sansom, Gorden VA Inf. 45th Bn. Co.E
Sansom, Gordon VA Cav. 34th Bn. Co.D
Sansom, Green F. TN 24th Inf. 2nd Co.G Sgt.
Sansom, Green F. TN 32nd Inf. Co.K
Sansom, Jacob MS 2nd Inf. (A. of 10,000) Co.A
Sansom, Jacob MS 42nd Inf. Co.D
Sansom, Jacob J. TN 32nd Inf. Co.K
Sansom, James GA Arty. Moore's Btty. Orderly
Sansom, James TN 32nd Inf. Co.K
Sansom, James D. AL 45th Inf. Co.I
Sansom, James E. TN 41st Inf. Co.H
Sansom, James H. MS 9th Cav. Co.G
Sansom, James H. MS 5th Inf. (St.Troops) Co.D Cpl.
Sansom, James L. MS 8th Inf. Co.E,H Capt.
Sansom, James T. GA Carlton's Co. (Troup Cty.Arty.)
Sansom, James T. GA 2nd Inf. Stanley's Co.
Sansom, J.L. MS Inf. 7th Bn. Co.A
Sansom, J.M. TX 12th Cav. Co.B Cpl.
Sansom, J.N. TX Cav. McCord's Frontier Regt. Co.B
Sansom, John FL 6th Inf. Co.F
Sansom, John GA Carlton's Co. (Troup Cty.Arty.)
Sansom, John GA 2nd Inf. Stanley's Co.
Sansom, John GA 2nd Inf. Co.H
Sansom, John GA 9th Inf. (St.Guards) Co.H
Sansom, John GA 36th (Broyles') Inf. Co.A 1st Lt.
Sansom, John MS 42nd Inf. Co.D
Sansom, John C. VA Inf. 45th Bn. Co.B Sgt.
Sansom, John C. VA 1st Cav.St.Line Co.A
Sansom, John F. AL 45th Inf. Co.I

Sansom, John L. MS 8th Inf. Co.E,H
Sansom, John W. TX 36th Cav. Co.D 1st Sgt.
Sansom, J.W. TX 1st Hvy.Arty. Co.H
Sansom, R.F. TX 20th Inf. Co.E
Sansom, Riley VA 16th Cav. Co.E
Sansom, Rufus F. AL 19th Inf. Co.D Cpl.
Sansom, Samuel F. TX 28th Cav. Co.I
Sansom, S.D. TN 17th Inf. Co.C
Sansom, T. AL 8th Inf. Co.F
Sansom, Thomas GA Phillips' Legion Co.B
Sansom, Thomas TX 8th Cav. Co.E
Sansom, Thomas C. LA 13th Bn. (Part.Rangers) Co.F
Sansom, W.C. MS 11th (Perrin's) Cav. Co.F 2nd Lt.
Sansom, W.C. MS 1st (Johnston's) Inf. Co.G
Sansom, W.C. MS 7th Inf. Co.H
Sansom, Wesley VA 36th Inf. 1st Co.B, 2nd Co.D
Sansom, William AL 19th Inf. Co.F
Sansom, William TN 32nd Inf. Co.K
Sansom, William C. MS Inf. 7th Bn. Co.A Sgt.Maj.
Sansom, William F. AL 33rd Inf. Co.A
Sansom, William M. TX 7th Cav. Co.H
Sansom, William T. AL 45th Inf. Co.I
Sansom, William W. TX 19th Inf. Co.G
Sansom, W.M. TX Inf. Currie's Co.
Sanson, B. LA Mil. 3rd Regt. French Brig. Co.3 Sgt.
Sanson, Benjamin AL Lt.Arty. Clanton's Btty.
Sanson, Elias M. TN 17th Inf. Co.C
Sanson, Gordon VA 129th Mil. Chambers' Co., Avis' Co.
Sanson, J.H. MS Cav. Jeff Davis Legion Co.E
Sanson, J.S. AL Inf. 1st Regt. Co.H
Sanson, Oren M. AL 19th Inf. Co.F Cpl.
Sanson, Peter LA Res.Corps
Sanson, T.H. AL 8th Inf. Co.H
Sanson, W.C. GA 44th Inf. Co.E
Sanson, William AR 20th Inf. Co.H
Sanson, William C. MS 1st (Patton's) Inf. Co.K
Sanson, W.T. AL Inf. 1st Regt. Co.H
Sansone, Giuseppe LA Mil. 6th Regt.Eur.Brig. (Italian Guards Bn.) Co.4 Cpl.
Sansoville, J.W. GA 43rd Inf. Co.L
Sansum, Andrew VA Cav. Ferguson's Bn. Spurlock's Co. Cpl.
Sansum, Hiram VA Inf. 45th Bn. Co.B
Sansum, Riley VA Cav. Ferguson's Bn. Spurlock's Co.
Sansy, I.R. Stewart's Corps A.Ord.Off.
Sant, Frank MS 13th Inf. Co.D
Sant, Franklin MS 3rd (St.Troops) Cav. Co.B Cpl.
Sant, James T. MS Cav. Vivion's Co.
Sant, J.C. MS 20th Inf. Co.E
Sant, John MO Inf. 5th Regt.St.Guard Co.D
Santa, Jose M. TX Cav. Benavides' Regt. Co.I
Santa Anna, Francisco TX Part.Rangers Thomas' Co.
Santabella, Manuel LA Mil. Cazadores Espanoles Regt. Co.2
Santana, Charles LA Miles' Legion Co.A
SanTanna, Juan TX 33rd Cav. Co.B
Santanno, Santiago Conf.Lt.Arty. Davis' Co.
Santapher, Jacob FL 6th Inf. Co.C

Santas, A.F. VA Lt.Arty. 1st Bn. Co.D
Santas, F. VA Arty. B.H. Smith's Co.
Sante, Monroe AR 23rd Inf. Co.D
Santee, Thomas MO Cav. 2nd Regt.St.Guard Co.D
Santen, Von F. SC Mil.Arty. 1st Regt. Co.C 1st Lt.
Santerfeil, William E. TN 41st Inf. Co.D
Santern, V. LA Mil. Orleans Guards Regt. Co.I
Santford, Robison AR Inf. Hardy's Regt. Co.G
Santford, T.A. AR 11th Inf. Co.D
Santhall, T.H. Johnston's A. Capt.,ACS
Santiago, Aneseto LA Mil. 5th Regt.Eur.Brig. (Spanish Regt.) Co.A
Santiago, Carpio LA Mil. 5th Regt.Eur.Brig. (Spanish Regt.) Co.A Cpl.
Santiago, D. LA Mil. 1st Chasseurs a pied Co.7
Santifitt, G. GA Inf. 18th Bn. Co.B
Santifitt, P.H. GA Inf. 18th Bn. Co.B
Santiford, Samuel B. AR Inf. Clayton's Co.
Santiford, Samuel B. MO 10th Inf. Co.F Sgt.
Santillana, Benito TX Trevino's Squad Part. Mtd.Vol.
Santina, J.A. GA 1st (Olmstead's) Inf. Stiles' Co.
Santina, J.A. GA Inf. 18th Bn. Co.A,B,C
Santina, J.F. GA 1st (Olmstead's) Inf. Stiles' Co., Co.G
Santina, J.F. GA Inf. 18th Bn. Co.B
Santina, W.H. GA Inf. 18th Bn. Co.A,B
Santina, William H. GA 1st (Olmstead's) Inf. Co.G, Screven's Co. Sgt.
Santini, J. LA Mil.Conf.Guards Regt. Co.F
Santte, B. LA Inf. 10th Bn. Co.G Cpl.
Santlen, James G. TX Cav. Baylor's Regt. Co.G
Sant Miers, John W. VA Cav. 35th Bn. Co.F
Santmyers, George VA 8th Bn.Res. Co.A
Santmyers, Isaac VA 49th Inf. Co.D
Santmyers, John B. VA 49th Inf. Co.D
Santmyers, John W. VA Cav. 41st Bn. Trayhern's Co.
Santmyers, John W. VA 97th Mil. Co.L
Santmyers, Thomas W. VA 17th Inf. Co.B
Santmyres, Alexander VA 33rd Inf. Co.K
Santmyres, D.M. VA 12th Cav. Co.I
Santmyres, Randolph VA 146th Mil. Co.G
Santon, Benj. AL 25th Inf.
Santon, J.E. LA 30th Inf. Co.F,G
Santon, N. LA Mil. Orleans Guards Regt. Co.I Sgt.
Santon, Robert H. GA 1st Reg. Co.K
Santon, W.H. LA Mil. McPherson's Btty. (Orleans Howitzers)
Santon, W.M. TN 61st Mtd.Inf. Co.D
Santoneh, --- NC Inf. Thomas Legion 2nd Co.A
Santoola, --- NC Inf. Thomas Legion 2nd Co.A
Santos, A.F. VA 3rd Inf.Loc.Def. Co.C 1st Lt.
Santos, A.F. VA 12th Inf. Co.H 1st Lt.
Santos, Alexander F. VA 6th Inf. Ferguson's Co. 1st Lt.
Santos, C. TX 17th Inf. Co.G
Santos, Charles A. VA 54th Mil. Co.A
Santos, Joe LA 2nd Cav. Co.E
Santos, John LA 2nd Cav. Co.E
Santos, Leonard LA Mil. 1st Native Guards
Santos, M. LA Mil. 5th Regt.Eur.Brig. (Spanish Regt.) Co.1
Santos, Natano TX Cav. Baird's Regt. Co.H

Santos, R.W. VA 54th Mil. Co.B
Santos, T. LA Mil. Orleans Guards Regt. Co.E
Santos, T. 15th Conf.Cav. Co.H
Santos, V. LA 2nd Cav. Co.E
Santos, Zeferino TX 3rd Inf. 1st Co.C
Santova, Joseph GA 47th Inf.
Santry, Joseph TN 2nd (Walker's) Inf. Co.K 2nd Lt.
Santry, Joseph 9th Conf.Inf. Co.A 1st Lt.
Santry, Matthew MO Lt.Arty. 3rd Btty. Cpl.
Santz, Ferdinand MS 3rd Inf. Co.E Music.
Santze, A. TX Inf. Timmons' Regt. Co.K
Sanus, James T. NC 2nd Cav. (19th St.Troops)
Sanway, William AR Inf. Cocke's Regt. Co.D
Sanxay, Richard S. VA 46th Inf. 2nd Co.A Lt.
Sanxay, R.S. VA Wise's Bn.Vol. Adj.
Sap, David TN 84th Inf. Co.D
Sap, M. AL Randolph Cty.Res. D.A. Self's Co.
Sap, Richard AL 12th Cav. Co.D
Sapa lutke 1st Creek Mtd.Vol. Co.A
Sapaugh, Christopher MO Lt.Arty. 13th Btty.
Sapaugh, John NC 12th Inf. Co.A Cpl.
Sapenfield, Andrew NC 48th Inf. Co.H
Sapenfield, D. MO St.Guard 1st Sgt.
Sapenfield, David NC 48th Inf. Co.H
Sapera, Joseph LA Mil. 5th Regt.Eur.Brig. (Spanish Regt.) Co.2
Saphell, William MO Lt.Arty. Parsons' Co.
Saphell, William MO 6th Inf. Co.I
Saphier, Frank MO 1st Inf. Co.I
Saphin, Binchard LA Mil. 2nd Regt. 3rd Brig. 1st Div.
Sa pin cully 1st Creek Mtd.Vol. Co.A
Sapington, Harrison KY 1st (Butler's) Cav. New Co.H
Sapington, Joseph W. MO Mtd.Inf. Boone's Regt.
Sapington, Reuben D. MS 31st Inf. Co.G
Sapirer, Louis LA 7th Cav. Co.B Cpl.
Sapley, J.A. TN 35th Inf. Co.B
Saporee, W.H. FL 7th Inf. Co.C
Sa port ta ke 1st Creek Mtd.Vol. Co.A
Sapp, --- GA Lt.Arty. Clinch's Btty.
Sapp, A. LA 18th Inf. Co.D
Sapp, Abram GA 49th Inf. Co.F
Sapp, Addison J.D. TX 13th Cav. Co.K
Sapp, A.G. NC 2nd Cav. (19th St.Troops) Co.F
Sapp, A.G. SC 1st (Butler's) Inf. Co.B
Sapp, Alexander GA Cav. 19th Bn. Co.B
Sapp, Alexander 10th Conf.Cav. Co.G
Sapp, Alexander W. GA 31st Inf. Co.E
Sapp, Alfred NC 21st Inf. Co.I
Sapp, Allen FL 6th Inf. Co.E
Sapp, Allen GA 54th Inf. Co.K,F
Sapp, Allen H. AL 17th Inf. Co.C
Sapp, Alpheus F. NC 22nd Inf. Co.E
Sapp, Alward AZ Cav. Herbert's Bn. Oury's Co. Sgt.
Sapp, Anthony FL 6th Inf. Co.E
Sapp, Asa FL 10th Inf. Davidson's Co.
Sapp, Asa C. FL 6th Inf. Co.A
Sapp, Augustus GA 66th Inf. Co.F
Sapp, Azariah G. NC 33rd Inf. Co.E,C
Sapp, Bartley FL 4th Inf. Co.E
Sapp, Bartley J. GA Cav. 2nd Bn. Co.F
Sapp, B.E. GA 4th (Clinch's) Cav. Co.E
Sapp, B.E. GA 7th Cav. Co.D

Sapp, B.E. GA Cav. 24th Bn. Co.A,C
Sapp, Benjamin GA 47th Inf. Co.G
Sapp, B. Harris AL 29th Inf. Co.F Capt.
Sapp, Blewford GA 27th Inf. Co.I
Sapp, C.E. GA 25th Inf. Co.I
Sapp, Celam GA 66th Inf. Co.D
Sapp, Clinton GA 47th Inf. Co.F
Sapp, Council FL 2nd Cav. Co.D
Sapp, Daniel L. MS 5th Inf. (St.Troops) Co.B
Sapp, David GA Cav. 22nd Bn. (St.Guards) Co.F
Sapp, David NC Mil. 66th Bn. J.H. Whitman's Co.
Sapp, David TN 28th (Cons.) Inf. Co.H Cpl.
Sapp, David VA 21st Cav. 2nd Co.C
Sapp, David L. MS 48th Inf. Co.A
Sapp, D.I. MO 4th Cav. Co.E
Sapp, D.W. AL 29th Inf. Co.F,I Sgt.
Sapp, E. GA 7th Cav. Co.B
Sapp, Edward GA 51st Inf. Co.A
Sapp, Elam GA 47th Inf. Co.G
Sapp, Eli GA 31st Inf. Co.I
Sapp, Elias FL 7th Inf. Co.C
Sapp, Elijah GA 47th Inf. Co.F
Sapp, Eliphaz Holt AL 5th Inf. New Co.B
Sapp, Enas GA 57th Inf. Co.G
Sapp, Enoch GA 4th (Clinch's) Cav. Co.G
Sapp, Enos GA Cav. 21st Bn. Co.C
Sapp, Everett GA 17th Inf. Co.K
Sapp, Everett GA 29th Inf. Co.A
Sapp, F.H. TX Cav. Terry's Regt. Co.K Capt.
Sapp, F.H. TX 4th Inf. (St.Troops) Co.H Capt.
Sapp, F.M. AL 8th Inf. Co.F
Sapp, Forsyth H. GA 31st Inf. Co.G
Sapp, Franklin F. GA 1st (Olmstead's) Inf. Co.D
Sapp, Furney GA 25th Inf. Co.B
Sapp, F.W. NC 2nd Cav. (19th St.Troops) Co.A
Sapp, George GA Cav. Pemberton's Co.
Sapp, George GA 17th Inf. Co.K
Sapp, George H. GA 3rd Cav. Co.B
Sapp, George R. GA 5th Inf. (St.Guards) Russell's Co.
Sapp, George W. FL 6th Inf. Co.E
Sapp, George W. FL 11th Inf. Co.K
Sapp, George W. GA 2nd Inf. Co.D
Sapp, G.L. MS Inf. 2nd St.Troops Co.E
Sapp, G.L. MS 5th Inf. (St.Troops) Co.B
Sapp, Hardy C. GA Cobb's Legion Co.E
Sapp, Harmon D. GA 51st Inf. Co.C 1st Lt.
Sapp, Hart B. NC 9th Bn.S.S. Co.B
Sapp, Hartwell B. NC 21st Inf. Co.E
Sapp, H.D. GA Lt.Arty. Guerard's Btty.
Sapp, H.D. GA 57th Inf. 1st Lt.
Sapp, Henry FL 1st Cav. Co.C
Sapp, Henry GA 4th (Clinch's) Cav. Co.G
Sapp, Henry GA 18th Inf. Co.D
Sapp, Henry NC 9th Bn.S.S. Co.B
Sapp, Henry H. FL 7th Inf. Co.C
Sapp, Henry M. GA Inf. 2nd Bn. Co.A Capt.
Sapp, Hiram GA Cav. 19th Bn. Co.B
Sapp, Hiram 10th Conf.Cav. Co.G
Sapp, Homer GA 50th Inf. Co.F
Sapp, H.T. TX 4th Inf. Co.H 1st Sgt.
Sapp, I. NC 1st Inf. Co.B Sgt.
Sapp, Isaac NC 48th Inf. Co.K
Sapp, Isaac R. GA 5th Res. Co.G
Sapp, J.A. GA 4th Inf.

Sapp, J.A. NC 2nd Cav. (19th St.Troops) Co.F
Sapp, Jackson GA 61st Inf. Co.B,K
Sapp, Jackson NC 7th Sr.Res. Fisher's Co.
Sapp, James FL 2nd Cav. Co.D 2nd Lt.
Sapp, James FL Inf. 2nd Bn. Co.B
Sapp, James TX 11th Inf. Co.H
Sapp, James A. GA 4th (Clinch's) Cav. Co.A
Sapp, James F. GA 25th Inf. Co.B
Sapp, James J. GA 1st (Ramsey's) Inf. Co.G
Sapp, James J. GA 31st Inf. Co.I 2nd Lt.
Sapp, Jason GA 29th Inf. Co.G
Sapp, Jason LA 16th Inf. Co.G
Sapp, Jasper FL 9th Inf. Co.K
Sapp, J.C. GA 2nd Inf. Co.D 1st Lt.
Sapp, J.D. FL 10th Inf. Co.A
Sapp, Jesse NC 9th Bn.S.S. Co.B
Sapp, Jesse VA 21st Cav. 2nd Co.C
Sapp, Jessee GA 26th Inf. Co.I
Sapp, Jesse E. MS 8th Inf. Co.G Cpl.
Sapp, Jesse W. NC 45th Inf. Co.K
Sapp, J.F. 2nd Conf.Eng.Troops Co.D Artif.
Sapp, J.H. GA 54th Inf. Co.K
Sapp, J.M. TX Cav. Mann's Regt. Co.A Sgt.
Sapp, John FL Sp.Cav. 1st Bn. Co.B
Sapp, John FL 2nd Cav. Co.I
Sapp, John FL Cav. 5th Bn. Co.F
Sapp, John FL 1st (Res.) Inf. Co.B
Sapp, John FL Inf. 2nd Bn. Co.C
Sapp, John FL 8th Inf. Co.A
Sapp, John FL 9th Inf. Co.E
Sapp, John FL 10th Inf. Co.H
Sapp, John GA 4th (Clinch's) Cav. Co.G
Sapp, John GA 2nd Inf. Co.D
Sapp, John LA Inf.Cons.Crescent Regt. Co.O
Sapp, John MO Searcy's Bn.S.S. Co.A
Sapp, John NC 9th Bn.S.S. Co.B
Sapp, John NC 21st Inf. Co.E
Sapp, John NC 45th Inf. Co.D
Sapp, John A. AL Cav. Barbiere's Bn. Brown's Co.
Sapp, John A. AL Cav. Lewis' Bn. Co.E
Sapp, John A. AL 17th Inf. Co.C
Sapp, John A. AL 27th Inf. Co.D
Sapp, John D. FL 1st Cav. Co.C
Sapp, John H. FL 4th Inf. Co.E
Sapp, John H. GA Lt.Arty. Fraser's Btty.
Sapp, John H. GA 10th Inf. 1st Co.K
Sapp, John H. NC 52nd Inf. Co.K
Sapp, John J. FL 2nd Inf. Co.G
Sapp, John M. LA 25th Inf. Co.I Cpl.
Sapp, John M. TX 20th Inf. Co.G Sgt.
Sapp, John O. LA 9th Inf. Co.D
Sapp, John T. TX Cav. Baylor's Regt. Co.E
Sapp, Joseph FL 7th Inf. Co.D
Sapp, Joseph GA Cav. 20th Bn. Co.G
Sapp, Joseph GA Cav. 21st Bn. Co.D
Sapp, Joseph KY 9th Cav. Co.B
Sapp, J.S. NC 1st Cav. (9th St.Troops) Co.G
Sapp, J.W. GA 8th Inf. Co.G
Sapp, J.W. GA 25th Inf. Co.I
Sapp, J.W. LA 1st Cav. Co.A
Sapp, J.Y. TX 12th Inf. Co.F
Sapp, Lemuel GA 21st Inf. Co.I
Sapp, Levi GA 7th Cav. Co.E
Sapp, Levi GA Cav. 21st Bn. Co.B
Sapp, L.L. GA 1st Reg. Co.H
Sapp, Luke GA Cav. 19th Bn. Co.B

Sapp, Luke GA 8th Inf. Co.G
Sapp, Luke 10th Conf.Cav. Co.G
Sapp, Luke L. GA 47th Inf. Co.G
Sapp, Maddison GA 17th Inf. Co.K
Sapp, Mark GA 8th Inf. Co.G
Sapp, Martin NC 48th Inf. Co.K
Sapp, M.C. AL 10th Inf. Co.H
Sapp, M.H. GA 3rd Cav. Co.B
Sapp, Michael A. NC 52nd Inf. Co.K
Sapp, Moses W. GA 9th Inf. Co.H
Sapp, Newell NC 9th Bn.S.S. Co.B Sgt.
Sapp, Newell NC 21st Inf. Co.E
Sapp, Newell W. NC 21st Inf. Co.E 1st Sgt.
Sapp, Newton FL 4th Inf. Co.E
Sapp, Newton TX 28th Cav. Co.K
Sapp, N.W. NC 9th Bn.S.S. Co.B Lt.
Sapp, Obadiah FL 9th Inf. Co.B
Sapp, Obediah AL 57th Inf. Co.K Cpl.
Sapp, Obediah FL 2nd Inf. Co.H
Sapp, Obediah TX 12th Cav. Co.K
Sapp, P. Allen AL 54th Inf. ACS
Sapp, P.C. GA 1st (Fannin's) Res. Co.H
Sapp, Pendleton GA 1st (Ramsey's) Inf. Co.G
Sapp, Pendleton GA 32nd Inf. Co.K
Sapp, Perry GA 47th Inf. Co.G
Sapp, Perry W. TX 5th Cav. Co.C
Sapp, Peter H. AL 29th Inf. Co.F
Sapp, Philip A. Gen. & Staff Asst.Comsy.
Sapp, Philip F. GA 61st Inf. Co.H,K
Sapp, Phulip A. AL Eufaula Lt.Arty.
Sapp, P.W. TX Waul's Legion Co.G
Sapp, P.W. Exch.Bn. 1st Co.B,CSA
Sapp, R. GA Lt.Arty. Fraser's Btty.
Sapp, R. NC 3rd Jr.Res. Co.K
Sapp, R. NC 4th Bn.Jr.Res. Co.D
Sapp, Raphael FL 6th Inf. Co.E
Sapp, Rayford FL 6th Inf. Co.E
Sapp, R.H. NC 2nd Cav. (19th St.Troops) Co.F
Sapp, R.H. SC Cav. 10th Bn. Co.D
Sapp, Richard GA 2nd Cav. Co.C
Sapp, Robert W. AL 27th Inf. Co.D
Sapp, R.S. NC 2nd Cav. (19th St.Troops) Co.F
Sapp, Russell FL 7th Inf. Co.C
Sapp, S. FL 2nd Inf. Co.H
Sapp, Salem GA 47th Inf. Co.G
Sapp, Seaborn GA Cobb's Legion Co.E
Sapp, Shadrack FL 7th Inf. Co.C
Sapp, Silas GA Inf. 1st Conf.Bn. Co.F
Sapp, Silas GA 25th Inf. Co.H
Sapp, Simeon E. FL 3rd Inf. Co.G
Sapp, S.T. GA 16th Inf. Co.A
Sapp, Thomas AL 29th Inf. Co.F
Sapp, Thomas MO 4th Inf. Co.C
Sapp, Thomas A. MO 3rd Cav. Co.K Capt.
Sapp, Thomas B. NC 48th Inf. Co.K
Sapp, Thomas H. NC 1st Cav. (9th St.Troops) Co.F
Sapp, W. GA 7th Cav. Co.G
Sapp, W. GA Cav. 24th Bn. Co.A
Sapp, W. LA 3rd Inf. Co.I
Sapp, W. LA Inf. Pelican Regt. Co.B
Sapp, W. TX 1st Hvy.Arty. Co.K
Sapp, W.A. GA 3rd Cav. Co.B
Sapp, W.A. GA Cav. Pemberton's Co.
Sapp, W.A. GA 5th Inf. (St.Guards) Russell's Co.
Sapp, W.A. TX Cav. Mann's Regt. Co.A

Sapp, Walton GA 66th Inf. Co.D
Sapp, Washington FL 6th Inf. Co.E
Sapp, W.B. GA 5th Res. Co.G Cpl.
Sapp, W.D. GA 1st (Symons') Res. Co.G
Sapp, William AL St.Res.
Sapp, William AL 4th Res. Co.I Sgt.
Sapp, William FL 7th Inf. Co.D
Sapp, William LA 25th Inf. Co.I
Sapp, William NC 9th Bn.S.S. Co.B
Sapp, William A. 3rd Conf.Cav. Co.D Cpl.
Sapp, William J. FL 8th Inf. Co.A
Sapp, William J. GA 8th Inf. Co.G Cpl.
Sapp, William M. GA 48th Inf. Co.D
Sapp, William P. AL 19th Inf. Co.D
Sapp, William R. GA 49th Inf. Co.K Sgt.
Sapp, William S. TX 12th Cav. Co.I
Sapp, W.M. TX 4th Inf. (St.Troops) Co.H
Sapp, W.P. AL 17th Bn.S.S. Co.A
Sapp, W.P. GA 3rd Res. Co.F
Sapp, W.S. MO 4th Inf. Co.C Sr.2nd Lt.
Sapp, W.W. GA 54th Inf. Co.K
Sappe, T. LA Lewis Regt. Co.G
Sapperfield, D. MO 4th Cav. Co.E
Sappinfield, John Frederic MO 8th Inf. Co.C
Sappingfield, William J. NC 42nd Inf. Co.A
Sappington, Benoni R. MO Cav. Freeman's Regt. Co.E
Sappington, C.W. MS Cav. Ham's Regt. Co.B,D
Sappington, David MO Searcy's Bn.S.S. Co.A
Sappington, Devilla MS 14th Inf. Co.K Cpl.
Sappington, D.M. GA 22nd Inf. Co.K
Sappington, George MO 4th Cav. Co.D
Sappington, George W. MO Mtd.Inf. Boone's Regt.
Sappington, George W. VA 2nd Inf. Co.H 1st Lt.
Sappington, Green H. MO Mtd.Inf. Boone's Regt. Co.A
Sappington, H. KY 3rd Cav. Co.I
Sappington, Hammond C. MO 2nd Inf. Co.A Sgt.
Sappington, Harrison KY Cav. Buckner Guards
Sappington, H.B. Morgan's,CSA
Sappington, Henson T. KY Morgan's Men Murphy's Co.
Sappington, H.P. KY 2nd Cav. Co.C
Sappington, James MS 3rd Inf. (St.Troops) Co.K
Sappington, James A.T. AL 50th Inf. Co.A Capt.
Sappington, James H. GA 44th Inf. Co.I
Sappington, James W.S. TN 47th Inf. Co.G
Sappington, J.A.T. AL 10th Inf. Co.G
Sappington, J.B. TN 12th (Cons.) Inf. Co.D
Sappington, J.B. TN 22nd Inf. Co.H
Sappington, J.B. TN 47th Inf. Co.C
Sappington, J.E. GA 13th Inf. Co.K
Sappington, J.H. GA Cav. 29th Bn. Co.D
Sappington, J.M. TN 3rd (Forrest's) Cav. Co.I
Sappington, J.M. TN 12th (Green's) Cav. Co.G
Sappington, John AR 1st Mtd.Rifles Co.A
Sappington, John G. GA 8th Inf. (St.Guards) Co.D
Sappington, John T. GA 44th Inf. Co.I
Sappington, Joseph MO 4th Cav. Co.D
Sappington, Joseph H. FL 1st Cav. Co.F 1st Lt.
Sappington, Joseph H. FL 1st Inf. Old Co.F

Sappington, J.W. GA 5th Inf. (St.Guards)
Everitt's Co. Sgt.
Sappington, J.W. GA Inf. City Bn. (Columbus)
Williams' Co.
Sappington, M.A. TX Cav. Bourland's Regt.
Co.D
Sappington, M.A. TX Inf. Rutherford's Co.
Sappington, Marcus MO Searcy's Bn.S.S. Co.A
Sappington, Mark MO 4th Cav. Co.D
Sappington, Mark MO Mtd.Inf. Boone's Regt.
Co.A
Sappington, N.A. GA 31st Inf. Co.D
Sappington, R. MS Cav. Jeff Davis Legion Co.B
Sappington, R.A. MS Cav. Ham's Regt. Co.B,D
1st Lt.
Sappington, Richard MS 1st Cav. Co.I
Sappington, Richard I. MO 4th Cav. Co.D
Sappington, R.J. MO 16th Inf. Co.I
Sappington, R.T. GA 8th Inf. (St.Guards) Co.G
1st Lt.
Sappington, T.C. GA 11th Inf. Co.I
Sappington, Thomas A. MO Mtd.Inf. Boone's
Regt. Co.A
Sappington, T.M. MO 6th Cav. Co.C
Sappington, Voltaire MS 14th Inf. Co.K
Sappington, W.G. TN 12th (Cons.) Inf. Co.D
Sappington, W.G. TN 22nd Inf. Co.H
Sappington, William A. GA 31st Inf. Co.D
Sappington, William D. MO 4th Cav. Co.D
Capt.
Sappington, William M. GA 8th Inf. (St.Guards)
Co.G
Sapps, A. NC 31st Inf. Co.I
Sapps, M. AL St.Res.
Sapps, M.C. AL 5th Cav. Co.H
Sapps, Riley GA 26th Inf. Co.I,H
Sap Sucker 1st Cherokee Mtd.Rifles Co.K
Sar, Pablo LA Mil. 4th Regt. 1st Brig. 1st Div.
Co.G
Saradet, J. LA 18th Inf. Co.B
Saradet, J. LA Inf.Crescent Regt. Co.C
Sarage, Taylor GA 34th Inf. Co.H
Saragosse, Arthur LA Mil. 1st Native Guards
Sarah, James O. VA 68th Inf. Co.B
Sarah, John F. VA 63rd Inf. Co.B
Saramiat, J. LA Mil. 1st Regt. French Brig. Co.8
Saramiat, Jn. Mie. LA Mil. 3rd Regt.Eur.Brig.
(Garde Francaise) Frois' Co.
Sarancy, J.B. TX 26th Cav. Co.H
Sarane, T.H. MS 31st Inf. Co.K
Sarasin, F.A. AR Willett's Co.
Sarasin, Louis TX 1st (McCulloch's) Cav. Co.B
Sarasin, Louis TX 3rd Inf. Co.K Capt.
Sarate, Vincente TX 3rd Inf. Co.F
Sarats, Peter V. TX 6th Inf. Co.K Cpl.
Saratt, Demosthenes, M. GA 35th Inf. Co.I
Saratt, John M. TX 7th Inf. Co.K
Saratt, William R. GA 35th Inf. Co.I
Sarazin, H. LA Lt.Arty. 6th Field Btty. (Grosse
Tete Flying Arty.)
Sarazin, H. LA 30th Inf. Co.A
Sarazin, Paul LA 30th Inf. Co.F
Sarazin, X. LA Lt.Arty. 6th Field Btty. (Grosse
Tete Flying Arty.)
Sarber, J.C. TX Cav. Wells' Regt. Co.G
Sarbno, A.L. MO Cav. Freeman's Regt. Co.B

Sarchet, Thomas P. GA Cav. 22nd Bn.
(St.Guards) Co.H
Sar co co nay 1st Creek Mtd.Vol. Co.E
Sar con ton na 1st Creek Mtd.Vol. Co.E
Sarcy, John AL 32nd Inf. Co.D
Sarda, Pedro LA Mil. 5th Regt.Eur.Brig.
(Spanish Regt.) Co.4
Sarda, Pedro LA Mil. 5th Regt.Eur.Brig.
(Spanish Regt.) Co.4
Sardee, J. MO 5th Cav. Co.K
Sardge, N.L. AL 49th Inf. Co.C
Sardi, Luis LA Mil. 5th Regt.Eur.Brig. (Spanish
Regt.) Co.7
Sardin, David MO Searcy's Bn.S.S.
Sardiner, C.B. TX Lt.Arty. Christmas' Btty. 2nd
Lt.
Sarenge, J.C. Forrest's Scouts,CSA
Sarfulley 1st Creek Mtd.Vol. Co.K
Sarfunnah 1st Creek Mtd.Vol. Co.A
Sargant, John MO 2nd Cav. 2nd Co.K
Sargant, Seborn H. GA 43rd Inf. Co.B
Sarge, John GA 34th Inf. Co.H
Sargeant, Augustine W. LA Inf. 11th Bn. Co.F
Sgt.
Sargeant, E.B. GA Philips' Legion Co.C,I
Sargeant, George VA Inf. 25th Bn. Co.H
Sargeant, George A. 1st Conf.Eng.Troops Co.D
Artif.
Sargeant, H. VA 18th Cav. Co.A
Sargeant, Harvey G. AL 16th Inf. Co.H
Sargeant, H.C. MS Lt.Arty. 14th Bn. Co.C
Sargeant, James K. KY 1st (Butler's) Cav. Co.C
Sargeant, James S. GA 66th Inf. Co.B
Sargeant, J.K. TX 21st Inf. Co.H,K
Sargeant, John C. GA 14th Inf. Co.D Sgt.
Sargeant, Johnson VA Inf. 23rd Bn. Co.D
Sargeant, Thomas MS 18th Inf. Co.D
Sargeant, W.B. MS 43rd Inf. Co.L
Sargeant, W.C. GA Cherokee Legion (St.Guards)
Co.A
Sargeant, William VA Inf. 23rd Bn. Co.D
Sargeant, William P. GA 43rd Inf. Co.B
Sargen, W.J. GA Siege Arty. 28th Bn. Co.A
Sgt.
Sargent, --- TX Cav. Mann's Regt. Co.H
Sargent, Aaron T. MS 2nd Inf. Co.C
Sargent, Abner O. MS 11th Inf. Co.B
Sargent, A.G. TX 11th (Spaight's) Bn.Vol. Co.D
Sargent, A.G. TX 21st Inf. Co.H
Sargent, A.T. MS 10th Cav. Co.C
Sargent, B. MS 2nd (Davidson's) Inf. Co.A
Sargent, Benj. F. GA 43rd Inf. Co.B
Sargent, C. AL 12th Inf. Co.H
Sargent, Campbell M. TN 1st (Turney's) Inf.
Co.I
Sargent, D. GA Inf. 1st Bn. (St.Guards) Co.D
Sargent, D. GA Inf. City Bn. (Columbus) Co.C
Sargent, D. TX Inf. 3rd St.Troops Co.E
Sargent, David R. GA 55th Inf. Co.D
Sargent, D.P.S. TN Cav. Shaw's Bn. Co.A
Sargent, Eli G. GA 24th Inf. Co.I
Sargent, Elijah VA Cav. Caldwell's Bn. Hankins'
Co.
Sargent, Ephraim SC 1st (Orr's) Rifles Co.L
Sargent, Ephraim SC Palmetto S.S. Co.I
Sargent, E.S. GA 24th Inf. Co.I
Sargent, Forist VA 64th Mtd.Inf. Co.H

Sargent, George VA Hvy.Arty. 19th Bn. Co.B
Sargent, G.M. TX 21st Cav. Co.F Cpl.
Sargent, G.W. TX Cav. Saufley's Scouting Bn.
Co.B
Sargent, H.D.C.G. MD Arty. 1st Btty.
Sargent, Henry VA 29th Inf. 1st Co.F
Sargent, H.F. GA 2nd Cav. (St.Guards) Co.C
Sargent, H.W. SC 1st Cav. Co.F,K
Sargent, H.W. SC 4th Inf. Co.I
Sargent, Jacob VA 20th Cav. Co.D
Sargent, James H. SC 1st (Orr's) Rifles Co.C
Sargent, James J. AL 16th Inf. Co.B
Sargent, James L. MS 2nd Inf. Co.C 2nd Lt.
Sargent, Jesse TN 48th (Nixon's) Inf. Co.E
Sargent, Jesse F. TN 54th Inf. Dooley's Co.
Sargent, Jesse S. TN Inf. Sowell's Detach.
Sargent, J. Henry TX 25th Cav. Co.H
Sargent, J. Henry Eng.Troops,CSA Lt.
Sargent, J.K. TX 11th (Spaight's) Bn.Vol. Co.D
Sargent, J.L. MS 10th Cav. Co.C 1st Lt.
Sargent, John MS 2nd Inf. Co.C
Sargent, John MS Cp.Guard (Cp. of Instr. for
Conscr.)
Sargent, John B. SC 2nd Rifles Co.H
Sargent, John L. GA 24th Inf. Co.I
Sargent, John M. MS 38th Cav. Co.A Cpl.
Sargent, John M. TN 3rd (Forrest's) Cav. Co.C
1st Sgt.
Sargent, Johnson VA Cav. Caldwell's Bn. Han-
kins' Co.
Sargent, John T. TX 35th (Brown's) Cav. Co.D
Sargent, J.R.K. KY 3rd Cav. Co.C
Sargent, J.W. GA 50th Inf.
Sargent, J.W. TN 6th (Wheeler's) Cav. Co.A
Ord.Sgt.
Sargent, M.H. TX 18th Inf. Co.G
Sargent, P. AL 14th Inf. Co.H
Sargent, Phillip O. MS 2nd Inf. Co.C
Sargent, Phillip O. TN Cav. 17th Bn. (Sanders')
Co.B
Sargent, P.O. MS 10th Cav. Co.F,C Cpl.
Sargent, P.P. LA Mil.Conf.Guards Regt. Co.I
Sgt.
Sargent, R.M. AL 5th Inf. Co.H
Sargent, Robert W. TN 48th (Nixon's) Inf. Co.E
Lt.
Sargent, Robert W. TN 54th Inf. Dooley's Co.
Sargent, Romulus D. MS 2nd Inf. Co.C Capt.
Sargent, R.W. TN 6th (Wheeler's) Cav. Co.A
Sargent, R.W. TN Inf. Sowell's Detach.
Sargent, Temp. MS 10th Cav. Co.C
Sargent, T.W. TX Cav. Saufley's Scouting Bn.
Co.B
Sargent, W. VA 18th Cav. Co.K
Sargent, W.B. TN 46th Inf. Co.D
Sargent, W.H. SC 12th Inf. Co.G
Sargent, Wilburn MS 2nd Inf. Co.B
Sargent, William KY 7th Cav. Co.G
Sargent, William A. MO St.Guards
Sargent, William B. MS 15th (Cons.) Inf. Co.K
Sargent, William F. TN 4th (McLemore's) Cav.
Co.K
Sargent, William H. SC Lt.Arty. Beauregard's
Co. Sgt.
Sargent, William J. MS 2nd Inf. Co.C
Sargent, William J. TN Cav. 2nd Bn. (Biffle's)
Co.D

Sargent, William P. AL 10th Inf. Co.A
Sargent, William P. GA 45th Inf. Co.B
Sargent, W.P. AL 58th Inf. Co.I
Sargo 1st Choctaw & Chickasaw Mtd.Rifles 3rd Co.F
Sar har fixico 1st Creek Mtd.Vol. Co.B
Sar he pah ke 1st Creek Mtd.Vol. Co.K
Sarinte, J. LA Mil. 3rd Regt. French Brig. Co.8
Sarjeant, Ephraim SC 4th Inf.
Sarjeant, J.E. GA Cav. 1st Bn.Res. Co.E
Sarjent, H.W. SC Lt.Arty. Beauregard's Co.
Sarjent, J.B. SC Lt.Arty. Beauregard's Co.
Sarjent, J.H. SC Lt.Arty. Beauregard's Co.
Sark, Frederick LA 10th Inf. Co.K
Sar ka te ho 1st Creek Mtd.Vol. Co.E
Sar kin tar ha 1st Creek Mtd.Vol. Co.E
Sark yar kah pe 1st Creek Mtd.Vol. Co.H
Sar lar ho 1st Creek Mtd.Vol. Co.H
Sar lar key 1st Creek Mtd.Vol. Co.L
Sar lar ti ke 1st Creek Mtd.Vol. Co.L
Sarlaw, Lemuel VA Hvy.Arty. 18th Bn. Co.B
Sarles, S.R. 7th Conf.Cav. Co.D
Sarles, Thomas L. GA 63rd Inf. Co.D 2nd Lt.
Sarles, Thomas L. VA 63rd Inf. Co.D 2nd Lt.
Sarling, S. GA Inf. 1st Loc.Troops (Augusta) Dearing's Cav.Co.
Sar loley 1st Creek Mtd.Vol. Co.M
Sar luppee 1st Creek Mtd.Vol. Co.L Cpl.
Sarmazy, Augustus LA 25th Inf. Co.C
Sarner, J.T. 8th (Wade's) Conf.Cav. Co.I
Sarney, D.M. GA 18th Inf. Co.H
Sarniquet, J. LA Mil. 3rd Regt.Eur.Brig. (Garde Franciase) Frois' Co.
Sarnour, J. LA C.S. Zouave Bn. Co.B
Sarnutter, Fixico 2nd Creek Mtd.Vol. Co.E
Sarod, J.L. AR 21st Mil. Co.G
Saron, Felix LA Mil. 2nd Regt. French Brig. Co.7 2nd Lt.
Sarongs, J. LA Inf. 10th Bn. Co.G
Sarow, William A. GA Inf. 9th Bn. Co.C
Sar par tah ke 1st Creek Mtd.Vol. Co.A
Sarpincal Ce 1st Creek Mtd.Vol. Co.K
Sar pi yeh 1st Creek Mtd.Vol. Co.L
Sar put tah ke 1st Creek Mtd.Vol. Co.A
Sarpy, L. LA Dreux's Cav. Co.A
Sarpy, L.D. LA Mil. Orleans Guards Regt. Co.D
Sarpy, P. LA Mil. 4th Regt. 2nd Brig. 1st Div. Co.D 2nd Lt.
Sarpy, P. LA Dreux's Cav. Co.A
Sarpy, Paul LA Lt.Arty. LeGardeur, Jr.'s Co. (Orleans Guard Btty.)
Sarpy, St.Marc LA Mil. Delery's Co. (St.Bernard Horse Rifles Co.)
Sarradit, Jean LA Mil. 2nd Regt. French Brig. Co.1
Sarragim, A. TX Inf. 4th Bn. (Oswald's) Co.A
Sarran, J. LA Mil. 1st Regt. French Brig. Co.4
Sarrano, A. LA Mil. 4th Regt. French Brig. Co.3
Sarrasqueta, Jose LA Mil. Cazadores Espanoles Regt. Co.5
Sarrat, Adolphus L. SC 18th Inf. Co.F
Sarrat, B. LA Mil. Orleans Guards Regt. Co.A Sgt.
Sarratt, A.A. SC Inf. Holcombe Legion Co.C,K 2nd Lt.
Sarratt, Anthony A. GA 36th (Villepigue's) Inf. Co.B

Sarratt, Daniel VA 45th Inf. Co.E Cpl.
Sarratt, F.C. SC Palmetto S.S. Co.M
Sarratt, Fernando C. SC 5th Inf. 1st Co.G
Sarratt, G.B. SC 1st Arty. Co.F
Sarratt, H.J. SC Palmetto S.S. Co.G
Sarratt, Irvin SC 7th Res. Co.C
Sarratt, Iverson G. SC 5th Inf. 1st Co.G
Sarratt, J.B. SC 7th Res. Co.C
Sarratt, J.G. SC 6th Cav. Co.F
Sarratt, J.M. SC Palmetto S.S. Co.M
Sarratt, J.M. Jackson's Co.,CSA
Sarratt, John SC Palmetto S.S. Co.M
Sarratt, John M. SC 5th Inf. 1st Co.G
Sarratt, Joseph Franklin KY 9th Mtd.Inf. Co.H
Sarratt, Joseph Franklin TX Inf. W. Cameron's Co.
Sarratt, L.D. GA 6th Cav. Co.E
Sarratt, L.W. TX 32nd Cav. Co.I
Sarratt, Obe C. SC 5th Inf. 1st Co.G
Sarratt, O.C. SC Palmetto S.S. Co.M
Sarratt, Tilman NC 34th Inf. Co.H Cpl.
Sarratt, Ugenis NC 15th Inf. Co.C Sgt.
Sarratt, W.A. SC 6th Cav. Co.F
Sarratt, W.A. SC Palmetto S.S. Co.M
Sarratt, William A. SC 5th Inf. 1st Co.G Sgt.
Sarrazin, A. LA Mil. 1st Native Guards
Sarre, H.W. AL 21st Inf. Co.K
Sarrel, G.H. GA 1st Troops & Def. (Macon) Co.G
Sarrell, James S. TX 17th Inf. Co.B
Sarrells, W.F. NC 60th Inf. Co.K
Sarrels, W.J. TX Cav. Wells' Regt. Co.I
Sarrett, H. GA 1st Inf. (St.Guards) Co.F
Sarrett, H.J. MS Cav. 1st Bn. (McNair's) St.Troops Co.E 1st Sgt.
Sarrett, James W. VA 45th Inf. Co.D
Sarrio, John W. 1st Chickasaw Inf. Kesner's Co. Cpl.
Sarrow, W.D. GA 37th Inf. Co.B
Sarsa, Evaristo LA Mil. 5th Regt.Eur.Brig. (Spanish Regt.) Co.3
Sarsfield, George LA 5th Inf. Co.I
Sarsfield, Louis LA Arty. Kean's Btty. (Orleans Ind.Arty.)
Sartain, A.B. AL St.Res.
Sartain, Alex KY 12th Cav. Co.A
Sartain, Anson NC 7th Sr.Res. Mitchell's Co.
Sartain, C. MS 3rd Inf. (St.Troops) Co.A
Sartain, C.A. TX 14th Inf. Co.D 2nd Lt.
Sartain, Carter MS 4th Inf. Co.D
Sartain, Crawford F. MS 8th Cav. Co.C
Sartain, Daniel B. AL 41st Inf. Co.A
Sartain, E.B. AL 9th Inf. Co.G
Sartain, Elija S. MS 7th Inf. Co.H
Sartain, Ezekial NC 3rd Bn.Sr.Res. Durham's Co.
Sartain, Francis M. TX 1st (McCulloch's) Cav. Co.H
Sartain, Francis M. TX Cav. Morgan's Regt. Co.B Cpl.
Sartain, George F. TX 9th Cav. Co.G 1st Lt.
Sartain, George P. MS 7th Inf. Co.H Cpl.
Sartain, George W. TX 14th Inf. Co.D
Sartain, H.C. TN 28th Cav. Co.C Cpl.
Sartain, Henry C. AL 8th (Hatch's) Cav. Co.K
Sartain, Humphrey H. AL 41st Inf. Co.A Capt.
Sartain, J.A. KY 2nd Mtd.Inf. Co.D

Sartain, Jackson MS 8th Cav. Co.C
Sartain, Jackson MS 4th Inf. Co.D
Sartain, James TX 28th Cav. Co.E,B
Sartain, James R. AL 41st Inf. Co.F
Sartain, J.C. VA Inf. 23rd Bn. Co.B
Sartain, J.F. TX 10th Cav. Co.A
Sartain, J.G. TX Cav. Morgan's Regt. Co.E
Sartain, Joel MS 4th Inf. Co.D Cpl.
Sartain, Joel MS 31st Inf. Co.D
Sartain, Joel VA 86th Mil. Co.F
Sartain, John MS 31st Inf. Co.D
Sartain, John MO 10th Cav. Co.I,H
Sartain, John L. VA Inf. 26th Bn. Co.I
Sartain, John W. VA 2nd Cav. Co.H
Sartain, Joseph TN 39th Mtd.Inf.
Sartain, J.R. AL 50th Inf. Co.K
Sartain, J.R. TN 38th Inf. 1st Co.K
Sartain, J.W. TN 38th Inf. Co.G Cpl.
Sartain, Lewis GA 16th Inf. Co.D
Sartain, Lewis V. VA 36th Inf. 1st Co.H, 2nd Co.D,K
Sartain, Lindsey MS 4th Inf. Co.D Ord.Sgt.
Sartain, Marcellous AR 7th Cav. Co.L
Sartain, Reuben Manly AL 5th Inf. Old Co.H
Sartain, S.H. TN Inf. 3rd Cons.Regt. Co.B Capt.
Sartain, S.H. TN 38th Inf. Co.G Capt.
Sartain, T.C. TN 2nd (Ashby's) Cav. Co.K 2nd Lt.
Sartain, W.H. MS 4th Inf. Co.D
Sartain, William TN 38th Inf. Co.G
Sartain, William VA 1st Cav. Co.B
Sartain, W.T. AL 50th Inf. Co.K
Sartain, W.T. TN Inf. 3rd Cons.Regt. Co.B
Sartain, W.T. TN 38th Inf. Co.G
Sartain, W.T. TN 38th Inf. 1st Co.K
Sartain, Zera NC 31st Inf. Co.E
Sartee 1st Creek Mtd.Vol. Co.A Bugler
Sartee 1st Creek Mtd.Vol. Co.M
Sarten, Christopher TN 55th (McKoin's) Inf. James' Co.
Sarter, --- SC Cav.Bn. Holcombe Legion Co.B
Sarter, Andrew J. GA 18th Inf. Co.F
Sarter, C.C. SC 18th Inf. Co.B Cpl.
Sarter, Christopher C. SC 1st Inf. Co.E
Sarter, Daniel R. SC 1st Inf. Co.E
Sarter, D.R. MS 12th Cav. Co.C
Sarter, G.W. MS 2nd St.Cav. Co.H
Sarter, G.W. MS Inf. 2nd St.Troops Co.K
Sarter, G.W. MS 10th Inf. Co.P
Sarter, G.W. MS 37th Inf. Co.H
Sarter, J.H. SC 7th Res. Co.K Sgt.
Sarter, John H. SC 1st Inf. Co.E
Sarter, John T. MS 10th Inf. Co.P
Sarter, John Y. SC 1st Inf. Co.E
Sarter, Laurenz SC 1st Inf. Co.E
Sarter, R.A. MS 10th Inf. New Co.G
Sarter, Reubin MS Conscr.
Sarter, Richard C. MS 11th Inf. Co.I Sgt.
Sarter, Robert W. SC 1st Inf. Co.E
Sarter, Thomas SC 1st Inf. Co.E
Sarter, W.D. MS 37th Inf. Co.H
Sarter, W.H. SC 5th St.Troops Co.M
Sarter, Will. H. SC 7th Res. Co.K
Sarthay 1st Creek Mtd.Vol. Co.E
Sar thle 1st Creek Mtd.Vol. Co.H
Sarthoie, --- LA Mil. French Co. of St.James

Sartin, Aaron H. TN 44th Inf. Co.B
Sartin, A.H. TN 44th (Cons.) Inf. Co.K Sgt.
Sartin, Alfred MS 2nd (Quinn's St.Troops) Inf. Co.A
Sartin, Basil AL Lt.Arty. 2nd Bn.
Sartin, Calvin D. MS 19th Inf. Co.B
Sartin, Charles J. TX 15th Cav. Co.I
Sartin, Christopher TN 44th (Cons.) Inf. Co.I
Sartin, Christopher J. NC 45th Inf. Co.G
Sartin, D. GA 16th Inf. Co.D
Sartin, David R. MS 38th Cav. Co.K
Sartin, D.B. AL 49th Inf. Co.A
Sartin, E.B. AL 8th Inf.
Sartin, Elijah S. MS 38th Cav. Co.K
Sartin, Ellis NC 13th Inf. Co.K
Sartin, Ellis NC 22nd Inf. Co.G
Sartin, George AL 18th Inf. Co.L
Sartin, George AL 58th Inf. Co.G
Sartin, George AR 20th Inf. Co.A
Sartin, Gilford GA 3rd Bn.S.S. Co.C
Sartin, Gilford GA 16th Inf. Co.D
Sartin, Granville C. MO Searcy's Bn.S.S.
Sartin, H.C. Mead's Conf.Cav. Co.I
Sartin, Henry MS 42nd Inf. Co.H
Sartin, Henry NC Walker's Bn. Thomas' Legion Co.G
Sartin, Henry TN 1st (Carter's) Cav. Co.H
Sartin, Hopkins L. TN 37th Inf. Co.F
Sartin, Isaiah MS Inf. 3rd Bn. Co.I
Sartin, J. MS St.Cav. 3rd Bn. (Cooper's) 1st Co.A
Sartin, James B. MS 38th Cav. Co.K
Sartin, James R. 3rd Conf.Cav. Co.G
Sartin, Jesse Y. AL Lt.Arty. 2nd Bn. Co.F
Sartin, J.G. MS 1st Lt.Arty. Co.F
Sartin, J.G. MS Horse Arty. Cook's Co.
Sartin, J.H. VA Inf. 1st Bn.Loc.Def. Co.C
Sartin, J.L. TN 1st (Carter's) Cav. Co.G
Sartin, J. Obed. MS 38th Cav. Co.K
Sartin, John VA Cav. 41st Bn. Co.G
Sartin, John F. MO Cav. 3rd Bn. Co.A
Sartin, John G. NC 21st Inf. Co.L
Sartin, John L. VA 46th Inf. 2nd Co.K
Sartin, John M. MS Bradford's Co. (Conf.Guards Arty.)
Sartin, John W. MS 38th Cav. Co.K
Sartin, John W. TX 1st Inf. Co.D
Sartin, John W. TX 9th (Young's) Inf. Co.F
Sartin, Joshua MO Cav. 3rd Bn. Co.A
Sartin, Joshua MO 10th Cav. Co.H
Sartin, J.R. AL 7th Inf. Co.G
Sartin, J.R. TX 32nd Cav. Co.C
Sartin, J.R. Mead's Conf.Cav. Co.C
Sartin, J.T. 1st Conf.Cav. 2nd Co.K
Sartin, J.W. TN Conscr. (Cp. of Instr.)
Sartin, Langford AL Cav. Moreland's Regt. Co.A Sgt.
Sartin, Lee MS St.Cav. 3rd Bn. (Cooper's) 1st Co.A
Sartin, Lewis AL 49th Inf. Co.B
Sartin, Lewis Exch.Bn. Co.D,CSA
Sartin, L.J. TN 1st (Carter's) Cav. Co.G
Sartin, M. AR 10th Mil. Co.B
Sartin, M.A. MS 9th Bn.S.S. Co.C Cpl.
Sartin, Martin A. MS 7th Inf. Co.H Cpl.
Sartin, Moses R. NC 22nd Inf. Co.G 1st Sgt.
Sartin, Richard NC Inf. 2nd Bn. Co.B

Sartin, Russell MS 42nd Inf. Co.H
Sartin, S.P. MS 1st Lt.Arty. Co.F
Sartin, S.P. MS Horse Arty. Cook's Co.
Sartin, Stephen NC 22nd Inf. Co.G
Sartin, Thomas H. AR 7th Inf. Co.H
Sartin, Thomas J.E. NC 13th Inf. Co.K
Sartin, T.J. AL 6th Cav. Co.C
Sartin, W. AL Cav. Moreland's Regt. Co.A Sgt.
Sartin, W. AL 48th Inf. Co.G
Sartin, W.A. TN 1st (Carter's) Cav. Co.K
Sartin, Washington AR 6th Inf. New Co.D
Sartin, Washington AR 12th Inf. Co.I
Sartin, W.C. TX 1st Inf. Co.D
Sartin, William MS 2nd (Quinn's St.Troops) Inf. Co.B
Sartin, William TN 1st (Carter's) Cav. Co.K
Sartin, William TN 44th Inf. Co.F
Sartin, William TN 44th (Cons.) Inf. Co.F
Sartin, William N. NC Walker's Bn. Thomas' Legion Co.G
Sartin, William N. TN 1st (Carter's) Cav. Co.H
Sartin, William S. AL Lt.Arty. Ward's Btty. Sgt.
Sartin, William S. AL Inf. 2nd Regt. Co.E
Sartin, W.M. MS St.Cav. 3rd Bn. (Cooper's) 1st Co.A
Sarting, J.T. KY Cav.
Sar to co thle 1st Creek Mtd.Vol. Co.B
Sarton, John AL 16th Inf. Co.E
Sarton, W.W. MS 9th Cav. Co.B
Sartor, Andrew J. Nitre & Min. Bureau War Dept.,CSA
Sartor, Bob W. SC 18th Inf. Co.B Bvt.2nd Lt.
Sartor, C.C. SC 7th Cav. Co.D
Sartor, D.R. SC 18th Inf. Co.B
Sartor, D.R. Gen. & Staff AASurg.
Sartor, D.T. SC 5th Inf. 2nd Co.D
Sartor, George W. GA 35th Inf. Co.I
Sartor, G.W. MS 41st Inf. Co.I
Sartor, John MS 41st Inf. Co.G
Sartor, John P. MS Cav. 1st Bn. (Miller's) Bowles' Co.
Sartor, John Y. SC Lt.Arty. Jeter's Co. (Macbeth Lt.Arty.)
Sartor, J.P. MS Inf. 2nd Bn. Co.K
Sartor, J.P. 8th (Wade's) Conf.Cav. Co.F
Sartor, J.W. SC Lt.Arty. Jeter's Co. (Macbeth Lt.Arty.)
Sartor, Lawrence SC 5th Inf. 2nd Co.D
Sartor, Lawrence SC 15th Inf. Co.B
Sartor, Lawrence SC Palmetto S.S. Co.A Cpl.
Sartor, Robert SC 5th Inf. 1st Co.D
Sartor, Thomas SC 15th Inf. Co.F
Sartor, W.C. FL Cav. 3rd Bn. Co.C
Sartor, W.C. 15th Conf.Cav. Co.E
Sartor, W.D. MS 44th Inf. Co.I Sgt.
Sartor, William SC 18th Inf. Co.B Capt.
Sartor, William D. AL 24th Inf. Co.D
Sartor, W.W. MS 6th Cav. Morgan's Co.
Sartor, W.W. MS 12th Cav. Co.C
Sartori, Constant TN 15th Inf. Co.K
Sartori, Joseph TN 15th Inf. Co.K
Sartwell, B.W. LA Inf. 9th Bn. Co.B
Sartwell, S. GA Inf. 19th Bn. (St.Guards) Co.D
Sartwell, William L. TX 5th Inf. Co.B
Sartwell, W.L. TX 8th Inf. Co.K,G
Sarvant, Benjamin LA 6th Inf. Co.C
Sarvant, Frank LA 6th Inf. Co.C

Sarvay, Rufus H. VA 46th Inf. 2nd Co.A Sgt.
Sarvay, William G. VA Lt.Arty. 13th Bn. Co.A
Sarver, --- VA Inf. 3rd Kanawha Regt. Capt.
Sarver, Adam A. VA 28th Inf. 2nd Co.C
Sarver, Ballard B. VA 28th Inf. Co.B
Sarver, Bartly VA 54th Inf. Co.K
Sarver, B.T. GA 38th Inf. Co.F
Sarver, Buchanan VA 11th Bn.Res. Co.B
Sarver, Buchanan VA 189th Mil. Co.C
Sarver, Daniel VA 54th Inf. Co.K
Sarver, David C. VA 28th Inf. 2nd Co.C
Sarver, Demarcus VA 7th Inf. Co.D
Sarver, Fleming A. VA 22nd Inf. Co.D
Sarver, George VA 11th Bn.Res. Co.B
Sarver, George VA 54th Inf. Co.K
Sarver, George VA 189th Mil. Co.C
Sarver, George W. VA 36th Inf. 2nd Co.H
Sarver, G.H. VA 1st Cav.St.Line Co.B
Sarver, H. GA 32nd Inf. Co.B
Sarver, H.B. VA 11th Bn.Res. Co.B
Sarver, Henly VA 36th Inf. 2nd Co.H
Sarver, Henry VA 11th Bn.Res. Co.D
Sarver, Henry VA 22nd Inf. Co.C
Sarver, Henry VA 24th Inf. Co.F
Sarver, Henry VA 30th Bn.S.S. Co.B
Sarver, Henry VA 189th Mil. Co.C
Sarver, Hiram VA 30th Bn.S.S. Co.B
Sarver, Hiram VA 54th Inf. Co.K
Sarver, Isaac AL 57th Inf.
Sarver, Isaac VA 54th Inf. Co.K
Sarver, Jacob VA 54th Inf. Co.K
Sarver, James VA 22nd Inf. Co.C
Sarver, James VA 22nd Inf. Co.K
Sarver, James VA 30th Bn.S.S. Co.F
Sarver, James VA 189th Mil. Co.C
Sarver, James B. VA 28th Inf. Co.B
Sarver, James E. KY 10th (Diamond's) Cav. Co.D
Sarver, James E. KY 5th Mtd.Inf. Co.F Lt.
Sarver, James L. VA 28th Inf. 2nd Co.C
Sarver, James M. VA 36th Inf. 2nd Co.H
Sarver, James W. TN 2nd (Robison's) Inf. Co.K
Sarver, J.B. VA Cav. 36th Bn. Co.A
Sarver, J.C. TX 11th (Spaight's) Bn.Vol. Co.B
Sarver, J.C. TX 13th Vol. 4th Co.D
Sarver, J.E. KY 1st Bn.Mtd.Rifles Co.E
Sarver, Jeremiah G. VA 36th Inf. 2nd Co.H Cpl.
Sarver, Jeremiah G. VA 86th Mil. Co.E
Sarver, J.M. VA Cav. 37th Bn. Co.H
Sarver, Joel G. VA 189th Mil. Co.C 1st Lt.
Sarver, John VA 22nd Cav. Co.F
Sarver, John VA Inf. 21st Bn. 1st Co.E, Co.A
Sarver, John VA 30th Bn.S.S. Co.B Cpl.
Sarver, John VA 54th Inf. Co.K
Sarver, John VA 64th Mtd.Inf. Co.A
Sarver, John VA 86th Mil. Co.B Sgt.
Sarver, John A. VA 46th Inf. 2nd Co.K
Sarver, John W. VA 7th Inf. Co.D
Sarver, Jonathan H. VA 11th Inf. Co.F
Sarver, Martin LA Inf. 16th Bn. (Conf.Guards Resp.Bn.) Co.B
Sarver, Michael A. VA 28th Inf. 2nd Co.C
Sarver, M.J. VA 22nd Inf. Co.G
Sarver, Philip M. VA 28th Inf. Co.B
Sarver, Samuel VA 86th Mil. Co.E

Sarver, William LA Inf. 16th Bn. (Conf.Guards Resp.Bn.) Co.B

Sarver, William VA Inf. 23rd Bn. Co.C

Sarver, William VA 45th Inf. Co.L

Sarver, William 3rd Conf.Eng.Troops Co.E Artif.

Sarver, William J. VA Lt.Arty. French's Co.

Sarver, William J. VA Arty. Wise Legion

Sarver, W.T. VA 8th Cav. Co.G 2nd Lt.

Sarvey, William J. LA 5th Inf. Co.D Sgt.

Sarvice, Alexander NC 28th Inf. Co.B

Sarvice, John R. NC 28th Inf. Co.B

Sarvice, S.T. NC 34th Inf. Co.H

Sarville, William MS 8th Inf. Co.B

Sarvis, A.G. SC 8th Inf. Co.K

Sarvis, Aoline LA 7th Cav. Co.B

Sarvis, E.A. NC 49th Inf. Co.G

Sarvis, J.A. SC 10th Inf. Co.B 2nd Lt.

Sarvis, J.M. SC Inf. Hampton Legion Co.F

Sarvis, John F. GA 64th Inf. Co.D

Sarvis, John F., Jr. SC 4th Cav. Co.A

Sarvis, John F., Sr. SC 4th Cav. Co.A

Sarvis, John F. SC Cav. 12th Bn. Co.A

Sarvis, John R. SC Inf. 9th Bn. Co.G

Sarvis, J.R. SC 3rd St.Troops Co.D

Sarvis, Moses F. SC 10th Inf. 2nd Co.G Capt.

Sarvis, S.H. SC 10th Inf. Co.M

Sarvis, S.S. SC Inf. 9th Bn. Co.A 2nd Lt.

Sarvis, S.S. SC 26th Inf. Co.A Bvt.2nd Lt.

Sarvis, Thomas L. SC Inf. 9th Bn. Co.G

Sarvis, T.L. SC 26th Inf. Co.K

Sarvis, W. MO 16th Inf. Co.G

Sarvis, William S. SC Inf. 9th Bn. Co.G

Sarvis, Wilson GA 4th (Clinch's) Cav. Co.A 1st Lt.

Sarvis, W.J. SC 7th Cav. Co.F

Sarvis, W.J. SC 10th Inf. Co.C Cpl.

Sarvis, W.V. GA 4th (Clinch's) Cav. Co.A

Sarvis, W.V. GA Lt.Arty. Clinch's Btty. Cpl.

Sar woh ley 1st Creek Mtd.Vol. Co.M

Sary, Philip LA 1st (Nelligan's) Inf. Co.I

Saryee 1st Creek Mtd.Vol. 1st Co.C

Sar yum kah 1st Creek Mtd.Vol. 2nd Co.C

Sar yum kala 1st Creek Mtd.Vol. 2nd Co.C

Sarzana, Pietro LA Mil. 6th Regt.Eur.Brig. (Italian Guards Bn.) Co.4

Sasa, --- TX Cav. Ragsdale's Bn. Co.A Cpl.

Sasher, Charles KY 3rd Bn.Mtd.Rifles Co.B

Sashnauss, J. GA 8th Inf. Co.C

Sasibery, W.J. GA 23rd Inf. Co.B 2nd Lt.

Sasmth, --- AL 12th Inf. Co.I

Sasnett, Fred G. GA 66th Inf. Co.B Cpl.

Sasnett, H.H. GA Brooks' Co. (Terrell Lt.Arty.)

Sasnett, H.H. GA 15th Inf. Co.E

Sasnett, James H. AL Mtd.Res. Logan's Co.

Sasnett, James J. AL 46th Inf. Co.B

Sasnett, Joshua NC 3rd Arty. (40th St.Troops) Co.H

Sasnett, J.R. GA Brooks' Co. (Terrell Lt.Arty.)

Sasnett, R.W. GA 7th Inf. Co.G

Sasnett, William GA 7th Inf. Co.G

Sasnett, William P. GA 15th Inf. Co.E Cpl.

Sasnowski, I.C. Gary's Brig. Ord.Sgt.

Saso, Luis LA Mil. 5th Regt.Eur.Brig. (Spanish Regt.) Co.7

Sass, G.H. SC 4th Cav. Co.K

Sass, G.H. SC 1st Regt. Charleston Guard Co.H

Sass, Homer GA 5th Inf. Co.F

Sass, W.J. GA 59th Inf.

Sassa, J. AL 17th Inf. Co.G

Sassamon, Christian C. NC 42nd Inf. Co.H

Sassar, James GA 45th Inf. Co.A

Sassard, J.A. SC Mil.Arty. 1st Regt. Tupper's Co.

Sassard, James SC Inf. 1st (Charleston) Bn. Co.A

Sassard, J.H. SC Mil.Arty. 1st Regt. Walter's Co.

Sasse, B. LA Mil. 3rd Regt. French Brig. Co.7

Sasse, Carl TX 24th Cav. Co.K

Sasse, F. TX 6th Inf. Co.B

Sasse, Frederic TX 24th Cav. Co.K

Sasse, Frederick TX Arty. 4th Bn. Co.B

Sasse, Frederick TX 8th Inf. Co.B

Sasseen, David R. TN 61st Mtd.Inf. Co.F

Sasseen, E.R. GA Inf. (Collier Guards) Collier's Co.

Sasseen, George GA Cav. Alexander's Co.

Sasseen, William AR 7th Inf. Co.I

Sassenberg, Fritz TX Waul's Legion Co.D

Sassenberg, William TX Waul's Legion Co.D

Sasser, A. GA 54th Inf. Co.D

Sasser, A.B. GA 8th Cav. Co.H Music.

Sasser, A.B. GA 62nd Cav. Co.I,H Music.

Sasser, Alen GA 12th (Wright's) Cav. (St.Guards) Stubbs' Co.

Sasser, Asa L. NC Mil. Clark's Sp.Bn. Co.D Capt.

Sasser, Augustus K. GA 2nd Cav. Co.G

Sasser, B.B. TX 35th (Brown's) Cav. Co.A

Sasser, B.B. TX 7th Field Btty.

Sasser, B.B. TX 13th Vol. 1st Co.B

Sasser, Benjamin NC 3rd Inf. Co.H

Sasser, Benjamin SC 1st (Orr's) Rifles Co.H

Sasser, Boaz W. NC 4th Inf. Co.D

Sasser, Bryan S. GA 21st Inf. Co.I

Sasser, Bryant GA 31st Inf. Co.K

Sasser, B.W. GA 8th Cav. Old Co.I

Sasser, B.W. GA 62nd Cav. Co.I

Sasser, B.W. NC 35th Inf. Co.I 2nd Lt.

Sasser, C. GA 5th Res. Co.A

Sasser, Calvin NC 51st Inf. Co.H Cpl.

Sasser, Cullen J. NC 18th Inf. Co.G

Sasser, Daniel V. MS 7th Inf. Co.B

Sasser, D.P. NC 18th Inf. Co.G

Sasser, D.V. MS 9th Bn.S.S. Co.C

Sasser, E. GA 8th Cav. Old Co.I

Sasser, Edward GA 62nd Cav. Co.I

Sasser, Edw. NC Mil. Clark's Sp.Bn. Co.D

Sasser, Edward B. NC 27th Inf. Co.A

Sasser, Enoch NC 8th Bn.Part.Rangers Co.B

Sasser, Enoch NC 66th Inf. Co.C

Sasser, F.E. GA 8th Cav. Co.H

Sasser, H. GA 2nd Inf. Co.A Capt.

Sasser, H. TN 20th Inf. Co.E

Sasser, Heli NC 51st Inf. Co.H

Sasser, Henry GA 12th (Wright's) Cav. (St.Guards) Stubbs' Co.

Sasser, Henry GA 54th Inf. Co.D Lt.

Sasser, Henry NC 31st Inf. Co.B

Sasser, Henry VA Inf. Mileham's Co.

Sasser, Henry F. NC 55th Inf. Co.G

Sasser, Henry G. AL 36th Inf.

Sasser, Henry P. TX 19th Inf. Co.D

Sasser, H.G. AL Cp. of Instr. Talladega

Sasser, H.H. AL 18th Inf. Co.B

Sasser, Hilliard NC 50th Inf. Co.E

Sasser, H.J. GA 17th Inf. Co.I

Sasser, Howel GA 12th (Wright's) Cav. (St.Guards) Stubbs' Co.

Sasser, Howel GA 2nd Inf. Co.K Sgt.

Sasser, Howell NC 8th Bn.Part.Rangers Co.D

Sasser, Howell NC Bass' Co.

Sasser, H.P. AL 31st Inf. Co.G

Sasser, Ira S. NC 18th Inf. Co.H Sgt.

Sasser, J. TN 20th Inf. Co.E

Sasser, Jacob GA 3rd Res. Co.B

Sasser, Jacob F. AL 57th Inf. Co.B

Sasser, James GA 59th Inf. Co.A

Sasser, James MS 7th Inf. Co.B Sgt.

Sasser, James A. NC 27th Inf. Co.C

Sasser, James J. AL 18th Inf. Co.B

Sasser, James J. FL 3rd Inf. Co.D

Sasser, J.B. AL 18th Inf. Co.B

Sasser, J.D. AL 36th Inf. Co.K

Sasser, J.D. AL Cp. of Instr. Talladega

Sasser, Jesse VA Inf. Mileham's Co.

Sasser, J.G. LA 2nd Inf. Co.C

Sasser, J.H. GA 8th Cav. Old Co.I, Co.H

Sasser, J.H. NC Mil. Clark's Sp.Bn. Co.D

Sasser, J.J. AL 17th Inf. Co.G

Sasser, J.L. LA 3rd Inf. Co.G

Sasser, John FL Inf. 2nd Bn. Co.E

Sasser, John GA 12th Inf. Co.A

Sasser, John 7th Conf.Cav. Co.F

Sasser, John 8th (Dearing's) Conf.Cav. Co.G

Sasser, John B. AL Eufaula Lt.Arty.

Sasser, John B. GA 28th Inf. Co.E

Sasser, John Hilleay GA 62nd Cav. Co.I,H

Sasser, John W. AL 17th Inf. Co.G

Sasser, Joseph GA 59th Inf. Co.A

Sasser, Joseph KY 4th Mtd.Inf. Co.K

Sasser, Joseph MS 7th Inf. Co.B

Sasser, Josiah FL 1st Inf. Old Co.E

Sasser, J.S. TN 14th (Neely's) Cav. Co.A Cpl.

Sasser, L. GA 3rd Inf.

Sasser, L. GA 54th Inf. Co.D

Sasser, Larkin P. NC 2nd Inf. Co.H

Sasser, Littleton GA 12th (Wright's) Cav. (St.Guards) Stubbs' Co.

Sasser, Littleton GA 2nd Inf. Co.K Lt.

Sasser, Littleton GA 3rd Res. Co.I Cpl.

Sasser, L.L. GA 5th Mil.

Sasser, L.M. AL 15th Inf. Co.G

Sasser, Madison GA 31st Inf. Co.K

Sasser, Matthew G. NC 51st Inf. Co.H Sgt.

Sasser, N.R. GA 46th Inf. Co.F

Sasser, O.C. NC 35th Inf. Co.I

Sasser, Philemon H. NC 2nd Cav. (19th St.Troops) Co.I 2nd Lt.

Sasser, Phil H. NC Lt.Arty. 3rd Bn. Co.C

Sasser, Phil H. NC 33rd Inf. Co.A 1st Lt.

Sasser, Philip E. NC 4th Inf. Co.F

Sasser, Philip H. NC 1st Arty. (10th St.Troops) Co.A 1st Sgt.

Sasser, P.L. TX 8th Cav. Co.K

Sasser, R.B. GA 62nd Cav. Co.H

Sasser, R.D. GA 54th Inf. Co.F

Sasser, Rigdon NC 27th Inf. Co.C

Sasser, S. AR 8th Inf. New Co.E

Sasser, Samuel D. AL 6th Inf. Co.F

Sasser, Samuel D. AL 7th Inf. Co.E

Sasser, Simon NC 51st Inf. Co.H
Sasser, Stephen MS 7th Inf. Co.B Sgt.
Sasser, Stephen TN Lt.Arty. McClung's Co.
Sasser, Stephen 14th Conf.Cav. Co.A
Sasser, Stephen L. NC 27th Inf. Co.K
Sasser, Sugars A. NC 4th Inf. Co.F
Sasser, Thomas GA 12th (Wright's) Cav.
   (St.Guards) Stubbs' Co.
Sasser, Thomas H. NC 5th Inf. Co.C
Sasser, Tippo H. NC 27th Inf. Co.K
Sasser, Tippo H. NC 35th Inf. Co.I Sgt.
Sasser, W. TN Lt.Arty. Winston's Co.
Sasser, W.G. MS Inf. 2nd St.Troops Co.O
Sasser, Wiley NC 50th Inf. Co.E Music.
Sasser, Wiley B. NC 66th Inf. Co.I
Sasser, William FL Milton Lt.Arty. Dunham's
   Co.
Sasser, William GA Cav. 12th Bn. (St.Guards)
   Co.C
Sasser, William GA 12th (Robinson's) Cav.
   (St.Guards) Co.F
Sasser, William MS 7th Inf. Co.B
Sasser, William NC 1st Arty. (10th St.Troops)
   Co.F
Sasser, William NC Inf. 13th Bn. Co.D
Sasser, William NC 66th Inf. Co.K
Sasser, William TX 8th Cav. Co.K
Sasser, William D. AL 57th Inf. Co.B
Sasser, William M. TX 10th Inf. Co.B
Sasser, William P. MS Cav. 24th Bn. Co.B
Sasser, William Z. FL 3rd Inf. Co.D Sgt.
Sasser, Wily NC 8th Bn.Part.Rangers Co.F
Sasser, W.P. AL 17th Inf. Co.G
Sasser, W.R. TX 1st Inf. Co.D
Sassers, Lewis H. AL 6th Inf. Co.A
Sassers, Louis TX 3rd Inf. Co.E
Sassers, Samuel D. AL 6th Inf. Co.F
Sasset, A. GA 2nd Inf. Co.K
Sassinot, L. LA 22nd Inf.
Sassmannshausen, Ludwig TX 36th Cav. Co.F
Sassnett, B.H. AL 1st Bn.Cadets Co.C
Sassnett, S. AL 8th Inf. Co.B
Sassnutt, Joshua NC Lt.Arty. 13th Bn. Co.F
Sasson, G.G. VA 14th Cav. 1st Co.F Sgt.
Sasson, W.T. AL 36th Inf. Co.K
Sassport, J. SC Mil. 1st Regt. (Charleston Res.)
   Co.B
Sassy, C. LA Mil. 1st Regt. 2nd Brig. 1st Div.
Sastram, Emile LA Pointe Coupee Arty.
Sastre, Jayme LA Mil. 5th Regt.Eur.Brig.
   (Spanish Regt.) Co.2
Sastre, Juan LA Mil. 5th Regt.Eur.Brig. (Spanish
   Regt.) Co.2
Satal, F.W. FL 3rd Inf. Co.A
Sa tan Kie 2nd Cherokee Mtd.Vol. Co.I
Satawhite, B.F. TX 28th Cav. Co.L
Satawhite, S.S. MS 22nd Inf. Co.H
Satawhite, William H. MS 22nd Inf. Co.H
Satberne, R.H. AL 10th Inf.
Satchel, H.M. MS 37th Inf. Co.I
Satchell, H. LA Mil. Beauregard Regt. Co.C
Satchell, James TX Cav. Waller's Regt. Menard's
   Co.
Satchell, John W. VA 39th Inf. Co.A
Satchell, Robert B. VA Hvy.Arty. 20th Bn. Co.B
Satchell, Thomas J. VA 39th Inf. Co.A
Satchell, Thomas P. VA 39th Inf. Co.F

Satchell, W. LA Mil. Beauregard Regt. Co.C
Satcher, Albert G. LA 9th Inf. Co.H
Satcher, Amos Watson SC 19th Inf. Co.D Cpl.
Satcher, Andrew J. MS 13th Inf. Co.E
Satcher, A.W. SC Inf.Bn. Co.D
Satcher, H. SC 19th Inf. Co.A
Satcher, Henry SC 15th Inf. Co.C
Satcher, Henry A. SC 1st Inf. Co.O
Satcher, Henry M. AL 39th Inf. Co.A Sgt.
Satcher, H.F. AL 15th Inf. Co.G Cpl.
Satcher, H.M. MS 37th Inf. Co.I
Satcher, H.M. SC 2nd Arty. Co.C
Satcher, H.M. SC 2nd St.Troops Co.B Cpl.
Satcher, Hugh MS 37th Inf. Co.E
Satcher, Isaiah SC 6th Cav. Co.B
Satcher, J. SC 5th Res. Co.K
Satcher, J.A. SC 2nd Arty. Co.E
Satcher, James SC 19th Inf. Co.A Sgt.
Satcher, James 7th Conf.Cav. Co.C
Satcher, James A. SC Inf.Bn. Co.C
Satcher, Jesse SC 2nd St.Troops Co.I
Satcher, J.H. SC 6th Inf. Co.D
Satcher, John MS 8th Inf. Co.F
Satcher, John M. AL 3rd Cav. Co.G
Satcher, Julius SC 2nd St.Troops Co.I
Satcher, J.W. AL 15th Inf. Co.I
Satcher, L.P. MS 9th Cav. Co.B
Satcher, L.P. MS Cav. 17th Bn. Co.B Cpl.
Satcher, L. Perry MS 1st Cav.Res. Co.H Sgt.
Satcher, L. Perry MS 14th Inf. Co.A
Satcher, L.W. MS 37th Inf. Co.I
Satcher, Perry A. MS Cav. 17th Bn. Co.B Cpl.
Satcher, Robert SC 19th Inf. Co.A
Satcher, S. SC 2nd St.Troops Co.B
Satcher, S.M. SC Inf.Bn. Co.D
Satcher, S.S. SC 2nd Inf. Co.K
Satcher, Stanmore M. SC 19th Inf. Co.D
Satcher, T. SC 19th Inf. Co.A
Satcher, Wood AL 50th Inf. Co.A Cpl.
Satcher, W.S. MS 38th Cav. Co.H
Satchers, Jeremiah AL 6th Inf. Co.A
Satchfield, Carter VA Inf. 44th Bn. Co.E
Satchfield, Frank VA Lt.Arty. Pegram's Co.
Satchfield, Frank VA 12th Inf. Co.K
Satchfield, Frank VA 41st Inf. Co.K,C
Satchfield, George W. VA Inf. 5th Bn. Co.B
Satchfield, George W. VA 53rd Inf. Co.E
Satchfield, Isham B. VA Hvy.Arty. 18th Bn.
   Co.C
Satchfield, John W. VA Lt.Arty. Pegram's Co.
Satchfield, John W. VA 12th Inf. Co.C,D
Satchill, Robert VA 54th Mil. Co.C,D
Satchwell, Solomon S. NC 25th Inf. Surg.
Satchwell, S.S. Gen. & Staff, Medical Dept.
   Surg.
Satchwell, William Benjamin NC 3rd Inf. Co.I
Sate, W.A. GA 1st Troops & Def. (Macon) Co.C
Sateb, J.H. GA 11th Inf. Co.C
Sateel, W.E. LA 16th Inf. Co.E
Sateer, George H. TN 8th Btty. Co.B
Saten, J.A. TX 8th Cav.
Saten, James W. GA 29th Inf. Co.K 1st Lt.
Sater, A.T. NC Snead's Co. (Loc.Def.)
Sater, George H. TN 4th Cav. Co.E
Sater, John T. MO Cav. Poindexter's Regt.
Saterfield, A. VA Lt.Arty. Penick's Co.
Saterfield, B. AR 17th (Lemoyne's) Inf. Co.E

Saterfield, B.D. AR 21st Inf. Co.I
Saterfield, B.F., Jr. GA 52nd Inf. Co.D
Saterfield, B.F., Sr. GA 52nd Inf. Co.D
Saterfield, Caswell SC 3rd Res. Co.H
Saterfield, Daniel SC 3rd Res. Co.H
Saterfield, D.D. SC 2nd Inf. Co.A
Saterfield, E.A. SC 18th Inf. Co.D
Saterfield, F.L. GA Inf. 8th Bn. Co.A
Saterfield, H.P. AR 45th Mil. Co.F
Saterfield, J. TN 1st (Carter's) Cav. Co.E
Saterfield, J.C. VA Arty. Young's Co.
Saterfield, J.F. SC 5th Mil. Beat.4
Saterfield, J.H. GA 52nd Inf. Co.D
Saterfield, J.S. KY 3rd Mtd.Inf. Co.A
Saterfield, J.T. NC 3rd Jr.Res. Co.C
Saterfield, J.W. GA Inf. 11th Bn. (St.Guards)
   Co.D
Saterfield, J.W. SC Inf. Holcombe Legion Co.A
Saterfield, M. TN 5th (McKenzie's) Cav. Co.A
Saterfield, Marian MS 12th Inf. Co.C
Saterfield, M.V. TN 1st (Carter's) Cav. Co.E
Saterfield, N.N. AR 45th Mil. Co.A
Saterfield, O.B. VA Arty. Young's Co.
Saterfield, Osborne B. VA Lt.Arty. 1st Bn. Co.C
Saterfield, P.M. AR 45th Mil. Co.A Cpl.
Saterfield, R.J. GA 52nd Inf. Co.D
Saterfield, S.J. GA Inf. 8th Bn. Co.A
Saterfield, S.R. AR 45th Mil. Co.F
Saterfield, Thomas KY 3rd Mtd.Inf. Co.A
Saterfield, T.N. GA Inf. 17th Bn. (St.Guards)
   Jefferson's Co.
Saterfield, William GA Phillips' Legion Co.E
Saterfield, William D. MS Cav. 1st Bn. (Miller's)
   Co.E
Saterfield, W.M. MO Cav. Coffee's Regt. Co.A
Saterwhite, Augustus P. LA 28th (Gray's) Inf.
   Co.D
Saterwhite, J.N. MO Inf. 3rd Bn. Co.B
Saterwhite, William AR 23rd Inf. Co.B
Sates, W. GA 28th Inf. Co.B
Satham, Robert AR 9th Inf. Old Co.B 2nd Lt.
Sathery, Jackson LA 3rd Inf. Co.E
Sa thla kah 1st Creek Mtd.Vol. 2nd Co.C
Sathle 1st Creek Mtd.Vol. 2nd Co.I
Satifield, J.S. GA 11th Cav. Co.E
Satis, Albert VA 22nd Inf. Swann's Co.
Satiswhet, Cicero AL 22nd Inf. Co.G
Satks, J.H. AR 24th Inf. Co.A
Satliff, Daniel NC 45th Inf. Co.H
Satmon, B.B. 8th (Wade's) Conf.Cav. Co.D
Satonchie, Pedro TX 22nd Cav. Co.F
Sattalings, James AL 40th Inf.
Sattarfield, L. AL Gid Nelson Lt.Arty.
Sattawhite, --- TX Cav. Mann's Regt. Co.D
Sattawhite, John AR 30th Inf. Co.A
Sattean, S.R. GA 54th Inf.
Sattefie, R.F.L. 2nd Conf.Eng.Troops Co.B
Sattele, Emile LA 6th Inf. Co.E
Sattenfield, Jacob NC 7th Inf. Co.G
Sattenhett, John AL Cp. of Instr. Talladega
Sattenwhite, J.W. TX 19th Inf. Co.C 1st Sgt.
Satter, H. VA 4th Cav. & Inf.St.Line 1st Co.I
Satter, Jacob LA Mil. Mech.Guard
Satter, Neill AL 33rd Inf. Co.E Cpl.
Satterfield, --- AL 28th Inf. Co.G
Satterfield, --- NC 7th Sr.Res. Williams' Co.

Satterfield, A. SC Lt.Arty. 3rd (Palmetto) Bn. Co.H
Satterfield, A. SC Inf. Hampton Legion Co.K
Satterfield, A.B. KY 12th Cav. Co.B,D
Satterfield, A.B. SC 16th Inf. Co.K
Satterfield, A.J. AR 18th (Marmaduke's) Inf. Co.I Cpl.
Satterfield, A.J. KY 1st (Helm's) Cav.
Satterfield, Alex AR Inf. Cocke's Regt. Co.K
Satterfield, Alexander TN 37th Inf. Co.K
Satterfield, Allen MO Cav. 3rd Regt.St.Guard Co.A
Satterfield, Allen T. GA 40th Inf. Co.B
Satterfield, Benjamin TN Cav. 12th Bn. (Day's) Co.D
Satterfield, Benjamin C. NC Walker's Bn. Thomas' Legion Co.G
Satterfield, Benjamin C. TN 1st (Carter's) Cav. Co.H
Satterfield, B.F. 1st Conf.Inf. 2nd Co.C
Satterfield, B.L. Gen. & Staff Asst.Surg.
Satterfield, B.W. GA 60th Inf. Co.E
Satterfield, C. SC 1st St.Troops Co.B
Satterfield, C. SC 5th Mil. Beat Co.4
Satterfield, Carter AR Inf. Clear Lake Ind.Guards
Satterfield, C.C. TN 50th Inf. Co.D
Satterfield, C.C. TN 50th (Cons.) Inf. Co.D
Satterfield, C.H. AL 46th Inf. Co.F
Satterfield, Columbus AR Inf. Cocke's Regt. Co.B
Satterfield, D. Sap. & Min. G.W. Maxson's Co.,CSA
Satterfield, Daniel D. SC 20th Inf. Co.A
Satterfield, David MS 32nd Inf. Co.A Cpl.
Satterfield, David 3rd Conf.Eng.Troops Co.F Artif.
Satterfield, DeMarcus VA 64th Mil. Powell's Co.
Satterfield, Dennis NC 45th Inf. Co.I
Satterfield, E. SC 5th St.Troops Co.C
Satterfield, E. SC 20th Inf. Co.F
Satterfield, E. SC Post Guard Senn's Co.
Satterfield, Edward F. MO 4th Cav. Co.I
Satterfield, Edward F. NC 24th Inf. Co.A 2nd Lt.
Satterfield, Edward M. GA 9th Inf. Co.G
Satterfield, Edward R. VA 10th Cav. Co.K
Satterfield, E.F. NC 55th Inf. Co.H 1st Lt.
Satterfield, F.M. AR 30th Inf. Co.G,D
Satterfield, Frederic G. GA 24th Inf. Co.C
Satterfield, George W. GA 40th Inf. Co.B 2nd Lt.
Satterfield, George W. VA 23rd Inf. Co.E
Satterfield, Gus TN 49th Inf. Co.I
Satterfield, G.W.R. NC Lt.Arty. 13th Bn. Co.D
Satterfield, Henry TN 19th Inf. Co.I
Satterfield, H.J. NC 5th Sr.Res. Co.C
Satterfield, H.M. 1st Conf.Cav. 1st Co.A
Satterfield, Hosea TN McClung's Btty.
Satterfield, Iras W. GA 24th Inf. Co.C
Satterfield, Isaac GA 1st Cav. Co.H
Satterfield, James GA 20th Inf. Co.F
Satterfield, James GA 23rd Inf. Co.H Cpl.
Satterfield, James MO Cav. 3rd Regt.St.Guard Co.A
Satterfield, James A. GA 52nd Inf. Co.G
Satterfield, James H. SC Inf. Hampton Legion Co.F Sgt.

Satterfield, James K. SC 2nd Rifles Co.E
Satterfield, James M. TX 9th Cav. Co.I
Satterfield, James M. VA 64th Mil. Powell's Co.
Satterfield, Jas. R. AL 8th Inf. Co.D
Satterfield, James T. GA 9th Inf. Co.B
Satterfield, James T. TN 26th Inf. Co.D
Satterfield, James W. TN 26th Inf. Co.C
Satterfield, James W. VA Inf. 22nd Bn. Co.B
Satterfield, J.B. AL 22nd Inf. Co.D
Satterfield, J.C. VA 1st (Farinholt's) Res. Co.E
Satterfield, Jefferson SC 13th Inf. Co.I
Satterfield, Jeremiah M. GA 9th Inf. Co.G
Satterfield, Jesse GA 1st Reg. Co.B
Satterfield, Jesse Cunningham's Ord.Detach. Black.
Satterfield, Jesse C. MO 3rd Cav. Co.K
Satterfield, Jesse C. MO 4th Cav. Co.K
Satterfield, Jesse C. MO Dismtd.Cav. Lawther's Temporary Regt.
Satterfield, Jesse F. GA 52nd Inf. Co.I
Satterfield, J.H. GA Cav. 6th Bn. (St.Guards) Co.E
Satterfield, J.H. GA Cav. 10th Bn. (St.Guards) Co.C
Satterfield, J.H. TN 30th Inf. Co.C 1st Sgt.
Satterfield, J.L. GA 23rd Inf. Co.I
Satterfield, J.L. TN 63rd Inf. Co.B
Satterfield, J.M. NC Lt.Arty. 13th Bn. Co.E
Satterfield, J.N. SC 7th Inf. Co.A
Satterfield, John GA 19th Inf. Co.K
Satterfield, John NC Hoskins' Co. (Loc.Def.)
Satterfield, John TN 8th Inf. Co.E
Satterfield, John TN 20th Inf. Co.K
Satterfield, John TN 49th Inf. Co.G
Satterfield, John Inf. Bailey's Cons.Regt. Co.C
Satterfield, John Exch.Bn. Co.D,CSA
Satterfield, John A. GA 38th Inf. Co.N
Satterfield, John B. GA 6th Cav. Co.E
Satterfield, John B. MS 18th Inf. Co.H
Satterfield, John B.O. SC Inf. Hampton Legion Co.E
Satterfield, John C. GA Inf. 11th Bn. (St.Guards) Co.A Cpl.
Satterfield, John D. GA 1st Reg. Co.B
Satterfield, John D. NC 17th Inf. (2nd Org.) Co.F
Satterfield, John D. NC 53rd Inf. Co.E
Satterfield, John G.J. GA 19th Inf. Co.K
Satterfield, John H. NC 45th Inf. Co.B
Satterfield, John R. AR 18th (Marmaduke's) Inf. Co.I
Satterfield, John S. TN 11th Inf. Co.H
Satterfield, John W. GA 4th Inf. Co.D
Satterfield, John W. GA 52nd Inf. Co.D
Satterfield, John W. TN 26th Inf. Co.D
Satterfield, John W. TN 61st Mtd.Inf. Co.F
Satterfield, John W. VA 11th Cav. Co.A Sgt.
Satterfield, John W. VA 67th Mil. Co.A
Satterfield, Joseph SC 2nd Rifles Co.K
Satterfield, J.R. AL St.Res. Elliby's Co.
Satterfield, J.R. NC Lt.Arty. 13th Bn. Co.D
Satterfield, J.S. AR 32nd Inf. Co.F
Satterfield, J.S. MS 4th Cav. Co.E Sgt.
Satterfield, J.S. MS Cav. Hughes' Bn. Co.E
Satterfield, J.T. NC 4th Bn.Jr.Res. Co.C
Satterfield, J.W. GA 11th Cav. Co.H
Satterfield, J.W. GA 30th Inf. Co.H

Satterfield, J.W. VA 13th Cav. Co.K
Satterfield, J.Y. GA 9th Inf. Co.B
Satterfield, Lemuel VA 20th Inf. Co.K
Satterfield, Lemuel VA 46th Inf. Co.F
Satterfield, Levi TN 18th Inf. Co.E
Satterfield, L.J.K.P. TN 61st Mtd.Inf. Co.F
Satterfield, L.M. MO 16th Inf. Co.B
Satterfield, Milton M. GA 9th Inf. Co.G
Satterfield, M.L. AR Lt.Arty. Zimmerman's Btty.
Satterfield, M.L. AR 24th Inf. Co.I
Satterfield, Moses C. GA 43rd Inf. Co.B
Satterfield, Nathaniel AR 18th (Marmaduke's) Inf. Co.I
Satterfield, N.N. AR 32nd Inf. Co.F
Satterfield, Noah AR 15th Mil. Co.I Sgt.
Satterfield, N.W. AR 35th Inf. Co.I
Satterfield, O. Benton VA 23rd Inf. Co.E
Satterfield, Onslav J. VA 14th Inf. Co.K
Satterfield, Orsmyn B. VA 1st Arty. 3rd Co.C
Satterfield, Peter TN 24th Bn.S.S. Co.C
Satterfield, P.F. AR Lt.Arty. Zimmerman's Btty.
Satterfield, P.L. AR 24th Inf. Co.I
Satterfield, Pleasant L. TN 39th Mtd.Inf. Co.I 1st Sgt.
Satterfield, P.M. AR 18th (Marmaduke's) Inf. Co.I
Satterfield, P.M. MO Cav. Fristoe's Regt. Co.F
Satterfield, R.A. VA 46th Inf. Co.F
Satterfield, Radford A. VA 3rd Hvy.Arty. Co.G
Satterfield, Radford A. VA 20th Inf. Co.K Cpl.
Satterfield, Radford A. VA 59th Inf. 3rd Co.C Sgt.
Satterfield, Reuben P. GA 9th Inf. Co.G
Satterfield, Reuben W. GA 7th Inf. Co.B Capt.
Satterfield, Reubin N. Conf.Cav. Clarkson's Bn. Ind.Rangers Co.H Sgt.
Satterfield, Richard NC 39th Inf. Co.I
Satterfield, R.J. 1st Conf.Inf. 2nd Co.C
Satterfield, R.N. MO Inf. Clark's Regt. Co.D
Satterfield, Robert F.L. MS 23rd Inf. Co.A
Satterfield, R.M. GA 7th Cav. Co.I
Satterfield, R.M. GA Cav. 24th Bn. Co.D
Satterfield, Robert E. KY 11th Cav. Co.B Sgt.
Satterfield, R.S. TN 4th (Murray's) Cav. Co.H
Satterfield, Samuel T. TN Cav. 7th Bn. (Bennett's) Co.B
Satterfield, S.C. TN Cav. 12th Bn. (Day's) Co.D Cpl.
Satterfield, S.R. AR 32nd Inf. Co.F Sgt.
Satterfield, S.S. TN 20th Inf. Co.K
Satterfield, S.T. TN 21st & 22nd (Cons.) Cav. Co.B
Satterfield, S.T. TN 22nd (Barteau's) Cav. Co.E Sgt.
Satterfield, Stephen M. GA 43rd Inf. Co.B
Satterfield, Thomas GA 6th Cav. Co.B Cpl.
Satterfield, Thomas GA Smith's Legion Cpl.
Satterfield, Thomas SC Hvy.Arty. 15th (Lucas') Bn. Co.B Music.
Satterfield, Thomas B. AL 10th Inf. Co.I
Satterfield, Thomas J. AR 17th (Lemoyne's) Inf. Co.B
Satterfield, W.D. NC 14th Inf. Co.G
Satterfield, W.E. MS 15th Inf. Co.B
Satterfield, W.H. GA 16th Inf. Co.C
Satterfield, Wiley TN 26th Inf. Co.C

Satterfield, William AR Inf. Cocke's Regt. Co.K
Satterfield, William MO 2nd Cav. Co.D,E
Satterfield, William SC Hvy.Arty. 15th (Lucas')
Bn. Co.B Sgt.
Satterfield, William SC 13th Inf. Co.I,G
Satterfield, William TN 21st Cav.
Satterfield, William TN 1st (Turney's) Inf. Co.G
Satterfield, William TX 23rd Cav. Co.I
Satterfield, William E. TN 14th Inf. Co.G
Satterfield, William H. GA 3rd Cav. (St.Guards)
Co.A Cpl.
Satterfield, William J. GA 9th Inf. Co.G
Satterfield, William P. NC 24th Inf. Co.A
Satterfield, William R. VA 20th Inf. Co.K
Satterfield, William R. VA 59th Inf. 3rd Co.C
Sgt.
Satterfield, Willis TN 8th Inf. Co.C
Satterfield, W.J. AR 32nd Inf. Co.F
Satterfield, W.M. GA Cav. 10th Bn. (St.Guards)
Co.C
Satterfield, W.M. GA 52nd Inf. Co.D
Satterfield, W.M.W. AR 27th Inf. Co.F
Satterfield, W.O. SC Lt.Arty. 3rd (Palmetto) Bn.
Co.H
Satterfield, W.O. SC 16th Inf. Co.K
Satterfield, W.R. VA 46th Inf. Co.F
Satterfield, W.S. MO 7th Inf. Co.I
Satterfield, W.T. GA Cav. Corbin's Co. Ens.
Satterlee, E. NC 6th Inf. Co.E
Satterly, Richard LA 5th Inf. Co.B
Sattersfield, John GA Smith's Legion
Satterthaitte, John NC 2nd Jr.Res. Co.I Cpl.
Satterthwaite, --- NC 3rd Bn.Sr.Res. Williams'
Co.
Satterthwaite, Benjamin F. NC 2nd Arty. (36th
St.Troops) Co.G Cpl.
Satterthwaite, B.F. NC Lt.Arty. 13th Bn.
Co.D,A Cpl.
Satterthwaite, George W. NC 37th Inf. Co.E
Satterthwaite, Henry D. NC 61st Inf. Co.B Sgt.
Satterthwaite, James H. NC 61st Inf. Co.B Cpl.
Satterthwaite, James H. NC 67th Inf.
Satterthwaite, Jeremiah NC 4th Inf. Co.E
Satterthwaite, Lewis E. NC 2nd Cav. (19th
St.Troops) Co.G Capt.
Satterthwaite, Luther E. NC 1st Arty. (10th
St.Troops) Co.G Cpl.
Satterthwaite, Major J. NC 13th Inf. Co.G
Satterthwaite, Seth A. NC 17th Inf. (2nd Org.)
Co.E
Satterthwaite, T.H. NC 1st Arty. (10th
St.Troops) Co.K Cpl.
Satterthwaite, Thomas H. NC 3rd Arty. (40th
St.Troops) Co.I Sr.1st Lt.
Satterthwaite, Thomas H. NC 61st Inf. Co.B 1st
Lt.
Satterthwaite, William A. NC 61st Inf. Co.B
Satterthwaite, William E. NC 2nd Cav. (19th
St.Troops) Co.G 1st Lt.
Satterwhite, --- TX Cav. 4th Regt.St.Troops Co.I
Satterwhite, A. GA Hvy.Arty. 22nd Bn. Co.B
Satterwhite, Alex GA 1st (Olmstead's) Inf. Co.G
Satterwhite, Benjamin VA 9th Cav. Co.B
Satterwhite, B.F. TX Cav. Morgan's Regt. Co.C
Satterwhite, B.W. AR 37th Inf. Co.I
Satterwhite, C.A. SC 7th Cav. Co.E Sgt.

Satterwhite, C.A. SC Cav.Bn. Holcombe Legion
Co.C Sgt.
Satterwhite, Charles NC 55th Inf. Co.K
Satterwhite, Charles M. AL Mil. 3rd Vol. Co.F
Satterwhite, David C. AL 22nd Inf. Co.G
Satterwhite, David M. TX 28th Cav. Co.I Cpl.
Satterwhite, David W. NC 12th Inf. Co.B
Satterwhite, D.S. GA 7th Inf. Co.G
Satterwhite, E.W. GA 11th Inf. Co.I
Satterwhite, E. Worell GA 47th Inf. Co.B
Satterwhite, F.M. TX 28th Cav. Co.L
Satterwhite, F.M. TX Cav. Morgan's Regt. Co.C
Satterwhite, Frank VA 30th Inf. Co.G
Satterwhite, H.E. AR 10th (Witt's) Cav. Co.C
Satterwhite, Isaac S.C. AL Lt.Arty. 20th Bn.
Co.A,B
Satterwhite, J. MS 28th Cav. Co.D
Satterwhite, J.A. NC Mallett's Bn.
Satterwhite, James VA 47th Inf. 2nd Co.K
Satterwhite, James A. GA 5th Inf. Co.F
Satterwhite, James A. NC 12th Inf. Co.D
Satterwhite, James E. GA 41st Inf. Co.E
Satterwhite, James E. NC 12th Inf. Co.B
Satterwhite, James S. AR 37th Inf. Co.I 2nd Lt.
Satterwhite, J.E. Conf.Arty. Lewis' Bn. Co.A
Sgt.
Satterwhite, Jeremiah E. VA Lt.Arty. J.D.
Smith's Co. Sgt.
Satterwhite, Jeremiah E. VA 34th Inf. Co.G
Satterwhite, J.F. NC 23rd Inf. Co.G
Satterwhite, J.M. GA 46th Inf. Co.E
Satterwhite, John AL 3rd Cav. Co.D
Satterwhite, John AL 21st Inf. Co.A
Satterwhite, John FL Inf. 2nd Bn. Co.E
Satterwhite, John MO Lt.Arty. Landis' Co.
Satterwhite, John NC McDugald's Co.
Satterwhite, John SC 5th St.Troops Co.C
Wagon M.
Satterwhite, John SC 9th Res. Co.F
Satterwhite, John SC Cav.Bn. Holcombe Legion
Co.C
Satterwhite, John VA 47th Inf. 2nd Co.K
Satterwhite, John G. VA Hvy.Arty. 10th Bn.
Co.A Cpl.
Satterwhite, John W. AL Mil. 4th Vol. Co.A
Satterwhite, John W. MO 6th Inf. Co.A
Satterwhite, Joseph M. NC 44th Inf. Co.A
Satterwhite, J.T. TX Waul's Legion Co.B
Satterwhite, Layfate GA 47th Inf. Co.B
Satterwhite, L.H. NC 8th Inf. Co.D Sgt.
Satterwhite, Michael NC 44th Inf. Co.A
Satterwhite, M.S. GA 11th Inf. Co.I
Satterwhite, Pascal SC 5th Inf. 2nd Co.D Cpl.
Satterwhite, Phil AL 43rd Inf. Co.G
Satterwhite, Philip AL 21st Inf. Co.A
Satterwhite, Philip AL Cp. of Instr. Talladega
Satterwhite, Richard SC 5th St.Troops Co.C Sgt.
Satterwhite, Robert M. NC 12th Inf. Co.B
Satterwhite, R.S. SC 3rd Inf. Co.B
Satterwhite, R.S. SC 9th Res. Co.F
Satterwhite, R.S. SC Inf. Holcombe Legion Co.G
Satterwhite, S.A. GA 41st Inf. Co.E
Satterwhite, Solomon T. NC 55th Inf. Co.K
Bvt.2nd Lt.
Satterwhite, Stephen A. AL Lt.Arty. 20th Bn.
Co.A,B
Satterwhite, Thomas AL Cav. Lewis' Bn. Co.A

Satterwhite, Thomas AL 43rd Inf. Co.G
Satterwhite, Thomas H. AR 33rd Inf. Co.B
Satterwhite, Thomas J. AL 57th Inf. Co.I
Satterwhite, T.P. VA 9th Cav. Co.H
Satterwhite, T.R. AR 37th Inf. Co.I
Satterwhite, W.D. GA 32nd Inf. Co.A
Satterwhite, W.E. GA 56th Inf. Co.K
Satterwhite, W.F. SC 1st (McCreary's) Inf. Co.B
Satterwhite, W.H. NC 55th Inf. Co.K Sgt.
Satterwhite, William AL 20th Inf. Co.C,G
Satterwhite, William GA 55th Inf. Co.G
Satterwhite, William VA 47th Inf. 2nd Co.K
Satterwhite, William H. AL Lt.Arty. 20th Bn.
Co.A,B
Satterwhite, Wm. J. AL 22nd Inf. Co.G
Satterwhite, William J. AL Cp. of Instr. Tal-
ladega
Satterwhite, William L. NC 12th Inf. Co.B
Satterwhite, William L. VA Hvy.Arty. 10th Bn.
Co.A 1st Lt.
Satterwhite, W.L. NC Jones' Co. (Supp.Force)
Satterwhite, W.N.B. NC Hvy.Arty. 10th Bn.
Co.B
Satterwhite, Y.M. AL 7th Cav. Co.H
Sattewhite, J.T. TX 19th Inf. Co.C
Sattifield, Green D. NC 15th Inf. Co.G
Sattle, William B. VA 11th Bn.Res. Co.C
Sattler, A. VA 13th Inf. Co.K
Sattler, Adolphe VA 3rd Res. Co.B
Sattler, Conrod VA Inf. 9th Bn. Duffy's Co.C
Sattler, Frank LA 1st Hvy.Arty. (Reg.) Co.G
Cpl.
Sattler, Frank TX 2nd Inf. Co.F Sgt.Maj.
Sattler, Frank Sig.Corps,CSA Cpl.
Sattler, Harman TX 19th Inf. Co.D
Sattler, J. LA 22nd Inf. Co.C
Sattler, John VA Inf. 9th Bn. Duffy's Co.C
Sattler, John VA 25th Inf. 2nd Co.C Cpl.
Sattler, T.H. TX 2nd Inf. Co.F Cpl.
Sattles, W.H. GA 2nd Res. Co.G Cpl.
Sattoon, J.B. LA Pointe Coupee Arty.
Sattoria, Antonia AL 1st Regt. Mobile Vol. Co.E
Satum, R.W. GA 50th Inf. Co.B Sgt.
Saturday, George W. GA 61st Inf. Co.B
Saturday, Jackson GA 49th Inf. Co.B
Saturduy Vann 1st Cherokee Mtd.Rifles Co.A
Saturman, Joseph LA 2nd Cav. Co.F Sgt.
Saturwhite, Stephen GA 60th Inf. Co.B Cpl.
Saturwhite, Thomas P. NC 2nd Inf. Co.F
Satyrwhite, William A. VA 30th Inf. Co.G
Satzeman, A. AL Mil. 2nd Regt.Vol. Co.A
Satzer, C.B. LA Inf. Pelican Regt. Co.G
Sauant, A. LA Mil. Orleans Guards Regt. Co.C
Sauber, Henry TX Conscr.
Saubert, Jean LA Mil. 2nd Regt. French Brig.
Co.7
Sauce, Andrew M. TN 28th Cav.
Sauce, Gravier LA 28th (Gray's) Inf. Co.G
Sauce, Marshall LA 28th (Gray's) Inf. Co.G
Sauceman, D.L. AR 5th Inf. Co.F
Sauceman, George A. MS 15th Inf. Co.E
Saucer, Benjamin F. AL 33rd Inf. Co.D Sgt.
Saucer, Christopher C. MS 21st Inf. Co.H
Music.
Saucer, John GA 1st (Ramsey's) Inf. Co.G
Saucer, John W. GA 55th Inf. Co.E Sgt.

Saucer, Lewis B. MS Lt.Arty. (The Hudson
   Btty.) Hoole's Co.
Saucer, Steven GA Res.Corps
Saucer, William J. AR 3rd Inf. Co.L,A
Saucer, William J. GA 4th (Clinch's) Cav. Co.C
   Sgt.
Saucer, William J. GA 26th Inf. Atkinson's Co.B
Saucerman, James TN 29th Inf. Co.I
Saucey, Henry J. GA 17th Inf. Co.I
Saucher, J. LA Inf.Crescent Regt. Co.H
Sauches, M. LA 7th Inf.
Saucier, A.F. LA 18th Inf. Co.C
Saucier, Aiken LA 10th Inf. Co.F 1st Sgt.
Saucier, Calvin A. MS 20th Inf. Co.E
Saucier, Clement LA Lt.Arty. LeGardeur, Jr.'s
   Co. (Orleans Guard Btty.)
Saucier, D. LA 22nd Inf. Co.B
Saucier, David MS 3rd Inf. Co.H Sgt.
Saucier, E. LA 22nd Inf. Co.E,A Sgt.
Saucier, E. LA 22nd (Cons.) Inf. Co.E Sgt.
Saucier, Edmond MS 3rd Inf. Co.H
Saucier, F.N. MS 3rd Inf. Co.F Cpl.
Saucier, J.H. AL 1st Bn.Cadets Co.A
Saucier, John MS 3rd Inf. Co.F Capt.
Saucier, John B. MS 3rd Inf. Co.H Sgt.
Saucier, Joseph LA 1st Hvy.Arty. (Reg.) Co.D
Saucier, Joseph MS 3rd Inf. Co.H
Saucier, Julien MS 3rd Inf. Co.H
Saucier, Lazare LA 1st Hvy.Arty. (Reg.) Co.I
Saucier, N.F. LA 18th Inf. Co.C
Saucier, N.F. MS 3rd Inf. Co.F
Saucier, P. LA Lt.Arty. LeGardeur, Jr.'s Co.
   (Orleans Guard Btty.)
Saucier, Pierre MS 3rd Inf. Co.H 3rd Lt.
Saucier, P.N. MS 3rd Inf. Co.H
Saucier, R. MS 20th Inf. Co.E
Saucier, Victor LA Mil. Chalmette Regt. Co.H
Saucier, Victor MS 3rd Inf. Co.F
Saucort, --- LA Mil. 2nd Regt. French Brig. Co.6
   Sgt.
Saucort, J.B. LA Mil. 2nd Regt. French Brig.
   Co.8
Saucs, Mike LA 1st Hvy.Arty. (Reg.) Co.H
Saudek, Joseph Gen. & Staff, Hvy.Arty.Corps
   Surg.
Saudlin, Jesse NC 1st Cav. (9th St.Troops) Co.I
Sauer, Antoine LA 14th Inf. Co.D,E
Sauer, C. TX 3rd Inf. 2nd Co.A
Sauer, Conradt VA Cav. 1st Bn. (Loc.Def.
   Troops) Co.B
Sauer, F. TX Inf. Timmons' Regt. Co.E
Sauer, F. TX Waul's Legion Co.D
Sauer, Frank LA C.S. Zouave Bn. Co.A
Sauer, Frederick TX 36th Cav. Co.H
Sauer, Gregory LA Mil. Fire Bn. Co.G
Sauer, Hermann TX 1st Hvy.Arty. Co.C
Sauer, J. LA Mil. 3rd Regt.Eur.Brig. (Garde
   Francaise) Co.2
Sauer, J. LA Mil. 3rd Regt. 2nd Brig. 1st Div.
   Co.H
Sauer, J. TX 5th Inf. (St.Troops) Martindale's
   Co.
Sauer, J.C. TX Inf. Timmons' Regt. Co.E
Sauer, J.C. TX Waul's Legion Co.D
Sauer, John MS Lt.Arty. Swett's Co. (Warren
   Lt.Arty.)
Sauer, Justis TX Res.Corps Co.A

Sauer, Lorenz TX 4th Field Btty.
Sauer, Vincent SC Lt.Arty. Walter's Co.
   (Washington Arty.)
Sauerbrey, Adolph Inf. School of Pract. Powell's
   Detach. Co.A
Sauerbrey, Charles NC 54th Inf. Co.F
Sauermilch, C. TX 6th Inf. Co.I
Sauermilch, Christian TX 8th Inf. Co.D
Sauffley, S.K. TN Douglass' Bn.Part.Rangers
   Coffee's Co.
Saufley, Benjamin VA 9th Bn.Res. Co.B
Saufley, G. VA 9th Bn.Res. Co.B
Saufley, Joseph F. VA 12th Cav. Co.H
Saufley, S.R. TN 11th (Holman's) Cav. Co.H
Saufley, William H. VA 12th Inf. Co.C
Saufley, W.P. TX Cav. Saufley's Scouting Bn.
   Maj.
Saufly, George VA 58th Mil. Co.C
Saufly, James TX Cav. Sutton's Co.
Saufly, James M. VA 52nd Inf. Co.G
Saufly, Joseph VA 58th Mil. Co.C
Saufly, Thomas TN 20th Inf. Co.B
Saufly, William M. VA 58th Mil. Co.C
Saufly, William McK. VA 12th Cav. Co.H
Saugrain, A.P. AR 27th Inf. Adj.
Sauker, John LA Mil. 1st Regt. 3rd Brig. 1st
   Div. Co.H
Saukesley, Daniel AL 55th Vol. Co.J
Saul AL 13th Inf. Co.C Laundress
Saul, Aaron T. VA 42nd Inf. Co.K Cpl.
Saul, C. KY 2nd (Woodward's) Cav. Co.F
Saul, C. LA Inf. 4th Bn. Co.E
Saul, C. NC 35th Inf. Co.K
Saul, Creed F. VA 21st Cav. 2nd Co.G
Saul, Creed T. VA 42nd Inf. Co.K
Saul, Edmond VA 22nd Cav. Co.K
Saul, Edward VA 51st Inf. Co.B
Saul, F. LA Inf. 1st Sp.Bn. (Rightor's) Co.A
Saul, George W. VA 48th Inf. Co.G Cpl.
Saul, George W. VA 64th Mtd.Inf. Co.B 1st
   Sgt.
Saul, George W.G. TN Lt.Arty. Burroughs' Co.
Saul, Isaac VA 57th Inf. Co.G
Saul, J. TN Lt.Arty. Rice's Btty.
Saul, James H. TN 39th Mtd.Inf. Co.H Cpl.
Saul, J.D. LA Lt.Arty. Bridges' Btty.
Saul, J.D. SC Arty. Manigault's Bn. 1st Co.A,D
Saul, J.H. VA 42nd Inf. Co.K
Saul, John GA Inf. 25th Bn. (Prov.Guard) Co.A
Saul, John GA 36th (Villepigue's) Inf. Co.D
Saul, John 1st Conf.Inf. 1st Co.D, 2nd Co.C
Saul, John J. MS 37th Inf. Co.K
Saul, John M. MS 13th Inf. Co.F Cpl.
Saul, Joseph D. LA Mil.Conf.Guards Regt. Co.G
Saul, J.P. VA 42nd Inf. Co.K
Saul, Michael Conf.Inf. Tucker's Regt. Co.B
   Sgt.
Saul, Moses NC 2nd Cav. (19th St.Troops) Co.I
Saul, R.M. MS 37th Inf. Co.K,A
Saul, S.A. TX Waul's Legion Asst.Surg.
Saul, T.H. LA Arty. 5th Field Btty. (Pelican
   Lt.Arty.)
Saul, Thomas, Jr. LA Mil.Cav. Cagnolatti's Co.
   (Chasseurs Jefferson)
Saul, William VA 42nd Inf. Co.K
Saul, William B. VA 63rd Inf. Co.E
Saul, William F. LA Washington Arty.Bn. Co.1

Saul, William F. LA Inf. 1st Sp.Bn. (Rightor's)
   New Co.C
Saul, William R. VA 37th Inf. Co.B
Saul, William S. TN Lt.Arty. Burroughs' Co.
   1st Sgt.
Saul, W.R. VA 42nd Inf. Co.K
Saules, Charles GA 2nd Bn.S.S. Co.A,E
Saules, J.B. NC 22nd Inf. Co.K
Saules, Musco SC 19th Inf. Co.K
Saules, William AR 19th (Dockery's) Inf. Co.A
Saulet, --- LA Mil. Orleans Guards Regt. Co.I
Saulet, A. LA Dreux's Cav. Co.A
Saulet, A. LA Mil. Orleans Guards Regt. Co.A
Saulet, P. LA 4th Inf. Co.F
Saulet, P. LA 30th Inf. Co.F
Saulet, P. LA Mil. Orleans Guards Regt. Co.H
Saulet, Zenon LA Mil. 1st Native Guards
Saulie, Adolph SC 1st Arty. Co.B
Saulmyers, John W. VA 18th Cav. Co.D
Saulnier, Sevigne LA 26th Inf. Co.E
Saulny, E. LA Mil. 1st Native Guards
Sauls, A. FL 2nd Cav. Co.K
Sauls, A. SC Lt.Arty. J.T. Kanapaux's Co.
   (Lafayette Arty.)
Sauls, Abraham J. FL 7th Inf. Co.A
Sauls, Abram SC 24th Inf. Co.D
Sauls, A.D. FL Lt.Arty. Dyke's Co.
Sauls, A.D. FL 1st (Res.) Inf. Co.L
Sauls, Alfred G. SC 3rd Cav. Co.C
Sauls, Andrew GA 25th Inf. Co.H
Sauls, Andrew NC 4th Inf. Co.D
Sauls, B. SC Inf. 1st (Charleston) Bn. Co.B
Sauls, B. SC 8th Bn.Res. Co.A
Sauls, B.B. NC Mil. Clark's Sp.Bn. A.R. Davis'
   Co. 1st Cpl.
Sauls, Benjamin AL 23rd Inf. Co.A
Sauls, Benjamin SC 5th Cav. Co.C
Sauls, Benjamin SC Part.Rangers Kirk's Co.
Sauls, Benjamin SC 2nd St.Troops Co.H
Sauls, Benjamin SC 11th Inf. Co.C
Sauls, Benjamin TN Hvy.Arty. Caruthers' Btty.
Sauls, Benjamin TN Conscr. (Cp. of Instr.)
Sauls, B.N. SC Cav. 19th Bn. Co.A
Sauls, C. GA 63rd Inf. Co.E
Sauls, C.A. AL Arty. 1st Bn. Co.F
Sauls, C.A. LA 1st Hvy.Arty. (Reg.) Co.F
Sauls, Caleb SC 1st Arty. Co.B
Sauls, Caleb SC 11th Inf. Bellinger's Co.
Sauls, Charles SC 2nd Cav. Co.C
Sauls, Charles SC 2nd St.Troops Co.H
Sauls, Charles SC 11th Inf. 1st Co.I, 2nd Co.I
Sauls, D. FL Inf. 2nd Bn. Co.D
Sauls, D. TN 84th Inf. Co.C
Sauls, Daniel FL 3rd Inf. Co.H
Sauls, Daniel FL 10th Inf. Co.K
Sauls, David FL 3rd Inf. Co.H
Sauls, David FL 5th Inf. Co.G
Sauls, David NC 1st Arty. (10th St.Troops) Co.E
Sauls, David C. MS 2nd St.Cav. Co.A Cpl.
Sauls, D.C. TN 3rd (Forrest's) Cav. Co.E
Sauls, D.C. TN 22nd Inf. Co.C
Sauls, D.W. AL 23rd Inf. Co.K
Sauls, E. FL 2nd Cav. Co.K
Sauls, Eason A. GA 51st Inf. Co.E
Sauls, Edmond VA 22nd Cav. Co.I
Sauls, Edwin M. NC 27th Inf. Co.K
Sauls, E.G. SC Inf. 6th Bn. Co.C

Sauls, E.G. SC 26th Inf. Co.I Music.
Sauls, E.G. SC Manigault's Bn.Vol. Co.E
Sauls, E.H. SC 26th Inf. Co.I
Sauls, E.S. SC 10th Inf. Co.H 2nd Lt.
Sauls, Ezekiel MO 1st Inf. Co.K
Sauls, F.E. MS 10th Inf. Old Co.K
Sauls, Fennel NC 1st Arty. (10th St.Troops)
  Co.G
Sauls, F.M. AL 48th Inf. Co.G,B
Sauls, Frederick NC 2nd Inf. Co.D
Sauls, G.A. SC Lt.Arty. J.T. Kanapaux's Co.
  (Lafayette Arty.)
Sauls, George SC 3rd Cav. Co.B
Sauls, George SC 11th Inf. 2nd Co.I
Sauls, George W. NC Snead's Co. (Loc.Def.)
Sauls, Gideon SC 1st Mtd.Mil. Screven's Co.
Sauls, Gideon SC Mil.Cav. 4th Regt. Howard's
  Co.
Sauls, Gideon SC 2nd St.Troops Co.D
Sauls, Gideon A. SC 3rd Cav. Co.C
Sauls, G.M. GA Siege Arty. 28th Bn. Co.I Sgt.
Sauls, Henry GA 2nd Cav. Co.C
Sauls, Henry GA 60th Inf. Co.G Music.
Sauls, Henry J. NC 1st Cav. (9th St.Troops)
  Co.H 2nd Lt.
Sauls, H.M. AL 49th Inf. Co.G
Sauls, H.M. SC Cav. 19th Bn. Co.A
Sauls, H.M. SC Part.Rangers Kirk's Co.
Sauls, Holliday KY 9th Mtd.Inf. Co.D
Sauls, Holloway GA 26th Inf. Co.E
Sauls, H.R. GA Cav. 29th Bn. Co.F
Sauls, H.W. MS 16th Inf. Co.G
Sauls, I.H. SC Inf. 6th Bn. Co.C
Sauls, Isaac L. MS 33rd Inf. Co.C
Sauls, J. FL 2nd Cav. Co.K
Sauls, J. GA 32nd Inf. Co.K
Sauls, J. SC 16th & 24th (Cons.) Inf. Co.I
Sauls, Jacob FL 3rd Inf. Co.G
Sauls, James FL 2nd Bn. Co.B
Sauls, James FL 9th Inf. Co.D
Sauls, James KY 9th Mtd.Inf. Co.D
Sauls, James SC 1st Mtd.Mil. Blakewood's Co.
Sauls, James SC 1st (Butler's) Inf. Co.G
Sauls, James SC 11th Inf. Bellinger's Co., 2nd
  Co.I
Sauls, James SC 24th Inf. Co.D
Sauls, James TX 30th Cav. Co.D Cpl.
Sauls, James B. NC 31st Inf. Co.D
Sauls, James H. GA Phillips' Legion Co.L
Sauls, James K. FL 5th Inf. Co.E
Sauls, James V. NC 1st Cav. (9th St.Troops)
  Co.B
Sauls, James V. NC 4th Cav. (59th St.Troops)
  Co.K 1st Lt.
Sauls, James V. NC Cav. 12th Bn. Co.A 1st Lt.
Sauls, James V. 8th (Dearing's) Conf.Cav. Co.A
  1st Lt.
Sauls, James W. AL 3rd Bn.Res. Co.C
Sauls, James W. SC 10th Inf. Co.E
Sauls, J.D. FL Lt.Arty. Dyke's Co.
Sauls, Jesse TN 18th (Newsom's) Cav. Co.E
Sauls, Jessee FL 5th Inf. Co.E
Sauls, Jessie AL Cav. Forrest's Regt.
Sauls, J.H. GA Lt.Arty. 14th Bn. Co.A
Sauls, J.H. SC 26th Inf. Co.I
Sauls, J.H. SC Manigault's Bn.Vol. Co.E
Sauls, J.J. NC 6th Cav. (65th St.Troops) Co.A

Sauls, J.J. SC 11th Inf. 1st Co.I
Sauls, J.M. GA 1st Reg. Co.K
Sauls, J.M. SC 24th Inf. Co.D
Sauls, J.N. SC 6th Inf. 2nd Co.K
Sauls, J.N. SC 9th Inf. Co.C
Sauls, John AL 15th Inf. Co.G
Sauls, John AL 48th Inf. Co.B
Sauls, John GA 7th Inf. Co.I
Sauls, John SC 1st Mtd.Mil. Screven's Co.
Sauls, John SC 3rd Cav. Co.A
Sauls, John SC Arty. Bachman's Co. (German
  Lt.Arty.)
Sauls, John SC 24th Inf. Co.D
Sauls, John A. AL 22nd Inf. Co.I
Sauls, John B. AL 51st (Part.Rangers) Co.B
Sauls, John B. GA 1st (Ramsey's) Inf. Co.B
Sauls, John E. SC 11th Inf. Co.D
Sauls, John H. GA Lt.Arty. Havis' Btty.
Sauls, John H. SC 11th Inf. 2nd Co.I
Sauls, John J. FL 3rd Inf. Co.C Sgt.
Sauls, John P. MS Cav. 24th Bn. Co.A,E
Sauls, John R.E. NC 56th Inf. Co.E
Sauls, Josiah NC 27th Inf. Co.A Cpl.
Sauls, Josiah SC 24th Inf. Co.D Sgt.
Sauls, J.W. AL 29th Inf. Co.I
Sauls, J.W. FL 11th Inf. Co.I
Sauls, K.Y. GA 26th Inf. Co.I
Sauls, Lawrence J. 7th Conf.Cav. Co.F Cpl.
Sauls, M.D. GA 4th (Clinch') Cav.
Sauls, M.D. GA 1st (Symons') Res. Co.F,H
Sauls, O.F. MS 33rd Inf. Co.B
Sauls, O.J. SC 11th Inf. Co.D 2nd Lt.
Sauls, Osbourn SC 2nd St.Troops Co.D
Sauls, Osbourn SC 11th Res. Co.I
Sauls, Patrick NC 3rd Inf. Co.A
Sauls, Perry FL Fernandez's Mtd.Co. (Supply
  Force)
Sauls, Ray TN 46th Inf. Co.G
Sauls, Reuben T. AL Inf. 1st Regt. Co.G
Sauls, Richard GA 51st Inf. Co.E
Sauls, Richard MS Inf. 7th Bn. Co.C
Sauls, Robert SC 1st Mtd.Mil. Screven's Co.
Sauls, Robert SC 3rd Cav. Co.C
Sauls, Robert SC 2nd St.Troops Co.D
Sauls, Rufus NC 1st Arty. (10th St.Troops) Co.E
Sauls, S. GA 6th Res. Co.I
Sauls, S. SC Cav. 19th Bn. Co.A
Sauls, S. SC Part.Rangers Kirk's Co.
Sauls, Samuel AL 10th Inf. Co.I Sgt.
Sauls, Samuel GA 25th Inf. Co.H
Sauls, Samuel TX 4th Cav. Co.I Bugler
Sauls, S.E.F. AL 48th Inf. Co.G
Sauls, Silas GA 11th Cav. (St.Guards) Smith's
  Co.
Sauls, Silas GA 1st (Symons') Res. Co.H
Sauls, S.V. GA Cav. 19th Bn. Co.C
Sauls, S.V. 10th Conf.Cav. Co.H
Sauls, T.B. AL Arty. 1st Bn. Co.F
Sauls, Theo NC 1st Arty. (10th St.Troops) Co.E
Sauls, Theophilis J. GA 2nd Inf. 1st Co.B
Sauls, Theophilus GA 6th Inf. Co.I
Sauls, Theophilus J. GA 26th Inf. Co.E,F
Sauls, Troy NC 1st Arty. (10th St.Troops) Co.E
Sauls, W.A. SC 1st Mtd.Mil. Screven's Co.
Sauls, Warren NC 4th Cav. (59th St.Troops)
  Co.K
Sauls, Warren NC 54th Inf. Co.D

Sauls, Washington GA Cav. 2nd Bn. Co.F
Sauls, Washington GA 5th Cav. Co.B
Sauls, W.D. GA 10th Cav. Co.A
Sauls, W.D. 7th Conf.Cav. Co.A Cpl.
Sauls, W.H. GA Phillips' Legion Co.M
Sauls, Wiley NC 14th Inf. Co.K
Sauls, William GA 62nd Cav. Co.E
Sauls, William NC 27th Inf. Co.K
Sauls, William TN 2nd (Smith's) Cav.
Sauls, William Alfred SC 3rd Cav. Co.C Cpl.
Sauls, William Alfred SC Mil.Cav. 4th Regt.
  Howard's Co.
Sauls, William C. NC 2nd Cav. (19th St.Troops)
  Co.H
Sauls, William H. GA Nav.Bn.
Sauls, William H. NC Bass' Co.
Sauls, William I. NC 18th Inf. Co.I
Sauls, William J. MS 7th Inf. Co.H
Sauls, William J. NC 3rd Cav. (41st St.Troops)
  Co.G
Sauls, William R. NC 27th Inf. Co.K
Sauls, William Riley NC 27th Inf. Co.K
Sauls, Willoughby NC 2nd Inf. Co.H
Sauls, Wilson FL 1st Inf. Old Co.F, New Co.C
Saulsberry, E. VA Cav. O'Ferrall's Bn. Co.C
Saulsberry, James VA Inf. 9th Bn. Duffy's Co.C
Saulsberry, Thomas J. AL Eufaula Lt.Arty.
Saulsbery, E. VA 62nd Mtd.Inf. 2nd Co.M Sgt.
Saulsbery, James NC 3rd Cav. (41st St.Troops)
  Co.K
Saulsbery, John NC 3rd Cav. (41st St.Troops)
  Co.K
Saulsburg, John SC 1st Mtd.Mil. Earnest's Co.
Saulsburg, T.W. SC 1st Mtd.Mil. Earnest's Co.
Saulsburry, C. GA Inf. 17th Bn. (St.Guards)
  Stocks' Co.
Saulsburry, F.M. TN 15th (Stewart's) Cav. Co.C
Saulsburry, James LA 28th (Gray's) Inf. Co.B
Saulsbury, E. VA 23rd Cav. Co.D Sgt.
Saulsbury, Edward LA 14th Inf. Co.C Cpl.
Saulsbury, Edward TN 1st (Carter's) Cav. Co.D
Saulsbury, Edwin GA Inf. 2nd Bn. Co.B
Saulsbury, Frank AL 4th Bn. (Love's) Cav. Co.C
Saulsbury, J. SC 11th Inf. Co.G
Saulsbury, James GA 3rd Res. Co.B
Saulsbury, James TN 39th Mtd.Inf. Co.H
Saulsbury, James L. GA 66th Inf. Co.D
Saulsbury, J.E. SC 6th Cav. Co.F
Saulsbury, J.E. SC 11th Inf. Co.G
Saulsbury, J.H. LA 13th Bn. (Part.Rangers)
  Co.A
Saulsbury, J.L. GA Cav. 9th Bn. (St.Guards)
  Co.B
Saulsbury, John A. SC Lt.Arty. 3rd (Palmetto)
  Bn. Co.D
Saulsbury, J.S. SC 11th Inf. Co.G
Saulsbury, L. GA 66th Inf. Co.B 1st Sgt.
Saulsbury, Mirabeau A. VA 16th Inf. 2nd Co.H,
  Co.G
Saulsbury, Richard MO 1st & 4th Cons.Inf.
  Co.D
Saulsbury, W. MS 7th Inf. Co.H
Saulsbury, William LA 13th Inf. Co.K
Saulsbury, William C. KY 4th Mtd.Inf. Co.F
  Sgt.
Saulsby, A. GA 24th Inf. Co.K
Saulsman, Charles AR 10th Mil. Co.B Fifer

Sault, Peter LA 7th Inf. Co.K
Sault, Peter TN 37th Inf.
Sault, Peter VA 13th Cav. Co.F
Sault, T.O. GA 4th Inf. Co.D
Saulter, Calvin LA 8th Inf. Co.F
Saulter, D. MS 2nd (Davidson's) Inf. Co.H
Saulter, James GA Arty. 11th Bn. (Sumter Arty.) Co.B
Saulter, James MS 10th Inf. Old Co.G, New Co.F
Saulter, John L. GA Cav. 7th Bn. (St.Guards) Co.B
Saulter, John P. GA 65th Inf. Co.F
Saulter, John T. GA 6th Inf. Co.F
Saulter, Lofton C. AL Lt.Arty. 2nd Bn. Co.E
Saulter, S. GA Inf. 1st Loc.Troops (Augusta) Barnes' Lt.Arty.Co.,Co.K
Saulter, Tilman L. AL 28th Inf. Co.H
Saulter, W.D. GA Lt.Arty. Howell's Co.
Saultz, Samuel TN Detailed Conscr. Co.A
Saulx, J.M. LA Mil. 3rd Regt.Eur.Brig. (Garde Francaise) Co.4
Sauly, C. KY 4th Mtd.Inf. Co.H
Saum, Daniel T. VA 10th Inf. Co.F
Saum, Eli VA 23rd Cav. Co.A
Saum, Eli VA Cav. 41st Bn. Co.A
Saum, Elias VA 2nd Inf. Co.K
Saum, Elias VA 146th Mil. Co.D
Saum, Elijah VA 8th Bn.Res. Co.D Sgt.
Saum, J.A. VA 23rd Inf. Co.I
Saum, Jacob VA 5th Inf. Co.K
Saum, Jacob VA 136th Mil. Co.E
Saum, James W. VA 23rd Cav. Co.L
Saum, John A. GA 64th Inf. Co.C
Saum, John A. VA 23rd Cav. Co.G
Saum, John A. VA 10th Inf. 1st Co.C 2nd Lt.
Saum, Joseph F. 1st Conf.Inf. Co.B
Saum, Mahlon G. VA 10th Inf. Co.F
Saum, William VA 2nd Inf. Co.K
Saum, William VA 136th Mil. Co.E
Saumage, Milton GA Mil. 8th Regt. Co.B
Sauminter, Daniel E. VA 51st Inf. Co.G
Saumpsell, David VA 51st Mil. Co.B
Saun, Allen MO Cav. Coleman's Regt. Co.F
Saunder, H.E. VA Arty. C.F. Johnston's Co. Cpl.
Saunder, T.B. MS 18th Cav. Co.G
Saunders, --- LA Mil. 1st Regt. 2nd Brig. 1st Div. Co.B
Saunders, --- MS 1st Cav. Co.F
Saunders, --- TX Cav. 4th Regt.St.Troops Co.A
Saunders, --- VA 2nd St.Res. Capt.
Saunders, A. 8th (Dearing's) Conf.Cav.
Saunders, A. GA Cav. 8th Bn. (St.Guards) Co.B
Saunders, A. SC 16th Inf. Cpl.
Saunders, A. SC 19th Inf. Co.G
Saunders, A. VA Conscr. Cp.Lee Co.A
Saunders, Aaron NC 14th Inf. Co.E
Saunders, Aaron NC 45th Inf. Co.H
Saunders, A.B. MS 21st Inf. Co.C
Saunders, A.C. VA 1st St.Res. Co.B
Saunders, A.D. NC 23rd Inf. Co.C
Saunders, Addison E. VA 17th Inf. Co.A 1st Sgt.
Saunders, Adison VA 42nd Inf. Co.H
Saunders, A.G. SC Inf. 7th Bn. (Enfield Rifles) Co.E 1st Lt.

Saunders, A.H. MS 1st Cav. Co.F
Saunders, A.H. MS Mtd.Men Foote's Co.
Saunders, A.J. AL 14th Inf. Co.D
Saunders, A.J. AR 1st (Dobbin's) Cav. Co.B
Saunders, A.J. AR 2nd Mtd.Rifles Hawkins' Co.
Saunders, A.J. GA 34th Inf. Co.F
Saunders, A.J. LA 15th Inf. Co.G
Saunders, A.J. TX 27th Cav. Co.A
Saunders, A.J. VA 5th Cav. Co.B
Saunders, A.J. 20th Conf.Cav. Co.B
Saunders, A.J.S. NC 43rd Inf.
Saunders, Al MS 1st Cav. Co.H
Saunders, Albert VA Hvy.Arty. Allen's Co.
Saunders, Albert A. NC 39th Inf. Co.I
Saunders, Alexander GA Inf. (Jasper & Butts Cty.Guards) Lane's Co.
Saunders, Alexander VA 19th Inf. Co.G
Saunders, Alexander VA 41st Mil. Co.D
Saunders, Alfred NC 7th Inf. Co.I 2nd Lt.
Saunders, Alfred Trans-MS Conf.Cav. 1st Bn. Co.E Lt.
Saunders, Alfred M. NC 37th Inf. Co.K Sgt.
Saunders, Allen J.S. NC 34th Inf.
Saunders, Amos A. AL 57th Inf. Co.H Sgt.
Saunders, Anderson A. LA 17th Inf. Co.K
Saunders, Anderson H. VA 56th Inf. Co.E Cpl.
Saunders, Anderson H. VA 57th Inf. Co.H Sgt.
Saunders, Anderson H. 1st Conf.Eng.Troops Co.E Cpl.
Saunders, Andrew C. GA 12th Inf. Co.D
Saunders, Andrew D. VA 55th Inf. Co.H Maj.
Saunders, Andrew J.M. TN 22nd Inf. Co.I
Saunders, A.P. MS 3rd Inf. (St.Troops) Co.D
Saunders, A.P. VA Lt.Arty. W.P. Carter's Co.
Saunders, Applewhite NC Loc.Def. Croom's Co.
Saunders, Armistead W. VA 8th Inf. Co.H
Saunders, Aron GA 25th Inf. Co.E
Saunders, Arthur L. VA 9th Cav. Co.K Cpl.
Saunders, Asa NC 1st Inf. Co.F
Saunders, Augustus MS 4th Inf.
Saunders, Augustus H. AL Lt.Arty. Hurt's Btty. Sgt.
Saunders, Austin KY 5th Mtd.Inf. Co.C
Saunders, Austin N. VA 41st Mil. Co.B
Saunders, A.V. Gen. & Staff, QM Dept. Capt.
Saunders, A.W. AR 36th Inf. Co.K Cpl.
Saunders, A.W. LA 15th Inf. Co.G
Saunders, A.W. VA 2nd Cav. Co.G
Saunders, B. FL Cav. 5th Bn. Co.I
Saunders, B. TX Cav. Saufley's Scouting Bn. Co.E
Saunders, B.A. NC 16th Inf. Co.H
Saunders, Bartlett GA Hvy.Arty. 22nd Bn. Co.C
Saunders, Bart W. KY 3rd Mtd.Inf. Co.E Sgt.
Saunders, B.B. AR 36th Inf. Co.K
Saunders, B.B. VA 56th Inf. Co.E
Saunders, Beman TX 27th Cav. Co.I
Saunders, Benjamin GA 62nd Cav. Co.L
Saunders, Benjamin MS 18th Cav. Co.A
Saunders, Benjamin VA 24th Cav. Co.K
Saunders, Benjamin 8th (Dearing's) Conf.Cav. Co.E
Saunders, Benjamin F. TN 2nd (Robison's) Inf. Co.H
Saunders, Benjamin F. VA 8th Inf. Co.H
Saunders, Beverly B. VA Inf. 5th Bn. Co.A
Saunders, B.F. GA Lt.Arty. Daniell's Btty.

Saunders, B.F. GA Arty. Maxwell's Reg.Lt.Btty.
Saunders, B.F. GA 1st Reg. Co.D
Saunders, B.F. GA Cobb's Legion Co.B
Saunders, B.F. KY Jessee's Bn.Mtd.Riflemen Co.C
Saunders, B.F. KY Part.Rangers Rowan's Co.
Saunders, B.F. MS 18th Cav. Co.K,L Capt.
Saunders, B.F. MS 3rd Inf. Co.K Capt.
Saunders, B.F. MS 23rd Inf. Co.K Capt.
Saunders, B.F. TX Cav. Bourland's Regt. Co.C
Saunders, B.G. NC 7th Inf. Co.E
Saunders, B.H. LA 7th Inf. Co.G
Saunders, B.H. MS 12th Cav. Co.H
Saunders, B.H. Eng.,CSA
Saunders, B.L. 20th Conf.Cav. Co.C
Saunders, B.M. VA 1st Bn.Res. Co.F
Saunders, Brantley H. NC 4th Cav. (59th St.Troops) Co.E 1st Lt.
Saunders, Britton NC 3rd Inf. Co.F
Saunders, Bryant GA 62nd Cav. Co.L
Saunders, Buckner VA Lt.Arty. Thornton's Co.
Saunders, C. VA 2nd Inf.Loc.Def. Co.F
Saunders, C.A. MS Res.Corps Withers' Co.
Saunders, Caleb MO 10th Inf. Co.E
Saunders, Calvin VA 14th Cav. 2nd Co.F
Saunders, Calvin E. LA 31st Inf. Co.E
Saunders, Cap AL 4th Inf. Co.D
Saunders, C.B. TX 4th Inf. Co.H
Saunders, C.C. VA Res.Forces Thurston's Co.
Saunders, C.D. MO Quantrill's Co.
Saunders, C.G. MS 5th Inf. (St.Troops) Co.D Jr.2nd Lt.
Saunders, C.H. KY 2nd Cav. Co.C
Saunders, C.H. KY 10th Cav. Co.B
Saunders, Charles AL Cav. Holloway's Co. Bugler
Saunders, Charles LA Mil. British Guard Bn. Kurczyn's Co.
Saunders, Charles SC 1st Arty. Co.G
Saunders, Charles A. VA 17th Cav. Co.F
Saunders, Charles C. VA 5th Inf. Co.G
Saunders, Charles E. VA 2nd Bn.Res. Co.B Cpl.
Saunders, Charles E. VA 23rd Inf. Co.D Cpl.
Saunders, Charles H. KY 5th Mtd.Inf. Co.C
Saunders, Charles H. VA Cav. 40th Bn. Co.B
Saunders, Charles J. NC 2nd Cav. (19th St.Troops) Co.E
Saunders, Charles W. NC 56th Inf. Co.H Cpl.
Saunders, Charles W. SC 1st (McCreary's) Inf. Co.I
Saunders, Christie VA Inf. 6th Bn.Loc.Def. Co.C
Saunders, Christopher VA 21st Inf. Co.H
Saunders, Christopher J. VA 6th Inf. Co.G
Saunders, Christopher W. VA 1st Inf. Co.A
Saunders, Christopher W. VA 12th Inf. Co.G
Saunders, Christopher W. VA Inf. 25th Bn. Co.F
Saunders, Clem KY 8th Cav. Co.H
Saunders, Commodore VA 41st Inf. Co.I Cpl.
Saunders, Crockett J. VA 24th Inf. Co.B 2nd Lt.
Saunders, C.T. AR 26th Inf. Co.G
Saunders, C.W. MS 1st Cav. Co.H
Saunders, C.W. Trans-MS Conf.Cav. 1st Bn. Co.E
Saunders, D. TX Inf. 1st Bn. (St.Troops) Co.E
Saunders, D. VA Mil. Scott Cty.

Saunders, Daniel VA 61st Inf. Co.B
Saunders, Daniel G. VA 28th Inf. Co.G
Saunders, Daniel J. VA 2nd Cav. Co.A,G
Saunders, Daniel Murray LA 19th Inf. Co.D
Saunders, Daniel T. VA Hvy.Arty. 10th Bn. Co.B
Saunders, Daniel W. MO Cav. Poindexter's Regt.
Saunders, David MS 38th Cav. Co.D
Saunders, David NC 20th Inf. Co.B
Saunders, David TX Lt.Arty. Hughes' Co.
Saunders, David VA Inf. 5th Bn. Co.C
Saunders, David N. VA 60th Inf. 2nd Co.H
Saunders, David S. NC 3rd Cav. (41st St.Troops) Co.E
Saunders, David W. Gen. & Staff Maj.,AAG
Saunders, D.J. GA 8th Inf. (St.Guards) Co.D
Saunders, D.J. KY 1st (Butler's) Cav. Co.F
Saunders, D.J. KY 1st (Helm's) Cav. New Co.A
Saunders, D.N. AL 15th Cav. Co.B
Saunders, D.P. VA 5th Cav. Co.E
Saunders, D.R. VA 14th Cav. Co.B
Saunders, Drewry W. VA 23rd Inf. Co.E
Saunders, D.S. TN 10th & 11th (Cons.) Cav. Co.K
Saunders, Dudley D. Gen. & Staff Surg.
Saunders, Duke H. GA Inf. 3rd Bn. Co.E
Saunders, E. AL Mil. 2nd Regt.Vol. Co.E
Saunders, E. AL 44th Inf. Co.K
Saunders, E. MS Cav. Street's Bn.
Saunders, E. VA Inf. 44th Bn. Co.B
Saunders, E.B. SC 11th Inf. Bellinger's Co.
Saunders, E.C. MS 12th Inf. Co.E
Saunders, Edgar J. VA 55th Inf. Co.F 2nd Lt.
Saunders, Edmond VA 55th Inf. Co.K
Saunders, Edmund A. VA 3rd Cav. Co.D
Saunders, Edward TN 55th (McKoin's) Inf. Co.I
Saunders, Edward G. MS 11th Inf. Co.E 1st Sgt.
Saunders, Edward H. VA Hvy.Arty. Coleman's Co. Sgt.
Saunders, E.E. KY 9th Cav. Co.D 1st Lt.
Saunders, E.E. LA 1st Res. Co.K
Saunders, E.F. MO Lt.Arty. Walsh's Co.
Saunders, E.J. FL 3rd Inf. Co.E
Saunders, E.J. MO 1st & 4th Cons.Inf. Co.C
Saunders, E.J. MO 4th Inf. Co.B
Saunders, E.J. VA 9th Cav.
Saunders, E.J. VA Mtd.Guard 1st Congr.Dist.
Saunders, E.J. VA 55th Inf. Co.K
Saunders, Eleand W. MS 18th Inf. Co.F
Saunders, Elijah AL 50th Inf. Co.C Cpl.
Saunders, Elijah MS Inf. 3rd Bn. (St.Troops) Co.F
Saunders, Elijah T. AL 5th Bn.Vol. Co.D,C
Saunders, Elton W. FL 5th Inf. Co.K
Saunders, E.M. NC 5th Inf. Co.I
Saunders, E.M. VA 8th Inf. Co.E
Saunders, E.T. VA Hvy.Arty. Allen's Co.
Saunders, E.T. VA 20th Inf. Co.C
Saunders, E.T. VA Loc.Def. Ezell's Co.
Saunders, E.T. Ord.Scouts & Guards Click's Co.,CSA
Saunders, Eugene L. VA 55th Inf. Co.F
Saunders, Ezell B. TN 13th Inf. Co.K
Saunders, F. KY 8th Mtd.Inf. Co.C
Saunders, F. MS 18th Cav. Co.A
Saunders, F.A. TX 15th Inf. Co.F

Saunders, Ferd MO Cav. Stallard's Co.
Saunders, F.F. MO 8th Inf. Co.C
Saunders, Fielden VA 22nd Cav. Co.D
Saunders, Fleming TN 9th (Ward's) Cav. Co.G
Saunders, Fleming VA 24th Inf. Co.D Capt.
Saunders, Fleming VA 42nd Inf. AQM
Saunders, Fleming Gen. & Staff, QM Dept. Capt.
Saunders, Fleming E. MS 22nd Inf. Co.H Cpl.
Saunders, F.M. MS 27th Inf. Co.A
Saunders, F.M. MS 36th Inf. Ch.Music.
Saunders, Francis K. TN 34th Inf. Co.D
Saunders, Francis M. AL 50th Inf. Co.C
Saunders, Francis M. AR 16th Inf. Co.C
Saunders, Francis M. TN 28th Inf. Co.I
Saunders, Frank LA C.S. Zouave Bn. Co.D Music.
Saunders, Frank TX 4th Inf. Co.D 1st Sgt.
Saunders, Frank TX Vol. Benton's Co.
Saunders, Frederick AR 4th Inf. Kelley's Co.
Saunders, Fredrick C. VA 24th Inf. Co.E 2nd Lt.
Saunders, F.T. TX 34th Cav. Co.B Sgt.
Saunders, G. GA 44th Inf. Co.E
Saunders, G. MS Inf. 2nd Bn. (St.Troops) Co.A
Saunders, G.A. TN 4th Inf. Co.B
Saunders, G.A. VA 7th Cav. Co.A
Saunders, George AL Arty. Williams' Bn. Co.C
Saunders, George SC Horse Arty. (Washington Arty.) Vol. Hart's Co.
Saunders, George SC 1st (McCreary's) Inf. Co.I
Saunders, George SC 1st Inf. Co.M Sgt.
Saunders, George TX 4th Inf. Co.D
Saunders, George TX Vol. Benton's Co.
Saunders, George VA Inf. 4th Bn.Loc.Def. Co.A
Saunders, George VA 8th Inf. Co.C
Saunders, George VA 45th Inf. Co.K
Saunders, George VA 115th Mil. Co.A
Saunders, George A. GA Cav. 1st Bn.Res. Co.C Sgt.
Saunders, George F. VA 1st Arty. Co.I
Saunders, Geo. F. VA 3rd Arty. Co.E
Saunders, George F. VA Lt.Arty. 38th Bn. Co.A
Saunders, George G. VA 58th Inf. Co.K Sgt.
Saunders, George H. MO Inf. 8th Bn. Co.B
Saunders, George H. VA 23rd Inf. Co.D 1st Sgt.
Saunders, George H. VA 32nd Inf. 2nd Co.K
Saunders, George L. VA 24th Cav. Co.E
Saunders, George L. VA Cav. 40th Bn. Co.D
Saunders, George M. VA Goochland Lt.Arty.
Saunders, George R. NC 11th (Bethel Regt.) Inf. Co.F
Saunders, George S. AR 26th Inf. Co.A 1st Lt.
Saunders, George T. VA Lt.Arty. E.J. Anderson's Co.
Saunders, George W. GA 1st (Olmstead's) Inf. Co.A
Saunders, George W. KY 10th Cav. Co.F 2nd Lt.
Saunders, George W. NC 7th Inf. Co.D
Saunders, George W. VA 2nd Arty. Co.H
Saunders, George W. VA 16th Inf. Co.B
Saunders, George W. VA 22nd Inf. Swann's Co.
Saunders, George W. VA Inf. 22nd Bn. Co.H
Saunders, George W. VA 28th Inf. Co.K
Saunders, George W. VA 36th Inf. Co.F

Saunders, George W. VA 41st Mil. Co.D 1st Lt.
Saunders, George W. VA 42nd Inf. Co.K
Saunders, George W.R. GA 45th Inf. Co.K
Saunders, G.F. 2nd Conf.Eng.Troops Co.H
Saunders, Gilbert G. NC 2nd Cav. (19th St.Troops) Co.C
Saunders, Gordon L. VA 24th Inf. Co.G
Saunders, Greenville AR 4th Inf. Kelley's Co.
Saunders, G.S. KY 1st (Butler's) Cav. Co.F Sgt.
Saunders, G.S. KY 1st (Helm's) Cav. New Co.A
Saunders, G.T. NC 18th Inf. Co.G
Saunders, Gustavus VA 24th Inf. Co.F
Saunders, G.W. AL 2nd Cav. Co.E
Saunders, G.W. AL 15th Inf. Co.E Cpl.
Saunders, G.W. GA 46th Inf. Co.E
Saunders, G.W. LA 25th Inf. Co.I
Saunders, G.W. MS 43rd Inf. Co.C
Saunders, G.W. TN Inf. 3rd Cons.Regt. Co.A
Saunders, G.W. TX 33rd Cav. Co.E
Saunders, G.W. VA 8th Cav. Co.A
Saunders, H. AR 11th Inf. Co.K
Saunders, H. KY 3rd Mtd.Inf. 1st Co.F
Saunders, H. MS 43rd Inf. Co.K
Saunders, H. NC 3rd Jr.Res. Co.B
Saunders, H. VA 11th Bn.Res. Co.C
Saunders, H.A. LA 4th Inf. Co.I
Saunders, H.A. MO Inf. 4th Regt.St.Guard Co.B Cpl.
Saunders, Halory M. MS 17th Inf. Co.A
Saunders, Harrison MS 7th Cav. Co.D
Saunders, H.C. KY 2nd (Woodward's) Cav. Co.B
Saunders, H.C. TN 10th & 11th (Cons.) Cav. Co.K
Saunders, H.C. TN Cav. Woodward's Co.
Saunders, Hector A. VA 8th Inf. Co.H
Saunders, Henry FL 2nd Cav. Co.G
Saunders, Henry MS 2nd St.Cav. Co.K
Saunders, Henry NC 16th Inf. Co.H
Saunders, Henry NC 61st Inf. Co.I
Saunders, Henry SC Lt.Arty. Walter's Co. (Washington Arty.)
Saunders, Henry VA 45th Inf. Co.K
Saunders, Henry VA 63rd Inf. Co.F
Saunders, Henry B. NC 14th Inf. Co.C
Saunders, Henry C. VA 51st Inf. Co.E Cpl.
Saunders, Henry G. VA 28th Inf. Co.D Jr.2nd Lt.
Saunders, Henry G. VA 34th Inf. Co.I 1st Lt.
Saunders, Henry J. VA 3rd (Archer's) Bn.Res. Co.C
Saunders, Henry L. FL Cav. 5th Bn. Co.A
Saunders, Henry M. GA 30th Inf. Co.E
Saunders, Henry T. NC 6th Cav. (65th St.Troops) Co.C
Saunders, Henry W. AL 4th Inf. Co.D
Saunders, Henry W. GA 45th Inf. Co.K
Saunders, Hezekiah C. MS 43rd Inf. Co.E
Saunders, H.H. AL 45th Inf. Co.B
Saunders, H.H. MS 27th Inf. Co.C
Saunders, H.H. MO Dismtd.Cav. Lawther's Temporary Regt. Co.A
Saunders, H.H. TX 34th Cav. Co.B
Saunders, Hiram MS Cav. 3rd Bn. (Ashcraft's) Co.F
Saunders, Hiram B. VA 23rd Inf. Co.D Capt.
Saunders, H.J. TN 12th (Green's) Cav. Co.G

Saunders, H.M. TN 49th Inf. Co.D
Saunders, Howard VA Lt.Arty. 13th Bn. Co.A
Saunders, H.T. AL 45th Inf. Co.K Lt.
Saunders, H.T. MS 1st Cav. Co.A
Saunders, H.T. MS 6th Inf. Co.I
Saunders, Hugh W. TN 2nd (Robison's) Inf.
  Co.B
Saunders, Humphrey D. AL 19th Inf. Co.I
Saunders, Irvin J. GA Cav. Nelson's Ind.Co.
  3rd Lt.
Saunders, Isaac J. VA 44th Inf. Co.D
Saunders, Isaac W. NC 45th Inf. Co.H
Saunders, Isaiah AL 1st Cav. 1st Co.B
Saunders, Isaiah GA 64th Inf. Co.B
Saunders, Isaiah MS 20th Inf. Co.G
Saunders, Iverson GA 66th Inf. Co.A Cpl.
Saunders, J. AR 38th Inf. Co.E
Saunders, J. GA 21st Inf. Co.A
Saunders, J. LA 9th Inf. Co.K
Saunders, J. MS 34th Inf. Co.I
Saunders, J. TX Inf. Timmons' Regt. Co.I
Saunders, J. VA 1st Inf. Co.D
Saunders, J. 10th Conf.Cav. Co.F
Saunders, J. 20th Conf.Cav. Co.E
Saunders, J.A. AR 18th (Marmaduke's) Inf.
  Co.A
Saunders, J.A. GA 48th Inf. Co.C
Saunders, J.A. LA Inf.Crescent Regt. Co.I
Saunders, J.A. MS 38th Cav. Co.D
Saunders, J.A. VA 7th Cav. Co.A
Saunders, J.A. VA Hvy.Arty. Allen's Co.
Saunders, J.A. VA 30th Bn.S.S. Co.C
Saunders, Jackson VA 42nd Inf. Co.H
Saunders, Jackson P. VA Inf. 26th Bn. Co.F,H
Saunders, Jacob NC Inf. 2nd Bn. Co.G
Saunders, Jacob VA 20th Inf. Co.F Cpl.
Saunders, Jacob VA 57th Inf. Co.A Cpl.
Saunders, Jacob B. TN 34th Inf. Co.G
Saunders, James AL Arty. 1st Bn. Co.D Drum.
Saunders, James AL 1st Bn.Cadets Co.A
Saunders, James AR 23rd Inf. Co.D
Saunders, James LA Arty. Castellanos' Btty. 1st
  Sgt.
Saunders, James MS 48th Inf. Co.E
Saunders, James NC 3rd Inf. Co.E
Saunders, James NC 17th Inf. (2nd Org.) Co.G
Saunders, James NC 52nd Inf. Co.H
Saunders, James TN 9th (Ward's) Cav. Co.C
  Cpl.
Saunders, James VA 4th Cav. Co.E
Saunders, James VA Cav. McNeill's Co.
Saunders, James VA 1st (Farinholt's) Res. Co.D
  Sgt.
Saunders, James VA 20th Inf. Co.K
Saunders, James VA 32nd Inf. 2nd Co.K Cpl.
Saunders, James VA 42nd Inf. Co.H
Saunders, James A. MO 16th Inf. Co.D
Saunders, James A. TN 63rd Inf. Co.C
Saunders, James A. VA Hvy.Arty. Allen's Co.
Saunders, James B. VA 38th Inf. Co.F
Saunders, James C. TN 13th Inf. Co.K
Saunders, James C. VA 58th Inf. Co.K
Saunders, James D. KY 4th Mtd.Inf. Co.F
Saunders, James D. MS 11th (Perrin's) Cav.
  Co.D
Saunders, James D. VA 8th Inf. Co.H
Saunders, James D. VA 41st Inf. 2nd Co.E

Saunders, James D. VA 57th Inf. Co.D
Saunders, James E. NC Lt.Arty. 3rd Bn. Co.B,C
  Cpl.
Saunders, James E. NC 17th Inf. (1st Org.) Co.D
Saunders, James F. KY 8th Mtd.Inf. Co.I
Saunders, James F. MO Cav. Williams' Regt.
  Co.C Cpl.
Saunders, James F. VA Arty. Bryan's Co.
Saunders, James G. GA 16th Inf.
Saunders, James G. VA 14th Inf. Co.B Cpl.
Saunders, James H. FL 2nd Inf. Co.B
Saunders, James H. GA 12th (Robinson's) Cav.
  (St.Guards) Co.A
Saunders, James H. GA 13th Inf. Co.G
Saunders, James H. KY 3rd Mtd.Inf. Co.E
Saunders, James H. MD 1st Inf. Co.G
Saunders, James H. TN 22nd Inf. Co.I
Saunders, James H. VA 24th Inf. Co.F
Saunders, James H. VA 46th Inf. 2nd Co.A
Saunders, James H. VA 109th Mil. 1st Co.A
  Cpl.
Saunders, James J. VA Hvy.Arty. 18th Bn. Co.C
Saunders, James K. VA 30th Bn.S.S. Co.C Sgt.
Saunders, James L. NC 23rd Inf. Co.C
Saunders, James L. TN Inf. 23rd Bn. Co.B
Saunders, James M. AL 37th Inf. Co.A
Saunders, James M. NC 3rd Cav. (41st
  St.Troops) Co.C
Saunders, James M. NC 6th Cav. (65th
  St.Troops) Co.C,G
Saunders, James M. VA 16th Inf. Co.D
Saunders, James M. VA 53rd Inf. Co.B Capt.
Saunders, James M. VA 59th Inf. 3rd Co.C
Saunders, James M. VA Inf. Tomlin's Bn. Co.A
  Sgt.
Saunders, James N. TN 2nd (Robison's) Inf.
  Co.K Sgt.
Saunders, James N. VA 8th Cav. Co.A Sgt.
Saunders, Jas. O. Gen. & Staff Asst.Surg.
Saunders, James P. VA 9th Cav. Co.D
Saunders, James P. VA 61st Inf. Co.F
Saunders, James R. NC 2nd Arty. (36th
  St.Troops) Co.F
Saunders, James R.N. GA 59th Inf. Co.E
Saunders, James S. VA 41st Inf. Co.K
Saunders, James S. VA 115th Mil. Co.A
Saunders, James T. VA Hvy.Arty. 19th Bn.
  Co.B
Saunders, James T. VA 16th Inf. Co.D
Saunders, James W. MS 2nd Inf. Co.F 1st Lt.
Saunders, James W. MD 3rd Inf. Co.B
Saunders, James W. NC 5th Cav. (63rd
  St.Troops) Co.D
Saunders, J. Archer VA 20th Inf. Co.C
Saunders, J.B. KY 3rd Mtd.Inf. Co.D
  Asst.Surg.
Saunders, J.B. MS 18th Cav. Co.C
Saunders, J.B. MO Cav. Stallard's Co.
Saunders, J.B. NC 4th Inf. Co.K
Saunders, J.B. Gen. & Staff Asst.Surg.
Saunders, J.C. AR 19th (Dockery's) Inf. Co.G
Saunders, J.C. GA Cav. 29th Bn. Co.B
Saunders, J.C. GA 45th Inf. Co.F
Saunders, J.D. AR 6th Inf. Co.C
Saunders, J.E. GA 18th Inf. Co.C
Saunders, J.E. TN 1st Hvy.Arty. 2nd Co.D
  Sr.1st Lt.

Saunders, J.E. VA Lt.Arty. Fry's Co.
Saunders, J.E. Johnson's Div. ADC
Saunders, Jefferson TX 21st Cav. Co.C
Saunders, Jesse AR 15th (N.W.) Inf. Co.K
Saunders, Jesse NC 3rd Inf. Co.F
Saunders, Jesse NC 4th Sr.Res. Co.G
Saunders, Jesse VA Lt.Arty. Penick's Co.
Saunders, Jesse VA 59th Inf. 3rd Co.E
Saunders, Jesse B. MO Cav. 3rd Bn. Co.D Sgt.
Saunders, Jesse H. NC 6th Cav. (65th St.Troops)
  Co.C
Saunders, Jesse R. NC 3rd Cav. (41st St.Troops)
  Co.C
Saunders, Jesse T. GA Inf. 3rd Bn. Co.E
Saunders, J.G. AL 61st Inf. Co.E
Saunders, J.G. TX Lt.Arty. Jones' Co.
Saunders, J.G. TX 2nd Inf. Co.A
Saunders, J.G. VA Mtd.Guard Congr.Dist.
Saunders, J.H. GA 38th Inf. 2nd Co.I
Saunders, J.H. GA 60th Inf. 2nd Co.A
Saunders, J.H. LA 8th Cav. Co.H
Saunders, J.H. MS 2nd Cav.Res. Co.I
Saunders, J.H. NC 6th Sr.Res. Co.I
Saunders, J.H. NC 57th Inf. Co.D 1st Sgt.
Saunders, J.H. VA 5th Cav. Co.G
Saunders, J.H. VA Mtd.Res. Rappahannock Dist.
  Sale's Co.
Saunders, J.H. VA 56th Inf. Co.K
Saunders, J.H. VA 63rd Inf. 1st Co.I
Saunders, J.J. AL 15th Inf. Co.E
Saunders, J.J. NC 1st Jr.Res. Co.G Sgt.
Saunders, J.J. NC 13th Inf. Co.C
Saunders, J.L. GA 1st (Ramsey's) Inf. Co.F
Saunders, J.L. KY 9th Mtd.Inf. Co.F
Saunders, J.L. 1st Conf.Cav. Co.I
Saunders, J.M. AR 38th Inf. Co.E Sgt.
Saunders, J.M. GA 3rd Cav. Co.A
Saunders, J.M. MS 10th Inf. New Co.I
Saunders, J.M. SC 11th Inf. Bellinger's Co.
Saunders, J.M. TN 10th (DeMoss') Cav. Co.F
Saunders, J.M. TN Cav. Napier's Bn. Co.C
Saunders, J.M. Trans-MS Conf.Cav. 1st Bn.
  Co.E
Saunders, J.M.H. AL 42nd Inf. Co.G
Saunders, J.N.F. GA 37th Inf. Co.G
Saunders, J.O. VA 5th Cav. Co.D
Saunders, Job C. GA 30th Inf. Co.A
Saunders, John AL 56th Part.Rangers Co.E
Saunders, John AR 5th Inf. Co.E
Saunders, John AR 26th Inf. Co.I
Saunders, John AR 26th Inf. Co.K
Saunders, John AR 38th Inf. Co.A,B
Saunders, John GA Cav. 1st Bn.Res. Co.C
Saunders, John GA 3rd Res. Co.E
Saunders, John LA 10th Inf. Co.D
Saunders, John MS 34th Inf. Co.K
Saunders, John MO Lt.Arty. McDonald's Co.
Saunders, John MO Inf. 4th Regt.St.Guard Co.D
Saunders, John MO 8th Inf. Co.F,B
Saunders, John MO 10th Inf. Co.E
Saunders, John NC 3rd Arty. (40th St.Troops)
  Co.D
Saunders, John NC 3rd Inf. Co.F
Saunders, John NC 8th Inf. Co.B
Saunders, John NC 17th Inf. (1st Org.) Co.I
Saunders, John NC 68th Inf.
Saunders, John NC Snead's Co. (Loc.Def.)

Saunders, John SC 1st Regt. Charleston Guard Co.I Cpl.
Saunders, John TN 16th (Logwood's) Cav. Co.E
Saunders, John TN 2nd (Walker's) Inf. Co.A
Saunders, John TN 18th Inf. Co.K
Saunders, John TX 9th Cav. Co.B
Saunders, John TX 3rd Inf. Co.I 1st Sgt.
Saunders, John VA 9th Cav. Co.H Bugler
Saunders, John VA Cav. 34th Bn. Co.F
Saunders, John VA Cav. Young's Co.
Saunders, John VA Hvy.Arty. 20th Bn. Co.E
Saunders, John VA 1st Bn.Res. Co.A
Saunders, John VA 8th Inf. Co.A
Saunders, John VA 36th Inf. Co.B
Saunders, John VA 47th Inf. Co.E
Saunders, John VA 59th Inf. 3rd Co.F
Saunders, John VA 166th Mil. Co.D
Saunders, John A. VA Cav. Mosby's Regt. (Part.Rangers) Co.B
Saunders, John A. VA Cav. Young's Co.
Saunders, John A. VA 13th Inf. Co.D
Saunders, John A. VA 23rd Inf. Co.D
Saunders, John A. Gen. & Staff Asst.Surg.
Saunders, John A.T. NC 6th Cav. (65th St.Troops) Co.C,G
Saunders, John B. AL 50th Inf. Co.C
Saunders, John B. TX Cav. Morgan's Regt. Co.E
Saunders, John B. TX 16th Inf. Co.B Cpl.
Saunders, Jno. B. Gen. & Staff A.Surg.
Saunders, John C. FL 6th Inf. Co.A Sgt.
Saunders, John C. KY 14th Cav. Co.D,E,C
Saunders, John C. NC 45th Inf. Co.G
Saunders, John C., Jr. VA 54th Mil. Co.A
Saunders, John C., Jr. Sig.Corps,CSA Cpl.
Saunders, John D. AL 3rd Cav. Co.G
Saunders, John D. AR 12th Inf. Bvt.2nd Lt.
Saunders, John D. VA 21st Inf. Co.E
Saunders, John D.H. GA 12th Inf. Co.D
Saunders, John E. VA 4th Cav. Co.K
Saunders, John F. VA 17th Cav. Co.F
Saunders, John G. MS 14th Inf. Co.I
Saunders, John H. VA 50th Inf. 1st Co.G
Saunders, John H. Gen. & Staff Surg.
Saunders, John J. MS 19th Inf. Co.K
Saunders, John J. VA Lt.Arty. Rives' Co.
Saunders, John J. VA 30th Inf. Co.F
Saunders, John K. KY 6th Cav. Co.H,F Ord.Sgt.
Saunders, John K. MO Inf. Clark's Regt. Co.G
Saunders, John K. NC 1st Arty. (10th St.Troops) Co.I
Saunders, John K. NC 2nd Arty. (36th St.Troops) Co.A
Saunders, John K. Conf.Cav. Clarkson's Bn. Ind.Rangers Co.E
Saunders, John M. AL 1st Regt.Conscr. Co.A
Saunders, John M. AL Conscr. Echols' Co.
Saunders, John M. NC 2nd Cav. (19th St.Troops) Co.A
Saunders, John M. NC 15th Inf. Co.M
Saunders, John M. VA 2nd Cav. Co.A,G
Saunders, John M. VA 2nd Cav. Co.C
Saunders, John M. VA 28th Inf. Co.F
Saunders, John O. NC 2nd Bn.Loc.Def.Troops Co.A Laborer
Saunders, John O. VA Cav. 41st Bn. Co.G
Saunders, John P. GA 1st Reg. Co.B

Saunders, John P. VA 1st Inf. Chambers' Co.
Saunders, John R. SC 6th Cav. Co.C
Saunders, John R. VA 6th Cav. Co.I
Saunders, John R. VA Lt.Arty. Clutter's Co. Bugler
Saunders, John R. VA Arty. Fleet's Co. Fifer
Saunders, John R. VA 55th Inf. Co.B Fifer
Saunders, John S. AL 39th Inf. Co.H
Saunders, John S. MS 42nd Inf. Co.B
Saunders, John S. VA Cav. 40th Bn. Co.A Sgt.
Saunders, John S. VA 115th Mil. Co.A
Saunders, Jno. S. Gen. & Staff, Arty. 1st Lt.
Saunders, John S. Gen. & Staff, Ord. Lt.Col.
Saunders, John T. TN 2nd (Robison's) Inf. Co.H
Saunders, John T. TN 15th Inf. Co.G 3rd Lt.
Saunders, John T. VA 56th Inf. Co.E
Saunders, John W. GA 62nd Cav. Co.L
Saunders, John W. GA 6th Inf. Co.D
Saunders, John W. MS 2nd Inf. Co.D
Saunders, John W. NC 5th Inf. Co.I
Saunders, John W. NC 33rd Inf. Co.E,C
Saunders, John W. SC Inf. 3rd Bn. Co.F
Saunders, John W. TN 15th Inf. Co.E
Saunders, John W. TN Inf. 23rd Bn. Co.B
Saunders, John W. VA 13th Cav. Co.H
Saunders, John W. VA 24th Cav. Co.K
Saunders, John W. VA Hvy.Arty. 20th Bn. Co.D
Saunders, John W. VA Inf. 5th Bn. Co.F
Saunders, John W. VA 6th Inf. Co.H
Saunders, John W. VA 15th Inf. Co.D
Saunders, John W. VA 32nd Inf. Co.A Sgt.
Saunders, John W. VA 48th Inf. Co.E
Saunders, John W. VA 51st Inf. Co.E
Saunders, John W. 8th (Dearing's) Conf.Cav. Co.E
Saunders, John Wesley MS 4th Inf. Co.F
Saunders, Joseph GA 62nd Cav. Co.L
Saunders, Joseph LA 4th Inf. Co.A
Saunders, Joseph MO Robertson's Regt.St.Guard Co.9
Saunders, Joseph VA 24th Cav. Co.I
Saunders, Joseph VA 24th Inf. Co.F
Saunders, Joseph VA 55th Inf. Co.K
Saunders, Joseph VA 59th Mil. Hunter's Co.
Saunders, Joseph 8th (Dearing's) Conf.Cav. Co.D
Saunders, Joseph B. MS 42nd Inf. Co.C
Saunders, Joseph C. AR 1st (Colquitt's) Inf. Co.B
Saunders, Joseph D. MS 17th Inf. Co.A
Saunders, Joseph H. AL 61st Inf. Co.K Sgt.
Saunders, Joseph H. GA 25th Inf. Co.E
Saunders, Joseph H. NC 1st Inf. (6 mo. '61) Co.D
Saunders, Joseph H. NC 33rd Inf. Co.A Lt.Col.
Saunders, Joseph J. VA 12th Inf. 2nd Co.I
Saunders, Joseph M. NC 32nd Inf. Co.I
Saunders, Joseph O. VA 157th Mil. Co.B
Saunders, Joseph P. VA 92nd Mil. Co.C
Saunders, Joseph S. GA 2nd Cav. Co.G 2nd Lt.
Saunders, Joseph W. VA 28th Inf. Co.D
Saunders, Joshua MS Wilkinson Cty. Minute Men Co.A
Saunders, Josiah N. VA Inf. 25th Bn. Co.B
Saunders, Josiah P. MS 13th Inf. Co.B,F
Saunders, J.P. AL Mil. 4th Vol. Moore's Co.
Saunders, J.P. MS 28th Cav. Co.G
Saunders, J.R. AL 19th Inf. Co.F Lt.

Saunders, J.R. FL Lt.Arty. Dyke's Co.
Saunders, J.R. SC Cav. Tucker's Co.
Saunders, J.R. TX 10th Cav. Co.D
Saunders, J.S. GA 1st (Fannin's) Res. Co.C
Saunders, J.S. GA 10th Inf.
Saunders, J.S. MS 2nd Inf.
Saunders, J.S. MO 10th Inf. Co.A
Saunders, J.S. TN 21st Inf. Co.C
Saunders, J.S. TX 13th Vol. Co.E
Saunders, J.S. VA 24th Cav. Co.A Sgt.
Saunders, J.S. VA 1st Bn.Res. Co.A
Saunders, J.S. Gen. & Staff Surg.
Saunders, J.T. AL Cp. of Instr. Talladega
Saunders, J.T. LA Conscr.
Saunders, J.T. TN Inf. 4th Cons.Regt. Co.I
Saunders, J.T. TX 9th Field Btty.
Saunders, J.T. TX 3rd (Kirby's) Bn.Vol. Co.B
Saunders, J.T. TX 17th Inf. Co.F
Saunders, J.V. MS 5th Inf. (St.Troops) Co.A
Saunders, J.W. KY 9th Mtd.Inf. Co.F
Saunders, J.W. NC Prov.Guard
Saunders, J.W. SC Arty. Manigault's Bn. 1st Co.B
Saunders, J.W. TN 7th (Duckworth's) Cav. Co.D
Saunders, J.W. TN 16th Inf. Co.E
Saunders, J.W. VA 1st Inf. Co.B
Saunders, J.W. VA 53rd Inf. Co.K
Saunders, J.W. 1st Conf.Cav. 2nd Co.G
Saunders, J.W. 8th (Wade's) Conf.Cav. Co.H
Saunders, Kemp H. AR 31st Inf. Co.A Cpl.
Saunders, Kemp P. NC 44th Inf. Co.K
Saunders, L. KY 3rd Mtd.Inf. Co.D
Saunders, L. LA 8th Inf. Co.F,D
Saunders, L. MS Lt.Arty. (Warren Lt.Arty.) Swett's Co.
Saunders, L. MS 3rd Inf. Co.B
Saunders, Lancaster K. NC 17th Inf. (2nd Org.) Surg.
Saunders, Lancaster K. Gen. & Staff, Medical Dept. Surg.
Saunders, Latitious A. VA 5th Cav. Co.E
Saunders, L.D. TN 31st Inf. Co.D Cpl.
Saunders, Leonard Gen. & Staff Asst.Surg.
Saunders, Leonidas H. AL Lt.Arty. Lee's Btty.
Saunders, Lewis TX 37th Cav. Co.E
Saunders, Lewis W. VA 30th Bn.S.S. Co.C Sgt.
Saunders, L.G. Conf.Cav. Wood's Regt. 2nd Co.D
Saunders, Liberty TN 11th Inf. Co.A
Saunders, L.J. TN 30th Inf. Co.K
Saunders, L.K. NC 17th Inf. (1st Org.) Asst.Surg.
Saunders, Logan H. NC 6th Cav. (65th St.Troops) Co.C
Saunders, Lovel VA 9th Cav. Co.K
Saunders, Lovell VA 41st Mil. Co.E
Saunders, Lowndes VA 2nd Cav. Co.A
Saunders, L.R. TN 3rd (Forrest's) Cav. Co.C
Saunders, L.T. AR Mtd.Vol. Baker's Co.
Saunders, Lucien L. GA 30th Inf. Co.A Surg.
Saunders, Lucien L. Gen. & Staff Surg.
Saunders, Lucius C. GA 17th Inf. Co.K
Saunders, Lunceford VA 46th Inf. 2nd Co.I
Saunders, L.V. VA Cav. O'Ferrall's Bn. Co.C Sgt.
Saunders, M. AL 53rd (Part.Rangers) Co.I

Saunders, M. AL 32nd Inf. Co.F
Saunders, M. FL 2nd Cav. Co.D
Saunders, Marcos B. TX 26th Cav. Co.B
Saunders, Marshall R. MS 12th Cav. Co.B 1st Sgt.
Saunders, Martin AL 57th Inf. Co.H
Saunders, Martin Rush MS 1st Lt.Arty. Co.A Artif.
Saunders, Mathew VA 57th Inf. Co.D
Saunders, Mathew T. Gen. & Staff 1st Lt.,Ord.Off.
Saunders, McB. VA Inf. 23rd Bn. Co.B
Saunders, McQueen FL 1st Cav. Co.C 1st Lt.
Saunders, M.D. 2nd Cherokee Mtd.Vol. Co.H
Saunders, M.E. MS 1st Cav. Co.B
Saunders, M.E. MS 7th Cav. Co.B
Saunders, Meda AR 5th Inf. Co.E
Saunders, Merrill TX Cav. Ragsdale's Bn. Co.E
Saunders, Micajah B. VA 24th Inf. Co.G
Saunders, Micazio VA 17th Cav. Co.D,E
Saunders, Michael AL Lt.Arty. 2nd Bn. Co.B
Saunders, Michael H. MS 2nd Inf. Co.B,L
Saunders, Miskell VA 41st Mil. Co.D
Saunders, M.J. MS 28th Cav. Co.G
Saunders, M.L. GA 17th Inf. Co.K
Saunders, M.L. MS 8th Cav. Co.A
Saunders, M.N. GA 17th Inf. Co.K
Saunders, M.O. MS Res.Corps Withers' Co.
Saunders, Mortimer VA Lt.Arty. Jackson's Bn.St.Line Co.A
Saunders, Mortimer F. VA 8th Inf. Co.H
Saunders, M.T. SC 7th Cav. Co.F
Saunders, N. TN 40th Inf. Co.C
Saunders, Nathaniel B. VA 23rd Inf. Co.D
Saunders, Nathaniel B. VA 59th Inf. 3rd Co.E Cpl.
Saunders, Nevil VA 8th Inf. Co.H
Saunders, N.L. GA 46th Inf. Co.A
Saunders, Noah NC 26th Inf. Co.I
Saunders, Noah VA Cav. Caldwell's Bn. Gent's Co.
Saunders, Noah VA Cav. McFarlane's Co.
Saunders, P. AR 10th Mil. Co.I Cpl.
Saunders, P. NC 23rd Inf. Co.H
Saunders, P. TN 30th Inf. Co.C 1st Sgt.
Saunders, P. Eng.,CSA Asst.Eng.
Saunders, P.A. GA 7th Inf.
Saunders, P.A. LA 2nd Inf. Co.D
Saunders, P.A. SC Inf. Hampton Legion
Saunders, Palmer VA 6th Inf. Co.G
Saunders, Parker VA 61st Inf. Co.F
Saunders, Patrick H. TX 19th Cav. Co.F Capt.
Saunders, P. Benjamin TX 17th Cons. Dismtd.Cav. Co.K
Saunders, Peter MS 31st Inf. Co.C Color Sgt.
Saunders, Peter MO Cav. Schnabel's Bn. 3rd Lt.
Saunders, Peter NC 1st Cav. (9th St.Troops) Co.A
Saunders, Peter J. MS 11th Inf. Co.A
Saunders, Peter R. VA 30th Inf. Co.F
Saunders, Peyton D. TX 27th Cav. Co.I
Saunders, Philip VA 58th Inf. Co.K
Saunders, P.J. TX 4th Cav. Co.A
Saunders, Pleasant KY 3rd Cav. Co.K
Saunders, Pleasant R. VA 28th Inf. Co.D
Saunders, P.M. MO 5th Cav. Co.D
Saunders, P.M. MO Cav. Stallard's Co.

Saunders, P.M. MO 1st Regt.St.Guards
Saunders, P.S. SC 9th Inf. Co.E
Saunders, Quenten T. NC Lt.Arty. 3rd Bn. Co.B
Saunders, R. MS 25th Inf. Co.I
Saunders, R. SC 4th St.Troops Co.A
Saunders, R. VA Cav. 40th Bn. Co.E
Saunders, R. Gen. & Staff AQM
Saunders, Raleigh W. VA Arty. J.W. Drewry's Co.
Saunders, Raleigh W. VA 8th Inf. Co.A
Saunders, Ransom W. NC 2nd Arty. (36th St.Troops) Co.G
Saunders, R.B. MS 40th Inf. Co.A
Saunders, R.B. MS Clayton's Co. (Jasper Defend.)
Saunders, R.B. TN 15th (Cons.) Cav. Co.G Capt.
Saunders, R.C. MS 3rd (St.Troops) Cav. Co.G
Saunders, R.C. MS 1st (King's) Inf. (St.Troops) Co.K
Saunders, R.C. MS 40th Inf. Co.A Sgt.
Saunders, R.C. MS Clayton's Co. (Jasper Defend.)
Saunders, R.C. VA 11th Inf. Co.G
Saunders, R.C. Gen. & Staff Capt.,AQM
Saunders, R.E. GA 1st (Olmstead's) Inf. Gordon's Co.
Saunders, R.E. GA 63rd Inf. Co.K,D Cpl.
Saunders, R.E. VA 9th Cav. Co.K
Saunders, R.H. GA 62nd Cav. Co.L
Saunders, R.H. TX Granbury's Cons.Brig. Co.G
Saunders, R.H. VA 24th Cav. Co.I
Saunders, R.H. VA Inf. 4th Bn.Loc.Def. Co.B
Saunders, R.H. VA 53rd Inf. Co.D
Saunders, Richard LA 9th Inf. Co.E
Saunders, Richard NC 1st Arty. (10th St.Troops) Co.I
Saunders, Richard NC 2nd Arty. (36th St.Troops) Co.A
Saunders, Richard VA 8th Inf. Co.D
Saunders, Richard VA 30th Inf. Co.A
Saunders, Richard VA 47th Inf. 3rd Co.H
Saunders, Richard B. NC 1st Inf. (6 mo. '61) Co.D 2nd Lt.
Saunders, Richard H. VA 47th Inf. 2nd Co.G
Saunders, Richard H. VA 59th Mil. Hunter's Co.
Saunders, Richard H. 8th (Dearing's) Conf.Cav. Co.D
Saunders, Richard S. VA 51st Inf. Co.E
Saunders, Richard W. VA 2nd Cav.
Saunders, Richard W. VA 4th Cav. Co.G
Saunders, R.J. TN Cav. 4th Bn. (Branner's) Co.D
Saunders, R.L. Conf.Cav. Wood's Regt. 2nd Co.F
Saunders, R.M. MS Clayton's Co. (Jasper Defend.)
Saunders, Ro. VA 3rd Inf.Loc.Def. Co.D
Saunders, Robert FL 2nd Cav. Co.D
Saunders, Robert MO Cav. Slayback's Regt. Co.F
Saunders, Robert NC 5th Inf. Co.H
Saunders, Robert VA Horse Arty. Shoemaker's Co.
Saunders, Robert VA Lt.Arty. Thompson's Co.
Saunders, Robert A. TX 16th Inf. Co.I
Saunders, Robert A. VA Lt.Arty. 38th Bn. Co.D

Saunders, Robert A. VA 28th Inf. Co.I
Saunders, Robert C. VA 11th Inf. Co.B Capt.
Saunders, Robert C. Gen. & Staff Maj.,QM
Saunders, Robert D. VA 9th Cav. Co.H
Saunders, Robert H. VA Lt.Arty. J.R. Johnson's Co.
Saunders, Robert H. VA 23rd Inf. Co.F Sgt.
Saunders, Robert M. TX 1st Inf. Co.F 2nd Lt.
Saunders, Robert R. NC 45th Inf. Co.B 2nd Lt.
Saunders, Robert S. AL Cav. Lewis' Bn. Co.D
Saunders, Robert T. VA 2nd Cav. Co.H 1st Lt.
Saunders, Robert T. VA 36th Inf. 2nd Co.I
Saunders, Robert W. TN 11th Inf. Co.A
Saunders, Robert W. VA Cav. Hounshell's Bn. Thurmond's Co.
Saunders, Robert W. VA Inf. 23rd Bn. Co.B 2nd Lt.
Saunders, Robert W. VA 28th Inf. Co.F 1st Lt.
Saunders, Robert W. VA 53rd Inf. Co.D
Saunders, Romulus VA 9th Cav. Co.D
Saunders, Romulus W. NC 2nd Cav. (19th St.Troops) Co.F 1st Lt.
Saunders, Ro. R. VA Inf. 25th Bn. Co.B
Saunders, R.P. LA 4th Inf. Co.D 2nd Lt.
Saunders, R.P. VA 32nd Inf. Co.C
Saunders, R.S. AL Cav. Barbiere's Bn. Goldsby's Co.
Saunders, R.S. AL 12th Inf. Co.D Lt.
Saunders, R.S. MS 18th Cav. Co.K
Saunders, R.S. VA Lt.Arty. W.P. Carter's Co.
Saunders, R.T. VA Inf. 23rd Bn. Co.B Sgt.
Saunders, R.T. VA 47th Inf. Co.C
Saunders, Rufus R. NC 16th Inf. Co.A
Saunders, Rufus R. NC Inf. Thomas Legion 1st Co.A
Saunders, R.W. LA Cav. Greenleaf's Co. (Orleans Lt.Horse)
Saunders, R.W. NC Lt.Arty. 13th Bn. Co.D
Saunders, R.W. SC 7th Cav. Co.F
Saunders, R.W. VA 36th Inf. Co.I 1st Lt.
Saunders, R.W.C. VA Courtney Arty. Cpl.
Saunders, S. TN 12th (Green's) Cav. Co.F
Saunders, S. Eng.,CSA
Saunders, S.A. SC 27th Inf. Co.I
Saunders, S.A. Anderson's Div. Hosp.Stew.
Saunders, Samuel AL 8th Cav. Co.G 1st Sgt.
Saunders, Samuel AL 17th Bn.S.S. Co.B
Saunders, Samuel AL 28th Inf. Co.E
Saunders, Samuel AL 39th Inf. Co.H
Saunders, Samuel VA Cav. 35th Bn. Co.F
Saunders, Samuel G. LA Washington Arty.Bn. Co.3 Sgt.
Saunders, Samuel H. TN Lt.Arty. Baxter's Co.
Saunders, Samuel H. VA Inf. 22nd Bn. Co.B
Saunders, Samuel H. VA 42nd Inf. Co.K Lt.Col.
Saunders, Samuel M. FL 3rd Inf. Co.G
Saunders, Samuel N. AR 7th Cav. Co.A
Saunders, Samuel T. VA 18th Inf. Co.D
Saunders, Samuel W. LA 1st (Nelligan's) Inf. Co.K 1st Sgt.
Saunders, S.D. GA 15th Inf. Co.K
Saunders, S.E. KY 3rd Mtd.Inf. Co.H
Saunders, Seth P. TN 55th (McKoin's) Inf. Joyner's Co. Cpl.
Saunders, Shepard NC 3rd Inf. Co.E
Saunders, Shields A. MO 2nd Cav. 3rd Co.K,A

Saunders, Silas G. VA 42nd Inf. Co.H
Saunders, Simon H. GA 5th Inf. Co.B
Saunders, Simon H., Jr. GA 53rd Inf. Co.I 2nd Lt.
Saunders, Simon H. Gen. & Staff Surg.
Saunders, S.J. TX 12th Inf. Co.E
Saunders, Smith VA Cav. Caldwell's Bn. Gent's Co.
Saunders, Smith VA Cav. McFarlane's Co.
Saunders, Smith VA Lt.Arty. Grandy's Co.
Saunders, S.N. AR 35th Inf. Co.H
Saunders, Solomon MS 20th Inf. Co.H
Saunders, S.P. KY 3rd Cav. Co.A
Saunders, S.P. TN 9th (Ward's) Cav. Co.B
Saunders, S.P. VA 110th Mil. Saunders' Co. Capt.
Saunders, S.S. GA Inf. 23rd Bn.Loc.Def. Cook's Co.
Saunders, S.S. MS 10th Inf. Old Co.D, New Co.E
Saunders, S.S. Conf.Lt.Arty. Richardson's Bn. Co.C
Saunders, Stephen FL Bonded Agriculturist
Saunders, Stephen NC 42nd Inf. Co.C Sgt.
Saunders, Stephen L. TN 34th Inf. Co.D
Saunders, Stephen P. VA 57th Inf. Co.C
Saunders, Stephen T. VA Lt.Arty. Montgomery's Co.
Saunders, Stephen T. VA 9th Inf. Co.I
Saunders, Sterling L. MS 21st Inf. Co.K
Saunders, Stewart TX 4th Inf. Co.D
Saunders, S.W. TX 11th Cav. Co.F 1st Sgt.
Saunders, S.Y. VA 20th Inf. Co.C
Saunders, T. AL Tuscaloosa Cadets Co.A
Saunders, T. AR 10th Mil. Co.B
Saunders, T. GA 27th Inf. Co.F
Saunders, T. MS 14th Inf. Co.A
Saunders, T. MS Blythe's Bn. (St.Troops) Co.A
Saunders, T. MO 12th Cav. Co.I
Saunders, T. VA Inf. 44th Bn. Co.B
Saunders, T.A. VA 46th Inf. Co.E
Saunders, Taliafero AL 6th Inf. Co.B
Saunders, T.B. GA Inf. 17th Bn. (St.Guards) Fay's Co. Cpl.
Saunders, T.B. TX Cav. McCord's Frontier Regt. Co.I
Saunders, T.B. 1st Conf.Eng.Troops
Saunders, Terrell LA 2nd Inf. Co.F
Saunders, T.G. TX Waul's Legion Co.B
Saunders, T.H. MS Res.Corps Withers' Co.
Saunders, T.H. TX Granbury's Cons.Brig. Co.G
Saunders, T.H. VA 4th Bn.Res. Co.A 2nd Lt.
Saunders, Thaddeus W. VA Lt.Arty. Cayce's Co.
Saunders, Theodore AL 7th Cav. Co.A
Saunders, Theodore MO 9th Inf. Co.H
Saunders, Thomas AL 2nd Cav. Co.E
Saunders, Thomas AL Lt.Arty. 2nd Bn. Co.B
Saunders, Thomas AL St.Arty. Co.C
Saunders, Thomas AL 1st Regt.Conscr. Co.B
Saunders, Thomas AL Mil. 2nd Regt.Vol. Co.B
Saunders, Thomas GA 10th Inf. Co.G
Saunders, Thomas GA 29th Inf. Co.A
Saunders, Thomas LA Arty. Moody's Co. (Madison Lt.Arty.)
Saunders, Thomas MS 11th (Perrin's) Cav. Co.H
Saunders, Thomas MS 2nd Inf. Co.D

Saunders, Thomas MS 5th Inf. (St.Troops) Co.C
Saunders, Thomas MS 20th Inf. Co.B
Saunders, Thomas MS 34th Inf. Co.K
Saunders, Thomas MO Cav. Snider's Bn. Co.B
Saunders, Thomas MO 10th Inf. Co.E
Saunders, Thomas VA Lt.Arty. Jeffress' Co.
Saunders, Thomas VA 111th Mil. Co.8
Saunders, Thomas VA 115th Mil. Co.A
Saunders, Thomas VA Mil. Scott Cty.
Saunders, Thomas 9th Conf.Inf. Co.B
Saunders, Thomas Conf.Inf. Tucker's Regt. Co.G
Saunders, Thomas A. TX 19th Cav. Co.F Sgt.
Saunders, Thomas B. GA 53rd Inf. Co.I 1st Sgt.
Saunders, Thomas B. VA 17th Inf. Co.K
Saunders, Thomas C. MS Inf. 2nd Bn. Co.C
Saunders, Thomas C. MS 48th Inf. Co.C
Saunders, Thomas D. VA 46th Inf. 2nd Co.K
Saunders, Thomas H. GA 10th Inf. Co.G
Saunders, Thomas H. VA 16th Inf. Co.D
Saunders, Thomas J. GA 48th Inf. Co.I
Saunders, Thomas J. MS 2nd Inf. Co.B,F
Saunders, Thomas J. NC 52nd Inf. Co.H
Saunders, Thomas J. TX Lt.Arty. H. Van Buren's Co.
Saunders, Thomas J. VA Lt.Arty. Clutter's Co.
Saunders, Thomas J. VA 19th Inf. Co.G
Saunders, Thomas J. VA 59th Mil. Hunter's Co.
Saunders, Thomas J.J. VA Arty. Fleet's Co.
Saunders, Thomas L. SC 3rd Cav. Co.H
Saunders, Thos. M. AL 15th Inf. Co.E
Saunders, Thomas M. Gen. & Staff Hosp.Stew.
Saunders, Thomas O. NC 8th Inf. Co.B
Saunders, Thomas S. NC 16th Inf. Co.H
Saunders, Thomas T. VA 2nd Cav. Co.F
Saunders, Thomas T. VA 58th Inf. Co.A
Saunders, Thomas W. MO Searcy's Bn.S.S. Co.C Sgt.
Saunders, Thornton VA 41st Mil. Co.E
Saunders, T.J. FL 2nd Cav. Co.E
Saunders, T.J. GA 12th (Robinson's) Cav. (St.Guards) Co.E
Saunders, T.J. TN 47th Inf. Co.C
Saunders, T.L. FL 2nd Cav. Co.D
Saunders, T.L. SC 3rd Cav. Co.H
Saunders, T.N. SC 1st (Butler's) Inf. Co.B
Saunders, Tom TN 21st Inf. Co.B
Saunders, T.P. KY Cav. Thompson's Co.
Saunders, T.S. GA 30th Inf. Co.A
Saunders, T.S. LA 2nd Cav. Co.C Sgt.
Saunders, V.W. VA 50th Inf. Co.K
Saunders, W. AR 1st Cav. Co.B
Saunders, W. LA 22nd (Cons.) Inf. Co.H
Saunders, W. MS Inf. 2nd Bn. (St.Troops) Co.A
Saunders, W. MS 3rd Inf. Co.B
Saunders, W. NC 5th Sr.Res. Co.K
Saunders, W. VA Cav. 40th Bn. Co.F
Saunders, W.A. VA 49th Inf. Co.H
Saunders, Walter H. VA Horse Arty. E. Graham's Co.
Saunders, Walter W. AL 4th Inf. Co.D
Saunders, Walton VA 55th Inf. Asst.Surg.
Saunders, Walton Gen. & Staff Asst.Surg.
Saunders, W.B. AL 5th Inf. New Co.G
Saunders, W.C. LA 6th Cav. Co.I
Saunders, W.D. GA 44th Inf. Co.F
Saunders, W.D. VA 13th Inf. Co.C
Saunders, W.E. TN 5th (McKenzie's) Cav. Co.A

Saunders, W.E. TX 14th Inf. Surg.
Saunders, W.E. VA Cav. Mosby's Regt. (Part.Rangers) Co.D
Saunders, Web MS 1st Cav. Co.H
Saunders, Wesley M. VA Lt.Arty. 38th Bn. Co.D
Saunders, Wesley M. VA 28th Inf. 1st Co.C
Saunders, Wesley W. VA Lt.Arty. J.R. Johnson's Co.
Saunders, W.F. MO 1st Inf. Co.C
Saunders, W.G. GA 1st (Olmstead's) Inf.
Saunders, W.H. AL Mobile Fire Bn. Mullany's Co.
Saunders, W.H. GA 1st (Olmstead's) Inf.
Saunders, W.H. VA 20th Inf. Co.C
Saunders, W.H. 15th Conf.Cav. Co.H
Saunders, W.H.H. AL Lt.Arty. Phelan's Co.
Saunders, Wiley AL 1st Cav. Co.I
Saunders, Wiley NC 42nd Inf. Co.B
Saunders, Wiley B. TN 63rd Inf. Co.A
Saunders, William GA 44th Inf. Co.K
Saunders, William GA Cobb's Legion Co.L
Saunders, William GA Inf. (Jasper & Butts Cty. Guards) Lane's Co.
Saunders, William MS 1st Inf. Co.D
Saunders, William MO 1st N.E. Cav. Co.D
Saunders, William MO 3rd Inf. Co.D Cpl.
Saunders, Wm. NC Mil. Clark's Sp.Bn. F.G. Simmons' Co.
Saunders, William NC 5th Inf. Co.A
Saunders, William NC 5th Inf. Co.I
Saunders, William NC 21st Inf. Co.H
Saunders, William NC 37th Inf. Co.K
Saunders, William TN 11th (Holman's) Cav. Co.H
Saunders, William TN Lt.Arty. Scott's Co.
Saunders, William TN 7th Inf. Co.E
Saunders, William, Jr. TX 26th Cav. 1st Co.G
Saunders, William TX 35th (Brown's) Cav. Co.H Capt.
Saunders, William TX Cav. Bourland's Regt. Co.C
Saunders, William TX 5th Inf. Co.D
Saunders, William TX 13th Vol. 2nd Co.A Capt.
Saunders, William VA Lt.Arty. Jeffress' Co.
Saunders, William VA Arty. B.H. Smith's Co.
Saunders, William VA 2nd Bn.Res. Sgt.
Saunders, William VA 8th Inf. Co.H
Saunders, William VA 22nd Inf. Co.A
Saunders, William VA 32nd Inf. 2nd Co.I
Saunders, William VA 38th Inf. Co.F
Saunders, William VA 59th Inf. 3rd Co.E Cpl.
Saunders, William VA 59th Mil. Riddick's Co.
Saunders, William VA 61st Inf. Co.F 1st Lt.
Saunders, William VA 115th Mil. Co.D
Saunders, William VA Murphy's Co.
Saunders, William Conf.Cav. Clarkson's Bn. Ind.Rangers Co.C
Saunders, William A. MS 19th Inf. Co.K
Saunders, William A. NC 2nd Cav. (19th St.Troops) Co.C
Saunders, William A. NC 39th Inf. Co.A
Saunders, William A. VA Arty. Fleet's Co. Cpl.
Saunders, William A. VA Lt.Arty. Woolfolk's Co. Cpl.
Saunders, William A. VA 53rd Inf. Co.I
Saunders, William A. VA 55th Inf. Co.B

Saunders, William B. NC 7th Inf. Co.E
Saunders, William C. AL 1st Regt.Conscr. Co.A
Saunders, William D. VA 21st Inf. Co.K,A Sgt.
Saunders, William D.B. VA 61st Inf. Co.E
Saunders, William D.H. TX 8th Inf. Co.F
Saunders, William E. AL 3rd Bn.Res. Co.A Cpl.
Saunders, William E. AL 37th Inf. Co.A Sgt.
Saunders, William E. MS Inf. 2nd St.Troops Co.G 2nd Lt.
Saunders, William E. TX Cav. 6th Bn. Surg.
Saunders, Wm. E. VA 46th Inf. 2nd Co.E Cpl.
Saunders, Wm. E. Gen. & Staff Surg.
Saunders, William F. NC 11th (Bethel Regt.) Inf. Co.F
Saunders, William G. VA 58th Inf. Co.K
Saunders, William H. AR 9th Inf. Co.C
Saunders, William H. MS Inf. 5th Bn. Co.B 2nd Lt.
Saunders, William H. MS 27th Inf. Co.K 1st Lt.
Saunders, William H. MO Cav. Slayback's Regt. Co.F
Saunders, William H. NC 14th Inf. Co.C
Saunders, William H. TN 2nd (Robison's) Inf. Co.H Capt.
Saunders, William H. TN 13th Inf. Co.K Cpl.
Saunders, William H. VA 9th Cav. Co.D
Saunders, William H. VA 1st Arty. Co.D
Saunders, William H. VA Lt.Arty. 1st Bn. Co.D
Saunders, Wm. H. VA Hvy.Arty. Allen's Co.
Saunders, William H. VA 23rd Inf. Co.E
Saunders, William J. AL 3rd Cav. Co.G
Saunders, William J. AL Inf. 2nd Regt. Co.D
Saunders, William J. GA 6th Inf. Co.A
Saunders, William J. NC 1st Arty. (10th St.Troops) Co.A 1st Lt.
Saunders, William J. NC 20th Inf. Co.A
Saunders, William J. VA 17th Cav. Co.H,F
Saunders, Wm. J. VA Mtd.Res. Rappahannock Dist. Sale's Co.
Saunders, William J. VA Arty. Dance's Co.
Saunders, William J. VA 60th Inf. 2nd Co.H
Saunders, William J. VA 115th Mil. Co.A
Saunders, William J. VA Res.Forces Thurston's Co.
Saunders, William K. NC 23rd Inf. Co.A
Saunders, William K. VA 44th Inf. Co.D
Saunders, William L. FL 3rd Inf. Co.G
Saunders, William L. NC 3rd Cav. (41st St.Troops) Co.C
Saunders, William L. NC 1st Arty. (10th St.Troops) Co.D 2nd Lt.
Saunders, William L. NC 46th Inf. Co.B Col.
Saunders, William L. TX 17th Cons.Distmd.Cav. Co.K
Saunders, William L. VA Lt.Arty. G.B. Chapman's Co.
Saunders, William L. VA 27th Inf. Co.D Sgt.
Saunders, William M. GA 13th Inf. Co.E
Saunders, William M. MS 24th Inf. Co.H
Saunders, William M. VA 30th Inf. Co.H Capt.
Saunders, William O. VA 24th Cav. Co.A 1st Lt.
Saunders, William O. VA Cav. 40th Bn. Co.A 2nd Lt.
Saunders, William P. GA Brooks' Co. (Terrell Lt.Arty.)

Saunders, William P. MS 20th Inf. Co.F
Saunders, William P. VA Lt.Arty. Thornton's Co.
Saunders, William R. AL Cav. Lewis' Bn. Co.D
Saunders, William R. GA 8th Inf. (St.Guards) Co.D
Saunders, William R. MS 17th Inf. Co.A
Saunders, William R. MS 42nd Inf. Co.I
Saunders, William R. NC 45th Inf. Co.G 1st Lt.
Saunders, William R. TN 34th Inf. Co.D Sgt.
Saunders, William R. VA 59th Inf. 3rd Co.F Sgt.
Saunders, William R. VA 60th Inf. 1st Co.H
Saunders, William T. AL 42nd Inf. Co.G
Saunders, William T. VA 55th Inf. Co.D
Saunders, Wm. T. Gen. & Staff Asst.Surg.
Saunders, William V. TN 11th Inf. Co.A
Saunders, William Wren VA 30th Inf. Co.F
Saunders, W.J. GA 2nd Inf. Co.I
Saunders, W.J. GA 4th Res. Co.E
Saunders, W.J. MS 1st (King's) Inf. (St.Troops) Co.K Cpl.
Saunders, W.J. Gen. & Staff, A. of TN Maj.
Saunders, W.L. KY 7th Cav. Co.B
Saunders, W.L. TX Cav. Gano's Squad. Co.B
Saunders, W.M. AR Lt.Arty. 5th Btty.
Saunders, W.M. FL 2nd Cav. Co.K 1st Lt.
Saunders, W.M. TN Cav. Napier's Bn. Co.D Cpl.
Saunders, Woodford LA 3rd Inf. Co.A
Saunders, Woodsy GA 11th Inf. Co.B
Saunders, W.P. VA 53rd Inf. Co.D
Saunders, Wren VA 24th Cav. Co.F
Saunders, Wren VA 47th Inf. 2nd Co.K
Saunders, Wright FL 2nd Cav. Co.E Cpl.
Saunders, Wright W. FL 5th Inf. Co.C
Saunders, W.S. KY 12th Cav. Co.G
Saunders, W.T. FL 2nd Cav. Co.D
Saunders, W.T. SC 7th Cav. Co.A
Saunders, W.T. SC Cav. Tucker's Co.
Saunders, W.T. TX Cav. Mann's Bn. Cox's Co.
Saunders, W.T. TX Inf. Timmons' Regt. Co.I
Saunders, W.W. LA 27th Inf. Co.E
Saunders, W.W. MS 1st (Patton's) Inf. Co.H
Saunders, W.W. 8th (Wade's) Conf.Cav. Co.I
Saunders, X.B. TX 16th Inf. Co.A Maj.
Saunders, Y.O. KY 9th Cav. Co.D
Saunders, Zachariah VA 9th Cav. Sandford's Co.
Saunders, Zachariah VA Cav. 15th Bn. Co.A Cpl.
Saunderson, Benjamin NC 2nd Jr.Res. Co.I
Saunderson, George L. VA 23rd Inf. Co.B
Saunderson, Henry SC 1st Arty. Co.H
Saunderson, James R. LA 2nd Inf. Co.F
Saunderson, John O. VA 13th Cav. Co.F
Saunderson, John T. VA 24th Cav. Co.B
Saunderson, John T. VA Cav. 40th Bn. Co.B
Saunderson, Richard H. VA 23rd Inf. Co.B
Saunderson, S.H. NC Gibbs' Co. (Loc.Def.)
Saunderson, T.H. MS Inf. 3rd Bn. Co.H
Saunderton, J. GA 47th Inf. Co.B
Saunderville, J.S. SC 12th Inf. Co.H Sgt.
Saundifer, I.W. MS 4th Cav. Co.G
Saune, J. LA Mil. 3rd Regt. French Brig. Co.7
Saunemann, C. TX Waul's Legion Co.A
Sauner, W.H. MS 10th Cav. Co.H
Sauner, W.H. Conf.Cav. Baxter's Bn. Co.A

Saunia, Eusat LA 16th Inf. Co.G
Saunican, A. LA Mil. French Co. of St.James
Saunier, Armand MS 16th Inf. Co.C
Saunier, Celestine AL 12th Inf. Co.A
Saunier, Don Louis LA 18th Inf. Co.B
Saunier, Felix LA 2nd Res.Corps Co.K
Saunier, Gideon LA 18th Inf. Co.B
Saunier, Leon LA Inf.Crescent Regt. Co.A
Saunneman, C. TX Inf. Timmons' Regt. Co.H
Saunsby, James MS Inf. 2nd Bn. Co.A Cpl.
Saunsby, James MS 48th Inf. Co.A Sgt.
Saunsby, James VA 26th Inf. 1st Co.B Cpl.
Saunsby, James 20th Conf.Cav. Co.F Sgt.
Saunter, A.D. NC 18th Inf. Co.G
Sauntmyres, Nuton VA 146th Mil. Co.H
Sau ny 1st Cherokee Mtd.Rifles Co.D
Saupe, Charles H. VA 3rd Bn.Valley Res. Co.B
Sauppe, Gustave TX 33rd Cav. Co.B
Sauppe, Gustavus TX 2nd Cav. Co.C
Saur, Fredrick TX Cav. McCord's Frontier Regt. 2nd Co.A
Saurage, Alex LA Mil.Cav.Squad. (Ind.Rangers Iberville)
Saurage, Alexander LA 2nd Cav. Co.I
Saurage, Herbert LA Mil.Cav.Squad. (Ind. Rangers Iberville)
Saurage, Horbert LA 2nd Cav. Co.I 1st Sgt.
Saurage, Norbut LA 2nd Cav. Co.I
Saurage, Oscar LA 2nd Cav. Co.I
Saurage, Sylvanie LA 27th Inf. Co.D
Saures, J.E. SC 5th Bn.Res. Co.B
Saures, Ysabel TX Cav. Benavides' Regt. Co.C
Saurin, Frank E. AL 3rd Inf. Co.F
Saurin, J.H. TN 7th (Duckworth's) Cav. Co.C
Saurin, Joseph AL 1st Regt. Mobile Vol. British Guard Co.A Sgt.
Saurin, Joseph MS 10th Inf. Old Co.K Sgt.
Sauroge, R. LA Mil. Orleans Guards Regt. Co.C
Saurris, Aubrey FL 1st Inf. Old Co.K
Sausaman, --- AR 15th Mil. Co.C
Sausaman, George MS Gage's Co. (Wigfall Guards)
Sauserman, James TN 39th Mtd.Inf. Co.H
Sauserman, William TN 39th Mtd.Inf. Co.H
Sausing, John TN 12th (Green's) Cav. Co.B Sgt.
Sausing, Ruffin Ready MS Inf. 1st St.Troops Co.G
Sausman, W.A. MS 3rd Inf. (St.Troops) Co.D Cpl.
Sausra, R.P. TX 20th Inf. Co.E
Saussaye, Alfred LA Mil. 1st Regt. French Brig. Co.6
Sausser, I.W. Eng.,CSA
Sausser, J.W. LA Inf. 11th Bn. Co.B
Saussey, R. Gen. & Staff Lt.,AAQM
Suassy, Clement H. GA Arty. (Chatham Arty.) Wheaton's Co.
Saussy, Clement H. GA 1st (Olmstead's) Inf. Claghorn's Co.
Saussy, Edward G. GA 1st (Olmstead's) Inf. Co.C,G
Saussy, George N. GA 1st (Olmstead's) Inf. Davis' Co.
Saussy, G.N. VA 6th Cav. 1st Co.E
Saussy, G. Nowlan MS Cav. Jeff Davis Legion Co.F

Saussy, J.R. GA Arty. (Chatham Arty.) Wheaton's Co.

Saussy, J.R. GA 1st (Olmstead's) Inf. Claghorn's Co.

Saussy, Robert GA Cav. Waring's Co.

Saussy, Robert MS Cav. Jeff Davis Legion Co.F 2nd Lt.

Saussy, Robert VA 6th Cav. 1st Co.E Sgt.

Saut, Thomas MS Inf. 1st Bn.St.Troops (30 days '64) Co.C

Sautell, Edward TN 4th (McLemore's) Cav. Co.A

Sauter, Daniel AL 48th Inf. Co.D

Sauter, E. AR 18th (Marmaduke's) Inf. Co.A

Sauter, Edward AL 48th Inf. Co.D

Sauter, Edward AR 26th Inf. Co.F 1st Sgt.

Sauter, John AR 32nd Inf. Co.B

Sauter, John TX 3rd Inf. Co.B

Sauter, Samuel AR 1st (Colquitt's) Inf. Co.D

Sauter, Tobias TX Conscr.

Sauters, J. TX 2nd Inf. Co.D

Sauters, J.A., Jr. TX 26th Cav. Co.F

Sautherland, J.W. SC 3rd Res. Co.I Sgt.

Sautherlin, W. AL 1st Cav. Co.G

Sauton, L.A. LA Inf.Cons. 18th Regt. & Yellow Jacket Bn. Co.A 2nd Lt.

Sauton, L.A. LA Inf.Crescent Regt. Co.D 2nd Lt.

Sautus, Cornelius LA 2nd Cav. Co.E

Sautz, Ferdinand MO 3rd Inf. Co.E

Sauvagean, Frank MS 3rd Inf. Co.K

Sauvagean, Frank MS 23rd Inf. Co.K

Sauvageot, Victor M. VA 27th Inf. Co.G

Sauve, --- LA 1st (Nelligan's) Inf. Asst.Surg.

Sauve, Felix LA Lt.Arty. LeGardeur, Jr.'s Co. (Orleans Guard Btty.)

Sauve, George LA Arty. Guyol's Co. (Orleans Arty.)

Sauve, George LA 10th Inf. Co.I 1st Lt.

Sauve, H. Gen. & Staff A.Surg.

Sauve, Henry LA 2nd Inf. Asst.Surg.

Sauve, Henry Gen. & Staff Asst.Surg.

Sauvergne, A. LA Inf.Crescent Regt. Co.A

Sauveur, Guillaume LA Mil. 4th Regt. French Brig. Co.5

Sauvinet, A.T. LA Mil. 1st Native Guards

Sauvinet, J.T. LA Mil. 1st Native Guards Cpl.

Sauvinet, S. LA Mil. 1st Native Guards Capt.

Savadge, F.S. NC Cav. 14th Bn. Co.I

Savage, A. AL 18th Inf. Co.L

Savage, A. GA 11th Cav. Co.A

Savage, A. NC 1st Arty. (10th St.Troops) Co.A

Savage, A. NC Mallett's Bn.

Savage, A. SC 11th Inf. 1st Co.I

Savage, Abner W. AL 40th Inf. Co.B

Savage, Abram SC 15th Inf. Co.H

Savage, A.C. MS 32nd Inf. Co.D

Savage, A.C. NC 21st Inf. Co.I

Savage, A.L. SC 3rd Cav. Co.B

Savage, Albert TN 1st (Carter's) Cav. Co.D

Savage, Alen GA 34th Inf. Co.I

Savage, Alexander VA 5th Cav. (12 mo. '61-2) Co.G Capt.

Savage, Alexander VA 13th Cav. Co.I Lt.Col.

Savage, A.M. AL Res. Moses' Co.

Savage, Andrew AL 58th Inf. Co.D

Savage, Andrew J. NC Mil. Clark's Sp.Bn. Rountree's Co.

Savage, Andrew W. TX 16th Cav. Co.I Cpl.

Savage, Aquilla TN 35th Inf. 2nd Co.D

Savage, Archibald AL 2nd Cav. Co.C

Savage, Asberry AL 18th Inf. Co.A

Savage, A.T. AL 22nd Inf. Co.C

Savage, Augustus NC 3rd Arty. (40th St.Troops) Co.G

Savage, A.W. TX Cav. Hardeman's Regt. Co.C Sgt.

Savage, B. MS 3rd Inf. (St.Troops) Co.H

Savage, Benjamin NC 7th Inf. Co.E

Savage, Benjamin O. NC 3rd Cav. (41st St.Troops) Co.G

Savage, Benjamin Z.T. AL 8th Cav. Co.I Sgt.

Savage, B.M. MS 11th (Cons.) Cav. Co.B

Savage, Braxton GA 53rd Inf. Co.B

Savage, B.W. SC 18th Inf. Co.B

Savage, Bythel NC 17th Inf. (2nd Org.) Co.E

Savage, C. GA 5th Res. Co.A

Savage, C. MS Cav. 3rd Bn. (Ashcraft's) Co.A

Savage, Calvin, Sr. NC 17th Inf. (2nd Org.) Co.E

Savage, Calvin N., Jr. NC 17th Inf. (2nd Org.) Co.E

Savage, C.C. FL 2nd Cav. Co.G

Savage, C.F. VA 45th Inf.

Savage, Charles AL 62nd Inf. Co.A

Savage, Charles NC 61st Inf. Co.G

Savage, Charles C. FL Cav. 5th Bn. Co.A

Savage, Charles E. MO 2nd Cav. Co.C

Savage, Charles L. TX 3rd Cav. Co.G

Savage, Charles W. GA 31st Inf. Co.K

Savage, C.L. TX 33rd Cav. Co.G

Savage, C.M. LA Inf.Crescent Regt. Co.A

Savage, Cornelius NC 30th Inf. Co.E

Savage, Cornelius F. VA 41st Inf. Co.I Cpl.

Savage, C.W. GA 2nd Cav. Co.A

Savage, C.W. VA 15th Inf. Co.A

Savage, D. GA 1st (Ramsey's) Inf. Co.I

Savage, D. NC 32nd Inf. Co.C

Savage, Daniel GA Cav. 21st Bn. Co.A

Savage, Daniel H. AL 45th Inf. Co.A

Savage, David NC 1st Inf. (6 mo. '61) Co.M

Savage, David NC 27th Inf. Co.C

Savage, David W. NC 52nd Inf. Co.C Sgt.

Savage, D.C. SC Hvy.Arty. Gilchrist's Co. (Gist Guard)

Savage, D.C. TN 8th Inf. Co.H

Savage, D.L. TX 11th Inf. Co.H

Savage, D.R. AL 33rd Inf. Co.K

Savage, E. TN 33rd Inf. Chap.

Savage, Ed. TX 4th Inf. Co.H

Savage, Edmund E. VA 1st Arty. Co.A

Savage, Edmund E. VA 32nd Inf. 1st Co.K

Savage, Edward LA 22nd Inf. Durrine, Jr.'s Co.

Savage, Edward NC 3rd Inf. Co.D Lt.Col.

Savage, Edward E. 15th Conf.Cav. Co.B

Savage, Edward W. MS 15th Inf. Co.K Sgt.

Savage, E.E. VA Lt.Arty. W.P. Carter's Co.

Savage, E.E. VA Inf. 4th Bn.Loc.Def. Co.B

Savage, E.F. VA Lt.Arty. 12th Bn. Co.B

Savage, E.G. AL 23rd Inf. Co.G

Savage, E.H. TN 1st Cav. Co.D

Savage, E.J. LA Inf.Cons.Crescent Regt. Co.H

Savage, E.L. TX 9th Cav. Co.C Sgt.

Savage, Eli TN 9th (Ward's) Cav. Co.B

Savage, Elisha A. NC 21st Inf. Co.F

Savage, F.J. NC 1st Arty. (10th St.Troops) Co.H

Savage, Francis M. AL 19th Inf. Co.I Sgt.

Savage, Francis M. AR Inf. 4th Bn. Co.C

Savage, Francis M. GA 6th Cav. Co.H Sgt.

Savage, Francis W. VA Hvy.Arty. 19th Bn. Co.B, 3rd Co.E Sgt.

Savage, Francis W. VA 39th Inf. Co.K Sgt.

Savage, Frank MS 23rd Inf. Co.K

Savage, Frederick E. KY 7th Cav.

Savage, G. MS Cav. Ham's Regt. Co.A

Savage, G.A. SC 1st Mtd.Mil. Kirk's Co.

Savage, George FL 9th Inf. Co.G QMSgt.

Savage, George TN 14th (Neely's) Cav. Co.E

Savage, George VA Lt.Arty. 13th Bn. Co.A

Savage, George VA 2nd St.Res. Co.I,F

Savage, George VA 3rd Inf.Loc.Def. Co.C

Savage, George A. SC 3rd Cav. Co.C

Savage, George A. SC Mil.Cav. 4th Regt. Howard's Co.

Savage, George B. VA Hvy.Arty. 19th Bn. Co.B, 3rd Co.E

Savage, George B. VA 39th Inf. Co.I

Savage, George F. VA 39th Inf. Co.A

Savage, George G. VA Hvy.Arty. 19th Bn. Co.B, 3rd Co.C Capt.

Savage, George G. VA 39th Inf. Co.K 2nd Lt.

Savage, George L. VA 2nd Arty. Co.D

Savage, George L. VA Inf. 22nd Bn. Co.D

Savage, George M. VA 1st St.Res. Co.F

Savage, George P. AL 43rd Inf. Co.F 1st Lt.

Savage, George W. NC 1st Inf. Co.C

Savage, George W. VA Lt.Arty. 12th Bn. Co.B

Savage, G.M. VA 3rd Inf.Loc.Def. Co.F

Savage, G.W. GA 53rd Inf. Co.A

Savage, G.W. TN 14th (Neely's) Cav. Co.I,E

Savage, G.W. TN Lt.Arty. Polk's Btty.

Savage, Haywood NC 27th Inf. Co.K

Savage, Henry GA 36th (Villepigue's) Inf. Co.C

Savage, Henry NC 18th Inf. Co.G Capt.

Savage, Henry 1st Conf.Inf. Co.A, 2nd Co.E Sgt.

Savage, Henry H. GA Siege Arty. 28th Bn. Co.C

Savage, Henry J. AL 3rd Cav. Co.D

Savage, Henry J. AL Mil. 4th Vol. Co.A

Savage, Henry M. TN Cav. Newsom's Regt. Co.D

Savage, H.G. Gen. & Staff Chap.

Savage, H.H. TN 8th Inf. Co.H

Savage, Hiram F. TX 16th Cav. Co.C

Savage, Hiram F. TX 22nd Cav. Co.B

Savage, Hiram T. TX 22nd Cav. Co.B

Savage, H.M. TN 14th (Neely's) Cav. Co.C

Savage, H.W. LA 3rd (Harrison's) Cav. Co.H

Savage, H.W. MS Cav. Ham's Regt. Co.H

Savage, I. MS 11th (Cons.) Cav. Co.H

Savage, I. VA Hvy.Arty. 19th Bn. Co.B

Savage, I.R. MS 2nd Cav.Res. Co.E Sgt.

Savage, J. AL 8th (Livingston's) Cav. Co.G 1st Lt.

Savage, J. TN Lt.Arty. Polk's Btty.

Savage, J.A. AL 58th Inf. Co.D

Savage, J.A. MS 2nd St.Cav. Co.H

Savage, J.A. MS St.Cav. 2nd Bn. (Harris') Co.C

Savage, J.A. MS 11th Inf. Co.C

Savage, James AL Lt.Arty. 2nd Bn. Co.B Cpl.

Savage, James AR Cav. Gordon's Regt. Co.B
Savage, James AR 19th (Dawson's) Inf. Co.F
Savage, James AR Inf. Hardy's Regt. Co.I,A
Savage, James GA 31st Inf. Co.K 1st Sgt.
Savage, James, Jr. GA 43rd Inf. Co.K
Savage, James, Sr. GA 43rd Inf. Co.K
Savage, James GA 53rd Inf. Co.B
Savage, James KY 2nd (Duke's) Cav. Co.C
Savage, James MS Lt.Arty. 14th Bn.
Savage, James MO 12th Cav. Co.I
Savage, James SC 15th Inf. Co.H Sgt.
Savage, James TN Cav. Newsom's Regt. Co.G
Savage, James TN 40th Inf. Co.H
Savage, James TN 51st (Cons.) Inf. Co.K
Savage, James TX 16th Cav. Co.I
Savage, James A. MS Cav. Ham's Regt. Co.I
Savage, James A.D. VA Hvy.Arty. 19th Bn. 3rd Co.E
Savage, James C. AL 5th Inf. New Co.I 1st Sgt.
Savage, James H. AL 19th Inf. Co.I Capt.
Savage, James K. TX 22nd Cav. Co.B
Savage, James K. VA 39th Inf. Co.D
Savage, James K. VA 115th Mil. Co.A Cpl.
Savage, James L. VA 16th Inf. 2nd Co.H Sgt.
Savage, James L. VA 39th Inf. Co.H Cpl.
Savage, James M. AR Cav. 1st Bn. (Stirman's) Co.G
Savage, James M. GA Inf. 1st Loc.Troops (Augusta) Co.F
Savage, James M. GA 63rd Inf. Co.A Band
Savage, James M. NC 1st Inf. (6 mo. '61) Co.A Cpl.
Savage, James M. TN Cav. Newsom's Regt. Co.D
Savage, James M. VA 41st Inf. Co.I
Savage, James Martin TN Cav. Newsom's Regt. Co.D
Savage, James Mc. NC 17th Inf. (2nd Org.) Co.I Cpl.
Savage, James R. TN Inf. 2nd Cons.Regt. Co.C
Savage, James R. TN 11th Inf. Co.G
Savage, James T. GA 20th Inf. Co.D
Savage, James T. VA 39th Inf. Co.I Orderly Sgt.
Savage, James T. 7th Conf.Cav. 1st Co.I, Co.H
Savage, James W. AL Lt.Arty. Phelan's Co.
Savage, James W. AR 1st Inf. Co.C
Savage, James W. FL 8th Inf. Co.G
Savage, James W. Sig.Corps,CSA
Savage, Jasper C. TN Cav. Newsom's Regt. Co.D
Savage, J.B. NC 3rd Arty. (40th St.Troops) Co.G
Savage, J.B. TN 8th Inf. Co.H
Savage, J.C. AL 9th Inf. Co.K Ord.Sgt.
Savage, Jeff. TN 11th (Holman's) Cav. Co.L
Savage, Jefferson L. AL 13th Inf. Co.K 1st Lt.,Adj.
Savage, Jerry AL 18th Inf. Co.A
Savage, Jerry AL 58th Inf. Co.D
Savage, Jesse NC 1st Inf. (6 mo. '61) Co.A
Savage, Jesse TN 16th Inf. Co.H
Savage, Jesse B. TN Cav. Shaw's Bn.
Savage, Jesse J. AL 13th Inf. Co.K Lt.
Savage, Jesse L. TN 19th Inf. Co.I
Savage, Jesse R. VA 16th Inf. Co.B
Savage, Jesse T. NC 44th Inf. Co.B

Savage, Jesse T. TN 5th Cav. Co.A
Savage, Jesse W. NC 33rd Inf. Co.E
Savage, Jethro VA 13th Cav. Co.C
Savage, J.F. MS 44th Inf. Co.B
Savage, J.G. AL 42nd Inf. Co.F
Savage, J.H. MS 3rd Cav.Res. Co.G
Savage, J.H. MS 18th Cav. Co.H
Savage, J.H. MS 2nd Inf. (A. of 10,000) Co.G Capt.
Savage, J.H. MS 9th Inf. New Co.H
Savage, J.H. MS 23rd Inf. Co.D
Savage, J.H. NC 2nd Inf. Co.A
Savage, J.H. TN 13th Inf. Co.C
Savage, J.H. TN 20th Inf. Co.C
Savage, J.H. VA 4th Cav. Co.I,F
Savage, J.L. GA 12th Cav. Co.E
Savage, J.L. NC 4th Cav. (59th St.Troops) Co.K
Savage, J.L. 8th (Dearing's) Conf.Cav. Co.A
Savage, J.M. AL 23rd Inf. Co.G
Savage, J.M. GA Lt.Arty. 12th Bn. 1st Co.A
Savage, J.M. GA 1st Reg. Co.F
Savage, J.M. TN 14th (Neely's) Cav. Co.C,D
Savage, Joel 7th Conf.Cav. Co.F
Savage, Joel 8th (Dearing's) Conf.Cav. Co.G
Savage, John AL Lt.Arty. 2nd Bn. Co.B Cpl.
Savage, John AL Seewell's Btty. (Mohawk Arty.)
Savage, John FL 5th Inf. Co.A
Savage, John FL 10th Inf. Co.E
Savage, John GA 24th Inf. Co.H
Savage, John LA 1st Hvy.Arty. (Reg.) Co.A
Savage, John LA C.S. Zouave Bn. Co.B Cpl.
Savage, John MS Cav. Ham's Regt. Co.A Sgt.
Savage, John MS 12th Inf. Co.I
Savage, John MS 43rd Inf. Co.L
Savage, John NC 13th Inf. Co.G
Savage, John NC 15th Inf. Co.G
Savage, John NC 30th Inf. Co.E
Savage, John SC Arty. Fickling's Co. (Brooks Lt.Arty.)
Savage, John SC 7th Res. Co.K Cpl.
Savage, John TN 8th Inf. Co.E Cpl.
Savage, John TN 15th Inf. Co.H
Savage, John VA 3rd Inf.Loc.Def. 1st Co.G
Savage, John C. VA 5th Cav. (12 mo. '61-2) Co.G
Savage, John H. MD 1st Cav. Co.E Sgt.
Savage, John H. NC 1st Arty. (10th St.Troops) Co.D,H
Savage, John H. NC 1st Arty. (10th St.Troops) Co.I
Savage, John H. NC 2nd Arty. (36th St.Troops) Co.A
Savage, John H. NC 3rd Arty. (40th St.Troops) Co.G
Savage, John H. SC 1st (McCreary's) Inf. Co.I
Savage, John H. SC 1st Inf. Co.M
Savage, John H. TN 21st (Wilson's) Cav. Co.E
Savage, John H. TN Cav. Newsom's Regt. Co.D
Savage, John H. TN 16th Inf. Col.
Savage, John H. VA 1st Arty. Co.I
Savage, John H. VA Hvy.Arty. 19th Bn. 2nd Co.C Cpl.
Savage, John H. VA 17th Inf. Co.A
Savage, John J. TX 22nd Cav. Co.B
Savage, John Jasper GA Cobb's Legion Co.E
Savage, John L. NC 3rd Cav. (41st St.Troops) Co.G

Savage, John L. NC Cav. 12th Bn. Co.A
Savage, John L. NC 43rd Inf. Co.E Cpl.
Savage, John M. TX 16th Cav. Co.G
Savage, John N. VA 13th Cav. Co.B
Savage, John N. VA 1st Arty. Co.E
Savage, John P. NC 1st Arty. (10th St.Troops) Co.E
Savage, John R. NC Coast Guards Galloway's Co.
Savage, John T. NC McDugald's Co.
Savage, John W. AL Lt.Arty. 2nd Bn. Co.F
Savage, John W. AL 44th Inf. Co.D
Savage, John W. LA Inf.Crescent Regt. Co.A
Savage, John W. MS Cav. Duncan's Co. (Tishomingo Rangers)
Savage, John W. MS 15th (Cons.) Inf. Co.K
Savage, John W. MS 23rd Inf. Co.D
Savage, John W. VA Hvy.Arty. 19th Bn. Co.B, 3rd Co.E 2nd Lt.
Savage, John W. VA 39th Inf. Co.H 1st Sgt.
Savage, John W. VA 39th Inf. Co.L
Savage, John W. VA 46th Inf. 4th Co.F
Savage, John Y. NC 3rd Cav. (41st St.Troops) Co.G 1st Lt.
Savage, Joseph AR 1st Mtd.Rifles Co.A
Savage, Joseph MS Lt.Arty. Yates' Btty.
Savage, Joseph NC 7th Inf. Co.E
Savage, Joseph A. AL 19th Inf. Co.I
Savage, Joseph B. NC 1st Arty. (10th St.Troops) Co.D
Savage, Joseph G. VA Hvy.Arty. 19th Bn. Co.B Sgt.
Savage, Joseph G. VA 39th Inf. Co.C
Savage, Joseph I. AR Cav. 15th Bn. (Buster's Bn.) Co.F
Savage, Joseph L. NC 1st Arty. (10th St.Troops) Co.H
Savage, Joseph S. AL 13th Inf. Co.K Sgt.
Savage, Joshua MS 1st (Johnston's) Inf. Co.B
Savage, Joshua H. MS 17th Inf. Co.K
Savage, Joshua H. MS 31st Inf. Co.D
Savage, J.P. AL 19th Inf. Co.I
Savage, J.T. AR 2nd Inf. Co.I
Savage, J.T. NC Mallett's Bn. Co.F
Savage, Julius TN 38th Inf. Co.G
Savage, J.W. AL 43rd Inf. Co.D
Savage, J.W. LA 18th Inf. Co.G
Savage, J.W. LA Inf.Crescent Regt. Co.E
Savage, J.W. LA Inf.Cons.Crescent Regt. Co.C
Savage, J.W. TN 40th Inf. Co.F
Savage, K.G. AL 1st Cav. 2nd Co.E
Savage, L. NC 2nd Jr.Res. Co.G
Savage, L.A. MO 2nd Inf. Co.B
Savage, L.A. TX 27th Cav. Co.K
Savage, Laban T. VA 16th Inf. Co.A
Savage, Lawrence J. LA 5th Inf. Co.F
Savage, L.D. AR 2nd Mtd.Rifles Co.H
Savage, L.D. AR 2nd Inf. Co.H
Savage, Leonard R. VA Hvy.Arty. 19th Bn. Co.B
Savage, Leonard R. VA 39th Inf. Co.A
Savage, Levi TN 9th (Ward's) Cav. Kirkpatrick's Co.
Savage, Levin H. TN Cav. Shaw's Bn. Hamilton's Co. Sgt.
Savage, L.J. AR 1st (Monroe's) Cav. Co.C
Savage, L.J. LA 1st Cav. Co.B 2nd Lt.

Savage, L.J. MS Cav. Ham's Regt. Co.C,A
Savage, L.N. TN 16th Inf. Co.A Capt.
Savage, L.O. AR 14th (Powers') Inf. Co.H Cpl.
Savage, Lott W. AL 19th Inf. Co.I
Savage, Lott W. Gen. & Staff Surg.
Savage, L.T. NC Lt.Arty. 13th Bn. Co.C
Savage, Lucius N. NC 2nd Cav. (19th St.Troops) Co.C Bugler
Savage, Luke W. TX 22nd Cav. Co.B
Savage, L.W. GA 6th Cav. Co.H
Savage, M. AL 6th Cav. Co.C
Savage, M. AL Cp. of Instr. Talladega Co.D
Savage, Marion AL 19th Inf. Co.I
Savage, Marshal AL 42nd Inf. Co.G
Savage, Marshall AL 51st (Part.Rangers) Co.E
Savage, M.D. GA 2nd Inf. Co.B
Savage, M.D. GA 13th Inf. Co.B
Savage, M.D. GA 19th Inf. Co.B
Savage, Merideth NC 5th Inf. Co.B
Savage, Michael MS 30th Inf. Co.H
Savage, Michael L. VA 9th Inf. Co.I
Savage, Moses AL 22nd Inf. Co.C
Savage, Moses KY 2nd (Duke's) Cav. Co.C
Savage, Moses LA Inf. 4th Bn. Co.C
Savage, Nathaniel L. AL 44th Inf. Co.C
Savage, N.R. VA 3rd Inf.Loc.Def. Co.A
Savage, Orran B. NC 5th Inf. Asst.Surg.
Savage, Orrin B. AL Rives Supp.Force 9th Congr.Dist.
Savage, O.W. AL 1st Regt. Mobile Vol. Co.E
Savage, O.W. AL 4th Res. Co.C
Savage, Owen LA 15th Inf. Co.A
Savage, Owen R. NC 4th Cav. (59th St.Troops) Co.C
Savage, Pat GA Inf. 1st City Bn. (Columbus) Co.B
Savage, Patrick TN 2nd (Walker's) Inf. Co.D
Savage, Patrick 9th Conf.Inf. Co.E
Savage, Patrick H. LA 21st (Patton's) Inf. Co.A 2nd Lt.
Savage, Paul SC 3rd Cav. Co.B
Savage, Paul T. VA 51st Inf. Co.B
Savage, Pendleton AL 12th Inf. Co.A
Savage, Philip TX 26th Cav. Co.C 2nd Lt.
Savage, Pleasant S. AL 38th Inf. Co.C
Savage, Preston VA 39th Inf. Co.A
Savage, R. AL 8th Inf. Co.F
Savage, R. GA 18th Inf. Co.D
Savage, R. NC 4th Cav. (59th St.Troops) Co.C
Savage, R.A. AL 1st Bn.Cadets Co.A Sgt.
Savage, R.A. NC 1st Arty. (10th St.Troops) Co.H
Savage, Randle AL 43rd Inf. Co.D
Savage, Richard FL 10th Inf. Co.E
Savage, Richard NC 2nd Arty. (36th St.Troops) Co.D
Savage, Richard B. FL 8th Inf. Co.G
Savage, Richard R. VA Hvy.Arty. 19th Bn. Co.B
Savage, Richard R. VA 39th Inf. Co.K
Savage, Richard S. AL 6th Inf. Co.M
Savage, Robert FL 10th Inf. Co.E
Savage, Robert TX 16th Cav. Co.I
Savage, Robert B. FL 8th Inf. Co.G
Savage, Robert M. MS 23rd Inf. Co.D 2nd Lt.
Savage, Robert R. AL 47th Inf. Co.E 1st Lt.
Savage, Robert T. VA 39th Inf. Co.D
Savage, Robert T. VA 39th Inf. Co.L

Savage, Robert W. NC McDugald's Co.
Savage, Roland TN Inf. 154th Sr.Regt. Co.C 1st Lt.
Savage, R.P. LA 17th Inf. Co.C
Savage, R.R. AL 1st Cav. Co.G Ord.Sgt.
Savage, R.R. AL 12th Cav. Co.G 1st Sgt.
Savage, R.S. AL 5th Inf. New Co.K
Savage, Russell GA 43rd Inf. Co.K
Savage, S. MS 10th Cav. Co.K
Savage, S. MS Cav. Ham's Regt. Co.H
Savage, Samuel B. TX 22nd Cav. Co.B 2nd Lt.
Savage, Samuel H. GA 12th Cav. Co.E
Savage, Samuel H. GA 6th Inf. Co.B
Savage, S.B. TX Cav. Martin's Regt. Co.D Capt.
Savage, Severn J. VA Hvy.Arty. 19th Bn. Co.B QMSgt.
Savage, Severn W. VA 39th Inf. Co.A
Savage, Simon VA 59th Mil. Hunter's Co.
Savage, S.L. VA 3rd Cav. Co.H
Savage, S.M. MS 10th Inf. Co.L, New Co.C
Savage, Solomon K. VA 41st Inf. Co.I
Savage, Southey L. VA 3rd Cav. Co.F 3rd Lt.
Savage, Starling TN 35th Inf. 2nd Co.D
Savage, Sylvester C. VA 39th Inf. Co.L
Savage, Sylvester C. VA 46th Inf. 4th Co.F
Savage, T. NC 2nd Jr.Res. Co.G
Savage, Taylor GA 43rd Inf. Co.D
Savage, Taylor GA 52nd Inf. Co.A
Savage, T.D. MS Inf. Comfort's Co.
Savage, Teagle J. Sig.Corps,CSA
Savage, Teakle J. VA 9th Inf. Co.K
Savage, T.F. MS 43rd Inf. Co.F
Savage, Thomas AL 41st Inf. Co.G
Savage, Thomas AR Lt.Arty. Thrall's Btty.
Savage, Thomas GA 43rd Inf. Co.K
Savage, Thomas LA Mil. Brenan's Co. (Co.A, Shamrock Guards)
Savage, Thomas TX Cav. Baird's Regt. Co.E
Savage, Thomas VA 3rd Inf. Co.H
Savage, Thomas A. NC 21st Inf. Co.I Sgt.
Savage, Thomas A. VA 9th Inf. Co.G
Savage, Thomas B. AL 15th Bn.Part.Rangers Asst.Surg.
Savage, Thos. B. Gen. & Staff Asst.Surg.
Savage, Thomas D. LA 7th Inf. Co.E
Savage, Thomas E. FL 8th Inf. Co.G
Savage, Thomas H. VA Hvy.Arty. 19th Bn. Co.B
Savage, Thomas H. VA Lt.Arty. Nelson's Co.
Savage, Thomas H. VA 39th Inf. Co.D Cpl.
Savage, Thomas H. VA 39th Inf. Co.I
Savage, Thomas H.B. VA Hvy.Arty. 19th Bn. Co.B
Savage, Thomas J. AL 21st Inf. Co.D 1st Lt.
Savage, Thomas J. MS 10th Inf. Old Co.B
Savage, Thomas J. NC 2nd Arty. (36th St.Troops) Co.B
Savage, Thomas K. VA 5th Cav. Co.C
Savage, Thomas L.P. AL 19th Inf. Co.I
Savage, Thomas N. TX 14th Cav. Co.F
Savage, Thomas O. VA Hvy.Arty. 19th Bn. Co.B
Savage, Thomas O. VA 39th Inf. Co.A
Savage, Thomas P. VA 5th Cav. (12 mo. '61-2) Co.G
Savage, Thomas P. VA 13th Cav. Co.I

Savage, Thomas T.P. GA 6th Cav. Co.H Sgt.
Savage, Thomas W. GA Cav. 1st Bn. Brailsford's Co.
Savage, Thomas W. GA 5th Cav. Co.H
Savage, Thomas W. VA 41st Inf. Co.I Cpl.
Savage, Timothy M. NC Hvy.Arty. 1st Bn. Co.B
Savage, T.J. NC Lt.Arty. 13th Bn. Co.B
Savage, T.M.A. MS Cav. Ham's Regt. Co.A
Savage, T.R. TX Cav. Hardeman's Regt. Co.A
Savage, Tyding NC 2nd Cav. (19th St.Troops) Co.I
Savage, Valentine AL Lt.Arty. 2nd Bn.
Savage, W. GA 62nd Cav. Co.L
Savage, W.A. LA 17th Inf. Co.C Cpl.
Savage, W.B. TN 13th Cav. Co.D
Savage, W.B. TN Lt.Arty. Polk's Btty. Sgt.
Savage, W.C. LA Mil. Orleans Fire Regt. Co.C
Savage, W.D. GA 13th Inf. Co.B
Savage, Wesley NC 24th Inf. Co.D
Savage, W.F. LA 4th Cav. Co.G
Savage, W.H. TN Arty. Marshall's Co.
Savage, W.I. TN 40th Inf. Co.H
Savage, William AL Pris.Guard Freeman's Co.
Savage, Wm. AL Cp. of Instr. Talladega
Savage, William NC 1st Cav. (9th St.Troops) Co.G
Savage, William NC 12th Inf. Co.C
Savage, William SC 7th Cav. Co.C
Savage, William SC 7th Res. Co.K
Savage, William SC Cav.Bn. Holcombe Legion Co.D
Savage, William TN 8th Inf. Co.H
Savage, William TN 14th Inf. Co.I
Savage, William TN 24th Inf. Co.A
Savage, William VA 9th Inf. Co.I
Savage, William A. GA Inf. 1st Loc.Troops (Augusta) Co.F
Savage, William A. TX 6th Cav. Co.D
Savage, William B. TN Cav. Newsom's Regt. Co.D
Savage, William E. NC 3rd Cav. (41st St.Troops) Co.K
Savage, William F. TN Cav. Shaw's Bn. Co.A
Savage, William H. NC 1st Inf. (6 mo. '61) Co.I
Savage, William H. NC 43rd Inf. Co.F
Savage, William H. NC 53rd Inf. Co.H
Savage, William J. AL 41st Inf. Co.G
Savage, William J. GA 14th Inf. Co.B
Savage, William L. NC 17th Inf. (2nd Org.) Co.I
Savage, William L. VA Lt.Arty. Brander's Co.
Savage, William M. AR 27th Inf. Co.E
Savage, William M. NC 1st Inf. Co.K
Savage, William M. TX Cav. Martin's Regt. Co.B
Savage, William N. NC 1st Arty. (10th St.Troops) Co.D
Savage, William N. NC 3rd Arty. (40th St.Troops) Co.G
Savage, William P. NC 1st Arty. (10th St.Troops) Co.I
Savage, William P. NC 2nd Arty. (36th St.Troops) Co.A
Savage, William R. NC 1st Inf. (6 mo. '61) Co.A
Savage, William R. NC 44th Inf. Co.B
Savage, William S. Conf.Cav. Wood's Regt. 2nd Co.G

Savage, William W. NC 17th Inf. (2nd Org.) Co.E
Savage, Willis VA 24th Cav. Co.I
Savage, Willis 8th (Dearing's) Conf.Cav. Co.D
Savage, Willis W. NC 5th Inf. Co.B
Savage, Willoughbey VA 4th Inf. Co.D
Savage, W.J. TN 33rd Inf. Co.B
Savage, W.M. AL 18th Inf. Co.G
Savage, W.M. SC 5th Cav. Co.K
Savage, W.S. MS 2nd Inf. (A. of 10,000) Co.G
Savage, Zachariah T. MS Inf. 5th Bn. Co.B
Savage, Zachariah T. MS 27th Inf. Co.K
Savage, Zebulon G. AR 1st Mtd.Rifles Co.I
Savage, Z.F. MS 14th (Cons.) Inf. Co.G
Savage, Z.F. MS 43rd Inf. Co.L
Savage, Z.T. MS 37th Inf. Co.K
Savageot, V.M. VA 10th Cav. Co.D
Savages, J.J. AR 35th Inf. Co.G
Saval, George TX 22nd Inf. Co.D
Savally, Henry GA 26th Inf. Co.B
Savan, R. AL 47th Inf. Co.H
Savanah, M. NC 5th Inf. Co.I
Savant, Ducis LA 2nd Res.Corps Co.I
Savant, Horthere LA 8th Inf. Co.F
Savant, Joseph LA Miles' Legion Co.D
Savant, O. LA Siege Train Bn. Co.D
Savant, Omer LA 8th Inf. Co.F Sgt.
Savant, Onile LA 3rd (Harrison's) Cav. Co.K
Savant, P.O. LA 16th Inf. Co.K
Savard, John LA Mil. Beauregard Bn. Co.C
Savarese, Saveris LA Mil. Cazadores Espanoles Regt. Co.F
Savario, John LA 28th (Thomas') Inf. Co.E
Savary, Charles AL Mil. Co.D 1st Lt.
Savary, Charles AL 8th Cav. Co.H Sgt.
Savary, Henry LA Mil. 1st Native Guards
Savary, Wiley P. TX 6th Inf. Co.D
Savassa, Augustus MS 44th Inf. Co.G
Savaye, R.S. AL Inf. 1st Regt. Co.C
Saveall, David AR 4th Inf. Co.F
Saveall, George GA 11th Cav. Co.I
Saveall, J.P. GA 30th Inf. Co.D
Savedge, George A. VA Lt.Arty. Hankins' Co.
Savedge, J.T. VA Lt.Arty. Hankins' Co.
Savedge, Richard R. VA Lt.Arty. Hankins' Co. Cpl.
Savedge, Richard R. VA 3rd Inf. 1st Co.I
Savedge, Travis VA Lt.Arty. Hankins' Co.
Savedge, Virginius A. VA 5th Cav. (12 mo. '61-2) Co.E
Savedge, Virginius A. VA 13th Cav. Co.G
Savedge, William H. VA 13th Cav. Co.G
Savedge, Winfield S. VA 13th Cav. Co.G
Savedge, Wingfield S. VA 5th Cav. (12 mo. '61-2) Co.E
Savell, James M. TX 13th Cav. Co.D
Savell, Jasper MS 33rd Inf. Co.A
Savell, J.B. GA Siege Arty. 28th Bn. Co.G
Savell, J.B. GA 55th Inf. Co.G
Savell, J.G.S. MS 5th Inf. Co.K
Savell, Joab GA 55th Inf. Co.B
Savell, John W. GA 55th Inf. Co.G,C
Savell, Joseph VA 33rd Inf. Co.F
Savell, M. MS 35th Inf. Co.E
Savell, P.J. TX Cav. (Loc.Def.) Durant's Co.
Savell, P.J. TX Cav. Madison's Regt. Co.B
Savell, Rolin B. MS 33rd Inf. Co.A

Savell, Samuel T. GA 51st Inf. Co.G
Savell, T.S. MD Arty. 3rd Btty.
Savell, William TN 5th (McKenzie's) Cav. Co.I
Savelle, A.M. MS 10th Inf. New Co.H
Savelle, John A. MS 10th Inf. New Co.H
Savells, A.G. MS 6th Inf. Co.C
Savells, Malachi NC 56th Inf. Co.A,I
Savells, S.W. KY 3rd Mtd.Inf. Co.C
Savells, Thomas P. NC 56th Inf. Co.A Capt.
Savelly, John W. MS Cav. Jeff Davis Legion Co.B
Savelly, William MS Cav. Jeff Davis Legion Co.B
Savely, Daniel TN 44th (Cons.) Inf.
Savely, John 8th (Wade's) Conf.Cav. Co.C
Savely, John 4th Conf.Inf. Co.E
Savely, J.W. TN 18th Inf. Co.B
Savely, R.E. 8th (Wade's) Conf.Cav. Co.C
Savely, Richard E. LA 8th Inf. Co.C
Savely, W.H. MS Cav. 4th Bn. Co.A Sgt.
Savely, W.H. 8th (Wade's) Conf.Cav. Co.C
Savely, W.S. MS Standefer's Co.
Saver, Barnabus VA 54th Inf. Co.K
Saver, James M. VA 48th Inf. Co.C
Saver, W.R. NC 35th Inf. Co.F
Saverance, Elias SC 14th Inf. Co.A
Saverance, G.W. SC 14th Inf. Co.A
Saverance, J.J.W. SC 14th Inf. Co.A
Saverance, Joseph J. SC 14th Inf. Co.A
Saverance, Paul A. SC 14th Inf. Co.A
Saverance, R.E. SC 8th Inf. Co.A
Saverance, Thomas G. SC Lt.Arty. 3rd (Palmetto) Bn. Co.C
Saverly, H.T. TN 1st (Feild's) Inf. Co.L
Saverly, H.T. TN Inf. Nashville Bn. Cattles' Co.
Saverly, John MS 2nd St.Cav. Co.G
Saverly, John S. TN 9th (Ward's) Cav. Co.B
Saverly, L. TN 1st (Feild's) Inf.
Saverly, William TN 9th (Ward's) Cav. Co.B
Savery, Ed O. LA Inf.Crescent Regt.
Savery, Harvey T. TX 6th Inf. Co.D
Savery, J.H. FL Lt.Arty. Abell's Co.
Savery, Phineas M. MO 2nd Cav. Co.C Capt.
Savery, P.M. MO St.Guard Capt.
Saves, A. LA Mil. 3rd Regt.Eur.Brig. (Garde Francaise) Co.7
Savey, J.N. AL Talladega Cty.Res. J. Henderson's Co.
Savier, J.B. AL Mil. 2nd Regt.Vol. Co.C
Savil, Alfred MS 44th Inf. Co.A
Savil, H. MS Cav. Williams' Co.
Savil, H.M. SC 5th St.Troops Co.K
Savile, H.M. SC 3rd Bn.Res. Co.C
Savill, A.G. MS 40th Inf. Co.B
Savill, A.J. MS 40th Inf. Co.B
Savill, E.B. MS 33rd Inf. Co.A
Savill, George E. VA Lt.Arty. Parker's Co. 2nd Lt.
Savill, James W. VA 114th Mil. Co.K Sgt.
Savill, J.K. GA 4th Cav. (St.Guards) Deadwyler's Co.
Savill, J.M. NC 1st Inf. (6 mo. '61) Co.C
Savill, Joseph VA 18th Cav. Co.K
Savill, Joseph VA 114th Mil. Co.B
Savill, Peter A. VA 114th Mil. Co.B
Savill, W.H. NC 1st Inf. (6 mo. '61) Co.C
Savill, William VA 18th Cav. Co.K

Saville, Albert VA 2nd Inf. Co.D
Saville, George MS Cav. Ham's Regt. Co.D Sgt.
Saville, George MS 11th Inf. Co.C Fifer
Saville, George VA 19th Cav.
Saville, George W. VA 18th Cav. Co.C
Saville, George W. VA 114th Mil. Co.E
Saville, H.M. SC 6th Res. Co.G
Saville, Isaac VA 114th Mil. Co.F
Saville, Jacob A. TN 63rd Inf. Co.B,G Cpl.
Saville, James H. VA 114th Mil. Co.E Cpl.
Saville, James M. NC 11th (Bethel Regt.) Inf. Co.H 2nd Lt.
Saville, James W. VA 11th Cav. Co.D
Saville, J.B. GA Siege Arty. 28th Bn. Co.G
Saville, J.C. NC 30th Inf. Co.K Cpl.
Saville, Jerry O. VA 62nd Mtd.Inf. 2nd Co.B
Saville, John VA 11th Cav. Co.B
Saville, John VA Lt.Arty. Arch. Graham's Co.
Saville, John VA 114th Mil. Co.E
Saville, John F. TN 63rd Inf. Co.G
Saville, John G. VA 11th Cav. Co.D
Saville, John O. VA 18th Cav. Co.C
Saville, John O. VA 114th Mil. Co.E
Saville, Joseph VA 14th Cav. Co.H
Saville, Joseph VA Rockbridge Cty.Res. Miller's Co.
Saville, Lewis Conf.Reg.Inf. Brooks' Bn. Co.F
Saville, Louis Conf.Reg.Inf. Brooks' Bn. Co.F
Saville, M.J. FL 1st Inf. New Co.G
Saville, Olover VA 114th Mil. Co.E
Saville, Perry VA 13th Inf. Co.I
Saville, Peter VA 62nd Mtd.Inf. 1st Co.G
Saville, Peter A. VA 18th Cav. Co.K
Saville, Robert AL 12th Inf. Co.A
Saville, Robert D. NC 11th (Bethel Regt.) Inf. Co.H Sgt.
Saville, Walker VA 18th Cav. Co.K
Saville, W.H. GA 46th Inf. Co.F
Saville, W.H. GA 48th Inf. Co.F
Saville, William VA 33rd Inf. Co.A
Saville, William VA 114th Mil. Co.G
Savilley, S.R. GA 47th Inf. Co.E
Savills, James KY 8th Mtd.Inf. Co.G
Savills, Marcus A. NC 32nd Inf. Co.I
Savills, Marcus A. VA 61st Inf. Co.C
Savills, Thomas NC 32nd Inf. Co.I
Savills, William F. NC 32nd Inf. Co.B 1st Lt.
Savin, Edward VA 2nd Inf. Co.K
Savin, Richard H. VA 40th Inf. Co.A Sgt.
Savin, William A. VA 40th Inf. Co.A
Savings, Newton AL 10th Inf. Co.I
Savini, Carlo LA Mil. Cazadores Espanoles Regt. Co.F
Savini, Luigi LA Mil. Cazadores Espanoles Regt. Co.F
Savinovich, Giorgio LA Mil. 4th Regt.Eur.Brig. Cognevich's Co.
Savins, James VA Cav. 14th Bn. Co.D
Savioi, Elias LA 26th Inf. Co.A
Saviors, James MO 8th Cav. Co.F Cpl.
Savirs, Theodore LA Mil. Assumption Regt. Capt.
Savoi, P. LA Mil. Chalmette Regt. Co.K Cpl.
Savoi, Thougene LA 28th (Gray's) Inf. Co.A
Savoie, Achille LA 2nd Cav. Co.H
Savoie, Alcide LA 2nd Res.Corps Co.K

Savoie, Bonneval LA 30th Inf. Co.H Cpl.
Savoie, Charles LA Conscr.
Savoie, Clerville LA Arty. Landry's Co.
 (Donaldsonville Arty.)
Savoie, D.L. LA 2nd Res.Corps Co.A
Savoie, Emile LA 2nd Cav. Co.C
Savoie, Esthival LA 18th Inf. Co.G
Savoie, Joseph LA 28th (Thomas') Inf. Co.A
Savoie, Jules LA Arty. Landry's Co. (Donaldson-
 ville Arty.)
Savoie, Jules LA Inf. 1st Sp.Bn. (Rightor's) Co.E
Savoie, Lezimo LA 2nd Cav. Co.C
Savoie, Marcellin LA 26th Inf. Co.H
Savoie, Pierre LA 28th (Thomas') Inf. Co.A
Savoie, Robert LA 18th Inf. Co.G 1st Sgt.
Savoie, Robert LA Inf.Cons. 18th Regt. & Yel-
 low Jacket Bn. Co.F
Savoir, D. LA 26th Inf. Co.A
Savoir, E. LA 7th Cav. Co.A
Savoir, Felix LA Mil. LaFourche Regt.
Savoir, H. LA Inf.Cons. 18th Regt. & Yellow
 Jacket Bn. Co.H
Savoir, H. LA 26th Inf. Co.A
Savoir, H.V. LA 18th Inf. Co.I
Savois, Jean LA 26th Inf. Co.E
Savois, Julien LA Inf.Cons. 18th Regt. & Yellow
 Jacket Bn. Co.A
Savois, Theodore LA Mil. LaFourche Regt.
Savoit, John Bt. LA Arty. King's Btty.
Savoit, John Bt. LA Inf.Cons.Crescent Regt.
 Co.H
Savom, J.F. AL 21st Inf.
Savon, D.L. LA Inf. 10th Bn.
Savon, Joseph LA 18th Inf. Co.I
Savory, David W. VA Hvy.Arty. 18th Bn. Co.C
Savory, David W. VA Horse Arty. E. Graham's
 Co.
Savory, D.W. Conf.Arty. Lewis' Bn. Co.C
Savory, O.A. VA 2nd Inf.Loc.Def. Co.F
Savory, O.A. VA Inf. 6th Bn.Loc.Def. Co.C
Savoy, C. Conf.Lt.Arty. Richardson's Bn. Co.B
Savoy, C.M. LA 18th Inf. Co.I
Savoy, Edward LA Inf. 16th Bn. (Conf.Guards
 Resp.Bn.) Co.B
Savoy, F. LA 2nd Cav. Co.A
Savoy, Onisime LA Inf. 16th Bn. (Conf.Guards
 Resp.Bn.) Co.B
Savoy, P. LA 22nd Inf. Co.E
Savoy, P. LA 22nd (Cons.) Inf. Co.E
Savoye, Victor LA Inf.Crescent Regt. Co.F Sgt.
Savoye, Victor LA Inf.Cons.Crescent Regt.
 Co.G,O 1st Sgt.
Savvage, T.A. TN 13th (Gore's) Cav. Co.A
Saw, George TX 15th Field Btty.
Saw, George H. TX 1st Field Btty.
Saw, George Henry TX 4th Field Btty.
Sawands, J. MS 1st (Percy's) Inf. Co.I
Sawdell, M.H. AL 26th (O'Neal's) Inf. Co.K
Sawel, J.L. AR 10th Inf. Co.C
Sawell, J.W. AR 5th Inf. Co.I Cpl.
Sawell, T.C. AL 37th Inf. Co.A Sgt.
Sawers, Henry TX 5th Cav. Co.H
Sawey, Roland TX 4th Cav. Co.B
Sawhardt, Nicholas MS 13th Inf. Co.G
Sawiers, H.F. MS 5th Cav. Co.H
Sawilske, Otto MS 18th Inf. Co.I Sgt.
Sawing, William A. NC 28th Inf.

Sawkey, T.L. AL 22nd Inf. Co.K
Sawlaw, Lemuel VA 62nd Mtd.Inf. 2nd Co.M
Sawles, Allen W. GA 46th Inf. Co.G,K
Sawles, J.W. FL 5th Inf. Co.C
Sawley, Ariostus GA 1st (Ramsey's) Inf. Co.K
Sawley, Jackson GA 1st Reg. Co.I
Sawley, J.W. AL 34th Inf. Co.B
Sawley, Randol G. GA 30th Inf. Co.F
Sawley, William T. GA 30th Inf. Co.F
Sawls, Christopher MS 7th Inf. Co.E
Sawls, James B. NC 3rd Cav. (41st St.Troops)
 Co.I
Sawn, J.R. AL 9th Inf. Co.B
Sawner, Isaac VA 79th Mil. Co.1
Sawrey, James NC 61st Inf. Co.F
Sawrie, John W. TN 6th Inf. Co.I
Sawrie, R.A. TN 12th (Green's) Cav. Co.H
Sawrie, Richard S. MO Cav. Wood's Regt. Co.C
Sawrie, William D.F. MO Cav. Wood's Regt.
 Co.C
Sawrie, William S. AR 2nd Inf. Co.F Adj.
Sawrie, William S. TN 1st (Feild's) Inf. Co.B
Sawrie, W.S. Govan's Brig. 1st Lt.
Sawtell, H.C. TN Cav. 16th Bn. (Neal's) Co.B
Sawtell, Isaac T. GA 64th Inf. Co.A
Sawtell, Isaac Y. Gen. & Staff Hosp.Stew.
Sawtell, James P. GA 2nd Inf. Co.D
Sawtell, J.B. LA Inf. 9th Bn. Co.C
Sawthoff, Foggy TX 1st (McCulloch's) Cav.
 Co.B
Sawyars, Samuel NC 17th Inf. (2nd Org.) Co.B
Sawyars, Timothy NC 17th Inf. (2nd Org.) Co.B
Sawyer, --- MS 11th Inf. Co.E
Sawyer, A. AL 5th Inf. New Co.C
Sawyer, A. AL 5th Inf. New Co.K
Sawyer, A. GA Cav. 16th Bn. (St.Guards) Co.D
Sawyer, Adison D. AL 61st Inf. Co.G
Sawyer, A.L. MS 6th Inf. Co.C
Sawyer, A.L. MS 40th Inf. Co.B
Sawyer, A.L. SC 5th Cav. Co.F
Sawyer, Albert VA 9th Inf. Co.I
Sawyer, Albert B. TX 2nd Cav. Co.E
Sawyer, Alex. T. AL 57th Inf. Co.F
Sawyer, Amelic S. VA Hvy.Arty. 18th Bn. Co.A
 Cpl.
Sawyer, Anciel SC Inf.Bn. Co.C
Sawyer, Ancil SC 19th Inf. Co.A
Sawyer, Andrew F. NC 2nd Inf. Co.G 1st Sgt.
Sawyer, Ansel MS 10th Inf. Old Co.B, New
 Co.G
Sawyer, Ansell LA 1st Hvy.Arty. (Reg.) Co.H
Sawyer, A.P. GA 7th Cav. Co.C
Sawyer, Archibald NC 12th Inf. Co.M
Sawyer, Archibald NC 21st Inf. Co.A
Sawyer, Archibald NC 32nd Inf. Co.B
Sawyer, B. AL 7th Cav. Co.K
Sawyer, Barney AL 62nd Inf. Co.H
Sawyer, Ben MS 44th Inf. Co.I Capt.
Sawyer, Benjamin F. AL 24th Inf. Co.K Lt.Col.
Sawyer, Benjamin R. NC 33rd Inf. Co.F
Sawyer, C. TN Cav. Napier's Bn. Co.A
Sawyer, C.A. GA Hvy.Arty. 22nd Bn. Co.F
Sawyer, Caleb T. VA Hvy.Arty. 20th Bn. Co.B
Sawyer, Caleb T. VA 38th Inf. 2nd Co.I
Sawyer, C.D. AL 33rd Inf. Co.K
Sawyer, C.G. AR 10th Inf. Co.D
Sawyer, Charles NC 8th Bn.Part.Rangers Co.A

Sawyer, Charles TN 10th (DeMoss') Cav. Co.D
Sawyer, Charles H.H. NC 12th Inf. Co.L
Sawyer, Charles H.H. NC 32nd Inf. Co.F,A
 Cpl.
Sawyer, C.M. LA Inf. 4th Bn. Co.E
Sawyer, C.M. MS 1st (Patton's) Inf. Co.A
Sawyer, Coston G. NC 32nd Inf. Co.I
Sawyer, Coston G. NC 56th Inf. Co.A
Sawyer, Coston J. TX Cav. Morgan's Regt.
 Co.A
Sawyer, D. TN Cav. Napier's Bn. Co.A
Sawyer, Daniel NC 33rd Inf. Co.F
Sawyer, Daniel TN 5th Inf. 2nd Co.K
Sawyer, Daniel A. NC 8th Inf. Co.A Capt.
Sawyer, David D. NC 17th Inf. (1st Org.) Co.E
Sawyer, D.C. GA 27th Inf. Co.C
Sawyer, Demsey FL 8th Inf. Co.H
Sawyer, Dionicius AL Rives' Supp.Force 9th
 Congr.Dist.
Sawyer, D.R. TN 10th (DeMoss') Cav. Co.D
Sawyer, D.R. TN Cav. Napier's Bn. Co.A
Sawyer, Drury SC 9th Inf. Co.K
Sawyer, D.S. SC Palmetto S.S. Co.F
Sawyer, E. AL 1st Inf. Co.C
Sawyer, E. AL Mil. 4th Vol. Co.I Sgt.
Sawyer, E. AR 11th Inf. Co.F
Sawyer, E. AR 11th & 17th Cons.Inf. Co.F
Sawyer, E. MS 2nd Cav. 2nd Co.G
Sawyer, Earl TX 27th Cav. Co.B
Sawyer, Earle AR 1st St.Cav. 3rd Lt.
Sawyer, Ebenezer W. NC 32nd Inf. Co.B Cpl.
Sawyer, Edwin VA 6th Inf. 2nd Co.B
Sawyer, E.H. AL 59th Inf. Co.C
Sawyer, Elcanah MS 5th Cav. Co.A
Sawyer, Eldridge AR Cav. Wright's Regt. Co.I
Sawyer, Elijah NC 12th Inf. Co.M
Sawyer, Elijah NC 32nd Inf. Co.B
Sawyer, Elijah NC 32nd Inf. Co.I
Sawyer, E.M.B. TX 15th Inf. Co.A Capt.
Sawyer, Enoch NC 32nd Inf. Co.I
Sawyer, Enoch VA 54th Mil. Co.E,F
Sawyer, E.P. MO Inf. Winston's Regt. Co.A
Sawyer, E.R. MS 44th Inf. Co.A
Sawyer, E.V. AL 36th Inf. Co.F
Sawyer, E.W. NC 3rd Cav. (41st St.Troops)
 Co.I
Sawyer, E.W. NC 66th Inf. Co.E
Sawyer, F.A. SC 1st Regt. Charleston Guard
 Co.A
Sawyer, F.H. LA Washington Arty.Bn. Co.2
Sawyer, F.M. GA 7th Inf. Co.B
Sawyer, Francis M. MS 19th Inf. Co.B,D
Sawyer, Fred KY 2nd Mtd.Inf. Co.D
Sawyer, G.A. NC 6th Inf. Co.H
Sawyer, George AL 59th Inf. Co.G
Sawyer, George NC 12th Inf. Co.M
Sawyer, George NC 17th Inf. (1st Org.) Co.A
Sawyer, George NC 32nd Inf. 1st Co.B
Sawyer, George NC 32nd Inf. 2nd Co.B
Sawyer, George SC 1st Arty. Co.F
Sawyer, George VA 6th Inf. 2nd Co.B
Sawyer, George C. SC 2nd Cav. Co.C
Sawyer, George R. SC 2nd St.Troops Co.G Sgt.
Sawyer, George W. NC 4th Cav. (59th
 St.Troops) Co.G Cpl.
Sawyer, George W. TX 16th Inf. Co.I

Sawyer, George W. VA 5th Cav. (12 mo. '61-2) Co.I
Sawyer, George W. VA 15th Cav. Co.I
Sawyer, Gideon L. VA 61st Inf. Co.C
Sawyer, Green B. GA 51st Inf. Co.C
Sawyer, H. GA 32nd Inf. Co.B
Sawyer, H. VA 54th Mil. Co.C,D
Sawyer, Halstead D. NC 56th Inf. Co.C
Sawyer, Harvey A. NC 2nd Inf. Co.G Capt.
Sawyer, Henry H. NC 3rd Arty. (40th St.Troops) Co.D
Sawyer, Henry H. NC 32nd Inf. Co.A
Sawyer, Henry W. NC 42nd Inf. Co.G
Sawyer, Hiram A. NC 2nd Inf. Co.G 2nd Lt.
Sawyer, Holman LA 13th Bn. (Part.Rangers) Co.A
Sawyer, Hor VA 54th Mil. Co.H
Sawyer, Horatio VA 16th Inf. 2nd Co.H
Sawyer, H.S. GA 6th Inf. Co.C
Sawyer, H.W. GA 5th Res. Co.A
Sawyer, I. MS Cav. Yerger's Regt. Co.A
Sawyer, I.L. VA 5th Cav. Co.A
Sawyer, I.M. MO 10th Cav. Co.K
Sawyer, Isaac NC 32nd Inf. Co.I
Sawyer, Isaac TN Inf. Spencer's Co.
Sawyer, Isaac J. NC Inf. Thomas Legion Co.H Cpl.
Sawyer, Isaac L. NC 17th Inf. (1st Org.) Co.L 3rd Lt.
Sawyer, Isaac L. VA 5th Cav. (12 mo.'61-2) Co.A
Sawyer, Isaac L. VA Cav. 14th Bn. Co.C
Sawyer, Isaac L. VA 15th Cav. Co.C
Sawyer, J. GA 15th Inf.
Sawyer, J. VA 6th Cav. Co.A
Sawyer, Jackson KY 3rd Cav.
Sawyer, Jacob SC 2nd St.Troops Co.G
Sawyer, Jacob VA 11th Cav. Co.B
Sawyer, James AL 45th Inf. Co.I
Sawyer, James GA 10th Mil. Co.B
Sawyer, James MO 9th Bn.S.S. Co.C
Sawyer, James MO 10th Inf. Co.G
Sawyer, James NC 56th Inf. Co.A Cpl.
Sawyer, James NC 64th Inf. Co.C
Sawyer, James SC 3rd Inf. Co.E
Sawyer, James TN 15th (Stewart's) Cav. Co.A
Sawyer, James TN 44th Inf. Co.E
Sawyer, James TN 47th Inf. Co.C
Sawyer, James TN Inf. Spencer's Co.
Sawyer, James TX Cav. Giddings' Bn. Weisiger's Co.
Sawyer, James A. MO 1st Cav. Co.K
Sawyer, James A. SC 21st Inf. Co.L Cpl.
Sawyer, James H. AL 26th (O'Neal's) Inf. Co.A
Sawyer, James H. AR 3rd Inf. Co.B Cpl.
Sawyer, James H. NC 12th Inf. Co.M
Sawyer, James H. NC 32nd Inf. Co.B 1st Lt.
Sawyer, James H. TX Cav. Madison's Regt. Co.A 3rd Lt.
Sawyer, James H. VA 31st Mil. Co.H Cpl.
Sawyer, James M. MS 20th Inf. Co.F
Sawyer, James M. MS 40th Inf. Co.H
Sawyer, James P. NC 25th Inf. Co.A 1st Sgt.
Sawyer, James P. SC 20th Inf. Co.I
Sawyer, James R. TN 10th (DeMoss') Cav. Co.A
Sawyer, James S. NC 32nd Inf. Co.I
Sawyer, James T. NC Cav. 5th Bn. Co.A

Sawyer, James T. NC Inf. 2nd Bn. Co.H
Sawyer, James T. NC 64th Inf. Co.G Sgt.
Sawyer, Jasper W. AL 12th Inf. Co.G
Sawyer, J.C. MO Inf. Winston's Regt. Co.A
Sawyer, J.D. AL 5th Inf. New Co.C
Sawyer, J.D. AR 3rd Inf. Co.K
Sawyer, Jerome B. NC 3rd Arty. (40th St.Troops) Co.D Sgt.
Sawyer, Jerome H. Gen. & Staff, Ord.Dept. Conscr.,Ch.Clerk
Sawyer, Jesse AR Cav. Wright's Regt. Co.I Sgt.
Sawyer, Jesse AR 18th Inf. Co.H Sgt.
Sawyer, Jesse NC 3rd Inf. Co.I
Sawyer, Jesse NC 17th Inf. (1st Org.) Co.L
Sawyer, Jesse NC 52nd Inf. Co.C
Sawyer, Jesse A. Sig.Corps,CSA
Sawyer, J.H. LA 4th Cav. Co.G
Sawyer, J.H. VA 3rd Inf.Loc.Def. Co.A
Sawyer, J.L. GA 3rd Res. Co.E
Sawyer, J.L. MS 6th Inf. Co.C
Sawyer, J.L. TN Cav. Napier's Bn. Co.A Cpl.
Sawyer, J.L.C. GA 7th Inf. Co.B
Sawyer, J.L.T. GA 45th Inf. Co.K
Sawyer, J.M. AR 2nd Vol. Co.D Ord.Sgt.
Sawyer, J.O. AR 8th Inf. New Co.E
Sawyer, Joel NC 32nd Inf. Co.B
Sawyer, Joel SC 23rd Inf. Co.G
Sawyer, Joel A. NC 39th Inf. Co.F 2nd Lt.
Sawyer, Joel S. NC 17th Inf. (1st Org.) Co.A
Sawyer, Joel S. NC 17th Inf. (2nd Org.) Co.B
Sawyer, Joel S. NC 56th Inf. Co.C Sgt.
Sawyer, John AL 30th Inf. Co.F Capt.
Sawyer, John AR 24th Inf. Co.G,F
Sawyer, John GA 10th Inf.
Sawyer, John NC 6th Cav. (65th St.Troops) Co.A
Sawyer, John NC 1st Arty. (10th St.Troops) Co.I
Sawyer, John NC 32nd Inf. Co.I
Sawyer, John NC 56th Inf. Co.A
Sawyer, John NC 64th Inf. Co.C
Sawyer, John NC 67th Inf. Co.B
Sawyer, John NC Inf. Thomas Legion Co.F
Sawyer, John SC 14th Inf. Co.D
Sawyer, John SC 21st Inf. Co.L
Sawyer, John SC 22nd Inf. Co.I
Sawyer, John SC 23rd Inf. Co.H Color Sgt.
Sawyer, John TN 4th Inf. Co.K
Sawyer, John TX 1st Inf. Co.C
Sawyer, John VA 45th Inf. Co.G
Sawyer, John A. NC Lt.Arty. 3rd Bn. Co.B
Sawyer, John A. VA 45th Inf. Co.G
Sawyer, John D. AL 61st Inf. Co.G 1st Sgt.
Sawyer, John F. NC Cav. 5th Bn. Co.A
Sawyer, John F. NC 12th Inf. Co.M
Sawyer, John F. NC 32nd Inf. Co.B
Sawyer, John H. NC 17th Inf. (1st Org.) Co.H
Sawyer, John H. NC 17th Inf. (2nd Org.) Co.G
Sawyer, John H. SC 4th Cav. Co.E
Sawyer, John L. VA 61st Inf. Co.I,K
Sawyer, John L. VA Inf. Cohoon's Bn. Co.C
Sawyer, John L.F. NC 4th Cav. (59th St.Troops) Co.G
Sawyer, John R. LA Red River S.S. Cpl.
Sawyer, John R. NC 8th Inf. Co.A
Sawyer, John R. NC 13th Inf. Co.G
Sawyer, John T. LA Mil. Orleans Fire Regt.
Sawyer, John T. MS 40th Inf. Co.H

Sawyer, John V. SC 2nd St.Troops Co.G Cpl.
Sawyer, John W. LA 13th Bn. (Part.Rangers) Co.A Cpl.
Sawyer, John W. NC 17th Inf. (1st Org.) Co.L
Sawyer, John W. SC 5th Cav. Co.F
Sawyer, John W. SC Cav. 14th Bn. Co.C
Sawyer, Joseph MS 43rd Inf. Co.C
Sawyer, Joseph NC 17th Inf. (1st Org.) Co.E
Sawyer, Joseph NC 32nd Inf. Co.I
Sawyer, Joseph NC 56th Inf. Co.C
Sawyer, Joseph TN 5th Inf. 2nd Co.K
Sawyer, Joseph VA 61st Inf. Co.C
Sawyer, Joseph 2nd Conf.Eng.Troops Co.A
Sawyer, Joseph H. TX 5th Inf. Co.K
Sawyer, J.P. MS 10th Cav. Co.B,D
Sawyer, J.R. LA 2nd Cav. Co.A
Sawyer, J.R. MS 31st Inf. Co.F
Sawyer, J.R. TN Cav. Napier's Bn. Co.A
Sawyer, J.S. TN 10th (DeMoss') Cav. Co.D Cpl.
Sawyer, Julian AL 62nd Inf. Co.I
Sawyer, Kader VA 3rd Inf. Co.A
Sawyer, Kenneth R.P. NC 8th Inf. Co.A Sgt.
Sawyer, L. AL 5th Inf. New Co.C
Sawyer, L. AL 62nd Inf. Co.I
Sawyer, L. AL 1st Bn. Hilliard's Legion Vol. Co.D
Sawyer, L. SC 8th Bn.Res. Co.A
Sawyer, L. SC Inf. Hampton Legion Co.A
Sawyer, Lawson F. AR 1st Inf. Co.G
Sawyer, Lemuel NC 1st Inf. Co.A
Sawyer, Lemuel NC 56th Inf. Co.A
Sawyer, Lemuel P. GA 51st Inf. Co.C
Sawyer, Levi SC 23rd Inf. Co.G Cpl.
Sawyer, Levin B. NC 24th Inf. Co.D
Sawyer, Lewis NC 1st Inf. Co.G
Sawyer, Lewis S. NC Inf. 2nd Bn. Co.H Cpl.
Sawyer, L.M. AR 37th Inf. Co.C 1st Lt.
Sawyer, Loring LA 5th Inf. New Co.A Lt.
Sawyer, M. VA Lt.Arty. 12th Bn. Co.B
Sawyer, M.A. GA 1st Reg. Co.B
Sawyer, M.A. NC Gibbs' Co. (Loc.Def.)
Sawyer, Madison M. VA Hvy.Arty. 20th Bn. Co.B Cpl.
Sawyer, Madison M. VA 38th Inf. 2nd Co.I Sgt.
Sawyer, Manuel NC 54th Inf. Co.C
Sawyer, Marcellus GA Siege Arty. 28th Bn. Co.C
Sawyer, Mark S. NC Lt.Arty. 13th Bn. Co.A
Sawyer, Marshall G. NC 32nd Inf. Co.H
Sawyer, Mathias M. NC 32nd Inf. Co.H
Sawyer, Maxey NC 4th Cav. (59th St.Troops) Co.G
Sawyer, McE. LA 13th Bn. (Part.Rangers) Co.A Sgt.
Sawyer, M.G. AR 10th Inf. Co.D Ord.Sgt.
Sawyer, Michael NC 3rd Arty. (40th St.Troops) Co.D
Sawyer, Miles NC 17th Inf. (2nd Org.) Co.B
Sawyer, Miller NC 32nd Inf. Co.I
Sawyer, M.L. TN 4th Inf. Co.C
Sawyer, Morrison VA 15th Cav. Co.I
Sawyer, N.C. GA 65th Inf. Co.A Cpl.
Sawyer, N.C. GA Smith's Legion Co.B Cpl.
Sawyer, Nelson VA 61st Inf. Co.C
Sawyer, Noah NC 32nd Inf. Co.I
Sawyer, Oscar AR 23rd Inf. Co.B

Sawyer, Peter C. GA Inf. 2nd Bn. Co.C
Sawyer, Ptolemy S. SC 20th Inf. Co.I
Sawyer, R. NC 27th Inf.
Sawyer, Ramsey AL 23rd Inf. Co.E
Sawyer, R.F. AL 30th Inf. Co.F
Sawyer, R.F.M. MS Cav. Polk's Ind.Co. (Polk
  Rangers)
Sawyer, R.S. AR 3rd Inf. Co.K Cpl.
Sawyer, Robert AL 8th Cav. Co.B
Sawyer, Robert W. NC 8th Inf. Co.C
Sawyer, Robert W. NC 8th Inf. Co.K Music.
Sawyer, Robison A. NC 33rd Inf. Co.I,H
Sawyer, Romant W. AL 61st Inf. Co.G
Sawyer, R.W. AL 1st Regt.Conscr. Co.D
Sawyer, S. NC Loc.Def.
Sawyer, S. TX 20th Inf. Co.I
Sawyer, Sam T. Gen. & Staff, QM Dept. Maj.
Sawyer, Samuel FL 7th Inf. Co.K Sgt.
Sawyer, Samuel GA 51st Inf. Co.H
Sawyer, Samuel LA 13th Bn. (Part.Rangers)
  Co.D Sgt.
Sawyer, Samuel LA 17th Inf. Co.C 1st Lt.
Sawyer, Samuel NC 12th Inf. Co.M
Sawyer, Samuel NC 17th Inf. (1st Org.) Co.E
Sawyer, Samuel NC 32nd Inf. Co.B
Sawyer, Samuel NC 56th Inf. Co.A
Sawyer, Samuel NC 68th Inf.
Sawyer, Samuel B. NC Cav. 5th Bn. Co.A
Sawyer, Samuel B. NC 39th Inf. Co.F
Sawyer, Samuel L. NC 12th Inf. Co.L
Sawyer, Samuel L. NC 32nd Inf. Co.F,A
Sawyer, Samuel S. NC 32nd Inf. Co.I
Sawyer, S.B. NC McLean's Bn.Lt.Duty Men
  Co.B
Sawyer, S.B. SC Cav. 14th Bn. Co.D
Sawyer, Selix NC 3rd Arty. (40th St.Troops)
  Co.D
Sawyer, Seymore NC Part.Rangers Swindell's
  Co.
Sawyer, S.H. MS 44th Inf. Co.I Sgt.
Sawyer, Simeon T. NC 12th Inf. Co.L
Sawyer, Simeon T. NC 32nd Inf. Co.F,A
Sawyer, S.S. AR 7th Inf. Co.A
Sawyer, S.V. SC 20th Inf. Co.I
Sawyer, Thomas AL 63rd Inf. Co.A
Sawyer, Thomas NC 7th Inf. Co.B
Sawyer, Thomas NC 17th Inf. (2nd Org.) Co.H
Sawyer, Thomas SC 10th Inf. Co.L
Sawyer, Thomas SC 21st Inf. Co.L
Sawyer, Thomas TN Jackson's Cav.
Sawyer, Thomas TN 4th Inf. Co.F
Sawyer, Thomas TN Inf. 23rd Bn. Co.E
Sawyer, Thomas TN Inf. Spencer's Co.
Sawyer, Thomas VA 6th Inf. 2nd Co.B
Sawyer, Thomas J. NC 3rd Arty. (40th
  St.Troops) Co.D
Sawyer, Thomas P. NC 39th Inf. Co.F
Sawyer, Thomas T. GA 10th Mil. Co.H
Sawyer, Thomas T. NC 1st Inf. (6 mo. '61) Co.E
Sawyer, Tillman T. NC 12th Inf. Co.L
Sawyer, Tillman T. NC 32nd Inf. Co.F,A
Sawyer, T.M. SC 14th Inf. Co.D
Sawyer, T.N. MS 44th Inf. Co.I 1st Sgt.
Sawyer, Tobias M. MO 1st Cav. Co.D
Sawyer, U.P. FL 1st Inf.
Sawyer, Valentine NC 33rd Inf. Co.F
Sawyer, W. GA 1st Reg. Co.B

Sawyer, W. GA 54th Inf. Co.A
Sawyer, W. SC 2nd Arty. Co.E
Sawyer, W. TX 1st Inf. Co.G
Sawyer, W.A. AL 53rd (Part.Rangers) Co.A
Sawyer, W.A. MO 8th Inf. Co.K
Sawyer, Washington NC 64th Inf. Co.D
Sawyer, Wash. J. NC 3rd Arty. (40th St.Troops)
  Co.I
Sawyer, W.B. 1st Conf.Cav. Co.E
Sawyer, W.E. AR 3rd Inf. Co.B Sgt.
Sawyer, W.E. SC 1st (Butler's) Inf.
Sawyer, W.E. SC 9th Inf. Co.K
Sawyer, W.E. SC Palmetto S.S. Co.F
Sawyer, Wesley NC Cav. 5th Bn. Co.A Cpl.
Sawyer, Wesley NC Inf. 2nd Bn. Co.H
Sawyer, Wesley NC 64th Inf. Co.G Sgt.
Sawyer, Wesley SC 9th Inf. Co.K
Sawyer, Wesley TN Cav. Jackson's Regt.
Sawyer, W.H. AL 53rd (Part.Rangers) Co.G
Sawyer, W.H. TN 12th (Green's) Cav. Co.A
Sawyer, Wilkes SC 1st (Hagood's) Inf. 2nd Co.A
Sawyer, Will I. NC 33rd Inf. Co.F
Sawyer, William AR 3rd Inf.
Sawyer, William FL 7th Inf. Co.K Cpl.
Sawyer, William GA Siege Arty. 28th Bn. Co.C
Sawyer, William GA Cherokee Legion
  (St.Guards) Co.G
Sawyer, William MO 10th Cav. Co.K Sgt.
Sawyer, William NC 56th Inf. Co.H
Sawyer, William NC 66th Inf. Co.H
Sawyer, William SC 14th Inf. Co.B
Sawyer, William VA Inf. Cohoon's Bn. Co.C
Sawyer, William A. NC 8th Inf. Co.K
Sawyer, William B. NC 3rd Arty. (40th
  St.Troops) Co.D
Sawyer, William B. NC 17th Inf. (1st Org.) Co.A
Sawyer, William B. NC 17th Inf. (2nd Org.)
  Co.B
Sawyer, William B. NC 32nd Inf. Co.B
Sawyer, William B. NC 33rd Inf. Co.F
Sawyer, William B. NC 56th Inf. Co.C
Sawyer, William C. NC 3rd Inf. Co.I
Sawyer, William E. AL 30th Inf. Co.F 1st Lt.
Sawyer, William E.P. TX 1st (Yager's) Cav.
  Co.H
Sawyer, William E.P. TX Cav. 8th (Taylor's)
  Bn. Co.E
Sawyer, William G. NC 7th Inf. Co.B Sgt.
Sawyer, William H. NC 1st Arty. (10th
  St.Troops) Co.B
Sawyer, William H. NC 33rd Inf. Co.F
Sawyer, William H.H. NC 12th Inf. Co.L
Sawyer, William H.H. NC 32nd Inf. Co.F,A
Sawyer, William H.T. GA 1st Reg. Co.H
Sawyer, William J. NC 3rd Inf. Co.I
Sawyer, William J. VA 61st Inf. Co.C
Sawyer, William J. Conf.Cav. Wood's Regt.
  Co.E
Sawyer, William S. LA Mil. Fire Bn. Co.G
Sawyer, Wm. T. Gen. & Staff Surg.
Sawyer, William W. AR 15th (Josey's) Inf. Co.E
  2nd Lt.
Sawyer, Wm. W. AR 23rd Inf. Co.B Capt.
Sawyer, William W. GA 6th Inf. Co.F
Sawyer, William W. VA 5th Cav. (12 mo. '61-2)
  Co.I
Sawyer, William W. VA Cav. 14th Bn. Co.B

Sawyer, William W. VA 15th Cav. Co.I
Sawyer, Willis TN Douglass' Bn.Part.Rangers
  Perkins' Co. Cpl.
Sawyer, Wilson GA Siege Arty. 28th Bn. Co.E
  Sgt.
Sawyer, Wilson GA 1st Reg. Co.I 1st Sgt.
Sawyer, Winfield S. SC 20th Inf. Co.I
Sawyer, W.L. TN 12th (Green's) Cav. Co.A
Sawyer, W.P. AR 3rd Inf. Co.B
Sawyer, W.P. LA 4th Cav. Co.G Cpl.
Sawyer, W.P. TN 4th (McLemore's) Cav. Co.D
Sawyer, W.R. TX 20th Inf. Co.H
Sawyer, Wright AL 36th Inf. Co.F
Sawyer, W.S. NC Inf. 2nd Bn. Co.A
Sawyer, W.T. NC Currituck Guard J.W.F.
  Bank's Co.
Sawyer, Zadock M. GA 51st Inf. Co.H
Sawyer, Zephniah H. GA 1st Inf.
Sawyer, Zion W. NC 3rd Inf. Co.I
Sawyer, Z.P. MO 4th Cav. Co.I
Sawyers, --- TN 53rd Inf. Co.B
Sawyers, A. VA Lt.Arty. Fry's Co.
Sawyers, A.A. TN 51st (Cons.) Inf. Co.I,C
Sawyers, A.A. TN 52nd Inf. Co.C 1st Sgt.
Sawyers, Abner AL 12th Cav. Co.C
Sawyers, A.F. NC 9th Bn.S.S. Co.A
Sawyers, A.F. NC 21st Inf. Co.B
Sawyers, A.J. GA Cav. 19th Bn. Co.E
Sawyers, A.J. 10th Conf.Cav. Co.K
Sawyers, Alexander AR 16th Inf. Co.G
Sawyers, Alexander T. AL 27th Inf. Co.H
  Music.
Sawyers, Alfred VA Lt.Arty. Turner's Co.
Sawyers, Alfred VA Arty. Wise Legion
Sawyers, Alfred C. VA 22nd Inf. Co.G
Sawyers, Allen GA 43rd Inf. Co.L,C
Sawyers, Andrew TN 39th Mtd.Inf. Co.I
Sawyers, Arthur NC 60th Inf. Co.H
Sawyers, B.B. NC 6th Inf. Co.H
Sawyers, C. TX 19th Inf. Co.K
Sawyers, C.D. AL 17th Inf. Co.F
Sawyers, C.H. TX 30th Cav. Co.C Cpl.
Sawyers, Charles TX 22nd Inf. Co.A
Sawyers, Columbus A. TX 36th Cav. Co.C
  Chap.
Sawyers, Cullen MS 38th Cav. Co.A
Sawyers, D. TN Inf. 3rd Cons.Regt. Co.D
Sawyers, Daniel J. AR 19th (Dawson's) Inf.
  Co.F
Sawyers, Denis AR 14th (Powers') Inf. Co.F 1st
  Lt.
Sawyers, E. AR 18th (Marmaduke's) Inf. Co.C
  Cpl.
Sawyers, E.J. MS 13th Inf. Co.E
Sawyers, Elbert H. TX 5th Inf. Co.C
Sawyers, Elder GA Inf. 1st City Bn. (Columbus)
  Co.F
Sawyers, Elder GA Inf. 19th Bn. (St.Guards)
  Co.A
Sawyers, Eldrige AR 2nd Inf. Co.K, New Co.E
Sawyers, Elisha P. MO 4th Cav. Co.I
Sawyers, E.R. MS 9th Inf. New Co.A
Sawyers, E.T. AR 2nd Inf. Co.B
Sawyers, Francis M. AR 19th (Dawson's) Inf.
  Co.F Sgt.
Sawyers, Frank TX 5th Cav. Co.I
Sawyers, Frank C. TX 12th Cav. Co.C

Sawyers, G.B. MS 9th Bn.S.S. Co.A
Sawyers, George MS 10th Inf. Co.P, New Co.G
Sawyers, George W. TN 1st (Turney's) Inf. Co.K Sgt.
Sawyers, G.M. TN 35th Inf. 2nd Co.I
Sawyers, G.M. TX 12th Inf. Co.K
Sawyers, Green B. MS 10th Inf. Old Co.B, New Co.G
Sawyers, G.T. AR 32nd Inf. Co.K
Sawyers, G.W. TN 53rd Inf. Co.D
Sawyers, H. TN 20th Inf. Co.H
Sawyers, H.A. AR Cav. Gordon's Regt. Co.F
Sawyers, Harrison H. AR 3rd Inf. Co.C
Sawyers, Harvey VA Lt.Arty. Turner's Co. Sgt.
Sawyers, Harvey VA Arty. Wise Legion Sgt.
Sawyers, Harvey P. VA Inf. 9th Bn. Duffy's Co.C
Sawyers, Harvey P. VA 25th Inf. 2nd Co.C
Sawyers, Henry VA 30th Bn.S.S. Co.E
Sawyers, Howe VA 24th Inf. Co.E
Sawyers, Isaac TN Inf. 23rd Bn. Co.E
Sawyers, Isaac J. VA 60th Inf. Co.C
Sawyers, J. TN Inf. 3rd Cons.Regt. Co.D
Sawyers, J.A. AR Cav. 1st Bn. (Stirman's) Co.D
Sawyers, Jac VA Cav. 34th Bn. Co.A
Sawyers, James MO 5th Inf. Co.D
Sawyers, James SC 2nd Rifles Co.H
Sawyers, James TN 15th (Cons.) Cav. Co.C
Sawyers, James TN 42nd Inf. 2nd Co.F
Sawyers, James TN 44th (Cons.) Inf. Co.K
Sawyers, James VA 21st Cav. Co.K
Sawyers, James C. TN 39th Mtd.Inf. Co.E
Sawyers, James M. TN 44th Inf. Co.K Cpl.
Sawyers, James M. TN 44th (Cons.) Inf. Co.A
Sawyers, James R. AL Eufaula Lt.Arty.
Sawyers, James S. VA 63rd Inf. Co.K
Sawyers, J.C. TX 12th Cav. Co.A
Sawyers, J.E. MO 9th Inf. Co.H
Sawyers, Jefferson E. TN 35th Inf. 3rd Co.F
Sawyers, Jeff. J. AL 2nd Cav. Co.A
Sawyers, Jeremiah M. VA Inf. 9th Bn. Duffy's Co.C
Sawyers, J.J. AR Cav. Gordon's Regt. Co.F
Sawyers, J.L. TN 42nd Inf. Co.C
Sawyers, J.L. 4th Conf.Inf. Co.H
Sawyers, J.M. AL 6th Cav. Co.A
Sawyers, J.M. LA 28th (Gray's) Inf. Co.C
Sawyers, John AR 19th (Dawson's) Inf. Co.K,F
Sawyers, John MO 8th Cav. Co.D
Sawyers, John NC 21st Inf. Co.H
Sawyers, John VA 188th Mil. Co.C
Sawyers, John Conf.Lt.Arty. 1st Reg.Btty. Cpl.
Sawyers, John Inf. School of Pract. Powell's Detach. Co.B
Sawyers, John C. MO 4th Cav. Co.I
Sawyers, John H. TN 3rd (Forrest's) Cav.
Sawyers, John H. VA 4th Inf. Co.D
Sawyers, John S. AR 1st Mtd.Rifles Co.K
Sawyers, John S. MO Cav. Coffee's Regt. Co.G
Sawyers, John S. TN 55th (McKoin's) Inf. McEwen, Jr.'s Co.
Sawyers, John S. VA Lt.Arty. Carpenter's Co. Cpl.
Sawyers, John S. VA 27th Inf. Co.A Cpl.
Sawyers, John T. SC 19th Inf. Co.F
Sawyers, Joseph A. VA Lt.Arty. Fry's Co. Cpl.
Sawyers, Joseph A. VA Lt.Arty. Turner's Co.

Sawyers, Joseph A. VA Arty. Wise Legion
Sawyers, Joseph R. NC 6th Inf. Co.H
Sawyers, J.R. TN 10th (DeMoss') Cav. Co.D
Sawyers, Julius T. GA 27th Inf. Co.C
Sawyers, Levi NC 6th Inf. Co.H
Sawyers, Lewis AL Arty. 1st Bn. Co.C
Sawyers, L.J.D. TN 9th Inf. Co.K 1st Sgt.
Sawyers, L.W. TN 37th Inf. Co.C
Sawyers, Moses VA 24th Inf. Co.C
Sawyers, Philip VA 50th Inf. Co.K
Sawyers, P.P. TN 35th Inf. 2nd Co.I
Sawyers, R.H. TX 12th Cav. Co.A Sgt.
Sawyers, Richard VA 51st Inf. Co.I
Sawyers, Richard L. VA 63rd Inf. Co.C,G
Sawyers, R.J. TN Conscr. (Cp. of Instr.)
Sawyers, Robert T. TX 5th Cav. Co.I
Sawyers, R.P. AL 1st Regt. Mobile Vol. Butt's Co.
Sawyers, Rufus TN 39th Mtd.Inf. Co.I
Sawyers, R.W. Stirman's S.S. Co.D,CSA
Sawyers, S.L. VA Lt.Arty. Fry's Co.
Sawyers, S.L. VA Arty. Wise Legion
Sawyers, Solomon NC 21st Inf. Co.H
Sawyers, Stanard L. VA Lt.Arty. Turner's Co.
Sawyers, Thomas TN 3rd (Forrest's) Cav.
Sawyers, Thomas 2nd Cherokee Mtd.Vol. Co.A
Sawyers, Thomas F. VA 24th Inf. Co.I
Sawyers, Thomas L. NC 13th Inf. Co.A
Sawyers, Tillman SC 19th Inf. Co.D
Sawyers, Watson W. VA Lt.Arty. G.B. Chapman's Co.
Sawyers, W.C. KY 9th Mtd.Inf. Co.F 2nd Lt.
Sawyers, W.C. TN Inf. 23rd Bn. Co.B 2nd Lt.
Sawyers, W.D. TN 20th Inf. Co.H
Sawyers, William AL Eufaula Lt.Arty.
Sawyers, William GA 57th Inf. Co.D Music.
Sawyers, William KY 13th Cav. Co.F
Sawyers, William VA 50th Inf. Co.K
Sawyers, William B. TN Cav. 12th Bn. (Day's) Co.B
Sawyers, William J. TN Holman's Bn. Part.Rangers Co.B
Sawyers, William M. TX 30th Cav. Co.D
Sawyers, William T. MO 1st Cav. Co.D
Sawyers, Willis TN 11th (Holman's) Cav. Co.D Sgt.
Sawyers, W.J. TN 11th (Holman's) Cav. Co.G
Sawyers, W.L. TN 42nd Inf. Co.C
Sawyers, W.L. 4th Conf.Inf. Co.H
Sawyers, W.P. FL 1st (Res.) Inf. Co.L
Sawyers, Zepheniah H. 1st Conf.Inf. 2nd Co.D
Sawyers, Z.M. GA Cav. 12th Bn. (St.Guards) Co.A
Sawyes, Dennis MO Cav. Fristoe's Regt. Co.E Sgt.
Sawyes, J. VA 21st Cav. 2nd Co.E
Sax, H. TX 30th Cav. Co.K
Saxby, W.W. MS 28th Cav. Co.A Bugler
Saxe, Benjamin GA 4th Inf. Co.G
Saxe, Patrick LA 13th Inf. Co.C
Saxen, A.C. GA 10th Cav. Co.B Sgt.
Saxley, W.W. MS 12th Inf. Co.I
Saxon, A.A. GA Lt.Arty. Daniell's Btty.
Saxon, A.B. GA Inf. (Jones Hussars) Jones' Co.
Saxon, A.C. GA 10th Cav. Co.B Sgt.
Saxon, Adam S. GA 52nd Inf. Co.G
Saxon, A.H. AL 8th Inf. Co.H

Saxon, A.J. TX 7th Cav. Co.H Cpl.
Saxon, Albert B. GA 63rd Inf. Co.F
Saxon, Alexander AL 22nd Inf. Co.H
Saxon, Alexander MS 14th Inf. Co.A
Saxon, Alferd C. 7th Conf.Cav. Co.B Sgt.
Saxon, Alford C. AL 13th Inf. Co.E Sgt.
Saxon, A.M. AL 4th (Russell's) Cav. Co.C 3rd Sgt.
Saxon, A.M. AL Inf. 2nd Regt. Co.K Capt.
Saxon, A.N. AL 38th Inf. Co.G
Saxon, Andrew VA Lt.Arty. Jackson's Bn.St.Line Co.A
Saxon, Andrew H. VA 5th Cav. Coakley's Co. Sgt.
Saxon, Asa S. TX 4th Cav. Co.E
Saxon, Aulsbury N. AL 22nd Inf. Co.H
Saxon, A.W. AL 22nd Inf. Co.I Sgt.
Saxon, Barney TN 1st Hvy.Arty. 2nd Co.D
Saxon, Ben TX 4th Cav. Co.B
Saxon, Benjamin AL 25th Inf. Co.G
Saxon, Benjamin FL 3rd Inf. Co.C
Saxon, Benjamin F. MS 48th Inf. Co.E
Saxon, B.F. LA Inf. 4th Bn. Co.D
Saxon, B.F. TX 7th Cav. Co.H
Saxon, B.F. 1st Conf.Cav. 1st Co.A, 2nd Co.A 1st Sgt.
Saxon, Charles H. TX 13th Cav. Co.I 2nd Lt.
Saxon, Charles S. Gen. & Staff, Ord.Dept.
Saxon, D.A. AL 53rd (Part.Rangers)
Saxon, David P. AL 13th Inf. Co.C,B
Saxon, David P. LA 13th Inf. Co.B Sgt.
Saxon, Davis AL 61st Inf. Co.B
Saxon, D.P. AR 19th (Dockery's) Inf. Co.F Capt.
Saxon, E.D. GA Inf. 27th Bn. Co.A
Saxon, Edward FL 5th Inf. Co.C
Saxon, Franklin E. FL 3rd Inf. Co.C
Saxon, George SC 4th Bn.Res. Co.E
Saxon, George SC 9th Res. Co.E
Saxon, George W. AL 2nd Bn. Hilliard's Legion Vol. Co.C
Saxon, George W. MS Inf. 2nd St.Troops Co.F
Saxon, George W. MS 35th Inf. Co.F
Saxon, Henry AL 4th Res. Co.E
Saxon, Henry GA Cav. 29th Bn. Co.F
Saxon, Henry GA 6th Mil.
Saxon, Henry C. TN 54th Inf. Hollis' Co.
Saxon, H.H. AL 10th Inf. Co.E
Saxon, H.O. FL Cav. 5th Bn. Co.F
Saxon, Irving MO Inf. 1st Bn. Co.C
Saxon, Israel G. Conf.Cav. Wood's Regt. Co.E
Saxon, J. MS 37th Inf. Co.F
Saxon, J.A. SC 1st Arty. Co.F
Saxon, Jack SC Inf. 1st (Charleston) Bn. Co.D
Saxon, Jack SC 27th Inf. Co.D
Saxon, James AL 9th Inf. Co.A Sgt.
Saxon, James AL Talladega Cty.Res. Breed's Co.
Saxon, James MS Lt.Arty. (Brookhaven Lt.Arty.) Hoskins' Btty.
Saxon, James A. AL 6th Inf. Co.H
Saxon, James A. MS 14th Inf. Co.A
Saxon, James H. AL 59th Inf. Co.A
Saxon, James H. AL 2nd Bn. Hilliard's Legion Vol. Co.C
Saxon, James M. AL 13th Inf. Co.K
Saxon, James N. LA 9th Inf. Co.D

Saxon, James R. FL 3rd Inf. Co.C
Saxon, James W. AL 13th Inf. Co.E
Saxon, James W. AL 44th Inf. Co.I
Saxon, J.F. MS 10th Cav. Co.A
Saxon, J.F. SC Inf. 1st (Charleston) Bn. Co.D
Saxon, J.F. SC 27th Inf. Co.D
Saxon, J.F. TN Cav. 17th Bn. (Sanders') Co.C
Saxon, J. Foster SC Inf. 3rd Bn. Co.C
Saxon, J. Frank MS 9th Cav. Co.F
Saxon, J.G. MS 14th Inf. Co.C
Saxon, J.M. 7th Conf.Cav. Co.B
Saxon, John AL 17th Inf. Co.G
Saxon, John LA Mil. 4th Regt. 1st Brig. 1st Div. Co.C
Saxon, John SC 4th Bn.Res. Co.E
Saxon, John SC 9th Res. Co.E
Saxon, John TN 1st Hvy.Arty. 2nd Co.D
Saxon, John A. AL 61st Inf. Co.B
Saxon, John C. AL 25th Inf. Co.G
Saxon, John F. GA 53rd Inf. Co.K
Saxon, John M.H.P. TN 54th Inf. Hollis' Co. 1st Sgt.
Saxon, John W. LA 17th Inf. Co.K
Saxon, John W. MS 14th Inf. Co.A Sgt.
Saxon, John W. MS 37th Inf. Co.E,C Cpl.
Saxon, Jonathan Y. GA 23rd Inf. Co.K
Saxon, Joshua TX Cav. Waller's Regt. Co.B Bugler
Saxon, J.S. SC 6th Cav. Co.G
Saxon, J.S. SC 14th Inf. Co.C
Saxon, J.T. GA Inf. 1st Conf.Bn. Co.B Cpl.
Saxon, J.T. SC 4th Bn.Res. Co.D
Saxon, J.W. TX 7th Cav. Co.H Sgt.
Saxon, L.A. AL 53rd Cav.
Saxon, Lewis AL 38th Inf. Co.B
Saxon, Lewis SC 4th Bn.Res. Co.E
Saxon, Lewis W. GA 10th Inf. Co.D
Saxon, Marion MS Inf. 3rd Bn. (St.Troops) Co.C
Saxon, M.C. GA Inf. (Jones Hussars) Jones' Co.
Saxon, M.D. MS 1st Lt.Arty. Co.K
Saxon, M.D. MS Arty. (Seven Stars Arty.) Roberts' Co.
Saxon, M.H. GA 7th Inf. Co.G
Saxon, M.J. AR Inf. Hardy's Regt. Co.G
Saxon, P.A. SC 4th Bn.Res. Co.D Cpl.
Saxon, P.A. SC 5th St.Troops Co.D
Saxon, Pearson A. SC Inf. 3rd Bn. Co.A
Saxon, Pressley H. AL 38th Inf. Co.G
Saxon, Prestley H. MS 14th Inf. Co.A
Saxon, Randall Gillum's Regt. Co.G
Saxon, Ransom Y. GA 3rd Inf. Co.A
Saxon, R.B. GA Cav. 29th Bn. Co.G
Saxon, R.C. GA Cav. 10th Bn. (St.Guards) Co.D Capt.
Saxon, R.C. GA 4th Res. Co.H Capt.
Saxon, R.C. GA 55th Inf. Adj.
Saxon, R.C. GA 63rd Inf. Co.I
Saxon, R.C. KY 1st (Butler's) Cav. Co.F
Saxon, R.C. Gen. & Staff 1st Lt.,Adj.
Saxon, R.M. GA 3rd Res. Co.E
Saxon, Robert SC 9th Res. Co.E
Saxon, Robert B. AL 44th Inf. Co.I Sgt.
Saxon, Robert C. KY 1st Inf.
Saxon, Robert H. TX 13th Cav. Co.B
Saxon, Robert L. TN 54th Inf. Hollis' Co.
Saxon, Robert N. TX 28th Cav. Co.I Cpl.
Saxon, Rufus J. GA 6th Inf. Co.G

Saxon, Samuel GA 23rd Inf. Co.K
Saxon, S.M. TX 15th Inf. Co.A
Saxon, S.R. SC 14th Inf. Co.C
Saxon, S.S. AL 3rd Res.
Saxon, Thomas LA 2nd Cav. Co.G
Saxon, Thomas SC 16th Inf. Co.A
Saxon, Thomas A. TX 2nd Cav. Co.C
Saxon, Thomas G. LA Scouts Vinson's Co.
Saxon, Thomas J. AL 47th Inf. Co.K
Saxon, Thomas J. GA 6th Inf. Co.G
Saxon, Thomas J. MS 14th Inf. Co.A
Saxon, Thomas J. MS 14th (Cons.) Inf. Co.D
Saxon, Thomas J. 1st Conf.Inf. 2nd Co.E Cpl.
Saxon, Thomas L. TX 2nd Inf. Co.E
Saxon, Thomas W. GA Phillips' Legion Co.D,K
Saxon, T.J. GA Arty. St.Troops Pruden's Btty.
Saxon, Walter T. FL 3rd Inf. Co.C Capt.
Saxon, W.B. GA 23rd Inf. Co.K
Saxon, W.C. AL 10th Inf. Co.E
Saxon, W.D. AL Cp. of Instr. Talladega Co.C
Saxon, W.E. AL 11th Inf. Co.E Sgt.
Saxon, W.H. AL 4th Res. Co.G
Saxon, W.H. GA 63rd Inf. Co.F
Saxon, William AL 47th Inf. Co.B,D
Saxon, William GA 60th Inf. Co.I
Saxon, William TN 12th (Cons.) Inf. Co.C Lt.
Saxon, William TN 22nd Inf. Co.A Cpl.
Saxon, William B. MS 14th Inf. Co.A
Saxon, William B. MS 14th (Cons.) Inf. Co.D
Saxon, William E. AL 41st Inf. Co.E Sgt.
Saxon, William H. GA Inf. 27th Bn. Co.A
Saxon, William H. 1st Conf.Inf. 2nd Co.E
Saxon, William J. AL 6th Inf. Co.L Sr.2nd Lt.
Saxon, William M. GA 6th Inf. Co.G
Saxon, William M. TX 2nd Inf. Co.E
Saxon, William P. SC 19th Inf. Co.G
Saxon, William T. GA 51st Inf. Co.E Sgt.
Saxon, William W. MS 1st Lt.Arty. Co.K
Saxon, W.T. GA 23rd Inf. Co.K
Saxon, W.W. MS Lt.Arty. (Jefferson Arty.) Darden's Co.
Saxson, G.W. TN 1st (Feild's) Inf. Co.G Cpl.
Saxson, T.J. GA Arty. St.Troops Pruden's Btty.
Saxson, William H. GA 12th Cav. Co.F
Saxton, A.C. SC Lt.Arty. Beauregard's Co.
Saxton, Allen AL Cav. 5th Bn. Hilliard's Legion Co.B
Saxton, Allen 10th Conf.Cav. Co.B
Saxton, Andrew TN 15th (Stewart's) Cav. Co.G
Saxton, B.B. TX 4th Cav. Co.B
Saxton, C.H. TX 4th Cav. Co.B
Saxton, Cicero GA 27th Inf. Co.D
Saxton, D. TN 7th (Duckworth's) Cav. Co.A
Saxton, E. MS 30th Inf. Co.D
Saxton, Flournoy MS 1st (Patton's) Inf. Co.B
Saxton, George KY 2nd Cav.
Saxton, George KY 9th Cav. Co.K
Saxton, George KY 9th Mtd.Inf. Co.H
Saxton, George SC 5th St.Troops Co.H
Saxton, George TN Cav. 9th Bn. (Gantt's) Co.F
Saxton, H. GA Mayer's Co. (Appling Cav.)
Saxton, Harvy VA 72nd Mil.
Saxton, Henry GA Inf. 1st Loc.Troops (Augusta) Co.D,B
Saxton, Henry B. VA 8th Cav. 2nd Co.D
Saxton, H.H. VA 8th Cav. Co.E
Saxton, Hiram AR Cav. Wright's Regt. Co.F

Saxton, Hiram AR 23rd Inf. Co.G
Saxton, J. MS Cav. Ham's Regt. Co.B,C Cpl.
Saxton, Jacob J. AL 38th Inf. Co.G
Saxton, J.D. SC Lt.Arty. Beauregard's Co.
Saxton, J.J. MS 22nd Cav. Co.C
Saxton, John GA 4th (Clinch's) Cav. Co.A
Saxton, John GA 12th Cav. Co.D
Saxton, John SC 5th St.Troops Co.H
Saxton, John Conf.Cav. Powers' Regt. Co.G
Saxton, John T. GA 1st (Ramsey's) Inf. Co.K
Saxton, J.W. TN Conscr. (Cp. of Instr.)
Saxton, M. AL 1st Bn.Cadets Co.A
Saxton, M. VA Inf. 5th Bn.Loc.Def. Co.B
Saxton, Madison MS 2nd St.Cav. Co.I
Saxton, Morgan Y. GA 46th Inf. Co.I
Saxton, N. VA 3rd Cav. Co.K
Saxton, Newton AL Lt.Arty. 20th Bn. Co.A
Saxton, Newton O. NC Walker's Bn. Thomas' Legion Co.A Sgt.
Saxton, R.A. TN 7th (Duckworth's) Cav. Co.E
Saxton, Randolph MS 30th Inf. Co.D
Saxton, R.C. KY 12th Cav. Co.E,F
Saxton, Robert VA Mil. Scott Cty.
Saxton, Simeon MO 4th Cav. Co.A
Saxton, Simeon MO Cav. Preston's Bn. Co.A
Saxton, S.J. AL 3rd Bn.Res. Jackson's Co.
Saxton, T.H. GA 51st Inf. Co.E
Saxton, T.J. AL 26th (O'Neal's) Inf. Co.D
Saxton, W.C. TX Inf. 1st St.Troops Saxton's Co. Capt.
Saxton, W.D. AL Cp. of Instr. Talladega
Saxton, William GA 10th Inf. Co.K
Saxton, William LA 1st Hvy.Arty. (Reg.) Co.D
Saxton, William VA 60th Inf. Co.G
Saxton, William B. AL Cav. 5th Bn. Hilliard's Legion Co.B
Saxton, William M. GA 48th Inf. Co.C Cpl.
Say, Albert SC 9th Inf. Co.F
Say, D.A. TX Cav. Martin's Regt. Co.E
Say, George W. GA 20th Inf. Co.K
Say, James AL 12th Cav. Co.B
Say, John AL 12th Cav. Co.D
Say, J.R. GA 16th Inf. Co.G Cpl.
Say, Martin GA Cherokee Legion (St.Guards) Co.B
Say, Patterson GA Cherokee Legion (St.Guards) Co.C
Say, R. GA 48th Inf. Co.I
Say, Sanford G. GA 6th Inf. Co.B
Say, William, Jr. GA Inf. Athens Reserved Corps
Say, William, Sr. GA Inf. Athens Reserved Corps
Sayall, Simeon KY 10th Cav. Co.H Cpl.
Sayart, T.B. MS 12th Inf. Co.H
Sayder, Cornelius AL 1st Inf. Co.K
Saye, Abraham R. SC 9th Inf. Co.F
Saye, Alexander GA 18th Inf. Co.H
Saye, Asbery W. GA Cherokee Legion (St.Guards) Co.D
Saye, Asbury W. MS 19th Inf. Co.K Sgt.
Saye, Bennett H. MO 9th Inf. Co.I
Saye, D.M. GA 18th Inf. Co.H Sgt.
Saye, Edwin R. TX 27th Cav. Co.G Sgt.
Saye, Ephriam T. GA 11th Inf. Co.A
Saye, E.W. GA 11th Cav. Co.B
Saye, George GA 18th Inf. Co.H
Saye, James N. GA 27th Inf. Co.D

Saye, J.D. GA 55th Inf. Co.D
Saye, J.F. GA 18th Inf. Co.F
Saye, John AL 1st Cav. Co.B,I
Saye, John AL 12th Cav. Co.B,I
Saye, John GA 18th Inf. Co.H
Saye, John GA 55th Inf. Co.D
Saye, John MO 11th Inf. Co.K
Saye, John R. GA 11th Inf. Co.A
Saye, Milton GA Inf. White's Co.
Saye, Richard W. GA Carlton's Co. (Troup Cty.Arty.)
Saye, Robert AL 12th Cav. Co.B
Saye, Robert GA 18th Inf. Co.H
Saye, Wesley B. MO 5th Inf. Co.C
Saye, William GA Cherokee Legion (St.Guards) Co.D
Saye, William L. GA 27th Inf. Co.D
Saye, William M. GA Phillips' Legion Co.C,I
Saye, W.N. GA 63rd Inf. Co.A
Saye, W.P. GA 55th Inf. Co.D
Sayer, A. MS 15th Inf. Co.F
Sayer, Bennett H. MO Inf. 8th Bn. Co.E
Sayer, Daniel P. GA 56th Inf. Co.G
Sayer, David W. GA 38th Inf. Co.F
Sayer, J. AL 26th (O'Neal's) Inf. Co.A
Sayer, J.A.B. SC Lt.Arty. J.T. Kanapaux's Co. (Lafayette Arty.) Teamster
Sayer, J.B. SC 2nd Bn.S.S. Co.B
Sayer, J.H. TX 33rd Cav. Co.D
Sayer, J.T. GA 56th Inf. Co.G
Sayer, J.W. MS 15th Inf. Co.F
Sayer, Matthew KY 5th Mtd.Inf. Co.F
Sayer, R.J. GA 56th Inf. Co.G
Sayer, William O. GA 38th Inf. Co.F
Sayer, William T. GA 38th Inf. Co.F
Sayers, A. MO Cav. 2nd Regt.St.Guard Maj.
Sayers, Abner VA 4th Inf. Co.C Cpl.
Sayers, A.D. TX 4th Cav. Co.A
Sayers, Anderson VA 54th Inf. Co.F
Sayers, Andrew TN 10th Inf. Co.D
Sayers, Augustus B. MO 3rd Cav. Co.F Cpl.
Sayers, Benjamin F. VA 2nd Inf.Loc.Def. Co.D
Sayers, B.F. VA Inf. 6th Bn.Loc.Def. Co.A
Sayers, Calvin 4th Conf.Inf. Co.C
Sayers, Cannard MO Inf. 4th Regt.St.Guard Co.C
Sayers, Charles AL 23rd Inf. Co.C
Sayers, Charles P. TN 11th Inf. Co.B Sgt.
Sayers, David GA 63rd Inf. Co.K
Sayers, David VA 8th Cav. Co.H
Sayers, David VA 51st Inf. Co.B
Sayers, David G. VA Cav. 34th Bn. Co.C Capt.
Sayers, D.J. LA 6th Cav. Co.A
Sayers, D.W. GA 7th Cav. Co.C
Sayers, D.W. GA Cav. 24th Bn. Co.B
Sayers, Edward B. Polk's Staff Capt.,Ch.Eng.
Sayers, E.H. AL 34th Inf. Co.A Sgt.
Sayers, E.H. GA 60th Inf. Co.H
Sayers, H. MO Robertson's Regt.St.Guard Co.3
Sayers, H. VA 45th Inf. Co.G
Sayers, Hough MO 8th Cav. Co.E
Sayers, James MO 10th Cav. Co.G
Sayers, James TN 6th (Wheeler's) Cav. Co.D
Sayers, James, Jr. VA 12th Inf. Co.D
Sayers, James VA 51st Inf. Co.B
Sayers, James VA 54th Inf. Co.F

Sayers, James A. VA 166th Mil. B.G. Lively's Co.
Sayers, James J. LA 9th Inf. Co.F
Sayers, James T. VA Inf. 23rd Bn. Co.F
Sayers, James W. LA 28th (Gray's) Inf. Co.C
Sayers, J.B. VA 4th Res. Co.E,G
Sayers, J.C. AL 53rd (Part.Rangers) Co.G
Sayers, J.D. AL 53rd (Part.Rangers) Co.G
Sayers, J.L. GA 1st (Fannin's) Res. Co.B,K
Sayers, Joel T. LA 19th Inf. Co.G
Sayers, John FL 10th Inf. Co.A
Sayers, John VA Inf. 23rd Bn. Co.D
Sayers, John F. LA 9th Inf. Co.F
Sayers, John G. TN Lt.Arty. Baxter's Co.
Sayers, John T., Jr. VA 4th Inf. Co.A 1st Lt.
Sayers, Joseph VA 51st Inf. Co.B
Sayers, Joseph D. TX 5th Cav. 1st Lt.,Adj.
Sayers, Joseph D. TX 12th Field Btty. Capt.
Sayers, Joseph D. Taylor's Corps Maj.,AAG
Sayers, Joseph D. Gen. & Staff 1st Lt.,Adj.
Sayers, Joseph T. 9th Conf.Inf. Co.D 1st Sgt.
Sayers, J.T. AL 53rd (Part.Rangers) Co.A
Sayers, L. KY 10th (Johnson's) Cav. Co.A
Sayers, L. LA 6th Cav. Co.A
Sayers, Marion VA 166th Mil. R.G. Lively's Co.
Sayers, M.S. 2nd Conf.Eng.Troops Co.D Artif.
Sayers, Nathan VA 45th Inf. Co.K
Sayers, N.O. VA 22nd Cav. Co.G
Sayers, Reuben VA 4th Res. Co.C
Sayers, Richard L. VA Mil. Grayson Cty.
Sayers, Robert MO Robertson's Regt.St.Guard Co.3
Sayers, Robert B. TN Lt.Arty. Baxter's Co.
Sayers, R.T. MO 1st Cav. Co.A
Sayers, Samuel M. GA 47th Inf. Co.B
Sayers, Samuel P. GA 30th Inf. Co.G
Sayers, Samuel R. VA 4th Inf. Co.A Surg.
Sayers, Samuel R. VA 27th Inf. Surg.
Sayers, Seth MO 10th Inf. Co.B
Sayers, S.R. Gen. & Staff Surg.
Sayers, T.A. VA 27th Inf. Surg.
Sayers, Thomas VA 22nd Cav. Co.G
Sayers, Thomas VA 51st Inf. Co.B
Sayers, Ths. AL 53rd (Part.Rangers) Co.A
Sayers, W.H. AL 2nd Cav. Co.G
Sayers, William AL 2nd Cav. Co.G
Sayers, William VA 4th Res. Co.E
Sayers, William VA 54th Inf. Co.F
Sayers, William B. TX 8th Cav. Co.D 1st Lt.,Adj.
Sayers, Wm. B. Gen. & Staff 1st Lt.,Adj.
Sayers, William David LA 16th Inf. Co.C
Sayers, W.M. TN 15th Inf. Co.G Cpl.
Sayers, W.P. GA 8th Inf. Co.I
Sayle, David P. MS Lt.Arty. Stanford's Co.
Sayle, D.L. MS Lt.Arty. 14th Bn. Co.C
Sayle, D.L. MS Lt.Arty. Merrin's Btty.
Sayle, Jesse T. MS Lt.Arty. Stanford's Co. Cpl.
Sayle, J.N. SC 2nd Res. Co.B Sgt.
Sayle, J.W. TN 4th (Murray's) Cav. Co.H
Sayle, J.W. TN 8th (Smith's) Cav. Co.C
Sayle, Robert TX 9th Cav. Asst.Surg.
Sayle, Samuel A. TN 27th Inf. Co.I Capt.
Sayle, W.A.C. AR 2nd Mtd.Rifles Asst.Surg.
Sayle, W.A.C. Gen. & Staff Asst.Surg.
Sayle, W.E. MS 29th Inf. Co.E Sgt.
Sayle, W.G. AR 36th Inf. Co.C

Sayler, John A. SC 1st St.Troops Co.C
Sayler, John B. SC 1st St.Troops Co.C
Sayler, John N. SC 1st St.Troops Co.C
Sayler, John R. MO Cav. Poindexter's Regt. Co.B
Sayler, John R. TN 61st Mtd.Inf. Co.A
Sayler, Sylveston MO Cav. Williams' Regt. Co.B
Saylers, John GA Inf. 23rd Bn.Loc.Def. Cook's Co.
Sayles, George LA Arty. Green's Co. (LA Guard Btty.)
Sayles, Green LA Arty. Green's Co. (LA Guard Btty.)
Sayles, J.D. MS 34th Inf. Co.E
Sayles, J.E. TN 5th Inf. 2nd Co.C Cpl.
Sayles, John TX Mil. Brig.Gen.
Sayles, L. NC 2nd Inf.
Sayles, Oren Robert MO 8th Inf. Co.E
Sayles, Thomas AR 1st Mtd.Rifles Co.K Cpl.
Sayles, Thomas AR 19th Inf. Co.F
Sayles, Thomas AR 25th Inf. Co.I Cpl.
Sayles, Thomas Conf.Inf. 8th Bn. Co.B
Sayles, W. LA C.S. Zouave Bn. Co.E
Sayles, William TX Cav. Martin's Regt. Co.H
Sayles, William H. MO 16th Inf. Co.C
Sayles, William T. VA 11th Cav. Co.A
Saylor, Abraham TX 15th Cav. Co.C
Saylor, B.W. TN 8th Cav. Co.H
Saylor, David VA 3rd Res. Co.K
Saylor, H.E. SC Inf. 1st (Charleston) Bn. Co.D Sgt.
Saylor, H.E. SC 27th Inf. Co.D Sgt.
Saylor, Henry TN Inf. 1st Bn. (Colms') Co.A
Saylor, H.H. TN 63rd Inf. Co.I
Saylor, Isaac SC 20th Inf. Co.E
Saylor, J. TX Cav. Wells' Regt. Co.E
Saylor, J.F. TN 61st Mtd.Inf. Co.A
Saylor, J.J. SC Inf. 1st (Charleston) Bn. Co.D
Saylor, J.K.P. TN 61st Mtd.Inf. Co.A
Saylor, J.N. GA 2nd Inf. Co.B Sgt.
Saylor, John NC 60th Inf. Co.H Cpl.
Saylor, John J. SC 27th Inf. Co.D Sgt.
Saylor, John N. SC 20th Inf. Co.E
Saylor, John R. MO Lt.Arty. 3rd Btty.
Saylor, John R. MO 5th Inf. Co.H
Saylor, J.R. AL 9th (Malone's) Cav. Co.B
Saylor, J.R. Lt.Arty. Dent's Btty.,CSA
Saylor, M.M. AL 12th Inf. Co.G
Saylor, Tedric SC 20th Inf. Co.E
Saylor, T.N. TN 61st Mtd.Inf. Co.A
Saylor, Washington D. SC 20th Inf. Co.E,N
Saylor, Wharton R. MO 2nd Inf. Co.A
Saylor, William SC Cav. 10th Bn. Co.C
Saylor, William I. SC 20th Inf. Co.E
Saylor, William P. SC 20th Inf. Co.E
Saylors, A. TN 25th Inf. Co.F
Saylors, A.A. TN Inf. 22nd Bn. Co.A
Saylors, Abraham TN Inf. 22nd Bn. Co.A
Saylors, Andrew TN 16th Inf. Co.K
Saylors, Andrew J. TX 22nd Cav. Co.F Cpl.
Saylors, Andy TN 13th (Gore's) Cav. Co.D
Saylors, B.W. TN 28th Inf. Co.K
Saylors, B.W. TN 28th (Cons.) Inf. Co.C
Saylors, Daniel W. AR 14th (Powers') Inf. Co.B
Saylors, David W. SC 12th Inf. Co.A
Saylors, Elisha L. TN 25th Inf. Co.E
Saylors, F.M. MS 23rd Inf. Co.E

Saylors, Isaac SC Cav. 19th Bn. Co.E
Saylors, James C. MS 23rd Inf. Co.E
Saylors, Jeremiah GA 1st Inf. (St.Guards) Co.B Sgt.
Saylors, Jerry GA 28th Inf. Co.G
Saylors, J.F. GA 11th Cav. Co.G
Saylors, J.F. GA 23rd Inf. Co.H
Saylors, J.H. GA 23rd Inf. Co.H
Saylors, J.M. TN Inf. 22nd Bn. Co.A
Saylors, J.M. TN 28th Inf. Co.K 2nd Lt.
Saylors, John B. SC 1st (Orr's) Rifles Co.L
Saylors, J.V. TN 3rd (Forrest's) Cav.
Saylors, M. MS Cav. Ham's Regt. Co.D
Saylors, William J. AR 14th (Powers') Inf. Co.B
Saylors, William J. AR 27th Inf. Co.K
Saylors, William J. SC 12th Inf. Co.A
Saylors, William R. AR 8th Inf. New Co.B 1st Sgt.
Saym, G.P. NC 2nd Jr.Res. Co.C
Sayner, James TX 3rd (Kirby's) Bn.Vol. Co.A
Saynes, R. VA Arty. Wise Legion
Saynord, Joseph T. AR 13th Inf. Co.E
Saynore, Joseph NC Home Guards Co.K
Sayors, William MO 2nd Cav. Co.D
Sayre, Augustin S. AL 3rd Inf. Co.F
Sayre, C. AL 8th Inf. Co.H
Sayre, Calvin L. Gen. & Staff Maj.
Sayre, Carey B. AL Lt.Arty. 2nd Bn. Co.E
Sayre, Cary B. AL 3rd Inf. Co.B
Sayre, Charles VA 17th Cav. Co.G
Sayre, Charles VA 19th Cav. Co.H
Sayre, Charles W. VA 36th Inf. 2nd Co.E
Sayre, Clayton V. AL 3rd Inf. Co.F Sgt.
Sayre, C.W. AL 1st Cav. Co.H Cpl.
Sayre, C.W. AL 51st (Part.Rangers) Co.H
Sayre, C.W. AL 3rd Inf. Co.C
Sayre, Daniel AL Rebels
Sayre, Daniel M. AL 3rd Inf. Co.C
Sayre, E.M. AL 1st Cav. Co.A
Sayre, Esra VA 36th Inf. Co.E Sgt.
Sayre, Francis S. TX 14th Cav. Co.K
Sayre, George H. AL 4th Inf. Co.D
Sayre, H.J. VA 19th Cav. Co.H Sgt.
Sayre, Howe VA Cav. 37th Bn. Co.H
Sayre, James KY Warsaw Gallatin Co.
Sayre, M.A. AL 21st Inf. Co.K Cpl.
Sayre, M. Hargrove AL 3rd Inf. Co.F
Sayre, Milton AL Cav. Callaway's Co.
Sayre, Nathan C. GA Inf. 27th Bn. Co.A,E Jr.2nd Lt.
Sayre, N.C. GA Inf. 1st Loc.Troops (Augusta) Dearing's Cav.Co.
Sayre, P.D. Adams' Staff 1st Lt.,Ord.Off.
Sayre, Phil D. AL 3rd Inf. Co.F 2nd Lt.
Sayre, P.T. AL Montgomery Guards 2nd Lt.
Sayre, R. Stokes GA Lt.Arty. 12th Bn. 1st Co.A QMS
Sayre, R. Stokes GA 63rd Inf. Co.A
Sayre, S.M. AL 4th Inf. Co.D
Sayre, S.M. Hosp.Stew.
Sayre, T. TX 14th Inf. Co.F
Sayre, Theopolus T. VA 37th Mil. Co.E
Sayre, Vanarandah VA 37th Mil. Co.A
Sayre, W. AL 7th Cav. Co.F
Sayre, William D. LA Washington Arty.Bn. Co.2
Sayre, W.N. GA Lt.Arty. 12th Bn. 1st Co.A
Sayres, --- Hosp.Stew.

Sayres, G. VA 5th Cav. Co.C
Sayres, J.F. TX Cav. Madison's Regt. Co.K
Sayres, L.W. KY 4th Mtd.Inf. Co.D
Sayres, Sanford Gen. & Staff Hosp.Stew.
Sayres, S.C. TX 13th Vol. 2nd Co.B
Sayres, W.C. KY 10th (Johnson's) Cav. Co.A
Says, Abraham LA 3rd (Harrison's) Cav. Co.K
Says, Benjamin VA Cav. 1st Bn. Co.C
Says, W.H. AR 3rd Cav. Co.B
Saysing, A. TN 61st Mtd.Inf. Co.C
Saysters, Amos N. MO Lawther's Part.Rangers
Sayton, Franklin A. NC 42nd Inf. Co.C Cpl.
Sbisa, Bernardo LA Mil. 5th Regt.Eur.Brig. (Spanish Regt.) Co.9
Sbiza, B. LA Mil. Orleans Guards Regt. Co.I
Scace, John NC 45th Inf. Co.E
Scachee Oonanooteh NC Inf. Thomas Legion Co.B
Scacheloskee NC Inf. Thomas Legion 2nd Co.A
Scaff, C.B. GA Inf. 1st Conf.Bn. Co.F
Scaff, C.B. GA 25th Inf. Co.H
Scaff, Charles S. VA 61st Inf. Co.B
Scaff, Ezekiel GA 49th Inf. Co.E
Scaff, James I. SC 14th Inf. Co.A
Scaff, John NC 17th Inf. (1st Org.) Co.I
Scaff, Jonathan B. VA 41st Inf. Co.F
Scaff, J.R. SC 21st Inf. Co.K
Scaff, Mathew SC 21st Inf. Co.K
Scaff, Richard P. VA 61st Inf. Co.C
Scaff, Riley SC 1st Inf. Co.I
Scaff, Riley SC 14th Inf. Co.A
Scaff, R.M. AR 30th Inf. Co.E
Scaff, Samuel SC 21st Inf. Co.K
Scaff, Thomas SC Lt.Arty. 3rd (Palmetto) Bn. Co.C,E
Scaff, W.C. AL 11th Inf. Co.F
Scaff, William VA 6th Inf. Co.D
Scaff, William E. NC 27th Inf. Co.F
Scafin, D. AL 21st Inf. Co.G
Scaggins, James J. AL 9th Inf. Co.A
Scaggs, Andrew KY 5th Mtd.Inf. Co.F
Scaggs, Benjamin F. AR 21st Inf. Co.E
Scaggs, C.C. KY 3rd Mtd.Inf. Co.B Sgt.
Scaggs, Clark VA 16th Cav. Co.H
Scaggs, Clark VA Cav. Ferguson's Bn. Ferguson's Co.
Scaggs, Clouney VA 14th Cav. Co.D,K
Scaggs, David MO 7th Cav. Co.G
Scaggs, E. AR 6th Inf. Old Co.F
Scaggs, Ed. O. MD 1st Cav. Co.B
Scaggs, E.V. TX 16th Cav. Co.G
Scaggs, F.M. MO Inf. Clark's Regt. Co.G
Scaggs, George R. VA 36th Inf. 1st Co.B, 2nd Co.D 1st Sgt.
Scaggs, G.W. AL 2nd Bn. Hilliard's Legion Vol. Co.F
Scaggs, G.W. MO 11th Inf. Co.F
Scaggs, H. KY 7th Mtd.Inf. Co.C
Scaggs, H.A. TN 3rd (Forrest's) Cav. Co.G,D
Scaggs, Headley MO 11th Inf. Co.K
Scaggs, H.H. VA 22nd Inf. Co.C
Scaggs, Humphrey VA 63rd Inf. Co.D
Scaggs, J. MD 1st Cav. Co.B
Scaggs, James AR Cav. Gordon's Regt. Co.H
Scaggs, James A. VA 21st Cav. Co.H 1st Sgt.
Scaggs, James M. VA 79th Mil. Co.3 Sgt.
Scaggs, James R. VA 21st Cav. Co.H

Scaggs, J.O. AR Inf. Cocke's Regt. Co.K
Scaggs, John AL 50th Inf. Co.B
Scaggs, John AR 18th (Marmaduke's) Inf. Co.B
Scaggs, John AR Inf. Cocke's Regt. Co.F
Scaggs, John KY 5th Mtd.Inf. Co.F
Scaggs, John MO 11th Inf. Co.K
Scaggs, John H. KY 4th Mtd.Inf. Co.F
Scaggs, John O. MO 1st N.E. Cav. Co.L
Scaggs, Joseph MO 4th Inf. Co.A
Scaggs, Joseph VA 1st Cav. Co.I
Scaggs, Joseph VA Inf. 45th Bn. Co.E
Scaggs, Joseph VA 129th Mil. Buchanon's Co. 2nd Lt.
Scaggs, Joseph P. AR 4th Inf. Co.B
Scaggs, J.P. AR 1st (Monroe's) Cav. Co.D
Scaggs, J.S. TX Cav. Baird's Regt. Co.A
Scaggs, Lemuel F. VA 16th Cav. Co.H
Scaggs, Lewis KY 5th Mtd.Inf. Co.K Cpl.
Scaggs, Lewis F. VA Cav. Ferguson's Bn. Ferguson's Co.
Scaggs, L.L. TX 18th Cav. Co.H
Scaggs, Louis F. GA 13th Cav. Co.H
Scaggs, Martin KY 5th Mtd.Inf. Co.F
Scaggs, Maston MO 9th Bn.S.S. Co.C
Scaggs, Peter KY 5th Mtd.Inf. Co.F,D
Scaggs, Robert MD 1st Cav. Co.K
Scaggs, Robert VA 1st Cav. 2nd Co.K
Scaggs, Sanford B. VA Cav. Hounshell's Bn. Co.A
Scaggs, S.H. MO 11th Inf. Co.F,K
Scaggs, S.P. GA 30th Inf. Co.G
Scaggs, Squire VA 16th Cav. Co.H Sgt.
Scaggs, Squire VA Cav. Ferguson's Bn. Ferguson's Co.
Scaggs, Thomas KY 5th Mtd.Inf. Co.K
Scaggs, Thomas MO Cav. Clardy's Bn. Farris' Co.
Scaggs, W.A. AR Cav. Harrell's Bn. Co.D
Scaggs, William MO 9th Bn.S.S. Co.C
Scaggs, William MO Inf. Clark's Regt. Co.G
Scaggs, William MO Cav. Williams' Regt. Co.K
Scaggs, William P. TN 3rd (Forrest's) Cav. Co.G
Scaggs, William P. TN 3rd (Lillard's) Mtd.Inf. Co.G
Scagliotti, C. LA 22nd Inf. Gomez's Co.
Scags, Aaron AR Cav. McGehee's Regt. Co.C
Scags, Franklin A. MO 1st N.E. Cav. Co.L
Scags, John MO 1st N.E. Cav. Co.M
Scahill, Thomas LA 1st Hvy.Arty. (Reg.) Co.A
Scaif, William J. SC 5th Inf. 1st Co.A Ord.Sgt.
Scaife, Benjamin H. SC 6th Inf. Co.F
Scaife, Charner T. SC 1st Inf.
Scaife, C.T. SC Lt.Arty. 3rd (Palmetto) Bn. Co.A Sgt.
Scaife, C.T. SC Lt.Arty. Jeter's Co. (Macbeth Lt.Arty.) 1st Sgt.
Scaife, Ferdinand SC 18th Inf. Co.A Lt.Col.
Scaife, Francis A. LA 12th Inf. Co.G Jr.2nd Lt.
Scaife, Hazel F. SC 1st Inf. Co.E Sgt.
Scaife, H.F. SC Lt.Arty. Jeter's Co. (Macbeth Lt.Arty.) 1st Lt.
Scaife, James W. AR 2nd Inf. Old Co.E Lt.Col.
Scaife, Jessie F. AL 3rd Bn. Hilliard's Legion Vol. Co.F
Scaife, J.F. AL 60th Inf. Co.D 1st Sgt.
Scaife, J.J. GA 60th Inf.

Scaife, Joel AL 17th Inf. Co.F
Scaife, John R. SC 6th Inf. 1st Co.F
Scaife, J.R. SC Lt.Arty. Jeter's Co. (Macbeth Lt.Arty.)
Scaife, J.T. AL 14th Inf. Co.I
Scaife, J.W. AR Inf. Cocke's Regt. Co.C Capt.
Scaife, J.W. GA 3rd Res. Co.K
Scaife, T.J. AR Inf. Cocke's Regt. Co.C 2nd Lt.
Scaife, William L. GA 31st Inf. Co.A N.C.S.
Scaife, William L. Gen. & Staff Asst.Surg.
Scaife, W.L. TX 9th (Young's) Inf. Asst.Surg.
Scaife, W.L. Gen. & Staff Asst.Surg.
Scailes, A.R. AL 26th (O'Neal's) Inf. Co.G
Scains, Adam LA 12th Inf. Co.I
Scajone, Damiano LA Mil. Cazadores Espanoles Regt. Co.F
Scalamara, P. LA Inf.Crescent Regt. Co.H
Scalamera, P. LA Inf.Cons.Crescent Regt. Co.A,C
Scale, J.H. VA Cav. 37th Bn. Co.H
Scale, N.W. VA Cav. 37th Bn. Co.H
Scale, Tom AL 4th (Roddey's) Cav. Co.F
Scale, Yewer D. AL 18th Inf. Co.B
Scaler, H.Y. TN Cav. Jackson's Co.
Scales, --- FL McBride's Co. (Indians)
Scales, A. MS 1st Cav.
Scales, Absalom W. TX 14th Cav. Co.B Asst.Surg.
Scales, Absolom TN 4th (McLemore's) Cav. Co.F
Scales, Alfred M. MS 2nd Inf. Co.C 1st Sgt.
Scales, Alfred M. NC 13th Inf. Co.H Col.
Scales, Alfred M. Gen. & Staff Brig.Gen.
Scales, Bedford C. GA 55th Inf. Co.I
Scales, Benjamin F. TX 14th Cav. Co.B
Scales, Calvin H. NC 45th Inf. Co.D 1st Lt.
Scales, C.F. SC 3rd Bn.Res. Co.A
Scales, C.H. NC 3rd Cav. (41st St.Troops) Co.C
Scales, Dabney M. MS 17th Inf. Co.G 1st Sgt.
Scales, David C. TN 11th Cav. Co.I
Scales, D.C. TN 3rd (Forrest's) Cav. Co.A
Scales, D.C. TN 20th Inf. Co.B
Scales, E. TN 51st (Cons.) Inf. Co.H
Scales, E.D. NC 2nd Cav. (19th St.Troops) Capt.,ACS
Scales, Edmund M. TX 15th Inf. 2nd Co.E
Scales, Edward AR 8th Inf. Co.K
Scales, Edward F. NC 13th Inf. Co.H
Scales, E.M. NC Snead's Co. (Loc.Def.)
Scales, E.P. TX 20th Inf. Co.A 1st Sgt.
Scales, Erasmus D. NC 13th Inf. ACS
Scales, G.B. MS Cav. Davenport's Bn. (St.Troops) Co.B
Scales, George LA 14th Inf.
Scales, George H. LA 25th Inf. Co.D Sgt.
Scales, George M. TX 11th (Spaight's) Bn.Vol. Co.F Comsy.Sgt.
Scales, G.W. AL 60th Inf. Co.B
Scales, Hamilton NC 22nd Inf. Co.H Capt.
Scales, H.B. Gen. & Staff AQM
Scales, Henry W. NC 13th Inf. Co.H
Scales, H.M. GA 1st Eng.Corps 2nd Lt.
Scales, I.S. GA 19th Inf. Co.I
Scales, J.A. TX 12th Cav. Co.E Sgt.
Scales, J.A. 1st Cherokee Mtd.Vol. 1st Co.C
Scales, James VA 42nd Inf. Co.H
Scales, James H. AL 62nd Inf. Co.E Sgt.

Scales, James H. TN 37th Inf.
Scales, Jas. H. Gen. & Staff 1st Lt.,Adj.
Scales, James M. TX 19th Cav. Co.I Sgt.
Scales, James P. MS 11th Inf. Co.K
Scales, James R. AL 41st Inf. Co.F
Scales, James R. VA 54th Inf. Co.H Capt.
Scales, James S. VA 16th Inf. Co.F
Scales, James T. NC 2nd Inf. Co.E Maj.
Scales, James T. VA 18th Inf. Co.A
Scales, James W. Gen. & Staff Surg.
Scales, J.C. AL 51st (Part.Rangers) Co.G
Scales, J.C. GA 19th Inf. Co.I
Scales, Jefferson NC 45th Inf. Co.D Sgt
Scales, J.G. GA 1st Inf. (St.Guards) Co.K
Scales, J.H. TN 35th Inf. Co.G
Scales, J.H. TX 5th Cav. Co.G
Scales, J.H. TX 20th Inf. Co.A
Scales, J.H. VA Conscr. Cp.Lee Co.A
Scales, J. Irving MS 30th Inf. Co.K Col.
Scales, Joab A. 2nd Cherokee Mtd.Vol. Co.F 1st Lt.,Adj.
Scales, Joel AL 6th Inf. Co.L
Scales, John LA Inf. Co.A
Scales, John TN 10th Inf. Co.B
Scales, John C. AL 41st Inf. Co.F
Scales, John L. LA 2nd Inf. Co.D Ord.Sgt.
Scales, John L. NC 13th Inf. Co.H 2nd Lt.
Scales, John L. NC 45th Inf. Co.D Capt.
Scales, John R. AL 48th Inf. Co.K
Scales, John R. TX 28th Cav. Co.D 1st Lt.
Scales, John S. GA Cav. 24th Bn. Co.B
Scales, John W. GA 4th Res. Co.E,K
Scales, Joseph GA 42nd Inf. Co.A Cpl.
Scales, Joseph A. NC 1st Arty. (10th St.Troops) Co.H
Scales, Joseph A.C. TX 19th Cav. Co.G
Scales, Joseph H. VA 54th Inf. Co.H Capt.
Scales, Joseph Henry NC 45th Inf. Co.C 1st Lt.
Scales, Joseph S. VA 64th Mil. Powell's Co.
Scales, J.P. MS 28th Cav. Co.B Capt.
Scales, J.R. TX 35th (Likens') Cav. Surg.
Scales, J.S. GA Lt.Arty. Ritter's Co.
Scales, J.S. GA 38th Inf. Co.H
Scales, J.T. SC 3rd Bn.Res. Co.A
Scales, J.W. Armstrong's Brig. Capt.
Scales, M.H. TN 45th Inf. Co.A
Scales, Michael VA 14th Cav. Co.D
Scales, Moore H. GA 2nd Inf. Co.A
Scales, Nathaniel M. NC 1st Inf. Co.B Asst.Surg.
Scales, N.E. NC 6th Inf. QM
Scales, N.E. Wilcox's Div. Maj.,Ch.QM
Scales, Nicholson D. NC 13th Inf. Co.H
Scales, N.M. Gen. & Staff A.Surg.
Scales, Noah TN Cav. Jackson's Co.
Scales, P.A. MS 10th Cav. Co.C
Scales, P.A. MS 2nd Inf. Co.C Capt.
Scales, P.D. TN Inf. 3rd Cons.Regt. Co.K CSSgt.
Scales, Peter MO 4th Inf. Co.B
Scales, Peter VA 64th Mil. Powell's Co.
Scales, Peter H. NC 21st Inf. Co.D
Scales, Peter N. VA 16th Inf. Co.F
Scales, Peter P. NC 45th Inf. Co.C Capt.
Scales, Pleasant D. TN 24th Inf. Co.D Comsy.Sgt.
Scales, Pleasant M. NC 45th Inf. Co.D

Scales, R.E. MS 2nd Inf. Co.C
Scales, Robert MS 2nd Part. Co.A
Scales, Robert MS 18th Cav. Co.E
Scales, Robert MS 18th Cav. Co.F
Scales, Robert MS Packer's Co. (Pope Guards) Sgt.
Scales, Robert TN 1st (Feild's) Inf. Co.D
Scales, Robert S. TN Lt.Arty. Baxter's Co.
Scales, R.S. TN 20th Inf. Co.D
Scales, Samuel SC 5th St.Troops Co.M
Scales, Samuel SC 7th Res. Co.E
Scales, Samuel SC Cav.Bn. Holcombe Legion Co.D
Scales, Samuel W. TN 37th Inf. Asst.Surg.
Scales, Sanford A. GA 55th Inf. Co.I 1st Lt.
Scales, S.H. TN Cav. Jackson's Co.
Scales, S.W. TN Cav. 1st Bn. (McNairy's) Co.C
Scales, S.W. TN 22nd (Barteau's) Cav. Co.B
Scales, S.W. Gen. & Staff Asst.Surg.
Scales, T. TN Cav. Napier's Bn. Co.B
Scales, Thomas SC 5th St.Troops Co.M
Scales, Thomas SC Cav.Bn. Holcombe Legion Co.D
Scales, Thomas Coyle TN Cav. Napier's Bn. Co.A
Scales, Thomas H. KY 10th Cav. 3rd Lt.
Scales, Thomas J. AL 36th Inf. Co.D
Scales, Thomas S. MS 11th Inf. Co.E 2nd Lt.
Scales, T.J. GA 4th Res. Co.K
Scales, T.O. AL 8th (Hatch's) Cav. Co.C
Scales, T. Sidney MS 13th Inf. Co.A
Scales, W. GA 2nd Res. Co.I
Scales, Walter W. MS 11th Inf. Co.E
Scales, Wesley GA 2nd Res. Co.I
Scales, W.F. GA 16th Inf. Co.I
Scales, W.G. TX 20th Inf. Co.A
Scales, William SC 18th Inf. Co.B
Scales, William TN 14th Cav. Co.B Capt.
Scales, William G. GA 19th Inf. Co.I
Scales, William G. TX 2nd Inf. Co.H
Scales, William H. AR 1st (Colquitt's) Inf. Co.C Capt.
Scales, William H. TN 44th (Cons.) Inf. Co.G
Scales, William H. TN 55th (McKoin's) Inf. Co.I
Scales, William W. AL 43rd Inf. Co.K
Scales, W.M. MS 1st Cav. Co.B
Scales, W.N. MS 5th Cav. Co.D Capt.
Scales, W.N. MS Cav. 6th Bn. Prince's Co.
Scales, W.N. MS 2nd Inf. (A. of 10,000) Co.H 1st Lt.
Scales, W.P. TN 41st Inf. Co.B Cpl.
Scales, W.T. KY 7th Mtd.Inf. Co.A
Scales, Y.D. MS 10th Cav. Co.H
Scales, Y.D. TN Cav. 1st Bn. (McNairy's) Co.C
Scales, Y.D. TN Conf.Cav. Baxter's Bn. Co.A
Scales, Yewer D. AL 16th Inf. Co.B
Scaley, Henry M. MS 9th Inf. Old Co.K, New Co.F 2nd Lt.
Scaley, James O. MS 11th Inf. Co.E
Scalf, Andrew TN 39th Mtd.Inf. Co.G
Scalf, Archibald KY 5th Mtd.Inf. Co.A,E
Scalf, David TN Sullivan Cty.Res. (Loc.Def.Troops) Witcher's Co.
Scalf, Henry SC 16th Inf. Co.C
Scalf, Hortrel VA 61st Inf. Co.G
Scalf, James TN 60th Mtd.Inf. Co.C
Scalf, Jesse R. TN 60th Mtd.Inf. Co.C

Scalf, Joseph SC 1st (Butler's) Inf. Co.E
Scalf, Martin M. TN 37th Inf. Co.F
Scalf, Nathan TN 60th Mtd.Inf. Co.C
Scalf, William VA 8th Inf. Co.F
Scallan, G. LA Cav. Benjamin's Co.
Scallan, N. LA Lt.Arty. 2nd Field Btty.
Scallan, V. LA Lt.Arty. 2nd Field Btty.
Scalles, J. FL 1st (Res.) Inf.
Scalley, Cornelius AL 3rd Cav. Co.E
Scalley, George W. MS 2nd Inf. Co.B
Scallien, Alcide LA 1st Hvy.Arty. (Reg.) Co.I
Scallion, G. LA 4th Cav. Co.C
Scallion, H.V. LA 2nd Inf. Co.E
Scallion, J.W. AR 1st (Dobbin's) Cav. Co.E
Scallion, T.D. MS 5th Cav. Co.H
Scallion, W.H. MS 5th Cav. Co.H
Scallions, A.D. AL 17th Inf. Co.A
Scallions, F.M. TX Waul's Legion Co.D
Scallions, George W. MS 29th Inf. Co.B
Scallions, John MS Lt.Arty. 14th Bn. Co.C
Scallions, J.P. TX Waul's Legion Co.C
Scallom, F.E. MS 12th Inf. Co.F
Scallom, Joseph A. MS 12th Inf. Co.F
Scallon, Jas. P. LA 6th Inf. Co.E
Scallorn, Anderson TX 16th Inf. Co.I
Scallorn, Andrew R. TX 36th Cav. Co.A Sgt.
Scallorn, George W. TX 16th Inf. Co.I Cpl.
Scallorn, Joab TX 21st Cav. Co.A
Scallorn, John M. TX 16th Inf. Co.I
Scallorn, John S. MS 42nd Inf. Co.I 1st Sgt.
Scallorn, Lemuel P. TX 36th Cav. Co.A
Scallorn, Newton TX 36th Cav. Co.A
Scallorn, N.J. MS 29th Inf. Co.C
Scallorn, S.W. TX 8th Cav. Co.F
Scallorn, Thomas J., Jr. TX 16th Inf. Co.I
Scallorn, William H. MS 42nd Inf. Co.I Sgt.
Scallorn, William M. TX 16th Inf. Co.I
Scally, C. AL 3rd Inf. Co.E
Scally, Cornelius AR 3rd Cav. Co.E
Scally, Henry P. MS 32nd Inf. Co.E
Scally, James TN Lt.Arty. Winston's Co. Sgt.
Scally, James K. MS 26th Inf. Co.B
Scally, J.N. MS 32nd Inf. Co.E Capt.
Scally, John N. MS 2nd Inf. Co.B 2nd Lt.
Scally, Michael LA Mil. 1st Regt. 3rd Brig. 1st Div. Co.E
Scally, P. LA 1st Cav. Co.F
Scally, Thomas GA Hvy.Arty. 22nd Bn. Co.E
Scally, Thomas GA 1st (Olmstead's) Inf. Guilmartin's Co.
Scally, William H. MS 32nd Inf. Co.E Cpl.
Scalman, Benjamin F. MS 14th Inf. Co.H
Sca lol le, Bill 1st Cherokee Mtd.Rifles McDaniel's Co.
Scalron, N. TX 33rd Cav. Co.K
Scameron, Solomon AL 24th Inf. Co.F
Scamia, Miguel LA 30th Inf. Co.D
Scammahorn, D.A. MO 3rd Inf. Co.B Cpl.
Scammands, Lafayette F. MS 2nd Part.Rangers Co.B
Scammans, L.T. LA Cav. Lott's Co. (Carroll Drag.)
Scammel, William J. Conf.Arty. Lewis' Bn. Co.B
Scammell, E.W. GA Cobb's Legion Co.D
Scammell, George G. GA 55th Inf. Co.A
Scammell, John N. VA 3rd Inf. 1st Co.I

Scammell, Joseph H. VA Arty. J.W. Drewry's Co.
Scammell, Ro VA 2nd St.Res. Co.I
Scammell, Robert M. VA 9th Inf. Co.C Cpl.
Scammell, W. AR Lt.Arty. 5th Btty.
Scammell, William AL Lt.Arty. 2nd Bn. Co.C
Scammell, William J. VA 1st Arty. Co.E
Scammell, William J. VA Hvy.Arty. 10th Bn. Co.D
Scanarotti, Joseph VA Arty. Wise Legion
Scandelon, Michael AL 12th Inf. Co.I
Scandlan, S.W. AR 7th Inf. Co.D Drum.
Scandland, William VA 4th Inf. Co.L
Scandlon, Patrick TN 21st Inf. Co.I
Scandret, Robert GA Inf. 14th Bn. (St.Guards) Co.H
Scane, Chamer C. TX 28th Cav. Co.I
Scane, Vardy TX 28th Cav. Co.I
Scanger, Carroll AL 18th Inf. Co.D
Scanin, G.W. LA 2nd Cav. Co.C
Scanlan, Alf LA Inf. 1st Sp.Bn. (Rightor's) Co.A
Scanlan, Alfred LA 10th Inf. Co.F 2nd Lt.
Scanlan, Daniel LA 14th Inf. Co.C Sgt.
Scanlan, Daniel TN 2nd (Walker's) Inf. Co.I
Scanlan, Daniel 9th Conf.Inf. Co.D
Scanlan, D.J. TN 10th Inf. Co.H
Scanlan, Dominic KY 9th Mtd.Inf. Co.G
Scanlan, E. MS 8th Inf. QM
Scanlan, Ed. R. TX 4th Inf. Co.A
Scanlan, Edward 1st Choctaw Bn.,CSA AQM
Scanlan, Edward Gen. & Staff Capt.,AQM
Scanlan, F.A. MS Lt.Arty. (Warren Lt.Arty.) Swett's Co. Sgt.
Scanlan, Frank LA 4th Inf. Co.E
Scanlan, G.J. TN 38th Inf. 1st Co.A 1st Sgt.
Scanlan, J. GA 5th Cav. Co.E
Scanlan, J.J. AL 4th (Roddey's) Cav. Co.F
Scanlan, John GA Cav. 21st Bn. Co.D
Scanlan, John LA 21st (Patton's) Inf. Co.F
Scanlan, John LA 22nd Inf. Durrive, Jr.'s Co.A
Scanlan, John SC Inf. 1st (Charleston) Bn. Co.F
Scanlan, John VA 19th Inf. Co.D
Scanlan, John S. LA 3rd Inf. Co.F Cpl.
Scanlan, M. LA Arty. Hutton's Co. (Crescent Arty.,Co.A)
Scanlan, Michael TN Lt.Arty. Tobin's Co.
Scanlan, Michael VA 21st Mil. Co.C
Scanlan, Michael VA 26th Inf. 2nd Co.B
Scanlan, Patrick LA 22nd (Cons.) Inf. Co.A
Scanlan, Patrick TN 2nd (Walker's) Inf. Co.A
Scanlan, Patrick TN 10th Inf. Co.A
Scanlan, Patrick 9th Conf.Inf. Co.B
Scanlan, R. MS 4th Cav. Co.D
Scanlan, R. MS Cav. Hughes' Bn. Co.C
Scanlan, S.E. SC 11th Inf. Co.A Artif.
Scanlan, Thomas GA 66th Inf. Co.A
Scanlan, Thomas LA 7th Inf. Co.D
Scanlan, Thomas VA 60th Inf. Co.F
Scanlan, Thomas M. MS 13th Inf. Co.D
Scanlan, T.M. MS 39th Inf. Co.D
Scanlan, T.T. LA 22nd Inf. D.H. Marks' Co. Sgt.
Scanlan, William VA 27th Inf. Co.C 1st Sgt.
Scanland, Benjamin VA 4th Cav. Co.L
Scanland, James VA 36th Inf. Co.F
Scanland, J.M. KY 2nd (Duke's) Cav. Co.H
Scanland, J.M.A. LA 6th Cav. Co.C

Scanland, J.M.A. LA Inf. 1st Sp.Bn. (Rightor's) Co.D
Scanland, John LA 1st (Nelligan's) Inf. Co.H
Scanland, John TX Cav. Wells' Bn. Co.A Capt.
Scanland, John VA 36th Inf. Co.F
Scanland, L. Dade VA 12th Cav. Co.I
Scanland, N. VA Inf. 7th Bn.Loc.Def. Co.C
Scanland, S.W. AR 38th Inf. Co.G
Scanland, W.H. LA 6th Cav. Co.C
Scanland, W.H.H. LA 19th Inf. Co.A
Scanlard, Pat TX Cav. Wells' Regt. Co.E
Scanlen, Owen SC 1st (Butler's) Inf. Co.C
Scanlin, Christopher MS 20th Inf. Co.C
Scanlin, Dennis LA Arty. Moody's Co. (Madison Lt.Arty.)
Scanlin, Edwin NC 55th Inf. Co.I
Scanlin, James 2nd Conf.Eng.Troops Co.D
Scanlin, Martin AL 15th Bn.Part.Rangers Co.B
Scanlin, Martin LA 1st (Strawbridge's) Inf. Co.I
Scanlin, Michael TN 21st Inf. Co.F
Scanlin, Patrick LA 10th Inf. Co.K
Scanlin, Patrick VA Cav. 35th Bn. Co.C
Scanlin, Richard GA Hvy.Arty. 22nd Bn. Co.D
Scanlin, Robert T. VA 13th Inf. Co.H
Scanlin, R.T. GA 64th Inf. Co.A
Scanlin, R.T. NC Cumberland Cty.Bn.Detailed Men Co.B Jr.2nd Lt.
Scanlin, Thomas VA 5th Inf. Co.L
Scanlin, Thomas VA 13th Inf. Co.I
Scanlin, Thomas VA 46th Inf. 2nd Co.I
Scanlin, Timothy MS 20th Inf. Co.C
Scanling, B. VA 33rd Inf. Co.I
Scanling, John T. TN 13th (Gore's) Cav. Co.G
Scanlins, Daniel MS 1st (King's) Inf. (St.Troops) Co.E
Scanlon, Bartholemew VA 33rd Inf. Co.I
Scanlon, Daniel VA 33rd Inf. Co.I
Scanlon, G. LA Mil. 3rd Regt. 3rd Brig. 1st Div. Co.D
Scanlon, J.D. LA 14th Inf. Co.C
Scanlon, John MS Inf. 1st Bn.St.Troops (12 mo. '62-3) Co.C
Scanlon, M. AL 56th Part.Rangers Co.B
Scanlon, M. LA Mil. Orleans Fire Regt. Co.G
Scanlon, M. TN 21st Inf. Co.E Sgt.
Scanlon, Michael GA 1st (Olmstead's) Inf. Co.A Cpl.
Scanlon, T. LA Mil. Orleans Fire Regt. Co.G
Scanlon, Thomas SC 1st (Butler's) Inf. Co.B
Scanlon, Thomas VA 18th Cav. Co.C
Scanlon, Thomas VA 12th Inf. Co.D
Scanlon, Thomas VA Inf. 25th Bn. Co.E
Scanlon, T.T. LA Inf. 7th Bn. Co.C
Scanlon, W. GA 1st (Olmstead's) Inf. Co.I
Scannarotte, Joseph VA Lt.Arty. Turner's Co.
Scannel, Frederick AL 15th Bn.Part.Rangers Co.B
Scannel, Jame LA Mil. 4th Regt. 3rd Brig. 1st Div. Co.H
Scannell, E. LA Mil. Moreau Guards Lt.
Scannell, Fred AL 8th Inf. Co.C
Scannell, Patrick LA 22nd Inf.
Scantlan, John Conf.Lt.Arty. 1st Reg.Btty.
Scantland, B.S. KY 1st Inf. Co.B
Scantland, John D. GA 64th Inf. Co.C
Scantland, L.A. VA 6th Cav. Co.K
Scantlin, F.M. TX 7th Cav. Co.A

Scantlin, G.W. AR 5th Mil. Co.E
Scantlin, Peter VA 3rd Res. Co.K
Scantlon, David H. VA 4th Inf. Co.C,D Music.
Scarbaugh, B.W. GA 4th Inf. Co.E
Scarber, John MS Clayton's Co. (Jasper Defend.)
Scarber, John NC Mil. Clark's Sp.Bn. A.B.
    Davis' Co.
Scarboroug, T.M. GA 16th Inf. Co.D
Scarborough, A. GA 16th Inf. Co.D
Scarberry, Alexander GA 52nd Inf. Co.H
Scarberry, Crede VA 57th Inf. Co.A
Scarberry, David VA 57th Inf. Co.B
Scarberry, Harland AR 25th Inf. Co.B
Scarberry, Isaac VA 57th Inf. Co.B
Scarberry, Joseph MS 26th Inf. Co.B
Scarberry, R.F. KY 3rd Cav. Co.C
Scarberry, Robert KY 3rd Mtd.Inf. Co.C
Scarberry, Thomas C. TN 37th Inf. Co.K
Scarberry, William TN Inf. 22nd Bn. Co.D
Scarberry, William VA 51st Inf. Co.A
Scarbor, John MS 2nd (Quinn's St.Troops) Inf.
    Co.D
Scarbor, William A. GA 28th Inf. Co.K
Scarboraugh, M. MS Cav. Terrell's Unatt.Co.
Scarborer, Christopher AL Lt.Arty. 2nd Bn.
    Co.B Cpl.
Scarborer, Silas AL Lt.Arty. 2nd Bn. Co.B
Scarboro, C.C. TN Lt.Arty. Phillips' Co. Cpl.
Scarboro, E.A. 1st Conf.Cav. 2nd Co.G
Scarboro, Eli O. NC 8th Sr.Res. Broadhurst's
    Co.
Scarboro, F.M. TN 37th Inf. Co.I
Scarboro, George D. NC 3rd Inf. Co.K
Scarboro, James GA Inf. 1st Loc.Troops
    (Augusta) Dearing's Cav.Co.
Scarboro, John NC Mil. Clark's Sp.Bn. Co.D
Scarboro, John NC Loc.Def. Griswold's Co.
Scarboro, John C. NC 1st Inf. Co.I Sgt.
Scarboro, Louis P. GA 3rd Inf. Co.A
Scarboro, R.H. NC 2nd Arty. (36th St.Troops)
    Co.B
Scarborogh, J.R. TX Vol. Teague's Co.
    (So.Rights Guards)
Scarborogh, T.P. TX 22nd Inf. Co.F
Scarborough, --- GA Lt.Arty. King's Btty.
Scarborough, A. LA Lt.Arty. 6th Field Btty.
    (Grosse Tete Flying Arty.)
Scarborough, A. LA 4th Inf. New Co.G
Scarborough, A. LA 27th Inf. Co.F
Scarborough, A. MS Rogers' Co. Cpl.
Scarborough, A.B. TX 22nd Inf. Co.F 2nd Lt.
Scarborough, Abner W. MS 15th Inf. Co.A Cpl.
Scarborough, Abram MS 3rd Inf. Co.A
Scarborough, Absalom GA Hvy.Arty. 22nd Bn.
    Co.D,C Sgt.
Scarborough, A.C. NC 14th Inf. Co.K Cpl.
Scarborough, A.C. NC 31st Inf. Co.H
Scarborough, Addison B. AL 61st Inf. Co.D 1st
    Lt.
Scarborough, A.J. LA 2nd Cav. Co.E
Scarborough, A.J. LA 2nd Inf. Co.A Sgt.
Scarborough, A.J. NC 31st Inf. Co.H
Scarborough, A.J. TX 4th Cav. Co.B
Scarborough, Albert GA 5th Inf. Co.E
Scarborough, Albert GA Inf. 10th Bn.
    Hosp.Stew.

Scarborough, Alfred M. GA Cav. 7th Bn.
    (St.Guards) Co.B
Scarborough, Allen MS 33rd Inf. Co.C 1st Lt.
Scarborough, Allen J. MS 22nd Inf. Co.A
Scarborough, Allen S. FL 9th Inf. Co.A Cpl.
Scarborough, A.M. AL Cp. of Instr. Talladega
Scarborough, A.M. GA 1st (Ramsey's) Inf. Co.E
Scarborough, A.M. SC 14th Inf. Co.A 2nd Lt.
Scarborough, A.M. TN Arty. Bibb's Co. 1st Lt.
Scarborough, Americus VA 46th Inf. 4th Co.F
Scarborough, Amos A. AL 24th Inf. Co.C
Scarborough, Andrew TN 59th Mtd.Inf. Co.G
Scarborough, Andrew J. TX 4th Cav. Co.B
    Capt.
Scarborough, Asa J. MS 36th Inf. Co.C Ens.
Scarborough, B. TX Cav. 1st Bn.St.Troops Co.F
    Cpl.
Scarborough, B.E. NC 31st Inf. Co.H
Scarborough, Benjamin LA 17th Inf. Co.C
Scarborough, Benjamin F. NC 28th Inf. Co.E
Scarborough, B.F. AL 18th Inf. Co.C
Scarborough, B.J. GA Inf. 1st Loc.Troops
    (Augusta) Co.C
Scarborough, B.J. SC 10th Inf. Co.K
Scarborough, B.O. LA 6th Inf. Co.A
Scarborough, B.S. TN 1st (Feild's) Inf. Co.B
Scarborough, C. Augustus AL Recruits
Scarborough, C.C. GA Inf. (Baldwin Inf.)
    Moore's Co.
Scarborough, C.D. NC 1st Jr.Res. Co.D
Scarborough, Charles A. AL Mil. 4th Vol. Co.H
Scarborough, Christopher C. LA 28th (Gray's)
    Inf. Co.I,G
Scarborough, C.L. LA 2nd Inf. Co.A
Scarborough, C.P. AL 28th Inf. Co.K
Scarborough, D. GA Siege Arty. 28th Bn. Co.K
Scarborough, Daniel GA 4th Res. Co.E,K
Scarborough, Daniel MS 8th Inf. Co.D
Scarborough, Daniel MS 37th Inf. Co.B
Scarborough, Daniel B. AR Inf. 1st Bn. Co.B
Scarborough, Darius MS Cav. 1st Bn. (McNair's)
    St.Troops Co.C
Scarborough, David LA 28th (Gray's) Inf. Co.A
Scarborough, David MS 3rd Inf. Co.A
Scarborough, David NC Hvy.Arty. 1st Bn. Co.A
Scarborough, David F. TX 19th Inf. Co.D
Scarborough, David G. MS 14th Inf. Co.H Sgt.
Scarborough, David J. GA 14th Inf. Co.H
Scarborough, David P. GA 3rd Cav. (St.Guards)
    Co.G
Scarborough, D.B. TX 9th (Nichols') Inf. Co.K
Scarborough, D.C. GA Inf. (Madison Cty. Home
    Guard) Milner's Co.
Scarborough, D.G. MS 14th (Cons.) Inf. Co.E
    Sgt.
Scarborough, D.M. MS 1st (King's) Inf.
    (St.Troops) Co.A Sgt.
Scarborough, Drury J. GA 14th Inf. Co.H
Scarborough, D.W. GA 1st (Fannin's) Res. Co.D
Scarborough, E. AR 12th Inf. Co.E
Scarborough, E. MS 6th Cav. Co.F
Scarborough, E.D. GA 32nd Inf. Co.E
Scarborough, Edward B. VA 40th Inf. Co.I
Scarborough, E.H. MS 11th (Perrin's) Cav.
    Co.K
Scarborough, E.H. MS 37th Inf. Co.I
Scarborough, Elisha MS 37th Inf. Co.D

Scarborough, E.M. AL 62nd Inf. Co.F
Scarborough, E.O. NC 1st Cav. (9th St.Troops)
    Co.I
Scarborough, E.R. SC 23rd Inf. Co.K
Scarborough, F.B. LA 2nd Cav. Co.I
Scarborough, F.G. LA 18th Inf. Co.E
Scarborough, F.G. LA Inf.Crescent Regt. Co.F
Scarborough, F.G. SC Lt.Arty. 3rd (Palmetto)
    Bn. Co.E
Scarborough, F.J. SC Lt.Arty. 3rd (Palmetto)
    Bn. Co.E
Scarborough, F.L. LA Lt.Arty. 1st Bn. Co.4
    Cpl.
Scarborough, Francis M. MS 6th Inf. Co.D
Scarborough, Franklin NC 44th Inf. Co.H 1st
    Sgt.
Scarborough, Franklin P. MS 15th Inf. Co.K
Scarborough, Frank P. MS 24th Inf. Co.C
Scarborough, Frederick B. GA 3rd Cav.
    (St.Guards) Co.G
Scarborough, Frederick B. GA 15th Inf. Co.F
Scarborough, Gadsden AL 10th Inf. Co.H
Scarborough, General J. GA 61st Inf. Co.D,K
Scarborough, George GA 48th Inf. Co.H
Scarborough, George TX 7th Cav. Co.H
Scarborough, George D. VA 46th Inf. 4th Co.F
Scarborough, George P. SC 14th Inf. Co.A
Scarborough, George W. TX Cav. Hardeman's
    Regt. Co.F 2nd Lt.
Scarborough, Gideon J.H. NC 54th Inf. Co.D
Scarborough, G.J. Trans-MS Conf.Cav. 1st Bn.
    Co.D
Scarborough, G.M. TX 1st Inf. Co.G
Scarborough, Green GA Inf. 3rd Bn. Co.E
Scarborough, Green L. AL 3rd Cav. Co.A Sgt.
Scarborough, Green L. Conf.Cav. Wood's Regt.
    Co.C Cpl.
Scarborough, G.T. VA 59th Inf. Asst.Surg.
Scarborough, G.W. GA 66th Inf. Co.A
Scarborough, G.W. MS 8th Inf. ACS
Scarborough, G.W. MS Inf. Lewis' Co.
Scarborough, H. SC 4th St.Troops Co.I
Scarborough, H.A. SC 23rd Inf. Co.K Lt.
Scarborough, Hardy AL 17th Inf. Co.F
Scarborough, Hardy GA Arty. 11th Bn. (Sumter
    Arty.) Co.A Sgt.
Scarborough, Haywood GA 3rd Inf. 1st Co.I
Scarborough, H.G. SC 2nd Inf. Co.E
Scarborough, Henry MS 2nd Cav. Co.F
Scarborough, Henry MS 16th Inf. Co.E
Scarborough, Henry SC Lt.Arty. Garden's Co.
    (Palmetto Lt.Btty.) Cpl.
Scarborough, Henry N. GA 57th Inf. Co.B
Scarborough, Henry P. MS 7th Inf. Co.D
Scarborough, H.F. GA Brooks' Co. (Terrell
    Lt.Arty.)
Scarborough, H.H. SC 23rd Inf. Co.K
Scarborough, H.J. LA 2nd Inf. Co.A
Scarborough, J. AL 38th Inf. Co.D
Scarborough, J. AR 24th Inf. Co.D
Scarborough, J. GA 45th Inf.
Scarborough, J. LA Lt.Arty. Holmes' Btty.
Scarborough, J.A. SC Lt.Arty. 3rd (Palmetto)
    Bn. Co.E
Scarborough, J.A.J. AL 2nd Cav. Co.I Bugler
Scarborough, James GA Lt.Arty. Milledge's Co.
Scarborough, James GA 3rd Inf. 1st Co.I

Scarborough, James GA 6th Inf. Co.F
Scarborough, James GA 8th Inf. Co.G
Scarborough, James LA 14th Inf. Co.I Cpl.
Scarborough, James MS Cav. Ham's Regt. Co.I
Scarborough, James MS Inf. 3rd Bn. Co.C Sgt.
Scarborough, James SC 1st St.Troops Co.K
Scarborough, James TN Cav. 16th Bn. (Neal's) Co.A
Scarborough, James TN 19th Inf. Co.D
Scarborough, James TN 25th Inf. Co.K
Scarborough, James TX 13th Cav. Co.D Sgt.
Scarborough, James A. SC 16th Inf. Co.A
Scarborough, James B. NC 26th Inf. Co.K
Scarborough, James C. GA Cav. 22nd Bn. (St.Guards) Co.H
Scarborough, James E. GA 10th Inf. Co.G
Scarborough, James H. GA 45th Inf. Co.K Cpl.
Scarborough, James H. SC Inf. Hampton Legion Co.C
Scarborough, James M. GA 61st Inf. Co.D,K
Scarborough, James M. MS 24th Inf. Co.C Sgt.
Scarborough, James S. AR 3rd Inf. Co.L
Scarborough, James S. VA 41st Inf. Co.A Cpl.
Scarborough, James W. GA 44th Inf. Co.E 2nd Lt.
Scarborough, James W. MS 15th (Cons.) Inf. Co.A
Scarborough, J.B. AR Inf. Hardy's Regt. Co.C Cpl.
Scarborough, J.B. GA Inf. Alexander's Co. Cpl.
Scarborough, J.C. MS 1st Lt.Arty. Co.F
Scarborough, J.C. TX 22nd Inf. Co.F
Scarborough, J.C. VA Courtney Arty.
Scarborough, J.E. GA 32nd Inf. Co.H
Scarborough, J.E. GA 63rd Inf. Co.E
Scarborough, Jerry GA 10th Inf. Co.G
Scarborough, Jesse GA 8th Inf. Co.G
Scarborough, Jesse MS Cav. Terrell's Unatt.Co. Sgt.
Scarborough, Jesse A. MS 6th Inf. Co.F Cpl.
Scarborough, Jesse C. NC 51st Inf. Co.G Sgt.
Scarborough, Jethro F.L. GA 14th Inf. Co.H
Scarborough, J.F. GA Brooks' Co. (Terrell Lt.Arty.)
Scarborough, J.F. LA 2nd Cav. Co.E 1st Lt.
Scarborough, J.F. LA 2nd Inf. Co.A 1st Lt.
Scarborough, J.F. TX 14th Inf. Co.F
Scarborough, J.H. GA 51st Inf. Co.I
Scarborough, J.H. TN 6th Inf. Co.B
Scarborough, J.J. SC Prov.Guard Hamilton's Co.
Scarborough, J.M. AL Cav. 24th Bn. Co.A
Scarborough, J.M. AL 53rd (Part.Rangers) Co.E
Scarborough, J.M. MS Cav. Jeff Davis Legion Co.D
Scarborough, J.M. TX 1st Inf. Co.G
Scarborough, J.M. TX Vol. Teague's Co. (So. Rights Guards)
Scarborough, J.N. GA 5th Res. Co.A
Scarborough, J.N. NC 31st Inf. Co.H
Scarborough, John GA 49th Inf. Co.K
Scarborough, John LA Pointe Coupee Arty.
Scarborough, John MS Cav. 1st Bn. (McNair's) St.Troops Co.B
Scarborough, John MS 3rd Inf. Co.H
Scarborough, John MS 8th Inf. Co.D
Scarborough, John TN 17th Inf. Co.I
Scarborough, John TX Cav. 6th Bn. Co.A

Scarborough, John VA 1st Arty. Co.E
Scarborough, John VA Hvy.Arty. 10th Bn. Co.D
Scarborough, John B. Gen. & Staff Asst.Surg.
Scarborough, John C. NC 14th Inf. Co.K
Scarborough, John C. VA Lt.Arty. Weisiger's Co.
Scarborough, John D. VA Inf. 5th Bn. Co.C
Scarborough, John D. VA 53rd Inf. Co.C Cpl.
Scarborough, John O. TN 50th Inf. Co.F Sgt.
Scarborough, John R. NC 6th Inf. Co.E
Scarborough, John R. SC 23rd Inf. Co.K
Scarborough, John R. TX 22nd Inf. Co.D Sgt.
Scarborough, John S. AL 6th Inf. Co.G Sgt.
Scarborough, John T. AL 17th Inf. Co.I Music.
Scarborough, John W. AL 2nd Cav. Co.C 1st Lt.
Scarborough, John W. AL Cp. of Instr. Talladega
Scarborough, Joseph TN 6th (Wheeler's) Cav. Co.B
Scarborough, Joseph H. TN 18th (Newsom's) Cav. Co.B
Scarborough, Joseph L. LA 1st (Nelligan's) Inf. Co.A
Scarborough, Josey GA Inf. 26th Bn. Co.A
Scarborough, Josh GA 5th Res. Co.G Cpl.
Scarborough, J.P. LA 2nd Cav. Co.E
Scarborough, J.S. LA 2nd Inf. Co.A Cpl.
Scarborough, J.T. LA 27th Inf. Co.F
Scarborough, J.W. AL 36th Inf. Co.B
Scarborough, J.W. LA 2nd Cav. Co.E 2nd Lt.
Scarborough, J.W. MS Cav. Jeff Davis Legion Co.C Cpl.
Scarborough, J.W. TN 50th Inf. Co.D
Scarborough, J.W. TX 25th Cav. Co.C
Scarborough, J.W. TX 9th (Nichols') Inf. Co.B
Scarborough, J.W. VA 13th Cav. Co.B
Scarborough, Kittrell W. GA 1st Inf.
Scarborough, L.B. SC 23rd Inf. Co.K Sgt.
Scarborough, L.D. TX 9th (Nichols') Inf. Co.H
Scarborough, Levy MS 3rd Inf. Co.A
Scarborough, Lovell GA 17th Inf. Co.E
Scarborough, L.T. MS 44th Inf. Co.G,I Cpl.
Scarborough, L.W. AR 20th Inf. Co.H Cpl.
Scarborough, L.W. SC Lt.Arty. Garden's Co. (Palmetto Lt.Btty.)
Scarborough, L.W. SC 2nd Inf. Co.E
Scarborough, M. FL 9th Inf. Co.F
Scarborough, Malcom F. NC 1st Inf. Co.I 1st Sgt.
Scarborough, Malta GA Lt.Arty. Anderson's Btty.
Scarborough, Martin AL 4th Inf. Co.K
Scarborough, Matthew M. FL 10th Inf. Co.F Sgt.
Scarborough, M.D. TX 14th Field Btty.
Scarborough, M.F. Gen. & Staff 2nd Lt.,Dr.M.
Scarborough, M.G. NC 31st Inf. Co.H
Scarborough, M.H. SC Lt.Arty. Garden's Co. (Palmetto Lt.Btty.)
Scarborough, Miles VA 9th Inf. Co.B
Scarborough, Miller GA 10th Inf. Co.G
Scarborough, Miller GA 49th Inf. Co.K
Scarborough, N.B. SC 23rd Inf. Co.K
Scarborough, N.J. GA 6th Inf. Co.C
Scarborough, N.J. TX 35th (Brown's) Cav. Co.A Music.

Scarborough, N.J. TX 13th Vol. 1st Co.B 2nd Music.
Scarborough, N.V. TX 24th & 25th Cav. (Cons.) Co.I
Scarborough, N.V. TX Waul's Legion Co.B
Scarborough, P.D. LA 13th Bn. (Part.Rangers) Co.E
Scarborough, Peter MS 3rd Inf. Co.A
Scarborough, Peter MS Inf. (Res.) Berry's Co.
Scarborough, P.F.D. GA Cav. 22nd Bn. (St.Guards) Co.F
Scarborough, P.L. TX Waul's Legion Co.F
Scarborough, P.S. AL 28th Inf. Co.D
Scarborough, R. VA Inf. 2nd Bn.Loc.Def. Co.F
Scarborough, R.B. GA Hvy.Arty. 22nd Bn. Co.D
Scarborough, R.H. NC Lt.Arty. 13th Bn. Co.B
Scarborough, R.H. SC Lt.Arty. 3rd (Palmetto) Bn. Co.E
Scarborough, R.H. SC 9th Inf. Co.F
Scarborough, Rhemer GA 9th Inf. Co.I
Scarborough, Richard LA Pointe Coupee Arty.
Scarborough, Richard MS 8th Inf. Co.D
Scarborough, Richmond C. MS 36th Inf. Co.I Cpl.
Scarborough, Robert VA 2nd Inf.Loc.Def. Co.H
Scarborough, Robert H. TN 14th Inf. Co.E
Scarborough, Robert M. TN 59th Mtd.Inf. Co.G Cpl.
Scarborough, Robert T. VA Hvy.Arty. 10th Bn. Co.D
Scarborough, R.S. VA 13th Cav. Co.K
Scarborough, Samuel GA 51st Inf. Co.B Cpl.
Scarborough, Samuel D. TN 14th Inf. Co.E Sgt.
Scarborough, Samuel F. GA 57th Inf. Co.B
Scarborough, Samuel R. MS 15th Inf. Co.A
Scarborough, Samuel W. NC 3rd Cav. (41st St.Troops) Co.E
Scarborough, S.B. TX Cav. 6th Bn. Co.D
Scarborough, S.D. GA 14th Inf. Sgt.
Scarborough, S.F. TX 24th & 25th Cav. Co.I
Scarborough, S.H. NC 31st Inf. Co.H
Scarborough, Shadrick GA 9th Inf. Co.I
Scarborough, Silas TX 15th Cav. Co.D
Scarborough, S.M. GA 54th Inf. Co.I
Scarborough, S.R. MS 40th Inf. Co.K
Scarborough, Stephen A. MS 8th Inf. Co.D
Scarborough, T. GA 5th Res. Co.H
Scarborough, T. TX 9th (Nichols') Inf. Co.B
Scarborough, T.C. LA 25th Inf. Co.K Capt.
Scarborough, T.C. TN Conscr. (Cp. of Instr.)
Scarborough, Tho. TX 36th Cav. Co.H
Scarborough, Thomas GA 10th Cav. (St.Guards) Co.F Bvt.2nd Lt.
Scarborough, Thomas TX 29th Cav. Co.I
Scarborough, Thomas B. AL 6th Inf. Co.G
Scarborough, Thomas J. MS 22nd Inf. Co.A
Scarborough, Thomas P. GA 6th Inf. Co.F
Scarborough, T.J. TX 24th & 25th Cav. (Cons.) Co.I
Scarborough, T.J. TX Waul's Legion Co.B
Scarborough, W.A. FL 10th Inf. Co.D
Scarborough, Warren GA 5th Res. Co.A
Scarborough, Washington D. GA 61st Inf. Co.D,K
Scarborough, Washington H. AR Inf. 1st Bn. Co.B

Scarborough, Washington P. TX Inf. Griffin's Bn. Co.C
Scarborough, W.B. FL 1st (Res.) Inf. Co.L
Scarborough, W.C. LA 2nd Inf. Co.A
Scarborough, W.D. SC Lt.Arty. 3rd (Palmetto) Bn. Co.E 2nd Lt.
Scarborough, W.F. TN 50th Inf. Co.D
Scarborough, W.G. TX 9th (Nichols') Inf. Co.K
Scarborough, W.H. SC 7th Cav. Co.I
Scarborough, W.H. SC Cav.Bn. Holcombe Legion Co.A
Scarborough, W.H. TX Cav. Hardeman's Regt. Co.F
Scarborough, Wiley J. MS 27th Inf. Co.F
Scarborough, William AL 61st Inf. Co.A
Scarborough, William AR 3rd Inf. Co.F
Scarborough, William GA Arty. (Macon Lt.Arty.) Slaten's Co.
Scarborough, William GA 48th Inf. Co.H
Scarborough, William LA 4th Cav. Co.A
Scarborough, William MS 6th Cav. Co.F Cpl.
Scarborough, William MS 22nd Inf. Co.A
Scarborough, William SC 2nd Inf. Co.C
Scarborough, William SC 21st Inf. Co.D
Scarborough, William TX 7th Cav. Co.H
Scarborough, William TX 9th (Nichols') Inf. Co.K
Scarborough, William TX 13th Vol. 3rd Co.I
Scarborough, William TX 20th Inf. Co.H
Scarborough, William TX Vol. Teague's Co. (So.Rights Guards)
Scarborough, William VA Horse Arty. G.W. Brown's Co. Cpl.
Scarborough, William B. GA 15th Inf. Co.F
Scarborough, William B. LA 28th (Gray's) Inf. Co.I
Scarborough, William D. NC 1st Inf. Co.I 1st Lt.
Scarborough, William H. GA 42nd Inf. Co.D
Scarborough, William J. AR 3rd Inf. Co.L,A Cpl.
Scarborough, William J. GA Cav. 22nd Bn. (St.Guards) Co.H
Scarborough, William J. GA 42nd Inf. Co.K
Scarborough, William M. GA 57th Inf. Co.B
Scarborough, William M. SC 14th Inf. Surg.
Scarborough, William R. MS 27th Inf. Co.H
Scarborough, William S. FL 1st Cav. Co.D
Scarborough, William S. NC 52nd Inf. Co.E
Scarborough, Wilson D. SC 9th Inf. Co.F
Scarborough, W.J. GA Lt.Arty. Guerard's Btty. Cpl.
Scarborough, W.J. MS 37th Inf. Co.I
Scarborough, W.M. Gen. & Staff Asst.Surg.
Scarborough, W.S. SC Lt.Arty. 3rd (Palmetto) Bn. Co.E
Scarborough, W.S. SC 23rd Inf. Co.K
Scarborough, W.T. AR 12th Bn.S.S. Co.D
Scarborough, W.T. AR 19th (Dockery's) Inf. Co.G
Scarborough, W.T. NC 1st Inf. Co.I
Scarborough, W.W. AR Inf. Hardy's Regt. Co.C
Scarborrough, Milton D. MS 6th Inf. Co.F
Scarborugh, John F. AL 39th Inf. Co.I
Scarbough, --- TX Cav. Steele's Command Co.D
Scarbough, A. MO Inf. 4th Regt.St.Guard Co.E 2nd Lt.

Scarbough, G.G. AL 62nd Inf. Co.C
Scarbough, J.H.T. AL 39th Inf. Co.B
Scarbough, W.M. AR 1st (Crawford's) Cav. Co.G
Scarbour, John W. GA 51st Inf. Co.B
Scarbourrough, George SC 21st Inf. Co.H
Scarbro, Micajah AL 2nd Bn. Hilliard's Legion Vol. Co.C
Scarbrock, F. LA 6th Cav. Co.I Sgt.
Scarbrough, --- AL 51st (Part.Rangers) Co.D
Scarbrough, A. GA 1st Reg. Co.H
Scarbrough, Aaron GA 1st (Olmstead's) Inf. Co.F
Scarbrough, A.B. AL 23rd Inf. Co.G
Scarbrough, A.B. AL 31st Inf. Co.D
Scarbrough, Alex. TN 46th Inf. Co.I Sgt.
Scarbrough, A.M. TN Inf. 3rd Bn. Co.C Cpl.
Scarbrough, Ambrose F. NC 23rd Inf. Co.C Capt.
Scarbrough, Aven AL 39th Inf. Co.F
Scarbrough, B.A.J. SC Inf. 7th Bn. (Enfield Rifles) Co.A
Scarbrough, Benjamin F. MS 14th Inf. Co.H
Scarbrough, B.F. AL 1st Cav. 2nd Co.B Cpl.
Scarbrough, C.F. TX 7th Inf. Co.I
Scarbrough, Charles GA 64th Inf. Co.F
Scarbrough, Charles A. AL 40th Inf. Co.F
Scarbrough, Charles P. AL 13th Inf. Co.B
Scarbrough, David P. AL 11th Inf. Co.B Sgt.
Scarbrough, D.C. KY 3rd Mtd.Inf. Co.B
Scarbrough, D.P. AL 7th Cav. Co.B Capt.
Scarbrough, E. AL 21st Inf. Co.I
Scarbrough, E. AL 27th Inf. Co.F
Scarbrough, Edmund D. NC 44th Inf. Co.H
Scarbrough, Francis Marion MO Inf. 1st Bn. Co.B
Scarbrough, George GA 28th Inf. Co.K
Scarbrough, George TX Cav. Wells' Bn. Co.A
Scarbrough, George T. TN 7th (Duckworth's) Cav. Co.G
Scarbrough, George W. TN 63rd Inf. Co.B
Scarbrough, G.M. TX Waul's Legion Co.H
Scarbrough, G.M. Exch.Bn. 1st Co.C,CSA
Scarbrough, G.P. TX Cav. 1st Regt.St.Troops Co.B
Scarbrough, H. GA Inf. 10th Bn. Sgt.
Scarbrough, H. 20th Conf.Cav. Co.A
Scarbrough, Haywood GA Lt.Arty. Milledge's Co.
Scarbrough, H.M. TX 22nd Inf. Co.D
Scarbrough, Hugh NC Walker's Bn. Thomas' Legion Co.H,B
Scarbrough, J.A. MS 8th Inf. Co.D
Scarbrough, James C. NC 50th Inf. Co.F
Scarbrough, James P. GA 57th Inf. Co.B
Scarbrough, James W. AL 37th Inf. Co.F Lt.
Scarbrough, J.C. GA 3rd Res. Co.A
Scarbrough, Jepp P. AL 62nd Inf. Co.K
Scarbrough, Jere MS 39th Inf. Co.G
Scarbrough, J.F. AL 58th Inf. Co.F
Scarbrough, J.G. TN 3rd (Forrest's) Cav. Co.F
Scarbrough, J.G. TN 13th Inf. Co.E,G Sgt.
Scarbrough, J.H.T. AL 22nd Inf. Co.H
Scarbrough, J.L. AL 31st Inf. Co.K
Scarbrough, J.L. AL 58th Inf. Co.H
Scarbrough, J. Lafayette MO 8th Inf. Co.A
Scarbrough, J.M. MO 11th Inf. Co.A,K,F

Scarbrough, J.M. TN 63rd Inf. Co.B
Scarbrough, John GA 30th Inf. Co.H
Scarbrough, John TN 43rd Inf. Co.B
Scarbrough, John TN 46th Inf. Co.I
Scarbrough, John TN 63rd Inf. Co.B
Scarbrough, John TX 12th Cav. Co.F
Scarbrough, John TX 15th Cav. Co.D
Scarbrough, John B. TN 12th (Green's) Cav. Co.I Asst.Surg.
Scarbrough, John C. VA 6th Inf. Weisiger's Co.
Scarbrough, John C. VA 16th Inf. Co.I
Scarbrough, John G. AL Lt.Arty. Hurt's Btty.
Scarbrough, John H. TN 43rd Inf. Co.H
Scarbrough, John Laurence TX 20th Cav. Co.A
Scarbrough, J.P. TN 46th Inf. Co.I Cpl.
Scarbrough, J.S. AL 31st Inf. Co.D
Scarbrough, J.W. AL 15th Inf. Co.I
Scarbrough, J.W. TX 14th Inf. Co.I
Scarbrough, L.A. TN 13th Inf. Co.E,G Cpl.
Scarbrough, L.D. TX 24th Cav. Co.E
Scarbrough, L.L. TX 13th Cav. Co.B
Scarbrough, L.M. GA 3rd Res. Co.F Sgt.
Scarbrough, L.T. AL 24th Inf. Co.K
Scarbrough, M. AL 21st Inf. Co.I
Scarbrough, Matthew A. AL Lt.Arty. 2nd Bn. Co.F
Scarbrough, M.D. LA 28th (Thomas') Inf. Co.F 1st Sgt.
Scarbrough, Miles NC 55th Inf. Co.I
Scarbrough, M.M. MS 39th Inf. Co.G
Scarbrough, P. MS 2nd St.Cav. 2nd Co.C
Scarbrough, R. TX 8th Cav. Co.C
Scarbrough, Robert P. AL Lt.Arty. Hurt's Btty. 1st Sgt.
Scarbrough, S. GA 12th Inf. Cpl.
Scarbrough, S.E. MS 31st Inf. Ch.Cook
Scarbrough, S.H. GA 28th Inf. Co.K
Scarbrough, Silas Constantine TX 20th Cav. Co.A
Scarbrough, S.M. GA 37th Inf. Co.E
Scarbrough, S.M. GA 54th Inf. Co.I
Scarbrough, T.E. TX 28th Cav. Co.D
Scarbrough, Thomas Benton MO Inf. 1st Bn. Co.B
Scarbrough, Thomas G. GA 37th Inf. Co.C
Scarbrough, Thomas Hicks TX 36th Cav. Co.H
Scarbrough, T.L. MS 44th Inf. Co.G,I Cpl.
Scarbrough, W.A. AL 31st Inf. Co.D
Scarbrough, W.C. AL 23rd Inf. Co.G Cpl.
Scarbrough, William AL Talladega Cty.Res. Breed's Co. Sgt.
Scarbrough, William MS 28th Cav. Co.A Sgt.
Scarbrough, William MS Inf. 3rd Bn. (St.Troops) Co.F
Scarbrough, William NC 23rd Inf. Co.C
Scarbrough, William TX Cav. 1st Regt.St.Troops Co.B 2nd Lt.
Scarbrough, William A. AL Lt.Arty. Hurt's Btty.
Scarbrough, William H. TN 63rd Inf. Co.B
Scarbrough, William Henry KY 3rd Mtd.Inf. Co.B
Scarbrough, William R. GA 57th Inf. Co.I
Scarbrough, William S. AL 20th Inf. Co.E 2nd Lt.
Scarbrough, William T. GA 32nd Inf. Co.H
Scarbrough, W.J. LA Inf. 4th Bn. Co.D
Scarbrough, W.P. TX 21st Inf. Co.C

473

Schacatie, J. SC Mil. 1st Regt. (Charleston Res.) Co.B

Scarbrough, W.S. TX Cav. 1st Regt.St.Troops Co.A

Scarbrugh, G. TX Cav. Wells' Regt. Co.A

Scarburgh, Americus VA 39th Inf. Co.L

Scarburgh, George D. VA 39th Inf. Co.L

Scarburgh, G.T. Lee's Div. Asst.Surg.

Scarbury, Richard TN 4th (Murray's) Cav. Co.F

Scarbury, William AR Inf. 2nd Bn. Co.A

Scarbury, Zach AR Lt.Arty. Rivers' Btty.

Scarce, Daniel KY 1st (Butler's) Cav. Co.A

Scarce, E.R. VA 57th Inf. Co.F

Scarce, E.R. VA Conscr. Cp.Lee Co.B

Scarce, J. VA Lt.Arty. Motley's Co.

Scarce, John, Sr. VA 57th Inf. Co.I

Scarce, Leonard VA 57th Inf. Co.I

Scarce, M.L. VA Conscr. Cp.Lee Co.A

Scarce, R. VA 57th Inf. Co.I

Scarce, Robert TN 14th Inf. Co.B

Scarf, John NC 2nd Arty. (36th St.Troops) Co.F

Scarf, John S. AL Lt.Arty. 2nd Bn. Co.E Cpl.

Scarff, J.E. AL 40th Inf. Co.K

Scarff, J.E.C. AL St.Arty. Co.A

Scargell, T.H. TX 26th Cav. Co.C Cpl.

Scarlet, --- VA 12th Cav. Co.B

Scarlet, Edward LA 20th Inf. Co.H

Scarlet, John W. VA 2nd Inf. Co.K

Scarlet, S. TN 28th (Cons.) Inf. Co.K

Scarlet, Stephen MO 3rd Cav. Co.B

Scarlet, Thomas TN 28th (Cons.) Inf. Co.K

Scarlet, William VA 7th Cav. Baylor's Co.

Scarlett, A.P. AR Cav. Gordon's Regt. Co.B Sgt.

Scarlett, A.P. AR 15th Mil. Co.D 1st Sgt.

Scarlett, Austin AR 31st Inf. Co.B

Scarlett, Bluford L. TN 16th Inf. Co.F

Scarlett, D.C. GA 4th (Clinch's) Cav. Co.A,K 2nd Lt.

Scarlett, D.C. GA Cav. Floyd's Co.

Scarlett, Felix NC 14th Inf. Co.A

Scarlett, George GA 4th (Clinch's) Cav. Co.B

Scarlett, George GA 47th Inf. Co.H

Scarlett, George W. NC 14th Inf. Co.G

Scarlett, G.S. GA 4th (Clinch's) Cav. Co.A,K

Scarlett, G.W. NC 48th Inf. Co.G

Scarlett, James TN 1st (Carter's) Cav. Co.K

Scarlett, James C. NC Inf. 13th Bn. Co.A

Scarlett, James C. NC 66th Inf. Co.A

Scarlett, James I. NC 14th Inf. Co.G Sgt.

Scarlett, John TN 13th (Gore's) Cav. Co.C

Scarlett, John TN 16th Inf. Co.K

Scarlett, John TN 43rd Inf. Co.G

Scarlett, John B. NC 27th Inf. Co.G

Scarlett, John P. GA 4th (Clinch's) Cav. Co.B 1st Lt.

Scarlett, John P. GA 26th Inf. Dent's Co.A 3rd Lt.

Scarlett, John W. NC 45th Inf. Co.H

Scarlett, J.P. AR Cav. Gordon's Regt. Co.B

Scarlett, J.S. NC 3rd Arty. (40th St.Troops) Co.G

Scarlett, J.S. NC Lt.Arty. 13th Bn. Co.E

Scarlett, Minor AR 10th Inf. Co.A

Scarlett, Moses TN 28th Inf. Co.B

Scarlett, Nathan AR 31st Inf. Co.F

Scarlett, Robert E. NC 45th Inf. Co.H

Scarlett, S. NC 1st Jr.Res. Co.C

Scarlett, Samuel J. NC 27th Inf. Co.G

Scarlett, S.H. NC 48th Inf. Co.G

Scarlett, Silas TN 28th Inf. Co.B

Scarlett, Stephen E. MO Lt.Arty. 4th (Harris') Field Btty.

Scarlett, Thomas TN 28th Inf. Co.B

Scarlett, Thomas C. NC 56th Inf. Co.D

Scarlett, William NC 44th Inf. Co.E

Scarlett, William R. NC Inf. 13th Bn. Co.A Sgt.

Scarlett, William R. NC 66th Inf. Co.A Sgt.

Scarlette, A.P. AR 3rd Cav. Co.K

Scarlock, T.V. LA Miles' Legion Co.D

Scarlot, Edward LA 13th Inf. Co.H

Scarlott, Jesse NC 38th Inf. Co.H

Scarlott, J.M. NC 38th Inf. Co.H

Scarlott, W.F. NC 23rd Inf. Co.H

Scarlott, William NC 38th Inf. Co.H

Scarls, W. TX 25th Cav. Co.A

Scarpa, J. AL Mil. 3rd Vol. Co.A

Scarpentier, Jean LA Mil. 1st Native Guards

Scarpentier, Joseph LA Mil. 1st Native Guards

Scarpeto, Owen 1st Seminole Mtd.Vol.

Scarpio, J. LA Mil. Lewis Guards

Scarpio, Joseph LA Mil. Orleans Fire Regt. Co.F

Scarr, Baylor GA 3rd Inf.

Scarritt, J.M. FL 2nd Inf. Co.A

Scarritt, J.M. GA Inf. (Loc.Def.) Whiteside's Nav.Bn. Co.C Cpl.

Scarso, Eugene KY 5th Cav. Co.I Cpl.

Scarver, Edgar AL 38th Inf. Co.D

Scatchell, J. TX 25th Cav.

Scate, F.B. TX Cav. 1st Bn.St.Troops Co.D

Scater, William AL 25th Inf. Co.A

Scates, Abe SC 5th Inf. 2nd Co.G

Scates, A.D. TN 31st Inf. Co.A

Scates, A.J. SC 2nd Inf. Co.D

Scates, Alfred VA 26th Inf. Co.H

Scates, Alfred VA 111th Mil. Co.5

Scates, Charles TN 10th Inf. Co.C

Scates, Clarence TN 14th Inf. Co.K,A

Scates, David H. TN 63rd Inf. Co.B

Scates, D.H. TN 12th (Cons.) Inf. Co.F 1st Lt.

Scates, D.H. TN 22nd Inf. Co.D 1st Lt.

Scates, George W. TX 6th Cav. Co.E

Scates, G.W. TX Cav. Border's Regt. Co.I

Scates, James M. VA 40th Inf. Co.D Capt.

Scates, James R. TX 35th (Brown's) Cav. Co.D Sgt.

Scates, James R. TX 13th Vol. 2nd Co.C Cpl.

Scates, Joel H. VA 53rd Inf. Co.I

Scates, John TX 6th Cav. Co.E

Scates, Joseph SC 17th Inf. Co.F

Scates, Joseph VA 40th Inf. Co.A

Scates, J. Pinkney SC Palmetto S.S. Co.K,H

Scates, Lewis SC 15th Inf. Co.F

Scates, Mathew SC 17th Inf. Co.F

Scates, Pinkney SC 6th Inf. 1st Co.I

Scates, Richard VA 9th Cav. Co.K

Scates, Richard J. VA 41st Mil. Co.E

Scates, Stewart SC Palmetto S.S. Co.M

Scates, Thomas H. NC 15th Inf. Co.K

Scates, W.H. SC Palmetto S.S. Co.H

Scates, W.H.C. VA 22nd Cav. Co.I

Scates, William SC 6th Inf. 1st Co.I

Scates, William F. TN 21st (Wilson's) Cav. Co.K 2nd Lt.

Scates, William J. SC Palmetto S.S. Co.K,M

Scates, Z.B. TN 21st (Wilson's) Cav. Co.K Sgt.

Scates, Zebulon B. VA 48th Inf. Co.D

Scatt, L.A. AL 48th Inf. Co.F

Scattergood, Benjamin F. AL 21st Inf. Co.E Sgt.

Scattergood, George W. GA Inf. 2nd Bn. Co.C Cpl.

Scattergood, Walter S. GA Inf. 2nd Bn. Co.C

Sceal, G.B. AL 3rd Inf. Co.K

Sceals, James M. GA 48th Inf. Co.I 1st Sgt.

Sceane, William MO Cav. Slayback's Regt. Co.K

Scearce, Anthony S. KY Cav. Buckner Guards

Scearce, Buck KY 5th Cav. Co.H

Scearce, Daniel KY 10th (Johnson's) Cav. Co.D 1st Sgt.

Scearce, David W. VA 38th Inf. Co.K

Scearce, George KY 3rd Mtd.Inf. Co.C

Scearce, James KY 5th Cav. Co.A

Scearce, Joseph VA 57th Inf. Co.I

Scearce, R.H. TN 9th Inf. Co.H

Scearce, Richard VA 38th Inf. Co.K

Scearce, Robert VA 57th Inf. Co.I

Scearce, Robert A. VA 57th Inf. Co.I

Scearce, Thomas VA 57th Inf. Co.I

Scearce, Wellington TN 22nd (Barteau's) Cav. Co.K 3rd Lt.

Scearcy, W.B. MS 32nd Inf. Co.F

Sceay, William A. GA Cherokee Legion (St.Guards) Co.D

Sceic, Christ LA Mil. 4th Regt. 3rd Brig. 1st Div. Co.C

Sceles, George NC 1st Cav. (9th St.Troops) Co.E

Scellars, William A. GA 35th Inf. Co.C

Scellen, John D. VA 9th Inf. Co.D 1st Lt.

Scellen, John D. VA Inf. 25th Bn. Co.B Sgt.

Scellers, J.E. FL Harrison's Co. (Santa Rosa Guards)

Scellers, J.G. FL Harrison's Co. (Santa Rosa Guards)

Scent, James AL Lt.Arty. Ward's Btty.

Scent, W. AL 49th Inf. Co.E

Scent, William M. AL Lt.Arty. Ward's Btty.

Scenter, J.B. AR 25th Inf. Co.H

Scercy, George W. MS 24th Inf. Co.I

Scersey, David W. NC 25th Inf. Co.E

Scersey, William H. NC 25th Inf. Co.E

Scessions, Ezra GA Inf. (Richmond Factory Guards) Barney's Co.

Scessions, Rubin GA Inf. (Richmond Factory Guards) Barney's Co.

Schaab, L. LA Mil. 3rd Regt.Eur.Brig. (Garde Francaise) Co.2

Schaad, Henry M. AL 44th Inf. Co.E Music.

Schaaf, B. VA 2nd St.Res. Co.H

Schaaf, George LA 27th Inf. Co.D

Schaaf, L. VA 2nd St.Res. Co.E

Schaaf, Philip AL 8th Inf. Co.G

Schaaf, William TX Comal Res.

Schaaf, William VA Cav. 1st Bn. Co.C

Schaaff, J.T. Gen. & Staff Capt.,ACS

Schaare, C. TX Waul's Legion Co.C

Schaare, Charles TX Cav. Ragsdale's Bn. Co.B

Schaarman, Philip NC 2nd Bn.Loc.Def.Troops Co.C

Schabel, W. LA 30th Inf. Co.A Sgt.

Schacatie, J. SC Mil. 1st Regt. (Charleston Res.) Co.B

Schacatie, W. SC Mil. 1st Regt. (Charleston Res.) Co.B

Schacht, Simon VA 13th Inf. Co.D Cpl.

Schachte, John SC Mil.Arty. 1st Regt. Co.A

Schachte, William SC Mil.Arty. 1st Regt. Co.A

Schackelford, J.R. MS 20th Inf. Co.C

Schackelford, J.W. MS Griffin's Co. (Madison Guards)

Schackelford, Levi AL 3rd Inf. Co.G

Schackleford, George S. VA 21st Inf. Co.B

Schackleford, J.J. MO 1st N.E. Cav.

Schackleford, John S. MO 2nd N.E. Cav. (Franklin's Regt.)

Schad, August VA 15th Inf. Co.K 1st Lt.

Schad, H. VA Inf. 1st Bn.Loc.Def. Co.F

Schad, Henry VA 24th Cav. Co.B

Schad, Mathias F. MS 22nd Inf. Co.I

Schadd, Adam VA 1st Inf. Co.B

Schadd, Henry VA Cav. 1st Bn. Co.C

Schadd, Henry M. AR 3rd Inf. Co.I Music.

Schadd, Martin AR 19th (Dockery's) Inf. Cons. Co.E,D

Schade, Anton TN Inf. 3rd Bn. Co.F

Schade, Charles H. VA 11th Inf. Co.H

Schade, Nicholas LA 3rd Inf. Co.A Cpl.

Schadelbauer, Carl TX 1st Hvy.Arty. Co.I

Schadle, Matthew AR 15th (Josey's) Inf. Co.G

Schadnell, S.C. AL 3rd Res. Co.A 2nd Lt.

Schadt, Adam AL 3rd Inf. Co.D

Schadt, J. LA Mil. 2nd Regt. 3rd Brig. 1st Div. Co.B

Schadt, William TX 1st Inf. Co.L

Schadwick, E. LA 17th Inf. Co.B

Schadwitz, Edward TX 3rd Inf. Co.K

Schaedel, John LA 20th Inf. Co.C Capt.

Schaedel, L. LA Mil. 3rd Regt. 3rd Brig. 1st Div. Co.A

Schaefer, A. TX 3rd Inf. 2nd Co.A

Schaefer, C. TX 4th Cav. Co.G

Schaefer, F. TX 3rd Inf. 2nd Co.A

Schaefer, Fr. TX 3rd Inf. Co.B 1st Sgt.

Schaefer, Francis C. NC 1st Arty. (10th St.Troops) Co.D 2nd Lt.

Schaefer, G.W. TX 3rd Inf. 2nd Co.A

Schaefer, Henry TX 7th Cav. Co.B Sgt.

Schaefer, J. LA Mil. Fire Bn. Co.D

Schaefer, Jacob AL Gorff's Co. (Mobile Pulaski Rifles)

Schaefer, John VA 5th Cav. (12 mo. '61-2) Winfield's Co. Bugler

Schaefer, John W. MD Arty. 4th Btty.

Schaefer, Paul O. GA 36th (Villepigue's) Inf. Co.F

Schaefer, Phillip GA Hvy.Arty. 22nd Bn. Co.C

Schaefer, P.O. GA Inf. 1st Loc.Troops (Augusta) Co.I

Schaefer, S. TX Arty. Douglas' Co. Cpl.

Schaefer, William TX Waul's Legion Co.B

Schaeferkoeter, William TX 3rd Inf. Co.K

Schaeffer, Anton LA 20th Inf. Co.F

Schaeffer, B. LA Mil. 4th Regt.Eur.Brig. Co.E

Schaeffer, Benjamin MD 1st Inf. Co.E

Schaeffer, Benjamin K. VA Lt.Arty. Brander's Co.

Schaeffer, B.K. KY Cav. 2nd Bn. (Dortch's) Adj.

Schaeffer, Brett R. Gen. & Staff Rec.Asst.Surg.

Schaeffer, Carl LA 20th Inf. Co.F

Schaeffer, Charles LA 4th Inf. Co.B

Schaeffer, Daniel LA 20th Inf. Co.C

Schaeffer, E. LA Mil. 4th Regt.Eur.Brig. Co.B

Schaeffer, Edouard Sap. & Min. Gallimard's Co.,CSA 2nd Sap.

Schaeffer, Emile LA 14th Inf. Co.H

Schaeffer, Frank B. VA 1st Arty. 1st Co.C Capt.

Schaeffer, Frank B. VA 1st Inf. Co.F Capt.

Schaeffer, Frank B. Gen. & Staff Capt.,Insp.Gen.

Schaeffer, Franz TX Inf. Griffin's Bn. Co.F

Schaeffer, Henry TN Lt.Arty. Winston's Co.

Schaeffer, H.W. MO Inf. 4th Regt.St.Guard Co.A

Schaeffer, J. LA Mil. 3rd Regt. 1st Brig. 1st Div. Co.H

Schaeffer, J. LA Mil. 4th Regt.Eur.Brig. Co.E

Schaeffer, John LA 4th Inf. Co.B

Schaeffer, John MO 1st Inf. Co.C

Schaeffer, Luther M. VA 4th Inf. Co.L

Schaeffer, M. LA Mil. 4th Regt.Eur.Brig. Co.E

Schaeffer, P.W. MD Line Sgt.

Schaeffer, Robert LA 11th Inf. Co.L

Schaeffer, T. LA Mil. 4th Regt.Eur.Brig. Co.B

Schaeffer, T.H. MD 1st Cav. Co.D

Schaeffer, W.G. LA Mil. Bragg's Bn. Schwartz's Co.

Schaer, Anthony AR Mil. Borland's Regt. Band Music.

Schaer, Joe AR 13th Mil. Co.A

Schaer, Joseph AR Mil. Borland's Regt. Band Prin.Music.

Schafar, Phillip VA Horse Arty. McClanahan's Co.

Schafer, August VA 136th Mil. Co.E

Schafer, C. LA Mil. 4th Regt.Eur.Brig. Co.A Sgt.

Schafer, E. LA Mil. 3rd Regt. 1st Brig. 1st Div. Co.I 1st Sgt.

Schafer, E.A. GA Lt.Arty. (Jackson Arty.) Massenburg's Btty.

Schafer, F. TX 4th Cav. Co.G

Schafer, Fred TX Comal Res. Co.H

Schafer, George LA 21st (Patton's) Inf. Co.I

Schafer, H. TX Inf. Timmons' Regt. Co.K

Schafer, Henry VA Hvy.Arty. 1st Co.E

Schafer, Jacob AL Mil. 2nd Regt.Vol. Co.B

Schafer, Peter GA 1st (Olmstead's) Inf. 1st Co.A

Schafer, Philip VA Lt.Arty. Clutter's Co.

Schafer, William AR 18th (Marmaduke's) Inf. Co.B

Schaferkotter, Henry LA 20th Inf. Co.A

Schaff, Nicholas LA 14th Inf. Co.D

Schaff, Philip GA Inf. (St.Guards) Hansell's Co.

Schaff, Philip MS Lt.Arty. (Brookhaven Lt.Arty.) Hoskins' Btty.

Schaffer, Adam F. MD Arty. 2nd Btty.

Schaffer, Andrew TX 7th Cav.

Schaffer, C.F. TX 19th Inf. Co.F Sgt.

Schaffer, Dr. TX 13th Vol. Bates' Regt. Co.H

Schaffer, E. VA Inf. 1st Bn.Loc.Def. Co.F

Schaffer, Edwin LA 1st Sap. & Min.

Schaffer, Ernest Inf. School of Pract. Powell's Detach. Co.C

Schaffer, F. LA Mil. Orleans Fire Regt. Co.H

Schaffer, F. VA 1st St.Res. Co.D

Schaffer, G. TX 2nd Field Btty.

Schaffer, George AL 1st Bn.Cadets Co.A

Schaffer, George LA 15th Inf. Co.C

Schaffer, Henry LA C.S. Zouave Bn. Co.F

Schaffer, H.W. LA Mil. 2nd Regt. 3rd Brig. 1st Div. Co.E

Schaffer, J. LA Mil. 2nd Regt. 3rd Brig. 1st Div. Co.E

Schaffer, J.A. GA 1st (Symons') Res. Co.B

Schaffer, Jacob TX Lt.Arty. Jones' Co.

Schaffer, J.H. TX Inf. Timmons' Regt. Co.H

Schaffer, John LA 13th Inf. Co.E,F

Schaffer, John LA Inf.Crescent Regt. Co.F

Schaffer, John LA Mil. Mech.Guard

Schaffer, John G. NC 2nd Inf. Co.I

Schaffer, John Philip VA 16th Inf. Co.E

Schaffer, L. LA Mil. Orleans Fire Regt. Co.H

Schaffer, P. LA 30th Inf. Co.A

Schaffer, Peter GA 1st Bn.S.S. Co.B Cpl.

Schaffer, Phillip SC 1st Arty. Co.A

Schaffer, Theodore VA 146th Mil. Co.D

Schaffer, Victor AL Lt.Arty. 2nd Bn. Co.E

Schaffer, Victor E. LA 15th Inf. Co.D 1st Sgt.

Schaffer, William MD Arty. 2nd Btty.

Schaffer, W.W. GA 1st Legion

Schaffler, Robert AR 15th (Josey's) Inf. Co.C

Schaffner, A. LA 3rd Inf. Co.F

Schaffner, A. LA 11th Inf. Co.K Capt.

Schaffner, Ch. TX 4th Inf. (St.Troops) Co.F

Schaffner, J. TX Waul's Legion Co.C

Schaffner, John TX Waul's Legion Co.B

Schaffner, Michael LA Arty. Kean's Btty. (Orleans Ind.Arty.)

Schaffner, Philip AL Arty. 1st Bn. Co.F

Schaffter, Aurelius VA Horse Arty. Shoemaker's Co. Ord.Sgt.

Schaffter, Florian LA Mil. 6th Regt.Eur.Brig. (Italian Guards Bn.) Co.5

Schafner, Christian TX Res.Corps Co.D

Schafver, Bennott TN 19th Inf. Co.I

Schahtmaw, H. AR Inf. 4th Bn. Co.A

Schaifer, E. TX 17th Field Btty.

Schaifer, G.W. LA 31st Inf. Co.F

Schaill, William SC 1st Arty. Co.E

Schainevert, Meril LA Inf.Cons. 18th Regt. & Yellow Jacket Bn. Co.I

Schairer, Jacob LA 3rd Inf. Co.A

Schakail, Michell LA Mil. 4th Regt. 1st Brig. 1st Div. Co.H

Schala, John SC 1st Regt. Charleston Guard Co.G

Schalabba, N. LA 22nd Inf. Gomez's Co.

Schalck, --- LA Mil. 2nd Regt. 2nd Brig. 1st Div. Co.A

Schaldelback, Julius VA 54th Mil. Co.G

Schalibo, Charles TX 1st Hvy.Arty. Co.C

Schalibo, F. TX 1st Hvy.Arty. Co.G

Schalibo, Henry TX 1st Hvy.Arty. Co.C, 2nd Co.F

Schalk, Chs. LA Mil. 3rd Regt. 3rd Brig. 1st Div. Co.H

Schall, Adam VA 5th Inf. Co.D

Schall, J. GA 3rd Res. Co.A

Schall, J.H. GA Inf. 14th Bn. (St.Guards) Co.A

Schaller, Charles LA 1st Hvy.Arty. (Reg.) Co.I

Schaller, F. MS 22nd Inf. Col.

Schaller, Joseph T. MS 1st Lt.Arty. Co.L
Schallert, Louis LA Mil. 3rd Regt. 1st Brig. 1st
  Div. Co.H Sgt.
Schally, Thomas MS Lt.Arty. (Jefferson Arty.)
  Darden's Co.
Schamber, Henry VA 6th Inf. Ferguson's Co.
Schamber, Henry VA 12th Inf. Co.H
Schamfeldt, James LA 11th Inf. Co.F
Schamlers, Eligha NC 16th Inf. Co.F
Schammahone, John Z. VA Lt.Arty. Arch.
  Graham's Co.
Schammel, John H. VA 1st Inf. Co.C
Schammer, Rufus LA 3rd Inf. Co.G
Schammerhorn, William H. Conf.Cav. Wood's
  Regt. Co.K
Schanawal, F. VA 3rd (Archer's) Bn.Res. Co.D
Schanb, Henry MD Cav. 2nd Bn. Sudler's Co.
Schandgrass, Henry LA Mil. 3rd Regt. 1st Brig.
  1st Div. Co.C
Schandorn, Joseph TX 4th Cav. Co.G
Schandua, Jean LA Mil. 6th Regt.Eur.Brig.
  (Italian Guards Bn.) Co.5
Schandua, Peter TX 6th Field Btty.
Schane, Herman MO Inf. 1st Bn. Co.C
Schane, Phillip GA Inf. 2nd Bn. (St.Guards)
  Co.B
Schanhan, M. VA 5th Cav. Co.G
Schank, B.B. VA 3rd (Archer's) Bn.Res. Co.B
Schank, George VA 3rd (Archer's) Bn.Res.
  Co.D
Schank, Peter TX Cav. 2nd Regt.St.Troops Co.E
Schanlan, Patrick VA Cav. 41st Bn. Co.C
Schanon, Thomas H. MO 10th Inf.
Schantz, Max LA Mil. Fire Bn. Co.D
Schantz, Peter LA 20th Inf. Old Co.B
Schantz, V. LA Mil. Fire Bn. Co.E
Schanze, Martine TX Cav. 3rd (Yager's) Bn.
  Co.C
Schanzie, Martin TX 1st (Yager's) Cav. Co.C
Schaper, Henry TX Waul's Legion Co.B
Schaper, William SC Arty.Bn. Hampton Legion
  Co.B
Schappaul, A. SC 5th Inf. 1st Co.F Music.
Schappaul, A. SC Palmetto S.S. Co.D Music.
Schaptoch, Simeon VA 1st Inf. Co.K
Scharborough, H. SC 5th Bn.Res. Co.B
Scharborough, M.H. SC 5th Bn.Res. Co.B
Scharch, Charles LA 4th Inf. Co.D
Scharch, George VA Second Class Mil. Wolff's
  Co.
Schardein, Philip TX St.Troops Edgar's Co. Sgt.
Schardt, John LA 12th Inf. Co.E,F
Schardt, M. VA 1st St.Res. Co.D
Scharenberg, Henry TX 4th Cav. Co.G Sgt.
Scharf, Henry AL 8th Inf. Co.G
Scharf, John LA Mil. 2nd Regt. 3rd Brig. 1st
  Div. Co.A
Scharfer, H. SC 1st Regt. Charleston Guard Co.F
Scharfer, H. SC Mil. 16th Regt. Stiles' Co.
Scharff, Benjamin MS 12th Inf. Co.A
Scharff, E. AL Lt.Arty. Goldthwaite's Btty.
  Bugler
Scharff, Emanuel AL 1st Cav. 1st Co.B
Scharff, Emanuel MS 19th Inf. Co.D
Scharff, John T. MD Arty. 1st Btty.
Scharff, Nicholas MS 12th Inf. Co.A

Scharlemon, Louis George VA Lt.Arty. Clutter's
  Co.
Scharlmeyer, William LA Mil. 4th Regt.
  Eur.Brig. Co.D
Scharlock, Charles E. SC 1st (Butler's) Inf. Co.C
  Drum.
Scharlock, E.C. SC Inf. 1st (Charleston) Bn.
  Co.F Music.
Scharlock, George SC 1st Regt. Charleston
  Guard Co.F
Scharlock, John AL Mil. 3rd Vol. Co.A
Scharlock, W.F. SC Inf. 1st (Charleston) Bn.
  Co.F Music.
Scharmitzky, L. LA 20th Inf. Co.F Music.
Scharnagle, Andrew LA Arty. Kean's Btty.
  (Orleans Ind.Arty.)
Scharnberg, F. TX 3rd Inf. 2nd Co.A
Scharnberg, G. TX 3rd Inf. 2nd Co.A
Scharniski, A. LA Arty. Watson Btty.
Scharniski, Ad LA Pointe Coupee Arty.
Scharp, A. AR 17th (Griffith's) Inf. Co.A
Scharp, Charles TX 1st Inf. Co.F Music.
Scharpe, H. SC Mil. 16th Regt. Sigwald's Co.
Scharpie, H. SC 1st Inf. Co.M
Scharre, Edward LA Mil. 4th Regt.Eur.Brig.
  Co.C
Schartiger, William VA Cav. McNeill's Co.
Schartle, J.W. SC Lt.Arty. Jeter's Co. (Macbeth
  Lt.Arty.) Cpl.
Schartt, Michael AL 15th Inf.
Schartz, William LA 20th Inf. Old Co.B, Co.C
Schartzer, Ai VA Lt.Arty. J.D. Smith's Co.
Schartzer, William A. VA Lt.Arty. J.D. Smith's
  Co.
Schasse, Conrad TX 5th Cav. Co.G
Schatz, Benjamin LA 1st Cav. Co.F
Schatz, E. TX 16th Inf. Co.E Sgt.
Schaub, G. LA Mil. Fire Bn. Co.A
Schaub, George KY 9th Mtd.Inf. Co.B 1st Lt.
Schaub, Henry TX 35th (Brown's) Cav. Co.A
Schaub, John TX 13th Vol. Co.C
Schaub, Martin TX 8th Field Btty.
Schaub, W.H. TN 7th (Duckworth's) Cav. Co.D
  1st Bugler
Schaub, W.H. NC 3rd Jr.Res. Co.C Sgt.
Schaub, William TX 13th Vol. Co.C
Schaube, Henry TX 26th Cav. Co.F
Schaube, W.H. NC 4th Bn.Jr.Res. Co.C
Schaudinhaus, Francis VA Lt.Arty. Pegram's Co.
Schaufele, Fred GA Inf. 18th Bn. (St.Guards)
  Co.B
Schaufele, Frederick GA 1st (Symons') Res.
  Co.K
Schaufenstein, Daniel LA 21st (Patton's) Inf.
  Co.F
Schauff, B. VA 1st St.Res. Co.C
Schauff, Benjamin TX 5th Inf. Co.A
Schauff, William VA 1st St.Res. Co.C
Schaufile, Frederick GA Inf. 1st Loc.Troops
  (Augusta) Co.K
Schaumberg, Christopher LA 22nd Inf. Co.B
Schaumberg, Christopher LA 22nd (Cons.) Inf.
  Co.B
Schaumbergen, Joseph Conf.Inf. 8th Bn.
Schaumburg, W.C. VA Inf. Hutter's Co. Cpl.
Schaumburg, Wright C. Gen. & Staff,
  Adj.Gen.Dept. Lt.Col.

Schauncey, Michael VA Lt.Arty. Woolfolk's Co.
Schaupp, William LA 1st (Nelligan's) Inf. Co.K
Schave, H. TX Waul's Legion Co.C
Schaw, A. AR 13th Mil. Co.A
Schawb, H. SC Mil. 16th Regt. Stiles' Co.
Schawbs, Ignace LA Mil. 2nd Regt. French Brig.
  Co.6
Schawreck, W. LA Mil. 2nd Regt. 2nd Brig. 1st
  Div. Co.E
Schawtz, Christopher TN 1st Cav. Co.G
Schaxnenai, N.L. LA Arty. 1st Field Btty.
Schay, Jacob NC Walker's Bn. Thomas' Legion
  Co.A
Scheafer, Emile MS 3rd Inf. Co.A
Scheaffer, Joseph AR 11th Inf. Co.G
Scheafmaker, William VA 5th Inf. Co.K
Scheahan, O. GA Inf. (Express Inf.) Witt's Co.
Schean, Crone 9th Conf.Inf. Co.G
Schean, D.G. GA N.C.S. Hosp.Stew.
Schean, John P. 9th Conf.Inf. Co.G
Schean, William TN 2nd (Walker's) Inf. Co.H
  Cpl.
Scheanks, F.A. MO Lt.Arty. H.M. Bledsoe's
  Co.
Schearon, William LA Mil. 3rd Regt. 1st Brig.
  1st Div. Co.K
Scheb, Alex MO 2nd Btty.
Schebasta, John TX 1st Hvy.Arty. Co.G
Schebasta, Joseph TX 1st Hvy.Arty. Co.G
Schechstripp, A. TX Inf. 1st St.Troops Steven-
  son's Co.F Cpl.
Scheck, A.H. NC 2nd Home Guards Music.
Scheck, Luther W. NC 21st Inf. Co.M Sgt.
Scheeks, Henry GA Lt.Arty. Milledge's Co.
Scheel, H. TX 5th Inf. (St.Troops) Martindale's
  Co.
Scheel, William TX 7th Cav. Co.B
Scheele, Hermann TX 1st (Yager's) Cav. Co.E
Scheele, M. LA Mil. 3rd Regt. 3rd Brig. 1st Div.
  Co.G
Scheeler, Henry TX Cav. 8th (Taylor's) Bn.
  Co.C
Scheen, John AL Inf. 1st Regt. Co.K
Scheen, John H. LA 28th (Gray's) Inf. Co.A
Scheetz, George MO 4th Inf. Co.K
Scheffe, Jacob LA 20th Inf. Co.C
Scheffel, E.W. LA 20th Inf. Old Co.B
Scheffel, Godfrie TX Res.Corps Co.B
Scheffenberger, Henry SC 1st (Butler's) Inf.
  Co.F
Scheffer, Theodore VA 11th Cav. Co.E
Scheffley, Fred SC Hvy.Arty. Gilchrist's Co.
  (Gist Guard) Music.
Schefler, C. TX 2nd Inf. Co.K
Scheftale, W. GA 1st (Olmstead's) Inf. Co.I
  Music.
Schegel, Andreas LA Mil. Mech.Guard
Schegmond, Constant LA 10th Inf. Co.F
Schehan, Matthew 9th Conf.Inf. Co.D
Schehin, Louis LA Mil. 2nd Regt. French Brig.
  Co.7
Scheib, Ph. LA Mil. Fire Bn. Co.C
Scheibel, Frederic LA 20th Inf. Co.D
Scheible, F. AL 1st Regt. Mobile Vol. Baas' Co.
Scheible, William AL 12th Inf. Co.C
Scheick, John Conf.Cav. Wood's Regt. 1st Co.A
Scheide, P. TX 7th Field Btty.

Scheidecker, Antoine LA C.S. Zouave Bn. Co.A
  Ord.Sgt.
Scheidle, Christian TX 4th Inf. Co.A
Scheidler, Caspar LA Mil. 4th Regt.Eur.Brig.
  Co.D
Scheidt, P. TX 4th Inf. (St.Troops) Co.F
Scheifele, Casper LA Mil.Cont.Regt. Lang's Co.
Scheifle, Math TN Inf. 3rd Bn. Co.F
Scheifler, D. TN Inf. 3rd Bn. Co.G
Scheile, William LA 25th Inf. Co.C
Scheiley, J.T. MS 1st Cav.Res. Co.G
Scheiley, T. MS 1st Cav.Res. Co.G
Schein, Albert GA 64th Inf. Co.A
Scheindler, William MS 48th Inf. Co.A Cpl.
Scheinneyder, Octave LA Mil. St.James Regt.
  Co.F
Scheip, A. LA Mil. Fire Bn. Co.D
Scheipey, Charles KY 2nd Mtd.Inf. Co.K Sgt.
Scheireman, Jacob AL 24th Inf. Co.D
Scheirmer, P. AL St.Arty. Co.D
Scheitmiller, M. LA Mil. 3rd Regt. 1st Brig. 1st
  Div. Co.H
Scheixnayde, R. LA Mil. Chalmette Regt. Co.C
  2nd Lt.
Scheixnaydre, F. LA Mil. Chalmette Regt. Co.C
  Cpl.
Scheixnaydre, M. LA Mil. Chalmette Regt. Co.C
  Sgt.
Scheixnaydre, W.M. LA Mil. Chalmette Regt.
  Co.C
Scheixsraydre, Furcy LA 1st Hvy.Arty. (Reg.)
  Co.D
Schekell, Marinus W. VA 1st Inf. Co.E
Scheles, W.G. TX 4th Cav. Co.H
Schelettre, Devers LA 2nd Cav. Co.D
Schelettre, Onezerine LA 2nd Cav. Co.D
Schell, A.B. Cheatham's Div. 1st Lt.
Schell, Abraham B. TN 2nd (Robison's) Inf. Co.I
  1st Lt.
Schell, A.J. Gen. & Staff Surg.
Schell, Alfred Conf.Inf. 8th Bn. Co.B
Schell, Elbert Clinton Gen. & Staff Asst.Surg.
Schell, H.A. Gen. & Staff Surg.
Schell, Henry A. MO 3rd Cav. Co.I
Schell, Joseph G. VA 1st Cav. Co.G
Schell, Philip MO 3rd Cav. Co.I
Schell, Richard VA 1st Arty. Co.I
Schell, William GA Arty. (Macon Lt.Arty.)
  Slaten's Co. Cpl.
Schell, William VA 1st Arty. Co.I
Schellenberger, F. LA Mil. 1st Regt. 2nd Brig.
  1st Div.
Schellentraeger, A.B. AL Lt.Arty. Phelan's Co.
  Bugler
Schellentraeger, Benhard AL 5th Inf. Old Co.H
  Music.
Scheller, C. TX 4th Inf. (St.Troops) Co.A
Scheller, John LA Mil. 1st Regt. 3rd Brig. 1st
  Div.
Scheller, John SC Arty.Bn. Hampton Legion
  Co.B
Schelles, Phillip FL Milton Lt.Arty. Dunham's
  Co.
Schelling, Eyre VA 12th Inf. Co.H
Schelling, H.A. MS 12th Inf. Co.G 2nd Lt.
Schellinger, F. Conf.Inf. 8th Bn. Co.D
Schellinger, J.C. TX 12th Cav. Co.E

Schellings, George VA 23rd Inf. Co.K Cpl.
Schelper, H. TX 3rd Inf. 2nd Co.C
Schelpert, Lewis GA 3rd Inf. Co.D 2nd Lt.
Schembri, Joseph LA 6th Inf. Co.G
Scheme, N. LA 31st Inf. Co.F
Schemmer, Henry TX 17th Inf. Co.H
Schemohon, John VA Lt.Arty. B.Z. Price's Co.
Schenberger, J.F. MD Arty. 2nd Btty.
Schenberger, John F. VA Inf. 1st Bn.Loc.Def.
  Co.F
Schench, Henry TX 26th Cav. Co.A
Schench, Samuel G. NC 67th Inf. 1st Lt.
Schenck, A. LA 6th Inf. Co.C
Schenck, A.T. MO Inf. 3rd Bn. Co.F Cpl.
Schenck, A.T. MO 6th Inf. Co.H Cpl.
Schenck, Charles VA 3rd Cav.
Schenck, Charles M. VA 5th Inf. Co.L
Schenck, Daniel R. AR 25th Inf. Co.F
Schenck, Daniel R. AR Inf. 8th Bn. Co.C
Schenck, Ernst GA Conscr.
Schenck, Franklin R. AL 58th Inf. Co.F 2nd Lt.
Schenck, Henry F. NC 56th Inf. Co.F Maj.
Schenck, J.A. TX Cav. 2nd Regt.St.Troops Co.E
Schenck, John C. AL 51st (Part.Rangers) Co.D
Schenck, John C. AL 7th Inf. Co.B
Schenck, N.W. Gen. & Staff, Subs.Dept. Capt.
Schenck, Samuel G. NC 1st Arty. (10th
  St.Troops) Co.K,G
Schene, Jacob LA Mil. Chalmette Regt. Co.A
Scheneck, Richard LA Mil. 3rd Regt. 1st Brig.
  1st Div. Co.K
Schener, Morris TX 1st (Yager's) Cav. Co.F
Schener, Philip V. VA 1st Inf. Co.G
Schenerman, Alois AL 1st Regt. Mobile Vol.
  Co.E Cpl.
Schenerman, F. AL 94th Mil. Co.A Ens.
Schenermann, J. LA Mil. 4th Regt.Eur.Brig.
  Co.E
Schenk, Henry C. VA 12th Cav. Co.C
Schenk, John M. SC 19th Inf. Co.C
Schenk, John W. VA 28th Inf. Co.F
Schenk, L. MS Inf. 3rd Bn. (St.Troops) Co.C
Schenk, Ro. B. VA 34th Inf. Co.H Sgt.
Schenks, D. AL 18th Inf. Co.F
Schenks, F.R. AL 18th Inf. Co.F
Schenks, Richard F. VA 28th Inf. Co.F Cpl.
Schenle, Matthias LA 11th Inf. Co.L
Scheper, H. SC Mil.Arty. 1st Regt. Harms' Co.
Scheper, W. SC Mil.Arty. 1st Regt. Harms' Co.
Scheper, W. SC Arty. Melchers' Co.
  (Co.B,German Arty.)
Schepert, H. LA Mil. 2nd Regt. 2nd Brig. 1st
  Div. Co.H
Schepmoes, J.D. LA Mil. 3rd Regt. 3rd Brig. 1st
  Div. Co.B 2nd Lt.
Schepner, Charles M. MS 28th Cav. Co.D
Schepp, P. LA Mil. French Co. of St.James
Schepp, Z. LA Mil. French Co. of St.James
Schepper, Henry VA 18th Inf. Co.B
Scherck, Abram MS 7th Inf. Co.C
Scherck, Isaac MS Inf. 3rd Bn. Co.E Jr.2nd Lt.
Scherck, Isaac Gen. & Staff, A. of TN
  Maj.,Asst.Ch.Comsy.
Scherck, Louis MS 16th Inf. Co.A
Scherer, George P. VA 5th Inf. Co.L Sgt.
Scherer, Henry TX 4th Field Btty.
Scherer, Jac. LA 20th Inf. Co.F

Scherer, Jacob AL 4th Inf. Co.D
Scherer, John B. VA 7th Bn.Res. Co.D
Scherer, John F. VA Lt.Arty. Parker's Co.
Scherer, Michael LA 21st (Patton's) Inf. Co.I
Scherer, Philip V. VA Lt.Arty. Parker's Co.
  Cpl.
Scherer, Riley TX 5th Inf. Co.B
Scherer, Samuel VA 5th Cav. (12 mo. '61-2)
  Co.I,A
Scherer, W. Dwight TX 13th Vol. 2nd Co.C
Scherf, Frederick MS 22nd Inf. Co.D Cpl.
Scherf, Henry LA 6th Inf. Co.H
Scherff, Fred LA 6th Inf. Co.H
Scherff, William TX 36th Cav. Co.F
Scherges, August MS 3rd Inf. Co.F
Scherhorn, H. LA Mil. Lafayette Arty.
Scherk, Daniel LA Mil. 4th Regt. 1st Brig. 1st
  Div. Co.K
Scherk, Windall LA Mil. 4th Regt. 1st Brig. 1st
  Div. Co.K
Scherman, John V. AL 4th Res. Co.A
Scherman, Junius VA Conscr. Cp.Lee Co.B
Scherman, P. AL Mil. 3rd Vol. Co.C
Schermann, Charles TX 1st Hvy.Arty. Co.C
Schermerhorn, Egmond P. VA 10th Cav. Co.I
Schermerhorn, Ira NC 26th Inf. Co.H
Schermerhorn, J. Crane AL 8th Inf. Co.D 1st
  Lt.
Schermerhorn, John P. VA 10th Cav. Co.K,I
  Cpl.
Schernborn, Charles E. VA 1st Inf. Co.B
Scherrer, C. LA Mil. Chalmette Regt. Co.E
Scherrer, F. LA Mil. Chalmette Regt. Co.E
Scherrer, Henry T. VA 15th Inf. Co.A
Scherrer, John TX Inf. 1st St.Troops Stevenson's
  Co.F
Scherrer, L. LA Mil. 4th Regt.Eur.Brig. Co.B
Scherrick, Charles LA Mil. 3rd Regt. 1st Brig.
  1st Div. Co.E
Schertz, Edward TX Cav. Border's Regt. Co.G
  Music.
Scherzinger, A. MS 19th Inf. Co.D
Scherry, G.J. SC 23rd Inf. Co.F
Schettley, Joseph LA Arty. Hutton's Co. (Cres-
  cent Arty.,Co.A)
Scheuber, Charles LA Inf. 4th Bn. Co.E
Scheuber, F. MS 12th Inf. Co.G
Scheuber, Frederick LA Inf. Crescent Regt.
  Co.G
Scheuber, William LA Inf. 4th Bn. Co.E
Scheuch, Christopher J. MO 2nd N.E. Cav.
  (Franklin's Regt.)
Scheuer, Emanuel TX Mtd. Coast Guards
  St.Troops Graham's Co.
Scheuer, Jonathan LA Arty. Landry's Co.
  (Donaldsonville Arty.) QMSgt.
Scheuer, L. LA Mil. 1st Regt. 2nd Brig. 1st Div.
  Co.E
Scheuerman, Aloysius AL 12th Inf. Co.C Sgt.
Scheuerman, Anthony AL 12th Inf. Co.C 1st Lt.
Scheuerman, F. LA Mil. Fire Bn. Co.E
Scheuerman, George TN Inf. 3rd Bn. Co.F
Scheuerman, H. AL 1st Regt. Mobile Vol. Co.E
Scheumburg, H. TX Inf. 1st St.Troops Steven-
  son's Co.F
Scheurer, A. LA Mil. 1st Regt. 2nd Brig. 1st
  Div. Co.I

Scheurer, E. TX Waul's Legion Co.C 1st Lt.

Scheurman, Anton AL 1st Regt. Mobile Vol. Co.E

Scheussler, L.G. GA 2nd Inf. Co.G

Scheussler, L.G. GA Inf. City Bn. (Columbus) William's Co. 1st Lt.

Scheustzer, William GA Cav. 8th Bn. (St.Guards) Co.A

Scheuterle, Thomas AL Gorff's Co. (Mobile Pulaski Rifles)

Schevenell, Joseph H. NC 25th Inf. Co.G Cpl.

Schevenell, Leonard NC 25th Inf. Co.G

Schevernell, Joseph H. GA Carlton's Co. (Troup Cty.Arty.)

Schevernell, Richard S. GA Inf. Athens Reserved Corps 1st Lt.

Schevetz, A. TX 5th Field Btty.

Schew, George LA Mil.Conf.Guards Regt. Co.K

Schew, J. LA Mil. Orleans Fire Regt. Co.A Jr.2nd Lt.

Schew, John LA Mil. 1st Regt. 3rd Brig. 1st Div. Co.A

Schewerman, G.I. MS 22nd Inf. Co.I

Schewrin, S. LA Mil.Cont.Regt. Mitchell's Co.

Schexnaider, L. LA 30th Inf. Locoul's Co.

Schexnaider, S. LA 30th Inf. Locoul's Co.

Schexnaider, T.F. LA 30th Inf. Locoul's Co.

Schexnaidre, L. LA Arty. 5th Field Btty. (Pelican Lt.Arty.)

Schexnaildre, A. LA Arty. Watson Btty.

Schexnaildre, Eugene LA Arty. Watson Btty. Cpl.

Schexnaildre, Francois LA Arty. Watson Btty. Sgt.

Schexnaildre, J. LA Arty. Watson Btty.

Schexnaildre, Jacob LA Ogden's Cav. Co.E

Schexnaildre, S. LA Arty. Watson Btty.

Schexnaildre, T. LA Ogden's Cav. Co.E

Schexnaildre, T. LA Arty. Watson Btty.

Schexnayder, C. LA Inf.Cons. 18th Regt. & Yellow Jacket Bn. Co.B

Schexnayder, M. LA Inf.Cons. 18th Regt. & Yellow Jacket Bn. Co.B

Schexnaydre, Octave LA 30th Inf. Co.G

Schexnaydre, Ozeine LA 30th Inf. Co.G

Schexnaydre, Theodole LA Inf.Cons. 18th Regt. & Yellow Jacket Bn. Co.D

Schexneider, L. LA 4th Cav. Co.E

Schexneildre, E. LA 1st Hvy.Arty. (Reg.) Co.G

Schexneyder, Valcin LA Mil. St.James Regt. Co.F

Schexsnaildre, Emile 14th Conf.Cav. Co.D

Schiber, Jacob GA 8th Cav. Co.A

Schiber, James GA 8th Cav. Co.A

Schiber, Ranson GA 8th Cav. Co.A

Schiciman, V. AL Mobile City Troop

Schick, George TN 15th Inf. Co.I Music.

Schick, J.A. VA Inf. 6th Bn.Loc.Def. Co.B

Schick, John TN 15th Cav.

Schick, John A. VA 2nd Inf.Loc.Def. Co.E

Schick, John L. TN 15th Inf. Co.I Music.

Schick, L. TX 3rd Inf. Co.B Cpl.

Schick, W. LA Mil. 4th Regt.Eur.Brig. Co.E

Schicke, H. TX 26th Cav.

Schicks, W. Henry SC 1st Inf. Co.I

Schicks, William H. GA Lt.Arty. Milledge's Co.

Schide, J.H. VA 46th Inf. Co.L

Schidner, D.I. GA Cav. Dorough's Bn.

Schidy, Phillip VA 47th Inf. Co.F

Schiedecker, A. KY 2nd Mtd.Inf. Co.K

Schiefer, H. TX 5th Field Btty.

Schiefer, H. TX Lt.Arty. Dege's Bn.

Schieffer, J. AR 11th & 17th Cons.Inf. Co.G

Schiefflin, John B. AL St.Arty. Co.A

Schiel, Robert TX 7th Cav. Co.B

Schield, A. MS 38th Cav. Co.A

Schield, M. AL Chas. A. Herts' Co.

Schiele, Jean Michel LA Mil. 1st Regt. French Brig. Co.7,10

Schiell, Mathias LA 1st (Nelligan's) Inf. Co.K

Schiell, Mitchell VA 6th Inf. 1st Co.E

Schier, Jacob LA Mil. 4th Regt. 3rd Brig. 1st Div. Co.C

Schier, Joseph TX 3rd Inf. Co.H

Schierholtz, Charles MS 28th Cav. Co.I Music.

Schierholz, Charles MS 3rd (St.Troops) Cav. Co.C

Schierman, V. AL Mil. 3rd Vol. Co.C

Schieseman, Ch. LA Mil. 3rd Regt. 1st Brig. 1st Div. Co.G

Schiewitz, Michael TX 6th Inf. Co.B

Schiff, Philip GA 29th Inf. Co.F Cpl.

Schiffer, Jacob AL 12th Inf. Co.C

Schiffer, John LA Mil. 1st Regt. 2nd Brig. 1st Div. Co.E

Schiffintain, Charles LA Mil. LaFourche Regt.

Schifft, B. LA Mil. 1st Chasseurs a pied Co.7

Schifland, F. SC Mil. 16th Regt. Bancroft, Jr.'s Co.

Schilcorn, William H. GA Inf. 2nd Bn. Co.F

Schilcott, Jonathan VA 146th Mil. Co.E

Schileiher, Frederick SC 1st (Butler's) Inf. Co.A

Schiller, Charles LA 22nd Inf. Wash. Marks' Co.

Schiller, F. FL 2nd Inf. Co.D

Schiller, F. LA Mil. 4th Regt. 2nd Brig. 1st Div. Co.F

Schiller, Ignatz TX Waul's Legion Co.D

Schiller, John B. LA Mil. British Guard Bn. Burrowes' Co.

Schiller, Louis SC 1st Cav. Co.C

Schiller, S. SC 1st Cav. Co.C

Schiller, Samuel TX 17th Inf. Co.K

Schiller, Vincent TX Inf. 1st St.Troops Stevenson's Co.F

Schiller, W.S. TX Inf. 1st St.Troops Stevenson's Co.F

Schillin, Daniel LA Washington Arty.Bn. Co.5

Schilling, A.B. GA Lt.Arty. 14th Bn. Co.A

Schilling, A.B. GA Lt.Arty. Havis' Btty.

Schilling, Alfred VA 27th Inf. Co.F 2nd Lt.

Schilling, Charles NC 27th Inf. Co.I

Schilling, Earnest TX Inf. 1st St.Troops Stevenson's Co.F

Schilling, Frederic LA 4th Inf. Co.B Sgt.

Schilling, H.T. LA Inf.Crescent Regt. Co.C Sgt.

Schilling, Jacob TN Hvy.Arty. Sterling's Co.

Schilling, J.G. LA 21st (Kennedy's) Inf. Co.B

Schilling, John L. NC 2nd Bn.Loc.Def.Troops Co.C 1st Sgt.

Schilling, L. TX Waul's Legion Co.A

Schilling, Michael LA 25th Inf. Co.H

Schilling, Philip LA 20th Inf. Co.C

Schilling, Robert VA Inf. 6th Bn.Loc.Def. Co.C

Schilling, William VA 27th Inf. Co.F Cpl.

Schillinger, Herm LA Mil. 3rd Regt. 3rd Brig. 1st Div. Co.H Cpl.

Schillinger, John L. MS 15th Inf. Co.F

Schilnick, John TX 17th Inf. Co.F

Schimerhorn, Jacob GA 12th Inf. Co.E

Schimmel, Louis KY 10th (Johnson's) Cav. Co.F 3rd Lt.

Schimmelpfennig, August TX 36th Cav. Co.F

Schimmerfinning, C. LA 20th Inf. Co.I

Schimpff, Francis P. TX 16th Cav. Co.H

Schimpff, Joseph AR 15th (Josey's) Inf. Co.G Cpl.

Schinault, Andrew J. TX 15th Cav. Co.F

Schinault, J.J. TN 16th (Logwood's) Cav. Co.G

Schinault, Temple VA Inf. 5th Bn. Co.D

Schinck, John TX 16th Inf. Co.H

Schindel, Charles F. VA 1st Cav. Co.C

Schindel, Samuel P. VA 11th Inf. Co.K Sgt.

Schindle, Charles F. VA Rockbridge Cty.Res. Miller's Co.

Schindle, John H. VA 11th Inf. Co.K

Schindler, Anthony LA 8th Inf. Co.B Band Sgt.

Schindler, C. LA Mil. 2nd Regt. French Brig. Co.8

Schindler, C. TX 1st Hvy.Arty. Co.B

Schindler, David R. KY 14th Cav. Co.B,D

Schindler, Henry LA Mil. Mech.Guard

Schindler, John TN 15th Inf. Co.K,I Sgt.

Schindler, Joseph LA 8th Inf. Co.B Band, Music.

Schindler, Louis LA 21st (Patton's) Inf. Co.I

Schine, Michael GA 1st (Olmstead's) Inf. Co.B

Schink, Christoph LA Mil. 4th Regt. 1st Brig. 1st Div. Co.K

Schinnate, Henry AL Vol. Rabby's Coast Guard Co. No.1

Schinner, F.M. SC Mil. 16th Regt. Steinmeyer, Jr.'s Co. Bvt.2nd Lt.

Schintzen, Louis LA 1st (Nelligan's) Inf. Co.G

Schipman, B.M. SC 2nd Inf. Co.I

Schipman, Harman SC 6th Cav. Co.F

Schipman, J.J. SC 8th Bn.Res. Co.A

Schipper, F. GA Inf. 2nd Bn. (St.Guards) Co.A

Schirer, John SC 25th Inf. Co.B

Schirlitz, A.C. MS Cav. Hughes' Bn. Co.B

Schirlnight, Artemas SC 10th Inf. Co.K

Schirm, John AL 11th Inf. Co.D

Schirm, William P. GA 4th (Clinch's) Cav. Co.A 1st Sgt.

Schirm, William P. GA Lt.Arty. Clinch's Btty. 1st Lt.

Schirmer, Charles W. Gen. & Staff, Ord. 1st Lt.

Schirmer, F.M. SC Lt.Arty. Walter's Co. (Washington Arty.) Cpl.

Schirmer, F.M. Gen. & Staff 2nd Lt.,Dr.M.

Schirmer, J.E. SC Arty. Manigault's Bn. 1st Co.A

Schirmer, Louis LA Arty. Kean's Btty. (Orleans Ind.Arty.) 1st Lt.

Schirmer, Philip AL 1st Regt. Mobile Vol. Co.E

Schirmer, W.H. SC Mil. 17th Regt. Buist's Co.

Schirmer, William R. GA Inf. 1st Loc.Troops (Augusta) Co.B

Schirmer, W.R. GA 1st (Symons') Res. Co.I

Schirska, --- NC Inf. Thomas Legion

Schirven, E.S. KY 5th Cav. Co.C

Schisand, Stephen P. NC 1st Inf. Co.K Sgt.

Schisano, Stephen P. VA 6th Inf. Ferguson's Co.
Schisler, Joseph VA Horse Arty. Lurty's Co.
Schism, Newton TN 45th Inf. Co.G
Schistel, William TN Inf. 3rd Bn. Co.G
Schlack, C.H. AL 4th (Russell's) Cav. Co.F Bugler
Schlack, C.H. AL 7th Inf. Co.D
Schlacter, A. LA Mil. 4th Regt.Eur.Brig. Co.E
Schlaer, F. LA Mil. Mooney's Co. (Saddlers Guards)
Schlake, Henry TX 15th Inf. Co.A
Schlandit, --- TX Cav. McCord's Frontier Regt. Co.A
Schlandt, Theo. TX Cav. Frontier Bn. Co.B
Schlanker, A. AR 17th (Griffith's) Inf. Co.A
Schlass, Thead LA Mil. 4th Regt.Eur.Brig. Co.B
Schlatchey, R. LA Mil. 1st Regt. 2nd Brig. 1st Div. Co.B
Schlater, William LA Inf.Cons.Crescent Regt. Co.E Cpl.
Schlatre, G. LA 1st Cav. Maj.
Schlatter, Charles L. GA 4th (Clinch's) Cav. Co.B
Schlatter, Charles L. GA 1st Bn.S.S. Co.D,A 2nd Lt.
Schlatter, Charles L. GA 26th Inf. Dent's Co.A,Co.B Sgt.Maj.
Schlatter, Charles L. GA Inf. (Brunswick Rifles) Harris' Ind.Co. Cpl.
Schlatter, C.L. GA Inf. 18th Bn. Co.C
Schlauch, F. LA Mil. Fire Bn. Co.E
Schlaughter, Gabriel VA 1st St.Res. Co.D
Schlegel, George MS 48th Inf. Co.E Sgt.
Schlegel, W. LA Mil. 4th Regt.Eur.Brig. Co.F
Schlegle, John MS 44th Inf. Co.B
Schleicher, F. TX 7th Cav. Co.B Bugler
Schleicher, Gustave Eng.,CSA Capt.
Schleicher, M. TX 3rd Inf. 2nd Co.A
Schleicher, M. TX Inf. 4th Bn. (Oswald's) Co.A
Schleigh, M.V. AR 35th Inf. Co.D 1st Sgt.
Schlein, F. GA 8th Inf. Co.I
Schleiser, Conrad VA Lt.Arty. 38th Bn. Co.C
Schlelger, H. SC Mil. 1st Regt. (Charleston Res.) Co.F
Schlemmer, Charles TX 2nd Inf. Co.F
Schleniger, G. LA Mil. 2nd Regt. 2nd Brig. 1st Div. Co.G
Schlenning, Harmon TX 3rd Inf. Co.B,K 2nd Lt.
Schlepegrill, F. TX Inf. 4th Bn. (Oswald's) Co.B
Schleppergrel, F. Gen. & Staff Asst.Surg.
Schleppergrell, F. TX 2nd Inf. Co.F
Schlesinger, Gustavus GA Cobb's Legion Co.B
Schlesinger, Henry TN 20th Inf. Co.A
Schlesinger, Jac LA 20th Inf. Co.F Music.
Schlessinger, J. AL 1st Regt. Mobile Vol. Co.C
Schlessinger, Jac LA 13th & 20th Inf. Band Music.
Schlessinger, S. AL 1st Regt. Mobile Vol. Co.C
Schleter, William AR 35th Inf. Co.C
Schletz, Frederic LA C.S. Zouave Bn. Co.B
Schlevoight, L. LA 22nd Inf. Co.B
Schlevoight, Louis AL Lt.Arty. 2nd Bn. Co.E
Schlevoight, Louis LA 22nd (Cons.) Inf. Co.B
Schlevoigt, Louis AL St.Arty. Co.D
Schley, C.C. GA 61st Inf. Maj.,Surg.

Schley, Chas. C. Gen. & Staff, Medical Dept. Surg.
Schley, Edward B. GA Inf. 2nd Bn. Co.A N.C.S Hosp.Stew.
Schley, Franz TX 24th Cav. Co.K
Schley, H.J. GA 63rd Inf. Co.K
Schley, J.H. AL 17th Inf. Co.A
Schley, Lake R. MD 1st Inf. Co.H
Schley, P.A. GA Lt.Arty. 12th Bn. 1st Co.A
Schley, Philip A. GA 63rd Inf. Co.A
Schley, Philip T., Jr. GA Inf. 2nd Bn. Co.A
Schley, Reuben GA 5th Res. Music.
Schley, Teneh Gen. & Staff AQM
Schley, Thomas GA 64th Inf. Co.I
Schley, T.P. GA Cav. Nelson's Ind.Co.
Schley, T.P. GA Cav. Ragland's Co.
Schley, V.W. TX 13th Vol. 2nd Co.H, 1st Co.H Sgt.
Schley, Wesley (Col'd) GA Inf. 2nd Bn. Co.A Music.
Schley, William AL 60th Inf. Co.D
Schley, William AL 3rd Bn. Hilliard's Legion Vol. Co.F
Schley, William MO Lt.Arty. 3rd Field Btty.
Schley, William C. Sig.Corps,CSA Lt.
Schleyer, H. SC Arty. Manigault's Bn. Co.E
Schleyer, Emil TX 2nd Cav. Co.C
Schleyer, Henry SC Hvy.Arty. Gilchrist's Co. (Gist Guard)
Schleyher, Oscar TX 3rd Inf.
Schlicer, G.W. VA 1st St.Res. Co.C
Schlichter, A.S. GA 6th Inf. (St.Guards) Co.K
Schlichting, W. LA Mil. 4th Regt.Eur.Brig. Co.C
Schlick, Albert TX 4th Cav. Co.G 2nd Lt.
Schlick, Rich TX 4th Cav. Co.G
Schlick, Richard TX 4th Cav. Co.G
Schliegemilk, S. GA Inf. 1st Bn. (St.Guards) Co.D
Schliephake, Henry T. MD 1st Inf. Co.H
Schliesar, G.W. VA Lt.Arty. 38th Bn. Co.C
Schliescher, George VA 1st Inf. Co.G
Schlim, C.W. TN Inf. 154th Sr.Regt. Co.A
Schlimmermeyer, Diedr. SC Arty. Bachman's Co. (German Lt.Arty.) Sgt.
Schlimmermeyer, Diedr. SC Arty.Bn. Hampton Legion Co.B Sgt.
Schline, C. TX 8th Inf. Co.G
Schlintz, Jacob TX Inf. Timmons' Regt. Co.K
Schliting, Henry TX 1st Hvy.Arty. Co.C
Schlittler, F. TX Inf. 1st St.Troops Shield's Co.B
Schlobaum, E.W. GA Hvy.Arty. 22nd Bn. Co.D
Schlobohm, Fred TX Waul's Legion Co.B
Schlobohm, William SC Arty. Bachman's Co. (German Lt.Arty.)
Schlobohm, William SC Arty.Bn. Hampton Legion Co.B
Schlobohmm, Albert NC 18th Inf. Co.A
Schloeter, Henry TX Cav. 8th (Taylor's) Bn. Co.C
Schlombert, John LA Herrick's Co. (Orleans Blues)
Schlondorff, H. SC Arty. Melchers' Co. (Co.B,German Arty.)
Schlondorff, W. SC Mil.Arty. 1st Regt. Harms' Co.

Schloper, Nich LA Mil. 4th Regt. 3rd Brig. 1st Div. Co.C
Schloss, Charles LA Mil. 3rd Regt. 1st Brig. 1st Div. Co.G
Schloss, Theo LA Mil. 4th Regt.Eur.Brig. Co.C Sgt.
Schlosser, Anton LA Mil. 3rd Regt. 3rd Brig. 1st Div. Co.H
Schlosser, Jacob AR 5th Inf. Co.A Music.
Schlosser, John LA Mil. 3rd Regt. 3rd Brig. 1st Div. Co.H
Schlosser, L. SC 1st Regt. Charleston Guard Co.G
Schlosser, Theodore MS 22nd Inf. Co.D
Schlotmann, F. TX 5th Inf. Martindale's Co.
Schlotmar, Hy. LA Mil. 2nd Regt. 3rd Brig. 1st Div. Co.A
Schlott, Louis TX 17th Inf. Co.H
Schlouck, John LA Miles' Legion Co.H
Schlue, M. LA 20th Inf. New Co.E
Schluentz, F. TX Waul's Legion Co.C
Schluentz, J. TX Waul's Legion Co.C
Schlueter, F. TN Hvy.Arty. Sterling's Co.
Schlueter, Henry TX 1st (Yager's) Cav. Co.E
Schlug, Jacob LA Mil. 1st Regt. French Brig. Co.7
Schlumbrecht, Charles LA Mil. Mooney's Co. (Saddlers Guards)
Schlumbrecht, Dick LA Mil. Chalmette Regt. Co.F
Schlunz, Dedlef TX 6th Inf. Co.K
Schlunz, J. TX 4th Inf. (St.Troops) Co.F
Schluphake, H. MD Weston's Bn. Co.D
Schlusted, F. GA Floyd Legion (St.Guards) Co.B
Schluter, --- TX Lt.Arty. Dege's Bn. Cpl.
Schluter, C. TX 6th Field Btty. Gunner
Schluter, Christian SC 12th Inf. Co.K
Schluter, George W. TX Cav. Crump's Regt. Co.B
Schluter, H. LA Mil.Conf.Guards Regt. Co.G
Schlutman, William LA Mil. 3rd Regt. 1st Brig. 1st Div. Co.A
Schluzer, Charles LA Mil. 3rd Regt. 1st Brig. 1st Div. Co.E
Schly, Frederick W. TX 5th Cav. Co.A
Schly, Ruben GA Inf. 27th Bn. (NonConscr.) Co.A Music.
Schmalbeck, F. LA Washington Arty.Bn. Co.1 Driver
Schmalfeld, F. TX 3rd Inf. 2nd Co.A
Schmalholtz, F.X. LA Inf. 1st Sp.Bn. (Rightor's) Co.A
Schmalholz, F.X. LA Mil. 1st Regt. 2nd Brig. 1st Div. Co.G
Schmaltz, J.E. LA Mil. 4th Regt.Eur.Brig. Co.F
Schmaltz, John E. LA Mil. 3rd Regt. 1st Brig. 1st Div. Co.D
Schmalz, Joseph LA Mil. 6th Regt. Eur.Brig. (Italian Guards Bn.) Co.5
Schmauch, Charles GA 1st (Olmstead's) Inf. 1st Co.A
Schmauch, Charles GA 1st Bn.S.S. Co.B
Schmeider, C. TX Inf. 1st St.Troops Martin's Co.A
Schmeit, C. GA 1st (Olmstead's) Inf.
Schmeitt, D.H. NC 66th Inf. Co.K
Schmelts, Charles TX 20th Inf. Co.B

Schmeltz, Henry TX 20th Inf. Co.H

Schmeltz, Nicholas SC 1st (Butler's) Inf. Co.C
Music.

Schmeltzer, G. TX 8th Cav. Co.D

Schmeltzer, Gustavus H. TX 5th Cav. Co.D 1st
Sgt.

Schmelzer, C. LA 21st (Patton's) Inf. Co.H

Schmennauer, G. LA 22nd Inf. Co.C

Schmer, G. GA Inf. 18th Bn. (St.Guards) Co.B

Schmer, George M. GA 48th Inf. Co.C

Schmer, G.M. GA Inf. 1st Loc.Troops (Augusta)
Co.K

Schmerber, N. TX Inf. 1st St.Troops Martin's
Co.A

Schmerle, J. Gen. & Staff Maj.Gen.

Schmerz, F. LA C.S. Zouave Bn. Co.B Cpl.

Schmetz, Alex TX Cav. Giddings' Bn. Co.A
Sgt.

Schmetzer, Louis SC Mil.Cav. Theo. Cordes'
Co.

Schmick, Henry AR 7th Inf. Co.A

Schmick, Henry S. AR 38th Inf. Co.E 2nd Lt.

Schmick, Isaac P. AR 38th Inf. Co.E 1st Lt.

Schmick, J.P. AR 45th Cav. Co.K Capt.

Schmick, J.P. AR 38th Inf. Co.E

Schmid, Adolphe LA Mil. 2nd Regt. French
Brig. Co.4

Schmid, B. VA 28th Inf. 2nd Co.C

Schmid, G.L. VA Hvy.Arty. 10th Bn. Co.B

Schmidt, --- LA Mil. 1st Regt. 2nd Brig. 1st Div.
Co.A

Schmidt, A. LA Mil. 4th Regt.Eur.Brig. Co.A

Schmidt, A. LA 5th Inf. Band Music.

Schmidt, A. SC Mil.Arty. 1st Regt. Harms' Co.

Schmidt, A. SC Arty. Melchers' Co.
(Co.B,German Arty.)

Schmidt, A. TX Inf. Timmons' Regt. Co.K

Schmidt, A. Conf.Lt.Arty. Richardson's Bn. Co.B

Schmidt, Adam VA Lt.Arty. Arch. Graham's Co.

Schmidt, Adolph AL 2nd Cav. Co.I Bugler

Schmidt, Adolph AL Lowndes Rangers Vol.
Fagg's Co. Bugler

Schmidt, Adolph Conf.Cav. Wood's Regt. Co.H
Music.

Schmidt, A.J. VA 3rd Inf.Loc.Def. Co.E

Schmidt, Albert TX 6th Inf. Co.K Sgt.

Schmidt, Albert J. LA Arty. Landry's Co.
(Donaldsonville Arty.)

Schmidt, Anton TN Inf. 3rd Bn. Co.G

Schmidt, August LA 15th Inf. Co.A

Schmidt, Augustin AL 3rd Res. Co.I

Schmidt, Augustus SC 1st Arty. Co.A

Schmidt, Augustus SC 1st (Butler's) Inf. Co.H

Schmidt, B. LA Mil. 4th Regt.Eur.Brig. Co.B

Schmidt, Balzer TX 4th Inf. Co.D

Schmidt, Bernhard 8th (Wade's) Conf.Cav. Co.A

Schmidt, Bernhart AL 51st (Part.Rangers) Co.G

Schmidt, C. GA 5th Cav. Co.I

Schmidt, C. LA Mil. 3rd Regt. 2nd Brig. 1st
Div.

Schmidt, C. LA Mil. Chalmette Regt. Co.B

Schmidt, C. TX 1st Hvy.Arty. Co.B

Schmidt, C. TX Waul's Legion

Schmidt, Carl LA Mil. 4th Regt. 2nd Brig. 1st
Div. Co.C

Schmidt, Carl TX 15th Field Btty.

Schmidt, C.C.L. LA Mil. 4th Regt. 3rd Brig. 1st
Div. Co.A Sgt.

Schmidt, C.E. LA Inf.Crescent Regt. Co.G

Schmidt, C.F. TN 12th (Cons.) Inf. Co.G

Schmidt, C.F. TN 22nd Inf. Co.G

Schmidt, Ch. LA Mil. 4th Regt.Eur.Brig. Co.E

Schmidt, Charles AL 1st Regt.Mobile Vol. Co.E

Schmidt, Charles AL 12th Inf. Co.C

Schmidt, Charles LA 1st (Nelligan's) Inf. Co.C

Schmidt, Charles LA Mil. 4th Regt. 1st Brig. 1st
Div. Co.H

Schmidt, Charles LA 21st (Patton's) Inf. Co.D,A
Cpl.

Schmidt, Charles TX 32nd Cav. Co.F

Schmidt, Charles TX Arty. 4th Bn. Co.B

Schmidt, Charles TX Lt.Arty. Hughes' Co.

Schmidt, Charles, 1st TX 2nd Inf. Co.F

Schmidt, Charles, 2nd TX 2nd Inf. Co.F

Schmidt, Charles TX 8th Inf. Co.B

Schmidt, Charles TX 17th Inf. Co.F

Schmidt, Charles TX Inf. Griffin's Bn. Co.F

Schmidt, Charles Conf.Cav. Wood's Regt. 1st
Co.D Music.

Schmidt, Christian GA Cav. 2nd Bn. Co.A

Schmidt, Christopher TX 4th Cav. Co.G

Schmidt, Chs. TX Inf. 4th Bn. (Oswald's) Co.B

Schmidt, Conrad VA 2nd Inf. Co.B

Schmidt, Cornelius LA 6th Inf. Co.G

Schmidt, C. William VA 10th Cav. Co.D

Schmidt, Daniel W. GA Arty. 11th Bn. (Sumter
Arty.) New Co.C

Schmidt, Daniel W. GA 9th Inf. Co.A

Schmidt, Dan'l. W. Gen. & Staff Asst.Surg.

Schmidt, David LA 20th Inf. Co.C

Schmidt, D.E. LA 21st (Kennedy's) Inf. Co.D

Schmidt, E.F. LA Washington Arty.Bn. Co.6
Can.

Schmidt, Ernst LA Mil.Cont.Regt. Roder's Co.
Sgt.

Schmidt, Eugene LA Arty. Guyol's Co. (Orleans
Arty.)

Schmidt, F. AL St.Arty. Co.D

Schmidt, F. LA Mil. Chalmette Regt. Co.A

Schmidt, F. TX 1st Hvy.Arty. Co.B

Schmidt, F. VA 46th Inf. 2nd Co.E

Schmidt, Felix LA 28th (Thomas') Inf. Co.C

Schmidt, F.N. AR 19th (Dawson's) Inf.

Schmidt, Fran Jos TX Conscr.

Schmidt, Frank LA 22nd Inf. Durrive, Jr.'s Co.A

Schmidt, Frank TX 1st Inf. Co.L

Schmidt, Franz LA Mil. Mech.Guard

Schmidt, Frederic LA 4th Inf. Co.B

Schmidt, Frederick TX Arty. 4th Bn. Co.B

Schmidt, Frederick TX 8th Inf. Co.B

Schmidt, Frederick W. TX 4th Field Btty. Sgt.

Schmidt, Fredrich TX 2nd Inf. Co.H

Schmidt, Fredrick TX 10th Inf. Co.G

Schmidt, Fried TX Inf. 1st St.Troops Sheldon's
Co.B

Schmidt, G. TX 14th Inf. Co.A

Schmidt, G.A. LA Mil. 3rd Regt. 3rd Brig. 1st
Div. Co.C

Schmidt, G.E. GA 3rd Inf. Co.F

Schmidt, George LA 13th Inf. Co.F 1st Sgt.

Schmidt, George LA 22nd Inf. Co.A

Schmidt, George LA Mil. Jackson Rifle Bn.

Schmidt, George TX Waul's Legion Co.B

Schmidt, George TX Res.Corps Co.B

Schmidt, George VA Inf. 6th Bn.Loc.Def. Co.B

Schmidt, George Conf.Inf. 8th Bn. Co.F

Schmidt, George W. TX 8th Inf. Co.K

Schmidt, G.H. LA Mil. Chalmette Regt. Co.B

Schmidt, Gust TN Inf. 3rd Bn. Co.F

Schmidt, Gustav TX 6th Inf. Co.K Cpl.

Schmidt, Gustav TX Res.Corps Co.A

Schmidt, Gustave TX Ford's Cav. Co.C

Schmidt, H. LA Mil. Squad. Guides d'Orleans
Cavalier

Schmidt, H. LA Mil. 3rd Regt. 3rd Brig. 1st Div.
Co.C

Schmidt, H., No.1 TN Inf. 3rd Bn. Co.G

Schmidt, H., No.2 TN Inf. 3rd Bn. Co.G

Schmidt, H. TX 4th Inf.(St.Troops) Co.F 1st Lt.

Schmidt, H. TX Inf. Timmons' Regt. Co.B Sgt.

Schmidt, Heinrich TX 3rd Inf. Co.K

Schmidt, Henry GA 1st (Olmstead's) Inf. 1st
Co.A

Schmidt, Henry GA 1st Bn.S.S. Co.B Cpl.

Schmidt, Henry GA Inf. 1st Loc.Troops
(Augusta) Co.B Cpl.

Schmidt, Henry LA 1st Hvy.Arty. (Reg.) Co.A

Schmidt, Henry LA 1st Hvy.Arty. (Reg.) Co.E

Schmidt, Henry LA Mil. 3rd Regt. 1st Brig. 1st
Div. Co.E 3rd Lt.

Schmidt, Henry LA Mil. 4th Regt. 2nd Brig. 1st
Div. Co.B

Schmidt, Henry LA C.S. Zouave Bn. Co.F

Schmidt, Henry SC Arty.Bn. Hampton Legion
Co.B

Schmidt, Henry TX Waul's Legion Co.D Cpl.

Schmidt, Henry Conf.Inf. 8th Bn. Co.D

Schmidt, Henry C. LA Arty. Green's Co. (LA
Guard Btty.)

Schmidt, Henry C. LA 1st (Nelligan's) Inf. 1st
Co.B

Schmidt, Henry Chris TX Detailed Conscr.

Schmidt, Henry D. Gen. & Staff Surg.

Schmidt, Henry R. LA 21st (Patton's) Inf.
Co.D,A Cpl.

Schmidt, Herman LA 20th Inf. Co.D

Schmidt, Herman LA 26th Inf. Co.C

Schmidt, Herman SC Arty. Bachman's Co.
(German Lt.Arty.) Cpl.

Schmidt, Hermann TX 8th Inf. Co.K

Schmidt, Hy. LA Mil. 4th Regt.Eur.Brig. Co.D

Schmidt, J. AR 18th (Marmaduke's) Inf. Co.A

Schmidt, J. LA Mil. Fire Bn. Co.D

Schmidt, J. TX Inf. 1st St.Troops Martin's Co.A

Schmidt, J. TX 3rd Inf. 2nd Co.A

Schmidt, J. TX 5th Inf. Martindale's Co.

Schmidt, Jacob MS 38th Cav. Co.A

Schmidt, Jacob VA 1st Inf. Co.K

Schmidt, J.B. LA Arty. Guyol's Co. (Orleans
Arty.)

Schmidt, J.B. LA Lt.Arty. LeGardeur, Jr.'s Co.
(Orleans Guard Btty.)

Schmidt, J.D. LA Mil. 1st Regt. 3rd Brig. 1st
Div.

Schmidt, Jean LA Mil. 1st Regt. French Brig.
Co.8

Schmidt, Jean LA C.S. Zouave Bn. Co.F

Schmidt, J.M. LA Inf. 1st Sp.Bn. (Rightor's)
Co.B

Schmidt, J.M. SC 11th Inf. Co.C 1st Sgt.

Schmidt, Johann S. AR 17th (Lemoyne's) Inf. Co.B Sgt.
Schmidt, John GA 1st (Olmstead's) Inf. 1st Co.A
Schmidt, John GA 1st Bn.S.S. Co.B
Schmidt, John LA Mil. 1st Regt. 3rd Brig. 1st Div.
Schmidt, John LA 6th Inf. Co.G
Schmidt, John LA 10th Inf. Co.B QMSgt.
Schmidt, John LA 11th Inf. Co.D
Schmidt, John LA 14th (Austin's) Bn.S.S. Co.B
Schmidt, John LA 20th Inf. Co.I
Schmidt, John LA 28th (Thomas') Inf. Co.C
Schmidt, John LA 31st Inf. Co.A
Schmidt, John LA Mil. Chalmette Regt. Co.I,G
Schmidt, John LA Miles' Legion Co.A
Schmidt, John MS 6th Inf. Co.D
Schmidt, John TN Arty. Stewart's Co.
Schmidt, John TX 2nd Cav. Co.E
Schmidt, John TX 35th (Brown's) Cav. Co.D,F
Schmidt, John TX 13th Vol. 1st Co.I
Schmidt, John TX Waul's Legion Co.C
Schmidt, John Gus TX Comal Res.
Schmidt, John Henry TX Arty. 4th Bn. Co.B
Schmidt, John Henry TX 8th Inf. Co.B
Schmidt, Joseph MS Inf. 2nd Bn. (St.Troops) Co.B
Schmidt, Joseph TX 17th Field Btty.
Schmidt, Karl NC 12th Inf. Co.F
Schmidt, Kasper AR 3rd Inf. Co.E
Schmidt, L. LA Mil. 1st Chasseurs a pied Co.2
Schmidt, L. SC Mil. 1st Regt. (Charleston Res.) Co.B
Schmidt, L. TX 6th Field Btty.
Schmidt, L. TX Lt.Arty. Dege's Bn. Co.A
Schmidt, Leonhard TX 36th Cav. Co.F
Schmidt, Lorenz LA 20th Inf. Co.A,B
Schmidt, Louis LA Mil. 4th Regt.Eur.Brig. Co.C
Schmidt, Louis TX 5th Field Btty.
Schmidt, Louis VA 7th Inf. Co.H
Schmidt, Ludwig GA 1st Reg. Co.G
Schmidt, Ludwig LA 21st (Patton's) Inf. Co.I
Schmidt, Ludwig TX 1st (Yager's) Cav. Co.E Sgt.
Schmidt, Ludwig TX Cav. 8th (Taylor's) Bn. Co.C Sgt.
Schmidt, M. LA Mil. 3rd Regt. 1st Brig. 1st Div. Co.G
Schmidt, M. TX 32nd Cav. Co.F
Schmidt, Martin TX 36th Cav. Co.F Sgt.
Schmidt, Mess SC 11th Inf. 1st Co.I, 2nd Co.I
Schmidt, N. LA 2nd Inf. Co.H Cpl.
Schmidt, Nic TX 3rd Inf. Co.B
Schmidt, Oscar LA Arty. Landry's Co. (Donaldsonville Arty.)
Schmidt, P. SC Mil.Arty. 1st Regt. Werner's Co.
Schmidt, Paul TX 3rd Inf. Co.K
Schmidt, Peter LA Mil. 3rd Regt. 1st Brig. 1st Div. Co.A Sgt.
Schmidt, P.F.C. GA Inf. 1st Loc.Troops (Augusta) Co.C
Schmidt, Philip LA 20th Inf. Co.D
Schmidt, Phillip LA Miles' Legion Co.A
Schmidt, Phillip TX Waul's Legion Co.B
Schmidt, R. AL 9th Inf. Co.G
Schmidt, R.D. NC 44th Inf. Co.C
Schmidt, R.H. LA Arty. Guyol's Co. (Orleans Arty.) Cpl.

Schmidt, S. TX 4th Cav. Co.C
Schmidt, Theo SC 2nd Inf. Co.K
Schmidt, Theodore VA 30th Inf. Co.A,B Music.
Schmidt, Theodore Conf.Cav. Wood's Regt. Co.K
Schmidt, V. LA Mil. Squad. Guides d'Orleans
Schmidt, Vincent LA 14th Inf. Co.F
Schmidt, W. AL Mil. Bligh's Co.
Schmidt, W. TX 5th Inf. Martindale's Co.
Schmidt, W.A. SC Lt.Arty. Parker's Co. (Marion Arty.)
Schmidt, W.A. SC Inf. 1st (Charleston) Bn. Co.E
Schmidt, W.B. LA Mil. Orleans Guards Regt. Co.F
Schmidt, William LA 21st (Patton's) Inf. Co.I
Schmidt, William, 2nd LA 21st (Patton's) Inf. Co.I
Schmidt, William LA Inf.Crescent Regt. Co.B
Schmidt, William TX 7th Cav. Co.B
Schmidt, Xavier TX 3rd Inf. Co.H
Schmidts, George LA 20th Inf. Co.F Sgt.
Schmidtt, David LA 8th Inf. Co.B
Schmidtt, Etna LA 8th Inf. Co.B
Schmiedekamp, B. TX 17th Inf. Co.H
Schmiedekampf, A. TX Inf. 1st St.Troops Martin's Co.A
Schmieding, Charls AR Part.Rangers F. Williams' Co.
Schmiedts, H. LA 20th Inf. Co.F
Schmiege, F. LA Mil. Orleans Fire Regt. Co.A
Schmierer, George TN 51st (Cons.) Inf. Co.G
Schmille, Fred LA 20th Inf. Co.I
Schmincke, Charles LA C.S. Zouave Bn. Co.D
Schminkey, Charles VA Lt.Arty. Clutter's Co.
Schmireker, H. LA Mil. Squad. Guides d'Orleans
Schmit, A. VA 2nd St.Res. Co.H
Schmit, Christian LA Mil. Bragg's Bn. Schwartz's Co.
Schmit, H. VA 2nd St.Res. Co.H
Schmit, Robert AL 21st Inf. Co.H
Schmith, Martin TX 7th Cav. Co.B
Schmitt, A. VA 2nd St.Res. Co.H
Schmitt, Adam TX 33rd Cav. Co.A
Schmitt, B. VA 27th Inf. Co.I
Schmitt, Bernadotte VA 146th Mil. Co.D
Schmitt, Edward VA 6th Inf. Co.A
Schmitt, Fred MS 46th Inf. Co.C
Schmitt, Fred VA 15th Inf. Co.K
Schmitt, Frederick LA 28th (Thomas') Inf. Co.D
Schmitt, George TN 26th Inf. Co.G
Schmitt, George TX 1st (McCulloch's) Cav. Co.E
Schmitt, George TX 2nd Cav. 2nd Co.F 1st Sgt.
Schmitt, George 1st Conf.Inf. 2nd Co.K
Schmitt, J. LA Mil. 1st Chasseurs a pied Co.4
Schmitt, Jean LA Mil. 6th Regt.Eur.Brig. (Italian Guards Bn.) Co.5
Schmitt, John AR Lt.Arty. Key's Btty.
Schmitt, John TN 35th Inf. 3rd Co.F
Schmitt, Joseph TX Arty. 4th Bn. Co.B
Schmitt, Joseph TX 8th Inf. Co.B
Schmitt, Joseph TX Conscr.
Schmitt, Lewis LA 15th Inf. Co.G
Schmitt, Mathias VA 3rd Bn. Valley Res. Co.B
Schmitt, Nicolas LA Mil. 1st Regt. French Brig. Co.6
Schmitt, Peter F. VA Lt.Arty. Garber's Co. Cpl.

Schmitt, Talleyrand VA Horse Arty. J.W. Carter's Co.
Schmitt, Tallyrand VA 136th Mil. Co.E
Schmitt, Theodore MS 18th Inf. Co.D
Schmitton, J.L.V. TN Inf. 2nd Cons.Regt. Co.F Cpl.
Schmitton, J.L.V. TN 11th Inf. Co.C Cpl.
Schmitton, J.O.L.V. TN 11th Inf. Co.C
Schmitz, --- LA Mil. 2nd Regt. French Brig. Co.3
Schmitz, Andrew TX 1st Hvy.Arty. Co.D Music.
Schmitz, Anthy R. AL Loc.Def. & Sp.Serv. Toomer's Co.
Schmitz, A.R. AL 4th Res. Co.G
Schmitz, Balthasar TX Conscr.
Schmitz, Charles LA 6th Inf. Co.G
Schmitz, Charles TX 4th Field Btty.
Schmitz, F. TX Lt.Arty. Dege's Bn.
Schmitz, Fred TX 6th Field Btty.
Schmitz, Frederick TX 3rd Inf. Co.H
Schmitz, George B. VA 24th Inf. Co.G
Schmitz, George S. MS 44th Inf. Co.C
Schmitz, Gerhard LA 20th Inf. Co.F
Schmitz, G.S. AL 19th Inf.
Schmitz, G.S. MS 8th Cav. Co.B
Schmitz, H.F. MS 29th Inf. Co.F
Schmitz, I.P. MS 24th Inf. Co.A
Schmitz, J. MS 8th Cav. Co.I
Schmitz, James H. MS 42nd Inf. Co.H
Schmitz, J.D. SC 20th Inf. Co.C
Schmitz, Peter TN 15th Inf. Co.K
Schmitzer, Ch. SC Mil.Arty. 1st Regt. Co.A Cpl.
Schmoke, Christian TX Inf. 1st St.Troops Stevenson's Co.F
Schmotzard, Joseph LA 7th Inf. Co.E
Schmozart, Joseph LA 7th Cav. Co.E
Schmucker, George E. VA 33rd Inf. Co.B Sgt.
Schmucker, Jacob L. VA 5th Inf. Co.K
Schmucker, Jacob L. VA 136th Mil. Co.C
Schmucker, John N. VA 31st Inf. Co.B
Schmucker, M. VA 12th Cav. Co.E
Schmucker, Samuel VA 136th Mil. Co.E
Schmucker, Samuel L. VA 62nd Mtd.Inf. 2nd Co.F
Schmucker, William VA 5th Inf. Co.A
Schmucker, William VA 136th Mil. Co.C Sgt.
Schmull, Frederick LA 21st (Patton's) Inf. Co.E
Schmutz, --- LA Mil. 3rd Regt.Eur.Brig. (Garde Francaise) Euler's Co. Cpl.
Schmutz, Charles AL Conscr.
Schmutz, Charles LA 20th Inf. Co.C
Schmutz, Ernst LA 20th Inf. Co.C
Schmutz, Louis LA Mil. 3rd Regt.Eur.Brig. (Garde Francaise) Co.4
Schmyth, Christopher TN 10th Inf. Co.I
Schnaars, D. SC Mil.Arty. 1st Regt. Harms' Co.
Schnaars, F. SC Mil.Arty. 1st Regt. Werner's Co.
Schnaars, F. SC Lt.Arty. Wagener's Co. (Co.A, German Arty.)
Schnaars, M. SC Mil.Arty. 1st Regt. Werner's Co.
Schnaars, M. SC Lt.Arty. Wagener's Co. (Co.A, German Arty.)
Schnaars, M. SC 1st (Butler's) Inf. Co.G Music.

Schnabal, August TX 1st Field Btty.

Schnabal, August TX St.Troops Edgar's Co.

Schnabbe, H. VA 1st St.Res. Co.D

Schnabel, J.A. MO 3rd Inf. 7th Div.St.Guard Co.Commander

Schnabel, J.A. MO Cav. Schnabel's Bn. Lt.Col.

Schnabel, John TX 17th Field Btty.

Schnabele, Henry VA 15th Inf. Co.K 2nd Lt.

Schnable, J.R. VA 2nd St.Res. Co.C

Schnackel H. MS 28th Cav. Co.K

Schnackenberg, D. SC Mil.Arty. 1st Regt. Werner's Co.

Schnackenberg, D. SC Lt.Arty. Wagener's Co. (Co.A,German Arty.)

Schnackenberg, D. SC Mil. 16th Regt. Lawrence's Co.

Schnapil, H. SC Mil. 16th Regt. Bancroft, Jr.'s Co.

Schnatz, C--- GA Arty. 9th Bn. Co.A

Schnaubert, Otto L. TX 8th Inf. Co.B Capt.

Schnaubert, Otto Ludwig TX Arty. 4th Bn. Co.B Lt.

Schnautz, F. LA Mil. 4th Regt.Eur.Brig. Co.E

Schnavis, George VA 1st Arty. Co.G,F

Schneberger, Francis H. LA 1st (Nelligan's) Inf. Co.I 1st Sgt.

Schnebly, C.A. AR 36th Inf. Co.C

Schnebly, John MO 4th Cav. Comsy.

Schnebly, M.J. AR 1st Mtd.Rifles Co.B Cpl.

Schneckenberger, John LA Mil. 4th Regt. Eur.Brig. Co.D

Schneckenberger, Joseph MS 17th Inf. Co.B

Schnee, Lewis GA 1st (Olmstead's) Inf. 1st Co.A

Schnee, Lewis GA 1st Bn.S.S. Co.B

Schneeder, Seman LA Inf.Cons.Crescent Regt.

Schneeder, Severin LA Inf. Weatherly's Bn. Co.A

Schneid, --- LA Mil.Squad. Guides d'Orleans

Schneidekamp, B. TX 17th Inf. Co.H

Schneider, --- LA Mil. 1st Regt. 2nd Brig. 1st Div. Co.A

Schneider, --- LA Mil. 2nd Regt. French Brig. Co.2

Schneider, A. LA Mil. 1st Regt. French Brig. Co.1

Schneider, A. VA Inf. 4th Bn.Loc.Def. Co.A

Schneider, Andreas LA Mil. Mech.Guard

Schneider, Anton GA 10th Inf. Co.G

Schneider, Antone VA Inf. 6th Bn.Loc.Def. Co.B

Schneider, August AL 8th Inf. Co.G

Schneider, B. TX 9th (Nichols') Inf. Co.G

Schneider, C. LA Mil. 2nd Regt. 2nd Brig. 1st Div. Co.E

Schneider, C. LA Mil. 4th Regt. French Brig. Co.1

Schneider, C. LA Mil. Fire Bn. Co.B

Schneider, C. TX 2nd Inf. Co.F

Schneider, C. LA Inf. 4th Bn. (Oswald's) Co.B

Schneider, Carl LA 20th Inf. Co.B

Schneider, Charles LA 20th Inf. New Co.B Sgt.

Schneider, Charles LA 21st (Kennedy's) Inf. Co.C

Schneider, Charles LA 21st (Patton's) Inf. Co.B

Schneider, Charles LA Inf. Jeff Davis Regt. Co.F

Schneider, Christ TX Cav. 8th (Taylor's) Bn. Co.C

Schneider, Christian TX 1st (Yager's) Cav. Co.E

Schneider, Conrad GA 1st (Symons') Res. Co.A

Schneider, Chr. LA Mil. 4th Regt.Eur.Brig. Co.D

Schneider, David LA C.S. Zouave Bn. Co.F

Schneider, E. LA Mil. 4th Regt. 2nd Brig. 1st Div. Co.D

Schneider, E.B.H. TX 1st Hvy.Arty. Co.C Capt.

Schneider, E.R. GA Inf. 1st Loc.Troops (Augusta) Co.K

Schneider, Ernest R. GA Inf. 18th Bn. (St.Guards) Co.B 3rd Lt.

Schneider, F. LA Mil. Fire Bn. Co.E Lt.

Schneider, F. TX Inf. 1st St.Troops Martin's Co.A

Schneider, F. TX 3rd Inf. 2nd Co.A

Schneider, F. VA 2nd St.Res. Co.M Sgt.

Schneider, Frank TX Waul's Legion Co.B

Schneider, Fred TX Inf. 1st St.Troops Sheldon's Co.B

Schneider, Frederick LA C.S. Zouave Bn. Co.F

Schneider, Frederick VA Lt.Arty. Page's Co.

Schneider, Frederick VA 15th Inf. Co.K

Schneider, Frederick VA 59th Inf. 3rd Co.F

Schneider, Fredrick 4th Conf.Inf.

Schneider, Fritz TX 13th Vol. 2nd Co.B

Schneider, G. LA 22nd Inf. Co.C

Schneider, G. NC 1st Cav. (9th St.Troops) Co.C

Schneider, G. SC Mil. 16th Regt. Sigwald's Co.

Schneider, G. TX Inf. 1st St.Troops Shield's Co.B Sgt.

Schneider, George AL 8th Inf. Co.G

Schneider, George LA Mil. 3rd Regt. 3rd Brig. 1st Div. Co.H

Schneider, George LA Mil. 4th Regt.Eur.Brig. Co.F

Schneider, George LA Mil. 4th Regt. 3rd Brig. 1st Div. Co.D

Schneider, George LA Mil. Fire Bn. Co.E

Schneider, Gustavus A. TX 15th Cav. Co.A Sgt.

Schneider, Henry LA Hvy.Arty. 2nd Bn. Co.D

Schneider, Henry LA Mil. 1st Regt. 3rd Brig. 1st Div. Co.A 1st Lt.

Schneider, Henry SC 15th Inf. Co.A

Schneider, Henry TX 17th Inf. Co.H

Schneider, Henry VA 15th Inf. Co.K

Schneider, Ire VA 2nd St.Res. Co.H

Schneider, J. GA Inf. 2nd Bn. (St.Guards) Co.A

Schneider, J. LA Mil. 1st Regt. 2nd Brig. 1st Div.

Schneider, J. LA Mil. 3rd Regt. 3rd Brig. 1st Div. Co.C

Schneider, J. LA Mil. 4th Regt.Eur.Brig. Co.A

Schneider, J. LA Mil. 4th Regt. French Brig. Co.6

Schneider, J. LA 14th Inf. Co.D

Schneider, J. LA Mil. Fire Bn. Co.E

Schneider, J. SC Mil.Arty. 1st Regt. Co.A

Schneider, J. TX 17th Inf. Co.F

Schneider, Jacob LA 14th Inf. Co.B

Schneider, Jacob TN Arty. Stewart's Co.

Schneider, Jacob TX 1st (Yager's) Cav. Co.E

Schneider, Jacob TX Cav. 8th (Taylor's) Bn. Co.C

Schneider, James TX 2nd Inf. Co.I

Schneider, J.B. LA Arty. Hutton's Co. (Crescent Arty.,Co.A)

Schneider, J.E. LA Mil. 2nd Regt. 3rd Brig. 1st Div. Co.H 3rd Lt.

Schneider, J.H. TX 20th Inf. Co.B

Schneider, John AL 8th Inf. Co.G

Schneider, John LA 4th Inf. Co.B Cpl.

Schneider, John LA Inf. 16th Bn. (Conf.Guards Resp.Bn.) Co.A Music.

Schneider, John LA Miles' Legion Co.A

Schneider, John TX 1st Hvy.Arty. Co.H

Schneider, John TX 15th Field Btty.

Schneider, John VA 2nd St.Res. Co.H

Schneider, Joseph LA 5th Inf. New Co.A

Schneider, Joseph TX 17th Field Btty.

Schneider, J.R. GA Inf. 1st Loc.Troops (Augusta) Co.K

Schneider, J.R. GA Inf. 18th Bn. (St.Guards) Adam's Co.

Schneider, Julius LA 20th Inf. Co.G,A

Schneider, L. TX 33rd Cav. Co.A

Schneider, Laurence LA 21st (Kennedy's) Inf. Co.C

Schneider, Martin LA 10th Inf. Co.I

Schneider, Martin NC 13th Inf. Co.A

Schneider, Mathias LA 4th Inf. Co.B

Schneider, Michael TX Conscr.

Schneider, P. TN Inf. Nashville Bn. Cattles' Co.

Schneider, P. TX 2nd Inf. Co.C

Schneider, Ph. LA Mil.Cont.Regt. Roder's Co. Ord.Sgt.

Schneider, Phillip TX Waul's Legion Co.F

Schneider, Simon LA 1st (Strawbridge's) Co.B

Schneider, Stephen LA Inf. 1st Sp.Bn. (Rightor's) Co.E

Schneider, Theodore LA 20th Inf. Co.D Capt.

Schneider, W. SC Lt.Arty. Wagener's Co. (Co.A,German Arty.)

Schneider, W.G. TX Inf. 1st St.Troops Shield's Co.B

Schneider, William AL Gorff's Co. (Mobile Pulaski Rifles)

Schneider, William LA Mil. Fire Bn. Co.A

Schneider, William H. MS 1st Lt.Arty. Co.E QMSgt.

Schneidey, Louis TX 33rd Cav. Co.A

Schneidmiller, Jacob LA Mil. 3rd Regt. 1st Brig. 1st Div. Co.C

Schneidmiller, John LA Mil. 3rd Regt. 1st Brig. 1st Div. Co.C Cpl.

Schneidre, B. LA Mil. 4th Regt. 2nd Brig. 1st Div. Co.E Jr.2nd Lt.

Schneiker, H. GA Inf. 1st Loc.Troops (Augusta) Co.K

Schnekeberg, John LA Mil. 3rd Regt. 1st Brig. 1st Div. Co.A

Schnekberger, Adam SC 1st (Butler's) Inf. Co.G

Schnell, Auguste LA 14th Inf. Co.D Sgt.

Schnell, Conrad SC 1st Regt. Charleston Guard Co.F

Schnell, Henry LA Mil. 4th Regt. 2nd Brig. 1st Div. Co.A

Schnell, Henry LA Mil. Chalmette Regt. Co.I

Schnell, John GA Inf. 3rd Bn. Co.F 2nd Lt.

Schnell, John GA 37th Inf. Co.B 1st Lt.

Schnell, Robert LA Mil. Chalmette Regt. Co.I

Schnell, Valentine GA 1st (Olmstead's) Inf. Co.I

Schnellenburg, Charles VA Inf. 4th Bn.Loc.Def.
Co.C
Schneller, Jacob LA Mil. 4th Regt.Eur.Brig.
Co.D
Schnepel, H. SC Mil.Arty. 1st Regt. Harms' Co.
Schnepel, H. SC Arty. Melchers' Co.
(Co.B,German Arty.)
Schnetker, William LA 28th (Thomas') Inf. Co.C
Schnetz, Alexander TX Conscr.
Schnibbe, C. SC Mil. 16th Regt. Eason's Co.
Cpl.
Schnibbe, Henry SC Sea Fencibles Symons' Co.
Schnible, C. SC Lt.Arty. Wagener's Co. (Co.A,
German Arty.)
Schnible, Charles LA C.S. Zouave Bn. Co.A
Schnider, Berd. LA Mil. 3rd Regt. 1st Brig. 1st
Div. Co.D
Schnider, Franzcis LA 10th Inf. Co.G
Schnider, G. LA Mil. 3rd Regt. 1st Brig. 1st Div.
Co.H
Schnider, George TN 7th Inf. Co.D
Schnider, George P. GA 12th (Robinson's) Cav.
(St.Guards) Co.K
Schnider, G.W. MD Cav. 2nd Bn. Co.D Sgt.
Schnider, John MO 6th Inf. Co.D
Schnider, Joseph LA 10th Inf. Co.G
Schnider, L. MO Thompson's Command
Schnider, M. Gen. & Staff, Comsy.Dept.
Schnider, P. MS 2nd (Quinn's St.Troops) Inf.
Co.H
Schnidler, Andreas LA Mil. Mech.Guard
Schniekard, F. TX 1st Hvy.Arty. Co.C Band
Music.
Schnier, W. TX 3rd Inf. 2nd Co.A Cpl.
Schnier, William TX Inf. 4th Bn. (Oswald's)
Co.A
Schnierle, H.E.V. SC Inf. 1st (Charleston) Bn.
Co.E
Schnierle, H.E.V. SC 27th Inf. Co.A
Schnierle, J.M. SC 1st Cav. Co.I
Schnierle, J.M. SC 23rd Inf. Adj.
Schnierlie, H. SC Mil. 1st Regt.Rifles Palmer's
Co.
Schniker, H. GA Inf. 18th Bn. (St.Guards) Co.B
Cpl.
Schnile, William SC Mil. 1st Regt. (Charleston
Res.) Co.D
Schnir, Anton LA Mil. Chalmette Regt. Co.I
Sgt.
Schnit, W. VA 2nd St.Res. Co.H
Schnitz, Joseph TX 3rd Inf. Co.G Sgt.
Schnocart, Joseph LA 17th Inf.
Schnuberger, --- LA Mil. Mech.Guard
Schnuberger, Jacob LA Mil. Mech.Guard
Schnurr, A. TN Hvy.Arty. Sterling's Co.
Schnurr, Andrew LA 17th Inf. Co.E
Schnurr, Martin 14th Conf.Cav. Co.G Black.
Schnyder, Michael TN Inf. 1st Cons.Regt. Co.B
Schoaltz, William SC 1st Arty. Co.H
Schoar, Anton LA Mil. 3rd Regt. 1st Brig. 1st
Div. Co.E
Schoat, Edward AR 17th (Lemoyne's) Inf. Co.F
Schobb, Fred TX 8th Inf. Co.E
Schober, C. TX Inf. 1st St.Troops Martin's Co.A
Schober, Jacob MS 9th Inf. New Co.C
Schober, Jacob MS 10th Inf. New Co.B
Schober, M. AL 32nd Inf. Band Music.

Schober, M. MS Cav. Buck's Co.
Schober, M. 1st Conf.Inf. 1st Co.G
Schobough, Christopher MO 8th Cav. Co.A
Schoch, Marcus LA Mil. 1st Regt. 3rd Brig. 1st
Div. Co.D
Schock, Henry LA 14th Inf. Co.F
Schock, John Conf.Inf. 8th Bn.
Schock, Philip AL Mil. 3rd Vol. Co.B
Schockey, Louis TN 15th Inf. Co.I Sgt.
Schoder, William VA 10th Cav.
Schodt, Charles TX 1st Inf. Co.L
Schodts, M. LA Mil. 3rd Regt.Eur.Brig. (Garde
Francaise) 1st Sgt.
Schoebel, John LA Mil. 4th Regt.Eur.Brig. Co.D
Schoeber, Fredrich W. NC 18th Inf. Co.A
Schoeber, Jacob GA 36th (Villepigue's) Inf.
Co.G
Schoeber, Michael GA 36th (Villepigue's) Inf.
Co.G Cpl.
Schoedel, L. LA Arty. Hutton's Co. (Crescent
Arty.,Co.A)
Schoeff, George LA 20th Inf. Co.A Sgt.
Schoeffer, Conrad LA Mil. 3rd Regt. 1st Brig.
1st Div. Co.C
Schoeffer, William TX 16th Inf. Co.E
Schoefield, James T. VA 38th Inf. Co.C 2nd Lt.
Schoemacher, Peter TX 3rd Inf. 1st Co.A
Schoembs, B. LA Mil. Fire Bn. Co.D
Schoenberg, Wolfe SC Horse Arty. (Washington
Arty.) Vol. Hart's Co.
Schoenberger, John LA 22nd Inf. Wash. Marks'
Co.
Schoenen, Henry TX 6th Inf. Co.K
Schoenert, A. TX 5th Cav. Co.D
Schoenert, Anton TX 12th Field Btty. Sgt.
Schoenfeld, --- LA Mil. Squad. Guides d'Orleans
Schoenpflug, Joseph LA 27th Inf. Co.D
Schoenstein, J.F. LA 22nd Inf. Wash. Marks'
Co. Sgt.
Schoepmoes, --- LA Mil. Beauregard Bn. Co.D
Schoesser, Ignaz NC 1st Arty. (10th St.Troops)
Co.D
Schoff, William VA 24th Cav. Co.G
Schoffield, Charles TX 8th Inf. Co.A
Schoffield, Samuel T. FL 2nd Cav.
Schoffill, Henry SC 9th Inf. Co.K
Schoffner, Gabriel MO Cav. 13th Regt.St.Guard
Co.D 2nd Lt.
Schoffner, J.T. MS 10th Inf. New Co.I
Schofield, Addison H. VA 3rd Inf. 2nd Co.I
Sgt.
Schofield, Benjamin VA 55th Inf. Co.L
Schofield, Benjamin VA 92nd Mil. Co.A
Schofield, C. TX St.Troops Teel's Co.
Schofield, Charles TX 2nd Field Btty.
Schofield, Charles TX Arty. 4th Bn. Co.A
Schofield, Corden A. AL 14th Inf. Co.B
Schofield, Ellis H. MO 1st N.E. Cav.
Schofield, Jacob GA 27th Inf. Co.B
Schofield, J.H. GA Inf. (Loc.Def.) Hamlet's Co.
Schofield, J.J. AL 17th Inf. Co.I
Schofield, John AL 14th Inf. Co.B
Schofield, John VA 23rd Inf. Co.H
Schofield, John H. GA Conscr.
Schofield, John R. AL 16th Inf. Co.A
Schofield, Joshua GA Inf. 2nd Bn. Co.C
Schofield, J.W. GA Inf. (Loc.Def.) Hamlet's Co.

Schofield, Marion MO 1st N.E. Cav. Co.I
Schofield, Marion MO 2nd N.E. Cav. (Franklin's
Regt.)
Schofield, M.S. Gen. & Staff Asst.Surg.
Schofield, R.C. VA 1st St.Res. Co.B
Schofield, R.J. FL 11th Inf. Co.C
Schofield, Robt. AL 23rd Inf. Co.K
Schofield, Robert C. VA Lt.Arty. E.J. Ander-
son's Co.
Schofield, Stephen KY 3rd Cav. Co.A
Schofield, William AL 3rd Inf. Co.H
Schofield, William MO 1st N.E. Cav. Co.I
Schofield, William H. MO McCullough's Regt.
Schofield, William H. SC 23rd Inf. Co.B
Schogel, N. LA Mil. 3rd Regt. 1st Brig. 1st Div.
Co.H
Schoggen, David J. MS 33rd Inf. Co.I
Schoggen, George W. MS 33rd Inf. Co.I
Schoggins, B.K. AL 1st Cav. 2nd Co.C Black.
Schoggins, John B. NC 58th Inf. Co.B Sgt.
Schoggins, William N. MS 28th Cav. Co.H
Scholas, C.C. NC 2nd Jr.Res.
Scholer, John TN 1st Hvy.Arty. Co.K, 2nd Co.C
Scholes, J.M. TN 10th (DeMoss') Cav. Co.G
Scholes, J.M. TN Cav. Napier's Bn. Co.D
Scholes, John T. TN 11th Inf. Co.I
Scholes, Milton R. TN 11th Inf. Co.I
Scholes, N.H. TN 11th Inf. Co.I 1st Sgt.
Scholes, Reuben MO 16th Inf. Co.C
Scholl, C. VA Cav. 35th Bn. Co.B
Scholl, Charles MD 1st Inf. Co.G
Scholl, Cyrus R. MO 10th Cav. Co.E 1st Sgt.
Scholl, Emile VA Lt.Arty. Brander's Co.
Scholl, Francis V. NC 46th Inf. Co.D
Scholl, Fredrick GA 40th Inf. Co.B
Scholl, George C. MO Cav. Wood's Regt. Co.B
1st Lt.
Scholl, Jacob AL 1st Bn. Hilliard's Legion Vol.
Co.A
Scholl, Jacob AL 60th Inf. Co.F
Scholl, Jessey MO Cav. Williams' Regt. Co.B
Scholl, John GA 1st (Symons') Res. Co.B
Scholl, John H. MD 1st Cav. Co.A 1st Sgt.
Scholl, John H. VA Cav. 35th Bn. Co.B
Scholl, John H. VA 1st Cav. 2nd Co.K
Scholl, Joseph LA 5th Inf. Co.H
Scholl, L. TX Cav. Baird's Regt. Co.C
Scholl, William M. MO 6th Cav. Co.K
Scholl, W.M. MO Cav. Williams' Regt. Co.B
Capt.
Schollasch, D. LA Mil. 4th Regt.Eur.Brig. Co.D
Cpl.
Schollick, John SC 1st Arty. Co.H
Schollmann, William TX 17th Inf. Co.H
Scholly, Michel LA Mil. 2nd Regt. 2nd Brig. 1st
Div. Co.I
Scholten, A. LA Arty. Guyol's Co. (Orleans
Arty.)
Scholten, A. LA Lt.Arty. LeGardeur, Jr.'s Co.
(Orleans Guard Btty.)
Scholtz, William TX Inf. 4th Bn. (Oswald's)
Co.A
Scholz, Anton LA 20th Inf. Old Co.B, Co.A
Scholz, H. TX 1st Hvy.Arty. Band Music.
Scholz, H. TX Inf. 4th Bn. (Oswald's) Co.A
Drum.

Scholz, Th. TX Inf. 4th Bn. (Oswald's) Co.A
 Sgt.
Schomberger, Nicholis VA Lt.Arty. Clutter's Co.
Schommer, Peter GA 42nd Inf.
Schonaltz, A. TX 17th Inf. Co.H Cpl.
Schonberger, Lewis J. VA Inf. 25th Bn. Co.F
Schonborn, L. VA 2nd St.Res. Co.H
Schoneberger, Casper TX 5th Inf. Co.B
Schonekalb, William LA Mil. 1st Regt. 2nd Brig.
 1st Div. Co.D
Schonemann, Charles TX 7th Cav. Co.B
Schonfeld, B. AL St.Arty. Co.C
Schonfeld, D. VA 1st St.Res. Co.A
Schonfeld, F.W. LA Mil.Conf.Guards Regt.
 Co.B
Schonfield, David VA Lt.Arty. Parker's Co.
Schonhoff, August TX Arty. 4th Bn. Co.A
Schoniane, D. LA Mil. 4th Regt. French Brig.
 Co.6 Cpl.
Schonigal, Gustave LA 1st (Nelligan's) Inf. Co.F
 1st Sgt.
Schonker, William VA 12th Cav. Co.A
Schonlakes, G. VA 2nd St.Res. Co.H
Schonnekas, F. LA Mil. 1st Regt. 3rd Brig. 1st
 Div. Co.A
Schonover, John VA 48th Inf.
Schonthall, J. SC 7th Res. Co.L
Schoock, A. TX Inf. 1st St.Troops Shield's Co.B
Schoock, Josiah VA 2nd St.Res. Co.K
Schoof, Charles LA Mil. Mooney's Co. (Saddlers
 Guards)
Schoof, John H. VA 1st St.Res. Co.F
School, J. VA Cav. 41st Bn. Co.B
School, M. MO 6th Cav. Co.D
Schoolar, George MS 6th Cav. Co.I
Schoolar, Henry K. MS 14th Inf. Co.K
Schoolar, H.K. MS 14th (Cons.) Inf. Co.F
Schoolar, James F. MS Inf. 2nd Bn. Co.C
Schoolar, James F. MS 48th Inf. Co.C
Schoolar, John W.H. MS 1st (Patton's) Inf. Co.C
Schoolar, Landon J. MS 14th Inf. Co.K
Schoolar, L.J. MS 14th (Cons.) Inf. Co.F
Schoolar, T.A. MS 10th Inf. Co.N, New Co.E
 Cpl.
Schoolar, W.A. AL Cp. of Instr. Talladega
Schoolar, Wm. A. AL Cp. of Instr. Talladega
Schoolcraft, E.P. VA 19th Cav. Co.G
Schoolcraft, George TX Cav. Baylor's Regt.
 Co.B
Schoolcraft, George VA 14th Cav. Co.M
Schoolcraft, George A. VA Cav. 36th Bn. Co.B
Schoolcraft, Henry MO 7th Cav. Co.A
Schoolcraft, Jacob VA 14th Cav. Co.M
Schoolcraft, Jacob VA Cav. 36th Bn. Co.B
Schoolcraft, James VA 14th Cav. Co.M
Schoolcraft, James VA 19th Cav. Co.G
Schoolcraft, James H. VA 19th Cav. Co.G
Schoolcraft, Peter J. VA 59th Inf. 2nd Co.B
Schooler, Benjamin H. TX 28th Cav. Co.A
 Black.
Schooler, C. MO 5th Cav. Co.B
Schooler, Charles W. VA 30th Inf. 1st Co.I
Schooler, Charles W. VA 47th Inf. 3rd Co.I Sgt.
Schooler, C.W. VA 9th Cav. Co.A
Schooler, Edward G. VA Lt.Arty. 12th Bn. Co.C
Schooler, Edward G. VA Goochland Lt.Arty.
Schooler, Edward G. VA Lt.Arty. Taylor's Co.

Schooler, G.B. MS 6th Cav. Co.C
Schooler, George W. AR Lt.Arty. Thrall's Btty.
Schooler, Henry T. LA 12th Inf. Co.A
Schooler, I.B. TN 1st Cav. Co.E
Schooler, J. TX Cav. Saufley's Scouting Bn.
 Co.C
Schooler, Jacob Conf.Lt.Arty. 1st Reg.Btty.
Schooler, Jacob Inf. School of Pract. Powell's
 Detach. Co.B
Schooler, James TN 2nd (Walker's) Inf. Co.D
 1st Lt.
Schooler, James B. NC Inf. Thomas Legion
 Co.K
Schooler, James B. Gen. & Staff Asst.Comsy.
Schooler, J.K. MS 35th Inf. Co.D
Schooler, John KY 7th Cav. Co.A
Schooler, John KY 11th Cav. Co.A
Schooler, John VA 9th Cav. Co.B
Schooler, John C. TX 27th Cav. Co.C
Schooler, John H. VA 24th Cav. Co.G,H
Schooler, John H. VA Lt.Arty. R.M. Anderson's
 Co.
Schooler, John H. VA 30th Inf. Co.C Cpl.
Schooler, John W.H. MS 35th Inf. Co.H
Schooler, J.W. TX 10th Cav. Co.C
Schooler, Nathan H. MO 3rd Inf. Co.C
Schooler, Peter D. VA 9th Cav. Co.A
Schooler, Richard VA Lt.Arty. Taylor's Co.
Schooler, R.L. TN 63rd Inf. Co.B
Schooler, Samuel TX 5th Inf. Co.K
Schooler, Samuel Gen. & Staff, Arty. Capt.
Schooler, Samuel J. LA 12th Inf. Co.A
Schooler, Thomas L. VA 30th Inf. Co.D
Schooler, William VA 47th Inf. 3rd Co.I
Schooler, William B. LA 12th Inf. Co.A
Schooler, William T. TX 7th Inf. Co.K Cpl.
Schooler, William T. TX 14th Inf. Co.B
Schooles, Albert VA 8th Inf. Co.F
Schooles, Samuel S. VA 8th Inf. Co.F
Schooley, D.F. SC 6th Res. Co.E
Schooley, George S. VA 6th Cav. Co.K
Schooley, J.T. TX 2nd Inf. Co.H
Schoolfield, Benjamin AR 20th Inf. Co.A Cpl.
Schoolfield, C.C. AR 2nd Mtd.Rifles Co.H
Schoolfield, David A. AR 20th Inf. Co.A
 Sgt.Maj.
Schoolfield, D.G. NC 7th Sr.Res. Co.C
Schoolfield, E.D. TX 3rd Inf. 2nd Co.C
Schoolfield, E.D. TX Conscr.
Schoolfield, Isaac C. VA 12th Inf. Co.E
Schoolfield, J.B. KY 2nd Bn.Mtd.Rifles Co.C
Schoolfield, J.J. KY Cav. Jenkins' Co. 1st Lt.
Schoolfield, J.J. KY Williams' Btty. 1st Lt.
Schoolfield, J.L. AR 1st (Monroe's) Cav. Co.D
Schoolfield, John J. KY 1st Bn.Mtd.Rifles Co.E
Schoolfield, John S. MO 10th Inf. Co.G
Schoolfield, J.P. AR 1st Mtd.Rifles Co.D
Schoolfield, J.P. AR 2nd Mtd.Rifles Co.H
Schoolfield, J.R. NC 3rd Jr.Res. Co.A
Schoolfield, J.R. NC 4th Bn.Jr.Res. Co.A
Schoolfield, L.H. MD 2nd Lt.Arty.
Schoolfield, O.P. TN 4th (Murray's) Cav. Co.K
 Capt.
Schoolfield, O.P. TN Inf. 22nd Bn. Co.F Capt.
Schoolfield, O.P. Johnston's Army Capt.
Schoolfield, P.A. TN 4th (Murray's) Cav. Co.K
 Cpl.

Schoolfield, P.A. TN Inf. 22nd Bn. Co.F Cpl.
Schoolfield, W.D. TX 35th (Brown's) Cav. Co.H
Schoolfield, W.D. TX 1st Inf. AQM
Schoolfield, W.D. TX 20th Inf. Co.H
Schoolfield, W.D. VA Cav. 41st Bn. Co.C Sgt.
Schoolfield, W.D. Gen. & Staff, QM Dept. Capt.
Schoolfield, William D. KY Cav. Jenkins' Co.
Schoolfield, William W.D. KY 4th Cav. Co.D,B
Schoolfield, W.J. TX 35th (Brown's) Cav. Co.H
Schoolhoffer, Philip AL 8th Inf. Co.K
Schooling, James W. KY 6th Cav. Co.A
 Sgt.Maj.
Schooling, John KY 6th Cav. Co.A Sgt.
Schooling, J.R. KY 6th Cav. Co.F 2nd Lt.
Schooling, Robert P. MO Inf. Perkins' Bn. Co.F
Schools, Albert VA Lt.Arty. Thornton's Co.
Schools, Albert VA 55th Inf. Co.D
Schools, Alexander C. VA 40th Inf. Co.E
Schools, Charles Henry VA 55th Inf. Co.D
Schools, Dawson VA 55th Inf. Co.K
Schools, G. GA 21st Inf. Co.B
Schools, George VA Inf. 5th Bn. Co.D Sgt.
Schools, George VA 12th Inf. Co.K
Schools, James LA 2nd Inf. Co.K
Schools, James A. VA 49th Inf. Co.C
Schools, John W. VA 9th Mil. Co.A
Schools, John W. VA 45th Inf. Co.K
Schools, John W. VA 55th Inf. Co.K
Schools, Joseph VA 55th Inf. Co.D
Schools, Lawrence VA 55th Inf. Co.D
Schools, Leonard VA 55th Inf. Co.A
Schools, Leonard VA 55th Inf. Co.D
Schools, Major F. VA 26th Inf. Co.I Cpl.
Schools, Nathan W. VA 24th Cav. Co.F
Schools, Nathan W. VA Cav. 40th Bn. Co.F
Schools, N.H. VA 23rd Cav. Co.B
Schools, R. VA 55th Inf. Co.D
Schools, Robert B. VA 26th Inf. Co.I
Schools, Samuel S. VA 9th Mil. Co.A
Schools, Tazwell VA Lt.Arty. Thornton's Co.
Schools, Temple VA 9th Mil. Co.A
Schools, Temple A. VA 26th Inf. Co.I
Schools, Thomas VA 26th Inf. Co.I
Schools, Waller G. VA 9th Mil. Co.A
Schools, Waller G. VA 26th Inf. Co.I
Schools, Wiley VA 47th Inf. Co.D
Schools, Wm. A. VA Mtd.Res. Rappahannock
 Dist. Sale's Co.
Schooly, D.F. SC 5th St.Troops Co.K
Schooly, D.W. SC 3rd Bn.Res. Co.C
Schoonmaker, T. GA 32nd Inf. Co.D
Schoonmaker, T.W. GA 46th Inf. Co.C Cpl.
Schoonmaker, William AR 7th Inf. Co.F 1st Sgt.
Schoonover, Benjamin VA 17th Cav. Co.I
Schoonover, Eli TX 4th Cav. Co.E
Schoonover, Francis M. TX Part.Rangers
 Thomas' Co.
Schoonover, J. Gen. & Staff Capt.,AQM
Schoonover, Jacob AR 38th Inf. Co.E AQM
Schoonover, Joseph VA 42nd Inf. Co.E
Schoonover, Paul VA 28th Inf. Co.I
Schoonover, William VA 6th Bn.Res. Co.H
Schoonover, William VA 28th Inf. Co.I
Schoonover, William VA 157th Mil. Co.A
Schoonover, William VA Mil. Scott Cty.
Schoope, James AL 56th Part.Rangers Co.K
Schopp, Christ LA Mil. Fire Bn. Co.D

Schopper, Henry LA Mil. 4th Regt. 1st Brig. 1st Div. Co.H 2nd Cpl.

Schoppert, John H. MD Cav. 2nd Bn. Co.D

Schoppert, Patrick C. AL 20th Inf. Co.E 2nd Lt.

Schoppert, Robert P. AL 11th Inf. Co.B Bvt.2nd Lt.

Schoppmann, Edward TX 1st Hvy.Arty. Co.C Adj.

Schorer, Jean LA 20th Inf. Co.D

Schorlett, M. AR 10th (Witt's) Cav. Co.A

Schorling, John LA Mil. 3rd Regt. 3rd Brig. 1st Div. Co.H

Schorn, C.A. NC 2nd Jr.Res. Co.E Sgt.

Schorne, E. TX 3rd Cav. Co.B

Schorr, G.F. LA Inf. Jeff Davis Regt. Co.F 2nd Lt.

Schorr, Thomas LA Lewis Regt. Co.B 2nd Lt.

Schorrie, Edward TX 1st (McCulloch's) Cav. Co.E

Schorrs, H. LA Mil. Fire Bn. Co.B

Schot, John LA Mil. 3rd Regt. 1st Brig. 1st Div. Co.E Sgt.

Schote, Edward AR 21st Inf. Co.E

Schott, Adam TN Inf. 3rd Bn. Co.F

Schott, Charles TX 2nd Inf. Co.B

Schott, Edmund LA 20th Inf. Old Co.B, Co.A

Schott, George AL Conscr.

Schott, Henry LA 1st (Strawbridge's) Inf. Co.I

Schott, Jacob AL Lt.Arty. Tarrant's Btty.

Schott, Jacob AL Cp. of Instr. Talladega

Schott, John LA Mil. Chalmette Regt. Co.K

Schott, John TX 8th Field Btty. Bugler

Schott, Nathaniel VA Lt.Arty. Douthat's Co.

Schott, Sebastian TX 6th Inf. Co.H

Schott, Stephen GA Cav. 29th Bn. Co.D

Schott, T. LA Mil. 4th Regt. French Brig. Co.1

Schott, V. TX 3rd Inf. 2nd Co.A

Schott, Valentine TX Inf. Griffin's Bn. Co.F

Schott, William AR 17th (Lemoyne's) Inf. Co.G

Schott, William TX Inf. 4th Bn. (Oswald's) Co.A

Schott, William TX 13th Vol. 2nd Co.C

Schottmiller, Fred TN 10th Inf. Co.D

Schottz, Richard MO 2nd N.E. Cav. (Franklin's Regt.) Co.B

Schoughenky, William Conf.Reg.Inf. Brooks' Bn. Co.F

Schouler, Michel LA Mil. 6th Regt.Eur.Brig. (Italian Guards Bn.) Co.5

Schouler, William LA 1st Hvy.Arty. (Reg.) Co.C

Schoulta, Ferd TX Cav. Waller's Regt. Co.A

Schoumaste, D. LA Mil. 3rd Regt. 2nd Brig. 1st Div. Co.K

Schouse, Edmond F. NC 22nd Inf. Co.M

Schoutz, Cornelius AL 59th Inf. Co.I

Schowalter, Joseph C.M. LA 1st (Nelligan's) Inf. Co.K

Schower, Nicola LA Mil. 4th Regt. 3rd Brig. 1st Div. Co.C

Schracker, L. LA Mil. 3rd Regt. 3rd Brig. 1st Div. Co.B

Schraded, A. LA Mil. 3rd Regt. 1st Brig. 1st Div. Co.C

Schrader, Ammi VA 25th Inf. 2nd Co.K

Schrader, A.T. TX 12th Field Btty.

Schrader, David VA 25th Inf. 2nd Co.K

Schrader, Ernest LA 11th Inf. Co.D

Schrader, Gustav TX 1st Hvy.Arty. Co.C

Schrader, H. VA Lt.Arty. Barr's Co.

Schrader, Henry TN Inf. 3rd Bn. Co.G Cpl.

Schrader, James C. MS 1st Lt.Arty. Co.I

Schrader, J.H. NC 3rd Inf. Co.I

Schrader, John AR 34th Inf. Co.E Sgt.

Schrader, John TX Lt.Arty. Hughes' Co.

Schrader, John TX Inf. Griffin's Bn. Co.F

Schrader, John C. AR Cav. 1st Bn. (Stirman's) Co.C

Schrader, John V. SC 19th Inf. Co.G

Schrader, J.T. MO 1st & 3rd Cons.Cav. Co.H

Schrader, Samuel E. VA 25th Inf. 2nd Co.K Cpl.

Schrader, Theodore MO Lt.Arty. Barret's Co.

Schrader, William LA Mil. 3rd Regt. 1st Brig. 1st Div. Co.I

Schrader, William TX 8th Inf. Co.A

Schraeder, Gustavus TX 4th Cav. Co.C

Schraeder, H.E. TX 6th Inf. Co.B Sgt.

Schraeder, William LA 28th (Thomas') Inf. Co.C

Schram, Louis F. GA 8th Cav. Co.K

Schram, Louis F. LA C.S. Zouave Bn. Co.B,D Cpl.

Schrame, J.H. KY 9th Cav. Co.G Cpl.

Schramer, John LA Arty. Landry's Co. (Donaldsonville Arty.)

Schramm, Edgar TX 36th Cav. Co.F Capt.

Schramm, Edgar E. TX 1st (McCulloch's) Cav. Co.B

Schramm, George F. TX 36th Cav. Co.D Cpl.

Schramm, Phillip GA Arty. 9th Bn. Co.A

Schramme, John H. KY 4th Cav. Co.G

Schrarcker, E. LA Mil. 3rd Regt. 3rd Brig. 1st Div. Co.B

Schrat, George LA Mil. Mech.Guard

Schrater, John TX 1st Hvy.Arty. Co.K

Schraub, Philip TX 1st Field Btty.

Schraut, Adam LA Mil. Mech.Guard

Schreader, H.E. TX St.Troops Hampton's Co.

Schreaves, George VA 32nd Inf. 1st Co.I

Schreck, Charles L. GA 63rd Inf. Co.B Cpl.

Schreck, C.L. GA 1st (Olmstead's) Inf. Gordon's Co.

Schreck, John Y. GA 63rd Inf. Co.F

Schreckhise, Daniel K. VA 52nd Inf. Co.G Sgt.

Schreefle, Gaspard LA 8th Inf. Co.B

Schref, James K. KY 7th Mtd.Inf. Co.H

Schreher, F. LA Mil. 4th Regt. 1st Brig. 1st Div. Co.H

Schreher, J. LA Mil. 4th Regt. 1st Brig. 1st Div. Co.H

Schreib, June TX 17th Inf. Co.H

Schreibble, Charles TX Waul's Legion Co.A

Schreiber, A. Gen. & Staff, Arty. & Ord. 1st Lt.

Schreiber, A. LA Mil. 1st Regt. French Brig. Co.3

Schreiber, A. LA Mil. Orleans Guards Regt. QM

Schreiber, Charles TX 1st Hvy.Arty. Co.G

Schreiber, Frederick GA 1st (Olmstead's) Inf. 1st Co.A

Schreiber, Frederick GA 1st Bn.S.S. Co.B

Schreiber, H. LA Mil. 3rd Regt.Eur.Brig. (Garde Francaise) Co.3

Schreiber, H. LA Mil. Chalmette Regt. Co.A

Schreiber, H. TX 1st Hvy.Arty. Co.G

Schreiber, John TX 26th Cav. Co.F

Schreiber, John Sig.Corps,CSA

Schreiber, John H. LA 6th Inf. Co.H

Schreiber, Julius LA 20th Inf. Co.B Music.

Schreiber, L. TX Inf. 4th Bn. (Oswald's) Co.B

Schreiber, L. TX Waul's Legion Co.F

Schreiber, Phillip LA Mil.Cont.Regt. Roder's Co.

Schreiber, Victor LA 18th Inf. Co.I

Schreiber, William LA Mil. Fire Bn. Co.C

Schreider, Charles LA 10th Inf. Co.K

Schreiner, A. LA Mil. 3rd Regt.Eur.Brig. (Garde Francaise) Co.3

Schreiner, C. AL St.Arty. Co.C

Schreiner, Charles TX 3rd Inf. Co.H Cpl.

Schreiner, Frederick TX 3rd Inf. Co.H 2nd Lt.

Schreiner, H., Sr. AL 1st Regt. Mobile Vol. Co.E

Schreiner, H. LA Mil. 3rd Regt. French Brig. Co.7

Schreiter, C. TX Waul's Legion Co.A

Schrekler, J.M. TX Cav. Border's Regt. Co.A

Schremper, Thomas GA 59th Inf. Co.C

Schrempf, A.N. TX 12th Inf. Co.A Music.

Schrempp, Joseph LA 1st Chasseurs a pied Co.3

Schremppe, E. LA 30th Inf. Co.A

Schrenk, E. LA Mil. 4th Regt.Eur.Brig. Co.A

Schrenk, J. LA Mil. 4th Regt.Eur.Brig. Co.A

Schrepple, John LA Mil. 3rd Regt. 3rd Brig. 1st Div. Co.E

Schrette, Henry LA 1st (Strawbridge's) Inf. Co.B

Schrewcraft, H. TN 9th (Ward's) Cav. Co.A

Schriber, Charles Inf. School of Pract. Powell's Detach. Co.A Cpl.

Schriber, Fredrick AL 1st Regt. Mobile Vol. Co.E

Schriber, L. TX Inf. Timmons' Regt. Co.D

Schrick, Charles LA 6th Inf. Co.D

Schrider, Jacob LA 14th Inf. Co.A Cpl.

Schrieber, Fritz AL 7th Cav. Co.F Bugler

Schrieber, Gaspard J. LA Mil. Beauregard Bn. Frobus' Co.

Schrieber, Lewis AL 1st Bn.Cadets Co.A Drum.

Schrieder, Ernest LA 14th (Austin's) Bn.S.S. Co.B

Schrieder, J.A. LA 22nd Inf. Co.F

Schrieider, George LA Mil.Cont.Regt. Roder's Co.

Schriek, Charles VA Inf. 25th Bn. Co.G

Schriener, F. AL 1st Regt. Mobile Vol. Baas' Co.

Schrier, John TX 36th Cav. Co.E

Schrier, M.B.L. TX 8th Cav. Co.E

Schrier, Wiley R. TX 36th Cav. Co.E

Schrier, William LA 13th Inf. Co.G

Schriever, H. SC Mil.Arty. 1st Regt. Werner's Co.

Schriever, H. SC Lt.Arty. Wagener's Co. (Co.A,German Arty.)

Schriever, Henry NC 2nd Arty. (36th St.Troops) Co.A

Schriever, Henry NC 18th Inf. Co.A

Schrieves, Cyrus VA 62nd Mtd.Inf. 2nd Co.I

Schrimer, C. AL 21st Inf.

Schrimp, F. LA Mil. 4th Regt. 2nd Brig. 1st Div. Co.C

Schrimp, Joseph LA Mil. 4th Regt. 2nd Brig. 1st Div. Co.C

Schrimpf, J.E. TX Inf. 1st St.Troops Lawrence's Co.D Sgt.

Schrimpsher, J.D. Mead's Conf.Cav. Co.E

Schrimpsher, Joshua TX 12th Inf. Co.A

Schrimpshew, A.J. Mead's Conf.Cav. Co.E

Schrimpshier, W.G. GA 46th Inf. Co.K

Schrimpshire, Jas. B. MS Inf. 7th Bn. Co.E

Schrimpshire, James V. GA 12th Inf. Co.H

Schrimpshun, W.G. GA Inf. 19th Bn. (St.Guards) Co.D

Schrimscher, Robert R. TX Waul's Legion Co.E

Schrimsher, G.R. AR 18th Inf. Co.C

Schrimsher, Henderson AL 50th Inf. Co.C

Schrimsher, J. TX Cav. Benavides' Regt. Co.F

Schrimsher, Jacob D. AL Lt.Arty. Ward's Btty.

Schrimsher, James E. AL Lt.Arty. Ward's Btty.

Schrimsher, John 2nd Cherokee Mtd.Vol. Co.G

Schrimsher, Robert J. TN 37th Inf. Co.E Sgt.

Schrimsher, R.R. TX 26th Cav. 1st Co.G

Schrimsher, R.R. TX 9th (Nichols') Inf. Atchison's Co.

Schrimsher, Thomas J. TN 37th Inf. Co.E Cpl.

Schrimsher, T.M. AL 35th Inf. Co.F 2nd Lt.

Schrimsher, Wesley TX 4th Cav. Co.F

Schrimsher, William F. AL 4th Inf. Co.F

Schrimshier, S.G. TX 30th Cav. Co.B Cpl.

Schriner, C. AL Mil. 3rd Vol. Co.C

Schriner, Francis AL Mil. 3rd Vol. Co.E

Schriner, Henry AL 1st Regt. Mobile Vol. Co.E

Schriner, Nicholas TN Lt.Arty. Scott's Co. Artif.

Schriner, Nicholas LA Mil. Bragg's Bn. Schwartz's Co.

Schrink, Johnathan NC 5th Sr.Res. Co.E

Schrinscher, John 1st Cherokee Mtd.Vol. 2nd Co.G QMSgt.

Schrioch, W.A. KY 2nd Cav. Co.K

Schrivener, William J. TX 13th Vol. Co.M

Schriver, Andrew TN 4th Inf. Co.F

Schriver, David LA 1st (Strawbridge's) Inf. Co.E

Schriver, David 7th Conf.Cav. Co.F

Schriver, Henry J. VA 7th Cav. Co.F

Schriver, Isaac VA 1st St.Res. Co.D 2nd Lt.

Schriver, John H. VA 7th Cav. Co.F

Schriver, Moses VA 1st St.Res. Co.D

Schroader, James W. KY 2nd Mtd.Inf. Co.E 2nd Lt.

Schrock, J.H.H. TX Conscr.

Schrock, J.M. MS 6th Inf. Co.C

Schrock, Joel A. SC 15th Inf. Co.D 1st Lt.

Schrock, Jonas MS 15th Inf. Co.C

Schrock, Thomas D. MS 24th Inf. Co.E Sgt.

Schrock, W.D.T. TX 13th Vol. 1st Co.B

Schroder, B. LA Ogden's Cav. Co.I

Schroder, B.F. LA 20th Inf. Co.F

Schroder, C. SC 25th Inf. Co.E

Schroder, E.F. SC Mil.Arty. 1st Regt. Werner's Co.

Schroder, F. SC 1st St.Troops Co.E

Schroder, Frank LA Mil. 1st Regt. 3rd Brig. 1st Div. Co.H

Schroder, F.W. SC 3rd Cav. Co.G

Schroder, H. SC Mil.Arty. 1st Regt. Werner's Co.

Schroder, H. SC Mil.Arty. 1st Regt. Harms' Co. 1st Cpl.

Schroder, H. SC Arty. Melchers' Co. (Co.B,German Arty.) Sgt.

Schroder, H. SC Lt.Arty. Wagener's Co. (Co.A, German Arty.)

Schroder, H. SC Inf. 1st (Charleston) Bn. Co.F

Schroder, H. SC 27th Inf. Co.C

Schroder, H. TX 7th Cav. Co.B Cpl.

Schroder, H.B. SC 3rd Cav. Co.G

Schroder, H.B. SC 1st Regt. Charleston Guard Co.G

Schroder, H.C. SC 3rd Cav. Co.G Sgt.

Schroder, Henry LA Mil. 3rd Regt. 3rd Brig. 1st Div. Co.H

Schroder, Henry TX Lt.Arty. Jones' Co.

Schroder, Isidore LA 8th Inf. Co.B

Schroder, J. GA 5th Cav. Co.C

Schroder, J. LA Ogden's Cav. Co.I

Schroder, J. SC 25th Inf. Co.E

Schroder, J.C.L. SC Mil.Arty. 1st Regt. Werner's Co.

Schroder, J.C.L. SC Lt.Arty. Wagener's Co. (Co.A,German Arty.) Cpl.

Schroder, J.F. SC 1st Regt. Charleston Guard Co.G

Schroder, John GA Cav. 2nd Bn. Co.E

Schroder, John SC 1st Regt. Charleston Guard Co.G

Schroder, John SC Sea Fencibles Symons' Co. Sgt.

Schroder, M. MS 37th Inf. Co.B

Schroder, Martin GA Cav. 2nd Bn. Co.F

Schroder, Martin GA 5th Cav. Co.B

Schroder, Nicholas H. SC Arty. Bachman's Co. (German Lt.Arty.)

Schroder, Nicolaus H. SC Arty.Bn. Hampton Legion Co.B

Schroder, R. LA Mil.Conf.Guards Regt. Co.K

Schroder, W. SC Mil.Arty. 1st Regt. Harms' Co.

Schroder, W. SC Arty. Melchers' Co. (Co.B,German Arty.)

Schrodts, John H. TN Arty. Akers' Btty. (Montgomery Hvy.Arty.) Asst.Eng.

Schroeder, A. LA Mil. Chalmette Regt. Co.E

Schroeder, A.E. LA Mil. 4th Regt. 1st Brig. 1st Div. Co.D

Schroeder, Antoine TX 5th Cav. Co.I

Schroeder, Aug LA Mil. 4th Regt.Eur.Brig. Co.D

Schroeder, C.F.H. LA 3rd Inf. Co.G

Schroeder, Charles TX 5th Cav. Co.A

Schroeder, Charles Conf.Inf. Tucker's Regt. Co.H

Schroeder, F. LA Millaudon's Co. (Jefferson Mtd.Guards,Co.B)

Schroeder, F. TX 4th Inf. (St.Troops) Co.F

Schroeder, F. TX 6th Inf. Co.I

Schroeder, Ferdinand TX Waul's Legion Co.D

Schroeder, Frederick LA Inf. 1st Sp.Bn. (Rightor's) Co.E

Schroeder, Frederick LA 22nd Inf. Durrive, Jr.'s Co.

Schroeder, Frederick TX 16th Inf. Co.D

Schroeder, Frederick, I TX 4th Field Btty.

Schroeder, Frederick, II TX 4th Field Btty.

Schroeder, Frederick, III TX 4th Field Btty.

Schroeder, G. AL Corps Cadets Ord.Sgt.

Schroeder, G. TX 6th Inf. Co.I

Schroeder, G.H. Gen. & Staff A.Ord.Off.

Schroeder, H. AL 1st Regt. Mobile Vol. Co.A

Schroeder, H. TX 1st Hvy.Arty. Band Music.

Schroeder, Henry LA Arty. Moody's Co. (Madison Lt.Arty.)

Schroeder, Henry LA Mil. 1st Regt. 3rd Brig. 1st Div. Co.F

Schroeder, Henry LA 25th Inf. Co.H

Schroeder, Henry TX 4th Field Btty.

Schroeder, Henry TX Inf. Riflemen Arnold's Co.

Schroeder, Henry B. VA 39th Inf. Co.B

Schroeder, J. LA Mil. Orleans Fire Regt. Co.A

Schroeder, Jacob LA Mil.Cont.Regt. Lang's Co.

Schroeder, John AL 40th Inf. Co.H

Schroeder, John LA Mil. Orleans Fire Regt. Co.F

Schroeder, John TX Waul's Legion Co.B

Schroeder, Louis TX 8th Field Btty.

Schroeder, N. LA Mil.Cont.Regt. Roder's Co.

Schroeder, Otto TX 4th Cav. Co.G Sgt.

Schroeder, P. LA Mil. Chalmette Regt. Co.D

Schroeder, R.B. LA Mil.Cont.Regt. Roder's Co.

Schroeder, T. TX 5th Field Btty.

Schroeder, T. TX Lt.Arty. Dege's Bn.

Schroeder, W.H. SC 11th Inf. Co.C

Schroeder, William LA Mil. 3rd Regt. 3rd Brig. 1st Div. Co.C

Schroeder, William LA Mil.Cont.Regt. Lang's Co.

Schroeder, William TX Waul's Legion Co.B

Schroeder, William Conf.Lt.Arty. 1st Reg.Btty.

Schroeder, William H. MS 10th Inf. Old Co.C, New Co.F

Schroepfer, J. TN Hvy.Arty. Sterling's Co.

Schroeter, Henry LA 4th Inf. Co.A

Schroff, Joseph LA Mil. 4th Regt.Eur.Brig. Co.D

Schroffel, John MS 19th Inf. Co.C

Schrogham, J.F. VA 7th Bn.Res. Co.D

Schrois, Theodore LA 1st Hvy.Arty. (Reg.) Co.G

Schroot, Clemens TX 4th Field Btty.

Schrotre, Charles SC Arty.Bn. Hampton Legion Co.A

Schrotter, William V. LA 1st (Nelligan's) Inf. Co.F

Schrotz, Joseph NC Lt.Arty. 13th Bn. Co.D Music.

Schroud, Phillip LA Miles' Legion Co.B

Schroyer, W.J. TN 12th (Green's) Cav. Co.I

Schruber, John LA 21st (Patton's) Inf. Co.H

Schrueske, W.W. TX Cav. Baird's Regt. Co.F

Schrugam, Dudley KY 2nd Mtd.Inf. Co.I Drum.

Schrum, Daniel MO Cav. Preston's Bn. Co.C

Schrum, David MO Cav. Preston's Bn. Co.C

Schrum, Nicholas J. TN Cav. 7th Bn. (Bennett's) Co.B

Schrum, William M. TN Cav. 7th Bn. (Bennett's) Co.B

Schubach, E. TX Cav. Baird's Regt. Co.G

Schubart, A. TN Arty.Corps Co.3 3rd Lt.

Schuber, F. LA Mil. Lafayette Arty.

Schuber, Frank LA Inf.Cons.Crescent Regt. Co.G Music.

Schuber, Jacob MS 21st Inf. Co.D

Schuber, Joseph MS 21st Inf. Co.D

Schuber, Joseph TX 14th Field Btty.

Schubert, August TX 5th Cav. Co.A
Schubert, August TX 5th Field Btty.
Schubert, E. TX 5th Field Btty.
Schubert, Edward LA C.S. Zouave Bn. Co.F
Schubert, F. TX 6th Inf. Co.B Bugler
Schubert, John TX 6th Inf. Co.D
Schubert, Louis LA 5th Inf. Co.C
Schubert, R. LA Mil.Cont.Regt. Roder's Co.
Schubert, W. TX 17th Inf. Co.H
Schubert, William TX 17th Inf. Co.H Cpl.
Schubert, William R. TX Cav. 3rd Regt.
    St.Troops Co.B
Schubort, E. TX Lt.Arty. Dege's Bn.
Schuceweiss, J.E. TX 26th Cav.
Schuch, Peter TX 1st (Yager's) Cav. Co.E
Schuch, Peter TX Cav. 8th (Taylor's) Bn. Co.C
    Black.
Schuchardt, C.F. TX 33rd Cav. Co.E Sgt.
Schuchert, L. SC Mil.Arty. 1st Regt. Werner's
    Co.
Schuchert, L. SC Lt.Arty. Wagener's Co.
    (Co.A,German Arty.)
Schuchert, Ludwig TX 6th Inf. Co.B
Schuckard, J.S. TX 20th Inf. Co.I
Schuckman, L. SC 1st Regt. Charleston Guard
    Co.G
Schuckman, L. SC Mil. 1st Regt. (Charleston
    Res.) Co.F Lt.
Schuckman, P. Sig.Corps,CSA
Schuckman, Ph. SC 3rd Cav. Co.G
Schue, M. LA Mil. 1st Regt. French Brig. Co.5
Schuech, L. TX 3rd Inf. 2nd Co.A, Co.B Cpl.
Schueler, August TX Cav. 8th (Taylor's) Bn.
    Co.C
Schueler, M. LA Mil. Chalmette Regt. Co.D
    Cpl.
Schueller, August TX 1st (Yager's) Cav. Co.E
Schuerer, E. TX Inf. Timmons' Regt. Co.K 1st
    Lt.
Schuessler, H.S. AL Cav. (St.Res.) Young's Co.
Schuessler, L.S. AL St.Troops
Schuette, Henry LA 20th Inf. Co.C
Schuffield, A. AL 23rd Inf. Co.C
Schuffield, J. AL 23rd Inf. Co.C
Schuffield, M. AL 23rd Inf. Co.C
Schuffle, William MO Cav. Jackman's Regt.
    Co.C
Schuffleberger, Gotlieb LA 13th Inf. Co.F
Schuga, Luis TX Cav. Baird's Regt. Co.H
Schuh, J.F. AL Mil. 4th Vol. Co.G
Schuh, Joseph LA Mil. 2nd Regt. 2nd Brig. 1st
    Div.
Schuhl, Jacob TX 7th Cav. Co.B
Schuhle, Jacob P. TX 6th Cav. Co.K
Schuhle, Peter KY 7th Cav. Co.B
Schuhlmeier, Lubolt TX Conscr.
Schuhmacher, J. TX Inf. 4th Bn. (Oswald's)
    Co.A
Schul, J. LA Mil.Conf.Guards Regt. Band
Schulae, J.B. NC 37th Inf. Co.D Sgt.
Schule, Peter KY 3rd Cav. Co.B
Schule, William LA Mil. 3rd Regt. 1st Brig. 1st
    Div. Co.A Sgt.
Schulein, Joseph AL 10th Inf. Co.E
Schulenkamp, Charles LA Mil. 3rd Regt. 1st
    Brig. 1st Div. Co.K

Schuler, Charles LA Mil. Chalmette Regt. Co.C
    1st Lt.
Schuler, F.F. LA 1st Cav. Co.G
Schuler, G. TN Inf. 3rd Bn. Co.G
Schuler, Henry LA 30th Inf. Co.E
Schuler, J.A. LA 3rd (Wingfield's) Cav. Co.B
Schuler, Jacob AR 1st (Colquitt's) Inf. Co.A 2nd
    Lt.
Schuler, Jacob LA 4th Inf. Co.B
Schuler, J.C. SC Mil. 16th Regt. Sigwald's Co.
Schuler, John TX 4th Inf. Co.B
Schuler, T. LA Mil. 1st Chasseurs a pied Co.7
Schulf, Archibald KY 3rd Mtd.Inf.
Schulken, Charles NC Hvy.Arty. 1st Bn. Co.A
Schulken, Engelhard NC 18th Inf. Co.A 2nd Lt.
Schulkey, Henry NC 8th Sr.Res. Jacob's Co.
Schull, Daniel VA Inf. 4th Bn.Loc.Def. Co.D
Schullein, Leopold GA 5th Inf. Co.I
Schuller, Charles J. TX 2nd Inf. Co.D
Schuller, Fred LA Inf.Crescent Regt. Co.I
Schuller, Jacob TX 2nd Inf. Co.F
Schuller, John TX 16th Inf. Co.F
Schuls, Frank TX Cav. Ragsdale's Bn. 1st Co.A
Schulsung, Albert LA 4th Inf. Co.B
Schulte, F. VA 1st St.Res. Co.B
Schulte, H. LA 21st (Patton's) Inf. Co.H
Schulte, J.H. SC 25th Inf. Co.B
Schulte, Joseph LA 20th Inf. Co.F
Schulteiss, E. SC 27th Inf. Co.C
Schulter, Frederic Conf.Lt.Arty. 1st Reg.Btty.
Schulter, Henry LA Mil. 2nd Regt. 2nd Brig. 1st
    Div. Co.I
Schulter, John SC Hvy.Arty. 15th (Lucas') Bn.
    Co.C
Schulter, John SC Arty. Childs' Co.
Schultheis, Peter LA 21st (Patton's) Inf. Co.I
Schultheiss, Em SC Inf. 1st (Charleston) Bn.
    Co.F
Schultheisse, Thomas E. AL 4th Inf. Co.A
Schults, J.H. AL 46th Inf. Co.C Cpl.
Schultz, A. TX 4th Inf. (St.Troops) Co.C
Schultz, A. TX 16th Inf. Music.
Schultz, A.A. AR Lt.Arty. Marshall's Btty.
Schultz, A.N. LA Mil. 3rd Regt. 3rd Brig. 1st
    Div. Co.B
Schultz, Aug TX 4th Cav. Co.G
Schultz, August AL 8th Inf. Co.G
Schultz, Benjamin F. MO 3rd Cav. Co.C Sgt.
Schultz, B.F. LA Inf.Cons.Crescent Regt. Co.I
Schultz, Brazillia AL 18th Inf. Co.H
Schultz, C.H. MS Inf. 1st Bn.St.Troops (30 days
    '64) Co.F
Schultz, Charles MS Inf. 2nd Bn. Co.E
Schultz, Charles 4th Conf.Eng.Troops Co.E
    Artif.
Schultz, D. AL Mil. T. Hunt's Co. 1st Cpl.
Schultz, D. AL 1st Regt. Mobile Vol. Baas' Co.
Schultz, D. AL 4th Res. Co.B
Schultz, Danl. E. AL Res. Belser's Co.
Schultz, Daniel E. AL Inf. 1st Regt. Co.B
Schultz, E. LA Mil. 4th Regt. French Brig. Co.2
Schultz, E.B. MO Inf. 1st Regt.St.Guard Co.E
    2nd Lt.
Schultz, Edward NC 22nd Inf. Co.I
Schultz, F. LA Mil. 3rd Regt. French Brig. Co.8
Schultz, Frank AL 23rd Bn.S.S. Co.G Sgt.
Schultz, Frank LA 1st (Strawbridge's) Inf. Co.H

Schultz, Fred TX 7th Cav. Co.B
Schultz, Frederick LA Inf. 1st Sp.Bn. (Wheat's)
    Old Co.D
Schultz, Fredrick GA Cav. 47th Regt. Co.C
Schultz, George LA 22nd Inf. Jones' Co.
Schultz, George TX 1st Hvy.Arty. Co.C
Schultz, Guerin LA Mil. Chalmette Regt. Co.C
Schultz, H. AL St.Arty. Co.D
Schultz, H. SC Mil.Arty. 1st Regt. Werner's Co.
Schultz, H. TX 7th Cav. Co.B
Schultz, Henry LA 6th Inf. Co.H
Schultz, Henry TX Cav. Waller's Regt. Co.E
Schultz, Henry TX 1st Inf. Co.L
Schultz, Henry TX 17th Inf. Co.H
Schultz, H.P. TX 1st Inf. Co.L Cpl.
Schultz, Hy LA Mil. Chalmette Regt. Co.A
Schultz, Isaiah AL 18th Inf. Co.H
Schultz, J. AL 60th Inf. Co.I
Schultz, J. LA Mil. 4th Regt. 1st Brig. 1st Div.
    Co.E
Schultz, Jacob LA Mil. Chalmette Regt. Co.C
Schultz, Jacob P. VA 22nd Inf. Co.F
Schultz, James TX Cav. Benavides' Regt. Co.H
Schultz, John AL 1st Regt. Mobile Vol. Co.E
Schultz, John LA Mil. 3rd Regt. 1st Brig. 1st
    Div. Co.A
Schultz, John LA 21st (Patton's) Inf. Co.A
Schultz, John LA 21st (Patton's) Inf. Co.H
Schultz, John VA 2nd Cav. Co.A,I
Schultz, John W. VA 5th Inf. Co.A
Schultz, Joseph LA 20th Inf. Old Co.B, Co.D,C
Schultz, Julius VA Inf. Lyneman's Co.
Schultz, L. LA 21st (Kennedy's) Inf. Co.B
Schultz, M. SC 1st Arty.
Schultz, Peter LA Mil. Chalmette Regt. Co.I
Schultz, T. LA Mil. 4th Regt. 1st Brig. 1st Div.
    Co.E
Schultz, T. VA 2nd St.Res. Co.M
Schultz, Theodore LA Inf.Crescent Regt. Co.H
Schultz, W. TX 33rd Cav. Co.E
Schultz, William TX 4th Inf. Co.F
Schultz, William TX 5th Inf. Co.F
Schultz, William VA Lt.Arty. J.S. Brown's Co.
Schultz, William A. AL 27th Inf. Co.G 1st Sgt.
Schultz, William C. SC Inf. 3rd Bn. Co.F
Schultze, C. LA Mil.Squad. Guides d'Orleans
Schultze, Charles AL Inf. 1st Regt. Co.I
Schultze, Charles TX 20th Inf. Co.A
Schultze, F. TX Waul's Legion Co.H
Schultze, F. Exch.Bn. 1st Co.C,CSA
Schultze, George SC 15th Inf. Co.A
Schultze, H. SC Lt.Arty. Wagener's Co. (Co.A,
    German Arty.)
Schultze, John VA Inf. 4th Bn.Loc.Def. Co.A
Schultze, John D. TN Inf. 3rd Bn. Co.F Cpl.
Schultze, W. TX 7th Cav. Co.B
Schulz, C. TX 17th Inf. Co.H
Schulz, Ernst LA 20th Inf. Co.A
Schulz, F.C. SC 1st Mtd.Mil. Anderson's Co.
    1st Lt.
Schulz, Frederick C. SC Lt.Arty. 3rd (Palmetto)
    Bn. Co.F Capt.
Schulz, G. TX 5th Inf. Martindale's Co.
Schulz, H. TX 17th Inf. Co.H
Schulz, H.E. TX 5th Inf. Martindale's Co.
Schulz, John LA 20th Inf. Co.C

Schulz, Joseph TX Waul's Legion Co.B 1st Cook
Schulz, Louis LA Mil. Chalmette Regt. Co.C
Schulz, Louis LA 20th Inf. Co.C
Schulz, Phlipp LA Mil. Mech.Guard
Schulz, W. TX 20th Inf. Co.I
Schulz, Will SC Arty. Bachman's Co. (German Lt.Arty.)
Schulz, William SC Arty.Bn. Hampton Legion Co.B
Schulz, William TX 4th Field Btty.
Schulz, William P. GA 1st (Olmstead's) Inf. 1st Co.A
Schulz, William P. GA 1st Bn.S.S. Co.B
Schulze, A. TX Waul's Legion Co.C
Schulze, Andreas F. Gen. & Staff A.Surg.
Schulze, August TX 36th Cav. Co.F Capt.
Schulze, Charles TX 17th Inf. Co.H Music.
Schulze, F. TX 3rd Inf. 2nd Co.A
Schulze, Frederick TX 36th Cav. Co.F 1st Lt.
Schulze, H. TX Inf. 4th Bn. (Oswald's) Co.A
Schulze, Henry TX Waul's Legion Co.D
Schulze, Herman TX 4th Field Btty.
Schulze, John TX Inf. Timmons' Regt. Co.K
Schulze, John TX Waul's Legion Co.C
Schultzt, --- TX 7th Cav. Co.B Hosp.Stew.
Schumacher, A. LA Arty. Watson Btty.
Schumacher, Alb H. SC Arty. Bachman's Co. (German Lt.Arty.)
Schumacher, Albrecht H. SC Arty.Bn. Hampton Legion Co.B
Schumacher, C. LA Mil. 3rd Regt.Eur.Brig. (Garde Francaise) Euler's Co. Ord.Sgt.
Schumacher, Ernst SC Arty. Bachman's Co. (German Lt.Arty.) Guidon
Schumacher, Ernst SC Arty.Bn. Hampton Legion Co.B
Schumacher, Frederick SC Arty.Bn. Hampton Legion Co.B
Schumacher, Gottlieb TX 1st (Yager's) Cav. Co.E Music.
Schumacher, Gottlieb TX Cav. 8th (Taylor's) Bn. Co.C
Schumacher, H. TX 3rd Inf. 2nd Co.A
Schumacher, H. TX 4th Inf. (St.Troops) Co.E
Schumacher, H. TX 12th Inf. Co.D
Schumacher, Henry AL 1st Bn.Cadets Co.A
Schumacher, J. LA Mil. 1st Chasseurs a pied Co.5
Schumacher, John H. SC Arty. Bachman's Co. (German Lt.Arty.)
Schumacher, John H. SC Arty.Bn. Hampton Legion Co.B
Schumacher, K. LA Pointe Coupee Arty.
Schumacher, Theodore SC Arty.Bn. Hampton Legion Co.B
Schumacher, William TX 36th Cav. Co.H
Schumacker, Chs. LA Mil. 5th Regt.Eur.Brig. (Spanish Regt.) Co.8
Schumacker, P. TX 3rd Inf. Co.B
Schumake, A. LA Mil. Chalmette Regt. Co.E
Schumaker, --- LA Mil. 2nd Regt. French Brig. Co.3
Schumaker, Anton TX Conscr.
Schumaker, Arnold LA Pointe Coupee Arty. Cpl.
Schumaker, Christian TX Conscr.

Schumaker, Dan MO 1st Cav. Co.I
Schumaker, F. LA Mil. 3rd Regt. 1st Brig. 1st Div. Co.D
Schumaker, H. 2nd Conf.Eng.Troops Co.C
Schumaker, John TN 1st (Feild's) Inf. Co.K
Schumaker, M. LA Mil. 3rd Regt. 1st Brig. 1st Div. Co.H
Schuman, Charles TX 36th Cav. Co.B
Schuman, Charles VA 1st Inf. Co.I Band
Schuman, Fred LA Mil. 1st Regt. 2nd Brig. 1st Div. Co.K
Schuman, George P. VA 10th Cav. Co.D
Schuman, H.E. TX Waul's Legion Co.E
Schuman, James W. GA 47th Inf. Co.E,C
Schuman, Lewis LA 1st (Strawbridge's) Inf. Co.A
Schuman, Simon LA 21st (Patton's) Inf. Co.I
Schuman, Theodore LA Maddox's Regt. Res.Corps Co.B
Schuman, V. TX Cav. Baird's Regt. Co.G
Schumann, Charles VA Inf. 25th Bn. Co.E Music.
Schumann, Fritz TX 7th Cav. Co.B
Schumann, Julius VA Inf. 25th Bn. Co.E Music.
Schument F. LA Mil. 1st Regt. French Brig. Co.5
Schument, J.P. LA Mil. 1st Regt. French Brig. Co.5
Schumlmeyer, William TX Conscr.
Schumm, Theodore AL Arty. 1st Bn. Co.D
Schumpart, J.P. SC 2nd St.Troops Co.B
Schumpent, J.J. SC 4th Bn.Res. Co.A
Schumpert, B.H.G. SC 3rd Inf. Co.E
Schumpert, Elisha K. SC 13th Inf. Co.G
Schumpert, George A. SC 19th Inf. Co.D
Schumpert, Jacob J. SC 20th Inf. Co.F
Schumpert, J.I. TX 17th Cons.Dismtd.Cav. Co.K
Schumpert, J.J. SC 2nd Inf. Co.F
Schumpert, John MS 10th Cav. Co.K
Schumpert, John MS Inf. 3rd Bn. Co.B Music.
Schumpert, John J. TX 17th Cav. Co.E
Schumpert, J.W. MS 10th Cav. Co.K
Schumpert, Mark MS 10th Cav. Co.K
Schumpert, M.L. SC 20th Inf. Co.F
Schumpert, O.L. SC 3rd Inf. Co.E
Schumpert, P.M. MS Inf. 3rd Bn. (St.Troops) Co.E Sgt.
Schumpert, Reuben F. GA Arty. 11th Bn. (Sumter Arty.) Co.A
Schumpherd, J. SC Cav.Bn. Holcombe Legion Co.C
Schumpherd, J.L. SC 7th Cav. Co.E
Schumput, T.D MS Conscr.
Schunaman, W.E. VA 2nd St.Res. Co.D
Schunelle, Frederic LA 26th Inf. Co.E
Schunemaker, C.J. TX Dismtd.Cav. Co.C
Schunemann, Conrad TX 36th Cav. Co.F
Schuner, Jacob TX Inf. 1st St.Troops Sheldon's Co.B
Schunk, Leo LA 13th Inf. Co.E
Schunta, J. TX 5th Inf. Martindale's Co.
Schupback, Fredrich LA 7th Inf. Co.D
Schuple, Peter LA Mil. 2nd Regt. 3rd Brig. 1st Div. Co.E
Schupp, Francis TX 11th (Spaight's) Bn.Vol. Co.E
Schuppe, A. TX 6th Inf. Co.B Cpl.

Schuppert, M. LA 14th Inf. Surg.
Schuppisser, H. TN Inf. 3rd Bn. Co.G
Schurloch, T.J. TX 27th Cav. Surg.
Schurman, Henry VA 15th Inf. Co.K Cpl.
Schurre, Ed TX 7th Cav. Co.B
Schursh, Joseph LA Arty. Kean's Btty. (Orleans Ind.Arty.)
Schurte, Joseph LA 1st (Strawbridge's) Inf. Co.A
Schurtz, --- LA Mil. 3rd Regt.Eur.Brig. (Garde Francaise)
Schussler, Francis TX 11th (Spaight's) Bn.Vol. Co.E
Schussler, John TX 1st (Yager's) Cav. Co.E
Schussler, Stephen, Jr. AL 6th Inf. Co.E
Schuster, A. TX Waul's Legion Co.C
Schuster, C.A. TX Waul's Legion Co.C
Schuster, F. TX 21st Inf. Co.B
Schuster, J.B. AL Mil. 3rd Vol. Co.A
Schuster, John AL 12th Inf. Co.C
Schutt, W.H. NC 4th Inf. Co.E Sgt.
Schutt, William H. NC 5th Sr.Res. Co.E 1st Sgt.
Schutte, Andrew VA 1st St.Res. Co.D
Schutte, B.D. LA Mil. 4th Regt.Eur.Brig. Co.B
Schutte, F. VA 2nd St.Res. Co.H
Schutte, H. LA Mil. 4th Regt.Eur.Brig. Co.E
Schutte, Henry LA Mil. Lafayette Arty.
Schutte, Henry VA Cav. 1st Bn. (Loc.Def. Troops) Co.C
Schutte, H.G. TX 1st Hvy.Arty. Co.B
Schutter, John GA Hvy.Arty. 22nd Bn. Co.C
Schutterle, George AL Gorff's Co. (Mobile Pulaski Rifles) Cpl.
Schutterle, John AL Gorff's Co. (Mobile Pulaski Rifles) Cpl.
Schutterlee, John AL 22nd Inf. Co.H
Schutterly, M. TX 1st Hvy.Arty. Co.C
Schutz, A. LA Dreux's Cav. Co.A
Schutz, A. LA Mil. Fire Bn. Co.B Jr.Lt.
Schutz, B. LA 20th Inf. Co.F
Schutz, Charles TX 7th Cav. Co.B
Schutz, E. VA 2nd St.Res. Co.H
Schutz, Fred GA 1st (Olmstead's) Inf. Co.G
Schutz, John SC Inf. Hampton Legion Co.F
Schutz, W. LA Mil. Fire Bn. Co.B Cpl.
Schutz, William TX 17th Inf. Co.H
Schüwitz, J. TX 7th Cav. Co.B
Schuyler, C.N. TN 3rd (Forrest's) Cav. Co.C
Schuyler, G.M. VA Lt.Arty. Fry's Co.
Schuyler, G.M. VA 46th Inf. 1st Co.K
Schvegman, Gerard LA Mil. 3rd Regt. 1st Brig. 1st Div. Co.C
Schwaab, F. GA 8th Inf. Co.C Band Music.
Schwab, Andreas TX 36th Cav. Co.F
Schwab, Andrew LA 1st (Strawbridge's) Inf.
Schwab, F. TX 26th Cav. Co.C
Schwab, George Conf.Inf. Tucker's Regt. Co.C
Schwab, Joe LA 4th Inf. Co.B
Schwab, Joseph LA Mil. Mech.Guard.
Schwab, Joseph TN 1st (Feild's) Inf. Co.C
Schwab, William KY 2nd Mtd.Inf. Co.C
Schwabb, John LA 13th Inf. Co.I
Schwabe, Edward TX 3rd Inf. Co.B
Schwabendiesen E. LA Mil. 4th Regt.Eur.Brig. Co.B Cpl.
Schwabenland, H. TX 7th Inf. Co.H
Schwable, William TN 15th Inf. Co.K

Schwacke, J.A. SC Mil.Arty. 1st Regt. Walter's Co.

Schwaegler, J. LA Mil. 3rd Regt.Eur.Brig. (Garde Francaise) Co.7

Schwaegler, L. LA Mil. 3rd Regt.Eur.Brig. (Garde Francaise) Co.7

Schwager, C. LA 21st (Patton's) Inf. Co.H

Schwager, G. LA 22nd Inf. Co.C

Schwager, Peter LA Mil. Orleans Fire Regt. Co.F

Schwagler, --- LA Mil. Beauregard Bn. Co.D

Schwake, Ang H. Gen. & Staff Hosp.Stew.

Schwake, Aug SC Mil.Arty. 1st Regt. Co.C

Schwake, F. TX 5th Inf. Martindale's Co.

Schwalb, Ph. LA Mil. Orleans Fire Regt. Co.A

Schwalbach, John P. VA 30th Inf. Co.B

Schwalby, F.W. TX 12th Inf. Co.D

Schwalby, J.A. TX 12th Inf. Co.D

Schwalenberg, Louis LA 28th (Thomas') Inf. Co.F

Schwall, George GA 48th Inf. Co.E

Schwall, George M. GA 12th (Wright's) Cav. (St.Guards) Wright's Co.

Schwaller, Frank TX 2nd Inf. Co.A

Schwalmeyer, Henry VA 15th Inf. Co.A

Schwalmeyer, J.T. VA 15th Inf. Co.A

Schwalmeyer, William C. VA 15th Inf. Co.H

Schwan, Augustus GA 42nd Inf. Co.F

Schwan, Francis MD Arty. 3rd Btty.

Schwan, J.G. LA Mil. 4th Regt.Eur.Brig. Co.F

Schwanbeck, George LA 30th Inf. Co.E

Schwance, S.L. TX 22nd Inf. Co.I

Schwander, P. TX Inf. Timmons' Regt. Co.H Capt.

Schwander, Peter TX Waul's Legion Co.A Capt.

Schwanemann, C. GA Inf. 18th Bn. Co.A

Schwang, S.L. TX Conscr.

Schwanig, --- LA Mil. 4th Regt. 3rd Brig. 1st Div. Co.B

Schwann, Y. LA Mil. 4th Regt. 1st Brig. 1st Div. Co.E

Schwantes, Ernst TX 36th Cav. Co.F 1st Sgt.

Schwarb, --- LA Mil. 3rd Regt.Eur.Brig. Euler's Co.

Schwarez, John TX 14th Field Btty.

Schwarez, P. TX 14th Field Btty.

Schwarner, James TX 25th Cav. Co.H

Schwarner, Robert KY 4th Mtd.Inf. Co.B

Schwarner, Robert MS Lt.Arty. (Issaquena Arty.) Graves' Co.

Schwarting, F. TX Inf. 1st St.Troops Sheldon's Co.B

Schwarting, Frederick TX 1st Inf. Co.L

Schwarting, William TX 1st (McCulloch's) Cav. Co.D

Schwarts, Benjamin MS 7th Inf. Co.C

Schwarty, Phillip SC Res. Co.F

Schwartz, A. AL 32nd Inf. Band Music.

Schwartz, A. GA 32nd Inf. Co.E

Schwartz, A. NC 18th Inf. Co.A

Schwartz, August TX 17th Inf. Co.H Cpl.

Schwartz, August Brig.Band B.R. Johnson's Brig. Music.

Schwartz, Augustus LA Mil.Cav.Squad. (Iberville Ind.Rangers)

Schwartz, C. GA 1st (Symons') Res. Co.A

Schwartz, Carl TX 1st (Yager's) Cav. Co.E

Schwartz, C.D. TX 20th Inf. Co.D

Schwartz, Charles LA 6th Inf. Co.H

Schwartz, Charles LA 10th Inf. Co.F

Schwartz, Charles MS Lt.Arty. (Jefferson Arty.) Darden's Co.

Schwartz, Charles TX Cav. 8th (Taylor's) Bn. Co.C

Schwartz, Charles TX 1st Hvy.Arty. Co.C

Schwartz, Charles VA Inf. 1st Bn. Co.D

Schwartz, Charles F. MS 16th Inf. Co.D Cpl.

Schwartz, Edward AL 21st Inf. Co.H

Schwartz, Ernest VA 9th Inf. Co.F

Schwartz, F. LA Mil. 2nd Regt. 3rd Brig. 1st Div. Co.B

Schwartz, Ferd 1st Conf.Inf. 1st Co.F

Schwartz, Francois LA Mil. Chalmette Regt. Co.C

Schwartz, Frank SC 1st (McCreary's) Inf. Co.G

Schwartz, George AL 8th Inf. Co.G 2nd Lt.

Schwartz, George VA 23rd Inf. Co.H

Schwartz, George VA 31st Mil. Co.F

Schwartz, George H. SC 3rd Inf. Co.H

Schwartz, George W. GA 10th Inf. Co.K

Schwartz, George W. SC 2nd Arty. Co.E Cpl.

Schwartz, Godfrey W. SC 13th Inf. Co.H

Schwartz, H. TX 1st Hvy.Arty. Co.K

Schwartz, H.C. SC 13th Inf. Co.H

Schwartz, Hry LA Mil. 4th Regt.Eur.Brig. Co.B

Schwartz, Isaac VA 17th Inf. Co.E

Schwartz, J. GA Siege Arty. Campbell's Ind.Co.

Schwartz, J. LA 25th Inf. Co.H

Schwartz, Jacob MS 7th Inf. Co.B

Schwartz, Jacob VA 15th Inf. Co.K

Schwartz, Jacob A. SC 12th Inf. Co.C

Schwartz, Jacques LA C.S. Zouave Bn. Co.F

Schwartz, J.B. SC 12th Inf. Co.C

Schwartz, J.G. MS Blythe's Bn. (St.Troops) Co.A

Schwartz, J.M. LA Mil. 2nd Regt. 3rd Brig. 1st Div. Co.H

Schwartz, J.M. LA Mil.Conf.Guards Regt. Co.G

Schwartz, John AL 1st Cav. 2nd Co.E

Schwartz, John LA C.S. Zouave Bn. Co.F

Schwartz, John Jacob VA 1st Cav. 2nd Co.D

Schwartz, John M. VA 12th Cav. Co.G Sgt.

Schwartz, Joseph LA Mil. Bragg's Bn. Schwartz's Co. Capt.

Schwartz, Karl T. TX Lt.Arty. Hughes' Co.

Schwartz, L. LA Mil. 4th Regt.Eur.Brig. Co.B

Schwartz, L. LA Mil. Orleans Guards Regt. Co.D

Schwartz, L. LA Prov.Regt. Legion Co.7 Capt.

Schwartz, Michel LA Mil. Bragg's Bn. Schwartz's Co.

Schwartz, Moses SC Arty. Melchers' Co. (Co.B,German Arty.)

Schwartz, Myer VA 1st St.Res. Co.D Cpl.

Schwartz, N. LA Mil. 2nd Regt. French Brig. Co.1

Schwartz, O. MS Cav. Buck's Co.

Schwartz, Otto LA 1st Cav. Co.A

Schwartz, P. LA Mil. 4th Regt.Eur.Brig. Co.B

Schwartz, Samuel SC 18th Inf. Co.A Cpl.

Schwartz, Thomas E. VA 12th Cav. Co.G

Schwartz, Thomas E. VA 4th Inf. Co.D

Schwartz, Valentine VA 15th Inf. Co.K Cpl.

Schwartz, Z. TX Inf. Cunningham's Co.

Schwartze, Augustus F. MD 1st Cav. Co.A,F Capt.

Schwartzer, M. LA 27th Inf. Co.A

Schwartzkoff, C. VA 54th Mil. Co.G

Schwarz, E.A. GA 1st (Olmstead's) Inf. Stiles' Co.

Schwarz, E. A. GA Inf. 18th Bn.

Schwarz, Emile A. GA Hvy.Arty. 22nd Bn. Co.C Sgt.

Schwarz, F. TX 33rd Cav. Co.E

Schwarz, Ferdinand GA 36th (Villepigue's) Inf. Co.F

Schwarz, Fred GA 5th Inf. Co.B

Schwarz, G. GA Inf. 18th Bn. (St.Guards) Co.B

Schwarz, Isaac TX 12th Inf. Co.A

Schwarz, Louis LA Mil. 4th Regt.Eur.Brig. Co.B Capt.

Schwarz, Samuel SC 1st Inf. Co.E

Schwarz, Theo. KY 14th Cav. Co.B

Schwarz, V. VA 2nd St.Res. Co.H Sgt.

Schwarz, William TX 5th Field Btty.

Schwarzbach, A. 4th Conf.Eng.Troops Co.E

Schwarzbach, Aug Sap. & Min. Kellersberg's Corps,CSA

Schwarzbach, Charles TX Lt.Arty. Jones' Co.

Schwarzbach, John TX Lt.Arty. Jones' Co.

Schwarzback, Ch. TX Inf. 4th Bn. (Oswald's) Co.B Cpl.

Schwarzenbach, Fredrick W. FL 6th Inf. Co.B

Schwarzhoff, Scipis TX 7th Cav. Co.B Capt.

Schwarzman, Gustavus A. Gen. & Staff, Adj.Gen.Dept. Capt.

Schwarzshild, A. LA Mil. Lafayette Arty. Sgt.

Schwatzs, Augustus TN 23rd Inf. 2nd Co.F,Co.D Music.

Schwceir, George TX 4th Inf. Co.F

Schwebber, G. LA Mil. 1st Regt. 2nd Brig. 1st Div. Co.D

Schwecart L. LA Mil. Fire Bn. Co.F

Schwecker, Fred LA Mil. 4th Regt. 1st Brig. 1st Div. Co.D

Schweckhart, S. LA Pointe Coupee Arty. Teamster

Schweduskey, Thomas E. Conf.Cav. Wood's Regt. Co.K Cpl.

Schweigert, George VA 10th Cav. 1st Co.E Black.

Schweigle, Charles MS 1st (King's) Inf. (St.Troops) Co.E

Schweikart, Fred TX 1st Hvy.Arty. Co.C Cpl.

Schweike, J.H. SC 1st Regt. Charleston Guard Co.A

Schweikert, G. SC 1st Regt. Charleston Guard Co.D

Schweikert, P. LA Mil. 2nd Regt. 3rd Brig. 1st Div. Co.A

Schwein, Henry GA 1st (Olmstead's) Inf. Co.I

Schweiss, Joseph LA 20th Inf. Old Co.B

Schweitzer, Charles LA 20th Inf. Co.C

Schweitzer, Charles TX 5th Inf. Co.B

Schweitzer, Francois LA Arty. Kean's Btty. (Orleans Ind.Arty.)

Schweitzer, Frederic LA 13th Inf. Co.F

Schweitzer, J. LA Mil. Cazadores Espanoles Regt. Co.D

Schweitzharat, J. LA Mil. 1st Regt. French Brig. Co.4

489

Sclater, William M. VA Arty. B.H. Smith's Co.

Schweizer, --- VA Lt.Arty. Page's Co.
Schwem, Daniel LA 3rd (Harrison's) Cav. Co.B
 Artif.
Schwencke, A. LA Mil. 1st Regt. French Brig.
 Co.4
Schwencke, H. LA Mil. 1st Regt. French Brig.
 Co.4
Schwenk, George AL 1st Regt. Mobile Vol.
 Co.C 1st Lt.
Schwenk, George AL 12th Inf. Co.C
Schwenn, John AL Mil. Gueringer's Co. Cpl.
Schwenterman, Frank LA 6th Inf. Co.G
Schwer, A. KY 1st Inf. Co.E
Schwer, H. LA Arty. Watson Btty.
Schwerburger, Wendelin TX 6th Inf. Co.D
Schwerdt, Henry LA Mil. 3rd Regt. 3rd Brig. 1st
 Div. Co.H 2nd Music.
Schwerdt, Henry LA 20th Inf. Band Music.
Schwerdt, Henry LA Inf.Crescent Regt. Co.I
Schwerdt, John LA 20th Inf. Band Music.
Schwern, F. SC 5th Res. Co.C
Schwers, William SC Arty. Bachman's Co.
 (German Lt.Arty.) 2nd Lt.
Schwers, William SC Arty.Bn. Hampton Legion
 Co.B Sgt.
Schwertz, R. LA Mil. 4th Regt.French Brig.
 Co.3 1st Lt.
Schwertzberger, A. LA Mil. 3rd Regt. 3rd Brig.
 1st Div. Co.D
Schwery, Jacob Sig.Corps,CSA
Schwetalsky, Lewis MS 37th Inf. Co.F
Schwickel, P. LA Mil. Irish Regt. Co.E
Schwickert, H. TX 16th Inf. Co.E
Schwimley, H. 15th Conf.Cav. Co.F
Schwimley, Henry AL City Troop (Mobile) Ar-
 rington's Co.A
Schwin, J.J. Conrad KY 1st Inf. Co.A
Schwin, William E. AL 62nd Inf. Co.G
Schwindler, William MS Inf. 2nd Bn. Co.A Cpl.
Schwindler, William VA 26th Inf. 1st Co.B Cpl.
Schwine, H. GA 25th Inf. Pritchard's Co.
Schwinford, John G. VA 136th Mil. Co.B
Schwing, Charles SC Horse Arty. (Washington
 Arty.) Vol. Hart's Co.
Schwing, Charles SC Arty.Bn. Hampton Legion
 Co.A
Schwing, George MS 16th Inf. Co.K
Schwing, George B. LA 2nd Cav. Co.I
Schwing, J.T. LA 2nd Cav. Co.I
Schwing, Samuel C. LA 1st Cav. Co.A
Schwing, William F. MS 19th Inf. Co.D Capt.
Schwitalsky, Louis MS 14th Inf. Co.A
Schwitzer, F. LA C.S. Zouave Bn. Co.B
Schwitzer, G.H. GA 64th Inf. Co.I
Schwitzer, H. LA C.S. Zouave Bn. Co.F
Schwitzer, Solomon LA C.S. Zouave Bn. Co.F
Schwoeder, C.J. TX Waul's Legion Co.B
Schwollenberg, Louis LA Mil. 1st Regt. 3rd
 Brig. 1st Div.
Schwop, Andre LA C.S. Zouave Bn. Co.F
Schwrar, J.M. TN Inf. 3rd Cons.Regt. Chap.
Schwrar, J.M. TN 4th Inf. Chap.
Schwrar, Jno. M. Gen. & Staff Chap.
Sciacalaga, Guiseppe LA Mil. Cazadores Es-
 panoles Regt. Co.F
Sciallona, Nicola LA Mil. 6th Regt.Eur.Brig.
 (Italian Guards Bn.) Co.1

Scibner, G.W. AR 27th Inf. Co.G
Scidmore, W.B. MO Cav. Fristoe's Regt. Co.F
Scidmore, Z.P. MO Cav. Fristoe's Regt. Co.F
Scifers, Isaac T. MO 16th Inf. Co.C
Scifers, William C. KY 2nd Cav. Co.C
Sciferth, A. Herman VA Arty. Paris' Co.
Sciffle, N. FL 2nd Inf. Co.L
Scifres, Claiborne W. KY 6th Mtd.Inf. Co.B
Scifres, Joseph M., Jr. KY 6th Mtd.Inf. Co.B
Scifres, Joseph M., Sr. KY 6th Mtd.Inf. Co.B
Scifres, J. Wesley KY 6th Mtd.Inf. Co.B
Scifres, Matthias D. KY 6th Mtd.Inf. Co.B Sgt.
Scifres, R.H. KY 6th Mtd.Inf. Co.H,B
Scifter, D.J. GA 22nd Inf. Co.B
Sciles, W.J. AR 45th Cav. Co.B
Scilinthner, Phillip TX Griffin's Bn. Co.E
Scillian, F.M. KY 3rd Mtd.Inf. Co.A
Scillian, Francis M. KY 3rd Cav. Co.A
Scimiluca, Michiele LA Mil. 6th Regt.Eur.Brig.
 (Italian Guards Bn.) Co.2
Sciminol, C.F. AR 38th Inf. Co.H
Scimmahorn, David TN Inf. 1st Cons.Regt. Co.C
Scimmons, J. GA Lt.Arty. Ritter's Co. Cpl.
Scims, William MO 9th (Elliott's) Cav. Co.H
Scincindwer, George L. VA Inf. 1st Bn.Loc.Def.
 Co.D
Scincindiver, J.M. VA Inf. 1st Bn.Loc.Def.
 Co.D
Scinclair, H.D. TN 9th Inf. Co.H
Scindzer, Cicerer TX 33rd Cav. Co.D
Scioneaux, Octave LA Mil. St.James Regt. Co.F
Scioneaux, Philogene LA 30th Inf. Co.F
Scioneaux, Silvanie LA Mil. St.James Regt. Co.F
Scionneaux, C. LA 30th Inf. Locoul's Co.
Scionneaux, Charles LA Mil. St.James Regt.
 Co.E
Scionneaux, Clem LA Mil. St.James Regt. Co.G
Scionneaux, Clid LA Mil. St.James Regt. Co.G
Scionneaux, Louis LA Mil. St.James Regt. Co.E
Scionneaux, Marcellin LA Mil. St.James Regt.
 Co.F
Scionneaux, Phil LA Mil. St.James Regt.
 Gaudet's Co.
Scipher, Thomas O. VA Inf. 23rd Bn. Co.E
Sciphers, Amos VA Inf. 23rd Bn. Co.E Cpl.
Scipio, Africanus GA Inf. 18th Bn. Co.B Cook
Sciples, George LA Mil. Cav.Squad. (Iberville
 Ind.Rangers)
Scipmore, R.J. LA Mil. 1st Regt. 2nd Brig. 1st
 Div. Co.E
Scipper, E. AL 1st Bn. Hilliard's Legion Vol.
 Co.G
Scipper, Edmund AL 53rd (Part.Rangers) Co.K
Scipper, J.H. AL 60th Inf. Co.H
Scipper, John NC 48th Inf. Co.I
Scipper, S. AL 17th Inf. Co.C
Scipple, P. MS Cav. Rhodes' Co. Part.Rangers
Scipple, P. 14th Conf.Cav. Co.F
Scirratt, James H. AL 11th Cav. Co.E Cpl.
Scirratt, J.H. TN 40th Inf. Co.E
Scirratt, J.L. TN 34th Inf. Co.B
Scirratt, John AL 11th Cav. Co.E
Scirratt, S.A. TN 34th Inf. Co.B
Scisemoore, George W. NC 34th Inf. Co.B
Scisk, John NC 29th Inf. Co.G
Scism, J.A. TX Cav. McCord's Frontier Regt.
 Co.F

Scism, James M. TN 29th Inf. Co.K
Scism, J.F. NC 34th Inf. Co.H
Scism, John A. TX 36th Cav. Co.D
Scism, William NC 34th Inf. Co.H
Scisom, Joseph AL 13th Bn. Part.Rangers Co.E
Scisom, S.L. GA 5th Inf. (St.Guards) Rucker's
 Co. Cpl.
Scison, Joseph AL 56th Part.Rangers Co.I
Scisson, E.M. AL Mil. 4th Vol. Co.E Cpl.
Scisson, Jeff W. KY 2nd (Duke's) Cav. Co.A
Scisson, John KY 2nd (Duke's) Cav. Co.A
Scisson, John A. NC 66th Inf. Co.I
Scisson, L.R. GA 38th Inf. Co.E
Scisson, Luther VA Inf. 45th Bn. Co.A
Scisson, Thomas GA 2nd Res. Co.E
Scisson, William D. GA 38th Inf. Co.E Sgt.
Scisson, William J. TN Cav. 17th Bn. (Sanders')
 Co.A
Scitze, David GA 65th Inf. Co.C
Scitze, David GA Smith's Legion Co.D
Scitze, Henry GA 65th Inf. Co.C
Scitze, Henry GA Smith's Legion Co.D
Sciute, Dominick MO 1st Inf. Co.D,E
Scivaley, D.W. TN Inf. Spencer's Co. Sgt.
Scivalley, George R. TN 41st Inf. Co.G
Scivalley, James V. TN 41st Inf. Co.G
Scivalley, Jasper N. TN 41st Inf. Co.G
Scivalley, John J. TN 41st Inf. Co.G
Scivally, D.W. TN 44th (Cons.) Inf. Co.B Sgt.
Scivally, J.J. TN 44th (Cons.) Inf. Co.B
Scivally, W.H. MS 12th Cav. Co.G
Scivally, William F. TN 1st (Turney's) Inf. Co.E
Sciveally, J.J. TN 17th Inf. Co.E
Sciveally, J.N. TN 17th Inf. Co.E
Sciveally, W.J. TN 17th Inf. Co.E Sgt.
Sciveally, Z.M. TN 17th Inf. Co.E
Sciver, James S. VA 136th Mil. Co.H
Scivicque, A.S. LA Inf. 9th Bn. Co.D
Scivicque, Charles LA Inf. 9th Bn. Co.D
Scizemore, Anderson VA Cav. 37th Bn. Co.K
Scizemore, Cleveland VA Cav. 37th Bn. Co.K
Scizemore, D.S. VA Cav. 37th Bn. Co.K
Scizemore, John VA Cav. 37th Bn. Co.K
Scizer, Charles VA 3rd Res. Co.K
Sckinger, Eugene LA Mil. 4th Regt. 3rd Brig. 1st
 Div. Co.G
Sclaggs, John MO 4th Inf. Co.A
Sclater, George T. VA 1st Bn.Res. Co.D
Sclater, H.S. VA Inf. 25th Bn. Co.D
Sclater, James VA 115th Mil. QMSgt.
Sclater, James B. VA Lt.Arty. 13th Bn. Co.A
Sclater, J.B. VA VMI
Sclater, John R. AL Lt.Arty. 2nd Bn. Co.C
 Capt.
Sclater, John R. AR Lt.Arty. 5th Btty. 2nd Lt.
Sclater, Lemuel H. VA Lt.Arty. R.M. Ander-
 son's Co. Sgt.
Sclater, Morton T. VA 14th Inf. Co.C Cpl.
Sclater, Richard A. VA 18th Inf. Co.E Music.
Sclater, Richard A. VA 32nd Inf. Co.A Music.
Sclater, Robert J. VA 44th Inf. Co.F Cpl.
Sclater, Thomas R. VA 32nd Inf. Co.A
Sclater, William VA Inf. 25th Bn. Co.C,H Sgt.
Sclater, William A. VA 44th Inf. Co.H
Sclater, William M. VA 1st Arty. Co.D
Sclater, William M. VA Lt.Arty. 1st Bn. Co.D
Sclater, William M. VA Arty. B.H. Smith's Co.

Sclater, William S. NC Moseley's Co. (Sampson Arty.)
Scloon, G.N. KY 1st (Butler's) Cav.
Scloss, A. TX 8th Inf. Co.G
Scluden, J.J.N. GA Lt.Arty. 12th Bn.
Scly, John W. 10th Conf.Cav. Co.E
Scmer, J.T. MO Lt.Arty. 1st Btty.
Scmitt, Arch 1st Squad. Cherokee Mtd.Vol. Co.A
Scn, G.H. TX 11th Inf. Co.I
Scoales, Noak W. VA 42nd Inf. Co.H Sgt.
Scobbee, S. KY 8th Cav. Co.E
Scobber, W.P. AL 31st Inf. Co.B
Scobee, A. KY Morgan's Men Co.D
Scobee, Alex KY 8th Cav. Co.D
Scobee, James KY 9th Cav. Co.G 1st Sgt.
Scobee, James MO 1st N.E. Cav. Price's Co.M, White's Co.
Scobee, J.W. Conf.Cav. 6th Bn. Co.G
Scobee, Rice P. KY 3rd Bn.Mtd.Rifles Co.D
Scobee, Stephen MO 1st N.E. Cav. Price's Co.M, White's Co.
Scobee, Stephen MO 9th Bn.S.S. Co.E
Scobey, Burchett D. TN 7th Inf. Co.K
Scobey, James E. TN 55th (McKoin's) Inf. Co.F Capt.
Scobey, Joseph B. TN 7th Inf. Co.I
Scoble, A. TX 25th Cav.
Scoble, A.W. TX Cav. Waller's Regt. Menard's Co.
Scobler, J. VA 46th Inf. Co.F
Scoborough, William H. KY 3rd Cav. Co.B
Scobry, James B. TN 1st Zouaves Co.B Capt.
Scoby, D.J. TN 47th Inf. Co.D
Scoby, J.A.H. TN 47th Inf. Co.D
Scoby, J.D. TN 5th Inf. 2nd Co.F
Scoby, John T. TN Lt.Arty. Huggins' Co.
Scoby, Joseph B. KY Cav. 2nd Bn. (Dortch's) Co.A 2nd Lt.
Scoby, M. TX Cav. Waller's Regt. Goode's Co.
Scoby, Robert E. AR 9th Inf. Co.D Cpl.
Scoby, W. MS 3rd Inf. (St.Troops) Co.D
Scoby, William MO 5th Inf. Co.K
Scoby, William A. AL 4th (Roddey's) Cav. Co.A
Scoby, William A. TN Greer's Regt.Part.Rangers Co.A
Scoby, William Monroe MO Inf. 1st Bn. Co.B
Scoby, W.W. MS 3rd Cav. Co.A,H Sgt.
Scocavitch, Jose SC Mil. 1st Regt. (Charleston Res.) Co.B
Scochland, R.H. AR 5th Inf. Co.B
Scodiera, J. LA 1st (Strawbridge's) Inf. Co.D
Scoff, F.M. TX 9th (Young's) Inf. Co.B Cpl.
Scoff, G.W. TX 9th (Young's) Inf. Co.B
Scoffield, B.B. GA 1st Troops & Defences (Macon) Co.C
Scoffield, J.H. VA 10th Cav. Co.D
Scoffield, R.T. AL 23rd Inf. Co.K
Scoffield, Thomas H. NC 17th Inf. (2nd Org.) Co.H Cpl.
Scoffill, William AR 2nd Cav. Webb's Co. Sgt.
Scofield, Cyrus J. TN 7th Inf. Co.H
Scofield, Elbert AL 18th Inf. Co.B
Scofield, Ephraim E. GA Inf. 1st Loc.Troops (Augusta) Co.A
Scofield, G.B. TX Cav. Border's Regt. Co.D
Scofield, Harrison GA 27th Inf. Co.B
Scofield, H.B. AL 25th Inf. Co.C Sgt.

Scofield, James AL 3rd Inf. Co.H
Scofield, James LA 6th Inf. Co.H
Scofield, James E. VA Inf. 25th Bn. Co.D
Scofield, J.C. TX Inf. 1st St.Troops Whitehead's Co.
Scofield, J.D. AL 25th Inf. Co.C
Scofield, Jeremiah LA 5th Inf. Co.B Cpl.
Scofield, J.M. AL 25th Inf. Co.C
Scofield, J.N. NC 4th Sr.Res. Co.D
Scofield, John AR 11th Inf. Co.F
Scofield, John GA 20th Inf. Co.A
Scofield, Joseph TX 6th Inf. Co.K
Scofield, J.S. GA Inf. 14th Bn. (St.Guards) Co.C
Scofield, Lawrence LA 6th Inf. Co.H
Scofield, Louis GA 3rd Bn. (St.Guards) Co.E
Scofield, Thomas KY 12th Cav. Co.C
Scofield, W.C. KY 7th Cav. Co.I Sgt.
Scofield, W.C. KY 7th Mtd.Inf. Co.A Sgt.
Scofield, William AR 26th Inf. Co.F
Scofield, William TX 1st Field Btty.
Scofield, William C. AR 32nd Inf. Co.G 1st Lt.
Scofield, W.J. AL 25th Inf. Co.C
Scofield, W.O. AR Army N. Sub.Dist. Maj.,AIG
Scofield, W.S. LA Siege Train Bn. Co.E
Scofill, Andrew J. GA 57th Inf. Co.F
Scofill, Bryant B. GA 57th Inf. Co.F
Scofill, James GA 57th Inf. Co.E
Scofill, James I. GA 57th Inf. Co.F
Scofill, Reece B. GA 57th Inf. Co.F,A Sgt.
Scogan, B.B. LA 3rd Inf. Co.H
Scogen, --- AR Lt.Arty. 5th Btty.
Scogen, B.B. LA Inf.Cons.Crescent Regt. Co.K
Scoggans, W.C. TX 11th Inf. Co.F
Scoggin, Aaron NC 45th Inf. Co.I Cpl.
Scoggin, A.J. GA 13th Inf. Co.B
Scoggin, Benjamin LA Inf. 11th Bn. Co.B
Scoggin, B.F. AR 19th (Dawson's) Inf. Co.I
Scoggin, Crispen M. MS 33rd Inf. Co.I
Scoggin, Davis G. TX 31st Cav. Co.C
Scoggin, E.B. AL 33rd Inf. Co.E Cpl.
Scoggin, Gillam TX 31st Cav. Co.C
Scoggin, H.H. TX 32nd Cav. Co.C
Scoggin, H.H. TX 11th Inf. Co.B
Scoggin, H.J. AL 20th Inf. Co.G
Scoggin, Isaac MO Cav. Coffee's Regt. Co.C
Scoggin, Jacob S. LA 16th Inf. Co.I
Scoggin, James NC 64th Inf. Co.F
Scoggin, James H. NC 12th Inf. Co.C
Scoggin, James J. TX 4th Cav. Co.H Cpl.
Scoggin, James L. VA 1st St.Res. Co.A Sgt.
Scoggin, James R. TN 53rd Inf. Co.A 1st Sgt.
Scoggin, James W. TN 13th (Gore's) Cav. Co.H
Scoggin, J.B. AR 19th (Dawson's) Inf. Co.I
Scoggin, J.G. TN 30th Inf. Co.C
Scoggin, J.M. AR 19th (Dawson's) Inf. Co.I
Scoggin, John NC 64th Inf. Co.F
Scoggin, John SC 3rd Bn.Res. Co.D
Scoggin, John TN 30th Inf. Co.C
Scoggin, John J. VA 12th Inf. Co.F Sgt.
Scoggin, Jonathan TX 17th Cav. Co.G
Scoggin, Joshua Y. TX 17th Cav. Co.A
Scoggin, J.W. TX 17th Cons.Dismtd.Cav. Co.G
Scoggin, Leonidas A. VA 20th Inf. Co.I
Scoggin, Polk TN 30th Inf. Co.C Cpl.
Scoggin, R.H. VA Hvy.Arty. Allen's Co. Sgt.
Scoggin, S. GA 32nd Inf. Co.H

Scoggin, T.W. SC 3rd Bn.Res. Co.D
Scoggin, W.A. TN 30th Inf. Co.C
Scoggin, W.G. AR 19th (Dawson's) Inf. Co.G 1st Sgt.
Scoggin, W.G. AR 19th (Dawson's) Inf. Co.I
Scoggin, W.G. AR Inf. Hutchinson's Co. (4th Vol.)
Scoggin, William D. AR 3rd Inf. Co.A 2nd Lt.
Scoggin, William E. GA 7th Inf. Co.D
Scoggin, William M. NC 34th Inf. Co.C
Scoggin, W.M. GA 19th Inf.
Scoggings, J.M. MS Cav. Ham's Regt. Co.E,C
Scoggins, A.C. MS 9th Inf. New Co.F, Old Co.H
Scoggins, B. AL 23rd Inf. Co.B
Scoggins, B.C. GA 35th Inf. Co.D
Scoggins, Berry GA 29th Inf. Co.C
Scoggins, Charles J. TN 53rd Inf. Co.A
Scoggins, Chatham D. GA 41st Inf. Co.K
Scoggins, Columbus TX Cav. Ragsdale's Bn. Co.B
Scoggins, C.R. LA 27th Inf. Co.E
Scoggins, Daniel AL 44th Inf. Co.G
Scoggins, D. Gris TX 2nd Cav. Co.I
Scoggins, Fenton T. VA 56th Inf. Co.E
Scoggins, George TN 8th (Smith's) Cav. Co.C
Scoggins, George W. GA 41st Inf. Co.C
Scoggins, George W. KY Cav. 2nd Bn. (Dortch's) Co.B
Scoggins, G.R. AL 2nd Cav. Co.H Sgt.
Scoggins, Green GA 52nd Inf. Co.H
Scoggins, Green B. GA 39th Inf. Co.G
Scoggins, G.W. GA 64th Inf. Co.A
Scoggins, H.B. AL Cav. Lewis' Bn. Co.A Cpl.
Scoggins, H.C. AL 29th Inf. Co.A
Scoggins, Henry L. AL 39th Inf. Co.C
Scoggins, Henry M. NC Cav. 12th Bn. Co.B
Scoggins, Henry M. 8th (Dearing's) Conf.Cav. Co.B
Scoggins, H.H. TX Cav. Border's Regt. Co.F
Scoggins, Hiram B. GA 65th Inf. Co.K
Scoggins, Hiram C. GA 12th Inf. Co.K
Scoggins, H.S. GA 1st (Fannin's) Res. Co.K
Scoggins, J. TN Inf. 4th Cons.Regt. Co.K
Scoggins, James AL 39th Inf. Co.C
Scoggins, James AR 1st (Colquitt's) Inf. Co.C
Scoggins, James GA Cav. 16th Bn. (St.Guards) Co.C Cpl.
Scoggins, James GA 1st (Fannin's) Res. Co.C
Scoggins, James NC 56th Inf. Co.E
Scoggins, James SC 1st Arty. Co.G
Scoggins, James SC 7th Res. Co.B
Scoggins, James TN 7th (Duckworth's) Cav. Co.E
Scoggins, James H. VA 59th Inf. 3rd Co.I
Scoggins, James M. MS 1st Lt.Arty. Co.L
Scoggins, James M. MS 48th Inf. Co.B
Scoggins, James O. NC Cav. 5th Bn. Co.A
Scoggins, James O. NC 56th Inf. Co.H
Scoggins, James S. TN 2nd (Robison's) Inf. Co.H
Scoggins, James W. NC 34th Inf. Co.C
Scoggins, J.B. GA 56th Inf. Co.K
Scoggins, Jesse TN 18th (Newsom's) Cav. Co.C
Scoggins, J.H. AL 5th Cav. Co.D
Scoggins, J.H. VA Inf. 28th Bn. Co.D
Scoggins, J.J. AL 22nd Inf. Co.H

Scoggins, J.J. GA 1st Cav. Co.B
Scoggins, J.J. NC 3rd Jr.Res. Co.C
Scoggins, J.J. NC 4th Bn.Jr.Res. Co.C
Scoggins, J.J.W. NC 50th Inf. Co.A
Scoggins, J.M. GA 10th Inf. Co.K
Scoggins, John GA 48th Inf. Co.F
Scoggins, John, Jr. NC 2nd Cav. (19th St.Troops) Co.I Cpl.
Scoggins, John A. SC 1st Arty. Co.I
Scoggins, John Hawkins TN 40th Inf. Co.A
Scoggins, John J. GA 6th Inf. Co.K
Scoggins, John L. AL 3rd Bn. Hilliard's Legion Vol. Co.D
Scoggins, John L. NC 34th Inf. Co.B
Scoggins, John M. GA 64th Inf. Co.C
Scoggins, John S. GA 38th Inf. Co.E
Scoggins, John S. TN 40th Inf. Co.K
Scoggins, Joseph NC Mallett's Bn. (Cp.Guard) Co.B Sgt.
Scoggins, Joseph SC 1st (Butler's) Inf. Co.I
Scoggins, J.R. LA 18th Inf. Co.B
Scoggins, J.R. TN 32nd Inf. Co.G
Scoggins, J.T. SC 5th Inf. 2nd Co.G
Scoggins, J.W. GA Tiller's Co. (Echols Lt.Arty.)
Scoggins, J.W. GA 64th Inf. Co.A
Scoggins, J.W. TX 24th & 25th Cav. (Cons.) Co.I
Scoggins, L.A. AL 7th Cav. Co.I
Scoggins, L.A. AL Cp. of Instr. Talladega
Scoggins, Lafayette AL 51st (Part.Rangers) Co.D Cpl.
Scoggins, Leonidas A. VA 59th Inf. 3rd Co.B
Scoggins, Levi W. MS 1st Lt.Arty. Co.L
Scoggins, Malcolm C. GA 38th Inf. Co.E
Scoggins, Martin V.B. TN 3rd (Lillard's) Mtd.Inf. Co.C
Scoggins, Michael H. GA 41st Inf. Co.D 3rd Lt.
Scoggins, Nathan M. AR 9th Inf. Co.A 1st Sgt.
Scoggins, Pleasant H. NC 47th Inf. Co.I
Scoggins, Reppso O. NC 47th Inf. Co.I
Scoggins, R.H. VA 59th Inf. 3rd Co.G
Scoggins, Richard W. GA 2nd Inf. Co.I
Scoggins, Robert D. MS 15th Inf. Co.A
Scoggins, Samuel TN 4th (Murray's) Cav. Co.H Sgt.
Scoggins, Samuel TN 8th (Smith's) Cav. Co.C 2nd Lt.
Scoggins, Samuel T. GA 64th Inf. Co.C
Scoggins, S.D. AL 51st (Part.Rangers) Co.D
Scoggins, Seburn GA 56th Inf. Co.B,D
Scoggins, S.H. 3rd Conf.Cav. Co.I
Scoggins, S.S. GA Cav. 1st Bn.Res. Co.E
Scoggins, Stephen NC 56th Inf. Co.E
Scoggins, Sylvanus GA 7th Inf. (St.Guards) Co.E
Scoggins, Theron A. VA 5th Cav. Co.H
Scoggins, Thomas TN 23rd Inf. 2nd Co.A
Scoggins, Thomas R. LA 22nd Inf. Jones' Co.
Scoggins, U.D. AL 11th Cav. Co.H
Scoggins, W.E. GA 1st Inf. Co.K
Scoggins, Wesley AL 39th Inf. Co.C
Scoggins, Wesley GA 32nd Inf. Co.C
Scoggins, W.H. MS Inf. 2nd St.Troops Co.B
Scoggins, William AR 7th Inf. Co.I
Scoggins, William GA 1st (Symons') Res. Co.K
Scoggins, William SC 5th Res. Co.G
Scoggins, William TN 25th Inf. Co.C 2nd Lt.

Scoggins, William A. GA Cav. 16th Bn. (St.Guards) Co.D
Scoggins, William E. GA 6th Inf. Co.K
Scoggins, William H. NC 24th Inf. Co.A
Scoggins, William J. GA 38th Inf. Co.E
Scoggins, William R. GA 52nd Inf. Co.H
Scoggins, W.J. MO 3rd & 5th Cons.Inf.
Scoggins, W.L. AR 10th Inf. Co.H
Scoggs, William A. MO 4th Cav. Co.I
Scogin, Benjamin T. TX 7th Inf. Co.D
Scogin, B.R. TX 4th Cav. Co.H
Scogin, C.S. AR 6th Inf. Old Co.D
Scogin, D.G. TX Cav. Benavides' Regt. Co.G
Scogin, E.B. AL 17th Inf. Co.F Cpl.
Scogin, Edward M. AR Lt.Arty. 5th Btty.
Scogin, Elisha H. GA 35th Inf. Co.I
Scogin, G.B. AL 15th Inf. Co.E
Scogin, Gillam M. GA 35th Inf. Co.D
Scogin, Henry H. AR Lt.Arty. 5th Btty.
Scogin, James A. AL 2nd Bn. Hilliard's Legion Vol. Co.B
Scogin, James H. GA 35th Inf. Co.I
Scogin, James S. LA 9th Inf. Co.C
Scogin, J.D. LA 2nd Cav. Co.B
Scogin, J.F. GA 13th Inf. Co.B
Scogin, J.H. AR 6th Inf. Old Co.D,H Capt.
Scogin, J.L. AL 60th Inf. Co.C
Scogin, J.M. AL 15th Inf. Co.E
Scogin, John GA Lt.Arty. Scogin's Btty. (Griffin Lt.Arty.) Capt.
Scogin, John GA 3rd Inf. Co.H Asst.Surg.
Scogin, Jno. Gen. & Staff, Medical Dept. Asst.Surg.
Scogin, John A. TX Cav. Benavides' Regt. Co.G
Scogin, John L. AL Stuart's Detach.Loc.Def.
Scogin, John T. GA 19th Inf. Co.I
Scogin, Joseph S. GA Cav. 7th Bn. (St.Guards) Co.C
Scogin, Laban B. GA 32nd Inf. Co.I,G
Scogin, Levi S. GA 35th Inf. Co.I
Scogin, L.G. TX Cav. 3rd Bn.St.Troops Maj.
Scogin, Lindsay H. GA 35th Inf. Co.I
Scogin, L.S. GA Cav. 6th Bn. (St.Guards) Co.F 1st Sgt.
Scogin, Millington M. GA 35th Inf. Co.D
Scogin, Monroe V. MS 13th Inf. Co.A
Scogin, Samuel M. LA 25th Inf. Co.C
Scogin, Toliver S. TX 4th Cav. Co.H
Scogin, Toliver W. LA 16th Inf. Co.I
Scogin, Toliver W. LA 25th Inf. Co.C
Scogin, W.G. AL 55th Vol. Co.E
Scogin, Wiley G. GA 35th Inf. Co.I
Scogin, William C. GA 35th Inf. Co.D 1st Lt.
Scogin, William H. AL 15th Inf. Co.E 2nd Lt.
Scogin, William J. LA 9th Inf. Co.C
Scogin, William J. TX 4th Cav. Co.H Sgt.
Scogin, William P. GA 35th Inf. Co.D
Scogin, W.J. AL 55th Vol. Co.E
Scogin, W.M. GA 34th Inf. Co.C
Scogin, Y.L. TX 24th Cav. Co.I
Scogins, L.H. GA 2nd Inf. Co.I
Scogins, L.J. GA 9th Inf. Co.B
Scogins, M.G. GA 9th Inf. Co.B
Scogins, T.N. GA 9th Inf. Co.B Sgt.
Scogins, W.G. AL 27th Inf. Co.K
Scogins, W.J. AL 27th Inf. Co.K
Scohfield, T.G. AL 7th Cav. Co.A

Scolamberger, C. LA Mil. 4th Regt. 1st Brig. 1st Div. Co.I Cpl.
Scolds, Robert GA Lt.Arty. Daniell's Btty.
Scolds, Robert GA Arty. Maxwell's Reg.Lt.Btty.
Scolds, Robert GA Reg.Lt.Arty. Maxwell's Bn. Co.B
Scoles, Henry MS 11th Inf. Co.E
Scoles, Jesse GA 7th Inf. Co.H
Scoles, Robert GA 42nd Inf. Co.C
Scoles, Robert LA 15th Inf. Co.A Cpl.
Scoles, Simeon GA 42nd Inf. Co.C
Scolle, J.W. MO Robertson's Regt.St.Guard Co.C
Scolley, John GA 64th Inf. Co.I
Scollorn, G.H. MS 18th Cav. Co.H
Sconce, B.F. GA 41st Inf. Co.A
Sconiers, J. AL 6th Cav. Co.I
Scontrino, Danisio LA Mil. 6th Regt.Eur.Brig. (Italian Guards Bn.) Co.3
Sconyears, James A. MS 3rd Inf. Co.I Ord.Sgt.
Sconyers, Andrew J. GA Cobb's Legion Co.F,L
Sconyers, Augustus H. GA 3rd Inf. Co.A Sgt.
Sconyers, C.D. LA 11th Inf. Co.G
Sconyers, F.M. AL 59th Inf. Co.C
Sconyers, Francis M. AL 2nd Bn. Hilliard's Legion Vol. Co.F
Sconyers, George W. AL 13th Inf. Co.H
Sconyers, Guilford D. GA 3rd Inf. Co.A
Sconyers, Harrison AL 13th Inf. Co.H
Sconyers, John AL 46th Inf. Co.A
Sconyers, L.B. GA 48th Inf. Co.H
Sconyers, Miles AL 2nd Bn. Hilliard's Legion Vol. Co.F
Sconyers, Richard GA Cobb's Legion Co.I
Sconyers, Thomas AL 13th Inf. Co.H
Sconyers, W.H. AL 53rd (Part.Rangers) Co.D
Sconyers, William D. GA 3rd Inf. Co.A
Sconyers, W.R. TX 20th Inf. Co.H
Scooler, G. LA Mil. Chalmette Regt. Co.D Sgt.
Scooler, Thornly A. MS 14th Inf. Co.K
Scooley, Edward VA 5th Cav. Co.B
Scoonover, Benjamin VA 14th Cav. Co.L
Scoonover, John C. VA 25th Cav. Co.C
Scoonover, John C. VA Inf. 21st Bn. 1st Co.D
Scoonover, J.W. TX 24th & 25th Cav. (Cons.) Co.I
Scoonover, P. TX 24th & 25th Cav. (Cons.) Co.I
Scoot, H. MS Rogers' Co.
Scoot, R.G. AR 6th Inf. Co.B
Scoot, W. MO 12th Inf. Co.G
Scoot, W.H. AL 54th Inf. Co.C Sgt.
Scopick, A. TX 5th Field Btty.
Scopie, H. TX Lt.Arty. Dege's Bn. Co.A
Scopini, Edward LA 25th Inf. Co.A
Scopini, N.F. LA 6th Cav. Co.F
Scorbin, William J. AR 3rd Inf. Co.A
Scorborough, J.R. LA 28th (Gray's) Inf. Co.B
Scorborough, Malta GA Lt.Arty. 14th Bn. Co.B,F
Scorbrough, M.G. TN 50th Inf. Co.I Sgt.
Scorce, Charles VA 32nd Inf. Co.C
Scorce, Ed. H. VA 38th Inf. Co.K
Scorefield, W.C. TX 5th Inf. Co.H
Scoregga, Chas. Gen. & Staff Lt.,AAQM
Scorn, Edward 1st Cherokee Mtd.Rifles Co.E Sgt.
Scorry, J.R. GA 10th Inf.

Scot, Edward L. TN 29th Inf. Co.C
Scot, Henry 1st Choctaw Mtd.Rifles Co.H
Scot, J.A.P. AL 61st Inf. Co.B
Scot, J.W. KY 2nd Bn.Mtd.Rifles Co.D
Scot, Thomas B. TN 54th Inf. Ives' Co.
Scot, Y. MO Cav. Ford's Bn. Co.C
Scotchler, Jacob LA 21st (Patton's) Inf. Co.G
Scote, John MO 1st N.E. Cav. Price's Co.M
Scothorn, A.G. LA 31st Inf. Co.D
Scothorn, H.L. LA Inf. 4th Bn. Co.E
Scothorn, J. LA 31st Inf. Co.D
Scothorn, W.S. LA 31st Inf. Co.D
Scotie, George B. SC Inf. Hampton Legion Co.D
　　Music.
Scotland, James Shecoe's Chickasaw Bn.Mtd.Vol.
　　Co.G 2nd Lt.
Scott 1st Cherokee Mtd.Vol. 2nd Co.H
Scott, --- AL 53rd (Part.Rangers) Co.E
Scott, --- GA 8th (Scott's) St.Troops Col.
Scott, --- KY Cav. Lt.
Scott, --- LA Mil. 1st Regt. 2nd Brig. 1st Div.
　　Co.C
Scott, --- SC 3rd Cav. Co.E Teamster
Scott, --- TX 1st (McCulloch's) Cav. Co.A
Scott, --- TX Cav. 4th Regt.St.Troops Co.E
Scott, --- TX Cav. Border's Regt. Co.K Sgt.
Scott, --- TX Cav. Good's Bn. Co.A
Scott, --- TX Cav. Mann's Regt. Co.C
Scott, --- TX Cav. Morgan's Regt. Co.K
Scott, --- TX 11th Inf. Co.E
Scott, --- VA Inf. 25th Bn. Co.A Cook
Scott, A. LA Btty. Co.E
Scott, A. LA Inf.Cons.Crescent Regt. Co.I
Scott, A. LA Mil. Irish Regt. Co.E
Scott, A. MS Cav. 24th Bn. Co.D
Scott, A. SC Inf. 7th Bn. (Enfield Rifles) Co.E
Scott, A. SC 9th Inf. Co.E
Scott, A. TX 5th Field Btty.
Scott, A. TX Lt.Arty. Dege's Bn. Co.A
Scott, A. VA 53rd Inf. Co.C
Scott, A.A. VA Burks' Regt.Loc.Def. Allen's
　　Co.
Scott, Aaron D. KY 2nd Cav. Co.B
Scott, Aaron G. GA Inf. 8th Bn. Co.E
Scott, A.B. GA 13th Inf. Co.B
Scott, A.B. KY 9th Cav. Co.A
Scott, A.B. TN Cav. 9th Bn. (Gantt's) Co.F,E
Scott, A.B. TN 8th Inf. Co.C
Scott, Abel S. VA 15th Inf. 2nd Lt., Adj.
Scott, Abner TX 31st Cav. Co.F Cpl.
Scott, Abraham A. NC 57th Inf. Co.H Cpl.
Scott, Abram Mc. NC Inf. Thomas Legion Co.H
Scott, Absalom KY 3rd Mtd.Inf. Co.I
Scott, Absolum L. TN Conscr. (Cp. of Instr.)
Scott, A.C., Jr. GA 5th Cav. Co.A
Scott, A.C. GA 20th Inf. Co.D
Scott, A.C. Trans-MS Conf.Cav. 1st Bn. Co.A
Scott, A.D. LA Mil. 1st Regt. 2nd Brig. 1st Div.
　　Co.B
Scott, A.D. TX 9th Cav. Co.B
Scott, Addison Madison AL 49th Inf. Co.C
Scott, Adolphus KY 2nd Cav. Co.B
Scott, A.F. GA Cobb's Legion Co.D
Scott, A.G. MS 6th Inf. Co.I 1st Sgt.
Scott, A.G. MS 14th Inf. Capt.,QM
Scott, A.G. MS 18th Inf. Co.A
Scott, A.G. TN 10th (DeMoss') Cav. Co.A

Scott, A.G. TX 18th Inf. Co.D
Scott, A.H. AL 4th Inf. Surg.
Scott, A.H. AR Cav. Gordon's Regt. Co.E 1st
　　Lt.
Scott, A.H. NC 1st Inf. Co.G
Scott, A.H. TX 4th Inf. Surg.
Scott, A.H. Trans-MS Conf.Cav. 1st Bn. Co.A,C
Scott, A. Howard Gen. & Staff Surg.
Scott, A.J. AL 38th Inf. Co.G
Scott, A.J. AR 1st (Dobbin's) Cav. Co.H
Scott, A.J. AR 14th (Powers') Inf. Co.A 2nd Lt.
Scott, A.J. AR 32nd Inf. Co.K Cpl.
Scott, A.J. AR 34th Inf. Co.E
Scott, A.J. AR 38th Inf. Co.C 1st Lt.
Scott, A.J. LA 2nd Inf. Co.H
Scott, A.J. LA 22nd Inf. Co.D
Scott, A.J. MS 2nd Part.Rangers Co.K
Scott, A.J. MS 28th Cav. Co.F
Scott, A.J. MS 15th Inf. Co.D
Scott, A.J. TN 41st Inf. Co.E
Scott, A.J. TX 3rd Cav. Co.A
Scott, A.J. TX 28th Cav. Co.D
Scott, A.J. Conf.Cav. Wood's Regt. Co.B
Scott, A.J. Brush Bn.
Scott, A.K. GA 19th Inf. Co.K
Scott, A.L. AL 9th Inf. Co.G,L
Scott, A.L. KY 12th Cav. Co.D
Scott, A.L. TN 3rd (Clack's) Inf. Co.F
Scott, A.L. TN 12th (Cons.) Inf. Co.F
Scott, A.L. TN 22nd Inf. Co.D
Scott, A.L. VA 10th Cav. Co.F,E Capt.
Scott, Albert A. VA 16th Inf. Co.C
Scott, Albert H. VA 14th Inf. Co.B
Scott, Albert J. VA 6th Bn.Res. Co.B
Scott, Albert S. VA 14th Inf. Co.A
Scott, Albert V. AL 44th Inf. Co.C
Scott, Alex NC 15th Inf. Co.F
Scott, Alex TN 8th Inf. Co.C
Scott, Alex TN 25th Inf. Co.C
Scott, Alex 20th Conf.Cav. Co.F
Scott, Alex 1st Cherokee Mtd.Rifles Co.E
Scott, Alexander AL 22nd Inf. Co.H
Scott, Alexander GA 31st Inf. Co.B
Scott, Alexander LA 10th Inf. Co.A Fifer
Scott, Alexander MS 15th Inf. Co.B
Scott, Alexander MO 10th Cav. Co.I
Scott, Alexander MO 2nd Inf. Co.H
Scott, Alexander MO 16th Inf.
Scott, Alexander SC Lt.Arty. 3rd (Palmetto) Bn.
　　Co.F
Scott, Alexander VA Inf. 1st Bn.Loc.Def. Co.D
Scott, Alexander C. GA Cav. 2nd Bn. Co.D
Scott, Alexander C. MS Lt.Arty. (Madison
　　Lt.Arty.) Richards' Co.
Scott, Alexander E. TX 27th Cav. Co.I
Scott, Alexander F. AL 3rd Bn.Res. Co.B
Scott, Alexander F. GA 51st Inf. Co.K
Scott, Alexander J. TX 1st Inf. Co.L
Scott, Alfred A. MS 18th Inf. Co.G
Scott, Alfred D. GA Cobb's Legion Co.I
Scott, Alfred H. LA 4th Inf. Co.C 2nd Lt.
Scott, Alfred M. MS Cav. 1st Bn. (Miller's)
　　Cole's Co.
Scott, Alfred N. FL 1st Inf. Old Co.D
Scott, Alfred W. AL 24th Inf. Co.G
Scott, Alfred W. NC Inf. 2nd Bn. Co.D Cpl.
Scott, Allan SC 1st Bn.S.S. Co.C Cook

Scott, Allen FL 1st Inf. Old Co.A,B
Scott, Allen FL 5th Inf. Co.C
Scott, Allen NC 22nd Inf. Co.L Cpl.
Scott, Allen SC Inf. 6th Bn. Co.A
Scott, Allen SC 26th Inf. Co.C
Scott, Allen SC 27th Inf. Co.G Cook
Scott, Allen SC Manigault's Bn.Vol. Co.D
Scott, Allen TN 15th Cav.
Scott, Allison NC 52nd Inf. Co.A
Scott, Almanzer U. MS 36th Inf. Co.A Sgt.
Scott, Alney 1st Conf.Cav. 2nd Co.A
Scott, Alonzo D. GA Inf. 10th Bn. Co.C
Scott, Alpheus A. AL 33rd Inf. Co.C Sgt.
Scott, Alx GA 4th (Clinch's) Cav. Co.D
Scott, A.M. AR Inf. Cocke's Regt. Co.C
Scott, A.M. FL 2nd Cav. Co.D
Scott, A.M. FL Cav. 5th Bn. Co.C QMSgt.
Scott, A.M. MS 1st Cav. Co.K
Scott, A.M. NC 4th Sr.Res. Co.D
Scott, A.M. TN 8th Inf. Co.B
Scott, A.M. TX 9th (Young's) Inf. Co.A
Scott, A.M. TX 9th (Young's) Inf. Co.G
Scott, Amos B. GA 31st Inf. Co.B
Scott, A.N. LA Mil. 1st Regt. 2nd Brig. 1st Div.
　　Co.B
Scott, Anderson AL 19th Inf. Co.K
Scott, Anderson AL 32nd Inf. Co.H
Scott, Anderson AL Cp. of Instr. Talladega
Scott, Anderson AR 3rd Inf. Co.I,C
Scott, Anderson TX 14th Inf. Co.C
Scott, Andrew FL 1st Cav. Co.A
Scott, Andrew NC Lt.Arty. 13th Bn. Co.A
Scott, Andrew TN 44th Inf. Co.E
Scott, Andrew TN 44th (Cons.) Inf. Co.B
Scott, Andrew VA Lt.Arty. 12th Bn. Co.D
Scott, Andrew A. TX 8th Inf. Co.F
Scott, Andrew D. SC 1st (McCreary's) Inf. Co.E
Scott, Andrew G. VA 27th Inf. Co.D
Scott, Andrew G. Gen. & Staff Maj.,QM
Scott, Andrew H. AR Cav. 1st Bn. (Stirman's)
　　Co.A
Scott, Andrew J. AL 9th Inf. Co.D Cpl.
Scott, Andrew J. AR 4th Inf. Co.F
Scott, Andrew J. GA 11th Cav. Co.H
Scott, Andrew J. GA Lt.Arty. Fraser's Btty.
Scott, Andrew J. GA 10th Inf. 1st Co.K
Scott, Andrew J. TN 48th (Nixon's) Inf. Co.G
Scott, Andrew J. VA 37th Inf. Co.K
Scott, Andrew P. VA 29th Inf. Co.B
Scott, Andrew T. GA Phillips' Legion Co.C
Scott, Andrew V. VA 23rd Inf. Co.C Capt.
Scott, Andrew W. MS 32nd Inf. Co.E
Scott, Angus GA 25th Inf. Co.E
Scott, A.O. AR 3rd Cav. Co.H Sgt.
Scott, A.P. GA Inf. 8th Bn. Co.C
Scott, A.P. MS 38th Cav. Co.H
Scott, A.P. MO 6th Cav. Co.E Sgt.
Scott, A.P. MO 16th Inf. Co.K
Scott, A.P. TN 21st Inf. Co.H
Scott, A.P. VA 6th Bn.Res. Co.A
Scott, A.Q. SC 1st Arty. Co.B
Scott, A.Q. SC 1st (McCreary's) Inf. Co.E
Scott, Archibald LA Arty. Green's Co. (LA
　　Guard Btty.)
Scott, Archibald LA Inf. 1st Sp.Bn. (Wheat's)
　　Co.B
Scott, Archibald SC 6th Cav. Co.A,D

Scott, Archibald W. LA 1st Hvy.Arty. (Reg.) Co.A
Scott, Armistead VA Conscr. Cp.Lee
Scott, Arnold B. NC 2nd Inf. Co.D
Scott, Arthur M. AR 15th (Josey's) Inf. Co.C
Scott, A.S. AR 8th Inf. Co.K
Scott, A.S. VA 18th Cav. 2nd Co.E Capt.
Scott, A.S. Gen. & Staff 1st Lt.,Adj.
Scott, Asa VA 5th Cav. Co.C
Scott, Asa VA Inf. 4th Bn.Loc.Def. Co.E
Scott, Asa VA 50th Inf. Co.K 2nd Lt.
Scott, Asa C. GA Phillips' Legion Co.D,C
Scott, Asa J. GA Inf. 4th Bn. (St.Guards) Co.A
Scott, Asa O. GA 11th Cav. Co.H
Scott, Asbury TN 25th Inf. Co.K
Scott, Asbury A. AL 6th Inf. Co.L 1st Lt.
Scott, Ashly W. TX 18th Cav. Co.K
Scott, A.U. MS 38th Cav. Co.F
Scott, Augustus F. TN 44th Inf. Co.H Cpl.
Scott, Augustus F. TN 44th (Cons.) Inf. Co.D
Scott, Aurelius NC 2nd Cav. (19th St.Troops) Co.C
Scott, Auville L. VA 28th Inf. Co.G
Scott, A.W. GA 43rd Inf. Co.F
Scott, A.W. MS 3rd Inf. (A. of 10,000) Co.G
Scott, A.W. NC 5th Cav. (63rd St.Troops) Co.I Cpl.
Scott, A.W. TN 10th (DeMoss') Cav. Co.A Sgt.
Scott, A. Winfield SC 15th Inf. Co.G
Scott, B. FL 10th Cav.
Scott, B. FL 5th Inf.
Scott, B. MO 10th Inf. Co.A
Scott, B. NC 67th Inf. Co.C
Scott, B.A. TX 1st Hvy.Arty. Co.A
Scott, B.A. TX 9th (Young's) Inf. Co.I
Scott, Barney J. AR 7th Inf. Co.C
Scott, B.B. KY 7th Cav. Co.C
Scott, B.B. KY 9th Cav. Co.A
Scott, B.C. AL 7th Inf. Co.E
Scott, B.C. GA QM Agent (Citizen Soldier)
Scott, B.C. LA 17th Inf. Co.A
Scott, B.C. MS Bradford's Co. (Conf.Guards Arty.)
Scott, Ben, Sr. TX Inf. Yarbrough's Co. (Smith Cty.Lt.Inf.)
Scott, Ben B. Morgan's Div. Asst.Surg.
Scott, Benagy NC 2nd Jr.Res. Co.H
Scott, Benjamin AL 44th Inf. Co.F
Scott, Benjamin AR 1st (Colquitt's) Inf. Co.C
Scott, Benjamin AR 8th Inf. New Co.B
Scott, Benjamin GA 26th Inf. Co.G
Scott, Benjamin MO 1st Cav.
Scott, Benjamin MO Robertson's Regt.St.Guard Co.12
Scott, Benjamin NC 3rd Cav. (41st St.Troops) Co.H
Scott, Benjamin SC 4th St.Troops Co.F
Scott, Benjamin SC Inf. 9th Bn. Co.C
Scott, Benjamin SC 26th Inf. Co.D
Scott, Benjamin B. KY 4th Mtd.Inf. Co.F
Scott, Benjamin D. VA 58th Inf. Co.A Cpl.
Scott, Benjamin F. AR 1st (Colquitt's) Inf. Co.E
Scott, Benjamin F. KY 4th Mtd.Inf. Co.H
Scott, Benjamin F. MS 2nd Part.Rangers Co.K,H
Scott, Benjamin F. MO Cav. 3rd Bn. Co.D
Scott, Benjamin F. SC 1st Mtd.Mil. Fripp's Co. Cpl.

Scott, Benjamin F. TN 32nd Inf. Co.C
Scott, Benjamin F. TX 6th Cav. Co.I
Scott, Benjamin F. 1st Conf.Inf. 2nd Co.F
Scott, Benjamin H. NC 35th Inf. Co.A
Scott, Benjamin I. VA 18th Inf. Co.G
Scott, Benjamin L. AL Inf. 1st Regt. Co.K
Scott, Benjamin L. NC 52nd Inf. Co.B
Scott, Benjamin M. AR Lt.Arty. 5th Btty. Cpl.
Scott, Benjamin M. GA 24th Inf. Co.B
Scott, Benjamin P. TN 33rd Inf. Co.D
Scott, Benjamin R. SC Lt.Arty. Parker's Co. (Marion Arty.)
Scott, Benjamin S. GA 45th Inf. Co.B Sgt.
Scott, Benjamin W. AL 38th Inf. Co.F
Scott, Benjamin W. NC Snead's Co. (Loc.Def.)
Scott, Benjamin W. VA 57th Inf. Co.G Cpl.
Scott, Benjamin Y. MS 41st Inf. Co.G
Scott, Ben M. AR 3rd Cav. Co.H Sgt.
Scott, Berry AR 2nd Cav. 1st Co.A
Scott, Berry B. SC Palmetto S.S. Co.K,M
Scott, Beverly D. LA 28th (Gray's) Inf. Co.C
Scott, Beverly S. VA 34th Inf. Co.K
Scott, B.F. AL 14th Inf. Co.G
Scott, B.F. AL 22nd Inf. Co.D
Scott, B.F. AR Stirman's S.S. Co.I,CSA
Scott, B.F. GA 1st (Symons') Res. Co.C Cpl.
Scott, B.F. GA 5th Inf. Co.E Sgt.
Scott, B.F. GA 6th Res. Co.A
Scott, B.F. GA Phillips' Legion Co.D
Scott, B.F. LA 2nd Cav. Co.G Sgt.
Scott, B.F. NC 28th Inf. Co.K
Scott, B.F. SC 3rd Cav. Co.H Sgt.
Scott, B.F. SC 6th Inf. 2nd Co.K Sgt.
Scott, B.F. SC 9th Inf. Co.D
Scott, B.F. SC 20th Inf. Co.G
Scott, B.F. TN 63rd Inf. Co.E
Scott, B.F. TX 12th Inf. Co.C 2nd Lt.
Scott, B.F. 14th Conf.Cav. Co.I
Scott, B.H. GA 45th Inf. Co.B
Scott, B.H. TN 3rd (Forrest's) Cav. Co.C
Scott, B.H. TX 3rd Cav. Co.A
Scott, Bill 1st Cherokee Mtd.Vol. 2nd Co.C
Scott, Billy 1st Creek Mtd.Vol. 2nd Co.D
Scott, B.K. TN 5th Inf. 2nd Co.I Cpl.
Scott, B.L. AR 3rd Cav. 3rd Co.E
Scott, B.L. GA 7th Cav. Co.D
Scott, B.L. GA Cav. 24th Bn. Co.C
Scott, B.L. NC 55th Inf. Co.A
Scott, Boston VA 22nd Cav. Co.H
Scott, Bowland C. MS 2nd Inf. Co.I
Scott, B.R. TN 22nd Inf. Co.D
Scott, Brantly R. MS 24th Inf. Co.F
Scott, B.S. AL 37th Inf. Co.F 1st Lt.
Scott, B.S. AR 2nd Inf. Co.A
Scott, B.S. AR 3rd Inf. Co.E
Scott, B.S. AR Inf. Cocke's Regt. Co.C Color-bearer
Scott, B.S. NC 52nd Inf. Co.B
Scott, B.S. TX 1st Hvy.Arty. 2nd Co.A
Scott, B.S. TX 15th Inf. 1st Co.E
Scott, B.T. TN 10th (DeMoss') Cav. Co.A 1st Sgt.
Scott, Burgess H. KY 2nd (Woodward's) Cav. Co.E,A
Scott, B.W. GA Cav. 19th Bn. Co.A
Scott, B.W. TN 1st (Carter's) Cav. Co.B Far.

Scott, B.W. TN 1st (Feild's) & 27th Inf. (Cons.) Co.I
Scott, B.W. 10th Conf.Cav. Co.F
Scott, B.Y. MS 9th Bn.S.S. Co.C
Scott, C. AL 48th Inf. Co.E
Scott, C. LA 27th Inf. Co.G
Scott, C.A. FL 1st (Res.) Inf. Co.F
Scott, C.A. 3rd Conf.Eng.Troops Co.B Artif.
Scott, C.A. Eng.Dept. Polk's Corps A. of TN Sap. & Min. Co.,CSA
Scott, Caleb W. TN Cav. 9th Bn. (Gantt's) Co.E,F
Scott, Calhoun MS 21st Inf. Co.D Sgt.
Scott, Calhoun MS 22nd Inf. Co.I
Scott, Calvin AL 48th Inf. Co.C
Scott, Calvin AR 1st (Monroe's) Cav. Co.C Sgt.
Scott, Calvin NC 28th Inf. Co.G 2nd Lt.
Scott, Campbell VA 37th Inf. Co.B
Scott, Capers SC 1st (Hagood's) Inf. 1st Co.G, 2nd Co.E
Scott, Capers SC 18th Inf. Co.F
Scott, Carr. B. VA Hvy.Arty. 18th Bn. Co.A
Scott, C.B. AL 33rd Inf. Co.E 1st Sgt.
Scott, C.B. LA Inf. 4th Bn. Co.A
Scott, C.B. TN 24th Bn.S.S. Co.A
Scott, C.B. TN Inf. 154th Sr.Regt. 2nd Co.B
Scott, C.C. GA 1st (Symons') Res. Co.C,H
Scott, C.C. MS 9th Inf. Co.G
Scott, C.C. MS 10th Inf. New Co.A
Scott, C.C. MO Inf. Perkins' Bn. Co.D
Scott, C.C. TX Cav. Baird's Regt. Co.E
Scott, C.C. TX Cav. Bourland's Regt. Co.D
Scott, C.E. VA 60th Inf. Co.I
Scott, C.H. AL Arty. 1st Bn. Co.F
Scott, C.H. MO 12th Cav. Co.G
Scott, C.H. VA 15th Cav. Co.A
Scott, Charles AL 43rd Inf. Co.G
Scott, Charles AL 47th Inf. Co.I
Scott, Charles KY 4th Cav. Co.B
Scott, Charles KY Lt.Arty. Cobb's Co.
Scott, Charles MS 2nd Part. Co.A
Scott, Charles MS 28th Cav. Co.D
Scott, Charles MS Lt.Arty. (Issaquena Arty.) Graves' Co. Sgt.
Scott, Charles MO 5th Cav. Co.B
Scott, Chas. MO 1st Inf. 2nd Co.A
Scott, Charles SC 5th St.Troops Co.M
Scott, Charles TN 2nd (Walker's) Inf. Co.C Cpl.
Scott, Charles TN 4th Inf. Co.I
Scott, Charles TN 10th Inf.
Scott, Charles TN 19th Inf. Co.I
Scott, Charles TN 24th Inf. Co.F Cpl.
Scott, Charles TN 34th Inf. Co.I
Scott, Charles TN 35th Inf. 3rd Co.F
Scott, Charles TX Cav. Morgan's Regt. Co.B
Scott, Charles VA Cav. 39th Bn. Co.D
Scott, Charles VA Lt.Arty. R.M. Anderson's Co.
Scott, Charles VA Lt.Arty. Cayce's Co.
Scott, Charles VA 3rd Res. Co.G,E
Scott, Charles VA 20th Inf. Co.G
Scott, Charles VA Inf. 25th Bn. Co.E
Scott, Charles VA 38th Inf. Co.H 2nd Lt.
Scott, Charles VA 51st Inf. Co.A
Scott, Charles A. MD 1st Inf. Co.C
Scott, Charles A. MD Westons' Bn. Co.A
Scott, Charles A. NC 4th Cav. (59th St.Troops) Co.D Ord.Sgt.

Scott, Charles A. NC Vol. Lawrence's Co.
Scott, Charles A. TN 4th Inf. Co.E
Scott, Charles A. VA 4th Cav. Co.K
Scott, Charles A., Jr. VA 19th Inf. Co.D
Scott, Charles A. VA 52nd Inf. Co.E
Scott, Charles A. 7th Conf.Cav. 1st Co.I, Co.H
Scott, Charles B. KY Cav. Buckner Guards
Scott, Charles B. MS Lt.Arty. (Jefferson Arty.)
  Darden's Co.
Scott, Charles C. VA 23rd Inf. Co.B Capt.
Scott, Charles C. VA 34th Inf. Co.F
Scott, Charles D. Conf.Inf. 8th Bn. Co.A
Scott, Charles G. VA 54th Mil. Co.B
Scott, Charles H. AL 53rd (Part.Rangers) Co.K
  Sgt.
Scott, Charles H. AL 31st Inf. Co.I 2nd Lt.
Scott, Charles H. GA 20th Inf. Co.B
Scott, Charles H. VA 5th (Cons.) Cav.
Scott, Charles H. VA 40th Inf. Co.D
Scott, Charles Hay VA Lt.Arty. Pollock's Co.
Scott, Charles J. GA 3rd Cav. (St.Guards) Co.G
  Cpl.
Scott, Charles J. GA 11th Cav. Co.A Sgt.
Scott, Charles L. AL 4th Inf. Maj.
Scott, Charles L. Gen. & Staff, Cav. Col.
Scott, Charles P. TX 8th Inf. Co.E
Scott, Charles R. MS 2nd Inf. Co.I
Scott, Charles R. TX 7th Cav. Co.A
Scott, Charles R.L. MO Cav. Williams' Regt.
  Co.F
Scott, Charles S. TN 3rd (Clack's) Inf. Co.E
  Cpl.
Scott, Charles T. VA 45th Inf. Co.K
Scott, Charles W. AL Inf. 1st Regt. Co.K
Scott, Charles W. FL 10th Inf. Co.K
Scott, Charles W. SC 5th Inf. 1st Co.E Capt.
Scott, Charles W. SC 5th Inf. 2nd Co.H
Scott, Charles W. SC 7th Res. Co.E Capt.
Scott, Charles W. VA Inf. 23rd Bn. Co.F
Scott, Charles W. VA 63rd Inf. Co.K
Scott, Charley MO 1st Inf. 2nd Co.A
Scott, Charley NC Bass' Co.
Scott, Christopher C. AR Lt.Arty. 5th Btty.
  Capt.
Scott, Christopher C. AR 1st (Colquitt's) Inf.
  Co.C
Scott, C.L. KY 1st Inf. Co.F
Scott, Clark SC 7th Inf. 1st Co.C
Scott, Clifton TX 20th Inf. Co.G
Scott, C.M. KY 10th (Johnson's) Cav. Co.A
Scott, C.M. MD Cav. 2nd Bn. 1st Sgt.
Scott, Cooper B. SC 1st (Butler's) Inf. Co.G
Scott, Crockett TN Cav. Newsom's Regt. Co.B
Scott, Crockett VA 8th Cav. Co.I
Scott, Crockett VA 22nd Inf. Co.D
Scott, C.T. MO Cav. 1st Regt.St.Guard Co.A
Scott, C.T. MO 6th Cav. Co.H
Scott, C.T. VA Second Class Mil. Wolff's Co.
Scott, C.W. AR 18th Inf. Co.K
Scott, C.W. FL Inf. 2nd Bn. Co.D
Scott, C.W. MS 1st (King's) Inf. (St.Troops)
  Co.F
Scott, C.W. SC 3rd Bn.Res. Co.A 1st Lt.
Scott, C.W. SC 5th St.Troops Co.M Sgt.
Scott, C.W. TX 8th Cav.
Scott, C.W. Exch.Bn. 3rd Co.B,CSA
Scott, C.Y. VA 48th Inf. Co.K

Scott, D. AL 59th Inf. Co.E
Scott, D. LA 22nd Inf. Co.C
Scott, D. MO Lt.Arty. Von Phul's Co.
Scott, D. NC 3rd Jr.Res. Co.A
Scott, D. TX Cav. 3rd (Yager's) Bn. Co.B
Scott, D.A. NC 4th Home Guards Co.K
Scott, D.A. TN 13th (Gore's) Cav. Co.B
Scott, Dangerfield VA Cav. 15th Bn. Co.D
Scott, Dangerfield VA 41st Mil. Co.B
Scott, Daniel GA Siege Arty. 28th Bn. Co.B
Scott, Daniel GA 6th Mil. Co.B
Scott, Daniel GA 8th Inf. (St.Guards) Co.G
  Jr.2nd Lt.
Scott, Daniel GA 42nd Inf. Co.F
Scott, Daniel KY 4th Cav. Co.G
Scott, Daniel KY 8th Cav. Co.I
Scott, Daniel SC 2nd Rifles Co.L
Scott, Daniel SC 8th Bn.Res. Co.A
Scott, Daniel D. VA 60th Inf. Co.E
Scott, Daniel G. AR 1st Mtd.Rifles Co.I
Scott, Daniel H. MS 23rd Inf. Co.H
Scott, Daniel L. MO 3rd Cav. Co.I 2nd Lt.
Scott, Daniel P. AL 19th Inf. Co.A Cpl.
Scott, Daniel W. TN 49th Inf. Co.A
Scott, Daniel W. Inf. Bailey's Cons.Regt. Co.G
Scott, David AL 6th Cav. Co.A
Scott, David AL 2nd Inf. Lt.
Scott, David AL 12th Inf. Co.I
Scott, David AL 43rd Inf. Co.G
Scott, David FL 9th Inf. Co.E
Scott, David FL 10th Inf.
Scott, David KY 1st (Helm's) Cav. Old Co.G
Scott, David MO Cav. 3rd Regt.St.Guard Co.B
Scott, David MO Inf. 4th Regt.St.Guard Co.A
Scott, David MO Inf. 8th Bn. Co.B
Scott, David MO 9th Inf. Co.F Jr.2nd Lt.
Scott, David NC 1st Inf. (6 mo. '61) Co.H
Scott, David NC 4th Bn.Jr.Res. Co.A
Scott, David, Jr. NC 53rd Inf. Co.D Capt.
Scott, David TN 1st (Feild's) Inf. Co.H
Scott, David TN 4th Inf.
Scott, David TN 8th Inf. Co.F
Scott, David TN 34th Inf. Co.I
Scott, David VA 6th Cav. Co.B
Scott, David VA Mil. Wythe Cty.
Scott, David 4th Conf.Inf. Co.F
Scott, David Brush Bn.
Scott, David A. VA 50th Inf. Co.C
Scott, David B. AL 4th Inf. Co.G 2nd Lt.
Scott, David B. SC Cav.Bn. Holcombe Legion
  Co.E
Scott, David C. TN 3rd (Clack's) Inf. Co.E
Scott, David J. NC 24th Inf. Co.B
Scott, David J. TX 22nd Cav. Co.E
Scott, David M. AL 62nd Inf. Co.A,K Sgt.
Scott, David M. MO 3rd Cav. Co.I,F Sgt.
Scott, David Mc. AL Mil. 4th Vol. Co.C
Scott, David P. MS 34th Inf. Co.A
Scott, David R. AL 6th Cav. Co.E Cpl.
Scott, David W. FL 1st Cav. Co.F Sgt.
Scott, David W. FL 5th Inf. Co.A
Scott, David W. TX 26th Cav. 2nd Co.G
Scott, David W. VA 3rd Cav. Co.C
Scott, David W.J. 4th Conf.Inf. Co.D
Scott, D.B. SC 7th Cav. Co.H
Scott, D.C. NC 5th Cav. (63rd St.Troops) Co.I
Scott, D.D. AR 1st (Monroe's) Cav. Co.K

Scott, D.E. AL 15th Bn.Part.Rangers Co.E
Scott, D.E. AL 31st Inf. Co.H Cpl.
Scott, D.E. FL Cav. 3rd Bn. Co.C
Scott, D.E. 15th Conf.Cav. Co.E
Scott, Demetrius TX 1st (Yager's) Cav. Co.B
Scott, Dennis TN 63rd Inf. Co.G
Scott, D.L. AR 2nd Mtd.Rifles Co.H
Scott, D.L. AR 15th (N.W.) Inf. Emergency Co.I
Scott, D.M. AR 15th (N.W.) Inf. Emergency
  Co.I
Scott, D.M.C. AL 1st Bn.Cadets Sgt.
Scott, D.R. TN 12th (Cons.) Inf. Co.F
Scott, Dren (Col'd) TN 50th Inf. Co.B Serv.
Scott, Duncan KY 2nd Mtd.Inf. Co.F
Scott, Duncan Morgan's Co.E,CSA Sgt.
Scott, Dunlop GA 8th Inf. Co.E Capt.
Scott, Dustin MO 10th Inf. Co.B
Scott, D.W. TX 28th Cav. 2nd Co.G
Scott, E. AL Cav. Hardie's Bn.Res. Co.A
Scott, E. AL Talladega Cty.Res. B. Stuart's Co.
Scott, E. SC Mil. 16th Regt. Triest's Co.
Scott, E. VA 7th Cav. Co.B
Scott, E.A. AL Inf. 2nd Regt. Co.C 1st Lt.
Scott, E.A. AR 26th Inf. Co.G
Scott, E.A. LA 3rd (Wingfield's) Cav. Co.I
  Maj.
Scott, E.A. MO 11th Inf. Co.D
Scott, E.B. SC 1st Mtd.Mil. Scott's Co. Capt.
Scott, E.B. SC 6th Inf. 2nd Co.K 2nd Lt.
Scott, E.B. SC 9th Inf. Co.D
Scott, E.B. VA 1st (Farinholt's) Res. Co.I Sgt.
Scott, Ebenezer T. AL 3rd Cav. Co.G
Scott, E.C. VA 1st (Farinholt's) Res. Co.K
Scott, E.D. TN 35th Inf. Co.B, 1st Co.D
Scott, Eddie M. MS 18th Inf. Co.K
Scott, Edgar VA Hvy.Arty. 18th Bn. Co.E
Scott, Edley TN 28th (Cons.) Inf. Co.F
Scott, Edmund G. FL 3rd Inf. Co.H
Scott, Edouard LA Conscr.
Scott, Edward FL 3rd Inf. Co.A
Scott, Edward NC 22nd Inf. Co.G Capt.
Scott, Edward TX 1st Hvy.Arty. 2nd Co.F
Scott, Edward TX 2nd Inf. Odlum's Co.
Scott, Edward, Jr. VA 4th Cav. Co.E
Scott, Edward, Sr. VA 4th Cav. Co.E
Scott, Edward 1st Cherokee Mtd.Rifles Co.E
Scott, Edward A. VA 3rd Cav. Co.K
Scott, Edward H. MO 6th Inf. Co.G Sgt.
Scott, Edward H. NC 24th Inf. Co.B Sgt.
Scott, Edward M. NC 1st Inf. Co.D Capt.
Scott, Edward P. VA Hvy.Arty. Epes' Co.
Scott, Edward P., Jr. VA 12th Inf. Co.F Capt.
Scott, Edward S. VA 3rd Cav. Co.E
Scott, Edward S. VA Lt.Arty. Jeffress' Co.
Scott, Edward T. FL 1st Inf. Old Co.A, New
  Co.B
Scott, Edward W. MS 21st Inf. Co.H Cpl.
Scott, Edward W. SC 1st (McCreary's) Inf. Co.C
Scott, Edwin A. LA Mil.Cav. Norwood's Co.
  (Jeff Davis Rangers) 1st Lt.
Scott, Edwin W. VA 41st Inf. Co.C
Scott, E.F. MO Cav. Wood's Regt. Co.I Sgt.
Scott, E.F. TN 48th (Voorhies') Inf. Co.F
Scott, E.H. MS 35th Inf. Co.B
Scott, E.H. MO Cav. Woodson's Co. 1st Lt.
Scott, E.I. TN 17th Cav. Co.E
Scott, E.L. TN 18th (Newsom's) Cav. Co.C

Scott, E.L. TX 2nd Inf. Co.F
Scott, Elbert TX Cav. Martin's Regt. Co.C
Scott, Eli MS 18th Cav. Co.F Cpl.
Scott, Eli SC 3rd St.Troops Co.B
Scott, Eli M. MS 41st Inf. Co.G
Scott, Eli M. MS 42nd Inf. Co.B
Scott, Eli P. TN 21st Cav. Co.A
Scott, Elias MO 6th Cav. Co.H
Scott, Elihu P. GA 40th Inf. Co.C Cpl.
Scott, Elijah NC 45th Inf. Co.E
Scott, Elijah NC 48th Inf. Co.H
Scott, Elijah TN 61st Mtd.Inf. Co.C
Scott, Elisha NC 55th Inf. Co.A
Scott, Elisha SC 3rd Bn.Res. Co.B
Scott, Elisha SC 6th Res. Co.I
Scott, Elisha TN 43rd Inf. Co.F
Scott, Elisha G. VA 2nd Cav. Co.B Sgt.
Scott, Elisha H. TN 4th (McLemore's) Cav. Co.A
Scott, Elisha L. NC Inf. Thomas Legion Co.C
Scott, E.M. LA Mil. Orleans Fire Regt. Hall's Co.
Scott, E.M. SC 1st Mtd.Mil. Earnest's Co.
Scott, E.M. SC 5th Cav. Co.G
Scott, E.M. SC Cav. 17th Bn. Co.B
Scott, E.M. TN 4th (McLemore's) Cav. Co.K
Scott, E.M. Adam's Staff 1st Lt.,ADC
Scott, Emmet R. MS 40th Inf. Co.B
Scott, Emmett B. LS 1st Cav. Co.K 2nd Lt.
Scott, Emory F. AL 3rd Inf. Co.C
Scott, Emsley NC 6th Sr.Res. Co.B
Scott, Enoch A. GA 31st Inf. Co.B
Scott, Enoch P. NC 22nd Inf. Co.M
Scott, E.P. TN 45th Inf. Co.D
Scott, E.P. Loc.Def. Scott's Co. Capt.
Scott, E.P. Gen. & Staff, A. of N.VA Capt.,AQM
Scott, E.R. MS Inf. 1st Bn.St.Troops (30 days '64) Co.G
Scott, Erastus N. TX 18th Cav. Co.F
Scott, Erastus W. AR 10th Inf. Co.F
Scott, Ervin MO 9th (Elliott's) Cav. Co.H
Scott, Eugene GA Inf. 27th Bn. Co.D
Scott, Evans W. SC Lt.Arty. Parker's Co. (Marion Arty.)
Scott, E.W. AR 32nd Inf. Co.K
Scott, E.W. MS 1st Lt.Arty.
Scott, E. William VA 10th Cav. Co.D Cpl.
Scott, Ezekiel MO Cav. Wood's Regt. Co.I
Scott, F. GA 4th (Clinch's) Cav. Co.D
Scott, F. KY 2nd (Duke's) Cav. Co.B
Scott, F. MO Cav. 6th Regt.St.Guard Co.G 3rd Lt.
Scott, F. VA 60th Inf. Co.A
Scott, F.A. KY Corbin's Men
Scott, F.A. MO Quantrill's Co. Sgt.
Scott, F.B. MO Cav. Freeman's Regt. Co.F
Scott, F.B. MO 1st & 4th Cons.Inf. Co.C
Scott, F.B. MO 4th Inf. Co.C
Scott, F.C. VA Burks' Regt.Loc.Def.
Scott, F. Calaway GA Phillips' Legion Co.O,C Sgt.
Scott, F.D. TX 2nd Inf. Co.C
Scott, Felix W. TX 14th Cav. Co.I
Scott, Fernandes VA 14th Cav. 1st Co.F
Scott, Fernando VA Cav. 36th Bn. Co.E Cpl.
Scott, F.G. TX 21st Inf. Co.E

Scott, F.J. SC 1st Inf. Co.A
Scott, F.L. TX 3rd Cav. Co.D 2nd Lt.
Scott, F.L. TX Cav. Bourland's Regt. Co.H,K
Scott, F.L. Brush Bn.
Scott, Floyd VA 22nd Cav. Co.C
Scott, F.M. GA 4th (Clinch's) Cav. Co.C
Scott, F.M. MS 3rd Inf. (A. of 10,000) Co.G
Scott, F.M. MO 12th Cav. Co.E Capt.
Scott, F.M. NC 5th Cav. (63rd St.Troops) Co.I
Scott, F.M. TN 2nd (Ashby's) Cav. Co.I
Scott, F.M., Jr. TX Cav. 1st Bn.St.Troops Co.D
Scott, F.M. TX 3rd Cav. Co.A
Scott, F.O. NC 2nd Jr.Res. Co.G
Scott, F.P. TN 22nd (Nixon's) Cav. Capt.
Scott, F.P. TN 3rd (Clack's) Inf. Co.K
Scott, F.R. MS Cav. Ham's Regt. Co.A
Scott, Francis LA 1st Hvy.Arty. (Reg.) Co.C Cpl.
Scott, Francis VA 60th Inf. Co.E
Scott, Francis VA 108th Mil. Co.F
Scott, Francis E. VA 48th Inf. Co.B 2nd Lt.
Scott, Francis F. VA 23rd Inf. Co.I
Scott, Francis H. VA 3rd Cav. Co.K Sgt.
Scott, Francis M. AR 15th (N.W.) Inf. Co.E
Scott, Francis M. GA 26th Inf. Atkinson's Co.B
Scott, Francis M. TX 19th Inf. Co.H
Scott, Francis Marion TN Cav. 4th Bn. (Branner's) Co.E
Scott, Francis P. GA 46th Inf. Co.C Cpl.
Scott, Francis W., Jr. VA 9th Cav. Co.B
Scott, Frank AL 8th Inf. Co.C
Scott, Frank KY 1st (Helm's) Cav. New Co.A
Scott, Frank KY Horse Arty. Byrne's Co.
Scott, Frank KY 4th Mtd.Inf. Co.D 1st Lt.
Scott, Frank NC 17th Inf. (2nd Org.) Co.I
Scott, Frank VA 4th Inf. Co.D
Scott, Frank VA 135th Mil. Co.C,I
Scott, Frank A. KY Jessee's Bn.Mtd.Riflemen Co.A
Scott, Frank Goode VA 2nd Cav. Co.G
Scott, Franklin LA 10th Inf. Co.B
Scott, Franklin NC 21st Inf. Co.A
Scott, Franklin TN 8th (Lillard's) Mtd.Inf. 1st Co.K
Scott, Franklin VA 6th Bn.Res. Co.D
Scott, Franklin J. NC 26th Inf. Co.E
Scott, Franklin L. TX 22nd Cav. Co.D Capt.
Scott, Franklin R. GA Lt.Arty. Fraser's Btty.
Scott, Fred SC Lt.Arty. 3rd (Palmetto) Bn. Co.F
Scott, Frederick LA 14th Inf. Co.F
Scott, Frederick SC 1st (Hagood's) Inf. 1st Co.G
Scott, Frederick J. SC Inf. 3rd Bn. Co.F
Scott, Frederick M. TN 54th Inf. Co.H
Scott, Frederick R. VA 12th Inf. Co.E
Scott, Fred R. Gen. & Staff, A. of N.VA Maj.,Comsy.Sub.
Scott, F.S. LA 1st Cav. Co.B
Scott, F.T. AR 11th Inf. Co.G Capt.
Scott, F.T. AR 11th & 17th Cons.Inf. Co.G Capt.
Scott, F.T. SC Lt.Arty. Garden's Co. (Palmetto Lt.Btty.)
Scott, F.T. SC 1st Bn.S.S. Co.A
Scott, F.T. SC 20th Inf. Co.G
Scott, F.T. SC 27th Inf. Co.E
Scott, F.T. VA Mtd.Guard 4th Congr.Dist.
Scott, F.T. VA 3rd (Archer's) Bn.Res. Co.D

Scott, Furman 4th Conf.Inf. Co.D
Scott, G. MS 28th Cav. Co.D
Scott, G.A. TN 11th (Holman's) Cav. Co.B
Scott, Garrett TX 4th Inf. Co.G
Scott, G. Boston VA 50th Inf. Co.K
Scott, G.C. AL 1st Regt.Home Guards
Scott, George AL 9th Inf. Co.A
Scott, George AL 24th Inf. Co.D
Scott, George AR 2nd Mtd.Rifles Co.A
Scott, George MD 1st Cav. Co.A
Scott, George MS Lt.Arty. (Madison Lt.Arty.) Richards' Co.
Scott, George MO 5th Cav. Co.A
Scott, George MO Inf. 1st Bn. Co.C
Scott, George MO 6th Inf. Co.K
Scott, George MO 10th Inf. Co.D
Scott, George SC 1st Arty. Co.D
Scott, George SC 1st Arty. Co.K
Scott, George SC 4th St.Troops Co.A
Scott, George TN 2nd (Ashby's) Cav. Co.B
Scott, George TN Cav. 5th Bn. (McClellan's) Co.C
Scott, George TN 7th (Duckworth's) Cav. Co.C
Scott, George TN 16th Inf. Co.F
Scott, George TN 50th Inf. Co.B Cpl.
Scott, George TX 17th Inf. Co.E 1st Lt.
Scott, George VA 3rd Res. Co.E
Scott, George VA 7th Bn.Res. Co.A
Scott, George VA 20th Inf. Co.E
Scott, George VA Inf. 26th Bn. Co.B
Scott, George VA 108th Mil. Co.C
Scott, Geo. Gen. & Staff, QM Dept. Capt.
Scott, George A.K. FL 10th Inf. Co.B
Scott, George C. KY 8th Cav. Co.B
Scott, George C. MS Lt.Arty. (Jefferson Arty.) Darden's Co.
Scott, George C. SC 15th Inf. Co.C
Scott, George C. Retributors Young's (5th) Co.
Scott, George D. Gen. & Staff Comsy.
Scott, George E. VA 58th Inf. Co.A
Scott, George F. MD Arty. 1st Btty. Cpl.
Scott, George H. SC 2nd Rifles Co.G
Scott, George H. TN 4th (McLemore's) Cav. Co.I
Scott, George J. AL 4th Res. Co.E
Scott, George J. AL 19th Inf. Co.A Sgt.
Scott, George J. TX 12th Inf. Co.D
Scott, George L. FL 2nd Inf. Co.E
Scott, George L. FL 9th Inf. Co.B
Scott, George L. TN 30th Inf. Co.F Ord.Sgt.
Scott, George L. TX Cav. Bourland's Regt. Surg.
Scott, George M. MS 22nd Inf. Co.I
Scott, George M. NC Inf. Thomas Legion Co.C
Scott, George M. TX 14th Field Btty
Scott, George M. TX 5th Inf. Co.C
Scott, George P. GA 20th Inf. Co.B
Scott, George R. GA Inf. 8th Bn. Co.E
Scott, George R. TN 38th Inf. Co.D 1st Lt.
Scott, George R. TX Cav. Ragsdale's Bn. Co.F
Scott, George S. AR 4th Inf. Co.F
Scott, George T. VA 1st Arty. Co.D
Scott, George T. VA Lt.Arty. 1st Bn. Co.D
Scott, George T. VA Arty. B.H. Smith's Co.
Scott, George T. Conf.Cav. Wood's Regt. Co.K
Scott, George V. TX 12th Inf. Co.F Sgt.

Scott, George V. VA Second Class Mil. Wolff's Co. 1st Lt.
Scott, George W. Gen. & Staff Surg.
Scott, George W. AR Cav. 6th Bn. Co.C
Scott, George W. FL Cav. 5th Bn. Lt.Col.
Scott, George W. FL 2nd Cav. Co.D Capt.
Scott, George W. GA 2nd Inf. Co.K Lt.
Scott, George W. GA 52nd Inf. Co.A
Scott, George W. KY 6th Mtd.Inf. Co.H
Scott, George W. LA Cav. Webb's Co.
Scott, George W. LA 12th Inf. Co.L Comsy.
Scott, George W. MS 38th Cav. Co.B
Scott, George W. MS 3rd Inf. Co.B
Scott, George W. MO 4th Cav. Co.I Lt.
Scott, George W. NC Cav. 12th Bn. Co.C
Scott, George W. NC Cav. 16th Bn. Co.G
Scott, George W. NC 1st Arty. (10th St.Troops) Co.G
Scott, George W. NC 13th Inf. Co.D
Scott, George W. NC 21st Inf. Co.A
Scott, George W. NC 33rd Inf. Co.C
Scott, George W. SC 3rd Cav. Co.E
Scott, George W. SC 7th Inf. Co.A Sgt.
Scott, George W. TN 4th Inf. Co.E
Scott, George W. TN 28th Inf. Co.C Cpl.
Scott, George W. TX 18th Cav. Co.B
Scott, George W. TX 25th Cav. Co.C
Scott, George W. TX 30th Cav. Co.G
Scott, George W. TX 1st Inf. Co.L
Scott, George W. TX 9th (Nichols') Inf. Co.K
Scott, George W. VA 4th Cav. Co.K
Scott, George W. VA 7th Cav. Co.I
Scott, George W. VA 9th Cav. Co.I
Scott, George W. VA 22nd Cav. Co.E
Scott, George W. VA 2nd Arty. Co.K
Scott, George W. VA Hvy.Arty. 18th Bn. Co.A
Scott, George W. VA Inf. 22nd Bn. Co.A
Scott, George W. VA 27th Inf. Co.D
Scott, George W. VA 30th Inf. Co.K
Scott, George W. VA 33rd Inf. Co.K
Scott, George W. VA 41st Inf. Co.A
Scott, George W. VA 45th Inf. Co.D
Scott, George W. VA 59th Inf. 2nd Co.A Sgt.
Scott, George W. VA 59th Inf. 3rd Co.F
Scott, George W. VA 60th Inf. 1st Co.H
Scott, George W. VA 136th Mil. Co.E
Scott, George W. 8th (Dearing's) Conf.Cav. Co.C
Scott, Geo. W. Gen. & Staff 1st Lt.,ADC
Scott, George W.F. MO Cav. Wood's Regt. Co.C
Scott, George Y. Conf.Cav. Wood's Regt. Co.K Sgt.
Scott, Geo. Y. Gen. & Staff 1st Lt.,ADC
Scott, G.H. TN Lt.Arty. Morton's Co.
Scott, G.H. TX 13th Vol. 2nd Co.B Cpl.
Scott, Gilberry M. FL 6th Inf. Co.F
Scott, Giles M. VA 20th Inf. Co.H
Scott, Giles M. VA 34th Inf. Co.F
Scott, G.J. TX 4th Inf. (St.Troops) Co.E
Scott, G.L. MS 5th Cav. Co.K
Scott, G.L. MS 18th Cav. Co.G
Scott, G.L. MS 33rd Inf. Co.D
Scott, G.M. TX 22nd Inf. Co.A
Scott, G.M. Gen. & Staff Hosp.Stew.
Scott, Golsborough TN Inf. 1st Bn. (Colms') Co.D
Scott, Govian MO 7th Cav. Co.F

Scott, G.R. KY 10th (Johnson's) Cav. Co.K
Scott, G.R. TN Inf. 3rd Cons.Regt. Co.B 1st Lt.
Scott, Grandison VA 6th Bn.Res. Co.I
Scott, Graves TX Cav. 1st Bn.St.Troops Co.F
Scott, Green KY 9th Mtd.Inf. Co.I
Scott, Green B. AR 14th (Powers') Inf. Co.A
Scott, Green B. GA Cherokee Legion (St.Guards) Co.B
Scott, Greenberry KY 5th Mtd.Inf. Co.I
Scott, Green M. GA Phillips' Legion Co.B,H
Scott, G.S. AL 46th Inf. Co.A
Scott, G.T. KY 7th Mtd.Inf. Co.K
Scott, Guigorard MS Arty. Byrne's Btty. Jr.1st Lt.
Scott, Gustavus AL Cav. (St.Res.) Young's Co.
Scott, Gustavus A. LA 1st Cav. Co.E Capt.
Scott, G.W. AL 5th Inf. New Co.H
Scott, G.W. AL 24th Inf. Co.K
Scott, G.W. AR 2nd Cav. 1st Co.A
Scott, G.W. AR 3rd Cav. 3rd Co.E
Scott, G.W. GA 12th (Wright's) Cav. (St.Guards) Stubb's Co.
Scott, G.W. GA 3rd Res. Co.C 1st Sgt.
Scott, G.W. GA 18th Inf. Co.K
Scott, G.W. LA Cav. Montgomery's Co.
Scott, G.W. LA Inf. McLean's Co.
Scott, G.W. MS 1st Lt.Arty. Co.I
Scott, G.W. MS 27th Inf. Co.F Sgt.
Scott, G.W. MS 44th Inf. Co.G,I
Scott, G.W. MO Cav. Snider's Bn. Co.E Sgt.
Scott, G.W. MO Cav. Williams' Regt. Co.B Cpl.
Scott, G.W. MO 10th Inf. Co.B
Scott, G.W. MO 11th Inf. Co.F
Scott, G.W. NC 31st Inf. Co.E
Scott, G.W. SC 5th Cav. Co.B Cpl.
Scott, G.W. SC Cav. 17th Bn. Co.C
Scott, G.W. SC Inf. Holcombe Legion Co.I
Scott, G.W. TN Arty. Stewart's Co.
Scott, G.W. TN Inf. 1st Cons.Regt. Co.C
Scott, G.W. TN 28th (Cons.) Inf. Co.A Cpl.
Scott, G.W. TN 46th Inf. Co.F 1st Lt.
Scott, G.W. VA 46th Inf. Co.L
Scott, G.W. Gen. & Staff, QM,Comsy.Dept. Capt.
Scott, G.W. Gen. & Staff Hosp.Stew.
Scott, G.Y. MS 2nd Cav.Res. Co.B
Scott, H. AL 11th Inf. Co.B
Scott, H. AR 3rd Cav. Co.D
Scott, H. GA Inf. Grubbs' Co.
Scott, H. LA 27th Inf. Co.G
Scott, H. MS 37th Inf. Co.H
Scott, H. TX 7th Cav. Co.G
Scott, H.A. KY 2nd (Woodward's) Cav. Co.A
Scott, H.A. KY 12th Cav. Co.A
Scott, H.A. TX 7th Field Btty.
Scott, H.A. TX 13th Vol. Co.E
Scott, H.A. Blake's Scouts,CSA
Scott, Hardy O. NC 27th Inf. Co.I Cpl.
Scott, Harod B. VA 19th Inf. Co.H
Scott, Harold F. VA 6th Bn.Res. Co.A
Scott, Harrison NC 1st Inf. Co.D
Scott, Harrison TN 25th Inf. Co.K
Scott, Harrison VA 108th Mil. Co.C
Scott, Harrison C. MS 17th Inf. Co.H
Scott, Harry 1st Cherokee Mtd.Rifles Co.I
Scott, Harry M. VA 8th Cav. Co.E

Scott, Hartwell G. GA 15th Inf. Co.E Cpl.
Scott, Harvey TX 20th Inf. Co.C
Scott, Harvey S. TN Cav. 9th Bn. (Gantt's) Co.E
Scott, Hasting SC 15th Inf. Co.D
Scott, Haywood NC 55th Inf. Co.A
Scott, H.B. AR 1st (Monroe's) Cav. Co.H
Scott, H.B. AR 37th Inf. Co.F
Scott, H.B. TN 3rd (Clack's) Inf. Co.E
Scott, H.B. TN Inf. 4th Cons.Regt. Co.C
Scott, H.B. TN 55th (Brown's) Inf. Co.C Sgt.
Scott, H.B. Gen. & Staff, Med.Dept. Asst.Surg.
Scott, H.C. GA Cav. 20th Bn. Co.C
Scott, H.C. GA 9th Inf. Co.K
Scott, H.C. MD AASurg.
Scott, H.C. MO 2nd Inf. Co.B
Scott, H.C. Gen. & Staff Surg.
Scott, H.E. TN 3rd (Clack's) Inf. Co.E
Scott, H.E. TN Inf. 4th Cons.Regt. Co.C
Scott, Henry AL Seawell's Btty. (Mohawk Arty.)
Scott, Henry GA Arty. 11th Bn. (Sumter Arty.) Co.D,B
Scott, Henry GA 1st (Ramsey's) Inf.
Scott, Henry GA 10th Inf. Co.F
Scott, Henry GA 46th Inf. Co.F
Scott, Henry GA Conscr.
Scott, Henry KY 14th Cav. Co.C,D
Scott, Henry KY 5th Mtd.Inf. Co.C
Scott, Henry LA 10th Inf. Co.A
Scott, Henry LA 25th Inf. Co.E
Scott, Henry LA Herrick's Co. (Orleans Blues)
Scott, Henry MS 20th Inf. Co.I
Scott, Henry MO Cav. Slayback's Regt. Co.G 1st Cpl.
Scott, Henry NC 8th Sr.Res. Co.C
Scott, Henry NC 33rd Inf. Co.F
Scott, Henry NC 55th Inf. Co.A
Scott, Henry SC 6th Cav. Co.B
Scott, Henry SC Inf. 7th Bn. (Enfield Rifles) Co.E
Scott, Henry TN 13th Inf. Co.L 1st Sgt.
Scott, Henry TN 28th (Cons.) Inf. Co.C 2nd Lt.
Scott, Henry TN 43rd Inf. Co.C
Scott, Henry TX 12th Cav. Co.K
Scott, Henry TX 21st Cav. Co.K
Scott, Henry TX 25th Cav. Co.D
Scott, Henry TX 30th Cav. Co.G
Scott, Henry TX 16th Inf. Co.D
Scott, Henry VA 26th Inf. Co.E
Scott, Henry 3rd Conf.Cav. Co.K
Scott, Henry A. GA 51st Inf. Co.K
Scott, Henry B. TX 13th Vol. Co.E 2nd Lt.
Scott, Henry B. VA 41st Mil. Surg.
Scott, Henry C. MD 1st Inf. Co.C Cpl.
Scott, Henry H. AL 19th Inf. Co.A
Scott, Henry M. LA 28th (Gray's) Inf. Co.C 1st Sgt.
Scott, Henry M. TN 28th Inf. Co.C Bvt.2nd Lt.
Scott, Henry Montague LA 8th Inf. Co.E
Scott, Henry R. GA 61st Inf. Co.I
Scott, Henry W. SC Lt.Arty. Garden's Co. (Palmetto Lt.Btty.)
Scott, Hercules VA 24th Inf. Co.G Capt.
Scott, Herman W. AR 4th Inf. Co.F Cpl.
Scott, Hezekiah VA 22nd Inf. Swann's Co.
Scott, Hezekiah K. GA 12th Inf. Co.H
Scott, H.F. GA Siege Arty. 28th Bn. Co.B
Scott, H.F. GA 1st Reg. Co.K

Scott, H.G. GA 8th Inf. Co.G
Scott, H. Hugh SC 1st Inf. Co.H
Scott, Hillard W. 4th Conf.Inf. Co.D
Scott, Hiram C. TX 16th Cav. Co.B
Scott, Hiram S. AL 24th Inf. Co.E
Scott, Hiram S. AL 28th Inf. Co.G
Scott, Hiram W. VA Inf. 21st Bn. 2nd Co.C
Scott, H.L. LA 3rd Inf. Co.H
Scott, H.L. TN 1st (Feild's) Inf. Co.L
Scott, H.L. TN Inf. Nashville Bn. Felts' Co.
Scott, H.L.W. TN 35th Inf. 1st Co.A
Scott, H.M. GA Cav. 9th Bn. (St.Guards) Co.B
Scott, H.M. GA 18th Inf. Co.A Hosp.Stew.
Scott, H.M. NC 21st Inf. Co.I
Scott, Hope B. GA 25th Inf. Co.G
Scott, Hope B. GA 47th Inf. Co.D
Scott, Houston AL Cav. Holloway's Co.
Scott, H.P. AL 4th (Russell's) Cav. Co.F
Scott, H.P. MS Cav. Davenport's Bn. (St.Troops) Co.C
Scott, H.P. MS 15th Inf. Co.D
Scott, H.P. MS Adair's Co. (Lodi Co.)
Scott, H.P. TN 20th (Russell's) Cav. Co.G
Scott, H.R. GA Lt.Arty. (Jackson Arty.) Massenburg's Btty.
Scott, H.R. SC 2nd Res.
Scott, H.R. SC 23rd Inf. Co.A,C
Scott, H.R. TX 30th Cav. Co.F
Scott, H.S. VA 64th Mtd.Inf. Co.H
Scott, H.T. GA Inf. 54th Regt. Co.C
Scott, H.T. SC 5th St.Troops Co.B
Scott, H.T. TX Inf. Houston Bn. Co.A Capt.
Scott, Hubbard L. KY 10th (Johnson's) Cav. Co.K
Scott, Hugh VA 8th Cav. Co.A
Scott, Hugh H. SC 2nd Cav. Co.I
Scott, Hugh H. SC Cav.Bn. Hampton Legion Co.A
Scott, Hugh T. GA 36th (Villepigue's) Inf. Co.I Sgt.
Scott, Hugh W. SC Lt.Arty. Garden's Co. (Palmetto Lt.Btty.)
Scott, Humphry P. NC Inf. Thomas Legion Co.C
Scott, H.W. AL 26th (O'Neal's) Inf. Co.F
Scott, H.W. MS 38th Cav. Co.D
Scott, H.W. NC 21st Inf. Co.I
Scott, H.W. SC 5th Cav. Co.G
Scott, H.W. SC Cav. 17th Bn. Co.B
Scott, H.W. SC 15th Inf. Co.F
Scott, H.W. VA 24th Cav. Co.G
Scott, I.J. VA Inf. 26th Bn. Co.B
Scott, I.M. MO 2nd Btty. Co.C 1st Lt.
Scott, Ira G. MS 17th Inf. Co.D,I
Scott, Irby G. GA 12th Inf. Co.G 1st Lt.
Scott, Irwin FL 9th Inf. Co.E
Scott, Irwin MO 2nd Cav. Co.B
Scott, Isaac AR 15th (N.W.) Inf. Emergency Co.I
Scott, Isaac FL Inf. 2nd Bn. Co.E
Scott, Isaac FL Res. Poe's Co.
Scott, Isaac KY 9th Cav. Co.H
Scott, Isaac TN 35th Inf. 1st Co.A
Scott, Isaac J. VA 108th Mil. Co.C, Lemans' Co.
Scott, Isaac M. MO 3rd Cav. Co.I,F
Scott, Isaac N. GA 7th Inf. Co.D
Scott, Isaac N. GA 44th Inf. Co.E
Scott, Isaac R. LA 6th Inf. Co.C

Scott, Isaac W. AL 3rd Bn.Res. Co.C
Scott, Isaah KY Horse Arty. Byrne's Co.
Scott, Israel LA Washington Arty.Bn. Co.1 Artif.
Scott, Israel S. MS 10th Inf. Co.O, New Co.B Sgt.
Scott, Iverson NC 5th Inf. Co.I
Scott, J. AL 11th Cav. Co.A
Scott, J. AL 44th Inf. Co.H
Scott, J. GA Arty. Lumpkin's Co.
Scott, J. GA Inf. Grubbs' Co.
Scott, J. LA 22nd Inf. Co.E
Scott, J. LA Mil. British Guard Bn. Coburn's Co. Sgt.
Scott, J. MO Lt.Arty. Von Phul's Co.
Scott, J. SC 6th Cav. Co.G
Scott, J. TN 3rd (Forrest's) Cav. Co.D
Scott, J. TX Cav. Border's Regt. Co.I
Scott, J. TX Cav. Border's Regt. Co.K
Scott, J. TX Cav. Terry's Regt. Co.K
Scott, J. TX 15th Inf. 1st Co.E
Scott, J. VA 1st Cav. Co.E
Scott, J. Inf. Bailey's Cons.Regt. Co.A Drum.
Scott, J.A. AL 51st (Part.Rangers) Co.C
Scott, J.A. AR 47th (Crandall's) Cav.
Scott, J.A. AR 1st Inf. Co.K 1st Sgt.
Scott, J.A. AR 6th Inf. Old Co.F
Scott, J.A. AR 23rd Inf. Co.F
Scott, J.A. AR 26th Inf. Co.G Sgt.
Scott, J.A. FL 2nd Cav. Co.E
Scott, J.A. GA 1st Inf. Co.E
Scott, J.A. LA Inf. 11th Bn. Co.A
Scott, J.A. MS 18th Cav. Co.D
Scott, J.A. MS 18th Cav. Co.F
Scott, J.A. MS 15th (Cons.) Inf. Co.F
Scott, J.A. NC Cav. 8th Regt. Co.F
Scott, J.A. SC 3rd Cav. Co.H
Scott, J.A. TN 6th (Wheeler's) Cav. Co.A
Scott, J.A. TX 12th Cav. Co.G
Scott, J.A. TX Cav. Terry's Regt. Co.E
Scott, J.A. TX 9th (Young's) Inf. Co.I
Scott, J.A. TX 13th Vol. 2nd Co.D
Scott, J.A. VA Lt.Arty. R.M. Anderson's Co.
Scott, J.A. VA Lt.Arty. Wimbish's Co. Sgt.
Scott, Jack 1st Cherokee Mtd.Vol. 1st Co.A, 2nd Co.C Cpl.
Scott, Jack W. TX 7th Inf. Co.C Music.
Scott, Jackson AL 4th Inf. Co.H
Scott, Jackson SC Lt.Arty. Beauregard's Co.
Scott, Jackson VA 24th Inf. Co.D
Scott, Jackson H. MO 8th Cav. Co.A
Scott, Jacob FL 2nd Cav. Co.A
Scott, Jacob FL Cav. 5th Bn. Co.E
Scott, Jacob MO 6th Cav. Co.E
Scott, Jacob E. AL 6th Inf. Co.D
Scott, Jacob W. GA 47th Inf. Co.D
Scott, James AL 6th Cav. Co.E
Scott, James AL 7th Cav. Co.I Sgt.
Scott, James AL 41st Inf. Co.C
Scott, James AL 41st Inf. Co.H
Scott, James AR 15th Mil. Co.A
Scott, James AR Inf. Hutchinson's Co. (4th Vol.)
Scott, James GA Hvy.Arty. 22nd Bn. Co.F
Scott, James GA 1st (Olmstead's) Inf. Read's Co.
Scott, James GA 5th Res. Co.B
Scott, James GA 11th Inf. Co.K
Scott, James GA 48th Inf. Co.H

Scott, James GA Floyd Legion (St.Guards) Co.H
Scott, James KY 7th Cav. Co.G
Scott, James LA 1st (Strawbridge's) Inf. Co.I,E,G
Scott, James LA Mil. 4th Regt. 1st Brig. 1st Div. Co.K
Scott, James LA 10th Inf. Co.C Capt.
Scott, James LA 15th Inf. Co.B
Scott, James LA Mil. C.S. Zouave Bn. Co.H
Scott, James MS 2nd St.Cav. Co.L
Scott, James MS 8th Cav. Co.D
Scott, James MS 12th Cav. Co.A
Scott, James MS 12th Inf. Co.F
Scott, James MO 1st Inf. Co.A
Scott, James MO Inf. Perkins' Bn. Co.D
Scott, James MO Robertson's Regt.St.Guard Co.3
Scott, James NC 3rd Inf. Co.I
Scott, James NC 7th Sr.Res. Davie's Co.
Scott, James NC 17th Inf. (1st Org.) Co.E
Scott, James NC 32nd Inf. Co.B
Scott, James NC 42nd Inf. Co.K Cpl.
Scott, James NC 44th Inf. Co.E
Scott, James NC 47th Inf. Co.H
Scott, James SC 1st Arty. Co.K
Scott, James SC 1st St.Troops Co.G
Scott, James SC 3rd St.Troops Co.B
Scott, James SC 16th Inf. Co.E
Scott, James SC 16th & 24th (Cons.) Inf. Co.F
Scott, James SC 24th Inf. Co.A
Scott, James SC Inf. Hampton Legion Co.E
Scott, James TN 2nd (Ashby's) Cav. Co.F
Scott, James TN Cav. 4th Bn. (Branner's) Co.F
Scott, James TN 6th (Wheeler's) Cav. Co.E
Scott, James TN 9th (Ward's) Cav. Co.F
Scott, James TN 9th (Ward's) Cav. Co.G
Scott, James TN 13th (Gore's) Cav. Co.I
Scott, James TN Lt.Arty. Winston's Co.
Scott, James TN 1st (Feild's) Inf. Co.K
Scott, James TN 8th Inf. Co.B
Scott, James TN 22nd Inf. Co.A
Scott, James TN 25th Inf. Co.A
Scott, James TN 35th Inf. 2nd Co.D
Scott, James TN 61st Mtd.Inf. Bundren's Co.
Scott, James TN 62nd Mtd.Inf. Co.G
Scott, James TX 26th Cav. Co.K
Scott, James TX 1st Inf. Co.C
Scott, James TX Inf. 1st Bn. (St.Troops) Co.B
Scott, James TX 11th Inf. Co.A
Scott, James TX 11th Inf. Co.H Cpl.
Scott, James TX 13th Vol. 2nd Co.D
Scott, James VA 21st Cav. 2nd Co.G
Scott, James VA Cav. Hounshell's Bn. Gwinn's Co.
Scott, James VA 12th Inf. Co.K
Scott, James VA 41st Mil. Co.D
Scott, James VA 53rd Inf. Co.I
Scott, James VA 55th Inf. Co.E
Scott, James VA 58th Inf. Co.D
Scott, James VA 59th Inf. 2nd Co.B
Scott, James Conf.Cav. 6th Bn. Co.G
Scott, James A. AL Inf. 1st Regt. Co.H
Scott, James A. AR 4th Inf. Co.C Sgt.
Scott, James A. AR 36th Inf. Co.G
Scott, James A. GA 15th Inf. Co.K
Scott, James A. GA 52nd Inf. Co.A
Scott, James A. KY 10th Cav. Unassign.Co.

Scott, James A. LA 1st Cav. Co.C Hosp.Stew.
Scott, James A. MS 7th Inf. Co.E
Scott, James A. MO 3rd Inf. Co.C
Scott, James A. NC Cav. 5th Bn. Co.D
Scott, James A. NC 6th Cav. (65th St.Troops) Co.D,B
Scott, James A. NC 6th Cav. (65th St.Troops) Co.E,D Sgt.
Scott, James A. NC Cav. 7th Bn. Co.E Sgt.
Scott, James A. NC 3rd Arty. (40th St.Troops) Co.G
Scott, James A. TN Cav. 2nd Bn. (Biffle's) Co.D
Scott, James A. TN 13th Inf. Co.D
Scott, James A. TN 48th (Voorhies') Inf. Co.C
Scott, James A. TX 2nd Cav. 2nd Co.F
Scott, James A. TX Cav. Martin's Regt. Co.C Sgt.
Scott, James A. VA 3rd Cav. Co.E
Scott, James A. VA 8th Cav. Co.A
Scott, James A. VA 2nd St.Res. Co.E 1st Lt.
Scott, James A. VA Inf. 26th Bn. Co.E Sgt.
Scott, James A. VA 46th Inf. Co.A 1st Lt.
Scott, James A. VA 57th Inf. Co.K
Scott, James A.C. AR 12th Inf. Co.H Sgt.
Scott, James B. AL 4th (Russell's) Cav. Co.G
Scott, James B. FL 9th Inf. Co.B
Scott, James B. TN 2nd (Smith's) Cav.
Scott, James B. TN 32nd Inf. Co.C
Scott, James B. TX 4th Inf. Co.G
Scott, James B. TX 6th Inf. Co.F
Scott, James B. TX 11th (Spaight's) Bn.Vol. Co.C Cpl.
Scott, James B. TX 21st Inf. Co.E
Scott, James C. AL 50th Inf.
Scott, James C. KY 1st (Butler's) Cav. Co.A Wagon M.
Scott, James C. MS Lt.Arty. (Madison Lt.Arty.) Richards' Co.
Scott, James C. MO 2nd Inf. Co.B
Scott, James C. NC 6th Inf. Co.B
Scott, James C. NC 7th Inf. Co.H
Scott, James C. TN 9th (Ward's) Cav. Co.G
Scott, James C. VA Lt.Arty. King's Co.
Scott, James D. GA Cobb's Legion Co.D Sgt.
Scott, James D. MS 42nd Inf. Co.C Cpl.
Scott, James D. TN 41st Inf. Co.C Capt.
Scott, James D. TX 18th Inf. Co.B
Scott, James D. VA 3rd Inf.Loc.Def. Co.E
Scott, James D. VA 58th Inf. Co.D
Scott, James D. VA Mil. 33rd Regt.
Scott, James E. AL 19th Inf. Co.K
Scott, James E. FL 1st Inf. New Co.C
Scott, James E. FL 3rd Inf. Co.H
Scott, James E. FL 4th Inf. Co.G Cpl.
Scott, James E. FL 10th Inf. Co.K
Scott, James E. GA 3rd Cav. (St.Guards) Co.A
Scott, James E. SC 7th Inf. 1st Co.D, 2nd Co.D
Scott, James E. VA 5th Cav. Co.K
Scott, James E. VA 5th Cav. (12 mo. '61-2) Co.I
Scott, James E. VA Cav. 14th Bn. Co.B
Scott, James E. VA 15th Cav. Co.I
Scott, James E. VA Lt.Arty. J.D. Smith's Co. Cpl.
Scott, James F. FL Inf. 2nd Bn. Co.E
Scott, James F. GA 44th Inf. Co.E
Scott, James F. MO 2nd Cav. Co.D Lt.
Scott, James F. TN 6th Inf. Co.E

Scott, James G. NC 3rd Cav. (41st St.Troops) Co.B 1st Sgt.
Scott, James G. NC 1st Inf. Co.D 2nd Lt.
Scott, James H. AL St.Res. Palmer's Co. 1st Sgt.
Scott, James H. GA 35th Inf. Co.B
Scott, James H. GA 36th (Villepigue's) Inf. Co.G
Scott, James H. GA Inf. 40th Bn. Co.B
Scott, James H. GA 41st Inf. Co.E
Scott, James H. KY 3rd Bn.Mtd.Rifles Co.D
Scott, James H. MS Cav. Buck's Co.
Scott, James H. SC 9th Inf. Co.B Cpl.
Scott, James H. TN 54th Inf. Co.E
Scott, James H. VA 5th Cav. (12 mo. '61-2) Co.A 1st Lt.
Scott, James H. VA Cav. 14th Bn. Co.D Capt.
Scott, James H. VA 108th Mil. Co.C, Lemans' Co.
Scott, James H. 1st Conf.Inf. 1st Co.G
Scott, James J. GA 6th Inf. Co.F
Scott, James J. TX Inf. Griffin's Bn. Co.C
Scott, James J. VA Lt.Arty. Montgomery's Co.
Scott, James L. GA Inf. 1st Loc.Troops (Augusta) Co.D
Scott, James L. GA 25th Inf. Co.K
Scott, James L. KY 4th Mtd.Inf. Co.E Sgt.
Scott, James L. MS 1st Lt.Arty. Co.I
Scott, James L. MS 5th Inf. Co.F
Scott, James L. TX 26th Cav. 1st Co.G
Scott, James L. TX 13th Vol. 2nd Co.A
Scott, James L. VA 8th Cav. Co.H Cpl.
Scott, James M. AL Lt.Arty. Ward's Btty.
Scott, James M. AL 17th Inf. Co.K
Scott, James M. AL 20th Inf. Co.B
Scott, James M. GA 4th Inf. Co.D
Scott, James M. LA 19th Inf. Co.H 2nd Lt.
Scott, James M. MS 2nd Inf. Co.I
Scott, James M. NC Walker's Bn. Thomas' Legion Co.C
Scott, James M. SC 1st (McCreary's) Inf. Co.H
Scott, James M. SC 7th Res. Co.E 1st Sgt.
Scott, James M. TN 10th Cav.
Scott, James M. TN 37th Inf. Co.D
Scott, James M. TX 14th Cav. Co.I Bugler
Scott, James M. TX 35th (Brown's) Cav. Co.E
Scott, James M. TX 9th Field Btty. Cpl.
Scott, James M. TX 12th Inf. Co.H
Scott, James M. VA 10th Cav. Co.F Sgt.
Scott, James M., Jr. VA Lt.Arty. Pollock's Co.
Scott, James M. VA 14th Inf. Co.A
Scott, James M. VA Inf. 23rd Bn. Co.F 2nd Lt.
Scott, James M. VA 50th Inf. Co.I
Scott, James N. TN 30th Inf. Co.C Cpl.
Scott, James O. LA Inf. 11th Bn. Co.F
Scott, James P. GA 1st Reg. Co.E
Scott, James P. NC 25th Inf. Co.F Sgt.Maj.
Scott, James P. TN 48th (Nixon's) Inf. Co.B Sgt.
Scott, James P. TN 48th (Voorhies') Inf. Co.A
Scott, James P. VA 3rd Res. Co.C 2nd Lt.
Scott, James P. VA Inf. 23rd Bn. Co.F
Scott, James R. AL 47th Inf. Co.A Cpl.
Scott, James R. GA Lt.Arty. Van Den Corput's Co.
Scott, James R. GA 16th Inf. Co.H
Scott, James R. SC 2nd Inf. Co.C
Scott, James R. TN 33rd Inf. Co.D Capt.

Scott, James R. VA 45th Inf. Co.D
Scott, James S. KY 6th Mtd.Inf. Co.D 2nd Lt.
Scott, James S. NC 27th Inf. Co.B
Scott, James S. TN 6th (Wheeler's) Cav. Co.H
Scott, James S. VA 10th Cav. Co.I
Scott, James S. VA Arty. Curtis' Co. Sgt.
Scott, James T. GA Phillips' Legion Co.A Sgt.
Scott, James T. KY 8th Cav. Co.I 1st Sgt.
Scott, James T. TX 25th Cav. Co.C
Scott, James T. VA 7th Cav. Co.B
Scott, James T. Gen. & Staff Surg.
Scott, James Thornwell SC 2nd Inf. Co.C 2nd Lt.
Scott, James U. MS 34th Inf. Co.F
Scott, James W. KY 2nd (Duke's) Cav. Co.I
Scott, James W. LA 2nd Inf. Co.F
Scott, James W. LA 8th Inf. Co.G
Scott, James W. MS 42nd Inf. Co.B Cpl.
Scott, James W. NC Hvy.Arty. 1st Bn. Co.B,D
Scott, James W. TN 27th Inf. Co.K
Scott, James W. VA Lt.Arty. 13th Bn. Co.C
Scott, James W. VA Cav. Mosby's Regt. (Part.Rangers)
Scott, James W. VA 58th Inf. Co.B
Scott, James Walter LA 19th Inf. Co.D 1st Lt.
Scott, Jamieson VA 27th Inf. Co.C
Scott, J.A.P. AL 47th Inf. Co.F
Scott, Jarrett TX 11th Cav. Co.I
Scott, Jasper MO 6th Cav. Co.E
Scott, J.B. AR Lt.Arty. Zimmerman's Btty.
Scott, J.B. AR 20th Inf. Co.E
Scott, J.B. TN 6th (Wheeler's) Cav. Co.E
Scott, J.B. TN 5th Inf. Co.B
Scott, J.B. TN 8th Inf. Co.H
Scott, J.B. TN 21st Inf. Co.A
Scott, J.B. TN 23rd Inf. Co.D
Scott, J.B. VA 54th Inf. Co.C
Scott, J.B. Mead's Conf.Cav. Co.A
Scott, J.B. 9th Conf.Inf. Co.H
Scott, J.C. AR Cav. Gunter's Bn. Co.F 3rd Lt.
Scott, J.C. GA 1st (Symons') Res. Co.C
Scott, J.C. TN 18th (Dawson's) Cav. Co.C
Scott, J.C. TX Cav. Waller's Regt. Co.A
Scott, J.C. TX 20th Inf. Co.G
Scott, J.C. VA 60th Inf. Co.I
Scott, J.C. Jackson's Co.,CSA
Scott, J.C.B. TX 1st Hvy.Arty. Co.K,A
Scott, J.D. LA 1st Hvy.Arty. (Reg.) Co.D,H 1st Lt.
Scott, J.D. MS Cav. Yerger's Regt. Co.C
Scott, J.D. MS 9th Inf. Old Co.K
Scott, J.D. TN 14th Cav. Co.D
Scott, J.D. TN Cav. Jackson's Co.
Scott, J.D. TN 51st (Cons.) Inf. Co.E 3rd Lt.
Scott, J.D. TX 11th Inf. Co.G
Scott, J.D. VA 40th Inf. Co.K
Scott, J.E. FL Inf. 2nd Bn. Co.D
Scott, J.E. MD 1st Cav. Co.C
Scott, J.E. SC 9th Inf. Co.D
Scott, J.E. SC 24th Inf. Co.A
Scott, J.E., Jr. SC 25th Inf. Co.C
Scott, J.E. TN 24th Bn.S.S. Co.B
Scott, J.E. TN 28th Inf. Co.C
Scott, J.E. TN 28th (Cons.) Inf. Co.A
Scott, J.E. TX Cav. Lilley's Co.
Scott, J.E. TX Cav. Mann's Regt. Co.G
Scott, J.E. TX 9th (Nichols') Inf. Co.K

Scott, J.E. TX 22nd Inf. Co.B Cpl.
Scott, J.E. Forrest's Scouts,CSA
Scott, J.E.B. TX 11th Inf. Co.C
Scott, J.E.D. TN 10th (DeMoss') Cav. Co.K
Scott, J.E.D. TN 21st & 22nd (Cons.) Cav. Co.F
Scott, Jefferson TN Cav. Newsom's Regt. Co.D
Scott, Jehu VA 54th Inf. Co.G
Scott, Jehue VA 1st (Farinholt's) Res. Co.B
Scott, Jephtha F. GA 20th Inf. Co.D
Scott, Jeptha GA 4th Res. Co.K
Scott, Jeremiah AL 21st Inf. Co.B
Scott, Jeremiah GA 48th Inf. Co.B
Scott, Jeremiah D. TX 1st (McCulloch's) Cav.
   Co.F Sgt.
Scott, Jeremiah D. TX 18th Cav. Co.D
Scott, Jeremiah R. GA 7th Inf. Co.D
Scott, Jerry TN 2nd (Walker's) Inf. Co.G
Scott, Jerry D. TX 1st (Yager's) Cav. Co.K
Scott, Jerry D. TX Cav. 8th (Taylor's) Bn. Co.B
   1st Sgt.
Scott, Jesse NC 3rd Arty. (40th St.Troops) Co.I
Scott, Jesse NC 4th Inf. Co.I 1st Sgt.
Scott, Jesse SC Inf. 3rd Bn. Co.G
Scott, Jesse TN 34th Inf. Co.I
Scott, Jesse TN 42nd Inf. Co.D
Scott, Jesse TN Conscr. (Cp. of Instr.) Co.B
Scott, Jesse VA 42nd Inf. Co.K
Scott, Jesse 1st Cherokee Mtd.Vol. 1st Co.E
Scott, Jesse 4th Conf.Inf. Co.K
Scott, Jesse A. AR 3rd Cav. Co.H Sgt.
Scott, Jesse F. GA 5th Inf. A.Surg.
Scott, Jesse G. TX 6th Inf. Co.F
Scott, Jesse G. VA 23rd Inf. Co.B Cpl.
Scott, Jesse H. TX 16th Cav. Co.C
Scott, Jesse M. NC 35th Inf. Co.I 2nd Lt.
Scott, Jesse M. SC 6th Cav. Co.B
Scott, Jesse W. AR Inf. 1st Bn. Co.F
Scott, J.E.W. VA 1st (Farinholt's) Res. Co.H
   Cpl.
Scott, J.F. AL 9th (Malone's) Cav. Co.F
Scott, J.F. AR 6th Inf. Co.A
Scott, J.F. AR 6th Inf. Old Co.F
Scott, J.F. AR 26th Inf. Co.G Sgt.
Scott, J.F. GA 18th Inf. Co.B
Scott, J.F. KY 7th Cav. Co.E
Scott, J.F. MS 35th Inf. Co.G
Scott, J.F. MO 9th (Elliott's) Cav. Co.E
Scott, J.F. MO Cav. Jackman's Regt. Co.H
   Capt.
Scott, J.F. SC 25th Inf. Co.K
Scott, J.F. TN 21st (Wilson's) Cav. Co.G
Scott, J.F. TN Lt.Arty. Kain's Co.
Scott, J.F. TN 48th (Nixon's) Inf. Surg.
Scott, J.F. TX 30th Cav. Co.F
Scott, J.F. TX 4th Inf. (St.Troops) Co.H
Scott, J.F. TX 5th Inf. Co.D
Scott, J.H. AL 32nd Inf. Band Music.
Scott, J.H. AL 48th Inf. Co.I Sgt.
Scott, J.H. GA Cav. 20th Bn. Co.C
Scott, J.H. GA 16th Inf. Co.C
Scott, J.H. GA 48th Inf. Co.I
Scott, J.H. LA Washington Arty.Bn. Co.5 Cpl.
Scott, J.H. LA Inf. 1st Sp.Bn. (Rightor's) Co.D
Scott, J.H. MO Cav. 3rd Bn. Co.H Sgt.
Scott, J.H. NC 1st Inf. Co.G
Scott, J.H. TN 48th (Nixon's) Inf. Co.K
Scott, J.H. TN 51st Inf. Co.C

Scott, J.H. TN 51st (Cons.) Inf. Co.I
Scott, J.H. VA 1st Cav. Co.D
Scott, J.H. VA 15th Cav. Co.K Capt.
Scott, J.H. VA 9th Bn.Res. Co.D
Scott, J.H. VA Inf. 26th Bn. Co.B
Scott, J.H. 8th (Wade's) Conf.Cav. Co.K
Scott, J.H.F. TN 50th Inf. Co.C
Scott, J.I. AR 18th (Marmaduke's) Inf. Co.C 1st
   Lt.
Scott, J.I. TN 6th Inf. Co.A
Scott, J.I. 3rd Conf.Inf. Co.C 1st Lt.
Scott, J.J. AR 35th Inf. Co.H
Scott, J.J. GA 1st Cav. Co.F
Scott, J.J. LA 6th Cav. Co.C
Scott, J.J. LA 13th Bn. (Part.Rangers) Co.C
Scott, J.J. LA 2nd Inf. Co.D
Scott, J.J. MS 1st Lt.Arty. Co.D
Scott, J.J. MO 16th Inf. Co.K
Scott, J.J. SC 5th Cav. Co.B
Scott, J.J. SC Cav. 17th Bn. Co.C
Scott, J.J. SC Inf. 7th Bn. (Enfield Rifles) Co.E
Scott, J.J. TN 18th (Newsom's) Cav. Co.A
Scott, J.J. TN Inf. Nashville Bn. Cattles' Co.
Scott, J.J. TX 10th Cav. Co.F
Scott, J.J. VA Lt.Arty. Wimbish's Co.
Scott, J. John SC Lt.Arty. Beauregard's Co.
Scott, J.K. AL 5th Inf. New Co.I
Scott, J.K. VA Cav. 37th Bn. Co.D
Scott, J.K.P. GA 4th Res. Co.H
Scott, J.K.P. MS 6th Cav. Co.B
Scott, J.K.P. MS Cav. Davenport's Bn.
   (St.Troops) Co.A
Scott, J.K.P. TN 3rd (Clack's) Inf. Co.F
Scott, J.K.P. TN 36th Inf. Co.E
Scott, J.K.P. TN 43rd Inf. Co.K
Scott, J.L. AL 48th Inf. Co.I
Scott, J.L. AR 1st (Monroe's) Cav. Co.D
Scott, J.L. MS 23rd Inf. Co.A
Scott, J.L. NC 45th Inf. Co.C
Scott, J.L. SC Inf. 6th Bn. Co.C Sgt.
Scott, J.L. SC 23rd Inf. Co.A,C
Scott, J.L. SC 25th Inf. Co.G
Scott, J.L. SC 26th Inf. Co.I Sgt.
Scott, J.L. SC Manigault's Bn.Vol. Co.E
Scott, J.L. TN 9th Inf. Co.E
Scott, J.L. Eng.Dept. Polk's Corps A. of TN Sap.
   & Min. Co.,CSA
Scott, J.L. Gen. & Staff Surg.
Scott, J.M. AL Cav. 5th Bn. Hilliard's Legion
   Co.A
Scott, J.M. AL 18th Inf. Co.C
Scott, J.M. AL 58th Inf. Co.E
Scott, J.M. AR Cav. Reves' Co.
Scott, J.M. AR 20th Inf. Co.C
Scott, J.M. GA 36th (Broyles') Inf. Co.I Cpl.
Scott, J.M. GA 44th Inf. Co.H Cpl.
Scott, J.M. GA Phillips' Legion Co.D
Scott, J.M. MS 1st Bn.S.S. Co.A
Scott, J.M. MS 25th Inf. Co.I
Scott, J.M. MS 31st Inf. Co.H
Scott, J.M. MO 12th Cav. Co.C
Scott, J.M. MO 1st Inf.
Scott, J.M. MO 9th Bn.S.S. Co.A
Scott, J.M. NC 4th Bn.Jr.Res. Co.A
Scott, J.M. NC 45th Inf. Co.H
Scott, J.M. SC 1st Inf. Co.A
Scott, J.M. SC 27th Inf. Co.B

Scott, J.M. TN Lt.Arty. Morton's Co.
Scott, J.M. TN 13th Inf. Co.B
Scott, J.M. TN 55th (Brown's) Inf. Co.H Sgt.
Scott, J.M. TX 28th Cav. Co.D 2nd Lt.
Scott, J.M. TX 13th Vol. 2nd Co.D
Scott, J.M. TX 22nd Inf. Co.A
Scott, J.M. VA Murphy's Co.
Scott, J.M. 3rd Conf.Cav. Co.K
Scott, J.M. 10th Conf.Cav. Co.A
Scott, J.N. GA 1st St.Line 1st Lt.
Scott, J.N. GA 4th Res. Co.B
Scott, J.N. KY 10th Cav. Martin's Co.
Scott, J.N. TX Cav. Morgan's Regt. Co.G Capt.
Scott, J.N. TX 20th Inf. Co.I
Scott, J.O. AR 14th (Powers') Inf. Co.F
Scott, J.O. GA Cav. 6th Bn. (St.Guards) Co.F
Scott, J.O. LA Inf.Cons.Crescent Regt. Co.K
Scott, Jo TN 11th Inf. Co.B
Scott, Jo. F. KY 1st Inf. Co.C
Scott, Joel T. GA 17th Inf. Co.F
Scott, Joel T. GA 20th Inf. Co.I 1st Lt.
Scott, Joel T. SC 7th Inf. Co.D
Scott, John AL 7th Cav. Co.I
Scott, John AL Cav. Holloway's Co.
Scott, John AL 40th Inf. Co.A
Scott, John AL 49th Inf. Co.K
Scott, John AL 62nd Inf. Co.F
Scott, John AR 1st Cav. Music.
Scott, John AR 4th Inf. Co.C 2nd Lt.
Scott, John AR 8th Inf. New Co.D
Scott, John AR 35th Inf. Co.F
Scott, John GA 2nd Res. Co.H
Scott, John GA 26th Inf. Co.G
Scott, John GA 48th Inf. Co.C
Scott, John GA 48th Inf. Co.H
Scott, John GA 63rd Inf. Co.H
Scott, John KY 12th Cav. Co.D
Scott, John KY Inf. Ficklin's Bn. Co.C
Scott, John LA 1st (Nelligan's) Inf. Co.A
Scott, John LA 1st (Strawbridge's) Inf. Co.C
Scott, John LA 2nd Inf. Co.E
Scott, John LA 9th Inf. Co.G
Scott, John LA 13th Inf. Co.A,F
Scott, John LA 18th Inf. Co.E
Scott, John LA Cons. 18th Regt. & Yellow
   Jacket Bn. Co.E
Scott, John LA 21st (Patton's) Inf. Co.D
Scott, John LA 22nd Inf. Co.A
Scott, John LA 22nd (Cons.) Inf. Co.A
Scott, John LA Conscr.
Scott, John MS 10th Cav. Co.E
Scott, John MS Cav. 24th Bn. Co.F
Scott, John MS 13th Inf. Co.G
Scott, John MS 20th Inf. Co.D
Scott, John MS 42nd Inf. Co.B
Scott, John MS 42nd Inf. Co.F
Scott, John MO 1st N.E. Cav. Co.A
Scott, John MO 1st N.E. Cav. Co.B
Scott, John MO 10th Cav. Co.D
Scott, John MO Cav. Wood's Regt. Co.A
Scott, John MO 1st Inf. 2nd Co.A
Scott, John MO 2nd Inf. Co.B
Scott, John MO 2nd Inf. Co.D
Scott, John MO 11th Inf. Co.K
Scott, John NC 3rd Jr.Res. Co.B
Scott, John NC 4th Bn.Jr.Res. Co.B
Scott, John NC 5th Inf. Co.A

Scott, John NC 5th Inf. Co.E Cpl.
Scott, John NC 21st Inf. Co.I
Scott, John NC 42nd Inf. Co.K
Scott, John SC Cav. 10th Bn. Co.B
Scott, John SC 1st (Butler's) Inf. Co.I
Scott, John SC 2nd Bn.S.S. Co.C
Scott, John SC 5th St.Troops Co.M
Scott, John SC 6th Inf. 2nd Co.D
Scott, John SC 17th Inf. Co.K
Scott, John SC 22nd Inf. Co.G
Scott, John SC 24th Inf. Co.A
Scott, John TN 16th Inf. Co.H
Scott, John TN 17th Inf. Co.G 2nd Lt.
Scott, John TN 23rd Inf.
Scott, John TN 35th Inf. Co.D
Scott, John TN 37th Inf. Co.C
Scott, John TN 48th (Nixon's) Inf. Co.K
Scott, John TN 54th Inf. Co.E Cpl.
Scott, John TN 62nd Mtd.Inf. Co.G
Scott, John TN 63rd Inf. Co.A
Scott, John TN Inf. 154th Sr.Regt. Co.F
Scott, John TX 1st (Yager's) Cav. Co.B
Scott, John TX Cav. 3rd (Yager's) Bn. Co.B
Scott, John TX 8th Cav. Co.L
Scott, John TX 24th Cav. Co.G
Scott, John TX 1st Hvy.Arty. 2nd Co.A
Scott, John TX 4th Field Btty. Bugler
Scott, John TX 2nd Inf. Co.G
Scott, John TX 3rd St.Troops Inf. Co.B
Scott, John TX 7th Inf. Co.B
Scott, John TX 13th Vol. 2nd Co.D
Scott, John TX 20th Inf. Co.H
Scott, John VA 5th Cav. Co.B
Scott, John VA 24th Bn.Part.Rangers Maj.
Scott, John VA Cav. 47th Bn. Co.A
Scott, John VA Hvy.Arty. 10th Bn.
Scott, John VA Hvy.Arty. 18th Bn. Co.A
Scott, John, Jr. VA Lt.Arty. Pollock's Co.
Scott, John VA Lt.Arty. Woolfolk's Co.
Scott, John VA Inf. 21st Bn. 1st Co.D
Scott, John VA 28th Inf. Co.E
Scott, John VA 34th Mil. Co.B
Scott, John VA 54th Mil. Co.A
Scott, John VA 58th Inf. Co.D
Scott, John Conf.Cav. 8th Bn. Co.E
Scott, John 8th (Wade's) Conf.Cav. Co.I
Scott, John 10th Conf.Cav. Co.A
Scott, John A. AL 54th Inf. Co.F Sgt.
Scott, John A. AR 14th (Powers') Inf. Co.A Adj.
Scott, John A. GA 34th Inf. Co.I
Scott, John A. GA Phillips' Legion Co.C,I
Scott, John A. GA Phillips' Legion Co.D
Scott, John A. KY 7th Mtd.Inf. Co.E
Scott, John A. MS 28th Cav. Co.D Cpl.
Scott, John A. MS 1st (Johnston's) Inf. Co.D Cpl.
Scott, John A. MS 8th Inf. Co.B
Scott, John A. MS 20th Inf. Co.A
Scott, John A. MS 21st Inf. Co.I
Scott, John A. MS 42nd Inf. Co.B,I
Scott, John A. TX 34th Cav. Co.F
Scott, John A. TX 35th (Brown's) Cav. Co.E
Scott, John A. VA Arty. Dance's Co. Sgt.
Scott, John A. VA 1st (Farinholt's) Res. Chap.
Scott, John A. VA 1st St.Res. Co.F
Scott, John A., Jr. VA 20th Inf. Co.G

Scott, John A. 4th Conf.Inf. Co.F
Scott, Jno. A. Gen. & Staff Chap.
Scott, John B. AL Lt.Arty. Goldthwaite's Btty. 1st Lt.
Scott, John B. AL Montgomery Guards
Scott, John B. AL Nitre & Min.Corps Young's Co.
Scott, John B. AR 18th Inf. Co.H
Scott, John B. GA 18th Inf. Co.K Cpl.
Scott, John B. KY 4th Mtd.Inf. Co.F
Scott, John B. NC 17th Inf. (1st Org.) Co.G
Scott, John B. NC 54th Inf. Co.F
Scott, John B. TX 22nd Inf. Co.D
Scott, John B. VA 53rd Inf. Co.G Cpl.
Scott, John C. MO Robertson's Regt.St.Guard Co.1
Scott, John C. SC 1st Cav. Co.G
Scott, John C. Forrest's Staff Capt.
Scott, John C. Forrest's Scouts,CSA
Scott, John D. GA 18th Inf. Co.A
Scott, John D. GA 35th Inf. Co.B,K
Scott, John D. LA 8th Inf. Co.E
Scott, John D. LA 22nd Inf. Co.A,E 2nd Lt.
Scott, John D. NC 2nd Inf. Co.D
Scott, John D. NC 44th Inf. Co.G Sgt.
Scott, John D. VA 14th Inf. Co.B
Scott, John E. AL 1st Bn.Cadets Co.C
Scott, John E. AL 46th Inf. Co.B Cpl.
Scott, John E. GA 1st (Olmstead's) Inf. Co.E
Scott, John E. MS 3rd Inf. Co.B 2nd Cpl.
Scott, John E. SC 3rd St.Troops Co.A
Scott, John E. VA 12th Inf. Co.E
Scott, John F. MO 3rd Cav. Co.D 1st Lt.
Scott, John F. NC 2nd Jr.Res. Co.A
Scott, John F. NC 7th Inf. Co.I
Scott, John F. NC 8th Inf. Co.F
Scott, John F. SC 7th Res. Co.E 2nd Lt.
Scott, John F. SC 18th Inf. Co.A
Scott, John F. TX Cav. Hardeman's Regt. Co.E
Scott, John F. VA Lt.Arty. Hankins' Co.
Scott, John F. Conf.Cav. Wood's Regt. Co.B
Scott, John G. KY Cav. 1st Bn. Co.B Capt.
Scott, John G. KY 4th Cav. Co.B Capt.
Scott, John G. KY 5th Cav. Co.B Capt.
Scott, John G. TX 1st Inf. Co.G
Scott, John G. TX 3rd Res. Col.
Scott, John G. VA Hvy.Arty. 19th Bn. Co.B
Scott, John G. VA 39th Inf. Co.C
Scott, John G. Gen. & Staff Surg.
Scott, John G. Gen. & Staff 1st Lt.,ADC
Scott, John H. GA 35th Inf. Co.A
Scott, John H. MS 3rd Inf. Co.A Color Cpl.
Scott, John H. MO 1st Cav. Co.K Sgt.
Scott, John H. MO 5th Cav. Co.F,K Sgt.
Scott, John H. NC 3rd Inf. Co.G
Scott, John Hide LA 27th Inf. Co.E
Scott, John J. AL 10th Inf. Co.C Music.
Scott, John J. AL St.Res. Palmer's Co.
Scott, John J. AL Cp. of Instr. Talladega Co.B
Scott, John J. LA Inf. 11th Bn. Co.G
Scott, John J. MS 18th Inf. Co.I Cpl.
Scott, John J. SC 7th Inf. 2nd Co.D
Scott, John J. TX 5th Cav. Co.B Capt.
Scott, John J. TX 16th Inf. Asst.Surg.
Scott, John K. GA 12th Inf. Co.H
Scott, John K. NC Inf. Thomas Legion Co.C
Scott, John K. VA 50th Inf. Co.D

Scott, John L. AL 41st Inf. Co.H
Scott, John L. GA 8th Inf. (St.Guards) Co.G
Scott, John L. LA 3rd (Wingfield's) Cav. Co.G,E
Scott, John L. LA Ogden's Cav.
Scott, John L. LA 31st Inf. Co.A Cpl.
Scott, John L. MS 4th Cav. Co.E
Scott, John L. NC 29th Inf. Co.D
Scott, John L. SC Cav. 4th Bn. Co.B
Scott, John L. TX 16th Cav. Co.C
Scott, John L. VA 13th Cav. Co.F
Scott, John L. VA 1st Bn.Res. Co.D
Scott, John L. VA Inf. 5th Bn. Co.B 1st Lt.
Scott, John L. 1st Conf.Inf. 2nd Co.D
Scott, John L. 3rd Conf.Eng.Troops Co.B Cpl.
Scott, John M. GA 42nd Inf. Co.A
Scott, John M. GA 47th Inf. Co.D Cpl.
Scott, John M. MS 9th Inf. Old Co.G, New Co.A Sgt.
Scott, John M. MO Lt.Arty. 1st Btty.
Scott, John M. SC 6th Cav. Co.B,D,G
Scott, John M. SC 15th Inf. Co.A
Scott, John M. TN 16th (Logwood's) Cav. Co.B
Scott, John M. TX 7th Cav. Co.G Lt.
Scott, John M. TX 22nd Inf. Co.A
Scott, John M. VA 2nd Cav. Co.I Cpl.
Scott, John M. VA Inf. 23rd Bn. Co.F 1st Lt.
Scott, John M. VA 36th Inf. 2nd Co.G Sgt.
Scott, John M. VA 63rd Inf. Co.K
Scott, John N. VA 10th Cav. Co.C
Scott, John O. KY 2nd Mtd.Inf. Asst.Surg.
Scott, Jno. Orlando Gen. & Staff Surg.
Scott, John P. AR 1st (Crawford's) Cav. Co.C
Scott, John P. AR 3rd Cav. Co.H
Scott, John P. GA 44th Inf. Co.E
Scott, John P. NC 12th Inf. Co.D
Scott, John P. NC 46th Inf. Co.A
Scott, John P. SC 14th Inf. Co.B Sgt.
Scott, John P. TX 17th Cav. 1st Co.I
Scott, John R. FL 4th Inf. Co.G 2nd Lt.
Scott, John R. FL 5th Inf. Co.C
Scott, John R. FL 6th Inf.
Scott, John R. GA Arty. 11th Bn. (Sumter Arty.) Co.A
Scott, John R. GA 2nd Bn.S.S. Co.A 1st Sgt.
Scott, John R. GA 5th Inf. Co.H,M Sgt.
Scott, John R. GA 31st Inf. Co.E
Scott, John R. GA Floyd Legion (St.Guards) Co.H
Scott, John R. NC 2nd Cav. (19th St.Troops) Co.H
Scott, John R. TN 43rd Inf. Co.F
Scott, John S. LA 1st Cav. Col.
Scott, John S. LA 1st Cav. Co.K Sgt.
Scott, John S. MS 6th Inf. Co.H 1st Sgt.
Scott, John S. MS 35th Inf. Co.C
Scott, John S. MO 1st N.E. Cav. Co.O
Scott, John S. SC Lt.Arty. Garden's Co. (Palmetto Lt.Btty.) Cpl.
Scott, John S. VA 1st Bn.Res. Co.H
Scott, John S. VA 7th Inf. Co.K
Scott, John S. VA 136th Mil. Co.E
Scott, John S. Gen. & Staff, Cav. Col.
Scott, John S.N. AL 54th Inf. Co.E
Scott, John T. AL 12th Inf. Co.K 1st Lt.
Scott, John T. AR 2nd Mtd.Rifles Co.A 1st Lt.
Scott, John T. GA 9th Inf. Co.K Sgt.
Scott, John T. GA 20th Inf. Co.B 2nd Lt.

Scott, John T. KY 4th Mtd.Inf. Co.A
Scott, John T. MS 1st (Johnston's) Inf. Co.D
Scott, John T. SC 5th Inf. Co.K
Scott, John T. TX 8th Cav. Co.G
Scott, John T. VA 14th Cav. Co.D,K Sgt.
Scott, John T. VA Cav. Hounshell's Bn.
  Holstead's Co.
Scott, John T. VA 39th Inf. Co.D
Scott, John T. VA 59th Inf. 2nd Co.B Sgt.
Scott, John T. Gen. & Staff, AG Dept. Capt.
Scott, John T.H. TN 30th Inf. Co.B Sgt.
Scott, John W. AL 15th Bn.Part.Rangers Co.A
Scott, John W. AL 56th Part.Rangers Co.A
Scott, John W. AL 41st Inf. Co.D
Scott, John W. AL 47th Inf. Co.F Sgt.
Scott, John W. AR Inf. 4th Bn. Co.B Sgt.
Scott, John W. GA 62nd Cav. Co.L
Scott, John W. GA Inf. 3rd Bn. Co.A
Scott, John W. GA 9th Inf. Co.D
Scott, John W. GA 43rd Inf. Co.G
Scott, John W. LA Inf. 4th Bn. Co.C
Scott, Jno. W. MD Weston's Bn. Co.B 3rd Sgt.
Scott, John W. MS 1st Lt.Arty. Co.K
Scott, John W. MS Inf. 3rd Bn. Co.G
Scott, John W. MS 9th Inf. Old Co.E
Scott, John W. MS 15th Inf. Co.D
Scott, John W. MS Adair's Co. (Lodi Co.)
Scott, John W. MO Lawther's Part.Rangers Sgt.
Scott, John W. MO 16th Inf. Co.G
Scott, John W. MO St.Guard
Scott, John W. NC 3rd Cav. (41st St.Troops)
  Co.C
Scott, John W. SC 1st (McCreary's) Inf. Co.E
Scott, John W. SC 18th Inf. Co.A
Scott, John W. TN 44th Inf. Co.H
Scott, John W. TN 44th (Cons.) Inf. Co.A Sgt.
Scott, John W. TX 2nd Cav. 1st Co.F
Scott, John W. TX 22nd Cav. Co.F
Scott, John W. TX Cav. Morgan's Regt. Co.I
Scott, John W. TX 10th Inf. Co.H Cpl.
Scott, John W. VA 24th Cav. Co.I
Scott, John W. VA Lt.Arty. J.D. Smith's Co.
Scott, John W. VA 16th Inf. 2nd Co.H
Scott, John W. VA 21st Inf. Co.B Sgt.
Scott, John W. VA Inf. 21st Bn. Co.A
Scott, John W. VA 20th Inf. Co.C
Scott, John W. VA 30th Inf. Co.E Capt.
Scott, John W. VA 39th Inf. Co.C
Scott, John W. VA 41st Inf. Co.A
Scott, John W. VA 51st Inf. Co.H
Scott, John W. VA 54th Inf. Co.C
Scott, John W. VA 57th Inf. Co.B
Scott, John W. VA 64th Mtd.Inf. Co.G
Scott, John W. 8th (Dearing's) Conf.Cav. Co.D
Scott, John W. President's Guard,CSA
Scott, John Y. SC Inf. 7th Bn. (Enfield Rifles)
  Co.B
Scott, John Z. VA 10th Cav. Co.F
Scott, Jonathan TN 25th Inf. Co.A
Scott, Jonathan J. MS 17th Inf. Co.C
Scott, Joseph AL Lt.Arty. 2nd Bn. Co.A
Scott, Joseph AL 16th Inf. Co.E
Scott, Joseph GA 44th Inf. Co.E
Scott, Joseph KY 3rd Cav. Co.C
Scott, Joseph KY 4th Cav.
Scott, Joseph KY 9th Cav. Co.A
Scott, Joseph LA 21st (Patton's) Inf. Co.D

Scott, Joseph LA 22nd (Cons.) Inf. Co.K
Scott, Joseph MO 4th Cav. Co.K,D
Scott, Joseph MO 2nd Inf.
Scott, Joseph MO 8th Inf. Co.A
Scott, Joseph NC 47th Inf. Co.I
Scott, Joseph TN 4th (McLemore's) Cav. Co.E
Scott, Joseph TX 2nd Inf. Co.E
Scott, Joseph TX 20th Inf. Co.B
Scott, Joseph VA 10th Cav. Co.A Music.
Scott, Joseph VA 11th Inf. Co.G
Scott, Joseph VA Inf. 26th Bn. Co.E Capt.
Scott, Joseph VA 55th Inf. Co.F
Scott, Joseph VA 60th Inf. Co.E
Scott, Joseph VA 61st Inf. Co.A
Scott, Joseph VA Mil. Washington Cty.
Scott, Joseph A. NC 2nd Cav. (19th St.Troops)
  Co.F
Scott, Joseph A. NC 4th Inf. Co.D
Scott, Joseph A. VA 9th Inf. 2nd Co.A
Scott, Joseph A. VA 11th Inf. Co.B 2nd Lt.
Scott, Joseph B. MS 6th Inf. Co.F Cpl.
Scott, Joseph B. MO 10th Cav. Co.E 2nd Lt.
Scott, Joseph C. KY 8th Cav. Co.E,D
Scott, Joseph C. MO 3rd Cav. Co.F
Scott, Joseph C. NC 33rd Inf. Co.E
Scott, Joseph D. GA 43rd Inf. Co.G
Scott, Joseph E. GA 2nd Cav. Co.H
Scott, Joseph F. AR 4th Inf. Co.I
Scott, Joseph F. KY 3rd Cav. Co.E
Scott, Joseph G. VA 6th Inf. Co.F Cpl.
Scott, Joseph H. AR 1st Mtd.Rifles Co.I
Scott, Joseph H. GA 3rd Cav. (St.Guards) Co.A
Scott, Joseph H. KY 4th Cav. Co.E
Scott, Joseph H. MS 3rd Inf. Co.B
Scott, Joseph H. SC 6th Inf. 2nd Co.H
Scott, Joseph H. VA 42nd Inf. Co.I
Scott, Joseph J. GA 17th Inf. Co.K
Scott, Joseph L. VA 19th Inf. Co.B
Scott, Joseph M. TX 6th Cav. Co.E
Scott, Joseph M. VA 14th Cav. Co.B
Scott, Joseph N. VA Cav. Hounshell's Bn. Co.F
Scott, Joseph P. FL 11th Inf. Co.C
Scott, Joseph T. TN Cav. 12th Bn. (Day's) Co.B
Scott, Joseph T. TN Arty. Ramsey's Btty.
Scott, Joseph T. TX 16th Cav. Co.B
Scott, Joseph T. VA 6th Bn.Res. Co.I
Scott, Joseph T. VA 37th Inf. Co.B
Scott, Joseph T. Gen. & Staff Medical Director
Scott, Joseph T. Gen. & Staff, KY Surg.
Scott, Joseph T.L. VA Mil. Scott Cty.
Scott, Joseph V. VA 3rd Inf. Co.E Lt.Col.
Scott, Joseph W. NC 47th Inf. Co.H Cpl.
Scott, Joseph William SC 15th Inf. Co.G
Scott, Josiah AL St.Arty. Co.A Cpl.
Scott, Josiah TN 20th Inf. Co.I
Scott, Josiah VA 58th Inf. Co.E
Scott, Josiah VA Mil. Washington Cty.
Scott, Josiah 1st Choctaw Mtd.Rifles Ward's Co.
Scott, Josiah B. GA Arty. 11th Bn. (Sumter
  Arty.) Co.A
Scott, Josiah B. GA 35th Inf. Co.G 2nd Lt.
Scott, Josiah B. VA Lt.Arty. King's Co.
Scott, J.P. FL Concsr.
Scott, J.P. GA Cav. Nelson's Ind.Co.
Scott, J.P. GA 1st (Symons') Res. Co.C
Scott, J.P. TX 28th Cav. Co.B Cpl.
Scott, J.R. AR 15th (N.W.) Inf. Emergency Co.I

Scott, J.R. GA 7th Inf. (St.Guards) Co.G
Scott, J.R. LA Mil.Conf.Guards Regt. Kirk's Co.
Scott, J.R. MS 6th Inf. Co.C 1st Cpl.
Scott, J.R. SC Lt.Arty. 3rd (Palmetto) Bn. Co.A
  Sgt.Maj.
Scott, J.S. AL 1st Cav. 2nd Co.A
Scott, J.S. AL 8th Cav. Co.I
Scott, J.S. AL Cav. Forrest's Regt.
Scott, J.S. AL 25th Inf. Co.H
Scott, J.S. GA 1st (Symons') Res. Co.H
Scott, J.S. NC 3rd Cav. (41st St.Troops) Co.F
Scott, J.S. SC 2nd Inf. Co.D
Scott, J.S. TN 12th (Green's) Cav. Co.F
Scott, J.S. TN 46th Inf. Co.F Sgt.
Scott, J.S. VA Hvy.Arty. 20th Bn. Co.C
Scott, Js 1st Cherokee Mtd.Vol. 1st Co.E
Scott, Js. W. AL 17th Inf. Co.F
Scott, J.T. AL 4th Inf. Co.A
Scott, J.T. AL 9th Inf. Co.G
Scott, J.T. AL 31st Inf. Co.H
Scott, J.T. GA 12th (Robinson's) Cav. (St.Guard)
  Co.E
Scott, J.T. GA Inf. 5th Bn. (St.Guards) Co.A
Scott, J.T. KY 3rd Mtd.Inf. Co.A Cpl.
Scott, J.T. MS Lt.Arty. 14th Bn. Co.C
Scott, J.T. MS 7th Inf. Co.H
Scott, J.T. MS 34th Inf. Co.A
Scott, J.T. SC 2nd Inf. Co.A
Scott, J.T. TN Cav. Nixon's Regt. Co.E 1st Lt.
Scott, J.T. TN Cav. Williams' Co. Bvt.2nd Lt.
Scott, J.T. TN 4th Inf. Co.B Cpl.
Scott, J.T. TX 12th Cav. Co.H
Scott, J.T. Hardee's Corps Capt.,AQM
Scott, Judson TX 9th (Young's) Inf. Co.D
Scott, Julius VA 5th Cav. Co.D
Scott, Julius VA 5th Cav. (12 mo. '61-2) Co.D
Scott, J.W. AL 6th Cav. Co.M
Scott, J.W. AL Mil. 2nd Regt.Vol. Co.A
Scott, J.W. AL 41st Inf. Co.H
Scott, J.W. AL 46th Inf. Co.F
Scott, J.W. AL Mil. 2nd Regt.Vol. Co.A
Scott, J.W. AR Inf. 8th Bn. Co.F
Scott, J.W. AR 19th (Dawson's) Inf. Co.G 1st
  Sgt.
Scott, J.W. AR 24th Inf. Co.H Cpl.
Scott, J.W. AR 34th Inf. Co.B
Scott, J.W. AR Inf. Hardy's Regt. Co.E
Scott, J.W. FL 1st (Res.) Inf. Co.K 1st Sgt.
Scott, J.W. GA Lt.Arty. Van Den Corput's Co.
Scott, J.W. GA 5th Res. Co.C
Scott, J.W. GA 11th Inf. Co.I
Scott, J.W. GA 28th Inf. Co.A Cpl.
Scott, J.W. GA 45th Inf. Co.H Cpl.
Scott, J.W. LA 5th Cav. Co.C
Scott, J.W. LA 1st (Nelligan's) Inf. Co.H
Scott, J.W. LA Inf. 1st Sp.Bn. (Rightor's) Co.D
Scott, J.W. LA 2nd Inf. Co.H
Scott, J.W. LA 25th Inf. Co.E Cpl.
Scott, J.W. MS 1st Cav. Co.K
Scott, J.W. MS 10th Inf. New Co.A
Scott, J.W. MS 33rd Inf. Co.F
Scott, J.W. MO 5th Cav. Co.A
Scott, J.W. MO 3rd Inf. Co.D
Scott, J.W. NC 22nd Inf. Co.F
Scott, J.W. NC 53rd Inf. Co.A 2nd Lt.
Scott, J.W. SC 2nd St.Troops Co.A
Scott, J.W. SC 5th St.Troops Co.M

Scott, J.W. SC 14th Inf. Co.I
Scott, J.W. TN 16th (Logwood's) Cav. Co.I Cpl.
Scott, J.W. TN 26th Cav. Co.K
Scott, J.W. TN 8th Inf. Co.C
Scott, J.W. TN 51st Inf. Co.C
Scott, J.W. TN 51st (Cons.) Inf. Co.I
Scott, J.W. TX 7th Cav. Co.D Cpl.
Scott, J.W. TX Cav. Border's Regt. Co.B
Scott, J.W. TX Inf. 3rd St.Troops Co.B
Scott, J.W. TX 12th Inf. Co.B
Scott, J.W. TX Granbury's Cons.Brig. Music.
Scott, J.W. VA Cav. McNeill's Co.
Scott, J.W. VA 3rd Inf.Loc.Def. Co.I
Scott, J.W. 4th Conf.Eng.Troops Co.E Cpl.
Scott, J.W.C. LA 9th Inf. Co.A
Scott, J. William MS 34th Inf. Co.F
Scott, J.W.W. MS 42nd Inf. Co.I
Scott, K.C. KY 7th Cav. Co.E
Scott, Kemp TX 14th Inf. Co.B
Scott, K.W. LA 18th Inf. Co.B
Scott, Kyle C. VA Lt.Arty. Carpenter's Co.
Scott, Kyle C. VA 27th Inf. Co.A
Scott, L. AL 33rd Inf. Co.D
Scott, L. LA Mil. 1st Regt. 2nd Brig. 1st Div. Co.E
Scott, L. SC 24th Inf. Co.A
Scott, L. TN 44th (Cons.) Inf.
Scott, L. TX Cav. Border's Regt. Co.K
Scott, L.A. AL 2nd Bn. Hilliard's Legion Vol. Co.E
Scott, L.A. AL 59th Inf. Co.B
Scott, L.A. MO Cav. 14th Regt.St.Guard Surg.
Scott, Lackey T. VA 1st Cav. Co.C
Scott, Lafayette TN 62nd Mtd.Inf. Co.G Cpl.
Scott, Lafayette VA 3rd Cav. Co.K
Scott, Langford J. SC 1st (Orr's) Rifles Co.L
Scott, Lanty K. VA Inf. 26th Bn. Co.E Sgt.
Scott, Larkin NC 26th Inf. Co.F
Scott, Larkin NC 61st Inf. Co.I
Scott, Larkin A. NC 48th Inf. Co.I
Scott, Larkin C. TX 1st (Yager's) Cav. Co.K
Scott, Larkin C. TX Cav. 8th (Taylor's) Bn. Co.B
Scott, Lawson AR 7th Inf. Co.E
Scott, Layfayette 1st Conf.Eng.Troops Co.I
Scott, L.B. AL 49th Inf. Co.G Cpl.
Scott, L.B. TN 9th Inf. Co.A Sgt.
Scott, L.B. TX 17th Inf. Co.G Cpl.
Scott, L.C. GA 13th Inf. Co.K
Scott, L.C. SC Mil. 16th Regt. Sigwald's Co.
Scott, L.D. GA 5th Cav. Co.F
Scott, L.D. TN 19th Inf. Co.B
Scott, L.E. GA Boddie's Co. (Troup Cty.Ind.Cav.)
Scott, Leander NC 42nd Inf. Co.K
Scott, Leath LA 1st Inf. Co.F
Scott, Lee SC 5th Cav. Co.K
Scott, Lee SC 5th Inf. 1st Co.K
Scott, Lee SC 7th Res. Co.A
Scott, Lemuel GA 24th Inf. Co.B
Scott, Lemuel T. AR 1st (Colquitt's) Inf. Co.E
Scott, Leonard TN Lt.Arty. Burrough's Co.
Scott, Leundous 1st Choctaw & Chickasaw Mtd.Rifles 2nd Co.K
Scott, Levi TX Cav. Madison's Regt. Co.F
Scott, Levi M. VA 48th Inf. Co.D

Scott, Levi V. MO 10th Inf. Co.G
Scott, Lewis GA 1st Cav. Co.A
Scott, Lewis VA 41st Mil. Co.D
Scott, Lewis C. VA 22nd Inf. Co.F
Scott, Lewis F. VA Cav. 15th Bn. Co.A
Scott, Lewis G. VA 5th Cav.
Scott, Lewis H. NC 44th Inf. Co.B
Scott, Lewis W. VA 9th Cav. Sandford's Co.
Scott, L.F. LA 27th Inf. Co.G Sgt.
Scott, L.F. VA 15th Cav. Co.A
Scott, L.H. NC 21st Inf. Co.I
Scott, L.J. MS 33rd Inf. Co.D 1st Lt.
Scott, L.L. MO 16th Inf. Co.K
Scott, L.M. KY Lt.Arty. Cobb's Co.
Scott, L.M. KY 3rd Mtd.Inf. 1st Co.F
Scott, L.M. TX 14th Inf. Co.B
Scott, L.N. SC 5th Cav. Co.G
Scott, Loftin B. NC 24th Inf. Co.A
Scott, Lorence N. SC Cav. 17th Bn. Co.B
Scott, Lorenzo D. NC 58th Inf. Co.B
Scott, Lots NC Vol. Lawrence's Co.
Scott, Lotte 7th Conf.Cav. Co.H
Scott, Louis SC 11th Inf. Co.G
Scott, Louis T. KY 1st Bn.Mtd.Rifles Co.D
Scott, L.S. AL 46th Inf. Co.F
Scott, Lucius C. NC 3rd Cav. (41st St.Troops) Co.F
Scott, Lucius M. TX 4th Cav. Co.F
Scott, Luther R. NC 6th Cav. (65th St.Troops) Co.D,B
Scott, L.V. SC 25th Inf. Co.K
Scott, L.W. MS 34th Inf. Co.F
Scott, M. AR 8th Inf. New Co.D
Scott, M. FL 2nd Cav. Co.H
Scott, M. GA 18th Inf. Co.K
Scott, M. KY 12th Cav. Co.D
Scott, M. NC 17th Inf. (2nd Org.) Co.L
Scott, M. SC 2nd Bn.S.S. Co.A
Scott, M. TN 15th (Cons.) Cav. Co.B Sgt.
Scott, M. TN 19th (Biffle's) Cav. Co.C
Scott, M. TN 19th & 20th (Cons.) Cav. Co.C
Scott, M.A. MS 9th Inf. New Co.K
Scott, Mack SC 1st Mtd.Mil. Earnest's Co.
Scott, Madison F. TX 14th Cav. Co.I
Scott, Madison H. GA 4th Inf. Co.K Cpl.
Scott, Maham AL Cav. Holloway's Co.
Scott, Manning AL 6th Cav. Co.D
Scott, Manning SC 15th Inf. Co.D
Scott, Marcellus TX 11th Inf. Co.G
Scott, Marcus NC Walker's Bn. Thomas' Legion Co.G
Scott, Marcus TN 1st (Carter's) Cav. Co.H
Scott, Marcus L. AR 9th Inf. Co.A
Scott, Marcus L. NC 29th Inf. Co.D
Scott, Marion SC 1st (Butler's) Inf. Co.B
Scott, Marion VA 59th Inf.
Scott, Marion C. GA 20th Inf. Co.G Sgt.
Scott, Marion J. SC 5th St.Troops Co.H
Scott, Mark GA 1st Cav. Co.A
Scott, Mark H. VA 45th Inf. Co.H Cpl.
Scott, Mark L. VA 4th Res. Co.I
Scott, Marshall TN 50th (Cons.) Inf. Co.K
Scott, Marshall A. TN Inf. 1st Bn. (Colms') Co.D
Scott, Martin KY 9th Cav. Co.D Cpl.
Scott, Martin P. Gen. & Staff, Med.Dept. Surg.
Scott, Martin V. TN 53rd Inf. Co.E

Scott, Mathew GA 1st Cav. Co.A
Scott, Matthew VA 4th Res. Co.H
Scott, Maxey O. MS Cav. Jeff Davis Legion Co.F
Scott, Mayhew M. MO Cav. Slayback's Regt. Co.G
Scott, M.C. AR 1st Mtd.Rifles Co.C
Scott, M.C. AR 2nd Mtd.Rifles Co.A Sgt.
Scott, M.C. AR 8th Cav. Co.F
Scott, M.C. AR 31st Inf. Co.I
Scott, M.C. TN 9th (Ward's) Cav. Co.A
Scott, Meredith NC Lt.Arty. 13th Bn. Co.A
Scott, Meredith VA Lt.Arty. 12th Bn. Co.D
Scott, M.F. 3rd Conf.Cav. Co.C
Scott, M.F. 3rd Conf.Cav. Co.K
Scott, M.G. GA Inf. 8th Bn. Co.F Cpl.
Scott, M.G. TN 4th Inf. Co.B Bvt.2nd Lt.
Scott, M.H. SC Inf. Holcombe Legion Co.E
Scott, Micajah TN 25th Inf. Co.A
Scott, Michael AR 23rd Inf. Co.E
Scott, Michael GA 1st (Olmstead's) Inf. Co.B
Scott, Michael VA Hvy.Arty. 18th Bn. Co.E
Scott, Michael VA 1st Inf. Chambers' Co.
Scott, Michael VA 2nd Inf. Co.K
Scott, Michael VA 46th Inf. Co.B
Scott, Michael VA 60th Inf. Co.F
Scott, Michael A. VA Harper's Res. Co.F
Scott, Michael W. NC 23rd Inf. Co.D
Scott, Millege L. SC 6th Cav. Co.B,D
Scott, Miller AL 6th Inf. Co.G
Scott, Milo TN 18th (Newman's) Cav. Co.C Cpl.
Scott, Milo W. TN Lt.Arty. Barry's Co.
Scott, Milton MS 12th Inf. Co.K
Scott, Milton TN 6th (Wheeler's) Cav. Co.K
Scott, Milton J. VA 24th Inf. Co.B
Scott, Milton N. Sig.Corps,CSA
Scott, Milus L. AL 41st Inf. Co.D
Scott, M.J. LA 2nd Inf. Co.D
Scott, M.J. LA Miles' Legion Co.E Sgt.
Scott, M.J. MO 9th (Elliott's) Cav. Co.G
Scott, M.L. AR 35th Inf. Co.E
Scott, M.L. FL Lt.Arty. Dyke's Co.
Scott, M.L. TN 6th (Wheeler's) Cav. Co.L Sgt.
Scott, M.L. TX Inf. 1st St.Troops Shield's Co.B
Scott, M.M. MS Lt.Arty. 14th Bn. Co.C
Scott, M.M. SC 25th Inf. Co.K
Scott, M.N. GA Cav. 29th Bn. Co.B
Scott, M.N. GA Siege Arty. Campbell's Ind.Co.
Scott, M.O. SC 2nd Inf. Co.I Sgt.
Scott, Morgan MO 4th Cav. Co.K,D Sgt.
Scott, Moses KY 2nd Cav.
Scott, Moses 1st Cherokee Mtd.Vol. 1st Co.A, 2nd Co.C
Scott, Moses A. VA Inf. 26th Bn. Co.G
Scott, Moses A. VA 59th Inf. 2nd Co.B
Scott, Moses Edward MO 8th Inf. Co.E
Scott, M.P. GA 40th Inf. Co.D
Scott, M.P. VA 15th Inf. Sgt.Maj.
Scott, M. Robert TX 1st (McCulloch's) Cav. Co.F
Scott, M.S. AR Lt.Arty. Hart's Btty.
Scott, M.S. SC 1st Bn.Res. 2nd Lt.
Scott, M.T. AR 11th Inf. Co.K
Scott, Nathaniel AR 23rd Inf. Co.A 2nd Lt.
Scott, Nathaniel NC 54th Inf. Co.D
Scott, Nathaniel J. GA 25th Inf. Co.G

Scott, Nathaniel W. GA 27th Inf. Co.F
Scott, N.B. MO 6th Cav. Co.E
Scott, N.B. TN 8th Inf. Co.C
Scott, N.B. TN 51st Inf. Co.C
Scott, N.B. TN 51st (Cons.) Inf. Co.I
Scott, N.B. TX 17th Inf. Co.C
Scott, N.D. FL 5th Inf. Co.H
Scott, Nelson NC 1st Arty. (10th St.Troops) Co.C
Scott, Newton SC 1st (Orr's) Rifles Co.D
Scott, Newton TN Cav. 17th Bn. (Sanders') Co.A
Scott, Newton J. AL 48th Inf. Co.B
Scott, N.G. AL 55th Vol. Co.G
Scott, N.G. KY 3rd Cav. Co.D
Scott, N.G. KY 3rd Mtd.Inf. Co.D
Scott, N.G. 8th (Wade's) Conf.Cav. Co.D
Scott, Nicholas E. GA 12th Inf. Co.G
Scott, Nimrod GA 11th Cav. Co.H
Scott, Nimrod GA Inf. 4th Bn. (St.Guards) Co.A Sgt.
Scott, N.J. LA 13th Bn. (Part.Rangers) Co.C 1st Lt.
Scott, N.L. GA 18th Inf. Co.K
Scott, N.M. MS 6th Inf. Co.C Sgt.
Scott, Noah GA 15th Inf. Co.A
Scott, Noah TX Cav. Lilley's Co. Cpl.
Scott, Noah TX 17th Inf. Co.E
Scott, Noah 2nd Cherokee Mtd.Vol. Co.F
Scott, Noah F. MS 33rd Inf. Co.I
Scott, O. TN 28th (Cons.) Inf. Co.F
Scott, O. TN 84th Inf. Co.B
Scott, Obed R. NC 1st Inf. Co.C 2nd Lt.
Scott, O.H.P. SC 25th Inf. Co.H
Scott, Oliver TX 17th Cons.Dismtd.Cav. 1st Co.G
Scott, Oliver TX 18th Cav. Co.K
Scott, Oliver TX 15th Inf. 2nd Co.F
Scott, Oliver VA 36th Inf. 2nd Co.C
Scott, Oliver H.P. SC 6th Cav. Co.B
Scott, Oliver P. GA 9th Inf. Co.K
Scott, O.P. AR Inf. Cocke's Regt. Co.F
Scott, O.S. AL 47th Inf. Co.I
Scott, Oscar D. GA 15th Inf. Co.K
Scott, Osceola P. TX 18th Cav. Co.E
Scott, Overton MO 10th Inf. Co.D
Scott, P.A. TN 46th Inf. Co.F Cpl.
Scott, Panill LA 6th Inf. Co.C Capt.
Scott, Paris MO 10th Inf. Co.K
Scott, Parish MO 11th Inf. Co.A
Scott, Patrick GA 3rd Cav. (St.Guards) Co.G
Scott, Patrick LA 6th Inf. Co.H
Scott, Patrick TX 3rd Inf. Co.D 2nd Lt.
Scott, Patrick VA Hvy.Arty. Patteson's Co.
Scott, Patrick Henry TX 23rd Cav. Co.K
Scott, Patrick J. MS Cav. Jeff Davis Legion Co.C
Scott, Patrick J. MS 13th Inf. Co.C
Scott, Paul LA 26th Inf. Co.I
Scott, P.B. NC 4th Cav. (59th St.Troops) Co.C
Scott, P.B. NC 29th Inf. Asst.Medical Director
Scott, P.B. NC Bass' Co.
Scott, P.B. TX 2nd Inf. Co.G
Scott, P.C. MO 6th Cav. Co.E
Scott, P.D. TX 7th Cav. Co.E
Scott, Perry TX 20th Inf. Co.C
Scott, Peter MS Cav. 3rd Bn. (Ashcraft's) Co.C

Scott, Peter F. VA Hvy.Arty. 19th Bn. 3rd Co.E
Scott, Peter H. MO 1st Inf. Co.G 1st Sgt.
Scott, Peter H. VA 3rd Cav. 2nd Co.I
Scott, Peyton AL 15th Bn.Part.Rangers Co.B
Scott, Peyton AL 24th Inf. Co.A
Scott, Peyton AL 56th Part.Rangers Co.B
Scott, P.F. Gen. & Staff,PACS Asst.Surg.
Scott, P.G. TX 1st Hvy.Arty. Co.A
Scott, P. Gay 1st Conf.Eng. Troops Co.E Sgt.
Scott, P.H. TN 5th Inf. 2nd Co.B
Scott, P.H. TN 46th Inf. Co.F
Scott, P.H. VA Mtd.Guard 4th Congr.Dist.
Scott, Philetus P. GA 47th Inf. Co.D
Scott, Philip C. KY 4th Cav. Co.E
Scott, Philip H. VA 13th Inf. Co.A
Scott, Philip T. TN 6th Inf. Co.I
Scott, Phillip A. LA 27th Inf. Co.F
Scott, Pinckney GA 48th Inf. Co.C
Scott, Pinckney SC 1st (Hagood's) Inf. 1st Co.G
Scott, Pinctney, Jr. GA 10th Inf. Co.D
Scott, Pleasant GA 11th Inf. Co.C
Scott, Pleasant S. NC 13th Inf. Co.A
Scott, P.M. AR 2nd Inf. New Co.E
Scott, P.M. AR 11th Inf. Co.K,B Sgt.
Scott, P.M. AR 11th & 17th Cons.Inf. Co.B Sgt.
Scott, P.M. TX 32nd Cav. Co.K
Scott, P.O. MO Inf. Clark's Regt. Co.A
Scott, Powhatan Gay VA 1st Arty. Co.D Cpl.
Scott, P.P. GA 1st Reg. Co.G
Scott, P.R. GA 31st Inf. Co.K
Scott, Preston B. KY 4th Mtd.Inf. Surg.
Scott, Preston Brown Gen. & Staff Surg.
Scott, P.W. AL Inf. 2nd Regt. Co.B
Scott, P.W. AL 42nd Inf. Co.B
Scott, R. AR Inf. 10th Bn. Lt.Col.
Scott, R. GA 1st Cav. Co.A
Scott, R. GA Phillips' Legion Co.D
Scott, R. LA 3rd (Harrison's) Cav. Co.B
Scott, R. LA Inf. 4th Bn. Co.D
Scott, R. LA Mil. Orleans Fire Regt. Co.H
Scott, R. MS 4th Cav. Co.H Cpl.
Scott, R. MS 41st Inf. Co.I
Scott, R. SC Mil. 16th Regt. Steinmeyer, Jr.'s Co.
Scott, R. SC Simons' Co.
Scott, R.A. AL 5th Cav. Co.E
Scott, R.A. GA 11th Cav. Co.B
Scott, R.A. MS 6th Cav. Co.A
Scott, R.A. NC 10th Regt. Co.D
Scott, Rankin VA 14th Cav. Co.K
Scott, R.B. MS 1st Cav. Co.K
Scott, R.C. GA Lt.Arty. Pritchard's Co. (Washington Arty.)
Scott, R.C. KY 2nd (Duke's) Cav. Co.A
Scott, R.C. LA 3rd Inf. Co.H
Scott, R.C. MS Lt.Arty. Stanford's Co. Cpl.
Scott, R.C. SC 5th Cav. Co.G
Scott, R.C. SC 1st St.Troops Co.I
Scott, R.C. SC 5th Res. Co.H
Scott, R.C. TN 1st (Feild's) Inf. Co.L
Scott, R.C. TN Inf. Nashville Bn. Cattles' Co.
Scott, R.C. VA 4th Cav.
Scott, R.C. VA Second Class Mil. Wolff's Co.
Scott, R.D. AR 27th Inf. Co.G
Scott, R.E. LA 8th Cav. Co.C
Scott, R.E. SC 24th Inf. Co.A
Scott, R.E. VA Lt.Arty. 12th Bn. Co.B

Scott, Reuben A. VA 10th Inf. Co.B Cpl.
Scott, Reuben S. NC 47th Inf. Co.I
Scott, Reuby. N. TX 18th Inf. Co.B
Scott, R.F. SC 3rd St.Troops Co.A
Scott, R.F. TN 3rd (Forrest's) Cav. Co.H
Scott, R.F. TN 4th Inf. Co.B
Scott, R.F. TX Cav. Bourland's Regt. Co.B
Scott, R.F. TX 14th Inf. Co.B 1st Sgt.
Scott, R.H. AL Inf. 1st Regt. Co.A
Scott, R.H. AL 59th Inf. Co.B
Scott, R.H. AR 32nd Inf. Co.C
Scott, R.H. TX Cav. Saufley's Scouting Bn. Co.D 1st Lt.
Scott, Richard LA 28th (Thomas') Inf.
Scott, Richard MS Cav. 24th Bn. Co.B
Scott, Richard MS Cav. Hughes' Bn. Co.B
Scott, Richard MS Lt.Arty. (Jefferson Arty.) Darden's Co.
Scott, Richard MS 9th Inf. New Co.H
Scott, Richard VA 25th Mil. Co.A
Scott, Richard VA 27th Inf. Co.E
Scott, Richard C. VA 41st Inf. 2nd Co.E
Scott, Richard H. TX Cav. Chisum's Regt. (Dismtd.) Co.F 1st Lt.
Scott, Richard H. VA 5th Cav. (12 mo. '61-2) Co.E
Scott, Richard H. VA 13th Cav. Co.K Sgt.
Scott, Richard L. TN 16th (Logwood's) Cav. Co.B
Scott, Richard L. VA Lt.Arty. Cayce's Co.
Scott, Richard L. VA Inf. 25th Bn. Co.E 1st Sgt.
Scott, Richard M. VA 23rd Inf. Co.C 1st Lt.
Scott, Richard P. GA 47th Inf. Co.D Cpl.
Scott, Riley TN 35th Inf. 3rd Co.F
Scott, R.J. LA 3rd (Harrison's) Cav. Co.C
Scott, R.J. LA 12th Inf. Co.K
Scott, R.J. MS 28th Cav. Co.E
Scott, R.J. TN 18th (Newsom's) Cav. Co.C
Scott, R.J. TN 42nd Inf. Co.D Sgt.
Scott, R. Jasper MS 36th Inf. Co.G
Scott, R.L. MS 2nd Part.Rangers Co.C
Scott, R.L. TN 15th (Cons.) Cav. Co.B
Scott, R.M. AR 12th Inf. Co.H 1st Lt.
Scott, R.M. LA 1st Hvy.Arty. (Reg.) 2nd Lt.
Scott, R.M. TN Inf. Nashville Bn. Cattles' Co.
Scott, R.M. VA 1st (Farinholt's) Res. Co.H Capt.
Scott, R.M. VA 4th Res. Co.E
Scott, R.M. VA Averett's Bn.Res. Capt.
Scott, R.M.K. TX 2nd Inf. Co.A
Scott, R.N. VA 8th Inf. Co.G Cpl.
Scott, Robert AR 45th Cav. Co.M
Scott, Robert AL Inf. 1st Regt. Co.B Cpl.
Scott, Robert AL 9th Inf. Co.K
Scott, Robert GA 36th (Broyles') Inf. Co.E
Scott, Robert LA 20th Inf. Co.K
Scott, Robert LA Maddox's Regt.Res.Corps Co.B
Scott, Robert LA Mil. Mooney's Co. (Saddlers Guards)
Scott, Robert MO 11th Inf. Co.F,K
Scott, Robert NC 22nd Inf. Co.A
Scott, Robert SC 6th Cav. Co.A
Scott, Robert SC 16th Inf. Co.A
Scott, Robert TN 2nd (Robison's) Inf. Co.E
Scott, Robert TX 3rd Cav. Co.A

Scott, Robert VA 4th Cav. Co.F
Scott, Robert VA Cav. Mosby's Regt. (Part.
  Rangers) Co.F,I
Scott, Robert VA Hvy.Arty. 18th Bn. Co.B
Scott, Robert VA 3rd Res. Co.F
Scott, Robert VA 41st Inf. 1st Co.E
Scott, Robert 3rd Conf.Eng.Troops Co.D
Scott, Robert B. GA 20th Inf. Co.E
Scott, Robert B. LA 7th Inf. Co.D Capt.
Scott, Robert B. MO Cav. Freeman's Regt. Co.A
Scott, Robert B. TN 1st Cav.
Scott, Robert C. GA 36th (Villepigue's) Inf.
  Co.F
Scott, Robert C. VA 151st Mil. Co.B Capt.
Scott, Robert C. VA 198th Mil.
Scott, Robert C. 1st Conf.Inf. 1st Co.F
Scott, Robert C. Gen. & Staff 1st Lt.,Ord.Off.
Scott, Robert C. GA Inf. 2nd Bn. (St.Guards)
  Old Co.D 1st Sgt.
Scott, Robert G. MS 1st (King's) Inf. (St.Troops)
  Co.A
Scott, Robert G. VA Lt.Arty. Kirkpatrick's Co.
  1st Lt.
Scott, Robert G. VA 3rd Inf. Co.H
Scott, Robert G. VA 14th Inf. Co.E
Scott, Robert H. AL 2nd Bn. Hilliard's Legion
  Vol. Co.E
Scott, Robert H. LA 8th Inf. Co.E Sgt.
Scott, Robert H. MS Cav. 24th Bn. Co.B
Scott, Robert J. 4th Conf.Inf. Co.K Sgt.
Scott, Robert M. AL 87th Regt. Co.H 1st Sgt.
Scott, Robert M. GA 24th Inf. Co.H
Scott, Robert M. GA 44th Inf. Co.H
Scott, Robert M. LA 8th Inf. Co.G
Scott, Robert M. LA 19th Inf. Co.D Sgt.
Scott, Robert M. MS 12th Inf. Co.D
Scott, Robert M. NC 2nd Cav. (19th St.Troops)
  Co.F
Scott, Robert M. TX 1st (Yager's) Cav. Co.K
Scott, Robert M. TX Cav. 8th (Taylor's) Bn.
  Co.B
Scott, Robert M. TX 11th Inf. Co.I
Scott, Robert P. GA Lt.Arty. Van Den Corput's
  Co.
Scott, Robert P. GA Inf. 3rd Bn. Co.A
Scott, Robert R. AL 8th Inf. Co.H 1st Lt.
Scott, Robert S. TX 10th Inf. Co.H Cpl.
Scott, Robert S. VA 30th Inf. Co.E
Scott, Robert T. AL Norwood's Cav.
Scott, Robert T. LA Inf. 4th Bn. Co.A Sgt.
Scott, Robert T. TN 11th Inf. Co.E
Scott, Robert T. TN 36th Inf. Co.D
Scott, Robert T. VA Arty. Wise Legion
Scott, Robert W. MS 2nd (Davidson's) Inf. Co.D
Scott, Rodger VA 6th Inf. Weisiger's Co.
Scott, Roger VA Courtney Arty.
Scott, Roger VA Lt.Arty. Weisiger's Co.
Scott, Roger VA 16th Inf. Co.I
Scott, Romelus LA 28th (Gray's) Inf. Co.K
Scott, R.P. TN 28th (Cons.) Inf. Co.C
Scott, R.S. AL 63rd Inf. Co.K
Scott, R.S. NC 3rd Cav. (41st St.Troops) Co.B
Scott, R.S. NC 11th (Bethel Regt.) Inf. Co.H
Scott, R.S. TN 13th Inf. Co.L 1st Lt.
Scott, R.S. Trans-MS Conf.Cav. 1st Bn. Co.C
Scott, R.T., Jr. AL 4th (Russell's) Cav. Co.C
Scott, R.T. VA Arty. Wise Legion

Scott, R.T. VA 8th Inf. Co.K Capt.
Scott, R. Taylor Gen. & Staff Maj.,QM
Scott, Rueben A. VA 97th Mil. Co.A 1st Lt.
Scott, Rufus VA 45th Inf. Co.D
Scott, Rufus C. SC Cav. 17th Bn. Co.B
Scott, Rufus H. AL 20th Inf. Co.C,G
Scott, Rufus H. MO 10th Cav. Co.I,H
Scott, Rutilius K. MS 7th Inf. Co.E 1st Sgt.
Scott, R.W. MS Cav. 24th Bn. Co.F
Scott, R.W. MS 32nd Inf. Co.B
Scott, R.W. TN 1st (Feild's) Inf. Co.B
Scott, R.W. TN 28th Inf. Co.K
Scott, R.W. TX 3rd Cav. Co.A
Scott, R.W. TX 2nd Inf. Co.G
Scott, R.W. Secret Serv. McDaniel's Co.
Scott, S. AL 2nd Bn. Co.A
Scott, S. MO Robertson's Regt.St.Guard Co.3
Scott, S. NC Cav. 16th Bn. Co.F
Scott, S. TN 1st Hvy.Arty. 2nd Co.C
Scott, S. TX Cav. Good's Bn. Co.A
Scott, S. TX 1st Hvy.Arty. Co.A
Scott, S. TX 13th Vol. Co.F
Scott, S. VA 21st Cav. 2nd Co.D
Scott, S. VA Lt.Arty. Barr's Co.
Scott, S.A. MO Cav. Freeman's Regt. Co.F
Scott, S.A. SC 26th Inf. Co.I
Scott, S.A. Trans-MS Conf.Cav. 1st Bn. Co.C
  Sgt.
Scott, Sam N. AL 13th Bn.Part.Rangers Co.E
Scott, Sam T. TX 3rd Cav. Co.A
Scott, Sampson TN 43rd Inf. Co.C
Scott, Samuel AL 6th Cav. Co.H
Scott, Samuel AR 7th Inf. Co.H Cpl.
Scott, Samuel FL Inf. 2nd Bn. Co.D
Scott, Samuel FL 11th Inf. Co.C
Scott, Samuel KY 2nd (Duke's) Cav. Co.A
Scott, Samuel KY 2nd Mtd.Inf. Co.B
Scott, Samuel KY 5th Mtd.Inf. Co.F
Scott, Samuel LA 17th Inf. Co.A
Scott, Samuel TN 4th (McLemore's) Cav. Co.E
Scott, Samuel TN 16th Inf. Co.K
Scott, Samuel TX 18th Cav. Co.H
Scott, Samuel VA 4th Res. Co.H
Scott, Samuel VA 51st Inf. Co.H
Scott, Samuel A. AR 20th Inf. Co.E Sgt.
Scott, Samuel A. GA 44th Inf. Co.E 1st Lt.
Scott, Samuel A. SC 2nd Res.
Scott, Samuel A. TX Cav. 4th Regt.St.Troops
  Co.G 2nd Lt.
Scott, Samuel A. TX Cav. Mann's Regt. Co.C
  2nd Lt.
Scott, Samuel B. MS 2nd Inf. Co.E
Scott, Samuel B. TN Lt.Arty. Lynch's Co. Cpl.
Scott, Samuel B. VA 2nd Arty. Co.E Sgt.
Scott, Samuel C. GA 31st Inf. Co.K Sgt.
Scott, Samuel C. LA 25th Inf. Co.C Capt.
Scott, Samuel C. TN Cav. 9th Bn. (Gantt's)
  Co.A
Scott, Samuel E. AR 23rd Inf. Co.F Cpl.
Scott, Samuel E. GA 4th (Clinch's) Cav. Co.D
  Cpl.
Scott, Samuel E. TX 3rd Cav. Co.C
Scott, Samuel F.M. FL 6th Inf. Co.D,F
Scott, Samuel H. GA Phillips' Legion Co.O
Scott, Samuel H. VA 57th Inf. Co.B
Scott, Samuel J. MS 9th Cav. Co.F
Scott, Samuel J. MS 11th Inf. Co.I

Scott, Samuel J. 1st Conf.Inf. 2nd Co.F
Scott, Samuel Joe VA 1st (Farinholt's) Res. Co.B
Scott, Samuel L. AR 7th Inf. Co.H
Scott, Samuel L. MS 7th Inf. Co.E,A
Scott, Samuel L. TX 37th Cav. Co.K Cpl.
Scott, Samuel L. TX Cav. Mann's Bn. Co.A
  Capt.
Scott, Samuel L. TX Cav. Mann's Regt. Co.A
  Capt.
Scott, Samuel L. TX 10th Inf. Co.A 2nd Lt.
Scott, Samuel L. TX 11th Inf. Co.C
Scott, Samuel M. AR 20th Inf. Co.E
Scott, Samuel M. SC 12th Inf. Co.A Cpl.
Scott, Samuel M. TN 36th Inf. Co.D
Scott, Samuel N. AL 56th Part.Rangers Co.I
Scott, Samuel P. VA Lt.Arty. King's Co.
Scott, Samuel P. VA 3rd Res. Co.F
Scott, Samuel P. VA 34th Inf. Co.I
Scott, Samuel P. VA Mil. Washington Cty.
Scott, Samuel S. AL 28th Inf. Co.G
Scott, Samuel S. KY 2nd Mtd.Inf. Co.H
Scott, Samuel S. LA 21st (Kennedy's) Inf. Co.D
Scott, Samuel S. TX 9th (Young's) Inf. Co.A
Scott, Samuel S. Gen. & Staff Surg.
Scott, Samuel T. TN Cav. 2nd Bn. (Biffle's)
  Co.C Sgt.
Scott, Samuel T. TN 6th (Wheeler's) Cav. Co.I
Scott, Samuel W. GA 12th Inf. Co.D
Scott, Samuel W. VA 42nd Inf. Co.F
Scott, Sandy TN 18th (Newsom's) Cav. Co.C
Scott, Sandy VA 3rd Res. Co.D
Scott, S.B. TX 10th Cav. Comsy.
Scott, S.D. AR 15th (N.W.) Inf. Co.B
Scott, S.D. LA 4th Inf. Co.D
Scott, S.D. TN 5th Inf. 2nd Co.B Sgt.
Scott, S.D. TN 46th Inf. Co.F
Scott, Seaburn S. AL 22nd Inf. Co.K
Scott, Seborn S. LA Inf. 4th Bn. Co.K
Scott, Seth H. NC 4th Inf. Co.F
Scott, Seth R. MS Lt.Arty. (Madison Lt.Arty.)
  Richards' Co.
Scott, S.F. GA 18th Inf. Co.B
Scott, S.F. TN 6th (Wheeler's) Cav. Co.D
Scott, S.H. AL 17th Inf. Co.B
Scott, S.H. GA 1st Cav. Co.A 3rd Lt.
Scott, Shadrach F. NC 21st Inf. Co.C 2nd Lt.
Scott, Shadrach F. TN Lt.Arty. Burrough's Co.
Scott, Shalem E. TX 30th Cav. Co.I Sgt.
Scott, Shelton F. TN Cav. 11th Bn. (Gordon's)
  Co.D
Scott, Sherod FL Inf. 2nd Bn. Co.E
Scott, Sherrod FL 11th Inf. Co.A
Scott, Sidney VA 14th Inf. Co.A Capt.
Scott, Sidney M. KY 4th Cav. Co.F
Scott, Silas MS 1st Lt.Arty. Co.G
Scott, Silas S. GA 17th Inf. Co.K
Scott, Simeon TX Cav. Baylor's Regt. Co.C
Scott, Simon TN 22nd Inf. Co.I
Scott, Simon 1st Choctaw Mtd.Rifles Ward's Co.
Scott, Simpson S. AL 41st Inf. Co.H
Scott, Sir Walter MS Cav. Shelby's Co. (Bolivar
  Greys)
Scott, S.J. MS 10th Cav. Co.A Cpl.
Scott, S.J. TN Cav. 17th Bn. (Sanders') Co.C
  Cpl.
Scott, S. Jefferson 1st Conf.Inf. 2nd Co.F
Scott, S.L. TX 1st Inf. Co.H

Scott, S.M. AL St.Res. Palmer's Co.
Scott, S.M. GA 18th Inf. Co.K
Scott, S.M. KY 7th Mtd.Inf. Co.G
Scott, Smith MO 5th Cav. Co.E
Scott, Smith MO Cav. Wood's Regt. Co.G
Scott, Smith MO 4th Inf. Co.C
Scott, Smith B. TX 6th Cav. Co.D
Scott, S.N. GA 7th Inf. (St.Guards) Co.G
Scott, S.N. TX 22nd Inf. Co.A
Scott, Solomon VA 25th Cav. Co.E,F
Scott, Solomon VA 6th Bn.Res. Co.E
Scott, Solomon VA 54th Inf. Co.F
Scott, S.P. MS Conscr.
Scott, S.P. TN 19th & 20th (Cons.) Cav. Co.E
Scott, S.P. TN 20th (Russell's) Cav. Co.H
Scott, Spencer B. Loring's Div. Capt.,ACS
Scott, Spencer M. GA Inf. 8th Bn. Co.C
Scott, S.R. LA Cav. Greenleaf's Co. (Orleans Lt.Horse)
Scott, S.S. AL Cp. of Instr. Talladega
Scott, S.S. AR 15th Mil. Co.A Cpl.
Scott, S.S. KY 4th Cav. Surg.
Scott, S.S. NC Arty. Surg.
Scott, S.S. VA Loc.Def. Sutherland's Co.
Scott, S.T. AL Lt.Arty. Kolb's Btty.
Scott, S.T. TN 1st Hvy.Arty. Co.K
Scott, S.T. TX 14th Inf. Co.B
Scott, Starkey AL Arty. 4th Bn. Hilliard's Legion Co.A
Scott, Starkey AL 60th Inf. Co.I
Scott, Starling AL 33rd Inf. Co.I
Scott, Stephen GA 31st Inf. Co.K Cpl.
Scott, Stephen MO 6th Cav. Co.A
Scott, Stephen NC 44th Inf. Co.E
Scott, Stephen L. MS 2nd Part.Rangers Co.A
Scott, Sterling TN 43rd Inf. Co.K
Scott, S.W. MS Cav. 1st Bn. (Montgomery's) St.Troops Cameron's Co.
Scott, S.W. MS 20th Inf. Co.A
Scott, S.W. MS 25th Inf. Co.C
Scott, S.W. MS St.Troops (Herndon Rangers) Montgomery's Ind.Co.
Scott, S.W. MO 16th Inf. Co.K
Scott, S.W. NC Mallett's Bn. (Cp.Guard) Co.D
Scott, S.W. TN 9th Inf. Co.E
Scott, S.W. TN 21st Inf. Co.A
Scott, S.W. Eng.Dept. Polk's Corps A. of TN Sap. & Min. Co.,CSA
Scott, T. GA Inf. 27th Bn. (NonConscr.) Co.A
Scott, T. GA Inf. Grubbs' Co.
Scott, T. GA Inf. (NonConscr.) Howard's Co.
Scott, T. LA 25th Inf. Co.F
Scott, T. LA Mil.Conf.Guards Regt. Co.E
Scott, T. TN 15th (Cons.) Cav. Co.I
Scott, T. VA 21st Cav. 2nd Co.D
Scott, T. VA Lt.Arty. Grandy's Co.
Scott, T. VA Murphy's Co.
Scott, T.A. LA 8th Cav. Co.E
Scott, T.A. TN Holman's Bn.Part.Rangers Co.A
Scott, T.A. TN 43rd Inf. Co.K
Scott, T.A. 3rd Conf.Eng.Troops Co.B Artif.
Scott, T.A. Eng.Dept. Polk's Corps A. of TN Sap. & Min. Co.,CSA
Scott, Talbert VA 40th Inf. Co.D
Scott, Tapp TN 40th Inf. Co.E
Scott, Tarlton W. VA 9th Inf. Co.B
Scott, T.B. KY 3rd Bn.Mtd.Rifles Co.C

Scott, T.B. MS 41st Inf. Co.I
Scott, T.B. SC 1st Cav. Co.G Sgt.
Scott, T.B. TX 5th Inf. Co.D
Scott, T.C. TN Inf. Sowell's Detach.
Scott, T.D. GA 1st Inf. (St.Guards) Co.E 2nd Lt.
Scott, T.E. SC 15th Inf. Co.F
Scott, T.F. MS 16th Inf. Co.C
Scott, T.F. MS Burt's Ind.Co. (Dixie Guards)
Scott, T.F. TN Inf. 1st Cons.Regt. Co.A
Scott, T.F. TN 6th Inf. Co.A QMS
Scott, T.G. NC 54th Inf. Co.B
Scott, T.H. GA Phillips' Legion Co.O
Scott, T.H. TX Inf. 1st Bn. Co.F
Scott, T.H. Gen. & Staff AASurg.
Scott, Thaddeus NC 33rd Inf. Co.B
Scott, Thaddeus B. GA 12th Inf. Co.E Capt.
Scott, Theophilus VA 41st Inf. Co.A
Scott, Thomas AL Lt.Arty. Ward's Btty.
Scott, Thomas AL 1st Inf. Co.B
Scott, Thomas AL 3rd Inf. Co.A
Scott, Thomas AL 26th (O'Neal's) Inf. Co.E
Scott, Thomas AR 2nd Cav. 1st Co.A
Scott, Thomas AR Cav. Wright's Regt. Co.C
Scott, Thomas AR Mil. Desha Cty.Bn. Capt.
Scott, Thomas GA 4th (Clinch's) Cav. Co.D
Scott, Thomas KY 1st Inf. Co.H 4th Sgt.
Scott, Thomas KY 3rd Mtd.Inf. Co.B
Scott, Thomas LA Inf. 4th Bn. Co.E
Scott, Thomas LA 6th Inf. Co.I Cpl.
Scott, Thomas MS 18th Cav. Co.B
Scott, Thomas MS Cav. Jeff Davis Legion Co.D
Scott, Thomas MS Lt.Arty. (Jefferson Arty.) Darden's Co.
Scott, Thomas MS 35th Inf. Co.B
Scott, Thomas MO 3rd Cav. Co.D
Scott, Thomas MO 4th Cav. Co.B
Scott, Thomas MO 7th Cav. Co.H
Scott, Thomas MO 16th Inf. Co.G
Scott, Thomas NC 6th Inf. Co.K
Scott, Thomas NC 21st Inf. Co.D
Scott, Thomas NC 21st Inf. Co.H
Scott, Thomas SC 1st (Butler's) Inf. Co.E
Scott, Thomas SC Palmetto S.S. Co.B
Scott, Thomas TN 1st (Carter's) Cav. Co.C
Scott, Thomas TN 6th (Wheeler's) Cav. Asst.Surg.
Scott, Thomas TN 12th (Green's) Cav. Co.G
Scott, Thomas TN 16th (Logwood's) Cav. Co.D Cpl.
Scott, Thomas TN 13th Inf. Co.K
Scott, Thomas TN 25th Inf. Co.I
Scott, Thomas TN 36th Inf. Co.E
Scott, Thomas TN 48th (Nixon's) Inf. Co.C
Scott, Thomas TN Conscr. (Cp. of Instr.)
Scott, Thomas TX 1st (McCulloch's) Cav. Co.C
Scott, Thomas TX 1st (Yager's) Cav. Co.H
Scott, Thomas TX Cav. 8th (Taylor's) Bn. Co.E
Scott, Thomas TX Cav. Mann's Regt. Co.G Cpl.
Scott, Thomas TX 1st Inf. Co.B
Scott, Thomas TX 22nd Inf. Co.B Sgt.
Scott, Thomas VA Cav. Caldwell's Bn. Taylor's Co.
Scott, Thomas VA 2nd Arty. Co.I Sgt.
Scott, Thomas VA Lt.Arty. Cayce's Co.
Scott, Thomas VA 25th Mil. Co.C

Scott, Thomas VA 45th Inf. Co.G
Scott, Thomas 1st Creek Mtd.Vol. Co.A
Scott, Thomas Sig.Corps,CSA
Scott, Thomas A. AL 47th Inf. Co.I
Scott, Thomas A. GA Inf. 27th Bn. Co.B
Scott, Thomas A. SC Inf. 7th Bn. (Enfield Rifles) Co.H
Scott, Thomas A. TN 11th (Holman's) Cav. Co.B
Scott, Thomas A. TN 4th Inf. Co.E
Scott, Thomas A. TN 45th Inf. Co.K
Scott, Thomas B. NC 45th Inf. Co.B
Scott, Thomas B. TN 48th (Nixon's) Inf. Co.I Cpl.
Scott, Thomas B. VA 3rd Inf. Co.C 1st Lt.
Scott, Thomas C. AR 3rd Cav. Co.D
Scott, Thomas C. GA 47th Inf. Co.E
Scott, Thomas C. NC 12th Inf. Co.E
Scott, Thomas C. SC Palmetto S.S. Co.K
Scott, Thomas F. LA 25th Inf. Co.C
Scott, Thomas F. MS 2nd Part.Rangers Co.C
Scott, Thomas F. MS 18th Inf. Co.A
Scott, Thomas F. VA 3rd Inf. Co.C
Scott, Thomas F. VA 52nd Inf. Co.E
Scott, Thomas G. AL 40th Inf. Co.D Sgt.
Scott, Thomas G. NC 28th Inf. Co.I
Scott, Thomas G. TX 13th Cav. Co.K 3rd Lt.
Scott, Thomas G. TX 17th Cons.Dismtd.Cav. Co.B
Scott, Thomas G. VA 16th Cav. Co.F
Scott, Thomas G. 4th Conf.Inf. Co.F
Scott, Thomas H. FL 6th Inf. Co.B
Scott, Thomas H. MD Arty. 1st Btty.
Scott, Thomas H. MS 33rd Inf. Co.H
Scott, Thomas H. TX 3rd Cav. Co.G
Scott, Thomas H. TX Inf. Chambers' Bn. Res.Corps Co.D
Scott, Thomas H. VA Hvy.Arty. Epes' Co.
Scott, Thomas J. AL 6th Inf. Co.E
Scott, Thomas J. AL 50th Inf. Co.E
Scott, Thomas J. AR 1st (Colquitt's) Inf. Co.B
Scott, Thomas J. AR 33rd Inf. Co.I
Scott, Thomas J. GA 16th Inf. Co.D Cpl.,Nurse
Scott, Thomas J. KY 8th Mtd.Inf. Co.H Capt.
Scott, Thomas J. MS Hamer's Co. (Salem Cav.)
Scott, Thomas J. MS 33rd Inf. Co.D 1st Sgt.
Scott, Thomas J. MS 34th Inf. Co.K
Scott, Thomas J. MO 3rd Cav. Co.E
Scott, Thomas J. MO 12th Inf. Co.I 1st Lt.
Scott, Thomas J. NC 29th Inf. Co.D Sgt.
Scott, Thomas J. SC 2nd Rifles Co.G
Scott, Thomas J. TX Cav. Martin's Regt. Co.B 1st Sgt.
Scott, Thomas J. TX Cav. Martin's Regt. Co.G
Scott, Thomas J. TX 9th Field Btty.
Scott, Thomas J. TX Inf. Whaley's Co.
Scott, Thos. J. Gen. & Staff Asst.Surg.
Scott, Thomas James NC 22nd Inf. Co.E Sgt.
Scott, Thomas Jeff MS 37th Inf. Co.K
Scott, Thomas L. AL Vol. Meador's Co.
Scott, Thomas L. VA Lt.Arty. Montgomery's Co.
Scott, Thomas L. VA Lt.Arty. Wimbish's Co.
Scott, Thomas L. VA 22nd Inf. Taylor's Co.
Scott, Thomas L. VA 60th Inf. Co.E
Scott, Thomas M. LA 12th Inf. Co.B Col.
Scott, Thomas M. NC 21st Inf. Co.I

Scott, Thomas M. TX 9th (Young's) Inf. Co.I Adj.

Scott, Thomas M. VA Hvy.Arty. 19th Bn. Co.B QMSgt.

Scott, Thomas M. Gen. & Staff Brig.Gen.

Scott, Thomas M. Gen. & Staff Capt.

Scott, Thomas M. Gen. & Staff, VA Sgt.,QM

Scott, Thomas N. TX 29th Cav. Co.D

Scott, Thomas P. TN 48th (Voorhies') Inf. Co.F

Scott, Thomas P. TX 2nd Cav. Co.G Cpl.

Scott, Thomas P. TX Cav. 2nd Regt.St.Troops Co.D

Scott, Thomas P. TX 3rd Cav. Co.K Sgt.

Scott, Thomas R. GA 52nd Inf. Co.A

Scott, Thomas S. AL 3rd Bn. Hilliard's Legion Vol. Co.A

Scott, Thomas S. TN 7th Inf. Co.E

Scott, Thomas S. VA Inf. 22nd Bn. Co.G Ord.Sgt.

Scott, Thomas T. MO 1st Inf. Co.G

Scott, Thomas W. AL 41st Inf. Co.D

Scott, Thomas W. AR 6th Inf. Co.H

Scott, Thomas W. KY 9th Cav. Co.A

Scott, Thomas W. TX 1st (McCulloch's) Cav. Co.H

Scott, Thomas W. VA 9th Inf. 2nd Co.H

Scott, Thomas W. VA 12th Inf. 1st Co.I Sgt.

Scott, Thomas W. VA 23rd Inf. Co.B 1st Lt.

Scott, Thomas W. VA 34th Inf. Co.K

Scott, Thomas W. VA 56th Inf. Co.G

Scott, Thomas W. Hebert's Staff Maj.

Scott, Thomas W. Gen. & Staff,PACS Chap.

Scott, Thomas Y. MS 21st Inf. Co.I

Scott, Thompson LA 31st Inf. Co.E Jr.2nd Lt.

Scott, T.I. Band Featherstone's Brig. Music.

Scott, Tilford TX Cav. 2nd Regt.St.Troops Co.H

Scott, Tilghman D. VA 2nd Cav. Co.F

Scott, Timothy SC Inf. 7th Bn. (Enfield Rifles) Co.F

Scott, T.J. AL 7th Inf. Co.G

Scott, T.J. AR 15th (Josey's) Inf. 1st Co.C

Scott, T.J. GA 1st Cav. Co.F

Scott, T.J. GA Cav. 1st Gordon Squad. (St.Guards) Reeves' Co.

Scott, T.J. GA 1st Inf.

Scott, T.J. GA 1st Inf. (St.Guards) Co.A

Scott, T.J. GA 3rd Bn.S.S. Co.C N.C.S. Hosp.Stew.

Scott, T.J. KY Cav.

Scott, T.J. LA 8th Cav. Co.G

Scott, T.J. LA 4th Inf. Co.G 3rd Lt.

Scott, T.J. MS 22nd Inf. Co.D Music.

Scott, T.J. MS 43rd Inf. Co.F

Scott, T.J. TX 10th Cav. Co.F

Scott, T.J. TX 12th Cav. Co.H

Scott, T.J. TX Cav. Hardeman's Regt. Co.A

Scott, T.J. TX 1st Hvy.Arty. Co.D

Scott, T.J. TX 15th Field Btty.

Scott, T.J. TX 7th Inf. Co.B

Scott, T.J. TX 9th (Nichols') Inf. Co.K

Scott, T.J. TX 9th (Young's) Inf. Co.D

Scott, T.J. 1st Conf.Cav. 2nd Co.K Sgt.

Scott, T.L. LA Hvy.Arty. 8th Bn. Co.C

Scott, T.L. MS St.Cav. 2nd Bn. (Harris') Co.C

Scott, T.L. MS Inf. 3rd Bn. (St.Troops) Co.B

Scott, T.L. TX Cav. Terry's Regt. Co.B Capt.

Scott, T.L. VA 1st Arty.

Scott, T.M. AL 41st Inf. Co.H

Scott, T.N. TN 11th (Holman's) Cav. Co.H

Scott, Toliver R. TX 18th Inf. Co.B

Scott, Tolly KY 3rd Bn.Mtd.Rifles Co.D

Scott, T.P. GA 1st Inf. Co.E

Scott, T.P. TX Cav. Wells' Regt. Co.K

Scott, T.R. GA Phillips' Legion Co.D

Scott, T.S. LA 3rd (Wingfield's) Cav. Co.E

Scott, T.S. TX Cav. 3rd Bn.St.Troops Co.E Capt.

Scott, T.T. AL 12th Cav. Co.E

Scott, T.T. AL 9th Inf. Co.F

Scott, Turner D. VA 6th Cav. Co.H 3rd Lt.

Scott, T.W. AR Lt.Arty. 5th Btty.

Scott, T.W. GA Siege Arty. 28th Bn. Co.H

Scott, T.W. MS 3rd Inf. (St.Troops) Co.C

Scott, T.W. TN 9th Inf. Co.A

Scott, T.W. TN 23rd Inf. Co.D

Scott, T.W. TX 28th Cav. Co.D Bugler

Scott, T.Y. VA 12th Cav. Co.F

Scott, W. AL 22nd Inf. Co.I

Scott, W. FL 7th Inf.

Scott, W. GA 4th (Clinch's) Cav. Co.D

Scott, W. LA Inf. 1st Sp.Bn. (Rightor's) Co.D

Scott, W. LA Mil.Cont.Regt. Roder's Co. Cpl.

Scott, W. MS 1st Cav.Res. Co.C

Scott, W. SC 1st Regt. Charleston Guard Co.F

Scott, W. SC 1st Bn.S.S. Co.B

Scott, W. SC Inf. 7th Bn. (Enfield Rifles) Co.E

Scott, W. SC 16th & 24th (Cons.) Inf. Music.

Scott, W. TX Cav. Baird's Regt. Co.E

Scott, W. TX Cav. Border's Regt. Co.K

Scott, W. TX Cav. Wells' Regt. Co.K

Scott, W. VA 5th Cav. Co.B

Scott, W. VA Cav. Mosby's Regt. (Part.Rangers) Co.D

Scott, W. VA Inf. 1st Bn.Loc.Def. Co.C

Scott, W.A. AL Mil. 4th Vol. Co.H

Scott, W.A. GA Lt.Arty. 12th Bn. 3rd Co.C Sr.2nd Lt.

Scott, W.A. KY 3rd Mtd.Inf. Co.A Sgt.

Scott, W.A. LA 27th Inf. Co.I

Scott, W.A. SC 2nd Inf. Co.E

Scott, W.A. TN 3rd (Clack's) Inf. Co.D

Scott, W.A. TN 8th Inf. Co.B

Scott, W.A. VA 1st St.Res. Co.B

Scott, W.A. 3rd Conf.Cav. Co.D

Scott, Wade SC 1st (Butler's) Inf. Co.B

Scott, Wainwright SC 8th Bn.Res. Co.A

Scott, Walter AL 4th (Russell's) Cav. Co.G

Scott, Walter AL 56th Part.Rangers Co.A

Scott, Walter AL Lt.Arty. 2nd Bn. Co.F

Scott, Walter AL 7th Inf. Co.A

Scott, Walter AL 40th Inf. Co.A

Scott, Walter AL 42nd Inf. Co.B

Scott, Walter LA 8th Inf. Co.G

Scott, Walter MO 4th Cav. Co.I Jr.2nd Lt.

Scott, Walter NC 1st Inf. Co.D

Scott, Walter NC 17th Inf. (1st Org.) Co.L

Scott, Walter NC 17th Inf. (2nd Org.) Co.B Comsy.Sgt.

Scott, Walter NC 44th Inf. Co.G

Scott, Walter SC 4th Cav. Co.B

Scott, Walter SC Cav.Bn. Holcombe Legion Co.E

Scott, Walter TN 14th (Neely's) Cav. Co.K

Scott, Walter TN 4th Inf. Co.G

Scott, Walter TX 30th Cav. Co.G

Scott, Walter VA 3rd (Archer's) Bn.Res. Co.E

Scott, Walter B. AL 4th Inf. Co.G

Scott, Walter B. VA 5th Cav. (12 mo. '61-2) Co.C

Scott, Walter M. TX 18th Cav. Co.E

Scott, Walter T. VA Lt.Arty. Pegram's Co.

Scott, Walter T. VA 12th Inf. Branch's Co.

Scott, Walter T. VA 16th Inf. Co.G

Scott, Walter W. AL 12th Inf. Asst.Surg.

Scott, Walter W. Gen. & Staff Asst.Surg.

Scott, Warner B. AL Lt.Arty. 2nd Bn. Co.E

Scott, Warren TX 22nd Inf. Co.I

Scott, Warren F. FL 5th Inf. Co.E

Scott, Warren M. LA 31st Inf. Co.C Capt.

Scott, Wash SC Inf. 7th Bn. (Enfield Rifles) Co.E

Scott, Washington SC 21st Inf. Co.F

Scott, Washington M. TX 13th Cav. Co.K Sgt.

Scott, Washington T. VA 3rd Cav. 2nd Co.I

Scott, Washington T. VA 3rd Inf. Co.C 1st Lt.

Scott, Wayman KY 2nd (Duke's) Cav. Co.A

Scott, W.B. AL Gid Nelson Lt.Arty.

Scott, W.B. AL Lt.Arty. Ward's Btty.

Scott, W.B. AL 18th Inf. Co.K,E

Scott, W.B. AL 22nd Inf. Co.A

Scott, W.B. AL Cp. of Instr. Talladega

Scott, W.B. AR 1st (Monroe's) Cav. Co.K

Scott, W.B. GA Cav. 8th Bn. (St.Guards) Co.B 1st Sgt.

Scott, W.B. GA Cav. Gartrell's Co.

Scott, W.B. GA Siege Arty. 28th Bn. Co.K

Scott, W.B. GA 54th Inf. Co.A

Scott, W.B. SC 2nd Inf. Co.A

Scott, W.B. TN 27th Inf. Co.F

Scott, W.B. VA 13th Cav. Co.H

Scott, W.C. AL 12th Cav. Co.C

Scott, W.C. AR 6th Inf. Old Co.F, Co.A

Scott, W.C., Jr. GA Cav. 6th Bn. (St.Guards) Co.F

Scott, W.C., Sr. GA Cav. 6th Bn. (St.Guards) Co.F

Scott, W.C. GA Cav. Gartrell's Co. Sgt.

Scott, W.C. MS 9th Inf. New Co.K

Scott, W.C. SC 2nd Cav. Co.G

Scott, W.C. SC 2nd Inf. Co.C,K

Scott, W.C. TN 11th (Holman's) Cav. Co.B

Scott, W.C. TN Holman's Bn.Part.Rangers Co.A

Scott, W.C. TX 12th Cav. Co.G Cpl.

Scott, W.C. TX 1st Inf. Co.E Cpl.

Scott, W.C. VA 26th Inf. Co.H

Scott, W.C. Gen. & Staff, QM Dept. Maj.,AQM

Scott, W.D. AL 9th Inf. Co.F

Scott, W.D. AL 44th Inf. Co.F

Scott, W.D. TN Cav. 9th Bn. (Gantt's) Co.A

Scott, W.E.B. LA Inf. 1st Sp.Bn. (Rightor's) Co.F

Scott, W.E.B. LA Mil. 4th Regt. 2nd Brig. 1st Div. Co.I 2nd Lt.

Scott, Weldon VA 3rd Cav. Co.G

Scott, Weldon VA 18th Inf. Co.C

Scott, Wellington W. MS 18th Inf. Co.A

Scott, Wesley 1st Creek Mtd.Vol. 1st Co.C

Scott, Wesley H. AL 42nd Inf. Co.B

Scott, W.F. AL 31st Inf. Co.F

Scott, W.F. AL 48th Inf. Co.I

Scott, W.F. AR 1st (Monroe's) Cav. Co.K

Scott, W.F. GA 12th (Robinson's) Cav. (St.Guards) Co.E
Scott, W.F. GA Inf. 8th Bn. Co.C
Scott, W.F. KY 4th Cav. Co.I,E
Scott, W.F. TN 16th Cav. Co.D
Scott, W.F. VA 14th Cav. 1st Co.F Cpl.
Scott, W.F. 10th Conf.Cav. Co.A
Scott, W.F.A. VA 3rd Inf. Co.C
Scott, W.G. KY 12th Cav. Co.B,D
Scott, W.G. MS 1st Bn.S.S. Co.A Cpl.
Scott, W.G. MS 22nd Inf. Co.A Cpl.
Scott, W.G. MS 25th Inf. Co.I
Scott, W.G. TX Cav. 1st Bn.St.Troops Co.D
Scott, W.H. AR 7th Cav. Co.H Capt.
Scott, W.H. AR 14th (Powers') Inf. Co.F
Scott, W.H. AR 26th Inf. Co.G
Scott, W.H. GA 9th Inf. Co.K
Scott, W.H. GA Cherokee Legion (St.Guards) Co.B
Scott, W.H. KY 10th Cav. Co.K
Scott, W.H. LA Inf. 11th Bn. Co.B
Scott, W.H. LA 12th Inf. Co.F
Scott, W.H. LA Inf.Cons.Crescent Regt. Co.K
Scott, W.H. LA 4th Bn.Eng.Troops Co.F
Scott, W.H. MD Arty. 3rd Btty.
Scott, W.H. SC 2nd Cav. Co.H
Scott, W.H. SC Lt.Arty. Garden's Co. (Palmetto Lt.Btty.)
Scott, W.H. SC 1st Inf. Co.A
Scott, W.H. SC 5th Bn.Res. Co.B
Scott, W.H. SC 7th Inf. Co.H 2nd Lt.
Scott, W.H. TN 9th Inf. Co.D 3rd Lt.
Scott, W.H. TN Inf. Nashville Bn. Cattles' Co.
Scott, W.H. TX Cav. Baird's Regt. Co.D
Scott, W.H. Bradford's Corps Scouts & Guards Co.A
Scott, W.H.H. MS 23rd Inf. Co.K
Scott, Whitfield TX 19th Cav. Co.H
Scott, Wiley W. NC Unassign.Conscr.
Scott, Will L. TN Lt.Arty. Scott's Co. Capt.
Scott, William AL
Scott, William AL Cav. 5th Bn. Hilliard's Legion Co.A
Scott, William AL Lt.Arty. Goldthwaite's Btty.
Scott, William AL Inf. 1st Regt. Co.D Cpl.
Scott, William AL Mil. 4th Vol. Co.G
Scott, William AL 5th Inf. Co.F
Scott, William AL 12th Inf. Co.K 2nd Lt.
Scott, William AL 17th Inf. Co.K
Scott, William AL 48th Inf. Co.H
Scott, William AL 49th Inf. Co.G
Scott, William AZ Cav. Herbert's Bn. Helm's Co.
Scott, William AR 2nd Inf. Co.D
Scott, William AR 5th Inf. Co.B
Scott, William AR 21st Inf. Co.E
Scott, William AR 38th Inf. Co.K
Scott, William FL Lt.Arty. Dyke's Co.
Scott, William FL 1st Inf. Old Co.I 2nd Lt.
Scott, William FL 5th Inf. Co.K
Scott, William FL 5th Inf. Adj.
Scott, William FL 9th Inf. Co.D 1st Lt.
Scott, William GA Cav. 1st Gordon Squad. (St.Guards) Co.A
Scott, William GA Cav. 20th Bn. Co.C
Scott, William GA Lt.Arty. Daniell's Btty.
Scott, William GA 36th (Villepigue's) Inf. Co.A

Scott, William KY 9th Cav. Co.D
Scott, William KY 9th Cav. Co.F Sgt.
Scott, William KY 3rd Bn.Mtd.Rifles Co.F
Scott, William KY 2nd Mtd.Inf.
Scott, William KY 3rd Mtd.Inf. Co.H
Scott, William KY 5th Mtd.Inf. Co.H 2nd Lt.
Scott, William KY 7th Mtd.Inf. Co.C
Scott, William LA Mil. 2nd Regt. 2nd Brig. 1st Div. Co.G
Scott, William LA C.S. Zouave Bn. Co.F
Scott, William MS 4th Cav. Co.C
Scott, William MS 18th Cav. Co.F
Scott, William MS 2nd Inf. Co.E
Scott, William MS 32nd Inf. Co.B
Scott, William MS 39th Inf. Co.I
Scott, William MO 1st N.E. Cav. Co.B
Scott, William MO Mtd.Inf. Boone's Regt.
Scott, William MO 1st Inf. Co.F
Scott, William MO 1st & 4th Cons.Inf. Co.F
Scott, William MO 6th Inf. Co.K
Scott, William MO St.Guard
Scott, William NC 1st Arty. (10th St.Troops) Co.G Cook
Scott, William NC 2nd Inf. Co.E
Scott, William NC 5th Inf. Co.K
Scott, William NC 13th Inf. Co.D
Scott, William NC 17th Inf. (1st Org.) Co.G
Scott, William NC 24th Inf. Co.E
Scott, William NC 31st Inf. Co.F
Scott, William NC 35th Inf. Co.A
Scott, William NC 48th Inf. Co.I
Scott, William SC 6th Cav. Co.A
Scott, William SC 6th Cav. Co.C
Scott, William SC 2nd Inf. Co.K
Scott, William SC 5th St.Troops Co.D 1st Sgt.
Scott, William SC 5th Bn.Res. Co.B
Scott, William SC 8th Inf. Co.A
Scott, William SC 9th Res. Co.B 1st Sgt.
Scott, William SC 16th Inf. Co.E Music.
Scott, William SC 27th Inf. Co.I
Scott, William TN 1st (Carter's) Cav. Co.C
Scott, William TN 7th (Duckworth's) Cav. Co.E
Scott, William TN 11th (Holman's) Cav. Co.B
Scott, William TN 12th (Green's) Cav. Co.I
Scott, William TN 18th (Newsom's) Cav. Co.C
Scott, William TN 19th (Biffle's) Cav. Co.C
Scott, William TN Cav. Newsom's Regt. Co.D
Scott, William TN 1st (Feild's) Inf. Co.G
Scott, William TN 24th Inf. Co.B
Scott, William TN 26th Inf. Co.K
Scott, William TN 43rd Inf. Co.F
Scott, William TN 44th Inf. Co.C
Scott, William TN 46th (Nixon's) Inf. Co.K
Scott, William TN 54th Inf. Co.E
Scott, William TN 63rd Inf. Co.F
Scott, William TX 4th Cav. Co.D
Scott, William TX 10th Cav. Co.F
Scott, William TX 26th Cav. Co.A,D
Scott, William TX 26th Cav. Co.C
Scott, William TX 37th Cav. 2nd Co.D
Scott, William TX Cav. Baird's Regt. Co.B
Scott, William TX Cav. Baird's Regt. Co.F
Scott, William TX Arty. 4th Bn. Co.A Music.
Scott, William TX 1st Inf. Co.B
Scott, William TX 1st Inf. Co.F
Scott, William TX 8th Inf. Co.A Music.
Scott, William TX 13th Vol. 3rd Co.A

Scott, William TX Inf. Griffin's Bn. Co.D
Scott, William VA 1st Cav. 1st Co.K
Scott, William VA 6th Cav. Co.B Cpl.
Scott, William VA 17th Cav. Co.A
Scott, William VA 19th Cav. Co.D
Scott, William VA Hvy.Arty. 19th Bn. 1st Co.E
Scott, William VA Arty. Bryan's Co.
Scott, William VA Courtney Arty.
Scott, William VA 19th Inf. Co.K
Scott, William VA 46th Inf. 1st Co.C
Scott, William VA 108th Mil. Co.A
Scott, William VA 151st Mil. Co.F
Scott, William 15th Conf.Cav. Co.E
Scott, William Conf.Cav. Baxter's Bn. Co.C
Scott, William 1st Conf.Inf. Co.A
Scott, William 1st Cherokee Mtd.Vol. 1st Co.E Cpl.
Scott, William Conf.Inf. Tucker's Regt. Co.C 1st Sgt.
Scott, William Gen. & Staff 1st Lt.,Adj.
Scott, William A. AL 12th Inf. Co.K Cpl.
Scott, William A. LA 14th Inf. Co.I,F Cpl.
Scott, William A. LA 17th Inf. Co.A Capt.
Scott, William A. MS 1st Lt.Arty. Co.A
Scott, William A. MS 18th Inf. Co.H
Scott, William A. NC 2nd Arty. (36th St.Troops) Co.B
Scott, William A. NC 34th Inf. Co.G
Scott, William A. TN 1st (Feild's) Inf. Co.K
Scott, William A. TN 7th Inf. Co.B
Scott, William A. TX 21st Cav. Co.K
Scott, William A. TX Cav. Chisum's Regt. (Dismtd.) Co.A
Scott, William A. VA 14th Cav. Co.D
Scott, William A. VA 10th Inf. Co.B
Scott, William A. VA Inf. 26th Bn. Co.E Cpl.
Scott, William A. VA 59th Inf. 2nd Co.B
Scott, William A. VA 64th Mtd.Inf. Franklin's Co.
Scott, William A.C. MS 35th Inf. Co.G Capt.
Scott, William B. AL 28th Inf. Co.G
Scott, William B. GA Inf. 8th Bn. Co.F,C Sgt.
Scott, William B. MS 42nd Inf. Co.B
Scott, William B. NC 52nd Inf. Co.B
Scott, William B. SC 5th St.Troops Co.H
Scott, William B. SC 9th Res. Co.I 1st Lt.
Scott, William B. TX 29th Inf. Co.G 1st Lt.
Scott, William B. VA 17th Cav. Co.D Cpl.
Scott, William B. VA 151st Mil. Co.C Cpl.
Scott, William B., Sr. 8th (Dearing's) Conf.Cav. Co.B
Scott, William B.F. NC 4th Cav. (59th St.Troops) Co.I
Scott, William B.F. NC Cav. 12th Bn. Co.B
Scott, William C. NC 7th Inf. Co.G Cpl.
Scott, William C. SC 1st Mtd.Mil. Fripp's Co.
Scott, William C. SC Lt.Arty. Parker's Co. (Marion Arty.)
Scott, William C. SC Lt.Arty. Walter's Co. (Washington Arty.)
Scott, William C. TN 4th (McLemore's) Cav. Co.A
Scott, William C. TX 6th Cav. Co.I 2nd Lt.
Scott, William C. VA Lt.Arty. Ellett's Co. Ord.Sgt.
Scott, William C. VA 13th Inf. Co.C Capt.
Scott, William C. VA 44th Inf. Col.

Scott, William D. NC 22nd Inf. Co.F
Scott, William D. SC 15th Inf. Co.K Music.
Scott, William D. TN 41st Inf. Co.E
Scott, William D. VA 6th Cav. Co.H
Scott, William D. VA 14th Cav. Co.D
Scott, William D. VA 39th Inf. Co.L
Scott, William D. VA 59th Inf. 2nd Co.B
Scott, William E. VA 1st Cav. 2nd Co.D
Scott, William E. VA Inf. 25th Bn. Co.A Cpl.
Scott, William E.B. AL Lt.Arty. 2nd Bn. Co.E
Scott, William F. AR 3rd Cav. Co.H
Scott, William F. GA 3rd Res. Co.C Capt.
Scott, William F. GA 34th Inf. Co.I
Scott, William F. GA 35th Inf. Co.G 2nd Lt.
Scott, William F. NC 2nd Inf. Co.A
Scott, William F. VA Cav. 36th Bn. Co.E Cpl.
Scott, William F. VA Inf. 23rd Bn. Co.F
Scott, William G. GA 4th Inf. Co.I
Scott, William G. NC 24th Inf. Co.A
Scott, William G. VA 51st Inf. Co.B
Scott, William H. AL Mil. 4th Vol. Co.A
Scott, William H. FL 2nd Cav. Co.E
Scott, William H. FL 6th Inf. Co.B 1st Lt.
Scott, William H. GA 10th Inf. Co.H 1st Lt.
Scott, William H. KY 5th Mtd.Inf. Co.B
Scott, William H. KY 6th Mtd.Inf. Co.D
Scott, William H. LA 1st (Strawbridge's) Inf. Co.E Capt.
Scott, William H. LA 12th Inf. Co.C
Scott, William H. MS 13th Inf. Co.G
Scott, William H. NC 2nd Home Guards Co.A Lt.
Scott, William H. NC 33rd Inf. Co.F
Scott, William H. NC 51st Inf. Co.D
Scott, William H. SC 4th Inf. Co.D
Scott, William H. SC 15th Inf. Co.A Sgt.
Scott, William H. TX 2nd Cav. Co.I Sgt.
Scott, William H. VA 4th Cav. Co.D
Scott, William H. VA 8th Cav. Co.L
Scott, William H. VA 14th Cav. Co.A Cpl.
Scott, William H. VA Lt.Arty. Pegram's Co. 2nd Lt.
Scott, William H. VA 2nd Inf.Loc.Def. Co.I 1st Lt.
Scott, William H. VA Inf. 2nd Bn.Loc.Def. Co.G Lt.
Scott, William H. VA 12th Inf. Co.E
Scott, William H. VA 13th Inf. 1st Co.B
Scott, William H. VA 14th Inf. Co.A Cpl.
Scott, William H. VA Inf. 25th Bn. Co.D
Scott, William H. VA 40th Inf. Co.K
Scott, William H. VA 63rd Inf. Co.C 2nd Lt.
Scott, William H. VA Mil. Grayson Cty.
Scott, William H. 1st Conf.Inf. 2nd Co.F
Scott, William H. 4th Conf.Inf. Co.D
Scott, William Henry MS 1st Lt.Arty. Co.A Music.
Scott, William J. AL Mil. 4th Vol. Co.H
Scott, William J. AR 4th Inf. Co.C
Scott, William J. GA 25th Inf. Co.F
Scott, William J. TX Unatt.Cav. 1st Lt.
Scott, William J. VA Inf. 4th Bn.Loc.Def. Co.E
Scott, William J. VA 60th Inf. Co.B
Scott, William Jason AL 51st (Part.Rangers) Co.A Sgt.
Scott, William Jason AL 2nd Inf. Co.A Sgt.

Scott, William Jason Conf.Inf. 1st Bn. 2nd Co.E 1st Lt.
Scott, William K. TX 22nd Cav. Co.F
Scott, William L. AL 3rd Inf. Co.G
Scott, William L. AL 20th Inf. Co.B
Scott, William L. AR 4th Inf. Co.C
Scott, William L. FL 2nd Cav. Co.E,G
Scott, William L. GA Lt.Arty. Van Den Corput's Co.
Scott, William L. GA Inf. 3rd Bn. Co.A
Scott, William L. LA 21st (Kennedy's) Inf. Co.F
Scott, William L. NC 15th Inf. Co.B
Scott, William L. NC 21st Inf. Co.M Lt.Col.
Scott, William L. TN 25th Inf. Co.B
Scott, William L. TX Cav. 2nd Regt.St.Troops Co.D
Scott, William L. VA Lt.Arty. Pollock's Co.
Scott, William L. VA 38th Inf. Co.H
Scott, William L. Gen. & Staff,PACS Surg.
Scott, William M. AR 3rd Cav. Co.C
Scott, William M. AR 33rd Inf. Co.I
Scott, William M. GA 1st Reg. Co.E
Scott, William M. GA 31st Inf. Co.G
Scott, William M. LA 31st Inf. Co.C Sgt.
Scott, William M. LA Inf.Cons.Crescent Regt. Co.G,N
Scott, William M. NC Lt.Arty. Thomas' Legion Levi's Btty. Cpl.
Scott, William M. SC Inf. Hampton Legion Co.D
Scott, William M. TX Cav. Chisum's Regt. Co.A
Scott, William M. TX 11th Inf. Co.I
Scott, William M. VA 6th Cav. Co.C
Scott, William M.B. TN Cav. 8th Bn. (Gantt's) Co.E
Scott, William Moore LA Inf.Crescent Regt. Co.I
Scott, William M.P. VA Lt.Arty. Lowry's Co.
Scott, William N. AL 4th Inf. Co.H
Scott, William N. AR 34th Inf. Co.B
Scott, William N. VA 20th Inf. Co.G
Scott, William O. LA 28th (Gray's) Inf. Co.B
Scott, William P. AL 3rd Cav. Co.B
Scott, William P. GA Inf. 10th Bn. Co.D
Scott, William P. GA 36th (Broyles') Inf. Co.D,G
Scott, William P. MO 1st Inf. Co.B
Scott, William P. MO 1st & 4th Cons.Inf. Co.D
Scott, William P. NC 8th Bn.Jr.Res. Co.C
Scott, William P. SC 10th Inf. Co.H
Scott, William P. TN 20th (Russell's) Cav. Co.F
Scott, William P. VA Lt.Arty. Kirkpatrick's Co. Lt.
Scott, William P. VA 4th Res. Co.A
Scott, William P. VA Wade's Regt.Loc.Def. Co.A
Scott, William R. AL 16th Inf. Co.F
Scott, William R. AR 24th Inf. Co.F
Scott, William R. GA 52nd Inf. Co.A
Scott, William R. MS 1st Lt.Arty. Co.K
Scott, William R. NC 1st Cav. (9th St.Troops) Co.F 1st Lt.
Scott, William R. NC 6th Inf. Co.K
Scott, William R. TN 44th (Cons.) Inf. Co.G
Scott, William R. TN 55th (McKoin's) Inf. McEwen, Jr.'s Co.
Scott, William R. TX 25th Cav. Co.C
Scott, William R.D. AR 15th (N.W.) Inf. Co.E
Scott, William R.J. TX 9th Cav. Co.H

Scott, William S. AR 25th Inf. Co.A
Scott, William S. GA 44th Inf. Co.H
Scott, William S. TX 11th Inf. Co.I
Scott, William S. Conf.Cav. Wood's Regt. 1st Co.A
Scott, William T. GA 6th Inf. Co.F
Scott, William T. GA 31st Inf. Co.E
Scott, William T. GA 38th Inf. Co.C
Scott, William T. GA 44th Inf. Co.E
Scott, William T. LA Inf. 11th Bn. Co.A 1st Sgt.
Scott, William T. MS 19th Inf. Co.D
Scott, William T. SC 1st (McCreary's) Inf. Co.G 1st Sgt.
Scott, William T. VA 6th Inf. Co.H
Scott, William T. VA 61st Inf. Co.A
Scott, William W. AL 53rd (Part.Rangers) Co.B
Scott, William W. AL Inf. 1st Regt. Co.D
Scott, William W. FL 10th Inf. Co.F Lt.Col.
Scott, William W. GA 3rd Cav. (St.Guards) Co.G 3rd Lt.
Scott, William W. GA 48th Inf. Co.C
Scott, William W. LA 14th Inf. Co.C,G,E Capt.
Scott, William W. TX 1st (Yager's) Cav. Co.K
Scott, William W. TX 7th Cav. Co.H
Scott, William W. TX Cav. 8th (Taylor's) Bn. Co.B
Scott, William W. TX Cav. Martin's Regt. Co.C
Scott, William W. VA 11th Inf. Co.B Sgt.
Scott, William W. VA 13th Inf. Co.A
Scott, William W. VA 34th Inf. Co.B
Scott, William W. VA 48th Inf. Co.B
Scott, William W. VA 57th Inf. Co.K
Scott, William W. Brush Bn.
Scott, Williamson GA 4th Res. Co.K
Scott, Willis TN Cav. Newsom's Regt.
Scott, Willis A. AL 39th Inf. Co.B
Scott, Willis L. AL 48th Inf. Co.I 1st Lt.
Scott, Willis T. MS Cav. 3rd Res. Co.F Sgt.
Scott, Wilson FL 1st Cav. Co.A
Scott, Wilson M. AR 4th Inf. Co.F
Scott, Winfield AL Lt.Arty. Tarrant's Btty.
Scott, Winfield GA Floyd Legion (St.Guards) Co.I
Scott, Winfield KY 3rd Bn.Mtd.Rifles Co.D
Scott, Winfield NC 1st Jr.Res. Co.D
Scott, Winfield VA 39th Inf. Co.H
Scott, Winfield VA 46th Inf. 4th Co.F
Scott, Winfield T. AL 61st Inf. Co.B
Scott, Winfrey Bond LA 19th Inf. Co.D Maj.
Scott, Winfrey G. AR 1st (Crawford's) Cav. Co.B 2nd Lt.
Scott, Winfrey G. AR 1st (Colquitt's) Inf. Co.E Cpl.
Scott, W.J. AL 40th Inf. Co.K
Scott, W.J. GA 35th Inf. Co.F
Scott, W.J. GA 45th Inf. Co.H
Scott, W.J. GA Phillips' Legion Co.D
Scott, W.J. LA 6th Cav. Co.A Capt.
Scott, W.J. MS 33rd Inf. Co.F
Scott, W.J. MO 11th Inf. Co.A
Scott, W.J. TN 21st Inf. Co.D
Scott, W.J. TX 16th Cav. Co.C
Scott, W.J.A. TN 15th (Stewart's) Cav. Co.B
Scott, W.L. GA 18th Inf. Co.K
Scott, W.L. KY 12th Cav. Co.D
Scott, W.L. LA 8th Inf. Co.K

Scott, W.L. MO 11th Inf. Co.F,K
Scott, W.L. TN 6th (Wheeler's) Cav. Co.D
Scott, W.L. TN Arty.Corps Co.6 3rd Lt.
Scott, W.L. TN 9th Inf. Co.G Sgt.
Scott, W.L. TN 13th Inf. Co.A
Scott, W.L. TX 2nd Inf. Co.G
Scott, W.M. AL 6th Cav. Co.E
Scott, W.M. AR 47th (Crandall's) Cav. McCoy's Co.
Scott, W.M. AR 3rd Inf. Co.C
Scott, W.M. AR 15th Mil. Co.A
Scott, W.M. GA Inf. 8th Bn. Co.C
Scott, W.M. LA 18th Inf. Co.C
Scott, W.M. MO 16th Inf. Co.G
Scott, W.M. TN 7th (Duckworth's) Cav. Co.L
Scott, W.M. TN 11th (Holman's) Cav. Co.B
Scott, W.M. TN 6th Inf. Co.A
Scott, W.M. TX 10th Cav. Co.F
Scott, W.M. VA 21st Cav. 2nd Co.G
Scott, W.M. VA Lt.Arty. Barr's Co. Cpl.
Scott, W.O. AR 3rd Cav. Co.B
Scott, Wolfford VA 45th Inf. Co.I
Scott, Wolford VA Mil. Carroll Cty.
Scott, W.P. FL 2nd Inf. Co.B
Scott, W.P. MS 35th Inf.
Scott, W.P. MO 11th Inf. Co.A
Scott, W.P. TN 19th & 20th (Cons.) Cav. Co.K
Scott, W.P. TX 12th Cav. Co.D
Scott, W.P. TX 2nd Inf. Co.B
Scott, W.P. Conf.Cav. Wood's Regt. 1st Co.M
Scott, W.P. VA 57th Inf. Co.A
Scott, W.P. Gen. & Staff Surg.
Scott, W.P.T. NC 3rd Jr.Res. Co.G Sgt.
Scott, W.R. AL 12th Inf. Co.E
Scott, W.R. KY 7th Cav. Co.A
Scott, W.R. MS 3rd Inf. (A. of 10,000) Co.G
Scott, W.R. MS 36th Inf. Co.K
Scott, W.R. MO 7th Cav. Co.G
Scott, W.R. TX Cav. Gano's Squad. Co.A Cpl.
Scott, W.R. TX 9th (Nichols') Inf. Co.B
Scott, W.R.D. AR 35th Inf. Co.H
Scott, W.S. GA 5th Res. Co.A,D Sgt.Maj.
Scott, W.S. KY 12th Cav. Co.B,D
Scott, W.S. MO Inf. 1st Bn. Co.C
Scott, W.S. TN 19th (Biffle's) Cav. Co.D
Scott, W.S. TX 1st Hvy.Arty. Co.G
Scott, W.T. AL 63rd Inf. Co.E
Scott, W.T. AL Cp. of Instr. Talladega
Scott, W.T. AR 15th Mil. Co.A
Scott, W.T. AR 35th Inf. Co.H
Scott, W.T. GA 7th Cav. Co.D
Scott, W.T. GA Cav. 24th Bn. Co.C
Scott, W.T. GA 2nd Inf. Co.H
Scott, W.T. LA Inf.Cons.Crescent Regt. Co.F Sr.2nd Lt.
Scott, W.T. LA Inf. Jeff Davis Regt. N.C.S. Sgt.Maj.
Scott, W.T. LA Supp.Force Co.A
Scott, W.T. SC 5th Inf. 2nd Co.A
Scott, W.T. TX 2nd Inf. Co.G
Scott, W.W. AL 15th Bn.Part.Rangers Co.A
Scott, W.W. AL 51st (Part.Rangers) Co.C
Scott, W.W. AL 63rd Inf. Co.D Sgt.
Scott, W.W. GA Inf. Fuller's Co.
Scott, W.W. LA 4th Inf. Co.G
Scott, W.W. MS 3rd (St.Troops) Cav. Co.H
Scott, W.W. MS 48th Inf. Asst.Surg.

Scott, W.W. NC 53rd Inf. Asst.Surg.
Scott, W.W. TN Inf. 22nd Bn. Co.E
Scott, W.W. TX 22nd Cav. Co.E
Scott, W.W. TX 28th Cav. Co.F
Scott, W.W. VA 4th Cav. Co.H
Scott, W.W. Gen. & Staff Hosp.Stew.
Scott, W.W.D. TN 17th Inf. Co.E Cpl.
Scott, Wyatt VA Hvy.Arty. Epes' Co.
Scott, Wyatt VA Mil. 42nd Regt.
Scott, Wyatt W. VA Arty. Kevill's Co.
Scott, Y. MO 6th Cav. Co.K
Scott, Z. TN 5th Inf. 2nd Co.D
Scott, Zachariah TN 9th (Ward's) Cav. Co.G
Scott, Z.J. MS 36th Inf. Co.K Surg.
Scott, Z.J. TX 32nd Cav. Co.B Capt.
Scott, Z.T. GA 44th Inf. Co.H
Scotte, John 1st Cherokee Mtd.Vol. 2nd Co.H
Scotte, P. VA Hvy.Ary. 20th Bn. Co.C
Scotten, Peter NC 6th Sr.Res. Co.A
Scotter, John T. MO Searcy's Bn.S.S.
Scotterr, Wm. MO St.Guard Lt.
Scotthorn, William B. MS 1st Lt.Arty. Co.H
Scotthorne, Henry LA 4th Inf.
Scottie, G.B. NC 57th Inf. Co.B 1st Sgt.
Scotton, James M. NC 22nd Inf. Co.M
Scotton, John NC 58th Inf. Co.E
Scotton, W.M. NC 1st Jr.Res. Co.F
Scotts, William TX Cav. 2nd Regt.St.Troops Co.C 3rd Lt.
Scotty, B. LA Mil. 3rd Regt. 1st Brig. 1st Div. Co.K
Scougers, John J. GA 2nd Inf. Co.H
Scouler, --- LA Mil.Squad. Guides d'Orleans
Scourer, Peter GA 43rd Inf. Co.C Conscr.
Scouyins, E. GA Inf. Grubbs' Co.
Scouyins, J. GA Inf. Grubbs' Co.
Scovel, E. AL 28th Inf. Co.D
Scovell, Benjamin F. MS 27th Inf. Co.L
Scovell, H.G. TX Waul's Legion Co.A
Scovell, Noah LA Red River S.S.
Scoven, Samuel G. GA 25th Inf. Co.K
Scover, R.H. GA Lt.Arty. Milledge's Co.
Scovil, Charles LA 4th Inf. Co.C
Scovil, Charles LA 4th Inf. Co.D,H
Scovill, Elliott C. NC 2nd Arty. (36th St.Troops) Co.G Sgt.
Scovill, James MS 9th Inf. New Co.D
Scovill, William T. LA 15th Inf. Co.E AQM
Scovill, W.N. SC 2nd Arty. Co.C
Scovill, W.T. Gen. & Staff Capt.,AQM
Scraggins, G.W. GA 12th Cav. Co.K
Scraggs, S.M. Hardee's Corps Comsy.Sgt.
Scraggs, Stephen C. TN Conscr. (Cp. of Instr.)
Scramble, H.M. Gen. & Staff Asst.Surg.
Scrams, John MS 9th Inf. New Co.D
Scranage, Charles H. LA 8th Inf. Co.I
Scranage, John W. VA 47th Inf. Co.B Sgt.
Scrance, Andrew NC 23rd Inf. Co.B
Scranton, --- AL 18th Inf. Co.F
Scranton, --- VA Mtd.Riflemen Balfour's Co.
Scranton, D.T. GA Inf. 1st Loc.Troops (Augusta) Dearing's Cav.Co.
Scranton, Henry H. GA 63rd Inf. Co.H Capt.
Scranton, Henry H. SC Arty.Bn. Hampton Legion Co.A Cpl.
Scranton, Henry H. VA Mtd.Riflemen Balfour's Co.

Scranton, L. AL Mobile Fire Bn. Mullany's Co. 1st Sgt.
Scranton, Lewis AL 21st Inf. Co.K
Scranton, Philemon A. GA Inf. 1st Loc.Troops (Augusta) Co.A
Scrape, A.A. TN 7th (Duckworth's) Cav. Co.D
Scrape, James TN 7th (Duckworth's) Cav. Co.D
Scraper 1st Cherokee Mtd.Rifles Co.F
Scraper 1st Cherokee Mtd.Vol. 1st Co.E, 2nd Co.C
Scraper Ahlee chah 1st Cherokee Mtd.Vol. 1st Co.F, 2nd Co.E
Scraper, Alexander 1st Cherokee Mtd.Vol. 1st Co.I
Scraper, Arch 1st Cherokee Mtd.Rifles Co.G 2nd Lt.
Scraper, Buck 1st Cherokee Mtd.Rifles Co.C
Scraper, George W. 1st Cherokee Mtd.Rifles Co.G Capt.
Scraper, Henry H. 1st Cherokee Mtd.Rifles Co.G Cpl.
Scraper, John 1st Cherokee Mtd.Rifles Co.F
Scraper, Luke 1st Cherokee Mtd.Vol. 1st Co.E, 2nd Co.C
Scraper, William 1st Cherokee Mtd.Rifles Co.G Sgt.
Scraps, S. GA 47th Inf. Co.B
Scratchin, Samuel GA 10th Mil.
Screech, Henry KY 13th Cav. Co.G
Screrlock, C. TN Cav. Jackson's Co.
Screven, B.S. GA Cav. 1st Bn. Winn's Co.
Screven, B.S. GA Cav. 20th Bn. Co.B Capt.
Screven, B.S. MS Cav. Jeff Davis Legion Co.G Capt.
Screven, J.B. GA Lt.Arty. Croft's Btty. (Columbus Arty.)
Screven, John GA 1st (Olmstead's) Inf. Screven's Co. Capt.
Screven, John GA Inf. 18th Bn. Co.A Maj.
Screven, John H. SC 1st Mtd.Mil. Screven's Co. Capt.
Screven, John H. Gen. & Staff, QM Dept. Maj.
Screven, R.D. Gen. & Staff 2nd Lt.,Inf.
Screven, T.F. GA 1st (Olmstead's) Inf. Stiles' Co. 3rd Lt.
Screven, Thomas E. SC 2nd Cav. Maj.
Screven, Thomas E. SC Cav.Bn. Hampton Legion Co.C Capt.
Screven, Thos. E. Gen. & Staff Lt.Col.
Screven, Thomas F. GA Inf. 18th Bn. Co.B,A Capt.
Screven, W.J. SC 3rd Cav. Co.H
Screw, Lewis NC 8th Bn.Part.Rangers Co.D
Screw, Lewis NC Bass' Co.
Screws, Allen GA 51st Inf. Co.G
Screws, Archibald MS 46th Inf. Co.E Cpl.
Screws, Benjamin H. AL Inf. 1st Regt. Co.F Sgt.
Screws, Benjamin H. AL 29th Inf. Co.K Capt.
Screws, Billy AL 60th Inf. Co.B
Screws, Curtice GA 62nd Cav. Co.B,H
Screws, E. GA 53rd Inf. Co.E
Screws, E.D. TN 12th (Green's) Cav. Co.H
Screws, F.M. GA 13th Cav. Co.F
Screws, George W. GA 2nd Cav. (St.Guards) Co.G
Screws, G.N. GA 13th Cav. Co.F

Screws, G.W. MO Cav. Ford's Bn. Co.A
Screws, Henry A. AL Lt.Arty. Hurt's Btty.
Screws, H.O. GA Siege Arty. 28th Bn. Co.B
Screws, H.O. GA 1st Reg. Co.K
Screws, H.P. AL 1st Bn. Hilliard's Legion Vol.
 Co.A
Screws, H.P. AL 29th Inf. Co.K
Screws, J. GA 1st (Symons') Res. Co.E
Screws, J. GA 8th Inf. Co.F
Screws, J. GA Inf. 27th Bn. Co.E
Screws, J. GA 55th Inf. Co.H
Screws, Jaber J. GA 12th (Wright's) Cav.
 (St.Guards) Wright's Co.
Screws, James GA 8th Inf. Co.F
Screws, James GA 62nd Cav. Co.F,H
Screws, James GA Lt.Arty. 14th Bn. Co.C
Screws, James GA Lt.Arty. Ferrell's Btty.
Screws, James NC 1st Inf. Co.K
Screws, James A. GA 48th Inf. Co.E
Screws, James H. MS 12th Inf. Co.B
Screws, James W. MS 4th Inf. Co.D
Screws, Jasper GA 2nd Cav. Co.C
Screws, Javis GA 28th Inf. Co.K
Screws, J.C. GA 62nd Cav. Co.B
Screws, Jessee G. GA 62nd Cav. Co.B Cpl.
Screws, J.G. GA 8th Cav. Co.B Cpl.
Screws, J.H. MS Cav. Gartley's Co. (Yazoo
 Rangers)
Screws, John T. AL 6th Inf. Co.C
Screws, John W. AL 15th Inf. Co.A Sgt.
Screws, J.T. GA 53rd Inf. Co.E
Screws, Newton GA 2nd Cav. Co.C
Screws, O. MS 7th Cav. Co.H
Screws, Robert W. VA 5th Cav. (12 mo. '61-2)
 Co.H Sgt.
Screws, Robert W. VA 13th Cav. Co.A
Screws, Samuel MS 7th Inf. Co.D
Screws, Samuel H. TX 8th Cav. Co.D
Screws, Stephen GA 47th Inf. Co.G
Screws, Thomas S. GA 28th Inf. Co.K
Screws, W.B. AL 29th Inf. Co.B
Screws, William GA 2nd Cav. Co.C
Screws, William GA Inf. 27th Bn. Co.A
Screws, William GA 48th Inf. Co.E
Screws, William NC 3rd Inf. Co.E
Screws, William NC 3rd Inf. Co.G
Screws, William P. AL 39th Inf. Co.E
Screws, William W. AL 2nd Bn. Hilliard's
 Legion Vol. Co.D 2nd Lt.
Screws, William W. AL 59th Inf. Co.G 2nd Lt.
Screws, W.W. AL 1st Bn. Hilliard's Legion Vol.
 Co.A
Scriber, Ab H. LA 5th Cav. Co.C Sgt.
Scriber, A.H. LA 13th Bn. (Part.Rangers) Co.D
Scriber, B.M. LA 27th Inf. Co.B Cpl.
Scriber, Henry VA 9th Inf. Co.F
Scriber, James P. MS 1st Lt.Arty. Co.H
Scriber, John D. LA 1st Inf.
Scriber, Robert L. AR 9th Inf. Co.K
Scriber, W. SC Mil. 16th Regt. Bancroft, Jr.'s
 Co.
Scriber, William LA 13th Bn. (Part.Rangers)
 Co.D
Scriber, William J. LA 5th Cav. Co.C
Scribes, Burling LA 5th Cav. Co.B
Scribner, --- VA 46th Inf. Co.F
Scribner, A.J. AR Cav. 1st Bn. (Stirman's) Co.D

Scribner, Andrew MO 9th Inf. Co.I
Scribner, Egbert A. VA Hvy.Arty. 18th Bn.
 Co.C
Scribner, G.W. AR 8th Cav. Co.D
Scribner, James MO 11th Inf. Co.B
Scribner, James D. VA 6th Inf. Ferguson's Co.
Scribner, James D. VA 12th Inf. Co.H Cpl.
Scribner, J.H. VA Arty. Wise Legion
Scribner, J.J. TX 13th Vol. Co.H
Scribner, J.W. VA Inf. 25th Bn. Co.G
Scribner, J.W. VA 46th Inf. Co.D Sgt.
Scribner, L. TN 6th (Wheeler's) Cav. Co.F
Scribner, N.A. VA Hvy.Arty. 18th Bn. Co.C
Scribner, Redden MO 4th Inf. Co.A 2nd Lt.
Scribner, Sylvester VA 3rd Inf. Co.E
Scribner, Sylvester B. VA 18th Inf. Co.C
Scribner, Sylvester B. Sig.Corps,CSA
Scribner, Thomas TN 37th Inf. Co.G
Scribner, V.L. VA Cav. 41st Bn. Co.E
Scribner, William AR Cav. 1st Bn. (Stirman's)
 Co.D
Scrigg, R. TN 15th (Stewart's) Cav. Co.F
Scrimager, Benjamin H. MO 3rd Cav. Co.F
Scrimager, William M. MO 3rd Cav. Co.F
Scrimger, George B. VA 41st Mil. Co.B
Scrimger, George W. VA 55th Inf. Co.A
Scrimger, James W. VA 41st Mil. Co.B
Scrimger, Thomas L. VA 40th Inf. Co.E
Scrimger, William H.H. VA 40th Inf. Co.E
Scrimpcher, J.M. MS 25th Inf. Co.D
Scrimpsher, Andrew J. AR 24th Inf. Co.G
Scrimpsher, D.L. AR Mil. Louis' Co.
Scrimpsher, W.F. AR 8th Inf. New Co.I
Scrimpsher, William A. AL 35th Inf. Co.F
Scrimpshire, N.M.B. MS Inf. 7th Bn. Co.E
Scrimpture, Henry TN 62nd Mtd.Inf. Co.H
Scrimscher, Robert W. MO Lt.Arty. 1st Btty.
Scrimsher, Benj. F. MO Inf. Perkins' Bn. Co.B
Scrimsher, D.L. AR 36th Inf. Co.B
Scrimsher, G.M. 2nd Conf.Inf. Co.D
Scrimsher, John J. MO Lt.Arty. Landis' Co.
Scrimsher, Robert MO 1st N.E. Cav.
Scrimsher, Robert W. MO 1st N.E. Cav.
Scrimsher, Robert W. MO 5th Inf. Co.H
Scrimsher, T.J. TN 36th Inf. Co.G
Scrimshew, S. AL 35th Inf. Co.F
Scrimshier, William AR 26th Inf. Co.C
Scrimshire, A.J.B. AR Lt.Arty. Hart's Btty.
Scrimshire, Henry GA Inf. 14th Bn. (St.Guards)
 Co.E
Scrimshire, Hercules D. AL 61st Inf. Co.B
Scrimshire, J.P.B. MS 14th Inf. Co.D
Scrimshire, R.W. GA Inf. 14th Bn. (St.Guards)
 Co.E
Scrimshire, Solomon B. AL 3rd Bn.Res. Co.C
 1st Sgt.
Scrimshire, Thomas GA Inf. 14th Bn.
 (St.Guards) Co.E
Scrimshire, Willis B. MS 14th Inf. Co.D
Scrinarneck, F. TX Inf. Timmons' Regt. Co.B
Scringer, W. VA Murphy's Co.
Scripture, A.W. MO Lt.Arty. 3rd Field Btty.
 Cpl.
Scrist, D.A. GA 23rd Inf.
Scritchfield, John MO 16th Inf. Co.K
Scritchfield, John W. LA 12th Inf. Co.A Sgt.
Scritchfield, William B. LA 12th Inf. Co.A

Scriven, Edwin GA 6th Inf. Sgt.
Scriven, E.W. GA 1st (Symons') Res. Co.G 1st
 Sgt.
Scriven, R.D. LA Inf. 1st Sp.Bn. (Rightor's)
 Co.A
Scriven, R.H. SC 2nd Inf. Co.I Sgt.
Scriven, R.H. SC Inf. Hampton Legion Co.A
Scriven, R.H. Sig.Corps,CSA Sgt.
Scriven, Richard D. Gen. & Staff Lt.,Adj.,
 Cons.Bureau
Scriven, Thomas J. NC 51st Inf. Co.D
Scrivener, Anderson MO Arty. Lowe's Co.
Scrivener, Benjamin T. AL Lt.Arty. 2nd Bn.
 Co.F
Scrivener, B.M. TX 19th Inf. Co.G Chap.
Scrivener, B.M. Gen. & Staff Chap.
Scrivener, Charles T. VA 9th Cav. Co.I
Scrivener, Charles T. VA 25th Mil. Co.B
Scrivener, David D. TX 36th Cav. Co.G
Scrivener, Henry NC Walker's Bn. Thomas'
 Legion Co.C
Scrivener, James AL Lt.Arty. 2nd Bn. Co.F
Scrivener, James O. VA 9th Cav. Co.I
Scrivener, James O. VA 25th Mil. Co.B
Scrivener, James P. VA 25th Mil. Co.B
Scrivener, John A. AL Eufaula Lt.Arty.
Scrivener, John J. MO 2nd Inf. Co.E
Scrivener, Reuben AL Lt.Arty. 2nd Bn. Co.F
Scrivener, Riley MS 43rd Inf. Co.A
Scrivener, W.H. VA 25th Mil. Co.B
Scrivenor, Anderson MO Inf. 3rd Bn. Co.C
Scrivner, A.J. MS 4th Cav. Co.E 2nd Lt.
Scrivner, Alex TN 11th Inf. Co.D
Scrivner, Charles MO 5th Inf. Co.G
Scrivner, D.M. MO 12th Cav. Co.E
Scrivner, E.J.P. MS Lt.Arty. Lomax's Co.
Scrivner, George Washington LA 28th (Gray's)
 Inf. Co.F
Scrivner, Isaiah J. TX 15th Inf. 2nd Co.H
Scrivner, James J. MS 30th Inf. Co.D
Scrivner, James P. MS 2nd Part.Rangers Co.A
Scrivner, J.H. VA Cav. 41st Bn. Co.C
Scrivner, J.M. MS 7th Cav. Co.A Cpl.
Scrivner, John TN 11th Inf. Co.D
Scrivner, John J. TX 15th Inf. 2nd Co.H
Scrivner, Joseph MS 2nd Part.Rangers Co.A
 Cpl.
Scrivner, Joseph MO 12th Cav. Co.E Cpl.
Scrivner, Joseph M.W. TX 7th Inf. Co.D
Scrivner, J.R. AL 3rd Res. Co.G
Scrivner, Leonidas Lafayette LA 28th (Gray's)
 Inf. Co.F
Scrivner, Vincent S. VA 31st Mil. Co.G
Scrivner, Wallace E. MS 15th Inf. Co.E Cpl.
Scrivner, William J. TX 15th Inf. 2nd Co.H Cpl.
Scroble, Steven NC 47th Inf. Co.H
Scrogger, Warner D. KY 10th Cav. Co.E
Scroggin, A.J. TX 23rd Cav. Co.E
Scroggin, B. TX 23rd Cav. Co.E
Scroggin, G.B. AL 5th Cav.
Scroggin, J. MO 2nd Inf. Co.D
Scroggin, James M. VA 6th Cav. Co.B
Scroggin, J.B. AL 3rd Bn. Hilliard's Legion Vol.
 Co.F
Scroggin, J.J. GA 56th Inf. Co.C
Scroggin, John VA 11th Cav. Co.E
Scroggin, John H. AL 40th Inf. Co.A

Scroggin, John S. VA 51st Mil. Co.A
Scroggin, J.T. TX 11th Cav. Co.D
Scroggin, Louis A. VA 17th Inf. Co.B
Scroggin, Peyton R. VA 17th Inf. Co.B
Scroggin, R.E. KY 5th Cav. Co.A
Scroggin, Sidney A. KY 5th Cav. Co.A
Scroggin, T.M. TX 9th Cav. Co.E
Scroggin, T.R. AL 2nd Cav. Co.I
Scroggin, William A. GA 56th Inf. Co.C
Scroggin, William W. AL 55th Vol.
Scroggin, W.S. VA 41st Inf. Co.C Sgt.
Scroggins, --- LA Mil.Crescent Cadets
Scroggins, Abner MS 32nd Inf. Co.A
Scroggins, Alexander TN 21st (Wilson's) Cav.
  Co.F
Scroggins, Allison AL 3rd Cav. Co.H
Scroggins, A.M. AL Cav. Hardie's Bn.Res.
  Co.E
Scroggins, Andy TN 59th Mtd.Inf. Co.K
Scroggins, Asa AR 8th Inf. New Co.H
Scroggins, Asa AR Inf. Cocke's Regt. Co.K
Scroggins, Burges H. TN 59th Mtd.Inf. Co.K
Scroggins, C. AR Cav. Harrell's Bn. Co.D
Scroggins, Chelsey AR 33rd Inf. Co.I
Scroggins, C.M. GA 13th Cav. Co.F Cpl.
Scroggins, C.R. VA 17th Inf. Co.B
Scroggins, Daniel GA 12th Cav. Co.C
Scroggins, Daniel MD Inf. 2nd Bn. Co.G
Scroggins, Daniel VA Hvy.Arty. 19th Bn. 2nd
  Co.C
Scroggins, Daniel W. TX 13th Vol. 2nd Co.D
Scroggins, Drury F. GA 43rd Inf. Co.I
Scroggins, Edward S. VA 41st Inf. Co.C
Scroggins, Elijah GA 43rd Inf. Co.I
Scroggins, Ezekiel TN 5th (McKenzie's) Cav.
  Co.F
Scroggins, F.A. GA 31st Inf. Co.A Sgt.
Scroggins, Fielden TX Cav. 6th Bn. Co.A
Scroggins, Franklin M. AR 31st Inf. Co.C
Scroggins, George B. AL 2nd Bn. Hilliard's
  Legion Vol. Co.F
Scroggins, George C. GA 41st Inf. Co.K
Scroggins, George H. MS 3rd Inf. Co.B
Scroggins, George R. AL 59th Inf. Co.D
Scroggins, George R. AL Arty. 4th Bn. Hilliard's
  Legion Co.B
Scroggins, George T. AL Inf. 1st Regt. Co.A
Scroggins, George W. AL 20th Inf. Co.G
Scroggins, George W. GA 46th Inf. Co.C
Scroggins, Giles AR 23rd Inf. Co.A,H
Scroggins, G.L. AL Inf. 1st Regt. Co.H
Scroggins, Glenn O. GA Phillips' Legion Co.D
Scroggins, Griffin AL Lt.Arty. Kolb's Btty.
Scroggins, G.T. AL 45th Inf. Co.C
Scroggins, G.W. AR 38th Inf. New Co.I
Scroggins, G.W. TN Cav. Clark's Ind.Co.
Scroggins, Harry TX 13th Vol. Co.H
Scroggins, H.B. AL Coosa Guards J.W. Suttles'
  Co.
Scroggins, H.C. TN 10th & 11th (Cons.) Cav.
  Co.K
Scroggins, Henry TN 10th (DeMoss') Cav. Co.B
Scroggins, Henry J. AL 2nd Cav. Co.B
Scroggins, Henry J. AL Arty. 1st Bn. Co.E
Scroggins, Hiram TN 10th (DeMoss') Cav. Co.B
Scroggins, H.M. NC 4th Cav. (59th St.Troops)
  Co.I

Scroggins, Isaac AR 27th Inf. Co.F,I
Scroggins, Isaac M. LA 3rd (Harrison's) Cav.
  Co.H
Scroggins, J. AL 6th Inf. Co.F
Scroggins, Jackson AR 31st Inf. Co.C
Scroggins, Jackson MS 1st Lt.Arty. Co.E
Scroggins, James MO 11th Inf. Co.B
Scroggins, James F. MS 3rd Inf. Co.B 1st Cpl.
Scroggins, James G. TX Cav. 6th Bn. Co.A Sgt.
Scroggins, James J. AL Inf. 1st Regt. Co.A
Scroggins, James M. MS Inf. 2nd Bn. Co.B
Scroggins, James W. TN 36th Inf. Co.B
Scroggins, J.B. TX 9th Cav. Co.E 1st Sgt.
Scroggins, J.C. AL 53rd (Part.Rangers) Co.G
Scroggins, J.C. TN 18th (Newsom's) Cav. Co.G
Scroggins, J.E. AL 53rd (Part.Rangers) Co.G
Scroggins, Jefferson AR Inf. Hardy's Regt. Co.K
Scroggins, Jerry J. AL 7th Inf. Co.E
Scroggins, Jessee AR 31st Inf. Co.D
Scroggins, J.H. AL 51st (Part.Rangers) Co.H
Scroggins, J.H. AR 2nd Cav. Co.G 1st Sgt.
Scroggins, J.H. AR 6th Inf. 1st Co.B Sgt.
Scroggins, J.M. AL 1st Bn.Cadets Co.A
Scroggins, J.M. MS 48th Inf. Co.B
Scroggins, J.M. MO Cav. 3rd Regt.St.Guard
  Co.C 1st Lt.
Scroggins, J.M. TX 12th Inf. Co.F
Scroggins, John H. GA 12th Inf. Co.B
Scroggins, John H. VA 12th Inf. Co.D
Scroggins, John S. VA Lt.Arty. Cutshaw's Co.
Scroggins, John W. VA 7th Inf. Co.B
Scroggins, J.R. AL 12th Cav. Co.F
Scroggins, J.R. AL 12th Inf. Co.F
Scroggins, J.R. AR 19th (Dawson's) Inf. Co.K
Scroggins, J.R. LA Inf.Cons. 18th Regt. & Yel-
  low Jacket Bn. Co.F
Scroggins, J.S. VA Lt.Arty. Carpenter's Co.
Scroggins, J.T. TX 23rd Cav. Co.I
Scroggins, J.W. GA Inf. 1st City Bn. (Columbus)
  Co.B Cpl.
Scroggins, L.D. AR 8th Inf. New Co.H
Scroggins, Lee A. VA 46th Inf. Co.D
Scroggins, Leroy AR 3rd Cav. Co.K
Scroggins, Leroy AR Cav. Gordon's Regt. Co.I
Scroggins, M. AL 51st (Part.Rangers) Co.D
Scroggins, M. GA 46th Inf. Co.E
Scroggins, Marcus D.L. MO 11th Inf. Co.B
Scroggins, M.M. TX 9th Cav. Co.E 1st Lt.
Scroggins, Newton J. MS 3rd Inf. Co.B
Scroggins, R. AR 7th Mil. Co.B
Scroggins, Richard AL 29th Inf. Co.G
Scroggins, Richard AR 34th Inf. Co.I
Scroggins, R.J. AR 10th (Witt's) Cav. Co.C
Scroggins, Robert H. AR 31st Inf. Co.C
Scroggins, R.R. AR 12th Inf. Co.G
Scroggins, Smith MS 32nd Inf. Co.A
Scroggins, Solomon AL 28th Inf. Co.B
Scroggins, T.C. AL 31st Inf. Co.B Cpl.
Scroggins, T.F. AR 10th Mil. Co.F
Scroggins, Thomas Mead's Conf.Cav. Co.K
Scroggins, Tho. B. AL 12th Inf. Co.I
Scroggins, Thomas G. GA 31st Inf. Co.A Sgt.
Scroggins, Thomas J. TX 6th Cav. Co.C
Scroggins, Thompson KY 2nd Mtd.Inf. Co.B
Scroggins, W.A. AR 30th Inf. Co.K
Scroggins, Warren C. AL Arty. 4th Bn. Hil-
  liard's Legion Co.B

Scroggins, W.C. AL 29th Inf. Co.G
Scroggins, W.H. AL Coosa Guards J.W. Suttles'
  Co.
Scroggins, W. Henry AL 59th Inf. Co.D
Scroggins, William AL 20th Inf. Co.G
Scroggins, William AR 38th Inf. Co.I
Scroggins, William MS 24th Inf. Co.L
Scroggins, William C. AL Arty. 1st Bn. Co.A
Scroggins, William H. AL Arty. 4th Bn. Hil-
  liard's Legion Co.B
Scroggins, William H. 3rd Conf.Inf. Co.A
Scroggins, William J. KY Cav. Chenoweth's
  Regt. Co.C
Scroggins, William J. MO 2nd Inf. Co.D
Scroggins, William S. KY Jessee's Bn.Mtd.
  Riflemen
Scroggins, William W. AL 11th Inf. Co.F
Scroggins, William W. AR 36th Inf. Co.F
Scroggins, William W. VA 12th Inf. Co.K
Scroggins, W.M. AL Inf. 1st Regt. Co.A
Scroggins, W.M. AL 34th Inf. Co.D
Scroggins, Wyle KY Cav. Chenoweth's Regt.
  Co.C
Scroggs, Amos NC 48th Inf. Co.C
Scroggs, B. LA Cav. Benjamin's Co.
Scroggs, David NC 48th Inf. Co.C Sgt.
Scroggs, David A. NC 6th Cav. (65th St.Troops)
  Co.B,F Bugler
Scroggs, David A. NC Cav. 7th Bn. Co.B
Scroggs, E.M. NC 62nd Inf. Co.B
Scroggs, Enos M. NC 62nd Inf. Co.B
Scroggs, Francies M. LA Res.Corps
Scroggs, Fielding F. VA Inf. 25th Bn. Co.B
Scroggs, J. MS 16th Inf. Co.D
Scroggs, James J. NC 6th Cav. (65th St.Troops)
  Co.B,F
Scroggs, James J. NC Cav. 7th Bn. Co.B
Scroggs, J.E. GA 44th Inf. Co.E
Scroggs, John LA 4th Regt.Eng.Troops Co.I
Scroggs, John NC 4th Inf. Co.C
Scroggs, John A. GA 24th Inf. Co.D
Scroggs, John A. NC 64th Inf. Co.I
Scroggs, John T. LA 14th Inf. Co.K
Scroggs, John W. NC 39th Inf. Co.I
Scroggs, Joseph E. NC 6th Cav. (65th St.Troops)
  Co.B,F Cpl.
Scroggs, Joseph E. NC Cav. 7th Bn. Co.B
Scroggs, Joseph H. GA Inf. (Mell Scouts) Wyly's
  Co.
Scroggs, M.F. TN 60th Mtd.Inf. Co.E
Scroggs, Newton M. GA 24th Inf. Co.D 3rd Lt.
Scroggs, Reese P. TN Lt.Arty. Lynch's Co.
  Wag.
Scroggs, Robert TN Cav. 16th Bn. (Neal's) Co.E
Scroggs, Robert M. NC 6th Cav. (65th
  St.Troops) Co.B,F
Scroggs, Robert M. NC Cav. 7th Bn. Co.B
Scroggs, W. NC Mallett's Co.
Scroggs, William A. NC 39th Inf. Co.I
Scroggy, W.B. KY 7th Cav. Co.C
Scroggy, William B. KY 6th Cav. Co.B,C,E
Scroggy, William L. NC 39th Inf. Co.C,G Cpl.
Scroghem, E.M. MO Lt.Arty. Von Phul's Co.
Scroghem, William T. MO Lt.Arty. 1st Field
  Btty. Bugler
Scrogin, Sidney A. KY 14th Cav.
Scrogin, T.A. AL Leighton Rangers

Scrogin, W.J. AL 34th Inf. Co.A
Scrogings, Humphrey AR 33rd Inf. Co.K
Scroginns, William GA 12th Cav. Co.C
Scrogins, George W. GA Inf. 9th Bn. Co.B
Scrogins, G.L. AL 45th Inf. Co.A
Scrogins, Jesse TN Cav. Newsom's Regt. Co.D
Scrogins, William H. GA 1st (Fannin's) Res. Co.K Sgt.
Scrogins, W.J. GA 35th Inf. Co.E
Scronce, Abram NC 23rd Inf. Co.B
Scronce, Andrew NC 18th Inf. Co.A
Scronce, C.B. NC 18th Inf. Co.A
Scronce, Ephraim NC 23rd Inf. Co.B
Scronce, J.C. MS 3rd Inf. (A. of 10,000) Co.C 1st Lt.
Scronce, S.E. TX 24th Cav. Co.I
Scronce, William A. NC 23rd Inf. Co.F
Scrothrone, Joseph VA 8th Bn.Res. Co.C
Scrots, G.A. 7th Conf.Cav. Co.G
Scrott, H. GA Inf. 18th Bn. Co.A
Scrott, Henry GA Hvy.Arty. 22nd Bn. Co.C
Scrott, Henry GA 1st (Olmstead's) Inf. Screven's Co.
Scrudgington, Alexander TN 29th Inf. Co.F
Scrudgington, James TN 29th Inf. Co.F
Scrudgington, John TN 29th Inf. Co.I
Scrugg, T.W. GA 11th Cav. Co.I
Scruggins, Adolph LA 2nd Cav. Co.D
Scruggins, G.L. LA 22nd Inf. Co.G
Scruggs, A. MS 3rd Cav. Co.F
Scruggs, A.B. AL 5th Cav. Co.K
Scruggs, A.B. Lt.Arty. Dent's Btty.,CSA
Scruggs, Abijah D. TN 59th Mtd.Inf. Co.E
Scruggs, Abraham E.T. VA 19th Inf. Co.C
Scruggs, A.D. NC 55th Inf. Co.D
Scruggs, A.G. TN 9th (Ward's) Cav. Co.B
Scruggs, A.J. SC 7th Res. Co.M
Scruggs, Albea E. VA 5th Cav. Co.B
Scruggs, Albert MS 15th Inf. Co.H
Scruggs, Albert NC 16th Inf. Co.D
Scruggs, Albert G. TN 21st Cav. Co.B,I
Scruggs, Albro VA 1st Bn.Res. Co.D
Scruggs, Alexander TN Cav. 12th Bn. (Day's) Co.D
Scruggs, Alexander W. TN Cav. 4th Bn. (Branner's) Co.E Lt.
Scruggs, Alfred SC Inf. Holcombe Legion Co.A
Scruggs, Alfred M. SC 9th Inf. Co.I Jr.2nd Lt.
Scruggs, Allen Franklin TX 20th Cav. Co.B
Scruggs, Allen S. SC 16th Inf. Co.A
Scruggs, A.M. SC Palmetto S.S. Co.H 2nd Lt.
Scruggs, Antony T. MS 17th Inf. Co.E
Scruggs, A.S. SC 1st St.Troops Co.K Cpl.
Scruggs, A.T. AL Cav. Moreland's Regt. Co.G Sgt.
Scruggs, A.T. MS 29th Inf. Co.E
Scruggs, A.T. TN 4th (McLemore's) Cav. Co.E
Scruggs, A.T. Gen. & Staff Surg.
Scruggs, Augustus R. GA 1st (Olmstead's) Inf. Co.H
Scruggs, A.W. TN 2nd (Ashby's) Cav. Co.I
Scruggs, A.W. TN Cav. 4th Bn. (Branner's) Co.E 1st Lt.
Scruggs, Ben F. TX 31st Cav. Co.I Jr.2nd Lt.
Scruggs, Benjamin NC 25th Inf. Co.E
Scruggs, Benjamin VA 3rd Lt.Arty. Co.C
Scruggs, Benjamin E. VA 23rd Inf. Co.A Sgt.

Scruggs, Berry KY 2nd (Duke's) Cav. Co.G
Scruggs, B.I. Lt.Arty. Dent's Btty.,CSA
Scruggs, B.O. SC Inf. Holcombe Legion Co.A,K
Scruggs, B. Pope AL 4th (Russell's) Cav. Co.C,B
Scruggs, Brookens C. TN 5th (McKenzie's) Cav. Co.H
Scruggs, C. SC 18th Inf. Co.K
Scruggs, C. SC Inf. Holcombe Legion Co.A
Scruggs, Calvin VA 2nd Cav. Co.K Cpl.
Scruggs, C.C. SC Inf. Holcombe Legion Co.A,K Capt.
Scruggs, C.F., Jr. KY 8th Cav. Co.D Sgt.
Scruggs, Charles VA Cav. 40th Bn.
Scruggs, Charles A. TX 17th Inf. Co.K
Scruggs, Charles L. VA 15th Cav. Co.B
Scruggs, Charles O. VA Lt.Arty. 38th Bn. Co.D Cpl.
Scruggs, Charles O. VA Lt.Arty. J.R. Johnson's Co.
Scruggs, Charles O. VA 28th Inf. 1st Co.C
Scruggs, Christopher C. SC 1st Inf. Co.E
Scruggs, C.K. TN 39th Mtd.Inf. Co.C
Scruggs, Clifton H. SC 12th Inf. Co.F
Scruggs, C.M. TN 17th Inf. Co.G
Scruggs, C.M. TN 42nd Inf. Co.C Cpl.
Scruggs, C.M. 4th Conf.Inf. Co.H
Scruggs, C.S.W. SC Inf. Holcombe Legion Co.A 1st Sgt.
Scruggs, Daniel SC Inf. Holcombe Legion Co.A
Scruggs, Daniel TX 17th Inf. Co.B
Scruggs, David AR 2nd Mtd.Rifles Co.D
Scruggs, D.C. TN 18th Inf. Co.B
Scruggs, D.E. LA Inf.Crescent Regt. Co.H Sgt.
Scruggs, D.E. VA Inf. 2nd Bn.Loc.Def. Co.A Lt.Col.
Scruggs, Dewit Clinton MS 14th Inf. Co.D
Scruggs, Dewit E. MS 37th Inf. Co.C
Scruggs, D.H. AR Cav. Gordon's Regt. Co.H
Scruggs, D.H. LA Washington Arty.Bn. Co.5
Scruggs, Drury NC 16th Inf. Co.D
Scruggs, Drury C. SC 5th Inf. 1st Co.G, 2nd Co.I
Scruggs, D.S. SC Inf. Holcombe Legion Co.K
Scruggs, Ed TN 1st (Feild's) Inf. Co.L
Scruggs, Edward Y. TX 10th Inf. Co.B
Scruggs, Edwin T. VA 3rd Lt.Arty. Co.C
Scruggs, E.F. MS 5th Inf. (St.Troops) Co.B
Scruggs, E.F. TN 39th Mtd.Inf. Co.A Cpl.
Scruggs, E.G. GA 48th Inf. Co.A Capt.
Scruggs, E.H. MS 3rd Inf. Co.B
Scruggs, E.L. VA Cav. 40th Bn.
Scruggs, Elijah GA 43rd Inf. Co.I
Scruggs, E.M. Gen. & Staff Hosp.Stew.
Scruggs, Ephraim TN Cav. 12th Bn. (Day's) Co.F Cpl.
Scruggs, E.R. AL 7th Inf. Co.K Sgt.Maj.
Scruggs, E.R. MS 2nd Part.Rangers Co.D 3rd Lt.
Scruggs, Fountain P. TN 55th (McKoin's) Inf. McEwen, Jr.'s Co. Cpl.
Scruggs, F.P. MS 17th Inf. Co.E
Scruggs, Frederick C. VA Hvy.Arty. 20th Bn. Co.D
Scruggs, Frederick H. VA 19th Inf. Co.C
Scruggs, G. AL Cav. Murphy's Bn. Co.D
Scruggs, G. TN 30th Inf. Co.K

Scruggs, G.C. AL Cav. Moreland's Regt. Co.G
Scruggs, George F. VA 1st Arty. Co.K
Scruggs, George F. VA Arty. L.F. Jones' Co.
Scruggs, George F. VA Lt.Arty. Snead's Co.
Scruggs, George F. VA 44th Inf. Co.C
Scruggs, George S. AL 6th Inf. Co.K
Scruggs, George W. MS 17th Inf. Co.E Cpl.
Scruggs, George W. TX 1st Inf. Co.I
Scruggs, G.S. TN 45th Inf. Co.B
Scruggs, Gutridge J. VA 4th Cav. Co.E
Scruggs, G.W. AL Cav. Moreland's Regt. Co.D
Scruggs, G.W. TX Inf. Cotton's Co.
Scruggs, G.W. VA 88th Mil.
Scruggs, Hamilton M. TX 1st (McCulloch's) Cav. Co.I
Scruggs, Hartwell VA Inf. 25th Bn. Co.B
Scruggs, H.C. TN 4th Inf. Co.C
Scruggs, Henry MO Inf. Perkins' Bn. Co.A
Scruggs, Henry VA 21st Inf. Co.D Cpl.
Scruggs, Henry F. AL 6th Inf. Co.K Cpl.
Scruggs, H.J. TN 29th Inf. Co.B Cpl.
Scruggs, H.M. TX 17th Inf. Co.K
Scruggs, Isom MS 28th Cav. Co.B
Scruggs, J. TX 20th Inf. Co.B
Scruggs, J.A. TX 22nd Inf. Chap.
Scruggs, J.A. Gen. & Staff Chap.
Scruggs, James AL 48th Inf. Co.D
Scruggs, James KY 2nd (Duke's) Cav. Co.G
Scruggs, James NC 13th Inf. Co.I Sgt.
Scruggs, James TN 4th (McLemore's) Cav. Co.F
Scruggs, James TN 29th Inf. Co.A
Scruggs, James TN 59th Mtd.Inf. Co.E
Scruggs, James TN 61st Mtd.Inf. Bundren's Co.
Scruggs, James TX 19th Cav. Co.D
Scruggs, James VA Inf. 4th Bn.Loc.Def. Co.F
Scruggs, James A. GA 48th Inf. Co.B,A
Scruggs, James A. TX 22nd Inf. Co.F Capt.
Scruggs, James E. MS 17th Inf. Co.B
Scruggs, James E. NC 1st Bn.Jr.Res. Co.B
Scruggs, James E. SC 5th Inf. 2nd Co.I
Scruggs, James E. TN 2nd (Robison's) Inf. Co.D
Scruggs, James E. VA 2nd Cav. Co.K
Scruggs, James E. VA 19th Inf. Co.C
Scruggs, James G. TX 26th Cav. Co.B
Scruggs, James H. AL Cav. Moreland's Regt. Co.G Cpl.
Scruggs, James H. VA 53rd Inf. Co.G
Scruggs, James H. 1st Cherokee Mtd.Vol. 2nd Co.K
Scruggs, James K. TN 28th Inf. Co.G
Scruggs, James M. MS 7th Inf. Co.H Capt.
Scruggs, James M. MS 9th Inf. Old Co.B, New Co.I Cpl.
Scruggs, James T. TN 32nd Inf. Co.E
Scruggs, James W. VA Loc.Def. Mallory's Co.
Scruggs, Jasper F. FL 1st Inf. New Co.C
Scruggs, J.B. MS 1st Cav. Co.K
Scruggs, J.B. MS 3rd Inf. Co.B
Scruggs, J.E. GA 48th Inf. Co.E
Scruggs, J. Emmett VA Mil. 85th Regt. Col.
Scruggs, Jesse TX Inf. 24th Bn. Co.B 2nd Lt.
Scruggs, Jesse M. NC 5th Sr.Res. Co.E
Scruggs, Jesse M. NC 12th Inf. Co.E
Scruggs, J.H. Gen. & Staff Capt.,AQM
Scruggs, J.J. VA 2nd Inf.Loc.Def. Co.K
Scruggs, J.J. VA Inf. 2nd Bn.Loc.Def. Co.B
Scruggs, J.M. Forrest's Staff Capt.

Scruggs, John SC 7th Res. Co.M
Scruggs, John TN Cav. 9th Bn. (Gantt's) Co.C
Scruggs, John TN Inf. 3rd Cons.Regt. Co.F
Scruggs, John TN 28th (Cons.) Inf. Co.E
Scruggs, John TN 35th Inf. 2nd Co.D 1st Sgt.
Scruggs, John TN 48th (Voorhies') Inf. Co.E
Scruggs, John TN 84th Inf. Co.A
Scruggs, John VA Hvy.Arty. 10th Bn. Co.C
Scruggs, John A. GA 20th Inf. Co.C
Scruggs, John A. TN 61st Mtd.Inf. Co.D 1st Sgt.
Scruggs, John A. VA Hvy.Arty. 19th Bn. Co.A
Scruggs, John A. VA Hvy.Arty. Kyle's Co.
Scruggs, John E. NC 16th Inf. Co.I
Scruggs, John E. VA 3rd Lt.Arty. Co.C
Scruggs, John H. VA 44th Inf. Co.C Cpl.
Scruggs, John J. SC Lt.Arty. 3rd (Palmetto) Bn. Co.A
Scruggs, John J. VA 44th Inf. Co.C
Scruggs, John J. VA 49th Inf. Co.I
Scruggs, John M. TX 17th Inf. Co.B
Scruggs, John M. VA Hvy.Arty. 19th Bn. Co.A
Scruggs, John M. VA Lt.Arty. 38th Bn. Co.D
Scruggs, John M. VA Hvy.Arty. Kyle's Co.
Scruggs, John P. SC 1st (McCreary's) Inf. Campbell's Co. Cpl.
Scruggs, John P. TX 1st (McCulloch's) Cav. Co.K
Scruggs, John P. TX 1st (Yager's) Cav. Co.I
Scruggs, John P. TX Cav. 8th (Taylor's) Bn. Co.D
Scruggs, John R. VA 2nd Cav. Co.H
Scruggs, John T. VA 21st Inf. Co.E
Scruggs, John W. AL 16th Inf. Co.I Cpl.
Scruggs, John W. GA 8th Inf. (St.Guards) Co.H
Scruggs, John W. MS Cav. Shelby's Co. (Bolivar Greys)
Scruggs, John W. VA 38th Inf. Co.H
Scruggs, Joseph MS 27th Inf. Co.H
Scruggs, Joseph A. VA 1st Cav. Co.G
Scruggs, Joseph L. GA 20th Inf. Co.C
Scruggs, Joseph L. GA Cobb's Legion Co.L
Scruggs, J.P. MS 5th Cav. Co.C
Scruggs, J.P. MS Cav. 6th Bn. Prince's Co.
Scruggs, J.P. SC Lt.Arty. 3rd (Palmetto) Bn. Co.A Sgt.
Scruggs, J.P. SC 6th Inf. 1st Co.I 2nd Lt.
Scruggs, J.P. SC Inf. Holcombe Legion Co.K Sgt.
Scruggs, J.P. SC Palmetto S.S. Co.H
Scruggs, J.S. VA Inf. Lyneman's Co.
Scruggs, J.T. GA Inf. 1st Loc.Troops (Augusta) Dearing's Cav.Co.
Scruggs, J.W. AL 18th Inf. Co.F
Scruggs, J.W. MS 20th Inf. Co.A
Scruggs, J.W. SC Inf. Holcombe Legion Co.K
Scruggs, J.W. SC Palmetto S.S. Co.H
Scruggs, J.W. TN 6th (Wheeler's) Cav. Co.K
Scruggs, J.W. TN Cav. 11th Bn. (Gordon's) Co.A
Scruggs, J.W. TN 29th Inf. Co.B
Scruggs, J.W.T. AL 17th Inf. Co.B
Scruggs, J.W.T. AL 18th Inf. Co.F
Scruggs, J.W.T. 2nd Conf.Eng.Troops Co.C Artif.
Scruggs, L. VA Inf. 4th Bn.Loc.Def. Co.F
Scruggs, L. VA 16th Inf. Co.B

Scruggs, Lafayett GA 11th Cav. Co.F
Scruggs, Lawrence H. AL 4th Inf. Co.I Lt.Col.
Scruggs, L.B. MS Cav. Shelby's Co. (Bolivar Greys)
Scruggs, Lem TX 10th Cav. Co.F
Scruggs, Lemuel D. SC Inf. Holcombe Legion Co.A,K Sgt.
Scruggs, Leroy VA 64th Mil. Campbell's Co.
Scruggs, Lewis MO 6th Cav. Co.I
Scruggs, Lewis SC Inf. Holcombe Legion Co.A
Scruggs, Lewis S. MS 17th Inf. Co.B Capt.
Scruggs, Lorenzo B. NC 28th Inf. Co.H
Scruggs, L.R. TX 3rd Cav. Co.B
Scruggs, L.S. GA Lt.Arty. (Arsenal Btty.) Hudson's Co. 1st Lt.
Scruggs, L.S. MS 19th Inf. QM
Scruggs, L.S. TN 3rd (Clack's) Inf. Co.B
Scruggs, L.S. Featherston's Brig. Maj.
Scruggs, M. KY 1st (Butler's) Cav. Co.C
Scruggs, Marcellus KY 3rd Cav. Co.C
Scruggs, Marion TN 1st (Turney's) Inf. Co.B
Scruggs, Marshall L. MO Cav. 3rd Bn. Co.A 2nd Lt.
Scruggs, Matt TN 16th Inf.
Scruggs, Matt TN 17th Inf. Co.G 1st Lt.
Scruggs, M.M. GA 22nd Inf. Co.G
Scruggs, N.H. AL 11th Cav. Co.H
Scruggs, N.H. TX 29th Cav. Co.K
Scruggs, Nicholas H. AR 15th (Josey's) Inf. Co.A
Scruggs, N.R. Hosp.Stew.
Scruggs, N.T. TX 17th Inf. Co.K
Scruggs, O.G. AR 2nd Inf. New Co.C
Scruggs, Oriley VA 16th Inf. Co.B
Scruggs, Oriley VA 64th Mil. Campbell's Co.
Scruggs, Palan L. MO 3rd Cav. Co.D
Scruggs, Peter SC 5th Inf. 2nd Co.G
Scruggs, P.K. MS 2nd Part.Rangers Co.D 3rd Lt.
Scruggs, Powhatan B. VA 38th Inf. Co.H Sgt.
Scruggs, R. GA 9th Regt.St.Troops Co.G Capt.
Scruggs, R. NC 3rd Jr.Res. Co.K
Scruggs, R.A. SC Inf. Holcombe Legion Co.A,K
Scruggs, R.A. VA 57th Inf. Co.A
Scruggs, R.D. SC 6th Inf. 1st Co.I
Scruggs, R.D. SC Inf. Holcombe Legion Co.K
Scruggs, R.G. TN 34th Inf. Co.K
Scruggs, Richard FL Cav. 3rd Bn. Co.A Cpl.
Scruggs, Richard LA 3rd Inf. Co.F
Scruggs, Richard LA 27th Inf. Co.I
Scruggs, Richard TN Cav. 12th Bn. (Day's) Co.F
Scruggs, Richard 15th Conf.Cav. Co.A
Scruggs, Richard A. GA 20th Inf. Co.C
Scruggs, Richard D. TN Cav. 12th Bn. (Day's) Co.B
Scruggs, Richard M. AR 3rd Cav. Co.F
Scruggs, Richard M. NC 25th Inf. Co.E
Scruggs, R.K. AL Lt.Arty. Clanton's Btty.
Scruggs, R.L. TN 4th (Murray's) Cav. Co.H
Scruggs, R.L. TN 8th (Smith's) Cav. Co.C 1st Lt.
Scruggs, R.M. SC Inf. Holcombe Legion Co.A,K Capt.
Scruggs, Robert AL 48th Inf. Co.D Cpl.
Scruggs, Robert NC 4th Bn.Jr.Res. Co.D
Scruggs, Robert NC 50th Inf. Co.I

Scruggs, Robert SC 18th Inf. Co.K
Scruggs, R.P. SC Inf. Holcombe Legion Co.A,K Cpl.
Scruggs, Samuel TN 1st (Turney's) Inf. Co.B
Scruggs, Samuel VA 2nd Cav. Co.K
Scruggs, Samuel A. VA Hvy.Arty. 19th Bn. Co.D
Scruggs, Samuel A. VA Hvy.Arty. Kyle's Co.
Scruggs, Samuel A. VA Loc.Def. Bosher's Co.
Scruggs, Samuel A. Marine Corps,CSA
Scruggs, Samuel M. VA 19th Inf. Co.C
Scruggs, Samuel S. VA Arty. Dance's Co.
Scruggs, Samuel S. VA 34th Inf. Co.H
Scruggs, Seth AL 5th Cav. Co.B
Scruggs, S.F. GA 5th Cav. Co.C Sgt.
Scruggs, S.J. GA 48th Inf. Co.E
Scruggs, Sol K. TX 8th Cav. Co.C 2nd Lt.
Scruggs, Solomon E. GA 5th Inf. Co.D
Scruggs, Solomon M. FL 3rd Inf. Co.H,A
Scruggs, Sterling AL 50th Inf. Co.D
Scruggs, Sterling A. VA Loc.Def. Bosher's Co.
Scruggs, T.H. AL 11th Cav. Co.I Cpl.
Scruggs, Thomas AL 4th (Russell's) Cav. Co.L
Scruggs, Thomas AL 19th Inf. Co.K
Scruggs, Thomas GA 6th Cav. Co.B
Scruggs, Thomas TN 6th Inf. Co.L Cpl.
Scruggs, Thomas TN 17th Inf. Co.B
Scruggs, Thomas TN Inf. 154th Sr.Regt. Co.E
Scruggs, Thomas VA Arty. C.F. Johnston's Co.
Scruggs, Thomas B. NC 13th Inf. Co.I Cpl.
Scruggs, Thomas J. VA 23rd Inf. Co.A
Scruggs, Tilleson SC Inf. Holcombe Legion Co.A
Scruggs, T.J. NC 1st Bn.Jr.Res. Co.B
Scruggs, T.L. TX 28th Cav. Co.D
Scruggs, T.M. MO 12th Cav. Co.B
Scruggs, Toliver D. NC 12th Inf. Co.E
Scruggs, T.S.J. TN 20th Inf. Co.D
Scruggs, T.S.J. TN 24th Inf. 1st Co.H
Scruggs, W.A. TX 33rd Cav. Co.D
Scruggs, W.A. TX 17th Inf. Co.K
Scruggs, Walter TN 44th (Cons.) Inf. Co.G
Scruggs, Walter C. AL 44th Inf. Co.E
Scruggs, Walter C. TN 55th (McKoin's) Inf. McEwen, Jr.'s Co.
Scruggs, W.B. TN Cav. Clark's Ind.Co.
Scruggs, W.C. AR 13th Mil. Co.A
Scruggs, W.C. GA 24th Inf. Co.E
Scruggs, W.C. TN 9th (Ward's) Cav. Co.B
Scruggs, W.D. AR Cav. Gordon's Regt. Co.H
Scruggs, W.D. SC Palmetto S.S. Co.M
Scruggs, W.F. TN 17th Inf. Co.G
Scruggs, W.H. TN 20th (Russell's) Cav. Co.D
Scruggs, W.H. TN 1st Hvy.Arty. 2nd Co.B
Scruggs, W.H. VA Hvy.Arty. Allen's Co.
Scruggs, W.H. Gen. & Staff, A. of N. VA Maj.,QM
Scruggs, W.H.M. FL Inf. 2nd Bn. Co.D
Scruggs, Wiley J. TN 2nd Cav. Orderly Sgt.
Scruggs, Wiley J. TN 2nd (Robison's) Inf. Co.C 1st Sgt.
Scruggs, William KY Cav. Malone's Regt. Co.A
Scruggs, William MS 28th Cav. Co.B
Scruggs, William NC 2nd Arty. (36th St.Troops) Co.I
Scruggs, William SC 7th Res. Co.M
Scruggs, Wm. SC 13th Inf. Co.E

Scruggs, William SC 16th Inf. Co.I
Scruggs, William SC 16th & 24th (Cons.) Inf. Co.D
Scruggs, William TN 12th (Green's) Cav. Co.A
Scruggs, William TN Cav. 12th Bn. (Day's) Co.E
Scruggs, William VA 1st Arty. Co.H
Scruggs, William VA Inf. 4th Bn.Loc.Def. Co.F
Scruggs, William A. TX 13th Cav. Co.G
Scruggs, William A. TX 36th Cav. Co.E
Scruggs, William B. TN 2nd (Robison's) Inf. Co.G
Scruggs, William B. VA Hvy.Arty. 20th Bn. Co.C 2nd Lt.
Scruggs, William Benjamin KY 2nd Cav. Co.F
Scruggs, William C. NC 16th Inf. Co.H
Scruggs, William D. SC 5th Inf. 1st Co.G
Scruggs, William D. VA 19th Inf. Co.C Sgt.
Scruggs, William E. VA 16th Inf. Co.F
Scruggs, William E. VA 49th Inf. Co.I Sgt.
Scruggs, William F. TN 44th Inf. Co.H
Scruggs, William F. TN 44th (Cons.) Inf. Co.D
Scruggs, William F. TN 61st Mtd.Inf. Co.F
Scruggs, William G. VA 56th Inf. Co.D
Scruggs, William H. AL 4th Inf.
Scruggs, William H. FL 3rd Inf. Co.H
Scruggs, William H. MS 1st (Johnston's) Inf. Co.A
Scruggs, William J. MS 20th Inf. Co.G Jr.2nd Lt.
Scruggs, William M. TN 21st Cav.
Scruggs, William M. TX 34th Cav. Co.C
Scruggs, William M. VA Hvy.Arty. 20th Bn. Co.A
Scruggs, William N. AL 6th Inf. Co.K 2nd Lt.
Scruggs, William P. TN 3rd (Clack's) Inf. Co.A
Scruggs, William P. VA Hvy.Arty. 18th Bn. Co.B
Scruggs, William R. VA Lt.Arty. Turner's Co. Sgt.
Scruggs, William R. VA Arty. Wise Legion Sgt.
Scruggs, William R. Gen. & Staff Hosp.Stew.
Scruggs, William S. MS 29th Inf. Co.E
Scruggs, William T. 1st Cherokee Mtd.Vol. 2nd Co.K
Scruggs, Wilson N. SC Inf. Holcombe Legion Co.A,K
Scruggs, W.L.M.A. SC 2nd Inf. Co.B
Scruggs, W.P. VA 2nd Cav. Co.K
Scruggs, W.R. VA Lt.Arty. Fry's Co.
Scruggs, W.R. Hosp.Stew.
Scruggs, W.W. SC Inf. Holcombe Legion Co.A,K
Scruggs, W.W. TX 28th Cav. Co.C
Scruggs, Y.J. MS Cav. 1st Bn. (Montgomery's) St.Troops Cameron's Co.
Scruggs, Young TN 1st (Feild's) Inf. Co.D
Scrugs, J.A. NC 2nd Jr.Res. Co.D
Scrugs, J.H. MO 6th Cav. Co.I
Scrugs, Nathaniel D. NC 62nd Inf. Co.E
Scrugs, R.M. SC 1st (Butler's) Inf. Co.E
Scrugs, Thomas GA Cav. Young's Co. (Alleghany Troopers) Cpl.
Scrumpshire, Thomas TN 59th Mtd.Inf. Co.C
Scrutchen, Samul GA Cav. 15th Bn. (St.Guards) Allen's Co.
Scrutchens, Benjamin B. VA 3rd Inf. Co.G

Scrutchens, Thomas GA Inf. (Collier Guards) Collier's Co.
Scrutchim, --- GA Inf. 25th Bn. (Prov.Guard) Co.D
Scruton, Frank S. Conf.Inf. 1st Bn. 2nd Co.E Cpl.
Scruton, F.S. AL Inf. 2nd Regt. Co.I
Scudamore, Edwin MS 12th Inf. Co.G
Scudamore, Robert MS 12th Inf. Co.G
Scudday, James A. GA Inf. 1st Loc.Troops (Augusta) Co.F
Scudday, James A. GA 6th Inf. Co.A
Scudday, James A. LA Arty. Green's Co. (LA Guard Btty.)
Scudday, James A. LA 1st (Nelligan's) Inf. 1st Co.B
Scudday, W.H. TX 30th Cav. Co.F
Scudder, Alexander M. GA Inf. Athens Reserved Corps
Scudder, Benjamin F. TN 16th Inf. Co.F Sgt.
Scudder, C. GA 19th Inf. Co.L
Scudder, C. GA 55th Inf. Co.B
Scudder, David GA 1st (Olmstead's) Inf.
Scudder, E. GA 5th Cav. Co.C
Scudder, Ephram GA Cav. 2nd Bn. Co.E
Scudder, Foulton VA Inf. 26th Bn. Co.B
Scudder, George F. GA 55th Inf. Co.F
Scudder, G.H. MS 38th Cav. Co.D Cpl.
Scudder, Ira KY 11th Cav. Co.B Comsy.Sgt.
Scudder, Ira KY 7th Mtd.Inf. Co.D Comsy.Sgt.
Scudder, Jacob M. GA Cobb's Legion Co.B
Scudder, J.B. MS 38th Cav. Co.D Jr.2nd Lt.
Scudder, John GA 55th Inf. Co.F
Scudder, Lewis B. GA Cobb's Legion Co.B
Scudder, Liberty GA 1st (Olmstead's) Inf.
Scudder, Richard F. TX Cav. Ragsdale's Bn. Co.B
Scudder, Samuel H. AR 2nd Inf. Co.G
Scudder, Samuel S. GA 7th Inf. Co.F
Scudder, S.S. GA Lt.Arty. 12th Bn. 3rd Co.C
Scudder, T. MO Lt.Arty. 3rd Field Btty.
Scudder, William GA 55th Inf. Co.F
Scudder, William H.H. GA Cobb's Legion Co.B
Scudders, Isaac M. TN Cav. 11th Bn. (Gordon's) Co.F Sgt.
Scudders, J.M. TN 6th (Wheeler's) Cav. Co.D
Scud dis 1st Cherokee Mtd.Rifles Co.I
Scuddy, J.W. TX 16th Inf. Co.B
Scuggs, Ed TN Inf. Nashville Bn. Cattles' Co.
Scuggs, E.L. AR Cav. Gordon's Regt. Co.B
Scull, Benjamin AR 6th Inf. Co.A
Scull, Benjamin F. AR 15th (Josey's) Inf. Co.B Surg.
Scull, B.F. Gen. & Staff Surg.
Scull, Chris AR 18th Inf. Co.K Sgt.
Scull, Fred W. AR 18th Inf. Co.K
Scull, G.R. FL Lt.Arty. Abell's Co.
Scull, Henry W. AR 15th (Josey's) Inf. Co.B Sgt.
Scull, James H. AR 15th (Josey's) Inf. Co.B Jr.2nd Lt.
Scull, J.H. AR 1st Field Btty. (McNally's Btty.) Lt.
Scull, Joseph G. NC Hvy.Arty. 1st Bn. Co.A,D
Scull, William TX Inf. Cunningham's Co.
Scull, William E. TX 8th Cav. Co.G

Scull, William J. FL Milton Lt.Arty. Dunham's Co. Asst.Surg.
Scull, W.J. Gen. & Staff Asst.Surg.
Scullen, John D. VA 1st Res.
Scullen, John J. LA 1st (Nelligan's) Inf. Co.E
Sculley, Bartley VA 15th Inf. Co.F
Sculley, Charles I. VA 14th Inf. Co.D Cpl.
Sculley, Marks GA 23rd Inf. Co.C
Sculley, Michael KY Cav. 2nd Bn. (Dortch's) Co.C
Scullin, Morgan R. AL 4th Inf. Co.B
Scullock, L.C. FL Cav. 5th Bn.
Scully, Charles TN 24th Inf. Co.G
Scully, Charles TX 1st Inf. Co.I
Scully, Christopher LA 20th Inf. Co.I
Scully, Daniel LA 1st Hvy.Arty. 2nd Bn. Co.A Capt.
Scully, James LA Mil. 1st Regt. 3rd Brig. 1st Div.
Scully, James MO Lt.Arty. 1st Btty.
Scully, James MO Lt.Arty. Landis' Co.
Scully, James TX Hvy.Arty. 2nd Co.F
Scully, James TX 2nd Inf. Odlum's Co.
Scully, Jeremiah LA 15th Inf. Co.H
Scully, John AR 35th Inf. Co.C
Scully, John LA 1st Hvy.Arty. (Reg.) Co.K
Scully, John Inf. School of Pract. Powell's Detach. Co.C
Scully, M. MO Lt.Arty. 1st Btty.
Scully, Mark LA 22nd Inf. Co.C
Scully, Michael LA 1st (Strawbridge's) Inf. Co.C
Scully, Michael LA 21st (Patton's) Inf. Co.C
Scully, P. GA Inf. 1st Loc.Troops (Augusta) Co.I
Scully, P. MD Cav. 2nd Bn. Co.F
Scully, Peter LA 1st Hvy.Arty. (Reg.) Co.F
Scully, Peter Inf. School of Pract. Powell's Detach. Co.C
Scully, Robert TN 21st Inf. Co.G
Scully, Simon AL 24th Inf. Co.B Sgt.
Scully, Thomas TN Lt.Arty. Tobin's Co.
Scully, Thomas TN 24th Inf. 2nd Co.G
Scully, W.A. TN Conscr. (Cp. of Instr.) Co.B
Scully, William A. NC Walker's Bn. Thomas' Legion Co.C
Scultatus, George VA Arty. Kevill's Co.
Scultatus, George VA 41st Inf. 1st Co.E
Sculthorp, Benjamin D. VA 21st Inf. Co.C
Sculthorp, James L. VA 21st Inf. Co.C
Sculthorp, John L. VA 21st Inf. Co.C
Sculthorpe, A.M. VA 34th Inf. Co.B Sgt.
Sculy, Thomas AR 15th (Josey's) Inf. Co.H
Scurbrough, W.A. AL 23rd Inf. Co.G 2nd Lt.
Scurley, Robert MS 22nd Inf. Sgt.
Scurlock, Alonzo C. TX 18th Cav. Co.A
Scurlock, C.T. 20th Conf.Cav. Co.C
Scurlock, Daniel TX 11th Inf. Co.D 1st Lt.
Scurlock, Henry F. FL Cav. 5th Bn. Co.E
Scurlock, James MS 43rd Inf. Co.I
Scurlock, James TN 35th Inf. Co.E
Scurlock, James W. TX 10th Cav. Co.I
Scurlock, J.F. LA Inf.Cons.Crescent Regt. Chap.
Scurlock, J.M. AL 3rd Res. Co.A
Scurlock, John MS Inf. 1st St.Troops Co.D Cpl.
Scurlock, John TX 6th Cav. Co.I
Scurlock, John H. TX 6th Cav. Co.I
Scurlock, J.W. TN 6th Inf. Co.G

Scurlock, Malcom V. TX 18th Cav. Co.A
Scurlock, O. 20th Conf.Cav. Co.C
Scurlock, Reuben J. TX 18th Cav. Co.C
Scurlock, Robert T. TN 2nd (Robison's) Inf. Co.K
Scurlock, R.T. TX 3rd Cav. Co.E
Scurlock, Sampson AL Arty. 1st Bn. Co.D
Scurlock, Samuel TN Lt.Arty. Winston's Co.
Scurlock, Samuel TN 25th Inf. Co.C
Scurlock, T.C. MS 14th (Cons.) Inf. Co.H Sgt.
Scurlock, Thaddeus C. MS 43rd Inf. Co.I
Scurlock, Thadeus C. MS Inf. 5th Bn. Co.A
Scurlock, Theodosius Joshua Gen. & Staff Surg.
Scurlock, Thomas B. MS Inf. 5th Bn. Co.A
Scurlock, Thomas B. MS 43rd Inf. Co.I
Scurlock, Thomas J. FL Cav. (Marianna Drag.) Smith's Co.
Scurlock, Thomas J. 15th Conf.Cav. Co.B
Scurlock, T.J. AR 20th Inf. Surg.
Scurlock, Walter L. FL Cav. 5th Bn. Co.E Sgt.
Scurlock, William C. AL 4th Inf. Co.G
Scurlock, William P. AL Arty. 1st Bn. Co.D Sgt.
Scurlock, W.L. TX 20th Inf. Co.E
Scurlocke, T.J. TX 3rd Cav. Co.H
Scurr, Benjamin MS 15th Inf. Co.G
Scurr, Benjamin MS Gage's Co. (Wigfall Guards)
Scurr, John W. MS 15th Inf. Co.G
Scurr, J.W. MS 12th Cav. Co.B
Scurr, Thomas MS 15th Inf. Co.G
Scurr, Wallace B. MS 15th Inf. Co.G
Scurr, W.B. MS Conscr.
Scurry, Alexander GA 4th Bn.S.S. Co.A Sgt.
Scurry, Alexander W. GA Inf. 3rd Bn. Co.G Cpl.
Scurry, David GA Inf. 3rd Bn. Co.G
Scurry, David GA 4th Bn.S.S. Co.A
Scurry, D.V. SC 9th Res. Co.F Sgt.
Scurry, E.M. SC 10th Inf. Co.H 1st Sgt.
Scurry, F. SC 7th Cav. Co.E
Scurry, Frederick SC Cav.Bn. Holcombe Legion Co.C
Scurry, G.R. SC 2nd Cav. Co.G
Scurry, G.R. SC 3rd Inf. Co.A,B
Scurry, Grant FL Lt.Arty. Dyke's Co.
Scurry, Grant FL Kilcrease Lt.Arty.
Scurry, James GA 1st (Symons') Res. Co.E
Scurry, James SC Hvy.Arty. 15th (Lucas') Bn. Co.A
Scurry, James R. GA Cav. Hall's Co.
Scurry, J.C. SC Cav. 19th Bn. Co.D
Scurry, J.C. SC Cav. Rodgers' Co.
Scurry, J.C. SC Inf. 6th Bn. Co.B
Scurry, J.C. SC 26th Inf. Co.H
Scurry, J.C. SC Post Guard Senn's Co.
Scurry, J.L. SC 5th Bn.Res. Co.F
Scurry, John G. VA 11th Inf. Co.A
Scurry, John J. SC Lt.Arty. 3rd (Palmetto) Bn. Co.C
Scurry, John R. AL 12th Cav. Co.F Capt.
Scurry, John R. AL 19th Inf. Co.D Surg.
Scurry, M.V. VA Cav. Mosby's Regt. (Part. Rangers) Co.E
Scurry, R.M. SC 2nd Arty. Co.B,K,D 1st Lt.
Scurry, Thomas J. AR 19th (Dockery's) Inf. Co.G Comsy.
Scurry, Thomas J. NC 3rd Inf. Co.H

Scurry, Thomas J. Gen. & Staff, QM Dept. Maj.
Scurry, W.G. SC 3rd St.Troops Co.A
Scurry, W.G. SC Inf. 6th Bn. Co.C
Scurry, W.G. SC 26th Inf. Co.I
Scurry, W.G. SC Manigault's Bn.Vol. Co.E
Scurry, William R. TX 4th Cav. Lt.Col.
Scurry, W.J.C. SC Lt.Arty. Gaillard's Co. (Santee Lt.Arty.)
Scurry, W.J.C. SC 1st (Hagood's) Inf. 1st Co.E
Scutchins, Thomas H. NC 17th Inf. (2nd Org.) Co.C
Scutchton, James H. TN Cav. 16th Bn. (Neal's) Co.E
Scutt, L.E. 15th Conf.Cav. Co.B
Scutten, William LA 10th Inf. Co.K
Scwarts, Henry VA 62nd Mtd.Inf. Co.C
Scwen, T.F. GA 18th Inf. Co.C Capt.
Scyle, P.W. SC 1st St.Troops Co.K
Scymour, Calvin M. VA 50th Inf. Co.A
Scyoc, Abel VA 19th Cav. Co.C
Scyoc, Abel VA 3rd Cav. & Inf.St.Line Co.D
Scyoc, William VA 19th Cav. Co.C
Scyoe, William H. VA 17th Cav. Co.F
Sczafranski, M. AL Mil. 2nd Regt.Vol. Co.A
Sea, A.C. GA 11th Cav. Co.E
Sea, Alfred B. SC 1st (McCreary's) Inf. Co.K
Sea, Andrew M. AR Lt.Arty. Wiggins' Btty. 2nd Lt.
Sea, Andrew M. TN Lt.Arty. Morton's Co. 2nd Lt.
Sea, Andrew M. Conf.Arty. Marshall's Co. 1st Sgt.
Sea, Edward KY 3rd Mtd.Inf. Co.B
Sea, H.H. GA 13th Inf. Co.B
Sea, John C. VA 136th Mil. Co.F
Sea, Madison NC 64th Inf. Co.I
Sea, Robert M. Gen. & Staff Lt.,Recruiting Off.
Sea, R.P. LA 1st Cav.
Sea, William NC 64th Inf. Co.I
Sea, William TN 2nd (Smith's) Cav. Rankin's Co.
Sea, William TN 4th (McLemore's) Cav. Co.H
Seabaugh, C. MO Lt.Arty. 4th (Harris') Field Btty.
Seabaugh, Charles C. MO 8th Cav. Co.B
Seabaugh, Eli MO 8th Cav.
Seabaugh, John MO 8th Cav. Co.B
Seabaugh, John MO Lt.Arty. 4th (Harris') Field Btty.
Seabaugh, John TN 12th Inf. Co.E
Seabaum, J.K. GA 12th Cav. Co.G Sgt.
Seabe, Augustus 14th Conf.Cav. Co.I Sgt.
Seaber, Charles AR 34th Inf. Co.K
Seaberry, Reuben FL 6th Inf. Co.A
Seaberry, Rol MS 36th Inf. Co.F Sgt.
Seaboch, George W. NC 28th Inf. Co.C
Seaboch, John P. NC 28th Inf. Co.C
Seaboch, William H. NC 28th Inf. Co.C
Seabolt, Abraham GA Cav. 6th Bn. (St.Guards) Co.B
Seabolt, Arch VA 25th Cav. Co.G
Seabolt, B.H. GA Inf. 11th Bn. (St.Guards) Co.A
Seabolt, Francis L. GA 52nd Inf. Co.G
Seabolt, George 2nd Cherokee Mtd.Vol. Co.K
Seabolt, George W. TN Arty. Ramsey's Btty. Cpl.

Seabolt, George W. Conf.Arty. Marshall's Co. Sgt.
Seabolt, G.W. TN 1st (Carter's) Cav. Co.H
Seabolt, Henry W. GA Smith's Legion Anderson's Co.
Seabolt, H.W. GA Inf. (Anderson Guards) Anderson's Co.
Seabolt, Jackson GA 52nd Inf. Co.G
Seabolt, James H. GA 52nd Inf. Co.G
Seabolt, James M. GA 52nd Inf. Co.C
Seabolt, Jerry 2nd Cherokee Mtd.Vol. Co.K
Seabolt, J.L. GA Inf. 11th Bn. (St.Guards) Co.A
Seabolt, John GA Inf. 11th Bn. (St.Guards) Co.A
Seabolt, John W. KY 8th Cav. Co.F
Seabolt, J.W. GA 23rd Inf. Co.K
Seabolt, J.W. TN 19th (Biffle's) Cav. Co.F
Seabolt, Peter GA Inf. 11th Bn. (St.Guards) Co.A
Seabolt, Travis S. NC 6th Inf. Co.D Cpl.
Seabolt, W.A. AR 34th Inf. Co.G
Seabolt, Wayman VA 6th Bn.Res. Co.D
Seaborn, B. MO 16th Inf. Co.H
Seaborn, B. Earle SC 4th Inf. QMSgt.
Seaborn, Benjamin C. TN 20th Inf. Co.I 1st Lt.
Seaborn, Benjamin L. TX 35th (Brown's) Cav. Co.D Cpl.
Seaborn, Christopher VA 24th Cav. Co.I
Seaborn, Christopher 8th (Dearing's) Conf.Cav. Co.D
Seaborn, David GA 61st Inf. Co.I
Seaborn, E. AR Cav. McGehee's Regt. Co.I
Seaborn, Ed AR 5th Inf.
Seaborn, Edward 3rd Conf.Inf. Co.E
Seaborn, George S. VA 13th Cav. Co.H
Seaborn, George W. AR 15th (Josey's) Inf. Co.F
Seaborn, G.W. AR 5th Inf.
Seaborn, G.W. MS 6th Inf. Co.A
Seaborn, G.W. MS 1st (King's) Inf. (St.Troops) Co.I
Seaborn, G.W. 3rd Conf.Inf. Co.E
Seaborn, James GA 12th Inf. Co.B
Seaborn, James SC 4th Inf. Co.E
Seaborn, James B. TX 35th (Brown's) Cav. Co.D
Seaborn, J.B. TN 62nd Mtd.Inf. Co.A
Seaborn, John GA 17th Inf. Co.F
Seaborn, O. LA Inf. 4th Bn. Co.D
Seaborn, Robert GA 17th Inf. Co.F
Seaborn, Samuel AR Cav. McGehee's Regt. Co.I
Seaborn, Thomas GA 27th Inf. Co.B
Seaborn, William R. SC Palmetto S.S. Co.B
Seaborn, William Robinson SC 4th Inf. Co.E
Seaborne, G.R. TN 30th Inf. Co.D
Seaborne, James B. TX 13th Vol. 1st Co.I
Seaborne, Oliver TN 11th Inf. Co.B
Seaborns, William AL 37th Inf. Co.H
Seabots, Chan Deneale's Regt. Choctaw Warriors Co.E
Seabott, McKinny GA 23rd Inf. Co.H
Seabough, Conrad MO Inf. 4th Regt.St.Guard Co.E Sgt.
Seabourn, A.J. TX Inf. 3rd St.Troops Co.C
Seabourn, F.M. TX Inf. 3rd St.Troops Co.C
Seabourn, John AR 32nd Inf. Co.I
Seabourn, M.L. TN 2nd (Ashby's) Cav. Co.A
Seabourn, M.L. TN Cav. 5th Bn. (McClellan's) Co.A
Seabourn, R.M. AR 5th Inf. Co.D

Seabourn, W.M. GA 12th Cav. Co.G Far.
Seabre, James VA 40th Inf. Co.F
Seabre, Joseph VA 40th Inf. Co.F
Seabrie, Henry LA 20th Inf. Co.D
Seabright, William VA 5th Inf. Co.K Cpl.
Seabring, John AL 14th Inf. Co.H
Seabrok, D.O. AL 21st Inf. Co.D,C
Seabrook, A.R. AL Mil. 2nd Regt.Vol. Co.B
Seabrook, Asa R. AL 38th Inf. Co.I
Seabrook, Ashe SC 1st Mtd.Mil. Kirk's Co. Cpl.
Seabrook, C.A. SC 3rd Cav. Co.I
Seabrook, C.A. SC Palmetto S.S. Adj.
Seabrook, C.A. Gen. & Staff Capt.,AAG
Seabrook, Cato A. SC 5th Inf. 1st Co.I Capt.
Seabrook, Charles J. VA 18th Inf. Co.G Sgt.
Seabrook, C. Pinckney SC 1st (McCreary's) Inf.
  Co.H 2nd Lt.
Seabrook, E.B. SC 1st Arty. Co.B
Seabrook, E.B. SC 3rd Cav. Co.I
Seabrook, E.B. SC Arty. Stuart's Co. (Beaufort
  Vol.Arty.)
Seabrook, Ed. TN 6th Inf. Co.D 1st Lt.
Seabrook, E.L. TX 20th Inf. Co.I
Seabrook, E.M. SC 1st Mtd.Mil. Kirk's Co. 1st
  Lt.
Seabrook, E.M. SC 3rd Cav. Co.H
Seabrook, E.M. Gen. & Staff Surg.
Seabrook, E.M. Gen. & Staff 1st Lt.,ADC
Seabrook, Esaw AL Lt.Arty. 2nd Bn. Co.E
Seabrook, E.W. Gen. & Staff Asst.Surg.
Seabrook, George W. GA Inf. 27th Bn. Co.C
Seabrook, George W. GA RR Guards
Seabrook, H. SC 4th Cav. Co.K
Seabrook, H. Anderson's Div. Capt.,Ord.Off.
Seabrook, Henry SC 2nd Bn.S.S. Co.C 2nd Lt.
Seabrook, J.A. SC 1st Mtd.Mil. Kirk's Co.
Seabrook, J.C. SC 3rd Cav. Co.I
Seabrook, J.C. SC 2nd Inf. Co.I
Seabrook, J.D. SC 1st Mtd.Mil. Kirk's Co.
Seabrook, J.D. SC 3rd Cav. Co.I,H
Seabrook, J.D. SC 11th Inf. Co.E
Seabrook, J.G. Gen. & Staff AASurg.
Seabrook, J.K. AL 21st Inf. Co.C
Seabrook, J.L. SC 3rd Cav. Co.I
Seabrook, J.L. SC 6th Cav. Co.F Sgt.
Seabrook, John L. SC 3rd Cav. Co.I Capt.
Seabrook, John S. AL 16th Inf. Co.A
Seabrook, John T. TN 4th Inf. Co.A
Seabrook, Joseph SC 4th Cav. Co.K
Seabrook, Joseph SC Lt.Arty. Parker's Co.
  (Marion Arty.)
Seabrook, Joseph M. SC 3rd Cav. Co.I Sgt.
Seabrook, J.P. AL Inf. 2nd Regt. Co.D
Seabrook, J.P. AL 38th Inf. Co.I,G
Seabrook, J.P. AL 38th Inf. Co.I 2nd Lt.
Seabrook, J.W. SC 1st Mtd.Mil. Kirk's Co.
Seabrook, J.W. Sig.Corps,CSA
Seabrook, L.B. SC 8th Bn.Res. Co.C
Seabrook, M. SC Inf. 1st (Charleston) Bn. Co.E
  Cook
Seabrook, M.M. SC 3rd Cav. Co.I
Seabrook, M.M. SC 6th Cav. Co.F Sgt.
Seabrook, P. SC 1st Cav. Co.G
Seabrook, Paul H. SC Mil.Cav. 4th Regt.
  Howard's Co.
Seabrook, Peter G. SC Lt.Arty. 3rd (Palmetto)
  Bn. Co.D

Seabrook, P.F. SC 25th Inf. Co.A
Seabrook, P.H. SC 23rd Inf. Co.B Capt.
Seabrook, R.J.E. SC 3rd Cav. Co.I
Seabrook, S. TX 39th Dismtd.Cav. Co.H
Seabrook, S.E. SC Inf. 1st (Charleston) Bn. Co.B
  Cpl.
Seabrook, S.E. SC 27th Inf. Co.B Cpl.
Seabrook, W.B. SC 11th Inf. Co.E
Seabrook, W.H. SC 1st Arty. Co.K 1st Lt.
Seabrook, Whitemarsh B. SC Cav.Bn. Hampton
  Legion Co.C
Seabrook, Whitemarsh H. SC 25th Inf. Co.H 1st
  Lt.
Seabrook, William SC 3rd Cav. Co.I
Seabrook, William SC Cav. Walpole's Co.
Seabrook, William SC 2nd St.Troops Co.H
Seabrook, William SC 8th Bn.Res. Fishburne's
  Co.
Seabrook, William SC 23rd Inf. Co.A Capt.
Seabrook, William C. SC Lt.Arty. 3rd (Palmetto)
  Bn. Co.D
Seabrook, William M. SC 11th Inf. Co.B
Seabrook, W.P. SC 1st Mtd.Mil. Kirk's Co.
Seabrook, W.P. SC 3rd Cav. Co.I,H
Seabrooks, J.S. AL Inf. 2nd Regt. Co.E
Seaburn, Edward AR 18th (Marmaduke's) Inf.
  Co.E
Seaburn, George W. AR 18th (Marmaduke's) Inf.
  Co.E
Seaburn, Henry TX 13th Vol. 2nd Co.B,C
Seaburn, J.R. TX 20th Inf. Co.G
Seaburn, William TX 13th Vol. Co.C
Seaburne, Charles GA 62nd Cav. Co.L
Seabury, A.L. VA 54th Mil. Co.C,D
Seabury, E.C. VA 2nd Cav. Co.B
Seabury, Kirk VA 11th Inf. Co.G Sgt.
Seabury, Robert N. VA 2nd Cav. Co.B
Seabury, William H. VA 54th Mil. Co.G
Seabury, William H. Sig.Corps,CSA
Seabury, William J. VA 2nd Cav. Co.B
Seacat, George W. VA 16th Cav. Co.A
Seacate, James VA 4th Res. Co.E,G
Seace, Alfred SC 1st (Hagood's) Inf. 1st Co.I
Seace, Calvin SC 1st (Hagood's) Inf. 1st Co.I
Seace, W.C. TN 3rd (Forrest's) Cav. Co.H
Seacer, H. AR 26th Inf. Co.C
Seachrist, Amos NC 14th Inf. Co.I
Seachrist, Andrew NC 6th Sr.Res. Co.G Cpl.
Seachrist, Andrew TX 13th Cav. Co.A
Seachrist, C. NC 1st Jr.Res. Co.C
Seachrist, Daniel NC 6th Sr.Res. Co.G
Seachrist, Daniel NC 14th Inf. Co.I
Seachrist, James NC 14th Inf. Co.I
Seachrist, Jesse NC 6th Sr.Res. Co.C,F
Seachrist, Lindsey NC 42nd Inf. Co.I
Seachrist, R. NC 1st Jr.Res. Co.C
Seacolt, E. GA 32nd Inf.
Seacott, George W. VA 37th Inf. Co.C
Seacrist, T.L. TN 19th (Biffle's) Cav. Co.E
Seacy, Monroe AL Cav. 4th Bn. (Love's) Co.C
Seadam, B.H. TX 14th Cav.
Seaden, W. MO 5th Cav. Co.H
Seadon, Gustavus A. VA 157th Mil. Co.B
Seaford, Albert C. NC 42nd Inf. Co.K
Seaford, C.M. NC 4th Cav. (59th St.Troops)
  Co.E

Seaford, Daniel A. NC 1st Arty. (10th St.Troops)
  Co.D
Seaford, Edmond NC 5th Inf. Co.K
Seaford, Eli NC 46th Inf. Co.B
Seaford, H. TX 1st Hvy.Arty. Co.B
Seaford, Henry A. NC 46th Inf. Co.B
Seaford, J.D. NC 5th Cav. (63rd St.Troops)
  Co.H
Seaford, John NC 42nd Inf. Co.K
Seaford, M.H. SC Inf. Hampton Legion Co.A
Seaford, Peter NC 5th Inf. Co.G
Seaford, Simeon NC 1st Arty. (10th St.Troops)
  Co.D
Seaford, Simeon NC 4th Sr.Res. Co.A
Seaford, Solomon NC 5th Inf. Co.G
Seaford, Thomas NC 20th Inf. Co.B
Seaford, Wiley M. NC 8th Inf. Co.K
Seager, Joseph, Jr. VA 1st Inf. Co.G
Seager, W.J. VA 3rd Inf.Loc.Def. Co.E
Seagers, Francis G. GA Cobb's Legion Co.H
Seagers, J.F. GA Lt.Arty. Daniell's Btty.
Seagers, J.F. GA Arty. Maxwell's Reg.Lt.Btty.
Seagers, Michael VA 1st Inf. Co.C 2nd Lt.
Seagers, Michael VA 1st St.Res. Co.D Capt.
Seagers, Mike TX Vol. Duke's Co.
Seagers, M.J. GA 1st Cav. Co.E,F
Seagers, R.I. MS 14th Inf. Co.F
Seaglar, H.H. SC 1st Arty. Co.E
Seagle, Adam NC 23rd Inf. Co.F
Seagle, A.J. NC 23rd Inf. Co.B Sgt.
Seagle, Andrew NC 11th (Bethel Regt.) Inf. Co.I
Seagle, Caleb NC 20th Inf. Co.E
Seagle, Charly NC 23rd Inf. Co.B
Seagle, Franklin V. FL 7th Inf. Co.D Music.
Seagle, Franklin V. FL Brig.Band,CSA Music.
Seagle, George NC 23rd Inf. Co.B
Seagle, George W. NC 1st Arty. (10th St.Troops)
  Co.C
Seagle, George W. NC 23rd Inf. Co.B Capt.
Seagle, Henry S. NC 8th Bn.Jr.Res. Co.B
Seagle, James M. TX Arty. Douglas' Co. Cpl.
Seagle, James M. TX Inf. Yarbrough's Co.
  (Smith Cty.Lt.Inf.) Ens.
Seagle, J.B. VA 4th Res. Co.E
Seagle, John NC 23rd Inf. Co.B
Seagle, John NC 58th Inf. Co.F
Seagle, John S. VA 45th Inf. Co.D
Seagle, Marcus NC 23rd Inf. Co.B
Seagle, Marion NC 23rd Inf. Co.B
Seagle, M.C. NC 2nd Jr.Res. Co.C
Seagle, Monroe NC 11th (Bethel Regt.) Inf. Co.I
  Music.
Seagle, M.V. NC 23rd Inf. Co.B Sgt.
Seagle, N.M. TX Arty. Douglas' Co. Sgt.
Seagle, Noah W. NC 23rd Inf. Co.B
Seagle, Philip NC 23rd Inf. Co.B Cpl.
Seagle, Polk D. NC 23rd Inf. Co.B Cpl.
Seagle, Thomas J. NC 23rd Inf. Co.B 1st Lt.
Seagle, T.J. TX Arty. Douglas' Co.
Seagle, William F. TN 35th Inf. 3rd Co.F
Seagle, William S. NC 55th Inf. Co.F
Seagler, Alfred A. NC 11th (Bethel Regt.) Inf.
  Co.I
Seagler, James SC 11th Inf. Co.H
Seagler, John N. MS 29th Inf. Co.A
Seagler, John S. LA 28th (Thomas') Inf. Co.F
Seagler, U. SC 11th Inf. Co.H

Seagler, William AL 3rd Bn.Res. Co.C
Seagler, William AL 33rd Inf. Co.I
Seagles, Elem NC 22nd Inf. Co.K
Seagles, O. VA Hvy.Arty. Wright's Co.
Seagles, T.A. GA 12th Cav. Co.G
Seagley, B.F. NC 22nd Inf. Co.B
Seagley, J.M. NC 22nd Inf. Co.B
Seagley, W.D. NC 22nd Inf. Co.B
Seago, A.K. GA 3rd Bn. (St.Guards) Co.D
Seago, Alexander GA 49th Inf. Co.F
Seago, Benjamin L. AL 36th Inf. Co.E
Seago, Benjamin L. Gen. & Staff Surg.
Seago, Benj. L. Gen. & Staff Asst.Surg.
Seago, B.J. MS 26th Inf. Co.A
Seago, D.R. NC 1st Jr.Res. Co.I
Seago, Eli M. GA 20th Inf. Co.F Lt.Col.
Seago, E.W. AL 45th Inf. Co.G Cpl.
Seago, George W. GA 1st (Cons.) Inf. Co.D
Seago, Henry M. MS 26th Inf. Co.A
Seago, James GA 1st Reg. Co.B
Seago, James F. GA Cobb's Legion Co.I
Seago, J.H. AL 45th Inf. Co.G
Seago, J.M. GA Inf. 5th Bn. (St.Guards) Co.E
Seago, John MS 26th Inf. Co.A Cpl.
Seago, Joseph AR 2nd Mtd.Rifles Hawkins' Co.
Seago, Joseph TX 27th Cav. Co.A
Seago, Josiah M. GA Cobb's Legion Co.I
Seago, Patrick H. NC 31st Inf. Co.B
Seago, Peter GA Inf. 1st Loc.Troops (Augusta) Dearing's Cav.Co.
Seago, Posey W. TX 3rd Cav. Co.I
Seago, Thomas NC 6th Inf. Co.B
Seago, Tim K. TX 3rd Cav. Co.I 1st Sgt.
Seago, T.N. AR Inf. 2nd Mtd.Rifles Co.B
Seago, William NC 31st Inf. Co.B
Seagoe, Thomas E. AR 23rd Inf. Co.I
Seagraves, A.L. GA 4th Res. Co.C
Seagraves, Alexander W. NC Mallett's Bn. (Cp.Guard) Co.B Cpl.
Seagraves, Andrew NC 7th Inf. Co.D
Seagraves, B. AL 37th Inf. Co.F
Seagraves, B.F. AR 13th Inf. Co.F
Seagraves, Calvin NC 1st Inf. Co.G
Seagraves, C.F. NC 32nd Inf. Co.E,F
Seagraves, Charles J. NC 5th Cav. (63rd St.Troops) Co.E
Seagraves, C.J. NC 11th (Bethel Regt.) Inf. Co.G
Seagraves, Frank NC 13th Inf. Co.F
Seagraves, Goodman TN 4th (McLemore's) Cav. Co.E
Seagraves, G.W. TN 15th (Cons.) Cav. Co.A
Seagraves, Henry C. GA Lt.Arty. Scogins' Btty. (Griffin Lt.Arty.)
Seagraves, Jacob A. NC 42nd Inf. Co.D
Seagraves, James NC 1st Inf. Co.G
Seagraves, James A. NC 47th Inf. Co.C
Seagraves, James M. NC Lt.Arty. 3rd Bn. Co.C
Seagraves, John NC 29th Inf. Co.K
Seagraves, Josiah GA Inf. White's Co.
Seagraves, J.P. GA 54th Inf. Co.B
Seagraves, Malzee GA Cherokee Legion (St.Guards) Co.H
Seagraves, M.L. TN 3rd (Clack's) Inf. Co.B Cpl.
Seagraves, R.F. AR 45th Cav. Co.G 1st Lt.

Seagraves, Seborn T. Trans-MS Conf.Cav. 1st Bn. Co.E
Seagraves, S.T. TN Cav. 7th Bn. (Bennett's) Co.A
Seagraves, Thomas D. GA 2nd Cav. Co.E
Seagraves, W. KY 4th Cav. Co.K
Seagraves, W. TN 3rd (Clack's) Inf. Co.D
Seagraves, Walter KY 5th Mtd.Inf. Co.K
Seagraves, Wilburn KY 5th Mtd.Inf. Co.K
Seagraves, William GA Adam's Bn. Co.A
Seagraves, William GA Inf. White's Co.
Seagraves, William KY 5th Mtd.Inf. Co.K
Seagraves, William L. KY 5th Mtd.Inf. Co.K
Seagreaves, Thomas NC 1st Inf. Co.G
Seagreen, Peter LA Mil. Barr's Ind.Co. (Blakesley Guards)
Seagrest, H.C. TX Inf. 1st St.Troops Wheat's Co.
Seagriff, Michael TX 1st Inf. Co.A
Seagrist, J.A. GA 62nd Cav. Co.K
Seagrist, Louis AL 63rd Inf. Co.D
Seahome, A.C. NC 1st Cav. (9th St.Troops) Co.I
Seahon, John F. TN 5th (McKenzie's) Cav. Co.F
Seahone, Joseph B. LA 13th Bn. (Part.Rangers) Co.F
Seahorn, C. AL 19th Inf. Co.H
Seahorn, Campbell R. TN 61st Mtd.Inf. Co.A
Seahorn, J.M. NC 8th Inf. Co.H
Seahorn, J.M. NC McLean's Bn.Lt.Duty Men Co.A
Seahorn, John AR 2nd Mtd.Rifles Co.C
Seahorn, J.W. TN 1st (Carter's) Cav. Co.H
Seahorn, Nicholas AR Inf. Hardy's Regt. Co.D
Seahorn, R.K. SC 5th Inf. 2nd Co.G
Seahorn, S.L. TN 1st (Carter's) Cav. Co.H
Seahorn, W.H. TN 1st (Carter's) Cav. Co.H
Seahorn, William AR Inf. Cocke's Regt. Co.K
Seahorn, William TN 21st (Wilson's) Cav. Co.G
Seahorn, William A. TN 63rd Inf. Co.D
Seahorn, William J. AR Inf. 2nd Bn. Co.C
Seahorn, W.J. TN 21st & 22nd (Cons.) Cav. Co.I
Seaib, A.M. GA 35th Inf. Co.I
Seaif, Thomas J. AR 1st (Dobbin's) Cav. Co.K
Seakell, J.M. AL Inf. 2nd Regt. Co.G
Seaker, J.M. MS 2nd Inf. Co.B
Seal, Alexander J. MS 42nd Inf. Co.K Cpl.
Seal, Amos MS Inf. 3rd Bn. (St.Troops) Co.G
Seal, Anthony MS 38th Cav. Co.C
Seal, Ben MS Inf. 2nd St.Troops Co.G
Seal, B.F. TX 11th (Spaight's) Bn.Vol. Co.G
Seal, C.D. MS 38th Cav. Co.C
Seal, Charles MS 38th Cav. Co.C
Seal, C.W. MS 38th Cav. Co.C
Seal, D. TX 24th Cav. Co.I Sgt.
Seal, David TX 2nd Cav. Co.E
Seal, D.B. MS 38th Cav. Co.C Capt.
Seal, Drury TN 5th (McKenzie's) Cav. Co.G
Seal, E. AL 3rd Inf. Co.H
Seal, E.B. MS 2nd (Quinn's St.Troops) Inf. Co.F
Seal, Edwin D. VA 6th Inf. Co.G
Seal, Eli MS 2nd (Quinn's St.Troops) Inf. Co.H Sgt.
Seal, Elijah M. MS 23rd Inf. Co.B 1st Sgt.
Seal, E.P. TX 24th & 25th Cav. (Cons.) Co.B
Seal, F. MS 38th Cav. Co.C 1st Lt.
Seal, Fielding VA 50th Inf. Cav.Co.B Cpl.

Seal, Fielding W. VA Lt.Arty. W.H. Chapman's Co.
Seal, Francis H. MS 3rd Inf. Co.G 2nd Lt.
Seal, Gustavus VA Inf. 4th Bn.Loc.Def. Co.C
Seal, H.M. AL 37th Inf. Co.K
Seal, Ira D. VA Lt.Arty. Thornton's Co.
Seal, J.A. MS 38th Cav. Co.C Cpl.
Seal, James VA Cav. Hounshell's Bn. Gwinn's Co.
Seal, James H. AL 47th Inf. Co.A
Seal, James L. MS 3rd Inf. Co.G Sgt.
Seal, James L. VA Inf. Mileham's Co.
Seal, J.E. MS 38th Cav. Co.C
Seal, Jerry MS 11th Inf. Co.C
Seal, J.G. VA 5th Inf. Lt.
Seal, J.J. MS 38th Cav. Co.C
Seal, J.L. MS 38th Cav. Co.C
Seal, J.L. TN 51st (Cons.) Inf. Co.K
Seal, J.M. TX 24th & 25th Cav. (Cons.) Co.E
Seal, John VA 1st Bn.Res. Co.H
Seal, John VA 97th Mil. Co.K
Seal, John J. VA 4th Cav. Co.C
Seal, John K. VA 50th Inf. Cav.Co.B Cpl.
Seal, John M. VA 31st Mil. Co.A
Seal, John N. AL 58th Inf. Co.B
Seal, John R. VA 6th Inf. Co.G
Seal, John R. Kemper's Staff
Seal, Joseph G. VA Inf. 5th Bn.Loc.Def. Co.F 1st Lt.
Seal, Joshua TN Inf. 1st Bn. (Colms') Co.C
Seal, Joshua W. MS Inf. 2nd St.Troops Co.F
Seal, J.K. AL 29th Inf. Co.E
Seal, J.T. TX Cav. Hardeman's Regt. Co.C Sgt.
Seal, J.T. VA 4th Cav. Co.C
Seal, J.W. KY 3rd Mtd.Inf. Co.L
Seal, J.W. TN 12th Inf. Co.E
Seal, J.W. TX 33rd Cav. Co.F
Seal, J.W. VA 7th Inf. Co.F
Seal, J.W. VA Mtd.Guard 8th Congr.Dist.
Seal, J.W. VA Mil. Greene Cty.
Seal, J.W. 15th Conf.Cav. Co.L
Seal, Lyttleton TN 15th (Stewart's) Cav. Co.G
Seal, M.D. MS 38th Cav. Co.C
Seal, Morgan VA 2nd Inf.Loc.Def. Co.B
Seal, Morgan VA Inf. 2nd Bn.Loc.Def. Co.D
Seal, Morgan VA 27th Inf. 2nd Co.H
Seal, R.G. GA 40th Inf.
Seal, Robert A. VA 1st Bn.Res. Co.H
Seal, Robert A. VA 7th Inf. Co.A Cpl.
Seal, Robert C. MO 9th (Elliott's) Cav. Co.D
Seal, Strother VA 7th Inf. Gibson's Co.
Seal, T. AR 4th Inf. Co.D
Seal, T.D. LA 2nd Inf. Co.B
Seal, T.G. MS 38th Cav. Co.C
Seal, Thomas LA 28th (Gray's) Inf. Co.C
Seal, Thomas MS 38th Cav. Co.C
Seal, Thomas C. SC 2nd Rifles Co.A Cpl.
Seal, T.J. MS 38th Cav. Co.C
Seal, W. AL 15th Cav. Co.I
Seal, W. MS 5th Inf. Co.C
Seal, W.B. MS 38th Cav. Co.C
Seal, W.F. MS 38th Cav. Co.C 1st Lt.
Seal, Willerby AL 3rd Res. Co.K
Seal, William VA 31st Mil. Co.C
Seal, William B. VA 6th Inf. Co.G
Seal, Williba AR 34th Inf. Co.K
Seal, W.M. AL 18th Inf. Co.I

Seale, A.C. MS 5th Cav. Co.G
Seale, Addison B. TX 2nd Inf. Co.B
Seale, A.F. TX 15th Inf. Co.I
Seale, A.H. MS Cav. Ham's Regt. Co.H 1st Sgt.
Seale, A.J. AL Cp. of Instr. Talladega
Seale, Alexander J. MS 17th Inf. Co.C
Seale, Andrew J. AL 36th Inf. Co.H
Seale, Anthony H.H. MS 17th Inf. Co.C
Seale, Barney MS Cav. Garland's Bn. Co.A
Seale, Barney 14th Conf.Cav. Co.A
Seale, B.B. AL 21st Inf. Co.C
Seale, Beaufort F. MS 11th Inf. Co.D
Seale, Benjamin B. AL 40th Inf. Co.F Band Music.
Seale, B.M. MS Inf. 1st Bn. Co.C
Seale, B.T. TX 21st Cav. Co.I
Seale, C.H. AL 17th Inf. Co.C
Seale, C.H. TX 15th Inf. Co.I Music.
Seale, Charles J. AR 3rd Inf. Co.B Lt.
Seale, C.W. TX 15th Inf. Co.I
Seale, David H. TN Lt.Arty. Burrough's Co.
Seale, David L. MS 11th Inf. Co.D Cpl.
Seale, David L. MS 40th Inf. Co.F 1st Sgt.
Seale, D.E. TX Waul's Legion Co.C
Seale, E.A. AL 15th Bn.Part.Rangers Co.E Cpl.
Seale, E.A. AL 17th Inf. Co.C
Seale, Eli LA 3rd (Wingfield's) Cav. Co.K
Seale, Eli MS 11th Inf. Co.D
Seale, Elias T. TX 13th Cav. Co.G Maj.
Seale, Elijah AL 3rd Res. Co.B
Seale, Elijah MS 2nd (Quinn's St.Troops) Inf. Co.F 1st Lt.
Seale, E.P. TX 25th Cav. Co.A
Seale, Ewing MS 7th Inf. Co.C
Seale, Festus VA 55th Inf. Co.A
Seale, Festus VA Res.Forces Clark's Co.
Seale, F.J. AL 62nd Inf. Co.C
Seale, F.W. MS 3rd (St.Troops) Cav. Co.C
Seale, George G. MS 11th Inf. Co.D
Seale, George G. MS 40th Inf. Co.F
Seale, George H. AL 33rd Inf. Co.H
Seale, George W. AL 20th Inf. Co.I
Seale, George W. MS 8th Inf. Co.F 2nd Lt.
Seale, Green B. AL 3rd Res. Co.B,K Cpl.
Seale, G.T. MS 41st Inf. Co.B
Seale, G.W. AL 15th Bn.Part.Rangers Co.C
Seale, G.W. AL 56th Part.Rangers Co.C
Seale, G.W. MS 10th Cav. Co.F
Seale, H. AL 4th Res. Co.F
Seale, H.B. AL 31st Inf. Co.K
Seale, Henry O. AL 17th Inf. Co.C Cpl.
Seale, H.T. AL 62nd Inf. Co.C,G
Seale, I.T. MS 40th Inf. Co.I
Seale, J. AL Mil. 4th Vol. Co.I
Seale, J.A. AL 7th Cav. Co.E 1st Lt.
Seale, J.A. AL 18th Inf. Co.F
Seale, James AR 3rd Inf. Co.B Sgt.
Seale, James MS 2nd (Quinn's St.Troops) Inf. Co.C Sgt.
Seale, James 14th Conf.Cav. Co.I
Seale, James A. AL 7th Cav. Co.E Capt.
Seale, James A. AL 10th Inf. Co.C
Seale, James H. LA 12th Inf. Co.H Capt.
Seale, James L. TN Lt.Arty. Burrough's Co. Cpl.
Seale, James P. MS 31st Inf. Co.D

Seale, James S. TX Granbury's Cons.Brig. Co.D Cpl.
Seale, James T. AL 18th Inf. Co.F
Seale, Jarvis AL 3rd Res. Co.H
Seale, Jasper J. 14th Conf.Cav. Co.B
Seale, Jerry MS 41st Inf. Co.L 1st Lt.
Seale, J.J. MS Cav. Garland's Bn. Co.B
Seale, J.J. TX 13th Cav. Co.G
Seale, J.M. AL 20th Inf. Co.D
Seale, J.M. MS Cav. Garland's Bn. Co.B
Seale, J.M. MS 41st Inf. Co.B
Seale, J.M. 14th Conf.Cav. Co.B
Seale, J.N. MS 41st Inf. Co.B Sgt.
Seale, John A. AL 23rd Inf. Co.H
Seale, John E. MS 40th Inf. Co.F Cpl.
Seale, John F. TX Lt.Arty. Hughes' Co. Cpl.
Seale, John K. TN Lt.Arty. Burrough's Co. Artif.
Seale, John L. TX 15th Field Btty. Cpl.
Seale, John P. LA 3rd (Harrison's) Cav. Co.D
Seale, John P. TX 27th Cav. Co.E
Seale, Joseph MS 7th Inf. Co.E Ch.Music.
Seale, Joshua AL 23rd Inf. Co.H
Seale, J.T. AR 6th Inf. Co.G
Seale, J.W. MS Lt.Arty. Turner's Co.
Seale, L.B. AL 21st Inf. Co.C
Seale, L.I. TX Cav. Baylor's Regt. Co. I
Seale, Louis P. TX 27th Cav. Co.E
Seale, Paschal 14th Conf.Cav. Co.B Cpl.
Seale, Paschal H. MS 7th Inf. Co.E
Seale, R.H. SC 11th Inf. Co.E
Seale, Robert AL 3rd Res. Co.B,K
Seale, Robert TN Lt.Arty. Burrough's Co.
Seale, Sanford S. AL 10th Inf. Co.C
Seale, S.H. AL 23rd Inf. Co.H Sgt.
Seale, Strother VA 49th Inf. Co.K
Seale, Thomas AL 18th Inf. Co.F
Seale, Thomas LA Res.Corps Scott's Co.
Seale, Thomas TX 10th Inf. Co.F
Seale, Thomas 14th Conf.Cav. Co.A
Seale, Thomas 14th Conf.Cav. Co.B
Seale, Thomas A. MS 40th Inf. Co.F Cpl.
Seale, Thomas J. 1st Conf.Inf. 2nd Co.H Sgt.
Seale, Thomas R. TX 27th Cav. Co.E
Seale, T.R. TX 13th Cav. Co.G
Seale, W.A. MS 41st Inf. Co.B
Seale, Westley Y. MS 35th Inf. Co.A
Seale, William 14th Conf.Cav. Co.B
Seale, William B. Medical Staff Hosp.Stew.
Seale, William F. TX 13th Cav. Co.G Capt.
Seale, William H. MS 35th Inf. Co.A
Seale, William T. MS 19th Inf. Co.D
Seale, Wilson AR 6th Inf. Co.G
Seale, W.L. TX 2nd Inf. Co.I
Seale, W.R. MS 40th Inf. Co.F Cpl.
Seales, A. GA 9th Inf. (St.Guards) Co.C
Seales, Allen B. AL 44th Inf. Co.C
Seales, Boyer TN 2nd (Ashby's) Cav. Co.B
Seales, B.W. LA 6th Inf. Co.K
Seales, D.E. VA Hvy.Arty. 20th Bn. Co.C
Seales, Francis M. AL 44th Inf. Co.C
Seales, Henry B. GA 48th Inf. Co.A
Seales, H.M. AL 31st Inf. Co.K
Seales, Holloway M. TN 11th Inf. Co.E
Seales, J. MS 2nd (Davidson's) Inf. Co.E
Seales, James Conf.Cav. Wood's Regt. 2nd Co.M
Seales, James K. AL 17th Inf. Co.K Music.

Seales, James S. TX 10th Inf. Co.G Cpl.
Seales, Jarvis MS Inf. 3rd Bn. Co.E
Seales, Jarvis MS 5th Inf. (St.Troops) Co.I Capt.
Seales, John MS 2nd (Davidson's) Inf. Co.E
Seales, John A. AL 31st Inf. Co.K
Seales, John D. AL 4th Res. Co.I Cpl.
Seales, John M. TX 1st (McCulloch's) Cav. Co.D
Seales, John T. LA 16th Inf. Co.B
Seales, John W. AL 44th Inf. Co.C
Seales, Joshua AL 31st Inf. Co.K
Seales, J.R. TX 5th Inf. Co.D
Seales, Peter SC 23rd Inf. Co.A
Seales, P.N. VA Cav. 32nd Bn. Co.B
Seales, Robert AL 31st Inf. Co.K Cpl.
Seales, S.H. AL Inf.
Seales, Thomas NC 18th Inf. Co.F
Seales, W.D. TN Inf. 1st Cons.Regt. Co.D
Seales, William MS 27th Inf. Co.E
Seales, William A. AL 6th Cav. Co.H
Seales, William A. GA 1st Inf. Co.F
Seales, William R. TX 11th Inf. Co.A
Seales, William S. President's Guard,CSA
Sealey, --- TX 24th & 25th Cav. (Cons.) Co.I
Sealey, A.H. GA 27th Inf. Co.K
Sealey, Amos TN 54th Inf. Dooley's Co.
Sealey, Amos C. TN Cav. 9th Bn. (Gantt's) Co.B,C,G
Sealey, David P. FL 5th Inf. Co.G
Sealey, Frank M. TN Cav. 9th Bn. (Gantt's) Co.C
Sealey, Frederick W. FL 3rd Inf. Co.H
Sealey, George TX Cav. Waller's Regt. Menard's Co. Cpl.
Sealey, George W. SC 1st Inf. Co.M
Sealey, Henry FL Cav. 5th Bn. Co.D
Sealey, James TX 3rd Inf. Co.G
Sealey, James B. FL 1st Inf. Old Co.I
Sealey, James W. FL 2nd Inf. Co.M
Sealey, J.E. FL Cav. 5th Bn. Co.D
Sealey, Jesse FL 5th Inf. Co.I
Sealey, J.H. AL 20th Inf. Co.I
Sealey, John FL 6th Inf. Co.K
Sealey, John GA Inf. (GA Defend.) Chapman's Co.
Sealey, John H. GA Siege Arty. 28th Bn. Co.C
Sealey, J.W. GA Cav. 12th Bn. (St.Guards) Co.E
Sealey, Neverson NC Hvy.Arty. 1st Bn. Co.D
Sealey, Nicholas T. NC 51st Inf. Co.E
Sealey, Paschal NC 39th Inf. Co.A
Sealey, S.E. FL Cav. 5th Bn. Co.D Cpl.
Sealey, Thomas SC 2nd St.Troops Co.I
Sealey, T.S. GA Cav. 12th Bn. (St.Guards) Co.A
Sealey, Wiley NC McDugald's Co.
Sealey, William S. FL 10th Inf. Co.E
Sealey, W.T. GA 30th Inf. Co.F
Sealing, Richard VA 1st St.Res. Co.E
Seall, Thomas E. LA 31st Inf. Co.G
Seally, William SC Inf. 3rd Bn. Co.F
Sealoch, Mason VA 34th Mil. Co.A
Sealock, Craven VA 49th Inf. Co.D
Sealock, George VA 12th Cav. Co.E
Sealock, John T. VA Lt.Arty. 38th Bn. Co.A Cpl.
Sealock, J.T. VA Cav. Mosby's Regt. (Part. Rangers) Co.D
Sealock, J.T. VA 49th Inf. 1st Co.G Cpl.

Sealock, Lewis VA 49th Inf. Co.D
Sealock, Thomas VA Lt.Arty. 38th Bn. Co.A
Seals, A. MS Inf. 3rd Bn. (St.Troops) Co.C
Seals, A. MS T. Williams' Co.
Seals, A. 20th Conf.Cav. Co.G
Seals, A.B. AL 45th Inf. Co.H
Seals, Abraham C. MS St.Cav. Perrin's Bn. Co.B
Seals, Absalum TN 11th Inf. Co.C
Seals, A.G. TX 8th Cav. Co.F
Seals, Alexander NC 46th Inf. Co.A
Seals, Alexander B. AL 34th Inf. Breedlove's Co.
Seals, Allen AL 30th Inf. Co.D,H
Seals, Ambrose MO 3rd Cav. Co.G
Seals, Andrew J. MS 21st Inf. Co.G
Seals, Archibald B. Gen. & Staff, QM Dept. Capt.,AQM
Seals, A.T. AL Lt.Arty. Tarrant's Btty.
Seals, A.W. GA 4th (Clinch's) Cav. Co.D
Seals, B.B. AL Cp. of Instr. Talladega
Seals, B.B. MS Cav. 6th Bn. Prince's Co.
Seals, Benjamin MS 6th Cav. Co.K
Seals, Benjamin B. AL City Guards Lockett's Co.
Seals, B.F. TX 21st Inf. Co.K
Seals, Bonager GA 38th Inf. Co.A,K
Seals, Burrel AR 7th Cav. Co.G
Seals, C. GA
Seals, C.A. TX 20th Inf. Co.B Sgt.
Seals, Charles B. LA 9th Inf. Co.I
Seals, Daniel MO 1st Cav. Co.E Jr.2nd Lt.
Seals, Daniel M. AL Vol. Lee, Jr.'s Co.
Seals, Edward R. GA Lt.Arty. Guerard's Btty.
Seals, Eli Driver MS Bradford's Co. (Conf. Guards Arty.)
Seals, Elijah AR 11th & 17th Cons.Inf. Co.A
Seals, Ewing MS 22nd Inf. Co.E
Seals, Felix P. AL 30th Inf. Co.D Sgt.
Seals, G.B. AR 27th Inf. Old Co.C, Co.D
Seals, George VA 25th Cav. Co.G
Seals, George W. MS Cav. Jeff Davis Legion Co.B
Seals, Green F. MS 18th Inf. Co.H Sgt.
Seals, G.W. GA 22nd Inf. Co.I
Seals, Harris SC 26th Inf. Co.D
Seals, Henry TN 22nd (Barteau's) Cav. Co.F
Seals, Henry B. GA 5th Inf. Co.F
Seals, Henry B. GA 15th Inf. Co.K
Seals, Houston MO 12th Inf. Co.C
Seals, Isaac TX 15th Inf. 2nd Co.H Cpl.
Seals, J.A. AL 8th (Hatch's) Cav. Co.H
Seals, J.A. GA Cav. 24th Bn. Co.D
Seals, Jackson B. AL 20th Inf. Co.D
Seals, Jacob TN 11th Inf. Co.C
Seals, James AL 12th Inf. Co.I
Seals, James AL 62nd Inf. Co.E
Seals, James SC 6th Cav. Co.C
Seals, James SC 5th Res. Co.B
Seals, James SC 23rd Inf. Co.G
Seals, James TX 19th Inf. Co.F
Seals, James A. AR 2nd Mtd.Rifles Hawkins' Co.
Seals, James A. MS 13th Inf. Co.F
Seals, James A. TX 27th Cav. Co.A
Seals, James D. AL 51st (Part.Rangers) Co.B
Seals, James M. MS 42nd Inf. Co.F 1st Lt.

Seals, James R. MS 8th Cav. Co.A
Seals, James S. TN 8th Inf. Co.K
Seals, Jarvis MS Inf. 1st St.Troops Co.E
Seals, Jarvis TN 37th Inf. Co.K
Seals, J.B. GA Inf. 1st City Bn. (Columbus) Co.B
Seals, J.C. GA 36th (Villepigue's) Inf. Co.F
Seals, J.C. MS Bradford's Co. (Conf.Guards Arty.)
Seals, J.C. MS 41st Inf. Co.B
Seals, J.C. 1st Conf.Inf. 1st Co.F
Seals, J.D. GA Cav. 7th Bn. (St.Guards) Co.G
Seals, J.D. GA 17th Inf. Co.E
Seals, J.E. TN 12th (Cons.) Inf. Co.D
Seals, J.E. TN 22nd Inf. Co.K
Seals, Jerry MS 6th Cav. Co.B,D 1st Sgt.
Seals, Jerry MS 8th Cav. Co.F 1st Sgt.
Seals, J.H. TX 24th & 25th Cav. (Cons.) Co.I
Seals, J.M. AR 12th Inf. Co.D
Seals, John MS 8th Inf. Co.B
Seals, John NC 18th Inf. Co.F
Seals, John SC 1st Cav. Co.G
Seals, John SC 2nd Cav. Co.G
Seals, John SC 5th Res. Co.C
Seals, John TX Cav. Madison's Regt. Co.E
Seals, John A. GA 7th Cav. Co.I
Seals, John A. MS 20th Inf. Co.F
Seals, John C. AR 27th Inf. Old Co.C, Co.D
Seals, John H. GA 3rd Bn. (St.Guards) Co.C
Seals, John K. VA Inf. Mileham's Co.
Seals, John M. AL 30th Inf. Co.D
Seals, John R. GA 2nd Cav. (St.Guards) Co.F
Seals, John R. SC 2nd Inf. Co.F
Seals, Joseph GA 5th Inf. Co.C
Seals, Joseph A. AL 9th Cav. Co.H
Seals, Joseph C. GA Lt.Arty. Pritchard's Co. (Washington Arty.) Cpl.
Seals, Joshua TN 14th Inf. Co.B
Seals, J.T. MS 4th Cav. Co.G
Seals, J.W. AL 58th Inf. Co.I
Seals, J.W. GA Inf. 1st Loc.Troops (Augusta) Dearing's Cav.Co.
Seals, J.W. TN 35th Inf. Co.E
Seals, L.A. AL Cav. Hardie's Bn.Res. Co.C
Seals, Linsey GA Inf. (Richmond Factory Guards) Barney's Co.
Seals, Marion I. GA 8th Inf. (St.Guards) Co.F
Seals, Marion J. GA Cherokee Legion (St.Guards) Co.B
Seals, N.A. TX 18th Inf. Co.H Cpl.
Seals, Nevel AL 30th Inf. Co.H
Seals, Peter NC 5th Cav. (63rd St.Troops) Co.A
Seals, Peter SC 4th St.Troops Co.F
Seals, Richmond T. AL Inf. 1st Regt. New Co.G, Old Co.G
Seals, R.J. AL 58th Inf. Co.I
Seals, R.L. AR 12th Inf. Co.D
Seals, R.W. MS 41st Inf. Co.B
Seals, S.V.B. AL 30th Inf. Co.H
Seals, T. AR 38th Inf. New Co.I
Seals, Thomas NC 23rd Inf. Co.D
Seals, Thomas TN 63rd Inf. Co.C
Seals, Thomas A. GA Cav. 10th Bn. (St.Guards) Co.D
Seals, Thomas A. NC 6th Inf. Co.A
Seals, Thomas J. MS 34th Inf. Co.F
Seals, W. AR 11th & 17th Cons.Inf. Co.A

Seals, W.B. GA 12th (Robinson's) Cav. (St.Guards) Co.I
Seals, W.D. AL 45th Inf. Co.A
Seals, W.H. AL 1st Cav. 2nd Co.E,H
Seals, William MS 21st Inf. Co.G
Seals, William NC Lt.Arty. 13th Bn. Co.A
Seals, William SC 26th Inf. Co.D
Seals, William VA Lt.Arty. 12th Bn. Co.D
Seals, William A. GA Lt.Arty. Guerard's Btty.
Seals, William A. 1st Conf.Inf. 2nd Co.F
Seals, William D. GA 15th Inf. Co.K Sgt.
Seals, William D. TN 8th Inf. Co.K
Seals, William H. TN 13th Inf. Co.K
Seals, William Henson MS Bradford's Co. (Conf.Guards Arty.) Cpl.
Seals, William S. GA Cav. 20th Bn. Co.C
Seals, W.J. TX 7th Cav. Co.G
Seals, W.R. AL Cav. 8th Regt. (Livingston's) Co.D
Seals, W.S. GA 8th Cav. New Co.E
Seals, Z.I. TX 20th Inf. Co.H
Seals, Z.J. 4th Conf.Eng.Troops Artif.
Sealy, A.H. AL 58th Inf. Co.H
Sealy, A.H. GA Inf. 27th Bn. (NonConscr.) Co.A
Sealy, Allen B. GA 51st Inf. Co.B
Sealy, Allen H. NC 31st Inf. Co.A
Sealy, Charles A. GA 44th Inf. Co.H
Sealy, Daniel TN 1st (Feild's) Inf. Co.H
Sealy, David LA Mil. LaFourche Regt.
Sealy, E. FL 1st (Res.) Inf. Co.E
Sealy, E. FL 5th Inf. Co.F
Sealy, Emcoin NC 50th Inf. Co.B
Sealy, G. TX 25th Cav.
Sealy, Garrett E. AL 41st Inf. Co.F
Sealy, George W. NC McDugald's Co. Cpl.
Sealy, H. VA 3rd Inf.Loc.Def. Co.K
Sealy, I. MS 2nd Cav.Res. Co.C
Sealy, Isham NC 50th Inf. Co.B
Sealy, James E. FL 2nd Cav. Co.E
Sealy, James F. GA 5th Inf. Co.F 3rd Lt.
Sealy, James O. AL 41st Inf. Co.F Sgt.
Sealy, J.H. AL 63rd Inf. Co.I
Sealy, J.J. FL Cav. 5th Bn. Co.D
Sealy, John GA 3rd Cav. Co.A
Sealy, John NC 55th Inf. Co.D
Sealy, John H. AL 3rd Res. Co.D
Sealy, John J. FL 2nd Cav. Co.E
Sealy, John R. NC 50th Inf. Co.B
Sealy, John W. TN Cav. 9th Bn. (Gantt's) Co.B
Sealy, J.T. TX 19th Inf. Co.I
Sealy, J.W. AL Randolph Cty.Res. D.A. Self's Co.
Sealy, Lambert D. LA 12th Inf. Co.H
Sealy, L.B. MS 11th (Perrin's) Cav. Co.I
Sealy, Malvin NC 50th Inf. Co.B
Sealy, Moore T. NC 31st Inf. Co.A. 2nd Lt.
Sealy, Nephison NC 51st Inf. Co.E
Sealy, Obediah E. LA 4th Cav. Co.E
Sealy, Peter J. GA 5th Inf. Co.F Sgt.
Sealy, Richard NC 8th Sr.Res. McLean's Co.
Sealy, R.T. GA 27th Inf. Co.G
Sealy, Sampson A. NC 18th Inf. Co.D
Sealy, Theodore GA Cav. 29th Bn. Co.F
Sealy, Thomas GA 27th Inf. Co.G
Sealy, Wiley NC 31st Inf. Co.A
Sealy, W.T. SC 3rd Bn.Res. Co.E 1st Lt.

Sealy, W.T. SC 5th St.Troops Co.A
Sealy, Z.B. GA 27th Inf. Co.K
Seaman, --- GA 1st (Olmstead's) Inf. Co.C
Seaman, A. VA Cav. 40th Bn. Co.F
Seaman, Andrew J. NC 33rd Inf. Co.A
Seaman, C.E. FL 1st Inf. Old Co.D, New Co.A
Seaman, Charles LA Mil. 3rd Regt. 1st Brig. 1st
  Div. Co.I
Seaman, Charles LA C.S. Zouave Bn. Co.F
Seaman, Charles TX 2nd Inf. Co.K
Seaman, Charles TX 6th Inf. Co.A,H Sgt.
Seaman, Charles VA Lt.Arty. Carpenter's Co.
Seaman, David W. VA 19th Cav. Co.C
Seaman, David W. VA 3rd Cav. & Inf.St.Line
  Co.D
Seaman, Edward AL 44th Inf. Co.B,I
Seaman, George LA Inf.Cons.Crescent Regt.
  Co.E Cpl.
Seaman, George W. KY 5th Mtd.Inf. Co.C 1st
  Lt.
Seaman, G.W. KY 2nd Cav. Co.C 1st Lt.
Seaman, G.W. KY 2nd Bn.Mtd.Rifles Co.C 1st
  Lt.
Seaman, H. LA Inf. Pelican Regt. Co.F
Seaman, H.D., Jr. LA Washington Arty.Bn.
  Co.4,6
Seaman, H.E. MS Cav. 17th Bn. Co.B 2nd Lt.
Seaman, Henry LA Inf. 4th Bn. Co.A
Seaman, Henry LA 5th Inf. Co.F
Seaman, Jacob VA Cav. McNeill's Co.
Seaman, James LA 1st Inf. Co.I
Seaman, James A. VA 33rd Inf. Co.F Sgt.
Seaman, J.B. MS 2nd St.Cav. Co.I
Seaman, John MS Cav. Buck's Co.
Seaman, John VA Mil. Scott Cty.
Seaman, John Conf.Inf. Tucker's Regt. Co.D
Seaman, M.S. MS 7th Cav. Co.H
Seaman, P.Y. AR 8th Cav. Peoples' Co.
Seaman, Robert N. LA 1st Hvy.Arty. (Reg.)
  Co.E Music.
Seaman, Robert N. LA 15th Inf. Co.A
Seaman, Samuel VA 25th Inf. 2nd Co.E
Seaman, S.W. NC McLean's Bn.Lt.Duty Men
  Co.B
Seaman, Thomas P. VA 14th Cav. Crawford's
  Co.
Seaman, Thomas P. VA 17th Cav. Co.F
Seaman, Thomas W. AR 1st (Colquitt's) Inf.
  Co.H
Seaman, W.H. LA Inf. 7th Bn. Co.C Sgt.
Seaman, William VA Cav. McNeill's Co.
Seaman, William H. LA Inf.Crescent Regt. Co.H
  Capt.
Seaman, William I. AL 3rd Inf. Co.I
Seaman, William J. MS 48th Inf. Co.F
Seaman, William L. VA 33rd Inf. Co.F
Seaman, W.J. MS Inf. 2nd Bn. Co.F
Seamands, Hiram J. VA 57th Inf. Co.H
Seamands, Joseph G. VA 57th Inf. Co.H
Seamands, Peyton H. VA 29th Inf. Co.H
Seamans, Charles VA Inf. Gregory's Co.
Seamans, J.B. AL 55th Vol. Co.D Cpl.
Seamans, J.H. AL 56th Part.Rangers Co.I
Seamans, John W. GA 18th Inf. Co.B
Seamans, King 1st Creek Mtd.Vol. Co.F 2nd Lt.
Seamans, Wiley T. VA 6th Cav. Co.G
Seamen, August VA Cav. McNeill's Co.

Seamen, Emanuel GA 4th Inf. Co.E
Seamens, J.C. AL 35th Inf. Co.C
Seamer, Peter AL 38th Inf. Co.K
Seamer, Richard LA 21st (Patton's) Inf. Co.D
Seamon, H.R. NC 23rd Inf. Co.H
Seamon, J. AL 94th Mil. Co.A
Seamon, John NC 42nd Inf. Co.F
Seamon, Losen NC 42nd Inf. Co.F
Seamon, Robert W. NC 7th Inf. Co.G
Seamonds, Charles VA 8th Cav. Co.E
Seamonds, William A. AR 25th Inf. Co.I
Seamone, John A. NC 20th Inf. Co.A
Seamone, William VA 13th Inf. Co.G
Seamons, Calvin MO 5th Inf. Co.I
Seamons, J.B. MS 25th Inf. Co.B
Seamons, Joshua AR 23rd Inf. Co.G
Seamons, W.J. AR 27th Inf. Co.I
Seamons, William T. TN 35th Inf. Co.C Sgt.
Seamont, James NC 4th Sr.Res. Co.A
Seamore, F.H. TN 50th Inf. Co.K
Seamore, George AR 15th Mil. Co.B
Seamore, Henry VA Hvy.Arty. Wright's Co.
Seamore, J. AL 30th Inf. Co.G
Seamore, Jesse MO 7th Cav. Co.H,F
Seamore, Jessie MO Lt.Arty. 4th (Harris') Field
  Btty.
Seamore, John TN 19th Inf. Co.G
Seamore, Joseph GA 34th Inf. Co.A
Seamore, Minson AL 58th Inf. Co.E
Seamore, William H. VA 9th Inf. Co.B Cpl.
Seams, John NC 50th Inf.
Seamster, C. VA 53rd Inf. Co.G
Seamster, Edward VA 3rd Inf. 2nd Co.K
Seamster, Henry VA Hvy.Arty. Wright's Co.
Seamster, J. VA 53rd Inf. Co.G
Seamster, James VA 20th Inf. Co.K
Seamster, James R. VA Hvy.Arty. Wright's Co.
Seamster, J.F. MS Cav. Ham's Regt. Co.E
Seamster, John A. VA 3rd Inf. 2nd Co.K
Seamster, Richard H. VA 26th Inf. Co.K
Seamster, Stephen MO 1st N.E. Cav. Co.E
Seamster, Timothy VA 59th Inf. 3rd Co.E,D
Seamster, William VA 26th Inf. Co.K
Seamster, William W. VA 59th Inf. 3rd Co.E
Seamus, Manl. LA Mil. 5th Regt.Eur.Brig.
  (Spanish Regt.) Co.8
Seanlon, E. LA Mil. Orleans Fire Regt. Co.G
Seans, John M. AL Mobile Fire Bn. Mullany's
  Co. Cpl.
Seapoch, Jacob SC 17th Inf. Co.F
Seapoch, Joseph SC 17th Inf. Co.F
Seapoch, Noah SC 17th Inf. Co.F
Seapock, Philip SC 17th Inf. Co.F
Seaps, John MS Cav. Davenport's Bn.
  (St.Troops) Co.C
Sear, Alexander VA 62nd Mtd.Inf. 2nd Co.E
  Cpl.
Sear, T.K. VA 1st (Farinholt's) Res. Co.K
Searamania, Giov LA Mil. 4th Regt.Eur.Brig.
  Cognevich's Co.
Searbery, William H. VA 42nd Inf. Co.F
Searborn, F.J. SC 8th Res.
Searcey, A. MS Cav. Davenport's Bn.
  (St.Troops) Co.C
Searcey, A.J. FL Cav. 3rd Bn. Co.C
Searcey, A.W. NC 60th Inf. Co.C
Searcey, Isham G. TX 12th Inf. Co.D 1st Lt.

Searcey, J.A. AR Lt.Arty. Marshall's Btty.
  Asst.Surg.
Searcey, Jas. J. Gen. & Staff 1st Lt.,Adj.
Searcey, James T. Conf.Arty. Palmer's Bn.
  Sgt.Maj.
Searcey, J.B. AR Cav. Wright's Regt. Co.C
Searcey, Jeremiah KY 2nd Mtd.Inf. Co.I
Searcey, John A. SC 1st Arty. Co.I,G
Searcey, J.P. AR 1st (Crawford's) Cav. Co.A
Searcey, O.L. GA 11th Inf. Co.F
Searcey, P. MS Cav. Davenport's Bn.
  (St.Troops) Co.C
Searcey, R. NC 60th Inf. Co.C
Searcey, R.C. NC Lt.Arty. Thomas' Legion
  Levi's Btty. 2nd Lt.
Searcey, Reuben VA Lt.Arty. Jackson's Bn.
  St.Line Co.A
Searcey, W.B. NC 60th Inf. Co.C Sgt.
Searcey, William MS 2nd Part.Rangers Co.K
Searcey, William O. GA 11th Inf. Co.D
Searcey, William W. TN 1st (Feild's) Inf. Co.I
Searcey, W.O. TN 3rd (Forrest's) Cav. Co.B
Searcy, A. TN Inf. 4th Cons.Regt. Col.
Searcy, Aaron GA 2nd Res. Co.B
Searcy, A.E. KY 4th Cav. Co.F
Searcy, A.H. MS Cav. Ham's Regt. Co.A
Searcy, A.H. NC 62nd Inf. Co.F
Searcy, A.J. AL Res. Co.B
Searcy, A.J. TX Cav. 6th Bn. Co.B
Searcy, Albert W. TX 27th Cav. Co.D 2nd Lt.
Searcy, Anderson TN 45th Inf. Co.C Col.
Searcy, A.P. TN 6th Inf. Co.B
Searcy, Asa L. AR 23rd Inf. Co.K
Searcy, A.T. AR 23rd Inf. Co.K
Searcy, Benjamin W. AL 39th Inf. Co.B Sgt.
Searcy, Bennett LA 3rd (Harrison's) Cav. Co.I
  Sgt.
Searcy, Bennett TX Cav. 6th Bn. Co.B Cpl.
Searcy, B.H. NC 62nd Inf. Co.F
Searcy, Britton AL Cav. 4th Bn. (Love's) Co.C
Searcy, B.W. AL Cav. 4th Bn. (Love's) Co.C
Searcy, B.W. GA 8th Cav. Co.G Sgt.
Searcy, B.W. GA 62nd Cav. Co.G Sgt.
Searcy, Daniel GA 20th Inf. Co.G
Searcy, Daniel D. TN 7th Inf. Co.I
Searcy, D.R. MS 6th Inf. Co.D Cpl.
Searcy, D.T. GA Phillips' Legion Co.D
Searcy, E.B. TN 3rd (Forrest's) Cav. Co.B
Searcy, Ed. B. TN 11th (Holman's) Cav. Co.A
Searcy, Edward S. MO 1st N.E. Cav. Co.D
Searcy, Elbert GA Cav. 16th Bn. (St.Guards)
  Co.G
Searcy, Elijah NC 62nd Inf. Co.F
Searcy, E.M.C. AL 39th Inf. Co.B
Searcy, F.M. AL 33rd Inf. Co.D
Searcy, George N. MO 2nd Cav. 3rd Co.K
Searcy, George W. AL 3rd Bn.Res. Appling's
  Co.
Searcy, George W. AL 17th Inf. Co.E
Searcy, Harvey G. GA Smith's Legion Ralston's
  Co.
Searcy, Henry C. Gen. & Staff 1st Lt.,ADC
Searcy, H. Clay TX 27th Cav. Co.D Sgt.Maj.
Searcy, Henry KY 4th Cav. Co.A
Searcy, Henry KY 8th Cav. Co.A
Searcy, Henry M. GA 6th Inf. Co.G Music.
Searcy, H.G. GA 6th Cav. Co.D

Searcy, H.P. NC 62nd Inf. Co.F
Searcy, Irwin MS 26th Inf. Co.H
Searcy, James GA Inf. 1st City Bn. (Columbus) Co.D
Searcy, James GA Inf. 19th Bn. (St.Guards) Co.B Cpl.
Searcy, James GA 20th Inf. Co.G
Searcy, James KY 6th Mtd.Inf. Co.G
Searcy, James LA 1st Cav. Co.I,F
Searcy, James MO 12th Cav. Co.H
Searcy, James TN 55th (McKoin's) Inf. Dillehay's Co. 2nd Lt.
Searcy, James F. NC 62nd Inf. Co.F
Searcy, James J. MO 9th Inf. Adj.
Searcy, James J. MO 16th Inf. Co.A
Searcy, James J. MO Searcy's Bn.S.S. Lt.Col.
Searcy, James K. MO 12th Inf. Co.I
Searcy, James K.P. AL 37th Inf. Co.H
Searcy, James M. KY 5th Cav. Co.H
Searcy, James M. MO Arty. Jos. Bledsoe's Co.
Searcy, James M. MO 4th Regt.St.Guard Co.F
Searcy, James N. MO St.Guard
Searcy, James S. TX 22nd Cav. Co.G
Searcy, James T. AL Lt.Arty. 2nd Bn. Co.F Cpl.
Searcy, James T. GA 8th Inf. (St.Guards) Co.D
Searcy, James W. AL 39th Inf. Co.B
Searcy, J.B. AR 26th Inf. Chap.
Searcy, J.B. Gen. & Staff Chap.
Searcy, J.D. GA 46th Inf. Co.I
Searcy, Jesse KY 1st (Butler's) Cav. Co.D
Searcy, Jesse KY 2nd Cav. Co.D
Searcy, Jessie AR 8th Inf. New Co.H 1st Lt.
Searcy, J.G. AL 22nd Inf. Co.H
Searcy, J.H. TX Cav. 6th Bn. Co.B Cpl.
Searcy, J.M. NC 62nd Inf. Co.K
Searcy, John AL 6th Inf. Co.K
Searcy, John GA 2nd Res. Co.B
Searcy, John GA 20th Inf. Co.G
Searcy, John MO 1st N.E. Cav. Co.H
Searcy, John A. MO 12th Cav. Co.A
Searcy, John A. Gen. & Staff AASurg.
Searcy, John D. NC 60th Inf. Co.I
Searcy, John G. AL 39th Inf. Co.B Sgt.
Searcy, John N. MS Lt.Arty. (The Hudson Btty.) Hoole's Co. Cpl.
Searcy, Joseph KY 6th Mtd.Inf. Co.G
Searcy, J.R. AL 8th Inf. Co.F Sgt.
Searcy, J.W. AL 22nd Inf. Co.H
Searcy, J.W. GA 27th Inf. Co.F Cpl.
Searcy, Kinchon T. TN 55th (McKoin's) Inf. Dillehay's Co.
Searcy, L.D. AL 22nd Inf. Co.H Cpl.
Searcy, Lemuel D. AL 37th Inf. Co.H
Searcy, Lemuel D. AL 39th Inf. Co.B Cpl.
Searcy, M.A. NC 62nd Inf. Co.F Drum.
Searcy, Marion C.J. AL 37th Inf. Co.H Capt.
Searcy, Mark W. AR 5th Inf. Co.A Cpl.
Searcy, M.W. TN Cav. 17th Bn. (Sanders') Co.A Cpl.
Searcy, N.A. AR 35th Inf. Old Co.F
Searcy, N.A. MO 9th Bn.S.S. Co.B 2nd Lt.
Searcy, N.A. MO 11th Inf. Co.H
Searcy, N.D. MO St.Guard
Searcy, Noah NC 39th Inf. Co.D
Searcy, O.C. TX Cav. Hardeman's Regt. Co.B
Searcy, Olen M. AL 51st (Part.Rangers) Co.E

Searcy, Olin M. AL 29th Inf. Co.K
Searcy, Oliver AL 57th Inf. Co.E
Searcy, Oliver C. TX 27th Cav. Co.D 1st Lt.
Searcy, Oliver C. TX Cav. Hardeman's Regt. Co.B
Searcy, P.F. NC 62nd Inf. Co.F
Searcy, R.C. VA Lt.Arty. Barr's Co. 1st Lt.
Searcy, Reuben C. TN 7th Inf.
Searcy, Reuben T. TN 7th Inf. Co.C Cpl.
Searcy, R.M. AL 34th Inf. Co.F
Searcy, R.S. TN 51st Inf. Co.G
Searcy, Stephen GA 36th (Villepigue's) Inf. Co.C
Searcy, Thomas TN Cav. Newsom's Regt. Co.E
Searcy, Thomas TN 6th Inf. Co.L
Searcy, Thomas TN 55th (Brown's) Inf. Ford's Co.
Searcy, Thomas B. GA 40th Inf. Co.B
Searcy, Thomas B. MO Searcy's Bn.S.S. Co.A
Searcy, Thomas W. GA 40th Inf. Co.B
Searcy, Tom TN 21st (Wilson's) Cav. Co.G
Searcy, W.B. KY 4th Cav. Co.F
Searcy, Wesley W. AL 39th Inf. Co.G
Searcy, W.H. GA 12th (Robinson's) Cav. (St.Guards) Co.I 1st Sgt.
Searcy, William AR 1st Cav. Co.I
Searcy, William GA 11th Cav. Co.G Sgt.
Searcy, William GA 1st Reg. Co.H
Searcy, William MO 1st N.E. Cav. Co.H
Searcy, William TX 12th Inf. Co.E
Searcy, William A. MS 6th Inf. Co.D
Searcy, William D. MO Cav. Jackman's Regt.
Searcy, William D. MO 6th Inf. Co.C
Searcy, William F. NC 39th Inf. Co.D
Searcy, William F. TN 28th Inf. Co.H
Searcy, William J. GA Arty. (Macon Lt.Arty.) Slaten's Co.
Searcy, William K. GA 46th Inf. Co.I Sgt.
Searcy, William M. MS 42nd Inf. Co.E
Searcy, William T. AR 8th Inf. New Co.H
Searcy, William W. AL 22nd Inf. Co.H
Searcy, William W. TN Cav. 11th Bn. (Gordon's) Co.D
Searcy, W.R. NC 62nd Inf. Co.K
Searcy, W.W. TN 6th (Wheeler's) Cav. Co.D
Searers, W.W. TN Cav. 12th Bn. (Day's) Co.C
Searey, William H. AL 6th Cav. Co.D,E
Seargeant, Andrew E. VA 23rd Inf. Co.D
Seargeant, Edward F. VA 23rd Inf. Co.D
Seargeant, H.H. AL 4th Inf. A.Surg.
Seargeant, James A. VA 23rd Inf. Co.D
Seargeant, James R. MS 2nd Inf. Co.B
Seargeant, James W. MO 12th Inf. Co.F
Seargeant, John M. VA 23rd Inf. Co.D
Seargeant, Nathaniel R. VA 19th Inf. Co.A
Seargeant, Silas J. SC 2nd Rifles Co.L,B
Seargeant, Thomas Gen. & Staff Cadet
Seargeant, William B. MS 23rd Inf. Co.B Cpl.
Seargeant, William H. AL 50th Inf. Co.K
Seargeant, William J. VA 23rd Inf. Co.D Capt.
Seargeant, William L. VA 23rd Inf. Co.D
Seargeant, William T. VA 23rd Inf. Co.D
Seargent, H. KY 3rd Mtd.Inf. Co.A
Seargent, Henry H. Gen. & Staff Asst.Surg.
Seargent, James TX 4th Inf. Co.H
Seargent, Joseph AL Inf. 2nd Regt. Co.K
Seargent, S.H. GA Inf. 40th Bn. Co.E
Seargent, Tandy T. VA 2nd Arty. Co.I

Seargent, Thomas TX 4th Inf. Co.H
Seargent, William S. TX Waul's Legion Co.C
Searight, Enoch SC Lt.Arty. Beauregard's Co.
Searight, James J. GA 52nd Inf. Co.A
Searight, J.H. SC 1st St.Troops Co.C
Searight, J.N. MS 5th Cav. Co.I
Searight, J.N. SC 1st St.Troops Co.F
Searight, Robert MS Inf. Comfort's Co.
Searing, R.B. LA Mil.Conf.Guards Regt. Co.A
Searing, T.F. LA Mil.Conf.Guards Regt. Co.H
Searl, Samuel MD 1st Inf. Co.G
Searle, E.B. TX 1st Inf. Co.C Sgt.
Searles, Chesley NC 47th Inf. Co.E
Searles, C.M. AL 25th Inf. Co.H
Searles, E. GA 7th Inf. Co.F
Searles, George VA 54th Mil. Co.C,D
Searles, James TN 47th Inf. Co.E
Searles, James M. LA Miles' Legion Co.G 1st Lt.
Searles, Jesse H. NC 2nd Inf. Co.K
Searles, J.F. TX Inf. Rutherford's Co. 3rd Lt.
Searles, John AR 20th Inf. Co.K
Searles, Major NC 5th Inf. Co.D
Searles, Marshall NC 61st Inf. Co.B
Searles, Richard VA 54th Mil. Co.C,D
Searles, R.P. TX 12th Inf. Co.B Sgt.
Searles, S. VA 21st Inf. Co.F
Searles, T.C. GA Inf. 9th Bn. Co.E
Searles, Thomas C. GA 37th Inf. Co.H
Searles, William A. NC 1st Arty. (10th St.Troops) Co.B
Searlls, G. KY 3rd Mtd.Inf. 1st Co.F
Searlls, George KY Lt.Arty. Cobb's Co. Sgt.
Searlor, A.B. AL 55th Vol. Co.C
Searls, E.A. SC 5th Inf. Co.F
Searls, Ellington TX 32nd Cav. Co.D
Searls, John H. AR 33rd Inf. Co.B
Searls, R. VA 54th Mil. Co.C,D
Searls, V.A. TX 32nd Cav. Co.D
Searly, W.N. MS 72nd Regt. Co.E
Searry, James TN 10th Inf. Co.H
Sears, --- AL 3rd Bn.Res. Co.H
Sears, A.B. TX 13th Vol. 2nd Co.D Sgt.
Sears, Abram KY 2nd Bn.Mtd.Rifles Co.B
Sears, A.H. AL 53rd (Part.Rangers) Co.C Sgt.
Sears, Albert MS 12th Cav. Co.A
Sears, Alexander NC 67th Inf. Co.H
Sears, A.N. TN 19th (Biffle's) Cav. Co.E
Sears, Andrew MO 1st Inf. 2nd Co.A
Sears, Andrew B. TX 37th Cav. Co.H
Sears, A.S. GA 27th Inf. Co.D 1st Sgt.
Sears, A.T. GA 46th Inf. Co.F
Sears, Augustus MO Searcy's Bn.S.S. Co.E
Sears, A.W. TX 15th Inf. Co.I Capt.
Sears, Barb NC 35th Inf. Co.D
Sears, Barry H. LA 19th Inf. Co.K 2nd Lt.
Sears, Belfield J. NC 56th Inf. Co.C
Sears, B.G. NC 6th Sr.Res. Co.K
Sears, Burrel GA 50th Inf. Co.C
Sears, Caswell J. AL 3rd Inf. Co.I Cpl.
Sears, Charles AL 23rd Inf. Co.C
Sears, Charles E. VA 5th Cav. Co.A
Sears, Charles E. VA 34th Inf. Co.A
Sears, Charles E. 7th Conf.Cav. 2nd Co.I
Sears, Claudius W. Gen. & Staff Brig.Gen.
Sears, Clem NC 54th Inf. Co.A
Sears, C.O. AL 45th Inf. Co.G,K Sgt.

Sears, C.W. MS 17th Inf. Co.G Capt.
Sears, C.W. MS 46th Inf. Col.
Sears, D. SC Inf. Hampton Legion Co.H
Sears, David LA 12th Inf. Co.K
Sears, Dewitt VA Lt.Arty. R.M. Anderson's Co.
Sears, E. GA St.Res.
Sears, E. NC 47th Inf.
Sears, E.A. TX Cav. Bourland's Regt. Co.H
Sears, E.G. TN 50th Inf. Co.A
Sears, E.H. AL 34th Inf. Co.A
Sears, Eli MO 5th Cav. Co.K
Sears, Elias GA 63rd Inf. Co.K
Sears, Eli T. AL Inf. 1st Regt. Co.K Sgt.
Sears, Franklin MO 6th Cav. Co.F
Sears, Gallenus VA 12th Cav. Co.G
Sears, George E. AR Cav. Anderson's Unatt.Bn.
    Co.C Jr.2nd Lt.
Sears, George Pinckney SC 4th Inf. Co.K
Sears, George R. TX 3rd Cav. Co.E
Sears, George W. AL 3rd Cav. Co.H
Sears, George W. GA 65th Inf. Co.C
Sears, George W. MO 5th Inf. Co.B
Sears, George W. NC 6th Inf. Co.I Music.
Sears, George W. NC 35th Inf. Co.D Music.
Sears, G.P. SC 25th Inf. Co.H
Sears, H. GA 4th (Clinch's) Cav. Co.E
Sears, H. GA St.Res.
Sears, H. MO Inf. 1st Regt.St.Guard Co.G
Sears, Hardy MO St.Guard
Sears, Harmon NC 6th Inf. Co.I 1st Sgt.
Sears, H.C. TX 9th Cav. Co.C
Sears, H.E. GA 30th Inf. Co.G
Sears, Henry MO 6th Cav. Co.F
Sears, Henry L. VA 34th Inf. Co.A Cpl.
Sears, Henry M. AR 3rd Cav. Co.K,B
Sears, Henry M. TN 23rd Inf. 1st Co.A, Co.B
Sears, H.M. TN 19th (Biffle's) Cav. Co.E 2nd
    Lt.
Sears, Henry S. VA 21st Mil. Co.D
Sears, Henry T. VA 26th Inf. 2nd Co.B
Sears, Hiram GA 50th Inf. Co.G
Sears, Hiram TN Lt.Arty. Baxter's Co. Sgt.
Sears, Isaac M. TX 13th Vol. 1st Co.F
Sears, J. TX Cav. Bourland's Regt. Co.H
Sears, J. VA 12th Cav. Co.G
Sears, J.A. TX 13th Vol. 2nd Co.D
Sears, James GA 50th Inf. Co.G
Sears, James C. NC Unassign.Conscr.
Sears, James E. TX 6th Cav. Co.G 2nd Lt.
Sears, James P. NC 47th Inf. Co.H
Sears, James W. TX 31st Cav. Co.G Cpl.
Sears, Jep. F. AR Inf. Hardy's Regt. Co.D
Sears, J.H. TX 30th Cav. Surg.
Sears, J.H. TX Cav. Bone's Co.
Sears, J.H. TX Cav. Terry's Regt. Co.I
Sears, J.H. Gen. & Staff Surg.
Sears, J.L. TN 63rd Inf. Co.H
Sears, J.M. AL Mil. 2nd Regt.Vol. Co.C Cpl.
Sears, J.M. TX 13th Vol. 2nd Co.D
Sears, J.N. SC Palmetto S.S. Co.L
Sears, John GA 4th (Clinch's) Cav. Co.I Cpl.
Sears, John GA Cav. 20th Bn. Co.G
Sears, John GA Cav. 21st Bn. Co.D
Sears, John GA 43rd Inf. Co.K Cpl.
Sears, John KY 2nd (Woodward's) Cav. Co.C
Sears, John TN 11th Inf. Co.K
Sears, John VA 7th Inf. Asst.Surg.

Sears, John VA 21st Mil. Co.E
Sears, John Brush Bn.
Sears, John C. VA 26th Inf. 2nd Co.B
Sears, John H. LA 9th Inf. Co.D
Sears, John H. TN 44th (Cons.) Inf. Co.I
Sears, John H. VA 2nd Cav. Co.C
Sears, John H. VA 24th Cav. Co.D 1st Lt.
Sears, John H. VA Cav. 40th Bn. Co.D 1st Lt.
Sears, John Henry VA 21st Mil. Co.E
    Asst.Surg.
Sears, John M. TX 31st Cav. Co.G
Sears, John R. VA 26th Inf. 2nd Co.B
Sears, John W. AL Jeff Davis Arty. Surg.
Sears, John W. GA 2nd Cav. Co.G
Sears, John W. VA Cav. 40th Bn. Co.C
Sears, John W. VA 39th Inf. Co.B,K
Sears, John W. Gen. & Staff Surg.
Sears, Joseph MO 6th Cav. Co.F
Sears, Joseph TX Inf. 1st Bn. Co.B
Sears, Joseph H. NC 17th Inf. (2nd Org.) Co.C
Sears, Joseph M. TN Lt.Arty. Baxter's Co.
Sears, Joseph Newton SC 4th Inf. Co.K
Sears, Joseph Presbry MO 5th Inf. Co.B
Sears, J.T. GA 43rd Inf. Co.F Cpl.
Sears, J.T. TN 2nd (Walker's) Inf. Co.G
Sears, J.T. VA 26th Inf. 2nd Co.B
Sears, J.W. GA 66th Inf. Co.H
Sears, L. VA Lt.Arty. Griffin's Co.
Sears, L.A. MO 3rd Inf. Co.F
Sears, Lewis MO Priests' Regt.
Sears, L.L. VA Lt.Arty. R.M. Anderson's Co.
Sears, Luke C. AR 24th Inf. Co.F
Sears, M. GA 6th Res. Co.I
Sears, M. 1st Conf.Cav. 2nd Co.A Ch.Bugler
Sears, Marion GA 50th Inf. Co.C
Sears, Marion MO Cav. 21st Regt.
Sears, Mathew GA 1st (Symons') Res. Co.H
Sears, Monroe KY 4th Mtd.Inf. Co.G,I
Sears, N. GA 7th Cav. Co.B
Sears, N.A. MO 3rd Inf. Co.F
Sears, Neadham GA Cav. 21st Bn. Co.C Cpl.
Sears, Newton VA 49th Inf. Co.C
Sears, O.H. Gen. & Staff Chap.
Sears, Perry W. MO 5th Inf. Co.B
Sears, Pres MO 5th Inf. Co.B
Sears, R. LA 3rd (Harrison's) Cav. Co.C
Sears, R.E. AL 45th Inf. Co.G
Sears, Richard LA 8th Inf. Co.G
Sears, Richard C. VA 26th Inf. 2nd Co.B
Sears, Richard K. VA 26th Inf. 2nd Co.B
Sears, Robert TX 3rd Cav. Co.E
Sears, Robert S. VA Hvy.Arty. 20th Bn. Co.D
Sears, Robert T. MO 1st Cav. Co.D
Sears, Robert T. VA 24th Cav. Co.C Capt.
Sears, Robert T. VA Cav. 40th Bn. Co.C 1st Lt.
Sears, R.T.D. NC 6th Sr.Res. Co.E
Sears, Samuel D. VA 3rd Res. Co.I 2nd Lt.
Sears, S.B. NC 35th Inf. Co.B
Sears, S.M. TX 14th Inf. Co.D 3rd Lt.
Sears, Solomon GA 63rd Inf. Co.K
Sears, Squire M. TX Cav. Morgan's Regt. Co.B
Sears, Th. TX Cav. Bourland's Regt. Co.H
Sears, Thomas A. VA 11th Inf. Co.G
Sears, Thomas C. MS 22nd Inf. Co.F 1st Sgt.
Sears, Thomas C. MS 26th Inf. Co.F
Sears, Thomas D. NC 4th Cav. (59th St.Troops)
    Co.G

Sears, Thomas G. SC Lt.Arty. Beauregard's Co.
Sears, Thomas H. VA 21st Mil. Co.D,E
Sears, Thomas J. KY 14th Cav. Co.D,C
Sears, Thomas J. KY Morgan's Men Murphy's
    Co.
Sears, T.P. AL 33rd Inf. Co.B
Sears, V.F. GA 52nd Inf. Co.B
Sears, W.C. GA 24th Inf. Co.C 1st Lt.
Sears, W.F. GA 43rd Inf. Co.F
Sears, W.G. NC 1st Jr.Res. Co.D
Sears, W.H. GA Siege Arty. 28th Bn. Co.B
Sears, W.H. MS 5th Cav. Co.K
Sears, William AL 55th Vol. Co.B
Sears, William TX 18th Inf. Co.H
Sears, William VA Cav. 36th Bn. Co.B
Sears, William VA 108th Mil. Co.B
Sears, William A. VA 21st Mil. Co.D,E
Sears, William A. VA 26th Inf. 2nd Co.B
Sears, William H. AL 22nd Inf. Co.F
Sears, William H. LA 28th (Gray's) Inf. Co.B
Sears, William J. GA 5th Inf. Co.G Capt.
Sears, William J. NC 17th Inf. (2nd Org.) Co.B
Sears, William J. NC 35th Inf. Co.D
Sears, William M. GA Cav. 1st Bn.Res. Co.C
Sears, William P. VA 28th Inf. Co.I,E
Sears, William R. NC 4th Cav. (59th St.Troops)
    Co.G
Sears, William T. TN 23rd Inf. 1st Co.A Cpl.
Sears, William T.J. AL 46th Inf. Co.B Jr.2nd
    Lt.
Sears, W.J. GA Inf. 5th Bn. (St.Guards) Co.D
    Capt.
Sears, W.J. TN 50th Inf. Co.A
Sears, W.T. TX 9th Cav. Co.C
Sears, Z.H. MS 2nd Cav. Sgt.
Searsay, W.A. FL Cav. 5th Bn. Co.E
Searsbourgh, J.H. TN 17th Cav. Co.B
Searsey, James J. MO Inf. Clark's Regt. Co.C
    Adj.
Searsey, John W. AL Eufaula Lt.Arty.
Searsey, Joseph AL 32nd Inf. Co.I
Searson, B.C. SC 7th Cav. Co.B
Searson, B.C. SC 1st Mtd.Mil. Green's Co.
Searson, R.P. SC 2nd Cav. Co.B 1st Sgt.
Searson, R. Plato SC Cav.Bn. Hampton Legion
    Co.C Cpl.
Searson, Thomas VA 11th Inf. Co.E
Searson, Thomas E., Jr. SC 3rd Cav. Co.A
Searson, Z.A. SC 7th Cav. Co.B
Searsy, James T. GA 45th Inf. Co.D 2nd Lt.
Seary, J.A. TX 33rd Cav. Co.B
Seary, Josiah AR 14th Preston's Co.H
Seary, Josiah MO Cav. Preston's Bn. Co.H
Seary, Pat LA Miles' Legion Co.F
Seary, Robert L. VA 2nd Arty. Co.E
Seary, Stephen LA Miles' Legion Co.F
Seary, William W. VA 2nd Arty. Co.E
Seas, A.N. SC 3rd Inf. Co.C
Seas, D.E. SC 1st Arty. Co.D
Seas, G.L. SC 3rd Inf. Co.C,A
Seascy, I.W. LA 27th Inf. Co.F
Sease, A. SC 3rd Cav. Co.D
Sease, Aca M. SC 13th Inf. Co.H Sgt.
Sease, A.N. SC Lt.Arty. 3rd (Palmetto) Bn. Co.F
Sease, A.N. SC 13th Inf. Co.H
Sease, C.W. SC 3rd Cav. Co.F
Sease, D.J. SC 15th Inf. Co.K Cpl.

Sease, Elias S. SC 5th Cav. Co.F
Sease, F.M. SC 15th Inf. Co.C
Sease, G. GA 12th (Wright's) Cav. (St.Guards) Brannen's Co.
Sease, G. SC 16th & 24th (Cons.) Inf. Co.I
Sease, George SC 24th Inf. Co.D
Sease, George W. GA 12th (Wright's) Cav. (St.Guards) Surg.
Sease, Jacob A. SC 14th Inf. Co.D
Sease, J.C. SC 1st Arty. Co.I
Sease, J.D. SC 1st (Hagood's) Inf. 1st Co.F, 2nd Co.G
Sease, John C. SC 13th Inf. Co.H Capt.
Sease, John L. SC Lt.Arty. Walter's Co. (Washington Arty.)
Sease, J. Wiley MS 30th Inf. Co.G
Sease, Miles SC 1st (Hagood's) Inf. 2nd Co.E
Sease, Miles SC 17th Inf. Co.G
Sease, M.L. SC 1st (Hagood's) Inf. 1st Co.K, 2nd Co.A Sgt.
Sease, Richard SC 20th Inf. Co.K Sgt.
Sease, Samuel SC 5th Res. Co.K Cpl.
Sease, Samuel SC 6th Inf. Co.E
Sease, W.E. SC 1st (Hagood's) Inf. 1st Co.K, 2nd Co.A
Sease, William D. SC Part.Rangers Kirk's Co.
Seastrank, L. MS St.Cav. 3rd Bn. (Cooper's) 1st Co.A
Seastrunk, H.T. TX 17th Cons.Dismtd.Cav. Co.C Cpl.
Seastrunk, James W. TX 17th Cav. Co.C Sgt.
Seastrunk, J.O. TX Cav. Border's Regt. Co.C
Seastrunk, Toler TX 17th Cav. Co.C
Seastrunk, W.E. MS 3rd Inf. Co.K Sgt.
Seastrunk, William MS St.Cav. 3rd Bn. (Cooper's) Little's Co.
Seastrunk, William W. MS 3rd Inf. Co.K
Seat, --- AL 4th (Russell's) Cav. Co.L 2nd Lt.
Seat, Abner NC 33rd Inf. Co.I Cpl.
Seat, Algeirn TN 30th Inf. Co.D
Seat, B.B. TX 5th Cav. Co.F Capt.
Seat, Charles TN 30th Inf. Co.D
Seat, Eli TN 38th Inf. 2nd Co.H
Seat, G.B. TN 14th (Neely's) Cav. Co.B
Seat, G.W. AR 7th Inf. Co.B
Seat, G.W. MO Cav. Coffee's Regt. Co.C
Seat, Hiram H. TN 7th Inf. Co.D
Seat, H.S. GA 13th Inf. Co.A
Seat, James GA 44th Inf. Co.H
Seat, James L. TN 7th Inf. Co.K
Seat, J.W. SC 15th Inf. Co.A
Seat, J.M. TN 38th Inf. 2nd Co.H Sgt.
Seat, John TN 4th (McLemore's) Cav. Co.G
Seat, John TN 7th Inf. Co.D
Seat, John TN 30th Inf. Co.D
Seat, John M. TN 44th (Cons.) Inf. Co.E
Seat, Joseph M. 3rd Conf.Eng.Troops Co.B
Seat, L.C. NC 18th Inf. Co.K
Seat, L.M. TN 37th Inf. Co.E
Seat, Ned T. NC 9th Bn.S.S. Co.A
Seat, N.T. NC 21st Inf. Co.B
Seat, R.B. KY 12th Cav. Co.F
Seat, R.B. TN 1st (Carter's) Cav.
Seat, Robert KY 12th Cav. Co.A
Seat, Robert TN 16th Inf. Co.H
Seat, Robert TN 38th Inf. 2nd Co.H
Seat, Robert A. VA 3rd Inf. 2nd Co.K

Seat, Robert B. TN 3rd (Forrest's) Cav.
Seat, R.P. TN 20th Inf. Co.K
Seat, S.B. TN Lt.Arty. Monsarrat's Co.
Seat, Thomas TN 30th Inf. Co.D
Seat, William TN 8th (Smith's) Cav.
Seat, William P. NC 33rd Inf. Co.I
Seat, William R. VA 3rd Cav. Co.C
Seat, Wood TN 8th (Smith's) Cav. Co.K
Seatch, D.A. GA 41st Inf. Co.C
Seate, C.M. MO 9th Bn.S.S. Co.A
Seater, R.Y. MS 1st (King's) Inf. (St.Troops) Co.F
Seaterick, Theodore LA 21st (Patton's) Inf. Co.H Cpl.
Seathmann, George MS 48th Inf. Co.E
Seaton, --- LA 3rd Inf. Co.E
Seaton, A.F. TN 44th Inf. Co.I
Seaton, Andrew F. TN 44th (Cons.) Inf. Co.A
Seaton, A.T. NC 17th Inf. (1st Org.) Co.G
Seaton, Barton TN 61st Mtd.Inf. Co.D
Seaton, Ben F. VA Mil. Scott Cty.
Seaton, Benjamin M. TX 10th Inf. Co.G
Seaton, Bennett H. AR Cav. Wright's Regt. Co.G
Seaton, B.H. AR 1st (Monroe's) Cav. Co.H
Seaton, C. MO 5th Cav. Co.D
Seaton, E.D. MS Lt.Arty. 14th Bn. Co.A
Seaton, Edward A. LA 10th Inf. Co.K 1st Lt.
Seaton, Elijah B. AL 49th Inf. Co.D
Seaton, Elisha TN Inf. 22nd Bn. Co.F
Seaton, Fleming W. VA 1st Arty. Co.I Cpl.
Seaton, Fleming W. VA Lt.Arty. 38th Bn. Co.B
Seaton, F.M. AR Mil. Desha Cty.Bn.
Seaton, F.M. MS 18th Cav. Co.E
Seaton, George MS 1st Cav. Co.C
Seaton, George MS 3rd Cav. Co.D
Seaton, Green TN 5th Inf. 2nd Co.B
Seaton, J. GA 25th Inf. Co.I
Seaton, J. TN 15th (Cons.) Cav. Co.D,E
Seaton, Jacob Marion TN 61st Mtd.Inf. Co.D
Seaton, James AL 50th Inf. Co.C
Seaton, James TX Cav. Giddings' Bn. Onins' Co.
Seaton, James C. TN 54th Inf. Co.C
Seaton, James H. VA 1st Cav. Co.H
Seaton, James M. TX 14th Cav. Co.B
Seaton, J.B. TN 5th Inf. 2nd Co.B Cpl.
Seaton, J.J. MS 1st Cav. Co.C
Seaton, John TN 48th (Nixon's) Inf. Co.K
Seaton, John TN 54th Inf. Co.E
Seaton, John TX Inf. 2nd St.Troops Co.C
Seaton, John W. TN 17th Inf. Co.D
Seaton, Joseph M. AL 49th Inf. Co.D
Seaton, J.T. TN 17th Inf. Co.D
Seaton, J.W. Forrest's Scouts T.N. Kizer's Co.,CSA
Seaton, Mark L. TN 61st Mtd.Inf. Co.D Cpl.
Seaton, M.V. VA Lt.Arty. Ellett's Co.
Seaton, M.V. VA 2nd Inf.Loc.Def. Co.D
Seaton, M.V. VA Inf. 6th Bn.Loc.Def. Co.A
Seaton, Nicholas AR 17th (Lemoyne's) Inf. Co.E
Seaton, Nicholas AR 21st Inf. Co.I
Seaton, Peter P. MS 2nd Inf. (A. of 10,000) Co.H
Seaton, Pinckney P. TN 5th (McKenzie's) Cav. Co.K
Seaton, Pleasant P. NC Walker's Bn. Thomas' Legion Co.F

Seaton, P.P. MS 28th Cav. Co.B
Seaton, R.N. TN 61st Mtd.Inf. Co.D Sgt.
Seaton, Robert V. TX 6th Cav. Co.K Cpl.
Seaton, S.B. TN 17th Inf. Co.D Sgt.
Seaton, S.N. MS Inf. 4th St.Troops Co.C
Seaton, Taliaferro H. Gen. & Staff, Ord.Dept.
Seaton, Thomas LA Lt.Arty. Fenner's Btty.
Seaton, Thomas LA Inf. 1st Sp.Bn. (Rightor's) Co.A
Seaton, W.A. Jackson's Co.,CSA
Seaton, W.B. MS Lt.Arty. 14th Bn. Co.A
Seaton, William MS 1st (Patton's) Inf. Co.A
Seaton, William MS 9th Inf. Co.G
Seaton, William MS 10th Inf. New Co.B
Seaton, William TN 17th Inf. Co.D
Seaton, William TN 61st Mtd.Inf. Co.D Sgt.
Seaton, William VA 6th Cav. Co.A
Seaton, William B. NC Inf. Thomas Legion Co.I
Seaton, William C. TN 54th Inf. Co.C
Seaton, William D. KY 10th Cav. Co.A
Seaton, William E. VA Courtney Arty. Cpl.
Seaton, William R. TN 48th (Nixon's) Inf. Co.E
Seaton, William R. TN 54th Inf. Dooley's Co.
Seaton, W.J. MS 1st Cav. Co.C
Seaton, W.M. TN 21st & 22nd (Cons.) Cav. Co.E
Seaton, W.P. LA 5th Inf. Co.H
Seaton, W.R. TN Inf. Sowell's Detach.
Seaton, W.S. VA Lt.Arty. 38th Bn. Co.B
Seaton, W.W. TN 21st (Wilson's) Cav. Co.H
Seaton, W.Y. TN 17th Inf. Co.D
Seatons, Elisha K. TN 4th (Murray's) Cav. Co.K
Seator, William TN 55th (Brown's) Inf. Co.E
Seats, A. SC 2nd Cav. Co.D
Seats, Ely TN Inf. 3rd Cons.Regt. Co.B
Seats, I. TN Inf. 4th Cons.Regt. Co.K
Seats, J. TN 42nd Inf. Co.C
Seats, J. 4th Conf.Inf. Co.H
Seats, J.G. AL 14th Inf. Co.E
Seats, J.M. GA 44th Inf. Co.H
Seats, John GA 20th Inf. Co.B
Seats, John Q. NC 46th Inf. Co.K
Seats, John T. GA 31st Inf. Co.D
Seats, John W. GA 1st (Ramsey's) Inf. Co.B
Seats, John W. GA 20th Inf. Co.B
Seats, John W. GA 59th Inf. Co.K
Seats, Joshua MO 1st & 4th Cons.Inf. Co.I
Seats, Joshua MO 4th Inf. Co.D
Seats, R.P. KY 7th Cav. Co.B
Seats, Stephen J. AL 37th Inf. Co.B
Seats, T. TN 42nd Inf. Co.C
Seats, T. 4th Conf.Inf. Co.H
Seats, Thomas GA 20th Inf. Co.B
Seats, W. GA 5th Inf. Co.L
Seats, Warren MO 16th Inf. Co.E
Seats, W.B. GA 3rd Cav. Co.A
Seats, W.B. GA 5th Inf. (St.Guards) Johnston's Co.
Seats, W.C. GA 46th Inf. Co.E 1st Sgt.
Seats, William MO 15th Cav. Co.C
Seats, William MO 16th Inf. Co.E
Seats, William NC 27th Inf. Co.B
Seats, William B. GA 20th Inf. Co.B
Seats, Willis C. GA Inf. 2nd Bn. Co.A
Seats, W.P. TN 42nd Inf. Co.D
Seats, W.W. TN 18th Inf. Co.C
Seats, W.W. TN 38th Inf. Co.I

Seatton, J.J. VA Cav. Mosby's Regt. (Part.Rangers) Co.E

524

Seatton, J.J. VA Cav. Mosby's Regt. (Part. Rangers) Co.E

Seaux, Eugene LA Mil. 1st Native Guards

Seaux, Isidore LA Mil. 1st Native Guards

Seav, S.S. AL 5th Bn.Vol.

Seaver, Benjamin FL 3rd Inf. Co.G

Seaver, E. FL 1st (Res.) Inf. Co.E

Seaver, Fulton TN 12th Cav. Co.A

Seaver, G.A. LA Mil.Conf.Guards Regt. Co.D Cpl.

Seaver, John H. VA 48th Inf. Co.C

Seaver, John R. LA 7th Inf. Co.E

Seaver, Joseph F. VA 46th Mil. Co.A

Seaver, Nathan TN 10th Inf. Co.A

Seaver, Thomas TN 37th Inf. Co.C

Seaver, William FL 5th Inf. Co.A

Seavers, Albert C. VA 6th Bn.Res. Co.A

Seavers, A.S. TN 12th Inf. Co.I

Seavers, Dickason TN Cav. 12th Bn. (Day's) Co.A

Seavers, Henry KY 2nd Bn.Mtd.Rifles Co.C

Seavers, Henry C. NC 4th Inf. Co.K

Seavers, James H. TN 6th Inf. Co.E

Seavers, J.N. FL 10th Inf. Co.A

Seavert, Jackson NC 18th Inf. Co.G

Seavey, Eb. E. MS Lt.Arty. (Brookhaven Lt.Arty.) Hoskins' Btty. QMSgt.

Seavey, James H. GA 3rd Bn. (St.Guards) Co.B Sgt.

Seavey, Willard H. MS 18th Inf. Co.H 2nd Lt.

Seavey, William GA 1st Cav. Co.A

Seavey, W.S. AR 8th Inf. Co.H

Seavies, Thomas TX 3rd Cav. Co.B

Seavil, T.F. VA Mil. Greene Cty.

Seavy, C.C. GA 19th Inf. Co.D 1st Lt.

Seavy, William LA Washington Arty.Bn. Co.5,6 2nd Lt.

Seavy, W.S.E. GA Inf. (Wright Loc.Guards) Holmes' Co.

Seaward, Joseph E. VA 6th Inf. Co.I Sgt.

Seaward, Mathew AR 24th Inf. Co.F

Seaward, Mathew AR Inf. Hardy's Regt. Co.D

Seaward, T.H. TX 7th Cav. Co.C

Seaweight, John VA 3rd Bn. Valley Res. Co.A Lt.

Seawell, B.S. AL Mil. 2nd Regt.Vol. Co.E

Seawell, B.S. AL 3rd Inf. Co.A

Seawell, B.W. LA Inf.Crescent Regt. Co.G Sgt.

Seawell, C.H. AL 8th Inf. Co.A 2nd Lt.

Seawell, Charles H. AL 4th Inf. Co.G

Seawell, Eli P. NC 26th Inf. Co.H

Seawell, F.H. NC 1st Arty. (10th St.Troops) Co.A AASurg.

Seawell, F.M. AR 21st Mil. Co.E

Seawell, James H. NC 3rd Cav. (41st St.Troops) Co.I

Seawell, James M. VA 3rd Cav. Co.B

Seawell, James T. MO Lt.Arty. 1st Field Btty.

Seawell, Jesse P. NC 26th Inf. Co.H

Seawell, J.J. AL 51st (Part.Rangers) Co.I Capt.

Seawell, John H. VA 5th Cav. Co.A Sgt.Maj.

Seawell, Joseph A. VA 26th Inf. Co.H

Seawell, Joseph H. AL 24th Inf. Co.D 2nd Lt.

Seawell, Joseph H. AL 61st Inf. AQM

Seawell, Jos. H. Gen. & Staff, QM Dept. Capt.,AQM

Seawell, Joseph P. NC 26th Inf. Co.H

Seawell, Leonard H. AL 4th Inf. Co.G

Seawell, M. Boswell VA 21st Mil. Co.C

Seawell, S.T. LA 16th Inf. Co.G 1st Lt.

Seawell, S.T. TX Cav. Ragsdale's Bn. Co.A Capt.

Seawell, S.W. NC 51st Mil. Maj.

Seawell, Virgil N. NC 18th Inf. Co.E

Seawell, Watt W. VA 26th Inf. Co.F

Seawell, W.B. AL Seawell's Btty. (Mohawk Arty.) Capt.

Seawell, W.B. LA 12th Lt.Arty. Capt.

Seawell, William A. AL 8th Inf. Co.H Sgt.

Seawell, William B. AL 13th Inf. Co.G 1st Lt.

Seawell, William F. VA 24th Cav. Co.D

Seawell, William F. VA Cav. 40th Bn. Co.D

Seawell, William F. VA 26th Inf. Co.A

Seawell, William H. VA 21st Mil. Lt.Col.

Seawell, William H. VA 21st Mil. Co.C

Seawell, Woodward AL 60th Inf. Co.E

Seawell, W.Q. AR 10th Inf. Co.E

Seaword, R.H. VA 13th Cav. Co.B

Seawright, A. 20th Conf.Cav. Co.C

Seawright, A.G. SC 1st (Hagood's) Inf. 1st Co.B

Seawright, A.G. SC 20th Inf. Co.D

Seawright, Alexander TN 5th Inf. 1st Co.C

Seawright, A.T. MS 32nd Inf. Co.B

Seawright, A.W. GA Inf. 17th Bn. (St.Guards) Stocks' Co. Sgt.

Seawright, E.J. FL 1st (Res.) Inf. Co.C Sgt.

Seawright, E.J. GA Inf. 25th Bn. (Prov.Guard) Co.F

Seawright, George A. AL 17th Inf. Co.K Sgt.

Seawright, Isaac Cowan SC 19th Inf. Co.I Cpl.

Seawright, James L. TN 7th (Duckworth's) Cav. Co.G

Seawright, James S. SC 20th Inf. Co.E

Seawright, J.B. SC 2nd Cav. Co.G

Seawright, J.B. SC 7th Inf. 1st Co.B

Seawright, J.H. SC 1st Cav. Co.I

Seawright, J.H. SC 2nd Inf. Co.E

Seawright, John SC 5th Res. Co.A Cpl.

Seawright, John H. SC 20th Inf. Co.E

Seawright, John H. TX 15th Cav. Co.F,B 2nd Lt.

Seawright, John L. TN 7th (Duckworth's) Cav. Co.G

Seawright, John N. SC 4th Bn.Res. Co.B 1st Lt.

Seawright, John R. AL 17th Inf. Co.K

Seawright, R.M. MS 38th Cav. Co.G

Seawright, R.W. SC 2nd Cav. Co.G Cpl.

Seawright, R.W. SC 7th Inf. 1st Co.B

Seawright, S. SC Cav. 19th Bn. Co.B

Seawright, S. SC 20th Inf. Co.M

Seawright, William MS 38th Cav. Co.G Cpl.

Seawright, William MS Inf. Comfort's Co.

Seawright, William SC 1st (Orr's) Rifles Co.G

Seawright, William SC 1st St.Troops Co.F

Seawright, William SC 5th Res. Co.A

Seawright, William TN 7th (Duckworth's) Cav. Co.G

Seawright, William L. GA Lt.Arty. Ritter's Co.

Seawright, William M. TX 10th Inf. Co.B Sgt.

Seawright, William R. GA 1st Cav. Co.D Capt.

Seawright, W.K. GA Cav. 1st Regt. Co.D Capt.

Seawright, W.L. GA Inf. 17th Bn. (St.Guards) Stocks' Co.

Seawright, W.M. VA Cav. 37th Bn. Co.B

Seawright, W.W. SC 1st St.Troops Co.A

Seay, --- VA 24th Cav. Lt.

Seay, --- Hosp.Stew.

Seay, A.B. SC 5th Inf. 1st Co.C, 2nd Co.K

Seay, A.B. SC Inf. Holcombe Legion Co.C

Seay, A.B. TX 4th Inf. Co.H

Seay, A.B. VA Cav. Mosby's Regt. (Part. Rangers) Lt.

Seay, Abraham VA Inf. 1st Bn. Co.B

Seay, Adam AL 57th Inf. Co.F

Seay, Adam P. VA Lt.Arty. Ancell's Co.

Seay, Adam P. VA Lt.Arty. Snead's Co.

Seay, A.G. AL 42nd Inf. Co.K

Seay, A.G. VA 1st Inf. Co.C

Seay, A.J. VA Lt.Arty. W.P. Carter's Co.

Seay, Albert VA Hvy.Arty. 19th Bn. Co.D

Seay, Albert W. AL 12th Inf. Co.K

Seay, Alexander B. VA 1st Arty. Co.D

Seay, Alexander R. VA 19th Inf. Co.D

Seay, Alfred SC 7th Res. Co.M

Seay, Alfred VA 46th Inf. Co.H

Seay, Alfred M. VA 2nd Cav. Co.E

Seay, Alfred M. VA 51st Inf. Co.G

Seay, Allen B. GA Arty. 9th Bn. Co.A,E

Seay, A.M. GA 39th Inf. Co.C

Seay, Andrew VA Hvy.Arty. Wright's Co.

Seay, Andrew J. VA Hvy.Arty. 18th Bn. Co.D

Seay, Andrew J. VA 14th Inf. Co.C

Seay, Andrew J. VA 20th Inf. Co.E

Seay, A.P. VA 5th Cav. Co.E

Seay, Austin GA Cherokee Legion (St.Guards) Co.D

Seay, Austin M. MS Inf. 2nd Bn. Co.C

Seay, Austin M. MS 48th Inf. Co.C

Seay, B.A. VA Hvy.Arty. 18th Bn. Co.C

Seay, Barnet GA 7th Inf. (St.Guards) Co.K Cpl.

Seay, Benjamin AL 45th Inf. Co.C

Seay, Benjamin NC 25th Inf. Co.C

Seay, Benjamin NC 62nd Inf. Co.A

Seay, Benjamin VA 20th Inf. Co.F

Seay, Benjamin VA 57th Inf. Co.A

Seay, Benjamin F. AL Vol. Lee, Jr.'s Co.

Seay, Bernard A. VA 14th Inf. Co.A Cpl.

Seay, B.H. MS Cav. 3rd Bn.Res. Co.C

Seay, Bluford VA 51st Inf. Co.E

Seay, Byrd H. VA 42nd Inf. Co.G

Seay, C. SC 3rd Inf. Co.K

Seay, C.C. Gen. & Staff Hosp.Stew.

Seay, C.H. VA Inf. 26th Bn. Co.E

Seay, Charles J. TN 4th Inf. Co.A

Seay, Charles J. TN 44th (Cons.) Inf. Adj.

Seay, Charles J. TN 55th (McKoin's) Inf. Co.F 1st Lt.

Seay, Charles J. VA 19th Inf. Co.I

Seay, Charles S. VA 14th Inf. Co.A

Seay, Charles S. VA Inf. 25th Bn. Co.A

Seay, C.J. TN 7th (Duckworth's) Cav. Co.B

Seay, C.J. TN Cav. Cox's Bn. Maj.

Seay, Collen C. Hosp.Stew.

Seay, Columbus AR 34th Inf. Co.B

Seay, C.T. VA 10th Cav. Co.K

Seay, Daniel NC 25th Inf. Co.C

Seay, Daniel NC Inf. Thomas Legion Co.E

Seay, Daniel VA Inf. 1st Bn. Co.E

Seay, Daniel B. VA 51st Inf. Co.E

Seay, Daniel E. SC 5th Cav. Co.F

Seay, Daniel E. SC Cav. 14th Bn. Co.C

Seay, Daniel E. SC 20th Inf. Co.K
Seay, Daniel R. AR 9th Inf. Co.D Capt.
Seay, David W. GA 46th Inf. Co.I
Seay, D.B. VA 3rd Res. Co.H
Seay, Dempsey GA 52nd Inf. Co.I
Seay, Dorsey H. GA 2nd Inf. Co.F
Seay, D.P. VA 28th Inf. Co.F
Seay, E.B. TX 2nd Inf. Co.I
Seay, Efford GA 21st Inf. New Co.E Cpl.
Seay, Efford NC Inf. 2nd Bn. Co.D Cpl.
Seay, Fleming P. VA 14th Inf. Co.C
Seay, Franklin SC 13th Inf. Co.F
Seay, Garrett W. TX 6th Inf. Co.F Sgt.
Seay, George A. GA Arty. 9th Bn. Co.E
Seay, George B. VA 18th Inf. Co.G Sgt.
Seay, George E. AR 2nd Mtd.Rifles Co.K
Seay, George E. TN 22nd (Barteau's) Cav. Co.E
    1st Lt.
Seay, George E. TN 2nd (Robison's) Inf. Co.H
Seay, George L. VA 21st Cav. Co.C
Seay, George P. VA 24th Cav. Co.G
Seay, George P. VA Inf. 25th Bn. Co.C
Seay, George R. TX 5th Cav. Co.I
Seay, George W. TN 6th (Wheeler's) Cav. Co.E
Seay, George W. VA 23rd Inf. Co.G
Seay, George W. VA 47th Inf. 2nd Co.K
Seay, George W. Sig.Corps,CSA
Seay, G.G. VA 2nd Cav. Co.C
Seay, Harley SC 1st Inf. Co.O Cpl.
Seay, Harley SC 2nd St.Troops Co.A 1st Lt.
Seay, Harley SC 20th Inf. Co.K 2nd Lt.
Seay, H.C. AL Inf. 1st Regt. Co.G
Seay, H.C. AL 45th Inf. Co.C
Seay, Henry AL 39th Inf. Co.I
Seay, Henry VA 2nd Cav. Co.H
Seay, Henry VA 13th Inf. Co.D
Seay, Henry D. NC 16th Inf. Co.L
Seay, Henry D. NC Inf. Thomas Legion Co.E
Seay, Herman L. VA 23rd Inf. Co.G
Seay, H.H. AL 2nd Cav. Co.D
Seay, Irving NC Inf. 2nd Bn. Co.D
Seay, Isaac VA Lt.Arty. 13th Bn. Co.C
Seay, Isaac VA 11th Inf. Co.H
Seay, Isaac N. KY 5th Mtd.Inf. Co.A
Seay, J. GA 63rd Inf. Co.I
Seay, J.A. TX 34th Cav. Co.B
Seay, Jackson GA 11th Cav. Co.E
Seay, Jacob VA Hvy.Arty. 19th Bn. Co.D
Seay, Jacob VA Hvy.Arty. Kyle's Co.
Seay, Jacob D. KY Cav. Buckner Guards
Seay, James AL 12th Inf.
Seay, James AR Inf. Cocke's Regt. Co.E
Seay, James GA 1st Inf. (St.Guards) Co.B
Seay, James GA 32nd Inf. Co.F Music.
Seay, James MS 6th Cav. Co.H Cpl.
Seay, James MS Inf. 2nd Bn. Co.C
Seay, James MS 48th Inf. Co.C
Seay, James NC 39th Inf. Co.K
Seay, James NC Inf. Thomas Legion 1st Co.A
Seay, James B. TX 16th Cav. Co.F
Seay, James B. VA 24th Inf. Co.H
Seay, James C. VA 19th Inf. Co.I
Seay, James F. VA Lt.Arty. Hardwicke's Co.
Seay, James F. VA 24th Inf. Co.H
Seay, James L. VA 13th Inf. Co.D
Seay, James L. VA 30th Inf. Co.I
Seay, James M. GA 11th Cav. Co.K

Seay, James M. SC 1st (Butler's) Inf. Co.A
Seay, James M. TN Inf. 3rd Cons.Regt. Co.H
Seay, James M. TN 19th Inf. Co.A Cpl.
Seay, James R. MS 14th Inf. Co.G
Seay, James T. VA Lt.Arty. Parker's Co.
Seay, J.B. GA 7th Inf. (St.Guards) Co.K
Seay, J.B. KY 3rd Mtd.Inf. Co.B
Seay, J.C. KY 7th Cav. Co.A
Seay, Jefferson NC 16th Inf. Co.L
Seay, Jefferson W. SC 7th Res. Co.M
Seay, Jesse E. VA 4th Inf. Co.D
Seay, J.F. TN Inf. 3rd Cons.Regt. Co.D 2nd Lt.
Seay, J.F. TN 4th Inf. Co.H 1st Sgt.
Seay, J.H. SC Inf. 1st (Charleston) Bn. Co.F
Seay, J.H. SC 5th Inf. 2nd Co.K
Seay, J.H. SC 7th Res. Co.L
Seay, J.H. SC 27th Inf. Co.C
Seay, J.H. VA 1st (Farinholt's) Res. Co.H
Seay, J. Hampden VA Lt.Arty. Lamkin's Co.
Seay, J.J. MS 12th Cav. Co.B
Seay, J.L. SC 7th Res. Co.L
Seay, J.L. SC 18th Inf. Co.K
Seay, J.L. VA Lt.Arty. 13th Bn. Co.C
Seay, J.L. VA Lt.Arty. R.M. Anderson's Co.
Seay, J.M. SC Inf. Holcombe Legion Co.C Sgt.
Seay, John AL 39th Inf. Co.I
Seay, John GA 3rd Cav. Co.E
Seay, John GA Inf. 3rd Bn. Co.B 1st Lt.
Seay, John GA 37th Inf. Co.A Capt.
Seay, John GA 52nd Inf. Co.D
Seay, John MS 8th Inf. Co.D
Seay, John MS 30th Inf. Co.I
Seay, John SC 1st (Hagood's) Inf. 2nd Co.D
Seay, John A. GA 2nd Inf. Co.K
Seay, John A. GA 36th (Broyles') Inf. Co.F
Seay, John B. GA 21st Inf. New Co.E
Seay, John B. NC Inf. 2nd Bn. Co.D
Seay, John C. SC 13th Inf. Co.K Cpl.
Seay, John F. VA Inf. 25th Bn. Co.E Sgt.
Seay, John G. VA 57th Inf. Co.A
Seay, John G. 1st Conf.Eng.Troops Co.G Artif.
Seay, John H. VA 30th Inf. Co.D
Seay, John J. AL 38th Inf. Co.F
Seay, John J. GA Cobb's Legion Co.C
Seay, John J. VA Lt.Arty. Lamkin's Co.
Seay, John K. SC 13th Inf. Co.E
Seay, John M. TN 50th (Cons.) Inf. Co.K
Seay, John P. TN 55th (McKoin's) Inf. Co.F
    Sgt.
Seay, John R. AL 7th Inf. Co.C
Seay, John R. AR Lt.Arty. Zimmerman's Btty.
Seay, John R. VA 20th Inf. Co.F
Seay, John R. VA 57th Inf. Co.A Sgt.
Seay, John Robert SC 9th Inf. Co.B Sgt.
Seay, John S. VA Hvy.Arty. 19th Bn. Co.D
Seay, Jno. W. VA Lt.Arty. R.M. Anderson's Co.
Seay, Joseph MS 28th Cav. Co.G
Seay, Joseph VA 1st Cav. Co.G
Seay, Joseph 4th Conf.Eng.Troops 2nd Lt.
Seay, Joseph A. VA 1st St.Res. Co.C
Seay, Jos. M. Gen. & Staff, QM Dept. Capt.
Seay, Josiah AR 8th Cav. Co.H
Seay, Josiah MO Cav. Fristoe's Regt. Co.H
Seay, Josiah VA 20th Inf. Co.F
Seay, J.R. KY 12th Cav. Co.A
Seay, J.R. KY 2nd Mtd.Inf. Co.A
Seay, J.R. MS 3rd Inf. Co.D

Seay, J. Robert SC 6th Inf. 2nd Co.C Sgt.
Seay, Junius H. VA 14th Inf. Co.A 1st Lt.
Seay, J.W. AL 45th Inf. Co.C
Seay, J.W. GA 9th Inf. (St.Guards) Co.H
Seay, J.W. KY 3rd Mtd.Inf. Co.B
Seay, L.P. GA 5th Res. Co.F
Seay, L.T. VA 1st Bn.Res. Co.A
Seay, Luther F. SC 13th Inf. Co.K
Seay, M. KY 2nd (Duke's) Cav. Co.D
Seay, M. VA 21st Inf. Co.F
Seay, M.A. MS 2nd St.Cav. Co.D
Seay, Marshall M. TX 36th Cav. Co.C
Seay, Mathew W. VA 57th Inf. Co.A Sgt.
Seay, Mat W. VA 20th Inf. Co.F
Seay, Meredith F. VA Lt.Arty. Snead's Co.
Seay, M.F. VA Hvy.Arty. Wright's Co.
Seay, Miles VA Hvy.Arty. Wright's Co.
Seay, M.J. VA Hvy.Arty. Wright's Co.
Seay, M.N. GA Cobb's Legion Co.K,G
Seay, Mountain SC 13th Inf. Co.K
Seay, Newton AR 10th Inf. Co.H 2nd Lt.
Seay, Osborne A. GA Cobb's Legion Co.B,G
Seay, Peter VA Lt.Arty. 13th Bn. Co.C
Seay, Peter TN 21st (Wilson's) Cav. Co.E
Seay, Philip G. VA 14th Inf. Co.C Jr.2nd Lt.
Seay, Presley TN 39th Mtd.Inf. Co.H
Seay, Pressley 3rd Conf.Cav. Co.F
Seay, Ransom GA 21st Inf. New Co.E
Seay, Ransom NC Inf. 2nd Bn. Co.D
Seay, Ransom T. GA Arty. 9th Bn. Co.A,E
Seay, R.B. SC Inf. 1st (Charleston) Bn. Co.G
Seay, R.B. SC 27th Inf. Co.K 2nd Lt.
Seay, R.D. VA Hvy.Arty. 18th Bn. Co.C
Seay, R.E. SC 13th Inf. Co.K
Seay, Reuben TX 22nd Inf. Co.K Sgt.
Seay, Reuben C. VA 20th Inf. Co.F 2nd Lt.
Seay, Reuben C. VA 57th Inf. Co.A 1st Lt.
Seay, Reuben F. GA Arty. 11th Bn. (Sumter
    Arty.) New Co.A, Co.C
Seay, Reuben F. GA 9th Inf. Co.A
Seay, Reubin AL 42nd Inf. Co.F
Seay, Rial B. SC 5th Inf. 1st Co.C Capt.
Seay, Richard A. TX 6th Cav. Co.I
Seay, Richard B. VA 11th Inf. Co.H
Seay, Richard B. VA 14th Inf. Co.C
Seay, Richard B. VA 18th Inf. Co.G 1st Sgt.
Seay, Richard D. VA 14th Inf. Co.A
Seay, Richard H. VA 23rd Inf. Co.B
Seay, R.L. VA 2nd Inf.Loc.Def. Co.F
Seay, R.L. VA Inf. 6th Bn.Loc.Def. Co.C
Seay, Robert VA Loc.Def. Bosher's Co.
Seay, Robert L. VA Inf. 25th Bn. Co.E
Seay, Robert M. KY 7th Mtd.Inf. Co.B Capt.
Seay, R.T. TX 7th Cav. Co.F
Seay, R.W. VA 3rd Res. Co.A
Seay, S.A. VA Averett's Bn.Res. 1st Lt.
Seay, Samuel, Jr. TN 1st (Feild's) Inf. Co.C
Seay, Samuel A. VA 12th Inf. Co.K
Seay, Samuel J. VA Lt.Arty. Huckstep's Co.
Seay, Samuel L. AR 32nd Inf. Co.B
Seay, Samuel R. KY 2nd Mtd.Inf. Co.A
Seay, Sanford G. GA 34th Inf. Co.F
Seay, Selden A. VA 1st (Farinholt's) Res. Co.H
    1st Lt.
Seay, Selden A. VA 14th Inf. Co.A Sgt.
Seay, S.F. VA 5th Cav. Co.E,G
Seay, S.G. GA 42nd Inf. Co.K

Seay, Sidney M. VA 14th Inf. Co.C
Seay, Silas M. VA Goochland Lt.Arty.
Seay, S.M. VA 5th Cav. Co.K
Seay, S.R. KY 2nd (Woodward's) Cav. Co.D
Seay, S.S. AL 26th (O'Neal's) Inf. Co.K 2nd Lt.
Seay, Starling NC 64th Inf. Co.I
Seay, T. MS 12th Cav. Co.B
Seay, T.H. TN 15th (Cons.) Cav. Co.G Sgt.
Seay, Thomas AR 6th Inf. Co.G 2nd Lt.
Seay, Thomas NC 16th Inf. Co.L
Seay, Thomas NC Inf. Thomas Legion Co.E
    Cpl.
Seay, Thomas VA 59th Inf. 3rd Co.E
Seay, Thomas A. VA Lt.Arty. Snead's Co.
Seay, Thomas B. GA 46th Inf. Co.I
Seay, Thomas G. TX 1st Inf. Co.G
Seay, Thomas H. GA Inf. 3rd Bn. Co.B
Seay, Thomas H. GA 37th Inf. Co.A
Seay, Thomas H. VA 14th Inf. Co.C
Seay, Thomas J. AL 15th Inf. Co.F Cpl.
Seay, Thomas J. AL 62nd Inf. Co.K 1st Sgt.
Seay, Thomas J. VA 24th Inf. Co.H
Seay, Thomas R. KY 2nd Mtd.Inf.
Seay, Van AL 15th Inf. Co.B
Seay, W.A. AR 24th Inf. Co.D
Seay, W.A. AR Inf. Hardy's Regt. Co.C Sgt.
Seay, Washington Hopkins AL 5th Inf. Old Co.H
    Music.
Seay, W.B. GA 2nd Inf. Co.K
Seay, W.C. VA 21st Inf. Co.F
Seay, W.D. GA 52nd Inf. Co.D
Seay, W.H. AL 2nd Cav. Co.D Cpl.
Seay, W.H. AL Lt.Arty. Phelan's Co.
Seay, W.H. VA 24th Cav. Co.G
Seay, W.H. VA Conscr. Cp.Lee Co.A
Seay, William AL 13th Bn.Part.Rangers Co.C,E
Seay, William AL 56th Part.Rangers Co.I
Seay, William AL 15th Inf. Co.F
Seay, William GA 23rd Inf. Co.E
Seay, William TN 8th (Smith's) Cav. Co.F
Seay, William VA 1st St.Res. Co.F
Seay, William A. GA 55th Inf. Co.K 1st Lt.
Seay, William A. TN 24th Inf. Co.K 1st Lt.
Seay, William A. VA 40th Inf. Co.B
Seay, William A. 4th Conf.Eng.Troops 2nd Lt.
Seay, William A. Frost's Brig. AAAG
Seay, William B. VA 20th Inf. Co.F
Seay, William B., Jr. VA 57th Inf. Co.A
Seay, William B., Sr. VA 57th Inf. Co.A
Seay, William D. VA Inf. 25th Bn. Co.E,A
Seay, William F. SC Inf. 7th Bn. (Enfield Rifles)
    Co.H
Seay, William G. VA 59th Inf. 3rd Co.E
Seay, William H. KY 7th Mtd.Inf. Co.B Capt.
Seay, William H. TN 4th Inf. Co.H
Seay, William H. VA Hvy.Arty. 18th Bn. Co.B
Seay, William H. VA Hvy.Arty. Kyle's Co.
Seay, William H. VA 1st Bn.Res. Co.D
Seay, William H. VA Inf. 25th Bn. Co.G
Seay, William J. GA 6th Inf. Co.B
Seay, William J. GA 23rd Inf. Co.B
Seay, William J. VA Lt.Arty. 12th Bn. Co.C
Seay, William M. KY 4th Cav.
Seay, William M. KY 1st Inf. Co.G
Seay, William M. VA 11th Inf. Co.E Sgt.
Seay, William P. VA Hvy.Arty. 10th Bn. Co.C

Seay, William T. TN Cav. 7th Bn. (Bennett's)
    Co.A
Seay, William T. VA 13th Inf. Co.D
Seay, William W. VA Inf. 22nd Bn. Co.E Cpl.
Seay, Wilson SC 13th Inf. Co.F,I Cpl.
Seay, W.J. AL 15th Inf. Co.F
Seay, W.J. 20th Conf.Cav. Co.C
Seay, W.M. TN Lt.Arty. Rice's Btty.
Seay, W.M. TX Cav. Madison's Regt. Co.C
Seay, W.M. TX Waul's Legion Co.A
Seay, W.M. VA 3rd Res. Co.H
Seay, W.N. GA Cav. Alexander's Co.
Seay, W.P. MS Cav. 4th Bn. Co.A
Seay, W.P. 8th (Wade's) Conf.Cav. Co.C
Seay, W.W. AL 38th Inf. Co.F
Seay, W.W. GA 12th (Robinson's) Cav.
    (St.Guards) Co.I
Seay, W.W. GA 20th Inf. Co.D
Seay, W.W. VA 2nd Inf.Loc.Def. Co.F
Seay, W.W. VA Inf. 6th Bn.Loc.Def. Co.C
Seay, Zachariah H. VA 1st St.Res. Co.B Sgt.
Seaymone, William H. VA Lt.Arty. 13th Bn.
    Co.C
Seays, Thomas C. AL 22nd Inf. Co.F
Seba, John MO 4th Cav. Co.F,G
Sebalt, Caleb GA Smith's Legion Co.D
Sebalt, George W. GA Smith's Legion Co.D
Sebasbin, William VA 50th Inf. Co.D
Sebasti, Edaristo LA Mil. 5th Regt.Eur.Brig.
    (Spanish Regt.) Co.4
Sebastian, B. MO 16th Inf. Co.G
Sebastian, C.B. LA 14th (Austin's) Bn.S.S. Co.A
    1st Sgt.
Sebastian, Charles AR 1st (Dobbin's) Cav. Co.H
Sebastian, Charles B. LA 11th Inf. Co.F Cpl.
Sebastian, Charles B. Conf.Cav. Raum's Co. Sgt.
Sebastian, G. SC 1st Regt. Charleston Guard
    Co.D
Sebastian, Geo. C. Gen. & Staff, QM Dept.
    Capt.,AQM
Sebastian, G.W. MO Cav. 2nd Regt.St.Guard
    Co.D
Sebastian, Henry NC 52nd Inf. Co.F Sgt.
Sebastian, James M. MO Cav. 3rd Regt.St.Guard
    Co.C
Sebastian, James M. MO 6th Inf. Co.D
Sebastian, J.D. AR Inf. Cocke's Regt. Co.E
    Cpl.
Sebastian, J.M. KY 9th Mtd.Inf. Co.E
Sebastian, J.M. TN Inf. 23rd Bn. Co.A
Sebastian, John B. LA Washington Arty.Bn.
    Co.5
Sebastian, John D. AR 15th (Josey's) Inf. Co.A
Sebastian, John D. TX Cav. Morgan's Regt.
    Co.E
Sebastian, John H. VA 25th Mil. Co.A
Sebastian, Joseph M. TN 8th Inf. Co.K
Sebastian, Leander VA 4th Res. Co.B
Sebastian, Lee VA 8th Cav. Co.C
Sebastian, Martin H. NC 52nd Inf. Co.F
Sebastian, N.C. MO 3rd Cav. Co.E
Sebastian, Posey GA 1st Inf. (St.Guards) Co.B
Sebastian, Robert F. TN Cav. Jackson's Co.
Sebastian, Samuel MO 2nd Cav. Co.C
Sebastian, Samuel MO 12th Cav. Co.C
Sebastian, T.B. MO 3rd Cav. Co.E

Sebastian, W.H. AR Inf. Cocke's Regt. Co.E
    Sgt.
Sebastian, W.H. TN 8th Inf. Co.K
Sebastian, William GA 1st Inf. (St.Guards) Co.B
Sebastian, William G. NC 52nd Inf. Co.F
Sebastian, William S. KY 5th Mtd.Inf. Co.A,G
    2nd Lt.
Sebastian, W.W. Conf.Cav. Wood's Regt. Co.L
    Sgt.
Sebastien, E.J. GA 34th Inf. Co.A
Sebastien, George C. Conf.Cav. Wood's Regt.
    QM
Sebastien, P. LA Mil. 4th Regt. 2nd Brig. 1st
    Div. Co.A
Sebastin, E.P. GA 39th Inf. Co.A
Sebastine, E.J. MS 28th Cav. Co.I
Sebastion, Benjamin MO 6th Cav. Co.F
Sebastion, E. GA 1st Inf. (St.Guards) Co.K
Sebastion, G. SC Mil. 16th Regt. Robinson's Co.
Sebastion, Jacob KY 5th Mtd.Inf. Co.A
Sebastion, J.C. MO Cav. 2nd Regt.St.Guard
    Co.D
Sebastion, J.M. TN 41st Inf. Co.A
Sebastion, John KY 5th Mtd.Inf. Co.E
Sebastion, T.J. MO Cav. 2nd Regt.St.Guard
    Co.D
Sebel, F. KY 3rd Cav. Co.I
Seber, Michel LA Mil. 2nd Regt. 2nd Brig. 1st
    Div. Co.I
Seber, Samuel TN 3rd (Lillard's) Mtd.Inf. Co.B
Seberger, Anthony LA 13th Inf. Co.K
Sebering, Fred LA Mil. 4th Regt. 1st Brig. 1st
    Div. Co.K
Seberling, A. VA 1st Cav. Co.C
Seberry, H.R. MS Regt.St.Troops Ruth's Co.
Sebert, Charles D. VA 1st Cav. Co.C
Sebert, H. VA 64th Mtd.Inf. Co.K
Sebert, J.F. VA 22nd Inf.
Sebert, Lanty L. VA 25th Inf. 2nd Co.I Cpl.
Sebert, Simon LA Mil. 3rd Regt. 2nd Brig. 1st
    Div. Co.C
Sebert, Valentine VA 10th Cav. Co.C
Sebley, W.B. TN 13th (Gore's) Cav. Co.G
Sebley, W.F. 15th Conf.Cav. Co.C
Sebly, J.L. TN 13th (Gore's) Cav. Co.G
Sebolin, --- 1st Choctaw & Chickasaw Mtd.Rifles
    2nd Co.C Cpl.
Sebolt, Caleb GA 65th Inf. Co.C
Sebolt, David 2nd Cherokee Mtd.Vol. Co.B
Sebolt, F.P. TN 51st (Cons.) Inf. Co.A
Sebolt, George W. GA 65th Inf. Co.C
Sebolt, George W. NC Walker's Bn. Thomas'
    Legion Co.G
Sebolt, James M. GA 52nd Inf. Co.C
Sebolt, John 1st Cherokee Mtd.Rifles Co.K Sgt.
Sebolt, J.W. TN 51st (Cons.) Inf. Co.A
Sebolt, L.K. GA 65th Inf. Co.C
Sebra, Joseph KY 4th Mtd.Inf. Co.A
Sebra, Joseph VA 37th Mil. 2nd Co.B
Sebralla, Charles TN Inf. 3rd Bn. Co.F
Sebree, Barnett KY Corbin's Men
Sebree, Charls VA 92nd Mil. Co.C
Sebree, Elmoton VA 40th Inf. Co.C
Sebree, G.J.O. KY 2nd Mtd.Inf. Co.E
Sebree, Jame KY 5th Cav.
Sebree, James KY 4th Cav. Riddle's Co.
Sebree, James H. KY 7th Cav. Co.B

Sebree, James W. VA 47th Inf. Co.F
Sebree, John KY 4th Cav. Co.G
Sebree, John KY 6th Cav. Co.I
Sebree, John A. KY 4th Mtd.Inf. Co.E
Sebree, John A. VA 40th Inf. Co.I
Sebree, John J. VA 40th Inf. Co.I Sgt.
Sebree, John T. KY 2nd Mtd.Inf. Co.E
Sebree, Joseph KY Cav. 2nd Bn. (Dortch's) Co.C
Sebree, Joseph KY 10th (Johnson's) Cav. Co.H
Sebree, Joseph KY 1st Inf. Co.G 3rd Cpl.
Sebree, Joseph KY Morgan's Men Co.D
Sebree, J.W. KY 2nd (Duke's) Cav. Co.F
Sebree, Moses VA 40th Inf. Co.C
Sebree, Robert KY 2nd Mtd.Inf. Co.E
Sebree, Thomas F. KY 2nd Mtd.Inf. Co.E
Sebree, Zion VA 40th Inf. Co.I
Sebrell, George W. VA 5th Cav. (12 mo. '61-2) Co.H
Sebrell, George W. VA Hvy.Arty. 18th Bn. Co.A
Sebrell, James E. VA Hvy.Arty. 18th Bn. Co.A Sgt.Maj.
Sebrell, Nathaniel H. VA Vol. Taylor's Co.
Sebrell, N.H. VA Lt.Arty. Grandy's Co.
Sebrell, N.H. Conf.Lt.Arty. Richardson's Bn. Co.C
Sebrens, John MS 39th Inf. Co.F
Sebring, James AL 14th Inf. Co.H
Sebring, William H. MO Cav. Wood's Regt. Co.A 1st Lt.
Sebring, William H. TN 2nd (Robison's) Inf. Co.E,D Cpl.
Sebron, John MS Inf. 3rd Bn. Co.A
Sebry, R.W. KY 2nd (Duke's) Cav.
Seburg, Jacob Conf.Reg.Inf. Brooks' Bn. Co.B
Seburn, Isaac F. VA 32nd Inf. 2nd Co.H
Seburn, J.R. TX 4th Inf. (St.Troops) Co.E
Secard, Appolinaire LA 2nd Cav. Co.K Cpl.
Secchi, Giovanni LA Mil. 6th Regt.Eur.Brig. (Italian Guards Bn.) Co.2
Seccombe, Thomas KY 1st Inf. Co.D
Secgers, Elijah J. GA 24th Inf. Co.A
Seche, D. LA Mil. 3rd Regt. French Brig. Co.1
Sechern, Charles E. KY 5th Cav.
Sechexneyder, M. LA 18th Inf. Co.E
Se chille 1st Creek Mtd.Vol. Co.B
Sechler, B.C. NC 57th Inf. Co.K
Sechler, G.A.J. NC 57th Inf. Co.K Capt.
Sechler, James P. NC 42nd Inf. Co.G
Sechler, Jesse NC 7th Inf. Co.C
Sechler, John F. NC 34th Inf. Co.D
Sechler, Joseph NC 5th Inf. Co.H
Sechneider, Jean LA 18th Inf. Co.A Sgt.
Sechrest, James D. KY 4th Cav. Co.G
Sechrest, Thomas MO 12th Cav. Co.H
Sechriest, Joshua MO 16th Inf. Co.A
Sechrist, Allen NC 35th Inf. Co.I
Sechrist, Ambros NC 14th Inf. Co.B
Sechrist, Ambrose NC 48th Inf. Co.H
Sechrist, Andrew NC 14th Inf. Co.B
Sechrist, Charles VA 33rd Inf. Co.I
Sechrist, Charles VA 146th Mil. Co.A
Sechrist, Conrad NC 14th Inf. Co.B
Sechrist, David 1st Conf.Eng.Troops Co.A
Sechrist, Eli R. NC 48th Inf. Co.H
Sechrist, Frederick VA 33rd Inf. Co.D

Sechrist, Frederick L. VA 114th Mil. Co.D 2nd Lt.
Sechrist, Harvey VA 33rd Inf. Co.I,A
Sechrist, Henry NC 48th Inf. Co.H
Sechrist, J.M. NC 45th Inf. Co.K
Sechrist, John L. VA 114th Mil. Co.D
Sechrist, M.S. NC 7th Sr.Res. Johnson's Co.
Sechrist, Noah NC 14th Inf. Co.H
Sechrist, Samuel H. VA 33rd Inf. Co.I
Sechrist, Samuel J.B. VA 114th Mil. Co.D Ord.Sgt.
Sechrist, William NC 48th Inf. Co.H
Secil, G.S. Gen. & Staff Capt.
Secinger, Clem. FL 9th Inf. Co.K
Secinger, Lemuel GA 1st (Symons') Res. Co.G
Seckendorf, M. SC 1st Regt. Charleston Guard Co.G
Seckenger, V.M. GA 54th Inf. Co.I
Seckeomey Tee cahlor hay Nah 1st Cherokee Mtd.Rifles Co.I
Seckinger, B.A. GA 32nd Inf. Co.K
Seckinger, Charles LA 30th Inf. Co.F,E
Seckinger, E. GA 5th Cav. Co.I
Seckinger, George W. GA 47th Inf. Co.I
Seckinger, Henry GA Cav. 2nd Bn. Co.A
Seckinger, Henry GA 5th Cav. Co.I
Seckinger, J.A. GA Inf. 18th Bn. Co.B
Seckinger, John A. SC 11th Inf. Co.E
Seckinger, Thomas GA 47th Inf. Co.I
Seckinger, W.R. GA 5th Cav. Co.I
Secleuthner, Charles TX 4th Field Btty.
Secor, C. AL 1st Bn.Cadets Co.A
Secord, Sauls GA 26th Inf. Co.E
Secord, Solomon GA 20th Inf. Surg.
Secord, Solomon Gen. & Staff Surg.
Se cowee, C. 1st Cherokee Mtd.Vol. 1st Co.D, 2nd Co.H
Secowie, Charles 1st Cherokee Mtd.Rifles Co.A
Se cow wee 1st Cherokee Mtd.Vol. 1st Co.F
Secoy, Benjamin F. AR 15th (Josey's) Inf. Co.E
Secoy, George MO 1st Inf. Co.K
Secoy, William H.H. MO 1st Inf. Co.G
Secrase, Robert AR Cav. Wright's Regt. Co.D
Secrece, Powell NC 46th Inf. Co.F
Secres, Daniel TX 6th Cav. Co.K
Secrese, Robert AR Cav. New's Regt. Co.B
Secress, Anderson AR 13th Inf. Co.E
Secress, Anderson KY 7th Mtd.Inf. 1st Co.K
Secress, Robert AR 13th Inf. Co.E
Secress, Robert KY 7th Mtd.Inf. 1st Co.K
Secrest, --- TX Cav. Mann's Regt. Co.H Cpl.
Secrest, --- TX Cav. Mann's Regt. Co.H Far.
Secrest, Abraham T. TX 27th Cav. Co.D,M
Secrest, A.F. TX Cav. Mann's Regt. Co.H Jr.2nd Lt.
Secrest, A.J. SC 4th Cav. Co.B
Secrest, A.J. SC 6th Res. Col.
Secrest, Andrew J. NC Hvy.Arty. 10th Bn. Co.C
Secrest, Andrew J. SC 6th Inf. Lt.Col.
Secrest, Coleman M. NC 15th Inf. Co.B
Secrest, F.C. TX 9th (Nichols') Inf. Co.F
Secrest, Felix TX Nolan's Mtd.Co. (Loc.Def.) 2nd Lt.
Secrest, Fielding C. TX 35th (Brown's) Cav. Co.D
Secrest, Fielding C. TX 13th Vol. 2nd Co.F Far.

Secrest, Hiram NC 43rd Inf. Co.B
Secrest, I. NC 2nd Jr.Res. Co.F
Secrest, I.L. TN 24th Inf. 1st Co.G, Co.B 1st Lt.
Secrest, J. NC 43rd Inf. Co.B
Secrest, J. SC Cav. 10th Bn. Co.A
Secrest, Jacob C. TX 9th (Nichols') Inf. Co.F
Secrest, Jacob G. TX 35th (Brown's) Cav. Co.D
Secrest, Jacob G. TX 13th Vol. 2nd Co.F
Secrest, J.C. SC 4th Cav. Co.B
Secrest, J.C. SC Cav. 10th Bn. Co.D
Secrest, J.C. SC 1st (Hagood's) Inf. Co.D
Secrest, J.C. SC 4th St.Troops Co.B
Secrest, J.E. TX 14th Inf. Co.C
Secrest, J.L. MS Cav. Jeff Davis Legion Co.C
Secrest, J.L. NC 2nd Jr.Res. Co.F
Secrest, J.M. TX Res.Corps Co.A
Secrest, John A. NC 15th Inf. Co.B
Secrest, John A. NC 26th Inf. Co.B
Secrest, J.S. TN 59th Mtd.Inf. Co.A
Secrest, J.T. MS Cav. Jeff Davis Legion Co.C
Secrest, Lafayette A. GA Inf. 1st Loc.Troops (Augusta) Co.F
Secrest, Lafayette A. NC 1st Arty. (10th St.Troops) Co.K
Secrest, Larkin D. TX 35th (Brown's) Cav. Co.H Lt.
Secrest, Larkin D. TX 13th Vol. 2nd Co.A Lt.
Secrest, L.C. NC 2nd Jr.Res. Co.F
Secrest, L.D. TX 26th Cav. 1st Co.G
Secrest, Leroy S. NC 26th Inf. Co.B Cpl.
Secrest, Milas S. NC Hvy.Arty. 10th Bn. Co.C
Secrest, Moses B. AR 4th Inf. Co.F
Secrest, Samuel T. NC 4th Sr.Res. Co.I 2nd Lt.
Secrest, S.M. NC 2nd Jr.Res. Co.F Sgt.
Secrest, S.W. TN 24th Inf. 1st Co.G
Secrest, Thomas TN 59th Mtd.Inf. Co.K
Secrest, Thomas A. NC 48th Inf. Co.A
Secrest, Thomas M. TN 37th Inf.
Secrest, Tilso NC Hvy.Arty. 10th Bn. Co.C
Secrest, W.F. TX 21st Inf. Co.C
Secrest, W.H. TN 24th Inf. 1st Co.G, Co.B
Secrest, Wiley MS Cav. Knox's Co. (Stonewall Rangers) Cpl.
Secrest, William L. AL 51st (Part.Rangers) Co.B
Secrest, William L. AL Inf. 1st Regt. Co.G Cpl.
Secrise, R.H. AR 8th Cav. Co.B
Secrist, A. VA 12th Cav. Co.F
Secrist, Barkley VA Burks' Regt.Loc.Def. Ammen's Co.
Secrist, C. NC 2nd Inf. Co.C
Secrist, Charles N. VA 2nd Inf. Co.B
Secrist, Daniel W. VA 10th Inf. Co.I Cpl.
Secrist, David VA 42nd Inf. Co.C
Secrist, David VA Burks' Regt.Loc.Def. Beckner's Co.
Secrist, David C. VA 10th Inf. Co.H
Secrist, John A. VA 10th Inf. Co.H Cpl.
Secrist, Martin V.B. VA 42nd Inf. Co.C
Secrist, Philip M. VA 10th Inf. Co.I Sgt.
Secrist, Samuel VA 58th Mil. Co.E
Secrist, Theopilus MO 12th Cav.
Secrist, Thomas J. VA 10th Inf. Co.H
Secrist, William A. NC 1st Inf. (6 mo. '61) Co.B
Sedars, Tiler W. AR 8th Inf. New Co.D
Sedars, James AR 12th Inf. Co.H

Sedberry, Bond E. NC 2nd Arty. (36th
    St.Troops) Co.B Sgt.
Sedberry, Bond E. NC Lt.Arty. 13th Bn. Co.B
    1st Sgt.
Sedberry, Bond E. NC 1st Inf. (6 mo. '61) Co.H
Sedberry, Daniel W. NC 52nd Inf. Co.E
Sedberry, George F. AL 3rd Inf. Co.I Sgt.
Sedberry, Henry O. NC 2nd Arty. (36th
    St.Troops) Co.B
Sedberry, Henry O. NC 1st Inf. (6 mo. '61)
    Co.H
Sedberry, H.O. NC Lt.Arty. 13th Bn. Co.B
Sedberry, J.D. TX 1st Inf. Co.A
Sedberry, J.L. TN 48th (Nixon's) Inf. Co.B 3rd
    Lt.
Sedberry, John A. NC 28th Inf. Co.E
Sedberry, John D. TX 19th Inf. Co.F 1st Sgt.
Sedberry, John L. TN 48th (Voorhies') Inf. Co.A
    2nd Lt.
Sedberry, John L. TN Inf. Sowell's Detach. 2nd
    Lt.
Sedberry, John S. NC 38th Inf. Co.E Sgt.
Sedberry, John S. TX 10th Inf. Co.H
Sedberry, John W. TX 15th Inf. Co.C Capt.
Sedberry, J.S. TX 15th Inf. Co.C
Sedberry, Meritt TX 15th Inf. Co.C
Sedberry, Michael K. TX 2nd Cav. 1st Co.F
Sedberry, Mike K. TX Cav. Morgan's Regt. Co.I
Sedberry, Robert H. AL 10th Inf. Co.I Music.
Sedberry, Shadrach P. MS 20th Inf. Co.F 2nd
    Lt.
Sedberry, T.D. TX 19th Inf. Co.F Capt.
Sedberry, William TX 19th Inf. Co.A
Sedberry, William B. NC 38th Inf. Co.E
Sedberry, William J. TX 3rd Cav. Co.G Cpl.
Sedberry, William R. TX 15th Inf. Co.K 2nd Lt.
Sedbeths, Geo. MO St.Guard
Sedden, Charles VA 4th Cav.
Sedden, Frank MD Cav. 2nd Bn. Co.C
Seddeth, George W. AR Lt.Arty. Thrall's Btty.
Seddeth, Spencer GA 44th Inf. Co.G
Seddlie, W.J.M. LA 3rd Inf. Co.C
Seddon, J.A. LA Mil. British Guard Bn. Bur-
    rowes' Co.
Seddon, James A. Gen. & Staff Secretary of War
Seddon, John VA Inf. 1st Bn. Co.D Maj.
Seddon, John Gen. & Staff Capt.,AAG
Seddreth, John TX 22nd Inf. Co.E
Sede, D. AL Shelby Cty.Res. J.M. Webster's
    Co.
Sederburg, Thaddeus MO 1st Inf. Co.B
Seders, Jacob VA 77th Mil. Co.B
Seders, James VA 77th Mil. Co.B
Sedgeley, W. LA Mil.Conf.Guards Regt. Co.E
Sedgewick, William J. VA 10th Cav. Co.A
Sedgley, J.T. TX 5th Inf. Co.E Cpl.
Sedgwick, J. VA 1st St.Res. Co.D
Sedgwick, John AL 14th Inf. Co.G
Sedgwick, Levy T. KY 2nd (Duke's) Cav.
    Co.A,I 2nd Lt.
Sedgwick, L.P. GA 2nd Cav. Lt.
Sedgwick, R.E. VA 1st St.Res. Co.K
Sedgwick, Richard VA 1st St.Res. Co.D
Sedgwick, W.F. FL 9th Inf. Co.D
Sedinger, James D. VA 8th Cav. Co.E 2nd Lt.
Sedley, Willis NC Invalid Corps Prov.Guard
    McDonough's Co.

Sedlick, M. MS 10th Inf. Old Co.D
Sedlon, J. AL 34th Inf. Co.A
Sedmear, Henry TX 16th Inf. Co.H
Sedotti, Francois LA Mil. 6th Regt.Eur.Brig.
    (Italian Guards Bn.) Sgt.
Sedson, James R.C. AL 3rd Inf. Co.G
Sedwick, B.F. VA 12th Cav. Co.G
Sedwick, Charles VA 4th Cav. Co.H
Sedwick, Charles VA 17th Inf. Co.H
Sedwick, Franklin VA 34th Mil. Co.A
Sedwick, George W. VA 97th Mil. Co.M
Sedwick, John F. VA 17th Inf. Co.K Cpl.
Sedwick, W.A. GA 12th Mil.
Sedwick, William VA 97th Mil. Co.M
Sedwick, William B. VA 12th Cav. Co.G
Sedwick, William D. VA 17th Inf. Co.H
See, A. SC 2nd St.Troops Co.A
See, A. TX 5th Inf. Co.D
See, Adam VA 25th Inf. 1st Co.F
See, Adam VA 62nd Mtd.Inf. 2nd Co.F
See, A.H. TX Cav. McCord's Frontier Regt. 1st
    Lt.,Adj.
See, A.J. KY 6th Cav. Co.I
See, Anderson P. TX 6th Cav. Co.A
See, Andrew TX Cav. 6th Bn. Co.E
See, Ben MO Inf. Clark's Regt. Co.B
See, Benjamin MO 1st N.E. Cav. Co.H
See, Benjamin F. KY 4th Mtd.Inf. Co.H Sgt.
See, C.H. AL 43rd Inf. Co.C
See, C.S.M. VA 5th Inf. Chap.
See, Cyrus VA 18th Cav. Co.B
See, Cyrus VA 14th Mil. Co.F
See, Cyrus St.C. VA 62nd Mtd.Inf. 1st Co.G
See, Daniel J. NC 18th Inf.
See, D.J. TX 17th Cons.Dismtd.Cav. 1st Co.G
See, D.J. TX 18th Cav. Co.I
See, D.P. SC 15th Inf. Co.C
See, Ervin SC 6th Inf. 2nd Co.I
See, George GA 2nd Inf. Co.B
See, George SC 27th Inf. Co.G
See, George VA 25th Inf. 1st Co.F
See, George VA 62nd Mtd.Inf. 2nd Co.F
See, George B. VA 52nd Inf. Co.G
See, George W. SC Hvy.Arty. Gilchrist's Co.
    (Gist Guard)
See, George W. SC 27th Inf. Co.F
See, George W. TN Cav. 7th Bn. (Bennett's)
    Co.A
See, George W. TN 22nd (Barteau's) Cav. Co.D
See, G.W. SC 1st Bn.S.S. Co.C
See, Hartwell H. GA 60th Inf. Co.A
See, Hartwell H. NC Inf. 2nd Bn. Co.E
See, Jackson FL 7th Inf. Co.A
See, Jacob W. VA 52nd Inf. Co.G
See, James B. MS 3rd (St.Troops) Cav. Co.A
See, J.B. SC 2nd Inf. Co.K
See, J.E. Brush Bn.
See, Jerome B. SC 20th Inf. Co.K
See, J.J.J. AL 18th Inf. Co.F
See, J.O. VA Cav. 37th Bn. Co.B
See, John GA 28th Inf. Co.E
See, John MO 6th Cav.
See, John MO Cav. Poindexter's Regt.
See, John VA 7th Cav. Co.K
See, John Conf.Reg.Inf. Brooks' Bn. Co.D
See, John C. VA 23rd Cav. Co.I
See, John D. TN 1st Hvy.Arty. 2nd Co.D

See, John F. MO Inf. Clark's Regt.
See, John L. TX Inf. Griffin's Bn. Co.A
See, John R. AR 20th Inf. Co.G
See, John T. GA 9th Inf. Co.H Sgt.
See, John W. GA 60th Inf. Co.A 1st Lt.
See, Joseph VA 21st Inf. Co.I
See, Joseph W. AR 16th Inf. Co.E
See, Leonard VA 14th Mil. Co.F
See, Levi SC 2nd St.Troops Co.A
See, Lewis W. MS 2nd Part.Rangers Co.G
See, Mack AR Cav. Harrell's Bn. Co.A
See, N.D. AL 31st Inf. Co.H
See, Nimrod MO 1st N.E. Cav. Co.H
See, Nimrod MO Inf. Clark's Regt. Co.B
See, Robert VA 25th Inf. 2nd Co.D
See, Samuel TX 12th Inf. Co.E
See, Silas R. VA 14th Mil. Co.F
See, William TX 11th Cav. Co.E
See, William H.H. TX Inf. Griffin's Bn. Co.A
See, William L. AR 7th Inf. Co.F Sgt.
See, William T. TN 22nd (Barteau's) Cav. Co.D
Seearey, Moses J. MO 10th Cav. Co.A
Seeba, C.F. SC 1st St.Troops Co.E Sgt.
Seebeck, C. SC Mil.Arty. 1st Regt. Harms' Co.
Seebeck, C. SC Arty. Melchers' Co. (Co.B,
    German Arty.) Cpl.
Seeber, George O. LA 12th Inf. Co.K
Seeber, John A. MO 1st & 4th Cons.Inf. Co.H
Seeber, John A. MO 4th Inf. Co.K
Seeber, William VA 8th Inf. Co.H
Seeberger, A. SC 3rd Cav. Co.G
Seeberger, Augustus SC Arty.Bn. Hampton
    Legion Co.A
Seeberger, H. 4th Conf.Eng.Troops Artif.
Seebey, Andrew LA 8th Inf. Co.D
Seeble, Francais VA 41st Inf. 2nd Co.G
Seebold, W.E. LA 1st Cav. Co.I
Seebolt, W.S. VA Cav. 34th Bn. Co.C
Seebra, Henry LA 2nd Inf.
Seebree, George W. KY 2nd Mtd.Inf. Co.C
Seebright, John H. VA 5th Inf. Co.A
Seebt, Jean Marie LA Mil. 1st Regt. French Brig.
    Co.7
See cah we 1st Cherokee Mtd.Rifles Co.G
Seed Catcher 1st Cherokee Mtd.Rifles Co.B Cpl.
Seed, J. AL 1st Regt. Mobile Vol. Baas' Co.
Seed, M.D. AR 38th Inf. New Co.I
Seedenburg, F.W. SC Mil. 16th Regt. Bancroft,
    Jr.'s Co.
Seeder, Anton LA Mil. 3rd Regt. 1st Brig. 1st
    Div. Co.H
Seederff, J. SC Mil. 16th Regt. Bancroft, Jr.'s
    Co.
Seeders, Ebenezer VA 77th Mil. Co.C
Seeders, John LA 4th Inf. Co.D
Seeders, Robert LA 4th Inf. Co.D
Seeders, Thomas F. VA Inf. 25th Bn. Co.E
Seedom, S.M. AR 13th Inf. Co.E
Seedorf, C.H. SC Mil.Arty. 1st Regt. Harms'
    Co.
Seedorff, J. SC Lt.Arty. Wagener's Co. (Co.A,
    German Arty.)
Seeds, Euphronius VA Hvy.Arty. 19th Bn. Co.A
Seeds, Euphronius 1st Conf.Eng.Troops Co.D
    Artif.
Seeds, O.H. Gen. & Staff Asst.Surg.

Seeds, Orin H. TX 13th Vol. 2nd Co.G
  Capt.,Asst.Surg.
Seeds, Thomas AL Inf. 2nd Regt. Co.F
Seeds, Thomas AL 38th Inf. Co.C
Seef, Thomas J. AL 36th Inf. Co.F
Seefred, Fred TN 47th Inf. Co.F
Seegar, B.E. FL Lt.Arty. Abell's Co.
Seegar, James J. LA 8th Inf. Co.G
Seegar, J.E. AL 15th Inf. Co.C Sgt.
Seegar, J.T. FL Cav. 5th Bn. Co.D 1st Lt.
Seegar, M.S. Trans-MS Conf.Cav. 1st Bn. Co.A
Seegars, J.A. AL 15th Inf. Co.D
Seegars, M.J. AL 15th Inf. Co.I
Seeger, C.F. TX 17th Inf. Co.H
Seeger, Christian TX 17th Inf. Co.H
Seeger, Fred VA 15th Inf. Co.K
Seeger, J.A. FL 1st (Res.) Inf.
Seegere, Charles LA Pointe Coupee Arty. Artif.
Seegers, John AL 12th Cav. Co.A
Seegers, R.W. SC Hvy.Arty. 15th (Lucas') Bn.
  Co.C
Seegfried, T.M. VA 5th Inf.
Seeggars, A.J. AL 33rd Inf. Co.A 1st Sgt.
Seegraves, J. TN 15th (Stewart's) Cav. Co.A
Seegraves, J.C. GA 16th Inf. Co.A
Seegum, E.M. MS 42nd Inf. Co.K
Seehagle, F. TX Inf. 1st St.Troops Sheldon's Co.
Seehaus, A. TX 4th Inf. (St.Troops) Co.A
Seehon, James LA 19th Inf. Co.D
Seekamp, Albert TX 26th Cav. Co.F, 2nd Co.G
Seekatz, William TX Conscr.
Seeker, Lewis VA Inf. 1st Bn.Loc.Def. Co.A
Seekford, Noah VA Res. Keyser's Co.
Seel, C. SC 25th Inf. Co.E
Seel, J.J. GA 41st Inf. Co.I
Seel, L. TX Inf. 4th Bn. (Oswald's) Co.B
Seel, R.F. FL Cav. 3rd Bn. Co.B
Seelan, John H. VA 15th Inf. Co.B
Seelbach, Henry TX 17th Cav. Co.H
Seelbach, William TX 17th Cav. Co.H
Seele, A.C.N. AL 1st Mil. 2nd Lt.
Seele, Jacob LA Mil. 4th Regt. 1st Brig. 1st Div.
  Co.D
Seeleman, Samuel NC 18th Inf. Co.A
Seeleutner, Th. TX Inf. 4th Bn. (Oswald's) Co.A
Seeley, A. NC 47th Inf. Co.K
Seeley, Alson B. NC 56th Inf. Co.C
Seeley, Charles LA Inf. 1st Sp.Bn. (Wheat's)
  New Co.E Sgt.
Seeley, Darwin G. TX 2nd Inf. Co.E
Seeley, George VA 7th Cav. Co.A
Seeley, James E. LA Arty. 1st Field Btty.
Seeley, J.H. FL 1st Inf. New Co.F
Seeley, John MO 8th Cav. Co.H
Seeley, John W. FL 1st Inf. Old Co.K, New
  Co.A
Seeley, Joseph H. AL Lt.Arty. Lee's Btty.
Seeley, J.T. MS Cav. Abbott's Co.
Seeley, J.W. MO 7th Cav. Co.K
Seeley, Milton MS Lt.Arty. English's Co.
Seeley, Milton MS 16th Inf. Co.I
Seeley, R.S. VA Lt.Arty. Ellett's Co.
Seeley, S.T. AL Mil. 2nd Regt.Vol. Co.E Sgt.
Seeley, T.E. MS 20th Inf. Co.E
Seeley, Thomas G. TN Cav. 2nd Bn. (Biffle's)
  Co.D
Seeley, Wiley SC McDonnell's Unatt.Co.

Seeley, William LA 1st (Strawbridge's) Co. Co.F
Seeley, William TX Inf. Chambers' Bn.
  Res.Corps Co.D
Seelhorst, Aug. TX 16th Inf. Co.C
Seelhorst, Aug TX Waul's Legion Co.B,A Sgt.
Seelhorst, E.W. Kellersberg's Corps Sap. &
  Min.,CSA
Seelhurst, Henry TX Inf. 1st St.Troops Co.F
Seelig, F. VA 54th Mil. Co.E,F
Seeligman, M. LA Mil. Lewis Guards
Seeligsen, Henry TX Cav. Waller's Regt. Co.E
  1st Sgt.
Seeligson, Edward TX Cav. Waller's Regt. Co.E
Seeligson, George TX Cav. Waller's Regt. Co.E
Seeligson, Luis TX Cav. Benavides' Regt. Co.G
Seeligthner, Phillip 4th Conf.Eng.Troops Artif.
Seelin, B. LA Mil. 4th Regt. 1st Brig. 1st Div.
  Co.C
Seeling, --- TX Lt.Arty. Jones' Co.
Seeling, E.H. TX 1st Hvy.Arty. Co.G
Seelinger, A. LA 22nd Inf. Durrive, Jr.'s Co.
Seels, A.W. GA Cav. Floyd's Co.
Seeluthmer, Philip TX Inf. Griffin's Bn. Co.E
Seely, A. MO Lt.Arty. 3rd Btty.
Seely, A.J. MS Inf. 2nd St.Troops Co.K
Seely, Amariah MO Arty. Lowe's Co. (Jackson
  Btty.)
Seely, E.B. MS 20th Inf. Co.E
Seely, George VA 1st Cav. Co.H
Seely, G.R. MS 20th Inf. Co.B
Seely, Green M. MS 20th Inf. Co.B
Seely, I.P. LA Mil. LaFourche Regt. Sgt.
Seely, Isaac TX 2nd Inf. Co.K
Seely, Isaac J. MS 20th Inf. Co.B
Seely, James R. MS 20th Inf. Co.B Sgt.
Seely, J. Horace VA 5th Inf. Co.L
Seely, J.N. MS 20th Inf. Co.B
Seely, Lambert D. LA Hvy.Arty. 2nd Bn. Co.B
Seely, Marion W. MS 20th Inf. Co.B
Seely, Samuel TX 15th Cav. Co.E
Seely, S.W. MS Inf. 2nd St.Troops Co.K 2nd
  Lt.
Seely, T.H. Exch.Bn. 1st Co.B,CSA
Seely, Thomas FL 6th Inf. Co.C
Seely, Thomas E. 14th Conf.Cav. Co.D
Seely, Thomas H. TX 2nd Cav. Co.K
Seely, W.E. MS Inf. 2nd St.Troops Co.K
Seely, William E. MS 41st Inf. Co.G
Seelye, Joseph W. AL 3rd Inf. Co.G
Seemer, J.M. VA 31st Mil. Co.B
Seemers, John VA 17th Inf. Co.B
Seemon, Adolph VA 24th Cav. Co.F
Seemore, A.C. GA Inf. 9th Bn. Co.D
Seemore, Charles E. GA Inf. 9th Bn. Co.D
Seemore, C.M. GA 38th Inf. Co.H
Seemore, J.A. GA 38th Inf. Co.H
Seemore, J.G. GA 38th Inf. Co.H
Seemore, Marshal M. GA 15th Inf. Co.I
Seemore, M.M. GA 38th Inf. Co.H
Seemore, W.G. GA Inf. 9th Bn. Co.D
Seemore, Z.G. GA Inf. 9th Bn. Co.D
Seemour, Jessee MO Cav. 1st Regt.St.Guard
  Co.B Cpl.
Seems, B.H. AL 47th Inf. Co.C
Seems, J.F. TN 31st Inf. Co.I
Se e muppe 1st Creek Mtd.Vol. Co.A
Seephen, C.S. SC 1st (Butler's) Inf. Co.A Cpl.

Seerey, Patrick LA 20th Inf. New Co.E
Seermann, F. LA Mil. 4th Regt.Eur.Brig. Co.A
Seernis, C.M. AL 3rd Inf. Co.G
Seers, George W.L. GA Inf. 19th Bn.
  (St.Guards) Co.B
Seers, James TX Cav. Baylor's Regt. Co.A
Seers, J.B. AL Randolph Cty.Res. Shepherd's
  Co.
Seers, John W. NC 4th Inf. Co.B
Seers, Lucas VA 157th Mil. Co.A
Seery, Patrick LA 11th Inf. Co.L,E
Seery, Peter TX 6th Inf. Co.A
Seery, Stephen LA 1st (Strawbridge's) Inf. Co.C
Seese, J. VA 18th Cav. Co.D
Seessel, H.C. TN 15th Inf. Co.I
Seester, I.A. AL 2nd Cav. Co.K
Seet, D.F. LA 2nd Inf. Co.K
Seet, Green M. AL 63rd Inf. Co.B
Seet, Robert E. NC 58th Inf. Co.I
Seeten, James M. Gen. & Staff 1st Lt.,Adj.
Seeth, J. TN 7th Cav. Co.L
Seeton, James AL 26th (O'Neal's) Inf. Co.C
Seeton, Jefferson AR 8th Inf. New Co.F
Seeton, Jefferson AR 14th (McCarver's) Inf.
  Co.B
Seeton, J.W. TN 51st (Cons.) Inf. Co.C
Seeton, J.W. TN 52nd Inf. Co.F Bvt.2nd Lt.
Seeton, William M. TX 14th Inf. Co.G 1st Lt.
Seets, Daniel L. TX 12th Inf. Co.H
Seets, John MS 26th Inf. Co.G
Seets, John B. TX 12th Inf. Co.H
Seever, F. VA 2nd St.Res. Co.C
Seever, George W. KY 5th Mtd.Inf. Co.C,A
Seever, Henry KY 5th Mtd.Inf. Co.C,A
Seever, James FL 5th Inf. Co.C
Seever, Peter KY Horse Arty. Byrne's Co.
Seever, William M. TX 8th Cav. Co.G
Seevers, Charles W. VA 13th Inf. Co.H Sgt.
Seevers, Robert E. VA 31st Mil. Co.B 1st Lt.
Seevey, Wm. H. VA Lt.Arty. Donald's Co.
Seevil, Marion AR 38th Inf. Co.C
Seewald, William H. AR 35th Inf. Co.C Fifer
Seewell, S.L. GA Cav. Dorough's Bn.
Sefen, G. TX 26th Cav. Co.D
Sefera, Flario LA Mil. 5th Regt.Eur.Brig.
  (Spanish Regt.) Co.A
Sefers, Michael AL St.Arty. Co.A Cpl.
Seffel, A., II TX 3rd Inf. Co.B
Seffel, J.A., I TX 3rd Inf. Co.B
Seffel, Stephen TX 33rd Inf. Co.I
Sefferan, M. SC Mil. 16th Regt. Bancroft, Jr.'s
  Co.
Sefferlin, Egyde TX 21st Cav. Co.K
Seffins, E.B. GA 2nd Cav. Co.D
Seffron, Thomas W. TN 13th Inf. Co.A 2nd Lt.
Seford, H. GA 26th Inf. Co.I
Sefton, Alexander LA 15th Inf. Co.F
Sefton, H.C. VA Lt.Arty. Woolfolk's Co.
Sefton, John VA Cav. 47th Bn. Co.A
Sefton, John B. LA 1st Hvy.Arty. (Reg.) Co.H
  Drum.
Sefton, John B. LA 15th Inf. Co.H,A Cpl.
Segain, F. LA 4th Inf. Co.F
Segar, Arthur S. VA 6th Inf. Co.G
Segar, Arthur S. VA 32nd Inf. Co.A
Segar, Arthur S. VA 38th Inf. Co.H 1st Lt.
Segar, Francis V. VA 34th Inf. Co.K

Segar, F. Valvian VA 9th Mil. Co.A Sgt.
Segar, Henry G. VA 34th Inf. Co.K
Segar, J. NC 12th Inf.
Segar, J.A. GA Inf. 9th Bn. Co.B
Segar, J.A. GA 37th Inf. Co.E
Segar, James M. MS 1st Bn.S.S. Co.B 2nd Lt.
Segar, Jesse VA Lt.Arty. Moore's Co.
Segar, Jesse S. VA Inf. 25th Bn. Co.E
Segar, John VA 6th Inf. Co.G
Segar, John A. VA 38th Inf. Co.H Sgt.
Segar, John F. VA 3rd Cav. Co.B
Segar, John F. VA 32nd Inf. 2nd Co.K Capt.
Segar, John R. VA 55th Inf. Co.C Cpl.
Segar, M. GA 5th Res. Co.B 2nd Lt.
Segar, S.D. GA Inf. 9th Bn. Co.B
Segar, S.D. GA 37th Inf. Co.E
Segar, Thomas VA Lt.Arty. Grandy's Co.
Segar, Thomas VA Vol. Taylor's Co.
Segar, Thomas C. VA 34th Inf. Co.K Sgt.
Segar, Travers VA 30th Inf. 1st Co.I
Segar, Travis VA 47th Inf. 3rd Co.I
Segar, William R. VA 109th Mil. Co.B, 2nd Co.A
Segarist, Frank Conf.Inf. 8th Bn. Co.F
Segars, B.J. MS 2nd Cav. Co.C
Segars, Burrell W. SC 4th Cav. Co.A
Segars, B.W. MS 2nd Cav. Co.C
Segars, B.W. SC Cav. 12th Bn. Co.A
Segars, Dove SC Inf. 7th Bn. (Enfield Rifles) Co.A,F Capt.
Segars, Francis J. GA 13th Cav. Co.D
Segars, G.R. GA 11th Cav. Co.A
Segars, James GA Inf. 4th Bn. (St.Guards) Co.F
Segars, James 1st Conf.Cav. 2nd Co.K
Segars, J.H. GA Arty. 9th Bn. Co.A
Segars, John SC 4th Cav. Co.A
Segars, John SC Cav. 12th Bn. Co.A
Segars, Kimsey GA 43rd Inf. Co.D
Segars, Love SC 1st Cav. Co.A
Segars, Martin GA 4th Cav. (St.Guards) McDonald's Co.
Segars, N. TX Inf. 1st St.Troops Whitehead's Co.
Segars, Phil VA 10th Inf. Co.I
Segars, Richard MS 2nd Cav. Co.C
Segars, Richard MS 13th Inf. Co.F
Segars, R.J. MS 15th Inf. Co.I
Segars, Robert J. MS 13th Inf. Co.F
Segars, Samuel E. SC 2nd Arty. Co.D
Segars, S.B. AL 5th Inf. New Co.A
Segars, Seth GA 43rd Inf. Co.D
Segars, Thomas GA 43rd Inf. Co.D
Segars, W.G. SC 23rd Inf. Co.A
Segars, Wiley GA 12th Inf. Co.D
Segars, William AL 23rd Inf. Co.H
Segars, William A. GA 43rd Inf. Co.D Sgt.
Segars, William Agisto AR 13th Inf.
Segars, William G. SC 4th St.Troops Co.K
Segars, William R. GA 13th Cav. Co.E
Segars, William R. GA Cobb's Legion Co.H
Segars, Willis GA 51st Inf. Co.D
Segaser, George TX 11th Cav. Co.A
Segassi, Jean LA Mil.Bn. French Vol. Co.8 Capt.
Segathe, Peter LA 11th Inf. Co.D
Segathe, Peter LA 14th (Austin's) Bn.S.S. Co.B
Sege, Charles MO Inf. 3rd Bn. Co.A

Sege, G. TX 4th Inf. (St.Troops) Co.F
Segearle, Joseph AL 1st Inf.
Segee, Celestine FL Inf. 2nd Bn. Co.A
Segely, Joseph AL 26th (O'Neal's) Inf. Co.F Cpl.
Seger, A.B. LA Mil. Algiers Bn. Capt.
Seger, B. LA Mil. Orleans Fire Regt. Co.I
Seger, Chars LA Mil. Mech.Guard
Seger, James M. MS 25th Inf. Co.A
Seger, J.S. VA 54th Mil. Co.B
Seger, P.S. AL 48th Inf. Co.B
Segers, E. AL 34th Inf. Co.E
Segers, Elijah KY 10th Cav. Co.F
Segers, G.P. AL 5th Bn.Vol. Co.C
Segers, Hiram P. AL 39th Inf. Co.D
Segers, James M. GA 34th Inf. Co.G
Segers, L.M. AL 5th Bn.Vol. Co.C
Segers, S.A. AL 5th Bn.Vol. Co.C
Segers, Simon P. AL 61st Inf. Co.I
Segers, S.P. FL 11th Inf. Co.C
Segers, William AL 61st Inf. Co.I
Segers, William R. AL Lt.Arty. Clanton's Btty.
Segerson, John MO 5th Inf. Co.H
Segganie, Felix LA Inf. 16th Bn. (Conf.Guards Resp.Bn.) Co.B Music.
Seggler, Joel E. GA Lt.Arty. Guerard's Btty.
Seggue, F.H. AL 10th Inf. Co.H
Seghers, E.D. LA 22nd (Cons.) Inf. Co.F 2nd Lt.
Seghers, Ed. D. LA Mil.Conf.Guards Regt. Co.E
Seghers, Edward D. LA 27th Inf. Co.D Lt.,Adj.
Seghus, J. LA Arty. 5th Field Btty. (Pelican Lt.Arty.)
Segilleh, Bigmeete NC Inf. Thomas Legion Co.B
Segilleh, Howeteiyeh NC Inf. Thomas Legion 2nd Co.A
Segineaux, Valiere LA 1st Cav. Co.A
Segister, A.N. MO Lawther's Part.Rangers
Seglan, S. LA Mil. 1st Regt. French Brig. Co.4
Seglar, Charles B. AL 3rd Bn.Res. Co.B
Seglar, D.J. SC 2nd Arty. Co.A
Seglar, Edward C. AL 33rd Inf. Co.A
Seglar, H.H. TN 19th Inf. Co.F
Segle, Lewis M. NC 1st Cav. (9th St.Troops) Co.G
Segler, Albert TX 4th Field Btty.
Segler, A.S. SC 22nd Inf. Co.I Capt.
Segler, C.P. SC 2nd Arty. Co.H
Segler, E.C. GA Inf. 1st City Bn. (Columbus) Co.A
Segler, Jabes T. MS 11th (Perrin's) Cav. Co.I
Segler, Joshua SC 2nd Arty. Co.E
Segler, J.P. SC 11th Res. Co.F Cpl.
Segler, Lewis T. MS 11th (Perrin's) Cav. Co.I
Segler, Martin MS 31st Inf. Co.E
Segler, Martin W. MS 31st Inf. Co.E
Segler, Matthew MS 7th Cav. Co.F Cpl.
Segler, T.F. AL Arty. 4th Bn. Hilliard's Legion Co.B,E
Segler, T.F. AL Lt.Arty. Kolb's Btty.
Segler, T.F. AL 59th Inf. Co.E
Segler, T.F. Gen. & Staff Hosp.Stew.
Segler, William R. MS 19th Inf. Co.E
Segley, Miles Thomas NC Hvy.Arty. 10th Bn. Co.C
Segman, James VA 6th Inf. Co.C

Segner, Antonio LA Mil. 5th Regt.Eur.Brig. (Spanish Regt.) Co.4
Segni, Bartole FL 8th Inf. Co.D Cpl.
Sego, A.H. TX 32nd Cav. Co.K
Sego, Calvin C. GA Cobb's Legion Co.A
Sego, Charles MO 6th Inf. Co.E
Sego, E.H. NC Mallett's Bn. (Cp.Guard) Co.B
Sego, G.W. AL 27th Inf. Co.C
Sego, G.W. TN 21st (Wilson's) Cav. Co.A
Sego, Jeremiah GA 57th Inf. Co.F
Sego, J.J. TN 55th (Brown's) Inf. Co.F
Sego, Jo. AL Cav. Moreland's Regt. Co.C
Sego, John TN 27th Inf. Co.F
Sego, John T. GA 50th Inf. Co.D
Sego, J.Q. AL Cav. Moreland's Regt. Co.D
Sego, J.T. GA Cav. Allen's Co.
Sego, Lawrence SC 1st Cav. Co.C
Sego, Leonidas SC 19th Inf. Co.B
Sego, O.J. GA Cav. Allen's Co.
Sego, Oliver J. GA 48th Inf. Co.I
Sego, Peter L. SC 1st Arty. Co.I
Sego, R.B. GA Cav. Allen's Co.
Sego, Telemachin M. GA 20th Inf. Co.K
Sego, Thomas TX 15th Cav. Co.G
Sego, Thomas A. SC 6th Cav. Co.B
Sego, Thomas W. AR 2nd Mtd.Rifles Co.B
Sego, T.P. TX 32nd Cav. Co.K
Sego, William GA 8th Cav. Co.H
Sego, William GA 62nd Cav. Co.H
Sego, William GA 10th Inf. Co.D
Sego, William TX 15th Cav. Co.G
Segoe, Malicha R. NC 43rd Inf. Co.H
Segoura, Gerard LA Conscr.
Segoura, Hervillien LA Conscr.
Segoura, Joseph O. LA Conscr.
Segraves, Alvin AR 35th Inf. Co.G
Segraves, A.W. NC Lt.Arty. 3rd Bn. Co.C
Segraves, B. MO Inf. Clark's Regt. Co.I
Segraves, C.N. GA 24th Inf. Co.F
Segraves, G. NC 1st Jr.Res. Co.D
Segraves, Hardy P. GA 16th Inf. Co.D
Segraves, Henry AL 37th Inf. Co.I
Segraves, J. GA 9th Inf. (St.Guards) Culp's Co.
Segraves, Jacob AR 38th Inf. Co.E
Segraves, Jacob A. NC Lt.Arty. 3rd Bn. Co.C
Segraves, James AR Inf. Hardy's Regt. Co.A
Segraves, James B. GA 4th Bn.S.S. Co.B
Segraves, James C. GA 37th Inf. Co.E
Segraves, Jesse TN 13th (Gore's) Cav. Co.I
Segraves, John G. GA Inf. 9th Bn. Co.B
Segraves, John G. GA 37th Inf. Co.E
Segraves, Joseph R. NC 26th Inf. Co.I
Segraves, Paschal NC 26th Inf. Co.D
Segraves, R.B. AR 33rd Inf. Co.H
Segraves, R.B. GA Inf. 9th Bn. Co.B
Segraves, R.B. GA 37th Inf. Co.E
Segraves, R.F. AR 36th Inf. Co.G 2nd Lt.
Segraves, Richard Conf.Cav. Clarkson's Bn. Ind.Rangers Co.C
Segraves, Rufus NC 3rd Cav. (41st St.Troops) Co.I Teamster
Segraves, Rufus NC 47th Inf. Co.H
Segraves, S.C. NC 31st Inf. Co.C
Segraves, Thomas F. AR Cav. Wright's Regt. Co.E Cpl.
Segraves, T.J. NC Snead's Co. (Loc.Def.)
Segraves, Valentine AR 38th Inf. Co.E

Segraves, Vincen MO 15th Cav. Co.G 1st Lt.
Segraves, Vincent AR 25th Inf. Co.A 1st Sgt.
Segraves, V.O. MO 15th Cav. Co.F
Segraves, W. NC Allen's Co. (Loc.Def.)
Segraves, W.D. GA 37th Inf. Co.E
Segraves, W.H. AR 26th Inf. Co.K
Segraves, W.H. NC 1st Inf. Co.G
Segraves, William GA 9th Inf. (St.Guards) Culp's
   Co.
Segraves, William D. GA Inf. 9th Bn. Co.B
Segraves, William H. AR 1st (Colquitt's) Inf.
   Co.K
Segraves, William H. MO Cav. Davies' Bn.
   Mehoe's Co.
Segraves, William J. GA Arty. 9th Bn. Co.D
Segres, James AL Arty. 1st Bn. Co.B
Segrest, C.B. AL 62nd Inf. Co.I
Segrest, Charles T. AL 61st Inf. Co.H
Segrest, David L. AL 61st Inf. Co.H
Segrest, D.M. AL 3rd Inf. Co.C
Segrest, D.T. MS 38th Cav. Co.B Sgt.
Segrest, George W. AL 3rd Inf. Co.C
Segrest, Henry AL 45th Inf. Co.G Sgt.
Segrest, H.G. AL 34th Inf. Co.F,E
Segrest, J.A. AL 45th Inf. Co.G Cpl.
Segrest, J.A. GA 8th Cav. Co.K
Segrest, James M. AL 34th Inf. Co.K
Segrest, John D. GA 55th Inf. Co.C
Segrest, J.R. 7th Conf.Cav. Co.K
Segrest, J.W. AL 1st Regt.Conscr. Co.E
Segrest, J.W. 7th Conf.Cav. Co.K
Segrest, L.L. MS St.Cav. 3rd Bn. (Cooper's)
   Little's Co.
Segrest, Louis MS 38th Cav. Co.B
Segrest, Nathan W. GA 55th Inf. Co.C
Segrest, Phillip AL 45th Inf. Co.G
Segrest, P.R. VA Inf. Lyneman's Co.
Segrest, S.A. 7th Conf.Cav. Co.D
Segrest, S.T. AL 3rd Inf. Co.C
Segrest, Thomas J. 20th Conf.Cav. Co.B
Segrest, T.J. MS 4th Cav. Co.C
Segrest, T.R. AL Lt.Arty. Clanton's Btty.
Segrest, U.D. SC 5th Cav. Co.I
Segrest, U.D. SC Cav. 14th Bn. Co.D
Segrey, Charles TX 26th Cav. Co.A
Segrist, B. MS Inf. 2nd Bn. (St.Troops) Co.A
   Cpl.
Segrist, Charles AL 13th Inf. Co.B 1st Sgt.
Segrist, David F. AL 4th Inf. Co.B
Segrist, David R. AL 4th Inf. Co.B,D
Segrist, D.P. Conf.Cav. Powers' Regt. Co.E
Segrist, H. MS Inf. 2nd Bn. (St.Troops) Co.F
Segrist, Jacob R. AL 1st Regt.Conscr. Co.B
Segrist, Jacob R. AL 4th Inf. Co.B
Segrist, Jerre W. AL 4th Inf. Co.B
Segrist, Noah AL 4th Res. Co.H
Segrist, Peter R. AL 4th Inf. Co.B
Segrist, P.J. AL 1st Regt. Co.B
Segrist, R.B. AL Lt.Arty. Clanton's Btty.
Segrist, R.F. AL 12th Inf. Co.F
Segrist, S. Absalom AL 4th Inf. Co.B
Segrist, W.E. LA 25th Inf. Co.K
Segrist, W.S. AL 9th Inf. Co.G
Segrove, J.T. AR Inf. Kuykendall's Co. Cpl.
Segroves, A.M. AR Cav. Davies' Bn. Co.E
Segroves, A.M. AR 30th Inf. Co.F
Segroves, James B. NC 7th Inf. Co.G

Segroves, Jesse W. NC 7th Inf. Co.G
Segroves, Joel H. NC 7th Inf. Co.G
Segroves, John T. AR Inf. 1st Bn. Co.D Cpl.
Segroves, J.T. AR Cav. Davies' Bn. Co.E
Segroves, S.H. AR 5th Inf. Co.H Cpl.
Segroves, Wesley NC 26th Inf. Co.D
Segroves, William NC 26th Inf. Co.D
Segroves, William TX 11th Inf. Co.C
Segsfoot, M.A. AL McQueen's Cav.
Seguela, --- LA Mil. 3rd Regt.Eur.Brig. (Garde
   Francaise) Co.5 1st Sgt.
Segui, Celestial H. FL 3rd Inf. Co.B
Segui, Charles D. FL 3rd Inf. Co.B 1st Lt.
Segui, John FL 8th Inf. Co.D
Segui, Thomas FL 3rd Inf. Co.E 1st Music.
Seguin, James LA Mil. Chalmette Regt. Co.H
Seguin, R. LA Mil. 1st Regt. French Brig. Co.4
Seguin, Valmon LA 4th Inf. Co.F
Segula, C. AL 21st Inf. Co.G
Se gu oyah Tahle yes kie 1st Cherokee Mtd.Rifles
   Co.K
Segur, Charles B. Gillum's Regt. Co.G Sgt.
Segur, E.L. GA 1st (Olmstead's) Inf. Screven's
   Co., Co.G
Segur, E.L. GA Inf. 18th Bn. Co.A Cpl.
Segur, Hampden S. GA 5th Inf. Co.A
Segur, Henry F. GA 63rd Inf. Co.B,D
Segur, H.F. GA 1st (Olmstead's) Inf. Gordon's
   Co., Stiles' Co.
Segur, H.F. GA Inf. 18th Bn. Co.B
Segur, J.W. AL 45th Inf. Co.G
Segura, A. LA Mil. 1st Native Guards
Segura, A. LA 18th Inf. Co.A
Segura, Alcebiave LA 7th Cav. Co.I
Segura, C. LA 18th Inf. Co.C
Segura, Juan TX 8th Inf. Co.C
Segura, Ulysses LA Inf. 10th Bn. Co.F
Segura, Wlysse LA 7th Cav. Co.I
Segure, E.L. 2nd Conf.Eng.Troops Co.D Artif.
Segure, H.F. 2nd Conf.Eng.Troops Co.D Sgt.
Seguro, H. LA Inf. 10th Bn. Co.C
Seguro, Teodoro TX Cav. 3rd (Yager's) Bn.
   Rhodes' Co.
Seguro, Tomas TX 3rd Inf. 1st Co.A
Segurs, Simeon FL Inf. 2nd Bn. Co.E
Segushue, Vanderlieu LA 6th Inf.
Segust, H. MS 4th Cav. Co.C
Sehaman, Valentine TX
Se he chi pe 1st Creek Mtd.Vol. 2nd Co.C Cpl.
Sehers, Henry LA 5th Inf. Co.E Sgt.
Sehlinger, Ch. LA Mil. Orleans Fire Regt. Co.I
Sehlinger, Fas. LA Mil. Orleans Fire Regt. Co.I
Sehlinger, Fg. LA Mil. Orleans Fire Regt. Co.I
Sehlte, J. LA Mil. 4th Regt. 1st Brig. 1st Div.
   Co.E
Sehon, C.M. AR 35th Inf. Co.C
Sehon, Henry LA Arty. Moody's Co. (Madison
   Lt.Arty.)
Sehon, Jno. L. Gen. & Staff, QM Dept. Maj.
Sehorn, A. Wallace VA 4th Inf. Co.A
Sehorn, Charles E. NC Cav. 5th Bn. Co.D
Sehorn, Jacob W. NC Walker's Bn. Thomas'
   Legion Co.G
Sehorn, Samuel L. NC Walker's Bn. Thomas'
   Legion Co.G
Sehorn, William H. NC Walker's Bn. Thomas'
   Legion Co.G

Sehorne, Charles E. NC 6th Cav. (65th
   St.Troops) Co.D
Sehrt, H.P.W. LA Mil. 4th Regt.Eur.Brig. Co.F
Seibe, Henry T. MS 16th Inf. Co.C
Seibel, H. MS 18th Inf. Co.D
Seibel, John TX 3rd Inf. Co.B
Seibel, Nic LA Mil. Fire Bn. Co.C
Seibels, E. Gen. & Staff Capt.,ACS
Seibels, Emmett SC 7th Inf. Maj.
Seibels, John J. AL 6th Inf. Col.
Seibenn, P. LA Mil. 4th Regt. 2nd Brig. 1st Div.
   Co.D
Seiber, Ferdinand TX Inf. 2nd St.Troops Co.G
Seiber, F.M. TX 14th Inf. Co.D
Seiber, Frederick, Jr. NC Inf. Thomas Legion
   Co.K
Seiber, Frederick, Sr. NC Inf. Thomas Legion
   Co.K
Seiber, George AL 48th Inf. Co.K
Seiber, George NC Inf. Thomas Legion Co.K
Seiber, Henry W. NC Inf. Thomas Legion Co.K
Seiber, J.C. AL 20th Inf. Co.K Cpl.
Seiber, J.C. AL 30th Inf. Co.B
Seiber, Jordan NC Inf. Thomas Legion Co.K
Seiber, Joseph NC Inf. Thomas Legion Co.K
Seiber, Philip NC Inf. Thomas Legion Co.K
Seiber, Samuel NC Inf. Thomas Legion Co.K
Seiber, Thomas NC Inf. Thomas Legion Co.K
Seiberger, A. LA Mil. Chalmette Regt. Co.K
Seibert, --- TX 5th Cav. Co.A
Seibert, Abraham VA 1st Cav. Co.B
Seibert, Adam LA Inf. Jeff Davis Regt. Co.F
Seibert, Adam VA 77th Mil. Co.C
Seibert, Charles J. VA 11th Cav. Co.D
Seibert, Eli VA 1st Cav. Co.B
Seibert, F. SC Inf. 1st (Charleston) Bn. Co.F
Seibert, F. SC 27th Inf. Co.C
Seibert, F. TX Inf. Houston's Bn. (Detailed Men)
   Co.C Capt.
Seibert, F. VA 2nd St.Res. Co.N 1st Lt.
Seibert, F. Gen. & Staff AQM
Seibert, Felix LA 28th (Thomas') Inf. Co.C
Seibert, Ferdinand TX 4th Field Btty. 1st Sgt.
Seibert, Frederick VA 1st St.Res. Co.E
Seibert, F.W. TX Cav. Benavides' Regt. Co.F
Seibert, George LA Mil. Orleans Fire Regt. Co.A
Seibert, H. LA Lt.Arty. Fenner's Btty.
Seibert, J. Conf.Reg.Inf. Brooks' Bn. Co.A
Seibert, Jacob LA Mil. 1st Regt. 3rd Brig. 1st
   Div. Co.E
Seibert, James W. VA 33rd Inf. Co.D
Seibert, J.B. VA 14th Cav. Co.A
Seibert, J.B. VA 67th Mil. Co.B Sgt.
Seibert, J. Beatty VA 11th Cav. Co.A 2nd Lt.
Seibert, J.C. TX Inf. Timmons' Regt. Co.B
Seibert, John TX Waul's Legion Co.E
Seibert, John B. VA 1st Cav. Co.B 1st Sgt.
Seibert, John H. VA 1st Cav. Co.F
Seibert, Joseph VA 1st Lt.Arty. Co.B
Seibert, Joseph VA Lt.Arty. J.S. Brown's Co.
Seibert, Joseph VA Lt.Arty. Taylor's Co. Cpl.
Seibert, Joseph L. VA 18th Cav. Co.F 1st Lt.
Seibert, Joseph M. VA 2nd Inf. Co.B
Seibert, Joseph S. VA 31st Mil. Co.G 1st Lt.
Seibert, J.W. VA 18th Cav. Co.F
Seibert, M. LA Mil. Fire Bn. Co.B
Seibert, Onesimus F. VA 1st Cav. Co.F

Seibert, P.W. VA 18th Cav. Co.H
Seibert, Rudolph MS Cav. Jeff Davis Legion Co.F
Seibert, W. VA 2nd St.Res. Co.C
Seibert, Wendel VA 1st Cav. Co.B
Seibil, Jacob AR 9th Inf. Co.A
Seibill, A. TX 37th Cav. Gray's Co.
Seible, Conrad LA Arty. Castellanos' Btty.
Seibles, E. SC 5th Cav. Co.D
Seibrecht, Henry J. SC 1st Arty. Co.C Sgt.
Seibrecht, L.P. LA Washington Arty. Bn. Co.5
Seibrecht, Phillip LA Washington Arty.Bn. Co.1
Seibt, J. VA Lt.Arty. 13th Bn. Co.A Artif.
Seicshneydre, Arthur LA Washington Arty.Bn. Co.3
Seicshneydre, Leonce LA Washington Arty.Bn. Co.3
Seidel, Charles W. GA 15th Inf. Co.C
Seidel, E. TX 4th Inf. (St.Troops) Co.F
Seidel, E. TX Waul's Legion Co.C Cpl.
Seidel, Ewld TX Inf. Timmons' Regt. Co.K Cpl.
Seidel, Frank TX 17th Inf. Co.B
Seidel, Herman TX 4th Cav. Co.C
Seidel, J.G. Conf.Cav. Wood's Regt. Co.H
Seidel, John Conf.Inf. 8th Bn. Co.C
Seidell, Hermann LA 8th Inf. Co.B
Seidelmann, L. TX Waul's Legion Co.D Music.
Seidenberg, Ernst TX 36th Cav. Co.H 1st Bugler
Seidenheimer, J. LA Mil. Fire Bn. Co.D
Seidenroth, Charles LA Mil. Orleans Fire Regt. Co.A
Seidenspinner, Joseph MS 21st Inf. Co.D
Seidentoff, William LA 1st (Nelligan's) Inf. Co.A
Seidenzahl, G. LA Mil. Mech.Guard
Seider, Jacob LA Nelligan's Inf. Co.C
Seiders, Thomas L. VA 22nd Inf. Co.A Cpl.
Seidler, Charles LA Inf. 9th Co.D
Seidler, Frederick MO 1st Inf. 2nd Co.A
Seidrich, Ignaz LA Mil.Cont.Regt. Lang's Co.
Seier, C. TX Inf. Timmons' Regt. Co.D
Seier, J. TX Waul's Legion Co.F
Seier, William TX Waul's Legion Co.C
Seifarth, C. SC Mil.Arty. 1st Regt. Co.C
Seifarth, C.C. SC Inf. 1st (Charleston) Bn. Co.B
Seifarth, Edward TX 2nd Inf. Co.F
Seifers, John B. VA 16th Cav. Co.H
Seifert, Adam VA Inf. 25th Bn. Co.E
Seifert, George T. VA 2nd St.Res. Co.K
Seifert, John AL Gorff's Co. (Mobile Pulaski Rifles)
Seifert, John AL 21st Inf. Co.H
Seiffert, Adam AL 5th Bn.Vol. Co.A
Seig, Francis L. GA 4th Inf. Co.K
Seig, J. MO Lt.Arty. 3rd Field Btty.
Seig, T.F. MO Lt.Arty. 3rd Btty.
Seige, J.A. LA 2nd Inf. Co.E
Seigel, Charles TN Lt.Arty. Morton's Co.
Seigel, Charles A. KY 8th Mtd.Inf. Co.K Cpl.
Seigel, Martin LA 1st (Strawbridge's) Inf. Co.D,F
Seigert, G. AL 1st Regt. Mobile Vol. Co.E
Seigert, G. AL 4th Res. Co.C
Seigfried, J.H. VA 15th Cav. Co.B
Seigfried, John TX 16th Inf. Co.F
Seigle, A. LA Mil. Fire Bn. Co.E
Seigle, George LA Mil. Fire Bn. Co.E

Seigle, H. NC 3rd Jr.Res. Co.E
Seigle, John Henry VA 53rd Inf. Co.D
Seigle, John M. MS Lt.Arty. (The Hudson Btty.) Hoole's Co.
Seigle, M. NC Cav. 14th Bn.
Seigle, Martin LA 21st (Kennedy's) Inf. Co.F
Seigle, Noah NC 26th Inf. Co.I
Seigle, Thomas L. NC 1st Arty. (10th St.Troops) Co.C 2nd Lt.
Seiglee, R.M. AL 58th Inf. Co.F
Seigler, A.J. VA 6th Cav. Co.C 2nd Lt.
Seigler, A.J. VA 23rd Cav. Co.B
Seigler, A.J. VA Cav. 41st Bn. Co.B
Seigler, Andrew Jackson SC 7th Inf. 1st Co.C, 2nd Co.C
Seigler, Aquilla S. SC 7th Inf. 1st Co.F
Seigler, A.S. SC 1st Bn.S.S. Co.A
Seigler, Bernard TX 3rd Inf. Co.I
Seigler, C.F. VA 2nd St.Res. Co.B
Seigler, David GA 6th Inf. Co.F
Seigler, David GA Inf. (Mitchell Home Guards) Brooks' Co.
Seigler, David J. SC 3rd Bn.Res. Co.B
Seigler, E.C. GA Inf. 1st City Bn. (Columbus) Co.C
Seigler, Elias SC Inf. Hampton Legion Co.B
Seigler, E.W. SC 7th Inf. 1st Co.F
Seigler, Fritz TX St.Troops Atkins' Co.
Seigler, George LA 25th Inf. Co.H
Seigler, Gibson H. SC 24th Inf. Co.K Cpl.
Seigler, H.G. SC 7th Inf. 1st Co.K 2nd Lt.
Seigler, H.G. SC 24th Inf. Co.K Cpl.
Seigler, H.H. TN 29th Inf. Co.B
Seigler, I. SC 16th & 24th (Cons.) Inf. Co.I
Seigler, Irvin SC 24th Inf. Co.C
Seigler, J. LA Mil. Chalmette Regt. Co.E
Seigler, Jacob SC 24th Inf. Co.C
Seigler, James SC 2nd St.Troops Co.F
Seigler, James SC 20th Inf. Co.C
Seigler, James TN 12th (Green's) Cav. Co.K
Seigler, J.E. GA Cav. 8th Bn. (St.Guards) Co.B Sgt.
Seigler, J.F. SC 20th Inf. Co.B
Seigler, J.J. AL 23rd Inf. Co.F
Seigler, John LA Mil. 4th Regt. 3rd Brig. 1st Div. Co.D
Seigler, John G. GA Cobb's Legion Co.B
Seigler, John M. FL Lt.Arty. Perry's Co.
Seigler, John R. GA 24th Inf. Co.B
Seigler, J.P. SC 2nd St.Troops Co.K
Seigler, L. AL 1st Cav. 2nd Co.E
Seigler, Leander GA 45th Inf. Co.G,I Cpl.
Seigler, M. FL Cav. 5th Bn. Co.G
Seigler, Samuel W. TN 43rd Inf. Co.K 1st Lt.
Seigler, Solomon VA 2nd Inf. Co.E
Seigler, Tandy M. SC 24th Inf. Co.K 2nd Lt.
Seigler, Thomas SC 24th Inf. Co.G
Seigler, Thomas TN 12th (Green's) Cav. Co.K
Seigler, T.M. SC 16th & 24th (Cons.) Inf. Co.I 1st Lt.
Seigler, W. SC 2nd Inf. Co.I
Seigler, W. SC 24th Inf. Co.C
Seigler, W.H. KY 7th Mtd.Inf. Co.L Cpl.
Seigler, William SC 2nd Inf. Co.C
Seigler, William SC 20th Inf. Co.C
Seigler, William A.J. SC 5th Res. Co.F
Seigler, W.Y. SC 6th Inf. 1st Co.C

Seigman, J.L. NC McLean's Bn.Lt.Duty Men Co.B
Seigman, R. GA Inf. (GA RR Guards) Porter's Co.
Seigman, T.F. TN 13th Inf. Co.G
Seigmondt, George A. AL 12th Inf. Co.A
Seigne, Huma LA 13th Inf. Co.D
Seignette, Carl LA 1st (Nelligan's) Inf. Co.B
Seignions, C.W. SC Mil. 1st Regt. (Charleston Res.) Co.D
Seignouret, A. LA Mil. 1st Regt. French Brig. Co.1
Seigurs, George D. GA Hvy.Arty. 22nd Bn. Co.C
Seiker, E.A. Gen. & Staff AASurg.
Seile, Charles SC 5th Cav. Co.D
Seile, Charles SC Cav. 17th Bn. Co.A
Seiler, Anthony F. LA Inf.Crescent Regt. Co.I Cpl.
Seiler, C. LA Mil. Orleans Guards Regt. Co.D
Seiler, Fred LA Cav. Greenleaf's Co. (Orleans Lt.Horse)
Seiler, Fred LA Mil. Orleans Guards Regt. Co.D
Seiler, John LA Inf.Crescent Regt. Co.I
Seiler, Joseph W. LA Mil. Lafayette Arty.
Seiler, L. TX 4th Inf. (St.Troops) Co.F
Seiler, William T. LA Inf.Crescent Regt. Co.I
Seilers, Samuel VA 19th Inf. Co.B
Seily, G.W. SC 1st (McCreary's) Inf. Co.G
Seimms, Frederick D. VA 1st Arty. 2nd Co.C
Seindblad, Charles AL St.Arty. Co.C
Seine, James TN 1st Cav.
Seins, William AR 13th Inf. Co.E
Seion, George W. VA 11th Cav. Co.E
Seip, F. LA Inf.Crescent Regt. Co.K 2nd Lt.
Seip, John TN 2nd (Robison's) Inf. Co.H,K
Seipples, Charles LA 2nd Cav. Co.I
Seirs, R.P. LA Mil. Lewis Guards
Seirs, W. TN 9th Inf. Co.I
Seis, Rafael TX Cav. Giddings' Bn. Co.A
Seischnaydre, A. LA 22nd Inf. Co.B
Seischnaydre, L. LA 22nd Inf. Co.B
Seisco, John TX 12th Cav. Co.G
Seiskind, P.A. LA Mil. 4th Regt.Eur.Brig. Co.E
Seiss, L. LA 18th Inf. Co.I
Seitenburg, Clemanee LA 22nd Inf.
Seither, F. LA Mil. Lewis Guards
Seither, Frederick LA Mil. Orleans Fire Regt. Co.F
Seither, J. LA Mil. Lewis Guards
Seither, Jacob LA 14th Inf. Co.K
Seither, Joseph LA Mil. Orleans Fire Regt. Co.F 2nd Lt.
Seithern, Jacob LA 1st (Nelligan's) Inf. Co.C
Seithman, George MS Inf. 2nd Bn. Co.E
Seitler, Joseph LA Arty. Castellanos' Btty.
Seitz, --- TX Cav. McCord's Frontier Regt. Co.K
Seitz, Anderson AL 11th Cav.
Seitz, A.T. TN 16th Inf. Co.I 3rd Lt.
Seitz, David GA 1st (Fannin's) Res. Co.K
Seitz, David N. NC 23rd Inf. Co.F
Seitz, D.C. AR 17th (Griffith's) Inf. Co.G
Seitz, D.C. AR 35th Inf. Co.K
Seitz, D.D. NC 4th Sr.Res. Co.C
Seitz, Emanuel VA 19th Cav. Co.C
Seitz, F. LA Mil. Orleans Fire Regt. Co.I
Seitz, G.J.M. AR 35th Inf. Co.K

Seitz, G.L. NC 23rd Inf. Co.F Cpl.
Seitz, Henry O. GA 11th Cav. Co.E Cpl.
Seitz, J. AL 1st Regt. Mobile Vol. Baas' Co.
Seitz, James AR 1st (Colquitt's) Inf. Co.C
Seitz, John AL 4th Res. Co.B
Seitz, John LA Mil.Cont.Regt. Lang's Co.
Seitz, John C. GA 1st Reg. Co.B
Seitz, Joseph LA Mil. 4th Regt. 2nd Brig. 1st
    Div. Co.G
Seitz, Julius NC 23rd Inf. Co.F
Seitz, S.A. AR 17th (Griffith's) Inf. Co.G Cpl.
Seitz, Laban M. NC 28th Inf. Co.C
Seitz, Lawson A. AR 35th Inf. Co.K Cpl.
Seitz, Levi NC 35th Inf. Co.K
Seitz, L.M. TX 12th Cav. Co.G Sgt.
Seitz, Marcus NC 28th Inf. Co.C
Seitz, S. LA Mil. Orleans Fire Regt. Co.A
Seitz, S.J. AR 5th Inf. Co.E
Seitz, Tucker AR Cav. Harrell's Bn. Co.B
Seitz, W.J. AL Lt.Arty. Tarrant's Btty.
Seitze, Henry GA Inf. 11th Bn. (St.Guards) Co.B
Seitze, Henry O. GA Inf. 11th Bn. (St.Guards)
    Co.B
Seitze, John GA Inf. 11th Bn. (St.Guards) Co.B
Seitzler, Joseph MS 1st Lt.Arty. Co.D
Seitzler, Wyley AR Cav. Wright's Regt. Co.C
    Cpl.
Seitzs, Charles H. MS 29th Inf. Co.I
Seiveigne, --- LA Mil. 1st Chasseurs a pied Co.1
Seiver, B. FL 1st (Res.) Inf. Co.D
Seiver, George W. VA 136th Mil. Co.A
Seiver, James S. VA 2nd Cav. Co.E
Seiver, John A. VA 14th Cav. Co.C
Seiver, John A. VA 162nd Mil. Co.B
Seiver, J.W. VA 10th Bn.Res. Co.D
Seiver, Samuel F. VA 20th Cav. Co.D
Seivers, Charles Conf.Reg.Inf. Brooks' Bn. Co.F
Seivers, Frederick TX 5th Inf. Co.B
Seivers, James MO 8th Inf. Co.H
Seivers, J.C. MS 39th Inf. Co.K
Seivert, John Conf.Reg.Inf. Brooks' Bn. Co.A
Seiwers, Joseph NC 33rd Inf. Co.I
Seix, Edmond VA 12th Cav. Co.K
Seix, Edward VA 33rd Inf. Co.K Sgt.
Seix, John S. VA 33rd Inf. Co.K 1st Lt.
Seixas, B.M. SC 20th Inf. Co.G
Seixas, C.L. VA 3rd Inf.Loc.Def. Co.D
Seixas, Henry O. LA Arty. Green's Co. (LA
    Guard Btty.)
Seixas, Henry O. LA 1st (Nelligan's) Inf. 1st
    Co.B
Seixas, J.M. LA Washington Arty.Bn. Co.5 2nd
    Lt.
Seixas, J.M. Gen. & Staff, A. of TN Maj.
Seiz, Antonis TX Cav. Ragsdale's Bn. Co.B
Seiz, Basilla TX Cav. Ragsdale's Bn. Co.B
Sejour, --- LA Mil. 1st Native Guards
Sejour, M. LA Mil. 1st Native Guards
Se ke ke 1st Creek Mtd.Vol. Co.M
Sekeles, Leopold MS 30th Inf. Co.B
Sekeles, Louis MS 2nd Inf. (A. of 10,000) Co.A
Sekinger, S.F. GA 5th Res. Co.E
Sel, Frank LA Pointe Coupee Arty.
Sel, Frank LA Arty. Watson Btty.
Sel, J. LA Mil. Orleans Guards Regt. Co.B
Sela, Jacob TX 27th Cav. Co.D,M
Selan, W. NC Inf. 2nd Bn. Co.A

Selards, David VA 16th Cav. Co.E
Selards, David VA Cav. Ferguson's Bn. Spur-
    lock's Co.
Selassi, Charles LA 4th Cav. Co.E
Selbe, Sherrod VA 18th Inf. Co.D
Selby, A. TN 2nd (Walker's) Inf. Co.D 1st Lt.
Selby, Armand LA 4th Inf. Co.C
Selby, Charles G. MO 5th Inf. Co.H Sr.2nd Lt.
Selby, Charles G. MO St.Guard
Selby, Daniel H. MS 35th Inf. Co.A
Selby, David P. NC Part.Rangers Swindell's Co.
Selby, Dixon S. NC 17th Inf. (1st Org.) Co.B
Selby, Edmond C. SC 2nd Inf. Co.F
Selby, George LA Inf.Crescent Regt. Co.C Cpl.
Selby, George B. NC 3rd Arty. (40th St.Troops)
    Co.I
Selby, George W. AL Nitre & Min. Corps
    Young's Co. Cpl.
Selby, George W. MS 16th Inf. Co.F Cpl.
Selby, H. TN 13th (Gore's) Cav. Co.H
Selby, Henry NC 33rd Inf. Co.F
Selby, Henry VA 10th Bn.Res. Co.B
Selby, Henry VA Rockbridge Cty.Res.
    Hutcheson's Co.
Selby, Isaiah TX 15th Cav. Co.G Cpl.
Selby, Jas. MD Weston's Bn. Co.B
Selby, James NC 3rd Arty. (40th St.Troops) Co.I
Selby, James VA 21st Inf. Co.B
Selby, James Conf.Inf. 8th Bn.
Selby, James B. AL Lt.Arty. 2nd Bn. Co.A Sgt.
Selby, James E. MS 17th Inf. Co.D 1st Lt.
Selby, James H. MS Lt.Arty. (The Hudson Btty.)
    Hoole's Co.
Selby, James J. MS 12th Cav. Co.B
Selby, James J. MS 37th Inf. Co.D
Selby, James O. AL 4th (Russell's) Cav. Co.E
Selby, James S. TN 13th (Gore's) Cav. Co.E
Selby, James S. TN 25th Inf. Co.I
Selby, James W. MO 2nd Inf. Co.H Capt.
Selby, J.C. MS 25th Inf. Co.B
Selby, J.D. MS 37th Inf. Co.D
Selby, J.E. MS 4th Cav. Co.G
Selby, J.E. MS Cav. Hughes' Bn. Co.F
Selby, J.H. MS Inf. 2nd St.Troops Co.D
Selby, Jim TX 23rd Cav. Co.A
Selby, J.J. MS St.Cav. Perrin's Bn. Co.C
Selby, J.J. MS 1st (Patton's) Inf. Halfacre's Co.
Selby, J.M. VA 15th Cav. Co.B
Selby, J.O. AL 4th Inf. Co.E Sgt.
Selby, John MD 1st Inf. Co.I
Selby, John NC Lt.Arty. 13th Bn. Co.D
Selby, John SC Inf. Holcombe Legion Co.F
Selby, John A. SC 8th Bn.Res. Co.A
Selby, John A. SC Vol. Simons' Co. Ord.Sgt.
Selby, John F. VA 4th Inf. Co.H
Selby, John N. NC 17th Inf. (1st Org.) Co.B
Selby, John W. NC 4th Inf. Co.I
Selby, Joseph VA 30th Bn.S.S. Co.E 1st Lt.
Selby, Joseph VA 21st Inf. Co.B 2nd Lt.
Selby, Milton NC 32nd Inf. Co.F,A
Selby, M.R. TX 9th Cav. Co.C
Selby, Norman C. VA 109th Mil. Co.B
Selby, O.E. MS 1st (Foote's) Inf. (St.Troops)
    Hobart's Co. Cpl.
Selby, P.H. MS 14th Inf. Co.G
Selby, Robert F. AL Nitre & Min. Corps
    Young's Co.

Selby, Robert H. TX 29th Cav. Co.E
Selby, Robert H. 1st Choctaw & Chickasaw
    Mtd.Rifles 1st Co.I
Selby, Samuel AL 4th (Russell's) Cav. Co.E
Selby, Samuel NC 2nd Jr.Res. Co.I 1st Lt.
Selby, T.B. VA Lt.Arty. Barr's Co.
Selby, T.H. MS 2nd Cav. Co.B Sgt.Maj.
Selby, Thomas B. MO Cav. Wood's Regt. Capt.
Selby, Thomas J. MS Lt.Arty. (The Hudson
    Btty.) Hoole's Co.
Selby, Thomas W. TX Cav. Martin's Regt. Co.E
    Cpl.
Selby, T.J. AL 4th (Russell's) Cav. Co.E
Selby, Warren C. MS 9th Inf. Old Co.B, New
    Co.C
Selby, W.D. AL 4th (Russell's) Cav. Co.E
Selby, William MS 37th Inf. Co.D 1st Sgt.
Selby, William MO Inf. 3rd Regt.St.Guard Co.H
    3rd Lt.
Selby, William TN 8th Inf. Co.F
Selby, William TX 15th Cav. Co.G
Selby, William A. AL Lt.Arty. 2nd Bn. Co.A
Selby, William C. MS 35th Inf. Co.A Sgt.
Selby, William H. VA 4th Inf. Co.H Cpl.
Selby, William H. VA 25th Inf. 2nd Co.H
Selby, William M. MS 14th Inf. Co.B Cpl.
Selby, William M. VA 34th Inf. Co.C
Selby, William T. NC 33rd Inf. Co.F
Selcer, William LA 21st (Kennedy's) Inf. Co.C
    Cpl.
Selcer, William 1st Conf.Cav. 2nd Co.K
Selden, Alfred F. VA 9th Cav. Co.H
Selden, Alfred F. VA Inf. 25th Bn. Co.C
Selden, Beverly R. VA 4th Cav. Co.E 1st Lt.
Selden, Braxton VA 9th Cav. Co.H Sgt.
Selden, C. VA 1st (Farinholt's) Res. Co.I
Selden, C.C. TN 7th (Duckworth's) Cav. Co.A
Selden, Charles Conf.Inf. Tucker's Regt.
    Asst.Surg.
Selden, Charles Gen. & Staff, Arty. 1st Lt.,MSK
Selden, Chas., Jr. Gen. & Staff 1st Lt.Arty.
Selden, Charles, Jr. VA Lt.Arty. R.M. Ander-
    son's Co.
Selden, Charles Gen. & Staff Asst.Surg.
Selden, C.P. VA 3rd Inf.Loc.Def. Co.I
Selden, D.H. VA Inf. 44th Bn. Co.E Sgt.
Selden, F.T. LA Mil.Cav. (Jeff Davis Rangers)
    Norwood's Co.
Selden, Harry H. Ewell's Staff Maj.
Selden, J.M. VA 10th Cav. 2nd Co.E 1st Sgt.
Selden, John VA 1st Arty. Co.H Sgt.
Selden, John, Jr. VA 1st Arty. Co.K Ord.Off.
Selden, John VA Lt.Arty. 1st Bn. Ord.Off.
Selden, John VA 2nd Inf. Co.G
Selden, John Cutsham's Arty.Bn. 1st
    Lt.,Ord.Off.
Selden, John A. Gen. & Staff, A. of N.VA
    Capt.,ACS
Selden, John A., Jr. VA 3rd Cav. Co.D ACS
Selden, Joseph AL Gid Nelson Lt.Arty. Capt.
Selden, Miles VA 5th Cav. AQM
Selden, Miles VA Hvy.Arty. 10th Bn.
    Capt.,AQM
Selden, Miles VA 49th Inf. AQM
Selden, Miles Gen. & Staff, QM Dept.
    Capt.,AQM
Selden, Miles C., Jr. Gen. & Staff 1st Lt.,ADC

Selden, M.L. TN 7th (Duckworth's) Cav. Co.A
Selden, R.C. Gen. & Staff MSK
Selden, R.D. Mumford's Cav.Brig. Sgt.
Selden, Richard C. VA 4th Cav. Co.E
Selden, Robert VA 4th Cav. Co.E
Selden, Robert C. VA 3rd Cav. Co.B
Selden, Robert C. VA 6th Inf. Co.G
Selden, Robert D. VA 3rd Cav. Co.D
Selden, R. Wallace VA 4th Cav. Co.E 1st Sgt.
Selden, Thomas W. VA Lt.Arty. 38th Bn. Co.A
Selden, W.A. Sig.Corps,CSA
Selden, W.B. Gen. & Staff 1st Lt.Arty.
Selden, W.D. VA 2nd St.Res. Co.I
Selden, William AL 5th Inf. New Co.D
Selden, William Gen. & Staff Surg.
Selden, Wm. A. Gen. & Staff Surg.
Selden, William H. VA 11th Inf. Co.G
Selden, William M. AL Gid Nelson Lt.Arty.
 Sr.2nd Lt.
Seldenridge, H. Samuel VA 135th Mil. Co.C
Seldenridge, Peter F. VA 135th Mil. Co.C
Seldner, Isaac VA 6th Inf. Co.H 1st Sgt.
Seldner, Samuel W. VA 1st St.Res. Co.A
Seldner, Samuel W. VA 54th Mil. Co.B
Seldomridge, A.D. VA 14th Cav. Co.K,D
Seldomridge, Peter F. VA 22nd Inf. Co.F
Seldomridge, Samuel H. VA Cav. 36th Bn. Co.A
 Cpl.
Seldon, Joseph N. NC 15th Inf. Co.A
Seldon, Miles VA 5th (Cons.) Cav. AQM
Seldon, N.W. VA Lt.Arty. R.M. Anderson's Co.
Seldon, William Cary VA 12th Cav. Co.B
Seldon, William D., Jr. VA Lt.Arty. Sturdivant's
 Co.
Selecman, George VA 4th Cav. Co.A
Selecman, George A. VA 4th Cav. Co.A
Selecman, J.H. VA 72nd Mil.
Selecman, Redmon VA 4th Cav. Co.A
Selecman, Thomas H. VA 4th Cav. Co.A
Selecman, William H. VA 4th Cav. Co.A Sgt.
Selectman, Silas R. MO Cav. 3rd Bn. Co.D 2nd
 Lt.
Selectman, S.R. MO Cav. 2nd Bn. Co.D 2nd Lt.
Selectman, T.H. GA 19th Inf. Co.A
Selenca, William AL 61st Inf. Co.B Sgt.Maj.
Selenger, Leobold LA 21st (Kennedy's) Inf.
 Co.A
Seler, Jessee KY 8th Mtd.Inf. Co.A
Selero, Neil AL 3rd Bn.Res. Co.H
Se lete ker 1st Creek Mtd.Vol. Co.F
Seley, G.F. MO 12th Cav. Co.C
Seley, William GA Hvy.Arty. 22nd Bn. Co.F
Self, Aaron SC 5th Inf. 2nd Co.I
Self, Aaron SC 6th Inf. 1st Co.I
Self, A.B. AL 30th Inf. Co.C
Self, Abner TN 35th Inf. Co.G, 1st Co.I
Self, Abraham TN 11th Inf. Co.C
Self, Abraham TN 49th Inf.
Self, A.D. LA 6th Cav. Co.K
Self, Adam M. TX 36th Cav. Co.D
Self, A.J. AL 12th Cav. Co.F
Self, A.J. GA 46th Inf. Co.A
Self, A.J. SC 18th Inf. Co.K
Self, Albert LA Hvy.Arty. 2nd Bn. Co.F
Self, Allen AL 1st Inf. Co.A
Self, Allen AR 7th Cav. Co.K
Self, A.N. TX Cav. 1st Bn.St.Troops Co.A

Self, Anderson NC 55th Inf. Co.F
Self, Andrew TN 61st Mtd.Inf. Co.C
Self, Andrew J. AL 11th Inf. Co.H
Self, Andrew J. GA 60th Inf. Co.G
Self, A.R. AL 12th Cav. Co.C Sgt.
Self, A.R. MS 44th Inf. Co.F
Self, Arthur D. LA Inf. 11th Bn. Co.C 2nd Lt.
Self, Asa J. TX 17th Cav. Co.B
Self, Baalam AR 4th Inf. Co.G
Self, Benjamin H. GA Inf. 3rd Bn. Co.C
Self, Berryman H. GA 37th Inf. Co.I
Self, Bevella A. AL Lt.Arty. Phelan's Co.
Self, Beverly Allen AL 5th Inf. Old Co.H
Self, B.H. AL 13th Bn.Part.Rangers Co.B
Self, B.H. NC 57th Inf. Co.G
Self, C. AR 6th Inf. Co.E
Self, Carter AL 12th Cav. Co.D
Self, Cephas NC 48th Inf. Co.I
Self, Chamock T. TX 31st Cav. Co.A
Self, Chapell B. AL 45th Inf. Co.A
Self, Charles T. AL 4th Inf.
Self, Columbus GA 6th Inf. Co.C
Self, C.T. TX 3rd Cav. Co.D
Self, Cyrus M. LA 28th (Gray's) Inf. Co.B
Self, Daniel R. 10th Conf.Cav. Co.E
Self, David GA 62nd Cav. Co.G,H
Self, David GA 12th Inf. Co.D
Self, David TX 19th Cav. Co.I
Self, David A. GA 21st Inf. Old Co.E
Self, David P. TX 17th Cons.Dismtd.Cav. Co.C
Self, David S. TX Inf. Griffin's Bn. Co.E
Self, David W. GA 6th Cav. Co.A
Self, David W. GA Smith's Legion Standridge's
 Co.
Self, D.F. TX 11th Cav. Co.F
Self, D.R. AL Cav. 5th Bn. Hilliard's Legion
 Co.E
Self, D.S. AR 30th Inf. Co.H
Self, D.S. TX 21st Inf. Co.D
Self, D.W. LA 17th Inf. Co.B Maj.
Self, E. AL Cp. of Instr. Talladega
Self, E.A. AL 8th (Hatch's) Cav. Co.K
Self, Eary MO 1st Cav. Co.E
Self, E.B. TX 37th Cav. Co.K
Self, Ebenezer TX 17th Cav. Co.B
Self, E.D. GA 39th Inf. Co.E
Self, Edmond AL Lt.Arty. 2nd Bn. Co.F
Self, Edmund L. VA 44th Inf. Co.I
Self, E.H. GA 65th Inf. Co.E
Self, E.H. TX 37th Cav. Co.K
Self, E.J. AR 6th Inf. Co.E
Self, Elias LA 3rd (Wingfield's) Cav. Co.E
Self, Elias LA 4th Inf. Old Co.G
Self, Elijah AL 21st Inf. Co.F
Self, Elijah AL 28th Inf. Co.E
Self, Elijah AL Cp. of Instr. Talladega
Self, Emeriah AL 5th Inf. Co.K
Self, F.D. LA 17th Inf. Co.B Capt.
Self, Felix G. TX 14th Cav. Co.H
Self, Fleet William VA 40th Inf. Co.C
Self, F.M. AR 32nd Inf. Co.G
Self, F.M. MO 7th Cav. Co.I,E
Self, F.M. TX 30th Cav. Co.E
Self, Francis M. GA 24th Inf. Co.D
Self, Francis W. VA 40th Inf. Co.K
Self, Frank FL 10th Inf. Co.H 1st Lt.
Self, Frank VA 8th Inf. Co.K

Self, Frank T. KY Cav. Buckner Guards Sgt.
Self, Franklin GA 6th Cav.
Self, F.S. GA 12th Cav. Co.K
Self, F.T. TN Cav. Clark's Ind.Co. Sgt.
Self, G. NC 2nd Jr.Res. Co.D
Self, Gabrel AR 7th Cav. Co.K Bvt.Lt.
Self, Gabriel AR 14th (Powers') Inf. Co.E
Self, George E. AL 28th Inf. Co.B
Self, George R. VA 1st Inf. Co.C
Self, George W. SC Inf. 7th Bn. (Enfield Rifles)
 Co.G
Self, George W. TX 22nd Cav. Co.G
Self, G.P. NC 2nd Jr.Res. Co.C
Self, G.W. LA 6th Cav. Co.K
Self, H. TX Cav. Border's Regt. Co.C
Self, H.C. KY 2nd Mtd.Inf. Co.K
Self, Henry AL 48th Inf. Co.F 1st Sgt.
Self, Henry GA Phillips' Legion Co.L
Self, Henry L. GA 1st Cav. Co.H
Self, H.G. AL 19th Inf. Co.C,K Cpl.
Self, Hiram L. VA 55th Inf. Co.E Sgt.
Self, H.K. AL 5th Cav. Co.K
Self, I.J. GA 8th Inf. Co.A
Self, Isaac AL 29th Inf. Co.C,I
Self, Isaac AR 7th Cav. Co.K
Self, Isaac AR 14th (Powers') Inf. Co.E
Self, Isaac R. NC 55th Inf. Co.F Sgt.
Self, Isaac T. AL 28th Inf. Co.D
Self, J. AL 27th Inf. Co.H
Self, J. GA 6th Inf. Co.C
Self, J. GA 39th Inf. Co.E
Self, J. LA 18th Inf. Co.I
Self, J. MO Cav. Slayback's Regt. Co.I
Self, J.A. GA 7th Inf. Co.H
Self, J.A. GA 60th Inf. Co.C
Self, Jackson AL Cp. of Instr. Talladega
Self, Jackson GA 7th Inf.
Self, Jacob VA Cav. Swann's Bn. Sweeny's Co.
 Cpl.
Self, Jacob C. GA 7th Inf. Co.H
Self, Jacob R. NC 55th Inf. Co.F
Self, James GA Cav. 20th Bn. Co.D
Self, James LA 28th (Thomas') Inf. Co.B
Self, James TX 1st Hvy.Arty. Co.K
Self, James A. GA 55th Inf. Co.B
Self, James D. TX 36th Cav. Co.D
Self, James E. TX 7th Cav. Co.I
Self, James H. LA Inf. 11th Bn. Co.E
Self, James H. LA Inf.Cons.Crescent Regt. Co.D
 Sgt.
Self, James M. GA 24th Inf. Co.D
Self, James T. GA 27th Inf. Co.B
Self, James T. GA Phillips' Legion Co.L
Self, James W. AR 20th Inf. Co.B
Self, James W. LA Inf. 11th Bn. Co.E
Self, Jasper N. AR Lt.Arty. Thrall's Btty.
Self, J.B. KY 10th (Johnson's) Cav. Co.K
Self, J.B. TX 11th Cav. Co.B
Self, J.C. AL 12th Cav. Co.D 3rd Lt.
Self, J.D. AR 8th Cav. Peoples' Co.
Self, Jehu C. GA 24th Inf. Co.D
Self, Jesse AL 48th Inf. Co.F
Self, Jesse AL Cp. of Instr. Talladega
Self, Jesse E. AL Lt.Arty. Hurt's Btty.
Self, Jesse F. GA 39th Inf. Co.E
Self, Jesse H. AL 43rd Inf. Co.I
Self, J.H. AL 18th Inf. Co.I

Self, J.H. AL 32nd & 58th (Cons.) Inf.
Self, J.H. AL 56th Inf. Co.A,H
Self, J.H. AR 4th Inf. Co.H
Self, J.M. AR 27th Inf. Co.C
Self, J.M. GA Cav. Corbin's Co.
Self, J.M. TX 9th (Nichols') Inf. Co.B
Self, J.M. TX 18th Inf. Co.K
Self, J.N. TX 32nd Cav. Co.I
Self, Job VA Lt.Arty. Ellett's Co.
Self, Job C. GA 6th Cav. Co.F
Self, Joel AR 1st (Dobbin's) Cav. Co.H
Self, Joel TN 40th Inf. Co.I
Self, John AL 7th Cav. Co.B
Self, John AL 58th Inf. Co.C
Self, John AR 24th Inf. Co.A Cpl.
Self, John GA 6th Cav. Co.I
Self, John GA 8th Inf.
Self, John GA 65th Inf. Co.C
Self, John GA Smith's Legion Co.D
Self, John NC 1st Bn.Jr.Res. Co.E
Self, John TX 1st Hvy.Arty. Co.K
Self, John VA Cav. 15th Bn. Co.B
Self, John VA Lt.Arty. Thornton's Co.
Self, John VA 30th Inf. Co.H
Self, John VA 33rd Inf. Co.F
Self, John VA 47th Inf. 2nd Co.K
Self, John A. AL 12th Cav. Co.C
Self, John B. GA 52nd Inf. Co.E
Self, John C. LA Inf.Cons.Crescent Regt. Co.F
Self, John C. NC 54th Inf. Co.F
Self, John C. TX 37th Cav. Co.K
Self, John D. GA 2nd Res. Co.D
Self, John L. AL 48th Inf. Co.F Sgt.
Self, John L. GA 41st Inf. Co.K
Self, John M. SC Inf. Hampton Legion Co.B
Self, John M. TX 22nd Cav. Co.C
Self, John N. AL 18th Inf. Co.I
Self, John N. GA 2nd Bn.S.S. Co.D Sgt.
Self, John R. TX 13th Vol. Co.E
Self, John W. AR 30th Inf. Co.H Bvt.2nd Lt.
Self, John W. SC Lt.Arty. 3rd (Palmetto) Bn. Co.B 2nd Lt.
Self, Jonathan AL Cp. of Instr. Talladega
Self, Jo. R. TN 29th Inf. Co.I 1st Sgt.
Self, Joseph AL 8th (Hatch's) Cav. Co.K
Self, Joseph NC 44th Inf. Co.A
Self, Joseph L. GA 21st Inf. Co.K
Self, Joseph L. GA 39th Inf. Co.K
Self, Joseph M. AR 15th Inf. Co.E
Self, Joshua MO 5th Cav. Co.D Black.
Self, Joshua MO Cav. Stallard's Co.
Self, J.P.T. TX 4th Inf. Co.I
Self, J.S. TN 61st Mtd.Inf. Co.C
Self, J.T. TX Waul's Legion Co.D
Self, Julian Conf.Inf. Tucker's Regt. Co.C
Self, J.W. MS 39th Inf. Co.F
Self, J.W. NC 2nd Jr.Res. Co.D
Self, J.W. SC 5th Inf. 2nd Co.I
Self, J.W. TN 11th Inf. Co.C
Self, J. Wesley SC 6th Inf. 1st Co.I
Self, K.C. KY 6th Mtd.Inf. Co.C
Self, Laban B. MS 43rd Inf. Co.D
Self, L.B. MS Cav. Russell's Co.
Self, Lemuel S. NC 34th Inf. Co.F Cpl.
Self, Levi VA 40th Inf. Co.C
Self, Levi H. LA 9th Inf. Co.I Sgt.
Self, Lorenzo VA 33rd Inf. Co.F

Self, Lott GA 6th Inf. Co.C
Self, Loyd AR 8th Inf. New Co.A
Self, M. GA 6th Inf. Co.C
Self, Mack AR 1st Mtd.Rifles Co.D
Self, Marabo GA 41st Inf. Co.A,F
Self, Marion LA Inf. 11th Bn. Co.E
Self, Melvin P. KY Cav. Buckner Guards
Self, M.M. TX 4th Inf. Co.F
Self, Moses NC 34th Inf. Co.H
Self, Moses VA 9th Cav. Co.K
Self, Moses A. VA 41st Inf. Co.C
Self, M.P. TN Cav. Clark's Ind.Co.
Self, Nathan AR 14th (Powers') Inf. Co.E
Self, Nathaniel GA 46th Inf. Co.A
Self, N.J. AR 30th Inf. Co.H
Self, Paul VA 47th Inf. 2nd Co.K
Self, P.C. GA 5th Res. Co.F
Self, R. AL 58th Inf. Co.A
Self, Raleigh D. LA Pointe Coupee Arty.
Self, R.B. MO Inf. 4th Regt.St.Guard Co.E
Self, Reece B. MO 8th Cav. Co.B
Self, Reuben AL 18th Inf. Co.I
Self, R.F. TX 21st Inf. Co.I
Self, R.J. MS 35th Inf. Co.D
Self, Richard F. TX Inf. Griffin's Bn. Co.A
Self, Robert NC 55th Inf. Co.F
Self, Robert VA 9th Cav. Sandford's Co.C
Self, Robert VA Cav. 15th Bn. Co.A
Self, R.P. AR 2nd Cav. Co.F
Self, Rufus NC 55th Inf. Co.F
Self, Rufus A. AL 29th Inf. Co.F
Self, S. SC 1st Inf. Co.N
Self, Samuel AL 29th Inf. Co.C
Self, Samuel AR 14th (Powers') Inf. Co.E
Self, Samuel GA Mil. 12th Regt. Co.K
Self, Samuel GA 50th Inf.
Self, Samuel MO Cav. Slayback's Regt. Co.I
Self, Samuel MO 8th Inf. Co.A
Self, Samuel MO 8th Inf. Co.B
Self, Samuel B. LA Inf. 11th Bn. Co.C
Self, Samuel B. LA Inf.Cons.Crescent Regt. Co.F
Self, Samuel E. GA Floyd Legion (St.Guards) Co.G
Self, Samuel H. VA 40th Inf. Co.K
Self, Silas N. VA 24th Cav. Co.H
Self, S.J. TN 47th Inf. Co.C
Self, S.N. VA Cav. 32nd Bn.
Self, Spencer GA 62nd Cav. Co.G,H
Self, Spencer M. TX 31st Cav. Co.D
Self, Stephen SC Inf. 7th Bn. (Enfield Rifles) Co.D
Self, Stephen VA 40th Inf. Co.C
Self, Thomas GA 11th Cav. Co.C
Self, Thomas TN 29th Inf. Co.I
Self, Thomas TN 61st Mtd.Inf. Co.C
Self, Thomas D. GA 39th Inf. Co.E
Self, Thomas P. AR 8th Cav. Peoples' Co.
Self, Tilman TX 1st Hvy.Arty. Co.K
Self, Timothy TX 9th Field Btty.
Self, T.J. GA 8th Inf. Co.E
Self, Vincent G. AL 29th Inf. Co.B
Self, W.A. TN 63rd Inf. Co.I
Self, W.B. LA 3rd (Wingfield's) Cav. Co.F Sgt.
Self, W.B. LA 4th Inf. Co.I Cpl.
Self, W.C. TX 1st Hvy.Arty. Co.K

Self, W.D. GA Inf. 2nd Bn. (St.Guards) New Co.D
Self, W.D. LA 4th Inf. Co.I
Self, W.D. TX 14th Inf. Co.E
Self, W.E. TX 17th Cons.Dismtd.Cav. Co.C
Self, W.F. GA 41st Inf. Co.F
Self, W.F. LA 17th Inf. Co.B
Self, W.F. SC 1st Inf. Co.N
Self, W.G. MS 23rd Inf. Co.L
Self, W.H. TN 15th (Stewart's) Cav. Co.D
Self, William AL 11th Inf.
Self, William AL 21st Inf. Co.F
Self, William AR 15th (Johnson's) Inf. Co.A Sgt.
Self, William AR 24th Inf. Co.K
Self, William AR Inf. Hardy's Regt. Co.H
Self, William NC 34th Inf. Co.F
Self, William NC 61st Inf. Co.D
Self, William NC 64th Inf. Co.N
Self, William TN 40th Inf. Co.I
Self, William A. AL 43rd Inf. Co.I
Self, William B. TX 15th Cav. Co.A 2nd Lt.
Self, William E. TX 17th Cav. Co.B
Self, William F. SC Inf. 7th Bn. (Enfield Rifles) Co.D
Self, William G. AL 20th Inf. Co.F
Self, William J. KY 6th Mtd.Inf. Co.C
Self, William J. LA Inf. 11th Bn. Co.E 2nd Lt.
Self, William J. NC 55th Inf. Co.F
Self, William J. TN 35th Inf. Co.H
Self, William J. TX 19th Inf. Co.F
Self, William J. VA Cav. 32nd Bn. Co.B
Self, William J. VA 30th Inf. Co.F
Self, William R. AL 5th Cav. Co.K
Self, William R. NC 6th Inf. Co.E Cpl.
Self, William R. NC 57th Inf. Co.E Cpl.
Self, William S. GA 3rd Bn.S.S. Co.C
Self, William T. AR 7th Cav. Co.A
Self, William T. VA 37th Mil. Co.A
Self, William T. VA 40th Inf. Co.C
Self, William W. GA 6th Cav. Co.A
Self, William W. GA Smith's Legion Standridge's Co.
Self, William W. MS 7th Inf. Co.I
Self, William W. NC 6th Cav. (65th St.Troops) Co.B
Self, Wilson AR 8th Inf. New Co.A
Self, W.J. LA Inf.Cons.Crescent Regt. Co.D Capt.
Self, W.J. VA 24th Cav. Co.H
Self, W.K. LA 17th Inf. Co.B
Self, W.L. AL 18th Inf. Co.I
Self, W.M. AL 51st (Part.Rangers) Co.E
Self, W.M. KY 10th (Johnson's) Cav. Co.K,A
Self, W.M.E. AL Cp. of Instr. Talladega Co.A
Self, W.S. AL 32nd & 58th (Cons.) Inf.
Self, W.S. AL 56th Inf. Co.A,H
Self, W.S. GA 16th Inf. Co.I
Self, W.W. AL 13th Cav. Co.C
Self, W.W. AL 18th Inf. Co.I
Self, W.Y. AL Inf. 1st Regt. Co.F
Self, W.Y. AL 62nd Inf. Co.F
Self, Zachius NC 48th Inf. Co.I
Selfe, C.W. MO 12th Inf. Co.A Cpl.
Selford, James Duff MS Inf. 1st Bn. Co.D Cpl.
Selfridge, D. GA 10th Cav. (St.Guards) Co.B
Selfridge, John R. GA 19th Inf. Co.G 1st Lt.

Selfridge, William MO Inf. Clark's Regt. Co.D
    Sgt.
Selfridge, William Conf.Cav. Clarkson's Bn.
    Ind.Rangers Co.H
Selig, Abraham GA 41st Inf. Co.E
Seligman, --- LA Mil. Orleans Guards Regt. Co.I
Seligman, A. AL 1st Regt. Mobile Vol. Co.C
    1st Sgt.
Seligman, Albert AL 4th Inf. Co.B Cpl.
Seligman, Henry VA 12th Inf. Co.C
Seligman, J. AL Mil. 4th Vol. Co.K
Seligman, Jacob VA 39th Mil. Co.B
Seligman, M. LA Mil. Lafayette Arty.
Seligman, S.B. GA 3rd Bn. (St.Guards) Co.D
Seligman, S.B. LA 11th Inf. Co.K Sgt.
Seligsberg, Abraham AL 8th Inf. Co.D
Selina, H.B. MS 36th Inf.
Selinger, Bernhard LA Mil. Mech.Guard
Selinger, Chass LA Mil. Mech.Guard
Selinger, John TN 10th Inf. Co.C
Selix, William VA 49th Inf. Cpl.
Selk, John TX 1st Hvy.Arty. Co.E
Selka, H.S. LA Mil. 4th Regt.Eur.Brig. Co.E
Selkirk, James TX 6th Inf. Co.D Capt.
Selkirk, James TX 6th & 15th (Cons.) Vol. Co.D
    Capt.
Selkirk, William TX 35th (Brown's) Cav. Co.D
Selkonie, --- NC Inf. Thomas Legion
Sell, Andrew NC 21st Inf. Co.K
Sell, Benjamin TN 1st Cav. Co.M
Sell, David NC 3rd Inf. Co.F
Sell, Ed. Emerick SC Mil. 16th Regt. Prender-
    gast's Co. 1st Lt.
Sell, E.E. SC Arty. Manigault's Bn. 1st Co.A
Sell, Frederick VA 18th Cav. Co.H
Sell, Henry TN 38th Inf. Co.F
Sell, Henry C. NC 14th Inf. Co.H Cpl.
Sell, Jacob NC 3rd Inf. Co.F
Sell, Jacob NC 52nd Inf. Co.I
Sell, John LA 20th Inf. Co.D
Sell, John MS 10th Cav. Co.I
Sell, John NC 4th Inf. Co.E
Sell, John NC 52nd Inf. Co.I
Sell, John VA Hvy.Arty. 19th Bn. 1st Co.E
Sell, John E. NC 28th Inf. Co.D
Sell, John J. NC 8th Inf. Co.H
Sell, John S. NC 8th Inf. Co.H
Sell, Joseph TN 60th Mtd.Inf.
Sell, J.P. NC 28th Inf. Co.D
Sell, J.S. NC 1st Jr.Res. Co.G
Sell, J.W. VA Cav. Swann's Bn.
Sell, M.A. NC 1st Jr.Res. Co.G
Sell, P. TX 26th Cav. Co.I
Sell, Peter TX Inf. Griffin's Bn. Co.F
Sell, Phillip NC 57th Inf. Co.F
Sell, Richmond NC 28th Inf. Co.D
Sell, Samuel NC 28th Inf. Co.D
Sell, Solomon NC 52nd Inf. Co.I
Sell, Valentine LA 20th Inf. Music.
Sell, William W. NC 45th Inf. Co.K
Sell, Worthy TX 24th Cav. Co.B
Sella leeseh Nichee NC Inf. Thomas Legion
    Co.B
Sella lee seh Sequoyeh NC Inf. Thomas Legion
    Co.B
Sella lee seh Wahteh NC Inf. Thomas Legion
    Co.B

Sellam, J.C., Jr. VA 3rd Inf.Loc.Def. Co.E Sgt.
Sellans, Thomas MO 3rd & 4th Cons.Cav. Co.H
Sellar, Lemuel NC 7th Sr.Res. Bradshaw's Co.
Sellards, Dory KY 5th Cav. Co.E
Sellards, Elias KY 5th Mtd.Inf. Co.E
Sellars, A.J. GA 56th Inf. Co.E
Sellars, Alison AL 28th Inf. Co.D
Sellars, Amos J. SC Inf. 9th Bn. Co.E
Sellars, Azariah R. NC 3rd Inf. Co.H Cpl.
Sellars, Benjamin F. MS 13th Inf. Co.E
Sellars, B.J. SC 4th Cav. Co.E
Sellars, Bryant NC 2nd Bn.Loc.Def.Troops Co.C
Sellars, B.T. SC 2nd St.Troops Co.D
Sellars, Calvin MS 1st Cav.Res. Co.H
Sellars, Calvin SC 7th Res. Co.A
Sellars, Calvin S. NC 3rd Inf. Co.H
Sellars, C.D. GA Lt.Arty. 12th Bn. 1st Co.A
Sellars, C.D. MO Cav. Ford's Bn. Co.C
Sellars, C.K. AL 3rd Bn.Res. Co.C
Sellars, Clinton D. GA 63rd Inf. Co.A
Sellars, David AL 57th Inf. Co.I 1st Sgt.
Sellars, David NC Hvy.Arty. 1st Bn. Co.B
Sellars, David NC 2nd Arty. (36th St.Troops)
    Co.D
Sellars, David L. GA 51st Inf. Co.G
Sellars, David S. NC 2nd Arty. (36th St.Troops)
    Co.B
Sellars, David W. GA 5th Inf. Co.G Sgt.
Sellars, David W. GA Conscr. Sgt.
Sellars, D.R. AR 35th Inf. Co.H
Sellars, Duncan C. NC 2nd Arty. (36th
    St.Troops) Co.B
Sellars, Duncan T. 1st Conf.Inf. 2nd Co.H
Sellars, E.A. AL 15th Inf. Co.L
Sellars, Edward GA 7th Cav. Co.K
Sellars, Edward GA Hardwick Mtd.Rifles Co.A
Sellars, E.K. SC 4th Inf. Co.B
Sellars, Eli B. TN 48th (Voorhies') Inf. Co.A
Sellars, Eli D. TN 7th Inf. Co.G Cpl.
Sellars, Elisha MS 43rd Inf. Co.K
Sellars, Emanuel H. AL 28th Inf. Co.D
Sellars, Ephraim GA Phillips' Legion Co.C
Sellars, F.E. TX 5th Cav. Co.A
Sellars, Flavers NC 2nd Arty. (36th St.Troops)
    Co.D
Sellars, Francis GA Mayer's Co. (Appling Cav.)
Sellars, George GA Hvy.Arty. 22nd Bn. Co.E
Sellars, George NC 2nd Arty. (36th St.Troops)
    Co.D
Sellars, George B. MS 21st Inf. Co.G
Sellars, George B. SC Palmetto S.S. Co.K,M
Sellars, H. AL 28th Inf. Co.D
Sellars, H. SC 11th Res. Co.E Cpl.
Sellars, Hardy AL 17th Inf. Co.G
Sellars, Hardy MS 27th Inf. Co.B
Sellars, Henry SC 2nd St.Troops Co.E
Sellars, H.O. TN 11th (Holman's) Cav. Co.E
Sellars, H.T. FL 6th Inf. Co.E
Sellars, Isaac TX 9th (Nichols') Inf. Co.F
Sellars, Jacob GA 34th Inf. Co.F
Sellars, Jacob B. GA 51st Inf. Co.E
Sellars, James GA 34th Inf. Co.I
Sellars, James TN Holman's Bn.Part.Rangers
    Co.B
Sellars, James C. MS 21st Inf. Co.G
Sellars, James O. 1st Conf.Inf. 2nd Co.H
Sellars, Jasper MS 12th Inf. Co.E

Sellars, J.B. SC 2nd Res.
Sellars, J.B. TN Inf. 3rd Cons.Regt. Co.A
Sellars, J.B. TN 35th Inf. Co.E
Sellars, J.C. AR 38th Inf. Co.B
Sellars, J.C. MS 6th Inf. Co.B
Sellars, J.C. SC 3rd St.Troops Co.D
Sellars, J.E. FL 2nd Cav. Co.F
Sellars, Jehill GA 6th Cav. Co.B
Sellars, Jessarine KY 3rd Mtd.Inf. Co.A
Sellars, J.H. TN 9th (Ward's) Cav. Co.A Lt.
Sellars, J.J. GA 51st Inf. Co.C
Sellars, J.J. TX 25th Cav. Co.D
Sellars, J.M. MS 1st Cav.Res. Co.C
Sellars, Joel NC 43rd Inf. Co.I
Sellars, John GA 6th Res. Co.H
Sellars, John GA 65th Inf. Co.H
Sellars, John NC 2nd Arty. (36th St.Troops)
    Co.D
Sellars, John TN Inf. 4th Cons.Regt. Co.A Cpl.
Sellars, John A. GA 17th Inf. Co.C 1st Sgt.
Sellars, John A. MS 27th Inf. Co.B
Sellars, John A. MS 29th Inf. Co.F
Sellars, John K. AR 26th Inf. Co.I
Sellars, John L. AR 15th (N.W.) Inf. Co.G
Sellars, John M. GA 47th Inf. Co.F Sgt.
Sellars, John R. GA 47th Inf. Co.D
Sellars, John T. NC 2nd Bn.Loc.Def.Troops
    Co.E Sgt.
Sellars, John W. NC Hvy.Arty. 1st Bn. Co.A
Sellars, John W. NC 2nd Arty. (36th St.Troops)
    Co.B Cpl.
Sellars, Joseph MS 8th Inf. Co.B
Sellars, Joseph H. GA 46th Inf. Co.B Sgt.
Sellars, Joseph L. NC 1st Arty. (10th St.Troops)
    Co.E Cpl.
Sellars, Joshua GA 1st Lt.Duty Men Co.A
Sellars, J.W. GA 46th Inf. Co.D
Sellars, L. NC 7th Sr.Res. Fisher's Co.
Sellars, Lafayette AR 15th (N.W.) Inf. Co.G
Sellars, L.B. TN 19th (Biffle's) Cav. Co.H
Sellars, Lemuel B. GA Mayer's Co. (Appling
    Cav.)
Sellars, Levi J. NC Hvy.Arty. 1st Bn. Co.B
Sellars, Melvin C. MS Lt.Arty. Turner's Co.
Sellars, M.L. TN Inf. 3rd Cons.Regt. Co.F
Sellars, M.L. TN 35th Inf. 2nd Co.A
Sellars, N.A. AR 5th Inf. Co.B
Sellars, N.A. TN 19th (Biffle's) Cav. Co.H
Sellars, Noah TN 27th Inf. Co.I
Sellars, Orin A. TN 42nd Inf. 1st Co.E
Sellars, Philip NC 43rd Inf. Co.I
Sellars, Pitman E. NC 51st Inf. Co.H
Sellars, R. MS Inf. 7th Bn. Co.B
Sellars, R.H. KY 7th Mtd.Inf. Co.A
Sellars, Richard MS 43rd Inf. Co.A
Sellars, Robert R. GA Lt.Arty. Milledge's Co.
Sellars, S. GA 50th Inf. Co.C
Sellars, S.A. GA 46th Inf. Co.B Lt.
Sellars, S.A. SC 10th Inf. Co.A
Sellars, Samuel SC 8th Inf. Co.C Cpl.
Sellars, S.E. AL 34th Inf. Co.B
Sellars, Seborn TN 50th Inf. Co.C
Sellars, S.M. GA 46th Inf. Co.C
Sellars, Stephen A. GA Siege Arty. 28th Bn.
    Co.D Sgt.
Sellars, S.W. AR 1st Mtd.Rifles Co.C
Sellars, S.W. AR Cav. Gordon's Regt. Co.C

Sellars, S.W. NC 7th Sr.Res. Bradshaw's Co.
Sellars, Thomas NC 8th Sr.Res. Broadhurst's Co.
Sellars, Thomas B. LA Inf.Cons.Crescent Regt.
    Co.D Sgt.
Sellars, T.J. MS 9th Inf. New Co.E Sgt.
Sellars, T.J. TN 20th Inf. Co.H
Sellars, Walter W. 1st Conf.Inf. 2nd Co.H
Sellars, W.C. TN 8th (Smith's) Cav. Co.D
Sellars, W.C. TN 18th Inf. Co.I
Sellars, W.C. TN 45th Inf. Co.G
Sellars, Wiley GA 51st Inf. Co.C
Sellars, Wiley GA Inf. (Mitchell Home Guards)
    Brooks' Co.
Sellars, William AL 45th Inf.
Sellars, William NC 2nd Arty. (36th St.Troops)
    Co.D
Sellars, William E. AL 34th Inf. Black's Co.
Sellars, William H. KY 2nd Mtd.Inf. Co.B
Sellars, William L. FL 3rd Inf. Co.I
Sellars, W.L. TX 9th Cav. Co.K Cpl.
Sellars, W.P. AL 15th Inf. Co.L
Sellars, W.W. TN 23rd Inf. Co.E
Sellbach, Gustave LA 20th Inf. Co.A
Selle, A. LA 22nd Inf. Co.E,C 1st Lt.
Selle, A. LA 22nd (Cons.) Inf. Co.E Capt.
Selleck, --- LA Mil. 2nd Regt. 2nd Brig. 1st Div.
    Co.A
Selleck, Clarence H. SC 2nd Inf. Co.K,F
Selleck, Clarence H. 3rd Conf.Cav. Co.F 1st
    Sgt.
Selleck, J.R.S. LA 5th Inf. Co.E
Selleck, M. LA 5th Inf. Co.E QM
Sellender, James H. KY 2nd Cav. Co.D
Sellens, H. AL 8th Cav. Co.G Cpl.
Seller, I. GA 57th Inf.
Seller, Jacob LA 21st (Kennedy's) Inf. Co.C
Seller, James TN 19th & 20th (Cons.) Cav. Co.C
Seller, James VA 58th Mil. Co.H
Seller, John LA Mil. 1st Regt. 3rd Brig. 1st Div.
    Co.H
Seller, John LA 21st (Kennedy's) Inf. Co.F
Seller, Joseph MS Cav. 1st Bn. (Montgomery's)
    St.Troops Cameron's Co. 2nd Lt.
Sellers, ---, 1st AL 22nd Inf. Co.B
Sellers, ---, 2nd AL 22nd Inf. Co.B
Sellers, --- FL Harrison's Co. (Santa Rosa
    Guards)
Sellers, --- TX Cav. 4th Regt.St.Troops Co.G
Sellers, --- TX Cav. Steele's Command Co.D
Sellers, --- TX Inf. Houston Bn. (Detailed Men)
    Capt.
Sellers, A. AL Mil. 2nd Regt.Vol. Co.D
Sellers, Aaron SC 6th Cav. Co.D
Sellers, Aaron V. MS 3rd (St.Troops) Cav. Co.F
Sellers, Abm. AL 32nd Inf. Co.F 1st Lt.
Sellers, Abraham NC 37th Inf. Co.D
Sellers, Abram AL 21st Inf. Co.A Sgt.
Sellers, Andrew AL 17th Inf. Co.G
Sellers, A.C. GA 12th Mil. Sgt.
Sellers, A.F. LA 25th Inf. Co.E
Sellers, A.J. AL 53rd (Part.Rangers) Co.D
Sellers, A.J. SC 26th Inf. Co.F Cpl.
Sellers, A.J. TN 19th (Biffle's) Cav. Co.K
Sellers, A.J. TN Inf. Harman's Regt. Co.K
Sellers, Alex AL 38th Inf. Co.I
Sellers, Alexander AL Inf. 2nd Regt. Co.D
Sellers, Alexander AL 32nd Inf. Co.D

Sellers, Aley NC 8th Sr.Res. Daniel's Co.
Sellers, Alva NC 18th Inf. Co.H
Sellers, Amariah NC 20th Inf. Co.I
Sellers, Amos NC 3rd Inf. Co.G
Sellers, Amos NC McDugald's Co.
Sellers, Anderson M. AL 53rd (Part.Rangers)
    Co.K
Sellers, Andrew W. SC 4th Cav. Co.A
Sellers, A.R. TX 4th Cav. Co.F
Sellers, Asher TN Hvy.Arty. Caruthers' Btty.
Sellers, Ben. TN Inf. Harman's Regt. Co.K
Sellers, Benjamin AL 61st Inf. Co.G
Sellers, Benjamin TX 7th Cav. Co.C
Sellers, Benjamin E. FL 6th Inf. Co.I
Sellers, Benjamin F. TX 18th Cav. Co.F
Sellers, Benjamin J. NC 7th Bn.Jr.Res. Co.B
Sellers, B.G. MS 6th Inf. Co.A
Sellers, B.G. MS 37th Inf. Co.B,F 1st Sgt.
Sellers, B.T. TN 1st (Feild's) Inf. Co.F
Sellers, C. AR 10th Mil. Co.I
Sellers, C. MS Inf. 1st Bn. Polk's Co.
Sellers, C. MS 2nd Inf. Co.A
Sellers, Calton E. FL 6th Inf. Co.D
Sellers, Calvin AL 22nd Inf. Co.B
Sellers, Calvin MS 8th Inf. Co.F
Sellers, Calvin VA 59th Inf. 3rd Co.F
Sellers, Calvin VA 60th Inf. 1st Co.H
Sellers, Calvin C. AL 13th Inf. Co.A 1st Lt.
Sellers, C.C. TX 30th Cav. Co.B
Sellers, Charles VA 2nd Inf.Loc.Def. Co.G
Sellers, Charles VA Inf. 2nd Bn.Loc.Def. Co.A
Sellers, Charles VA 13th Inf. Co.G
Sellers, Christopher W. AR Lt.Arty. Rivers'
    Btty. QMSgt.
Sellers, C.K. AL 3rd Bn.Res. Jackson's Co.
Sellers, Columbus MS Inf. 7th Bn. Co.F
Sellers, Curren TN Cav. 9th Bn. (Gantt's) Co.A
    Cpl.
Sellers, D.A. NC 66th Inf. Co.K
Sellers, Daniel NC 20th Inf. Co.I
Sellers, Daniel NC 55th Inf. Co.C
Sellers, Daniel VA 10th Cav. Co.H
Sellers, Daniel A. NC Inf. 13th Bn. Co.D
Sellers, Daniel B. AL 17th Inf. Co.B
Sellers, Daniel C. AL Mil. 4th Vol. Co.A
Sellers, Daniel Rice AL 49th Inf. Co.B
Sellers, David NC 1st Inf. Co.C
Sellers, David SC 4th St.Troops Co.K
Sellers, David SC 5th Bn.Res. Co.C
Sellers, David G. NC 51st Inf. Co.B
Sellers, David More AL 49th Inf. Co.B
Sellers, D.B. MO 16th Inf. Co.H
Sellers, D.C. AL 3rd Cav. Co.C
Sellers, D.C. MS 7th Cav. Co.G
Sellers, D.C. TN 14th (Neely's) Cav. Co.A
Sellers, D.G. NC 3rd Arty. (40th St.Troops)
    Co.A
Sellers, D.L. MS 2nd Part.Rangers Co.K
Sellers, Doctor Burton MO 8th Inf. Co.H
Sellers, D.T. NC 57th Inf. Co.I
Sellers, D.V. MS 4th Cav. Co.A
Sellers, D.V. MS 46th Inf. Co.B
Sellers, E.E. AL 20th Inf. Co.A
Sellers, E.E. TX 1st Hvy.Arty. Co.K
Sellers, Eli GA 47th Inf. Co.D
Sellers, Eli NC 37th Inf. Co.C
Sellers, Elias N. MS Inf. 2nd Bn. Co.D

Sellers, Elias N. MS 48th Inf. Co.D
Sellers, Elijah AL Mil. 4th Vol. Co.H
Sellers, Elijah AL 36th Inf. Co.B
Sellers, Elijah NC 2nd Inf. Co.F
Sellers, Elijah SC 4th Cav. Co.A
Sellers, Elijah SC Cav. 12th Bn. Co.A
Sellers, Elijah B. TX 27th Cav. Co.D,E
Sellers, Elisha GA 25th Inf. Co.E
Sellers, Elisha NC 2nd Arty. (36th St.Troops)
    Co.G
Sellers, Elisha T. LA 12th Inf. Co.I 1st Lt.
Sellers, E.M. MO 16th Inf. Co.A
Sellers, E.T. AR 34th Inf. Co.G
Sellers, Eugene TX 26th Cav. Co.A
Sellers, Evander D. AL 15th Inf. Co.L
Sellers, F.C. KY 12th Cav. Co.C
Sellers, Felix H. NC 25th Inf. Co.G
Sellers, F.F. AL 1st Inf. Co.G
Sellers, F.G. MS 48th Inf. Co.K 2nd Lt.
Sellers, Flavious NC Hvy.Arty. 10th Bn. Co.B
    Music.
Sellers, Francis GA 4th Inf. Co.E
Sellers, Franklin J. FL 6th Inf. Co.F
Sellers, Franklin M. GA 53rd Inf. Co.I Cpl.
Sellers, G. AL 19th Inf. Co.B
Sellers, G.C. NC 6th Inf. Co.C
Sellers, G.D. SC 20th Inf. Co.B
Sellers, George NC 37th Inf. Co.D
Sellers, George SC 6th Inf. 1st Co.I
Sellers, George VA 14th Cav. Co.I
Sellers, George Sig.Corps,CSA
Sellers, George L. NC 51st Inf. Co.A
Sellers, George N. NC 6th Cav. (65th St.Troops)
    Co.C,G Cpl.
Sellers, George N. NC Cav. 7th Bn. Co.C Cpl.
Sellers, George W. GA 17th Inf. Co.E
Sellers, George W. NC 20th Inf. Co.K Cpl.
Sellers, G.L. LA 1st Hvy.Arty. (Reg.) Co.G,B
Sellers, G.L. MS 1st Cav. Co.E
Sellers, G.T. GA 25th Inf. Co.C
Sellers, G.W. GA 51st Inf. Co.E
Sellers, G.W. MS Inf. 2nd St.Troops Co.D
Sellers, G.W. MS 5th Inf. (St.Troops) Co.B
Sellers, G.W. SC 13th Inf. Co.H
Sellers, H. AL 8th Inf. Co.G Cpl.
Sellers, Hardy AL 27th Inf. Co.B
Sellers, Hardy SC Cav. 12th Bn. Co.A
Sellers, Hardy SC Lt.Arty. Kelly's Co. (Chester-
    field Arty.)
Sellers, Hardy J. SC 4th Cav. Co.A
Sellers, Hartney AL 36th Inf. Co.H
Sellers, H.B. VA 14th Cav. Co.I
Sellers, Henry MS Lt.Arty. Turner's Co.
Sellers, Henry SC Palmetto S.S. Co.M
Sellers, Henry TN 22nd Inf. Co.C
Sellers, Henry VA 13th Inf. Co.G
Sellers, Henry P. 3rd Conf.Eng.Troops
Sellers, H.H. Gen. & Staff Lt.Col.,AAG
Sellers, H.J. SC 8th Inf. Co.B
Sellers, H.M. 2nd Conf.Eng.Troops Co.A
Sellers, Honore LA 28th (Thomas') Inf. Co.A
Sellers, Hubert F. NC 18th Inf. Co.H
Sellers, Hugh M. AL 17th Inf. Co.A
Sellers, I.D. TN 19th (Biffle's) Cav. Co.C
Sellers, I.M. GA Smith's Legion Co.A
Sellers, Irvin MS Inf. 7th Bn. Co.G
Sellers, Isaac AL 32nd Inf. Co.G

Sellers, Isaac TN Cav. 9th Bn. (Gantt's) Co.A Cpl.
Sellers, Isaac TX Waul's Legion Co.D
Sellers, Ivan H. TN 4th Inf. Co.A
Sellers, J. VA 7th Cav. Co.I
Sellers, J.A. GA 51st Inf.
Sellers, J.A. SC 6th Cav. Co.D
Sellers, Jacob NC 62nd Inf. Co.I
Sellers, Jacob VA 3rd (Chrisman's) Bn.Res. Co.A
Sellers, Jacob B. VA 7th Bn.Res. Co.A
Sellers, Jacob S. VA 10th Cav. Co.H
Sellers, James GA Inf. 1st Bn. (St.Guards) Co.C 3rd Lt.
Sellers, James GA 29th Inf. Co.C
Sellers, James MS 6th Inf. Co.H 1st Lt.
Sellers, James TN 18th (Newsom's) Cav. Co.I
Sellers, James VA 33rd Inf. Co.E
Sellers, James A. NC 39th Inf. Co.B Sgt.
Sellers, James A. NC 62nd Inf. Co.B
Sellers, James B. NC 2nd Arty. (36th St.Troops) Co.G
Sellers, James C. NC McDugald's Co.
Sellers, James D. AL 5th Inf. New Co.D
Sellers, James D. TN 9th Cav. Co.F
Sellers, James E. TX Cav. Baylor's Regt. Co.H
Sellers, James H. KY 4th Cav. Co.D
Sellers, James L. TN 1st (Feild's) Inf. Co.H
Sellers, James M. AL 37th Inf. Co.B
Sellers, James M. GA 47th Inf. Co.F
Sellers, James M. SC Lt.Arty. 3rd (Palmetto) Bn. Co.F
Sellers, James M. TN 44th Inf. Co.C
Sellers, James M. VA 10th Inf. Co.I Sgt.
Sellers, James O. MS 3rd Inf. Co.K
Sellers, James P. SC 7th (Ward's) Bn.St.Res. Co.B
Sellers, James R. LA 16th Inf. Co.C
Sellers, James R. MS 3rd Inf. Co.K Sgt.
Sellers, James R. NC 18th Inf. Co.H
Sellers, James R.E. AL 37th Inf. Co.E
Sellers, Jasper AL 59th Inf. Co.G Cpl.
Sellers, Jasper MS 10th Inf. Old Co.F
Sellers, J.C. AR 38th Inf. Co.G
Sellers, J.C. TN 19th (Biffle's) Cav. Co.K
Sellers, J.C. TN 6th Inf. Co.B
Sellers, J.D. GA 25th Inf. Co.C
Sellers, J.D. MO 16th Inf. Co.A
Sellers, J.D. SC 2nd Arty. Co.B
Sellers, J.D. SC 8th Inf. Co.B
Sellers, J.D. TX 4th Cav. Co.B
Sellers, J.E. MS 4th Cav. Co.A Sgt.
Sellers, J.E. MS 38th Cav. Co.G
Sellers, J.E. MS Cav. Stockdale's Bn. Co.A Cpl.
Sellers, J.E. MS 46th Inf. Co.B Cpl.
Sellers, J.F. TN Inf. 3rd Bn. Co.C 1st Lt.
Sellers, J.H. KY 2nd (Duke's) Cav. Co.A
Sellers, J.H. TN 1st (Carter's) Cav. Co.E Sgt.
Sellers, Jimpsey M. GA 47th Inf. Co.F
Sellers, J.J. AL 63rd Inf. Co.E
Sellers, J.J. NC 1st Jr.Res. Co.A
Sellers, J.J. TN 1st (Carter's) Cav. Co.E
Sellers, J.J. TN 49th Inf. Co.D Cpl.
Sellers, J.J. Inf. Bailey's Cons.Regt. Co.L Cpl.
Sellers, J.L. TX 1st Hvy.Arty. Co.K

Sellers, J.M. AL 2nd Bn. Hilliard's Legion Vol. Co.D
Sellers, J.M. AL 6th Inf. Co.K
Sellers, J.M. AR 19th Inf. Co.C
Sellers, J.M. GA Mayer's Co. (Appling Cav.)
Sellers, J.M. GA 10th Inf. Co.I Sgt.
Sellers, J.M. GA 65th Inf. Co.H
Sellers, J.M. TN Inf. 22nd Bn. Co.B
Sellers, J.M. TN 44th (Cons.) Inf. Co.K
Sellers, J.N. MS 7th Cav. 1st Co.H Sgt.
Sellers, J.N. TN 14th (Neely's) Cav. Co.A Sgt.
Sellers, J.O. TX 1st Hvy.Arty. Co.G
Sellers, Jo. B. SC 5th Bn.Res. Co.C
Sellers, Joel AL Cav. 4th Bn. (Love's) Co.A
Sellers, Joel AL 59th Inf. Co.G
Sellers, Joel NC 3rd Arty. (40th St.Troops) Co.G,C
Sellers, John FL 11th Inf. Co.K
Sellers, John GA 1st (Symons') Res. Co.G
Sellers, John GA 35th Inf. Co.A Cpl.
Sellers, John KY 5th Cav. Co.E
Sellers, John KY 7th Cav. Co.D
Sellers, John KY 10th Cav. Co.E
Sellers, John NC 2nd Arty. (36th St.Troops) Co.G 1st Sgt.
Sellers, John NC 20th Inf. Co.B
Sellers, John NC 61st Inf. Co.G
Sellers, John NC McDugald's Co.
Sellers, John A. AL 27th Inf. Co.B
Sellers, John A. GA 38th Inf. Co.A
Sellers, John A. MS Inf. 2nd Bn. Co.D
Sellers, John A. MS 48th Inf. Co.D
Sellers, John A. MS K. Williams' Co. (Gray's Port Greys)
Sellers, John A. NC 39th Inf. Co.B
Sellers, John C. AL 61st Inf. Co.G
Sellers, John D. MS 8th Inf. Co.C
Sellers, John E. GA 17th Inf. Co.E
Sellers, John E. SC 4th Cav. Co.A 1st Sgt.
Sellers, John E. SC Cav. 12th Bn. Co.A Sgt.
Sellers, John F. FL Cav. 5th Bn. Co.A
Sellers, John J. GA 26th Inf. Co.F
Sellers, John J. TN Cav. 9th Bn. (Gantt's) Co.C,G
Sellers, John Jasper AL 49th Inf. Co.B
Sellers, John M. LA 16th Inf. Co.G Cpl.
Sellers, John M. LA Mil. Chalmette Regt. Co.C Cpl.
Sellers, John M. NC 2nd Arty. (36th St.Troops) Co.G
Sellers, John M. NC 62nd Inf. Co.I
Sellers, John M. TN 6th (Wheeler's) Cav. Co.E Cpl.
Sellers, John P. VA 97th Mil. Co.H
Sellers, John Peter VA 10th Inf. Co.I,B
Sellers, John R. VA 10th Inf. Co.I,B
Sellers, John S. AR Cav. J.H. Bull's Co.
Sellers, John S. SC Inf. Hampton Legion Co.B
Sellers, John S. Gen. & Staff Capt.,AQM
Sellers, John W. NC 2nd Arty. (36th St.Troops) Co.G Music.
Sellers, John W. NC 54th Inf. Co.C
Sellers, John W. SC 1st (Hagood's) Inf. 1st Co.D Capt.
Sellers, John W. TN 37th Inf. Co.F
Sellers, Jordan NC 3rd Inf. Co.K

Sellers, Jorden NC 5th Cav. (63rd St.Troops) Co.C
Sellers, Joseph NC 35th Inf. Co.B
Sellers, Joseph NC 58th Inf. Co.A
Sellers, Joseph TN Inf. Harman's Regt. Co.K
Sellers, Joseph B. SC 4th St.Troops Co.K
Sellers, Joseph C. NC 51st Inf. Co.G
Sellers, Joseph D. GA 17th Inf. Co.E
Sellers, Joseph D. NC 3rd Inf. Co.F
Sellers, Joseph E. KY 5th Cav. Co.A
Sellers, Joseph H. KY 4th Cav. 2nd Lt.
Sellers, Jos. H. TN 9th (Ward's) Cav. Co.A 3rd Lt.
Sellers, Joseph N. GA 44th Inf. Co.B
Sellers, Joseph S. AL 51st (Part.Rangers) Co.B
Sellers, Joseph W. FL 11th Inf. Co.C
Sellers, Joseph W. LA 31st Inf. Co.G
Sellers, Joseph W. MS 8th Inf. Co.C
Sellers, Joshua GA 59th Inf. Co.A
Sellers, Josiah AL 1st Bn. Hilliard's Legion Vol. Co.B
Sellers, J.W. AL 7th Cav. Co.G
Sellers, J.W. MS 7th Cav. Co.B
Sellers, J.W. NC 31st Inf. Co.B
Sellers, J.W. SC 25th Inf. Co.F Capt.
Sellers, J.W. TN 21st Inf. Co.C Sgt.
Sellers, J.W. TX 30th Cav. Co.C
Sellers, J.W. TX Cav. McCord's Frontier Regt. Co.C
Sellers, Killis AL 36th Inf. Co.K
Sellers, Leander R. NC 6th Cav. (65th St.Troops) Co.C,G
Sellers, Leander R. NC Cav. 7th Bn. Co.C Far.
Sellers, Lemuel NC 57th Inf. Co.A
Sellers, L.H. AL 23rd Inf. Co.B
Sellers, L.H. AL 46th Inf. Co.C
Sellers, L.H. MS 37th Inf. Co.F
Sellers, Littleton GA 59th Inf. Co.A
Sellers, L.J. SC Inf. Hampton Legion Co.G
Sellers, Lorenzo NC 2nd Arty. (36th St.Troops) Co.G
Sellers, Louis KY 10th (Johnson's) Cav. Co.A
Sellers, M. VA Patrol Guard 11th Congr.Dist. (Mtd.)
Sellers, Martin H. AL 25th Inf. Co.K
Sellers, Mathew AL 3rd Res. Co.C
Sellers, Mathew AL 6th Inf. Co.A
Sellers, Matt TX 30th Cav. Co.C
Sellers, M.C. SC 6th Cav. Co.K
Sellers, M.C. SC 28th Inf. Co.F
Sellers, M.H. SC 1st (Hagood's) Inf. 1st Co.D 2nd Lt.
Sellers, M.H. SC 25th Inf. Co.F Capt.
Sellers, Michael SC Palmetto S.S. Co.M
Sellers, Micha H. TN Cav. Welcker's Bn. Kincaid's Co.
Sellers, Milton VA 58th Mil. Co.H
Sellers, M.J. MS 1st Lt.Arty. Co.F
Sellers, M.K. MS 4th Cav. Co.A
Sellers, M.M. SC Cav. 19th Bn. Co.D
Sellers, M.M. SC Cav. (St.Troops) Rodgers' Co.
Sellers, M.N. MS 3rd Inf. Co.B
Sellers, M.N. MS 36th Inf. Co.B
Sellers, Morgan VA 7th Cav. Co.I
Sellers, Morgan VA 58th Mil. Co.H
Sellers, Morgan VA Guards & Scouts Rockingham Cty.

Sellers, M.S. AL 15th Inf. Co.F
Sellers, N. TX 5th Cav. Co.F Sgt.
Sellers, Needham AL 22nd Inf. Co.I
Sellers, Newton NC 48th Inf. Co.I
Sellers, N.K. MS 46th Inf. Co.B
Sellers, N.M. TN 5th (McKenzie's) Cav. Co.B
  Sgt.
Sellers, Osborn J. FL 11th Inf. Co.C,F
Sellers, P.A. NC 6th Sr.Res. Co.G
Sellers, P.A. SC 8th Inf. Co.B
Sellers, P.B. AL 7th Cav. Co.H
Sellers, Peter TX 30th Cav. Co.C
Sellers, Peter TX 1st Hvy.Arty. Co.G
Sellers, Philip SC 8th Inf. Co.B 1st Lt.
Sellers, Philip TN 51st (Cons.) Inf. Co.A
Sellers, Pleasant AR 33rd Inf. Co.D
Sellers, R. AL 22nd Inf. Co.B
Sellers, R. SC 7th Res. Co.L
Sellers, R.A. SC Inf. 1st (Charleston) Bn. Co.F
Sellers, R.A. SC 3rd Inf. Co.G
Sellers, R.A. SC 27th Inf. Co.C
Sellers, Ramon F. GA 48th Inf. Co.F
Sellers, Raymond G. NC 30th Inf. Co.C
Sellers, Reuben VA 146th Mil. Co.B
Sellers, Richard MS 12th Cav. Co.F
Sellers, Richard NC 20th Inf. Co.K
Sellers, Richard NC 50th Inf. Co.E Sgt.
Sellers, Richard SC 6th Cav. Co.D
Sellers, Richard C. SC 8th Inf. Co.B Sgt.
Sellers, Rilah AL Arty. 1st Bn. Co.F
Sellers, Riley AL 61st Inf. Co.K
Sellers, Rily GA 38th Inf. 2nd Co.I
Sellers, R.L. GA 65th Inf. Co.H
Sellers, R.L. GA Smith's Legion Co.A
Sellers, R.M. GA 11th Inf. Co.B
Sellers, Robert NC Walker's Bn. Thomas' Legion
  2nd Co.D
Sellers, Robert A. NC 3rd Arty. (40th St.Troops)
  Co.G
Sellers, Robin R. NC 26th Inf. Co.K
Sellers, Rollin R. NC 3rd Arty. (40th St.Troops)
  Co.G,C
Sellers, S. TN Inf. 2nd Cons.Regt. Co.I
Sellers, S. TN 50th (Cons.) Inf. Co.C
Sellers, S. VA 9th Bn.Res. Co.A
Sellers, Sampson SC 17th Inf. Co.H
Sellers, Samuel AL 13th Inf. Co.A Capt.
Sellers, Samuel MO 16th Inf. Co.H
Sellers, Samuel SC 6th Cav. Co.K Sgt.
Sellers, Samuel A. GA 20th Inf. Co.K
Sellers, Samuel A. VA 10th Inf. Co.I Capt.
Sellers, Samuel H. NC 30th Inf. Co.C
Sellers, Samuel H. NC 47th Inf. Co.A
Sellers, Samuel S. SC Inf. 9th Bn. Co.D
Sellers, Samuel S. SC 26th Inf. Co.E
Sellers, S.G. AL 51st (Part.Rangers) Co.B
Sellers, Sidney P. AL Mil. 4th Vol. Co.A
Sellers, Sidney P. AL 13th Inf. Co.A
Sellers, Simeon M. TX 13th Cav. Co.G
Sellers, S. Jasper AL 2nd Bn. Hilliard's Legion
  Vol. Co.D Cpl.
Sellers, S.M. GA 5th Inf. (St.Guards) Johnston's
  Co.
Sellers, S.R. TX 1st Hvy.Arty. Co.K Sgt.
Sellers, Stephen D. SC Lt.Arty. Kelly's Co.
  (Chesterfield Arty.)
Sellers, Stephen S. TX 5th Cav. Co.I

Sellers, T. LA Ogden's Cav. Co.G
Sellers, T. TN 19th (Biffle's) Cav. Co.I
Sellers, T.B. SC 26th Inf. Co.E
Sellers, T.B. SC Inf. Hampton Legion Co.G
Sellers, T.E. TN 19th (Biffle's) Cav. Co.K
Sellers, T.G. MS Inf. 1st Bn. Co.C
Sellers, T.G. MS Inf. 2nd Bn. Co.L Lt.
Sellers, T.G. MS 48th Inf. Co.L,K 2nd Lt.
Sellers, Theodore N. VA 58th Mil. Co.B
Sellers, Theoli TX 13th Vol. Co.E
Sellers, Thomas AL 6th Inf. Co.A
Sellers, Thomas AR 27th Inf. New Co.B
Sellers, Thomas FL 6th Inf. Co.I
Sellers, Thomas SC 6th Cav. Co.K
Sellers, Thomas TN 19th & 20th (Cons.) Cav.
  Co.C
Sellers, Thomas TN Inf. Harman's Regt. Co.K
Sellers, Thomas A. NC 2nd Arty. (36th
  St.Troops) Co.G
Sellers, Thomas B. AR 34th Inf. Co.K
Sellers, Thomas B. LA Inf. 11th Bn. Co.G Sgt.
Sellers, Thomas E. AR 1st (Crawford's) Cav.
  Co.A
Sellers, Thomas G. MS St.Cav. Perrin's Bn.
  Co.F 2nd Lt.
Sellers, Thomas W. MO 2nd Cav. Co.G
Sellers, T.M. MS Lt.Arty. (Issaquena Arty.)
  Graves' Co.
Sellers, T.R. TX 24th & 25th Cav. (Cons.) Co.E
Sellers, T.W. AR 1st Vol. Co.F
Sellers, T.W. AR 4th Inf.
Sellers, Van J. KY 2nd (Duke's) Cav. Co.A 2nd
  Lt.
Sellers, Van J. TN 9th (Ward's) Cav. Co.G 2nd
  Lt.
Sellers, Vilmont LA 28th (Thomas') Inf. Co.A
Sellers, V.W. MS Cav. Jeff Davis Legion Co.C
Sellers, W. SC 7th (Ward's) Bn.St.Res. Co.F
Sellers, W.A. MS 8th Inf. Co.C
Sellers, W.A. MS 37th Inf. Co.F
Sellers, W.A. TN 19th (Biffle's) Cav. Co.K
Sellers, W.A. TN 19th & 20th (Cons.) Cav.
  Co.C
Sellers, W.B. SC 6th Cav. Co.D Cpl.
Sellers, W.B. SC 8th Inf. Co.B
Sellers, W.C. AL Vol. Goldsmith's Ind.Co.
Sellers, W.F. TX 7th Cav. Co.C
Sellers, W.H. KY 2nd Mtd.Inf. Co.D
Sellers, W.H. TX 5th Inf. Co.A Adj.
Sellers, W.H. VA Mil. Carroll Cty.
Sellers, W.H. VA 4th St.Line Love's Co.
Sellers, W.I. GA 9th Cav. Cpl.
Sellers, Wilkerson KY 13th Cav. Co.D Capt.
Sellers, William AL 15th Inf. Co.E
Sellers, Wm. AL 22nd Inf. Co.B
Sellers, William AR 33rd Inf. Co.E
Sellers, William LA 12th Inf. Co.I Music.
Sellers, William MO 16th Inf. Co.A
Sellers, William NC 5th Inf. Co.C
Sellers, William NC 6th Inf. Co.E
Sellers, William NC 35th Inf. Co.B
Sellers, William NC 37th Inf. Co.D
Sellers, William SC 6th Cav. Co.D Sgt.
Sellers, William SC 8th Inf. Co.C
Sellers, William TN 18th (Newsom's) Cav. Co.I
Sellers, William VA 9th Bn.Res. Co.D
Sellers, William E. AL 12th Inf. Co.K

Sellers, William H. GA 47th Inf. Co.F Cpl.
Sellers, William H. KY 4th Mtd.Inf. Co.E
Sellers, William H. NC 2nd Arty. (36th
  St.Troops) Co.E Cpl.
Sellers, William H. TX Cav. Mann's Regt. Co.H
Sellers, William J. AL 53rd (Part.Rangers) Co.K
Sellers, William J. GA 1st (Symons') Res. Co.G
  Sgt.
Sellers, William J. NC 25th Inf. Co.C Music.
Sellers, William L. FL 5th Inf. Co.B
Sellers, William L. GA 50th Inf. Co.E
Sellers, William M. AL 13th Inf. Co.C
Sellers, William R. NC 2nd Arty. (36th
  St.Troops) Co.G
Sellers, William R. SC 4th Cav. Co.A
Sellers, William R. SC Cav. 12th Bn. Co.A
Sellers, William R. SC 8th Inf. Co.B
Sellers, William W. AR 15th (Josey's) Inf. Co.C
Sellers, William W. NC 51st Inf. Co.G
Sellers, Williamson TX 17th Cav. Co.A
Sellers, Williamson TX 17th Cons.Dismtd.Cav.
  Co.A
Sellers, W.J. AL 17th Inf. Co.A
Sellers, W.L. GA Inf. 1st City Bn. (Columbus)
  Co.B
Sellers, W.M. AR 1st (Monroe's) Cav. Co.L
Sellers, W.P. SC 6th Cav. Co.D
Sellers, W.R. TN 19th & 20th (Cons.) Cav. Co.E
Sellers, W.R. TN 15th Inf. Co.C
Sellers, Wright FL 11th Inf. Co.C
Sellers, W.S. TN 16th (Logwood's) Cav. Co.E
Sellers, W.S. TX 30th Cav. Co.C
Sellers, Young M. AL 6th Inf. Co.K
Sellert, N.E. AL 51st (Part.Rangers) Co.B
Selles, Anto. LA Mil. 5th Regt.Eur.Brig.
  (Spanish Regt.) Co.8
Selles, F. LA 22nd Inf. Co.E
Selles, F. LA 22nd (Cons.) Inf. Co.E Sgt.
Selles, Miguel LA Mil. 5th Regt.Eur.Brig.
  (Spanish Regt.) Co.6
Selles, Miguel LA Mil. Cazadores Espanoles
  Regt. Co.5
Selles, Stephen R. MS 8th Inf. Co.F
Sellevant, Riley B. FL 7th Inf. Co.E
Selley, George W. TN 5th Inf. Co.E
Sellick, James B. AL 11th Inf. Co.K
Sellick, James B. AL 28th Inf. Co.C,A Lt.
Sellier, A. LA Arty. Guyol's Co. (Orleans Arty.)
Sellier, Charles F. FL 1st Inf. Old Co.A,B Cpl.
Sellier, Charles F. FL Lt.Arty. Dyke's Co. Cpl.
Sellier, Romain MS 3rd Inf. Co.H
Sellin, Francis TX 8th Field Btty.
Selling, J.G. VA 27th Inf. Co.E
Selling, W.W. TX Inf. Timmons' Regt. Co.H
Sellinger, Andrew LA 7th Inf. Co.D
Sellinger, Leopold LA Arty. 1st Field Btty.
Sellis, Alex AL 22nd Inf. Co.B
Sellis, J.W. VA 6th Cav. Co.G
Sellis, W.A. TN 19th (Biffle's) Cav. Co.I
Sellison, F. AL 6th Inf. Co.A
Sellman, Benjamin T. MS 2nd Inf. Co.E
Sellman, George W. TX 25th Cav. Co.B Sgt.
Sellman, H. GA Inf. 19th Bn. (St.Guards) Co.F
Sellman, Henry C. VA Cav. 35th Bn. Co.B
Sellman, James C. MD 1st Inf. Co.C
Sellman, James C., Jr. MD Weston's Bn. Co.A
Sellman, James W. GA 30th Inf. Co.C 2nd Lt.

Sellman, John MD 1st Cav. Co.A
Sellman, John H. VA 1st Cav. Co.K
Sellman, William MS 22nd Inf. Co.B
Sellman, William L. VA Cav. 1st Bn. Co.B
Sellman, Willis R. MS 4th Cav. Co.E
Sellman, W.R. MS 1st (King's) Inf. (St.Troops)
  Co.B
Sellors, H. AL 8th (Hatch's) Cav. Co.G
Sells, A.J. TN 13th (Gore's) Cav. Co.A
Sells, A.J. TN 8th Inf. Co.B
Sells, A.S. GA 43rd Inf. Co.F
Sells, Benjamin TN 1st (Carter's) Cav. Co.M
Sells, Benjamin TN Sullivan Cty.Res.
  (Loc.Def.Troops) White's Co.
Sells, C.D. VA 50th Inf. Co.D
Sells, D. GA 48th Inf. Co.K
Sells, Daniel GA Inf. 1st City Bn. (Columbus)
  Co.D
Sells, Daniel GA 27th Inf. Co.F
Sells, D.J. VA 50th Inf. Co.D
Sells, F.L.S. MO 15th Cav. Co.M
Sells, Frederick VA 33rd Inf. Co.G
Sells, George W. VA 50th Inf. Co.D
Sells, G.W. MO 10th Inf. Co.L Cpl.
Sells, G.W. MO 12th Inf. Co.I Sgt.
Sells, G.W. TN 63rd Inf. Co.K
Sells, H. GA Cav. Alexander's Co.
Sells, H.D. TX Granbury's Cons.Brig. Co.K
Sells, Henry TN 25th Inf. Co.H
Sells, Henry C. TX Cav. Martin's Regt. Co.G
Sells, Henry D. TX 25th Cav. Co.C,F,A
  Sgt.Maj.
Sells, H.J. TN 13th (Gore's) Cav. Co.B
Sells, H.T. GA 10th Cav. (St.Guards) Co.C
Sells, John GA Inf. 1st City Bn. (Columbus)
  Co.F
Sells, John TN 60th Mtd.Inf. Co.G
Sells, John H. TN 1st (Turney's) Inf. Co.I
Sells, Jonathan TN 60th Mtd.Inf. Co.E
Sells, Jonathan M. TN Sullivan Cty.Res.
  (Loc.Def.Troops) Witcher's Co. Sgt.
Sells, Jones GA 43rd Inf. Co.H
Sells, J.W. TN 13th (Gore's) Cav. Co.B
Sells, L. GA 13th Cav. Co.G
Sells, L.A. TN 63rd Inf. Co.F
Sells, M.L. GA 4th Cav. (St.Guards) White's Co.
Sells, Peter G. AL 33rd Inf.
Sells, Peter J. AL 18th Bn.Vol. Co.B
Sells, Samuel TN 63rd Inf. Co.K
Sells, Samuel TX Cav. Waller's Regt. Co.A Sgt.
Sells, Spencer MO 16th Inf. Co.C
Sells, T. GA 13th Cav. Co.K
Sells, Thomas W. TX 25th Cav. Co.H Sgt.
Sells, William TN 1st (Turney's) Inf. Co.B
Sells, William F. VA 50th Inf. Co.D
Sells, William H. GA 34th Inf. Co.F
Sellwood, Henry FL 9th Inf. Co.E,H
Selman, Amos AL St.Res. Palmer's Co.
Selman, Benjamin G. AR 6th Inf. Co.C 1st Lt.
Selman, Benjamin T. MS 17th Inf. Co.C
Selman, B.F. GA 9th Inf. (St.Guards) Co.E
Selman, B.F. MS 2nd (Davidson's) Inf. Co.H
Selman, B.L. AL 23rd Inf. Co.H Capt.
Selman, B.T. TX 1st Inf. Co.I
Selman, Calvin M. AL 24th Inf. Co.D
Selman, Calvin M. AL 28th Inf. Co.A
Selman, Calvin M. AL 41st Inf. Co.E

Selman, D.F. GA Smith's Legion Co.F
Selman, F.M. TX 9th (Young's) Inf. Co.A
Selman, George C. GA 9th Inf. (St.Guards) Co.E
  Capt.
Selman, George W. TX 17th Cons.Dismtd.Cav.
  Co.B Sgt.
Selman, George W. TX 9th (Nichols') Inf. Co.D
Selman, J. VA 51st Mil. Co.E
Selman, James GA 65th Inf. Co.D
Selman, James W. GA 35th Inf. Co.I 2nd Lt.
Selman, J.C. TX 28th Cav. Co.E
Selman, J.F. GA Floyd Legion (St.Guards) Co.E
Selman, J.G. TX 9th (Nichols') Inf. Co.C
Selman, J.G. TX Waul's Legion Co.C Cpl.
Selman, J.H. GA 6th Cav. Co.E
Selman, J.J. AL 14th Inf. Co.H Cpl.
Selman, John TX 22nd Cav. Co.B
Selman, John A. VA 34th Mil. Co.C
Selman, John C. MS 1st Lt.Arty. Co.K
Selman, John D. AL 41st Inf. Co.I
Selman, J.T. AL Cav. (St.Res.) Young's Co.
Selman, J.T. GA Floyd Legion (St.Guards) Co.E
Selman, J.W. GA 1st Cav. Co.G
Selman, J.W., Jr. GA Floyd Legion (St.Guards)
  Co.E
Selman, J.W., Sr. GA Floyd Legion (St.Guards)
  Co.E
Selman, O.W. GA 50th Inf. Co.D
Selman, Robert MS 1st Lt.Arty. Co.K
Selman, Robert TX Cav. Giddings' Bn. Carr's
  Co.
Selman, T.B. TX 28th Cav. Co.E
Selman, T.B. 2nd Conf.Eng.Troops Co.C Artif.
Selman, T.D. LA 16th Inf. Co.D,A
Selman, T.H. GA 30th Inf. Co.C
Selman, Thomas B. AL 17th Inf. Co.A
Selman, T.J. TX 4th Inf. Co.E Capt.
Selman, W.E. TX 4th Cav. Co.K
Selman, W.H.B. AL 14th Inf. Co.H
Selman, William R. GA 30th Inf. Co.C Sgt.
Selman, W.J. GA 65th Inf. Co.D
Selman, W.J. GA Smith's Legion Co.F
Selman, W.L. GA 28th Inf. Co.C Sgt.Maj.
Selman, W.L. GA Floyd Legion (St.Guards)
  Co.E
Selman, W.R. GA 7th Inf. (St.Guards) Co.B
  Cpl.
Selman, W.W. AL 14th Inf. Co.H Capt.
Selman, W.W. TX 4th Cav. Co.K
Selmar, J.T. AL Talladega Cty.Res. R.N. Ware's
  Cav.Co.
Selmon, G.W. TX 24th & 25th Cav. (Cons.)
  Co.B Sgt.
Selmon, J.T. 8th (Wade's) Conf.Cav. Co.I
Selmon, Thos. VA 44th Bn. Co.A
Selmon, Thos. H. VA Inf. 44th Bn. Co.D
Selola, --- NC Inf. Thomas Legion
Selony, Jules P. LA 12th Inf. Co.E
Selor, Jh. Chs. LA Mil. 3rd Regt.Eur.Brig.
  (Garde Francaise) Co.6
Selosky, Louis VA Hvy.Arty. 19th Bn. 1st Co.E
Selph, A.P. TN 14th (Neely's) Cav. Co.B
Selph, Benjamin D. VA 52nd Inf. Co.E
Selph, Benjamin F. FL 9th Inf. Co.I
Selph, Charnie GA 49th Inf. Co.B
Selph, C. McRae LA Washington Arty.Bn.
  Capt.

Selph, C. McRae Gen. & Staff Capt.,AAG
Selph, Dudley LA Washington Arty.Bn. Co.2
Selph, Dudley MS Cav. 24th Bn. Co.B Cpl.
Selph, Ezekiel GA 49th Inf. Co.B
Selph, F.M. FL Inf. 2nd Bn. Co.C Lt.
Selph, Francis M. FL 5th Inf. Co.F 2nd Lt.
Selph, G.A. TN 14th (Neely's) Cav. Co.E
Selph, G.W. GA 61st Inf. Co.C
Selph, James GA 8th Cav. New Co.I
Selph, J.M. GA 41st Inf. Co.F
Selph, John AL 19th Inf. Co.B
Selph, John GA 11th Cav. (St.Guards) Tillman's
  Co. 1st Lt.
Selph, John GA 61st Inf. Co.C
Selph, John J. FL 3rd Inf. Co.B
Selph, John L. AR 19th (Dockery's) Inf. Co.E
Selph, John M. AR 36th Inf. Co.H
Selph, John W. GA 61st Inf. Co.C
Selph, L.E. LA 3rd (Wingfield's) Cav. Co.H
Selph, Montgomery C. MS 2nd Inf. Co.D,F Sgt.
Selph, P.J. MS 2nd Cav.Res. Co.I
Selph, T.H. GA 61st Inf. Co.C
Selph, Thomas GA 49th Inf. Co.B
Selph, T.J. AR 36th Inf. Co.H
Selph, W.A. LA Inf. 1st Sp.Bn. (Rightor's) Co.F
  Jr.2nd Lt.
Selph, W.A. MS 38th Cav. Co.G Capt.
Selph, William GA 49th Inf. Co.B
Selph, William TN 6th Inf. Co.I
Selph, William B. MS Inf. 3rd Bn. Co.F
Selph, William J. VA 52nd Inf. Co.E
Selser, E.A. MS 12th Inf. Co.K
Selser, J.M. MS Scouts Montgomery Co.
Selsor, J.P. TN 1st (Carter's) Cav. Co.E
Seltner, Alvis LA 1st Hvy.Arty. (Reg.) Co.E
Selton, C.P. NC 49th Inf. Co.K
Selton, O.A. GA 8th Cav.
Seltzer, Henry GA 1st (Symons') Res. Co.C
  Cpl.
Seltzer, J. LA Mil.Squad. Guides d'Orleans
Seltzer, P. LA 22nd Inf. Gomez Co.
Selvage, Edwin MD 1st Cav. Co.D Cpl.
Selvage, Edwin MD 1st Inf. Co.D 1st Cpl.
Selvage, Isaac KY 5th Mtd.Inf. Co.K
Selvage, James M. AL 49th Inf.
Selvage, J.D. AR 51st Mil. Co.H
Selvage, John AL 49th Inf. Co.D
Selvage, John TN Cav. 16th Bn. (Neal's) Co.D
Selvage, Joseph M.C. TN 3rd (Lillard's)
  Mtd.Inf. Co.H
Selvage, Peter AL 49th Inf. Co.D
Selvage, R. TN 15th (Stewart's) Cav. Co.D
Selvage, W.H. AR 15th (N.W.) Inf. Co.D
Selvage, William AL 49th Inf. Co.D Sgt.
Selvage, William H. TN 43rd Inf. Co.F
Selvedge, J.D. TX 14th Inf. Co.E
Selvedge, J.H. AR 1st Cav. Co.B
Selvedge, Samuel H. TN 3rd (Lillard's) Mtd.Inf.
  Co.C Sgt.
Selven, William W. AL 4th Inf. Co.B Sgt.
Selvenridge, Samuel VA 8th Cav. Co.L
Selvera, Manuel TX 8th Inf. Co.H
Selves, John GA 54th Inf. Co.C Sgt.
Selvey, D.C. MS Cav. Gamblin's Co.
  (St.Troops)
Selvey, William H. VA Lt.Arty. Donald's Co.

Selvey, William M. VA Lt.Arty. G.B. Chapman's Co.

Selvidge, James H. AR 2nd Mtd.Rifles Co.D Bugler

Selvidge, J.H. TX 7th Cav. Co.I

Selvidge, J.J. AR 1st Cav. Co.E

Selvidge, J.J. AR 30th Inf. Co.K

Selvidge, John TN Inf. 31st Bn.

Selvidge, John H. AR 2nd Mtd.Rifles Co.D

Selvidge, Joseph M. TN 62nd Mtd.Inf. Co.K Sgt.

Selvidge, Michael K. TX 31st Cav. Co.A

Selvidge, M.K. TX Arty. Douglas' Co.

Selvidge, R.J. TN 12th (Green's) Cav. Co.G

Selvidge, Wm. AL 48th Inf. Co.D Sgt.

Selvidge, W.R. AR 11th Inf. Co.E 1st Lt.

Selvidge, W.R. AR 11th & 17th Cons.Inf. Co.E Capt.

Selvis, --- MS Cav. 1st Choctaw Bn.

Selvius, Uriah VA 7th Bn.Res. Co.A

Selvous, Isaac VA 8th Bn.Res. Co.C

Selvy, James L. MO 12th Cav. Co.C 2nd Lt.

Selvy, Jasper N. NC 22nd Inf. Co.G

Selvy, Jasper S. NC 37th Inf. Co.H

Selvy, Wm. GA 11th Cav. Co.C

Selvy, William GA Inf. 4th Bn. (St.Guards) Co.D

Selwin, George VA 9th Inf. Co.C

Sely, John GA Arty. 11th Bn. (Sumter Arty.) Cpl.

Selzel, John M. TX 9th Field Btty.

Selzer, Frederick GA 1st (Olmstead's) Inf. 1st Co.A

Selzer, Frederick GA 1st Bn.S.S. Co.B

Selzner, John LA Mil. Chalmette Regt. Co.G

Sem, James AL Conscr.

Semamus, Joshua VA 45th Inf. Co.I

Semanall, Joshua VA Mil. Carroll Cty.

Semans, P.G. AR Cav. 28th Regt. Co.G

Semare, Joshua LA 1st Bn. Co.C

Semarton, A.C. LA 28th (Gray's) Inf. Co.I

Semawakika 1st Seminole Mtd.Vol.

Sembler, William, Jr. AR 30th Inf. Co.G,D

Sembler, William, Sr. AR 30th Inf. Co.G

Semen, John J. VA 1st Cav. Co.F

Semen, Jonah VA 27th Inf. 1st Co.H

Semen, Richard D. VA 27th Inf. 1st Co.H

Semer, James VA 5th Cav.Arty. & Inf.St.Line Co.I Sgt.

Semer, O. LA Inf.Cons. 18th Regt. & Yellow Jacket Bn. Co.G

Seminere, Joseph TX 13th Vol. Co.I

Semington, C. TN 12th (Green's) Cav. Co.C Sgt.

Semino, A. LA 18th Inf. Co.I

Semis, James A. AR 13th Inf. Co.B Sgt.

Semitch, W.S. MS 12th Inf. Co.B

Semitierre, Joseph LA Conscr.

Semke, John SC Mil.Arty. 1st Regt. Werner's Co.

Semken, D. SC Mil.Arty. 1st Regt. Werner's Co.

Semken, J. SC Mil.Arty. 1st Regt. Werner's Co.

Semken, J. SC Lt.Arty. Wagener's Co. (Co.A,- German Arty.)

Semken, William SC Mil.Arty. 1st Regt. Werner's Co. Sgt.

Semken, William SC Lt.Arty. Wagener's Co. (Co.A,German Arty.) Sgt.

Semker, A.D. VA Inf. 54th Bn. Hosp.Stew.

Semkie, D. SC 1st Regt. Charleston Guard Co.G

Semkie, J. SC 1st Regt. Charleston Guard Co.G

Semler, A. LA Inf. Pelican Regt. Co.F

Semler, August T. LA Inf. 4th Bn. Co.A

Semler, H. MS 8th Inf. Co.D

Semloch, S.V. AL Young's Arty.

Semmens, J.H. GA 8th Inf. Co.A

Semmers, H.W. AL 62nd Inf. Co.F

Semmes, Abner G. Gen. & Staff 1st Lt.,Ord.Off.

Semmes, A.G. MS 10th Inf. Old Co.D

Semmes, A.G. MS 37th Inf. Co.H

Semmes, A.J. Gen. & Staff Surg.

Semmes, Alexander J. LA 8th Inf. Surg.

Semmes, Alfonzo T. MS Part.Rangers Smyth's Co.

Semmes, Andrew G. MS 18th Inf. Co.G Bvt.2nd Lt.

Semmes, B.J. TN Inf. 154th Sr.Regt. Co.L Sgt.

Semmes, B.J. Gen. & Staff Capt.,ACS

Semmes, C.C. VA 5th Cav. Co.B,D

Semmes, C.C. VA Hvy.Arty. 19th Bn. 3rd Co.C 1st Lt.

Semmes, Charles W. VA Lt.Arty. Brander's Co. 1st Sgt.

Semmes, D.R. VA 3rd Inf.Loc.Def. Co.F

Semmes, F.C. MS Conscr.

Semmes, J.M. MS 28th Cav. Co.F

Semmes, John T. MS 1st (King's) Inf. (St.Troops) Co.F 1st Sgt.

Semmes, J.T. Conf.Cav. Wood's Regt. 2nd Co.M

Semmes, J.W. Gen. & Staff Capt.,AQM

Semmes, Lewis L. MD Inf. 2nd Bn. Co.B

Semmes, Oliver J. Conf.Lt.Arty. 1st Reg.Btty. Capt.

Semmes, O.S. Inf. School of Pract. Co.B 2nd Lt.

Semmes, Paul J. GA 2nd Inf. Col.

Semmes, Paul J. Gen. & Staff,PACS Brig.Gen.

Semmes, Peter KY 1st Bn.Mtd.Rifles Co.F

Semmes, P. Warfield LA 1st (Nelligan's) Inf. Co.C Adj.

Semmes, P. Warfield LA Inf. 1st Sp. Bn. (Rightor's) New Co.C 2nd Lt.

Semmes, P. Warfield VA Lt.Arty. Jackson's Bn.St.Line Co.A 1st Lt.

Semmes, P. Warfield 3rd Conf.Eng.Troops Co.B Sr.2nd Lt.

Semmes, Raphael Gen. & Staff Brig.Gen.

Semmes, R.J. Gen. & Staff Capt.,ADC

Semmes, S.S. LA 1st (Strawbridge's) Inf. Co.E Capt.,QM

Semmes, S.S. Gen. & Staff, QM Dept. AQM

Semmes, Thomas J. LA Mil.Conf.Guards Regt. Co.H 1st Lt.

Semmes, T.M. AR 3rd Inf. Co.K Adj.

Semmes, William Conf.Cav. Wood's Regt. 2nd Co.M

Semmins, W.D. GA 7th Cav. Co.D

Semmler, Fritz TX 8th Inf. Co.K

Semmler, H. AL 23rd Inf. Co.G

Semmons, N. MS 18th Cav. Co.G

Semms, J.A. AL 4th Cav. Co.F

Semms, Philip B. GA 64th Inf. Co.I 2nd Lt.

Semn, Thomas M. MS 44th Inf. Co.G

Semnes, John LA 28th (Gray's) Inf. Co.B

Semns, T.S. MS 1st Inf. Maj.

Semo, U. LA 7th Cav. Co.D

Semon, Semon VA 9th Inf. Co.F Music.

Semonas, James S. VA 45th Inf. Co.E

Semonds, George SC Mil. Co.A

Semone, James NC 14th Inf. Co.I

Semones, Absalom VA 45th Inf. Co.A

Semones, Benjamin M. VA 10th Cav. Co.K Sgt.

Semones, B.T. VA 10th Cav. Co.K

Semones, J.A. VA 10th Cav. Co.K QMSgt.

Semones, James S. VA 24th Inf. Co.C,K

Semones, John C. TN Cav. 4th Bn. (Branner's) Co.C Black.

Semones, John P. VA 24th Inf. Co.D

Semones, John W. VA 24th Inf. Co.C

Semones, J.S. VA 10th Cav. Co.K

Semones, J.T. VA 10th Cav. Co.K

Semones, Lewis P. VA 24th Inf. Co.C

Semones, Nathaniel L. VA 24th Inf. Co.C

Semones, Peter H. VA 57th Inf. Co.G

Semones, Samuel M. VA 24th Inf. Co.D

Semones, William G. VA 24th Inf. Co.D

Semones, Wilson F. VA 24th Inf. Co.C

Semonis, A. VA 22nd Cav. Co.G

Semonis, John KY 2nd (Duke's) Cav. Co.H

Semonis, John KY 11th Cav. Co.F

Semonius, Absalom VA 54th Inf. Co.G

Semonius, John TN 2nd (Ashby's) Cav. Co.D

Semons, A.M. TX 2nd Cav. Co.B

Semons, J.B. 2nd Conf.Inf. Co.B

Semons, J.D. VA 51st Inf. Co.H

Semons, William MO 2nd & 6th Cons.Inf. Co.C

Semorah, Holcan TX 2nd Cav. Co.I

Semore, Calvin TN 3rd (Lillard's) Mtd.Inf. Co.B

Semore, Jesse KY 2nd (Woodward's) Cav. Co.A,B

Semper, Charles S. LA 1st Hvy.Arty. (Reg.) Co.G N.C.S. Sgt.Maj.

Sempie, --- SC 27th Inf. Co.C Cook

Semple, Charles KY 2nd Mtd.Inf. Co.K 1st Lt.

Semple, Charles KY 9th Mtd.Inf. Co.D 1st Lt.

Semple, Charles Gen. & Staff Capt.,ACS or MSK

Semple, D.M. VA Lt.Arty. 12th Bn. Co.B

Semple, E.A. Gen. & Staff Surg.

Semple, E.A. Gen. & Staff, Inf. 2nd Lt.

Semple, Edward A. AL 3rd Inf. Surg.

Semple, Edward A. NC 57th Inf. Co.A Capt.

Semple, Edward A. Osborne's Staff Capt., Insp.Gen.

Semple, George W. VA 32nd Inf. 1st Co.K 1st Lt.

Semple, G.W. VA Arty. L.F. Jones' Co.

Semple, G.W. VA 3rd Inf.Loc.Def. Co.B, 2nd Co.G

Semple, G.W. Gen. & Staff Surg.

Semple, Henry C. AL Lt.Arty. Goldthwaite's Btty. Capt.

Semple, Henry C. Gen. & Staff, Arty.Bn. Maj.

Semple, J. Gen. & Staff, Cav. 2nd Lt.,Dr.M.

Semple, James AL 51st (Part.Rangers) Co.I 1st Lt.

Semple, James VA 13th Cav. Co.F

Semple, James VA 24th Inf. Co.H

Semple, James Conf.Arty. Nelson's Bn. Surg.

Semple, James Gen. & Staff Surg.

Semple, John P. AL 5th Inf. New Co.D

Semple, John T. LA 1st Cav. Co.C

Semple, John T. LA 1st Hvy.Arty. (Reg.) Co.C

Semple, J.T. MS Cav. Semple's Co.
Semple, R. Arty. Braxton's Bn.Res.,CSA
  Hosp.Stew.
Semple, R.B. VA Lt.Arty. 12th Bn. Co.B
Semple, Richard B. VA Lt.Arty. Pollock's Co.
Semple, Robert MS Cav. Semple's Co. Capt.
Semple, Robert MS Wilkinson Cty. Minute Men
  Lt.Col.
Semple, Robert B. VA Lt.Arty. Pollock's Co.
Semple, Wellington TX 1st (Yager's) Cav. Co.D
  Cpl.
Semple, W.H. AR 15th Inf.
Semple, W.W. MS 4th Cav. Co.I Cpl.
Semple, W.W. Gen. & Staff 1st Lt.
Sempson, Charles W. MS 8th Inf. Co.D
Sempson, Gabriel 1st Choctaw & Chickasaw
  Mtd.Rifles Maytubby's Co.
Sempson, John C. SC 1st (Butler's) Inf. Co.L
Sems, A.J. MS 12th Inf. Co.H 1st Lt.
Sems, Allen VA 79th Mil. Co.2
Sems, H. AL Cav. Moreland's Regt. Co.C
Sems, H.J. GA Arty. Lumpkin's Co.
Sems, J. GA Arty. Lumpkin's Co.
Sems, John N. AL 51st (Part.Rangers) Co.C
Sems, W.J. GA Arty. Lumpkin's Co.
Semsenbacker, John LA 20th Inf. New Co.E
Sena, Franc A. LA Mil. 2nd Regt. 2nd Brig. 1st
  Div. Co.I
Senac, Antony LA Mil. 1st Native Guards
Senac, Francois LA Mil. 4th Regt. 1st Brig. 1st
  Div. Co.I
Senac, J. LA Mil. 3rd Regt.Eur.Brig. (Garde
  Francaise) Co.4
Senaca, Jesse L. VA 6th Inf. Co.F
Senage, James MO 12th Cav. Co.I
Senaker, Archimadus D. VA 63rd Inf. Co.B
  Hosp.Stew.
Senaker, David B. VA 63rd Inf. Co.B
Senaker, William VA 25th Cav. Co.D
Senalois, --- TX Cav. Ragsdale's Bn. Co.B
Senaret, A. LA Mil. 1st Regt. French Brig. Co.6
Senaret, Antoine LA Mil. 2nd Regt. French Brig.
  Co.5
Se nar ter 1st Creek Mtd.Vol. Co.F
Senat, Anto. LA Mil. 5th Regt.Eur.Brig.
  (Spanish Regt.) Co.6
Senat, B. LA Mil. 3rd Regt.Eur.Brig. (Garde
  Francaise) Co.4
Senat, Louis LA Mil. 3rd Regt.Eur.Brig. (Garde
  Francaise) Co.4
Senate, Richard AL 4th Res. Co.K
Senate, William TN 2nd (Walker's) Inf. Co.K
Senate, William 9th Conf.Inf. Co.A
Senate, William L.J. NC 61st Inf. Co.H
Senaydar, W.S. LA 18th Inf. Co.D
Senaydar, W.S. LA Inf.Cons. 18th Regt. & Yel-
  low Jacket Bn. Co.D
Sence, John H. VA Arty. Wise Legion 1st Sgt.
Senchenlagr, J. LA Mil. 2nd Regt. 3rd Brig. 1st
  Div. Co.C
Sencindiver, George VA 12th Cav. Co.A
Sencindiver, George VA 67th Mil. Co.D
Sencindiver, J. VA 67th Mil. Co.A
Sencindiver, Jacob VA 67th Mil. Col.
Sencindiver, James L. VA 12th Cav. Co.A
Sencindiver, J.L. VA 67th Mil. Co.A
Sencindiver, J.M. VA 7th Cav. Glenn's Co.

Sencindiver, J.M. VA 67th Mil. Co.A Capt.
Sencindiver, Samuel VA 12th Cav. Co.A
Sencindiver, Samuel VA 67th Mil. Co.A
Send, Benjamin LA Mil. 2nd Regt. French Brig.
  Co.7
Sendemer, Frederick TX 36th Cav. Co.F Cpl.
Senders, H. MS 36th Inf. Co.I
Sene, T. LA Mil. 1st Native Guards
Senebaugh, W.H. AL 8th Inf. Co.D
Seneca, D.W. VA 6th Inf. Co.D
Seneca, Joseph LA 18th Inf. Co.E
Seneca, Joseph LA Inf.Cons. 18th Regt. & Yel-
  low Jacket Bn. Co.E
Seneca, Milton P. VA 5th Cav. (12 mo. '61-2)
  Co.A
Seneca, Milton P. VA Cav. 14th Bn. Co.C
  Bvt.2nd Lt.
Seneca, Milton P. VA 15th Cav. Co.C 2nd Lt.
Seneca, William H. VA 6th Inf. Co.F
Senechal, A. TX 27th Cav. Co.G
Senechal, Elick TX 27th Cav. Co.G
Senechal, Louis TX 1st Hvy.Arty. Co.G
Seneker, E. VA 21st Cav. Co.F
Seneker, Jacob S. TN 59th Mtd.Inf. Co.F Sgt.
Seneker, John H. NC 56th Inf. Co.G Sgt.
Seneker, Robert A. TN 59th Mtd.Inf. Co.F Cpl.
Seneker, W.R. TN 60th Mtd.Inf. Co.G
Senell, Benjamin GA 47th Inf. Co.I
Senell, Frank FL 6th Inf. Co.D
Senentz, Louis LA Mil. 1st Regt.French Brig.
  Co.6 Cpl.
Sener, Henry C. VA Lt.Arty. Pollock's Co.
Sener, Joseph W. VA 30th Inf. Co.A Capt.
Seneschal, Alexander TX 2nd Inf. Co.B
Senet, Charles LA 15th Inf. Co.E
Senette, Felix LA Arty. 1st Field Btty.
Senette, Marius LA 2nd Bn.
Senette, William VA 62nd Mtd.Inf. 2nd Co.K
  Cpl.
Seney, William MO 5th Inf. Co.B
Seney, William 1st Creek Mtd.Vol. Co.G
Senf, R. VA 2nd St.Res. Co.H Cpl.
Senff, Ed. H. LA 25th Inf. Co.I 2nd Lt.
Senger, J.B. LA Mil. Orleans Fire Regt. Co.A
Senger, Joseph VA 58th Mil. Co.E
Senger, Samuel GA 1st (Olmstead's) Inf. Gor-
  don's Co.
Senger, Samuel GA 63rd Inf. Co.B
Sengletary, B.F. SC 2nd Res.
Sengstack, H.H. Moody's Brig. AAG
Sengstacks, Henry H. AL 3rd Inf. Co.A
Sengstak, Henry Herman AL Lt.Arty. 2nd Bn.
  Co.D Capt.
Seniago, J.B. TN Inf. 3rd Bn. Co.E
Seniard, Alex AR 11th Inf. Co.E
Seniath, J.S. SC Mil. 16th Regt. Sigwald's Co.
Seniff, Herman VA 77th Mil. Co.C
Senile, J.C. TX Cav. Waller's Regt. Co.F Capt.
Senior, S.M. VA Arty. C.F. Johnston's Co.
Senior, Thomas MD 1st Cav. Co.K
Senior, Thomas VA 1st Cav. 2nd Co.K
Senior, Thomas VA 1st Inf. Co.I
Seniors, John G. MO 10th Cav. Co.I
Seniors, John G. MO 5th Inf. Co.A Cpl.
Senitierre, Adolph LA Conscr.
Senleslen, A.J. AR 37th Inf.
Senly, J.H. AL 48th Inf. Co.K

Senn, A.C. SC 1st Inf. Co.O
Senn, Alvan C. SC 5th Cav. Co.F
Senn, Alvan. C. SC Cav. 14th Bn. Co.C
Senn, Adam D. SC 20th Inf. Co.H
Senn, D. SC 1st Inf. Co.O
Senn, D. SC 3rd Inf. Co.B
Senn, Daniel AL Inf. 1st Regt. Co.E Cpl.
Senn, Daniel AR 3rd Inf. Co.B
Senn, Daniel D. GA 46th Inf. Co.G
Senn, David AL Inf. 1st Regt. Co.F
Senn, Dederick SC Inf. 3rd Bn. Co.F
Senn, Dennis A. SC 13th Inf. Co.D
Senn, D.L. SC 2nd Cav. Co.H
Senn, E. GA Inf. 1st City Bn. (Columbus) Co.B
Senn, F.S. GA Cav. 1st Bn.Res. Co.A
Senn, F.S. GA 45th Inf. Co.A
Senn, G. SC 1st (Hagood's) Inf. 2nd Co.H
Senn, George SC 2nd Inf. Co.F
Senn, George SC 9th Res. Co.F
Senn, George SC 20th Inf. Co.F
Senn, George W. SC 13th Inf. Co.D
Senn, Grant SC 3rd Inf. Co.E
Senn, Grant SC 18th Inf. Co.E
Senn, H. AR Inf. Hardy's Regt. Co.C
Senn, H. GA Cav. 12th Bn. (St.Guards) Co.D
Senn, Henry AL Inf. 1st Regt. Co.F
Senn, Henry GA Cav. 29th Bn. Co.D
Senn, Henry SC 4th St.Troops Co.A
Senn, Henry SC 5th Bn.Res. Co.D
Senn, Isham AL Inf. 1st Regt. Co.E
Senn, J. GA Inf. City Bn. (Columbus) Co.C
Senn, Jacob SC 2nd St.Troops Co.G
Senn, Jacob SC 20th Inf. Co.K,H
Senn, James P. SC 13th Inf. Co.D
Senn, J.D. SC 13th Inf. Co.D
Senn, Jesse SC 5th St.Troops Co.C
Senn, Jesse SC 9th Res. Co.F
Senn, Joel E. SC 20th Inf. Co.H Cpl.
Senn, John LA Mil. 1st Regt. 2nd Brig. 1st Div.
  Co.H 1st Lt.
Senn, John LA 6th Inf. Co.C
Senn, John P. SC 13th Inf. Co.D
Senn, J.T. GA Inf. 1st Bn. (St.Guards) Co.A
Senn, K.L. GA Conscr.
Senn, K.M. SC 13th Inf. Co.D
Senn, Lemuel AL 1st Inf. Co.F
Senn, Levi E. SC 5th Cav. Co.F
Senn, Levi E. SC Cav. 14th Bn. Co.C
Senn, Lovick J. SC 5th Cav. Co.F
Senn, Lovick J. SC Cav. 14th Bn. Co.C
Senn, M.A. SC Inf. Hampton Legion Co.K
Senn, Nathaniel AL Inf. 1st Regt. Co.E
Senn, Nicholaus LA Mil. 4th Regt.Eur.Brig.
  Co.C
Senn, R.D. SC Post Guard Senn's Co. Capt.
Senn, Robert N. SC 20th Inf. Co.H
Senn, Rufus D. SC Inf. 3rd Bn. Co.F Comsy.
Senn, Rufus D. Gen. & Staff Capt.
Senn, S. SC 20th Inf. Co.H
Senn, Samuel SC 3rd Inf. Co.G
Senn, Samuel SC 20th Inf. Co.K
Senn, Stephen J. GA 64th Inf. Co.G
Senn, Thomas F. SC 13th Inf. Co.D
Senn, W.A. SC Inf. Holcombe Legion Co.G
Senn, William AL 18th Inf. Co.H
Senn, William AL 46th Inf. Co.H
Senn, William TN Inf. 3rd Bn. Co.G

Senn, William A. SC 5th St.Troops Co.C
Senn, William A. SC 9th Res. Co.F
Senn, William R. SC 20th Inf. Co.H
Senn, William T. GA 8th Inf. (St.Guards) Co.G
Senn, William T. GA 42nd Inf. Co.F
Sennate, Robert NC 17th Inf. (1st Org.) Co.H
Senne, Henry TX 5th Inf. Co.B
Senne, James SC 1st (Butler's) Inf. Co.E
Senne, K.S. AL 57th Inf.
Senne, William SC 1st (Butler's) Inf. Co.E
Senneca, John C. VA 54th Mil. Co.E,F
Sennenger, Jacques GA 3rd Inf. 1st Co.I
Senner, Henry MO 1st Inf. Co.C,K
Senner, Henry MO 1st & 4th Cons.Inf. Co.K
Sennett, Henry VA 25th Inf. 2nd Co.E Cpl.
Sennett, Isham NC 1st Inf. Co.G
Sennett, Michael LA 13th Inf. Co.D
Sennett, Milo G. MO 10th Cav. Co.I 2nd Lt.
Sennett, Richard NC 1st Inf. Co.G
Sennette, John NC 52nd Inf. Co.C
Sennette, Robert LA 18th Inf. Co.B
Sennette, Robert LA Scouts Vinson's Co. Cpl.
Senniff, Hermon L. VA 11th Cav. Co.D
Senninger, --- LA Mil. 3rd Regt.Eur.Brig. (Garde
     Francaise) Co.9
Senninger, J. LA Mil. 3rd Regt.Eur.Brig. (Garde
     Francaise)
Sennit, Michael LA 11th Inf. Co.H
Sennix, C.D. AR 12th Inf. Co.C Sgt.
Sennott, Henry VA Cav. Mosby's Regt.
     (Part.Rangers) Co.B
Sennott, John LA 1st Hvy.Arty. (Reg.) Co.I
Sennott, Thomas LA Mil. British Guard Bn. Bur-
     rowes' Co.
Sensabaugh, David TN 60th Mtd.Inf. Co.B
Sensabaugh, Jacob TN Miller's Co.
     (Loc.Def.Troops)
Sensabaugh, John S. NC 29th Inf. Co.E
Sensabaugh, Leon F. Gen. & Staff Surg.
Sensabaugh, M.H. Gen. & Staff Asst.Surg.
Sensabaugh, Robert M. 3rd Conf.Eng.Troops
     Co.D
Sensabaugh, Thomas VA 14th Cav. Co.H
Sensabaugh, William TX 7th Inf. Co.F
Sensabaugh, William C. TN 60th Mtd.Inf. Co.B
     Cpl.
Sense, Harman TX 20th Inf. Co.A
Sense, Joel E. VA 94th Inf. Co.G
Sensebaugh, D. VA Lt.Arty. Carpenter's Co.
Sensebaugh, William TX 5th Inf. Co.E
Sensely, Lawrence LA C.S. Zouave Bn. Co.A
Sensen, A. TX Inf. 1st St.Troops Lawrence's
     Co.D
Sensendiver, John L. VA 7th Cav. Glenn's Co.
     Cpl.
Senseney, Anthony E. VA Lt.Arty. Cutshaw's
     Co.
Senseney, Edward VA 11th Cav. Co.E
Senseney, Edward D. VA 136th Mil. Co.H Sgt.
Senseney, H.R. VA Cav. 47th Bn. Co.A
Senseny, A.E. VA 6th Cav. Co.D
Senseny, A.E. VA Lt.Arty. Carpenter's Co.
Sensibaugh, David VA 25th Inf. 2nd Co.H
Sensibaugh, D.H. TX 22nd Inf. Co.I
Sensibaugh, Jacob VA 25th Inf. 2nd Co.H
Sensibaugh, John VA 25th Inf. 2nd Co.H
Sensibaugh, Samuel VA 25th Inf. 2nd Co.H

Sensibaugh, Thomas VA 25th Inf. 2nd Co.D
Sensing, A.B. TN 49th Inf. Co.B Sgt.
Sensing, A.B. Inf. Bailey's Cons.Regt. Co.D Sgt.
Sensing, A.R. TN 2nd (Walker's) Inf. Co.B
Sensing, A.R. TN 13th Inf. Co.H
Sensing, G.W. TN 49th Inf. Co.B Cpl.
Sensing, G.W. Inf. Bailey's Cons.Regt. Co.D
     Cpl.
Sensing, J.D. TN 51st Inf. Co.B Cpl.
Sensing, J.H. TN 11th Inf. Co.C
Sensing, J.P. TN 13th Inf. Co.H
Sensintaffar, Rufus F. MO 9th Inf. Co.A
Sensney, A.E. VA 18th Cav. Co.D Cpl.
Sensney, Cornelius VA 18th Cav. Co.D
Senson, A.H. TX 27th Cav. Co.F
Senson, Eduardo LA Mil. 5th Regt.Eur.Brig.
     (Spanish Regt.) Co.A Cpl.
Senstrum, James GA 6th Cav. 1st Co.K
Sentall, John D. AL 13th Inf. Co.F
Sentel, Augustus AL Cav. 5th Bn. Hilliard's
     Legion Co.C
Sentel, Augustus D. AL Cav. 5th Bn. Hilliard's
     Legion Co.C
Sentel, David J. NC Cav. 7th Bn. Co.E
Sentel, Guilford NC 62nd Inf. Co.E
Sentel, James L. NC 62nd Inf. Co.E
Sentel, John B. TX 10th Cav. Co.E
Sentel, P.J. NC 6th Cav. (65th St.Troops) Co.D
Sentel, W.B. NC 6th Cav. (65th St.Troops) Co.D
Sentell, Augustus 10th Conf.Cav. Co.C
Sentell, Augustus D. 10th Conf.Cav. Co.C
Sentell, Charles M. GA Inf. 27th Bn. Co.A Cpl.
Sentell, F.M. NC 6th Cav. (65th St.Troops)
     Co.D Sgt.
Sentell, Francis M. NC Cav. 7th Bn. Co.D
Sentell, Henry AL 5th Inf. New Co.I
Sentell, Henry V. LA 9th Inf. Co.D
Sentell, James C. SC 7th Inf. 1st Co.F, 2nd Co.F
     1st Lt.
Sentell, James M. GA Arty. 9th Bn. Co.B Cpl.
Sentell, James M. LA 9th Inf. Co.D Cpl.
Sentell, Jasper NC 6th Cav. (65th St.Troops)
     Co.D
Sentell, Jasper NC Cav. 7th Bn. Co.D,E
Sentell, J.B. TX Conscr.
Sentell, J.J. AL 5th Inf. Old Co.A
Sentell, J.J. GA Cherokee Legion (St.Guards)
     Co.B Capt.
Sentell, J.N. NC 64th Inf. Co.B
Sentell, John SC 5th Res. Co.D 3rd Lt.
Sentell, John SC 7th Inf. 1st Co.K Cpl.
Sentell, John B. AR 1st (Crawford's) Cav. Co.C
     Sr.2nd Lt.
Sentell, John F. GA 44th Inf. Co.H
Sentell, John R. AL 11th Inf. Co.D
Sentell, J.R. SC 7th Inf. 2nd Co.G
Sentell, Lewis AL 3rd Res. Co.B
Sentell, N.W. LA 6th Cav. Co.C Capt.
Sentell, Oscar SC 7th Inf. 1st Co.K
Sentell, R.A. AL Arty. 1st Bn. Co.A
Sentell, Samuel AR 9th Inf. Co.K,C
Sentell, S.M. LA 17th Inf. Co.H
Sentell, Thomas J. GA Arty. 9th Bn. Co.B
Sentell, William M. LA 28th (Gray's) Inf. Co.B
     2nd Lt.
Sentell, William R. NC Cav. 7th Bn. Co.E,D

Sentell, William W. GA Arty. 9th Bn. Co.B
     Capt.
Senteny, Pembroke S. MO 2nd Inf. Co.A
     Lt.Col.
Senter, A.F. VA 50th Inf. Co.H Cpl.
Senter, Andrew VA 51st Inf. Co.I
Senter, Andrew Jackson MO 6th Inf. Co.I 1st
     Lt.
Senter, A.R. MS 24th Inf. Co.F Sgt.
Senter, Caleb O. NC 52nd Inf. Co.H
Senter, Calvin H. VA 51st Inf. Co.I Capt.
Senter, Calvin H. VA Mil. Grayson Cty.
Senter, C.D. Sap. & Min. Kellersberg's
     Corps,CSA Artif.
Senter, Charles NC 31st Inf. Co.I
Senter, Daniel B. VA 51st Inf. Co.I
Senter, David C. TN 13th Inf. Co.D,A
Senter, Drewry E. VA 51st Inf. Co.I
Senter, Enoch D. VA 50th Inf. Co.H
Senter, Felix VA 50th Inf. Co.H Sgt.
Senter, H.P. TN 14th (Neely's) Cav. Co.B
Senter, H.P. TX 22nd Inf. Co.I
Senter, J. AR 18th (Marmaduke's) Inf. Co.A
Senter, J. NC 1st Bn.Jr.Res. Co.D
Senter, James B. AR 2nd Mtd.Rifles Co.C Sgt.
Senter, James O. TN 30th Mtd.Inf. Co.I 1st Sgt.
Senter, James P. TX Cav. Waller's Regt. Co.A
     1st Sgt.
Senter, J.F. TX 22nd Inf. Co.I
Senter, J.M. Gen. & Staff, Comsy.Dept. Capt.
Senter, J.M.F. KY 3rd Mtd.Inf. Co.B
Senter, John GA 39th Inf. Co.C 1st Lt.
Senter, John NC 26th Inf. Co.A
Senter, John A. MS 24th Inf. Co.F
Senter, John A. NC 2nd Arty. (36th St.Troops)
     Co.D
Senter, John R. GA 1st (Ramsey's) Inf. Co.K
Senter, John W. NC 50th Inf. Co.H
Senter, Jonas NC 34th Inf. Co.E
Senter, Joseph AL Mil. 3rd Vol. Co.E Cpl.
Senter, Joseph NC 26th Inf. Co.A
Senter, J.R. GA 45th Inf. Co.D
Senter, J.V. KY 3rd Mtd.Inf. Co.B Sgt.
Senter, Levi B. VA Mil. Grayson Cty.
Senter, M.F. TN 20th Inf. Co.K Cpl.
Senter, M.G. TN 14th (Neely's) Cav. Co.B
Senter, M.J. NC 31st Inf. Co.I
Senter, N.A. TN 14th (Neely's) Cav. Co.B 1st
     Lt.
Senter, P.H. TX 11th Cav. Co.E Sgt.
Senter, P.H. TX 22nd Inf. Co.I
Senter, Randall J. NC 2nd Inf. Co.C
Senter, Robert T. MS 24th Inf. Co.F
Senter, Seaburn W. TN 3rd (Lillard's) Mtd.Inf.
     Co.A Sgt.
Senter, Stephen SC 16th Inf. Co.D 1st Lt.
Senter, W.F. TN 15th Cav. Co.D
Senter, William NC 21st Inf. Co.C
Senter, William Conway TX 20th Cav. Co.F
     Sgt.
Senter, William E. VA 21st Cav. Co.C
Senter, William F. MO 11th Inf. Co.C Sgt.
Senter, William H. NC 8th Sr.Res. Williams' Co.
     1st Lt.
Senter, William J. MS 24th Inf. Co.F
Senter, William T. VA Lt.Arty. King's Co.
Senter, W.N. NC 5th Sr.Res. Co.B

Senter, W.T. TN 14th (Neely's) Cav. Co.B
Senter, W.T. TN 47th Inf. Co.G
Senterfeit, Benjamin G. AL 6th Cav. Co.K
Senterfeit, Henry J. AL 6th Inf. Co.M
Senterfeit, J. AL 53rd (Part.Rangers) Co.I
Senterfeit, Jasper G. AL 6th Inf. Co.M
Senterfeit, M.T. FL Cav. 3rd Bn. Co.D
Senterfeit, M.T. 15th Conf.Cav. Co.I
Senterfeit, Robert FL Cav. 3rd Bn. Co.D
Senterfeit, Robert 15th Conf.Cav. Co.I
Senterfeit, W.D. AL 53rd (Part.Rangers) Co.I
    Sgt.
Senterfeit, Elsie SC 19th Inf. Co.F
Senterfiet, Stephen SC 19th Inf. Co.F
Senterfit, Levi GA 50th Inf. Co.D
Senterfit, Samuel GA 50th Inf. Co.D
Senterfit, W.D. 10th Conf.Cav. Co.D
Senterfitt, M.M. TX 17th Inf. Co.D
Sentic, J.W. AL Talladega Cty.Res. J.T. Smith's
    Co. Sgt.
Senticum, Rufus Gen. & Staff Asst.Surg.
Sentill, R.A. AL 34th Inf. Co.F
Sentle, David J. NC 6th Cav. (65th St.Troops)
    Co.E
Sentle, William G. NC Cav. 7th Bn. Co.E
Sentle, William M. NC 6th Cav. (65th St.Troops)
    Co.E,D
Sentmanat, Charles LA Mil. 1st Native Guards
    Capt.
Sentmires, John MO Inf. 6th Regt.St.Guard Co.D
Sentmires, John MO St.Guard
Senton, Joseph VA Cav. 40th Bn. Co.A
Senton, Robert D. AR 1st Mtd.Rifles
Sentor, A.A. AR 30th Inf. Co.K 1st Sgt.
Sentry, Nathaniel H. MS 2nd Cav. Co.B
Senturia, Nicholas LA Mil. 4th Regt. 1st Brig.
    1st Div. Co.G
Senuppe 1st Creek Mtd.Vol. Co.K
Senzer, George VA 12th Inf. Co.H
Seobell, Lwa LA Mil. 4th Regt.Eur.Brig. Cog-
    nevich's Co.
Seot, Robert A. GA 14th Inf. Co.E Bvt.2nd Lt.
Separd, J. TX Cav. 3rd Regt.St.Troops
    Townsend's Co.
Separk, Joseph H. NC 12th Inf. Co.F 1st Lt.
Sepeachey, W.J. MS 30th Inf. Co.K
Sepeda, Teodosa TX 3rd Inf. Co.F
Seperment, John LA 2nd Cav. Co.B
Sephans, Charles AR 30th Inf. Co.L
Sephas, Robert MO 1st Inf.
Sephas, Robert MO 7th Regt.St.Guards
Sephas, William MS 4th Inf. Co.A
Sephold, J.H. AL 1st Inf. Co.C
Sephton, William TN 10th Inf. Co.E
Sepoch, N. SC Inf. Hampton Legion Co.K
Sepp, J.A. AR 6th Inf. Co.G
Seppelt, Joe LA Mil. 3rd Regt. 1st Brig. 1st Div.
    Co.F
Seppes, Joseph AL 17th Inf. Co.K
Seppora, J.A. MS 4th Cav. Co.B
Sepps, Campbell VA 8th Cav. Co.L
Septer, John H. MD Inf. 2nd Bn. Co.D
Sepulvera, Antonio TX 3rd Inf. 1st Co.C
Se que ah 1st Cherokee Mtd.Rifles Co.K
Sequeeeskih NC Inf. Thomas Legion Co.C Sgt.
Sequest, Henry G. AL 24th Inf. Co.E Sgt.
Sequi, G. AL 21st Inf. Co.G 2nd Lt.

Sequi, G. AL Mobile Fire Bn. Mullany's Co.
Sequoyah 1st Cherokee Mtd.Rifles Co.D
Serafin, Castro AL 21st Inf. Co.G
Serafin, Marselino LA Mil. 5th Regt.Eur.Brig.
    (Spanish Regt.) Co.A
Seraingen, M.B. FL 5th Inf. Co.I
Seraner, Zachariah T. MS 12th Cav. Co.C
Seranger, William G. KY 5th Cav. Co.B
Serango, Jacob KY 5th Cav. Co.D
Serat, G.G. AR 35th Inf. Co.A
Serat, H. SC 5th Inf. 1st Co.I
Serat, Henry NC 64th Inf. Co.F
Serat, James VA Mil. Stowers' Co.
Serat, John TN Cav. Welcker's Bn. Co.A
Seratt, Crockett TN 39th Mtd.Inf. Co.K
Seratt, J.Q. AL Cav. Hardie's Bn.Res. Co.C
Seratt, J.R. TN 48th (Nixon's) Inf. Co.F
Seratt, Obet A. NC 64th Inf. Co.F
Seratt, S.P. AL 22nd Inf. Co.D
Serbantes, Juan TX Cav. Benavides' Regt. Co.E
    Cpl.
Serber, Alford TN 63rd Inf. Co.A
Serber, Andrew TN Lt.Arty. Burrough's Co.
Serber, Palser VA Inf. 23rd Bn. Co.A
Serbot, Phillip W. VA 12th Cav. Co.F
Serboudet, J. LA Mil. 4th Regt. French Brig.
    Co.6
Serbough, C.W. VA Cav. 41st Bn. Co.E
Sercax, George LA Mil. 3rd Regt. 1st Brig. 1st
    Div. Co.F
Sercey, George AL 12th Inf. Co.D,E
Sercey, Henry NC 34th Inf. Co.C
Sercey, Prince MS Cav. Yerger's Regt. Co.A
Sercy, A.J. AL Res. Co.B
Sercy, George W. AL 58th Inf. Co.E
Sercy, James AL 11th Inf. Co.E
Sercy, James AL 38th Inf. Co.E
Sercy, J.B. AR 26th Inf. Chap.
Sercy, Robert C. VA Horse Arty. Jackson's Co.
Sercy, William AL 38th Inf. Co.E
Sercy, Wn. M. AL Hubbard's Cav.
Serda, Eugenio TX 33rd Cav. 1st Co.H
Serda, Eujenio TX Cav. Benavides' Regt. Co.A
Serda, Pedro LA 30th Inf. Co.D
Sere, Leon GA Inf. 1st Loc.Troops (Augusta)
    Co.B
Sere, Leon LA Lt.Arty. LeGardeur, Jr.'s Co.
    (Orleans Guard Btty.)
Sere, Ln. AL Mil. Orleans Guards Regt. Co.F
    Sgt.
Sere, Vr. LA Mil. Orleans Guards Regt. Co.F
Sereey, O. TX Cav. Cater's Bn. Co.I 1st Lt.
Serell, J. GA 1st Reg. Co.C
Serenar, Zack MS 6th Cav. Morgan's Co.
Sereni, Vincenzo LA Mil. Cazadores Espanoles
    Regt. Co.F
Seres, John TN Conscr. (Cp. of Instr.)
Seret, Samuel TX 14th Cav. Co.G
Serey, Robert MO 2nd & 6th Cons.Inf. Co.F
    Cpl.
Serf, T.H. GA Phillips' Legion Co.B
Serford, W.J. LA Mil. 2nd Regt. 3rd Brig. 1st
    Div. Co.K
Sergeant, --- SC Inf. 1st (Charleston) Bn. Co.A
Sergeant, A.B. SC 4th Inf. Co.D
Sergeant, Andrew H. TX 4th Inf. Co.F Cpl.
Sergeant, Cooper AL 29th Inf. Co.B

Sergeant, Daniel NC 45th Inf. Co.I Cpl.
Sergeant, Elijah LA Arty. Fuller's Regt.
Sergeant, Elijah VA 16th Cav. Co.C
Sergeant, G.A. VA Hvy.Arty. Read's Co.
Sergeant, Henry H. VA 1st Inf. Asst.Surg.
Sergeant, H.H. AL 48th Inf. A.Surg.
Sergeant, James MO 11th Inf. Co.A
Sergeant, James VA 64th Mtd.Inf. Co.K
Sergeant, James R. AL 1st Cav. Co.C
Sergeant, J.G.A. KY 1st (Helm's) Cav. New
    Co.G
Sergeant, John A. TX 13th Vol. 2nd Co.F
Sergeant, Johnson VA 16th Cav. Co.C
Sergeant, L.F. SC 2nd Rifles Co.B
Sergeant, N. TN 31st Inf. Co.G
Sergeant, Robert W. NC 13th Inf. Co.D Cpl.
Sergeant, W.B. AL 1st Cav. Co.B
Sergeant, William AL 29th Inf. Co.B
Sergeant, William KY Cav. 2nd Bn. (Dortch's)
    Co.B
Sergeant, William VA 16th Cav. Co.C
Sergeant, William VA 27th Inf. Co.E
Sergeant, William VA 64th Mtd.Inf. Co.H,K
Sergeant, William B. VA 56th Inf. Co.D Sgt.
Sergeant, W.J. VA 23rd Cav. Co.E
Sergeant, W.M. GA 27th Inf. Co.E
Sergeant, W.N. AL 26th (O'Neal's) Inf. Co.F
Sergener, Abraham R. VA 64th Mtd.Inf. Co.B
Sergent, --- MS Arty. Byrne's Btty.
Sergent, George SC Mil. 16th Regt. Jones' Co.
Sergent, J.H. TX 24th & 25th Cav. (Cons.) Co.H
Sergent, J.M. SC Mil. Charbonnier's Co.
Sergent, J.R. TN 13th Inf. Co.I
Sergent, Peter K. GA 23rd Inf. Co.F Lt.
Sergent, Thomas M. VA 60th Inf. Co.F
Sergent, William KY 1st (Butler's) Cav. Co.A
Sergenter, Stephen TN 2nd (Ashby's) Cav. Co.C
Serges, H. LA Mil. Fire Bn. Co.A 1st Lt.
Sergle, F.J. NC Arty.
Sergle, J. TN 39th Mtd.Inf. Co.D
Serientine, A. LA 22nd Inf.
Series, J.M. AL 30th Inf. Co.D
Serigny, B. LA Mil. 1st Regt. French Brig. Co.2
Serigny, J.B. LA Mil. 1st Regt. French Brig.
    Co.7 Maj.
Serils, L.V. TN 17th Inf. Co.B
Serinanask, T. TX Cav. Timmons' Regt. Co.B
Serinano, B.B. LA Mil. 5th Regt.Eur.Brig.
    (Spanish Regt.) Co.1
Seris, Barthelemy LA Mil. 6th Regt.Eur.Brig.
    (Italian Guards Bn.) Co.5
Seris, R.M. Gen. & Staff Maj.,CS
Serjacques, A. LA Mil. 4th Regt.Eur.Brig. Co.A
Serjacques, C.W.L. LA Mil. 4th Regt.Eur.Brig.
    Co.A
Serles, Ellington SC 5th Res. Co.F
Serles, H. NC 35th Inf. Co.K
Serles, James KY 12th Cav.
Serles, James TN 1st Cav.
Serles, J.F. TX Inf. 3rd St.Troops Co.A
Serlon, J.W. TX 6th Cav. Co.H
Serlyn, Anthony NC 11th (Bethel Regt.) Inf.
    Co.C
Serman, M. TX 15th Field Btty.
Sermans, Mathew GA Lt.Arty. Anderson's Btty.
Sermon, A.D. AL 24th Inf. Co.I
Sermon, J.A. GA 10th Inf. Co.G

Sermon, J.R. AL 33rd Inf. Co.D
Sermon, W.H. LA 3rd (Wingfield's) Cav.
Sermons, B. GA 54th Inf. Co.E
Sermons, David W. NC 33rd Inf. Co.I,H
Sermons, Elias NC 17th Inf. (2nd Org.) Co.K
Sermons, H.T. 20th Conf.Cav. Co.B
Sermons, J. GA 50th Inf. Co.G
Sermons, J.C. GA 54th Inf. Co.E
Sermons, J.F.M. TX 21st Inf. Co.H
Sermons, J.H. TX Cav. Wells' Regt. Co.I
Sermons, John W. MS 7th Inf. Co.E
Sermons, Jonathan MS 7th Inf. Co.E
Sermons, J.P. MS 1st Lt.Arty. Co.F
Sermons, Lorenzo GA Lt.Arty. 14th Bn. Co.B
Sermons, Lorenzo GA Lt.Arty. Anderson's Btty.
Sermons, L.R. GA 50th Inf. Co.G
Sermons, Matthew GA Lt.Arty. 14th Bn. Co.B
Sermons, Sylvester TX 11th (Spaight's) Bn.Vol. Co.D
Sermons, Thaddeus 20th Conf.Cav. Co.B
Sermons, William C. MS 33rd Inf. Co.D
Serna, Antonio TX Cav. 3rd (Yager's) Bn. Rhodes' Co.
Serna, Blas TX 33rd Cav. Co.B
Serna, Ignacio F. TX 1st (McCulloch's) Cav. Co.B
Serna, Ignacio F. TX 33rd Cav. Co.A
Sernix, Andrea LA Mil. 5th Regt.Eur.Brig. (Spanish Regt.) Co.5
Serns, Isaac GA 2nd Inf. Co.A
Seron, Adolph Conf.Inf. Tucker's Regt. Co.C
Seron, D.T. NC 44th Inf.
Seroyer, A.D. 8th (Wade's) Conf.Cav. Co.B
Seroyer, Charles P. AL Cav. Falkner's Co.
Seroyer, C.P. 8th (Wade's) Conf.Cav. Co.B
Serpas, A. LA Mil. Chalmette Regt. Co.K
Serpas, Francis LA Mil. Chalmette Regt. Co.I
Serpas, J. LA Mil. Chalmette Regt. Co.K
Serpas, John LA 28th (Thomas') Inf. Co.G
Serpas, Raphael LA 28th (Thomas') Inf. Co.G Cpl.
Serpell, G.M. MD 1st Cav. Co.B Cpl.
Ser pi che chee 1st Creek Mtd.Vol. Co.F
Serra, Adolph AL City Troop (Mobile) Arrington's Co.A
Serra, Angiguel LA 28th (Thomas') Inf. Co.G
Serra, Ansiguel LA 22nd (Cons.) Inf. Co.G
Serra, Charles P. FL 1st Inf. Old Co.K, New Co.G
Serrantine, A. LA Arty. Guyol's Co. (Orleans Arty.)
Serrantine, A. SC Arty. Manigault's Bn. 1st Co.B,D
Serrat, Jonathan VA 21st Cav. Co.K
Serrate, L.D. 3rd Conf.Inf. Co.A
Serratt, Anthony A. GA 36th (Broyles') Inf. Co.B 1st Sgt.
Serratt, Crocket TN 63rd Inf. Co.K
Serratt, Henry J. NC Cav. 5th Bn. Co.A
Serratt, Henry M. SC 6th Cav. Co.F
Serratt, John AR 10th Inf. Co.E
Serratt, L.A.J. GA 36th (Broyles') Inf. Co.B
Serratt, Levi W. KY 9th Mtd.Inf. Co.H
Serratt, Levi Willson TX Inf. W. Cameron's Co.
Serratt, M.W. AR 30th Inf. Co.G
Serratt, N.M. AR 11th & 17th Cons.Inf. Co.C Sgt.

Serratt, Thomas AR 30th Inf. Co.G,D
Serre, Faustin LA Mil. St.James Regt. Co.E
Serre, Frank MO Lt.Arty. Barret's Co.
Serre, J. LA Mil. 4th Regt. French Brig. Co.6
Serrel, Doctor AL 31st Inf. Co.F
Serrel, R. TX 5th Field Btty.
Serrell, David AL 25th Inf. Co.A
Serrell, Peres LA 28th (Thomas') Inf. Co.D
Serrels, B.F. MS 18th Cav. Co.H
Serres, Pierre LA Mil. 2nd Regt. French Brig. Co.2
Serret, Baltazar LA 27th Inf. Co.D
Serret, Firmin LA 27th Inf. Co.D Cpl.
Serret, Gustave LA 4th Inf. Co.H
Serrett, A.L. TN 5th Inf. 2nd Co.C
Serrett, Gustave LA 2nd Cav. Co.C Sgt.
Serrett, John L. VA 28th Inf. Co.K
Serrett, Obediah W. NC Cav. 5th Bn. Co.A
Serrett, Simeon NC Inf. Thomas Legion Co.E
Serrett, William VA 28th Inf. Co.H
Serriat, Ch. LA Mil. Orleans Guards Regt. Co.F
Serrigue, H. LA Mil. 3rd Regt. French Brig. Co.7 2nd Lt.
Serrill, Richard O. TX 6th Inf. Co.D
Serrim, G.W. Forrest's Scouts A. Harvey's Co.,CSA
Serritt, Cicero GA 56th Inf. Co.A
Serrot, Remi LA Mil. 2nd Regt. French Brig. Co.4
Serry, E. LA Mil. Beauregard Regt. Co.C
Sers, Abel LA Inf.Cons.Crescent Regt. Co.G
Sers, Adolphe LA 18th Inf. Co.C
Sers, Felix LA 18th Inf. Co.C Sgt.
Sers, Justin E. LA 18th Inf. Co.C
Sers, Leon LA Lt.Arty. 2nd Field Btty.
Sersea, John AL 32nd Inf. Co.K
Sertain, Sidney NC 1st Inf. Co.G
Serton, Thompson Choctaw Cav. 1st (McCurtain') Bn. Co.C,CSA Capt.
Seruntim, A. LA Lt.Arty. Bridges' Btty.
Servalien, James GA 41st Inf. Co.B
Servance, R. MS Inf. 3rd Bn. (St.Troops) Co.F
Servance, William AL Auburn Home Guards Vol. Darby's Co.
Servant, Richard B. VA 32nd Inf. Co.A 1st Lt.
Servantez, Casania TX 8th Inf. Co.I
Servantos, Manuel TX Conscr.
Servants, R. MS 6th Cav. Co.F
Servary, Louis F. LA Arty. Green's Co. (LA Guard Btty.)
Servat, Paul TX 25th Cav. Co.I,G
Servau, Paul LA Mil. 1st Native Guards
Serveaunt, Frank LA 28th (Thomas') Inf. Co.A Cpl.
Serveboube, J. LA Mil. 3rd Regt. French Brig. Co.8
Servener, J.T. AL 10th Inf. Co.E
Server, G.W. TX Bean's Bn.Res.Corps Wilson's Co.
Server, H.C. TX 15th Inf. Co.B
Server, James TX 4th Cav. Co.D
Servia, Valentin LA Mil. 5th Regt.Eur.Brig. (Spanish Regt.) Co.4
Service, L.C. SC Mil. 1st Regt. (Charleston Res.) Sgt.Maj.
Service, L.C. SC 5th Res. Co.I

Service, Robert LA Mil. Irish Regt. O'Brien's Co.
Service, Thomas SC 5th St.Troops Co.F
Servies, T. NC 49th Inf. Co.G
Servill, M.L. AL 55th Vol. Co.A
Serville, G. LA Mil. 4th Regt. French Brig. Co.6
Servilly, G. LA Mil. 3rd Regt. French Brig. Co.7
Servis, John Gill MS 1st (Johnston's) Inf. Co.C 2nd Lt.
Servis, Thomas O. NC 5th Cav. (63rd St.Troops) Co.F
Serwell, N.L. NC 2nd Cav. (19th St.Troops) Co.A
Sesan, Paul LA 30th Inf. Co.F
Ses a pochee 1st Creek Mtd.Vol.
Se se pin che 1st Creek Mtd.Vol. Co.C
Sesford, W.K. SC 4th St.Troops
Sesion, John LA 3rd (Wingfield's) Cav. Co.B Sgt.
Sesler, James VA 36th Inf. Co.F
Sesler, John VA 14th Cav. Co.G
Sesler, Mark VA 8th Cav. Co.C
Sesler, Sam AL 18th Inf. Co.B
Sesler, Samuel VA 4th Res. Co.D
Sesler, Thomas VA 63rd Inf. Co.D
Sesler, William H. AR 1st (Colquitt's) Inf. Co.F
Seson, Samuel TX 20th Inf. Co.A
Sessams, E. MS Inf. 3rd Bn. (St.Troops) Co.E
Sessams, Richard H. 7th Conf.Cav. 2nd Co.I
Sesselcamp, William NC 2nd Inf. Co.K
Sessell, William A. TX 25th Cav. Co.D Sgt.
Sessenns, R.T. AR 21st Mil. Co.E
Sessens, E.J. GA Cav. 9th Bn. (St.Guards) Co.E Cpl.
Sesser, Isaac VA 10th Inf. Co.H
Sesser, J.S. MS 7th Cav. Co.G Cpl.
Sesser, J.W. AL Cav. Moreland's Regt. Co.E
Sessiell, Albert NC 12th Inf. Co.A
Sessims, J.F. MS 11th (Perrin's) Cav. Co.H
Sessims, Thomas MS 11th (Perrin's) Cav. Co.H
Sessims, W.T. NC 17th Inf. (2nd Org.) Co.I
Sessino, M. NC 2nd Inf.
Session, Bengimon AL 33rd Inf. Co.G
Session, I.J. TX Inf. Griffin's Bn. Co.E
Session, J.N. GA Cav. 15th Bn. (St.Guards) Allen's Co.
Session, R.A.J. MS Wilkinson Cty. Minute Men Co.B Capt.
Session, Reubin GA 2nd Res. Co.B
Session, T.J. AL Cav. (St.Res.) Young's Co.
Session, William S. AR Cav. Wright's Regt. Co.E
Sessions, A. FL 1st (Res.) Inf. Co.I
Sessions, Abner FL 10th Inf. Co.F
Sessions, Abner D. GA 6th Inf. Co.I Cpl.
Sessions, A.T. GA Lt.Arty. 12th Bn. 3rd Co.B 2nd Lt.
Sessions, A.T. GA 1st (Ramsey's) Inf. Co.E Cpl.
Sessions, B.F. GA 51st Inf. Co.F Sgt.
Sessions, C. FL 1st (Res.) Inf. Co.I
Sessions, C.C. AL 21st Inf. Co.E
Sessions, C.C. Gen. & Staff Hosp.Stew.
Sessions, Christopher C. AL 37th Inf. Co.B
Sessions, C.L. AL 33rd Inf. Co.D 1st Sgt.
Sessions, D.A.J. GA 51st Inf. Co.B Capt.
Sessions, Daniel R. SC 10th Inf. Co.B

Sessions, D.S. FL 2nd Cav. Co.I
Sessions, E.G. TX 4th Inf. Co.I
Sessions, E.R. TX 25th Cav.
Sessions, Erasmus AL 43rd Inf. Co.B
Sessions, F. MS 5th Inf. (St.Troops) Co.A Sgt.
Sessions, F.M. AL 1st Cav. 2nd Co.A,F,G
Sessions, F.M. MS 1st (Percy's) Inf. Co.A
Sessions, Francis M. AL 1st Inf. Co.G
Sessions, Francis M. GA 55th Inf. Co.E Cpl.
Sessions, Francis M. MS 36th Inf. Co.A
Sessions, Frank MS 3rd Inf. (St.Troops) Co.A Sgt.
Sessions, Frederick L. AL 1st Regt.Conscr. Co.G
Sessions, Fred L. AL 37th Inf. Co.I
Sessions, G.A. TX Inf. Timmons' Regt. Co.A Cpl.
Sessions, G.A. TX Waul's Legion Co.B Cpl.
Sessions, George K. SC 28th Inf. Co.E
Sessions, George R. FL 10th Inf. Co.F Sgt.
Sessions, George W. AL 5th Inf. New Co.K
Sessions, George W. AL 6th Inf. Co.M
Sessions, George W. AL 42nd Inf. Co.C
Sessions, G.W. GA 51st Inf. Co.A
Sessions, G.W. SC Arty. Manigault's Bn. 1st Co.B
Sessions, Henri W. TX 6th Inf. Co.H
Sessions, Henry MS 8th Cav. Co.B Cpl.
Sessions, H.F. GA 5th Res. Co.A,D Cpl.
Sessions, Howard MS 4th Cav. Co.C
Sessions, Isaac W. AL 37th Inf. Co.F Sgt.
Sessions, J. LA 57th Inf. Co.F
Sessions, James AL 3rd Cav. Co.I
Sessions, James AL Cav. Lenoir's Ind.Co.
Sessions, James AK Inf. 1st Regt. Co.B
Sessions, James W.B. TX 21st Cav. Co.K
Sessions, Jasper AL 37th Inf. Co.F
Sessions, J.D. SC 7th Cav. Co.F Cpl.
Sessions, J.D. SC Cav. Tucker's Co.
Sessions, Jesse H. TX 18th Cav. Co.K
Sessions, J.F. MS 7th Inf. Co.K Capt.
Sessions, J.F. Conf.Cav. Powers' Regt. Co.E Capt.
Sessions, J.F. Inf.Med.Staff
Sessions, J.G. MS St.Cav. 3rd Bn. (Cooper's) 1st Co.A Jr.2nd Lt.
Sessions, J.G. MS Cav. Powers' Regt. Co.I
Sessions, J. Grisby SC 6th Inf. 2nd Co.C Cpl.
Sessions, J.H. MS 1st Cav. Co.E
Sessions, J.H. TX 25th Cav. Co.D
Sessions, J.J. AL 8th Inf. Co.F
Sessions, J.L. TX Cav. Hardeman's Regt. Co.E
Sessions, J.M. LA Ogden's Cav. Co.C
Sessions, J.M. LA Mil.Cav. Norwood's Co. (Jeff Davis Rangers)
Sessions, J.M. SC Arty. Manigault's Bn. 1st Co.B
Sessions, J.M. TX 25th Cav. Co.D
Sessions, J.M. TX Granbury's Cons.Brig. Co.K
Sessions, Joe MS Page's Co. (Lexington Guards)
Sessions, John AL 37th Inf. Co.I
Sessions, John GA 8th Inf. Co.C
Sessions, John LA Arty. Moody's Co. (Madison Lt.Arty.)
Sessions, John B. GA 36th (Villepigue's) Inf. Co.A Cpl.
Sessions, John D. AL Cav. Gachet's Co.

Sessions, John G. SC Inf. Hampton Legion Co.D
Sessions, John N. TX 10th Inf. Co.E
Sessions, John R. FL 3rd Inf. Co.G,B
Sessions, Jonathan MS 13th Inf. Co.B Cpl.
Sessions, Joseph MS Inf. (Res.) Berry's Co.
Sessions, Joseph B. TX 18th Cav. Co.K
Sessions, Joseph F. MS 18th Inf. Co.K Capt.
Sessions, Joseph G. MS 36th Inf. Co.A
Sessions, Joseph M. Gen. & Staff Surg.
Sessions, Joseph W. FL 10th Inf. Co.D,F
Sessions, Joseph W. NC 4th Cav. (59th St.Troops) Asst.Surg.
Sessions, J.T. SC 7th Cav. Co.F
Sessions, J.W. LA Inf. 11th Bn. Co.B
Sessions, J.W. LA Inf.Cons.Crescent Regt. Co.K
Sessions, J.W. SC 7th (Ward's) Bn.St.Res. Co.B Lt.
Sessions, J.W. 14th Conf.Cav. Co.G
Sessions, J.W.B. TX 25th Cav. Co.D
Sessions, Laurin T. SC 10th Inf. Co.B
Sessions, L.D. SC Inf. 9th Bn. Co.D
Sessions, L.D. SC 26th Inf. Co.E
Sessions, L.D. TX 28th Cav. Co.B
Sessions, L.M.C. FL Lt.Arty. Dyke's Co.
Sessions, Lorenzo D. TX 17th Cav. 1st Co.I
Sessions, L.S. GA 1st (Olmstead's) Inf. Screven's Co.
Sessions, L.S. GA 8th Inf. Co.B
Sessions, L.S. GA Inf. 18th Bn. Co.A
Sessions, L.S. SC 7th Cav. Co.F
Sessions, Luellen L. FL 3rd Inf. Co.G
Sessions, Mezenar R. FL 5th Inf. Co.E
Sessions, P.C. GA Inf. 18th Bn. Co.A
Sessions, P.C. SC 1st Mtd.Mil.
Sessions, P.C. SC 26th Inf. Co.K Cpl.
Sessions, Percival W. SC Arty. Gregg's Co. (McQueen Lt.Arty.) Bugler
Sessions, Percival W. SC Arty. Manigault's Bn. 1st Co.C Bugler
Sessions, Percival W. SC 1st (Orr's) Rifles Co.H Band Music.
Sessions, Phillip LA 8th Inf. Co.A
Sessions, Phillip LA 31st Inf. Co.A
Sessions, Phillip K. MS 25th Inf. Co.A
Sessions, P.K. 2nd Conf.Inf. Co.A
Sessions, R.D. LA Inf. 4th Bn. Co.F
Sessions, R.G. SC 7th Cav. Co.F
Sessions, Robert J. GA 12th Inf. Co.D Cpl.
Sessions, Robert J. GA 38th Inf. Co.G
Sessions, Robert S. TX Inf. Griffin's Bn. Co.B
Sessions, Rufus TX 2nd Cav. Co.I
Sessions, Samuel R. FL 4th Inf. Co.C
Sessions, Samuel T. FL 10th Inf. Co.F
Sessions, Sherrod W. GA 51st Inf. Co.A
Sessions, Silas SC Inf. 9th Bn. Co.A
Sessions, S.M. SC Cav. Tucker's Co.
Sessions, S.N. SC Cav. Tucker's Co.
Sessions, S.N. SC Hvy.Arty. 15th (Lucas') Bn. Co.A
Sessions, Solomon SC 1st Arty. Co.K
Sessions, S.W. GA Cav. 29th Bn. Co.H
Sessions, T.B. AL 60th Inf. Co.H Sgt.
Sessions, T.C. AL 31st Inf. Co.G
Sessions, T.C. SC 7th Inf. 1st Co.L
Sessions, T.G. 8th (Wade's) Conf.Cav. Co.I
Sessions, T.H. LA 4th Inf. Co.K 2nd Lt.
Sessions, Thadeus C. AL 36th Inf. Co.G

Sessions, Thomas AL 57th Inf. Co.G
Sessions, Thomas FL 1st Inf. Old Co.B
Sessions, Thomas SC 4th St.Troops Co.C
Sessions, Thomas SC 5th Bn.Res. Co.D
Sessions, Thomas B. AL 1st Bn. Hilliard's Legion Vol. Co.B Sgt.
Sessions, Thomas W. TX Inf. Griffin's Bn. Co.B
Sessions, T.J. AL St.Res. Elliby's Co.
Sessions, T.J. SC 7th Cav. Co.A
Sessions, T.J. SC Cav. Tucker's Co.
Sessions, T.J. TX 4th Inf. Co.I
Sessions, T.S. SC 7th Cav. Co.A
Sessions, T.S. SC Cav. Tucker's Co.
Sessions, T.V. GA 5th Res. Co.G
Sessions, T.W. TX 21st Inf. Co.G
Sessions, W.B. TX 25th Cav. Co.D
Sessions, W.D. AL 37th Inf. Co.B
Sessions, W.E. GA 51st Inf. Co.F
Sessions, W.H. AL 37th Inf. Co.F
Sessions, William AR 24th Inf. Co.G
Sessions, William SC 10th Inf. Co.M
Sessions, Wm. TN Cav. 25th Bn. Co.D
Sessions, William B. TX 21st Cav. Co.K
Sessions, William H. LA 31st Inf. Co.K
Sessions, W.J. SC Arty. Manigault's Bn. 1st Co.B
Sessions, W.M. GA Mayer's Co. (Appling Cav.)
Sessions, W.S. AR Inf. Hardy's Regt. Co.F Cpl.
Sessler, J.B. VA Burks' Regt.Loc.Def. Sprinkle's Co. 2nd Lt.
Sessler, John W. VA 54th Inf. Co.E
Sessler, William H.H. VA 4th Inf. Co.L
Sessler, Zedeiah VA 54th Inf. Co.E Cpl.
Sessom, A.D. TN 51st Inf. Co.C Cpl.
Sessom, A.D. TN 51st (Cons.) Inf. Co.I
Sessom, David E. TX 3rd Inf. Co.I
Sessom, D.G. TN 12th (Green's) Cav. Co.E
Sessom, Ed. B. TX 3rd Inf. Co.I
Sessom, J.G. TX Waul's Legion Co.B
Sessom, J.L.H. TN 51st Inf. Co.C AASurg.
Sessom, J.L.H. TN 51st (Cons.) Inf. Co.I
Sessom, John TX 3rd Inf. Co.I
Sessom, S.D. TN 51st (Cons.) Inf. Co.I
Sessom, W.C. TN 12th (Green's) Cav. Co.E
Sessoms, Albert NC 20th Inf. Co.F Cpl.
Sessoms, Alexander NC 2nd Arty. (36th St.Troops) Co.B
Sessoms, Alexander NC 2nd Arty. (36th St.Troops) Co.C Sgt.
Sessoms, Amos NC 24th Inf. Co.F
Sessoms, Arthur NC 46th Inf. Co.I
Sessoms, A.S. NC 4th Cav. (59th St.Troops) Co.I
Sessoms, A.S. NC Cav. 12th Bn. Co.B
Sessoms, A.S. 8th (Dearing's) Conf.Cav. Co.B
Sessoms, Blakely NC 2nd Arty. (36th St.Troops) Co.B
Sessoms, Calton NC 30th Inf. Co.A
Sessoms, Daniel B. NC 53rd Inf. Co.D Cpl.
Sessoms, David NC 56th Inf. Co.B Cpl.
Sessoms, D.B. FL Cav. 5th Bn. Co.D
Sessoms, Dickson NC 51st Inf. Co.K
Sessoms, H.F. NC 2nd Jr.Res. Co.G
Sessoms, I. NC 3rd Jr.Res. Co.I
Sessoms, Isaac NC 46th Inf. Co.I
Sessoms, Isaiah NC 46th Inf. Co.I
Sessoms, James NC 20th Inf. Co.K

Settle, James G. VA 7th Inf. Co.B

Sessoms, James G. NC 2nd Arty. (36th
St.Troops) Co.C
Sessoms, James R. NC 7th Bn.Jr.Res. Co.C
Sessoms, John NC 2nd Arty. (36th St.Troops)
Co.I Music.
Sessoms, John NC 8th Sr.Res. Callihan's Co.
Sessoms, John NC 54th Inf. Co.C Sgt.
Sessoms, John W. NC 68th Inf. AQM
Sessoms, Jordan NC 2nd Jr.Res. Co.A
Sessoms, Joseph H. NC 3rd Cav. (41st
St.Troops) Co.G
Sessoms, Jos. W. Gen. & Staff A.Surg.
Sessoms, Love D. NC 61st Inf. Co.A
Sessoms, Marshall NC 2nd Jr.Res. Co.A
Sessoms, Micajah A. NC 20th Inf. Co.F
Sessoms, Nathan H. NC 3rd Arty. (40th
St.Troops) Co.G
Sessoms, Neill NC 2nd Arty. (36th St.Troops)
Co.C
Sessoms, Neill NC Lt.Arty. 13th Bn. Co.A
Sessoms, Neill VA Lt.Arty. 12th Bn. Co.D
Sessoms, Owen NC 20th Inf. Co.F
Sessoms, Sherwood NC 2nd Arty. (36th
St.Troops) Co.C
Sessoms, Solomon NC 3rd Arty. (40th
St.Troops) Co.H
Sessoms, Theophilus NC 20th Inf. Co.F Cpl.
Sessoms, Thomas NC 3rd Arty. (40th St.Troops)
Co.K
Sessoms, Thomas NC 23rd Inf. Co.D
Sessoms, Thomas S. NC 2nd Arty. (36th
St.Troops) Co.I
Sessoms, Uriah NC 2nd Jr.Res. Co.A
Sessoms, William NC 2nd Arty. (36th St.Troops)
Co.C
Sessoms, William NC 8th Inf. Co.E
Sessoms, William NC 20th Inf. Co.F 2nd Lt.
Sessoms, William NC 46th Inf. Co.H
Sessoms, William J. NC 3rd Inf. Co.C
Sessoms, William W. NC 8th Inf. Co.C
Sessoms, W.W. 2nd Conf.Eng.Troops Co.G
Artif.
Sesson, G.W. AR 30th Inf. Co.D
Sesson, Paul LA Inf.Cons. 18th Regt. & Yellow
Jacket Bn. Co.C 1st Sgt.
Sessons, Robert V. GA Inf. 14th Bn. (St.Guards)
Co.E Ord.Sgt.
Sessum, John L.H. MS 14th Inf. Asst.Surg.
Sessum, Jno. L.H. Gen. & Staff A.Surg.
Sessum, R.F. TX Cav. Chisum's Regt. (Dismtd.)
Co.B
Sessum, R.F. TX 20th Bn.St.Troops Co.A
Sessum, W.R. TX Cav. Chisum's Regt.
(Dismtd.) Co.B
Sessums, B.D. TX 7th Cav. Co.G 2nd Lt.
Sessums, B.D. TX 35th (Brown's) Cav. Co.K
Sessums, Blake T. LA 31st Inf. Co.C
Sessums, Cader MS 8th Inf. Co.B
Sessums, Ellis MS 11th (Perrin's) Cav. Co.K
Sessums, Ellis MS St.Cav. Perrin's Bn. Co.E
Sessums, G. TX Cav. Steele's Command Co.D
Sessums, George TX 7th Cav. Co.G
Sessums, Jacob MS 46th Inf. Co.I
Sessums, James AR 2nd Inf. Co.G
Sessums, John MS 8th Inf. Co.I
Sessums, John MS 46th Inf. Co.I
Sessums, John E. NC 8th Sr.Res. Bryan's Co.

Sessums, J.S. TX 24th & 25th Cav. (Cons.) Co.I
Sessums, Napoleon T. LA 31st Inf. Co.C
Sessums, Nathan H. NC 1st Arty. (10th
St.Troops) Co.D
Sessums, Pader MS 46th Inf. Co.I
Sessums, Peter TX 7th Cav. Co.G
Sessums, R.T. AR 31st Inf. Co.G
Sessums, S.D. MS Inf. 2nd St.Troops Co.G
Capt.
Sessums, Solomon MS 8th Inf. Co.B
Sessums, W.C. MS 46th Inf. Co.I 1st Sgt.
Sessums, William T. NC 44th Inf. Co.K
Sessums, Wilson NC 15th Inf. Co.I
Sessums, W.M. TX 13th Vol. 2nd Co.D
Seston, Charles A. TN 11th Inf. Co.B
Setberry, Haro. KY 1st (Helm's) Cav. Old Co.G
Setel, Dellolier LA Mil. French Co. of St.James
Seth, Benjamin F. LA 16th Inf. Co.C Cpl.
Seth, E. TN 3rd (Forrest's) Cav. Co.D
Seth, Ester TX 23rd Cav. Co.K
Seth, F.O. LA 6th Cav. Co.D
Seth, Isaac LA 28th (Gray's) Inf. Co.D
Seth, Jacob AR 1st Mtd.Rifles Co.E
Seth, Stephen AR 19th (Dawson's) Inf. Co.E
Seth, Thomas SC 21st Inf. Col.
Sethcot, J.C. SC 18th Inf. Co.E
Setlemires, John W. MS 23rd Inf. Co.G
Setlemires, S.B. MS 23rd Inf. Co.G
Setler, George W. VA 49th Inf. 3rd Co.G
Setlers, Samuel P. KY 3rd Cav. Co.C
Setley, S.J. GA Inf. 14th Bn. (St.Guards) Co.E
Setliff, B.F. TN 17th Inf. Co.G
Setliff, Thomas P. GA 2nd Inf. Co.H
Setliff, Thomas P. 1st Conf.Inf. Co.B
Setliff, William D. NC 45th Inf. Co.E
Seto, No.1 1st Creek Mtd.Vol. Co.A
Seto 1st Creek Mtd.Vol. Co.K
Seton, George FL 3rd Inf. AQM
Seton, George S. Gen. & Staff, QM Dept.
Asst.QM
Seton, William Francis AL Lt.Arty. 2nd Bn.
Co.D
Setser, Adam NC 26th Inf. Co.F
Setser, Eli NC 26th Inf. Co.I
Setser, Emanuel G. NC 25th Inf. Co.D 1st Lt.
Setser, Emanuel M. AR 15th (N.W.) Inf. Co.F
Setser, Ephraim D. NC 58th Inf. Co.E
Setser, H.F. NC 12th Inf. Co.C
Setser, Jacob M. NC Inf. Thomas Legion Co.E
Setser, Joseph NC 26th Inf. Co.F
Setser, Joshua NC 58th Inf. Co.E
Setser, J.W. 2nd Cherokee Mtd.Vol. Co.C
Setser, Larkin J. NC 22nd Inf. Co.A
Setser, Mathias B. NC Cav. 7th Bn. Co.B
Setser, Matthias B. NC 6th Cav. (65th St.Troops)
Co.G Sgt.
Setser, M.Y. 7th Conf.Cav. Co.G
Setser, P. TX 1st Inf. Co.A
Setser, Reuben NC 7th Inf. Co.A
Setser, T.D. NC 26th Inf. Co.F
Setser, Thomas R. NC 6th Cav. (65th St.Troops)
Co.B,F Far.
Setser, Thomas R. NC Cav. 7th Bn. Co.B
Setser, Thomas W. NC 26th Inf. Co.F
Setser, W.A. 2nd Cherokee Mtd.Vol. Co.C
Setser, W.E. NC 26th Inf. Co.F
Setser, William NC 56th Inf. Co.E

Setsler, George A. SC 13th Inf. Co.E Sgt.
Setsler, J.R. TX 22nd Inf. Co.H 1st Sgt.
Setsor, Lafayette TN 19th Inf. Co.K
Settel, Thomas GA Inf. White's Co.
Settells, J. Frank KY 1st (Helm's) Cav. Old
Co.G Bugler
Settelmeier, M. LA Mil. Fire Bn. Co.A
Settels, W.T. KY 1st (Helm's) Cav. Old Co.G
Setterfield, W.H. GA 20th Inf. Co.B
Setters, John H. KY 2nd Bn.Mtd.Rifles Co.B
Setters, John H. KY 5th Mtd.Inf. Co.C
Setters, Parker KY Cav. 2nd Bn. (Dortch's)
Co.D Cpl.
Setters, S.S. KY 11th Cav. Co.C
Settgast, William TX 5th Cav. Co.H
Settigg, Charles LA 28th (Thomas') Inf.
Settine, Emanuel NC 4th Sr.Res. Co.K
Settipp, G.W. NC 6th Inf. Co.C
Settle, A. VA Cav. Mosby's Regt. (Part.Rangers)
Co.B
Settle, Alfred KY 6th Mtd.Inf. Co.E Music.
Settle, Andrew W. NC 45th Inf. Co.G
Settle, Archibald G. TN 2nd (Smith's) Cav. Adj.
Settle, Benjamin TN 9th (Ward's) Cav. Co.A
Settle, Benjamin F. VA 4th Cav. Co.D Sgt.
Settle, Benjamin F. VA 19th Inf. Co.H
Settle, Berryman J. VA 28th Inf. Co.I
Settle, Bransom VA 34th Mil. Co.B
Settle, Broadus VA 6th Cav. Co.B
Settle, C.C. KY 6th Mtd.Inf. Co.E
Settle, C.F. TX 5th Inf. Co.A Sgt.
Settle, C.F. VA 4th Res. Co.E
Settle, Charles B. VA 28th Inf. Co.D
Settle, Charles H. VA 28th Inf. Co.D,I
Settle, David GA 8th Inf. Co.K
Settle, David NC 13th Inf. Co.H 2nd Lt.
Settle, D.G. AR 20th Inf. Co.C Sgt.
Settle, E.B. TX 5th Inf. ACS
Settle, E.B. Gen. & Staff, Comsy.Dept. Capt.
Settle, E.F. VA 8th Bn.Res. Co.A
Settle, E.H. GA Arty. 11th Bn. (Sumter Arty.)
Settle, F. Gen. & Staff Capt.,ACS
Settle, Fielding VA 28th Inf. Co.D
Settle, F.M. TX 13th Vol. 2nd Co.H Artif.
Settle, Francis M. TX 7th Field Btty. QMSgt.
Settle, Franklin B. KY 6th Mtd.Inf. Co.E Sgt.
Settle, Frederick VA 40th Inf. Co.E 2nd Lt.
Settle, G.B. NC 1st Inf. Co.H
Settle, George F. SC 5th St.Troops Co.F
Settle, George W. VA 6th Cav. Co.B
Settle, George W. VA 17th Inf. Co.B
Settle, G.F. SC 7th Res. Co.G
Settle, G.F. SC Palmetto S.S. Co.D
Settle, Gid VA 34th Mil. Co.B
Settle, Gideon VA 12th Cav. Co.G
Settle, Hannibal C. TX 7th Field Btty. Bugler
Settle, H.C. NC 1st Arty. (10th St.Troops) Co.A
Settle, Henry C. GA 6th Inf. Co.K
Settle, Henry P. VA Inf. 21st Bn. 2nd Co.E
Settle, H.G. TX 5th Inf. Co.A Sgt.
Settle, Isaac M. VA 6th Cav. Co.A Cpl.
Settle, J.A. AR 6th Inf. Co.B
Settle, Jackson VA 7th Inf. Co.B
Settle, Jacob VA 49th Inf. 3rd Co.G
Settle, James VA 34th Mil. Co.B
Settle, James A. VA 48th Inf. Co.D
Settle, James G. VA 7th Inf. Co.B

Settle, James H. MS 10th Cav. Co.H
Settle, James K.P. MO Cav. Poindexter's Regt.
Settle, James K.P. MO Lt.Arty. 1st Field Btty.
Settle, James M. GA 31st Inf. Co.D
Settle, James S. GA 38th Inf. Co.H
Settle, J.B. KY 9th Cav. Co.G
Settle, J.C. TN Cav. 11th Bn. (Gordon's) Co.G
Settle, Jerdean VA 48th Inf. Co.D
Settle, J.H. Conf.Cav. Baxter's Bn. Co.A
Settle, J.L. SC Palmetto S.S. Co.D
Settle, J.M. AR 6th Inf. Co.B
Settle, J.M. TX 11th Cav. Co.D Cpl.
Settle, J.M. TX Cav. Bourland's Regt. Co.G,H,I
Settle, Joel S. TN 28th Inf. Co.B,I
Settle, Joel S. TN 28th (Cons.) Inf. Co.D
Settle, John MO 9th (Elliott's) Cav. Co.D
Settle, John SC 5th Inf. 1st Co.C
Settle, John TN 27th Inf.
Settle, John VA 146th Mil. Co.H
Settle, John A. TX 2nd Cav. ACS
Settle, Jno. A. Gen. & Staff Capt.,ACS
Settle, John F.C. GA 2nd Cav. Co.C
Settle, John H. TX 6th Cav. Co.E 2nd Lt.
Settle, John H. VA 34th Mil. Co.A
Settle, John L. MO Cav. Poindexter's Regt.
Settle, John L. MO Inf. Perkins' Bn. Co.E 1st Sgt.
Settle, John M. 1st Conf.Cav. 2nd Co.A
Settle, John S. TN 14th Inf. Co.D 2nd Lt.
Settle, John S.T. VA 28th Inf. Co.D
Settle, John T. MS 9th Inf. Old Co.A 1st Sgt.
Settle, John W. VA 28th Inf. Co.I
Settle, Joseph N. VA 28th Inf. Co.I
Settle, J.R. MS Cav. Ham's Regt. Co.A
Settle, J.T. AL Cav. Forrest's Regt. 2nd Lt.
Settle, J.T. MS 10th Cav. Co.H
Settle, J.T. TN 18th (Newsom's) Cav. Co.A 1st Lt.
Settle, J.T. Conf.Cav. Baxter's Bn. Co.A
Settle, Judson VA 49th Inf. 3rd Co.G
Settle, J.W. VA 18th Cav. Co.D
Settle, Lafayette MS 9th Inf. Old Co.A
Settle, L.D. MS 15th (Cons.) Inf. Co.K 2nd Lt.
Settle, L.D. MS 32nd Inf. Co.D Sgt.
Settle, Leftwich H. VA 28th Inf. Co.D
Settle, Leroy B. TN 7th Inf. Co.H
Settle, L.J. MO Cav. Snider's Bn. Co.B
Settle, M.G. TX Inf. 1st Bn. (St.Troops) Lt.Col.
Settle, M.G. TX Inf. Chambers' Bn.Res.Corps Co.B Capt.
Settle, Milton KY 3rd Mtd.Inf. Co.D
Settle, Montgomery MO 9th Inf. Co.B
Settle, Moore TX Inf. 1st Bn. (St.Troops) QMSgt.
Settle, Ottaway J. GA Lt.Arty. Milledge's Co.
Settle, Otway J. GA 3rd Inf. 1st Co.I
Settle, Reuben 1st Conf.Cav. 1st Co.A
Settle, Richard J. NC 45th Inf. Co.I
Settle, Richard J. VA 48th Inf. Co.D
Settle, Russell VA 49th Inf. 3rd Co.G
Settle, R.W. TX 11th Cav. Co.B
Settle, Sanford VA 48th Inf. Co.D
Settle, Sidney L. TN 28th Inf. Co.K,E
Settle, S.L. MS 32nd Inf. Co.D Cpl.
Settle, Tal. F. MS 23rd Inf. Co.D 1st Sgt.
Settle, T.B. MS 23rd Inf. Co.D
Settle, T.B. MS 32nd Inf. Co.D Sgt.

Settle, T.C. TN 8th Inf. Co.K Sgt.
Settle, T.F. MS 15th (Cons.) Inf. Co.K 3rd Sgt.
Settle, T.G. TN 8th Inf. Co.G Sgt.
Settle, Thomas GA 9th Inf. (St.Guards) Culp's Co.
Settle, Thomas NC 13th Inf. Co.I Capt.
Settle, Thos. NC 21st Inf. Col.
Settle, Thomas B. GA 31st Inf. Co.D Capt.
Settle, Thomas L. VA 11th Cav. Surg.
Settle, Thomas L. Gen. & Staff Surg.
Settle, Thornton TX 17th Field Btty.
Settle, T.L. VA 7th Cav. Asst.Surg.
Settle, Turner VA 34th Mil. Co.B
Settle, W.H. TX Cav. Bourland's Regt. Co.H
Settle, William AR 2nd Inf. Co.D
Settle, William SC 4th Cav. Co.H 2nd Lt.
Settle, William SC Cav. 10th Bn. Co.D 2nd Lt.
Settle, William SC 5th Inf. Co.C
Settle, William SC Palmetto S.S. Co.D
Settle, William A. KY 6th Mtd.Inf. Co.E Music.
Settle, William H. TX Cav. 2nd Regt.St.Troops Co.I
Settle, William H. TX 15th Cav. Co.H
Settle, William R. VA 45th Inf. Co.B
Settle, W.W. GA 31st Inf. Co.D
Settlemayer, J. LA Arty. Castellanos' Btty.
Settlemire, Cyrus NC 6th Inf. Co.A
Settlemire, David NC 11th (Bethel Regt.) Inf. Co.D
Settlemire, George NC 5th Sr.Res. Co.E
Settlemire, G.N. NC 35th Inf. Co.K
Settlemire, J.M. NC 22nd Inf. Co.A
Settlemire, Phillip NC 32nd Inf. Co.G
Settlemoer, J.W. MS 2nd Cav. Co.L
Settlemoir, James W. MS 23rd Inf. Co.G
Settlemoir, John A. NC 46th Inf. Co.K
Settlemoir, Sampson B. MS 32nd Inf. Co.E
Settlemoir, Sidney NC 26th Inf. Co.I
Settlemon, Sidney NC 58th Inf. Co.H
Settlemore, N.P. NC 3rd Jr.Res. Co.E
Settlemyer, A.M. NC 12th Inf. Co.A
Settlemyer, Daniel S. NC 12th Inf. Co.A
Settlemyer, J.A. SC Palmetto S.S. Co.D
Settlemyer, John C. NC 12th Inf. Co.A
Settlemyer, M.E. SC Palmetto S.S. Co.D
Settlemyre, George P. NC 8th Bn.Jr.Res. Co.C
Settlemyre, J.A. SC 5th Inf. 1st Co.F
Settlemyre, Langdon S. NC 35th Inf. Co.K Cpl.
Settlemyre, M.E. SC 5th Inf. 1st Co.F
Settlemyre, Noah P. NC 8th Bn.Jr.Res. Co.B
Settler, George TN 50th Inf. Co.K Sgt.
Settler, George TN 50th (Cons.) Inf. Co.G Sgt.
Settler, Jack 1st Creek Mtd.Vol. Co.K
Settles, George W. TN 50th Inf. Co.H Jr.2nd Lt.
Settles, G.M. AL 31st Inf. Co.I
Settles, Henry P. VA 64th Mtd.Inf. Co.E
Settles, James VA 9th Cav. Co.A,C
Settles, James W. MO 3rd Inf. Co.H Sgt.
Settles, J.M. MO Inf. Clark's Regt. Co.A
Settles, Joseph KY 8th Cav. Co.G
Settles, Joseph MO 2nd Inf. Co.A
Settles, Josiah TX 18th Inf. Co.D
Settles, Minor MO 4th Cav. Co.F
Settles, Patrick H. TN 50th Inf. Co.H
Settles, Thomas J. AR 2nd Inf. Co.D
Settles, Thornton MO 9th Inf. Co.G

Settles, Tipton C. TN Cav. Shaw's Bn. Hamilton's Co.
Settles, W.M. GA 3rd Cav. (St.Guards) Co.K
Settley, Samuel GA Inf. (Loc.Def.) Hamlet's Co.
Settliffe, B.F. TN Lt.Arty. McClung's Co.
Setton, Andrew TN 19th & 20th (Cons.) Cav. Co.C
Setton, Felix G. Gen. & Staff AASurg.
Setton, Henry S. KY 4th Mtd.Inf.
Setton, T.J. TX 24th Cav. Co.F
Settoon, Archa LA Ogden's Cav. Co.E
Settoon, Archey 14th Conf.Cav. Co.D
Settoon, Henry LA 1st Cav. Co.H
Settoon, John LA 7th Inf. Co.K
Settoon, Tobias LA 28th (Thomas') Inf. Co.E
Settoon, William A. LA 16th Inf. Co.D
Settoon, William B. LA 7th Inf. Co.K
Settoon, William G. LA Pointe Coupee Arty.
Settro, J.R. LA 1st Cav. Robinson's Co.
Setz, Dizan LA Mil. Orleans Fire Regt. Hall's Co.
Setze, A.J. GA 1st (Ramsey's) Inf. Co.D Lt.
Setze, A.J. Gen. & Staff 1st Lt.,Adj.
Setze, Alphonse J. GA 7th Cav. Co.C 1st Lt.
Setze, Alphonse J. GA Cav. 24th Bn. Co.B 1st Lt.
Setze, John SC Lt.Arty. Walter's Co. (Washington Arty.)
Setze, John Conf.Inf. Tucker's Regt. Co.G
Setzer, A. SC 21st Inf. Co.C
Setzer, A. SC 25th Inf. Co.I
Setzer, Alfred NC 38th Inf. Co.F
Setzer, Calvin NC 46th Inf. Co.K
Setzer, Carr NC 46th Inf. Co.K
Setzer, C.B. LA Inf. 4th Bn. Co.E
Setzer, C.C. NC 3rd Jr.Res. Co.G Sgt.
Setzer, Columbus D. NC 8th Bn.Jr.Res. Co.C Sgt.
Setzer, Daniel NC 46th Inf. Co.K
Setzer, Daniel A. NC 46th Inf. Co.K
Setzer, David NC 4th Sr.Res. Co.C
Setzer, David NC 12th Inf. Co.A
Setzer, D.P. AR 25th Inf. Co.C Color Sgt.
Setzer, Evan A. GA 43rd Inf. Co.I 1st Sgt.
Setzer, Franklin A. NC 28th Inf. Co.C Sgt.
Setzer, George M. VA 18th Inf. Co.F Cpl.
Setzer, Jacob NC 12th Inf. Co.A
Setzer, James H. NC 4th Sr.Res. Co.C Cpl.
Setzer, James P. NC 49th Inf. Co.I
Setzer, Jason D. NC 6th Inf. Co.G
Setzer, J.H. NC Mallett's Co.
Setzer, J. Noah NC 12th Inf. Co.A
Setzer, John GA 19th Inf. Co.G
Setzer, John NC 57th Inf. Co.E
Setzer, John F. NC 2nd Cav. (19th St.Troops) Co.B
Setzer, John F. NC 23rd Inf. Co.F
Setzer, John H. NC 57th Inf. Co.E
Setzer, John S. NC 32nd Inf. Co.D,E
Setzer, M. GA 8th Inf. (St.Guards) Co.K
Setzer, Marcus NC 12th Inf. Co.A
Setzer, Marcus NC 38th Inf. Co.F
Setzer, Marcus L. GA Lt.Arty. Scogin's Btty. (Griffin Lt.Arty.)
Setzer, M.E. NC 57th Inf. Co.E
Setzer, Milford R. NC 42nd Inf. Co.D Sgt.
Setzer, M.Y. NC Cav. 16th Bn. Co.E

Setzer, Otto Inf. School of Pract. Powell's Detach. Co.D

Setzer, P.S. NC 57th Inf. Co.E

Setzer, Samuel H. MO 3rd Inf. Co.B Sgt.

Setzer, Wilborne S. NC 46th Inf. Co.K

Setzer, William A. NC 57th Inf. Co.E

Setzer, William L. MO 3rd Inf. Co.B 1st Lt.

Setzes, B. LA Mil. French Co. of St.James

Setzler, George MS 1st Cav. Co.I

Setzler, George A. SC 13th Inf. Co.D

Setzler, Jacob SC 2nd St.Troops Co.F

Setzler, Jacob SC Post Guard Senn's Co.

Setzler, John TX 10th Cav. Co.B

Setzler, John J. AL 3rd Cav. Co.F

Setzler, J.T. SC Lt.Arty. 3rd (Palmetto) Bn. Co.G

Setzler, J.T. SC 3rd Inf. Co.H

Setzler, L.T. TX 10th Cav. Co.B

Setzler, Marion F. SC 13th Inf. Co.D Cpl.

Setzler, Simeon A. TX 22nd Inf. Co.H

Setzler, Wade H. SC 20th Inf. Co.F Cpl.

Setzler, W.H. TX 10th Cav. Co.B Cpl.

Setzler, William F. AL 3rd Cav. Co.F

Seubille, Joseph LA 2nd Res.Corps Co.D

Seugstack, Charles P. VA 1st Inf. Co.E

Seuler, Andrew AL 17th Inf. Lt.

Seum, George AL 31st Inf. Co.I

Seurop, Victor TX 13th Vol. 2nd Co.G Black.

Seurs, John VA 3rd Cav. & Inf.St.Line Co.A

Seus, C. TX 2nd Inf. Co.F

Seuse, G.W. GA 54th Inf. Co.I

Seuter, Charles W. GA 1st (Ramsey's) Inf. Co.K

Seuter, George W. NC 25th Inf. Co.G

Seuter, Neil A. TN 27th Inf. Co.K 1st Lt.

Seutz, Jonathan NC 22nd Inf. Co.E

Seuzenean, C. LA 22nd (Cons.) Inf. Co.B,E

Seuzenean, Chs. LA Mil. Orleans Guards Regt. Co.E

Seuzenean, J. LA 22nd (Cons.) Inf. Co.E

Seuzenean, O. LA 22nd (Cons.) Inf. Co.E Sgt.

Seuzeneau, F. LA Mil. Orleans Guards Regt. Co.A,G

Seuzeneau, J. LA 22nd Inf. Co.E

Seuzeneau, O. LA 22nd Inf. Co.E Sgt.

Sevacri, H. MS 10th Inf. Old Co.A

Sevallos, Antonio Conf.Lt.Arty. Davis' Co.

Sevane, Geo. S. FL 5th Inf. Co.D 2nd Lt.

Sevanino, Castella TX Cav. Benavides' Regt. Co.C

Sevanowich, L. SC 1st Regt. Charleston Guard Co.D

Sevar, George W. FL 6th Inf. Co.D

Sevard, Henry NC 1st Cav. (9th St.Troops) Co.A

Sevario, Henry LA 1st Cav. Co.H

Sevart, Franklin NC 2nd Cav. (19th St.Troops) Co.A

Sevary, Frederick LA 1st (Nelligan's) Inf. 1st Co.B Cpl.

Sevaston, John NC Inf. 13th Bn. Co.C

Seveall, James P. GA 11th Cav. Co.A

Sevear, James AR 17th (Lemoyne's) Inf. Co.A

Sevedge, J.T.F. AR 19th (Dockery's) Inf. Co.H

Seveignes, Jules TN Lt.Arty. Tobin's Co.

Sevely, N.C. AL 19th Inf. Co.I

Seven Fields 1st squad. Cherokee Mtd.Vol. Co.A

Seven Filds 1st Cherokee Mtd.Vol. Co.J

Seven, George 1st Cherokee Mtd.Rifles Co.D Sgt.

Sevens, J.N. MS 1st Inf. Co.C

Sevenson, H.S. AL Cav. Barbiere's Bn. Bowie's Co.

Sever, Charles NC 61st Inf. Co.G

Sever, Charles SC 1st (Butler's) Inf. Co.F

Sever, Charles VA 9th Inf. 2nd Co.A

Sever, George KY 4th Cav. Co.E

Sever, James FL 5th Inf. Co.C

Sever, Jefferson TX 6th Inf. Co.G

Sever, W.H. FL Conscr.

Sever, W.R. TN 5th Inf. Co.A

Sever, W.W. FL Sp.Cav. 1st Bn. Co.A

Severain, Francois LA Mil. 1st Native Guards

Severan, Joseph LA 16th Inf. Co.G

Severance, C. VA 2nd St.Res. Co.G

Severance, Matthew S. GA 26th Inf. Co.B

Severance, R.M. SC Conscr.

Severance, R.M. SC Prov.Guard Hamilton's Co. Sgt.

Severe, A.M. MO Cav. 5th Regt.St.Guard Co.B 2nd Lt.

Severe, Francis AL 12th Inf. Co.I

Severe, Jacob TX 5th Cav. Co.I Music.

Severe, James VA 3rd Inf.Loc.Def. Co.E

Severe, James VA Inf. 4th Bn.Loc.Def. Co.D

Severe, John VA Inf. 28th Bn. Co.D

Severe, John VA 59th Inf. 3rd Co.I

Severe, John M. AR 30th Inf. Co.I

Severe, Moses W. MO Cav. 9th Regt.St.Guard Co.D Capt.

Severe, Obed. VA Inf. 4th Bn.Loc.Def. Co.D

Severe, Samuel MS Cav. 4th Bn. Roddey's Co. Cpl.

Severe, William J. AR 30th Inf. Co.I

Severence, Robert MS Cav. Jeff Davis Legion Co.B

Severene, Charles GA 46th Inf. Co.A

Severich, Charles E. LA 1st Cav. Robinson's Co. 2nd Lt.

Severin, --- TX 4th Inf. (St.Troops) Co.F

Severin, A. TN 2nd (Ashby's) Cav. Co.H

Severin, Francois LA Mil. 1st Native Guards

Severing, C. KY 1st Inf. Co.A

Severing, C.A. AL 32nd Inf. Co.F

Severing, Charles A. KY 2nd Mtd.Inf. Co.E

Severink, Peter NC Pris.Guards Howard's Co.

Severio, William LA Ogden's Cav. Co.A

Severio, William 14th Conf.Cav. Co.D

Severise, Andrew Conf.Inf. Tucker's Regt. Co.A

Severn, Adam TN Cav. 4th Bn. (Branner's) Co.A

Severns, Thomas J. LA 2nd Inf. Co.B,F Cpl.

Severon, Thomas AL Lt.Arty. 2nd Bn. Co.B

Severous, E. SC 3rd Inf. Co.B

Severs, Andrew J. VA 8th Bn.Res. Co.C Sgt.

Severs, C. SC 1st Regt. Charleston Guard Co.G

Severs, F.B. 1st Creek Mtd.Vol. Co.B Capt.

Severs, George W. GA Smith's Legion Co.D

Severs, Jacob TN Cav. 12th Bn. (Day's) Co.E

Severs, Jacob TX 3rd (Kirby's) Bn.Vol. Co.B Drum Maj.

Severs, James MO 8th Inf. Co.K

Severs, J.P. AL 55th Vol. Co.A

Severs, J.P. MS 25th Inf. Co.D

Severs, J.P. 2nd Conf.Inf. Co.D

Severs, Peter KY 9th Cav. Co.B

Severs, S. TN 12th (Cons.) Inf. Co.I

Severs, William MS 18th Cav. Co.K

Severs, Winton W. TN Cav. 13th Bn. (Day's) Co.A

Severson, Chas. S. Gen. & Staff, QM Dept. Maj.

Severt, Enoch NC 37th Inf. Co.A

Severt, John NC 37th Inf. Co.A

Severt, Silas NC 37th Inf. Co.A

Severt, Wiley NC 37th Inf. Co.A

Sevette, J.M. TN 21st (Wilson's) Cav. Co.H

Sevetty, James MO Inf. 4th Regt.St.Guard Co.D

Sevetus, L. SC 25th Inf. Co.E

Sevey, George A. VA 135th Mil. Co.A

Sevey, Henry H. VA 135th Mil. Co.A

Sevey, James A. VA Inf. 26th Inf. Co.E

Sevey, William S.E. LA 5th Inf. Co.D 2nd Lt.

Seveze, M. LA Mil. 2nd Regt. French Brig. Co.8

Sevier, A.H. AR 30th Inf. Co.L 1st Lt.

Sevier, Ambrose H. Churchill's Brig. 1st Lt., ADC

Sevier, Andrew J. MS 12th Inf. Co.K

Sevier, Bailey P. TX 19th Cav. Co.C

Sevier, B.P. TX 12th Cav. Co.E

Sevier, Bushy head 1st Cherokee Mtd.Rifles Co.C Sgt.

Sevier, Charles TX 12th Cav. Co.E

Sevier, Edward NC Cav. 5th Bn. Co.A QMS

Sevier, Edward NC 8th Cav. (65th St.Troops) Co.I

Sevier, Edward NC 64th Inf. Comsy.Sgt.

Sevier, E.F. TN 26th Inf. Co.I

Sevier, Francis MD Cav. 2nd Bn. Co.A

Sevier, Francis A. TX 1st (Yager's) Cav. Co.H

Sevier, Francis A. TX 8th (Taylor's) Bn. Co.E

Sevier, Frank TX 12th Cav. Co.E

Sevier, George LA Ogden's Cav. Co.C

Sevier, George 14th Conf.Cav. Co.G

Sevier, George J. TN 2nd (Ashby's) Cav. Co.E

Sevier, George P. MS 12th Inf. Co.K

Sevier, George W. AR 4th Inf. Co.G 1st Sgt.

Sevier, George W. MS 1st Lt.Arty. Co.K Sgt.

Sevier, George W. MS Inf. Lewis' Co.

Sevier, G.W. MS Cav. 24th Bn. Co.B 1st Sgt.

Sevier, G.W. TN 4th (Murray's) Cav. Co.D

Sevier, G.W. 1st Conf.Cav. 2nd Co.C

Sevier, Henry C. MS 1st Lt.Arty. Co.K

Sevier, Henry D. AR 3rd Cav. Co.I

Sevier, James AR 21st Inf. Co.D

Sevier, James TN 11th Inf. Co.G,B,D

Sevier, James C. AR 4th Inf. Co.G

Sevier, John TX Cav. 8th (Taylor's) Bn. Co.A

Sevier, John TX 12th Cav. Co.A

Sevier, John 14th Conf.Cav. Co.G

Sevier, John A. TX 1st (Yager's) Cav. Co.G

Sevier, John C. LA 3rd (Harrison's) Cav. Co.A

Sevier, John C. Conf.Cav. Wood's Regt. 1st Co.A

Sevier, John F. TX 1st (Yager's) Cav. Co.H

Sevier, Joseph 1st Conf.Cav. 2nd Co.G

Sevier, J.R. AR 1st Mtd.Rifles Sgt.

Sevier, J.V. LA Ogden's Cav. Co.B

Sevier, L. TX 20th Inf. Co.G,E

Sevier, Michal R. AR 3rd Cav. Co.I

Sevier, M.N. MO Cav. Hicks' Co.

Sevier, M.W. MO Cav. 14th Regt.St.Guard Co.B Capt.

Sevier, Peter C. AR 33rd Inf. Co.E
Sevier, R.A. TN 62nd Mtd.Inf. Co.I
Sevier, T.B. TN Cav. 16th Bn. (Neal's) Co.D
Sevier, T.F. TN 1st (Feild's) Inf. Co.A Lt.Col.
Sevier, T.F. TN 1st (Feild's) & 27th Inf. (Cons.) Lt.Col.
Sevier, T.F. Stewart's Corps Lt.Col.
Sevier, Thomas R. MO 6th Inf. Co.D
Sevier, V.B. TN 9th Inf. Co.B 2nd Lt.
Sevier, W. TN Inf. 2nd Cons.Regt. Co.I
Sevier, W.C. MO Cav. Freeman's Regt. Co.L
Sevier, W.C. TX Cav. Baird's Regt. 2nd Lt.
Sevier, William MO 16th Inf. Co.I
Sevier, William J. AR 3rd Cav. Co.I
Sevier, William Val TN Cav. 4th Bn. (Branner's) Co.D
Sevier, William Vol TN 2nd (Ashby's) Cav. Co.E Capt.,AQM
Sevier, W.P. MO 9th Bn.S.S. Co.C Cpl.
Sevier, W. Vol. Gen. & Staff, QM Dept. Capt.
Sevier, W.W. TX 12th Cav. Co.E Bugler
Seviere, John 2nd Cherokee Mtd.Vol. Co.F
Seviere, John T. TX Cav. 8th (Taylor's) Bn. Co.E
Sevierre, William TN 50th Inf. Co.F
Sevierre, William TN 50th (Cons.) Inf. Co.F
Sevill, James AL 18th Inf. Co.K
Sevilla, Valentin LA Mil. 5th Regt.Eur.Brig. (Spanish Regt.) Co.A
Seville, A. James AL 12th Inf. Co.A
Sevillers, --- AL 25th Inf. Co.F
Sevills, J.R. TX Cav. Giddings' Bn. Maddox's Co. Sgt.
Sevilly, Stephen V. AL 57th Inf. Co.E
Seviltra, --- TX Cav. Ragsdale's Bn. 2nd Co.C
Sevin, Aurelien LA 30th Inf. Co.H Sgt.
Sevin, Felix P. LA 18th Inf. Co.G Cpl.
Sevin, F.P. LA Inf.Cons. 18th Regt. & Yellow Jacket Bn. Co.F 2nd Cpl.
Sevin, John VA 15th Inf. Co.K 1st Sgt.
Sevin, Joseph LA 26th Inf. Co.I
Sevin, Nicholas LA 26th Inf. Co.D
Sevin, Onesippe LA Inf.Cons. 18th Regt. & Yellow Jacket Bn. Co.F
Sevin, Onezipe LA 18th Inf. Co.G
Sevin, Prosper LA Mil. LaFourche Regt.
Sevin, Trevil LA Mil. LaFourche Regt.
Seviney, William MO Inf. Perkins' Bn. Co.A
Sevino, D.P. VA 36th Inf. Beckett's Co.
Sevir, A. MS 3rd Inf. (St.Troops) Co.K
Seviss, S.W. MO St.Guard
Sevons, H.A. TN 63rd Inf. Co.K
Sevor, A.G. MS Cav. Terrell's Unatt.Co.
Sevor, William FL 11th Inf. Co.I
Sevy, A.R. VA 19th Cav. Co.A
Sevy, A.R. VA Inf. 23rd Bn. Co.H
Sevy, Cain H. VA Inf. 26th Bn. Co.E
Sevy, George A. VA Inf. 26th Bn. Co.E
Sevy, George W. VA Inf. 26th Bn. Co.E
Sevy, Henry H. VA Inf. 26th Bn. Co.E
Sevy, Jacob VA 60th Inf. Co.C
Sevy, James H. VA 60th Inf. Co.C Cpl.
Sevy, Zebulon VA 60th Inf. Co.C
Sewald, C. TX 33rd Cav. Co.E
Sewall, E.W. TX 12th Cav. Co.H
Sewall, F.M. MS 11th Inf. Co.C
Sewall, J.A. LA 6th Cav. Co.C

Sewall, J.H. GA 11th Cav. Co.D Cpl.
Sewall, Jonas AL 31st Inf. Co.G
Sewall, Joseph C. VA 17th Inf. Co.D
Sewall, K. TX 20th Inf. Co.G
Sewall, R.E. LA 3rd (Harrison's) Cav. Co.G Capt.
Sewall, Robert S. AL 32nd Inf. Co.G 1st Sgt.
Sewall, R.S. AL Inf. 2nd Regt. Co.D
Sewall, R.S. AL 38th Inf. Co.I
Sewall, Rufus E. LA 1st (Nelligan's) Inf. Co.A 1st Sgt.
Sewall, T. MS 27th Inf. Co.I
Sewa nokee 1st Creek Mtd.Vol. 2nd Co.D
Seward, Albert H. VA 1st Arty. Co.E
Seward, Algernon TN 42nd Inf. Co.C,E
Seward, Allen FL 10th Inf.
Seward, A.M. AR 6th Inf. New Co.F
Seward, A.M. AR 12th Inf. Co.C Sgt.
Seward, A.N. TN 13th Inf. Co.B Cpl.
Seward, A.R. FL 1st Cav. Co.K
Seward, Benjamin R. TN 9th (Ward's) Cav. Co.I
Seward, B.R. TN 24th Inf. Co.B
Seward, C.D. TX 5th Inf. Co.I
Seward, E.C. TN 42nd Inf. Co.C Sgt.
Seward, E.C. 4th Conf.Inf. Co.H
Seward, Edmund W. VA 55th Inf. Co.B Cpl.
Seward, Edward C. VA 26th Inf. Co.G
Seward, Edward W. TN 37th Inf. Co.E
Seward, Edward W. VA Lt.Arty. Clutter's Co. Jr.2nd Lt.
Seward, Edward W. VA Arty. Fleet's Co. Sgt.
Seward, E.S. MS 27th Inf. Co.I
Seward, E.T. TN 51st Inf. Co.B
Seward, F. MS 12th Inf.
Seward, F. Sap. & Min.,CSA
Seward, Felix J. FL 7th Inf. Co.E Sgt.
Seward, Frank R. VA Lt.Arty. Hankins' Co.
Seward, George H. MD Cav. 2nd Bn. Co.C
Seward, George W. SC Hvy.Arty. 15th (Lucas') Bn. Co.C
Seward, George W. SC Arty. Childs' Co.
Seward, G.S. TN 51st Inf. Co.B
Seward, Hansell H. GA 26th Inf. 1st Co.G
Seward, Hansell H. GA 29th Inf. Co.E
Seward, Hiram A. VA Horse Arty. E. Graham's Co.
Seward, Hiram A. VA 109th Mil. Co.B, 2nd Co.A
Seward, H.R. TX 8th Inf.
Seward, I.W. GA 12th Mil.
Seward, J.A. AR 32nd Inf. Co.C
Seward, J.A. GA 1st Cav.
Seward, James A. AR Cav. McGehee's Regt. Co.C Sgt.
Seward, James A. MS 1st Lt.Arty. Co.L,E
Seward, James E. VA Hvy.Arty. 10th Bn. Co.E
Seward, James R. AL 49th Inf. Co.H Cpl.
Seward, James R. FL 7th Inf. Co.E
Seward, James R. VA 13th Cav. Co.G
Seward, James T. VA 24th Cav. Co.C
Seward, James T. VA Cav. 40th Bn. Co.C
Seward, James T. VA 9th Mil. Co.B
Seward, J.B. Exch.Bn. Co.F,CSA Sgt.
Seward, J.D. AR 8th Inf. New Co.H
Seward, J.D. AR 23rd Inf. Co. Co.I
Seward, J.E. VA Inf. 1st Bn.Loc.Def. Co.D Sgt.

Seward, Jeremiah MO Cav. Freeman's Regt. Wolf's Co.
Seward, J.L. TN 15th (Cons.) Cav. Co.I 2nd Lt.
Seward, J.L. TN 42nd Inf. Co.C Sgt.
Seward, J.L. 4th Conf.Inf. Co.H Sgt.
Seward, John GA 18th Inf. Co.K
Seward, John LA 15th Inf. Co.D
Seward, John B. VA Arty. Fleet's Co.
Seward, John B. VA Lt.Arty. Woolfolk's Co.
Seward, John B. VA 55th Inf. Co.B
Seward, John G. VA 92nd Mil. Co.C
Seward, John L. VA Hvy.Arty. Coleman's Co.
Seward, John L. VA Lt.Arty. Hankins' Co.
Seward, John L. VA 3rd Inf. 1st Co.I
Seward, John W. AR 23rd Inf. Co.C Capt.
Seward, John W. VA 12th Inf. Co.F
Seward, John W. VA 26th Inf. Co.G
Seward, J.P. MO 1st & 4th Cons.Inf. Co.C
Seward, J.R. TX 4th Inf. Co.H
Seward, J.R. VA 39th Mil. Co.B
Seward, J.W. GA Employee Comsy.
Seward, J.W. VA 54th Mil. Co.C,D
Seward, L.A. LA Mil. British Guard Bn. Coburn's Co.
Seward, Louis A. VA 55th Inf. Co.F
Seward, Markus A. VA 109th Mil. Co.B, 2nd Co.A
Seward, M.T. AR 8th Inf. New Co.A Cpl.
Seward, M.W. KY 1st (Helms) Cav. Co.B
Seward, M.W. KY 2nd (Woodward's) Cav. Co.A
Seward, M.W. TN Cav. Woodward's Co. Cpl.
Seward, Patrick AL 9th Inf. Co.B 1st Lt.
Seward, Peter E. VA 9th Cav. Co.F
Seward, R. TN 12th (Green's) Cav. Co.E
Seward, R.A. TN 16th (Logwood's) Cav. Co.G
Seward, Richard A. FL 7th Inf. Co.E
Seward, Richard H. VA 12th Inf. Co.F
Seward, R.M. VA 21st Inf. Co.G
Seward, Robert B. VA 26th Inf. Co.G
Seward, Samuel T. VA 1st Arty. Co.E
Seward, Samuel T. VA Hvy.Arty. 10th Bn. Co.E
Seward, S.H. LA Mil.Conf.Guards Regt. Co.C
Seward, Simon E.V. VA 13th Cav. Co.E
Seward, Taylor AR Cav. McGehee's Regt. Co.C
Seward, Thomas C. VA 24th Cav. Co.C
Seward, Thomas C. VA Cav. 40th Bn. Co.C
Seward, Thomas C. VA 9th Mil. Co.B
Seward, Thomas W.B. VA 12th Inf. Co.F
Seward, Walter F. VA 55th Inf. Co.A
Seward, William H. VA 53rd Inf. Co.F
Seward, William M. NC 3rd Inf.
Seward, W.L. TN Arty. Marshall's Co.
Seward, Zachariah FL 7th Inf. Co.E Sr.2nd Lt.
Seward, Zack P. TN 1st (Feild's) Inf. Co.I
Sewart, A. AL Cav. Barbiere's Bn.
Sewart, J.M. GA Conscr.
Sewart, John NC Mil. 66th Bn. J.H. Whitman's Co.
Sewart, L. LA Mil. 4th Regt. 1st Brig. 1st Div. Co.E
Sewart, L.A. LA Mil. 4th Regt. 1st Brig. 1st Div. Co.E 1st Sgt.
Sewel, --- TX 13th Vol. Co.G
Sewel, A.J. GA Inf. 1st Bn. (St.Guards) Co.D
Sewel, Arington Conf.Cav. Clarkson's Bn. Ind.Rangers Co.A
Sewel, C. TX Waul's Legion Co.D Cpl.

Sewel, C.T. LA 3rd (Wingfield's) Cav. Co.E
Sewel, D. GA 11th Cav. Co.K
Sewel, J. TN 39th Mtd.Inf. Co.F
Sewel, James W. GA 8th Inf. (St.Guards) Co.F
Sewel, James W. VA 17th Inf. Co.C
Sewel, Jesse AL 20th Inf. Co.C
Sewel, Jesse F. TN 25th Inf. Co.D Cpl.
Sewel, John F. GA Inf. 1st Conf.Bn. Co.D
Sewel, Jonathan C. TN 25th Inf. Co.D Sgt.
Sewel, L.W. TN 38th Inf. Co.F
Sewel, M.D. TN 19th (Biffle's) Cav. Co.I
Sewel, M.L. MS 25th Inf. Co.D
Sewel, Newton AL 7th Inf. Co.B
Sewel, Thomas A. GA Cobb's Legion Co.E Far.
Sewell, A. GA 2nd Cav. (St.Guards) Co.F
Sewell, A. MO Inf. Clark's Regt. Co.E
Sewell, Aaron J. GA 36th (Broyles') Inf. Co.E
Sewell, Aaron M. GA 39th Inf. Co.H
Sewell, Abraham J. GA 52nd Inf. Co.K Cpl.
Sewell, A.C. GA Inf. 25th Bn. (Prov.Guard) Co.B
Sewell, A.F. GA Phillips' Legion Co.F
Sewell, A.G. TN 21st (Wilson's) Cav. Co.F,B Sgt.
Sewell, A.G. TN 27th Inf. Co.B Sgt.
Sewell, A.J. FL 1st (Res.) Inf. Co.B
Sewell, A.J. GA Inf. City Bn. (Columbus) Co.C Sgt.
Sewell, A.K. TN 21st (Wilson's) Cav. Co.F,B
Sewell, Alexander MO 1st Cav. Co.C
Sewell, Alvin D. GA 36th (Broyles') Inf. Co.E
Sewell, Amos B. AL 28th Inf. Co.G Sgt.
Sewell, Andrew J. TX 18th Cav. Co.I
Sewell, Angus C. GA 5th Inf. Co.B
Sewell, Asbury GA 1st Cav. Co.B Sgt.
Sewell, Asbury GA Cav. 13th Regt. Co.F
Sewell, A.V. TX 20th Cav. Co.E
Sewell, B.B. TX 32nd Cav. Co.K 2nd Lt.
Sewell, B.W. TX 14th Inf. Co.G
Sewell, C. AL Talladega Cty.Res. D.B. Brown's Co.
Sewell, C. TX 35th (Brown's) Cav.
Sewell, C. TX Inf. Timmons' Regt. Co.E
Sewell, C. TX Waul's Legion Co.D Cpl.
Sewell, Charles AL 62nd Inf. Co.B,I
Sewell, Charles FL 1st Inf. New Co.G
Sewell, Charles W. NC 3rd Inf. Co.G
Sewell, Christopher A. GA 36th (Broyles') Inf. Co.E
Sewell, Clement B. AL 49th Inf. Co.H Sgt.
Sewell, Columbus T. GA Phillips' Legion Co.M,B Black.
Sewell, Cornelius TX 9th (Nichols') Inf. Co.A
Sewell, C.P. GA 2nd Cav. (St.Guards) Co.F
Sewell, C.P. GA Phillips' Legion Co.D
Sewell, C.T. 14th Conf.Cav. Co.G
Sewell, Daniel H. NC 3rd Inf. Co.E
Sewell, Daniel W. TN 7th Inf. Co.A
Sewell, David GA Inf. 4th Bn. (St.Guards) Co.C
Sewell, E. GA 1st Cav. Co.B
Sewell, E. TX 9th (Nichols') Inf. Co.G
Sewell, Ed. TX Waul's Legion Co.A
Sewell, E.G. TN 12th (Green's) Cav. Co.E
Sewell, Eli AL Inf. 1st Regt. Co.I
Sewell, Ervin GA 36th (Broyles') Inf. Co.E
Sewell, Floreston P. GA 22nd Inf. Co.C
Sewell, F.M. GA 43rd Inf. Co.D Cpl.

Sewell, Francis M. AL 17th Bn.S.S. Co.A
Sewell, Francis M. AL 19th Inf. Co.H
Sewell, George S. AR 2nd Mtd.Rifles Co.A
Sewell, George W. Al Lt.Arty. 20th Bn. Co.A,B
Sewell, George W. GA Inf. 4th Bn. (St.Guards) Co.C Sgt.
Sewell, George W. GA 41st Inf. Co.D Sgt.
Sewell, George W. KY 5th Mtd.Inf. Co.D 1st Sgt.
Sewell, George W. VA 3rd Inf.Loc.Def. Co.H Capt.
Sewell, George W. VA 11th Inf. Co.A
Sewell, G.G. TN 13th (Gore's) Cav. Co.B
Sewell, G.W. TX 18th Cav. Co.I
Sewell, G.W. VA Lt.Arty. Ellett's Co.
Sewell, H. GA 40th Inf. Co.F
Sewell, Henry AL Mtd.Res. Logan's Co.
Sewell, Henry GA 11th Cav. Co.D Cpl.
Sewell, Henry GA Inf. 4th Bn. (St.Guards) Co.C
Sewell, Henry NC 1st Arty. (10th St.Troops) Co.I
Sewell, Henry NC 2nd Arty. (36th St.Troops) Co.A
Sewell, Henry C. GA Inf. 8th Bn. Co.B
Sewell, Henry C. VA 6th Cav. Co.K
Sewell, Henry D. TN 16th Inf. Co.A
Sewell, Henry K. AL 30th Inf. Co.I
Sewell, Henry T. NC 17th Inf. (1st Org.) Co.D
Sewell, H.F. AL 10th Inf. Co.B Sgt.
Sewell, H.W. TX 26th Cav. Co.C
Sewell, I.A. LA 3rd (Harrison's) Cav. Co.G
Sewell, Isaac GA Phillips' Legion Co.M,B
Sewell, Isaac H. GA 5th Inf. Co.A
Sewell, Isaac P. GA 3rd Inf. Co.G
Sewell, Isaac R. GA 13th Cav. Co.F
Sewell, Isaac S. TN 13th (Gore's) Cav. Co.B
Sewell, J. AR 21st Mil. Co.A
Sewell, J. GA 1st Cav. Co.B
Sewell, J.A. AR 19th (Dockery's) Inf. Co.K
Sewell, J.A. GA 22nd Inf. Co.C Cpl.
Sewell, J.A. GA 60th Inf. Co.H Sgt.
Sewell, J.A. GA 66th Inf. Co.H
Sewell, Jacob L. TX 15th Cav. Co.I Cpl.
Sewell, James AR 4th Inf. Co.K
Sewell, James LA 1st Cav. Co.H
Sewell, James VA Cav. 35th Bn. Co.F
Sewell, James A. AR 12th Bn.S.S. Co.D Sgt.
Sewell, James A. MS 31st Inf. Co.A
Sewell, James H. AR 19th (Dockery's) Inf. Co.A
Sewell, James H. LA Cav. Cole's Co.
Sewell, James H. TX 7th Inf. Co.F
Sewell, James M. GA 9th Inf. Co.H
Sewell, James M. GA Phillips' Legion Co.D,K
Sewell, James R. GA Inf. 4th Bn. (St.Guards) Co.C Sgt.
Sewell, James W. GA Inf. 25th Bn. (Prov.Guard) Co.B
Sewell, Jasper AL 7th Inf. Co.B
Sewell, Jasper AL 20th Inf. Co.B
Sewell, Jasper TN Cav. Newsom's Regt. Co.H
Sewell, J.E. AL 33rd Inf. Co.H
Sewell, J.E. GA Phillips' Legion Co.E
Sewell, Jesse AR Inf. Hardy's Regt. Co.D
Sewell, Jesse A. TX 37th Cav. Co.A 1st Sgt.
Sewell, Jesse Assa TX 20th Cav. Co.C
Sewell, Jesse P. GA 30th Inf. Co.H
Sewell, J.F. GA 6th Cav. Co.E

Sewell, J.G. TX 2nd Inf. Co.D
Sewell, J.H. GA 1st Cav. Co.B
Sewell, J.H. GA Inf. 25th Bn. (Prov.Guard) Co.C
Sewell, J.H. GA 64th Inf. Co.F
Sewell, J.H. TN Cav. Nixon's Regt. Co.I Cpl.
Sewell, J.H. Battle's Brig. Capt.,AQM
Sewell, J.J. AR 33rd Inf. Co.G
Sewell, J.N. GA Phillips' Legion Co.D,K
Sewell, J.N. TX 37th Cav. Co.H
Sewell, John AR 10th (Witt's) Cav. Co.C
Sewell, John AL 28th Inf. Co.K
Sewell, John AR 7th Inf. Co.F
Sewell, John AR 19th (Dockery's) Inf. Co.A
Sewell, John AR 11th Cav. Co.D
Sewell, John GA Inf. 25th Bn. (Prov.Guard) Co.A
Sewell, John MS 8th Cav. Co.F
Sewell, John MS Inf. 5th Bn. Co.C
Sewell, John MS 41st Inf. Co.A
Sewell, John TN 8th (Smith's) Cav. Co.K
Sewell, John TX 32nd Cav. Co.D
Sewell, John Exch.Bn. 2nd Co.A,CSA
Sewell, John A. GA 2nd Inf. Co.B
Sewell, John A. GA 52nd Inf. Co.K Sgt.
Sewell, John C. GA Inf. 4th Bn. (St.Guards) Co.C
Sewell, John F. GA 30th Inf. Co.H
Sewell, John H.P. VA 21st Mil. Co.B
Sewell, John M. GA 46th Inf. Co.I
Sewell, John P. TN 48th (Voorhies') Inf. Co.K Cpl.
Sewell, John R. GA 2nd Inf. Co.B
Sewell, John R. GA Phillips' Legion Co.D,K
Sewell, John R. TN 1st Cav. Co.E,G
Sewell, John W. GA Inf. 25th Bn. (Prov.Guard) Co.A
Sewell, John W. GA 36th (Villepigue's) Inf. Co.D
Sewell, John W. GA 41st Inf. Co.K 1st Sgt.
Sewell, John W. GA Phillips' Legion Co.M
Sewell, John W. Conf.Inf. 1st Bn. 2nd Co.A Sgt.
Sewell, John W.A. GA Phillips' Legion Co.M
Sewell, Jonas AL 53rd (Part.Rangers) Co.E
Sewell, Joseph AR 58th Mil. Co.E
Sewell, Joseph NC 31st Inf. Co.G
Sewell, Joseph B. AL 28th Inf. Co.G
Sewell, Joseph G. TN 13th (Gore's) Cav. Co.B
Sewell, Joseph H. TN 1st (Feild's) Inf. Co.A Sgt.
Sewell, Joseph W. GA 46th Inf. Co.I
Sewell, Joseph W. TN 48th (Voorhies') Inf. Co.A
Sewell, J.P. AR 1st (Monroe's) Cav. Co.K Bvt.2nd Lt.
Sewell, J.R. GA 2nd Cav. (St.Guards) Co.F,A
Sewell, J.S. AL 4th Res. Co.E
Sewell, J.S. AL 30th Inf. Co.E
Sewell, J.S. 8th (Wade's) Conf.Cav. Co.K
Sewell, J.V. AL 47th Inf. Co.A Comsy.Sgt.
Sewell, J.W. GA 1st Cav. Co.K
Sewell, J.W. GA 1st (Fannin's) Res. Co.F
Sewell, J.W. TN 48th (Nixon's) Inf. Co.B
Sewell, J.W. TN Inf. Sowell's Detach.
Sewell, J. Wesley GA Inf. 2nd Bn. Co.B
Sewell, Land AL 30th Inf. Co.E

Sewell, Larkin D. GA Inf. 4th Bn. (St.Guards) Co.C Sgt.
Sewell, Layton AL 41st Inf. Co.D
Sewell, Levi GA Inf. 4th Bn. (St.Guards) Co.C
Sewell, Levi F. GA Phillips' Legion Co.D
Sewell, Lewis J. MO 5th Inf. Co.D
Sewell, Littleton GA 7th Inf. (St.Guards) Co.L
Sewell, M. GA 1st Cav. Co.B
Sewell, Marcus L. AL 4th Inf. Co.G Cpl.
Sewell, Marion GA 1st Cav. Co.K
Sewell, Marion W. MS 15th Inf. Co.D
Sewell, M.H. NC Cumberland Cty.Bn. Detailed Men Co.B
Sewell, Milton AL 5th Bn.Vol. Co.B
Sewell, M.L. 2nd Conf.Inf. Co.D
Sewell, N. AL 29th Inf. Co.D
Sewell, N.A. TX 28th Cav. Co.E
Sewell, Newton AL 20th Inf. Co.B
Sewell, Newton AL 30th Inf. Co.E
Sewell, Newton LA 1st Cav. Co.H
Sewell, Newton A. LA 1st Cav. Co.H
Sewell, Newton A. LA Cav. Cole's Co.
Sewell, Octavius A. TX 17th Cav. Co.K
Sewell, P.A. GA Inf. 25th Bn. (Prov.Guard) Co.B
Sewell, Pierce GA 2nd Cav. (St.Guards) Co.F
Sewell, Pinckney A. GA 42nd Inf. Co.I
Sewell, Pinkney A. GA 5th Inf. Co.B
Sewell, P.W. TX 35th (Brown's) Cav. Co.B
Sewell, Ransome GA Inf. 10th Bn. Co.C
Sewell, R.B. TX 9th (Nichols') Inf. Co.D Cpl.
Sewell, R.B. TX Waul's Legion Co.F Ord.Sgt.
Sewell, Richard F. TX 2nd Cav. Co.G
Sewell, Riley GA Inf. (Franklin Cty.Guards) Kay's Co.
Sewell, Robert AR 1st (Colquitt's) Inf. Co.A Capt.
Sewell, S. GA 13th Inf. Co.B
Sewell, Samuel MS 21st Inf. Co.F
Sewell, Samuel C. GA 42nd Inf. Co.I
Sewell, Samuel D. GA 34th Inf. Co.G
Sewell, Samuel P. GA 30th Inf. Co.H
Sewell, S.C. GA 6th Cav. Co.E Cpl.
Sewell, S.H. KY 8th Cav. Co.B
Sewell, S.N. NC 3rd Inf. Co.C
Sewell, Spencer GA 15th Inf. Co.B
Sewell, Stephen H. TN 13th (Gore's) Cav. Co.B Cpl.
Sewell, S.W. GA 64th Inf. Co.F
Sewell, T.C. TX Cav. 1st Regt.St.Troops Co.G
Sewell, T.H. MO 2nd Cav. Co.C
Sewell, Thomas NC 3rd Arty. (40th St.Troops) Co.F
Sewell, Thomas NC Inf. 13th Bn. Co.D
Sewell, Thomas NC 24th Inf. Co.C
Sewell, Thomas NC 51st Inf. Co.A
Sewell, Thomas TN Inf. 1st Cons.Regt. Co.I
Sewell, Thomas TX 3rd Cav. Co.F
Sewell, Thomas VA Lt.Arty. Cooper's Co.
Sewell, Thomas E. NC 3rd Inf. Co.E
Sewell, Thomas H. NC 17th Inf. (1st Org.) Co.D
Sewell, Thomas H. NC 17th Inf. (2nd Org.) Co.C Cpl.
Sewell, Thomas J. LA Cav. Cole's Co.
Sewell, Thos. J. LA Ogden's Cav. Co.C
Sewell, Thomas L. TN Inf. 1st Bn. (Colms') Co.A

Sewell, Thomas M. GA 41st Inf. Co.D
Sewell, Thomas W. GA Phillips' Legion Co.D,K
Sewell, T.J. 14th Conf.Cav. Co.G
Sewell, T.L. GA Inf. 14th Bn. (St.Guards) Co.E
Sewell, T.L. GA Inf. Hamlet's Co.
Sewell, Uriah AL 37th Inf. Co.A
Sewell, W.A. GA 2nd Cav. (St.Guards) Co.A
Sewell, W.A. TX 35th (Brown's) Cav. 2nd Co.B 1st Sgt.
Sewell, Wade L. AL 63rd Inf. Co.B
Sewell, W.B. TN 21st (Wilson's) Cav. Co.B 1st Sgt.
Sewell, W.D. MS 31st Inf. Co.A
Sewell, W.F. GA 5th Cav. Co.A
Sewell, W.F. GA Lt.Arty. (Arsenal Btty.) Hudson's Co.
Sewell, W.F. GA 41st Inf. Co.D
Sewell, W.H.H. GA 13th Cav. Co.F
Sewell, W.I. AL 30th Inf. Co.E
Sewell, William AR 33rd Inf. Co.G
Sewell, William GA 7th Inf. Co.D
Sewell, William GA 20th Inf. Co.I
Sewell, William MO Inf. Clark's Regt. Co.E
Sewell, William TN 7th Inf. Co.A
Sewell, William TX Inf. Yarbrough's Co. (Smith Cty.Lt.Inf.)
Sewell, William F. GA Cav. 2nd Bn. Co.D
Sewell, William F. GA 15th Inf. Co.B
Sewell, William J. GA 64th Inf. Co.E
Sewell, William J. NC 17th Inf. (1st Org.) Co.D
Sewell, William J. NC 31st Inf. Co.G Cpl.
Sewell, Wm. Jasper MO Inf. Clark's Regt. Co.E
Sewell, William M. GA 30th Inf. Co.H Sgt.
Sewell, William Marion TX 20th Cav. Co.C
Sewell, William N. GA 42nd Inf. Co.I Cpl.
Sewell, William P. GA 55th Inf. Co.K
Sewell, William P. GA Inf. (Loc.Def.) Whiteside's Nav.Bn. Co.B
Sewell, William T. VA 21st Mil. Co.B
Sewell, William W. MS 14th Inf. Co.K
Sewell, W.J. TN 14th (Neely's) Cav. Co.D
Sewell, W.J. TN 22nd Inf. Co.B
Sewell, W.J. Conf.Cav. Clarkson's Bn. Ind. Rangers Co.A,F
Sewell, W.P. GA 13th Cav. Co.F Bugler
Sewell, W.R. TX 11th Inf. Co.B
Sewell, W.W. AL 30th Inf. Co.E
Sewell, W.W. LA Washington Arty.Bn. Co.5 Cpl.
Sewells, J.S. AL 4th Res. Co.E
Sewels, Marion J. AL 20th Inf. Co.B
Sewer, John TX 16th Inf. Co.H
Sewer, W. AL 4th Inf. Co.H
Sewers, Isaac VA 97th Mil. Co.K
Sewers, Robert LA 4th Cav. Co.I Sgt.
Sewett, W.R. AR 30th Inf. Co.E
Se wih ke 1st Creek Mtd.Vol. Co.A
Sewill, Ed TX Inf. Timmons' Regt. Co.G
Sewill, Isaac N. TX 14th Cav. Co.B
Sewter, Andrew Conf.Cav. Clarkson's Bn. Ind.Rangers Co.A
Sexchenaildre, E. MS Lt.Arty. (The Hudson Btty.) Hoole's Co.
Sexneider, Cleophas LA 18th Inf. Co.E
Sexneider, Lawrence LA 18th Inf. Co.E
Sexon, J.S. GA 25th Inf. Co.C Sgt.
Sexon, Newton J. SC 16th Inf. Co.A

Sexon, Thomas SC 16th & 24th (Cons.) Inf. Co.E
Sexsmith, Truman MD Cav. 2nd Bn. Co.C
Sexsmith, William T. AR 3rd Inf. Co.H
Sexston, Joseph AR 21st Inf. Co.E
Sexston, William AR 21st Inf. Co.E
Sexston, William P. AR 21st Inf. Co.E
Sext, J. GA 1st Inf. Co.I
Sexton, A. FL 1st (Res.) Inf. Sgt.
Sexton, A.C. AL 1st Bn. Hilliard's Legion Vol. Co.D
Sexton, A.C. AL 17th Inf. Co.A
Sexton, A. Jackson VA 45th Inf. Co.C
Sexton, Albert F.H. VA 4th Inf. Co.D Sgt.
Sexton, Alexander AR 32nd Inf. Co.F
Sexton, Alfred FL 6th Inf. Co.D,E
Sexton, Alsey NC 31st Inf. Co.C
Sexton, Andrew TN 18th (Newsom's) Cav. Co.I
Sexton, Andrew TN Cav. Newsoms' Regt. Co.F
Sexton, Andrew J. GA 14th Inf. Co.K
Sexton, Andrew J. VA 51st Inf. Co.K Sgt.
Sexton, Archibald VA 50th Inf. Co.D
Sexton, Augustine NC 31st Inf. Co.C
Sexton, B. AL 10th Inf. Co.B
Sexton, Barton MO Cav. Fristoe's Regt. Co.E
Sexton, Benjamin VA Inf. 21st Bn. 2nd Co.E
Sexton, Benjamin F. AL Lt.Arty. 2nd Bn. Co.F
Sexton, Benjamin F. VA 4th Inf. Co.D
Sexton, Benjamin F. VA 64th Mtd.Inf. Co.E
Sexton, Benjamin H. TN 37th Inf. Co.K Cpl.
Sexton, Berry KY 13th Cav. Co.B Cpl.
Sexton, Blackburn GA 12th Cav. Co.D
Sexton, B.W. SC 18th Inf. Co.C Cpl.
Sexton, C. SC 12th Inf. Co.F,H
Sexton, Calvin NC 22nd Inf. Co.F
Sexton, Campbell VA 50th Inf. Co.A
Sexton, Charles GA Lt.Arty. 14th Bn. Co.D
Sexton, Charles GA Lt.Arty. King's Btty.
Sexton, Charles GA Inf. Clemons' Co.
Sexton, Charles SC 1st (Butler's) Inf. Co.G
Sexton, Charles 1st Choctaw & Chickasaw Mtd.Rifles Co.A
Sexton, Charles M. VA 4th Inf. Co.D
Sexton, Charles W. VA 6th Bn.Res. Co.G
Sexton, Charley GA Cav. 6th Bn. (St.Guards) Co.C
Sexton, Clark VA 50th Inf. Co.B
Sexton, Cornelius SC 17th Inf. Co.A
Sexton, Cornelius SC 24th Inf. Co.H
Sexton, Cornelius P. SC 5th Cav. Co.K
Sexton, Dan TN 33rd Inf. Co.E
Sexton, Daniel AR 14th (Powers') Inf. Co.E
Sexton, Daniel SC 24th Inf. Co.H
Sexton, David LA 1st (Strawbridge's) Inf. Co.A
Sexton, David VA Cav. 37th Bn. Co.D
Sexton, David VA 37th Inf. Co.D
Sexton, David VA 48th Inf. Co.C
Sexton, David D. SC 13th Inf. Co.C
Sexton, D.C. GA 27th Inf. Co.D
Sexton, D.D. AL 4th Res. Co.A
Sexton, D.F. AL 4th Cav. Co.K 2nd Lt.
Sexton, Duncan M. NC 15th Inf. Co.F 1st Lt.
Sexton, Duncan McL. NC Hvy.Arty. 10th Bn. Co.B Sgt.
Sexton, Edmond NC 2nd Cav. (19th St.Troops) Co.G

553

Sexton, N.B. VA Lt.Arty. King's Co. 1st Sgt.

Sexton, Edward LA 1st (Strawbridge's) Inf. Co.A
Sexton, E.J. AL 1st Bn. Hilliard's Legion Vol.
  Co.D
Sexton, E.J. AL 60th Inf. Co.I
Sexton, Elbert G. TN 50th Inf. Co.H Capt.
Sexton, Eli VA 51st Inf. Co.K
Sexton, Elijah MS 2nd Cav. Co.F
Sexton, Elijah MS 2nd (Davidson's) Inf. Co.C
Sexton, Elijah P. NC 60th Inf. Co.H Drum.
Sexton, E.T. SC 18th Inf. Co.C
Sexton, Ezekiel NC 39th Inf. Co.E
Sexton, F.B. FL 2nd Cav. Co.A
Sexton, F.C. GA 10th Cav. (St.Guards) Co.A
Sexton, Flornoy MS 48th Inf. Co.L
Sexton, Francis M. SC 5th Cav. Co.K Cpl.
Sexton, Francis P. FL Cav. (Marianna Drag.)
  Smith's Co.
Sexton, Friley B. FL Cav. 5th Bn. Co.E
Sexton, George NC 60th Inf. Co.H Fifer
Sexton, George TN 15th Inf. Co.D
Sexton, George W. AL 37th Inf. Co.H
Sexton, George W. AR Mil. Desha Cty.Bn.
Sexton, George W. KY 9th Cav. Co.F
Sexton, George W. NC 12th Inf. Co.H
Sexton, Gibson 1st Choctaw & Chickasaw
  Mtd.Rifles Co.G
Sexton, Green NC 15th Inf. Co.F Sgt.
Sexton, Green TN 14th (Neely's) Cav. Co.F
Sexton, G.W. AL 1st Bn. Hilliard's Legion Vol.
  Co.D
Sexton, G.W. AL 21st Inf. Co.D
Sexton, G.W. AL 60th Inf. Co.I
Sexton, G.W. KY Morgan's Men Co.E
Sexton, G.W. VA 50th Regt. Co.D
Sexton, Halter H. KY 5th Mtd.Inf. Co.F Sgt.
Sexton, Hardin VA 51st Inf. Co.K
Sexton, Hardy VA 51st Inf. Co.K
Sexton, Harris S. 1st Choctaw Mtd.Rifles Co.I
  2nd Lt.
Sexton, H.D. TN 6th Inf. Co.G Cpl.
Sexton, Henry AL 3rd Res. Co.G Cpl.
Sexton, Henry MO Cav. Freeman's Regt. Co.A
Sexton, Henry A. VA 64th Mtd.Inf. Co.E
Sexton, Henry A. VA Mil. Scott Cty.
Sexton, H.H. KY 13th Cav. Co.A Sgt.
Sexton, Hiram NC Inf. 2nd Bn. Co.H
Sexton, Hiram VA 25th Cav. Co.C
Sexton, Hiram VA 37th Inf. Co.D
Sexton, H.L. TN 46th Inf. Co.B
Sexton, H.M. KY 12th Cav. Co.G
Sexton, Horace H. AL Lt.Arty. 2nd Bn. Co.F
Sexton, Hugh AL 1st Regt. Mobile Vol. British
  Guard Co.A
Sexton, H.W. GA 2nd Cav. Co.A
Sexton, H.W. GA 10th Cav. (St.Guards) Co.H
  Cpl.
Sexton, I. TN 19th & 20th (Cons.) Cav. Co.D
Sexton, I.P. LA 17th Inf. Co.D
Sexton, J. GA 5th Res. Co.C
Sexton, J.A. GA Inf. Clemons' Co.
Sexton, J.A. SC 9th Res. Co.H
Sexton, J.A.B. AR 45th Mil. Co.C
Sexton, Jabers SC 3rd Bn.Res. Co.E
Sexton, Jackson TX 30th Cav. Co.C
Sexton, Jackson 1st Choctaw & Chickasaw
  Mtd.Rifles 3rd Co.H

Sexton, Jackson Deneale's Regt. Choctaw War-
  riors Co.C
Sexton, Jacob 1st Choctaw & Chickasaw
  Mtd.Rifles Co.A
Sexton, James AL 41st Inf. Co.G
Sexton, James LA 11th Inf. Co.A
Sexton, James LA 13th Inf. Co.A
Sexton, James LA Mil. Bonnabel Guards
Sexton, James MO 1st N.E. Cav. Co.F
Sexton, James NC 38th Inf. Co.B
Sexton, James SC 3rd Bn.Res. Co.E
Sexton, James SC 5th St.Troops Co.L
Sexton, James VA 51st Inf. Co.K
Sexton, James A. NC 3rd Cav. (41st St.Troops)
  Co.D
Sexton, James A. NC Hvy.Arty. 10th Bn. Co.B
  Cpl.
Sexton, James A. TX 10th Inf. Co.C
Sexton, James G. MS 48th Inf. Co.H
Sexton, James H. MS 24th Inf. Co.G
Sexton, James H. MS 27th Inf. Co.C
Sexton, James L. AR 38th Inf. Co.A,F Capt.
Sexton, James L. MO 15th Cav. Maj.
Sexton, James M. MS 24th Inf. Co.H
Sexton, James M. TN 7th Inf. Co.B
Sexton, James R. TX Cav. Madison's Regt.
  Co.D
Sexton, James W. FL 6th Inf. Co.E
Sexton, J.B. FL 11th Inf. Co.C
Sexton, J.B. TN 50th Inf. Co.B
Sexton, J.C. SC Palmetto S.S. Co.D
Sexton, J.C. TN Cav. 12th Bn. (Day's) Co.G
Sexton, J.C. TX 13th Vol. Co.H
Sexton, J.D. MS 7th Cav. Co.B 2nd Lt.
Sexton, J.D. MS 2nd (Davidson's) Inf. Co.C
Sexton, J.E. MO Cav. Freeman's Regt. Co.E
  Capt.
Sexton, Jeff MO 1st & 4th Cons.Inf. Co.D
Sexton, Jefferson TN 61st Mtd.Inf. Co.I
Sexton, Jefferson 1st Choctaw & Chickasaw
  Mtd.Rifles Co.A 2nd Lt.
Sexton, Jeremiah MO 1st N.E. Cav.
Sexton, Jeremiah MO Lt.Arty. 3rd Btty.
Sexton, Jeremiah MO 5th Inf. Co.H
Sexton, J.F. MS 6th Inf. Co.F
Sexton, J.F. SC 11th Inf. Co.K
Sexton, J.G. MS Inf. 2nd Bn. Co.H
Sexton, J.L. AL 25th Inf. Co.K
Sexton, J.M. TN 10th (DeMoss') Cav. Co.D
  Cpl.
Sexton, J.M. TN Cav. Napier's Bn. Co.A Cpl.
Sexton, J.M. TN 20th Inf. Co.H
Sexton, Joel TN 44th Inf. Co.C
Sexton, John AL 1st Regt. Mobile Vol. British
  Guard Co.A
Sexton, John AL Pris.Guard Freeman's Co.
Sexton, John MO 1st N.E. Cav. Co.L
Sexton, John NC Inf. 2nd Bn. Co.F
Sexton, John NC 12th Inf. Co.H
Sexton, John NC 52nd Inf. Co.G
Sexton, John NC 60th Inf. Co.H
Sexton, John TN 20th (Russell's) Cav. Co.K
Sexton, John VA 8th Cav. Co.C
Sexton, John GA 37th Inf. Co.D
Sexton, John 1st Cherokee Mtd.Vol. Co.G
Sexton, John B. FL Inf. 2nd Bn. Co.E

Sexton, John B. SC Inf. 7th Bn. (Enfield Rifles)
  Co.B
Sexton, John E. MO 8th Cav. Co.F,G
Sexton, John F. KY 8th Cav. Co.I
Sexton, John F. MS 1st Lt.Arty. Co.F
Sexton, John F. MS 1st (Percy's) Inf. Co.A
Sexton, John G. NC 60th Inf. Co.H
Sexton, John H. AL Arty. 1st Bn. Co.E
Sexton, John H. GA 43rd Inf. Co.F
Sexton, John H. VA 51st Inf. Co.K
Sexton, John M. AL 28th Inf. Co.A
Sexton, John M. GA 42nd Inf. Co.A 1st Sgt.
Sexton, John M. NC 62nd Inf. Co.H
Sexton, John M. TN 50th Inf. Co.H
Sexton, John M. AL 4th Inf. Co.A
Sexton, John T. KY 5th Mtd.Inf. Co.H
Sexton, John T. NC 32nd Inf. Co.H
Sexton, John T. TN 50th Inf. Co.B Sgt.
Sexton, John W. TN Lt.Arty. Lynch's Co.
Sexton, John W. VA Cav. 35th Bn. Co.C Sgt.
Sexton, John W. VA 17th Inf. Co.C
Sexton, John W. VA 51st Inf. Co.K
Sexton, Jonathan NC 22nd Inf. Co.F
Sexton, Joseph AR 17th (Lemoyne's) Inf. Co.F
Sexton, Joseph GA 1st (Symons') Res. Co.B
Sexton, Joseph KY 13th Cav. Co.A
Sexton, Joseph KY 5th Mtd.Inf. Co.F
Sexton, Joseph NC 37th Inf. Co.A
Sexton, Joseph C. VA 4th Inf. Co.A
Sexton, Joseph C. Gen. & Staff, A. of N.VA
  Maj.,CS
Sexton, Joseph E. MO Inf. 8th Bn. Co.B
Sexton, Joseph W. NC Walker's Bn. Thomas'
  Legion Co.C
Sexton, Joseph W. VA 6th Bn.Res. Co.A
Sexton, J.P. AL 34th Inf. Co.B
Sexton, J.S. LA 27th Inf. Co.B
Sexton, J.S. TX Cav. 6th Bn. Co.B
Sexton, J.T. AR 10th Inf. Co.B
Sexton, J.T. NC 32nd Inf. Co.C
Sexton, J.T. TN 50th (Cons.) Inf. Co.A Sgt.
Sexton, J.W. SC 3rd Inf. Co.D
Sexton, L. MO Cav. 1st Regt.St.Guard Co.B
Sexton, Lafayette MO 7th Cav. Co.A
Sexton, Legrand VA 6th Bn.Res. Co.D
Sexton, Levi NC 5th Sr.Res. Co.D Sgt.
Sexton, Levi VA 51st Inf. Co.K
Sexton, Levi G. KY 2nd Bn.Mtd.Rifles Co.A
Sexton, Levy G. KY 5th Mtd.Inf. Co.H Cpl.
Sexton, Linsday Conf.Reg.Inf. Brooks' Bn. Co.E
Sexton, Lorensy D. VA 51st Inf. Co.K
Sexton, M. AL 8th Inf. Co.I
Sexton, M. TN 38th Inf. Co.G
Sexton, Marcus W. SC 13th Inf. Co.C
Sexton, Marion NC 37th Inf. Co.A
Sexton, Martin V. VA 51st Inf. Co.K
Sexton, M.B. TX 9th (Young's) Inf. Co.G Sgt.
Sexton, McLean TX 11th Cav. Co.C
Sexton, Michael TN 2nd (Walker's) Inf. Co.H
Sexton, Michael 9th Conf.Inf. Co.F
Sexton, Morehead NC Inf. 2nd Bn. Co.F
Sexton, M.V. TX 25th Cav. Co.D
Sexton, M.Y. GA Inf. 8th Bn. Co.B Capt.
Sexton, Nathan 1st Choctaw & Chickasaw
  Mtd.Rifles Co.G 2nd Lt.
Sexton, Nathaniel KY 13th Cav. Co.H Cpl.
Sexton, N.B. VA Lt.Arty. King's Co. 1st Sgt.

Sexton, Neill TX Cav. 6th Bn. Co.B
Sexton, Newton O. NC Walker's Bn. Thomas'
  Legion Co.A Sgt.
Sexton, Newton O. TN 3rd (Lillard's) Mtd.Inf.
  Co.D
Sexton, N.W. SC 18th Inf. Co.C
Sexton, Oliver M. SC Arty. Gregg's Co.
  (McQueen Lt.Arty.)
Sexton, Oliver M. SC Arty. Manigault's Bn. 1st
  Co.C Bugler
Sexton, O.M. AR 15th (Johnson's) Inf. Co.C
Sexton, O.M. Gen. & Staff Hosp.Stew.
Sexton, P. 2nd Conf.Inf. Co.K
Sexton, Patrick LA 7th Inf. Co.B
Sexton, Patrick MS 1st Lt.Arty. Co.E
Sexton, Patrick MS 29th Inf. Co.E
Sexton, Patrick VA Hvy.Arty. 20th Bn. Co.E
Sexton, Phillip MS 25th Inf. Co.K
Sexton, Phillip MO 1st Inf. Co.C
Sexton, Pinkney NC Inf. 2nd Bn. Co.H
Sexton, Presley KY 5th Cav. Co.A
Sexton, Presley KY 5th Mtd.Inf. Co.A
Sexton, R.A. TN 7th Cav.
Sexton, R.A. TN 14th (Neely's) Cav. Co.F
Sexton, R.A. TN Inf. Harman's Regt. Co.K
Sexton, Raleigh TN 3rd (Lillard's) Mtd.Inf.
  Co.D
Sexton, Randall R. NC 31st Inf. Co.C
Sexton, R.C. AR 19th (Dockery's) Inf. Co.H
  Cpl.
Sexton, Reuben NC 37th Inf. Co.A
Sexton, Reuben A. TN 50th Inf. Co.H
Sexton, Reuben F. GA 36th (Broyles') Inf. Co.C
Sexton, Robert AR 26th Inf. Co.C
Sexton, Robert TN 7th Inf. Co.B
Sexton, Robert VA 8th Inf. Co.E
Sexton, Robert VA Inf. 21st Bn. 2nd Co.E
Sexton, Robert VA 64th Mtd.Inf. Co.E
Sexton, Robert VA 72nd Mil.
Sexton, Robert B. VA 48th Inf. Co.C 2nd Lt.
Sexton, Robert K. NC 1st Inf. Co.A
Sexton, S. AL 48th Inf. Co.K
Sexton, S. SC Inf. 1st (Charleston) Bn. Co.F
Sexton, Samuel LA Miles' Legion Co.B
Sexton, Samuel NC 1st Inf. Co.G
Sexton, Samuel SC Inf. 1st (Charleston) Bn.
  Co.F
Sexton, Samuel SC 9th Res. Co.H
Sexton, Samuel SC 18th Inf. Co.E
Sexton, Samuel I. NC 64th Inf. Co.C
Sexton, Samuel J. NC Inf. 2nd Bn. Co.H
Sexton, Seth R. FL 6th Inf. Co.E
Sexton, S.H. TN 19th Inf. Co.H
Sexton, Simon NC 27th Inf. Co.F
Sexton, Solomon M. VA 4th Inf. Co.D Sgt.
Sexton, S.T. GA Lt.Arty. 14th Bn. Co.D Cpl.
Sexton, S.T. GA Lt.Arty. King's Btty. Cpl.
Sexton, Stephen KY 13th Cav. Co.A
Sexton, Stephen KY 5th Mtd.Inf. Co.A
Sexton, T.C. TN 14th (Neely's) Cav. Co.F
Sexton, Thomas AL 28th Inf. Co.G
Sexton, Thomas AL 43rd Inf. Co.D
Sexton, Thomas AR 23rd Inf. Co.B Cpl.
Sexton, Thomas TN 7th (Duckworth's) Cav.
  Co.E
Sexton, Thomas VA 6th Bn.Res. Co.C
Sexton, Thomas C. VA 4th Inf. Co.D

Sexton, Thomas J. TN 46th Inf.
Sexton, Thornton NC 37th Inf. Co.A
Sexton, T.J. MS Cav. 6th Bn. Prince's Co.
Sexton, T.J. SC 8th Inf. Co.A
Sexton, T.J. VA 8th Inf. Co.E
Sexton, T.J. 2nd Cherokee Mtd.Vol. Co.A
Sexton, T.K. VA 21st Cav. 2nd Co.E
Sexton, Uriah KY 2nd Bn.Mtd.Rifles Co.D
Sexton, W. GA 2nd Cav. Co.A
Sexton, W. KY Morgan's Men Co.E
Sexton, W.A. MS 15th Bn.S.S. Co.B Sgt.
Sexton, W.C. SC 13th Inf. Co.C
Sexton, W.C. AL 54th Inf. Co.G
Sexton, W.H. AL 23rd Inf. Co.F
Sexton, W.H. AR 34th Inf. Co.B
Sexton, Wiley TX 2nd Cav. Co.G
Sexton, William AL 32nd Inf. Co.I
Sexton, William AR 12th Bn.S.S. Co.B
Sexton, William AR 15th (N.W.) Inf. Co.H
Sexton, William AR 17th (Lemoyne's) Inf. Co.F
Sexton, William KY 9th Cav. Co.F Sgt.
Sexton, William KY 13th Cav. Co.H
Sexton, William, Jr. KY 5th Mtd.Inf. Co.H Sgt.
Sexton, William LA 20th Inf. Co.G
Sexton, William MS 8th Inf. Co.C
Sexton, William MO Inf. Perkins' Bn.
Sexton, William NC 12th Inf. Co.H
Sexton, William NC 17th Inf. (1st Org.) Co.H
Sexton, William NC 17th Inf. (2nd Org.) Co.G
Sexton, William NC 32nd Inf. Co.H
Sexton, William NC 56th Inf. Co.C
Sexton, William TN 19th Inf. Co.H
Sexton, William TN 44th Inf. Co.C
Sexton, William TN 44th (Cons.) Inf. Co.K
Sexton, William TN 61st Mtd.Inf. Co.D
Sexton, William TX 13th Vol. 1st Co.K
Sexton, William VA Lt.Arty. Jeffress' Co. Artif.
Sexton, William VA Inf. 1st Bn. Co.A
Sexton, William A. AL 33rd Inf. Co.A
Sexton, William D. NC 60th Inf. Co.H
Sexton, William D. VA 51st Inf. Co.K,A
Sexton, William E. NC 17th Inf. (2nd Org.)
  Co.D
Sexton, William E. VA 54th Mil. Co.E,F
Sexton, William G. GA Arty. 9th Bn. Co.D
Sexton, William H. AL 47th Inf. Co.H
Sexton, William H. GA 41st Inf. Co.H
Sexton, William H. NC 1st Inf. Co.H
Sexton, William J. TN 59th Mtd.Inf. Co.E
Sexton, William Madison TX 20th Cav. Co.D
Sexton, William R. TN 32nd Inf. Co.C 1st Sgt.
Sexton, William T. GA Inf. 8th Bn. Co.B
Sexton, Williamson L. GA 35th Inf. Co.F
Sexton, Willis 1st Choctaw & Chickasaw
  Mtd.Rifles Co.A
Sexton, Witt TN 29th Inf. Co.I Music.
Sexton, W.L. SC 17th Inf. Co.A
Sexton, W.M. AR 1st S.S. Co.B
Sexton, W.M. GA 19th Inf. Co.D
Sexton, W.S. GA 5th Res. Co.C
Sexton, W.S. GA Inf. 25th Bn. (Prov.Guard)
  Co.G
Sexton, W.W. TN Cav. Williams' Co.
Sey, Walter TN 50th Inf. Co.E
Seybert, Andrew C. VA 62nd Mtd.Inf. 2nd Co.D
  Sgt.
Seybert, Andrew C. VA 162nd Mil. Co.A

Seybert, Eli VA 62nd Mtd.Inf. 2nd Co.D
Seybert, Eli VA 162nd Mil. Co.C
Seybert, John W. VA 31st Inf. Co.E
Seybert, William VA 31st Inf. Co.H
Seybert, William VA 162nd Mil. Co.A
Seybt, George W. SC Inf. 1st (Charleston) Bn.
  Co.A Sgt.
Seybt, G.W. SC Mil.Arty. 1st Regt. Tupper's
  Co.
Seybt, G.W. SC 27th Inf. Co.I 1st Sgt.
Seydel, Adolph GA 1st (Olmstead's) Inf. Co.I
Seydler, Julius TX 5th Field Btty.
Seyers, F. KY 6th Mtd.Inf. Co.B
Seyers, R. AL Randolph Cty.Res. B.C. Raney's
  Co.
Se yert toh 1st Creek Mtd.Vol. 2nd Co.C
Seyes, T. SC 1st Regt. Charleston Guard Co.D
Seyfried, R. TX Inf. 4th Bn. (Oswald's) Co.B
Seyle, --- SC Inf. 1st (Charleston) Bn. Co.A
Seyle, Charles C. FL 7th Inf. Co.I 1st Lt.
Seyle, J.H. SC Mil. 1st Regt. (Charleston Res.)
  Co.C
Seyle, S.H. SC 25th Inf. Co.A,B
Seyle, W.J. SC 27th Inf. Co.I
Seyles, P.W. SC 3rd Res. Co.B
Seyles, W.J. SC Mil. 16th Regt. Jones' Co.
Seymee, John S. AL 42nd Inf. Co.H
Seymer, James J. AL 11th Inf. Co.H
Seymer, John MS 12th Cav. Co.D
Seymere, George LA 15th Inf. Co.D
Seymon, Joseph NC 6th Sr.Res. Co.E
Seymoor, A. TX 30th Cav. Co.D Cpl.
Seymoore, Z.G. GA 37th Inf. Co.G
Seymore, A. VA 1st (Farinholt's) Res. Co.D
Seymore, A.F. GA Conscr.
Seymore, Alfred TN 61st Mtd.Inf. Bundren's Co.
Seymore, Allen GA Cherokee Legion (St.Guards)
  Co.G
Seymore, Andrew J. GA 13th Cav. Co.G
Seymore, B.L. AR 2nd Cav. Co.D
Seymore, B.L. AR 6th Inf. Co.C
Seymore, Charles AL 3rd Inf. Co.G Sgt.
Seymore, Daniel TN 3rd (Forrest's) Cav. Co.C
Seymore, D.P. TX 32nd Cav. Co.D
Seymore, Edmond TN 19th Inf. Co.B
Seymore, F.M. AR 1st Cav. Co.I
Seymore, G. GA 16th Inf.
Seymore, G.A. GA 46th Inf. Co.G
Seymore, George W. VA Inf. Gregory's Co.
Seymore, G.W. GA Phillips' Legion Co.E Cpl.
Seymore, G.W. TN 1st (Carter's) Cav. Co.E
Seymore, H. TN 1st (Carter's) Cav. Co.E
Seymore, Henry VA 38th Inf. Co.H
Seymore, Henry C. GA 8th Inf. (St.Guards)
  Co.D
Seymore, H.H. GA Phillips' Legion Co.E
Seymore, Isaiah NC 8th Bn.Part.Rangers Co.D
  Sgt.
Seymore, Isaiah NC Bass' Co. Sgt.
Seymore, J.A. AR 2nd Cav. Co.D
Seymore, J.A. GA 11th Cav.
Seymore, J.A. TN 3rd (Forrest's) Cav. Co.B
Seymore, Jabrid NC 5th Inf. Co.C
Seymore, James MS Cav. Powers' Regt. Co.G
Seymore, James NC 27th Inf. Co.C
Seymore, James SC 1st Arty. Co.D
Seymore, James SC 17th Inf. Co.B

Seymore, James VA Inf. 5th Bn. Co.E
Seymore, James E. AR 1st (Dobbin's) Cav. Co.I 3rd Lt.
Seymore, Jardin W. AR 2nd Inf. Co.K
Seymore, J.H. GA 29th Inf. Co.B
Seymore, John MO 12th Inf. Co.D
Seymore, John NC 27th Inf. Co.C
Seymore, John SC 1st Arty. Co.K
Seymore, John R. AL 18th Inf. Co.A Cpl.
Seymore, John R. GA 27th Inf. Co.B Sgt.
Seymore, J.T. AL Cp. of Instr. Talladega Co.C,A,E
Seymore, J.W. GA Arty. Lumpkin's Co.
Seymore, L. SC 4th St.Troops Co.I
Seymore, L. 15th Conf.Cav. Co.H
Seymore, L.E. AR 2nd Cav. Co.D
Seymore, Mat TX Lt.Arty. Jones' Co.
Seymore, Miles NC 32nd Inf. Co.H
Seymore, Peter NC 32nd Inf. Co.H
Seymore, R.H. GA Phillips' Legion Co.E
Seymore, Richard VA 12th Inf. Co.K
Seymore, R.L. TX 32nd Cav. Co.D
Seymore, R.T. GA 11th Cav. Co.G
Seymore, R.W.A. TN 1st (Carter's) Cav. Co.E
Seymore, S. MS 27th Inf. Co.F
Seymore, Samuel AL 9th (Malone's) Cav. Co.B
Seymore, Thomas VA 30th Inf. Co.D
Seymore, T.R. AR 2nd Cav. Co.D
Seymore, W. AR Pine Bluff Arty.
Seymore, W.A. GA 6th Inf. Co.G
Seymore, Watkins LA 7th Cav. Co.C
Seymore, W.B. AL 9th (Malone's) Cav. Co.B
Seymore, W.C. Eng.,CSA
Seymore, W.H. GA Cav. 24th Bn. Co.B
Seymore, William GA 32nd Inf. Co.A
Seymore, William MS 9th Cav. Co.C
Seymore, William B. AR 2nd Cav. Co.D Bvt.2nd Lt.
Seymore, William H. NC 56th Inf. Co.A 2nd Lt.
Seymore, William J. GA 14th Inf. Co.C
Seymour, A. VA 18th Cav. 2nd Co.E
Seymour, Abe VA 18th Cav. Co.H
Seymour, Abel VA Cav. McNeill's Co. Sgt.
Seymour, Abel (of Aaron) VA 25th Inf. 1st Co.K
Seymour, Abel (of Moses) VA 25th Inf. 1st Co.K
Seymour, Abner VA 6th Inf. Co.I
Seymour, Alfred TN 2nd (Ashby's) Cav. Co.B
Seymour, Asa GA Inf. 14th Bn. (St.Guards) Co.A
Seymour, Asa F. GA Inf. 2nd Bn. Co.B
Seymour, A.W. VA 77th Mil. Co.C
Seymour, B.F. VA 13th Cav. Co.I
Seymour, Bobb H. MS 21st Inf. Co.I
Seymour, B.P. SC Mil. 16th Regt. Jones' Co.
Seymour, C. TN Inf. 154th Sr.Regt. Co.L
Seymour, Charles TX 5th Cav. Co.A
Seymour, Charles VA 7th Cav. Co.F
Seymour, Charles L. VA Horse Arty. D. Shanks' Co. Sgt.
Seymour, C.M. TX 1st Hvy.Arty. Co.B Color-bearer
Seymour, C.M. TX 2nd Inf. Co.H
Seymour, D. NC 61st Inf. Co.D
Seymour, Daniel AR 18th (Marmaduke's) Inf. Co.A Cpl.
Seymour, Daniel VA 77th Mil. Blue's Co.
Seymour, Daniel H. VA 11th Cav. Co.D

Seymour, David NC 32nd Inf. Co.I
Seymour, Edward H. GA 66th Inf. Co.G Sgt.
Seymour, Edward K. VA 6th Inf. Co.F
Seymour, Eli H. GA 13th Cav. Co.E
Seymour, Elihu GA 9th Inf. (St.Guards) DeLaperriere's Co.
Seymour, E.M. TN Inf. 1st Cons.Regt. Co.A
Seymour, E.M. TN 6th Inf. Co.D
Seymour, E.T. TN 51st Inf. Co.B
Seymour, E.T. TN 51st (Cons.) Inf. Co.I 1st Sgt.
Seymour, E.W. LA 15th Inf. Co.D
Seymour, F. MS 1st Cav.Res. Co.G
Seymour, Felix VA 14th Mil. Co.A
Seymour, Felix VA 25th Inf. 1st Co.K
Seymour, F.T. TN 6th Inf. Co.D
Seymour, F.W. LA Mil. Beauregard Bn.
Seymour, F.W. LA Mil.Conf.Guards Regt. Co.C
Seymour, G.B. TN 2nd (Ashby's) Cav. Co.B Cpl.
Seymour, George AL Arty. 1st Bn. Co.A
Seymour, George LA 5th Inf. Co.D Capt.
Seymour, George LA 10th Inf. Co.A
Seymour, George B. TN 61st Mtd.Inf. Bundren's Co.
Seymour, George F. MS 1st Lt.Arty. Co.L
Seymour, George H. LA 21st (Patton's) Inf. Co.C Sgt.
Seymour, Geo. S. Gen. & Staff Asst.Surg.
Seymour, George W. AL 7th Cav.
Seymour, George W. GA Inf. 2nd Bn. Co.B
Seymour, George W. TX 5th Cav. Co.A
Seymour, George W. VA 18th Inf. Co.D
Seymour, George Washington AL 49th Inf. Co.B
Seymour, G.S. GA 2nd Inf. Co.K
Seymour, G.W. GA 2nd Inf. Co.H
Seymour, G.W. GA 8th Inf. (St.Guards) Co.C Cpl.
Seymour, H. GA Inf. Ezzard's Co.
Seymour, Henry MS 3rd Inf. Co.A
Seymour, Henry C. KY 2nd Cav. Co.E,C
Seymour, Isaac G. LA 6th Inf. Col.
Seymour, Isiah GA 9th Inf. (St.Guards) Co.D
Seymour, J. GA Arty. Lumpkin's Co.
Seymour, J. GA Inf. 1st Bn.
Seymour, Jackson GA Siege Arty. Campbell's Ind.Co.
Seymour, Jacob VA 47th Inf. 2nd Co.G
Seymour, James LA 3rd Inf. Co.B
Seymour, James LA 15th Inf. Co.B
Seymour, James TN 2nd (Ashby's) Cav. Co.B
Seymour, James TX 13th Vol. 2nd Co.H
Seymour, James VA Cav. 34th Bn. Co.D
Seymour, James 20th Conf.Cav. Co.B
Seymour, James 2nd Cherokee Mtd.Vol. Co.H
Seymour, James H. TN 2nd (Ashby's) Cav. Co.B
Seymour, James S. VA 8th Cav.
Seymour, J.E. AR 1st (Monroe's) Cav. Co.G Sgt.
Seymour, Jerome SC 6th Inf. 2nd Co.D
Seymour, Jerome SC 9th Inf. Co.H
Seymour, J.I. AL Cp. of Instr. Talladega Co.C,A,E
Seymour, J.L. AL 32nd Inf. Co.I
Seymour, J.M. TX 2nd Inf. Co.C,F 2nd Lt.
Seymour, J.N. GA Cav. 20th Bn. Co.G
Seymour, J.N. GA Cav. 21st Bn. Co.D

Seymour, John AR 5th Inf. Co.A Sgt.
Seymour, John MS 3rd Inf. Co.E,A
Seymour, John VA 18th Cav. Co.H
Seymour, John VA Inf. 23rd Bn. Co.H
Seymour, John VA 25th Inf. 1st Co.K
Seymour, John VA 77th Mil. Blue's Co.
Seymour, John J. SC 15th Inf. Co.E
Seymour, John M. VA 7th Cav. Co.F
Seymour, John P. TN 13th Inf. Co.I
Seymour, John R. GA 13th Cav. Co.E
Seymour, John W. VA 18th Cav. 2nd Co.E Cpl.
Seymour, Jonathan VA 11th Cav. Co.D 2nd Lt.
Seymour, Jonathan VA 77th Mil. Co.C
Seymour, Joseph NC Inf. Thomas Legion Co.K
Seymour, J.R. MO Inf. 5th Regt.St.Guard Co.B
Seymour, J.S. TX 18th Cav. Co.F
Seymour, J.T. AL 4th Inf. Co.A
Seymour, J.T. AL Cp. of Instr. Talladega Co.C,A,E
Seymour, J.W. GA 9th Inf. (St.Guards) Co.H
Seymour, J.W. Conf.Cav. Wood's Regt. Co.M
Seymour, L. MS Cav. 17th Bn. Co.A
Seymour, Leonidas B. NC 50th Inf. Co.E
Seymour, L.M. AL 6th Cav. Co.E
Seymour, L.S. GA 2nd Inf. Co.K
Seymour, Math NC 15th Inf. Co.M
Seymour, Matthew NC 32nd Inf. Co.I
Seymour, Morgan VA 8th Bn.Res. Co.A
Seymour, O.L. VA Inf. 44th Bn. Co.D
Seymour, R. MS Cav. 17th Bn. Co.A
Seymour, R. VA Inf. 25th Bn. Co.D
Seymour, R.A. MO Beck's Co.
Seymour, Robert P. TN 10th Inf. Co.F 1st Lt.
Seymour, R.W., Jr. SC Mil. 1st Regt.Rifles Palmer's Co.
Seymour, S. GA 23rd Inf. Co.A
Seymour, Samuel J. LA Mil. Orleans Fire Regt. Hall's Co.
Seymour, S.C. SC 3rd Cav. Co.H
Seymour, S.C. SC Mil. 1st Regt.Rifles Palmer's Co.
Seymour, Shelly LA Edward's Bn. Co.B A.Adj.
Seymour, Silas C. NC 4th Cav. (59th St.Troops) Co.G 2nd Sgt.
Seymour, Syct MS Cav. 17th Bn. Co.E
Seymour, T.J. AL 40th Inf. Co.G
Seymour, V. AL 58th Inf. Co.E
Seymour, W. Conf.Reg.Inf. Brooks' Bn. Co.A
Seymour, Walker W. VA 51st Mil. Co.E
Seymour, Watkins MS 18th Inf.
Seymour, W.H. AL 14th Inf. Co.K Sgt.
Seymour, William GA 16th Inf. Co.B
Seymour, William LA Mil. Irish Regt. O'Brien's Co. Jr.2nd Lt.
Seymour, William MS 28th Cav. Co.C
Seymour, William MS 1st (King's) Inf. (St.Troops) Co.E
Seymour, William TN 1st Cav.
Seymour, William VA Lt.Arty. Cayce's Co.
Seymour, William D. AL 4th Inf. Co.A
Seymour, William D. NC Inf. 2nd Bn. Co.H
Seymour, William D. VA 54th Mil. Co.G
Seymour, William H. LA 21st (Patton's) Inf. Co.C Sgt.
Seymour, William H. NC 32nd Inf. Co.H Sgt.
Seymour, William Porter GA 45th Inf. Co.K
Seymour, William R. VA Cav. McNeill's Co.

Seymour, William T. AR 17th (Lemoyne's) Inf.
Co.C
Seymour, William T. AR 21st Inf. Co.C
Seymour, W.J. Gen. & Staff, AG Dept. Capt.
Seymour, W.K. TX Cav. McCord's Frontier
Regt. Co.H
Seymour, W.P. AL 51st (Part.Rangers) Co.H
Seymour, W.S. LA 4th Inf. Co.A
Seymoure, L. MS 9th Cav. Co.A Cpl.
Seymoure, L. SC 5th Bn.Res. Co.B Cpl.
Seymure, R. MS 9th Cav. Co.A
Seysler, Edward MO 6th Inf. Co.I Music.
Seyssler, Edward MO Lt.Arty. Parsons' Co.
Bugler
Seyssler, Edward Conf.Inf. 1st Bn. 2nd Co.E
Music.
Seyton, Henry GA 41st Inf.
Seyton, John S. AL 43rd Inf. Co.F
Seywood, H. MO Robertson's Regt.St.Guard
Co.1
Sha, Dennis TN 19th Inf. Co.G
Sha, J. AL 15th Inf. Co.B
Shaad, Jacob LA 5th Inf. Co.G
Shaaf, Mathew VA Cav. 1st Bn. Co.C
Shaaff, Arthur GA 1st Bn.S.S. Co.A Maj.
Shaaff, Francis K. AL 15th Inf. Co.A Capt.
Shaaff, Francis K. KY 1st Inf. Co.D
Shaaff, John T. LA 1st Hvy.Arty. (Reg.) Co.C
Capt.
Shaaff, John T. Gen. & Staff AACS
Shachno, Charles GA Inf. 1st Loc.Troops
(Augusta) Co.A
Shack, John MS 27th Inf. Co.E
Shack, John D. MS 1st Lt.Arty. Co.G
Shackeford, R. MS Cav. 3rd Bn. (Ashcraft's)
Co.C
Shackel, James P. AL 16th Inf. Co.E
Shackelford, A.D. GA 6th Cav. Co.L 1st Sgt.
Shackelford, Adam KY 9th Mtd.Inf. Co.K
Shackelford, A.G. AR 8th Inf. New Co.I
Shackelford, Albert F. VA 21st Mil. Co.C
Shackelford, Alexander VA 5th Cav. Co.A Cpl.
Shackelford, Andrew J. AL 43rd Inf. Co.I
Shackelford, Anthony B. AL 46th Inf. Co.B,D
Shackelford, August W. FL 3rd Inf. Co.H
Shackelford, Benjamin F. MO Cav. 3rd Bn.
Co.C
Shackelford, B.F. SC 10th Inf. Co.M
Shackelford, B. Howard VA 17th Inf. Co.K
Capt.
Shackelford, Calvin TN 30th Inf. Co.B
Shackelford, C.C., Jr. Conf.Cav. Wood's Regt.
2nd Co.D
Shackelford, Charles Morgan's,CSA
Shackelford, Charles R. MS 26th Inf. Co.H
Shackelford, Charles W. GA 13th Cav. Co.E,K
2nd Lt.
Shackelford, Charles W. GA Cobb's Legion
Co.C
Shackelford, C.M. AL 45th Inf. Co.K
Shackelford, C.R. MO Robertson's Regt.
St.Guard Co.4
Shackelford, C.W. MS 41st Inf. Co.L
Shackelford, Daniel NC 61st Inf. Co.G 2nd Lt.
Shackelford, D.H. MS 5th Inf. Co.K
Shackelford, D.P. MS 10th Inf. Old Co.A
Shackelford, E. TX 5th Inf. Co.D Music.

Shackelford, E.D. VA Cav. Mosby's Regt.
(Part.Rangers) Co.E
Shackelford, E.H. GA 6th Inf. Co.F Capt.
Shackelford, F. AL 2nd Cav. Co.F
Shackelford, F. AL 8th Inf. Co.B Sgt.
Shackelford, F. AR 6th Inf. New Co.F
Shackelford, Fountain G. VA 36th Inf. Co.F
Sgt.
Shackelford, Francis M. NC 21st Inf. Co.F Cpl.
Shackelford, Francis R. Gen. & Staff Maj.,CS
Shackelford, F.W. SC 5th Cav. Co.E
Shackelford, F.W. SC Bn.St.Cadets Co.B
Shackelford, Geo. MD Weston's Bn. Co.B
Shackelford, George MS 26th Inf. Co.H
Shackelford, Geo. D. MO 5th Div.St.Guard
Maj.,AAG
Shackelford, George E. VA 34th Inf. Co.A
Shackelford, George S. VA 24th Cav. Co.C 2nd
Lt.
Shackelford, George S. VA Cav. 40th Bn. Co.C
Shackelford, George W. AL 43rd Inf. Co.I,K
Shackelford, George W. VA 21st Mil. Co.B
Shackelford, George W. VA 26th Inf. Co.A
Shackelford, G.M. TX 14th Inf. Co.C Sgt.
Shackelford, G.W. AL 2nd Cav. Co.F
Shackelford, G.W. MS Cav. Davenport's Bn.
(St.Troops) Co.B
Shackelford, G.W. TX 3rd Cav. Co.G
Shackelford, H. MO St.Guard W.H. Taylor's
Co.
Shackelford, H.D. AR Inf. Hardy's Regt. Co.B
Shackelford, H.D. NC Loc.Def. Lee's Co.
(Silver Greys)
Shackelford, Henry GA Lt.Arty. 12th Bn. 2nd
Co.D
Shackelford, Henry C. VA Cav. 40th Bn. Co.F
Shackelford, Henry C. VA 21st Mil. Co.C
Shackelford, Henry D. GA 40th Inf. Co.E Cpl.
Shackelford, Henry H. VA 34th Inf. Co.A
Shackelford, H.H. MS 8th Cav. Co.F Capt.
Shackelford, H.J. MS 38th Cav. Co.H
Shackelford, Hodges VA Cav. 40th Bn. Co.F
Shackelford, J. KY Arty. Corbett's Co.
Shackelford, J. VA 5th Cav. Co.G
Shackelford, J.A. VA 5th Cav. Co.G
Shackelford, James MO 9th Inf. Co.C
Shackelford, James VA 26th Inf. Co.F
Shackelford, James B. TN 27th Inf. Co.I 1st Sgt.
Shackelford, James C. GA 7th Inf. (St.Guards)
Co.I
Shackelford, James J. KY 3rd Cav. Co.H 2nd
Lt.
Shackelford, James M. MS Inf. 2nd Bn. Co.C
Shackelford, James M. MS 48th Inf. Co.C
Shackelford, James M. VA 34th Inf. Co.A
Shackelford, James R. TX Inf. Griffin's Bn.
Co.B Cpl.
Shackelford, James R. VA 26th Inf. Co.D
Shackelford, James T. NC 61st Inf. Co.G Sgt.
Shackelford, James T. Gen. & Staff Asst.Surg.
Shackelford, James W. AL 46th Inf. Co.B
Shackelford, James W. VA 24th Cav. Co.C
Shackelford, James W. VA Cav. 40th Bn. Co.C
Shackelford, J.B. SC Inf. Hampton Legion Co.A
Shackelford, J.C. MO 1st Cav. Co.A
Shackelford, Jesse H. AL 11th Inf. Co.G
Shackelford, J.F. AL Cav. Barlow's Co.

Shackelford, J.F. MS Inf. (Res.) Berry's Co.
Cpl.
Shackelford, J.F. VA 48th Inf. Capt.,Asst.Surg.
Shackelford, J.G. KY 9th Mtd.Inf. Co.G 2nd Lt.
Shackelford, J.G. KY Logan Co.
Shackelford, J.H. NC 3rd Jr.Res. Co.C 2nd Lt.
Shackelford, J.H. NC 4th Bn.Jr.Res. Co.C 2nd
Lt.
Shackelford, J.H.B. GA 1st Inf. (St.Guards)
Co.A
Shackelford, J.L. SC 18th Inf. Co.E Bvt.2nd Lt.
Shackelford, J.M. AR 6th Inf. New Co.F
Shackelford, J.M. VA 4th Cav. Co.C
Shackelford, Joel W. VA Lt.Arty. Armistead's
Co.
Shackelford, Joel W. VA 61st Mil. Co.B
Shackelford, John TX 13th Vol. 2nd Co.C
Shackelford, John VA 42nd Inf. Co.A
Shackelford, John C. AL 46th Inf. Co.B Cpl.
Shackelford, John C. KY 14th Cav. Co.C
Shackelford, John E. VA Lt.Arty. Armistead's
Co.
Shackelford, Jno. F. Gen. & Staff Asst.Surg.
Shackelford, John H. MO 3rd Inf. Co.H
Shackelford, John H. NC 21st Inf. Co.F
Shackelford, John H. TX 36th Cav. Co.K Cpl.
Shackelford, John H. TX 17th Inf. Co.K
Shackelford, John J. AL 43rd Inf. Co.I
Shackelford, John M. GA Inf. 10th Bn. Co.C,E
Sgt.
Shackelford, John M. MS Inf. 2nd Bn. Co.C 1st
Lt.
Shackelford, John M. MS 48th Inf. Co.C Capt.
Shackelford, John W. MS 11th Inf. Co.K
Shackelford, John W. NC 3rd Cav. (41st
St.Troops) Co.H Sgt.
Shackelford, John W., Jr. VA 21st Mil. Co.B
Shackelford, John W., Sr. VA 21st Mil. Co.B
Shackelford, John W. VA 34th Inf. Co.A
Shackelford, Jonathan SC 18th Inf. Co.E
Shackelford, Joseph AL 1st Cav. 1st Co.K
Shackelford, Joseph AL 2nd Cav. Co.F 1st Lt.
Shackelford, Joseph AL 4th (Roddey's) Cav.
Co.G Capt.
Shackelford, Joseph AL 4th (Roddey's) Cav.
Chap.
Shackelford, Joseph GA 41st Inf. Co.I
Shackelford, Joseph P. MO 2nd Inf. Co.F,I
Shackelford, J.T. GA 8th Inf. Co.A
Shackelford, J.W. GA 3rd Bn. (St.Guards) Co.C
Shackelford, Lee MS 37th Inf. Co.A
Shackelford, Leonard W. MS 26th Inf. Co.H
Shackelford, Levi AL Lty.Arty. Lee's Btty. Sgt.
Shackelford, Lloyd W. AL 6th Inf. Co.B Cpl.
Shackelford, L.W. MS Cav. Davenport's Bn.
(St.Troops) Co.B
Shackelford, M.A. GA 3rd Bn. (St.Guards) Co.F
Shackelford, Matt AL 2nd Cav. Co.F 2nd Lt.
Shackelford, Mordiaca GA 34th Inf. Co.G
Shackelford, M.S. MO 3rd Inf. Co.H
Shackelford, N.A. Gen. & Staff Asst.Surg.
Shackelford, N.C. AL Cav. Barlow's Co.
Shackelford, N.C. 15th Conf.Cav. Co.C
Shackelford, Pinckney SC 18th Inf. Co.E
Shackelford, Pleasant C. NC 60th Inf. Co.K 3rd
Lt.
Shackelford, R. MS 28th Cav. Co.C

Shackelford, R.C. GA 6th Cav. Co.C
Shackelford, R.C. GA Smith's Legion Stiff's Co.
Shackelford, Richard D. VA Lt.Arty. B.Z.
    Price's Co.
Shackelford, Richard N. GA 41st Inf. Co.G
Shackelford, R.J. MS 5th Inf. Co.K
Shackelford, Robert MO 9th Inf. Co.C
Shackelford, Robert L. VA 61st Mil. Co.G
Shackelford, R.L. GA 3rd Bn. (St.Guards) Co.F
Shackelford, R.M. GA Inf. 1st Loc.Troops
    (Augusta) Co.E,B
Shackelford, R.M. KY 9th Mtd.Inf. Co.G
Shackelford, Robert C. AL 7th Inf. Co.C
Shackelford, Robert L. GA 2nd Res. Co.A 1st
    Sgt.
Shackelford, R.W. SC 3rd St.Troops
Shackelford, Samuel VA 42nd Inf. Co.A
Shackelford, S.B. LA 18th Inf. Co.C 1st Lt.
Shackelford, S.P. SC 21st Inf. Co.I
Shackelford, T.A. LA 1st Hvy.Arty. (Reg.)
    Co.D
Shackelford, T.G. TX 21st Cav. Co.D
Shackelford, T.H. AL 54th Inf. Lt.Col.
Shackelford, T.H. 4th Conf.Inf. Co.E Capt.
Shackelford, Thomas TX Cav. Madison's Regt.
    Co.F
Shackelford, Thomas C. SC 10th Inf. Co.B
Shackelford, Thomas J. AL 43rd Inf. Co.I Sgt.
Shackelford, Thomas J. GA Cobb's Legion Co.C
Shackelford, T.J. AR 6th Inf. New Co.F
Shackelford, T.W. GA Inf. 1st Loc.Troops
    (Augusta) Barnes' Lt.Arty.Co.
Shackelford, W.A.H. MS 26th Inf. Co.H Capt.
Shackelford, W.D. GA Inf. 2nd Bn. (St.Guards)
    Co.A
Shackelford, W.G. GA Cav. 10th Bn.
    (St.Guards) Co.D
Shackelford, W.H. AL 30th Inf. Co.I
Shackelford, W.H.H. KY 1st Inf. Co.A
Shackelford, William LA 14th (Austin's) Bn.S.S.
    Co.A
Shackelford, William MS 6th Cav. Co.B Cpl.
Shackelford, William TX Cav. Martin's Regt.
    Co.B
Shackelford, William VA 21st Mil. Co.A
Shackelford, William, Sr. VA 21st Mil. Co.D,E
Shackelford, William F. VA 26th Inf. Co.A
Shackelford, William H. GA Lt.Arty. Milledge's
    Co. Cpl.
Shackelford, William H. GA 3rd Inf. 1st Co.I
Shackelford, William H. TN 27th Inf. Co.I
Shackelford, William H. VA Lt.Arty.
    Armistead's Co.
Shackelford, William J. AL 10th Inf. Co.K
Shackelford, William M. TX 2nd Inf. Co.H Cpl.
Shackelford, William N. TX Inf. Griffin's Bn.
    Co.B
Shackelford, W.P. AL 19th Inf. Co.C
Shackelford, W.S. MO 5th Cav. Co.I
Shackelford, W.S. MO 10th Cav. Co.I
Shackelford, Zachariah L. VA 26th Inf. Co.A
Shackelton, G.J. MS 29th Inf. Co.C
Shackelton, R.S. TN 47th Inf. Co.C
Shackency, H.M. TN Inf. 4th Cons.Regt. Co.I
Shackett, Richard KY 2nd (Woodward's) Cav.
    Co.E
Shackford, Ephraim J. MS 12th Inf. Co.E

Shackford, J.B. SC 26th Inf. Co.C
Shackford, W. VA 5th Cav. Co.H
Shackford, W.E. VA 5th Cav. Co.F